CONCISE MAJOR 21ST-CENTURY WRITERS

CONCISE MAJOR 21ST-CENTURY WRITERS

A Selection of Sketches from *Contemporary Authors*

Tracey L. Matthews, Project Editor

Volume 1: A-Cl

THOMSON

GALE

Detroit • New York • San Francisco • New Haven, Conn. • Waterville, Maine • London • Munich

Concise Major 21st-Century Writers

Project Editor
Tracey L. Matthews

Editorial
Michelle Kazensky, Josh Kondek, Lisa Kumar,
Julie Mellors, Joyce Nakamura, Mary Ruby

Composition and Electronic Capture
Carolyn A. Roney

Manufacturing
Rita Wimberley

Library of Congress Control Number: 2006929297

ISBN 0-7876-7539-3 (hardcover : set), ISBN 0-7876-7540-7 (v. 1), ISBN 0-7876-7541-5 (v. 2),
ISBN 0-7876-7542-3 (v. 3), ISBN 0-7876-7543-1 (v. 4), ISBN 0-7876-7544-X (v. 5)

Printed in the United States of America
10 9 8 7 6 5 4 3 2 1

Contents

Introduction

Concise Major 21st-Century Writers (*CMTFCW*) is an abridgement of the 2004 eBook-only edition of Thomson Gale's *Major 21st-Century Writers* (*MTFCW*), a set based on Thomson Gale's award-winning *Contemporary Authors* series. *CMTFCW* provides students, educators, librarians, researchers, and general readers with a concise yet comprehensive source of biographical and bibliographical information on 700 of the most influential and studied authors at the turn of the twenty-first century as well as emerging authors whose literary significance is likely to increase in the coming decades.

CMTFCW includes sketches on approximately 700 authors who made writing literature their primary occupation and who have had at least part of their oeuvre published in English. Thus novelists, short story writers, nonfiction writers, poets, dramatists, genre writers, children's writers, and young adult writers of about sixty nationalities and ethnicities are represented. Selected sketches of authors that appeared in the 2004 edition of *MTFCW* are completely updated to include information on their lives and works through 2006. About thirty authors featured in *CMTFCW* are new to this set evidencing Thomson Gale's commitment to identifying emerging writers of recent eras and of many cultures.

How Authors Were Chosen for *CMTFCW*

The preliminary list of authors for *MTFCW* was sent to an advisory board of librarians, teaching professionals, and writers whose input resulted in informal inclusion criteria. In consultation with the editors, the list was narrowed to 700 authors for the concise edition plus criteria were established for adding authors. Criteria our editors used for adding authors not previously published in the last edition of *MTFCW* include:

- Authors who have won major awards

- Authors whose works are bestsellers

- Authors whose works are being incorporated into curricula and studied at the high school and/or college level

Broad Coverage in a Single Source

CMTFCW provides detailed biographical and bibliographical coverage of the most influential writers of our time, including:

- *Contemporary Literary Figures*: Mitch Albom, Sherman Alexie, Maya Angelou, Margaret Atwood, Dan Brown, Michael Chabon, J.M. Coetzee, Don DeLillo, Joan Didion, Dave Eggers, Gabriel Garcia Marquez, Nadine Gordimer, Khaled Hosseini, Toni Morrison, Joyce Carol Oates, Thomas Pynchon, J.K. Rowling, Salman Rushdie, Amy Tan, and John Updike, among many others.

- *Genre Writers*: Ray Bradbury, Tom Clancy, Philip K. Dick, Neil Gaiman, Sue Grafton, Dennis Lehane, Stephen King, Walter Mosley, Christopher Paolini, Anne Rice, Nora Roberts, Art Spiegelman, and Jane Yolen, among many others.

- *Novelists and Short Story Writers*: James Baldwin, Charles Baxter, Peter Carey, Carlos Fuentes, Graham Greene, Sebastian Junger, Sue Monk Kidd, John le Carré, Yann Martel, Rick Moody, Chuck Palahniuk, and Zadie Smith, among many others.

- *Dramatists*: Edward Albee, Samuel Beckett, Athol Fugard, Tony Kushner, David Mamet, Arthur Miller, Neil Simon, Tom Stoppard, Wendy Wasserstein, Alfred Uhry, Paula Vogel, and Tennessee Williams, among many others.

- *Poets*: Gwendolyn Brooks, Allen Ginsburg, Louise Glück, Jorie Graham, Seamus Heaney, Ted Kooser, Mary Oliver, Kenneth Rexroth, Adrienne Rich, Derek Walcott, and C.K. Williams, among many others.

How Entries Are Organized

Each *CMTFCW* biography begins with a series of rubrics that outlines the author's personal history, including information on the author's birth, death, family life, education, career, memberships, and awards. The *Writings* section lists a bibliography of the author's works along with the publisher and year published. The *Sidelights* section provides a biographical portrait of the author's development; information about the critical reception of the author's works; and revealing comments, often by the author, on personal interests, motivations, and thoughts on writing. The *Biographical/Critical Sources* section features a useful list of books, articles, and reviews about the author and his or her work. This section also includes citations for all material quoted in the *Sidelights* essay.

Other helpful sections include *Adaptations*, which lists the author's works that have been adapted by others into various media, including motion pictures, stage plays, and television or radio broadcasts, while the *Work in Progress* section lists titles or descriptions of works that are scheduled for publication by the author.

Using the Indexes

CMTFCW features a Nationality/Ethnicity index as well as a Subject/Genre index. More than sixty nations are represented in the Nationality/Ethnicity index, reflecting the international scope of this set and the multinational status of many authors. The Subject/Genre index covers over fifty genres and subject areas of fiction and nonfiction frequently referenced by educators and students, including social and political literature, environmental issues, and science fiction/science fantasy literature.

Citing *CMTFCW*

Students writing papers who wish to include references to information found in *CMTFCW* may cite sources in their bibliographies using the following format. Teachers adhering to other bibliographic formats may request that their students alter the citation below, which should only serve as a guide:

"Margaret Atwood." *Concise Major 21st-Century Writers.* Ed. Tracey L. Matthews. Detroit: Thomson Gale, 2006, pp. 214-223.

Comments Are Appreciated

CMTFCW is intended to serve as a useful reference tool for a wide audience, so your comments about this work are encouraged. Suggestions for authors to include in future editions of *CMTFCW* are also welcome. Send comments and suggestions to: *Concise Major 21st-Century Writers*, Thomson Gale, 27500 Drake Rd., Farmington Hills, MI 48331-3535; call at 1-248-699-4253; or fax at 1-248-699-8070.

Concise Major 21st-Century Writers
Advisory Board

In preparation for the first edition of *Major 20th-Century Writers* (MTCW), the editors of *Contemporary Authors* conducted a telephone survey of librarians and mailed a survey to more than 4,000 libraries to help determine the kind of reference resource the libraries wanted. Once it was clear that a comprehensive, yet affordable source of information on twentieth-century writers was needed to serve small and medium-sized libraries, a wide range of resources was consulted: national surveys of books taught in American high schools and universities; British secondary school syllabi; reference works such as the *New York Library Desk Reference, Reading Lists for College-Bound Students: The Books Most Recommended by America's Top Colleges, The List of Books, E.D. Hirsch's Cultural Legacy*, and volumes in Thomson Gale's Literacy Criticism and Dictionary of Literary Biography series. From these resources and with advice of an international advisory board, the author list for the first edition of *MTCW* was finalized, the sketches edited, and the volume published.

For the eBook edition of *Major 21st-Century Writers* (MTFCW), the editors compiled a preliminary author list based largely upon a list of authors included in the second print edition of *MTCW* with recommendations based on new inclusion criteria. This list was sent to an advisory board of librarians, authors, and teaching professionals in both the United States and Britain. In addition to vetting the submitted list, the advisors suggested other noteworthy writers. Recommendations made by the advisors ensure that authors from all nations and genres are represented.

Concise Major 21st-Century Writers (CMTFCW) is an abridgement of the eBook-only edition of *MTFCW*. The editors built upon the work of past advisors of the eBook edition to create a concise version and added authors who have earned increased recognition since the publication of *MTFCW*. The advisory board for *MTFCW* played a major role in shaping the author list for *CMTFCW*, and the editors wish to thank them for sharing their expertise. The twenty-seven member advisory board includes the following individuals:

- **Carl Antonucci,** Director of Library Services, Capital Community College, Hartford, Connecticut

- **Barbara Bibel,** Reference Librarian, Oakland Public Library, Oakland, California

- **Beverly A. Buciak,** Librarian, Brother Rice High School, Chicago, Illinois

- **Mary Ann Capan,** District Library Media Specialist, Sherrard Jr. Sr. High School, Sherrard, Illinois

- **Linda Carvell,** Head Librarian, Lancaster Country Day School, Lancaster, Pennsylvania

- **Anne Christensen,** Librarian II, Phoenix Public Library, Phoenix, Arizona

- **Peggy Curran,** Adult Services Librarian, Naperville Public Library, Naperville, Illinois

- **Eva M. Davis,** Youth Services Manager, Ann Arbor District Library, Ann Arbor, Michigan

- **Thomas Eertmoed,** Librarian, Illinois Central College, East Peoria, Illinois

- **Lucy K. Gardner,** Director, Howard Community College, Columbia, Maryland

- **Christine C. Godin,** Director of Learning Resources, Northwest Vista College, San Antonio, Texas

- **Francisca Goldsmith,** Senior Librarian, Berkeley Public Library, Berkeley, California

- **Nancy Guidry,** Reference Librarian, Bakersfield College, Bakersfield, California

- **Jack Hicks,** Administrative Librarian, Deerfield Public Library, Deerfield, Illinois

- **Charlie Jones,** School Library Media Specialist, Plymouth High School Library Media Center, Canton, Michigan

- **Carol M. Keeler,** Upper School Media Specialist, Detroit Country Day School, Beverly Hills, Michigan

- **Georgia Lomax,** Managing Librarian, King County Library System, Covington, Washington

- **Mary Jane Marden,** Librarian, M.M. Bennett Library, St. Petersburg College, Pinellas Park, Florida

- **Frances Moffett,** Materials Selector, Fairfax County Public Library, Chantilly, Virginia

- **Ruth Mormon,** Upper School Librarian, The Meadows School, Las Vegas, Nevada

- **Bonnie Morris,** Upper School Media Specialist, Minnehaha Academy, Minneapolis, Minneapolis

- **Nancy Pinkston,** English Teacher, Sherrard Jr. Sr. High School, Sherrard, Illinois

- **Robert Reginald,** Head of Technical Services and Collection Development, California State University, San Bernadino, California

- **Janet P. Sarratt,** Library Media Specialist, John E. Ewing Middle School, Gaffney, South Carolina

- **Brian Stableford,** 0.5 Lecturer in Creative Writing, University College, Winchester (formerly King Alfred's College), Reading, England

- **Stephen Weiner,** Director, Maynard Public Library, Maynard, Massachusetts

- **Hope Yelich,** Reference Librarian, College of William and Mary, Williamsburg, Virginia

Concise Major 21st-Century Writers

VOLUME 1: A-Cl

Abbey, Edward 1927-1989

Abe, Kobo 1924-1993

Achebe, Chinua 1930-

Ackroyd, Peter 1949-

Adams, Alice 1926-1999

Adams, Douglas 1952-2001

Affabee, Eric
See Stine, R.L.

Aghill, Gordon
See Silverberg, Robert

Albee, Edward 1928-

Albom, Mitch 1958-

Aldiss, Brian W. 1925-

Aldrich, Ann
See Meaker, Marijane

Alegría, Claribel 1924-

Alexie, Sherman 1966-

Allan, John B.
See Westlake, Donald E.

Allen, Paula Gunn 1939-

Allen, Roland
See Ayckbourn, Alan

Allende, Isabel 1942-

Allison, Dorothy E. 1949-

Alvarez, A. 1929-

Alvarez, Julia 1950-

Amado, Jorge 1912-2001

Ambrose, Stephen E. 1936-2002

Amichai, Yehuda 1924-2000

Amis, Kingsley 1922-1995

Amis, Martin 1949-

Anand, Mulk Raj 1905-2004

Anaya, Rudolfo A. 1937-

Anderson, Laurie Halse 1961-

Anderson, Poul 1926-2001

Andrews, Elton V.
See Pohl, Frederik

Angelou, Maya 1928-

Anouilh, Jean 1910-1987

Anthony, Peter
See Shaffer, Peter

Anthony, Piers 1934-

Archer, Jeffrey 1940-

Archer, Lee
See Ellison, Harlan

Ard, William
See Jakes, John

Arenas, Reinaldo 1943-1990

Arias, Ron 1941-

Arnette, Robert
See Silverberg, Robert

Aronson, Marc 1948-

Ashbery, John 1927-

Ashbless, William
See Powers, Tim

Asimov, Isaac 1920-1992

Atwood, Margaret 1939-

Axton, David
See Koontz, Dean R.

Ayckbourn, Alan 1939-

Bachman, Richard
See King, Stephen

Bainbridge, Beryl 1934-

Baker, Nicholson 1957-

Baker, Russell 1925-

Baldacci, David 1960-

Baldwin, James 1924-1987

Ballard, J.G. 1930-

Bambara, Toni Cade 1939-1995

Banat, D.R.
See Bradbury, Ray

Banks, Iain M. 1954-

Banks, Russell 1940-

Baraka, Amiri 1934-

Barclay, Bill
See Moorcock, Michael

Barclay, William Ewert
See Moorcock, Michael

Barker, Clive 1952-

Barnes, Julian 1946-

Baron, David
See Pinter, Harold

Barrington, Michael
See Moorcock, Michael

Barthelme, Donald 1931-1989

Bashevis, Isaac
See Singer, Isaac Bashevis

Bass, Kingsley B., Jr.
See Bullins, Ed

Baxter, Charles 1947-

Beagle, Peter S. 1939-

Beattie, Ann 1947-

Beauvoir, Simone de 1908-1986

Beckett, Samuel 1906-1989

Beldone, Phil "Cheech"
See Ellison, Harlan

Bell, Madison Smartt 1957-

Bellow, Saul 1915-2005

Benchley, Peter 1940-2006

Benitez, Sandra 1941-

Berendt, John 1939-

Berger, Thomas 1924-

Berry, Jonas
  See Ashbery, John

Berry, Wendell 1934-

Bethlen, T.D.
  See Silverberg, Robert

Binchy, Maeve 1940-

Bird, Cordwainer
  See Ellison, Harlan

Birdwell, Cleo
  See DeLillo, Don

Blade, Alexander
  See Silverberg, Robert

Blais, Marie-Claire 1939-

Bliss, Frederick
  See Card, Orson Scott

Block, Francesca Lia 1962-

Bloom, Amy 1953-

Blount, Roy, Jr. 1941-

Blue, Zachary
  See Stine, R.L.

Blume, Judy 1938-

Bly, Robert 1926-

Boland, Eavan 1944-

Böll, Heinrich 1917-1985

Boot, William
  See Stoppard, Tom

Borges, Jorge Luis 1899-1986

Bowles, Paul 1910-1999

Box, Edgar
  See Vidal, Gore

Boyle, Mark
  See Kienzle, William X.

Boyle, T. Coraghessan 1948-

Brackett, Peter
  See Collins, Max Allan

Bradbury, Edward P.
  See Moorcock, Michael

Bradbury, Ray 1920-

Bradley, Marion Zimmer 1930-1999

Bragg, Rick 1959-

Brashares, Ann 1967-

Breslin, Jimmy 1930-

Brink, André 1935-

Brodsky, Iosif
Alexandrovich 1940-1996

Brodsky, Joseph
  See Brodsky, Iosif Alexandrovich

Brodsky, Yosif
  See Brodsky, Iosif Alexandrovich

Brookner, Anita 1928-

Brooks, Cleanth 1906-1994

Brooks, Gwendolyn 1917-2000

Brooks, Terry 1944-

Brown, Dan 1964-

Brown, Dee Alexander 1908-2002

Brown, Rita Mae 1944-

Brown, Sterling Allen 1901-1989

Brownmiller, Susan 1935-

Bruchac, Joseph, III 1942-

Bryan, Michael
  See Moore, Brian

Buckley, William F., Jr. 1925-

Buechner, Frederick 1926-

Bukowski, Charles 1920-1994

Bullins, Ed 1935-

Burke, Ralph
  See Silverberg, Robert

Burns, Tex
  See L'Amour, Louis

Busiek, Kurt

Bustos, F.
  See Borges, Jorge Luis

Butler, Octavia E. 1947-2006

Butler, Robert Olen 1945-

Byatt, A.S. 1936-

Cabrera Infante,
Guillermo 1929-2005

Cade, Toni
  See Bambara, Toni Cade

Cain, G.
  See Cabrera Infante, Guillermo

Caldwell, Erskine 1903-1987

Calisher, Hortense 1911-

Calvino, Italo 1923-1985

Camp, John 1944-

Campbell, Bebe Moore 1950-

Capote, Truman 1924-1984

Card, Orson Scott 1951-

Carey, Peter 1943-

Carroll, James P. 1943-

Carroll, Jonathan 1949-

Carruth, Hayden 1921-

Carter, Nick
  See Smith, Martin Cruz

Carver, Raymond 1938-1988

Cavallo, Evelyn
  See Spark, Muriel

Cela, Camilo José 1916-2002

Cela y Trulock, Camilo José
  See Cela, Camilo José

Cesaire, Aimé 1913-

Chabon, Michael 1963-

Chang, Iris 1968-2004

Chapman, Lee
  See Bradley, Marion Zimmer

Chapman, Walker
  See Silverberg, Robert

Charby, Jay
  See Ellison, Harlan

Chávez, Denise 1948-

Cheever, John 1912-1982

Chevalier, Tracy 1962-

Childress, Alice 1920-1994

Chomsky, Noam 1928-

Cisneros, Sandra 1954-

Cixous, Hélène 1937-

Clancy, Tom 1947-

Clark, Carol Higgins 1956-

Clark, Curt
  See Westlake, Donald E.

Clark, John Pepper
  See Clark Bekederemo, J.P.

Clark, Mary Higgins 1929-

Clark Bekederemo, J.P. 1935-

Clarke, Arthur C. 1917-

Clarke, Austin C. 1934-

Clavell, James 1925-1994

Cleary, Beverly 1916-

Clifton, Lucille 1936-

Clinton, Dirk
    See Silverberg, Robert

Clowes, Daniel 1961-

VOLUME 2: Co-Gr

Codrescu, Andrei 1946-

Coe, Tucker
    See Westlake, Donald E.

Coetzee, J.M. 1940-

Coffey, Brian
    See Koontz, Dean R.

Coleman, Emmett
    See Reed, Ishmael

Collins, Billy 1941-

Collins, Max Allan 1948-

Colvin, James
    See Moorcock, Michael

Condé, Maryse 1937-

Connell, Evan S., Jr. 1924-

Conroy, Pat 1945-

Cook, Roy
    See Silverberg, Robert

Cooper, J. California

Cooper, Susan 1935-

Coover, Robert 1932-

Cormier, Robert 1925-2000

Cornwell, Patricia 1956-

Corso, Gregory 1930-2001

Cortázar, Julio 1914-1984

Courtney, Robert
    See Ellison, Harlan

Cox, William Trevor
    See Trevor, William

Craig, A.A.
    See Anderson, Poul

Creeley, Robert 1926-2005

Crews, Harry 1935-

Crichton, Michael 1942-

Crowley, John 1942-

Crutcher, Chris 1946-

Cruz, Victor Hernández 1949-

Culver, Timothy J.
    See Westlake, Donald E.

Cunningham, E.V.
    See Fast, Howard

Cunningham, J. Morgan
    See Westlake, Donald E.

Cunningham, Michael 1952-

Curtis, Price
    See Ellison, Harlan

Cussler, Clive 1931-

Cutrate, Joe
    See Spiegelman, Art

Dahl, Roald 1916-1990

Dale, George E.
    See Asimov, Isaac

Danticat, Edwidge 1969-

Danziger, Paula 1944-2004

Davies, Robertson 1913-1995

Davis, B. Lynch
    See Borges, Jorge Luis

Deighton, Len 1929-

Delany, Samuel R. 1942-

DeLillo, Don 1936-

Demijohn, Thom
    See Disch, Thomas M.

Denis, Julio
    See Cortázar, Julio

Denmark, Harrison
    See Zelazny, Roger

dePaola, Tomie 1934-

Derrida, Jacques 1930-

Desai, Anita 1937-

DeWitt, Helen 1957-

Dexter, Colin 1930-

Dexter, John
    See Bradley, Marion Zimmer

Dexter, N.C.
    See Dexter, Colin

Dexter, Pete 1943-

Diamond, Jared 1937-

Dick, Philip K. 1928-1982

Didion, Joan 1934-

Dillard, Annie 1945-

Disch, Thomas M. 1940-

Disch, Tom
    See Disch, Thomas M.

Doctorow, E.L. 1931-

Domecq, H. Bustos
    See Borges, Jorge Luis

Domini, Rey
    See Lorde, Audre

Dorris, Michael 1945-1997

Douglas, Leonard
    See Bradbury, Ray

Douglas, Michael
    See Crichton, Michael

Dove, Rita 1952-

Doyle, John
    See Graves, Robert

Doyle, Roddy 1958-

Dr. A.
    See Asimov, Isaac

Dr. Seuss
    See Geisel, Theodor Seuss

Drabble, Margaret 1939-

Gibson, William 1948-

Gibson, William2 1914-

Gilchrist, Ellen 1935-

Ginsberg, Allen 1926-1997

Ginzburg, Natalia 1916-1991

Giovanni, Nikki 1943-

Glück, Louise 1943-

Godwin, Gail 1937-

Golden, Arthur 1956-

Golding, William 1911-1993

Goodkind, Terry 1948-

Gordimer, Nadine 1923-

Goryan, Sirak
  See Saroyan, William

Gottesman, S.D.
  See Pohl, Frederik

Gould, Stephen Jay 1941-2002

Goytisolo, Juan 1931-

Grafton, Sue 1940-

Graham, Jorie 1950-

Grant, Skeeter
  See Spiegelman, Art

Grass, Günter 1927-

Graves, Robert 1895-1985

Graves, Valerie
  See Bradley, Marion Zimmer

Gray, Alasdair 1934-

Gray, Francine du Plessix 1930-

Gray, Spalding 1941-2004

Greeley, Andrew M. 1928-

Green, Brian
  See Card, Orson Scott

Greene, Graham 1904-1991

Greer, Richard
  See Silverberg, Robert

Gregor, Lee
  See Pohl, Frederik

Grisham, John 1955-

Grumbach, Doris 1918-

VOLUME 3: Gu-Ma

Guest, Judith 1936-

Gump, P.Q.
  See Card, Orson Scott

Guterson, David 1956-

Haddon, Mark 1962-

Hailey, Arthur 1920-2004

Halberstam, David 1934-

Hall, Donald 1928-

Hall, Radclyffe 1886-1943

Hamilton, Franklin
  See Silverberg, Robert

Hamilton, Jane 1957-

Hamilton, Mollie
  See Kaye, M.M.

Hamilton, Virginia 1936-2002

Handke, Peter 1942-

Hardwick, Elizabeth 1916-

Hargrave, Leonie
  See Disch, Thomas M.

Harjo, Joy 1951-

Harris, E. Lynn 1957-

Harris, Robert 1957-

Harris, Thomas 1940-

Harson, Sley
  See Ellison, Harlan

Hart, Ellis
  See Ellison, Harlan

Harvey, Jack
  See Rankin, Ian

Hass, Robert 1941-

Havel, Vaclav 1936-

Hawkes, John 1925-1998

Hawking, S.W.
  See Hawking, Stephen W.

Hawking, Stephen W. 1942-

Haycraft, Anna
  See Ellis, Alice Thomas

Hayes, Al
  See Grisham, John

Hazzard, Shirley 1931-

Head, Bessie 1937-1986

Heaney, Seamus 1939-

Hébert, Anne 1916-2000

Hegi, Ursula 1946-

Heinlein, Robert A. 1907-1988

Heller, Joseph 1923-1999

Hellman, Lillian 1906-1984

Helprin, Mark 1947-

Hempel, Amy 1951-

Henley, Beth 1952-

Herbert, Frank 1920-1986

Hersey, John 1914-1993

Hiaasen, Carl 1953-

Highsmith, Patricia 1921-1995

Hijuelos, Oscar 1951-

Hill, John
  See Koontz, Dean R.

Hillenbrand, Laura 1967-

Hillerman, Tony 1925-

Hinojosa, Rolando 1929-

Hinton, S.E. 1950-

Hoban, Russell 1925-

Hochhuth, Rolf 1931-

Høeg, Peter 1957-

Hoffman, Alice 1952-

Hollander, Paul
  See Silverberg, Robert

Homes, A.M. 1961-

hooks, bell 1952-

Hosseini, Khaled 1965-

Houellebecq, Michel 1958-

Houston, Jeanne Wakatsuki 1934-

Howard, Maureen 1930-

Howard, Warren F.
  See Pohl, Frederik

Hoyle, Fred 1915-2001

Hubbell, Sue 1935-

Hudson, Jeffrey
  See Crichton, Michael

Hughes, Ted 1930-1998

Humes, Edward

Hwang, David Henry 1957-

Ionesco, Eugene 1912-1994

Irving, John 1942-

Isaacs, Susan 1943-

Isherwood, Christopher 1904-1986

Ishiguro, Kazuo 1954-

Ives, Morgan
  See Bradley, Marion Zimmer

Jakes, John 1932-

James, Mary
  See Meaker, Marijane

James, P.D. 1920-

James, Philip
  See Moorcock, Michael

Janowitz, Tama 1957-

Jarvis, E.K.
  See Ellison, Harlan

Jarvis, E.K.2
  See Silverberg, Robert

Jenkins, Jerry B. 1949-

Jhabvala, Ruth Prawer 1927-

Jiang, Ji-li 1954-

Jimenez, Francisco 1943-

Jin, Ha 1956-

Johnson, Adam 1967-

Johnson, Angela 1961-

Johnson, Charles 1948-

Jones, Diana Wynne 1934-

Jones, Edward P. 1950-

Jones, Gayl 1949-

Jones, LeRoi
  See Baraka, Amiri

Jong, Erica 1942-

Jorgensen, Ivar
  See Ellison, Harlan

Jorgenson, Ivar2
  See Silverberg, Robert

Judd, Cyril
  See Pohl, Frederik

Junger, Sebastian 1962-

Karageorge, Michael A.
  See Anderson, Poul

Karr, Mary 1955-

Kastel, Warren
  See Silverberg, Robert

Kaufman, Moises 1963-

Kavanagh, Dan
  See Barnes, Julian

Kaye, M.M. 1908-2004

Kaye, Mollie
  See Kaye, M.M.

Keillor, Garrison 1942-

Kelly, Lauren
  See Oates, Joyce Carol

Keneally, Thomas 1935-

Kennedy, William 1928-

Kennilworthy Whisp
  See Rowling, J.K.

Kerr, M.E.
  See Meater, Marijane

Kerry, Lois
  See Duncan, Lois

Kesey, Ken 1935-2001

Keyes, Daniel 1927-

Kidd, Sue Monk

Kienzle, William X. 1928-2001

Kincaid, Jamaica 1949-

King, Stephen 1947-

King, Steve
  See King, Stephen

Kingsolver, Barbara 1955-

Kingston, Maxine Hong 1940-

Kinnell, Galway 1927-

Kinsella, Thomas 1928-

Kinsella, W.P. 1935-

Kizer, Carolyn 1925-

Knight, Etheridge 1931-1991

Knowles, John 1926-2001

Knox, Calvin M.
  See Silverberg, Robert

Knye, Cassandra
  See Disch, Thomas M.

Koch, Kenneth 1925-2002

Kogawa, Joy 1935-

Kolb, Edward W. 1951-

Kolb, Rocky
  See Kolb, Edward W.

Koontz, Dean R. 1945-

Kooser, Ted 1939-

Kosinski, Jerzy 1933-1991

Kozol, Jonathan 1936-

Krakauer, Jon 1954-

Kumin, Maxine 1925-

Kundera, Milan 1929-

Kunitz, Stanley 1905-

Kushner, Tony 1956-

L'Amour, Louis 1908-1988

L'Engle, Madeleine 1918-

La Guma, Alex 1925-1985

Lahiri, Jhumpa 1967-

Lamb, Wally 1950-

Lange, John
  See Crichton, Michael

Laredo, Betty
  See Codrescu, Andrei

Laurence, Margaret 1926-1987

Lavond, Paul Dennis
  See Pohl, Frederik

Leavitt, David 1961-

le Carré, John 1931-

Lee, Don L.
    See Madhubuti, Haki R.

Lee, Harper 1926-

Lee, Stan 1922-

Le Guin, Ursula K. 1929-

Lehane, Dennis 1965-

Leonard, Elmore 1925-

LeSieg, Theo.
    See Geisel, Theodor Seuss

Lessing, Doris 1919-

Lester, Julius 1939-

Lethem, Jonathan 1964-

Levi, Primo 1919-1987

Levin, Ira 1929-

Levon, O.U.
    See Kesey, Ken

Leyner, Mark 1956-

Lindbergh, Anne Morrow 1906-2001

Lively, Penelope 1933-

Lodge, David 1935-

Logan, Jake
    See Smith, Martin Cruz

Long, David 1948-

Loos, Anita 1893-1981

Lorde, Audre 1934-1992

Louise, Heidi
    See Erdrich, Louise

Lowry, Lois 1937-

Lucas, Craig 1951-

Ludlum, Robert 1927-2001

Lynch, B. Suarez
    See Borges, Jorge Luis

M.T.F.
    See Porter, Katherine Anne

Macdonald, Anson
    See Heinlein, Robert A.

MacDonald, John D. 1916-1986

Mackay, Shena 1944-

MacKinnon, Catharine A. 1946-

MacLeish, Archibald 1892-1982

MacLeod, Alistair 1936-

Maddern, Al
    See Ellison, Harlan

Madhubuti, Haki R. 1942-

Maguire, Gregory 1954-

Mahfouz, Naguib 1911-

Mailer, Norman 1923-

Makine, Andreï 1957-

Malabaila, Damiano
    See Levi, Primo

Malamud, Bernard 1914-1986

Malcolm, Dan
    See Silverberg, Robert

Malouf, David 1934-

Mamet, David 1947-

Mara, Bernard
    See Moore, Brian

Marchbanks, Samuel
    See Davies, Robertson

Marías, Javier 1951-

Mariner, Scott
    See Pohl, Frederik

Markandaya, Kamala 1924-2004

Markham, Robert
    See Amis, Kingsley

Marshall, Allen
    See Westlake, Donald E.

Marshall, Paule 1929-

Martel, Yann 1963-

Martin, Webber
    See Silverberg, Robert

Mason, Bobbie Ann 1940-

Mason, Ernst
    See Pohl, Frederik

Mass, William
    See Gibson, William2

Massie, Robert K. 1929-

Mathabane, Mark 1960-

Matthiessen, Peter 1927-

Maupin, Armistead 1944-

Mayo, Jim
    See L'Amour, Louis

VOLUME 4: Mc-Sa

McBride, James 1957-

McCaffrey, Anne 1926-

McCall Smith, Alexander 1948-

McCann, Edson
    See Pohl, Frederik

McCarthy, Cormac 1933-

McCourt, Frank 1930-

McCreigh, James
    See Pohl, Frederik

McCullough, Colleen 1937-

McCullough, David 1933-

McDermott, Alice 1953-

McEwan, Ian 1948-

McGuane, Thomas 1939-

McInerney, Jay 1955-

McKie, Robin

McKinley, Robin 1952-

McLandress, Herschel
    See Galbraith, John Kenneth

McMillan, Terry 1951-

McMurtry, Larry 1936-

McNally, Terrence 1939-

McPhee, John 1931-

McPherson, James Alan 1943-

Meaker, M.J.
    See Meaker, Marijane

Meaker, Marijane 1927-

Mehta, Ved 1934-

Members, Mark
    See Powell, Anthony

Méndez, Miguel 1930-

Merchant, Paul
    See Ellison, Harlan

Merrill, James 1926-1995

Merriman, Alex
    See Silverberg, Robert

Merwin, W.S. 1927-

Michener, James A. 1907-1997

Miéville, China 1973-

Miller, Arthur 1915-

Millett, Kate 1934-

Millhauser, Steven 1943-

Milosz, Czeslaw 1911-2004

Min, Anchee 1957-

Mitchell, Clyde
    See Ellison, Harlan

Mitchell, Clyde2
    See Silverberg, Robert

Momaday, N. Scott 1934-

Monroe, Lyle
    See Heinlein, Robert A.

Moody, Anne 1940-

Moody, Rick 1961-

Moorcock, Michael 1939-

Moore, Alan 1953-

Moore, Brian 1921-1999

Moore, Lorrie
    See Moore, Marie Lorena

Moore, Marie Lorena 1957-

Mora, Pat 1942-

Morgan, Claire
    See Highsmith, Patricia

Mori, Kyoko 1957-

Morris, Mary McGarry 1943-

Morrison, Chloe Anthony Wofford
    See Morrison, Toni

Morrison, Toni 1931-

Morrow, James 1947-

Mortimer, John 1923-

Mosley, Walter 1952-

Motion, Andrew 1952-

Mowat, Farley 1921-

Mukherjee, Bharati 1940-

Munro, Alice 1931-

Murdoch, Iris 1919-1999

Murray, Albert L. 1916-

Myers, Walter Dean 1937-

Myers, Walter M.
    See Myers, Walter Dean

Nafisi, Azar 1950-

Naipaul, Shiva 1945-1985

Naipaul, V.S. 1932-

Narayan, R.K. 1906-2001

Naylor, Gloria 1950-

Nemerov, Howard 1920-1991

Newt Scamander
    See Rowling, J.K.

Ngugi, James T.
    See Ngugi wa Thiong'o

Ngugi wa Thiong'o 1938-

Nichols, John 1940-

Nichols, Leigh
    See Koontz, Dean R.

North, Anthony
    See Koontz, Dean R.

North, Milou
    See Dorris, Michael

North, Milou2
    See Erdrich, Louise

Nosille, Nabrah
    See Ellison, Harlan

Novak, Joseph
    See Kosinski, Jerzy

Nye, Naomi Shihab 1952-

O'Brian, E.G.
    See Clarke, Arthur C.

O'Brian, Patrick 1914-2000

O'Brien, Edna 1932-

O'Brien, Tim 1946-

O'Casey, Brenda
    See Ellis, Alice Thomas

O'Faolain, Sean 1900-1991

O'Flaherty, Liam 1896-1984

Oates, Joyce Carol 1938-

Oates, Stephen B. 1936-

Oe, Kenzaburo 1935-

Okri, Ben 1959-

Olds, Sharon 1942-

Oliver, Mary 1935-

Olsen, Tillie 1912-

Ondaatje, Michael 1943-

Osborne, David
    See Silverberg, Robert

Osborne, George
    See Silverberg, Robert

Osborne, John 1929-1994

Oz, Amos 1939-

Ozick, Cynthia 1928-

Packer, Vin
    See Meaker, Marijane

Paglia, Camille 1947-

Paige, Richard
    See Koontz, Dean R.

Pakenham, Antonia
    See Fraser, Antonia

Palahniuk, Chuck 1962-

Paley, Grace 1922-

Paolini, Christopher 1983-

Parfenie, Marie
    See Codrescu, Andrei

Park, Jordan
  See Pohl, Frederik

Parker, Bert
  See Ellison, Harlan

Parker, Robert B. 1932-

Parks, Gordon 1912-2006

Pasternak, Boris 1890-1960

Patchett, Ann 1963-

Paton, Alan 1903-1988

Patterson, James 1947-

Payne, Alan
  See Jakes, John

Paz, Octavio 1914-1998

Peretti, Frank E. 1951-

Petroski, Henry 1942-

Phillips, Caryl 1958-

Phillips, Jayne Anne 1952-

Phillips, Richard
  See Dick, Philip K.

Picoult, Jodi 1966-

Piercy, Marge 1936-

Piers, Robert
  See Anthony, Piers

Pinsky, Robert 1940-

Pinta, Harold
  See Pinter, Harold

Pinter, Harold 1930-

Plimpton, George 1927-2003

Pohl, Frederik 1919-

Porter, Katherine Anne 1890-1980

Potok, Chaim 1929-2002

Powell, Anthony 1905-2000

Powers, Richard 1957-

Powers, Tim 1952-

Pratchett, Terry 1948-

Price, Reynolds 1933-

Prose, Francine 1947-

Proulx, E. Annie 1935-

Puig, Manuel 1932-1990

Pullman, Philip 1946-

Pygge, Edward
  See Barnes, Julian

Pynchon, Thomas, Jr. 1937-

Quindlen, Anna 1953-

Quinn, Simon
  See Smith, Martin Cruz

Rampling, Anne
  See Rice, Anne

Rand, Ayn 1905-1982

Randall, Robert
  See Silverberg, Robert

Rankin, Ian 1960-

Rao, Raja 1909-

Ravenna, Michael
  See Welty, Eudora

Reed, Ishmael 1938-

Reid, Desmond
  See Moorcock, Michael

Rendell, Ruth 1930-

Rensie, Willis
  See Eisner, Will

Rexroth, Kenneth 1905-1982

Rice, Anne 1941-

Rich, Adrienne 1929-

Rich, Barbara
  See Graves, Robert

Richler, Mordecai 1931-2001

Ríos, Alberto 1952-

Rivers, Elfrida
  See Bradley, Marion Zimmer

Riverside, John
  See Heinlein, Robert A.

Robb, J.D.
  See Roberts, Nora

Robbe-Grillet, Alain 1922-

Robbins, Tom 1936-

Roberts, Nora 1950-

Robertson, Ellis
  See Ellison, Harlan

Robertson, Ellis2
  See Silverberg, Robert

Robinson, Kim Stanley 1952-

Robinson, Lloyd
  See Silverberg, Robert

Robinson, Marilynne 1944-

Rodman, Eric
  See Silverberg, Robert

Rodríguez, Luis J. 1954-

Rodriguez, Richard 1944-

Roquelaure, A.N.
  See Rice, Anne

Roth, Henry 1906-1995

Roth, Philip 1933-

Rowling, J.K. 1965-

Roy, Arundhati 1960-

Rule, Ann 1935-

Rushdie, Salman 1947-

Russo, Richard 1949-

Rybczynski, Witold 1943-

Ryder, Jonathan
  See Ludlum, Robert

Sábato, Ernesto 1911-

Sacco, Joe 1960-

Sacks, Oliver 1933-

Sagan, Carl 1934-1996

Salinger, J.D. 1919-

Salzman, Mark 1959-

Sanchez, Sonia 1934-

Sanders, Noah
  See Blount, Roy, Jr.

Sanders, Winston P.
  See Anderson, Poul

Sandford, John
  See Camp, John

Saroyan, William 1908-1981

Sarton, May 1912-1995

Sartre, Jean-Paul 1905-1980

Satterfield, Charles
  See Pohl, Frederik

Saunders, Caleb
  See Heinlein, Robert A.

VOLUME 5: Sc-Z

Schaeffer, Susan Fromberg 1941-

Schulz, Charles M. 1922-2000

Schwartz, Lynne Sharon 1939-

Scotland, Jay
    See Jakes, John

Sebastian, Lee
    See Silverberg, Robert

Sebold, Alice 1963-

Sedaris, David 1957-

Sendak, Maurice 1928-

Seth, Vikram 1952-

Shaara, Jeff 1952-

Shaara, Michael 1929-1988

Shackleton, C.C.
    See Aldiss, Brian W.

Shaffer, Peter 1926-

Shange, Ntozake 1948-

Shapiro, Karl Jay 1913-2000

Shepard, Sam 1943-

Shepherd, Michael
    See Ludlum, Robert

Shields, Carol 1935-2003

Shreve, Anita 1946-

Siddons, Anne Rivers 1936-

Silko, Leslie 1948-

Sillitoe, Alan 1928-

Silverberg, Robert 1935-

Silverstein, Shel 1932-1999

Simic, Charles 1938-

Simon, David 1960-

Simon, Neil 1927-

Simpson, Louis 1923-

Singer, Isaac
    See Singer, Isaac Bashevis

Singer, Isaac Bashevis 1904-1991

Škvorecký, Josef 1924-

Smiley, Jane 1949-

Smith, Martin
    See Smith, Martin Cruz

Smith, Martin Cruz 1942-

Smith, Rosamond
    See Oates, Joyce Carol

Smith, Wilbur 1933-

Smith, Zadie 1976-

Snicket, Lemony 1970-

Snodgrass, W.D. 1926-

Snyder, Gary 1930-

Solo, Jay
    See Ellison, Harlan

Solwoska, Mara
    See French, Marilyn

Solzhenitsyn, Aleksandr I. 1918-

Somers, Jane
    See Lessing, Doris

Sontag, Susan 1933-2004

Soto, Gary 1952-

Soyinka, Wole 1934-

Spark, Muriel 1918-

Sparks, Nicholas 1965-

Spaulding, Douglas
    See Bradbury, Ray

Spaulding, Leonard
    See Bradbury, Ray

Spencer, Leonard G.
    See Silverberg, Robert

Spender, Stephen 1909-1995

Spiegelman, Art 1948-

Spillane, Mickey 1918-

Stack, Andy
    See Rule, Ann

Stacy, Donald
    See Pohl, Frederik

Stancykowna
    See Szymborska, Wislawa

Stark, Richard
    See Westlake, Donald E.

Steel, Danielle 1947-

Steig, William 1907-

Steinem, Gloria 1934-

Steiner, George 1929-

Steiner, K. Leslie
    See Delany, Samuel R.

Stephenson, Neal 1959-

Sterling, Brett
    See Bradbury, Ray

Sterling, Bruce 1954-

Stine, Jovial Bob
    See Stine, R.L.

Stine, R.L. 1943-

Stone, Robert 1937-

Stone, Rosetta
    See Geisel, Theodor Seuss

Stoppard, Tom 1937-

Straub, Peter 1943-

Styron, William 1925-

Swenson, May 1919-1989

Swift, Graham 1949-

Swithen, John
    See King, Stephen

Symmes, Robert
    See Duncan, Robert

Syruc, J.
    See Milosz, Czeslaw

Szymborska, Wislawa 1923-

Talent Family, The
    See Sedaris, David

Talese, Gay 1932-

Tan, Amy 1952-

Tanner, William
    See Amis, Kingsley

Tartt, Donna 1964-

Taylor, Mildred D. 1943-

Tenneshaw, S.M.
    See Silverberg, Robert

Terkel, Studs 1912-

Theroux, Paul 1941-

Thomas, D.M. 1935-

Thomas, Joyce Carol 1938-

Thompson, Hunter S. 1937-2005

Thornton, Hall
    See Silverberg, Robert

Tiger, Derry
    See Ellison, Harlan

Tornimparte, Alessandra
    See Ginzburg, Natalia

Tremblay, Michel 1942-

Trevor, William 1928-

Trillin, Calvin 1935-

Trout, Kilgore
    See Farmer, Philip José

Turow, Scott 1949-

Tyler, Anne 1941-

Tyree, Omar

Uchida, Yoshiko 1921-1992

Uhry, Alfred 1936-

Uncle Shelby
    See Silverstein, Shel

Updike, John 1932-

Urban Griot
    See Tyree, Omar

Uris, Leon 1924-2003

Urmuz
    See Codrescu, Andrei

Vance, Gerald
    See Silverberg, Robert

Van Duyn, Mona 1921-2004

Vargas Llosa, Mario 1936-

Verdu, Matilde
    See Cela, Camilo José

Vidal, Gore 1925-

Vile, Curt
    See Moore, Alan

Vine, Barbara
    See Rendell, Ruth

Vizenor, Gerald Robert 1934-

Vogel, Paula A. 1951-

Voigt, Cynthia 1942-

Vollmann, William T. 1959-

Vonnegut, Kurt, Jr. 1922-

Vosce, Trudie
    See Ozick, Cynthia

Wakoski, Diane 1937-

Walcott, Derek 1930-

Walker, Alice 1944-

Walker, Margaret 1915-1998

Wallace, David Foster 1962-

Walley, Byron
    See Card, Orson Scott

Ware, Chris 1967-

Warren, Robert Penn 1905-1989

Warshofsky, Isaac
    See Singer, Isaac Bashevis

Wasserstein, Wendy 1950-2006

Watson, James D. 1928-

Watson, John H.
    See Farmer, Philip José

Watson, Larry 1947-

Watson, Richard F.
    See Silverberg, Robert

Ways, C.R.
    See Blount, Roy, Jr.

Weldon, Fay 1931-

Wells, Rebecca

Welty, Eudora 1909-2001

West, Edwin
    See Westlake, Donald E.

West, Owen
    See Koontz, Dean R.

West, Paul 1930-

Westlake, Donald E. 1933-

White, Edmund 1940-

Wideman, John Edgar 1941-

Wiesel, Elie 1928-

Wilbur, Richard 1921-

Williams, C.K. 1936-

Williams, Juan 1954-

Williams, Tennessee 1911-1983

Willis, Charles G.
    See Clarke, Arthur C.

Wilson, August 1945-2005

Wilson, Dirk
    See Pohl, Frederik

Wilson, Edward O. 1929-

Winterson, Jeanette 1959-

Wolf, Naomi 1962-

Wolfe, Gene 1931-

Wolfe, Tom 1931-

Wolff, Tobias 1945-

Woodiwiss, Kathleen E. 1939-

Woodson, Jacqueline 1964-

Wouk, Herman 1915-

Wright, Charles 1935-

Wright, Judith 1915-2000

Xingjian, Gao 1940-

Yolen, Jane 1939-

York, Simon
    See Heinlein, Robert A.

Zelazny, Roger 1937-1995

Zindel, Paul 1936-2003

A

ABBEY, Edward 1927-1989

PERSONAL: Born January 29, 1927, in Home, PA; died of internal bleeding due to a circulatory disorder, March 14, 1989, in Oracle, AZ; buried in a desert in the southwestern United States; son of Paul Revere (a farmer) and Mildred (a teacher; maiden name, Postlewaite) Abbey; married Jean Schmechalon, August 5, 1950 (divorced, 1952); married Rita Deanin, November 20, 1952 (divorced, August 25, 1965); married Judith Pepper, 1965 (died, July 4, 1970); married Renee Dowling, February 10, 1974 (divorced, 1980); married Clarke Cartwright, May 5, 1982; children: (with Deanin) Joshua Nathanael, Aaron Paul; (with Pepper) Susannah Mildred; (with Cartwright) Rebecca Claire, Benjamin Cartwright. *Education:* University of New Mexico, B.A., 1951, M.A., 1956; attended University of Edinburgh. *Politics:* "Agrarian anarchist." *Religion:* Piute.

CAREER: Writer. Park ranger and fire lookout for National Park Service in the southwest United States, 1956-71; University of Arizona, Tuscon, teacher of creative writing, beginning 1981, became full professor, 1988. *Military service:* U.S. Army, 1945-46.

AWARDS, HONORS: Fulbright fellow, 1951-52; Wallace Stegner Creative Writing Fellowship, Stanford University, 1957; Western Heritage Award for Best Novel, 1963, for *Fire on the Mountain;* Guggenheim fellow, 1975; American Academy of Arts and Letters award, 1987 (declined).

WRITINGS:

NOVELS

Jonathan Troy, Dodd (New York, NY), 1956.
The Brave Cowboy, Dodd (New York, NY), 1958, reprint published as *The Brave Cowboy: An Old Tale in a New Time,* University of New Mexico Press (Albuquerque, NM), 1977.

Fire on the Mountain, Dial (New York, NY), 1962.
Black Sun, Simon & Schuster (New York, NY), 1971, published as *Sunset Canyon,* Talmy (London, England), 1972.
The Monkey Wrench Gang, Lippincott (Philadelphia, PA), 1975.
Good News, Dutton (New York, NY), 1980.
Confessions of a Barbarian (bound with *Red Knife Valley* by Jack Curtis), Capra (Santa Barbara, CA), 1986, revised edition published as *Confessions of a Barbarian: Selections from the Journals of Edward Abbey, 1951-1989,* edited and with an introduction by David Petersen, Little, Brown (Boston, MA), 1994.
The Fool's Progress, Holt (New York, NY), 1988.
Hayduke Lives!, Little, Brown (Boston, MA), 1990.

NONFICTION

Desert Solitaire: A Season in the Wilderness, illustrated by Peter Parnall, McGraw (New York, NY), 1968, reprint published as *Desert Solitaire,* University of Arizona Press (Tucson, AZ), 1988.
Appalachian Wilderness: The Great Smoky Mountains, photographs by Eliot Porter, Dutton (New York, NY), 1970.
(With Philip Hyde) *Slickrock: The Canyon Country of Southeast Utah,* Sierra Club, 1971.
(With others) *Cactus Country,* Time-Life (New York, NY), 1973.
The Journey Home: Some Words in Defense of the American West, illustrated by Jim Stiles, Dutton (New York, NY), 1977.
Back Roads of Arizona, photographs by Earl Thollander, Northland Press, 1978, published as *Arizona's Scenic Byways,* 1992.
The Hidden Canyon: A River Journey, photographs by John Blaustein, Viking (New York, NY), 1978.
(With David Muench) *Desert Images: An American Landscape,* Chanticleer (New York, NY), 1979.
Abbey's Road: Take the Other, Dutton (New York, NY), 1979.

(Self-illustrated) *Down the River,* Dutton (New York, NY), 1982.

(With John Nichols) *In Praise of Mountain Lions,* Albuquerque Sierra Club (Albuquerque, NM), 1984.

Beyond the Wall: Essays from the Outside, Holt (New York, NY), 1984.

(Editor and illustrator) *Slumgullion Stew: An Edward Abbey Reader,* Dutton (New York, NY), 1984, published as *The Best of Edward Abbey,* Sierra Club Books (San Francisco, CA), 1988.

One Life at a Time, Please, Holt (New York, NY), 1988.

Vox Clamantis in Deserto: Some Notes from a Secret Journal, Rydal Press (Santa Fe, NM), 1989, published as *A Voice Crying in the Wilderness: Essays from a Secret Journal,* illustrated by Andrew Rush, St. Martin's Press (New York, NY), 1990.

The Serpents of Paradise: A Reader, edited by John Macrae, Holt (New York, NY), 1995.

OTHER

(Essayist) Thomas Miller, *Desert Skin,* University of Utah Press (Salt Lake City, UT), 1994.

Earth Apples: The Poetry of Edward Abbey, collected and introduced by David Peterson, illustrated by Michael McCurdy, St. Martin's Press (New York, NY), 1994.

Also author of introductions for books, including *Walden,* by Henry D. Thoreau, G.M. Smith (Salt Lake City, UT), 1981; *Ecodefense: A Field Guide to Monkeywrenching,* edited by Dave Foreman, Ned Ludd Books, 1987; *The Land of Little Rain,* by Mary Austin, Viking (New York, NY), 1988; and *Wilderness on the Rocks,* by Howie Wolke, Ned Ludd Books, 1991. Contributor to books, including *Utah Wilderness Photography: An Exhibition,* Utah Arts Council, 1978; *Images from the Great West,* edited by Marnie Walker Gaede, Chaco Press (La Cañada, CA), 1990; *Late Harvest: Rural American Writing,* edited by David R. Pichaske, Paragon House (New York, NY), 1991; and *The Best of Outside: The First 20 Years,* Vintage Departures (New York, NY), 1998. A collection of Abbey's manuscripts is housed at the University of Arizona, Tucson.

ADAPTATIONS: The Brave Cowboy was adapted for film and released as *Lonely Are the Brave,* starring Kirk Douglas and Walter Matthau, 1962; *Fire on the Mountain* was adapted for film, 1981.

SIDELIGHTS: Edward Abbey was best known for his hard-hitting, frequently bitter, and usually irreverent defense of the world's wilderness areas. Anarchistic and outspoken, he was called everything from America's crankiest citizen to the godfather of modern environmental activism. Abbey himself strenuously resisted any attempt to classify him as a naturalist, environmentalist, or anything else. "If a label is required," Burt A. Folkart quoted him as saying in the *Los Angeles Times,* "say that I am one who loves the unfenced country." His favorite places were the deserts and mountains of the American West, and the few people who won his respect were those who knew how to live on that land without spoiling it. The many targets of his venom ranged from government agencies and gigantic corporations responsible for the rape of the wild country, to cattle ranchers grazing their herds on public lands, to simple-minded tourists who, according to Abbey, defile the solitude with their very presence.

Born on a small farm in Appalachia, Abbey hitchhiked west in 1946, following one year of service in the U.S. Army. Captivated by the wide-open spaces of Arizona, New Mexico, and Utah, he stayed there, studying philosophy and English at the University of New Mexico. His first novel, *Jonathan Troy,* shows the influence of the philosophical works he was reading in college, including the writings of William Godwin, Pierre-Joseph Proudhon, Karl Marx, and Michael Bakunin. Published in 1954, *Jonathan Troy* is the story of a self-involved young man who yearns to escape his Pennsylvania home for the open spaces of the West. He finally realizes his dream, but not without overcoming many problems first. The greatest difficulty is the loss of his anarchist father, Nat, who is wrongly killed by a rookie policeman. Jonathan's dreams are also imperiled by a shallow young woman who tries to trap him into marriage. He is threatened by his friendship with his English teacher, who reinforces in him his father's radical politics. Ultimately, Jonathan sees that life in the East has become impossible for him, and the story ends with him heading West, lured by the promise of a new way of life there. The novel is notable for its depiction of the conflict between wilderness and civilization, a theme that would always be central to Abbey's work. It is also distinguished by "Abbey's descriptions of an industrial wreckage visited on the Pennsylvania coal country," remarked an essayist for the *Dictionary of Literary Biography.* "These descriptions are important because they mark the first expressions of Abbey's environmental awareness. The dialogue is the weak element of the novel, particularly Jonathan's ponderous interior monologues."

Abbey's next novel, *The Brave Cowboy,* enjoyed somewhat greater success than *Jonathan Troy*—particularly after it was adapted into the film *Lonely Are the Brave.*

The novel features Jack Burns, a nineteenth-century-style cowboy whose rugged individualism has become anachronistic in modern New Mexico. Burns rides his horse into modern Duke City, intent on helping his friend Paul Bondi, a draft resister serving a jail term. Burns undertakes this rescue by getting arrested so that he will be imprisoned with Bondi. The plot twists when Bondi will not follow Burns into the night and to freedom. Burns then runs for Mexico, pursued by the authorities, in a compelling chase story that includes his bringing down a helicopter with a small-caliber rifle. In a similar story, *Fire on the Mountain,* Abbey explores the struggles of John Vogelin as he attempts to prevent the White Sands Missile Range from encroaching on his ranch land in southern New Mexico.

Desert Solitaire, published in 1968, is drawn from Abbey's experiences as a forest ranger and fire lookout. His first nonfiction work was also one of his greatest successes. *Desert Solitaire* opens with a truculent preface, in which the author expresses his hope that serious critics, librarians, and professors will intensely dislike his book. In the body of the book, which compresses many of Abbey's experiences with the Park Service and Forest Service into the framework of one cycle of the seasons, readers find both harsh criticism and poetic description, all related to the landscape of the West and what mankind is doing to it. Freeman Tilden, reviewing *Desert Solitaire* in *National Parks,* recommended the book, "vehemence, egotism, bad taste and all. Partly because we need angry young men to remind us that there is plenty we should be angry about. . . . Partly because Abbey is an artist with words. There are pages and pages of delicious prose, sometimes almost magical in their evocation of the desert scene. . . . How this man can write! But he can do more than write. His prehension of the natural environment—of raw nature—is so ingenuous, so implicit, that we wonder if the pre-Columbian aborigines didn't see their environment just that way."

In a review of *Desert Solitaire* for the *New York Times Book Review,* Pulitzer Prize-winning writer Edwin Way Teale noted that Abbey's work as a park ranger brought him to the wilderness before the invasion of "the parked trailers, their windows blue tinged at night while the inmates, instead of watching the desert stars, watch TV and listen to the canned laughter of Hollywood." Calling the book "a voice crying in the wilderness, for the wilderness," Teale warned that it is also "rough, tough and combative. The author is a rebel, an eloquent loner. In his introduction, he gives fair warning that the reader may find his pages 'coarse, rude, bad-tempered, violently prejudiced.' But if they are all these, they are

many things besides. His is a passionately felt, deeply poetic book. It has philosophy. It has humor. It has sincerity and conviction. It has its share of nerve tingling adventure in what he describes as a land of surprises, some of them terrible." Teale concluded: "Abbey writes with a deep undercurrent of bitterness. But as is not infrequently the case, the bitter man may be the one who cares enough to be bitter and he often is the one who says things that need to be said. In *Desert Solitaire* those things are set down in lean, racing prose, in a close-knit style of power and beauty. Rather than a balanced book, judicially examining in turn all sides, it is a forceful presentation of one side. And that side needs presenting. It is a side too rarely presented. There will always be others to voice the other side, the side of pressure and power and profit."

While it never made the best-seller lists, *Desert Solitaire* is credited as being a key source of inspiration for the environmental movement that was growing in the late 1960s. Abbey's no-holds-barred book awakened many readers to just how much damage was being done by government and business interests to so-called "public" lands, as did the many other essay collections he published throughout his career. But an even greater influence may have come from his 1975 novel, *The Monkey Wrench Gang.* Receiving virtually no promotion, it nonetheless became an underground classic, selling half a million copies. Within the comic story, which follows the misadventures of four environmentalist terrorists, is a serious message: peaceful protest is inadequate; the ecology movement must become radicalized. The ultimate goal of the Monkey Wrench Gang—blowing up the immense Glen Canyon Dam on the Colorado River—is one Abbey seemed to endorse, and his book provides fairly explicit instructions to anyone daring enough to carry it out. The novel is said to have inspired the formation of the real-life environmental group Earth First!, which impedes the progress of developers and loggers by tactics such as sabotaging bulldozers and booby-trapping trees with chainsaw-destroying spikes. Their term for such tactics: monkeywrenching.

National Observer reviewer Sheldon Frank called *The Monkey Wrench Gang* a "sad, hilarious, exuberant, vulgar fairy tale filled with long chase sequences and careful conspiratorial scheming. As in all fairy tales, the characters are pure cardboard, unbelievable in every respect. But they are delightful." A contributor to the London *Times* observed that the book is "less a work of fiction . . . than an incitement to environmentalists to take the law into their own hands, often by means of vandalizing whatever they considered to be themselves examples of vandalism and overkill."

The Monkey Wrench Gang is possibly Abbey's best-known work, but the author's personal favorite of his more than twenty books was the bulky, largely autobiographical novel *The Fool's Progress*. "From the outset of this cross-country story it seems almost impossible to separate Edward Abbey from his narrator," observed Howard Coale in the *New York Times Book Review*. "The harsh, humorous, damn-it-all voice of Henry Lightcap is identical to the voice in the author's many essays." In Coale's opinion, the book was too "self-involved" to be a really successful work of fiction, although it contained some excellent descriptive passages. Other commentators agreed that the book was flawed. John Skow wrote in *Time*, "Abbey . . . is feeling sorry for his hero and probably for himself too. What saves the book is that he is skilled enough to pull sympathetic readers into his own mood of regret." "Abbey is not for everybody," summarized Kerry Luft in his *Chicago Tribune* assessment. "He's about as subtle as a wrecking ball. Some might call him sexist or downright misogynistic and point out that his female characters tend to be shallow stereotypes. I can only agree. But for those readers with the gumption and the stomach to stay with him, Abbey is a delight."

Abbey's last act contributed to his legend as a rugged individualist. When he realized he was terminally ill, he left the care of his doctors and checked himself out of the hospital. Following instructions he had set down years earlier in his journal, his wife and friends took him into the desert so that he could die under the stars. After one night went by and he was still alive, Abbey was taken back to his cabin home until the end came. Then his body was taken back into the desert and buried illegally there in a secret location.

Shortly before his death, Abbey had completed a sequel to *The Monkey Wrench Gang*, titled *Hayduke Lives!* Published posthumously, *Hayduke Lives!* finds most of the cast of the earlier novel settled comfortably into middle-class lives, only to be galvanized into action again by the reappearance of their leader, thought to be long dead. Critical assessment of the sequel varied widely. Grace Lichtenstein, reviewing it in the *Washington Post Book World*, found "the entire theme of ecotage" to be "shopworn," while *Chicago Tribune* editor David E. Jones stated that "the fun-loving bawdiness [of the original] is still there, and the camaraderie and dedication," along with "an unexpected darker side."

Excerpts from Abbey's journals and a collection of his essays were also published posthumously. *Confessions of a Barbarian: Selections from the Journals of Edward Abbey, 1951-1989* includes 368 pages from the writer's copious journals. His acid pen ranges over subjects such as aging, suicide, music, and literature. Assessing the book in *Backpacker*, Peter Lewis observed that Abbey proves his ability to "inspire and infuriate. . . . It's spirited stuff. Some of the highlights center around his closely observed, tack-sharp sketches of places he knew and loved. Abbey was as nimble as they come when summoning emotions surrounding a landscape, and the desert Southwest has had few who could better sing its praises." Roland Wulbert concurred in *Booklist* that Abbey is "both compelling and infuriating," and added, "His journals show that he didn't so much find a voice as mature the one he always had."

The Serpents of Paradise: A Reader is a collection of essays, travel pieces, and works of fiction by Abbey, organized to parallel events in Abbey's own life. His fiction is represented by excerpts from *The Brave Cowboy, The Fool's Progress,* and *The Monkey Wrench Gang,* while the nonfiction is drawn from *Desert Solitaire* and numerous other sources. The pieces here reveal Abbey as "a true independent, a self-declared extremist and 'desert mystic,'" as well as "a hell of a good writer," observed Donna Seaman in *Booklist*. "Irreverent about man and reverent toward nature, Abbey wielded his pen as a weapon in the battle for freedom and wilderness and against arrogance and greed." A *Publishers Weekly* reviewer commented that *The Serpents of Paradise* "makes for a splendid summary of his best work—though it does not slight his faults," which include "occasional outbursts of xenophobia and old-fashioned sexism," as well as "gleefully overweening destructive fantasies. . . . Anyone who doesn't already know his work will find this volume, culled from more than a dozen books of fiction and nonfiction, an addictive introduction."

Reflecting in the *New York Times Book Review* on Abbey's body of work, Edward Hoagland called him "the nonpareil 'nature writer' of recent decades." Hoagland went on: "He was uneven and self-indulgent as a writer and often scanted his talent by working too fast. But he had about him an authenticity that springs from the page and is beloved by a rising generation of readers." "*Desert Solitaire* stands among the towering works of American nature writing," stated Lichtenstein. "Abbey's polemic essays on such subjects as cattle subsidies and Mexican immigrants, scattered through a half-dozen volumes, remain so angry, so infuriating yet so relevant that they still provoke arguments among his followers. As for his outdoors explorations, no one wrote more melodic hymns to the red rocks and rivers of the Southwest; no one ever defended them with more elan. It is in those nonfiction odes to the wilderness, by turns cantankerous and lyrical . . . that Abbey lives, forever."

Speaking for himself in the essay "A Writer's Credo," Abbey declared, "I write to entertain my friends and exasperate our enemies. I write to record the truth of our time as best I can see it. To investigate the comedy and tragedy of human relationships. To oppose, resist, and sabotage the contemporary drift toward a global technocratic police state, whatever its ideological coloration. I write to oppose injustice, to defy power, and to speak for the voiceless. I write to make a difference."

BIOGRAPHICAL AND CRITICAL SOURCES:

BOOKS

Abbey, Edward, *Confessions of a Barbarian: Selections from the Journals of Edward Abbey, 1951-1989,* edited by David Petersen, original drawings by Abbey, Little, Brown (Boston, MA), 1994.

Abbey, Edward, *One Life at a Time,* Holt (New York, NY), 1988.

Balassi, William, and others, editors, *This Is about Vision: Interviews with Southwestern Writers,* University of New Mexico Press (Albuquerque, NM), 1990.

Berry, Wendell, *What Are People For?,* North Point (San Francisco, CA), 1990.

Bishop, James, Jr., with Charles Bowden, *Epitaph for a Desert Anarchist: The Life and Legacy of Edward Abbey,* Atheneum (New York, NY), 1994.

Calahan, James M., *Edward Abbey: A Life,* University of Arizona Press (Tucson, AZ), 2001.

Contemporary Literary Criticism, Thomson Gale (Detroit, MI), Volume 36, 1986, Volume 59, 1990.

Dictionary of Literary Biography, Volume 256: *Twentieth-Century Western Writers, Third Series,* Thomson Gale (Detroit, MI), 2002.

Foreman, Dave, *Confessions of an Eco-Warrior,* Harmony Books (New York, NY), 1991.

Hafen, Lyman and Milo McCowan, *Edward Abbey: An Interview at Pack Creek Ranch,* Vinegar Tom (Santa FE, NM), 1991.

Hepworth, James, and Gregory McNamee, editors, *Resist Much, Obey Little: Some Notes on Edward Abbey,* Dream Garden (Salt Lake City, UT), 1985.

Loeffler, Jack, *Adventures with Ed—A Portrait of Abbey,* University of New Mexico Press (Albuquerque, NM), 2002.

McCann, Garth, *Edward Abbey,* Boise State University (Boise, ID), 1977.

McClintock, James, *Nature's Kindred Spirits: Aldo Leopold, Joseph Wood Krutch, Edward Abbey, Annie Dillard, and Gary Snyder,* University of Wisconsin Press (Madison, WI), 1994.

Quigley, Peter, editor, *Coyote in the Maze: Tracking Edward Abbey in a World of Words,* University of Utah Press (Salt Lake City, UT), 1998.

Ronald, Ann, *The New West of Edward Abbey,* University of New Mexico Press (Albuquerque, NM), 1982.

St. James Encyclopedia of Popular Culture, St. James Press (Detroit, MI), 2000.

Scribner Encyclopedia of American Lives, Volume 2: *1986-1990,* Scribner (New York, NY), 1999.

Stegner, Wallace, and Richard W. Etulain, *Conversations with Wallace Stegner on Western History and Literature,* revised edition, University of Utah Press (Salt Lake City, UT), 1990.

PERIODICALS

Albuquerque Journal, November 4, 2001, "Book Attempts to Release Edward Abbey from Myth," p. F8.

America, April 9, 2001, Thomas J. McCarthy, "The Ultimate Sanctum," p. 6.

Audubon, July, 1989, pp. 14, 16.

Backpacker, December, 1994, Peter Lewis, review of *Confessions of a Barbarian,* p. 115.

Best Sellers, June 15, 1971.

Booklist, August, 1994, John Mort, review of *Earth Apples: The Poetry of Edward Abbey,* p. 2018; September 15, 1994, Roland Wulbert, review of *Confessions of a Barbarian,* p. 100; March 1, 1995, Donna Seaman, review of *The Serpents of Paradise: A Reader,* p. 1173.

Canadian Dimension, May, 2001, Louis Proyect, "Lonely Are the Brave," p. 43.

Chicago Tribune, February 14, 1988, section 14, p. 3; November 29, 1988; March 15, 1989; February 12, 1990.

Chicago Tribune Book World, November 30, 1980, section 7, p. 5.

Christian Science Monitor, July 27, 1977.

Growth and Change, summer, 1995, Nathanael Dresser, "Cultivating Wilderness: The Place of Land in the Fiction of Ed Abbey and Wendell Berry," p. 350.

Harper's, August, 1971; February, 1988, pp. 42-44.

Library Journal, January 1, 1968; July, 1977; August, 1994, Frank Allen, review of *Earth Apples: The Poetry of Edward Abbey,* p. 90; September 1, 1994, Tim Markus, review of *Confessions of a Barbarian,* p. 181; February 15, 1995, Cathy Sabol, review of *The Serpents of Paradise,* p. 155.

Los Angeles Times, October 22, 1980.

Los Angeles Times Book Review, June 17, 1979; May 16, 1982, p. 1; November 29, 1987, p. 10; January 24, 1988, p. 12; May 15, 1988, p. 14; November 20, 1988, p. 3; September 2, 1989, p. 8; January 7, 1990, p. 1; March 26, 1995, p. 6.

Nation, May 1, 1982, pp. 533-535.

National Observer, September 6, 1975, p. 17.

National Parks, February, 1968, pp. 22-23.

National Review, August 10, 1984, pp. 48-49.

New Yorker, July 17, 1971.

New York Times, June 19, 1979; March 15, 1989; May 11, 1997, Lesley Hazleton, "Arguing with a Ghost in Yosemite," p. XX37; February 10, 2002, T. Coraghessan Boyle, "A Voice Griping in the Wilderness," p. 8; April 29, 2002, Blaine Harden, "A Friend, Not a Role Model: Remembering Edward Abbey, Who Loved Words, Women, Beer and the Desert," p. E1.

New York Times Book Review, January 28, 1968, p. 7; July 31, 1977, pp. 10-11; August 5, 1979, pp. 8, 21; December 14, 1980, p. 10; May 30, 1982, p. 6; April 15, 1984, p. 34; December 16, 1984, p. 27; February 28, 1988, p. 27; May 1, 1988; December 18, 1988, p. 22; May 7, 1989, Edward Hoagland, "Standing Tough in the Desert," pp. 44-45; February 4, 1990, p. 18; July 8, 1990, p. 28; January 27, 1991, p. 32; December 11, 1994, Tim Sandlin, review of *Confessions of a Barbarian,* p. 11; June 11, 1995, p. 18; March 17, 1996, p. 32.

Publishers Weekly, October 5, 1984, p. 85; August 12, 1988, p. 439; November 11, 1988, pp. 34-36; July 25, 1994, p. 44; September 12, 1994, p. 75; January 23, 1995, review of *The Serpents of Paradise,* p. 52.

Seattle Times, January 20, 2002, Anne Stephenson, "Straight-on Look at Writer Edward Abbey," p. J9.

Southwest Review, winter, 1976, pp. 108-111; winter, 1980, pp. 102-105.

Time, November 28, 1988, p. 98.

Washington Post, December 31, 1979; January 5, 1988.

Washington Post Book World, March 24, 1968; June 25, 1979; May 30, 1982, p. 3; April 1, 1984, p. 9; April 3, 1988, p. 12; December 31, 1989, p. 12; January 28, 1990, p. 5; April 1, 1990, p. 8; April 22, 1990, p. 12; June 10, 1990, p. 15.

Western American Literature, fall, 1966, pp. 197-207; May, 1989, pp. 37-43; May, 1993, Paul T. Bryant, "The Structure and Unity of *Desert Solitaire,*" pp. 3-19.

Wilson Library Bulletin, March, 1994, Preston Hoffman, review of *Hayduke Lives!* (sound recording), p. 116.

Zephyr, April-May, 1999, interview with Edward Abbey.

ONLINE

Edward Abbey, http://www.abbeyweb.net/ (July 20, 2003).

OTHER

Edward Abbey: A Voice in the Wilderness (documentary film), 1993.

OBITUARIES:

PERIODICALS

Chicago Tribune, March 15, 1989.

Detroit Free Press, March 15, 1989.

Los Angeles Times, March 16, 1989; May 22, 1989.

New York Times, March 15, 1989.

Times (London), March 28, 1989.

Washington Post, March 17, 1989.

*   *   *

ABE, Kobo 1924-1993

PERSONAL: Born March 7, 1924, in Tokyo, Japan; died of heart failure, January 22, 1993, in Tokyo, Japan; son of Asakichi (a doctor) and Yorimi Abe; married Machi Yamada (an artist), March, 1947; children: Neri (daughter). *Education:* Tokyo University, M.D., 1948.

CAREER: Novelist and playwright. Director and producer of the Kobo Theatre Workshop in Tokyo, Japan, beginning in 1973.

MEMBER: American Academy of Arts and Sciences.

AWARDS, HONORS: Post-war literature prize, 1950; Akutagawa prize, 1951, for *Kabe-S karumashi no hanzai;* Kishida prize for drama, 1958; Yomiuri literature prize, 1962; special jury prize from Cannes Film Festival, 1964, for film *Woman in the Dunes;* Tanizaki prize for drama, 1967; L.H.D., Columbia University, 1975.

WRITINGS:

NOVELS IN ENGLISH TRANSLATION

Daiyon Kampyoki, Kodan-sha (Tokyo, Japan), 1959, translated by E. Dale Saunders as *Inter Ice Age Four,* Knopf (New York, NY), 1970.

Suna no onna, Shincho-sha (Tokyo, Japan), 1962, translated by E. Dale Saunders as *The Woman in the Dunes,* Knopf (New York, NY), 1964, adapted screenplay with Hiroshi Teshigahara published under same title, Phaedra (New York, NY), 1966, 2nd edition, 1971.

Tanin no kao, Kodan-sha (Tokyo, Japan), 1964, translated by E. Dale Saunders as *The Face of Another,* Knopf (New York, NY), 1966, Vintage (New York, NY), 2003.

Moetsukita chizu, Shincho-sha (Tokyo, Japan), 1967, translated by E. Dale Saunders as *The Ruined Map,* Knopf (New York, NY), 1969, Vintage (New York, NY), 2001.

Hakootoko, Shincho-sha (Tokyo, Japan), 1973, translation published as *The Box Man,* Knopf (New York, NY), 1975.

Mikkai, 1977, translated by Juliet W. Carpenter as *Secret Rendezvous,* Knopf (New York, NY), 1979.

The Ark Sakura, translated by Juliet W. Carpenter, Knopf (New York, NY), 1988.

The Kangaroo Notebook, translated by Maryellen Toman Mori, Knopf (New York, NY), 1996.

OTHER NOVELS

Owarishi michino shirubeni (title means "The Road Sign at the End of the Road"), Shinzenbi-sha, 1948.

Kabe-S karumashi no hanzai (title means "The Crimes of S. Karma"), Getsuyo-syobo, 1951.

Kiga domei (title means "Hunger Union"), Kodan-sha (Tokyo, Japan), 1954.

Kemonotachi wa kokyo o mezasu (title means "Animals Are Forwarding to Their Natives"), Kodan-sha (Tokyo, Japan), 1957.

Ishi no me (title means "Eyes of Stone"), Shincho-sha (Tokyo, Japan), 1960.

Omaenimo tsumi ga aru (title means "You Are Guilty Too"), Gakusyukenkyusha, 1965.

Enomoto Buyo, Tyuokaron-sha, 1965.

PLAYS IN ENGLISH TRANSLATION

Tomodachi, Enemoto Takeaki, Kawade-syobo, 1967, translated by Donald Keene as *Friends,* Grove (New York, NY), 1969.

Bo ni natta otoko, Shincho-sha (Tokyo, Japan), 1969, translated by Donald Keene as *The Man Who Turned into a Stick* (produced in New York City at Playhouse 46, May, 1986), University of Tokyo Press (Tokyo, Japan), 1975.

Three Plays, translated with an introduction by Donald Keene, Columbia University Press (New York, NY), 1993.

OTHER PLAYS

Seifuku (title means "The Uniform"), Aokisyoten, 1955.

Yurei wa kokoniiru (title means "Here Is a Ghost"), Shincho-sha (Tokyo, Japan), 1959.

Abe Kobe gikyoku zenshu (title means "The Collected Plays of Kobo Abe"), Shincho-sha (Tokyo, Japan), 1970.

Mihitsu no koi (title means "Willful Negligence"), Shincho-sha (Tokyo, Japan), 1971.

Ai no megane wa irogarasu (title means "Love's Spectacles Are Colored Glass"), Shincho-sha (Tokyo, Japan), 1973.

Midoriiro no stocking (title means "Green Stocking"), Shincho-sha (Tokyo, Japan), 1974.

Ue (title means "The Cry of the Fierce Animals"), Shincho-sha (Tokyo, Japan), 1975.

OTHER WORKS

Suichu toshi (short stories; title means "The City in Water"), Togen-sha, 1964.

Yume no tobo (short stories; title means "Runaway in the Dream"), Tokuma-syoten, 1968.

Uchinaro henkyo (essays; title means "Inner Border"), Tyuokoron-sha, 1971.

Abe Kobo zensakuhin (title means "The Collected Works of Kobo Abe"), fifteen volumes, Shincho-sha (Tokyo, Japan), 1972–73.

Han gekiteki ningen (collected lectures; title means "Anti-Dramatic Man"), Tyuokoron-sha, 1973.

Hasso no shuhen (lectures; title means "Circumference of Inspiration"), Shincho-sha (Tokyo, Japan), 1974.

Warau Tsuki (short stories; title means "The Laughing Moon"), Shincho-sha (Tokyo, Japan), 1975.

Ningen sokkuri, Shincho hunko (Tokyo, Japan), 1976.

Shi ni isogu kujiratachi, Shincho-sha (Tokyo, Japan), 1986.

Beyond the Curve (short stories), translated by Juliet W. Carpenter, Kodansha America (New York, NY), 1991.

Tobu otoko (title means "The Flying Man"), Shincho-sha (Tokyo, Japan), 1994.

Abe Kobo zenshu, twenty-nine volumes, Shincho-sha (Tokyo, Japan), 1997.

Also author of *Chinnyusha,* 1952, *Sabakareru kiroku* (title means "Judgment Book of Films"), 1978, and *Toshi e no kairo,* 1980.

SIDELIGHTS: Kobo Abe, Japanese novelist and writer of film scenarios, "occupied a central position among avant-garde artists in Japan," according to *Dictionary of Literary Biography* contributor J. Thomas Rimer. From the early 1950s to his death in 1993, Abe attracted international recognition for his fictional work that explored the postwar Japanese experience in bleak and sometimes surreal terms. His fiction bears little resemblance to the traditional literature of Abe's native country. With its existential themes and what *Saturday Review* contributor Thomas Fitzsimmons described as its "bizarre situations loaded with metaphysical overtones," Abe's work has more in common with that of Samuel Beckett and Franz Kafka, to whom he is often compared.

Abe's preoccupation with modern man's sense of displacement originated during his childhood. Abe grew up in the ancient Manchurian city of Mukden, which was seized from China by the Japanese in 1931. According to *Washington Post* reviewer David Remnick, Abe "was fascinated by the Chinese quality of the town and was appalled by the behavior of the Japanese army during occupation. As a testament to his ambivalence about Japan, he changed his name from Kimfusa to the more Chinese rendering, Kobo. Abe was in high school during the war, and though he once said, 'I longed to be a little fascist,' he never accepted the extreme nationalism of his country in the 1940s. When he heard of Japan's imminent defeat in late 1944, he was 'overjoyed.'" The author's strong feelings against nationalism remained with him, and he once told Remnick, "Place has no role for me. I am rootless." Many critics believe that Abe's alienation from his own country is also the key to his international popularity. As Hisaaki Yamanouchi noted in his book *The Search for Authenticity in Modern Japanese Literature,* "It enabled him to create a literary universe which transcends the author's nationality. He is probably the first Japanese writer whose works, having no distinctly Japanese qualities, are of interest to the Western audience because of their universal relevance."

Abe's first novel to be translated into English was *Suna no onna (The Woman in the Dunes).* In this story, a schoolteacher and amateur entomologist goes to the country for a weekend of insect hunting. He stumbles upon a primitive tribe living in sandpits and becomes their prisoner. Escape is his obsession for a time, but when it is finally possible, he has lost the desire to return to his former identity. Critics praise Abe for both his metaphysical insights and his engrossing description of life in the sandpits. "The story can be taken at many levels," reported a *Times Literary Supplement* reviewer.

"It is an allegory, it shares elements with *Pincher Martin* and Kafka; . . . and it also has the suspense, the realism, and the obsessive regard for detail of a superb thriller. . . . It is a brilliantly original work, which cannot easily be fitted into any category or given any clear literary ancestors. The claustrophobic horror, the sense of physical degradation and bestiality, are conveyed in a prose as distinct and sharp as the sand grains which dominate the book."

The central theme of *The Woman in the Dunes*—loss of identity—reoccurs in most of Abe's subsequent novels. *Moetsukita chizu,* translated as *The Ruined Map,* uses the conventions of detective novels as a framework. Flight and pursuit merge as a private investigator gradually takes on the persona of the very man he has been hired to track down. Earl Mine found *The Ruined Map*'s "combination of the macabre and the realistic" similar to that of *The Woman in the Dunes.* "Although less hallucinatory in its effect, *The Ruined Map* is in the end more terrifying." observed Mine. "Abe has a remarkable talent for creating fables of contemporary experience that manage to be at once rooted in minute detail and expressive of man's plight; but in none of his previous work have the detail and the larger meaning combined so perfectly. The sheer force of accumulating realities is what drives man to madness, what leads him to abscond from himself since he cannot otherwise abscond from the modern world. It is astonishing how successfully Abe renders this effacing of human consciousness in the very mind that is lost." Shane Stevens also reserved high praise for *The Ruined Map,* calling it in the *New York Times Book Review* "a brilliant display of pyrotechnics, a compelling tour de force that seems to have been built lovingly, word by word, sentence by sentence, by a master jeweler of polished prose."

Although Abe's attitudes and concerns were far from those of a typical Japanese writer, some reviewers point out that the author's work was not completely outside his cultural tradition. *The Face of Another* and *Secret Rendezvous* are both presented in the form of journals and letters, a style that dates back to the tenth century in Japan. Furthermore, pointed out William Currie in *Approaches to the Modern Japanese Novel,* "Abe shows a meticulous care for concrete detail worthy of the most confirmed naturalist or realist. His precision and concreteness give the impression of reality to the dream or nightmare. In this regard, Abe, who is sometimes considered thoroughly Western in his approach to literature, is solidly in the Japanese tradition with his emphasis on the concrete and the particular."

A *New Republic* contributor referred to another aspect in which Abe's writing differs from most Western literature. "The Japanese seem to embrace the unspeakable openly, as a form of release, accepting the facets of the imagination Americans often skirt—even in the most lurid popular fiction," stated the writer in his review of Abe's novel *Mikkai,* translated as *Secret Rendezvous. Secret Rendezvous* relates the story of a man's search for his wife, who has been taken to the hospital although she was not sick. The man discovers that the hospital is run by an "incestuous circle of rapists, voyeurs, thirteen-year-old nymphomaniacs, test-tube babies and centaurs." Abe's graphic descriptions of their activities drew negative reactions from many Western critics. Sidney DeVere Brown declared in *World Literature Today,* "The novel would be pornography but for the sterile laboratory in which the explicit scenes are placed." D.J. Enright protested in the *New York Review of Books:* "The paths whether of pursuit or of flight lead through turds, urine, phlegm, vomit, the stench of dead animals. A master of the seedy, Abe seems ambitious to erect it into a universal law." Concluded the *New Republic* reviewer: "Kobo Abe delights in the excessive and the perverse. With its surrealistic setting, its claustrophobic atmosphere, and its increasingly distressing scenes of sexual decadence and violence, *Secret Rendezvous* disturbs rather than titillates."

Doug Lang defended *Secret Rendezvous,* however. His *Washington Post Book World* review calls the plot incoherent, but continues, "fortunately, the novel does not depend on plot for its momentum. It depends much more on the ever-expanding circles of [the protagonist's] nightmarish experience, as Abe propels his main character to the outer perimeters of his existence, where he is confronted with the terrifying absurdity of his life. . . . The hospital is a metaphor for modern Japanese life. . . . *Secret Rendezvous* is very convincing. There is passion in it and a great deal of very bleak humor. Abe's view of things is not a pretty one, but it is well worth our attention." Howard Hibbitt concluded in *Saturday Review* that Abe is the master of the "philosophical thriller" and summarized the strengths of his novels: "Brilliant narrative, rich description and invention, [and] vital moral and intellectual concerns."

Abe's novel *The Ark Sakura* also is considered a dark book. It is about a hermit's preparations for nuclear disaster. Pig, who prefers to be called Mole, constructs an underground "ark" using the profits he made disposing of wastes through the toilet. He invites some outcasts he meets to become his crew, but a group of militant senior citizens has other ideas about whom he should select. "Abe's depiction of the deadly game of survival is hilarious but at the same time leaves us with a chilling sense of apprehension about the brave new world

that awaits us in the future," noted Kevin Keane in the *Los Angeles Times Book Review.* In *The New York Times Book Review,* Edmund White said, "*The Sakura Ark* may be a grim novel, but it is also a large, ambitious work about the lives of outcasts in modern Japan and such troubling themes as ecological destruction, old age, violence and nuclear war."

Other reviewers found the book disappointing. "The idea behind the story, to start with, is interesting enough, the development is not," claimed Louis Allen in the *Times Literary Supplement.* "*The Ark Sakura* is a small disaster," wrote Ivan Gold in the *Washington Post.* "A clumsy translation, marked by solecisms, gibberish and pseudoprose, does not sufficiently distract from the flimsiness beneath."

Beyond the Curve is the first collection of Abe's short fiction published in English. The stories imaginatively merge real and surreal events to explore such themes as human isolation and the fragility of identity. Herbert Mitgang observed in *The New York Times* that "the endings [of the stories] are often left dangling, forcing the reader to stretch his imagination, which isn't a bad endorsement for any book." A critic for the *Economist* felt that the collection "shows Mr. Abe at his best, full of wry humour and images of self-defeat, and obsessed with the idea that alienation is the natural condition of contemporary man." A reviewer for *Publishers Weekly* found that with this gathering of tales, "Abe confirms his reputation as one of Japan's most significant modern writers."

Abe is less-well known in the West for his plays, though these brought him critical acclaim in Japan. Such theater works often mine the same absurdist ground as his novels and stories. *Three Plays,* a 1993 translation including *Involuntary Homicide, Green Stockings,* and *The Ghost Is Here,* demonstrate the "universality to Abe's works," according to Yoshio Iwamoto in *World Literature Today.* The translations of Abe's theatrical works could "only enhance his already considerable reputation in the West," Iwamoto further commented. Tony Dallas, writing in the *Antioch Review,* found "this witty, lyrical, eminently theatrical collection a welcome change from the confessional realism that pervades most contemporary American drama."

Abe's last novel was *The Kangaroo Notebook.* In this strange, surrealistic work, the narrator wakes up one morning to find radishes sprouting from his legs; his experiences get more horrific as he tries to find someone who can help him. David R. Slavitt concluded in the *New York Times Book Review* that *The Kangaroo Notebook* "is essentially an account of a dream experience, and the trouble with nightmares as a mode of literature is that there is nothing much for a protagonist to do. . . . Weirdness just piles up on other weirdness, higher and higher, but there is never an end to it and we never arrive at a reasonable vista." Iwamoto, writing in *World Literature Today,* found the novel a good summing of Abe's oeuvre in that it "refigures with imaginative vigor those ingredients that have become trademarks in the novelist-playwright's works: metamorphosis, the theme of alienation and the problem of personal identity, and the journey motif through a labyrinthine modern dystopia." Iwamoto further thought that though *The Kangaroo Notebook* "lacks the mesmerizing power" of some of Abe's earlier work, "what is evident is the author's still vivid and playful imagination at work conveying his essentially nihilistic vision of life in an absurd and meaningless modern world." A contributor for *Publishers Weekly* found that Abe "deftly blends antic comedy with metaphysical dread while maintaining the internal logic" of its narrative. And Nancy Pearl, reviewing the same work in *Booklist,* praised Abe's "triumphant last novel" as a "supremely fitting end of an illustrious writing career."

BIOGRAPHICAL AND CRITICAL SOURCES:

BOOKS

Contemporary Literary Criticism, Thomson Gale (Detroit, MI), Volume 8, 1978, Volume 22, 1982, Volume 53, 1989, Volume 81, 1994.

Dictionary of Literary Biography, Volume 182: *Japanese Fiction Writers since World War II,* Thomson Gale (Detroit, MI), 1997, pp. 3-10.

Janiera, Armando Martins, *Japanese and Western Literature,* Tuttle (Boston, MA), 1970.

Shields, Nancy K., *Fake Fish: The Theater of Kobo Abe,* Weatherhill (New York, NY), 1996.

Tsurutu, Kinya, editor, *Approaches to the Modern Japanese Novel,* Sophia University (Tokyo, Japan), 1976.

Yamanouchi, Hisaaki, *The Search for Authenticity in Modern Japanese Literature,* Cambridge University Press (New York, NY), 1978.

PERIODICALS

Antioch Review, fall, 1994, Tony Dallas, review of *Three Plays,* p. 651.

Atlantic, October, 1979.

Booklist, April 15, 1996, Nancy Pearl, review of *The Kangaroo Notebook,* p. 1419.

Chicago Tribune Book World, October 7, 1979.

Commonweal, December 21, 1979.

Economist (U.S.), August 3, 1991, "Sand and Tendrils," p. 82.

Globe and Mail (Toronto, Ontario, Canada), May 7, 1988.

International Fiction Review, summer, 1979.

Los Angeles Times Book Review, April 17, 1988, Kevin Keane, review of *The Ark Sakura.*

New Republic, September 22, 1979, review of *Secret Rendezvous.*

New York Review of Books, January 14, 1964; September 27, 1979, D.J. Enright, review of *Secret Rendezvous.*

New York Times, September 27, 1966; June 3, 1969; December 31, 1974; May 25, 1986; March 23, 1991, Herbert Mitgang, review of *Beyond the Curve.*

New York Times Book Review, September 18, 1966; August 3, 1969, Shane Stevens, review of *The Ruined Map;* December 8, 1974; September 9, 1979; April 10, 1988; Edmund White, review of *The Ark Sakura;* March 17, 1991; April 28, 1996, David R. Slavitt, review of *The Kangaroo Notebook,* p. 31.

New York Times Magazine, November 17, 1974.

Publishers Weekly, February 22, 1991, review of *Beyond the Curve,* p. 212; March 11, 1996, review of *The Kangaroo Notebook,* p. 44.

Saturday Review, September 5, 1964; September 10, 1966; October 11, 1969; September 26, 1970.

Spectator, March 18, 1972.

Times (London, England), August 4, 1988.

Times Literary Supplement, March 18, 1965, review of *The Woman in the Dunes;* March 6, 1969; September 3, 1971; March 17, 1972; August 12, 1988, Louis Allen, review of *The Ark Sakura.*

Tribune Books (Chicago, IL), April 24, 1988.

Washington Post, January 20, 1986.

Washington Post Book World, February 21, 1971; October 28, 1979, Doug Lang, review of *Secret Rendezvous;* March 27, 1988; April 21, 1991.

World Literature Today, winter, 1981; summer, 1994, Yoshio Iwamoto, review of *Three Plays,* p. 637; winter, 1997, Yoshio Iwamoto, review of *The Kangaroo Notebook,* p. 228.

ONLINE

Salon.com, http://www.salon.com/ (March 28, 1997).

OBITUARIES:

PERIODICALS

Chicago Tribune, January 24, 1993, sec. 2, p. 6.
Los Angeles Times, January 23, 1993, p. A22.
Times (London, England), January 25, 1993, p. 19.
Washington Post, January 23, 1993, p. C4.

* * *

ACHEBE, Albert Chinualumogu
  See ACHEBE, Chinua

* * *

ACHEBE, Chinua 1930-
  (Albert Chinualumogu Achebe)

PERSONAL: Pronounced "CHIN-yoo-uh ah-CHAY-bee." Born November 16, 1930, in Ogidi, Nigeria; son of Isaiah Okafo (an Anglican churchman and teacher) and Janet N. Iloegbunam Achebe; married Christiana Chinwe Okoli, September 10, 1961; children: Chinelo (daughter), Ikechukwu (son), Chidi (son), Nwando (daughter). *Education:* Church Mission Society School; a colonial government secondary school in which English was enforced; Government College Umuahia, 1944-47; and University College, Ibadan, 1948-53, B.A. (under London University) 1953; studied broadcasting at the British Broadcasting Corporation, London, 1956. *Hobbies and other interests:* Music.

ADDRESSES: Home—P.O. Box 53 Nsukka, Anambra State, Nigeria. *Office*—Institute of African Studies, University of Nigeria, Nsukka, Anambra State, Nigeria; and c/o Bard College, P.O. Box 41, Annandale on Hudson, NY, 12504. *E-mail*—achebe@bard.edu.

CAREER: Writer. Nigerian Broadcasting Company (NBC), Lagos, Nigeria, talk show producer, 1954-57, controller of Eastern Region in Enugu, Nigeria, 1958-61, founder and director of Voice of Nigeria, 1961-66; University of Nigeria, Nsukka, senior research fellow, 1967-72, professor of English, 1976-81, professor emeritus, 1985—; Anambra State University of Technology, Enugu, pro-chancellor and chair of council, 1986-88; University of Massachusetts-Amherst, professor, 1987-88. Served on diplomatic missions for Biafra during the Nigerian Civil War, 1967-69. Visiting professor of English at University of Massachusetts-Amherst, 1972-75, and University of Connecticut, Afro-American Studies department, 1975-76. University of California, Los Angeles, Regents' lecturer, 1984; Cambridge University, Clare Hall, visiting fellow and Ashby lecturer, 1993; Charles P. Stevenson Professor of Languages and Literatures at Bard College, Annandale-on-Hudson, NY, 1993—; lecturer at universities in Nigeria and the United States; speaker at events in numerous countries throughout the world. Chair, Citadel Books Ltd., Enugu, Nigeria, 1967; founding editor, Heinemann African Writers series, 1962-72, director, Heinemann Educational Books Ltd., Ibadan, Nigeria, 1970—; director, Nwamife Publishers Ltd., Enugu, Nigeria, 1970—. Founder and publisher, *Uwa Ndi Igbo: A Bilingual Journal of Igbo Life and Arts,* 1984—. Governor, Newsconcern International Foundation, 1983. Member, University of Lagos Council, 1966, East Central State Library Board, 1971-72, Anambra State Arts Council, 1977-79, and National Festival Committee, 1983; director, Okike Arts Centre, Nsukka, 1984—. Deputy national president of People's Redemption Party, 1983; president of town union, Ogidi, Nigeria, beginning 1986; goodwill ambassador for U.N. Population Fund, 1999.

MEMBER: International Social Prospects Academy (Geneva), Writers and Scholars International (London), Writers and Scholars Educational Trust (London), Commonwealth Arts Organization (member of executive committee, 1981—), Association of Nigerian Authors (founder; president, 1981-86), Ghana Association of Writers (fellow), Royal Society of Literature (London), Modern Language Association of America (honorary fellow), American Academy and Institute of Arts and Letters (honorary member).

AWARDS, HONORS: Margaret Wrong Memorial Prize, 1959, for *Things Fall Apart;* Rockefeller travel fellowship to East and Central Africa, 1960-1961; Nigerian National Trophy, 1961, for *No Longer at Ease;* UNESCO fellowship for creative artists for travel to United States and Brazil, 1963; Jock Campbell/ *New Statesman* Award, 1965, for *Arrow of God;* Commonwealth Poetry Prize, 1972, for *Beware, Soul-Brother, and Other Poems;* Neil Gunn international fellow, Scottish Arts Council, 1975; Lotus Award for Afro-Asian Writers, 1975; Nigerian National Merit Award, 1979; named to the Order of the Federal Republic of Nigeria, 1979; Commonwealth Foundation senior visiting practitioner award, 1984; *A Man of the People* was cited in Anthony Burgess's 1984 book *Ninety-nine Novels: The Best in England since 1939;* Booker Prize nomination, 1987, for *Anthills of the Savannah,* Champion Award,

1996. D.Litt., Dartmouth College, 1972, University of Southampton, 1975, University of Ife, 1978, University of Nigeria, Nsukka, 1981, University of Kent, 1982, Mount Allison University, 1984, University of Guelph, 1984, and Franklin Pierce College, 1985, Ibadan University, 1989, Skidmore College, 1991, City College of New York, 1992, Fichburg State College, 1994, Harvard University, 1996, Binghamton University, 1996, Bates College, 1996, Trinity College, Connecticut, 1999; D.Univ., University of Stirling, 1975, Open University, 1989; LL.D., University of Prince Edward Island, 1976, Georgetown University, 1990, Port Harcourt University, 1991; D.H.L., University of Massachusetts-Amherst, 1977, Westfield College, 1989, New School for Social Research, 1991, Hobart and William Smith College, 1991, Marymount Manhattan College, 1991, Colgate University, 1993; nominated for Nobel prize in literature, 2000; German Booksellers Peace Prize for promoting human understanding through literature, 2002.

WRITINGS:

NOVELS

Things Fall Apart, Heinemann (London, England), 1958, Obolensky (New York, NY), 1959, abridged and annotated edition published as *Things Fall Apart: An Adapted Classic,* adapted by Sandra Widner, Globe Fearon (Lebanon, IN), 2000; *Things Fall Apart: With Related Readings,* Paradigm (St. Paul, MN), 2002.

No Longer at Ease, Heinemann (London, England), 1960, Obolensky, 1961, second edition, Fawcett (Uncasville, CT), 1988.

Arrow of God, Heinemann (London, England), 1964, John Day (New York, NY), 1967.

A Man of the People, John Day (New York, NY), 1966, published with an introduction by K.W.J. Post, Doubleday (New York, NY), 1967.

Anthills of the Savannah, Anchor Books (New York, NY), 1988.

Things Fall Apart has been translated into 45 languages.

JUVENILE

Chike and the River, Cambridge University Press (Cambridge, England), 1966.

(With John Iroaganachi) *How the Leopard Got His Claws,* Nwankwo-Ifejika (Enugu, Nigeria), 1972, bound with *Lament of the Deer,* by Christopher Okigbo, Third Press (New York, NY), 1973.

The Flute, Fourth Dimension Publishers (Enugu, Nigeria), 1978.

The Drum, Fourth Dimension Publishers (Enugu, Nigeria), 1978.

POETRY

Beware, Soul-Brother, and Other Poems, Nwankwo-Ifejika (Engigu, Nigeria), 1971, Doubleday (New York, NY), 1972, revised edition, Heinemann (London, England), 1972.

Christmas in Biafra, and Other Poems, Doubleday (New York, NY), 1973.

(Editor with Dubem Okafor) *Don't Let Him Die: An Anthology of Memorial Poems for Christopher Okigbo,* Fourth Dimension Publishers (Enigu, Nigeria), 1978.

(Coeditor) *Aka Weta: An Anthology of Igbo Poetry,* Okike (Nsukka, Nigeria), 1982.

Another Africa, poems and essays, Anchor Books (New York, NY), 1997.

OTHER

The Sacrificial Egg, and Other Stories, Etudo (Onitsha, Nigeria), 1962.

(Contributor) *The Insider; Stories of War and Peace from Nigeria,* Nwankwo-Ifejika (Enigu, Nigeria), 1971.

Girls at War (short stories), Heinemann (London, England), 1972, Fawcett (Uncasville, CT), 1988.

Morning Yet on Creation Day (essays), Doubleday (New York, NY), 1975.

(Contributor) *In Person—Achebe, Awoonor, and Soyinka at the University of Washington,* University of Washington (Seattle, Washington), 1975.

Editor, with Jomo Kenyatta and Amos Tutuola, *Winds of Change: Modern Stories from Black Africa,* Longman (London, England)), 1977.

Editor, with Dubem Okafor, *Don't Let Him Die: An Anthology of Memorial Poems for Christopher Okigbo,* Fourth Dimension Publishers (Enugu, Nigeria), 1978.

The Trouble with Nigeria (essays), Fourth Dimension Publishers (Enigu, Nigeria), 1983, Heinemann (London, England), 1984.

(Editor with C.L. Innes) *African Short Stories,* Heinemann (London, England), 1984.

The World of the Ogbanje, Fourth Dimension (Enugu, Nigeria), 1986.

Hopes and Impediments: Selected Essays 1965-1987, Heinemann (London, England), 1988.

The University and the Leadership Factor in Nigerian Politics, Abic Books (Enigu, Nigeria), 1988.

The African Trilogy, (fiction), Picador (London, England), 1988.

A Tribute to James Baldwin: Black Writers Redefine the Struggle: Proceedings of a Conference at the University of Massachusetts at Amherst, April 22-23, 1988 Featuring Chinua Achebe, University of Massachusetts Press (Amherst, MA), 1989.

(Co-Editor) *Beyond Hunger in Africa: Conventional Wisdom and an African Vision,* Currey (London, England), 1990.

(Editor with C.L. Innes and contributor) *The Heinemann Book of Contemporary African Short Stories,* Heinemann (London, England), 1992.

The Voter, Viva Books (Johannesburg), 1994.

(With others) *The South Wind and the Sun,* edited by Kate Turkington, Thorold's Africana Books (Johannesburg), 1996.

Another Africa (poems and essay, with photographs by Robert Lyons), Anchor Books (New York, NY), 1997.

Order and Chaos (with others), Great Books Foundation (Chicago, IL), 1997.

Conversations with Chinua Achebe, University Press of Mississippi (Jackson, MS), 1997.

Home and Exile, Oxford University Press (New York, NY), 2000.

Also author of essay collection *Nigerian Topics,* 1988. Contributor to anthologies, including *Modern African Stories,* edited by Ellis Ayitey Komey and Ezekiel Mphahlele, Faber (London), 1964; *Africa Speaks: A Prose Anthology with Comprehension and Summary Passages,* Evans, 1970; and *The Short Century: Independence and Liberation Movements in Africa, 1945-1994,* edited by Okwui Enwezor, Prestel, 2001. Author of foreword, *African Rhapsody: Short Stories of the Contemporary African Experience,* 1994. Founding editor, "African Writers Series," Heinemann, 1962-72; editor, *Okike: A Nigerian Journal of New Writing,* 1971—; editor, *Nsukkascope,* a campus magazine.

ADAPTATIONS: Things Fall Apart was adapted for the stage and produced by Eldred Fiberesima in Lagos, Nigeria; it was also adapted for radio and produced by the British Broadcasting Corporation in 1983, and for television in English and Igbo and produced by the Nigerian Television Authority in 1985.

WORK IN PROGRESS: Our Shared Future, a series of books focused on the issues affecting children around the world, for UNICEF, edited with Toni Morrison.

SIDELIGHTS: Since the 1950s, Nigeria has witnessed "the flourishing of a new literature which has drawn sustenance both from traditional oral literature and from the present and rapidly changing society," wrote Margaret Laurence in her book *Long Drums and Cannons: Nigerian Dramatists and Novelists.* Thirty years ago, Chinua Achebe, who rejected the British name "Albert" and took his indigenous name "Chinua" in college in 1948, was among the founders of this new literature and over the years many critics have come to consider him the finest of the Nigerian novelists. His achievement has not been limited to his native country or continent (his work has been published in some 50 languages). As Laurence maintained, "Chinua Achebe's careful and confident craftsmanship, his firm grasp of his material and his ability to create memorable and living characters place him among the best novelists now writing in any country in the English language."

On the level of ideas, Achebe's "prose writing reflects three essential and related concerns," observed G.D. Killam in his book *The Novels of Chinua Achebe,* "first, with the legacy of colonialism at both the individual and societal level; secondly, with the *fact* of English as a language of national and international exchange; thirdly, with the obligations and responsibilities of the writer both to the society in which he lives and to his art." Over the past century, African nations have been caught in struggles for identity between tradition, colonialism, and independence. These conflicts, deepened by the continuing presence of economic colonialism and neocolonialism among European educated rulers, has prevented many nations from raising themselves above political and social chaos to achieve true independence. "Most of the problems we see in our politics derive from the moment when we lost our initiative to other people, to colonizers," Achebe noted in a book of essays. He went on to explain: "What I think is the basic problem of a new African country like Nigeria is really what you might call a 'crisis in the soul.' We have been subjected—we have subjected ourselves too—to this period during which we have accepted everything alien as good and practically everything local or native as inferior." "We had all been duped," he wrote. "No independence was given . . . Europe had only made a tactical withdrawal on the political front and while we sang our anthem . . . she was securing her grip behind us in the economic field. And our leaders in whose faces we hurled our disenchantment neither saw nor heard because they were not leaders at all but marionettes."

In order to recognize the virtues of precolonial Nigeria, chronicle the ongoing impact of colonialism on native cultures, and expose present-day corruption, Achebe desired to clearly communicate these concerns first to his fellow countrymen but also to those outside his country. Unlike Kenyan writer Ngugi wa Thiongo and others, who chose to return to writing in their native languages, Achebe judged the best channel for these messages to be English, the language of colonialism. He did so because he wished to repossess the power of description from those, like Conrad, Joyce Cary, and Rider Haggard, who had, as he said, secured "an absolute power over narrative" that cast Africans as beasts, savages, and idiots. He explained that language need not to be viewed as an enemy, "but as a tool." Through repossession, he could "help [his] society regain belief in itself and put away the complexes of the years of denigration and self-abasement." He was taking up a long fight against European writers who were "bloody racists" in their descriptions of Africans and Africa.

Achebe's transformation of language to achieve his particular ends distinguishes his writing from that of other English-language novelists. To repossess description of Nigeria in English, he translates Ibo proverbs and weaves them into his stories with Ibo vocabulary, images, and speech patterns. "Among the Ibo the art of conversation is regarded very highly," he wrote in his novel *Things Fall Apart*, "and proverbs are the palm-oil with which words are eaten." "Proverbs are cherished by Achebe's people as . . . the treasure boxes of their cultural heritage," explained Adrian A. Roscoe in *Mother Is Gold: A Study in West African Literature.* "When they disappear or fall into disuse . . . it is a sign that a particular tradition, or indeed a whole way of life, is passing away." Achebe's use of proverbs also has an artistic aim, as Bernth Lindfors suggested in *Folklore in Nigerian Literature.* "Proverbs can serve as keys to an understanding of his novels," commented the critic, "because he uses them not merely to add touches of local color but to sound and reiterate themes, to sharpen characterization, to clarify conflict, and to focus on the values of the society."

Although he has also written poetry, short stories, and essays—both literary and political—Achebe is best known for his novels: *Things Fall Apart, No Longer at Ease, Arrow of God, A Man of the People,* and *Anthills of the Savannah.* Anthony Daniels wrote of Achebe's novels in the *Spectator,* "In spare prose of great elegance, without any technical distraction, he has been able to illuminate two emotionally irreconcilable facets of modern African life: the humiliations visited on Africans by colonialism, and the . . . worthlessness of what replaced colonial rule." Set in this historical context, the novels develop the theme of what happens to a society when change outside distorts and blocks the natural change from within and offer, as Eustace Palmer observed in *The Growth of the African Novel,* "a powerful presentation of the beauty, strength and validity of traditional life and values and the disruptiveness of change." Even as he resists the rootless visions of postmodernist globalisation, Achebe does not appeal for a return to the ways of the past.

Things Fall Apart and *Arrow of God*—Achebe's first novels—focus on Nigeria's early experience with colonialism, from first contact with the British to widespread British administration. "With remarkable unity of the word with the deed, the character, the time and the place, Chinua Achebe creates in these two novels a coherent picture of coherence being lost, of the tragic consequences" of European colonialism, suggested Robert McDowell in a special issue of *Studies in Black Literature* dedicated to Achebe's work. "There is an artistic unity of all things in these books, which is rare anywhere in modern English fiction."

Things Fall Apart was published in 1958, early in the Nigerian renaissance. Achebe explained why he began writing at this time in an interview with Lewis Nkosi in *African Writers Talking: A Collection of Radio Interviews:* "One of the things that set me thinking was Joyce Cary's novel set in Nigeria, *Mr. Johnson,* which was praised so much, and it was clear to me that this was a most superficial picture . . . not only of the country, but even of the Nigerian character. . . . I thought if this was famous, then perhaps someone ought to try and look . . . from the inside." Charles R. Larson, in *The Emergence of African Fiction,* said of Achebe's success, both in investing his novel of Africa with an African sensibility and in making this view available to African readers: "In 1964 . . . *Things Fall Apart* became the first novel by an African writer to be included in the required syllabus for African secondary school students throughout the English-speaking portions of the continent." As Simon Gikandi recalled in a special issue of *Research in African Literatures,* "Once I had started reading *Things Fall Apart* . . . I could not cope with the chapter a day policy. I read the whole novel over one afternoon and it is not an exaggeration to say that my life was never to be the same again. . . . In reading *Things Fall Apart,* everything became clear: the yam was important to Igbo culture, not because of what we were later to learn to call use-value . . . but because of its location at the nexus of a symbolic economy in which material wealth was connected to spirituality and ideology and desire." Later in the 1960s, the novel "became recognized by African and non-African literary critics as the first 'classic' in English from tropical Africa," added Larson.

The novel tells the story of an Ibo village of the late 1800s and one of its great men, Okonkwo. Although the son of a ne'er-do-well, Okonkwo has achieved much in his life. He is a champion wrestler, a wealthy farmer, a husband to three wives, a title-holder among his people, and a member of the select *egwugwu* who represent ancestral spirits at tribal rituals. "The most impressive achievement of *Things Fall Apart*" maintained David Carroll in his book *Chinua Achebe,* "is the vivid picture it provides of Ibo society at the end of the nineteenth century." He explained: "Here is a clan in the full vigor of its traditional way of life, unperplexed by the present and without nostalgia for the past. Through its rituals the life of the community and the life of the individual are merged into significance and order."

In *Things Fall Apart,* the order of the village is disrupted with the appearance of the white man in Africa and with the introduction of his religion. "The conflict in the novel, vested in Okonkwo, derives from the series of crushing blows which are levelled at traditional values by an alien and more powerful culture causing, in the end, the traditional society to fall apart," observed Killam. Okonkwo is unable to counter the changes that accompany colonialism. In the end, in frustration, he kills an African employed by the British, and then commits suicide, a sin against the tradition to which he had long remained true. The novel thus presents "two main, closely intertwined tragedies," wrote Arthur Ravenscroft in his study *Chinua Achebe,* "the personal tragedy of Okonkwo . . . and the public tragedy of the eclipse of one culture by another." Achebe reclaims the power of description from the colonial writer by depicting both tragedies from within Ibo culture.

Although the author emphasizes the message in his novels, he also receives praise for his artistic achievement. As Palmer commented, the work "demonstrates a mastery of plot and structure, strength of characterization, competence in the manipulation of language and consistency and depth of thematic exploration which is rarely found in a first novel." Achebe also achieves balance in recreating the tragic consequences of colonial damage to his culture. Killam noted that "in showing Ibo society before and after the coming of the white man he avoids the temptation to present the past as idealized and the present as ugly and unsatisfactory." And, Killam concluded, Achebe's "success proceeds from his ability to create a sense of real life and real issues in the book and to see his subject from the point of view which is neither idealistic nor dishonest."

Arrow of God, the second novel, takes place in the 1920s after the British have established a presence in Nigeria. The "arrow of god" in the title is Ezeulu, the chief priest of the god Ulu, a deity created to unite Umuaro, a federation of six Ibo villages. As chief priest, Ezeulu is responsible for initiating rituals that structure village life and maintain the unity of the federation, a position with a great deal of political as well as spiritual power. In fact, the central theme of this novel, as Laurence pointed out, is power: "Ezeulu's testing of his own power and the power of his god, and his effort to maintain his own and his god's authority in the face of village factions and of the [Christian] mission and the British administration." "This, then, is a political novel in which different systems of power are examined and their dependence upon myth and ritual compared," wrote Carroll.

In Ezeulu, Achebe presents a study of loss of power in the face of colonial manipulation whose depth he does not understand. After the village council rejects his advice to avoid conflict with a neighboring village, Ezeulu finds himself at odds with his own people and praised by British administrators. The British, seeking a candidate to install as village chieftain, make him an offer, which he refuses and is therefore imprisoned. Caught in the middle with no allies, Ezeulu becomes more and more uncompromising and finally dooms the villages in his rigid opposition to the council. "As in Achebe's other novels," observed Gerald Moore in *Seven African Writers,* "it is the strong-willed man of tradition who cannot adapt, and who is crushed by his virtues in the war between the new, more worldly order, and the old, conservative values of an isolated society." The artistry displayed in *Arrow of God,* Achebe's second portrait of cultures in collision, has drawn a great deal of attention, adding to the esteem in which the writer is held. Charles Miller commented in a *Saturday Review* article that Achebe's "approach to the written word is completely unencumbered with verbiage. He never strives for the exalted phrase, he never once raises his voice; even in the most emotion-charged passages the tone is absolutely unruffled, the control impeccable." Concluded Miller, "It is a measure of Achebe's creative gift that he has no need whatever for prose fireworks to light the flame of his intense drama."

Achebe's three other novels—*No Longer at Ease, A Man of the People,* and *Anthills of the Savannah*—examine Africa in the era of independence. This is an

Africa less and less under obvious European administration, but still deeply controlled by it, an Africa struggling to regain its footing in order to stand on its own two feet. Standing in the way of realizing its goal of true independence is the persistence of European values pervasive in modern Africa, an obstacle Achebe continues to scrutinize in each of these novels. Tejumola Olaniyan commented in *Research in African Literatures,* "The postcolonial state was determined by, and is an expression of, the political superstructure elaborated by colonial power, and not an outgrowth of the autonomous evolution of the people. . . . The postcolonial state has been unable to escape the logic of its origin in the colonial state: absence of legitimacy with the governed, dependence on coercion, lack of political accountability, a bureaucracy with an extraverted mentality, disregard for the cultivation of a responsive civic community, uneven horizontal integration into the political community such that the government is most felt in the cities, extraction of surplus from the interior to overfeed the capital, and many more!"

In *No Longer at Ease,* set in Nigeria just prior to independence, Achebe extends his history of the Okonkwo family. The central character is Obi Okonkwo, grandson of the tragic hero of *Things Fall Apart.* Obi Okonkwo has been raised a Christian and educated in England. Like many of his peers, he has left the bush behind for a position as a civil servant in Lagos, Nigeria's largest city. "*No Longer at Ease* deals with the plight of [this] new generation of Nigerians," observed Palmer, "who, having been exposed to education in the western world and therefore largely cut off from their roots in traditional society, discover, on their return, that the demands of tradition are still strong, and are hopelessly caught in the clash between the old and the new," the demands the logic of colonialism continues to make on the ruling class.

Many faced with this internal conflict between individualistic and communal values succumb to corruption. Obi is no exception. "The novel opens with Obi on trial for accepting bribes," noted Killam, "and the book takes the form of a long flashback." "In a world which is the result of the intermingling of Europe and Africa . . . Achebe traces the decline of his hero from brilliant student to civil servant convicted of bribery and corruption," wrote Carroll. "It reads like a postscript to the earlier novel [*Things Fall Apart*] because the same forces are at work but in a confused, diluted, and blurred form." In *This Africa: Novels by West Africans in English and French,* Judith Illsley Gleason pointed out how the imagery of each book depicts the changes in the Okonkwo family and the Nigeria they

represent. She wrote, "The career of the grandson Okonkwo ends not with a machete's swing but with a gavel's tap," but the legacy that destroys him is the same.

A Man of the People is satire, and in this "novel of disenchantment," Achebe further casts his eye on African politics, taking on, as Moore noted, "the corruption of Nigerians in high places in the central government." The author's eyepiece is the book's narrator Odili, a schoolteacher; the object of his scrutiny is the Honorable M.A. Nanga, Member of Parliament, Odili's former teacher and a popular bush politician who has risen to the post of Minister of Culture in his West African homeland.

At first, Odili is charmed by the politician but eventually he recognizes the extent of Nanga's abuses and decides to oppose the minister in an election. Odili is beaten, both physically and politically, his appeal to the people heard but ignored because he too has left his roots behind for abstract intellect. The novel demonstrates, according to Shatto Arthur Gakwandi in *The Novel and Contemporary Experience in Africa,* that "the society has been invaded by a wide range of values which have destroyed the traditional balance between the material and the spiritual spheres of life, which has led inevitably to the hypocrisy of double standards." Odili is both victim and perpetrator of these double standards.

Despite his political victory, Nanga, along with the rest of the government, is ousted by a coup. "The novel is a carefully plotted and unified piece of writing," wrote Killam. "Achebe achieves balance and proportion in the treatment of his theme of political corruption by evoking both the absurdity of the behavior of the principal characters while at the same time suggesting the serious and destructive consequences of their behavior to the commonwealth." The seriousness of the fictional situation portrayed in *A Man of the People* became real very soon after the novel was first published in 1966 when Nigeria itself was racked by a coup.

Two decades passed between the publications of *A Man of the People* and Achebe's 1988 novel, *Anthills of the Savannah.* During this time, rather than flee abroad as he might have done, Achebe became involved in the political struggle between Nigeria and the seceding nation of Biafra, a struggle marked by five coups, a civil war, elections marred by violence, and a number of attempts to return to civilian rule. He worked throughout the war as Biafran Minister of Information. Judging that novels could not express the horrors of the struggle, he wrote poetry, short stories, and essays that mourned and celebrated the attempted revolution.

Anthills of the Savannah is Achebe's return to the novel, and as Nadine Gordimer commented in the *New York Times Book Review,* "it is a work in which 22 years of harsh experience, intellectual growth, self-criticism, deepening understanding and mustered discipline of skill open wide a subject to which Mr. Achebe is now magnificently equal." It is a return to the themes of independent Africa informing Achebe's earlier novels but it gives the most significant role to women, who invent a new kind of storytelling, offering a glimmer of hope at the end of the novel. "This is a study of how power corrupts itself and by doing so begins to die," wrote *Observer* contributor and fellow Nigerian Ben Okri. "It is also about dissent, and love."

Three former schoolmates have risen to positions of power in an imaginary West African nation, Kangan. Ikem is editor of the state-owned newspaper; Chris is the country's minister of information; Sam is a military man who has become head of state. Sam's quest to have himself voted president for life sends the lives of these three and the lives of all Kangan citizens into turmoil. Neal Ascherson in the *New York Review of Books,* commented that the novel becomes "a tale about responsibility, and the ways in which men who should know better betray and evade that responsibility."

The turmoil comes to a head in the novel's final pages. All three of the central characters are dead. Ikem, who spoke out against the abuses of the government, is murdered by Sam's secret police. Chris, who flees into the bush to begin a journey of transformation among the people, is shot attempting to stop a rape. Sam is kidnapped and murdered in a coup. "The three murders, senseless as they are, represent the departure of a generation that compromised its own enlightenment for the sake of power," wrote Ascherson. At Achebe's 70th birthday celebration at Bard College, Wole Soyinka commented that "Achebe never hesitates to lay blame for the woes of the African continent squarely where it belongs." And, as Okri observed, "The novel closes with the suggestion that power should reside not within an elite but within the awakened spirit of the people."

Anthills of the Savannah was well-received and earned Achebe a nomination for the Booker Prize. Larson, in *Tribune Books,* estimated that "No other novel in many years has bitten to the core, swallowed and regurgitated contemporary Africa's miseries and expectations as profoundly as *Anthills of the Savannah.*"

Achebe's next book, *Hopes and Impediments: Selected Essays 1965-1987,* essays and speeches written over a period of twenty-three years, is perceived in many ways to be a logical extension of ideas in *Anthills of the Savannah.* In this collection, however, he is not addressing the way Africans view themselves but rather how Africa is viewed by the outside world. The central theme is the corrosive impact of the racism that pervades Western traditional appraisal of Africa. The collection opens with an examination of Joseph Conrad's 1902 novella *Heart of Darkness;* Achebe criticizes Conrad for projecting an image of Africa as "the other world"—meaning non-European and, therefore, uncivilized. Achebe argues that to this day, the Condradian myth persists that Africa is a dark and bestial land. The time has come, Achebe states, to sweep away this racism in favor of new myths and socially "beneficent fiction" which will enable Africans and non-Africans alike to redefine the way they look at the continent. "I am a political writer," he said, and "My politics is concerned with universal communication across racial and cultural boundaries as a means of fostering respect for all people. . . . As long as one people sits on another and are deaf to their cry, so long will understanding and peace elude us."

Achebe continues this critique, after a long silence while he recovered from a serious car crash that left him paralyzed from the waist down, in *Home and Exile,* a memoir in the form of three essays, where he extends his attack on linguistic colonialism in its many forms: "the subject of naming, especially naming to put down, appears in a variety of forms in the course of his deliberations." For instance, he repossesses for the Ibo the word "nation" rather than "tribe." Adebayo, in an article in *Research in African Literatures,* contended that Achebe "resents the colonial categorization of non-Western nationalities as tribes distinguished by primordial affiliations and primitive customs. By sheer force of logic and weight of evidence, Achebe demonstrates that his own people . . . do not share most of the notorious attributes of tribal groups, particularly blood ties and a centralized authority." As Richard Feldstein wrote in a *Literature and Psychology* review, "*Home and Exile* calls for overwriting colonial narratives by painstakingly reviewing their articulation as well as their accumulated details while instituting a counter-discourse of repossession. Repossession . . . calls for the process of re-storying marginalized indigenes who have been silenced by the trauma of dispossession. Repossession presents counter-discursive 'stories,' along with new ways of telling them."

In his writings, Achebe has created a significant body of work in which he offers a close and balanced examination of contemporary Africa and the historical forces that have shaped it. "His distinction is to have [looked back] without any trace either of chauvinistic idealism or of neurotic rejection," maintained Moore. Achebe's writing reverberates beyond the borders of Nigeria and beyond the arenas of anthropology, sociology, and political science. As literature, it deals with universal qualities. And, as Killam writes in his study: "Achebe's novels offer a vision of life which is essentially tragic, compounded of success and failure, informed by knowledge and understanding, relieved by humour and tempered by sympathy, embued with an awareness of human suffering and the human capacity to endure." Concluded the critic, "Sometimes his characters meet with success, more often with defeat and despair. Through it all the spirit of man and the belief in the possibility of triumph endures." In 1990, only weeks after attending a celebration for his 60th birthday, Achebe was paralyzed in an accident in Nigeria, but has continued to publish, teach, and appear in public. He moved to the United States for therapy, and has lived there, "a reluctant refugee," according to Oluwole Adujare in an *African News Service* review, during a dark time of Nigerian dictatorship.

BIOGRAPHICAL AND CRITICAL SOURCES:

BOOKS

Achebe, Chinua, *Things Fall Apart,* Heinemann (London, England), 1958, Obolensky (New York, NY), 1959.

Awoonor, Kofi, *The Breast of the Earth,* Doubleday (New York, NY), 1975.

Awosika, Olawale, *Form and Technique in the African Novel,* Sam Bookman (Ibadan), 1997.

Baldwin, Claudia, *Nigerian Literature: A Bibliography of Criticism,* G.K. Hall (Boston, MA), 1980.

Carroll, David, *Chinua Achebe,* Macmillan (New York, NY), 1990.

Champion, Ernest A., *Mr. Baldwin, I Presume: James Baldwin-Chinua Achebe, a Meeting of the Minds,* University Press of America (Lanham, MD), 1995.

Contemporary Literary Criticism, Thomson Gale (Detroit, MI), Volume 1, 1973; Volume 3, 1975; Volume 5, 1976; Volume 7, 1977; Volume 11, 1979; Volume 26, 1983; Volume 51, 1988; Volume 75, 1993.

Contemporary Novelists, 7th edition, St. James Press (Detroit, MI), 2001.

Ezenwa-Ohaeto, *Chinua Achebe: A Biography,* Indiana University Press, 1997.

Gakwandi, Shatto Arthur, *The Novel and Contemporary Experience in Africa,* Africana Publishing, 1977.

Gikandi, Simon, *Reading Chinua Achebe: Language and Ideology in Fiction,* Heinemann, 1991.

Gleason, Judith Illsley, *This Africa: Novels by West Africans in English and French,* Northwestern University Press, 1965.

Gurnah, Abdulrazak, editor, *Essays on African Writing: A Re-evaluation,* Heinemann, 1993.

Ihekweazu, Edith, editor *Eagle on Iroko: Selected Papers from the Chinua Achebe International Symposium, 1990,* Heinemann Education Books (Ibadan), 1996.

Indrasena Reddy, K., *The Novels of Achebe and Ngugi: A Study in the Dialectics of Commitment,* Prestige Books (New Delhi), 1994.

International Symposium for Chinua Achebe's 60th Birthday, Heinemann Educational Books (Ibadan), 1996.

Kambaji, Christopher Tshikala, *Chinua Achebe: A Novelist and a Portraitist of His Society,* Vantage Press (New York, NY), 1994.

Killam, G. D., *The Novels of Chinua Achebe,* Africana Publishing, 1969.

Kim, Soonsik, *Colonial and Post-Colonial Discourse in the Novels of Yaeom Sang-Saeop, Chinua Achebe, and Salman Rushdie,* P. Lang (New York City), 1996.

King, Bruce, *Introduction to Nigerian Literature,* Africana Publishing, 1972.

King, Bruce, *The New English Literatures: Cultural Nationalism in a Changing World,* Macmillan, 1980.

Larson, Charles R., *The Emergence of African Fiction,* Indiana University Press, 1972.

Laurence, Margaret, *Long Drums and Cannons: Nigerian Dramatists and Novelists,* Praeger (New York, NY), 1968.

Lindfors, Bernth, *Folklore in Nigerian Literature,* Africana Publishing, 1973.

Lindfors, Bernth, *Conversations with Chinua Achebe,* University Press of Mississippi (Jackson, MS), 1997.

McEwan, Neil, *Africa and the Novel,* Humanities Press (Atlantic Highlands, NJ), 1983.

Moore, Gerald, *Seven African Writers,* Oxford University Press (New York, NY), 1962.

Moses, Michael Valdez, *The Novel and the Globalization of Culture,* Oxford University Press (New York, NY), 1995.

Muoneke, Romanus Okey, *Art, Rebellion and Redemption: A Reading of the Novels of Chinua Achebe,* Peter Lang (New York, NY), 1994.

Njoku, Benedict Chiaka, *The Four Novels of Chinua Achebe: A Critical Study,* Peter Lang (New York, NY), 1984.

Nkosi, Lewis, interview with Achebe in *African Writers Talking: A Collection of Radio Interviews,* edited by Cosmo Pieterse and Dennis Duerden, Africana Publishing, 1972.

Ogbaa, Kalu, *Gods, Oracles and Divination,* Africa World Press (Trenton, NJ), 1992.

Ojinma, Umelo, *Chinua Achebe: New Perspectives,* Spectrum Books Ltd. (Ibadan), 1991.

Okoye, E.M., *The Traditional Religion and Its Encounter with Christianity in Achebe's Novels,* 1987.

Okpu, B.M., *Chinua Achebe: A Bibliography,* Libriservice, 1984.

Omotoso, Kole, *Achebe or Soyinka?: A Reinterpretation and a Study in Contrasts,* Hans Zell Publishers, 1992.

Palmer, Eustace, *The Growth of the African Novel,* Heinemann, 1979.

Parker, Michael, *Postcolonial Literatures: Achebe, Ngugi, Desai, Wolcott,* St. Martin's Press (New York, NY), 1995.

Petersen, K. H., *Chinua Achebe: A Celebration,* Heinemann, Dangeroo Press, 1991.

Podis, Leonard A., and Yakubu Saaka, editors, *Challenging Hierarchies: Issues and Themes in Colonial and Postcolonial African Literature,* P. Lang (New York), 1998.

Ravenscroft, Arthur, *Chinua Achebe,* Longmans, 1969.

Roscoe, Adrian A., *Mother Is Gold: A Study in West African Literature,* Cambridge University Press, 1971.

Simola, Raisa, *World Views in Chinua Achebe's Works,* P. Lang (New York City), 1995.

Wren, Robert M., *Achebe's World: The Historical and Cultural Context of the Novels,* Three Continents (Washington, DC), 1980.

PERIODICALS

Africa News Service, May 24, 1999; October 16, 2000; November 27, 2000; September 13, 2002; February 14, 2003.

Africa Today, March, 1995, p. 93.

America, June 22-29, 1991; July 20, 1996; October 14, 2000, p. 24.

Ariel, April, 1992, p. 7.

Black Issues Book Review, September, 2000, p. 54.

Bloomsbury Review, January, 1996, p. 21.

Bookbird, spring, 1998, p. 6.

Booklist, March 1, 1997, p. 1168; August, 1997, p. 1842; January 1, 1998, p. 835; May 15, 2000, p. 1721.

Boston Globe, March 9, 1988.

Callaloo, fall, 1999, p. 1054.

Children's Literature Association Quarterly, winter, 1997, p. 160.

Choice, March, 1995, p. 1059.

Christian Century, April 18, 2001, p. 26.

Christian Science Monitor, November 16, 2000, p. 16.

CLA Journal, March, 1992, p. 303.

College Literature, October, 1992, special issue; winter, 1999, p. 69.

Commonweal, December 1, 1967.

Commonwealth Essays and Studies, fall, 1990.

Ebony, February, 1999, p. 96.

Economist, October 24, 1987.

Emerge, June, 2000, p. 68.

English Journal, March, 1995, p. 49.

Entertainment Weekly, September 26, 1997, p. 74.

Explicator, summer, 2002, p. 229.

Guardian, April 4, 1998, p. TW5; November 18, 2000, p. 6.

Harper's Bazaar, January, 1999, p. 66.

Journal of Commonwealth Literature, spring, 2001, p. 75.

Library Journal, September 15, 1997, p. 74; February 15, 1998, p. 184; May 15, 1998, p. 135; April 15, 2000, p. 87.

Listener, October 15, 1987.

Literature and Psychology, spring-summer, 2002, p. 131.

London Review of Books, October 15, 1981; August 7, 1986; June 22, 1989, pp. 16-17.

Los Angeles Times Book Review, February 28, 1988.

Modern Fiction Studies, fall, 1991.

Nation, October 11, 1965; April 16, 1988.

National Post, July 8, 2000, p. B11.

New Statesman, January 4, 1985; September 25, 1987.

New Statesman and Society, July 22, 1988, pp. 41-2; February 9, 1990, p. 30; November 17, 1995, p. 40.

New York Review of Books, March 3, 1988.

New York Times, August 10, 1966; February 16, 1988; August 29, 1999, p. WK2; November 6, 2000, pp. B1 and E1.

New York Times Book Review, December 17, 1967; May 13, 1973; August 11, 1985; February 21, 1988; November 12, 1989, p. 55; August 13, 2000, p. 15.

Observer (London), September 20, 1987.

People, January 11, 1999, p. 35; January 25, 1999, p. 33.

Philadelphia Enquirer, August 16, 2000.

Publications of the Modern Language Association of America, January, 1995, p. 30.

Publishers Weekly, February 21, 1994, p. 249; August 4, 1997, p. 54; May 8, 2000, p. 211.

Research in African Literatures 30 (2), 1999; fall, 2001, special issue.

Saturday Review, January 6, 1968.

School Library Journal, December, 1992, p. 146.

Social Education, November-December, 1997, p. 380.

Spectator, October 21, 1960; September 26, 1987; February 24, 2001, p. 39.

Studies in Black Literature: Special Issue; Chinua Achebe, spring, 1971.

Times Educational Supplement, January 25, 1985.

Times Higher Education Supplement, July 16, 1999, p. 22.

Times Literary Supplement, February 3, 1966; March 3, 1972; May 4, 1973; February 26, 1982; October 12, 1984; October 9, 1987.

Tribune Books (Chicago), February 21, 1988.

UNESCO Courier, June, 2001, Amy Otchet "Chinua Achebe: No Longer at Ease in Exile" (interview with Chinua Achebe), p. 47.

Variety, September 21, 1998, p. 110.

Village Voice, March 15, 1988.

Wall Street Journal, February 23, 1988.

Washington Post, February 16, 1988.

Washington Post Book World, February 7, 1988.

World Literature Today, summer, 1985.

World Literature Written in English, November, 1978.

ONLINE

Pegasos, http://www.kirjasto.sci.fi/ (December 4, 2003), "Author's Calendar."

University Scholars Programme, National University of Singapore, http://www.scholars.nus.edu/ (December 4, 2003).

*   *   *

ACKROYD, Peter 1949-

PERSONAL: Born October 5, 1949, in London, England; son of Graham and Audrey (Whiteside) Ackroyd. *Education:* Clare College, Cambridge, M.A., 1971; attended Yale University, 1971-73.

ADDRESSES: *Home*—London, England. *Agent*—Anthony Sheil Associates Ltd., 43 Doughty St., London WC1N 2LF, England.

CAREER: Poet, novelist, playwright, and essayist. *Spectator,* London, England, literary editor, 1973-77, managing editor, 1977-81; *Times,* London, England, television critic, 1977-81; chief book reviewer, 1986—.

MEMBER: Royal Society of Literature (fellow).

AWARDS, HONORS: W. Somerset Maugham Award, 1984, for *The Last Testament of Oscar Wilde;* Whitbread Award, and *Guardian* Fiction Prize, both 1985, both for *Hawksmoor;* Heinemann Award for nonfiction, Royal Society of Literature, 1985, for *T.S. Eliot: A Life;* James Tait Black Memorial Prize for Best Biography, University of Edinburgh, 1998, for *The Life of Thomas More.*

WRITINGS:

POETRY

Ouch, Curiously Strong Press (London, England), 1971.

London Lickpenny (also see below), Ferry Press (London, England), 1973.

Country Life (also see below), Ferry Press (London, England), 1978.

The Diversions of Purley, and Other Poems (contains poems from *London Lickpenny* and *Country Life*), Hamish Hamilton (London, England), 1987.

NOVELS

The Great Fire of London, Hamish Hamilton (London, England), 1982.

The Last Testament of Oscar Wilde, Harper (New York, NY), 1983.

Hawksmoor, Hamish Hamilton (London, England), 1985, Harper (New York, NY), 1986.

Chatterton, Grove (New York, NY), 1988.

First Light, Viking Penguin (New York, NY), 1989.

English Music, Knopf (New York, NY), 1992.

The House of Doctor Dee, Hamish Hamilton (London, England), 1993, Penguin (New York, NY), 1994.

Dan Leno and the Limehouse Golem, Sinclair-Stevenson (London, England), 1994, published as *The Trial of Elizabeth Cree: A Novel of the Limehouse Murders,* Nan A. Talese (New York, NY), 1995.

Milton in America, Nan A. Talese (New York, NY), 1997.

The Plato Papers: A Prophecy, Nan A. Talese (New York, NY), 2000.

The Clerkenwell Tales, Chatto & Windus (London, England), 2003, Nan A. Talese (New York, NY), 2004.

NONFICTION

Notes for a New Culture: An Essay on Modernism, Barnes & Noble (New York, NY), 1976.

Dressing Up: Transvestism and Drag: The History of an Obsession, Simon & Schuster (New York, NY), 1979.

Ezra Pound and His World, Scribner (New York, NY), 1981.

T.S. Eliot: A Life, Simon & Schuster (New York, NY), 1984.

(Editor) *PEN New Fiction,* Quartet Books (London, England), 1984.

(Author of introduction) *Dickens' London: An Imaginative Vision,* Headline (London, England), 1987.

Dickens, Sinclair-Stevenson (London, England), 1990, HarperPerennial (New York, NY), 1992.

Introduction to Dickens, Sinclair-Stevenson (London, England), 1991, Ballantine (New York, NY), 1992.

(Author of introduction) Frank Auerbach, *Recent Works,* Marlborough (New York, NY), 1994.

Blake, Sinclair-Stevenson (London, England), 1995.

(Editor) Oscar Wilde, *The Picture of Dorian Gray,* G.K. Hall (Thorndike, ME), 1995.

The Life of Thomas More, Chatto & Windus (London, England), 1998.

London: The Biography, Chatto & Windus (London, England), 2000.

The Collection (nonfiction and fiction), Chatto & Windus (London, England), 2001.

Dickens (based on documentary film; also see below), British Broadcasting Corporation (London, England), 2002.

Albion: The Origins of the English Imagination, Nan A. Talese (New York, NY), 2003.

Chaucer, Nan A. Talese (New York, NY), 2005.

OTHER

The Mystery of Charles Dickens (play), produced in New York, NY, 2002.

(And narrator) *Dickens* (documentary film), British Broadcasting Corporation, 2002, Public Broadcasting Service, 2003.

Escape from Earth (juvenile fiction), DK Publishing (New York, NY), 2003.

The Beginning (juvenile fiction), DK Publishing (New York, NY), 2003.

Contributor of short story "The Inheritance" to anthology *London Tales,* edited by Julian Evans, Hamish Hamilton, 1983. Contributor of book reviews to periodicals, including the *New York Times Book Review.*

SIDELIGHTS: Hailed as an accomplished and versatile writer, Peter Ackroyd has authored works ranging from poems to novels, criticism to biography. He was published first as a poet, his book *London Lickpenny* prompting a *Times Literary Supplement* reviewer to deem Ackroyd "a delicate and insistent stylist" whose words make "not only an odd poetry, but a poetry out of the oddness of the world." Ackroyd came to literary prominence, however, as a biographer, and his well-received volumes on literary giants T.S. Eliot and Charles Dickens have been complemented by novels which frequently fictionalize the lives of famous historical personalities such as Oscar Wilde and Thomas Chatterton. Glen M. Johnson, writing in the *Dictionary of Literary Biography,* explained that "as his career has developed, Ackroyd has sought 'a new way to interanimate' biography and fiction." In addition to fusing history and fiction, his novels also consider the nature of time and art, often involving their protagonists in situations that transcend time and space. Ackroyd once commented: "My own interest isn't so much in writing historical fiction as it is in writing about the nature of history as such. . . . I'm much more interested in playing around with the idea of time."

In 1982 Ackroyd published his first novel, *The Great Fire of London,* which revolves around a film production of Dickens' novel *Little Dorrit.* Ackroyd's tale presents itself as a continuation of the Dickens novel, which concerns a young girl's trials and tribulations in Victorian England. Beginning with a summary of Dickens' work, *The Great Fire of London* then introduces its own cast of Dickensian characters, including Spenser Spender, a filmmaker who plans the adaptation of *Little Dorrit;* Sir Frederick Lustlambert, a bureaucrat who arranges the film's financing; and Rowan Phillips, a Dickens scholar who has written the film's script. Another important figure is Little Arthur, an adult so named because he ceased growing at age eight. Little Arthur is proprietor of an amusement park near Marshalsea Prison, a key setting in *Little Dorrit.* When Arthur's park closes, he loses his grasp on reality and commits murder. Once apprehended, he is sentenced to Marshalsea Prison, where Spender is filming his adaptation. Spender's insistence on realism eventually sparks the disaster of the novel's title, a raging inferno resulting from a mishap on the film set.

Galen Strawson, in his review of *The Great Fire of London* in the *Times Literary Supplement,* described Ackroyd's novel as an extension of Dickens' novel. "Ackroyd is clearly intrigued by the idea of past fiction working great changes in present (fictional) reality," Strawson wrote, "and he misses few chances to make further connections and to elaborate the network of co-incidences." Strawson was also impressed with Ackroyd's insights into human nature, writing that the novelist is "continually alive . . . to that hidden presence in many people's lives which he calls 'the vast sphere of unremembered wishes,' and to the effects it has on their conscious thoughts and actions."

Ackroyd followed *The Great Fire of London* with *The Last Testament of Oscar Wilde,* a novel purporting to be Wilde's autobiography, written during the final months of the author's life in Paris, where he had fled in self-imposed exile after serving two years in a British prison for indecency. Many critics praised Ackroyd's duplication of Wilde's own writing style and commended the work for its compelling insights into the personality of the notorious Irish writer. Toronto *Globe and Mail* critic William French, for instance, declared that Ackroyd "does an uncanny job of assuming Wilde's persona." Similarly, London *Times* reviewer Mary Cosh, who called Ackroyd's novel "a brilliant testament in its own right," lauded the writer for fashioning a well-rounded portrait of Wilde. Cosh wrote: "Not only does Peter Ackroyd exert a masterly command of language and ideas that credibly evokes Wilde's sharp wit in epigram or paradox, but he captures the raw vulnerability of the man isolated behind his mask."

When *The Last Testament of Oscar Wilde* was published in 1983, Ackroyd was already working on *T.S. Eliot: A Life.* In researching this biography, Ackroyd encountered imposing obstacles: he was forbidden by Eliot's estate from quoting Eliot's correspondence and unpublished verse, and he was allowed only minimum citations of the published poetry. Critics generally agreed, however, that Ackroyd nonetheless produced a worthwhile account of the modernist poet. As A. Walton Litz wrote in the *New York Times Book Review:* "Given all these restrictions, Peter Ackroyd has written as good a biography as we have any right to expect. He has assimilated most of the available evidence and used it judiciously." Rosemary Dinnage, who reviewed *T.S.*

Eliot in the *New York Review of Books,* also praised Ackroyd's difficult feat, observing that he "illuminates Eliot's poetry and criticism more acutely than many a ponderous academic volume." And *Newsweek*'s Paul Gray contended that Ackroyd's biography "does more than make the best of a difficult situation; it offers the most detailed portrait yet of an enigmatic and thoroughly peculiar genius." In the end, Ackroyd acknowledged that his inability to quote Eliot's letters or work made for a better book. "I had to be much more inventive about how I brought him to life," he explained.

In his biography *Dickens,* Ackroyd's intent was not to provide the definitive account of the writer's life, but rather to "rescue the character" of Dickens, as Verlyn Klinkenborg wrote in the *Smithsonian,* and thereby cross "the boundary between Dickens' fiction and his life." Klinkenborg further asserted that Ackroyd "does this not only to show how the novels illuminate the life, but also to understand the transforming powers of Dickens' imagination." Yet James R. Kincaid of the *New York Times Book Review* lamented that *Dickens* utilizes none of the twentieth-century conventions for understanding biography: "post-structuralist suspicions have made no inroads, and even Freud causes no alarm." Despite this, Kincaid allowed that *Dickens* sets itself apart from other biographies on the author and "demands our attention precisely (and only) because it is so open to the strange."

After several more novels, Ackroyd returned to biography with *Blake,* an account of visionary poet and artist William Blake (1757-1827). Blake's life appeared outwardly unremarkable. A London native, he was happily married, lived modestly, and worked hard. But many of Blake's contemporaries considered him insane; he spoke of his grandiose visions and hallucinations as if they were commonplace, often astounding acquaintances by relating his conversations with devils and angels. Blake was an engraver by trade whose illustration style was composed of intricate scenes of battling angels and fallen men, and he boldly compared his writing to John Milton's *Paradise Lost.* "Ackroyd does Blake the considerable service of taking his visions as seriously and soberly as he [Blake] did," stated a reviewer in the *Economist,* who added that Blake "has found the gentlest of biographers." In addition, Ackroyd's knowledge of London history serves to accentuate the biography, continued the reviewer, since he is familiar with the places that Blake would have known and which are the most likely locales for some of his prose. Charles Moore of the *Spectator* commented that Blake's eccentricities, one of which he called a "magnificent lack of embarrassment," were in fact the result of what Ackroyd deemed the "peculiar kind of lucidity which springs from those who have nothing left to lose."

Ackroyd's *The Life of Thomas More* focuses on More (1479-1535), the lawyer and statesman who was beheaded for refusing to support Henry VIII's divorce from Catherine of Aragon and the king's subsequent marriage to Anne Boleyn, and who was subsequently declared a saint by the Catholic Church. "Ackroyd makes him a man," wrote Bryce Christensen in *Booklist,* "with all the paradoxes, ironies, and complexities that mortality entails." Ackroyd traces More's life, from his baptism to his execution. Included are descriptions of his upbringing, education, and the people he interacted with, including his friend, the humanist Erasmus.

Andrew Sullivan wrote in the *New York Times Book Review* that Ackroyd sees More "not as an early individualist (as in Robert Bolt's gorgeously anachronistic play, *A Man for All Seasons*), or as an early ultramontane absolutist (in the vein of much nineteenth-century Roman Catholic hagiography), or even as a twisted and conflicted bigot (as in Richard Marius's biography, *Thomas More*). Rather, Ackroyd sees More simply as a particularly sensitive, and elegantly playful, representative of a vibrant, late-medieval, Catholic England." Sullivan claimed that Ackroyd "has an ear and a nose for physicality, and he deploys his expertise in the history of London to illustrate this faith. Rather than condescending to medieval Catholicism, Ackroyd empathetically observes it." A *Kirkus Reviews* contributor called *The Life of Thomas More* "a limpidly written and superbly wrought portrait of a complex hero."

In 2000 Ackroyd expanded his nonfiction writing to include a "biography of place" with his widely acclaimed work *London: The Biography*. This work has been followed by an even more expansive study: *Albion: The Origins of the English Imagination*. "Albion" is the name given ancient England, a name that evokes the island's mythic past. Calling *Albion* "fresh and fascinating," *America* contributor Joseph J. Feeney explained that in this work Ackroyd "turns to the inner springs of English[—as opposed to British, Scots, Welsh, or Irish—]creativity to ask, quite simply, what it means—what it has meant for centuries—to be an English writer, painter or composer." From *Beowulf* to the Arthurian legends, to the writings of Jonathan Swift, John Milton, J.R.R. Tolkien, and Daniel Defoe, to the musical compositions of Ralph Vaughn Williams, and the English penchant for the sea, dreams, gardening, and all things gothic, Ackroyd contends that the uniquely visionary—and often melancholy—English imagination is cyclical

rather than linear; "no art can be viewed in isolation since all the arts are part of the same continuum going back to Anglo-Saxon times," explained *Library Journal* contributor Denise J. Stankovics. *Contemporary Review* critic George Wedd added that this imagination is guided by the English landscape, a "spirit of place" which embodies "an acute appreciation of living on an island which is different from its neighbours—cold, stormy and dark and only to be reached across an often stormy ocean." Feeney praised *Albion* as "a grand success in its originality, its detail and its insights," while in *New Statesman* Will Self maintained that *Albion* is more a reflection of its author's own view of time and history than a scholarly study. Calling Ackroyd "an encyclopedist, universalist, [and] a cultural critic on the grand scale," Self concluded: "It doesn't matter whether his argument stands up to criticism, because I don't think that he's advancing one at all. Rather, he's taking us by the hand and leading us for a stroll around the tumultuous rookeries of his effortlessly acquired erudition."

Winner of the Whitbread Award, *Hawksmoor* fuses the detective and horror story genres. One of the work's two principal characters is Nicholas Hawksmoor, a police detective trying to solve a series of grisly murders at various eighteenth-century churches in London. Alternating with the account of Hawksmoor's progress are chapters on Victorian architect Nicholas Dyer. Dyer adheres to certain demonic principles and consecrates his churches with human blood sacrifices to please Satanic creatures. Dyer's nemesis is renowned architect Christopher Wren, his superior, who contends that science and rational thought will bring an end to superstition. Hawksmoor is also faithful to rationalism, and when he fails to perceive the connection between the two sets of murders, he finds himself slowly going insane.

Like Ackroyd's earlier novels, *Hawksmoor* impressed critics as a daring, technically innovative work. *Newsweek*'s Peter S. Prescott called it "a fascinating hybrid, a tale of terrors that does double duty as a novel of ideas." Similarly, *Time*'s Christopher Porterfield, who noted that Ackroyd possesses "a gift for historical pastiche," acknowledged "the eerie interplay between the earlier age and our own," and commended *Hawksmoor* as "a fictional architecture that is vivid, provocative, and as clever as . . . the devil." Another of the novel's many enthusiasts was Joyce Carol Oates, who wrote in the *New York Times Book Review* that *Hawksmoor* is "primarily a novel of ideas, a spirited debate between those who believe . . . that 'the highest Passion is Terrour' and those who believe . . . that the new science of rationalism and experimental method will eventually eradicate superstition." Oates deemed Ackroyd a "virtuoso" and lauded *Hawksmoor* as "an unfailingly intelligent work of the imagination."

Ackroyd executed another multiple-narrative story with *Chatterton,* a novel revolving around eighteenth-century poet Thomas Chatterton, who committed suicide at age seventeen. In Ackroyd's novel, Chatterton appears through an autobiographical document that suggests he may have faked his death. The document is owned by Charles Wychwood, a minor poet obsessed with an old portrait whose subject might have been Chatterton. The painting, however, is dated 1802, thus serving as further indication that Chatterton might not have died in 1770. Another story line concerns the creation of an actual painting, Henry Wallis's "The Death of Chatterton." But this painting, too, is misleading, for Wallis finished it in 1856, long after Chatterton's death, and relied on another young man, writer George Meredith, to represent Chatterton. Further discrepancies of authenticity and originality abound in the novel—a writer steals plots from second-rate Victorian novels, and an artist's secretary completes his employer's canvases. Even Chatterton confesses to chicanery of a sort, having attributed his own poems to fictitious fifteenth-century clergyman Thomas Rowley.

With *Chatterton,* Ackroyd strengthened his reputation as a unique and compelling storyteller. Dennis Drabelle, in his review for the *Washington Post Book World,* called Ackroyd's work a "witty, tricky new novel," and "a contrivance of the highest order." Denis Donoghue, writing in the *New York Times Book Review,* was similarly enthusiastic, describing *Chatterton* as "a wonderfully vivid book," and "superb." London *Times* reviewer Victoria Glendinning praised the novel as "agile and entertaining." She added that in the novel Ackroyd "has at least three balls in the air, and [he] keeps them up there."

The interconnectedness of time past, present, and future is central to *The House of Doctor Dee,* a historical novel concerning the Elizabethan-era intellectual John Dee, a purported practitioner of black magic and alchemy. Dee alternates narrative duties with Matthew Palmer, the modern-day inheritor of Dee's house in London, whose curiosity sparks an investigation into the house's lurid history. Much of the book's detail concerns the milieu of fifteenth-century London's buildings and history, one of Ackroyd's favorite subjects. *Spectator* reviewer Francis King noted the differing styles of the two narrators—Dee writes in an Elizabethan dialect while Matthew writes in a more modern voice—and called the contrast

"fascinating." As Matthew learns more about the house's previous owner, paranormal occurrences abound—not the least of which is Matthew's discovery that he is embroiled in an ancient plot concerning an immortal homunculus. Soon Dee's and Matthew's paths cross, and as they become aware of each other through visions and research, both are eventually redeemed in "a timeless London," stated Eric Korn of the *Times Literary Supplement,* "for time can be deconstructed by any magician or novelist."

Multiple narratives again are the crux of *Dan Leno and the Limehouse Golem,* published in the United States as *The Trial of Elizabeth Cree: A Novel of the Limehouse Murders.* In 1881 a seedy district in London suffers a gruesome series of murders some residents believe is the work of a golem. Exhibiting Ackroyd's penchant for infusing fiction with historical figures, the suspects include Karl Marx, George Gissing, and Dan Leno, one of the era's popular comedians. Ackroyd also weaves throughout his narrative the pages of a diary that may or may not be written by the murderer him or herself; the diary hints that the killer is actually John Cree, whose wife Elizabeth, a former vaudeville cross-dresser, is hanged for poisoning him during the opening pages of the novel. An air of growing oppression builds throughout the work, as people (both real and fictitious), the squalor of 1880s London, and the tangled storyline weigh increasingly heavily upon reader's imaginations.

Reviewing *The Trial of Elizabeth Cree* for the *Spectator,* David Sexton proclaimed that Ackroyd "manages these parallel narratives expertly. . . . He just loves to feel all London's past coming up behind him." Valerie Martin agreed in the *New York Times Book Review,* noting that the suspects in the work are all "men of ideas . . . obsessed with the need for social reform," and stated that the book is "not so much a novel of ideas as a novel about some men who had ideas." "Ackroyd's methods are both subtle and outrageous," Martin concluded. "Everything and everyone in [*The Trial of Elizabeth Cree*] . . . is so intimately connected that one reads with a sense of the world becoming progressively smaller and tighter. . . . The tone is agitated and compelling, by turns macabre and inventive, and this novel is a fine addition to Mr. Ackroyd's impressive body of work."

Placing blind English writer John Milton squarely in the North American colonies is "Ackroyd's joke" in *Milton in America,* according to *Times Literary Supplement* reviewer Treve Broughton. Milton perceived the exodus of his countrymen to New England as a kind of purgatory second only to death, and he is recorded as referring to America as "a savage desert." In Ackroyd's novel, the fictional Milton finds himself aboard a ship bound for New England in order to avoid capture by British authorities for publishing pamphlets critical of the Crown (the real Milton was in fact imprisoned for the same transgression). He becomes what Broughton termed a "hero in exile and visionary of the New World, accepting the adulation of his fellow passengers and generally talking up a storm." A shipwreck ends Milton's dreams of a grandiose landing in Boston, however; instead he finds himself aground in the New England wilderness, where he eventually founds his own colony. Broughton praised the work for its allusions and creativity, although he commented that the narrative sometimes fails from a lack of "conviction and pace." The critic called Ackroyd's Milton "a wonderful creation: as exasperating and exhilarating as we have come to expect of an Ackroyd hero." Citing parallels to Milton's *Paradise Lost,* John Clute viewed the work with a more critical eye. "Blindness governs the telling of the book, and is its final message," Clute stated in the *New Statesman.* "Milton's own blindness, as he stumbles into a paradise he will soon be instrumental in losing, is matched by the virtuoso blindness of the text itself, most of which comprises letters, recounted anecdotes, reveries, heresay." *Milton in America,* Clute concluded, "is a hard book to judge."

Ackroyd's fantasy novella *The Plato Papers* is set in the year 3700, and includes fifty-five short chapters of meditations, essays, and dialogues. The Plato of the story lives in a utopian London and is also a philosopher and teacher. "The Age of Witspell," has replaced "The Age of Mouldwarp," the scientific period that collapsed in the year 2300. Through his papers, Plato tries to educate Londoners about previous ages and encourages them to learn from history how the past can clarify the present. He works from the scraps of information that have survived into Witspell, and misses the mark when he credits Charles Dickens with writing a fictional work titled *On the Origins of Species by Means of Natural Selection,* and writes that Brother Marx was a comedian who wrote about gender, class, and race.

"*The Plato Papers* is a significant comic achievement," wrote Nick Gevers in *Infinity Plus* online. "But one is always aware in these passages that Plato is the fool whose japes conceal wisdom; every statement he makes about our time is symbolically or spiritually true at the core of its misprision. His scholarly madness is always close to true vision. And so, as Plato is vouchsafed a full and accurate experience of Mouldwarp, in which he

can wander its streets and speak with its souls of its benighted, activity-besotted, inwardly blind inhabitants, the novel's tone darkens." John Sutherland noted in the *New York Times Book Review* that *The Plato Papers* reminded him of Walter M. Miller, Jr.'s *A Canticle for Leibowitz,* although "the initial impression is surprise. One did not expect this book." Calling *The Plato Papers* "unlike anything else Peter Ackroyd . . . has written," Sutherland added that "the most enjoyable section of the book is the opening one, which is replete with jokes—some extremely funny."

Ackroyd, who has embarked on yet another literary endeavor with several volumes of earth history in the "Voyages through Time" series, once commented: "I think of myself primarily as a novelist. The other activities are marginal but related—certainly I think my novels and biographies are connected, although not in ways I myself could interpret. I leave that to the critics." Donna Seaman summed up her *Booklist* review of *Albion* by dubbing its author "a master extrapolator and wonderfully epigrammatic stylist fluent in many disciplines," a description Ackroyd's still evolving career proves out.

BIOGRAPHICAL AND CRITICAL SOURCES:

BOOKS

Contemporary Literary Criticism, Thomson Gale (Detroit, MI), Volume 34, 1985, Volume 52, 1989.
Dictionary of Literary Biography, Volume 155: *Twentieth-Century Literary Biographers,* Thomson Gale (Detroit, MI), 1995.

PERIODICALS

America, January 19, 1985; December 22, 2003, Joseph J. Feeney, review of *Albion: The Origins of the English Imagination,* p. 23.
Antioch Review, summer, 1985.
Booklist, October 1, 1998, Bryce Christensen, review of *The Life of Thomas More;* January 1, 2000, review of *The Plato Papers,* p. 871; September 15, 2003, Donna Seaman, review of *Albion,* p. 197; December 15, 2003, Jennifer Mattson, review of *In the Beginning,* p. 749.
Books, September-October, 1993, p. 8; summer, 1995, p. 22.
Choice, March, 1999, review of *The Life of Thomas More,* p. 1329.

Christian Science Monitor, February 1, 1985; January 10, 1990, Merle Rubin, review of *First Light,* p. 13; February 25, 1991, Merle Rubin, review of *Dickens,* p. 13; December 10, 1998, Merle Rubin, "Thomas More's Devotion to a Higher Law," p. 16; January 20, 2000, review of *The Plato Papers,* p. 16.

Contemporary Review, May, 2003, George Wedd, "Peter Ackroyd and the Englishman's Imagination," p. 305.

Economist, September 29, 1984; November 11, 1995; December 4, 1999, review of *The Plato Papers,* p. 4.

English Review, April, 2003, Victoria Kingston, "Face to Face" (interview), pp. 21-24.

Globe and Mail (Toronto, Ontario, Canada), January 7, 1984; June 26, 1999, review of *The Plato Papers,* p. D15.

Guardian, September 12, 1993, p. 28.

Kirkus Reviews, September 15, 1998, review of *The Life of Thomas More;* December 1, 1999, review of *The Plato Papers,* p. 1824; August 1, 2003, review of *Albion,* p. 997.

Library Journal, January, 2000, review of *The Plato Papers,* p. 154; December, 2002, Nancy R. Ives, review of *The Collection,* p. 125; September 15, 2003, Denise J. Stankovics, review of *Albion,* p. 57.

London Review of Books, November 17, 1983; December 22, 1994, pp. 20-22.

Los Angeles Times Book Review, December 2, 1984; February 14, 1988; October 25, 1992, pp. 3, 11; June 25, 1995, p. 12; January 16, 2000, review of *The Plato Papers,* p. 11.

Maclean's, February 17, 1986.

New Republic, December 17, 1984; January 18, 1993, pp. 29-32.

New Statesman, March 19, 1976; November 30, 1979; January 29, 1982; October 12, 1984; September 9, 1994, p. 39; September 27, 1985; November 4, 2002, Will Self, review of *Albion,* p. 50.

Newsweek, November 26, 1984; February 24, 1986.

New Yorker, March 25, 1985; November 23, 1992, pp. 142-143.

New York Review of Books, April 30, 1981; December 20, 1984.

New York Times, August 21, 1995, p. B3.

New York Times Book Review, December 16, 1984; January 19, 1986; January 17, 1988; January 13, 1991, pp. 1, 24; October 11, 1992, Alison Lurie, "Hanging out with Hogarth," p. 7; November 9, 1992, Christopher Lehmann-Haupt, "An Entertainment for the Library"; April 16, 1995, p. 7; August 21, 1995, Richard Bernstein, "The Limehouse Kill-

ings and Much, Much More"; April 14, 1996, Penelope Fitzgerald, "Innocence and Experience"; September 14, 1997, review of *Blake,* p. 44; October 25, 1998, Andrew Sullivan, "Public Man, Public Faith"; February 6, 2000, John Sutherland, "After Mouldwarp," p. 7.

New York Times Magazine, December 22, 1991, pp. 27-36.

Observer (London, England), August 29, 1993, p. 51; September 11, 1994; March 14, 1999, review of *The Life of Thomas More,* p. 14; March 28, 1999, review of *The Plato Papers,* p. 13.

Publishers Weekly, December 25, 1987, pp. 59-60; December 6, 1999, review of *The Plato Papers,* p. 55; August 11, 2003, review of *Albion,* p. 267; October 27, 2003, review of *The Beginning,* p. 71.

School Library Journal, January, 2004, Courtney Lewis, review of *In the Beginning,* p. 138.

Smithsonian, January, 1993, pp. 131-132.

Spectator, September 29, 1984; September 28, 1985; September 11, 1993, p. 27; September 10, 1994; September 23, 1995, pp. 36-37; August 9, 2003, Sebastian Smee, review of *The Clerkenwell Tales,* p. 38.

Time, December 3, 1984; February 24, 1986; May 29, 1995, p. 72.

Times (London, England), April 14, 1983; September 27, 1984; September 26, 1985; February 19, 1987; June 8, 1987; September 3, 1987.

Times Literary Supplement, May 3, 1974; December 7, 1979; August 28, 1981; January 29, 1982; April 15, 1983; September 21, 1984; November 30, 1984; September 27, 1985; September 11, 1987; September 10, 1993, p. 20; September 9, 1994, p. 21; August 30, 1996, p. 23.

Tribune Books (Chicago, IL), November 18, 1984; November 1, 1992, p. 6.

Voice Literary Supplement, December, 1984; December 1992, p. 6.

Wall Street Journal, April 9, 1996, Robert M. Adams, review of *Blake,* p. A16; May 6, 1997, Paul Dean, review of *Milton in America,* p. A20; October 22, 1998, Perez Zagorin, review of *The Life of Thomas More,* p. A20.

Washington Post Book World, December 9, 1984; February 16, 1986; January 24, 1988.

ONLINE

Infinity Plus Web site, http://www.iplus.zetnet.co.uk/ (August 12, 2000).

ADAMS, Alice 1926-1999
(Alice Boyd Adams)

PERSONAL: Born August 14, 1926, in Fredericksburg, VA; died May 27, 1999, in San Francisco, CA; daughter of Nicholson Barney (a professor) and Agatha Erskine (a writer; maiden name, Boyd); married Mark Linenthal, Jr. (a professor), 1946 (divorced, 1958); children: Peter. *Education:* Radcliffe College, B.A., 1946.

CAREER: Writer. Has held various office jobs, including secretary, clerk, and bookkeeper. Instructor at the University of California—Davis, 1980, University of California—Berkeley, and Stanford University.

AWARDS, HONORS: O. Henry Awards, Doubleday, 1971-82 and 1984-96, for short stories; National Book Critics Circle Award nomination, 1975, for *Families and Survivors;* National Endowment for the Arts fiction grant, 1976; Best American Short Stories Awards, 1976, 1992, 1996; Guggenheim fellowship, 1978; O. Henry Special Award for Continuing Achievement, 1982; Academy and Institute Award in Literature, American Academy and Institute of Arts and Letters, 1992.

WRITINGS:

Careless Love, New American Library (New York, NY), 1966, published as *The Fall of Daisy Duke,* Constable (London, England), 1967.
Families and Survivors (novel), Knopf (New York, NY), 1975.
Listening to Billie (novel), Knopf (New York, NY), 1978.
Beautiful Girl (short stories), Knopf (New York, NY), 1979.
Rich Rewards (novel), Knopf (New York, NY), 1980.
To See You Again (short stories), Knopf (New York, NY), 1982.
Molly's Dog (short stories), Evert (Concord, NH), 1983.
Superior Women (novel), Knopf (New York, NY), 1984.
Return Trips (short stories), Knopf (New York, NY), 1985.
Roses, Rhododendron: Two Flowers, Two Friends (nonfiction), Redpath Press (Minneapolis, MN), 1987.
Second Chances (novel), Knopf (New York, NY), 1988.
After You've Gone (short stories), Knopf (New York, NY), 1989.

Mexico: Some Travels and Some Travelers There, introduction by Jan Morris, Prentice-Hall (New York, NY), 1990.
Caroline's Daughters (novel), Knopf (New York, NY), 1991.
Almost Perfect (novel), Knopf (New York, NY), 1993.
A Southern Exposure (novel), Knopf (New York, NY), 1995.
Medicine Men, Knopf (New York, NY), 1997.
The Last Lovely City (short stories), Knopf (New York, NY), 1999.
After the War (novel), Knopf (New York, NY), 2000.
The Stories of Alice Adams, Knopf (New York, NY), 2002.

Contributor of short stories to anthologies, including *Best American Short Stories,* 1976, and *Prize Stories: The O. Henry Awards,* 1971-82 and 1984-88. Contributor to periodicals, including *New Yorker, Atlantic, Shenandoah, Crosscurrents, Grand Street, Mademoiselle, Virginia Quarterly Review, New York Times Book Review, Vogue, Redbook, McCall's,* and *Paris Review.*

SIDELIGHTS: In many of her short stories and novels, Alice Adams wrote about women struggling to find their place in the world. Adams challenged her female characters, whether they lived alone or with a man, to establish meaningful lives and to work creatively both with life's blessings and its disappointments. Robert Phillips wrote in *Commonweal:* "The usual Adams character does not give in to his or her fate, but attempts to shape it, however misguidedly. . . . Women become aware not only of missed opportunities, but also of life's endless possibilities." While men occupy important positions in the female characters' lives, Adams's books tended to focus on the women's own struggles with identity. "The conflict—not the outward conflict between men and women, but the private and inward conflict of individual women—runs through all Adams's work," noted Stephen Goodwin in the *Washington Post Book World.* "Her women value men, but prize their own independence." Adams's women generally find true contentment in work and the freedom to make their own choices. According to William L. Stull in the *Dictionary of Literary Biography Yearbook,* "each of her novels concerns a woman's search for satisfying work as a means to economic, artistic, and finally political independence." *Contemporary Southern Writers* essayist Annette Petrusso pointed out that Adams's "repeated exploration of personal change can relate to a larger social context—the post World War II era when more women pursued self-realization, for example, and more casual discussion of personal sexual experiences."

Adams's first novel, *Careless Love,* about a woman seeking a man who is more exciting than either her husband or her extramarital lover, "has a more sentimental tone" than the author's subsequent works, according to Petrusso. Stull, however, felt Adams intended the book as a work of satire rather than sentiment, but he noted that in several of Adams's writings, it was "hard to determine whether her overall attitude toward her characters is sympathetic or satirical." To him, Adams is at her best when she "wields a subtle irony tempered by empathy," something that he thinks happened most often in her short stories but occurred in her novels as well. As Petrusso remarked, "While Adams is usually compassionate in her portrayal of her female characters, she can also explore the ironies in their lives."

After *Careless Love,* Adams firmly established herself as a novelist with *Families and Survivors* and *Listening to Billie.* The first follows the ups and downs of two sisters during three decades of their lives. The second details a character buffeted by the suicides of her husband and her father and her struggle to deal with their deaths. It was in these novels, noted Sheila Weller in *Ms.* magazine, that Adams first revealed herself as "a wonderfully old-fashioned writer." She revealed, continued Weller, the qualities that underlie her fiction: "the Dickensian coincidence, the solemn omniscience, the sense of lives destined to intertwine." In addition to laying the foundation for her fiction, Adams also honed a style to serve her thematic concerns in these early novels. "In a prose style that was somehow both grave (even ominous) and unlabored almost to the point of being dashed off," observed Weller, "she showed how time burnishes character, how we come to accrue what we refer to as the 'lessons' of life." Adams succeeded, in Weller's words, in creating a "powerful wistfulness." For Petrusso, these two books "define [Adams's] maturity as a novelist."

In *Rich Rewards,* Adams focuses on a middle-aged woman who spent her life in a series of disappointing and often addictive relationships with men. At the novel's beginning, the heroine, Daphne, having recently broken off a relationship with an abusive lover, intends to immerse herself in her work as an interior decorator. She becomes embroiled in a friend's troubled marriage and eventually finds herself reunited with a lover from her youth. According to Larry T. Blades in *Critique,* "*Rich Rewards* chronicles the maturation of Daphne from a woman who devotes her life to punishing and humiliating sexual encounters into a woman who can establish a productive love relationship because she has first learned to respect herself." In the *New York Times*

Book Review, Anne Tyler called it "a marvelously readable book. It's mysterious in the best sense—not a setup, artificial mystery but a real one, in which we wonder along with the heroine just what all the chaotic events are leading up to." Chicago *Tribune Books* contributor Lynne Sharon Schwartz called *Rich Rewards* "a stringent story elegantly told, and enhanced by a keen moral judgment. . . . As in her earlier novels, . . . Adams is concerned with the shards of broken families and with the quickly severed ties that spring up in place of families. But in *Rich Rewards* the harshness latent in such tenuous relations is more overt than before. . . . It takes a sort of magician to render hope from the brew of pain, muddle, and anomie that Alice Adams has managed charmingly to concoct. Once again she brings it off with panache."

Superior Women concerns the relationship among four young women during their years at Radcliffe and afterwards. The novel has frequently been compared to Mary McCarthy's *The Group,* which described the lives of eight women who attended Vassar in the 1930s. As in *The Group, Superior Women* follows its characters through graduation and into the outside world, showing how political and social events affected their lives. This technique met with some criticism. "The effects of viewing a whole age through gauze in this fashion is pretty deadening," claimed Michael Wood in the *London Review of Books.* Jonathan Yardley, a *Washington Post Book World* contributor, stated: "What we . . . have is a shopping list of public events, causes and fads. As the women leave Radcliffe and enter the world, Adams dutifully trots them through everything from civil rights to Watergate." And yet other critics found Adams's usual style, allied with a swifter pace, produced a highly satisfactory work. John Updike wrote in the *New Yorker,* "The novel . . . reads easily, even breathlessly; one looks forward, in the chain of coincidences, to the next encounter, knowing that this author always comes to the point from an unexpected angle, without fuss." And Barbara Koenig Quart remarked in *Ms.* that Adams's talent holds the reader through any weak points: "Not at all systematically, to be sure, and with fairly thin references to the extraordinary events of those turbulent decades, still, Adams holds us firmly with a lively narrative pace. She creates an almost gossipy interest in what happens to her characters; and she can't write a bad sentence, though hers is the kind of fine unobtrusive style that you notice only if you're looking for it." Some reviewers were uncertain whether *Superior Women* was "a serious, satiric novel," "lighter, spicier fare," or "somehow both at once," related Stull, who maintained that Adams's "intention seems deeply divided, a have-your-romance-and-mock-it-too attitude."

Adams's novel *Second Chances* portrays the lives of men and women who face the onset of their sixties and the stigma of "old age." Like Adams's other characters, they worry about relationships and suffer losses, but in this book a marriage dissolving through death forces them to evaluate their own lives. Adams once told Mervyn Rothstein in an interview for the *New York Times:* "The novel grew out of the fact I was getting toward being sixty myself. It struck me that sixty is not middle-age. I do not know a lot of people who are 120. . . . I began looking at people who are ten to fifteen years older. The book is for me a kind of exploration." *Second Chances* also gave Adams a chance to speak truthfully about aging. In an interview with Kim Heron for the *New York Times Book Review,* she once noted, "I have the perception that people talk about old age in two ways. One is to focus on the horrors of it, not that they should be underestimated, and the other is to romanticize it."

The book starts with a group of long-term friends, all of them examining changes in their relationships. The scene soon changes to memory, and the reader is filled in on the characters' sometimes highly intricate lives. Barbara Williamson related in the *Washington Post Book World* that "the backward and forward motion of time in the novel happily captures the way old people tell wistful, probably falsified tales of when they were young and beautiful. And the stories of their youth are the liveliest parts of the novel." But Williamson also found that the characters' very gracefulness inhibited Adams's attempts to portray old age truthfully: "The picture presented in this novel seems too kind, too pretty. Old age, we suspect, is not a gentle stroll on the beach at twilight with kind and caring friends. Where, we ask, is the 'rage against the dying of the light'?" But *Los Angeles Times Book Review* contributor Joanna Barnes praised the depiction of the pain that exists in all relationships, whether among the young or the old. Barnes wrote: "In a larger sense, it is the nature of friendship under Adams's delicate examination here. She recreates, too, the haunting undertone of the loneliness present in all human intercourse, that separateness which, despite the presence of kindly acquaintances and lovers, can never be bridged nor breached."

In *Almost Perfect,* Adams created "an oddly affecting morality tale that tastes like good medicine with no more than the requisite spoonful of darkly humorous sugar," in the words of *World Literature Today* contributor B.A. St. Andrews. In her tale, the author places familiar characters and issues in a familiar setting; as Anita Shreve wrote in the *Washington Post Book World,* "Once again we are on familiar Adams territory: atop the hills of San Francisco, inside the well-appointed interiors of the successful and near-successful, and enmeshed in a constellation of interconnecting and constantly observed relationships." The central relationship here is that of Stella Blake, a journalist, and Richard Fallon, a commercial artist. At first Richard seems almost perfect, as does Stella's relationship with him. Soon, however, Stella's condition in life and work improves, while Richard's gets worse. Their relationship soon suffers strains and other relationships around them grow more complicated. Through these relationships, observed Shreve, "Adams explores the consequences of hate, love and just plain bitchiness in a universe in which everyone seems to be connected to everyone else." Moreover, Lawrence Thornton noted in the *New York Times Book Review,* "Ms. Adams's chronicle of Richard's descent into psychotic depression is minutely recorded. And it is the double trajectory—Stella's rise to success and self-esteem against Richard's self-destruction—that gives the novel its compelling signature."

Reviewers of *Almost Perfect* found much to praise in its author's use of character and setting. "A lot goes on in the two-year span of the novel," wrote Victoria Jenkins in Chicago's *Tribune Books,* "and it's all marvelously well told—full of revealing detail, smart dialogue and astute observation. Adams's characters are drawn with such precision and complexity that it's easy to imagine forgetting that they are characters in fiction and to mistakenly remember them as real people." Jenkins also lauded Adams's style. "*Almost Perfect* has a breathless, gossipy tone. The story is told in the present tense from the points of view of many different characters with many parenthetical asides. We're drawn in as though we're part of the circle of friends, confided in and gossiped to." And as Thornton wrote, "Adams explores the tension of [Stella and Richard's] deteriorating relationship with something approaching the novelist's equivalent of perfect pitch. She paces the story by means of highly concentrated episodes and uses the present tense effectively to increase the sense of urgency."

In *Caroline's Daughters,* the title character and her third husband return to San Francisco from a long stay in Europe. Upon her arrival home, Caroline finds each of her five daughters in some degree of crisis. Caroline's daughters range in age from twenty-five to forty-one. Caroline's first husband died in World War II, leaving her to take care of their daughter, Sage, by herself. The three middle daughters were fathered by her second husband, a doctor. Liza is married with children and hopes to write a book. Fiona is a restaurateur and Jill a lawyer and high-class call girl. The youngest girl's father is Caroline's current husband. Named Portia, she is struggling to find her place.

Adams wove together the lives of this mother and her daughters and suggests that the daughters need their mother more than she needs them. As Christopher Lehmann-Haupt commented in the *New York Times,* "What Ms. Adams's witty scenes add up to is any number of things: a portrait of San Francisco, a profile of the 1980's, a still life of women after liberation." In fact, in the opinion of *Women's Review of Books* contributor Barbara Rich, "One of the delights of the book is the way in which it illuminates the superficial sheen of the Reagan years, and how it reflects back upon the principals' lives." Even so, noted Hilma Wolitzer in the *Los Angeles Times Book Review,* "Despite its contemporary style, and its current setting and concerns, *Caroline's Daughters* is a roomy and tantalizing old-fashioned read."

Ellen Pall believed that this book has much to offer its readers. "*Caroline's Daughters* is crammed with plot," she wrote. "Careers rise and fall, affairs begin and end, people fall in and out of love and fortunes are won and lost as the lives of the sisters intertwine in gratifyingly shocking ways." And, added Wolitzer, "There is enough intrigue here to keep things animated and suspenseful, and enough sensual detail—more often related to food and clothing than to sex—to create a lush atmosphere." Dispelling the fear that a novel with so many characters and so much happening would become far too complex for the reader, Rich countered, "If the cast of characters and their convoluted scripts sound overwhelming, they may well have been in the hands of a less skillful writer. Alice Adams knows exactly where she is going, and why. She delivers a fluid, meaty, sexy and rewarding novel." Pall's praise for Adams's craftsmanship was more tempered. "Fluent though the prose is, it is otherwise unremarkable," she wrote, "and a few of the characters seem to have sprung more from the pages of glossy magazines than the depths of the author's imagination or experience. And the very end of the novel feels artificial and arbitrary. Nevertheless," she believed, "this is an immensely satisfying book."

In *A Southern Exposure,* Adams departed from San Francisco and moved to the sandhills of North Carolina just prior to World War II, when the Depression still dominated American life. A New England couple, Harry and Cynthia Baird, leave their home for a new life in the South and settle in a small community peopled by a famous poet, his depressed wife, her psychiatrist, and a wealthy gossip, among others. In following the town's many social encounters, Adams crafted a portrait of people and place. Lee Smith, writing in the *New York Times Book Review,* noted that "sex and race" are "two of the major if understated themes in this novel." A *Publishers Weekly* reviewer commented that the novel's "melodramas feel witty, given Adam's intelligent characterization, and are at equal pitch with her descriptions of Pinehill's flush, distracting beauty." *Booklist* contributor Nancy Pearl added, "Adams's perfect pitch for dialogue has never been put to better use." Smith concluded, *A Southern Exposure* "is rich and sweet, like candy; you read away feeling guilty because you're enjoying it so much, and then it's over."

Adams returned to San Francisco for *Medicine Men,* which recounted the struggles of recently widowed Molly Bonner and her best friend, Felicia Flood. Molly is dating Dr. Dave Jacobs and is diagnosed with a life-threatening brain tumor. Jacobs guides Molly through her treatment, but brings to their relationship his professional tendency to control his patients and dismiss their fears. Felicia is the unfortunate paramour of the self-aggrandizing, misogynistic Dr. Raleigh Sanders. The tale is an indictment of the male-dominated medical establishment, an affirmation of the common sense and strength of friendship between women, and an absorbing yarn about complicated personal lives in a high-powered professional medical setting. For Deborah Mason, writing in the *New York Times Book Review,* Adams's portrayal of a hopelessly insensitive and inept medical establishment was "overkill." On the other hand, a *Booklist* contributor noted that "this 'medical' novel transcends any of the genre's stock characters and hackneyed situations to become a trenchant psychological exploration of physical and emotional pain and recovery." And Ellen Howards declared in *Boston Book Review* that "medicine aside, this is an entirely enjoyable novel to read just for the sake of Adams's interwoven story lines and sharp, natural wit."

Beautiful Girl was Adams's first published collection of short stories. Although half of the stories had won the O. Henry Prize, the tales did not fully satisfy *New York Times Book Review* critic Katha Pollitt. While praising Adams's gifts as a storyteller, Pollitt lamented the ubiquitous presence of one "recognizable type" of heroine in the collection: "I kept waiting for Miss Adams to flash an ironic smile toward these supremely sheltered, idle, unexamined people. . . . She never does." *Hudson Review* contributor Dean Flowers believed that in *Beautiful Girl,* Adams portrays difficult problems with too much ease: "At their best these stories explore complex relationships in a quick, deceptively offhand manner. They tend to begin with a tense problem (a wife dying, a divorce impending, a moment of wrath, an anxious move to a new place) and unravel gradually, without much climax except a muted sense of recovered balance and diminished expectation. . . . One feels neither gladness nor sorrow in such conclusions, but rather an implicit appeal of stylish melancholy." Still, the intensity of her characters' feelings can belie the author's seemingly neat appraisals of their lives. Susan Schindehette commented in the *Saturday Review* of *Return Trips:* "It is Adams's gift to reveal the tremendous inner workings beneath the apparent tranquility and make characters come to life in her spare, elegant style."

Adams moved to California in the 1950s, and the state and its residents figure prominently in her work. *To See You Again* is a "collection of nineteen short stories [that] may surprise readers who have been led to think that all fictional California women are angst-ridden, sex-crazed or mellowed-out," wrote Paul Gray in *Time.* Some reviewers took issue with the book's even tone. While Benjamin DeMott admired the irony and understatement in the collection, he noted in the *New York Times Book Review:* "Life in this book is indeed lived . . . in easygoing obedience to the key emotional imperative of the age (Change Your Life). None of Miss Adams's people ever tears a passion to tatters. . . . But these stories do suffer from a lack of tonal variety." Mary Morris, in a *Tribune Books* article, stated that Adams "has spared us the fights, she has spared us the asking of the unaskable, the struggle to love. And in the end she has also spared us what we want most, the drama." Morris claimed "the protagonists' inability to achieve involvement" frustrated the reader. Adams's characters in *To See You Again* "don't reach out, they don't fight back. What they do is leave, remember or fantasize." But the strength of the book, Linda Pastan wrote in *American Book Review,* lies in "the cumulative effect" that makes "the reader feel as though he knows the San Francisco of Alice Adams in the special way one knows a place inhabited by friends."

Adams earned ample praise with her third collection of stories, *Return Trips,* which "shows a master writer at the height of her powers," says Stull. He related: "The title is apt in every way, from the dedication [to Adams's son, Peter Adams Linenthal] to the travel motifs that link these fifteen accounts of women recalling or revisiting people and places that shaped their lives." All the stories in the collection depict women struggling along on a physical or spiritual journey. According to Isabel Raphael in the London *Times:* "To make a return trip, [Adams] seems to be saying, you must leave where you are, and there is no guarantee that things will be

the same when you come back, or that you yourself will be unaffected by the journey. But with a solid experience of love in your life on which to base a sense of identity, you will not lose your way." And Elaine Kendall concluded in the *Los Angeles Times* that in *Return Trips,* "unburdened by complex rigging, her imagination sails swiftly and gracefully over a sea of contemporary emotional experience, sounding unexpected depths."

Adams's next collection of short stories appeared in 1989 as *After You've Gone.* As Ron Carlson explained in the *New York Times Book Review,* "The fourteen short romances in Alice Adams's new collection are—with two exceptions—about women. These women are professionals . . . who live in the upscale world of gracious houses in cities from California to Maryland." The stories are also about the aftermath of lost relationships. Catherine Petroski detailed the themes of these stories in *Tribune Books,* "Several stories of uneasy coexistence . . . deal pointedly with the difficulties people have in sustaining relationships and why, given the difficulties, they persist in them." She added, "The other major strain running through the collection is the theme of old friendships." Carlson expressed disappointment with these works. "Reading the stories becomes like reading about people in stories and not—as in the best realistic fiction—about people we know." Yet, in Petroski's opinion, "Adams's new collection of short stories, her fourth, is the work of a writer at the height of her powers—lucid, confident, refined, adept, provocative, perspicacious, startling and satisfying."

Another book of short stories, *The Last Lovely City,* came out in 1999. The world of this collection, according to *New York Times Book Review* contributor Susan Bolton, was "an essentially female place" that was "both densely populated and lonely," given the troubled relationships Adams's characters have had with men in these tales of "love lost and found and usually lost again." A couple on the brink of divorce discuss a reconciliation, which may be ill-advised; a widowed doctor changes his life drastically after he realizes that his young woman friend does not reciprocate his desire. Bolton praised Adams's portrayals of these people: "Her characters are as specifically executed as their names; their inner voices speak as loudly as their real ones." These characters are not easy to love, Bolton averred, but added, "perhaps that is Adams's point: when we search for love, we are not always lovable."

In her final novel, *After the War,* published a year after her death, Adams revisited the characters she introduced in *A Southern Exposure.* The place is Pinehill,

North Carolina, the year is 1944, and World War II is raging. Readers are once again caught up in the lives of Cynthia and Harry Baird and their neighbors, which include a New York Jewish couple, active members of the Communist Party. To the themes of racism and sexual infidelity are added the threats of communism and military combat. Beth E. Andersen, reviewing *After the War* for *Library Journal,* wrote: "Adams is a genius at affectionately tweaking the stereotypes of a Southern gentility struggling mightily to understand the ways of the world." A *Publishers Weekly* critic similarly praised the novelist's "deep acquaintance with her milieu" and with period details that allow "a smooth reference to the atomic bomb and the musical *Oklahoma* in the same sentence."

In 2002 Knopf reprised Adams's prolific career—six story collections and eleven novels—by republishing fifty-three of her tales in *The Stories of Alice Adams.* About this compilation, and her literary achievement, a *Publishers Weekly* reviewer wrote: "Taken together, these stories betray the changing mores of the past half-century; taken in sequence, they trace the changes in the American short story over the past forty years, some of those changes wrought by Adams herself." The variety of Adams's richly portrayed female protagonists is here in abundance: mothers and daughters, sisters and best friends, wives and lovers, independent women embroiled in messy relationships. Andersen, reviewing the collection in *Library Journal,* noted Adams's gift for creating "the familiar landscapes of interior life with pitch-perfect diction," adding that, "with her pen Adams indeed became the master of the encapsulated moment."

BIOGRAPHICAL AND CRITICAL SOURCES:

BOOKS

Contemporary Literary Criticism, Thomson Gale (Detroit, MI), Volume 6, 1976, Volume 13, 1980, Volume 46, 1988.
Contemporary Southern Writers, St. James Press (Detroit, MI), 1999.
Dictionary of Literary Biography Yearbook: 1986, Thomson Gale (Detroit, MI), 1987.

PERIODICALS

American Book Review, July, 1983.
Atlanta Journal Constitution, January 2, 1990, p. B3; November 17, 1991, p. K6; August 1, 1993, p. N10.

Belles Lettres, winter, 1989, p. 7; winter, 1993, p. 37.
Booklist, December 15, 1978; January 15, 1982; June 15, 1984; July, 1985; August, 1995, p. 1907; February 15, 1997, p. 971; August, 2000, Brad Hooper, review of *After the War;* July, 2002, review of *The Stories of Alice Adams,* p. 1795.
Books and Bookmen, March, 1985; February, 1986.
Boston Book Review, May 1, 1997.
Boston Globe, April 7, 1991, p. A18; October 30, 1991, p. 60; July 28, 1993, p. 23.
Chicago Tribune, September 1, 1985.
Christian Science Monitor, February 20, 1975; October 16, 1985, p. 22; June 17, 1988, p. 20.
Commonweal, March 25, 1983, p. 188.
Critique, summer, 1986.
Globe and Mail (Toronto, Ontario, Canada), November 10, 1984.
Harvard Magazine, February, 1975.
Hudson Review, summer, 1979; spring, 1985.
Kirkus Reviews, September 1, 2002, review of *The Stories of Alice Adams,* p. 1246.
Library Journal, October 1, 2000, Beth E. Andersen, review of *After the War,* p. 146; August, 2002, Beth E. Andersen, review of *The Stories of Alice Adams,* p. 147.
Listener, January 29, 1976.
London Review of Books, February 21, 1985.
Los Angeles Times, April 13, 1982; August 19, 1985; October 10, 1989, p. V3.
Los Angeles Times Book Review, November 16, 1980; September 14, 1986, p. 14; May 8, 1988, p. 13; October 14, 1990, p. 14; March 10, 1991, p. 3; July 11, 1993, p. 3.
Ms., September, 1980, p. 18; September, 1984, p. 28.
New England Review, autumn, 1986.
New Leader, March 27, 1978.
New Republic, February 4, 1978.
New Statesman, January 16, 1976.
Newsweek, February 3, 1975.
New Yorker, February 10, 1975; November 5, 1984, p. 160; August 2, 1993, p. 83.
New York Times, January 30, 1975; January 10, 1978; April 11, 1982, p. 7; August 21, 1985, p. C17; May 19, 1988; March 21, 1991, p. C21.
New York Times Book Review, March 16, 1975; February 26, 1978; January 14, 1979; September 14, 1980, p. 13; April 11, 1982; September 23, 1984, p. 9; September 1, 1985; September 21, 1986, p. 42; May 1, 1988, p. 11; October 8, 1989, p. 27; April 7, 1991, p. 12; December 1, 1991, p. 20; July 11, 1993, p. 7; December 4, 1994, p. 88; April 13, 1997, p. 26; February 14, 1999, p. 16.
Observer (London, England), January 18, 1976; August 14, 1988, p. 41.

People, April 3, 1978.

Publishers Weekly, January 16, 1978; July 31, 1995, p. 65; August 14, 2000, review of *After the War,* p. 329; September 2, 2002, review of *The Stories of Alice Adams,* p. 50.

Rapport, number 3, 1992, p. 24.

Rolling Stone, April 20, 1978.

San Francisco Review of Books, spring, 1985, p. 19; number 1, 1988, p. 35.

Saturday Review, November-December, 1985, p. 73.

Spectator, December 3, 1988, p. 35.

Story Quarterly, number 11, 1980.

Time, December 26, 1977; April 19, 1982.

Times (London, England), January 9, 1986.

Times Literary Supplement, January 16, 1976; January 31, 1986, p. 112; July 28, 1988, p. 840.

Tribune Books (Chicago, IL), September 14, 1980; May 2, 1982; May 1, 1988, p. 7; September 3, 1989, p. 4; March 10, 1991, p. 1; July 18, 1993, p 3; August 15, 1993, p. 8.

Village Voice, January 9, 1978.

Washington Post, October 24, 1989, p. C3; November 21, 1991, p. D3.

Washington Post Book World, February 23, 1975; January 13, 1978; January 21, 1979; October 12, 1980, p. 9; May 9, 1982; September 2, 1984, p. 3; September 15, 1985, p. 5; May 6, 1988; March 10, 1991, p. 1; June 27, 1993, p. 1.

West Coast Review of Books, March, 1978; November, 1984, p. 26.

Women's Review of Books, February, 1985, p. 14; July, 1991, p. 41; December, 1993, p. 23; September, 1997, p. 19.

World Literature Today, spring, 1994, p. 369.

OBITUARIES:

PERIODICALS

Detroit News, May 29, 1999.

ONLINE

Salon.com, http://www.salon.com/ (March 7, 2000).

*   *   *

ADAMS, Alice Boyd
See ADAMS, Alice

ADAMS, Douglas 1952-2001
(Douglas Noel Adams)

PERSONAL: Born March 11, 1952, in Cambridge, England; died of an apparent heart attack, May 11, 2001, in Santa Barbara, CA; son of Christopher Douglas (a management consultant) and Janet (a nurse; maiden name, Donovan, present surname, Thrift) Adams; married Jane Elizabeth Belson, 1991; children: Polly Jane Rocket. *Education:* St. John's College, Cambridge, B.A. (with honors), 1974, M.A. *Hobbies and other interests:* Purchasing equipment for recreations he would like to take up, playing acoustic guitar, scuba diving, fiddling with computers.

CAREER: British Broadcasting Corporation (BBC), London, producer and scriptwriter for "Hitchhiker's Guide to the Galaxy" radio and television series, beginning 1978, script editor for television series "Doctor Who," 1978-80; writer, 1978-2001.

MEMBER: Cambridge Footlights Club, which also produced *Monthy Python's* John Cleese, Eric Idle, and Graham Chapman.

AWARDS, HONORS: Best Books for Young Adults List, American Library Association (ALA), 1980, for *The Hitchhiker's Guide to the Galaxy*; The Hitchhiker's Guide to the Galaxy was voted "one of the nation's 21 best-loved novels" by the British public as part of the BBC's The Big Read, 2003.

WRITINGS:

"THE HITCHHIKER'S GUIDE TO THE GALAXY" SERIES

The Hitchhiker's Guide to the Galaxy, Pan Books (London, England), 1979, Harmony (New York, NY), 1980.

The Restaurant at the End of the Universe, Pan Books (London, England), 1980, Harmony (New York, NY), 1982.

Life, the Universe and Everything, Harmony (New York, NY), 1982.

So Long, and Thanks for All the Fish, Pan Books (London, England), 1984, Harmony (New York, NY), 1985.

The Hitchhiker's Trilogy (omnibus volume), Harmony (New York, NY), 1984.

The Original Hitchhiker's Radio Scripts, edited with an introduction by Geoffrey Perkins, Harmony (New York, NY), 1985.

The Hitchhiker's Quartet (omnibus volume), Harmony (New York, NY), 1986.

More Than Complete Hitchhiker's Guide, Longmeadow Press (New York, NY), 1987, revised edition published as the *More Than Complete Hitchhiker's Guide Fifty-one Point Eighty,* 1989, unabridged edition, 1994.

Mostly Harmless, Crown (New York, NY), 1992.

The Illustrated Hitchhiker's Guide to the Galaxy, Crown (New York, NY), 1994.

The Ultimate Hitchhiker's Guide, unabridged and complete version, Wings Books (New York, NY), 1996.

(Creator and author of introduction) Terry Jones, *Douglas Adams's Starship Titanic: A Novel,* Harmony Books (New York, NY), 1997.

The Hitchhiker's Guide to the Galaxy: The Authorized Collection, adapted by John Carnell, illustrated by Steve Leialoha, DC Comics, 1997.

Neil Richards, *Douglas Adams's Starship Titanic: The Official Strategy Game,* Three Rivers Press, 1998.

The Salmon of Doubt: Hitchiking the Galaxy One Last Time, Harmony Books (New York, NY), 2002.

Also author of scripts for the "Hitchhiker's Guide to the Galaxy" radio and television programs, BBC-TV, and "Dr. Who" episodes (1978-1980); author, with Steve Meretzky, of interactive computer program.

OTHER

(With others) *Not 1982: Not the Nine o'Clock News Rip-Off Annual,* Faber (London, England), 1981.

(With John Lloyd) *The Meaning of Liff,* Pan Books (London, England), 1983, Harmony (New York, NY), 1984.

(Editor, with Peter Fincham) *The Utterly Utterly Merry Comic Relief Christmas Book,* Fontana (London, England), 1986.

Dirk Gently's Holistic Detective Agency (novel), Simon & Schuster (New York, NY), 1987.

The Long Dark Tea-Time of the Soul (novel), Heinemann, 1988, Simon & Schuster (New York, NY), 1989.

(With Mark Carwardine) *Last Chance to See* (nonfiction), Crown (New York, NY), 1990.

(With Lloyd) *The Deeper Meaning of Liff: A Dictionary of Things There Aren't Words for Yet—but There Ought to Be,* Crown (New York, NY), 1990.

Two Complete Novels (*Dirk Gently's Holistic Detective Agency* and *The Long Dark Tea-Time of the Soul*), Wings Books, 1994.

Dirk Gently's Holistic Detective Agency: Two Complete Novels (contains *Dirk Gently's Holistic Detective Agency* and *The Long Dark Tea-Time of the Soul*), Random House (New York, NY), 1995.

Contributor to *The Great Ape Project: Equality Beyond Humanity,* edited by Peter Singer, St. Martin's, 1993, and *Tales from the Jungle: A Rainforest Reader,* edited by Daniel R. Katz and Miles Chapin, Crown (New York, NY), 1995. Also author of episodes of "Doctor Who" for BBC-TV; coauthor of interactive computer program, "Bureaucracy" and CD-Rom game, "Starship Titanic."

ADAPTATIONS: Hitchhiker's Guide has been produced as a stage play, Liverpool (1979); producer Ivan Reitman holds the movie rights to the *Hitchhiker* trilogy; a film version of *The Hitchhiker's Guide to the Galaxy* is to be written by Karey Kirkpatrick and directed by Jay Roach. The screenplay will be based on a draft by Douglas, who was working on it at the time of his death and will be credited as an executive producer. A BBC radio broadcast of *The Restaurant at the End of the Universe, Life, the Universe, and Everything,* and *So Long, and Thanks For All the Fish* is planned for 2004.

The film version of *The Hitchhiker's Guide to the Galaxy* opened on April 29, 2005. The film was written by Adams and Karey Kirkpatrick, directed by Garth Jenning, and released by Touchstone Pictures and Spyglass Entertainment.

SIDELIGHTS: When Douglas Adams first dreamed up the cosmic satire *The Hitchhiker's Guide to the Galaxy,* he had no idea his radio series would become so popular as to inspire several novels, a television series, and even an interactive computer game. As the author once commented: "I never set out to be a novelist, because I thought I was just a scriptwriter. When I was asked by Pan Books to turn my radio scripts of *The Hitchhiker's Guide to the Galaxy* into a book, I thought that there were two ways of doing it. I could either do the normal script-novelization hack job, which involves going through the script putting 'he said' or 'she said' (and in the case of my books, 'it said' as well) at the end of each line, or I could have a go at doing it properly. I decided to see if I could do it properly." Adams's first attempt at a novel proved immensely successful, garnering favorable reviews and selling 100,000 copies in its first month alone.

The Hitchhiker's Guide to the Galaxy, as well as its sequels, *The Restaurant at the End of the Universe; Life, the Universe and Everything; So Long, and Thanks for All the Fish;* and *Mostly Harmless,* is "inspired lunacy that leaves hardly a science fictional cliché alive," as *Washington Post Book World* contributor Lisa Tuttle described it. The novels chronicle in stream-of-consciousness style the adventures of Arthur Dent, a hapless and continually bewildered Englishman, wearing his dressing gown throughout the adventures, and his friend Ford Prefect, an alien who has been posing as an unemployed actor for fifteen years. When Ford warns Arthur that Earth is minutes away from demolition to make room for an interstellar bypass, the two hitch a ride on a space vehicle, narrowly escaping the calamity. Traveling through the galaxy with the aid of a computer travel guide, Prefect and Dent encounter a motley array of characters, including Marvin, a terminally depressed robot; Zaphod Beeblebrox, the three-armed, two-headed president of the galaxy; and Slartibartfast, a planet designer whose specialty is fjords.

Many reviewers praised the *Hitchhiker* series for a sense of humor uncommon to most science fiction, and some have likened it to Alice's bewildering travels through Wonderland. Noting that "humorous science fiction novels have notoriously limited audiences," Gerald Jonas of the *New York Times Book Review* declared that *Hitchhiker's Guide* "is a delightful exception." The second *Hitchhiker* volume similarly impressed *Washington Post Book World's* Ron Goulart: "Adams has a gift for sending up the sacred precepts of sf and those who took his vastly successful *The Hitchhiker's Guide to the Galaxy* to their hearts will want to perform similar acts with this sequel." As Richard Brown explained in the London *Times,* "much of the comedy arises from a variety of pseudo-high-tech mis-information"; countering the traditional idea of science as benefactor, Adams portrays science as the embodiment of Murphy's Law—anything that can malfunction, will. Thus while he faults *Hitchhiker* for a "sometimes damagingly sophomoric" tone, John Clute of the *Magazine of Fantasy and Science Fiction* nevertheless remarked that "there is enough joy throughout, enough tooth to the zaniness, and enough rude knowingness about media-hype versions of science fiction, to make *Hitchhiker* one of the genre's rare genuinely funny books." Richard Dawkins commented in his "Lament," that he had been surprised to learn how deeply read in science Adams was: "You can't understand many of the jokes in Hitchhiker if you don't know a lot of advanced science."

Although the plots of the *Hitchhiker* novels are science fictional, Adams asserted, "I'm not a science fiction writer, but a comedy writer who happens to be using the conventions of science fiction for this particular thing." Critics have likewise observed a wider scope in the author's satire. As London *Times* reviewer Philip Howard stated, "Adams has fun with the trendy manners of our time, from worship of the motor car to jogging, and from the pedantry of committee meetings, Point of Order Madam Chairperson, to religious enthusiasm and, engagingly, Sci-Fi itself." Citing Adams's "surreal, comic creativity," *Listener* contributor Peter Kemp saw "hints from Lewis Carroll and Edward Lear" in the *Hitchhiker* books: "There are logical extensions of mad premises, grotesque creatures with crazily evocative names, chattering objects, moments of satiric farce, and picturesquely absurd landscapes." Others have compared him to Jonathan Swift and Kurt Vonnegut. "Adams tries to make fun of almost every possible concern of humans from their quest for knowledge and power to their obsession with prolonging life," *Dictionary of Literary Biography Yearbook* contributor Michael Adams observed. As a result, his humor targets not only science fiction clichés, but "bureaucracies, bad poets, literary critics, scientific theories, nightclub entertainers, religion, philosophy, labor unions, economists, tax laws, clichés . . . structural linguists, rock 'n' roll, sentimentality, cricket commentators, and Paul McCartney's wealth."

While they are noted for their humor and satire, "it is not just the comic techniques that make Adams's novels worth reading," Robert Reilly asserted in *Twentieth-Century Science Fiction Writers.* "The characters, who may at first appear as mere parodies of science-fiction stereotypes, grow throughout the series into fairly well-rounded comic persons." Michael Adams concurred with this assessment, noting that "one of Adams's main virtues is his gift for characterization. The adventures of Arthur and his friends are entertaining not only for all the last-second escapes from disaster but for how the characters respond to the whims of fate." The author explained to James Brown of the *Los Angeles Times* that many of *Hitchhiker's* characters, including the protagonist, are based on people Adams knows. "Arthur Dent is to a certain extent autobiographical," the novelist said. "He moves from one astonishing event to another without fully comprehending what's going on. He's the Everyman character—an ordinary person caught up in some extraordinary events."

While critics and the author alike found the fourth novel of the Hitchhiker "trilogy" an overextension of the series—the humorist told the *Bloomsbury Review* that "that book was a mistake"—critics praised the fifth novel, *Mostly Harmless.* Carolyn Cushman said in *Locus,* "This time, Adams sinks his teeth into a basic human problem looking for a purpose in life and uses it as a theme, giving *Mostly Harmless* a coherence lacking in the other novels in the series. And it's funny to boot." A reviewer for *Analog Science Fiction and Fact* called it "a hit of bubbly seltzer in a dour, dour world. . . . Adams's cockeyed logic is bound to make you smile."

After the fourth Hitchhiker novel, Adams discovered another venue for his satire. *Dirk Gently's Holistic Detective Agency* introduces a time-machine, a spaceship, an Electric Monk, and Samuel Taylor Coleridge's ghost in solving the murder of a computer executive. Featuring Dirk Gently, a detective who unravels mysteries (usually missing cat cases) by examining the "interconnectedness of all things," the novel is full of coincidence and humor. While "the plot is inventive and often surprising," *Chicago Tribune* writer Christopher Farley found that "at points there is just too much of it." Douglas E. Winter similarly faulted the novel, commenting in the *Washington Post* that the excess of events overshadows the characters: "Missing are the outrageous characterizations that charmed the 'Hitchhiker' books; indeed, save for the quirky Dirk himself, Adams's cast is a wan and almost antiseptic assortment sent over by Central Casting."

In contrast, Toronto *Globe and Mail* reviewer H.J. Kirchhoff maintained that *Dirk Gently's Holistic Detective Agency* "is Adams's best novel. That is, his characters are more fully delineated than in the *Hitchhiker* books, the settings more credible and the plot more . . . well, linear." And Farley admitted that "in the end, Adams succeeds because he is flat-out funny. It will make you laugh, and that's the bottom line, even if his line isn't necessarily the shortest distance between two points." "Following a tradition which stretches from Laurence Sterne to P.G. Wodehouse," John Nicholson similarly concluded in the London *Times,* "what signifies most here is the quality of the writing, the asides and allusions, and—above all—the jokes. Mr. Adams scores very high on all counts."

Dirk Gently returns in *The Long Dark Tea-Time of the Soul,* "a clever and funny novel about an English detective, an American girl in a bad mood and a Norse god who sells his soul to an advertising executive," as Cathleen Schine summarized in the *New York Times Book Review.* After failing to prevent the murder of his only client, Dirk turns his attention to a mysterious explosion at an airport check-in counter; the two seemingly unrelated events, as the "holistic" detective knows, have some connection. Along the way, "with a skewed imagination and ironic wit, Douglas Adams romps through

modern life's paranoias and absurdities," Jess Bravin remarked in the *Chicago Tribune.* The author's "humor, crisp and intelligent, and his prose—elegant, absurdly literal-minded understatements or elegant, absurdly literal-minded overstatements—are a pleasure to read," Schine claimed.

Nevertheless, the critic believed that "in spite of all the nimble plots, the skillful writing and the underlying wit of his work, Mr. Adams is a bit banal." Marc Conly, however, found that the author's "social awareness and the accuracy of his barbs keep the narrative of *The Long Dark Tea-Time of the Soul* from becoming too frothy," as he wrote in the *Bloomsbury Review.* "Douglas Adams is a dismayed idealist in jester's clothing. His portrayal of modern society, and his unrelenting dissection of the modern style of self-centeredness, make us think, make us laugh, and make us look forward to his next book." "Adams is concerned less with the intricacies of detective novels than with the promulgation of ideas," Bravin similarly contended. With *Tea-Time,* the critic concluded, "Adams affirms his standing as one of England's top exporters of irreverence."

The Deeper Meaning of Liff: A Dictionary of Things There Aren't Words for Yet—but There Ought to Be takes "geographical names with no current meaning and matches them with objects, feelings, actions for which no word exists," wrote a reviewer for the London *Observer,* explaining the content of the "funny, highly perceptive book." However, in his review for *The Spectator,* Richard Ingrams said, "The book might have passed muster as a cheap paperback, but as a hardback, it seems unduly pretentious."

With zoologist Mark Carwardine, Adams traveled to Indonesia, Zaire, New Zealand, China, and Mauritius to research *Last Chance to See.* The book covers people, places, and animals the pair saw on their journeys. All the animals are endangered in some way. *Atlantic* reviewer Jack Beatty asserted that "*Last Chance* makes us care about some hard-pressed animals. . . . It renders this service to nature not through the instrumentalities of science but through those of humanism—rhetoric, irony, cadence, and wit." Commented Beth Levine in the *New York Times Book Review,* "Don't expect any great insights here, but *Last Chance to See* is enjoyable and accessible, and its details on the heroic efforts being made to save these animals are inspirational."

Adams found it very difficult to write and had once to be confined to a hotel room by his publisher to make him finish a novel. "I would never sit down and write for pleasure because it's too much like hard work," he told the *Times* of London, so the pleasure his work continues to give thousands of readers is the more admirable. He had moved to Santa Barbara, California, and was working on the script for a movie, when he died unexpectedly. Unfinished written work and other papers, essays, and speeches have been collected in *The Salmon of Doubt.*

BIOGRAPHICAL AND CRITICAL SOURCES:

BOOKS

Bestsellers 89, Issue 3, Thomson Gale (Detroit, MI), 1989.

Contemporary Literary Criticism, Volume 27, Thomson Gale (Detroit, MI), 1984.

Dictionary of Literary Biography Yearbook: 1983, Thomson Gale (Detroit, MI), 1984.

Gaiman, Neil, *Don't Panic: The Official Hitchhiker's Guide to the Universe Companion,* Pocket Books (New York, NY), 1988.

Richards, Neil, *Douglas Adams Starship Titanic: The Official Strategy Guide,* Three Rivers Press (New York, NY), 1998.

Twentieth-Century Science Fiction Writers, St. James Press (Detroit, MI), 1986.

PERIODICALS

Analog Science Fiction and Fact, September, 1993, p. 164.

Atlantic, March, 1991, p. 131.

Bangkok Post, May 23, 2001.

Bloomsbury Review, December, 1982; May-June, 1989, Marc Conly, interview with Adams.

Booklist, April 15, 2002, p. 1386.

Chicago Tribune, October 28, 1982; March 13, 1985; March 17, 1985; August 25, 1987; March 31, 1989.

Chicago Tribune Book World, October 12, 1980.

Fantasy Review, April, 1985.

Globe and Mail (Toronto), April 4, 1987; June 27, 1987.

GQ 61, December, 1991, Carolina Upcher, interview with Adams.

Greenman Review, August 2, 2002.

Guardian, July 23, 1992, p. 33.

Illustrated London News, September, 1982.

Interzone 66, December, 1992, Stan Nicholls, interview with Adams.

Kirkus Reviews, April 15, 2002, p. 508.

Kliatt Young Adult Paperback Book Guide, July, 1999, p. 5.

Listener, December 18-25, 1980, June 25, 1987.

Locus, October, 1992, p. 37.

London Times, June 18, 1987.

London Times Literary Supplement, September 24, 1982.

Los Angeles Times, April 19, 1985; June 13, 1987; March 17, 1989, May 13, 2001, p. B12.

Los Angeles Times Book Review, December 7, 1980; February 3, 1985; February 3, 1991, p. 4.

Magazine of Fantasy and Science Fiction, February, 1982.

New Scientist, August 18, 2001, p. 47.

Newsweek, November 15, 1982; April 13, 1998.

New York Times, April 9, 1998; May 15, 2001.

New York Times Book Review, January 25, 1981; March 12, 1989; March 17, 1991, p. 22; November 1, 1992.

Observer, December 2, 1990, p. 64; August 12, 2001, p. 15; May 12, 2002.

People, January 10, 1983; May 20, 1991, p. 79.

Publishers Weekly, January 14, 1983, Jennifer Crichton, interview with Adams, p. 47; February 1, 1991, Michele Field, interview with Adams, p. 62; April 15, 2002, p. 43.

Quadrant, September, 2002, p. 84.

Religious Studies Review, January, 1999, p. 99.

Science Fiction Studies, March, 1988, p. 61.

Spectator, December 15, 1990, p. 35.

Times (London, England), February 7, 1981; September 9, 1982; December 13, 1984; June 18, 1987; November 5, 1988.

Times Literary Supplement, September 24, 1982; May 24, 2002, p. 23.

VOYA, April, 1993, p. 33.

Washington Post, July 23, 1987; March 16, 1989.

Washington Post Book World, November 23, 1980; December 27, 1981; March 24, 1991, p. 4.

ONLINE

BBC-H2G2-Hitchhiker's Guide to the Galaxy, http://www.bbc.co.uk/h2g2/ (December 2, 2003).

Douglas Adams Home Page, http://www.douglasadams.com/ (December 2, 2003).

Floor 42 (fansite), http://www.floor42.com/ (December 2, 2003).

Guardian, http://books.guardian.co.uk/ (December 2, 2003), review of *The Salmon of Doubt.*

OBITUARIES:

PERIODICALS

Los Angeles Times, May 13, 2001, p. B12.

New York Times, May 15, 2001, pp. A21, A23, and E-1.
Times (London, England), May 14, 2001.
Washington Post, May 13, 2001, p. C8.

ONLINE

Guardian, http://booksguardian.co.uk/.

*   *   *

ADAMS, Douglas Noel
See ADAMS, Douglas

*   *   *

AFFABEE, Eric
See STINE, R.L.

*   *   *

AGHILL, Gordon
See SILVERBERG, Robert

*   *   *

ALBEE, Edward 1928-
(Edward Franklin Albee III)

PERSONAL: Surname pronounced *All*-bee; born March 12, 1928, probably in VA; adopted son of Reed A. (part-owner of Keith-Albee theater circuit) and Frances (Cotter) Albee; partner and lifelong friend of composer and music critic William Flanagan (1951-59), playwright Terence McNally (1959-63), decorator William Pennington (1963-71), and artist, Jonathon Thomas (1971—). *Education:* Rye Country Day School, Lawrence, New Jersey, 1940-43, Valley Forge Military Academy, Pennsylvania, 1946-47 (expelled from both), Choate School, Connecticut, 1944-46 (where he first wrote—a play, a novel, poems, and short stories), Trinity College, Hartford, CT, 1946-47, Columbia University, 1949. *Hobbies and other interests:* Travel, playing the harpsichord.

ADDRESSES: Office—14 Harrison St., New York, NY 10013.

CAREER: Writer, producer, and director of plays. Served in the U.S. Army. Worked as continuity writer for WNYC-radio, office boy for Warwick & Legler (ad-vertising agency), record salesman for G. Schirmer, Inc. (music publishers), and counterman in luncheonette of Manhattan Towers Hotel; messenger for Western Union, 1955-58. Producer, with Richard Barr and Clinton Wilder, New Playwrights Unit Workshop, 1963—; director of touring retrospective of his one-act plays including, *The Zoo Story, The American Dream, Fam and Yam, The Sandbox, Box, Quotations from Chairman Mao Tse-Tung, Counting the Ways,* and *Listening,* produced as *Albee Directs Albee,* 1978-79; co-director of Vivian Beaumont Theatre at Lincoln Center for the Performing Arts, New York, NY, 1979-81. Founder of William Flanagan Center for Creative Persons in Montauk, NY, 1971. Lecturer at colleges, including Brandeis University, Johns Hopkins University, and Webster University. Cultural exchange visitor to Latin American countries and the U.S.S.R. for U.S. State Department, 1961, 1963. President of Edward F. Albee Foundation. Resident playwright, Atlantic Center for the Arts, New Smyrna Beach, Florida, 1982. Regents Professor of Drama, University of California at Irvine, 1983-85. Instructor/Artist-in-Residence, University of Houston, 1988—.

MEMBER: PEN American Center, National Academy of Arts and Letters, Dramatists Guild, National Endowment grant-giving council Dramatists Guild Council, governing commission of New York State Council for the Arts, Theater Hall of Fame.

AWARDS, HONORS: Berlin Festival Award, 1959, for *The Zoo Story,* and 1961, for *The Death of Bessie Smith;* Vernon Rice Memorial Award, and Obie Award, 1960, and Argentine Critics Circle Award, 1961, all for *The Zoo Story; The Death of Bessie Smith* and *The American Dream* were chosen as best plays of the 1960-61 season by Foreign Press Association, 1961; Lola D'Annunzio Award, 1961, for *The American Dream;* selected as most promising playwright of 1962-63 season by New York Drama Critics, 1963; New York Drama Critics Circle Award, Foreign Press Association Award, Antoinette Perry Award (Tony), Outer Circle Award, *Saturday Review* Drama Critics Award, and *Variety* Drama Critics' Poll Award, 1963, and *Evening Standard* Award, 1964, all for *Who's Afraid of Virginia Woolf?;* Tony Award nominee for best play, 1964, for *The Ballad of the Sad Café;* with Richard Barr and Clinton Wilder, recipient of Margo Jones Award, 1965, for encouraging new playwrights; Tony Award nominee both for author, and best play, 1965, for *Tiny Alice;* Pulitzer Prize and Tony Award nominee for best play, 1967, for *A Delicate Balance;* Pulitzer Prize and Tony Award nominee for best play, 1975, for *Seascape;* D.Litt., Emerson College, 1967, and Trinity College, 1974; American Academy and Institute of Arts and Letters Gold Medal, 1980; inducted into Theater Hall of Fame, 1985; Pulitzer Prize and New York Drama Critics Circle Award for *Three Tall Women*, 1994; Obie Award for Sustained Achievement in the American Theater, 1994; Kennedy Center Honoree, 1996; National Medal of Arts, 1996; Tony Award for best play, 2002, for *The Goat, or Who Is Sylvia?*

WRITINGS:

PLAYS, EXCEPT AS NOTED

The Zoo Story, The Death of Bessie Smith, The Sandbox: Three Plays (*The Zoo Story*, first produced [in German] in Berlin at Schiller Theater Werkstatt, September 28, 1959, produced off-Broadway at Provincetown Playhouse, January 14, 1960; *The Death of Bessie Smith*, first produced in Berlin at Schlosspark Theater, April 21, 1960, produced off-Broadway at York Playhouse, February 28, 1961; *The Sandbox*, first produced in New York City at Jazz Gallery, May 15, 1960, produced off-Broadway at Cherry Lane Theatre, February, 1962, directed by author), Coward McCann (New York, NY), 1960, published with *The American Dream* (also see below) as *The Zoo Story and Other Plays*, J. Cape, 1962, and as *The American Dream; and Zoo Story: Two Plays*, Plume (New York, NY), 1997.

(Author of libretto with James Hinton, Jr.) *Bartleby* (opera; adaptation of story by Herman Melville; music by William Flanagan), produced off-Broadway at York Playhouse, January 24, 1961.

The American Dream, with introduction by the author (produced off-Broadway at York Playhouse, January 24, 1961), Coward McCann (New York, NY), 1961.

Fam and Yam (produced in Westport, CT, at White Barn Theatre, August 27, 1960), Dramatists Play Service (New York, NY), 1961.

Who's Afraid of Virginia Woolf? (produced on Broadway at Billy Rose Theatre, October 13, 1962), Atheneum (New York, NY), 1962.

The Ballad of the Sad Café (adaptation of novella of same title by Carson McCullers; produced on Broadway at Martin Beck Theatre, October 30, 1963), Houghton Mifflin (Boston, MA), 1963, Scribner Classics (New York, NY), 2001.

Tiny Alice (produced on Broadway at Billy Rose Theatre, December 29, 1964), Atheneum (New York, NY), 1965.

Malcolm (adaptation of novel of same title by James Purdy; produced on Broadway at Sam S. Shubert Theatre, January 11, 1966), Atheneum, 1966.

A Delicate Balance (produced on Broadway at Martin Beck Theatre, September 22, 1966), Atheneum (New York, NY), 1966, Plume (New York, NY), 1997.

Breakfast at Tiffany's (musical; adaptation of story of same title by Truman Capote; music by Bob Merrill), produced in Philadelphia, PA, 1966, produced on Broadway at Majestic Theatre, December, 1966.

Everything in the Garden (based on play by Giles Cooper; produced on Broadway at Plymouth Theatre, November 29, 1967), Atheneum (New York, NY), 1968.

Box [and] *Quotations from Chairman Mao Tse-Tung* (two interrelated plays; first produced at Studio Arena Theatre, Buffalo, NY; produced on Broadway at Billy Rose Theatre, September 30, 1968), Atheneum (New York, NY), 1969.

All Over (produced on Broadway at Martin Beck Theatre, January 26, 1971; produced in London by Royal Shakespeare Company at Aldwych Theatre, January 31, 1972), Atheneum (New York, NY), 1971.

Seascape (produced on Broadway at Sam S. Shubert Theatre, January 26, 1975, directed by author), Atheneum (New York, NY), 1975.

Counting the Ways [and] *Listening: Two Plays* (*Counting the Ways*, first produced in London by National Theatre Company, 1976, produced by Hartford Stage Company, Hartford, CT, January 28, 1977; *Listening: A Chamber Play* [produced as radio play by British Broadcasting Corp. (BBC), 1976], first produced on stage by Hartford Stage Company, Hartford, January 28, 1977), Atheneum (New York, NY), 1977.

The Lady from Dubuque (produced on Broadway at Morosco Theatre, January 31, 1980), Atheneum (New York, NY), 1980.

Lolita (adaptation of novel of same title by Vladimir Nabokov), first produced in Boston at Wilbur Theatre, January 15, 1981, produced on Broadway at Brooks Atkinson Theatre, March 19, 1981, published as *Lolita: A Play*, Dramatists Play Service (New York, NY), 1984.

1981–82 *The Plays* (four volumes), Atheneum (New York, NY).

Alice, A Delicate Balance, Box and Quotations from Chairman Mao Tse-tung, Atheneum (New York, NY), 1982.

Counting the Ways, Listening, All Over, Atheneum (New York, NY), 1982.

Everything in the Garden, Malcolm, The Ballad of the Sad Café, Atheneum (New York, NY), 1982.

The Man Who Had Three Arms, first produced in Miami, FL, at New World Festival, June 10, 1982, directed by the author; produced in Chicago, IL at Goodman Theater, October 4, 1982, directed by the author.

Edward Albee: An Interview and Essays, edited by Julian N. Wasserman, University of St. Thomas, 1983.

Finding the Sun (first produced in 1983, New York premiere at the Signature Theatre Company, February, 1994), Dramatists Play Service (New York, NY), 1994.

Envy in *Faustus in Hell,* (produced Princeton, NJ, 1985).

Marriage Play, first produced at the English Theatre in Vienna, 1987, American premiere at the McCarter Theater in Princeton, NJ, February 22, 1992; *Edward Albee's Marriage Play,* Dramatists Play Service (New York, NY), 1995.

Selected Plays of Edward Albee, Doubleday (Garden City, NY), 1987.

Conversations with Edward Albee, edited by Philip C. Kolin, University Press of Mississippi (Jackson, MS), 1988.

Straight through the Night (novel), Soho (New York, NY), 1989.

Three Tall Women (two-act play; first produced at the English Theatre in Vienna, June, 1991, New York City premiere at the Vineyard Theatre, February 13, 1994), Dutton (New York, NY), 1995.

The Lorca Play, (produced at the Alley Theatre, Houston, TX, April 24, 1992).

Fragments: A Sit Around (premiered at Ensemble Theater of Cincinnati, Cincinnati, OH, November, 1993, New York opening at Signature Theatre Company, 1994), published as *Edward Albee's Fragments: A Sit-Around,* Dramatists Play Service (New York, NY), 1995.

The Play about the Baby, (first produced at Almeida Theatre, London, September 1, 1998; Houston, TX, Alley Theatre, April 11, 2000; New York, February 1, 2001), Dramatists Play Service (New York, NY), 2002, Overlook Press (Woodstock, NY), 2003.

From Idea to Matter: Nine Sculptors . . . , Anderson Gallery (Richmond, VA), 2000.

(With Sam Hunter) *Tony Rosenthal* (literary criticism), Rizzoli (New York, NY), 2000.

(With Carson McCullers) *The Ballad of the Sad Café: Carson McCullers's Novella Adapted to the Stage,* Scribner Classics (New York, NY), 2001.

Occupant, (produced at the John Golden Theatre, New York, 2002).

The Goat, or Who Is Sylvia? (first produced at the John Golden Theatre in New York, March 10, 2002), Overlook Press (Woodstock, NY), 2003.

Peter and Jerry, Hartford Stage (Hartford, CT), 2004.

AUTHOR OF INTRODUCTION

Noel Coward, *Three Plays by Noel Coward: Blithe Spirit, Hay Fever,* [and] *Private Lives,* Delta (New York, NY), 1965.

Phyllis Johnson Kaye, editor, *National Playwrights Directory,* 2nd edition, Eugene O'Neill Theater Center (Waterford, CT), 1981.

(With Sabina Lietzmann) *New York,* Vendome Press (New York, NY), 1981.

Louise Nevelson: Atmospheres and Environments, Clarkson N. Potter (New York, NY), 1981.

Three Tall Women: A Play in Two Acts, Dutton (New York, NY), 1994.

Also author of screenplays, including an adaptation of *Le Locataire* (title means "The Tenant"), a novel by Roland Topor, an adaptation of his *The Death of Bessie Smith,* one about the life of Nijinsky, one about Stanford White and Evelyn Nesbitt, and *A Delicate Balance,* American Film Theater, 1973. Contributor to anthologies, including *American Playwrights on Drama,* edited by Horst Frenz, Hill & Wang, 1965; *The Off-Broadway Experience,* edited by Howard Greenberger, Prentice-Hall, 1971. Also contributor to periodicals, including *Harper's Bazaar, Saturday Review,* and *Dramatists Guild Quarterly.*

ADAPTATIONS: Who's Afraid of Virginia Woolf? was adapted and filmed by Warner Bros. in 1966.

Albee's play *Who's Afraid of Virginia Woolf?* was revived on Broadway at the Longacre Theater in a production directed by Anthony Page and starring Kathleen Turner and Bill Irwin.

SIDELIGHTS: Reviewing the numerous commentaries written about Edward Albee's plays, C.W.E. Bigsby noted in *Edward Albee: A Collection of Critical Essays* that in comparison to Albee "few playwrights . . . have been so frequently and mischievously misunderstood, misrepresented, overpraised, denigrated, and precipitately dismissed." Capsulizing the changing tone of Albee criticism since the early-1960s (when his first play appeared), Bigsby offered this overview: "Canonized after . . . *The Zoo Story,* [Albee] found himself in swift succession billed as America's most promising playwright, leading dramatist, and then, with astonishing suddenness, a 'one-hit' writer. . . . The progression was essentially that suggested by George in [Albee's] *Who's Afraid of Virginia Woolf?,* 'better, best, bested.'"

To symbolize the curve of Albee's reputation as a dramatist, Bigsby chose a phrase from a play designated by many critics as a dividing line in the playwright's career. T.E. Kalem, for example, in *Time* remarked: "Albee almost seems to have lived through two careers, one very exciting, the other increasingly depressing. From *The Zoo Story* through *The American Dream* to *Who's Afraid of Virginia Woolf?*, he displayed great gusto, waspish humor and feral power. In the succeeding . . . years, he has foundered in murky metaphysics, . . . dabbled in adaptations, . . . and gone down experimental blind alleys." Confusing him with more nihilist European absurdist playwrights, many critics have failed to understand the autobiographical sources of his writing and the more hopeful nature of his message, as Lincoln Konkle pointed out in the *Dictionary of Literary Biography* entry on Albee. Matthew C. Roudané has declared, "Albee's is an affirmative vision of human experience. . . . In the midst of a dehumanizing society, Albee's heroes, perhaps irrationally, affirm living."

However, many critics have praised these same plays. Albee continues to win awards; he has received three Pulitzer Prizes since *Virginia Woolf,* one in 1967 for *A Delicate Balance,* one in 1975, for *Seascape,* and, in 1994, a third for his autobiographical drama *Three Tall Women.* His three Pulitzer Prizes place him in the ranks of such notable dramatists as Tennessee Williams, holder of two Pulitzers, Robert E. Sherwood, a three-time winner, and four-time honoree Eugene O'Neill.

Although stylistically varied, Albee's plays are thematically connected. Gerald Weales in *The Jumping Off Place: American Drama in the 1960s* noted: "Each new Albee play seems to be an experiment in form, in style, . . . and yet there is unity to his work as a whole. This is apparent in the devices and the characters that recur, modified according to context, but it is most obvious in the repetition of theme, in the basic assumptions about the human condition that underlie all his work."

Reviewing Albee's touring retrospective of eight of his one-act plays, "Albee Directs Albee," Sylvie Drake of the *Los Angeles Times* observed: "This condensation of work reveals Albee's consistent and enduring concern with loss. . . . 'Pain is understanding,' says someone in [Albee's play] 'Counting the Ways.' 'It's really loss.' Yes. These plays are *all* about loss." In her analysis of Albee's plays Drake also discovered the following themes: "the chasm between people, [and] their inability to connect except through pain."

John MacNicholas, writing in the *Dictionary of Literary Biography,* said the development of these themes in Albee's plays started with his first play, *The Zoo Story.* According to Brian Way in *American Theatre,* this play, a tale of a fairly prosperous married man and his confrontation on a Central Park bench with a totally alienated young drifter, "is an exploration of the farce and agony of human isolation." George Wellwarth, in *The Theater of Protest and Paradox: Development in the Avant-Garde Drama,* explained the play's thematic content in more detail: "[Albee] is exemplifying or demonstrating a theme. That theme is the enormous and usually insuperable difficulty that human beings find in communicating with each other. More precisely, it is about the maddening effect that the enforced loneliness of the human condition has on the person who is cursed (for in our society it undoubtedly is a curse) with an infinite capacity for love."

Albee's thematic preoccupation with loss of contact between individuals is tied to the playwright's desire to make a statement about American values, as Weales pointed out. "In much of his work," according to the critic, "there is a suggestion . . . that the emptiness and loneliness of the characters are somehow the result of a collapse of values in the Western world, in general, in the United States, in particular." Albee finds the feelings of loss and emptiness prevalent in the society that surrounds him.

Following *The Zoo Story,* three Albee plays opened in New York during 1960-61. All of these—*The Sandbox, The American Dream,* and *The Death of Bessie Smith*—"attack certain features in American society," according to MacNicholas. *The Death of Bessie Smith,* for example, deals with the death of the black singer who bled to death after an automobile accident, apparently because she was denied care at a nearby all-white hospital. *The American Dream* and *The Sandbox* share the same characters—Mommy, Daddy, and Grandma. MacNicholas feels that these two plays "form a continuum in subject matter and technique; both attack indifference to love, pity, and compassion. In both, . . . the characters . . . live in a kind of moral narcosis."

Allen Lewis, in *American Plays and Playwrights of the Contemporary Theatre,* commented: "*The American Dream* is a wildly imaginative caricature of the American family. . . . [In this play] Albee is the angry young man, tearing apart the antiseptic mirage of American middle-class happiness." The American family of the play is comprised of characters known only as "Mommy" (a domineering shrew), "Daddy" (a weak, henpecked husband), and "Grandma" (an older version of "Mommy"). Set in the family's stuffy apartment, the play includes the story of the couple's adoption of a "bumble of joy" whom they destroy after discovering his various defects. (For example, they cut out his tongue when he says a dirty word.) As he grows up, Mommy and Daddy complain that the baby has no head on his shoulders, is spineless, and has feet of clay. They complain again when he dies after having already been paid for. Near the end of the play, the baby's twin appears. He is a handsome young man who describes himself as a "clean-cut midwest farm boy type, almost insultingly good-looking in a typically American way." "The young man," as Frederick Lumley noted in *New Trends in Twentieth Century Drama,* "feels that he is incomplete, he doesn't know what has happened to something within him, but he has no touch, he is unable to make love, to see anything with pity; in fact he has no feeling." Continuing his interpretation of the play, Lewis stated: "The American Dream [of the title] is the young man who is all appearance and no feelings. . . . He says: 'I cannot touch another person and feel love. . . . I have no emotions. . . . I have now only my person . . . my body, my face. . . . I let people love me. . . . I feel nothing.'"

In his preface to *The American Dream,* Albee explains the play's content: "The play is an examination of the American Scene, an attack on the substitution of artificial for real values in our society, a condemnation of complacency, cruelty, emasculation and vacuity; it is a stand against the fiction that everything in this slipping land of ours is peachy-keen." According to MacNicholas, Albee continues his critique of American society in his first three-act play, *Who's Afraid of Virginia Woolf?* Many critics note a relationship between this play and *The American Dream.* Martin Esslin, writing in *The Theatre of the Absurd,* commented: "A closer inspection reveals elements which clearly . . . relate [*Virginia Woolf*] to Albee's earlier work. . . . George and Martha [a couple in the play] (there are echoes here of George and Martha Washington) have an imaginary child which they treat as real, until in the cold dawn of that wild night [in which the action of the play takes place] they decide to 'kill' it by abandoning their joint fantasy. Here the connection to *The American Dream* with its horrid dream-child of the ideal all-American boy becomes clear. . . . Is the dream-child which cannot become real among people torn by ambition and lust something like the American ideal itself?"

Drake found George and Martha of *Virginia Woolf* directly related to Mommy and Daddy of *The American Dream.* Lumley described this evolution: "The Mommy

and Daddy of . . . *Virginia Woolf* are this time given names, Martha and George, thus becoming individuals instead of abstract characters. . . . They have been unable to have children; so that their love is mixed-up sexual humiliation, a strong love-hate relationship which makes them want to hurt and claw and wound each other because they know each other and cannot do without one another." In the *Arizona Quarterly,* James P. Quinn described the combination of social criticism and the theme of human isolation in *Virginia Woolf:* "In [the play] the author parodies the ideals of western civilization. . . . Thus, romantic love, marriage, sex, the family, status, competition, power all the 'illusions' man has erected to eliminate the differences between self and others and to escape the . . . burden of his freedom and loneliness come under attack."

Critics noted the continuation of theme and social awareness throughout Albee's work. For example, Harold Clurman, in his *Nation* review of *All Over,* wrote: "Albee is saying [in this play] that despite all the hasty bickering, the fierce hostility and the mutual misunderstandings which separate us, we need one another. We cry out in agony when we are cut off." Bigsby, commenting on the same play, concluded: "Albee's concern in *All Over* is essentially that of his earlier work. He remains intent on penetrating the bland urbanities of social life in an attempt to identify the crucial failure of nerve which has brought individual men and whole societies to the point of not merely soulless anomie but even of apocalypse."

Bigsby also found similar characteristics in Albee's play *Box,* calling it "a protest against the dangerously declining quality of life—a decline marked . . . by the growth of an amoral technology with a momentum and direction of its own." MacNicholas noted Albee's preoccupation with loss in *A Delicate Balance:* "[The play] concerns itself with loss: not loss which occurs in one swift traumatic stroke, but that which evolves slowly in increments of gentle and lethal acquiescence."

Then, in what several critics have referred to as phoenix-like fashion, Albee was seemingly reborn as a popular and critically successful artist during the 1993-94 New York theater season in off-and off-off-Broadway houses similar in spirit to the fringe theaters Albee and his contemporaries helped nourish in the 1960s, during the early days of avant-garde American playwriting. One such artistic enclave, the Signature Theatre, a non-profit company in lower Manhattan, brought Albee aboard as its playwright-in-residence and dedicated an entire season to his works, proving that at least some producers remembered his allegedly forgotten plays. The lineup included a variety of full-length dramas and one-acts, old and new. Among them were *Finding the Sun,* a long 1983 one-act in twenty-two vignettes, involving the interaction of eight characters on a New England beach; *Marriage Play,* Albee's 1987 sparring match between a long-wed husband and wife that elicited several comparisons to *Virginia Woolf*; and *Fragments: A Sit Around.*

Rounding off the list were two one-act collections. The first, *Listening: A Chamber Play,* and *Counting the Ways* were originally presented in London at the National Theatre in 1976, then in America at the Hartford Stage Company in Connecticut. These plays represent Albee's experimental writing in the middle part of his career. In a *New York Times* review, Ben Brantley suggested that both "are essentially linguistic chamber works. . . . Though they are radically different in tone, their preoccupation with the slipperiness of language and perception and with the opacity of what truly lies behind it is much the same. The questions posed reverberate without answers and are often as unapologetically naked as 'Who am I?' 'Who are you?' and 'Do you love me?'"

The next short play bill, collectively entitled *Sand,* was directed by Albee himself and included three representative pieces, *Box* (1968), *The Sandbox* (1960), and *Finding the Sun* (1983). While the Signature season provided him a rare opportunity to revisit several old works and try out new ideas, it was the 1994 New York premiere of his 1991 play *Three Tall Women* a few blocks north at the Vineyard Theater that earned Albee his greatest accolades since *Virginia Woolf,* including a third Pulitzer Prize and the New York Drama Critics Circle Award.

Autobiographical in content, *Three Tall Women* is an examination of the life of a wealthy, boisterous, strong-minded woman nearly a century old. The first act consists of a conversation between this often cantankerous dowager, known only as A; her sympathetic, middle-aged caretaker, B; and C, her twenty-six-year-old lawyer. These are Albee's "three tall women" in their first incarnation. A's physical condition is deteriorating rapidly—she is frequently incontinent and has recently broken an arm that will not heal—and her mental state is precarious. As she attempts to put her affairs in order with C and reminisces about her experiences, she alternates between an amazing perceptiveness and scandalous wit, and amnesic episodes accompanied by childlike tantrums. She can't remember if she is ninety-one or ninety-two, or whether close friends are alive or dead, but can relate tales from her courtship and early years of marriage in great detail.

The fifty-two-year-old B has become inured to the abuse A frequently heaps upon her, and to the personal tasks she must help the older woman perform. In her own climbing years B waxes philosophically about the natural aging process. C is both attracted to and repulsed by the behavior of her elders. She giggles at A's anecdotes of her early sexual escapades (though A claims to have been the "wild one" her behavior was prudish by C's youthful standards), then she is shocked at A's casual, overt racism, bigotry, and insensitivity. The first act ends with A lying in bed lamenting the breakdown in her relationships with her own mother, whom she cared for in her old age, and her homosexual son, who couldn't stand her intolerance and left her when he was still a teenager. Her rambling diatribe ends suddenly, and upon examining her, B announces A has suffered a stroke.

A transformation occurs between acts, and when the curtain rises on the second half of *Three Tall Women,* a mannequin representation of A occupies the bed while the actresses playing A, B, and C are revealed as the same woman at three different stages of life, all attending what will soon be her own deathbed. This partition of the elderly A's life allows the playwright the opportunity to examine his character from three distinct, yet similar points of view.

C remembers her glory days, when she and her sister worked as department store models and cavorted innocently, and not so innocently, with boys, all the while waiting for "the man of my dreams." Hers is the voice of youth and naivete, silly yet romantically appealing. B, the realist, has fresher adult memories of the man of her dreams, including both her and her husband's extramarital affairs. She also recalls, quite vividly, opening her son's mail and finding admiring notes from older men, then arguing with him, and watching him exit her life for the next twenty years. A remembers the six agonizing years it took for her husband to die of cancer, and how she sold her jewelry a little at a time to meet expenses, replacing it with replicas to maintain appearances. In the final moments of the play, the three tall women, multiple facets of the same spirit, share what they feel has been their happiest moment. For the youthful C it is uncertain. It may have been her confirmation or, better yet, perhaps they are still to come. B's happiest moment is the here and now, "half of being adult done," she says, "the rest ahead of me. Old enough to be a *little* wise, past being *really* dumb." As they all join hands A reveals her happiest moment will be "coming to the end of it; yes. . . . That's the happiest moment. When it's all done. When we stop. When we can stop."

Following the success of *Three Tall Women* in New York, Albee admitted in interviews that the play's main character was directly inspired by his own adoptive mother, Frances Cotter Albee, who expelled the eighteen-year-old Albee from his family's home for his homosexuality, and later removed him from her will. As Albee told David Richards of the *New York Times,* "The play is a kind of exorcism. . . . I didn't end up any more fond of the woman after I finished it than when I started. But it allowed me to come to terms with the long unpleasant life she led and develop a little respect for her independence. She was destructive, but she had lots of reasons to be. It's there on the stage, all the good stuff and the bad stuff." Though elements of his own life and family had crept into his plays before, notably in *The American Dream* and *Finding the Sun,* Albee did not feel free enough to write particularly about his mother until after her death at the age of ninety-two in 1990. In the *New Yorker,* John Lahr suggested that the "last great gift a parent gives to a child is his or her own death, and the energy underneath *Three Tall Women* is the exhilaration of a writer calling it quits with the past." Robert Brustein asserted in the *New Republic* that "*Three Tall Women* is a mature piece of writing . . . in which Albee seems to be coming to terms not only with a socialite foster parent, . . . but with his own advancing age."

The rest of the 1990s and the early 2000s continued with further productions but many mixed reviews. *A Delicate Balance* was revived in 1996 to win Tonys for best revival, direction and actor. It also ran successfully in London. *The Play about the Baby,* appearing 1998 through 2001, brought such mixed reactions that it appeared both on best-of-the-year-in-theater and worst-of-the-year-in-theater lists. *The Goat or Who Is Sylvia?* was Albee's first play on Broadway after the 1983 production of *The Man Who Had Three Arms,* and Albee warned that it would be his most controversial play because it dealt with bestiality. According to Konkle, its real theme is the mercurial nature of love. *The Goat,* despite divided responses, received the 2002 Tony and Drama Desk Awards for best new play of the year.

As Konkle concluded, Albee, with a career spanning six decades, has influenced some of the most important twentieth-century playwrights, such as Tom Stoppard and David Mamet. More directly, he has supported young artists through the Playwrights Unit and the Flanagan Center. He has received many honorary doctorates, and his plays have been produced all over the world. Many drama critics and scholars credit him with "practically   inventing   Off-Broadway singlehandedly. . . . He has enjoyed success but not

made that his priority, so that he could expand the possibilities of theater and drama and continue to post tough moral and philosophical questions to his audiences."

BIOGRAPHICAL AND CRITICAL SOURCES:

BOOKS

Amacher, Richard E., *Edward Albee,* Twayne (New York, NY), 1969.

Amacher, Richard E., and Margaret Rule, *Edward Albee at Home and Abroad: A Bibliography 1958-June 1968,* AMS Press (New York, NY), 1970.

Bigsby, C.W. E., *Albee,* Oliver & Boyd, 1969.

Bigsby, C.W. E., editor, *Edward Albee: A Collection of Critical Essays,* Prentice-Hall, 1975.

Bloom, Harold, editor, *Edward Albee,* Chelsea House, 1987.

Brown, John Russell, and Bernard Harris, editors, *American Theatre,* Edward Arnold, 1967.

Bryer, Jackson R., editor, *The Playwright's Art: Conversations with Contemporary American Dramatists,* Rutgers University Press (New Brunswick, NJ), 1995.

Cohn, Ruby, *Edward Albee,* University of Minnesota Press (Minneapolis, MN), 1969.

Contemporary Literary Criticism, Thomson Gale (Detroit, MI), Volume 1, 1973, Volume 2, 1974, Volume 3, 1975, Volume 5, 1976, Volume 9, 1978, Volume 11, 1979, Volume 13, 1980, Volume 25, 1983, Volume 53, 1989, Volume 86, 1995.

Debusscher, Gilbert, *Edward Albee: Tradition and Renewal,* American Studies Center (Brussels, Belgium), 1967.

De La Fuente, Patricia, editor, *Edward Albee, Planned Wilderness: Interviews, Essays, and Bibliography,* Living Author Series, Number 3, Pan American University (Edinburgh, TX), 1980.

Dictionary of Literary Biography, Volume 7: *Twentieth-Century American Dramatists,* Part I, Thomson Gale (Detroit, MI), 1981.

Downer, Alan S., editor, *American Drama and Its Critics: A Collection of Critical Essays,* University of Chicago Press (Chicago, IL), 1965.

Esslin, Martin, *The Theatre of the Absurd,* Doubleday (New York, NY), 1969.

Giantvalley, Scott, *Edward Albee: A Reference Guide,* G.K. Hall, 1987.

Green, Charles Lee, *Edward Albee: An Annotated Bibliography 1968-1977,* AMS Press (New York, NY), 1980.

Gussow, Mel, *Edward Albee: A Singular Journey,* Simon & Schuster, 1999.

Hayman, Ronald, *Edward Albee,* Heinemann (London, England), 1971, Ungar (New ork, NY), 1973.

Hirsch, Foster, *Who's Afraid of Edward Albee,* Creative Arts (Berkeley, CA), 1978.

Kolin, Philip C., and J. Madison Davis, editors, *Critical Essays on Edward Albee,* G.K. Hall (Boston, MA), 1986.

Kolin, Philip C., editor, *Conversations with Edward Albee,* University Press of Mississippi (Jackson, MS), 1988.

Konkle, Lincoln, *Dictionary of Literary Biography, Vol. 266: Twentieth-Century American Dramatists, Fourth Series,* Thomson Gale (Detroit, MI), 2002.

Lewis, Allan, *American Plays and Playwrights of the Contemporary Theatre,* Crown (New York, NY), 1965.

Lumley, Frederick, *New Trends in Twentieth Century Drama,* 4th edition, Oxford University Press, 1972.

Mayberry, Bob, *Theatre of Discord: Dissonance in Beckett, Albee, and Pinter,* Fairleigh Dickinson University Press, 1989.

McCarthy, Gerald, *Edward Albee,* Macmillan (London, England), 1987.

Paolucci, Anne, *From Tension to Tonic: The Plays of Edward Albee,* Southern Illinois University Press (Carbondale, IL), 1972.

Roudané, Matthew Charles, *Understanding Edward Albee,* University of South Carolina Press (Columbia, SC), 1987.

Roudané, Matthew Charles, *Who's Afraid of Virginia Woolf?: Necessary Fictions, Terrifying Realities,* Twayne Publishers, 1990.

Rutenberg, Michael E., *Edward Albee: Playwright in Protest,* Avon, 1969.

Singh, C.P., *Edward Albee: The Playwright of Quest,* Mittal Publications (Delhi, India), 1987.

Stenz, Anita M., *The Poet of Loss,* Mouton (The Hague, Netherlands), 1978.

Tyce, Richard, *Edward Albee: A Bibliography,* Scarecrow (Metuchen, NY), 1986.

Vos, Nelvin, *Eugene Ionesco and Edward Albee: A Critical Essay,* Eerdmans (Grand Rapids, MI), 1968.

Wagner, Walter, editor, *The Playwrights Speak,* Delacorte (New York, NY), 1967.

Weales, Gerald, *The Jumping Off Place: American Drama in the 1960's,* Macmillan (New York, NY), 1969.

Wellwarth, George, *The Theater of Protest and Paradox: Development in the Avant-Garde Drama,* New York University Press (New York, NY), 1964.

PERIODICALS

Advocate, March 13, 2001, p. 56; April 16, 2002, p. 58.

America, April 2, 1994, p. 18.

American Book Collector, March-April, 1983, p. 37.

American Drama, spring, 1993, special issue; fall 1995, p. 51.

American Theater, September, 1994, p. 38; September 1996, p. 24.

Arizona Quarterly, autumn, 1974.

Asia Africa Intelligence Wire, November 30, 2002.

Atlantic Monthly, April, 1965.

Back Stage, December 8, 2000, p. 56.

Back Stage West, January 18, 2001, p. 10.

Booklist, June 1, 2000, p. 1808.

Books, July, 1966.

Chicago Tribune, March 26, 1979; September 26, 1982; April 9, 1995, sec. 13, p. 2.

Chicago Tribune Book World, September 26, 1982.

Christian Science Monitor, November 10, 1993, p. 12; April 13, 2001, p. 18; April 26, 2002, p. 18.

CLA Journal, 1984, p. 210.

Commonweal, January 22, 1965; April 10, 1992, p. 18; December 3, 1993, p. 17.

Contemporary Drama, spring, 1970, p. 151.

Daily Variety, May 8, 2002, p. 1; August 13, 2002, p. 1; September 10, 2002, p. 15.

Dance Magazine, October, 2002, p. 56.

Detroit News, June 27, 1982.

Educational Theatre Journal, March, 1973, pp. 71 and 80.

Explicator, 1988, p. 46.

Gay and Lesbian Review Worldwide, July-August, 2002, p. 50.

Hollywood Reporter, February 27, 2002, p. 44; March 11, 2002, p. 30.

Houston Chronicle, March 17, 2002, p. 12.

Hudson Review, spring, 1965; winter, 1966-67.

Journal of Evolutionary Psychology, August, 1985, p. 302.

Life, October 28, 1966; May 26, 1967; February 2, 1968.

London Magazine, March, 1969.

Los Angeles Times, October 18, 1978; April 21, 1994, pp. F1, F6; January 8, 2001, p. B6; January 15, 2001, p. F1; August 18, 2002, p. F44.

Modern Drama, December, 1967, p. 274.

Nation, December 18, 1967; March 25, 1968; April 12, 1971; February 23, 1980; April 18, 1981; March 14, 1994, p. 355.

National Observer, December 4, 1967.

New Criterion, June, 2002, p. 54.

New Leader, December 18, 1967; April 19, 1971.

New Republic, January 23, 1965; April 17, 1971; February 2, 1975; April 11, 1981; April 4, 1994, pp. 26, 28; June 17, 1996; April 15, 2002, p. 24.

Newsday, March 26, 1971.

New Statesman, January 23, 1970.

Newsweek, January 4, 1965; March 18, 1968; April 5, 1971; February 10, 1975; March 30, 1981.

New York, May 6, 1996, p. 86; March 25, 2002, p. 133; July 8, 2002, p. 47.

New Yorker, January 22, 1966; April 3, 1971; March 3, 1980; May 30, 1981; May 16, 1994, pp. 102-05; May 27, 1996, p. 138; February 19, 2001, p. 228.

New York Magazine, November, 1993, p. 70.

New York Times, December 27, 1964; January 21, 1965; January 13, 1966; August 16, 1966; September 18, 1966; September 24, 1966; October 2, 1966; August 20, 1967; November 26, 1967; April 4, 1971; April 18, 1971; January 27, 1975; February 4, 1977; May 23, 1978; January 27, 1980; March 1, 1981; March 20, 1981; March 29, 1981; February 23, 1992; November 20, 1993, p. A11; December 1, 1993, p. C17; February 14, 1994, pp. C13, C16; February 20, 1994, p. 5; April 13, 1994, p. C15; August 28, 1994, p. WC1; May 5, 1996, p. H4; June 16, 1996, p. H33; July 25, 1999; April 12, 2000, p. B2, E2; December 6, 2000, p. B1, E1; September 24, 2000; January 28, 2001; February 2, 2001, p. B1, E1; April 8, 2001; February 25, 2002, p. B1, E1; March 11, 2002, p. B1, E1; June 30, 2002, p. 5.

New York Times Magazine, February 25, 1962. p. 30, 64, 66.

New York World Journal Tribune, September 22, 1966; October 2, 1966.

Observer Review, January 19, 1969.

Paris Review, fall, 1966.

People Weekly, February 25, 1980; April 6, 1981.

Pittsburgh Press, February 3, 1974.

Prairie Schooner, fall, 1965; spring, 1966, p.139.

Progressive, August, 1996, Richard Farr, interview with Albee, pp. 60-67.

Recherches Anglaises et Américaine, number 5, summer, 1972, p. 85.

Reporter, December 28, 1967.

San Francisco Chronicle, March 20, 2002, p. D2; November 27, 2002, p. D1.

Saturday Review, June 4, 1966; April 17, 1971; March 8, 1975; May, 1981.

South Central Review, spring, 1990, p. 50.

Studies in Contemporary Satire, 1987, p. 30.

Theatre Arts, March, 1961.

Theatre Survey, November 1993, Rakesh Solomon, interview with Albee on directing *Who's Afraid of Virginia Woolf?,* p. 95.

Time, April 5, 1971; February 10, 1975; May 20, 1996, p. 77.

Transatlantic Review, summer, 1963.

Tri-Quarterly, 1966, p. 182.

Tulane Drama Review, spring, 1963; summer, 1965.

Twentieth-Century Literature: A Scholarly and Critical Journal, spring, 1982, p. 14.

Variety, March 4, 1991, p. 66; January 20, 1992, p. 147; November 8, 1993, p. 30; February 14, 1994, p. 61; November 6, 1995, p. 80; October 27, 1997; April 17, 2000, p. 36; March 13, 2001, p. 47; March 18, 2002, p. 32; May 13, 2002, p. 35; October 14, 2002, p. 38; February 3, 2003, p. 42 and 71.

Village Voice, December 7, 1967; March 21, 1968; October 31, 1968.

Wall Street Journal, December 20, 2000, p. A20; March 13, 2002, p. A16.

Washington Post, February 18, 1979; August 14, 1994.

World Literature Today, autumn, 1995, pp. 799-800.

Writer's Digest, October, 1980.

ONLINE

John F. Kennedy Center for the Performing Arts, http://www.kennedy-center.org/ (December 1, 2003).

University of Houston Web site, http://www.uh.edu/ (December 1, 2003).

OTHER

Edward Albee (video), edited and presented by Melvyn Bragg, London Weekend Television in association with RM Arts, Films for the Humanities, 1996.

*   *   *

ALBEE, Edward Franklin, III
See ALBEE, Edward

*   *   *

ALBOM, Mitch 1958-
(Mitch David Albom)

PERSONAL: Born May 23, 1958, in Passaic, NJ; son of Ira (a corporate executive) and Rhoda (an interior designer) Albom; married Janine Sabino (a singer), 1995. *Education:* Brandeis University, B.A. (sociology), 1979; Columbia University, M.J., 1981, M.B.A., 1982.

ADDRESSES: Home—Franklin, MI. *Office*—Detroit Free Press, 321 West Lafayette, Detroit, MI 48226-2721. *E-mail*—mitch@albom.com.

CAREER: Journalist and author. *Queens Tribune,* Flushing, NY, editor, 1981-82; contributing writer for *Sport, Philadelphia Inquirer,* and *Geo,* 1982-83; *Fort Lauderdale News and Sun Sentinel,* Fort Lauderdale, FL, sports columnist, 1983-85; *Detroit Free Press,* Detroit, MI, sports columnist, 1985—; WLLZ-radio, Farmington Hills, MI, sports director, beginning 1985, cohost of *Sunday Sports Albom,* 1988-99; WDIV-TV, Detroit, broadcaster and commentator, beginning 1987; *Monday Sports Albom* (originally *Sunday Sports Albom;* syndicated weekly sports talk show), host, 1999—. *The Mitch Albom Show* (nationally syndicated sports talk show), host, beginning c. 1995; *Sports Reporters,* ESPN, panelist. Composed song for television movie *Christmas in Connecticut,* 1992. Dream Team (charity), founder, 1989; A Time to Help (volunteer organization), founder, 1998. Member of board of directors, Caring Athletes Team for Children's and Henry Ford Hospitals, Forgotten Harvest, and Michigan Hospice.

MEMBER: Baseball Writers of America, Football Writers of America, Tennis Writers of America.

AWARDS, HONORS: Award for best sports news story in the United States, 1985; named number-one Michigan sports columnist, Associated Press (AP) and United Press International (UPI), 1985, 1986, 1987, and 1988; named number-one U.S. sports columnist, AP Sports Editors, 1987, 1988, 1989, 1990, 1991, 1992, 1993, 1994, 1995, 1996, 1997, and 1998; named number-one Michigan sports columnist, National Association of Sportswriters and Broadcasters, 1988 and 1989; National Headliners Award as number-two outstanding writer, 1989; awards for best feature, AP Sports Editors, including 1993; named National Hospice Organization Man of the Year, 1999; numerous other awards.

WRITINGS:

The Live Albom: The Best of Detroit Free Press *Sports Columnist Mitch Albom,* Detroit Free Press (Detroit, MI), 1988.
(With Bo Schembechler) *Bo: The Bo Schembechler Story,* Warner Books (New York, NY), 1989.
Live Albom II, foreword by Ernie Harwell, Detroit Free Press (Detroit, MI), 1990.
Live Albom III: Gone to the Dogs, Detroit Free Press (Detroit, MI), 1992.
Fab Five: Basketball, Trash Talk, the American Dream, Warner Books (New York, NY), 1993.
Live Albom IV, foreword by Dave Barry, Detroit Free Press (Detroit, MI), 1995.

Tuesdays with Morrie: An Old Man, a Young Man, and Life's Greatest Lesson, Doubleday (New York, NY), 1997.
The Five People You Meet in Heaven, Hyperion (New York, NY), 2003.

Contributor to periodicals, including *Gentlemen's Quarterly, Sports Illustrated, New York Times,* and *Sport;* contributor to *MSNBC.com.*

ADAPTATIONS: *Tuesdays with Morrie: An Old Man, a Young Man, and Life's Greatest Lesson* was adapted as an Emmy Award-winning television movie, aired by American Broadcasting Companies, Inc. (ABC), 1999, and as a play produced in New York, NY, 2002. *Bo: The Bo Schembechler Story* and *Tuesdays with Morrie* were adapted as audio books.

SIDELIGHTS: Mitch Albom, a journalist for the *Detroit Free Press,* has earned national attention and awards for penning sports columns distinguished by insight, humor, and empathy. Many of his columns have been collected in books that include *The Live Albom: The Best of Mitch Albom, Live Albom II, Live Albom III: Gone to the Dogs,* and *Live Albom IV.* Disdaining the questionable ethical conduct, drug problems, and overinflated egos often found in the sports world, Albom highlights instances of athletic courage and determination while providing fact-based commentary on a team's performance.

After stints in New York and Florida, Albom arrived in Detroit, Michigan, in 1985 as a staff member of the *Detroit Free Press.* Introducing himself to his new audience in his first column, he explained that readers could expect "some opinion, some heart, some frankness. Some laughs. Some out of the ordinary." Albom also made a good first impression with area sports fans by rejecting the negative stereotype—a crime-ridden and dying city—that Detroit held for the nation. "Some people apparently look at a new job in Detroit as something to be endured or tolerated," he told his audience, going on to say: "I, for one, am thrilled to be here. For sports, they don't make towns any better than this one."

One of Albom's most distinguished traits as a columnist has been his sympathy with disappointed fans when local professional teams struggle unsuccessfully for championships. He commiserated with area readers in 1988 when Detroit's basketball team, the Pistons, battled to the National Basketball Association (NBA) finals and pushed Los Angeles to a full seven-game series, only to lose the last game by three points. He reasoned in one column, included in *The Live Albom:* "They went further than any Pistons team before them. They came onto the stage as brutes and left with an entire nation's respect—for their courage, for their determination, for their talent. . . . They took on all comers. . . . They could beat any team in the league. They just couldn't beat them all." A year earlier, when the underdog Red Wings reached the National Hockey League (NHL) semifinals but lost, Albom reported how, on the long flight home, the players dealt with this defeat. Upon learning that a devoted fan had flown to Edmonton to watch the game, Detroit players chipped in to reimburse him for his ticket. They also joined in on a chorus of that fan's favorite cheer. Witnessing this, Albom wrote, "Amazing. Here were these bruising, scarred, often toothless men, on the night of a season-ending loss, singing a high school cheer. Simply because it made an old guy happy. Many people will remember goals and saves and slap shots from this season. I hope I never forget that cheer."

With columns such as these, Albom earned a loyal following and a reputation as a blue-collar sports fan. His success in print carried over to other media, including radio and television. He joined the staff of rock station WLLZ in 1985, initially serving as sports director. In 1988 he and cohost Mike Stone began a weekly program, *The Sunday Sports Albom.* Guests included both local and national sports figures and the program's format allowed calls by listeners. His stellar guest list was evidence of the comfortable rapport Albom shared with many area athletes and coaches. This accord extended beyond interviews; in 1987 he was even a good luck charm for Detroit's Red Wings. As he explained in a column reprinted in *The Live Albom,* "I am not sure when my car and the fortunes of the Red Wings actually became intertwined. I do know [coach] Jacques Demers and I have now driven to five playoff games together and Detroit has won all five, and now even Demers, who is not superstitious, is asking me what time we're leaving."

Albom's relationship with former University of Michigan football coach Bo Schembechler led to a collaboration on Schembechler's autobiography, *Bo: The Bo Schembechler Story.* Respected as a top college coach for his Big Ten championships and frequent bowl appearances, Schembechler reputedly had a quick temper and churlish personality. In *Bo,* Albom presents Schembechler as a sincere family man whose surly demeanor was a deliberate act and who inspired love and respect from his football players. Albom credits Schembechler with turning the Michigan football program around. Al-

bom notes a greater accomplishment, however: Schembechler ran a program free from rules violations and saw his athletes graduate. *New York Times Book Review* contributor Charles Salzberg concluded that while *Bo* does not offer much new information about Schembechler, the work strengthened Schembechler's position as a role model for college athletes.

While Albom soon reigned as the darling of the Detroit sports scene, he also became involved with his share of controversy. He raised the ire of a Detroit Tigers pitcher with a column, and eleven months later had a bucket of ice water dumped over his head in the Tigers' clubhouse because the pitcher blamed his disintegrating effectiveness on Albom's commentary. Albom also broke the 1988 story of the after-curfew bar visits of several Red Wings players, reporting that, when confronted with the news, the coach "looked as if he was going to cry." Albom added that this black mark on the team's accomplishments was "not the story I wanted to write. Not the one you wanted to read." In these instances, a prediction Albom made in his first column came true: "I try to be honest. . . . This is not always a pretty job. Sometimes you have to write that the good guys lost, or that somebody's favorite baseball hero in the whole world just checked into the rehab clinic. Still, sports are the only show in town where no matter how many times you go back, you never know the ending. That's special."

Albom expanded his writing beyond the realm of sports with his 1997 publication *Tuesdays with Morrie: An Old Man, a Young Man, and Life's Greatest Lesson.* The book, which was the top-selling nonfiction title of 1998, sprang from Albom's weekly visits with his former professor, Morrie Schwartz. While a student at Brandeis University, Albom was strongly influenced by the unconventional Schwartz, who urged his students to disdain high-paying careers and follow their hearts instead. Upon graduating, Albom promised to keep in touch with his teacher, but he neither called nor visited Schwartz for the next sixteen years. Watching television one night, he saw Schwartz on the ABC television program *Nightline.* The professor had been diagnosed with amyotrophic lateral sclerosis (ALS), commonly known as Lou Gehrig's disease. A hasty trip to Massachusetts to see his old mentor led to a weekly meeting over the next fourteen weeks until Schwarz's died. Albom was struck by the realization that although he was young, healthy, and wildly successful, his old, dying teacher was a much happier, more peaceful person. He began to write a book based on their conversations, in part to help defray Schwartz's medical expenses.

Tuesdays with Morrie is "a slender but emotionally weighty account of Albom's final seminar with

Schwartz," in the words of *People* contributor William Plummer. Albom relates the way in which, without even realizing it, he had slowly abandoned his youthful ideals, becoming cynical, spiritually shallow, and materialistic. Working around the clock to maintain his career left him little time for reflection. Schwartz helped his former student to refocus his life and in chapters that focus on fear, aging, greed, family, forgiveness, and other topics, "the reader hears Morrie advise Mitch to slow down and savor the moment . . . to give up striving for bigger toys and, above all, to invest himself in love," explained Plummer. "Familiar pronouncements, of course, but what makes them fresh is Morrie's eloquence, his lack of self-pity . . . and his transcendent humor, even in the face of death."

"One gets whiffs of Jesus, the Buddha, Epicurus, Montaigne and Erik Erikson" from Schwartz's discourses, related Alain de Botton in the *New York Times Book Review.* Yet Botton objected that the "true and sometimes touching pieces of advice" dispensed by Schwartz "don't add up to a very wise book. Though Albom insists that Schwartz's words have transformed him, it's hard to see why. . . . Because Albom fails to achieve any real insight into his own . . . life, it's difficult for the reader to trust in his spiritual transformation." In contrast, a *Publishers Weekly* reviewer maintained: "Far from being awash in sentiment, the dying man retains a firm grasp on reality," and called *Tuesdays with Morrie* "an emotionally rich book and a deeply affecting memorial to a wise mentor." In a review for the *Columbia Journalism Review,* Dante Chinni commented that *Tuesdays with Morrie* "made Albom something akin to the Kahlil Gibran of disease and spirituality, quoted all over the Internet as a source of inspiration." The book did open doors for the sports journalist, who became a sought-after speaker and was even asked by fellow columnist Dave Barry to join a literary rock band called the Rock Bottom Remainders, which includes Stephen King, Barry, and Amy Tan on its roster.

Albom followed *Tuesdays with Morrie* with his first novel, 2003's *The Five People You Meet in Heaven.* As he told *Publishers Weekly,* the novel is based on stories his Uncle Eddie told him as a child. In the novel, Eddie is a grizzled old man, a war veteran who works as a maintenance man at a fairground. Both he and the people who employ him think little of his worth as a person, and it is not until Eddie dies saving the life of a little girl that the value of his life becomes clear. In heaven, Eddie meets five people who help him gain understanding about life's meaning. A *Publishers Weekly* reviewer commented that, "One by one, these mostly unexpected characters remind him that we all live in a

vast web of interconnection with other lives; that all our stories overlap; that acts of sacrifice seemingly small or fruitless do affect others; and that loyalty and love matter to a degree we can never fathom."

Albom continues to write on difficult moral questions— among them euthanasia, medical marijuana, and questions of personal responsibility and law suits—in his newspaper columns and to talk about them on his syndicated radio programs. As Chinni noted in the *Columbia Journalism Review,* "Albom is not a typical sportswriter or a typical anything, for that matter. . . . *Tuesdays with Morrie* . . . put him in a league of his own." Albom described his role to Chinni: "Communicator. . . . That's all. . . . I'm talking about a lot of things that I'm writing about and I'm writing about a lot of things that I think about. For me it's sort of one job with a lot of tentacles."

BIOGRAPHICAL AND CRITICAL SOURCES:

BOOKS

Albom, Mitch, *The Live Albom,* Detroit Free Press, 1988, pp. 12, 208, 218.
Albom, Mitch, *Live Albom II,* Detroit Free Press, 1990, pp. 33, 35, 44.

PERIODICALS

Back Stage, November 29, 2002, p. 32; January 17, 2003, p. 9.
Book, September, 2000, p. 10.
Books, December, 1998, p. 22.
Bookwatch, February, 1998, p. 11.
Christian Science Monitor, April 30, 1998, Robin Whitten, review of audio version of *Tuesdays with Morrie: An Old Man, a Young Man, and Life's Greatest Lesson,* p. B4.
Columbia Journalism Review, September, 2001, Dante Chinni, review of *Tuesdays with Morrie,* p. 18.
Detroit Free Press, March 30, 1993, p. C1; August 27, 2003.
Hollywood Reporter, November 23, 2002, p. 7.
Image, winter, 1998, p. 395.
Kirkus Reviews, July 1, 1997, p. 993.
Kliatt, May, 1998, p. 56.
Knight-Ridder/Tribune News Service, June 9, 1999, p. K3422; October 16, 2001, p. K0231; November 13, 2002, p. K5785; August 27, 2003, p. K7744.

Lancet, October 17, 1998, Faith McLellan, "A Teacher to the Last," p. 1318.

Los Angeles Business Journal, April 24, 2000, p. 65; December 11, 2000, p. 53; August 5, 2002, p. 39; September 30, 2002, p. 47.

Modern Healthcare, February 10, 2003, p. 34.

Multichannel News, January 29, 2001, p. 20.

New York, December 2, 2002, p. 78.

New York Times Book Review, November 19, 1989, Charles Salzberg, review of *Bo: The Bo Schembechler Story,* p. 44; November 23, 1997, Alain de Botton, review of *Tuesdays with Morrie,* p. 20.

People, January 12, 1998, William Plummer, "Memento Morrie: Morrie Schwartz, While Dying, Teaches Writer Mitch Albom the Secrets of Living," p. 141.

Publishers Weekly, October 5, 1990, review of audio version of *Bo,* p. 73; June 30, 1997, review of *Tuesdays with Morrie,* p. 60; March 2, 1998, review of audio version of *Tuesdays with Morrie,* p. 30; October 9, 2000, Daisy Maryles and Dick Donahue, "Three Years+ with Morrie," p. 22; July 28, 2003, review of *The Five People You Meet in Heaven,* p. 18; August 18, 2003, Tracy Cochran, "Everyone Matters" (interview).

Quest, March-April, 1998, p. 42.

Sports Illustrated, May 15, 1995, "Record Albom," p. 22; December 20, 1999, "Morrie Glory: His Bestseller Now a Hit TV Movie, Sportswriter Mitch Albom Continues His Crossover Act," p. 28; March 5, 2001, p. 16.

Tikkun, March, 2001, p. 75.

Tribune Books (Chicago, IL), December 12, 1993, p. 3.

TV Guide, December 4, 1999, "These Days with Morrie," p. 39.

Wall Street Journal, March 14, 1988, Bradley A. Stertz, "It's Probably Not Too Smart for Us to Publicize This Kind of Revenge," p. 29.

Writer's Digest, September, 2001, p. 38.

Writing!, April-May, 2003, p. 11.

ONLINE

Albom Online, http://www.albom.com/ (March 19, 2004).

*   *   *

ALBOM, Mitch David
    See ALBOM, Mitch

ALDISS, Brian W. 1925-
    (Brian Wilson Aldiss, C.C. Shackleton)

PERSONAL: Born August 18, 1925, in East Dereham, Norfolk, England; son of Stanley (an outfitter) and Elizabeth May (Wilson) Aldiss; married second wife, Margaret Christie Manson, December 11, 1965 (died, 1997); children: (first marriage) Clive, Caroline Wendy; (second marriage) Timothy Nicholas, Charlotte May. *Education:* Attended Framlingham College, 1936-39; West Buckland School, 1939-42. *Hobbies and other interests:* Amateur theatricals.

ADDRESSES: Home—Hambledon, 39 St. Andrews Rd., Old Headington, Oxford OX3 9DL, England. *Agent*—Michael Shaw, Curtis Brown, Haymarket House, 28/29 Haymarket, London SW1Y 4SP, England; Robin Straus, 229 East 79th St., New York, NY 10021. *E-mail*—aldiss@dial.pipex.com.

CAREER: Bookseller, writer, editor, actor, and critic. *Oxford Mail,* Oxford, England, literary editor, 1957-69; Penguin Books, Ltd., London, England, editor of science fiction novels, 1961-64; *Guardian,* London, art correspondent, 1971-78; Avernus Publishing, London, managing director, 1988—. Judge for Booker-McConnell Prize, 1981. *Military service:* British Army, five years, served with Royal Corps of Signals; attached to Indian Army, 1945-46; received Burma Star.

MEMBER: Royal Society of Literature, International Institute for the Study of Time, International Association for the Fantastic in the Arts (permanent special guest), World Science Fiction Society (president, 1982-84), British Science Fiction Association (president, 1960-64), Science Fiction Writers of America, Science Fiction Research Association, Society of Authors (chair, 1977-78), PEN, Arts Council of Great Britain (literature panelist, 1978-80), Cultural Exchanges Committee (chair).

AWARDS, HONORS: Observer short story prize, 1955, for "Not for an Age," and 1956, for "Tradesman's Exit"; named most promising new author of the year at the World Science Fiction Convention, 1958; Hugo Award for best short fiction, World Science Fiction Convention, 1962, for "Hothouse"; British Science Fiction Association Award as Britain's Most Popular Science Fiction Author, 1964; Nebula Award for best novella, Science Fiction Writers of America, 1965, for *The Saliva Tree, and Other Strange Growths;* Ditmar Award for world's best contemporary science fiction author, 1970; British Science Fiction Association Award, 1972, for *The Moment of Eclipse;* British Science Fiction Association Special Award, 1972, and Eurocon III Merit Award, 1976, both for *Billion Year Spree: The History of Science Fiction;* James Blish Award for excellence in science fiction criticism, 1977; Ferrara Silver Comet, 1977, for *Science Fiction Art;* Prix Jules Verne, 1977, for *Non-Stop;* Science Fiction Research Association Pilgrim Award, 1978; John W. Campbell Memorial Award for best novel of 1982, British Science Fiction Association Award for best fiction of 1982, and Kurd Lasswitz Award for best foreign novel, 1984, all for *Helliconia Spring;* first International Association for the Fantastic in the Arts distinguished scholarship award, 1986; British Science Fiction Association Award for best novel, 1986, for *Helliconia Winter;* Hugo Award for best nonfiction, 1987, Locus Award for best nonfiction, 1987, and J. Lloyd Eaton Award, 1988, all for *Trillion Year Spree: The History of Science Fiction;* World SF President's Award, 1988; fellow, Royal Society of Literature, 1990; Kafka Award, 1991; Grand Master Award, Science Fiction Writers of America, 2000; Honorary D.Litt. awarded by University of Reading, 2000; Vision Award, Science Fiction Writers of Macedonia, 2001.

WRITINGS:

NOVELS

The Brightfount Diaries, Faber & Faber (London, England), 1955.

Non-Stop, Faber & Faber (London, England), 1958, published as *Starship,* Criterion (New York, NY), 1959.

Equator, Digit Books (London, England), 1958, reprinted, House of Stratus (London, England), 2001, published as *Vanguard from Alpha,* Ace (New York, NY), 1959.

Bow down to Nul, Ace, 1960, published as *The Interpreter,* Digit Books (London, England), 1961.

The Male Response, Ballantine (New York, NY), 1961.

The Primal Urge, Ballantine (New York, NY), 1961.

Long Afternoon of Earth, Signet (New York, NY), 1962, published as *Hothouse,* Faber & Faber (London, England), 1962, with new introduction by Joseph Milicia, Gregg Press (Boston, MA), 1976.

The Dark Light Years, Harcourt (New York, NY), 1964.

Greybeard, Harcourt (New York, NY), 1964.

Earthworks, Faber & Faber (London, England), 1965, Doubleday (New York, NY), 1966.

An Age, Faber & Faber (London, England), 1967, published as *Cryptozoic!,* Doubleday (New York, NY), 1968.

Report on Probability A, Faber & Faber (London, England), 1968, Doubleday (New York, NY), 1969.

A Brian Aldiss Omnibus, Sidgwick & Jackson (London, England), 1969.

Barefoot in the Head: A European Fantasia, Faber & Faber (London, England), 1969, Doubleday (New York, NY), 1970.

The Hand-Reared Boy (also see below), Weidenfeld & Nicolson (London, England), 1969, McCall (New York, NY), 1970.

A Soldier Erect (also see below), Coward (New York, NY), 1971, published as *A Soldier Erect; or, Further Adventures of the Hand-Reared Boy,* Weidenfeld & Nicolson (London, England), 1971.

Brian Aldiss Omnibus 2, Sidgwick & Jackson (London, England), 1971.

Frankenstein Unbound (also see below), Random House (New York, NY), 1973.

The Eighty-Minute Hour: A Space Opera, Doubleday (New York, NY), 1974.

The Malacia Tapestry, Jonathan Cape (London, England), 1976, HarperCollins (New York, NY), 1977.

Brothers of the Head, illustrated by Ian Pollock, Pierrot (New York, NY), 1977.

A Rude Awakening (also see below), Weidenfeld & Nicolson (London, England), 1978, Random House (New York, NY), 1979.

Enemies of the System: A Tale of Homo Uniformis, Harper (New York, NY), 1978.

Life in the West, Weidenfeld & Nicolson (London, England), 1980, Carroll & Graf (New York, NY), 1990.

Moreau's Other Island, Jonathan Cape (London, England), 1980, published as *An Island Called Moreau,* Simon & Schuster (New York, NY), 1981.

Helliconia Spring, Atheneum (New York, NY), 1982.

Helliconia Summer, Atheneum (New York, NY), 1983.

Helliconia Winter, Atheneum (New York, NY), 1985.

The Helliconia Trilogy (contains *Helliconia Spring, Helliconia Summer,* and *Helliconia Winter*), Atheneum (New York, NY), 1985.

The Horatio Stubbs Saga (contains *The Hand-Reared Boy, A Soldier Erect,* and *A Rude Awakening*), Panther (London, England), 1985.

The Year before Yesterday: A Novel in Three Acts, F. Watts (New York, NY), 1987.

Ruins, Century Hutchinson (London, England), 1987.

Forgotten Life, Gollancz (London, England), 1988, Atheneum (New York, NY), 1989.

Dracula Unbound, HarperCollins (New York, NY), 1991.

Remembrance Day, HarperCollins (New York, NY), 1992.

Somewhere East of Life: Another European Fantasia, HarperCollins (New York, NY), 1994.

(With Roger Penrose) *White Mars; or The Mind Set Free, or, The Mind Set Free: A Twenty-first-Century Utopia,* St. Martin's Press (New York, NY), 1999.

The Cretan Teat, House of Stratus, 2002.

The Super-State, Orbit (London, England), 2002.

NONFICTION

Cities and Stones: A Traveller's Yugoslavia, Faber & Faber (London, England), 1965.

The Shape of Further Things, Doubleday (New York, NY), 1970.

Billion Year Spree: The History of Science Fiction, Doubleday (New York, NY), 1973.

Science Fiction Art, New English Library (London, England), 1975.

Science Fiction As Science Fiction, Bran's Head (Frome, Somerset, England), 1978.

This World and Nearer Ones: Essays Exploring the Familiar, Weidenfeld & Nicolson (London, England), 1979, Kent State University Press (Kent, OH), 1981.

Pile: Petals from St. Klaed's Computer, illustrations by Mike Wilkis, Jonathan Cape (London, England), 1979, Holt (New York, NY), 1980.

The Pale Shadow of Science, Serconia (Seattle, WA), 1985.

. . . And the Lurid Glare of the Comet, Serconia (Seattle, WA), 1986.

(With David Wingrove) *Trillion Year Spree: The History of Science Fiction,* Atheneum (New York, NY), 1986.

Bury My Heart at W.H. Smith's: A Writing Life (autobiography), Hodder & Stoughton (London, England), 1990.

The Detached Retina: Aspects of SF and Fantasy, Syracuse University Press (Syracuse, NY), 1995.

The Twinkling of an Eye: My Life as an Englishman, Little, Brown (London, England), 1998, St. Martin's Press (New York, NY), 1999.

When the Feast Is Finished, Little, Brown (London, England), 1999.

STORY COLLECTIONS

Space, Time, and Nathaniel, Faber & Faber (London, England), 1957.

The Canopy of Time, Faber & Faber (London, England), 1959.

No Time like Tomorrow, Signet (New York, NY), 1959.

Galaxies like Grains of Sand, Signet (New York, NY), 1960, with new introduction by Norman Spinrad, Gregg Press (Boston, MA), 1977.

The Airs of Earth, Faber & Faber (London, England), 1963.

Starswarm, Signet (New York, NY), 1964, with new introduction by Joseph Milicia, Gregg Press (Boston, MA), 1978.

Best Science Fiction Stories of Brian Aldiss, Faber & Faber (London, England), 1965, revised edition, 1971, published as *Who Can Replace a Man?,* Harcourt (New York, NY), 1966.

The Saliva Tree, and Other Strange Growths, Faber & Faber (London, England), 1966.

The Future Makers: A Selection of Science Fiction, Sidgwick & Johnson (London, England), 1968.

Intangibles Inc., and Other Stories: Five Novellas, Faber & Faber (London, England), 1969.

Neanderthal Planet, Avon (New York, NY), 1969.

The Moment of Eclipse, Faber & Faber (London, England), 1971, Doubleday (New York, NY), 1972.

The Book of Brian Aldiss, DAW Books, 1972, published as *Comic Inferno,* New English Library (London, England), 1973.

Last Orders and Other Stories, Jonathan Cape (London, England), 1977.

New Arrivals, Old Encounters, HarperCollins (New York, NY), 1979.

Foreign Bodies, Chopman (Singapore), 1981.

Seasons in Flight, Jonathan Cape (London, England), 1984, Atheneum (New York, NY), 1986.

The Magic of the Past, Kerosina Books (Worcester Park, Surrey, England), 1987.

Best SF Stories of Brian W. Aldiss, Gollancz (London, England), 1988, published as *Man in His Time: The Best Science Fiction Stories of Brian W. Aldiss,* Atheneum (New York, NY), 1989.

Science Fiction Blues: The Show That Brian Aldiss Took on the Road, Avernus Publishing (London, England), 1988.

A Romance of the Equator: The Best Fantasy Stories of Brian W. Aldiss, Gollancz (London, England), 1989, Atheneum (New York, NY), 1990.

A Tupolev Too Far: And Other Stories, HarperCollins (New York, NY), 1993.

The Secret of This Book: Twenty Odd Stories, HarperCollins (New York, NY), 1995.

Common Clay: Twenty Odd Stories, St. Martin's Press (New York, NY), 1996.

Supertoys Last All Summer Long: And Other Stories of the Future, St. Martin's Griffin, (New York, NY), 2001.

Contributor of short stories to books, including *The Inner Landscape,* Allison & Busby (London, England), 1969, and *Pulphouse Science-Fiction Short Stories,* Pulphouse, 1991.

EDITOR

Penguin Science Fiction, Penguin (New York, NY), 1961.

More Penguin Science Fiction: An Anthology, Penguin (New York, NY), 1962.

Best Fantasy Stories, Faber & Faber (London, England), 1962.

Science Fiction Horizons, numbers 1-2, Arno Press, 1964–65.

Yet More Penguin Science Fiction, Penguin (New York, NY), 1964.

Introducing Science Fiction: A Science Fiction Anthology, Faber & Faber (London, England), 1964.

(With Harry Harrison) *Nebula Award Stories II,* Doubleday (New York, NY), 1967.

(With Harry Harrison) *All about Venus: A Revelation of the Planet Venus in Fact and Fiction,* Dell (New York, NY), 1968, published as *Farewell Fantastic Venus! A History of the Planet Venus in Fact and Fiction,* Macdonald (London, England), 1968.

(With Harry Harrison) *The Astounding Analog Reader,* two volumes, Doubleday (New York, NY), 1973.

Penguin Science Fiction Omnibus: An Anthology, Penguin (New York, NY), 1973.

Space Opera: An Anthology of Way-Back-When Futures, Weidenfeld & Nicolson (London, England), 1974, Doubleday (New York, NY), 1975.

(With Harry Harrison) *Hell's Cartographers: Some Personal Histories of Science Fiction Writers,* Doubleday (New York, NY), 1975.

Space Odysseys, Weidenfeld & Nicolson (London, England), 1975, Doubleday (New York, NY), 1976.

Evil Earths, Weidenfeld & Nicolson (London, England), 1975, Avon (New York, NY), 1979.

Galactic Empires, two volumes, Weidenfeld & Nicolson (London, England), 1976, St. Martin's Press (New York, NY), 1977.

(With Harry Harrison) *Decade: The 1940s,* Macmillan (London, England), 1977, St. Martin's Press (New York, NY), 1978.

(With Harry Harrison) *Decade: The 1950s,* Macmillan (London, England), 1977, St. Martin's Press (New York, NY), 1978.

(With Harry Harrison) *Decade: The 1960s,* Macmillan (London, England), 1977.

Perilous Planets, Weidenfeld & Nicolson (London, England), 1978, Avon (New York, NY), 1980.

Mary Shelley: The Last Man, Hogarth Press, 1985.

The Penguin World Omnibus of Science Fiction, Penguin Books (New York, NY), 1986.

My Madness: The Selected Writings of Anna Kavan, Picador (New York, NY), 1990.

H.G. Wells, *The Island of Doctor Moreau,* C.E. Tuttle, 1993.

Mini Sagas from the Daily Telegraph Competition, Sutton, 1997.

Also coeditor of "SF Master" series, New English Library, 1976-79; editor of four books of mini-sagas by Alan Sutton, 1985, 1988, 1997, and 2001. Also editor, with Harry Harrison, *Best Science Fiction,* Putnam (New York, NY), annually, 1967-76.

OTHER

Frankenstein Unbound (radio play based on the novel of the same title), British Broadcasting Corp. (BBC Radio), 1974, abridged version released as a sound recording by Alternate World Recordings, 1976, produced as *Roger Corman's Frankenstein Unbound,* Warner Brothers, 1990.

Pile: Petals from St. Klaed's Computer (poetry), illustrated by Mike Wilks, Jonathan Cape (London, England), 1979, Holt (New York, NY), 1980.

Farewell to a Child (poetry), Priapus Press (Berkhamsted, England), 1982.

(Author of foreword) Robert Crossley, *Olaf Stapledon: Speaking for the Future,* Syracuse University Press (Syracuse, NY), 1994.

At the Caligula Hotel and Other Poems, Sinclair-Stevenson, 1995.

(Versifier) Makhtumkuli, *Songs from the Steppes of Central Asia: The Collected Poems of Makhtumkuli: Eighteenth-Century Poet-Hero of Turkmenistan,* based on translations by Youssef Azemoun, Society of Friends of Makhtumkuli, 1995.

Author of plays *SF Blues, Drinks with the Spider King,* and *Monsters of Everyday.* Contributor of articles and reviews to periodicals under pseudonym C.C. Shackleton. Also author of chapbooks *The Dark Sun Rises,* a collection of poetry; *A New (Governmental) Father Christmas,* and *Researches and Churches in Serbia,* all published by Avernus Media.

ADAPTATIONS: The title story and its two sequels collected in *Supertoys Last All Summer Long: And Other Stories of the Future* were adapted for film by Steven Spielberg and released in 2001 as *A.I.,* directed by Spielberg and starring Haley Joel Osment.

SIDELIGHTS: Brian W. Aldiss is a prolific British author who has published criticism, essays, travelogues, short stories, and traditional novels, but who remains best known for his science-fiction writing. Since the appearance of his first science-fiction novel, *Non-Stop,* in 1958, Aldiss has garnered virtually every major award in the field, including a Hugo Award for "Hothouse," a Nebula Award for *The Saliva Tree and Other Strange Growths,* a John W. Campbell Memorial Award for *Helliconia Spring,* and a James Blish Award for excellence in science fiction criticism.

Aldiss was born in 1925, in East Dereham, Norfolk, England, where his parents were shopkeepers. He attended what he called "an inadequate boarding school and an even more inadequate public school," according to Willis E. McNelly in *Science Fiction Writers.* He was drafted into the British Army to serve in India, Burma, and Indonesia during World War II. After being discharged, he married, had two children, and worked in a bookstore in Oxford. This employment allowed him to continue his education on his own and gave him time to write. He has been a professional writer since his first book, *The Brightfount Diaries,* was published in 1955.

Unlike many of his colleagues, Aldiss approaches science fiction from a humanist point of view, focusing on character and theme rather than gadget-oriented technology. He demands an authorial autonomy that is rare in the field, and he typically discards worn-out formulas in favor of riskier, creative experiments. In the year 2000, his fellows recognized his outstanding achievement in science fiction by awarding him the title of 1999 Grand Master of Science Fiction.

As a critic, Aldiss campaigns for the acceptance of science fiction as a legitimate genre. He argues that science fiction is not just a fad, but will remain a permanent fixture in literature. According to Jonathan White in *Publishers Weekly,* Aldiss believes that science fiction has the potential to evolve, while other genres inevitably disappear after running their courses. The author explained to White: "I don't look upon science fiction as a genre at all; rather, it *contains* genres. For a bit it was the space opera that was in vogue. Then the catastrophe novel. For every kind of story that gets used up, another will always take its place." His comprehensive history of this genre, *Trillion Year Spree: The History of Science Fiction,* written with David Wingrove, testifies to his vision of science fiction as a serious literary endeavor.

Aldiss has himself experimented with different types of science fiction. *An Age,* for example, deals with the theme of time travel, but it is also "an amalgam . . .

of detective story, psychological thriller, and visionary fantasy," wrote a *Times Literary Supplement* reviewer.- *The Eighty-Minute Hour* "joyously resurrects old SF stereotypes," but it does so with "an amused self-consciousness, stylistic flair and dexterity, and a double-edged humor based in the comic multiple meanings of language," declared Richard Mathews in his *Aldiss Unbound: The Science Fiction of Brian W. Aldiss.* Two of the author's books, *Report on Probability A* and *Barefoot in the Head: A European Fantasia,* are experimental works which are meant to challenge the reader intellectually, Aldiss told White. *Barefoot in the Head* describes a war fought with hallucinogenic drugs, while *Report on Probability A* is "a kind of fantasy *nouveau roman* of voyeurism," as a *Chicago Tribune Book World* reviewer called it. Aldiss once commented that *Report on Probability A* marks his "commitment to bringing art and artistic concerns into SF." Neither novel was accepted with much critical or public enthusiasm upon publication, but both, especially the repeatedly reissued *Report on Probability A,* have enjoyed some success since then. After exploring the many features of the genre in over a dozen books, Aldiss felt he had "written himself out of science fiction," related Mathews. He ventured into what he terms "ordinary fiction" with the novel *The Hand-Reared Boy* and its two sequels, *A Soldier Erect* and *A Rude Awakening.* Mathews claimed that the adjective "ordinary," far from having any negative connotation, is "used in its best sense" because the book, which records the "male rites of passage before [World War II], is one with which any man can identify." It is, the reviewer suggested, far from ordinary in its ability to reach its audience. *The Hand-Reared Boy* is the story of Horatio Stubbs's experiences at a private (or, in British usage, public) boarding school for boys in England. Its sequel, *A Soldier Erect,* follows Stubbs into military service. Mathews found that "these novels are significant in marking [Aldiss's] return to standard fiction devices, without the aid of stylistic inventions or SF gimmicks." The third volume, *A Rude Awakening,* follows Horatio Stubbs, the young central character, to conflict in Sumatra.

The frankness of Aldiss's approach to this trilogy, which strongly emphasizes Horatio's sexual exploits, inspired strong reactions from critics, who found the characters either refreshing or vulgar. A *Times Literary Supplement* reviewer noted that *The Hand-Reared Boy* may seem like "an erotic fantasy. Yet it rings true—however surprising to young readers educated at day-schools." And Valentine Cunningham remarked in the *Times Literary Supplement* that "even a taste for the tasteless has a way of sliding into tastefulness" in *A Rude Awakening,* the last Horatio book. The reviewer felt that the post-war wisdom Horatio expresses toward the end of the book is the most tasteful part, though in Cunningham's opinion, Aldiss wades through too many "bodily fluids" before offering anything of literary substance to his text. *New York Times Book Review* critic Martin Levin also had mixed feelings about the Horatio Stubbs trilogy. Reviewing *The Hand-Reared Boy,* Levin believed that the "disarming keynote" of an otherwise sexually preoccupied book is the "spirit of joyful exuberance" with which Horatio recalls his childhood memories. Levin expressed little tolerance for Horatio's "zest for whoring [which] declines only during bouts of dysentery," but he praised Aldiss's portrayal of war in the China-Burma-India theater. The vividness of this part of the book comes from the author's personal experiences in Asia during the Second World War. "Mr. Aldiss brings to life this long-dead war, with its vanished mystique and its forgiven and forgotten enemies," declared Levin. Balancing out the blunt corporeal language and situations of this trilogy, this aspect of the Horatio novels has helped mitigate criticism of these publicly well-received books. The first two novels topped Britain's best-seller lists. Paul Fussell, in his book *Wartime,* summed up the trilogy as collected in *The Horatio Stubbs Saga:* "Aldiss's trilogy is not the best writing to come out of the war but it does offer the most clear-sighted view, necessarily comic."

Aldiss's *Forgotten Life,* published in 1988, contains descriptions of life in wartime Burma and Sumatra which echo those of the Asian war theater in the Horatio books, but any similarities between this and those earlier works end there. *Forgotten Life* deals with the relationships between mature people, rather than with the maturation processes of a single character. It is concerned with three people, explained *Glasgow Herald* contributor Ian Bell: Clement Winter, an Oxford psychoanalyst who is struggling "for an emotional life of his own"; his wife Sheila, a successful science fiction/ fantasy novelist, who is "living half her life in a fantasy world"; and Clement's brother Joseph, who is striving "to form a lasting relationship free from the rejection he endured at his mother's hands." Jonathan Keates claimed in an *Observer* review that "the true protagonist here is Joseph," whose tale is told when Clement reads his brother's journals after the latter's death. "Aldiss's skill," continued Keates, "lies in sustaining [Joseph] in a continuing duel with Clement." Contrary to this opinion, *Punch* critic Simon Brett wrote that "too great a percentage of the book is devoted to [Joseph]. And the author has created a self-regarding style for Joseph's writings which, while entirely appropriate for the character, does become a little wearing for the reader."

The organization of the book is complex, shifting in viewpoint as it involves the reader in Joseph's journal,

Clement's life in North Oxford, the brothers' childhood lives, and the present-day relationships between Clement and his brother's mistress, and Sheila and her American editor. *Times Literary Supplement* contributor John Melmoth observed that this approach "fails to cohere," making it a "frustrating experience." But Isabel Quigley wrote in the London *Financial Times* that "all these shifts of viewpoint, method, sympathy, place and time . . . [form a] whole and achieves a pattern, likeable, solid and satisfying." Sophia Watson, a *Literary Review* critic, similarly remarked that *Forgotten Life* is "a good read," but she did not believe it should be considered a major work of fiction. Bell of the *Glasgow Herald* felt more strongly about the novel's merits, however, maintaining that "this is a fine and satisfying novel of a type which Mr. Aldiss, masterly SF writer that he is, should try more often."

Despite praise for his mainstream fiction, the author has concentrated most of his efforts on science fiction. His most ambitious work in this genre is the much-praised "Helliconia" trilogy, which Gerald Jonas wrote in the *New York Times Book Review* "truly deserves the label 'epic.'" The novels—*Helliconia Spring, Helliconia Summer,* and *Helliconia Winter*—are set on a world in a binary star system. The 2,592-year orbit of Helliconia's sun Batalix around the larger sun Freyr "subjects Helliconia to a Great Year whose seasons last for centuries," summarized Colin Greenland in a *Times Literary Supplement* review of *Helliconia Summer.* The extremity of the weather on the planet dictates to a great extent the rise and fall of civilizations, the relationship between the humans and a-human "Phagors," and the biology of the planet's inhabitants (including humans).

Helliconia Spring starts at the end of Helliconia's 600-year-long barbaric ice age and follows the story of Yuli and his descendants as they begin to reestablish civilization in the town of Embruddock, which Yuli renames Oldorando. As the town grows, the men vie for power and battle the Phagors, while the women, led by the sorceress Shay Tal, establish an academy of science and discover how their planet behaves in its solar system. In a review of *Helliconia Spring,* Greenland of the *Times Literary Supplement* also raised the objection that the plot of the novel depends too much on coincidence and is "overburdened with slabs of undigested science." But these are complaints which critics like Carolyn See of the *Los Angeles Times* believed to be outweighed by the book's strengths. "For use of climate as character, for making the very long view palatable to the reader, for creating an entire universe that pulses and hums and crackles with life, Aldiss deserves full marks," concluded See.

In the trilogy's second book, *Helliconia Summer,* the author focuses on a time period of only a few months. The Phagors have been subjugated (at least temporarily), and the story focuses on Jandal Anganol, King of Borlien, and the intrigue and politics between his country and neighboring Oldorando. It is a tale which, according to London *Times* critic Nicholas Shakespeare, "smacks less of science fiction than medieval romance," though the plot also follows the society's progress as the priesthood becomes more and more involved in scientific studies.

The concluding book of the series, *Helliconia Winter,* "combines the best of the Helliconia volumes—the breadth, scope, and historical sweep of *Spring* with the finely crafted details and narrow focus of *Summer,*" said *Fantasy Review* contributor Michael R. Collins. In a review of *Helliconia Winter,* Greenland wrote that the trilogy signifies "fatalism, fundamentality, the brute biology of it all. Everything comes back to nature, which endures." As civilization struggles to survive the oncoming winter, the reader follows the adventures of Luterin Shokerandit as he goes to war, is imprisoned in the Great Wheel of Kharnabar, and survives the "Fat Death," a disease transmitted by ticks which infest the Phagors and cause the victim's body to change drastically. Strangely enough and unknown to the Helliconians, the virus actually has a beneficial side effect which allows humankind to survive the harsh winter.

While all this is taking place, the importance of the space station Avernus—which was also mentioned in the earlier books—is made more apparent to the reader in *Helliconia Winter.* The purpose of the station is to transmit messages back to Earth about every event that occurs on Helliconia's surface. Greenland felt that Aldiss's inclusion of the events on Avernus and Earth do not add to the story of Helliconia. This parallel story seems "like a dissonant dream, almost trivial beside the main drama," Greenland wrote. In contrast, an *Extrapolation* reviewer held that the stories of Earth and Helliconia present a unifying theme of hope for humanity which is finally brought together in the last book. "The endless pictures coming from Helliconia [are] an example from which humanity might learn," suggested the reviewer, concluding that as the people on Earth achieve a "new consciousness" which provides "humanity with a new unity instead of the old isolation," the highly technological station Avernus, which is also, in turn, a place of isolation for its caretakers, is replaced by higher, empathic communications. Humanity finds peace and understanding at last through the unification of the people of Earth with the Helliconians.

In a *Los Angeles Times* article, Sue Martin expressed her feeling that overall the trilogy is only "semicompel-

ling" because there are "no real twists" in the plot. Many critics, however, wrote that the Helliconia trilogy was a considerable achievement. "Though science fiction often has this scope," asserted Greenland, "it has never had this grandeur." Jonas felt these books comprised "a splendid work of imagination that weds grandeur of concept to a mastery of detail and a sense of style unmatched in modern science fiction." Aldiss said in *Publishers Weekly* that the importance of these books to him was that they signified his attempt "to get on my horse again and write a big, solid novel that *no* one could say wasn't SF." According to his own definition of science fiction quoted in the *New York Times Book Review,* this meant that he had written a work which attempted "to build some sort of philosophical and metaphysical framework around the immense changes of our times brought about by technological development." The trilogy addresses all these aspects by including a scope of time encompassing thousands of years, the description of technology and its effect on Avernus and Earth, and, in *Science Fiction and Fantasy Book Review* contributor Willis E. McNelly's words, the "artistic, intellectual, theological, even teleological sustenance" which Helliconia offers to Earth.

The trilogy is thought of as the author's most ambitious effort to give science fiction credibility as a form of serious literature. *Fantasy Review* contributor Collins remarked that "only an author such as Aldiss, who has immersed himself in questions of stasis and change, entropy, ecological balance, and definitions of what it is to be human—and has explored their possibilities for almost three decades—could have completed such a vision" as the Helliconia trilogy.

Aldiss's 1994 novel *Somewhere East of Life: Another European Fantasia* was described by a reviewer for the *Times Literary Supplement* as "a reckoning of accounts and an examination of conscience, both personal and political." The protagonist is Roy Burnell, an early twenty-first-century architectural historian who has had ten years of his memory stolen to be made into illicit tapes. The novel follows him as he searches throughout the East for his missing memories. Jonas wrote in the *New York Times Book Review,* "The story [Aldiss] has to tell is funny and disturbing, depressing and heartening by turns, and worth reading under any label." *Somewhere East of Life* is the fourth book in Aldiss's "Squire" quartet.

In the novel *White Mars; or The Mind Set Free,* called "a paean to rationalism and scientific truth" by a *Library Journal* contributor, Aldiss explores the ramifications of attempts to construct a utopian society on the Martian colonies following a Terran economic collapse. "Led by the philosopher Tom Jeffries," explained a *Publishers Weekly* contributor, "the citizens of the colony . . . devote their time to debating ethical and political theory at enormous length." The colonists adopt the principles of communal property, group childcare, and rejection of gun violence and drug culture. The title is both a nod to the successful trilogy of Martian novels by Kim Stanley Robinson and a reference to the international treaties that have kept Antarctica an unspoiled wilderness. At one point the colonists debate the morality of transforming the Martian desert into a more earth-like environment. "Humankind has matured, Aldiss suggests," declared John Mort in *Booklist,* "so that, given a brand-new start, it would behave in a brand-new way."

Discussing Aldiss's science fiction work in general, critic Robert E. Colbert wrote in *Extrapolation* that Aldiss's "concern for the dearth of ordinary human feeling in so much genre science fiction, its lack of warmth and compassion, is clear. And the specific literary benefits of the reintroduction of such concerns are also clear: an art which renders situations, depicts characters, closer to the more immediate human concerns can only benefit artistically." A number of critics have written that for these reasons, Aldiss's contributions to science fiction have done much to improve its respectability. According to Greenland, Aldiss "continues to represent the acceptable face of science fiction to those literati who still cannot bring themselves to acknowledging the genre."

Aldiss is also a prolific short-story writer and has had many of his stories published in various collections. A *Publishers Weekly* reviewer said the stories in *A Romance of the Equator: The Best Fantasy Stories of Brian W. Aldiss* "are carefully crafted word pictures that should be read slowly and savored." That is not to say they are light reading. Jonas wrote in the *New York Times Book Review* that "despite some attempts at humor, which I found strained, the prevailing mood in these fictions is melancholy, a sadness that comes from contemplating the mess that human beings usually make of themselves."

Aldiss experiments with styles in the sinister *A Tupolev Too Far: And Other Stories.* According to Gary K. Wolfe of *Locus,* the "juxtaposition of the mundane with the exotic . . . may be the hallmark of the book. Aldiss repeatedly convinces us we're in a mainstream story, then sends us right over the edge." *Times Literary Supplement* critic Julian Ferraro said the stories in *The Secret of This Book: Twenty Odd Stories* "vary greatly

in terms of tone, subject-matter and genre." He added, "Aldiss alternates between contemporary and fantastic settings, often combining elements of both to good effect." The strange, eclectic tales of *Common Clay: Twenty Odd Stories* have autobiographical elements and, observed a *Kirkus Reviews* critic, convey "the unnerving sense that there's always something else going on just beyond the reader's immediate apprehension."

Of Aldiss's 2001 collection, *Supertoys Last All Summer Long: And Other Stories of the Future,* Mark Greener of *Vector* wrote, "A new short-story collection from one of Europe's leading sf writers is always welcome—and *Supertoys* is no exception. It is, quite simply, stunning." The title story and two of its sequels, which tell the tale of David, an android who thinks he is a "real boy," were adapted by Steven Spielberg for the film, *A.I.* Of the collection, Greener concluded, "This isn't a book to just read. It's a book to linger over, to savour, to relish."

Some insight on Aldiss is gained from his first autobiography, *Bury My Heart at W.H. Smith's: A Writing Life.* In it he tells anecdotes about his writing career, friends, and travels. However, as David V. Barrett noted in *New Statesman and Society,* "This is less a book about Brian Aldiss than about what writing has meant to him throughout his life, and his love affair with words." Barrett concluded, "This is a salutary book for aspiring writers to read, whatever their chosen literary field." Aldiss has since published *When the Feast Is Finished,* in which he explores the life of his late wife Margaret, who died of pancreatic cancer, and *The Twinkling of an Eye: My Life as an Englishman,* which surveys his own varied life and career. A *Publishers Weekly* contributor commented of *The Twinkling of an Eye,* "The quirky blend of classical learning, poetic language and exotic landscapes that animate Aldiss's fiction . . . also suffuse this book, which eschews a linear chronology in favor of a more Proustian narrative." Roland Green of *Booklist* concluded, "This is a large chronicle of large achievements, related with eloquence, wit, and a decent reticence about certain colleagues." He continued, "May Aldiss enjoy enough more years to justify a second volume."

Aldiss once explained in *Contemporary Novelists:* "I write every day and always have done—not invariably for publication. . . . To be able to write is a slice of great golden fortune."

BIOGRAPHICAL AND CRITICAL SOURCES:

BOOKS

Aldiss, Margaret, compiler, *Brian W. Aldiss: A Bibliography, 1954-1988,* Borgo Press (San Bernardino, CA), 1989.

Aldiss, Margaret, *The Work of Brian W. Aldiss: An Annotated Bibliography and Guide,* edited by Boden Clark, Borgo (San Bernardino, CA), 1992.

Bleiler, E. F., editor, *Science Fiction Writers,* Scribner (New York, NY), 1982.

Contemporary Authors Autobiography Series, Volume 2, Thomson Gale (Detroit, MI), 1985.

Contemporary Literary Criticism, Thomson Gale (Detroit, MI), Volume 5, 1976, Volume 14, 1980, Volume 40, 1986.

Contemporary Novelists, 7th edition, St. James Press (Detroit, MI), 2001.

Dictionary of Literary Biography, Volume 14: *British Novelists since 1960,* Thomson Gale (Detroit, MI), 1983.

Drabble, Margaret, editor, *Oxford Companion to British Literature,* 6th edition, Oxford University Press, 2000.

Fussell, Paul, *Wartime,* Oxford University Press (New York, NY), 1989.

Hatherley, Frank, Margaret Aldiss, and Malcolm Edwards, editors, *A Is for Brian: A Sixty-fifth Birthday Present for Brian W. Aldiss from His Family, Friends, Colleagues, and Admirers* (limited edition), Avernus Publishing (London, England), 1990.

Mathews, Richard, *Aldiss Unbound: The Science Fiction of Brian W. Aldiss,* Borgo (San Bernardino, CA), 1977.

Modern British Literature, Volume 1, St. James Press (Detroit, MI), 2000.

Platt, Charles, editor, *Dream Makers: The Uncommon People Who Write Science Fiction,* Berkley Publishing (New York, NY), 1980.

Short Story Criticism; Criticism of the Works of Short Story Writers, Volume 36, Thomson Gale (Detroit, MI), 1988.

PERIODICALS

Analog Science Fiction and Fact, December 15, 1989, Tom Easton, review of *Last Orders and Other Stories,* p. 183; August, 1994, Tom Easton, review of *A Tupolev Too Far: And Other Stories,* p. 165; September, 2000, Tom Easton, review of *White Mars; or, The Mind Set Free,* p. 135.

Booklist, March 15, 1996, Carl Hays, review of *Common Clay,* p. 1244; April 15, 1999, Roland Green, review of *The Twinkling of an Eye: My Life as an Englishman,* p. 1501; March 15, 2000, John Mort, review of *White Mars,* p. 1334.

Chicago Tribune Book World, January 25, 1981, review of *Report on Probability A;* February 28, 1982.

Extrapolation, winter, 1982, review of *Helliconia Spring;* spring, 1986, Robert E. Colbert, review of *Helliconia Winter;* fall, 1996, Donald M. Hassler, review of *The Detached Retina,* p. 285.

Fantasy Review, April, 1985, Michael R. Collins, review of *Helliconia Winter.*

Financial Times (London, England), October 1, 1988, Isabel Quigley, review of *Forgotten Life.*

Foundation, winter, 1985-1986.

Glasgow Herald, October 8, 1988, Ian Bell, review of *Forgotten Life.*

Kirkus Reviews, January 1, 1996, review of *Common Clay,* p. 30.

Library Journal, May 15, 1989, Marcia R. Hoffman, review of *Forgotten Life,* p. 87; May 15, 1993, Ann Donovan, review of *Remembrance Day,* p. 95; March 15, 1996, Sue Hamburger, review of *Common Clay,* p. 99; March 15, 2000, John Mort, review of *White Mars,* p. 1334; April 15, 2000, review of *White Mars,* p. 128; September 1, 2001, Michael Rogers, "Nebula Award Stories," p. 241; January, 2002, Michael Rogers, "Nebula Award Two," p. 160.

Listener, March 25, 1971; July 22, 1976.

Literary Review, September, 1988, Sophia Watson, review of *Forgotten Life.*

Locus, February, 1991, p. 61; October, 1993, Gary K. Wolfe, review of *A Tupolev Too Far,* p. 57.

London Magazine, March, 1982.

Los Angeles Times, February 12, 1981; February 25, 1982, Carolyn See, review of *Helliconia Spring;* June 12, 1985, Sue Martin, review of *Helliconia Winter.*

Los Angeles Times Book Review, August 18, 1985; March 17, 1991, Sheery Gershon Gottlieb, review of *Dracula Unbound;* June 30, 1991, p. 6.

Nature, February 22, 2001.

New Statesman, November 2, 1973.

New Statesman and Society, August 10, 1990, David V. Barrett, review of *Bury My Heart at W.H. Smith's: A Writer's Life,* p. 38; August 12, 1994, John Clute, review of *Somewhere East of Life: Another European Fantasia,* p. 36.

New York Times, February 17, 1981.

New York Times Book Review, April 19, 1970, Martin Levin, review of *The Hand-Reared Boy;* August 22, 1971, Martin Levin, review of *A Soldier Erect;* September 12, 1976; February 26, 1984, Gerald Jonas, review of *Helliconia Spring,* section 7, p. 31; April 28, 1985, Gerald Jonas, review of *Helliconia Winter;* April 30, 1989, Samuel Hynes, review of *Forgotten Life and Other Stories,* p. 10; May 21, 1989, p. 26; July 15, 1990, Gerald Jonas, review of *A Romance of the Equator: Best Fantasy Stories,*

p. 13; March 17, 1991, Gerald Jonas, review of *Dracula Unbound,* p. 22; September 11, 1994, Gerald Jonas, review of *Somewhere East of Life,* p. 46; May 9, 1999, Gerald Jonas, review of *The Twinkling of an Eye,* p. 27.

Observer, September 25, 1988, Jonathan Keates, review of *Forgotten Life;* December 17, 1989, p. 46.

People, February 11, 1991, David Hiltbrand, review of *Dracula Unbound,* p. 22.

Publishers Weekly, April 19, 1985, Jonathan White, review of *Helliconia Winter;* February 15, 1990, Sybil Steinberg, review of *A Romance of the Equator,* p. 71; April 6, 1990, Sybil Steinberg, review of *Life in the West,* p. 102; December 7, 1990, review of *Dracula,* p. 76; May 10, 1993, review of *Remembrance Day,* p. 50; January 17, 1994, p. 416; August 8, 1994, review of *Somewhere East of Life,* p. 392; February 12, 1996, review of *Common Clay,* p. 63; March 22, 1999, review of *The Twinkling of an Eye,* p. 81; February 14, 2000, review of *White Mars,* p. 177; June 11, 2001, review of *Supertoys Last All Summer Long: And Other Stories of Future Time,* p. 67.

Punch, September 30, 1988, Simon Brett, review of *Forgotten Life.*

Science Fiction and Fantasy Book Review, June, 1982, Willis E. McNelly, review of *Helliconia Spring.*

Science Fiction Studies, Volume 1, number 2, 1973; July, 2000, pp. 339-342.

Spectator, November 10, 1973; May 27, 1978; May 8, 1980; August 22, 1980.

Times (London, England), December 8, 1983, Nicholas Shakespeare, review of *Helliconia Summer.*

Times Literary Supplement, September 21, 1967, review of *An Age;* January 22, 1970, review of *The Hand-Reared Boy;* May 19, 1978, Valentine Cunningham, review of *A Rude Awakening;* March 7, 1980; December 2, 1983, Colin Greenland, review of *Helliconia Spring* and *Helliconia Winter;* September 30, 1988, John Melmoth, review of *A Forgotten Life;* August 24, 1990, p. 901; September 23, 1994, review of *Somewhere East of Life,* p. 24; November 10, 1995, Julian Ferraro, review of *The Secret of This Book: Twenty Odd Stories,* p. 24; January 22, 1999, p. 31.

Tribune Books (Chicago, IL), July 31, 1994, p. 5.

Vector, March-April, 2001, Mark Greener, review of *Non-Stop* and *Supertoys Last All Summer Long,* and L.J. Hurst, review of *White Mars.*

Washington Post Book World, March 22, 1981; August 28, 1988; April 29, 1990, p. 8; December 30, 1990; April 24, 1994.

ONLINE

Official Brian W. Aldiss Web site, http://www.brianwaldiss.com/ (August 5, 2004).

ALDISS, Brian Wilson
   See ALDISS, Brian W.

* * *

ALDRICH, Ann
   See MEAKER, Marijane

* * *

ALEGRÍA, Claribel 1924-
   (Claribel Joy Alegría)

PERSONAL: Born May 12, 1924, in Esteli, Nicaragua; daughter of Daniel Alegría (a medical doctor) and Ana Maria Vides; married Darwin J. Flakoll (a journalist), 1947 (died, 1995); children: Maya, Patricia, Karen, Erik. *Education:* Received George Washington University, B.A. (philosophy and letters), 1948.

ADDRESSES: Home—Apt. Postal A 36, Managua, Nicaragua. *Office*—c/o Curbstone Press, 321 Jackson St., Willimantic, CT 06226.

CAREER: Poet, novelist, and essayist.

AWARDS, HONORS: Cenizas de Izalco was a finalist in the Seix Barral competition, Barcelona, Spain, 1964; Casa de las Americas poetry award, 1978, for *Sobrevivo;* honorary doctorate degree from Eastern Connecticut State University.

WRITINGS:

Anillo de silencio (poetry; title means "Ring of Silence"; also see below), Botas (Mexico), 1948.

Suite de amor, angustia y soledad (poetry), Brigadas Liricas (Mendoza, Argentina), 1950.

Vigilias (poetry; also see below), Ediciones Poesia de America (Mexico City, Mexico), 1953.

Acuario (poetry; also see below), Editorial Universitaria (Santiago, Chile), 1955.

Tres cuentos (children's stories; title means "Three Stories"), illustrations by Agustin Blancovaras, El Salvador Ministerio de Cultura (San Salvador, El Salvador), 1958.

Huesped de mi tiempo (poetry; also see below), Americalee (Buenos Aires, Argentina), 1961.

(Editor and translator, with husband, Darwin J. Flakoll) *New Voices of Hispanic America,* Beacon Press (Boston, MA), 1962.

Via unica (poetry; title means "One Way"; includes *Auto de fe* and *Comunicacion a larga distancia*), Alfa (Montevideo, Uruguay), 1965.

(With Darwin J. Flakoll) *Cenizas de Izalco* (novel), Seix Barral (Barcelona, Spain), 1966, translated by Darwin J. Flakoll as *Ashes of Izalco,* Curbstone Press/Talman (Willimantic, CT), 1989.

(Translator, with Darwin J. Flakoll) Miguel Angel Asturias, *The Cyclone,* Peter Owen (London, England), 1967.

(Translator, with Darwin J. Flakoll) Morris West, *El hereje,* Pomaire (Barcelona, Spain), 1969.

(Translator, with Darwin J. Flakoll) *Unstill Life: An Introduction to the Spanish Poetry of Latin America,* edited by Mario Benedetti, Harcourt, Brace & World (New York, NY), 1969.

Aprendizaje (title means "Apprenticeship"; includes poetry from *Anillo de silencio, Vigilias, Acuario, Huesped de mi tiempo,* and *Via unica*), Universitaria de El Salvador (San Salvador, El Salvador), 1970.

(Translator, with Darwin J. Flakoll) Mario Benedetti, editor, *Unstill Life: An Introduction to the Spanish Poetry of Latin America,* Harcourt (New York, NY), 1970.

Pagare a cobrar y otros poemas, Ocnos (Barcelona, Spain), 1973.

El deten (novel; also see below), Lumen (Barcelona, Spain), 1977.

Sobrevivo (poetry; title means "I Survive"), Casa de las Americas (Havana, Cuba), 1978.

(With Darwin J. Flakoll) *La encrucijada salvadorena* (historical essays), CIDOB (Barcelona, Spain), 1980.

(Author of introduction) *Homenaje a El Salvador,* edited by Alberto Corazon, Visor (Madrid, Spain), 1981.

(Editor and translator, with Darwin J. Flakoll) *Nuevas voces de norteamerica* (bilingual edition), Plaza y Janes (Barcelona, Spain), 1981.

Suma y sigue (anthology), Visor (Madrid, Spain), 1981.

(Editor, with Darwin J. Flakoll) *Nuevas voces de norteamerica* (anthology; parallel text in English and Spanish), Plaza & Janes (Barcelona, Spain), 1981.

(Translator, with Darwin J. Flakoll) Robert Graves, *Cien poemas* (anthology), Lumen (Barcelona, Spain), 1982.

Flores del volcan/Flowers from the Volcano (anthology; parallel text in English and Spanish), translated by Carolyn Forche, University of Pittsburgh Press (Pittsburgh, PA), 1982.

(With Darwin J. Flakoll) *Nicaragua: La revolucion sandinista; Una cronica politica, 1855-1979* (history), Ediciones Era (Mexico), 1982.

(With Darwin J. Flakoll) *No me agarran viva: La mujer salvadorena en lucha,* Ediciones Era (Mexico), 1983, translated by Amanda Hopkinson as *They Won't Take Me Alive: Salvadoran Women in Struggle for National Liberation,* Women's Press (London, England), 1987.

Poesia viva (anthology), Blackrose Press (London, England), 1983.

Album familiar (novel; title means "Family Album"; also see below), Editorial Universitaria Centroamericana (San Jose, Costa Rica), 1984.

Para romper el silencio: Resistencia y lucha en las carceles salvadorenas (title means "Breaking the Silence: Resistance and Struggle in Salvadoran Prisons"), Ediciones Era (Mexico), 1984.

Pueblo de Dios y de mandinga: Con el asesoriamiento cientifico de Slim (also see below), Ediciones Era (Mexico), 1985.

(Translator, with Darwin J. Flakoll) Carlos Fonseca, *Viva Sandino,* Vanguardia (Managua, Nicaragua), 1985.

Pueblo de dios y de mandinga (contains *El deten, Album familiar,* and *Pueblo de dios y de mandinga*), Editorial Lumen (Barcelona, Spain), 1986, translated by Amanda Hopkinson as *Family Album,* Curbstone Press (Willimantic, CT), 1991.

Despierta, mi bien, despierta (title means "Wake up, My Love, Wake up"), UCA Editores (San Salvador, El Salvador), 1986.

Luisa en el pais de la realidad/Luisa in Realityland (parallel text in English and Spanish), translated by Darwin J. Flakoll, Curbstone Press/Talman (Willimantic, CT), 1987.

(Editor and translator, with Darwin J. Flakoll) *On the Front Line: Guerilla Poems of El Salvador,* Editorial Nueva Nicaragua (Managua, Nicaragua), 1988.

Y este poema rio, Editorial Nueva Nicaragua (Managua, Nicaragua), 1988.

Mujer del rio/Woman of the River (poetry; parallel text in English and Spanish), translated by Darwin J. Flakoll, University of Pittsburgh Press (Pittsburgh, PA), 1989.

Fuga de Canto Grande, UCA Editores, 1992, translated by Darwin J. Flakoll as *Tunnel to Canto Grande,* Curbstone Press (Willimantic, CT), 1996.

Fugues (parallel text in English and Spanish), translated by Darwin J. Flakoll, Curbstone Press (Willimantic, CT), 1993.

Somoza: expediente cerrado: la historia de un ajusticiamiento, Editorial el Gato Negro (Managua, Nicaragua), 1993, translation published as *Death of Somoza,* Curbstone Press (Willimantic, CT), 1996.

Variaciones en clave de mi, Libertarias/Prodhufi (Madrid, Spain), 1993.

Clave de mi, EDUCA (San Jose, Costa Rica), 1996.

(Editor with Darwin J. Flakoll) *Blood Pact and Other Stories,* translated by Daniel Balderston and others, Curbstone Press (Willimantic, CT), 1997.

El niño que buscaba a ayer (title means "The Boy Who Searched for Yesterday"), 1997.

Umbrales = Thresholds: Poems, translated by Darwin J. Flakoll, Curbstone Press (Willimantic, CT), 1997.

Saudade = Sorrow (poems), translated by Carolyn Forche, Curbstone Press (Willimantic, CT), 1999.

In *Soltando Amarras = Casting Off* (poems), translated by Margaret Sayers Peden, Curbstone Press (Willimantic, CT), 2003.

Una vida en poemas (poems), Editorial Hispamer (Managua, Nicaragua), 2003.

Contributor to books including *Lives on the Line: The Testimony of Contemporary Latin American Authors,* edited by Doris Meyer, University of California Press (Berkeley, CA) 1988; and *You Can't Drown the Fire: Latin American Women Writing in Exile,* edited by Alicia Portnoy, Cleis Press (Pittsburgh, PA), 1988; contributor to periodicals such as *Casa de las Americas* and *Massachusetts Review.*

SIDELIGHTS: Considered one of the most prolific and significant voices in late twentieth-century Latin-American literature, Claribel Alegría, a poet, novelist, and testimony writer, was born in Nicaragua and spent her childhood in exile in El Salvador. Alegría lived in the United States, Mexico, Chile, Uruguay, and Majorca, Spain, before returning to her native Nicaragua upon the victory of the Sandinista Front for National Liberation (FSLN) in 1979. According to Jan Clausen in the *Women's Review of Books,* Alegría represents a writer of "an educated class which is relatively privileged by Central American standards, yet has suffered enough at the hands of repressive oligarchs who represent North American imperial interests to be acutely sensitized to the plight of workers and campesinos."

Alegría's mother loved to read poetry, her father loved to recite it, and both loved to recite it to their young daughter. She, in turn, loved to create it, and her mother insisted she dictate it to her while she wrote it down. Although she learned to read French from her grandfather who had an extensive library containing many books written in French, Alegría had no real interest in literature other than poetry. As a child, she dreamt of becoming an actress or a performer of tragic theater and as an adolescent, of becoming a scientist or a doctor. When she was fourteen, she read Rainer Maria Rilke's 1903 *Letters to a Young Poet,* which made such an impression on her that she decided there and then that poetry would become her life's pursuit; her first poems were published in *Repertorio Americano* when she was seventeen. At the age of eighteen, she was admitted to a girls' finishing school in Hammond, Louisiana, and in 1944, she was awarded a scholarship to summer school at Loyola University in New Orleans. There she met poet Juan Ramon Jiménez who lived in Washington, D.C., but who had read some of her poems in *Repertorio Americano.* He invited her to move to Washington, D.C., where he could mentor her while she attended college. She forfeited a four-year scholarship elsewhere, enrolled at Georgetown University, acquired a job as a translator at the Pan-American Union, pursued her degree in philosophy and letters, and studied writing verse under Jiménez's mentorship. Within three years, Jiménez had chosen twenty-two of her poems, which were published as *Anillo de silencio.*

Political discord, however, galvanized Alegría's desire to become a writer. She told Marjorie Agosin in *Americas* that it was not until the Cuban Revolution in the early 1950s that she began to write about more serious topics. "I was living in Paris," she explained, and "Carlos Fuentes and other friends . . . encouraged me to write down those memories" precipitated by the revolution. For Alegría, this meant writing "about what was happening around me, to go outside of my bourgeois family." Her first prose novel, *Cenizas de Izalco* (*Ashes of Izalco*), was the result; it went on to become one of the Salvadoran education system's official texts.

Often employing feminist and political themes, Alegría's novels are sometimes classified as "resistance narratives." *Ashes of Izalco* is a love story cowritten with her husband, Darwin J. Flakoll, that recounts the repressive aspects of small-town life in El Salvador. The narrative focuses on events that occurred in 1932, the year the Salvadoran government massacred hundreds of political dissidents in Alegría's adopted hometown of Santa Ana. Focusing on a daughter's discovery of her mother's love affair, the novel provides little direct discourse on the massacre itself. Some critics have interpreted the detachment of Alegría's characters from their political surroundings as a commentary on the United States' involvement in the war-torn countries of El Salvador and Nicaragua.

With *Despierta, mi bien, despierta* ("Wake up, My Love, Wake Up"), Alegría focuses on Lorena, an upper-middle-class Salvadoran woman who is married to a member of the oligarchy in 1980. Although her social class affords her many privileges, she is lonely and bored, and her marriage is dull. When she has an affair with a young guerrilla poet, however, she becomes more attuned to the political and social situation in her country. Seymour Menton observed in *World Literature Today* that "the novel ends melodramatically with Lorena's discovering her lover's severed head on her car seat."

Linda Gregory in the *American Book Review* praised the way Alegría's language in her novel *Luisa in Realityland,* "delights and astounds in its presence as words, sounds, and images." A novel that blends poetry and prose in telling about the coming of age of a young girl in El Salvador, *Luisa in Realityland* employs the techniques of magic realism to blend traditional Central American fables with actual historic events in order to emphasize Latin America's cultural heritage. The novel "moves the reader through a narrative mixing present with past, dreams with reality, the personal with the political," commented Gregory, who concluded that the work is a "complexly textured piece of literature which is as concerned with modes of perception as with that which is perceived and just as dependent on the resonance between images as on the images themselves."

Despite her prolific and acclaimed prose output, Alegría considers poetry, which she has been writing since 1948, to be her primary passion. But her verse was not widely known among English-speaking North Americans until the publication in 1982 of *Flowers from the Volcano*, a bilingual collection of poetry drawn from more than two decades of work. Helene J.F. De Aguilar, in a *Parnassus* essay, quoted translator Carolyn Forche from her preface to this collection: "In her poems, we listen to the stark cry of the human spirit, stripped by necessity of its natural lyricism, deprived of the luxuries of cleverness and virtuosity enjoyed by poets of the north." Calling the poems neither easy nor comfortable, a *Publishers Weekly* contributor wrote that although the poems "ask us to share the loss of friends and country, to stand witness to torture and violent death," there is a spirit of hope in them as well, "of belief in the power of the word and in the value of one human memory."

Like *Flowers from the Volcano*, Alegría's poetry collection *Woman of the River* is concerned with political turmoil, repression of citizens, and torture in Central America. Alegría's later poetry collection, *Fugues,* translated by her husband Darwin J. Flakoll, was faulted by one critic for its failure to match the level of insight and accomplished imagery revealed in her previous vol-

umes. Others critics, however, emphasized the distinctly personal voice of *Fugues,* arguing that the collection presents a deliberate contrast with her previous work in its use of classical imagery and concern with the theme of death from an individual, rather than political, perspective.

With *On the Front Line: Guerrilla Poems of El Salvador,* a bilingual anthology of poetry, Alegría turned to translation and editorship, again in collaboration with her husband. Reviewers have observed that while the terror of war provides the dark background to the poems, the central focus of the verse is human and life-affirming.

In *No me agarran viva: La mujer salvadorena en lucha,* translated in a 1987 English version as *They Won't Take Me Alive: Salvadoran Women in Struggle for National Liberation,* Alegría recounts the life of Eugenia, a Salvadoran guerilla leader who was killed by army troops in 1981. Through interviews with Eugenia's family and friends, Alegría offers a portrait of a committed, brave woman who lost numerous friends in battles with the government. Some critics faulted the book for being overly doctrinaire and one-dimensional. Writing in the *New Statesman,* Jane Dibblin observed that the work is "stiff with political jargon" but remarked that Alegría's verse nonetheless "challenges and lingers in the mind."

When Flakoll, to whom Alegría had been married for forty-seven years, died in 1995, the poet told Agosin she felt "mutilated." Yet this loss became the source of yet another poetry collection, *Saudade = Sorrow,* published in a bilingual edition with an English translation by Forche. The book was welcomed as a sensitive, tender, and powerful collection that, according to Forche, records "the passage of the human soul through searing grief and separation." *Bloomsbury Review* critic Cristian Salazar hailed *Sorrow* as a "gorgeous and brave" work that "pulses with the rhythm of grief and grieving." A writer for *Kirkus Reviews* observed that "these simple lyrics of solitude and sorrow, with their haiku-like brevity, at their best achieve the purity and clarity of classical verse." The book was chosen for the Academy of American Poets Book Club catalog, and the American Bookseller Association selected it for its Book Sense program.

When reviewing *In Soltando Amarras = Casting Off*—a natural sequel to *Saudade = Sorrow,* in which she immortalizes her dead husband as she struggles with her loss—Juana Ponce de Leon commented in *School Li-*

brary Journal that Alegría "comes from a culture where the living stay in constant conversation with the dead. With an ease and laughter that register clearly over our long-distance telephone connection, she says, 'Since I was very young the two main themes in my writing have been love and death. When I was young, however, death was distant. Now death is near, especially since Bud passed away. Now death is my friend. I speak to her.'" Ponce de Leon added that, in *In Soltando Amarras,* "the past looms large as the future diminishes. The poems illuminate the open road that lies before the prize-winning poet and evoke the feelings that go with charting new terrain."

BIOGRAPHICAL AND CRITICAL SOURCES:

BOOKS

Alegría, Claribel, *Saudade = Sorrow,* translated by Carolyn Forche, Curbstone Press (Willimantic, CT), 1999.

Boschetto-Sandoval, Sandra M., *Claribel Alegría and Central American Literature: Critical Essays,* Ohio University Center for International Studies (Athens, OH), 1994.

Contemporary Literary Criticism, Volume 75, Thomson Gale (Detroit, MI), 1993.

Dictionary of Literary Biography, Volume 145: *Modern Latin-American Fiction Writers, Second Series,* Thomson Gale (Detroit, MI), 1994.

Encyclopedia of World Literature in the Twentieth Century, St. James Press (Detroit, MI), 1999.

PERIODICALS

American Book Review, July, 1988, Linda Gregory, review of *Luisa in Realityland.*

Americas, February, 1999, interview with Marjorie Agosin, p. 48.

Bloomsbury Review, March-April, 2000, Cristian Salazar, review of *Saudade = Sorrow.*

Library Journal, February 15, 2000, Judy Clarence, review of *Sorrow,* p. 166.

New Statesman, April 24, 1987, Jane Dibblin, review of *No me agarran viva: La mujer salvadorena en lucha,* p. 28.

Parnassus, spring, 1985, Helene J.F. De Aguilar, review of *Flowers from the Volcano.*

Publishers Weekly, October 22, 1982, review of *Flowers from the Volcano;* October 18, 1993, review of *Fugues,* p. 69; October 25, 1999, review of *Sorrow,* p. 78.

School Library Journal, June, 2003, Juana Ponce de Leon, "Acetylene Rose" (interview), p. 30.

Times Educational Supplement, May 29, 1987, p. 23.

Women's Review of Books, October, 1984.

World Literature Today, spring, 1988, Seymour Menton, review of *Despierta, mi bien, despierta.*

*   *   *

ALEGRÍA, Claribel Joy
  See ALEGRÍA, Claribel

*   *   *

ALEXIE, Sherman 1966-
  (Sherman Joseph Alexie, Jr.)

PERSONAL: Born October 7, 1966, in Spokane, WA; son of Sherman Joseph and Lillian Agnes (Cox) Alexie. *Ethnicity:* Native American *Education:* Attended Gonzaga University, 1985-87; Washington State University, B.A., 1991.

ADDRESSES: Home—P.O. Box 376, Wellpinit, WA 99040. *Agent*—Hanging Loose Press, 231 Wyckoff St., Brooklyn, NY 11217.

CAREER: Writer, c. 1992—; song writer and music composer; director of films, including *The Business of Fancydancing,* 2003.

AWARDS, HONORS: Poetry fellow, Washington State Arts Commission, 1991; National Endowment for the Arts grant, 1992; Slipstream chapbook contest winner, 1992, for *I Would Steal Horses;* American Book Award, 1996, for *Reservation Blues;* three-time World Heavyweight Championship Poetry Bout winner; nominated for Independent Spirit Award for best first screenplay, c. 1998, Outstanding Achievement in Writing award, First Americans in the Arts, 1999, and Florida Film Critics Circle Award, all for *Smoke Signals;* Outstanding Screenwriting Award, OUTFEST, 2003, for *The Business of Fancydancing; Los Angeles Times* Book Prize for fiction finalist, 2003, for *Ten Little Indians;* O. Henry Prize, 2005, for the short story "What You Pawn I Will Redeem."

WRITINGS:

The Business of Fancydancing (poems), Hanging Loose Press (Brooklyn, NY), 1992.

I Would Steal Horses (poems), Slipstream, 1992.

First Indian on the Moon (poems), Hanging Loose Press (Brooklyn, NY), 1993.

The Lone Ranger and Tonto Fistfight in Heaven (short stories), Atlantic Monthly Press (New York, NY), 1993.

Old Shirts and New Skins (poems), UCLA American Indian Studies Center (Los Angeles, CA), 1993.

Water Flowing Home (poems), Limberlost Press (Boise, ID), 1994.

Seven Mourning Songs for the Cedar Flute I Have Yet to Learn to Play (poems), Whitman College Press, 1994.

Reservation Blues (novel), Grove/Atlantic (New York, NY), 1994, published as *Coyote Spring*, Atlantic (New York, NY), 1995.

(With Jim Boyd) *Reservation Blues: The Soundtrack* (recording), Thunderwolf Productions, 1995.

The Indian Fighter (radio script), National Public Radio, 1995.

Because My Father Was the Only Indian Who Saw Jimi Hendrix Play the Star-spangled Banner at Woodstock (radio script), aired on *This American Life*, National Public Radio, 1996.

Indian Killer, Atlantic Monthly Press (New York, NY), 1996.

The Summer of Black Widows, Hanging Loose Press (Brooklyn, NY), 1996.

The Man Who Loves Salmon (poems), Limberlost Press (Boise, ID), 1998.

Smoke Signals: Introduction, Screenplay, and Notes, Miramax (New York, NY), 1998.

One Stick Song (poems), Hanging Loose Press (Brooklyn, NY), 2000.

The Toughest Indian in the World (stories), Atlantic Monthly Press (New York, NY), 2000.

(Author of introduction) Gwendolyn Cates and Richard W. West, *Indian Country,* Grove/ Atlantic (New York, NY), 2001.

(Editor) *Scribner's Best of the Fiction Workshops,* Simon & Schuster (New York, NY), 2002.

(Author of foreword, with Robert Hershon) *The CLMP Directory of Literary Magazines and Presses,* Manic D Press, 2002.

(Author of introduction) Percival Everett, *Watershed,* Beacon Press (Boston, MA), 2003.

The Business of Fancydancing (screenplay), Hanging Loose Press (Brooklyn, NY), 2003.

(With others) *The Business of Fancydancing: Music from the Movie* (soundtrack), 2003.

Ten Little Indians: Stories, Grove Press (New York, NY), 2003.

Contributing editor, *Contentville,* 2000—. Contributor to periodicals, including *New York Times Magazine,* *Ploughshares, Left Bank, Seattle Weekly, New Yorker,* and *New York Times;* contributor to poetry anthologies, including *Voices of the City,* Hanging Loose Press, 2003; contributor to recordings, including *Talking Rain: Spoken Word and Music from the Pacific Northwest,* 1995, *Honor: A Benefit for the Honor the Earth Campaign,* 1996, *Jack Hammer Lobotomy,* 1991, and *Roadkillbasa,* 1994.

WORK IN PROGRESS: Tattoo Tears, a collection of short stories; *House Fire,* a novel.

SIDELIGHTS: Drawing heavily upon his experiences as a native Spokane/Coeur d'Alene tribal member who grew up and still lives on the Spokane Indian Reservation in Wellpinit, Washington, writer, performer, and filmmaker Sherman Alexie has garnered high praise for his poems and short stories of contemporary Native American reservation life, among them *The Business of Fancydancing,* a poetry collection Alexie has since adapted into a film. Alexie, who performs many of his poems at poetry slams, festivals, and other venues, has received praise for the energy and emotion he brings to his work.

When Alexie was a child, his mother supported the family by working at the Wellpinit Trading Post and selling her hand-sewn quilts, while his alcoholic father was absent from the home much of the time. Alexie spent most of his childhood reading every book in the Wellpinit school library, and in the eighth grade he decided to attend Reardan High School, located thirty-two miles outside the reservation. His achievements in high school secured his admission to Spokane's Jesuit Gonzaga University in 1985, where pressure to succeed led him to begin abusing alcohol. Alexie transferred to Washington State University in 1987 to be with his high-school girlfriend, and it was there that he began writing poetry and short fiction. In 1990 Alexie's works were published in *Hanging Loose* magazine, and this success gave him the will and incentive to quit drinking, which he did that same year.

In his short-story and poetry collections, Alexie delineates the despair, poverty, and alcoholism that often pervade the lives of Native Americans living on reservations. He has been lauded for writings that evoke sadness and indignation yet leave readers with a sense of respect and compassion for characters who are in seemingly hopeless situations. Involved with crime, alcohol, or drugs, Alexie's protagonists struggle to survive the constant battering of their minds, bodies, and spirits by white American society and by their own self-hatred and sense of powerlessness. As Alexie asserted in *The Lone Ranger and Tonto Fistfight in Heaven*: Native Americans "have a way of surviving. But it's almost like Indians can easily survive the big stuff. Mass murder, loss of language and land rights. It's the small things that hurt the most. The white waitress who wouldn't take an order, Tonto, the Washington Redskins." While he depicts the lives of Native Americans who attempt to escape their situation through alcohol and other forms of self-abuse, Alexie also finds a mental, emotional, and spiritual outlet in his writing, which he refers to as "fancydancing."

A key characteristic of Alexie's writing is his irony, surfacing in dark humor buoyed by his exquisite sense of timing. His poetry collections *The Business of Fancydancing, First Indian on the Moon,* and *Old Shirts and New Skins* reveal this irony by exposing the "fraudulent illusions that tempt us all in America today," noted Andrea-Bess Baxter in *Western American Literature*. Alexie, commented Baxter, has a "talent for frequently turning history upside down" by placing historical characters such as Crazy Horse and Christopher Columbus in modern contexts with ironic twists. For example, in one instance Crazy Horse comes to life in the Smithsonian but is misidentified as an anonymous Hopi male; in another Columbus is cast as a real estate agent. Carl L. Bankston III, reviewing Alexie's oeuvre for the *Bloomsbury Review*, wrote that the author "combines a gift for startling associations and a fluid ease of literary style with an intimate familiarity with the quotidian facts of modern reservation life. As a result, his poems are simultaneously documentaries of tribal existence and revelations of the spirit and inner significance of that existence."

Commenting on *The Business of Fancydancing*, Alexie's first published poetry collection, Leslie Ullman in *Kenyon Review* wrote that the author "weaves a curiously soft-blended tapestry of humor, humility, pride and metaphysical provocation out of the hard realities . . . : the tin-shack lives, the alcohol dreams, the bad luck and burlesque disasters, and the self-destructive courage of his characters." Noted Bankston in his review of *The Business of Fancydancing,* "The most impressive quality of Alexie's writing is his ability to let poetry appear unexpectedly from . . . themes of everyday life in an unadorned, conversational idiom. There is no straining after effect."

Alexie introduces several characters in his poetry that resurface later in his short-story collection *Tonto and the Lone Ranger Fistfight in Heaven* and his novel *Res-*

ervation Blues. These include Big Mom, mystical matriarch and "the best fry bread cook" on the reservation; Thomas Builds-the-Fire, a young storyteller; and Thomas's friends Victor Joseph and Junior Polatkin. In *Reservation Blues* the young friends, now in their thirties, come into possession of legendary blues musician Robert Johnson's magical guitar, which provides Victor with a measure of unnatural talent and the boys with something to do: form a rock band. Their trials and tribulations bring together Native and Anglo worlds in a resounding crash, as Verlyn Klinkenborg notes in the *Los Angeles Times Book Review*. Klinkenborg found that Alexie writes effectively for "a divided audience, Native American and Anglo. He is willing to risk didacticism whenever he stops to explain the particulars of the Spokane, and, more broadly, the Native American experience to his readers. But Alexie never sounds didactic. His timing is too good for that. *Reservation Blues* never misses a beat, never sounds a false note." Abigail Davis in *Bloomsbury Review* declared that "this first novel by Sherman Alexie comes as close to helping a non-Native American understand the modern Indian experience as any attempt in current literature. The reader closes the book feeling troubled, hurt, hopeful, profoundly thoughtful, and somehow exhausted, as if the quest of the characters had been a personal experience." Frederick Busch in the *New York Times Book Review,* however, saw Alexie's work as falling short in the novel form. "Though there is wonderful humor and profound sorrow in this novel, and brilliant renditions of each, there is not enough structure to carry the dreams and tales that Mr. Alexie needs to portray and that we need to read. . . . But the talent is real, and it is very large, and I will gratefully read whatever he writes, in whatever form."

In an interview with John and Carl Bellante for the *Bloomsbury Review*, Alexie commented on his progression from poems to short stories to novels as occurring "pretty naturally because . . . my poems are stories. It felt natural for me to evolve to a larger form. Not to say it wasn't difficult for me at first, though. . . . I had this thing about going beyond one page, typewritten. I'd get to the bottom of a page and freak out, because I wouldn't know what to do next. But the stories kept getting bigger and bigger. . . . They began to demand more space than a poem could provide."

Comparing Alexie's novels to his short stories, Ken Foster suggested in the *San Francisco Chronicle* that the author's longer works have "an odd, aggressive, middlebrow sensibility to them." Conversely, according to Foster, the 2000 short-story collection *The Toughest Indian in the World* "blessedly lacks" such qualities.

The nine stories in the collection retrace Alexie's familiar territory of Native-white conflict while sustaining "a consistently dark comic tone," in Foster's opinion. The author "doesn't feel the need to instruct his readers in the details of contemporary American Indian culture, and why should he? The lives he portrays are so finely detailed . . . that even the most culturally sheltered reader is transported."

The title story in *The Toughest Indian in the World* finds its narrator, a Native journalist who feels all-too-assimilated in the white world, deciding to reconnect with his heritage by seducing a young Native fighter. At the end of the story, "the narrator is no more gay than he was at the start," noted Foster, "and yet the attraction between these two men, on this particular night, seems apt and true." In "Dear John Wayne" a young Navajo woman engages in a brief affair with the cowboy star during the 1950s filming of John Ford's epic western *The Searchers*. Interracial themes also figure in "South by Southwest," about a white drifter who takes a down-and-out Indian with him on a "nonviolent killing spree" across the West. What *Denver Post* contributor Ron Franscell found impressive in these two entries is the way Alexie "puts himself inside the heads and hearts of non-Indians. The result is tender, touching and erotic." *The Toughest Indian in the World* "proves once again that [Alexie is] the real deal: a master stylist, a born storyteller as well as a writer of inspired formal innovations and experiments," declared Emily White in a *Seattle Weekly* review.

While Alexie has been the recipient of numerous awards and grants, White commented that the author "nevertheless manifests a palpable hostility toward whiteness; it's clear that the idea of the great melting pot he is paid by publishers and grant committees actually makes his blood boil." Indeed, being a mass-market author is not in Alexie's plans either: "Good art doesn't come out of assimilation—it comes out of tribalism," he was quoted as saying in the *Denver Post*.

Alexie broke further barriers when he helped create the first all-Indian movie. *Smoke Signals,* for which he wrote the screenplay based on his short stories, was produced, directed, and acted by Native American talent. The plot follows a young man living an aimless life in Idaho. Victor Joseph, who has lost contact with his Native roots, embarks on a journey to "discover his past and accept his present," as *Los Angeles Magazine* writer James Greenberg put it. The finished film took top honors at the Sundance Film Festival; on the occasion of its 1998 wide release, Alexie told a *Time* inter-

viewer that he hoped *Smoke Signals* would open doors for Indian filmmakers. He pointed to African-American director Spike Lee as a role model: "Spike didn't necessarily get films made as much as he inspired filmmakers to believe in themselves. That's what's going to happen here. These 13-year-old Indian kids who've been going crazy with their camcorders will finally see the possibilities."

BIOGRAPHICAL AND CRITICAL SOURCES:

PERIODICALS

Bloomsbury Review, September, 1992; May-June, 1993, p. 5; May-June, 1994; July-August, 1995.
Chicago Tribune, September 27, 1993.
Denver Post, May 21, 2000, Ron Franscell, "Alexie's Tribal Perspective Universal in Its Appeal."
Kenyon Review, summer, 1993, p. 182.
Kirkus Reviews, August 1, 1996.
Kliatt, May, 1994, p. 23.
Library Journal, November 15, 1993; October 15, 1994, p. 72; August, 1996, p. 109.
Los Angeles, July, 1998, review of *Smoke Signals,* p. 107.
Los Angeles Times Book Review, June 18, 1995.
New Yorker, May 10, 1993.
New York Times Book Review, October 11, 1992; October 17, 1993; July 16, 1995, p. 9; May 21, 2000, Joanna Scott, "American Revolutions."
New York Times Magazine, October 4, 1992; January 18, 1998, p. 16.
Prairie Schooner, spring, 1996, p. 70.
Publishers Weekly, July 29, 1996, p. 70; April 17, 2000, review of *The Toughest Indian in the World,* p. 52.
San Francisco Chronicle, May 21, 2000, Ken Foster, review of *The Toughest Indian in the World.*
School Library Journal, July, 1993, p. 112.
Seattle Weekly, May 11-17, 2000, Emily White, review of *The Toughest Indian in the World.*
Time, June 29, 1998, review of *Smoke Signals* and interview, p. 69.
Western American Literature, fall, 1994, p. 277.
World Literature Today, spring, 1994.

ONLINE

Sherman Alexie Web site, http://www.shermanalexie.com/ (April 7, 2004).

ALEXIE, Sherman Joseph, Jr.
　　See ALEXIE, Sherman

*   *   *

ALLAN, John B.
　　See WESTLAKE, Donald E.

*   *   *

ALLEN, Paula Gunn 1939-

PERSONAL: Born 1939, in Cubero, NM; daughter of E. Lee (a businessman and politician) and Ethel (Francis); married (divorced); children: three. *Education:* University of Oregon, B.A., 1966, M.F.A., 1968; University of New Mexico, Ph.D., 1975.

ADDRESSES: Office—c/o Author Mail, Harper San Francisco, 10 East 53rd Street, New York, NY 10022. *E-mail*—shimanna@mcn.org.

CAREER: Fort Lewis College, Durango, CO, lecturer; San Francisco State University, San Francisco, CA, director of Native-American studies program; University of New Mexico, Albuquerque, lecturer; University of California, Berkeley, lecturer, professor of Native American Studies/Ethnic Studies; University of California, Los Angeles, professor of literature, 1990-99.

AWARDS, HONORS: National Endowment for the Arts fellowship, 1978; postdoctoral fellow in American Indian Studies, University of California, Los Angeles, 1981; postdoctoral fellowship grant, Ford Foundation-National Research Council, 1984; American Book Award, Before Columbus Foundation, 1990, for *Spider Woman's Granddaughters: Traditional Tales and Contemporary Writing by Native American Women;* Susan Koppelman Award, Popular and American Culture Associations, and Native American Prize for Literature, both 1990.

WRITINGS:

POETRY

The Blind Lion, Thorp Springs Press (Berkeley, CA), 1974.
Coyote's Daylight Trip, La Confluencia (Albuquerque, NM), 1978.

A Cannon between My Knees, Strawberry Press (New York, NY), 1981.
Star Child: Poems, Blue Cloud Quarterly (Marvin, SD), 1981.
Shadow Country, University of California American Indian Studies Center (Los Angeles, CA), 1982.
Wyrds, Taurean Horn (San Francisco, CA), 1987.
Skins and Bones, West End (Albuquerque, NM), 1988.
Life Is a Fatal Disease: Collected Poems, 1962-1995, West End (Albuquerque, NM), 1997.

EDITOR

From the Center: A Folio of Native American Art and Poetry, Strawberry Press (New York, NY), 1981.
Studies in American Indian Literature: Critical Essays and Course Designs, Modern Language Association of America (New York, NY), 1983.
Spider Woman's Granddaughters: Traditional Tales and Contemporary Writing by Native American Women, Beacon Press (Boston, MA), 1989.
(And author of introduction) *The Voice of the Turtle: American Indian Literature, 1900-1970,* Ballantine (New York, NY), 1994.
Song of the Turtle: American Indian Fiction, 1974-1994, Ballantine (New York, NY), 1995.
(With Carolyn Dunn Anderson) *Hozho: Walking in Beauty: Native American Stories of Inspiration, Humor, and Life,* Contemporary Books (Chicago, IL), 2001.

OTHER

Sipapu: A Cultural Perspective, University of New Mexico Press (Albuquerque, NM), 1975.
The Woman Who Owned the Shadows (novel), Spinsters Ink (San Francisco, CA), 1983.
(Author of foreword) Brian Swann, *Song of the Sky: Versions of Native American Songs and Poems,* Four Zoas Night House (Boston, MA), 1985.
Grandmothers of the Light: A Medicine Woman's Sourcebook, Beacon Press (Boston, MA), 1991.
Indian Perspectives, Southwest Parks and Monuments Association (Tucson, AZ), 1992.
The Sacred Hoop: Recovering the Feminine in American Indian Traditions (essays), Beacon Press (Boston, MA), 1986, reissued with new preface, 1992.
(With Patricia Clark Smith) *As Long As the Rivers Flow: Nine Stories of Native Americans,* Scholastic (New York, NY), 1996.

Off the Reservation: Reflections on Boundary-Busting Border-Crossing Loose Canons, Beacon Press (Boston, MA), 1998.

Pocahontas: Medicine Woman, Spy, Entrepreneur, Diplomat, HarperSanFrancisco (San Francisco, CA), 2003.

Contributor to *I Tell You Now: Autobiographical Essays by Native American Writers,* edited by Brian Swann and Arnold Krupat, University of Nebraska Press (Lincoln, NE), 1987; and *Columbus and Beyond: Views from Native Americans,* edited by Randolph Jorgen, Southwest Parks and Monuments Association (Tucson, AZ), 1992.

SIDELIGHTS: Paula Gunn Allen is a registered member of the Laguna Pueblo tribe, but her heritage has been enriched by many nationalities. Her father, E. Lee Francis, was born of Lebanese parents at Seboyeta, a Spanish/Mexican land grant village north of Laguna Pueblo. He spoke only Arabic and Spanish until he learned English at the age of ten. He owned the Cubero Trading Company and later served as Lieutenant Governor of New Mexico from 1967 through 1970. Allen's mother, Ethel, was of mixed Laguna Pueblo, Sioux, and Scots ancestry.

Allen grew up in Cubero, New Mexico, where she attended Catholic school. According to Kathy J. Whitson in the book *Native American Literatures,* Allen noted: "Sometimes I get in a dialogue between what the Church taught me, what the nuns taught me, what my mother taught me, what my experience growing up where I grew up taught me. Often you can't reconcile them. I can't reconcile them." In contrast, Allen found stability and what Whitson called the "thematic bedrock" in her New Mexican upbringing: "the land, the family, the road."

Allen married while in college and had two children before divorcing. After the divorce, she went back to school and studied writing. Her work as a writer was initially inspired by the success of N. Scott Momaday, a Native American writer whose novel *House Made of Dawn* has been widely recognized and acclaimed in mainstream American culture.

Although Allen has a diverse ethnic heritage, it is her American Indian roots that inform and direct her work. In an interview with Robin Pogrebin of the *New York Times Book Review,* Allen characterized Native Americans as "something other than victims—mostly what we are is unrecognized." To help remedy this situation,

Allen compiled *The Sacred Hoop: Recovering the Feminine in American Indian Traditions,* a collection of seventeen essays covering topics that range from the status of lesbians in Native American cultures, to literature's roots in the soil of tradition and ritual. In the *Los Angeles Times Book Review,* Quannah Karvar complimented the volume's "power and insight as a commentary on the perceptions and priorities of contemporary Native American women." Allen has also gained recognition as a poet. Her first published collection of poems, *The Blind Lion,* appeared in 1974, followed by *Skins and Bones* in 1988 and *Life Is a Fatal Disease: Collected Poems, 1962-1995,* published in 1997.

Allen's novel, 1983's *The Woman Who Owned the Shadows,* received a generally favorable review from Alice Hoffman in the *New York Times Book Review.* "In those sections where the author forsakes the artifice of her style," declared the critic, "an absorbing, often fascinating world is created." The novel's heroine, Ephanie, is emotionally wounded as a young girl and struggles to mend her fractured core "guided," according to Hoffman, "by the traditional tales of spirit women." After several unsuccessful attempts to fit into male-dominated white society, Ephanie attempts suicide, only to cut herself down from the rope by which she is hanging. Struck by a sudden appreciation for life, Ephanie begins her journey toward community and self-acceptance by learning what her woman-centered tribal heritage can mean for her. Within this tradition she finds the Spider Woman, known also as Thought Woman, who "enlightens Ephanie and helps her to enter the shadows of her psyche and to own them, to dream her own dreams and to own them," said Marcia G. Fuchs in *Twentieth-Century Western Writers.*

The Woman Who Owned the Shadows uses a variety of narrative elements, including Native American folklore, letters, dreams, and therapy transcripts to tell Ephanie's story. While some critics, like Hoffman, found this compilation to be forced, others believed it to be effective and enjoyable. "Allen continues her cultural traditional in her novel by using it in the same way in which the traditional arts have always functioned for the Laguna Pueblo. She has extended traditional storytelling into the modern form of the novel by weaving in the tribal history, cultural traditions, and mythology of the Laguna Pueblo to create a form of curing ceremony for her readers," noted Annette Van Dyke in *Lesbian Texts and Contexts: Radical Revisions.*

A few critics have suggested that the novel represents a vision quest, not only for Ephanie but for her readers, who learn that self-acceptance requires a feeling of connection with the past. Allen affirmed the notion that writing the novel was also a kind of vision quest: "That's what I am searching for, to pull the vision out of me, because it is here, I know it is. . . . That's what a vision quest is for, you know. You go out . . . and you find out who you are. Well, a writer goes into the wilderness and finds out who she is," she remarked in a 1987 interview with Annie O. Eysturoy published in *This Is about Vision: Interviews with Southwestern Writers.*

In 1989 Allen edited *Spider Woman's Granddaughters: Traditional Tales and Contemporary Writing by Native American Women,* which Karvar called "a companion in spirit" to the author's book of essays *The Sacred Hoop.* In *Spider Woman's Granddaughters,* Allen gives space not only to contemporary authors such as Vickie L. Sears, but also to legends of old deities such as the Pueblos' mother goddess of corn. She also includes the words of Pretty Shield, a Crow native who told her life story to ethnographer Frank B. Linderman early in the twentieth century. In the *New York Times Book Review,* Ursula K. Le Guin praised the organization of the book, noting that Allen has arranged the pieces "so that they interact to form larger patterns, giving the book an esthetic wholeness rare in anthologies."

With the 1991 publication of *Grandmothers of the Light: A Medicine Woman's Sourcebook,* Allen again focuses attention on the central role of women in many Native American cultures. A collection of twenty-one stories from the oral tradition of a variety of tribes, the book is divided into three sections that provide information for those seeking to possess something of the goddesses' supernatural and creative powers. In the *Voice Literary Supplement,* Suzanne Ruta asserted that "*goddesses* is probably the wrong word for these divinities, who don't dazzle or attack from distant thrones. Like the cultures that nourished them, they're down to earth, egalitarian, democratic, and resourceful, plunging their arms into the clay, the corn dough, the ashes, to come up with what's needed to create or sustain life."

Many of the stories are told in Allen's own voice as she combines them with her own critical insights into their meaning and their relevance to historical events. While some have noted the lack of critical references in Allen's nonfiction writing, reception generally has been positive. The tribes represented in the stories cover a wide geographic area, including the Navajo, the Cherokee, the Lakota, and the Mayan. While Allen admits that these tribes have very different cultures, she asserts that they all share similar worldviews with respect to the

need for balance between the "mundane" and spiritual worlds. This notion of balance, she asserts, is the product of woman-centered societies where models of shared obligations replace struggles for power between men and women. Lucy Patrick said in a *Library Journal* review of *Grandmothers of the Light* that the "recovery of respect for complementary polarity and gynecratic tribal values are central to [Allen's] vision of the interrelationship of the human and supernatural worlds." One of Allen's continuing efforts is to counter the popular notion that Native American culture has been lost in today's world.

In *Off the Reservation: Reflections on Boundary-Busting, Border-Crossing Loose Canons,* Allen draws on her own mixed heritage of mixed Laguna and Lebanese origins to examine contemporary American culture. The collection of essays range widely, from political to spiritual to ecological issues, and are often very personal, as when she considers her Lebanese roots, or describes her return to Laguna Pueblo after a long absence. Writing in *Library Journal,* Faye Powell described the collection as "thought-provoking and informative." A *Booklist* reviewer called the essays "intelligent work from a renegade spirit."

In Allen's 2003 publication, *Pocahontas: Medicine Woman, Spy, Entrepreneur, Diplomat,* she examines the legend of the Native American woman and represents her as other than the tragic and forlorn historical figure who fell in love with Captain John Smith. *Library Journal*'s John Burch criticized the book's lack of "authoritative biographical information," stating "it is the native perspective that apparently gives [Allen] license to construct an image of Pocahontas as a 'shaman priestess, sorcerer, adept pf high degree' without any cited evidence." A *Publishers Weekly* reviewer, however, enjoyed Allen's interpretation of history, and pointed out that Allen's Pocahontas "is a real visionary, a prodigiously gifted young woman fervently devoted to the spiritual traditions of her people." This reviewer praised *Pocahontas,* commenting, "When casting Pocahontas as 'the embodiment of . . . dual culture transformation,' her role, and the book, are at their clearest and are made manifest by Allen's often lyrical and powerful writing."

Allen's "powerful writing" has entranced, enriched, and educated, according to many reviewers, while also offering up many aspects of Native American heritage to culturally enrich readers and add valuable morsels to the collective American history. In *Paula Gunn Allen,* Elizabeth I. Hanson asserted that Allen combines the sacredness of the past with the reality of the present as a means of self-renewal. "Like Allen's own vision of self," said Hanson, "contemporary Native Americans exist not in a romantic past but instead in a community which extends throughout the whole of American experience."

BIOGRAPHICAL AND CRITICAL SOURCES:

BOOKS

Bataille, Gretchen M., and Kathleen M. Sands, editors, *American Indian Women: Telling Their Lives,* University of Nebraska Press (Lincoln, NE), 1984.

Bataille, Gretchen M., and Laurie Lisa, editors, *Native American Women: A Biographical Dictionary,* 2nd edition, Routledge (London, England), 2001.

Bruchac, Joseph, *Survival This Way: Interviews with American Indian Poets,* University of Arizona Press (Tucson, AZ), 1987, pp. 1-24.

Coltelli, Laura, editor, *Winged Words: American Indian Writers Speak,* University of Nebraska Press (Lincoln, NE), 1990, pp. 11-39.

Contemporary Literary Criticism, Volume 84, Thomson Gale (Detroit, MI), 1995.

Contemporary Women Poets, St. James Press (Detroit, MI), 1998.

Crawford, C. F., John F. William Balassi, and Annie O. Eysturoy, *This Is about Vision: Interviews with Southwestern Writers,* University of New Mexico Press (Albuquerque, NM), 1990, pp. 95-107.

Encyclopedia of World Biography, 2nd edition, Thomson Gale (Detroit, MI), 1998.

Green, Carol Hurd, and Mary Grimley Mason, editors, *American Women Writers,* Continuum (New York, NY), 1994.

Hanson, Elizabeth J., *Paula Gunn Allen,* Boise State University (Boise, ID), 1990.

Jay, Karla and Joanne Glasgow, editors, *Lesbian Texts and Contexts: Radical Revisions,* New York University Press (New York, NY), 1990, pp. 339-354.

Keating, Ana Louise, *Women Reading Women Writing: Self-Invention in Paula Gunn Allen, Gloria Anzaldua, and Audre Lorde,* Temple University Press (Philadelphia, PA), 1996.

Lincoln, Kenneth, *Native American Renaissance,* University of California Press (Los Angeles, CA), 1983, pp. 183-221.

Literature Lover's Companion, Prentice Hall Press (New York, NY), 2001.

Milton, John R., *Four Indian Poets,* [South Dakota], 1974.

Moss, Maria, *We've Been Here Before: Women in Creation Myths and Contemporary Literature of the Native American Southwest,* Lit (Münster, Germany), 1993.

Native North American Literature, Thomson Gale (Detroit, MI), 1994.

Pollack, Sandra, and Denise Knight, editors, *Contemporary Lesbian Writers of the United States: A Bio-Bibliographical Critical Sourcebook,* Greenwood Press (Westport, CT), 1993.

Riggs, Thomas, editor, *Reference Guide to American Literature,* 4th edition, St. James Press (Detroit, MI), 2000.

Ruoff, A. La Vonne Brown, *American Indian Literatures: An Introduction, Bibliographic Review, and Selected Bibliography,* Modern Language Association (New York, NY), 1990, pp. 92-94.

Scanlon, Jennifer, editor, *Significant Contemporary American Feminists,* Greenwood Press (Westport, CT).

Twentieth-Century Western Writers, 2nd edition, edited by Geoff Sadler, St. James Press (Detroit, MI), 1991.

Van Dyke, Annette, *The Search for a Woman-Centered Spirituality,* New York University Press (New York, NY), 1992.

Whitson, Kathy J., *Native American Literatures: An Encyclopedia of Works, Characters, Authors, and Themes,* American Bibliographic Center-Clio (Santa Barbara, CA).

PERIODICALS

American Book Review, December, 1992-January, 1993, p. 12.

Belles Lettres, summer, 1990, pp. 40, 42.

Booklist, July, 1994, p. 1917; September 15, 1991, pp. 101-102; March 15, 1998, review of *Spider Woman's Granddaughters: Traditional Tales and Contemporary Writing by Native American Women,* p. 1235; October 1, 1998, review of *Off the Reservation: Reflections on Boundary-Busting Border-Crossing Loose Canons,* p. 303.

Choice, November, 1983, p. 427; September, 1986, p. 114.

Journal of American Folklore, April-June, 1990, pp. 245-247.

Kirkus Reviews, August 1, 1991, p. 976.

Kliatt, November, 2001, review of *Hozho: Walking in Beauty: Native American Stories of Inspiration, Humor, and Life,* p. 23.

Library Journal, January, 1986, p. 89; September 15, 1991, p. 84; November 15, 1998, Faye Powell, review of *Off the Reservation,* p. 74; October 1, 2003, John Burch, review of *Pocahontas: Medicine Woman, Spy, Entrepreneur, Diplomat,* p. 88.

Los Angeles Times, October 19, 1990, pp. E1, E7.

Los Angeles Times Book Review, January 25, 1987, p. 11; July 9, 1989, p. 10.

MELUS, summer, 1983, pp. 3-25.

New York Times Book Review, June 3, 1984, p. 18; May 14, 1989, p. 15.

North Dakota Quarterly, spring, 1989, pp. 149-161.

Parabola, November, 1986, pp. 102, 104; November, 1989, pp. 98, 102.

Publishers Weekly, July 5, 1991, p. 51; October 26, 1998, review of *Off the Reservation,* p. 51; September 1, 2003, review of *Pocahontas,* p. 76.

Village Voice, September 19, 1989, p. 57.

Voice Literary Supplement, November, 1991, p. 26.

Women's Review of Books, March, 1984, p. 8; July, 1989, p. 8; September, 1989, pp. 29-31.

World Literature Today, spring, 1990, pp. 344-345; summer, 1997, Robert L. Berner, review of *Life Is a Fatal Disease: Collected Poems, 1962-1995,* p. 631.

*   *   *

ALLEN, Roland
See AYCKBOURN, Alan

*   *   *

ALLENDE, Isabel 1942-

PERSONAL: Surname is pronounced "Ah-*yen*-day"; born August 2, 1942, in Lima, Peru; daughter of Tomas (a Chilean diplomat) and Francisca (Llona Barros) Allende; married Miguel Frias (an engineer), September 8, 1962 (divorced, 1987); married William Gordon (a lawyer), July 17, 1988; children: (first marriage) Paula (deceased), Nicolas; Scott (stepson). *Ethnicity:* "Hispanic." *Education:* Educated privately.

ADDRESSES: Home—15 Nightingale Lane, San Rafael, CA 94901. *Agent*—Carmen Balcells, Diagonal 580, Barcelona 21, Spain.

CAREER: United Nations Food and Agricultural Organization, Santiago, Chile, secretary, 1959-65; *Paula* magazine, Santiago, journalist, editor, and advice columnist, 1967-74; *Mampato* magazine, Santiago, journalist, 1969-74; television interviewer for Canal 13/ Canal 7 (television station), 1970-75; worked on movie newsreels, 1973-78; *El Nacional,* Caracas, Venezuela, journalist, 1974-75, columnist, 1976-83; Colegio Marroco, Caracas, administrator, 1979-82; writer. Guest teacher at Montclair State College, Montclair, NJ, spring, 1985, and University of Virginia, fall, 1988; Gildersleeve Lecturer, Barnard College, spring, 1988; teacher of creative writing, University of California, Berkeley, spring, 1989.

AWARDS, HONORS: Panorama Literario Award (Chile), 1983; Grand Prix d'Evasion (France), 1984; Author of the Year and Book of the Year Awards (Germany), 1984; Point de Mire (Belgium), 1985; Colima Award for Best Novel (Mexico), 1985; Author of the Year Award (Germany), 1986; Quality Paperback Book Club New Voice Award nomination, 1986, for *The House of the Spirits; Los Angeles Times* Book Prize nomination, 1987, for *Of Love and Shadows;* XV Premio Internazionale (Italy), and Mulheres best foreign novel award (Portugal), 1987; *Eva Luna* was named one of *Library Journal's* Best Books of 1988, awarded an American Book Award, Before Columbus Foundation, 1989, Freedom to Write Pen Club Award, 1991, and XLI Bancarella Literature Award (Italy), and Brandeis University Major Book Collection Award, both 1993.

WRITINGS:

Civilice a su troglodita: Los impertinentes de Isabel Allende (humor), Editorial Lord Cochran (Santiago, Chile), 1974.

La Casa de los espíritus, Plaza y Janés (Barcelona, Spain), 1982, HarperLibros (New York, NY), 1995, translation by Magda Bogin published as *The House of the Spirits,* Knopf (New York, NY), 1985.

La Gorda de porcelana (juvenile; title means "The Fat Porcelain Lady"), Alfaguara (Madrid, Spain), 1984.

De amor y de sombra, Plaza y Janés (Barcelona, Spain), 1984, HarperLibros (New York, NY), 1995, translation by Margaret Sayers Peden published as *Of Love and Shadows,* Knopf (New York, NY), 1987.

Eva Luna, translation by Margaret Sayers Peden published under same title, Knopf (New York, NY), 1988, HarperLibros (New York, NY), 1995.

Cuentos de Eva Luna, Plaza y Janés (Barcelona, Spain), 1990, HarperCollins (New York, NY), 1995, translation by Margaret Sayers Peden published as *The Stories of Eva Luna,* Atheneum (New York, NY), 1991.

El Plan infinito, Editorial Sudamericana (Buenos Aires, Argentina), 1991, translation by Margaret Sayers Peden published as *The Infinite Plan,* HarperCollins (New York, NY), 1993.

Paula (autobiography), Plaza y Janés (Barcelona, Spain), 1994, translation by Margaret Sayers Peden, HarperCollins (New York, NY), 1995.

(With others) *Salidas de madre,* Planeta (Santiago, Chile), 1996.

Afrodita: Recetas, cuentos y otros afrodisiacos, Harper-Collins (New York, NY), 1997, translation by Margaret Sayers Peden published as *Aphrodite: A Memoir of the Senses,* HarperFlamingo (New York, NY), 1998.

Hija de la fortuna, Plaza y Janés (Barcelona, Spain), 1999, translation by Margaret Sayers Peden published as *Daughter of Fortune: A Novel,* Harper-Collins (New York, NY), 1999.

(And author of foreword) *Conversations with Isabel Allende,* edited by John Rodden, translations from the Spanish by Virginia Invernizzi and from the German and Dutch by John Rodden, University of Texas (Austin, TX), 1999.

Retrato en sepia, Plaza y Janés (Barcelona, Spain), 2000, translation by Margaret Sayers Peden published as *Portrait in Sepia,* HarperCollins (New York, NY), 2001.

La Ciudad de las bestias, Rayo (New York, NY), 2002, translation by Margaret Sayers Peden published as *City of the Beasts* (young adult), HarperCollins (New York, NY), 2002.

Mi país inventado, Areté (Barcelona, Spain), 2003, translation by Margaret Sayers Peden published as *My Invented Country: A Nostalgic Journey through Chile,* HarperCollins (New York, NY), 2003.

El Reino del dragón de oro, Montena Mondadori (Barcelona, Spain), translation by Margaret Sayers Peden published as *Kingdom of the Golden Dragon,* HarperCollins (New York, NY), 2004.

Zorro, translated by Margaret Sayers Peden, HarperCollins (New York, NY) 2005.

Author of several plays and stories for children. Also contributor to *Los Libros tienen sis propios espíritus: Estudios sobre Isabel Allende,* edited by Marcello Coddou, Universidad Veracruzana, 1986; *Paths of Resistance: The Art and Craft of the Political Novel,* edited by William Zinsser, Houghton Mifflin, 1989; and *El Amor: Grandes escritores latinoamericanos,* Ediciones Instituto Movilizador, 1991.

ADAPTATIONS: The House of the Spirits was filmed in English by Bille August in 1993, starring Meryl Streep, Jeremy Irons, Antonio Banderas, and Vanessa Redgrave. Allende's young adult trilogy has been optioned for adaptation by Walden Media.

SIDELIGHTS: When Chilean President Salvador Allende was assassinated in 1973 as part of a military coup against his socialist government, it had a profound effect on his niece, novelist Isabel Allende. "I think I have divided my life [into] before that day and after that day," Allende told *Publishers Weekly* interviewer Amanda Smith. "In that moment, I realized that everything was possible—that violence was a dimension that was always around you." At first, Allende and her family did not believe that a dictatorship could last in Chile; they soon found it too dangerous to remain in the country, however, and fled to Venezuela. Although she had been a noted journalist in Chile, Allende found it difficult to get a job in Venezuela and did not write for several years; but after receiving word from her grandfather, a nearly one-hundred-year-old man who had remained in Chile, she began to write again in a letter to him. "My grandfather thought people died only when you forgot them," the author explained to Harriet Shapiro in *People.* "I wanted to prove to him that I had forgotten nothing, that his spirit was going to live with us forever." Allende never sent the letter to her grandfather, who soon died, but her memories of her family and her country became the genesis of *The House of the Spirits,* her first novel. "When you lose everything, everything that is dear to you . . . memory becomes more important," Allende commented to *Mother Jones* writer Douglas Foster. With *The House of the Spirits,* the author added, "[I achieved] the recovery of those memories that were being blown by the wind, by the wind of exile."

Following three generations of the Trueba family and their domestic and political conflicts, *The House of the Spirits* "is a novel of peace and reconciliation, in spite of the fact that it tells of bloody, tragic events," claimed *New York Times Book Review* contributor Alexander Coleman. "The author has accomplished this not only by plumbing her memory for the familial and political textures of the continent, but also by turning practically every major Latin American novel on its head," the critic continued. The patriarch of the family, Esteban Trueba, is a strict, conservative man who exploits his workers and allows his uncompromising beliefs to distance him from his wife and children, even in the face of tremendous events.

Allende's grand scope and use of fantastic elements and characters have led many critics to place *The House of the Spirits* in the tradition of the Latin American novel of "magic realism," and they compare it specifically to Nobel-winner Gabriel García Márquez's *One Hundred Years of Solitude*. "Allende has her own distinctive voice, however," noted a *Publishers Weekly* reviewer; "while her prose lacks the incandescent brilliance of the master's, it has a whimsical charm, besides being clearer, more accessible and more explicit about the contemporary situation in South America." In contrast, *Village Voice* contributor Enrique Fernandez believed that "only the dullest reader can fail to be distracted by the shameless cloning from *One Hundred Years of Solitude*. . . . Allende writes like one of the many earnest minor authors that began aping Gabo after his success, except she's better at it than most." "Allende is very much under the influence of Gabriel García Márquez, but she is scarcely an imitator," remarked *Washington Post Book World* critic Jonathan Yardley, concluding that "she is most certainly a novelist in her own right and, for a first novelist, a startlingly skillful, confident one."

While *The House of the Spirits* contains some of the magic realism so characteristic of late-twentieth-century Latin-American fiction, it is counterbalanced by the political realities that Allende recounts. *Times Literary Supplement* reviewer Antony Beevor stated that whereas the early chapters of *The House of the Spirits* seem "to belong firmly in the school of magical realism," a closer reading "suggests that Isabel Allende's tongue is lightly in her cheek. It soon becomes clear that she has taken the genre to flip it over," the critic elaborated. "The metaphorical house, the themes of time and power, the *machista* violence and the unstoppable merry-go-round of history: all of these are reworked and then examined from the other side—from a woman's perspective." Other critics, however, faulted Allende for trying to combine the magical and the political. Richard Eder of the *Los Angeles Times* felt that the author "rarely manages to integrate her magic and her message," while *Nation* contributor Paul West said that the political story is "the book Allende probably wanted to write, and would have had she not felt obliged to toe the line of magical realism." But others maintained that the contrast between the fantastic and political segments is effective, as Harriet Waugh of *Spectator* explained: "[The] magic gradually dies away as a terrible political reality engulfs the people of the country. Ghosts, the gift of foretelling the future and the ability to make the pepper and salt cellars move around the dining-room table cannot survive terror, mass-murder and torture."

Although *The House of the Spirits* includes political approaches similar to other Latin-American works, it also contains "an original feminist argument that suggests [a] women's monopoly on powers that oppose the violent 'paternalism' from which countries like Chile continue to suffer," according to *Chicago Tribune* contributor Bruce Allen. Alberto Manguel likewise considered important Allende's "depiction of woman as a colonial object," as he wrote in the Toronto *Globe and Mail*, a depiction reinforced by Esteban Trueba's cruel treatment of his wife, daughter, and female workers. But despite the concentration on female characters and "the fact that Esteban rapes, pillages, kills and conspires, he never entirely loses the reader's sympathy," commented Waugh. "It is a remarkable achievement to make the old monster lovable not just to his wife, daughter, and granddaughter, and the other women in his life, but also to the reader," Philip Howard contended in the London *Times*. "It is a fair-minded book, that pities and understands people on both sides of the politics." Allen concurred: "The most remarkable feature of this remarkable book is the way in which its strong political sentiments are made to coexist with its extravagant and fascinating narrative. . . . Despite its undeniable debt to *One Hundred Years of Solitude*," the critic concluded, *The House of the Spirits* "is an original and important work; along with García Márquez's masterpiece, it's one of the best novels of the postwar period, and a major contribution to our understanding of societies riddled by ceaseless conflict and violent change. It is a great achievement, and it cries out to be read."

With *Of Love and Shadows*, which *Detroit Free Press* contributor Anne Janette Johnson called "a frightening, powerful work," Allende "proves her continued capacity for generating excellent fiction. She has talent, sensitivity, and a subject matter that provides both high drama and an urgent political message." The novel begins "matter-of-factly, almost humorously," with the switching of two identically named babies, as Charles R. Larson described it in the *Detroit News*. The story becomes more complex, however, when one of the babies grows up to become the focus of a journalist's investigation; after a reporter and photographer expose the political murder of the girl, they are forced to flee the country. "And so," Larson observed, "Allende begins with vignettes of magical realism, only to pull the rug out from under our feet once we have been hooked by her enchanting tale. What she does, in fact, is turn her story into a thriller." "Love and struggle a la *Casablanca*—it's all there," Gene H. Bell-Villada likewise stated in the *New York Times Book Review*. "Allende skillfully evokes both the terrors of daily life under military rule and the subtler form of resistance in the hidden corners and 'shadows' of her title." But while political action comprises a large part of the story, "above all, this is a love story of two young people sharing the fate of their historical circumstances, meeting the challenge of discovering the truth, and determined to live their life fully, accepting their world of love and shadows," *Christian Science Monitor* reviewer Marjorie Agosin declared. With *Of Love and Shadows* "Allende has mastered the craft of being able to intertwine the turbulent political history of Latin America with the everyday lives of her fictional characters caught up in recognizable, contemporary events."

"Fears that Isabel Allende might be a 'one-book' writer, that her first success . . . would be her only one, ought to be quashed by *Eva Luna*," asserted Abigail E. Lee in the *Times Literary Supplement*. "The eponymous protagonist and narrator of this, her third novel, has an engaging personality, a motley collection of interesting acquaintances and an interesting angle on political upheavals in the unnamed Latin-American republic in which she lives." Born illegitimate and later orphaned, Eva Luna becomes a scriptwriter and storyteller who becomes involved with a filmmaker—Rolf Carle, an Austrian emigré haunted by his Nazi father—and his subjects, a troop of revolutionary guerrillas. "In *Eva Luna*, Allende moves between the personal and the political, between realism and fantasy, weaving two exotic coming-of-age stories—Eva Luna's and Rolf Carle's—into the turbulent coming of age of her unnamed South American country," Elizabeth Benedict summarized in Chicago's *Tribune Books*. Switching between the stories of the two protagonists, *Eva Luna* is "filled with a multitude of characters and tales," recounted *Washington Post Book World* contributor Alan Ryan. Allende's work is "a remarkable novel," the critic elaborated, "one in which a cascade of stories tumbles out before the reader, stories vivid and passionate and human enough to engage, in their own right, all the reader's attention and sympathy."

Perhaps due to this abundance of stories and characters, John Krich thought that "few of the cast of characters emerge as distinctive or entirely believable," as he commented in the *New York Times Book Review*. "Too often, we find Eva Luna's compatriots revealed through generalized attributions rather than their own actions. . . . Is this magic realism *à la* García Márquez or Hollywood magic *à la* Judith Krantz? We can only marvel at how thin the line becomes between the two, and give Ms. Allende the benefit of the doubt." London *Times* writer Stuart Evans, however, praised Allende's "range of eccentric or idiosyncratic characters who are always credible," and added: "Packed with action, prodigal in invention, vivid in description and metaphor, this cleverly plotted novel is enhanced by its flowing prose and absolute assurance." "*Eva Luna* is a great

read that *El Nobel* [García Márquez] couldn't hope to write," claimed Dan Bellm in the *Voice Literary Supplement,* for the women "get the best political debate scenes, not the men." Lee also saw a serious political side to the novel, noting "an interesting juxtaposition in *Eva Luna* of feminism and revolutionary politics. . . . In all the depictions of women and their relationships with men, though, one feels not a militant or aggressive feminism—rather a sympathetic awareness of the injustices inherent in traditional gender roles." The critic continued, remarking that *Eva Luna* "is an accomplished novel, skillfully blending humour and pathos; its woman's perspective on Latin American is a refreshing one, but it is enjoyable above all for its sensitivity and charm." "Reading this novel is like asking your favorite storyteller to tell you a story and getting a hundred stories instead of one . . . and then an explanation of how the stories were invented . . . and then hearing the storyteller's life as well," concluded Ryan. "Does it have a happy ending? What do you think?"

Daughter of Fortune differs from Allende's previous works in that it moves away from Chile and takes place in the setting of the 1849 California gold rush. The novel also includes a greater cultural mix than her previous works, with British, American, and Chinese characters. The main character, Eliza Somers, who spends several years disguised as a boy, raises questions about the nature of gender and identity, according to Sophia A. McClennan in the *Review of Contemporary Fiction*. Cecilia Novella remarked in *Américas* that Allende "provides us with a masterly description of that part of North America that was to become California at the height of the gold rush, painting a vivid picture of boisterous activity, chaos, avarice, unrelieved drudgery, and the broad range of lifestyles, habits and dissolute ways of those drawn there by the gleaming precious metal."

Portrait in Sepia tells the story of Aurora del Valle, who is filled with questions about the mysterious beginnings of her life. When she is five years old, she is sent to live with her grandmother, Paulina, who previously appeared in *Daughter of Fortune*. Paulina, who is wealthy and powerful, provides for her every material need but refuses to answer her questions about the past. Her confusion lingers until adulthood, and perhaps drives her to art: she is a talented photographer. After Paulina dies, she feels more free to explore her own and her family's past, examining her memories as well as those of relatives. At the end of the novel, Allende reveals that one of Aurora's cousins is Clara del Valle, a character from *The House of the Spirits*. Thus, as Teresa R. Arrington noted in *World Literature Today*, "Allende has produced two prequels years after the original novel, thus forming a chronologically out-of-sequence trilogy. The three novels represent a transnational saga that shows us how major historical events across the world can affect the lives of several generations of an extended Chilean family." In *Book,* Beth Kephart observed, "Allende's imagination is a spectacle unto itself—she infects her readers with her own colossal dreams."

In *City of the Beasts* Allende departed from her previous works for adults and wrote a story for young adults. In *Booklist,* she told Hazel Rochman, "The idea of writing for young adults wasn't mine; it was something that my three grandchildren had been asking me to do for a long time." Alexander Cold, the main character in the novel, was modeled after Allende's grandson, Alejandro Frias. Another character, Nadia Santos, was inspired by her two granddaughters, Andrea and Nicole. In the novel, Alexander is sent to stay with his grandmother in the Amazon while his mother receives chemotherapy in Texas. His grandmother is researching a mysterious "beast" that is terrifying everyone in the jungle, and she is part of a group of adventurers that includes a self-centered professor, some photographers, a government doctor, soldiers, local tribespeople, and a guide, Cesar Santos, who brings his daughter, Nadia. Alexander and Nicole must face dangers both physical and supernatural and struggle with both good and evil, but through shamanic techniques taught by the local tribe, they find their own inner strength and emerge transformed. A *Publisher's Weekly* reviewer said of *City of the Beasts,* "Reluctant readers may be intimidated by the thickness of this volume, but the plot moves at a rapid pace, laced with surprises and ironic twists." The reviewer then examined Allende's creation process: "The action and the outcome seem preordained, cleverly crafted to deliver the moral, but many readers will find the author's formula successful with its environmentalist theme, a pinch of the grotesque, and a larger dose of magic."

Allende's 2003 novel *My Invented Country: A Nostalgic Journey through Chile* is a memoir. The book examines Chile and Allende's place in it closely, tracing her relationship to the country and its people since the September 11, 1973, military coup that overthrew Chile's democracy. She relates stories of her family, historical tales of Chile, and considers how the country has influenced her writing. Allende "paints a fascinating picture of an unusual country," stated Gloria Maxwell in *Library Journal.* "She is unflinchingly honest about detailing Chilean adherence to a class system, the people's fixation with machismo, and their inherent conservatism and clannishness." Allende had a rich source of material at her disposal for the crafting of this book.

"Each country has its customs, its manias, its complexes," she writes. "I know the idiosyncrasies of mine like the back of my hand." Another *Library Journal* reviewer, Sheila Kasperek, observed that *My Invented Country* "provides a fuller understanding of her works," and in *Booklist,* Donna Seaman maintained that "Allende's conjuring of her 'invented,' or imaginatively remembered, country is riveting in its frankness and compassion, and her account of why and how she became a writer is profoundly moving."

Allende has shared many memories, both real and fictional, with her readers. She has examined political issues, related stories of her "interesting" childhood, enthralled readers with magical ideas, and shared the beauties of her homeland. The large topical span of Allende's writings makes it difficult to classify the author as a particular type. However, when *San Francisco Chronicle* writer Heather Knight asked Allende how she would like to be remembered after her death, Allende did not mention any of her acclaimed books. Instead, she responded, "I'd like to be remembered by my grandchildren as a grandma who gave them unconditional love, stories, and laughter."

BIOGRAPHICAL AND CRITICAL SOURCES:

BOOKS

Bloom, Harold, editor, *Isabel Allende,* Chelsea House (Philadelphia, PA), 2003.
Coddou, Marcelio, editor, *Los Libros tienen sus propios espíritus: Estudios sobre Isabel Allende,* Universidad Veracruzana (Veracruz, Mexico), 1986.
Contemporary Hispanic Biography, Volume 1, Thomson Gale (Detroit, MI), 2003.
Contemporary Literary Criticism, Thomson Gale (Detroit, MI), Volume 39, 1986, Volume 57, 1990, Volume 97, 1997.
Feal, Rosemary G., and Yvette E. Miller, editors, *Isabel Allende Today: An Anthology of Essays,* Latin American Literary Review Press (Pittsburgh, PA), 2002.
Hart, Patricia, *Narrative Magic in the Fiction of Isabel Allende,* Fairleigh Dickinson University Press (Teaneck, NJ), 1989.
Levine, Linda Gould, *Isabel Allende,* Twayne Publishers (New York, NY), 2002.
Lindsay, Claire, *Locating Latin American Women Writers: Cristina Peri Rossi, Rosario Ferré, Albalucía, and Isabel Allende,* Peter Lang (New York, NY), 2003.

Postlewate, Marisa Herrera, *How and Why I Write: Redefining Women's Writing and Experience,* Peter Lang (New York, NY), 2004.

Ramblado-Minero, Maria de la Cinta, *Isabal Allende's Writing of the Self: Trespassing the Boundaries of Fiction and Autobiography,* E. Mellen Press (Lewiston, NY), 2003.

Rojas, Sonia Riquelme, and Edna Aguirre Rehbein, editors, *Critical Approaches to Isabel Allende's Novels,* P. Lang (New York, NY), 1991.

Zapata, Celia Correas, *Isabel Allende: Life and Spirits,* translation by Margaret Sayers Peden, Arte Público Press (Houston, TX), 2002.

PERIODICALS

Américas, November-December, 1995, p. 36; September, 1999, Cecilia Novella, review of *Daughter of Fortune,* p. 61; October, 2001, Barbara Mujica, review of *Portrait in Sepia,* p. 63.

Architectural Digest, April, 1995, p. 32.

Atlanta Journal-Constitution, December 2, 2000, Greg Changnon, review of *Portrait in Sepia,* p. C4.

Book, November-December, 2001, Beth Kephart, review of *Portrait in Sepia,* p. 60.

Booklist, February 1, 1998, p. 875; August, 1999, Brad Hooper, review of *Daughter of Fortune,* p. 1984; September 1, 2001, Brad Hooper, review of *Portrait in Sepia,* p. 3; November 15, 2002, Hazel Rochman, review of *City of the Beasts,* p. 590, and interview with Allende, p. 591; April 1, 2003, Donna Seaman, review of *My Invented Country: A Nostalgic Journey through Chile,* p. 1354.

Chicago Tribune, May 19, 1985.

Christian Science Monitor, June 7, 1985; May 27, 1987.

Detroit Free Press, June 7, 1987.

Detroit News, June 14, 1987.

Globe and Mail (Toronto, Ontario, Canada), June 24, 1985; June 27, 1987.

Guardian, November 13, 1999, Alex Clark, review of *Daughter of Fortune,* p. 10; November 30, 2002, Carol Birch, review of *City of the Beasts,* p. 33.

Kirkus Reviews, October 1, 2002, review of *City of the Beasts,* p. 1462; April 1, 2003, review of *My Invented Country,* p. 514.

Library Journal, August, 1999, Barbara Hoffert, review of *Daughter of Fortune,* p. 134; October 15, 2001, Barbara Hoffert, review of *Portrait in Sepia,* p. 105; June 1, 2003, Sheila Kasperek, review of *My Invented Country,* p. 118; October 15, 2003, Gloria Maxwell, review of *My Invented Country,* p. 115.

Los Angeles Times, February 10, 1988.

Los Angeles Times Book Review, June 16, 1985; May 31, 1987.

Mother Jones, December, 1988.

Ms., May-June, 1995, p. 75.

Nation, July 20-27, 1985.

New Leader, November-December, 2001, Philip Graham, review of *Portrait in Sepia,* p. 38.

New Statesman, July 5, 1985.

Newsweek, May 13, 1985.

New York Review of Books, July 18, 1985.

New York Times, May 2, 1985; May 20, 1987; February 4, 1988.

New York Times Book Review, May 12, 1985; July 12, 1987; October 23, 1988; May 21, 1995, p. 11.

People, June 10, 1985; June 1, 1987; June 5, 1995, p. 34; April 20, 1998, p. 47.

Publishers Weekly, March 1, 1985; May 17, 1985; January 19, 1998, p. 360; August 23, 1999, review of *Daughter of Fortune* p. 41; July 16, 2001, review of *Portrait in Sepia,* p. 1142; June 24, 2002, review of *City of the Beasts,* p. 58; April 28, 2003, review of *My Invented Country,* p. 57; June 30, 2003, review of *City of the Beasts.*

Review of Contemporary Fiction, summer, 2000, Sophia A. McClennan, review of *Daughter of Fortune,* p. 184.

St. Louis Post-Dispatch, October 28, 2001, Jan Garden Castro, review of *Portrait in Sepia,* p. G11.

San Francisco Chronicle, October 19, 2001, Heather Knight, review of *City of the Beasts,* p. 1.

Spectator, August 3, 1985.

Sunday Telegraph (London, England), October 14, 2001, Jenny McCartney, review of *Portrait in Sepia,* p. NA.

Time, May 20, 1985.

Times (London, England), July 4, 1985; July 9, 1987; March 22, 1989; March 23, 1989.

Times Literary Supplement, July 5, 1985; July 10, 1987; April 7-13, 1989.

Tribune Books (Chicago, IL), October 9, 1988.

U.S. News and World Report, November 21, 1988.

Village Voice, June 7, 1985.

Voice Literary Supplement, December, 1988.

Wall Street Journal, March 20, 1998.

Washington Post Book World, May 12, 1985; May 24, 1987; October 9, 1988.

World Literature Today, winter, 2002, Teresa R. Arrington, review of *Portrait in Sepia,* p. 115.

World Press Review, April, 1995, p. 47.

ALLISON, Dorothy E. 1949-

PERSONAL: Born April 11, 1949, in Greenville, SC; daughter of Ruth Gibson Allison (a waitress and cook); companion of Alix Layman (a printer); children: Wolf Michael. *Education:* Florida Presbyterian College (now Eckerd College), B.A., 1971; New School for Social Research, M.A.

ADDRESSES: Home—Box 112, Monte Rio, CA 95462. *Agent*—Frances Goldin, 305 East 11th St., New York, NY 10003.

CAREER: Writer. Founder: Independent Spirit Award, administered by Astraea Foundation; serves on the advisory boards of National Coalition against Censorship, Feminists for Free Expression, and James Tiptree, Jr. Memorial Award.

MEMBER: PEN International (advisory board member), Authors Guild, Authors League of America, National Writers Union.

AWARDS, HONORS: Lambda literary awards, best lesbian small press book and best lesbian fiction, both 1989, for *Trash;* National Book Award finalist, 1992, and Ferro Grumley and Bay Area Book Reviewers awards for fiction, all for *Bastard out of Carolina*; Gay and Lesbian Book Award, American Library Association, 1995, for *Skin: Talking about Sex, Class, and Literature*; *Two or Three Things I Know for Sure* was named a notable book of the year by the *New York Times Book Review;* Lambda literary award for fiction, 1998, for *Cavedweller.*

WRITINGS:

The Women Who Hate Me (poems), Long Haul Press, 1983.
Trash (stories), Firebrand Books (Ithaca, NY), 1988, expanded edition, Penguin Books (New York, NY), 2002.
The Women Who Hate Me: Poetry, 1980-1990, Firebrand Books (Ithaca, NY), 1991.
Bastard out of Carolina (novel), Dutton (New York, NY), 1992.
Skin (essays), Firebrand Books (Ithaca, NY), 1993, published as *Skin: Talking about Sex, Class, and Literature,* 1994.

Two or Three Things I Know for Sure (autobiography), Dutton (New York, NY), 1995.
Cavedweller (novel), Dutton (New York, NY), 1998.

Author of introduction, *The Redneck Way of Knowledge: Down Home Tales,* by Blanche McCrary Boyd, Vintage (New York, NY), 1995, and *Nightwood,* by Djuna Barnes, Modern Library (New York, NY), 2000; author of foreword, *My Dangerous Desires: A Queer Girl Dreaming Her Way Home,* by Amber L. Hollibaugh, Duke University Press (Durham, NC), 2000. Work represented in anthologies, including *Building Feminist Theory: Essays from "Quest,"* edited by Charlotte Bunch and others, Longman (New York, NY), 1981; *Lesbian Words: State of the Art,* edited by Randy Turoff, Masquerade Books (New York, NY), 1995; *Ida Applebroog: Nothing Personal, Paintings 1987-1997,* by Ida Applebroog, Distributed Art Publishers (New York, NY), 1998; *This Is What Lesbian Looks Like,* edited by Kris Kleindienst, Firebrand Books (Ithaca, NY), 1999; *The Beacon Best of 1999: Creative Writing by Women and Men of All Colors,* edited by Ntozake Shange, Beacon Books (New York, NY), 1999; *The Mammoth Book of Modern Lesbian Short Stories,* edited by Emma Donoghue, Carroll & Graf (New York, NY), 1999; and *The Vintage Book of International Lesbian Fiction: An Anthology,* edited by Naomi Holoch and Joan Nestle, Random/Vintage (New York, NY), 1999.

ADAPTATIONS: Bastard out of Carolina was adapted for film by Showtime, directed by Angelica Huston, 1996, and as a sound recording by Penguin-HighBridge Audio, 1993. *Two or Three Things I Know for Sure* was produced as a short documentary, *Two or Three Things and Nothing for Sure* by Tina Di Feliciantonlo and Jane Wagner for the PBS series *POV* in 1998, and was also adapted as a sound recording by Nova Audio Books, 1995. *Cavedweller* was adapted as a sound recording, Brilliance/Nova, 1998, and was adapted for the stage by Kate Moira Ryan in a production directed by Michael Grief at the New York Theater Workshop in 2003.

WORK IN PROGRESS: A science-fiction trilogy.

SIDELIGHTS: Dorothy E. Allison became a recognized poet and short story writer in the 1980s with her collections *The Women Who Hate Me* and *Trash*. But it was not until the publication of her novel *Bastard out of Carolina* that Allison garnered mainstream attention as a writer. In this National Book Award-nominated work, as well as in more recent publications, Allison has secured her reputation as a writer who deals frankly and boldly with issues of gender, class, and sexual orientation. To quote Mark Shechner in the *Buffalo News*, Allison is an author "we have come to admire . . . and come moreover to depend on to remind us that there are hard places in this world that we are obliged to know something about."

In an essay published in the *New York Times Book Review*, Allison commented on the importance of literature that deals honestly with difficult themes of poverty, violence against children, and sexual orientation: "We are the ones they make fiction of—we gay and disenfranchised and female—and we have the right to demand our full, nasty, complicated lives." In an interview with Dan Cryer for *Newsday*, the author said: "I have a certain advocacy. . . . I don't believe in a writer who doesn't have politics, convictions. I do believe I'm writing about a huge part of the population that is essentially ignored or disdained, and I'm trying to take it seriously." This intense engagement with her subject matter has brought Allison a wide audience that includes literary critics and casual readers alike.

Allison was born in 1949 in Greenville, South Carolina, to a poor, unmarried fifteen-year-old girl. When Allison was five, her stepfather—her mother having since married—began sexually abusing her. The abuse lasted for several years before Allison was finally able to tell a relative; the relative informed Allison's mother, who put a stop to it. Nonetheless, the family stayed together. In her *Newsday* interview, Allison recalled that growing up poor and abused "was about being angry, helpless, held in contempt. It makes you want to eat your own soul, despise the world."

When she was eighteen, Allison left home to attend college in Florida. She was introduced to feminism, which she embraced, and which—as she noted in a *New York Times Book Review* essay—"gave me a vision of the world totally different from everything I had ever assumed or hoped. The concept of a feminist literature offered the possibility of pride in my sexuality." Later, she attended graduate school in New York City. However, it was not until after this period, in the early 1980s, that she began writing seriously. She published poetry and short story collections, and she began work on *Bastard out of Carolina*.

The incest, abuse, and poverty Allison experienced as a child figure heavily in *Bastard out of Carolina*, a fictional portrayal of a young girl's life in a poor Southern family. Ruth Anne Boatwright, the protagonist, relates how she earned her nickname, "Bone," when she was prematurely born—the size of a knucklebone—after her mother had an automobile accident. Allison admitted in an interview with Lynn Karpen in the *New York Times Book Review* that these introductory details are largely autobiographical. The author further commented, "A lot of the novel is based on real experience, but not the entire thing. The characters are modeled on members of my family and on stories I heard when I was growing up." In her *Newsday* interview she described Bone as "an alternative version of me. A little smarter, a little cleaner, a little less damaged."

Bone's illegitimacy, her plain looks, and her lack of talent for gospel singing make her an outcast among her peers, but she finds shelter among the women of her family. She particularly admires her Aunt Raylene, a former carnival worker who once had a love affair with another woman. Bone's mother, Anney, attempts to establish a more traditional home for herself and her daughter by marrying the son of a wealthy local family. Daddy Glen, Anney's new husband, is kind to his wife, but takes out his frustrations by physically and sexually assaulting Bone. Anney refuses to acknowledge these acts until a brutal confrontation occurs, which leaves Bone feeling, at the age of thirteen, that her life is over. A *Booklist* reviewer noted, however, that at this turning point of adolescence, Bone, like Mark Twain's Huckleberry Finn, realizes that in order to live her life she must move on to new territory.

Reviewers of *Bastard out of Carolina* commended Allison for her realistic, unsentimental, and often humorous portrayal of her eccentric characters, and in 1992 the novel was nominated for a National Book award. In *Publishers Weekly*, a reviewer stated that Allison "doesn't condescend to her 'white trash' characters; she portrays them with understanding and love." A *Washington Post Book World* contributor complained that *Bastard out of Carolina* "has a tendency to bog down in its own heat, speech and atmosphere," but also acknowledged that Allison "has a superb ear for the specific dialogue of her characters." George Garrett, writing in the *New York Times Book Review*, praised the novel for being "as richly various, with its stories and memories and dreams, as a well-made quilt." Garrett further declared that Allison's "technical skill in both large things and details, so gracefully executed as to be always at the service of the story and its characters and thus almost invisible, is simply stunning."

Allison followed *Bastard out of Carolina* with a collection of essays, *Skin: Talking about Sex, Class, and Literature,* and a memoir, *Two or Three Things I Know for*

Sure. Reviewers reacted positively to both works, again praising the author's spare, straightforward writing style and expressing admiration for her hard-won success. Commenting on *Skin* in the *Los Angeles Times Book Review,* Carla Tomaso noted, "one marvels at the incredible achievement this is for someone born poor and despised in the South." Susie Bright, reviewing *Skin* in the *New York Times Book Review,* maintained that the "tautness of Ms. Allison's storytelling comes from her ability to describe cruelty and desperate measures with such grace that it leaves a sensual impression unmistakable to the literary touch."

Allison's literary success has brought her widespread media attention and made her a popular draw on the lecture circuit. In an interview with Alexis Jetter for the *New York Times Magazine,* she spoke about the importance of storytelling in her life. "I believe that storytelling can be a strategy to help you make sense of your life," she told Jetter. "It's what I've done."

A *Christian Century* contributor wrote that the theme of Allison's *Cavedweller* is redemption, "the need for it, the courage it requires, and the time and effort that may be necessary to achieve it." *Entertainment Weekly* reviewer Margot Mifflin called the book "a sprawling, bighearted, Southern-fried slab of family drama." *Advocate* writer Carol Anshaw found the work "a woman's book through and through, filled with women's suffering, women's strength, women's survival."

In *Cavedweller,* Delia Byrd, a singer with a rock and roll band, returns to her Georgia hometown with Cissy, her daughter by a rock star lover who had been killed in a motorcycle accident. Delia had fled more than ten years earlier to escape an abusive husband and had left behind her daughters Amanda and Dede, now teenagers. Delia works to earn the town's respect, first cleaning houses, then by managing the town's beauty shop, as she reclaims her daughters and also nurses their father, Clint, who is dying of cancer.

Writing in *Lambda Book Report,* Deborah Peifer described Amanda and Dede as "lost girls, raised by their bitterly religious grandmother, a woman who smiles only at another's misfortune. Amanda has become her grandmother, religious and filled with hate for sin and sinners; Dede is prepared to take life on, no matter what it offers. Delia and her daughters are the heart of this novel, and their journeys, through hate and rage to love, acceptance, the possibility of redemption, with many and varied detours along the way, form its soul."

Time contributor R.Z. Sheppard wrote that Allison "has a grip on the elementary physics of gender: women are centripetal, the force that binds. Men are centrifugal; for all their good intentions, they feel best when whirling away from the center."

Nation contributor JoAnn Wypijewski wrote that "'grief' peppers the pages of a story that's harder than *Bastard,* harder because the air of high Southern Gothic (the home terror, the family tragedy worthy of Flannery O'Connor) is trapped in the past, harder because the poverty is far more familiar and far better managed, harder because its central figures aren't at all the 'characters' Northerners find so comforting in 'Southern writing,' harder because it has a happy ending."

When Cissy is fifteen, her exploring takes her to the caves that are both threatening and comforting as she attempts to understand her sexuality and attraction to lesbian friends. Allison told *Salon.com* interviewer Laura Miller that she began writing the book by picturing Cissy in the cave. "The notion was of somebody in such trouble that the only place she was going to feel safe was in this hole in the ground. And I had the notion of a woman who, in order to redeem herself, basically buries herself alive." Wypijewski felt that it is at this point that Cissy "begins to emerge as something other than the novel's neutral slate. Allison uses an omniscient narrator in this book, unlike the hopeful-angry girl-voice of *Bastard,* but the perspective seems to be Delia's until past halfway though, when ever so slowly it shifts to Cissy. In a sense, this child has always monitored the action."

Valerie Sayers wrote in the *New York Times Book Review* that *Cavedweller* "is not a novel interested in formal invention, in ironic distance, or even in elegant prose. It doesn't give two cents for post-modern preening or cold intellectual approaches. It is clear-eyed about the economic forces that shape these women's lives, but it is also unabashedly emotional and hopeful about their futures. It reaches back to the conventions of straightforward storytelling and pays close attention to the way women get by, the way they come to forgive one another, the way they choose who they will be."

In an essay for *Library Journal,* David Hellman identified *Bastard out of Carolina* as a "grit-lit classic." He described the genre as being "full of pluck . . . [with] the abrasive quality of sand in your shoes. Like tableside grits, it is also comfort food for those who love it, nasty and unfamiliar stuff to those who don't." Allison herself recognizes the uncomfortable notes she strikes so well in her work. The *Buffalo News* quoted her as saying: "I know that some authors write for truth. I know that others write for justice. And some might even write for love. But I'm here to tell you there is another reason authors write fiction, and that reason is revenge." Whatever her motives, Allison emerged in the late twentieth century as one of the premiere practitioners of realistic fiction depicting the plight of the poor, the lesbian, and the class-conscious intellectual.

BIOGRAPHICAL AND CRITICAL SOURCES:

BOOKS

Allison, Dorothy, *Two or Three Things I Know for Sure* (autobiography), Dutton (New York, NY), 1995.

Contemporary Novelists, seventh edition, St. James Press (Detroit, MI), 2001.

Contemporary Southern Writers, St. James Press (Detroit, MI), 1999.

Gilmore, Leigh, *The Limits of Autobiography: Trauma and Testimony,* Cornell University Press (Ithaca, NY), 2001.

PERIODICALS

Advocate, April 7, 1992, p. 70; March 9, 1993, p. 66; May 17, 1994, p. 72; September 5, 1995, p. 63; March 17, 1998, Carol Anshaw, review of *Cavedweller,* p. 62.

Booklist, June 15, 1992, review of *Bastard out of Carolina,* p. 1814.

Christian Century, March 10, 1999, review of *Cavedweller,* p. 291.

Christian Science Monitor, March 11, 1998, review of *Cavedweller,* p. 15.

College Literature, spring, 1998, Katrina Irving, "'Writing It down So That It Would Be Real': Narrative Strategies in Dorothy Allison's *Bastard out of Carolina,*" p. 94.

Contemporary Literature, summer, 1998, Deborah Horvitz, "'Sadism Demands a Story': Oedipus, Feminism, and Sexuality in Gayl Jones's *Corregidora* and Dorothy Allison's *Bastard out of Carolina,*" p. 238.

Entertainment Weekly, April 3, 1998, Margot Mifflin, review of *Cavedweller,* p. 89.

Kirkus Reviews, January 15, 1998, review of *Cavedweller,* p. 70.

Lambda Book Report, July, 1998, Deborah Peifer, review of *Cavedweller,* p. 24.

Library Journal, March 1, 1992, p. 116; March 1, 1998, review of *Cavedweller,* p. 125.

Los Angeles Times Book Review, January 1, 1995, p. 3; July 30, 1995, p. 6; March 15, 1998, review of *Cavedweller,* p. 8.

Ms., September-October, 1995, p. 80; May, 1998, review of *Cavedweller,* p. 85.

Nation, December 28, 1992, p. 815; July 5, 1993, p. 20; March 30, 1998, JoAnn Wypijewski, review of *Cavedweller,* p. 25.

New Statesman & Society, January 8, 1993, p. 41.

Newsweek, March 30, 1998, Jeff Giles, "Return of the Rebel Belle: A New Novel from Dorothy Allison, Author of *Bastard out of Carolina,*" p. 66.

New York Times Book Review, July 5, 1992, p. 3; June 26, 1994, p. 15; September 25, 1994, p. 29; August 13, 1995, p. 16; March 15, 1998, Valerie Sayers, "Back Home in Dixie," p. 19; June 20, 1999, review of *Cavedweller,* p. 24.

New York Times Magazine, December 17, 1995, Alexis Jetter, "The Roseanne of Literature," p. 54.

Observer (London, England), August 30, 1998, review of *Cavedweller,* p. 16.

People Weekly, April 6, 1998, Alison M. Rosen, review of *Cavedweller,* p. 31.

Progressive, January, 1995, p. 38; July, 1995, p. 30.

Publishers Weekly, November 18, 1988, p. 74; March 22, 1991, p. 77; January 27, 1992, p. 88; February 1, 1993, p. 12; May 29, 1995, p. 72; January 19, 1998, review of *Cavedweller,* p. 369.

Rapport, May, 1999, review of *Cavedweller,* p. 33.

Southern Literary Journal, fall, 2000, Vincent King, "Hopeful Grief: The Prospect of a Postmodernist Feminism in Allison's *Bastard out of Carolina,*" p. 122.

Time, April 13, 1998, R.Z. Sheppard, review of *Cavedweller,* p. 221.

Times Literary Supplement, March 8, 1991, p. 18; August 28, 1998, review of *Cavedweller,* p. 21.

Washington Post Book World, May 3, 1992, review of *Bastard out of Carolina,* p. 11; April 5, 1998, review of *Cavedweller,* p. 1; May 9, 1999, review of *Cavedweller,* p. 10.

Women's Review of Books, September, 1994, p. 10; December, 1995, p. 14.

ONLINE

Curve Magazine, http://www.curvemag.com/ (September 7, 2001), Kathleen Wilkinson, "Dorothy Allison: The Value of Redemption."

Dorothy Allison Home Page, http://www.previewport. com/Home/ (September 7, 2001).

Gay.com, http://www.content/gay.com/ (September 7, 2001), Mary Ann Stover, "Dorothy Allison Weaves Tales from the Heart."

Printed Matter, http://www.dcn.davis.ca.us/ (February 8, 1998), Elisabeth Sherwin, "Patron Saint of Battered Women Writes, Forgives."

Salon.com, http://www.salon.com/ (March 31, 1998), Laura Miller, "The *Salon.com* Interview: Dorothy Allison."

*   *   *

ALVAREZ, A. 1929-
(Alfred Alvarez)

PERSONAL: Born August 5, 1929, in London, England; son of Bertie and Katie (Levy) Alvarez; married Ursula Graham Barr, 1956 (divorced, 1961); married Audrey Anne Adams, 1966; children: (first marriage) Adam Richard; (second marriage) Luke Lyon, Kate. *Education:* Attended Corpus Christi College, Oxford, B.A., 1952, M.A., 1956. *Hobbies and other interests:* Rock climbing, poker, classical music.

ADDRESSES: Agent—c/o Aitken and Stone Ltd., 29 Fernshaw Rd., London SW10 0TG, England. *E-mail*—aalvarez\@compuserve.com.

CAREER: Oxford University, Corpus Christi College, Oxford, England, senior research scholar, 1952-55, and tutor in English, 1954-55; Princeton University, Princeton, NJ, Procter visiting fellow, 1953-54; Rockefeller Foundation, New York, NY, visiting fellow, 1955-56, 1958; *Observer,* London, England, poetry editor and critic, 1956-66; freelance writer, 1956; *Journal of Education,* poetry critic and editor, London, 1957; Gauss Seminarian and visiting lecturer, Princeton University, 1957-58; D.H. Lawrence fellow, University of New Mexico, 1958; drama critic, *New Statesman,* London, England, 1958-60; visiting professor at Brandeis University, Waltham, MA, 1960-61, and State University of New York—Buffalo, NY, 1966; Penguin Modern European Poets in Translation, advisory editor, 1965-75; *Voices* program, presenter, Channel 4 Television, 1982.

MEMBER: Climbers' Club, Alpine Club.

AWARDS, HONORS: Rockefeller fellowship, 1955-56; Vachel Lindsay Prize for Poetry (Chicago, IL), 1961.

WRITINGS:

(Poems), Fantasy Press (Oxford, England), 1952.

Stewards of Excellence: Studies in Modern English and American Poets, Scribner (New York, NY), 1958, published as *The Shaping Spirit: Studies in Modern English and American Poets,* Chatto & Windus (London, England), 1958.

The End of It, privately printed, 1958.

The School of Donne, Chatto & Windus (London, England), 1961, Pantheon (New York, NY), 1962.

(Editor and author of introduction) *The New Poetry,* Penguin (Harmondsworth, England), 1962, revised edition, 1966.

Under Pressure: The Writer in Society, Eastern Europe and the U.S.A., Penguin (Baltimore, MD), 1965, published as *Under Pressure: The Artist and Society, Eastern Europe and the U.S.A.,* Penguin (Harmondsworth, England), 1965.

Lost (poems), Turret Books (London, England), 1968.

Beyond All This Fiddle: Essays, 1955-1967, Allen Lane (London, England), 1968, Random House (New York, NY), 1969.

(With Roy Fuller and Anthony Thwaite) *Penguin Modern Poets 18* (poems), Penguin (Harmondsworth, England), 1970.

Apparition (poems), University of Queensland Press (St. Lucia, Australia), 1971.

The Savage God: A Study of Suicide, Weidenfeld & Nicolson (London, England), 1971, Random House (New York, NY), 1972.

The Legacy, Poem-of-the-Month Club (London, England), 1972.

Samuel Beckett, Viking (New York, NY), 1973, published as *Beckett,* Fontana (London, England), 1973.

Hers (novel), Weidenfeld & Nicolson (London, England), 1974, Random House (New York, NY), 1975.

Autumn to Autumn, and Selected Poems, 1953-1976, Macmillan (London, England), 1978.

(Editor, with David Skilton) Thomas Hardy, *Tess of the D'Urbervilles,* Penguin (Harmondsworth, England), 1978.

Hunt (novel), Simon & Schuster (New York, NY), 1978.

Life after Marriage: Love in an Age of Divorce, Simon & Schuster (New York, NY), 1982, published as *Life after Marriage: Scenes from Divorce,* Macmillan (London, England), 1982.

The Biggest Game in Town, Houghton Mifflin (Boston, MA), 1983.

Offshore: A North Sea Journey, Houghton Mifflin (Boston, MA), 1986.

(With Charles Blackman) *Rainforest,* Macmillan (Melbourne, Australia), 1988.

Feeding the Rat: Profile of a Climber, Bloomsbury (London, England), 1988, Atlantic Monthly Press (New York, NY), 1989.

Day of Atonement (novel), J. Cape (London, England), 1991.

(Editor) *The Faber Book of Modern European Poetry,* Faber (London, England), 1992.

Night: An Exploration of Night Life, Night Language, Sleep and Dreams, Norton (New York, NY), 1995.

Where Did It All Go Right? (autobiography), Morrow (New York, NY), 1999.

Poker: Bets, Bluffs, and Bad Beats, edited by Kelly Duane, Chronicle Books (San Francisco, CA), 2001.

Feeding the Rat: A Climber's Life on the Edge, Thunder Mouth Press (New York, NY), 2001.

The Biggest Game in Town, Chronicle Books (San Francisco, CA), 2002.

New and Selected Poems, Waywiser (London, England), 2002.

The Writer's Voice, Norton (New York, NY), 2005.

Also author of screenplay *The Anarchist,* 1969. Contributor to *Observer, New Yorker, Cosmopolitan, Daily Telegraph Magazine, Times, New York Review of Books,* and other periodicals. Advisory editor, "Penguin Modern European Poets" series, 1966-75.

SIDELIGHTS: A. Alvarez first made a name for himself in literary circles with his work as critic, particularly with his meditation on suicide, *The Savage God: A Study of Suicide,* but his career moved in a more creative direction in the late 1960s when, as he once explained, he "had grown weary of writing books about other people's books, so effectively [I] gave up criticism in order to concentrate on [my] own creative work." Since then, he has published several poetry collections and a handful of novels, in which, according to Carol Simpson Stern in *Contemporary Novelists,* "his passion for language and curiosity about the human condition find expression." Though she found some fault in these creative writings, she concluded that Alvarez "writes well and is always eminently readable."

Alvarez published his first poems in 1952, while still at Corpus Christi College at Oxford, and six years later, he privately published a collection called *The End of It.* Three years later, he won a poetry prize for a group of poems about the breakup of his first marriage, which, remarked John Ferns in the *Dictionary of Literary Biography,* "are written in a style that combines natural

and violent images to express states of alienation and separation . . . and attempts to capture almost suicidal states of isolation."

However, Alvarez did not fully embrace creative writing until the late 1960s. By the beginning of the next decade, he was established "as a recognized, if minor, contemporary British poet," Ferns related. Despite these early successes, Alvarez has never produced a large body of poetry. Stern wrote in *Contemporary Poets* that the "published poetry of A. Alvarez is slight indeed in volume, but it is rich in its economy." His body of work is consistent in its preoccupation with themes of love, separation, and death.

Alvarez's later poems often concern mates divided by fears. Noted Stern in *Contemporary Poets,* "They are poems of ephemera, in which an emotion is briefly isolated, felt, and wafted away, leaving the persona with a sense of perplexity and regret." The collection *Autumn to Autumn, and Selected Poems, 1953-1976,* contains one new, seven-sequence poem along with poems that had appeared over the previous two decades. Alvarez stated that *Autumn to Autumn* "contains all the poems I want to preserve." The new work, depicting a cycle of loss and renewal, is full of "delicate, lyric particularity and subtle rhythms," observed Ferns, "reminiscent in places of Lawrence and the Thomas Hardy of the 1912-1913 poems." Stern, in *Contemporary Poets,* also commented that some of the earlier poems in the collection "recall Plath's stridency and savage treatment of love's anger." Derek Sanford of *Books and Bookmen* further praised this work as "good, very good, strictly minor poetry, much of which poets with bigger names might justifiably be proud."

Alvarez first turned to fiction writing in the early 1970s with *Hers,* a novel about a middle-aged woman married to an older university professor, who has an affair with one of her husband's students. Stern, in *Contemporary Novelists,* found that Alvarez's "portrait of the professor Charles is both entertaining and honest." *Hers,* drawing upon some of Alvarez's personal experiences, also shares themes of his poetry in his characters' inability to forge meaningful communication; when Charles discovers his wife's affair, he cannot even speak his own words and instead quotes Shakespeare's *Othello.*

Alvarez's other novels, *Hunt* and *Day of Atonement,* are written in the thriller tradition. In *Hunt* he tells the story of Conrad Jessup, whose quest for excitement leads him to the discovery of a murdered body and a charge by the police that he is the killer. Jessup, once released, seeks the real killer and so becomes involved in a game of international intrigue. Stern, in her *Contemporary Novelists* essay, deemed the plot "slow and obvious." A *Contemporary Review* critic, though, declared of the book, "Taut, disturbing and expertly constructed, this is a novel not to be missed."

Day of Atonement finds a married couple, Joe and Judy Constantine, implicated after their friend Tommy Apple mysteriously dies. The Constantines are hounded by drug traffickers and the police alike, and Joe finds that a questionable favor he once did for Tommy now endangers his relationship to Judy. Stern, in *Contemporary Novelists,* looked on *Day of Atonement* in a far more favorable light than *Hunt.* "At one level," she remarked, "the book is a who-dunnit. . . . At another, it is a rich exploration of friendship, love, guilt, and reparation." She also found that the characters are "compelling" and that the dialogue "rings true." Stern also praised Alvarez's portrayal of the underworld: "His sense of detail, the excitement, and the people is unerring."

Where Did It All Go Right? is Alvarez's exploration of his life. He describes himself as "not quite an Englishman . . . a Jew with a Spanish surname disguised as a true Brit." His forebears had enjoyed success in business, and although this was followed by reverses of fortune, Alvarez grew up in a world of privilege; he was attended by servants and educated at elite schools. He still felt like an outsider, though, because of being Jewish. He writes of this feeling, of his sometimes difficult relationship with his family, of his happy second marriage, and of his literary career and friendships, especially his role in promoting the poetry of Sylvia Plath, John Berryman, and Robert Lowell. He also details his experiences in World War II and his penchant for dangerous hobbies—boxing, rock climbing, stunt flying—leading an *Economist* reviewer to call him "the Hemingway of poetry." The reviewer described Alvarez's autobiography as "a good read, with lots of page-turning anecdote."

Independent on Sunday contributor William Scammell deemed *Where Did It All Go Right?* an "engaging but exasperating memoir." Scammell remarked of Alvarez, "As a critic he deserves honor for championing the unhappy few, for his fighting spirit—and sometimes deserves flaying for his glibness and exhibitionism." Stephen Pile, writing in the *New Statesman,* found both faults and virtues in the book. "The greatest fault in this autobiography," Pile observed, "is that he gives us, for example, little sense of his life as a poet, novelist or a writer of rather good non-fiction books about divorce, poker and life on North Sea oil rigs. . . . He is also frustratingly silent on his bizarre first marriage," to D.H. Lawrence's granddaughter Ursula, whom Alvarez had known for only seven weeks before they wed. Pile continued, "The greatest virtue of this book lies in the vivid pen portraits he gives of the leading poets of the second half of the twentieth century." Similarly, Ian Sansom, critiquing for the *London Review of Books,* pointed out, "There are in fact more than enough highly polished little gems about family and friends and twentieth-century writers, artists and critics to merit the price of the book." Pile added, "What stops this being the club-room ramblings of a senior contributor is that they are expertly written with irony and humor." Michael Schmidt, writing in the daily *Independent,* praised Alvarez's "unostentatious rightness of style. . . . He believes in this world—its people and passions—and he brings it wonderfully alive."

After nearly twenty-five years since his last book of poems, *Autumn to Autumn and Selected Poems 1953-1976,* Alvarez followed up with *New and Selected Poems.* Maintaining the theme of love, which was mixed with death and separation in his last poetry collection, this time around Alvarez delves into the purity of love, not only between individuals, but between man and the world as a whole. "The new poems . . . lack the bustle and energy of the earlier . . . but the best make up for it with a Keatsian appreciation of the sensual possibilities of the world and of human love," commented Martin Crucefix of *Poetry London.* Christopher Levenson of *World Literature Today* commented that for Alvarez, the collection is "surprisingly traditional, even neoclassical." However, he continued, "The evidence of these later poems, which infuse his characteristic wit and imagery with greater colloquial ease, suggests there may be even better things to come."

Alvarez is still primarily known as a critic, but his literary contributions in other capacities are undeniable. As his criticism delves into topics of concern to both literary circles and to contemporary society, his creative work also explores relevant issues, such as suicide, religious prejudice, infidelity, divorce, and crime. In both his poetry and his fiction, Alvarez finds "his own colloquial, modern voice," observed Stern in *Contemporary Poets.* His novels, like his poetry, "offer lyrical descriptions of the urban wasteland or the mood of the day," she wrote. She also maintained in *Contemporary Novelists* that "Alvarez is a writer one wants to read."

BIOGRAPHICAL AND CRITICAL SOURCES:

BOOKS

Alvarez, A., *Where Did It All Go Right?,* Morrow (New York, NY), 1999.

Contemporary Literary Criticism, Thomson Gale (Detroit, MI), Volume 5, 1976, Volume 13, 1980.

Contemporary Novelists, 6th edition, St. James Press (Detroit, MI), 1996.

Contemporary Poets, 6th edition, St. James Press (Detroit, MI), 1996.

Dictionary of Literary Biography, Thomson Gale (Detroit, MI), Volume 14: *British Novelists since 1960,* 1983, Volume 40: *Poets of Great Britain and Ireland since 1960,* 1985.

Fraser, G. S., *The Modern Writer and His World,* Deutsch (London, England), 1964.

Hamilton, Ian, *The Modern Poet,* Macdonald (London, England), 1968, Horizon Press (New York, NY), 1969.

PERIODICALS

Books and Bookmen, April, 1968; June, 1978.

Book World, August 10, 1969; April 25, 1972.

Christian Science Monitor, January 4, 1962; August 2, 1969.

Contemporary Review, July, 1978, review of *Hunt.*

Detroit News, February 14, 1982.

Economist (U.S.), November 13, 1999, "English Writers: Wish Him Well," p. 11.

Guardian, February 24, 1961.

Independent (London, England), September 18, 1999, Michael Schmidt, "Hearts Are Trumps in a Long-Winning Streak," p. 11.

Independent on Sunday (London, England), October 24, 1999, William Scammell, "Been There, Donne That," p. 13.

Insight on the News, April 24, 1995, p. 25.

Listener, February 29, 1968.

London Review of Books, August 24, 2000, Ian Sansom, "What's This?," pp. 19-20.

Los Angeles Times, February 3, 1982.

Los Angeles Times Book Review, April 20, 1986; April 30, 1989.

New Review (London, England), March, 1978.

New Statesman, March 22, 1968; November 19, 1971; April 14, 1978; June 2, 1978; September 27, 1999, Stephen Pile, review of *Where Did It All Go Right?,* p. 85.

New Statesman & Society, February 3, 1995, p. 38.

Newsweek, February 1, 1982.

New Yorker, March 31, 1974.

New York Times, July 5, 1969; April 7, 1972; March 19, 1975; January 30, 1979; January 25, 1982; March 1, 1982; May 6, 1983.

New York Times Book Review, July 20, 1969; August 17, 1969; April 16, 1972; March 30, 1975; June 1, 1975; February 11, 1979; February 1, 1981; January 31, 1982; May 8, 1983; May 18, 1986.

Observer, March 3, 1968; December 20, 1970; May 7, 1978.

Poetry, November, 1959.

Poetry London, spring, 2003, Martin Crucefix, review of *New and Selected Poems.*

Saturday Review, August 2, 1969; April 5, 1975.

Spectator, December 18, 1971.

Sunday Times, July 7, 2002.

Time, February 8, 1982; May 30, 1983.

Times Literary Supplement, May 9, 1958; March 3, 1961; February 29, 1968, November 26, 1971; November 8, 1974; April 21, 1978; June 2, 1978; July 2, 1982; October 10, 1986; July 22, 1988.

Washington Post, July 5, 1986.

Washington Post Book World, February 14, 1982; May 29, 1983; June 25, 1989.

World Literature Today, July-September, 2003, p. 100.

*   *   *

ALVAREZ, Alfred
See ALVAREZ, A.

*   *   *

ALVAREZ, Julia 1950-

PERSONAL: Born March 27, 1950, in New York, NY; married Bill Eichner (a physician and farmer), June 3, 1989. *Education:* Attended Connecticut College, 1967-69; Middlebury College, B.A. (summa cum laude), 1971; Syracuse University, M.F.A., 1975; attended Bread Loaf School of English, 1979-80.

ADDRESSES: Agent—Susan Bergholz Literary Services, 17 West 10th St., No. 5B, New York, NY 10011-8769.

CAREER: Writer and educator. Poet-in-the-Schools in KY, DE, and NC, 1975-78; Phillips Andover Academy, Andover, MA, instructor in English, 1979-81; University of Vermont, Burlington, visiting assistant professor of creative writing, 1981-83; George Washington University, Washington, DC, Jenny McKean Moore Visiting Writer, 1984-85; University of Illinois at Urbana, assistant professor of English, 1986-88; Middlebury College, Middlebury, VT, associate professor, 1988-

1996, professor of English, 1996-98, writer-in-residence, 1998—. Owner of Café Alta Gracia, an organic coffee farm in the Dominican Republic.

MEMBER: PEN (National Members Council, 1997-1999), Sigma Tau Delta (honorary member).

AWARDS, HONORS: Benjamin T. Marshall Poetry Prize, Connecticut College, 1968 and 1969; prize from Academy of American Poetry, 1974; creative writing fellowship, Syracuse University, 1974-75; Kenan grant, Phillips Andover Academy, 1980; poetry award, La Reina Press, 1982; exhibition grant, Vermont Arts Council, 1984-85; Robert Frost Poetry fellowship, Bread Loaf Writers' Conference, 1986; Third Woman Press Award, first prize in narrative, 1986; award for younger writers, General Electric Foundation, 1986; National Endowment for the Arts grant, 1987-88; syndicated fiction prize, PEN, for "Snow"; grant from Ingram Merrill Foundation, 1990; Josephine Miles Award, PEN Oakland, 1991, notable book designation, American Library Association, 1992, and "Twenty-one Classics for the Twenty-first Century" designation, New York Librarians, all for *How the García Girls Lost Their Accents*; notable book designation, 1994, American Library Association; National Book Critics Circle Award finalist, 1995; Best Books for Young Adults designation, 1995, American Library Association, all for *In the Time of the Butterflies*; Jessica Nobel-Maxwell Poetry Prize, 1995, American Poetry Review; Doctor of Humane Letters, City University of New York, John Jay College, 1996; Alumni Achievement Award, 1996, Middlebury College; Dominican Republic Annual Book Fair, 1997, dedicated to Alvarez's body of work; selected "Woman of the Year," *Latina Magazine,* 2000; Sor Juana Award, 2002; Hispanic Heritage Award, Hispanic Heritage Awards Foundation, 2002; Américas Award for Children's and Young Adult Literature, Consortium of Latin American Studies Programs, 2002, and Pura Belpré Award, American Library Association, 2004, both for *Before We Were Free.*

WRITINGS:

NOVELS

How the García Girls Lost Their Accents, Algonquin Books (Chapel Hill, NC), 1991.
In the Time of the Butterflies, Algonquin Books (Chapel Hill, NC), 1994.
¡Yo!, Algonquin Books (Chapel Hill, NC), 1997.
In the Name of Salomé, Algonquin Books (Chapel Hill, NC), 2000.

POETRY

(Editor) *Old Age Ain't for Sissies,* Crane Creek Press (Sanford, NC), 1979.
The Housekeeping Book, illustrations by Carol MacDonald and Rene Schall, Burlington (Burlington, VT), 1984.
Homecoming, Grove Press (New York, NY), 1984, revised edition, Plume (New York, NY), 1996.
The Other Side/El Otro Lado, Dutton (New York, NY), 1995.
Seven Trees, Kat Ran Press (North Andover, MA), 1998.
The Woman I Kept to Myself, Algonquin Books (Chapel Hill, NC), 2004.

OTHER

Something to Declare (essays), Algonquin Books (Chapel Hill, NC), 1998.
The Secret Footprints (picture book), illustrations by Fabian Negrin, Knopf (New York, NY), 2000.
How Tía Lola Came to Stay (juvenile), Knopf (New York, NY), 2001.
A Cafecito Story, Chelsea Green Publishers (White River Junction, VT), 2001, bilingual edition published as *A Cafecito Story/El cuento del cafecito,* Chelsea Green Publishers (White River Junction, VT), 2002.
Before We Were Free (young adult), Knopf (New York, NY), 2002.

Contributor to anthologies, including *The One You Call Sister: New Women's Fiction,* edited by Paula Martinac, Cleis Press (Pittsburgh, PA), 1989; *The Best American Poetry 1991,* edited by David Lehman, Scribner's (New York, NY), 1991; *Poems for a Small Planet: Contemporary American Nature Poetry,* edited by Robert Pack and Jay Parini, Middlebury College Press (Middlebury, VT), 1993; *Mondo Barbie,* edited by Lucinda Ebersole and Richard Peabody, St. Martin's Press (New York, NY), 1993; *Growing up Female: Short Stories by Women Writers from the American Mosaic,* edited by Susan Cahill, Penguin (New York, NY), 1993; *A Formal Feeling Comes: Poems in Form by Contemporary Women,* edited by Annie Finch, Story Line Press, 1994; and *New Writing from the Caribbean,* Macmillan (New York, NY), 1994.

Contributor of fiction to periodicals, including *Caribbean Writer, Commonwoman, Greensboro Review, High Plains Literary Review, Green Mountain Review, New*

Mexico Humanities Review, Story, and *Syracuse Magazine.* Contributor of poetry to periodicals, including *Barataria Review, Burlington Review, Caribbean Writer, Florilegia, George Washington Review, Green Mountain Review, Helicon Nine, Jar, Kentucky Poetry Review, Kenyon Review, Latinos in the U.S. Review, Poetry, Poetry Miscellany, Wind,* and *Womanspirit.* Contributor of translations to *Barataria Review, Bitter Oleander, Pan American Review, Pulse: The Lamar Review,* and *Tower.* Editor of *Special Reports/Ecology,* 1971.

ADAPTATIONS: In the Time of the Butterflies was adapted as a television movie starring Salma Hayek for Showtime in 2001.

WORK IN PROGRESS: Finding Miracles, a young adult novel, for Knopf; *A Gift of Thanks: The Legend of Altagracia,* a picture book, expected 2005.

SIDELIGHTS: Julia Alvarez, who was born in New York City but raised until the age of ten in the Dominican Republic, is a distinguished novelist and poet. Alvarez was forced to flee with her family from the Dominican Republic in 1960 after the discovery of her father's involvement in a plot to overthrow dictator Rafael Trujillo. Since that time she has lived in the United States, but has retained ties to the Dominican Republic and visits the nation frequently. Much of her fiction and poetry can be viewed as semi-autobiographical, dealing both with the immigrant experience and bicultural identity. *Seattle Times* reporter Irene Wanner described Alvarez as "a lyrical writer with passions for individuals, particularly women, who affect history. Her chosen but difficult genre is intensely rewarding."

Alvarez's first book-length work of fiction, *How the García Girls Lost Their Accents,* is often referred to as a novel. Actually, it consists of fifteen interrelated stories detailing the experiences of four sisters and their family both before and after their exile from the Dominican Republic, and their subsequent life in New York City. The book begins with a series of episodes in which the sisters are already Americanized: sex and drugs and mental breakdowns all figure into life as the girls live it in the late 1960s and early 1970s. The book's central portion concerns the difficult periods of adjustment experienced by the García sisters while growing up as immigrants in vast, fast-paced New York City. It closes with a collection of tales recalling the way of life experienced by the sisters while youngsters,

both in the Dominican Republic and as newcomers to the United States. Donna Rifkind, writing in the *New York Times Book Review,* noted that the volume's reverse chronology constitutes "a shrewd idea," and she declared that Alvarez has "beautifully captured the threshold experiences of the new immigrant, where the past is not yet a memory and the future remains an anxious dream." At the same time, Rifkind felt that the depiction of the four sisters' experiences in the United States is less successful and that "Alvarez has not yet quite found a voice." Stephen Henighan in the Toronto *Globe and Mail* characterized *How the García Girls Lost Their Accents* as a "humane, gracefully written novel."

In her second novel, *In the Time of the Butterflies,* Alvarez recalls a grim incident in Dominican history: the untimely deaths in 1960 of three sisters—the Mirabals—who had denounced Rafael Trujillo's dictatorship. Alvarez chooses to portray these events from a subjective fictional perspective rather than as historical biography. According to Roberto Gonzalez Echevarria, writing in the *New York Times Book Review,* "by dealing with real historical figures in this novel, Ms. Alvarez has been much more ambitious than she was in her first, as if she needed to have her American self learn what it was really like in her native land." *In the Time of the Butterflies* is constructed in four sections, one for each of the dead sisters and one for their surviving sibling. It is through the surviving sister that the reader obtains background on the others; she recalls their love affairs and marriages as well as the activist actions that led to their deaths. *Nation* reviewer Ilan Stavans stated that, although Alvarez's subject matter is not unique, "her pen lends it an authenticity and sense of urgency seldom found elsewhere." Stavans went on to deem *In the Time of the Butterflies* "enchanting" and added that the book serves as "a wonderful examination of how it feels to be a survivor." *Progressive* contributor Elizabeth Martinez felt that Alvarez "moves [her] characters forward in the shadow of impending doom, yet never victimizes, never negates human complexity." Although Elsa Walsh noted in the *Washington Post Book World* that *In the Time of the Butterflies* is not without flaws—Trujillo is depicted only as a caricature—she praised the novel as "at once personal and political, both sweet and sweeping in scale."

In Alvarez's third novel, *¡Yo!,* the author returns to the four sisters portrayed in *How the García Girls Lost Their Accents.* The title of the book is a triple-entendre. "Yo" is Spanish for "I"; it is a call for attention, and it is also the nickname of the book's central character, Yolanda García. Like Alvarez herself, Yolanda has become a successful novelist who bases much of her fiction on her own life experiences. However, it is not Yolanda who tells the story in *¡Yo!*, but rather the people who have known her. Each of the sixteen chapters in the novel presents the voice of a different character, including Yolanda's sisters, her parents, a former professor, her husband, a lover, and even an obsessed fan. A *Publishers Weekly* reviewer found *¡Yo!* to be a "splendid sequel" to *How the García Girls Lost Their Accents,* and observed that "Alvarez's command of Latino voices has always been impeccable, but here she is equally adept at conveying the personalities of a geographically diverse group of Americans."

In the Name of Salomé is in many ways Alvarez's most ambitious work of fiction. Based on the historical figures Salomé Ureña and her daughter, Camila, the novel explores the lives of two women dedicated to revolutionary causes and the bond between them that exists despite the mother's early death. Salomé is a Dominican political poet of national stature; Camila is a college professor at Vassar whose ties to the Caribbean are enhanced by her attempts to put her mother's papers in order. The story spans a century, alternating between Salomé's first-person recollections and Camila's third-person, reverse chronological narrative. "It's this long view, this hundred-year reach, that makes *In the Name of Salomé* original and illuminating," maintained Suzanne Ruta in the *New York Times Book Review.* Ruta added that the book, despite its anecdotal nature, "delivers a strong sense of who these people were." In a *Creative Loafing Online* review, Amy Rogers wrote: "*In the Name of Salomé* takes readers on an epic journey from pre-Revolutionary Cuba to the world of academia, from the mid-19th century to the late 20th, and from the political and moral sensibilities that once limited modern women to those that now liberate them. . . . A family saga that imagines the lives of real-life Dominican poet Salomé Ureña and her daughter, Camila Henriquez Ureña, it is a work both dense and deeply layered with intertwining stories." *Christian Science Monitor* contributor Kendra Nordin concluded: "This novel gives the impression of sitting at the feet of an old woman recounting her long life in jumbled order, but with emphasis on important moments, passionate impressions, wisdom learned and shared."

Alvarez's poetry has also received considerable critical attention. *Homecoming* combines a series of poems about the everyday chores of housekeeping with forty-one autobiographical sonnets. "This vivid and engaging collection proves [Alvarez] to be a talented poet," noted Christine Stenstrom in *Library Journal.* Another collection of poetry, *The Other Side/El Otro Lado,* is titled after its centerpiece, a twenty-one-canto poem about Alvarez's residency at a Dominican artists' colony and her experiences with the people she meets in a nearby fishing village. Sandra M. Gilbert, writing in *Poetry,* stated: "A novelist as well as a poet, Alvarez produces memoristic narratives in a range of sometimes quite complex forms along with prose poems, love poems, and elegiac lyrics."

In *The Woman I Kept to Myself,* Alvarez "writes candidly of epic concerns and everyday realities in this unfailingly lucid collection of autobiographical poems," according to Donna Seaman in *Booklist.* Discussing the work on her home page, Alvarez stated, "For me, poetry is that cutting edge of the self, the part which moves out into experience ahead of every other part of the self. It's a way of saying what can't be put into words, our deepest and most secret and yet most universal feelings."

In 2000 Alvarez produced her first work for young readers, a picture book titled *The Secret Footprints.* She followed that with the middle-grade reader *How Tía Lola Came to Stay,* about a young Dominican boy who experiences culture shock when his family moves from New York City to Vermont. In *School Library Journal,* Maria Otero-Boisvert remarked, "Alvarez does an excellent job of capturing the social unease of the child of immigrants who is unsure of where he belongs." *Before We Were Free,* a young adult novel, focuses on the life of Anita, a twelve-year-old girl in the Dominican Republic under the Trujillo regime. When Anita's father is arrested for plotting to overthrow the dictator, the girl and her mother are forced into hiding. According to Lauren Adams in *Horn Book, Before We Were Free,* is "a realistic and compelling account of a girl growing up too quickly while coming to terms with the cost of freedom." For the work, Alvarez received the 2004 Pura Belpré Award.

In her review of *In the Time of the Butterflies,* Walsh declared that the versatile Alvarez has joined "a growing list of ethnic writers breaking into mainstream American literature, but as with the best and most authentic side of diversity, her voice is a universal one." Insisting that "the experience of enduring the disorientations of learning a new culture" informs all of Alvarez's work, *New York Times Book Review* correspondent Christina Cho commended the author for a "graceful fusion of lush imagery and poetic economy."

Alvarez once commented: "I think of myself at ten years old, newly arrived in this country, feeling out of place, feeling that I would never belong in this world of

United States of Americans who were so different from me. Back home in the Dominican Republic, I had been an active, lively child, a bad student full of fun with plentiful friends. In New York City I was suddenly thrown back on myself. I looked around the schoolyard at unfriendly faces. A few of the boys called me a name. I didn't know what it meant, but I knew it couldn't be anything good from the ugly looks on their faces.

"And then, magic happened in my life. I didn't even recognize it as magic until years later: it looked like schoolwork, a writing assignment. An English teacher asked us to write little stories about ourselves. I began to put into words some of what my life had been like in the Dominican Republic. Stories about my gang of cousins and the smell of mangoes and the iridescent, vibrating green of hummingbirds. Since it was my own little world I was making with words, I could put what I wanted in it. I could make things up. If I needed more yellow in that mango, I could put it in. Set amapola blooming in January. Make the sun shine on a cloudy day. If I needed to make a cousin taller, I could make her grow two inches with an adjective so she could reach that ripe yellow mango on the tree. The boys in the schoolyard with ugly looks on their faces were not allowed into this world. I could save what I didn't want to lose—memories and smells and sounds, things too precious to put anywhere else.

"I found myself turning more and more to writing as the one place where I felt I belonged and could make sense of myself, my life, all that was happening to me. I realized that I had lost the island we had come from, but with the words and encouragement of my teacher, I had discovered an even better world: the one words can create in a story or poem. 'Language is the only homeland,' the exiled Polish poet, Czeslaw Milosz, has said. And that was where I landed when we left the Dominican Republic, not in the United States but in the English language."

BIOGRAPHICAL AND CRITICAL SOURCES:

BOOKS

Contemporary Literary Criticism, Volume 93, Thomson Gale (Detroit, MI), 1996.

Dictionary of Hispanic Biography, Thomson Gale (Detroit, MI), 1996.

Dictionary of Literary Biography, Volume 282: *New Formalist Poets,* Thomson Gale (Detroit, MI), 2003.

Encyclopedia of World Biography, 2nd edition, Thomson Gale (Detroit, MI), 1998.

Notable Hispanic American Women, 2nd edition, Thomson Gale (Detroit, MI), 1998.

Novels for Students, Thomson Gale (Detroit, MI), Volume 5, 1999, Volume 9, 2000.

Sirias, Silvio, *Julia Alvarez: A Critical Companion,* Greenwood (Westport, CT), 2001.

PERIODICALS

Americas, March, 1995, Barbara Mujica, review of *In the Time of the Butterflies,* p. 60; January, 2001, Ben Jacques, "Julia Alvarez: Real Flights of Imagination," p. 22, and Barbara Mujica, review of *In the Name of Salomé,* p. 60.

Americas Review, Ibis Gomez-Vega, review of *¡Yo!,* pp. 242-245.

Antioch Review, summer, 1991, review of *How the García Girls Lost Their Accents,* pp. 474-475.

Atlanta Journal-Constitution, March 23, 2003, Teresa K. Weaver, "Books: Writer Alvarez's 'Rays of Light' Sometimes Irritate the Powerful," p. C1.

Belles Lettres, spring, 1995, Janet Jones Hampton, review of *In the Time of the Butterflies,* pp. 6-7.

Bilingual Review, January-April, 2001, Ricardo Castells, "The Silence of Exile in *How the García Girls Lost Their Accents,*" pp. 34-42.

Black Issues Book Review, March, 2001, Milca Esdaille, "Same Trip, Different Ships," p. 40.

Bloomsbury Review, March, 1992, pp. 9-10.

Booklist, July, 1994, Brad Hooper, review of *In the Time of the Butterflies,* p. 1892; September 15, 1996, Brad Hooper, review of *¡Yo!,* p. 180; August, 1998, Donna Seaman, review of *Something to Declare,* p. 1952; March 15, 2000, Veronica Scrol, review of *In the Name of Salomé,* p. 1292; August, 2000, Connie Fletcher, review of *The Secret Footprints,* p. 2143, and Isabel Schon, reviews of *In the Time of the Butterflies* and *¡Yo!,* p. 2154; February 15, 2001, Hazel Rochman, review of *How Tía Lola Came to Stay,* p. 1138; August, 2002, Hazel Rochman, review of *Before We Were Free,* p. 1945; March 1, 2004, Donna Seaman, review of *The Woman I Kept to Myself,* p. 1126.

bookWOMEN, October-November, 2002, "Beyond Words."

Boston Globe, June 28, 2000, Vanessa E. Jones, "Writing Her Book of High Grace."

Callaloo, summer, 2000, William Luis, review of "A Search for Identity in Julia Alvarez's *How the García Girls Lost Their Accents,*" p. 839.

Christian Science Monitor, October 17, 1994, Katherine A. Powers, review of *In the Time of the Butterflies,* p. 13; October 29, 1998, Kendra Nordin, review of *Something to Declare,* p. B7; July 6, 2000, Kendra Nordin, "Recalling the Dreams of a Caribbean Past."

Commonweal, April 10, 1992, review of *How the García Girls Lost Their Accents,* pp. 23-25.

E, May-June, 2002, Starre Vartan, review of *A Cafecito Story,* p. 60.

Entertainment Weekly, August 14, 1992, review of *How the García Girls Lost Their Accents,* p. 56.

Globe and Mail (Toronto), August 31, 1991, p. C6.

Hispanic, June, 1991, David D. Medina, review of *How the García Girls Lost Their Accents,* p. 55; December, 1994, Mary Bats Estrada, review of *In the Time of the Butterflies,* p. 82; March, 1997, Monica Hsu, review of *¡Yo!,* pp. 68-69.

Horn Book, September-October, 2002, Lauren Adams, review of *Before We Were Free,* pp. 563-565.

Intertexts, spring, 1999, Ibis Gomez-Vega, "Hating the Self in the 'Other' or How Yolanda Learns to See Her Own Kind in Julia Alvarez's *How the García Girls Lost Their Accents,*" pp. 85-98.

Journal of Adolescent and Adult Literacy, March, 2003, Susan Carlile, review of *How Tía Lola Came to Stay,* p. 528.

Kirkus Reviews, June 15, 2002, review of *Before We Were Free,* p. 876.

Knight-Ridder/Tribune News Service, August 9, 2000, Mary Ann Horne, review of *In the Name of Salomé,* p. K3161.

Lambda Book Report, October, 2000, Karen Helfrich, "Living in the Shadows," p. 28.

Latin American Literature and Arts Review, Volume 54, 1997, Heather Rosaria-Sievert, "Conversation with Julia Alvarez," pp. 31-37.

Library Journal, May 1, 1991, Ann H. Fisher, review of *How the García Girls Lost Their Accents,* p. 102; April 1, 1996, Christine Stenstrom, review of *Homecoming: New and Selected Poems,* p. 84; October 1, 1996, Janet Ingraham, review of *¡Yo!,* p. 124; August, 1998, Nancy Shires, review of *Something to Declare,* p. 88; July, 1999, review of *¡Yo!,* p. 76; May 1, 2000, Eleanor J. Bader, review of *In the Name of Salomé,* p. 151; September 1, 2000, "Noah's Ark Choices," p. 168; February 15, 2004, Diane Scharper, review of *The Woman I Kept to Myself,* pp. 129-130.

Los Angeles Times, January 20, 1997, p. E3; March 23, 1997, Maria Elena Fernandez, "Two Sides of an American Identity," p. E1.

Los Angeles Times Book Review, February 26, 1995, p. 8.

Melus, spring, 1998, Julie Barak, "'Turning and Turning in the Widening Gyre': A Second Coming into Language in Julia Alvarez's *How the García Girls Lost Their Accents,*" p. 159; winter, 2002, Charlotte Rich, "Talking Back to El Jefe: Genre, Polyphony, and Dialogic Resistance in Julia Alvarez's *In the Time of Butterflies,*" pp. 165-184; winter, 2003, Catherine E. Wall, "Bilingualism and Identity in Julia Alvarez's Poem 'Bilingual Siesta'," pp. 125-144.

Mosaic, June, 2003, Kelli Lyon Johnson, "Both sides of the Massacre: Collective Memory and Narrative on Hispaniola," pp. 75-91.

Ms., September-October, 1994, Ava Roth, review of *In the Time of the Butterflies,* pp. 79-80; March-April, 1997, Julie Phillips, review of *¡Yo!,* p. 82; August-September, 2000, Dylan Siegler, review of *In the Name of Salomé,* p. 85.

Nation, December 30, 1991, pp. 863-864; November 7, 1994, Ilan Stavans, review of *In the Time of the Butterflies,* pp. 552-556.

New England Review & Breadloaf Quarterly, winter, 1986, pp. 231-232.

Newsweek, April 20, 1992, Susan Miller, review of *How the García Girls Lost Their Accents,* p. 78; October 17, 1994, Susan Miller, review of *In the Time of the Butterflies,* pp. 77-78.

New York Times Book Review, October 6, 1991, Donna Rifkind, review of *How the García Girls Lost Their Accents,* p. 14; December 18, 1994, Roberto Gonzalez Echevarria, review of *In the Time of the Butterflies,* p. 28; July 15, 1995, Philip Gambone, review of *The Other Side/El Otro Lado,* p. 20; February 9, 1997, Abby Frucht, review of *¡Yo!,* p. 19; September 20, 1998, Christina Cho, review of *Something to Declare*; July 16, 2000, Suzanne Ruta, "Daughters of Revolution," p. 24; December 2, 2001, Linnea Lannon, review of *How Tía Lola Came to Stay,* p. 83.

New York Times Magazine, March 23, 1997, pp. 67-68.

People Weekly, January 20, 1997, Clare McHugh, review of *¡Yo!,* p. 33; September 21, 1998, Laura Jamison, review of *Something to Declare,* p. 49.

Poetry, August, 1996, p. 285.

Postscript, Volume 16, 1999, Richard Vela, "Daughter of Invention: The Poetry of Julia Alvarez," pp. 33-42.

Prairie Schooner, summer, 2000, Maria Garcia Tabor, "The Truth according to Your Characters," pp. 151-156.

Progressive, July, 1995, p. 39.

Publishers Weekly, April 5, 1991, Sybil Steinberg, review of *How the García Girls Lost Their Accents,* p. 133; July 11, 1994, review of *In the Time of the*

Butterflies, p. 62; April 24, 1995, p. 65; March 18, 1996, review of *Homecoming,* p. 67; October 14, 1996, review of *¡Yo!,* p. 62; December 16, 1996, Jonathan Bing, "Julia Alvarez: Books That Cross Borders," p. 38; May 15, 2000, review of *In the Name of Salomé,* p. 86. April 5, 1991; July 11, 1994; April 24, 1995; March 18, 1996; October 14, 1996; December 16, 1996; July 13, 1998, review of *Something to Declare,* p. 67; September 21, 1998; May 15, 2000; August 14, 2000, review of *The Secret Footprints,* p. 354; February 26, 2001, review of *How Tía Lola Came to Stay,* p. 87; July 22, 2002, review of *Before We Were Free,* p. 180; March 22, 2004, review of *The Woman I Kept to Myself,* p. 82.

Quill and Quire, May, 2000, review of *In the Name of Salomé,* p. 23.

San Francisco Chronicle, February 5, 1997, Patricia Holt, "Reality Continues in Fiction in *Yo,*" p. E1.

School Library Journal, September 1, 1991, Pam Spencer, review of *How the García Girls Lost Their Accents,* p. 292; April, 1997, Dottie Kraft, review of *¡Yo!,* p. 166; April, 1999, Francisca Goldsmith, review of *Something to Declare,* p. 162; September, 2000, Barbara Scotto, review of *The Secret Footprints,* p. 213; April, 2002, Maria Otero-Boisvert, review of *How Tía Lola Came to Stay,* p. S63; August, 2002, Kathleen Isaacs, review of *Before We Were Free,* p. 182.

Seattle Times, July 23, 2000, Irene Wanner, review of *In the Name of Salomé.*

Sojourners, May, 2001, Jim Wallis, review of *In the Name of Salomé,* p. 53.

Tribune Books (Chicago, IL), January 26, 1997, section 14, p. 2.

USA Today Magazine, March, 1999, Steven G. Kellman, review of *Something to Declare,* p. 80.

Washington Post Book World, November 27, 1994, Elsa Walsh, "Arms and the Women," p. 7; January 19, 1997, p. 9; June 11, 2000, Joanne Omang, "Revolutionary Fervor," p. X03.

Women's Review of Books, July, 1991, p. 39; May, 1995, Ruth Behar, review of *In the Time of the Butterflies,* pp. 6-7; November, 1998, Rosellen Brown, review of *Something to Declare,* pp. 7-8; September, 2002, Judith Grossman, "La musa de la patria," p. 5.

Women's Studies, February, 2000, Shara McCallum, "Reclaiming Julia Alvarez: *In the Time of the Butterflies,*" pp. 93-117.

World & I, December, 2000, Linda Simon, "Poetry and Patria: In Her Fourth Novel, Alvarez Explores Personal and Political Exigencies in the Lives of Two Passionate Women," pp. 232-236; November, 2002, Linda Simon, "Mixed Breed—A Profile of Julia Alvarez."

World Literature Today, summer, 1992, review of *How the García Girls Lost Their Accents,* p. 516; autumn, 1995, Kay Pritchett, review of *In the Time of the Butterflies,* p. 789; autumn, 1997, Cynthia Tompkins, review of *¡Yo!,* p. 785; winter, 2001, Fernando Valerio-Holguin, review of *In the Name of Salomé,* p. 113.

ONLINE

Café Alta Gracia Web site, http://www.cafealtagracia. com/ (April 20, 2004).

Creative Loafing Online, http://web.cin.com/ (July 26, 2001), Amy Rogers, "Magical History."

Frontera Magazine, http://www.fronteramag.com/ issue5/ (July 26, 2001), Marny Requa, "The Politics of Fiction."

Julia Alvarez Home Page, http://www.alvarezjulia.com/ (April 10, 2004).

Middlebury College Online, http://www.middlebury. edu/ (April 10, 2004), "Julia Alvarez."

*   *   *

AMADO, Jorge 1912-2001

PERSONAL: Born August 10, 1912, in Itabuna, Bahia, Brazil; died of heart and lung failure, August 6, 2001, in Salvador, Bahia, Brazil; son of Joao Amado de Faria (a plantation owner) and Eulalia (Leal) Amado; married Matilde Garcia Rosa, 1933 (divorced, 1944); married Zelia Gattai, July 14, 1945; children: Joao Jorge, Paloma. *Education:* Federal University of Rio de Janeiro, J.D., 1935. *Hobbies and other interests:* Reading, gardening, cats, poker.

CAREER: Writer. *Diario da Bahia,* Bahai, Brazil, reporter, 1927; imprisoned for political reasons, 1935; exiled, 1937, 1941-43, 1948-52; federal deputy of Brazilian parliament, 1946-48; *Para Todos* (cultural periodical), Rio de Janeiro, Brazil, editor, 1956-59.

MEMBER: Brazilian Association of Writers, Brazilian Academy of Letters.

AWARDS, HONORS: Stalin International Peace Prize, 1951; National Literary Prize (Brazil), 1958; Calouste Gulbenkian Prize, Academie du Monde Latin, 1971; Italian-Latin American Institute Prize, 1976; Nonnino literary Prize (Italy), 1983; candidate for Neustadt International Prize for Literature, 1984; Neruda Prize, and Volterra Prize (Italy), 1989; Sino del Duca Prize (Paris), and Mediterranean Prize, 1990; named commander, Legion d'Honneur (France).

WRITINGS:

IN ENGLISH TRANSLATION

Jubiaba, J. Olympio, 1935, translated by Margaret A. Neves under same title, Avon (New York, NY), 1984.

Mar morto, J. Olympio, 1936, translated by Gregory Rabassa as *Sea of Death,* Avon (New York, NY), 1984.

Capitaes da areia, J. Olympio, 1937, translated by Gregory Rabassa as *Captains of the Sands,* Avon (New York, NY), 1988.

Terras do sem fim, Livraria Martins Editôra (São Paulo, Brazil), 1942, translated by Samuel Putnam as *The Violent Land,* Knopf (New York, NY), 1945, revised edition, 1965.

São Jorge dos Ilheus, Livraria Martins Editôra (São Paulo, Brazil), 1944, translated by Clifford E. Landers as *The Golden Harvest,* Avon (New York, NY), 1992.

Gabriela, cravo e canela, Livraria Martins Editôra (São Paulo, Brazil), 1958, translated by James L. Taylor and William L. Grossman as *Gabriela, Clove, and Cinnamon,* Knopf (New York, NY), 1962.

Os velhos marinheiros, Livraria Martins Editôra (São Paulo, Brazil), 1961, translated by Harriet de Onis as *Home Is the Sailor,* Knopf (New York, NY), 1964.

A morte e a morte de Quincas Berro Dagua, Sociedade dos Cem Bibliofilos do Brasil, 1962, translated by Barbara Shelby as *The Two Deaths of Quincas Wateryell,* Knopf (New York, NY), 1965.

Os pastores da noite, Livraria Martins Editôra (São Paulo, Brazil), 1964, translated by Harriet de Onis as *Shepherds of the Night,* Knopf (New York, NY), 1966.

Dona Flor e seus dois maridos: Historia moral e de amor, Livraria Martins Editôra (São Paulo, Brazil), 1966, translated by Harriet de Onis as *Dona Flor and Her Two Husbands: A Moral and Amorous Tale,* Knopf (New York, NY), 1969.

Tenda dos milagres, Livraria Martins Editôra (São Paulo, Brazil), 1969, translated by Barbara Shelby as *Tent of Miracles,* Knopf (New York, NY), 1971, with introduction by Ilan Stavans, University of Wisconsin Press (Madison, WI), 2003.

Bahia (bilingual Portuguese-English edition), Graficos Brunner, 1971.

Tereza Batista cansada de guerra, Livraria Martins Editôra (São Paulo, Brazil), 1972, translated by Barbara Shelby as *Tereza Batista: Home from the Wars,* Knopf (New York, NY), 1975.

O gato malhado e a andorinha Sinha, Editora Record (Rio de Janeiro, Brazil), 1976, translated by Barbara Shelby Merello as *The Swallow and the Tom Cat: A Love Story,* Delacorte (New York, NY), 1982.

Tieta do agreste, pastora de cabras; ou, A volta da filha prodiga: Melodramatico folhetim em cinco sensacionais episodios e comovente epilogo, emoçáo e suspense!, Editora Record (Rio de Janeiro, Brazil), 1977, translated by Barbara Shelby Merello as *Tieta, the Goat Girl; or, The Return of the Prodigal Daughter: Melodramatic Serial Novel in Five Sensational Episodes, with a Touching Epilogue, Thrills, and Suspense!,* Knopf (New York, NY), 1979, with introduction by Moacyr Scliar, University of Wisconsin Press (Madison, WI), 2003.

Farda, fardao, camisola de dormir: Fabula para acender uma esperanca, Editora Record (Rio de Janeiro, Brazil), 1979, translated by Helen R. Lane as *Pen, Sword, Camisole: A Fable to Kindle a Hope,* D.R. Godine (Boston, MA), 1985.

The Miracle of the Birds, Targ Editions, 1982.

Tocaia grande, Editora Record (Rio de Janeiro, Brazil), 1984, translated by Gregory Rabassa as *Showdown,* Bantam (New York, NY), 1988.

O sumiço da santa: Uma história de feitiçaria, Editora Record (Rio de Janeiro, Brazil), 1988, translated by Gregory Rabassa as *The War of the Saints,* Bantam (New York, NY), 1993.

OTHER

O pais do carnaval (title means "Carnival Land"; also see below), Schmidt, 1932.

Suor (title means "Sweat"; also see below), [Brazil], 1933, 2nd edition, J. Olympio, 1936.

Cacau (title means "Cocoa"; also see below), [Brazil], 1934, 3rd edition, J. Olympio, 1936.

A B C de Castro Alves (title means "The Life of Castro Alves"), Livraria Martins Editôra (São Paulo, Brazil), 1941.

Vida de Luiz Carlos Prestes, o cavaleiro da esperanca (title means "The Life of Luiz Carlos Prestes"), Livraria Martins Editôra (São Paulo, Brazil), 1942.

O pais do carnaval; Cacau; Suor, Livraria Martins Editôra (São Paulo, Brazil), 1944.

Obras (collected works), seventeen volumes, Livraria Martins Editôra (São Paulo, Brazil), beginning 1944.

Bahia de Todos os Santos: Guia das ruas e dos misterios da cidade do Salvador (title means "Bahia: A Guide to the Streets and Mysteries of Salvador"), Livraria Martins Editôra (São Paulo, Brazil), 1945.

Seara vermelha (title means "Red Harvest"), Livraria Martins Editôra (São Paulo, Brazil), 1946.

Homens e coisas do Partido Comunista (title means "Men and Facts of the Communist Party"), Ediçoes Horizonte, 1946.

O amor de Castro Alves (title means "Castro Alves's Love"), Ediçoes do Povo, 1947, published as *O amor do soldado* (title means "The Soldier's Love"), Livraria Martins Editôra (São Paulo, Brazil), 1958.

O mundo da paz: Uniao Sovietica e democracias populares (title means "The World of Peace: The Soviet Union and Popular Democracies"), Editorial Vitoria, 1952.

Os subterraneos da liberdade (title means "The Subterraneans of Freedom"; contains "Os asperos tempos," "Agonia da noite," and "A luz no tunel"), Livraria Martins Editôra (São Paulo, Brazil), 1954, essays published separately, 1961–1963.

Jorge Amado: Trinta años de literatura (title means "Jorge Amado: Thirty Years of Literature"), Livraria Martins Editôra (São Paulo, Brazil), 1961.

O poeta Ze Trindade (title means "Ze Trindade: A Poet"), J. Ozon, 1965.

Bahia boa terra Bahia (title means "Bahia Sweet Land"), Image (Rio de Janeiro, Brazil), 1967.

O compadre de Ogun, Sociedade dos Cem Bibliofilos do Brasil, 1969.

Jorge Amado, povo e terra: Quarenta anos de literatura (title means "Jorge Amado, His Land and People: Forty Years of Literature"), Livraria Martins Editôra (São Paulo, Brazil), 1972.

(With others) *Brandao entre o mar e o amor* (title means "Swinging between Love and Sea"), Livraria Martins Editôra (São Paulo, Brazil), 1973.

(With others) *Gente boa* (title means "The Good People"), Editora Brasilial (Rio de Janeiro, Brazil), 1975.

(With Luis Viana Filho and Jeanine Warnod) *Porto Seguro recriado por Sergio Telles* (title means "Porto Seguro in the Painting of Sergio Telles"), Bolsa de Arte (Rio de Janeiro, Brazil), 1976.

Conheca o escritor brasileiro Jorge Amado: Textos para estudantes com exercicios de compreensão e dabate (title means "Know the Writer Jorge Amado: Texts for Students"), edited by Lygia Marina Moraes, Editora Record (Rio de Janeiro, Brazil), 1977.

O menino grapiuna, Editora Record (Rio de Janeiro, Brazil), 1981.

A bola e o goleiro, Editora Record (Rio de Janeiro, Brazil), 1984.

Conversaciones con Alice Raillard, Emece Editores, 1992.

Navegacao de cabotagem: Apontamentos para um livro de memorias que jamais escreverei, Editora Record (Rio de Janeiro, Brazil), 1992.

Discursos, Fundáçáo Casa de Jorge Amado (Salvador, Brazil), 1993.

A descoberta da América pelos turcos: Romancinho, illustrated by Pedro Costa, Editora Record (Rio de Janeiro, Brazil), 1994.

Bahia amada Amado, ou, O amor à liberdade y à liberdade no amor, edited by Maureen Bisilliat, Empresa das Artes (Sao Paulo, Brazil), 1996.

(With Arnaldo Jabor and Roberto Damatta) *Carnaval,* photographs by Claudio Edinger, Dórea Books and Art (São Paulo, Brazil), 1996, Distributed Art Publishers, 1997.

(With Antonio Riserio and Renato Pinagiro) *Mágica bajia* (bilingual Portuguese-Spanish text), Fundáçáo Casa de Jorge Amado (Salvador, Brazil), 1997.

O Milagre dos pássaros, Editora Record (Rio de Janeiro, Brazil), 1997.

(With Gilberbert Chaves and Paloma Jorge Amado Costa) *Rua Alagoinhas 33, Rio Vermelho: A Casa de Zélia e Jorge Amado,* Fundação Casa de Jorge Amado (Savador, Brazil), 1999.

(Author of text with Padre Antonio Vieira and Wilson Rocha) *Salvador,* edited, with photographs by Mario Cravo Neto, Aries Editorial (Salvador, Brazil), 1999.

Author's works have been translated into French, Spanish, Russian, and numerous other languages.

ADAPTATIONS: Gabriela, Clove, and Cinnamon was adapted for film as *Gabriela,* Metro-Goldwyn-Mayer/ United Artists, 1984; *Dona Flor and Her Two Husbands: A Moral and Amorous Tale* was adapted for the stage as *Sarava.*

SIDELIGHTS: Ranked by some critics as Brazil's greatest twentieth-century novelist, Jorge Amado certainly was the most widely read. His depictions of the social, political, and cultural aspects of Brazil's northwestern Bahia region have been translated into as many as fifty languages. Amado wrote with the eye of a social realist; his early work was politically inflammatory and evoked a poverty-stricken land afflicted by brutal government management. In his later novels Amado mellowed his political approach—still depicting the underclass, but with informed compassion and humor.

Amado was born the son of immigrant farmers on a cacao plantation in southern Bahia. When he was old enough to work, he spent his summer holidays toiling in the cacao groves with other area laborers. These early episodes among Brazil's impoverished proved an invaluable learning experience for Amado and provided a foundation for much of his writing. In an interview with Berta Sichel for *Américas,* he once elaborated on the importance these people hold for him and his work: "I am a writer who basically deals with social themes, since the source material for my creation is Brazilian reality. . . . [Many of my] novels narrate the life of the people, everyday life, the struggle against extreme poverty, against hunger, the large estates, racial prejudice, backwardness, underdevelopment. The hero of my novels is the Brazilian people. My characters are the most destitute, the most needy, the most oppressed—country and city people without any power other than the strength of the mestizo people of Brazil. They say that I am a novelist of whores and vagabonds, and there is truth in that, for my characters increasingly are antiheroes. I believe that only the people struggle selflessly and decently, without hidden motives."

Appreciating Amado's concern for social realism requires an understanding of the sociopolitical climate in which he first began to write. Following a global economic crisis that had shattered the coffee industry and forced an unprecedented number of Brazilians into poverty, Brazil's 1930 presidential election was rife with revolution. When liberal challenger Getulio Vargas met with apparent defeat, he headed an armed rebellion against the state—gaining control of civilian and military establishments, dissolving the congress, and issuing a decree of absolute power for his government. Initially, the overthrow of the old order produced a renaissance of sorts among Brazil's writers. Vargas had championed achievement and reform, and the writers were quick to adopt this spirit of social renewal. The new critical literature of Brazil lay bare the squalor of its lower classes and offered solutions for a nation restless for change.

Amado's early novels, often termed works of social protest, were published amid these turbulent times. *O pais do carnaval, Suor,* and *Cacau,* all written during the early 1930s, depict a destitute and violent Brazil and offer answers to many of the prevailing social problems. For many critics though, these early works hold little literary merit. In his assessment of this first phase

in Amado's literary career, Fred P. Ellison wrote in *Brazil's New Novel: Four Northeastern Masters,* "Character, plot, and literary form are consistently neglected. . . . In fact, there is reason to believe that Amado purposely slighted artistic qualities in attempting to draft social documents."

If Amado was indeed attempting to affect social change, he was not alone. As nationwide impatience with the economic plight grew, Vargas's support waned. Several political factions—notably the Communist Party and the fascist Integralistas—began to exert a marked influence among Brazilians. In 1935 a short-lived rebellion broke out, and Vargas subsequently declared martial law. Communists and others labeled seditionists were hunted down relentlessly, and a censorship department was created to suppress all forms of dissent. Amado's inflammatory early novels, though given little regard by critics, attracted the suspicious eye of the Vargas regime. Their author was imprisoned as a member of the Communist Party in 1935, exiled on several later occasions, and, in 1937 following a national ban, two thousand of his books were burned in a plaza by the Brazilian military.

The Vargas crackdown did not silence the writer's call for reform so much as alter his form of protest. Starting with his 1935 book *Jubiaba,* Amado began to display a greater concern for technique, often cloaking social themes within psychological studies. This new style found its greatest success in *Terras do sem fin (The Violent Land).* Published in 1942, *The Violent Land* depicts the brutal land-battles that ensue when two neighboring estates rush for the last, precious cacao groves in northern Brazil. Bertram D. Wolfe noted similarities between the Brazilian power wars Amado characterized in *The Violent Land* and those that took place during the expansion of the American West. He wrote in the *New York Herald Tribune Weekly Book Review:* "To the raw violence and action of one of our gold-rush, claim-jumping, frontier tales, this novel adds an exuberant, tropical lyricism. . . . It is one of the most important novels to have come North in some time, and, because of its frontier character and crowded action, one of the most accessible to the American reader." Ellison termed the book "Amado's masterpiece, a story of almost epic grandeur," and attributed its success to Amado's avoidance of the propaganda in his earlier work: *"The Violent Land* shows what Amado can achieve when art is not encumbered with the millstone of political argument." Although Amado continued for several years to write novels of social realism, none ever earned the literary acclaim given *The Violent Land.*

In 1958, with the publication of *Gabriela, cravo e canela (Gabriela, Clove, and Cinnamon),* Amado's writing took another significant shift. As in his earlier work, the underclasses of Brazil's Bahia region continued to dominate Amado's novels. Beginning with *Gabriela,* however, the examination of their afflictions gave way to romantic and humorous themes. In the *New York Times Book Review,* Juan de Onis attributed this shift in tone to Amado's alignment with the contemporary European rejection of Communism. "*Gabriela,*" Onis wrote, "represents undoubtedly the artistic liberation of Senhor Amado from a long period of ideological commitment to Communist orthodoxy."

Gabriela, cravo e canela is named for a spirited migrant worker who is discovered by an Ilheus bar owner and elevated to social respectability. Gabriela's healthy sexual appetite is instrumental in liberating the growing Bahian town from its restrictive social values. For most critics, Amado's foray into the lighter side of Brazilian life proved highly successful. "It is in *Gabriela* that [Amado] really finds himself," wrote Harriet de Onis in the *Saturday Review.* "One hardly knows what to admire most: the dexterity with which Amado can keep half a dozen plots spinning; the gossamer texture of the writing; or his humor, tenderness, and humanity." Onis described Amado's stylistic evolution thusly: "In his earlier novels on the cacao region, . . . Amado tended to paint caricatures rather than characters. . . . In striking contrast to these flat symbols, the characters in *Gabriela* are created in-the-round; they live, breathe and feel as genuine individuals—and none more so than Gabriela herself." The critic also noticed a change in the tone of Amado's writing. For example, the earlier novel *The Violent Land,* wrote Onis, "is spun out with grim, humorless indignation. In *Gabriela,* however, irony, satire and plain high spirits illuminate every page."

With the critical acclaim that Amado's new style attracted came a growing popularity. The 1960s found him enjoying best-seller status with several novels, notably *Dona Flor e seus dois maridos* (*Dona Flor and Her Two Husbands*). Like most of Amado's later novels, *Dona Flor* blends elements of burlesque with the surreal. Critic David Gallagher granted credit for the success of this strange brew to Amado's convincing characters. "*Dona Flor and Her Two Husbands* is a remarkable novel for the coolness with which the author is able to impose his extraordinary characters on us," Gallagher wrote in the *New York Times Book Review.* "Like them, we learn to take exoticism and magic in our stride."

The novel presents the life of the virtuous Dona Flor who, after her disreputable first husband dies in drunken revelry, weds an upstanding and meticulous pharmacist.

When the ghost of her first husband appears—with his exceptional lovemaking skills still effective on Dona Flor—she is ambivalent about her dilemma. She appreciates the security that her new husband provides but longs for his predecessor's passion. A *Time* magazine critic charged *Dona Flor* with overblown sentimentalism, calling the book "a love letter to Bahia." The reviewer claimed that Amado "romanticizes his Bahians into virile lovers, darkly sensual *morenas* [women], whores and neighbors, all larger than life. . . . In lavishing details of color, touch and taste, Amado so ignores the canons of construction that at times he seems embarked on little more than an engaging shaggy-dog story." Gallagher held a similar opinion of Amado's prose: "It is a pity that Amado mars his achievement by often writing flatly, without discipline or tension. His refreshing exuberance is diminished by the novel's almost aggressive repetitiveness. Cut to half its size, it would have been a better book."

Amado continued to produce international best-sellers despite such charges of prosaic deficiency and claims that machismo elements dominated his later work; in *Myth and Ideology in Contemporary Brazilian Fiction,* Daphne Patai criticized the author for his "evident commitment to the status quo in that most fundamental of issues: men's domination of women." His 1984 work *Tocaia grande,* translated as *Showdown,* was no exception. Tracing the lively history of a town founded on the Brazilian frontier, the novel proves to be an epic patchwork of the nation's heritage. "*Showdown* is a second look at the terrain Amado covered in *The Violent Land,*" commented Pat Aufderheide in the *Washington Post Book World.* "It has the plot drive that has kept people reading the latest Amado novel all these years; it's loaded with sex and violence; and the picaresque characters all share their inner lives with the reader through Amado's omniscient narration." Paul West, writing in the *New York Times Book Review,* called *Showdown* "a vital novel, more complex than it seems at first, written in a long series of ebullient lunges, none of them stylish or notably elegant or eloquent, but in sum haunting and massive. . . . [Amado] creates something fecund and funny, tender and burly, as if his lively social conscience, under pressure, . . . yet again had to take the side of the human race."

Through the 1990s to his death in 2001, Bahia's leading literary authority continually painted a lyrical image of his homeland, aggrandizing Brazil's downtrodden in rollicking tales of passion and mystique. Two of his later novels, *Tent of Miracles* and *Tieta, the Goat Girl; or, The Return of the Prodigal Daughter,* were reprinted in honor of the writer, and "continue his undying concern for the future of Brazil," according to Sophia A. McClennen in *Review of Contemporary Fiction.* "Rich in narrative structure and remarkable in the description of Brazilian plenitude, these novels are smart, witty, and fun," McClennen continued, adding that the fictions characterize Amado's transition, after the mid-twentieth century, "from more overtly political narrative to writing that was full of excess, sensual delight, and the richness of everyday life."

In summation of Amado's writing, Ellison wrote: "In the works of this most controversial of modern Brazilian writers, unevenness is the salient characteristic. Amado seems to write solely by instinct. Of conscious art intellectually arrived at, the result of reflection and high craftsmanship, there is relatively little. Yet his novels have a mysterious power to sweep the reader along. Serious defects in artistry are overcome by the novelist's ability to weave a story, to construct vivid scenes, and to create fascinating characters." In his interview with Sichel, Amado once revealed the source of his inspiration: "I consider myself to be a writer with a commitment, a writer who is for the people and against their enemies, who develops his work around the reality of Brazil, discussing the country's problems, touching on the dramatic existence of the people and their struggle."

BIOGRAPHICAL AND CRITICAL SOURCES:

BOOKS

Chamberlain, Bobby J., *Jorge Amado,* Twayne (New York, NY), 1990.

Contemporary Literary Criticism, Thomson Gale (Detroit, MI), Volume 13, 1980, Volume 40, 1986, Volume 106, 1998.

Curran, Mark J., *Jorge Amado e a literature de cordel,* Fundaçáo Cultural do Estado da Bahia, 1981.

Dictionary of Literary Biography, Volume 113: *Modern Latin-American Fiction Writers,* Thomson Gale (Detroit, MI), 1992.

Ellison, Fred P., *Brazil's New Novel: Four Northeastern Masters,* University of California Press (Berkeley, CA), 1954.

Patai, Daphne, *Myth and Ideology in Contemporary Brazilian Fiction,* Fairleigh Dickinson University Press (Rutherford, NJ), 1983.

Peden, Margaret Sayers, editor, *The Latin American Short Story: A Critical History,* Twayne (Boston, MA), 1983.

Tati, Miecio, *Amado: Vida e obra,* Itatiaia, 1960.

Tavares, Paulo, *O baiano Jorge Amado e sua obra,* Record (Rio de Janeiro, Brazil), 1985.

PERIODICALS

Américas, May-June, 1984; September-October, 1992, p. 60.

Booklist, August, 1992, 1993; September 15, 1993, p. 100.

Book World, August 24, 1969.

Hispania, May, 1968; September, 1978.

Kirkus Reviews, October 15, 1993.

Library Journal, August, 1992, p. 144; December, 1993.

Los Angeles Times Book Review, February 28, 1988; March 27, 1988.

Nation, June 5, 1967.

New York Review of Books, May 4, 1967; February 26, 1970.

New York Times, October 1, 1977; January 12, 1985; January 24, 1988.

New York Times Book Review, September 16, 1962; November 28, 1965; January 22, 1967; August 17, 1969; October 24, 1971; September 21, 1975; July 1, 1979; October 28, 1984; May 19, 1985; February 7, 1988; November 28, 1993, p. 20.

Publishers Weekly, November 21, 1980.

Review of Contemporary Fiction, spring, 2004, Sophia A. McClennen, review of *Tent of Miracles,* p. 143.

Saturday Review, September 15, 1962; January 8, 1966; February 4, 1967; August 16, 1969; August 28, 1971.

Times Literary Supplement, July 2, 1970; October 2, 1981; November 12, 1982; January 20-26, 1989.

Tribune Books (Chicago, IL), September 9, 1979; January 24, 1988.

Variety, March 31, 1997, Bill Hinchberger, "Jorge Amado Writes from Heart, Home," p. 56.

Washington Post, December 29, 1984.

Washington Post Book World, September 12, 1971; January 10, 1988.

World Literature Today, winter, 1996, Nelson H. Vieira, review of *A descoberta da América pelos turcos: Romancinho,* p. 173.

OBITUARIES:

PERIODICALS

Chicago Tribune, August 7, 2001, section 2, p. 8.

Los Angeles Times, August 8, 2001, p. B10.

Time, August 20, 2001, p. 13.
Times (London, England), August 8, 2001.
New York Times, August 7, 2001, p. A15.
Washington Post, August 8, 2001, p. B6.

*   *   *

AMBROSE, Stephen E. 1936-2002
(Stephen Edward Ambrose)

PERSONAL: Born January 10, 1936, in Decatur, IL; died of lung cancer, October 13, 2002, in Bay Saint Louis, MS; son of Stephen Hedges (a family physician) and Rosepha (Trippe) Ambrose; married Judith Dorlester, 1957 (died, 1966); married Moira Buckley, 1967; children: (first marriage) Stephanie (Tubbs), Barry Halleck; (adopted) Andrew, Grace, Hugh. *Ethnicity:* "English." *Education:* University of Wisconsin, B.S., 1957, Ph.D., 1963; Louisiana State University, M.A., 1958. *Politics:* Republican. *Religion:* Congregationalist.

CAREER: Louisiana State University, New Orleans, (now University of New Orleans), assistant professor, 1960-64, professor, 1971-89, Alumni Distinguished Professor of History, 1982-95, Boyd Professor of History, 1989-95, professor emeritus, 1995-2002; Johns Hopkins University, Baltimore, MD, associate professor of history, 1964-69; U.S. Naval War College, Newport, RI, Ernest J. King Professor of Maritime History, 1969-70; Kansas State University, Manhattan, KS, Dwight D. Eisenhower Professor of War and Peace, 1970-71; founder of Eisenhower Center, 1983, director, 1983-95, director emeritus, 1995-2002; founder and president of National D-Day Museum, New Orleans, 2000-02. Visiting assistant professor, Louisiana State University, Baton Rouge, 1963-64; Mary Ball Washington Professor, University College, Dublin, Ireland, 1981-82; visiting professor, University of California, Berkeley, 1986; Howard Johnson Visiting Professor of Military History, Army War College, 1989; senior fellow, Rutgers Center for Historic Analysis, 1993. Interviewee on television documentary *Lewis & Clark: The Journey of the Corps of Discovery,* produced by Ken Burns and Dayton Duncan, 1997. Historical consultant on feature film *Saving Private Ryan,* directed by Steven Spielberg, 1998. *Military service:* Reserve Officer Training Corps.

MEMBER: American Committee on World War II (member, board of directors), American Historical Association, American Military Institute (member, board of directors; member, board of trustees, 1971-74), Organization of American Historians, Conference on History of Second World War (member of American Committee), SANE (member, board of directors), Society for American Historians of Foreign Relations, Southern Historical Association, Lewis and Clark Heritage Trail Foundation (member, board of directors), Big Blue Athletic Association, Chi Psi.

AWARDS, HONORS: Freedom Foundation National Book Award, for *Eisenhower: Soldier, General of the Army, President-Elect, 1890-1952.*

WRITINGS:

Halleck: Lincoln's Chief of Staff, Louisiana State University Press (Baton Rouge, LA), 1962.
Upton and the Army, Louisiana State University Press (Baton Rouge, LA), 1964.
Duty, Honor, and Country: A History of West Point, Johns Hopkins Press (Baltimore, MD), 1966.
Eisenhower and Berlin, 1945: The Decision to Halt at the Elbe, Norton (New York, NY), 1967, reprinted, 2000.
The Supreme Commander: The War Years of General Dwight D. Eisenhower, Doubleday (New York, NY), 1970.
Rise to Globalism: American Foreign Policy since 1938, Penguin (New York, NY), 1971, 8th edition (with Douglas G. Brinkley), 1997.
General Ike: Abeline to Berlin (for children), Harper (New York, NY), 1973.
Crazy Horse and Custer: The Parallel Lives of Two American Warriors, illustrations by Kenneth Francis Dewey, Doubleday (New York, NY), 1975.
(With Richard H. Immerman) *Ike's Spies: Eisenhower and the Espionage Establishment,* Doubleday (New York, NY), 1981.
(With Richard H. Immerman) *Milton S. Eisenhower: Educational Statesman,* Johns Hopkins University Press (Baltimore, MD), 1983.
Eisenhower: Soldier, General of the Army, President-Elect, 1890-1952 (Book of the Month Club choice; also see below), Simon & Schuster (New York, NY), 1983, abridged version published as *Eisenhower: Soldier and President,* 1990.
Eisenhower: The President (also see below), Simon & Schuster (New York, NY), 1984.
Pegasus Bridge: 6 June 1944, Allen & Unwin (London, England), 1984, Simon & Schuster (New York, NY), 1985.
(Author of introduction) *Hitler's Mistakes,* Morrow (New York, NY), 1987.

Nixon: The Education of a Politician, 1913-1962, Simon & Schuster (New York, NY), 1987.

Nixon: The Triumph of a Politician, 1962-1972 (Book of the Month Club alternate), Simon & Schuster (New York, NY), 1989.

(Author of introduction) *Handbook on German Military Forces,* Louisiana State University Press (Baton Rouge, LA), 1990.

Nixon: The Ruin and Recovery of a Politician, 1973-1990, Simon & Schuster (New York, NY), 1991.

Band of Brothers: E Company, 506th Regiment, 101st Airborne, from Normandy to Hitler's Eagle's Nest, Simon & Schuster (New York, NY), 1992, 2001.

D-Day, June 6, 1944: The Climactic Battle of World War II, Simon & Schuster (New York, NY), 1994.

Undaunted Courage: Meriwether Lewis, Thomas Jefferson, and the Opening of the American West, Simon & Schuster (New York, NY), 1996.

Americans at War (essays), University Press of Mississippi (Jackson, MS), 1997.

Citizen Soldiers: The U.S. Army from the Normandy Beaches to the Bulge to the Surrender of Germany, Simon & Schuster (New York, NY), 1997.

The Victors: Eisenhower and His Boys—The Men of World War II, Simon & Schuster (New York, NY), 1998.

Lewis & Clark: Voyage of Discovery, photographs by Sam Abell, National Geographic Society (Washington, DC), 1998.

Comrades: Brothers, Fathers, Heroes, Sons, Pals, illustrated by Jon Friedman, Simon & Schuster (New York, NY), 1999.

Nothing like It in the World: The Men Who Built the Transcontinental Railroad, 1863-1869, Simon & Schuster (New York, NY), 2000.

The Good Fight: How World War II Was Won, Atheneum (New York, NY), 2001.

The Wild Blue: The Men and Boys Who Flew the B-24s over Germany, Simon & Schuster (New York, NY), 2001.

To America: Personal Reflections of an Historian, Simon & Schuster (New York, NY), 2002.

(With Douglas E. Brinkley) *The Mississippi and the Making of a Nation: From the Louisiana Purchase to Today,* photography by Sam Abell, National Geographic (Washington, DC), 2002.

This Vast Land: A Young Man's Journal of the Lewis and Clark Expedition, Simon & Schuster (New York, NY), 2003.

EDITOR

A Wisconsin Boy in Dixie, University of Wisconsin Press (Madison, WI), 1961.

Institutions in Modern America: Innovation in Structure and Process, Johns Hopkins Press (Baltimore, MD), 1967.

(Assistant editor) Alfred Chandler, editor, *The Papers of Dwight David Eisenhower: The War Years,* five volumes, Johns Hopkins Press (Baltimore, MD), 1970.

(With James A. Barber, Jr.) *The Military and American Society,* Free Press (New York, NY), 1972.

Dwight D. Eisenhower, *The Wisdom of Dwight D. Eisenhower: Quotations from Ike's Speeches and Writings, 1939-1969,* Eisenhower Center, 1990.

(With Gunter Bischof) *Eisenhower and the German POWs: Facts against Falsehood,* Louisiana State University Press (Baton Rouge, LA), 1992.

C.L. Sulzberger, *American Heritage New History of World War II,* revised version, Viking (New York, NY), 1997.

(With Douglas G. Brinkley) *Witness to America: An Illustrated Documentary History of the United States from the Revolution to Today,* HarperCollins (New York, NY), 1999.

OTHER

Author of television documentary, *Eisenhower: Supreme Commander,* British Broadcasting Corporation, 1973. Author of biweekly column, *Baltimore Evening Sun,* beginning 1968. Contributor to *The Harry S. Truman Encyclopedia,* edited by Richard S. Kirkendall, G.K. Hall, 1989; *What If? The World's Foremost Military Historians Imagine What Might Have Been: Essays,* edited by Robert Cowley, Putnam, 1999; and *No End Save Victory: Perspectives on World War II,* edited by Robert Cowley, Putnam, 2001. Authenticator, *New Standard Encyclopedia,* 1994. Contributor of reviews and articles to numerous journals and newspapers, including *American Heritage, American History Illustrated, American Historical Review, Foreign Affairs, Harvard Magazine, Historic New Orleans Collection Quarterly, Journal of Contemporary History, Times Literary Supplement, New York Times Book Review, Prologue: Quarterly of the National Archives, Quarterly Journal of Military History,* and *U.S. News and World Report.* Contributing editor of *Quarterly Journal of Military History.* Member of board of editors of *Military Affairs.*

Duty, Honor, and Country: A History of West Point has been translated into Spanish; *Eisenhower: The President, Eisenhower: Soldier, General of the Army, President-Elect, 1890-1952,* and *Pegasus Bridge: 6 June 1944,* have been translated into French; *Crazy Horse and Custer: The Parallel Lives of Two American War-*

riors has been translated into German and Italian; *The Supreme Commander: The War Years of General Dwight D. Eisenhower* has been translated into Norwegian, Spanish, and Romanian; *Eisenhower: Soldier and President* has been translated into French, German, and Russian; and *Rise to Globalism: American Foreign Policy since 1938* has been translated into Arabic, Norwegian, Romanian, Spanish, and Turkish. An abridged edition of *Ike's Spies: Eisenhower and the Espionage Establishment* was translated into French and published under the title *Les Services Secrets d'Eisenhower.*

ADAPTATIONS: Band of Brothers was adapted for a ten-part Home Box Office (HBO) miniseries, 2001.

SIDELIGHTS: Stephen E. Ambrose was a "military historian and biographer whose books recounting the combat feats of American soldiers and airmen fueled a national fascination with the generation that fought World War II," according to *New York Times* writer Richard Goldstein. Historian and biographer, Ambrose wrote about generals, presidents, explorers, major military battles, railroads, and foreign policy in his three dozen books, always demonstrating an uncommon ability to bring history and historical actors to vivid life. Ambrose had already had a productive and distinguished career as an author when events of the late 1990s increased his fame. *Undaunted Courage: Meriwether Lewis, Thomas Jefferson, and the Opening of the American West* became a best-seller, and Ambrose served as a historical consultant on Steven Spielberg's 1998 film, *Saving Private Ryan.*

Ambrose, who retired in 1995 from a professorship at the University of New Orleans, was also well known for his multi-volume biographies of presidents Dwight D. Eisenhower and Richard M. Nixon. Ambrose labored for nearly twenty years on the Eisenhower volumes and ten years on the Nixon volumes, both times with results that critics praised for their meticulous research and balance. Unfortunately, toward the end of his life, Ambrose's success was somewhat eclipsed by accusations of plagiarism in his 2001 book *The Wild Blue: The Men and Boys Who Flew the B-24s over Germany.* Although he survived the scandal by saying he had properly footnoted the passages, Ambrose did not escape being grouped with several other academics accused of plagiarism in a rash of scandals in academia during that same time. Nevertheless, he continued to be praised for his role in helping to popularize the study of World War II in America. He died in 2002 from lung cancer; the posthumous *This Vast Land: A Young Man's Journal of the Lewis and Clark Expedition* was published in 2003.

Ambrose grew up in Whitewater, Wisconsin. A high-school football captain and prom king, he went to the University of Wisconsin in Madison, where he decided to major in history. After earning his B.A. in 1957, Ambrose moved on to a master's degree program at Louisiana State University, and then returned to the University of Wisconsin to earn a Ph.D. in history in 1963. During graduate school Ambrose published a biography of General Henry Halleck, who had served as chief of staff to President Abraham Lincoln. A few years later, while Ambrose was working as an assistant professor at Louisiana State University, he received a phone call from an admirer of the book. The caller was former President Dwight D. Eisenhower.

"I was flabbergasted," Ambrose once told *New York Times Book Review* contributor Herbert Mitgang. President Eisenhower told Ambrose that he liked the author's book, had thought about writing a work on Halleck himself, and invited Ambrose to come to his Gettysburg, Pennsylvania, home to talk; he also asked Ambrose if he would be interested in working on the Eisenhower papers. Ambrose recalled: "I told him, 'General, I'd prefer to write your biography.' He replied, 'I'd like to have you any way I can.'" So began Ambrose's long association with the life and career of President Eisenhower, an association that allowed him to produce a multi-volume set of edited papers; a biography of Milton S. Eisenhower, the president's brother; two books on Eisenhower's military career, *Eisenhower and Berlin, 1945: The Decision to Halt at the Elbe* and *The Supreme Commander: Eisenhower;* an analysis of Eisenhower's relationship with the espionage community; and a two-volume biography.

In the introduction to *Eisenhower: Soldier, General of the Army, President-Elect, 1890-1952,* Ambrose describes Eisenhower as "decisive, well disciplined, courageous, dedicated . . . intensely curious about people and places, often refreshingly naive, fun-loving—in short a wonderful man to know or be around." Despite his clear liking for the former president, most reviewers felt that Ambrose developed an even-handed portrait of the man who is widely perceived to have been, in the words of *Time* reviewer Donald Morrison, both a "canny leader who brilliantly outmaneuvered subordinates and statesmen," and a "mediocre President . . . slow of wit and out of touch with the currents of upheaval swirling beneath the calm surface of the 1950s." In reconciling these two views, Ambrose "provided the most complete and objective work yet on the general who became President," wrote Drew Middleton in the *New York Times Book Review. New Yorker* contributor Naomi Bliven said that the biography "offers the beguiling mixture of nostalgia and illumination we find in old newsreels, along with an abundance of themes for reflection."

Reviewers praised Ambrose's reassessment of a president who had been reviled as a bumbling, inefficient leader, a president who, in the words of reviewer Richard Rhodes of Chicago's *Tribune Books,* "golfed too much, knew little and did nothing." Ambrose acknowledges such public perception, wrote Henry Brandon in the *Washington Post Book World,* but his biography portrays Eisenhower as "a man in charge if not always in control, a born leader and a deft pilot who knows how to weather storms." In volume two, *Eisenhower: The President,* Ambrose highlights the fact that "Ike," as he was affectionately known, kept his country out of war for eight turbulent years, stood up to a burgeoning military-industrial complex, and managed to maintain domestic economic prosperity.

Though most reviewers praised Ambrose for his equanimity, some thought that he failed to advance a compelling interpretation of the voluminous data he compiled. *Los Angeles Times Book Review* contributor Kenneth Reich complained that the book was too restrained. "It seems sad," he wrote, "when someone has obviously put in so much effort yet fails to go beyond evenhandedness. . . . [This] biography of Eisenhower emerges as a dull parade of data." Ivan R. Dee, writing in the Chicago *Tribune Books,* said that the problem was that "a reader can arrive at opposite judgments about Eisenhower's performance based upon the evidence Ambrose presents." Dee pointed to Eisenhower's handling of civil rights, the U-2 spying incident, and Middle Eastern politics as examples of Eisenhower's failed leadership which Ambrose does not acknowledge.

After nearly twenty years of writing about one of America's best-loved presidents, Ambrose turned his attention to a man he said had once been "the most hated and feared man in America," President Richard M. Nixon. A number of writers had penned psychological portraits of Nixon that attempted to account for his seeming cruelty, his terrific drive to succeed, his failure to admit fault for the Watergate controversy, and his subsequent resignation in the face of impeachment proceedings. But in 1987 Ambrose began a comprehensive three-volume work on Richard Nixon, undertaking a carefully researched, scholarly biography on one of the most controversial presidents of the twentieth century. Reviewing the first volume, *Nixon: The Education of a Politician, 1913-1962, Washington Post Book World* re-

viewer Richard Harwood echoed the praise of many critics, noting Ambrose's ability to "examine with a surgeon's neutrality all the clichés and stereotypical assumptions about the character of this strange and fascinating man." Political analyst Sidney Blumenthal wrote in the *New Republic* that "Ambrose has written the standard, a middle point of reference, around which all Nixonia may be organized."

In the trilogy, Ambrose follows Nixon from his humble beginnings in Yorba Linda, California, to his academic success at Duke University, to his bitter 1950 senate campaign, to his troubled tenure as Eisenhower's vice president, and finally to the rise and fall of his own presidency. Along the way, Ambrose debunks many of the myths about Nixon, picturing Nixon's childhood as happy, not sad, writing that Nixon's opponents initiated much of the mud-slinging for which he became known, and demonstrating that the political dirty work Nixon performed while vice president was done at President Eisenhower's insistence. The third volume, *Nixon: Ruin and Recovery,* focuses on the resuscitation of the former president's reputation throughout the 1980s. *Spectator* reviewer Anthony Howard wrote that Ambrose "crowned the edifice of his impressive trilogy with an admirably fair-minded last volume covering easily the most controversial aspect of what was already a singularly resilient political career." Throughout the three volumes, Ambrose does not excuse Nixon for the excesses that characterized his political career, nor does he attempt to provide an explanation of what motivated Nixon to behave as he did; instead, he shows what happened and lets the reader decide.

Ambrose's reluctance to offer insights into Nixon's motivations frustrated some critics. *New York Times* reviewer Christopher Lehmann-Haupt complained that "there is something passive about the way Mr. Ambrose tells Mr. Nixon's story. He seems always confined by context, praising his subject for this, condemning him for that. He lacks the lift of a driving thesis." Ronald Steel, writing in the *New York Times Book Review,* echoed this appraisal, suggesting that Ambrose "is better at providing information than at delving into the dark recesses of character." And Gary Wills, whose own *Nixon Agonistes* attempted to probe the dark recesses of Nixon's character, thought that Ambrose's concern for the facts made him overlook an essential undercurrent in Nixon's life.

Edward Z. Friedenberg saw Ambrose's hesitancy to pass judgment on Nixon in a slightly different light. Writing in the Toronto *Globe and Mail,* he claimed that

"Ambrose seems largely content to explain the hostility Nixon aroused in terms of his personality," but contended that "Nixon's enemies hated not merely the man but his (and his country's) policies." According to Friedenberg, Ambrose's equanimity led him to excuse the most sinister elements of Nixon's presidency: his policy toward Vietnam and his drive to do whatever it might take to win that conflict. R.W. Apple, Jr. wrote in the *New York Times Book Review,* however, that "it is Mr. Ambrose's achievement to immerse himself in Mr. Nixon's life and keep his cool. . . . The result is a portrait that is all its subject is not: evenhanded and thoroughly reliable." Ambrose himself told *New York Times Book Review* contributor Alex Ward, "I make no claim to finding the key to the man—he's so complicated that it would take Shakespeare to do him justice."

Ambrose again focused on World War II in *Band of Brothers: E Company, 506th Regiment, 101st Airborne, from Normandy to Hitler's Eagle's Nest,* detailing that company's numerous engagements and exploits. Ambrose based his book on the stories he collected from the surviving members of the company as part of his work for the Eisenhower Center at the University of New Orleans. The soldiers told Ambrose of their pre-dawn drop behind enemy lines on D-Day and of their eventual capture of German leader Adolf Hitler's private retreat, "Eagle's Nest." The result, wrote *New York Times Book Review* contributor and combat veteran Harry G. Summers, Jr., is "a harrowing story" that captures "the true essence of a combat rifle company." *Times Literary Supplement* reviewer M.R.D. Foot asserted that the book "is full of insights into the nature of comradeship, as well as brutally frank description: noise, stench, discomfort, hunger and fear are all there, tied together in a masterly narrative flow."

Ambrose continued with World War II subject matter in *D-Day, June 6, 1944: The Climactic Battle of World War II.* Ambrose drew on soldiers' oral histories on file at the Eisenhower Center and accounts from other eyewitnesses to tell the story of the landing of Allied troops on June 6, 1944, in the famous invasion along the coast of France's Normandy region. He deals with the strategies and personalities of the commanders, Eisenhower and German Field Marshal Erwin Rommel, but the stories of ordinary soldiers form the heart of the book. "The descriptions of individual ordeals on the bloody beach of Omaha make this book outstanding," praised Raleigh Trevelyan in the *New York Times Book Review.* Trevelyan noted that Ambrose cites Cornelius Ryan's 1959 work, *The Longest Day,* as an inspiration for his book. "Like that account, *D-Day, June 6, 1944* is mostly about people, but goes even further in evoking the hor-

ror, the endurance, the daring and, indeed, the human failings at Omaha Beach and other places along the Calvados coastline," Trevelyan observed. *New Leader* contributor William L. O'Neill found it "unlikely" that any other historian "will produce a book like *D-Day, June 6, 1944,* with its wealth of detail, absorbing vignettes, and rich anecdotal material." Ambrose, he added, "brings to his new work the narrative drive, thorough research and muscular prose he is justly famous for." In the *National Forum,* Leah Rawls Atkins pronounced the book "the definitive account of America's landing on the French coast," adding that "*D-Day* is not a quick read, but it is a satisfying one. The bloody tales of carnage are thankfully relieved by Ambrose's selection of humorous anecdotes and perceptive quotations that linger in the reader's mind."

Undaunted Courage brought Ambrose additional accolades. He had long been fascinated by Meriwether Lewis and William Clark's exploratory journey from St. Louis to the Pacific Ocean. He had read the pair's journals in 1975, and since then had visited numerous sites along Lewis and Clark's trail. He had wanted to write about the expedition for years, and decided to do so after becoming convinced there was sufficient fresh material available to warrant a new biography of Lewis (he found out another well-regarded historian was planning a book on Clark). *Undaunted Courage,* therefore, is a comprehensive study of Lewis as well as of his 1804-1806 trek with Clark and their party to the Pacific and back, through an expanse of land the United States had just acquired from France in the Louisiana Purchase. President Thomas Jefferson hoped the land would contain an all-water route to the Pacific; Lewis and Clark found that no such route existed, but they did bring back a plethora of information about the new territory. The expedition turned out to be the pinnacle of Lewis's life; he was a failure as the subsequent governor of the Louisiana territory, and he suffered from alcohol abuse and depression, committing suicide at age thirty-five in 1809. Though some historians have suggested Lewis was murdered, Ambrose finds no evidence that Lewis's death was anything other than a suicide.

"A remarkably balanced historian, Ambrose is neither a revisionist nor an apologist," remarked Malcolm Jones, Jr., in his *Newsweek* review of *Undaunted Courage.* For instance, Jones noted, Ambrose shows that Lewis was not always honest with the Native Americans the party encountered, but still maintained a degree of respect for them. "Here and elsewhere, Ambrose weighs shortcomings against positive attributes and ultimately presents us with a convincing hero," the critic averred. In the *New York Times Book Review,* Alvin M. Josephy, Jr. reported that Lewis emerges "as an outstanding explorer and hero, fair, energetic, beloved by his men and greatly self-disciplined, but also occasionally impetuous and arrogant, and possessed of a flaring temper that could get him into trouble." *Yale Review* contributor Howard Lamar likewise praised Ambrose's portrait of Lewis: "Ambrose with good reason not only rescues Meriwether Lewis from two centuries of obscurity but presents him as a fascinating, complex, strong, contradictory individual. What Ambrose has done is to make Lewis a real person, a hero who was at once a frontiersman and near poet." What's more, Lamar related, Ambrose "portrays Thomas Jefferson as a more shrewd, highly political, and tough figure than we usually encounter in American texts . . . standing midway between the opposite categories of dreamer and schemer." In *Wild West,* Dale Walker lauded Ambrose's analysis of Lewis's relationship with Jefferson, his mentor; this "has never been explored so deeply," Walker asserted. Walker also complimented Ambrose's "meticulous reconstruction" of Lewis and Clark's journey, saying, "all the joys and miseries of that greatest exploration in our history come to life in the author's measured prose." Lamar summed up the book by declaring that the well-known story of the expedition "is so well told by Ambrose that it seems a fresh, new saga. *Undaunted Courage* may well remain the most effectively narrated American adventure story to appear in this decade."

Ambrose's association with the story of Lewis and Clark continued as he contributed text to a photography book covering the pair's route, and he subsequently appeared in Ken Burns's documentary film about the expedition. He also returned to the subject of World War II, writing *Citizen Soldiers: The U.S. Army from the Normandy Beaches to the Bulge to the Surrender of Germany* and *The Victors: Eisenhower and His Boys—The Men of World War II. Citizen Soldiers* chronicles the final eleven months of the war in Europe through interviews with the men who served on the front lines, who had often been neglected by the historians who focused primarily on their leaders. "Almost no one except the surviving participants has any comprehension of the vicious, unrelenting, blood-stained conflict that continued through every day and every night of the eleven months from D-Day to the German surrender on V-E Day," observed Charles W. Bailery in a *Washington Monthly* review of the book. "*Citizen Soldiers* fills that gap. In the process, Ambrose has produced not only an authoritative history but a powerful and painful anti-war testament as well." Carlo D'Este, writing in the *New York Times Book Review,* thought that "in Ambrose's capable hands, the bloody and dramatic battles fought in northwest Europe in 1944-45 come alive as never before."

Among other things, D'Este noted, Ambrose details how not only bullets and grenades but also frostbite and disease were dangerous enemies of ordinary soldiers, and he decries the military's racial segregation and some aspects of the Army's inefficiency. Added Malcolm Jones, Jr., in *Newsweek:* "Without ever questioning the necessity of fighting, Ambrose provides one of the best looks yet at the dark side of the 'good' war." D'Este concluded, "*Citizen Soldiers* is an unforgettable testament to the World War II generation."

In *The Victors,* Ambrose drew on his previous World War II books to produce a portrait of the U.S. Army, from Eisenhower's appointment to lead the forces in Europe through the end of the war. "Ambrose fans will have a distinct sense of deja vu," remarked Nathaniel Tripp in the *New York Times Book Review.* "Still, there is a lot to be said for having it all under one cover, for combining Ambrose's compelling portrait of Eisenhower's leadership with the vivid experiences of the infantrymen, and following the campaign from conception to conclusion." This has a downside as well, Tripp contended, because "in the compression of thousands of pages from his earlier books into just under 400 here, many illuminating and insightful details have been lost and jingoism comes to the fore." *National Review* contributor Josiah Bunting III, however, felt that Ambrose had done exactly what he set out to do: to demonstrate "that the essential goodness of a moral, democratic society makes of its citizens military defenders who will triumph over enemies whose soldiers are the product of totalitarian, racist, and authoritarian regimes. Ambrose accomplishes this with great power."

As a kind of addendum to his other books on history, Ambrose wrote *Comrades: Brothers, Fathers, Heroes, Sons, Pals.* Described by Kevin Hymel of *Military History* as "a quick 140-page read that is hard to put down," the book explores "a common thread shared among players in military history: their camaraderie." Discussing Dwight D. Eisenhower, Ambrose portrays both the president's warm friendship with his brother Milton and his often strained relationship with General George S. Patton. Eisenhower respected and needed Patton's military talents, but was often irritated by the general's behavior. With regard to Richard M. Nixon, Ambrose suggests that Nixon's failure to develop close friendships with those around him may have contributed to his downfall. In an autobiographical vein, Ambrose takes a look at camaraderie in his own life and the bonds he has formed with friends and relatives, particularly his own father. Other friendships discussed in the book include those between Lewis and Clark, and between George Custer of Little Big Horn fame and his brothers. Hymel found *Comrades* to be "a fresh look at most of his [Ambrose's] favorite personalities, revealing new insights," and concluded by suggesting: "Read it and then pass it to your father or your son." Gilbert Taylor of *Booklist* described the volume as "quickly perusable, congenial confessions for the author's huge readership."

In a change of pace from military and political history, Ambrose offered *Nothing like It in the World: The Men Who Built the Transcontinental Railroad, 1863-1869.* In chapters that alternate between the construction of the Central Pacific line in the West and the Union Pacific line in the East, Ambrose paints a broad and comprehensive picture that encompasses the planning of the transcontinental railroad, the financing of its construction, and the day-to-day labor of the workers who made it a reality. The volume also covers the impact of the railroad on the settling of America. Nancy Spillman of *Booklist* characterized the work as relating "a spellbinding combination of entrepreneurial foresight, Herculean human fortitude, and prescient political wisdom." Henry Kisor of the *New York Times Book Review* stated: "Ambrose's scholarship seems impeccable, supported by copious notes and an extensive bibliography. He writes a brisk, colloquial, straightforward prose that not only is easy to read but also bears the reader on shoulders of wonder and excitement." Kisor concluded: "*Nothing like It in the World* may be a popular history, but it is also a complex one, and the several maps of the route as well as a section of contemporary photographs greatly aid the reader's understanding of its builders' grand accomplishment."

Ambrose again turned to World War II for his subject matter with both *The Good Fight: How World War II Was Won,* a volume for young adults, and *The Wild Blue: The Men and Boys Who Flew the B-24s over Germany.* Reviewing *The Good Fight* for *School Library Journal,* Cindy Darling stated: "Whenever a celebrated historian produces a volume for young people, one wonders if he will write for them or merely condense and chop. Ambrose does write for them, in a beautifully abbreviated style." Arranged chronologically, moving from the origins of World War II through the Marshall Plan, *The Good Fight* consists of a series of one-page essays complemented by fact boxes, numerous photographs, and maps. Randy Meyer of *Booklist* credited it with being "an excellent balance between the big picture and the humanizing details," and went on to praise Ambrose's style as "authoritative and warm." However, in an article for the *Atlantic Monthly* titled "The Real War—Stephan Ambrose's GIs Are Plaster Saints Engaged in a Sanctified Crusade," Benjamin Schwarz offered a very different opinion of *The Good Fight.* According to Schwartz, "Ambrose's version of events retroactively imposes an elevated meaning on the American side of the war. . . . *The Good Fight* is littered with lofty cant." Schwartz also disagreed with Ambrose's interpretations on numerous specific counts, such as the Normandy invasion, which Ambrose depicts as an attempt by the United States "to free France from Nazi tyranny," while Schwartz defined it as primarily an effort "to establish a literal and figurative beachhead in Western Europe." Schwartz concluded with a broader criticism of the author's work, stating that "the great problem with Ambrose's books—especially this one—is that they fail to treat history as tragic, ironic, paradoxical, and ambiguous. If readers are old enough to study an event that involved the deaths of more than sixty million people, they are old enough to learn that one studies history not to simplify issues but to illuminate their complexities."

In *The Wild Blue,* Ambrose recounts the experiences of the men who flew B-24 bombers over Nazi Germany in the Allied attempt to cripple the Axis war machine. Rather than attempting to chronicle the experience of all the men involved in the campaign, Ambrose focuses on a single bomber crew commanded by future Senator and presidential candidate George McGovern. McGovern and his crew flew a total of thirty-five missions, the maximum number allowed. Lev Raphael of the *Knight-Ridder/Tribune News Service* stated: "Ambrose does a good job of putting readers in the middle of combat, and makes us appreciate how exhausting and dangerous it was for crews, who had a survival rate of fifty percent." Although Sean McCann of *Book* faulted Ambrose for failing to examine the larger question of the effectiveness of the Allied campaign of strategic bombing, he also commented that "in a remarkable string of vivid histories . . . Ambrose has done more than anyone else to remind us of the heroic struggles American soldiers endured during World War II and of the valiant cause for which they fought." In January of 2002, *The Wild Blue* received a barrage of attention, although not the kind of attention Ambrose hoped for. The author later admitted to plagiarizing passages found in *The Wild Blue.* The material was taken from Dr. Thomas Childers's 1995 book, *The Wings of Morning.* Ambrose issued an apology and stated that future editions of the book would be corrected. Childers, a longtime fan of Ambrose's work, accepted the apology and told *People,* "I thought it was a classy thing to do." The attention led to further investigations of plagiarism in Ambrose's work. The author told a *Time,* contributor that from that point on he would "cite and have quotation marks around anything I take out of secondary works."

Later that same year, Ambrose, a long-time smoker, was diagnosed with lung cancer. He died in the fall of

2002, just as his memoir, *To America: Personal Reflections of a Historian,* and his illustrated history, *The Mississippi and the Making of a Nation: From the Louisiana Purchase to Today,* were published. In the first book, Ambrose blends personal history with reflections on topics in American history from the Battle of New Orleans to the Vietnam War. A contributor for *Publishers Weekly* felt that there are too few personal recollections in this book: "readers looking for [Ambrose's] life story will have to take notes and write it themselves." Similarly, a *Kirkus Reviews* critic found the book to be a "blend of memoir, canned book-talks, and synopses" providing a "breezy, self-congratulatory survey of the author's career." *Book* contributor Terry Teachout called *To America* an "informal, almost chatty quasi-memoir," but regretted that the author "says nothing about the charges of plagiarism that darkened his final months, or the widespread feeling among colleagues that his work became less serious as it grew more popular." For *Booklist*'s Gilbert Taylor, however, the memoir was more successful. Taylor felt that "Ambrose reveals his beliefs and attitudes in this reflective ramble." Reviewing Ambrose's collaborative effort with Douglas C. Brinkley, *The Mississippi and the Making of a Nation,* *Library Journal* contributor Charlie Cowling noted that the book relates the history of the river from the early nineteenth century up to modern times, and "promises to appeal to a wide range of readers." Taylor, writing in *Booklist,* concluded, "Variegated and ruminative about the Mississippi's physical and literary centrality to American history, Ambrose and Brinkley's exploration will justly attract great attention." And a critic for *Publishers Weekly* had further praise for the same title, commenting that "this absorbing book should please any lay enthusiast of American history."

At the time of his death, Ambrose was at work on another treatment of the Lewis and Clark story, this time approaching it from a fictional angle in a book written for young adults. Published in 2003, *This Vast Land: A Young Man's Journal of the Lewis and Clark Expedition* is Ambrose's only work of fiction. It purports to be the journal of the youngest member of the Lewis and Clark party, that of seventeen-year-old George Shannon, and is written in a "voice that is both strong and authentic," according to *Horn Book* contributor Betty Carter. Shannon is, Carter further noted, "far from a one-dimensional character," and it is through him that readers experience the hardships of the expedition. *Booklist*'s Roger Leslie found the book "very easy reading," and went on to commend the fact that Ambrose's protagonist ultimately rejects the prejudice of some of the other white explorers, offering "a positive message about diversity." *Kliatt*'s Paula Rohrlick felt that events depicted in Shannon's journal in brief entries, while "giving the narrative a choppy feel," "are often dramatic and the descriptions are colorful and frequently earthy." And Mary Mueller of *School Library Journal* wrote that *This Vast Land* would be a "good choice for older teens who are interested in this fascinating expedition."

BIOGRAPHICAL AND CRITICAL SOURCES:

BOOKS

Ambrose, Stephen E., *Eisenhower: Soldier, General of the Army, President-Elect, 1890-1952,* Simon & Schuster (New York, NY), 1983.
Authors and Artists for Young Adults, Volume 44, Thomson Gale (Detroit, MI), 2002.
Contemporary Literary Criticism, Volume 145, Thomson Gale (Detroit, MI), 2001.

PERIODICALS

Atlantic Monthly, June, 2001, Benjamin Schwartz, "The Real War—Stephan Ambrose's GIs Are Plaster Saints Engaged in a Sanctified Crusade," p. 100.
Book, July, 2001, Sean McCann, review of *The Wild Blue: The Men and Boys Who Flew the B-24s over Germany,* p. 64; January-February, 2003, Terry Teachout, review of *To America: Personal Reflections of a Historian,* p. 75.
Booklist, June 1, 1999, Gilbert Taylor, review of *Comrades: Brothers, Fathers, Heroes, Sons, Pals,* p. 1752; March 1, 2001, Nancy Spillman, review of *Nothing like It in the World: The Men Who Built the Transcontinental Railroad, 1863-1869,* p. 1295; July, 2001, Randy Meyer, review of *The Good Fight: How World War II Was Won,* p. 2008; September 15, 2002, Gilbert Taylor, review of *The Mississippi and the Making of America: From the Louisiana Purchase to Today,* p. 178; November 1, 2002, Gilbert Taylor, review of *To America,* p. 450; April 1, 2003, Will Manley, "Who Makes History?," p. 1357; September 1, 2003, Roger Leslie, review of *This Vast Land: A Young Man's Journal of the Lewis and Clark Expedition,* p. 77
Chicago Tribune, March 24, 1985.
Commonweal, April 24, 1998, p. 13.
Fortune, August 8, 1994, p. 108.
Globe and Mail (Toronto, Ontario, Canada), March 16, 1985; July 25, 1987; November 4, 1989.
Horn Book, January-February, 2004, Betty Carter, review of *This Vast Land,* p. 78.

Kirkus Reviews, October 15, 2002, review of *To America,* p. 1511; August 1, 2003, review of *This Vast Land,* p. 101.

Kliatt, September, 2003, Paula Rohrlick, review of *This Vast Land,* p. 5.

Knight-Ridder/Tribune News Service, Lev Raphael, review of *The Wild Blue,* p. K5470.

Library Journal, October 15, 2002, Charlie Cowling, review of *The Mississippi and the Making of America,* p. 83; January, 2003, Randall M. Miller, review of *To America,* p. 130.

London Review of Books, July 4, 1985, pp. 5-6.

Los Angeles Times, February 13, 1981; January 10, 2002.

Los Angeles Times Book Review, November 4, 1984, Kenneth Reich, review of *Eisenhower: The President;* June 21, 1987, p. 12; October 15, 1989; November 24, 1991, pp. 4, 11.

Maclean's, June 6, 1994, p. 56.

Military History, April, 2000, Kevin Hymel, review of *Comrades,* p. 68.

Nation, February 28, 1972.

National Forum, fall, 1994, Leah Rawls Atkins, review of *D-Day, June 6, 1944,* p. 45; spring, 2001, Pat Kaetz, review of *Nothing like It in the World,* p. 39.

National Review, December 21, 1998, Josiah Bunting III, review of *The Victors,* p. 60.

New Leader, March 5, 1990, pp. 16-17; June 6, 1994, William L. O'Neill, review of *D-Day, June 6, 1944,* p. 12.

New Orleans Magazine, December, 1998, p. 56.

New Republic, July 6, 1987, Sidney Blumenthal, review of *Nixon: The Education of a Politician, 1913-1962,* pp. 30-34.

Newsweek, April 27, 1987; February 19, 1996, p. 70; August 26, 1996, p. 46; November 17, 1997, Malcolm Jones, Jr., review of *Citizen Soldiers,* p. 89.

New Yorker, July 1, 1985, Naomi Bliven, review of *Eisenhower: Soldier, General of the Army, President-Elect, 1890-1952,* pp. 95-97.

New York Review of Books, May 6, 1971.

New York Times, April 23, 1987; November 9, 1989; January 11, 2002.

New York Times Book Review, October 4, 1970, p. 5; September 19, 1983, Drew Middleton, review of *Eisenhower: Soldier, General of the Army, President-Elect, 1890-1952;* December 9, 1984, pp. 1, 46-47; April 28, 1985; April 26, 1987; November 12, 1989, pp. 1, 65-66; November 24, 1991, pp. 3, 25; September 6, 1992, Harry G. Summers, review of *Band of Brothers,* p. 11; May 29, 1994, Raleigh Trevelyan, review of *D-Day, June 6, 1944,* p. 1; March 10, 1996, Alvin M. Josephy, Jr., review of *Undaunted Courage,* p. 9; December 21, 1997,

Carlo D'Este, review of *Citizen Soldiers,* p. 10; November 22, 1998, Nathaniel Tripp, review of *The Victors,* p. 14; September 17, 2000, Henry Kisor, "Working on the Railroad."

People, July 1, 1996, p. 101; November 3, 1997, p. 17; January 19, 1998, p. 34; January 21, 2002, p. 15.

Publishers Weekly, January 22, 1996, p. 50; August 27, 2001, Daisy Maryles, Dick Donahue, "Into the Wild Blue," p. 17; September 30, 2002, review of *The Mississippi and the Making of America,* p. 62; November 11, 2002, review of *To America,* p. 54; August 25, 2003, review of *This Vast Land: A Young Man's Journal of the Lewis and Clark Expedition,* p. 66.

School Library Journal, May, 2001, Cindy Darling, review of *The Good Fight,* p. 161; September 2003, Mary Mueller, review of *This Vast Land,* p. 209.

Spectator, July 4, 1987, pp. 32-33; February 1, 1992, Anthony Howard, review of *Nixon: Ruin and Recovery,* p. 32.

Time, October 3, 1983, Donald Morrison, review of *Eisenhower: Soldier, General of the Army, President-Elect, 1890-1952,* pp. 79-80; May 4, 1987, p. 101; November 6, 1989, pp. 100-102; November 24, 1997, p. 108; January 21, 2002, p. 130.

Times Literary Supplement, June 1, 1967, p. 486; November 5, 1971, p. 1398; February 8, 1985, p. 135; December 25, 1987, p. 1424; August 21, 1992, M.R.D. Foot, review of *Band of Brothers,* p. 20.

Tribune Books (Chicago, IL), October 16, 1983, Richard Rhodes, review of *Eisenhower: Soldier, General of the Army, President-Elect, 1890-1952;* October 7, 1984, Ivan R. Dee, review of *Eisenhower: The President,* pp. 1, 24; April 12, 1987, p. 3; July 19, 1992, p. 6.

U.S. News & World Report, January 21, 2002, Jay Tolson, "Whose Own Words?," p. 52.

Wall Street Journal, January 22, 2002, Mark Lewis, "Don't Indict Popular History," p. A20.

Washington Monthly, December, 1997, Charles W. Bailery, review of *Citizen Soldiers,* p. 49.

Washington Post Book World, September 11, 1983, Henry Brandon, review of *Eisenhower: Soldier, General of the Army, President-Elect, 1890-1952,* pp. 1, 4; September 30, 1984; May 3, 1987, Richard Harwood, review of *Nixon: The Education of a Politician, 1913-1962;* November 12, 1989, pp. 1, 13; November 10, 1991, p. 5.

Wild West, December, 1996, Dale Walker, review of *Undaunted Courage,* p. 74.

Yale Review, October, 1997, Howard Lamar, review of *Undaunted Courage,* p. 146.

ONLINE

Official Stephen E. Ambrose Web site, http://www.stephenambrose.com/ (August 12, 2004).

OBITUARIES:

PERIODICALS

Chicago Tribune, October 14, 2002, section 2, p. 7.
Daily Variety, October 14, 2002, p. 4.
New York Times, October 14, 2002, Richard Goldstein, "Stephen Ambrose, Historian Who Fueled New Interest in World War II, Dies at 66," p. B2.
People, October 28, 2002, "Last Stand," p. 82.
Time, October 28, 2002, p. 23.
Times (London, England), October 14, 2002.
Washington Post, October 14, 2002, p. B7.

ONLINE

CNN Online, http://www.cnn.com/ (October 14, 2002).

*   *   *

AMBROSE, Stephen Edward
See AMBROSE, Stephen E.

*   *   *

AMICHAI, Yehuda 1924-2000

PERSONAL: First name sometimes transliterated as "Yehudah"; born 1924, in Germany; immigrated to Palestine, 1936; naturalized Israeli citizen; died September 25, 2000; children: David, Emanuella.

CAREER: Poet and writer. *Military service:* British Army during World War II; member, Israeli defense forces, 1948, during Arab-Israeli war.

MEMBER: American Academy and Institute of Arts and Letters (foreign honorary member).

AWARDS, HONORS: Israel's Prize for Poetry, 1982.

WRITINGS:

IN ENGLISH

Lo me-'akhshav, Lo mi-kan (novel), [Tel Aviv, Israel], 1963, translation by Shlomo Katz published as *Not of This Time, Not of This Place,* Harper (New York, NY), 1968.

Selected Poems, translation from the Hebrew by Assia Gutmann, Cape Goliard Press, 1968, published as *Poems,* introduction by Michael Hamburger, Harper (New York, NY), 1969.

Selected Poems of Yehuda Amichai, translation from the original Hebrew by Gutmann, Harold Schimmel, and Ted Hughes, Penguin (London, England), 1971, published as *The Early Books of Yehuda Amichai,* Sheep Meadow Press (Riverdale, NY), 1988.

Songs of Jerusalem and Myself (poetry), translation from the Hebrew by Schimmel, Harper (New York, NY), 1973.

Travels of a Latter-Day Benjamin of Tudela, translation from the Hebrew by Ruth Nevo, House of Exile (Toronto, Ontario, Canada), 1976.

Amen (poetry), translation from the Hebrew by the author and Hughes, Harper (New York, NY), 1977.

On New Year's Day, Next to a House Being Built, Sceptre Press (Knotting, England), 1979.

Time: Poems, Harper (New York, NY), 1979.

(Editor with Allen Mandelbaum) Avoth Yeshurun, *The Syrian-African Rift, and Other Poems,* translation by Schimmel, Jewish Publication Society (Philadelphia, PA), 1980.

Love Poems (also see below), translation from the Hebrew by Glenda Abramson and Tudor Parfitt, Harper (New York, NY), 1981.

(Editor with Mandelbaum) Dan Pagis, *Points of Departure,* translation from the Hebrew by Stephen Mitchell, Jewish Publication Society (Philadelphia, PA), 1982.

The Great Tranquility: Questions and Answers, translation from the Hebrew by Abramson and Parfitt, Harper (New York, NY), 1983, reprinted, Sheep Meadow Press (Riverdale, NY), 1997.

The World Is a Room, and Other Stories, Jewish Publication Society (Philadelphia, PA), 1984.

Travels (bilingual edition), English translations by Nevo, Sheep Meadow Press (Philadelphia, PA), 1986.

The Selected Poetry of Yehudah Amichai, translation from the Hebrew by Mitchell and Chana Bloch, Harper (New York, NY), 1986, revised and expanded edition, University of California Press (Berkeley, CA), 1996.

Poems of Jerusalem: A Bilingual Edition (also see below), Harper (New York, NY), 1988.

Even a Fist Was Once an Open Palm with Fingers: Recent Poems, selected and translated by Barbara and Benjamin Harshav, HarperCollins (New York, NY), 1991.

Poems of Jerusalem; and, Love Poems: Bilingual Edition, Sheep Meadow Press (Riverdale, NY), 1992.

I Am Sitting Here Now, Land Marks Press (Huntington Woods, MI), 1994.

Poems: English and Hebrew, Shoken (Jerusalem), 1994.

Yehuda Amichai, A Life of Poetry, 1948-1994, Translated by Barbara and Benjamin Harshave, HarperCollins (New York, NY), 1994.

Exile at Home (poetry), photographs by Frederic Brenner, Harry N. Abrams (New York, NY), 1998.

Open Closed Open: Poems, translated from the Hebrew by Chana Bloch and Chana Kronfeld, Harcourt (New York, NY), 2000.

OTHER

Akhshav uva-yamim ha-aherim (poetry; title means "Now and in Other Days"), [Tel Aviv, Israel], 1955.

Ba-ginah ha-tsiburit (poetry; title means "In the Park"), [Jerusalem], 1958–59.

Be-merhak shete tikvot (poetry), [Tel Aviv, Israel], 1958.

Be-ruah ha-nora'ah ha-zot (stories), Merhavya, 1961.

Masa' le-Ninveh (play; title means "Journey to Nineveh"), 1962.

Shirim, 1948-1962 (title means "Poetry, 1948-1962"), [Jerusalem], 1962–63.

'Akshav ba-ra'ash, 1968.

Mah she-karah le-Roni bi-Nyu York, 1968.

Pa 'amonim ve-rakavot, 1968.

Ve-lo 'al menat li-zekor (poetry), 1971.

Mi yitneni malon (title means "Hotel in the Wilderness"), 1972, reprinted, Bitan (Tel Aviv, Israel), 2003.

Me-ahore kol zeh mistater osher gadol (poetry), 1974.

Translator of German works into Hebrew.

Amichai's works have been translated into thirty-seven languages, including French, Swedish, Chinese, and Spanish.

SIDELIGHTS: In the later years of his life, Yehuda Amichai came to be recognized as one of Israel's finest poets. His poems—written in Hebrew—have been translated into thirty-seven languages, and whole volumes have been published in English, French, German, Swedish, Spanish, and Catalan. In an online review for the *East Bay Express,* Stephen Kessler noted that Amichai had "long been one of the planet's preeminent poets. . . . Jewish down to the bones, his humanity is broadly universal, obsessed as Amichai [was] with time and death, war and peace, love and memory, joy and suffering." *New Republic* essayist C.K. Williams found in Amichai's oeuvre "the shrewdest and most solid of poetic intelligences."

Born in Germany in 1924, Amichai left that country at age twelve with his family and journeyed to Palestine. During the 1948 Arab-Israeli war he fought with the Israeli defense forces. The rigors and horrors of his service in this conflict, and in World War II, inform his poetry, although, to quote Kessler, the political slant is "elusive," addressing the issues of Arab-Israeli relations in metaphorical, rather than ideological, terms. By the mid-1960s Amichai was "already regarded in many circles in Israel as the country's leading poet," to quote Robert Alter in the *New York Times Magazine.* Amichai's reputation outside of Israel soon soared, Alter explaining that the author was "accorded international recognition unprecedented for a modern Hebrew poet."

In his novel *Not of This Time, Not of This Place,* Amichai struggled with "the torment of being buried alive in the irrelevant past." The novel's hero is torn between returning to the German town where he grew up and staying in Jerusalem and "immersing himself in a love affair with an outsider who has had no part in it." In his review of the novel for the *New Yorker,* Anthony West explained: "The alternatives are both impossibilities. The past is still going on back in Germany, and it is inescapable in Israel: the knowledge of what men are and what they can do that was acquired in the years of Hitler's 'final solution' cannot be discarded or ignored, and it is no easier to live with when one is in the country of the ex-butchers than it is in that of the ex-victims."

While serving in the British Army, Amichai was influenced by modern English and American poetry, and, according to Alter, the author's early work bears a resemblance to the poetry of Dylan Thomas and W.H. Auden. "[German poet Rainer] Rilke," wrote Alter, "is another informing presence for him, occasionally in matters of style—he has written vaguely Rilkesque elegies—but perhaps more as a model for using a language of here and now as an instrument to catch the glimmerings of a metaphysical beyond." Although Amichai's native language was German, he read Hebrew fluently by the time he immigrated to Palestine.

Chad Walsh commented in the *Washington Post Book World* that "a Jewish poet, like a Greek, has the enormous advantage of an immense history and tradition which he can handle with an easy familiarity, and play with as a foil to the homogenized culture that is spreading over the globe like a universal parking lot. This combination of the old and the new speaks very powerfully in Amichai's poetry and makes him, as it were, a contemporary simultaneously of King David the psalmist and [popular television news journalist] Eric Sevareid." Amichai once raised a similar point about the ease with which he handled different cultures and traditions in an interview published in the *American Poetry Review:* "I grew up in a very religious household. . . . So the prayers, the language of prayer itself became a kind of natural language for me. . . . I don't try—like sometimes poets do—to 'enrich' poetry by getting more *cultural* material or more *ethnic* material into it. It comes very naturally." Other critics noted the writer's talent for bridging the gap between the personal and the universal. Grace Shulman, writing in the *Nation,* observed: "Amichai has a rare ability for transforming the personal, even private, love situation, with all its joys and agonies, into everybody's experience, making his own time and place general."

The Selected Poetry of Yehuda Amichai brings together poems published between 1955 and 1985, the poet's early work translated by Stephen Mitchell and his later work by Chana Bloch. In a *New York Times Book Review* assessment of the collection, Edward Hirsch described the Amichai of the 1950s and 1960s as "more formal and metaphysical . . . a tender ironist influenced by W.H. Auden . . . and by such poets as John Donne and George Herbert." In contrast, the Amichai of the 1970s and 1980s, according to Hirsch, is "in some ways a sparer and more informal poet whose colloquial free verse rhythms seem modeled, perhaps, on William Carlos Williams and whose profuse imagery and lightning-flash analogies may be compared to Deep Imagism."

According to Hirsch, one of Amichai's central works is a long autobiographical poem that has been translated into English as both *Travels* and *Travels of a Latter-Day Benjamin of Tudela.* Hirsch described the poem as a "miniature Jewish version of Wordsworth's *Prelude,* charting the growth of a poet's soul from the vantage point of middle age." *Travels* traces the poet's life by comparing it to that of major figures from Jewish history. Hirsch wrote that the poem "dramatizes [Amichai's] sense of being poised between his father's life and his son's, his struggle to feel worthy and whole, . . . and his assessment of the way his own life is tied to the fate of Israel." Furthermore, Hirsch stated that Amichai "is a representative man with unusual gifts who in telling his own story also relates the larger story of his people."

Amichai's collection titled *Yehuda Amichai, A Life of Poetry 1948-1994,* is a comprehensive work covering verse written during the Arab-Israeli war through poetry "beautifully translated" by Benjamin and Barbara Har-

shov, noted a *Publishers Weekly* contributor. While Amichai "historically belongs to the 1948 generation in Israeli literature," wrote Gila Ramras-Rauch for *World Literature Today,* she placed Amichai's work "in effect . . . with the Statehood Generation of the 1960s . . . stripping the language of its heavy historical gear and enhancing its accessibility to contemporary readers." Elizabeth Gunderson commented in *Booklist* that Amichai has the ability to "take on the burden of history, but the load rarely strains his work or makes him appear omnipotently beyond the reaches of human skirmishes." With any lifetime oeuvre, critics seem tempted to define periods in an artist's work. However, Ramras-Rauch found this difficult to do in Amichai's case: "From its inception it was not the poetry of a young man. His daring images, his subtle irony, his subdued tone have been his hallmarks."

Open Closed Open, published in Israel in 1998 and in English translation in 2000, has been described as Amichai's magnum opus. The sequence of twenty-five poems was characterized in *Publishers Weekly* as "a searching late book from a writer who acknowledges the high stakes of writing and of life as lived daily." To quote *New Republic* contributor Williams, the book "comprises a sustained outburst of inspiration, and it has a . . . complicated relation to wisdom and to matters of the spirit." In works rich in simile and metaphor, Amichai employs the rich spiritual tradition of the Jews—and the modern anxieties of the Jewish state—to comment on the wider human emotions of religious doubt, parental love, and commitment to the world. As Kessler observed: "The poignancy of our earthly sojourn, its ephemeral sweetness, the pregnancy of the smallest human gestures, the haunted beauty and richness of the most mundane things and events—none of this is lost on the poet. He dares to tackle cosmic themes in domestic terms." Williams concluded: "To sojourn with Amichai in the vast, rugged, sympathetic domain of his imagination is to be given leave to linger in one of those privileged moments when we are in a confidential and confident engagement with our own spirits, when we know with certainty that such a process of imaginative self-investigation is proper and just, regardless of the substance or the occasion of our thoughts."

BIOGRAPHICAL AND CRITICAL SOURCES:

BOOKS

Abramson, Glenda, editor, *The Experienced Soul: Studies in Amichai,* Westview Press (Boulder, CO), 1997.

Abramson, Glenda, *The Writing of Yehuda Amichai: A Thematic Approach,* State University of New York Press (Albany, NY), 1989.

Alter, Robert, *After the Tradition: Essays on Modern Jewish Writing,* Dutton (New York, NY), 1969.

Amichai, Yehuda, *Not of This Time, Not of This Place,* Harper (New York, NY), 1968.

Cohen, Joseph, *Voices of Israel: Essays on and Interviews with Yehuda Amichai, A.B. Yehoshua, T. Carmi, Aharon Appelfeld, and Amos Oz,* State University of New York Press (Albany, NY), 1990.

Contemporary Literary Criticism, Thomson Gale (Detroit, MI), Volume 9, 1978, Volume 22, 1982, Volume 57, 1990.

Lapon-Kandelshein, Essi, *To Commemorate the Seventieth Birthday of Yehuda Amichai: A Bibliography of His Work in Translation,* Institute for the Translation of Hebrew Literature (Ramat Gan, Israel), 1994.

PERIODICALS

American Poetry Review, November-December, 1987.

Booklist, October 1, 1994, p. 230; March 15, 2000, Donna Seaman, review of *Open Closed Open,* p. 1313.

Commentary, May, 1974.

Hudson Review, autumn, 1991.

Kenyon Review, winter, 1988.

Library Journal, July, 1969; July, 1977.

Nation, May 29, 1982.

New Republic, March 3, 1982; July 3, 2000, C.K. Williams, "We Cannot Be Fooled, We Can Be Fooled," p. 29.

New Yorker, May 3, 1969.

New York Times Book Review, August 4, 1965; July 3, 1977; November 13, 1983; August 3, 1986, Edward Hirsch, "In Language Torn from Sleep," p. 14.

New York Times Magazine, June 8, 1986, Robert Alter, "Israel's Master Poet," p. 40.

Publishers Weekly, August 29, 1994, p. 66; March 27, 2000, review of *Open Closed Open,* p. 71.

Tikkun, May-June, 1994, p. 96.

Times Literary Supplement, October 17, 1986.

Village Voice, July 2, 1985; April 14, 1987.

Virginia Quarterly Review, autumn, 1987.

Washington Post Book World, February 15, 1970.

World Literature Today, spring, 1995, pp. 426-427.

ONLINE

East Bay Express Online, http://www.eastbayexpress.com/ (September 24, 2000), Stephen Kessler, "Theology for Atheists."

OBITUARIES:

PERIODICALS

New Republic, October, 9, 2000, p. 28.

Poetry, December, 2000, p. 232.

Times (London, England), October, 13, 2000, p. 25.

*   *   *

AMIS, Kingsley 1922-1995

(Kingsley William Amis, Robert Markham, William Tanner)

PERSONAL: Born April 16, 1922, in London, England; died after suffering severe injuries in a fall, October 22, 1995, in London, England; son of William Robert (an office clerk) and Rosa Annie (Lucas) Amis; married Hilary Ann Bardwell, 1948 (divorced, 1965); married Elizabeth Jane Howard (a novelist), 1965 (divorced, 1983); children: (first marriage) Philip Nicol William, Martin Louis, Sally Myfanwy. *Education:* St. John's College, Oxford, B.A. (first class honors in English), 1947, M.A., 1948. *Hobbies and other interests:* Music (jazz, Mozart), thrillers, television, science fiction.

CAREER: University College of Swansea, Swansea, Glamorganshire, Wales, lecturer in English, 1949-61; Cambridge University, Peterhouse, Cambridge, England, fellow, 1961-63; full-time writer, 1963-95. Princeton University, visiting fellow in creative writing, 1958-59; Vanderbilt University, visiting professor of English, 1967-68. Appeared (as guest) in the film *Tell Me Lies,* 1968. *Military service:* British Army, Royal Signal Corps, 1942-45; became lieutenant.

MEMBER: Authors' Club (London, England), Bristol Channel Yacht Club, Garrick Club.

AWARDS, HONORS: Somerset Maugham Award, 1955, for *Lucky Jim;* Booker-McConnell Prize nomination, Great Britain's Book Trust, and *Yorkshire Post* Book of the Year Award, both 1974, for *Ending Up;* fellowship, St. John's College, Oxford, 1976; Commander of the Order of the British Empire, 1981; fellowship, University College of Swansea, 1985; Booker-McConnell Prize for Fiction, Great Britain's Book Trust, 1986, for *The Old Devils;* Cholmondeley Award, 1990; knighted, 1990.

WRITINGS:

NOVELS

Lucky Jim, Doubleday (New York, NY), 1954, abridged edition, edited by D.K. Swan, illustrations by William Burnard, Longmans (London, England), 1963, abridged edition with glossary and notes by R.M. Oldnall, Macmillan (New York, NY), 1967.

That Uncertain Feeling, Gollancz (London, England), 1955, Harcourt (New York, NY), 1956.

I Like It Here, Harcourt (New York, NY), 1958.

Take a Girl Like You, Gollancz (London, England), 1960, Harcourt (New York, NY), 1961.

One Fat Englishman, Gollancz (London, England), 1963, Harcourt (New York, NY), 1964.

(With Robert Conquest) *The Egyptologists,* J. Cape (London, England), 1965, Random House (New York, NY), 1966.

The Anti-Death League, Harcourt (New York, NY), 1966, Gollancz (London, England), 1978.

(Under pseudonym Robert Markham) *Colonel Sun: A James Bond Adventure,* Harper (New York, NY), 1968.

I Want It Now, J. Cape (London, England), 1968, collected edition, 1976, Harcourt (New York, NY), 1969.

The Green Man, J. Cape (London, England), 1969, Harcourt (New York, NY), 1970.

Girl, 20, J. Cape (London, England), 1971, Harcourt (New York, NY), 1972.

The Riverside Villas Murder, Harcourt (New York, NY), 1973.

Ending Up, Harcourt (New York, NY), 1974.

The Alteration, J. Cape (London, England), 1976, Viking (New York, NY), 1977.

Jake's Thing (also see below), Hutchinson (London, England), 1978, Viking (New York, NY), 1979.

Russian Hide-and-Seek: A Melodrama, Hutchinson (London, England), 1980, Penguin (New York, NY), 1981.

Stanley and the Women (also see below), Hutchinson (London, England), 1984, Summit Books (New York, NY), 1985.

The Old Devils (also see below), Hutchinson (London, England), 1986, Summit Books (New York, NY), 1987.

The Crime of the Century, Dent (New York, NY), 1987.

A Kingsley Amis Omnibus (includes *Jake's Thing, Stanley and the Women,* and *The Old Devils*), Hutchinson (London, England), 1987.

Difficulties with Girls, Summit Books (New York, NY), 1988.

The Folks That Live on the Hill, Hutchinson (London, England), 1990.

The Russian Girl, Viking (New York, NY), 1994.

You Can't Do Both, limited edition, Hutchinson (London, England), 1994.

The Biographer's Moustache, Flamingo (London, England), 1995.

POEMS

Bright November, Fortune Press (London, England), 1947.

A Frame of Mind: Eighteen Poems, School of Art, Reading University (Reading, England), 1953.

Poems, Oxford University Poetry Society (Oxford, England), 1954.

Kingsley Amis, Fantasy Press (Oxford, England), 1954.

A Case of Samples: Poems, 1946-1956, Gollancz (London, England), 1956, Harcourt (New York, NY), 1957.

(With Dom Moraes and Peter Porter) *Penguin Modern Poets 2,* Penguin (New York, NY), 1962.

The Evans Country, Fantasy Press (Oxford, England), 1962.

A Look Round the Estate: Poems 1957-1967, J. Cape (London, England), 1967, Harcourt (New York, NY), 1968.

Collected Poems: 1944-1979, Hutchinson (London, England), 1979, Viking (New York, NY), 1980.

OTHER

Socialism and the Intellectuals, Fabian Society (London, England), 1957.

New Maps of Hell: A Survey of Science Fiction, Harcourt (New York, NY), 1960.

My Enemy's Enemy (short stories; also see below), Gollancz (London, England), 1962, Harcourt (New York, NY), 1963.

Reading His Own Poems (recording), Listen, 1962.

(With Thomas Blackburn) *Poems* (recording), Jupiter (London, England), 1962.

(Under pseudonym William Tanner) *The Book of Bond; or, Every Man His Own 007,* Viking (New York, NY), 1965.

The James Bond Dossier, New American Library (New York, NY), 1965.

Lucky Jim's Politics, Conservative Political Centre (London, England), 1968.

What Became of Jane Austen? and Other Questions (essays), J. Cape (London, England), 1970, Harcourt (New York, NY), 1971, published as *What Became of Jane Austen and Other Essays,* Penguin (New York, NY), 1981.

Dear Illusion (short stories; also see below), Covent Garden Press (London, England), 1972.

On Drink (also see below), illustrations by Nicolas Bentley, J. Cape (London, England), 1972, Harcourt, 1973.

First Aid for ABA Conventioneers (excerpt from *On Drink*), Harcourt (New York, NY), 1973.

Rudyard Kipling and His World, Scribner (New York, NY), 1975.

Interesting Things, edited by Michael Swan, Cambridge University Press (Cambridge, England), 1977.

Harold's Years: Impressions of the Harold Wilson Era, Charles River Books (Boston, MA), 1977.

The Darkwater Hall Mystery (also see below), illustrations by Elspeth Sojka, Tragara Press (Edinburgh, Scotland), 1978.

(Editor) *The New Oxford Book of English Light Verse,* Oxford University Press (Oxford, England), 1978.

An Arts Policy? (with a foreword by Hugh Thomas), Centre for Policy Studies (London, England), 1979.

(Editor) *The Faber Popular Reciter,* Faber & Faber (London, England), 1979.

Collected Short Stories (includes "My Enemy's Enemy," "Dear Illusion," and "The Darkwater Hall Mystery"), Hutchinson (London, England), 1980, Penguin (New York, NY), 1983, revised edition, 1987.

Every Day Drinking, illustrations by Merrily Harper, Hutchinson (London, England), 1983.

How's Your Glass? A Quizzical Look at Drinks and Drinking, Weidenfeld & Nicolson (London, England), 1984, with cartoons by Michael Heath, Arrow, 1986.

The Amis Anthology, Century Hutchinson (London, England), 1988.

The Amis Collection: Selected Non-Fiction, 1954-1990, Hutchinson (London, England), 1990.

The Pleasure of Poetry, Cassell (London, England), 1990.

Kingsley Amis, in Life and Letters, edited by Dale Salwak, Macmillan (Basingstoke, England), 1990, St. Martin's (New York, NY), 1991.

Memoirs, Summit Books (New York, NY), 1991.

We Are All Guilty (for children), Viking Children's Books (New York, NY), 1992.

Mr. Barrett's Secret and Other Stories, Hutchinson (London, England), 1993.

The Biographer's Mustache, HarperCollins (New York, NY), 1995.

The King's English: A Guide to Modern Usage, St. Martin's Press (New York, NY), 1998.

The Letters of Kinsley Amis, edited by Zachary Leader, HarperCollins (New York, NY), 2000.

Also author of a science fiction radio play, *Something Strange,* and of television plays *A Question about Hell,* 1964, *The Importance of Being Harry,* 1971, *Dr. Watson and the Darkwater Hall Mystery,* 1974, and *See What You've Done,* 1974. Also editor of *Spectrum: A Science Fiction Anthology,* Amereon. Author of column on beverages in *Penthouse.* Editor of and contributor to literary anthologies. Contributor to periodicals, including *Spectator, Encounter, New Statesman, Listener, Observer,* and *London Magazine.*

ADAPTATIONS: Lucky Jim was adapted as a motion picture, written by Jeffrey Dell and Patrick Campbell, directed by John Boulting, starring Sharon Acker and Ian Carmichael, British Lion, 1957; *That Uncertain Feeling* was adapted as a motion picture as *Only Two Can Play,* written by Bryan Forbes, directed by Sidney Gilliat, starring Peter Sellers, Mai Zetterling, Virginia Maskell, and Richard Attenborough, Columbia, 1962; *Take a Girl Like You* was adapted as a motion picture, written by George Melly, directed by Jonathan Miller, starring Hayley Mills and Oliver Reed, Columbia, 1970; *That Uncertain Feeling* was adapted as a television miniseries, 1985; one of Amis's novels formed the basis of the television movie *Haunted: The Ferryman,* 1986; *Jake's Thing* was recorded on audiocassette, Books on Tape, 1988; *Ending Up* was adapted for television, 1989; *The Old Devils* was adapted as a play, 1989; *The Green Man* was adapted for television, 1990; *Stanley and the Women* was adapted as a television miniseries, 1991; *The Old Devils* was adapted as a television miniseries, 1992; *Take a Girl Like You* was adapted for television, 2001; *Lucky Jim* was adapted for television by Jack Rosenthal, 2003.

SIDELIGHTS: "I think of myself like a sort of mid-or late-Victorian person," said Kingsley Amis in *Contemporary Literature,* "not in outlook but in the position of writing a bit of poetry (we forget that George Eliot also wrote verse), writing novels, being interested in questions of the day and occasionally writing about them, and being interested in the work of other writers and occasionally writing about that. I'm not exactly an entertainer pure and simple, not exactly an artist pure and simple, certainly not an incisive critic of society, and certainly not a political figure though I'm interested in politics. I think I'm just a combination of some of those things."

Though an eclectic man of letters, Amis was best known as a prolific novelist who, in the words of Blake Morrison in the *Times Literary Supplement,* had the "ability to go on surprising us." He won critical acclaim in

1954 with the publication of his first novel, *Lucky Jim.* After producing three other comic works, Amis was quickly characterized as a comic novelist writing in the tradition of P.G. Wodehouse and Evelyn Waugh. Critics ranked him among the foremost "Angry Young Men," a school of British writers who disdained post-World War II British society throughout the 1950s. However, "Amis," stated *Los Angeles Times* writer William D. Montalbano, "rejected the label as 'a very boring journalistic phrase.'"

After his early works, Amis produced a spate of novels that differed radically in genre and seriousness of theme. He kept "experimenting with ways of confounding the reader who hopes for a single focus," claimed William Hutchings in *Critical Quarterly,* though Clancy Sigal suggested in *National Review* that Amis simply had "the virtue, rare in England, of refusing to accept an imposed definition of what a Serious Writer ought to write about." His place in British literature was recognized in 1986, when his novel *The Old Devils* won the Booker Prize, Britain's highest literary award. In 1990, he was knighted by Queen Elizabeth II.

Jim Dixon, the protagonist of *Lucky Jim,* is, according to Anthony Burgess in *The Novel Now: A Guide to Contemporary Fiction,* "the most popular anti-hero of our time." Though a junior lecturer at a provincial university, Jim has no desire to be an intellectual—or a "gentleman"—because of his profound, almost physical, hatred of the social and cultural affectations of university life. This characteristic of Jim has led several critics to conclude that he is a philistine, and, moreover, that beneath the comic effects, Amis was really attacking culture and was himself a philistine. Brigid Brophy, for example, wrote in *Don't Never Forget: Collected Views and Reviews* that the "apex of philistinism" is reached "when Jim hears a tune by the composer whom either he or Mr. Amis . . . thinks of as 'filthy Mozart.'" Ralph Caplan, however, claimed in Charles Shapiro's *Contemporary British Novelists* that *Lucky Jim* "never [promises] anything more than unmitigated pleasure and insight, and these it keeps on delivering. The book [is] not promise but fulfillment, a commodity we confront too seldom to know how to behave when it is achieved. This seems to be true particularly when the achievement is comic. Have we forgotten how to take humor straight? Unable to exit laughing, the contemporary reader looks over his shoulder for Something More. The trouble is that by now he knows how to find it."

Critics generally have seen the three novels that follow *Lucky Jim* as variations on this theme of appealing to common sense and denouncing affectation. Discussing

Lucky Jim, That Uncertain Feeling, I Like It Here, and *Take a Girl Like You* in the *Hudson Review,* James P. Degnan stated: "In the comically outraged voice of his angry young heroes—e.g., Jim Dixon of *Lucky Jim* and John Lewis of *That Uncertain Feeling*—Amis [lampoons] what C.P. Snow . . . labeled the 'traditional culture,' the 'culture of the literary intellectuals,' of the 'gentleman's world.'" James Gindin noted in *Postwar British Fiction* that the similarity of purpose is reflected in a corresponding similarity of technique: "Each of the [four] novels is distinguished by a thick verbal texture that is essential comic. The novels are full of word play and verbal jokes. . . . All Amis's heroes are mimics: Jim Dixon parodies the accent of Professor Welch, his phony and genteel professor, in *Lucky Jim;* Patrick Standish, in *Take a Girl Like You,* deliberately echoes the Hollywood version of the Southern Negro's accent. John Lewis, the hero of *That Uncertain Feeling,* also mimics accents and satirically characterizes other people by the words and phrases they use."

The heroes in these four novels are in fact so much alike that Brophy charged Amis with "rewriting much the same novel under different titles and with different names for the characters," although Walter Allen insisted in the *Modern Novel* that the "young man recognizably akin to Lucky Jim, the Amis man as he might be called, . . . has been increasingly explored in depth." Consistent with her assessment of Jim Dixon in *Lucky Jim,* Brophy saw the other three Amis heroes also as "militant philistines," a view that was not shared by Caplan, Burgess, or Degnan. Caplan explained that though the Amis hero in these novels is seemingly anti-intellectual, he is nonetheless "always cerebral," and Burgess pointed out that the hero "always earns his living by purveying culture as teacher, librarian, journalist, or publisher." Representing a commonsensical approach to life, the Amis protagonist, according to Degnan, is an inversion of a major convention of the hero "as 'sensitive soul,' the convention of the 'alienated' young man of artistic or philosophical pretensions struggling pitifully and hopelessly against an insensitive, middle-class, materialistic world. . . . In place of the sensitive soul as hero, Amis creates in his early novels a hero radically new to serious contemporary fiction: a middle-class hero who is also an intellectual, an intellectual who is unabashedly middle-brow. . . . Suspicious of all pretentiousness, of all heroic posturing, the Amis hero . . . voices all that is best of the 'lower middle class, of the non-gentlemanly' conscience."

Degnan, however, did believe that Patrick Standish in *Take a Girl Like You* came dangerously close to "the kind of anti-hero—e.g., blase, irresponsible, hedonistic—that Amis's first three novels attack," and that this weakened the satirical aspect of the novel. Echoing this observation in *The Reaction against Experiment in the English Novel, 1950-1960,* Rubin Rabinovitz detected an uncertainty as to what "vice and folly" really are and who possesses them: "In *Take a Girl Like You* Amis satirizes both Patrick's lechery and Jenny's persistence in preserving her virginity. . . . The satire in *Lucky Jim* is not divided this way: Jim Dixon mocks the hypocrisy of his colleagues in the university and refuses to be subverted by it. [In *Lucky Jim*] the satire is more powerful because the things being satirized are more boldly defined."

After *Take a Girl Like You,* Amis produced several other "straight" novels, as *Time*'s Christopher Porterfield described them, as well as a James Bond spy thriller, written under the pseudonym of Robert Markham, called *Colonel Sun: A James Bond Adventure;* a work of science fiction, *The Anti-Death League;* and a ghost story, *The Green Man.* When Gildrose Productions, the firm to which the James Bond copyright was sold after Ian Fleming's death, awarded the first non-Fleming sequel to Amis, the literary world received the news with a mixture of apprehension and interest. Earlier, Amis had done an analysis of the nature of Fleming's hero, *The James Bond Dossier,* and he appeared to be a logical successor to Bond's creator. But the reactions to *Colonel Sun* were not entirely positive. Though Clara Siggins stated in *Best Sellers* that Amis "produced an exciting narrative with the expertise and verve of Fleming himself," S.K. Oberbeck claimed in the *Washington Post Book World* that the changes Amis made "on Bond's essential character throw the formula askew. . . . In humanizing Bond, in netting him back into the channel of real contemporary events, Amis somehow deprives him of the very ingredients that made his barely believable adventures so rewarding." Similarly, David Lodge, discussing the book in *The Novelist at the Crossroads and Other Essays on Fiction and Criticism,* considered *Colonel Sun* "more realistic" yet "duller" than most of the Fleming novels, because "the whole enterprise, undertaken, apparently, in a spirit of pious imitation, required Amis to keep in check his natural talent for parody and deflating comic realism."

Amis's comic spirit, so prominent in his first four novels and muted in *Colonel Sun,* is noticeably absent from *The Anti-Death League,* which was published two years before the Bond adventure. Bernard Bergonzi commented in *The Situation of the Novel* that in *The Anti-Death League,* Amis "has written a more generalised kind of fiction, with more clearly symbolic implications, than in any of his earlier novels. There is still a

trace of sardonic humor, and his ear remains alert to the placing details of individual speech; but Amis has here abandoned the incisive social mimicry, the memorable responses to the specificity of a person's appearance or the look of a room that have previously characterized his fiction."

The story concerns a British army officer who becomes convinced that a nonhuman force of unlimited malignancy, called God, is responsible for a pattern of seemingly undeserved deaths. Bergonzi viewed the work as a provocative, anti-theological novel of ideas and maintained that it "represents Amis's immersion in the nightmare that flickers at the edges of his earlier fiction." He did, however, find one shortcoming in the novel: "*The Anti-Death League . . .* is intensely concerned with the questions that lead to tragedy—death, cruelty, loss of every kind—while lacking the ontological supports—whether religious or humanistic—that can sustain the tragic view of life." A *Times Literary Supplement* reviewer admitted that the rebellion against the facts of pain and death "seems rather juvenile, like kicking God's ankle for doing such things to people," but declared: "[Amis] takes the argument to more audacious and hopeful lengths. . . . We do care about his creatures; the agents intrigue us and the victims concern us. The handling is vastly less pompous than the theme: oracular, yes, but eloquent and earthly and even moving."

Amis followed *The Anti-Death League* with *The Green Man* and *Girl, 20,* a comic novel with serious overtones. Paul Schleuter in *Saturday Review* viewed *Girl, 20* as a harmonious addition to Amis's body of work. He wrote: "[Amis's] talent for creating humorous situations, characters, and dialogue is as fresh as ever. . . . Amis also has a distinct undercurrent of pathos, darkness, and trauma. The result is not really a 'new' Amis so much as a more mature examination of human foibles and excesses than was the case in his earlier novels." But Amis's next novel, *The Riverside Villas Murder,* "offers no comfort to those who look for consistency in [his] work," according to a *Times Literary Supplement* reviewer.

A departure from Amis's previous works, *The Riverside Villas Murder* is a detective story, though there was some debate among critics as to whether it is should be read "straight" or as a parody of the genre. Patrick Cosgrave, for example, claimed in *Saturday Review/World* that the book is "a straight detective story, with a murder, several puzzles, clues, a great detective, and an eminently satisfying and unexpected villain. So bald a statement is a necessary introduction in order to ensure that nobody will be tempted to pore over *The Riverside Villas Murder* in search of portentiousness, significance, [or] ambiguity. . . . The book is straight detection because Amis intended it to be such: It is written out of a great love of the detective form and deliberately set in a period—the Thirties—when that form was . . . most popular." The *Times Literary Supplement* reviewer, however, considered the book "something more and less than a period detective story. Mr. Amis is not one to take any convention too seriously, and on one plane he is simply having fun." Patricia Coyne, writing in *National Review,* and *Time*'s T.E. Kalem expressed similar opinions. Coyne described the story as "a boy discovers sex against a murder-mystery backdrop," and Kalem concluded that by making a fourteen-year-old boy the hero of the novel, "Amis cleverly combines, in mild parody, two ultra-British literary forms—the mystery thriller with the boyhood adventure yarn."

Amis followed *The Riverside Villas Murder* with a straight novel, *Ending Up,* before producing *The Alteration,* which *Time*'s Paul Gray said "flits quirkily between satire, science fiction, boy's adventure, and travelogue. The result is what *Nineteen Eighty-Four* might have been like if Lewis Carroll had written it: not a classic, certainly, but an oddity well worth an evening's attention." According to Bruce Cook in *Saturday Review, The Alteration* belongs to a rare subgenre of science fiction: "the so-called counterfeit-or alternative-world novel." Though set in the twentieth century, in 1976, the book has as its premise that the Protestant Reformation never occurred and, as a result, that the world is essentially Catholic. The plot centers on the discovery of a brilliant boy soprano, the Church's plans to preserve his gift by "altering" his anatomy through castration, and the debate on the justice of this decision.

Thomas R. Edwards noted in the *New York Review of Books* that though "Amis isn't famous for his compassion," in *The Alteration* he "affectingly catches and respects a child's puzzlement about the threatened loss of something he knows about only from descriptions." John Carey insisted in the *New Statesman* that the book "has almost nothing expectable about it, except that it is a study of tyranny." The tyranny to which Carey referred was the destructive power of the pontifical hierarchy to emasculate life and art, which he saw as the theme of the novel.

From *The Alteration* to *Jake's Thing,* Amis again made the transition from science fiction to "comic diatribe," according to V.S. Pritchett in the *New York Review of*

Books. Pritchett considered *Jake's Thing* "a very funny book, less for its action or its talk than its prose. . . . Mr. Amis is a master of laconic mimicry and of the vernacular drift." A reviewer wrote in *Choice* that this is "the Amis of *Lucky Jim,* an older and wiser comic writer who is making a serious statement about the human condition."

The story focuses on Jake Richardson, a sixty-year-old reader in early Mediterranean history at Oxford who in the past has been to bed with well over a hundred women but now suffers from a loss of libido. Referred to sex therapist Dr. Proinsias (a Celtic name, pronounced "Francis") Rosenberg, Jake, said *Nation*'s Amy Wilentz, "is caught up in the supermarket of contemporary life. The novel is filled with encounter groups, free love, women's liberation, and such electronic contrivances as the 'nocturnal mensurator,' which measures the level of a man's arousal as he sleeps." Christopher Lehmann-Haupt of the *New York Times* noted that Amis "makes the most of all the comic possibilities here. Just imagine sensible, civilized Jake coming home from Dr. Rosenberg's office with . . . assignments to study 'pictorial pornographic material' and to 'write out a sexual fantasy in not less than six hundred words.' Consider Jake struggling to find seventy-three more words, or contemplating the nudes in *Mezzanine* magazine, which 'had an exotic appearance, like the inside of a giraffe's ear or a tropical fruit not much prized by the locals.'"

But for all the hilarity, there is an undercurrent of seriousness running through the novel. "It comes bubbling up," wrote Lehmann-Haupt, "when Jake finally grows fed up with Dr. Rosenberg and his experiments." Wilentz argued that the novel expresses "outrage at, and defeat at the hands of, modernity, whose graceless intrusion on one's privacy is embodied in Dr. Rosenberg's constantly repeated question, 'I take it you've no objection to exposing your genitals in public?'" Malcolm Bradbury shared this interpretation, writing in the *New Statesman:* "Amis, watching [history's] collectivising, behaviourist, depersonalizing progress, would like nice things to win and certain sense to prevail. Indeed, a humanist common sense—along with attention to farts—is to his world view roughly what post-Heideggerian existentialism is to Jean-Paul Sartre's."

After the problems of libido in *Jake's Thing,* wrote Morrison in the *Times Literary Supplement, Russian Hide-and-Seek* "signals the return of the young, uncomplicated, highly sexed Amis male; . . . the more important connection, however, is with Amis's earlier novel, *The Alteration.*" Another example of the "alternative world" novel, *Russian Hide-and-Seek* depicts an England, fifty years hence, that has been overrun by the Soviet Union; oddly enough, though, the Soviets have abandoned Marxism and returned to the style of Russia under the czars. Paul Binding described the book in the *New Statesman* as "at once a pastiche of certain aspects of nineteenth-century Russian fiction and an exercise in cloak-and-dagger adventure. The two genres unite to form a work far more ambitious than those earlier *jeux*—a fictional expression of the author's obsessive conviction that, whatever its avatar, Russian culture is beastly, thriving on conscious exploitation, enamoured of brutality."

Amis placed himself at the center of political controversy with his next novel, *Stanley and the Women*. Well received upon publication in England, the book was rejected by publishing houses in the United States twice because of objections to its main character's misogyny, said some sources. "When rumors that one of Britain's most prominent and popular postwar novelists was being censored Stateside by a feminist cabal hit print [in early 1985], the literary flap echoed on both sides of the Atlantic for weeks," reported *Time's* Paul Gray. After the book found an American publisher, a critical debate ensued, with some reviewers condemning its uniformly negative depiction of women and others defending the book's value nonetheless.

In a *Washington Post Book World* review, Jonathan Yardley charged that "Amis has stacked the deck against women, reducing them to caricatures who reinforce the damning judgments made by Stanley and his chums." Though Yardley felt that "much else in the novel is exceedingly well done," he also felt that its "cranky misogynism" is too prominent to be ignored. Indeed, Stanley casts himself as the victim of a gang of female villains: a self-centered ex-wife; a current wife who stabs herself and accuses Stanley's emotionally unstable son; and a psychiatrist who deliberately mishandles the son's case and blames Stanley for the son's schizophrenia. On the other hand, "the men in the novel hardly fare any better," remarked Michiko Kakutani of the *New York Times*. In her view, similar to that of Susan Fromberg Schaeffer in the *New York Times Book Review, Stanley and the Women* proves Amis to be "not just a misogynist, but a misanthrope as well. Practically every character in the novel is either an idiot or a scheming hypocrite." Amis, who observed that British women took less offense from the book, claimed it is not anti-female; *Time* presented his statement that "all comedy, . . . all humor is unfair. . . . There is a beady-eyed view of women in the book, certainly. . . . But a novel is not a report or a biographical statement

or a confession. If it is a good novel, it dramatizes thoughts that some people, somewhere, have had."

Viewing the book from this perspective, some critics found it laudable. *Spectator* contributor Harriet Waugh argued, "It does have to be admitted . . . that Mr. Amis's portrayal of Stanley's wives as female monsters is funny and convincing. Most readers will recognise aspects of them in women they know. . . . [Amis] has written a true account of the intolerableness of women in relation to men." Such a tract, she felt, is comparable in many respects to novels by women that show women "downtrodden" by men. Wrote Gray, "Amis has excelled at rattling preconceptions ever since the appearance of his classically comic first novel. . . . Is this novel unfair to women? Probably. Is the question worth asking? No. . . . The females in the world of this book all commit 'offences' . . . at least in the eyes of Stanley, who is . . . nobody's idea of a deep thinker." In the *Times Literary Supplement,* J.K.L. Walker concluded, "*Stanley and the Women* reveals Kingsley Amis in the full flood of his talent and should survive its ritual burning in William IV Street unscathed."

The author's next novel, *The Old Devils,* "manifests little of the female bashing that made the satiric *Stanley and the Women* . . . so scandalous. In fact, dissatisfied wives are given some tart remarks to make about their variously unsatisfactory husbands. . . . Even so, these concessions never denature Amis's characteristic bite," wrote Gray. In a London *Times* review, Victoria Glendinning thought: "This is vintage Kingsley Amis, fifty percent alcohol, with splashes of savagery about getting old, and about the state of the sex-war in marriages of thirty or more years' standing." Reviewers admired most the book's major female character; Amis gives her a relationship with her daughter "so close, candid and trusting that the most ardent feminist must applaud," noted Martin Champlin in the *Los Angeles Times Book Review.* Her husband, Alun, an aggressive womanizer, drew the most disfavor. In what Gray felt was the author's "wisest and most humane work," both sexes enjoy their best and worst moments. "This is one of Amis's strengths as a novelist, not noticeably to the fore in recent work but making a welcome return here: 'bad' characters are allowed their victories and 'good' characters their defeats. Yet Amis comes down against Alun in a firmly 'moral' conclusion," commented Morrison in the *Times Literary Supplement.* Alun's funeral near the close of the book is balanced with "the reconciliation of two of the feuding older generation, and the marriage of two of the younger," such that the ending has "an almost Shakespearean symmetry," stated Morrison. But the mood, he warned, is not exactly one of celebration. He explained that the character Amis seems to most approve of "belongs in that tradition of the Amis hero who would like to believe but can't," whose "disappointed scepticism" keeps him from seeing a romantic encouragement behind a pleasant scene. "Finally," reflected Bryan Appleyard in the London *Times,* "it is this sense of an empty, somewhat vacuous age which seems to come close to the heart of all [Amis's] work. His novels are no-nonsense, well-made, good-humored products. They are about the struggle to get by in the gutter and their heroes seldom roll over to gaze at the stars. Like Larkin he is awestruck by the *idea* of religion but he cannot subscribe. Instead, his novels are happily committed to the obliteration of cant without thought of what to put in its place."

For *The Old Devils,* Amis received the Booker-McConnell Prize for Fiction, the most prestigious book award in England. Among critics who felt the prize was well deserved was Champlin, who referred to "its sheer storytelling expertise, and its qualities of wit, humanity, and observation." In the *New York Times Book Review,* William H. Pritchard recognized *The Old Devils* as Amis's "most ambitious and one of his longest books, . . . neither a sendup nor an exercise in some established genre. It sets forth, with full realistic detail, a large cast of characters at least six of whom are rendered in depth. . . . *The Old Devils* is also Mr. Amis's most inclusive novel, encompassing kinds of feeling and tone that move from sardonic gloom to lyric tenderness."

Critics celebrated Amis's return to the satiric comic-novel again in *Difficulties with Girls,* a sort of sequel to his 1960 work *Take a Girl Like You.* "In returning to the characters of . . . *Take a Girl Like You,*" wrote *New York* magazine contributor Rhoda Koenig, "Amis has also . . . reverted to his style of that period, the sprightly, needling tone he had only six years after *Lucky Jim.*" Patrick Standish has not changed much from the "dedicated sexual predator" who married the girl he raped after getting her drunk at a party, declared Judith Grossman in the *New York Times Book Review.* He has left his job as a high school teacher and entered the world of publishing, which provides him with just as many opportunities for sexual conquests. When his wife, Jenny, discovers the latest of these, she leaves him; then, discovering she is pregnant, she returns. "Amis is one of the best chroniclers we have of the lost world [of 1950s-era male chauvinism]," Michael Wood wrote in the *Times Literary Supplement,* "in large part because he knows it's not lost at all, but lies around us everywhere. . . . Amis is not a praiser of the old world, but he is very suspicious of the new one. Maybe it's not

even there; maybe it's just a phantom bred of our lame trendiness, our cult of tolerance."

The Folks That Live on the Hill again looks at problems in modern life—alcoholism, prostate surgery, divorce—in a serio-comic vein. "Formally," commented *New Statesman and Society* contributor Anthony Quinn, "it's another funny-sad comedy of social and sexual manners, cast in the old-farts-ensemble mould of *Ending Up* and *The Old Devils.*" It tells of the struggles of retired librarian Harry Caldecote to resolve the problems of different members of his extended family—his son's financial irresponsibility, his brother's suffering marriage, and the various problems of relatives of his ex-wives. "Mr. Amis is, however, less interested in exploring Harry's burden of obligation toward others than in focusing on the novel's different characters as they undergo their troubles," Pritchard explained in the *New York Times Book Review.* Although critics noted that *The Folks That Live on the Hill* covers ground that Amis had written about before, many found, as did Quinn, that "Amis is still *funny.* The knack of capturing the false starts and dead ends of everyday chatter, the gift for mimicry, the elaborate expressions of outrage—time has withered none of these. You wince as he drives a coach and horses over the liberal consensus, but you find yourself cackling like a maniac."

Amis reviewed his own career in *Memoirs,* published four years before his death. "Television interviewers and others who expected him to be uniformly reactionary on every issue," wrote Merle Rubin in the *Christian Science Monitor,* "were often surprised to discover that he was not an advocate of capital punishment, a racist, or an America-basher, after all." However, many reviewers criticized the work, claiming that it lacked focus and personal insight. "The faint hope might have been that, in writing directly about himself, the irascible old shag would come over as . . . cuddlier than his usual public image makes him seem," said *London Review of Books* critic Ian Hamilton. "To any such tender expectations, though, Amis offers here a close-to-gleeful 'In a pig's arse, friend'—i.e. you bastards will get nothing out of me, or not much and what you do get you won't like." "Amis," Craig Brown wrote in the *Times Literary Supplement,* "has created his autobiographical persona along the lines of one of his most comically pitiless characters."

In his novel *The Russian Girl,* Amis returned to skewer one of his prime targets: the halls of academe. Richard Vaisey is an academic at a British university who specializes in Russian literature. Like other Amis protagonists, he is also oversexed and unhappily married—to Cordelia, whose good points are that she is good in bed and independently wealthy. Vaisey is approached by an expatriate Russian poet named Anna Danilova, who is circulating a petition to have her brother released from prison in Russia. "Anna Danilova is a terrible poet but sweet, gentle and deferential," explained Diane Roberts in the *Atlanta Journal-Constitution.* "Richard must choose between Cordelia (and money) and Anna (and true love)." "Amis, the old master, somehow orchestrates all these themes, and several more, into a wonderful new concert of plot and language," Gary Abrams declared in the *Los Angeles Times Book Review,* "that provokes both belly laughs and twinges of discomfort over the silly messes we humans make while blundering through life." "*The Russian Girl,*" wrote *New York Times Book Review* contributor Christopher Buckley, "is . . . vintage Amis: smooth, dry and not overpriced."

Amis died unexpectedly late in 1995, while he was being treated in St. Pancras Hospital, London, after having crushed several vertebrae in his back in a severe fall. A posthumous publication, *The King's English: A Guide to Modern Usage,* represented a last foray into nonfiction for an author who had written works of literary criticism, political commentary, and history dating back to *Socialism and the Intellectuals,* published by the Fabian Society in 1957. The publication gave occasion for a new round of obituaries-cum-reviews, many of them appreciative commentaries regarding Amis's vigorous stance with regard to proper English usage—the subject of the book itself. Several critics noted that by choosing the title he did—taken from that of a definitive 1906 volume by British lexicographer Henry Watson Fowler and his brother George Francis Fowler—Amis, perhaps in a final act of audacity, raised the stakes to an almost insurmountable height. For Roger Draper of the *New Leader,* the author's gambit failed: "In appropriating the title *The King's English . . .* for his posthumously published effort, the English comic novelist Kingsley Amis gives the impression of having aspired to a very high standard—and, perhaps inevitably, fell short of it. Amis' opus is largely a collection of crochets and jokes."

Those "crochets and jokes," however, are precisely what endeared the book to other reviewers, particularly in England. Several British critics, in fact, had known Amis, and they peppered their reviews with personal reminiscences. "Kingsley loved to present his prejudices outrageously," wrote James Michie in the *Spectator.* "I remember him clinching an argument with me about Milton by a simple mime, one hand pinching his

nose, the other pulling a lavatory chain. There's plenty of gratuitous provocation here." Thus, as Michie went on to note, Amis lambasted the seemingly innocuous "continental crossed seven" as "gross affectation" or even "straightforward ignorance." The old anti-feminist issues were much in evidence as well, a fact noted both by Michie and E.S. Turner in the *Times Literary Supplement.* "Women will not expect to find much for their comfort in these pages," wrote Turner, "though Lady Thatcher is commended for saying 'There is no alternative' (and not 'no other alternative'). Women, it seems, know nothing about etymology, but 'can be trusted with revision and kindred tasks.'" Though some may find Amis's social views objectionable, Sebastian Faulks suggested in the *New Statesmen* that his knowledge of the language itself was above reproach: "Kingsley Amis wrote in a style that was as close to actual speech as one can get without talking, or without foregoing effects only written language can produce; yet it was based on a classical education and a life-long exploration of grammar and etymology."

Amis's death prompted many retrospectives and assessments of his career. His first novel, *Lucky Jim,* was still widely regarded as his masterpiece at the time of his death. "It established him as a master of invective and a man well able to raise a guffaw from his readers, especially the male ones," wrote a London *Times* obituary writer. "For the next forty years Amis produced a regular flow of books which established him as the leading British comic novelist of his generation. The tone varied considerably, but Amis picked his targets carefully and his aim was deadly accurate. He wrote about what he knew well and made sure that he did not too much like what he saw around him."

BIOGRAPHICAL AND CRITICAL SOURCES:

BOOKS

Allen, Walter, *The Modern Novel,* Dutton (New York, NY), 1984.

Allsop, Kenneth, *The Angry Decade,* P. Owen (London, England), 1958.

Amis, Kingsley, *Memoirs,* Summit Books (New York, NY), 1991.

Bell, Robert H., editor, *Critical Essays on Kingsley Amis,* G.K. Hall (Boston, MA), 1998.

Bergonzi, Bernard, *The Situation of the Novel,* University of Pittsburgh Press (Pittsburgh, PA), 1970.

Bradford, Richard, *Lucky Him,* Peter Owen, 2002.

Brophy, Brigid, *Don't Never Forget: Collected Views and Reviews,* Holt (New York, NY), 1967.

Burgess, Anthony, *The Novel Now: A Guide to Contemporary Fiction,* Norton (New York, NY), 1967.

Contemporary Literary Criticism, Thomson Gale (Detroit, MI), Volume 1, 1973, Volume 2, 1974, Volume 3, 1975, Volume 5, 1976, Volume 8, 1978, Volume 13, 1980, Volume 40, 1987, Volume 44, 1988.

Dictionary of Literary Biography, Thomson Gale (Detroit, MI), Volume 15: *British Novelists, 1930-1959,* 1983, Volume 27: *Poets of Great Britain and Ireland, 1945-1960,* 1984, Volume 100: *Modern British Essayists, Second Series,* 1990, Volume 139: *British Short-Fiction Writers, 1945-1980,* 1994.

Feldman, Gene, and Max Gartenberg, editors, *The Beat Generation and the Angry Young Men,* Citadel (Kent, England), 1958.

Fussell, Paul, *The Anti-Egotist: Kingsley Amis, Man of Letters,* Oxford University Press, 1994.

Gardner, Philip, *Kingsley Amis,* Twayne (Boston, MA), 1981.

Gindin, James, *Postwar British Fiction,* University of California Press (Berkeley, CA), 1962.

Jacobs, Eric, *Kingsley Amis: A Biography,* Hodder and Stoughton (London, England), 1995.

Johnson, William, compiler, *Focus on the Science Fiction Film,* Prentice-Hall (Englewood Cliffs, NJ), 1972.

Karl, Frederick R., *The Contemporary English Novel,* Farrar, Straus (New York, NY), 1962.

Laskowski, William E., *Kingsley Amis,* Twayne Publishers (Boston, MA), 1998.

Lodge, David, *Language of Fiction,* Columbia University Press (New York, NY), 1966.

Lodge, David, *The Novelist at the Crossroads and Other Essays on Fiction and Criticism,* Cornell University Press (Ithaca, NY), 1971.

Moseley, Marritt, *Understanding Kingsley Amis,* University of South Carolina Press (Columbia, SC), 1993.

Nemerov, Howard, *Poetry and Fiction: Essays,* Rutgers University Press (New Brunswick, NJ), 1963.

Rabinovitz, Rubin, *The Reaction against Experiment in the English Novel, 1950-1960,* Columbia University Press (New York, NY), 1967.

Salwak, Dale, *Kingsley Amis, Modern Novelist,* Barnes & Noble (Lanham, MA), 1992.

Shapiro, Charles, editor, *Contemporary British Novelists,* Southern Illinois University Press (Carbondale, IL), 1963.

Wilson, Edmund, *The Bit between My Teeth: A Literary Chronicle of 1950-1965,* Farrar, Straus (New York, NY), 1965.

PERIODICALS

America, May 7, 1977.

Atlanta Journal-Constitution, July 24, 1994, Diane Roberts, review of *The Russian Girl,* p. N10.

Atlantic Monthly, April, 1956; April, 1958; July, 1965; June, 1968; June, 1970; February, 1977; November, 1985, Phoebe-Lou Adams, review of *Stanley and the Women,* p. 143; September, 2000, review of *The Letters of Kingsley Amis,* pp. 110-118; May, 2002, review of *Lucky Jim,* pp. 103-108.

Best Sellers, May 15, 1968, Clara Siggins, review of *Colonel Sun: A James Bond Adventure;* April 4, 1969.

Bloomsbury Review, March, 1992, p. 2.

Booklist, March 1, 1994, John Mort, review of *The Russian Girl,* p. 1139; June 1, 1998, Joanne Wilkinson, review of *The King's English: A Guide to Modern Usage,* p. 1691.

Books and Bookmen, December, 1965; July, 1968; January, 1969; September, 1969; October, 1978.

Bookseller, November 11, 1970.

Boston Globe, May 22, 1994, p. B18; September 7, 1994, p. 74.

British Book News, June, 1981.

Chicago Tribune, August 1, 1989.

Chicago Tribune Book World, October 13, 1985.

Choice, November, 1979, review of *Jake's Thing.*

Christian Science Monitor, January 16, 1958; September 24, 1970; September 11, 1985; March 10, 1987; October 7, 1991, Merle Rubin, review of *Memoirs,* p. 13.

Commonweal, March 21, 1958.

Contemporary Literature, winter, 1975.

Critical Quarterly, summer, 1977, William Hutchings.

Critique, spring-summer, 1966; Volume 9, number 1, 1968; summer, 1977.

Economist, March 9, 1991, "'I'm a Great Man for Tyrannies': A Conversation with Kingsley Amis," pp. 89-90.

Encounter, November, 1974; January, 1979; September-October, 1984.

Entertainment Weekly, June 3, 1994, Vanessa Friedman, review of *The Russian Girl,* p. 53.

Essays in Criticism, January, 1980.

Guardian (Manchester, England), February 2, 1954; August 23, 1955; November 30, 1956.

Harper's Bazaar, May, 1989, David Lida, review of *Difficulties with Girls,* pp. 76-77.

Hudson Review, summer, 1972; winter, 1973-74; winter, 1974-75; winter, 1980-81.

Library Journal, July, 1970; May 15, 1998, Robert Kelly, review of *The King's English,* p. 84.

Life, May 3, 1968; March 14, 1969; August 28, 1970.

Listener, November 9, 1967; January 11, 1968; November 26, 1970; May 30, 1974; October 7, 1976; May 22, 1980; October 23, 1980; May 24, 1984; October 16, 1986.

London Magazine, January, 1968; August, 1968; October, 1968; January, 1970; January, 1981; October, 1986.

London Review of Books, June 7-20, 1984; September 18, 1986; December 4, 1986; April 2, 1987; September 29, 1988, pp. 14, 16; March 22, 1990, p. 20; March 21, 1991, Ian Hamilton, review of *Memoirs,* p. 3; November 16, 1995, p. 8.

Los Angeles Times, September 25, 1985, Richard Eder, review of *Stanley and the Women,* p. 8; July 6, 1989.

Los Angeles Times Book Review, May 4, 1980; April 26, 1987, Martin Champlin, review of *The Old Devils;* June 12, 1994, Gary Abrams, review of *The Russian Girl,* p. 3.

Nation, January 30, 1954; August 20, 1955; April 28, 1969; May 5, 1969; October 5, 1970; April 7, 1979, Amy Wilentz, review of *Jake's Thing.*

National Observer, September 15, 1969; June 29, 1977.

National Review, June 18, 1968; June 3, 1969; August 25, 1970; October 27, 1973, Patricia Coyne, review of *The Riverside Villas Murder;* February 1, 1974; March 14, 1975; October 27, 1983; February 22, 1985; May 8, 1987; August 1, 1994, Thomas Mallon, review of *The Russian Girl,* pp. 62-63; September 14, 1998, John Derbyshire, review of *The King's English,* pp. 66-67.

New Leader, September 21, 1970; December 6, 1976; June 29-July 13, 1998, Roger Draper, review of *The King's English,* pp. 3-4.

New Republic, March 24, 1958; September 19, 1970; October 12, 1974; May 28, 1977; November 26, 1977; February 25, 1985; May 30, 1987; October 3, 1994, Stanislaw Baranczak, review of *The Russian Girl,* pp. 36-39.

New Statesman, January 30, 1954; August 20, 1955; January 18, 1958; September 24, 1960; November 28, 1963; July 7, 1967; December 1, 1967; October 11, 1968; November 21, 1975; October 8, 1976, John Carey, review of *The Alteration;* September 15, 1978; April 13, 1979, Malcolm Bradbury, review of *Jake's Thing;* May 23, 1980, Paul Binding, review of *Russian Hide and Seek,* p. 784; December 5, 1980, John Lucas, review of *Collected Short Stories,* p. 30; September 19, 1986; March 21, 1997, Sebastian Faulks, review of *The King's English,* pp. 51-52; March 21, 1997, pp. 51-52; November 29, 1999, Walter Allen, review of *Lucky Jim,* p. 62; May 29, 2000, D.J. Taylor, "Will They

Survive?" (literary reputations of Kingsley and Martin Amis), p. 41.

New Statesman and Society, March 30, 1990, Anthony Quinn, review of *The Folks That Live on the Hill,* p. 38; October 5, 1990, Anthony Quinn, review of *The Amis Collection: Selected Non-Fiction, 1954-1990,* p. 44; March 29, 1991, Michael Horovitz, review of *Memoirs,* p. 38; September 16, 1994, Alan Brien, review of *You Can't Do Both,* p. 37; September 8, 1995, Susan Jeffreys, review of *The Biographer's Moustache,* pp. 37-38; December 15, 1995, D.J. Taylor, "The Amis Legacy," pp. 63-64.

Newsweek, March 2, 1964; May 8, 1967; May 6, 1968; September 14, 1970; September 30, 1974; January 17, 1977; February 4, 1985, "Kingsley and the Women," p. 80.

New York, April 17, 1989, Rhoda Koenig, review of *Difficulties with Girls,* p. 73.

New Yorker, March 6, 1954; March 24, 1958; April 26, 1969; September 13, 1969; October 21, 1974; March 14, 1977; August 20, 1979; April 27, 1987; June 12, 1989, pp. 121-124.

New York Review of Books, October 6, 1966; August 1, 1968; March 9, 1972; March 20, 1975; April 15, 1976; March 3, 1977, Thomas R. Edwards, review of *The Alteration;* May 17, 1979, V.S. Pritchett, review of *Jake's Thing;* March 26, 1987, David Lodge, review of *The Old Devils,* pp. 15-17; June 9, 1994, John Banville, review of *The Russian Girl,* p. 29.

New York Times, January 31, 1954; February 26, 1956; February 23, 1958; April 25, 1967; April 25, 1968; March 12, 1969; August 17, 1970; January 6, 1972; May 11, 1979, Christopher Lehmann-Haupt, review of *Jake's Thing;* September 14, 1985, Michiko Kakutani, review of *Stanley and the Women,* p. 12; October 8, 1985, Edwin McDowell, "Calm Reaction to Disputed Amis Book," section C, p. 9; November 8, 1986; February 25, 1987; March 28, 1989, Michiko Kakutani, review of *Difficulties with Girls,* section C, p. 19.

New York Times Book Review, April 28, 1963; July 25, 1965; April 28, 1968; May 19, 1968; March 23, 1969; August 23, 1970; November 11, 1973; October 20, 1974; April 18, 1976; January 30, 1977; May 13, 1979; January 13, 1985, John Gross, "Hoopla and Hullabaloo on the London Literary Scene," p. 3; June 13, 1985; September 22, 1985, Susan Fromberg Schaeffer, review of *Stanley and the Women,* p. 9; March 22, 1987, Malcolm Bradbury, "The Comic Bad Men of English Letters," p. 15; April 2, 1989, Judith Grossman, review of *Difficulties with Girls,* p. 11; July 1, 1990, William H. Pritchard, review of *The Folks That Live on the Hill,* p. 5; September 8, 1991, Joel Conarroe, review of *Memoirs,* p. 7; May 15, 1994, Christopher Buckley, review of *The Russian Girl,* p. 11.

Observer (London, England), October 10, 1976; December 12, 1976; February 12, 1978; July 23, 1978.

Observer Review, November 12, 1967; October 6, 1968.

Paris Review, winter, 1975.

Poetry, spring, 1968; July, 1969.

Publishers Weekly, October 28, 1974; March 21, 1994, review of *The Russian Girl,* p. 51.

Punch, April 24, 1968; August 28, 1968; October 12, 1968; October 22, 1969; November 18, 1970; October 4, 1978.

Saturday Review, February 20, 1954; May 7, 1955; February 25, 1956; July 27, 1957; March 8, 1958; April 6, 1963; April 5, 1969; February 5, 1977, Bruce Cook, review of *The Alteration;* May-June, 1985.

Saturday Review/World, May 8, 1973, Patrick Cosgrave, review of *The Riverside Villas Murder.*

Southern Review, autumn, 1996, Russell Fraser, "Lucky Jim as I Remember Him," pp. 783-792.

Southwest Review, fall, 2002, David Galef, "The Importance of Being Amis, Revisited," pp. 554-565.

Spectator, January 29, 1954; September 2, 1955; January 17, 1958; September 23, 1960; October 11, 1969; October 9, 1976; June 2, 1984, Harriet Waugh, review of *Stanley and the Women;* September 13, 1986; November 29, 1986; December 6, 1986; December 14, 1991, pp. 40-42; March 22, 1997, James Michie, review of *The King's English,* pp. 43-44.

Sunday Times (London, England), September 28, 1986.

Time, May 27, 1957; August 31, 1970; September 10, 1973, T.E. Kalem, review of *The Riverside Villas Murder;* September 30, 1974; January 3, 1977, Paul Gray, review of *The Alteration;* June 12, 1978; September 20, 1985; September 30, 1985, Paul Gray, review of *Stanley and the Women,* pp. 74-75; March 9, 1987, Paul Gray, review of *The Old Devils,* p. 77; September 16, 1991, John Elson, review of *Memoirs,* p. 74; July 18, 1994, Paul Gray, review of *The Russian Girl,* p. 58.

Times (London, England), May 15, 1980; December 31, 1980; May 17, 1984; May 24, 1984; December 15, 1984; September 4, 1986; September 11, 1986; October 23, 1986; December 12, 1987; March 26, 1988; March 31, 1990.

Times Educational Supplement, March 14, 1997, p. A9.

Times Literary Supplement, February 12, 1954; September 16, 1955; January 17, 1958; September 21, 1962; November 23, 1967; March 28, 1968; September 24, 1971; April 6, 1973, review of *The Riverside Villas Murder;* October 8, 1976; September 22, 1978, review of *The Anti-Death League;* May 16, 1980; October 24, 1980, Blake Morrison, review of *Russian Hide-and-Seek;* November 27, 1981; May 25, 1984, J.K.L. Walker, review of *Stanley and the Women;* September 12, 1986; December 26, 1986; September 23-29, 1988, Michael Wood, review of *Difficulties with Girls,* p. 1039; March 30-April 5, 1990, Lorna Sage, review of *The Folks That Live on the Hill,* p. 339; October 5-11, 1990, Peterley Kemp, review of *The Amis Collection,* pp. 1061-1062; March 8, 1991, Craig Brown, review of *Memoirs,* p. 9; November 22, 1991, Lachlan MacKinnon, review of *We Are All Guilty,* p. 24; May 30, 1997, E.S. Turner, review of *The King's English,* p. 32.

Tribune Books (Chicago, IL), March 8, 1987.

Vanity Fair, May, 1987.

Village Voice, October 25, 1973.

Washington Post, September 10, 1973; May 30, 1994, p. C2.

Washington Post Book World, May 5, 1968; August 8, 1968; October 20, 1968; September 1, 1985, Jonathan Yardley, review of *Stanley and the Women,* p. 3; March 1, 1987; March 26, 1989.

Wilson Library Bulletin, May, 1958; May, 1965.

World, May 8, 1973.

World Literature Today, summer, 1977; winter, 1977; summer, 1996, Carter Kaplan, review of *The Biographer's Moustache,* pp. 689-690.

Yale Review, autumn, 1969; summer, 1975.

OBITUARIES:

PERIODICALS

Entertainment Weekly, November 3, 1995, p. 19.

Los Angeles Times, August 6, 1991, section E, p. 1.

Time, November 6, 1995, p. 87.

*   *   *

AMIS, Kingsley William
See AMIS, Kingsley

*   *   *

AMIS, Martin 1949-
(Martin Louis Amis)

PERSONAL: Born August 25, 1949, in Oxford, England; son of Kingsley William (a writer) and Hilary (Bardwell) Amis; married Antonia Phillips, 1984 (divorced); married Isabel Fonseca, 1998; children: two sons and two daughters. *Education:* Exeter College, Oxford, B.A. (English; with honors), 1971.

ADDRESSES: Agent—The Wylie Agency, 250 West 57th St., Ste. 2114, New York, NY 10107.

CAREER: Novelist and essayist. *Times Literary Supplement,* London, editorial assistant, 1972-75, fiction and poetry editor, 1974; *New Statesman,* London, assistant literary editor, 1975-77, literary editor, 1977-79; writer, 1980—; *Observer* (London), special writer, 1980—. Actor in the film *A High Wind in Jamaica,* 1965.

AWARDS, HONORS: Somerset Maugham Award, National Book League, 1974, for *The Rachel Papers;* James Tait Black Memorial Prize for Biography, 2000, for *Experience;* National Book Critics Circle Award in criticism category, 2001, for *The War Against Cliché: Essays and Reviews, 1971-2000.*

WRITINGS:

FICTION

The Rachel Papers (novel), J. Cape (London, England), 1973, Knopf (New York, NY), 1974.

Dead Babies (novel), J. Cape (London, England), 1975, published as *Dark Secrets,* Panther, 1977.

(With others) *My Oxford,* edited and introduced by Ann Thwaite, Robson Books (London), 1977, revised edition, 1986.

Success (novel), J. Cape (London, England), 1978.

(Contributor) Caroline Hobhouse, editor, *Winter's Tales 25,* Macmillan (London), 1979, St. Martin's (New York, NY), 1980.

Other People: A Mystery Story (novel), J. Cape (London, England), 1981.

Money: A Suicide Note (novel), J. Cape (London, England), 1984, Viking, 1985.

London Fields (novel), J. Cape (London, England), 1989.

Time's Arrow; or, the Nature of the Offence, Harmony (New York, NY), 1991.

The Information (novel), Harmony (New York, NY), 1995.

Night Train (novel), Harmony (New York, NY), 1998.

Heavy Water and Other Stories, Harmony Books (New York, NY), 1999.

Yellow Dog, Miramax (New York, NY), 2003.

Vintage Amis (various past writings and excerpts and new short story), Vintage (New York, NY), 2004.

NONFICTION

Invasion of the Space Invaders (autobiographical), with an introduction by Stephen Spielberg, Hutchinson (London, England), 1982.

The Moronic Inferno and Other Visits to America (articles, reviews and interviews), Harcourt (New York, NY), 1986.

Einstein's Monsters (essay and short stories), Harmony (New York, NY), 1987.

Visiting Mrs. Nabokov and Other Excursions (essays), J. Cape (London, England), 1993, Harmony (New York, NY), 1994.

Experience (memoirs), Talk Miramax (New York, NY), 2000.

The War against Cliché: Essays and Reviews, 1971-2000, J. Cape (London, England), 2001.

Koba the Dread: Laughter and the Twenty Million, Miramax/Talk Books (New York, NY), 2002.

Also author of screenplays *Mixed Doubles,* 1979, and *Saturn 3,* 1980. Contributor of short stories to *Encounter, Penthouse, Granta 13, London Review of Books,* and *Literary Review.* Contributor of articles and reviews to numerous periodicals, including *Times Literary Supplement, Observer, New Statesman, New York Times,* and *Sunday Telegraph.*

SIDELIGHTS: With the publication of *The Rachel Papers* at age twenty-four, Martin Amis established himself as one of the leading British writers of the late-twentieth century. Regularly compared to works by writers such as Vladimir Nabokov and Saul Bellow, Amis's books are often filled with wordplay and are self-conscious works of fiction. In fact, John Greenya reported in the *Detroit News* that Amis was "called by one critic 'the nearest thing to a Nabokov that the punk generation has to show.'" The reason, noted Charles Champlin in the *Los Angeles Times,* is that Amis is "a writer with what can only be called a furious command of words, a social commentator of lethal invention and savage wit." Bellow himself compared Amis's stylistic skills to Gustave Flaubert and James Joyce in a *New York Times Magazine* profile. Amis's biting, yet moralistic satire has also drawn comparisons to the work of Jonathan Swift and Angus Wilson. Margaret Drabble suggested in the *New York Times Book Review* "that Amis is so horrified by the world he sees in the process of formation that he feels compelled to warn us all about it."

Inevitably, Amis has also been compared to his father, Kingsley Amis, the late British comic novelist of the post-World War II generation. "Both father and son write of intellectual phonies and pretenders, assorted degenerates and a rotted-out youth in an England of depraved popular culture and not the slightest social or moral structure," wrote Richard Eder in the *Los Angeles Times Book Review.* Eder continued that, like his father, "Martin Amis is dark, satirical and gifted with irascibility. But what we get under the satire is not a sense of protest but of contempt." Blake Morrison noted in the *Times Literary Supplement* that Amis takes his satire to another level of nastiness, making it "the comedy of the grotesque." In many ways, Amis's works occupy a place well beyond the imposing shadow of his father's works.

In 1973 Amis entered the British literary scene with *The Rachel Papers,* a novel that "caused a stir in Britain—and, it may be, a dreadful thrill of excitement at what may by some be regarded as the spectacle of a crusadingly nasty adolescent unburdening himself in print," said Karl Miller in the *New York Review of Books.* In the *New Leader,* Pearl K. Bell elaborated: "*The Rachel Papers* offers a candid, groin-level view of teen-age sex, circa 1970, in Swinging Britain. Amis' hero, Charles Highway, is no slouch at telling us exactly what-he-did-and-then-she-did. But since he is also a precocious and totally self-absorbed intellectual, this indefatigable swordsman is more interested in what he thought, pretended, felt, and above all what he *wrote* in his journal about his sexual happenings, than he is in the act itself." Assessments of the novel's faults take up limited space in reviews that recognize Amis's uncannily mature comic talent. Clive Jordan, for instance, remarked in *Encounter* that "Amis directs a determined, dead-pan stare at his chosen patch of the lush teenage jungle, teeming with characters who are about as appealing as bacilli on a face flannel, described with the detached, excessively detailed physicality common to satirists down the ages. What holds the attention are not these limited characters, but the author's verbally inventive scrutiny of them." Many U.S. readers first became aware of Amis when his novel *The Rachel Papers* was shown to have been plagiarized by U.S. novelist Jacob Epstein in Epstein's *Wild Oats.*

Amis's novel *Success* is the "first of three fictions, a series of turmoils, in which orphan and double meet," observed Karl Miller in *Doubles: Studies in Literary History.* Terry Service, bereft of his father—a man who murdered his own wife and baby daughter—sets himself against his upper-class foster brother Gregory Riding. As they begin with opposite fortunes, so they end, Gregory having fallen from what seemed to be a charmed position of wealth and sexual opportunity, Terry rising to a higher level of success. "At the crossing-point of their two lives lies the smashed body of Ursula, Gregory's sister, successful at the second attempt in a suicide nurtured in an incestuous childhood with Gregory, and triggered by a more recent relationship with Terry," Neil Hepburn noted in the *Listener.*

To Wolcott, *Success* is "a doomsday reverie, in which Terry represents the brutal, heartless spirit of Urban Apocalypse," while Miller called it a "comedy of orphan malice and adolescent trauma." "The malice these brothers level at women is nearly equal to their hatred of themselves," Jay Parini wrote in the *New York Times Book Review.* Jonathan Yardley, writing in the *Washington Post,* guessed that Amis means to express his contempt for both young men.

A profusion of doubles complicates Amis's second turmoil, *Other People: A Mystery Story.* Mary Lamb, an amnesiac, faintly recalls her past as bad girl Amy Hide, who nearly died after being attacked by a sadistic psychopath. Two voices tell her story; its ending suggests a return to the beginning for a second take. Mary's social worker may be sincere, or may be her abductor, setting her up for more abuse. Numerous ambiguities throughout the book make the mystery hard to solve, according to some reviewers, while others, like Miller, felt that "its obscurities may be considered a necessary element." Amis provides the answer to this long riddle in literary allusions too subtle for some readers to decipher, but *Encounter* contributor Alan Brownjohn recognized the voice of Amis throughout, musing on his own godlike power to manipulate his characters. When read this way, *Other People* appears to be an analysis of the process of making fiction. Extending the analogy, Charles Nichol declared in the *Saturday Review,* "Not all readers will agree with Martin Amis that writing a novel is necessarily a sado-masochistic process, but the force and brilliance of his speculation are undeniable."

Amis elicits sympathy for another unlikely character in *Money: A Suicide Note.* Narrator John Self lost his mother when he was seven years of age and later received a bill from his father to cover the cost of his upbringing. Obsessed with money and overcome by his appetites, Self, said John Gross in the *New York Times,* "embodies . . . just about everything your mother told you not to play with." Yardley elaborated in the *Washington Post* that *Money* "is one long drinking bout, interrupted only briefly by a period of relative sobriety; it contains incessant sexual activity, much of it onanistic; it has a generous supply of sordid language. . . ; and it has an unkind word for just about every race, creed or nationality known to exist." According to *Time* reviewer R.Z. Sheppard, Self demonstrates that "a culture geared to profit from the immediate gratification of egos and nerve endings is not a culture at all, but an addiction. As an addict, he discovers that bad habits and ignorance are the bars of self-imprisonment." *Listener* contributor Angela Huth deemed *Money* "a grim book; a black study of the humiliations and degradations of an alcoholic, a warning of the corruptibility of money and the emptiness of a life with no culture to fall back on." In any other novel, Self's indecencies might cause offense, said Yardley, but in this case, Amis "has created a central character of consummate vulgarity and irresistible charm."

The Moronic Inferno and Other Visits to America shows the same fascinated disdain Amis holds for U.S. culture through essays, reviews, and interviews about and with American writers. Reviewers mentioned the negative slant of these pieces, most of which first appeared in the London *Observer.* London *Times* reviewer Fiona MacCarthy suggested that Amis "is answering some devastating inner urge to reach out and describe in minute detail the worst side of America, the false, silly, double-thinking land of violence, vulgarity, of grid-lock and decay. He ignores have-a-nice-day America completely. Almost all his cast of characters have absolutely dreadful days. At best, Truman Capote in the grip of a grand hangover." Perhaps anticipating charges of anti-Americanism, Amis claims in the introduction to his book that the cultural ailment diagnosed in *The Moronic Inferno* is not "a peculiarly American condition. It is global and perhaps eternal." His America is "primarily a metaphor . . . for mass, gross, ever-distracting human infamy."

In *Einstein's Monsters,* a collection of short stories centered on the danger of a nuclear holocaust, Amis continues his "attack on the apocalyptic folly of the age," as Hepburn once called it. "In addition to high verbal energy and flashes of satiric genius, the stories hum with resentment and loathing of a man who fears for his natural patrimony, the earth, the sky and time itself," Sheppard wrote in a *Time* review. Bruce Cook, writing in the *Washington Post Book World,* commented on the author's emotional intensity: "Usually a writer with a cool, commanding manner (utterly unflappable in . . . *The Moronic Inferno*) he comes unglued before us here, attributing his high excitement over the nuclear issue to his impending fatherhood and to a relatively late reading of Jonathan Schell's *The Fate of the Earth.*" Speaking to John Blades in the *Chicago Tribune,* Amis said Schell's book helped him identify the

previously felt but unnamed concern that distinguishes his generation from all others: "We are at the evolutionary crisis point, it seems to me. We're in a new moral universe. We can unmake the world. Extinction is a possibility." He feels that rabid consumerism and many other "present-day peculiarities have to do with this damaged set of time we have. We don't think into the future. People behave as if there were no future." Meanwhile, Amis maintains in the volume's opening essay, the generation that invented and proliferated the A-bomb (or "Z-bomb," in his view) does not give the matter much thought. "The argument is really with our fathers," he told Ruth Pollack Coughlin of the *Detroit News.* "But it's also about our children. And all the unborn children."

Amis's *London Fields* is "a mordant allegory of *fin de millenaire* entropy in the post-Thatcherite toilet" of late 1990s Great Britain, according to Graham Fuller in the *Village Voice.* The London of this novel . . . is heading toward some undefined but seemingly inevitable apocalypse. Amis's characters are all headed toward a more personal apocalypse. Nicola Six is a beautiful, self-destructive, thirty-four-year-old woman who, having foreseen that she will be murdered on her thirty-fifth birthday, sets out to be killed on her own terms. She lures two married men, Keith and Guy, into a bizarre sex triangle. Keith is a coarse pub regular with no morals, but with the ambition to be a champion at darts. Guy is a handsome, wealthy British gentleman. One of these two men will kill Nicola; the other will be taken along for a ride. A third man, Sam, a Jewish-American writer who is dying of an incurable disease, is attracted to the triangle for its story value.

As a novel, *London Fields* received mixed critical attention. For some, Amis was to be commended for capturing a decaying world on the edge of destruction and raising it up as a mirror to our own times. "*London Fields* is a virtuoso depiction of a wild and lustful society," commented Bette Pesetsky in the *New York Times Book Review.* "In an age of attenuated fiction, this is a large book of comic and satirical invention." According to Jonathan Yardley in the *Washington Post Book World,* "Amis plunges like Dickens reincarnate into the life of the city, wallowing in its messiness and nastiness and desperation." Yet, as Martyn Harris suggested in *New Statesman and Society,* in his preoccupation with creating a setting and scenes of decay and decadence, the author slights some of the other elements of his novel: "Amis isn't interested in character, plot, motivation. . . . In denying motive Amis denies his characters the capacity for change, which in turn rules out the manipulation of reader sympathy—the strongest lever in fiction." Harris continued, "Instead of character the book offers chronocentrism—the conceit that your own age is more special, more scary, more apocalyptic than any other."

The Information reflects a change in Amis's perspective as a writer. It is a novel about two middle-aged friends and how their careers, each headed in a different direction, affect them and their friendship. Richard Tull and Gwyn Barry are middle-aged writers. In addition to looking at their stage of life, the book is also about how writers react to success and failure. As Gail Caldwell wrote in a *Boston Globe* review, "*The Information* is a novel about literary envy, the kind that most writers swear isn't their own affliction, though they all seem to know someone else who's succumbed. It is a frighteningly funny, erudite and mostly compelling novel, dragging you along through London's rough side and Tull's sewers and staircases of consciousness until you beg for mercy. Tull will go to any length, almost, to torment his rival." This literary battle, argued *Vanity Fair* contributor Michael Shnayerson, is at the novel's core: "*The Information* lampoons a publishing world driven by vacuous best-sellers and foolish prizes; for all the grim fun it makes of male midlife confusion, the literary crisis is real, Amis is saying, and must be met."

In the novel failing author Tull has written two experimental novels which received only an inkling of critical attention, while his four more-recent works remain unpublished. His most recent work places such demands on its readers that the few who have attempted it have been rendered physically ill. Barry, on the other hand, has of late achieved fame, wealth, and critical acclaim with a best-selling novel. Tull does not take his friend's good fortune well. In fact, he begins to plot Barry's downfall. Through a variety of far-fetched schemes, Tull attempts to destroy Barry's career, his marriage, and his life. Caldwell wrote that Amis's main character is "an intelligence of enough dimension and humanity, however soiled, to make us stay for the whole performance. Richard Tull is smart, he is demented, sometimes he is even deeper than his depression. . . . His sullied passion is what fuels him, and the wicked mind that spawned him is what fuels" *The Information*.

The Information "drags a bit around the middle," commented Christopher Buckley in the *New York Times Book Review,* "but you're never out of reach of a sparkly phrase, stiletto metaphor or drop-dead insight into the human condition. And there is the humor; Mr. Amis goes where other humorists fear to tread." "*The Information* is quite good," wrote *Washington Post Book World* contributor David Nicholson. "There is, however, a wonderful sidesplitting smaller book trapped inside it. *The Information* would have been far better had Amis allowed it to come out." *New York Times* reviewer Michiko Kakutani found in the novel "Amis's own idiosyncratic vision and his ability to articulate that vision in wonderfully edgy, street-smart prose." Kakutani suggested that Amis "has written just the sort of novel his bumbling hero dreams in vain of writing: an uncompromising and highly ambitious novel that should also be a big popular hit."

For some reviewers, the strength of *The Information* went beyond its style and humor. Kakutani also contended that the novel "marks a giant leap forward in Mr. Amis's career. Here, in a tale of middle-aged angst and literary desperation, all the themes and stylistic experiments of Mr. Amis's earlier fiction come together in a symphonic whole." Amis's "Nabokovian devices are not only employed to frame the story of a failed novelist," added Kakutani, "but are also cunningly used to open out his hilarious tale of envy and revenge into a glittering meditation on the nervous interface between the real world and the world of art." Chris Heath also saw the book in a larger context. In *Details* he noted, "Only in the smallest way is *The Information* about what happens when Richard Tull and Gwyn Barry start scheming around each other. It's about messier, more troubling matters: competitiveness and jealousy and vanity, the vacuum of middle age, the need to be remembered, the ways we corrupt innocence. It is also, in all its side alleys, simply about describing the modern world in all its vain, grotesque minutiae." Yardley called Amis "a force unto himself among those of his generation now writing fiction in English; there is, quite simply, no one else like him."

Reviewed in the *New York Times Book Review* by Patrick McGrath, *Night Train* refers to suicide as a one-way train ride "speeding your way to darkness." Comparing this work to earlier novels such as *Money* and *London Fields,* McGrath believed that in his 1998 book Amis "probes deep into the question of human motivation," a refinement of his views on suicide. In *Night Train* the narrator is "tough and battered" female cop Mike Hoolihan, who is called in to investigate the apparent suicide of Jennifer Rockwell, the daughter of a former boss. Dan DeLuca in the *Philadelphia Inquirer* considered *Night Train* a "disappointing" novel, concluding, "By the end . . . we may know who killed Jennifer Rockwell, but we still don't know who she is, why she died, or why we should care." On the other hand, Mike Hanna in the *Denver Post* viewed the novel more favorably, writing that people like Rockwell "conceal their problems so well that no one notices until it is too late."

Amis's novel *Yellow Dog* delves into sex, violence, gender, and the media via the story of Xan Meo. An ideal husband, Meo suffers a serious head injury that transforms him into an abusive, primitive man filled with rage and uncontrollable lust. In the novelist's view, this primitive outlook on life and sex exists just beneath the surface of all men, and Meo is not the only example Amis provides to make his point. His satiric, comic novel includes other Jekyll-and-Hyde characters which Xan meets throughout the course of his uncivilized adventures: Clint Smoker, a tabloid journalist, writes about illicit sex and outrageous scandal, while the king of England has a Chinese mistress and works to keep a pornographic video of his fifteen-year-old daughter off the Internet. In an interview with Kimberly Cutter for *Women's Wear Daily* Amis noted, "I think the real duty of a novelist is to interpret how the world feels at a particular point. And that's what I've done here."

Characteristically, *Yellow Dog* met with a wide variety of responses from reviewers. *Nation* contributor Keith Gessen wrote that the novel features "a rogues' gallery of disappointing predictability" and contended that the second half of the novel falls apart. Sean McCann, writing in *Book,* wrote that the second part of the novel "takes a header into a series of contrived plot devices," although *Library Journal* contributor David Hellman commented that "All of these disparate plots connect in an intelligent and hilarious fashion." Many reviewers also found *Yellow Dog*'s structure awkward and convoluted and without a satisfying conclusion. Writing in *Time,* Lev Grossman noted, "It tries to be structurally clever, but several of its strands either get tangled up with another or fail to tangle up properly." Nevertheless, Grossman added, "through it all one feels that Amis writes the way he does not to show that he can, but because what he has to say is just too important for prose that is less than painfully acerbic, relentlessly intelligent, and pitilessly funny." Donna Seaman, writing in *Booklist,* commented of *Yellow Dog* that, "A sloppy, maddening, hilarious, and oddly touching amalgam of Evelyn Waugh and John Waters, Amis' wicked burlesque evinces his disgust with the herd mentality and surprisingly tender regard for women." While George Walden, writing in *New Statesman,* noted that the novel has some problems, including Amis's "obtrusive style," the critic concluded: "When Amis is really swinging, who cares about the obtrusion?"

Published five years after the death of his father, the memoir *Experience* focuses not only on the Kingsley-Martin relationship, but also on the younger Amis's connections with relatives, spouses, children, friends, and associates. Many topics get his attention, from the

tragic examination of the grisly murder of his cousin to the bemusing British press's apparent fascination with Amis's lengthy and expensive dental work.

Experience takes a non-linear view of the author's life. "One moment he's six, the next he's 26," an *Economist* review quipped. "Here his parents are divorced, an article later married. The point is the parallels and connections. His book is cross-hatched with them, running across from fathers to sons and back; between marriages and books, between books and books, between births and deaths." The best part of the memoir, continued the critic, "is Kingsley Amis, or rather Martin-and-Kingsley Amis." The author "captures his father's pettiness and phobias, his searing intelligence and wit, his chaste erotic dreams" about Queen Elizabeth II, noted *National Review* critic Joyce Hackett. At the same time, Hackett felt "his asides to the un-famous, especially the women in his life, fall utterly flat."

As the author reveals the complex bond between two generations of fiery writers, the son's understanding of his father, even in the elder man's failing health, "comes across movingly," said the *Economist* critic. To the critic, Amis's look at his father's last days in the hospital "are the most sustained, the least 'stop-go' in the book." Indeed, in his portrayals of his father, mother, sister, and other close family members, the reviewer concluded, "Martin Amis, the bad boy, turns out to be an exemplary family man."

In two separate *New York Times* reviews, John Leonard and Michiko Kakutani took different views of Amis's recollections. On the negative side, Leonard labeled *Experience* "a portmanteau of personal history, ancestor worship and promiscuous opinionizing, . . . a piñata of literary gossip that Amis beats with a stick, causing many names to drop." Kakutani had fewer such reservations, calling *Experience* "remarkable" as a coming-of-age chronicle, as well as the author's "most fully realized book yet—a book that fuses his humor, intellect and daring with a new gravitas and warmth, a book that stands, at once, as a loving tribute to his father and as a fulfillment of his own abundant talents as a writer."

In addition to his fiction and general essays, Amis has worked as a literary critic. Almost three decades of reviews, as well as essays ranging from poker and chess to the sexual allure of former British Prime Minister Margaret Thatcher, are collected in the *The War against Cliché: Essays and Reviews, 1971-2000.* Much of Amis's critical literary focus is reflected in the book's title. Amis places a heavy emphasis on style and berates cliché; even so, for Amis cliché means more than style. As noted by a contributor to the *Economist,* "Cliché, he holds, is not just fossilized language, it is any sort of stock response—emotional, political or literary. It is, in short, thoughtlessness, and the avoidance of cliché is therefore not just a requirement for a stylist, but a duty for the moralist." Robert L. Kelly, writing in the *Library Journal,* noted, "His evaluations are lively, scholarly, and, on rare, occasion, numbing—though probably less so for those few who know as much about literature as Amis." *Booklist* contributor Donna Seaman called the collection "a great feast for serious readers." Writing in *World Literature Today,* William Hutchings summarized, "*The War against Cliché* will survive repeated readings well."

In *Koba the Dread: Laughter and the Twenty Million* Amis continues in the nonfiction mode as he ponders the life and the atrocities of the late Soviet dictator Josef Stalin and recalls his own father's affiliation with communism in the 1930s. Stalin exterminated millions of people, massacring those he believed to be dissidents. Amis writes in length about the life of "Koba," the nickname given to Stalin and taken from a Robin Hood-like hero in a Russian folk tale. The core of the book focuses on the many horrors Stalin oversaw as leader of the former Soviet Union. Amis also devotes considerable time to pondering why his father, like many other intellectuals, was enamored with communism when, says Amis, it became relatively clear early on that Soviet-style communism had evolved into a murderous regime. According to Peter Wilby in the *New Statesman,* Amis addresses another bothersome question: "And why, even now, are so many on the left reluctant to acknowledge how flawed and monstrous it was?" In trying to answer this question, Amis also delves into why there appears to be less stigma or personal remorse expressed regarding those associated with Stalin and the KGB than those who supported Hitler and the Nazis. This discrepancy led to the book's subtitle *Laughter and the Twenty Million,* by which Amis means that it has been possible for many to joke about Stalin and the USSR but never about Hitler and the Holocaust.

Several reviewers noted that Amis's treatise on Stalin contains factual errors, such as mistakenly identifying Ivan the IV as the first Russian leader to take the title czar when it was Ivan the III. A contributor to *Bookseller* noted, however, that such mistakes are less important because the book is not really a work of history. "*Koba the Dread* is a historical mediation, avowedly using secondary sources," the contributor noted. "His-

torical accuracy is not Mr. Amis' primary concern; and nor, one may guess, was it that of his editor, who would have been occupied largely with the literary quality of the work." As for Amis's prose, David Pryce-Jones wrote in *Commentary,* "Amis also has his own way of postponing the truth, in his case by means of overblown language. To speak, for example, of the 'glandular sensuality' of Stalin's malevolence, or to describe Stalin as a 'bellowed rebuttal' of some Marxist thesis, is to blur meaning." Writing in *Maclean's,* Sue Ferguson had a more favorable view of Amis's style, commenting, "What Amis brings to the subject is a rambling prose that, at points, captures in creative, penetrating ways the sheer immensity of Stalin's crimes." A *Publishers Weekly* contributor noted that many readers may not be interested in the author's "private quarrels, but in the bulk of the book he relates passionately a story that needs to be told." In a review in *Library Journal,* Robert H. Johnston called the book "passionate and intensely personal" and also noted that "it will appeal to admirers of Amis's literary panache."

BIOGRAPHICAL AND CRITICAL SOURCES:

BOOKS

Amis, Martin, *Experience,* Talk Miramax (New York, NY), 2000.
Contemporary Literary Criticism, Thomson Gale (Detroit, MI), Volume 4, 1975, Volume 9, 1978, Volume 38, 1987, Volume 62, 1992.
Dern, John A., *Martians, Monsters, and Madonna: Fiction and Form in the World of Martin Amis,* Peter Lang (New York, NY), 1999.
Dictionary of Literary Biography, Volume 14: *British Novelists since 1960,* Thomson Gale (Detroit, MI), 1983.
Diedrick, James, *Understanding Martin Amis,* University of South Carolina Press (Columbia, SC), 1995.
Miller, Karl, *Doubles: Studies in Literary History,* Oxford University Press (New York, NY), 1985.

PERIODICALS

American Spectator, May, 1987.
Atlanta Journal-Constitution, March 4, 1990, p. N8.
Book, November-December 2003, Sean McCann, review of *Yellow Dog,* p. 69.
Booklist, January 15, 1994, p. 894; January 1, 1999, Jim O'Laughlin, review of *Heavy Water and Other Stories,* p. 827; June 1, 2000, Brad Hooper, review

of *Experience,* p. 1795; November 15, 2001, Donna Seaman, review of *The War against Cliché: Essays and Reviews, 1971-2000,* p. 540; May 1, 2002, Brad Hooper, review of *Koba the Dread: Laughter and the Twenty Million,* p. 1442; September 15, 2003, Donna Seaman, review of *Yellow Dog,* p. 179.

Bookseller, "Blue Pencil Please," p. 18.

Boston Globe, February 18, 1990, p. B41; March 25, 1990, p. B37; April 30, 1995, p. B15; May 31, 1995, p. 59.

Chicago Tribune, April 21, 1985; February 23, 1986; June 11, 1987; September 1, 1987; May 14, 1995.

Christian Science Monitor, September 4, 1987, p. B4; April 11, 1990, p. 12; May 17, 1995, p. 14.

Commentary, October 2002, David Pryce-Jones, review of *Koba the Dread,* p. 71.

Cosmopolitan, August, 1978.

Denver Post, March 9, 1998.

Details, June, 1995, p. 92.

Detroit News, June 16, 1985; June 14, 1987.

Economist, May 27, 2000, review of *Experience,* p. 88; May 26, 2001, review of *The War against Cliché,* p. 5.

Encounter, February, 1974; February, 1976; September, 1978; May, 1981.

Esquire, November, 1980; November, 1986; January, 1987; October, 1987; February, 1999, Sven Birkerts, "The Twentieth Century Speaks," p. 64.

Globe and Mail (Toronto, Ontario, Canada), January 26, 1985; September 6, 1986; June 6, 1987.

History Today, November 2002, S.A. Smith, review of *Koba the Dread,* p. 89.

Interview, June, 1985; May, 1995, p. 122.

Knight-Ridder/Tribune News Service, June 21, 2000, Margaria Fichtner, "Martin Amis Pens Autobiography," p. K1583; July 24, 2002, Charles Matthews, review of *Koba the Dread,* p. 1504.

Library Journal, October 1, 2001, Robert L. Kelly, review of *The War against Cliché,* p. 96; June 1, 2002, Robert H. Johnston, review of *Koba the Dread,* p. 169; October 15, 2003, David Hellman, review of *Yellow Dog,* p. 95.

Listener, August 15, 1974; October 30, 1975; April 13, 1978; March 5, 1981; September 27, 1984; April 30, 1987, p. 28; September 21, 1989, p. 30.

London Magazine, February-March, 1974.

London Review of Books, May 7-20, 1981; September 20-October 3, 1984; July 24, 1986, p. 5; May 7, 1987, p. 11; September 28, 1989, p. 7; September 12, 1991, p. 11.

Los Angeles Times, June 28, 1987; September 27, 1987; March 29, 1990, p. E1.

Los Angeles Times Book Review, March 31, 1985, p. 3; June 28, 1987, p. 13; March 4, 1990, p. 3; November 10, 1991, p 3; April 30, 1995, p. 3.

Maclean's, June 26, 2000, Barry Came, "Look Back in Love," p. 48; August 19, 2002, Sue Ferguson, review of *Koba the Dread,* p. 52.

Nation, April 23, 1990, p. 565; December 30, 1991, p. 852; December 8, 2003, Keith Gessen, review of *Yellow Dog,* p. 50.

National Review, August 14, 1987, p. 44; November 20, 1987, p. 60; May 28, 1990, p. 46; May 29, 1995, p. 61.

New Criterion, February, 1987; May, 1990.

New Leader, May 13, 1974.

New Republic, May 6, 1985, p. 34; January 26, 1987, p. 36; April 30, 1990, p. 45; August 28, 2000, review of *Experience,* p. 45.

New Statesman, November 16, 1973; October 17, 1975; March 13, 1981; October 1, 1993, p. 39; March 24, 1995, p. 24; September 2, 2002, Peter Wilby, review of *Koba the Dread,* p. 14; September 8, 2003, George Walden, review of *Yellow Dog,* p. 48.

New Statesman and Society, May 29, 1987, p. 24; September 22, 1989, p. 34; September 27, 1991, p. 55.

Newsweek, May 6, 1974; March 25, 1985, p. 80; March 5, 1990, p. 62; May 8, 1995, p. 66; June 26, 2000, "Growing up with Kingsley," p. 66.

New Yorker, June 24, 1974; August 10, 1981; June 10, 1985; April 15, 1991, p. 25; May 25, 1992, p. 85; March 6, 1995, p. 96.

New York Magazine, April 29, 1974; October 21, 1991, p. 117; May 29, 1995, p. 38.

New York Review of Books, July 18, 1974.

New York Times, March 15, 1985, p. 36; February 13, 1990, p. C17; July 5, 1990, p. C11; October 22, 1991, p. C17; January 31, 1995, p. C13; May 2, 1995, p. C17; May 23, 2000, Michiko Kakutani, review of *Experience;* May 28, 2000, John Leonard, review of *Experience.*

New York Times Book Review, May 26, 1974; February 8, 1976; July 26, 1981; March 24, 1985, p. 36; May 17, 1987, p. 28; September 6, 1987, p. 8; March 4, 1990, p. 1; December 2, 1990, p. 1; November 17, 1991, p. 15; February 27, 1994, p. 17; April 23, 1995, Christopher Buckley, "The Inflammation," review of *The Information,* p. 1; February 1, 1998; January 31, 1999, A.O. Scott, "Trans-Atlantic Flights," p. 5.

New York Times Magazine, February 4, 1990, p. 32.

Observer (London, England), December 2, 1984, p. 19; April 7, 1985, p. 21; September 24, 1989, p. 47; September 22, 1991, p. 59; November 24, 1991, p. 2; October 17, 1993, p. 16; March 26, 1995, p. 17.

Philadelphia Inquirer, February 1, 1998.

Publishers Weekly, February 8, 1985; May 22, 2000, review of *Experience,* p. 81; May 20, 2002, review of *Koba the Dread,* p. 55; October 13, 2003, review of *Yellow Dog,* p. 55.

Punch, October 10, 1984, p. 82; May 27, 1987, p. 66.

Quill and Quire, September, 1987, p. 86.

Rolling Stone, May 17, 1990, p. 95.

San Francisco Review of Books, April, 1991, p. 32.

Saturday Review, June, 1981.

Spectator, November 24, 1973; April 15, 1978; March 21, 1981; October 20, 1984; July 12, 1986, p. 29; December 6, 1986, p. 33; May 2, 1987, p. 31; September 23, 1989, p. 36; July 20, 1991, p. 25; September 28, 1991, p. 37; October 16, 1993, p. 38.

Sunday Times (London, England), March 8, 1981; September 26, 1982.

Time, March 11, 1985, p. 70; June 22, 1987, p. 74; February 26, 1990, p. 71; May 1, 1995, p. 90; February 8, 1999, R.Z. Sheppard, "Bitter Sweets," p. 70; November 3, 2003, Lev Grossman, review of *Yellow Dog,* p. 76.

Time Out, March 27, 1981.

Times (London, England), September 27, 1984; August 14, 1986; April 30, 1987; July 25, 1987.

Times Educational Supplement, November 5, 1993, p. 12.

Times Literary Supplement, October 17, 1975; March 6, 1981; November 26, 1982; October 5, 1984; July 18, 1986, p. 785; May 1, 1987, p. 457; September 29, 1989, p. 1051; September 20, 1991, p. 21; October 15, 1993, p. 21.

Tribune Books (Chicago, IL), May 29, 1988, p. 6; March 4, 1990, p. 1; May 6, 1990, p. 8; November 24, 1991, p. 3; May 14, 1995, p. 5.

Vanity Fair, March, 1990, p. 62; May, 1995, p. 132.

Village Voice, January 26, 1976; June 10-June 16, 1981; February 24, 1987, p. 43; December 1, 1987, p. 66; April 24, 1990, p. 75.

Voice Literary Supplement, October, 1991, p. 31.

Wall Street Journal, April 24, 1985; March 13, 1990, p. A14; December 23, 1991, p. A7; February 14, 1994, p. A16; April 25, 1995, p. A18; May 1, 1995, p. A12.

Washington Post, April 28, 1985; January 7, 1987; September 16, 1987; November 26, 1991, p. B1; February 9, 1994, p. B2; February 6, 1995, p. C2.

Washington Post Book World, March 24, 1985 p. 3; July 5, 1987, p. 4; June 5, 1988; February 18, 1990, p. 3; October 27, 1991, p 1; May 7, 1995, p 3.

World Literature Today, spring, 1982; winter 2001, Daniel R. Bronson, review of *Experience,* p. 126;

summer-autumn, 2002, William Hutchings, review of *The War against Cliché,* p. 77.

Women's Wear Daily, October 21, 2003, Kimberly Cutter, "Amis Amiss," p. 4.

*   *   *

AMIS, Martin Louis
   See AMIS, Martin

*   *   *

ANAND, Mulk Raj 1905-2004

PERSONAL: Born December 12, 1905, in Peshawar, India; died of pneumonia September 28, 2004, in Pune, India; son of Lal Chand (a coppersmith and soldier) and Ishwar (Kaur) Anand; married Kathleen Van Gelder (an actress), 1939 (divorced, 1948); married Shirin Vajifdar (a classical dancer), 1949; children: one daughter. *Education:* University of Punjab, B.A. (with honors), 1924; University College, London, Ph.D., 1929; additional study at Cambridge University, 1929-30.

CAREER: Novelist, essayist, and lecturer. Helped found the Progressive Writer's Movement in India, 1938; lecturer in literature and philosophy at London County Council Adult Education Schools, and broadcaster and scriptwriter in films division for British Broadcasting Corp., 1939-45; lecturer at various Indian universities, 1948-63; Tagore Professor of Fine Arts at University of Punjab, 1963-66; visiting professor at Institute of Advanced Studies in Simla, 1967-68; president of Lokayata Trust (an organization developing community and cultural centers in India), beginning 1970. Editor, *MARG* (Indian art quarterly), Bombay, India, beginning 1946. *Military service:* Fought with Republicans in Spanish Civil War, 1937-38.

MEMBER: Indian National Academy of Letters (fellow), Indian National Academy of Art (fellow), Indian National Council of Arts, Sahitya Academy (fellow), Lalit Kala Academy (fellow).

AWARDS, HONORS: Leverhulme fellow, 1940-42; International Peace Prize, World Council of Peace, 1952, for promoting understanding among nations; Padma Bhusan Award from the President of India, 1968; honorary doctorates from Indian universities in Delhi, Benares, Andhra, Patiala, and Shantiniketan.

WRITINGS:

Persian Painting, Faber (London), 1930.

Curries and Other Indian Dishes, Harmsworth (London), 1932.

The Golden Breath: Studies in Five Poets of the New India, Dutton (New York, NY), 1933.

The Hindu View of Art, Allen &Unwin (London), 1933, 2nd edition published as *The Hindu View of Art with an Introductory Essay on Art and Reality by Eric Gill,* Asia Publishing House, 1957, 3rd edition, Arnold Publishers (New Delhi), 1988.

Apology for Heroism: A Brief Autobiography of Ideas, Drummond (London), 1934, published as *Apology for Heroism: An Essay in Search of Faith,* Drummond, 1946.

Letters on India, Routledge (London), 1942.

India Speaks (play), first produced in London at the Unity Theatre, 1943.

Homage to Tagore, Sangam (Lahore, India), 1946.

(With Krishna Hutheesing) *The Bride's Book of Beauty,* Kutub-Popular (Bombay), 1947, published as *The Book of Indian Beauty,* Tuttle (Rutland, VT), 1981.

On Education, Hind Kitabs (Bombay), 1947.

The Story of India (juvenile history), Kutub-Popular, 1948.

The King-Emperor's English; or, The Role of the English Language in Free India, Hind Kitabs (Bombay), 1948.

Lines Written to an Indian Air: Essays, Nalanda (Bombay), 1949.

The Indian Theatre, illustrated by Usha Rani, Dobson (London), 1950, Roy (New York, NY), 1951.

The Story of Man (juvenile natural history), Sikh (New Delhi), 1954.

The Dancing Foot, Publications Division, Indian Ministry of Information &Broadcasting (New Delhi), 1957.

Kama Kala: Some Notes on the Philosophical Basis of Hindu Erotic Sculpture, Skilton (London), 1958, Lyle Stuart (New York, NY), 1962.

(Author of introduction and text) *India in Color,* McGraw (New York City), 1958.

(With Stella Kramrisch) *Homage to Khajuraho,* MARG Publications (Bombay), 1960, 2nd edition, 1962.

More Indian Fairy Tales, Kutub, 1961.

Is There a Contemporary Indian Civilisation?, Asia Publishing House (Bombay), 1963.

The Third Eye: A Lecture on the Appreciation of Art, edited by Diwan Chand Sharma, University of Punjab (Patiala), 1963.

(With Hebbar) *The Singing Line,* Western Printers &Publishers, 1964.

(With others) *Inde, Napal, Ceylan* (French guidebook), Editions Vilo (Paris), 1965.

The Story of Chacha Nehru (juvenile), Rajpal, 1965.

Bombay, MARG Publications, 1965.

Design for Living, MARG Publications, 1967.

The Volcano: Some Comments on the Development of Rabindranath Tagore's Aesthetic Theories and Art Practice, Maharaja Sayajirao University of Baroda, 1967.

The Humanism of M.K. Gandhi, Three Lectures, University of Punjab, 1967.

(With others) *Konorak,* MARG Publications, 1968.

Indian Ivories, MARG Publications, 1970.

(Author of text) *Ajanta,* photographs by R.R. Bhurdwaj, MARG Publications/ McGraw, 1971.

Roots and Flowers: Two Lectures on the Metamorphosis of Technique and Content in the Indian-English Novel, Karnatak University (Dharwar), 1972.

Mora, National Book Trust (New Delhi), 1972.

Album of Indian Paintings, National Book Trust, 1973.

Author to Critic: The Letters of Mulk Raj Anand, edited by Saros Cowasjee, Writers Workshop (Calcutta), 1973.

Folk Tales of Punjab, Sterling (New Delhi), 1974.

Lepakshi, MARG Publications, c. 1977.

(With others) *Persian Painting, Fifteenth Century,* Arnold-Heinemann/MARG Publications (India), 1977.

Seven Little-Known Birds of the Inner Eye, Tuttle, 1978.

The Humanism of Jawaharlal Nehru, Visva-Bharati (Calcutta), 1978.

The Humanism of Rabindranath Tagore, Marathwada University (Aurangabad, India), 1979.

Album of Indian Paintings, Auromere, 1979.

Maya of Mohenjo-Daro (juvenile), 3rd edition, Auromere, 1980.

Conversations in Bloomsbury (reminiscences), Wildwood House (London), 1981.

Madhubani Painting, Publications Division, Ministry of Information and Broadcasting, 1984, Oxford University Press (Oxford), 1995.

Ghandhian Thought and Indo-Anglican Novelists, Chanakya Publications (India), 1984.

Poet-Painter: Paintings by Rabindranath Tagore, Abhinav Publications (New Delhi), 1985.

Pilpali Sahab: The Story of a Childhood under the Raj (autobiography), Arnold-Heinemann, 1985.

Homage to Jamnalal Bajaj: A Pictorial Biography, Allied (Ahmedabad), 1988.

Amrita Sher Gill, National Gallery of Modern Art (New Delhi), 1989.

Pilpali Sahab: The Story of a Big Ego in a Small Body, Arnold Publishers, 1990.

Caliban and Gandhi: Letters to "Bapu" from Bombay, (correspondence), Arnold Publishers, 1991.

Indian Folk Tales, Publications Division, Ministry of Information and Broadcasting, Government of India, 1991.

Kama Yoga: Some Notes on the Philosophical Basis of "Erotic" Art of India, Arnold Publishers, 1991.

Little Plays of Mahatma Gandhi, Arnold Publishers, 1991.

Old Myth and New Myth: Letters from Mulk Raj Anand to K.V.S. Murti, (correspondence), Writers Workshop, 1991.

Shahid, Urdu Akadmi, 1995.

Tales Told By an Idiot: Selected Short Stories, Jaico Publishing House, 1999.

English Writer Mulk Raj Anand Reads from His Fiction, (sound recording made on December 20, 2000), Archive of World Literature on Tape, 2000.

Also author of *Kama Yoga,* Aspect (Edinburgh), and *Chitralakshana,* National Book Trust.

NOVELS

Untouchable, preface by E.M. Forster, Wishart (London), 1935, revised edition, Bodley Head (London), 1970.

The Coolie, Lawrence & Wishart, 1936, published as *Coolie,* Penguin (London), 1945, Liberty Press (New York, NY), 1952, new revised edition, Bodley Head, 1972.

Two Leaves and a Bud, Lawrence &Wishart, 1937, Liberty Press, 1954.

Lament on the Death of a Master of Arts, Naya Sansar (Lucknow, India), 1938.

The Village, J. Cape (London), 1939.

Across the Black Waters, J. Cape, 1940.

The Sword and the Sickle, J. Cape, 1942.

The Big Heart, Hutchinson, 1945, revised edition, Arnold-Heinemann (New Delhi), 1980.

Private Life of an Indian Prince, Hutchinson, 1953, revised edition, Bodley Head, 1970.

The Old Woman and the Cow, Kutub-Popular, 1960, published as *Gauri,* Arnold-Heinemann, 1987.

The Road, Kutub, 1961, Oriental University Press (London), 1987.

Death of a Hero: Epitaph for Maqbool Sherwani, Kutub-Popular, 1963, Arnold-Heinemann, 1988.

"THE SEVEN AGES OF MAN" SERIES

Seven Summers: The Story of an Indian Childhood, Hutchinson, 1951.

Morning Face, Kutub-Popular, 1968.

Confession of a Lover, Arnold-Heinemann, 1984.

The Bubble, Arnold-Heinemann, 1984.

STORY COLLECTIONS

The Lost Child and Other Stories (also see below), J.A. Allen (London), 1934.

The Barber's Trade Union and Other Stories (includes the stories from *The Lost Child and Other Stories*), J. Cape, 1944.

Indian Fairy Tales: Retold, Kutub-Popular, 1946, 2nd edition, 1966.

The Tractor and the Corn Goddess and Other Stories, Thacker (Bombay), 1947, reprinted, Arnold-Heinemann, 1987.

Reflections on the Golden Bed and Other Stories, Current Book House (Bombay), 1954, reprinted, Arnold Publishers, 1984.

The Power of Darkness and Other Stories, Jaico (Bombay), 1959.

More Indian Fairy Tales, Kutub-Popular, 1961.

Lajwanti and Other Stories, Sterling, 1973.

Between Tears and Laughter, Sterling, 1973.

Selected Short Stories of Mulk Raj Anand, edited by M.K. Naik, Arnold-Heinemann, 1977.

EDITOR

Marx and Engels on India, Socialist Book Club (Allahabad, India), 1933.

(With Iqbal Singh) *Indian Short Stories,* New India (London), 1946.

Ananda Kentish Coomaraswamy, *Introduction to Indian Art,* Theosophical Publishing, 1956.

Annals of Childhood, Kranchalson (Agra, India), 1968.

Experiments: Contemporary Indian Short Stories, Kranchalson, 1968.

Grassroots (short stories), Kranchalson, 1968.

Contemporary World Sculpture, MARG Publications, 1968.

Homage to Jaipur, MARG Publications, 1977.

Homage to Amritsar, MARG Publications, 1977.

Tales from Tolstoy, Arnold-Heinemann, 1978.

Alampur, MARG Publications, 1978.

Homage to Kalamkari, MARG Publications, 1979.

Splendours of Kerala, MARG Publications, 1980.

Golden Goa, MARG Publications, 1980.

Splendours of the Vijayanagara, MARG Publications, 1980.

Treasures of Everyday Art, MARG Publications, 1981.

Maharaja Ranjit Singh as Patron of the Arts, MARG Publications, 1981, Humanities (New York, NY), 1982.

(With Lance Dane) *Kama Sutra of Vatsyayana* (from a translation by Richard Burton and F.F. Arbuthnot), Humanities, 1982.

(With S. Balu Rao) *Panorama: An Anthology of Modern Indian Short Stories,* Sterling (New Delhi), 1986.

Chacha Nehru, Sterling, 1987.

Aesop's Fables, Sterling, 1987.

(And author of background essay) *The Historic Trial of Mahatma Gandhi,* National Council of Educational Research and Training (New Delhi), 1987.

The Other Side of the Medal, Sterling, 1989.

Sati: A Writeup of Raja Ram Mohan Roy about Burning of Widows Alive, B.R. Publishing (New Delhi), 1989.

Annihilation of Caste: An Undelivered Speech, by B.R. Ambedkar, Arnold Publishers, 1990.

(With Eleanor Zelliot) *An Anthology of Dalit Literature: Poems,* Gyan Publishing House, 1992.

Splendours of Himachal Heritage, Abhinav Publications (New Delhi), 1997.

OTHER

(Contributor) *Bharata Natyam,* by Sunil Kothari, Marg Publications, 1997.

Editor of numerous magazines and journals, beginning 1930.

SIDELIGHTS: Mulk Raj Anand is considered by many critics to be one of India's best writers. Along with R.K. Narayan and Raja Rao, he has established the basic forms and themes of Indian literature that is written in English. Through his socially conscious novels and short stories, Anand attacks religious bigotry, established institutions, and the Indian state of affairs. At the same time, he has greatly enriched his country's literary heritage. In *World Literature Today,* Shyam M. Asani comments that "Anand writes about Indians much as Chekhov writes about Russians, or Sean O'Faolain or Frank O'Connor about the Irish."

Anand's first novel, *Untouchable,* is based on an incident in his own life. Injured by a stone, the young Anand was carried home by the lower-caste Bakha, who was abused by Anand's mother for "polluting" her son. *Untouchable* conveys all of these facts along with

an understanding of the dual nature of the untouchables' mindset, for while the untouchable Bakha is reviled by all Hindus because he cleans latrines, he still has pride. As Shyamala A. Narayan notes in *Contemporary Novelists,* "The distinction of Anand's writings lies in capturing Bakha's work ethic—Bakha tackles his odious job with a conscientiousness that invests his movements with beauty."

Saros Cowasjee of *Journal of Commonwealth Literature* applauds *Untouchable* on many levels. "The novel is not only a powerful social tract but also a remarkable technical feat," Coswasjee writes. "The action takes place within the compass of a single day, but the author manages to build round his hero Bakha . . . a spiritual crisis of such breadth that it seems to embrace the whole of India." *Untouchable* was indeed a revelation to readers who remained unaware of life in a caste society, and sparked critical debate and commentary. But the novel also functions emotionally; E.M. Forster, who wrote the preface to the novel, notes: "It has gone straight to the heart of its subject and purified it."

Anand continued to explore his interest in social themes with his next few novels, which relate the hardships of working-class Indians. *Coolie* centers around Munoo, an orphan boy who dies of tuberculosis brought on by malnutrition. Munoo is not an untouchable but he is just as much a victim of the unfairness of Indian society as he finds himself at the mercy of his various employers. Ronald Dewsbury of *Life and Letters Today* even maintains that in *Coolie,* "Anand does show that under the present system India is at its worst." Cowasjee also finds that "Munoo is a most attractive character, with his warm-heartedness, his love, and comradeship, his irrepressible curiosity and zest for life." These attributes again demonstrate Anand's ability to bring out the positive human characteristics in people whom mainstream Indian society would rather ignore.

Anand also explores the lives of poor Indians in *The Village,* the first volume of a trilogy about a young Sikh named Lal Singh. *The Village,* writes Kate O'Brien in the *Spectator,* "gives a vivid picture of a life that is poor and terrible, but in many aspects extremely dignified . . . its theme is universal." Anand writes about women, also underprivileged members of Indian society, in *The Old Woman and the Cow,* and about exploited coppersmiths whose existence is threatened by mechanization in *The Big Heart.* Anand's novels show increasing development over the years. Krishan Nanda Shinha, in his *Mulk Raj Anand,* comments that "while the earlier novels show a sense of horror and disgust against social and economic ills, the novels of the middle period show a greater concern for and with the human heart. It is, however, in the later novels that a healthy synthesis of the social and personal concerns is achieved. . . . While the later novels retain the passion for social justice, they sound greater emotional depths."

In *Private Life of an Indian Prince,* Anand demonstrates this synthesis, producing a piece of fiction, based on his own experience with lost love, that convincingly explores the psychological workings of its hero. This novel concerns the destruction of a young prince who, shortly after India achieves independence in the 1940s, holds out against a union with the rulers of three other princely states. He is encouraged to make this choice by his mistress, an illiterate peasant woman, and ends by losing the mistress, the state, and his sanity. In this novel, Anand skillfully balances the demands of drawing a realistic portrayal of the prince and maintaining characters and situations that remain true to the historical backdrop. Cowasjee calls *Private Life of an Indian Prince* "a great historical novel that is at the same time a work of art," comparing it to "a Dostoevskian novel on the grand scale."

In addition to these novels, Anand has intermittently worked on a proposed seven-volume series of autobiographical novels known as the "Seven Ages of Man." Anand has completed four volumes thus far, and his depiction of childhood in *Seven Summers* and *Morning Face* have earned him comparisons to Tolstoy. Anand plans to finish this series, but despite what the future brings for his work, as Cowasjee writes, "his reputation is secure." Not only has Anand successfully "dispel[led] the myth built around the Indian character: the myth about 'contentment' in the midst of poverty," the value of his novels, according to Margaret Berry in her *Mulk Raj Anand: The Man and the Novelist,* "is the witness they offer of India's agonizing attempt to break out of massive stagnation and create a society in which men and women are free and equal."

Anand once told *CA:* "I believe in the only ism possible in our age—humanism. I feel that man can grow into the highest consciousness from insights into the nature of human experience derived through creative art and literature. The piling up of these insights may make a man survive at some level of the quality of life, in our tragic age. I believe in co-existence among human beings and co-discovery of cultures. I believe the world must end the arms race and get five percent disarmament to give resources for building basic plenty throughout the world by the year 2000. I believe, though

man has fallen very low at various times in history, he is not so bad that he will not survive on this planet—as long as the earth does not grow cold. I always dream the earth is not flat, but round."

BIOGRAPHICAL AND CRITICAL SOURCES:

BOOKS

Amirthanayagam, Guy, editor, *Asian and Western Writers in Dialogue: New Cultural Identities,* Macmillan, 1982, pp. 142-158.

Berry, Margaret, *Mulk Raj Anand: The Man and the Novelist,* Oriental Press, 1971.

Contemporary Literary Criticism, Thomson Gale (Detroit), Volume 23, 1983, Volume 93, 1996.

Contemporary Novelists, St. James (Detroit), sixth edition, 1996.

Cowasjee, Saros, *So Many Freedoms: A Study of the Major Fiction of Mulk Raj Anand,* Oxford University Press (Delhi), 1977.

Fisher, Marlene, *Wisdom of the Heart,* Sterling, 1980.

Gautam, G. L., *Mulk Raj Anand's Critique of Religious Fundamentalism: A Critical Assessment of His Novels,* Kanti Publications (Delhi), 1996.

George, C. J., *Mulk Raj Anand, His Art and Concerns: A Study of His Non-Autobiographical Novels,* Atlantic (New Delhi), 1994.

Gupta, G.S. Balarama, editor, *Studies in Indian Fiction in English,* JIWE Publications (Gulbarga, India), 1987, pp. 128-141.

Iyengar, K.R. Srinivasa, *Indian Writing in English,* Asia Publishing House, 1962.

Kaul, Premila, *The Novels of Mulk Raj Anand: A Thematic Study,* Sterling, 1983.

Kirpal, Viney, editor, *The New Indian Novel in English: A Study of the 1980s,* Allied Publishers, 1990, pp. 11-23.

Lindsay, Jack, *The Lotus and the Elephant,* Kutub-Popular, 1954.

McLeod, A. L., editor, *Subjects Worthy of Fame: Essays in Commonwealth Literature in Honour of H.H. Anniah Gowda,* Sterling, 1989, pp. 17-26.

Naik, M. K., *Mulk Raj Anand,* Arnold-Heinemann, 1973.

Nasimi, Reza Ahmad, *The Language of Mulk Raj Anand, Raja Rao and R.K. Narayan,* Capital Publishing (Delhi), 1989, pp. 5-28.

Niven, Alastair, *The Yoke of Pity,* Arnold-Heinemann, 1978.

Packham, Gillian, *Mulk Raj Anand: A Checklist,* Centre for Commonwealth Literature and Research (Mysore), 1983.

Patil, V.T. and H.V. Patil, *Gandhism and Indian English Fiction: The Sword and the Sickle, Kanthapura, and Waiting for the Mahatma,* Devika Publications (Delhi, India), 1997.

Prasad, Shaileshwar Sati, *The Insulted and the Injured: Untouchables, Coolies, and Peasants in the Novels of Mulk Raj Anand,* Janaki Prakashan, 1997.

Rajan, P. K., *Mulk Raj Anand: A Revaluation,* Arnold Associates (New Delhi), 1994.

Riemenschneider, D., *The Ideal of Man in Anand's Novels,* Kutub-Popular, 1969.

Sharma, Ambuj Kumar, *The Theme of Exploitation in the Novels of Mulk Raj Anand,* H.K. Publishers (New Delhi), 1990.

Sinha, Krishna Nandan, *Mulk Raj Anand,* Twayne, 1972.

PERIODICALS

Ariel, July, 1991, pp. 27-48.
Contemporary Indian Literature, December, 1965.
Indian Literature, Volume XIII, number 1, 1970, pp. 147-149.
International Fiction Review, January, 1977, pp. 18-22.
Journal of American Folklore, October-December, 1951, p. 439.
Journal of Commonwealth Literature, July, 1968, pp. 52-64.
Life and Letters Today, autumn, 1936, pp. 208, 210.
Literary Criterion, Volume XVIII, number 4, 1983, pp. 1-12.
Literary Half-Yearly, July, 1986, pp. 105-123.
Literature East and West, Volume XVII, numbers 2-4, 1973, pp. 199-211.
Modern Asian Studies, October, 1974, pp. 473-489.
New Statesman, January 1, 1982, p. 21.
Scrutiny, June, 1935.
Spectator, April 28, 1939, p. 730.
World Literature Today, summer, 1978; spring, 1983, p. 348; summer, 1992, pp. 580-581.
World Literature Written in English, April, 1974, pp. 109-122; November, 1975; spring, 1980; summer, 1982, pp. 336-341.

ONLINE

Independent Online, http://news.independent.co.uk/ (September 29, 2004).

OBITUARIES:

PERIODICALS

Chicago Tribune, October 2, 2004, Section 2, p. 10.

Independent (London, England), September 29, 2004, p. 32.
Los Angeles Times, October 1, 2004, p. B8.
New York Times, September 30, 2004, p. C14.
Times (London, England), September 30, p. 65.
Washington Post, October 3, 2004, p. C10.

*   *   *

ANAYA, Rudolfo A. 1937-
(Rudolfo Alfonso Anaya)

PERSONAL: Born October 30, 1937, in Pastura, New Mexico; son of Martin (a laborer) and Rafaelita (Mares) Anaya; married Patricia Lawless (a counselor), July 21, 1966. *Ethnicity:* "Mexican American/Chicano." *Education:* Attended Browning Business School, 1956-58; University of New Mexico, B.A. (Education), 1963, M.A. (English), 1969, M.A. (guidance and counseling), 1972. *Hobbies and other interests:* Reading, travel, apple orchards.

ADDRESSES: Home—5324 Canada Vista N.W., Albuquerque, NM, 87120. *Office*—Department of English, University of New Mexico, Albuquerque, NM 87131.

CAREER: Public school teacher in Albuquerque, NM, 1963-70; University of Albuquerque, Albuquerque, NM, director of counseling, 1971-73, associate professor, 1974-88, professor of English, 1988-93 (retired), professor emeritus, 1993—. Teacher, New Mexico Writers Workshop, summers, 1977-79. Lecturer, Universidad Anahuac, Mexico City, Mexico, summer, 1974; lecturer at other universities, including University of Haifa, Israel, Yale University, University of Michigan, Michigan State University, University of California—Los Angeles, University of Indiana, and University of Texas at Houston. Quebec Writers Exchange, Trois Rivières, 1982; Brazil International Seminar, 1984. Board member, El Norte Publications/Academia; consultant. Founder and first President, Rio Grande Writers Association. Professor emeritus, University of New Mexico, 1993—.

MEMBER: Modern Language Association of America, American Association of University Professors, National Council of Teachers of English, Trinity Forum, Coordinating Council of Literary Magazines (vice president, 1974-80), Rio Grande Writers Association (founder and first president), La Academia Society, La Compania de Teatro de Albuquerque, Multi-Ethnic Literary Association (New York, NY), Before Columbus Foundation (Berkeley, CA), Santa Fe Writers Co-op, Sigma Delta Pi (honorary member).

AWARDS, HONORS: Premio Quinto Sol literary award, 1971, for *Bless Me, Ultima;* University of New Mexico Mesa Chicana literary award, 1977; City of Los Angeles award, 1977; New Mexico Governor's Public Service Award, 1978 and 1980; National Chicano Council on Higher Education fellowship, 1978-79; National Endowment for the Arts fellowships, 1979, 1980; Before Columbus American Book Award, Before Columbus Foundation, 1980, for *Tortuga;* New Mexico Governor's Award for Excellence and Achievement in Literature, 1980; literature award, Delta Kappa Gamma (New Mexico chapter), 1981; honorary doctorates from universities including University of New Mexico, 1981, and 1996, Marycrest College, 1984, College of Santa Fe, 1991, University of New England, 1992, California Lutheran University, 1994, and University of New Hampshire, 1997; Corporation for Public Broadcasting script development award, 1982, for "Rosa Linda"; Award for Achievement in Chicano Literature, Hispanic Caucus of Teachers of English, 1983; Kellogg Foundation fellowship, 1983-85; Mexican Medal of Friendship, Mexican Consulate of Albuquerque, NM, 1986; PEN Center West Award for *Albuquerque,* 1992; Erna S. Fergusson award for exceptional accomplishment, University of New Mexico Alumni Association, 1994; Art Achievement award, Hispanic Heritage Celebration, 1995; El Fuego Nuevo Award, 1995; Tomas Rivera Mexican American Children's Book Award, 1995, for *The Farlitos of Christmas* and 2000, for *My Land Sings;* Distinguished Achievement Award, Western Literature Association, and Premio Fronterizo, Border Book Festival, both 1997; Arizona Adult Author Award, Arizona Library Association, and De Coleres Hispanic Literature Award, both 2000; National Medal of Arts in literature, Wallace Stegner Award, Center for the American West, National Hispanic Cultural Center Literary Award, and Bravos Award, Albuquerque Arts Alliance, all 2001; National Association of Chicano scholar, and Champion of Change Award, both 2002.

WRITINGS:

Bless Me, Ultima (novel; also see below), Tonatiuh International, 1972.

Heart of Aztlan (novel), Editorial Justa (Berkeley, CA), 1976.

Bilingualism: Promise for Tomorrow (screenplay), Bilingual Educational Services, 1976.

(Editor, with Jim Fisher, and contributor) *Voices from the Rio Grande,* Rio Grande Writers Association Press (Albuquerque, NM), 1976.

(Contributor) Charlotte I. Lee and Frank Galati, editors, *Oral Interpretations,* 5th edition, Houghton (Boston, MA), 1977.

(Contributor) *New Voices 4 in Literature, Language and Composition,* Ginn (Oxford, England), 1978.

(Author of introduction) Sabine Ulibarri, *Mi abuela fumaba puros,* Tonatiuh International, 1978.

(Contributor) *Anuario de letras chicanas,* Editorial Justa (Berkeley. CA), 1979.

(Contributor) *Grito del sol,* Quinto Sol Publications, 1979.

Tortuga (novel), Editorial Justa (Berkely, CA), 1979.

The Season of La Llorona (one-act play), first produced in Albuquerque, NM, at El Teatro de la Compania de Albuquerque, October 14, 1979.

(Translator) *Cuentos: Tales from the Hispanic Southwest, Based on Stories Originally Collected by Juan B. Rael,* edited by Jose Griego y Maestas, Museum of New Mexico Press (Santa Fe, NM), 1980.

(Editor, with Antonio Marquez) *Cuentos Chicanos: A Short Story Anthology,* University of New Mexico Press (Albuquerque, NM), 1980.

(Editor, with Simon J. Ortiz) *A Ceremony of Brotherhood, 1680-1980,* Academia Press, 1981.

The Silence of the Llano (short stories), Tonatiuh/Quinto Sol International, 1982.

The Legend of La Llorona (novel), Tonatiuh/Quinto Sol International, 1984.

The Adventures of Juan Chicaspatas (epic poem), Arte Publico, 1985.

A Chicano in China (nonfiction, travel), University of New Mexico Press (Albuquerque, NM), 1986.

The Farolitos of Christmas: A New Mexican Christmas Story (juvenile), New Mexico Magazine, 1987.

Lord of the Dawn: The Legend of Quetzalcóatl, University of New Mexico Press (Albuquerque, NM), 1987.

(Editor) *Voces: An Anthology of Nuevo Mexicano Writers,* University of New Mexico Press (Albuquerque, NM), 1987.

Who Killed Don Jose (play), first produced in Albuquerque, NM, at La Compania Menval High School Theatre, July, 1987.

The Farolitos of Christmas (play), first produced in Albuquerque, NM, at La Compania Menval High School Theatre, December, 1987.

(Contributor) *Flow of the River = Corre el Rio,* Hispanic Culture Foundation, 1988.

Selected from "Bless Me, Ultima," Literary Volumes of New York City, 1989.

(Editor, with Francisco Lomeli) *Aztlan: Essays on the Chicano Homeland,* El Norte, 1989.

(Editor) *Tierra: Contemporary Fiction of New Mexico* (short story collection), Cinco Puntos, 1989.

Alburquerque (novel), University of New Mexico Press (Albuquerque, NM), 1992.

Los Matachines (play), produced at La Casa Teatro, Albuquerque, December 10, 1992.

(Author of introduction) Howard Bryan, *Incredible Elfego Baca,* Clear Light (Santa Fe, NM), 1993.

(Author of introduction) *Growing Up Chicana/o* (anthology), Morrow (New York, NY), 1993.

(Contributor) *Man on Fire: Luis Jimenez = El Hombre en Llamas,* translated by Margarita B. Montalvo, Albuquerque Museum, 1994.

The Anaya Reader, Warner Books, 1995.

(Author of foreword) *Writing the Southwest,* edited by David K. Dunaway, NAL/Dutton, 1995.

Zia Summer (novel), Warner Books, 1995.

(Editor) *Blue Mesa Review, Volume 8: Approaching the Millenium,* Blue Mesa Review/Creative Writing Center, University of New Mexico (Albuquerque, NM), 1996.

(Author of foreword) *Dictionary of Hispanic Biography,* Gale (Detroit, MI), 1996.

(Author of introduction) David L. Witt, *Spirit Ascendant: The Art and Life of Patrocino Barela,* Red Crane Books (Santa Fe, NM), 1996.

Jalamanta: A Message from the Desert (novel), Warner Books, 1996.

(With others) *Muy Macho: Latin Men Confront Their Manhood,* edited by Ray Gonzales, Anchor (New York, NY), 1996.

Rio Grande Fall (novel), Warner Books, 1996.

Abelardo Baeza, *Keep Blessing Us, Ultima: A Teaching Guide for "Bless Me, Ultima" by Rudolfo Anaya,* Easkin Press (Austin, TX), 1997.

Billy the Kid (play), produced at La Casa Teatro, July 11, 1997.

Angie (play), produced at La Casa Teatro, July 10, 1998.

Conversations with Rudolfo Anaya, edited by Bruce Dick and Silvio Sirias, University Press of Mississippi (Jackson, MS), 1998.

(With others) *The Floating Borderlands: Twenty-five Years of U.S. Hispanic Literature,* edited by Lauro Flores, University of Washington Press (Seattle, WA), 1999.

(With others) *Saints and Sinners: The American Catholic Experience through Stories, Memoirs, Essays, and Commentary,* edited by Greg Tobin, Doubleday (New York, NY), 1999.

Shaman Winter, Warner Books, 1999.

Elegy on the Death of Cesar Chavez (epic poem), illustrations by Gaspar Enriquez, Cinco Puntos Press, 2000.

FOR CHILDREN

The Farlitos of Christmas, illustrated by Edward Gonzalez, Hyperion (New York, NY), 1995.

Maya's Children, illustrated by Maria Baca, Hyperion (New York, NY), 1996.

Farolitos for Abuelo, illustrated by Edward Gonzales, Hyperion (New York, NY), 1998.

My Land Sings: Stories from the Rio Grande, illustrated by Amy Cordova, Morrow (New York, NY), 1999.

Roadrunner's Dance, illustrated by David Diaz, Hyperion (New York, NY), 2000.

Author of unproduced play "Rosa Linda," for the Corporation for Public Broadcasting; author of unpublished and unproduced dramas for the Visions Project, KCET-TV (Los Angeles). Contributor of short stories, articles, essays, and reviews to periodicals in the United States and abroad, including *La Luz, Bilingual Review-Revista Bilingue, New Mexico Magazine, La Confluencia, Contact II, Before Columbus Review, L'Umano Avventura, 2 Plus 2,* and *Literatura Uchioba;* contributor to *Albuquerque News.* Editor, *Blue Mesa Review;* associate editor, *American Book Review,* 1980-85, and *Escolios;* regional editor, *Viaztlan* and *International Chicano Journal of Arts and Letters;* member of advisory board, *Puerto Del Sol Literary Magazine.* Anaya's manuscript collection is available at the Zimmerman Museum, University of New Mexico, Albuquerque.

WORK IN PROGRESS: Jamez Spring (novel), *The Santero's Miracle* (children's book), and *Serafina's Stories* (young adult book), all expected 2004.

SIDELIGHTS: Best known for his first novel, *Bless Me, Ultima,* Rudolfo A. Anaya's writing stems from his New Mexican background and his fascination with the oral tradition of Chicano stories in Spanish *cuentos.* He grew up listening to *cuentistas,* oral storytellers, and wanted to bring their magic into his writing. The mystical nature of these folk tales, together with events from his own life, have had a significant influence on his novels, which portray the experiences of Chicanos in the American Southwest. But the novelist's books are also about faith and the loss of faith. As Anaya explained in *Contemporary Authors Autobiography Series,* his education at the University of New Mexico intensified his questions about his religious beliefs, and this, in turn, led him to write poetry and prose in order to "fill the void." "I lost faith in my God," Anaya wrote, "and if there was no God there was no meaning, no secure road to salvation. . . . The depth of loss one feels is linked to one's salvation. That may be why I write. It is easier to ascribe those times and their bittersweet emotions to my characters."

Bless Me, Ultima, "a unique American novel that deserves to be better known," in *Revista Chicano-Riquena* contributor Vernon Lattin's words, leans heavily on Anaya's background in folklore in its depiction of the war between the evil Tenorio Trementina and the benevolent *curandera* (healer) Ultima. Several critics, such as *Latin American Literary Review*'s Daniel Testa, have praised Anaya's use of old Spanish-American, specifically Chicano, tales in his book. "What seems to be quite extraordinary," averred Testa, "is the variety of materials in Anaya's work. He intersperses the legendary, folkloric, stylized, or allegorized material with the detailed descriptions that help to create a density of realistic portrayal."

The novel is also a *bildungsroman* about a young boy, named Antonio, who grows up, as Anaya did, in a small village in New Mexico around the time of World War II. Most of Antonio's maturation is linked with a struggle with his religious faith and his trouble in choosing between the nomadic way of life of his father's family, and the agricultural lifestyle of his mother's. Reviewers of *Bless Me, Ultima* have lauded Anaya for his depiction of these dilemmas in the life of a young Mexican-American. For example, in *Chicano Perspectives in Literature: A Critical and Annotated Bibliography,* authors Francisco A. Lomeli and Donaldo W. Urioste called this work "an unforgettable novel . . . already becoming a classic for its uniqueness in story, narrative technique and structure." And *America* contributor Scott Wood remarked: "Anaya offers a valuable gift to the American scene, a scene which often seems as spiritually barren as some parched plateau in New Mexico."

Anaya's next novel, *Heart of Aztlan,* influenced by Anaya's involvement in the Chicano movement of the 1960s, is a more political work about a family that moves from a rural community to the city; but as with its predecessor, Anaya mixes in some mystical elements along with the book's social concern for the Chicano worker in capitalist America. Reception of this second book was somewhat less enthusiastic than it was for *Bless Me, Ultima.* Marvin A. Lewis observed in *Revista*

Chicano-Requena that "on the surface, the outcome [of *Heart of Aztlan*] is a shallow, romantic, adolescent novel which nearly overshadows the treatment of adult problems. The novel [has] redeeming qualities, however, in its treatment of the urban experience and the problems with racism inherent therein, as well as in its attempt to define the mythic dimension of the Chicano experience." Similarly, *World Literature Today* critic Charles R. Larson felt that *Heart of Aztlan,* along with *Bless Me, Ultima,* "provide[s] us with a vivid sense of Chicano Life since World War II."

Anaya himself says that he was working, in cathartic writings before *Bless Me, Ultima,* without models or mentors for delineating Chicano experiences: "I was still imitating a style and mode not indigenous to the people and setting I knew best. I was desperately seeking my natural voice, but the process by which I formed it was long and arduous." At university, he, along with other Mexican-American students, had been "unprepared by high school to compete. . . . The thought was still prevalent in the world of academia that we were better suited as janitors than scholars." He had to learn English which "was still a foreign language to us," and with the attitudes of teachers who believed learning meant changing to be like them. His life of writing has been a journey of discovery: how to present the reality of Chicano people in the United States from within that experience.

Tortuga, Anaya's third novel, continues in the mythical vein of the author's other works and has been called "Anaya's most accomplished novel" by Antonio Marquez in *The Magic of Words.* The novel concerns a young boy who must undergo therapy for his paralysis and wear a body cast, hence his nickname "Tortuga," which means turtle. "Tortuga," however, also "refers . . . to the 'magic mountain' (with a nod here to Thomas Mann) that towers over the hospital for paralytic children," according to Angelo Restivo in *Fiction International.* While staying at the Crippled Children and Orphans Hospital, Tortuga becomes more spiritually and psychologically mature, and the novel ends when he returns home after his year-long ordeal. As with the novelist's other books, *Tortuga* is a story about growing up; indeed, *Bless Me, Ultima, Heart of Aztlan,* and *Tortuga* form a loosely-tied trilogy that depicts the Chicano experience in the southwestern United States over a period of several decades. As the author once commented these novels "are a definite trilogy in my mind. They are not only about growing up in New Mexico, they are about life."

All of Anaya's novels, including the award-winning quartet *Alburquerque* (the original spelling of the city's name), *Zia Summer, Rio Grande Fall,* and *Shaman Winter,* attempt to find the answers to life's questions, doing so from the perspective of his own personal cultural background and thus offering an opportunity to Mexican-American students of all ages to educate themselves about their culture, heritage, and history. "If we as Chicanos do have a distinctive perspective on life," he told Juan D. Bruce-Novoa in *Chicano Authors: Inquiry by Interview,* "I believe that perspective will be defined when we challenge the very basic questions which mankind has always asked itself: What is my relationship to the universe, the cosmos? Who am I and why am I here? If there is a Godhead, what is its nature and function? What is the nature of mankind?" These questions echo the doubts, realizations, and experiences the author has had in his life, and that he links closely to mythology alive in the land and peoples of the Americas, especially in the Mexican/Spanish and Native American cultures which flow together in Anaya. He explained to Bruce-Novoa, "All literature, and certainly Chicano literature, reflects, in its more formal aspects, the mythos of the people, and the writings speak to the underlying philosophical assumptions which form the particular world view of culture. . . . In a real sense, the mythologies of the Americas are the only mythologies of all of us, whether we are newly arrived or whether we have been here for centuries. The land and the people force this mythology on us. I gladly accept it; many or most of the American newcomers have resisted it."

As well as novels, Anaya has written plays and screenplays, two epic poems and other poems, short stories, essays, documentaries, and children's stories. His first epic poem, a mock-heroic piece written in the language of "vatos locos," or crazy barrio Chicanos who jest at almost everything, continues the search for self-definition. In 2000 Anaya published *Elegy on the Death of Cesar Chavez,* another epic poem which celebrates the life and struggles of the famed Chicano labor leader.

Anaya commented: "With fear throbbing in my heart I said goodbye to my mother and father and went off to my first day at school. First grade in Santa Rosa, New Mexico. I didn't know a word of English. But, as time progressed, I learned to read. I wrote great book reviews and illustrated them. I read the Nancy Drew and Hardy Boys mysteries. I read cowboy stories. I read comic books. I had a comic book collection three feet high. I loved stories. Stories are what the old people told. I was raised on the folk tales of the Hispanic New Mexicans.

"I really fell in love with reading when I was a student at the University of Mexico. I read everything in those days when a liberal education meant preparing the student in world literature—multicultural literature.

"I began to write poetry. The Beatnik era was full of poetry and rebellion, and some of that energy became mine. I began to write what I knew best, my childhood, my family, community, place. More like Thomas Wolfe than Hemingway.

"I discovered in the arduous, creative process that the story must be personal. My place. The history, language, and culture of my community.

"I wrote every night, descending into the world of my dreams, the mythos, the images of the unconscious, the world of symbols. My history was tied to the history of my community.

"In the 1970s, the Chicago Movement was born—we gave it birth. We began to write *us.* Identity. The movement spread across the country and continues to this day.

"I don't have a favorite novel. They are all children born of blood, pain, joy, and revelation—the dark world coming into light. Some are fuller of soul, some are weaker in style, but they are all children to be loved.

"We write for ourselves and for others. Messages. A sharing. We write to say we exist. The reader reads and also shouts I too exist! We are all together in the structure, which we call creativity. The structure is a house. We all live there. Some write, some do carpentry, plumbing or doctoring. We all live and share what we do. If it wasn't for those guys, I wouldn't have a house to live in. If it weren't for me, they wouldn't have a book of revelation to read. It all works out in the end."

BIOGRAPHICAL AND CRITICAL SOURCES:

BOOKS

Baeza, Abelardo, *Keep Blessing Us, Ultima: A Teaching Guide for Bless Me, Ultima by Rudolfo Anaya,* Easkin Press (Austin, TX), 1997.
Bruce-Novoa, Juan D., *Chicano Authors: Inquiry by Interview,* University of Texas Press (Austin, TX), 1980, pp. 183-202.

Chavez, John R., *The Lost Land, The Chicano Image of the Southwest,* University of New Mexico Press (Albuquerque, NM), 1984.

Chicano Literature: A Reference Guide, Greenwood Press (Westport, CT), 1985.

Contemporary Authors Autobiography Series, Volume 4, Thomson Gale (Detroit, MI), 1986.

Contemporary Literary Criticism, Volume 23, Thomson Gale (Detroit, MI), 1983.

Dennis, Philip A., and Wendell Aycock, *Literature and Anthropology,* Texas Tech University Press (Lubbock, TX), 1989, pp. 193-208.

Dick, Bruce, and Silvio Sirias, *Conversations with Rudolfo Anaya,* University Press of Mississippi (Jackson, MS), 1998.

Dictionary of Literary Biography, Volume 82: *Chicano Writers, First Series,* Thomson Gale (Detroit, MI), 1989, pp. 24-35.

Fabre, Genvieve, *European Perspectives on Hispanic Literature of the United States,* Arte Publico Press, 1988, pp. 55-65.

Gonzales-Berry, Erlinda, *Paso por Aqui: Critical Essays on the New Mexican Literary Tradition, 1542-1988,* University of New Mexico Press (Albuquerque, NM), 1989, pp. 243-54.

Gonzales, Cesar A., *Rudolfo Anaya: Focus on Criticism* (includes bibliography by Teresa Marquez), Lalo Press (Tempe, AZ), 1990.

Gonzales, Cesar A., *A Sense of Place: Rudolfo A. Anaya: An Annotated Bio-Bibliography,* University of California Press (Berkeley, CA), 1999.

Hispanic Literature Criticism, Thomson Gale (Detroit, MI), 1994.

Jimenez, Francisco, editor, *The Identification and Analysis of Chicano Literature,* Bilingual Press (New York, NY), 1979.

Kanellos, Nicolas, editor, *Understanding the Chicano Experience through Literature,* Mexican American Studies, University of Houston Press (Houston, TX), 1981.

Lattin, Vernon E., editor, *Contemporary Chicano Fiction: A Critical Survey,* Bilingual Press/Editorial Bilinguumlal (Binghamton, NY), 1986.

Lomeli, Francisco A., and Donaldo W. Urioste, *Chicano Perspectives in Literature: A Critical and Annotated Bibliography,* Apparition, 1976.

Olmos, Margarite Fernandez, *Rudolfo A. Anaya: A Critical Companion,* Greenwood Press (Westport, CT), 1999.

Reference Guide to American Literature, 3rd edition, St. James Press (Detroit, MI), 1994, p. 57.

Robinson, Cecil, *Mexico and the Hispanic Southwest in American Literature,* University of Arizona Press (Tucson, AZ), 1977.

Ryan, Bryan, *Hispanic Writers,* Thomson Gale (Detroit, MI), 1991.

Vassallo, Paul, editor *The Magic of Words: Rudolfo A. Anaya and His Writings,* University of New Mexico Press (Albuquerque, NM), 1982.

PERIODICALS

Agenda: A Journal of Hispanic Issues, July, 1977, p. 46; November, 1979, pp. 4 and 33.

Albuquerque Monthly, November, 1981, pp. 26-28.

America, January 27, 1973, p. 72.

American Book Review, March-April, 1979.

American Literature, January, 1979, p. 625.

Americas Review: A Review of Hispanic Literature and Art of the USA, fall-winter, 1996, p. 201.

Aztlan, spring, 1987, pp. 59-68.

Bilingual Review, January-April, 1982, pp. 82-87.

Bloomsbury Review, September-October, 1993, pp. 3, 18.

Booklist, February 1, 1996, p. 915; September 1, 1996, p. 66; May 1, 1997, p. 1500; October 1, 1997, p. 94; April 15, 1998, p. 1389; August 1999, p. 2043; May 1, 2000, p. 1594; December 15, 2000, pp. 811 and 823.

Caribe, spring, 1976, p. 113.

Center for Children's Books Bulletin, August, 1997, p. 387.

Children's Book & Play Review, January, 2001, p. 13.

Children's Book Review Service, August, 1997, p. 164; October, 1999, p. 188.

Children's Bookwatch, June, 1997, p. 6; February, 2001, p. 3.

Commonweal, November 5, 1999, p. 24.

Critica, fall, 1986, p. 21.

Critique, 1980, pp. 55-64.

De Colores, 1975, p. 22; fall, 1977, p. 30; spring, 1980, p. 111.

Emergency Librarian, May, 1996, p. 56.

Empire, March, 1980, p. 24.

Environment, March, 1999, p. 8.

Fiction International, number 12, 1980, p. 283.

Hispanic, September, 1994, p. 90; January, 1999, p. 106.

Horn Book Guide, November-December, 1995, p. 727; spring, 1996, p. 53; fall, 1997, p. 257; spring, 2001, pp. 27 and 139.

Hungry Mind Review, fall, 1999, p. 34.

Journal for Youth Services in Libraries, summer 1996, p. 414.

Kirkus Reviews, July 15, 1996, p. 1004; December 1, 1998, p. 1696; July 1, 1999, p. 1050; September 15, 1999, p. 1496.

La Confluenzia, July, 1977, p. 61.

La Luz, May, 1973.

Latin American Literary Review, spring-summer, 1977, pp. 64 and 70; spring-summer, 1978, p.70.

Library Journal, February 1, 1996, p. 64; September 1, 1996, p. 213; January 1997, p. 51.

Los Angeles Times Book Review, August 30, 1992, p. 8.

MELUS, spring, 1978, p. 71; spring, 1984, pp. 27-32, winter, 1984, pp. 47-57.

Mester, November, 1974, p. 27.

Nation, July 18, 1994, p. 98.

New Mexico Humanities Review, summer, 1979, pp. 5-12.

New York Times Book Review, October 11, 1981, p. 15; November 29, 1992, pp. 22; 36-37; July 2, 1995, p. 15; December 17, 1995, p. 28.

Ploughshares, June 1978, p. 190.

PMLA, January, 1987, pp. 10, 15-17.

Publishers Weekly, May 25, 1992; March 21, 1994, p. 24; April 10, 1994, p. 56; June 5, 1995, p. 41; January 1, 1996, p. 58; July 29, 1996, p. 73; October 6, 1997, p. 58; September 27, 1999, p. 60; October 11, 1999, p. 77; November 20, 2000, p. 68.

Reading Teacher, October, 2001, p. 208.

Revista Chicano-Riquena, spring, 1978, p. 50; summer, 1981, p. 74.

San Francisco Review of Books, June, 1978, pp. 9-12, 34.

School Library Journal, June, 1997, p. 78; September, 1999, p. 218; October, 1999, p. 64; September, 2000, p. 184; January 1, 2001, p. 136.

Skipping Stones, May-August 2001, p. 9.

Sojourners, May, 2001, p. 51.

Southwestern American Literature, 1974, p. 74.

Stone Soup, July-August, 2002, p. 8.

University of Albuquerque Alumni Magazine, January, 1973.

University of New Mexico Alumni Magazine, January, 1973.

Western American Literature, summer, 1997, p. 179.

World Literature Today, spring, 1979, p. 245; spring, 1996, p. 403; autumn 1996, p. 957.

*   *   *

ANAYA, Rudolfo Alfonso
    See ANAYA, Rudolfo A.

*   *   *

ANDERSON, Laurie Halse 1961-

PERSONAL: Born October 23, 1961, in Potsdam, NY; daughter of Frank A., Jr. (a Methodist minister) and Joyce (in management) Halse; married Gregory H. Anderson (chief executive officer of Anderson Financial Systems), June 19, 1983 (divorced, 2002); married Scott Larrabee (a construction company owner), June 5, 2004; children: Stephanie, Meredith; (stepchildren) Jessica, Christian. *Education:* Onondaga County Community College, A.A., 1981; Georgetown University, B.S. L.L., 1984. *Politics:* Independent *Religion:* Society of Friends (Quaker) *Hobbies and other interests:* American history, advocating for children and teens.

ADDRESSES: Office—P.O. Box 906, Mexico, NY 13114. *E-mail*—laurie@writerlady.com.

CAREER: Former journalist for *Philadelphia Inquirer* and other newspapers; writer and speaker at numerous schools, conventions, and other gatherings, beginning 1998.

MEMBER: Society of Children's Book Writers and Illustrators, Authors Guild, PEN American Center.

AWARDS, HONORS: "Pick of the Lists," American Booksellers Association, 1996, for *Ndito Runs;* National Book Award finalist in Young People's Literature, 1999, Edgar Allan Poe Award nomination, Printz Honor Medal Book Award nomination, *Los Angeles Times* Book Prize nomination, Golden Kite award nomination, Society of Children's Book Writers and Illustrators, *School Library Journal* Best Book citation, *Booklist*'s Top Ten First Novels listee, and *Horn Book* Fanfare Honor listee, all 1999, and American Library Association (ALA) Honor listee for excellence in literature for young adults, 2000, all for *Speak;* Henry Bergh ASPCA Award for Children's Books, 2000, for *Fight for Life;* ALA Best Books for Young Adults selection, Parents' Guide to Children's Media Award, "Pick of the Lists," American Booksellers Association, 100 Best Books of Fall selection, Jefferson Cup Honor Book, and New York Public Library Book for the Teen Age designation, all 2000, Free Library of Philadelphia/Drexel University Children's Literature Citation, 2002, Rebecca Caudill Young Readers' Book Award, 2003, and Great Lakes Great Books Award, all for *Fever 1793;* Children's Book Council Children's Choice title, 2002, for *Say Good-Bye;* New York Public Library Book for the Teen Age designation, and Barnes & Noble Best Teen Book of the Year listee, 2002, and ALA Top Ten Best Books for Young Adults designation, 2003, all for *Catalyst;* Once upon a World Award, Simon Weisenthal Center, Chapman Award for Shared Reading, and Teacher's Choice Award, International Reading Association, 2003, and Storytelling World Honor designation, 2004, all for *Thank You, Sarah!;* Fayettevill-Manlius Hall of Distinction honoree, 2004.

WRITINGS:

Speak, Farrar, Straus (New York, NY), 1999.
Fever 1793, Simon & Schuster (New York, NY), 2000.
(With Ward K. Swallow) *The Shy Child: Helping Children Triumph over Shyness,* Warner Books (New York, NY), 2000.
Saudi Arabia (part of "A Ticket To" series), Carolrhoda Books, 2001.
Catalyst, Viking (New York, NY), 2002.
Prom, Viking (New York, NY), 2005.

Short stories have appeared in anthologies, including *Dirty Laundry,* Viking (New York, NY), 1998; and *Love and Sex,* Simon & Schuster, (New York, NY), 2001.

"WILD AT HEART" SERIES

Fight for Life: Maggie, Pleasant Company (Middleton, WI), 2000.
Homeless: Sunita, Pleasant Company (Middleton, WI), 2000.
The Trickster, Pleasant Company (Middleton, WI), 2000.
Manatee Blues, Pleasant Company (Middleton, WI), 2000.
Say Good-Bye, Pleasant Company (Middleton, WI), 2001.
Storm Rescue, Pleasant Company (Middleton, WI), 2001.
Teacher's Pet, Pleasant Company (Middleton, WI), 2001.
Trapped, Pleasant Company (Middleton, WI), 2001.
Fear of Falling, Pleasant Company (Middleton, WI), 2001.
Time to Fly, Pleasant Company (Middleton, WI), 2002.
Masks, Pleasant Company (Middleton, WI), 2002.
End of the Race, Pleasant Company (Middleton, WI), 2002.

PICTURE BOOKS

Ndito Runs, illustrated by Anita Van der Merwe, Henry Holt (New York, NY), 1996.
Turkey Pox, illustrated by Dorothy Donohue, Albert Whitman, 1996.
No Time for Mother's Day, illustrated by Dorothy Donohue, Albert Whitman, 1999.
The Big Cheese of Third Street, illustrated by David Gordon, Simon & Schuster (New York, NY), 2002.

Thank you, Sarah: The Woman Who Saved Thanksgiving, illustrated by Matt Faulkner, Simon & Schuster (New York, NY), 2002.

ADAPTATIONS: Thank You, Sarah! and *The Big Cheese of Third Street* were adapted for video by Spoken Arts. Several of the author's books have been adapted as audio books.

SIDELIGHTS: Laurie Halse Anderson became a finalist for the prestigious National Book Award with her first work of fiction for young adults, *Speak.* The 1999 novel won an array of honors for Anderson, the author of three earlier picture books for younger readers, for its searing portrayal of a fourteen-year-old girl who becomes mute after a sexual assault. Nancy Matson, writing for *CNN.com,* hailed Anderson as "a gifted new writer whose novel shows that she understands (and remembers) the raw emotion and tumult that marks the lives of teenagers."

The inspiration for *Speak,* Anderson's first book aimed at teenage readers, which was published in 1999, came from a bad dream that woke the author one night in the summer of 1996. She had been plagued by nightmares all of her life, Anderson explained in the *ALAN Review.* "Since I can't afford extensive psychotherapy, I write down my nightmares. . . . After an hour of scribbling in my journal or pounding the keyboard, the most horrific night-vision is reduced to a pile of sentences. And I can go back to sleep." On that night in 1996, Anderson was roused by the sound of a girl crying. Upon checking on her daughters and finding them undisturbed, she realized it had all been a dream. Wide awake by then, she went to her desk to write, but could still hear the girl's sobbing in her head. "Once the word processor blinked awake, she stopped," Anderson wrote in the *ALAN Review.* "She made a tapping noise and blew into a microphone. 'Is this thing on?' she asked. 'I have a story to tell you.' That is how I met Melinda Sordino, the protagonist of *Speak.* "

Melinda recounts her tale in short chapters, and *Speak* is divided into the four marking periods of a school year. As it opens, Melinda's first day of high school is off to a disastrous start. No one will sit next to her on the bus, and the other students make derisive remarks about her when they are not shunning her completely. As the story unfolds, Melinda reveals the reason behind the ostracism: at an end-of-summer drinking party hosted by a group of older students, she drank too much and was sexually assaulted by a popular senior. A call made to 911 from the house brought the police, and the party was broken up. Some kids were arrested, and Melinda's "odd" behavior that night reveals to others that she was the caller.

As the weeks of her freshman year wear on, Melinda has no friends. When she sees her rapist in the halls, the young man continues to taunt her by winking at her; Melinda can only refer to him as "IT." She has told no one about the crime, and finds it increasingly difficult to communicate. She bites her lip incessantly, and her busy parents do not seem to notice the scabs or even that anything is wrong. At times, Melinda's narrative recounts dialogue, which takes the form of an exchange between someone else, and Melinda's "Me," which is rarely followed by any lines. She feels stifled. "All that crap you hear on TV about communication and expressing feelings is a lie," Melinda scoffs. "Nobody really wants to hear what you have to say."

"While Melinda's smart and savvy interior narrative slowly reveals the searing pain of that 911 night, it also nails the high-school experience cold," a *Horn Book* reviewer noted. Melinda's friends from middle school have dispersed into different cliques, and her former best friend changes her name from Rachel to Rachelle and hangs out only with the foreign-exchange students. Everyone else is hostile to her. Despite the trauma, Melinda emerges as a wry observer of high school life. As narrator she analyzes the various school cliques, which she tags by various names: Eurotrash, Country Clubbers, Jocks, Future Fascists of America, Suffering Artists, Thespians, Goths, and Marthas, among others. As *Speak* progresses, Melinda makes one friend, Heather, who recently moved to town and knows nothing about the 911 call. But Melinda is only nominally interested in being friends with the girl, who wants to be a Martha, one of the "the do-gooder bunch who collect food cans for the less fortunate and decorates the teachers' lounge," as Nancy Matson explained on *CNN.com*. The Marthas, however "are not a whit less brutal than any of the other high school cliques," Matson observed.

Melinda finds some solace in her art class, where her sympathetic teacher seems to be the only one who realizes that something is amiss in her life. As Melinda's grades decline over the marking periods, she grows increasingly withdrawn and even begins to find refuge by hiding in a closet at school. Her voice manages to assert itself in other ways besides her internal narrative: through her tree project for art class, for instance, or a piece of graffiti she begins on the wall of a bathroom stall, "Ten Guys to Stay Away From." When her ex-best

friend begins dating "IT," Melinda finally begins to realize what the real cost of her silence may be. In a nightmarish denouement, she finds herself in danger again, and at last finds the voice to scream.

Reviewers of *Speak* were generous in their praise. "In a stunning first novel, Anderson uses keen observations and vivid imagery to pull readers into the head of an isolated teenager," a *Publishers Weekly* reviewer wrote. Paula Rohrlick of *Kliatt* noted that "Melinda's voice is bitter, sardonic and always believable," and predicted that the heroine's "bleak, scathingly honest depiction of the world of high school will ring true for many." A reviewer writing in the *Bulletin of the Center for Children's Books* observed that "Anderson doesn't overburden Melinda with insight or with artistic metaphors," and concluded by calling the novel "a gripping account of personal wounding and recovery." Writing for *School Library Journal*, Dina Sherman stated that *Speak* "is a compelling book, with sharp, crisp writing that draws readers in, engulfing them in the story." A contributor to *Horn Book* predicted that the novel "will hold readers from first word to last." Writing in *Kirkus Reviews*, a reviewer commended Anderson for her engaging story and strong characters, but pointed out that "it is its raw and unvarnished look at the dynamics" among the teenagers portrayed in *Speak* "that makes this a novel that will be hard for readers to forget."

At the time that she had the nightmare that brought Melinda alive, Anderson had been reading *Reviving Ophelia*, a best-selling study from Nebraska psychologist Mary Pipher about preteen girls and the difficulties they face. "I had been processing all this information about adolescence and girls, and remembered all too vividly what it was like," Anderson told Jennifer M. Brown in a *Publishers Weekly* interview. "*Speak* is the least deliberately written book I've ever done." As the author wrote in the *ALAN Review*, she grew very attached to her heroine, whom she refers to as "Mellie," over the course of writing her story. "The ending of the book was the hardest. In fact, I had to do it three times to get it right. My patient, very smart editor, Elizabeth Mikesell, gently pushed me to do it over until I found the right ending. I was not happy about it at the time, but she was right. I was too protective of Mellie. I didn't want her to get hurt again. I couldn't stand the thought of leaving her unprotected." In fact, as Anderson told a *Book Bag* contributor, she felt so close to her character that it was sometimes hard to remember that she existed only on paper. Anderson noted, "When my editor called me to say she wanted to publish the book, I was really bummed because I wanted to call Melinda and tell her, she was so real to me!"

Anderson has also written a historical novel for teens, *Fever 1793*, which appeared in 2000. The work is set in postrevolutionary times during a yellow fever outbreak. Matilda Cook is fourteen that summer, and her family owns a coffeehouse in Philadelphia, which was also the capital of the United States at the time. When Matilda is separated from her mother and her grandfather succumbs to the epidemic, she is saved by the freed slave who works at the coffeehouse. Through her, the teen becomes involved in the Free African Society, and by the end of the novel Matilda has emerged as the almost-adult proprietor of the coffeehouse. "Readers will be drawn in by the characters and will emerge with a sharp and graphic picture of another world," opined *School Library Journal* reviewer Kathleen Isaacs.

In *Catalyst* Anderson tells the story of eighteen-year-old Kate Malone whose life becomes unraveled after her application to attend college at MIT is rejected. Extremely disappointed, Kate begins a deep struggle with her good and bad sides while she runs the household of her Preacher father, a chore she has been doing for some time since her mother died nine years earlier. Writing in *Publishers Weekly,* a reviewer commented that some readers "may be confused about what makes her tick." Nevertheless, the reviewer noted that "the universal obstacles she faces and the realistic outcome will likely hold readers' attention." Anderson's 2003 book, *Thank You Sarah: The Woman Who Saved Thanksgiving,* focuses on the true-life story of Sarah Hale, an overachieving woman in the mid-1800s who juggled duties as a magazine editor, mother, teacher, and feminist. Hale is largely credited with saving the holiday of Thanksgiving. For nearly four decades Hale wrote letters to various U.S. presidents asking that Thanksgiving be made a national holiday, finally having her request granted by Abraham Lincoln. Writing in the *School Library Journal,* Louise L. Sherman commented, "Anderson turns a little-known historical tidbit into a fresh, funny, and inspirational alternative to the standard Thanksgiving stories." The book received the 2003 Once upon a World Award given by the Simon Weisenthal Center and was recommended by the Amelia Bloomer Project on its third annual list of feminist books for young readers.

Anderson's first picture book was *Ndito Runs,* published in 1996. Illustrated by Anita Van der Merwe, the story depicts a typical morning's journey for Ndito, a Kenyan girl whose path to school traverses some of her country's characteristically stunning landscape. Ndito imagines herself as the various animals she encounters, such as the crane and the dik-dik. Anderson also wrote a second picture book that appeared in 1996. *Turkey Pox,* illustrated by Dorothy Donohue, follows Charity, a youngster girl who looks forward to spending the Thanksgiving holiday with her beloved grandmother. In their haste to depart Charity's harried family does not take notice of her face. It is only when they are in the car that they realize she has a case of chicken pox. The discovery forces them to return home, and a snowstorm further complicates matters. The disconsolate Charity is cheered when her intrepid Nana arrives, having hitched a ride with snowplowers and bringing along her roasted turkey. The family then decorates the bird with cherries to resemble poor Charity's face. In another story about Charity and her busy family, *No Time for Mother's Day,* the girl is confounded by the holiday and what she might give her mother as a present. After following her parent around on a very busy Saturday, Charity realizes what her mom really needs is a day of peace and quiet. "The message about modern life and how to make it just a bit simpler should hit close to home," wrote Ilene Cooper in *Booklist.*

BIOGRAPHICAL AND CRITICAL SOURCES:

BOOKS

Anderson, Laurie Halse, *Speak,* Farrar, Straus (New York, NY), 1999.

PERIODICALS

ALAN Review, spring-summer, 2000, Laurie Halse Anderson, "Speaking Out," pp. 25-26.

Booklist, March 15, 1996, Hazel Rochman, review of *Ndito Runs,* p. 1268; September 1, 1996, Carolyn Phelan, review of *Turkey Pox,* p. 35; February 15, 1999, Ilene Cooper, review of *No Time for Mother's Day,* p. 1073; September 15, 1999, Debbie Carton, review of *Speak;* November 15, 1999, Stephanie Zvirin, review of *Speak,* p. 618; May 1, 2000, Lauren Peterson, review of *Fight for Life: Maggie,* p. 1665; October 1, 2000, Frances Bradburn, review of *Fever 1793,* p. 332; April 1, 2001, Stephanie Zvirin, review of *Fever 1793,* p. 1486; December 15, 2002, Ilene Cooper, review of *Thank You, Sarah: The Woman Who Saved Thanksgiving,* p. 764.

Bulletin of the Center for Children's Books, November, 1996, Janice Del Negro, review of *Turkey Pox,* pp. 89-90; April, 1999, review of *No Time for Mother's Day,* pp. 271-272; October, 1999, review of *Speak,* p. 45.

Children's Book Review Service, April, 1996, p. 97.

Horn Book, fall, 1996, p. 246; September, 1999, review of *Speak,* p. 605; September, 2000, Anita K. Burkam, review of *Fever 1793,* p. 562.

Kirkus Reviews, September 19, 1999, review of *Speak,* p. 1496.

Kliatt, September, 1999, Paula Rohrlick, review of *Speak,* p. 4.

New York Times Book Review, November 19, 2000, Constance Decker Thompson, review of *Fever 1793,* pp. 45-46.

Publishers Weekly, review of *Ndito Runs,* March 18, 1996, pp. 68-69; September 20, 1996, review of *Turkey Pox,* p. 87; September 13, 1999, review of *Speak,* p. 85; December 20, 1999, Jennifer M. Brown, "In Dreams Begin Possibilities," p. 24; July 31, 2000, review of *Fever 1793,* p. 96; July 22, 2002, review of *Catalyst,* p. 180.

School Library Journal, May, 1996, Tom S. Hurlburt, review of *Ndito Runs,* p. 84; October, 1996, Lisa Marie Gangemi, review of *Turkey Pox,* p. 84; April, 1999, Roxanne Burg, review of *No Time for Mother's Day,* p. 85; October, 1999, Dina Sherman, review of *Speak,* p. 144; July, 2000, Janie Schomberg, review of *Fight for Life,* p. 100; August, 2000, Kathleen Isaacs, review of *Fever 1793,* p. 177; December, 2000, Ronni Krasnow, review of *Homeless: Sunita,* p. 138; January, 2001, Carol Johnson Shedd, review of *Saudi Arabia,* p. 112; July, 2001, Jennifer Ralston, review of *Say Good-Bye,* p. 102; October, 2002, Lynn Bryant, review of *Catalyst,* p. 154; December, 2002, Louise L. Sherman, review of *Thank You, Sarah,* p. 116.

Voice of Youth Advocates, December, 2000, Christine M. Hill, "Laurie Halse Anderson Speaks: An Interview," pp. 325-327; December, 2000, Dr. Stefani Koorey, review of *Fever 1793,* p. 344.

ONLINE

authors4teens.com, http://www.authors4teens.com/ (May 24, 2001), interview with Anderson.

Book Bag Web site, http://www.bookreport.com/ (May 24, 2001), interview with Anderson.

CNN.com, http://www.cnn.com/ (May 24, 2001), Nancy Matson, review of *Speak.*

Laurie's Bookshelf, http://www.writerlady.com/ (May 24, 2001).

Publishers Weekly Online, http://www.publishers weekly.com/ (May 24, 2001), Laurie Halse Anderson, "The Books That Changed My Life."

ANDERSON, Poul 1926-2001
(Poul William Anderson, A.A. Craig, Michael A. Karageorge, Winston P. Sanders)

PERSONAL: Born November 25, 1926, in Bristol, PA; died of prostate cancer, July 31, 2001, in Orinda, CA; son of Anton William and Astrid (Hertz) Anderson; married Karen J.M. Kruse, December 12, 1953; children: Astrid May. *Education:* University of Minnesota, B.S., 1948.

CAREER: Freelance writer, except for occasional temporary jobs, beginning 1948.

MEMBER: Institute for Twenty-first Century Studies, Science Fiction Writers of America (president, 1972-73), American Association for the Advancement of Science, Mystery Writers of America (northern California regional vice chair, 1959) Scowrers (secretary, 1957-62), Baker Street Irregulars, Elves, Gnomes, and Little Men's Science Fiction Chowder and Marching Society, Society for Creative Anachronism.

AWARDS, HONORS: First annual Cock Robin Mystery Award, 1959, for *Perish by the Sword;* Guest of Honor, World Science Fiction Convention, 1959; Hugo Award, World Science Fiction Convention, for best short fiction, 1961, for "The Longest Voyage," 1964, for "No Truce with Kings," 1969, for "The Sharing of Flesh," 1972, for "The Queen of Air and Darkness," 1973, for "Goat Song," 1979, for "Hunter's Moon," and 1982, for "The Saturn Game"; Nebula Award, Science Fiction Writers of America, 1971, for "The Queen of Air and Darkness," 1972, for "Goat Song," and 1981, for "The Saturn Game"; August Derleth Award, British Fantasy Society, 1974, for *Hrolf Kraki's Saga;* Mythopoeic Award, 1975; J.R.R. Tolkien Memorial Award and Gandalf Award, 1978; Grand Master of Fantasy, World Science Fiction Convention, 1978; Grandmaster, Science Fiction and Fantasy Writers of America, 1997; Grand Master Award, Science Fiction Writers of America, 1998; Strannik Award, Congress of Fantasy Writers, 1999; inducted into the Science Fiction Fantasy Hall of Fame, 2000; John W. Campbell Award, 2001, for *Genesis.*

WRITINGS:

Perish by the Sword (novel), Macmillan (New York, NY), 1959.

Murder in Black Letter (novel), Macmillan (New York, NY), 1960.

The Golden Slave (novel), Avon (New York, NY), 1960.

Rogue Sword (novel), Avon (New York, NY), 1960.

Murder Bound (novel), Macmillan (New York, NY), 1962.

Is There Life on Other Worlds? (nonfiction), Crowell (New York, NY), 1963.

Thermonuclear Warfare (nonfiction), Monarch (New York, NY), 1963.

The Infinite Voyage: Man's Future in Space (nonfiction), Macmillan (New York, NY), 1969.

The Road of the Sea Horse, Zebra (New York, NY), 1980.

SCIENCE FICTION NOVELS

Vault of the Ages (for children), Winston (Philadelphia, PA), 1952.

Brain Wave, Ballantine (New York, NY), 1954, reprinted, Ballantine (New York, NY), 1985, I Books (New York, NY), 2005.

The Broken Sword, Abelard-Schuman (New York, NY), 1954, revised with an introduction by Lin Carter, Ballantine (New York, NY), 1971.

No World of Their Own (bound with *The 1,000 Year Plan* by Isaac Asimov), Ace Books (New York, NY), 1955, published separately as *The Long Way Home,* Gregg (Boston, MA), 1978.

Planet of No Return, Ace Books (New York, NY), 1956, published as *Question and Answer,* Ace (New York, NY), 1978.

Star Ways, Avalon (New York, NY), 1957, published as *The Peregrine,* Ace Books (New York, NY), 1978.

War of the Wing-Men, Ace Books (New York, NY), 1958, published as *The Man Who Counts,* Ace Books (New York, NY), 1978.

The Snows of Ganymede, Ace Books (New York, NY), 1958.

Virgin Planet, Avalon (New York, NY), 1959.

The Enemy Stars, Lippincott (Philadelphia, PA), 1959, expanded edition, Baen Books (New York, NY), 1987.

The War of Two Worlds, Ace Books (New York, NY), 1959.

We Claim These Stars! (bound with *The Planet Killers* by Robert Silverberg), Ace Books (New York, NY), 1959, expanded edition, Baen Books (New York, NY), 1987.

Earthman, Go Home! (bound with *To the Tombaugh Station* by Wilson Tucker), Ace Books (New York, NY), 1960.

The High Crusade, Doubleday (Garden City, NY), 1960, reprinted, I Books (New York, NY), 2003.

Twilight World, Torquil (New York, NY), 1960.

Mayday Orbit (bound with *No Man's World* by Kenneth Bulmer), Ace Books (New York, NY), 1961.

Three Hearts and Three Lions, Doubleday (Garden City, NY), 1961, reprinted, I Books (New York, NY), 2004.

The Makeshift Rocket, Ace Books (New York, NY), 1962.

After Doomsday, Ballantine (New York, NY), 1962.

Shield, Berkley Publishing (New York, NY), 1963.

Let the Spacemen Beware! (bound with *The Wizard of Starship Poseidon* by Kenneth Bulmer), Ace Books (New York, NY), 1963, published separately as *The Night Face,* Ace Books (New York, NY), 1978.

Three Worlds to Conquer, Pyramid Publications (New York, NY), 1964.

The Star Fox, Doubleday (Garden City, NY), 1965.

The Corridors of Time, Doubleday (Garden City, NY), 1965.

Ensign Flandry, Chilton (Philadelphia, PA), 1966, reprinted, I Books (New York, NY), 2003.

World without Stars, Ace Books (New York, NY), 1966.

Satan's World, Doubleday (Garden City, NY), 1969.

The Rebel Worlds, Signet (New York, NY), 1969, published as *Commander Flandry,* Severn House (London, England), 1978.

A Circus of Hells, Signet (New York, NY), 1970.

Tau Zero, Doubleday (Garden City, NY), 1970.

The Byworlder, NAL (New York, NY), 1971.

Operation Chaos, Doubleday (Garden City, NY), 1971.

The Dancer from Atlantis, Signet (New York, NY), 1971.

There Will Be Time, Doubleday (Garden City, NY), 1972.

Hrolf Kraki's Saga, Ballantine (New York, NY), 1973.

The Day of Their Return, Doubleday (Garden City, NY), 1973.

The People of the Wind, Signet (New York, NY), 1973.

Fire Time, Doubleday (Garden City, NY), 1974.

A Knight of Ghosts and Shadows, Doubleday (Garden City, NY), 1974, published as *Knight Flandry,* Severn House (London, England), 1980.

A Midsummer Tempest, Doubleday (Garden City, NY), 1974.

(With Gordon Ecklund) *Inheritors of Earth,* Chilton (Radnor, PA), 1974.

The Worlds of Poul Anderson (contains *Planet of No Return, The War of Two Worlds,* and *World without Stars*), Ace Books (New York, NY), 1974.

(With Gordon Dickson) *Star Prince Charlie* (for children), Putnam (New York, NY), 1975.

The Winter of the World, Doubleday (Garden City, NY), 1975.

Mirkheim, Berkley (New York, NY), 1977.

The Avatar, Berkley (New York, NY), 1978.

Two Worlds (contains *Question and Answer* and *World without Stars*), Gregg (Boston, MA), 1978.

The Merman's Children, Berkley (New York, NY), 1979.

A Stone in Heaven, Ace Books (New York, NY), 1979.

The Devil's Game, Pocket Books (New York, NY), 1980.

The Road of the Sea Horse, Zebra Books (New York, NY), 1980.

Conan the Rebel #5, Bantam (New York, NY), 1980.

(With Mildred D. Broxon) *The Demon of Scattery,* Ace Books (New York, NY), 1980.

The Last Viking: Book One, The Golden Horn, Zebra Books (New York, NY), 1980.

The Sign of the Raven, Zebra Books (New York, NY), 1980.

Cold Victory, Pinnacle Books (New York, NY), 1982.

The Gods Laughed, Pinnacle Books (New York, NY), 1982.

Maurai and Kith, Tor Books (New York, NY), 1982.

New America, Pinnacle Books (New York, NY), 1983.

The Long Night, Pinnacle Books (New York, NY), 1983.

Orion Shall Rise, Pocket Books (New York, NY), 1983.

Agent of Vega, Ace Books (New York, NY), 1983.

Conflict, Pinnacle Books (New York, NY), 1983.

Time Patrolman, Pinnacle Books (New York, NY), 1983.

Bat-Twenty-One, Bantam (New York, NY), 1983.

(With Gordon Dickson) *Hoka!,* Simon & Schuster (New York, NY), 1983.

(With wife, Karen Anderson) *The Unicorn Trade,* Tor Books (New York, NY), 1984.

Dialogue with Darkness, Tor Books (New York, NY), 1985.

The Game of Empire, Pocket Books (New York, NY), 1985.

The Psychotechnic League, Tor Books (New York, NY), 1985.

(With wife, Karen Anderson) *The King of Ys,* Baen (New York, NY), Book 1: *Roma Mater,* 1986, Book 2: *Gallicenae,* 1988, Book 3: *Dahut,* 1988, Book 4: *The Dog and the Wolf,* 1988, four volumes revised and published together, Simon & Schuster (New York, NY), 1996.

The Year of the Ransom, Walker & Co. (New York, NY), 1988.

(With Larry Niven and Dean Ing) *Man-Kzin Wars,* Baen Books (New York, NY), 1988.

Conan the Rebel #17, Ace Books (New York, NY), 1989.

No Truce with Kings (bound with *Ship of Shadows* by Fritz Leiber), Tor Books (New York, NY), 1989.

The Boat of a Million Years, Tor Books (New York, NY), 1989, reprinted, Orb Books (New York, NY), 2004.

The Shield of Time, Tor Books (New York, NY), 1990.

(With Larry Niven, Jerry Pournelle, and S.M. Sterling) *Man-Kzin Wars III,* Baen Books (New York, NY), 1990.

Inconstant Star (contains *Man-Kzin Wars* and *Man-Kzin Wars III*), Baen Books New York, NY), 1991.

How to Build a Planet, Pulphouse (Eugene, OR), 1991.

Kinship with the Stars, Tor Books (New York, NY), 1991.

Murasaki: A Novel in Six Parts, Bantam (New York, NY), 1992.

A Harvest of Stars, Tor Books (New York, NY), 1993.

The Stars Are Also Fire, Tor Books (New York, NY), 1994.

Harvest the Fire, Tor Books (New York, NY), 1995.

The Fleet of Stars, Tor Books (New York, NY), 1997.

War of the Gods, Tor Books (New York, NY), 1997.

Starfarers, Tor Books (New York, NY), 1998.

Operation Luna, Tor Books (New York, NY), 1999.

Genesis, Tor Books (New York, NY), 2000.

Mother of Kings, Tor Books (New York, NY), 2001.

Going for Infinity, Tor Books (New York, NY), 2002.

For Love and Glory, Tor Books (New York, NY), 2004.

SHORT STORY COLLECTIONS

(With Gordon Dickson) *Earthman's Burden,* Gnome Press (New York, NY), 1957.

Guardians of Time, Ballantine (New York, NY), 1960, revised edition, Pinnacle Books (New York, NY), 1981.

Strangers from Earth: Eight Tales of Vaulting Imagination, Ballantine (New York, NY), 1961.

Orbit Unlimited, Pyramid Publications (New York, NY), 1961.

Un-Man and Other Novellas (bound with *The Makeshift Rocket*), Ace Books (New York, NY), 1962.

Trader to the Stars, Doubleday (Garden City, NY), 1964.

Time and Stars, Doubleday (Garden City, NY), 1964.

Agent of the Terran Empire (includes *We Claim These Stars!*), Chilton (Philadelphia, PA), 1965, reprinted, I Books (New York, NY), 2004.

Flandry of Terra (includes *Earthman, Go Home!* and *Mayday Orbit*), Chilton (Philadelphia, PA), 1965, reprinted, I Books (New York, NY), 2004.

The Trouble Twisters, Doubleday (Garden City, NY), 1966.

The Horn of Time, Signet (New York, NY), 1968.

Beyond the Beyond, Signet (New York, NY), 1969.

Seven Conquests: An Adventure in Science Fiction, Macmillan (New York, NY), 1969, published as *Conquests,* Granada (London, England), 1981.

Tales of the Flying Mountains, Macmillan (New York, NY), 1970.

The Queen of Air and Darkness and Other Stories, Signet (New York, NY), 1973.

The Many Worlds of Poul Anderson, Chilton (Philadelphia, PA), 1974, published as *The Book of Poul Anderson,* DAW Books (New York, NY), 1975.

Homeward and Beyond, Doubleday (Garden City, NY), 1975.

Homebrew, National Education Field Service Association Press (Cambridge, MA), 1976.

The Best of Poul Anderson, Pocket Books (New York, NY), 1976.

The Earth Book of Stormgate, Berkley (New York, NY), 1978.

The Night Face and Other Stories, Gregg (Boston, MA), 1978.

The Dark between the Stars, Berkley (New York, NY), 1980.

Explorations, Tor Books (New York, NY), 1981.

Fantasy, Tor Books (New York, NY), 1981.

Winners, Tor Books (New York, NY), 1981.

Starship, Tor Books (New York, NY), 1982.

Past Times, Tor Books (New York, NY), 1984.

(With wife, Karen Anderson) *The Unicorn Trade,* Tor Books (New York, NY), 1984.

Dialogue with Darkness, Tor Books (New York, NY), 1985.

(Editor, with Martin H. Greenberg and Charles G. Waugh) *Time Wars,* Tor Books (New York, NY), 1986.

Space Folk, Baen Books (New York, NY), 1989.

The Saturn Game (published with *Iceborne,* by Gregory Benford and Paul A. Carter), Tor Books (New York, NY), 1989.

The Longest Voyage (published with *Slow Lightning,* by Fritz Lieber), Tor Books (New York, NY), 1991.

Alight in the Void, Tor Books (New York, NY), 1991.

Loser' Night, Pulphouse (Eugene, OR), 1991.

The Time Patrol (contains "Star of the Sea"), Tor Books (New York, NY), 1991.

The Armies of Elfland (contains "The Queen of Air and Darkness"), Tor Books (New York, NY), 1992.

OTHER

(Editor) *West by One and by One: An Anthology of Irregular Writings by the Scowrers and Molly Magu-* *ires of San Francisco and the Trained Cormorants of Los Angeles County,* privately printed (San Francisco, CA), 1965.

(Adaptor) Christian Molbech, *The Fox, the Dog, and the Griffin,* Doubleday (Garden City, NY), 1966.

(Editor) *Nebula Award Stories Four,* Doubleday (Garden City, NY), 1969.

(Author of introduction) *The Best of L. Sprague de Camp,* Ballantine (New York, NY), 1978.

(Translator) *The Method of Holding the Three Ones: A Taoist Manual of Meditation of the Fourth Century, A.D.,* Humanities Press (Atlantic Highlands, NJ), 1980.

(Editor, with Martin H. Greenberg and Charles G. Waugh) *Mercenaries of Tomorrow,* Critic's Choice (New York, NY), 1985.

(Editor, with Martin H. Greenberg and Charles G. Waugh) *Terrorists of Tomorrow,* Critic's Choice (New York, NY), 1986.

(Editor, with wife, Karen Anderson) *The Night Fantastic* (anthology), DAW (New York, NY), 1991.

All One Universe (contains short stories, essays, and a play), Tor Books (New York, NY), 1996.

Contributor to books, including *All about the Future,* edited by Martin Greenberg, Gnome Press (New York, NY), 1955; *The Day the Sun Stood Still: Three Original Novellas of Science Fiction,* Thomas Nelson (Nashville, TN), 1972; *Science Fiction: Today and Tomorrow,* edited by Reginald Bretnor, Harper (New York, NY), 1974; *The Craft of Science Fiction,* edited by Reginald Bretnor, Harper (New York, NY), 1976; *Turning Points: Essays on the Art of Science Fiction,* edited by Damon Knight, Harper (New York, NY), 1977; *Swords against Darkness,* edited by Andrew J. Offutt, Zebra Books (New York NY), Volume 1, 1977, Volume 3, 1978, Volume 4, 1979; *The Blade of Conan,* edited by L. Sprague de Camp, Ace Books (New York, NY), 1979; *Space Wars* (short stories), edited by Charles Waugh and Martin H. Greenberg, Tor Books (New York, NY), 1988; and *Three in Time: Classic Novels of Time Travel.*

Also contributor to anthologies, including *Possible Worlds of Science Fiction,* edited by Groff Conklin, Vanguard, 1951; *A Treasury of Great Science Fiction,* edited by Anthony Boucher, Doubleday (Garden City, NY), 1959; *The Hugo Winners,* edited by Isaac Asimov, Doubleday (Garden City, NY), 1962; *Space, Time, and Crime,* edited by Miriam Allen de Ford, Paperback Library (New York, NY), 1964; *Masters of Science Fiction,* Belmont Books (New York, NY), 1964; *The Science Fiction Hall of Fame,* edited by Ben Bova, Doubleday (Garden City, NY), 1973; and *The Future at*

War, edited by Reginald Bretnor, Ace Books (New York, NY), 1979. Contributor of short stories, some under pseudonyms A.A. Craig and Winston P. Sanders, to *Magazine of Fantasy and Science Fiction, Galaxy, Analog Science Fiction/Science Fact, Isaac Asimov's Science Fiction Magazine,* and other publications.

Anderson's manuscript collection is housed at the University of Southern Mississippi, Hattiesburg.

ADAPTATIONS: The High Crusade was produced as a film in 1994.

SIDELIGHTS: Although often referred to as a writer of "hard" science fiction—science fiction with a scrupulously accurate scientific basis—Poul Anderson was also known for his creation of plausible fantasy worlds, often based on Nordic mythology. His "recognition of the inevitability of sorrow and death and of the limitations of human powers (but not human spirit) in the face of the immense inhumanity of the universe," Russell Letson of the *Science Fiction and Fantasy Book Review* believed, "lifts Anderson's fiction above its flaws." "It is increasingly clear," wrote Michael W. McClintock in the *Dictionary of Literary Biography,* "that [Anderson] is one of the five or six most important writers to appear during the science-fiction publishing boom of the decade following the end of World War II."

The novel *Tau Zero* is considered one of Anderson's best works of hard science fiction. It presents a simple scientific possibility—a space ship uncontrollably accelerating at a steady one gravity—and develops the consequences in a relentlessly logical and scientifically plausible manner. Sandra Miesel, writing in her *Against Time's Arrow: The High Crusade of Poul Anderson,* found the novel's structure a key to its effectiveness. "To convey the numbing immensities of the time and distance traversed [during the novel]," Miesel noted, "Anderson begins slowly, letting a few hours elapse at the normal rate in the first chapter. Thereafter, the tempo quickens at an exponential rate until eons fleet by in heartbeats and the reader unquestioningly accepts all the marvels described." James Blish called *Tau Zero* "the ultimate 'hard' science fiction novel." In his review of the book for the *Magazine of Fantasy and Science Fiction,* Blish went on to say that "everybody else who has been trying to write this kind of thing can now fold up his tent and creep silently away. . . . Overall, [*Tau Zero*] is a monument to what a born novelist and poet can do with authentic scientific materials. And as is usual with recent Anderson, the poet is as important as the novelist."

Anderson's scientific accuracy is reflected in the carefully constructed backgrounds he created for his stories. He set about fifty of his science fiction novels and short stories in a consistent "future history" of his own devising. This history concerns the exploration of outer space by the *Technic Civilization,* and each story explores a different event within this history. Although other science fiction writers have also used the future history idea, McClintock said Anderson "utilized it more extensively—and arguably to better advantage—than any other writer."

In his fantasy works, too, Anderson constructed imaginary worlds that are logical and coherent. These worlds are often based on Nordic sagas or contain elements from Nordic history. His prize-winning story "The Queen of Air and Darkness" is set in an arctic wilderness that is, Miesel stated, "a scientifically plausible Elfland." The story is included in an eight-tale collection published under the title *The Armies of Elfland,* which *Kliatt* contributor Karen L. Ellis called an "entertaining anthology." In *Operation Chaos,* Miesel noted, magic is "a perfectly rational, orderly activity." The novel *The Merman's Children* is based on a medieval Danish ballad about the decline of the world of Faerie. Set in Denmark in the Middle Ages, the novel tells of the struggle between the mermen and the Christian church. The conflict arises because the mermen, an older and less developed species, do not possess souls.

The three adventures in *The Shield of Time* also showed Anderson's interest in ancient and medieval history. They take place in 200 B.C., the Pleistocene era, and twelfth-century Naples. For this book, Anderson resurrected the "Time Patrol" (a squad he first created in the 1950s), whose job it is to travel through time to make sure history is not tampered with. "Anderson play[s] nicely with the idea that history may pivot on one lone individual, though the identity of that individual may not be at all obvious," noted Tom Easton in *Analog: Science Fiction/Science Fact.* Tom Whitmore remarked in *LOCUS:* "Anderson has looked closely at several historical points where a small nudge would have made a big difference, and his historical settings (as always) feel grittily believable. But the story struck me as ultimately futile." A new novella, "Star of the Sea," and Anderson's other stories about the Time Patrol are compiled in the book *The Time Patrol.* The stories relate the people and places throughout history that agent Manse Everard encounters during his career. "There is an indefinable 'period' feel to the earlier tales, a 1950s sensibility different from the bleak [vision of] the stories from the 1980s," Russell Letson wrote in *LOCUS.*

In his fiction, Anderson dealt with "overpopulation, conflict between cultures, humankind's biological imperatives, and depleted natural resources," wrote Michael Pottow in the *Science Fiction and Fantasy Book Review,* "but in the final analysis each of the stories is about people." A recurring theme in his work is the importance of individual liberty and free will. Anderson once admitted to Jeffrey M. Elliot in *Science Fiction Voices #2:* "If I preach at all, it's probably in the direction of individual liberty, which is a theme that looms large in my work." Miesel saw Anderson as primarily concerned with the question, "How should mortal man in a finite universe act? Rejecting passivity, [Anderson] asserts that free action is both possible and necessary. . . . Mortals must resist entropy in both its guises, tyrannical stasis or anarchic chaos. The fight is all the more valiant for its utter hopelessness."

In *Quadrant,* Hal G.P. Colebatch elaborated on the author's use of conflict in his fiction. While Anderson "has many a good-versus-evil epic," he stated, "his stories very frequently contain what may be the more complex and potentially greater tragedy of a conflict of goods. It is typical (though by no means invariable) the villains or antagonists try to do the right thing and are even kindly by their own lights. This is a refreshing change from the hide-bound conventions of much adventure and fantasy writing."

In *Harvest of Stars,* pilot Kyra Davis travels to North America to rescue her boss, Anson Guthrie, who now exists as a downloaded personality. The continent is governed by religious fanatics known as Avantists, aiming to take over Fireball Enterprises. The book also introduces Earth's intelligent nonhuman species, the Keiki, and the bioengineered human species, the Lunarians. Critics claim the book changes from an adventure to a vision. In the *New York Times Book Review,* Gerald Jones wrote: "*Harvest of Stars* is overwritten, underimagined and fatally flawed with self-satisfied musings on life-according-to-Guthrie that read suspiciously like the author's own self-justifications." Letson noted in *LOCUS:* "[The book] has more of Anderson's strengths than his weaknesses," including "a *genuinely* poetic feeling for the physical universe" and "a capacity for the elegiac and the tragic that are rare in sf."

As *The Stars Are Also Fire* opens, Dagny Beynac, a descendant of Anson Guthrie, works to preserve peace on the Moon where she lives with her genetically adapted children. In the second part, two individuals search for the secret to unlocking the Peace Authority's control of their way of life. The two intertwined stories in the book span centuries and multiple worlds. *Harvest the Fire* features the rivalry between humans and cyber-

netic organisms, while in *The Fleet of Stars,* Anson Guthrie returns to Earth as a personality downloaded onto his spacecraft's computer. On Earth he seeks the secret that keeps artificial intelligences in power. *Publishers Weekly* called the book "an exciting culmination to an ambitious saga about the future of human evolution."

Anderson provided a running commentary to connect nine stories, six essays, a play, and two other pieces that compose *All One Universe.* Noted a reviewer for *Publishers Weekly,* "Readers tolerant of potpourri may go for this, but Anderson's most pungent work it isn't." However, a reviewer commented in *Rapport,* "On the whole, *All One Universe* is a collection which does its creator proud while delighting his fans."

As the twentieth century drew to a close, Anderson continued to produce novels for sci-fi and fantasy readers. *Starfarers,* a 1998 release, is set in the new millennium. A deep-space message uncovers the existence of galaxy-faring aliens, and a starship is sent to take Earth representatives to meet the extraterrestrial neighbors. The space-time continuum, however, deems that the decade spent by the crew aboard ship will translate into thousands of years back on Earth. The voyage is a success, but "when and if the crew returns," noted Eric Robbins in *Booklist,* "it is a gamble that they will come back to a recognizable home planet." Robbins praised the work of "master storyteller" Anderson in his review, an opinion that was echoed by a *Publishers Weekly* contributor, who deemed it a "spectacular novel written in [Anderson's] classic manner" and, comparing the book favorably to *Tau Zero,* called *Starfarers* the author's "best work in some time."

In *Genesis,* another well-received entry, the author "flings his long-time audience [beyond *Starfarers*] into a far-future extrapolation of human destiny that sings praises to the power of human love," according to a *Publishers Weekly* reviewer. Astronaut Christian Brannock volunteers to have his personality uploaded into an artificial-intelligence machine that will travel the galaxy on a billion-year exploration. The virtual Brannock's return to a vastly evolved Earth brings him into contact with the meaning of human existence. Jackie Cassada of *Library Journal* pointed to that theme as giving *Genesis* a "surreal, allegorical feel." The fantasy-skewed *Mother of Kings,* a Norse epic, was released corresponding with Anderson's death from prostate cancer in August 2001.

The occasion of Anderson's death brought revelations into the author's standing among his fans and peers. As David Kipen quoted her in a *San Francisco Chronicle* piece, Anderson's widow, Karen, said that in the waning hours of her husband's life, "messages poured in from strangers who told how they had learned honor and courage from his writing, courtesy and kindness from his personal example." Such tributes, she added, "cannot be awarded, but only earned."

When asked to comment on the role of science fiction in relation to other types of literature, Anderson once told *CA:* "I have written quite a lot of it, and am proud to have done so, because science fiction is and always has been part of literature. Its long isolation, strictly a twentieth-century phenomenon, is ending; its special concepts and techniques are becoming common property, employed not only by the mass media but by some of our most respected writers; in turn, it is shedding artistic parochialism and thus starting to communicate beyond a small circle of enthusiasts." He continued, "This is good, because the particular concerns of science fiction never have been parochial; they have included, or tried to include, all of space, time, and fate. Not that I wish to make exaggerated claims. I merely set forth that science fiction is one human accomplishment, among countless others, which has something to offer the world. Lest even this sound too pompous let me say that at the very least it is often a lot of fun."

BIOGRAPHICAL AND CRITICAL SOURCES:

BOOKS

Benson, Gordon, Jr., *Poul Anderson, Myth-Master and Wonder-Weaver: An Interim Bibliography (1947-1982),* G. Benson, Jr. (Albuquerque, NM), 1982, 5th revised edition published as *Poul Anderson, Myth-Master and Wonder-Weaver: A Working Bibliography,* Borgo Press (San Bernardino, CA), 1990.
Contemporary Authors Autobiography Series, Volume 2, Thomson Gale (Detroit, MI), 1985.
Contemporary Literary Criticism, Volume 15, Thomson Gale (Detroit, MI), 1980.
Dictionary of Literary Biography, Volume 8: *Twentieth-Century American Science-Fiction Writers,* Thomson Gale (Detroit, MI), 1981.
Elliot, Jeffrey M., *Science Fiction Voices #2,* Borgo Press (San Bernardino, CA), 1979.
Miesel, Sandra, *Against Time's Arrow: The High Crusade of Poul Anderson,* Borgo (San Bernardino, CA), 1978.
Peyton, Roger C., *A Checklist of Poul Anderson,* privately printed, 1965.

Platt, Charles, *Dream Makers, Volume 2: The Uncommon Men and Women Who Write Science Fiction,* Berkley (New York, NY), 1983.
Stever, David, and Andrew Adams Whyte, *The Collector's Poul Anderson,* privately printed, 1976.
Walker, Paul, *Speaking of Science Fiction: The Paul Walker Interviews,* Luna Publications (Oradell, NY), 1978.

PERIODICALS

Algol, summer-fall, 1978.
Analog: Science Fiction/Science Fact, February, 1991, p. 176; December, 1993, p. 163; March, 1996, p. 146; January, 1998, review of *War of the Gods,* p. 145; November 1, 1998, Tom Easton, review of *Starfarers,* p. 132; March, 1999, Tom Easton, review of *Starfarers,* p. 132; October, 1999, review of *Operation Luna,* p. 132; June, 2000, Tom Easton, review of *Genesis,* p. 132.
Booklist, October 1, 1995, p. 254; February 15, 1996, p. 981; November 1, 1998, Eric Robbins, review of *Starfarers,* p. 477; July, 1999, Roland Green, review of *Operation Luna,* p. 1929; February 15, 2000, Roland Green, review of *Genesis,* p. 1090.
Books and Bookmen, August, 1972.
Globe and Mail (Toronto, Ontario, Canada), November 18, 1989.
Kirkus Reviews, August 15, 1995, p. 1146; December 1, 1995, p. 1671; October 1, 1998, review of *Starfarers,* p. 1420; June 1, 1999, review of *Operation Luna,* p. 840; September 1, 2001, review of *Mother of Kings,* p. 1252.
Kliatt, September, 1991, p. 19; September, 1992, p. 18; January, 1995, p. 12.
Library Journal, October 15, 1995, p. 91; November 15, 1996, p. 42; October 15, 1998, Jackie Cassada, review of *Starfarers,* p. 103; June 15, 1999, Jackie Cassada, review of *Operation Luna,* p. 111; February 15, 2000, Jackie Cassada, review of *Genesis,* p. 202; October 15, 2001, Jackie Cassada, review of *Mother of Kings,* p. 12.
LOCUS, August, 1990, p. 27; May, 1991, p. 45; October, 1991, p. 19; June, 1993, p. 29; November, 1994, p. 25; June, 1999, review of *Operation Luna,* p. 25.
Los Angeles Times, March 15, 2000, Michael Harris, review of *Genesis,* p. E3.
Luna Monthly, June, 1972.
Magazine of Fantasy and Science Fiction, March, 1971; December, 1971; December, 1992, p. 31; February, 1998, Robert Killheffer, review of *Three in Time: Classic Novels of Time Travel,* p. 42; March, 1998, Mike Resnick, review of *Tau Zero,* p. 82.

National Review, January 2, 1964.

New York Times Book Review, October 28, 1979; September 12, 1993, p. 36.

Publishers Weekly, September 20, 1991, p. 124; July 26, 1993, p. 62; July 18, 1994, p. 239; January 22, 1996, p. 61; February 24, 1997, p. 69; September 28, 1998, review of *Starfarers,* p. 76; July 5, 1999, review of *Operation Luna,* p. 63; February 14, 2000, review of *Genesis,* p. 179; September 10, 2001, review of *Conan the Rebel* and *Mother of Kings,* pp. 66-67.

Quadrant, June, 2001, Hal G.P. Colebatch, "Poul Anderson: An Appreciation," p. 56.

Rapport, Volume 19, number 3, 1996, p. 31; Volume 20, number 3, 1998, review of *War of the Gods,* p. 26.

School Library Journal, April, 1992, p. 170.

Science Fiction and Fantasy Book Review, April, 1982.

Science Fiction Chronicle, April, 1998, review of *War of the Gods,* p. 53; October, 1998, review of *Starfarers,* p. 51; August, 1999, review of *Operation Luna,* p. 39.

Science Fiction Review, May, 1978.

Tribune Books (Chicago, IL), December 30, 1990, p. 6; October 27, 1991, p. 6.

Voice of Youth Advocates, February, 1995, p. 343; June, 1999, review of *Starfarers,* p. 119.

Washington Post Book World, February 24, 1980; May 29, 1983; August 26, 1990, p. 8; March 31, 1991, p. 12; January 24, 1999, review of *Starfarers,* p. 8.

Wilson Library Bulletin, January, 1995, p. 90.

OBITUARIES:

PERIODICALS

Daily Telegraph (London, England), August 7, 2001.

Guardian (London, England), August 4, 2001, p. 20.

Los Angeles Times, August 3, 2001, p. B10.

New York Times, August 3, 2001, p. A23.

San Francisco Chronicle, August 3, 2001, p. A24.

Times (London, England), September 3, 2001, p. 17.

*   *   *

ANDERSON, Poul William
See ANDERSON, Poul

*   *   *

ANDREWS, Elton V.
See POHL, Frederik

ANGELOU, Maya 1928-
(Marguerite Annie Johnson)

PERSONAL: Surname is pronounced "Ahn-ge-low"; born Marguerite Annie Johnson, April 4, 1928, in St. Louis, MO; daughter of Bailey (a doorman and naval dietician) and Vivian (a registered nurse, professional gambler, and a rooming house and bar owner; maiden name, Baxter) Johnson; married Tosh Angelos, 1950 (divorced); married Paul Du Feu, December, 1973 (divorced, 1981); children: Guy. *Education:* Attended public schools in Arkansas and California; studied music privately, dance with Martha Graham, Pearl Primus, and Ann Halprin, and drama with Frank Silvera and Gene Frankel; studied cinematography in Sweden.

ADDRESSES: Home—Winston-Salem, NC. *Agent*—c/o Dave La Camera, Lordly and Dame, Inc., 51 Church Street, Boston, MA 02116.

CAREER: Author, poet, scriptwriter, playwright, performer, actress, and composer. *Arab Observer* (English-language newsweekly), Cairo, Egypt, associate editor, 1961-62; University of Ghana, Institute of African Studies, Legon-Accra, Ghana, assistant administrator of School of Music and Drama, 1963-66; freelance writer for *Ghanaian Times* and Ghanaian Broadcasting Corporation, 1963-65; *African Review,* Accra, feature editor, 1964-66. Lecturer at University of California, Los Angeles, 1966; writer-in-residence at University of Kansas, 1970; distinguished visiting professor at Wake Forest University, Wichita State University, and California State University, Sacramento, 1974; Reynolds Professor of American Studies at Wake Forest University, 1981—; visiting professor, universities in the United States; lecturer at various locations in the United States. Southern Christian Leadership Conference, northern coordinator, 1959-60; appointed member of American Revolution Bicentennial Council by President Gerald R. Ford, 1975-76; member of the Presidential Commission for International Women's Year, 1978-79; Board of Governors, University of North Carolina, Maya Angelou Institute for the Improvement of Child & Family Education at Winston-Salem State University, Winston-Salem, NC, 1998. Writer of poems for Hallmark greeting cards and gifts, 2002—.

Appeared in *Porgy and Bess* on twenty-two nation tour sponsored by the U.S. Department of State, 1954-55; appeared in Off-Broadway plays, *Calypso Heatwave,* 1957, and Jean Genet's *The Blacks,* 1960; produced and performed in *Cabaret for Freedom,* Off-Broadway,

1960; appeared in *Mother Courage* at University of Ghana, 1964; appeared in *Medea* in Hollywood, 1966; television narrator, interviewer, and host for African American specials and theater series, 1972—; made Broadway debut in *Look Away,* 1973; directed film, *All Day Long,* 1974; appeared in television miniseries *Roots,* 1977; directed play, *And Still I Rise,* Oakland, CA, 1976; directed play, *Moon on a Rainbow Shawl,* by Errol John, London, 1988; appeared as Aunt June in film, *Poetic Justice,* 1993; appeared as Lelia Mae in television film, *There Are No Children Here,* 1993; appeared in advertising for the United Negro College Fund, 1994; appeared as Anna in film, *How to Make an American Quilt,* 1995; narrator of the film *The Journey of the August King,* 1995; narrator of the video *Elmo Saves Christmas,* 1996; appeared in the film *Down in the Delta,* 1998; appeared in film *The Amen Corner* and television series *Down in the Delta,* both 1999; appeared as Conjure Woman in the television special *The Runaway,* 2000; appeared as herself in various television specials.

MEMBER: American Film Institute (member of board of trustees, 1975—), Directors Guild of America, Equity, American Federation of Television and Radio Artists, Women's Prison Association (member of advisory board), National Commission on the Observance of International Women's Year, Harlem Writer's Guild, Horatio Alger Association of Distinguished Americans, W.E.B. DuBois Foundation, National Society of Collegiate Scholars, National Society for the Prevention of Cruelty to Children.

AWARDS, HONORS: National Book Award nomination, 1970, for *I Know Why the Caged Bird Sings;* Yale University fellow, 1970; Pulitzer Prize nomination, 1972, for *Just Give Me a Cool Drink of Water 'fore I Diiie;* Tony Award nomination, 1973, for performance in *Look Away;* Rockefeller Foundation scholar in Italy, 1975; named Woman of the Year in Communications, *Ladies' Home Journal,* 1976; Emmy Award nomination, 1977, for performance in *Roots;* appointed first Reynolds Professor of American Studies at Wake Forest University, 1981; Matrix Award in the field of books, Women in Communication, Inc., 1983; North Carolina Award in Literature, 1987; Langston Hughes Award, City College of New York, 1991; Horatio Alger Award, 1992; Inaugural poet for President Bill Clinton, 1993; Grammy, Best Spoken Word Album, 1994, for recording of "On the Pulse of Morning"; etiquette award, National League of Junior Cotillions, 1993; Medal of Distinction, University of Hawaii Board of Regents, 1994; President's Award, Collegiate of Language Association for Outstanding Achievements, 1996; Southern Chris-

tian Leadership Conference of Los Angeles and Martin Luther King, Jr., Legacy Association National Award, 1996; named to the New York Black 100 list, Schomburg Center and The Black New Yorkers, 1996; distinguished merit citation, National Conference of Christians and Jews, 1997; Homecoming Award, Oklahoma Center for Poets and Writers, 1997; North Carolina Woman of the Year Award, North Carolina Black Publishers Association, 1997; Presidential & Lecture Series Award, University of North Florida, 1997; Cultural Keeper Awards, Black Caucus of the American Library Association, 1997; Humanitarian Contribution Award, Boston, MA, 1997; Alston/Jones International Civil and Human Rights Award, 1998; Christopher Award, New York, NY, 1998; American Airlines Audience, Gold Plaque Choice Award, Chicago International Film Festival, 1998, for *Down in the Delta;* Sheila Award, Tubman African American Museum, 1999; Lifetime Achievement Award for Literature, 1999; named one of the 100 best writers of the twentieth century, *Writer's Digest,* 1999; National Medal of Arts, 2000; Grammy award, 2002, for recording of *A Song Flung Up to Heaven;* recipient of over fifty honorary degrees from colleges and universities.

WRITINGS:

AUTOBIOGRAPHY

I Know Why the Caged Bird Sings, Random House (New York, NY), 1970, reprinted, 2002.
Gather Together in My Name, Random House (New York, NY), 1974, reprinted, 1990.
Singin' and Swingin' and Gettin' Merry like Christmas, Random House (New York, NY), 1976.
The Heart of a Woman, Random House (New York, NY), 1981.
All God's Children Need Traveling Shoes, Random House (New York, NY), 1986.
A Song Flung up to Heaven, Random House (New York, NY), 2002.
I Know Why the Caged Bird Sings: The Collected Autobiographies of Maya Angelou (omnibus edition of all six autobiographies), Modern Library (New York, NY), 2004.

POETRY

Just Give Me a Cool Drink of Water 'fore I Diiie, Random House (New York, NY), 1971.
Oh Pray My Wings Are Gonna Fit Me Well, Random House (New York, NY), 1975.

And Still I Rise, Random House (New York, NY), 1978, new version published as *Still I Rise,* illustrated by Diego Rivera, edited by Linda Sunshine, Random House (New York, NY), 2001.

Shaker, Why Don't You Sing?, Random House (New York, NY), 1983.

Poems, four volumes, Bantam (New York, NY), 1986.

Now Sheba Sings the Song (illustrated poem), illustrations by Tom Feelings, Dutton (New York, NY), 1987.

I Shall Not Be Moved, Random House (New York, NY), 1990.

On the Pulse of Morning, Random House (New York, NY), 1993.

The Complete Collected Poems of Maya Angelou, Random House (New York, NY), 1994.

A Brave and Startling Truth, Random House (New York, NY), 1995.

Phenomenal Woman: Four Poems Celebrating Women, Random House (New York, NY), 1995, new edition published as *Phenomenal Woman,* paintings by Paul Gaugin, edited by Linda Sunshine, Random House (New York, NY), 2000.

Also author of *The Poetry of Maya Angelou,* 1969. Contributor of poems in *The Language They Speak Is Things to Eat: Poems by Fifteen Contemporary North Carolina Poets* and to *Mary Higgins Clark, Mother,* Pocket Books (New York, NY), 1996.

ESSAYS

Lessons in Living, Random House (New York, NY), 1993.

Wouldn't Take Nothing for My Journey Now, Random House (New York, NY), 1993.

Even the Stars Look Lonesome, Random House (New York, NY), 1997.

Hallelujah! The Welcome Table, Random House (New York, NY), 2004.

CHILDREN'S PICTURE BOOKS

Mrs. Flowers: A Moment of Friendship (selection from *I Know Why the Caged Bird Sings*) illustrated by Etienne Delessert, Redpath Press (Minneapolis, MN), 1986.

Life Doesn't Frighten Me (poem), edited by Sara Jane Boyers, illustrated by Jean-Michel Basquiat, Stewart, Tabori & Chang (New York, NY), 1993.

(With others) *Soul Looks Back in Wonder,* illustrated by Tom Feelings, Dial (New York, NY), 1993.

My Painted House, My Friendly Chicken, and Me, photographs by Margaret Courtney-Clarke, Crown (New York, NY), 1994.

Kofi and His Magic, photographs by Margaret Courtney-Clarke, Crown (New York, NY), 1996.

Angelina of Italy, illustrated by Lizzy Rockwell, Random House (New York, NY), 2004.

Izak of Lapland, illustrated by Lizzy Rockwell, Random House (New York, NY), 2004.

Renie Marie of France, illustrated by Lizzy Rockwell, Random House (New York, NY), 2004.

Mikale of Hawaii, illustrated by Lizzy Rockwell, Random House (New York, NY), 2004.

PLAYS

(With Godfrey Cambridge) *Cabaret for Freedom* (musical revue), produced at Village Gate Theatre, New York, 1960.

The Least of These (two-act drama), produced in Los Angeles, 1966.

(Adapter) Sophocles, *Ajax* (two-act drama), produced at Mark Taper Forum, Los Angeles, 1974.

(And director) *And Still I Rise* (one-act musical), produced in Oakland, CA, 1976.

(Author of poems for screenplay) *Poetic Justice* (screenplay), Columbia Pictures, 1993.

(Author of lyrics, with Alistair Beaton) *King,* book by Lonne Elder, III, music by Richard Blackford, London, 1990.

Also author of the play *Gettin' up Stayed on My Mind,* 1967, a drama, *The Best of These,* a two-act drama, *The Clawing Within,* 1966, a two-act musical, *Adjoa Amissah,* 1967, and a one-act play, *Theatrical Vignette,* 1983.

FILM AND TELEVISION SCRIPTS

Georgia, Georgia (screenplay), Independent-Cinerama, 1972.

(And director) *All Day Long* (screenplay), American Film Institute, 1974.

(Writer of script and musical score) *I Know Why the Caged Bird Sings,* CBS, 1979.

Sister, Sister (television drama), National Broadcasting Co., Inc. (NBC-TV), 1982.

(Writer of poetry) *John Singleton, Poetic Justice* (motion picture), Columbia Pictures, 1993.

Composer of songs, including two songs for movie *For Love of Ivy,* and composer of musical scores for both her screenplays. Author of *Black, Blues, Black,* a series of ten one-hour programs, broadcast by National Educational Television (NET-TV), 1968. Also author of *Assignment America,* a series of six one-half-hour programs, 1975, and of *The Legacy* and *The Inheritors,* two television specials, 1976. Other documentaries include *Trying to Make It Home* (Byline series), 1988, and *Maya Angelou's America: A Journey of the Heart* (also host). Public Broadcasting Service Productions include *Who Cares about Kids, Kindred Spirits, Maya Angelou: Rainbow in the Clouds,* and *To the Contrary.* Writer for television series *Brewster Place,* Harpo Productions.

RECORDINGS

Miss Calypso (audio recording of songs), Liberty Records, 1957.

The Poetry of Maya Angelou (audio recording), GWP Records, 1969.

An Evening with Maya Angelou (audio cassette), Pacific Tape Library, 1975.

I Know Why the Caged Bird Sings (audio cassette with filmstrip and teacher's guide), Center for Literary Review, 1978, abridged version, Random House (New York, NY), 1986.

Women in Business (audio cassette), University of Wisconsin, 1981.

Making Magic in the World (audio cassette), New Dimensions, 1988.

On the Pulse of Morning (audio production), Ingram, 1993.

Wouldn't Take Nothing for My Journey Now (audio production), Ingram, 1993.

Phenomenal Woman (audio production), Ingram, 1995.

Been Found, 1996.

OTHER

Conversations with Maya Angelou, edited by Jeffrey M. Elliot, Virago Press (London, England), 1989.

Maya Angelou (four-volume boxed set), Ingram (London, England), 1995.

(With Mary Ellen Mark) *Mary Ellen Mark: American Odyssey,* Aperture (New York, NY), 1998.

Contributor to books, including *Poetic Justice: Filmmaking South Central Style,* Delta, 1993; *Bearing Witness: Contemporary Works by African American Women Artists,* Rizzoli International Publications, 1996; *The Journey Back: A Survivor's Guide to Leukemia,* Rainbow's End Company, 1996; *The Challenge of Creative Leadership,* Shephard-Walwyn, 1998; and *Amistad: "Give Us Free": A Celebration of the Film by Stephen Spielberg,* Newmarket Press, 1998.

Author of forewords to *African Canvas: The Art of African Women,* by Margaret Courtney-Clarke, Rizzoli (New York, NY), 1991; *Dust Tracks on the Road: An Autobiography,* by Zora Neale Hurston, HarperCollins (New York, NY), 1991; *Caribbean & African Cooking,* by Rosamund Grant, Interlink (Northampton, MA), 1993; *Double Stitch: Black Women Write about Mothers & Daughters,* HarperCollins, 1993; *African Americans: A Portrait,* by Richard A. Long, Crescent Books (New York, NY), 1993; and *Essence: Twenty-five Years Celebrating Black Women,* edited by Patricia M. Hinds, Harry N. Abrams (New York, NY), 1995; author of introduction to *Not without Laughter,* by Langston Hughes, Scribner (New York, NY), 1995; author of preface to *Mending the World: Stories of Family by Contemporary Black Writers,* edited by Rosemarie Robotham, BasicCivitas Books (New York, NY), 2003.

Author, with Charlie Reilly and Amiri Bakara, *Conversations with Amiri Bakara.* Short stories are included in anthologies, including *Harlem* and *Ten Times Black.* Contributor of articles, short stories, and poems to national periodicals, including *Harper's, Ebony, Essence, Mademoiselle, Redbook, Ladies' Home Journal, Black Scholar, Architectural Digest, New Perspectives Quarterly, Savvy Woman,* and *Ms.* Magazine.

ADAPTATIONS: I Know Why the Caged Bird Sings was adapted as a television movie by Columbia Broadcasting System, Inc. (CBS-TV), 1979; *And Still I Rise* was adapted as a television special by Public Broadcasting Service (PBS-TV), 1985; *I Know Why the Caged Bird Sings* was produced for audio cassette and compact disk, Ingram, 1996.

SIDELIGHTS: As a young black woman growing up in the South, and later in wartime San Francisco, Maya Angelou faced racism from whites and poor treatment from many men. She found that, in this position, few things in life came easily to her. But instead of letting forces beyond her control overcome her, Angelou began to forge art from her early experiences and to change the world as she'd once known it. She became a singer, dancer, actress, composer, and Hollywood's first female black director. She became a writer, editor, essayist, playwright, poet, and screenwriter. She became known, as Annie Gottlieb wrote in the *New York Times Book Review,* as a person who "writes like a song, and like the truth. The wisdom, rue and humor of her storytelling are borne on a lilting rhythm completely her own."

Angelou also became a civil rights activist—she worked at one time for Dr. Martin Luther King and once staged a protest at the United Nations—as well as an educator. By 1975, wrote Carol E. Neubauer in *Southern Women Writers: The New Generation,* "Angelou had become recognized not only as a spokesperson for blacks and women, but also for all people who are committed to raising the moral standards of living in the United States." She did so by writing about herself, by fighting for civil and women's rights, and by providing an amazing example of the human potential to rise above defeat. Angelou explained this herself in an interview with George Plimpton in the *Paris Review:* "In all my work, in the movies I write, the lyrics, the poetry, the prose, the essays, I am saying that we may encounter many defeats—maybe it's imperative that we encounter the defeats—but we are much stronger than we appear to be, and maybe much better than we allow ourselves to be."

Angelou was born in St. Louis, Missouri, and lived her early years in Long Beach, California. As she related in *I Know Why the Caged Bird Sings,* the first book of her six-volume memoirs, she was just three years old when her parents divorced. Her father sent Angelou and her four-year-old brother alone by train to the home of his mother in Stamps, Arkansas. In Stamps, a segregated town, "Momma" (as Angelou and her brother Bailey called their grandmother) took care of the children and ran a lunch business and a store. The children were expected to stay clean and sinless, and to do well in school. Although she followed the example of her independent and strong-willed grandmother, and was a healthy child, Angelou felt ugly and unloved. When her mother, who lived in St. Louis, requested a visit from the children, Angelou was shocked by her mother's paler complexion, and by the red lipstick her grandmother would have thought scandalous. Angelou was almost as overwhelmed by her mother's wildness and determination as she was by her beauty.

Life in St. Louis was different from that in Stamps; Angelou was unprepared for the rushing noises of city life and the Saturday night parties. Then, when she was just seven-and-a-half years old, something terrible happened. In one of the most evocative (and controversial) moments in *I Know Why the Caged Bird Sings,* Angelou

described how she was first lovingly cuddled, then raped by her mother's boyfriend. When the man was murdered by her uncles for his crime, Angelou felt responsible, and she stopped talking. She and her brother were sent back to Stamps. Angelou remained mute for five years, but she developed a love for language and the spoken word. She read and memorized books, including the works of black authors and poets Langston Hughes, W.E.B. Du Bois, and Paul Lawrence Dunbar. Even though she and Bailey were discouraged from reading the works of white writers at home, Angelou read and fell in love with the works of William Shakespeare, Charles Dickens, and Edgar Allan Poe. When Angelou was twelve and a half, Mrs. Flowers, an educated black woman, finally got her to speak again. Mrs. Flowers, as Angelou recalled in *Mrs. Flowers: A Moment of Friendship,* emphasized the importance of the spoken word, explained the nature of and importance of education, and instilled in her a love of poetry. Angelou graduated at the top of her eighth-grade class.

When race relations made Stamps a dangerous place for Angelou and her brother, "Momma" took the children to San Francisco, where Angelou's mother was working as a professional gambler. World War II was raging, and while San Franciscans prepared for air raids that never came, Angelou prepared for the rest of her life by attending George Washington High School and by taking lessons in dance and drama on a scholarship at the California Labor School. When Angelou, just seventeen, graduated from high school and gave birth to a son, she began to work as well. She worked as the first female and black street car conductor in San Francisco. As she explained in *Singin' and Swingin' and Gettin' Merry like Christmas,* she also "worked as a shake dancer in night clubs, fry cook in hamburger joints, dinner cook in a Creole restaurant and once had a job in a mechanic's shop, taking the paint off cars with my hands." For a time, Angelou also managed a couple of prostitutes.

Angelou married a white ex-sailor, Tosh Angelos, in 1950. The pair did not have much in common, and Angelou began to take note of the reaction of people—especially African Americans—to their union. After they separated, Angelou continued her study of dance in New York City. She returned to San Francisco and sang in the Purple Onion cabaret. There, Angelou garnered the attention of talent scouts. From 1954 to 1955, she was a member of the cast of a touring production of *Porgy and Bess;* she visited twenty-two countries before leaving the tour to return to her son. During the late 1950s, Angelou sang in West Coast and Hawaiian nightclubs. After some time living in a houseboat commune in Sausalito, California, she returned to New York.

In New York, Angelou continued her stage career with an appearance in an Off-Broadway show, *Calypso Heatwave.* Then, with the encouragement of writer John Killens, she joined the Harlem Writers Guild and met James Baldwin and other important writers. It was during this time that Angelou had the opportunity to hear Dr. Martin Luther King speak. Inspired by his message, she decided to become a part of the struggle for civil rights. So, with comedian Godfrey Cambridge, she wrote, produced, directed, and starred in *Cabaret for Freedom* in 1960, a benefit for Dr. King's Southern Christian Leadership Conference (SCLC). Given the organizational abilities she demonstrated as she worked for the benefit, she was offered a position as the northern coordinator for Dr. King's SCLC. She appeared in Jean Genet's play, *The Blacks,* which won an Obie Award, in 1960.

Angelou began to live with Vusumzi Make, a South African freedom fighter; with Angelou's son Guy, they relocated to Cairo, Egypt. There, Angelou found work as an associate editor at the *Arab Observer.* As she recalled in *The Heart of a Woman,* she learned a great deal about writing there, but Vusumzi could not tolerate the fact that she was working. After her relationship with him ended, Angelou went on to Ghana, in West Africa, in 1962. She later worked at the University of Ghana's School of Music and Drama as an assistant administrator. She worked as a freelance writer and was a feature editor at *African Review.* As she related in *All God's Children Need Traveling Shoes,* Angelou also played the title role in *Mother Courage* during this time.

Angelou returned to the United States in the mid-1960s and found a position as a lecturer at the University of California in Los Angeles in 1966. She also played a part in the play *Medea* in Hollywood. In this period, she was encouraged by author James Baldwin and Random House publishers to write an autobiography. Initially, Angelou declined offers, and went to California for the production of a series of ten one-hour programs that she'd written, "Black, Blues, Black," which were broadcast in 1968. But eventually Angelou changed her mind and wrote *I Know Why the Caged Bird Sings.* The book, which chronicles Angelou's childhood and ends with the birth of her son Guy, bears what Selwyn R. Cudjoe in *Black Women Writers* calls a burden: "to demonstrate the manner in which the Black female is violated . . . in her tender years and to demonstrate the 'unnecessary insult' of Southern girlhood in her movement to adolescence." *I Know Why the Caged Bird Sings* won immediate success and a nomination for a National Book Award.

Although Angelou did not write *I Know Why the Caged Bird Sings* with the intention of writing other autobiographies, she eventually wrote five more, which may be read with the first as a series. Most critics have judged the subsequent autobiographies in light of the first, and *I Know Why the Caged Bird Sings* remains the most highly praised. *Gather Together in My Name* begins when Angelou is seventeen and a new mother; it describes a destructive love affair, Angelou's work as a prostitute, her rejection of drug addiction, and the kidnapping of her son. *Gather Together in My Name* was not as well received by critics as *I Know Why the Caged Bird Sings.* As Mary Jane Lupton reported in *Black American Literature Forum,* in this 1974 autobiography, "the tight structure" of *I Know Why the Caged Bird Sings* "appeared to crumble; childhood experiences were replaced by episodes which a number of critics consider disjointed or bizarre." Lupton thought, however, that there is an important reason why Angelou's later works are not as tight as the first, and why they consist of episodes: these "so-called 'fragments' are reflections of the kind of chaos found in actual living. In altering the narrative structure, Angelou shifts the emphasis from herself as an isolated consciousness to herself as a black woman participating in diverse experiences among a diverse class of peoples."

Singin' and Swingin' and Gettin' Merry like Christmas is Angelou's account of her tour in Europe and Africa with *Porgy and Bess.* Much of the work concerns Angelou's separation from her son during that time. In *The Heart of a Woman,* Angelou describes her acting and writing career in New York and her work for the civil rights movement. She recalls visits with great activists Dr. Martin Luther King, Jr., and Malcolm X, and the legendary singer Billie Holiday. She also tells of her move to Africa, and her experiences when her son was injured in a serious car accident; the book ends with Guy's move into a college dormitory at the University of Ghana. "Angelou's message is one blending chorus: Black people and Black women do not just endure, they triumph with a will of collective consciousness that Western experience cannot extinguish," wrote Sondra O'Neale in *Black Women Writers. All God's Children Need Traveling Shoes* once again explores Guy's accident; it moves on from there to recount Angelou's travels in West Africa and her decision to return, without her son, to America.

It took Angelou fifteen years to write the final volume of her autobiography, *A Song Flung up to Heaven,* after *All God's Children Need Traveling Shoes* was published. The book covers four years, from the time Angelou returned from Ghana in 1964 through the moment when she sat down at her mother's table and began to write *I Know Why the Caged Bird Sings* in 1968. Angelou hesitated so long to start the book and took so long to finish it, she told *Knight Ridder/Tribune News Service* interviewer Sherryl Connelly, because so many painful things happened to her, and to the entire African-American community, in those four years. "I didn't know how to write it," she said. "I didn't see how the assassination of Malcolm [X], the Watts riot, the breakup of a love affair, then [the assassination of Dr.] Martin [Luther] King [Jr.], how I could get all that loose with something uplifting in it." Malcolm X's and King's assassinations were particularly painful for Angelou because in both cases the men were killed shortly after Angelou had agreed to work for them; it was, in fact, the offer of a job with Malcolm X that brought Angelou back from Africa. *A Song Flung up to Heaven* deals forthrightly with these events, and "the poignant beauty of Angelou's writing enhances rather than masks the candor with which she addresses the racial crisis through which America was passing," Wayne A. Holst wrote in *Christian Century*. But as Angelou intended, "not everything in [*A Song Flung up to Heaven*] is bleak," Cassandra Spratling commented in a review for *Knight Ridder/ Tribune News Service*. "Tales of parties with writers and other friends; her bond with a woman with whom her Ghanian manfriend cheated; and descriptions of her closeness with the late writer James Baldwin lighten the story."

Angelou's poetry has often been lauded more for its content—praising black beauty, the strength of women, and the human spirit; criticizing the Vietnam War; demanding social justice for all—than for its poetic virtue. Yet *Just Give Me a Cool Drink of Water 'fore I Diiie,* which was published in 1971, was nominated for a Pulitzer Prize in 1972. This volume contains thirty-eight poems, some of which were published in *The Poetry of Maya Angelou*. According to Carol Neubauer in *Southern Women Writers,* "the first twenty poems describe the whole gamut of love, from the first moment of passionate discovery to the first suspicion of painful loss." In the other poems, "Angelou turns her attention to the lives of black people in America from the time of slavery to the rebellious 1960s. Her themes deal broadly with the painful anguish suffered by blacks forced into submission, with guilt over accepting too much, and with protest and basic survival."

As Angelou wrote her autobiographies and poems, she continued her career in film and television. She was the first black woman to get a screenplay (*Georgia, Georgia*) produced in 1972. She was honored with a nomination for an Emmy award for her performance in *Roots*

in 1977. In 1979, Angelou helped adapt her book, *I Know Why the Caged Bird Sings,* for a television movie of the same name. Angelou wrote the poetry for the 1993 film *Poetic Justice* and played the role of Aunt June. She also played Lelia Mae in the 1993 television film *There Are No Children Here* and appeared as Anna in the feature film *How to Make an American Quilt* in 1995. Also in 1995, Angelou's poetry helped to commemorate the fiftieth anniversary of the United Nations. She had elevated herself to what Richard Grenier in *National Review* called a "dizzying height of achievement." As a title from an article by Freda Garmaise in *Gentleman's Quarterly* proclaimed, "Maya-ness" was "next to godliness."

One of the most important sources of Angelou's fame in the early 1990s was President Bill Clinton's invitation to write and read the first inaugural poem in decades. Americans all across the country watched the six-foot-tall, elegantly dressed woman as she read her poem for the new president on January 20, 1993. "On the Pulse of Morning" begins "A Rock, a River, a Tree" and calls for peace, racial and religious harmony, and social justice for people of different origins, incomes, genders, and sexual orientations. It recalls the civil rights movement and Dr. Martin Luther King, Jr.'s famous "I have a dream" speech as it urges America to "Give birth again/To the Dream" of equality. Angelou challenged the new administration and all Americans to work together for progress: "Here, on the pulse of this new day,/You may have the grace to look up and out/ And into your sister's eyes, and into/Your brother's face, your country/And say simply/Very simply/With hope—Good morning."

While some viewed President Clinton's selection of Angelou as a tribute to the poet and her lifelong contribution to civil rights and the arts, Angelou had her own ideas. She told Catherine S. Manegold in an interview for the *New York Times:* "In all my work, what I try to say is that as human beings we are more alike than we are unalike." She added, "It may be that Mr. Clinton asked me to write the inaugural poem because he understood that I am the kind of person who really does bring people together."

During the early 1990s, Angelou wrote more poetry and several books for children. *Now Sheba Sings the Song* is just one poem inspired by the work of artist Tom Feelings; the lines or phrases are isolated on each page with eighty-four of Tom Feelings' sepia-toned and black-and-white drawings of black women. *I Shall Not Be Moved* is a collection that takes its title from a line in one of the book's poems. *Phenomenal Woman,* a collection of four poems, takes its title from a poem which originally appeared in *Cosmopolitan* magazine in 1978; the narrator of the poem describes the physical and spiritual characteristics and qualities that make her attractive.

Angelou dedicated *Wouldn't Take Nothing for My Journey Now,* a collection of twenty-four short essays, to Oprah Winfrey, the television talk-show host who celebrated Angelou's sixty-fifth birthday with a grand party. The essays in this book contain declarations, complaints, memories, opinions, and advice on subjects ranging from faith to jealousy. Genevieve Stuttaford, writing in *Publishers Weekly,* described the essays as "quietly inspirational pieces." Anne Whitehouse of the *New York Times Book Review* observed that the book would "appeal to readers in search of clear messages with easily digested meanings." Yet not all critics appreciated this collection. Richard Grenier of *National Review* concluded that the book "is of a remarkably coherent tone, being from first page to last of a truly awesome emptiness."

Although Angelou's autobiographies are written, in part, for young people, they are beyond the comprehension of most young children. But with the publication of *Mrs. Flowers: A Moment of Friendship,* children can access one of the stories that Angelou tells in *I Know Why the Caged Bird Sings.* Another book for children, *Life Doesn't Frighten Me,* consists of one poem. Each line or phrase is accompanied by the dynamic, abstract, colorful paintings of the late artist Jean-Michel Basquiat. The poem lists scary things that the narrator should be afraid of, and Basquiat's art illustrates those terrors vividly, but, with the refrain of "They don't frighten me at all," "fear is answered with dancing energy and daring imagination and laughter," Hazel Rochman explained in *Booklist.* "Pairing Angelou's reassuring poem with Basquiat's unsettling, childlike images was a stroke of genius," wrote *Artforum International* contributor Dan Cameron.

In *My Painted House, My Friendly Chicken, and Me,* with photographs by Margaret Courtney-Clarke, a young African girl introduces herself and discusses her life. She tells about her friend, a pet chicken to whom she tells all of her best secrets. She displays her beautiful home, and explains how her mother has carefully painted it. The girl also explains how, although she must go to school wearing uniforms her father has purchased in town, she loves to wear her traditional beads and clothing. She expresses a wish that she and the reader can be friends despite the physical and cultural distance that separates them.

Kofi and His Magic is a second picture book by Angelou and Courtney-Clark which allows young readers to get to know an African child, another culture, and another worldview. Through Angelou's text and Courtney-Clarke's colorful photographs, a West African boy named Kofi shows off his beautiful earth-toned home and tells of his life. Kofi's town, Bonwire, is famous for its Kente cloth production. He explains how, even though he is still quite young, he is a trained weaver of Kente cloth. Then, Kofi takes readers on a journey to visit other nearby towns and people, and finally, to see the ocean (which he initially thinks is a big lake). At the end of the book, after Kofi returns to Bonwire, he reveals why he calls himself a magician. Kofi's magic involves allowing the reader to imagine that she or he can visit Kofi and become his friend: the reader must only close her eyes and open her mind for the magic to work.

As Angelou has been busy furthering her career, critics and scholars have attempted to keep up with her, and to interpret her continuing work. While many critics have pointed out that the message in Angelou's prose is universal, Mary Jane Lupton has called attention to the theme of motherhood in Angelou's work. In five volumes of autobiography, Angelou "moves forward: from being a child, to being a mother; to leaving the child; to having the child, in the fifth volume, achieve his independence." In her interview with George Plimpton in the *Paris Review,* Angelou agreed with him that the love of her child was a "prevailing theme" in her autobiographical work.

Some critics have argued that Angelou's poetry is inferior to her prose. Unlike her autobiographical work, Angelou's poetry has not received much of what William Sylvester of *Contemporary Poets* would call "serious critical attention." In Sylvester's opinion, however, Angelou's poetry is "sassy." When "we hear her poetry, we listen to ourselves." In addition, as Lynn Z. Bloom pointed out in *Dictionary of Literary Biography,* "Angelou's poetry becomes far more interesting when she dramatizes it in her characteristically dynamic stage performances." Colorfully dressed, Angelou usually recites her poems before spellbound crowds.

Angelou takes her writing very seriously. She told Plimpton, "Once I got into it I realized I was following a tradition established by Frederick Douglass—the slave narrative—speaking in the first-person singular talking about the first-person plural, always saying I meaning 'we.' And what a responsibility. Trying to work with that form, the autobiographical mode, to change it, to make it bigger, richer, finer, and more inclusive in the twentieth century has been a great challenge for me."

While many critics have described Angelou's ability to write beautiful prose as a natural talent, Angelou has emphasized that she must work very hard to write the way she does. As she has explained to Plimpton and others, very early each morning she goes to a sparse hotel room to concentrate, to lie on the bed and write. She spends the morning on first draft work, and goes home in the afternoon to shower, cook a beautiful meal, and share it with friends. Later that night, she looks at what she's written, and begins to cut words and make revisions. Critics who suggest writing is easy for her, Angelou explained to Plimpton, "are the ones I want to grab by the throat and wrestle to the floor because it takes me forever to get it [a book] to sing. I work at the language."

BIOGRAPHICAL AND CRITICAL SOURCES:

BOOKS

Angelou, Maya, *Gather Together in My Name,* Random House (New York, NY), 1974.

Angelou, Maya, *Singin' and Swingin' and Gettin' Merry like Christmas,* Random House (New York, NY), 1976.

Angelou, Maya, *The Heart of a Woman,* Random House (New York, NY), 1981.

Angelou, Maya, *All God's Children Need Traveling Shoes,* Random House (New York, NY), 1986.

Angelou, Maya, *I Know Why the Caged Bird Sings,* Bantam (New York, NY), 1993.

Angelou, Maya, *Lessons in Living,* Random House (New York, NY), 1993.

Angelou, Maya, *Even the Stars Look Lonesome,* Random House (New York, NY), 1997.

Angelou, Maya, *A Song Flung up to Heaven,* Random House (New York, NY), 2002.

Bloom, Harold, editor, *Maya Angelou's I Know Why the Caged Bird Sings,* Chelsea House Publishers (New York, NY), 1995.

Braxton, Joanne M., editor, *Maya Angelou's I Know Why the Caged Bird Sings: A Casebook,* Oxford University Press (New York, NY), 1999.

Concise Dictionary of American Literary Biography Supplement: Modern Writers, 1900-1998, Thomson Gale (Detroit, MI), 1998.

Contemporary Black Biography, Volume 15, Thomson Gale (Detroit, MI), 1997.

Contemporary Heroes and Heroines, Book 1, Thomson Gale (Detroit, MI), 1990.

Contemporary Poets, seventh edition, St. James Press (Detroit, MI), 2001.

Contemporary Popular Writers, St. James Press (Detroit, MI), 1997.

Contemporary Southern Writers, St. James Press (Detroit, MI), 1999.

Contemporary Women Poets, St. James Press (Detroit, MI), 1998.

Dictionary of Literary Biography, Volume 38: *Afro-American Writers after 1955: Dramatists and Prose Writers,* Thomson Gale (Detroit, MI), 1985.

Encyclopedia of World Biography, second edition, seventeen volumes, Thomson Gale (Detroit, MI), 1998.

Evans, Mari, editor, *Black Women Writers (1950-1980): A Critical Evaluation,* Anchor Press-Doubleday (New York, NY), 1984.

Inge, Tonette Bond, editor, *Southern Women Writers: The New Generation,* University of Alabama Press (Tuscaloosa, AL), 1990.

King, Sarah E., *Maya Angelou: Greeting the Morning,* Millbrook Press (Brookfield, CT), 1994.

Kirkpatrick, Patricia, compiler, *Maya Angelou,* Creative Education (Mankato, MN), 2003.

Lisandrelli, Elaine Slivinski, *Maya Angelou: More than a Poet,* Enslow Publishers (Berkeley Heights, NJ), 1996.

Literature and Its Times: Profiles of 300 Notable Literary Works and the Historical Events That Influenced Them, Volume 4: *World War II to the Affluent Fifties (1940s-1950s),* Thomson Gale (Detroit, MI), 1997.

Newsmakers 1993, Issue 4, Thomson Gale (Detroit, MI), 1993.

Notable Black American Women, Book 1, Thomson Gale (Detroit, MI), 1992.

Poetry Criticism, Volume 32, Thomson Gale (Detroit, MI), 2001.

St. James Encyclopedia of Popular Culture, five volumes, St. James Press (Detroit, MI), 2000.

St. James Guide to Young Adult Writers, second edition, St. James Press (Detroit, MI), 1999.

Spain, Valerie, *Meet Maya Angelou,* Random House (New York, NY), 1994.

Women Filmmakers and Their Films, St. James Press (Detroit, MI), 1998.

Writers for Young Adults, three volumes, Scribner's (New York, NY), 1997.

PERIODICALS

Artforum International, December, 1993, Dan Cameron, review of *Life Doesn't Frighten Me,* p. 74.

Black American Literature Forum, summer, 1990, Mary Jane Lupton, "Singing the Black Mother: Maya Angelou and Autobiographical Continuity," pp. 257-276.

Black Issues Book Review, March, 2001, Maitefa Angaza, "Maya: A Precious Prism," p. 30; March-April, 2002, Elsie B. Washington, review of *A Song Flung up to Heaven,* pp. 56-57.

Book, March-April, 2002, Beth Kephart, review of *A Song Flung up to Heaven,* p. 72.

Booklist, January 1, 1994, Hazel Rochman, review of *Life Doesn't Frighten Me,* pp. 829-830; October 1, 1994, Hazel Rochman, review of *My Painted House, My Friendly Chicken, and Me,* p. 329; August, 1997, Donna Seaman, review of *Even the Stars Look Lonesome,* p. 1842; January 1, 2002, Gillian Engberg, review of *A Song Flung up to Heaven,* p. 774.

Christian Century, June 19, 2002, Wayne A. Holst, review of *A Song Flung up to Heaven,* pp. 35-36.

Ebony, February, 1999, review of *Down in the Delta,* p. 96.

Essence, December, 1992, Marcia Ann Gillespie, interview with Angelou, pp. 48-52; August, 1998, Lisa Funderberg, interview with Angelou and Congresswoman Eleanor Holmes Norton, pp. 70-76.

Five Owls, September, 1995, p. 2.

Gentlemen's Quarterly, July, 1995, Freda Garmaise, "Maya-ness Is Next to Godlinesss," p. 33.

Herizons, winter, 2003, Heather Marie, review of *A Song Flung Up to Heaven,* pp. 40-41.

Jet, December 21, 1998, review of *Down in the Delta,* p. 58.

Kirkus Reviews, January 1, 2002, review of *A Song Flung up to Heaven,* p. 25.

Kliatt, July, 2002, Janet Julian, review of *Even the Stars Look Lonesome,* p. 58.

Knight Ridder/Tribune News Service, November 5, 1997, Fon Louise Gordon, review of *Even the Stars Look Lonesome,* p. 1105K5928; March 14, 2002, Leigh Dyer, "Shrugging off Criticism, Angelou Relishes Getting Her Words before So Many," p. K0392; April 3, 2002, Cassandra Spratling, "Maya Angelou, Still Rising: Turbulent Times Mark the Celebrated Author's Latest Memoir," p. K7652; April 10, 2002, Sherryl Connelly, "Maya Angelou, a Life Well Chronicled," p. K2443; April 30, 2002, Lamar Wilson, review of *A Song Flung up to Heaven,* p. K4586.

Library Journal, October 1, 1995, p. 102; September 15, 1997, Ann Burns, review of *Even the Stars Look Lonesome,* p. 74; March 15, 2002, Amy Strong, review of *A Song Flung up to Heaven,* pp. 79-80.

Mother Jones, May-June, 1995, Ken Kelley, interview with Angelou, pp. 22-25.

National Post, July 20, 2002, Marcie Good, "Inspiration for Hire: Hallmark Has Hired Poet Maya Angelou," p. SP1.

National Review, November 29, 1993, Richard Grenier, review of *Wouldn't Take Nothing for My Journey Now,* p. 76.

New Republic, May 20, 2002, John McWhorter, review of *A Song Flung up to Heaven,* p. 35.

New York Times, January 20, 1993, Catherine S. Manegold, "A Wordsmith at Her Inaugural Anvil," pp. C1, C8.

New York Times Book Review, June 16, 1974, Annie Gottlieb, review of *Gather Together in My Name;* December 19, 1993, Anne Whitehouse, review of *Wouldn't Take Nothing for My Journey Now,* p. 18; June 5, 1994, p. 48.

Paris Review, fall, 1990, Maya Angelou, and George Plimpton, "The Art of Fiction CXIX: Maya Angelou," pp. 145-167.

People, January 11, 1999, review of *Down in the Delta,* p. 35.

Poetry, August, 1976, Sandra M. Gilbert, review of *Oh Pray My Wings Are Gonna Fit Me Well.*

Publishers Weekly, September 20, 1993, review of *Life Doesn't Frighten Me,* p. 71; September 27, 1993, Genevieve Stuttaford, review of *Wouldn't Take Nothing for My Journey Now,* pp. 53-54; September 12, 1994, review of *My Painted House, My Friendly Chicken, and Me,* p. 91; August 4, 1997, review of *Even the Stars Look Lonesome,* pp. 54-55.

School Library Journal, October, 1987, Joseph Harper, review of *Now Sheba Sings the Song,* p. 146; May, 1995, p. 57; July, 2002, Karen Sokol, review of *A Song Flung up to Heaven,* p. 144.

Smithsonian, April, 2003, Lucinda Moore, interview with Angelou, p. 96.

Southern Literary Journal, fall, 1998, Marion M. Tangum, "Hurston's and Angelou's Visual Art: The Distancing Vision and the Beckoning Gaze," p. 80.

Variety, September 21, 1998, Joe Leydon, review of *Down in the Delta,* p. 110.

ONLINE

Official Maya Angelou Web site, http://www.maya angelou.com/ (April 24, 2004).

*   *   *

ANOUILH, Jean 1910-1987
(Jean Marie Lucien Pierre Anouilh)

PERSONAL: Surname pronounced "Ahn-wee"; born June 23, 1910, in Bordeaux, France; died of a heart attack, October 3, 1987, in Lausanne, Switzerland; son of François (a tailor) and Marie-Magdeleine (a pianist;

maiden name, Soulue) Anouilh; married Monelle Valentin (divorced); married Nicole Lancon, July 30, 1953; children: (first marriage) Catherine; (second marriage) Caroline, Nicolas, Marie-Colombe. *Education:* College Chaptal, baccalaureate; Sorbonne, University of Paris, law student, 1931-32.

CAREER: Writer, 1929-87. Advertising copywriter, author of publicity scripts and comic gags for films, 1929-32; secretary to theatrical company Comédie des Champs-Elysees, Paris, France, 1931-32. Also directed several films in France. *Military service:* Served in the French Army during the 1930s.

AWARDS, HONORS: Grand Prix du Cinema Francais, 1949, for film *Monsieur Vincent;* Antoinette Perry ("Tony") Award and citation from the cultural division of the French Embassy, both 1955, both for *Thieves' Carnival* (New York production); New York Drama Critics Circle Award for best foreign play of 1956-57, and nominee for the Antoinette Perry ("Tony") Award for best play, 1957, both for *Waltz of the Toreadors;* nominee for the Antoinette Perry ("Tony") Award for best play, 1958, for *Time Remembered;* Prix Dominique for the direction of film *Madame M.,* 1959; *Evening Standard* newspaper drama award and Antoinette Perry ("Tony") Award for best foreign play of the year, both 1961, both for *Becket; or, The Honor of God; Evening Standard* newspaper drama award for best play of the year, 1963, for *Poor Bitos;* first prize for best play of the year, Syndicate of French Drama Critics, 1970, for *Cher Antoine; ou, l'amour raté* and *Les poissons rouges; ou, mon père, ce héros;* Paris Critics Prize, 1971, for *Ne réveillez pas madame.*

WRITINGS:

PLAYS

(With Jean Aurenche) *Humulus le muet,* Éditions Françaises Nouvelles (Grenoble, France), 1929.
L'hermine, first produced at Théâtre de l'Oeuvre, Paris, France, 1932.
Mandarine, first produced at Théâtre de l'Athénée, Paris, France, 1933.
Y'avait un prisonnier, first produced at Théâtre des Ambassadeurs, Paris, France, 1935.
Le voyageur sans bagage (first produced at Théâtre des Mathurins, Paris, France, 1937; English translation by Lucienne Hill produced in New York at ANTA Theatre, 1964), translation by John Whiting pub-

lished as *Traveller without Luggage,* Methuen (London, England), 1959, edition edited by Diane Birckbichler, Ann Dubé, and Walter Meiden published under original title, Holt, Rinehart (New York, NY), 1973.
La sauvage (first produced at Théâtre des Mathurins, Paris, France, 1938), translation by Lucienne Hill published as *Restless Heart,* Methuen (London, England), 1957.
Le bal des voleurs (first produced at Théâtre des Arts, Paris, France, 1938; produced at Théâtre des Quatre Saisons, New York, NY, 1938; English version produced as *Thieves' Carnival* at Cherry Lane Theatre, New York, 1955), Éditions Françaises Nouvelles (Grenoble, France), 1945, translation by Lucienne Hill published as *Thieves' Carnival,* Samuel French (New York, NY), 1952.
Le rendez-vous de Senlis (first produced at Théâtre de l'Atelier, Paris, France, 1938; produced as *Dinner with the Family,* at Gramercy Arts Theatre, New York, NY, 1961), Éditions de la Table Ronde (Paris, France, France), 1958, translation by Edwin Owen Marsh published as *Dinner with the Family,* Methuen (London, England), 1958.
Léocadia (first produced at Théâtre de l'Atelier, Paris, France, 1939; produced as *Time Remembered,* at Morosco Theater, New York, NY, 1957; translation by Stephanie L. Debner and Jeffrey Hatcher produced as *To Fool the Eye,* Guthrie Theater, Minneapolis, MN, 2000), Appleton (New York, NY), 1965, translation by Patricia Moyes published as *Time Remembered,* Methuen (London, England), 1955, Coward (New York, NY), 1958, edition edited by Bettina L. Knapp and Alba della Fazia published under original title, Appleton-Century-Crofts (New York, NY), 1965.
Eurydice (first produced at Théâtre de l'Atelier, Paris, France, 1941; produced in English at Coronet Theatre, Hollywood, CA, 1948), annotation by Rambert George, Bordas (Paris, France), 1968, translation by Kitty Black published as *Point of Departure,* Samuel French (New York, NY), 1951, second English translation published as *Legend of Lovers,* Coward (New York, NY), 1952.
Antigone (first produced at Théâtre de l'Atelier, Paris, France, 1944; produced in English at Cort Theatre, New York, NY, 1946), Éditions de la Table Ronde (Paris, France), 1946, translation by Lewis Galantiere, Random House (New York, NY), 1946, new edition edited by Raymond Laubreaux, Didier (Paris, France), 1977, excerpts published as *Antigone: Extraits,* Bordas (Paris, France), 1968.
Roméo et Jeannette, first produced at Théâtre de l'Atelier, Paris, France, 1946, translation by Miriam John produced as *Jeannette,* at Maidman Playhouse, New York, NY, 1960.

L'invitation au château (first produced at Théâtre de l'Atelier, Paris, France, 1947; produced as *Ring around the Moon,* at Martin Beck Theatre, New York, NY, 1950), Éditions de la Table Ronde (Paris, France), 1948, edited by D.J. Conlon, Cambridge University Press (Cambridge, England), 1962, translation by Christopher Fry published as *Ring around the Moon,* Oxford University Press (New York, NY), 1950, French (London, England), 1976.

Épisode de la vie d'un auteur, first produced in Paris, France, at Comédie des Champs-Elysees, 1948; translation produced as *Episode in the Life of an Author* in Buffalo, NY, at Studio Arena Theatre, September, 1969.

Ardèle; ou, la Marguerite (first produced with *Épisode de la vie d'un auteur,* in Paris, France, at Comédie des Champs-Elysees, 1948; produced as *Cry of the Peacock,* at Mansfield Theatre, New York, NY, 1950), Éditions de la Table Ronde (Paris, France), 1949, Le Livre de Poche (Paris, France), 1970, translation by Lucienne Hill published as *Ardèle,* Methuen (London, England), 1951.

Cécile; ou, l'École des pères (first produced in Paris, France, at Comédie des Champs-Elysees, 1949), Éditions de la Table Ronde (Paris, France), 1954.

La répétition; ou, l'amour puni (first produced at Théâtre Marigny, Paris, France, 1950; produced in New York at Ziegfield Theatre, 1952), La Palatine (Geneva, Switzerland), 1950, critical edition, Bordas (Paris, France), 1970, translation by Pamela Hansford Johnson and Kitty Black published as *The Rehearsal,* Coward (New York, NY) 1961.

Colombe (first produced at Théâtre de l'Atelier, Paris, France, 1951; adaptation by Denis Cannan produced at Longacre Theatre, New York, NY, 1954), Livre de Poche, 1963, translation by Denis Cannan published by Methuen (London, England), 1954.

Monsieur Vincent (dialogue), Beyerische Schuelbuch-Verlag, 1951.

La valse des toréadors (English translation produced at Coronet Theatre, New York, NY, 1957), Éditions de la Table Ronde (Paris, France), 1952, translation by Lucienne Hill published as *The Waltz of the Toreadors,* Elek, 1956, Coward (New York, NY) 1957.

L'alouette (first produced at Théâtre Montparnasse, Paris, France, 1953; adaptation by Lillian Hellman produced as *The Lark* at Longacre Theatre, New York, NY, 1955), Éditions de la Table Ronde (Paris, France), 1953, edited by Merlin Thomas and Simon Lee, with exercises and vocabulary by Bert M.P. Leefmans, Appleton (New York, NY), 1956, translation by Christopher Fry published as *The Lark,* Methuen (London, England), 1955, Oxford University Press (New York, NY), 1956, translation by Lillian Hellman published as *The Lark,* Random House (New York, NY), 1956.

Médée (first produced at Théâtre de l'Atelier, Paris, France, 1953; also see below), Éditions de la Table Ronde (Paris, France), 1953.

Ornifle; ou, le courant d'air (first produced in Paris, France, at Comédie des Champs-Elysees, 1955), Éditions de la Table Ronde (Paris, France), 1955, translation by Lucienne Hill published as *Ornifle: A Play,* Hill & Wang (New York, NY), 1970.

Pauvre Bitos; ou, le dîner de têtes (first produced at Théâtre Montparnasse, Paris, France, 1956; produced in English in New York at Classic Stage Repertory, 1969), Éditions de la Table Ronde (Paris, France), 1958, translation by Lucienne Hill published as *Poor Bitos,* Coward (New York, NY) 1964.

L'hurluberlu; ou, le réactionnaire amoureux (first produced in Paris, France, dat Comédie des Champs-Elysees, 1959; produced in English at ANTA Theatre, New York, NY, 1959), Éditions de la Table Ronde (Paris, France), 1959, translation by Lucienne Hill published as *The Fighting Cock,* Coward (New York, NY) 1960.

Becket; ou, l'honneur de Dieu (first produced at Théâtre Montparnasse-Gaston Baty, Paris, France, 1959; produced as *Becket,* at St. James Theatre, New York, NY, 1960), Éditions de la Table Ronde (Paris, France), 1959, translation by Lucienne Hill published as *Becket; or, The Honor of God,* Coward (New York, NY) 1960, with a foreword by André Aciman, Riverhead Books (New York, NY), 1995.

Madame de. . . (produced with *Traveller without Luggage* at Arts Theatre, London, England, 1959), translation by John Whiting published by Samuel French (London, England), 1959.

La petite Molière, first produced at Festival of Bordeaux, France, 1960.

La grotte (first produced at Théâtre Montparnasse, Paris, France, 1961; produced in English at Playhouse in the Park, Cincinnati, OH, June, 1967), Éditions de la Table Ronde (Paris, France), 1961, translation by Hill published as *The Cavern,* Hill & Wang (New York, NY), 1966.

La foire d'empoigne (first produced in Paris, France, 1962), Éditions de la Table Ronde (Paris, France), 1961.

L'orchestre (first produced in Paris, France, 1962; produced in English in Buffalo, at Studio Arena Theatre, September, 1969), translation by Miriam John published as *The Orchestra,* French (New York, NY), 1975.

Fables, Éditions de la Table Ronde (Paris, France), 1962.

Le boulanger, la boulangère et le petit mitron (first produced in Paris, France, at Comédie des Champs-

Elysées, November 13, 1968; English translation by Lucienne Hill produced at University Theatre, Newcastle, England, fall, 1972), Éditions de la Table Ronde (Paris, France), 1969.

Cher Antoine; ou, l'amour raté (first produced in Paris, France, at Comédie des Champs-Elysées, October 1, 1969; produced in English in Cambridge, MA, at Loeb Drama Center of Harvard University, July 20, 1973), Éditions de la Table Ronde (Paris, France), 1969, translation by Lucienne Hill published as *Dear Antoine; or, The Love That Failed,* Hill & Wang, 1971.

Le Théâtre; ou, la vie comme elle est, first produced in Paris, France, at Comédie des Champs-Elysées, 1970.

Ne réveillez pas madame (first produced at Comédie des Champs-Elysées, October 21, 1970), Éditions de la Table Ronde (Paris, France), 1970.

Les poissons rouges; ou, mon père, ce héros (first produced at Théâtre de l'Oeuvre, c. 1970), Éditions de la Table Ronde (Paris, France), 1970.

Tu étais si gentil quand tu étais petit (first produced at Théâtre Antoine, January 18, 1972), Éditions de la Table Ronde (Paris, France), 1972.

Le directeur de l'opera, Éditions de la Table Ronde (Paris, France), 1972, translation by Lucienne Hill published as *The Director of the Opera,* Methuen (London, England), 1973.

Monsieur Barnett (bound with Claude Brulé's *Le siècle des lumières*), L'Avant-scène du théâtre (Paris, France), 1975.

L'arrestation: Pièce en deux parties, Éditions de la Table Ronde (Paris, France), 1975, translation by Lucienne Hill published as *The Arrest: A Drama in Two Acts,* Samuel French (New York, NY), 1978.

Le scénario, Éditions de la Table Ronde (Paris, France), 1976.

Chers Zoiseaux (four-act comedy), Éditions de la Table Ronde (Paris, France), 1977.

La culotte, Éditions de la Table Ronde (Paris, France), 1978.

Le nombril (produced in English under the title *Number One* at Queen's Theatre, London, England, April 24, 1984), Éditions de la Table Ronde (Paris, France), 1981, translation by Michael Frayn published as *Number One,* French (New York, NY), 1985.

OEdipe, ou, Le roi boiteux: d'après Sophocle, Éditions de la Table Ronde (Paris, France), 1986.

Thomas More, ou, L'homme libre, Éditions de la Table Ronde (Paris, France), 1987.

Vive Henri IV!, ou, La Galigaï, Éditions de la Table Ronde (Paris, France), 2000.

Also author of plays published in French periodicals, including *Attile le magnifique,* 1930, *Le petit bonheur,* 1935, *L'incertain,* 1938, *Oreste,* 1945, *Jezebel,* 1946, and *Le songe du critique,* 1961.

TRANSLATOR

(And editor) William Shakespeare, *Trois Comédies* (contains *As You Like It, Winter's Tale,* and *Twelfth Night*), Éditions de la Table Ronde (Paris, France), 1952.

(With wife Nicole Anouilh) Graham Greene, *L'amant complaisant* (translation of *The Complacent Lover*), Laffont, 1962.

(With Claude Vincent) Oscar Wilde, *Il est importand dêtre aimé* (tranlsation of *The Importance of Being Earnest*), produced in Paris, France, 1964.

William Shakespeare, *Richard III,* produced at Théâtre Montparnasse, Paris, France, 1964.

OMNIBUS VOLUMES IN FRENCH

Pièces roses: Le bal des voleurs, Le rendez-vous de Senlis, Léocadia, Éditions Balzac (Paris, France), 1942, 2nd edition, with addition of *Humulus le muet,* Éditions de la Table Ronde (Paris, France), 1958.

Pièces noires: L'hermine, La sauvage, Le voyageur sans bagage, Eurydice, Éditions Balzac (Paris, France), 1942, Éditions de la Table Ronde (Paris, France), 1966.

Nouvelles pièces noires: Jézabel, Antigone, Roméo et Jeannette, [and] *Médée,* Éditions de la Table Ronde (Paris, France), 1946, 1967.

Antigone [and] *Médée,* Le Club Francais du Livre, 1948.

Pièces brillantes: L'invitation au château, Colombe, La répétition; ou, l'amour puni, [and] *Cécile; ou, l'École des pères,* Éditions de la Table Ronde (Paris, France), 1951, 1965.

Deux pièces brillantes: L'invitation au château [and] *La répétition; ou, l'amour puni,* Le Club Français du Livre, 1953.

La sauvage [and] *Le bal des voleurs,* Colmann-Levy, 1955.

Antigone [and] *L'alouette,* Livre Club de Libraire, 1956.

Pièces grinçantes (includes *Ardèle; ou, la Marguerite, La valse des toréadors, Ornifle; ou, le courant d'air,* and *Pauvre Bitos; ou, le dîner de têtes*), Éditions de la Table Ronde (Paris, France), 1956.

Une piece rose, deux pièces noires (includes *Le bal des voleurs, La sauvage,* and *Eurydice*), Club des Libraires de France, 1956.

Le rendez-vous de Senlis [and] *Leocadia,* Éditions de la Table Ronde (Paris, France), 1958.

Le voyageur sans bagage [and] *Le bal des voleurs,* Éditions de la Table Ronde (Paris, France), 1958.

Antigone, Becket, [and] *Cécile,* Éditions de la Table Ronde (Paris, France), 1959.

La sauvage [and] *L'invitation au château,* Éditions de la Table Ronde (Paris, France), 1960.

Pièces costumées (includes *L'alouette, Becket; ou, l'honneur de Dieu,* and *La foire d'empoigne*), Éditions de la Table Ronde (Paris, France), 1960.

Théâtre complet, six volumes, Éditions de la Table Ronde (Paris, France), 1961–63.

Deux pièces roses: Le bal des voleurs [and] *Le rendez-vous de Senlis,* Le Club Francais du Livre, 1963.

Sauvage [and] *L'Invitation au château,* Éditions de la Table Ronde (Paris, France), 1965.

Le rendez-vous de Senlis [and] *Léocadia,* Éditions de la Table Ronde (Paris, France), 1967.

Ardèle; ou, la Marguerite suivi de La valse des toréadors, Éditions de la Table Ronde (Paris, France), 1970.

Nouvelles pièces grinçantes (contains *L'hurluberlu; ou, le réactionnaire amoreux, La grotte, L'orchestre, Le boulanger, la boulangere, et le petit mitron,* and *Les poissons rouges; ou, mon père, ce héros*), Éditions de la Table Ronde (Paris, France), 1970.

Eurydice, suivi de Roméo et Jeannette, Éditions de la Table Ronde (Paris, France), 1971.

Pièces baroques (includes *Cher Antoine, Ne réveillez pas madame, Le directeur de l'opera*), Éditions de la Table Ronde (Paris, France), 1974.

Monsieur Barnett [and] *L'Orchestre,* Éditions de la Table Ronde (Paris, France), 1975.

Pièces secrets (includes *Tu étais si gentil quand tu étais petit, L'arrestation,* and *Le scénario*), Éditions de la Table Ronde (Paris, France), 1977.

La Foire d'empoigne [and] *Cécile: ou, l'École des pères,* Gallimard (Paris, France), 1979.

La belle vie [and] *Épisode de la vie d'un auteur,* Éditions de la Table Ronde (Paris, France), 1980.

Pièces farceuses, Éditions de la Table Ronde (Paris, France), 1984.

OMNIBUS VOLUMES IN ENGLISH

Antigone [and] *Eurydice,* Methuen (London, England), 1951.

. . . *Plays,* three volumes, Hill & Wang (New York, NY), Volume 1: *Five Plays* (contains *Antigone, Eurydice, The Ermine, The Rehearsal,* and *Roméo and Jeannette*), 1958, Volume 2: *Five Plays* (contains *Restless Heart, Time Remembered, Ardèle, Made-* moiselle Colombe, and *The Lark*), 1959, Volume 3: *Seven Plays* (contains *Thieves' Carnival, Medea, Cecile; or, The School for Fathers, Traveler without Luggage, The Orchestra, Episode in the Life of an Author,* and *Catch as Catch Can*), 1967.

Ardèle [and] *Colombe,* Methuen (London, England), 1959.

Leocadia [and] *Humulus le muet,* Harrap, 1961.

Ardèle [and] *Pauvre Bitos,* Dell (New York, NY), 1965.

The Collected Plays, Methuen, Volume 1 (contains *The Ermine, Thieves' Carnival, Restless Heart, Traveller without Luggage,* and *Dinner with the Family*), 1966, Volume 2 (contains *Time Remembered, Point of Departure, Antigone, Roméo and Jeannette,* and *Medea*), 1967.

Euridice [and] *Médée,* edited and with an introduction and notes by E. Freeman, Blackwell (New York, NY), 1984.

Jean Anouilh: Five Plays, with an introduction by Ned Chaillet, Methuen (New York, NY), 1987.

Ring Round the Moon appeared in *Three European Plays,* edited by E. Martin Browne, Penguin, 1958.

FILMS

(With Jean Aurenche; and director) *Le voyageur sans bagage,* based on the play by Anouilh, 1944, released in United States as *Identity Unknown,* Republic, 1945.

(With Jean Bernard-Luc and Maurice Cloche) *Monsieur Vincent,* 1947; released in United States, Lopert, 1949.

(With Leonardo Bercovici, Forrest Judd, and David Robinson) *Monsoon,* based on Anouilh's play *Roméo et Jeannette,* United Artists, 1952.

La mort de Belle (also known as *The End of Belle*), 1961, released in United States as *The Passion of Slow Fire,* Trans-Lux Distributing, 1962.

Also author of the films (with André Cerf and J.J. Thoren) *La citadelle du silence,* based on the story by T.H. Robert, 1937, released in United States as *The Citadel of Silence,* 1939; (with Jean Aurenche and others) *Vous n'avez rien à dáclarer?,* 1937, released in United States as *Confessions of a Newlywed,* 1941; (with Jean Aurenche and others) *Dégourdis de la 11ème,* 1937; (with Leo Mittler and Victor Trivas) *Les otages,* 1938, released in United States as *The Mayor's Dilemma,* 1940; (with Jean Aurenche) *Cavalcade d'amour,* 1940; (uncredited; with Jacques Viot) *Marie-Martine,* 1943; (with Julien Duvivier and Guy Morgan) *Anna*

Karenina, based on the novel by Leo Tolstoy, 1948; (with Jean Bernard-Luc) *Pattes blanches,* 1949; (with Michel Audiard) *Caroline chérie,* based on the novel by Cécil Saint-Laurent, 1950, released in United States as *Dear Caroline,* 1954; (with Monelle Valentin; and director) *Deux sous de violettes* (also known as *Two Pennies Worth of Violets*), 1951; (with André Barsacq) *Le rideau rouge* (also known as *Ce soir on joue Macbeth, Crimson Curtain,* and *Les rois d'une nuit*), 1952; (with Cécil Saint-Laurent) *Un caprice de Caroline chérie* (also known as *Caroline Cherie*), based on the novel by Cécil Saint-Laurent, 1953; *Le chevalier de la nuit* (also known as *Knight of the Night*), 1954; *La ronde,* based on the play by Arthur Schnitzler, 1964; (with Sébastien Japrisot) *Piège pour Cendrillon* (also known as *A Trap for Cinderella*), 1965; and *A Time for Loving,* 1971.

OTHER

(With Pierre Imbourg and Andre Warnod) *Michel-Marie Poulain,* Braun, 1953.

(With Georges Neveux) *Le loup* (ballet), score by Henri Dutilleux, Éditions Ricordi, 1953.

(With Leon Thoorens and others) *Le dossier Molière,* Gerard, 1964.

La vicomtesse d'Eristal n'a pas reçu son balai mécanique: Souvenirs d'un jeune homme, Éditions de la Table Ronde (Paris, France), 1987.

En marge du théâtre, edited and with noted by Efrin Knight, Éditions de la Table Ronde (Paris, France), 2000.

Also author of ballet *Les demoiselles de la nuit,* score by Jean-Rene Francaix, 1948. Author of (with others) *Robert Brasillach et la gétération perdue,* 1987. Contributor to anthologies, including *Contemporary Drama,* Scribner, 1956; *One-Act: Eleven Short Plays of the Modern Theatre,* Grove, 1961; *Joan of Arc: Fact, Legend, and Literature,* Harcourt, 1964; and *Masterpieces of Modern French Theatre,* Macmillan, 1967.

Also author of teleplays, including (with Nicole Anouilh) *Comme il vous plaira,* based on the play *As You Like It* by William Shakespeare, for French television, 1972; *Histoire du chevalier Des Grieux et de Manon Lescaut* (miniseries), based on the play by Abbé Prévost, 1978; and *La belle vie,* for French television, 1979.

ADAPTATIONS: *Le rendez-vous de Senlis* was adapted as the film *Quartieri alti* (also known as *In High Places*), 1945; *Antigone* was filmed for the television program *The Kaiser Aluminum Hour,* c. 1956; *L'alouette* was adapted for German television as *Jeanne oder Die Lerche,* 1956 and 1966; *L'alouette* was adapted for television and presented as *The Lark,* in the "Hallmark Hall of Fame" series, 1956-57; *La répétition ou L'amour puni* was adapted for television, 1958; *Colombe* was adapted for television, 1958 and 1960; *The Waltz of the Toreadors* was filmed for television, 1959; *Madame de . . .* was filmed in 1959; *Thieves' Carnival* was filmed for television, 1959; *Léocadia* was adapted for television and presented by Compass Productions as *Time Remembered* for the "Hallmark Hall of Fame" series, 1961; *Eurydice, Le rendez-vous de Senlis, Becket; ou, l'honneur de Dieu, La valse des torédors, Le voyageur sans bagages* and *La grotte* were adapted for German television, 1961-63; *La valse des toréadors* was filmed with the title *Waltz of the Toreadors,* Continental Distributing, 1962; *Dinner with the Family* was filmed for television, 1962; *Becket; ou, l'honneur de Dieu* was filmed with the title *Becket,* Paramount Pictures, 1963, and television, 1964; *La foire d'empoigne* was adapted for television as *Catch as Catch Can,* 1964; *Colombe* was adapted for television, 1965; an extract from *Antigone* adapted as *I Was Happy Here* (also known as *Passage of Love* and *Time Lost and Time Remembered*), 1965; *La répétition ou L'amour puni* was adapted for Swedish television as *Repetitionen,* 1968; *Die Katze* appeared on West German television, 1968; *Le rendez-vous de Senlis* was adapted for Belgian television as *Het rendez-vous van Senlis,* 1968; *Monsieur Barnette, avec l'orchestre* was adapted for Swedish television as *Monsieur Barnett,* 1968, and for West German television as *Mister Barnett,* 1969; *Colombe* was produced as an opera at Opéra Comique, Paris, France, c. 1970; *L'invitation au château* was adapted for television as *Einladung ins Schloss* (also known as *Ring Round the Moon*), 1970; *Cher Antoine; ou, l'amour raté* was adapted for West German television as *Cher Antoine oder Die verfehlte Liebe,* 1970; *Traveller without Luggage* was adapted for NET Playhouse in 1971; *Ornifle ou le courant d'air* was adapted for West German television as *Ornifle oder Der erzürnte Himmel,* 1972; *Antigone* was produced in English for "Playhouse New York," Public Broadcasting System, 1972, and adapted for television, 1974; *Le bal des voleurs* was adapted for Belgian television as *Het Dievenbal,* 1977; *The Rehearsal* was adapted for British television, 1977; *Le Scénario* was adapted for television, 1978; *Le songe du critique* was filmed for the television program *Le petit Théâtre d'Antenne 2,* c. 1978; *Le diable amoureux* was adapted for television, 1991; *Colombe* was adapted for television, 1996; *Skovránok* appeared on Slovak television, 1999; *Le voyageur sans bagages* was adapted for Czech television as *Cestující bez zavazadel,* 2000; *L'alouette* was adapted for Romanian television as *Ciocârlia,* 2002; *Le voyageur sans bagage* was adapted for French television, 2004.

SIDELIGHTS: Jean Anouilh was ranked among France's most successful playwrights for more than forty years. One of several theatrical craftsmen whose work marked an exceptionally rich era in French theatre, Anouilh authored numerous dramas that have been performed all over the world. His plays often feature heroes who are forced to desperate confrontations with "a world fueled by cowardice, revenge and hatred," to quote *Washington Post* contributor Richard Pearson. This expressed horror at mankind's predicament led Anouilh to pen many grim dramas (he called them "black plays" and "grating plays"), but it also spawned humorous pieces that have been compared to the works of Molière. In *Jean Anouilh: Stages in Rebellion,* Branko Alan Lenski wrote: "For thirty years, through bedroom as well as metaphysical farces, Anouilh has been providing us with his orchestration of the eternal debate between the body and the soul. . . . [His] voice rises in indignation before certain historical crimes and yet always remains stylized, elegant and perfectly allied to the action on the stage." Sylvie Drake put it more succinctly in the *Los Angeles Times.* Anouilh, Drake concluded, "was a man of ideas who skillfully disguised them as entertainments."

Anouilh held strong views on the purpose of the theatre. He saw drama as a temporary escape from awareness of the inevitability of death, and he therefore strove to make his work highly theatrical. A London *Times* reviewer found Anouilh's plays "compellingly watchable," with "dialogue which could be spoken easily and effectively on stage." *Nation* correspondent Harold Clurman also observed that the playwright desired "to do little more than purvey material for enjoyable theatregoing. But that is only a disguise: Anouilh [possessed] an artistic individuality, deep-rooted in his personality and in the nature of the French nation." Lenski wrote that Anouilh was "the type of playwright who [poured] all his life into his plays, crying, laughing, vituperating, battling, confessing. . . . Such theatre often exhibits cheap sentimentality, is talkative, abounds in locker-room jokes, relies on vaudeville gimmicks—yet in so doing it is only true to life." The effect of such entertainment, Jack Kroll concluded in *Newsweek,* is "like a child being held by a sage and cynical uncle who talks seductively of the bittersweet pleasure-pains of life."

Anouilh enjoyed grouping his plays into categories. He did it, he said, to satisfy the public's need for classifications—but it also helped to organize his prolific oeuvre. His categories included *pièces noires* (black plays), *pièces roses* (rosy plays), *nouvelles pièces noires* (new black plays), *pièces brillantes* (brilliant plays), *pièces grinçantes* (grating plays), *pièces costumées* (costume plays), and *pièces baroques* (baroque plays). In *Jean Anouilh,* author Alba M. Della Fazia wrote: "In plays classified as 'black,' 'pink,' 'brilliant,' 'jarring,' and 'costumed,' Anouilh treats an assortment of themes that range from the soul of man to the world of men, from the heroism of the individual to the mediocrity of the masses. Some of the plays are heavy and dismal, some are light and fanciful, but all reveal the author's profound and often painful insight into the human condition."

The *pièces noires* and the *pièces roses* are similar in content—both are concerned with human survival in an inhospitable environment. In the *pièces noires,* society triumphs over the hero's ideals, forcing the hero to seek a tragic form of escape. Lenski observed that the central characters in the *pièces noires* "are deaf to arguments in favor of a humble sort of happiness. They want all or nothing at all, and the lower they stand, the greater their claims on the Ideal, the louder their plea for help." In the *pièces roses,* the hero escapes not through death but through fantasy, illusion, and changing personality. In *The World of Jean Anouilh,* author Leonard Cabell Pronko contended that although the characters of the *pièces roses* are unheroic in their compromise with happiness, "they at least possess the noble desire for the purity of life that dares to be what it is without excuses. But they are satisfied with a happiness that Anouilh later satirizes as illusory and unworthwhile." In his book titled *Jean Anouilh,* Lewis W. Falb concluded: "Anouilh may choose to present his observations in the guise of amusing fables, but one must not be deceived by their often pleasing surfaces; the vision underlying them is brutal and unpleasant. . . . But in his theatre, even at his most misanthropic, Anouilh offers a glimpse of an ideal, which, although faint or parodied, is not forgotten."

Over time Anouilh gradually became more grim in his theatrical treatments of humanity. Harold Hobson noted in *Drama* magazine that these *pièces grinçantes* "certainly caused audiences and critics to say that Anouilh was a man who hated life itself." *New York Times* contributor Gerald Jonas described these "grating plays" as productions in which "moments of realism, even tragedy, alternate with moments of corrosive humor. In such plays, judgments about events on the stage and the motivations of the principals must be constantly revised in the light of new revelations. Anyone in the audience who does not feel a certain discomfort as the evening progresses is probably not paying attention." Pronko claimed that the picture "is one of compromise, and the outlook seems more pessimistic than ever. We can find no hole in the fabric of an absurd universe through which to bring in some meaning." Della Fazia, too, stated that the effect of the plays "is 'jarring' because two irreconcilables—comedy and tragedy—clash on a battlefield strewn with the castoff armor of humanity's defense mechanisms."

In his *The Theatre of Jean Anouilh,* H.G. McIntyre wrote: "It is hardly an exaggeration to say that there is only one central theme running through the whole of Anouilh's work—the eternal and universal conflict between idealism and reality. All his other themes are related to this, either as expressions of the idealistic rejection of life or as explorations of the various obstacles to idealism and self-realization in an imperfect world." Lenski felt that Anouilh judged reality "from the height of the ideal and inevitably, seen from high up, the world seems a very sad place to live. At the same time, in showing reality in black coloring, Anouilh places the ideal into proper perspective." According to Joseph Chiari in *The Contemporary French Theatre: The Flight from Naturalism,* the pessimism of Anouilh is "the revolt of a sensitive being appalled and wounded by the cruelty of life and expressing man's despair at never being able to know his true self or to meet another self in a state of purity. . . . His heroes and heroines are alone, and when they hope to escape from their loneliness through another they generally realize that there is no escape, that life soils everything and that unless they choose to live a lie, death is the only solution—or failing death, the acceptance of suffering as a refining fire which will consume the dross into the ashes of a life devoted to an ideal."

This tendency to champion nonconformity gave Anouilh's work a political edge, especially during World War II. During the Nazi occupation of France, Anouilh produced the play *Antigone,* a reworking of the classical story of a young woman who dies because she defies the state. With *Antigone,* Bryan Appleyard wrote in the London *Times,* Anouilh "confronted the ironic contrast between the life of the imagination and the life of the world." Resistance critics hailed the work as a position statement, but Nazi collaborators also praised it for the pragmatic, reasoned arguments it offered in favor of capitulation. A *Times* contributor claimed, however, that *Antigone* "remains the quintessential French play of the 1940s. It combines moving if ambiguous references to the politics of the Resistance with a metaphysical despair that went straight to many an adolescent heart." After the war, Anouilh continued to pen dramas about

martyrs; his best-known plays include *Becket; or, The Honor of God,* the story of an English archbishop murdered for his steadfast adherence to church law, and *The Lark,* a treatment of the life of Joan of Arc. Pronko noted that these works show a conflict between "the hero's or the heroine's aspirations and the world of compromise that they must face and in contact with which they would become sullied. . . . Contrasted to them are the mediocre who consent to play the game, and who seek happiness by hiding the truth of life's absurdity from themselves."

Anouilh died of a heart attack at the age of seventy-seven. Ironically, given his predilection for viewing himself as an entertainer, he was eulogized as a playwright of ideas. Pronko called Anouilh "a writer who [was] bound to the cause of man's freedom." Likewise, Falb praised the author for his "rich statement of a personal vision, a lucid yet entertaining exploration of themes that involve the anxieties and preoccupations of contemporary audiences." Still, Chiari maintained that it was "human reality and not systems or concepts which Anouilh [was] after, and that is why his characters, full of human contradictions, are emotionally alive. It is in fact not what they think, but above all what they feel which is the main factor." In comedies that force audiences to laugh uncomfortably at their own absurdities, and in tragedies that highlight the venality of life, Anouilh strove to reveal his deepest torments. In the process, to quote Bettina L. Knapp in *Books Abroad,* he "has given the world some very great plays."

BIOGRAPHICAL AND CRITICAL SOURCES:

BOOKS

Archer, Marguerite, *Jean Anouilh,* Columbia University Press (New York, NY), 1971.
Bogard, Travis and William I. Oliver, editors, *Modern Drama: Essays in Criticism,* Oxford University Press (New York, NY), 1965.
Brustein, Robert, *Seasons of Discontent: Dramatic Opinions, 1959-1965,* Simon & Schuster (New York, NY), 1965.
Chiari, Joseph, *Landmarks of Contemporary Drama,* Herbert Jenkins (London, England), 1965.
Chiari, Joseph, *The Contemporary French Theatre: The Flight from Naturalism,* Gordian Press (New York, NY), 1970.
Cole, Toby, editor, *Playwrights on Playwrighting,* Hill & Wang (New York, NY), 1961.

Curtis, Anthony, *New Developments in the French Theatre: A Critical Introduction to the Plays of Jean-Paul Sartre, Simone de Beauvoir, Albert Camus, and Jean Anouilh,* Curtain Press (London, England), 1948.

Della Fazia, Alba M., *Jean Anouilh,* Twayne (New York, NY), 1969.

Encyclopedia of World Biography, second edition, seventeen volumes, Thomson Gale (Detroit, MI), 1998.

Falb, Lewis W., *Jean Anouilh,* Ungar (New York, NY), 1977.

Fowlie, Wallace, *Dionysus in Paris: A Guide to Contemporary French Theater,* World (Cleveland, OH), 1960.

Gassner, John, *Theatre at the Crossroads: Plays and Playwrights of the Mid-Century American Stage,* Holt (New York, NY), 1960.

Gassner, John, *Dramatic Soundings: Evaluations and Retractions Culled from Thirty Years of Drama Criticism,* Crown (New York, NY), 1968.

Grossvogel, David I., *The Self-Conscious Stage in Modern French Drama,* Columbia University Press (New York, NY), 1958.

Harvey, John, *Anouilh: A Study in Theatrics,* Yale University Press (New Haven, CT), 1964.

International Dictionary of Theatre, Volume 2: *Playwrights,* St. James Press (Detroit, MI), 1993.

Jolivet, Phillippe, *Le Théâtre de Jean Anouilh,* Michel Brient (Paris, France), 1963.

Kelly, K. W., *Jean Anouilh: An Annotated Bibliography,* Scarecrow (Metuchen, NJ), 1973.

Lenski, Branko Alan, *Jean Anouilh: Stages in Rebellion,* Humanities Press (Atlantic Heights, NJ), 1975.

Luppé, Robert de, *Jean Anouilh,* Éditions Universitaires (Paris, France), 1959.

Marsh, Edward Owen, *Jean Anouilh,* British Book Centre (London, England), 1953.

McIntyre, H. G., *The Theatre of Jean Anouilh,* Barnes & Noble (New York, NY), 1981.

Picon, Gaetan, *Contemporary French Literature: 1945 and After,* Ungar (New York, NY), 1974.

Pronko, Leonard Cabell, *The World of Jean Anouilh,* University of California Press (Berkeley, CA), 1961.

Smith, H. A., *Contemporary Theater,* Arnold, 1962.

Thody, Philip Malcolm Waller, *Anouilh,* Oliver & Boyd (Edinburgh, Scotland), 1968.

PERIODICALS

Back Stage, February 3, 1995, Eric Grode, review of *The Rehearsal,* p. 38; November 29, 1996, Irene Backalenick, review of *The Rehearsal,* p. 40.

Books Abroad, autumn, 1976, Bettina L. Knapp.

College English, March, 1955.

Financial Post, February 8, 1992, John Burgess, review of *Becket,* section S, p. 12.

Journal of European Studies, March-June, 1993, Mary Ann Frese Witt, "Fascist Ideology and Theater under the Occupation: The Case of Anouilh," pp. 49-69.

Nation, October 8, 1973, Harold Clurman.

New Republic, February 11, 1957.

Newsweek, September 24, 1973, Jack Kroll.

New York Times, November 7, 1979; October 13, 1985, Gerald Jonas, review of *The Waltz of the Toreadors,* section H, p. 4; October 17, 1985, Frank Rich, review of *The Waltz of the Toreadors,* section C, p. 16; May 29, 1989.

Plays and Players, April, 1974.

Romance Notes, fall, 1978.

Times (London, England), April 23, 1984.

Variety, May 3, 1999, Charles Isherwood, review of *Ring Round the Moon,* p. 94; October 30, 2000, Peter Ritter, review of *To Fool the Eye,* p. 36.

Yale French Studies, winter, 1954-55.

OBITUARIES:

PERIODICALS

Chicago Tribune, October 6, 1987.

Drama, 1st quarter, 1988, Harold Hobson.

Los Angeles Times, October 7, 1987, Sylvie Drake.

New York Times, October 5, 1987.

Time, October 19, 1987, p. 74.

Times (London, England), October 5, 1987.

Variety, October 7, 1987, pp. 107-108.

Village Voice, October 20, 1987.

Washington Post, October 5, 1987, Richard Pearson.

*   *   *

ANOUILH, Jean Marie Lucien Pierre
See ANOUILH, Jean

*   *   *

ANTHONY, Peter
See SHAFFER, Peter

ANTHONY, Piers 1934-
(Robert Piers, a joint pseudonym)

PERSONAL: Born Piers Anthony Dillingham Jacob, August 6, 1934, in Oxford, England; immigrated to United States, 1940, naturalized U.S. citizen, 1958; son of Alfred Bennis and Norma (Sherlock) Jacob; married Carol Marble, June 23, 1956; children: Penelope Carolyn, Cheryl. *Education:* Goddard College, B.A., 1956; University of South Florida, teaching certificate, 1964. *Politics:* Independent. *Hobbies and other interests:* Tree farming, archery.

ADDRESSES: Home—Inverness, FL. *Agent*—c/o Author Mail, Tor Books, 175 5th Ave., New York, NY 10010. *E-mail*—PiersAnthony@hipiers.com.

CAREER: Novelist. Electronic Communications, Inc., St. Petersburg, FL, technical writer, 1959-62; freelance writer, 1962-63, 1966—; Admiral Farragut Academy, St. Petersburg, teacher of English, 1965-66. *Military service:* U.S. Army, 1957-59.

MEMBER: Authors Guild, Authors League of America, National Writers Union.

AWARDS, HONORS: Science fiction award, Pyramid Books/*Magazine of Fantasy and Science Fiction*/Kent Productions, 1967, for *Sos the Rope;* British Fantasy Award, 1977, for *A Spell for Chameleon;* EPPIE, Friend of E-Publishing award, 2003.

WRITINGS:

SCIENCE FICTION

Chthon, Ballantine (New York, NY), 1967.
(With Robert E. Margroff) *The Ring,* Ace Books (New York, NY), 1968.
Macroscope, Avon (New York, NY), 1969.
(With Robert E. Margroff) *The E.S.P. Worm,* Paperback Library (New York, NY), 1970.
Prostho Plus, Berkley Publishing (New York, NY), 1973.
Race against Time, Hawthorne (New York, NY), 1973.
Rings of Ice, Avon (New York, NY), 1974.
Triple Detente, DAW Books (New York, NY), 1974.
Phthor (sequel to *Chthon*), Berkley Publishing (New York, NY), 1975.

(With Robert Coulson) *But What of Earth?,* Laser (Toronto, Ontario, Canada), 1976, corrected edition, Tor Books (New York, NY), 1989.
(With Frances T. Hall) *The Pretender,* Borgo Press (San Bernadino, CA), 1979.
Mute, Avon (New York, NY), 1981.
Ghost, Tor Books (New York, NY), 1986.
Shade of the Tree, Tor Books (New York, NY), 1986.
(Editor, with Barry Malzberg, Martin Greenberg, and Charles G. Waugh) *Uncollected Stars* (short stories), Avon (New York, NY), 1986.
Total Recall, Morrow (New York, NY), 1989.
Balook, illustrated by Patrick Woodroffe, Underwood-Miller (Novato, CA), 1990.
Hard Sell, Tafford (Houston, TX), 1990.
(With Roberto Fuentes) *Dead Morn,* Tafford (Houston, TX), 1990.
MerCycle, illustrated by Ron Lindahn, Tafford (Houston, TX), 1991.
(With Philip José Farmer) *Caterpillar's Question,* Ace Books (New York, NY), 1992.
Killobyte, Putnam (New York, NY), 1993.
The Willing Spirit, Tor Books (New York, NY), 1996.
Volk Internet 1996, Xlibris (Philadelphia, PA), 1997.
(With Clifford Pickover) *Spider Legs,* Tor Books (New York, NY), 1998.
(With J.R. Goolsby and Alan Riggs) *Quest for the Fallen Star,* Tor Books (New York, NY), 1998.
(With Julie Brady) *Dream a Little Dream,* Tor Books (New York, NY), 1999.
(With Jo An Taeusch) *The Secret of Spring,* Tor Books (New York, NY), 2000.
(With Ron Leming) *The Gutbucket Quest,* Tor Books (New York, NY), 2000.
Realty Check, Xlibris (Philadelphia, PA), 2000.

"OMNIVORE" SERIES; NOVELS

Omnivore, Ballantine (New York, NY), 1968, reprinted, Mundania Press (Cincinnati, OH), 2004.
Orn, Avon (New York, NY), 1971, Mundania Press (Cincinnati, OH), 2004.
Ox, Avon (New York, NY), 1976, Mundania Press (Cincinnati, OH), 2005.

"BATTLE CIRCLE" SERIES; NOVELS

Sos the Rope, Pyramid (New York, NY), 1968.
Var the Stick, Faber (London, England), 1972.
Neq the Sword, Corgi (London, England), 1975.
Battle Circle (contains *Sos the Rope, Var the Stick,* and *Neq the Sword*), Avon (New York, NY), 1978.

"CLUSTER" SERIES; NOVELS

Cluster, Avon (New York, NY), 1977, published as *Vicinity Cluster,* Panther (London, England), 1979.
Chaining the Lady, Avon (New York, NY), 1978.
Kirlian Quest, Avon (New York, NY), 1978.
Thousandstar, Avon (New York, NY), 1980.
Viscous Circle, Avon (New York, NY), 1982.

"TAROT" TRILOGY

God of Tarot, Jove (New York, NY), 1979.
Vision of Tarot, Berkley Publishing (New York, NY), 1980.
Faith of Tarot, Berkley Publishing (New York, NY), 1980.
Tarot (contains *God of Tarot, Vision of Tarot,* and *Faith of Tarot*), Ace Books (New York, NY), 1988.

"BIO OF A SPACE TYRANT" SERIES; NOVELS

Refugee, Avon (New York, NY), 1983.
Mercenary, Avon (New York, NY), 1984.
Politician, Avon (New York, NY), 1985.
Executive, Avon (New York, NY), 1985.
Statesman, Avon (New York, NY), 1986.

FANTASY NOVELS

Hasan, Borgo Press (San Bernardino, CA), 1977.
(With Robert Kornwise) *Through the Ice,* illustrated by D. Horne, Underwood-Miller (Novato, CA), 1989.
(With Mercedes Lackey) *If I Pay Thee Not in Gold,* Baen (New York, NY), 1993.

"MAGIC OF XANTH" SERIES; FANTASY NOVELS

A Spell for Chameleon, Del Rey (New York, NY), 1977.
The Source of Magic, Del Rey (New York, NY), 1979.
Castle Roogna, Del Rey (New York, NY), 1979.
The Magic of Xanth (contains *A Spell for Chameleon, The Source of Magic,* and *Castle Roogna*), Doubleday (New York, NY), 1981, published as *Piers Anthony: Three Complete Xanth Novels,* Wings Books (New York, NY), 1994.
Centaur Aisle, Del Rey (New York, NY), 1982.
Ogre, Ogre, Del Rey (New York, NY), 1982.

Night Mare, Del Rey (New York, NY), 1983.
Dragon on a Pedestal, Del Rey (New York, NY), 1983.
Crewel Lye: A Caustic Yarn, Del Rey (New York, NY), 1985.
Golem in the Gears, Del Rey (New York, NY), 1986.
Vale of the Vole, Avon (New York, NY), 1987.
Heaven Cent, Avon (New York, NY), 1988.
Man from Mundania, Avon (New York, NY), 1989.
(With Jody Lynn Nye) *Piers Anthony's Visual Guide to Xanth,* illustrated by Todd Cameron Hamilton and James Clouse, Avon (New York, NY), 1989.
Isle of View, Morrow (New York, NY), 1990.
Question Quest, Morrow (New York, NY), 1991.
The Color of Her Panties, Avon (New York, NY), 1992.
Demons Don't Dream, Tor Books (New York, NY), 1993.
Harpy Thyme, Tor Books (New York, NY), 1994.
Geis of the Gargoyle, Tor Books (New York, NY), 1995.
Roc and a Hard Place, Tor Books (New York, NY), 1995.
Yon Ill Wind, Tor Books (New York, NY), 1996.
Faun and Games, Tor Books (New York, NY), 1997.
Zombie Lover, Tor Books (New York, NY), 1998.
Xone of Contention, Tor Books (New York, NY), 1999.
The Dastard, Tor Books (New York, NY), 2000.
Swell Foop, Tor Books (New York, NY), 2001.
Up in a Heaval, Tor Books (New York, NY), 2001.
Cube Route, Tor Books (New York, NY), 2003.
Currant Events, Tor Books (New York, NY), 2004.
Pet Peeve, Tor Books (New York, NY), 2005.

"INCARNATIONS OF IMMORTALITY" SERIES; FANTASY NOVELS

On a Pale Horse, Del Rey (New York, NY), 1983.
Bearing an Hourglass, Del Rey (New York, NY), 1984.
With a Tangled Skein, Del Rey (New York, NY), 1985.
Wielding a Red Sword, Del Rey (New York, NY), 1986.
Being a Green Mother, Del Rey (New York, NY), 1987.
For Love of Evil, Morrow (New York, NY), 1988.
And Eternity, Morrow (New York, NY), 1990.

"DRAGON'S GOLD" SERIES; FANTASY NOVELS

(With Robert E. Margroff) *Dragon's Gold,* Tor Books (New York, NY), 1987, Mundania Press (Cincinnati, OH), 2004.
(With Robert E. Margroff) *Serpent's Silver,* Tor Books (New York, NY), 1988, Mundania Press (Cincinnati, OH), 2005.

(With Robert E. Margroff) *Chimaera's Copper,* Tor Books (New York, NY), 1990.

(With Robert E. Margroff) *Orc's Opal,* Tor Books (New York, NY), 1990.

(With Robert E. Margroff) *Mouvar's Magic,* Tor Books (New York, NY), 1992.

(With Robert E. Margroff) *Three Complete Novels* (contains *Dragon's Gold, Serpent's Silver,* and *Chimaera's Copper*), Wings Books (New York, NY), 1993.

"APPRENTICE ADEPT" SERIES; SCIENCE-FICTION/ FANTASY NOVELS

Split Infinity, Del Rey (New York, NY), 1980.
Blue Adept, Del Rey (New York, NY), 1981.
Juxtaposition, Del Rey (New York, NY), 1982.
Double Exposure (contains *Split Infinity, Blue Adept,* and *Juxtaposition*), Doubleday (New York, NY), 1982.
Out of Phaze, Ace Books (New York, NY), 1987.
Robot Adept, Ace Books (New York, NY), 1988.
Unicorn Point, Ace Books (New York, NY), 1989.
Phaze Doubt, Ace Books (New York, NY), 1990.

"MODE" SERIES; SCIENCE FICTION/FANTASY NOVELS

Virtual Mode, Putnam (New York, NY), 1991.
Fractal Mode, Putnam (New York, NY), 1992.
Chaos Mode, Putnam (New York, NY), 1993.
DoOon Mode, Tor Books (New York, NY), 2001.

"JASON STRIKER" SERIES; MARTIAL ARTS NOVELS

(With Roberto Fuentes) *Kiai!,* Berkley Publishing (New York, NY), 1974.

(With Roberto Fuentes) *Mistress of Death,* Berkley Publishing (New York, NY), 1974.

(With Roberto Fuentes) *The Bamboo Bloodbath,* Berkley Publishing (New York, NY), 1974.

(With Roberto Fuentes) *Ninja's Revenge,* Berkley Publishing (New York, NY), 1975.

(With Roberto Fuentes) *Amazon Slaughter,* Berkley Publishing (New York, NY), 1976.

"GEODYSSEY" SERIES; HISTORICAL SCIENCE FICTION

Isle of Woman, Tor Books (New York, NY), 1993.
Shame of Man, Tor Books (New York, NY), 1994.

Hope of Earth, Tor Books (New York, NY), 1997.
Muse of Art, Tor Books (New York, NY), 1999.

"CHROMAGIC" SERIES; NOVELS

Key to Havoc, Mundania Press (Cincinnati, OH), 2003.
Key to Chroma, Mundania Press (Cincinnati, OH), 2003.
Key to Destiny, Mundania Press (Cincinnati, OH), 2004.

OTHER

Steppe (science fiction/history), Millington (London, England), 1976, Tor Books (New York, NY), 1985.

Anthonology (short stories), Tor Books (New York, NY), 1985.

Bio of an Ogre: The Autobiography of Piers Anthony to Age Fifty, Ace Books (New York, NY), 1988.

Pornucopia (erotic fantasy), Tafford (Houston, TX), 1989.

Firefly (novel), Morrow (New York, NY), 1990.

Tatham Mound (historical fiction), Morrow (New York, NY), 1991.

Alien Plot (short stories), Tor Books (New York, NY), 1992.

Letters to Jenny (nonfiction), Tor Books (New York, NY), 1993.

(Editor, with Richard Gilliam) *Tales from the Great Turtle,* Tor Books (New York, NY), 1994.

How Precious Was That While: An Autobiography, Tor Books (New York, NY), 2001.

The Magic Fart (erotica), Mundania Books (Cincinnati, OH), 2003.

Also author of novel *The Unstilled World.* Contributor to *Science against Man,* edited by Anthony Cheetham, Avon (New York, NY), 1970; *Nova One: An Anthology of Original Science Fiction,* edited by Harry Harrison, Delacorte Press (New York, NY), 1970; *Again, Dangerous Visions,* edited by Harlan Ellison, Doubleday (New York, NY), 1972; *Generation,* edited by David Gerrold, Dell (New York, NY), 1972; and *The Berkley Showcase,* edited by Victoria Schochet and John Silbersack, Berkley Publishing (New York, NY), 1981. Also contributor, with Robert E. Margroff under joint pseudonym Robert Piers, of a short story to *Adam Bedside Reader.* Contributor of short stories to periodicals, including *Analog, Fantastic, Worlds of If, Worlds of Tomorrow, Amazing, Magazine of Fantasy and Science*

Fiction, SF Age, Vegetarian Times, Twilight Zone, Books and Bookmen, Writer, Gauntlet, Chic, Far Point, Starburst, Vertex, and *Pandora.*

ADAPTATIONS: Macroscope, A Spell for Chameleon, The Source of Magic, Castle Roogna, Through the Ice, Chaos Mode, Virtual Mode, and *Fractal Mode* have been adapted to audio cassette.

WORK IN PROGRESS: Novels in the "Magic of Xanth" series; *Climate of Change,* a novel in the "Geodyssey" series.

SIDELIGHTS: Prolific author Piers Anthony is widely known in the science-fiction and fantasy genres for his many popular series—including the ongoing "Magic of Xanth" novels—and his various novels and collections; he has published more than one hundred books since 1967. "I am an SF writer today," he told Cliff Biggers in a *Science Fiction* interview, "because without SF and writing I would be nothing at all today."

Within a childhood affected by illness and isolation, Anthony escaped by immersing himself in books. "From the time I was thirteen, I had been hooked on science fiction," Anthony recalled in an interview with the *Science Fiction Radio Show* (*SFRS*) published in *The Sound of Wonder.* "It's what I did for entertainment. It was a whole different world, multiple worlds, each one of them better than the one I knew. And so when I thought about writing [science fiction], I thought I could be original because I had read everything in the field."

Among the traumatic events of Anthony's youth were his family's moves to Spain when he was five and to the United States the following year, the loss of his cousin to cancer at age fifteen, and his parents' divorce when he was eighteen. As members of the Quaker faith, his parents were involved with the British Friends Service Committee during the Spanish Civil War, and Anthony spent the first years of his life in England under the care of his grandparents and a nanny. When he and his sister joined his parents after the war, they "seemed like acquaintances rather than close kin," the author recounted in an essay for *Something about the Author Autobiography Series* (*SAAS*). The family soon moved to the United States, where Anthony found it difficult to fit in. He often had to deal with bullies at school, and this compounded the alienation he suffered because of his parents' divorce. "The dominant emotion of my later childhood was fear," he recalled in his essay. "Fear of bigger kids at school, of a monster in the forest, and

fear of the corpse. Fear, really, of life. I hated being alone, but others neither understood nor cared, so I was alone a lot. That is, often physically, and almost always emotionally. Today when I get a letter from a reader who feels almost utterly alone, I understand, because I remember."

In addition, the young Anthony had difficulty at school. "Everyone in my immediate family was academically gifted except me," he explained in *SAAS*. "I was the dunce who made up for it all, pulling the average down." It wasn't until he was an adult that he discovered his academic problems had been due to some type of learning disability. "In my day things like learning disabilities or dyslexia didn't exist, just stupid or careless children," he wrote. Nevertheless, encouraged by his parents, who read and told stories to him, Anthony became a regular reader. "I think that nightly reading, and the daytime storytelling when we worked together outside, was the most important influence on my eventual choice of career. I knew that books contained fascinating adventures, and those stories took me away from my dreary real life," he recalled.

Anthony began to write at age twenty, deciding in college to make writing his career. He told Holly Atkins of the *St. Petersburg Times,* "I did not know I wanted to be a writer until I needed to decide on my college major. I thought about it overnight and realized that writing was it. From that point my ambition never changed, though for several years I had to take mundane jobs to support my family. Finally my wife went to work, so that I could stay home and write full time; that's when I started selling stories, and later novels. Now I write all the time that is available." After eight years of submitting stories to magazines, Anthony sold his first piece, "Possible to Rue," to *Fantastic* in 1962. In the next several years he worked variously as a freelance writer and English teacher, but finally decided to devote all of his time to writing. His first published novel, *Chthon,* came out in 1967. It received numerous award nominations and caught the attention of both critics and readers in the science fiction genre.

The novel traces the escape efforts of Aton Five, a man imprisoned on the planet Chthon and forced to work in its garnet mines. A *Publishers Weekly* reviewer commented that Anthony has combined language, myth, suspense, and symbolism to create "a bursting package, almost too much for one book, but literate, original and entertaining." Those elements—and Anthony's liberal use of them—would become his trademark. In a detailed analysis of *Chthon* and its sequel, *Phthor,* in his study *Piers Anthony,* Michael R. Collings noted Anthony's many references to mythological symbols. Literary references are present as well, exemplified by the resemblance of the prison caverns of Chthon to Dante's depiction of Hell in *The Inferno.* To *Books and Bookmen* contributor Leo Harris, in *Chthon,* "Anthony has created a whole new world, a dream universe which you find yourself living in and, after a while, understanding. Very poetic and tough and allegorical it all is, and it will rapidly have thee in thrall." While *Chthon* focuses on Aton's life, *Phthor* follows Aton's son, Arlo, who symbolizes Thor of Norse mythology. "The mythologies embedded in *Chthon* and *Phthor* go far beyond mere ornamentation or surface symbolism," Collings related. "They define the thematic content of the novels. Initially, there is a clear demarcation between myth and reality. Yet early in *Chthon* Anthony throws that clear demarcation into question."

Anthony won a prize in a contest jointly sponsored by Pyramid Books, Kent Productions, and the *Magazine of Fantasy and Science Fiction* for *Sos the Rope,* the first entry in the "Battle Circle" series, which is Anthony's first trilogy. *Sos the Rope* is based on a chapter of his 1956 B.A. thesis novel titled "The Unstilled World." The titles of *Sos the Rope* and the other installments in the series are characters' names; the trilogy's warriors are named after their weapons. The first novel explores the efforts of a group of radiation survivors led by Sos as they attempt to rebuild their society after the Blast. Yet the resulting Empire soon becomes a malevolent force and Sos sets out to destroy it. The novel speaks against the dangers of centralized civilization and overpopulation: millions of shrews, like the Biblical plague of locusts, invade the area and consume every living creature within their reach. Eventually the horde destroys itself with its enormity and its wholesale pillaging. The shrews' rampage and ultimate demise serve as a metaphor for humanity's overcrowding and abuse of the environment. Humankind, like the shrews, will be decimated when it outgrows the Earth's ability to sustain it. In *Var the Stick* and *Neq the Sword,* the "Battle Circle" story is completed. Collings observed similarities to the epic works of Homer, Virgil, and John Milton in "Battle Circle," which "investigates the viability of three fundamental forms of epic: the Achilean epic of martial prowess; the Odyssean epic of wandering; and the Virgillian/Miltonic epic of self-sacrifice and restoration."

The "Omnivore" trilogy provided a forum for Anthony to further his exploration of the dangers humankind continues to inflict upon itself, and introduced his support of vegetarianism. "Like 'Battle Circle,' *Chthon,*

and *Phthor,*" Collings observed, "'Omnivore' deals with control—specifically, with controlling the most dangerous omnivore of all, man." Three interplanetary explorers, the herbivorous Veg, carnivorous Cal, and omnivorous Aquilon, play out Anthony's views. The three journey to the planet Nacre, reporting back to investigator Subble and subsequently revealing to readers their adventures and clues to the secret threatening to destroy Earth. In the sequel, *Orn,* the three explorers venture to the planet Paleo, which resembles the Earth of sixty-five million years past, and encounter Orn, a creature whose racial memory endows it with the knowledge of its ancestors and enables it to survive the changes bombarding its planet. In *Ox,* the final volume of the trilogy, Veg, Cal, and Aquilon gradually uncover the existence of a sentient supercomputer while exploring alternative worlds. As with Anthony's other books, reviewers noted that the "Omnivore" volumes contain substantial discussions of technical and scientific issues. A *Publishers Weekly* reviewer described *Ox* as "a book for readers willing to put a lot of concentration into reading it."

The similarly challenging *Macroscope,* described by Collings as "one of Anthony's most ambitious and complex novels," seeks to place humanity in its proper context within the galaxy. The book enhanced Anthony's reputation but, due to a publisher's error, was not submitted for consideration for the important Nebula Award and lost one crucial source of publicity. Nevertheless, *Macroscope* was a milestone in Anthony's career. In a *Luna Monthly* review, Samuel Mines observed, " *Macroscope* recaptures the tremendous glamour and excitement of science fiction, pounding the reader into submission with the sheer weight of its ideas which seem to pour out in an inexhaustible flood."

Beginning with the "Cluster" series, Anthony began expanding beyond trilogies. "Cluster" became a series of five novels, while "Magic of Xanth" has grown to about thirty titles and been supplemented by the companion book *Piers Anthony's Visual Guide to Xanth.* "Magic of Xanth" and the "Apprentice Adept" series, which had seven entries published between 1980 and 1990, were originally planned as trilogies. In the case of the "Xanth" books, Anthony attributes his decision to continue the series to reader response. "We did a third [Xanth novel], and said, 'Let's wrap it up as a trilogy and not do any more,'" Anthony remarked to *SFRS.* "Then the readers started demanding more, and more, and more, and finally both the publisher and the author were convinced. It's hard to say 'No' when the readers are begging for more."

A Spell for Chameleon, the first of the "Xanth" books, marked Anthony's branching-out from science fiction into fantasy. Although one early work, *Hasan*, was fantasy, it was *Chameleon*, his second fantasy novel, that established Anthony in the genre. The switch to fantasy came as a result of Anthony's much-publicized split with his first publisher, Ballantine Books. The author told *SFRS*, Ballantine "was sending me statements-of-account that were simply not true. I sent a letter demanding a correct statement and correct payments. Rather than do that, they blacklisted me for six years." Anthony moved to Avon Books; six years later, with a new administration at Ballantine, he found himself invited back and wanted to give Ballantine another chance. His contract at Avon, however, prohibited him from writing science fiction for another publisher, so he decided to try fantasy. Anthony knew and liked the fantasy editor at Ballantine, Lester del Rey; Ballantine's Del Rey imprint went on to publish the first nine "Xanth" novels as well as the early "Apprentice Adept" and "Incarnations of Immortality" entries. Anthony differentiates between his science fiction and fantasy works in their content as well as their popularity. "For the challenge and sheer joy of getting in and tackling a difficult problem and surmounting it, science fiction is better," Anthony explained to *SFRS*. "But if I need money, fantasy is better." He later added, "I talk about writing fantasy in the sense of doing it for the money, but I also enjoy it. If I didn't enjoy it, I wouldn't do it for the money."

The "Xanth" series was still continuing over two decades after its first book appeared. The novels in the series are generally less complex and easier to read than Anthony's earlier works, and they appeal to younger readers as well as adults. *A Spell for Chameleon*, a 1978 Hugo Award nominee, introduces Bink, who tackles another recurring topic in Anthony's novels: maturity and control. The first "Xanth" installment chronicles Bink's growing-up; his son, Dor, and subsequent generations of the family feature in later books. The land of Xanth closely resembles Anthony's longtime home state of Florida in size and shape, and its place names are often wittily twisted versions of Floridian ones. In Xanth, everyone and everything—even a rock or tree—has a magical talent, except Bink. *Chameleon* follows Bink on his quest to discover his talent or face exile to the boring, powerless land of Mundania. In the process, Bink gains not only knowledge of his talent but emotional maturity as well. Bink sets out on another adventure in *The Source of Magic*, in which he is assigned to discover the source of all magic in Xanth. In *Castle Roogna*, Bink's son Dor travels 800 years back in time to rescue his nurse's boyfriend. Throughout each book, Bink and Dor encounter innumerable illusions and feats of magic. "Anthony apparently decided to invest his

magical land of Xanth with every fantastical conception ever invented," a reviewer for *Isaac Asimov's Science Fiction Magazine* remarked. "It has quests, enchanted castles, riddles, unicorns, griffins, mermaids, giants (not to mention invisible giants), zombies, ghosts, elves, magicians, man-eating trees, enchantresses, and a host of inventions from Anthony's own fertile mind."

"The Magic of Xanth" continues with *Centaur Aisle, Ogre, Ogre,* and *Night Mare,* the next "trilogy" of "Xanth" books. The first of these finds Dor filling in for Xanth's King Trent while he and Queen Iris take a trip to Mundania, a good experience for Dor since he will one day become king. When the king and queen fail to return, Dor sets out on another adventure. Anthony once again explores the process of maturing, as Dor leads a search party through Xanth and into Mundania, and falls in love with Princess Irene. In *Ogre, Ogre* the half-human, half-ogre Smash must protect the half-human, half-nymph Tandy. A stupid, insensitive creature at the beginning of the tale, Smash gradually acquires more human traits until he finally realizes that he is in love with Tandy.

Other entries in the series further develop Anthony's portrait of the fantastic land of Xanth, with storylines including the rescue of the kingdom by a creature responsible for delivering bad dreams (*Night Mare*), the adventures of three-year-old Princess Ivy, lost and wandering in the forest with newfound friends Hugo and the Gap Dragon (*Dragon on a Pedestal*), the diminutive Golem's quest to rescue a lost baby dragon and prove himself worthy of attention (*Golem in the Gears*), Prince Dolph's protest against the Adult Conspiracy that keeps children ignorant of adult matters (*Heaven Cent*), Princess Ivy's trip to Mundania in search of Good Magician Humfrey (*Man from Mundania*), and the search of Gloha, Xanth's only half-harpy/half-goblin, for advice from Magician Trent to further a quest for her true love (*Harpy Thyme*). In the opinion of *Fantasy Review* contributor Richard Mathews, the "Xanth" series "ranks with the best of American and classic fantasy literature."

Anthony's use of puns and other language tricks is a hallmark of the "Xanth" novels. "In Xanth," Collings noted, Anthony "incorporates much of this interest in language in furthering the plot and in establishing the essence of his fantasy universe. In Xanth, language is literal, especially what in Mundania would be called metaphors." As a result, the critic continued, "breadfruit bears loaves of bread; shoetrees bear shoes in varying sizes and styles; nickelpedes are like centipedes, only five times larger and more vicious; and sunflowers are flowers whose blossoms are tiny suns blazing at the top of the stalk—a potent weapon if an enemy looks directly at them." In a *Voice of Youth Advocates* review of *Ogre, Ogre,* Peggy Murray observed that the "sophomoric humor and bad puns" in Anthony's stories "have tremendous appeal with YA fantasy readers." In fact, Anthony's readers sent him some of the puns used in *Harpy Thyme. Sarasota Herald Tribune* writer Cindy Cannon commented of Anthony's "Xanth" wordplay, "Where else will you hit an imp ass, eat pun-kin pies, see a river bank lien or meet a character named Ann Arky?" She summed up the series by saying, "I can't think of a better place to meet up with centaurs, merfolk, zombies, ghosts, magically-talented humans and assorted half-breeds of every shape and kind than in one of Piers Anthony's many Xanth novels."

Cluster, the first novel in the series of the same name, was published in the same year as the first "Xanth" book. Intergalactic travel and adventure are the subjects of the "Cluster" books, in which Anthony introduces the concept of Kirlian transfer, a type of out-of-body travel that requires much less energy than the outmoded "mattermission." The Kirlian transfer and other innovations are fundamental to the outcomes of the First and Second Wars of Energy, described in the first two "Cluster" volumes, and to the battle of an intergalactic force against the space amoeba in *Kirlian Quest.* "More than anything, the Cluster series is an exercise in enjoyment" for Anthony, Collings remarked. The author apparently relishes the opportunity to create bizarre beings and situations unlike any the reader has experienced.

The original "Cluster" trilogy led to *Tarot,* published in three volumes as *God of Tarot, Vision of Tarot,* and *Faith of Tarot.* In fact, Anthony originally wrote *Tarot* as the ending to *Kirlian Quest* and intended that the two be published as one volume. Anthony emphasized in his interview with *SFRS* that *Tarot* is not a trilogy, but "a quarter-million-word novel." The novel was published not only in three parts, but in two different years. "It bothered me because I feel that this is the major novel of my career," Anthony remarked in *SFRS.* "Split into three parts and published in two years—it washed me out totally. I had no chance to make a run for any awards or anything like that. It was simply gone." He resents referrals to the book as a trilogy because this term implies that each volume is a full novel, when in fact each is one-third of a novel. Brother Paul, a character introduced in the "Cluster" trilogy and featured in *But What of Earth?,* is the central figure in *Tarot,* in which Anthony attempts to develop a definition of God.

Collings acknowledged that the "brutality, horror, and disgust" present in the book, while expressed in many other Anthony novels, are combined in *Tarot* with religious references, a controversial strategy that offended some readers. *Tarot* "is certainly not for the squeamish, nor is it altogether for those who enjoyed the first installment of Tarot civilization in the Cluster novels. Anthony himself admits this," Collings noted.

Anthony returned to pure fantasy in the "Incarnations of Immortality" series, which begins with *On a Pale Horse* and is set in "a world very much like ours, except that magic has been systematized and is as influential as science," a *Publishers Weekly* reviewer related. The abstract concepts of Time, War, Nature, Fate, and Death are all real people—the Incarnations—and all are involved in the battle of Satan against God. Diana Pharaoh Francis, a contributor to *Contemporary Popular Writers,* observed that *On a Pale Horse* "may be the best of Anthony's fantasy novels. . . . The characterization and dramatization are superbly handled and engage the reader. Besides clever social commentary, it provides a good read." In *Bearing an Hourglass,* a grief-stricken man agrees to take on the role of Chronos, the Incarnation of Time, and soon finds himself locked in a battle with Satan. *Booklist* reviewer Roland Green commented that "even people who may disagree with [Anthony's] ideas will recognize" that the religious and ethical aspects of the series are "intelligently rendered." Subsequent volumes feature the Incarnations of Fate (*With a Tangled Skein*), War (*Wielding a Red Sword*), Nature (*Being a Green Mother*), Evil (*For Love of Evil*), and finally, Good (*And Eternity*). "This grand finale showcases Anthony's multiple strengths" including his humor, characterizations, and themes, a *Library Journal* reviewer concluded.

Virtual Mode is a novel "to which teens relate well," Anthony remarked. Published in 1991, *Virtual Mode* introduces the "Mode" series, in which characters traverse the universe through the use of "skew paths" anchored by other people. As the anchors change, the paths and destinies of the travelers are affected and new stories are presented. In *Virtual Mode,* Darius of Hlahtar ventures to Earth to bring the girl he loves, the suicidal Colene, back to his universe. Together Darius and Colene discover that they must build a skew path to complete the journey. *Publishers Weekly* writer Sybil Steinberg described Colene as "a clearly defined character, virtues, flaws and all" who is "brought fully to life in this skillful, enjoyable book."

Another work with appeal to teen readers is *MerCycle,* Anthony's story about five people recruited to pedal bicycles under the waters of the Gulf of Mexico on a secret mission to save the Earth from collision with a meteor. The novel was originally written in 1971 but then shelved after Anthony was unable to find a publisher for it. After he was established as a best-selling author, Anthony returned to the manuscript and revised it extensively. The story deals heavily with themes of human nature and survival: the bicyclists experience being "out of phase" and "phased in" to other Earth life, are kept unaware of their mission, and meet up with Chinese mermaids. "The result," reported a *New York Times Book Review* critic, "is an engaging tall tale, spun out of the most unpromising raw material." Also of interest to youths is *Tatham Mound.* The story of fifteen-year-old Throat Shot, a sixteenth-century native of the land that would eventually become the state of Florida, *Tatham Mound* is based on an actual Indian burial mound discovered in north Florida and features historically accurate reconstructions of Spanish explorer Hernando de Soto's march across the region and his battles with the Indian tribes of the area. A *Library Journal* reviewer found *Tatham Mound* a "heartfelt tribute to a lost culture" and a "labor of both love and talent."

Likewise based on history, but spanning eight million years, are the works in the "Geodyssey" series. *Isle of Woman* is made up of a series of vignettes that center on two prehistoric families who are reborn into succeeding centuries up to twenty-first-century America. *Library Journal* contributor Jackie Cassada called *Isle of Woman* Anthony's "most ambitious project to date." *Shame of Man* explores evolution one generation at a time, beginning with families of gorillas and chimpanzees on through the species of homo sapiens that has evolved by 2050 A.D. Called "speculative fiction" by *Voice of Youth Advocates* reviewer Kim Carter, *Shame of Man* encompasses more than twenty-five years of Anthony's research in "history, archaeology, anthropology, and human nature," as well as showcasing some of the author's personal theories on these subjects.

Virtual Mode, Tatham Mound, and *Shame of Man* exemplify Anthony's desire to produce works of lasting value along with those written simply for entertainment. While he wants readers to enjoy his work, the author hopes also to provoke contemplation of the serious issues he presents. "I'd like to think I'm on Earth for some purpose other than just to feed my face," Anthony remarked to *SFRS.* "I want to do something and try to leave the universe a better place than it was when I came into it."

In *How Precious Was That While,* a sequel to his earlier volume of autobiography, *Bio of an Ogre,* Anthony "tacitly and emphatically acknowledges that his readers mean more to him than critics, publishers or editors," according to a *Publishers Weekly* reviewer. He is devoted to his many readers, and often spends two days a week answering their letters. The book also contains many of Anthony's strong opinions, including his continuing distrust and dislike of Dallas, Texas, because President John F. Kennedy was assassinated there. Anthony also takes on publishing executives with whom he has had disagreements over the years. *Booklist* critic Roland Green called the autobiography "a frank, eye-opening memoir."

Two years after the publication of *How Precious Was That While,* Anthony began yet another book series. The fantasy series titled "Chromagic" includes the books *Key to Havoc, Key to Chroma,* and *Key to Destiny.*

Evaluating Anthony's career in the *St. James Guide to Fantasy Writers,* Andy Sawyer drew attention to the author's loyalty to his fans, remarking that Anthony's "large body of fantasy is viewed (together with his growing propensity for 'series' novels) as a surrender to commercial pressures and fashionable trends. To some extent this may be so, although this judgment would neglect the part played by Anthony's own writings in creating the market for a particular form of fantasy. In fact, he has created a fiercely loyal readership (whom he frequently addresses directly in lengthy afterwords to his novels) and much of this loyalty is due to his provision of a type of escapism which embodies an easily grasped symbolism." Writing in *Twentieth-Century Young Adult Writers,* Lesa Dill concluded: "While entertaining his readers with his inventive word play, numerous literary allusions, apt symbolism, humorous satire, and wild adventures, Anthony effectively conveys his personal convictions about man's responsibilities in and to the universe."

BIOGRAPHICAL AND CRITICAL SOURCES:

BOOKS

Collings, Michael R., *Piers Anthony,* Starmont House (Mercer Island, WA), 1983.
Contemporary Literary Criticism, Volume 35, Gale (Detroit, MI), 1985, pp. 34- 41.
Contemporary Popular Writers, St. James Press (Detroit, MI), 1997.
Lane, Daryl, William Vernon, and David Carson, *The Sound of Wonder: Interviews from "The Science Fiction Radio Show,"* Volume 2, Oryx (Phoenix, AZ), 1985.

St. James Guide to Fantasy Writers, St. James Press (Detroit, MI), 1996.

St. James Guide to Science Fiction Writers, 4th edition, St. James Press (Detroit, MI), 1996.

Something about the Author Autobiography Series, Volume 22, Gale (Detroit, MI), 1996.

Twentieth-Century Young Adult Writers, St. James Press (Detroit, MI), 1994.

PERIODICALS

Analog, January, 1989, p. 182; August, 1992, pp. 165-166.

Booklist, July, 1984, p. 1497; May 1, 1999, Patricia Monaghan, review of *Muse of Art,* p. 1582; October 15, 1999, Roland Green, review of *Xone of Contention,* p. 424; April 15, 2000, Ray Olson, review of *The Gutbucket Quest,* p. 1527; October 15, 2000, Roland Green, review of *The Dastard,* p. 426; March 1, 2001, Roland Green, review of *DoOon Mode,* p. 1232; September 1, 2001, Roland Green, review of *How Precious Was That While,* p. 42; October 1, 2001, Roland Green, review of *Swell Foop,* p. 304; October 1, 2005, Frieda Murray, review of *Pet Peeve,* p. 43.

Books and Bookmen, April, 1970, pp. 26-27.

Computimes (Malaysia), May 3, 2001, "An Old Sci-Fi Book with Foresight."

Fantasy and Science Fiction, August, 1986, pp. 37-40.

Fantasy Review, March, 1984, pp. 24-25.

Horn Book, October 6, 1989, p. 84.

Isaac Asimov's Science Fiction Magazine, September, 1979, p. 18.

Kirkus Reviews, August 15, 1993, p. 1034; August 1, 2001, review of *Swell Foop,* p. 1075; July 15, 2005, review of *Pet Peeve,* p. 769.

Kliatt, November, 1992, p. 13.

Library Journal, December, 1989, p. 176; August, 1991, p. 150; September 15, 1993, p. 108; October 15, 1998, p. 104; January, 1999, p. 166; October 15, 1999, Jackie Cassada, review of *Xone of Contention,* p. 111; May 15, 2000, Jackie Cassada, review of *The Gutbucket Quest,* p. 129; October 15, 2000, Jackie Cassada, review of *The Dastard,* p. 108; April 15, 2001, Jackie Cassada, review of *DoOon Mode,* p. 137; November 15, 2002, Jackie Cassada, review of *Up in a Heaval,* p. 106.

Luna Monthly, September, 1970, p. 22.

New York Times Book Review, April 20, 1986, p. 27; September 13, 1992, p. 28.

Publishers Weekly, June 5, 1967, p. 180; July 26, 1976, p. 78; September 2, 1983, p. 72; July 25, 1986, p. 174; August 29, 1986, p. 388; May 29, 1987, p. 73; February 10, 1989, p. 58; August 11, 1989, p. 444; August 25, 1989, p. 58; April 20, 1990, p. 61; May 11, 1990, p. 251; August 10, 1990, p. 431; December 21, 1990, p. 57; January 4, 1991, p. 61; October 18, 1991, p. 55; July 20, 1992, p. 237; November 29, 1993, pp. 57-58; September 5, 1994, p. 96; September 21, 1998, p. 79; December 14, 1998, p. 61; April 26, 1999, p. 61; September 27, 1999, review of *Xone of Contention,* p. 78; March 6, 2000, review of *The Secret of Spring,* p. 88; May 1, 2000, review of *The Gutbucket Quest,* p. 55; October 2, 2000, review of *The Dastard,* p. 64; March 5, 2001, review of *DoOon Mode,* p. 66; July 23, 2001, review of *How Precious Was That While,* p. 59; August 27, 2001, review of *Swell Foop,* p. 59; November 4, 2002, review of *Up in a Heaval,* p. 67.

St. Petersburg Times (St. Petersburg, FL), July 13, 2001, p. P5; March 11, 2002, Holly Atkins, "Fantasy Flourishes in Florida Forests," p. D4.

Sarasota Herald Tribune, November 26, 2000, p. E4; July 23, 2001, p. 59.

Science Fiction, November, 1977, p. 60.

Voice of Youth Advocates, April, 1983, p. 44; December, 1992, p. 290; August, 1994, p. 152; February, 1995, p. 343.

Writer, August, 1989, pp. 11-13, 35.

Writer's Digest, January, 1991, p. 32.

ONLINE

Piers Anthony Home Page, http://www.hipiers.com/ (April 25, 2004).

*   *   *

ARCHER, Jeffrey 1940-
(Jeffrey Howard Archer)

PERSONAL: Born April 15, 1940, in Mark, Somerset, England; son of William (a professional soldier) and Lola (a journalist; maiden name, Cook) Archer; married Mary Weeden (a chemist), 1966; children: two sons. *Education:* Attended Brasenose College, Oxford, 1963-66; received diploma from Oxford University. *Politics:* Conservative *Hobbies and other interests:* Theater, watching Somerset play cricket, art, auctioneering for charity.

ADDRESSES: Home—93 Albert Embankment, London SE1 7TY, England. *Agent*—St. Martin's Press, 175 Fifth Avenue, New York, NY, 10010.

CAREER: Writer. Conservative member of British Parliament, 1969-74; deputy chair, British Conservative Party, 1985-86. Member, Greater London Council for Havering, 1966-70.

MEMBER: Royal Society of Arts (fellow), Oxford University Athletics Club (president, 1965), Somerset Amateur Athletics Association (former president), Marylebone Cricket Club.

AWARDS, HONORS: Created Life Peer, 1992.

WRITINGS:

NOVELS

Not a Penny More, Not a Penny Less, Doubleday (New York, NY), 1976.
Shall We Tell the President?, Viking (New York, NY), 1977.
Kane and Abel, Simon & Schuster (New York, NY), 1980.
The Prodigal Daughter, Linden Press (New York, NY), 1982.
First among Equals, Linden Press (New York, NY), 1984.
A Matter of Honor, Linden Press (New York, NY), 1986.
As the Crow Flies, HarperCollins (New York, NY), 1991.
Honor among Thieves, HarperCollins (New York, NY), 1993, published as *Honour among Thieves,* HarperCollins (London, England), 1993.
The Fourth Estate, HarperCollins (New York, NY), 1996.
The Eleventh Commandment, HarperCollins (New York, NY), 1998.
Sons of Fortune, St. Martin's Press (New York, NY), 2003.
False Impression, St. Martin's Press (New York, NY), 2006.

"PRISON DIARY" TRILOGY

A Prison Diary, St. Martin's Press (New York, NY), 2003.
Purgatory, St. Martin's Press (New York, NY), 2004.
Heaven, St. Martin's Press (New York, NY), 2004.

SHORT STORIES

A Quiver Full of Arrows, Linden Press (New York, NY), 1982.
A Twist in the Tale, HarperCollins (New York, NY), 1989.
(Editor, with Simon Bainbridge) *Fools, Knaves, and Heroes: Great Political Short Stories,* Norton (New York, NY), 1991.
Twelve Red Herrings, HarperCollins (New York, NY), 1994.
The Collected Short Stories, HarperCollins (New York, NY), 1998.
To Cut a Long Story Short, HarperCollins (New York, NY), 2000.

FOR CHILDREN

By Royal Appointment, Octopus (London, England), 1980.
Willy Visits the Square World, Octopus (London, England), 1980.
Willy and the Killer Kipper, Hodder & Stoughton (London, England), 1981.
The First Miracle, HarperCollins (New York, NY), 1994.

PLAYS

Beyond Reasonable Doubt (produced on London's West End, 1987), Samuel French (London, England), 1989.
(With others) *Gemma Levine's Faces of the '80s,* Collins (New York, NY), 1987.
Exclusive, produced on London's West End, 1989.
The Accused (produced at the Theatre Royal, Haymarket, London, 2000), Methuen (London, England), 2000.

ADAPTATIONS: Not a Penny More, Not a Penny Less was adapted for British television, serialized on British radio, and made into a sound recording; *Kane and Abel* was made into a miniseries for Columbia Broadcasting System (CBS-TV), 1985. Steven Spielberg purchased the film rights to *A Matter of Honor.*

WORK IN PROGRESS: Mallory (novel); *Mallory: Walking off the Map* (screenplay).

SIDELIGHTS: It has been said that Jeffrey Archer's career is reflected in his fiction—or, in some cases, that his fiction is reflected in his career. Both have attracted much public attention and have become the center of much controversy. A man of boundless energy—at Oxford University, he was a world-class sprinter, representing Great Britain in international competition—Archer walked the corridors of power with England's politicians after becoming the youngest member of the House of Commons in 1969, being appointed deputy chairman of the Conservative Party in 1985, and elevated to the House of Lords in 1992. He has also earned a reputation as a popular author in both England and America: A writer for *Books* magazine declared Archer to be "Britain's top-selling novelist." Bill Bryson, writing for *New York Times Magazine,* commented that "The great contradiction of Jeffrey Archer's life is that the one thing he has tried hardest to do—become a successful politician—is the one thing he has most signally failed to accomplish." His writing, however, tells a different story: all his short stories and novels have been international best sellers.

Archer founded his own company, Arrow Enterprises, after leaving university. Drawing on his experiences in fundraising and public relations for the university as well as his own tremendous energy, he quickly earned a fortune. He once commented: "I think energy is a God-given gift, in the way the ability to play a violin, the ability to sing, the ability to paint is a gift. People underestimate energy. If you have one gift plus energy, you'll go to the very top. I've always said the formula is: one gift plus energy, you'll be a king; energy and no gift, you're a prince; a gift and no energy, you're a pauper. I think energy is much underestimated. You will see it in the truly successful. It's the one thing Maria Callas, Pablo Picasso, and Margaret Thatcher have in common."

In 1969, Archer put his money to work by running for, and winning by a landslide, a seat in Parliament. Then only twenty-nine years old, he took his place in the House of Commons as one of its youngest members. For five years he served as a Conservative politician, enjoying political power and personal wealth. In 1974, however, Archer's dream of a political career fell apart. He had borrowed over 250,000 pounds sterling and invested it in a Canadian industrial cleaning company called Aquablast. The directors of the company embezzled the funds and Aquablast collapsed with over eight million dollars in debts. "I lost every penny," Archer told Bryson. "The shares were 3.20 pounds on one day and seven pence the next day. I never had a chance." Although Archer was a victim of the fraud, he felt obliged to not seek reelection and to devote himself to repaying his debts of 620,000 dollars. He left Parliament, borrowed a room in Oxford, and went to work writing a book loosely based on his experiences.

Not a Penny More, Not a Penny Less tells about four men—a doctor, a college professor, an art dealer, and a member of the aristocracy—who invest a million dollars in a company set up to exploit oil in the North Sea. The businessperson who runs the company proves to be dishonest, however, and the members of the quartet determine to get their money back by cheating him in return. *Not a Penny More, Not a Penny Less* went on to become an instant best seller in the United States (where it was first published) after having been turned down by a dozen British publishers. Its success surprised Archer, among others, and he once commented that he had "absolutely" no previous experience as a writer and no previous ambitions to become an author. "I'd been to university and was certainly educated, but I'd never done any writing at all, which makes me think that probably there are a lot of storytellers out there, or, more important, people who could do a second career and haven't thought about it. . . . I am by nature a person who enjoys other people's company. But I didn't mind being on my own during that time, because I needed to readjust, and I needed to put some work in to make up for my own stupidity."

Although *Not a Penny More* did not earn enough to pay off all Archer's debts, its success encouraged him to write more. *Shall We Tell the President?,* Archer's second novel, did not make the best-seller lists in the United States, but it did generate a great deal of controversy. Set in the early 1980s, it tells of a plan to assassinate President Edward Kennedy. American reviewers were outraged by what they perceived as Archer's callousness. Jacqueline Kennedy Onassis, President John F. Kennedy's widow, resigned her position as an editor with Viking, although she had no direct connection with the book. "The new editions in the bookshops," Archer once commented, "have Florentyna Kane"—the heroine of his novel *The Prodigal Daughter*—"as the president, not Edward Kennedy." Skillful marketing of the book and its paperback and movie rights netted Archer around 750,000 dollars—enough to pay off all his debts.

Archer's next novel, *Kane and Abel,* is also partially based on real people. It tells the story of William Kane, a Boston banker, and Abel Rosnovski, a Polish immigrant and hotelier, and their ferocious hatred for each other. Kane earns Rosnovski's hostility when his bank withholds crucial help from the Pole's American benefactor after the stock market crash of 1929. The bene-factor then commits suicide, and Rosnovski launches a vendetta against Kane that lasts for decades. "I met two such men in New York," Archer once said. "They were very close friends, unlike Kane and Abel, who were enemies. But they came from totally different backgrounds. One was a Polish aristocrat, and the other was one of America's most successful multimillionaires. They both told me their [stories]. I was quite interested in that, but I thought it would be much more interesting if they were deadly enemies. So I wrote the book with them as background material, but my own story." *Kane and Abel* sold more than a quarter million copies in hardcover and eight times that in paperback.

The Prodigal Daughter, a sequel about Rosnovski's daughter, followed *Kane and Abel* in 1982. It tells how Florentyna Rosnovski—now married to Kane's son Richard—becomes the first woman president of the United States. "I wanted to write the story of the first woman president of the United States," Archer once admitted. "I wanted an Englishman to write it, so that the Americans would realize that we're still awake over here. And you must remember that it was written some time before Geraldine Ferraro was chosen to be a vice-presidential candidate [in the 1984 election]. People laughed at me to begin with. They said it could never happen." However, like *Kane and Abel, The Prodigal Daughter* topped best-seller lists in Great Britain and the United States.

Archer established a precedent in *The Prodigal Daughter* by creating two versions of the story: one for his British audience and another for his American fans. For instance, he made changes in the novel to simplify the American political system. "The British, of course," he once explained, "find reading *The Prodigal Daughter* a fairly simple way of learning about the American system."

More sweeping changes are apparent in the two versions of Archer's *First among Equals,* which tells about the competition between four British candidates for the office of Prime Minister. One of the main characters in the British version of the book is almost totally absent in the American counterpart, and each version of the book has a different prologue and ending. "The Americans do seem interested," once commented. "They have a desire to learn about other countries. *First among Equals* is a very simple way of understanding our strange parliamentary system."

As the Crow Flies tells the story of Charlie Trumper, a man of working-class origins who serves in World War I and then rises to become the founder and head of a chain of department stores. Ken Gross, reviewing the book for *People,* praised Archer's choice of theme and his execution of it. The author "doesn't possess the prose skills of a Fitzgerald or the thundering moral outrage of Dostoevsky. But he tells a nice story." The reviewer concluded that the novel "is like a long, languid, comforting soak in a warm tub." Maggie Scarf, writing in the *New York Times Book Review* about the same book, made a similar comment: "If [Archer's] writing does appear somewhat naive at times . . . it nevertheless conveys the message that what is right will be rewarded and what is evil will inevitably be punished." "Jeffrey Archer may not be portraying the world as it is," she concluded, "but he is giving us an uncomplicated view of life that was deeply comfortable and gratifying. Archer's simpler world is, in many ways, far preferable to the one we inhabit."

In *Honor among Thieves,* published in England as *Honour among Thieves,* Archer tried his hand at the international spy-novel genre. The book's complicated plot focuses on Iraqi president Saddam Hussein's plan to steal the original Declaration of Independence and burn it on live television. Sent to foil Hussein's plot are a Yale University law professor Scott Bradley and model-turned-Mossad agent Hannah Kopec. Simon Louvish, in a review of *Honour among Thieves* for *New Statesman and Society,* asserted that the book "appears to have been written by a committee of ten year olds as an assignment" and accused Archer of maintaining some pulp magazine prejudices. "But who needs the muse," he concluded, "if the cash tills sing so well unaided?" On the other hand, Gene Lyons stated in *Entertainment Weekly* that in *Honor among Thieves,* Archer "has an undeniable flair for . . . ingeniously plotted, grandiose tales of derring-do." However, he also complained that the story is too formulaic. Archer, however, described his method of writing fiction. "I'm a storyteller," the author once said. "I never know what's going to be in the next line, the next paragraph, or the next page. And if I did, you would. If I don't know what's on the next page, how can you know?"

Archer's success in writing helped bring him back into politics. In 1985, Margaret Thatcher, prime minister of Great Britain and a reputed Archer fan (as well as a main character in *First among Equals*), appointed the author to the post of deputy chair of the Conservative party. A purely honorary job, the position nonetheless recognized Archer's devotion to the Conservatives and exploited his huge popularity and his fund-raising prowess.

Unfortunately by late 1986, Archer was embroiled in the first of a series of scandals that would shadow him through the remainder of the century and also put an end to his political career. Despite lawsuits, an arrest, and other unwelcomed notoriety, Archer also managed to publish several novels. His *The Fourth Estate* was praised by *Entertainment Weekly* reviewer Rhonda Johnson as a story that "turns raw male ambition into fast and furious fun," with the critic noting the close resemblance of the two leads to real-life moguls Rupert Murdoch and the late Robert Maxwell. With *The Eleventh Commandment* ("thou shalt not get caught"), Archer's tenth novel, CIA assassin Connor Fitzgerald kills a Colombian presidential candidate, sparking a chain of events that could lead to a new Cold War. The focus "is on global politics, with all the double-dealing and skullduggery inherent in that arena," as *Booklist* critic George Cohen noted. In following Fitzgerald through a complex maze of conspiracy, disguise, and danger, a *Kirkus Reviews* contributor dubbed the book "Archerland Deluxe." A reviewer for *Publishers Weekly,* while noting the book's "occasional giddiness," said, "From the first line . . . Archer . . . navigates a nonstop, rocketing ride." The reviewer added that Archer delivers a "slam-bang climax" in *The Eleventh Commandment.*

In 2000, Archer's short-story collection *To Cut a Long Story Short* was published. Several of these stories are based on actual events. A reviewer for *Publishers Weekly* called the work a "collection of fourteen cleverly twisting tales. . . . If most of the stories fail to produce a lasting effect, they are characteristically fluid and occasionally satisfying." Brad Hooper in *Booklist* called *To Cut a Long Story Short* "very successful," adding that in this collection the author's "expertise in [short-story writing] is displayed in compelling fashion."

In July of 2001, Archer was served with a four-year jail sentence after being convicted of perjury and perverting the course of justice during a libel trial he had initiated against a British newspaper. He served two years of that sentence before being released and has published three volumes of memoirs about the experience. The first, *A Prison Diary,* records the weeks he spent with forty-nine other prisoners in the "lifer's wing" in a high-security prison that houses some of Britain's most violent criminals. Locked in a cell for eighteen hours a day under unbearable conditions, he kept his sanity by writing prolifically in his diary. Reviewing the book for the *Houston Chronicle,* Elizabeth Bennett commented that "Archer's material can't be taken as gospel, of course." As a reviewer for *Publishers Weekly* pointed out, the author "is a convicted perjurer, and his second-hand stories come from the mouths of murderers and other felons." *Purgatory* and *Heaven* complete the period from his transfer from prison to jail and his eventual release on parole in July of 2003.

BIOGRAPHICAL AND CRITICAL SOURCES:

BOOKS

Contemporary Popular Writers, St. James Press (Detroit, MI), 1997.

PERIODICALS

Booklist, May 15, 1998, George Cohen, review of *The Eleventh Commandment,* p. 1563; November 15, 1998, Joe Collins, review of *The Collected Short Stories,* p. 565; November 15, 2000, Brad Hooper, review of *To Cut a Long Story Short,* p. 586.
Books, July-August, 1993, pp. 8-9.
Chicago Tribune, August 8, 1982; September 10, 1985; January 3, 1989; August 26, 1994, sec. 3, pp. 1, 4.
Entertainment Weekly, July 30, 1993, Gene Lyons, review of *Honor among Thieves,* p. 51; June 14, 1996, Rhonda Johnson, review of *The Fourth Estate,* p. 55.
Globe and Mail (Toronto, Ontario, Canada), September 13, 1986.
Guardian, July 11, 1993, p. 28.
Kirkus Reviews, June 15, 1994, pp. 786-787; May 1, 1998, review of *The Eleventh Commandment.*
Los Angeles Times, August 19, 1982; October 24, 1982; March 11, 1983; July 21, 1984; January 22, 1989.
Los Angeles Times Book Review, April 27, 1980.
New Statesman and Society, July 2, 1993, Simon Louvish, review of *Honour among Thieves,* p. 38; May 10, 1996, Jonathan Sale, review of *The Fourth Estate,* p. 39.
New York Times, August 30, 1984, Michiko Kakutani, review of *First among Equals,* p. 21; November 10, 1984, Jennifer Dunning, review of *First among Equals,* p. 15; October 10, 1985, Joseph Lelyveld, "Tory Plot: Can Life Copy Jeffrey Archer's Fiction?" p. 4; July 30, 1993.
New York Times Book Review, October 23, 1977; May 4, 1980; July 6, 1980; July 11, 1982; November 28, 1982; June 19, 1983; February 19, 1989, p. 23; June 9, 1991, p. 52; August 15, 1993, p. 18; July 7, 1996, p. 15.
New York Times Magazine, November 25, 1990, pp. 35, 75-78.
Observer, September 18, 1988, p. 43; June 9, 1991, p. 59; July 17, 1994, p. 18.

People, August 5, 1991, Ken Gross, review of *As the Crow Flies,* pp. 25-26.

Publishers Weekly, November 4, 1988, Sybil Steinberg, review of *A Twist in the Tale,* p. 72; April 26, 1991, Michele Field, interview, "Jeffrey Archer: The Events of His Life Rival the Circumstances of His Bestselling Novels," pp. 42-43; June 21, 1993, review of *Honor among Thieves,* pp. 86-87; June 20, 1994, review of *Twelve Red Herrings,* p. 96; May 4, 1998, review of *The Eleventh Commandment,* p. 203; October 12, 1998, review of *The Collected Short Stories,* p. 57; December 11, 2000, review of *To Cut a Long Story Short,* p. 65; June 16, 2003, review of *A Prison Diary,* p. 60; May 10, 2004, review of *Purgatory,* p. 44.

Quill and Quire, May, 1991, p. 29.

Spectator, July 10, 1993, p. 31; July 16, 1994, p. 28.

Time, July 28, 1986, John Skow, review of *Matter of Honor,* p. 64; November 10, 1986, Sara C. Medina, "More Scandalous than Fiction," p. 50; July 26, 1993, John Skow, review of *Honor among Thieves,* p. 72.

Times (London, England), October 27, 1986.

Times Literary Supplement, September 10, 1976; October 28, 1977; November 21, 1980; December 5, 1986; June 28, 1991, p. 18.

Tribune Books (Chicago, IL), April 27, 1980.

Washington Post, March 7, 1980; April 16, 1986; July 27, 1986; January 26, 1989.

Washington Post Book World, July 23, 1982; August 5, 1984.

ONLINE

Houston Chronicle.com, http://www.chron.com/ (September 19, 2003), Elizabeth Bennett, "Prison Offers New Material for Writer."

*   *   *

ARCHER, Jeffrey Howard
    See ARCHER, Jeffrey

*   *   *

ARCHER, Lee
    See ELLISON, Harlan

*   *   *

ARD, William
    See JAKES, John

ARENAS, Reinaldo 1943-1990

PERSONAL: Born July 16, 1943, in Holguin, Cuba; immigrated to the United States, 1980; died of an apparent overdose of drugs and alcohol, December 7, 1990, in New York, NY; son of Antonio and Oneida (Fuentes) Arenas. *Education:* Attended Universidad de la Habana, 1966-68, and Columbia University.

CAREER: Writer. Jose Marti National Library, Havana, Cuba, researcher, 1963-68; Instituto Cubano del Libro (Cuban Book Institute), Havana, Cuba, editor, 1967-68; *La Gaceta de Cuba* (official Cuban monthly literary magazine), Havana, Cuba, journalist and editor, 1968-74; imprisoned by the Castro government, c. 1974-76, served time in State Security Prison, 1974, El Murro (prison), Havana, Cuba, 1974, and Reparto Flores (rehabilitation camp), 1976; visiting professor of Cuban literature at International University of Florida, 1981, Center for Inter-American Relations, 1982, and Cornell University, 1985; guest lecturer at Princeton University, Georgetown University, Washington University (St. Louis, MO), Stockholms Universitet, Cornell University, and universities of Kansas, Miami, and Puerto Rico.

MEMBER: Center for Inter-American Relations.

AWARDS, HONORS: First mention in Cirilo Villaverde contest for best novel from the Cuban Writers' Union, 1965, for *Celestino antes del alba;* French Prix Medici, best foreign novel, 1969, for *Celestino antes del alba;* named best novelist published in France by *Le Monde,* 1969, for *El mundo alucinante;* fellow of the Cintas Foundation, 1980, John Simon Guggenheim Memorial Foundation, 1982, and Wilson Center Foundation, 1988.

WRITINGS:

Celestino antes del alba (novel), Union de Escritores, 1967, translation by Andrew Hurley published as *Singing from the Well,* Viking (New York, NY), 1987.

El mundo alucinante (novel), Diogenes, 1969, translation by Gordon Brotherston published as *Hallucinations: Being an Account of the Life and Adventures of Friar Servando Teresa de Mier,* Harper (New York, NY), 1971, new translation by Andrew Hurley published as *The Ill-Fated Peregrinations of Fray Servando,* Avon (New York, NY), 1987.

Con los ojos cerrados (short stories), Arca, 1972.

El palacio de las blanquisimas mofetas [France], 1975, translation by Andrew Hurley published as *Palace of the White Skunks,* Viking (New York, NY), 1990.

La vieja rosa (novel), Libreria Cruz del Sur, 1980, translation by Andrew Hurley, Grove (New York, NY), 1989.

Termina el desfile (short stories), Seix Barral, 1981.

El Central (poetry), Seix Barral, 1981, translation by Anthony Kerrigan published as *El Central: A Cuban Sugar Mill,* Avon (New York, NY), 1984.

Otra vez el mar (novel), Argos, 1982, translation by Andrew Hurley published as *Farewell to the Sea,* Viking (New York, NY), 1986, reprinted in Spanish, Tusquets Editores (Barcelona, Spain), 2002.

Arturo, la estrella mas brillante, Montesinos, 1984, translation published by Grove (New York, NY), 1989.

Necesida de libertad (essays), Kosmos, 1985.

Persecucion: Cinco piezas de teatro experimental (plays), Ediciones, 1986.

La loma del angel (novel), translation by Alfred MacAdam published as *Graveyard of the Angels,* Avon (New York, NY), 1987.

El portero (novel), Presses de la Renaissence, 1988, translation published as *The Doorman,* 1991.

El asalto (novel), 1990, translation by Andrew Hurley published as *The Assault,* Viking (New York, NY), 1994.

El color del verano (novel), Ediciones Universal, 1991, translation by Andrew Hurley published as *The Color of Summer; or, The New Garden of Earthly Delights,* Viking (New York, NY), 2000.

Antes que anochezca (autobiography), 1992, translation by Dolores Koch published as *Before Night Falls: A Memoir,* Viking (New York, NY), 1993.

Necesidad de libertad, Ediciones Universal (Miami, FL), 2001.

Inferno (complete poems), Editorial Lumen, Random House Mondadori (Barcelona, Spain), 2001.

Mona and Other Tales (short stories), selected and translated by Dolores M. Koch, Vintage Books (New York, NY), 2001.

Contributor of articles and short stories to numerous periodicals, including *El Universal* and *Miami Herald.* Editorial advisor to *Mariel Magazine, Noticias de arte, Unveiling Cuba, Caribbean Review,* and *Linden Lane Magazine.* Author's writings included in *Caliente!: The Best Erotic Writing in Latin American Fiction,* Penguin/Putnam, 2002. Works have been translated into various languages, including English, French, Dutch, German, Italian, Japanese, Portuguese, and Turkish.

Author's papers are housed in the Manuscripts Division, Department of Rare Books and Special Collections, at Princeton University.

ADAPTATIONS: Author's memoir *Before Night Falls* was adapted for film by Julian Schnabel, 2000.

SIDELIGHTS: Internationally acclaimed writer Reinaldo Arenas was one of more than 140,000 Cuban citizens who left their Latin American homeland for the United States in 1980 during a mass exodus known as the Mariel boat lift. Cuban president Fidel Castro exported to the Florida coast certain natives of Cuba, including common criminals, artists, members of the literati, and other perceived adversaries of the state, in an effort to squelch opposition to his Communist regime. In an interview with F.O. Geisbut for *Encounter,* Arenas explained that, as a writer and a homosexual, he was considered "an enemy of the revolution," guilty of a twofold crime against his country. The author was imprisoned by the Castro government, he further explained to Geisbut, for his alleged display of disrespect "for the rules of the official literature [and] of conventional morality." Arenas reached the U.S. mainland on May 5, 1980, with nothing but pajamas and a spare shirt. His manuscripts were confiscated by the Cuban government before he left the island.

As a teenager, Arenas had joined the resistance movement against the regime of Fulgencio Batista y Zaldivar, then president of Cuba. The author explained in the *Encounter* interview that the Cuban people wanted to topple Batista's totalitarian government and thus fought "against the tyrant in power rather than for Fidel Castro," the young revolutionary leader who had led an unsuccessful revolt against the president in 1953. By 1959 Batista had fled Cuba, and, within two years, Castro established a Communist state there, replacing the previous Batista dictatorship with his own brand of totalitarianism.

It was in an atmosphere of fierce social and political scrutiny that Arenas composed his first novel, *Celestino antes del alba,* in the mid-1960s. Translated in 1987 as *Singing from the Well,* the book is an evocation of the fantastic visions experienced by a mentally impaired boy growing up in Cuba's rural poverty. Illegitimate and raised in the turbulent environment created by his cruel grandparents, the child has trouble distinguishing fantasy from reality and imagines, among other things, that he can fly to the safety of the clouds when threatened by his axe-wielding grandfather. The boy finds consolation through his relationship with his cousin (or alter ego), a poet named Celestino who carves verses on trees. While several critics reported difficulty differentiating between dream sequences and periods of realism in the book, most regarded *Singing from the Well* as a novel of hope and an exceptional literary debut for Arenas. One *Times Literary Supplement* reviewer commented, "There is . . . a great deal of social significance in the child's pathetic longing for affection in so unsympathetic an environment." Commenting on his first novel in an interview with Ana Roca for *Americas,* Arenas referred to the story as "the revolt of a poet who wants to create in a completely violent medium."

Arenas's second novel, *El mundo alucinante,* also blends the fantastic with the real, this time in the form of a fictionalized biography. Translated in 1971 as *Hallucinations: Being an Account of the Life and Adventures of Friar Servando Teresa de Mier,* the book chronicles the life of nineteenth-century Mexican monk and adventurer, Fray Servando Teresa de Mier, who suffered torture and persecution in his fight for Mexico's independence from Spain. Imprisoned for suggesting that Mexico was a Christian country prior to the arrival of the Spanish, Servando is sentenced to a lifelong quarantine in Spain. He manages an unbelievable series of escapes from his captors, only to fight in an ultimately doomed revolution. "Servando's real crime," theorized Alan Schwartz in *Washington Post Book World,* "is his refusal to be demoralized in a world completely jaded and dedicated to the exploitation of power and wealth."

Arenas defended *Hallucinations* against claims by several critics that the surrealistic rendering of Servando's exploits should have more closely approximated the monk's actual adventures. "True realism," the author told Roca, "is fantasy, the fantastic, the eclectic. It knows no bounds." Arenas further maintained that the depiction of Servando he envisioned could only be accomplished by weaving historical fact with fantasy: "My aim was to portray this compelling personality as a part of the American myth, the New World myth . . . part raving madman and part sublime, a hero, an adventurer, and a perennial exile." Schwartz felt that any flaws in Arenas's "ambitious technique" were "overshadowed by [the author's] madcap inventiveness, the acid satire, and the powerful writing."

The antirevolutionary implications of *Hallucinations* led to the banning of the book in Cuba by the Castro government. "What emerges [from the novel]," asserted a *Times Literary Supplement* reviewer, "is at least as much a disenchanted view of Man himself as of revolution in the abstract." Servando finds that the movement for Mexican independence meets with only token victory. By the end of the book, the ghosts of the old regime greet the new revolutionary leaders with a haunt-

ing, "We welcome you." Arenas implies that, as in Cuba, the new regime in Mexico will only perpetuate an unjust order. Yet in spite of the apparent bleakness of its vision, the *Times Literary Supplement* reviewer allowed, "The narrative . . . is an accomplished and bizarrely entertaining piece of work."

The manuscript of Arenas's 1982 novel, *Otra vez el mar,* translated as *Farewell to the Sea,* was twice confiscated by the Cuban authorities. After being arrested in 1974 for his supposed social deviancy, the author spent time in a reeducation camp; following unsuccessful attempts to reconstruct the novel's plot while in jail, Arenas finally rewrote the book for the third time soon after reaching the United States in 1980. In the *Encounter* interview, Arenas described *Farewell to the Sea* as a depiction of "the secret history of the Cuban people."

Set on a beach resort just outside of Havana, the novel describes Cuba's tumultuous political events and the impact those events had on the nation's citizenry. Hector and his unnamed wife reflect on their lives, hopes, and disappointments since the fall of the Batista government. The first portion of the book is a lengthy interior monologue in which the woman expresses her feelings of emptiness and her desire for, as well as distance from, her husband. Speaking of life under Castro as well as life in a passionless marriage, she muses, "The terrible becomes merely monotonous." Hector's thoughts are documented in the second section through a long sequence of dreamlike poetry revealing his outrage over Cuba's failed revolution and his own homosexual longings. After engaging in a sexual encounter with a boy from a nearby beach cottage, Hector hurls seething invectives at his young lover: "You will live your whole life pleading, begging pardon of the whole world for a crime you haven't committed, and doesn't even exist. . . . You will be the world's shame." Hector's verbal abuse leads to the boy's suicide.

While several critics were disappointed by what Michael Wood, writing in the *New York Review of Books,* termed an overly "obsessive and . . . prolix" anticommunist demeanor in the book, virtually every critic acknowledged the power and beauty of Arenas's words. In an article for *Saturday Review,* Anthony DeCurtis called *Farewell to the Sea* "a stunning literary tour-de-force." And Jay Cantor stated in the *New York Times Book Review,* "Mr. Arenas is not interested in ordinary realistic drama. He wants to give the reader the secret history of . . . emotions, the sustaining victories of pleasure and the small dishonesties that callous the soul."

El color del verano—translated as *The Color of Summer; or, The New Garden of Earthly Delights*—is the phantasmagorical story of a Caribbean dictator celebrating fifty years in power by resurrecting his dead enemies so that they may pay homage to him before he kills them again. When he resurrects a famous woman poet, she refuses to participate in the pro-government farce and makes a run for the Florida coast. Told by a huge cast of real and imaginary characters, each of whom has multiple names, *The Color of Summer* is a "verbal whirlpool, spinning out stories, prayers, lists, tongue twisters, letters, taxonomies, lectures, vignettes, aphorisms, dreams, confessions, diatribes, and farces," as Lee Siegel wrote in the *New York Times Book Review*. In *Booklist,* Brad Hooper explained that "this character-rich novel wraps its social and political criticism in an absurdly hilarious skin." In addition to being a biting attack on the Cuban regime's authoritarianism, its imprisonment of gays, and its suppression of liberty, the novel is also, as Sophia McLennan noted in the *Review of Contemporary Fiction,* a novel of "emotional intensity. . . . Fantastic humor is combined artfully with a profound sense of sadness, loss, and suffering." Jack Shreve of *Library Journal* called the book "magnificent," and "hilarious and savagely sarcastic." "The book is a pained affirmation of the uncanny pleasure of maintaining hope when all is profoundly hopeless," concluded Siegel.

Having emerged from a totalitarian milieu that he describes in *Encounter* as one holding that "there's nothing more dangerous than new ideas," Arenas garnered worldwide attention and praise as an eminent writer who—in the tradition of fantastic Latin American fiction—depicts the reality of life in contemporary Cuba. Commenting in the Toronto *Globe and Mail* on the effect of the author's writings, Alberto Manguel observed, "Reinaldo Arenas' Cuba is a dreamworld of repeatedly frustrated passions." The critic further theorized that the writer's works have turned Castro into a "literary creation," rendering the dictator "immortal" and "condemn[ing him] to repeat [his] sins for an eternity of readers."

Arenas once commented, "Being an isolated child growing up on a farm very far from people and civilization and under very poor conditions was an important motivating factor in my becoming a writer. In my books I try to communicate my happiness and my unhappiness, my solitude and my hope.

"Since the publication of my novel *El mundo alucinante* in Mexico in 1969, all of my writings have been prohibited in Cuba. In spite of Marxist censorship, however, I managed to keep on writing and was able to send four other novels out of Cuba. Though many of my works have been published all over the world and translated into French, English, Dutch, German, Italian, Japanese, Portuguese, and Turkish, I have not been able to receive any royalties, because Cuba does not have a copyright law." At the time of his death, Arenas had several works under contract for publication, including the novel *Journey to Havana.*

Despite his death in 1990, Arenas's works continue to be published. In 2002, Editorial Lumen of Spain published a complete collection of his poems titled *Inferno.* In addition, the Spanish publisher Tusquets has begun republishing all of the author's works, some of which have been out of print for years. A collection of fourteen stories and one essay by Arenas was also published in 2001 under the title *Mona and Other Tales.* The stories which are available in English for the first time, range from tales of Cuban landmark events, such as Castro's revolutionary takeover of Cuba, to stories about children who, as described by Juliet Sarkessian in the *Gay & Lesbian Review Worldwide,* "struggle to survive in a world that always disappoints their hopes." Ulrich Baer, writing in *Library Journal,* commented, "Several pieces burst with his enormously brave and productive defiance of any form of thought control, be it political repression or aesthetic convention." *Review of Contemporary Fiction* contributor Mark Axelrod noted that Arenas's prose is distinguished by its "versatility" and concluded, "Even a cursory reading of Arenas would indicate that one is reading the work of someone totally in control of his material, whose prose, even in English, is as lyrical as he had planned and as subtle as he had envisioned."

BIOGRAPHICAL AND CRITICAL SOURCES:

BOOKS

Arenas, Reinaldo, *El mundo alucinante* (novel), Diogenes, 1969, translation by Gordon Brotherston published as *Hallucinations: Being an Account of the Life and Adventures of Friar Servando Teresa de Mier,* Harper (New York, NY), 1971, new translation by Andrew Hurley published as *The Ill-Fated Peregrinations of Fray Servando,* Avon (New York, NY), 1987.

Arenas, Reinaldo, *Otra vez el mar* (novel), Argos, 1982, translation by Andrew Hurley published as *Farewell to the Sea,* Viking (New York, NY), 1986.

Arenas, Reinaldo, *Arturo, la estrella mas brillante,* Montesinos, 1984, translation published by Grove (New York, NY), 1989.

Bejar, Edurdo, *La textualidad de Reinaldo Arenas*, [Madrid, Spain], 1988.

Contemporary Literary Criticism, Volume 41, Thomson Gale (Detroit, MI), 1987.

Nazario, Felix Lugo, *La alucinacion y los recursos literarios en las novelas de Reinaldo Arenas*, Ediciones Universal Libreria & Dist., 1995.

Paulson, Michael G., *The Youth and the Beach: A Comparative Study of Thomas Mann's Der Tod in Venedig (Death in Venice) and Reinaldo Arenas's Otra vez el mar (Farewell to the Sea)*, Ediciones Universal (Miami, FL), 1993.

Rozencvaig, Perla, *The Work of Reinaldo Arenas*, [Mexico], 1986.

Soto, Francisco, *Reinaldo Arenas: The Pentaonia*, University Press of Florida, 1994.

Soto, Francisco, *Reinaldo Arenas*, Twayne (Boston, MA), 1998.

PERIODICALS

Americas, September, 1981; January-February, 1982.

Booklist, June 1, 2000, Brad Hooper, review of *The Color of Summer; or, The New Garden of Earthly Delights*, p. 1807.

Chicago Tribune, January 26, 1986.

Chicago Tribune Book World, September 5, 1971.

Encounter, January, 1982, F.O. Geisbut, interview with Reinaldo Arenas.

Gay & Lesbian Review Worldwide, January-February, 2002, Juliet Sarkessian, review of *Mona and Other Tales*, p. 38.

Globe and Mail (Toronto, Ontario, Canada), June 21, 1986.

Hispanic Review 53, autumn, 1985.

Library Journal, July, 2000, Jack Shreve, review of *The Color of Summer*, p. 136; June 1, 2001, Marcela Valdes, review of *The Palace of the Whitest Skunk*, p. S59; October 1, 2001, Ulrich Baer, review of *Mona and Other Tales*, p. 144.

Listener, April 22, 1971.

New York Review of Books, March 27, 1986, Michael Wood, review of *Farewell to the Sea;* March 7, 1991; November 18, 1993.

New York Times Book Review, August 29, 1971; November 24, 1985, Jay Cantor, review of *Farewell to the Sea;* January 20, 1991; October 24, 1993; October 15, 2000, Lee Siegel, "A Disappearing Novel."

Publishers Weekly, May 22, 2000, review of *The Color of Summer*, p. 72.

Review of Contemporary Fiction, spring, 2001, Sophia McLennan, review of *The Color of Summer*, p. 186; summer, 2002, Mark Axelrod, review of *Mona and Other Tales*, p. 239.

San Francisco Review of Books, May-June, 1985.

Saturday Review, November-December, 1985, Anthony DeCurtis, review of *Farewell to the Sea*.

School Library Journal, April, 2002, Rafael Ocasio, review of *Inferno*, p. S48.

Times Literary Supplement, April 30, 1970; May 7, 1971; May 30, 1986, review of *Singing from the Well*.

Washington Post Book World, September 5, 1971, Alan Schwartz, review of *Hallucinations: Being an Account of the Life and Adventures of Friar Servando Teresa de Mier.*

*   *   *

ARIAS, Ron 1941-
(Ronald Francis Arias)

PERSONAL: Born November 30, 1941, Los Angeles, CA; son of Armando (an army officer) and Emma Lou (a homemaker; maiden name, Estrada) Arias; married Joan Londerman (a business executive), April 1, 1966; children: Michael. *Education:* Attended Oceanside-Carlsbad College (now Mira Costa College), 1959-60, University of Barcelona (Spain), 1960, University of California—Berkeley, 1960-61, and National University (Buenos Aires, Argentina), 1962; University of California—Los Angeles, B.A., 1967, M.A., 1968. *Politics:* Independent

ADDRESSES: Office—People Magazine, Time and Life Building, Rockefeller Center, New York, NY 10020. *Agent*—Reid Boates, P.O. Box 328, 274 Cooks Cr., Pittstown, NJ 08867.

CAREER: Buenos Aires Herald, Buenos Aires, Argentina, reporter, 1962; community development volunteer with Peace Corps in Cuzco, Peru, 1963-64; writer for Copley Newspapers and for national and international wire services, 1960s; *Caracas Daily Journal*, Caracas, Venezuela, reporter, 1968-69; Inter-American Development Bank, Washington, DC, editor for agency publications, 1969-71; San Bernardino Valley College, San Bernardino, CA, instructor, 1971-80, associate professor of English, until 1985; Crafton Hills College, Yucaipa, CA, instructor in English and journalism, 1980-84; *People* magazine, New York, NY, senior writer, 1986—. Member of the board of directors of the National Endowment for the Arts coordinating council of literary magazines, 1979-80.

AWARDS, HONORS: Scholarship to study journalism in Buenos Aires, Argentina, from Inter-American Press Association, 1962; Machris Award for journalistic excellence from Los Angeles Press Club, 1968; writer's fellowship from California Arts Commission, 1973; Chicano Literary Contest first place award in fiction from University of California—Irvine, 1975, for short story "The Wetback"; Modern Language Association fellowship, 1975; National Book Award nomination for fiction, 1976, for *The Road to Tamazunchale;* Latino Literary Hall of Fame Award for biography, 2003, for *Moving Target.*

WRITINGS:

The Road to Tamazunchale (novel), West Coast Poetry Review, 1975.
Five against the Sea (nonfiction), New American Library, 1989, revised, Bristol Fashion Publications (Harrisburg, PA), 2002.
(With Mehmet Oz and Lisa Oz) *Healing from the Heart: A Leading Heart Surgeon Explores the Cutting Edge of Alternative Medicine,* Dutton (New York, NY), 1998.
(With Mehmet Oz and Lisa Oz) *Healing from the Heart: A Leading Surgeon Combines Eastern and Western Traditions to Create the Medicine of the Future,* Dutton (New York, NY), 1999.
Moving Target: A Memoir of Pursuit, Bilingual Press (Tempe, AZ), 2003.

Also author of short stories; author of play *The Interview,* adapted from the author's short story, 1979; author of screenplays, including *Jesus and the Three Wise Guys;* author of television scripts.

Work represented in anthologies, including *The Chicanos: Mexican-American Voices,* edited by Ed Ludwig and James Santibanez, Penguin Books, 1971; *First Chicano Literary Contest Winners,* edited by Juan Villegas, Spanish and Portuguese Department, University of California, 1975; and *Cuentos Chicanos: A Short Story Anthology,* edited by Rudolfo A. Anaya and Antonio Marquez, revised edition, University of New Mexico Press, 1984. Contributor to periodicals, including the *New York Times, Quarry West, Bilingual Review/Revista Bilingue, Latin American Literary Review, Journal of Ethnic Studies, Revista Chicano-Riqueña, Nuestro, Christian Science Monitor, Nation,* and *Los Angeles Times.*

Arias' works have been translated into Spanish.

WORK IN PROGRESS: Researching Latin America and third-world situations and themes.

SIDELIGHTS: Ron Arias is a journalist and short-story writer whose widely acclaimed debut novel, *The Road to Tamazunchale,* distinguished him as a leading Chicano writer of "magic realism," a literary form popularized by Gabriel García Márquez that blends reality with fantasy. His memoir *Moving Target,* which chronicles Arias's long search for his father, received the 2003 Latino Literary Hall of Fame Award for biography.

Arias is best known for his novel *The Road to Tamazunchale.* Influenced by García Márquez's *One Hundred Years of Solitude,* Arias related to Juan Bruce-Novoa in *Chicano Authors: Inquiry by Interview* the novel's effect on him: "For me, García-Márquez transformed, *deepened* reality in so many of its aspects—tragic, humorous, adventurous, wondrous. The work was alive, entertaining at every word. There was nothing sloppy, facile, overly clever, belabored, preachy—all the things I detest in literature." Arias's own style of magic realism is a mixture of precise, journalistic descriptions and stream-of-consciousness writing, which often centers on magical figures who can manipulate reality. Bruce-Novoa contended that even more important than Arias's stylistic affinities with magic realism are his achievements as "a skilled, patient craftsman, with a healthy sense of irony about himself and the world. . . . [H]e shares the current—we could say modern—sense of literature as one enormous text, interrelated and consciously self-referential."

The Road to Tamazunchale, which was nominated for a National Book Award, is about the final days of a retired encyclopedia salesman named Fausto Tejada. In order to understand and accept his impending death, Fausto makes an imaginative journey to Tamazunchale, a Mexican village that in the book symbolizes the final resting place after death. The story opens with an ailing and despondent Fausto peeling off his skin; not until his niece Carmela enters the room does the reader learn that Fausto has actually been playing with a wad of Kleenex. Still, the incident functions as the first in a series of events in which the boundaries between reality and illusion, past and present, and life and death are clouded: Fausto travels to sixteenth-century Lima; he helps an Inca shepherd move his flock off the Los Angeles freeway; he leads hundreds of men across the Mexican-American border; he finds himself in a play called "The Road to Tamazunchale"; and, finally, he joins friends and neighbors on a cosmic picnic where he is reunited with his deceased wife. The events culminate with Fausto accepting his inevitable demise, though exactly when this occurs is ambiguous. As quoted in *Chicano Literature: A Reference Guide,* Vernon Lattin explained in *American Literature* that even after Fausto apparently dies, "the novel continues for one more chapter without suggestions of distortion or logical violation. Fausto and his friends continue as in the past: there is no funeral or burial; the logic of the world and the dichotomy of life and death have been transcended, and the road to Tamazunchale has become a sacred way for Everyman to follow."

The Road to Tamazunchale earned favorable reviews. In the *School Library Journal,* reviewer Dolores M. Koch called the book "A profoundly human novel that deals creatively with death." Calling Arias's novel "skillful and imaginative," *Los Angeles Times Book Review* contributor Alejandro Morales defended the book's status as a Chicano classic because of its "magical realistic imagination, its precise crisp prose, its relationship to the 'new reality' of Spanish American fiction and its compassionate treatment of death, its central theme." Morales concluded that Arias offers "a new social reality and a new vision of the American literary mosaic in which [he himself] must now be recognized." Eliud Martinez lauded Arias in the *Latin American Literary Review* for examining universal themes and capturing distinctly Chicano speech patterns. Moreover, Martinez asserted, "no Chicano novel before *Tamazunchale* has tapped the artistic resources of the modern and contemporary novel (and the arts) in a comparable way, deliberately and intuitively."

Arias himself once commented: "My Mexican family heritage and continuing travel abroad, especially in Latin-American countries for magazine story assignments, are strong inspirations for my writing. My work in the Peace Corps with the Andean poor also gave me an abiding insight into the world of basic survival, which is the theme of my own favorite writing projects." He has explored his own heritage in the book *Moving Target,* a memoir that recounts his fourteen-year-long search for his father—the "moving target" referred to in the title—who was known to be a prisoner of war during World War II and the Korean War.

BIOGRAPHICAL AND CRITICAL SOURCES:

BOOKS

Bruce-Novoa, Juan, *Chicano Authors: Inquiry by Interview,* University of Texas Press (Austin, TX), 1980.

Dictionary of Literary Biography, Volume 82, *Chicano Writers, First Series,* Thomson Gale (Detroit, MI), 1989.

Martinez, Julio A., and Francisco A. Lomeli, editors, *Chicano Literature: A Reference Guide,* Greenwood Press (Westport, CT), 1985.

Von Bardeleban, Renate, Dietrich Briesemeister, and Juan Bruce-Novoa, editors, *Missions in Conflict: Essays on U.S.-Mexican Relations and Chicano Culture,* Günter Narr Verlag (Tübingen, Germany), 1986.

PERIODICALS

American Literature, number 50, 1979.

Americas Review, fall-winter, 1994, Andrea O'Reilly Herrera, review of *The Road to Tamazunchale,* p. 114.

Latin American Literary Review, number 4, 1976; number 5, 1977.

Library Journal, October 1, 1998, Charles Wessel, review of *Healing from the Heart,* p. 125.

Los Angeles Times Book Review, April 12, 1987.

New Mexico Humanities Review, Volume 3, number 1, 1980.

Revista Chicano-Riqueña, Volume 5, number 4, 1977; Volume 10, number 3, 1982.

School Library Journal, June, 2003, Dolores M. Koch, review of *The Road to Tamazunchale,* p. 35.

*   *   *

**ARIAS, Ronald Francis
    See ARIAS, Ron**

*   *   *

**ARNETTE, Robert
    See SILVERBERG, Robert**

*   *   *

ARONSON, Marc 1948-

PERSONAL: Born 1948; married Marina Budhos (an author); children: two sons. *Education:* Earned a Ph.D. in American history.

ADDRESSES: Home—New York, NY. *Agent*—c/o Author Mail, Clarion Books, 215 Park Ave., New York, NY 10020. *E-mail*—marc@marcaronson.com.

CAREER: Writer and editor. Editor of books for children and young adults; Harper & Row, New York, NY, and later, Henry Holt Books for Young Readers, New

York, NY, became senior editor; Carus Publishing, Chicago, IL, editorial director and vice president of nonfiction development, 2000-04; *Zooba.com,* managing editor, 2001-02; acquisition editor for Candlewick Press and for other publishing houses; writer. Instructor in publishing courses at New York University, Simmons College, and Radcliffe Publishing program.

AWARDS, HONORS: Publishers Weekly Best Book of the Year and *New York Times* Notable Book citations, both 1998, both for *Art Attack: A Short Cultural History of the Avant-Garde; Boston Globe-Horn Book* Award for nonfiction, 2000, Blue Ribbon Award, *Bulletin of the Center for Children's Books,* 2000, and Robert F. Sibert Award for "most distinguished informational book for children," American Library Association, 2001, all for *Sir Walter Ralegh and the Quest for El Dorado.*

WRITINGS:

NONFICTION

(With Thomas Leonard and Cynthia Crippen) *Day by Day: The Seventies,* two volumes, Facts on File (New York, NY), 1988.
(With Ellen Meltzer) *Day by Day: The Eighties,* two volumes, Facts on File (New York, NY), 1995.
Art Attack: A Short Cultural History of the Avant-Garde, Clarion Books (New York, NY), 1998.
Exploding the Myths: The Truth about Teenagers and Reading, Scarecrow Press (Lanham, MD), 2000.
Sir Walter Ralegh and the Quest for El Dorado, Clarion Books (New York, NY), 2000.
(Editor, with Michael Cart and Marianne Carus) *911: The Book of Help,* Cricket Books (Chicago, IL), 2002.
Beyond the Pale: New Essays for a New Era, Scarecrow Press (Lanham, MD), 2003.
Witch-Hunt: Mysteries of the Salem Witch Trials, Atheneum (New York, NY), 2003.
John Winthrop, Oliver Cromwell, and the Land of Promise, Clarion Books (New York, NY), 2004.
The Real Revolution: The Global Story of American Independence, Clarion Books (New York, NY), 2005.

Contributor to *The Holocaust in Literature for Youth,* edited by Edward T. Sullivan, Scarecrow Press (Lanham, MD), 1999. Contributor to periodicals, including *New York Times Book Review* and *Los Angeles Times Book Review.*

WORK IN PROGRESS: Prejudice: A History, for Atheneum, publication expected in 2006.

SIDELIGHTS: Marc Aronson writes nonfiction titles for young adults that have been praised for the author's engrossing prose style and unique approach to source materials. For example, in *Art Attack: A Short Cultural History of the Avant-Garde,* Aronson explains that throughout history avant-garde artists have challenged the world with their personal visions, and that young artists, even adolescents, have often taken the greatest risks to bring their art to the public. "What an exciting invitation to a brisk but rigorous survey that connects Marcel Duchamp, the Russian avant-garde and Mondrian to Charles Ives and the Sex Pistols!" observed a reviewer in the *New York Times Book Review.* Indeed, it is through such cross-cultural and cross-generic connections that *Art Attack* manages to offer fresh insights into the history of twentieth-century art despite its brevity, according to reviewers. Throughout the volume, art movements and the work of individual artists are explored in conjunction with the evolution of twentieth-century music. "In fact, what is unique and appealing in Aronson's cultural history is his placing of experimental and popular music within the art world," remarked Shirley Wilton in *School Library Journal.* Thus, Aronson juxtaposes the artwork of the Dadaists and rap music, Jean-Michel Basquiat's expressive scribbles and the jazz innovations of Philip Glass. The result is "an exceptional resource," Wilton concluded.

Aronson turned to the more distant past in *Sir Walter Ralegh and the Quest for El Dorado,* a work for which he was named the first winner of the Robert F. Sibert Award for the "most distinguished informational book for children published in 2000." Ralegh (as the man himself rendered his name) was both an exceptional figure, in his talents, ambition, and willingness to take large risks, and representative of his times, in that his talents, ambition, and willingness to take risks were all pointed towards exploring and conquering the New World. Ralegh's intelligence and drive took him from rural obscurity to courtier in Queen Elizabeth's court to fame and fortune through his journeys to South America. The resulting story of his life is an exciting tale. "Aronson not only details Ralegh's career as soldier, sailor, explorer, writer, and schemer but consistently discusses causes, effects, and the broader significance of events large and small," commented a reviewer for *Kirkus Reviews.* Aronson's skills as a writer of histories for young people were extolled by reviewers. Ilene Cooper, writing in *Booklist,* noted that at just over 200 pages, there is not space enough to discuss every topic presented by the multifaceted life of Sir Walter

Ralegh, but added that "the book is beautifully researched, and it is written with wit and passion." A reviewer for the *Los Angeles Times* praised Aronson's portrait of Ralegh as "both provocative and tantalizing, revealing his subject as a person of canny wit and magnetism with all-too-human shortcomings." In conclusion, Cooper dubbed *Sir Walter Ralegh and the Quest for El Dorado* "sweeping, multilayered nonfiction."

Aronson's experience as a publisher, editor, and critic comes to the fore in *Exploding the Myths: The Truth about Teens and Reading,* a collection of his speeches and articles that touches on the development of young adult literature as well as its major controversies. In a review for *Booklist,* Hazel Rochman found the author's style "clear, chatty, and tough" while pointing out that Aronson "shows that teenagers today are often more open to challenge and diversity in narrative and format than their adult guardians are." *School Library Journal* contributor Vicki Reutter called *Exploding the Myths* a "thought-provoking collection [that] should be not missed." A related work, *Beyond the Pale: New Essays for a New Era,* "reveals the wider context of Aronson's particular concerns as a publisher, writer, and reader of young adult literature," wrote Cathryn M. Mercier in *Horn Book. Beyond the Pale* contains fourteen essays covering such topics as multicultural book prizes and the challenges of reaching teenage male readers. "This excellent book should be required reading for anyone who cares about young adults and their literature," stated Ellen A. Greever in *School Library Journal.*

In 2002 Aronson coedited *911: The Book of Help,* a "highly personal, often affecting roundup of essays, short stories, and poems inspired by the events of September 11th," according to a reviewer in *Publishers Weekly.* The contributors to *911* include award-winning children's and young adult authors such as Katherine Paterson, Walter Dean Myers, Sharon Creech, Naomi Shihab Nye, Margaret Mahy, Russell Freedman, and Marion Dane Bauer. "Some of the best essays put the attacks in historical or autobiographical perspective," Roger Sutton noted in *Horn Book.* Claire Rosser, reviewing the work in *Kliatt,* felt that *911* "would be an excellent resource for teachers of writing, helping students realize the power of words to educate, inspire, to express deepest feelings."

In *Witch-Hunt: Mysteries of the Salem Witch Trials,* Aronson examines the events surrounding the infamous series of trials in Massachusetts in 1692. In *Witch-Hunt,* Aronson dispels misinformation about the trials, and he looks at the contentious social, economic, and religious issues facing the Salem community. According to Andrew Medlar in *School Library Journal,* the author "actively encourages the rethinking of past notions of the events leading up to the accusations and hearings." A *Publishers Weekly* contributor stated that Aronson "uses primary source documents and trial records to help tease out the facts of the highly charged court atmosphere," and *Booklist* critic Stephanie Zvirin remarked that the author produces "a dense, wide-angle view of the tragedy that evaluates causative theories ranging from deceit and outright fraud to spoiled food that caused hallucinations." Aronson also draws parallels to the "counterculture of the 1960s, modern terrorism, and current tensions between western countries and Islamic fundamentalists," a *Kirkus Reviews* critic noted.

The 2004 work *John Winthrop, Oliver Cromwell, and the Land of Promise* "charts a parallel history between seventeenth-century Great Britain and colonial New England, as represented by emblematic figures Oliver Cromwell and John Winthrop," wrote *Horn Book* reviewer Peter D. Sieruta. Both Cromwell and Winthrop were influential Puritan leaders: Cromwell deposed King Charles I of England, and Winthrop served as the first governor of the Massachusetts Bay Colony. In the work, "Aronson shows how events of the 1630s and '40s have affected political thought ever since," noted a *Kirkus Reviews* critic. According to *Booklist* contributor GraceAnne A. DeCandido, Aronson illuminates "the reality of religious faith and the cataclysmic clash of beliefs that created fertile ground for ideas about democracy and equality."

BIOGRAPHICAL AND CRITICAL SOURCES:

PERIODICALS

Booklist, July, 1998, Stephanie Zvirin, review of *Art Attack: A Short Cultural History of the Avant-Garde;* August, 2000, Ilene Cooper, review of *Sir Walter Ralegh and the Quest for El Dorado,* p. 2130; March 15, 2001, Hazel Rochman, review of *Exploding the Myths: The Truth about Teenagers and Reading,* p. 1406; November 1, 2003, Stephanie Zvirin, review of *Witch-Hunt: Mysteries of the Salem Witch Trials,* p. 488; June 1, 2004, GraceAnne A. DeCandido, review of *John Winthrop, Oliver Cromwell, and the Land of Promise,* p. 1751.

Horn Book, September-October, 2000, Peter D. Sieruta, review of *Sir Walter Ralegh and the Quest for El Dorado,* p. 593; September-October, 2002, Roger Sutton, review of *911: The Book of Help,* pp. 593-

594; January-February, 2004, Cathryn M. Mercier, review of *Beyond the Pale: New Essays for a New Era*, pp. 107-108; July-August, 2004, Peter D. Sieruta, review of *John Winthrop, Oliver Cromwell, and the Land of Promise*, p. 465.

Kirkus Reviews, May 15, 2000, review of *Sir Walter Ralegh and the Quest for El Dorado*, p. 710; July 1, 2002, review of *911*, p. 950; October 15, 2003, review of *Witch-Hunt*, p. 1268; May 1, 2004, review of *John Winthrop, Oliver Cromwell, and the Land of Promise*, p. 437.

Kliatt, November, 2002, Claire Rosser, review of *911*, p. 29.

Los Angeles Times, October 22, 2000, review of *Sir Walter Ralegh and the Quest for El Dorado*, p. 6.

New York Times Book Review, February 14, 1999, review of *Art Attack*, p. 26.

Publishers Weekly, August 27, 2001, Jason Britton, "Marcato/Cricket Books," p. 23; July 29, 2002, review of *911*, p. 74; December 1, 2003, review of *Witch-Hunt*, p. 58; May 24, 2004, "Understanding History," p. 64.

Reading Teacher, March, 2003, review of *911*, p. 589.

School Library Journal, June, 1995, Linda Diane Townsend, review of *Day by Day: The Eighties*, pp. 144-145; July, 1998, Shirley Wilton, review of *Art Attack*, p. 102; December, 2000, review of *Sir Walter Ralegh and the Quest for El Dorado*, p. 52; May, 2001, Vicki Reutter, review of *Exploding the Myths*, p. 179; September, 2002, Wendy Lukehart, "One Year Later," pp. 44-46, and Joanne K. Cecere, review of *911*, pp. 241-242; November, 2003, Ellen A. Greever, review of *Beyond the Pale*, p. 175; December, 2003, Andrew Medlar, review of *Witch-Hunt*, pp. 163; April, 2004, Wendy Lukehart, review of *Art Attack*, p. 64.

ONLINE

Marc Aronson Web site, http://www.marcaronson.com/ (August 19, 2004).

*   *   *

ARRLEY, Richmond
    See DeLANY, Samuel R.

*   *   *

ASHBERY, John 1927-
(John Lawrence Ashbery, Jonas Berry)

PERSONAL: Born July 28, 1927, in Rochester, NY; son of Chester Frederick (a farmer) and Helen (a biology teacher) Ashbery. *Education:* Harvard University, B.A.,

1949; Columbia University, M.A., 1951; graduate study at New York University, 1957-58.

ADDRESSES: Office—Department of Languages and Literature, Bard College, P.O. Box 5000, Annandale-on-Hudson, NY 12504-5000. *Agent*—Georges Borchardt, Inc., 136 East 57th St., New York, NY 10022.

CAREER: Writer, critic, and editor. Worked as reference librarian for Brooklyn Public Library, Brooklyn, NY; Oxford University Press, New York, NY, copywriter, 1951-54; McGraw-Hill Book Co., New York, NY, copywriter, 1954-55; New York University, New York, NY, instructor in elementary French, 1957-58; *Locus Solus,* Lans-en-Vercors, France, editor, 1960-62; *New York Herald-Tribune,* European edition, Paris, France, art critic, 1960-65; *Art International,* Lugano, Switzerland, art critic, 1961-64; *Art and Literature,* Paris, editor, 1963-66; *Art News,* New York, NY, Paris correspondent, 1964-65, executive editor in New York, NY, 1965-72; *New York Magazine,* art critic, 1975-80; *Partisan Review,* poetry editor, 1976-80; *Newsweek,* art critic, 1980-85. Brooklyn College of the City University of New York, Brooklyn, professor of English and codirector of M.F.A. program in creative writing, 1974-90, distinguished professor, 1980-90, distinguished emeritus professor, 1990; Harvard University Charles Eliot Norton Professor of Poetry, 1989-90; Bard College, Charles P. Stevenson, Jr. Professor of Languages and Literature, 1990—. Has read his poetry at the Living Theatre, New York, NY, and at numerous universities, including Yale University, University of Chicago, and University of Texas.

MEMBER: American Academy and Institute of Arts and Letters, American Academy of Arts and Sciences, Academy of American Poets (chancellor, 1988-99).

AWARDS, HONORS: Discovery Prize co-winner, Young Men's Hebrew Association, 1952; Fulbright scholarships to France, 1955-56 and 1956-57; Yale Series of Younger Poets Prize, 1956, for *Some Trees;* Poets' Foundation grants, 1960 and 1964; Ingram-Merrill Foundation grants, 1962 and 1972; Harriet Monroe Poetry Award, *Poetry,* 1963; Union League Civic and Arts Foundation Prize, *Poetry,* 1966; National Book Award nomination, 1966, for *Rivers and Mountains;* Guggenheim fellowships, 1967 and 1973; National Endowment for the Arts grants, 1968 and 1969; National Institute of Arts and Letters Award, 1969; Shelley Memorial Award, Poetry Society of America, 1973, for *Three Poems;* Frank O'Hara Prize, Modern Poetry Association,

1974; Harriet Monroe Poetry Award, University of Chicago, 1975; Pulitzer Prize, National Book Award, and National Book Critics Circle Award, all 1976, all for *Self-Portrait in a Convex Mirror;* Levinson Prize, *Poetry,* 1977; Rockefeller Foundation grant in playwriting, 1978; D.Litt., Southampton College of Long Island University, 1979; Phi Beta Kappa Poet, Harvard University, 1979; English-Speaking Union Poetry Award, 1979; American Book Award nomination, 1982, for *Shadow Train;* Academy of American Poets fellowship, 1982; Mayor's Award of Honor for Arts and Culture, City of New York, 1983; Charles Flint Kellogg Award in Arts and Letters, Bard College, 1983; National Book Critics Circle award nomination, and *Los Angeles Times* Book Award nomination, both 1984, both for *A Wave;* named Poet of the Year, Pasadena City College, 1984; Bollingen Prize (corecipient), 1985, for body of work; Wallace Stevens fellowship, Yale University, 1985; MacArthur Foundation fellowship, 1985-90; *Los Angeles Times* Book Award nomination, 1986, for *Selected Poems;* Common Wealth Award, Modern Language Association of America, 1986; Lenore Marshall award, *Nation,* 1986, for *A Wave;* Creative Arts Award in Poetry, Brandeis University, 1989; Ruth Lilly Poetry Prize, *Poetry,* 1992; Robert Frost Medal, Poetry Society of America, 1995; Grand Prix, Biennales Internationales de Poesie, 1996; Gold Medal for Poetry, American Academy of Arts and Letters, 1997; Walt Whitman citation of merit, New York State Writers Institute; Signet Society Medal for Achievement in the Arts, Harvard University, 2001; named New York State poet, 2001-02; Wallace Stevens Award, 2002.

WRITINGS:

Turandot and Other Poems (chapbook), Tibor de Nagy Gallery, 1953.
Some Trees (poems), foreword by W.H. Auden, Yale University Press (New Haven, CT), 1956, Ecco Press (Hopewell, NJ), 1978.
The Poems, Tiber Press (New York, NY), 1960.
The Tennis Court Oath (poems), Wesleyan University Press (Middletown, CT), 1962.
Rivers and Mountains (poems), Holt (New York, NY), 1966.
Selected Poems, J. Cape (London, England), 1967.
Sunrise in Suburbia, Phoenix Bookshop (New York, NY), 1968.
Three Madrigals, Poet's Press, 1969.
(With James Schuyler) *A Nest of Ninnies* (novel), Dutton (New York, NY), 1969.
Fragment (poem; also see below), Black Sparrow Press (Santa Barbara, CA), 1969.

Evening in the Country, Spanish Main Press, 1970.
The Double Dream of Spring (includes "Fragment," originally published in book form), Dutton (New York, NY), 1970.
The New Spirit, Adventures in Poetry, 1970.
(With Lee Hawood and Tom Raworth) *Penguin Modern Poets 19,* Penguin (New York, NY), 1971.
Three Poems, Viking (New York, NY), 1972.
The Serious Doll, privately printed, 1975.
(With Joe Brainard) *The Vermont Notebook* (poems), Black Sparrow Press (Santa Barbara, CA), 1975, reprinted, Granary Books (Calais, VT), 2001.
Self-Portrait in a Convex Mirror (poems), Viking (New York, NY), 1975.
Houseboat Days (poems), Viking (New York, NY), 1977, reprinted, Farrar, Straus (New York, NY), 1999.
As We Know (poems), Viking (New York, NY), 1979.
Shadow Train: Fifty Lyrics, Viking (New York, NY), 1981.
(With others) *R.B. Kitaj: Paintings, Drawings, Pastels,* Smithsonian Institution (Washington, DC), 1981.
(With others) *Apparitions* (poems), Lord John Press (Northridge, CA), 1981.
Fairfield Porter: Realist Painter in an Age of Abstraction, New York Graphic Society (New York, NY), 1983.
A Wave (poems), Viking (New York, NY), 1984.
Selected Poems, Viking (New York, NY), 1985.
April Galleons, Penguin (New York, NY), 1987.
The Ice Storm, Hanuman Books, 1987.
Reported Sightings: Art Chronicles, 1957-1987 (art criticism), edited by David Bergman, Knopf (New York, NY), 1989.
Three Poems (different text than 1972 volume with same title), Ecco Press (New York, NY), 1989.
Haibun, illustrations by Judith Shea, Collectif Génération (Colombes, France), 1990.
Flow Chart (poem), Knopf (New York, NY), 1991.
Hotel Lautreamont, Knopf (New York, NY), 1992.
Three Books (poems), Penguin (New York, NY), 1993.
And the Stars Were Shining, Farrar, Straus (New York, NY), 1994.
Can You Hear, Bird, Farrar, Straus (New York, NY), 1995.
Pistils (essays), photographs by Robert Mapplethorpe, Random House (New York, NY), 1996.
Wakefulness, Farrar, Straus (New York, NY), 1998.
The Mooring of Starting Out: The First Five Books of Poetry, Ecco Press (Hopewell, NJ), 1998.
Girls on the Run, Farrar, Straus (New York, NY), 1999.
Other Traditions: The Charles Eliot Norton Lectures, Harvard University Press (Cambridge, MA), 2000.

Your Name Here: Poems, Farrar, Straus (New York, NY), 2000.

As Umbrellas Follow Rain, Qua Books (Lennox, MA), 2001.

Chinese Whispers: Poems, Farrar, Straus (New York, NY), 2002.

Where Shall I Wander?, HarperCollins (New York, NY), 2005.

Selected Prose , edited by Eugene Richie, University of Michigan Press (Ann Arbor, MI), 2005.

Works have been anthologized in *New American Poetry, 1945-1960,* Grove (New York, NY), 1960; *A Controversy of Poets,* edited by Paris Leary and Robert Kelly, Doubleday/Anchor (New York, NY), 1964; *L'Avant-Garde aujourd'hui,* [Brussels, Belgium], 1965; *Anthology of New York Poets,* Random House (New York, NY), 1969; *The Voice That Is Great within Us: American Poetry of the Twentieth Century,* Bantam (New York, NY), 1970; *Contemporary American Poetry,* Houghton Mifflin (Boston, MA), 1971; *Fifty Modern American and British Poets, 1920-1970,* edited by Louis Untermeyer, McKay (New York, NY), 1973; and *Shake the Kaleidoscope: A New Anthology of Modern Poetry,* Simon & Schuster (New York, NY), 1973.

Contributor of poetry to periodicals, including *New York Review of Books, Partisan Review, Harper's,* and *New Yorker;* contributor of art criticism to periodicals, including *Art International* and *Aujourd'hui;* contributor of literary criticism to *New York Review of Books, Saturday Review, Poetry, Bizarre* (Paris, France), and other periodicals.

PLAYS

The Heroes (one-act; also see below; produced Off-Broadway, 1952; produced in London, England, 1982), in *Artists' Theater,* edited by Herbert Machiz, Grove (New York, NY), 1969.

The Compromise (three-act; also see below; produced in Cambridge, MA, at the Poet's Theater, 1956), in *The Hasty Papers,* Alfred Leslie, 1960.

The Philosopher (one-act; also see below), in *Art and Literature,* number 2, 1964.

Three Plays (contains *The Heroes, The Compromise,* and *The Philosopher*), Z Press (Calais, VT), 1978.

EDITOR

(With others) *The American Literary Anthology,* Farrar, Straus (New York, NY), 1968.

(With Thomas B. Hess) *Light,* Macmillan (New York, NY), 1969.

(With Thomas B. Hess) *Painters Painting,* Newsweek (New York, NY), 1971.

(With Thomas B. Hess) *Art of the Grand Eccentrics,* Macmillan (New York, NY), 1971.

(With Thomas B. Hess) *Avant-Garde Art,* Macmillan (New York, NY), 1971.

Penguin Modern Poets 24: Ken Ward Elmslie, Kenneth Hoch, James Schuyler, Penguin (New York, NY), 1974.

Richard F. Sknow, *The Funny Place,* O'Hara (Chicago, IL), 1975.

Bruce Marcus, *Muck Arbour,* O'Hara (Chicago, IL), 1975.

(Translator from the French) Max Jacob, *The Dice Cup: Selected Prose Poems,* SUN (New York, NY), 1979.

(With David Lehman) *The Best American Poetry, 1988,* Scribner (New York, NY), 1989.

Coeditor, *One Fourteen,* 1952-53.

OTHER

(Translator) Jean-Jacques Mayoux, *Melville,* Grove (New York, NY), 1960.

(Translator, as Jonas Berry, with Lawrence G. Blochman) *Murder in Montmartre,* Dell (New York, NY), 1960.

(Translator, as Jonas Berry, with Lawrence G. Blochman) Genevieve Manceron, *The Deadlier Sex,* Dell (New York, NY), 1961.

(Translator) Marcel Allain and Pierre Souvestre, *Fantomas,* Morrow (New York, NY), 1986.

(Translator) Pierre Martory, *Every Question but One,* Groundwater Press/ InterFlo Editions, 1990.

(Translator, with others) Pierre Reverdy, *Selected Poems,* Wake Forest University Press (Winston-Salem, NC), 1991.

(Translator) Pierre Martory, *The Landscape Is behind the Door,* Sheep Meadow Press (Riverdale-on-Hudson, NY), 1994.

John Ashbery in Conversation with Mark Ford, Dufour Editions (Chester Springs, PA), 2003.

Collaborator with Joe Brainard on C Comic Books; collaborator with Elliott Carter on musical setting *Syringa,* produced in New York, NY, 1979. Poetry recordings include *Treasury of 100 Modern American Poets Reading Their Poems,* Volume 17, Spoken Arts; *Poetry of John Ashbery,* Jeffrey Norton, and *John Ashbery* ("Voice of the Poet" series), Random Audio, 2001. Translator, from the French, of the works of Raymond Roussel, Andre Breton, Pierre Reverdy, Arthur Cravan, Max Jacob, Alfred Jarry, Antonin Artaud, Noel Vexin, and others.

ADAPTATIONS: Ashbery's verse has been set to music by Ned Rorem, Eric Salzman, Paul Reif, and James Dashow.

SIDELIGHTS: Award-winning poet John Ashbery is recognized as one of the leading lights of twentieth-century American letters. Ashbery's poetry challenges its readers to discard all presumptions about the aims, themes, and stylistic scaffolding of verse in favor of a literature that reflects upon the limits of language and the volatility of consciousness. In *New Criterion,* William Logan noted: "Few poets have so cleverly manipulated, or just plain tortured, our soiled desire for meaning. [Ashbery] reminds us that most poets who give us meaning don't know what they're talking about." *Dictionary of Literary Biography* contributor Raymond Carney likewise contended that Ashbery's work "is a continuous criticism of all the ways in which literature would tidy up experience and make the world safe for poetry." *New York Times Book Review* essayist Stephen Koch characterized Ashbery's voice as "a hushed, simultaneously incomprehensible and intelligent whisper with a weird pulsating rhythm that fluctuates like a wave between peaks of sharp clarity and watery droughts of obscurity and languor."

Ashbery's style, once considered avant-garde, has since become "so influential that its imitators are legion," Helen Vendler observed in the *New Yorker.* Although even his strongest supporters admit that his poetry is often difficult to read and willfully difficult to understand, Ashbery has become, as James Atlas noted in the *New York Times Sunday Magazine,* "the most widely honored poet of his generation." Ashbery's position in American letters is confirmed by his unprecedented sweep of the literary "triple crown" in 1976, when *Self-Portrait in a Convex Mirror* won the Pulitzer Prize, the National Book Award, and the National Book Critics Circle Prize. However, as Nicholas Jenkins suggested in the *New York Times Book Review,* Ashbery has been resistant to his canonization. "For him," the critic contended, "prizes and fame seem little more than sweetly scented warning signs that his strategies have become too easily legible, that his poems are in danger of being embalmed. . . . Certainly no other poet has been more diligent about finding new ways of 'starting out' again—of continuously emerging from the shadow of his own previous work."

A key element of Ashbery's success is his openness to change; it is both a characteristic of his development as a writer and an important thematic element in his verse. "It is a thankless and hopeless task to try and keep up with Ashbery, to try and summarize the present state of his art," Carney observed, adding, "He will never stand still, even for the space (or time) of one poem. Emerson wrote that 'all poetry is vehicular,' and in the case of Ashbery the reader had better resign himself to a series of unending adjustments and movements. With each subsequent book of poetry we only know that he will never be standing still, for that to him is death." In a *Washington Post Book World* review of *Shadow Train,* David Young noted: "You must enjoy unpredictability if you are to like John Ashbery. . . . We must be ready for anything in reading Ashbery because this eclectic, dazzling, inventive creator of travesties and treaties is ready to and eager to include anything, say anything, go anywhere, in the service of an esthetic dedicated to liberating poetry from predictable conventions and tired traditions." And in the *New York Times Book Review,* J.M. Brinnon maintained that *Self-Portrait in a Convex Mirror* is "a collection of poems of breathtaking freshness and adventure in which dazzling orchestrations of language open up whole areas of consciousness no other American poet has even begun to explore. . . . The influence of films now shows in Ashbery's deft control of just those cinematic devices a poet can most usefully appropriate. Crosscut, flashback, montage, close-up, fade-out—he employs them all to generate the kinetic excitement that starts on the first page of his book and continues to the last."

As Brinnon's analysis suggested, Ashbery's verse has taken shape under the influence of films and other art forms. The abstract expressionist movement in modern painting, stressing nonrepresentational methods of picturing reality, is an especially important presence in his work. "Modern art was the first and most powerful influence on Ashbery," Helen McNeil declared in the *Times Literary Supplement.* "When he began to write in the 1950s, American poetry was constrained and formal while American abstract-expressionist art was vigorously taking over the heroic responsibilities of the European avant garde. . . . Ashbery remarks that no one now thinks it odd that Picasso painted faces with eyes and mouth in the wrong place, while the hold of realism in literature is such that the same kind of image in a poem would still be considered shocking."

True to this influence, Ashbery's poems, according to Fred Moramarco, are a "verbal canvas" upon which the poet freely applies the techniques of expressionism. Moramarco, writing in the *Journal of Modern Litera-*

ture, felt that Ashbery's verse, "maligned by many critics for being excessively obscure, becomes less difficult to understand when examined in relation to modern art. *The Tennis Court Oath* is still a book that arouses passions in critics and readers, some of whom have criticized its purposeful obscurity. For me it becomes approachable, explicable, and even downright lucid when read with some of the esthetic assumptions of Abstract Expressionism in mind. . . . [Jackson] Pollock's drips, Rothko's haunting, color-drenched, luminous, rectangular shapes, and Gottlieb's spheres and explosive strokes are here, in a sense, paralleled by an imagistic scattering and emotional and intellectual verbal juxtaposition."

In reviewing "Self-Portrait in a Convex Mirror," a long poem inspired by a painting by the Renaissance artist Francesco Parmigianino, Moramarco was "struck by Ashbery's unique ability to explore the verbal implications of painterly space, to capture the verbal nuances of Parmigianino's fixed and distorted image. The poem virtually resonates or extends the painter's meaning. It transforms visual impact to verbal precision." And Jonathan Holden believed that "Ashbery is the first American poet to successfully carry out the possibilities of analogy between poetry and 'abstract expressionist' painting. He has succeeded so well for two reasons: he is the first poet to identify the *correct* correspondences between painting and writing; he is the first poet to explore the analogy who has possessed the *skill* to *produce* a first-rate 'abstract expressionist' poetry, a poetry as beautiful and sturdy as the paintings of Willem de Kooning." In the *American Poetry Review,* Holden added that "it is Ashbery's genius not only to be able to execute syntax with heft, but to perceive that syntax in writing is the equivalent of 'composition' in painting: it has an intrinsic beauty and authority almost wholly independent of any specific context."

Ashbery's experience as an art critic in France and America has strengthened his ties to abstract expressionism and instilled in his poetry a sensitivity to the interrelatedness of artistic media. His poetry is open-ended and multivarious because life itself is, he told Bryan Appleyard in the London *Times:* "I don't find any direct statements in life. My poetry imitates or reproduces the way knowledge or awareness come to me, which is by fits and starts and by indirection. I don't think poetry arranged in neat patterns would reflect that situation. My poetry is disjunct, but then so is life."

Ashbery's verbal expressionism has attracted a mixed critical response. James Schevill, in a *Saturday Review* article on *The Tennis Court Oath,* wrote: "The trouble

with Ashbery's work is that he is influenced by modern painting to the point where he tries to apply words to the page as if they were abstract, emotional colors and shapes. . . . Consequently, his work loses coherence. . . . There is little substance to the poems in this book." In the *New York Times Book Review,* X.J. Kennedy praised the same title: "'Attempt to use words abstractly,' [Ashbery] declares, 'as an artist uses paint'. . . . If the reader can shut off that portion of the brain which insists words be related logically, he may dive with pleasure into Ashbery's stream of consciousness." Appleyard related the view of some critics that, "however initially baffling his poetry may seem, it is impossible to deny the extraordinary beauty of its surface, its calm and haunting evocation of a world of fragmentary knowledge." Moramarco contended that Ashbery's technique has an invigorating effect: "We become caught up in the rich, vitalized verbal canvas he has painted for us, transported from the mundane and often tedious realities of our daily lives to this exotic, marvelous world. . . . Literature and art can provide these moments of revitalization for us, and although we must always return to the real world, our esthetic encounters impinge upon our sensibilities and leave us altered."

Many critics have commented on the manner in which Ashbery's fluid style has helped to convey a major concern in his poetry: the refusal to impose an arbitrary order on a world of flux and chaos. In his verse, Ashbery attempts to mirror the stream of perceptions of which human consciousness is composed. His poems move, often without continuity, from one image to the next, prompting some critics to praise his expressionist technique and others to accuse him of producing art that is unintelligible, even meaningless.

"Reality, for Ashbery, is elusive, and things are never what they seem to be. They cannot be separated from one another, isolated into component parts, but overlap, intersect, and finally merge into an enormous and constantly changing whole," Paul Auster suggested in *Harper's.* "Ashbery's manner of dealing with this flux is associative rather than logical, and his pessimism about our ever really being able to know anything results, paradoxically, in a poetry that is open to everything."

In the *American Poetry Review,* W.S. Di Piero stated that Ashbery "wonders at the processes of change he sees in people, in the seasons, in language, but his perception of the things about him also persuades him that nothing has ever really changed. If all things, all thought and feeling, are subject to time's revisions, then what can we ever know? What events, what feelings can we ever trust? In exploring questions such as these, Ashbery has experimented with forms of dislocated language as one way of jarring things into order; his notorious twisting of syntax is really an attempt to straighten things out, to clarify the problems at hand." David Kalstone, in his book *Five Temperaments,* commented: "In his images of thwarted nature, of a discontinuity between past and present, Ashbery has tuned his agitation into a principle of composition. From the start he has looked for sentences, diction, a syntax which would make these feelings fully and fluidly available." "Robbed of their solid properties, the smallest and surest of words become part of a new geography," Kalstone wrote of *The Double Dream of Spring* in the *New York Times Book Review.* To explore this "new geography," Kalstone added, the reader must immerse himself in Ashbery's language and "learn something like a new musical scale."

Closely related to Ashbery's use of language as a "new musical scale" is his celebration of the world's various motions and drives. Under the poet's care, the most ordinary aspects of our lives leap into a new reality, a world filled with the joyous and bizarre. In his book, *The Poem in Its Skin,* Paul Carroll found that "one quality most of Ashbery's poems share is something like the peculiar excitement one feels when stepping with Alice behind the Looking Glass into a reality bizarre yet familiar in which the 'marvelous' is as near as one's breakfast coffee cup or one's shoes. His gift is to release everyday objects, experiences and fragments of dreams or hallucinations from stereotypes imposed on them by habit or preconception or belief: he presents the world as if seen for the first time." In a review of *Self-Portrait in a Convex Mirror* for *Harper's,* Paul Auster contended that "few poets today have such an uncanny ability to undermine our certainties, to articulate so fully the ambiguous zones of our consciousness. We are constantly thrown off guard as we read his poems. The ordinary becomes strange, and things that a moment ago seemed clear are cast into doubt. Everything remains in place, and yet nothing is the same." Edmund White, appraising *As We Know* in *Washington Post Book World,* observed: "As David Shapiro has pointed out in his critical study, all [of Ashbery's] long poems tend to end on a joyful note, though one harmonized with doubt and anguish." In the conclusion of "Litany" he "rejects the equation of life and text in order to acknowledge the rich messiness of experience."

Several critics have suggested that this joyful quality is sometimes contradicted by an intellectualism and obscurity present in Ashbery's verse. Victor Howes, re-

viewing *Houseboat Days* for the *Christian Science Monitor,* recognized the rich diversity of the poet's work, but asked, "does he touch the heart? Does he know the passions? My dear. My dear. Really, sometimes you ask too much." J.A. Avant of *Library Journal* argued that in *The Double Dream of Spring,* "emotion has been intellectualized to the extent that it is almost nonexistent." And Pearl K. Bell commented in the *New Leader:* "Long stretches of 'Self-Portrait' read like the bland prose of an uninspired scholar, complete with references and quotations. Bleached of feeling and poetic surprise, the words gasp for air, stutter, go dead." In a *New York Review of Books* article on *The Double Dream of Spring,* Robert Mazzocco asserted that "in Ashbery there has always been a catlike presence, both in the poems themselves and in the person these poems reveal: tender, curious, cunning, tremendously independent, sweet, guarded. Above all, like a cat, Ashbery is a born hunter. . . . But the one prime act of the cat—to spring, to pounce, to make the miraculous leap—Ashbery, for me, has yet to perform."

In *The Poem in Its Skin,* Carroll examined Ashbery's "Leaving the Atocha Station," and felt that "several close readings fail to offer a suspicion of a clue as to what it might be all about." Carroll admitted his annoyance: "The poem makes me feel stupid. . . . [The] narrative skeleton is fleshed out by skin and features made from meaningless phrases, images and occasional sentences. In this sense, 'Leaving the Atocha Station' out-Dadas Dada: it is totally meaningless. . . . The most obvious trait is the general sense that the reader has wandered into somebody else's dream or hallucination." After suggesting several ways to read the poem, Carroll concluded that "the reader should feel free to do whatever he wants with the words in this poem. . . . I also suspect some readers will respond to Ashbery's invitation that the reader too become a poet as he rereads" the poem. As Ashbery explained in *Poetry,* a poem is "a hymn to possibility . . . a general, all-purpose model which each reader can adapt to fit his own set of particulars." In the *New York Review of Books,* Irvin Ehrenpreis commented on Ashbery's assessment of the participatory nature of poetry: "The poem itself must become an exercise in re-examining the world from which the self has become alienated. We must confront its language with the same audacity that we want when confronting the darkened world within us and without. To offer a clear meaning would be to fix the reader in his place, to turn him away from the proper business of poetry by directing him to an apparent subject. . . . The act of reading must become the purpose of the poem."

Calling the poet a "late Romantic," Adam Kirsch declared in *New Republic:* "Ashbery, like God, is most easily defined by negatives. His poems have no plot, narrative, or situation; no consistent emotional register or tone; no sustained mood or definite theme. They do not even have meaningful titles. So complete is Ashbery's abandonment of most of what we come to poetry for that his achievement seems, on first acquaintance, as though it must be similarly complete: a radical new extension of poetry's means and powers, or an audacious and wildly successful hoax." In a review of *As We Know* for the *Chicago Tribune Book World,* Joseph Parisi granted that Ashbery's "'subject matter' remains incomprehensible, to be sure," but the critic nevertheless insisted: "As these streams of everyday and extraordinary objects flow past us in no apparent order, but always in wondrously lyrical lines, the poems make their own curious kind of sense. After all, isn't this how we perceive 'reality'? . . . Ashbery's poems imply the improbability of finding ultimate significance amid the evanescence and transience of modern life. If, however, in the process of these poems the old order is lost or irrelevant, the longing for it or some kind of meaning is not." Reflecting upon the critical response to his poem, "Litany," Ashbery once told *CA,* "I'm quite puzzled by my work too, along with a lot of other people. I was always intrigued by it, but at the same time a little apprehensive and sort of embarrassed about annoying the same critics who are always annoyed by my work. I'm kind of sorry that I cause so much grief."

Di Piero described the reaction of critics to Ashbery's style as "amusing. On the one hand are those who berate him for lacking the Audenesque 'censor' (that little editing machine in a poet's head which deletes all superfluous materials) or who accuse him of simply being willfully and unreasonably perverse. On the other hand are those reviewers who, queerly enough, praise the difficulty of Ashbery's verse as if difficulty were a positive literary value in itself, while ignoring what the poet is saying." Vendler offered this summary in the *New Yorker:* "It is Ashbery's style that has obsessed reviewers, as they alternately wrestle with its elusive impermeability and praise its power of linguistic synthesis. There have been able descriptions of its fluid syntax, its insinuating momentum, its generality of reference, its incorporation of vocabulary from all the arts and sciences. But it is popularly believed, with some reason, that the style itself is impenetrable. . . . An alternative view says that every Ashbery poem is about poetry." Kirsch commented: "Ashbery proves, better than any other poet, that a certain style of 'difficulty' is not at all as difficult as it may seem. . . . Difficulty is only possible within a system of conventions, including the convention of meaning. . . . When a poet leaves conventions behind (which is not the same thing as playing

with them or transcending them), a vast territory of verbiage is opened up, and he can journey anywhere."

This alternative view emphasizes Ashbery's concern with the nature of the creative act, particularly as it applies to the writing of poetry. This is, Peter Stitt noted, a major theme of *Houseboat Days,* a volume acclaimed by Marjorie Perloff in *Washington Post Book World* as "the most exciting, most original book of poems to have appeared in the 1970s." Ashbery shares with the abstract expressionists of painting "a preoccupation with the art process itself," Stitt maintained in the *Georgia Review.* "Ashbery has come to write, in the poet's most implicitly ironic gesture, almost exclusively about his own poems, the ones he is writing as he writes about them. The artist becomes his own theoretical critic, caught in the critical lens even at the moment of conception." Roger Shattuck made a similar point in the *New York Review of Books:* "Nearly every poem in *Houseboat Days* shows that Ashbery's phenomenological eye fixes itself not so much on ordinary living and doing as on the specific act of composing a poem. Writing on Frank O'Hara's work, Ashbery defined a poem as 'the chronicle of the creative act that produces it.' Thus every poem becomes an ars poetica of its own condition." Ashbery's examination of creativity, according to Paul Breslin in *Poetry,* is a "prison of self-reference" which detracts from the poet's "lyrical genius." *New Leader* reviewer Phoebe Pettingell commented that Ashbery "carries the saw that 'poetry does not have subject matter because it is the subject' to its furthest limit. Just as we feel we are beginning to make sense of one of his poems, meaning eludes us again. . . . Still, we are somehow left with a sense that the conclusion is satisfactory, with a wondering delight at what we've heard. . . . *Houseboat Days* is evidence of the transcendent power of the imagination, and one of the major works of our time."

Ashbery's poetry, as critics have observed, has evolved under a variety of influences besides modern art, becoming in the end the expression of a voice unmistakably his own. Among the influences seen in his verse are the Romantic tradition in American poetry that progressed from Whitman to Wallace Stevens, the so-called "New York School of Poets" featuring contemporaries such as Frank O'Hara and Kenneth Koch, and the French surrealist writers with whom Ashbery has dealt in his work as a critic and translator. In *The Fierce Embrace,* Charles Molesworth traced Ashbery's development: "The first few books by John Ashbery contained a large proportion of a poetry of inconsequence. . . . Subject matter, or rather the absence of it, helped form the core of his aesthetic, an aesthetic that refused to maintain a consistent attitude toward any fixed phenomena. The poems tumbled out of a whimsical, detached amusement that mixed with a quizzical melancholy. . . . Slowly, however, it appears as if Ashbery was gaining confidence for his true project, and, as his work unfolds, an indulging reader can see how it needed those aggressively bland 'experiments' in nonsense to protect its frailty." Ashbery's "true project," Molesworth believed, is *Self-Portrait in a Convex Mirror.* Many reviewers agreed with Molesworth that this volume, especially the long title poem, is Ashbery's "masterpiece."

Essentially a meditation on the painting "Self-Portrait in a Convex Mirror," the narrative poem focuses on many of the themes present in Ashbery's work. "I have lived with John Ashbery's 'Self-Portrait in a Convex Mirror' as with a favorite mistress for the past nine months," Laurence Lieberman declared in his *Unassigned Frequencies.* "Often, for whole days of inhabiting the room of its dream, I have felt that it is the only poem—and Ashbery the only author—in my life. It is what I most want from a poem. Or an author." Lieberman enthused that "when I put this poem down I catch myself in the act of seeing objects and events in the world as through different—though amazingly novel other eyes: the brilliantly varied other life of surfaces has been wonderfully revivified, and I take this transformation to be an accurate index of the impact of Ashbery's poetry upon the modus operandi of my perception." Like Molesworth, Lieberman believed that Ashbery's early work, though "unreadable," was an "indispensable detour that precipitated, finally, the elevated vision of Ashbery's recent work. . . . Following his many years of withdrawal and seclusion, a period of slow mellowing, this exactly appointed occasion has been granted to him."

Like other critics, Lieberman felt that Ashbery was once overly concerned with examining the nature of art and creativity, with escaping into his poems and "producing forms that achieved a semblance of ideal beauty." In "Self-Portrait," Lieberman contended, "Ashbery forecloses irrevocably on the mortgage of an *ars poetica* which conceives the poem as 'exotic refuge,' and advances to an aesthetic which carries a full burden of mirroring the age's ills." Unlike Parmigianino, who retreated into his hermitage, Ashbery ventures out from "the comfortable sanctuary of the dream" to confront the world. "His new art achieves a powerful re-engagement with the human community," Lieberman concluded. "That is his honorable quest."

Ashbery's second epic poem, *Flow Chart,* was published in 1991. One might assume, as Alfred Corn noted

in *Poetry,* that "such a poet might . . . [now] reflect the golden serenity that comes in the latter years of a life that has achieved its aims. No. Or not simply, yes. In fact, *Flow Chart* shows us a John Ashbery at his most achingly vulnerable." Corn continued, "It is impossible to be certain this early on, but the reach of *Flow Chart* suggests that it is Ashbery's most important book, and certainly his most human." Lawrence Joseph declared in *Nation* that the poem, "more than any of his other books, portrays the essence of Ashbery's process. . . . *Flow Chart* is a catalogue, which Ashbery presents as endlessly expansive and open to interpretation, encompassing within its subject matter—well, as much as the poet may imagine." Helen Vendler, writing in *New Yorker,* attempted to capture the poem in its entirety: "What is John Ashbery's . . . *Flow Chart?* A two-hundred-and-fifteen-page lyric; a diary; a monitor screen registering a moving EEG; a thousand and one nights; Penelope's web unraveling; views from Argus' hundred eyes; a book of riddles; a ham-radio station; an old trunk full of memories; a rubbish dump; a Bartlett's *Familiar Quotations;* a Last Folio; a vaudeville act. . . . It makes Ashbery's past work (except for those poems in *The Tennis Court Oath. . .*) seem serenely classical, well ordered, pure, shapely, and above all, *short.*"

As with Ashbery's other poetry, *Hotel Lautreamont,* was met with mixed critical response. In the *National Review,* James Gardner qualified his criticism by noting: "The appreciation of a poem by John Ashbery requires an act of faith, a surrender of the ordinary faculties of judgment. What you are to admire is a certain deposit of psychic life in each of these poems, a shifting, disengaged record of the poet's spiritual state at the moment of setting the words down on paper." Gardner concluded: "There was a time when I had more patience for this sort of thing than I now have. It is no longer enough." As Nicholas Everett noted in the *Times Literary Supplement,* "Those who expect poetry to evoke a specific experience or event, real or fictional, will always find Ashbery's work frustrating or just dull." He added, "Besides, the essential subjects of Ashbery's poetry—subjectivity and time. . . —are themselves general and elusive; and though in passing it says a good deal about them, its means are in the end mimetic rather than discursive." Tom Sleigh in the *New York Times Book Review* found Ashbery "extremely forgiving, a poet, like Wordsworth, of superb passages who doesn't insist that one dig out the gold in every line." However, Sleigh admitted, "This isn't to say that he's wired like other poets."

Can You Hear, Bird was Ashbery's seventeenth volume of poetry. According to John Boening in *World Litera-*

ture Review, "The poems in *Can You Hear, Bird* range across all manner of forms and styles, moods and voices. Some are more engaging than others (almost all Ashbery poems, even those which 'do' nothing for us or leave us disoriented, are engaging)." Stephen Yenser raved in the *Yale Review:* "There is nowhere that Ashbery's poetry can't sail, one feels, and nothing it can't do, apart of course from 'doing' anything." Yenser continued, "Reading Ashbery—like reading the Gertrude Stein of *Tender Buttons*—is a continually surprising, exciting venture that proves the endlessness of the resources that we call 'language.'" Mark Ford, writing in the *Times Literary Supplement,* compared Ashbery's poetry to Walt Whitman's. "Like Whitman's, it is essentially a means of involving the reader in the poem on what Whitman calls 'equal terms'. . . . Ashbery's evasions might be seen as motivated by a similar desire to achieve a greater—and more democratic—intimacy by short-circuiting conventional modes of address."

The poems in *Girls on the Run* were inspired by the art work and writings of Henry Darger (1892-1973), a mentally ill recluse whose fantastic sketches and paintings of little girls only came to light after his death. Once again, Ashbery uses Darger's work only as a point of departure for his own vivid and free-flowing imaginings, described by David Kirby in the *New York Times Book Review* as "a tank of literary laughing gas that exhilarates and confounds in roughly equal measures." The "characters" in *Girls on the Run* include Tidbit, Rags the Dog, Uncle Margaret, and Dimples, but these creations come and go through the pieces with no discernable plot or motivation to compel them onward. As *Art in America* contributor Raphael Rubinstein saw it, *Girls on the Run* "is, in an odd way, closer in spirit to Ashbery's earlier work. . . . Despite expressing a degree of nostalgia for childhood diversions, this new poem is perhaps more radical in its unpredictability than anything Ashbery has yet written." Calling the volume "beautiful, comic, and mysterious" in his review for *World Literature Today,* Michael Leddy cited references to Homer and classical myth that run through both Darger's work and Ashbery's poem, and notes that the work's "large cast gives a good sense of the poem's many dimensions." *Booklist* reviewer Donna Seaman felt that the work in *Girls on the Run* "has captured the peculiar energy of Darger's disturbing creation" in "a virtuoso interpretative performance."

In more recent Ashbery works, such as *Girls on the Run, Wakefulness,* and *Chinese Whispers,* some critics have noted an infusion of elegy as the poet contemplates aging and death. In *Nation,* Calvin Bedient stated: "For all his experimentation, Ashbery writes (as the im-

portant writers have always done) about happiness and woe. If the woe he knows is treated comically, it's still woe." The critic added: "Ashbery's brilliantly eccentric images are bees released to find a hidden (mythic) hive. His humor is the knowledge that they will perish en route. . . . Even if his pathos is by now well worn, it's no fuzzy pair of slippers. His poetry is almost as full of strange voices as Caliban's island, and as full of magic, a gracefully humorous pathos, a pathetic humor like no other shuddering laughter in the world." While praising the poems in *Chinese Whispers* for their "light touch and consistent pacing," *Library Journal* reviewer Barbara Hoffert noted that in "these autumnal pieces a sense of calm predominates" as "things repeatedly fall, ebb, dissipate, or descend." However, autumnal does not mean lackluster. Characterizing Ashbery's work after the late 1990s as "equal parts cracked drawing-room dialogue, 4-H Americana, withering sarcasm, and sleeve-worn pathos," a *Publishers Weekly* contributor noted that in *Chinese Whispers* Ashbery's poems seem "brilliantly tossed off."

Much as he has throughout his career, Ashbery continues to foster a variety of reactions among readers. In an online review for *Men's Journal,* Mark Levine contended that Ashbery "remains the most outrageously daring verbal mapmaker of the modern imagination. Bawdy, feverish, irreverent, and beset by melancholy, his poems inhabit a range of textures and emotions you won't find in another living writer." Nicholas Jenkins concluded in the *New York Times Book Review* that Ashbery's poetry "appeals not because it offers wisdom in a packaged form, but because the elusiveness and mysterious promise of his lines remind us that we always have a future and a condition of meaningfulness to start out toward." Dubbing him "a poet of our time," *World Literature Today* reviewer Ashley Brown found Ashbery's writing "disarmingly colloquial," but possessing a "rhythmic pattern . . . as unpredictable as his images." Lauding the poet's contribution to American letters, Jenkins characterized Ashbery's work as "a poetry whose beauties are endless."

BIOGRAPHICAL AND CRITICAL SOURCES:

BOOKS

Ashton, Dore, *The New York School: A Cultural Reckoning,* Viking (New York, NY), 1973.

Blasing, Mutlu Konuk, *Politics and Form in Postmodern Poetry: O'Hara, Bishop, Ashbery, and Merrill,* Cambridge University Press (New York, NY), 1995.

Bloom, Harold, *John Ashbery,* Chelsea House (New York, NY), 1985.

Carroll, Paul, *The Poem in Its Skin,* Follett (New York, NY), 1968.

Cazé, Antoine, *John Ashbery,* Belin (Paris, France), 2000.

Contemporary Literary Criticism, Thomson Gale (Detroit, MI), Volume 2, 1974, Volume 3, 1975, Volume 4, 1975, Volume 6, 1976, Volume 9, 1978, Volume 13, 1980, Volume 15, 1980, Volume 25, 1983, Volume 41, 1988, Volume 77, 1993.

Contemporary Poets, 6th edition, St. James Press (Detroit, MI), 1996.

Dictionary of Literary Biography, Thomson Gale (Detroit, MI), Volume 5: *American Poets since World War II,* 1978, Volume 165: *American Poets since World War II, Fourth Series,* 1996.

Dictionary of Literary Biography Yearbook, 1981, Thomson Gale (Detroit, MI), 1982.

Herd, David, *John Ashbery and American Poetry: Fit to Cope with Our Occasions,* St. Martin's Press (New York, NY), 2001.

Hoeppner, Edward Haworth, *Echoes and Moving Fields: Structure and Subjectivity in the Poetry of W.S. Merwin and John Ashbery,* Bucknell University Press (Lewisburg, PA), 1994.

Howard, Richard, *Alone with America: Essays on the Art of Poetry in the United States since 1950,* Atheneum (New York, NY), 1969.

Kalstone, David, *Five Temperaments: Elizabeth Bishop, Robert Lowell, James Merrill, Adrienne Rich, John Ashbery,* Oxford University Press (New York, NY), 1977.

Kelly, Lionel, editor, *Poetry and the Sense of Panic: Critical Essays on Elizabeth Bishop and John Ashbery,* Rodopi (Atlanta, GA), 2000.

Kermani, David K., *John Ashbery: A Comprehensive Bibliography,* Garland Publishing (New York, NY), 1976.

Koch, Kenneth, *Rose, Where Did You Get That Red?,* Random House (New York, NY), 1973.

Kostelanetz, Richard, editor, *The New American Arts,* Horizon Press (New York, NY), 1965.

Kostelanetz, Richard, *The Old Poetries and the New,* University of Michigan Press (Ann Arbor, MI), 1979.

Leary, Paris and Robert Kelly, editors, *A Controversy of Poets,* Doubleday (New York, NY), 1965.

Lehman, David, editor, *Beyond Amazement: New Essays on John Ashbery,* Cornell University Press (Ithaca, NY), 1980.

Lehman, David, editor, *John Ashbery,* Cornell University Press (Ithaca, NY), 1979.

Lehman, David, *The Last Avant-Garde: The Making of the New York School of Poets,* Doubleday (New York, NY), 1999.

Lieberman, Laurence, *Unassigned Frequencies: American Poetry in Review, 1964-1977,* University of Illinois Press (Champaign, IL), 1977.

Meyers, John Bernard, editor, *The Poets of the New York School,* University of Pennsylvania Press (Philadelphia, PA), 1969.

Molesworth, Charles, *The Fierce Embrace: A Study of Contemporary American Poetry,* University of Missouri Press (Columbia, MO), 1979.

Packard, William, editor, *The Craft of Poetry,* Doubleday (New York, NY), 1964.

Perloff, Marjorie, *Poetic License: Essays on Modernist and Postmodernist Lyric,* Northwestern University Press (Evanston, IL), 1990.

Ross, Andrew, *The Failure of Modernism: Symptoms of American Poetry,* Columbia University Press (New York, NY), 1986.

Schultz, Susan M., editor, *The Tribe of John Ashbery and Contemporary Poetry,* University of Alabama Press (Tuscaloosa, AL), 1995.

Shapiro, David, *John Ashbery: An Introduction to the Poetry,* Columbia University Press (New York, NY), 1979.

Shaw, Robert B., editor, *American Poetry since 1960: Some Critical Perspectives,* Carcanet Press (Manchester, England), 1973.

Shoptaw, John, *On the Outside Looking Out: John Ashbery's Poetry,* Harvard University Press (Cambridge, MA), 1994.

Stepanchev, Stephen, *American Poetry since 1945: A Critical Survey,* Harper (New York, NY), 1965.

Sutton, Walter, *American Free Verse: The Modern Revolution in Poetry,* New Directions (New York, NY), 1973.

Ward, Geoff, *Statutes of Liberty: The New York School of Poets,* St. Martin's Press (New York, NY), 1993.

PERIODICALS

American Poetry Review, August, 1973; September, 1978; July, 1979; July, 1981; May-June, 1984, pp. 29-33; March, 2002, Donald Revell, "Invisible Green V," p. 23; March-April, 2004, Fred Moramarco, "Across the Millennium: The Persistence of John Ashbery," p. 39.

Architectural Digest, June, 1994, p. 36.

Art in America, February, 2000, Raphael Rubinstein, review of *Girls on the Run,* p. 37.

Booklist, May 1, 1981; March 15, 1999, Donna Seaman, review of *Girls on the Run,* p. 1271; October 1, 2000, Donna Seaman, review of *Your Name Here,* p. 313.

Chicago Tribune Book World, January 27, 1980; July 26, 1981.

Christian Science Monitor, September 6, 1962; March 9, 1970; October 12, 1977; December 3, 1979.

Commentary, February, 1973.

Confrontation, fall, 1974, pp. 84-96.

Contemporary Literature, winter, 1968; spring, 1969; summer, 1992, pp. 214-242.

Encounter, April, 1980.

Esquire, January, 1978.

Georgia Review, winter, 1975; winter, 1978; summer, 1980.

Harper's, April, 1970; November, 1975.

Hudson Review, spring, 1970; autumn, 1975; autumn, 1976; spring, 1978; autumn, 1980; winter, 1981.

Journal of Modern Literature, September, 1976.

Library Journal, January 1, 1970; August, 2000, Graham Christian, review of *Your Name Here,* p. 109; August, 2001, Laurie Selwyn, review of *John Ashbery,* p. 186; October 15, 2002, Barbara Hoffert, review of *Chinese Whispers,* p. 77.

Listener, August 18, 1977.

London Review of Books, April 23, 1992, p. 20.

Michigan Quarterly Review, summer, 1981, pp. 243-255.

Nation, December 12, 1966; April 14, 1969; September 3, 1977; November 11, 1978; May 29, 1989; April 20, 1992, p. 531; June 1, 1998, Calvin Bedient, review of *Wakefulness,* p. 27.

National Review, February 15, 1993, p. 50.

New Criterion, June, 1998, William Logan, "Soiled Desires," p. 61.

New Leader, May 26, 1975; November 7, 1977; January 29, 1981.

New Republic, June 14, 1975; November 29, 1975; November 26, 1977; December 29, 1979; October 16, 1989; June 17, 1991; September 28, 1998, Adam Kirsch, review of *Wakefulness,* p. 38; January 1, 2001, Mark Ford, "Life without End," p. 30.

New Statesman, June 16, 1967; January 4, 1980; April 24, 1981; July 22, 1994, p. 45.

Newsweek, September 26, 1977.

New York, May 20, 1991, pp. 46-52.

New York Arts Journal, November, 1977.

New Yorker, September 1, 1956; March 24, 1969; March 16, 1981; August 3, 1992; December 13, 1993; February 14, 1994; February 28, 1994.

New York Quarterly, winter, 1972.

New York Review of Books, April 14, 1966; December 14, 1973; October 16, 1975; March 23, 1978; January 24, 1980; July 16, 1981.

New York Times, April 15, 1956.

New York Times Book Review, July 15, 1962; February 11, 1968; May 4, 1969; June 8, 1969; July 5, 1970; April 9, 1972; August 2, 1975; November 13, 1977; January 6, 1980; September 6, 1981; May 23, 1993; October 23, 1994, p. 3; January 4, 1998, Nicholas Jenkins, review of *The Mooring of Starting Out: The First Five Books of Poetry;* April 11, 1999, David Kirby, review of *Girls on the Run,* p. 24; November 12, 2000, Taylor Antrim, review of *Other Traditions.*

New York Times Sunday Magazine, May 23, 1976; February 3, 1980.

Observer (London, England), December 9, 1979; December 16, 1979.

Paris Review, winter, 1983, pp. 30-59.

Parnassus, fall-winter, 1972; fall-winter, 1977; spring-summer, 1978; fall-winter, 1979.

Partisan Review, fall, 1972; summer, 1976.

Poet and Critic, Volume 11, number 3, 1979.

Poetry, July, 1957; September, 1962; December, 1966; October, 1970; August, 1972; October, 1980; May, 1988; December, 1991, p. 169; October, 1994, p. 44; May, 2002, p. 107.

Poetry Review, August, 1985, pp. 20-25.

Publishers Weekly, March 28, 1994; September 25, 1995, p. 49; January 21, 2002, review of *As Umbrellas Follow Rain,* p. 87; August 19, 2002, review of *Chinese Whispers,* p. 81.

Saturday Review, June 16, 1956; May 5, 1962; August 8, 1970; July 8, 1972; September 17, 1977.

Sewanee Review, April, 1976; April, 1978; July, 1980.

Southern Review, April, 1978.

Spectator, November 22, 1975.

Time, April 26, 1976.

Times (London, England), August 23, 1984.

Times Literary Supplement, September 14, 1967; July 25, 1975; September 1, 1978; March 14, 1980; June 5, 1981; October 8, 1982; February 12, 1993, p. 10; May 17, 1996, p. 26.

Twentieth-Century Literature, summer, 1992, pp. 125-151.

Verse, spring, 1991, pp. 61-72.

Village Voice, January 19, 1976; October 17, 1977; December 26, 1977.

Village Voice Literary Supplement, October, 1981.

Virginia Quarterly Review, autumn, 1970; winter, 1973; spring, 1976; spring, 1979; spring, 1980.

Washington Post Book World, May 11, 1975; October 30, 1977; December 11, 1977; November 25, 1979; June 7, 1981; December 10, 1995, p. 8.

Western Humanities Review, winter, 1971.

World Literature Review, autumn, 1996, p. 961.

World Literature Today, autumn, 1999, Michael Leddy, review of *Girls on the Run,* p. 740; July-September, 2003, Ashley Brown, review of *Chinese Whispers,*

p. 101, John Boening, review of *The Vermont Notebooks,* p. 111.

Yale Review, October, 1969; June, 1970; winter, 1981; spring, 1990; April, 1993; January, 1996.

ONLINE

Men's Journal Online, http://www.mensjournal.com/ (November 6, 2000), Mark Levine, "Lingo Here Awhile."

* * *

ASHBERY, John Lawrence
See ASHBERY, John

* * *

ASHBLESS, William
See POWERS, Tim

* * *

ASIMOV, Isaac 1920-1992
(George E. Dale, Dr. A, Paul French)

PERSONAL: Born January 2, 1920, in Petrovichi, USSR; immigrated to United States, 1923, naturalized citizen, 1928; died of complications related to AIDS, April 6, 1992, in New York, NY; son of Judah (a candy store owner) and Anna Rachel (Berman) Asimov; married Gertrude Blugerman, July 26, 1942 (divorced, November 16, 1973); married Janet Opal Jeppson (a psychiatrist), November 30, 1973; children: David, Robyn Joan. *Education:* Columbia University, B.S., 1939, M.A., 1941, Ph.D., 1948.

CAREER: Writer. Boston University School of Medicine, Boston, MA, instructor, 1949-51, assistant professor, 1951-55, associate professor, 1955-79, professor of biochemistry, 1979-92. Worked as a civilian chemist at U.S. Navy Air Experimental Station, Philadelphia, PA, 1942-45. *Military service:* U.S. Army, 1945-46.

MEMBER: Authors League of America, Science Fiction Writers of America, National Association of Science Writers, American Chemical Society, Zero Population Growth, Population Institute, National Organization of Non-Parents, Sigma Xi, Mensa.

AWARDS, HONORS: Guest of honor, Thirteenth World Science Fiction Convention, 1955; Edison Foundation National Mass Media Award, 1958; Blakeslee Award for nonfiction, 1960; special Hugo Award for distinguished contributions to the field, 1963; special Hugo Award for best all-time science-fiction series, 1966, for *Foundation, Foundation and Empire,* and *Second Foundation;* James T. Grady Award, American Chemical Society, 1965; American Association for the Advancement of Science-Westinghouse award for science writing, 1967; Nebula Award, Science Fiction Writers of America, and Hugo Award for best novel, both 1973, both for *The Gods Themselves;* Nebula Award, and Hugo Award for best short story, both 1977, both for "The Bicentennial Man"; Glenn Seabord Award, International Platform Association, 1979; Hugo Award for best novel, 1983, for *Foundation's Edge;* Science Fiction Writers of America Grand Master Award, 1986; Hugo Award for best nonfiction book, 1995, for *I. Asimov;* inducted into Science Fiction and Fantasy Hall of Fame, 1997.

WRITINGS:

SCIENCE FICTION

Pebble in the Sky (novel; also see below), Doubleday (New York, NY), 1950, reprinted, R. Bentley, 1982.

I, Robot (short stories), Gnome Press, 1950, reprinted, Fawcett (New York, NY), 1970.

The Stars, Like Dust (novel; also see below), Doubleday (New York, NY), 1951, published as *The Rebellious Stars* with *An Earth Gone Mad* by R.D. Aycock, Ace Books (New York, NY), 1954, reprinted under original title, Fawcett (New York, NY), 1972.

Foundation (also see below), Gnome Press, 1951, published as *The 1,000 Year Plan* with *No World of Their Own* by Poul Anderson, Ace Books (New York, NY), 1955, reprinted under original title, Ballantine (New York, NY), 1983.

(Under pseudonym Paul French) *David Starr, Space Ranger* (juvenile; also see below), Doubleday (New York, NY), 1952, reprinted under name Isaac Asimov, Twayne Publishers (Boston, MA), 1978.

Foundation and Empire (also see below), Gnome Press, 1952, reprinted, Ballantine (New York, NY), 1983.

The Currents of Space (novel; also see below), Doubleday (New York, NY), 1952, reprinted, Fawcett (New York, NY), 1971.

Second Foundation (also see below), Gnome Press, 1953, reprinted, Ballantine (New York, NY), 1983.

(Under pseudonym Paul French) *Lucky Starr and the Pirates of the Asteroids* (juvenile; also see below), Doubleday (New York, NY), 1953, reprinted under name Isaac Asimov, Twayne Publishers (Boston, MA), 1978.

The Caves of Steel (novel; also see below), Doubleday (New York, NY), 1954, reprinted, Fawcett (New York, NY), 1972.

(Under pseudonym Paul French) *Lucky Starr and the Oceans of Venus* (juvenile), Doubleday (New York, NY), 1954, reprinted under name Isaac Asimov, Twayne Publishers (Boston, MA), 1978.

The Martian Way and Other Stories (also see below), Doubleday (New York, NY), 1955, reprinted, Ballantine (New York, NY), 1985.

The End of Eternity (novel; also see below), Doubleday (New York, NY), 1955, reprinted, Fawcett (New York, NY), 1971.

(Contributor) Groff Conklin, editor, *Science Fiction Terror Tales by Isaac Asimov and Others*, Gnome Press, 1955.

(Under pseudonym Paul French) *Lucky Starr and the Big Sun of Mercury* (juvenile), Doubleday (New York, NY), 1956, published under name Isaac Asimov as *The Big Sun of Mercury*, New English Library, 1974, reprinted under name Isaac Asimov under original title, Twayne (Boston, MA), 1978.

The Naked Sun (novel; also see below), Doubleday (New York, NY), 1957, reprinted, Fawcett (New York, NY), 1972.

(Under pseudonym Paul French) *Lucky Starr and the Moons of Jupiter* (juvenile), Doubleday (New York, NY), 1957, reprinted under name Isaac Asimov, Twayne (Boston, MA), 1978.

Earth Is Room Enough: Science Fiction Tales of Our Own Planet (also see below), Doubleday (New York, NY), 1957.

The Robot Novels (contains *The Caves of Steel* and *The Naked Sun*; also see below), Doubleday (New York, NY), 1957.

(Under pseudonym Paul French) *Lucky Starr and the Rings of Saturn* (juvenile), Doubleday (New York, NY), 1958, reprinted under name Isaac Asimov, Twayne Publishers (Boston, MA), 1978.

Nine Tomorrows: Tales of the Near Future, Doubleday (New York, NY), 1959.

Triangle: "The Currents of Space," "Pebble In the Sky," and "The Stars, Like Dust," Doubleday (New York, NY), 1961, published as *An Isaac Asimov Second Omnibus*, Sidgwick & Jackson (London, England), 1969.

The Foundation Trilogy: Three Classics of Science Fiction (contains *Foundation, Foundation and Empire,* and *Second Foundation*), Doubleday (New York,

NY), 1963, published as *An Isaac Asimov Omnibus*, Sidgwick & Jackson (London, England), 1966, reprinted, Doubleday (New York, NY), 1982.

The Rest of the Robots (short stories and novels; includes *The Caves of Steel* and *The Naked Sun*), Doubleday (New York, NY), 1964, published as *Eight Stories from the Rest of the Robots*, Pyramid Books, 1966.

Fantastic Voyage (novelization of screenplay by Harry Kleiner), Houghton Mifflin (Boston, MA), 1966.

Through a Glass Clearly, New English Library, 1967.

Asimov's Mysteries (short stories), Doubleday (New York, NY), 1968.

Nightfall and Other Stories, Doubleday, 1969, published in two volumes, Panther Books (London, England), 1969, published as *Nightfall: Twenty SF Stories*, Rapp Whiting, 1971.

The Best New Thing (juvenile), World Publishing (New York, NY), 1971.

The Gods Themselves (novel), Doubleday (New York, NY), 1972.

The Early Asimov; or, Eleven Years of Trying (short stories), Doubleday (New York, NY), 1972.

(Contributor) Groff Conklin, editor, *Possible Tomorrows by Isaac Asimov and Others*, Sidgwick & Jackson (London, England), 1972.

An Isaac Asimov Double: "Space Ranger" and "Pirates of the Asteroids," New English Library (London, England), 1972.

A Second Isaac Asimov Double: "The Big Sun of Mercury" and "The Oceans of Venus," New English Library (London, England), 1973.

The Third Isaac Asimov Double, Times Mirror (New York, NY), 1973.

The Best of Isaac Asimov (short stories), Doubleday (New York, NY), 1974.

Have You Seen These?, NESFA Press, 1974.

Buy Jupiter and Other Stories, Doubleday (New York, NY), 1975.

The Heavenly Host (juvenile), Walker (New York, NY), 1975.

The Bicentennial Man and Other Stories, Doubleday (New York, NY), 1976.

The Collected Fiction of Isaac Asimov, Volume 1: *The Far Ends of Time and Earth* (contains *Pebble in the Sky, Earth Is Room Enough,* and *The End of Eternity*), Doubleday (New York, NY), 1979, Volume 2: *Prisoners of the Stars* (contains *The Stars, Like Dust, The Martian Way and Other Stories,* and *The Currents of Space*), Doubleday (New York, NY), 1979.

Three by Asimov, Targ Editions, 1981.

The Complete Robot (also see below), Doubleday (New York, NY), 1982.

Foundation's Edge (novel), Doubleday (New York, NY), 1982.

The Winds of Change and Other Stories, Doubleday (New York, NY), 1983.

(With wife, Janet Asimov) *Norby, the Mixed-up Robot* (juvenile; also see below), Walker (New York, NY), 1983.

The Robots of Dawn (novel), Doubleday (New York, NY), 1983.

The Robot Collection (contains *The Caves of Steel, The Naked Sun,* and *The Complete Robot*), Doubleday (New York, NY), 1983.

(With Janet Asimov) *Norby's Other Secret* (juvenile; also see below), Walker (New York, NY), 1984.

Isaac Asimov's Magical World's of Fantasy, Crown (New York, NY), 1985.

Robots and Empire (novel), Doubleday (New York, NY), 1985.

(With Janet Asimov) *Norby and the Invaders* (juvenile; also see below), Walker (New York, NY), 1985.

(With Janet Asimov) *Norby and the Lost Princess* (juvenile; also see below), Walker (New York, NY), 1985.

The Best Science Fiction of Isaac Asimov, Doubleday (New York, NY), 1986.

The Alternative Asimovs (contains *The End of Eternity*), Doubleday (New York, NY), 1986.

(With Janet Asimov) *The Norby Chronicles* (contains *Norby, the Mixed-up Robot* and *Norby's Other Secret*), Ace Books (New York, NY), 1986.

Foundation and Earth (novel), Doubleday (New York, NY), 1986.

(With Janet Asimov) *Norby and the Queen's Necklace* (juvenile; also see below), Walker (New York, NY), 1986.

(With Janet Asimov) *Norby: Robot for Hire* (contains *Norby and the Lost Princess* and *Norby and the Invaders*), Ace Books (New York, NY), 1987.

Fantastic Voyage II: Destination Brain, Doubleday (New York, NY), 1987.

(With Janet Asimov) *Norby Finds a Villain* (juvenile; also see below), Walker (New York, NY), 1987.

(With Janet Asimov) *Norby through Time and Space* (contains *Norby and the Queen's Necklace* and *Norby Finds a Villain*), Ace Books (New York, NY), 1988.

Azazel, Doubleday (New York, NY), 1988.

Nemesis, Doubleday (New York, NY), 1988.

Prelude to Foundation, Doubleday (New York, NY), 1988.

(With Theodore Sturgeon) *The Ugly Little Boy/The Widget, the Wadget, and Boff,* Tor Books (New York, NY), 1989.

Franchise (juvenile), Creative Education (Mankato, MN), 1989.

(With Janet Asimov) *Norby down to Earth* (juvenile), Walker (New York, NY), 1989.

All the Troubles of the World (juvenile), Creative Education (Mankato, MN), 1989.

(With Janet Asimov) *Norby and Yobo's Great Adventure* (juvenile), Walker (New York, NY), 1989.

Sally (juvenile), Creative Education (Mankato, MN), 1989.

Robbie (juvenile), Creative Education (Mankato, MN), 1989.

(Editor, with Martin Greenberg) *Visions of Fantasy: Tales from the Masters,* Doubleday (New York, NY), 1989.

The Asimov Chronicles, three volumes, Ace Books (New York, NY), 1990.

Invasions, New American Library (New York, NY), 1990.

(With Janet Asimov) *Norby and the Oldest Dragon* (juvenile), Walker (New York, NY), 1990.

Isaac Asimov: The Complete Stories, Doubleday (New York, NY), 1990.

Robot Visions, New American Library (New York, NY), 1991.

(With Janet Asimov) *Norby and the Court Jester* (juvenile), Walker (New York, NY), 1991.

(With Robert Silverberg) *The Positronic Man,* Doubleday (New York, NY), 1993.

Gold: The Final Science Fiction Collection, Harper-Prism (New York, NY), 1995.

Isaac Asimov's I-Bots: History of I-Botics: An Illustrated Novel, HarperPrism (New York, NY), 1997.

Also editor or coeditor of numerous science fiction and fantasy anthologies.

MYSTERY NOVELS

The Death Dealers, Avon Publications (New York, NY), 1958, published as *A Whiff of Death,* Walker (New York, NY), 1968.

Tales of the Black Widowers, Doubleday (New York, NY), 1974.

Murder at the ABA: A Puzzle in Four Days and Sixty Scenes, Doubleday (New York, NY), 1976, published as *Authorised Murder: A Puzzle in Four Days and Sixty Scenes,* Gollancz (London, England), 1976.

More Tales of the Black Widowers, Doubleday (New York, NY), 1976.

The Key Word and Other Mysteries, Walker (New York, NY), 1977.

Casebook of the Black Widowers, Doubleday (New York, NY), 1980.

The Union Club Mysteries, Doubleday (New York, NY), 1983.

Computer Crimes and Capers, Academy Chicago Publishers (Chicago, IL), 1983.

Banquets of the Black Widowers, Doubleday (New York, NY), 1984.

The Disappearing Man and Other Mysteries, Walker (New York, NY), 1985.

The Best Mysteries of Isaac Asimov, Doubleday (New York, NY), 1986.

Puzzles of the Black Widowers, Doubleday (New York, NY), 1990.

(With Martin H. Greenburg, Martin Harry, and Charles Waugh) *Isaac Asimov Presents the Best Crime Stories of the Nineteenth Century,* Barricade (New York, NY), 1995.

Also editor, with others, of numerous mystery anthologies.

ADULT NONFICTION

(With William C. Boyd and Burnham S. Walker) *Biochemistry and Human Metabolism,* Williams Wilkins, 1952, 3rd edition, 1957.

The Chemicals of Life: Enzymes, Vitamins, Hormones, Abelard-Schuman (London, England), 1954.

(With William C. Boyd) *Races and People,* Abelard-Schuman (London, England), 1955.

(With Burnham S. Walker and Mary K. Nicholas) *Chemistry and Human Health,* McGraw (New York, NY), 1956.

Inside the Atom, Abelard-Schuman (London, England), 1956, revised and updated edition, 1966.

Only a Trillion (essays), Abelard-Schuman (London, England), 1958, published as *Marvels of Science: Essays of Fact and Fancy on Life, Its Environment, Its Possibilities,* Collier Books (New York, NY), 1962, reprinted under original title, Ace Books (New York, NY), 1976.

The World of Carbon, Abelard-Schuman (London, England), 1958, revised edition, Collier Books (New York, NY), 1962.

The World of Nitrogen, Abelard-Schuman (London, England), 1958, revised edition, Collier Books (New York, NY), 1962.

The Clock We Live On, Abelard-Schuman (London, England), 1959, revised edition, 1965.

Words of Science and the History behind Them, Houghton Mifflin (Boston, MA), 1959, revised edition, Harrap (London, England), 1974.

Realm of Numbers, Houghton Mifflin (Boston, MA), 1959.

The Living River, Abelard-Schuman (London, England), 1959, published as *The Bloodstream: River of Life,* Collier Books (New York, NY), 1961.

The Kingdom of the Sun, Abelard-Schuman (London, England), 1960, revised edition, 1963.

Realm of Measure, Houghton Mifflin (Boston, MA), 1960.

The Wellsprings of Life, Abelard-Schuman, (London, England), 1960, New American Library (New York, NY), 1961.

The Intelligent Man's Guide to Science, two volumes, Basic Books (New York, NY), 1960, Volume 1 published separately as *The Intelligent Man's Guide to the Physical Sciences,* Pocket Books (New York, NY), 1964, Volume 2 published separately as *The Intelligent Man's Guide to the Biological Sciences,* Pocket Books (New York, NY), 1964, revised edition published as *The New Intelligent Man's Guide to Science,* 1965, published as *Asimov's Guide to Science,* 1972, revised edition published as *Asimov's New Guide to Science,* 1984.

The Double Planet, Abelard-Schuman (London, England), 1960, revised edition, 1967.

Realm of Algebra, Houghton Mifflin (Boston, MA), 1961.

Life and Energy, Doubleday (New York, NY), 1962.

Fact and Fancy (essays), Doubleday (New York, NY), 1962.

The Search for the Elements, Basic Books (New York, NY), 1962.

The Genetic Code, Orion Press (New York, NY), 1963.

The Human Body: Its Structure and Operation (also see below), Houghton Mifflin (Boston, MA), 1963.

View from a Height, Doubleday (New York, NY), 1963.

The Human Brain: Its Capacities and Functions (also see below), Houghton Mifflin (Boston, MA), 1964, revised and expanded edition, Penguin (New York, NY), 1994.

A Short History of Biology, Natural History Press for the American Museum of Natural History, 1964, reprinted, Greenwood Press (Westport, CT), 1980.

Quick and Easy Math, Houghton Mifflin (Boston, MA), 1964.

Adding a Dimension: Seventeen Essays on the History of Science, Doubleday (New York, NY), 1964.

(With Stephen H. Dole) *Planets for Man,* Random House (New York, NY), 1964.

Asimov's Biographical Encyclopedia of Science and Technology, Doubleday (New York, NY), 1964, 2nd revised edition, 1982.

A Short History of Chemistry, Doubleday (New York, NY), 1965.

Of Time and Space and Other Things (essays), Doubleday (New York, NY), 1965.

An Easy Introduction to the Slide Rule, Houghton Mifflin (Boston, MA), 1965.

The Noble Gasses, Basic Books (New York, NY), 1966.

The Neutrino: Ghost Particle of the Atom, Doubleday (New York, NY), 1966.

Understanding Physics, three volumes, Walker (New York, NY), 1966.

The Genetic Effects of Radiation, U.S. Atomic Energy Commission (Washington, DC), 1966.

The Universe: From Flat Earth to Quasar, Walker (New York, NY), 1966, 3rd edition published as *The Universe: From Flat Earth to Black Holes—and Beyond,* 1980.

From Earth to Heaven (essays), Doubleday (New York, NY), 1966.

Environments out There, Abelard-Schuman (London, England), 1967.

Is Anyone There? (essays), Doubleday (New York, NY), 1967.

Science, Numbers and I (essays), Doubleday (New York, NY), 1968.

Photosynthesis, Basic Books (New York, NY), 1968.

Twentieth-Century Discovery (essays), Doubleday (New York, NY), 1969, revised edition, Ace Books (New York, NY), 1976.

The Solar System and Back (essays), Doubleday (New York, NY), 1970.

The Stars in Their Courses (essays), Doubleday (New York, NY), 1971, revised edition, Ace Books (New York, NY), 1976.

The Left Hand of the Electron (essays), Doubleday (New York, NY), 1972.

Electricity and Man, U.S. Atomic Energy Commission (Washington, DC), 1972.

Worlds within Worlds: The Story of Nuclear Energy, three volumes, U.S. Atomic Energy Commission (Washington, DC), 1972.

A Short History of Chemistry, Heinemann (London, England), 1972.

Today and Tomorrow and . . . , Doubleday (New York, NY), 1973.

The Tragedy of the Moon, Doubleday (New York, NY), 1973.

Asimov on Astronomy (essays), Doubleday (New York, NY), 1974.

Our World in Space, foreword by Edwin E. Aldrin, Jr., New York Graphic Society (New York, NY), 1974.

Asimov on Chemistry (essays), Doubleday (New York, NY), 1974.

Of Matters Great and Small, Doubleday (New York, NY), 1975.

Science Past, Science Future, Doubleday (New York, NY), 1975.

Eyes on the Universe: A History of the Telescope, Houghton Mifflin (Boston, MA), 1975.

The Ends of the Earth: The Polar Regions of the World, Weybright Talley, 1975.

Asimov on Physics (essays), Doubleday (New York, NY), 1976.

The Planet That Wasn't (essays), Doubleday (New York, NY), 1976.

The Collapsing Universe, Walker (New York, NY), 1977.

Asimov on Numbers (essays), Doubleday (New York, NY), 1977.

The Beginning and the End (essays), Doubleday (New York, NY), 1977.

Quasar, Quasar, Burning Bright (essays), Doubleday (New York, NY), 1978.

Life and Time, Doubleday (New York, NY), 1978.

The Road to Infinity (essays), Doubleday (New York, NY), 1979.

A Choice of Catastrophes: The Disasters That Threaten Our World, Simon & Schuster (New York, NY), 1979.

The Shaping of England, Houghton Mifflin (Boston, MA), 1969.

Constantinople: The Forgotten Empire, Houghton Mifflin (Boston, MA), 1970.

The Land of Canaan, Houghton Mifflin (Boston, MA), 1970.

Visions of the Universe, preface by Carl Sagan, Cosmos Store, 1981.

The Sun Shines Bright (essays), Doubleday (New York, NY), 1981.

Exploring the Earth and the Cosmos: The Growth and Future of Human Knowledge, Crown (New York, NY), 1982.

Counting the Eons, Doubleday (New York, NY), 1983.

The Roving Mind, Prometheus Books (Amherst, NY), 1983, revised edition, 1997.

The Measure of the Universe, Harper (New York, NY), 1983.

X Stands for Unknown, Doubleday (New York, NY), 1984.

The History of Physics, Walker (New York, NY), 1984.

Isaac Asimov on the Human Body and the Human Brain (contains *The Human Body: Its Structure and Operation* and *The Human Brain: Its Capacities and Functions*), Bonanza Books (New York, NY), 1984.

The Exploding Suns: The Secrets of the Supernovas, Dutton (New York, NY), 1985, updated edition, Plume (New York, NY), 1996.

Asimov's Guide to Halley's Comet, Walker (New York, NY), 1985.

The Subatomic Monster, Doubleday (New York, NY), 1985.

(With Karen Frenkel) *Robots: Machines in Man's Image,* Robot Institute of America, 1985.

Isaac Asimov's Wonderful Worldwide Science Bazaar: Seventy-two Up-to-Date Reports on the State of Everything from Inside the Atom to Outside the Universe, Houghton Mifflin (Boston, MA), 1986.

The Dangers of Intelligence and Other Science Essays, Houghton Mifflin (Boston, MA), 1986.

Far As Human Eye Could See (essays), Doubleday (New York, NY), 1987.

The Relativity of Wrong: Essays on the Solar System and Beyond, Doubleday (New York, NY), 1988.

Asimov on Science: A Thirty-Year Retrospective, Doubleday (New York, NY), 1989.

Asimov's Chronology of Science and Technology: How Science Has Shaped the World and How the World Has Affected Science from 4,000,000 B.C. to the Present, Harper (New York, NY), 1989, updated and illustrated edition, 1994.

The Secret of the Universe, Doubleday (New York, NY), 1989.

The Tyrannosaurus Prescription and One Hundred Other Essays, Prometheus Books (Amherst, NY), 1989.

Out of the Everywhere, Doubleday (New York, NY), 1990.

Atom: Journey across the Subatomic Cosmos, New American Library (New York, NY), 1991.

Frontiers: New Discoveries about Man and His Planet, Outer Space, and the Universe, New American Library (New York, NY), 1991.

Asimov's Chronology of the World, HarperCollins (New York, NY), 1991.

Asimov's Guide to Earth and Space, Random House (New York, NY), 1991.

(With Frederick Pohl) *Our Angry Earth,* Tor Books (New York, NY), 1991.

Frontiers II: More Recent Discoveries about Life, Earth, Space, and the Universe, Truman Valley Books/Dutton (New York, NY), 1993.

Aliens and Extraterrestrials: Are We Alone? (revised and updated edition of *Is There Life on Other Planets?*), Gareth Stevens (Milwaukee, WI), 1995.

JUVENILE NONFICTION

Building Blocks of the Universe, Abelard-Schuman (London, England), 1957, revised and updated edition, 1974.

Breakthroughs in Science, Houghton Mifflin (Boston, MA), 1960.

Satellites in Outer Space, Random House (New York, NY), 1960, revised edition, 1973.

Words from the Myths, Houghton Mifflin (Boston, MA), 1961.

Words in Genesis, Houghton Mifflin (Boston, MA), 1962.

Words on the Map, Houghton Mifflin (Boston, MA), 1962.

Words from Exodus, Houghton Mifflin (Boston, MA), 1963.

The Kite That Won the Revolution (juvenile), Houghton Mifflin (Boston, MA), 1963, revised edition, 1973.

The Greeks: A Great Adventure, Houghton Mifflin (Boston, MA), 1965.

The Roman Republic, Houghton Mifflin (Boston, MA), 1966.

The Moon, Follett (New York, NY), 1966.

To the Ends of the Universe, Walker (New York, NY), 1967, revised edition, 1976.

Mars, Follett (New York, NY), 1967.

The Roman Empire, Houghton Mifflin (Boston, MA), 1967.

The Egyptians, Houghton Mifflin (Boston, MA), 1967.

The Near East: Ten Thousand Years of History, Houghton Mifflin (Boston, MA), 1968.

Asimov's Guide to the Bible, Doubleday (New York, NY), Volume 1: *The Old Testament,* 1968, Volume 2: *The New Testament,* 1969.

The Dark Ages, Houghton Mifflin (Boston, MA), 1968.

Words from History, Houghton Mifflin (Boston, MA), 1968.

Stars, Follett (New York, NY), 1968.

Galaxies, Follett (New York, NY), 1968.

ABC's of Space, Walker (New York, NY), 1969, published as *Space Dictionary,* Scholastic (New York, NY), 1970.

Great Ideas of Science, Houghton Mifflin (Boston, MA), 1969.

ABC's of the Ocean, Walker (New York, NY), 1970.

Light, Follett (New York, NY), 1970.

What Makes the Sun Shine?, Little, Brown (Boston, MA), 1971.

ABC's of the Earth, Walker (New York, NY), 1971.

ABC's of Ecology, Walker (New York, NY), 1972.

Ginn Science Program, Ginn (New York, NY), intermediate levels A, B, and C, 1972, advanced levels A and B, 1973.

Comets and Meteors, Follett (New York, NY), 1972.

The Sun, Follett (New York, NY), 1972.

More Words of Science, Houghton Mifflin (Boston, MA), 1972.

The Story of Ruth, Doubleday (New York, NY), 1972.

The Shaping of France, Houghton Mifflin (Boston, MA), 1972.

The Shaping of North America from Earliest Times to 1763, Houghton Mifflin (Boston, MA), 1973.

Jupiter, the Largest Planet, Lothrop (New York, NY), 1973, revised edition, 1976.

Please Explain, Houghton Mifflin (Boston, MA), 1973.

Earth: Our Crowded Spaceship, John Day (New York, NY), 1974.

The Birth of the United States, 1763-1816, Houghton Mifflin (Boston, MA), 1974.

Our Federal Union: The United States from 1816 to 1865, Houghton Mifflin (Boston, MA), 1975.

The Solar System, Follett (New York, NY), 1975.

Alpha Centauri, the Nearest Star, Lothrop (New York, NY), 1976.

Mars, the Red Planet, Lothrop (New York, NY), 1977.

The Golden Door: The United States from 1865 to 1918, Houghton Mifflin (Boston, MA), 1977.

Animals of the Bible, Doubleday (New York, NY), 1978.

Saturn and Beyond, Lothrop (New York, NY), 1979.

Extraterrestrial Civilizations (speculative nonfiction), Crown (New York, NY), 1979.

Isaac Asimov's Book of Facts, Grosset (New York, NY), 1979.

Venus: Near Neighbor of the Sun, Lothrop (New York, NY), 1981.

In the Beginning: Science Faces God in the Book of Genesis, Crown (New York, NY), 1981.

The Edge of Tomorrow, T. Doherty (New York, NY), 1985.

(With James Burke and Jules Bergman) *The Impact of Science on Society,* National Aeronautics and Space Administration (NASA), 1985.

Futuredays: A Nineteenth-Century Vision of the Year 2000, Holt (New York, NY), 1986.

Beginnings: The Story of Origins—Of Mankind, Life, the Earth, the Universe, Walker (New York, NY), 1987.

Franchise, Creative Education (Mankato, IL), 1988.

All the Troubles of World, Creative Education (Mankato, IL), 1988.

(With Frank White) *Think about Space: Where Have We Been and Where Are We Going?,* Walker (New York, NY), 1989.

Little Treasury of Dinosaurs, Crown (New York, NY), 1989.

Unidentified Flying Objects, Dell (New York, NY), 1990.

(With Frank White) *The March of the Millennia: A Key to Looking at History,* Walker (New York, NY), 1990.

Ancient Astronomy, Dell (New York, NY), 1991.

Also author of volumes in the "How Did We Find Out" series, Walker (New York, NY), beginning 1972.

"NEW LIBRARY OF THE UNIVERSE" SERIES

Ferdinand Magellan: Opening the Door to World Exploration, Gareth Stevens (Milwaukee, WI), 1991.

Henry Hudson: Arctic Explorer and North American Adventurer, Gareth Stevens (Milwaukee, WI), 1991.

A Distant Puzzle: The Planet Uranus (revised edition of *Uranus, the Sideways Planet*), Gareth Stevens (Milwaukee, WI), 1994.

Cosmic Debris: The Asteroids (revised edition of *The Asteroids*), Gareth Stevens (Milwaukee, WI), 1994.

Death from Space: What Killed the Dinosaurs? (revised and updated edition of *Did Comets Kill the Dinosaurs?*), Gareth Stevens (Milwaukee, WI), 1994.

(With Greg Walz-Chojnacki) *The Moon* (revised edition of *Earth's Moon*), Gareth Stevens (Milwaukee, WI), 1994.

(With Francis Reddy) *The Red Planet: Mars* (revised edition of *Mars*), Gareth Stevens (Milwaukee, WI), 1994.

(With Francis Reddy) *Mysteries of Deep Space: Black Holes, Pulsars, and Quasars* (revised edition of *Quasars, Pulsars, and Black Holes*), Gareth Stevens (Milwaukee, WI), 1994.

(With Greg Walz-Chojnacki) *Our Planetary System* (revised edition of *Our Solar System*), Gareth Stevens (Milwaukee, WI), 1994.

(With Francis Reddy) *The Sun and Its Secrets* (revised edition of *Sun*), Gareth Stevens (Milwaukee, WI), 1994.

(With Greg Walz-Chojnacki) *UFOs: True Mysteries or Hoaxes?* (revised edition of *Unidentified Flying Objects*), Gareth Stevens (Milwaukee, WI), 1995.

Astronomy in Ancient Times (revised and updated), Gareth Stevens (Milwaukee, WI), 1995.

The Birth of Our Universe (revised and updated edition of *How Was the Universe Born?*), Gareth Stevens (Milwaukee, WI), 1995.

Discovering Comets and Meteors (revised edition of *Comets and Meteors*), Gareth Stevens (Milwaukee, WI), 1995.

(With Greg Walz-Chojnacki) *Our Vast Home: The Milky Way and Other Galaxies* (revised edition of *Our Milky Way and Other Galaxies*), Gareth Stevens (Milwaukee, WI), 1995.

(With Francis Reddy) *Exploring Outer Space: Rockets, Probes, and Satellites* (revised edition of *Rockets, Probes, and Satellites,* Gareth Stevens (Milwaukee, WI), 1995.

(With Greg Walz-Chojnacki) *Science Fiction: Visions of Tommorow?* (revised edition of *Science Fiction, Science Fact*), Gareth Stevens (Milwaukee, WI), 1995.

(With Greg Walz-Chojnacki) *Pollution in Space* (revised edition of *Space Garbage*), Gareth Stevens (Milwaukee, WI), 1995.

(With Greg Walz-Chojnacki) *Space Colonies* (revised edition of *Colonizing the Planets and Stars*), Gareth Stevens (Milwaukee, WI), 1995.

(With Francis Reddy) *Space Explorers* (revised edition of *Piloted Space Flights*), Gareth Stevens (Milwaukee, WI), 1995.

(With Francis Reddy) *Star Cycles: The Life and Death of Stars* (revised edition of *Birth and Death of Stars*), Gareth Stevens (Milwaukee, WI), 1995.

(With Francis Reddy) *A Stargazer's Guide* (revised edition of *Space Spotter's Guide*), Gareth Stevens (Milwaukee, WI), 1995.

(With Francis Reddy) *Our Planet Earth* (revised edition), Gareth Stevens (Milwaukee, WI), 1995, revised by Richard Hantula as *Earth*, 2002.

(With Francis Reddy) *The Ringed Planet: Saturn* (revised edition of *Saturn*), Gareth Stevens (Milwaukee, WI), 1995.

(With Greg Walz-Chojnacki) *Planet of Extremes—Jupiter* (revised edition of *Jupiter*), Gareth Stevens (Milwaukee, WI), 1995.

(With Francis Reddy) *Nearest Sun: The Planet Mercury* (revised edition of *Mercury*), Gareth Stevens (Milwaukee, WI), 1995.

A Distant Giant: The Planet Neptune (revised edition of *Neptune*), Gareth Stevens (Milwaukee, WI), 1996.

(With Greg Walz-Chojnacki) *A Double Planet?: Pluto and Charon* (revised edition of *Pluto*), Gareth Stevens (Milwaukee, WI), 1996, revised by Richard Hantula, 2002.

(With Francis Reddy) *Earth's Twin: The Planet Venus* (revised edition of *Venus*), Gareth Stevens (Milwaukee, WI), 1996.

(With Francis Reddy) *Global Space Programs* (revised edition of *The World's Space Programs*), Gareth Stevens (Milwaukee, WI), 1996.

(With Francis Reddy) *Folklore and Legend of the Universe* (revised edition of *Mythology and the Universe*), Gareth Stevens (Milwaukee, WI), 1996.

(With Greg Walz-Chojnacki) *The Twenty-first Century in Space* (revised edition of *The Future in Space*), Gareth Stevens (Milwaukee, WI), 1996.

(With Greg Walz-Chojnacki) *Modern Astronomy* (revised edition of *Astronomy Today*), Gareth Stevens (Milwaukee, WI), 1996.

(With Greg Walz-Chojnacki) *Astronomy Projects* (revised edition of *Projects in Astronomy)*, Gareth Stevens (Milwaukee, WI), 1996.

Isaac Asimov's New Library of the Universe Index, Gareth Stevens (Milwaukee, WI), 1996.

OTHER

Opus 100 (selections from author's first one hundred books), Houghton Mifflin (Boston, MA), 1969.

Asimov's Guide to Shakespeare, two volumes, Doubleday (New York, NY), 1970, published in one volume, Avenel Books, 1981.

Unseen World (teleplay), American Broadcasting Co. (ABC-TV), 1970.

(Under pseudonym Dr. A) *The Sensuous Dirty Old Man,* Walker (New York, NY), 1971.

Isaac Asimov's Treasury of Humor: A Lifetime Collection of Favorite Jokes, Anecdotes, and Limericks with Copious Notes on How to Tell Them and Why, Houghton Mifflin (Boston, MA), 1971.

(With James Gunn) *The History of Science Fiction from 1938 to the Present* (filmscript), Extramural Independent Study Center, University of Kansas, 1971.

Asimov's Annotated "Don Juan," Doubleday (New York, NY), 1972.

Asimov's Annotated "Paradise Lost," Doubleday (New York, NY), 1974.

Lecherous Limericks, Walker (New York, NY), 1975.

"The Dream," "Benjamin's Dream," and "Benjamin's Bicentennial Blast": Three Short Stories, Printing Week in New York (New York, NY), 1976.

More Lecherous Limericks, Walker (New York, NY), 1976.

Familiar Poems Annotated, Doubleday (New York, NY), 1977.

Still More Lecherous Limericks, Walker (New York, NY), 1977.

Asimov's Sherlockian Limericks, New Mysterious Press, 1978.

(With John Ciardi) *Limericks Too Gross,* Norton (New York, NY), 1978.

Opus 200 (selections from the author's second hundred books), Houghton Mifflin (Boston, MA), 1979.

In Memory Yet Green: The Autobiography of Isaac Asimov, 1920-1954, Doubleday (New York, NY), 1979.

In Joy Still Felt: The Autobiography of Isaac Asimov, 1954-1978, Doubleday (New York, NY), 1980.

The Annotated "Gulliver's Travels," C.N. Potter, 1980.

Asimov on Science Fiction, Doubleday (New York, NY), 1981.

Change!: Seventy-one Glimpses of the Future (forecasts), Houghton Mifflin (Boston, MA), 1981.

(With John Ciardi) *A Grossery of Limericks,* Norton (New York, NY), 1981.

Would You Believe?, Grosset (New York, NY), 1981.

(With Ken Fisher) *Isaac Asimov Presents Superquiz,* Dembner, 1982.

More—Would You Believe?, Grosset (New York, NY), 1982.

(Editor, with George R. Martin) *The Science Fiction Weight-Loss Book,* Crown (New York, NY), 1983.

(Editor, with Martin H. Greenberg and Charles G. Waugh) *Isaac Asimov Presents the Best Horror and Supernatural of the Nineteenth Century,* Beaufort Books, 1983.

(Editor) *Thirteen Horrors of Halloween,* Avon (New York, NY), 1983.

(Editor, with Martin H. Greenberg and George Zebrowski, and author of introduction) *Creations: The Quest for Origins in Story and Science,* Crown (New York, NY), 1983.

(With Ken Fisher) *Isaac Asimov Presents Superquiz 2,* Dembner, 1983.

Opus 300 (selections from the author's third hundred books), Houghton Mifflin (Boston, MA), 1984.

Isaac Asimov's Limericks for Children, Caedmon, 1984.

(Editor) *Living in the Future* (forecasts), Beaufort Books, 1985.

Isaac Asimov, Octopus Books, 1986.

(Editor) *Sherlock Holmes through Time and Space,* Bluejay Books, 1986.

The Alternate Asimovs, Doubleday (New York, NY), 1986.

Other Worlds of Isaac Asimov, edited by Martin H. Greenberg, Avenel, 1986.

Past, Present, and Future, Prometheus Books (Amherst, NY), 1987.

Robot Dreams, edited by Byron Preiss, Berkley (New York, NY), 1987.

(With Janet Asimov) *How to Enjoy Writing: A Book of Aid and Comfort,* Walker (New York, NY), 1987.

Asimov's Annotated Gilbert and Sullivan, Doubleday (New York, NY), 1988.

(Editor, with Jason A. Schulman) *Isaac Asimov's Book of Science and Nature Quotations,* Weidenfeld & Nicolson (London, England), 1988.

Asimov's Galaxy: Reflections on Science Fiction, Doubleday (New York, NY), 1989.

Foundation's Friends: Stories in Honor of Isaac Asimov, edited by Martin H. Greenberg, Tom Doherty (New York, NY), 1989.

(Compiler, with Martin H. Greenberg) *Cosmic Critiques: How and Why Ten Science Fiction Stories Work,* Writer's Digest, 1990.

(Contributor) *The John W. Campbell Letters with Isaac Asimov and A.E. van Vogt,* A.C. Projects, 1991.

Isaac Asimov Laughs Again, HarperCollins (New York, NY), 1991.

I. Asimov: A Memoir, Doubleday (New York, NY), 1994.

I, Robot: The Illustrated Screenplay, Warner (New York, NY), 1994.

Yours, Isaac Asimov: A Lifetime of Letters, Doubleday (New York, NY), 1995.

Magic: The Final Fantasy Collection, HarperPrism (New York, NY), 1996.

The Best of Isaac Asimov's Super Quiz, Barricade (New York, NY), 1996.

Isaac Asimov's I-Bots: History of I-Botics: An Illustrated Novel, HarperPrism (New York, NY), 1997.

Isaac Asimov's Christmas, Ace Books (New York, NY), 1997.

Isaac Asimov's Solar System, Ace Books (New York, NY), 1999.

Isaac Asimov's Father's Day, Ace Books (New York, NY), 2001.

Isaac Asimov's Halloween, Ace Books (New York, NY), 2001.

Isaac Asimov Collected Short Stories, Peterson Publishing (North Mankato, MN), 2001.

It's Been a Good Life, edited by Janet Jeppson Asimov, Prometheus (Amherst, NY), 2002.

Also author of *The Adventures of Science Fiction,* Ameron Ltd. Author of "Science" column in *Magazine of Fantasy and Science Fiction,* 1958-92. Contributor of stories to numerous science-fiction anthologies, and to many science-fiction magazines, including *Astounding Science Fiction, Amazing Stories, Fantastic Adventures, Science Fiction,* and *Future Fiction;* contributor of short story under pseudonym George E. Dale to *Astounding Science Fiction.* Contributor of articles to science journals and periodicals. Editorial director, *Isaac Asimov's Science Fiction Magazine.*

ADAPTATIONS: A sound recording of William Shatner reading the first eight chapters of *Foundation* was produced as *Foundation: The Psychohistorians,* Caedmon, 1976, and of Asimov reading from the same novel was produced as *The Mayors,* Caedmon, 1977; the film *The Ugly Little Boy* was adapted from Asimov's short story of the same title, Learning Corporation of America, 1977; *I, Robot* was adapted for film, 20th Century Fox, 2004.

SIDELIGHTS: Isaac Asimov was "the world's most prolific science writer," according to David N. Samuelson in *Twentieth-Century Science-Fiction Writers,* and he "has written some of the best-known science fiction ever published." Considered one of the three greatest writers of science fiction in the 1940s—along with Robert Heinlein and A.E. van Vogt—Asimov remained throughout his life a potent force in the genre. Stories such as "Nightfall" and "The Bicentennial Man," and novels such as *The Gods Themselves* and *Foundation's Edge* have received numerous honors and are recognized as among the best science fiction ever written. As one of the world's leading writers on science, explaining everything from nuclear fusion to the theory of numbers, Asimov illuminated for many the mysteries of science and technology. He was a skilled raconteur as well, who enlivened his writing with incidents from his own life. "In his autobiographical writings and comments," stated James Gunn in *Isaac Asimov: The Foundations of Science Fiction*, "Asimov continually invites the reader to share his triumphs, to laugh at his blunders and lack of sophistication, and to wonder, with him, at the rise to prominence of a bright Jewish boy brought to this country from Russia at the age of three and raised in a collection of Brooklyn candy stores."

Asimov's interest in science fiction began when he first noticed several of the early science-fiction magazines for sale on the newsstand of his family's candy store. Although as a boy he read and enjoyed numerous volumes of nonfiction as well as many of the literary "classics," Asimov recalled in his first autobiography, *In Memory Yet Green,* that he still longed to explore the intriguing magazines with their glossy covers. But his father refused, maintaining that fiction magazines are "junk! . . . Not fit to read. The only people who read magazines like that are bums." And bums represented "the dregs of society, apprentice gangsters."

In August of 1929, a new magazine appeared on the scene called *Science Wonder Stories.* Asimov knew that as long as science-fiction magazines had titles like *Amazing Stories,* he would have little chance of convincing his father of their worth. However, the new periodical had the word "science" in its title, and he said, "I had read enough about science to know that it was a mentally nourishing and spiritually wholesome study. What's more, I knew that my father thought so from our occasional talks about my schoolwork." When confronted with this argument, the elder Asimov consented. Soon Isaac began collecting even those periodicals that didn't have "science" in the title. He noted: "I planned to maintain with all the strength at my disposal the legal position that permission for one such magazine implied permission for all the others, regardless of title. No fight was needed, however; my harassed father conceded everything." Asimov rapidly developed into an avid fan.

Asimov first tried writing stories when he was eleven years old. He had for some time been reading stories and then retelling them to his schoolmates, and had also

started a book like some of the popular boys' series volumes of the 1920s: "The Rover Boys," "The Bobbsey Twins," and "Pee Wee Wilson." Asimov's story was called "The Greenville Chums at College," patterned after *The Darewell Chums at College,* and it grew to eight chapters before he abandoned it. Asimov, in *In Memory Yet Green,* described the flaw in his initial literary venture: "I was trying to imitate the series books without knowing anything but what I read there. Their characters were small-town boys, so mine were, for I imagined Greenville to be a town in upstate New York. Their characters went to college, so mine did. Unfortunately, a junior high school youngster living in a shabby neighborhood in Brooklyn knows very little about small-town life and even less about college. Even I, myself, was forced eventually to recognize the fact that I didn't know what I was talking about."

Despite initial discouragements, Asimov continued to write. His first published piece appeared in his high school's literary semiannual and was accepted, he once admitted, because it was the only funny piece anyone wrote, and the editors needed something funny. In the summer of 1934 Asimov had a letter published in *Astounding Stories* in which he commented on several stories that had appeared in the magazine. His continuing activities as a fan prompted him to attempt a science fiction piece of his own; in 1937, at the age of seventeen, he began a story titled "Cosmic Corkscrew." The procedure Asimov used to formulate the plot was, he later said, "typical of my science fiction. I usually thought of some scientific gimmick and built a story about that."

By the time he finished the story on June 19, 1938, *Astounding Stories* had become *Astounding Science Fiction.* Its editor was John W. Campbell, who was to influence the work of some of the most prominent authors of modern science fiction, including Arthur C. Clarke, Robert Heinlein, Poul Anderson, L. Sprague de Camp, and Theodore Sturgeon. Since Campbell was also one of the best-known science fiction writers of the thirties and *Astounding* one of the most prestigious publications in its field at the time, Asimov was shocked by his father's suggestion that he submit "Cosmic Corkscrew" to the editor in person: mailing the story would cost twelve cents while subway fare, round trip, was only ten cents. In the interest of economy, therefore, Asimov agreed to make the trip to the magazine's office, fully expecting to leave the manuscript with a secretary.

It was Campbell's habit to invite many young writers to discuss their work with him, and when Asimov arrived he was shown into the editor's office. Campbell talked with him for over an hour and agreed to read the story; two days later Asimov received the manuscript back in the mail. It had been rejected, but Campbell offered extensive suggestions for improvement and encouraged the young man to keep trying. This began a pattern that was to continue for several years, with Campbell guiding Asimov through his formative beginnings as a science-fiction writer.

Asimov's association with the field of science fiction was a long and distinguished one. He has been credited with the introduction of several innovative concepts into the genre, including the formulation of the "Three Laws of Robotics." Asimov maintained that the idea for the laws was given to him by Campbell; Campbell, on the other hand, said that he had merely picked them out of Asimov's early robot stories. In any case, it was Asimov who first formally stated the three laws: "1. A robot may not injure a human being or, through inaction, allow a human being to come to harm. 2. A robot must obey the orders given it by human beings except where such orders would conflict with the First Law. 3. A robot must protect its own existence as long as such protection does not conflict with the First or Second Laws." Asimov said that he used these precepts as the basis for "over two dozen short stories and three novels . . . about robots," and he felt that he was "probably more famous for them than for anything else I have written, and they are quoted even outside the science-fiction world. The very word 'robotics' was coined by me." The three laws gained general acceptance among readers and among other science-fiction writers; Asimov, in his autobiography, wrote that they "revolutionized" science fiction and that "no writer could write a *stupid* robot story if he used the Three Laws. The story might be bad on other counts, but it wouldn't be stupid." The laws became so popular, and seemed so logical, that many people believed real robots would eventually be designed according to Asimov's basic principles.

Also notable among Asimov's science-fiction works is the "Foundation" series. This group of short stories, published in magazines in the 1940s and then collected into a trilogy in the early 1950s, was inspired by Edward Gibbon's *Decline and Fall of the Roman Empire.* It was written as a "future history," a story being told in a society of the distant future which relates events of that society's history. The concept was not invented by Asimov, but there can be little doubt that he became a master of the technique. *Foundation, Foundation and Empire,* and *Second Foundation* have achieved special standing among science-fiction enthusiasts. In 1966 the World Science Fiction Convention honored them with a special Hugo Award as the best all-time science-fiction

series. Decades after its original publication Asimov's future-history series remained popular, and in the 1980s Asimov added a new volume, *Foundation's Edge,* and eventually linked the "Foundation" stories with his robot novels in *The Robots of Dawn, Robots and Empire, Foundation and Earth,* and *Prelude to Foundation.*

Asimov's first stories written specifically for a younger audience were his "Lucky Starr" novels. In 1951, at the suggestion of his Doubleday editor, he began working on a series of science-fiction stories that could easily be adapted for television. "Television was here; that was clear," he wrote in *In Memory Yet Green.* "Why not take advantage of it, then? Radio had its successful long-running series, 'The Lone Ranger,' so why not a 'Space Ranger' modeled very closely upon that?" *David Starr: Space Ranger,* published under the pseudonym Paul French, introduced David 'Lucky' Starr, agent of the interplanetary law enforcement agency the Council of Science. Accompanying Lucky on his adventures is sidekick John Bigman Jones, a short, tough man born and raised on the great agricultural farms of Mars. Together the two of them confront and outwit space pirates, poisoners, mad scientists, and interstellar spies— humans from the Sirian star system, who have become the Earth's worst enemies.

Although the "Lucky Starr" series ran to six volumes, the television deal Asimov and his editor envisioned never materialized. "None of us dreamed that for some reason . . . television series would very rarely last more than two or three years," Asimov wrote. "We also didn't know that a juvenile television series to be called *Rocky Jones: Space Ranger* was already in the works." Another problem the series faced was in the scientific background of the stories. "Unfortunately," stated Jean Fiedler and Jim Mele in *Isaac Asimov,* "Asimov had the bad luck to be writing these stories on the threshold of an unprecedented exploration of our solar system's planets, an exploration which has immensely increased our astronomical knowledge. Many of his scientific premises, sound in 1952, were later found to be inaccurate." In subsequent editions of the books Asimov included forewords explaining the situation to new readers.

Asimov's first nonfiction book—the beginning of what would number several hundred works for adults and younger readers—was a medical text titled *Biochemistry and Human Metabolism,* begun in 1950 and written in collaboration with William Boyd and Burnham Walker, two of his colleagues at the Boston University School of Medicine. He had recognized his ability as an explainer early in life, and he enjoyed clarifying scientific principles for his family and friends. He also discovered that he was a most able and entertaining lecturer who delighted in his work as a teacher. He once told *New York Times* interviewer Israel Shenker that his talent lay in the fact that he could "read a dozen dull books and make one interesting book out of them." The result was that Asimov was phenomenally successful as a writer of science books for the general public. Asimov later added: "I'm on fire to explain, and happiest when it's something reasonably intricate which I can make clear step by step. It's the easiest way I can clarify things in my own mind."

Toward the end of his career particularly, Asimov was concerned with a variety of subjects that went far beyond the scientific, and wrote on such diverse topics as the Bible, mythology, William Shakespeare, ecology, and American history. Asimov additionally wrote several volumes of autobiography, beginning with *In Memory Yet Green* in 1979 and culminating in *I. Asimov: A Memoir,* a 1994 work composed of 166 short chapters that discuss key elements which shaped the author's life. Michael Swanwick characterized the work as "quintessential Asimov," and Michael White commented that Asimov "was our era's great artist of explanation, a master of the declarative sentence and the lockstep paragraph, and both his fiction and his nonfiction conspire to convince you that the world makes more sense than you thought it did." In 1995 Stanley Asimov presented a significant contribution to the literary biography of his brother by publishing *Yours, Isaac Asimov: A Lifetime of Letters.* Organized thematically, the volume presents excerpts from thousands of letters and notes written by Isaac Asimov over the course of his life.

The years immediately preceding and following the author's death witnessed the publication of anthologies and collections of Asimov's fictional and prose writings. In 1990, for example, a collection titled *Robot Visions* appeared, encompassing all of Asimov's short stories and essays concerning robots. In 1995 the posthumous collection *Magic: The Final Fantasy Collection* was published, collecting numerous pieces for the first time. Many of the short stories in the anthology feature the comic adventures of George and the feckless supernatural being Azazel; and the volume additionally contains Asimov's critical writings on such noted fantasy writers as J.R.R. Tolkien, Robert E. Howard, and L. Sprague de Camp.

When Asimov died in 1992 he received numerous tributes highlighting the breadth of his curiosity and acknowledging his profound impact in enlarging the pos-

sibilities of the science fiction genre. Over the following decade, Asimov's second wife, Janet Jeppson Asimov, condensed her husband's autobiographies—numbering some 2,000 pages—into a single 300-page volume titled *It's Been a Good Life,* which was published in 2002. Arranged topically rather than chronologically, the work is divided into chapters that treat such topics as education, war, religion, family, writing, sexism, and his own illnesses. In addition to Asimov's words, Jepson Asimov includes excerpts from her correspondence with her husband, an account of his final days alive, and an epilogue in which she explains that he had contracted the AIDS virus from a blood transfusion during an 1983 triple-bypass operation, a fact he kept secret. Among the work's enthusiasts was *Booklist*'s Roland Green, who dubbed it a "good introduction" to Asimov's career, and a *Publishers Weekly* reviewer, who predicted that this "readable and idiosyncratic self-portrait" would likely attract new readers to Asimov's works.

BIOGRAPHICAL AND CRITICAL SOURCES:

BOOKS

Asimov, Isaac, *The Bicentennial Man and Other Stories,* Doubleday (New York, NY), 1976.

Asimov, Isaac, *In Memory Yet Green: The Autobiography of Isaac Asimov, 1920-1954,* Doubleday (New York, NY), 1979.

Asimov, Isaac, *In Joy Still Felt: The Autobiography of Isaac Asimov, 1954-1979,* Doubleday (New York, NY), 1980.

Boerst, William J., *Isaac Asimov: Writer of the Future,* Morgan Reynolds, 1998.

Children's Literature Review, Volume 12, Thomson Gale (Detroit, MI), 1987.

Clareson, Thomas D., editor, *Voices for the Future: Essays on Major Science-Fiction Writers,* Popular Press, 1976.

Contemporary Literary Criticism, Thomson Gale (Detroit, MI), Volume 1, 1973, Volume 3, 1975, Volume 9, 1978, Volume 19, 1981, Volume 26, 1983.

Dictionary of Literary Biography, Volume 8: *Twentieth-Century American Science-Fiction Writers,* Thomson Gale (Detroit, MI), 1981.

Fiedler, Jean, and Jim Mele, *Isaac Asimov,* Ungar, 1982.

Greenberg, Martin H., and Joseph D. Olander, editors, *Isaac Asimov,* Taplinger, 1977.

Gunn, James, *Isaac Asimov: The Foundations of Science Fiction,* Oxford University Press (New York, NY), 1982.

Isaac Asimov: An Annotated Bibliography of the Asimov Collection at Boston University, Greenwood Press (Westport, CT), 1995.

Judson, Karen, *Isaac Asimov: Master of Science Fiction,* Enslow Publishers, 1998.

Miller, Marjorie Mithoff, *Isaac Asimov: A Checklist of Works Published in the United States,* Kent State University Press (Kent, OH), 1972.

Patrouch, Joseph F., Jr., *The Science Fiction of Isaac Asimov,* Doubleday (New York, NY), 1974.

Platt, Charles, *Dream Makers: The Uncommon People Who Write Science Fiction,* Berkley (New York, NY), 1980.

Schweitzer, Darrell, *Science Fiction Voices 5,* Borgo Press (San Bernardino, CA), 1981, pp. 7-14.

Slusser, George E., *Isaac Asimov: The Foundations of His Science Fiction,* Borgo Press (San Bernardino, CA), 1979.

Touponce, William F., *Isaac Asimov,* Twayne (Boston, MA), 1991).

Twentieth-Century Science-Fiction Writers, 2nd edition, St. James Press (Detroit, MI), 1986.

Wollheim, Donald A.,*The Universe Makers,* Harper (New York, NY), 1971.

PERIODICALS

Analog: Science Fiction/Science Fact, December 15, 1994, p. 167; May, 1998, review of *Isaac Asimov's I-Bots,* p. 144; September, 1998, Tom Easton, review of *The Roving Mind,* p. 133.

Booklist, July, 1993; January 1, 2000, Mary Ellen Quinn, review of *Asimov's Chronology of Science and Technology,* p. 966; May 1, 2000, Shelle Rosenfeld, review of *Caves of Steel,* p. 1608; February 15, 2002, Roland Green, review of *It's Been a Good Life,* p. 984.

Books and Bookmen, July, 1968; February, 1969; July, 1973.

Chicago Tribune Book World, March 4, 1979; January 19, 1986.

Chicago Tribune Magazine, April 30, 1978.

Facts on File World News Digest, May 2, 2002, p. 327.

Fantasy Newsletter, April, 1983.

Fantasy Review, September, 1985.

Globe and Mail (Toronto, Ontario, Canada), August 10, 1985.

Hastings Center Report, March, 1998, review of *The Roving Mind,* p. 45.

Isis, March, 2003, Errol Vieth, review of *It's Been a Good Life,* pp. 183-185.

Library Journal, March 1, 2002, Robert L. Kelly, review of *It's Been a Good Life,* p. 98.

Magazine of Fantasy and Science Fiction, October, 1966; September, 1980; July, 1991; February, 1992.

Nation, March 5, 1983.

New Scientist, March 2, 2002, review of *It's Been a Good Life,* p. 46.

New York Review of Books, September 12, 1977; October 24, 1985.

New York Times, October 18, 1969; January 1, 1980; December 17, 1984; February 26, 1985.

New York Times Book Review, November 17, 1968; January 28, 1973; January 12, 1975; May 30, 1976; June 25, 1978; February 25, 1979; December 16, 1979; December 19, 1982; October 20, 1985; May 8, 1994, p. 25.

Publishers Weekly, April 17, 1972; September 2, 1983; March 7, 1994; September 11, 1995, p. 67; January 28, 2002, review of *It's Been a Good Life,* p. 279.

School Library Journal, February, 1992.

Science Books and Films, special edition, 1998, review of *The Caves of Steel,* p. 18.

Science Fiction and Fantasy Book Review, December, 1982; June, 1983; November, 1983; May 8, 1994.

Science Fiction Chronicle, July, 1998, review of *Isaac Asimov's I-Bots,* p. 41.

Science Fiction Review, winter, 1982; spring, 1984; winter, 1985.

Time, February 26, 1979; November 15, 1982.

Times Literary Supplement, October 5, 1967; December 28, 1967.

Washington Post, April 4, 1979.

Washington Post Book World, April 1, 1979; May 25, 1980; September 26, 1982; September 27, 1983; August 25, 1985.

ONLINE

Issac Asimov Home Page, http://www.asimovonline.com/ (April 15, 2003).

OTHER

Isaac Asimov Talks: An Interview (sound recording), Writer's Voice, 1974.

OBITUARIES:

PERIODICALS

Chicago Tribune, April 7, 1992, sec. 1, p. 13.

Detroit Free Press, April 7, 1992, p. 1B.

Los Angeles Tribune, April 7, 1992, p. 1A.
New York Times, April 7, 1992, p. B7.
Times (London, England), April 7, 1992, p. 19.
Washington Post, April 7, 1992.

*   *   *

ATWOOD, Margaret 1939-
(Margaret Eleanor Atwood)

PERSONAL: Born November 18, 1939, in Ottawa Ontario, Canada; daughter of Carl Edmund (an entomologist) and Margaret Dorothy (Killam) Atwood; married Graeme Gibson (a writer); children: Jess (daughter). *Education:* University of Toronto, B.A., 1961; Radcliffe College, A.M., 1962; Harvard University, graduate study, 1962-63 and 1965-67. *Politics:* "William Morrisite." *Religion:* "Immanent Transcendentalist."

ADDRESSES: Home—Toronto, Ontario, Canada. *Agent*—c/o Random House, 1745 Broadway New York, NY 10019.

CAREER: Writer. University of British Columbia, Vancouver, Canada, lecturer in English literature, 1964-65; Sir George Williams University, Montreal, Quebec, Canada, lecturer in English literature, 1967-68; York University, Toronto, Ontario, Canada, assistant professor of English literature, 1971-72; House of Anansi Press, Toronto, editor and member of board of directors, 1971-73; University of Toronto, writer-in-residence, 1972-73; University of Alabama, Tuscaloosa, writer-in-residence, 1985; New York University, New York, NY, Berg Visiting Professor of English, 1986; Macquarie University, North Ryde, Australia, writer-in-residence, 1987. Worked variously as a camp counselor and waitress.

MEMBER: PEN International, Amnesty International, Writers' Union of Canada (vice chair, 1980-81), Royal Society of Canada (fellow), Canadian Civil Liberties Association (member of board, 1973-75), Canadian Centre, American Academy of Arts and Sciences (honorary member), Anglophone (president, 1984-85).

AWARDS, HONORS: E.J. Pratt Medal, 1961, for *Double Persephone;* President's Medal, University of Western Ontario, 1965; YWCA Women of Distinction Award, 1966 and 1988; Governor General's Award, 1966, for *The Circle Game,* and 1986, for *The Handmaid's Tale;* first prize in Canadian Centennial Commission Poetry Competition, 1967; Union Prize for poetry, 1969; Bess Hoskins Prize for poetry, 1969 and 1974; City of Toronto Book Award, Canadian Booksellers' Association Award, and Periodical Distributors of Canada Short Fiction Award, all 1977, all for *Dancing Girls and Other Stories;* St. Lawrence Award for fiction, 1978; Radcliffe Medal, 1980; *Life before Man* selected a notable book of 1980, American Library Association; Molson Award, 1981; Guggenheim fellowship, 1981; named Companion of the Order of Canada, 1981; International Writer's Prize, Welsh Arts Council, 1982; Book of the Year Award, Periodical Distributors of Canada/Foundation for the Advancement of Canadian Letters, 1983, for *Bluebeard's Egg and Other Stories;* Ida Nudel Humanitarian Award, 1986; named Woman of the Year, *Ms.* magazine, 1986; Toronto Arts Award for writing and editing, 1986; *Los Angeles Times* Book Award, 1986, and Arthur C. Clarke Award for Best Science Fiction, and Commonwealth Literature Prize, both 1987, all for *The Handmaid's Tale;* Canadian Council for the Advancement and Support of Education silver medal, 1987; Humanist of the Year award, 1987; Royal Society of Canada fellow, 1987; named *Chatelaine* magazine's Woman of the Year; City of Toronto Book Award, Coles Book of the Year Award, Canadian Booksellers' Association Author of the Year Award, Book of the Year Award, Foundation for Advancement of Canadian Letters citation, Periodical Marketers of Canada Award, and Torgi Talking Book Award, all 1989, all for *Cat's Eye;* Harvard University Centennial Medal, 1990; Order of Ontario, 1990; Trillium Award for Excellence in Ontario Writing, and Periodical Marketers of Canada Book of the Year Award, both 1992, both for *Wilderness Tips and Other Stories;* Commemorative Medal for 125th Anniversary of Canadian Confederation; Trillium Award, Canadian Authors' Association Novel of the Year Award, Commonwealth Writers' Prize for Canadian and Caribbean Region, and *Sunday Times* Award for Literary Excellence, all 1994, and Swedish Humour Association's International Humourous Writer Award, 1995, all for *The Robber Bride;* Chevalier dans l'Ordre des Arts et des Lettres (France), 1994; named best local author, *NOW* magazine readers' poll, 1995 and 1996; Trillium Award, 1995, for *Morning in the Burned House;* Norwegian Order of Literary Merit, 1996; Booker Prize shortlist, and Giller Prize, both 1996, both for *Alias Grace;* International IMPAC Dublin Literary Award shortlist, Dublin City Library, 1998; Booker Prize, 2000, International IMPAC Dublin Literary Award nomination, and Dashiell Hammett Prize, International Association of Crime Writers (North American branch), 2001, all for *The Blind Assassin;* Booker prize shortlist and Governor General's literary award nominee, both 2003, both for *Oryx and Crake;* Enlightenment Award, Edinburgh International Book Festival,

2005; recipient of numerous honorary degrees, including Trent University, 1973, Concordia University, 1980, Smith College, 1982, University of Toronto, 1983, Mount Holyoke College, 1985, University of Waterloo, 1985, University of Guelph, 1985, Victoria College, 1987, University of Montreal, 1991, University of Leeds, 1994, Queen's University, 1974, Oxford University, 1998, and Cambridge University, 2001; Enlightenment Award, Edinburgh International Book Festival, 2005.

WRITINGS:

POETRY

Double Persephone, Hawkshead Press (Ontario, Canada), 1961.

The Circle Game, Cranbrook Academy of Art (Bloomfield Hills, MI), 1964, revised edition, House of Anansi Press (Toronto, Ontario, Canada), 1978.

Kaleidoscopes Baroque: A Poem, Cranbrook Academy of Art (Bloomfield Hills, MI), 1965.

Talismans for Children, Cranbrook Academy of Art (Bloomfield Hills, MI), 1965.

Speeches for Doctor Frankenstein, Cranbrook Academy of Art (Bloomfield Hills, MI), 1966.

The Animals in That Country, Little, Brown (Boston, MA), 1968.

The Journals of Susanna Moodie, Oxford University Press (Toronto, Ontario, Canada), 1970.

Procedures for Underground, Little, Brown (Boston, MA), 1970.

Power Politics, House of Anansi Press (Toronto, Ontario, Canada), 1971, Harper (New York, NY), 1973.

You Are Happy, Harper & Row (New York, NY), 1974.

Selected Poems, 1965- 1975, Oxford University Press (Toronto, Ontario, Canada), 1976, Simon & Schuster (New York, NY), 1978.

Marsh Hawk, Dreadnaught Press (Toronto, Ontario, Canada), 1977.

Two-headed Poems, Oxford University Press, 1978, Simon & Schuster (New York, NY), 1981.

Notes Toward a Poem That Can Never Be Written, Salamander Press (Toronto, Ontario, Canada), 1981.

True Stories, Oxford University Press (Toronto, Ontario, Canada), 1981, Simon & Schuster (New York, NY), 1982.

Snake Poems, Salamander Press (Toronto, Ontario, Canada), 1983.

Interlunar, Oxford University Press (Toronto, Ontario, Canada), 1984.

Selected Poems II: Poems Selected and New, 1976-1986, Oxford University Press (Toronto, Ontario, Canada), 1986.

Morning in the Burned House, Houghton Mifflin (Boston, MA), 1995.

Eating Fire: Selected Poetry, 1965-1995, Virago Press (London, England), 1998.

Also author of *Expeditions,* 1966, and *What Was in the Garden,* 1969.

NOVELS

The Edible Woman, McClelland & Stewart (Toronto, Ontario, Canada), 1969, Little, Brown (Boston, MA), 1970, reprinted, Anchor Press (New York, NY), 1998.

Surfacing, McClelland & Stewart (Toronto, Ontario, Canada), 1972, Simon & Schuster (New York, NY), 1973, reprinted, Anchor Press (New York, NY), 1998.

Lady Oracle, Simon & Schuster (New York, NY), 1976, reprinted, Anchor Press (New York, NY), 1998.

Life before Man, Simon & Schuster (New York, NY), 1979, reprinted, Anchor Press (New York, NY), 1998.

Bodily Harm, McClelland & Stewart (Toronto, Ontario, Canada), 1981, Simon & Schuster (New York, NY), 1982, reprinted, Anchor Press (New York, NY), 1998.

Encounters with the Element Man, William B. Ewert (Concord, NH), 1982.

Unearthing Suite, Grand Union Press (Toronto, Ontario, Canada), 1983.

The Handmaid's Tale, McClelland & Stewart (Toronto, Ontario, Canada), 1985, Houghton Mifflin (Boston, MA), 1986, reprinted, Chelsea House Publishers (Philadelphia, PA), 2001.

Cat's Eye, McClelland & Stewart (Toronto, Ontario, Canada), 1988, Doubleday (Garden City, NY), 1989.

The Robber Bride, Doubleday (New York, NY), 1993.

Alias Grace, Doubleday (New York, NY), 1996.

The Blind Assassin, Random House (New York, NY), 2000.

Oryx and Crake, Nan A. Talese (New York, NY), 2003.

The Tent, Nan A. Talese/Doubleday (New York, NY), 2006.

STORY COLLECTIONS

Dancing Girls and Other Stories, McClelland & Stewart (Toronto, Ontario, Canada), 1977, Simon & Schuster (New York, NY), 1982, reprinted, Anchor Press (New York, NY), 1998.

Bluebeard's Egg and Other Stories, McClelland & Stewart (Toronto, Ontario, Canada), 1983, Anchor Doubleday (New York, NY), 1998.

Murder in the Dark: Short Fictions and Prose Poems, Coach House Press (Toronto, Ontario, Canada), 1983.

Wilderness Tips and Other Stories, Doubleday (New York, NY), 1991.

Good Bones, Coach House Press (Toronto, Ontario, Canada), 1992, published as *Good Bones and Simple Murders,* Doubleday (New York, NY), 1994.

A Quiet Game: And Other Early Works, edited and annotated by Kathy Chung and Sherrill Grace, Juvenilia Press (Edmonton, Alberta, Canada), 1997.

The Tent, Doubleday (New York, NY), 2006.

OTHER

The Trumpets of Summer (radio play), Canadian Broadcasting Corporation (CBC- Radio), 1964.

Survival: A Thematic Guide to Canadian Literature, House of Anansi Press (Toronto, Ontario, Canada), 1972.

The Servant Girl (teleplay), CBC-TV, 1974.

Days of the Rebels, 1815- 1840, Natural Science Library, 1976.

The Poetry and Voice of Margaret Atwood (recording), Caedmon (New York, NY), 1977.

Up in the Tree (juvenile), McClelland & Stewart (Toronto, Ontario, Canada), 1978.

(Author of introduction) Catherine M. Young, *To See Our World,* GLC Publishers, 1979, Morrow (New York, NY), 1980.

(With Joyce Barkhouse) *Anna's Pet* (juvenile), James Lorimer, 1980.

Snowbird (teleplay), CBC-TV, 1981.

Second Words: Selected Critical Prose, House of Anansi Press (Toronto, Ontario, Canada), 1982, 2000.

(Editor) *The New Oxford Book of Canadian Verse in English,* Oxford University Press (Toronto, Ontario, Canada), 1982.

(Editor, with Robert Weaver) *The Oxford Book of Canadian Short Stories in English,* Oxford University Press (Toronto, Ontario, Canada), 1986.

(With Peter Pearson) *Heaven on Earth* (teleplay), CBC-TV, 1986.

(Editor) *The Canlit Foodbook,* Totem Books (New York, NY), 1987.

(Editor, with Shannon Ravenal) *The Best American Short Stories, 1989,* Houghton Mifflin (Boston, MA), 1989.

For the Birds, illustrated by John Bianchi, Firefly Books (Richmond Hill, Ontario, Canada), 1991.

(Editor, with Barry Callaghan; and author of introduction) *The Poetry of Gwendolyn MacEwen,* Exile Editions (Toronto, Ontario, Canada), Volume 1: *The Early Years,* 1993, Volume 2: *The Later Years,* 1994.

Princess Prunella and the Purple Peanut (juvenile), illustrated by Maryann Kovalski, Workman (New York, NY), 1995.

Strange Things: The Malevolent North in Canadian Literature (lectures), Oxford University Press (Toronto, Ontario, Canada), 1996.

Some Things about Flying, Women's Press (London, England), 1997.

(With Victor-Levy Beaulieu) *Two Solicitudes: Conversations* (interviews), translated by Phyllis Aronoff and Howard Scott, McClelland & Stewart (Toronto, Ontario, Canada), 1998.

(Author of introduction) *Women Writers at Work: The "Paris Review" Interviews,* edited by George Plimpton, Random House (New York, NY), 1998.

Negotiating with the Dead: A Writer on Writing (lectures), Cambridge University Press (New York, NY), 2002.

Rude Ramsay and the Roaring Radishes (juvenile), illustrated by Dusan Petricic, Key Porter Books (Toronto, Ontario, Canada), 2003.

(With others) *Story of a Nation: Defining Moments in Our History,* Doubleday Canada (Toronto, Ontario, Canada), 2001.

(Author of introduction) Chisitan Bok, editor, *Ground Works: Avant-Garde for Thee,* House of Anansi Press (Toronto, Ontario, Canada), 2002.

Moving Targets: Writing with Intent, House of Anansi Press (Toronto, Ontario, Canada), 2004.

Bashful Bob and Doleful Dorinda (juvenile), illustrated by Dusan Petricic, Key Porter Kids (Toronto, Ontario, Canada), 2004.

(With others) *New Beginnings: Sold in Aid of the Indian Ocean Tsunami Earthquake Charities,* Bloomsbury (New York, NY), 2005.

Writing with Intent: Essays, Reviews, Personal Prose, 1983-2005, Carroll & Graf (New York, NY), 2005.

The Penelopiad (part of the Knopf "Myth Series"), Knopf (Toronto, Ontario, Canada), 2005.

Curious Pursuits: Occasional Writing, 1970-2005, Virago (London, England), 2005.

Contributor to anthologies, including *Five Modern Canadian Poets,* 1970, *The Canadian Imagination: Dimensions of a Literary Culture,* Harvard University Press, 1977, and *Women on Women,* 1978. Contributor to periodicals, including *Atlantic, Poetry, New Yorker, Harper's, New York Times Book Review, Saturday Night, Tamarack Review,* and *Canadian Forum.*

ADAPTATIONS: Reflections: Progressive Insanities of a Pioneer, a six-minute visual interpretation of Atwood's poem by the same name, was produced by Cinematics Canada, 1972 and by Universal as *Poem as Imagery: Progressive Insanities of a Pioneer,* 1974. *The Journals of Susanna Moodie* was adapted as a screenplay, Tranby, 1972; *Surfacing* was adapted for film, Pan-Canadian, 1979; *The Handmaid's Tale* was filmed by Cinecom Entertainment Group, 1989, and was adapted as an opera by Danish composer Poul Ruders, for the Royal Danish Opera Company. *The Atwood Stories,* adaptations of Atwood's fiction, appeared as six half-hour episodes on W Network. *Alias Grace* was being adapted for film by Working Title Films. Union Pictures planned to produce a four-part miniseries based on *The Blind Assassin.* Many of Atwoods books are available as sound Recordings, including *The Tent,* Doubleday, 2005.

SIDELIGHTS: As a poet, novelist, story writer, and essayist, Margaret Atwood holds a unique position in contemporary Canadian literature. Her books have received critical acclaim in the United States, Europe, and her native Canada, and she has been the recipient of numerous literary awards. Atwood's critical popularity is matched by her popularity with readers. She is a frequent guest on Canadian television and radio and her books are often bestsellers.

Atwood first came to public attention as a poet in the 1960s with her collections *Double Persephone,* winner of the E.J. Pratt Medal, and *The Circle Game,* winner of a Governor General's award. These two books marked out the terrain her subsequent poetry has explored. *Double Persephone* concerns "the contrast between the flux of life or nature and the fixity of man's artificial creations," as explained by a *Dictionary of Literary Biography* contributor. *The Circle Game* takes this opposition further, setting such human constructs as games, literature, and love against the instability of nature. Human constructs are presented as both traps and shelters; the fluidity of nature as both dangerous and liberating. Sherrill Grace, writing in *Violent Duality: A Study of Margaret Atwood,* identified the central tension in all of Atwood's work as "the pull towards art on one

hand and towards life on the other." This tension is expressed in a series of "violent dualities," as Grace termed it. Atwood "is constantly aware of opposites—self/other, subject/ object, male/female, nature/man—and of the need to accept and work within them," Grace explained. "To create, Atwood chooses violent dualities, and her art re-works, probes, and dramatizes the ability to see double."

Linda W. Wagner, writing in *The Art of Margaret Atwood: Essays in Criticism,* asserted that in Atwood's poetry "duality [is] presented as separation." This separation leads her characters to be isolated from one another and from the natural world, resulting in their inability to communicate, to break free of exploitative social relationships, or to understand their place in the natural order. "In her early poetry," Gloria Onley wrote in the *West Coast Review,* Atwood "is acutely aware of the problem of alienation, the need for real human communication and the establishment of genuine human community—real as opposed to mechanical or manipulative; genuine as opposed to the counterfeit community of the body politic."

Wagner, commenting on the *The Circle Game,* noted that "the personae of those poems never did make contact, never did anything but lament the human condition." Wagner added, "Relationships in these poems are sterile if not destructive." In a review of *True Stories* Robert Sward of *Quill and Quire* explained that many reviewers of the book have exaggerated the violence and given "the false impression that all thirty-eight poems . . . are about torture."

Suffering is common for the female characters in Atwood's poems, although they are never passive victims. In her later works, her characters take active measures to improve their situations. Atwood's poems, *West Coast Review* contributor Onley maintained, concern "modern woman's anguish at finding herself isolated and exploited (although also exploiting) by the imposition of a sex role power structure." Atwood explained to Judy Klemesrud in the *New York Times* that her suffering characters come from real life: "My women suffer because most of the women I talk to seem to have suffered." Although she became a favorite of feminists, Atwood's popularity in the feminist community was unsought. "I began as a profoundly apolitical writer," she told Lindsy Van Gelder of *Ms.,* "but then I began to do what all novelists and some poets do: I began to describe the world around me."

Atwood's 1995 book of poetry, *Morning in the Burned House,* "reflects a period in Atwood's life when time seems to be running out," observed John Bemrose in

Maclean's. Noting that many of the poems address grief and loss, particularly in relationship to her father's death and a realization of her own mortality, Bemrose added that the book "moves even more deeply into survival territory." Bemrose further suggested that in this book, Atwood allows the readers greater latitude in interpretation than in her earlier verse: "Atwood uses grief . . . to break away from that airless poetry and into a new freedom."

Atwood's feminist concerns also emerge clearly in her novels, particularly in *The Edible Woman, Surfacing, Life before Man, Bodily Harm,* and *The Handmaid's Tale.* These novels feature female characters who are, as Klemesrud reported, "intelligent, self-absorbed modern women searching for identity . . . . [They] hunt, split logs, make campfires and become successful in their careers, while men often cook and take care of their households."

The Edible Woman tells the story of Marian McAlpin, a young woman engaged to be married, who rebels against her upcoming nuptials. Her fiancé seems too stable, too ordinary, and the role of wife too fixed and limiting. Her rejection of marriage is accompanied by her body's rejection of food; she cannot tolerate even a spare vegetarian diet. Eventually Marian bakes a sponge cake in the shape of a woman and feeds it to her fiancé because, she explains, "You've been trying to assimilate me." After the engagement is broken off, she is able to eat some of the cake herself.

Reaction to *The Edible Woman* was divided. Nevertheless, many critics noted Atwood's at least partial success. Tom Marshall, writing in his *Harsh and Lovely Land: The Major Canadian Poets and the Making of a Canadian Tradition,* called *The Edible Woman* "a largely successful comic novel, even if the mechanics are sometimes a little clumsy, the satirical accounts of consumerism a little drawn out." A *Dictionary of Literary Biography* contributor described *The Edible Woman* as "very much a social novel about the possibilities for personal female identity in a capitalistic consumer society."

In *Life before Man* Atwood dissects the relationships between three characters: Elizabeth, a married woman who mourns the recent suicide of her lover; Elizabeth's husband, Nate, who is unable to choose between his wife and his lover; and Lesje, Nate's lover, who works with Elizabeth at a museum of natural history. All three characters are isolated from one another and unable to experience their own emotions. The fossils and dinosaur bones on display at the museum are compared throughout the novel with the sterility of the characters' lives. As Laurie Stone noted in the *Village Voice, Life before Man* "is full of variations on the theme of extinction."

Life before Man is what Rosellen Brown of *Saturday Review* called an "anatomy of melancholy." Comparing the novel's characters to museum pieces and commenting on the analytical examination to which Atwood subjects them, Peter S. Prescott wrote in *Newsweek* that, "with chilly compassion and an even colder wit, Atwood exposes the interior lives of her specimens." Writing in the *New York Times Book Review,* Marilyn French made clear that in *Life before Man,* Atwood "combines several talents—powerful introspection, honesty, satire and a taut, limpid style—to create a splendid, fully integrated work." The novel's title, French believed, relates to the characters' isolation from themselves, their history, and from one another. They have not yet achieved truly human stature. "This novel suggests," French wrote, "that we are still living life before man, before the human—as we like to define it—has evolved." Prescott raised the same point. The novel's characters, he wrote, "do not communicate; each, in the presence of another, is locked into his own thoughts and feelings. Is such isolation and indeterminacy what Atwood means when she calls her story 'Life before Man'?" This concern is also found in Atwood's previous novels, French argued, all of which depict "the search for identity . . . a search for a better way to be—for a way of life that both satisfies the passionate, needy self and yet is decent, humane and natural."

Atwood further explores this idea in *Bodily Harm.* In this novel, Rennie Wilford is a Toronto journalist who specializes in light, trivial pieces for magazines. She is, Anne Tyler explained in the *Detroit News,* "a cataloguer of current fads and fancies." Following a partial mastectomy, which causes her lover to abandon her, Rennie begins to feel dissatisfied with her life. She takes on an assignment to the Caribbean island of St. Antoine in an effort to get away from things for a while. Her planned magazine story, focusing on the island's beaches, tennis courts, and restaurants, is distinctly facile in comparison to the political violence she finds on St. Antoine. When Rennie is arrested and jailed, the experience brings her to a self-realization about her life. "Death," Nancy Ramsey remarked in the *San Francisco Review of Books,* "rather than the modern sense of ennui, threatens Rennie and the people around her, and ultimately gives her life a meaning she hadn't known before."

Anatole Broyard in the *New York Times,* claimed that "the only way to describe my response to [*Bodily Harm*] is to say that it knocked me out. Atwood seems to be able to do just about everything: people, places, problems, a perfect ear, an exactly right voice and she tosses off terrific scenes with a casualness that leaves you utterly unprepared for the way these scenes seize you." Tyler called Atwood "an uncommonly skillful and perceptive writer," and went on to state that, because of its subject matter, *Bodily Harm* "is not always easy to read. There are times when it's downright unpleasant, but it's also intelligent, provocative, and in the end—against all expectations—uplifting."

In *The Handmaid's Tale* Atwood turns to speculative fiction, creating the dystopia of Gilead, a future America in which fundamentalist Christians have killed the president and members of Congress and imposed their own dictatorial rule. In this future world, polluted by toxic chemicals and nuclear radiation, few women can bear children; the birthrate has dropped alarmingly. Those women who can bear children are forced to become Handmaids, the official breeders for society. All other women have been reduced to chattel under a repressive religious hierarchy run by men.

The Handmaid's Tale is a radical departure from Atwood's previous novels. Her strong feminism was evident in earlier books, but *The Handmaid's Tale* is dominated by the theme. As Barbara Holliday wrote in the *Detroit Free Press,* Atwood "has been concerned in her fiction with the painful psychic warfare between men and women. In *The Handmaid's Tale . . .* she casts subtlety aside, exposing woman's primal fear of being used and helpless." Atwood's creation of an imaginary world is also new. As Mary Battiata noted in the *Washington Post, The Handmaid's Tale* is the first of Atwood's novels "not set in a worried corner of contemporary Canada."

Atwood was moved to write her story only after images and scenes from the book had been appearing to her for three years. She eventually became convinced that her vision of Gilead was not far from reality. Some of the anti-female measures she had imagined for the novel actually exist. "A law in Canada," Battiata reported, "[requires] a woman to have her husband's permission before obtaining an abortion." Atwood, speaking to Battiata, pointed to repressive laws in the totalitarian state of Romania as well: "No abortion, no birth control, and compulsory pregnancy testing, once a month." *The Handmaid's Tale* does not depend upon hypothetical scenarios, omens, or straws in the wind, but upon documented occurrences and public pronouncements; all matters of record." Stephen McCabe of the *Humanist* called the novel "a chilling vision of the future extrapolated from the present."

Yet, several critics voiced a disbelief in the basic assumptions of *The Handmaid's Tale.* Mary McCarthy, in her review for the *New York Times Book Review,* complained that "I just can't see the intolerance of the far right . . . as leading to a super-biblical puritanism." And although acknowledging that "the author has carefully drawn her projections from current trends," McCarthy asserted that "perhaps that is the trouble: the projections are too neatly penciled in. The details . . . all raise their hands announcing themselves present. At the same time, the Republic of Gilead itself, whatever in it that is not a projection, is insufficiently imagined." Richard Grenier of *Insight* observed that the Fundamentalist-run Gilead does not seem Christian: "There seems to be no Father, no Son, no Holy Ghost, no apparent belief in redemption, resurrection, eternal life. No one in this excruciatingly hierarchized new clerical state . . . appears to believe in God." Grenier also found it improbable that "while the United States has hurtled off into this morbid, feminist nightmare, the rest of the democratic world has been blissfully unaffected."

Despite what he saw as a flaw, French saw *The Handmaid's Tale* as being "in the honorable tradition of *Brave New World* and other warnings of dystopia. It's imaginative, even audacious, and conveys a chilling sense of fear and menace." Prescott compared the novel to other dystopian books. It belongs, he wrote, "to that breed of visionary fiction in which a metaphor is extended to elaborate a warning." Prescott went on to note, "Wells, Huxley and Orwell popularized the tradition with books like *The Time Machine, Brave New World* and *1984*— yet Atwood is a better novelist than they." Christopher Lehmann-Haupt identified *The Handmaid's Tale* as a book that goes far beyond its feminist concerns. Writing in the *New York Times,* the critic explained that the novel "is a political tract deploring nuclear energy, environmental waste, and anti-feminist attitudes. But it [is] so much more than that—a taut thriller, a psychological study, a play on words." Van Gelder saw the novel in a similar light: "[It] ultimately succeeds on multiple levels: as a page-turning thriller, as a powerful political statement, and as an exquisite piece of writing."

In *The Robber Bride,* Atwood again explores women's issues and feminist concerns, this time concentrating on women's relationships with each other—both positive and negative. Inspired by the Brothers Grimm's fairy tale "The Robber Bridegroom," the novel chronicles the relationships of college friends Tony, Charis, and Roz with their backstabbing classmate Zenia. Now middleaged women, the women's paths and life choices have diverged, yet Tony, Charis, and Roz have remained friends. Throughout their adulthood, however, Zenia's manipulations have nearly destroyed their lives and cost them husbands and careers. Lorrie Moore, writing in the *New York Times Book Review,* called *The Robber Bride* "Atwood's funniest and most companionable book in years," adding that its author "retains her gift for observing, in poetry, the minutiae specific to the physical and emotional lives of her characters." About Zenia, Moore commented, "charming and gorgeous, Zenia is a misogynist's grotesque: relentlessly seductive, brutal, pathologically dishonest," postulating that "perhaps Ms. Atwood intended Zenia, by the end, to be a symbol of all that is inexplicably evil: war, disease, global catastrophe." Judith Timson commented in *Maclean's* that *The Robber Bride* "has as its central theme an idea that feminism was supposed to have shoved under the rug: there are female predators out there, and they will get your man if you are not careful."

Atwood maintained that she had a feminist motivation in creating Zenia. The femme fatale all but disappeared from fiction in the 1950s due to that decade's sanitized ideal of domesticity; and in the late 1960s came the women's movement, which in its early years encouraged the creation of only positive female characters, Atwood asserted in interviews. She commented that "there are a lot of women you have to say are feminists who are getting a big kick out of this book," according to interviewer Sarah Lyall in the *New York Times.* "People read the book with all the wars done by men, and they say, 'So, you're saying that women are crueler than men,'" the novelist added. "In other words, that's normal behavior by men, so we don't notice it. Similarly, we say that Zenia behaves badly, and therefore women are worse than men, but that ignores the helpfulness of the other three women to each other, which of course gives them a power of their own."

Francine Prose, reviewing *The Robber Bride* for the *Washington Post Book World,* recommended the book "to those well-intentioned misguided feminists or benighted sexists who would have us believe that the female of the species is 'naturally' nicer or more nurturing than the male." Prose found the book "smart and entertaining" but not always convincing in its blend of exaggerated and realistic elements. *New York Times* critic Michiko Kakutani also thought Atwood has not achieved the proper balance in this regard: "Her characters remain exiles from both the earthbound realm of realism and the airier attitudes of allegory, and as a result, their story does not illuminate or entertain: it grates."

Alias Grace represents Atwood's first venture into historical fiction, but the book has much in common with her other works in its contemplation of "the shifting notions of women's moral nature" and "the exercise of power between men and women," wrote *Maclean's* contributor Diane Turbide. Based on a true story Atwood had explored previously in a television script titled *The Servant Girl, Alias Grace* centers on Grace Marks, a servant who was found guilty of murdering her employer and his mistress in northern Canada in 1843. Some people doubt Grace's guilt, however, and she serves out her sentence of life in prison, claiming not to remember the murders. Eventually, reformers begin to agitate for clemency for Grace. In a quest for evidence to support their position, they assign a young doctor, versed in the new science of psychiatry, to evaluate her soundness of mind. Over many meetings, Grace tells the doctor the harrowing story of her life—a life marked by extreme hardship. Much about Grace, though, remains puzzling; she is haunted by flashbacks of the supposedly forgotten murders and by the presence of a friend who had died from a mishandled abortion. The doctor, Simon Jordan, does not know what to believe in Grace's tales.

Several reviewers found Grace a complicated and compelling character. "Sometimes she is prim, naive, sometimes sardonic; sometimes sardonic because observant; sometimes observant because naive," commented Hilary Mantel in the *New York Review of Books.* Turbide added that Grace is more than an intriguing character: she is also "the lens through which Victorian hypocrisies are mercilessly exposed."

Prose, however, writing in the *New York Times Book Review,* thought the historical trivia excessive. "The book provides, in snippets, a crash course in Victorian culture. Prose added, "Rather than enhancing the novel's verisimilitude, these mini-lessons underline the distance between reader and subject." She also noted that some readers "will admire the liveliness with which Ms. Atwood toys with both our expectations and the conventions of the Victorian thriller."

"Dying octogenarian Iris Chasen's narration of the past carefully unravels a haunting story of tragedy, corruption, and cruel manipulation," summarized Beth E. Andersen in a *Library Journal* review of Atwood's *The Blind Assassin.* The novel, which earned its author the Booker Prize, involves multiple story lines. It is Iris's memoir, retracing her past with the wealthy and conniving industrialist Richard Griffen and the death of her sister Laura, her husband, and her daughter. Iris "reveals at long last the wrenching truth about herself and Laura amid hilariously acerbic commentary on the inanities of contemporary life," wrote Donna Seaman in *Booklist*. Interspersed with these narrative threads are sections devoted to Laura's novel, *The Blind Assassin,* published after her death. Seaman called the work a "spellbinding novel of avarice, love, and revenge." Andersen noted that some readers may guess how the story will pan out before the conclusion, but argued that "nothing will dampen the pleasure of getting there." Michiko Kakutani in the *New York Times* called *The Blind Assassin* an "absorbing new novel" that "showcases Ms. Atwood's narrative powers and her ardent love of the Gothic." Kakutani also noted that Atwood writes with "uncommon authority and ease."

Atwood has remained a noted writer of short stories as well as novels. *Wilderness Tips and Other Stories,* published in 1991, is a collection of ten "neatly constructed, present-tense narratives," reported Merle Rubin in the *Christian Science Monitor*. While finding Atwood's writing style drab and unappealing, Rubin nevertheless praised the author for her "ability to evoke the passing of entire decades . . . all within the brief compass of a short story." The tales in Atwood's 1992 collection, *Good Bones* —published in 1994 as *Good Bones and Simple Murders*—"occupy that vague, peculiar country between poetry and prose," stated John Bemrose in *Maclean's*. Describing Atwood as "storyteller, poet, fabulist and social commentator rolled into one," Bemrose claimed that "the strongest pieces in *Good Bones* combine a light touch with a hypnotic seriousness of purpose." In the *New York Times Book Review,* Jennifer Howard labeled *Good Bones and Simple Murders* a "sprightly, whimsically feminist collection of miniatures and musings, assembled from two volumes published in Canada in 1983 and 1992." A *Publishers Weekly* reviewer, who characterized the entries as "postmodern fairy tales, caustic fables, inspired parodies, witty monologues," declared each piece to be "clever and sharply honed."

Survival: A Thematic Guide to Canadian Literature is Atwood's most direct presentation of her strong support of Canadian nationalism. In this work, she discerns a uniquely Canadian literature, distinct from its American and British counterparts, and discusses the dominant themes to be found in it. Canadian literature, she argues, is primarily concerned with victims and with the victim's ability to survive. Atwood, Onley explained, "perceives a strong sado-masochistic patterning in Canadian literature as a whole. She believes that there is a national fictional tendency to participate, usually at some level as Victim, in a Victor/Victim basic pattern." Nevertheless, "despite its stress on victimization," a *Dictionary of Literary Biography* contributor wrote,

"this study is not a revelation of, or a reveling in, [masochism]." What Atwood argues, Onley asserted, that is, "every country or culture has a single unifying and informing symbol at its core: for America, the Frontier; for England, the Island; for Canada, Survival."

Several critics find that Atwood's own work exemplifies this primary theme of Canadian literature. Her examination of destructive gender roles and her nationalistic concern over the subordinate role Canada plays to the United States are variations on the victor/victim theme. Atwood believes a writer must consciously work within his or her nation's literary tradition, and her own work closely parallels the themes she sees as common to the Canadian literary tradition. *Survival* "has served as the context in which critics have subsequently discussed [Atwood's] works," stated a *Dictionary of Literary Biography* contributor.

In her novel *Oryx and Crake,* Atwood returns to themes from *The Handmaid's Tale*. "Once again she conjures up a dystopia, where trends that started way back in the twentieth century have metastasized into deeply sinister phenomena," wrote Michiko Kakutani in the *New York Times*. The story begins with a character called Snowman, the lone survivor of an Armageddon-like catastrophe. He wanders the streets trying to survive and finds that bioengineered animals are the only living creatures remaining. As the novel progresses, Snowman recalls his days as a boy and his childhood friend named Crake. Eventually, we learn that Crake became a scientist, one who was involved in the secret project that caused the global catastrophe. Kakatuni called the novel "at times intriguing." Referring to *Oryx and Crake* as a "scorching new novel," *Science* contributor Susan M. Squier wrote, "Atwood imagines a drastic revision of the human species that will purge humankind of all of our negative traits." Squier went on to note that "in *Oryx and Crake* readers will find a powerful meditation on how education that separates scientific and aesthetic ways of knowing produces ignorance and a wounded world."

Atwood also writes for children, and while much of her writing for adults is known to be quite dark, her books for juveniles are far more whimsical. For example, *Rude Ramsay and the Roaring Radishes* features a text of "alliterative 'R' sounds, making it a challenging read-aloud," noted Denise Parrott in *Resource Links*. The story, illustrated by Dusan Petricic, revolves around Rude Ramsay, a red-nosed rat named Ralph, and their new friend Rilla. A *Kirkus Reviews* contributor noted that "Atwood's prose is both amusing and enlightening in its use of rich vocabulary." Atwood and Petricic also worked together on *Bashful Bob and Doleful Dorinda,* a takeoff on the Cinderella tale. "Atwood's hilarious tale will amuse listeners of almost any age with its alliteration and clever wordplay," wrote Patricia Morley in the *Canadian Book Review Annual.* Bill Richardson, writing in the Toronto *Globe & Mail,* concluded: "I think the virtue in this cascade of consonants is the joy that lives in the sound of the words, the merely phonetic exuberance that's at least as important, at a certain age, as meaning."

Atwood has also continued to write about writing. Her lectures *Negotiating with the Dead: A Writer on Writing* were published under the same title in 2002. She has also released several collections. These include the 2004 publication *Moving targets: Writing with Intent, 1982-2004* and the 2005 collection *Curious Pursuits: Occasional Writing, 1970-2005.* Each collection is representative of Atwood's oeuvre. Although the author has been labeled a Canadian nationalist, a feminist, and even a gothic writer, it seems reasonable to say that, given the range and volume of her work, Atwood incorporates and transcends these categories.

BIOGRAPHICAL AND CRITICAL SOURCES:

BOOKS

Beran, Carol L.,*Living over the Abyss: Margaret Atwood's Life before Man,* ECW Press (Toronto, Ontario, Canada), 1993.

Bloom, Harold, editor, *Margaret Atwood,* Chelsea House (Philadelphia, PA), 2000.

Bouson, J. Brooks,*Brutal Choreographies: Oppositional Strategies and Narrative Design in the Novels of Margaret Atwood,* University of Massachusetts Press (Amherst, MA), 1993.

Contemporary Literary Criticism, Gale (Detroit, MI), Volume 2, 1974, Volume 3, 1975, Volume 4, 1975, Volume 8, 1978, Volume 13, 1980, Volume 15, 1980, Volume 25, 1983, Volume 44, 1987.

Cooke, John, *The Influence of Painting on Five Canadian Writers: Alice Munro, Hugh Hood, Timothy Findley, Margaret Atwood, and Michael Ondaatje,* Edwin Mellen (Lewiston, NY), 1996.

Cooke, Nathalie, *Margaret Atwood: A Biography,* ECW Press (Toronto, Ontario, Canada), 1998.

Davidson, Arnold E., *Seeing in the Dark: Margaret Atwood's Cat's Eye,* ECW Press (Toronto, Ontario, Canada), 1997.

Davidson, Arnold E., and Cathy N. Davidson, editors, *The Art of Margaret Atwood: Essays in Criticism,* House of Anansi Press (Toronto, Ontario, Canada), 1981.

Dictionary of Literary Biography, Volume 53: *Canadian Writers since 1960,* Gale (Detroit, MI), 1986.

Gibson, Graeme, *Eleven Canadian Novelists,* House of Anansi Press (Toronto, Ontario, Canada), 1973.

Grace, Sherrill, *Violent Duality: A Study of Margaret Atwood,* Véhicule Press (Montreal, Quebec, Canada), 1980.

Grace, Sherrill, and Lorraine Weir, editors, *Margaret Atwood: Language, Text, and System,* University of British Columbia Press (Vancouver, British Columbia, Canada), 1983.

Hengen, Shannon, *Margaret Atwood's Power: Mirrors, Reflections, and Images in Select Fiction and Poetry,* Second Story Press (Toronto, Ontario, Canada), 1993.

Howells, Coral Ann,*Margaret Atwood,* St. Martin's Press (New York City), 1996.

Irvine, Lorna, *Collecting Clues: Margaret Atwood's Bodily Harm,* ECW Press (Toronto, Ontario, Canada), 1993.

Lecker, Robert, and Jack David, editors, *The Annotated Bibliography of Canada's Major Authors,* ECW Press (Toronto, Ontario, Canada), 1980.

Marshall, Tom, *Harsh and Lovely Land: The Major Canadian Poets and the Making of a Canadian Tradition,* University of British Columbia Press (Vancouver, British Columbia, Canada), 1978.

McCombs, Judith, and Carole L. Palmer, *Margaret Atwood: A Reference Guide,* G.K. Hall (Boston, MA), 1991.

Michael, Magali Cornier, *Feminism and the Postmodern Impulse: Post-World War II Fiction,* State University of New York Press (Albany, NY), 1996.

Nicholson, Colin, editor, *Margaret Atwood: Writing and Subjectivity: New Critical Essays,* St. Martin's Press (New York, NY), 1994.

Nischik, Reingard M., editor, *Margaret Atwood: Works and Impact,* Camden House (Rochester, NY), 2000.

Rao, Eleanora, *Strategies for Identity: The Fiction of Margaret Atwood,* P. Lang (New York, NY), 1993.

Sandler, Linda, editor, *Margaret Atwood: A Symposium,* University of British Columbia (Vancouver, British Columbia, Canada), 1977.

Stein, Karen F., *Margaret Atwood Revisited,* Twayne (New York, NY), 1999.

Sullivan, Rosemary, *The Red Shoes: Margaret Atwood Starting Out,* HarperFlamingo Canada (Toronto, Ontario, Canada), 1998.

Thompson, Lee Briscoe, *Scarlet Letters: Margaret Atwood's The Handmaid's Tale,* ECW Press (Toronto, Ontario, Canada), 1997.

Twigg, Alan, *For Openers: Conversations with Twenty-four Canadian Writers,* Harbour Publishing (Madeira Park, British Columbia, Canada), 1981.

Woodcock, George, *The Canadian Novel in the Twentieth Century,* McClelland & Stewart (Toronto, Ontario, Canada), 1975.

PERIODICALS

Book World, November 7, 2004, Elizabeth Ward, review of *Rude Ramsay and the Roaring Radishes,* p. 12.

Booklist, June 1, 2000, Donna Seaman, review of *The Blind Assassin,* p. 1796; January 1, 2004, review of *Oryx and Crake,* p. 776; March 1, 2005, Donna Seaman, review of *Writing with Intent: Essays, Reviews, Personal Prose, 1983-2005,* p. 1130..

Bookseller, February 4, 2005, review of *Curious Pursuits: Occasional Writing, 1970-2005,* p. 36.

Canadian Book Review Annual, 2004, Patricia Morley, review of *Bashful Bob and Doleful Dorinda,* p. 465.

Christian Science Monitor, December 27, 1991, Merle Rubin, review of *Wilderness Tips and Other Stories,* p. 14.

Contemporary Literature, winter, 2003, Susan Strehle, review of *Negotiating with the Dead: A Writer on Writing,* pp. 737-42.

Detroit News, April 4, 1982, Anne Tyler, review of *Bodily Harm.*

Globe & Mail (Toronto, Ontario, Canada), December 11, 2004, Bill Richardson, review of *Bashful Bob and Doleful Dorinda,* p. D18; January 21, 2006, Aritha van Herk, review of *The Tent,* p. D4.

Humanist, September- October, 1986, Stephen McCabe, review of the *Handmaid's Tale,* p. 31.

Insight, March 24, 1986, Richard Grenier, review of *The Handmaid's Tale.*

Kirkus Reviews, August 15, 2004, review of *Rude Ramsay and the Roaring Radishes,* p. 802; October 1, 2005, review of *The Tent,* p. 1057.

Library Journal, August 9, 2000, Beth E. Andersen, review of *The Blind Assassin;* March 15, 2005, Nancy R. Ives, review of *Writing with Intent: Essays, Reviews, Personal Prose, 1983-2005,* p. 84.

London Review of Books, November 17, 2005, Thomas Jones, review of *The Penelopiad,* p. 23.

Maclean's, January 15, 1979, review of *Two-Headed Poems,* p. 50; October 15, 1979, review of *Life Before Man,* p. 66; March 30, 1981, Mark Able, review of *True Stories,* p. 52; September 16, 1991, John Bemrose, review of *Wilderness Tips and Other Stories,* p. 58; October 5, 1992, John Bem-rose, review of *Good Bones,* p. S10; October 4, 1993, Judith Timson, review of *The Robber Bride,* p. 55; February 6, 1995, John Bemrose, review of *Morning in the Burned House,* p. 85; September 23, 1996, Diane Turbide, "Amazing Atwood," pp. 42-45; July 1, 1999, Margaret Atwood, "Survival, Then and Now," p. 54.

Ms., January, 1987, Lindsy Van Gelder, "Margaret Atwood," p. 48.

Newsweek, February 18, 1980, Peter S. Prescott, review of *Life Before Man,* p. 108; February 17, 1986, Peter S. Prescott, review of *The Handmaid's Tale,* p. 70.

New Yorker, September 18, 2000, John Updike, review of *The Blind Assassin,* p. 142.

New York Review of Books, December 19, 1996, Hilary Mantel, "Murder and Memory."

New York Times, March 6, 1982, Anatole Broyard, review of *Bodily Harm,* pp. 13(N), 21(LC); March 28, 1982, Judy Klemesrud, "Canada'a 'High Preistess of Angst,'" p. 21; September 15, 1982; January 27, 1986, Christopher Lehmann-Haupt, review of *The Handmaid's Tale,* p. C24; February 17, 1986; November 5, 1986; October 26, 1993, Michiko Kakutani, review of *The Robber Bride,* p. C20; November 23, 1993, Sarah Lyall, " An Author Who Lets Women Be Bad Guys," pp. C13, C16; September 3, 2000, Thomas Mallon, review of *The Blind Assassin;* September 8, 2000, Michiko Kakutani, review of *The Blind Assassin*; May 13, 2003, Michiko Kakutani, review of *Oryx and Crake,* p. E9.

New York Times Book Review, February 3, 1980, Marilyn French, review of *Life Before Man,* p. 1; February 9, 1986, Mary McCarthy, review of *The Handmaid's Tale,* p. 1; October 31, 1993, Lorrie Moore, review of *The Robber Bride,* pp. 1, 22; December 11, 1994, Jennifer Howard, review of *Good Bones and Simple Murders,* p. 22; December 29, 1996, Francine Prose, review of *Alias Grace,* p. 6; December 7, 2003, review of *Oryx and Crake,* p. 69.

O, the Oprah Magazine, November, 2005, Vince Passaro, review of *The Penelopiad,* p. 184.

Publishers Weekly, July 24, 2000, review of *The Blind Assassin,* p. 67; July 24, 2000, " *PW* Talks to Margaret Atwood," p. 68; August 23, 2004, review of *Rude Ramsay and the Roaring Radishes,* p. 54.

Quill and Quire, April, 1981, Robert Sward, review of *True Stories*; September, 1984.

Resource Links, December 2003, Denise Parrott, review of *Rude Ramsay and the Roaring Radishes,* p. 1; April, 2005, Adriane Pettit, review of *Bashful Bob and Doleful Dorinda,* p. 1.

San Francisco Review of Books, summer, 1982, Nancy Ramsey, review of *Bodily Harm,* p. 21.

Saturday Night, July-August, 1998, Rosemary Sullivan, "The Writer-Bride," p. 56.

Saturday Review, February 2, 1980, Rosellen Brown, review of *Life Before Man,* p. 33.

School Library Journal, November, 2004, Caroline Ward, review of *Rude Ramsay and the Roaring Radishes,* p. 90.

Science, November 14, 2003, Susan M. Squier, review of *Oryx and Crake,* p. 1154.

Studies in the Novel, spring, 2004, Earl G. Ingersoll, review of *Negotiating with the Dead: A Writer on Writing,* p. 126.

Village Voice, January 7, 1980, Laurie Stone, review of *Life Before Man.*

Washington Post, April 6, 1986, Mary Battiata, review of *The Handmaid's Tale.*

Washington Post Book World, November 7, 1993, Francine Prose, review of *The Robber Bride,* p. 1.

West Coast Review, January, 1973, Gloria Onley, "Margaret Atwood: Surfacing in the Interests of Survival."

ONLINE

Atwood Society Web site, http://www.mscd.edu/~atwoodso/ (March 9, 2006).

*   *   *

ATWOOD, Margaret Eleanor
    See ATWOOD, Margaret

*   *   *

AXTON, David
    See KOONTZ, Dean R.

*   *   *

AYCKBOURN, Alan 1939-
    (Roland Allen)

PERSONAL: Surname is pronounced Ache-born; born April 12, 1939, in London, England; son of Horace (a concert musician) and Irene (Worley) Ayckbourn; married Christine Roland, May 9, 1959 (divorced, 1997); married Heather Elizabeth Stoney, 1997; children: Steven Paul, Philip Nicholas. *Education:* Attended Haileybury and Imperial Service College, Hertfordshire, England, 1952-57.

ADDRESSES: Office—Stephen Joseph Theatre, Westborough, Scarborough, North Yorkshire YO11 1JW, England. *Agent*—Casarotto Ramsay Ltd., National House, 60-66 Wardour St., London W1 4ND, England.

CAREER: Stephen Joseph Theatre-in-the-Round Company (now Stephen Joseph Theatre Company), Scarborough, England, stage manager and actor, 1957-59, writer and director, 1959-61; Victoria Theatre, Stoke-on-Trent, England, actor, writer, and director, 1961-64; British Broadcasting Corporation (BBC), Leeds, Yorkshire, England, drama producer, 1965-70; Stephen Joseph Theatre, writer and artistic director, 1970—; professor of contemporary theatre, St. Catherine's College, Oxford University, 1992. Visiting playwright and director, Royal National Theatre, London, 1977, 1980, 1986-88. Also acted with several British repertory companies.

AWARDS, HONORS: London *Evening Standard* best comedy award, 1973, for *Absurd Person Singular,* best play awards, 1974, for *The Norman Conquests,* 1977, for *Just between Ourselves,* and 1987, for *A Small Family Business; Plays and Players* award, 1989, for *Henceforward . . . Vaudeville,* and 1990, for *Man of the Moment,* best new play awards, 1974, for *The Norman Conquests,* and 1985, for *A Chorus of Disapproval;* named "playwright of the year" by Variety Club of Great Britain, 1974; Antoinette Perry ("Tony") Award nomination for best play and (with Peter Hall) for outstanding direction, both 1979, both for *Bedroom Farce;* London *Evening Standard* Award, Olivier Award, and *DRAMA* award, all 1985, all for *A Chorus of Disapproval;* appointed commander, Order of the British Empire, 1987; Director of the Year Award, *Plays and Players,* 1987, for production of Arthur Miller's *A View from the Bridge;* Drama-Logue Critics Award, 1991, for *Henceforward . . . Vaudeville;* TMA/Martini Regional Theatre Award for Best Show for Children Young People, 1993, for *Mr. A's Amazing Maze Plays;* lifetime achievement award, Writers' Guild of Great Britain, Birmingham Press Club Personality of the Year Award, and John Ederyn Hughes Rural Wales Award for Literature, all 1993; named Yorkshire Man of the Year award, and Mont Blanc de la Culture Award for Europe, both 1994; Best West End Play award, Writers' Guild of Great Britain, 1996, for *Communicating Doors;* knighted, 1997; Lloyds Private Banking Playwright of the Year honor, 1997, and Molière award for best comedy (Paris, France), 2003, both for *Things We Do for Love;* London *Sunday Times* Award for Literary Excellence, 2001. Honorary degrees include D.Litt. from University of Hull, 1981, University of Keele, 1987, University of Leeds, 1987, University of Bradford, 1994, and University of Manchester, 2000;

honorary fellow of University of Bretton, 1982, and University of Cardiff, 1995; and Doctor of University from University of York, 1992, and Open University, 1998.

WRITINGS:

PLAYS

(Under pseudonym Roland Allen) *The Square Cat,* first produced in Scarborough, England, at Library Theatre, June, 1959.

(Under pseudonym Roland Allen) *Love after All,* first produced in Scarborough, England, at Library Theatre, December, 1959.

(Under pseudonym Roland Allen) *Dad's Tale,* first produced in Scarborough, England, at Library Theatre, December 19, 1960.

(Under pseudonym Roland Allen) *Standing Room Only,* first produced in Scarborough, England, at Library Theatre, July 13, 1961.

Xmas v. Mastermind, first produced in Stoke-on-Trent, England, at Victoria Theatre, December 26, 1962.

Mr. Whatnot, first produced in Stoke-on-Trent, England, at Victoria Theatre, November 12, 1963, revised version produced in London, England, at Arts Theatre, August 6, 1964.

Relatively Speaking (first produced as *Meet My Father* in Scarborough, England, at Library Theatre, July 8, 1965, produced in the West End at Duke of York's Theatre, March 29, 1967), Samuel French (London, England), 1968.

The Sparrow, first produced in Scarborough, England, at the Library Theatre, July 13, 1967.

We Who Are about To. . . (one-act; includes *Countdown;* first produced in London, England, at Hampstead Theatre Club, February 6, 1969; also see below), published in *Mixed Doubles: An Entertainment on Marriage,* Methuen (London, England), 1970.

How the Other Half Loves (first produced in Scarborough, England, at Library Theatre, July 31, 1969, produced in the West End at Lyric Theatre, August 5, 1970), Samuel French (London, England), 1971.

Mixed Doubles: An Entertainment on Marriage (includes *Countdown,* and *We Who Are about To . . . ;* first produced in the West End at Comedy Theatre, April 9, 1969), Methuen (London, England), 1970.

The Story so Far, produced in Scarborough, England, at Library Theatre, August 20, 1970, revised version as *Me Times Me Times Me,* produced on tour

March 13, 1972, second revised version as *Family Circles* (produced in Richmond, England, at Orange Tree Theatre, November 17, 1978), Samuel French (London, England), 1997.

Ernie's Incredible Illucinations (first produced in London, England, 1970), Samuel French (London, England), 1969.

Time and Time Again (first produced in Scarborough, England, at Library Theatre, July 8, 1971, produced in the West End at Comedy Theatre, August 16, 1972), Samuel French (London, England), 1973.

Absurd Person Singular (first produced in Scarborough, England, at Library Theatre, June 26, 1972, produced in the West End at Criterion Theatre, July 4, 1973), Samuel French (London, England), 1974.

Mother Figure (one-act; first produced in Horsham, Sussex, England, at Capitol Theatre, 1973, produced in the West End at Apollo Theatre, May 19, 1976; also see below), published in *Confusions,* Samuel French (London, England), 1977.

The Norman Conquests (trilogy; composed of *Table Manners, Living Together,* and *Round and Round the Garden;* first produced in Scarborough, England, at Library Theatre, June, 1973, produced in the West End at Globe Theatre, August 1, 1974), Samuel French (London, England), 1975.

Absent Friends (first produced in Scarborough, England, at Library Theatre, June 17, 1974, produced in the West End at Garrick Theatre, July 23, 1975), Samuel French (London, England), 1975.

Service Not Included (television script), produced by British Broadcasting Corporation (BBC), 1974.

Confusions (one-acts; includes *Mother Figure, Drinking Companion, Between Mouthfuls, Gosforth's Fete,* and *A Talk in the Park;* first produced in Scarborough, England, at Library Theatre, September 30, 1974, produced in the West End at Apollo Theatre, May 19, 1976), Samuel French (London, England), 1977.

(Author of book and lyrics) *Jeeves* (musical; adapted from stories by P.G. Wodehouse), music by Andrew Lloyd Webber, first produced in the West End at Her Majesty's Theatre, April 22, 1975.

Bedroom Farce (first produced in Scarborough, England, at the Library Theatre, June 16, 1975, produced on the West End at Prince of Wales's Theatre, November 7, 1978, produced on Broadway at Brooks Atkinson Theatre, 1979; also see below), Samuel French (London, England), 1977.

Just between Ourselves (first produced in Scarborough, England, at Library Theatre, January 28, 1976, produced in the West End at Queen's Theatre, April 22, 1977; also see below), Samuel French (London, England), 1978.

Ten Times Table (first produced in Scarborough, England, at Stephen Joseph Theatre-in-the-Round, January 18, 1977, produced in the West End at Globe Theatre, April 5, 1978; also see below), Samuel French (London, England), 1979.

Joking Apart (first produced in Scarborough, England, at Stephen Joseph Theatre-in-the-Round, January 11, 1978, produced in the West End at Globe Theatre, March 7, 1979), Samuel French (London, England), 1979.

(Author of book and lyrics) *Men on Women on Men* (musical), music by Paul Todd, first produced in Scarborough, England, at Stephen Joseph Theatre-in-the-Round, June 17, 1978.

Sisterly Feelings (first produced in Scarborough, England, at Stephen Joseph Theatre-in-the-Round, January 10, 1979, produced in the West End at Olivier Theatre, June 3, 1980; also see below), Samuel French (London, England), 1981.

Taking Steps (first produced in Scarborough, England, at Stephen Joseph Theatre-in-the-Round, September 27, 1979, produced in the West End at Lyric Theatre, September 2, 1980), Samuel French (London, England), 1981.

(Author of book and lyrics) *Suburban Strains* (musical; first produced in Scarborough, England, at Stephen Joseph Theatre-in-the-Round, January 20, 1980, produced in London, England, at Round House Theatre, February 2, 1981), music by Paul Todd, Samuel French (London, England), 1981.

Season's Greetings (first produced in Scarborough, England, at Stephen Joseph Theatre-in-the-Round, September 24, 1980, revised version first produced in Greenwich, England, at Greenwich Theatre, January 27, 1982, produced in the West End at Apollo Theatre, March 29, 1982), Samuel French (London, England), 1982.

(Author of book and lyrics) *Me, Myself, and I* (musical), music by Paul Todd, first produced in Scarborough, England, at Stephen Joseph Theatre-in-the-Round, June, 1981.

Way Upstream (first produced in Scarborough, England, at Stephen Joseph Theatre-in-the-Round, October, 1981, produced in London, England, at National Theatre, October 4, 1982), Samuel French (London, England), 1983.

(Author of book and lyrics) *Making Tracks* (musical), music by Paul Todd, first produced in Scarborough, England, at Stephen Joseph Theatre-in-the-Round, December 16, 1981.

Intimate Exchanges (first produced in Scarborough, England, at Stephen Joseph Theatre-in-the-Round, June 3, 1982, produced in the West End at the Ambassadors Theatre, August 14, 1984), Samuel French (London, England), 1985.

It Could Be Any One of Us, first produced in Scarborough, England, at Stephen Joseph Theatre-in-the-Round, 1983.

A Chorus of Disapproval (first produced in Scarborough, England, at Stephen Joseph Theatre-in-the-Round, 1984, produced in the West End at the Lyric Theatre, 1986), Samuel French (London, England), 1985, screenplay adaptation by Ayckbourn and Michael Winner, Southgate Entertainment, 1989.

The Westwoods, first produced in Scarborough, England, at Stephen Joseph Theatre-in-the-Round, 1984, produced in London, England, at Etcetera Theatre, May 31, 1987.

Woman in Mind (first produced in Scarborough, England, at Stephen Joseph Theatre-in-the-Round, 1985, produced in the West End at Vaudeville Theatre, 1986), Faber (London, England), 1986, Samuel French (London, England), 1987.

A Small Family Business (first produced at Royal National Theatre, June 5, 1987), Faber (London, England), 1987, Samuel French (New York, NY), 1988.

Henceforward. . . (first produced in Scarborough, England, at Stephen Joseph Theatre-in-the-Round, July 30, 1987, produced in the West End at Vaudeville Theatre, November 21, 1988), Faber (London, England), 1989.

Man of the Moment, first produced in Scarborough, England, at Stephen Joseph Theatre-in-the-Round, August 10, 1988, produced in London, England, 1990.

(Adaptor) Will Evans and Valentine, *Tons of Money: A Farce,* Samuel French (London, England), 1988.

Mr. A's Amazing Maze Plays (first produced in Scarborough, England, at Stephen Joseph Theatre-in-the-Round, 1988), Faber (London, England), 1989.

The Revengers' Comedies, first produced in Scarborough, England, at Stephen Joseph Theatre-in-the-Round, 1989.

Body Language (first produced in Scarborough, England, at Stephen Joseph Theatre-in-the-Round, May 16, 1990), Samuel French (London, England), 2001.

Callisto 5 (produced in Scarborough, England, 1990), Samuel French (London, England), 1995.

My Very Own Story: A Play for Children (produced in Scarborough, England, 1991), Samuel French (London, England), 1995.

Wildest Dreams, first produced in Scarborough, England, 1991.

Ernie's Incredible Illucinations, published together with *A Day in the Life of Tich Oldfield,* by Alan England, Thornes, 1991.

A Cut in the Rates, Samuel French (London, England), 1991.

Time of My Life, first produced in Scarborough, England, April 21, 1992.

Dreams from a Summer House, first produced in Scarborough, England, August 26, 1992.

(Adaptor) Henry Becque, *Wolf at the Door,* translated by David Walker, Samuel French (London, England), 1993.

Communicating Doors, first produced in Scarborough, England, February 2, 1994.

Haunting Julia, first produced in Scarborough, England, April 20, 1994.

The Musical Jigsaw Play, first produced in Scarborough, England, December 1, 1994.

A Word from Our Sponsor, first produced in Scarborough, England, April 20, 1995.

This Is Where We Came In, Samuel French (London, England), 1995.

By Jeeves, music by Andrew Lloyd Webber, first produced in Scarborough, England, then Duke of York Theatre, London, England, 1996.

The Champion of Paribanou, first produced in Scarborough, England, December 4, 1996.

Things We Do for Love, first produced in Scarborough, England, April 24, 1997, produced in London, England, 1998.

Family Circles: A Comedy, Samuel French (London, England), 1997.

It Could Be Any One of Us: A Comedy, Samuel French (London, England), 1998.

A Word from Our Sponsor: A Musical Play, Samuel French (London, England), 1998.

Comic Potential (produced in Scarborough, England, 1998, produced in London, England, 1999), Faber (London, England), 1999.

House, first produced in Scarborough, England, 1999, produced in London, England, at the National Theater, August 9, 2000.

Garden, first produced in London, England, at the National Theater, August 9, 2000.

Virtual Reality, first produced in Scarborough, England, at Stephen Joseph Theatre, 2000.

Whenever, music by Denis King, first produced in Scarborough, England, at Stephen Joseph Theatre, December 5, 2000.

Damsels in Distress: GamePlan (first produced in Scarborough, England, at Stephen Joseph Theatre, May 29, 2001, produced in London, England, 2002), Faber (London, England), 2002.

Damsels in Distress: FlatSpin (first produced in Scarborough, England, at Stephen Joseph Theatre, July 3, 2001, produced in London, England, 2002), Faber (London, England), 2002.

Damsels in Distress: RolePlay (first produced in Scarborough, England, at Stephen Joseph Theatre, September 4, 2001), Faber (London, England), 2002.

Snake in the Grass, first produced in Scarborough, England, at Stephen Joseph Theatre, May 30, 2002.

The Jollies (first produced in Scarborough, England, at Stephen Joseph Theatre, December 3, 2002), Faber (London, England), 2002.

Sugar Daddies, first produced in Scarborough, England, at Stephen Joseph Theatre, July, 22, 2003.

Orvin—Champion of Champions (first produced in Scarborough, England, at Stephen Joseph Theatre, August 8, 2003), Faber (London, England), 2003.

My Sister Sadie (first produced in Scarborough, England, at Stephen Joseph Theatre, December 2, 2003), Faber (London, England), 2003.

Drowning on Dry Land, first produced in Scarborough, England, at Stephen Joseph Theatre, 2004.

Private Fears in Public Places, first produced in Scarborough, England, at Stephen Joseph Theatre, August, 12, 2004.

Miss Yesterday, produced 2004.

OMNIBUS VOLUMES

Three Plays (contains *Absurd Person Singular, Absent Friends,* and *Bedroom Farce*), Grove (New York, NY), 1979.

Joking Apart and Other Plays (includes *Just between Ourselves,* and *Ten Times Table*), Chatto & Windus (London, England), 1979.

Sisterly Feelings and Taking Steps, Chatto & Windus (London, England), 1981.

Alan Ayckbourn: Plays 1, Faber (London, England), 1995.

Alan Ayckbourn: Plays 2, Faber (London, England), 1998.

OTHER

The Crafty Art of Playmaking, Palgrave Macmillan (London, England), 2003.

ADAPTATIONS: A Chorus of Disapproval was produced as a feature film, 1989; numerous plays by Ayckbourn have been adapted for BBC radio presentation.

SIDELIGHTS: "Alan Ayckbourn is the most performed of contemporary British dramatists; his plays are a staple of repertory theaters, frequently translated, and usually highly successful," according to *Dictionary of Literary Biography* contributor Trevor R. Griffiths. In a career that began in 1959, British playwright Ayckbourn has penned over three score plays that humorously dissect the British middle class, and, by extension, explore the quotidian adventures and misadventures of the bourgeois worldwide. Ayckbourn is generally considered Great Britain's most successful living playwright, with his comedies appearing regularly in London's West End theatres, earning the author handsome royalties as well as an international reputation. London *Times* reviewer Anthony Masters observed that Ayckbourn's work since the mid-1960s "is rich in major and minor masterpieces that will certainly live and are now overdue for revival." A prolific writer who often crafts his dramas just shortly before they are due to be staged, Ayckbourn extracts wry and disenchanted humor from the dull rituals of English middle-class life. *Nation* contributor Harold Clurman wrote that the dramatist is "a master hand at turning the bitter apathy, the stale absurdity which most English playwrights now find characteristic of Britain's lower-middle-class existence into hilarious comedy." *Dictionary of Literary Biography* essayist Albert E. Kalson described a typical Ayckbourn play as an "intricately staged domestic comedy with a half-dozen intertwined characters who reflect the audience's own unattainable dreams and disappointments while moving them to laughter with at least a suggestion of a tear." In the London *Times,* Andrew Hislop commented that the plays, translated into two dozen languages, "are probably watched by more people in the world than those of any other living dramatist."

Kalson suggested that Ayckbourn's work "is rooted in the Home Counties, his characters' speech patterns reflecting his upbringing." Indeed, although Ayckbourn was born in London, he was raised in a succession of small Sussex towns by his mother and her second husband, a provincial bank manager. Ayckbourn told the *New York Times* that his childhood was not comfortable or cheery. "I was surrounded by relationships that weren't altogether stable, the air was often blue, and things were sometimes flying across the kitchen," he said. *New York Times* contributor Benedict Nightingale found this youthful insecurity reflected in Ayckbourn's writings, since the characters "often come close to destroying each other, though more commonly through insensitivity than obvious malice." At age seventeen Ayckbourn determined that he wanted to be an actor. After several years with small repertory companies, during which he learned stage-managing as well as acting techniques, he took a position with the Stephen Joseph Theatre-in-the-Round Company in Scarborough, England. According to Kalson, his continuing association with that group "eventually turned a minor actor into a major playwright." Nightingale was philosophical about Ayckbourn's creative development. "If he had been a

happier man," the critic writes, "he wouldn't have wanted to write plays. If he had been a more successful actor, he would have had no need to do so. If he'd known happier people in his early life, his plays wouldn't be so interesting. And if he had not been an actor at all, it would have taken him much longer to learn how to construct his plots, prepare his effects and time his jokes."

Ayckbourn began his tenure at Scarborough as an actor and stage manager. He has described the company as "the first of the fringe theatres," with interests in experimental theatre-in-the-round work and other so-called underground techniques. As he gained experience, Ayckbourn began to agitate for larger roles. The group leader, Stephen Joseph, had other ideas, however. In *Drama,* Ayckbourn reminisced about his earliest attempts at playwriting. Joseph told him, "If you want a better part, you'd better write one for yourself. You write a play, I'll do it. If it's any good. . . . Write yourself a main part." Ayckbourn appreciated the latter advice especially, calling it "a very shrewd remark, because presumably, if the play had not worked at all, there was no way I as an actor was going to risk my neck in it." Ayckbourn actually wrote several plays that were staged at Scarborough, England, in the early 1960s—pseudonymous works such as *The Square Cat, Love after All, Dad's Tale,* and *Standing Room Only.* According to Ian Watson in *Drama,* these "belong to Ayckbourn's workshop period, and today he is careful to ensure that nobody reads them, and certainly nobody produces them."

Eventually Ayckbourn gave up acting when he discovered his particular muse: the fears and foibles of Britain's middle classes. As he began to experience success outside of Scarborough, however, he continued to craft his work specifically for that company and its small theatre-in-the-round. A large majority of his plays have debuted there, despite the lure of the West End. "My plays are what one would expect from someone who runs a small theater in a community such as Scarborough," Ayckbourn told the *Chicago Tribune.* "That means the cost for the play is about the budget for one production in the company's season, and the subject matter offers the audience a chance to see something they know, to laugh at jokes they've heard before." Kalson likewise noted that the playwright "bears in mind the requirements of the Scarborough audience, many of them his neighbors, upon whom he depends for the testing of his work. He will neither insult nor shock them, respecting their desire to be entertained. He provides them with plays about the life he observes around him, sometimes even his own." *Los Angeles*

Times correspondent Sylvie Drake wrote: "Ayckbourn is a blithe spirit. He has been writing plays for actors he knows in a theater in Scarborough, England, without much concern for the rest of the world. Since that 'rest of the world' admires nothing more than someone with the audacity to pay it no attention, it promptly embraced his idiosyncratic comedies and totally personal style."

Ayckbourn's early plays "succeeded in resuscitating that most comatose of genres, the 'farcical comedy,'" according to Nightingale in *New Statesman*. In *Modern Drama*, Malcolm Page similarly characterized the early works as "the lightest and purest of comedies, giving [Ayckbourn] the reputation of being the most undemanding of entertainers." Plays such as *Relatively Speaking, How the Other Half Loves,* and *Absurd Person Singular* "abound with the basic element of theatrical humor, that is incongruity, the association of unassociable elements," wrote Guido Almansi in *Encounter.* Typically revolving around extramarital affairs or class conflicts, the comedies begin with a peculiar situation that grows inexorably out of control, with mistaken identities, unclarified misunderstandings, and overlooked clues. *New York Times* commentator Walter Goodman observed: "How Mr. Ayckbourn contrives to get his people into such states and persuade us to believe that they are reasonable is a secret of his comic flair." With the enthusiastic reception for *Relatively Speaking,* concluded Oleg Kerensky in *The New British Drama: Fourteen Playwrights since Osborne and Pinter,* Ayckbourn established himself "as a writer of ingenious farcical comedy, with an ear for dialogue and with a penchant for complex situations . . . and ingenious plots." That reputation led some critics to question Ayckbourn's lasting contribution to the theatre, but subsequent plays have clarified the author's more serious intentions. Kalson concluded: "Beyond the easy jokes, the mistaken identities, the intricate staging, Ayckbourn was learning a craft that would enable him, always within the framework of bourgeois comedy, to illuminate the tedium, the pain, even the horror of daily life recognizable not only in England's Home Counties, . . . or in gruffer, heartier northern England, . . . but all over the world."

Throughout his years of playwriting, Ayckbourn has taken risks not easily reconciled with popular comedy. Some American critics have labeled him "the British Neil Simon," but in fact his characters often must contend with an undercurrent of humiliation, mediocrity, and embarrassment that Simon does not address. In the *Chicago Tribune,* Howard Reich wrote: "The best of Ayckbourn's work . . . is funny not only for what its characters say but because of what they don't. Between the wisecracks and rejoinders, there breathe characters who are crumbling beneath the strictures of British society." Ayckbourn may pillory the manners and social conventions of the middle classes, but he also concerns himself with the defeats that define ordinary, often hopeless, lives. According to Alan Brien in *Plays and Players,* the author "shows . . . that what is funny to the audience can be tragic to the characters, and that there is no lump in the throat to equal a swallowed laugh which turns sour." *New York* magazine contributor John Simon suggested that Ayckbourn "extends the range of farce, without cheating, to cover situations that are not farcical—the fibrillations of the heart under the feverish laughter. And he keeps his characters characters, not walking stacks of interchangeable jokebooks." As Guido Almansi noted in *Encounter,* the playwright "knows how to operate dramatically on what seems to be utterly banal: which is certainly more difficult than the exploitation of the sublime."

A favorite Ayckbourn theme is the pitfalls of marriage, an institution in which the playwright finds little joy. *New Yorker* correspondent Brendan Gill contended that the author "regards human relationships in general and the marriage relationship in particular as little more than a pailful of cozily hissing snakes." Richard Eder elaborated in the *New York Times:* "His characters are simply people for whom the shortest distance between two emotional points is a tangle; and who are too beset by doubts, timidities and chronic self-complication to have time for anything as straightforward as sex." Harold Hobson also observed in *Drama* that behind Ayckbourn's foolery "he has this sad conviction that marriage is a thing that will not endure. Men and women may get instant satisfaction from life, but it is not a satisfaction that will last long. . . . It is when Ayckbourn sees the tears of life, its underlying, ineradicable sadness, that he is at his superb best." *Bedroom Farce* and *Absurd Person Singular* both tackle the thorny side of marriage; the two plays are among Ayckbourn's most successful. In *New Statesman,* Nightingale concluded that in both works Ayckbourn "allows his people to have feelings, that these feelings can be hurt, and that this is cause for regret. . . . There are few sadder things than the slow destruction of youthful optimism, not to mention love, trust and other tender shoots: Mr. Ayckbourn makes sure we realise it."

Throughout his career Ayckbourn has demonstrated a reluctance to be limited by conventional staging techniques. This tendency, born in the Scarborough theatre-in-the-round atmosphere, has become an abiding factor in the playwright's work. Some Ayckbourn plays juxtapose several floors of a house—or several different houses—in one set; others offer alternative scenes decided at random by the actors or by a flip of a coin. According to J.W. Lambert in *Drama,* Ayckbourn's "ingenuity in thus constructing the plays positively makes the head spin if dwelt upon; but of course it should not be dwelt upon, for however valuable the challenge may have been to his inventive powers, it is to us only an incidental pleasure. The value of the work lies elsewhere—in its knife-sharp insights into the long littleness of life and in its unflagging comic exhilaration." Page likewise insisted that while his staging skills "are frequently dazzling, Ayckbourn claims our attention for his insights about people: he prompts us to laugh, then to care about the character and to make a connection with ourselves, our own behavior, and possibly beyond to the world in which we live."

The Norman Conquests, first produced in 1973, combines Ayckbourn's theme of the frailty of relationships with an experimental structure. The piece is actually a trilogy of plays, any one of which can be seen on its own for an understanding of the story. Together, however, the three parts cover completely several hours in the day of an unscrupulous character named Norman, whose "conquests" are generally restricted to the seduction of women. In the *Chicago Tribune,* Richard Christiansen suggested that the three plays "fit together like Chinese boxes. Each comedy has the same cast of characters, the same time frame and the same house as a setting; but what the audience sees on stage in the dining room in one play may happen off stage in the living room in another, and vice versa. Though each play can be enjoyed on its own, much of the fun relies on the audience knowing what is going on in the other two plays." Almansi wrote: "As we view the second and then the third play of the trilogy, our awareness of what is going on in the rest of the house and likewise the satisfaction of our curiosity grow concurrently. We enjoy guessing what preceded or what will follow the entrance or the exit of the actor from the garden to the lounge, or from the latter to the kitchen, and we slowly build up a complete picture of the proceedings, as if we were Big Brother enjoying a panoptic and all-embracing vision. I dare surmise that this innovation will count in the future development of theatrical technique." Gill commented that despite its length, the farce "is likely to make you laugh far more often than it is likely to make you look at your watch."

Some critics have noted a gradual darkening of Ayckbourn's vision over the years. The author's plays, wrote Page, "challenge an accepted rule of contemporary comedy: that the audience does not take home the sorrows of the characters after the show. This convention—a matter of both the dramatist's style and the audience's expectations—verges on breakdown when Ayckbourn shifts from farce to real people in real trouble." London *Times* reviewer Bryan Appleyard similarly contended that in more recent Ayckbourn dramas "the signs are all there. Encroaching middle age and visionary pessimism are beginning to mark [his] work." This is not to suggest that the author's plays are no longer funny; they simply address such themes as loneliness, adultery, family quarrels, and the twists of fate with candor and sincerity. "Up to now, we have thought of Ayckbourn as the purveyor of amusing plays about suburban bumblers," noted Dan Sullivan in a *Los Angeles Times* review of Ayckbourn's futuristic comedy *Henceforward.* "Here we see him as a thoughtful and painfully honest reporter of the crooked human heart—more crooked every year, it seems." Appleyard observes that Ayckbourn "appears to be entering a visionary middle age and the long-term effect on his plays is liable to be stronger polarization. Villains will really be villains . . . and heroes may well at last begin to be heroes." Indeed, Ayckbourn seems to have become interested in the acceleration of moral decay in his country; plays such as *Way Upstream, A Chorus of Disapproval,* and *A Small Family Business* explore small communities where extreme selfishness holds sway. In the *Chicago Tribune,* for instance, Matthew Wolf called *A Small Family Business* "a strong study of one man's seduction into a milieu of moral filth." Christiansen concluded that the cumulative effect of these plays puts Ayckbourn "into his rightful place as an agile and insightful playwright in the front ranks of contemporary theatre."

Drama essayist Anthony Curtis declared that Ayckbourn's career "is shining proof that the well-made play is alive and well." Now in his fifth decade as a playwright, Ayckbourn continues to craft at least one full-length work a year; he also directs his own and others' works in Scarborough and at London's National Theatre. In *Drama,* Michael Leech observed: "There are those who compare [Ayckbourn] to a latterday Molière, those who say he is a mere play factory, others who might opine that he veers violently between the two extremes. Certainly he is one of our most prolific and gifted writers of comedy, with characters pinned to the page with the finesse and exactness of a collector of unusual butterflies. . . . And he can look back on a body of work that for most writers would be a life-time's effort." London *Times* commentator Andrew Hislop found Ayckbourn "at the summit of his career. . . . The security of his Scarborough nest has enabled him to continue his work remarkably unaffected by those who have overpraised him, comparing him to Shakespeare, and those who have unjustly reviled him, regarding him as a vacuous, right-wing boulevardier." Certainly Ayckbourn has more champions than critics, both in England and abroad. Hobson, for one, concluded that the public responds to Ayckbourn's work "because he is both a highly comic writer and, dramatically speaking, a first-class conjuror. The tricks he plays in some of his work are stupendous. They are miracles of human ingenuity."

Certainly it is understandable that one might become bored writing comedies for decades, but Ayckbourn manages to keep it fresh with new and innovative ideas. His two plays, *House* and *Garden* are linked in a very interesting manner. They were written to be performed simultaneously, with only one cast who must run between sets, back and forth from the "house" to the "garden." Daniel Okrent of *Entertainment Weekly* felt that Ayckbourn "has topped himself with an act of unprecedented theatrical invention," with these two plays. Chris Jones of *Variety* thought that the plays were "funny and complex," and added that, "the concept allows Ayckbourn to explore the perils of miscommunication by allowing the audience to fill in the gaps in its knowledge."

Ayckbourn continued to dazzle with his 2001 trilogy, *Damsels in Distress.* As James Inverne commented in *Time International,* "trickery is afoot" in this series of plays. The first, *GamePlan,* is "a disturbing drama of teenage prostitution [that] turns into hide-the-corpse farce," according to Inverne. The second play, *FlatSpin,* is a "lonely-gal romance [that] becomes a spy thriller," as Inverne further explained, and the third in the series, *RolePlay,* is a "meet-the-parents dinner comedy [that] morphs into a piercing study of social class." For Inverne *Damsels in Distress* was an "uneven but enjoyable triptych." *Variety*'s Wolf found the same plays an "ambitious trilogy," but also a work in which Ayckbourn "is at both his near-best and his laziest." Wolf went on to conclude that *RolePlay,* like much of the rest of the trilogy, "shows a writer perched uneasily between critiquing a milieu and selling out to it." Other British reviewers had higher praise for the group of plays, and despite this positive critical reception, the production had difficulty making costs. Ayckbourn had harsh words for the London production schedule of his plays which focused primarily on *RolePlay,* relegating the other two to one performance weekly. The playwright vowed never to stage another play in London's West End again.

Scarborough, England, continues to be Ayckbourn's home and principle theater. All of his plays since *Damsels in Distress* have premiered and run there primarily, including his 2003 *Sugar Daddies* and the 2004 *Drowning on Dry Land.* In the former play, Sasha comes to the aid of Father Christmas with startling results. Ben Walsh, writing in the London *Independent,* found *Sugar Daddies* a "menacing, yet humorous piece that explores the unsavoury underbelly of English society." *Drowning on Dry Land* focuses on the golden boy, Charlie Conrad, a man whose life seems perfect. Yet no one really seems to know why Charlie has risen so far. In his sixty-sixth play, Ayckbourn turns his eye on the media and their illusory celebrity creations such as Charlie. Lynne Walker, reviewing the play in the *Independent,* chided Ayckbourn for forgetting, as she felt, that "twists and turns in a storyline do need to be plausible rather than just the vehicle for a sequence of ideas, no matter how cunning they are in themselves."

Ayckbourn has also authored a how-to for playwrights, the 2003 title *The Crafty Art of Playmaking.* Here he lays out a set of one-hundred-and-one "Obvious Rules" in which he tries to cover all aspects of stage production. Reviewing the work in *Library Journal,* Susan L. Peters felt that the "overall tone is breezy, lighthearted, and fun," and that Ayckbourn's "experiences are well worth the price of the book." Writing in *Back Stage West,* Dany Margolies praised Ayckbourn, noting that the playwright and director "has welcomed us into his head and heart as he explains his methods of writing and directing, using ample examples from his more than sixty." Ayckbourn's "Obvious Rule No. 101" states: "No one ever set out to do a show with the intention of giving you a bad time."

Ayckbourn told the *Los Angeles Times* that his ambition is to write "totally effortless, totally truthful, unforced comedy shaped like a flawless diamond in which one can see a million reflections, both one's own and other people's." He also commented in the London *Times* that the best part of his work "is not the clapping, it's the feeling at the end of the evening, that you have given the most wonderful party and those five hundred strangers who came in are feeling better. . . . I don't know, but they are sort of unified into a whole and that is marvelous. That's really like shutting the door on a good party and thinking—that went well!"

BIOGRAPHICAL AND CRITICAL SOURCES:

BOOKS

Allen, Paul, *Grinning at the Edge,* Methuen (London, England), 2002.

Ayckbourn, Alan, *The Crafty Art of Playmaking,* Palgrave Macmillan (London, England), 2003.

Contemporary Dramatists, 6th edition, Thomson Gale (Detroit, MI), p. 19.

Contemporary Literary Criticism, Thomson Gale (Detroit, MI), Volume 5, 1976, Volume 8, 1978, Volume 18, 1981, Volume 33, 1985.

Dictionary of Literary Biography, Thomson Gale (Detroit, MI), Volume 13: *British Dramatists since World War II,* 1982, pp. 15-32, Volume 245: *British and Irish Dramatists since World War II,* 2001, pp. 23-36.

Elsom, John, *Post-War British Theatre,* Routledge & Kegan Paul (Boston, MA), 1976.

Encyclopedia of World Literature in the Twentieth Century, St. James Press (Detroit, MI), 1999.

Hayman, Ronald, *British Theatre since 1955: A Reassessment,* Oxford University Press (New York, NY), 1979.

Joseph, Stephen, *Theatre in the Round,* Barrie Rockcliff, 1967.

Kerensky, Oleg, *The New British Drama: Fourteen Playwrights since Osborne and Pinter,* Hamish Hamilton (London, England), 1977.

Modern British Literature, Volume 1, St. James Press (Detroit, MI), 2000.

Taylor, John Russell, *The Second Wave: British Drama for the Seventies,* Methuen (London, England), 1971.

Taylor, John Russell, *Contemporary English Drama,* Holmes Meier (London, England), 1981.

Watson, Ian, *Alan Ayckbourn: Bibliography, Biography, Playography, Theatre Checklist, No. 21,* T.Q. Publications, 1980.

Watson, Ian, *Conversations with Ayckbourn,* Macmillan (London, England), 1981.

White, Sidney Howard, *Alan Ayckbourn,* Twayne (Boston, MA), 1985.

PERIODICALS

Back Stage, November 16, 2001, Julius Novick, review of *By Jeeves,* p. 34.

Back Stage West, December 7, 2000, David Sheward, review of *House* and *Garden,* p. 14; April 3, 2003, Dany Margolies, review of *The Crafty Art of Playmaking,* p. 7.

Chicago Tribune, July 17, 1982; July 15, 1983; August 2, 1987.

Commonweal, May 3, 1991.

Drama, autumn, 1974; spring, 1979; summer, 1979; January, 1980; October, 1980; first quarter, 1981; second quarter, 1981; autumn, 1981; spring, 1982; summer, 1982; Volume 162, 1986.

Encounter, December, 1974; April, 1978.

Entertainment Weekly, March 2, 2001, Daniel Okrent, review of *House* and *Garden,* p. 60; November 9, 2001, review of *By Jeeves,* p. 101.

Europe Intelligence Wire, October 9, 2002, Aleks Sierz, "Alan Ayckbourn Proves He Is a Dramatist to Be Taken Seriously"; October 24, 2002, Nigel Reynolds, "I'll Boycott the West End, Says Angry Ayckbourn."

Guardian, August 7, 1970; August 14, 1974.

Independent (London, England), February 7, 2004, Ben Walsh, review of *Sugar Daddies,* p. 12; May 13, 2004, Lynne Walker, review of *Drowning on Dry Land,* p. 16.

Library Journal, May 1, 2003, Susan L. Peters, review of *The Crafty Art of Playmaking,* p. 115.

Listener, May 23, 1974.

Los Angeles Times, January 20, 1983; March 6, 1984; March 30, 1987; October 28, 1987.

Modern Drama, March, 1983.

Nation, March 8, 1975; December 27, 1975; April 21, 1979; April 8, 1991; June 8, 1992.

New Leader, June 1, 1992.

New Republic, November 9, 1974; September 11, 1989.

New Statesman, May 31, 1974; July 5, 1974; December 1, 1978; June 13, 1980.

Newsweek, October 21, 1974.

New York, October 28, 1974; December 22, 1975; April 16, 1979; April 2, 1984; November 13, 1989; February 25, 1991; March 4, 1991; May 18, 1992.

New Yorker, October 21, 1974; December 22, 1975; April 9, 1979; February 25, 1991; May 11, 1992; June 3, 2002, Nancy Franklin, review of *House* and *Garden;* July 7, 2003, Leo Carey, review of *The Crafty Art of Playmaking,* p. 17.

New York Times, October 20, 1974; February 16, 1977; April 4, 1977; March 25, 1979; March 30, 1979; March 31, 1979; May 1, 1979; October 16, 1981; May 29, 1986; June 15, 1986; June 25, 1986; October 3, 1986; October 29, 1986; November 26, 1986; July 20, 1987; April 15, 1988; June 5, 1988.

Observer, February 13, 1977; March 4, 1979.

Plays and Players, September, 1972; September, 1975; January, 1983; May, 1983; April, 1987.

Sunday Times (London, England), June 3, 1973; June 8, 1980.

Sunday Times Magazine, February 20, 1977.

Time, May 9, 1979; August 13, 1984; June 11, 1990; March 4, 1991; November 11, 1991; February 7, 1994; June 13, 1994.

Time International, November 25, 2002, James Inverne, "Farce by the Book," p. 75.

Times (London, England), January 5, 1976; January 19, 1980; February 4, 1981; February 2, 1982; June 7,

1982; August 18, 1982; October 6, 1982; October 10, 1983; May 4, 1984; June 4, 1985; April 9, 1986; September 5, 1986; November 5, 1986; December 15, 1986; June 1, 1987; June 8, 1987; June 27, 1987; February 10, 1988; November 23, 1988.

Tribune, February 13, 1981.

Variety, February 18, 1991; May 4, 1992; August 3, 1992; August 16, 1993; November 8, 1993; December 27, 1993; February 12, 2001, Chris Jones, review of *House* and *Garden,* p. 47; March 12, 2001, Chris Jones, review of *By Jeeves,* p. 47; November, 2001, Charles Isherwood, review of *By Jeeves,* p. 33; May 27, 2002; October 14, 2002, Matt Wolf, review of *Damsels in Distress,* p. 38; August 4, 2003, Matt Wolf, "Legit's Energizer Bunny," pp. 41-42.

Wall Street Journal, August 2, 1994.

Washington Post, July 10, 1977.

ONLINE

Official Alan Ayckbourn Web site, http://www.alanayckbourn.net/ (July 22, 2004).

B

BACHMAN, Richard
See KING, Stephen

* * *

BAINBRIDGE, Beryl 1934-
(Beryl Margaret Bainbridge)

PERSONAL: Born November 21, 1934, in Liverpool, England; daughter of Richard (a salesperson) and Winifred (Baines) Bainbridge; married Austin Davies (an artist), April 24, 1954 (divorced, 1959); children: Aaron Paul, Johanna Harriet, Ruth Emmanuella. *Education:* Attended Merchant Taylor's School and Arts Educational Schools, Ltd. *Politics:* Socialist. *Religion:* "Lapsed Catholic." *Hobbies and other interests:* Painting, reading, sleeping, smoking.

ADDRESSES: Home—42 Albert St., Camden Town, London NW1 7NU, England.

CAREER: Novelist and actress. Actress in England on radio and television, and in repertory theaters in Windsor, Salisbury, Dundee, Liverpool, and London, England, 1943-72; writer, 1956-68, 1972—; *Evening Standard* (newspaper), London, England, weekly columnist, 1986-92. Has also worked in a wine-bottling factory and as a clerk for Gerald Duckworth and Company (publishers). Host of British Broadcasting Corporation television series *English Journey,* 1983, and *Forever England,* 1986.

MEMBER: Royal Society of Literature (fellow).

AWARDS, HONORS: Booker Prize nomination, 1973, for *The Dressmaker,* 1992, for *An Awfully Big Adventure,* and 2001, for *According to Queeney;* Booker Prize

nomination and *Guardian* Fiction Award, both 1974, both for *The Bottle Factory Outing;* Whitbread Award, 1977, for *Injury Time;* Litt.D. from University of Liverpool, 1986; Booker Prize nomination, and Whitbread Award, both 1996, both for *Every Man for Himself;* Booker Prize nomination, W.H. Smith Fiction Prize, *Commonwealth* Eurasian section winner, and James Tait Black Memorial Prize for Best Novel, all 1999, all for *Master Georgie;* named Dame of the British Empire, 2000; David Cohen British Literature prize (shared with Thom Gunn), 2003, for lifetime achievement.

WRITINGS:

FICTION

A Weekend with Claud (novel), Hutchinson (London, England), 1967, revised edition published as *A Weekend with Claude,* Duckworth (London, England), 1981.
Another Part of the Wood (novel), Hutchinson (London, England), 1968, revised edition, Duckworth (London, England), 1979, Braziller (New York, NY), 1980.
Harriet Said (novel), Duckworth (London, England), 1972, Braziller (New York, NY), 1973.
The Dressmaker (novel), Duckworth (London, England), 1973, Carroll & Graf (New York, NY), 1996, published as *The Secret Glass,* Braziller (New York, NY), 1973.
The Bottle Factory Outing (novel), Braziller (New York, NY), 1974, reprinted, Carroll & Graf (New York, NY), 1994.
Sweet William (novel; also see below), Braziller (New York, NY), 1975.

A Quiet Life (novel; also see below), Duckworth (London, England), 1976, Braziller (New York, NY), 1977.

Injury Time (novel), Braziller (New York, NY), 1977.

Young Adolf (novel), Duckworth (London, England), 1978, Braziller (New York, NY), 1979.

Winter Garden (novel), Duckworth (London, England), 1980, Braziller (New York, NY), 1981.

Watson's Apology (novel; also see below), Duckworth (London, England), 1984, McGraw-Hill (New York, NY), 1985.

Mum and Mr. Armitage (short stories; contains "Mum and Mr. Armitage Clap Hands," "Here Comes Charlie," "People for Lunch," and "The Worst Policy"; also see below), Duckworth (London, England), 1985, McGraw-Hill (New York, NY), 1987.

Filthy Lucre; or, The Tragedy of Andrew Ledwhistle and Richard Soleway (novel), Duckworth (London, England), 1986.

Watson's Apology [and] *Mum and Mr. Armitage, and Other Stories,* McGraw-Hill (New York, NY), 1988.

An Awfully Big Adventure (novel; also see below), Duckworth (London, England), 1989, HarperCollins (New York, NY), 1991.

The Birthday Boys (novel), Duckworth (London, England), 1993, Carroll & Graf (New York, NY), 1994.

Collected Stories, Penguin (London, England), 1994.

Every Man for Himself (novel), Duckworth (London, England), 1996, Carroll & Graf (New York, NY), 1996.

Master Georgie (novel), Duckworth (London, England), 1996, Carroll & Graf (New York, NY), 1998.

According to Queeney, Little, Brown (Boston, MA), 2001.

NONFICTION

English Journey; or, The Road to Milton Keynes, Duckworth (London, England), 1984, Carroll & Graf (New York, NY), 1997.

Forever England: North and South, Duckworth (London, England), 1987.

Something Happened Yesterday, Duckworth (London, England), 1993.

TELEVISION SCRIPTS

Sweet William (based on her novel of the same title), British Broadcasting Corp. (BBC), 1979.

A Quiet Life (based on her novel of the same title), BBC, 1980.

(With Phillip Seville) *The Journal of Bridget Hitler,* BBC, 1980.

(With Udayan Prasad) *According to Beryl,* BBC, 2001.

Also author of *Tiptoe through the Tulips,* 1976; *Blue Skies from Now On,* 1977; *The Warrior's Return,* 1977; *It's a Lovely Day Tomorrow,* 1977; *Words Fail Me,* 1979; *Somewhere More Central,* 1981; and *Evensong,* 1986.

OTHER

(Editor) *New Stories 6* (anthology), Hutchinson (London, England), 1981.

Contributor to books, including *Bananas,* edited by Emma Tennant, and *Winter's Tales 26,* edited by A.D. Maclean; contributor to periodicals, including *Spectator, Listener, Times Literary Supplement,* and London *Sunday Times Magazine.*

ADAPTATIONS: Sweet William, The Dressmaker, and *An Awfully Big Adventure* were produced as films.

SIDELIGHTS: Beryl Bainbridge was counted among Great Britain's "half-dozen most inventive and interesting novelists" by *New York Review of Books* contributor Julian Symons. Since beginning her fiction-writing career in the 1960s, Bainbridge has gone on to win critical acclaim and a wide readership on two continents for her chronicles of the lives and neuroses of the English lower middle classes. Reviewers have cited Bainbridge for her satiric but naturalistic portrayals of the drab and desperate British poor, and her depiction of "the hidden springs of anarchy that bedevil the least adventurous of us, booby-trapping our lives and making them the occasion of violent and dangerous humor," according to *Spectator* contributor Harriet Waugh. Bainbridge's tales of urban wildness often stray into the realm of violence and nightmare, where trapped spirits collide with thwarted ambition and the bosom of the family offers more grief than relief. *Newsweek* correspondent Margo Jefferson commented that "Bainbridge's books are melancholy, provincial landscapes in which violence, like a thunderstorm, always threatens, sometimes strikes." *New York Times* columnist Anatole Broyard suggested that Bainbridge "has established herself as the high priestess of the rueful. She has opened a thrift shop in English literature, a home for frayed, faded, out-of-fashion and inexpensive people. The name of her shop might be Things Out of Joint. . . . Bainbridge's people have all missed the train, or boat, the main chance. They are stranded in themselves, left behind by a world rushing toward the gratification of desire."

Fiction writing is Bainbridge's second career; during her teen and early adult years she worked as an actress on the radio and in repertory theaters. At age sixteen she met and fell in love with her future husband, artist Austin Davies. They were married in 1954, although Bainbridge had misgivings about the match. While awaiting the birth of her first child in 1956, Bainbridge began to write a novel. She derived the plot from a newspaper story about two girls who murdered their mother, and drew on her own childhood experiences to enhance and alter the details. The resulting work, *Harriet Said,* was completed in 1958 but remained unpublished until 1972. Barbara C. Millard noted in the *Dictionary of Literary Biography:* "When Bainbridge submitted the manuscript to publishers in 1959, she received outraged response, including the comment that the book was 'too indecent and unpleasant even for these lax days.'" Editors were aghast at the novelist's tale of juvenile sexuality, voyeurism, and murder; their response so daunted Bainbridge that she returned to the stage. In 1959, her marriage ended, she moved with her two young children to London and started writing again. In 1967, her second novel, *A Weekend with Claud,* became her first book to be published.

"Bainbridge's publishing history is perhaps the kind of thing you'd expect of a writer who is preoccupied with the idea of isolation," noted Karl Miller in the *New York Review of Books.* "It may be that this portrayer of shyness and constraint, who appears to be no punctuator, found it difficult to cope with the embarrassment of a debut, and of getting herself properly published." Indeed, Bainbridge eventually revised her first two published books, *A Weekend with Claud* and *Another Part of the Wood.* In the London *Times,* Bainbridge attributed her success as an author to her acquaintance, in 1970, with Anna Haycraft, fiction editor for Gerald Duckworth and Company: "She had read my two published books, didn't like them all that much ('rotten' was the word she used) and wanted to know if I had written anything else. I showed her *Harriet Said.* . . . Duckworth published it, employed me in the office for a year, put me on a monthly salary . . . and suggested I write another novel as soon as possible." Bainbridge added that Haycraft helped her to find her authorial voice: "It was she who told me to abandon the flowery and obscure style of my two later books and return to the simpler structure of the first. She pointed out that, in my case, clarity came from writing from my own experience. . . . I gradually learnt the best way, for

me, of expressing what I wanted to say, and wrote a novel a year from then on."

Critics have suggested that although *A Weekend with Claud, Another Part of the Wood,* and *Harriet Said* lack the polish of more recent Bainbridge works, they nonetheless demonstrate a burgeoning talent at work. *New York Times Book Review* contributor Gail Godwin observed that *Harriet Said* "certainly ranks in content with the more celebrated thrillers of corrupt childhood, but it has literary and psychological virtues as well. The architecture of its narrative would have satisfied Poe: every incident advances the design. The language, though simple, often has the effect of poetry . . . [and] there are also several remarkable passages which reveal, so accurately, adolescence's frequent, unpredictable swing between mature and infantile behavior." Assessing *A Weekend with Claud,* Millard wrote: "The novel lacks the author's characteristic crispness; its fuzzy prose is rescued only by the pointed imagery which projects an exact vision of the despair and folly of love and lovemaking." A *Washington Post* reviewer found *Another Part of the Wood* "a scrupulously detailed, wryly witty and ultimately harrowing study of manners in the British middle and working classes, of the effects of dependency on a variety of weak people and of the lies we all tell ourselves to make life bearable and the deadly passions that lie buried under the dull surface of our daily banalities. . . . This slow-moving book does acquire a cumulative momentum, pointing toward an effective, quietly powerful end, and much of the detail work is exquisite."

The Dressmaker, published in the United States as *The Secret Glass,* remains one of Bainbridge's best-known works. Set in Liverpool during World War II, the novel explores the painful and claustrophobic existence of a young woman who lives with her two unmarried aunts. Millard suggested that the book "depicts the cramped, impoverished lives of working-class Liverpudlians during the darker days of 1944. The psychological realism of the novel goes beyond reminiscence and proves Bainbridge a master of detail and atmosphere." Godwin felt that *The Dressmaker* "will attract readers not for its suspense-entertainment but for its sharp character study and unrelenting Naturalism. . . . The author is painstaking in her evocation of era and perceptive about the world of manners in working-class Liverpool" and "has much to tell us about those pressure cookers of family life and limited means." A *Times Literary Supplement* reviewer wrote: "To have disinterred so many nasty things in the woodshed and yet evoked a workaday image of Liverpudlian optimism and resilience, in so few claustrophobic pages, is a remarkable achievement.

Miss Bainbridge's imagination pushes her towards nightmare, and her eye for detail is macabre; but because she writes with taut, matter-of-fact simplicity this seems as authentic as any contemporary image the camera has preserved of that mercifully vanished past."

The Bottle Factory Outing draws on Bainbridge's experience of working in just such a factory. The central characters are factory workers Brenda and Freda. Brenda, a shy young woman, is being stalked by the plant manager; the more outgoing Freda is in love with the manager's nephew, but her pursuit of him is doomed. She ends up murdered at the company picnic, and Brenda discovers Freda's body. "The catastrophe is only the beginning of Freda's strange voyage in Brenda's care, as survivor and victim change roles," Millard related. *Contemporary Novelists* essayist Val Warner dubbed the novel a "flamboyant black comedy" and praised Bainbridge's "rare lyricism" and "Joycean acceptance of her characters." Millard noted that the author uses much theatrical symbolism—role-playing, rehearsals, and so forth—and that "such a motif aptly conveys Bainbridge's central theme, the conflict between self-knowledge and self-deception, between the person and the role, between reality and fantasy."

Sweet William, like *The Bottle Factory Outing,* finds Bainbridge dealing with "the human tendency toward self-deception and self-parody," according to Millard. In this book, a young woman named Ann becomes caught in the web spun by the title character, a playwright who is deceptive and amoral. Ann's love for William leads her to give up everything else in her life, while he goes through a string of lovers. It emerges, however, that Ann can be deceptive, too. "The novel asserts that possessiveness and selfishness are invariably intermingled with love," Millard observed. Warner particularly praised the pivotal characterization of Ann's mother because "it was in reaction against her vicious pettiness that the daughter was vulnerable to William."

A Quiet Life reflects much of Bainbridge's life in its tale of the sometimes difficult relationships between family members. Framed within the story of a brother and sister meeting to divide an inheritance, the novel is largely in flashback form, as the brother, Alan, remembers events that occurred shortly after World War II. "At the end of the novel it is clear that Alan has remembered only what he could bear and has transformed or forgotten what he could not," Millard reported. Warner commented that in *A Quiet Life* Bainbridge focuses "devastatingly . . . on what children become in reaction to their parents." Also, according to Millard, the novel provides an example of "Bainbridge's skill at defining theme through black comedy."

Injury Time is also semiautobiographical in its focus on love affairs at midlife. Binny is a forty-year-old single mother in love with a married man; they try to give an elegant dinner party, but it ends up being crashed by bank robbers on the run. The novel's absurd action, which Bainbridge has said is based on things that happened to her, is a catalyst for character study. "Using multiple points of view, Bainbridge returns to the problems people have distinguishing reality from their own invented scenarios," Millard explained. Observed Warner: "Beneath the black comedy . . . the meaner and more generous impulses of the two main characters come through, in all their ambivalence."

Bainbridge's eye for telling details is again evident in *An Awfully Big Adventure.* To write this story she drew on her girlhood growing up in Liverpool. Like the author, the novel's protagonist, Stella, works as the assistant stage manager of a local repertory theater. Innocent yet determined to become worldly, Stella unwittingly influences the fate of all the older members of the company as they stage a production of *Peter Pan.* The novel brims with the dark humor typical of Bainbridge, including a scene in which Stella traumatizes an audience full of children by failing to revive Tinkerbell at the end of the play. *Times Literary Supplement* reviewer Lindsay Duguid commented that, "despite the grim setting and the characteristically bleak view of human nature, there is a mellowness about *An Awfully Big Adventure* which may come partly from the autobiographical element, but which is perhaps also due to its being set in the past. However sharp the details of poverty, . . . the retrospective picture has inevitably a blurred sepia halo." Duguid argued that while the novel's themes and settings are similar to those in her previous works, she invests the novel's subjects with a "new richness and complexity." Writing in the *Women's Review of Books,* Francine Prose remarked that the most striking characteristic of *An Awfully Big Adventure* "is how sympathetic its characters are without being, exactly, likeable." Prose called the novel "a joy to read; the narrative jogs along swiftly, turning and circling back on itself, pushed forward by the momentum of the characters' separate ambitions, quirks, desires and frustrated imbroglios." While faulting the conclusion as somewhat predictable and melodramatic, she asserted that such "minor reservations" do not detract from Bainbridge's "terse wit, her precision, her economy of style and, above all, the absolutely unique sensibility with which she observes and records the unjust, upsetting, clumsy and terribly moving comedy of errors that we call human relations."

As a writer Bainbridge has been frequently inspired by history and her own travels. Her novel *Young Adolf,* for instance, describes a family reunion in Liverpool between Adolf Hitler and his half-brother Alois, who did indeed live in England. Broyard contended in the *New York Times* that the book "has all the improbability of history. It is funny in a way that will make you shudder, sad in a way that will astonish you with unwanted feelings of sympathy. In making Hitler human, Miss Bainbridge has reminded us once again that it is persons, not abstract forces, that engender our disasters." *Christian Science Monitor* contributor Bruce Allen likewise asserted that the novel's best effects "rise out of Bainbridge's genius for finding latent menace in the dreariest everydayness." Noting that the fictional Hitler "is less . . . an embryonic monster than a subtle revelation of the social enfeeblement that let him grow and prosper," Warner called *Young Adolf* "Bainbridge's most ambitious book, with the tension deriving from our knowledge of what is to come, historically. Against this appalling factual scenario, details like the brown shirt made for the penniless Adolf by his sister-in-law . . . are intensely black comedy."

The novel *Watson's Apology* is based on a notorious Victorian murder case in which minister and schoolmaster J.S. Watson beat his wife, Anne, to death after years of increasingly unhappy wedlock; they had barely known each other when they married. According to Merle Rubin in Chicago's *Tribune Books,* Bainbridge uses the framework of documents surrounding the murder trial to weave "her fictional fabrication: thickly detailed, redolent of the specific time and place, and suffused in the grimly desperate atmosphere of a misbegotten marriage." James Lasdun, in *Encounter,* wrote that Bainbridge's "achievement is to show how very ordinary and unmysterious were the forces at play upon Mr. Watson and his wife. . . . What propelled them towards tragedy was an accumulation of the kinds of mutual disappointments that could afflict any marriage under similar circumstances." The Watsons' story, opined Michelle Slung in the *Washington Post Book World,* is "creepy, sad and suspenseful, all at once," and Bainbridge tells it in "tantalizing style." *New York Times Book Review* critic Marilyn Stasio deemed *Watson's Apology* "an extraordinarily lively work of the imagination because the facts themselves remain so obdurately dull," although the critic added: "For all [Bainbridge's] compassion for poor Watson's unarticulated miseries, she's a bit miserly with her sympathy for Anne."

The basis of *The Birthday Boys* is the South Pole expedition launched in 1911 by Robert Falcon Scott. An Englishman, Scott was determined to reach the pole before his rival, Norwegian Roald Amundsen. In January of 1912 he and his party did reach the pole, despite a series of unfortunate incidents, only to find that Amundsen had been and gone a month before. On their return trip, Scott and his entire party perished from cold and hunger. For years, they were held up by the British as examples of gallantry and courage, but it has more recently been argued that Scott's stubbornness and lack of preparation contributed greatly to the tragedy that befell his party. Using Scott's journal as a starting point, Bainbridge fashioned journals in the voices of the other team members to create her version of their fatal adventure.

Reviewing *The Birthday Boys* for the *New York Times,* Michiko Kakutani suggested that in this "affecting novel" Bainbridge creates a parable for the sort of brave, foolish optimism that flourished in Victorian England but died during World War I. The author "recounts their journey . . . with both sympathy and unflinching candor, capturing the boyish idealism and impetuosity that initially impel their journey, and the weariness and terror that gradually overtake them during their mission's final days." Furthermore, wrote Kakutani, Bainbridge renders their hardships with a verisimilitude so palpable that one "has the sensation of sharing the characters' experiences in that dangerously beautiful landscape firsthand. *The Birthday Boys* is a riveting tale by an enormously versatile writer." *New York Times Book Review* contributor Gary Krist added that in giving voice to Scott and his party, Bainbridge provides "some of the most convincing and slyly revealing first-person narrative I've ever read." While she subtly questions the heroic image of Scott and casts a jaundiced eye on "the whole ethos of action, conquest and empire," Bainbridge also creates a novel "that succeeds on many levels besides the political, most notably the visceral level of the adventure story," Krist averred.

Again focusing on the Edwardian era, Bainbridge's *Every Man for Himself* plumbs the depths of the 1912 sinking of the *Titanic.* As a *Kirkus Reviews* writer commented, this real-life tragedy "is not played for the usual melodrama but used . . . as the backdrop for the coming-of-age story of a well-connected, uncertain young man." The young man, Morgan, has been rescued from poverty by his aunt's fortuitous marriage to millionaire J.P. Morgan. This rescue is not entirely secure, however; although Morgan's formidable uncle expects him to find some sort of gainful employment, the young man is cast adrift with plenty of time and opportunity for drinking and getting into mischief. Once again, reviewers noted Bainbridge's ability to evoke character and history with a few deft passages. A *Publishers Weekly* contributor applauded *Every Man for Himself* as a "meticulously observed account that almost offhandedly convinces the reader that this is exactly what it must have been like aboard the doomed liner." For John Updike, writing in the *New Yorker,* such telling details do not come so neatly, however. "Bainbridge writes with a kind of betranced confidence," wrote Updike, "seeming to lose all track of her story only to pop awake for a stunning image or an intense exchange," and "her sudden details make a surreal effect."

Another historical novel, *Master Georgie* draws readers to Liverpool and the Crimea of the mid-nineteenth century. The title refers to George Hardy, a doctor and amateur photographer from a wealthy family. His story has three narrators, all of whom are dependent upon George. Myrtle, an orphan taken in by George's parents, grows up to become his lover and bears him children when his wife cannot. Pompey Jones, a boy of the streets, becomes George's photographic assistant and also his lover. Dr. Potter, the third narrator, is George's scholarly but impoverished brother-in-law. All three accompany George to the Crimean War, which was the first conflict to be photographed. It also was a very poorly executed war, and its most famous moment was the suicidal charge of a group of light cavalry, immortalized by Alfred, Lord Tennyson as "The Charge of the Light Brigade."

Master Georgie joins *The Birthday Boys* and *Every Man for Himself* to form what *Time* reviewer Elizabeth Glieck viewed as "an ambitious trilogy of novels that dissect great examples of human folly." Glieck went on to write that saying that Bainbridge writes historical novels "is like saying that Jane Austen wrote domestic comedies." Bainbridge's characters witness history but sometimes falsify it, explained the critic, citing George's composition of war scene photographs. By the same token, through their complicated relationships they sometimes deceive themselves, each other, and their repressive Victorian society. Glieck dubbed *Master Georgie* "a deadpan tale of secrets and lies," while in *Commonweal,* Daniel M. Murtaugh considered the book "a very rich novel," although "not an ingratiating one on the first reading." He advised, "Go back and read it again, and it will astonish you."

In addition to her novels, Bainbridge has also adapted several of her books for the screen and has served as a host-commentator on two British Broadcasting Corporation travel serials. She once explained that she writes to work out her own "personal obsessions," because she believes that writing, "like old photographs, gives a record by which past experience can be remembered."

New York Review of Books essayist Frank Kermode characterized Bainbridge's ability as "an odd and . . . fantastic talent," while in the *New York Times Book Review,* Guy Davenport made the observation that Bainbridge "has her comic eye on cultural confusion. She makes us see that it goes deeper than we think and touches more widely than we had imagined. The most appalling muddles can still be laughed at, and laughter is a kind of understanding."

BIOGRAPHICAL AND CRITICAL SOURCES:

BOOKS

Contemporary Literary Criticism, Thomson Gale (Detroit, MI), Volume 4, 1975, Volume 5, 1976, Volume 8, 1978, Volume 10, 1979, Volume 14, 1980, Volume 18, 1981, Volume 22, 1982, Volume 62, 1991.
Contemporary Novelists, 7th edition, St. James Press (Detroit, MI), 2001.
Dictionary of Literary Biography, Volume 14: *British Novelists since 1960,* Thomson Gale (Detroit, MI), 1983.
Finney, Gail, editor, *Look Who's Laughing: Gender and Comedy,* Gordon & Breach (Langhorne, PA), 1994.
Meyers, Helene, *Femicidal Fears: Narratives of the Female Gothic Experience.* Southwestern University Press (Georgetown, TX), 2002.
Wenno, Elisabeth, *Ironic Formula in the Novels of Beryl Bainbridge,* Acta Universitatis Gothoburgensis (Goteborg, Sweden), 1993.

PERIODICALS

Albion, Volume XI, 1979.
Antioch Review, fall, 1979.
Atlantic, March, 1979; May, 1994, p. 144; December, 1996; December, 1998, p. 116.
Best Sellers, March, 1982, p. 447.
Birmingham Post, October 6, 2001, p. 53.
Booklist, November 1, 1996.
Books and Bookmen, January, 1974; December, 1977; November, 1978; February, 1980.
Boston Globe, April 10, 1994, p. B18.
British Book News, January, 1985, p. 46.
Chicago Tribune, June 9, 1994, section 5, p. 5; December 7, 1998, p. 3.
Christian Science Monitor, April 9, 1979.
Commonweal, November 6, 1998, p. 26.

Courier Mail (Brisbane, Australia), March 2, 2002, p. M5.

Daily Post (Liverpool, England), September 19, 2001, p. 12.

Daily Telegraph (London, England), August 25, 2001, p. 6; September 17, 2002, p. 3.

Detroit News, April 29, 1979; April 27, 1980.

Encounter, February, 1975; February, 1976; February, 1985, pp. 42, 44-47; May, 1986, pp. 55-58.

Financial Times, September 22, 2001, p. 4.

Guardian (Manchester, England), June 1, 2002, p. 24.

Hudson Review, winter, 1977-78.

Independent (London, England), September 5, 2001, p. 7; October 15, 2002, p. 16.

Independent Sunday (London, England), September 1, 2002, p. 16.

Kirkus Reviews, August 15, 1996.

Library Journal, September, 1996.

Listener, November 29, 1973; November 20, 1980; January 11, 1990, p. 25.

London, January, 1978; April-May, 1979.

London Review of Books, November 20, 1980; June 7, 1984, pp. 20-22; November 15, 1984, p. 23; January 25, 1990, p. 19; January 30, 1992, p. 16.

Los Angeles Times, July 12, 1983; April 19, 1991, p. E10; August 13, 2001, p. E3; August 19, 2001, p. 11.

Los Angeles Times Book Review, May 18, 1980; April 25, 1982; September 9, 1984, p. 2; January 12, 1986; August 7, 1994, p. 10.

Milwaukee Journal Sentinel, July 22, 2001, p. 6.

Ms., December, 1974; August, 1977.

National Review, September 17, 1976.

New Leader, September 2, 1974; May 5, 1980.

New Republic, September 28, 1974; May 24, 1975; March 25, 1978; June 16, 1979; August 21, 1995, p. 31.

New Review, November, 1977.

New Statesman, November 1, 1974; November 10, 1978; December 21-28, 1979; September 11, 1981, pp. 17-18; November 29, 1985, p. 35; January 5, 1990, pp. 38-39; August 27, 1993, p. 13; May 1, 1998, p. 59.

Newsweek, August 12, 1974; March 19, 1979; April 7, 1979; May 9, 1994, p. 68.

New Yorker, April 25, 1977; November 25, 1985, p. 163; September 14, 1987, p. 134; July 25, 1994, p. 81; October 14, 1996.

New York Review of Books, May 16, 1974; July 15, 1976; April 5, 1979; July 17, 1980; October 25, 1984, pp. 46-49.

New York Times, August 21, 1974; May 26, 1975; March 17, 1976; March 1, 1978; March 7, 1979; May 18, 1979; March 5, 1980; March 13, 1981;

September 6, 1984; July 11, 1987, p. 18; March 8, 1991, p. C27; April 12, 1994, p. C24; August 5, 1999, p. E10.

New York Times Book Review, September 30, 1973; September 15, 1974; June 8, 1975; May 16, 1976; March 20, 1977; February 26, 1978; March 11, 1979; April 13, 1980, p. 14; March 1, 1981, p. 9; March 21, 1982, pp. 10, 25; September 23, 1984, p. 24; October 20, 1985, pp. 7, 9; July 11, 1987, p. 18; March 17, 1991, p. 24; July 11, 1993, p. 32; April 17, 1994, p. 15; October 16, 1994, p. 44; December 4, 1994, p. 70; April 30, 1995, p. 36; June 11, 1995, p. 58; December 22, 1996; August 30, 1998; August 19, 2001, p. 18; July 28, 2002, p. 16.

Observer (London, England), September 20, 1981, p. 26; August 18, 1985, p. 18; December 29, 1985; October 5, 1986, p. 25; December 17, 1989, p. 46; September 16, 1990, p. 55; August 19, 2001, Lynn Barber, interview with Bainbridge; August 26, 2001, p. 15; September 30, 2001, p. 18; October 6, 2002, p. 18.

Paris Review, winter, 2001, Shusha Guppy, interview with Bainbridge.

Phoebe, fall, 1991, p. 12.

Publishers Weekly, March 15, 1976; April 9, 1979; August 26, 1996; April 10, 1998, p. 365; November 9, 1998; January 6, 2002, p. 17.

Saturday Review, July 26, 1975; April 2, 1977.

School Library Journal, October, 1994, p. 158.

Seattle Times, July 28, 2002, p. K9.

Soviet Literature, number 11, 1984, pp. 141-149.

Spectator, November 2, 1974; October 11, 1975; October 9, 1976; October 1, 1977; November 11, 1978; December 8, 1979; November 1, 1980; April 28, 1984; November 3, 1984; August 22, 1987, p. 28; December 9, 1989, p. 37; November 28, 1992, p. 42; August 18, 2001, p. 36.

Time, November 11, 1974; May 16, 1994, p. 86; November 30, 1998, p. 22.

Times (London, England), September 3, 1981; April 5, 1984; August 17, 1984; October 4, 1984; March 29, 2003, Thom Gunn, interview with Bainbridge, p. 1.

Times Literary Supplement, October 6, 1972; September 28, 1973; November 1, 1974; October 3, 1975; November 3, 1978; December 1, 1978; February 29, 1980; October 31, 1980; August 14, 1981; September 11, 1981; October 5, 1984; December 20, 1985, p. 1463; October 17, 1986, p. 1168; April 24, 1987; December 15, 1989, p. 1385; December 20, 1991, p. 24; January 6, 1995, p. 20.

Tribune Books (Chicago, IL), April 8, 1979; January 12, 1986; January 6, 1991, p. 4.

Voice Literary Supplement, October, 1985, p. 5.

Wall Street Journal, July 13, 1994, p. A12.

Washington Post, April 8, 1980; March 5, 1981; April 18, 1991, p. D3; August 19, 2001, p. T7.

Washington Post Book World, December 4, 1977; August 20, 1978; April 15, 1979; September 23, 1984; November 17, 1985, pp. 14-15; July 26, 1987, pp. 3, 6; April 10, 1994, p. 7.

Women's Review of Books, July, 1991, p. 37; January 1999, p. 5.

Yale Review, winter, 1978.

ONLINE

BBC Audio Interviews, http://www.bbc.co.uk/bbcfour/audiointerviews/ (February 5, 1998), Christopher Cook, interview with Bainbridge.

RTE Interactive, http://www.rte.ie/arts/ (September 20, 2001), "According to Beryl."

*　　　*　　　*

BAINBRIDGE, Beryl Margaret
See BAINBRIDGE, Beryl

*　　　*　　　*

BAKER, Nicholson 1957-

PERSONAL: Born January 7, 1957, in New York, NY; son of Douglas and Ann (Nicholson) Baker; married Margaret Brentano, 1985; children: Alice, Elias. *Education:* Attended Eastman School of Music, 1974-75; Haverford College, B.A., 1980.

ADDRESSES: Agent—Melanie Jackson Agency, 915 Broadway, Suite 1009, New York, NY 10010.

CAREER: Worked variously as an oil analyst, word processor, and technical writer, 1980-87; full-time writer, 1987—. Founder of the nonprofit organization American Newspaper Repository.

AWARDS, HONORS: National Book Critics Circle Award, 2001, for *Double Fold: Libraries and the Assault on Paper.*

WRITINGS:

NOVELS

The Mezzanine, Weidenfeld & Nicolson (London, England), 1988.

Room Temperature, Grove Weidenfeld (New York, NY), 1990.

Vox, Random House (New York, NY), 1992.

The Fermata, Random House (New York, NY), 1994.

The Everlasting Story of Nory, Random House (New York, NY), 1998.

A Box of Matches, Random House (New York, NY), 2003.

Checkpoint, Knopf (New York, NY), 2004.

Vintage Baker, Vintage Books (New York, NY), 2004.

NONFICTION

U and I, Random House (New York, NY), 1991.

The Size of Thoughts: Essays and Other Lumber, Random House (New York, NY), 1996.

Double Fold: Libraries and the Assault on Paper, Random House (New York, NY), 2001.

Contributor of stories and essays to periodicals, including *Atlantic* and *New Yorker.*

SIDELIGHTS: Critically acclaimed author Nicholson Baker is known for writing comic novels that are essentially plotless. A Baker book, in fact, can consist almost entirely of digression, with virtually no plot, action, dialogue, or characterization. This offbeat approach comes naturally to Baker, although at first he tried to make his work more conventional. "I had a whole elaborate plot worked out with [my first novel]," the author told Harry Ritchie in the London *Sunday Times.* "But I'd start writing, and if the plot were, say, a foot long, I'd find I'd covered an eighth of an inch. So I got rid of the plot. I felt enormous relief that I didn't have to pretend to do something that didn't interest me."

Baker's first novel, *The Mezzanine,* celebrates the trivia of daily existence. The slim volume revolves around the largely uneventful lunch hour of the protagonist, a young office worker named Howie who uses his lunch break to buy shoelaces, eat a hot dog and a cookie, and read from second-century Roman emperor Marcus Aurelius's *Meditations.* "What Howie observes of his equally worn laces—it made the variables of private life seem suddenly graspable and law-abiding—could also be said of Baker's technique," David Dowling wrote in *Contemporary Novelists.* "Whether it is a record player arm, a doorknob, a straw or a shoelace, his disquisitions make one feel the private life matters, can have logic, and even beauty. Sometimes his examinations have the aridity of a consumer magazine report, but mostly Baker surprises and charms with images which are both ingenious metaphors for the emotional subject, and exact in their own right."

Robert Taylor of the *Boston Globe* noted, "The plot might in summary sound either banal or absurdist, when in fact it is a constant delight." The substance of the novel is derived not from the plot, but from the inner workings of Howie's mind. Through Baker's fascination with minutiae, Howie muses about a myriad of everyday objects and occurrences, including how paper milk cartons replaced glass milk bottles, the miracle of perforation (to which he gives a loving tribute), and the nature of plastic straws, vending machines, paper-towel dispensers, and popcorn poppers.

"What makes Howie's ruminations so mesmerizing is the razor-sharp insight and droll humor with which Mr. Baker illuminates the unseen world," said *New York Times Book Review* contributor Robert Plunket. Barbara Fisher Williamson, writing in *Washington Post Book World,* called Baker's descriptions of ordinary items "verbal ballets of incredible delicacy." Brad Leithauser, in the *New York Review of Books,* cited Baker's precision by quoting a passage from *The Mezzanine:* "The upstairs doorknobs in the house I grew up in were made of faceted glass. As you extended your fingers to open a door, a cloud of flesh-color would diffuse into the glass from the opposite direction. The knobs were loosely seated in their latch mechanism, and heavy, and the combination of solidity and laxness made for a multiply staged experience as you turned the knob: a smoothness that held intermediary tumbleral fallings-into-position. Few American products recently have been able to capture that same knuckly, orthopedic quality." Though some critics considered Baker's technique a gimmick, many praised his mastery of observation. Plunket said *The Mezzanine*'s "135 pages probably contain more insight into life as we live it than anything currently on the best-seller lists." Williamson called it "the most daring and thrilling first novel since John Barth's 1955 *The Floating Opera,* which it somewhat resembles. It is innovative and original. . . . It is wonderfully readable, in fact gripping, with surprising bursts of recognition, humor, and wonder."

Baker wrote *Room Temperature* similarly. Again, the book contains little plot: Mike, the narrator, is feeding his new baby girl. The book takes place during the twenty minutes necessary for the baby, nicknamed the Bug, to finish her bottle. During this time Mike's ruminations include nose-picking, breathing, the comma, childhood, love, and eating peanut butter straight from the jar, digressions that again display what *Washington Post* writer Michael Dirda called a "flair for noticing what we all know but don't quite remember or acknowledge." According to Dirda, *Room Temperature* is like *The Mezzanine* in "its microscopic approach to ordinary life, but is altogether more lighthearted, airier." The phrase "room temperature" describes the feel of the baby's bottle and also Mike's world, that of warm daydreams. Comparing *Room Temperature* with *The Mezzanine, Times Literary Supplement* contributor Lawrence Norfolk said the meanderings in *Room Temperature* are "brought closer to the meditations of the character, becoming credible as part of Mike's psychology rather than his author's cleverness. Not word-play but thought-process." Taylor called the work "a big novel unfolding out of small devices so subtly one is scarcely aware of its magnitude until the final page." Dirda described the book as "less sheerly innovative than its more clinical, austere predecessor, . . . yet nevertheless a real charmer, a breath of fresh air, a show-stopping coloratura aria made up of the quirks of memory and the quiddities of daily life."

Critics have compared Baker's writing, noted for its warmth and power of observation, to that of novelist John Updike, who plays a supporting role in Baker's first nonfiction book, *U and I.* This tribute to Updike is experimental and deliberately nonacademic; early in the book, Baker surprisingly says he has read less than half of Updike's work and does not intend to read any more until he has finished writing *U and I.* Calling his method "memory criticism," Baker strives to discover how Updike truly influenced him only through what he spontaneously remembers and forgets about the author and his work. Lewis Burke Frumkes, in the *New York Times Book Review,* described *U and I* as a "fascinating if unsteady journey of literary analysis and self-discovery, shuttling back and forth between soaring, manic moments of unabashed hero-worship and sober, even critical appraisals of the man who, he says, has haunted, inspired and influenced him beyond any other." *Times Literary Supplement* contributor Galen Strawson, however, maintained that "the *I* engulfs the *U.* In the end, *U and I* is almost all about Baker." Strawson added, "[Baker] has very little of interest to say about Updike." But according to Chicago *Tribune Books* critic Joseph Coates, *U and I* contains "a host of offhand, and sometimes startling, critical observations," making it a "provocative and compelling book for any serious reader of contemporary fiction."

Baker returned to fiction with *Vox* and *The Fermata.* In *Vox,* an *Economist* reviewer wrote, Baker "turns his hand to something that should be really interesting:

sex." The story centers on one phone call between a man and a woman. The two characters in this short novel both call an adult party line, then decide to converse privately, a dialogue *Time*'s Richard Stengel called "the ultimate in '90s safe sex: voices, not hands, caress each other." Readers learn very little about the characters, at least physically, as the book focuses only on what these two strangers say to one another. The conversation is sexual in nature, with some critics referring to this novel as soft porn. But Stengel said to call it just that would miss the point. Stengel preferred to call *Vox* "an anatomically correct, technology-assisted love story." He also praised Baker for his obvious love relationship with language. "*Vox* is as much about wordplay," Stengel wrote, "as it is about foreplay."

In *The Fermata,* Baker continues with a discussion of sexuality. In a *Seattle Times* review, Michael Upchurch described this novel as "an X-rated sci-fi fantasy that leaves 'Vox' seeming like mere fiber-optic foreplay." The word *fermata* refers to a so-called fold in time, which the book's socially shy protagonist, Arno Strine, uses to stop time and thus freeze the motions of other characters. Dowling, writing in *Contemporary Novelists,* found the author "freezing" spots of time "so that they, or more precisely those [spots] on the bodies of women in the vicinity, can be examined minutely. The device gives the text its typical baroque lassitude, but the hero, despite protesting: 'My curiosity has more love and tolerance in it than other men's does,' comes across as smug, and his eroticism as unpleasantly voyeuristic." Dowling further faults the narrative for taking an "adolescent male fantasy" approach, but adds that despite these flaws, *The Fermata* "contains some exquisite apercus such as . . . the color of those older Tercels and Civics whose paint had consequently oxidized into state of frescoesque, unsaturated beauty, like M&Ms sucked for a minute and spit back out into the palm for study." However, Upchurch said the novel had an undeniable "warmth and generous spirit," and concluded that *The Fermata* confirmed Baker "as one of our most gifted and original writers."

The Size of Thoughts: Essays and Other Lumber is a collection of essays under the categories of "Thought," "Machinery," "Reading," "Mixed," "Library Science," and "Lumber." Baker examines life's simplicities such as toenail clippers and the all-but-forgotten library index card catalog. Some critics said this collection again exemplifies Baker's passion for language. Jennie Yabroff, writing for the online publication *Hot Wired,* compared Baker to "a hip lit professor who seduces his class into reading deconstructivist criticism by referencing MTV." He "spices up his readings with outrageous metaphors," Yabroff added, to keep his readers involved. Sven Birkerts, for the *New York Times Book Review,* said Baker settles on "something commonplace yet structurally intricate [such as the nail clippers] and then, with magnified detailing and sly humor" proceeds to take his readers into "hitherto unimagined panoramas." His "incessantly effervescing prose," Birkerts wrote, "tunes" the reader's mind.

Baker returned to fiction with his novel *The Everlasting Story of Nory,* which relates the childhood story of Eleanor Winslow, a nine-year-old American girl who attends school in England. Again, Baker manipulates language to set the story apart. Baker demonstrates through his young protagonist, Eric Lorberer wrote in the *Review of Contemporary Fiction,* "how both the scientist and the surrealist inhabit a child's consciousness." Nory entices the reader with her self-defined concepts of the world, her stories, and her own peculiar language in her attempt to find meaning. Carol Herman, in *Insight on the News,* refers to *Nory* as a literary gem that "presents the fears, dreams and ideas of a prepubescent schoolgirl whose preoccupations are more innocent than erotic and as such all the more stunning." Though Baker has a young daughter, Herman found that the author did not write from a father's perspective. Rather, he let Nory speak for herself.

Baker stirred much controversy with *Double Fold: Libraries and the Assault on Paper,* in which he rails against the commonplace destruction of index-card files, newspapers, and other paper documents at many modern libraries across the United States. Although he admits computerized files may be more efficient, the demise of the actual paper products, especially the newspapers and old books, saddens him. According to Margaria Fichtner, writing for the *Knight-Ridder/Tribune News Service,* Baker blames the loss of "at least 925,000 books," many rare, on modernization. Baker has invested his own money in a non-profit organization, American Newspaper Repository, through which he attempts to preserve as many old newspapers as he can. In his book, he scolds many large libraries, including the Library of Congress, for their practices. Librarians, such as Francine Fialkoff in her *Library Journal* article, defended such library modernization practices; she said Baker just "doesn't get it." Though Fialkoff bemoaned Baker's negativity, other critics praised him for publicizing the loss of original publications. Baker won the National Book Critics Circle Award for his effort.

In an interview, Baker told Jeffrey Freymann-Weyr of *National Public Radio* that he wrote *A Box of Matches* "only by the light of a fire," because he did not want "to let incandescent light intrude on my consciousness." This 2003 novel focuses on the little things. "I want the books to be about things that you don't notice when you're noticing them," Baker told Freymann-Weyr. Protagonist Emmett, a forty-four-year-old married man, lights a fire every morning, using only one match each time, then sits down to think. He will perform this ceremony for thirty-three days, one day for every match in a box. Emmett, wrote Walter Kirn in the *New York Times Book Review,* is "something of a homebody Thoreau, camped out in the Walden Woods of his own living room." The book captures Emmett's often-funny ruminations. "There is gentle humor at work here," Michael Upchurch wrote for the *Seattle Times.* Some critics have described the humor as melancholic. Someone going through a mid-life crisis worries a lot and reminisces. "There's nothing else like" *A Box of Matches,* wrote Upchurch, except another book by Baker. David Gates in *Newsweek* praised *A Box of Matches* as one of Baker's most "satisfying" books yet.

Baker attracted attention with his next book, *Checkpoint,* which is made up completely of a conversation between two old high school friends, one of whom, Jay, wants to kill President George Bush because of the war in Iraq. The other friend, Ben, tries to talk him out of it. The two friends have not seen each other for many years, and Ben is successful while Jay has lost his job and has become obsessed with his assassination plots. Although Baker has Jay base much of his argument for assassination on real facts about the war, his ideas for completing the task tend to be fantastical. Writing in the *Christian Science Monitor,* Ron Charles noted, "Jay's argument swings wildly from an insane rant to caustic political analysis. Though most of his weapons— Bush-seeking bullets and a giant uranium ball—are clearly delusional, his final plan is pedestrian and deadly. While largely agreeing with his friend's recitation of Bush's sins, [Ben] struggles to calm [Jay] and get him to abandon his illegal plot." Writing a month before the book appeared in stores, Charles noted that the book could be seen as a threat and lead to Baker being investigated but that the U.S. Justice Department and the FBI would not comment on whether or not Baker was of interest to them. As for Baker, he told David Gates of *Newsweek,* "I don't think I should stand behind any part of the book. These are the miseries, these are the doubts that you have. I had Jay say them as forcefully as I could, because I think the left has to think about this a little more carefully. And it also seemed like, if I'm going to get myself in trouble in a book, why shouldn't I just be indiscriminately outrageous?"

BIOGRAPHICAL AND CRITICAL SOURCES:

BOOKS

Contemporary Novelists, 6th edition, St. James Press (Detroit, MI), 1996.
Saltzman, Arthur M., *Understanding Nicholson Baker,* University of South Carolina Press (Columbia, SC), 1999.

PERIODICALS

America, June 4, 2001, Peter Heinegg, "Bureaucrat, Spare That Book!," p. 27.
Atlantic, January-February, 2003, Thomas Mallon, review of *A Box of Matches,* pp. 190-193.
Booklist, March 15, 1998, Donna Seaman, review of *The Everlasting Story of Nory,* pp. 1178-1179; February 15, 2001, Mark Knoblauch, review of *Double Fold: Libraries and the Assault on Paper,* p. 1087.
Boston Globe, December 14, 1988, Robert Taylor, review of *The Mezzanine;* April 18, 1990, Robert Taylor, review of *Room Temperature,* p. 70.
Christian Science Monitor, July 30, 2004, Ron Charles, "It's Only Fiction, but Is It Legal?," p. 11.
Columbia Journalism Review, July, 2001, James Boylan, review of *Double Fold,* p. 67.
Economist, April 4, 1992, review of *Vox,* p. 109.
Entertainment Weekly, March 11, 1994, p. 28; January 17, 2002, Troy Patterson, review of *A Box of Matches,* p. 85.
Esquire, February, 1994, p. 76.
Guardian (Manchester, England), April 5, 1990.
Harper's Bazaar, February, 1994, p. 84.
Independent (London, England), September 6, 1989.
Insight on the News, August 31, 1998, Carol Herman, review of *The Everlasting Story of Nory,* p. 36.
Knight-Ridder/Tribune News Service, April 11, 2001, Margaria Fichtner, "Writer's Anger Is Painful, and His Book about Library Discards Is Disturbing," p. K4872.
Library Journal, January, 1994, p. 157; May 1, 1998, Kay Hogan, review of *The Everlasting Story of Nory,* p. 135; May 15, 2001, Francine Fialkoff, "Baker's Book Is Half-Baked," p. 102; June 15, 2002, "Baker-Inspired Backlash at LC?," p. 11.
Los Angeles Times, April 19, 1990.
Los Angeles Times Book Review, April 1, 1990, p. 6.
Micrographics and Hybrid Imaging Systems Newsletter, September, 2001, "Fighting Back against the Double Scold," p. 7.

New Republic, May 28, 2001, Alexander Star, review of *Double Fold,* p. 38.

New Statesman, April 6, 1990, p. 38.

Newsweek, April 16, 2001, Malcolm Jones, "Paper Tiger: Taking Librarians to Task," p. 57; January 13, 2002, David Gates, review of *A Box of Matches,* p. 60; August 9, 2004, David Gates, "Target," p. 50.

New York Review of Books, August 17, 1989, Brad Leithauser, review of *The Mezzanine,* p. 15; April 7, 1994, p. 14; June 20, 1996, p. 65.

New York Times Book Review, February 5, 1989, p. 9; April 15, 1990, p. 17; April 14, 1991, Lewis Burke Frumkes, review of *U and I,* p. 12; February 13, 1994, p. 13; April 14, 1996, Sven Birkerts, review of *The Size of Thoughts,* p. 12; February 2, 2003, Walter Kirn, review of *A Box of Matches,* pp. 7, 10.

Observer (London, England), April 1, 1990.

Philadelphia Inquirer, April 15, 1990.

Publishers Weekly, November 29, 1993, p. 52; February 7, 1994, p. 42; March 30, 1998, review of *The Everlasting Story of Nory,* p. 66; April 2, 2001, review of *Double Fold,* p. 53; October 14, 2002, Jeff Zaleski, review of *A Box of Matches,* p. 62.

Review of Contemporary Fiction, fall, 1998, Eric Lorberer, review of *The Everlasting Story of Nory,* p. 242.

San Francisco Chronicle, July 8, 1990, p. 3.

San Jose Mercury News, March 18, 1990, p. 20.

Searcher, June, 2001, review of *Double Fold,* p. 6.

Seattle Times, February 27, 1994, Michael Upchurch, review of *The Fermata,* p. F2; January 12, 2003, Michael Upchurch, review of *A Box of Matches,* p. L10.

Sunday Times (London, England), September 3, 1989; April 8, 1990, p. H8.

Time, February 3, 1992, Richard Stengel, "1-900-Aural Sex," review of *Vox,* p. 59; May 11, 1998, R.Z. Sheppard, review of *The Everlasting Story of Nory,* p. 80.

Times Literary Supplement, September 15, 1989, p. 998; April 27, 1990, Lawrence Norfolk, review of *Room Temperature,* p. 456; April 19, 1991, Galen Strawson, review of *U and I,* p. 20; April 5, 1996, p. 22.

Tribune Books (Chicago, IL), April 28, 1991, Joseph Coates, review of *U and I,* p. 7.

Washington Post, May 7, 1990, Michael Dirda, review of *Room Temperature,* p. C3; September 23, 1990.

Washington Post Book World, November 13, 1988, Barbara Fisher Williamson, review of *The Mezzanine,* p. 7.

Wilson Quarterly, summer, 2001, James Morris, review of "*Double Fold,*" p. 125.

ONLINE

Hot Wired Web site, http://www.hotwired.lycos.com/ (February 15, 2003), Jennie Yabroff, "Lumbering Genius."

National Pubic Radio Web site, http://www.npr.org/ (January 15, 2003), Jeffrey Freymann-Weyr, "Nicholson Baker: A Life in Detail."

*   *   *

BAKER, Russell 1925-
(Russell Wayne Baker)

PERSONAL: Born August 14, 1925, in Loudoun County, VA; son of Benjamin Rex (a stonemason) and Lucy Elizabeth (a schoolteacher; maiden name, Robinson) Baker; married Miriam Emily Nash, March 11, 1950; children: Kathleen Leland, Allen Nash, Michael Lee. *Education:* Johns Hopkins University, B.A., 1947.

ADDRESSES: Office—c/o New York Times, 229 W. 43rd St., New York, NY 10036.

CAREER: Sun, Baltimore, MD, member of staff, 1947-53, London bureau chief, 1953-54; *New York Times,* member of Washington, DC, bureau, 1954-62, author of nationally syndicated "Observer" column for the *New York Times,* 1962—. Host of PBS television series "Masterpiece Theatre," 1993—. *Military service:* U.S. Naval Reserve, 1943-45.

MEMBER: American Academy and Institute of Arts and Letters (elected, 1984); American Academy of Arts and Sciences (fellow).

AWARDS, HONORS: Frank Sullivan Memorial Award, 1976; George Polk Award, 1979, for commentary; Pulitzer Prize, 1979, for distinguished commentary (in "Observer" column), and 1983, for *Growing Up;* Elmer Holmes Bobst prize, 1983, for nonfiction; American Academy and Institute of Arts and Letters, 1984; Howland Memorial Prize, Yale University, and Fourth Estate Award, National Press Club, all 1989; H.L.D., Hamilton College, Princeton University, Johns Hopkins University, Franklin Pierce College, Yale University, Long Island University, and Connecticut College; LL.D., Union College; D.Litt, Wake Forest University, University of Miami, Rutgers University, Columbia University; H.H. D., Hood College.

WRITINGS:

COLLECTIONS

No Cause for Panic, Lippincott (Philadelphia, PA), 1964.

Baker's Dozen, New York Times (New York, NY), 1964.

All Things Considered, Lippincott (Philadelphia, PA), 1965.

Poor Russell's Almanac, Doubleday (New York, NY), 1972.

So This Is Depravity, Congdon & Lattes (New York, NY), 1980.

The Rescue of Miss Yaskell and Other Pipe Dreams, Congdon & Weed (New York, NY), 1983.

AUTOBIOGRAPHY

Growing Up, Congdon & Weed (New York, NY), 1982.

The Good Times, Morrow (New York, NY), 1989.

Looking Back, New York Review of Books (New York, NY), 2002.

OTHER

(Author of text) *Washington: City on the Potomac,* Arts, 1958.

An American in Washington, Knopf (New York, NY), 1961.

Our Next President: The Incredible Story of What Happened in the 1968 Elections (fiction), Atheneum (New York, NY), 1968.

The Upside-Down Man (children's book), McGraw-Hill (New York, NY), 1977.

(Editor) *The Norton Book of Light Verse,* Norton (New York, NY), 1986.

There's a Country in My Cellar, Morrow, 1990.

(Editor) *Russell Baker's Book of American Humor,* Norton (New York, NY), 1993.

(With William Knowlton Zinsser) *Inventing the Truth: The Art and Craft of Memoir,* Houghton Mifflin (Boston, MA), 1995.

Also coauthor of musical play *Home Again,* 1979. Contributor to books, including John Brannon Albright, *Better Times,* Dolphin Books, 1975. Contributor to periodicals, including *Saturday Evening Post, New York Times Magazine, Sports Illustrated, Ladie's Home Journal, Holiday, Theatre Arts, Mademoiselle, Life, Look,* and *McCall's.*

ADAPTATIONS: One of Baker's columns, "How to Hypnotize Yourself into Forgetting the Vietnam War," was dramatized and filmed by Eli Wallach for *The Great American Dream Machine,* PBS, 1971.

SIDELIGHTS: Noted humorist Russell Baker has charmed readers for years with his witty, literate observations of the foibles and follies of contemporary life. Baker began his career as a journalist for the Baltimore *Sun* and the *New York Times,* where he enjoyed a reputation as a skilled reporter and astute political commentator. The author is perhaps best known for his "Observer" column, which has appeared in the *New York Times* since 1962 and in syndication in hundreds of other papers across the country. Regarded by *Washington Post Book World* critic Robert Sherrill as "the supreme satirist" of the late twentieth century, Baker has been credited with taking newspaper humor and turning it into "literature—funny, but full of the pain and absurdity of the age," according to *Time*'s John Skow.

Armed with a sense of humor described by *Washington Post* writer Jim Naughton as "quick, dry, and accessibly cerebral," Baker has taken aim at a wide range of targets, including the presidency, the national economy, and the military. In one "Observer" column, Baker spoofed the government's MX-missile plan, a proposal to transport nuclear weapons around the country using the nation's railroads. Baker took the idea even further by proposing the MX-Pentagon plan, a system of mobile Pentagon replicas, complete with a phony president and secretary of defense, that would criss-cross the United States and confuse the nation's enemies. In another essay, Baker suggested that the reason Congress voted against a bill requiring truth-in-advertising labels on defective used cars was the politicians' fear that the same fate would someday befall them: "Put yourself in your Congressman's shoes. One of these days he is going to be put out of office. Defeated, old, tired, 120,000 miles on his smile and two pistons cracked in his best joke. They're going to put him out on the used-Congressman lot. Does he want to have a sticker on him stating that he gets only eight miles on a gallon of bourbon? That his rip-roaring anti-Communist speech hasn't had an overhaul since 1969? That his generator is so decomposed it hasn't sparked a fresh thought in fifteen years?"

Though many of Baker's columns concern themselves with the dealings of pompous politicians and the muddled antics of government bureaucrats, not all of the author's essays are political in nature. All manner of human excesses, fads, and trendy behavior have come under Baker's scrutiny; among the topics he has satirized are Super Bowl Sunday, the Miss America pageant, and television commercials. Other selections have touched on the author's anger over the physical and moral decay of urban America. In "Such Nice People," Baker examines fellow New Yorkers' reactions to the deterioration of their city, finding a thin veneer of civility masking a barely suppressed rage. "In a city like this," he wrote, "our self-control must be tight. Very tight. So we are gentle. Civilized. Quivering with self-control. So often so close to murder, but always so self-controlled. And gentle." *Spectator* critic Joe Mysak applauded this type of essay, judging its significance to be "closer to the grain of American life" than Baker's politically tinged writings, and columns of this sort moved Sherrill to write that, "when it comes to satire of a controlled but effervescent ferocity, nobody can touch Baker." In addition to having his column appear in newspapers, Baker has published several compilations of selected "Observer" columns.

Baker has also written a fictional story of the 1968 presidential election, *Our Next President,* as well as a children's book, *The Upside-Down Man.* In *Russell Baker's Book of American Humor,* published in 1993, Baker presents a collection of humorous literary pieces, both fiction and nonfiction, from the past 200 years. The book includes one-line snippets as well as poems, short stories, and excerpts from longer essays from the likes of Mark Twain, Garrison Keillor, Mae West, Tom Wolfe, Fran Lebowitz, Abraham Lincoln, Annie Szymanski, and P.J. O'Rourke, among others. Christopher Buckley, writing in the *New York Times Book Review,* called the collection "mostly funny . . . generous and big-hearted," while *Washington Post Book World* contributor Burling Lowrey remarked that the pieces in the book "prove the validity of two familiar axioms: (1) We should always treat light things seriously and serious things lightly; and (2) All first-rate humor is subversive." Baker has also edited *The Norton Book of Light Verse* and coauthored *Inventing the Truth: The Art and Craft of Memoir.*

Along with his writings in the "Observer" and his other humorous literary endeavors, Baker is known for his memoirs, *Growing Up* and *The Good Times.* The former chronicles Baker's adventures as a youngster in Depression-era Virginia, New Jersey, and Baltimore, while the latter recounts his career as a journalist, from his early work on the crime beat at the Baltimore *Sun* to his days as a Washington correspondent with the

New York Times. Both books earned critical and popular acclaim for their gentle humor and warm, retrospective narratives.

Described by Mary Lee Settle in the *Los Angeles Times Book Review* as "a wondrous book, funny, sad, and strong," *Growing Up* explores the often difficult circumstances of Baker's childhood with a mix of humor and sadness. His father, a gentle, blue-collar laborer fond of alcohol, died in an "acute diabetic coma" when Baker was five. Baker's mother, Lucy Elizabeth, suddenly widowed and impoverished, accepted her brother's offer to live with his family in New Jersey. Before moving, Lucy left her youngest daughter, Audrey, in the care of wealthier relatives who could provide the infant with a more comfortable existence than she. In *Growing Up,* Baker bore witness to his mother's pain and ambivalence over the decision: "It was the only deed of her entire life for which I ever heard her express guilt. Years later, in her old age, she was still saying, 'Maybe I made a terrible mistake when I gave up Audrey.'"

The family lived off the kindness of relatives for years, finally settling in Baltimore, where Lucy eventually remarried. Baker got his first taste of journalistic life at a young age when, at his mother's insistence, he began selling copies of the *Saturday Evening Post.* Lucy exerted a strong influence over Baker's life, serving as "goad, critic, and inspiration to her son," in the words of *New York Times Book Review* critic Ward Just. The loving but tempestuous relationship that existed between mother and son threaded its way through the work, so that *Growing Up* becomes as much the mother's story as the son's. Baker portrays Lucy as a driven woman, haunted by her life of poverty and obsessed with the idea that her son would achieve success. "I would make something of myself," Baker wrote in *Growing Up,* "and if I lacked the grit to do it, well then she would make me make something of myself." *Spectator* critic Peter Paterson saw the work as "a tribute" to the women in Baker's life, first and foremost to Lucy, "who dominates the book as she dominated her son's existence."

Baker's fully drawn portraits of his mother and other relatives were a result of his extensive research efforts. To gather information for his book, Baker interviewed dozens of family members, collecting a trove of facts about historical America in the process. In a *Washington Post* interview, the writer once said, "I was writing about a world that seemed to have existed 200 years ago. I had one foot back there in this primitive countrylife where women did the laundry running their knuckles on scrub boards and heated irons on coal stoves. That was an America that was completely dead." In a review of *Growing Up, Washington Post Book World* reviewer Jonathan Yardley wrote that Baker "passed through rites that for our culture are now only memories, though cherished ones, from first exposure to the miracle of indoor plumbing to trying on his first pair of long pants," and Settle found Baker's descriptions of such scenes "as funny and as touching as Mark Twain's."

Many critics also lauded Baker's ability to translate his personal memories into a work of universal experience. *New Statesman* critic Brian Martin admired the author's "sharp eye for the details of ordinary life," while Yardley offered even stronger praise, affirming that Baker "has accomplished the memorialist's task: to find shape and meaning in his own life, and to make it interesting and pertinent to the reader. In lovely, haunting prose, he has told a story that is deeply in the American grain, one in which countless readers will find echoes of their own, yet in the end is very much his own."

The Good Times continues Baker's story, recounting the author's coming of age as a journalist during the 1950s and 1960s. Hired in 1947 as a writer for the Baltimore *Sun,* Baker developed a reputation as a fast, accurate reporter and eventually earned a promotion to the post of London bureau chief. In the opinion of *New York Times* reviewer Frank Conroy, the time spent in London made Baker a better reporter and a better writer. Conroy determined that Baker's "ability to take the best from the Brits—who in general write better than we do . . . was perhaps the key event in his growth as a writer." Though Baker enjoyed London, he moved on to become the *Sun*'s White House correspondent, a decision he soon regretted. Once in Washington, Baker found the work boring, the atmosphere stifling, and his writing style unappreciated. Writing in *The Good Times,* Baker acknowledged: "I had swapped the freedom to roam one of the world's great cities and report whatever struck my fancy. And what had I got in return? A glamorous job which entitled me to sit in a confined space, listening to my colleagues breathe."

Frustrated at the *Sun,* Baker jumped at an offer to write for the *New York Times* Washington bureau, although he insisted on covering the Senate, hoping to capture the human side of the country's leaders. But in time even Congress, with its fawning politicians and controlled press briefings, proved disappointing. Recalling his dissatisfaction with the work, Baker told *Time,* "I began to wonder why, at the age of thirty-seven, I was wearing

out my hams waiting for somebody to come out and lie to me." When the *Sun* attempted to regain Baker's services with the promise of a column, the *Times* promptly countered the offer with its own column, a proposal which convinced Baker to stay.

The Good Times is filled with Baker's portrayals of political heavyweights like John Kennedy, Lyndon Johnson, and Richard Nixon. Baker also profiled some of his fellow journalists, saving his harshest criticisms for those reporters who compromised their professional integrity by letting themselves become seduced by savvy politicians. Complimenting Baker on his balanced characterizations, Just reported that the author's "level gaze is on full display here in the deft, edged portraits" of his Congressional contacts, while William French of the Toronto *Globe and Mail* stated that "Baker's thumbnail sketches of the Washington movers and shakers of his time are vivid."

Many critics viewed *The Good Times* favorably, including Just who called the book "a superb autobiography, wonderfully told, often hilarious, always intelligent and unsparing." Some reviewers, however, felt that Baker's trademark sense of modesty is used to excess in the book. In Conroy's opinion, Baker takes too little credit for his early success, "ascribing much to luck and his ability to touch-type." Naughton was more critical of Baker's style, asserting that "his humility weakens the book." Other reviewers observed that, because of its subject matter, *The Good Times* necessarily evokes different feelings from its predecessor, *Growing Up.* "Some readers may find that this sequel lacks the emotional tug of the original," Robert Shogan stated in the *Los Angeles Times Book Review,* "what *The Good Times* offers instead is an insider's view of modern American journalism that illuminates both the author and his trade." Along those lines, Yardley added that "Baker seems to understand that it is one thing to write for public consumption about the distant years of childhood, and quite another to write about the unfinished stories of marriage and parenthood." He concluded, "In the end, though, *The Good Times* is every bit as much a personal document as was *Growing Up.*"

Looking Back is a collection of essays, each of which originally appeared in the *New Yorker.* They are reflections on American public figures, among them Lyndon Johnson, William Randolph Hearst, Joe DiMaggio, Barry Goldwater, and Martin Luther King. Reviewing the book for the *New York Review of Books,* a contributor noted that, "With an elegiac yet shrewd sense of their accomplishments both enduring and ephemeral, he traces the impressions they left on twentieth-century America—and on him."

Describing his writing career to Naughton, Baker downplayed his talents, stating, "I've just had the good luck to escape the meaner reviewers." Readers of his work attribute Baker's success to things altogether different. Skow noted that while Baker most often uses humor to make his point, he "can also write with a haunting strain of melancholy, with delight, or . . . with shame and outrage." In addition, Baker's consistency and clarity are mentioned as strengths. "There is just a lucidity and a sanity about him that is so distinctive," U.S. Senator Daniel Patrick Moynihan told *Time*. "He writes clearly because he thinks clearly." Finally, summarizing the opinions of many critics, Mysak declared: "For a look at how we live now . . . Baker has no superiors, and few peers."

BIOGRAPHICAL AND CRITICAL SOURCES:

BOOKS

Baker, Russell, *So This Is Depravity,* Congdon & Lattes, 1980.
Baker, Russell, *Growing Up,* Congdon & Weed (New York, NY), 1982.
Baker, Russell, *The Rescue of Miss Yaskell and Other Pipe Dreams,* Congdon & Weed (New York, NY), 1983.
Baker, Russell, *The Good Times,* Morrow (New York, NY), 1989.
Contemporary Literary Criticism, Volume 31, Thomson Gale (Detroit, MI), 1985.

PERIODICALS

Chicago Tribune, January 16, 1987.
Detroit Free Press, June 27, 1989.
Detroit News, November 7, 1982; July 9, 1989.
Economist, January 22, 1994, p. 97.
Entertainment Weekly, December 31, 1993, p. 62.
Globe and Mail (Toronto, Ontario, Canada), January 19, 1985; June 24, 1989.
Library Journal, May 1, 1989.
Los Angeles Times, December 7, 1980; January 22, 1984; March 17, 1988.
Los Angeles Times Book Review, October 10, 1982; November 30, 1986; June 11, 1989.
New Statesman, March 16, 1984.
Newsweek, September 29, 1980; November 8, 1982.
New Yorker, March 8, 1993, p. 33.
New York Review of Books, August 6, 2004.

New York Times, January 30, 1972; October 6, 1982; May 23, 1989.
New York Times Book Review, January 30, 1972; October 18, 1982; May 28, 1989; July 8, 1990; February 20, 1994, p. 22.
New York Times Magazine, September 12, 1982.
People, December 20, 1982; October 4, 1993, p. 12.
Publishers Weekly, January 24, 1972; April 28, 1989.
Spectator, February, 1984; March, 1984.
Time, January 19, 1968; January 17, 1972; June 4, 1979; November 1, 1982; October 4, 1993, p. 81.
Times Literary Supplement, April 6, 1984.
Tribune Books (Chicago, IL), January 16, 1987; May 21, 1989.
Washington Post, July 25, 1989.
Washington Post Book World, October 5, 1980; October 3, 1982; October 9, 1983; January 18, 1987; May 28, 1989; December 5, 1993, p. 3.

*　　*　　*

BAKER, Russell Wayne
See BAKER, Russell

*　　*　　*

BALDACCI, David 1960-

PERSONAL: Born in 1960, in Richmond, VA; married, wife's name, Michelle; children: Spencer, Collin. *Education:* Virginia Commonwealth University, B.A.; University of Virginia, J.D.

ADDRESSES: Home—Northern Virginia. *Agent*—Aaron Priest Literary Agency, 708 3rd Ave., 23rd Floor, New York, NY 10017.

CAREER: Writer. Former trial and corporate lawyer in Washington, DC. Board member of Virginia Commonwealth University, Library of Virginia, Multiple Sclerosis Society, and Virginia Blood Services.

AWARDS, HONORS: W.H. Smith's Thumping Good Read Award for fiction, 1997, for *Absolute Power.*

WRITINGS:

Absolute Power, Warner (New York, NY), 1996.
Total Control, Warner (New York, NY), 1997.

The Winner, Warner (New York, NY), 1997.
The Simple Truth, Warner (New York, NY), 1998.
Saving Faith, Warner (New York, NY), 1999.
Wish You Well, Warner (New York, NY), 2000.
Last Man Standing, Warner (New York, NY), 2001.
The Christmas Train, Warner (New York, NY), 2002.
Split Second, Warner (New York, NY), 2003.
Hour Game, Warner (New York, NY), 2004.

Contributor to periodicals, including *Panorama Magazine* (Italy), *UVA Lawyer, Welt am Sonntag* (Germany), *Tatler Magazine* (United Kingdom), *New Statesman,* and *USA Today Magazine.* Also author of unproduced screenplays. Also author of the short story "The Mighty Johns," published in an anthology of the same title, 2002, and of the novella *Office Hours.*

ADAPTATIONS: Absolute Power was adapted as a screenplay by William Goldman, Castle Rock, 1997; rights to *Total Control* have been sold to Columbia/TriStar; *McCourt & Stein,* a television series pilot based on a novel by Baldacci was developed by the USA cable network, 2002.

WORK IN PROGRESS: Second book in a series that began with *Split Second.*

SIDELIGHTS: Author of bestselling legal thrillers, David Baldacci turned a successful career in the law into an even more lucrative writing industry. With over thirty million copies of his novels in print in thirty languages, Baldacci is not only a hot literary property, but he also takes chances in genre. After producing back-to-back "turbo-thrillers," as a reviewer for *Publishers Weekly* dubbed titles such as *Absolute Power* and *The Simple Truth,* Baldacci changed pace with mainstream literary efforts including *Wish You Well* and *The Christmas Train.* But suspense mixed with gripping plots is what the author does best. Returning to that format with the 2003 *Split Second,* Baldacci created a thriller "sustained by the pulse-pounding suspense his fans have come to expect," according to Kristine Huntley writing in *Booklist.*

Regularly hitting the bestseller lists around the world, Baldacci's work has been praised by many for its turn-the-page readability, and criticized by others for overly complex plots, simplified characterizations, and an uncanny ability to switch point of view in mid-scene. Reviewing his mainstream novel, *Wish You Well,* in *Book,* Don McLeese complained that "Baldacci commits so many literary crimes that he risks disbarment from the

world of letters." Yet a contributor for *Publishers Weekly* found that same book "an utterly captivating novel" that offers readers "bone-deep emotional truth." Often compared to writer John Grisham for his use of the legal world in his thrillers, Baldacci counts among his readers former President Bill Clinton, who called Baldacci's 1999 *The Simple Truth* his favorite novel of the year. A self-confessed writing junkie, Baldacci told an interviewer for the *Warner Book,* Web site "If I'm not writing, I'm not comfortable. I can write anywhere under any circumstances. I can write in a plane or a train or a boat. In a corner, with a screaming child in my lap, I've done all those things. If you wait for the perfect place to write, you'll never write anything because there's no such place."

Born in Virginia in 1960, Baldacci grew up with a simple philosophy, instilled by his father, a first generation Italian-American who worked as a foreman for a trucking firm. As Baldacci explained to Jeff Zaleski in *Publishers Weekly,* his father advised him that "If I work hard and respect others, life turns out okay." From his part-Cherokee mother he inherited high cheekbones and numerous stories of Appalachia and rural Virginia. A love of stories was with him from an early age, and he began writing in high school. "I love to read," Baldacci noted in his *Warner Books* Web site interview. "I wanted to make other people feel the magic of a good story and so I took up my pen too. I've always been a storyteller, since I was a child."

While an undergraduate at Virginia Commonwealth College and studying law at the University of Virginia, Baldacci continued writing in his spare time. Then when he became a full-time trial and corporate lawyer in Washington, DC, Baldacci still managed to find time, late at night, to write. "It was my private passion," Baldacci commented on his author's Web site. He also noted on the *Warner Books Web site* that just being a lawyer taught him "a great deal about fiction writing." Models for him included John Irving, Patricia Highsmith, Elmore Leonard, William Styron, and Tom Wolfe, among others. He was also an avid reader of thrillers and began to think that he could do just as well if not better than those writers. So, after spending a number of years crafting short stories and screenplays, Baldacci turned his hand to writing a thriller.

He quickly came up with a high-concept storyline and first chapter, enough to attract the interest of agent Aaron Priest. It subsequently took Baldacci two years to write the full manuscript, working late into the night after his full day as a lawyer. Finished, the manuscript sold in one day for five million dollars. Baldacci's nine years as a lawyer had come to an end.

Baldacci's first book, *Absolute Power,* presents "the mother of all presidential cover-ups," according to a critic for *Kirkus Reviews.* In this debut thriller, the career break-in artist, Luther Whitney, is in the middle of robbing the house of a fabulously wealthy woman when a man on the other side of a secret wall begin to make love to said woman. Whitney is amazed when he figures out the man is no less than the president of the United States—and not the woman's husband. His amazement turns to shock, though, when the love play turns violent and the woman of the house uses a letter opener to fend off the president, who then calls for his Secret Service agents. They kill the woman, and Whitney witnesses the whole thing through a one-way mirror. Leaving the house, Whitney takes proof of the murder: the letter opener the woman used. Whitney becomes the subject of a manhunt when he tries to blackmail the president and in on the run for his life. When Whitney is killed, lawyer Jack Graham, former fiance of the thief's daughter, sets out to show the president for what he is and to reveal the cover up.

Resident on bestseller charts for over a year, *Absolute Power* was also adapted as a feature film starring Clint Eastwood. Reviewers, meanwhile, came down on both sides of the critical divide. The *Kirkus Reviews* contributor felt that despite its high-flying opening, the book did not live up to its promise: "For all its arresting premise, an overblown and tedious tale of capital sins." Writing in the *New York Times Book Review,* Jean Hanff Korelitz found that the book's "lack of suspense may result from the fact that Jack, its apparent hero, remains at the periphery of the story until it is nearly over." *Booklist*'s Gilbert Green noted that Baldacci's book "has plenty of commercial potential," but could use some "polishing in plot and story structure." More positive was the assessment of a reviewer for *Publishers Weekly* who called *Absolute Power* a "sizzler of a first novel," and praised Baldacci as a "first-rate storyteller who grabs readers by their lapels right away and won't let go until they've finished this enthralling yarn."

Baldacci's second novel, *Total Control,* opens with a plane crash that takes the life of Jason, husband of attorney Sidney Archer. Soon, however, she learns that her husband was not on board the plane after all and that she and her young daughter are now in danger for their lives, as Jason has disappeared with a load of high-tech corporate secrets in his briefcase. He has also supposedly sent himself a computer disk with encrypted information on it, and those seeking Jason are on her track too. Aided by a veteran of the FBI, Sidney tries to get to the bottom of this intrigue before her own time runs out in this suspense thriller that involves corporate wrongdoing and the Federal Reserve System.

Once again Baldacci's novel soared to the top of bestseller charts and was sold for adaptation as a mini series for a seven-figure number. At the same time, critical response was mixed. Gene Lyons, writing in *Entertainment Weekly,* complained of a "lumbering prose style that reads like a software manual translated from Japanese," while a contributor for *Publishers Weekly* called it a "windy thriller" with "plenty of lumpy prose." On the other hand, *Booklist* contributor Donna Seaman thought *Total Control* "is even more suspenseful" than Baldacci's first novel, and that it "is also far more interesting in terms of the questions it raises about how much technology controls us."

Baldacci continued his string of blockbusters with 1997's *The Winner* about a rigged national lottery and the plucky heroine who breaks the corruption wide open. LuAnn Tyler is a young, unwed mother when she wins one hundred million dollars in the national lottery, only she does not really "win" the money, for the lottery has been rigged by her employer, the evil and mysterious Mr. Jackson. The one condition is, LuAnn must leave the country and not return. But after a decade of lonely exile, LuAnn comes back and settles in Virginia. Jackson tracks her down, for with a newspaper investigation of the national lottery scam, he cannot afford witnesses around to tell tales. LuAnn, however, is not just a docile heroine; she turns from "hunted to huntress," as a critic for *Publishers Weekly* explained. This same contributor went on to note that despite "workaday" prose and a "mercilessly melodramatic" plot, the book "is flat-out fun to read." Similarly, *Booklist*'s Gilbert Taylor called the novel "undemanding fun," and praised Baldacci's "pedal-to-the-metal plotting."

Baldacci brings back the lawyer aspect of his tales with his fourth novel, *The Simple Truth,* in which ex-cop John Fiske and law clerk Sara Evans set out to find out the truth behind the death of John's brother and to uncover the mystery behind a twenty-five year-old murder. Fiske's brother Michael, a clerk at the Supreme Court, was attempting to help a man in prison, Rufus Harms, who claims he is the victim of a conspiracy. Now it appears that Michael Fiske has been a victim of the same people who framed Harms and quickly the body count rises as the depths of this conspiracy are uncovered. Critically, this was one of Baldacci's best-received titles. A reviewer for *Publishers Weekly* felt it was the author's "most generously textured novel" to date, and Paula Chin, writing in *People,* found that Baldacci "ratchets up the suspense." Writing in *Booklist,* Gilbert Taylor commented that readers, "repeaters and new ones alike, will be clamoring to ride along" on this narrative train.

After four hits, Baldacci had gotten not only his rhythm, but also his formula. As he noted on the *Warner Books Web site,* he tends to write about the legal world "because I know a lot about it. Also, in coming up with plots I look for classical dilemmas, interesting confrontations, ordinary people close to powerful epicenters. Political situations, lawyers, Washington, all allow for those creative elements." Baldacci also explained his choice of characters. "In my novels I try to have at least one character represent the 'every person'. It's a way to allow the reader to relate to the events taking place in the novel and also to have someone to root for (or against) as the case may be. Most stories need a moral linchpin as well, and there's always one of these (seen via a character) in my stories."

Baldacci's fifth novel, *Saving Faith* was yet another "high-concept premise," as a *Publishers Weekly* critic noted. Here there is an off-the-books CIA team fighting turf battles with the FBI, and Faith Lockhart, a lobbyist, is caught in the middle. On the run from ruthless killers from the CIA, Faith has only her wits and the help of FBI agent Brooke Reynolds, to parry the strikes of assassins who do not want the secret of CIA manipulation of Congressional voting leaked. "Baldacci's prose can still break the jaws of subvocalizers," commented a *Publishers Weekly* reviewer, but, according to the same critic, "the novel moves fast. . . and its players and suspense are strong." Taylor, writing in *Booklist,* found the plot "more than a little improbable," but also remarked that the author makes the book work "with solid suspense, pithy dialogue, and plenty of hot but tender sex scenes."

With his sixth novel, *Wish You Well,* Baldacci left suspense behind for the time, writing a mainstream literary novel that found a readership with both the young and old. Employing stories learned from his mother, he focuses on the rural world of Appalachia in a tale of a young girl who loses her writer father in a traffic accident but gains a new world when she and her younger brother are sent to stay with their great grandmother. With her mother in a coma after the accident, siblings Louisa and Oz are sent off to the family farm in southwestern Virginia. Here twelve-year-old Louisa learns hard truths about the land and comes to love the difficult new life. But this idyll is endangered when corporate interests threaten to seize her great grandmother's farm. Set in 1940, the novel won praise from *Library Journal*'s Kathy Piehl who called it "affecting" and "richly textured." Jaye Munger also found the novel "hauntingly beautiful" in a *Redbook* review, while *Kliatt*'s Judith H. Silverman thought it provided an "excellent portrait of race and class distinction of the time and place, and of a young woman growing up."

With his 2001 novel, *Last Man Standing,* Baldacci returned to thrillers with a story about the FBI's elite Hostage Rescue Team. Web London, a member of the HRT, is living with the ghosts of his former team members, all killed in an ambush which he managed to avoid. Shaken by the experience and investigating the drug dealers who staged it, he also undergoes therapy for his guilt feelings at surviving when all his friends were killed. His psychiatrist, Claire Daniels, tries to get the bottom of Web's problem, and ultimately uncovers facts that bring many of the plot's threads together. A reviewer for *Publishers Weekly* felt that Baldacci offered up another "exciting thriller, but one that hasn't forsaken the ambitions of *Wish You Well.*" Moreover, according to this contributor, the author also created "characters that readers will demand to see back in a sequel." Kristine Huntley observed in *Booklist* that Baldacci's legion of fans "will be happy to see him back in thriller-writing mode."

That mode did not last long. In the 2002 novel, *The Christmas Train* Baldacci veered once again into mainstream fiction. "It's the classic travel adventure tale," Baldacci explained on the *Warner Books Web site.* "A runaway screwball comedy on a train, separated by intense moments of personal strife, quiet introspection, romantic mayhem and puzzling mysteries." When journalist Tom Langdon sets out on a train journey across the country to visit his girlfriend in Los Angeles for Christmas, he meets a raft of strange, zany characters on board, one of whom turns out to be his one-time love, Eleanor Carter. A *Publishers Weekly* contributor noted that the book "is loaded with cool train lore . . . and plenty of romance and good cheer." Huntley, writing in *Booklist,* also commended the novel as a "heartwarming holiday story."

Baldacci's ninth novel, *Split Second,* marked another return to the suspense thriller format when two discredited Secret Service agents investigate the kidnapping of a presidential candidate and the assassination of another. These crimes were, in fact, what sent these agents' careers in a tailspin, for they happened on their watch. Agent Michelle Maxwell averted her eyes one second from John Bruno and he was spirited away. Almost a decade earlier Agent Sean King, protecting candidate Clyde Ritter, was not quick enough to keep the man from being killed. Retiring from the Secret Service, King has set up a law practice, but now he and Maxwell come together when they begin to see parallels in the two incidents. Soon they are in over their heads in an investigation that leads in many directions at once. A reviewer for *Publishers Weekly* commended the author for creating "people that readers care about."

However, the same contributor felt that *Split Second* was "Baldacci's weakest thriller in years." Similarly, a critic for *Kirkus Reviews* commented adversely on the book's "jerry-built conclusion that beggars credibility and offers few surprises."

In 2004 Baldacci published *Hour Game,* a thriller about a serial killer in Virginia who leaves a watch behind with each of his murder victims. The watches are set to the hour corresponding with that victim's position on the killer's hit list. Each killing is a copy of an infamous murder from history, and it seems as if the murderer is trying to improve on the notorious crimes of the past. Sean King and Michelle Maxwell are investigating another crime in the area, a simple burglary, when they are pulled in to help find and stop the serial killer. Their investigation becomes more difficult when a copycat killer also begins to operate in the area.

Baldacci is less concerned with what reviewers have to say about his work than what his fans do, and his readership, as measured at the cash register, continues to give him top marks. Baldacci, who is also involved in several charitable and literacy efforts, has strong advice for other would-be authors. As he told Lewis Burke Frumkes in an interview for the *Writer,* aspiring writers should "take a few years and learn how to write well. Learn the craft. Don't finish anything. Read everything you can and practice. Try to build a character to the point at which you can see the person and how he moves and acts. Practice writing dialogue until a reader would say it sounds like two people talking. Then start with a short story, and after you've done that for a few years, try to construct a novel that is a major work."

BIOGRAPHICAL AND CRITICAL SOURCES:

PERIODICALS

Book, November, 2000, Don McLeese, review of *Wish You Well,* p. 72.
Booklist, November 1, 1995, Gilbert Taylor, review of *Absolute Power,* p. 434; November 15, 1996, Donna Seaman, review of *Total Control,* p. 548; October 15, 1997, Gilbert Taylor, review of *The Winner,* p. 362; September 1, 1998, Gilbert Taylor, review of *The Simple Truth,* p. 5; October 1, 1999, Gilbert Taylor, review of *Saving Faith,* p. 307; July, 2000, Brad Hooper, review of *Wish You Well,* p. 1972; November 1, 2001, Kristine Huntley, review of *Last Man Standing,* p. 442; November 1,

2002, Kristine Huntley, review of *The Christmas Train,* p. 450; August, 2003, Kristine Huntley, review of *Split Second,* p. 1924.
Entertainment Weekly, November 22, 1996, review of *Absolute Power,* p. 131; February 21, 1997, Gene Lyons, review of *Total Control,* pp. 120-121.
Kirkus Reviews, October 15, 1995, review of *Absolute Power,* p. 1444; September 15, 1998, review of *The Simple Truth,* p. 1302; October 1, 2002, review of *The Christmas Train,* p. 1441; July 15, 2003, review of *Split Second,* pp. 921.
Kliatt, January, 2002, Judith H. Silverman, review of *Wish You Well,* pp. 8-9.
Library Journal, January, 1997, Kathy Piehl, review of *Total Control,* p. 142; September 1, 2000, Kathy Piehl, review of *Wish You Well,* p. 248.
Los Angeles Times, David Rosenzweig, "Jury Rules against Southland Publisher," p. C2.
M2 Best Books, May 22, 2002, "Federal Court Blocks Anthology Publication."
Maclean's, February 17, 1997, Brian D. Johnson, review of *Absolute Power,* p. 72.
Mother Earth News, February-March, 2002, review of *Wish You Well,* p. 18.
Nation, March 17, 1997, Stuart Klawans, review of *Absolute Power* (film), pp. 43-44.
New Republic, March 17, 1997, Stanley Kauffmann, review of *Absolute Power* (film), pp. 28-29.
Newsweek, February 17, 1997, David Ansen, review of *Absolute Power* (film), p. 67.
New York Times Book Review, February 25, 1996, Jean Hanff Korelitz, review of *Absolute Power,* p. 21.
People, February 19, 1996, William Plummer, review of *Absolute Power,* p. 31; May 12, 1997, "David Baldacci," p. 135; January 26, 1998, William Plummer, review of *The Winner,* p. 33; December 21, 1998; Paula Chin, review of *The Simple Truth,* p. 45; November 17, 2003, Sherryl Connelly, review of *Split Second,* p. 21.
Publishers Weekly, October 16, 1995, review of *Absolute Power,* p. 42; December 2, 1996, review of *Total Control,* p. 41; April 14, 1997, Paul Nathan, "Building Momentum," p. 26; October 6, 1997, review of *The Winner,* p. 73; October 5, 1998, review of *The Simple Truth,* p. 78; November 8, 1999, review of *Saving Faith,* p. 50; November 22, 1999, Daisy Maryles and Dick Donahue, "Baldacci's Savings," p. 16; July 17, 2000, review of *Wish You Well,* p. 171; November 5, 2001, review of *Last Man Standing,* p. 42; December 10, 2001, Jeff Zaleski, "A Return to Thrillers," p. 47; October 7, 2002, review of *The Christmas Train,* p. 52; August 18, 2003, review of *Split Second,* pp. 58-59.
Redbook, December, 2001, Jaye Munger, review of *Wish You Well,* p. G3.

Variety, February 10, 1997, Todd McCarthy, review of *Absolute Power,* p. 62.

Writer, June, 1997, Lewis Burke Frumkes, "A Conversation with . . . David Baldacci," pp. 11-13.

Writer's Digest, January, 1997, Audrey T. Hingley, "After 11 Years and 10,000 Discarded Pages, He's an Overnight Success," pp. 30-32.

ONLINE

BookPage, http://www.bookpage.com/ (December, 2002).

Official David Baldacci Web site, http://www.david-baldacci.com/ (May 16, 2004).

Warner Books Web site, http://www.twbookmark.com/ (May 16, 2004).

*   *   *

BALDWIN, James 1924-1987
(James Arthur Baldwin)

PERSONAL: Born August 2, 1924, in New York, NY; died of stomach cancer, December 1 (some sources say November 30), 1987, in St. Paul de Vence, France; son of David (a clergyman and factory worker) and Berdis Emma (Jones) Baldwin. *Education:* Graduate of De Witt Clinton High School, New York, NY, 1942.

CAREER: Writer, 1944-87. Youth minister at Fireside Pentecostal Assembly, New York, NY, 1938-42; variously employed as handyman, dishwasher, waiter, and office boy in New York, NY, and in defense work in Belle Meade, NJ, 1942-46. Lecturer on racial issues at universities in the United States and Europe, 1957-87. Director of play, *Fortune and Men's Eyes,* in Istanbul, Turkey, 1970, and film, *The Inheritance,* 1973.

MEMBER: Congress on Racial Equality (member of national advisory board), American Academy and Institute of Arts and Letters, Authors League, International PEN, Dramatists Guild, Actors' Studio, National Committee for a Sane Nuclear Policy.

AWARDS, HONORS: Eugene F. Saxton fellowship, 1945; Rosenwald fellowship, 1948; Guggenheim fellowship, 1954; *Partisan Review* fellowship, National Institute of Arts and Letters grant for literature, and National Institute of Arts and Letters Award, all 1956; Ford Foundation grant, 1959; National Conference of Christians and Jews Brotherhood Award, 1962, for *Nobody Knows My Name: More Notes of a Native Son;* George Polk Memorial Award, 1963, for magazine articles; Foreign Drama Critics Award, 1964, for *Blues for Mister Charlie;* D.Litt. from the University of British Columbia, Vancouver, 1964; National Association of Independent Schools Award, 1964, for *The Fire Next Time;* American Book Award nomination, 1980, for *Just above My Head;* named Commander, Legion of Honor (France), 1986.

WRITINGS:

FICTION

Go Tell It on the Mountain (novel), Knopf (New York, NY), 1953.

Giovanni's Room (novel; also see below), Dial (New York, NY), 1956, reprinted, Modern Library (New York, NY), 2001.

Another Country (novel), Dial (New York, NY), 1962.

Going to Meet the Man (short stories), Dial (New York, NY), 1965.

Tell Me How Long the Train's Been Gone (novel), Dial (New York, NY), 1968.

If Beale Street Could Talk (novel), Dial (New York, NY), 1974.

Little Man, Little Man: A Story of Childhood (for children), M. Joseph (London, England), 1976, Dial (New York, NY), 1977.

Just above My Head (novel), Dial (New York, NY), 1979.

Harlem Quartet (novel), Dial (New York, NY), 1987.

Contributor to *American Negro Short Stories,* Hill & Wang (New York, NY), 1966.

NONFICTION

Autobiographical Notes, Knopf (New York, NY), 1953.

Notes of a Native Son (essays), Beacon Press (Boston, MA), 1955.

Nobody Knows My Name: More Notes of a Native Son (essays), Dial (New York, NY), 1961.

The Fire Next Time, Dial (New York, NY), 1963, reprinted, Holt, Rinehart (Austin, TX), 2000.

(Author of text) Richard Avedon, *Nothing Personal* (photographic portraits), Atheneum (New York, NY), 1964.

(With others) *Black Anti-Semitism and Jewish Racism,* R.W. Baron, 1969.

(With Kenneth Kaunda) Carl Ordung, editor, *Menschenwürde und Gerechtigkeit* (essays delivered at the fourth assembly of the World Council of Churches), Union-Verlag, 1969.

(With Margaret Mead) *A Rap on Race* (transcribed conversation), Lippincott (Philadelphia, PA), 1971.

No Name in the Street (essays), Dial (New York, NY), 1972.

(With Françoise Giroud) *Cesar: Compressions d'or,* Hachette (Paris, France), 1973.

(With Nikki Giovanni) *A Dialogue* (transcribed conversation), Lippincott (Philadelphia, PA), 1973.

The Devil Finds Work (essays), Dial (New York, NY), 1976.

(With others) John Henrik Clarke, editor, *Harlem, U.S.A.: The Story of a City within a City,* Seven Seas (Berlin, Germany), 1976.

The Evidence of Things Not Seen, Holt (New York, NY), 1985.

The Price of the Ticket: Collected Nonfiction 1948-1985, St. Martin's (New York, NY), 1985.

(With others) Michael J. Weber, editor, *Perspectives: Angles on African Art,* Center for African Art, 1987.

PLAYS

The Amen Corner (first produced in Washington, DC, at Howard University, 1955; produced on Broadway at Ethel Barrymore Theatre, April 15, 1965), Dial (New York, NY), 1968, reprinted, Vintage (New York, NY), 1998.

Giovanni's Room (based on novel of same title), first produced in New York, NY, at Actors' Studio, 1957.

Blues for Mister Charlie (first produced on Broadway at ANTA Theatre, April 23, 1964), Dial (New York, NY), 1964.

One Day, When I Was Lost: A Scenario (screenplay; based on *The Autobiography of Malcolm X* by Alex Haley), M. Joseph (London, England), 1972, Dial (New York, NY), 1973.

A Deed for the King of Spain, first produced in New York, NY, at American Center for Stanislavski Theatre Art, January 24, 1974.

Also author of *The Welcome Table,* 1987.

OTHER

Jimmy's Blues: Selected Poems, M. Joseph (London, England), 1983, St. Martin's Press (New York, NY), 1985.

Early Novels and Stories, Library of America (New York, NY), 1998.

Collected Essays, Library of America (New York, NY), 1998.

Going to Meet the Man (sound recording), Koch Jazz (New York, NY), 2002.

(With Sol Stein) *Native Sons: A Friendship That Created One of the Greatest Works of the Twentieth Century: Notes of a Native Son* (correspondence), One World (New York, NY), 2004.

Vintage Baldwin, Vintage (New York, NY), 2004.

Contributor of book reviews and essays to numerous periodicals in the United States and abroad, including *Harper's, Nation, Esquire, Playboy, Partisan Review, Mademoiselle,* and *New Yorker.*

ADAPTATIONS: The Amen Corner was adapted as a musical stage play, *Amen Corner,* by Garry Sherman, Peter Udell and Philip Rose, and produced on Broadway at the Nederlander Theater, November 10, 1983. *Go Tell It on the Mountain* was dramatized under the same title for the Public Broadcasting System's *American Playhouse* series, January 14, 1985. A musical play based on Baldwin's life, *A Prophet among Them,* was written by Wesley Brown and first produced in 2001.

SIDELIGHTS: A novelist and essayist of considerable renown, James Baldwin bore articulate witness to the unhappy consequences of American racial strife. Baldwin's writing career began in the last years of legislated segregation; his fame as a social observer grew in tandem with the civil rights movement as he mirrored blacks' aspirations, disappointments, and coping strategies in a hostile society. *Tri-Quarterly* contributor Robert A. Bone declared that Baldwin's publications "have had a stunning impact on our cultural life" because the author "succeeded in transposing the entire discussion of American race relations to the interior plane; it is a major breakthrough for the American imagination." In his novels, plays, and essays alike, Baldwin explored the psychological implications of racism for both the oppressed and the oppressor. Bestsellers such as *Nobody Knows My Name: More Notes of a Native Son* and *The Fire Next Time* acquainted wide audiences with his highly personal observations and his sense of urgency in the face of rising black bitterness. As Juan Williams noted in the *Washington Post,* long before Baldwin's death, his writings "became a standard of literary realism. . . . Given the messy nature of racial hatred, of the half-truths, blasphemies and lies that make up American life, Baldwin's accuracy in reproducing that world stands as a remarkable achievement. . . . Black people reading Baldwin knew he wrote the truth. White people reading Baldwin sensed his truth about the lives of black people and the sins of a racist nation."

Critics accorded Baldwin high praise for both his style and his themes. "Baldwin has carved a literary niche through his exploration of 'the mystery of the human being' in his art," observed Louis Hill Pratt in *James Baldwin.* "His short stories, novels, and plays shed the light of reality upon the darkness of our illusions, while the essays bring a boldness, courage, and cool logic to bear on the most crucial questions of humanity with which this country has yet to be faced." In the *College Language Association Journal,* Therman B. O'Daniel called Baldwin "the gifted professor of that primary element, genuine talent. . . . Secondly he is a very intelligent and deeply perceptive observer of our multifarious contemporary society. . . . In the third place, Baldwin is a bold and courageous writer who is not afraid to search into the dark corners of our social consciences, and to force out into public view many of the hidden, sordid skeletons of our society. . . . Then, of course, there is Baldwin's literary style which is a fourth major reason for his success as a writer. His prose . . . possesses a crystal clearness and a passionately poetic rhythm that makes it most appealing." *Saturday Review* correspondent Benjamin De Mott concluded that Baldwin "retains a place in an extremely select group: That composed of the few genuinely indispensable American writers. He owes his rank partly to the qualities of responsiveness that have marked his work from the beginning. . . . Time and time over in fiction as in reportage, Baldwin tears himself free of his rhetorical fastenings and stands forth on the page utterly absorbed in the reality of the person before him, strung with his nerves, riveted to his feelings, breathing his breath."

Baldwin's central preoccupation as a writer lay in "his insistence on removing, layer by layer, the hardened skin with which Americans shield themselves from their country," according to Orde Coombs in the *New York Times Book Review.* The author saw himself as a "disturber of the peace"—one who revealed uncomfortable truths to a society mired in complacency. Pratt found Baldwin "engaged in a perpetual battle to overrule our objections and continue his probe into the very depths of our past. His constant concern is the catastrophic failure of the American Dream and the devastating inability of the American people to deal with that calamity." Pratt uncovered a further assumption in Baldwin's work; namely, that all of mankind is united by virtue of common humanity. "Consequently," Pratt stated, "the ultimate purpose of the writer, from Baldwin's perspec-

tive, is to discover that sphere of commonality where, although differences exist, those dissimilarities are stripped of their power to block communication and stifle human intercourse." The major impediment in this search for commonality, according to Baldwin, is white society's entrenched moral cowardice, a condition that through longstanding tradition equates blackness with dark impulses, carnality, and chaos. By denying blacks' essential humanity so simplistically, the author argued, whites inflict psychic damage on blacks and suffer self-estrangement—a "fatal bewilderment," to quote Bone. Baldwin's essays exposed the dangerous implications of this destructive way of thinking; his fictional characters occasionally achieve interracial harmony after having made the bold leap of understanding he advocated. In the *British Journal of Sociology,* Beau Fly Jones claimed that Baldwin was one of the first black writers "to discuss with such insight the psychological handicaps that most Negroes must face; and to realize the complexities of Negro-white relations in so many different contexts. In redefining what has been called the Negro problem as white, he has forced the majority race to look at the damage it has done, and its own role in that destruction."

Dictionary of Literary Biography essayist John W. Roberts felt that Baldwin's "evolution as a writer of the first order constitutes a narrative as dramatic and compelling as his best story." Baldwin was born and raised in Harlem under very trying circumstances. His stepfather, an evangelical preacher, struggled to support a large family and demanded the most rigorous religious behavior from his nine children. Roberts wrote: "Baldwin's ambivalent relationship with his stepfather served as a constant source of tension during his formative years and informs some of his best mature writings. . . . The demands of caring for younger siblings and his stepfather's religious convictions in large part shielded the boy from the harsh realities of Harlem street life during the 1930s." As a youth Baldwin read constantly and even tried writing; he was an excellent student who sought escape from his environment through literature, movies, and theatre. During the summer of his fourteenth birthday he underwent a dramatic religious conversion, partly in response to his nascent sexuality and partly as a further buffer against the ever-present temptations of drugs and crime. He served as a junior minister for three years at the Fireside Pentecostal Assembly, but gradually he lost his desire to preach as he began to question blacks' acceptance of Christian tenets that had, in essence, been used to enslave them.

Shortly after he graduated from high school in 1942, Baldwin was compelled to find work in order to help support his brothers and sisters; mental instability had incapacitated his stepfather. Baldwin took a job in the defense industry in Belle Meade, New Jersey, and there, not for the first time, he was confronted with racism, discrimination, and the debilitating regulations of segregation. The experiences in New Jersey were closely followed by his stepfather's death, after which Baldwin determined to make writing his sole profession. He moved to Greenwich Village and began to write a novel, supporting himself by performing a variety of odd jobs. In 1944 he met author Richard Wright, who helped him to land the 1945 Eugene F. Saxton fellowship. Despite the financial freedom the fellowship provided, Baldwin was unable to complete his novel that year. He found the social tenor of the United States increasingly stifling even though such prestigious periodicals as the *Nation, New Leader,* and *Commentary* began to accept his essays and short stories for publication. Eventually, in 1948, he moved to Paris, using funds from a Rosenwald Foundation fellowship to pay his passage. Most critics feel that this journey abroad was fundamental to Baldwin's development as an author.

"Once I found myself on the other side of the ocean," Baldwin once told the *New York Times,* "I could see where I came from very clearly, and I could see that I carried myself, which is my home, with me. You can never escape that. I am the grandson of a slave, and I am a writer. I must deal with both." Through some difficult financial and emotional periods, Baldwin undertook a process of self-realization that included both an acceptance of his heritage and an admittance of his bisexuality. Bone noted that Europe gave the young author many things: "It gave him a world perspective from which to approach the question of his own identity. It gave him a tender love affair which would dominate the pages of his later fiction. But above all, Europe gave him back himself. The immediate fruit of self-recovery was a great creative outburst. First came two [works] of reconciliation with his racial heritage. *Go Tell It on the Mountain* and *The Amen Corner* represent a search for roots, a surrender to tradition, an acceptance of the Negro past. Then came a series of essays which probe, deeper than anyone has dared, the psychic history of this nation. They are a moving record of a man's struggle to define the forces that have shaped him, in order that he may accept himself."

Many critics view Baldwin's essays as his most significant contribution to American literature. Works such as *Notes of a Native Son, Nobody Knows My Name, The Fire Next Time, No Name in the Street,* and *The Evidence of Things Not Seen* "serve to illuminate the condition of the black man in twentieth-century America," according to Pratt. Highly personal and analytical, the essays probe deeper than the mere provincial problems of white versus black to uncover the essential issues of self-determination, identity, and reality. "An artist is a sort of emotional or spiritual historian," Baldwin told *Life* magazine. "His role is to make you realize the doom and glory of knowing who you are and what you are. He has to tell, because nobody else *can* tell, what it is like to be alive." *South Atlantic Quarterly* contributor Fred L. Standley asserted that this quest for personal identity "is indispensable in Baldwin's opinion and the failure to experience such is indicative of a fatal weakness in human life." C.W.E. Bigsby elaborated in *The Fifties: Fiction, Poetry, Drama:* "Baldwin's central theme is the need to accept reality as a necessary foundation for individual identity and thus a logical prerequisite for the kind of saving love in which he places his whole faith. For some this reality is one's racial or sexual nature, for others it is the ineluctable fact of death. . . . Baldwin sees this simple progression as an urgent formula not only for the redemption of individual men but for the survival of mankind. In this at least black and white are as one and the Negro's much-vaunted search for identity can be seen as part and parcel of the American's long-standing need for self-definition."

Inevitably, however, Baldwin's assessments of the "sweet" and "bitter" experiences in his own life led him to describe "the exact place where private chaos and social outrage meet," according to Alfred Kazin in *Contemporaries.* Eugenia Collier described this confrontation in *Black World:* "On all levels personal and political . . . life is a wild chaos of paradox, hidden meanings, and dilemmas. This chaos arises from man's inability—or reluctance to face the truth about his own nature. As a result of this self-imposed blindness, men erect an elaborate facade of myth, tradition, and ritual behind which crouch, invisible, their true selves. It is this blindness on the part of Euro-Americans which has created and perpetuated the vicious racism which threatens to destroy this nation." In his essays on the 1950s and early 1960s, Baldwin sought to explain black experiences to a white readership as he warned whites about the potential destruction their psychic blindness might wreak. *Massachusetts Review* contributor David Levin noted that the author came to represent "for 'white' Americans, the eloquent, indignant prophet of an oppressed people, a voice speaking . . . in an all but desperate, final effort to bring us out of what he calls our innocence before it is (if it is not already) too late. This voice calls us to our immediate duty for the sake of our own humanity as well as our own safety. It demands that we stop regarding the Negro as an abstraction, an invisible man; that we begin to recognize each

Negro in his 'full weight and complexity' as a human being; that we face the horrible reality of our past and present treatment of Negroes—a reality we do not know and do not want to know." In *Ebony* magazine, Allan Morrison observed that Baldwin evinced an awareness "that the audience for most of his nonfiction writings is white and he uses every forum at his disposal to drive home the basic truths of Negro-white relations in America as he sees them. His function here is to interpret whites to themselves and at the same time voice the Negro's protest against his role in a Jim Crow society."

Because Baldwin sought to inform and confront whites, and because his fiction contains interracial love affairs—both homosexual and heterosexual—he came under attack from the writers of the Black Arts Movement, who called for a literature exclusively by and for blacks. Baldwin refused to align himself with the movement; he continued to call himself an "American writer" as opposed to a "black writer" and continued to confront the issues facing a multi-racial society. Eldridge Cleaver, in his book *Soul on Ice,* accused Baldwin of a hatred of blacks and "a shameful, fanatical fawning" love of whites. What Cleaver saw as complicity with whites, Baldwin saw rather as an attempt to alter the real daily environment with which American blacks have been faced all their lives. Pratt noted, however, that Baldwin's efforts to "shake up" his white readers put him "at odds with current white literary trends" as well as with the Black Arts Movement. Pratt explained that Baldwin labored under the belief "that mainstream art is directed toward a complacent and apathetic audience, and it is designed to confirm and reinforce that sense of well-being. . . . Baldwin's writings are, by their very nature, iconoclastic. While Black Arts focuses on a black-oriented artistry, Baldwin is concerned with the destruction of the fantasies and delusions of a contented audience which is determined to avoid reality." As the civil rights movement gained momentum, Baldwin escalated his attacks on white complacency from the speaking platform as well as from the pages of books and magazines. *Nobody Knows My Name* and *The Fire Next Time* both sold more than a million copies; both were cited for their predictions of black violence in desperate response to white oppression. In *Encounter,* Colin MacInnes concluded that the reason "why Baldwin speaks to us of another race is that he still believes us worthy of a warning: he has not yet despaired of making us feel the dilemma we all chat about so glibly, . . . and of trying to save us from the agonies that we too will suffer if the Negro people are driven beyond the ultimate point of desperation."

Retrospective analyses of Baldwin's essays highlight the characteristic prose style that gives his works literary merit beyond the mere dissemination of ideas. In *A World More Attractive: A View of Modern Literature and Politics,* Irving Howe placed the author among "the two or three greatest essayists this country has ever produced." Howe claimed that Baldwin "has brought a new luster to the essay as an art form, a form with possibilities for discursive reflection and concrete drama. . . . The style of these essays is a remarkable instance of the way in which a grave and sustained eloquence—the rhythm of oratory, . . . held firm and hard—can be employed in an age deeply suspicious of rhetorical prowess." "Baldwin has shown more concern for the painful exactness of prose style than any other modern American writer," noted David Littlejohn in *Black on White: A Critical Survey of Writing by American Negroes.* "He picks up words with heavy care, then sets them, one by one, with a cool and loving precision that one can feel in the reading. . . . The exhilarating exhaustion of reading his best essays—which in itself may be a proof of their honesty and value—demands that the reader measure up, and forces him to learn."

Baldwin's fiction expanded his exploration of the "full weight and complexity" of the individual in a society prone to callousness and categorization. His loosely autobiographical works probed the milieus with which he was most familiar—black evangelical churches, jazz clubs, stifling Southern towns, and the Harlem ghetto. In *The Black American Writer: Fiction,* Brian Lee maintained that Baldwin's "essays explore the ambiguities and ironies of a life lived on two levels—that of the Negro and that of the man—and they have spoken eloquently to and for a whole generation. But Baldwin's feelings about the condition—alternating moods of sadness and bitterness—are best expressed in the paradoxes confronting the haunted heroes of his novels and stories. The possible modes of existence for anyone seeking refuge from a society which refuses to acknowledge one's humanity are necessarily limited, and Baldwin has explored with some thoroughness the various emotional and spiritual alternatives available to his retreating protagonists." Pratt felt that Baldwin's fictive artistry "not only documents the dilemma of the black man in American society, but it also bears witness to the struggle of the artist against the overwhelming forces of oppression. Almost invariably, his protagonists are artists. . . . Each character is engaged in the pursuit of artistic fulfillment which, for Baldwin, becomes symbolic of the quest for identity."

Love, both sexual and spiritual, was an essential component of Baldwin's characters' quests for self-realization. John W. Aldridge observed in the *Saturday Review* that sexual love "emerges in his novels as a kind of universal anodyne for the disease of racial separatism, as a means not only of achieving personal identity but also of transcending false categories of color and gender." Homosexual encounters emerged as the principal means to achieve important revelations; as Bigsby explained, Baldwin felt that "it is the homosexual, virtually alone, who can offer a selfless and genuine love because he alone has a real sense of himself, having accepted his own nature." Baldwin did not see love as a "saving grace," however; his vision, given the circumstances of the lives he encountered, was more cynical than optimistic. In his introduction to *James Baldwin: A Collection of Critical Essays,* Kenneth Kinnamon wrote: "If the search for love has its origin in the desire of a child for emotional security, its arena is an adult world which involves it in struggle and pain. Stasis must yield to motion, innocence to experience, security to risk. This is the lesson that . . . saves Baldwin's central fictional theme from sentimentality. . . . Similarly, love as an agent of racial reconciliation and national survival is not for Baldwin a vague yearning for an innocuous brotherhood, but an agonized confrontation with reality, leading to the struggle to transform it. It is a quest for truth through a recognition of the primacy of suffering and injustice in the American past." Pratt also concluded that in Baldwin's novels, "love is often extended, frequently denied, seldom fulfilled. As reflections of our contemporary American society, the novels stand as forthright indictments of the intolerable conditions that we have accepted unquestioningly as a way of life."

Black family life—the charged emotional atmosphere between parents and children, brothers and sisters—provided another major theme in Baldwin's fiction. This was especially apparent in his first and best-known novel, *Go Tell It on the Mountain,* the story of a Harlem teenager's struggles with a repressive father and with religious conversion. According to Roberts, *Go Tell It on the Mountain* "proved that James Baldwin had become a writer of enormous power and skill. [It] was an essential book for Baldwin. Although clearly a fictional work, it chronicles two of the most problematic aspects of his existence as a young man: a son's relationship to his stepfather and the impact of fundamentalist religion on the consciousness of a young boy." In her work titled *James Baldwin,* Carolyn Wedin Sylvander praised Baldwin's family chronicle particularly because the author "is dealing comprehensively and emotionally with the hot issue of race relations in the United States at a time . . . when neither white ignorance and prejudice nor black powerlessness is conducive to holistic depictions of black experience." Indeed, the overt confrontation between the races that character-

izes Baldwin's later work was here portrayed as a peripheral threat, a danger greater than, but less immediate than, the potential damage inflicted by parents on children. Sylvander wrote: "It is painfully, dramatically, structurally clear throughout *Go Tell It on the Mountain* that the struggles every individual faces—with sexuality, with guilt, with pain, with love—are passed on, generation to generation." Littlejohn described Baldwin's treatment of this essential American theme as "autobiography-as-exorcism, . . . a lyrical, painful, ritual exercise whose necessity and intensity the reader feels." Pratt likewise stated that *Go Tell It on the Mountain* "stands as an honest, intensive, self-analysis, functioning simultaneously to illuminate self, society, and mankind as a whole."

In addition to his numerous books, Baldwin was one of the few black authors to have had more than one of his plays produced on Broadway. Both *The Amen Corner,* another treatment of storefront pentecostal religion, and *Blues for Mister Charlie,* a drama based on the racially-motivated murder of Emmett Till in 1955, had successful Broadway runs and numerous revivals. Standley commented in the *Dictionary of Literary Biography* that in both plays, "as in his other literary works, Baldwin explores a variety of thematic concerns: the historical significance and the potential explosiveness in black-white relations; the necessity for developing a sexual and psychological consciousness and identity; the intertwining of love and power in the universal scheme of existence as well as in the structures of society; the misplaced priorities in the value systems in America; and the responsibility of the artist to promote the evolution of the individual and the society." In *The Black American Writer: Poetry and Drama,* Walter Meserve offered remarks on Baldwin's abilities as a playwright. "Baldwin tries to use the theatre as a pulpit for his ideas," Meserve stated. "Mainly his plays are thesis plays—talky, over-written, and cliche dialogue and some stereotypes, preachy, and argumentative. Essentially, Baldwin is not particularly dramatic, but he can be extremely eloquent, compelling, and sometimes irritating as a playwright committed to his approach to life." Meserve added, however, that although the author was criticized for creating stereotypes, "his major characters are the most successful and memorable aspects of his plays. People are important to Baldwin, and their problems, generally embedded in their agonizing souls, stimulate him to write. . . . A humanitarian, sensitive to the needs and struggles of man, he writes of inner turmoil, spiritual disruption, the consequence upon people of the burdens of the world, both White and Black."

Baldwin's oratorical prowess—honed in the pulpit as a youth—brought him into great demand as a speaker during the civil rights era. Sylvander observed that national attention "began to turn toward him as a spokesperson for blacks, not as much because of his novels as his essays, debates, interviews, panel discussions." Baldwin embraced his role as racial spokesman reluctantly and grew increasingly disillusioned as the American public "disarmed him with celebrity, [fell] in love with his eccentricities, and institutionalized his outrage . . . into prime-time entertainment," to quote Aldridge. Nor was Baldwin able to feel that his speeches and essays were producing social change—the assassinations of three of his associates, Medgar Evers, Martin Luther King, Jr., and Malcolm X, shattered his remaining hopes for racial reconciliation. Kinnamon remarked that by 1972, the year Baldwin published *No Name in the Street,* "the redemptive possibilities of love seemed exhausted in that terrible decade of assassination, riot, and repression. . . . Social love had now become for Baldwin more a rueful memory than an alternative to disaster." *London Magazine* contributor James Campbell also noted that by 1972 "Baldwin the saviour had turned into Baldwin the soldier. What [observers] failed to notice was that he was still the preacher and the prophet, that his passion and rage were mingled with detachment, and that his gloomy prognostications were based on powerful observation and an understanding of the past which compelled their pessimism."

Many critics have taken Baldwin to task for the stridency and gloom that overtook his writings. "To function as a voice of outrage month after month for a decade and more strains heart and mind, and rhetoric as well," declared Benjamin De Mott in the *Saturday Review.* "The consequence is a writing style ever on the edge of being winded by too many summonses to intensity." *New Republic* correspondent Nathan Glazer likewise stated that Baldwin had become "an accusing voice, but the accusation is so broad, so general, so all-embracing, that the rhetoric disappears into the wind." Stephen Donadio offered a similar opinion in the *Partisan Review:* "As his notoriety increased, his personality was oversimplified, appropriated, and consumed. . . . Mr. Baldwin created a situation in which the eye of the audience was fixed on the author as a performer, and the urgency of the race problem in America became a backdrop for elaborate rhetorical assaults which could be dutifully acknowledged but forgotten with a sigh."

Baldwin's passionate detractors were offset by equally passionate defenders, however. Sylvander wrote: "Wading through vehement and sometimes shallow reactions to the deep water of the statements and works themselves, one is struck repeatedly by the power of Baldwin's prose, and by our continuing need, as readers and

as citizens, for his steadying apocalyptic vision. Finally, in his fantastic, experientially various, wide-ranging, searching, and committed life, one can find a vigorous model for venturing beyond charted areas." Charles Newman made two points in *James Baldwin: A Collection of Critical Essays.* First, Newman noted that Baldwin's experience is "unique among our artists in that his artistic achievements mesh so precisely with his historical circumstances. He is that nostalgic type—an artist speaking for a genuinely visible revolution." Second, Newman maintained that as an observer of this painful revolution, "almost alone [Baldwin] continued to confront the unmanageable questions of modern society, rather than creating a nuclear family in which semantic fantasies may be enacted with no reference to the larger world except that it stinks." Kinnamon concluded: "James Baldwin has always been concerned with the most personal and intimate areas of experience and also with the broadest questions of national and global destiny—and with the intricate interrelationships between the two. Whatever the final assessment of his literary achievement, it is clear that his voice—simultaneously that of victim, witness, and prophet—has been among the most urgent of our time."

At the time of his death from cancer late in 1987, Baldwin was still working on two projects—a play, *The Welcome Table,* and a biography of Martin Luther King, Jr. Although he lived primarily in France, he had never relinquished his United States citizenship and preferred to think of himself as a "commuter" rather than as an expatriate. The publication of his collected essays *The Price of the Ticket: Collected Nonfiction 1948-1985,* and his subsequent death sparked reassessments of his career and comments on the quality of his lasting legacy. "Baldwin has become a kind of prophet, a man who has been able to give a public issue all its deeper moral, historical, and personal significance," remarked Robert F. Sayre in *Contemporary American Novelists.* "Certainly one mark of his achievement, . . . is that whatever deeper comprehension of the race issue Americans now possess has been in some way shaped by him. And this is to have shaped their comprehension of themselves as well." Sylvander asserted that what emerges from the whole of Baldwin's work is "a kind of absolute conviction and passion and honesty that is nothing less than courageous. . . . Baldwin has shared his struggle with his readers for a purpose—to demonstrate that our suffering is our bridge to one another."

Perhaps the most telling demonstration of the results of Baldwin's achievement came from other black writers. Orde Coombs, for instance, concluded: "Because he existed we felt that the racial miasma that swirled around us would not consume us, and it is not too much to say that this man saved our lives, or at least, gave us the necessary ammunition to face what we knew would continue to be a hostile and condescending world." Playwright Amiri Baraka phrased a similar assessment even more eloquently in his funeral eulogy to Baldwin. "This man traveled the earth like its history and its biographer," Baraka said. "He reported, criticized, made beautiful, analyzed, cajoled, lyricized, attacked, sang, made us think, made us better, made us consciously human. . . . He made us feel . . . that we could defend ourselves or define ourselves, that we were in the world not merely as animate slaves, but as terrifyingly sensitive measurers of what is good or evil, beautiful or ugly. This is the power of his spirit. This is the bond which created our love for him." In a posthumous profile for the *Washington Post,* Williams wrote: "The success of Baldwin's effort as the witness is evidenced time and again by the people, black and white, gay and straight, famous and anonymous, whose humanity he unveiled in his writings. America and the literary world are far richer for his witness. The proof of a shared humanity across the divides of race, class and more is the testament that the preacher's son, James Arthur Baldwin, has left us."

In 2004, Sol Stein, a novelist, playwright, and poet, published *Native Sons: A Friendship That Created One of the Greatest Works of the Twentieth Century: Notes of a Native Son,* to honor his late friend. The previously unpublished correspondence included in this volume, according to Donna Seaman in a review for *Booklist,* offers a revealing look at the process behind their collaboration on Baldwin's classic, *Notes of a Native Son.* "Baldwin's letters are extremely moving as he parses civil rights issues, and reports on the writing life in Paris and on Corsica, his nervous breakdown, and the woes of his family," Seaman commented, adding that "Stein's involving commentary is rich in fascinating literary history and sharp observations on racism, anti-Semitism, and their biracial friendship." In *Kirkus Reviews,* Wendy Smith wrote that the correspondence "captures the kinship between a child of Russian-Jewish immigrants and the gay stepson of a preacher," yearning to make America a place where they could fit in.

BIOGRAPHICAL AND CRITICAL SOURCES:

BOOKS

Balakian, Nona, and Charles Simmons, editors, *The Creative Present: Notes on Contemporary Fiction,* Doubleday (New York, NY), 1963.

Bigsby, C.W.E., *Confrontation and Commitment: A Study of Contemporary American Drama,* University of Missouri Press (Columbia, MO), 1967.

Bigsby, C.W.E., editor, *The Black American Writer,* Volume I: *Fiction,* Volume II: *Poetry and Drama,* Everett/Edwards, 1969.

Bobia, Rosa, *The Critical Reception of James Baldwin in France,* Peter Lang (New York, NY), 1997.

Bone, Robert, *The Negro Novel in America,* Yale University Press (New Haven, CT), 1965.

Brustein, Robert, *Seasons of Discontent: Dramatic Opinions 1959-1965,* Simon & Schuster (New York, NY), 1965.

Burgess, Anthony, *The Novel Now: A Guide to Contemporary Fiction,* Norton (New York, NY), 1967.

Champion, Ernest A., *Mr. Baldwin, I Presume: James Baldwin—Chinua Achebe, A Meeting of the Minds,* University Press of America (Lanham, MD), 1995.

Chapman, Abraham, editor, *Black Voices: An Anthology of Afro-American Literature,* New American Library (New York, NY), 1968.

Cleaver, Eldridge, *Soul on Ice,* McGraw-Hill, 1968.

Cohn, Ruby, *Dialogue in American Drama,* Indiana University Press (Bloomington, IN), 1971.

Concise Dictionary of American Literary Biography: The New Consciousness, 1941-1968, Thomson Gale (Detroit, MI), 1987.

Contemporary Authors Bibliographical Series, Volume I: *American Novelists,* Thomson Gale (Detroit, MI), 1986.

Contemporary Literary Criticism, Thomson Gale (Detroit, MI), Volume I, 1973, Volume II, 1974, Volume III, 1975, Volume IV, 1975, Volume V, 1976, Volume VIII, 1978, Volume XIII, 1980, Volume XV, 1980, Volume XVII, 1981, Volume XLII, 1987, Volume L, 1988.

Cook, M. G., editor, *Modern Black Novelists: A Collection of Critical Essays,* Prentice-Hall (Englewood Cliffs, NJ), 1971.

Culture for the Millions, Van Nostrand, 1959.

Dance, Daryl, *Black American Writers: Bibliographical Essays,* St. Martin's (New York, NY), 1978.

Dictionary of Literary Biography, Thomson Gale (Detroit, MI), Volume II: *American Novelists since World War II,* 1978, Volume VIII: *Twentieth-Century American Dramatists,* 1981, Volume XXXIII: *Afro-American Fiction Writers after 1955,* 1984.

Dictionary of Literary Biography Yearbook: 1987, Thomson Gale (Detroit, MI), 1988.

Eckman, Fern Marja, *The Furious Passage of James Baldwin,* M. Evans, 1966.

French, Warren, editor, *The Fifties: Fiction, Poetry, Drama,* Everett/Edwards, 1970.

Frost, David, *The Americans,* Stein & Day, 1970.

Gayle, Addison, Jr., *The Way of the World: The Black Novel in America,* Anchor Press (New York, NY), 1975.

Gibson, Donald B., editor, *Five Black Writers: Essays on Wright, Ellison, Baldwin, Hughes, and LeRoi Jones,* New York University Press (New York, NY), 1970.

Gottfried, Ted, *James Baldwin: Voice from Harlem,* F. Watts (New York, NY), 1997.

Harris, Trudier, *New Essays on "Go Tell It on the Mountain,"* Cambridge University Press (New York, NY), 1995.

Hesse, H. Ober, editor, *The Nature of a Humane Society,* Fortress, 1976.

Hill, Herbert, editor, *Anger and Beyond,* Harper (New York, NY), 1966.

Howe, Irving, *A World More Attractive: A View of Modern Literature and Politics,* Horizon Press, 1963.

Hyman, Stanley Edgar, *Standards: A Chronicle of Books for Our Time,* Horizon Press, 1966.

Jothiprakash, R., *Commitment as a Theme in African American Literature: A Study of James Baldwin and Ralph Ellison,* Wyndham Hall Press (Bristol, IN), 1994.

Kazin, Alfred, *Contemporaries,* Little, Brown (Boston, MA), 1962.

Kazin, Alfred, *Bright Book of Life: American Novelists & Storytellers from Hemingway to Mailer,* Little, Brown (Boston, MA), 1973.

Kenan, Randall, *James Baldwin,* Chelsea House (New York City), 1994.

King, Malcolm, *Baldwin: Three Interviews,* Wesleyan University Press (Middletown, CT), 1985.

Kinnamon, Kenneth, editor, *James Baldwin: A Collection of Critical Essays,* Prentice-Hall (Englewood Cliffs, NJ), 1974.

Klein, Marcus, *After Alienation: American Novels in Mid-Century,* World Publishing (Cleveland, OH), 1964.

Leeming, David Adams, *James Baldwin: A Biography,* H. Holt and Co. (New York, NY), 1995.

Littlejohn, David, *Black on White: A Critical Survey of Writing by American Negroes,* Viking (New York, NY), 1966.

Lumley, Frederick, *New Trends in Twentieth-Century Drama: A Survey Since Ibsen and Shaw,* Oxford University Press (New York, NY), 1967.

Macebuh, Stanley, *James Baldwin: A Critical Study,* Joseph Okpaku, 1973.

Major, Clarence, *The Dark and Feeling: Black American Writers and Their Work,* Joseph Okpaku, 1974.

Moore, Harry T., editor, *Contemporary American Novelists,* Southern Illinois University Press (Carbondale, IL), 1964.

O'Daniel, Therman B., *James Baldwin: A Critical Evaluation,* Howard University Press, 1977.

Panichas, George A., *The Politics of Twentieth-Century Novelists,* Hawthorn, 1971.

Podhoretz, Norman, *Doings and Undoings,* Farrar, Straus (New York, NY), 1964.

Pratt, Louis Hill, *James Baldwin,* Twayne, 1978.

Rosenblatt, Roger, *Black Fiction,* Harvard University Press (Cambridge, MA), 1974.

Sheed, Wilfrid, *The Morning After,* Farrar, Straus (New York, NY), 1971.

Simon, John, *Uneasy Stages: Chronicle of the New York Theatre,* Random House (New York, NY), 1975.

Sontag, Susan, *Against Interpretation and Other Essays,* Farrar, Straus, 1966.

Standley, Fred, and Nancy Standley, *James Baldwin: A Reference Guide,* G.K. Hall (Boston, MA), 1980.

Standley, Fred, and Nancy Standley, editors, *Critical Essays on James Baldwin,* G.K. Hall (Boston, MA), 1981.

Sylvander, Carolyn Wedin, *James Baldwin,* Frederick Ungar (New York, NY), 1980.

Tachach, James, *James Baldwin,* Lucent Books (San Diego, CA), 1996.

Turner, Darwin T., *Afro-American Writers,* Appleton (New York, NY), 1970.

Washington, Bryan R., *The Politics of Exile: Ideology in Henry James, F. Scott Fitzgerald, and James Baldwin,* Northeastern University Press (Boston, MA), 1995.

Weatherby, William J., *Squaring Off: Mailer vs. Baldwin,* Mason/Charter, 1977.

Williams, John A., and Charles F. Harris, editors, *Amistad I: Writings on Black History and Culture,* Random House (New York, NY), 1970.

Williams, Sherley Anne, *Give Birth to Brightness: A Thematic Study in Neo-Black Literature,* Dial (New York, NY), 1972.

PERIODICALS

Advocate, March 4, 2003, p. 61; April 27, 2004, p. 34.

America, March 16, 1963.

American Scholar, winter, 1994, p. 102.

ANQ, summer, 2002, Steven Weisenburger, "The Shudder and the Silence: James Baldwin on White Terror," p. 3.

Atlanta Constitution, May 19, 1976.

Atlantic, July, 1961; July, 1962; March, 1963; July, 1968; June, 1972.

Atlas, March, 1967.

Back Stage West, September 18, 2003, Paul Birchall, "Down from the Mountaintop at the Elephant Asylum Theater," p. 12.

Black Scholar, December, 1973-January, 1974.

Black World, June, 1972; December, 1974.

Booklist, July, 2004, Donna Seamnan, review of *Native Sons: A Friendship That Created One of the Greatest Works of the Twentieth Century: Notes of a Native Son,* p. 1810.

Books and Bookmen, August, 1968; September, 1972; December, 1979.

Book Week, May 31, 1964, September 26, 1965.

British Journal of Sociology, June, 1966.

Bulletin of Bibliography, January-April, 1965, May-August, 1968.

Cappers, July 20, 2004, p. 16.

Chicago Tribune, September 16, 1979; October 10, 1979; November 15, 1985; December 16, 1987; November 15, 1989.

Christian Science Monitor, July 19, 1962.

College Language Association Journal, number 7, 1964; number 10, 1966; March, 1967.

Commentary, November, 1953; January, 1957; December, 1961; June, 1968; December, 1979; December, 1985.

Commonweal, May 22, 1953; December 8, 1961; October 26, 1962; December 7, 1962; October 12, 1973; June 24, 1977.

Critical Quarterly, summer, 1964.

Critique, winter, 1964-65.

Cross Currents, summer, 1961.

Detroit Free Press, December 2, 1987; December 8, 1987.

Ebony, October, 1961.

Ecumenical Review, October, 1968.

Encounter, August, 1963; July, 1965.

English Journal, May, 1973.

Esquire, July, 1968.

Essence, January, 2001, p. 60.

Freedomways, summer, 1963.

Free Inquiry, fall, 2000, p. 69.

Globe & Mail (Toronto, Ontario, Canada), January 11, 1986.

Harper's, March, 1963; September, 1968.

Hollins Critic, December, 1965.

Hudson Review, autumn, 1964; autumn, 1968.

Intellectual Digest, July, 1972.

Jet, August 16, 2004, p. 20.

Kirkus Reviews, May 15, 2004, Wendy Smith, review of *Native Sons.*

Library Journal, June 15, 2004, Ron Ratliff, review of *Native Sons,* p. 70.

Life, May 24, 1963, June 7, 1968; June 4, 1971; July 30, 1971.

Listener, July 25, 1974.

London Magazine, December, 1979-January, 1980.

Lone Star Book Review, January-February, 1980.

Look, July 23, 1968.

Los Angeles Times Book Review, December 1, 1985.

Mademoiselle, May, 1963.

Massachusetts Review, winter, 1964.

MELUS, winter, 2001, Stefanie Dunning, "Parallel Perversions: Interracial and Same Sexuality in James Baldwin's *Another Country*"; spring, 2003, p. 87.

Midcontinent American Studies Journal, fall, 1963.

Mississippi Quarterly, fall, 2000, p. 515.

Muhammad Speaks, September 8, 1973; September 15, 1973; September 29, 1973; October 6, 1973.

Nation, July 14, 1962; November 17, 1962; March 2, 1963; December 13, 1965; April 10, 1972; June 10, 1968; July 3, 1976; November 3, 1979.

National Observer, March 6, 1967; June 3, 1968.

National Review, May 21, 1963; July 7, 1972.

Negro American Literature Forum, spring, 1969; winter, 1972.

Negro Digest, June, 1963; October, 1966; April, 1967.

New Leader, June 3, 1968; May 27, 1974; May 24, 1976.

New Republic, December 17, 1956; August 7, 1961; August 27, 1962; November 27, 1965; August 17, 1968; June 15, 1974; November 24, 1979; December 30, 1985.

New Statesman, July 13, 1962; July 19, 1963; December 4, 1964; November 3, 1972; June 28, 1974; February 25, 1977; November 29, 1985.

Newsweek, February 4, 1963; June 3, 1969; May 27, 1974.

New Yorker, June 20, 1953; November 25, 1961; August 4, 1962; July 8, 1974; November 26, 1979.

New York Herald Tribune Book Review, June 17, 1962.

New York Review of Books, May 28, 1964; December 17, 1964; December 9, 1965; June 29, 1972; June 13, 1974; December 6, 1979; January 21, 1988.

New York Times, May 3, 1964; April 16, 1965; May 31, 1968; February 2, 1969; May 21, 1971; May 17, 1974; June 4, 1976; September 4, 1977; September 21, 1979; September 23, 1979; November 11, 1983; January 10, 1985; January 14, 1985; June 22, 1989.

New York Times Book Review, February 26, 1956; July 2, 1961; June 24, 1962; December 12, 1965; June 2, 1968; June 23, 1968; May 28, 1972; May 19, 1974; May 2, 1976; September 23, 1979; May 24, 1984; December 9, 1987.

New York Times Magazine, March 7, 1965.

Nickel Review, February 27, 1970.

Observer, November 24, 1985; April 6, 1986.

Partisan Review, summer, 1963; winter, 1966.

People, January 7, 1980.

Philadelphia Inquirer, December 2, 1987; December 9, 1987; December 14, 1987.

Progressive, August, 1972.

Queen's Quarterly, summer, 1965.

ReVision, spring, 2003, p. 12.

San Francisco Chronicle, June 28, 1962.

Saturday Review, December 1, 1956; July 1, 1961; July 7, 1962; February 2, 1963; February 8, 1964; May 2, 1964; November 6, 1965; June 1, 1968; May 27, 1972; June 15, 1974; January 5, 1980.

Sight and Sound, autumn, 1976.

South Atlantic Quarterly, summer, 1966.

Southern Humanities Review, winter, 1970.

Southern Review, summer, 1985.

Spectator, July 12, 1968; July 6, 1974; January 11, 1986; April 26, 1986.

Studies in Short Fiction, summer, 1975; fall, 1977.

Time, June 30, 1961; June 29, 1962; November 6, 1964; June 7, 1968; June 10, 1974.

Times (London, England), May 15, 1986; January 19, 1987; January 22, 1987; December 2, 1987; January 31, 1989.

Times Educational Supplement, December 27, 1985.

Times Literary Supplement, July 26, 1963; December 10, 1964; October 28, 1965; July 4, 1968; April 28, 1972; November 17, 1972; June 21, 1974; December 21, 1979; August 2, 1984; January 24, 1986; September 19, 1986.

Tri-Quarterly, winter, 1965.

Twentieth-Century Literature, April, 1967.

Village Voice, October 29, 1979; January 12, 1988.

Vogue, July, 1964.

Washington Post, September 23, 1979; October 15, 1979, September 9, 1983, September 25, 1983, August 14, 1989.

Washington Post Book World, September 11, 1977; September 23, 1979; October 27, 1985; December 9, 1987.

Western Humanities Review, spring, 1968.

World Literature Today, spring, 1980.

Yale Review, October, 1966.

OBITUARIES:

PERIODICALS

Chicago Tribune, December 2, 1987.

Los Angeles Times, December 2, 1987.

New York Times, December 2, 1987; December 9, 1987.

Times (London, England), December 2, 1987.

USA Today, December 2, 1987.

Washington Post, December 2, 1987.

BALDWIN, James Arthur
See BALDWIN, James

*   *   *

BALLARD, James Graham
See BALLARD, J.G.

*   *   *

BALLARD, J.G. 1930-
(James Graham Ballard)

PERSONAL: Born November 15, 1930, in Shanghai, China; son of James (a chemist and business executive) and Edna (Johnstone) Ballard; married Helen Mary Matthews, 1953 (died 1964); children: James, Fay, Beatrice. *Education:* Studied medicine at King's College, Cambridge, 1949-51.

ADDRESSES: Home—36 Old Charlton Rd., Shepperton, Middlesex, TW17 8AT, England. *Agent*—Margaret Hanbury, 27 Walcot Sq., London SE11 44B, England.

CAREER: Novelist and author of short fiction. Institute for Research in Art and Technology, trustee. *Military service:* Royal Air Force, 1954-57; became pilot.

AWARDS, HONORS: Guardian Fiction Prize, and nomination for Booker Prize, both 1984, and James Tait Black Memorial Prize, 1985, all for *Empire of the Sun;* European Science Fiction Society Award for short story writer, 1984.

WRITINGS:

NOVELS

The Wind from Nowhere (also see below), Berkley Publishing (New York, NY), 1962.

The Drowned World (also see below), Berkley Publishing (New York, NY), 1962.

The Burning World, Berkley Publishing (New York, NY), 1964, revised as *The Drought,* J. Cape (London, England), 1965.

The Drowned World [and] *The Wind from Nowhere,* Doubleday (New York, NY), 1965.

The Crystal World, Farrar, Straus & Giroux (New York, NY), 1966.

Crash, J. Cape (London, England), 1972, Farrar, Straus & Giroux (New York, NY), 1973, reprinted, 2000.

Concrete Island, Farrar, Straus & Giroux (New York, NY), 1974.

High-rise, J. Cape (London, England), 1975, Holt (New York, NY), 1977.

The Unlimited Dream Company, Holt (New York, NY), 1979.

Hello America, J. Cape (London, England), 1981.

Empire of the Sun, Simon & Schuster (New York, NY), 1984.

The Day of Creation, Gollancz (London, England), 1987, Farrar, Straus & Giroux (New York, NY), 1988, reprinted, Picador USA (New York, NY), 2001.

Running Wild, Hutchinson (London, England), 1989.

The Kindness of Women, Farrar, Straus & Giroux (New York, NY), 1991.

Rushing to Paradise, Picador USA (New York, NY), 1995.

Cocaine Nights, Counterpoint (Washington, DC), 1996.

Super-Cannes, Flamingo (London, England), 2000, Picador USA (New York, NY), 2001.

Millennium People, Flamingo (London, England), 2003.

STORY COLLECTIONS

The Voices of Time and Other Stories, Berkley Publishing (New York, NY), 1962.

Billenium and Other Stories, Berkley Publishing (New York, NY), 1962.

The Four-dimensional Nightmare, Gollancz (London, England), 1963, revised edition, 1974, published as *The Voices of Time,* Phoenix (London, England), 1998.

Passport to Eternity and Other Stories, Berkley Publishing (New York, NY), 1963.

Terminal Beach, Berkley Publishing (New York, NY), 1964, revised edition published as *The Terminal Beach,* Gollancz, 1964.

The Impossible Man and Other Stories, Berkley Publishing (New York, NY), 1966.

The Disaster Area, J. Cape (London, England), 1967.

By Day Fantastic Birds Flew through the Petrified Forests, Esographics for Firebird Visions, 1967.

The Day of Forever, Panther Books, 1967, revised edition, 1971.

The Overloaded Man, Panther Books, 1968.

The Atrocity Exhibition, J. Cape (London, England), 1970, published as *Love and Napalm: Export U.S.A.,* Grove Press (New York, NY), 1972.

Vermilion Sands, Berkley Publishing (New York, NY), 1971.

Chronopolis and Other Stories, Putnam (New York, NY), 1971.

Low-flying Aircraft and Other Stories, J. Cape (London, England), 1976.

The Best of J.G. Ballard, Futura Publications, 1977, revised edition published as *The Best Short Stories of J.G. Ballard,* Holt (New York, NY), 1978.

The Venus Hunters, Granada, 1980.

Myths of the Near Future, J. Cape (London, England), 1982.

Memories of the Space Age, Arkham House (Sauk City, WI), 1988.

War Fever, Farrar, Straus & Giroux (New York, NY), 1990.

The Complete Short Stories, Flamingo (London, England), 2001.

OTHER

(Editor, with others) *Best Science Fiction from "New Worlds,"* Medallion, 1968.

The Assassination Weapon (play; produced in London, England), 1969.

(Author of introduction) *Salvador Dali,* Ballantine (New York, NY), 1974.

(Author of introduction) Brian Ash, editor, *The Visual Encyclopaedia of Science Fiction,* Pan Books, 1977.

A User's Guide to the Millennium: Essays and Reviews, Picador (New York, NY), 1996.

Contributor to *The Inner Landscape,* Allison & Busby, 1969; and *Re/Search: J.G. Ballard,* edited by V. Vale and Andre Juno, Re/Search Publishing, 1984. Also contributor to publications, including *New Worlds, Ambit, Guardian, Transatlantic Review, Triquarterly, Playboy, Encounter,* and *Evergreen Review.*

ADAPTATIONS: Empire of the Sun was adapted as a film by Tom Stoppard and Menno Meyjes (uncredited), produced and directed by Steven Spielberg, Warner Bros., 1987; *Crash* was adapted as a film, written and directed by David Cronenberg, starring Holly Hunter and James Spader, Fine Line, 1996; "Low-flying Aircraft" was adapted by Swedish director Solveig Nordlund into a Portuguese-language film; *Running Wild* and *Super-Cannes* have both been optioned for film.

SIDELIGHTS: J.G. Ballard uses the language and symbols of science fiction to "explore the collective unconscious, the externalized psyche, which is plainly visible around us and which belongs to us all," as David Pringle stated in his study *Earth Is the Alien Planet: J.G. Ballard's Four-dimensional Nightmare.* Ballard's obsessive characters, searching "for a reality beyond 'normal' life," as Douglas Winter described it in the *Washington Post Book World,* attempt to manifest their private visions in landscapes that reflect their own mental states. Whether he uses post-holocaust or electronic media landscapes, what characterizes this surreal fusion of environment and the unconscious, Ballard wrote in an essay for *New Worlds,* "is its redemptive and therapeutic power. To move through these landscapes is a journey of return to one's innermost being."

This idea is echoed by Joseph Lanz who, in *Re/Search: J.G. Ballard,* also pointed out the neurotic nature of Ballard's characters. Ballard's science fiction, Lanz wrote, "replaces the intergalactic journey with excursions into the convoluted psyche. In Ballard's realm, neurosis is an ultracivilized version of primitive ritual where object and subject meld into an alchemical union. The outside world is just a projection of private fetishes." Pringle claimed that Ballard's characters "are driven by obsessions" and often choose "to strand themselves in some bizarre terrain which reflects their states of mind." Ballard addressed this question in an interview with Douglas Reed in *Books and Bookmen.* "My psychological landscapes," he explained, "are the sort that might be perceived by people during major mental crises—not literally, of course, but they represent similar disturbed states of mind." Speaking with Thomas Frick for *Paris Review,* Ballard further explained his intentions: "I quite consciously rely on my obsessions in all my work. . . . I deliberately set up an obsessional state of mind."

This obsessional quality is reflected in Ballard's recurring use of a few powerful symbols—symbols that have become so closely associated with his work that some critics label them "Ballardian." Sand dunes, abandoned buildings, crashed automobiles, low-flying airplanes, drained swimming pools, and beaches are found in story after story. They are used, Charles Platt wrote in *Dream Makers: The Uncommon People Who Write Science Fiction,* "as signposts, keys to the meaning of technology, the structure of the unconscious, and the promise of the Future." Noting the repetitive use of these symbols, Galen Strawson observed in the *Times Literary Supplement* that "sometimes it seems as if Ballard's oeuvre is just the systematic extrapolation . . . of an initial fixed set of possibilities, obsessions, and palmary symbols."

Ballard's richly metaphoric prose and his emphasis on psychological and technological themes make him a unique and important figure on the contemporary literary scene. Malcolm Bradbury, writing in the *New York Times Book Review,* stressed the psychological insights in Ballard's work. Ballard is, Bradbury believed, "an explorer of the displacements produced in modern consciousness by the blank ecology of stark architecture, bare high-rises, dead super-highways, and featureless technology." In similar terms, Emma Tennant wrote in the *New Statesman* that "Ballard's talent . . . is to show us what we refuse to see—the extraordinary mixture of old ideas and modern architecture, the self-contradictory expectation of 'human' responses in a landscape constructed to submerge all traces of identity—and to prove that it is only by knowing ourselves that we can understand the technology we have created."

Ballard began his writing career in the 1950s, selling his short stories to science-fiction magazines in his native England and in the United States. Encouraged by E.J. Carnell, the editor of *New Worlds,* to follow his own inclinations, Ballard soon adopted a distinctive style and choice of subject matter. "By the late 1950s," Robert Silverberg wrote in *Galactic Dreamers: Science Fiction as Visionary Literature,* Ballard "was dazzling and perplexing science-fiction readers with his dark and hypnotic stories and novels, typified by intelligent though passive characters in the grips of inexplicable cosmic catastrophes."

The catastrophes and ruined landscapes of Ballard's fiction find their roots in his childhood, which was spent in Shanghai during World War II. The son of a British businessman, Ballard was a child when the war began and the Japanese conquered the city. After several months of separation from his parents, during which he wandered the city alone, he was reunited with his family in a prisoner-of-war camp. The startling inversions brought about by the war and occupation, the empty or ruined buildings, the sudden evacuations, and the societal instability are all echoed in his fiction. He told Platt that the abandoned buildings and drained swimming pools found in his fiction are based on Shanghai's luxury hotels, which were closed for the duration of the war. Ballard told Platt about going to visit a friend whose building had been evacuated during the night: "I remember going there and suddenly finding that the building was totally empty, and wandering around all those empty flats with the furniture still in place, total silence, just the odd window swinging in the wind." "Conventional life," he added, "places its own glaze over everything, a sort of varnish through which the reality is muffled. In Shanghai, what had been a conventional world for me was exposed as no more than a stage set whose cast could disappear overnight; so I saw the fragility of everything, the transience of everything, but also, in a way, the *reality* of everything."

In 1984's *Empire of the Sun* Ballard deals directly with his childhood experiences. "Perhaps," he mused to Frick, "I've always been trying to return to the Shanghai landscape, to some sort of truth that I glimpsed there." The semi-autobiographical novel of a young boy on his own in war-torn Shanghai, *Empire of the Sun* received high praise from reviewers, and made the British best-seller lists. Reviewing the novel for *Newsweek*, David Lehman and Donna Foote placed the book "on anyone's short list of outstanding novels inspired by the second world war . . . [It] combines the exactness of an autobiographical testament with the hallucinatory atmosphere of twilight-zone fiction." Although *Empire of the Sun* is more realistic than Ballard's other writings, John Gross in the *New York Times* was reluctant to describe it as a "conventional novel . . . because many of the scenes in it are so lurid and bizarre, so very nearly out of this world. Among other things, they help to explain why in his work up till now Mr. Ballard should have been repeatedly drawn to apocalyptic themes." Lehman and Foote wrote, "It's ironic that *Empire of the Sun* . . . has earned him accolades denied to his earlier 'disaster novels,' since it has more in common with them than immediately meets the eye. Like its predecessors, the book explores the zone of 'inner space' that Ballard sees as 'the true domain of science-fiction.'" Winter saw *Empire of the Sun* as something new for Ballard, "a union of apparent irreconcilables—autobiography, naturalistic storytelling, and surrealism. Ballard has not only transcended science fiction, he has pushed at the limits of fiction itself, producing a dream of his own life that is both self-critique and story, an entertainment that enriches our understanding of the fact and fantasy in all our lives."

The Kindness of Women, a sequel to *Empire of the Sun*, traces four decades of the author's life and times, beginning with his medical studies in the 1950s to the death of his wife in a freak accident and his relationships with the various women for whom the book is named. "The main thrust of Ballard's writing," wrote Nick Kimberley in *New Statesman & Society*, "is to weld us, his characters, to what we are not—the world we live in."

In his first four novels, Ballard depicts global catastrophes that destroy modern civilization: high winds in *The Wind from Nowhere*, melting ice caps in *The Drowned World*, drought in *The Burning World*, and a

spreading, cancerous mutation in *The Crystal World*. These catastrophes alter the perceptions of Ballard's protagonists who, feeling a kinship with the destruction around them, respond by embracing it. Ballard's heroes, wrote Platt, are "solitary figures, courting the apocalypse and ultimately seduced by it. To them, a private, mystical union with a ruined world [is] more attractive than the pretense of a 'normal' lifestyle among organized bands of survivors."

Although some critics viewed these early novels as pessimistic because of their seemingly passive and self-destructive characters, Ballard disagrees. "I haven't got any sort of 'deathwish,'" he told Reed. "This aspect of my work parallels the self-destructive but curiously consistent logic of people enduring severe mental illness. There is a unique set of laws governing their actions, laws as constant as those controlling sane behavior but based on different criteria." Speaking to Platt on the same topic, Ballard claimed his work is not pessimistic. "It's a fiction of psychological fulfillment," he clarified. "The hero of *The Drowned World*, who goes south toward the sun and self-oblivion, is choosing a sensible course of action that will result in absolute psychological fulfillment for himself. . . . All my fiction describes the merging of the self in the ultimate metaphor, the ultimate image, and that's psychologically fulfilling." Graeme Revell, writing in *Re/Search: J.G. Ballard*, saw these books as "'transformation' rather than 'disaster' stories, involving not a material solution, but one of psychic fulfillment for the hero. . . . The hero is the only one who pursues a meaningful course of action—instead of escaping or trying to adapt to the material environment, he stays and comes to terms with the changes taking place within it and, by implication, within himself."

Ballard's early novels, particularly *The Drowned World* and *The Crystal World*, "helped make his name as a topographer of post-cataclysmic landscape," according to a reviewer for the *Times Literary Supplement*. This reputation changed in the late 1960s when Ballard became a leading spokesman for "New Wave" science fiction, a genre introducing experimental literary techniques and more sophisticated subject matter. In his fiction Ballard now began to explore the media landscape through a nonlinear writing style, entering his most experimental period. Many of his stories from this period are found in *The Atrocity Exhibition*. In this collection of related stories, Ballard explained to Reed, he writes of "a doctor who's had a mental break-down. He has been shocked and numbed by events like the deaths of the Kennedys and Marilyn Monroe. To make sense of the modern world he wants to immerse himself in its most destructive elements. He creates a series of psycho-dramas that produce grim paradoxes." As a critic for the *Times Literary Supplement* saw it, *The Atrocity Exhibition* "presents extreme examples of the private psyche being invaded by public events." In a preface to the U.S. edition of the book, William S. Burroughs called it "profound and disquieting. . . . The nonsexual roots of sexuality are explored with a surgeon's precision."

Because of objections to some of the book's content—in particular, the stories "Why I Want to Fuck Ronald Reagan" and "The Assassination of John Fitzgerald Kennedy Considered as a Downhill Motor Race," as well as certain unflattering references to consumer activist Ralph Nader—two U.S. publishers accepted and then rejected the book before Grove Press released it in 1972. Called by Joseph W. Palmer of *Library Journal* an "ugly, nauseating, brilliant, and profound" book, *The Atrocity Exhibition* might well be considered "a long poem on metaphysical themes," Jerome Tarshis claimed in the *Evergreen Review*. "That is the difficult part; the horrifying part is that this philosophical investigation is conducted in terms of violent death and perverse sexuality." This opinion was echoed by Paul Theroux in the *New York Times Book Review*. *The Atrocity Exhibition*, Theroux wrote, "is a kind of toying with horror, a stylish anatomy of outrage. . . . It is not [Ballard's] choice of subject, but his celebration of it, that is monstrous."

The sex and violence of *The Atrocity Exhibition* are also found in three other Ballard novels—*Crash, Concrete Island,* and *High-rise*—each of which presents an urban disaster and deals with the perverse violence of modern society. *Crash,* an attempt to discover the "true significance of the automobile crash," as one character states, tells the story of crash victim James Ballard and photographer Vaughan, a man obsessed with the idea of dying in an auto crash with Elizabeth Taylor, the two of them receiving identical wounds to their genitalia. It is, wrote a *Times Literary Supplement* critic, "a fetishist's book. . . . Ballard's endless reiteration of crashes—of the famous, on acid, with dummies, on film—begins to seem like a frantic litany, grotesque mantras in a private meditation." John Fletcher of the *Dictionary of Literary Biography* called *Crash* "an unsentimental scrutiny of the dehumanized eroticism and the brutality [Ballard] . . . feels are inseparable from the new technologies."

Critical reaction to *Crash* was sometimes harsh. D. Keith Mano wrote in the *New York Times Book Review* that the novel is "the most repulsive book I've yet to come across. . . . Ballard choreographs a crazed, mor-

bid roundelay of dismemberment and sexual perversion. *Crash* is well written: credit given where due. But I could not, in conscience, recommend it." A critic for the *Times Literary Supplement* believed that with *The Atrocity Exhibition* and *Crash,* Ballard has "produced a compendium of twentieth-century pathological imagery which earned him the disparaging reputation of being the intellectual of avant-garde science-fiction." Revell observed that *The Atrocity Exhibition* and *Crash* seemed to many critics to be "some kind of perverse aberration in the career of their author. . . . These new works developed previously latent ideas to a malignancy which burst out of the confines of science-fiction. The fiction seemed to have become real, too real, and there were dangerous questions: moral, existential, even political."

The idea for *Crash* originated in a scene from *The Atrocity Exhibition*. One of the psycho-dramas staged by Ballard's protagonist in that book is an art exhibit consisting of crashed cars. Before beginning *Crash,* Ballard also staged an exhibit of crashed cars at the New Arts Laboratory in London. "I had an opening party at the gallery," *Studio International* quoted Ballard as saying. "I'd never seen 100 people get drunk so quickly. Now, this had something to do with the cars on display. I also had a topless girl interviewing people on closed circuit TV, so that people could see themselves being interviewed around the crashed cars by this topless girl. This was clearly too much. I was the only sober person there. Wine was poured over the crashed cars, glasses were broken, the topless girl was nearly raped. . . . It was not so much an exhibition of sculpture as almost of experimental psychology using the medium of the fine art show. People were unnerved, you see. There was enormous hostility." Ironically, two weeks after completing *Crash,* Ballard was involved in a serious car accident in which his car rolled over and into the oncoming traffic lane. "This is," Ballard told James Goddard of *Cypher,* "an extreme case of nature imitating art."

Concrete Island again concerns a car crash. In this novel Robert Maitland has an accident on the freeway and is stranded on an isolated strip of land between the interweaving lanes of an interchange. Because of his injuries, Maitland cannot climb the embankment to get out. After a time he finds survival more important than escape and comes to accept his situation. Martin Levin in the *New York Times Book Review* noted that "Ballard plays two themes in this compact little book. The external theme is the Robinson Crusoe gambit. . . . The internal theme is the search-for-self motif." *Concrete Island,* wrote a *Times Literary Supplement* reviewer, "is a most intelligent and interesting book" in which Ballard "reveals undertones of savagery and desolation beneath a metaphor of apparent neutrality. . . . [Ballard is] our foremost iconographer of landscape."

Ballard's novel *High-rise* is set in a forty-story apartment block, the residents of which revert to tribal savagery after a power failure, transforming their building into a re-creation of man's prehistoric past. The apartments are ruled, Fletcher explained, "by the brutally simple law of the jungle: to survive one must prey on others and keep out of the way of those who would prey upon oneself." In a review for *Listener,* Neil Hepburn found the novel "well stocked with bizarre and imaginative strokes . . . but requiring such an effort for the suspension of disbelief as to become tiresome." Mel Watkins saw little merit in *High-rise,* claiming in his *New York Times Book Review* appraisal that it "exploits both technology and human emotion in a compulsively vulgar manner." According to Pringle, however, *High-rise* "makes the point that the high-rise building is not so much a machine for living in as a brutal playground full of essentially solitary children. It is a concrete den which encourages every anti-social impulse in its inhabitants rather than serving as a physical framework for a genuine social structure."

In the novel *Rushing to Paradise* Ballard reexamines the dark side of human nature. His main character—obsessive doctor Barbara Rafferty—becomes an ecological crusader and founder of an albatross sanctuary after losing her right to practice medicine. But the opportunistic doctor's intentions are far from selfless: she seeks to establish a utopian colony of women who will bear female children after being impregnated by disposable males. As a London *Observer* reviewer put it, "*Rushing to Paradise* is full of passive witnesses who will not admit the significance of the dramas unfolding in front of their eyes. This is a violent novel, but it also possesses an eerie calm, a glassy formality of texture which is as frightening as it is beautiful."

The violent underpinnings of seemingly placid communities is the focus of the novels *Cocaine Nights* and *Super-Cannes*. In *Cocaine Nights* Ballard posits a dystopian society deadened by leisure. Scores of retirement communities line the Costa del Sol in Spain, full of early-retired people with no purpose or will left in their lives. When his brother is charged with firebombing a house and killing five people in the sleepy town of Estrella de Mar, travel writer Charles Prentice goes down to investigate. In a story that is more of a detective novel than Ballard's previous disaster novels, Prentice uncovers a wide-ranging plot, masterminded by local tennis pro Bobby Crawford, to energize and mobilize the lazy retirees by introducing random violence into their lives.

Rex Roberts of *Insight on the News* called *Cocaine Nights* "one of the author's most accessible novels," even though its theme is the typically Ballardian one of "palpable evil lurking beneath [a] placid surface, a hidden world of drugs, illicit sex and violence." While Roberts claimed that "Ballard seems more moralist than nihilist," a reviewer for *Publishers Weekly* called *Cocaine Nights* "fairly mild," although he credited Ballard for painting a "bleak picture of trouble in paradise [that] has the ring of truth." A.O. Scott, writing in the *New York Times Book Review,* maintained that the book contains "a curious blend of deadpan detachment and almost comical self-consciousness." He quoted Bobby Crawford's explanation of why Estrella de Mar has more culture than the surrounding towns on the Costa del Sol: "Crime and creativity go together, and always have done. The greater the sense of crime, the greater the civic awareness and richer the civilization. Nothing else binds a community together." In the end, Smith said, Ballard overreaches with this idea: "Just as explaining a joke kills the humor, so does theorizing transgression blunt the thrill."

Super-Cannes also explores the sinister forces that wage violence on a supposedly utopian society. The setting is the high-tech office mecca of Eden-Olympia, a new development outside the French city of Cannes. Paul Sinclair, an airplane pilot who suffered injuries in a plane crash, moves to the soulless office park with his new wife, Jane, a doctor he met while convalescing. The former occupant of their house in Eden-Olympia was Dr. Greenwood, a seemingly benevolent figure who died after gunning down ten people and then shooting himself. He was also Jane's former lover. While Jane works long hours in Eden-Olympia's medical building, Paul obsesses about Greenwood and the reason for his killing spree. His investigations lead him to Wilder Penrose, Eden-Olympia's resident psychiatrist, who "believes that Eden-Olympia is a model for a future where leisure has been replaced by work and indulgence in premeditated violence is the surest way for members of the corporate elite to stay sane," according to a critic in the *Economist.* Paul uncovers a diabolical plot that indicates Penrose manipulated Greenwood into abusing the orphans in his care, and that Greenwood's murder spree was an attempt to rid Eden-Olympia of Penrose and other high-ranking administrators who had succumbed to his ideas.

John Gray, reviewing *Super-Cannes* for the *New Statesman,* commented that the book "presents a clairvoyantly lucid vision of what the future will be like." Gray wrote that if the novel "has a lesson, it is that the hyper-capitalism that is emerging in Europe cannot function without manufacturing psychopathology. It needs to satisfy repressed needs for intimacy and excitement, and it will not shrink from trying to apply to that task the same efficiency that has worked so well in the rest of the economy." "Ballard quickly and effectively makes the point that corporatism has crushed our souls," observed Barbara Hoffert in *Library Journal,* adding that the novel's "final pages" are "persuasive and gripping."

"*Cocaine Nights* and *Super-Cannes* rely on an idea central to Ballard's fiction: that forbidden activity can provide extreme liberation," wrote Sam Gilpin in *London Review of Books.* Furthermore, Gilpin continued, "in both novels there is a manipulative figure who orchestrates the vice and justifies it intellectually." Speaking of *Super-Cannes,* Helen Brown wrote in *Books Online* that "the novel asks us if we can be programmed to meet the abstract targets of the multinationals without compromising our humanity. Can we protest against it without resorting to even greater violence and madness?"

Introducing *Millennium People* to readers as a "wonderfully warped new novel," an *Economist* contributor detailed the novel's plot: deranged pediatrician Richard Gould has inflamed the Volvo-driving, yuppie upscale masses to commit acts of gratuitous violence as a way of combating social unrest. When his wife dies in a senseless accident, psychologist David Markham is converted to Gould's mantra and, as the level of violence accelerates, ultimately helps fire-bomb England's National Film Theatre, joined in this act of violence by several well-dressed residents of an upscale gated community. "With its allusions to the 11 September attacks on the World Trade Center," the novel will hold meaning for some readers, maintained *Spectator* critic Steve King; however, "others will no doubt be appalled by its characters' insistence on the life-affirming delights of terrorism, though it's hard to say how seriously Ballard wants us to take all this." As the author himself explained to *Bookseller* interviewer Benedicte Page, "I am interested in whether there is something in the air we breathe that encourages a very small minority of people to carry out violent acts of terrorism, I won't say as a cry for help, but as an act of last resort—an act of desperation." Noting references to the writing of Joseph Conrad, *New Statesman* critic John Gray argued that *Millennium People* is "a mesmerising novel" that "could be read as a Conradian fable of loss and dereliction set on the banks of the Thames." Noting that the novel "dissects the perverse psychology that links terrorists

with their innocent victims," Gray added: "This is news from the near future, another despatch from one of the supreme chroniclers of our time."

BIOGRAPHICAL AND CRITICAL SOURCES:

BOOKS

Aldiss, Brian, and Harry Harrison, editors, *SF Horizons,* two volumes, Arno Press, 1975.

Burns, Alan, and Charles Sugnet, editors, *The Imagination on Trial: British and American Writers Discuss Their Working Methods,* Allison & Busby, 1981.

Clareson, Thomas D., editor, *SF: The Other Side of Realism—Essays on Modern Fantasy and Science-fiction,* Bowling Green University (Louisville, KY), 1971.

Clareson, Thomas D., editor, *Voices for the Future: Essays on Major Science-fiction Writers,* Bowling Green University (Louisville, KY), Volume I, 1976, Volume II, 1979.

Contemporary Fiction in America and England, 1950-1970, Thomson Gale (Detroit, MI), 1976.

Contemporary Literary Criticism, Thomson Gale (Detroit, MI), Volume 3, 1975, Volume 6, 1976, Volume 14, 1980, Volume 36, 1986.

Dictionary of Literary Biography, Volume 14: *British Novelists since 1960,* two volumes, Thomson Gale (Detroit, MI), 1983.

Goddard, James, and David Pringle, editors, *J.G. Ballard: The First Twenty Years,* Bran's Head Books, 1976.

James, Langdon, editor, *The New Science-Fiction,* Hutchinson, 1969.

Neilson, Keith, editor, *Survey of Science-Fiction Literature,* Salem Press, 1979.

Platt, Charles, *Dream Makers: The Uncommon People Who Write Science Fiction,* Berkley Publishing (New York, NY), 1980.

Pringle, David, *Earth Is the Alien Planet: J.G. Ballard's Four-dimensional Nightmare,* Borgo Press (San Bernardino, CA), 1979.

Pringle, David, *J.G. Ballard: A Primary and Secondary Bibliography,* G.K. Hall (Boston, MA), 1984.

Rose, Mark, *Alien Encounters: Anatomy of Science Fiction,* Harvard University Press (Cambridge, MA), 1981.

Ross, Lois, and Stephen Ross, *The Shattered Ring: Science Fiction and the Quest for Meaning,* John Knox Press, 1970.

Short Story Criticism, Volume 1, Thomson Gale (Detroit, MI), 1988.

Silverberg, Robert, editor, *The Mirror of Infinity,* Harper (New York, NY), 1970.

Silverberg, Robert, editor, *Galactic Dreamers: Science Fiction as Visionary Literature,* Random House (New York, NY), 1977.

Vale, V., and Andrea Juno, editors, *Re/Search: J.G. Ballard,* Re/Search Publishing (San Francisco, CA), 1984.

PERIODICALS

Booklist, May 1, 1998, review of *Cocaine Nights,* p. 1500.

Books and Bookmen, April, 1971; March, 1977.

Bookseller, June 20, 2003, Benedicte Page, review of *Millennium People,* p. 27.

Chicago Tribune, December 11, 1987.

Cypher, October, 1973.

Economist (U.S.), October 14, 2000, review of *Super-Cannes,* p. 106; October 4, 2003, review of *Millennium People,* p. 92.

Evergreen Review, spring, 1973.

Foundation, November, 1975, Volume 9, "Some Words about *Crash!*" pp. 44-54; February, 1982.

Globe and Mail (Toronto, Ontario, Canada), November 7, 1987.

Guardian, September 11, 1970; September 13, 2000, Stephen Moss, "Mad about Ballard."

Hudson Review, winter, 1973-74.

Independent, November 10, 2001, Gareth Evans, "A Crash Course in the Future," p. 10.

Insight on the News, September 21, 1998, Rex Roberts, review of *Cocaine Nights,* p. 36.

Kirkus Reviews, March 15, 1996, p. 413; March 1, 1998, review of *Cocaine Nights,* p. 282.

Library Journal, July, 1970; June 15, 1996, p. 64; October 15, 2000, Barbara Hoffert, review of *Super-Cannes,* p. 105.

Listener, December 11, 1975, Neil Hepburn, review of *High-Rise.*

London Review of Books, February 2, 1989; November 16, 2000, Sam Gilpin, "Vaguely on the Run," p. 22.

Los Angeles Times, October 20, 1988.

Los Angeles Times Book Review, October 20, 1985; May 1, 1988; October 27, 1991, p. 3; May 19, 1996, p. 11.

Magazine Litteraire, April, 1974.

Magazine of Fantasy and Science-fiction, September, 1976.

New Review, May, 1974.

New Statesman, May 10, 1974; November 15, 1975; December 20, 1999, Martin Amis, review of *High-Rise,* p. 126; September 11, 2000, John Gray, review of *Super-Cannes,* p. 53; November 19, 2001, Sebastian Shakespeare, review of *The Complete Short Stories,* p. 55; September 8, 2003, John Gray, review of *Millennium People,* p. 50.

New Statesman & Society, September 27, 1991, Nick Kimberley, "The Sage of Shepperton," p. 52.

Newsweek, January 28, 1985, David Lehman and Donna Foote, review of *Empire of the Sun.*

New Worlds, November, 1959; May, 1962; July, 1966; October, 1966.

New York Review of Books, January 25, 1979.

New York Times, May 11, 1977; October 13, 1984, John Gross, "A Survivor's Narrative," p. 18; April 5, 1988, John Gross, "Fable of Man as a River-borne Creator-Destroyer," p. C17.

New York Times Book Review, September 23, 1973; December 1, 1974; December 9, 1979; November 11, 1984, John Calvin Batchelor, "A Boy Saved by the Bomb," p. 11; May 15, 1988; October 16, 1988, Gregory Benford, "Buicks and Madmen," p. 22; December 17, 1989; November 10, 1991, David R. Slavitt, "The Monster He Became," p. 22; November 5, 1995, p. 26; May 26, 1996, p. 14; July 12, 1998, A.O. Scott, "Pinter on the Beach," p. 16; March 7, 1999, review of *War Fever* and *The Day of Creation,* p. 28; November 25, 2001, Geoff Nicholson, review of *Super-Cannes,* p. 29.

Observer (London, England), September 4, 1994, p. 16.

Paris Review, winter, 1984, Thomas Frick, interview with Ballard, pp. 133-160.

Penthouse, September, 1970; April, 1979.

Publishers Weekly, March 11, 1988; July 25, 1991; February 26, 1996, p. 90; April 13, 1998, review of *Cocaine Nights,* p. 54; September 3, 2001, review of *Super-Cannes,* p. 58.

Rolling Stone, November 19, 1987.

Science-Fiction Studies, July, 1976, Charles Nicol, "J.G. Ballard and the Limits of Mainstream SF," pp. 150-157.

Search and Destroy, number 10, 1978.

Spectator, September 17, 1994, p. 38; September 13, 2003, Steve King, review of *Millennium People,* p. 60.

Studio International, October, 1971.

Thrust, winter, 1980.

Time, November 13, 1989.

Times (London, England), September 20, 1984; September 10, 1987; November 3, 1988; November 8, 1990; November 8, 2001, Giles Whittell, "Terrorism, the British Psyche, and the M25" (interview), p. S5.

Times Literary Supplement, July 9, 1970; November 30, 1973; April 26, 1974; December 5, 1975; November 30, 1979; June 12, 1981; September 14, 1984;

September 11, 1987; January 13, 1989; November 23, 1990; March 17, 1995, p. 22; April 12, 1996, p. 32; January 2, 1998, review of *The Voices of Time,* p. 20; December 13, 2001, Christopher Taylor, review of *The Complete Short Stories,* p. 20; September 7, 2003, Bharat Tandon, review of *Millennium People,* pp. 6-7.

Transatlantic Review, spring, 1971.

Tribune Books (Chicago, IL), April 10, 1988; December 22, 1991, p. 5; June 4, 1995, p. 3.

Vector, January, 1980.

Washington Post, February 21, 1989.

Washington Post Book World, November 25, 1979; October 28, 1984; July 26, 1987; April 17, 1988; June 12, 1988; May 21, 1995, p. 2; August 2, 1998, review of *Cocaine Nights,* p. 5; February 27, 1999, review of *War Fever* and *The Day of Creation,* p. 6.

Writer, June, 1973.

ONLINE

Books Online, http://www.booksonline.co.uk/ (September 10, 2000), Helen Brown, "Sex as a Means of Sedation."

Fine Line Features Web site, http://www.flf.com/ (January 30, 2002), interview with Ballard.

J.G. Ballard Web site, http://www.jgballard.com/ (March 14, 2001).

Spike Online, http://www.spikemagazine.com/ (August 31, 2001), David B. Livingstone, "Prophet with Honor"; (August 31, 2001) Chris Hall, "Flight and Imagination" (interview with Ballard).

OTHER

The Unlimited Dream Company (film), Royal College of Art School of Films, 1983.

*   *   *

BAMBARA, Toni Cade 1939-1995
(Toni Cade)

PERSONAL: Surname originally Cade, name legally changed in 1970; born March 25, 1939, in New York, NY; died of colon cancer, December 9, 1995, in Philadelphia, PA; daughter of Helen Brent Henderson Cade; children: Karma (daughter). *Education:* Queens College (now Queens College of the City University of New York), B.A., 1959; University of Florence, studied at Commedia dell'Arte, 1961; student at Ecole de Mime Etienne Decroux in Paris, 1961, New York, 1963; City College of the City University of New York, M.A., 1964; additional study in linguistics at New York University and New School for Social Research. Also attended Katherine Dunham Dance Studio, Syvilla Fort School of Dance, Clark Center of Performing Arts, 1958-69, and Studio Museum of Harlem Film Institute, 1970.

CAREER: Freelance writer and lecturer. Social investigator, New York State Department of Welfare, 1959-61; director of recreation in psychiatry department, Metropolitan Hospital, New York, NY, 1961-62; program director, Colony House Community Center, New York, NY, 1962-65; English instructor in Seek Program, City College of the City University of New York, New York, NY, 1965-69, and in New Careers Program of Newark, NJ, 1969; assistant professor, Livingston College, Rutgers University, New Brunswick, NJ, 1969-74; visiting professor of African-American studies, Stephens College, Columbia, MO, 1975; Atlanta University, visiting professor, 1977, research mentor and instructor, School of Social Work, 1977, 1979. Founder and director of Pamoja Writers Collective, 1976-85. Production artist-in-residence for Neighborhood Arts Center, 1975-79, Stephens College, 1976, and Spelman College, 1978-79. Production consultant, WHYY-TV, Philadelphia, PA. Conducted numerous workshops on writing, self-publishing, and community organizing for community centers, museums, prisons, libraries, and universities. Lectured and conducted literary readings at many institutions, including the Library of Congress, Smithsonian Institute, Afro-American Museum of History and Culture, and for numerous other organizations and universities. Humanities consultant to New Jersey Department of Corrections, 1974, Institute of Language Arts, New York Institute for Human Services Training, 1978, and Emory University, 1980. Art consultant to New York State Arts Council, 1974, Georgia State Arts Council, 1976, 1981, National Endowment for the Arts, 1980, and the Black Arts South Conference, 1981.

MEMBER: National Association of Third World Writers, Screen Writers Guild of America, African-American Film Society, Sisters in Support of South African Sisterhood.

AWARDS, HONORS: Peter Pauper Press Award, 1958; John Golden Award for Fiction from Queens College (now Queens College of the City University of New York), 1959; Theatre of Black Experience Award, 1969;

Rutgers University research fellowship, 1972; Black Child Development Institute service award, 1973; Black Rose Award from Encore, 1973; Black Community Award from Livingston College, Rutgers University, 1974; award from the National Association of Negro Business and Professional Women's Club League; George Washington Carver Distinguished African-American Lecturer Award from Simpson College; *Ebony's* Achievement in the Arts Award; Black Arts Award from University of Missouri; American Book Award, 1981, for *The Salt Eaters;* Best Documentary of 1986 Award from Pennsylvania Association of Broadcasters and Documentary Award from National Black Programming Consortium, both 1986, for *The Bombing of Osage;* nominated for Black Caucus of the American Library Association Literary Award, 1997, for *Deep Sightings and Rescue Missions: Fiction, Essays, and Conversations.*

WRITINGS:

Gorilla, My Love (short stories), Random House (New York, NY), 1972, reprinted, Vintage (New York, NY), 1992.

The Sea Birds Are Still Alive (short stories), Random House (New York, NY), 1977.

The Salt Eaters (novel), Random House (New York, NY), 1980, reprinted, Vintage (New York, NY), 1992.

(Author of preface) Cecelia Smith, *Cracks,* Select Press, 1980.

(Author of foreword) Cherrie Moraga and Gloria Anzaldua, editors, *This Bridge Called My Back: Radical Women of Color,* Persephone Press (Watertown, MA), 1981.

(Author of foreword) *The Sanctified Church: Collected Essays by Zora Neale Hurston,* Turtle Island (Berkeley, CA), 1982.

If Blessing Comes (novel), Random House (New York, NY), 1987.

Raymond's Run (juvenile; also see below), Creative Education (Mankato, MN), 1990.

Deep Sightings and Rescue Missions: Fiction, Essays, and Conversations, edited by Toni Morrison, Pantheon (New York, NY), 1996.

SCREENPLAYS

Zora, produced by WGBH-TV, 1971.

The Johnson Girls, produced by National Educational Television, 1972.

Transactions, produced by School of Social Work, Atlanta University, 1979.

The Long Night, produced by American Broadcasting Companies, Inc. (ABC), 1981.

Epitaph for Willie, produced by K. Heran Productions, Inc., 1982.

Tar Baby (based on Toni Morrison's novel), produced by Sanger/Brooks Film Productions, 1984.

Raymond's Run, produced by Public Broadcasting System (PBS), 1985.

The Bombing of Osage, produced by WHYY-TV, 1986.

Cecil B. Moore: Master Tactician of Direct Action, produced by WHYY-TV, 1987.

(With others) *W.E.B. Du Bois: A Biography in Four Voices,* produced by PBS, 1997.

EDITOR

(And contributor, under name Toni Cade) *The Black Woman: An Anthology,* New American Library (New York, NY), 1970.

(And contributor) *Tales and Stories for Black Folks,* Doubleday (New York, NY), 1971.

(With Leah Wise) *Southern Black Utterances Today,* Institute for Southern Studies (Durham, NC), 1975.

CONTRIBUTOR

Addison Gayle, Jr., editor, *Black Expression: Essays by and about Black Americans in the Creative Arts,* Weybright, 1969.

Jules Chametsky, editor, *Black and White in American Culture,* University of Massachusetts Press, 1970.

Ruth Miller, *Backgrounds to Blackamerican Literature,* Chandler Publishing, 1971.

Janet Sternburg, editor, *The Writer on Her Work,* Norton (New York, NY), 1980.

Paul H. Connolly, editor, *On Essays: A Reader for Writers,* Harper (New York, NY), 1981.

Florence Howe, editor, *Women Working,* Feminist Press (Old Westbury, NY), 1982.

Mari Evans, editor, *Black Women Writers (1950-1980): A Critical Evaluation,* Doubleday, 1984.

Baraka and Baraka, editors, *Confirmations,* Morrow (New York, NY), 1984.

Claudia Tate, editor, *The Black Writer at Work,* Howard University Press (Washington, DC), 1984.

Fictions for Our Times: Listener Favorites Old and New: Selected Shorts: A Celebration of the Short Story (compact disc), Symphony Space (New York, NY), 2004.

Contributor to *What's Happnin, Somethin Else,* and *Another Eye,* all readers published by Scott, Foresman, 1969-70. Contributor of articles and book and film reviews to *Massachusetts Review, Negro Digest, Liberator, Prairie Schooner, Redbook, Audience, Black Works, Umbra, Onyx,* and other periodicals. Guest editor of special issue of *Southern Exposure,* summer, 1976, devoted to new southern black writers and visual artists.

ADAPTATIONS: Three of Bambara's short stories, "Gorilla, My Love," "Medley," and "Witchbird," have been adapted for film.

SIDELIGHTS: Toni Cade Bambara was a well-known and respected civil rights activist, professor of English and of African-American studies, editor of anthologies of black literature, and author of short stories and novels. Throughout her career, Bambara used her art to convey social and political messages about the welfare of the African-American community and of African-American women especially. According to Alice A. Deck in the *Dictionary of Literary Biography,* the author was "one of the best representatives of the group of Afro-American writers who, during the 1960s, became directly involved in the cultural and sociopolitical activities in urban communities across the country." However, Deck pointed out that "Bambara is one of the few who continued to work within the black urban communities (filming, lecturing, organizing, and reading from her works at rallies and conferences), producing imaginative reenactments of these experiences in her fiction. In addition, Bambara established herself over the years as an educator, teaching in colleges and independent community schools in various cities on the East Coast." For Bambara, the duties of writer, social activist, teacher, and even student combined to influence her perspective. "It's a tremendous responsibility—responsibility and honor—to be a writer, an artist, a cultural worker . . . whatever you call this vocation," she explained in an interview in *Black Women Writers at Work.* "One's got to see what the factory worker sees, what the prisoner sees, what the welfare children see, what the scholar sees, got to see what the ruling-class mythmakers see as well, in order to tell the truth and not get trapped." Bambara made it her objective to describe the urban black community without resorting to stereotype or simplification. A deep understanding of the complexities of African-American life informs all of her work.

Born Toni Cade in New York City in 1939, Bambara credited her mother with providing a nurturing environment for her budding creativity. Growing up in Harlem, Bedford-Stuyvesant, and Queens, and in Jersey City, New Jersey, she was encouraged to explore her imagination, to daydream, and to follow her inner motives. She published her first short story at the age of twenty, a piece called "Sweet Town." The name "Bambara," which she later appended to her own, was discovered as part of a signature on a sketchbook she found in her great-grandmother's trunk. Bambara received a bachelor's degree in theater arts and English from Queens College in 1959. In the following decade, she served as a social worker and director of neighborhood programs in Harlem and Brooklyn, published short stories in periodicals, earned a master's degree and spent a year at the Commedia dell'Arte in Milan, Italy, and directed a theater program and various publications funded by the City College Seek program. This wide variety of experience inevitably found its way into her fiction and influenced her political sensibility as well.

Bambara's first book-length publication was *The Black Woman: An Anthology,* a collection of essays that was envisioned as a response to the so-called "experts" who had been conducting studies on the status of black American women. One of the first of its kind, the anthology provided an arena for black women's opinions not only on racism and sexism but also on a wealth of other equally important issues. She followed this work with *Tales and Stories for Black Folks,* a sourcebook intended to stimulate an interest in storytelling among young African-American students. The two anthologies and her first volume of fiction, *Gorilla, My Love,* were all published while she held a professorship at Livingston College, a division of Rutgers University.

Bambara's first two books of fiction, *Gorilla, My Love* and *The Sea Birds Are Still Alive,* are collections of her short stories. Susan Lardner remarked in the *New Yorker* that the stories in these two works, "describing the lives of black people in the North and the South, could be more exactly typed as vignettes and significant anecdotes, although a few of them are fairly long. . . . All are notable for their purposefulness, a more or less explicit inspirational angle, and a distinctive motion of the prose, which swings from colloquial narrative to precarious metaphorical heights and over to street talk, at which Bambara is unbeatable." In a review of *Gorilla, My Love,* for example, a writer remarked in the *Saturday Review* that the stories "are among the best portraits of black life to have appeared in some time. They are written in a breezy, engaging style that owes a good deal to street dialect." A critic writing in *Newsweek* made a similar observation, describing Bambara's second collection of short stories, *The Sea Birds Are Still Alive,* in this manner: "Bambara directs her vigorous sense and sensibility to black neighborhoods in big cities, with occasional trips to small Southern towns. . . . The stories start and stop like rapid-fire conversations conducted in a rhythmic, black-inflected, sweet-and-sour language." In fact, according to Anne Tyler in the *Washington Post Book World*, Bambara's particular style of narration is one of the most distinctive qualities of her writing. "What pulls us along is the language of her characters, which is startlingly beautiful without once striking a false note," declared Tyler. "Everything these people say, you feel, ordinary, real-life people are saying right now on any street corner. It's only that the rest of us didn't realize it was sheer poetry they were speaking."

In terms of plot, Bambara tended to avoid linear development in favor of presenting "situations that build like improvisations of a melody," according to a *Newsweek* reviewer. Commenting on *Gorilla, My Love,* Bell Gale Chevigny observed in the *Village Voice* that despite the "often sketchy" plots, the stories were always "lavish in their strokes—there are elaborate illustrations, soaring asides, aggressive sub-plots. They are never didactic, but they abound in far-out common sense, exotic home truths." Numerous reviewers also remarked on Bambara's sensitive portrayals of her characters and the handling of their situations, portrayals marked by an affectionate warmth and pride. Laura Marcus wrote in the *Times Literary Supplement* that Bambara "presents black culture as embattled but unbowed. . . . Bambara depicts black communities in which ties of blood and friendship are fiercely defended." Deck expanded on this idea, remarking that "the basic implication of all of Toni Cade Bambara's stories is that there is an undercurrent of caring for one's neighbors that sustains black Americans. In her view the presence of those individuals who intend to do harm to people is counterbalanced by as many if not more persons who have a genuine concern for other people." C.D.B. Bryan admired this expression of the author's concern for other people, declaring in the *New York Times Book Review* that "Bambara tells me more about being black through her quiet, proud, silly, tender, hip, acute, loving stories than any amount of literary polemicizing could hope to do. She writes about love: a love for one's family, one's friends, one's race, one's neighborhood and it is the sort of love that comes with maturity and inner peace." According to Bryan, "all of Bambara's stories share the affection that their narrator feels for the subject, an affection that is sometimes terribly painful, at other times fiercely proud. But at all times it is an affection that is so genuinely genus *homo sapiens* that her stories are not only black stories."

In 1980, Bambara published her first novel, a generally well-received work titled *The Salt Eaters*. Written in an almost dream-like style, *The Salt Eaters* explores the relationship between two women with totally different backgrounds and lifestyles brought together by a suicide attempt by one of the women. John Leonard, who described the book as "extraordinary," wrote in the *New York Times* that *The Salt Eaters* "is almost an incantation, poem-drunk, myth-happy, mud-caked, jazz-ridden, prodigal in meanings, a kite and a mask. It astonishes because Toni Cade Bambara is so adept at switching from politics to legend, from particularities of character to prehistorical song, from LaSalle Street to voodoo. It is as if she jived the very stones to groan." In a *Times Literary Supplement* review, Carol Rumens stated that *The Salt Eaters* "is a hymn to individual courage, a sombre message of hope that has confronted the late twentieth-century pathology of racist violence and is still able to articulate its faith in 'the dream'." And John Wideman noted in the *New York Times Book Review*: "In her highly acclaimed fiction and in lectures, Bambara emphasizes the necessity for black people to maintain their best traditions, to remain healthy and whole as they struggle for political power. *The Salt Eaters,* her first novel, eloquently summarizes and extends the abiding concerns of her previous work." After serving as writer-in-residence at Spelman College during the 1970s, Bambara relocated to Philadelphia, where she continued to write both fiction and film scripts. One of her best-known projects for film, *The Bombing of Osage,* explored a notorious incident in which the administration of Philadelphia Mayor Wilson Goode, himself an African American, used lethal force against a group of militant black citizens. The author's later books included another adult novel, *If Blessing Comes,* and a juvenile work, *Raymond's Run,* about a pair of siblings who like to run foot races. While never completely relinquishing her fiction work, however, Bambara became more and more involved with film. As she commented in *Black Women Writers at Work,* "I've always considered myself a film person. . . . There's not too much more I want to experiment with in terms of writing. It gives me pleasure, insight, keeps me centered, sane. But, oh, to get my hands on some movie equipment."

BIOGRAPHICAL AND CRITICAL SOURCES:

BOOKS

Black Literature Criticism, Thomson Gale (Detroit, MI), 1990.

Butler-Evans, Elliott, *Race, Gender, and Desire: Narrative Strategies in the Fiction of Toni Cade Bambara, Toni Morrison, and Alice Walker,* Temple University Press (Philadelphia, PA), 1989.

Contemporary Literary Criticism, Volume 29, Thomson Gale (Detroit, MI), 1984.

Dictionary of Literary Biography, Volume 38: *Afro-American Writers after 1955: Dramatists and Prose Writers,* Thomson Gale (Detroit, MI), 1985.

Notable Black American Women, Thomson Gale (Detroit, MI), 1992.

Parker, Bell, and Beverly Guy-Sheftall, *Sturdy Black Bridges: Visions of Black Women in Literature,* Doubleday (New York, NY), 1979.

Prenshaw, Peggy Whitman, editor, *Women Writers of the Contemporary South,* University Press of Mississippi, 1984.

Tate, Claudia, editor, *Black Women Writers at Work,* Continuum (New York, NY), 1983.

PERIODICALS

Black World, July, 1973.
Books of the Times, June, 1980.
Chicago Tribune Book World, March 23, 1980.
Drum, spring, 1982.
First World, Volume 2, number 4, 1980.
Los Angeles Times, December 15, 1995, p. A51.
Los Angeles Times Book Review, May 4, 1980.
Ms., July, 1977; July, 1980.
National Observer, May 9, 1977.
Newsweek, May 2, 1977.
New Yorker, May 5, 1980.
New York Times, October 11, 1972; October 15, 1972; April 4, 1980.
New York Times Book Review, February 21, 1971; May 2, 1971; November 7, 1971; October 15, 1972; December 3, 1972; March 27, 1977; June 1, 1980; November 1, 1981.
Saturday Review, November 18, 1972; December 2, 1972; April 12, 1980.
Sewanee Review, November 18, 1972; December 2, 1972.
Times Literary Supplement, September 27, 1985.
Village Voice, April 12, 1973.
Washington Post, December 13, 1995, P. D5.
Washington Post Book World, November 18, 1973; March 30, 1980.

*   *   *

BANAT, D.R.
See BRADBURY, Ray

*   *   *

BANKS, Iain
See BANKS, Iain M.

BANKS, Iain M. 1954-
(Iain Banks, Iain Menzies Banks)

PERSONAL: Born February 16, 1954, in Fife, Scotland; son of Thomas Menzies (an admiralty officer) and Euphemia (an ice skating instructor; maiden name, Thomson) Banks. *Education:* University of Stirling, B.A., 1975. *Politics:* Socialist. *Religion:* Atheist. *Hobbies and other interests:* "Hillwalking, eating and drinking, and talking to friends."

ADDRESSES: Home—31 South Bridge, Flat 3, Edinburgh EH1 1LL, Scotland. *Agent*—c/o Macmillan Publishers Ltd., 4 Little Essex St., London WC2R 3LF, England.

CAREER: Writer. Nondestructive testing technician in Glasgow, Scotland, 1977; International Business Machines Corp. (IBM), Greenock, Scotland, expediter-analyzer, 1978; solicitor's clerk in London, England, 1980-84.

MEMBER: Amnesty International, Campaign for Nuclear Disarmament.

WRITINGS:

UNDER NAME IAIN BANKS

The Wasp Factory, Houghton Mifflin (Boston, MA), 1984.

Walking on Glass, Macmillan (London, England), 1985, Houghton Mifflin (Boston, MA), 1986.

The Bridge, Macmillan (London, England), 1986.

Espedair Street, Macmillan (London, England), 1987.

Canal Dreams, Doubleday (New York, NY), 1991.

The Crow Road, Abacus (London, England), 1993.

Complicity, Doubleday (New York, NY), 1995.

Whit, or Isis amongst the Unsaved, Little, Brown (London, England), 1995.

A Song of Stone, Villard (New York, NY), 1998.

Inversions, Orbit (London, England), 1998, Pocket Books (New York, NY), 2000.

The Business: A Novel, Little, Brown (London, England), 1999.

(Editor, with Beverley Ballin Smith) *In the Shadow of the Brochs: The Iron Age in Scotland,* Stroud & Charleston, 2002.

SCIENCE FICTION

Consider Phlebas, St. Martin's Press (New York, NY), 1987.

The Player of Games, St. Martin's Press (New York, NY), 1989.

The State of the Art, M.V. Ziesing (Willimantic, CT), 1989.

Use of Weapons, Bantam (New York, NY), 1992.

Against a Dark Background, Spectra, 1993.

Feersum Endjinn, Bantam (New York, NY), 1995.

Excession, Orbit (London, England), 1996, Bantam (New York, NY), 1997.

Look to Windward, Orbit (London, England), 2000, Pocket Books (New York, NY), 2001.

SIDELIGHTS: Scottish novelist Iain M. Banks has sparked considerable controversy in British and American literary circles with his unique and highly imaginative brand of fiction. While the author is credited with crossing and redefining the boundaries of the thriller, fantasy, and science-fiction genres, he is probably best known for his macabre tales of horror, which have been compared by reviewers to the psychologically probing fiction of Franz Kafka and Edgar Allan Poe. Although Banks's books have received widely mixed reviews, many critics have conceded that the writer possesses a distinctive talent for structuring bold and compelling stories.

Banks was born in 1954, in Fife, Scotland, the son of an admiralty officer. He studied at Stirling University, and served as an extra in a battle scene for *Monty Python and the Holy Grail,* then filming nearby. He spent much of 1975 hitchhiking throughout Europe and North Africa, and then settled in London, where he worked as a accounting clerk at a law firm. In a biography published on his Web site, the author explained that this job involved "drawing up narratives for enormous legal bills—arguably a good grounding in fiction writing."

Banks first captured the attention of critics in 1984 with his highly acclaimed novel, *The Wasp Factory.* A bizarre tale of murder and perversity, *The Wasp Factory* centers on Frank Cauldhame, a disturbed adolescent who narrates the sordid story of his life. Living on a remote Scottish island with his reclusive ex-professor father, Frank has developed a taste for killing children and ritualistically mutilating animals and insects. The book's plot turns on the escape from an asylum of Frank's insane half-brother, Eric, who was committed for his sadistic indulgences, which included setting dogs on fire and choking babies with maggots. Eric's return to the Cauldhame cottage and Frank's revelation of his father's ghastly secret bring the novel to its climax.

The Wasp Factory takes its title from a device that Frank concocted specifically for the systematic torture and execution of wasps, a process which, according to Frank, can reveal the future if correctly interpreted. In the novel Frank muses, "Everything we do is part of a pattern we at least have some say in. . . . The Wasp Factory is part of the pattern because it is part of life and—even more so—part of death. Like life it is complicated, so all the components are there. The reason it can answer questions is because every question is a start looking for an end, and the Factory is about the End—death, no less."

Some critics were outraged by the sadistic streak that runs through Banks's narrator. Commenting on the apparent delight Frank takes in his ghoulish acts of cruelty, Patricia Craig, writing in the *Times Literary Supplement,* deemed the book "a literary equivalent of the nastiest brand of juvenile delinquency." But in an article for *Punch,* Stanley Reynolds defended Banks's novel as "a minor masterpiece . . . red and raw, bleeding and still maybe even quivering . . . on the end of the fork." Much controversy surrounds the question of the author's intent in composing such a grizzly and fantastic tale; critics have attributed Banks's motivation to several varied forces, including the desire to expose the dark side of humanity, to experiment in the avant-garde, or simply to shock and revolt readers. Reynolds suggested that *The Wasp Factory* "is not an indictment of society" but "instead a toy, a game." This assessment was disputed by several other critics, including *Washington Post Book World* contributor Douglas E. Winter, who judged the novel "a literate, penetrating examination of the nature of violence and the dwindling value of life in the modern world."

Reviewers generally considered Banks's skillful use of black humor and mesmerizing narrative power more than enough compensation for the novel's few cited structural flaws, mainly the implausibility of plot and character. Winter felt that "Banks indulges too often in . . . insight beyond the years of his young narrator." Rosalind Wade echoed that sentiment in *Contemporary Review,* claiming that the tale "strain[s] credulity to the breaking point"; she nevertheless dubbed *The Wasp Factory* "a first novel of unusual promise."

Banks's second novel, *Walking on Glass,* consists of three separate but ultimately interwoven stories, each of which, upon interpretation, sheds light on the others.

Two of the tales are set in London, the first detailing young Graham Park's obsessive pursuit of the mysterious Sara ffitch and the second focusing on temperamental Steven Grout's paranoid belief that "They" are out to get him. The last story concerns Quiss and Ajayi, prisoners in a surreal castle who are doomed to play "One-Dimensional Chess" and "Spotless Dominoes" until they can correctly answer the riddle, "What happens when an unstoppable force meets an immovable object?" Banks ties the three narratives together in the book's closing pages, making *Walking on Glass* "a brilliant mind-boggler of a novel . . . [with] real kick," according to Jack Sullivan in the *Washington Post Book World.*

Banks followed *Walking on Glass* with another complex story titled *The Bridge,* about an amnesiac's fantasy life. Following an accident, Orr (the central character, whose real name is Alexander Lennox), awakens in the world of the "Bridge," a land of social segregation arranged around an expansive railway that literally divides the classes. Dream and reality clash as Orr tries to make his escape. While some critics faulted Banks for his sketchy account of the narrator's life prior to the accident, the author was once again praised for his technical acumen. *The Bridge* drew comparisons to what Justin Wintle, in an article for *New Statesman,* termed "Banks's Kafka-Orwellian polity." Wintle further ventured that through his writings, the author strives "to make a point of pointlessness."

In 1987 Banks published his first science fiction novel, *Consider Phlebas,* one of two books he released that year. He refined his skill in the genre with his follow-up novel, *The Player of Games.* Although a few reviewers characterized both of these novels as overly extravagant, Tom Hutchinson, writing in the London *Times,* called *The Player of Games* "tremendous."

Gerald Jonas, a critic for the *New York Times Book Review,* noted that Banks's "passion for overwriting" was evident in another science fiction offering, *Use of Weapons,* but admitted that the flashback-laden narrative was worth reading just to get to the surprising denouement. Yet another science fiction novel, *Feersum Endjinn,* featured sections narrated by a character who can only spell phonetically, leading to sentences such as "Unlike evrybody els I got this weerd wirin in mi brane so I cant spel rite, juss-2 do eveythin foneticly." Gerald Jonas, again writing in the *New York Times Book Review,* explained: "I confess that I groaned inwardly each time this narrator took over. But despite the effort required, I was so caught up in the story and so eager to solve the

puzzle that I never for a moment considered giving up." *Analog* reviewer Tom Easton similarly noted that at times the book is "irritating," but went on to declare that "Banks proves quite convincingly that his imagination can beggar anyone else's. Wow. . . . If you can stand orthographic-phonetic-rebus overkill, yool find a grate deel hear 2 luv." Carl Hays concluded in *Booklist:* "Banks' skill at high-tech speculation continues to grow. Every page of this, his most ingenious work yet, seems to offer more dazzling, intriguing ideas." Summarizing Banks's work in the science fiction genre, Charles Shaar Murray wrote in *New Statesman:* "What comes through most clearly is just how much Banks loves SF. . . . He stuffs each novel to bursting point with everything he adores about the genre, and with everything his literary ancestors unaccountably left out. [His work proves] that 'fun' SF doesn't need to be either dumb or reactionary."

As his career has progressed, Banks's mainstream work has drawn increasingly positive reviews, despite his continued use of brutality and labyrinthine plots. In *Canal Dreams,* for example, he starts with a Japanese concert cellist whose fear of flying leads her to travel on her world tours by such unusual means as oil tankers. On one such cruise, she stumbles into the middle of a terrorist action, is raped, and then transformed into a grenade-carrying warrior. A *Publishers Weekly* writer called *Canal Dreams* a "stunning, hallucinatory, semi-surreal fable" and a "wrenching story, which can be read as a parable of the feminine principle reasserting itself and taking revenge on earth-destroying males." *Booklist* contributor Peter Robertson was so impressed with Banks's achievement in *Canal Dreams* that he declared, "Banks joins Martin Amis and Ian McEwan among the vanguard of the new British subversive novelist."

Banks's whodunit, *Complicity,* was, like much of his work, a cult bestseller in Britain but little known in North America. The plot centers on a hermit in Scotland who enjoys visiting revenge on criminals who have gone undetected and are thus unpunished. Following the trail is an investigative journalist, but this "hero" is anything but, and instead reveals himself as a tortured masochist with a drug problem. *Complicity* proved to be, according to a *St. James Guide to Horror, Ghost, and Gothic Writers* contributor, "certainly his most horrific book."

A Song of Stone was described as "a morality tale and, ultimately, a passion play with startlingly twisted passions," by Thomas Gaughan in *Booklist.* Its plot shares a similarity with one of the stories in *Walking on Glass:*

a couple are held hostage at a castle. But Abel and Morgan, of noble birth, belong there, and have been taken into captivity by a group of soldiers while a mysterious war rages elsewhere. Abel narrates the tale, and wonders if the desperate band has deserted the army. The brutality with which they treat Abel and Morgan is horrendous, and the contemptuous Abel considers himself above such savagery. His elitist attitude, however, proves false, as the degradation of his days fills him with a rage that causes him to harbor barbaric thoughts himself. A *Publishers Weekly* review of the novel compared Banks to J.G. Ballard and Anthony Burgess. Banks's "impeccable prose undulates with a poetry and sensuality that transform the most ordinary movements of his tale into resonant images of beauty and terror," its reviewer stated. Barbara Hoffert, writing in *Library Journal,* called the novel "worthy, but nearly unbearable to read" for its "images [that] are astonishingly grim and forceful."

Much of Banks's science fiction is set in a utopian world known as "The Culture"; there is even a fanzine by that name devoted to his novels in the genre. In *Inversions,* Banks imagines a world without technology. The work seems at first to be two unrelated tales: the first centering upon Vosill, the female physician to a king. She becomes embroiled in court intrigues and finds herself in love with the monarch. The figure in the second tale, a bodyguard named DeWar, is also devoted to his employer. A *Publishers Weekly* review remarked that "the story of Vosill and DeWar and their unspoken connection unfolds with masterful subtlety," and predicted it would further enhance Banks's "reputation for creating challenging, intelligent stories." The author also won praise from Jackie Cassada in *Library Journal,* who stated that *Inversions* "demonstrates his considerable talent for subtle storytelling."

Look to Windward, published in North America in 2001, returns readers to the world of "The Culture." In this novel, government agents from the Culture unintentionally initiate a civil war on the planet Chel, which results in the deaths of billions of Chelgrians. Quilan, an ambassador from Chel, is sent to the Masaq' Orbital in an effort to avenge the killings. *Library Journal*'s Jackie Cassada called the book a "literate and challenging tale by one of the genre's master storytellers." Although Roland Green, reviewing the title in *Booklist,* characterized it as "no more than a thinking reader's space opera," a *Publishers Weekly* contributor praised "Banks's fine prose, complex plotting and well-rounded characters," and noted that readers "will find themselves fully rewarded when the novel reaches its powerful conclusion."

Banks skewers global multinational corporations in *The Business.* The work centers upon Kathryn Telman, who has worked as an executive for a very large, very secretive, but omnipresent corporation for much of her adult life. Known only as "The Business," it stretches back more than 2,000 years and appears to control much of the planet's resources. Kathryn was recruited when still a child in a Scotland slum; educated and groomed for an executive position, she now closes lucrative high-tech deals for her employer. Her personal life, however, is a bit more directionless: a prince from the tiny Himalayan nation of Thulahn courts her, but she is uninterested, favoring a romance with a married colleague instead. But when a few top executives at "The Business" become determined to buy a United Nations seat, and try to oust Thulahn's representative permanently, Kathryn is transferred to his small country in order to take care of the groundwork. To her surprise, she falls in love with the country and its peaceful way of life. A *Kirkus Reviews* contributor found *The Business* to be a novel "sprinkled with erudite puns" and described it as "smart, breezy entertainment." Other reviews were similarly positive. "Banks offers a hilarious look at international corporate culture and the insatiable avarice that drives it," stated a *Publishers Weekly* reviewer, "but he suggests the positive potential of globalization, too."

BIOGRAPHICAL AND CRITICAL SOURCES:

BOOKS

Banks, Iain, *The Wasp Factory,* Houghton Mifflin (Boston, MA), 1984.
Banks, Iain, *Feersum Endjinn,* Bantam (New York, NY), 1995.
Contemporary Literary Criticism, Volume 34, Thomson Gale (Detroit, MI), 1985.
St. James Guide to Horror, Ghost, and Gothic Writers, first edition, St. James Press (Detroit, MI), 1998.

PERIODICALS

Analog, December, 1995, Tom Easton, review of *Feersum Endjinn,* pp. 183-184; October, 2000, Tom Easton, review of *Inversions,* p. 131.
Booklist, August, 1991, p. 2097; January 15, 1995, Emily Melton, review of *Complicity,* p. 899; July, 1995, p. 1865; February 1, 1997, Dennis Winters, review of *Excession,* p. 929; August, 1998, Thomas Gaughan, review of *A Song of Stone,* p. 1958; June 1, 2001, Roland Green, review of *Look to Windward,* p. 1855.

Books and Bookmen, February, 1984, pp. 22-23.

British Book News, April, 1984, p. 238.

Contemporary Review, April, 1984, Rosalind Wade, review of *The Wasp Factory,* pp. 213-224.

Globe and Mail (Toronto, Ontario, Canada), October 19, 1985.

Guardian, August 7, 1999, Colin Hughes, "Doing the Business," p. S6.

Kirkus Reviews, September 15, 2000, review of *The Business,* p. 1300.

Library Journal, August, 1991, Jackie Cassada, review of *Canal Dreams,* p. 150; June 15, 1995, p. 98; July, 1998, Barbara Hoffert, review of *A Song of Stone,* p. 132; February 14, 2000, Jackie Cassada, review of *Inversions,* p. 202; November 1, 2000, Marc Kloszewski, review of *The Business,* p. 132; August, 2001, Jackie Cassada, review of *Look to Windward,* p. 171.

Los Angeles Times, August 19, 1984, Charles Champlin, review of *The Wasp Factory,* p. 1; February 5, 1986.

Los Angeles Times Book Review, September 15, 1991, p. 6.

Magazine of Fantasy and Science Fiction, February, 1996, Charles De Lint, review of *Whit, or Isis amongst the Unsaved,* p. 37.

New Scientist, March 20, 1993.

New Statesman, April 5, 1985, Grace Ingoldby, review of *Walking on Glass,* p. 32; July 18, 1986; July 26, 1996, pp. 47-48.

New Statesman & Society, August 12, 1988; April 24, 1992, Brian Morton, review of *The Crow Road,* p. 37; September 3, 1993, John Williams, review of *Complicity,* p. 41; September 15, 1995, Roz Kaveney, review of *Whit,* p. 34.

New York Times Book Review, March 2, 1986, Samuel R. Delany, review of *Walking on Glass,* p. 37; May 3, 1992, Gerald Jonas, review of *Use of Weapons,* p. 38; February 19, 1995, Catherine Texier, review of *Complicity,* p. 26; September 10, 1995, Gerald Jonas, review of *Feersum Endjinn,* p. 46; January 7, 1996, p. 32; November 1, 1998, Margot Mifflin, review of *A Song of Stone,* p. 23; December 17, 2000, Peter Bricklebank, review of *The Business,* p. 23.

Observer (London, England), March 10, 1985; July 13, 1986; August 23, 1987.

Publishers Weekly, June 28, 1991, review of *Canal Dreams,* p. 88; November 7, 1994, review of *Complicity,* p. 66; January 27, 1997, review of *Excession,* p. 82; August 3, 1998, review of *A Song of Stone,* p. 73; January 3, 2000, review of *Inversions,* p. 61; September 25, 2000, review of *The Business,* p. 85; May 28, 2001, review of *Look to Windward,* p. 55.

Punch, February 29, 1984, Stanley Reynolds, review of *The Wasp Factory,* p. 42.

Sunday Times (London, England), February 12, 1984.

Times (London, England), February 16, 1984; March 7, 1985; September 24, 1988.

Times Literary Supplement, March 16, 1984; November 13, 1987; September 10, 1993, Will Eaves, review of *Complicity,* p. 22; September 1, 1995, Nicholas Lezard, review of *Whit,* p. 20; June 14, 1996; August 13, 1999, Robert Potts, review of *The Business,* p. 21.

Voice Literary Supplement, April, 1986.

Washington Post, March 17, 1986.

Washington Post Book World, September 9, 1984; July 31, 1988; October 29, 1989, p. 8; February 19, 1995, p. 7.

ONLINE

James Thin-Iain Banks Page, http://www.jthin.co.uk/banks1.htm/ (January 2, 2001), "Iain Banks—Biography."

*   *   *

BANKS, Iain Menzies
See BANKS, Iain M.

*   *   *

BANKS, Russell 1940-
(Russell Earl Banks)

PERSONAL: Born March 28, 1940, Newton, MA; son of Earl and Florence Banks; married Darlene Bennett, June, 1960 (divorced, February, 1962); married Mary Gunst (a poet), October 29, 1962 (marriage ended, 1977); married Kathy Walton (an editor), 1982 (divorced, 1988); married Chase Twitchell (a poet), 1989; children: Leona Stamm, Caerthan, Maia, Danis (all daughters). *Education:* Attended Colgate University, 1958; University of North Carolina, A.B., 1967.

ADDRESSES: Home—Princeton, NJ. *Agent*—Ellen Levine Literary Agency, Suite 1801, 15 East 26th St., New York, NY 10010.

CAREER: Writer, 1975—. Mannequin dresser, Montgomery Ward, Lakeland, FL, 1960-61; plumber in New Hampshire, 1962-64; Lillabulero Press, Inc., Chapel

Hill, NC, publisher and editor; Northwood Narrows, NH, publisher and editor, 1966-75; instructor at Emerson College, Boston, MA, 1968, 1971, University of New Hampshire, Durham, 1968-75, New England College, Henniker, NH, 1975, 1977-82, Princeton University, Princeton, NJ, 1981—. Has also taught at New York University, Sarah Lawrence College, and Columbia University. Played the role of Dr. Robeson in the film version of *The Sweet Hereafter* (see below).

MEMBER: International PEN, Coordinating Council of Literary Magazines (member of board of directors, 1967-73), American Academy of Arts and Sciences (fellow), Phi Beta Kappa.

AWARDS, HONORS: Woodrow Wilson fellowship, 1968; Guggenheim fellowship, 1976; St. Lawrence Award for Fiction, St. Lawrence University and *Fiction International,* 1975; NEA Fellowships, 1977, 1983; American Book Award, Before Columbus Foundation, 1982, for *The Book of Jamaica;* American Academy and Institute of Arts and Letters Award for work of distinction, 1986; John Dos Passos Award, 1986; Fels Award; O. Henry Memorial Award; Ingram Merrill Award; Best American Short Story Award; Pulitzer Prize finalist, 1986, for *Continental Drift,* and 1998, for *Cloudsplitter.*

WRITINGS:

POEMS

(With William Matthews and Newton Smith) *15 Poems,* Lillabulero Press (Chapel Hill, NC), 1967.

30/6, Quest (New York, NY), 1969.

Waiting to Freeze, Lillabulero Press (Northwood Narrows, NH), 1969.

Snow: Meditations of a Cautious Man in Winter, Granite Press (Hanover, NH), 1974.

SHORT STORIES

Searching for Survivors, Fiction Collective (New York, NY), 1975.

The New World, University of Illinois Press (Urbana, IL), 1978.

Trailerpark, Houghton (Boston, MA), 1981, new edition, HarperCollins (New York, NY), 1996.

Success Stories, Harper & Row (New York, NY), 1986.

The Angel on the Roof: The Stories of Russell Banks, HarperCollins (New York, NY), 2000.

NOVELS

Family Life, Avon (New York, NY), 1975, revised edition, Sun & Moon (Los Angeles, CA), 1988.

Hamilton Stark, Houghton (Boston, MA), 1978, new edition, HarperCollins (New York, NY), 1996.

The Book of Jamaica, Houghton (Boston, MA), 1980.

The Relation of My Imprisonment, Sun & Moon (College Park, MD), 1984.

Continental Drift, Harper & Row (New York, NY), 1985.

Affliction, HarperCollins (New York, NY), 1990.

The Sweet Hereafter, HarperCollins (New York, NY), 1991.

Rule of the Bone, HarperCollins (New York, NY), 1995.

Cloudsplitter, HarperCollins (New York, NY), 1998.

Darling, HarperCollins (New York, NY), 2004.

OTHER

(With Paul C. Metcalf) *Paul Metcalf—A Special Issue,* Lillabulero Press (Northwood Narrows, NH), 1973.

(Editor, with Michael Ondaatje and David Young) *Brushes with Greatness: An Anthology of Chance Encounters with Greatness,* Coach House (Toronto, Ontario, Canada), 1989.

(With Arturo Patten) *The Invisible Stranger: The Patten, Maine, Photographs of Arturo Patten,* HarperCollins (New York, NY), 1999.

Contributor to *Portfolio/1967: Poems,* Lillabulero Press, 1967; *Antaeus, No. 45-56: The Autobiographical Eye,* Ecco Press, 1982; *The Pushcart Prize X: Best of the Small Presses,* Pushcart Press, 1985; and *Mark Twain,* Knopf, 2001. Author of introduction, Nathaniel Hawthorne, *The Scarlet Letter,* Folio Society, 1992; coauthor, with William Matthews, of *Lillabulero: A Journal of Contemporary Writing.*

Contributor of essays to numerous periodicals, including *Transition, New York Times Book Review, Washington Post, American Review, Vanity Fair, Esquire, Harper's, Antaeus, Partisan Review, New England Review, Fiction International,* and *Boston Globe Magazine.*

Banks has made several audio recordings, including *Russell Banks Reads Excerpts from Continental Drift,* American Audio Prose Library (Columbia, MO), 1986; *Russell Banks Interview with Kay Bonetti,* American Audio Prose Library (Columbia, MO), 1986; *Weekend Edition, Sunday, 5-22-1988,* National Public Radio (Washington, DC), 1988; *Russell Banks Reads from His Novel Affliction, and Talks about Working Class Heroes,* 1991; *Russell Banks Reads from The Sweet Hereafter, and Talks about Snow as Metaphor, and Community Response to Tragedy,* Moveable Feast (New York, NY), 1994. Also, "The Gully," *Continental Drift, Rule of the Bone,* and *Cloudsplitter* have been released as audio books. His work has been translated into French, Spanish, Portuguese, Hebrew, and Japanese.

ADAPTATIONS: The Sweet Hereafter was adapted for the screen in a 1997 version directed by Atom Egoyan. A film version of *Affliction,* also released in 1997, was directed by Paul Schrader and starred Nick Nolte, Willem Dafoe, Sissy Spacek, and James Coburn.

WORK IN PROGRESS: A screenplay for director Francis Ford Coppola's adaptation of *On the Road* by Jack Kerouac.

SIDELIGHTS: Russell Banks is a native New Englander who has drawn on his experiences in the region's small towns, many of which have been hard-hit by economic decline, to create fiction that captures the lives of Northeastern people. As Banks has continued to add to the body of his novels, "he has ever more clearly emerged as a writer from the white working class," noted Fred Pfeil in the *Voice Literary Supplement,* "writing directly about the rage and damage, the capitulations, self-corruptions, and small resistances of subordinated lives." Banks offered his own view of the character of his fiction in an interview in the *New York Times Book Review.* "I grew up in a working-class family," he explained. For this reason, "I have a less obstructed path as a writer to get to the center of their lives. Part of the challenge of what I write is uncovering the resiliency of that kind of life, and part is in demonstrating that even the quietest lives can be as complex and rich, as joyous, conflicted and anguished, as other, seemingly more dramatic lives." These characteristics support Pfeil's belief that "Banks has now become . . . the most important living white male American on the official literary map, a writer we, as readers and writers, can actually learn from, whose books help and urge us to change."

Trailerpark and *Hamilton Stark* both take place in New Hampshire. Both works feature desperate, not always admirable, lead characters. In *Trailerpark,* the inhabitants of the trailers gathered in the poor part of town include a demented woman who raises dozens of guinea pigs, a drug pusher, and other outcasts. *New York Times Book Review* writer Ivan Gold found fault with Banks's omnipresent narrator in this collection—the "imprecise crackerbarrel tone and the equally arbitrary departure from it are accompanied by sometimes illuminating, more often disorienting, leaps in time," he remarked. However, in his *Washington Post Book World* review, Jonathan Yardley saw the collection as individual pieces of art: "Each [is] uncommonly good, and the whole of *Trailerpark* is greater than the sum of its parts; it is an odd, quirky book that offers satisfactions different from those provided by the conventional, or even unconventional, novel." Yardley further stated that he saw in *Trailerpark* "brief stories of hope and disappointment, of infidelity and murder, of betrayal and alienation. They are bleak stories set in a bleak place, yet there is a wicked comic edge to them. Banks has a terrific eye, mordant yet affectionate, for the bric-a-brac and the pathos of the American dream."

With *Hamilton Stark,* the author presents a title character with very few redeeming qualities. *Newsweek* critic Margo Jefferson described him as "a misanthropic New Hampshire pipefitter [who is] frequently drunk and abusive. He hurls furniture into the fields surrounding his house, then fires his rifle at it for sport. . . . He rejects love of any sort, finding hate the more interesting emotion. . . . To his neighbors he is possibly a madman." Nevertheless, at least two people find Stark fascinating: Stark's grown daughter and the book's narrator, each of whom is trying to write a novel about this quirky character. While the narrator's novel is about Hamilton Stark, Banks's novel is about the narrator, "the way *The Great Gatsby* is more about Nick Carroway than Jay Gatsby," as Terence Winch pointed out in a *Washington Post Book World* review. Winch also speculates that Banks is portraying Hamilton Stark himself as the narrator, "or a version of the narrator. . . . But ultimately these issues—Who is Hamilton Stark? Or who is the narrator? And are they the same person?—are academic." What is important, said the critic, is that "Banks has skillfully used his repertoire of contemporary techniques to write a novel that is classically American—a dark, but sometimes funny, romance with echoes of Poe and Melville."

The Book of Jamaica and *Continental Drift* both concern themselves with travel and self-discovery. In the former, a thirty-five-year-old New Hampshire college professor travels to the Caribbean to finish a novel and finds himself so drawn to the island of Jamaica that he decides to live there among its people. In the beginning, the unnamed narrator "finds daunting mysteries and complexities at every turn," according to *New York Times Book Review* critic Darryl Pinckney. But "what he lacks in intuition and skepticism he makes up for with a self-lacerating sensitivity of which he is quite proud." *Washington Post* reviewer James W. Marks believed that "the most distinctive feature of the novel is Banks' rigorous exploitation of point of view. A melange of voices results from the novel's medium-is-the-message: 'You will see what you want to see.' Shifts in point of view define the structure and specify the stages in the hero's progress." Marks concluded that despite some "self-conscious sermonizing" in the book, the author "deserves praise for the novel's weight of thought; he has read much and pondered long."

Much critical attention greeted the publication of *Continental Drift,* often acknowledged as one of Banks's most ambitious novels. The story covers the lives of two characters who are worlds apart culturally and geographically, but who share the same dreams of bettering their lives by moving to a new home. For thirty-year-old Bob Dubois, a New Hampshire oil-burner repairman with a wife, two daughters, and a girlfriend, the solution to his aimless life lies in moving the family to Florida, where he hopes to gain a partnership in his brother's liquor store. At the same time, Vanise Dorsinville, a Haitian woman who looks after her infant son and her nephew, longs to emigrate to America to start a new life. Within these parameters, Banks has constructed tragic, interlocking stories in a novel "that will surely imprint [the author's] name on the roster of important contemporary novelists. The physical world with its natural beauties and blights is played off against what Banks sees as an abandonment of enduring social values by modern man for the seductive promises of material success," as Ralph B. Sipper commented in the *Los Angeles Times Book Review.* "It is clear that the electronic age has freed man's mind," continued Sipper. "What has happened to his heart is a question that [*Continental Drift*] explores."

In his *New York Review of Books* article, Robert Towers described *Continental Drift* as Banks's most potentially "commercial" novel and notes that "admirers of [the author's] early fiction, which resisted conventional narrative, may find this objectionable, but his new book strikes me as the most interesting he has yet produced. [The novel] is an absorbing and powerful book that ambitiously attempts to 'speak' to the times." *Nation* critic James Marcus also found Banks's move away from experimental fiction a successful one, declaring that, in *Continental Drift,* the author has "developed a vigorous, unornamented style which moves easily between

narrative and authorial aside. This facility allows a double-edged view of Bob, as an eloquently fleshed-out character and as a type, a subject for speculation. Banks steps onstage repeatedly to discuss Bob's character, intelligence and sexuality, but these lectures don't seem condescending; nor does Banks outfit Bob with the usual bloodless accouterments of the common man—sentimental honesty or sentimental ingenuity. Average, yes, but also solid, painful and real."

Banks's novel *Affliction* is a "gripping, most beautiful, grim and wide-sweeping novel," wrote Carol Ascher in the *Women's Review of Books.* "The book is a requiem for a working-class manhood, no longer viable if it ever had been, that careens between decency, even sweetness, and brutal violence." The novel is Rolfe Whitehouse's attempt to reconstruct the recent events of his older brother Wade's life in order to understand his disappearance. Wade is in his forties and works as a jack-of-all-trades in his hometown, a small town in New Hampshire. He takes after his father in his tendencies to excessive drinking and abusive behavior. These have cost him his first marriage and the affection of his daughter. Wade becomes obsessed by the death of a visiting union official in a hunting accident.

Eric Larsen commented in the *Los Angeles Times Book Review,* "The book has at its heart a firm, lean, real, observed, honest story; but all around that heart, as if it's felt just not to be sufficient in itself, are built-up thicknesses and protections of the derivative, inflated and excessive, of the posturing and often just plain false-toned." Fred Pfeil held these same characteristics as among *Affliction*'s strengths, maintaining that "Banks avoids the twin dangers of a mere 'sociological' accuracy on the one hand and a voyeuristic sensationalism on the other, through a wise combination of elevation and distancing techniques."

With *Affliction,* observed Sven Birkerts in the *New Republic,* Banks returned to fiction that is both geographically and spiritually closer to home. "Where [*Continental Drift*] charted a grand scheme of cultural migration, seeking to isolate the larger as well as the human-sized circulations of malaise," wrote Birkerts, "*Affliction* stays rooted in place, hews to a single scale. Its study is the deeper ramifications of blood and kinship; it roots in to find the wellsprings of the will to violence." Birkerts concluded, "Bank's idiom is now vigorous and gritty, perfectly suited to the life of his characters and place. With his last few books, but with *Affliction* especially, he joins that group of small-town realists—writers like William Kennedy, Andre Dubus, and Larry Woiwode—

who have worked to sustain what may in time be seen as our dominant tradition. Like them, Banks unfolds the sufferings of the ordinary life, of those who must worry, who can't be happy."

In *The Sweet Hereafter,* "Russell Banks has used a small town's response to tragedy to write a novel of compelling moral suspense," Richard Eder pointed out in the *Los Angeles Times Book Review.* The town is Sam Dent, a small burg in the Adirondack Mountains of upstate New York. The tragedy is an accident; a school bus swerves off a snowy road and falls into a quarry pond. Fourteen of the town's children die, and several other people are injured. Banks tells the story of the tragedy and its aftermath through four narrators in sequence. The narrators are Dolores Driscoll, the bus driver; Billy Ansel, a garage owner who has lost his two daughters; Mitchell Stevens, a New York lawyer who comes to capitalize on the town's misfortune; and Nicole Burnell, a promising teenager left paralyzed by the accident. The four accounts follow the town through its process of dealing with this tragedy.

Rule of the Bone is Russell Banks's nod to Mark Twain, J.D. Salinger, and other chroniclers of wayward youth. Bone, a Huck Finn for the 1990s, is a mall rat from a working-class family in upstate New York. He runs away from his dysfunctional family and sets off in search of new role models. He first tries a gang of bikers and eventually finds a Rastafarian who lives in a bus. This Jamaican, I-Man, becomes to Bone what Jim became to Huck Finn, and the two set off on a journey to Jamaica. In Bone's travels, the reader learns of what his world has and lacks. "Banks gives the entire story over to a child," observes Ann Hulbert in the *New Republic,* "and the result is brutally, often fantastically, picaresque." *Atlanta Journal-Constitution* contributor Hal Crowther says Bone's story is "a tour de force of a monologue, it's a guidebook to an underworld we never visit, and it answers our first question—what's lurking in the brain beneath that ghastly mohawk?"

For some reviewers, *Rule of the Bone* succeeds not because it pays homage to previous coming-of-age novels, but because it gives voice to a new generation of Huck Finns and Holden Caufields. As Hal Crowther put it, "Russell Banks has a singular gift for articulating the feelings of characters who would pass for inarticulate in the world. He trades in stunted lives and undernourished spirits; he gives them voices. And he knows there's beauty in a spirit almost crushed that somehow finds the soil and light to grow in." Gail Caldwell offered a similar view in a *Boston Globe* article. "Banks

has the voice just right: Bone alternately manages to irritate, endear and outrage, just like thousands of other misbegotten kids through the ages. The end of the novel, after a few ludicrously unmoving events, is lovely in its simplicity. What Russell Banks has given us in his fiction is the truth—sometimes creepily intimate—about what's going on in the underpasses of America's highways." Caldwell added that Banks "also writes better about race, from a white man's perspective, than most of his peers."

In *Cloudsplitter,* "Banks' most ambitious and fully realized novel since *Continental Drift,*" as reviewed by Michiko Kakutani of the daily *New York Times,* Banks attempts to tell the difficult story of John Brown, a radical abolitionist who sought to bring a violent end to the practice of slavery with a raid on a government armory at Harpers Ferry, West Virginia, in 1859. Kakutani maintained that the novel "makes for some highly entertaining—and at times affecting—reading."

In 2000 Banks published *The Angel on the Roof: The Stories of Russell Banks,* a collection that includes twenty-two works from earlier in Banks's career as well as nine new pieces. The works presented illustrate "a master writer at his best," thought *Library Journal* reviewer Robert E. Brown. As in his earlier fiction, Banks writes about the quiet desperation of common men and women in these "almost unbearably poignant, unflinching glimpses into the dark recesses of life," as a reviewer for *Publishers Weekly* described them. However, that reviewer continued, the stories are also "illuminated by Banks's unfailing compassion."

Banks's empathy with his often ordinary characters is mirrored by his ordinary surroundings, as described in a summer, 2000, profile by Allen St. John in *Book* magazine. Visiting Banks at his home, "a brick-red, ranch-style house that has served as a home away from home to visiting writers like Richard Ford," St. John observed the strikingly common neighborhood in which the writer lived: "The street, in Princeton, New Jersey, lined by tiny split-levels and neatly groomed yards, has the markings of a place where lawn flamingos once roamed free." Banks himself joked that the place "looks like it belongs to a midlevel Mafia *caporegime,*" and St. John noted that "the only clue that this isn't a button man's abode" is "the 'Wade Whitehouse for Sheriff' bumper sticker on the Subaru wagon."

Not only the environment in which he lives and works, but also the attitude of Banks himself, reflects a closeness and familiarity with the thoughts of ordinary people. "When I began," he told St. John, "my audience was largely late middle age, people who bought literary books that were recommended in *The New York Times.* As I've gotten older, my audience has become much younger and more diverse in terms of class and race and background, cultural and otherwise. I'm enormously pleased by this."

BIOGRAPHICAL AND CRITICAL SOURCES:

BOOKS

Niemi, Robert, *Russell Banks,* HarperPerennial (New York, NY), 1996.
Novels for Students, Thomson Gale (Detroit, MI), 2002.

PERIODICALS

America, May 2, 1992, p. 391.
Atlantic Monthly, February, 1985.
Bloomsbury Review, November-December, 1989, p. 7; March, 1992, p. 3.
Book, July/August, 2000, Allen St. John, "Russell Banks: Telling Stories," pp. 38-41.
Booklist, January 1, 1999, review of *Cloudsplitter,* p. 778; March 15, 1999, review of the audio version of *Cloudsplitter,* p. 1350.
Book World, February 27, 1999, review of *Cloudsplitter,* p. 6.
Boston Globe, September 10, 1989, p. 100; October 4, 1989, p. 69; August 25, 1991, p. M15; January 19, 1992, p. A14; May 14, 1995, p. 33; May 28, 1995, p. B30.
Chicago Tribune, March 17, 1985.
Chicago Tribune Book World, July 6, 1980.
Christian Science Monitor, September 20, 1989, p. 13; September 24, 1991, p. 14.
Commonweal, October 24, 1986, p. 570.
Entertainment Weekly, February 12, 1999, review of *Cloudsplitter,* p. 75.
Globe and Mail (Toronto, Canada), February 13, 1999, review of *Affliction,* p. D-15.
Hungry Mind Review, summer, 1999, review of *Rule of the Bone,* p. 46.
Journal-Constitution (Atlanta, GA), September 17, 1989, p. L10; May 14, 1995, p. M11.
Kliatt Young Adult Paperback Book Guide, May, 1999, review of the audio version of *Cloudsplitter,* p. 52.
Library Journal, June 1, 2000, review of *The Angel on the Roof,* p. 206.

Listener, October 10, 1985, p. 29; September 13, 1990, p. 34.
Los Angeles Times, August 20, 1989, p. B10; September 30, 1991, p. E1.
Los Angeles Times Book Review, February 17, 1985, p. 5; June 22, 1986, p. 3; August 20, 1989, p. 10; September 1, 1991, p. 3; May 21, 1995, p. 3.
Maclean's, September 18, 1989, p. 68.
Nation, February 10, 1972; April 27, 1985, p. 505; September 13, 1986, p. 226; December 16, 1991, p. 786; June 12, 1995, p. 826.
New Republic, April 1, 1985, p. 38; September 11, 1989, p. 38; May 29, 1995, p. 40.
New Statesman, September 5, 1986, p. 28; September 21, 1990, p. 41.
Newsweek, June 26, 1978; February 25, 1985, p. 86; June 2, 1986, p. 72; September 18, 1989, p. 76; September 16, 1991, p. 62.
New York, May 8, 1995, p. 70.
New Yorker, April 15, 1985, p. 126; October 28, 1991, p. 119.
New York Review of Books, April 11, 1985, p. 36; December 7, 1989, p. 46.
New York Times, February 27, 1985, p. 18; May 31, 1986, p. 13; September 8, 1989, p. C26; September 6, 1991, p. C21; May 19, 1995, p. B8; June 1, 2000, Janet Maslin, "The Grit of Daily Life Meets Spiritual Epiphany."
New York Times Book Review, April 20, 1975; May 18, 1975; July 2, 1978; February 25, 1979; June 1, 1980; November 22, 1981; April 1, 1984; March 24, 1985, p. 11; September 17, 1989, p. 7; December 7, 1989, p. 46; September 15, 1991, p. 1; May 7, 1995, p. 13; June 18, 1995, p. 3; February 22, 1998, p. 9; February 7, 1999, review of *Cloudsplitter,* p. 24; June 25, 2000, A.O. Scott, "Cold Comfort."
New York Times Magazine, September 10, 1989, p. 53.
Publishers Weekly, March 15, 1985; June 14, 1999, review of *The Invisible Stranger,* p. 63.
Quill and Quire, October, 1989, p. 27.
Saturday Review, May, 1980; October, 1981.
Time, September 4, 1989, p. 66; June 5, 1995, p. 65.
Times Educational Supplement, August 27, 1999, review of *Cloudsplitter,* p. 21.
Times Literary Supplement, October 25, 1985, p. 1203; October 26, 1990, p. 1146; April 17, 1992, p. 20.
Tribune Books (Chicago), September 3, 1989, p. 1; September 15, 1991, p. 1.
Voice Literary Supplement, September, 1989, p. 25.
Washington Post, April 18, 1980.
Washington Post Book World, July 2, 1978; October 4, 1981; April 29, 1984; March 3, 1985, p. 3; Septem-

ber 24, 1989, p. 7; September 8, 1991, p. 3; October 13, 1991, p. 15; August 16, 1992, p. 12.
Women's Review of Books, April, 1990, p. 21.
Yale Review, January, 1999, review of *Cloudsplitter,* p. 139.

ONLINE

HarperCollins, http://www.harpercollins.com/ (April 23, 2002), author bio of Banks.
Salon.com, http://www.salon.com/ (April 23, 2002), Jonathan Miles, review of *The Angel on the Roof.*

OTHER

Russell Banks (video), UWTV (Seattle, WA), 1998.

*   *   *

BANKS, Russell Earl
   See BANKS, Russell

*   *   *

BARAKA, Amiri 1934-
   (Fundi, a joint pseudonym, Everett LeRoi Jones, LeRoi Jones)

PERSONAL: Born Everett LeRoi Jones, October 7, 1934, in Newark, NJ; name changed to Imamu ("spiritual leader") Ameer ("blessed") Baraka ("prince"); later modified to Amiri Baraka; son of Coyette Leroy (a postal worker and elevator operator) and Anna Lois (Russ) Jones; married Hettie Roberta Cohen, October 13, 1958 (divorced, August, 1965); married Sylvia Robinson (Bibi Amina Baraka), 1966; children: (first marriage) Kellie Elisabeth, Lisa Victoria Chapman; (second marriage) Obalaji Malik Ali, Ras Jua Al Aziz, Shani Isis, Amiri Seku, Ahi Mwenge. *Education:* Attended Rutgers University, 1951-52; Howard University, B.A., 1954; Columbia University, M.A. (philosophy); New School for Social Research, M.A. (German literature).

ADDRESSES: Office—Department of Africana Studies, State University of New York, Long Island, NY 11794-4340. *Agent*—Joan Brandt, Sterling Lord Literistic, 660 Madison Ave., New York, NY 10021.

CAREER: State University of New York at Stony Brook, assistant professor, 1980-83, associate professor, 1983-85, professor of African studies, 1985—. Instruc-

tor, New School for Social Research (now New School University), New York, NY, 1962-64; visiting professor, University of Buffalo, summer, 1964, Columbia University, fall, 1964, and 1966-67, San Francisco State University, 1967, Yale University, 1977-78, George Washington University, 1978-79, and Rutgers University, 1988. Founded *Yugen* magazine and Totem Press, 1958; coeditor and founder of *Floating Bar* magazine, 1961-63; editor of *Black Nation.* Founder and director, Black Arts Repertory Theatre/School, 1964-66; director of Spirit House (black community theater; also known as Heckalu Community Center), 1965-75, and head of advisory group at Treat Elementary School, both in Newark; Kimako Blues People (community arts space), co-director. Founder, Congress of African People, 1970-76. Member, Political Prisoners Relief Fund, and African Liberation Day Commission. Candidate, Newark community council, 1968. National Black Political Assembly, former secretary general and co-governor; National Black United Front, member; Congress of African People, co-founder and chair; League of Revolutionary Struggle, member. *Military service:* U.S. Air Force, 1954-57; weather-gunner; stationed for two and a half years in Puerto Rico with intervening trips to Europe, Africa, and the Middle East.

MEMBER: All-African Games, Pan African Federation, Black Academy of Arts and Letters, Black Writers' Union, United Brothers (Newark), Newark Writers Collective.

AWARDS, HONORS: Longview Best Essay of the Year award, 1961, for "Cuba Libre"; John Whitney Foundation fellowship for poetry and fiction, 1962; *Village Voice* Best American Off-Broadway Play ("Obie") award, 1964, for *Dutchman;* Guggenheim fellowship, 1965-66; Yoruba Academy fellow, 1965; second prize, International Art Festival (Dakar), 1966, for *The Slave;* National Endowment for the Arts grant, 1966; D.H.L. from Malcolm X College, 1972; Rockefeller Foundation fellow (drama), 1981; Poetry Award, National Endowment for the Arts, 1981; New Jersey Council for the Arts award, 1982; American Book Award, Before Columbus Foundation, 1984, for *Confirmation: An Anthology of African-American Women;* Drama Award, 1985; PEN-Faulkner Award, 1989; Langston Hughes Medal, 1989, for outstanding contribution to literature; Ferroni award (Italy), and Foreign Poet Award, 1993; Playwright's Award, Winston-Salem Black Drama Festival, 1997; appointed poet laureate of State of New Jersey (position abolished, 2003).

WRITINGS:

PLAYS

(Under name LeRoi Jones) *A Good Girl Is Hard to Find,* produced in Montclair, NJ, 1958.

(Under name LeRoi Jones) *Dante* (one act; excerpted from novel *The System of Dante's Hell;* also see below), produced in New York, NY, 1961, produced as *The Eighth Ditch,* 1964.

(Under name LeRoi Jones) *Dutchman,* (also see below; produced Off-Broadway, 1964; produced in London, 1967), Faber & Faber (London, England), 1967.

(Under name LeRoi Jones) *The Baptism: A Comedy in One Act* (also see below; produced Off-Broadway, 1964, produced in London, 1970-71), Sterling Lord, 1966.

(Under name LeRoi Jones) *The Toilet* (also see below; produced with *The Slave: A Fable* Off-Broadway, 1964), Sterling Lord, 1964.

Dutchman [and] The Slave: A Fable, Morrow (New York, NY), 1964.

(Under name LeRoi Jones) *J-E-L-L-O* (one act comedy; also see below; produced in New York, NY, by Black Arts Repertory Theatre, 1965), Third World Press, 1970.

(Under name LeRoi Jones) *Experimental Death Unit #1* (one act; also see below), produced Off-Broadway, 1965.

(Under name LeRoi Jones) *The Death of Malcolm X* (one act; produced in Newark, NJ, 1965), published in *New Plays from the Black Theatre,* edited by Ed Bullins, Bantam (New York, NY), 1969.

(Under name LeRoi Jones) *A Black Mass* (also see below), produced in Newark, NJ, 1966.

Slave Ship (also see below; produced as *Slave Ship: A Historical Pageant* at Spirit House, 1967; produced in New York, NY, 1969), Jihad, 1967.

Madheart: Morality Drama (one act; also see below), produced at San Francisco State College, 1967.

Arm Yourself, or Harm Yourself, A One-Act Play (also see below; produced at Spirit House, 1967), Jihad, 1967.

Great Goodness of Life (A Coon Show) (one act; also see below), produced at Spirit House, 1967; produced Off-Broadway at Tambellini's Gate Theater, 1969.

The Baptism [and] The Toilet, Grove (New York, NY), 1967.

Home on the Range (one act comedy; also see below), produced at Spirit House, 1968; produced in New York, NY, 1968.

Junkies Are Full of SHHH . . . , produced at Spirit House, 1968; produced with *Bloodrites* (also see below), Off-Broadway, 1970.

Board of Education (children's play), produced at Spirit House, 1968.

Resurrection in Life (one-act pantomime), produced as *Insurrection* in Harlem, NY, 1969.

Four Black Revolutionary Plays: All Praises to the Black Man (contains *Experimental Death Unit #1, A Black Mass, Great Goodness of Life (A Coon Show),* and *Madheart*), Bobbs-Merrill (New York, NY), 1969.

Black Dada Nihilism (one act), produced Off-Broadway, 1971.

A Recent Killing (three acts), produced Off-Broadway, 1973.

Columbia the Gem of the Ocean, produced in Washington, DC, 1973.

The New Ark's A-Moverin, produced in Newark, NJ, 1974.

The Sidnee Poet Heroical, in Twenty-nine Scenes (one act comedy; also see below; produced Off-Broadway, 1975), Reed & Cannon, 1979.

S-1: A Play with Music (also see below), produced in New York, NY, 1976.

(With Frank Chin and Leslie Siko) *America More or Less* (musical), produced in San Francisco, CA, 1976.

The Motion of History (four-act; also see below), produced in New York, NY, 1977.

The Motion of History and Other Plays (contains *Slave Ship* and *S-1*), Morrow (New York, NY), 1978.

What Was the Relationship of the Lone Ranger to the Means of Production? (one-act; also see below; produced in New York, NY, 1979), Anti-Imperialist Cultural Union, 1978.

Dim Cracker Party Convention, produced in New York, NY, 1980.

Boy and Tarzan Appear in a Clearing, produced Off-Broadway, 1981.

Money: Jazz Opera, produced Off-Broadway, 1982.

Song: A One-Act Play about the Relationship of Art to Real Life, produced in Jamaica, NY, 1983.

General Hag's Skeezag, 1992.

Also author of plays *Police,* published in *Drama Review,* summer, 1968; *Rockgroup,* published in *Cricket,* December, 1969; *Black Power Chant,* published in *Drama Review,* December, 1972; *The Coronation of the Black Queen,* published in *Black Scholar,* June, 1970; *Vomit and the Jungle Bunnies, Revolt of the Moonflowers,* 1969, *Primitive World,* 1991, *Jackpot Melting,* 1996, *Election Machine Warehouse,* 1996, *Meeting Lillie,* 1997, *Biko,* 1997, and *Black Renaissance in Harlem,* 1998.

Plays included in anthologies, including Woodie King and Ron Milner, editors, *Black Drama Anthology* (includes *Bloodrites* and *Junkies Are Full of SHHH. . .*),

New American Library, 1971; and Rochelle Owens, editor, *Spontaneous Combustion: Eight New American Plays* (includes *Ba-Ra-Ka*), Winter House, 1972.

SCREENPLAYS

Dutchman, Gene Persson Enterprises, Ltd., 1967.
Black Spring, Jihad Productions, 1968.
A Fable (based on *The Slave: A Fable*), MFR Productions, 1971.
Supercoon, Gene Persson Enterprises, Ltd., 1971.

POETRY

April 13 (broadside), Penny Poems (New Haven, CT), 1959.
Spring and So Forth (broadside), Penny Poems (New Haven, CT), 1960.
Preface to a Twenty Volume Suicide Note, Totem/Corinth, 1961.
The Disguise (broadside), [New Haven, CT], 1961.
The Dead Lecturer (also see below), Grove (New York, NY), 1964.
Black Art (also see below), Jihad, 1966.
Black Magic (also see below), Morrow (New York, NY), 1967.
A Poem for Black Hearts, Broadside Press, 1967.
Black Magic: Sabotage; Target Study; Black Art; Collected Poetry, 1961-1967, Bobbs-Merrill (New York, NY), 1969.
It's Nation Time, Third World Press, 1970.
Spirit Reach, Jihad, 1972.
Afrikan Revolution, Jihad, 1973.
Hard Facts: Excerpts, People's War, 1975, 2nd edition, Revolutionary Communist League, 1975.
Spring Song, Baraka, 1979.
AM/TRAK, Phoenix Bookshop, 1979.
Selected Poetry of Amiri Baraka/LeRoi Jones (includes Poetry for the Advanced), Morrow (New York, NY), 1979.
In the Tradition: For Black Arthur Blythe, Jihad, 1980.
Reggae or Not!, Contact Two, 1982.
LeRoi Jones—Amiri, Thunder's Mouth Press, 1991.
Transbluency: The Selected Poems of Amiri Baraka/LeRoi Jones (1961-1995), Marsilio, 1995.
Funk Lore: New Poems, 1984-1995, Sun & Moon Press, 1996.
Beginnings and Other Poems, House of Nehesi (Fredericksburg, VA), 2003.

ESSAYS

Cuba Libre, Fair Play for Cuba Committee (New York, NY), 1961.
Blues People: Negro Music in White America, Morrow (New York, NY), 1963, reprinted, Greenwood Press (Westport, CT), 1980, published as *Negro Music in White America,* MacGibbon & Kee (London, England), 1965.
Home: Social Essays (contains "Cuba Libre," "The Myth of a 'Negro Literature,'" "Expressive Language," "The Legacy of Malcolm X, and the Coming of the Black Nation," and "State/meant"), Morrow (New York, NY), 1966, Ecco Press (Hopewell, NJ), 1998.
Black Music, Morrow (New York, NY), 1968.
Raise, Race, Rays, Raze: Essays since 1965, Random House (New York, NY), 1971.
Strategy and Tactics of a Pan-African Nationalist Party, Jihad, 1971.
Kawaida Studies: The New Nationalism, Third World Press, 1972.
Crisis in Boston!, Vita Wa Watu People's War, 1974.
Daggers and Javelins: Essays, 1974-1979, Morrow (New York, NY), 1984.
(With wife, Amina Baraka) *The Music: Reflections on Jazz and Blues,* Morrow (New York, NY), 1987.
Jesse Jackson and Black People, 1996.
The Essence of Reparation, House of Nehesi (Fredericksburg, VA), 2003.

Contributor of essays to *Lorraine Hansberry, A Raisin in the Sun;* and *The Sign in Sidney Brustein's Window,* Vintage Books (New York, NY), 1995.

EDITOR

January 1st 1959: Fidel Castro, Totem, 1959.
Four Young Lady Poets, Corinth, 1962.
(And author of introduction) *The Moderns: An Anthology of New Writing in America,* 1963, published as *The Moderns: New Fiction in America,* 1964.
(And co-author) *In-formation,* Totem, 1965.
Gilbert Sorrentino, *Black & White,* Corinth, 1965.
Edward Dorn, *Hands Up!,* Corinth, 1965.
(And contributor) *Afro-American Festival of the Arts Magazine,* Jihad, 1966, published as *Anthology of Our Black Selves,* 1969.
(With Larry Neal and A.B. Spellman) *The Cricket: Black Music in Evolution,* Jihad, 1968, published as *Trippin': A Need for Change,* New Ark, 1969.

(And contributor, with Larry Neal) *Black Fire: An Anthology of Afro-American Writing*, Morrow (New York, NY), 1968.

A Black Value System, Jihad, 1970.

(With Billy Abernathy under pseudonym Fundi) *In Our Terribleness (Some Elements of Meaning in Black Style)*, Bobbs-Merrill (New York, NY), 1970.

(And author of introduction) *African Congress: A Documentary of the First Modern Pan-African Congress*, Morrow (New York, NY), 1972.

(With Diane Di Prima) *The Floating Bear, A Newsletter, No.1-37, 1961-1969*, McGilvery, 1974.

(With Amina Baraka) *Confirmation: An Anthology of African-American Women*, Morrow (New York, NY), 1983.

OTHER

The System of Dante's Hell (novel; includes the play *Dante*), Grove (New York, NY), 1965.

(Author of introduction) David Henderson, *Felix of the Silent Forest*, Poets Press, 1967.

Striptease, Parallax, 1967.

Tales (short stories), Grove (New York, NY), 1967.

(Author of preface) *Black Boogaloo (Notes on Black Liberation)*, Journal of Black Poetry Press, 1969.

Focus on Amiri Baraka: Playwright LeRoi Jones Analyzes the 1st National Black Political Convention (sound recording), Center for Cassette Studies, 1973.

Three Books by Imamu Amiri Baraka (LeRoi Jones), (contains *The System of Dante's Hell*, *Tales*, and *The Dead Lecturer*), Grove (New York, NY), 1975.

Selected Plays and Prose of Amiri Baraka/LeRoi Jones, Morrow (New York, NY), 1979.

The Autobiography of LeRoi Jones/Amiri Baraka, Freundlich, 1984, Lawrence Hill Books (Chicago, IL), 1997.

(Author of introduction) Martin Espada, *Rebellion Is the Circle of a Lover's Hand*, Curbstone Press, 1990.

(Author of introduction) *Eliot Katz, Space, and Other Poems*, Northern Lights, 1990.

The LeRoi Jones/Amiri Baraka Reader, Thunder's Mouth Press, 1991.

Thornton Dial: Images of the Tiger, Harry N. Abrams (New York, NY), 1993.

Jesse Jackson and Black People, Third World Press, 1994.

Shy's Wise, Y's: The Griot's Tale, Third World Press, 1994.

(With Charlie Reilly) *Conversations with Amiri Baraka* (also see below), University Press of Mississippi (Jackson, MS), 1994.

Eulogies, Marsilio Publishers (New York, NY), 1996.

The Fiction of LeRoi Jones/Amiri Baraka, foreword by Greg Tate, Lawrence Hill, 2000.

Works represented in anthologies, including *A Broadside Treasury, For Malcolm, The New Black Poetry, Nommo*, and *The Trembling Lamb*. Contributor to *Black Men in Their Own Words*, 2002; contributor to periodicals, including *Evergreen Review, Poetry, Downbeat, Metronome, Nation, Negro Digest*, and *Saturday Review*. Editor with Diane Di Prima, *The Floating Bear*, 1961-63.

Baraka's works have been translated into Japanese, Norwegian, Italian, German, French, and Spanish.

SIDELIGHTS: Amiri Baraka, who published under his birth name LeRoi Jones until 1967, is known for his strident social criticism and an incendiary style that has made it difficult for some audiences and critics to respond with objectivity to his works. Baraka's art stems from his African-American heritage. Throughout his career his method in poetry, drama, fiction, and essays has been confrontational, calculated to shock and awaken audiences to the political concerns of black Americans during the second half of the twentieth century. Baraka's own political stance has changed several times, thus dividing his oeuvre into periods; a member of the avant garde during the 1950s, Baraka became a black nationalist, and more recently a Marxist with socialist ideals. In the wake of the September 11, 2001, bombings of the World Trade Center, Baraka was accused of adding anti-Semite to his political outlook when in his poem "Somebody Blew up America" he suggested that New York's Jews had been warned in advance not to enter the doomed buildings on that fateful day; public outcry became so great that the State of New Jersey took action to abolish the position of poet laureate Baraka then held. Baraka, for his part, threatened legal action.

Throughout his career Baraka has stirred controversy, some praising him for speaking out against oppression and others arguing that he fosters hate. Critical opinion has been sharply divided between those who feel, with *Dissent* contributor Stanley Kaufman, that Baraka's race and political moment have created his celebrity, and those who feel that Baraka stands among the most important writers of the twentieth century. In *American Book Review*, Arnold Rampersad counted Baraka with Phyllis Wheatley, Frederick Douglass, Paul Laurence Dunbar, Langston Hughes, Zora Neale Hurston, Richard Wright, and Ralph Ellison "as one of the eight fig-ures . . . who have significantly affected the course of African-American literary culture."

Baraka did not always identify with radical politics, nor did he always channel his writing into use as their tool. He was born in Newark, New Jersey, and enjoyed a middle-class education. During the 1950s he attended Rutgers University and Howard University. Then he spent three years in the U.S. Air Force, where he was stationed for most of that time in Puerto Rico. When he returned to New York City, he attended Columbia University and the New School for Social Research. Baraka lived in Greenwich Village's lower east side where he made friends with Beat poets Allen Ginsberg, Frank O'Hara, and Gilbert Sorrentino. The white avant garde—primarily Ginsberg, O'Hara, and leader of the Black Mountain poets Charles Olson—and Baraka be-lieved that writing poetry is a process of discovery rather than an exercise in fulfilling traditional expecta-tions of what poems should be. Baraka, like the projec-tivist poets, believed that a poem's form should follow the shape determined by the poet's own breath and in-tensity of feeling. In 1958 Baraka founded *Yugen* maga-zine and Totem Press, important forums for new verse. His first play, *A Good Girl Is Hard to Find,* was pro-duced at Sterington House in Montclair, New Jersey, that same year.

Preface to a Twenty Volume Suicide Note, Baraka's first published collection of poems, appeared in 1961. M.L. Rosenthal wrote in *The New Poets: American and Brit-ish Poetry since World War II* that these poems show Baraka's "natural gift for quick, vivid imagery and spontaneous humor." The reviewer also praised the "sar-donic or sensuous or slangily knowledgeable passages" that fill the early poems. While the cadence of blues and many allusions to black culture are found in the po-ems, the subject of blackness does not predominate. Throughout, rather, the poet shows his integrated, Bo-hemian social roots. For example, the poem "Notes for a Speech" states, "African blues / does not know me . . . Does / not feel / what I am," and the book's last line is "You are / as any other sad man here / ameri-can."

With the rise of the civil rights movement Baraka's works took on a more militant tone, and he began a re-luctant separation from his Bohemian beginnings. His trip to Castro's Cuba in July of 1959 marked an impor-tant turning point in his life. His view of his role as a writer, the purpose of art, and the degree to which eth-nic awareness deserved to be his subject changed dra-

matically. In Cuba he met writers and artists from third world countries whose political concerns included the fight against poverty, famine, and oppressive govern-ments. They felt he was merely being self-indulgent, "cultivating his soul" in poetry while there were social problems to solve in America. In *Home: Social Essays,* Baraka explains how he tried to defend himself against these accusations, and was further challenged by Jaime Shelley, a Mexican poet, who had said, "'In that ugli-ness you live in, you want to cultivate your soul? Well, we've got millions of starving people to feed, and that moves me enough to make poems out of.'" Soon Baraka began to identify with third world writers and to write poems and plays with strong ethnic and political mes-sages.

Dutchman, a play of entrapment in which a white woman and a middle-class black man both express their murderous hatred on a subway, was first performed Off-Broadway in 1964. The one-act play makes many refer-ences to sex and violence and ends in the black man's murder. While other dramatists of the time were using the techniques of naturalism, Baraka used symbolism and other experimental techniques to enhance the play's emotional impact. Lula, the white woman, represents the white state, and Clay, the black man in the play, represents ethnic identity and non-white manhood. Lula kills Clay after taunting him with sexual invitations and insults such as "You ain't no nigger, you're just a dirty white man. Get up, Clay. Dance with me, Clay." The play established Baraka's reputation as a playwright and has been often anthologized and performed. Con-sidered by many to be the best play of the year, it won the *Village Voice* Obie Award in 1964. Later, Anthony Harvey adapted it for a film made in Britain, and in the 1990s it was revived for several productions in New York City. Darryl Pinckney commented in the *New York Times Book Review* that *Dutchman* survived the test of time better than other protest plays of the 1960s due to its economic use of vivid language, its surprise ending, and its quick pacing.

The plays and poems following *Dutchman* expressed Baraka's increasing disappointment with white America and his growing need to separate from it. He wrote in *Cuba Libre* that the Beat generation had become a coun-terculture of drop-outs who did not generate very mean-ingful politics. Baraka felt there had to be a more effec-tive alternative to disengagement from the political, legal, and moral morass the country had become. In *The Dead Lecturer* Baraka explored the alternatives, finding no room for compromise: if he identified with an ethnic cause, he would find hope of meaningful ac-tion and change; but if he remained in his comfortable assimilated position, writing "quiet" poems, he would remain "a dead lecturer." Critics observed that as Baraka's poems became more politically intense, they left behind some of the flawless technique of the earlier poems. *Nation* review contributor Richard Howard wrote: "These are the agonized poems of a man writing to save his skin, or at least to settle in it, and so urgent is their purpose that not one of them can trouble to be perfect."

To make a clean break with the Beat influence, Baraka turned to writing fiction in the mid-1960s, penning *The System of Dante's Hell,* a novel, and *Tales,* a collection of short stories. The novel echoes the themes and structures found in his earlier poems and plays. The stories, like the poems in *Black Magic,* also published in 1967, are "'fugitive narratives' that describe the harried flight of an intensely self-conscious Afro-American artist/intellectual from neo-slavery of blinding, neutralizing whiteness, where the area of struggle is basically within the mind," Robert Elliot Fox wrote in *Conscientious Sorcerers: The Black Postmodernist Fiction of LeRoi Jones/Baraka, Ishmael Reed, and Samuel R. Delany.* The role of violent action in achieving political change is more prominent in these stories. Unlike Shakespeare's Hamlet, who deliberates at length before taking violent action, Baraka sought to stand with "the straight ahead people, who think when that's called for, who don't when they don't have to," as he explained in *Tales.* The role of music in black life is seen more often in these books, also. In the story "Screamers," the screams from a jazz saxophone galvanize the people into a powerful uprising.

Baraka's classic history *Blues People: Negro Music in White America,* published in 1963, traces black music from slavery to contemporary jazz. The blues, a staple of black American music, grew out of the encounter between African and American cultures in the South to become an art form uniquely connected to both the African past and the American soil. Finding indigenous black art forms was important to Baraka at this time, as he was searching for a more authentic ethnic voice for his own poetry. From this important study Baraka became known as an articulate jazz critic and a perceptive observer of social change. As Clyde Taylor stated in *Amiri Baraka: The Kaleidoscopic Torch,* "The connection he nailed down between the many faces of black music, the sociological sets that nurtured them, and their symbolic evolutions through socio-economic changes, in *Blues People,* is his most durable conception, as well as probably the one most indispensable thing said about black music."

Baraka will also be long remembered for his other important studies, *Black Music,* which expresses black na-

tionalist ideals, and *The Music: Reflections on Jazz and Blues,* which expresses his Marxist views. In *Black Music* John Coltrane emerges as the patron saint of the black arts movement after replacing "weak Western forms" of music with more fluid forms learned from a global vision of black culture. Though some critics have maintained that Baraka's essay writing is not all of the same quality, Lloyd W. Brown commented in *Amiri Baraka* that Baraka's essays on music are flawless: "As historian, musicological analyst, or as a journalist covering a particular performance Baraka always commands attention because of his obvious knowledge of the subject and because of a style that is engaging and persuasive even when the sentiments are questionable and controversial."

After Black Muslim leader Malcolm X was killed in 1965, Baraka moved to Harlem and became a black nationalist. He founded the Black Arts Repertory Theatre/School in Harlem and published the collection *Black Magic.* Poems in *Black Magic* chronicle Baraka's divorce from white culture and values and also display his mastery of poetic techniques. As Taylor observed, "There are enough brilliant poems of such variety in *Black Magic* and *In Our Terribleness* to establish the unique identity and claim for respect of several poets. But it is beside the point that Baraka is probably the finest poet, black or white, writing in this country these days." There was no doubt that Baraka's political concerns superseded his just claims to literary excellence, and the challenge to critics was to respond to the political content of the works. Some critics who felt the best art must be apolitical, dismissed Baraka's newer work as "a loss to literature." Kenneth Rexroth wrote in *With Eye and Ear* that Baraka "has succumbed to the temptation to become a professional Race Man of the most irresponsible sort. . . . His loss to literature is more serious than any literary casualty of the Second War." In 1966 Bakara moved back to Newark, New Jersey, and a year later changed his name to the Bantuized Muslim appellation Imamu ("spiritual leader," later dropped) Ameer (later Amiri, "blessed") Baraka ("prince").

A new aesthetic for black art was being developed in Harlem and Baraka was its primary theorist. Black American artists should follow "black," not "white" standards of beauty and value, he maintained, and should stop looking to white culture for validation. The black artist's role, he wrote in *Home: Social Essays,* is to "aid in the destruction of America as he knows it." Foremost in this endeavor was the imperative to portray society and its ills faithfully so that the portrayal would move people to take necessary corrective action.

By the early 1970s Baraka was recognized as an influential African American writer. Randall noted in *Black*

World that younger black poets Nikki Giovanni and Don L. Lee (later Haki R. Madhubuti) were "learning from LeRoi Jones, a man versed in German philosophy, conscious of literary tradition . . . who uses the structure of Dante's *Divine Comedy* in his *System of Dante's Hell* and the punctuation, spelling and line divisions of sophisticated contemporary poets." More importantly, Arnold Rampersad wrote in the *American Book Review*, "More than any other black poet . . . he taught younger black poets of the generation past how to respond poetically to their lived experience, rather than to depend as artists on embalmed reputations and outmoded rhetorical strategies derived from a culture often substantially different from their own."

After coming to see black nationalism as a destructive form of racism, Baraka denounced it in 1974 and became a third world socialist. Hatred of non-whites, he declared in the *New York Times,* "is sickness or criminality, in fact, a form of fascism." Beginning in 1974 he produced a number of Marxist poetry collections and plays, his newly adopted political goal the formation of socialist communities and a socialist state. *Daggers and Javelins* and the other books produced during this period lack the emotional power of the works from the black nationalist period, contended many critics. However, some reviewers agreed with his new politics, exiled Filipino leftist intellectual E. San Juan praising Baraka's work of the late 1970s. San Juan wrote in *Amiri Baraka: The Kaleidoscopic Torch* that Baraka's 1978 play *What Was the Relationship of the Lone Ranger to the Means of Production?* was "the most significant theatrical achievement of 1978 in the Western hemisphere." Joe Weixlmann responded in the same book to the tendency to categorize the radical Baraka instead of analyze him: "At the very least, dismissing someone with a label does not make for very satisfactory scholarship. Initially, Baraka's reputation as a writer and thinker derived from a recognition of the talents with which he is so obviously endowed. The subsequent assaults on that reputation have, too frequently, derived from concerns which should be extrinsic to informed criticism."

In more recent years, recognition of Baraka's impact on late twentieth-century American culture has resulted in the publication of several anthologies of his literary oeuvre. *The LeRoi Jones/Amiri Baraka Reader* presents a thorough overview of the writer's development, covering the period from 1957 to 1983. The volume presents Baraka's work from four different periods and emphasizes lesser-known works rather than the author's most-famous writings. Although criticizing the anthology for offering little in the way of original poetry, *Sul-*

fur reviewer Andrew Schelling termed the collection "a sweeping account of Baraka's development." A *Choice* contributor also praised the volume, calling it "a landmark volume in African American literature." *Transbluency: The Selected Poems of Amiri Baraka/LeRoi Jones (1961-1995),* published in 1995, was hailed by Daniel L. Guillory in *Library Journal* as "critically important." And Donna Seaman, writing in *Booklist,* commended the "lyric boldness of this passionate collection."

Baraka's legacy as a major poet of the second half of the twentieth century remains matched by his importance as a cultural and political leader. His influence on younger writers was significant and widespread, and as a leader of the Black Arts movement of the 1960s Baraka did much to define and support black literature's mission into the next century. His experimental fiction of the 1960s is yet considered some of the most significant contribution to black fiction since that of Jean Toomer, who wrote during the Harlem Renaissance of the 1920s. Writers from other ethnic groups have credited Baraka with opening "tightly guarded doors" in the white publishing establishment, noted Murice Kenney in *Amiri Baraka: The Kaleidoscopic Torch,* adding: "We'd all still be waiting the invitation from the *New Yorker* without him. He taught us how to claim it and take it."

BIOGRAPHICAL AND CRITICAL SOURCES:

BOOKS

Allen, Donald M., and Warren Tallman, editors, *Poetics of the New American Poetry,* Grove (New York, NY), 1973.

Anadolu-Okur, Nilgun, *Contemporary African American Theater: Afrocentricity in the Works of Larry Neal, Amiri Baraka, and Charles Fuller,* Garland (New York, NY), 1997.

Baraka, Amiri, *Tales,* Grove (New York, NY), 1967.

Baraka, Amiri, *Black Magic: Sabotage; Target Study; Black Art; Collected Poetry, 1961-1967,* Bobbs-Merrill (New York, NY), 1969.

Baraka, Amiri, *The Autobiography of LeRoi Jones/ Amiri Baraka,* Freundlich Books, 1984.

Baraka, Amiri, and Charlie Reilly, *Conversations with Amiri Baraka,* University Press of Mississippi (Jackson, MS), 1994.

Baraka, Amiri, and Larry Neal, editors, *Black Fire: An Anthology of Afro-American Writing,* Morrow (New York, NY), 1968.

Benston, Kimberly A., editor, *Baraka: The Renegade and the Mask,* Yale University Press (New Haven, CT), 1976.

Benston, Kimberly A., editor, *Imamu Amiri Baraka (LeRoi Jones): A Collection of Critical Essays,* Prentice-Hall, 1978.

Bigsby, C.W.E., *Confrontation and Commitment: A Study of Contemporary American Drama, 1959-1966,* University of Missouri Press, 1968.

Bigsby, C.W.E., *The Second Black Renaissance: Essays in Black Literature,* Greenwood Press (Westport, CT), 1980.

Bigsby, C.W.E., editor, *The Black American Writer, Volume II: Poetry and Drama,* Everett/Edwards, 1970, Penguin (Harmondsworth, England), 1971.

Birnebaum, William M., *Something for Everybody Is Not Enough,* Random House (New York, NY), 1972.

Black Literature Criticism, Thomson Gale (Detroit, MI), 1991.

Brown, Lloyd W., *Amiri Baraka,* Twayne (New York, NY), 1980.

Concise Dictionary of American Literary Biography, Volume 1: *The New Consciousness,* Thomson Gale (Detroit, MI), 1987.

Contemporary Literary Criticism, Thomson Gale (Detroit, MI), Volume 1, 1973, Volume 2, 1974, Volume 3, 1975, Volume 5, 1976, Volume 10, 1979, Volume 14, 1980, Volume 33, 1985.

Cook, Bruce, *The Beat Generation,* Scribner (New York, NY), 1971.

Dace, Letitia, *LeRoi Jones (Imamu Amiri Baraka): A Checklist of Works by and about Him,* Nether Press, 1971.

Debusscher, Gilbert, and Henry I. Schvey, editors, *New Essays on American Drama,* Rodopi, 1989.

Dictionary of Literary Biography, Thomson Gale (Detroit, MI), Volume 5: *American Poets since World War II,* 1980, Volume 7: *Twentieth-Century American Dramatists,* 1981, Volume 16: *The Beats; Literary Bohemians in Postwar America,* 1983, Volume 38: *Afro-American Writers after 1955: Dramatists and Prose Writers,* 1985.

Dukore, Bernard F., *Drama and Revolution,* Holt (New York, NY), 1971.

Elam, Harry Justin, *Taking It to the Streets: The Social Protest Theater of Luis Valdez and Amiri Baraka,* University of Michigan Press (Ann Arbor, MI), 1997.

Ellison, Ralph, *Shadow and Act,* New American Library (New York, NY), 1966.

Emanuel, James A., and Theodore L. Gross, editors, *Dark Symphony: Negro Literature in America,* Free Press (New York, NY), 1968.

Fox, Robert Elliot, *Conscientious Sorcerers: The Black Postmodernist Fiction of LeRoi Jones/Baraka, Ishmael Reed, and Samuel R. Delany,* Greenwood Press (Westport, CT), 1987.

Frost, David, *The Americans,* Stein & Day, 1970.

Gayle, Addison, *The Way of the New World: The Black Novel in America,* Anchor/Doubleday (New York, NY), 1975.

Gayle, Addison, editor, *Black Expression: Essays by and about Black Americans in the Creative Arts,* Weybright & Talley, 1969.

Gwynne, James B., editor, *Amiri Baraka: The Kaleidoscopic Torch,* Steppingstones Press, 1985.

Harris, William J., *The Poetry and Poetics of Amiri Baraka: The Jazz Aesthetic,* University of Missouri Press, 1985.

Haskins, James, *Black Theater in America,* Crowell (New York, NY), 1982.

Henderson, Stephen E., *Understanding the New Black Poetry: Black Speech, and Black Music as Poetic References,* Morrow (New York, NY), 1973.

Hill, Herbert, *Soon, One Morning,* Knopf (New York, NY), 1963.

Hill, Herbert, editor, *Anger, and Beyond: The Negro Writer in the United States,* Harper (New York, NY), 1966.

Hudson, Theodore, *From LeRoi Jones to Amiri Baraka: The Literary Works,* Duke University Press, 1973.

Inge, M. Thomas, Maurice Duke, and Jackson R. Bryer, editors, *Black American Writers: Bibliographic Essays; Richard Wright, Ralph Ellison, James Baldwin, and Amiri Baraka,* St. Martin's Press (New York, NY), 1978.

Jones, LeRoi, *Blues People: Negro Music in White America,* Morrow (New York, NY), 1963.

Jones, LeRoi, *The Dead Lecturer,* Grove (New York, NY), 1964.

Jones, LeRoi, *Home: Social Essays,* Morrow (New York, NY), 1966.

Keil, Charles, *Urban Blues,* University of Chicago Press (Chicago, IL), 1966.

King, Woodie, and Ron Milner, editors, *Black Drama Anthology,* New American Library (New York, NY), 1971.

Knight, Arthur, and Kit Knight, editors, *The Beat Vision,* Paragon House, 1987.

Kofsky, Frank, *Black Nationalism and the Revolution in Music,* Pathfinder, 1970.

Lacey, Henry C., *To Raise, Destroy, and Create: The Poetry, Drama, and Fiction of Imamu Amiri Baraka (LeRoi Jones),* Whitson Publishing Company, 1981.

Lewis, Allan, *American Plays and Playwrights,* Crown (New York, NY), 1965.

Littlejohn, David, *Black on White: A Critical Survey of Writing by American Negroes,* Viking (New York, NY), 1966.

O'Brien, John, *Interviews with Black Writers,* Liveright (New York, NY), 1973.

Olaniyan, Tejumola, *Scars of Conquest/Masks of Resistance: The Invention of Cultural Identities in African, African-American, and Caribbean Drama,* Oxford University Press (New York, NY), 1995.

Ossman, David, *The Sullen Art: Interviews with Modern American Poets,* Corinth, 1963.

Rexroth, Kenneth, *With Eye and Ear,* Herder & Herder, 1970.

Rosenthal, M. L., *The New Poets: American and British Poetry since World War II,* Oxford University Press (New York, NY), 1967.

Sollors, Werner, *Amiri Baraka/LeRoi Jones: The Quest for a "Populist Modernism,"* Columbia University Press (New York, NY), 1978.

Stepanchev, Stephen, *American Poetry since 1945,* Harper (New York, NY), 1965.

Weales, Gerald, *The Jumping-off Place: American Drama in the 1960s,* Macmillan (New York, NY), 1969.

Whitlow, Roger, *Black American Literature: A Critical History,* Nelson Hall (New York, NY), 1973.

Williams, Sherley Anne, *Give Birth to Brightness: A Thematic Study in Neo-Black Literature,* Dial (New York, NY), 1972.

PERIODICALS

American Book Review, February, 1980; May-June, 1985.

African-American Review, summer-fall, 2003, special Baraka issue.

Atlantic, January, 1966; May, 1966.

Avant Garde, September, 1968.

Black American Literature Forum, spring, 1980; spring, 1981; fall, 1982; spring, 1983; winter, 1985.

Black Issues Book Review, Robert Fleming, "Trouble Man," p. 22.

Black World, April, 1971; December, 1971; November, 1974; July, 1975.

Booklist, January 1, 1994, p. 799; February 15, 1994, p. 1052; October 15, 1995, p. 380.

Book Week, December 24, 1967.

Book World, October 28, 1979.

Boundary 2, number 6, 1978.

Callaloo, summer, 2003, Matthew Rebhorn, "Flying Dutchman: Maosochism, Minstrelsy, and the Gender Politics of Amiri Baraka's 'Dutchman'," p. 796.

Chicago Defender, January 11, 1965.

Chicago Tribune, October 4, 1968.

Commentary, February, 1965.

Contemporary Literature, Volume 12, 1971; winter, 2001, Michael Magee, "Tribes of New York," p. 694.

Detroit Free Press, January 31, 1965.

Detroit News, January 15, 1984; August 12, 1984.

Dissent, spring, 1965.

Ebony, August, 1967; August, 1969; February, 1971.

Educational Theatre Journal, March, 1968; March, 1970; March, 1976.

Esquire, June, 1966.

Essence, September, 1970; May, 1984; September, 1984; May, 1985.

Jazz Review, June, 1959.

Journal of Black Poetry, fall, 1968; spring, 1969; summer, 1969; fall, 1969.

Library Journal, January, 1994, p. 112; November, 1995, pp. 78-79.

Los Angeles Free Press, Volume 5, number 18, May 3, 1968.

Los Angeles Times, April 20, 1990.

Los Angeles Times Book Review, May 15, 1983; March 29, 1987.

Nation, October 14, 1961; November 14, 1961; March 13, 1964; April 13, 1964; January 4, 1965; March 15, 1965; January 22, 1968; February 2, 1970; November 18, 2002, Art Winslow, "Prosody in Motion," p. 11.

Negro American Literature Forum, March, 1966; winter, 1973.

Negro Digest, December, 1963; February, 1964; Volume 13, number 19, August, 1964; March, 1965; April, 1965; March, 1966; April, 1966; June, 1966; April, 1967; April, 1968; January, 1969; April, 1969.

Newsweek, March 13, 1964; April 13, 1964; November 22, 1965; May 2, 1966; March 6, 1967; December 4, 1967; December 1, 1969; February 19, 1973.

New York, November 5, 1979.

New Yorker, April 4, 1964; December 26, 1964; March 4, 1967; December 30, 1972; October 14, 2002, Nick Paumgarten, "Goodbye, Paramus."

New York Herald Tribune, March 25, 1964; April 2, 1964; December 13, 1964; October 27, 1965.

New York Post, March 16, 1964; March 24, 1964; January 15, 1965; March 18, 1965.

New York Review of Books, May 22, 1964; January 20, 1966; July 2, 1970; October 17, 1974; June 11, 1984; June 14, 1984.

New York Times, April 28, 1966; May 8, 1966; August 10, 1966; September 14, 1966; October 5, 1966; January 20, 1967; February 28, 1967; July 15, 1967; January 5, 1968; January 6, 1968; January 9,

1968; January 10, 1968; February 7, 1968; April 14, 1968; August 16, 1968; November 27, 1968; December 24, 1968; August 26, 1969; November 23, 1969; February 6, 1970; May 11, 1972; June 11, 1972; November 11, 1972; November 14, 1972; November 23, 1972; December 5, 1972; December 27, 1974; December 29, 1974; November 19, 1979; October 15, 1981; January 23, 1984; February 9, 1991.

New York Times Book Review, January 31, 1965; November 28, 1965; May 8, 1966; February 4, 1968; March 17, 1968; February 14, 1971; June 6, 1971; June 27, 1971; December 5, 1971; March 12, 1972; December 16, 1979; March 11, 1984; July 5, 1987; December 20, 1987.

New York Times Magazine, February 5, 1984.

Salmagundi, spring-summer, 1973.

Saturday Review, April 20, 1963; January 11, 1964; January 9, 1965; December 11, 1965; December 9, 1967; October 2, 1971; July 12, 1975.

Skeptical Inquirer, January-February, 2003, Kevin Christopher, "Baraka Buys Bunk," p. 8.

Studies in Black Literature, spring, 1970; Volume 1, number 2, 1970; Volume 3, number 2, 1972; Volume 3, number 3, 1972; Volume 4, number 1, 1973.

Sulfur, spring, 1992.

Sunday News (New York, NY), January 21, 1973.

Time, December 25, 1964; November 19, 1965; May 6, 1966; January 12, 1968; April 26, 1968; June 28, 1968; June 28, 1971.

Times Literary Supplement, November 25, 1965; September 1, 1966; September 11, 1969; October 9, 1969; August 2, 1991.

Tribune Books (Chicago, IL), March 29, 1987.

Village Voice, December 17, 1964; May 6, 1965; May 19, 1965; August 30, 1976; August 1, 1977; December 17-23, 1980; October 2, 1984.

Washington Post, August 15, 1968; September 12, 1968; November 27, 1968; December 5, 1980; January 23, 1981; June 29, 1987.

Washington Post Book World, December 24, 1967; May 22, 1983.

ONLINE

Academy of American Poets Web site, http://www.poets. org/ (July 19, 2001), "Amiri Baraka."

*   *   *

BARCLAY, Bill
See MOORCOCK, Michael

BARCLAY, William Ewert
See MOORCOCK, Michael

*   *   *

BARKER, Clive 1952-

PERSONAL: Born 1952, in Liverpool, England; son of Len (dock worker) and Joan (nurse) Barker; children: Nicole. *Education:* Received degree from University of Liverpool.

ADDRESSES: Home—Los Angeles, CA. *Office*—Stealth Press, 128 East Grant St., 4th Fl., Lancaster, PA 17602-2854.

CAREER: Illustrator, painter, actor, playwright, screenwriter, and author. Founder of Dog Company (theatre group) and Seraphim Productions (producer of Barker's novels, films, plays, CD-ROMs, comic books, and paintings). Director of short films, including *Salome,* 1973, and *The Forbidden,* 1978; director of feature-length films, including *Hellraiser,* 1987, *Nightbreed,* 1990, *Lord of Illusions,* 1995, and *Tortured Souls,* 2004. Executive producer of films, including *Hellbound: Hellraiser II,* 1989, *Hellraiser III: Hell on Earth,* 1992, *Candyman,* 1992, *Candyman II: Farewell to the Flesh,* 1995, and *Gods and Monsters,* 1998. *Exhibitions:*Barker's paintings and drawings have appeared at Bess Cutler Gallery, New York, NY, 1993; South Coast Plaza branch, Laguna Art Museum, Costa Mesa, CA, 1995; and Pacific Design Center, West Hollywood, CA, 2002.

AWARDS, HONORS: Two British Fantasy awards from British Fantasy Society; World Fantasy Award for best anthology/collection from World Fantasy Convention, 1985, for *Clive Barker's Books of Blood;* Bram Stoker Award, Horror Writers Association, 2004, for *Days of Magic, Nights of War.*

WRITINGS:

SHORT FICTION

Clive Barker's Books of Blood, Volume One (contains "The Book of Blood," "In the Hills, the Cities," "The Midnight Meat Train," "Pig Blood Blues," "Sex, Death, and Starshine," and "The Yattering and Jack"), introduction by Ramsey Campbell, Sphere (London, England), 1984, Berkley (New York, NY), 1986.

Clive Barker's Books of Blood, Volume Two (contains "Dread," "Hell's Event," "Jaqueline Ess: Her Will and Testament," "New Murders in the Rue Morgue," and "The Skins of the Fathers"), Sphere (London, England), 1984, Berkley (New York, NY), 1986.

Clive Barker's Books of Blood, Volume Three (contains "Confessions of a [Pornographer's] Shroud," "Human Remains," "Rawhead Rex," "Scape-Goats," and "Son of Celluloid"), Sphere (London, England), 1984, Berkley (New York, NY), 1986.

Books of Blood, Volumes 1-3, Weidenfeld & Nicolson (London, England), 1985, published in one volume, Scream/Press (Santa Cruz, CA), 1985.

Clive Barker's Books of Blood, Volume Four (contains "The Age of Desire," "The Body Politic," "Down, Satan!," "The Inhuman Condition," and "Revelations"), Sphere (London, England), 1985, published as *The Inhuman Condition: Tales of Terror,* Poseidon (New York, NY), 1986.

Clive Barker's Books of Blood, Volume Five (contains "Babel's Children," "The Forbidden," "In the Flesh," and "The Madonna"), Sphere (London, England), 1985, published as *In The Flesh: Tales of Terror,* Poseidon (New York, NY), 1986.

Clive Barker's Books of Blood, Volume Six (includes "How Spoilers Breed," "The Last Illusion," "The Life of Death," "On Jerusalem Street," and "Twilight at the Towers"), Sphere (London, England), 1985.

Books of Blood, Volumes 4-6, Weidenfeld & Nicolson (London, England), 1986.

The Hellbound Heart (novella), published in *Night Visions 3,* edited by George R.R. Martin, Dark Harvest (Arlington Heights, IL), 1986, published separately, Simon & Schuster (New York, NY), 1988.

Cabal (includes novella "Cabal," and stories "How Spoilers Breed," "The Last Illusion," "The Life of Death," and "Twilight at the Towers"), Poseidon (New York, NY), 1988.

London, Volume One: Bloodline, Fantaco (Albany, NY), 1993.

1993–1994 *Saint Sinner,* Marvel Comics (New York, NY).

Clive Barker's A-Z of Horror, compiled by Stephen Jones, HarperPrism (New York, NY), 1997.

Books of Blood (contains volumes 1-6), Stealth Press (Lancaster, PA), 2001.

Tapping the Vein, Checker Book Co. (Centerville, OH), 2002.

NOVELS

The Damnation Game, Weidenfeld & Nicolson (London, England), 1985, Putnam (New York, NY), 1987.

Weaveworld, Poseidon (New York, NY), 1987, illustrated by the author, Collins (London, England), 1987.

The Great and Secret Show: The First Book of the Art, Harper (New York, NY), 1989.

Imajica, HarperCollins (New York, NY), 1991, published in two volumes as *Imajica I: The Fifth Dominion* and *Imajica II: The Reconciliation,* Harper (New York, NY), 1995, published in one volume with new illustrations, 2002.

The Thief of Always: A Fable, illustrated by Clive Barber, HarperCollins (New York, NY), 1992.

Everville: The Second Book of the Art (sequel to *The Great and Secret Show*), HarperCollins (New York, NY), 1994.

Sacrament, HarperCollins (New York, NY), 1996.

Galilee, HarperCollins (New York, NY), 1998.

Coldheart Canyon: A Hollywood Ghost Story, HarperCollins (New York, NY), 2001.

"ABARAT QUARTET"; FOR CHILDREN; SELF-ILLUSTRATED

Abarat, HarperCollins (New York, NY), 2002.

Days of Magic, Nights of War, Joanna Cotler Books (New York, NY), 2004.

SCREENPLAYS

(With James Caplin) *Underworld,* Limehouse Pictures, 1985.

Rawhead Rex (adapted from his short story of the same title), Empire, 1986.

(And director) *Hellraiser* (adapted from his novella *The Hellbound Heart*), New World, 1987.

(And director) *Nightbreed* (adapted from his novella *Cabal*), Twentieth Century-Fox, 1990.

(And director and producer) *Lord of Illusions* (adapted from his short story "The Last Illusion"), United Artists, 1995.

(With Bernard Rose) *The Thief of Always* (adapted from his novel of the same title), Universal Pictures, 1998.

(And producer) *Saint Sinner,* Sci Fi Channel, 2002.

OTHER

(Author of introduction) Ramsey Campbell, *Scared Stiff: Tales of Sex and Death,* Scream/Press (Santa Cruz, CA), 1987.

(Author of introduction) *Night Visions Four* (anthology), Dark Harvest (Arlington Heights, IL), 1987.

(Author of introduction) *Taboo,* edited by Stephen R. Bissette, SpiderBaby Grafix and Publications (Wilmington, VT), 1988.

Theatre Games, Heinemann (London, England), 1988.

(Illustrator) Fred Burke, *Clive Barker: Illustrator,* edited by Steve Niles, Arcane/ Eclipse (Forestville, CA), 1990.

Clive Barker's Nightbreed: The Making of the Film, Fontana (London, England), 1990.

(Author of introduction) *H.R. Giger's Necronomicon,* Morpheus International (Beverly Hills, CA), 1991.

(Author of introduction) Stephen King, *Salem's Lot* ("Stephen King Collectors Editions"), New American Library/Dutton (New York, NY), 1991.

Clive Barker's Shadows in Eden (autobiography), edited by Stephen Jones, Underwood-Miller (San Francisco, CA), 1991.

Pandemonium: The World of Clive Barker (autobiography), Eclipse (Forestville, CA), 1991.

(Illustrator) Fred Burke, *Illustrator II: The Art of Clive Barker,* edited by Amacker Bullwinkle, Eclipse (Forestville, CA), 1993.

Incarnations: Three Plays, HarperPrism (New York, NY), 1995.

Forms of Heaven: Three Plays, HarperPrism (New York, NY), 1996.

(Author of introduction) *Dark Dreamers,* photographs by Beth Gwinn, commentary by Stanley Wiater, Cemetery Dance (Abingdon, MD), 2001.

(Editor, with others) *Clive Barker's Hellraiser: Collected Best II,* Checker (Centerville, NY), 2003.

Author of plays, including *Frankenstein in Love, The History of the Devil, Subtle Bodies,* and *The Secret Life of Cartoons.* Work represented in anthologies, including *Cutting Edge* and *I Shudder at Your Touch: Twenty-two Tales of Sex and Horror.* Has written stories for comic books, including *Razorline* for Marvel Comics. Also co-creator, with Todd McFarlane, of *Tortured Souls,* a serial novella combined with action figures, and film, produced by Universal. Contributor to periodicals, including *American Film* and *Omni.*

ADAPTATIONS: Barker's short story "The Forbidden" was adapted as the film *Candyman* in 1992; the short stories "In the Hills, the Cities" and "Son of Celluloid" were adapted for the Organic Theater in 1994. Film rights to Barker's "Arabat Quartet" novel series were purchased by the Walt Disney Company. A television series is being adapted from *Lord of Illusions.*

WORK IN PROGRESS: Further novels in the "Arabat Quartet"; book three in the "Book of the Art" trilogy; a sequel to *Galilee.*

SIDELIGHTS: "Renaissance man" is a tag often associated with Clive Barker, and for good reason. Since exploding into the publishing scene in the mid-1980s with six volumes of horror short stories known as the "Books of Blood," Barker steadily expanded his reach to the point where he became the driving force behind a creative empire. He has written short stories, novellas, novels, plays, and screenplays. He has directed, produced, and acted in films and plays. His drawings and paintings have appeared in books, comic books, art galleries, and museums. Others have adapted his work for the stage, the screen, for comic books, and for audiobooks. Still others have been inspired by his worlds and characters to create new films and comic books, carrying his creations even farther.

Due to the success of the six volumes of his "Books of Blood" series in both Great Britain and the United States, Barker has been hailed for his combination of unprecedented ugliness and literary touch. "I have seen the future of the horror genre, and his name is Clive Barker," Stephen King was quoted as saying in *Publishers Weekly* following the publication of one of the first books in the series. "What Barker does makes the rest of us look like we've been asleep for 10 years." Fellow Briton Ramsey Campbell offered a similar view as quoted in *Books and Bookmen,* terming Barker "the first true voice of the next generation of horror writers." Barker continues to make publishing history with his "Abarat Quartet," targeted for young adults as a competitor to J.K. Rowling's "Harry Potter" books and bankrolled to the tune of $8 million by the Walt Disney Studio for film, multimedia, and theme park rights.

Journalists who meet Barker observe that despite his nightmarish imagination, he seems very well adjusted: smiling, personable, and boyishly enthusiastic. In fact, Barker did not always intend to write horrific short stories. Born in Liverpool, England, in 1952, not far from the Penny Lane made famous by those other famous Liverpudlians, the Beatles, Barker came of age in an England still struggling to find its place in the postwar world. His father was a dock worker and his mother worked as a nurse. He developed a taste for the macabre and for fantastic literature as a youth, enjoying the works of authors Herman Melville, Ray Bradbury, C.S. Lewis, and Kenneth Grahame, among others. Speaking with Mikal Gilmore in *Rolling Stone,* Barker recalled, "I never read much material that didn't have some element of the extraordinary or the fantastic in it. Of course my parents were not really in sympathy with the surreal. I suppose that made it into a vice, which wasn't altogether a bad thing." Art also captured his attention as a youth. Increasingly he came to think of himself as an imaginer. "The whole point is to make your imagination work in the most potent way possible," Barker told S.C. Ringgenberg in an interview for *Comics Journal*. "Pretty early in my life I realized that I could do that and enjoy doing that, that it gave me, I suppose, a sense of power to do it. It was recognized by my parents, although not necessarily liked by them."

Barker's parents would have liked him to focus more on academics than fantasy. As the author told Ringgenberg, although his parents valued creativity, "they [came] from a generation where art was thought of as being practically indulgent, and in their hearts they probably still do." After studying English and philosophy at college in Liverpool, Barker moved to London, where he worked in the theater, did illustrations, and sometimes lived on welfare. As he told Ringgenberg, "Right from [the] start I was unemployed—*gainfully* unemployed, in the sense that I was writing plays and painting pictures." The theatre-going public soon saw the curtain go up on such Barker-penned fantasy plays as *The History of the Devil* and *Frankenstein in Love.* "The pieces were . . . very often surreal," Barker told Ringgenberg, "very often dark, and, I like to think, stimulating and a little controversial, which never hurts. By the age of 30 it was pretty apparent I wasn't going to make any money from this stuff." At this point, he decided to concentrate on the short fiction he had begun writing, but which only friends had seen.

After reading *Dark Forces,* a 1980 anthology edited by Stephen King's agent, Kirby McCauley, Barker perceived an audience for a new, more audacious kind of horror writing, and he quickly penned the first three volumes in the "Books of Blood" series. Initially Barker's fiction was only published in England, but his work caused such a stir among fantasy fans in North America that U.S. publishers soon produced their own editions. "I was completely unprepared for the fact that these things would find such favor," Barker told Ringgenberg. "I always thought that the work that I did was too off the beaten track really to find wide popular appeal. I remain astonished by that." Barker's "Books of Blood" series ultimately stretched to six volumes published between 1984 and 1986, firmly establishing him on both sides of the Atlantic as a major force in the new wave of horror writers.

Barker's stories, reviewers warn, are relentlessly graphic. Many consider such lack of restraint to be his trademark and his chief innovation. The author "never averts his gaze, no matter how gruesome the scene," explained Beth Levine in *Publishers Weekly.* "He fol-

lows every story through to its logical end, never flinching from detail. The result is mesmerizing, disturbing and elating, all at once." The story "In the Hills, the Cities" depicts an ancient quarrel between a pair of Yugoslavian towns: the townspeople abjure their individuality and form themselves into two lumbering giants who do battle. The title character of "Rawhead Rex," a flesh-eating monster, lingers indulgently over his evening meal, a freshly killed child, and especially enjoys the kidneys. As Mikal Gilmore wrote in *Rolling Stone,* "Barker's willingness to enter the sensibilities of his characters—to make their terrible desires comprehensible, even sympathetic—raises questions about both his work and modern horror in general. Namely, does it merely appeal to the meanness of the modern spirit?"

Barker and his admirers would respond that tales of terror can be valid as works of art and as social commentary. "I feel that horror literature is touching upon the big issues time and time again," the author told *Omni:* "death and life after death, sex after death, insanity, loneliness, anxiety. Horror writers are addressing the deepest concerns of the human condition." In remarks quoted in *Publishers Weekly* he rejected the common view of horror fiction as a defender of social and cultural norms, in which the monster is an outsider who is reassuringly destroyed. "I don't believe that's true of the world," he said. "We can't destroy the monster because the monster is us." Yet, as he explained to Richard Harrington of the *Washington Post,* these social and cultural norms try to block this realization. "We're attracted and repulsed, but our culture doesn't allow us to say, 'I like these guys; they are a part of me.' We define our humanity because we are not monsters—and that's a lie, a complete lie." The role of the horror writer, in Barker's view, is to expose this lie.

As Michael Morrison suggested in *Fantasy Review,* Barker's stories become a strongly worded commentary on human nature. In "Jaqueline Ess: Her Will and Testament," an embittered, suicidal woman discovers that psychokinetic powers can liberate her from the tyranny of men but not from her own hatred of life. In "The Skins of the Fathers," the monsters who approach a small town to reclaim their half-human child seem less repugnant than the cold, tough Americans who oppose them. Writers such as Barker, said Kim Newman in *New Statesman,* "raise the possibility that horror fiction is the most apt form for dealing with the subject of life in the late 20th century."

While he relishes horror stories, Barker has not confined himself to a single genre. By broadening his approach to handling the themes of his work, he has proven that for him there is more than gore. He told *Books and Bookmen* that he believes his work belongs to a broader category—"imaginative fiction"—which is a valid part of the larger literary tradition. "Mainstream" writers, Barker contended, readily use the techniques of imaginative fiction, though they may not admit it. Along with these techniques, Barker's works also show a deep interest in and respect for the power of the human imagination. As he told Robert W. Welkos in the *Los Angeles Times,* "Something that profoundly touches the imagination carries more weight in your present mental geography than things that actually happen to you." This power of imagination is a key element of Barker's novels.

Barker's first novel, *The Damnation Game,* "a tour-de-force of gruesome supernatural horror" in the words of Chris Morgan of *Fantasy Review,* made the *New York Times* best-seller list within a week of its publication in 1987. The story is one of betrayal and vengeance involving two mythic figures, the Thief and the Cardplayer. Just after World War II in war-torn Warsaw, Poland, the Thief betrays the Cardplayer. Forty years later the Thief has become Joseph Whitehead, the wealthy head of a London drug company. The centuries-old Cardplayer, also known as Mamoulian, tracks down his nemesis and looks to exact revenge on Whitehead as payment for his betrayal.

As in his short stories, in *The Damnation Game* Barker combines unflinching horror with a literary sensibility. Morgan noted that "the most startling features of his work are the fact that he allows no depth of nastiness, cruelty or perversion to go unplumbed and the beautifully figurative and allusive nature of his prose style." Colin Greenland drew a similar conclusion, commenting in *British Book News* that "Barker is generous with the gore and grue . . . , but he is also a highly literate fantasist, and makes powerful use of the subtleties and ambiguities inherent in the situation." Barker also draws on his experience in a variety of creative forms. "The author's experience with short stories, and also with stage and film plays," noted Greenland, "shows strongly in his organization of the action by tableaux." This is not always used to the best effect, suggested Greenland. "At times he is apt to load more emotional or symbolic weight onto a scene than its position in the plot will easily bear, but he never loses his grip on the reader's nerve-ends."

Some reviewers found that Barker's first novel lacked the depth required of true literature. In his review of *Damnation Game, New York Times Book Review* con-

tributor Alan Caruba found that Barker's "unremitting devotion to the most sickening imagery" overwhelms any deeper meaning the story might have. The critic added, "The absence of meaning in all this is the flaw that runs through what might have been an allegory of evil, an extended commentary on the various addictions that entrap people." Laurence Coven conceded in the *Washington Post Book World* that Barker's "overkill deprives us of a sense of anticipation, and . . . suspense." Yet, he also observed, "Time after time Barker makes us shudder in revulsion. In pure descriptive power there is no one writing horror fiction now who can match him. And to his credit, Barker does not write in a social vacuum. His terrors arise, at least in part, from a profound sadness and misery he perceives in the human condition."

In his 1987 novel *Weaveworld,* Barker pushes his writing even farther beyond the bounds of horror toward the fantasy genre, to what the author himself calls "the fantastique." "The fantastique," he explained to Richard Harrington in the *Washington Post,* "at its heart is a genre, or a collection of genres, which grow because of the ambiguities, because they're not about fixed moral codes; they're about shifting moral codes." *Weaveworld* is still punctuated by Barker's characteristically graphic writing, but, as Colin Greenland related in the *Times Literary Supplement,* the book "is almost classically a romance, a heraldic adventure in which figures possessed by principles, of love or greed or despair, pursue one another headlong with spells or pistols through a vague locality full of numinous things." *Weaveworld* is the story of a magic carpet, but one unlike those of the Arabian Nights which transport people from one place to another. This magic carpet contains within its weave a mystical realm created by the last of a race of magicians as a means to escape from sinister intruders, both mortal and supernatural.

In creating his story of this magical-carpet world and its contact with our own world, Barker follows the example of the weaver, bringing together many different threads to create a complex, intertwined whole. He also projects the dreamy, imaginative state of anyone who, in contemplating the complex design of a well-made rug, gets lost in its weave. As Phil Normand put it in the *Bloomsbury Review, Weaveworld* "is a tapestry of themes and characters. Beyond the chase-and-capture plot," he added, "we are called to rejoice in the strength of dream. This is a book of fantasy *about* fantasy, the struggle for man's dominion over the ungovernable casts of the imagination. It is about finding a place as close as breath where all things have a special purpose and meaning." Reviewer John Calvin Batchelor recognized the fantasy elements of Barker's novel, but found that the author's fantasy resonates into contemporary times. "Barker reveals his prodigious talent for erecting make-believe worlds in the midst of [British Prime Minister Margaret] Thatcher's tumbledown kingdom of Windsorian privilege and secretly policed ghettos," Batchelor wrote in the *New York Times Book Review.* "Reaching into its degraded and strangely fertile streets, he creates a fantastic romance of magic and promise that is at once popular fiction and utopian conjuring."

The Great and Secret Show and *Everville* are the first two installments in Barker's "Book of the Art" trilogy. The Art is a magical power that gives those who wield it control in our world and the dimensions beyond. As with his other novels, Barker finds dramatic tension and a spotlighted canvas on which to compose his thematic concerns in bringing together the mundane and the supernatural. In *The Great and Secret Show,* Randolf Jaffe—a postman in the dead-letter office at the Omaha post office—discovers the existence of a secret dream-sea that lies beyond the world as we know it. On further investigation, he learns of the Art and sets out to master it. In the course of his quest, Jaffe enlists the help of scientist Richard Fletcher, but the partnership eventually devolves into a rivalry over who will be the first to possess the Art. Ken Tucker, in a *New York Times Book Review* piece, called *The Great and Secret Show* "a cross between 'Gravity's Rainbow' and J.R.R. Tolkien's 'Lord of the Rings,' allusive and mythic, complex and entertaining."

While Tucker recognized that Barker set high goals for the novel, the reviewer found that the author had come up short. "From 'The Great and Secret Show,' it is clear that Mr. Barker's intention is to force the horror genre to encompass a kind of dread, and existential despair, that it hasn't noticeably evinced until now," Tucker commented. "This is a tall order, one that this novel, which is skillful and funny but ultimately overwrought, doesn't quite accomplish." *Washington Post* reviewer David Foster Wallace also noted Barker's execution. He contended, "Barker demands that the reader take him seriously but declines to do the artistic work necessary to make his story believable or even coherent."

For reviewer Barry Schechter, however, *The Great and Secret Show* is worthy of praise, both for its author's craft and its thematic concerns. In a *Chicago Tribune* piece, Schechter observed that Barker "proves himself an expert tactician, smoothly deploying over 40 characters and any number of careening, converging plots. He renders it all in a precise, ironic, measured style that

avoids both campy humor and pretentious solemnity." He added, "A Britisher, Barker seems fascinated by the contrast between the American Dream and the atrophying American imagination: Even his self-created gods are hemmed in by lack of imagination and the trashy Hollywood images cluttering their minds." In conclusion, Schechter commented, "At a time of literary minimalism, read-my-lips political discourse and a moribund pop culture, 'The Great and Secret Show' is a maelstrom of fresh air."

Everville: The Second Book of the Art begins in 1848 with a party of pioneers setting out from Missouri to travel the Oregon Trail to the Northwest Territory. These pioneers face all of the hardships that have made their historical counterparts part of American legend. Yet, this is the work of Clive Barker: An otherworldly beast enters the mix and helps the party to found a new town on a border, not between territories, but between our world and the dream-sea introduced in *The Great and Secret Show.* The clock then moves forward to present-day Oregon, where a rift is opening between the two worlds and with consequences that threaten to be disastrous. The story that results, according to Elizabeth Hand in the *Washington Post Book World,* is "less a classic struggle between Good and Evil than it is a race to see who will put his (or her, or its) finger in the dike, and who will help the walls come tumbling down and loose the awful" creatures from the other world upon us.

As with many sequels, *Everville* faces the challenge of connecting with its predecessor and yet still having enough of its own elements to stand alone. Hand found that the novel's fast-paced action and the many characters and themes made it dependent on its previous volume. "Barker's strength is not really in his plotting," she observed. "*Everville* rolls along like an out-of-control juggernaut, and a reader who hasn't been primed by reading *The Great and Secret Show* should prepare to hang on for dear life or risk being crushed." Yet, in the opinion of Bruce Allen in the *New York Times Book Review,* this effort on the part of readers is well rewarded. "Readers who'll hang on for the wild ride throughout this exhilarating trilogy-in-progress may be surprised by the depths and heights thus encountered," he suggested. "Barker is much more than a genre writer, and his extravagantly unconventional inventions are ingenious refractions of our common quest to experience and understand the mysterious world around us and the mysteries within ourselves."

In novels such as *Imajica, Sacrament,* and *Galilee,* as well as in the children's horror story *The Thief of Always,* Barker continues to explore his vision of the fantastique that arises where the real and imagined collide, and how this vision sheds light on the human condition. A failed murder inspired by jealousy becomes entwined with a failed attempt to unite our world with a supernatural otherworld in *Imajica*. This 1991 dark fantasy is "rich in plot twists, byzantine intrigues and hidden secrets," noted Stefan Dziemianowicz in the *Washington Post Book World*. "*Imajica* is a Chinese puzzle box constructed on a universal scale. Not only has Barker imagined a commonplace world in which wonders lurk beneath the most banal surfaces, he has also taken the issues of our time—AIDS, the intransigence of sexual and racial politics, censorship, political repression, class struggle—and turned them into the stuff of myth."

Sacrament is the tale of Will Rabjohns, a wildlife photographer who is attacked and left for dead by a polar bear in northern Canada. In a coma, Rabjohns relives pivotal moments from his childhood. After he returns to consciousness and recovers, he travels to San Francisco and his native England to reconcile some personal metaphysical issues. A contributor to *Kirkus Reviews* characterized the novel variously as "suspenseful, intellectually exciting, wildly melodramatic, turgid, and bombastic." The reviewer added, "Barker's novel is charged—in its complex development and surprising resolution—with very real, very human emotion. A weirdly absorbing and entertaining tale that offers more disturbing delights from one of our most inventive and risk-taking writers."

Barker's novel *Galilee* is a saga that pits two families in a centuries-old struggle. A reviewer for *Publishers Weekly* reported that "the novel's scale is smaller than that of previous Barker efforts—missing are the titanic battles of form vs. chaos, good vs. evil, the riot of wonders and terrors. But it's less cluttered, too, despite abundant inspiration and invention." A *Kirkus Reviews* writer termed *Galilee* "a black comedy of miscegenation and its discontents that has to be a sendup of both the Harlequin romance and the American Southern Gothic novel."

In 2001 Barker released his first novel in three years, *Coldheart Canyon*, a Hollywood Babylon fantasy-chiller. The story follows movie star Todd Pickett, a character who "bears the strongest resemblance to Tom Cruise that is legally possible," as *New York Times* reviewer Janet Maslin remarked. Sadly for Todd, his sex appeal is fading as he ages, so on the advice of a studio head, he opts for plastic surgery. Of course, complications ensue: "Barker wouldn't have a story if the chemical peel didn't go horribly awry," Maslin noted. Seek-

ing to hide his deformities, Todd takes refuge in an old Los Angeles mansion that was once the site of wild parties and is now haunted by the ghosts of Hollywood past. Todd encounters the house's mistress, Katya Lupi, who must be at least one hundred years old yet appears as youthful and nubile as she did in her days as a silent-screen vamp. As Katya turns her seductive powers toward Todd, the book reveals the mansion as a netherworld that features sadistic sex between all manner of creatures, both real and imagined.

Coldheart Canyon runs an epic-length 600 pages, surprising even its author, who revealed to *Clive Barker Revelations* online interviewers Phil and Sarah Stokes that the original concept "was really going to be a very simple book about a rather narcissistic actor in Hollywood who encounters some ghosts . . . and as I got into it I realised these ghosts are sort of really interesting, and I want to write about them because they represent old Hollywood and here I have a chance not only to talk about new Hollywood but also to talk about old Hollywood and to contrast their methodologies."

Barker's depiction of Tinseltown scandal and gothic horror caught the eye of reviewers, including Maslin, who said *Coldheart Canyon* "unfolds with genuine momentum, the vigorous style of a fully engaged storyteller." *USA Today* contributor Robert Allen Papinchak likewise enjoyed the book, saying that "lush, musky prose and crisp, staccato dialogue propel the ghost story as assuredly as the perfumed breezes of the Santa Ana winds that open and close this endlessly entertaining novel."

In 2001 Barker also announced that he was beginning work on a novel series suitable for younger readers, the series to be called the "Abarat Quartet." Film rights to the still-unwritten books were promptly bought by family-friendly Walt Disney Company. Barker voiced high expectations for this series; as he told Phil and Sarah Stokes, "Abarat" "is bigger than we thought it was going to be. . . . Originally I thought it was going to be a sort of Narnia size, now it turns out to be more sort of a Harry Potter size!" Working from a plethora of self-painted illustrations of the characters—a technique the author often employs—Barker toyed with the idea of the fictional place called Abarat for many years. "It began with a painting," noted Jeff Jensen in *Entertainment Weekly*. "A portrait of a cranky old man in a canary suit, six squished hats stacked atop his head." For Barker, this portrait began his journey into the world of Abarat. For seven years Barker continued to paint the characters forming in his imagination, pictures that are both "whimsical and weird," according to Jensen, "Cirque du Soleil meets circus freak show." According to Jensen, the resulting first novel of the quartet is a "blend of *Alice in Wonderland* and *The Lion, the Witch, and the Wardrobe.*"

Indeed, Barker has long wanted to concoct a children's epic that would be a tip of the hat to C.S. Lewis and his "Chronicles of Narnia," but his publishers initially resisted the idea. Finally he got his chance at such a large-scale children's book, in the self-illustrated *Abarat* fashioning a tale of Candy Quackenbush, a heroine partly modeled after Barker's adopted daughter, Nicole. Candy is fed up with her quiet life in Chickentown, Minnesota, and longs for adventures. Cutting class one day and walking in the fields near town, she gets her wish. Diving into a mysterious sea that suddenly appears, she is transported to the magical world of Abarat with its twenty-five islands, one for every hour of the day, plus an extra one called Time outside of Time. As she travels from island to island in the bizarre archipelago, Candy is thrust into a battle for power between Christopher Carrion, the Lord of Midnight, and his arch-rival, Rojo Pixler of Commexo City. Slowly Candy begins to understand that her journey to Abarat is not merely some incredible accident, but actually her destiny. Included in the first "Abarat" novel are over one hundred of Barker's "quirky, grotesque, and campy" illustrations, as *Booklist*'s Sally Estes described the artwork.

Abarat presents a "beautiful and frightening world," according to Alison Ching in *School Library Journal,* who prophesied that the quartet "is sure to be a rollicking, epic ride." Estes had praise for the novel, calling it a "multilayered adventure story" reminiscent of "Oz, Wonderland, and Narnia . . . [as well as] Aldous Huxley's *Brave New World.*" A critic for *Kirkus Reviews* similarly found *Abarat* "an intriguing creation deserving of comparison to Oz." However, the same reviewer found a "peculiar lifelessness to all this imaginative fecundity." A contributor for *Publishers Weekly* also felt that Barker's "imagination runs wild as he conjures up striking imagery." For this critic, the novel is "unwieldy," but also full of "thrills and chills." The second installment of the quartet, *Days of Magic, Nights of War,* continues Candy's adventures as Carrion and Pixler's efforts to launch all-out war against each other help the young heroine learn her purpose in Barker's amazing fantasy world.

In addition to his printed works, Barker has continued to display a broad range of artistic talents. Most visible to the public eye have been the movies for which Barker has served as screenwriter, director, or executive producer. Barker's *Hellraiser* and *Candyman* have attracted a cult following and have taken on a life of their own. With his 1995 *Lord of Illusions* he brought his own short story, "The Last Illusion," to the screen. In 1999 he broke into a more serious mode by producing the critically acclaimed *Gods and Monsters,* which examines the complex personal life of aging homosexual film director James Whale, who made the 1930s horror classic *Frankenstein.*

In his movies, his writings, and his other creations, Barker has been credited with pushing the horror genre to new levels of gory violence. Yet, as he expanded his creative powers and as his audience has grown, he has been able to compose a broader understanding of horror. Barker suggested to Mikal Gilmore in *Rolling Stone* that an interest in horror can be natural and healthy. "Within the circle of your skull you have an immense imaginative freedom," he told Gilmore. "For Christ's sake, use it to understand your response to death . . . eroticism . . . all the things that come to haunt you and attract you and repulse you in your dreams. Because as soon as you relinquish control and lay your head down on the pillow, those things are going to come anyway." Reflecting the opinion of many critics, *Guardian* contributor China Mieville noted: "Barker is one of the few writers who has altered an entire field: more than anyone since [H. P.] Lovecraft, he has changed the shape, the corporeality of horror."

BIOGRAPHICAL AND CRITICAL SOURCES:

BOOKS

Badley, Linda, *Writing Horror and the Body: The Fiction of Stephen King, Clive Barker, and Anne Rice,* Greenwood Press (Westport, CT), 1996.

Barbieri, Suzanne J., *Clive Barker: Mythmaker for the Millennium,* British Fantasy Society (Stockport, Lancashire, England), 1994.

Bestsellers '90, issue 3, Thomson Gale (Detroit, MI), 1990.

Contemporary Literary Criticism, Volume 52, Thomson Gale (Detroit, MI), 1989.

Hoppenstand, Gary, editor, *Clive Barker's Short Stories: Imagination as Metaphor in the Books of Blood and Other Works,* McFarland (Jefferson, NC), 1994.

Jones, Stephen, editor, *Clive Barker's Shadows in Eden* (bibliography), Underwood-Miller (Lancaster, PA), 1991.

McCauley, Kirby, editor, *Dark Forces: New Stories of Suspense and Supernatural Horror,* Bantam (New York, NY), 1980.

St. James Encyclopedia of Popular Culture, St. James Press (Detroit, MI), 2000.

St. James Guide to Horror, Ghost, and Gothic Writers, St. James Press (Detroit, MI), 1998.

PERIODICALS

Advocate, September 28, 1999, review of *The Essential Clive Barker,* p. 98.

American Theatre, May-June, 1993, p. 6.

Billboard, July 21, 2001, Christa Titus, "Unlikely Couple Weaving Musical Magic into Barker's Art," p. 78.

Bloomsbury Review, September-October, 1987, Phil Normand, review of *Weaveworld,* p. 21.

Booklist, October 15, 1992, p. 379; February 1, 1994, p. 989; September 15, 1994, p. 83; June 1, 1996, p. 1628; November 15, 1999, review of *The Essential Clive Barker,* p. 608; August, 2001, Ray Olson, review of *Coldheart Canyon,* p. 2049; September 1, 2002, Sally Estes, review of *Abarat,* p. 120; June 1, 2003, Ray Olson, review of *Clive Barker's Hellraiser: Collected Best II,* p. 1724.

Books and Bookmen, July, 1985; September, 1987.

Bookwatch, April, 1999, review of *The History of the Devil* (audio version), p. 10.

British Book News, December, 1985, Colin Greenland, review of *The Damnation Game,* p. 742.

Chicago Tribune, September 15, 1987; February 5, 1990, section 5, p. 3; February 19, 1990, section 5, p. 3; December 29, 1992, section 5, p. 3; May 23, 1993, section 13, p. 22; August 25, 1995, p. 7H.

Comics Journal, September, 1994, S.C. Ringgenberg, "A Man for All Seasons: Clive Barker Interview."

Detroit Free Press, December 23, 1988.

Entertainment Weekly, September 25, 1992, p. 43; September 15, 1995, p. 87; October 4, 2002, Jeff Jensen, review of *Abarat,* p. 21.

Fantasy Review, February, 1985; June, 1985, p. 15; August, 1985; September, 1985, p. 16; October, 1986, p. 19; April, 1987, Chris Morgan, review of *The Damnation Game,* p. 32.

Guardian, October 17, 1986; October 19, 2002, China Mieville, review of *Abarat.*

Journal of Popular Culture, winter, 1993, p. 35.

Kirkus Reviews, August 1, 1987, p. 1085; May 15, 1996, review of *Sacrament;* May 11, 1998, review of *Galilee;* October 15, 1999, review of *The Essential Clive Barker,* p. 1603; August 1, 2001, review of *Coldheart Canyon,* p. 1043; September 1, 2002, review of *Abarat,* p. 1303.

Kliatt, November, 2002, Michele Winship, review of *Abarat,* p. 6.

Library Journal, January, 1990, p. 145; December, 1991; February, 1993; July, 1996, p. 152; November 1, 1999, review of *The Essential Clive Barker,* p. 80; August, 2001, Nancy McNicol, review of *Coldheart Canyon,* p. 156; February 1, 2002, Michael Rogers, review of *Books of Blood,* p. 138.

Locus, December, 1992, p. 17; January, 1993, p. 19; November, 1994, p. 17.

Los Angeles Magazine, October, 2002, "Buzz Cuts," p. 26.

Los Angeles Times, February 19, 1990, p. F4; October 11, 1992, p. CAL3; August 22, 1995, p. F1; August 25, 1995, p. F10.

Los Angeles Times Book Review, August 10, 1986; June 14, 1987; October 11, 1992, p. 3.

Magazine of Fantasy and Science Fiction, August, 1987; May, 1990, p. 44; April, 1993, p. 26; July, 1999, review of *Galilee,* p. 37.

New Statesman, July 18, 1986, p. 29; October 5, 1990, p. 30; December 7, 1990, p. 34; March 22, 1996, p. 38.

New Theater Quarterly, February, 1990, p. 5.

New York, May 26, 1986.

New York Times, September 20, 1987; February 17, 1990, p. A19; August 25, 1995, p. C6; October 25, 2001, Janet Maslin, "Sex with Dead Film Stars Means Breakfast for One"; February 1, 2002, Michael Rogers, review of *Books of Blood,* p. 138.

New York Times Book Review, September 21, 1986, p. 26; February 15, 1987, p. 20; June 21, 1987, p. 22; November 22, 1987, p. 32; December 18, 1988; February 11, 1990, Ken Tucker, review of *The Great and Secret Show,* p. 11; November 20, 1994, Bruce Allen, review of *Everville,* p. 18.

Notes on Contemporary Literature, November, 1994, p. 7.

Observer (London, England), December 27, 1987, p. 17; December 17, 1989, p. 46; February 14, 1993, p. 59.

Omni, October, 1986.

Orlando Business Journal, August 24, 2001, Alan Byrd, "Clive Barker and Disney: Now There's an E-Ticket Ride," p. 3.

People, June 15, 1987; September 18, 1995, p. 27; November 5, 2001, Bernard Welt, review of *Coldheart Canyon,* p. 51.

Publishers Weekly, December 13, 1985; July 4, 1986; December 22, 1989, p. 44; September 28, 1992; September 12, 1994, p. 78; May 27, 1996, p. 63; July 1, 1996, p. 30; May 11, 1998, p. 49; April 12, 1999, review of *The History of the Devil* (audio version), p. 32; October 11, 1999, review of *The*

Essential Clive Barker, p. 57; March 26, 2001, review of *Dark Dreamers,* p. 68; July 23, 2001, review of *Coldheart Canyon,* p. 55; February 4, 2002, review of *The Thief of Always,* p. 78; February 11, 2002, review of *Books of Blood,* p. 167; June 24, 2002, review of *Abarat,* p. 58; August 11, 2003, review of *Clive Barker's Hellraiser: Collected Best II,* p. 259.

Rolling Stone, February 11, 1988.

School Library Journal, October, 2002, Alison Ching, review of *Abarat,* pp. 154-155.

Time, March 19, 1990, p. 84.

Times (London, England), October 17, 1986.

Times Literary Supplement, February 12, 1988, Colin Greenland, review of *Weaveworld,* p. 172.

Tribune Books (Chicago, IL), September 14, 1986; April 26, 1987.

USA Today, August 25, 1995, p. D12.

USA Weekend, October 9-11, 1987; January 26, 1990, p. 8; June 24, 1994, p. 4.

Variety, August 21, 1995, p. 67.

Video, April, 1988.

Village Voice, December 2, 1986, p. 63.

Washington Post, September 30, 1987; November 17, 1988; February 19, 1990, David Foster Wallace, review of *The Great and Secret Show,* p. D3; September 11, 1992, p. B1.

Washington Post Book World, August 24, 1986, p. 6; June 28, 1987, p. 10; September 27, 1987; October 27, 1991, p. 8; February 28, 1993, p. 6; December 18, 1994, Elizabeth Hand, review of *Everville,* p. 5.

ONLINE

Clive Barker Official Web site, http://www.clivebarker. com/ (June 4, 2003).

Clive Barker Revelations, http://www.clivebarker.dial. pipex.com/ (April 7, 2004), Phil Stokes and Sarah Stokes, "Open Roads. . . . What Price Wonderland?"

January Magazine, http://www.januarymagazine.com/ (June 4, 2003), Linda Richards, "Clive Barker Biography."

USA Today, http://www.usatoday.com/ (October 26, 2001), Robert Allen Papinchak, "Clive Barker Fills 'Canyon' with Secrets, Dead Souls."

*   *   *

BARNES, Julian 1946-
(Julian Patrick Barnes, Dan Kavanagh, Edward Pygge)

PERSONAL: Born January 19, 1946, in Leicester, England; son of Albert Leonard (a French teacher) and Kaye (a French teacher) Barnes; married Pat Kavanagh (a literary agent), 1979. *Education:* Magdalen College, Oxford, B.A. (with honors), 1968.

ADDRESSES: Agent—Peters, Fraser, and Dunlop Ltd., Drury House, 34-43 Russell St., London WC2B 5HA, England.

CAREER: Freelance writer, 1972—. Lexicographer for *Oxford English Dictionary Supplement,* Oxford, England, 1969-72; *New Statesman,* London, England, assistant literary editor, 1977-78, television critic, 1977-81; *Sunday Times,* London, deputy literary editor, 1979-81; *Observer,* London, television critic, 1982-86; London correspondent for *New Yorker* magazine, 1990-94.

AWARDS, HONORS: Somerset Maugham Prize, 1980, for *Metroland;* Booker Prize nomination, 1984, Geoffrey Faber Memorial Prize, and Prix Medicis, all for *Flaubert's Parrot;* American Academy and Institute of Arts and Letters award, 1986, for work of distinction; Prix Gutembourg, 1987; Premio Grinzane Carour, 1988; Prix Femina for *Talking It Over,* 1992; Shakespeare Prize (Hamburg), 1993; Officier de l'Ordre des Arts et des Lettres; shortlisted for Booker Prize, 1998, for *England, England.*

WRITINGS:

NOVELS

Metroland, St. Martin's Press (New York, NY), 1980.

Before She Met Me, Jonathan Cape (London, England), 1982, McGraw-Hill (New York, NY), 1986.

Flaubert's Parrot, Jonathan Cape (London, England), 1984, Knopf (New York, NY), 1985.

Staring at the Sun, Jonathan Cape (London, England), 1986, Knopf (New York, NY), 1987.

A History of the World in Ten and One-Half Chapters, Knopf (New York, NY), 1989.

Talking It Over, Knopf (New York, NY), 1991.

The Porcupine, Knopf (New York, NY), 1992.

Letters from London, Vintage (New York, NY), 1995.

England, England, Knopf (New York, NY), 1999.

Love, etc., Knopf (New York, NY), 2001.

In the Land of Pain, Jonathan Cape (London, England), 2002, Knopf (New York, NY), 2003.

The Lemon Table, Jonathan Cape (London, England), 2004.

Arthur & George, Jonathan Cape (London, England), 2005.

UNDER PSEUDONYM DAN KAVANAGH; CRIME NOVELS

Duffy, Jonathan Cape (London, England), 1980, Pantheon (New York, NY), 1986.

Fiddle City, Jonathan Cape (London, England), 1981, Pantheon (New York, NY), 1986.

Putting the Boot In, Jonathan Cape (London, England), 1985.

Going to the Dogs, Pantheon (New York, NY), 1987.

OTHER

(Contributor) Charles Hobson, *Flaubert & Louise: Letters and Impressions,* Limestone (San Francisco, CA), 1988.

Cross Channel (short stories), Knopf (New York, NY), 1996.

Something to Declare (essays), Picador (London, England), 2002.

The Pedant in the Kitchen (nonfiction), Atlantic Books, 2003.

Contributing editor, under pseudonym Edward Pygge, to *New Review,* c. 1970s. Regular contributor to *Times Literary Supplement* and *New York Review of Books.*

ADAPTATIONS: *Talking It Over* was adapted for film in 1996; *Metroland* was adapted for film in 1999.

SIDELIGHTS: "Julian Barnes," wrote *Dictionary of Literary Biography* contributor Merritt Moseley, "is one of the most celebrated, and one of the most variously rewarding, of Britain's younger novelists." His work, the critic continued, "has been acclaimed by readers as different as Carlos Fuentes and Philip Larkin; reviewers and interviewers sum him up with praise such as Mark Lawson's claim that he 'writes like the teacher of your dreams: jokey, metaphorical across both popular and unpopular culture, epigrammatic.'" In addition to novels such as *Flaubert's Parrot, A History of the World in Ten and One-Half Chapters,* and *The Porcupine,* Barnes has also won a reputation as a writer of innovative detective fiction and an essayist. "Since 1990," Moseley concluded, "he has been the London correspondent of the *New Yorker* magazine, contributing 'Letters from London' every few months on subjects such as the royal family and the quirkier side of British politics." Barnes was also one of many writers—among them Stephen King and Annie Proulx—invited to read from their works at the first-ever New Yorker Festival in 2000.

Barnes published four novels, *Metroland, Before She Met Me,* and the detective novels *Duffy* and *Fiddle City*—both written under the pseudonym Dan Kavanagh—before he completed *Flaubert's Parrot,* his first great success. Critics have acclaimed these early books for their comic sensibility and witty language. *Metroland* tells the story of two young men who "adopt the motto *epater la bourgeoisie,*" explained *New Statesman* contributor Nicholas Shrimpton. "But this grandiose ambition is promptly reduced to the level of 'epats,' a thoroughly English field-sport in which the competitors attempt to shock respectable citizens for bets of sixpence a time." "After this vision of the Decadence in short trousers," the reviewer concluded, "it is hard to take the idea of outrage too solemnly." *Before She Met Me* is the tale of an older man who falls into an obsession about his actress wife's former screen lovers. The book, stated Anthony Thwaite in the *Observer,* presents an "elegantly hardboiled treatment of the nastier levels of obsession, full of controlled jokes when almost everything else has got out of control."

Barnes's detective fiction also looks at times and characters for whom life has gotten out of control. The title character of *Duffy* is a bisexual former policeman who was blackmailed out of his job. "The thrillers are active, louche, violent, thoroughly plotted," stated Moseley. "*Duffy* shows the result of serious research into the seamy world of London's sex industry; in *Duffy,* as in its successors, the crime tends to be theft or fraud rather than murder, though Barnes successfully imbues the book with a feeling of menace." *Fiddle City,* for instance, takes place at London's Heathrow airport and looks at the smuggling of drugs and other illegal items.

It was with the publication of *Flaubert's Parrot,* though, that Barnes scored his greatest success to date. The novel tells of Geoffrey Braithwaite, a retired English doctor, and his obsession with the great French novelist Gustave Flaubert. After his wife's somewhat mysterious death, Braithwaite travels to France in search of trivia concerning Flaubert; his chief aim is to find the stuffed parrot that the writer kept on his desk for inspiration while writing *Un coeur simple,* the story of a peasant woman's devotion to her pet. Barnes "uses Braithwaite's investigations to reflect on the ambiguous truths of biography, the relationship of art and life, the impact of death, the consolations of literature," explained Michael Dirda in the *Washington Post Book World.*

Far from a straightforward narrative, *Flaubert's Parrot* blends fiction, literary criticism, and biography in a manner strongly reminiscent of Vladimir Nabokov's

Pale Fire, according to many critics. *Newsweek* reviewer Gene Lyons called it "too involuted by half for readers accustomed to grazing contentedly in the bestseller list," but recommended it to readers "of immoderate literary passions." Other reviewers stressed that, while a complex and intellectual work, *Flaubert's Parrot* is also "endlessly fascinating and very funny," in the words of London *Times* contributor Annabel Edwards. Dirda concluded that this "delicious potpourri of quotations, legends, facts, fantasies, and interpretations of Flaubert and his work . . . might seem dry, but Barnes' style and Braithwaite's autumnal wisdom make the novel into a kind of Stoic comedy. . . . Anyone who reads *Flaubert's Parrot* will learn a good deal about Flaubert, the making of fiction, and the complex tangle of art and life. And—not least important—have a lot of rather peculiar fun too."

Of Barnes's more recent works, *A History of the World in Ten and One-Half Chapters* and *The Porcupine* are probably best known to U.S. readers. *A History of the World in Ten and One-Half Chapters* "builds on Barnes' reputation as one of Britain's premier postmodernists," stated *Village Voice Literary Supplement* contributor Rob Nixon. "The anti-novel that emerges attempts to double as a novel of ideas—never Brit lit's forté. . . . The principal concern of the novel, which begins with corruption on the Ark and ends in the tedium of heaven (pretty much like life with lots of shopping), is to debunk religion and that most seductive of theologies, History." Barnes conceives of history in the book as a series of different, mostly unrelated events, and the connections individuals invent to link them together. "One of Barnes's characters rather improbably describes her supposed mental condition—imagining that she has survived a nuclear disaster, which, as it turns out, she has—as 'Fabulation. You keep a few true facts and spin a new story about them,'" declared Frank Kermode in the *London Review of Books*. "This is what Barnes himself, in this book, attempts. He fabulates this and that, stitches the fabulations together, and then he and we quite properly call the product a novel." "As a 'historian,'" stated Anthony Quinn in the *New Statesman and Society,* "he is unlikely to dislodge Gibbon or Macaulay; but as satirist and story-teller he has few equals at present."

The Porcupine is a short novel set in a fictional Eastern European country in the post-Communist era. "Stoyo Petkanov, the former president, a cross between [former Rumanian premier] Nicolae Ceaucescu and Bulgaria's Georgi Dimitrov," explained *New York Times Book Review* contributor Robert Stone, "is on trial in the courts of the shakily democratic successor government." His

prosecutor is Peter Solinsky, born into a family prominent under the Communists. Solinsky is shaken by Petkanov's sincere belief in the principles of Communism. Contrasting them with the poverty and lack of respect that the reforms have brought, Solinsky begins to turn away from his new democratic ideals. "In the end," Mary Warner Marien declared in the *Christian Science Monitor,* "nothing is resolved except a clearer vision of the stupendous obstacles facing the former communist country." "Admirers of the earlier, Francophile Julian Barnes may regret that in his latest work . . . the author of *Flaubert's Parrot* and *Talking It Over* has shed his brilliance and dandyism to become a rather somber recorder of his times," stated *London Review of Books* contributor Patrick Parrinder. "The grayness seems inherent in his subject-matter, but it has not infected his acute and spiny prose."

England, England, a darkly satiric novel set in the twenty-first century, incorporates conflicting world situations and their connectedness to greed for power and money. Protagonist and businessman Sir Jack Pitman plots to replace England with a replica island—a Disneyland-type fantasy world—intending to reap huge financial rewards. John Kennedy, writing for the *Antioch Review,* concluded that the book falls short because the characters are underdeveloped. Even so, he commended Barnes's writing style, adding that he "cleverly puts his finger upon a central issue: how do we find our personal uniqueness and salvation when 'memory is identity' and everywhere history and heritage are being manipulated for profit." Philip Landon, in the *Review of Contemporary Fiction,* dubbed *England, England* "a novel of downright Swiftian darkness and ferocity." Comparing the fantasy island to Lilliput, Landon called the work a "stinging caricature" that "chills with the bleakness of its cultural panorama."

Commenting on *Love, etc.* for *Yomiuri Shimbun/Daily Yomiuri,* a reviewer called Barnes a "sensitive writer, whose specialty is a down-to-earth lucidity about the sad paradoxes of love and marriage." *Love, etc.* is a ten-years-later look into the lives of the characters of *Talking It Over,* although reading the latter is not a prerequisite to enjoying the former. Steven Rea, reviewing the book for *Knight-Ridder/Tribune News Service,* noted that *Love, etc.* "is penned in confession mode—in the voices of its protagonists, a knotty triangle of love, loathing, trust and betrayal known as Stuart, Gillian and Oliver." He called Barnes's prose "lively, lucid, ricocheting with wryly observed commentary on the human condition," adding that Barnes "pokes and prods into the dark corners of contemporary relationships." Dale Peck in the *New Republic,* however, found the writing clever but the story ultimately "soulless." As Peck explained, "Barnes is a terribly smart man, a terribly skilled writer . . . [but] intelligence and talent in the service of a discompassionate temperament are precisely the opposite of what one seeks from a novelist, or a novel."

In a departure from his longer fictional works, Barnes experimented with the short-story form in 1996's *Cross Channel*. A collection of ten short stories that span centuries, each tale is also linked by its depiction of a Brit heading for the far bank of the Channel, lured by the pleasures of neighboring France. Drawing on the similarities between the British and their Gallic cousins, Barnes's "imagination seems to work comfortably in a historical context, building fiction on bits of fact," according to Chicago's *Tribune Books* reviewer Bruce Cook. Among the stories—each set on French soil—are "Junction," which revolves around the perception of the French-born Channel-spanning railroad's builders' perception of their British co-workers during the railroad's 1840s construction. "Melon" finds a cross-cultural cricket match interrupted by the French Revolution, much to the dismay of the story's high-born protagonist who had hoped to sideline the populace's rush to rebel by sparking a far more healthy interest in sport. And in "Inferences," an older-than-middle-aged English musical composer now living in France awaits the performance of his latest composition on the radio, hoping to surprise his young mistress with its magnificence.

Slipping back and forth between the centuries, Barnes's "prose slips quietly back from its modern cadences into those of the early nineteenth century, into the cherished foreignness of the past," noted Michael Wood in a *New York Times Book Review* critique of *Cross Channel*. The author also slips back and forth between outlook, between the way the British view the French and vice versa, understanding the French perspective yet clearly aligned with the British. "*Cross Channel* reconfirms Barnes' sympathy for those characters whose Englishness accompanies them, like a sensible mackintosh, into the unpredictable depths of France," quipped critic Gerald Mangan in his review of the collection for the *Times Literary Supplement*. Praising the volume for its sensitive portrayal of a myriad of cultural subtleties, Cook had particular praise for the dry wit that imbues the collection. Barnes "may indeed be a comic writer at heart—and that may be why he appeals to French readers," surmised the critic. "His humor is the sort that translates well. It travels."

Returning again to the short-fiction format in *The Lemon Table*, Barnes combines eleven unique short stories that focus on individuals whose lives are connected through the unnerving themes of death and aging. As readers plunge into the lives of the characters, dark secrets are revealed, along with chilling answers to much-feared questions. Barbara Love in *Library Journal* called *The Lemon Table* a "superb collection" and added: "This is Barnes at his best." A reviewer for *Publishers Weekly* commented that the short tales "are as stylish as any of Barnes's creations, while also possessed of a pleasing heft. . . . the reader is taken for a delightful ride."

BIOGRAPHICAL AND CRITICAL SOURCES:

BOOKS

Contemporary Literary Criticism, Volume 42, Thomson Gale (Detroit, MI), 1987.
Contemporary Novelists, 6th edition, St. James Press (Detroit, MI), 1996.
Dictionary of Literary Biography Yearbook, Thomson Gale (Detroit, MI), 1994.
Moseley, Merritt, *Understanding Julian Barnes,* University of South Carolina Press (Columbia, SC), 1997.
Sesto, Bruce, *Language, History, and Metanarrative in the Fiction of Julian Barnes,* Peter Lang Publishing (New York, NY), 2001.

PERIODICALS

Antioch Review, winter, 2000, John Kennedy, review of *England, England,* p. 117.
Booklist, July, 1995, p. 1856; June 1, 2004, p. 1697.
Chicago Tribune, January 3, 1993, p. 3.
Christian Science Monitor, January 20, 1993, p. 13.
Commonweal, May 8, 1992, pp. 22-24.
Financial Times, September 16, 2002, James Haldane, "Reversibility, etc.," review of *Love, etc.,* p. 4.
Independent, July 13, 1991, pp. 34-36.
Journal of Literature and Theology, June, 1991, pp. 220-232.
Kirkus Reviews, November 1, 2002, p. 1585.
Knight-Ridder/Tribune News Service, March 28, 2001, Steven Rea, review of *Love, etc.,* p. K6406.
Library Journal, March 15, 1996, p. 98; June 1, 2004, p. 128.
London Review of Books, June 22, 1989, p. 20; February 11, 1993, pp. 18-19.
Los Angeles Time Book Review, March 17, 1985; November 8, 1992, p. 3.
National Review, August 30, 1999, Roger Kimball, "Faux Britannia," p. 48.

New Republic, April 2, 2001, Dale Peck, "Literature's Cuckold," review of *Love, etc.,* p. 32.

New Statesman, March 28, 1980, p. 483.

New Statesman and Society, June 23, 1989, p. 38; November 13, 1992, pp. 34-35; January 16, 1996, pp. 39-40; June 4, 2001, Jason Cowley, "Blame It on Amis, Barnes and McEwan," p. 36.

Newsweek, April 29, 1985.

New York Review of Books, March 21, 1996, p. 22.

New York Times, February 28, 1985; March 30, 1987, p. C16; July 5, 1990, pp. C11, C15; April 16, 1996, p. B2; May 11, 1999, Michiko Kakutani, "England As Theme Park, with Doubled Everything," p. E7.

New York Times Book Review, March 10, 1985; December 13, 1992, p. 3; April 21, 1996, p. 12.

New York Times Magazine, November 22, 1992, pp. 29, 68-72, 80.

Observer (London, England), April 18, 1982, p. 31; July 7, 1991, pp. 25-26.

Publishers Weekly, November 3, 1989, pp. 73-74; February 19, 1996, p. 204; April 12, 1999, review of *England, England,* p. 54, December 23, 2002, review of *In the Land of Pain,* p. 60; May 10, 2004, review of *The Lemon Table,* p. 33; August 9, 2004, review of *The Lemon Table,* p. 47.

Review of Contemporary Fiction, fall, 1999, Philip Landon, review of *England, England,* p. 174; summer, 2001, Philip Landon, review of *Love, etc.,* p. 167.

Spectator, January 26, 2002, Alberto Manguel, review of *Something to Declare,* p. 46.

Sunday Times (London, England), June 18, 1989, p. G9.

Time, April 8, 1985.

Times (London, England), March 21, 1980; October 4, 1984; November 7, 1985.

Times Literary Supplement, March 28, 1980; April 23, 1982; January 6, 1984, pp. 4214-4215; October 5, 1984, p. 1117; January 19, 1996, p. 24.

Tribune Books (Chicago, IL), April 21, 1996, p. 3.

Village Voice Literary Supplement, November, 1989, p. 5.

Wall Street Journal, December 11, 1992, p. A10.

Washington Post Book World, March 3, 1985; November 15, 1992.

Yale Review, summer, 1988, pp. 478-491.

Yomiuri Shimbun/Daily Yomiuri, April 2, 2001.

ONLINE

Julian Barnes Home Page, http://www.julianbarnes. com/ (August 4, 2004).

Salon.com, http://www.salon.com/ (May 13-17, 1996).

BARNES, Julian Patrick
See BARNES, Julian

*   *   *

BARON, David
See PINTER, Harold

*   *   *

BARRINGTON, Michael
See MOORCOCK, Michael

*   *   *

BARTHELME, Donald 1931-1989

PERSONAL: Born April 7, 1931, in Philadelphia, PA; died of cancer, July 23, 1989, in Houston, TX; son of Donald (an architect) and Helen (Bechtold) Barthelme; married (marriage ended); married, wife's name Birgit (marriage ended); married, wife's name Helen (marriage ended); married, wife's name Marion; children: (second marriage) Anne Katherine.

CAREER: Author of short fiction and novels. Worked as a newspaper reporter for the *Houston Post,* Houston, TX, and managing editor of *Location* magazine; Contemporary Arts Museum, Houston, TX, director, 1961-62; distinguished visiting professor of English, City College of the City University of New York, 1974-75. *Military service:* U.S. Army; served in Korea and Japan.

MEMBER: American Academy and Institute of Arts and Letters, Authors League of America, Authors Guild, PEN.

AWARDS, HONORS: Guggenheim fellowship, 1966; *Time* magazine's Best Books of the Year list, 1971, for *City Life;* National Book Award for children's literature, 1972, for *The Slightly Irregular Fire Engine or the Hithering Thithering Djinn;* Morton Dauwen Zabel Award from the National Institute of Arts and Letters, 1972; Jesse H. Jones Award from Texas Institute of Letters, 1976, for *The Dead Father;* nominated for National Book Critics Circle Award, PEN/Faulkner Award for Fiction, *Los Angeles Times* Book Prize, all for *Sixty Stories,* all 1982.

WRITINGS:

Come Back, Dr. Caligari (stories), Little, Brown (Boston, MA), 1964.

Snow White (novel), Atheneum (New York, NY), 1967.

Unspeakable Practices, Unnatural Acts (stories), Farrar, Straus (New York, NY), 1968.

City Life (stories), Farrar, Straus (New York, NY), 1970.

The Slightly Irregular Fire Engine or the Hithering Thithering Djinn (for children), Farrar, Straus (New York, NY), 1971.

Sadness (stories), Farrar, Straus (New York, NY), 1972.

Guilty Pleasures (parodies and satire), Farrar, Straus (New York, NY), 1974.

The Dead Father (novel), Farrar, Straus (New York, NY), 1975, with an introduction by Donald Antrim, 2004.

Amateurs (stories), Farrar, Straus (New York, NY), 1976.

Great Days (stories; also see below), Farrar, Straus (New York, NY), 1979.

Sixty Stories, Putnam (New York, NY), 1981, Penguin (New York, NY), 2003.

Overnight to Many Distant Cities (stories), Putnam (New York, NY), 1983.

Great Days (play; based on his story of the same title), produced at American Place Theater, New York, 1983.

Paradise (novel), Putnam (New York, NY), 1986.

Sam's Bar, Doubleday (New York, NY), 1987.

Forty Stories, Putnam (New York, NY), 1987.

The King, with wood engravings by Barry Moser, Harper (New York, NY), 1990.

The Teachings of Don B.: Satires, Parodies, Fables, Illustrated Stories, and Plays of Donald Barthelme, edited by Kim Herzinger, with an introduction by Thomas Pynchon, Turtle Bay Books (New York, NY), 1992.

Not-Knowing: The Essays and Interviews of Donald Barthelme, Random House (New York, NY), 1997.

Regular contributor to the *New Yorker.*

SIDELIGHTS: Donald Barthelme was an original and influential American writer of short fiction. Richard Gilman, in a representative statement reprinted in *The Confusion of Realms,* called Barthelme "one of a handful of American writers who are working to replenish and extend the art of fiction instead of trying to add to the stock of entertainments, visions and human documents that fiction keeps piling up." Lois Gordon elaborated upon this idea in her Twayne volume, *Donald Barthelme.* Barthelme, she claimed, "rejects traditional chronology, plot, character, time, space, grammar, syntax, metaphor, and simile, as well as the traditional distinctions between fact and fiction. What used to orga-

nize reality—time, space, and the structure of language—is now often disjointed, and *language,* and the difficulties in 'using' it, becomes the very subject of his art. Most obvious is . . . its refusal to be an orderly reflection of, and comment upon, a stable, external world." The collections *Sixty Stories* and *Forty Stories* contain most of the short fiction for which Barthelme is remembered.

Bizarre incidents abound in Barthelme's world: a thirty-five year old man is placed by some inexplicable error in a sixth-grade class, a woman attempts to open a car rental agency in a city whose every building is a church, the nonsense poet Edward Lear invites friends to witness his death. But such experiences are all pointedly disengaged from the voice that recounts them and from the audience's emotional sympathies. Even the characters in the stories take the wildest dislocations for granted. When King Kong, "now an adjunct professor of art history at Rutgers," breaks through a window in "The Party," the guests simply utter "loud exclamations of fatigue and disgust, examining the situation in the light of their own needs and emotions, hoping that the ape was real or papiermache according to their temperaments, or wondering whether other excitements were possible out in the crisp, white night." As Maurice Couturier noted in *Donald Barthelme,* the writer's idiom is marked by a "high degree of impersonality. . . . 'Sadness' and 'equanimity' appear to refer to essences which the characters accidentally happen to run across. Man is like a chance visitor in a world teeming with universals." Charles Molesworth, writing in *Donald Barthelme's Fiction: The Ironist Saved from Drowning,* stated: "For the typical Barthelme character, it is just the variousness of the world that spells defeat, since the variety is both a form of plenitude and the sign of its absence. The realm of brand names, historical allusions, 'current events,' and fashionable topics exists in a world whose fullness results from the absence of any strong hierarchical sense of values, and the causal randomness of such things both blurs and signals how any appeal to a rigorous, ordering value system would be futile."

Underlying what Molesworth called Barthelme's three chief subjects—"the futility of work in a post-industrial society, the emotional disorientation of divorce (in both literal and metaphoric terms), and the impotent double-mindedness of the artist"—many critics perceive a horrified fascination with the dreck of cultural disintegration: advertising slogans, facts from the public media, objects arrayed like trash on a junkpile, and opinions and actions unmoored from any system of belief that might give them meaning. Barthelme's contradictory attitude toward the cultural debris his work both celebrates and deplores is best revealed in an often-cited passage from *Snow White,* in which the "stuffing" of ordinary language is compared to trash by virtue of its leading qualities: "(1) an 'endless' quality and (2) a 'sludge' quality." The proportion of "stuffing" in language, the novel contends, is constantly increasing. "We may very well reach a point," Barthelme wrote, "where it's one hundred percent. Now at such a point, you will agree, the question turns from a question of disposing of this 'trash' to a question of appreciating its qualities."

In many stories, Barthelme concentrates on a single bit of cultural junk and speculates on its range of implications. But even in his best stories, he was constantly in danger of being engulfed by the cultural dreck—second-hand language, second-hand beliefs, second-hand emotions—he took as his subject, so that his work sometimes appeared to be a symptom of cultural malaise rather than a response to it. Molesworth believed that "Barthelme's work can be read as an attack on the false consciousness generated by meretricious sources of information that are accepted as commonplace in the modern, technologized, urban society of mass man." But he adds, "This is . . . to read the stories as more morally pointed than they are intended." In *The Metafictional Muse: The Works of Robert Coover, Donald Barthelme, and William H. Gass,* Larry McCaffery wrote: "If there is a sense of optimism in [Barthelme's] work, it does not derive from the familiar modernist belief that art offers the possibility of escape from the disorders of the modern world or that art can change existing conditions; Barthelme overtly mocks these beliefs along with most other modern credos. Instead, Barthelme posits a less lofty function for art with his suggestion that it is valuable simply because it gives man a chance to create a space in which the deadening effects of ordinary living can be momentarily defied."

Other critics have applied a variety of labels to Barthelme in an attempt to place him accurately in the context of contemporary fiction. Alfred Kazin called him an "antinovelist"; Frederick R. Karl a "minimalist"; Jack Hicks and McCaffery, a "metafictionist." Molesworth, titling him "perhaps the final post-Enlightenment writer," located him on the frontier between modernism and post-modernism: "An absurdist like [Samuel] Beckett maintains the world is fundamentally ambiguous, whereas a playful surrealist like [Richard] Brautigan suggests it is ambivalent. For Barthelme, it is both. . . . Nowhere does Barthelme's fiction wholly reject or wholly assent to the contemporary world."

Following Barthelme's death in 1989, *The King,* a novel, and *The Teachings of Don B.: Satires, Parodies,*

Fables, Illustrated Stories, and Plays of Donald Barthelme, a collection, were published. In *The King* Barthelme offered a farcical version of the King Arthur legend set in England during the Second World War. The legendary quest for the Grail is here presented as the competition between Nazi Germany and the Allies to develop the atomic bomb. Ultimately, "Arthur renounces the Grail-bomb as immoral," the reviewer for the *New Yorker* commented, transforming the farce into "a pacifist tract, a rueful travesty . . . and a dazzlement of style." On the other hand, writing in the *New Statesman & Society,* Robert Carver found that *The King,* "for all its wit and playful inventiveness, reads like a series of stories strung together. . . . It reads embarrassingly off-key and banal."

The pieces gathered in *The Teachings of Don B.,* as James Marcus explained in the *New York Times Book Review,* are "a superb cross section of what Thomas Pynchon, in his fine introduction, calls *Barthelmismo.*" Writing in *Studies in Short Fiction,* Gary R. Grund found that *The Teachings of Don B.* "show Barthelme at his most creative and decreative, irreducible, fragmented, and undigested." Marcus concluded that the collection "is a small education in laughter, melancholy and the English language."

By offering an alternative to the short story organized in terms of a traditional plot, characters, conflict, and resolution, Barthelme's fiction persuasively demonstrates the comparatively superficial dependence of the short story on these conventions. Because his own work, however, has typically resisted new descriptive categories, it is easier to define the formal tradition with which he is breaking than to say exactly what he is creating in its place. But the leading characteristic of all Barthelme's work is clearly its antithetical stance toward its materials, a stance that, without necessarily expressing hostility toward the world, frees the stories from commitment to the truth of any representation of that world.

Gordon suggested that Barthelme's most striking formal technique is a "shifting from one voice of authority to another, or manipulation or literalization of metaphor or cliche, or creation of open-ended or seemingly nonfixed situations" that "is noticeably *dislocating* (or disorienting)." She added that "because of the open-ended quality of his language—which always begins with a logical albeit extraordinarily unusual connection before it splits and widens into its several, moving parts—one never feels he 'finishes' a Barthelme story." As Molesworth wrote, "For Barthelme the highest success is not if the story strikes us as true, but rather if it shows us how it works."

Evaluations of Barthelme's achievement as a writer usually highlight his ability to work on the extreme fringes of literary convention. Herbert Mitgang, writing in the *New York Times,* called him "among the leading innovative writers of modern fiction," while John Barth described him in the *New York Times Book Review* as "the thinking man's—and woman's—Minimalist."

BIOGRAPHICAL AND CRITICAL SOURCES:

BOOKS

Barthelme, Donald, *Snow White,* Atheneum (New York, NY), 1967.

Bellamy, Joe David, editor, *The New Fiction: Interviews with Innovative American Writers,* University of Illinois Press (Champaign, IL), 1974.

Bruss, Paul, *Victims: Textual Strategies in Recent American Fiction,* Bucknell University Press (Cranbury, NJ), 1981.

Contemporary Fiction in America and England, 1950-1970, Thomson Gale (Detroit, MI), 1976.

Contemporary Literary Criticism, Thomson Gale (Detroit, MI), Volume 1, 1973, Volume 2, 1974, Volume 3, 1975, Volume 5, 1976, Volume 6, 1976, Volume 8, 1978, Volume 13, 1980, Volume 23, 1983, Volume 46, 1987, Volume 59, 1990.

Couturier, Maurice and Regis Durand, *Donald Barthelme,* Methuen (New York, NY), 1982.

Devil in the Fire: Retrospective Essays on American Literature and Culture, Harper's Magazine Press (New York, NY), 1972.

Dickstein, Morris, *Gates of Eden: American Culture in the Sixties,* Basic Books (New York, NY), 1977.

Dictionary of Literary Biography, Volume 2: *American Novelists since World War II,* Thomson Gale (Detroit, MI), 1978.

Dictionary of Literary Biography Yearbook: 1980, Thomson Gale (Detroit, MI), 1981.

Fiction and the Figures of Life, Knopf (New York, NY), 1970.

Gilman, Richard, *The Confusion of Realms,* Random House (New York, NY), 1969.

Gordon, Lois, *Donald Barthelme,* Twayne (New York, NY), 1981.

Graff, Gerald, *Literature against Itself: Literary Ideas in Modern Society,* University of Chicago Press (Chicago, IL), 1979.

Harris, Charles B., *Contemporary American Novelists of the Absurd,* College and University Press, 1971.

Hendin, Josephine, *Vulnerable People: A View of American Fiction since 1945,* Oxford University Press (New York, NY), 1978.

Hicks, Jack, *In the Singer's Temple: Prose Fictions of Barthelme, Gaines, Brautigan, Piercy, Kesey, and Kosinski,* University of North Carolina Press (Chapel Hill, NC), 1981.

Karl, Frederick R., *American Fictions, 1940-1980: A Comprehensive History and Critical Evaluation,* Harper (New York, NY), 1983.

Kazin, Alfred, *Bright Book of Life: American Novelists and Story Tellers from Hemingway to Mailer,* Atlantic/Little, Brown (Boston, MA), 1973.

Klinkowitz, Jerome, and others, editors, *Donald Barthelme: A Comprehensive Bibliography and Annotated Secondary Checklist,* Shoe String (Hamden, CT), 1977.

Klinkowitz, Jerome, *Literary Disruptions: The Making of a Post-Contemporary American Fiction,* 2nd edition, University of Illinois Press (Champagne, IL), 1980.

Klinkowitz, Jerome, *The American 1960s: Imaginative Arts in a Decade of Change,* Iowa State University Press (Ames, IA), 1980.

Klinkowitz, Jerome, *The Self-Apparent Word: Fiction as Language/Language as Fiction,* Southern Illinois University Press (Carbondale, IL), 1984.

Maltby, Paul, *Dissident Postmodernists: Barthelme, Coover, Pynchon,* University of Pennsylvania Press (Philadelphia, PA), 1991.

McCaffery, Larry, *The Metafictional Muse: The Works of Robert Coover, Donald Barthelme, and William H. Gass,* University of Pittsburgh Press (Pittsburgh, PA), 1982.

Molesworth, Charles, *Donald Barthelme's Fiction: The Ironist Saved from Drowning,* University of Missouri Press (Columbia, MO), 1982.

Patteson, Richard F., editor, *Critical Essays on Donald Barthelme,* G.K. Hall (New York, NY), 1992.

Peden, William, *The American Short Story,* Houghton (Boston, MA), 1975.

Roe, Barbara L., *Donald Barthelme: A Study of the Short Fiction,* Twayne (New York, NY), 1992.

Sakrajda, Mira, *Postmodern Discourses of Love: Pynchon, Barth, Coover, Gass, and Barthelme,* Peter Lang (New York, NY), 1997.

Scholes, Robert, *Fabulation and Metafiction,* University of Illinois Press (Champagne, IL), 1971.

Stengel, Wayne B., *The Shape of Art in the Short Stories of Donald Barthelme,* Louisiana State University Press (Baton Rouge, LA), 1985.

Tanner, Tony, *City of Words: American Fiction, 1950-1970,* Harper (New York, NY), 1971.

Trachtenberg, Stanley, *Understanding Donald Barthelme,* University of South Carolina Press (Columbia, SC), 1990.

Weaver, Gordon, editor, *The American Short Story, 1945-1980: A Critical History,* Twayne (New York, NY), 1983.

Werner, Braig Hansen, *Paradoxical Resolutions: American Fiction since James Joyce,* University of Illinois Press (Champaign, IL), 1982.

PERIODICALS

America, December 10, 1981, Samuel Coale, review of *Sixty Stories,* p. 404; December 22, 1990, Alan R. Davis, review of *The King,* p. 517.
American Book Review, December, 1989, pp. 3, 18, 25.
Antioch Review, spring, 1970; spring, 1987, p. 247.
Atlanta Constitution, November 30, 1987, p. B2.
Books, April, 1967; April, 1988, p. 16.
Books and Bookmen, February, 1974.
Book Week, May 21, 1967; February 4, 1979.
Boston Globe, October 4, 1987, p. C3.
Boundary 2, fall, 1976; spring, 1977.
Chicago Review, number 1, 1973.
Chicago Tribune, November 27, 1986; October 23, 1987, p. 3.
Chicago Tribune Book World, January 28, 1979; September 27, 1981; October 17, 1982.
Christian Science Monitor, June 1, 1967.
Commentary, November, 1975; August, 1976.
Commonweal, December 29, 1967; June 21, 1968; November 8, 1991, Paul Giles, "Dead, but Still with Us: Barthelme's Fading Catholic Intuitions," pp. 637-640.
Critique: Studies in Modern Fiction, number 3, 1969; number 3, 1975; fall, 1984, p. 11.
Denver Quarterly, winter, 1979.
Detroit News, October 4, 1981; December 11, 1983.
Fantasy Review, March, 1987, p. 32.
Fiction International, number 4/5, 1975.
Georgia Review, summer, 1974; winter, 1993, Irvin Malin, review of *The Teachings of Don B.: The Satires, Parodies, Fables, Illustrated Stories, and Plays of Donald Barthelme,* pp. 819-820.
Harper's, January, 1973.
Hudson Review, autumn, 1967; autumn, 1988, p. 549; spring, 1991, Tom Wilhelmus, review of *The King* and *Visionary Historians,* pp. 125-132.
International Fiction Review, Number 6, 1979.
Journal of Narrative Theory, spring, 1982.
Kenyon Review, spring, 1967.
Language and Style, spring, 1975.
Library Journal, December 15, 1976.
Life, May 26, 1967.
Linguistics in Literature, Number 2, 1977.
Listener, December 6, 1973; April 7, 1988, p. 30.
London Review of Books, July 7, 1988, p. 20.
Los Angeles Times, December 7, 1983, Art Seidenbaum, review of *Overnight to Many Distant Cities,* p. 22.

Los Angeles Times Book Review, October 18, 1981; October 24, 1982; November 2, 1986, p. 3; October 18, 1987, p. 3.
Magazine of Fantasy & Science Fiction, December, 1990, Orson Scott Card, review of *The King,* p. 90.
Michigan Quarterly Review, spring, 1977.
Milwaukee Journal, February 4, 1973.
Minnesota Review, fall, 1971; fall, 1977.
Modern Fiction Studies, spring, 1982, pp. 129-143.
Nation, June 19, 1967; April 7, 1979; October 17, 1981, Charles Newman, review of *Sixty Stories,* pp. 381-382; August 6, 1983, Richard Gilman, review of *Great Days,* pp. 124-125.
National Review, March 28, 1975.
New Leader, February 26, 1979.
New Orleans Review, summer, 1981.
New Republic, May 2, 1964; June 3, 1967; December 14, 1974; February 17, 1979.
New Statesman, December 7, 1973.
New Statesman & Society, March 1, 1991, Robert Carver, review of *The King,* p. 38.
Newsweek, May 22, 1967; May 6, 1968; November 25, 1974; October 12, 1981, Walter Clemons, review of *Sixty Stories,* pp. 100-101; November 3, 1986, Peter S. Prescott, review of *Paradise,* p. 76.
New Yorker, June 27, 1983, Edith Oliver, review of *Great Days,* p. 75; July 9, 1990, review of *The King,* p. 92.
New York Review of Books, April 30, 1964; August 24, 1967; April 25, 1968; December 14, 1972; December 11, 1975.
New York Times, April 24, 1968; January 31, 1979; October 24, 1981, Anatole Broyard, review of *Sixty Stories,* p. 13; February 18, 1982, Herbert Mitgang, "Barthelme Face-to-Face with His Own Fiction," section C, p. 15; June 18, 1983; December 9, 1983, p. C33; October 22, 1986, Michiko Kakutani, review of *Paradise,* section C, p. 24; October 25, 1987, p. 14; May 31, 1988, section C, p. 21.
New York Times Book Review, September 27, 1964; May 21, 1967; May 12, 1968; November 7, 1971; September 3, 1972; November 5, 1972; December 23, 1973; December 19, 1976; February 4, 1979; October 4, 1981, John Romano, review of *Sixty Stories,* pp. 9-10; October 10, 1982, review of *Sixty Stories,* p. 35; December 18, 1983, Joel Conarroe, review of *Overnight to Many Distant Cities,* pp. 8, 22; October 26, 1986, Jane Perlez, interview with Barthelme, Elizabeth Jolley, review of *Paradise,* p. 7; October 25, 1987, Caryn James, review of *Forty Stories,* p. 14; April 23, 1989, p. 34; September 3, 1989, John Barth, "Thinking Man's Minimalist: Honoring Barthelme," p. 9; December 6, 1992, James Marcus, review of *The Teachings of Don B.,* p. 30.

New York Times Magazine, August 16, 1970.

Observer (London, England), April 3, 1988, p. 42; February 10, 1991, p. 54.

Orbis Litterarum, number 38, 1983.

Partisan Review, number 3, 1973.

Philological Quarterly, fall, 1983.

Prospects, number 1, 1975.

Publishers Weekly, March 18, 1968; November 11, 1974.

Quill & Quire, January, 1987, p. 33; January, 1988, review of *Forty Stories,* p. 30.

Resources for American Literary Study, number 7, 1977.

Review of Contemporary Fiction, spring, 1991, Barry Lewis, review of *The King,* pp. 341-342; summer, 1991, special issue dedicated to Barthelme's work; summer, 1998, Monique Dufour, review of *Not-Knowing,* p. 226.

Saturday Review, May 9, 1970; November 25, 1972; March 3, 1979; September, 1981, Carey Horwitz, review of *Sixty Stories,* p. 59.

Sewanee Review, summer, 1970.

Southwest Review, spring, 1982.

Spectator, December 8, 1973; February 16, 1991, p. 26.

Studies in Short Fiction, winter, 1981; summer, 1984, pp. 277-279; spring, 1994, Gary R. Grund, review of *The Teachings of Don B.,* pp. 257-258.

Style, summer, 1975.

Time, May 26, 1967; November 11, 1974; September 21, 1981, John Skow, review of *Sixty Stories,* p. 82.

Times Literary Supplement, June 17, 1977; May 13, 1988, John Clute, review of *Forty Stories,* p. 532.

Tribune Books (Chicago, IL), May 7, 1989, p. 9; June 10, 1990, p. 3; December 13, 1992, p. 3.

Tri Quarterly, winter, 1973; spring, 1974; spring, 1975.

Twentieth Century Literature, January, 1972.

Village Voice, January 17, 1984, pp. 38-39; February 3, 1987, p. 51.

Virginia Quarterly Review, spring, 1975.

Wall Street Journal, May 1, 1990, Richard Locke, review of *The King,* section A, p. 16.

Washington Post Book World, November 5, 1972; November 3, 1974; November 28, 1976; February 11, 1979; October 25, 1981; November 27, 1983, pp. 3, 10; October 11, 1987, p. 8.

World Literature Today, spring, 1987, p. 285; spring, 1993, Robert Murray Davis, review of *The Teachings of Don B.,* p. 393.

Xavier Review, number 1, 1980-81.

Yale Review, spring, 1976.

OBITUARIES:

PERIODICALS

Chicago Tribune, July 26, 1989.

Detroit Free Press, July 25, 1989.

Los Angeles Times, July 25, 1989.

New Yorker, August 14, 1989, pp. 23-24.

New York Times, July 24, 1989, section C, p. 10, section D, p. 11.

Times (London, England), July 25, 1989.

Washington Post, July 25, 1989.

*   *   *

BASHEVIS, Isaac
See SINGER, Isaac Bashevis

*   *   *

BASS, Kingsley B., Jr.
See BULLINS, Ed

*   *   *

BAXTER, Charles 1947-
(Charles Morley Baxter)

PERSONAL: Born May 13, 1947, in Minneapolis, MN; son of John Thomas and Mary Barber (Eaton) Baxter; married Martha Ann Hauser (a teacher), July 12, 1976; children: Daniel John. *Education:* Macalester College, B.A., 1969; State University of New York at Buffalo, Ph.D., 1974.

ADDRESSES: Home—Minneapolis, MN. *Office*—Department of English, University of Minnesota, 210G Lind Hall, 207 Church St. SE, Minneapolis, MN 55455. *E-mail*—baxte029@umn.edu.

CAREER: High school teacher in Pinconning, MI, 1969-70; Wayne State University, Detroit, MI, assistant professor, 1974-79, associate professor, 1979-85, professor of English, 1985-89; Warren Wilson College, faculty member, beginning 1986; University of Michigan, Ann Arbor, visiting faculty member, 1987, professor of English, 1989-99, adjunct professor of creative writing, 1999-2003; University of Minnesota, Minneapolis, Edelstein-Keller Senior Fellow in Creative Writing, 2003—.

AWARDS, HONORS: Faculty research fellowship, Wayne State University, 1980-81; Lawrence Foundation Award, 1982, and Associated Writing Programs Award Series in Short Fiction, 1984, both for *Harmony of the*

World; National Endowment for the Arts fellowship, 1983, Michigan Council for the Arts fellowship, 1984; Faculty Recognition Award, Wayne State University, 1985 and 1987; Guggenheim fellowship, 1985-86; Michigan Council of the Arts grant, 1986; Arts Foundation of Michigan Award, 1991; Lawrence Foundation Award, 1991; *Reader's Digest* Foundation fellowship, 1992; Michigan Author of the Year Award, Michigan Foundation, 1994; *Harvard Review* Award and O. Henry Prize, both 1995; Award in Literature, American Academy of Arts and Letters, 1997; finalist, National Book Award in Fiction, 2000, for *The Feast of Love.*

WRITINGS:

Chameleon (poetry), illustrated by Mary E. Miner, New Rivers Press (New York, NY), 1970.
The South Dakota Guidebook, New Rivers Press (New York, NY), 1974.
Harmony of the World (short stories), University of Missouri Press (Columbia, MO), 1984.
Through the Safety Net (short stories), Viking (New York, NY), 1985.
First Light (novel), Viking (New York, NY), 1987.
Imaginary Paintings and Other Poems, Paris Review Editions (Latham, NY), 1990.
A Relative Stranger (short stories), Norton (New York, NY), 1990.
Shadow Play (novel), Norton (New York, NY), 1993.
Believers (short stories and novella), Pantheon (New York, NY), 1997.
Burning down the House: Essays on Fiction, Graywolf Press (St. Paul, MN), 1997.
(Editor) *The Business of Memory: The Art of Remembering in an Age of Forgetting,* Graywolf Press (St. Paul, MN), 1999.
The Feast of Love (novel), Pantheon (New York, NY), 2000.
(Editor, with Peter Turchi) *Bringing the Devil to His Knees: The Craft of Fiction and the Writing Life,* University of Michigan Press (Ann Arbor, MI), 2001.
Saul and Patsy (novel), Pantheon (New York, NY), 2003.
(Editor, with Edward Hirsch and Michael Collier) *A William Maxwell Portrait: Memories and Appreciations,* Norton (New York, NY), 2004.

Poems have been featured in numerous anthologies, including *The Fifth Annual Best Science Fiction,* edited by Harry Harrison and Brian Aldiss, Putnam (New York, NY), 1972; *Toward Winter,* edited by Robert Bonazzi,

New Rivers Press (New York, NY), 1972; *The Pushcart Prize Anthology XVI,* Pushcart Press (Wainscott, NY), 1991; and *Best American Short Stories,* 1982, 1986, 1987, 1989, and 1991. Contributor to periodicals, including *Minnesota Review, Kayak, Prairie Schooner, Antioch Review, Michigan Quarterly Review, Georgia Review, New England Review, Centennial Review, New York Times,* and *Journal of Modern Literature.* Associate editor, *Minnesota Review,* 1967-69, and *Criticism;* editor of *Audit/Poetry,* 1973-74.

Baxter's works have been translated into Japanese, Swedish, German, Russian, Romanian, French, Spanish, Catalan, Italian, Portugese, and Chinese.

SIDELIGHTS: Charles Baxter initially caught critics' attention with his poetry and criticism, but it is the graceful prose and human understanding of his short stories and novels that have gained him entry into the pantheon of leading American writers of the twentieth century. In the words of Chuck Wachtel in *Nation,* "Baxter is a remarkable storyteller" who, in each new book, "has offered his readers an increasingly significant, humane and populous reflection, one in which we keep finding things we have sensed the presence of but have not before seen." Another *Nation* critic, Theodore Solotaroff, noted that Baxter "has the special gift of capturing the shadow of genuine significance as it flits across the face of the ordinary." Baxter's sharply drawn, unique characters—one of his hallmarks—elicited praise from Jonathan Yardley in the *Washington Post Book World:* "Unlike so many other young American writers . . . Baxter cares about his people, recognizes the validity and dignity of their lives, grants them humor and individuality."

Born in Minnesota and a longtime resident of Michigan, Baxter has created a fictional world that embraces the Midwest. As a reviewer for *Ploughshares* explained, the author portrays "in luminous, precise language, solid Midwestern citizens, many of whom reside in the fictional town of Five Oaks, Michigan, whose orderly lives are disrupted, frequently by an accident or incident or a stranger." The reviewer added: "The limits of geography tend to elicit introspection, and when even a small calamity befalls Baxter's characters, they brood over surprisingly large issues of morality and theodicy, grappling with good and evil and the mysteriousness of existence."

Baxter's first volume of short stories, *Harmony of the World,* includes the award-winning title story as well as several others. "Harmony of the World," originally published in the *Michigan Quarterly Review,* is about a young pianist who decides to become a newspaper critic after one of his performances elicits a particularly scathing review from a music teacher. His affair with a somewhat untalented singer and the events that bring both of their lives to a crisis are the means through which Baxter explores "the ache of yearning for perfection, in love and art, a perfection human beings can never attain, however close they come to apprehending it," to quote Laurence Goldstein in the *Ann Arbor News.* Goldstein praised Baxter for the "imaginative sympathy and marvelous craft" of his short stories, a view shared by Peter Ross of the *Detroit News:* "There are no weak spots in *Harmony of the World,* no falterings of craft or insight. Baxter's influences are many and subtle, but his voice is his own and firmly in control. . . . *Harmony of the World* is a serious collection by a serious writer; it deserves as much attention, study and praise as anything being written today."

Baxter's second collection of short stories, *Through the Safety Net,* was published just one year after *Harmony of the World* and was received with great enthusiasm by critics. "It's a nice surprise that a second collection is so speedily upon us and that it improves on the first," wrote Ron Hansen in the *New York Times Book Review. Through the Safety Net* is an exploration of the inevitable perils of everyday life. Baxter's characters—among them an unsuccessful graduate student, a five-year-old boy trying to understand his grandmother's death, and a spurned lover who becomes obsessed with the object of his desire—spend their energies trying to escape pain and loss, but inevitably fail. In the title story, Diana visits a psychic only to be told that she is headed for a great calamity. "What kind? The Book of Job kind," the psychic tells her. "I saw your whole life, your house, car, that swimming pool you put in last summer, the career, your child, and the whole future just start to radiate with this ugly black flame from the inside, poof, and then I saw you falling, like at the circus, down from the trapeze. Whoops, and down, and then down through the safety net. Through the ground." In another narrative, a psychopath, lamenting his lack of fame, remarks: "If you are not famous in America, you are considered a mistake. They suspend you in negative air and give you bad jobs working in basements pushing mops from eight at night until four in the morning."

Yardley characterized the people in Baxter's stories as individuals without purpose, "amiably retreating from life's challenges . . . though the forms of their retreats and the motives for them vary." A *Publishers Weekly* reviewer found the stories "flawed by a fondness for

excessive detail, implausible turns and mere trickiness," but conceded that they contained "bright flashes of unmistakable talent." Baxter's careful attention to detail was praised by a *New York Times* critic: "An extraordinarily limber writer, Mr. Baxter makes his characters' fears palpable to the reader by slowly drawing us into their day-to-day routine and making us see things through their eyes." The stories in *Through the Safety Net,* concluded Hansen, are "intelligent, original, gracefully written, always moving, frequently funny and—that rarest of compliments—wise."

When Baxter's first novel, *First Light,* was published in 1987, it immediately garnered praise for its unique structure. Prefaced by a quote from Danish philosopher Sören Kierkegaard—"Life can only be understood backwards, but it must be lived forwards"—the novel presents events in reverse chronological order. Thus, each chapter is a step further back into the past of the characters. At the outset of *First Light,* Hugh Welch and his sister Dorsey are uneasy adults reunited for a Fourth of July celebration. Their strained, distant relationship is clearly a source of anguish to them both. As the novel progresses, Hugh and Dorsey become younger and younger, and the many layers of their life-long bond are slowly uncovered. "We see their youth and childhoods revealed, like rapidly turning pages in a snapshot album," observed Michiko Kakutani in the *New York Times.* By the time the novel ends, Hugh is a young child being introduced to his newborn baby sister. "In reading of these events," Kakutani wrote, "we see why Dorsey and Hugh each made the choices they did, how their childhood dreams were translated into adult decisions." The combination of Baxter's unique narrative structure and fine characterization results in "a remarkably supple novel that gleams with the smoky chiaroscuro of familial love recalled through time," concluded Kakutani.

Although *First Light* was Baxter's first published novel, it was not his first attempt at the novel form. His first three novels, he remarked in the *New York Times,* are "apprentice" efforts he would never consider publishing. "I did take a brief episode out of one of them but, for the most part, I can't stand to look at them now, so I wouldn't want anyone else to." Describing the structure of *First Light,* he commented: "The technique resembles those little Russian dolls that fit into each other—you open them up and they keep getting smaller and smaller. What I am trying to say is that grownups don't stop being the people they were many years before, in childhood."

Baxter's 1990 collection of short stories, *A Relative Stranger,* features characters "constantly having odd encounters with strangers that disrupt their quiet, humdrum lives and send them skidding in unexpected new directions," Kakutani stated in a *New York Times* review. In one story, a man's attempt to help an insane, homeless man sparks the jealousy of his wife and son. In another, a woman who is secretly in love with her husband's best friend develops an irrational fear of burglars. Describing the couple's suburban home as one of many "little rectangular temples of light," the friend scoffs at the wife's fear. "Nothing here but families and fireplaces and Duraflame logs and children of God," he tells the husband. "Not the sort of place," he continues, "where a married woman ought to be worried about prowlers."

Recommending *A Relative Stranger* in *Nation,* Theodore Solotaroff commented: "Baxter is well on his way to becoming the next master of the short story." *A Relative Stranger* was also praised by Kakutani: "All the stories in this collection attest to Mr. Baxter's ability to orchestrate the details of mundane day-to-day reality into surprising patterns of grace and revelation, his gentle but persuasive knack for finding and describing the fleeting moments that indelibly define a life. . . . We finish the book with the satisfaction of having been immersed in a beautifully rendered and fully imagined world."

Baxter's 1993 novel, *Shadow Play,* revolves around Wyatt Palmer, a man whose chaotic childhood has left him unable to deal with emotions. Instead, he focuses on maintaining a neatly ordered life with his understanding wife and two children. Wyatt's job as an assistant city manager leads him to cross paths with a former high school classmate interested in starting a chemical company in their economically depressed hometown. The former classmate, Jerry Schwartzwalder, asks Wyatt to bend the rules in order to help him launch his new company. In exchange for his cooperation, Jerry offers Wyatt's unstable foster brother, Cyril, a job at the plant. When Cyril shows signs of a fatal disease caused by exposure to toxins, Wyatt becomes enraged and vows to take revenge. According to *New York Times Book Review* contributor Lorrie Moore, *Shadow Play* is reminiscent of "The Lottery," by Shirley Jackson. Like Jackson's story, Baxter's novel "takes large themes of good and evil and primitive deal making, and situates them in municipal terms and local ritual. He is interested in those shadowy corners of civilization in which barbarity manages to nestle and thrive. The America of this book has become a kind of hell." Or, as Winston Groom, the author of *Forrest Gump,* put it in the *Los Angeles Times Book Review,* "Baxter has created a scenario in which alienation and anxiety are the norm, a kind of dubious universe where people are neither good nor evil but instead are driven by 20th-century pragmatism into a twilight zone of utter practicality."

In unfolding Wyatt's story of conflict in small-town America, Baxter brings to bear many of his talents as a storyteller. "To convey this sense of abandonment and emptiness without losing the reader is not easy," observed R.Z. Sheppard in *Time.* "*Shadow Play* could have turned into another clever existential dead end. But Baxter fills the void with a hundred human touches, a style as intimate as chamber music, and a hero who rouses himself to reject the banality that hoohah happens." A *Publishers Weekly* critic also drew a musical analogy to describe Baxter's command of style. The story of how Wyatt deals with his emotional handicaps is told in "language so carefully honed it sings." The reviewer continued that the author's "metaphors and apercus are striking and luminous, and several scenes—notably Wyatt and Cyril's final bonding—are unforgettable." Baxter's achievement, in the opinion of Lorrie Moore, is that "he has steadily taken beautiful and precise language and gone into the ordinary and secret places of people—their moral and emotional quandaries, their typically American circumstances, their burning intelligence, their negotiations with what is tapped, stunted, violent, sustaining, decent or miraculous in their lives."

Jane Smiley, writing in Chicago's *Tribune Books,* conceded the eloquence of Baxter's writing and the wisdom of his observations, but she found "Wyatt himself is something of a cipher, a blank at the center whose moral odyssey is less than compelling. . . . The very vividness" of the fictional characters' "eccentricities finally limits the broader appeal of their situation." Moore drew a different conclusion. She maintained that "one of Mr. Baxter's great strengths as a writer has always been his ability to capture the stranded inner lives of the Middle West's repressed eccentrics. And here, in his second novel, he is full throttle." For a contributor to the *Yale Review,* the situations represented in *Shadow Play* achieve broad appeal because they demonstrate that Baxter "has a feeling for nuance, for what's being said and not said, for the complexities of social class and social privilege, for the resonance of personal history, for how much we are the authors—and the products—of our experience." The reviewer continued: "He's not only generous to his characters, but compassionate, endlessly patient, and tolerant of their human frailties and flaws." Richard Locke concluded in the *Wall Street Journal,* "After a decade of so much play-it-safe fiction of photorealistic gloom, it's a pleasure to encounter a novel in the great tradition of American moral realism touched by shards of gnostic faith and glints of transcendental light."

While some reviewers hailed *Shadow Play* as the book that would thrust Baxter into the national literary limelight, Baxter himself refused to set such high expectations. "When *First Light* came out, I was full of the American Dream," he recalled in the *Detroit News*. "I thought the birds of money were going to land in a huge flock on the roof, and I'd be proclaimed from housetop to housetop. It was foolish, and that's what young writers are. . . . I'm trying not to get my hopes up. I worked on [*Shadow Play*] so long, I just want it to do well. I just want people to like it and to find it interesting and find it has some meaning to their lives."

Baxter published another collection of short stories, with a novella, in 1997. A *Publishers Weekly* reviewer described *Believers* as "ambitious and accomplished," adding that "the shorter works here tackle slippery themes and subjects—fleeting moments of truth; the ambiguities of daily life and the defenses through which ordinary men and women attempt to clarify them." These stories are "Michigan stories," commented Frederick Busch in the *Los Angeles Times Book Review*. "They occur in the lives of those with intelligence, leisure in which to use it, walls behind which they may retreat and time enough for contemplation." "The book's self-scrutinizers," Busch added, "those who believe and those who cannot . . . are the middle class in the middle of the nation." Like Baxter's readers, they often experience "failures of will, of nerve, of ethics, of feeling," Busch suggested. "But . . . they are like us in that their souls do not only sink: They strive to climb."

Believers "will remind us that [Baxter] is an exemplary writer because he works in persuasive solidities, in what is actual," concluded Busch. Chuck Wachtel offered greater praise in his *Nation* review. "Rarely . . . have I been stopped by what I read and moved so deeply as I was in the novella and stories that make up *Believers*. Baxter, a master craftsman, knows that craft is more than something to be good at."

Baxter's National Book Award-nominated *The Feast of Love* begins with a character—named Charles Baxter—whose chronic insomnia leads him to a deserted park bench in Ann Arbor, Michigan. It is there that the fictional Baxter encounters a neighbor named Bradley who offers his own life story of two marriages—and two divorces—as grist for a new novel. After initial resistance, Baxter delves into Bradley's past and present,

where each of his former wives, as well as his coworkers, help to enlarge the emerging group portrait. "*The Feast of Love* is as precise, as empathetic, as luminous as any of Baxter's past work," declared Jacqueline Carey in the *New York Times Book Review*. "It is also rich, juicy, laugh-out-loud funny and completely engrossing." A *Publishers Weekly* critic felt that Baxter's particular gift in the novel "is to catch the exact pitch of a dozen voices in an astutely observed group of contemporary men and women." Carey also noted the old-fashioned sense of community underlying the work. "In *The Feast of Love*, Charles Baxter shows us the hard-won generosity of spirit that day-to-day dealings with other human beings require," she stated. "He builds a community right on the page before us, using a glittering eye, a silvery tongue—and just a little moonlight."

Similar to *The Feast of Love, Saul and Patsy* focuses on married life in the Midwest, in this case on a newlywed couple who settle in a small town and find themselves moth-balled in their comfortable, middle-class neighborhood. At least Saul, the Jewish, former city-dwelling husband, feels stifled, "shipwrecked in the plainspoken, poker-faced Midwest," explained *Atlantic* contributor James Marcus, although the critic was quick to add that the novel is also "a valentine to the Midwest, whose terrain the author describes with almost luminarist ardor." Calling Baxter "a master of the distributed plot, the deceptively looping situation that discloses its tensions gradually," *Book* critic Sven Birkerts praised the novel's depiction of the "inevitably mine-studded marital terrain" traversed by his transplanted couple as they negotiate the role of outsider. Praising Baxter's characters, which include a troubled, obsessive teen, and a plot that rises to a tense and tragic denouement, *Booklist* reviewer Donna Seaman dubbed Baxter's protagonists "magnetic, his humor incisive, his decipherment of the human psyche felicitous, and his command of the storyteller's magic absolute."

In addition to authoring fiction, Baxter has also served as editor of anthologies which focus on various aspects of the writing process. *The Business of Memory: The Art of Remembering in an Age of Forgetting*, for instance, explores the art of memoir and the process by which artists of all sorts recover and interpret memories. In *Library Journal*, Julia Burch wrote of the work: "These are self-conscious and beautifully written essays that deftly explore the act of memoir-making and the art of storytelling." A *Publishers Weekly* correspondent likewise found the essays "often engaging and occasionally quite inspired."

In both his short stories and novels, Baxter's exploration of his characters' inner desires and outward realities has struck a chord in critics and readers alike. "If there is a consistent theme in Baxter's work, it is the difficulty people have in accommodating themselves to a world that is complex, mysterious, and demanding, that offers rewards that glitter all the more brightly because so few attain them," Yardley summarized in the *Washington Post Book World.* "Whether he's writing about an overly self-conscious intellectual or an inarticulate street person," concluded Kakutani, "Mr. Baxter is able to map out their emotions persuasively and delineate the shape of their spiritual confusion." Praising the fluid beauty of the author's style, John Saari wrote in the *Antioch Review:* "Many writers today feel no depth of compassion for their characters. Baxter, in contrast, is adept at portraying his characters as human beings, even when some of them are not the best examples."

A self-described insomniac, Baxter also admitted in *Ploughshares* that he likes a routine and will sometimes fixate on even the slightest intrusions or variations from his schedule. Noting that he is "conscious of pattern-making" in his day-to-day life, the author added: "I think if you are somewhat compulsive or habitual in your ordinary life, it gives you some latitude to be wild in your creative work."

BIOGRAPHICAL AND CRITICAL SOURCES:

BOOKS

Baxter, Charles, *Through the Safety Net,* Viking (New York, NY), 1985.

Baxter, Charles, *A Relative Stranger,* Norton (New York, NY), 1990.

Contemporary Literary Criticism, Thomson Gale (Detroit, MI), Volume 45, 1987, Volume 78, 1993.

Contemporary Popular Writers, St. James Press (Detroit, MI), 1997.

Dictionary of Literary Biography, Volume 130: *American Short-Story Writers since World War II,* Thomson Gale (Detroit, MI), 1993.

PERIODICALS

Ann Arbor News, May 16, 1982.

Antioch Review, fall, 1985, p. 498; summer, 1993, p. 465.

Atlantic, September, 2003, James Marcus, review of *Saul and Patsy,* p. 152.

Book, September-October, 2003, Sven Birkerts, review of *Saul and Patsy,* p. 74.

Booklist, April 15, 2000, Grace Fill, review of *The Feast of Love,* p. 1522; August, 2003, Donna Seaman, review of *Saul and Patsy,* p. 1924.

Detroit Free Press, December 23, 1992.

Detroit News, May 20, 1984; December 28, 1992, p. 1D.

Entertainment Weekly, September 12, 2003, Thom Geier, review of *Saul and Patsy,* p. 156.

Hudson Review, spring, 1991, p. 133.

Kirkus Reviews, July 1, 2003, review of *Saul and Patsy,* p. 869.

Library Journal, April 15, 1990, p. 96; December, 1992, p. 184; September 15, 1993, p. 136; May 1, 1999, Julia Burch, review of *The Business of Memory: The Art of Remembering in an Age of Forgetting,* p. 76; September 1, 2003, David W. Henderson, review of *Saul and Patsy,* p. 204.

Los Angeles Times Book Review, July 6, 1986, p. 10; December 6, 1987, p. 3; September 29, 1991; March 21, 1993, p. 5; March 30, 1997, p. 10.

Nation, December 30, 1991, p. 862; April 7, 1997, p. 33.

New England Review, summer, 1992, p. 234.

New York Times, June 26, 1985; August 24, 1987; September 7, 1987; September 4, 1990; September 29, 1991.

New York Times Book Review, August 25, 1985, p. 1; October 4, 1987, p. 18; October 23, 1988, p. 60; October 21, 1990, p. 18; February 14, 1993, p. 7; May 7, 2000, Jacqueline Carey, "The Ex Files."

People, February 1, 1993, p. 22; February 24, 1997, p. 65.

Ploughshares, fall, 1999, Don Lee, "About Charles Baxter: A Profile."

Publishers Weekly, May 24, 1985; October 19, 1992, p. 57; December 7, 1992, p. 45; February 24, 1997, p. 65; March 29, 1999, review of *The Business of Memory: The Art of Remembering in an Age of Forgetting,* p. 76; March 6, 2000, review of *The Feast of Love,* p. 79; July 28, 2003, review of *Saul and Patsy,* p. 76.

Southern Review, April, 1991, p. 465.

Time, September 7, 1987, p. 81; September 14, 1987; January 25, 1993, p. 70.

Tribune Books (Chicago, IL), January 17, 1993, p. 4.

Wall Street Journal, February 5, 1993, p. A9.

Washington Post Book World, July 10, 1985; January 17, 1993, p. 3.

Yale Review, July, 1993, p. 122.

*   *   *

BAXTER, Charles Morley
See BAXTER, Charles

BEAGLE, Peter S. 1939-
(Peter Soyer Beagle)

PERSONAL: Born April 20, 1939, in New York, NY; son of Simon (a teacher) and Rebecca (a teacher; maiden name, Soyer) Beagle; married Enid Elaine Nordeen, May 8, 1964 (divorced, July, 1980); married Padma Hejmadi (a writer and artist), September 21, 1988; children: (first marriage) Victoria Lynn Nordeen, Kalisa Nordeen, Daniel Nordeen. *Education:* University of Pittsburgh, B.A., 1959; Stanford University, graduate study, 1960-61. *Politics:* "Anarcho/monarchist." *Religion:* Jewish animist *Hobbies and other interests:* Singing, playing the guitar, writing and performing music, reading, animals, walking, swimming.

ADDRESSES: Home—Berkeley, CA. *Agent*—Sebastian Agency, 172 East 6th St., St. Paul, MN 55101. *E-mail*—unclefox1@juno.com.

CAREER: Author, editor, screenwriter, journalist, and musician, 1960—. University of Washington, Seattle, visiting professor, 1988.

MEMBER: American Civil Liberties Union (vice chair, Santa Cruz Chapter, 1968-69), Friends of Davis (California activist group), Society for American Baseball Research.

AWARDS, HONORS: Wallace Stegner writing fellowship, 1960-61; Guggenheim Foundation Award, 1972-73; National Endowment for the Arts grant, 1977-78; Guest of Honor, Seventh World Fantasy Convention, 1981; Mythopoeic Award, 1987, for *The Folk of the Air;* Locus Award, Mythopoeic Award for adult literature, and *New York Times Book Review* notable book nomination, all 1994, all for *The Innkeeper's Song;* Locus Award for Best Anthology, 1996, for *Peter S. Beagle's Immortal Unicorn, Volume One,* 1996; Locus Awards for Best Novella, 1998, for *Giant Bones,* and 1998, for *The Unicorn Sonata;* Mythopoeic Award and World Fantasy Award, both 2000, both for *Tamsin;* various short-story awards.

WRITINGS:

FANTASY FICTION

A Fine and Private Place (also see below), Viking (New York, NY), 1960, illustrated by Darrell Sweet, New American Library (New York, NY), 1992.

The Last Unicorn (also see below), Viking (New York, NY), 1968, anniversary edition, illustrated by Mel Grant, Penguin (New York, NY), 1991.

Lila the Werewolf (novella; also see below), illustrated by Courtlandt Johnson, Capra Press (Santa Barbara, CA), 1974, revised edition, 1976.

The Fantasy Worlds of Peter S. Beagle (omnibus; includes *A Fine and Private Place, The Last Unicorn, Lila the Werewolf,* and "Come, Lady Death"), illustrated by Courtlandt Johnson, Capra Press (Santa Barbara, CA), 1974.

The Folk of the Air, Ballantine Books/Del Rey (New York, NY), 1986.

The Innkeeper's Song, Roc (New York, NY), 1993.

The Unicorn Sonata, illustrated by Robert Rodriguez, Turner (Atlanta, GA), 1996.

Giant Bones (short stories), illustrated by Tony DiTerlizzi, Roc (New York, NY), 1997.

Tamsin, Roc (New York, NY), 1999.

A Dance for Emilia, Roc (New York, NY), 2000.

NONFICTION

I See by My Outfit (memoir), Viking (New York, NY), 1965.

The California Feeling (memoir), photographs by Michael Bey and Ansel Adams, Doubleday (Garden City, NY), 1969.

(With Harry N. Abrams) *American Denim: A New Folk Art,* photographs by Baron Wolman and the Denim Artists, Abrams/Warner (New York, NY), 1975.

(With Pat Derby) *The Lady and Her Tiger* (biography), Dutton (New York, NY), 1976.

The Garden of Earthly Delights (art criticism), illustrations from the paintings of Hieronymous Bosch, Viking (New York, NY), 1981.

(With Pat Derby) *In the Presence of Elephants* (biography), photographs by Genaro Molina, Capra Press (Santa Barbara, CA), 1995.

PLAYS AND SCREENPLAYS

The Zoo (television script), Columbia Broadcasting System, 1973.

(With Adam Kennedy) *The Dove* (film script), E.M.I., 1974.

The Greatest Thing That Almost Happened (television script), Charles Fries, 1977.

(With Chris Conkling) *The Lord of the Rings, Part One* (animated film script), United Artists, 1978.

The Last Unicorn (animated film script), Marble Arch/Rankin-Bass, 1982.

The Last Unicorn (play; adaptation of his novel), produced in Seattle, WA, 1988.

The Midnight Angel (opera libretto; based on his short story "Come, Lady Death"), music by David Carlson, produced by the Glimmerglass Opera, Cooperstown, NY, the Opera Theater, St. Louis, MO, and the Sacramento Opera, Sacramento, CA, 1993.

Also author of "Sarek" (television script), *Star Trek—The Next Generation,* season three, 1990. Also author of film scripts for *A Fine and Private Place* and for a live-action movie version of *The Last Unicorn.* Author of scripts for *Camelot* and *The Story of Moses,* both 1996. Author of script for *A Whale of a Tale,* a television special featuring characters from the film *The Little Mermaid* for Walt Disney Studios.

OTHER

(Author of introduction) J.R.R. Tolkien, *The Tolkien Reader,* Houghton Mifflin (Boston, MA), 1966.

(Author of introduction) Robert Nathan, *Evening Song,* Capra Press (Santa Barbara, CA), 1973.

(Author of introduction) Robert Nathan, *Portrait of Jennie,* Amereon Ltd, 1976.

(Author of foreword) Abraham Soyer, *Adventures of Yemima and Other Stories,* translated by Rebecca Beagle and Rebecca Soyer, illustrated by Raphael Soyer, Viking (New York, NY), 1979.

(Author of foreword) Avram Davidson, *The Best of Avram Davidson,* Doubleday (New York, NY), 1979.

(Author of foreword) Edgar Pangborn, *Davy,* Macmillan Collier Nucleus, 1990.

(Author of foreword) Avram Davidson, *Adventures in Unhistory: Conjectures on the Factual Foundation of Several Ancient Legends,* Owlswick Press, 1993.

(Editor, with Janet Berliner and Martin H. Greenberg) *Peter S. Beagle's Immortal Unicorn, Volume One,* HarperCollins (New York, NY), 1995.

The Rhinoceros Who Quoted Nietzsche and Other Odd Acquaintances (short stories and essays), Tachyon Publishers, 1997.

(Editor, with Janet Berliner and Martin H. Greenberg) *Peter S. Beagle's Immortal Unicorn, Volume Two,* HarperCollins (New York, NY), 1999.

Also contributor of short stories to anthologies, including *New Worlds of Fantasy* and *New Worlds of Fantasy,* Volume 3, edited by Terry Carr, Ace Books, 1967 and 1971, respectively; *Phantasmagoria,* edited by Jane Mobley, Anchor Books, 1977; *The Fantastic Imagina-* tion: *An Anthology of High Fantasy,* edited by Robert H. Boyer and Kenneth J. Zahorski, Avon (New York, NY), 1977; *Dark Imaginings: A Collection of Gothic Fantasy,* edited by Robert H. Boyer and Kenneth J. Zahorski, Dell (New York, NY), 1978; *After the King,* edited by Martin H. Greenberg, Tor (New York, NY), 1992; *Space Opera,* edited by Anne McCaffrey and Elizabeth Anne Scarborough, DAW (New York, NY), 1996; *Modern Classics of Fantasy,* edited by Gardner Dozois, St. Martin's Press (New York, NY), 1997; and *Knights in Madness,* edited by Peter Haining, Ace Books (New York, NY), 2000. Work also appears in a volume of *Prize Stories: The O. Henry Awards.* Contributor of introductions to *Forgotten Worlds* by Abraham Soyer, *The Boss in the Wall: A Treatise on the House Devil* by Avram Davidson and Grania Davis, *The Fellowship of the Ring* by J.R.R. Tolkien, and *The Avram Davidson Treasury* by Avram Davidson. Contributor of recipes to *Serve It Forth: Cooking with Anne McCaffrey,* edited by Anne McCaffrey, 1996. Contributor of short fiction and articles to periodicals, including *Atlantic, Harper's, Holiday, Ladies' Home Journal, Mademoiselle, Saturday Evening Post, Seventeen, Today's Health, Venture, West,* and others. Beagle's works have been translated into over fifteen languages. His papers are housed in a permanent collection at the University of Pittsburgh.

ADAPTATIONS: The Last Unicorn is the subject of "Captain Cully," a short play by Aaron Shepard directed to middle graders and junior high school students that appears in the book *Stories on Stage. A Fine and Private Place* was adapted as a musical by Erik Haagensen (book and lyrics) and Richard Isen (music) and published by Samuel French, 1992. *The Last Unicorn, Lila the Werewolf,* and "Come, Lady Death" were released as audio cassettes read by the author. Beagle also released a recording, *Peter S. Beagle—Live!,* in 1991.

SIDELIGHTS: An American author who is considered a master fantasist as well as a distinguished writer of nonfiction, Peter S. Beagle is celebrated for his originality, inventiveness, skill with plot and characterization, and rich, evocative literary style. In addition to novels, he has written short stories, poetry, essays, and screenplays for film and television and has edited and contributed to anthologies. Beagle is also an accomplished folk singer, guitarist, and songwriter who has released a live album and has written the libretto for an opera based on one of his short stories. He is perhaps best known as the author of *The Last Unicorn,* a fantasy that describes the quest of the title character to discover the last of her species. Using the classic fairy tale as his basic structure, Beagle created a work that is credited with breathing new life into the fantasy genre through its blend of comedy, tragedy, pathos, literary allusions, and contemporary culture. *The Last Unicorn* is usually acknowledged as a landmark, a post-modern touchstone that has been compared favorably with such works as J.R.R. Tolkien's *The Lord of the Rings* and Ursula K. Le Guin's *A Wizard of Earthsea.* In his other fantasies, Beagle continues to marry the traditional fairy story, fable, and legend to realistic concerns, most notably the state of the human condition and the thin line between fantasy and reality, life and death. Although he generally is not considered a writer for the young, Beagle has written two books, *The Unicorn Sonata* and *Tamsin,* that feature thirteen-year-old girls as main characters. Some of his other fantasies are also popular with young adults, especially *The Last Unicorn* and his first novel, *A Fine and Private Place.* Youthful audiences enjoy the lively talking animals and supernatural characters in Beagle's works as well as his fiction's humor, action, and romance. In addition, young people appreciate much of Beagle's nonfiction, especially *I See by My Outfit,* an account of Beagle's trip from New York to California by motor scooter; *American Denim: A New Folk Art,* a history of blue jeans; and *In the Presence of Elephants,* one of two books written with and about Pat Derby, a California animal trainer and activist who is the founder of PAWS (Performing Animals' Welfare Society), an organization for abused or neglected animals in show business.

As a writer, Beagle is regarded a lyrical, elegant, and economical stylist who fills his works with eloquent language and colorful images and metaphors. He often mixes slang, Yiddish phrases, and pop culture references with the language of high fantasy and romance; he also favors disparate narrative techniques and, on occasion, multiple points of view. In addition, Beagle includes humor, wit, and, perhaps most notably, irony in his books; his inclusion of irony in his fantasies is often acknowledged as a new feature in the genre. As a fantasist, Beagle has been compared to such authors as Lewis Carroll, George MacDonald, Hans Christian Andersen, C.S. Lewis, Lord Dunsany, James Thurber, and Robert Nathan. The author is praised consistently for his relevant portrayals of people of various ages and ethnic backgrounds as well as for making the otherworldly seem familiar and real. Thematically, Beagle addresses such subjects as renewal and rebirth, the nature of truth, the power of love and friendship, good versus evil, the difficulties of aging, and the importance of magic and wonder in readers' lives, issues thought to give his books depth and authenticity. Critics have noted that Beagle sometimes overwrites and that some of his

works are disappointing, thin, overlong, or incoherent. However, most observers have agreed that Beagle is a gifted writer whose books have helped to transform the fantasy novel while contributing greatly to a variety of other genres. Writing in *Booklist,* John Mort called Beagle "the class act of fantasy writing, the only one to remind me of Tolkien and, in his darker moments, Dined. . . . Gentle yet biting, far-fetched and altogether common, Beagle's fairy tales invoke comparisons with those associated with yet another great name, the Brothers Grimm."

Born in New York City, Beagle is the son of two teachers, Simon and Rebecca Soyer Beagle. At age seventy-three, his mother translated a collection of fairy tales her father had written in Hebrew more than forty years before; Beagle did the foreword to the book. He grew up in the Bronx, and wrote in an article in *Holiday* magazine, "As far as New York is concerned, I grew up at the end of the world. The subways end, and the buses run by appointment only." Beagle's neighborhood was lined with trees and surrounded by hills. While he was going to elementary school in the East Bronx, there was, he said, "the ghost of a farm just across the street from us, a jungly, terrifying place owned by a half-mad old man who threw stones at us when we tried to sneak up on him at lunch hour. Less and less these days, but still more than the rest of New York, the Bronx reminds you that it was wild country once."

Beagle once remembered that, as a boy, "I read early and I was read to early. Animals were an immediate intense interest. I know I was comfortable with animals long before I was comfortable with most human beings." Beagle lived near the Bronx Zoo and spent many hours there as a child. He wrote in *Today's Health,* "I was shy, overweight, ill-conditioned, asthmatic, and allergic to everything. . . . My parents gave me a great deal of affection, but not many other people did. I came home from school and read books. I remember that I had a long-lived bout being a wolf—and, as late as high school—an imaginary lion friend named Cyrano. Thinking about that time now, I realize that in its own painful way, it was invaluable for me. I learned to be alone. Nobody who wants to be a writer can do without that skill. I learned to entertain myself and to look after myself, in a sloppily efficient sort of way. And I taught myself not to care what anyone else thought about me. I can remember making that decision, very consciously, around the sixth grade. I also lost the ability to cry, but you pay for everything."

At an early age, Beagle decided to become a writer. In an interview with Dan Tooker and Roger Hofheins in their *Fiction! Interviews with Northern California Nov-*

elists, Beagle stated, "I started [to write] when I was seven, literally. My parents were remarkable. They never told me that writing was not a fit profession for a young man. I can remember writing stories in class. I wanted to imitate sounds. I love sounds. I was always excited by the sound of words and I wanted to copy that. I would imitate other writers. I haven't altogether lost that. *The Last Unicorn* starts off imitating a half dozen people: James Stephens, Thurber, T.H. White. And Lord Dunstan is always somewhere in the background."

At the Bronx High School of Science, Beagle's friends and acquaintances were almost all from the North and West Bronx and were Jewish, like himself. He wrote in *Holiday* magazine, "We were intelligent, hungrily so, having been the family prodigies, the block's 'walking dictionaries' long enough to be sick of it, and, for many of us, high school was the first contact we had had with people like ourselves." Beagle and his friends traded records, read their plays to one another, and showed each other their poetry and art. They went to the theater, to movies, and to museums—"to all the places," Beagle recalled, "that had bored us so when our parents used to take us there." He added, "And we talked—lord, how we learned to talk!—constantly, perpetually. . . . We all began running away from home about then; rarely in the classic sense—Tom Sawyer never had College Boards—but within ourselves."

Beagle was a frequent contributor to his school's literary magazine. His work attracted the attention of the fiction editor at *Seventeen* magazine. As a teenager, Beagle was befriended by poet Louis Untermeyer, who passed him on to his literary agent, Elizabeth Otis, who was also the agent for novelist John Steinbeck, author of *The Grapes of Wrath*. At nineteen, Beagle completed a novel that Otis placed with the Viking Press: that work, *A Fine and Private Place,* was published when the author was just twenty-one.

Set in a Bronx cemetery, *A Fine and Private Place* features Jonathan Rebeck, a fifty-three-year-old druggist who had gone bankrupt twenty years before. After giving up on the world, Rebeck went to live in an isolated mausoleum, where he has survived on food stolen from a nearby deli by a tough-talking raven. Rebeck has gotten to know the ghosts of the recently deceased. However, his relationship with them lasts for only a short while, since they soon forget their lives and fall into an endless sleep. Two of these ghosts are Michael Morgan and Laura Durand, a couple who meet in the cemetery, fall in love, and decide that they want to avoid their

fate. Rebeck decides to help the couple and does so with the help of Mrs. Gertrude Klapper, a widow who visits her husband's grave in the cemetery. The story ends with multiple happy endings, including Rebeck moving out of the cemetery into the land of the living.

A Fine and Private Place has been noted as a funny and tender story that demonstrates that love is stronger than death and includes an especially amusing character, the scene-stealing raven. Beagle was also lauded for the assurance he displayed as a writer, especially one just out of his teens. Writing in *Saturday Review,* Granville Hicks stated that *A Fine and Private Place* "seems to me quite as important as many solemn and pretentious novels I have read. . . . [Beagle] persuades the reader to play his game of make-believe, and then rewards him with an admirably sustained performance. For so young a writer, he is amazingly sure of himself, and it will be interesting to see what he writes next." Harold Jaffe of *Commonweal* commented that Beagle seemed to be saying that death "is life without feeling. A familiar enough admonition, certainly, but I have never felt its authenticity in quite the same way." Writing in the *New York Times Book Review,* Edmund Fuller concluded, "A disembodied love in our literary climate is about as original as a young man can be. . . . The great thing is that *A Fine and Private Place* has wit, charm, and individuality—with a sense of style and structure notable in a first novel. . . . The publishers evoke E.B. White and Robert Nathan in comparison. I think Peter DeVries might be closer. Be that as it may; watch Beagle." In 1992, *A Fine and Private Place* was adapted into a musical comedy by Erik Haagensen and Richard Isen.

In his senior year of high school, Beagle entered a story and a poem in the Scholastic Writing Awards Contest. His poem won first prize: a college scholarship. Beagle went to the University of Pittsburgh. While at the university, Beagle was taught by the Irish short story writer and translator Frank O'Connor, who disliked the genre of fantasy. Beagle wrote a short story, "Come, Lady Death" to see whether he could sneak it by O'Connor. The story, later published, is now recognized as one of Beagle's best early efforts; it was also turned into an opera with a libretto by Beagle and music by David Carlson. As a college sophomore, Beagle won first place in a short story contest sponsored by *Seventeen* magazine. He graduated from the University of Pittsburgh with a bachelor's degree in creative writing and a minor in Spanish.

Beagle then spent a year in Europe. In an article for *Holiday* magazine, he recalled this period as "a lonesome, stupid time, and if I learned anything from it, it doesn't show." In 1960, Beagle returned to the United States to attend grad school at Stanford University in California after being enrolled there by his agent; he stayed at Stanford for a year on a Wallace Stegner Writing Fellowship. In 1963, Beagle and a friend, Phil Signuick, took an eventful cross-country journey from New York to California on their mopeds, a trip documented in the memoir *I See by My Outfit.* In 1964, Beagle married Enid Elaine Nordeen, the mother of his two daughters, Victoria and Kalisa, and his son, Danny. Beagle wrote in the *Saturday Evening Post,* "Before they came, I think, I slept through my relationships with others, as I did through my childhood and my schooling." Enid and her children also brought animals back into Beagle's life; eventually, the family acquired seventy-five creatures—including a quail, a parrot, a squirrel, a chipmunk, an iguana, a shrew, and a kinkajou, as well as dogs, cats, horses, birds, ferrets, and others.

In 1968, Beagle produced *The Last Unicorn.* In this work, a nameless unicorn is prompted to leave her enchanted forest after she overhears some hunters state that she is the last of her kind; the fact is confirmed by a butterfly from a far-away land who talks in a combination of twentieth-century slang, song lyrics, and a more courtly form of speech. After the unicorn sets off to look for her missing species, she is captured by Mommy Fortuna, a sorceress who runs Mommy Fortuna's Midnight Carnival and who weaves spells that make people believe that they are seeing mythical beasts when they are actually seeing domestic and wild animals. The unicorn is freed by Schmendrick the Magician, a bumbling wizard who botches simple tricks but can, on occasion, perform true feats of magic. Schmendrick has had a spell placed on him that causes him to remain immortal until he becomes competent. He and the unicorn are joined by Molly Grue, a cynical, middle-aged scullery maid who has been a Maid Marian figure to Captain Cully, a Robin Hood wannabe who lives with a group of distinctly unmerry men. The trio go to Hagsgate, a wasteland where time has stopped and imagination has been destroyed. The kingdom is ruled by King Haggard, who lives in a castle by the sea with his son, Prince Lir, an ineffectual hero, and the Red Bull, an evil being created by Haggard. The king has imprisoned the unicorns because he wishes to possess all of their beauty. He has fashioned the Red Bull, a creature that sees only unicorns, to hunt them down and trap them in the sea.

In order to gain access to the castle, the unicorn is turned into a human by Schmendrick. As Lady Amalthea, the unicorn forgets her immortal nature, and she and Prince Lir fall in love. Schmendrick and Molly try to find the lost unicorns before Amalthea loses her memory and becomes a mortal permanently. After the pair discover the trapped prisoners, the unicorn reverts back to her original form. When she is charged by the Red Bull, Prince Lir selflessly throws himself in front of the creature to save the unicorn's life. His sacrifice gives the unicorn the power to drive the Red Bull into the sea, thus freeing her brethren. At the end of the story, King Haggard's kingdom is destroyed by a tidal wave, Prince Lir becomes King Lir, Schmendrick and Molly go off to find other adventures, and the unicorn goes back to her world, knowing good and evil, love, and mortality; her innocence has been replaced with experience.

The Last Unicorn often is lauded as a masterpiece of fantasy writing, a novel that can be read purely as an adventure story or as an exploration of the purpose of life. It is considered both a parody of its traditional sources—the fairy tale, the quest story, the romance, and others—and a reestablishment of the fantasy genre. At the time of its publication, *The Last Unicorn* was an instant success and became a best seller. Most reviewers had high praise for the novel. For example, Rochelle Girson of *Saturday Review* stated that Beagle "has extraordinary inventive powers, and they make every page a delight. . . . Beagle is a true magician with words, a master of prose and an deft practitioner in verse. He has been compared, not unreasonably, with Lewis Carroll and J.R.R. Tolkien, but he stands squarely and triumphantly on his own feet." Subsequent critics have continued to praise Beagle and his creation. A critic in *St. James Guide to Fantasy Writers* commented that *The Last Unicorn* "remains the book for which Beagle will always be known and to which all his later work will be compared. . . . It is one of the enduring classics of American fantasy." Writing in *Imaginary Worlds: The Art of Fantasy,* Lin Carter stated that *The Last Unicorn* "is in a class by itself," while Jon Pennington, writing in *Mythlore,* called the novel "a new type of fantasy that is a powerful vision for our modern world." Pennington concluded that Beagle "recombines the archetypal patterns of fairy tales into a vision that is specifically modern. And American."

The Last Unicorn has always had a loyal and supportive audience among young people. Initially, the novel especially appealed to hippies, artists, musicians, and fans of such authors as Tolkien and the science fiction writer Robert Heinlein; it became recognized as a cult classic. Many Web sites devoted to the book and to the animated film version produced by Marble Arch/Rankin-Bass in 1981 have since appeared. In addition to the film, *The Last Unicorn* has been adapted for the stage and as a short play for children. Beagle has noted that he wrote *The Last Unicorn* as an homage to the authors he loved and whose style he wanted to emulate, such as Lord Dunsany, James Stephens, James Thurber, and T.H. White. In an interview with David Van Becker in *San Jose Studies,* Beagle said that, with *The Last Unicorn,* "I was deliberately taking the classic fairy-tale structure, the classic fairy-tale characters, and trying to do something else with them. I was saddling myself and aiding myself both with the proper forms."

After the publication of *The Last Unicorn,* Beagle did not produce another fantasy novel for another eighteen years. In the meantime, he produced screenplays for film and television, including *The Last Unicorn* and *The Lord of the Rings, Part One* (with Chris Conkling), as well as writing short stories, novellas, nonfiction, forewords, and articles. In 1969, he produced *The California Feeling,* a memoir that describes Beagle's year-long trek across California with photographer friend Michael Bry; the pair traveled in a 1957 Volkswagen bus they named Renata Tebaldi. Beagle also began performing regularly as a folk singer: in 1973, he began a part-time engagement as the dinner entertainment at L'Oustalou, a French restaurant in Santa Cruz, California, a gig that lasted for twelve years. As a singer/guitarist, he performs songs in English, French, German, and Yiddish, including several of his own compositions. Beagle has also released a live album of one of his concerts.

In 1980, Beagle's marriage to Enid Elaine Nordeen ended. In 1985, he moved to Seattle, Washington, but returned to California after a few years. In 1986, he released his next work of fantasy, *The Folk of the Air.* This novel features Joe Farrell, a wandering musician and talented lute player who first appeared in Beagle's novella *Lila the Werewolf* in 1974. Joe goes to Avicenna, a college town on the California coast. He moves in with his friend Ben, a college buddy now living with Sia, an attractive older woman who is a practicing psychologist. Joe runs into a former girlfriend, Julie Tanikawa, who is involved in the League for Archaic Pleasures, a role-playing group that reenacts medieval battles and celebrations. Joe becomes involved and learns that the League is real, not a game; its members actually become the characters that they portray. While attending a meeting, Joe and Julie watch Aiffe, a teenage witch, summon up Nicholas Bonner, a young man who was sent into limbo five centuries earlier. Bonner has a vendetta against Sia, who is actually an ancient goddess of immense power. Finally, Joe realizes that Sia is the only thing that can protect them all from destruction, and she and Bonner engage in a magical duel to the death.

The Folk of the Air is perhaps Beagle's most highly disputed work. Due perhaps to the high level of expectation surrounding its publication, the novel received a mixed reception. However, its multiculturalism and prose style were praised consistently. Observers also noted the similarity of Avicenna to Berkeley, California, and the League for Archaic Pleasures to the real-life Society for Creative Anachronism. The year after the publication of *The Folk of the Air,* Beagle married Padma Hejmadi, a writer and artist of Indian descent.

In 1993, Beagle produced *The Innkeeper's Song,* a novel that is often considered among his best; based on a song written by Beagle, it is the author's favorite among his own works. In this book, three women—one black, one brown, and one paler than a corpse—take a room at a village inn, the Gaff and Slasher. Two of the women, Lal, a mercenary, and Nyaterneri, a warrior priestess, are the former pupils of a magician, The Man Who Laughs. The third woman, Lukassa, has been called back from the dead by Lal. The Man Who Laughs is being pursued by Arshadin, a former protégé who has sold his blood and soul to the Others for immortality. Arshadin intends to kill the wizard, turn him into an evil ghost, and send him to the Others in return for his blood. Young Tikat, a weaver's son, searches for his betrothed, Lukassa, after he views her death and resurrection. Rosseth, the stable boy at the Gaff and Slasher, also becomes involved, as does Karsh, the bad-tempered innkeeper, and Nyaterneri's familiar, a cranky, shapeshifting fox. Finally, Arshadin turns The Man Who Laughs into a ghost, but Lukassa makes a deal with the Others that saves the wizard. Beagle uses ten different viewpoints to tell the story, which addresses the issues of the nature of life, death, and love.

Writing in *Locus,* Gary K. Wolfe stated, "*The Last Unicorn* may always be Beagle's best fantasy, but *The Innkeeper's Song . . .* is his best *novel.*" Writing in the *New York Times Book Review,* Gerald Jonas opined that, as a commercial genre, fantasy "has come to mean endlessly recycled adventures of sword-wielding heroes and spell-casting wizards, recounted in pseudopoetic prose as dreary and predictable as the characters and settings. This makes the achievement of Peter S. Beagle in *The Innkeeper's Song* all the more remarkable. In his capable hands, even the most timeworn material shines again." In an interview with Ed Bryant in *Prime Time Replay,* Beagle called *The Innkeeper's Song* "my first grown-up book." *Giant Bones,* a collection of six stories published in 1997, is set in the same land as *The Innkeeper's Song* and includes a story, "Lal and Soukyan," that features some of the same characters.

The Unicorn Sonata, a novel published in 1996, is the first of Beagle's works to feature a young adult protagonist. Josephine "Joey" Rivera is a thirteen-year-old Latina girl living in contemporary Los Angeles. A natural musician, she helps to clean up Papas Music store in exchange for lessons in music theory. One day, a strange young man, Indigo, comes into the store to try and sell his beautiful horn for gold, but he disappears before the transaction can take place. Later, Joey hears a distant melody and follows it down the street. She accidentally crosses the Divide, an invisible border, and enters a mystical place called Shei'rah. Joey encounters many mythological creatures, including the Eldest, unicorns whose music is one of the foundations of Shei'rah. The Eldest are being weakened by a mysterious disease that is stealing their sight. Crossing between her world and Shei'rah, Joey works furiously to transcribe the music of the Eldest before it is lost. At the same time, she tries to save her beloved Mexican grandmother, Abuelita, from the retirement home.

Joey learns that Indigo is actually an Eldest who prefers to live on Earth as a human being. Selling his horn will permit him to live well, although its loss will prohibit him from going home to Shei'rah. In addition, Joey discovers that Indigo's greed for gold was the cause of the blindness that affects the unicorns. Joey takes Abuelita, a wise healer, to Shei'rah to help cure the plague, and she recalls an old folk remedy for blindness that uses gold as its chief ingredient. Finally, Indigo decides to relinquish his selfish plans in order to save the Eldest. Writing in *Library Journal,* Susan Hamburger stated, "This enchanting story of seeking a true home is highly recommended." Ray Olson of *Booklist* commented, "America's finest gentle fantasist manages to point up the best qualities of both real life and fantasy, of both Earth and Shei'rah." A critic in *Publishers Weekly* called *The Unicorn Sonata* "a charming fantasy" before concluding that "the characterizations are grand, enhanced by graceful prose laced with exquisite detail, and through both literary creativity and folkloric expertise where unicorns are concerned." Beagle, who has become recognized as an expert on unicorns, is also the editor, with Janet Berliner and Martin H. Greenberg, of two collections of short stories featuring the mythical beast, *Peter S. Beagle's Immortal Unicorn, Volume One* and *Volume Two.*

Tamsin, a novel that blends history, folklore, and the supernatural, is the second of Beagle's works to feature a teenager as its main character and the first to use one as its narrator. Jenny Gluckstein, a petulant, rebellious thirteen-year-old New Yorker, moves to England with her divorced mother Sally, who is to marry Evan McHugh, an agricultural biologist. Evan is responsible for restoring and managing the rundown Stourhead Farm—a place beset by strange accidents, noises, and smells—in Dorset, England. When Jenny's cat chases a Persian ghost cat, it leads her to a secret chamber and its owner, Tamsin Willoughby, a twenty-year-old girl who died three hundred years before. The daughter of the farm's original builder, Tamsin is in mourning for her lover, Edric, a poor musician, and is fearful of a figure that she calls the Other One. Jenny meets a variety of preternatural creatures, including the Black Dog, who warns her of danger; the billy-blind, who gives advice to her; and the Pooka, an untrustworthy, unsympathetic shape-shifter. Jenny learns that Tamsin and Edric will be tormented eternally if she does not help them; she must decide whether she is brave and unselfish enough to aid the ghostly lovers.

By piecing together Tamsin's memories and information gathered from local historians, Jenny discovers that the Other One is the evil George Jeffreys, the "hanging judge" who presided over the Bloody Assizes and sent hundreds of people to violent deaths in the aftermath of the Monmouth Rebellion in 1685. Jeffreys, who wanted to marry Tamsin, was responsible for Edric's disappearance. Jenny narrates the tale in retrospect as a nineteen-year-old in brash contemporary language; Beagle also includes Tamsin's refined Jacobean English and the earthy dialect of old Dorset. A reviewer in *Publishers Weekly* stated, "Like his enchanting *The Last Unicorn,* Beagle's newest fantasy features characters so real they leap off his pages and into readers' souls. . . . Fantasy rarely dances through the imagination in more radiant garb than this." John Mort of *Booklist* added, "Although nowhere labeled as such, *Tamsin* is a fine young adult novel. . . . [It] may be the best of its kind this year." Although some reviewers were less than enchanted by Jenny's whiny persona in the beginning of *Tamsin,* most acknowledge that she is one of Beagle's most convincing characterizations. For example, Teri Smith of *Crescent City Book Views* commented, "Beagle creates a moody, spoiled, opinionated thirteen year old and makes us believe in and care for her. . . . Beagle's characters will stay in your heart forever."

Beagle has continued to contribute works to several genres, and much of his writing appeals to young people. For example, he has written forewords to books by J.R.R. Tolkien as well as a story and teleplay, "Sarek," as an episode of the television series *Star Trek: The Next Generation.* He also has given readings, lectures, and concerts at universities; has conducted writing workshops at academic institutions; and has appeared at fantasy conventions. In assessing his work as a writer, Beagle once said that he creates fantasy because "the fantastic turn of vision suits both my sense of the world as a profoundly strange and deceptive place, and my deepest sense of poetry, which is singing." Beagle confided to Van Becker of *San Jose Studies* that he sees himself as a traditional storyteller, "a descendant of Scheherazade. . . . a long line of people who made up stories in the bazaar." Writing in *Holiday* magazine, Beagle said, "My life is a slow process of making things real, making them continue to exist when my back is turned. It is my worst failing, this dangerous solipsism, but it is also one reason why I write: to create the world line-by-line, to find a way in, a handhold. For all I know, no one else in the world has this problem, but I wonder, 'Could we all go on treating people the way we do if we believed that they were real?' Lizard and louse, man and tiger, we are all here together, barely alive in the dark, clinging to the earth and trying to stay warm. Either we all have souls, or none of us do." Writing in the *St. James Guide to Fantasy Writers,* Beagle concluded, "I write what I would love to read if someone else had written it. But no one else quite does what I do, so I have to. That's really all the statement I can honestly make."

BIOGRAPHICAL AND CRITICAL SOURCES:

BOOKS

Carter, Lin, *Imaginary Worlds: The Art of Fantasy,* Ballantine (New York, NY), 1973.

Contemporary Literary Criticism, Thomson Gale (Detroit, MI), Volume 7, 1977, Volume 104, 1998.

Dictionary of Literary Biography Yearbook: 1980, Thomson Gale (Detroit, MI), 1981.

Hark, Ina Rae, "The Fantasy Worlds of Peter Beagle," *Survey of Modern Fantasy Literature,* edited by Frank N. Magill, Salem Press, 1983.

Olderman, Raymond M, *Beyond the Waste Land: A Study of the American Novel in the Nineteen-Sixties,* Yale University Press, 1972.

St. James Guide to Fantasy Writers, St. James Press (Detroit, MI), 1996.

St. James Guide to Young Adult Writers, 2nd edition, St. James Press (Detroit, MI), 1999.

Tooker, Dan, and Roger Hofheins, *Fiction! Interviews with Northern California Novelists* (amended by Peter S. Beagle), Harcourt (New York, NY), 1972.

Tymn, Marshall B., Kenneth J. Zahorski, and Robert H. Boyer, *Fantasy Literature: A Core Collection and Reference Guide,* Bowker (New York, NY), 1979.

Zahorski, Kenneth J., *Peter S. Beagle* (Starmont Reader's Guide, no. 44), Starmount House, 1988.

PERIODICALS

Booklist, July, 1997, John Mort, review of *Giant Bones,* p. 1806; August, 1996, Ray Olson, review of *The Unicorn Sonata,* p. 1853; August, 1999, John Mort, review of *Tamsin,* p. 1984; August, 2000, Ray Olson review of *A Dance for Emilia,* p. 2124.

Commonweal, June 28, 1968, Harold Jaffe, review of *A Fine and Private Place* and *The Last Unicorn,* p. 447.

Holiday, December, 1964, Peter S. Beagle, "Good-bye to the Bronx;" August, 1965, Peter S. Beagle, "My Last Heroes."

Library Journal, September 15, 1996, Susan Hamburger, review of *The Unicorn Sonata,* p. 100; October 15, 1999, Jackie Cassada review of *Tamsin,* p. 110.

Locus, September, 1993, Gary K. Wolfe, review of *The Innkeeper's Song,* pp. 23-24.

Mythlore, summer, 1989, John Pennington, "Innocence and Experience and the Imagination in the World of Peter Beagle," pp. 10-16.

New York Times Book Review, June 5, 1962, Edmund Fuller, "Unique Recluse"; November 14, 1993, Gerald Jonas, review of *The Innkeeper's Song,* p. 74.

Publishers Weekly, August 5, 1986, review of *The Unicorn Sonata,* p. 430; August 9, 1999, review of *Tamsin,* p. 348; October 2, 2000, review of *A Dance for Emilia,* p. 63.

San Jose Studies, February, 1975, David Van Becker, "Time, Space, and Consciousness in the Fantasy of Peter S. Beagle."

Saturday Evening Post, December, 1966, Peter S. Beagle, "On Being the Man of the House."

Saturday Review, March 30, 1958, Rochelle Girson, review of *The Last Unicorn,* pp. 21-22; May 28, 1960, Granville Hicks, "Visit to a Happy Hunting Ground," p. 18.

Today's Health, October, 1974, Peter S. Beagle, "Kids and Kinkajous: The Special Blessing of Growing up with Animals."

ONLINE

Crescent City Book Views, http://crescentblues.com/ (December 6, 2001), Teri Smith, review of *Tamsin.*

Green Man Review, http://www.greenmanreview.com/ (December 6, 2001), Naomi de Bruyn, review of *A Dance for Emilia.*

Infinity Plus, http://www.iplus.zetnet.co.uk/ (December 6, 2001), Nick Gevers, review of *Tamsin.*

Last Unicorn, http://utd500.utdallas.edu/ (November, 2001), Peter S. Beagle, commentary on *The Last Unicorn;* Marc Hairston, commentary on *The Last Unicorn.*

Prime Time Replay, http://www.omnimag.com/ (October 3, 1996), Ed Bryant, interview with Beagle for Omni Visions; Don Thompson, press release on *The Unicorn Sonata.*

Rambles Online, http://www.rambles.net/ (August 19, 1999), review of *Tamsin.*

SciFi.com, http://www.scifi.com/ (December 6, 2001), interview with Beagle.

Under the Covers, http://mtnimage.com/ (August 19, 1999), Harriet Klausner, review of *Tamsin.*

*   *   *

BEAGLE, Peter Soyer
    See BEAGLE, Peter S.

*   *   *

BEATTIE, Ann 1947-

PERSONAL: Born September 8, 1947, in Washington, DC; daughter of James A. and Charlotte (Crosby) Beattie; married David Gates (a psychiatrist), 1972 (divorced, 1980); married Lincoln Perry (an artist). *Education:* American University, B.A., 1969; University of Connecticut, M.A., 1970, graduate study, 1970-72.

ADDRESSES: Agent—c/o Janklow Nesbit, 598 Madison Ave., New York, NY 10022.

CAREER: Fiction writer. University of Virginia, Charlottesville, visiting writer and lecturer, 1975-77, 1980, Edgar Allan Poe Professor of Creative Writing, 2001—. Harvard University, Briggs-Copeland Lecturer in English, 1977-78; Northwestern University, writer-in-residence at Center for the Writing Arts, 1994.

MEMBER: American Academy and Institute of Arts and Letters, PEN, Authors Guild, Authors League of America.

AWARDS, HONORS: Guggenheim fellowship, 1978; Award in Literature, American Academy and Institute of Arts and Letters, 1980; Distinguished Alumni Award, American University, 1980; honorary doctorates from American University, 1983, Colby College, 1991; PEN/Malamud Award for Excellence in Short Fiction, 2001.

WRITINGS:

Distortions (short stories), Doubleday (New York, NY), 1976, reprinted, Vintage Books (New York, NY), 1991.

Chilly Scenes of Winter (novel), Doubleday (New York, NY), 1976, reprinted, Vintage Books (New York, NY), 1991.

Secrets and Surprises (short stories), Random House (New York, NY), 1979.

Falling in Place (novel), Random House (New York, NY), 1980.

The Burning House (short stories), Random House (New York, NY), 1982.

Love Always (novel), Random House (New York, NY), 1985.

Spectacles, Workman Publishing (New York, NY), 1985.

Where You'll Find Me, and Other Stories, Linden Press/ Simon & Schuster (New York, NY), 1986.

Alex Katz (art criticism), Abrams (New York, NY), 1987.

Picturing Will (novel), Random House (New York, NY), 1989.

What Was Mine (short stories), Random House (New York, NY), 1991.

(With Bob Adelman) *Americana,* Scribner (New York, NY), 1992.

(With Andy Grundberg) *Flesh Blood: Photographers' Images of Their Own Families,* New York Picture Project (New York, NY), 1992.

(Selector) *The American Story: Short Stories from the Rea Award,* edited by Michael M. Rea, Ecco Press (Hopewell, NJ), 1993.

Another You, Knopf (New York, NY), 1995.

My Life, Starring Dara Falcon, Knopf (New York, NY), 1997.

(Author of introduction) Mary M. Kalergis, *With This Ring: A Portrait of Marriage,* Chrysler Museum Library (Norfolk, VA), 1997.

Park City: New and Selected Stories, Knopf (New York, NY), 1998.

Perfect Recall (short stories), Scribner (New York, NY), 2001.

The Doctor's House (novel), Scribner (New York, NY), 2002.

Contributor of essay to *Maine: The Seasons,* 2001. Contributor of short stories to periodicals, including *Esquire, Gentlemen's Quarterly,* and *New Yorker.*

Follies: New Stories (novel), Scribner (New York, NY), 2005.

ADAPTATIONS: Chilly Scenes of Winter was adapted as the movie *Head over Heels,* United Artists, 1979, and reedited and released as *Chilly Scenes of Winter,* 1982; Beattie's short story "A Vintage Thunderbird" was adapted by Robert Clem as a short film, 1983. Beattie recorded four stories from *The Burning House* for American Audio Prose Library, 1987, and recorded *Picturing Will* for Dove Books on Tape, 1990.

SIDELIGHTS: Novelist and short-story writer Ann Beattie "has become perhaps our most authoritative translator-transcriber of the speech patterns, nonverbal communications, rituals, and tribal customs of those members (white, largely middle class) of a generation who came of age around 1970—who attended or dropped out of college, smoked dope, missed connections, lived communally, and drifted in and out of relationships with a minimum of self-recognized affect or commitment," commented Robert Towers in the *New York Review of Books*. Beattie portrays people who feel "that their lives are entirely out of control, that they lack power and cannot be expected to take responsibility for the consequences of their actions," Margaret Atwood observed in the *Washington Post Book World*, adding, "Adrift in a world of seemingly pointless events . . . these characters cry out for meaning and coherence, but their world hands them nothing more resonant than popular song titles and T-shirt slogans." In exploring these lives of suburban angst, Beattie has been compared to such American authors as John Cheever, John Updike, Joseph Heller, and J.D. Salinger, all of whom chronicled the angst of a previous generation.

Beattie first honed her craft writing short stories for the *New Yorker,* and many of these short stories are included in the five collections of her work published between 1976 and 1991: *Distortions, Secrets and Surprises, The Burning House, Where You'll Find Me, and Other Stories,* and *What Was Mine.* These collections reflect not only the characteristic concerns and style of their author, but also the evolution of Beattie's fiction. Reviewers tend to hold up *Distortions, The Burning House,* and *What Was Mine* as milestones in the author's development as a short-story writer. As *New York Times* reviewer Anatole Broyard noted of her earliest work: "In spite of a style that virtually eliminates personality, she still manages to haunt the reader with her work. The things her characters say and do are rather like the inexplicable noises very old houses make in the middle of the night. You wake up in alarm when you hear them—what can *that* be?—then reason asserts itself and you go uneasily back to sleep."

Margaret Atwood hailed *The Burning House,* Beattie's third story collection, in the *New York Times Book Review.* "A new Beattie is almost like a fresh bulletin from the front," noted Atwood: "We snatch it up, eager to know what's happening out there on the edge of that shifting and dubious no man's land known as interpersonal relations." In following the relationships in these stories, Beattie shows that "there are no longer any ties that bind, not securely, not definitively: jobs, marriages, the commitments of love, even the status of parent or child—are all in a state of flux." Atwood added that "freedom, that catchword of sixties America, has translated into free fall, or a condition of weightlessness, and the most repeated motifs in the book are variants of this."

Perfect Recall collects eleven long stories portraying older people in sexless alliances. In the *New York Times* Jennifer Schuessler noted that Beattie is "still writing about the shifting kinship structures of late-twentieth-century America, but in a richer, more expansive, even elegiac register," which she dubbed "freewheeling and soulful." Also writing in the *New York Times,* Michiko Kakutani noted that even as the stories in *Perfect Recall* "have become more structured, her authorial stance has shifted as well, her embrace of indirection and omission giving way to a more concerted effort to connect the emotional dots." While Kakutani viewed this change in style as a weakness, Schuessler praised Beattie's evolving approach as "so vivid and beguiling . . . that it isn't until you look again that you realize how rarely she reaches for metaphors or other figures of speech, and how little she needs to." Nancy Schapiro, in the *St. Louis Post-Dispatch,* gave the collection qualified praise, writing that "Beattie mixes comedy and tragedy in a cohesive way." Still, Schapiro maintained that the stories may be too long, stretching "slight subjects beyond what they can well sustain." Enthusiasts of *Perfect Recall* also included *Los Angeles Times* reviewer Bernadette Murphy, who wrote that Beattie has "followed that tradition of portraying families in disintegration" into the new century with "a keen eye, a cutting sense of humor and wonderful depth." *Booklist*'s Brad Hooper also praised the 2000 collection as exhibiting the "primary attraction of Beattie's fiction: people with whom we identify placed in recognizably human situations." "In the end," Schuessler concluded, "these sparkling stories succeed not as diagnoses of the state of our unions, but as stories, pure and simple—slices of life whose larger significance you can't quite pin down, about people who seem as real as any friend of a friend of a friend you've ever heard something interesting about."

Reviewers such as Jonathan Yardley of the *Washington Post Book World* characterized Beattie as a "miniaturist . . . whose strength is brevity and who seems most sure of herself when loose ends are left untied; as a result," contended Yardley, "she is more suited to the form of the story than that of the novel." Others have seen promise in Beattie's novels *Chilly Scenes of Winter, Falling in Place, Love Always,* and *Picturing Will. Chilly Scenes of Winter* offers Beattie's first extended look at the 1960s generation that finds itself lost and disillusioned in the 1970s. In an interview with Bob Miner, Beattie said: "I *was* going out of my way in the novel to say something about the '60s having passed. It just seems to me to be an attitude that most of my friends and most of the people I know have. They all feel sort of let down, either by not having involved themselves more in the '60s now that the '70s are so dreadful, or else by having involved themselves to no avail. Most of the people I know are let down—they feel cheated—and these are the people I am writing about."

Beattie's second novel, *Falling in Place,* was published in 1980. At the center of the work is a suburban family descending into chaos. As John Clavin Batchelor explained in the *Village Voice,* the novel "weaves a trap from which [the central] family cannot escape; their home is destroyed in the end by their own sloth, envy, selfishness, and lack of grace." Although, like Beattie's earlier fiction, the novel is peopled by characters adrift from the 1960s and treats some of the author's characteristic concerns, Richard Locke argued in the *New York Times Book Review* that *Falling in Place* "is stronger, more accomplished, larger in every way than anything [Beattie has] done." The critic commented that "there's a new urgency to the characters' feelings and a much greater range and number of characters and points of view." Moreover, Locke pointed out, "These characters are not just quickly sketched-in; no fewer than five have distinct points of view: we learn and come to feel a lot about them and about the way they see the world."

Falling in Place drew critical attention for its almost journalistic depiction of Beattie's world. *New York Review of Books* contributor Robert Towers remarked that the author's realistic style recalls other media. "On a page-by-page basis the novel held my interest as an exceptionally good documentary film or television program might." Jack Beatty, however, found fault with Beattie's characteristic view of the world. He maintained in a *New Republic* review that "Beattie's sociological realism is superficial, a reflective realism of accurate detail—what songs are in, what clothes, what expressions—rather than the kind of critical realism whose exemplar is *Buddenbrooks.*" Pearl K. Bell, writing in *Commentary,* was especially critical of Beattie's style. "Making no comic gestures, taking everything in with her customary neutrality and giving it all back,"

wrote Bell, "Miss Beattie seems oblivious to her readers, unperturbed by their inevitable irritation and boredom." Locke countered, however, that *Falling in Place* "establishes Ann Beattie not merely as the object of a cult or as an 'interesting' young novelist, but as a prodigiously gifted and developing writer who has started to come of age."

In her next novel, *Love Always,* Beattie's "theme is a somber one, the failure of love between parents and children, between husbands and wives, between couples of every sexual persuasion," observed *New York Times* reviewer Christopher Lehmann-Haupt. The novel tells the story of Nicole Nelson, the fourteen-year-old star of the soap opera *Passionate Intensity.* Nicole takes a vacation from the Hollywood sets to visit her Aunt Lucy Spencer, who writes a pseudo-advice column for an offbeat magazine in Vermont. These two and the other characters, including Nicole's agent and Lucy's friends and colleagues, all become intertwined in a chaotic free-for-all that ricochets toward the moment when Nicole's mother dies offstage in an accident. In the end, concluded John Updike in the *New Yorker, Love Always* "is sadder than satire, for it is about the emptiness not of these lives but of our lives."

Love Always "is clearly Beattie; as intelligent as ever about contemporary pain and oddness, but less composed and quite a bit funnier," noted Richard Eder in the *Los Angeles Times Book Review.* He added that the author's "use of comedy is exuberant, sometimes uncontrolled, occasionally precious." Lehmann-Haupt offered a similar view, suggesting that "Beattie's narrative technique is essentially Keystone comedy, with sudden jump-cuts from one character's point of view to another and outrageous collisions among the various subplots of the comedy." However, in the opinion of Elizabeth Rosner in the *San Francisco Review of Books,* Beattie's humor is not enough. "Instead of the tightly woven display of wit and satire Beattie seems to have intended," Rosner wrote, "the book is a loose collection of plotlines going nowhere." She concluded, "This novel is missing both intensity and passion, and the weak humor it contains is inadequate to take their place."

The novel *Picturing Will* "is a bitter-sweet story that captures the psychological terrain of parenthood with the sure hand and accuracy of a photographer," observed Tim Falconer in *Quill & Quire.* "In fact, photography is a central image in the book." The book follows Jody, a small-town portrait photographer with artistic aspirations, her young son, Will, her lover, Mel, and her ex-husband, Wayne. As the novel progresses, Will's mother becomes captivated by her emerging career as an artist and his father drops out of the picture; only his "stepfather" comes forward to give him the love and affection expected of a parent. In its portrayal of Will and his family, Merle Rubin commented in the *Christian Science Monitor,* the novel "focuses on the peculiarities of the parent-child relationship in a world of splintered families and parents whose attitudes run the gamut from intense empathy to outright refusal of responsibility." The events of the novel make clear, in Rubin's words, "that adults . . . cannot always calculate the effect they have on children; that a child's unfathomable mixture of imagination and ignorance, vulnerability and resilience, exposes him to danger and hurt while protecting him in unexpected ways."

T. Coraghessan Boyle presented his evaluation of *Picturing Will* in the *New York Times Book Review,* noting that Beattie "has created a surprising, lyrical and deeply affecting work that is both radical in its movement and perfectly attuned to its telling." "Her style," Boyle added, "has never been better suited to a longer work, and she writes out of a wisdom and maturity that are timeless. But look to the details, the small things. They are everything here." Boyle characterized *Picturing Will* as Beattie's "best novel since *Chilly Scenes of Winter* . . . and its depth and movement are a revelation."

Published in 2002, *The Doctor's House* began as a novella and developed into a novel told from several viewpoints. The story follows Andrew and Nina and their experiences growing up as children of an abusive father. For their mother, the doctor's estranged wife, marital infidelity drives her to drink. Because the doctor never gets to speak for himself, readers must determine for themselves the trustworthiness of the portrait these three narrators create. "It's a challenge to glean the truth," wrote *Booklist*'s Donna Seaman, adding that the novel's structure creates "an aura of almost sacred mystery." A *Publishers Weekly* contributor expressed dissatisfaction with Beattie's technique, noting that the narrators' "gossip, self-pity and self-deception undermine the trauma." A *Kirkus Reviews* contributor also complained that, while the novel is "smartly written . . . one balks at the time spent in the company of these relentlessly unhappy people." Like *Library Journal* reviewer Starr E. Smith, who praised Beattie's "forceful prose," an *Economist* writer noted that the novelist "conjures up a wholly believable world, cruel and unattractive as that world might be." With *The Doctor's House* Beattie continues to demonstrate "her gift for revealing the dark truths at the core of human relationships," summed up Jo Ann Beard in a review for *O* magazine.

In her short stories and novels, Beattie continues to chronicle the lives of those people who came of age in the 1960s, following them throughout the 1970s, 1980s, and 1990s and the new century. "Beattie's power and influence . . . arise from her seemingly resistless immersion in the stoic bewilderment of a generation without a cause," explained John Updike in the *New Yorker,* "a generation for whom love as well as politics is a consumer item too long on the shelves and whose deflationary mood is but dimly brightened by the background chirping of nostalgia-inducing pop tunes and the faithful attendance of personable pet dogs." "Beattie is a master of indirection," Boyle maintained. "Her stories are propelled not so much by event as by the accumulation of the details that build a life as surely as the tumble and drift of sediment builds shale or sandstone. Pay attention to the small things, she tells us. All the rest will fall in place." Thus, Murphy maintained in the *Los Angeles Times,* "Those who approach Beattie's work with the attention she demands and a willingness to engage in equal measure their brains, intuitions and hearts will . . . be rewarded in some indefinable, but life-affirming way."

BIOGRAPHICAL AND CRITICAL SOURCES:

BOOKS

Contemporary Literary Criticism, Thomson Gale (Detroit, MI), Volume 8, 1978, Volume 13, 1980, Volume 18, 1981, Volume 40, 1986, Volume 63, 1991.
Contemporary Novelists, 7th edition, St. James Press (Detroit, MI), 2001.
Dictionary of Literary Biography: Volume 218: *American Short-Story Writers since World War II, Second Series,* Thomson Gale (Detroit, MI), 1999.
Montresor, Jaye Berman, editor, *The Critical Response to Ann Beattie,* Greenwood Press (Westport, CT), 1993.
Murphy, Christina, *Ann Beattie,* G.K. Hall (Boston, MA), 1986.
Rainwater, Catherine, and William J. Scheick, editors, *Contemporary American Women Writers: Narrative Strategies,* University Press of Kentucky (Lexington, KY), 1985, pp. 9-25.
Short Story Criticism, Volume 11, Thomson Gale (Detroit, MI), 1992.

PERIODICALS

America, May 12, 1990, P.H. Samway, interview with Beattie, pp. 469-471; October 12, 1991, p. 253.
American Spectator, April, 1990, p. 45

Atlantic, December, 1976, p. 114; June, 1980, p. 93.

Book, March-April, 2002, Penelope Mesic, review of *The Doctor's House,* p. 72.

Booklist, November 15, 2000, Brad Hooper, review of *Perfect Recall,* p. 586; December 1, 2001, Donna Seaman, review of *The Doctor's House,* p. 605.

BookPage, February, 2002, review of *The Doctor's House,* p. 18.

Boston Globe, April 20, 1987, p. 23; January 21, 1990, p. B49; February 3, 1990, p. 9; May 26, 1991, p. A13.

Christian Science Monitor, September 29, 1976, p. 19; January 31, 1979, p. 19; October 23, 1979, Maggie Lewis, "The Sixties: Where Are They Now? Novelist Ann Beattie Knows," pp. B6-B10; June 4, 1980, p. 17; February 9, 1983, p. 15; August 26, 1985, p. 21; November 10, 1986, p. 30; February 5, 1990, p. 12.

Commentary, February, 1977, p. 62; February, 1979, p. 71; July, 1980, pp. 59-61; March, 1983, Joseph Epstein, "Anne Beattie and the Hippoisie," pp. 54-58.

Commonweal, September 6, 1985, p. 474; May 18, 1990, p. 322.

Contemporary Literature, winter, 1990, Steven R. Centola, interview with Beattie, pp. 405-422.

Detroit Free Press, March 10, 2002, review of *The Doctor's House,* p. 4G.

Economist, March 9, 2002, review of *The Doctor's House.*

Entertainment Weekly, March 1, 2002, review of *The Doctor's House,* p. 74.

Esquire, July, 1985, Richard Ford, "Beattie Eyes," pp. 107-108.

Five Points, spring-summer, 1997, Robert W. Hill, "Ann Beattie," pp. 26-60.

Georgia Review, winter, 1999, Erin McGraw, review of *Park City,* p. 775.

Globe and Mail (Toronto, Ontario, Canada), March 17, 2001, review of *Perfect Recall,* p. D16; March 2, 2002, review of *The Doctor's House,* p. D3.

Horizon, Volume 25, 1982, Jay Parini, "A Writer Comes of Age," pp. 22-24.

Hudson Review, spring, 1977, p. 150; fall, 1977, Peter Glassman, review of *Distortions,* p. 447; summer, 1983, p. 359; winter, 1999, review of *Park City,* p. 759.

Kirkus Reviews, December 1, 2001, review of *The Doctor's House,* p. 1622.

Library Journal, December, 2000, Mary Szczesiul, review of *Perfect Recall,* p. 194; January, 2002, Starr E. Smith, review of *The Doctor's House,* p. 148.

Literary Review, Volume 27, number 2, Larry McCaffery and Gregory Sinda, "A Conversation with Ann Beattie," pp. 165-177.

London, March, 1983, p. 87.

London Review of Books, December 5, 1985, p. 22.

Los Angeles Times, January 18, 1990, Josh Getlin, "Novelist Focuses on Childhood Isolation," pp. E14-E15; May 2, 1991, p. E7; December 28, 2000, Bernadette Murphy, review of *Perfect Recall,* p. E3.

Los Angeles Times Book Review, June 9, 1985, p. 3; October 12, 1986, p. 2; July 19, 1987, p. 6; January 21, 1990, p. 3.

Maclean's, June 23, 1980, p. 52; July 1, 1985, p. 65; February 26, 1990, p. 54; August 19, 1991, p. 43.

Michigan Quarterly Review, summer, 1993, James Plath, "Counternarrative: An Interview with Ann Beattie," pp. 359-379.

Ms., December, 1976, p. 45; January, 1979, p. 42; July, 1980, p. 28; July, 1985, p. 16.

Nation, October 30, 1982, p. 441.

New England Review, Volume 1, 1979, Blanche H. Gelfant, "Ann Beattie's Magic Slate or the End of the Sixties," pp. 374-384.

New Republic, June 7, 1980, p. 34; July 15, 1985, p. 42.

Newsweek, August 23, 1976, p. 76; January 22, 1979, p. 76; May 5, 1980, p. 86; June 17, 1985, p. 81; January 22, 1990, p. 62.

New York, January 22, 1990, p. 30.

New Yorker, November 29, 1976, John Updike, "Seeresses," pp. 164-166; June 9, 1980, p. 148; August 5, 1985, p. 80; December 10, 2001, review of *Perfect Recall,* p. 106.

New York Review of Books, May 15, 1980, p. 32; July 18, 1985, p. 40; May 31, 1990, p. 33; August 15, 1991, pp. 9-11.

New York Times, August 24, 1976, p. 33; January 3, 1979; January 14, 1979, Gail Godwin, review of *Falling in Place,* p. 14; May 11, 1980, Joyce Maynard, "Visiting Ann Beattie," p. 14; September 25, 1982, p. 16; September 26, 1982, Margaret Atwood, review of *The Burning House,* p. 1; May 27, 1985, p. 13; October 1, 1986, p. C23; January 4, 1990, p. C20; April 23, 1991, p. C16; September 24, 1995, Sven Birkerts, review of *Another You,* p. 12; January 2, 2001, Michiko Kakutani, review of *Perfect Recall,* p. E9; January 14, 2001, Jennifer Schuessler, review of *Perfect Recall,* p. 7; February 26, 2002, Michiko Kakutani, review of *The Doctor's House,* p. E7; March 10, 2002, Rand Richards Cooper, review of *The Doctor's House,* p. 11.

New York Times Book Review, August 15, 1976, p. 14; May 11, 1980, Richard Locke, "Keeping Cool," pp. 1, 38-39; June 2, 1985, p. 7; October 12, 1986, p. 10; June 28, 1987, p. 24; January 7, 1990, p. 1;

May 31, 1990, p. 33; May 26, 1991, p. 3; May 11, 1997, p. 10; June 28, 1998, Lorrie Moore, "A House Divided," p. 15; July 25, 1999, review of *Park City,* p. 24; December 5, 1999, review of *Park City,* p. 105; January 14, 2001, Jennifer Schuessler, review of *Perfect Recall,* p. 7; June 3, 2001, review of *Perfect Recall,* p. 26; December 2, 2001, review of *Perfect Recall,* p. 66; February 17, 2002, review of *The Doctor's House,* p. 22; March 3, 2002, Scott Veale, review of *Perfect Recall,* p. 20; March 10, 2002, Rand Richards Cooper, review of *The Doctor's House,* p. 11; March 24, 2002, review of *The Doctor's House,* p. 18; June 2, 2002, review of *The Doctor's House,* pp. 22-23; March 2, 2003, Scott Veale, review of *The Doctor's House,* p. 28.

O, February, 2002, Jo Ann Beard, review of *The Doctor's House,* p. 114.

Partisan Review, Volume 50, 1983, Pico Iyer, "The World according to Beattie," pp. 548-553.

Ploughshares, fall, 1995, Don Lee, "About Ann Beattie," pp. 231-235.

Publishers Weekly, November 20, 2000, review of *Perfect Recall,* p. 44; November 19, 2001, review of *Perfect Recall,* p. 34; December 17, 2001, review of *The Doctor's House,* p. 63.

Quill & Quire, February, 1990, p. 27; May, 1991, p. 30.

Rapport, Volume 21, 2000, review of *Perfect Recall,* p. 18.

Review of Contemporary Fiction, spring, 1999, Brian Evenson, review of *Park City,* p. 184; fall, 2002, Suzanne Scanlon, review of *The Doctor's House,* pp. 141-142.

St. Louis Post-Dispatch (St. Louis, MO), January 7, 2001, Nancy Schapiro, "Beattie's Short Stories Are Long on Local Detail," p. F10; April 14, 2002, Nancy Schapiro, review of *The Doctor's House,* p. F10.

San Francisco Chronicle, February 21, 2001, Heidi Benson, "Ann Beattie Makes Eye Contact," p. C1; February 17, 2002, Jane Ganahl, "Ann Beattie; You Can't Pin a Label on This 'Lifer'," p. 2.

San Francisco Review of Books, summer, 1985, p. 18.

Saturday Review, August 7, 1976, p. 37.

Southern Review, winter, 1992, David Wyatt, "Ann Beattie," pp. 145-159.

Story Quarterly, Volume 7-8, 1979, G.E. Murray, "A Conversation with Ann Beattie," pp. 62-68.

Time, May 12, 1980, p. 79; July 1, 1985, p. 60; January 22, 1990, p. 68.

Times Literary Supplement, March 27, 1981, p. 333; October 25, 1985, p. 1203; August 14, 1987, p. 873.

Tribune Books (Chicago, IL), October 5, 1986, p. 3; May 24, 1987, p. 4; January 31, 1988, p. 7; January 28, 1990, p. 3; May 5, 1991, p. 5; July 19, 1992, p. 8; February 25, 2001, review of *Perfect Recall,* p. 3.

Us Weekly, January 22, 2001, Michael Tyrell, review of *Perfect Recall,* p. 39.

Victoria, February, 2002, Michele Slung, "Romancing the Word," pp. 38-39.

Village Voice, August 9, 1976, Bob Miner, "Ann Beattie: I Write Best When I Am Sick," pp. 33-34; March 26, 1979, p. 86; June 2, 1980, p. 38.

Vogue, January, 1990, p. 106.

Voice Literary Supplement, November, 1982, p. 6.

Wall Street Journal, January 19, 2001, Gabriella Stern, review of *Perfect Recall,* p. W9.

Washington Post, February 4, 1990, p. F1.

Washington Post Book World, October 3, 1976, p. F5; January 7, 1979, p. E1; May 25, 1980, p. 1; September 19, 1982, p. 3; May 26, 1985, p. 3; January 28, 1990, p. 5; May 12, 1991, p. 8; October 24, 1999, review of *Park City,* p. 10; February 4, 2001, review of *Perfect Recall,* p. 15; February 10, 2002, review of *The Doctor's House,* p. T06; March 17, 2002, review of *Perfect Recall,* p. 12.

Weber Studies, spring, 1990, Neila C. Seshachari, "Picturing Ann Beattie: A Dialogue," pp. 12-36.

Webster Review, fall, 1985, Barbara Schapiro, "Ann Beattie and the Culture of Narcissism," pp. 86-101.

Women's Review of Books, April, 1984, p. 5.

World Literature Today, spring, 1999, Deirdre Neilen, review of *Park City,* p. 333; winter, 1999, review of *My Life, Starring Dara Falcon,* p. 145.

Yale Review, summer, 1977, David Thorburn, review of *Chilly Scenes of Winter,* pp. 585-586; Volume 85, 1997, Lorin Stein, "Fiction in Review," pp. 156-166.

OTHER

Ann Beattie Interview with Kay Bonetti (sound recording), American Audio Prose Library (Columbia, MO), 1987.

* * *

BEAUVOIR, Simone de 1908-1986
(Simone Lucie Ernestine Marie Bertrand de Beauvoir)

PERSONAL: Born January 9, 1908, in Paris, France; died of a respiratory ailment April 14, 1986, in Paris, France; daughter of Georges Bertrand (an advocate to the Paris Court of Appeal) and Françoise de Beauvoir; children: (adopted) Sylvie Le Bon. *Education:* Sorbonne, University of Paris, licencie es lettres and agrege des lettres (philosophy), 1929. *Religion:* Atheist.

CAREER: Philosopher, novelist, autobiographer, nonfiction writer, essayist, editor, lecturer, and political activist. Instructor in philosophy at Lycée Montgrand, Marseilles, France, 1931-33, Lycée Jeanne d'Arc, Rouen, France, 1933-37, and Lycéee Moliére and Lycée Camille-See, both Paris, France, 1938-43. Founder and editor, with Jean-Paul Sartre, of *Les temps modernes,* beginning 1945.

MEMBER: International War Crimes Tribunal, Ligue du Droit des Femmes (president), Choisir.

AWARDS, HONORS: Prix Goncourt, 1954, for *Les mandarins;* Jerusalem prize, 1975; Austrian state prize, 1978; Sonning prize for European Culture, 1983; LL.D. from Cambridge University.

WRITINGS:

L'invitee (novel), Gallimard (Paris, France), 1943, reprinted, 1977, translation by Yvonne Moyse and Roger Senhouse published as *She Came to Stay,* Secker & Warburg (London, England), 1949, World Publishing (New York, NY), 1954, reprinted, Flamingo, 1984.

Pyrrhus et Cineas (philosophy; also see below), Gallimard (Paris, France), 1944.

Les bouches inutiles (play in two acts; first performed in Paris), Gallimard (Paris, France), 1945, translation published as *Who Shall Die?,* River Press, 1983.

Le sang des autres (novel), Gallimard (Paris, France), 1946, reprinted, 1982, translation by Yvone Moyse and Roger Senhouse published as *The Blood of Others,* Knopf (New York, NY), 1948, reprinted, Pantheon (New York, NY), 1984.

Tous les hommes sont mortel (novel), Gallimard (Paris, France), 1946, reprinted, 1974, translation by Leonard M. Friedman published as *All Men Are Mortal,* World Publishing (New York, NY), 1955.

Pour une morale de l'ambiguite (philosophy; also see below), Gallimard (Paris, France), 1947, reprinted, 1963, translation by Bernard Frechtman published as *The Ethics of Ambiguity,* Philosophical Library, 1948, reprinted, Citadel (New York, NY), 1975.

Pour une morale de l'ambiguite [and] *Pyrrhus et Cineas,* Schoenhof's Foreign Books, 1948.

L'existentialisme et la sagesse des nations (philosophy; title means "Existentialism and the Wisdom of the Ages"), Nagel, 1948.

L'Amerique au jour le jour (diary), P. Morihien, 1948, translation by Patrick Dudley published as *America Day by Day,* Duckworth (London, England), 1952, Grove (New York, NY), 1953, new edition translated by Carol Cosman, foreword by Douglas Brinkley, University of California Press (Berkeley, CA), 1999.

Le deuxième sexe, two volumes, Gallimard (Paris, France), 1949, translation by H.M. Parshley published as *The Second Sex,* Knopf (New York, NY), 1953, reprinted, Random House (New York, NY), 1974, Volume 1 published as *A History of Sex,* New English Library (London, England), 1961, published as *Nature of the Second Sex,* 1963.

The Marquis de Sade (essay; translation of *Faut-il bruler Sade?*; also see below; originally published in *Les temps modernes*), translation by Annette Michelson, Grove (New York, NY), 1953, published as *Must We Burn de Sade?,* Nevill (London, England), 1953, reprinted, New English Library (London, England), 1972.

Les mandarins (novel), Gallimard (Paris, France), 1954, reprint published in two volumes, 1972, translation by Leonard M. Friedman published as *The Mandarins,* World Publishing (New York, NY), 1956, reprinted, Flamingo, 1984.

Privileges (essays; includes *Faut-il bruler Sade?*), Gallimard (Paris, France), 1955.

La longue marche: essai sur la Chine, Gallimard (Paris, France), 1957, translation by Austryn Wainhouse published as *The Long March,* World Publishing (New York, NY), 1958.

Memoires d'une jeune fille rangée (autobiography), Gallimard (Paris, France), 1958, reprinted, 1972, translation by James Kirkup published as *Memoirs of a Dutiful Daughter,* World Publishing (New York, NY), 1959, reprinted, Penguin, 1984.

Brigitte Bardot and the Lolita Syndrome, translated by Bernard Frechtman, Reynal (London, England), 1960, published with foreword by George Amberg, Arno (New York, NY), 1972.

La force de l'age (autobiography), Gallimard (Paris, France), 1960, reprinted, 1976, translation by Peter Green published as *The Prime of Life,* World Publishing (New York, NY), 1962.

(With Gisele Halimi) *Djamila Boupacha,* Gallimard (Paris, France), 1962, translated by Peter Green, Macmillan (London, England), 1962.

La force des choses (autobiography), Gallimard (Paris, France), 1963, reprinted, 1977, translation by Richard Howard published as *The Force of Circumstance,* Putnam (New York, NY), 1965.

Une mort tres douce (autobiography), Gallimard (Paris, France), 1964, with English introduction and notes by Ray Davison, Methuen Educational (London, England), 1986, translation by Patrick O'Brian published as *A Very Easy Death,* Putnam (New York, NY), 1966, reprinted, Pantheon (New York, NY), 1985.

(Author of introduction) Charles Perrault, *Bluebeard and Other Fairy Tales of Charles Perrault,* Macmillan (London, England), 1964.

(Author of preface) Violette Leduc, *La batarde,* Gallimard (Paris, France), 1964.

Les belles images (novel), Gallimard (Paris, France), 1966, translated by Patrick O'Brian, Putnam (New York, NY), 1968, with introduction and notes by Blandine Stefanson, Heinemann Educational (London, England), 1980.

(Author of preface) Jean-François Steiner, *Treblinka,* Simon & Schuster (New York, NY), 1967.

La femme rompue (three novellas; includes *L'age de discretion*), Gallimard (Paris, France), 1967, translation by Patrick O'Brian published as *The Woman Destroyed* (includes *Age of Discretion* and *Monologue*), Putnam (New York, NY), 1969, reprinted, Pantheon (New York, NY), 1987.

La vieillesse (nonfiction), Gallimard (Paris, France), 1970, translation by Patrick O'Brian published as *The Coming of Age,* Putnam (New York, NY), 1972, published as *Old Age,* Weidenfeld & Nicolson (London, England), 1972.

Tout compte fait (autobiography), Gallimard (Paris, France), 1972, translation by Patrick O'Brian published as *All Said and Done,* Putnam (New York, NY), 1974.

Quand prime le spirituel (short stories), Gallimard (Paris, France), 1979, translation by Patrick O'Brian published as *When Things of the Spirit Come First: Five Early Tales,* Pantheon (New York, NY), 1982.

Le ceremonie des adieux: suivi de entretiens avec Jean-Paul Sartre (reminiscences), Gallimard (Paris, France), 1981, translation published as *Adieux: A Farewell to Sartre,* Pantheon (New York, NY), 1984.

(Editor and contributor) *Lettres au Castor et a quelques autres,* Gallimard (Paris, France), 1983, Volume 1: *1926-1939,* Volume 2: *1940-1963.*

Lettres a Sartre, French and European Publications, 1990, Volume 1: *1930-1939,* Volume 2: *1940-1963.*

Journal de guerre, septembre 1939-janvier 1941, Gallimard (Paris, France), 1990.

(Editor) *Witness to My Life: The Letters of Jean-Paul Sartre to Simone de Beauvoir,* translated by Norman MacAfee and Lee Fahnestock, Macmillan (New York, NY), 1992.

A Transatlantic Love Affair: Letters to Nelson Algren, compiled and annotated by Sylvie le Bon de Beauvoir; translation by Ellen Gordon Reeves, New Press (New York, NY), 1998.

ADAPTATIONS: The Mandarins was adapted for film by Twentieth Century-Fox, 1969; *The Blood of Others* was adapted for a film by Home Box Office, starring Jodie Foster, 1984.

SIDELIGHTS: At Simone de Beauvoir's funeral on April 19, 1986, flowers from all over the world filled the corner of the Montparnasse cemetery where she was laid to rest next to Jean-Paul Sartre (1905-1980). Banners and cards from the American-based Simone de Beauvoir Society, women's studies groups, women's health centers and centers for battered women, diverse political organizations, and publishing houses attested to the number of lives the author had touched during her seventy-eight years. Five thousand people, many of them recognizable figures from the political, literary, and film worlds, made their way along the boulevard du Montparnasse past Beauvoir's birthplace, past the cafes where she, Sartre, and their friends had discussed their ideas and written some of their manuscripts, to the cemetery.

Beauvoir was a perceptive witness to the twentieth century, a witness whose works span the period from her early childhood days before World War I to the world of the 1980s. Born in Paris in 1908, in the fourteenth "arrondissement" or district where she continued to live throughout most of her life, Beauvoir was raised by a devout Catholic mother from Verdun and an agnostic father, a lawyer who enjoyed participating in amateur theatrical productions. The contrast between the beliefs of the beautiful, timid, provincial Françoise de Beauvoir and those of the debonair Parisian Georges de Beauvoir led the young Simone to assess situations independently, unbiased by the solid parental front presented by the more traditional families of many of her classmates. As family finances dwindled during World War I, Beauvoir observed the uninspiring household chores that fell upon her mother and decided that she herself would never become either a homemaker or a mother. She had found such pleasure in teaching her younger sister Helene everything she herself was learning at school that she decided to pursue a teaching career when she grew up.

Beauvoir and her best friend Zaza "Mabille"—Beauvoir often assigned fictional names to friends and family members described in her autobiographical writings—

sometimes discussed the relative merits of bringing nine children into the world, as Zaza's mother had done, and of creating books, an infinitely more worthwhile enterprise, the young Beauvoir believed. As the girls matured, Beauvoir observed the degree to which Zaza's mother used her daughter's affection and commitment to Christian obedience to manipulate Zaza's choice of career and mate. When Zaza, tormented by her parents' refusal to grant her permission to marry Maurice Merleau-Ponty, the "Jean Pradelle" of the memoirs, died at age twenty-one, Beauvoir felt her friend had been assassinated by bourgeois morality. Many of Beauvoir's early fictional writings attempted to deal on paper with the emotions stirred by her recollection of the "Mabille" family and of Zaza's death. Only many years later did she learn that Merleau-Ponty, who became a well-known philosopher and writer and remained a close friend of Beauvoir's and Sartre's, was unacceptable to the "Mabilles" because he was illegitimate.

Despite her warm memories of going to early morning mass as a little girl with her mother and of drinking hot chocolate on their return, Beauvoir gradually pulled away from the traditional values with which Françoise de Beauvoir hoped to imbue her. She and her sister began to rebel, for example, against the restrictions of the Cours Adeline Desir, the private Catholic school to which they were being sent. Weighing the pleasures of this world against the sacrifices entailed in a belief in an afterlife, the fifteen-year-old Beauvoir opted to concentrate on her life here on earth. Her loss of faith erected a serious barrier to communication with her mother.

Beauvoir was convinced during several years of her adolescence that she was in love with her cousin Jacques Champigneulles ("Jacques Laiguillon" in her memoirs), who introduced her to books by such French authors as Andre Gide, Alain-Fournier, Henry de Montherlant, Jean Cocteau, Paul Claudel, and Paul Valery; these books scandalized Beauvoir's mother, who had carefully pinned together pages of volumes in their home library that she did not want her daughters to read. Jacques Champigneulles, however, seemed unwilling to make a commitment either to Beauvoir or to anything else, and the Beauvoir sisters were totally disillusioned when this bright bohemian opted to marry the wealthy and generously dowried sister of one of his friends.

Because family finances did not allow Georges de Beauvoir to provide dowries, his daughters became unlikely marriage prospects for young middle-class men, and

both Simone and Helene were delighted to have this excuse for continuing their studies and pursuing careers. Even as a young girl, Beauvoir had a passion for capturing her life on paper. In the first volume of her autobiography, *Memoires d'une jeune fille rangée* (*Memoirs of a Dutiful Daughter*), she looked back with amusement at her determination, recorded in her adolescent diary, to "tell all"; yet her memoirs, her fiction, her essays, her interviews, and her prefaces do indeed record events, attitudes, customs, and ideas that help define approximately seven decades of the twentieth century.

It was through Rene Maheu, a Sorbonne classmate called "Andre Herbaud" in the memoirs, that Beauvoir first met Sartre in a study group for which she was to review the works and ideas of German philosopher Gottfried Wilhelm von Leibniz. In Sartre Beauvoir found the partner of whom she had dreamed as an adolescent. As she remarked in *Memoirs of a Dutiful Daughter,* "Sartre corresponded exactly to the ideal I had set for myself when I was fifteen: he was a soulmate in whom I found, heated to the point of incandescence, all of my passions. With him, I could always share everything." And so she did, for fifty-one years, from the time they became acquainted at the Sorbonne in 1929 until his death on April 15, 1980.

Together Sartre and Beauvoir analyzed their relationship, deciding that they enjoyed an indestructible essential love but that they must leave themselves open to "contingent loves" as well in order to expand their range of experience. Although marriage would have enabled them to receive a double teaching assignment instead of being sent off to opposite ends of the country, they were intent upon escaping the obligations that such a bourgeois institution would entail. That neither had a particular desire for children was an added reason to avoid marriage. A daring and unconventional arrangement during the early 1930s, their relationship raised consternation in conservative members of Beauvoir's family.

Except for a brief period during World War II, Beauvoir and Sartre never lived together, but spent their days writing in their separate quarters and then came together during the evenings to discuss their ideas and to read and criticize one another's manuscripts. As both became well known in the literary world, they found it increasingly difficult to maintain their privacy; as *La force des choses* (*The Force of Circumstance*) records, they had to alter their routine and avoid certain cafes during the years after the war in order to protect themselves from the prying eyes of the public.

Sartre's autobiography, *Les mots* (*The Words*), published in 1963, dealt only with the early years of his life. Beauvoir's autobiographical writings provide a much more complete and intimate account of the adult Sartre. In several volumes of reminiscences, Beauvoir described their mutual reluctance to leave their youth behind and become part of the adult world, their struggles to set aside adequate time for writing, the acceptance of their works for publication, their travels, their friendships, their gradually increasing commitment to political involvement; her final autobiographical volume, *Le ceremonie des adieux: suivi de entretiens avec Jean-Paul Sartre* (*Adieux: A Farewell to Sartre*), recreates her anguish in witnessing the physical and mental decline of a lifelong companion who had been one of the most brilliant philosophers of the twentieth century.

For Beauvoir, writing was not only a way of preserving life on paper but also a form of catharsis, a means of working out her own problems through fiction. Her early short stories, written between 1935 and 1937 and originally rejected by two publishers, were brought out by Gallimard in 1979. The tales in *Quand prime le spirituel* (*When Things of the Spirit Come First: Five Early Tales*) capture Beauvoir's infatuation with Jacques, the tragedy of Zaza's death, the young philosophy teacher's ambivalence about the impact her ideas and her lifestyle might have on her impressionable lycée students in Marseille and Rouen, and her sense of excitement as she saw the world opening up before her. Beauvoir identifies strongly with her central character Marguerite who, in the final paragraphs of the book, perceives the world as a shiny new penny ready for her to pick up and do with as she wishes.

Experimenting with nontraditional relationships, Sartre and Beauvoir formed a trio with Beauvoir's lycée student Olga Kosakiewicz in 1933. The anguish experienced by Beauvoir as a result of this intimate three-way sharing of lives led to the writing of her first published work, *L'invitee* (*She Came to Stay*). In this novel the author relives the hothouse atmosphere generated by the trio, and she choses to destroy the judgmental young intruder, the fictional Xaviere, on paper, but to dedicate her novel to Olga. The real-life situation resolved itself less dramatically after Olga became interested in Jacques-Laurent Bost, a former student of Sartre's, and broke away from the trio; the four principals remained lifelong friends, however. In *Simone de Beauvior,* Judith Okely suggested that *She Came to Stay* reflects not only the Beauvoir-Sartre-Olga trio but also the young Simone's rivalry with her mother for her father's affections.

Beauvoir's second novel, *Le sang des autres* (*The Blood of Others*), focuses on the dilemma of dealing with the consequences of one's acts. The liberal Jean Blomart, shaken by the accidental death of a young friend he inspired to participate in a political demonstration, struggles throughout much of the narrative to avoid doing anything that may inadvertently harm another human being, his "search for a saintly purity," as Carol Ascher labeled it in *Simone de Beauvoir: A Life of Freedom.* The female protagonist, Helene Bertrand, intent on protecting her own happiness in a world turned upside down by war and the German Occupation, is shaken out of her inertia by the cries of a Jewish mother whose small daughter is being wrenched away from her by the Gestapo. Helene seeks an active and ultimately fatal involvement in terrorist Resistance activities orchestrated by Jean Blomart, who has decided finally that violence is perhaps the only rational response to Hitler's insanity. Infused with the euphoria of Resistance camaraderie, the novel highlights a question that is also central to Sartre's play *Les mains sales* (*Dirty Hands*)—the relationship between intellectuals and violence.

As Beauvoir and Sartre became better known, the label "existentialist" was regularly attached to their writings. At first Beauvoir resisted the use of the term, but she and Sartre gradually adopted it and began to try to explain existentialist philosophy to the public. In *Pour une morale de l'ambiguite* (*The Ethics of Ambiguity*), published in 1947, she defines existentialism as a philosophy of ambiguity, one emphasizing the tension between living in the present and acting with an eye to one's mortality; she also attempts to answer critics who accused existentialists of wallowing in absurdity and despair. In the four essays published as *L'existentialisme et la sagesse des nations* ("Existentialism and the Wisdom of the Ages"), Beauvoir argues for the importance of a philosophical approach to modern life. Here she defends existentialism against accusations of frivolity and gratuitousness and explains that existentialists consider man neither naturally good nor naturally bad: "He is nothing at first; it is up to him to make himself good or bad depending upon whether he assumes his freedom or denies it." Emphasizing the fact that man can be "the sole and sovereign master of his destiny," Beauvoir insists that existentialist philosophy is essentially optimistic; in *Simone de Beauvoir and the Limits of Commitment,* however, Anne Whitmarsh sees the author's existentialism as "a stern ethical system."

With the end of the war came the opportunity to travel once again. Beauvoir spent four months in the United States in 1947, lecturing on U.S. college campuses about the moral problems facing writers in postwar Europe. She recorded her impressions through journal entries dating from January 25 to May 19, 1947, in *L'Ame-rique au jour le jour* (*America Day by Day*), which was dedicated to author Richard Wright and his wife Ellen. Her perceptive eye took in a great variety of detail but saw everything through a lens whose focus was influenced by certain preconceived notions. Terry Keefe, in her *Simone de Beauvoir: A Study of Her Writings,* found the value of the book in the record it presents of Beauvoir's "excitement and disappointment at a historical moment when many Europeans knew little about America and were eager to expose themselves to its impact, for better or worse." Consistently critical of capitalist traditions and values, *America Day by Day* can be paired with Beauvoir's account of her 1955 trip to China, *La longue marche: essai sur la Chine* (*The Long March*), in which she euphorically accepts everything in communist China. While praising Beauvoir's ability to evoke settings and glimpses of life in China, Keefe saw *The Long March* as "first and foremost a long, extremely serious attempt to explain the situation of China in 1955-56 and justify the direction in which the new regime [was] guiding the country."

Ready after the war to begin her purely autobiographical works, Beauvoir realized she first needed to understand the extent to which being born female had influenced the pattern of her life. She therefore spent hours at the National Library in Paris seeking documentation for each section of the book that was to become the battle-cry of feminism in the latter half of the twentieth century. When *Le deuxiéme sexe* (*The Second Sex*) appeared in 1949, reactions ranged from the horrified gasps of conservative readers to the impassioned gratitude of millions of women who had never before encountered such a frank discussion of their condition. The opening statement of the section on childhood, "One is not born a woman, one becomes one," became familiar throughout the world, and the book advised women to pursue meaningful careers and to avoid the status of "relative beings" implied, in its author's view, by marriage and motherhood.

Before turning to her memoirs, Beauvoir wrote the novel that won her the prestigious Prix Goncourt. *Les mandarins* (*The Mandarins*) presents the euphoria of Liberation Day in Paris and the subsequent disillusionment of French intellectuals who had been temporarily convinced that the future was theirs to fashion as they saw fit, but who found themselves gradually dividing into factions as the glow of Resistance companionship and of victory over the Nazis dimmed. Beauvoir always denied that *The Mandarins* was a roman à clef, with Robert Dubreuilh, Henri Perron, and Anne Dubreuilh representing Sartre, Albert Camus, and herself; nonethe-

less, echoes of the developing rift between Sartre and Camus, of the discussions of staff members of *Les temps modernes*—the leftist review founded by Sartre, Beauvoir, and their associates—and of the concern of French intellectuals over the revelation of the existence of Soviet work camps are clearly audible throughout the novel. Moreover, Lewis Brogan is certainly a fictionalized portrait of Chicago author Nelson Algren, who became one of Beauvoir's "contingent loves" during her 1947 trip to the United States and to whom the novel is dedicated. Whether or not the work is a roman à clef, it is generally regarded, in Ascher's words, as Beauvoir's "richest, most complex, and most beautifully wrought novel."

The first volume of Beauvoir's autobiography appeared in 1958. In *Memoirs of a Dutiful Daughter* the author chronicles the warmth and affection of the early years of her life, her growing rebellion against bourgeois tradition, and her sense of emancipation when she moved from the family apartment on the rue de Rennes to a rented room at her grandmother's. Highlighted in these pages are her close association with her sister, her relationship with Zaza, and her infatuation with Jacques. In *Simone de Beauvoir on Woman,* Jean Leighton focused on the portrait of Zaza in *Memoirs of a Dutiful Daughter,* finding that she "epitomizes . . . traditional feminine qualities. Next to Simone de Beauvoir she is the most vivid person in the book."

Beauvoir dedicated the second volume of her autobiography, *La force de l'age* (*The Prime of Life*), to Sartre. The first half of the narrative tells the story of their lives from 1929 to 1939, recounting the exhilarating sense of freedom they experienced as they pooled their money to travel throughout France and to London, Italy, Germany, and Greece. Here the memoir looks back on the experiment of the trio, on the illness that put Beauvoir in a clinic for several weeks, on her insistence upon living in the present and trying to ignore the menacing news filtering through from Adolph Hilter's Germany. The second half of the book begins in 1939, as the German occupation of France was about to begin, and ends with Liberation Day in Paris in August of 1944. These pages provide one of the most vivid accounts of life in France during World War II, as the reader witnesses the lines of people waiting for gas masks, the sirens and descents into metro stations during air raids, and the struggle to find enough food to survive. These were the years when leftist intellectuals remained in close contact with one another, when Albert Camus, actress Maria Casares, writers Michel Leiris and Raymond Queneau, theatrical director Charles Dullin, and artist Pablo Picasso joined Beauvoir, Sartre,

Olga, and Bost in "fiestas" that provided occasional nights of relaxation amidst the bombings and the anticipation of the Allied landing. The emotions of Liberation Day were unforgettable for Beauvoir, who asserted: "No matter what happened afterward, nothing would take those moments away from me; nothing has taken them away; they shine in my past with a brilliance that has never been tarnished."

What did become tarnished, however, were Beauvoir's hopes of participating in the creation of a brave new world, preferably one in which socialism would solve the problems of society. The third volume of autobiography, *The Force of Circumstance,* begins with the Liberation and covers the period from 1944 to early 1963. Despite the success of her books and her increasing political involvement, Beauvoir penned *The Force of Circumstance* with a heavy heart because of the anguish associated with the Algerian war. These were also the years during which she began to reflect upon aging and death, began to realize that there were certain activities in which she was engaging for perhaps the last time. The final sentence in the memoir's epilogue has been widely discussed: "I can still see . . . the promises with which I filled my heart when I contemplated that gold mine at my feet, a whole life ahead of me. They have been fulfilled. However, looking back in amazement at that gullible adolescent I once was, I am stupefied to realize to what extent I have been cheated." For Konrad Bieber in his *Simone de Beauvoir, The Force of Circumstance* is "a remarkable monument to the crucial years of the cold war. . . . A whole era, with its ups and downs, its hopes and disillusionments, is seen through the temperament of a highly gifted writer."

Nineteen sixty-three was a time of personal crisis for Beauvoir both because of her vision of the state of the modern world and because of the death of her mother. Deeply affected by her mother's valiant struggle against cancer, Beauvoir shared with her readers the pain of helplessly watching a life ebb away. In *Une mort tres douce (A Very Easy Death),* a slender volume dedicated to her sister, the author recaptured the warmth of her childhood relationship with her mother and reactivated her admiration for this woman who had always "lived against herself" yet could still appreciate a ray of sunlight or the song of the birds in the tree outside her hospital window. Looking back at her interaction with her mother, Beauvoir realized the full impact of Françoise de Beauvoir's unhappy childhood, of the unfortunate social restraints that kept her mother from finding a satisfying outlet for the energy and vitality which she had passed on to her daughters but which she had never been able to use appropriately herself. Sartre considered

A Very Easy Death Beauvoir's best work; Marks, who commented on its "excruciating lucidity," called the book the only one of the author's writings "in which the hectic rhythm which she projects on the world is abruptly interrupted and the interruption prolonged."

Adieux: A Farewell to Sartre, a companion piece to *A Very Easy Death,* records Beauvoir's efforts to cope with the anguish of watching age and illness take their toll on her companion of fifty years. It is dedicated to "those who have loved Sartre, who love him and who will love him." Beauvoir's subsequent publication of Sartre's *Lettres au Castor et a quelques autres* further attempts to share the quality of their relationship with her readers. "Castor" was a nickname invented by her Sorbonne classmate Rene Maheu, who noted the similarity between the name Beauvoir and the English word "beaver" (*castor* in French) and who considered it an appropriate appellation for the hard-working Beauvoir. The two volumes of Sartre's letters cover a period from 1926 to 1963 and include detailed references to his involvements with other women. Some feminist critics have viewed *Adieux* as Beauvoir's revenge on her partner for the pain inflicted upon her by his numerous "contingent" affairs. *Philosophy and Literature* essayist Hazel Barnes disagreed, considering these passages "both factual reporting and a tribute" and noting "the profound respect which Sartre and Beauvoir had for each other, something deeper than the obvious affection, companionship and commonality of values, more bedrock than love."

Beauvoir's correspondence to Sartre, published in 1990 as *Letters a Sartre,* provides readers with what Jerome Charyn in the *Los Angeles Times Book Review* termed "an incredible gift." Beauvoir herself had claimed these letters were lost, but they were found stashed away in a cupboard in her apartment after her death. The letters are explicit in their detail of Beauvoir's relationship with Sartre as well as with several women who were also Sartre's lovers. Their graphic portrayal of Beauvoir's unconventional personal life led some critics to posit their damage to her reputation as a dedicated feminist. "This is nonsense," stated Elaine Showalter in the *London Review of Books.* "Beauvoir's feminist credentials come from her writing, and from her years of staunch, courageous and generous support of abortion legislation, battered women's shelters, women's publishing, and the cause of women's liberation around the world. . . . To have had a less-than-perfect personal life weighs no more against her intellectual achievements than it would against those of a man."

During the mid-1960s Beauvoir also returned to fiction with *Les belles images.* This novel describes a milieu quite alien to Beauvoir: that of the mid-century techno-crats, and centers on Laurence, a bright, attractive ca-reer woman, comfortably married and the mother of two daughters. Laurence suddenly finds herself caught between two generations as she attempts to help her es-tranged mother cope with the loss of her wealthy lover and to answer the probing questions of her own ten-year-old daughter about poverty and misery. As she gradually develops the sensitivity she has been taught by her mother to restrain, she despairs of ever changing anything in her own life, yet vows in the concluding lines of the novel that she will raise her daughters to express their feelings. Laurence is an incarnation of the contemporary superwoman juggling commitments to career, family, and aging parents until she falls apart under the strain of such responsibilities.

In *La vieillesse* ("Old Age") Beauvoir turns her atten-tion to old age, presenting a companion piece to *The Second Sex;* the title was euphemistically translated as *The Coming of Age* in the United States. The work fo-cuses upon the generally deplorable existence of most elderly people, and defines one of the as-yet-unresolved dilemmas of the late twentieth century. Bieber saw in *The Coming of Age* an example of Beauvoir's "bound-less empathy" and of her understanding of human frailty; Ascher, in contrast, found it "shocking for its lack of feeling for the special plight of old women" and asserted that for the author the universal is male, at least among the elderly.

Several critics have taken Beauvoir to task for her ap-parently negative presentation of women and their val-ues. Leighton sees the female protagonists in Beau-voir's fiction as "finely etched portraits of various types of femininity" who "personify in a compelling way the pessimistic and anti-feminine bias of *The Second Sex.*" Evans discerned an assumption in Beauvoir's works that "traditionally male activities (the exercise of ratio-nality, independent action, and so on) are in some sense superior, and are instances almost of a higher form of civilization than those concerns—such as child care and the maintenance of daily life—that have traditionally been the preserve of women." Whitmarsh was critical of the author's confining her political commitment to the ethical and the literary rather than extending her ac-tivities to the practical aspects of everyday politics, while Okely found that many of Beauvoir's generaliza-tions are based on her limited experience in a small Pa-risian intellectual circle and do not apply as readily to cultures that are neither western, white, nor middle class.

Interviews granted by Beauvoir gave her the opportu-nity to clarify many of her ideas and to answer her crit-ics. Betty Friedan's *It Changed My Life* contains a dia-logue with Beauvoir, to whom Friedan looked for answers to the questions raised by the American femi-nist groups forming in the 1970s. In her introduction to this dialogue, Friedan acknowledges her debt to Beau-voir: "I had learned my own existentialism from her. It was *The Second Sex* that introduced me to that approach to reality and political responsibility that . . . led me to whatever original analysis of women's existence I have been able to contribute." When they spoke, how-ever, the two women disagreed completely about the vi-ability of motherhood for women seeking their indepen-dence and about the possibility of providing salaries for homemakers in order to enhance their self-image. In *It Changed My Life,* Friedan expresses disappointment over what she saw in Beauvoir as detachment from the lives of real women, and concluded: "I wish her well. She started me out on a road on which I'll keep moving. . . . There are no gods, no goddesses. . . . We need and can trust no other authority than our own personal truth."

Most appraisals of Beauvoir's writings focused on *The Second Sex,* called by Philip Wylie in the *New York Times* "one of the few great books of our era." How-ever, Bertrand Poirot-Delpech, who noted in *Le Monde* that Beauvoir is "a much less minor novelist than one might think," described *The Mandarins* as one of the best sources of documentation on the committed intel-lectuals of the cold war period. Michel Contat, also writing for *Le Monde,* saw *All Men Are Mortal* as Beau-voir's most powerful philosophical work, "the most daring, the most scandalous and the most strangely pas-sionate interrogation launched by this great rationalist intellectual against the human condition."

BIOGRAPHICAL AND CRITICAL SOURCES:

BOOKS

Arp, Kristina, *The Bonds of Freedom: Simone de Beauvoir's Existentialist Ethics,* Open Court Pub-lishing, 2001.

Ascher, Carol, *Simone de Beauvoir: A Life of Freedom,* Beacon Press (Boston, MA), 1981.

Bergoffen, Debra B., *The Philosophy of Simone de Beauvoir: Gendered Phenomenologies, Erotic Gen-erosities,* State University of New York Press (Al-bany, NY), 1996.

Bieber, Konrad, *Simone de Beauvoir,* Twayne (New York, NY), 1979.

Bree, Germaine, *Women Writers in France: Variations on a Theme,* Rutgers University Press (Rutgers, NJ), 1973.

Brombert, Victor, *The Intellectual Hero,* Lippincott (Philadelphia, PA), 1961.

Brophy, Brigid, *Don't Never Forget: Collected Views and Reviews,* Holt (New York, NY), 1966.

Card, Claudia, editor, *The Cambridge Companion to Simone de Beauvoir,* Cambridge University Press (New York, NY), 2003.

Contemporary Literary Criticism, Thomson Gale (Detroit, MI), Volume 1, 1973, Volume 2, 1974, Volume 4, 1975, Volume 8, 1978, Volume 14, 1980, Volume 31, 1985, Volume 44, 1987, Volume 50, 1988, Volume 71, 1992.

Corbin, Laurie, *The Mother-Mirror: Self-representation and the Mother-Daughter Relation in Colette, Simone de Beauvoir, and Marguerite Duras,* P. Lang (New York, NY), 1996.

Cottrell, Robert D., *Simone de Beauvior,* Ungar (New York, NY), 1975.

Dictionary of Literary Biography, Volume 72: *French Novelists, 1930-1960,* Thomson Gale (Detroit, MI), 1988.

Dictionary of Literary Biography Yearbook: 1986, Thomson Gale (Detroit, MI), 1987.

Evans, Mary, *Simone de Beauvoir: A Feminist Mandarin,* Tavistock, 1985.

Fallaize, Elizabeth, editor, *Simone de Beauvoir: A Critical Reader,* Routledge (New York, NY), 1998.

Francis, Claude, and Fernande Gontier, *Simone de Beauvoir: A Life . . . A Love Story,* Librairie Academique Perrin, 1985.

Friedan, Betty, *It Changed My Life,* Random House (New York, NY), 1976.

Fullbrook, Kate, and Edward Fullbrook, *Simone de Beauvoir and Jean-Paul Sartre: The Remaking of a Twentieth-Century Legend,* Basic Books (New York, NY), 1994.

Fullbrook, Kate, and Edward Fullbrook, *Simone de Beauvoir: A Critical Introduction,* Polity Press, 1997.

Hatcher, Donald L., *Understanding "The Second Sex,"* P. Lang (New York, NY), 1984.

Jeanson, Francis, *Simone de Beauvoir ou l'entreprise de vivre,* Editions du Seuil (Paris, France), 1966.

Keefe, Terry, *Simone de Beauvoir: A Study of Her Writings,* Barnes & Noble (New York, NY), 1983.

Keefe, Terry, *Simone de Beauvoir,* St. Martin's Press (New York, NY), 1998.

Lamblin, Bianca, *A Disgraceful Affair: Simone de Beauvoir, Jean-Paul Sartre, and Bianca Lamblin,* Northeastern University Press (Boston, MA), 1996.

Leighton, Jean, *Simone de Beauvoir on Woman,* Associated University Presses, 1975.

Lundgren-Gothlin, Eva, *Sex and Existence: Simone de Beauvoir's "The Second Sex,"* Wesleyan University Press (Hanover, NH), 1996.

Madsen, Axel, *Hearts and Minds: The Common Journey of Simone de Beauvoir and Jean-Paul Sartre,* Morrow (New York, NY), 1977.

Mahon, Joseph, *Existentialism, Feminism, and Simone de Beauvoir,* St. Martin's Press, 1997.

Marks, Elaine, *Simone de Beauvior: Encounters with Death,* Rutgers University Press (Rutgers, NJ), 1973.

Moi, Toril, *Simone de Beauvoir: The Making of an Intellectual Woman,* Blackwell (Cambridge, MA), 1994.

Nedeau, Maurice, *The French Novelist since the War,* Methuen (London, England), 1967.

Okely, Judith, *Simone de Beauvoir,* Pantheon (New York, NY), 1986.

Pilardi, Jo-Ann, *Simone de Beauvoir Writing the Self: Philosophy Becomes Autobiography,* Greenwood Press (New York, NY), 1998.

Sartre, Jean-Paul, *The Words,* translation by Bernard Fechtman, Braziller (New York, NY), 1964.

Schwarzer, Alice, *After "The Second Sex": Conversations with Simone de Beauvoir,* Pantheon (New York, NY), 1984.

Simons, Margaret A., *Feminist Interpretations of Simone de Beauvoir,* Pennsylvania State University Press (University Park, PA), 1995.

Vintges, Karen, *Philosophy as Passion: The Thinking of Simone de Beauvoir,* Indiana University Press (Bloomington, IN), 1996.

Whitmarsh, Anne, *Simone de Beauvoir and the Limits of Commitment,* Cambridge University Press (New York, NY), 1981.

PERIODICALS

Antioch Review, Volume 31, number 4, 1971-72.

Booklist, September 15, 1990, p. 143.

Catholic Forum, October, 1965.

Chicago Tribune Book World, March 20, 1983.

Contemporary French Civilization, spring, 1984.

Dalhousie Review, autumn, 1970.

Feminist Studies, summer, 1979.

Fontaine, October, 1945.

Forum for Modern Languages Studies, April, 1975.

France-Dimanche, April 27, 1986.

French Review, April, 1979.

Globe & Mail (Toronto, Ontario, Canada), April 19, 1986.

Hecate, Volume 7, number 2, 1981.

La Vie en Rose, March 16, 1984.

Le Monde, March 20, 1948, April 16, 1986.
London Review of Books, June 14, 1990, p. 6.
Los Angeles Times, April 25, 1984.
Los Angeles Times Book Review, May 24, 1992, p. 2.
Nation, June 8, 1958; June 27, 1959; June 14, 1975.
New Statesman, June 6, 1959; January 5, 1968; December 13, 1991.
Newsweek, June 8, 1959; February 9, 1970.
New Yorker, February 22, 1947.
New York Review of Books, July 20, 1972.
New York Times, June 2, 1974; May 6, 1984; April 15, 1986.
New York Times Book Review, May 18, 1958; June 7, 1959; March 3, 1968; February 23, 1969; July 21, 1974; November 7, 1982; May 24, 1987; July 19, 1992; January 9, 1994.
Paris-Match, April 25, 1986.
Paris Review, spring/summer, 1965.
Philosophy and Literature, Volume 9, number 1, 1985.
Saturday Review, May 22, 1956.
Time, March 20, 1966; May 22, 1972.
Times (London, England), January 21, 1982; August 12, 1982; May 11, 1984.
Times Literary Supplement, June 5, 1959; May 5, 1966; March 30, 1967; April 4, 1980; December 25, 1981; July 30, 1982; January 21, 1983; September 14, 1990, p. 963.
Washington Post Book World, August 18, 1974; May 20, 1984.

OBITUARIES:

PERIODICALS

Chicago Tribune, April 15, 1986.
Detroit Free Press, April 15, 1986.
Los Angeles Times, April 15, 1986.
Newsweek, April 28, 1986.
New York Times, June 2, 1974.
Observer, April 20, 1986.
Publishers Weekly, May 2, 1986.
Time, April 28, 1986.
Times (London, England), April 15, 1986.
USA Today, April 15, 1986.
Washington Post, April 15, 1986.

*   *   *

BEAUVOIR, Simone Lucie Ernestine Marie Bertrand de
   See BEAUVOIR, Simone de

BECKETT, Samuel 1906-1989
   (Samuel Barclay Beckett)

PERSONAL: Born April 13, 1906, in Foxrock, Dublin Ireland; died of respiratory failure December 22, 1989, in Paris, France; son of William Frank (a quantity surveyor) and Mary Jones (an interpreter for the Irish Red Cross; maiden name, Roe) Beckett; married Suzanne Dechevaux-Dumesnil (a pianist), March 25, 1961. *Education:* Attended Portora Royal School, County Fermanagh, Ireland; Trinity College, Dublin, B.A. (French and Italian), 1927, M.A., 1931.

CAREER: Writer. École Normale Superieure, Paris, France, lecturer in English, 1928-30; Trinity College, Dublin, Dublin, Ireland, lecturer in French, 1930-32; assistant to author James Joyce, c. early 1930s; worked as a farmhand near Roussillon, France, during World War II. *Military service:* Involved in French resistance, 1940-43; storekeeper and interpreter for Irish Red Cross Hospital, St. Lo, France, 1945-46; decorated.

AWARDS, HONORS: Hours Press (Paris) award for best poem concerning time, 1930, for *Whoroscope: Poem on Time;* London *Evening Standard* Award for Most Controversial Play, 1955, for *Waiting for Godot;* Italia Prize, 1957, for *All That Fall,* and 1959, for *Embers; Village Voice* Off-Broadway awards for best new play, 1958, for *Endgame,* and 1964, for *Play,* for distinguished play, 1960, for *Krapp's Last Tape,* and for best foreign play, 1962, for *Happy Days;* Litt.D., Trinity College, Dublin, 1959; International Publishers prize, 1961 (shared with Jorge Luis Borges), for body of work; Prix Filmcritice, 1965, and Tours film prize, 1966, both for *Film;* Nobel Prize for Literature, 1969; Grand Prix National du Theatre (France), 1975.

WRITINGS:

NOVELS

Murphy, Routledge & Kegan Paul (London, England), 1938, Grove (New York, NY), 1957, French translation by Beckett, Bordas (Paris, France), 1947, reissued as *Demented Particulars: The Annotated Murphy,,* edited by C.J. Ackerley, preface by S.E. Gontarski, Journal of Beckett Studies Books (Tallahassee, FL), 1998.
Molloy (fragment of early version; originally published in *transition,* 1950, together with fragment of *Malone Dies* under collective title, "Two Fragments";

also see below), Minuit (Paris, France), 1951, English translation by Beckett and Patrick Bowles, Grove (New York, NY), 1955.

Malone meurt, Minuit (Paris, France), 1951, English translation by Beckett published as *Malone Dies,* Grove (New York, NY), 1956.

Watt, Olympia Press (Paris, France), 1953, Grove (New York, NY), 1959, revised and translated into French by the author, Minuit (Paris, France), 1968.

L'Innommable, Minuit (Paris, France), 1953, English translation by Beckett published as *The Unnamable,* Grove (New York, NY), 1958.

Three Novels: Molloy, Malone Dies, [and] The Unnamable, Grove (New York, NY), 1959, with an introduction by Gabriel Josipovici, Knopf (New York, NY), 1997.

Comment c'est, Minuit (Paris, France), 1961, English translation by Beckett published as *How It Is,* Grove (New York, NY), 1964.

Imagination morte imaginez, Minuit (Paris, France), 1965, English translation by Beckett published as *Imagination Dead Imagine,* Calder & Boyars (London, England), 1965.

Mercier et Camier, Minuit (Paris, France), 1970, translation by Beckett published as *Mercier and Camier,* Calder & Boyars (London, England), 1974, Grove (New York, NY), 1975.

Dream of Fair to Middling Women, edited by Eoin O'Brien and Edith Fournier, Arcade Publishing (New York, NY), 1993.

Nohow On: Three Novels, edited by S.E. Gontarski, Grove (New York, NY), 1996.

SHORT FICTION

More Pricks than Kicks, Chatto & Windus (London, England), 1934, reprinted, Calder & Boyars (London, England), 1966.

Nouvelles et textes pour rien (fiction; contains "L'Expulse," "Le Calmant," and "La Fin"), Minuit (Paris, France), 1955, translation by Beckett and others published as *No's Knife: Collected Shorter Prose, 1947-1965* (also see below), Calder & Boyars (London, England), 1967, published as *Stories and Texts for Nothing,* Grove (New York, NY), 1967.

Assez, Minuit (Paris, France), 1966.

Ping, Minuit (Paris, France), 1966.

Tete-mortes (includes *Imagination morte imaginez, Ping,* and *Assez*), Minuit (Paris, France), 1967.

L'Issue, Georges Visat, 1968.

Sans, Minuit (Paris, France), 1969, translation by Beckett published as *Lessness,* Calder & Boyars (London, England), 1971.

Sejour, Georges Richar, 1970.

Premier amour, Minuit (Paris, France), 1970, translation by Beckett published as *First Love,* Calder & Boyars (London, England), 1973.

The North, Enitharmon Press, 1972.

First Love and Other Shorts, Grove (New York, NY), 1974.

Fizzles, Grove (New York, NY), 1976.

For to End Yet Again and Other Fizzles, Calder & Boyars (London, England), 1976.

All Strange Away, Gotham Book Mart (New York, NY), 1976.

Four Novellas, Calder & Boyars (London, England), 1977, published as *The Expelled and Other Novellas,* Penguin (Harmonsdworth, England), 1980.

Six Residua, Calder & Boyars (London, England), 1978.

Mal vu mal dit, Minuit (Paris, France), 1981, translation by Beckett published as *Ill Seen Ill Said,* Grove (New York, NY), 1982.

Worstward Ho, Grove (New York, NY), 1983.

As the Story Was Told, Riverrun Press (New York, NY), 1990.

Stirrings Still, Blue Moon Books, 1991.

Nohow On (novella), Riverrun Press (New York, NY), 1993.

Collected Shorter Prose, 1945-1988, Riverrun Press (New York, NY), 1995.

Samuel Beckett, The Complete Short Prose, 1929-1989, edited and with introduction by S.E. Gontarski, Grove (New York, NY), 1995.

Also author of short story "Premier amour."

PLAYS

Le Kid, produced in Dublin, Ireland, 1931.

En Attendant Godot (first produced in Paris, France, 1953), Minuit (Paris, France), 1952, English translation by Beckett published as *Waiting for Godot* (first produced in London, England, 1955; produced in Miami Beach, 1956; produced on Broadway, 1956), Grove (New York, NY), 1954, revised edition, 1994.

All That Fall (radio play; produced on BBC Third Programme, 1957), Grove (New York, NY), 1957, revised, 1968–69.

Fin de partie (one-act; first produced with *Acte sans paroles* in London, England, 1957), French European Publications, 1957, English translation by Beckett produced as *Endgame* in New York, NY, 1958.

Acte sans paroles (mime for one player; first produced with *Fin de partie* in London, England, 1957), music by John Beckett, English translation by Beckett produced as *Act without Words* in New York, NY, 1959.

From an Abandoned Work (produced on BBC Third Programme, 1957), published in *Evergreen Review,* Volume 1, number 3, 1957, Faber & Faber, 1958.

Krapp's Last Tape, first produced in London, England 1958, produced in Provincetown, RI, 1960.

Embers, first produced on BBC Third Programme, 1959.

Acte sans paroles II, produced in London, England, 1960, English translation produced as *Act without Words II.*

Happy Days (first produced in New York, NY, 1961), Grove (New York, NY), 1961, French translation by Beckett as *Oh les beaux jours* (produced in Paris, France, 1963), Minuit (Paris, France), 1963, 2nd edition, French European Publications, 1975.

Play, produce in London, England, 1964.

Eh, Joe? and Other Writings (television play; produced by New York Television Theatre, 1966; also see below), Faber & Faber (London, England), 1967.

Va et vient (produced in Berlin, Germany, 1966), published in *Comedie et actes divers,* Calder & Boyars (London, England), 1967, English version produced as *Come and Go,* Dublin, Ireland, 1968.

Breath, produced in Oxford, England, 1970.

Le depeupleur, French European Publications, 1970, translation by Beckett published as *The Lost Ones* (produced in New York, NY, 1975), Grove (New York, NY), 1972.

Not I (produced in New York, NY, 1972), Faber & Faber (London, England), 1971.

That Time (produced in London, England, 1976), Faber & Faber (London, England), 1976.

Footfalls (produced in London, England, 1976), Faber & Faber (London, England), 1976.

A Piece of Monologue, produced in New York, NY, 1979.

Company (monologue), Grove (New York, NY), 1980.

Rockabye, produced in Buffalo, NY, 1981.

Texts for Nothing, produced in New York, NY, 1981.

Ohio Impromptu, produced in Columbus, OH, 1981.

Eleutheria (new edition), Minuit (Paris, France), 1995, published in English as *Eleutheria: A Play in Three Acts,* Foxrock (New York, NY), 1995.

The Shorter Plays (includes revised texts for *Footfalls, Come and Go,* and *What Where*), edited and introduction by S.E. Gontarski, Grove (New York, NY), 1999.

OMNIBUS EDITIONS OF PLAYS

Fin de partie [and] *Acte sans paroles,* Minuit (Paris, France), 1957, English translation by Beckett published as *Endgame* [and] *Act without Words,* Grove (New York, NY), 1958.

Krapp's Last Tape [and] *Embers,* Faber & Faber (London, England), 1959, published as *Krapp's Last Tape and Other Dramatic Pieces* (also contains *All that Fall, Act without Words,* and *Act without Words II*), Grove (New York, NY), 1960.

Play and Two Short Pieces for Radio (contains *Play, Words and Music* [first published in *Evergreen Review,* November-December, 1962], and *Cascando* [first published in *Dublin Magazine,* October-December, 1936; also see below]), Faber & Faber (London, England), 1964.

Comedie et actes divers (contains *Comedie, Va et vient, Cascando, Paroles et musiques* [French translation by Beckett of *Words and Music*], *Dis Joe* [French translation by Beckett of *Eh, Joe?;* also see below], and *Acte sans paroles II*), Minuit (Paris, France), 1966.

Cascando and Other Short Dramatic Pieces, Grove (New York, NY), 1968.

Breath and Other Shorts, Faber & Faber (London, England), 1971.

Ends and Odds: Eight New Dramatic Pieces, Faber & Faber (London, England), 1977.

Rockabye and Other Short Pieces, Grove (New York, NY), 1981.

Catastrophe et autres dramaticules: cette fois, solo, berceuse, impromptu d'Ohio, Minuit (Paris, France), 1982.

Three Occasional Pieces, Faber & Faber (London, England), 1982.

Collected Shorter Plays, Grove (New York, NY), 1984.

Ohio Impromptu, Catastrophe, and What Where, Grove (New York, NY), 1984.

The Complete Dramatic Works, Faber & Faber (London, England), 1986.

Samuel Beckett's Company-Compagnie and a Piece of Monologue—Solo: A Bilingual Variorum Edition, Garland (New York, NY), 1993.

Dramaticulesg, Riverrun Press (New York, NY), 1995.

OTHER

Whoroscope: Poem on Time, Hours Press (Paris), 1930.

Proust (criticism), Chatto & Windus (London, England), 1931, Grove (New York, NY), 1957.

Echo's Bones and Other Precipitates (poems), Europa Press (Paris, France), 1935.

A Samuel Beckett Reader, edited by John Calder, Calder & Boyars (London, England), 1967.

(With Georges Duthuit and Jacques Putnam) *Bram van Velde* (criticism), Falaise (Paris, France), 1958, English translation by Olive Chase and Beckett, Grove (New York, NY), 1960.

Henri Hayden, Waddington Galleries, 1959.

Poems in English, Calder & Boyars (London, England), 1961, Grove (New York, NY), 1962.

(With Georges Duthuit) *Proust and Three Dialogues* (criticism), Calder & Boyars (London, England), 1965.

Poemes, Minuit (Paris, France), 1968.

Abandonne, Georges Visat, 1972.

Au loin un oiseau, Double Elephant Press, 1973.

An Examination of James Joyce, M.S.G. House, 1974.

Pour finir encore, French and European Publications, 1976.

I Can't Go On: A Selection from the Works of Samuel Beckett, edited by Richard Seaver, Grove (New York, NY), 1976.

Collected Poems in English and French, Grove (New York, NY), 1977, revised as *Collected Poems, 1930-1978,* Calder & Boyars (London, England), 1984.

Disjecta: Miscellaneous Writings and a Dramatic Fragment, edited by Ruby Cohn, Calder & Boyars (London, England), 1983, Grove (New York, NY), 1984.

Collected Shorter Prose, 1945-1980, Calder & Boyars (London, England), 1984.

Happy Days: The Production Notebook, edited by James Knowlson, Faber & Faber (London, England), 1985, Grove (New York, NY), 1986.

(Translator with Edouard Roditi and Denise Levertov) Alain Bosquet, *No Matter No Fact,* New Directions (New York, NY), 1988.

Collected Poems in English, Grove (New York, NY), 1989.

Endgame: Production Notebook, revised edition, Grove (New York, NY), 1993.

Collected Poems, 1930-1989, Riverrun Press (New York, NY), 1995.

No Author Better Served: The Correspondence of Samuel Beckett and Alan Schneider, edited by Maurice Harmon, Harvard University Press (Cambridge, MA), 1998.

Beckett Short (short writings and excerpts), Calder (New York, NY), 1999.

(Translator) *Beckett in Black and Red: The Translations for Nancy Cunard's Negro (1934),* edited by Alan Warren Friedman, University Press of Kentucky (Lexington, KY), 2000.

Contributor to books, including *Our Examination round His Factification for Incamination of Work in Progress,* Shakespeare Co. (Paris, France), 1929, New Directions (New York, NY), 1939, 2nd edition, 1962; contributor to periodicals, including *transition, New Review, Evergreen Review, Contempo, Les Temps Modernes, Merlin,* and *Spectrum.*

ADAPTATIONS: Film, a mime adaptation by Mariu Karmitz, of *Play),* was produced by M.K. Productions and starred Buster Keaton, M.K. Productions, 1966. Many of Beckett's works have been adapted for radio and television broadcast. Film versions of nineteen of Beckett's plays were presented at the "Beckett of Film" festival in Dublin, Ireland, February 1-8, 2001, and are available in DVD format from Ambrose Video. His works have also been produced on CD and audiotape.

SIDELIGHTS: Most discussions of Samuel Beckett's work take a tone seldom applied to others writers. As a *Time* reviewer noted: "Some chronicle men on their way up; others tackle men on their way down. Samuel Beckett stalks after men on their way out." Most literary critics agree that there is difficulty in communicating the unique power of Beckett's writing. Along with the work of Eugene Ionesco, Jean Genet, and Harold Pinter, Beckett's stark plays are said to compose the "Theatre of the Absurd." But to so label Beckett's work is to disqualify one of his own first premises: that, since no human activity has any intrinsic meaning, it is pointless to ascribe traditional or categorical significance to the existence of an object or the performance of a deed. Perhaps Beckett himself stated his dilemma most succinctly in *L'Innommable:* "Dans ma vie, puisqu'il faut l'appeler ainsi, il y eut trois choses, l'impossibilite de parler, l'impossibilite de me taire, et la solitude." ("One must speak; man cannot possibly communicate with his fellows, but the alternative—silence—is irreconcilable with human existence.") According to the *Time* contributor, "Beckett's champions argue that his threnodies in dusky twilight represent the existential metaphor of the human condition, that the thin but unwavering voices of his forlorn characters speak the ultimate statement of affirmation, if only because the merest attempt at communication is itself affirmation."

But in case the reader of Beckett criticism should come to regard this question as the black and white one of "despair" versus "optimism," Richard N. Coe added new terms to the argument in his *Beckett:* "To class Beckett himself as the simple incarnation of 'despair' is a drastic oversimplification. To begin with, the concept of 'despair' implies the existence of a related concept 'hope,' and 'hope' implies a certain predictable continuity in time—which continuity Beckett would seriously question. 'Despair,' with all its inherent moral overtones, is a term which is wholly inadequate to describe Beckett's attitude towards the human condition; nor is this condition, in the most current sense of the definition, 'absurd.' It is literally and logically impossible. And in this central concept of 'impossibility,' his thought has most of its origins—as does also his art."

For some critics, like John Gassner in his *Theatre at the Crossroads,* the scholarly complexity of the critical response to Beckett's work has been overwrought. Gassner wrote: "To a parvenu intelligentsia, it would seem that a work of art exists not for its own sake but only for the possibilities of interpreting it." Nevertheless, some critics believe that Beckett's theater is most meaningful when considered within the context of a recognizable literary tradition. Kenneth Allsop noted in his *The Angry Decade* that Beckett's "harsh, desolate, denuded style is entirely and unmistakably his own, but his literary 'form' . . . derives from his years [working with] . . . James Joyce. That is only a partial explanation. He is in a monolithic way the last of the Left Bank Mohicans of the Twenties; the others of the *avant-garde* died or deserted or prospered, but Beckett was a loyal expatriate." In the *New York Times Book Review* J.D. O'Hara saw Beckett's work as exponential to the philosophy of Descartes: "In Beckett's world of post-Cartesian dualism, the mind has no connection to the body, its values worth nothing there, and so it cannot logically concern itself with the body's problems." John Fletcher concluded in *Samuel Beckett's Art* that "whatever the truth of the matter, one thing is certain. Beckett has ranged freely among the writings of the philosophers, where he has found confirmation and justification of the metaphysical obsessions that haunt his work: the gulf set between body and mind, the epistemological incertitude. His genius has achieved the transmutation of such speculative problems into art." But, according to Coe, one must keep in mind that "Beckett has renounced his claim to erudition. The main theme of his work is impotence, of mind just as much as of body."

Most critics agree that the 1954 English-language publication of *Waiting for Godot* established Beckett's prominence in the United States; in *Contemporary Theatre,* H.A. Smith dubbed the work "the most comprehensively and profoundly evocative play" of the mid-twentieth century. As Allsop maintained, "*Godot* is a hymn to extol the moment when the mind swings off its hinges. . . . Beckett is unconcerned with writing requiems for humanity, for he sees life as polluted and pointless: he merely scrawls its obituary, without bitterness or compassion because he cannot really believe it is worth the words he is wasting." Gassner also found the play to be a straightforward pronouncement, but he did not accept it as a prediction of certain doom. "To all this tohu and bohu about the profundity and difficulty of the play," he wrote, "my reply is simply that there is nothing painfully or exhilaratingly ambiguous about *Waiting for Godot* in the first place. It presents the view that man, the hapless wanderer in the universe, brings his quite wonderful humanity—his human capacity for hope, patience, resilience, and, yes, for love of one's kind, too, as well as his animal nature—to the weird journey of existence. He is lost in the universe and found in his own heart and in the hearts of his fellow men."

Kenneth Tynan wrote in his *Curtains* that the implications of *Waiting for Godot* are significant within the spectrum of mid-twentieth-century theater. He wrote: "A special virtue attaches to plays which remind the drama of how much it can do without and still exist. By all known criteria, Beckett's *Waiting for Godot* is a dramatic vacuum. Pity the critic who seeks a chink in its armour, for it is all chink. It has no plot, no climax, no *denouement;* no beginning, no middle, and no end. Unavoidably, it has a situation, and it might be accused of having suspense. . . . *Waiting for Godot* frankly jettisons everything by which we recognise theatre. It arrives at the custom-house, as it were, with no luggage, no passport, and nothing to declare; yet it gets through, as might a pilgrim from Mars. It does this, I believe, by appealing to a definition of drama much more fundamental than any in the books. A play, it asserts and proves, is basically a means of spending two hours in the dark without being bored. . . . It forced me to re-examine the rules which have hitherto governed the drama; and, having done so, to pronounce them not elastic enough."

Some critics found 1957's *Endgame* to be an even more powerful expression of Beckett's negativism. Gassner wrote: "Nothing happens in *Endgame* and that nothing is what matters. The author's feeling about nothing also matters, not because it is true or right but because it is a strongly formed attitude, a felt and expressed viewpoint. . . . The yardsticks of dialectical materialism and moralism are equally out in appraising the play. Dialectical materialism could only say that *Endgame* is decadent. Moralism and theology would say that the play is sinful, since nothing damns the soul so much as despair of salvation. Neither yardstick could tell us that this hauntingly powerful work of the imagination is art."

Although critics discuss his plays more frequently than his novels, Beckett himself was said to have considered his novels to be his major works. A *Times Literary Supplement* reviewer, in his discussion of *Imagination Dead Imagine,* summarized Beckett's work thus: "[This novel] certainly describes two people in an imaginary situation and it is equally certainly a work of large implications and a desolate, cruel beauty. It might not seem so, however, if it had not been apparent for some time that Mr. Beckett's prose narratives compose a single, long saga of exclusion and heroic relinquishment as well as of the desperate, perhaps unavailing, pursuit of finality." In his *Puzzles and Epiphanies* Frank Kermode offered this analysis of the novels: "In Beckett's plays the theatrical demand for communicable rhythms and relatively crude satisfactions has had a beneficent effect. But in the novels he yields progressively to the magnetic pull of the primitive, to the desire to achieve, by various forms of decadence and deformation, some Work that eludes the intellect, avoids the spread nets of habitual meaning. Beckett is often allegorical, but he is allegorical in fitful patches, providing illusive toeholds to any reader scrambling for sense."

The fact that most of Beckett's important work was originally written in French is far more than coincidentally significant to his stylistic achievement. Coe explained: "Beckett, in the final analysis, is trying to say what cannot be said; he must be constantly on his guard, therefore, never to yield to the temptation of saying what the words would make him say. Only when language is, as it were, defeated, bound hand and foot; only when it is so rigorously disciplined that each word describes exactly and quasiscientifically the precise concept to which it is related and no other, only then, by the progressive elimination of that which precisely is, is there a remote chance for the human mind to divine the ultimate reality which is not. And this relentless, almost masochistic discipline, which reaches its culmination in *Comment c'est,* Beckett achieves by writing in a language which is not his own—in French."

Although unpublished for sixty years, Beckett's first novel, *Dream of Fair to Middling Women,* was published in the United States in 1993. The author composed the book as a young man of twenty-six during a summer spent in Paris. The protagonist of *Dream* is the adventurous Belacqua, and the story centers on his varied experiences in Dublin and Paris. Beckett's style here, according to Colm Toibin in the *London Review of Books,* "is a rambling stream of consciousness, full of asides and associations, with a tone of half-seriousness and oblique mockery. . . . The writing is self-conscious: it reads as though the writer wrote it merely to read it himself." Beckett himself described *Dream* as "the chest into which I threw my wild thoughts." And, as O'Hara commented in the *New York Times Book Review,* "he reused them, often word for word." In the end, George Craig asserted in the *Times Literary Supplement,* while *Dream of Fair to Middling Women* "is Beckett's earliest venture, and it shows. . . . something important is going on: the search for [his] voice."

Similarly, Beckett's first play, *Eleutheria*—the title means "freedom" in Greek—collected dust in the author's trunk for nearly fifty years before being published in 1995. The dark, three-act comedy concerns a privacy-obsessed writer who tries in vain to escape from his family and friends, spending most of the play fighting off their efforts to mend what is left of his life. *Eleutheria* was written just prior to *Waiting for Godot,* but it demands more complex staging; seventeen characters and two sets are shown simultaneously in the first two acts before one disappears into the orchestra pit in the final act. Because of its stage requirement, it was not produced in the 1950s when *Godot* burst onto the contemporary theatrical scene.

Because it was well known that Beckett did not want *Eleutheria* published, its appearance prompted considerable controversy, with some people appalled that the author's final request for its suppression—from his deathbed, no less—was ignored. Jonathan Kalb noted in *American Theatre* that the play is neither "a hidden masterpiece" nor "a catastrophe," but rather "a fascinating, rare instance of Beckettian excess. . . . At times windy, redundant, even confusing, it will certainly take its proper place as a minor, formative work that is buoyed by eloquent and hilarious passages and the tantalizing seeds of great themes, devices, and characters to come." As Mel Gussow put it in the *New York Times Book Review,* "*Waiting for Godot* is revolutionary; *Eleutheria* is evolutionary."

Beckett's works continue to be dissected by critics and his plays, especially "Waiting for Godot," are performed around the world; in 2003, for example, *Happy Days,* was performed in London's West End and *Endgame* was staged in Korea. Nearly all of Godot's plays have also been adapted for film, the most ambitious endeavor in this area being the "Beckett on Film" project, which filmed nineteen plays. "One of the things with all the Beckett plays, per the Beckett estate, is that you have to stick to the text," Michael Lindsay-Hogg, who directed the film version of "Waiting for Godot," told Charles Lyons in *Variety.*

In 2003 the city of Dublin, Ireland, where Beckett was born, held a fiftieth-anniversary celebration of Beckett's *Waiting for Godot.* Whether or not Beckett would have appreciated the celebration, few would argue that the author's work will continue to impact the literary consciousness for years to come. As Kalb noted, "Thirteen years after his death and 50 years after the premiere of *Waiting for Godot,*—a play that made boredom (of a sort) respectable in the theatre—Samuel Beckett is still something of an incalculable quantity."

BIOGRAPHICAL AND CRITICAL SOURCES:

BOOKS

Abbott, H. Porter, *Beckett Writing Beckett: The Author in the Autograph,* Cornell University Press (Ithaca, NY), 1996.

Acheson, James, *Samuel Beckett's Artistic Theory and Practice: Criticism, Drama, and Early Fiction,* St. Martin's Press (New York, NY), 1997.

Allsop, Kenneth, *The Angry Decade,* Copp, 1958.

Armstrong, William A., and others, editors, *Experimental Drama,* G. Bell, 1963.

Baker, Phil, *Beckett and the Mythology of Psychoanalysis,* St. Martin's Press (New York, NY), 1997.

Beckett, Samuel, *L'Innommable,* Minuit (Paris, France), 1953.

Brater, Enoch, *The Drama in the Text: Beckett's Late Fiction,* Oxford University Press (New York, NY), 1994.

Brown, John Russell, and Bernard Harris, *Contemporary Theatre,* Stratford-upon-Avon Studies 4, Edward Arnold, 1962.

Bryden, Mary, editor, *Samuel Beckett and Music,* Clarendon Press (Oxford, England), 1998.

Bryden, Mary, *Samuel Beckett and the Idea of God,* St. Martin's Press (New York, NY), 1998.

Butler, Lance St. John, *Critical Essays on Samuel Beckett,* Ashgate Publishing Co. (Brookfield, VT), 1994.

Coe, Richard N., *Beckett,* Oliver & Boyd, 1964.

Cohn, Ruby, *Samuel Beckett: The Comic Gamut,* Rutgers University Press (Rutgers, NJ), 1962.

Contemporary Literary Criticism, Thomson Gale (Detroit, MI), Volume 1, 1973, Volume 2, 1974, Volume 3, 1975, Volume 4, 1975, Volume 6, 1976, Volume 9, 1978, Volume 10, 1979, Volume 11, 1979, Volume 14, 1980, Volume 18, 1981, Volume 29, 1984, Volume 57, 1990, Volume 59, 1990, Volume 83, 1994.

Cronin, Anthony, *Samuel Beckett: The Last Modernist,* HarperCollins (New York, NY), 1996.

Danziger, Marie A., *Text/Countertext: Fear, Guilt, and Retaliation in the Postmodern Novel,* Peter Lang (New York, NY), 1996.

Davies, Paul, *The Ideal Real: Beckett's Fiction and Imagination,* Associated University Presses (Cranbury, NJ), 1994.

Dictionary of Literary Biography, Thomson Gale (Detroit, MI), Volume 13: *British Dramatists since World War II,* 1982, Volume 15: *British Novelists, 1930-1959,* 1983.

Dillon, Brian, *Beckett's Blurry Signature,* Department of Liberal Arts, Nova University (Ft. Lauderdale, FL), 1995.

Esslin, Martin, *The Theatre of the Absurd,* Doubleday-Anchor (New York, NY), 1961.

Fletcher, John, *Samuel Beckett's Art,* Barnes & Noble (New York, NY), 1967.

Gassner, John, *Theatre at the Crossroads,* Holt (New York, NY), 1960.

Gordon, Lois G., *The World of Samuel Beckett, 1906-1946,* Yale University Press (New Haven, CT), 1996.

Guicharnaud, Jacques, and June Beckelman, *Modern French Theatre from Giraudoux to Beckett,* Yale University Press (New Haven, CT), 1961.

Harding, James M., *Adorno and "A Writing of the Ruins": Essays on Modern Aesthetics and Anglo-American Literature and Culture,* State University of New York Press (Albany, NY), 1997.

Hoffman, Frederick J., *Samuel Beckett: The Language of Self,* Southern Illinois University Press, 1962.

Kenner, Hugh, *Samuel Beckett,* J. Calder, 1962.

Kenner, Hugh, *A Reader's Guide to Samuel Beckett,* Syracuse University Press (Syracuse, NY), 1996.

Kermode, Frank, *Puzzles and Epiphanies,* Chilmark, 1962.

Kim, Hwa Soon, *The Counterpoint of Hope, Obsession, and Desire for Death in Five Plays by Samuel Beckett,* Peter Lang (New York, NY), 1996.

Knowlson, James, *Damned to Fame: The Life of Samuel Beckett,* Bloomsbury (New York, NY), 1996.

Kostelanetz, Richard, editor, *On Contemporary Literature,* Avon (New York, NY), 1954.

Lumley, Frederick, *New Trends in Twentieth-Century Drama,* Oxford University Press (Oxford, England), 1967.

Minihan, John, and Aidan Higgins, *Samuel Beckett: Photographs,* George Braziller (New York, NY), 1996.

Murphy, P. J., *Critique of Beckett Criticism: A Guide to Research in English, French, and German,* Camden House (Columbia, SC), 1994.

O'Hara, J. D., *Samuel Beckett's Hidden Drives: Structural Uses of Depth Psychology,* University Press of Florida, 1997.

Oppenheim, Lois, *Directing Beckett,* University of Michigan Press (Ann Arbor, MI), 1994.

Oppenheim, Lois, Marius Buning and The International Beckett Symposium, *Beckett On and On,* Fairleigh Dickinson University Press (Madison, NJ), 1996.

Piette, Adam, *Remembering and the Sound of Words: Mallarmae, Proust, Joyce, Beckett,* Clarendon Press (New York, NY), 1996.

Pilling, John, *The Cambridge Companion to Beckett,* Cambridge University Press (New York, NY), 1994.

Pilling, John, *Beckett before Godot,* Cambridge University Press (New York, NY), 1997.

Pultar, Geoneul, *Technique and Tradition in Beckett's Trilogy of Novels,* University Press of America (Lanham, MD), 1996.

Simpson, Alan, *Beckett and Behan and a Theatre in Dublin,* Routledge & Kegan Paul (London, England), 1962.

Tindall, William York, *Samuel Beckett,* Columbia University Press (New York, NY), 1964.

Tynan, Kenneth, *Curtains,* Atheneum (New York, NY), 1961.

Wellwarth, George, *Theatre of Protest and Paradox,* New York University Press (New York, NY), 1964.

Wolosky, Shira, *Language Mysticism: The Negative Way of Language in Eliot, Beckett, and Celan,* Stanford University Press (Stanford, CA), 1995.

PERIODICALS

American Scholar, winter, 1992, p. 124.

American Theatre, January, 2003, Jonathan Kalb, "Stardust Melancholy: Does the Filming of Samuel Beckett's Complete Works Compromise His Theatrical Legacy?," p. 42.

Atlantic, August, 1967.

Carleton Miscellany, winter, 1967.

Christian Science Monitor, July 27, 1967.

Comparative Literature, winter, 1965.

Connoisseur, July, 1990, p. 56.

Critique, spring, 1963; winter, 1964-65.

Economist, January 6, 1990, p. 90.

English Review, February 2001, Paul Williams, "Samuel Beckett's Engame," p. 17.

Esquire, September, 1967; May, 1990, p. 87.

Explicator, spring, 2002, p. 159.

Hudson Review, spring, 1967.

Journal of European Studies, December, 2002, p. 351.

Kenyon Review, March, 1967.

Kirkus Reviews, February 15, 1993, p. 162.

Life, February 2, 1968.

Listener, August 3, 1967.

Livres de France, January, 1967.

London Magazine, August, 1967.

London Review of Books, November 9, 1989, p. 26; April 8, 1993, p. 14.

Manchester Guardian, April 21, 1966.

Nation, October 3, 1987, p. 349; December 19, 1988, p. 26; April 30, 1990, p. 611; May 6, 1996, p. 16.

New Republic, December 12, 1988, p. 26; October 22, 1990, p. 30.

New Statesman, February 14, 1964; March 25, 1966; July 14, 1967.

New Statesman & Society, July 6, 1990, p. 46; October 11, 1991, p. 22; January 8, 1993, p. 42.

New York, September 28, 1987, p. 133; July 11, 1988, p. 46.

New York Review of Books, March 19, 1964; December 7, 1967; December 8, 1988, p. 30; August 13, 1992, p. 17; December 16, 1993, p. 42.

New York Times, July 21, 1964; February 27, 1966; April 19, 1966; July 20, 1967; September 14, 1967.

New York Times Book Review, June 12, 1988, p. 18; June 13, 1993, p. 11; April 17, 1994, p. 24; June 25, 1995, p. 9; May 26, 1996, p. 4.

Observer (London, England), July 16, 1967; July 15, 1990, p. 53; July 22, 1990, p. 52; November 1, 1992, p. 62.

Partisan Review, spring, 1966.

Publishers Weekly, September 26, 1994, p. 12.

Punch, August 2, 1967.

Saturday Review, October 4, 1958.

Studies in Twentieth-Century Literature, summer, 2003, p. 219; winter, 2003, p. 6.

Time, July 14, 1967; November 21, 1988, p. 58.

Times Literary Supplement, December 21, 1962; January 30, 1964; June 30, 1966; July 20, 1990, p. 782; November 27, 1992, p. 25.

Tri-Quarterly, winter, 1967.

Tulane Drama Review, summer, 1967.

Variety, November 6, 2000, Charles Lyons, "Helmer Weights 'Godot,'" p. 71.

Village Voice, April 6, 1967; July 13, 1967; June 20, 1995, p. 69.

Washington Post Book World, May 23, 1993, p. 8.

World Literature Today, winter, 1994, p. 125; autumn, 1995, p. 761.

OBITUARIES:

PERIODICALS

Chicago Tribune, December 27, 1989.

Los Angeles Times, December 27, 1989.

Maclean's, January 8, 1990, p. 47.

Newsweek, January 8, 1990, p. 43.

New York Times, December 27, 1989.

People, January 8, 1990, p. 46.

Time, January 8, 1990, p. 69.

*   *   *

BECKETT, Samuel Barclay
See BECKETT, Samuel

*   *   *

BELDONE, Phil "Cheech"
See ELLISON, Harlan

BELL, Madison Smartt 1957-

PERSONAL: Born August 1, 1957, in Nashville, TN; son of Henry Denmark (an attorney) and Allen (a farmer; maiden name, Wigginton) Bell; married Elizabeth Spires (a poet), June 15, 1985; children: Celia. *Education:* Princeton University, B.A. (summa cum laude), 1979; Hollins College, M.A., 1981.

ADDRESSES: Home—Baltimore, MD. *Office*—Department of English, Goucher College, Towson, MD 21204. *Agent*—Jane Gellman, 250 West 57th St., New York, NY 10107. *E-mail*—mbell\@goucher.edu.

CAREER: Security guard at Unique Clothing Warehouse (boutique), 1979; production assistant for Gomes-Lowe Associates (commercial production house), 1979; sound man for Radiotelevisione Italiana (Italian national network), 1979; Franklin Library (publishing firm), New York, NY, picture research assistant, 1980, writer of reader's guides, 1980-83; Berkley Publishing Corp., New York, NY, manuscript reader and copy writer, 1981-83; Goucher College, Towson, MD, assistant professor of English, 1984-86, writer-in-residence, 1988—. Visiting writer, Poetry Center, 92nd Street Y, New York, NY, 1984-86, Iowa Writers Workshop, 1987-88, and Johns Hopkins Writing Seminars, 1989-93. Director of 185 Corporation (media arts organization), 1979-84.

MEMBER: PEN American Center, Authors Guild, Authors League of America, Poets and Writers, Phi Beta Kappa.

AWARDS, HONORS: Ward Mathis Prize, 1977, for short story "Triptych," Class of 1870 Junior Prize, 1978, Francis LeMoyne Page Award, 1978, for fiction writing, and Class of 1859 Prize, 1979, all from Princeton University; Lillian Smith Award, 1989; Guggenheim fellowship, 1991; Maryland State Arts Council Individual Artist Award, 1991-92; George A. and Eliza Gardner Howard Foundation Award, 1991-92; National Endowment for the Arts fellowship, 1992; National Book Award finalist, 1995, PEN/Faulkner Award finalist, Maryland Library Association Award, and Anisfield-Wolf Award, all 1996, all for *All Souls' Rising;* selected as one of the "Best American Novelists under Forty," *Granta,* 1996; Andrew James Purdy Fiction Award, Hollins College.

WRITINGS:

NOVELS

The Washington Square Ensemble, Viking (New York, NY), 1983.

Waiting for the End of the World, Ticknor & Fields (New York, NY), 1985.
Straight Cut, Ticknor & Fields (New York, NY), 1986.
The Year of Silence, Ticknor & Fields (New York, NY), 1987.
Soldier's Joy, Ticknor & Fields (New York, NY), 1989.
Doctor Sleep, Harcourt (San Diego, CA), 1991.
Save Me, Joe Louis, Harcourt (New York, NY), 1993.
All Souls' Rising, Pantheon (New York, NY), 1995.
Ten Indians, Pantheon (New York, NY), 1996.
Master of the Crossroads, Pantheon (New York, NY), 2000.
Anything Goes, Pantheon (New York, NY), 2002.

OTHER

History of the Owen Graduate School of Management (nonfiction), Vanderbilt University (Nashville, TN), 1985.
Zero db (short fiction), Ticknor & Fields (New York, NY), 1987.
(With others) *George Garrett: An Interview,* Northouse & Northouse (Dallas, TX), 1988.
Waiting for the End of the World (screenplay), Cine Paris, 1988.
The Safety Net (screenplay), New Horizons, 1990.
Barking Man and Other Stories (contains "Holding Together," "Black and Tan," "Customs of the Country," "Finding Natasha," "Dragon's Seed," "Barking Man," "Petit Cachou," "Witness," "Move on Up," and "Mr. Potatohead in Love,") Ticknor & Fields (New York, NY), 1990.
Choc en Retour (screen adaptation of *Straight Cut*), Thomas Kuchenreuther (Munich, Germany), 1993.
New Millennium Writings, Spring & Summer 1996, New Messenger Books (Nashville, TN), 1996.
Narrative Design: A Writer's Guide to Structure, Norton (New York, NY), 1997.
(Author of introduction) George Garrett, *The King of Babylon Shall Not Come against You* (novel), Harcourt (New York, NY), 1998.

Contributor of short fiction to periodicals and anthologies, including *Best American Short Stories, New Writers of the South, New Stories from the South, Atlantic, Harper's, Best of Intro, Editors' Choice, Louder Than Words, A Pocketful of Prose, Sound of Writing, Elvis in Oz, That's What I Like about the South, Antaeus, Boulevard, Cosmopolitan, Literary Review* (London, England), *Ploughshares, Columbia, Crescent Review, Northwest Review, Lowlands Review, Poughkeepsie Review, Stories, Tennessee Illustrated, Switch, Southern*

Review, Witness, Hudson Review, and *North American Review.* Contributor of reviews and essays to *Harper's, Antaeus, Chronicles, Switch, World and I, A Wake for the Living, Critical Essays on Peter Taylor, New York Times Magazine, USA Today, Philadelphia Inquirer, London Standard, North American Review, Boston Globe, Southern Magazine, New York Times Book Review, Village Voice,* and *Los Angeles Times Book Review.* Work included in anthologies, including *It's Only Rock and Roll,* edited by Janice Eidus and John Kastan, D. Godine; and *Sudden Fiction (Continued),* edited by Robert Shapard and James Thomas. Contributor of essay to *Joyful Noise: The New Testament Revisited,* edited by Rick Moody and Darcey Steinke, Little, Brown, and to *Outside the Law: Narratives on Justice in America,* edited by Susan Richards Shreve and Porter Shreve, Beacon Press. Author of readers' guides, Franklin Library, 1979-83.

Several of Bell's works have been translated into other languages, including German, Danish, Spanish, Portuguese, Japanese, French, and Dutch.

SIDELIGHTS: "Madison Smartt Bell has been called a postmodernist, a minimalist, a prose poet of aloneness, and the best writer of his generation," stated Donna Seaman in *Booklist.* "His distinctively riling fiction sizzles with tension and menace." Bell, who had published six novels and two short-story collections by the time he was thirty-five years old, usually writes about society's misfits. Most of his main characters are petty criminals, drifters, and lost souls whose lives Seaman describes as "fateful and apocalyptic."

Save Me, Joe Louis exemplifies the themes and situations found in much of Bell's fiction. In this novel, Macrae, an AWOL Southerner, and Charlie, an unstable ex-con, forge a dangerous partnership soon after meeting in New York City. Together they embark on a small-time crime spree that eventually leads them to flee for Macrae's backcountry homeland. There, the relationship sours and violence erupts. Macrae and Charlie are typical of Bell's protagonists in that there is little to like about them; many commentators find that one of the great strengths of Bell's writing is his ability to generate characters for such people. Andy Solomon wrote in the *Chicago Tribune* that Bell "moves among modern thieves and lepers with charity. His is a Robert Browning empathy that creates no character so defiled that Bell cannot ask, 'What is at the heart of this man that is in me as well?' In Macrae, Bell once again takes a character you'd be disturbed to find living anywhere near your neighborhood, then moves relentlessly against

the grain of popular thought to find the embers of Macrae's humanity beneath the ashes of his pain." Reviewing the novel for *Booklist,* Seaman called *Save Me, Joe Louis* "a work of ferocious intensity and poetic nihilism" in which Bell examines the "soul's disturbing capacity for both good and evil and the pointlessness of unexamined lives lived wholly by instinct and rage."

Rage is at the center of *All Souls' Rising,* an epic history of Haiti's war for independence, which broke out shortly after the French revolution in the late 1700s. The strange alliances, hatred, and tensions among Haiti's rich white ruling class, the poor whites, the free mulattoes, and the island's mistreated slave population culminated in a fifteen-year bloodbath. In just the first few months of the revolution, 12,000 people perished and nearly 200 plantations were burned. Writing in the *New York Times Book Review,* John Vernon described Bell's historical novel as a "carefully drawn roadmap through hell." "*All Souls' Rising,*" he continued, "is historical fiction in the monumental manner, heavily prefaced, prologued, glossaried and chronologized. It admirably diagrams the complex muddle of eighteenth-century Haiti, a slave society constructed along clearly racist lines but with surprising alliances. Haitian whites, split into royalists and revolutionaries, alternately compete for and spurn the loyalties of free mulattoes, for whom gradations of color are of central importance. . . . This bizarre and rich stew is the perfect stuff of fiction, whose subject is never reality but competing realities."

Countless atrocities were committed on all sides in the Haitian revolution, and Bell's book details many examples. For some reviewers, the gore was too much. Brian Morton expressed little enthusiasm for the novel, stating in the *New Statesman* that *All Souls' Rising* "is an ugly book about ugly times. The author can claim historical veracity. . . . But there are undercurrents that recall the violent pornography of another triple-barrelled American novelist, Bret Easton Ellis." Vernon also found the scenes of mutilation, rape, and violence relentless and warned that such repeated gore may numb the novel "into a handbook of splatter-punk. To his credit," Vernon continued, "Bell knows that violence may be the writer's hedge against mawkishness, but it also threatens to become mere slush, the sentimentality of gore." Still, Vernon found much to praise, especially Bell's ability to humanize all types of characters and concluded that while there are flaws in the novel, they are overshadowed by its power and intelligence: "*All Souls' Rising,* refreshingly ambitious and maximalist in its approach, takes enormous chances, and consequently will haunt readers long after plenty of flawless books have found their little slots on their narrow shelves."

A *Publishers Weekly* reviewer expressed unreserved enthusiasm for *All Souls' Rising,* deeming it an "astonishing novel of epic scope." The reviewer argued that "Bell avoids the sense of victory that mars so many novels about revolution." After the many scenes of massacre, rape, and violence, the critic continued, "there can be no question of a winner of the battle for Haitian liberation. Surviving it was feat enough. In Bell's hands, the chaos . . . that surrounds these characters somehow elucidates the nobility of even the most craven among them."

Discussing *All Souls' Rising,* with Ken Ringle of the *Washington Post,* Bell compared Haiti's race conflict with conditions in the contemporary United States. "Haiti's was a full-blown race war," he explained, "over issues we've never really come to terms with in this country. Now we're having our own race war. But it's a slow-motion race war, disguised as crime in the streets. And nobody, black or white, wants to admit what's happening."

Bell's next novel, *Ten Indians,* centers on a white, middle-aged therapist for children named Mike Devlin who creates in the black ghetto of Baltimore a school for Tae Kwon Do, which ends up drawing people from two rivaling drug gangs—one member becomes involved with Devlin's seventeen-year-old daughter, Michelle. A reviewer for *Publishers Weekly* said that in the novel, which switches between first-and third-person narratives, "Devlin's motivations . . . remain personally unclear, if admirable in the abstract," but the reviewer called Bell "a natural storyteller." John Skow, in a review for *Time,* noted that "the working out, told partly from Devlin's viewpoint and partly, in convincing street language, from that of the drug dealers and their women, is spare and cinematic," and concluded, "Good ending, good novel." In a review of *Ten Indians,* *Booklist*'s Michael Cart mentioned that the novel "would be a wonderful book for mature young adult readers" because it "captures the mix of literary quality and right-on relevance that, if put into the right readers' hands, can change lives—one individual at a time. It can, in fact, translate good intentions into redeeming reality."

Anything Goes, which centers on a bass player in a bar band, reflects a world Bell has some personal experience with. He has collaborated with poet Wyn Cooper, who came to fame as the author of the lyrics of the Sheryl Crow song *All I Wanna Do.* The two have collaborated on a CD, *Anything Goes,* which contains the songs mentioned in Bell's book. The CD garnered the duo a recording contract and a second album, titled *Forty Words for Fear.*

BIOGRAPHICAL AND CRITICAL SOURCES:

PERIODICALS

Atlanta Journal-Constitution, April 22, 1990, p. N8; January 13, 1991, p. N10; June 13, 1993, p. N8; November 26, 1995, p. C1.

Booklist, April 15, 1993, pp. 1468-1469; September 1, 1995, p. 4; January 1, 1997, p. 834.

Boston Globe, May 23, 1993, p. B40; October 22, 1995, p. B38.

Chicago Tribune, January 13, 1991, section 14, p. 1; May 30, 1993, section 14, p. 6; October 22, 1995, section 14, p. 1.

Entertainment Weekly, November 10, 1995, p. 55.

Harper's, August, 1986.

Library Journal, October 1, 1995, p. 118.

Los Angeles Times, September 16, 1985; September 15, 1986; February 20, 1987; November 3, 1987.

Los Angeles Times Book Review, February 27, 1983; September 30, 1990, p. 12; January 20, 1991, p. 8; July 11, 1993, p. 7.

New Statesman, February 9, 1996, pp. 37-38.

New York Times Book Review, February 20, 1983; August 18, 1985; October 12, 1986; February 15, 1987; November 15, 1987; December 27, 1987; April 8, 1990, p. 11; January 6, 1991, p. 11; June 20, 1993, p. 9; November 24, 1994; October 29, 1995, p. 12.

Publishers Weekly, August 28, 1995, p. 102; November 6, 1995, p. 58; August 26, 1996, p. 75.

Time, October 28, 1996, p. 110.

Times (London, England), November 14, 1985; November 19, 1987.

Times Literary Supplement, August 26, 1983; November 22, 1985; November 6, 1987.

Tribune Books (Chicago, IL), November 22, 1987.

Washington Post, October 25, 1986; January 24, 1991, p. B3; November 28, 1995, pp. C1-C2; March 19, 1996.

Washington Post Book World, February 16, 1983; September 1, 1985; October 26, 1986; February 1, 1987; November 22, 1987; April 15, 1990, p. 7; June 24, 1993, p. C2; November 5, 1995, p. 4.

ONLINE

Goucher College Web site, http://www.faculty.goucher.edu/ (January 15, 2000).

BELLOW, Saul 1915-2005
(Solomon Bellow)

PERSONAL: Born Solomon Bellows, June 10, 1915 (some sources say July 10, 1915), in Lachine, Quebec, Canada; came to United States, c. 1924; died April 5, 2005, in Brookline, MA; son of Abraham (a Russian emigré and businessman) and Liza (Gordon) Bellow; married Anita Goshkin (a social worker), December 31, 1937 (divorced); married Alexandra Tschacbasov, February 1, 1956 (divorced); married Susan Glassman (a teacher), 1961 (divorced); married Alexandra Ionesco Tuleca (a mathematician), 1974 (divorced); married Janis Freedman (a professor), 1989; children: (first marriage) Gregory, (second marriage) Adam, (third marriage) Daniel, (fifth marriage) Naomi-Rose. *Education:* Attended University of Chicago, 1933-35; Northwestern University, B.S. (with honors), 1937; graduate study at University of Wisconsin, 1937.

CAREER: Author and educator. Worked on WPA Writers' Project, writing biographies of authors; Pestalozzi-Froebel Teachers College, Chicago, IL, instructor, 1938-42; Encyclopaedia Britannica, Inc., Chicago, member of editorial department of "Great Books" project, 1943-46; University of Minnesota at Minneapolis, member of English department, 1946, assistant professor, 1948-49, associate professor of English, 1954-59; Boston University, Boston, MA, professor of English, beginning 1993. New York University, New York, NY, visiting lecturer, 1950-52; Princeton University, Princeton, NJ, creative writing fellow, 1952-53; Bard College, Annandale-on-Hudson, NY, faculty member, 1953-54; University of Puerto Rico, Rio Piedras, visiting professor of English, 1961; University of Chicago, Chicago, celebrity-in-residence, 1962, became Grunier Distinguished Services Professor, member of committee on social thought, 1962-93, chair, 1970-76. Presented Jefferson Lecture for National Endowment for the Humanities in 1977; Tanner Lecturer at Oxford University. Fellow, Academy for Policy Study, 1966, and Brandford College of Yale University. *Military service:* U.S. Merchant Marine, 1944-45.

MEMBER: Authors League of America, American Academy of Arts and Letters, PEN, Yaddo Corporation.

AWARDS, HONORS: Guggenheim fellowship in Paris and Rome, 1948; National Institute of Arts and Letters grant, 1952; National Book Awards, 1954, for *The Adventures of Augie March,* 1965, for *Herzog,* and 1971, for *Mr. Sammler's Planet;* O. Henry Award, 1956, for

"The Gonzaga Manuscripts," and 1980, for "A Silver Dish"; Ford grants, 1959, 1960; Friends of Literature Fiction Award, 1960; James L. Dow Award, 1964; Prix International de Litterature (France), 1965, for *Herzog;* Jewish Heritage Award, B'nai B'rith, 1968; Croix de Chevalier (France), 1968; Formentor Prize, 1970; Pulitzer Prize, 1976, for *Humboldt's Gift;* Nobel Prize for Literature, 1976; Gold Medal, American Academy of Arts and Letters, 1977; Emerson-Thoreau Medal, American Academy of Arts and Sciences, 1977; Neil Gunn International fellowship, 1977; Brandeis University Creative Arts Award, 1978; Commander, Legion of Honor (France), 1983; Malaparte prize (Italy), 1984; Commander, Order of Arts and Letters (France), 1985; National Medal of Arts, 1988, for "outstanding contributions to the excellence, growth, support and availability of the arts in the United States"; Lifetime Achievement Award, National Book Award, 1990. D.Litt from Northwestern University, 1962, Bard College, 1963, New York University, 1970, Harvard University, 1972, Yale University, 1972, McGill University, 1973, Brandeis University, 1974, Hebrew Union College, 1976, and Trinity College, Dublin, 1976.

WRITINGS:

NOVELS

Dangling Man, Vanguard (New York, NY), 1944, reprinted, Penguin (New York, NY), 1988.
The Victim, Vanguard (New York, NY), 1947.
The Adventures of Augie March (also see below), Viking (New York, NY), 1953, with an introduction by Lionel Trilling, Modern Library (New York, NY), 1965, with an introduction by Martin Amis, Knopf (New York, NY), 1995, with an introduction by Christopher Hitchens, Viking (New York, NY), 2003.
Henderson the Rain King (also see below), Viking (New York, NY), 1959, reprinted, Penguin (New York, NY), 1996.
Herzog (early drafts published in *Esquire,* July, 1961, and July, 1963, in *Commentary,* July, 1964, and in *Saturday Evening Post,* August 8, 1964; also see below), Viking (New York, NY), 1964, reprinted, Penguin (New York, NY), 2003.
Mr. Sammler's Planet (originally appeared in a different form in *Atlantic;* also see below), Viking (New York, NY), 1970, with an introduction by Stanley Crouch, Penguin (New York, NY), 1996.
Humboldt's Gift, Viking (New York, NY), 1975, with illustrations by Herb Tauss, Franklin Library (Franklin, PA), 1980, reprinted, Penguin (New York, NY), 1996.

The Dean's December, Harper (New York, NY), 1982, with illustrations by Robert Heindel, Franklin Library (Franklin Center, PA), 1982, reprinted, Penguin (New York, NY), 1998.

More Die of Heartbreak, Morrow (New York, NY), 1987.

Ravelstein, Viking (New York, NY), 2000.

SHORT STORIES

Mosby's Memoirs, and Other Stories (contains "Leaving the Yellow House," "The Old System," "Looking for Mr. Green," "The Gonzaga Manuscripts," and "A Father-to-Be"; also see below), Viking (New York, NY), 1968, reprinted, Penguin (New York, NY), 1996.

Him with His Foot in His Mouth, and Other Stories (contains "Cousins," "A Silver Dish," "What Kind of Day Did You Have?," and "Zetland: By a Character Witness"), Harper (New York, NY), 1984, reprinted, Penguin (New York, NY), 1998.

Collected Stories, preface by Janis Bellow, introduction by James Wood, Viking (New York, NY), 2001.

Contributor of short stories to anthologies, including *Partisan Reader: Ten Years of Partisan Review, 1934-1944,* edited by William Phillips and Philip Rahv, introduction by Lionel Trilling, Dial (New York, NY), 1946; *Nelson Algren's Own Book of Lonesome Monsters,* edited by Nelson Algren, Geis, 1963; and *How We Live: Contemporary Life in Contemporary Fiction,* edited by Penny Chapin Hills and L. Rust Hills, Macmillan (New York, NY), 1968.

PLAYS

The Last Analysis, a Play (first produced on Broadway, 1964); first version published as *Bummidge,* revised version, Viking (New York, NY), 1965.

Under the Weather (three one-act comedies: *Orange Souffle* first published in *Esquire,* January, 1965; *A Wen* published in *Esquire,* October, 1965; and *Out from Under*), first produced in London, England, 1966; produced on Broadway, 1966.

Also author of play *The Wrecker,* published in *New World Writing 6* (also see below), 1954.

OTHER

Seize the Day; With Three Short Stories and a One-Act Play (novella; also contains stories "Father-to-Be," "The Gonzaga Manuscripts," and "Looking for Mr.

Green," and play, *The Wrecker*), Viking (New York, NY), 1956, play published separately as *Seize the Day,* 1961, with introduction by Alfred Kazin, Fawcett (New York, NY), 1968, with an introduction by Cynthia Ozick, Penguin (New York, NY), 1996.

(Translator of title story) Isaac Bashevis Singer, *Gimpel the Fool, and Other Stories,* Noonday Press, 1957.

(Author of text, with C. Zervos) Jesse Reichek, *Dessins,* Cahiers d'Art (Paris, France), 1960.

(Editor, with Keith Botsford [first three volumes also with Jack Ludwig]) *The Noble Savage,* five volumes, Meridian.

Recent American Fiction; A Lecture Presented under the Auspices of the Gertrude Clarke Whitall Poetry and Literature Fund, Library of Congress (Washington, DC), 1963.

(Editor and author of introduction) *Great Jewish Short Stories,* Dell (New York, NY), 1963.

Acceptance Speech by Saul Bellow, Author of "Herzog," Fiction Winner National Book Awards, March 9, 1965, privately printed, 1965.

Like You're Nobody: The Letters of Louis Gallo to Saul Bellow, 1961-1962, plus Oedipus Schmoedipus, the Story That Started It All, New Dimensions Press (New York, NY), 1966.

The Portable Saul Bellow (contains *Henderson the Rain King* and *Seize the Day,* plus selections from *The Adventures of Augie March, Herzog, Mr. Sammler's Planet,* "Leaving the Yellow House," "The Old System," and "Mosby's Memoirs"), introduction by Gabriel Josipovici, Viking (New York, NY), 1974.

To Jerusalem and Back: A Personal Account (memoirs), Viking (New York, NY), 1976.

The Nobel Lecture (first published in *American Scholar,* 1977), Targ Editions, 1979.

Herzog (sound recording of Bellow reading excerpts from novel), Caedmon (New York, NY), 1978.

A Theft (novella; also see below), Penguin (New York, NY), 1989.

The Bellarosa Connection (novella; also see below), Penguin (New York, NY), 1989.

Something to Remember Me By: Three Tales (novellas; contains *A Theft* and *The Bellarosa Connection*), Viking (New York, NY), 1991.

It All Adds Up: From the Dim Past to the Uncertain Future (essays), Viking (New York, NY), 1994.

Conversations with Saul Bellow, edited by Gloria L. Cronin and Ben Siegel, University Press of Mississippi (Jackson, MS), 1994.

The Actual (novella), Viking (New York, NY), 1997.

Novels, 1944-1953 (selections), Library of America (New York, NY), 2003.

Also author of "Deep Readers of the World, Beware!," 1959, and *The Future of the Moon,* 1970. Contributor to books, including *The Open Form: Essays for Our Time,* edited by Alfred Kazin, Harcourt (New York, NY), 1961; *The Great Ideas Today,* six volumes, edited by Robert M. Hutchins and Mortimer J. Adler, Atheneum (New York, NY), 1961-66; *To the Young Writer,* edited by A.L. Bader, University of Michigan Press (Ann Arbor, MI), 1963; *First Person Singular: Essays for the Sixties,* edited by Herbert Gold, Dial (New York, NY), 1963; *Saul Bellow and the Critics,* edited by Irving Malin, New York University Press (New York, NY), 1967; *The Art and the Public* (essays), edited by James E. Miller, Jr., and Paul D. Herring, University of Chicago Press (Chicago, IL), 1967; and *Technology and the Frontiers of Knowledge,* Doubleday (New York, NY), 1975. Also contributor to periodicals, including *Partisan Review, Hudson Review, Sewanee Review, New Yorker, New Republic, Nation, New Leader, Saturday Review, Holiday, Reporter, Horizon, Esquire, Commentary,* and *New York Times Book Review.* Founder and coeditor of *Noble Savage,* 1960-62; founder, *News from the Republic of Letters,* 1997.

Author of forewords to books by others, including *Winter Notes on Summer Impressions,* by Feodor Dostoevsky, Criterion Books, 1955; *The Closing of the American Mind,* Allan Bloom, Simon & Schuster, 1987; and *Tales of Grabowski: Transformations, Escape, and Other Stories,* by John Auerbach, Toby, 2003. Author of afterword, *Con Man: A Master Swindler's Own Story,* J.R. Weil, as told to W.T. Brannon, Broadway Books (New York, NY), 2004.

A collection of Bellow's manuscripts, including most of his novels, correspondence, and memorabilia, is housed at the Regenstein Library, University of Chicago. The Humanities Research Center, University of Texas at Austin, holds several manuscripts of *Seize the Day.*

ADAPTATIONS: The Wrecker was televised in 1964; a sound recording of the Chicago Radio Theatre presentation of the plays *Orange Souffle* and *The Wrecker* was produced by All-Media Dramatic Workshop, 1978; a television adaptation of *Seize the Day,* featuring Robin Williams and a cameo appearance by Bellow, was produced by Public Broadcasting Service, 1987.

SIDELIGHTS: Pulitzer Prize-and Nobel Prize-winning novelist Saul Bellow is considered a leading figure in twentieth-century American literature. In his writing and teaching, Bellow champions human and moral possibilities in the face of personal and social struggle. He also takes to task intellectuals, artists, and social commentators who focus on value-free function, technique, practice, and experimentation. In a *Times Literary Supplement* article, Julian Symons compared Bellow to two British "other-sayers," George Orwell and Wyndham Lewis. "In the United States," wrote Symons, "Saul Bellow has . . . been saying unpopular things about American culture in general, and about the relationship between the society and its literature in particular." Continues Symons: "When he says American intellectuals are becoming more and more alike, and 'often as philistine as the masses from which they have emerged' he has to be listened to."

In his 1976 Nobel Prize for Literature acceptance speech, Bellow reaffirmed his conviction that art was more important than science in exploring significant values in twentieth-century human experience. Following Marcel Proust, Bellow explained in his speech, "Only art penetrates what pride, passion, intelligence and habit erect on all sides—the seeming realities of this world. There is another reality, the genuine one, which we lose sight of. This other reality is always sending us hints, which, without art, we can't receive. Proust calls these hints our 'true impressions.' . . . The value of literature lies in these intermittent true impressions. . . . What [Joseph] Conrad said was true: art attempts to find in the universe, in matter as well as in the facts of life, what is fundamental, enduring, essential." To Bellow, the novel is "a sort of latter-day lean-to, a hovel in which the spirit takes shelter"; as such, the novel performs the same function that Robert Frost claimed for poetry; it provides "a momentary stay against confusion," and in a world where confusion has become king, momentary stillnesses and humble sanctuaries for the spirit are not insignificant contributions.

Joseph, the Kafkaesque protagonist and Dostoevskian underground figure of *Dangling Man,* Bellow's first novel, exists between the military nightmare of World War II and civilian economic opportunism, between the material world of action and the ideal world of thought, between detachment and involvement, life and death. A compulsive diarist and a man condemned to an existential freedom without moral precedent, Joseph is, as Tony Tanner described him in *Saul Bellow,* "a man up to his neck in modern history. Joseph oscillates between corrosive inertia and compulsive self-inquiry, wrestling with irresolvable paradoxes of world and spirit which have a drastically deleterious effect on his character and bring him to the point of futility and exhaustion." As Joseph mismanages his freedom and perceives ever more vividly the disparity between his "ideal constructions" and the "craters of the spirit" that the real world places daily in his path, he grows less confident of his ability to understand the universe or to discern his proper identity in it. Finally, in quasi-optimistic desperation, Joseph decides that he will find no answers in his detached state; thus he insists that his draft board subject him immediately to the same fate his countrymen are enduring. Marcus Klein viewed this movement toward community as part of a pattern in the contemporary American novel, a "strategy of accommodation." In *After Alienation: American Novels in Mid-Century* Klein observed, "Joseph must give himself to idiopathic freedom, and that way is madness, or submit to the community's ordinary, violent reality. He hurries his draft call. He surrenders."

Asa Leventhal, in Bellow's *The Victim,* is a good man, a middle-aged, happily married Jew who has unknowingly caused the gentile Kirby Allbee to lose his job. In his subsequent decline, Allbee becomes a drunk, loses his wife in an auto accident, and blames Leventhal—and by extension all Jews—for his wretchedness. Because he has always felt very tentative about his place in the scheme of things, Leventhal is susceptible to Allbee's unwarranted accusations and subsequent persecutions. Determining what he owes to himself and what he owes to others—that is, how he should live as a good man—becomes Leventhal's primary concern and the integrating principle in the novel.

The Victim develops on two levels, the realistic and the symbolic. At the realistic levels, its themes are guilt, fear of failure, anti-Semitism, and existential responsibility; these themes are embodied in the characterizations, the dialogue, and patterns of metaphor, especially those involving tickets and acting. These matters expand, however, to become questions of Death and Evil at the symbolic level. Bellow draws heavily on classical mythology for the encounters of Leventhal with death, and on the American myth of guilt and redemption, Nathaniel Hawthorne's *The Scarlet Letter,* for his confrontation with guilt in the person of Allbee.

A *bildungsroman,* or novel of education, and a quest novel, *The Adventures of Augie March* traces Augie's erratic pursuit of a worthwhile fate. Telling his own story "free style," Augie relives his experiences for the reader, from his boyhood in Chicago and his wanderings in Michigan, Mexico, and the African Sea to his maturity as a husband and import businessman in Paris. Augie encounters a Chaucerian pilgrimage of Bellovian characters, and from each Augie learns something about "bitterness in his chosen thing" and thus something about his search for a worthwhile fate. He does not find the fate he imagined, but he does affirm the validity of

the search: "Columbus too," says Augie, "thought he was a flop, probably, when they sent him back in chains. Which didn't prove there was no America."

Despite Bellow's admission that he went "too far" and violated formal unity, *The Adventures of Augie March* does have a firm organizing principle, the tension of opposites. Refusing to lead a disappointed life, Augie seeks a worthwhile fate in accordance with what he calls the "axial lines of life," which lead one to "truth, love, peace, bounty, usefulness, harmony." Augie is a free and optimistic spirit, but Bellow exposes him to characters, ideas, and situations inimical to his freedom and his optimism. The figure Kayo Obermark supplies a name for the negative factors, *moha,* the limitations imposed by the finite and imperfect, "the Bronx cheer of the conditioning forces." Einhorn's and Georgie's handicaps, Simon's monomania and loveless marriage, the superficiality of the Magnuses, the varied victimizations of Jimmy Klein and Mim Villars, the limited love of Stella, the lost children everywhere—all testify to the power of *moha* and assail the fortress of Augie's dream of happiness on the axial lines of life. But Augie stands firm in his optimism, earning the book's affirmative vision through his awareness of life's dark side and his resilience in the face of it. "It is important to keep in mind," observed Brigitte Scheer-Schaezler in her study *Saul Bellow,* "that Augie's desire for life in the sun is not motivated by a shunning of action or a rejection of consciousness but arises from his knowledge of darkness, the darkness which he says has widened his outlook." "Indeed," said Sarah Blacher Cohen in the *Saul Bellow Journal,* "Augie is the picaresque apostle who, meeting up with errant humanity, eagerly listens to their confessions and generously pardons their sins, even blessing them for their anti-trespasses."

Whereas Augie defines his humanity through his charm, striving, and compassion, Tommy Wilhelm in *Seize the Day* defines his humanity through his slovenliness, selfishness, and suffering—and, most importantly, through his desire to be better than he is. "The shrill quality of the marriage relationship between Tommy and his wife," Robert Detweiler wrote in *Saul Bellow: A Critical Essay,* "may echo Bellow's own situation at the time. He worked on the story while living in a desert shack in Nevada and waiting out the residency requirements for a divorce."

An antihero, Wilhelm has messed up his life. By changing his name (Saul Bellow was born Solomon Bellows), dropping out of school, and failing in business, Tommy has embarrassed and alienated his father, Dr. Adler, a selfish retired physician. Out of his foolish pride, Wilhelm has quit a good job and now can find no other. His mismanagement of his life has led to estrangement from his wife and painful separation from his two boys. In loneliness and desperation, Wilhelm has turned for companionship and advice to a kind of surrogate father, Dr. Tamkin, a quack psychologist, aspiring poet, slick operator in the stock market, and mainline Bellovian reality-instructor. On the titular day depicted in *Seize the Day,* Wilhelm's serial miscalculations and bad judgments bring him to his knees. His father and wife turn deaf ears to his appeals for help, Tamkin abandons him after misguiding him into losing his last savings in the stock market, and Tommy ends the day crying unceasingly in a funeral home over the body of a stranger. Writing in *Saul Bellow: A Collection of Critical Essays,* M. Gilbert Porter observed that "the unity of effect achieved in *Seize the Day* results from the skillful blending of all the elements of fiction in tightly constructed scenic units functioning very much like poetic images built around a controlling metaphor," the image of Wilhelm drowning.

At age fifty-five the manic gentile Henderson, in Bellow's *Henderson the Rain King,* stands six feet four and weighs two hundred and thirty pounds. He has an M.A. from a prestigious eastern university, a second wife, seven children, a three-million-dollar estate, and a voice within him crying, "I want, I want, I want," testifying both to his unhappiness and his yet-unfulfilled aspiration. Although he has most of the things Madison Avenue equates with human happiness, Henderson feels a central element is missing from his life. His vigorous but bumbling quest to discover that element leads him through whimsical pig-farming, gratuitous violence, and antisocial behavior to Africa, where through exotic experiences with African tribes he determines that he can "burst the spirit's sleep" and still the voice within him by serving others as a physician, in emulation of his hero, Sir Wilfred Grenfill. In the final scene, Henderson's dance around the New York-bound plane with a lion cub and a Persian orphan during the refueling stop in symbolic Newfoundland is a rhapsodic celebration of his movement toward community and his confirmed new vision of the possibilities of life over death: "God does not shoot dice with our souls," cries the joyful Henderson, "and therefore grun-tu-molani. . . . I believe there is justice, and that much is promised." According to Walter Clemons and Jack Kroll in a *Newsweek* interview with the author, "Of all his characters, Bellow has said, Henderson, the quixotic seeker of higher truth, is most like himself."

The theme of the novel is a recurrent one in Bellow's fiction: that the world is tough and mysterious, that man is subject to great errors and subsequent pain, but that he yearns for nobility and joy and feels in his deepest soul that such things are possible. "*Henderson the Rain King* is clearly Bellow's most full-blown comic novel," wrote Sarah Blacher Cohen in *Saul Bellow's Enigmatic Laughter.* "The dreaded nightmare experiences of the earlier realistic novels are transformed into the playful and dreamlike episodes of romance. The comic flaws which the early heroes were often too obtuse to notice are magnified in Henderson, who both flamboyantly exhibits them and exorcizes them through his own jocose language."

One man's frantic attempts to formulate a synthesis to shore up his disintegrating life is the substance of Bellow's 1964 novel, *Herzog.* Herzog seeks clarity and justice as a professor of history with a Ph.D. and an impressive professional bibliography. But with the discovery that his wife, Madeleine, and his good friend Gersbach have made him a cuckold and abandoned him to his isolated personal fate, Herzog finds himself lost in the modernist waste land of cynical "reality instructors" and existential nothingness, "down in the mire of post-Renaissance, post-humanistic, post-Cartesian dissolution, next door to the void." Such hostile territory is particularly hard on a sensitive intellectual whose sensibilities are at war with his intellect. With his feelings, he resists the negations of the reality instructors, but the chaotic evidence of his personal life makes an intellectual assent to their conclusions almost irresistible. His final transcendence of their teachings and his own anguish in the pastoral setting of Ludeyville testifies to the power Herzog discovers in simple being and the "law of the heart"; at peace at last, he says, "I am pretty well satisfied to be, to be just as it is willed, and for as long as I may remain in occupancy."

Some critics have argued that the stress and resolution in *Herzog* is typical of the Bellow canon. "It is this problem," Alfred Kazin said in *Contemporaries,* "first of representing all that a man intends and plans and then of getting him not merely to recognize the countervailing strength of life but to humble himself before it, that is the real situation in all Bellow's novels." Where Kazin found acceptance and submission, Ihab Hassan, in *Radical Innocence: Studies in the Contemporary American Novel,* saw affirmation in the protagonist as the sequel to his conflict between self and the world: "the movement is from acid defeat to acceptance, and from acceptance to celebration. The querulous and ill-natured hero becomes prodigal and quixotic. In this process something of the dignity that the fictional hero has lost to history is restored to him."

Bellow's seventh novel, *Mr. Sammler's Planet,* is an indignant depiction of contemporary America from the perspective of one of Bellow's most formidable "men thinking," Sammler, a Krakow-born Anglophile in his seventies and a Jewish survivor of a Nazi pogrom in Poland. His war injuries have left him with a tempered detachment and vision in only one eye. Thus Sammler sees outward and inward. His good right eye records characters, actions, and events in the world around him. His blind left eye subjects current events to introspective analysis, the historical and philosophical perspective. "The damaged eye seemed to turn in another direction, to be preoccupied separately with different matters." The novel oscillates from action to reflection as Sammler tries to make sense of a planet that seems to be coming unglued. Within that general strategy there are complementary movements from past to present, from public to private, from life to death. Three obliquely related plots provide the structural matrix of the narrative: 1) a pickpocket who plies his trade on the Forty-second Street bus and exposes himself to Sammler to warn him not to interfere; 2) a book manuscript on space travel and inhabitation of the moon, stolen from its author by Sammler's daughter, Shula; and 3) the slow dying of Dr. Gruner from an aneurysm in his brain.

Bellow told Jane Howard in an interview for *Life* that *Mr. Sammler's Planet* is his own favorite work: "I had a high degree of excitement writing it . . . and finished it in record time. It's my first thoroughly nonapologetic venture into ideas. In *Herzog* . . . and *Henderson the Rain King* I was kidding my way to Jesus, but here I'm baring myself nakedly." The novel and this statement about it marked a shift in proportion in Bellow's art, as abstraction began to overshadow concretion. The change has elicited mixed responses. Robert R. Dutton, in *Saul Bellow,* called the novel "Bellow's highest technical achievement," and Scheer-Schaezler, in support of what she called "enlarged vision," described the book as representative of "Bellow's effort to turn the novel into a medium of inquiry. In Bellow's most recent novels, experiences are not so much being undergone as discussed in a probing approach that may well be called essayistic." In the same vein, Nathan A. Scott, Jr. declared approvingly in *Three American Moralists: Mailer, Bellow, Trilling* that Bellow's "insistently didactic intention has had the effect of making rhetoric itself—rather than action and character—the main source of the essential energies in his fiction. And there is perhaps no other comparable body of work in the literature of the contemporary novel so drenched in ideas and speculations and theories, even commandments."

Humboldt's Gift is the story of intellectual Chicagoan Charlie Citrine, a Pulitzer prize-winning biographer and dramatist. Citrine approaches the completion of his

sixth decade in the company of the nimbus of his deceased poetic mentor, Von Humboldt Fleisher, and the nemesis of his self-appointed materialistic advisor, Rinaldo Cantabile, both manic manipulators. The dead poet speaks to Citrine of his obligation to his creative spirit, art as power. The minor-league Mafioso Cantabile urges capitalistic enterprise, art as profit. Citrine ultimately frees himself from both figures, and at the end walks from the new grave he has provided for Humboldt into an ambivalently emerging spring to begin a meditative life away from the distractions of dissident voices and grotesque behavior. Charlie's compulsive flights into metaphysical explanations have to contend with the corrective pragmatism of his earthy mistress, Renata: "I prefer to take things as billions of people have throughout history. You work, you get bread, you lose a leg, kiss some fellows, have a baby, you live to be eighty and bug hell out of everybody, or you get hung or drowned. But you don't spend years trying to dope your way out of the human condition. . . . I think when you're dead you're dead, and that's that." Such views led Renata to abandon the hyperintellectual Citrine and choose an undertaker for a husband. Charlie resists Renata's reality-instructor text by clinging to a message from the dead poet: "Remember: we are not natural beings but supernatural beings," a spiritual reinforcement of Charlie's natural impulses that represents Humboldt's real gift to his protege.

The humor that dominates *Humboldt's Gift* is absent in Bellow's ninth novel, *The Dean's December.* As a journalist turned academic, Dean Albert Corde has accompanied his Rumanian-born wife, Minna, to Bucharest to attend her dying mother, Valeria. Isolated in his room or cruising the streets as a "hungry observer" and a "moralist of seeing," Corde observes Bucharest and reflects on Chicago, a city whose "whirling lives" typify the chaotic American reality. The communist and the capitalist cities are grim places of different but related forms of disorder, injustice, repression, and destruction. They are yoked by violence together, for death is everywhere: "I imagine, sometimes," Corde thinks, "that if a film could be made of one's life, every other frame would be death." This macabre mood is sustained throughout the novel even though at the end, after Valeria's death, Corde is comforted briefly by a renewed closeness to his wife that somehow has its counterpart in his closeness to the heavens in the great telescope of the Mount Palomar Observatory. He is cold there, he tells his guide as they descend: "But I almost mind coming down more"—that is, coming down to earth, where robbery, rape, murder, prejudice, and political injustice mock the human quest for order, beauty, love, and justice.

Some of the darkness of *The Dean's December* grew out of Bellow's personal experience. Bellow told William Kennedy in *Esquire* that he wrote the novel "in a year and a half . . . and had no idea it was coming. One of these things that came over me. My wife's mother was dying in Bucharest, and I went with her to give her some support, which in that place one badly needs. The old mother died while we were there." Part of the grimness grew out of actual conditions and events, like a sensational Chicago rape case and the Cabrini Green housing project in Chicago, but most of the pessimism came from Bellow's increasing conviction that the decline of civilization is magnified in American cities. Malcolm Bradbury wrote in *The Modern American Novel* that *The Dean's December* "confirms the later Bellow as the novelist of a world which has lost cultural bearings, moved into an age of boredom and terror, violence and indifference, private wealth and public squalor." Bellow himself has been very explicit about his intentions in the novel. He told Matthew C. Roudane in an interview for *Contemporary Literature* that the decaying city has its counterpart in an "inner slum": "What I [mean is] there is a correspondence between outer and inner, between the brutalized city and the psyche of its citizens. Given their human resources I don't see how people today can experience life at all. Politicians, public figures, professors address 'modern problems' solely in terms of employment. They assume that unemployment causes incoherence, sexual disorders, the abandonment of children, robbery, rape and murder. Plainly, they have no imagination of these evils. They don't even *see* them." Ironically, an exchange of styles seems to occur, in effect, between Corde and Bellow. The passionate intensity that allows Corde's journalism to rise to the stature of art—as Bellow describes it here—leads Bellow's prose in the novel as a whole to assume the condition of journalism, the documentary, or, as Roudane observed, "a nonfiction novelistic style," an extension of the essayistic prose that has become increasingly prominent in Bellow's more recent novels.

Bellow returns to the comic mode in his tenth novel, *More Die of Heartbreak,* a turgid, almost plotless story of two academics connected less by their blood kinship than by their similarly oblique relations to women and to everyday reality. The narrator is thirty-five-year-old Kenneth Tractenberg, a professor of Russian literature at a university in the Midwest. His beloved uncle, Benn Crader, is an internationally respected botanist whose specialty is Arctic lichens and whose patterns of practical misjudgment make him think of himself as "a phoenix who runs with arsonists." Kenneth, though, admires his uncle for reasons that are not clear. Kenneth's philandering father offers his son a sarcastic but perhaps accurate explanation: "you're one of those continuing-education types and you think Benn still has something

to teach you." Although intelligent and ceaselessly introspective, Kenneth and Uncle Benn are curious naifs. Kenneth is at great pains to marry Treckie, the mother of his illegitimate daughter and a woman who rejects him to live with a sadist and travel the flea-market circuits. Uncle Benn marries a spoiled rich girl, Matilda Layamon, whose physician father maneuvers to recover Benn's lost inheritance from crooked Uncle Vilitzer so that Matilda can continue to live a life of pampered ease. Benn escapes both the solicitousness of Kenneth and the machinations of the Layamons, finally, by retreating to the North Pole to study lichens.

Critical response to *More Die of Heartbreak* has been characterized by qualified praise and reluctantly held reservations. "Kenneth's free-ranging mind allows Bellow to put just about everything real and imaginable into this novel," noted Robert Wilson in *USA Today*. "Even so, Kenneth does not seem to me to be among the best of Bellow's characters, nor this among the best of Bellow's comic novels. Kenneth wore me out, especially when his divagations took us so far from the plot that it was barely a memory." Clemons, writing in *Newsweek,* found the supporting characters more appealing than the principals: "It's a slight drawback to *More Die of Heartbreak* that the innocents in the foreground, Uncle Benn and Kenneth, are upstaged by their captivating adversaries. . . . Our time with Benn and Kenneth is well spent for the sake of the rascals to whom they introduce us."

The title of *The Actual,* Bellow's 1997 novella, refers to Amy Wustrin, high school sweetheart of the middle-aged narrator Harry Trellman. The diffident Harry never pursued her while they were in school, and as an adult Harry traveled the world on business and rarely saw Amy. She married a bold, brash lawyer, Jay Wustrin, but now Jay is dead, Harry has returned to their native Chicago, and he now has his chance: "Half a century of feeling is invested in her, of fantasy, speculation, absorption, of imaginary conversation," he tells the reader. However, Harry's feelings for Amy are a counterpoint to the central narrative, which involves aging tycoon Sigmund Adletsky, who is bored and, as the *New Republic*'s James Wood wrote, "asks Harry to act as a kind of intellectual informer for him—to provide the old man with advice, entertainment, cultural scraps." In a surprising twist, "it is Adletsky, whom Harry assumed to be uninterested in such things, who brings [Harry and Amy] together." Wood went on to observe: "That Bellow's characters wear their moral age so visibly, as a tree stump is ringed in years, tells us something about his metaphysics. In his fictional world—and *The Actual* is a fine example—people do not stream with motives.

They are embodied souls." Hence the central activity in the story takes place internally, rather than externally.

Richard Canning in *New Statesman* described Harry as "the latest of Saul Bellow's great observer-narrators," who like Augie March and Moses Herzog "draws back from outright misanthropy in the face of the 'commonplace person' around him—but chiefly by reflecting on the consolations of being quite distinct from them." Canning went on to note that, "In proving true to his first love, Trellman acts on his belief that people don't change"; Amy, on the other hand, is a great question, and the reader is left unsure of her affections. Louis Begley of the *New York Times Book Review* concluded that *The Actual* "is not a young man's piece of fiction, and our expectations for it must be adjusted accordingly. It is instead something far more rare: the work of a great master still locked in unequal combat with Eros and Time."

Bellow's novel *Ravelstein* raised a fuss in literary and academic circles not so much because of its story, but because of the actual events behind the story. The book, many agreed, is a fictionalized tale of the relationship between Bellow and his friend Allan Bloom, author of the best-selling book *The Closing of the American Mind.* Bloom, a hero among conservatives, died in 1992, reportedly of liver failure. In *Ravelstein,* however, Ravelstein, secretly a homosexual, dies of an AIDS-related illness. This idea that the novel is principally an "outing" of Bellow's late friend upset Bellow, who told *Time* interviewer Andrea Sachs: "This is a problem that writers of fiction always have to face in this country. People are literal minded, and they say 'Is it true? If it is true, is it factually accurate? If it isn't factually accurate, why isn't it factually accurate?' Then you tie yourself into knots, because writing a novel in some ways resembles writing a biography, but it really isn't. It is full of invention." "There is a character based on Bloom . . . in *Ravelstein,*" commented Louis Menand in the *New York Review of Books.* "Everyone knows this, since Bellow himself has said it. But it is odd how quick people have been to read the book as a memoir—as an essentially plotless, meditative, lightly fictionalized tribute to an unusual man and an unusual friendship. . . . The inner novel is not about Ravelstein. Ravelstein is, in fact, the least novelized character in the book." *Perspectives on Political Science* contributor David K. Nichols also thought that many readers missed the point of the book. "The biggest mistake that reviewers make is their failure to appreciate both the political and intellectual weight of *Ravelstein,*" Nichols wrote. "It is a book about ideas, and it is also a very political book."

Bellow's novel is narrated by Chick, Ravelstein's close friend. Ravelstein repeatedly asks Chick to write his bi-

ography and Chick promises to one day do so. "Chick realizes a memoir won't be an easy task," commented Stephen Goode in *Insight on the News,* in part because Chick doesn't understand the genius Ravelstein's theories, and to the extent that he does understand them, he doesn't necessarily agree with them. But when Chick gets suddenly ill while on vacation, he remembers his promise to his friend and also remembers his courage in the face of debilitating, life-threatening illness. He writes Ravelstein's story, but it turns out as more of a memoir of their friendship and of Chick's own life than as a biography of Ravelstein. The story "does not progress in a linear fashion," Curt Leviant wrote in *Midstream;* "rather it shifts and curves and folds around itself, following the forward and rearward thrusts of memory."

Critics responded enthusiastically to *Ravelstein.* David W. Henderson in *Library Journal* called the book "at once witty, erudite, and compassionate." A *Kirkus Reviews* critic described the work as the "work of a master, who has lost none of his unique ability to entertain, enthrall, and enlighten." Goode concluded that *Ravelstein* "isn't Bellow working with all stops pulled out. But it is a poignant, beautifully wrought book that says a lot about the mysteries of genuine friendship and what others can mean to us."

Although he has always been better known for his fictional explorations of contemporary life, Bellow has also confronted social issues through essays published in various periodicals and through lectures. Many of these are reprinted in Bellow's first collection of nonfiction writing, *It All Adds Up: From the Dim Past to the Uncertain Future.* "Here, in these nonfiction writings," Mark Harris noted in Chicago's *Tribune Books,* "Bellow draws upon those powers of observation basic to his fiction: his minutely detailed descriptions of people and places and striking conclusions about wonders of the world he has seen in many places." *Spectator* contributor Tom Shone also observed a kinship between these essays and Bellow's fiction: "Like his novels, Saul Bellow's journalism throngs with memorable grotesques."

New York Times Book Review contributor Peter S. Prescott found that "the best entries in *It All Adds Up* are autobiographical—sharp vignettes of the author at a certain time and in a specific place—or memories of friends and colleagues like John Berryman, John Cheever and Isaac Rosenfeld." Mordecai Richler offered a similar view in the *National Review,* writing that "a couple of the most enjoyable pieces in *It All*

Adds Up are memoirs of Chicago. His prodigious gifts as a novelist beyond dispute, Mr. Bellow turns out to be a first-rate reporter as well." *Christian Science Monitor* reviewer Merle Rubin also observed that "some of Bellow's pronouncements betray a sort of dismissive irritability toward the claims of feminists, homosexuals, and multiculturalists." Yet, as Richler concluded, *It All Adds Up* can be read as a "thoughtful, provocative, and only occasionally querulous addendum to the work of a novelist who has given us more aesthetic bliss than most."

BIOGRAPHICAL AND CRITICAL SOURCES:

BOOKS

Bellow, Saul, *Herzog,* Viking (New York, NY), 1964.

Bigler, Walter, *Figures of Madness in Saul Bellow's Longer Fiction,* Peter Lang (New York, NY), 1998.

Bloom, Harold, editor, *Saul Bellow,* Chelsea House (New York, NY), 1982.

Bradbury, Malcolm, *Saul Bellow,* Methuen (New York, NY), 1982.

Bradbury, Malcolm, *The Modern American Novel,* Oxford University Press, 1983.

Cohen, Sarah Blacher, *Saul Bellow's Enigmatic Laughter,* University of Illinois Press (Champaign, IL), 1974.

Concise Dictionary of American Literary Biography: The New Consciousness, 1941-1968, Thomson Gale (Detroit, MI), 1987.

Contemporary Novelists, 7th edition, St. James Press (Detroit, MI), 2001.

Detweiler, Robert, *Saul Bellow: A Critical Essay,* Eerdmans (Grand Rapids, MI), 1967.

Dictionary of Literary Biography, Thomson Gale (Detroit, MI), Volume 2: *American Novelists since World War II, First Series,* 1978, Volume 28: *Twentieth Century American-Jewish Fiction Writers,* 1984.

Dutton, Robert R., *Saul Bellow,* Twayne (Boston, MA), 1971, revised edition, 1982.

Friedrich, Marianne, *Character and Narration in the Short Fiction of Saul Bellow,* Peter Lang (New York, NY), 1996.

Goldman, L. H., *Saul Bellow's Moral Vision: A Critical Study of the Jewish Experience,* Irvington, 1983.

Hassan, Ihab, *Radical Innocence: Studies in the Contemporary American Novel,* Harper (New York, NY), 1966.

Hollahan, Eugene, *Saul Bellow and the Struggle at the Center,* AMS Press (New York, NY), 1996.

Kazin, Alfred, *Contemporaries,* Little, Brown (Boston, MA), 1962.

Klein, Marcus, *After Alienation: American Novels in Mid-Century,* World Publishing, 1965.

Kramer, Michael P., editor, *New Essays on "Seize the Day,"* Cambridge University Press (New York, NY), 1998.

McCadden, Joseph F., *The Flight from Women in the Fiction of Saul Bellow,* University Press of America (Lanham, MD), 1980.

Reference Guide to American Literature, 3rd edition, St. James Press (Detroit, MI), 1994.

Reference Guide to Short Fiction, 1st edition, St. James Press (Detroit, MI), 1994.

Rovit, Earl H., editor, *Saul Bellow: A Collection of Critical Essays,* Prentice-Hall (Englewood Cliffs, NJ), 1975.

Scheer-Schaezler, Brigitte, *Saul Bellow,* Ungar (New York, NY), 1972.

Scott, Nathan A., Jr., *Three American Moralists: Mailer, Bellow, Trilling,* University of Notre Dame Press (Notre Dame, IN), 1968.

Tanner, Tony, *Saul Bellow,* Oliver & Boyd, 1965.

Trachtenberg, Stanley, *Critical Essays on Saul Bellow,* G.K. Hall (Boston, MA), 1979.

Wasserman, Harriet, *Handsome Is: Adventures with Saul Bellow: A Memoir,* Fromm, 1997.

PERIODICALS

American Enterprise, September, 2000, Leon Aron, review of *Ravelstein,* p. 56.

American Literature, Volume 43, number 2, 1971; July, 1989, p. 47.

American Prospect, June 5, 2000, Mark Greif, review of *Ravelstein,* p. 46.

American Spectator, September, 1987, p. 43.

Antioch Review, summer, 1982, p. 266; winter, 2001, Kathleen Wildman, review of *Ravelstein,* p. 118.

Atlantic, January, 1965; October, 1995, Martin Amis, review of *The Adventures of Augie March,* p. 114; May, 2000, review of *Ravelstein,* p. 128; December, 2003, Martin Amis, "The Supreme American Novelists: A Tribute to Saul Bellow," pp. 111-114.

Book, November-December, 2001, Paul Evans, review of *Collected Stories,* pp. 64-65.

Booklist, May 1, 1997, Brad Hooper, review of *The Actual,* p. 1460; February 15, 2000, Brad Hooper, review of *Ravelstein,* p. 1051; September 1, 2001, Brad Hooper, review of *Collected Stories,* p. 3.

Boston Globe, April 17, 1994, p. A14.

Chicago Review, Volume 23, number 4, 1972; Volume 32, number 4, 1981, p. 92.

Chicago Tribune, March 2, 1990, section 5, p. 1; April 18, 1990, section 5, p. 1; May 25, 1993, section 2C, p. 1; June 19, 1994, section 10, p. 8.

Christian Science Monitor, November 1, 1985, p. B11; July 3, 1987, p. B1; April 28, 1994, p. 14.

College English, Volume 34, 1973.

College Language Association Journal, Volume 10, 1967.

Commentary, June, 1994, p. 37; October, 1997, Hillel Halkin, review of *The Actual,* p. 46; July, 2000, Norman Podhoretz, "Bellow at 85, Roth at 67," p. 35; September, 2003, Algis Valiunas, "Bellow's Progress," pp. 51-55.

Commonweal, December 4, 1987, p. 715.

Comparative Literature Studies, Volume 3, number 2, 1966.

Contemporary Literature, Volume 25, number 3, 1984.

Critical Quarterly, Volume 15, 1973.

Economist (U.S.), November 15, 1997, review of *The Actual,* p. 14.

Esquire, February, 1982; April, 2000, Sven Birkerts, review of *Ravelstein,* p. 70.

Essays in Literature, Volume 5, 1979.

Gay and Lesbian Review, fall, 2000, Adam Feldman, review of *Ravelstein,* p. 46.

Georgia Review, winter, 1978.

Guardian, September 10, 1997, pp. T2-3.

Harper's, August, 1974; September, 1997, pp. 33-35.

Historical Reflections, Volume 3, number 2, 1976.

Humanitas, fall, 2000, Juliana Geran Pilon, review of *Ravelstein,* p. 108.

Indian Journal of American Studies, Volume 8, number 2, 1978.

Insight on the News, May 29, 2000, Stephen Goode, review of *Ravelstein,* p. 26; February 25, 2002, David Skinner, review of *Collected Stories,* pp. 26-27.

International Fiction Review, January, 2003, G. Neelakantan, "Beast in Chicago: Saul Bellow's Apocalypse in *The Dean's December,*" pp. 66-75.

Journal of American Studies, Volume 7, 1973; Volume 9, 1975; Volume 15, 1981.

Judaism, Volume 22, 1972.

Kirkus Reviews, February 15, 2000, review of *Ravelstein,*p. 190; September 15, 2001, review of *Collected Stories,* p. 1322.

Library Journal, May 1, 1997, Amy Boaz, review of *The Actual,* p. 136; April 15, 2000, David W. Henderson, review of *Ravelstein,* p. 121; July, 2003, review of *The Republic of Letters,* p. SS20.

Life, April 3, 1970.

Listener, February 13, 1975.

London Review of Books, November 12, 1987, p. 3; March 30, 1989, p. 21; January 11, 1990, p. 11.

Los Angeles Times Book Review, November 17, 1985, p. 14; June 14, 1987, p. 1; March 19, 1989, p. 3.

Maclean's, July 14, 1997, John Bemrose, review of *The Actual,* p. 61.

Mature Outlook, Volume 1, number 3, 1984.

Midstream, May-June, 2003, Curt Leviant, review of *Ravelstein,* p. 42; September-October, 2003, Jerome Charyn, "Inside the Hornet's Head," pp. 17-22.

Modern Age, winter, 1984, p. 55.

Modern Fiction Studies, Volume 12, 1966-67; Volume 17, 1971; Volume 19, 1973; Volume 25, 1979.

Modern Language Studies, winter, 1986, p. 71.

Nation, February 9, 1970; May 15, 1989, p. 674; November 27, 1989, p. 652; August 8, 1994, p. 168; February 26, 1996, p. 34; May 15, 2000, Christopher Hitchens, review of *Ravelstein,* p. 9; May 29, 2000, John Leonard, review of *Ravelstein,* p. 25; June 23, 2003, Leonard Kriegel, "Wrestling with Augie March," p. 27.

National Review, July 17, 1987, p. 49; March 5, 1990, p. 52; August 1, 1994, p. 58; July 28, 1997, Mitt Beauchesne, review of *The Actual,* p. 62.

New England Review, Volume 1, 1972.

New Leader, July 14, 1997, Bill Christophersen, review of *The Actual,* p. 18.

New Republic, January 1, 1990, p. 37; May 2, 1994, p. 37; June 16, 1997, James Wood, review of *The Actual,* pp. 41-45; April 17, 2000, Andrew Sullivan, review of *Ravelstein,* p. 12.

New Statesman, October 23, 1987, p. 28; August 29, 1997, Richard Canning, review of *The Actual,* p. 48; November 29, 1999, Malcolm Bradbury, review of *The Victim,* p. 84; December 10, 2001, Stephen Amidon, review of *Collected Stories,* pp. 49-50.

New Statesman and Society, March 31, 1989, p. 35; October 20, 1989, p. 46; August 29, 1997, p. 48.

Newsweek, September 1, 1975; June 8, 1987; February 7, 2000, Malcolm Jones, review of *Ravelstein,* p. 69.

New York, June 8, 1987.

New Yorker, September 15, 1975; July 27, 1987, p. 89; May 1, 1989, p. 111; May 16, 1994, p. 109; August 24, 1998, pp. 96-108; October 6, 2003, Joan Acocella, review of *The Adventures of Augie March, Dangling Man,* and *The Victim,* p. 113.

New York Review of Books, July 16, 1987, p. 3; April 27, 1989, p. 50; October 12, 1989, p. 34; May 25, 2000, Louis Menand, review of *Ravelstein,* pp. 17-18.

New York Times, May 21, 1987, p. 21; April 11, 1994, p. C15; October 11, 2003, Edward Rothstein, review of *The Adventures of Augie March,* p. B9.

New York Times Book Review, February 15, 1959; May 9, 1971; October 27, 1985, p. 50; May 24, 1987,

p. 1; March 5, 1989, p. 3; October 1, 1989, p. 11; April 10, 1994, p. 9; May 25, 1997, p. 14; April 23, 2000, Jonathan Wilson, review of *Ravelstein*, p. 6.

New York Times Magazine, November 21, 1978; April 15, 1984, p. 52.

Observer (London, England), December 2, 1984, p. 19; April 2, 1989, p. 45; October 8, 1989, p. 46; September 11, 1994, p. 23.

Partisan Review, Volume 26, number 3, 1959.

People, September 8, 1975.

Perspectives on Political Science, winter, 2003 (*Ravelstein* issue).

Playboy, May, 1997, pp. 59-70.

Publishers Weekly, March 3, 1989, p. 59; March 24, 1997, review of *The Actual*, p. 57; February 28, 2000, review of *Ravelstein*, p. 57; October 22, 2001, review of *Collected Stories*, p. 47.

Rolling Stone, March 4, 1982.

Salmagundi, Volume 30, 1975 (special Bellow issue).

Saturday Review, February 7, 1970.

Saturday Review of Literature, August 22, 1953; September 19, 1953; September 19, 1964.

Saul Bellow Journal, 1981-1990.

Saul Bellow Newsletter, Volume 1, number 1, 1981.

Shofar, fall, 2001, Michael Greenstein, "Secular Sermons and American Accents: The Nonfiction of Bellow, Ozick, and Roth," p. 4.

Southwest Review, Volume 62, 1977.

Spectator, October 31, 1987, p. 36; April 15, 1989, p. 29; October 14, 1989, p. 34; September 17, 1994, p. 35; December 8, 2001, Diana Hendry, review of *Collected Stories*, pp. 57-58.

Studies in American Fiction, spring, 2000, Martin Corner, "The Novel and Public Truth: Saul Bellow's *The Dean's December,*" p. 113.

Studies in Literature and Language, winter, 1987, p. 442.

Studies in Short Fiction, summer, 1974, p. 297.

Studies in the Literary Imagination, Volume 17, number 2, 1984 (special Bellow issue), p. 59.

Studies in the Novel, Volume 1, number 3, 1969; Volume 15, number 3, 1983, p. 249; fall, 2000, Martin Corner, "Moving Outwards: Consciousness, Discourse, and Attention in Saul Bellow's Fiction," p. 369.

Studies in the Twentieth Century, Volume 14, 1974.

Time, May 9, 1994, p. 80; April 24, 2000, Andrea Sachs, review of *Ravelstein,* p. 70.

Times Literary Supplement, October 23, 1987, p. 71; March 24, 1989, p. 299; October 27, 1989, p. 1181; November 6, 1992, p. 20; September 23, 1994, p. 25.

Tribune Books (Chicago, IL), May 31, 1987, p. 1; March 5, 1989, p. 1; October 8, 1989, p. 3; April 10, 1994, p. 1.

Twentieth Century Literature, Volume 18, number 4, 1972.

USA Today, June 5, 1987.

U.S. News & World Report, May 19, 1997, interview with Bellow, p. 76.

Voice Literary Supplement, March, 1990, p. 11.

Washington Post Book World, June 7, 1987, p. 1; December 3, 1989, p. 3; March 27, 1994, p. 3.

Western Humanities Review, Volume 14, 1960.

Wilson Quarterly, winter, 2001, Christopher Hitchens, "The Great American Augie," p. 22.

World and I, August, 2000, Bernard Rogers, "Bellow's Gift," p. 219.

World Literature Today, autumn, 1992, p. 721; winter, 1998, Marvin J. LaHood, review of *The Actual*, p. 132; autumn, 2000, Rita D. Jacobs, review of *Ravelstein*, p. 813; spring, 2002, John L. Brown, review of *Collected Stories*, pp. 149-150.

ONLINE

Nobel e-Museum, http://www.nobel.se/ (April 24, 2004), "Saul Bellow—Biography."

OBITUARIES:

ONLINE

CNN.com, http://www.cnn.com/ (April 6, 2005).

*   *   *

BELLOW, Solomon
  See BELLOW, Saul

*   *   *

BENCHLEY, Peter 1940-2006
(Peter Bradford Benchley)

PERSONAL: Born May 8, 1940, in New York, NY; died February 11, 2006, in Princeton, NJ; son of Nathaniel Goddard (an author) and Marjorie (Bradford) Benchley; married Wendy Wesson, September 19, 1964; children: Tracy, Clayton, Christopher. *Education:* Harvard University, B.A. (cum laude), 1961. *Hobbies and other interests:* Diving, tennis, wildlife, the theater, films.

CAREER: Author. *Washington Post,* Washington, DC, reporter, 1963; *Newsweek,* New York, NY, associate editor, 1963-67; The White House, Washington, DC, staff assistant to the President, 1967-69; freelance writer and television news correspondent, beginning in 1969. Writer, narrator, and host of television series *The American Sportsman,* 1974-83; co-creator of television series *Dolphin Cove,* 1989; host of television series *Expedition Earth,* ESPN, 1990-93; executive producer of miniseries *Beast,* NBC, 1996; host of radio series *Ocean Reports,* 1997-2000; creator, co-executive producer of television series *Peter Benchley's Amazon,* 1999-2000. Co-writer, co-producer, co-creator, and narrator for "World of Water" film series, New England Aquarium, 1998. Member of board of directors, Sea-Web; member of board of advisors, Bermuda Underwater Exploration Institute. Spokesperson for the University of Miami's Rosenstiel School of Marine and Atmospheric Science's Center for Sustainable Fisheries, 2001-06. *Military service:* U.S. Marine Corps Reserve, 1962-63.

MEMBER: Century Association, Coffee House, Spee Club, Hasty Pudding Institute of 1770.

WRITINGS:

NOVELS

Jaws (also see below), Doubleday (New York, NY), 1974, special abbreviated edition published as *Selected from Jaws,* Literacy Volunteers of New York City, 1990.
The Deep (also see below), Doubleday (New York, NY), 1976.
The Island (also see below), Doubleday (New York, NY), 1979.
The Girl of the Sea of Cortez, Doubleday (New York, NY), 1982.
Tiburon, Distibooks International, 1983.
Q Clearance, Random House (New York, NY), 1986.
Rummies, Random House (New York, NY), 1989.
Beast, Random House (New York, NY), 1991.
Three Complete Novels (contains *Jaws, Beast,* and *The Girl of the Sea of Cortez*), Random House Value Publishing (New York, NY), 1994.
White Shark, Random House (New York, NY), 1994.
Peter Benchley's Creature, St. Martin's (New York, NY), 1998.

SCREENPLAYS

(With Carl Gottlieb) *Jaws* (based on his novel of the same title), Universal, 1975.

(With Tracy Keenan Wynn) *The Deep* (based on his novel of the same title), Columbia, 1977.
The Island (based on his novel of the same title), Universal, 1980.

OTHER

Time and a Ticket (nonfiction), Houghton (New York, NY), 1964.
Jonathan Visits the White House (juvenile), McGraw (New York, NY), 1964.
(Editor, with Judith Gradwohl, and contributor and author of introduction) *Ocean Planet: Writings and Images of the Sea,* H.N. Abrams/Times Mirror Magazines (New York, NY), 1995.
Shark Trouble: True Stories about Sharks and the Sea, Random House (New York, NY), 2002.

Also author of introduction for *Secrets of the Ocean Realm,* Carroll & Graf (New York, NY), 1997. Contributor to periodicals, including *Holiday, New Yorker, Diplomat, Moderator, Vogue, New York Herald-Tribune, New York Times Magazine,* and *National Geographic.*

ADAPTATIONS: Beast was adapted as a television mini-series entitled *The Beast,* NBC-TV, 1996; *Peter Benchley's Creature* was adapted as a television mini-series, ABC-TV, 1998. *Q Clearance* was recorded on audiotape, Recorded Books, 1989; *White Shark* was recorded on audiotape, Random House, 1995.

SIDELIGHTS: Ever since he began exploring the Atlantic with his father, Peter Benchley was been fascinated by the sea. In 1974 the young writer turned that fascination to profit with a novel that was on the *New York Times* best-seller list for more than forty weeks. *Jaws* "put sharks on the map and made him the most successful first novelist in literary history," according to Jennifer Dunning in the *New York Times Book Review.* Most of Benchley's novels involved the ocean in one way or another. His first three—*Jaws, The Deep,* and *The Island*—are stories of high adventure in which an unexpected menace lurks in the water; his fourth—*The Girl of the Sea of Cortez*—is less dramatic and more lyrical, a sort of poetic fable with an environmental theme.

Peter Benchley inherited more than just a love of the sea from his father: his literary talents were a family legacy as well. His grandfather was the celebrated humorist Robert Benchley, and his father, Nathaniel, who was also a writer, encouraged his son's interest by offering him, at fifteen, a small salary if he would write every day for a summer. By the time Peter was twenty-one, he had a literary agent from the same institution that represented his dad. Though Peter de-emphasized the role his heritage played in launching his career, Doubleday editor Thomas Congdon became increasingly aware of its importance when he and Benchley were discussing the proposal for *Jaws*.

Most of the money in publishing is made by authors with proven track records, while first novels by unknown writers are generally ignored. But the financial risk of publishing Benchley's first book of adult fiction was mitigated by his famous literary name. "I didn't realize it at the time," Congdon told the *Miami Herald*, "but Benchley did have a track record—his father and his grandfather."

Benchley's proposal also fit the formula of a best seller. "First, its subject was something-about-which-the-general-public-knows-a-little-but-wants-to-know-more," explained a *Miami Herald* reporter. "Secondly, it conjured up a race memory: the external menace. Such situations as a fire in a skyscraper or a jumbo jet with a dead pilot at the controls. Such appeal to our survival instincts." Not only did *Jaws* catapult to the top of the best-seller lists, it also became an enormously successful motion picture—so successful that it spawned three sequels: *Jaws II, Jaws 3-D,* and *Jaws the Revenge*. None of these equaled the original film's intensity, however. Still, Benchley estimated that the combined revenue from the movie rights, paperback rights, and magazine and book club syndications provided him with enough income to write freely for ten years.

Despite its unqualified popularity, *Jaws* drew fire from some critics for what they perceived as weak characterization, contrived sub-plotting, and inappropriate allusions to Herman Melville's classic fish tale, *Moby Dick*. "Benchley claims he wanted to keep this a serious novel, as well as a best-seller, and that was probably his mistake," asserted Michael Rogers in the *Rolling Stone*. "None of the humans are particularly likable or interesting; the shark was easily my favorite character—and one suspects, Benchley's also." Writing in the *New Statesman*, John Sparling similarly said that the "characterisation of the humans is fairly rudimentary. . . . The shark, however, is done with exhilarating and alarming skill and every scene in which it appears is imagined at a special pitch of intensity." Other critics, including John Skow, were even less appreciative. "Nothing works," wrote Skow in *Time*, "not a hokey as-

signation between [the police chief's] wife and a predatory ichthyologist, and especially not an eat-'em up ending that lacks only Queequeg's coffin to resemble a bathtub version of *Moby Dick*."

When asked how he felt about having his novel compared to Melville's, Benchley told *Palm Springs Life*: "I'm embarrassed. It isn't that kind of book, really. . . . It's a novel, and I think it's a good one, but it's a story not an allegory. I mean it's nice being a little bit rich and a little bit famous, but dammit, I didn't intend to rank with Melville."

One critic in tune with Benchley's intentions was Gene Lyons. "What one gets from Benchley, and this, I think, is the essence of his commercial genius, is *escape*," Lyons wrote in the *New York Times Book Review*. "Instead of wallowing among the commonplaces of our culture's self-doubt, [his protagonists are] lucky enough to have An Adventure. But for the mundane accidents of fate, it might have been you or me."

Though the plots of Benchley's adventures occasionally strain the limits of credibility, their backgrounds are always carefully researched. In an author's note to *The Island*, his gruesome tale of seventeenth-century-style pirates holed up on an island near the Bahamas, Benchley wrote that he "consulted scores of books, and while I have endeavored to avoid any resemblance to real characters, I have tried equally hard to be faithful to historical reality." *Chicago Tribune Book World* contributing critic Lloyd Sachs felt he succeeded: "Benchley has certainly done his homework on pirate lore—his portrait of the murderous but honorable buccaneer Jean-David Nau and his tenth-generation pirates, who are on the brink of extinction, is convincing and entertaining and more than a little affecting. Benchley succeeds in making their plight touching and funny with one small detail: that they have come to prize 6-12 insect repellent more than just about anything."

With the appearance of *The Island*—Benchley's third adventure novel—*Washington Post* reporter Joseph McLellan concluded that Benchley "writes according to a formula. The formula moreover is a simple one: take a lot of salt water and put into it—something unexpected and menacing. Anybody can do it, and in the wake of *Jaws*, quite a few have tried. The problem (the writer's problem, not the reader's) is that nobody seems to do it quite as well as Benchley."

Despite a successful track record as an adventure novelist, Benchley abandoned his "formula" when he wrote *The Girl of the Sea of Cortez*. An idyllic tale of a young girl's fascination with the sea and its inhabitants, this book moves much more slowly than Benchley's thrillers—and that is too slowly, according to some critics. "This could be a refreshing deviation [from the style of his previous novels], but Benchley doesn't tell a story," noted Lola D. Gillebaard in the *Los Angeles Times Book Review.* "His words describe rather than dramatize. Though his descriptions are often lyrical, this reader yearned for more conflict, more 'and then what happened?'" Writing in the *Washington Post Book World,* Thomas Gifford expressed a similar view: "When Benchley sticks to the manta ray, the girl, and the memories of her late father . . . , he is often effective, even poignant, moving. But out of water he is quickly beached and gasping his last. The problem is the plot." Tony Bednarczyk, on the other hand, thought that "the continual unveiling of thoughts, feelings, discoveries and wonderment about the underwater world," is what makes *The Girl of the Sea of Cortez* a success. Benchley's "book is dedicated to the infinite and mysterious wisdom of Nature," Bednarczyk concluded in *Best Sellers.* "It is not to be missed."

Benchley continued to tackle new genres and subjects with his next work, *Q Clearance,* which he described as "a spy comedy." Set in the post-Reagan era, the novel features Timothy Burnham, a speechwriter or "ventriloquist" for the salty-speaking President Ben Winslow. After Burnham involuntarily gains "Q clearance" because of a promotion, he receives confidential information—which is to be destroyed—concerning nuclear energy. Thereafter Burnham must endure the strong censure of his very liberal wife and children. Calling *Q Clearance* a "prime example of that vanishing literary species, the comic novel," *Los Angeles Times* contributor Elaine Kendall noted that the book's appeal rests in the "merciless sendup of various bureaucrats easily recognizable to anyone who reached the age of reason during the past four administrations."

Kendall also appreciated the humor in Benchley's 1989 novel, *Rummies,* deeming the book "more satirical, less reverent, and far wittier" than many others on the same subject. Dan Wakefield summed up the book's theme in the *Washington Post:* "At its best and most convincing . . . it is about the successful treatment of an Ivy League, up-scale, Eastern intellectual establishment alcoholic." At his family's insistence, Scott Preston, an editor for a large New York publishing house, enters a substance abuse center. There he encounters an assortment of people he considers unlike himself in every way, but he comes to realize that he has more in common with them than he does with anyone else; "Preston is made miserably aware that all differences of educa-

tion and background vanish in the brotherhood of addiction," Kendall explained in the *Los Angeles Times.* "His evolution from a know-it-all, above-it-all, self-deluding lush to a vulnerable human being . . . is told in moving passages," Wakefield added. When a former glamour/movie star is murdered at the facility, the other patients become involved in solving the crime and working to see justice done; but Wakefield asserted that "the real drama" is still in witnessing Preston change from an out-of-control drinker into a recovered person. In his review of *Rummies* for the *Chicago Tribune,* David E. Jones declared that "Benchley's credentials as a storyteller . . . are only reinforced by this effort."

The publication of *Beast* in 1991 and *White Shark* in 1994 marked the author's return to a familiar formula: "lethal creatures, relentless pursuers, and vast quantities of saline solution," as Stefan Kanfer remarked in *Time.* In *Beast,* the setting is Bermuda and the menace is a giant squid. This story of a tentacled killing machine offers, according to Bill Kent in the *New York Times Book Review,* "a crude simplification of the way humans exploit marine life. The book's environmental subtext, in which Mr. Benchley argues that the best cure for our abuse of natural habitats is to leave well enough alone, saves this novel from being too much a copy of his earlier success." Clearly, noted Chicago *Tribune Books* reviewer James Kaufmann, "Benchley . . . did not set out to write cutting edge literary fiction, and criticizing the book for not being what it never tried to be is unfair. Still," he concluded, "*Beast* is an immensely enjoyable reading experience." *White Shark* did not fare as well with the critics. The novel centers on a Nazi-engineered superweapon—code-named "White Shark"—that "looks more like Arnold Schwarzenegger than any fish," chided Christopher Lehmann-Haupt in the *New York Times.* The steel-toothed mechanical soldier apparently sank to the ocean floor at the close of World War II, but more than fifty years later, off the coast of Bermuda, it erupts from its airtight shell and begins to wreak havoc on all things edible.

A year after *White Shark,* Benchley was able to redeem himself in the critics' eyes with a surprising departure from his "tear 'em up" sea fiction. The 1995 essay collection *Ocean Planet: Writings and Images of the Sea* (labeled a coffee table book by some) was edited by Benchley and Judith Gradwohl, director of the Smithsonian Institute's Environmental Awareness Program. It features an introduction by Benchley and short writings by an impressive array of environmentalists, travel writers, and novelists, Benchley among them. Published as a companion volume to the Smithsonian's "Ocean Planet" exhibit, the work includes stunning photography, little-known facts and statistics, and entertaining sea lore.

Benchley's nonfiction book *Shark Trouble* is, in a way, an attempt to make up for the shark hysteria he had caused with earlier books. Benchley began by chiding the media for naming 2001 "the year of the shark attack." He noted that there were no more attacks that summer than any other year, but the media made it seem like a bad year for shark attacks through its hype. Benchley wrote, "for every human being killed by a shark, roughly ten million sharks are killed by humans." However, he did insist that sharks should be deeply respected and offers many tips on when and where to go into the ocean. He also warned of dangerous sea creatures other than sharks and included his own family stories of encounters with these creatures. "*Shark Trouble* helps us see that all the planet's creatures are interconnected, interdependent, magnificent in their own right," said Polly Paddock of *Knight-Ridder Tribune News Service.*

BIOGRAPHICAL AND CRITICAL SOURCES:

BOOKS

Authors in the News, Volume 2, Thomson Gale (Detroit, MI), 1976.
Contemporary Literary Criticism, Thomson Gale (Detroit, MI), Volume 4, 1975, Volume 8, 1978.

PERIODICALS

Atlanta Journal-Constitution, June 14, 2002, Teresa K. Weaver, "Book Buzz: Benchley Back in Shark Waters," p. E1.
Best Sellers, August, 1982, Tony Bednarczyk, review of *The Girl of the Sea of Cortez.*
Booklist, April 15, 2002, Donna Seaman, review of *Shark Trouble: True Stories and Lessons about the Sea,* p. 1362.
Boston Herald, July 25, 2001, "It's a Benchley Summer," p. 20.
Chicago Tribune, November 17, 1989, David E. Jones, review of *Rummies.*
Chicago Tribune Book World, May 13, 1979; August 8, 1982; June 8, 1986.
Detroit News, May 6, 1979.
Entertainment Weekly, June 3, 1994, p. 50; December 30, 1994, p. 120.
Fortune, August 26, 1991, p. 113; August 8, 1994, p. 107.
Kirkus Reviews, May 1, 1991, p. 551; April 1, 1994, p. 410.

Knight-Ridder/Tribune News Service, June 5, 2002, Jeff Guin, review of *Shark Trouble,* p. K748, Joe Steinman, review of *Shark Trouble,* p. K568; July 3, 2002, Polly Paddock, review of *Shark Trouble,* p. K5952.
Library Journal, February 1, 1994, p. 109; June 1, 1995, p. 152.
Locus, May, 1994, p. 21.
Los Angeles Times, July 4, 1986; November 24, 1989.
Los Angeles Times Book Review, August 22, 1982; April 16, 1995, p. 8; December 3, 1995, p. 5.
Miami Herald, June 8, 1975.
New Statesman, May 17, 1974; June 22, 1979.
Newsweek, May 10, 1976.
New Yorker, February 18, 1974.
New York Times, January 17, 1974; May 30, 1994, p. 13.
New York Times Book Review, February 3, 1974; May 16, 1976; May 13, 1979; July 8, 1979; May 9, 1982; December 17, 1989; July 7, 1991, p. 7; June 5, 1994, p. 22; April 23, 1995, p. 14.
Palm Springs Life, April, 1975.
PR Newswire, September 5, 2001, p. 5806.
Rolling Stone, April 11, 1974, Michael Rogers, review of *Jaws.*
Time, February 4, 1974; July 5, 1982; July 1, 1991, p. 70.
Tribune Books (Chicago), July 7, 1991, p. 7; June 28, 1992, p. 8; June 19, 1994, p. 3; July 23, 1995, p. 8.
Washington Post, September 1, 1978; April 30, 1979; October 19, 1989.
Washington Post Book World, June 13, 1982; June 8, 1986; June 30, 1991, p. 4.

*   *   *

BENCHLEY, Peter Bradford
See BENCHLEY, Peter

*   *   *

BENITEZ, Sandra 1941-
(Sandra Ables Benitez)

PERSONAL: Born March 26, 1941, in Washington, DC; daughter of James Q. (a diplomat, road builder, comptroller, and writer) and Marta A. (an executive secretary and translator; maiden name, Benitez) Ables; married second husband, James F. Kondrick (a writer and game inventor), May 25, 1980; children: (first marriage) Christopher Charles Title, Jonathon James Title. *Education:* Truman State University, B.S., 1962, M.A., 1974.

ADDRESSES: Home and office—6075 Lincoln Dr., No. 210, Edina, MN 55436. *Agent*—Ellen Levine Literary Agency, Inc., 15 E. 26th St., Ste. 1801, New York, NY 10010-1505.

CAREER: Gaunt High School, Affton, MO, ninth-grade Spanish and English teacher, 1963-68; Northeast Missouri State University, Kirksville, teaching assistant, 1974; Wilson Learning Corporation, Eden Prairie, MN, freelance Spanish/English translator, 1975-76, marketing liaison in international division, 1977-80; fiction writer and creative writing teacher for The Loft and the University of Minnesota, Duluth, Split Rock Arts Program, 1980—. Loft Inroads Program, Hispanic mentor, 1989-92. COMPAS Writers-in-the-Schools Roster Artist, St. Paul, MN; member of the National Writers' Voice Project Reading Tour, 1994-95; University of Minnesota, Keller-Edelstein Distinguished Writer-in-Residence, 1997; University of San Diego, member of Knapp (chair, 2001).

MEMBER: Authors Guild, The Loft, Poets and Writers.

AWARDS, HONORS: Loft Mentor Award for fiction, 1987; Loft-McKnight Award for fiction, 1988; Jerome Foundation Travel and Study Grant, 1989; Minnesota State Arts Board fellowship, 1991; Minnesota Hispanic Heritage Month Award, 1992; Loft-McKnight Award of Distinction for prose, 1993; Barnes and Noble Discover Great New Writers Award, 1993, and Minnesota Book Award for fiction, 1994, both for *A Place Where the Sea Remembers;* Edelstein-Keller Writer of Distinction, 1997; American Book Award, Before Columbus Foundation, 1998, for *Bitter Grounds;* Bush Artists fellowship, 1999; *Book Sense '76* Pick, *Star Tribune* "Talking Volumes" selection, 2002, both for *The Weight of All Things;* All-city book read award, 2002, for *A Place Where the Sea Remembers.*

WRITINGS:

A Place Where the Sea Remembers, Coffee House Press (Minneapolis, MN), 1993.

Mickey Pearlman, editor, *"Home Views," A Place Called Home: Twenty Writing Women Remember,* St. Martins Press (New York, NY), 1996.

Bitter Grounds, Hyperion (New York, NY), 1997.

Marilyn Kallet and Judith Ortiz Cofer, editors, *"Fire, Wax, Smoke," Sleeping with One Eye Open: Women Writers and the Art of Survival,* University of Georgia Press (Athens, GA), 1999.

The Weight of All Things, Hyperion (New York, NY), 2000.

Night of the Radishes, Hyperion (New York, NY), 2003.

Work has been published in British, Dutch, German, Spanish, and French.

Work represented in several anthologies. Contributor of numerous English and Spanish articles to periodicals.

SIDELIGHTS: Sandra Benitez draws upon her experiences living in Mexico and El Salvador to craft novels that reveal how domestic life is compromised by politics in Latin America. In Benitez's novels, political discord dissolves family and friendship ties, it leaves young children orphaned and vulnerable, and it infects generation after generation. The larger social framework of Latin America becomes understandable when presented from the viewpoint of so-called "ordinary" characters with whom the reader can develop a rapport. To quote a *Publishers Weekly* writer in a review of *The Weight of All Things,* Benitez—who published her first novel at the age of fifty-two—"gives voice to the silenced."

Benitez's first novel, *A Place Where the Sea Remembers,* was published in 1993. The book reveals the aspirations and disillusionment felt by people living in the Mexican village of Santiago. Candelario Marroquin is fired from his job one afternoon and, upon returning home, discovers that his wife is pregnant. Now Candelario is unable to keep his promise to his wife's sister to take in her baby that was conceived as the result of a rape. A quarrel between the sisters ensues which triggers a series of events that touches the lives of many of the residents of Santiago. Some reviewers complimented Benitez on her ability to create a distinctive society by interweaving the stories of her characters. "Throughout *A Place Where the Sea Remembers,* Ms. Benitez's descriptions of people and places are crisp, and the staccato rhythms of her prose are just right for this dark fable of a story. She has built a little world . . . and filled it with people we care for, we root for, and whose flaws we are willing to forgive," wrote Chris Bohjalian in the *New York Times Book Review.* Cristina Garcia of the *Washington Post Book World* felt that *A Place Where the Sea Remembers* "is a quietly stunning book that leaves soft tracks in the heart." The work won Benitez the Barnes and Noble Discover Great New Writers Award in 1993, as well as a Minnesota Book Award for fiction in 1994.

In 1997 Benitez published *Bitter Grounds,* a story that follows two connected Salvadoran families through the political events of the 1930s through the 1970s. One family owns a coffee plantation; the other works in their employment. Benitez keeps her focus on the women of these families through three generations and shows despite their disparate circumstances, how they are linked by a complex mix of servitude and friendship. The author gives a careful sensory picture of their combined experiences, such as the making of sweet and salt tamales, and a ubiquitous radio soap opera called "Las Dos." The story concentrates on individual experiences, but the violence of continuous political upheaval in El Salvador is inescapable, beginning with the flight of Nahuat-descended Mercedes from the massacre in her Indian village. Political allegiances and class divisions threaten to end the generations-old relationship between the families, as each generation produces daughters who rebel against their places in the world.

Bitter Grounds received enthusiastic reviews and was admired for its cultural and social nuances, as well as for its careful treatment of a controversial political situation. Writing for *Booklist,* Grace Fill called the novel "a beautiful work of fiction that reveals the complicated roots of human drama and lays bare the truth of a troubled nation." Suzanne Ruta commended Benitez in *Entertainment Weekly,* admiring her "savory details. . . . comic touches. . . . [and] delicate, domestic look at violent history." A *Publishers Weekly* reviewer found the work "surprisingly free of propaganda" and commented that the "Spanish-sprinkled, elegant prose is mesmerizing in its simplicity and frankness." Mary Margaret Benson noted the book's "rich and fluid" prose in her review for *Library Journal* and called it a "welcome addition to the growing body of Latina literature."

The Weight of All Things offers a chilling portrait of a young boy caught up in an incomprehensible war. Nine-year-old Nicolas de la Virgen Veras accompanies his mother to the funeral of a martyred Catholic hero, Archbishop Romero. Soldiers fire on the large crowd, killing Nicolas's mother, who has tried to shield him from the flying bullets. Unaware that his mother is dead, and not just wounded, the bewildered boy makes his way home to his grandfather—only to discover that the war has arrived in his rural town as well. According to Michael Porter in the *New York Times Book Review,* through Nicolas's eyes "we see the war as a morass of fear and confusion, punctuated by acts of brutality and selfless kindness." In *Book* magazine, Mimi O'Connor praised the work for its "straightforward and evocative prose" that offers "a deeply affecting and startling portrait" of

a country caught in the throes of war. In *Publishers Weekly,* a critic noted that the novel "seamlessly blends fact with imagination, evoking the trauma of war more vividly than any newspaper account." And Andrea Caron Kempf concluded in the *Library Journal:* "With its deceptively simple narrative, *The Weight of All Things* tells a powerful story."

Benitez once told *CA:* "I came to writing late. I was thirty-nine before I gathered enough courage to begin. When I hear other writers talk about writing, I'm amazed by those who say they always knew they had to write. When I was a girl, I never wished to do it. Being a writer was something magical I never dreamed I could attain. But while growing up, I frequently had a book in my lap, and so I was linked, even then, to writing and to the spell that stories cast.

"Over the years, I didn't know a writing life was lying in store for me. I had to live and grow before I caught the faint call at the age of thirty-nine. Since then, I've worked hard at being faithful to the call. For writing is an act of faith. We must keep faith each day with our writing if we want to be called writers.

"Since I've been writing, I've searched what's in my heart and it's from *that* core that I write and not from what seems marketable. I am a Latina American. In my heart are stored the stories of my Puerto Rican and Missourian heritage and of a childhood lived in Mexico and El Salvador. When I write, I have to suppress the knowledge that mainstream America often ignores the stories of 'la otra America.' Over the years, I've learned to write from the heart, to persevere despite the setbacks of a host of rejections.

"In the end, I've learned these things about writing: it's never too late to begin; we know all we need to know in order to do it; persistence and tenacity will take us all the way; and there are angels on our shoulders. Be still to catch their whisperings."

BIOGRAPHICAL AND CRITICAL SOURCES:

PERIODICALS

Book, January-February, 2001, Mimi O'Connor, review of *The Weight of All Things,* p. 79.
Booklist, September 15, 1997, Grace Fill, review of *Bitter Grounds,* p. 207.

Boston Globe, December 29, 1993.

Christian Science Monitor, January 21, 1998, Kathleen Kilgore, "Mayan and Modern Worlds Vie in El Salvador Tale," p. 13.

Entertainment Weekly, October 31, 1997, Suzanne Ruta, review of *Bitter Grounds,* p. 100.

Hispanic Times Magazine, May-June, 1997, Robert Kendall, review of *A Place Where the Sea Remembers,* p. 39.

Library Journal, September 1, 1997, Mary Margaret Benson, review of *Bitter Grounds,* p. 214; December, 2000, Andrea Caron Kempf, review of *The Weight of All Things,* p. 184.

Los Angeles Times, October 28, 1997, Kevin Baxter, "Rediscovering Roots through Her Writing," p. E3.

Minneapolis-St. Paul Magazine, November, 1999, Alicia Fedorczak, "The Stories of Her Life," p. 50.

New York Times Book Review, October 31, 1993; March 25, 2001, Michael Porter, review of *The Weight of All Things,* p. 22.

Publishers Weekly, August 11, 1997, review of *Bitter Grounds,* p. 384; December 11, 2000, review of *The Weight of All Things,* p. 64.

St. Louis Post-Dispatch, September 7, 1997, Susan C. Hegger, "Melodrama with Latin Accent," p. C5.

Washington Post Book World, September 5, 1993.

Women's Review of Books, June, 1998, Barbara Belejack, review of *Bitter Grounds,* p. 100.

*   *   *

BENITEZ, Sandra Ables
   See BENITEZ, Sandra

*   *   *

BERENDT, John 1939-

  (John Lawrence Berendt)

PERSONAL: Born December 5, 1939, in Syracuse, NY; son of Ralph Sidney and Carol (Deschere) Berendt. *Education:* Harvard University, A.B., 1961.

ADDRESSES: Home—135 West 87th St., New York, NY 10024. *Agent*—International Creative Management, 40 West 57th St., New York, NY 10019.

CAREER: Writer. *Esquire,* New York, NY, associate editor, 1961-69; *Holiday,* New York, NY, senior staff editor, 1969; associate producer for *David Frost Show,* 1969-71, and *Dick Cavett Show,* 1973-75; *New York Magazine,* New York, NY, editor, 1977-79; *Esquire,* columnist, 1982-94.

MEMBER: PEN, Century Association.

AWARDS, HONORS: Pulitzer Prize finalist for general nonfiction, 1995, for *Midnight in the Garden of Good and Evil.*

WRITINGS:

Midnight in the Garden of Good and Evil: A Savannah Story (nonfiction), Random House (New York, NY), 1994.

(Author of introduction) Lady Chablis and Theodore Bouloukos, *Hiding My Candy: The Autobiography of the Grand Empress of Savannah,* Pocket Books (New York, NY), 1997.

(Author of introduction) Paula H. Deen, *The Lady and Sons: Savannah Country Cookbook,* Random House (New York, NY), 1998.

(Author of introduction) Arthur Conan Doyle, *The Adventures and Memoirs of Sherlock Holmes,* Modern Library (New York, NY), 2001.

(Guest editor) *The Best American Crime Writing: 2003 Edition: The Year's Best True Crime Reporting,* edited by Otto Penzler and Thomas H. Cook, Vintage (New York, NY), 2003.

City of Fallen Angels, Penguin (New York, NY), 2005.

Author of column in *Esquire,* 1982-94. Contributor to periodicals.

ADAPTATIONS: Midnight in the Garden of Good and Evil was adapted to film, directed by Clint Eastwood, and released by Warner Bros., 1997.

SIDELIGHTS: John Berendt, a journalist who has served as an editor with both *Esquire* and *New York* magazines, is the author of *Midnight in the Garden of Good and Evil: A Savannah Story.* An account of life in Savannah, Georgia, as observed by Berendt in the 1980s, the book provides portraits of Savannah's more colorful citizens, notably the transvestite performer Lady Chablis and various members of the storytelling Married Woman's Card Club. In addition, *Midnight in the Garden of Good and Evil* reports on a real-life, high-profile murder case in which Jim Williams, a respected antiques dealer, was accused of the murder of his youthful companion, Danny Hansford. Berendt, who has also worked in television as an associate producer for the *David Frost Show* and the *Dick Cavett Show,* lived part-time in Savannah for eight years while writing the book.

The details of the Hansford killing and the four ensuing murder trials occupy the second half of *Midnight in the Garden of Good and Evil.* Williams, who was eventually acquitted, died in 1990 with the distinction of being the only Georgian to be tried by the state four times for the same murder. "In recounting the tale of Williams's trials, [Berendt] frequently veers off and includes overheard conversations, funny vignettes and bits of historical and architectural data—a method that a lesser observer might have botched but that works wonderfully here," commented Glenna Whitley in the *New York Times Book Review.* One of Williams's strategies to fight off a conviction is to employ Minerva, a voodoo priestess. As Jean Hanff Korelitz remarked in the *Times Literary Supplement,* "When Minerva's roots and spells fail to stop Williams's subsequent trials, he none the less puts her on a kind of retainer, and has her called to appear as a defence witness to put curses on the D.A., the judge, and the jury . . . the results are uncertain, but Williams is philosophical: 'She'll never cost me fraction of what I've had to pay my lawyers.'"

Midnight in the Garden of Good and Evil has been appraised by critics as a quirky, fascinating work. A reviewer in *Publishers Weekly* commended Berendt for his "smart, sympathetic observations." In *Newsweek,* Malcolm Jones Jr. noted that the author "has fashioned a Baedeker to Savannah that, while it flirts with condescension, is always contagiously affectionate. Few cities have been introduced more seductively." Whitley, who in the *New York Times Book Review* described the book as "a peculiar combination of true crime and travelogue," stated that "Berendt's writing is elegant and wickedly funny." In the *Times Literary Supplement,* Korelitz summed up *Midnight in the Garden of Good and Evil* as "a strange but satisfying brew."

Midnight in the Garden of Good and Evil ultimately "smashed the 186-week record in February [1998] for staying on the *New York Times* nonfiction best seller list" noted Marcel Dufresne for the *Columbia Journalism Review.* In late August of 1998, Berendt suffered a mild heart attack while visiting Savannah. He was hospitalized for four days. One year later, Berendt hosted a travel forum for Savannah, as tourism to Savannah had "increased forty-six percent after [his] book hit the bestseller list" wrote a *Publishers Weekly* contributor. In

1998, during an interview for the *Writer,* he stated that "Savannah is a beautiful place that has been completely overlooked by the rest of the country and writers. The story would not have worked as well in a different setting." When asked "What advice would you give writers?" Berendt responded "Writing is never easy—even for professionals. 'Write and keep on writing' is the best advice I can give." As for his own aspirations, Berendt told Dave Weich in an online interview for *Powells.com:* "I want to write another book that's as much fun to write as [*Midnight in the Garden of Good and Evil*]. I don't have any illusion that the next book I write will be anywhere near as successful—it's impossible. So what I really want is for the book to be engrossing and fun and exciting."

BIOGRAPHICAL AND CRITICAL SOURCES:

PERIODICALS

Architectural Digest, May, 1995, p. 56.
Columbia Journalism Review, May-June, 1998, Marcel Dufresne, "Why *Midnight* May Be Darker than You Think," p. 78.
Entertainment Weekly, September 18, 1998, p. 16.
Library Journal, January, 1994, p. 139.
Los Angeles Times, December 30, 1993, p. E4.
Los Angeles Times Book Review, January 23, 1994, p. 6.
Newsweek, February 28, 1994, Malcom Jones, Jr., review of *Midnight in the Garden of Good and Evil,* p. 62.
New York Times Book Review, March 20, 1994, Glenna Whitley, review of *Midnight in the Garden of Good and Evil,* p. 12.
People, April 11, 1994, p. 108; September 21, 1998, p. 131.
Publishers Weekly, December 13, 1993, p. 58; July 26, 1999, "Midnight Strikes Again," p. 20.
Time, April 3, 1995, p. 79.
Times Literary Supplement, July 29, 1994, Jean Hanff Korelitz, review of *Midnight in the Garden of Good and Evil,* p. 7.
Washington Post, February 24, 1994, p. C1.
Washington Post Book World, February 6, 1994, p. 3.
Writer, January, 1998, Kristine F. Anderson, "A Conversation with . . . John Berendt," p. 17.

ONLINE

Powells.com, http://www.powells.com/ (July 14, 1999), David Weich, "Midday in the Annex with John Berendt."

BERENDT, John Lawrence
  See BERENDT, John

                    *   *   *

BERGER, Thomas 1924-
  (Thomas Louis Berger)

PERSONAL: Born July 20, 1924, in Cincinnati, OH; son of Thomas Charles and Mildred (Bubbe) Berger; married Jeanne Redpath (an artist), June 12, 1950. *Education:* University of Cincinnati, B.A. (honors), 1948; Columbia University, graduate study, 1950-51.

ADDRESSES: Office—P.O. Box 11, Palisades, NY 10964-0011. *Agent*—Don Congdon Associates, 156 Fifth Ave., New York, NY 10010.

CAREER: Novelist, short-story writer, and playwright. Rand School of Social Science, librarian, 1948-51; *New York Times Index,* staff member, 1951-52; *Popular Science Monthly,* associate editor, 1952-53; *Esquire* (magazine), film critic, 1972-73; University of Kansas, writer-in-residence, 1974; Southampton College Distinguished Visiting Professor, 1975-76; Yale University, lecturer, 1981, 1982; University of California—Davis, Regent's Lecturer, 1982. *Military service:* U.S. Army, 1943-46.

MEMBER: Authors Guild, Authors League of America, Phi Alpha Theta (honorary member).

AWARDS, HONORS: Dial fellowship, 1962; Western Heritage Award, and Richard and Hinda Rosenthal Award, National Institute of Arts and Letters, both 1965, both for *Little Big Man;* Ohioana Book Award, 1982, for *Reinhart's Women;* Pulitzer Prize nomination, 1984, for *The Feud;* Litt.D., Long Island University, 1986.

WRITINGS:

NOVELS

Crazy in Berlin, Scribner (New York, NY), 1958.
Reinhart in Love, Scribner (New York, NY), 1962.
Little Big Man, Dial (New York, NY), 1964.
Killing Time, Dial (New York, NY), 1967.
Vital Parts, Baron (New York, NY), 1970.

Regiment of Women, Simon & Schuster (New York, NY), 1973.
Sneaky People, Simon & Schuster (New York, NY), 1975.
Who Is Teddy Villanova?, Delacorte (New York, NY), 1977.
Arthur Rex: A Legendary Novel, Delacorte (New York, NY), 1978.
Neighbors, Delacorte (New York, NY), 1980.
Reinhart's Women, Delacorte (New York, NY), 1981.
The Feud, Delacorte (New York, NY), 1983.
Nowhere, Delacorte (New York, NY), 1985.
Being Invisible, Little, Brown (Boston, MA), 1987.
The Houseguest, Little, Brown (Boston, MA), 1988.
Changing the Past, Little, Brown (Boston, MA), 1989.
Orrie's Story, Little, Brown (Boston, MA), 1990.
Meeting Evil, Little, Brown (Boston, MA), 1992.
Robert Crews, Morrow (New York, NY), 1994.
Suspects, Morrow (New York, NY), 1996.
The Return of Little Big Man, Little, Brown (Boston, MA), 1999.
Best Friends, Simon & Schuster (New York, NY), 2003.
Adventures of the Artificial Woman, Simon & Schuster (New York, NY), 2004.

OTHER

Other People (play), first produced at Berkshire Theatre Festival, 1970.
Granted Wishes (short stories), Lord John Press (Northridge, CA), 1984.
(With Sidney L. Sondergard and William C. Bradford) *An Index of Characters in Early Modern English Drama: Printed Plays, 1500-1660,* Cambridge University Press (New York, NY), 1998.
(Editor, with Laurie E. Maguire) *Textual Formations and Reformations,* University of Delaware Press (Newark, DE), 1999.
(Editor, with Jill L. Levenson and Barry Gaines) William Shakespeare, *Romeo and Juliet, 1597,* Oxford University Press (New York, NY), 2000.

Also author of play *The Burglars,* published in *New Letters,* fall, 1988. Contributor of short stories to periodicals, including *Gentleman's Quarterly, American Review, Penthouse, Playboy, Saturday Evening Post,* and *Harper's.*

ADAPTATIONS: Little Big Man was adapted as a film starring Dustin Hoffman, 1970; *Neighbors* was adapted as a film starring John Belushi, Universal, 1981.

SIDELIGHTS: "Thomas Berger belongs, with Mark Twain and [H. L.] Mencken and Philip Roth, among our first-rate literary wiseguys," wrote John Romano in the *New York Times Book Review.* "Savvy and skeptical, equipped with a natural eloquence and a knack for parody, he has been expertly flinging mud at the more solemn and self-important national myths" for much of his career. Other critics offer similar assessments of Berger's talent, rating him as one of the leading American satiric novelists. Brom Weber called Berger in the *Saturday Review* "one of the most successful satiric observers of the ebb and flow of American life after World War II. His prolificacy promises a continued development of the tragicomic mode of vision." *National Review* contributor Guy Davenport called Berger "the best satirist in the United States, the most learned scientist of the vulgar, the futile, and the lost, and the most accurate mimic in the trade." Davenport elaborated his praise, calling Berger "a comedian whose understanding of humanity is devilishly well informed and splendidly impartial. Nothing is exempt from the splash of his laughter. The result is an amazing universality."

Berger, who has said he writes to celebrate the creative possibilities of language, works in a variety of traditional fiction genres. His aim is not to produce parody, satire, or to diagnose social ills, though critics have recognized all these features in most of his novels. Critics have especially emphasized the comic social commentary in the books; and in at least two of his novels—*Killing Time* and *Sneaky People*—Berger makes serious comments on modern society. But the author's forte is the kind of mock-heroism found in one of his best-known novels, *Little Big Man.* While the 1970 motion-picture adaptation of the novel was a box-office success, many critics claimed it does not do justice to Berger's creation. Michael Harris stated in the *Washington Post Book World* that the novel *Little Big Man,* "unfortunately obscured by the movie, is nothing less than a masterpiece. American history itself provided Berger with his types—a set of buckskin-fringed waxworks bedizened with legend—and in blowing the myths up to ridiculous proportions he paradoxically succeeded in reclaiming history." Gerald Green, writing in *Proletarian Writers of the Thirties,* maintained that "the glory of *Little Big Man* lies in the way Berger imposes his comic view of life on a deadly accurate portrait of the Old West. . . . It is the truest kind of humor, a humor that derives from real situations and real people. Who can resist Berger's Cheyennes who refer to themselves haughtily as 'The Human Beings?' Or his description of the way an Indian camp smells? Or the Indians' disdain for time, schedules, anything contiguous—a trait which causes them to hate the railroad?"

Although *Little Big Man* was not an immediate success when it was first published in 1964, "its reputation has spread and solidified since then," according to R.V. Cassill of the *New York Times Book Review.* "On the strength of this prodigious work alone," Cassill continued, "the author's reputation can rest secure." *Atlantic's* David Denby believed the book to be "probably as close as sophisticated men can come to a genuine folk version of the Old West. Its central character, Jack Crabb, is not so much a hero as an Everyman—an essentially passive recorder of vivid experience. American history happens to him, runs over him, and fails to break him. . . . Crabb himself is decent, competent, hopeful, and neither outstandingly courageous or weak; life is sordid, absurd, and as Crabb always survives, surprisingly persistent in its ability to make him suffer. . . . Crabb just wants to survive."

In *The Return of Little Big Man,* published in 1999, Berger offers a sequel to his 1964 classic. Crabb picks up his earlier narrative with the aftermath of the Battle of the Little Bighorn in 1876 and ends it with the Columbian Exposition in Chicago in 1893. In between, he relates a new set of adventures, chief among them his involvement with classic Western characters such as Wyatt Earp, Bat Masterson, and Doc Holliday. He also enjoys an extended, and eventually heartbreaking, affair with Amanda Teasdale, whom he first meets in Dodge City, Kansas, in the late 1870s. Though he deeply loves the social justice-minded Amanda, Jack eventually realizes that he lacks the requisite emotional tools to make the relationship last. Verlyn Klinkenborg, writing in the *New York Times Book Review,* felt that the affair with Amanda is the central element in the novel: "If Jack's main struggle in *Little Big Man* is with the mentality represented by George Custer, his struggle in *The Return of Little Big Man* is with that embodied by Amanda Teasdale."

Though affirming that *Little Big Man* remains a classic of twentieth-century postwar literature, critics generally concluded that the novel's sequel did not measure up to its predecessor. David Ulin, writing in Chicago's *Tribune Books,* remarked on his "sense that Berger is not merely revisiting previously explored territory, but in some ways attempting to recreate his earlier novel, without giving this one anything new." Klinkenborg also expressed doubts that the sequel "offers the same radical freshness" as the original novel. Ulin, however, had praise for some of the novel's components, particularly the affair between Jack and Amanda. "Their scenes together are marked by a quickening of the narrative," wrote Ulin, who added that "by opening Jack up to [an unexpected emotional vulnerability,] Berger achieves a deeper truth than in all his historical reconstructions combined." Since Jack is still relatively young at the close of this narrative, reviewers also noted that Berger has set the stage for future works continuing Jack's life story.

Another Berger character who is, more than anything else, a survivor, is Carlo Reinhart, protagonist of *Crazy in Berlin, Reinhart in Love, Vital Parts,* and *Reinhart's Women.* Jib Fowles commented in the *New Leader* that both "Reinhart and Crabb were people that Berger obviously liked having around. . . . Reinhart was neither a comedian nor a scapegoat, but he was never far from things comic or painful. . . . Like most of us, Reinhart could not qualify as a hero or anti-hero; he got through, and Berger set it all down in wry and superbly-told accounts." Reinhart lives in the twentieth century, and the four books in which he appears take him from his youthful days in World War II—*Crazy in Berlin*—to his middle years in the late 1970s—*Reinhart's Women.* A *Newsweek* reviewer noted that "Berger loves Carlo Reinhart, and he makes us love him, and he does this without resorting to tricks. . . . Reinhart is an unlikely hero: fat, 'bloated with emptiness,' scorned by women and animals, looked through as though he were polluted air, in debt, a voyeur, 'redundant in the logistics of life,' he nonetheless is a splendid man. He is novel, quick to forgive and hope."

Who Is Teddy Villanova? is Berger's exploitation of what *New York Times* contributor John Leonard called "the pulp detective story, in which, of course, nothing is as it seems and nothing ever makes any sense. The story, moreover, is populated entirely by people who talk like books, usually, but not always, nineteenth-century books by such Englishmen as Thomas Babington Macaulay and John Ruskin." Writing in the *New York Times Book Review,* Leonard Michaels commented on Berger's style, comparing it to that of writer S.J. Perelman—"educated, complicated, graceful, silly, destructive in spirit, and brilliant—and it is also something like Mad Comics—densely, sensuously detailed, unpredictable, packed with gags. Beyond all this, it makes an impression of scholarship—that is, Berger seems really to know what he jokes about. This includes not only Hammett and Chandler, but also Racine, Goethe, Ruskin, Elias Canetti, New York and the way its residents behave. . . . His whole novel . . . is like a huge verbal mirror. Its reflections are similar to what we see in much contemporary literature—hilarious and serious at once."

Having exposed the humor of American life from the Old West in *Little Big Man* to the twentieth century in the "Reinhart" series, Berger turns in *Arthur Rex* to a parody of time-honored myth and literature. *New Republic* reviewer Garrett Epps called the book "a massive retelling of the Camelot legend" and said that *Arthur Rex* "may be Berger's most ambitious book, at least in size and literary scale." Commenting in the *New York Times Book Review* on Berger's method in the retelling of the King Arthur morality tale, John Romano explained that the novelist paints his mythical landscapes "in his droll, relentlessly straight-faced prose, so as to empty them of romance, and let the brutal/crummy facts stare out. His pages swarm with bawdy puns and slapstick and bookish in-jokes; but even at his most absurd, his intrinsic tone is that of a hard-nosed realist who won't let the myths distort his essentially grouchy idea of the way things are."

In *Neighbors* Berger returned to the present suburban neighborhood and, according to *New York Times* contributor Christopher Lehmann-Haupt, "parodies all the rituals of neighborliness—the competitiveness, the bonhomie, the striving for civility in the face of what seems to be barbarism—and compresses into a single day a lifetime of over-the-back-fence strife." Paul Gray, in a review for *Time,* called *Neighbors* "a tour de force, [Berger's] most successfully sustained comic narrative since *Little Big Man.* . . . Like the best black humor of the 1960s, *Neighbors* offers a version of reality skewed just enough to give paranoia a good name."

Writing in the *New York Times Book Review,* Thomas Edwards believed that *Neighbors* "raises yet again the embarrassing question of why Thomas Berger isn't more generally recognized as one of the masters of contemporary American fiction." Isa Kapp wrote in the *New Republic:* "It is a mystery of literary criticism, that Thomas Berger, one of the most ambitious, versatile, and entertaining of contemporary novelists, is hardly ever mentioned in the company of America's major writers. He is a wit, a fine caricaturist, and his prose crackles with Rabelaisian vitality." Edwards postulated, "No doubt the trouble has something to do with obtuse notions that funny writing can't really be serious, that major talents devote themselves to [big] subjects and elaborate fictional techniques, that Mr. Berger is too eclectic and unpredictable to be important. . . . But *Neighbors* proves once again that Thomas Berger is one of our most intelligent, witty and independent-minded writers, that he knows, mistrusts and loves the texture of American life and culture as deeply as any novelist alive, and that our failure to read and discuss him is a national disgrace."

The Feud relates the unwinding of small events into a sprawl of disaster. The owner of a hardware store sees a fire hazard in a customer's unlit cigar; discussion over this perceived threat ends when Reverton, the owner's cousin, forces the customer to apologize at gunpoint. The gun, it turns out, is harmless, but the series of revenges that follow are not; businesses, lives, and futures are destroyed before the novel's end. Berger makes the story comic as well as sad; thus the usual conventions of the feud novel gain new life from Berger, according to many reviewers. "What makes Thomas Berger's version so fresh is the innocent bewilderment of most of the people involved," Anne Tyler noted in the *New York Times Book Review*. Epps, writing in the *Washington Post Book World*, believed: "In presenting this pageant of ignorance, rage, and deceit, Berger is harsh but never cruel. In all their variety, his novels have consistently presented a serious view of humanity as a race utterly spoiled by something that looks a lot like Original Sin. This merciless vision frees Berger somehow to love even his less prepossessing creations."

Critical assessments of *Nowhere* and *Being Invisible* generally rate both as limited successes in comparison to Berger's other novels. A cross between a spy-thriller and an updated *Gulliver's Travels, Nowhere* allows Berger to joke about private eyes while examining human nature, remarked David W. Madden in the *San Francisco Review of Books*. Lehmann-Haupt, in the *New York Times,* viewed the novel as a courageous attempt "to poke fun at every excess of the world from the cold war to racial prejudice" via text troubled by the same kinds of excesses it ridicules. More important to Madden is Berger's "ability of consistently exploring new fictional possibilities" while at the same time returning to characters and themes seen in his earlier novels.

"There is a certain type of scene that no writer does better than Mr. Berger," maintained *New York Times Book Review* contributor Francine Prose: "the depiction of the instant when the most routine social encounter becomes—suddenly and without provocation or warning—pure hell; the simplest exchange of banalities turns sour, then surly, then rancorous, then violent." Accordingly, *Being Invisible* has its "moments of random brutality." The fact that Fred Wagner, the anti-hero of *Being Invisible,* can disappear at will gives his story some "marvelous ironies," including Fred's distaste "for the voyeurism, the petty crime, the guilty, secret delights" available to him when he vanishes, Prose related. In this "fantasy of the white male as victim," as *Being Invisible* was described by *Los Angeles Times* reviewer Carolyn See, Fred is "outnumbered by jerks—pushy, stupid, self-satisfied," noted Prose.

According to MacDonald Harris of the *Washington Post Book World,* Berger excels when observing quarrels "from the sidelines." "In *The Houseguest,*" noted Harris, Berger "takes up the Quarrel again, and treats it in a way that is more complicated, more subtle, and more odd than anything in his previous work." The antagonist in this case is a charming visitor who gradually takes control of a well-to-do family's household. At first the Graves family do not resist this control, because the antagonist serves them as handyman and gourmet cook. But after the outsider steals from them and tricks their daughter into having sex with him, Graves family members decide to kill him. He not only survives their violent attacks but solidifies his place in the household by providing the amenities the Graveses have grown to expect.

Harris found *The Houseguest* the most interesting of Berger's novels "because it seems to suggest something more subtle going on under the surface" through an allegory that points to relations between the privileged and underprivileged. Since neither class behaves admirably, it is clear that "Berger will not take sides," Art Seidenbaum related in the *Los Angeles Times Book Review*. Seidenbaum called the author's noncommittal stance a weakness, but other critics found it consistent with the view of humanity expressed in Berger's other books. In *The Houseguest,* said Harris, Berger remains "ready to strain our credence with . . . the loutish realism of his events. His humor is Rabelaisian: larger than life, improbable and always on the edge of vulgarity; his penchant for stripping off the dirty underwear of life is unrelenting."

Like *Arthur Rex,* Berger's novel *Orrie's Story* harkens back to an ancient myth, updates it, and provides the author a forum for his modern concerns. This time Berger's source is the *Oresteia,* the Greek tragedy that recounts the story of Orestes. A wife kills her husband; a son, Orestes, kills his mother; then Orestes flees from the Furies, but finds justice and redemption in the big city. For Berger, the well-known story offers a fitting framework for his dark comic satire. He includes all of the characters, only the names have been slightly altered, the setting and events updated, and the themes slightly twisted.

According to *Washington Post Book World* editor Nina King, Berger's adaptation was unsuccessful: *Orrie's Story* "is decidedly unsteady. It is also grim, colorless, flat." King also argued that the events in the novel do not develop in any purposeful way. "In *The Oresteia,* cause leads inexorably to effect, fate must work itself out, and 'men shall learn wisdom—by affliction schooled,'" she noted, countering that, "In *Orrie's Story,* randomness is all." Yet, Michael Harris found more to the novel. *Orrie's Story* resembles those earlier comedies of mutual incomprehension, *Sneaky People* and *The Feud,* in which the omniscient author reveals that all of his characters "are riddled with lust and chicanery *and* with a wacky but genuine innocence," Harris noted in the *Los Angeles Times Book Review.* "Every one of them is a type, right down to his or her innermost fantasies." By connecting these modern characters and their stories with those of Greek tragedy, Berger draws the parallels. "What he did with types," concluded Harris of the novelist, "he can do with archetypes just as well."

In *Meeting Evil* Berger attempts to push readers and critics alike to see his dark writing in a new light. As Laurel Graeber explained in a *New York Times Book Review* interview, "Berger is always annoyed that the public finds his novels funny." As the novelist told Graeber, "I think some people dismiss me as a clown who makes fun of serious things. . . . I've been trying in recent years to be grimmer and grimmer and grimmer. . . . I wanted to write a book no one could call comic." That book, Graeber pointed out, is *Meeting Evil,* which begins as real estate agent John Felton, an ordinary guy with a wife and two children, makes the mistake of answering the doorbell during breakfast one morning. At the door, John finds Richie, a motorist in need of help, or so Richie says. What John does not know is that he is at this moment meeting evil.

As Louis B. Jones pointed out in the *New York Times Book Review,* Berger "throws a nice guy together with a scoundrel for a day-long crime spree, and thereby submits niceness to a day-long test." Jones continued, "In a trip by turns scary and farcical, intended to examine the nature of evil itself, Mr. Berger arrives at a . . . paradox of our century: that innocence consorts, mysteriously, with evil." This may occur because each person comprises both good and evil, an idea that emerges in *Meeting Evil* as Berger raises the possibility that Richie is just the darker side of John. Joseph Coates remarked upon this quality in his *Chicago Tribune Book World* review, while also noting Berger's ability to keep characters and readers struggling with this issue. "To the last line and beyond," Coates continued, "this brilliant and troubling book keeps in suspense the question of 'who was the greater criminal to the other'—a question Richie typically forces John to face and resolve, if either he or we can."

In *Robert Crews* Berger again updates a literary classic, this time creating a Robinson Crusoe story for the 1990s. Robert Crews is a middle-aged man who has never had to worry about money, thanks to his inherited wealth. As a result, he has spent an aimless life in a drunken stupor feeling sorry for himself. A fishing trip with what pass for friends comes to an abrupt end when the small plane carrying Crews and his fishing party goes down in a lake somewhere in a north country forest. Crews is the only survivor. "Just as in the original tale," suggested Thomas M. Disch in the *Washington Post Book World,* there is a strong didactic component. "The moral of Berger's story is drawn from the most successful theology of the present time, the recovery movement." The struggle for survival in nature proves just what Crews needs. He slowly and painfully develops the skills needed to stay alive, and eventually he meets his Friday in the person of a woman escaping from her abusive husband.

Crews's newfound skills and redemption come too easily for some reviewers. For Philip Graham in Chicago's *Tribune Books,* Crews "mysteriously develops a woodsman's competence too quickly, leaving behind decades of heavy drinking with no apparent ill effects." James Knudsen wrote in *World Literature Today* that, "Although the narrator steps in to tell us that Crews has changed from his old ways, we never come to understand *how* he changed." Still, Knudsen admitted that "despite its problems, *Robert Crews* is immaculately written and entertaining."

In *Suspects* Berger returns to a more straightforward narrative—straightforward, that is, within Berger's universe. The story begins with the murder of Donna Howland, whom Richard Bernstein in the *New York Times* described as "a sexy but prudish housewife in an anonymous American city," who is killed along with her baby daughter, Amanda, "both of them sliced up in an act of gothic horror suggesting a peculiar American dementia." Detectives Nick Moody and Dennis LeBeau—both "artfully named," Bernstein pointed out—begin their investigation, and naturally their attention focuses on those closest to the deceased. There is Larry, Donna's philandering husband, and Larry's half-brother, Lloyd, a brooding and apparently unstable drifter who bore a deep passion for Donna. The solution to the murders may seem obvious, but Joe Queenan in the *New York Times Book Review* assured readers that it is not. "All these odd goings-on are described in such a matter-of-fact way," Queenan wrote, "that it takes a long time to realize how profoundly odd the whole book is."

Bernstein concluded that, "Here and there, *Suspects* glints like a mirror in the sun, showing its author's obviously big talent, but it is not a major work in Mr.

Berger's large oeuvre. The light doesn't glint quite often enough." Michael Dirda in the *Washington Post Book World* gave the novel higher marks, while suggesting that it pales in comparison to Berger's more powerful novels: "*Suspects* really is a good, engrossing book, a bit meandering but smooth, professional, and better than any television police show it might resemble. . . . So if *Suspects* isn't in the same class as, say, *Killing Time,* which it loosely resembles . . . any Berger fan will still want to read the new book." Queenan conceded that, while "The Fraternal Order of Police" may not care for the book, "*Suspects* is an engrossing, often hilarious offering from one of our most persistently strange writers."

Berger's novel *Best Friends* introduces Roy Courtright and Sam Grandy, who have known each other since childhood. Roy is the wealthy owner of a classic car business and a compulsive womanizer, and his success is built on inherited wealth. Sam's life is very different; a spendthrift, he often runs short of money and is dependent on his wife, Kirsten. Though Roy's dealings with women make him seem superficial, he does have a great loyalty to Sam, who has become bloated and dull since the days of their youth. Roy repeatedly gives Sam money when he needs it. He feels some contempt for his friend, yet he repeatedly sets those feelings aside, grateful to his friend for the years of friendship. Roy is intrigued by Kirsten, but because she is Sam's wife, he keeps his distance from her, which is remarkable behavior for him. Then Sam suffers a series of heart attacks. As he becomes increasingly ill, Kirsten and Roy are drawn together. Sympathy turns to lust, and revelations about Sam's opinion of his friend change the relationship between the two, with surprising results.

Roy's point of view dominates *Best Friends,* and his "shallow, amoral view of the world" is used effectively by Berger, according to Ellen Emry Heltzel in the *Seattle Times.* The use of "Roy's vacuity to its fullest effect" is both "the book's strength and its weakness," related Heltzel. "Either you relate to these people as they stumble blindly through life, or you want to spank them for their childish ways. In the end, *Best Friends* is a mundane cautionary tale about the unexamined life." *New York Times* writer Richard Eder ranked *Best Friends* as one of the author's best efforts, calling it "a tautly drawn tragicomedy taking one more mythical swipe at contemporary life." He added: "Not often are the scruples, veiled steps, retreats and advances of an adulterous affair so shrewdly and erotically portrayed." Dorman T. Shindler, a contributor to the *Denver Post,* found the book "slight on plot, but featuring some very strong and well-drawn characters." He added that it

"focuses on the values of friendship, the sometimes fragile nature of a marital relationship and the duality inherent in everyone's personality." Robert E. Brown, a reviewer for *Library Journal,* concluded that Berger "succeeds with characterization, detail, ethical complication, and nuance, and the result is outstanding."

BIOGRAPHICAL AND CRITICAL SOURCES:

BOOKS

Cohen, Sarah Blacher, editor, *Comic Relief,* University of Illinois Press (Champaign, IL), 1978.
Contemporary Literary Criticism, Thomson Gale (Detroit, MI), Volume 3, 1975, Volume 5, 1976, Volume 8, 1978, Volume 11, 1979, Volume 18, 1981, Volume 38, 1986.
Dictionary of Literary Biography, Volume 2: *American Novelists since World War II,* Thomson Gale (Detroit, MI), 1978.
Dictionary of Literary Biography Yearbook: 1980, Thomson Gale (Detroit, MI), 1981.
Landon, Brooks, *Thomas Berger,* Twayne (Boston, MA), 1989.
Madden, David W., editor, *Proletarian Writers of the Thirties,* Southern Illinois University Press (Carbondale, IL), 1968.
Madden, David W., *Critical Essays on Thomas Berger,* G.K. Hall (New York, NY), 1995.
Mitchell, Burroughs, *The Education of an Editor,* Doubleday (New York, NY), 1980.
Schulz, Max F., *Black Humor Fiction of the Sixties: A Pluralistic Definition of Man and His World,* Ohio State University Press (Columbus, OH), 1973.

PERIODICALS

American Book Review, March-April, 1982.
American Heritage, May, 1999, Andrew Ward, interview with Berger, p. 89.
Antaeus, number 61, 1988.
Armchair Detective, number 14, 1981.
Atlantic, March, 1971; September, 1973; April, 1999, review of *The Return of Little Big Man,* pp. 112-113.
Audience, Volume 2, number 4, 1972.
Booklist, February 1, 1999, Ray Olson, review of *The Return of Little Big Man,* p. 940; March 15, 2003, Brendan Driscoll, review of *Best Friends,* p. 1252.

Chicago Tribune Book World, April 13, 1980; September 27, 1981; December 18, 1981; May 29, 1983; May 20, 1984; May 19, 1985; June 16, 1985.

Denver Post, May 25, 2003, Dorman T. Shindler, review of *Best Friends,* p. EE2.

Harper's, April, 1970.

Hollins Critic, December, 1983.

Library Journal, January, 1994, p. 157; February 15, 1999, Nathan Ward, review of *The Return of Little Big Man,* p. 181; October 1, 2000, Michael Rogers, review of *Neighbors,* p. 153; May 1, 2003, Robert E. Brown, review of *Best Friends,* p. 153.

Los Angeles Times, May 11, 1987; May 18, 1990.

Los Angeles Times Book Review, November 1, 1981; May 15, 1983; April 3, 1988; September 24, 1989.

Nation, August 20, 1977; May 3, 1980; June 11, 1983.

National Review, November 14, 1967; April 21, 1970; October 10, 1975.

New Leader, November 6, 1967; November 12, 1973; May 23, 1977.

New Republic, October 7, 1978; April 26, 1980; May 23, 1983.

Newsweek, April 20, 1977; May 3, 1980; June 11, 1983.

New Yorker, October 21, 1967.

New York Review of Books, May 26, 1977.

New York Times, September 13, 1996, p. B17; June 1, 2003, Richard Eder, review of *Best Friends,* p. 7.

New York Times Book Review, October 11, 1964; September 17, 1967; March 29, 1970; May 13, 1973; April 20, 1975; March 20, 1977; April 17, 1977; November 12, 1978; April 6, 1980; September 27, 1981; June 6, 1982; June 20, 1982; May 8, 1983; April 7, 1985; May 5, 1985; April 2, 1987; April 12, 1987; April 17, 1988; March 6, 1994, p. 7; September 29, 1996, p. 19; December 8, 1996, p. 82; May 9, 1999, p. 14.

Philological Quarterly, Volume 62, number 1, 1983.

Publishers Weekly, January 4, 1999, review of *The Return of Little Big Man,* p. 73.

San Francisco Review of Books, summer, 1985.

Saturday Review, March 21, 1970; July 31, 1973; May-June, 1985.

Seattle Times, June 22, 2003, Ellen Emry Heltzel, review of *Best Friends,* p. K14.

South Dakota Review, Volume 4, number 2, 1966.

Studies in American Humor, spring, 1983; fall, 1983.

Studies in Medievalism, Volume 2, number 4, 1983.

Time, December 21, 1970; April 7, 1980; October 12, 1981; May 23, 1983; June 17, 1985.

Times Literary Supplement, September 3, 1982; February 10, 1984; February 21, 1986; June 17, 1988; July 22, 1988.

Tribune Books (Chicago, IL), July 12, 1992, Joseph Coates, "The Laureate of the Ludicrous," p. 6; May 9, 1999, p. 3.

Virginia Quarterly Review, winter, 1997, p. 23.

Voice Literary Supplement, May, 2003, Jonathan Lethem, "Uncertainty Principle: Berger's Ambivalent Usurpations."

Washington Post Book World, April 20, 1975; September 17, 1978; June 27, 1982; May 15, 1983; August 26, 1984; July 7, 1985; April 19, 1987; April 17, 1988; September 29, 1996, p. 5.

Washington Times, June 1, 2003, Rex Roberts, review of *Best Friends,* p. B8.

Western American Literature, Volume 8, numbers 1-2, 1973; Volume 22, number 4, 1988.

World and I, October, 2003, Brooks Landon, "A Secret Too Good to Keep: Thomas Berger Profile."

Yale Review, winter, 1981.

*   *   *

BERGER, Thomas Louis
See BERGER, Thomas

*   *   *

BERRY, Jonas
See ASHBERY, John

*   *   *

BERRY, Wendell 1934-
(Wendell Erdman Berry)

PERSONAL: Born August 5, 1934, in Henry County, KY; married Tanya Amyx, May 29, 1957; children: Mary Dee, Pryor Clifford. *Education:* University of Kentucky, A.B., 1956, M.A., 1957.

ADDRESSES: Home—P.O. Box 1, Port Royal, KY 40058.

CAREER: Writer and farmer. Stanford University, Stanford, CA, Wallace Stegner writing fellow, 1958-59, lecturer, 1959-60, visiting professor, 1968-69; New York University, New York, NY, lecturer, 1962-64; University of Kentucky, Lexington, member of faculty, 1964-70, distinguished professor of English, 1971-72, professor of English, 1973-77, 1987-93; farmer, 1993—.

AWARDS, HONORS: Guggenheim fellow, 1961-62; *Poetry* magazine, Vachel Lindsay Prize, 1962, Bess Hokin Prize, 1967, for six poems; Rockefeller Foundation grant, 1967; first-place awards, Borestone Mountain Poetry Awards, 1969, 1970, 1972; literary award, National Institute of Arts and Letters, 1971; Friends of American Writers Award, 1975, for *The Memory of Old Jack;* Jean Stein Award, American Academy of Arts and Letters, 1987; Lannan Foundation Award for nonfiction, 1989; University of Kentucky Libraries Award for intellectual excellence, 1993; Aiken-Taylor Award for Poetry, *Sewanee Review,* 1994; T.S. Eliot Award, Ingersoll Foundation, 1994; *Writer* award, 2004, for body of work; O. Henry Prize, 2005, for short story "The Hurt Man;" honorary doctorates from Centre College, Transylvania College, Berea College, University of Kentucky, Santa Clara University, and Eureka College.

WRITINGS:

FICTION

Nathan Coulter: A Novel, Houghton Mifflin (Boston, MA), 1960, revised edition, North Point Press (Berkeley, CA), 1985.

A Place on Earth: A Novel, Harcourt (New York, NY), 1967, revised edition, North Point Press (Berkeley, CA), 1983, reprinted, Counterpoint Press (Washington, DC), 2001.

The Memory of Old Jack, Harcourt (New York, NY), 1974.

The Wild Birds: Six Stories of the Port William Membership, North Point Press (Berkeley, CA), 1986.

Remembering: A Novel, North Point Press (Berkeley, CA), 1988.

Fidelity: Five Stories, Pantheon (New York, NY), 1992.

Watch with Me: And Six Other Stories of the Yet-Remembered Ptolemy Proudfoot and His Wife, Miss Minnie, neé Quinch, Pantheon (New York, NY), 1994.

Two More Stories of the Port William Membership, Gnomon Press (Frankfort, KY), 1997.

Jayber Crow: The Life Story of Jayber Crow, Barber, of the Port William Membership as Written by Himself, Counterpoint Press (Washington, DC), 2000.

That Distant Land: The Collected Stories of Wendell Berry, Counterpoint Press (Washington, DC), 2002.

Three Short Novels (contains *Nathan Coulter, Remembering,* and *A World Lost*), Counterpoint Press (Washington, DC), 2002.

Hannah Coulter: A Novel, Shoemaker & Hoard (Washington, DC), 2004.

POETRY

November Twenty-six Nineteen Hundred Sixty-three, Braziller (New York, NY), 1964.

The Broken Ground, Harcourt (New York, NY), 1964.

Openings: Poems, Harcourt (New York, NY), 1968.

Findings, Prairie Press (Iowa City, IA), 1969.

Farming: A Handbook, Harcourt (New York, NY), 1970.

The Country of Marriage, Harcourt (New York, NY), 1973.

An Eastward Look (also see below), Sand Dollar Books (Berkeley, CA), 1974.

Reverdure: A Poem, Press at Colorado College (Colorado Springs, CO), 1974.

Horses, Larkspur Press (Monterey, KY), 1975.

To What Listens, Best Cellar Press (Crete, NE), 1975.

Sayings and Doings (also see below), Gnomon Press (Frankfort, KY), 1975.

The Kentucky River: Two Poems, Larkspur Press (Monterey, KY), 1976.

There Is Singing around Me, Cold Mountain Press (Austin, TX), 1976.

Clearing, Harcourt (New York, NY), 1977.

Three Memorial Poems, Sand Dollar Books (Berkeley, CA), 1977.

The Gift of Gravity, illustrated by Timothy Engelland, Deerfield Press (Old Deerfield, MA), 1979.

A Part, North Point Press (Berkeley, CA), 1980.

The Salad, North Point Press (Berkeley, CA), 1980.

Wendell Berry Reading His Poems (sound recording), Archive of Recorded Poetry and Literature (Washington, DC), 1980.

The Wheel, North Point Press (Berkeley, CA), 1982.

Collected Poems, 1957-1982, North Point Press (Berkeley, CA), 1985.

Sabbaths, North Point Press (Berkeley, CA), 1987.

Sayings and Doings [and] *An Eastward Look,* Gnomon Press (Frankfort, KY), 1990.

Entries: Poems, Pantheon (New York, NY), 1994.

The Farm, Larkspur Press (Monterey, KY), 1995.

The Selected Poems of Wendell Berry, Counterpoint Press (Washington, DC), 1998.

A Timbered Choir: The Sabbath Poems, 1979-1997, Counterpoint Press (Washington, DC), 1998.

Given: New Poems, Shoemaker & Hoard (Washington, DC), 2005.

NONFICTION

The Rise, University of Kentucky Library Press (Lexington, KY), 1968.

The Long-Legged House, Harcourt (New York, NY), 1969, portions reprinted as *A Native Hill,* introduction by Raymond D. Peterson, Santa Rosa Junior College (Santa Rosa, CA), 1976, original version reprinted, Shoemaker & Hoard (Washington, DC), 2004.

The Hidden Wound, Houghton Mifflin (Boston, MA), 1970, reprinted with new afterword, North Point Press (Berkeley, CA), 1989.

(With Ralph Eugene Meatyard and A. Gassan) *Ralph Eugene Meatyard,* Gnomon Press (Frankfort, KY), 1970.

The Unforeseen Wilderness: An Essay on Kentucky's Red River Gorge, photographs by Ralph Eugene Meatyard, University Press of Kentucky (Lexington, KY), 1971, revised and expanded edition published as *The Unforeseen Wilderness: Kentucky's Red River Gorge,* North Point Press (Berkeley, CA), 1991.

A Continuous Harmony: Essays Cultural and Agricultural, Harcourt (New York, NY), 1972, reprinted, Shoemaker & Hoard (Washington, DC), 2003.

Civilizing the Cumberland: A Commentary (bound with *Mountain Passes of the Cumberland* by James Lane Allen), King Library Press (Lexington, KY), 1972.

The Unsettling of America: Culture and Agriculture, Sierra Club Books (San Francisco, CA), 1977.

Recollected Essays, 1965-1980, North Point Press (Berkeley, CA), 1981.

The Gift of Good Land: Further Essays, Cultural and Agricultural, North Point Press (Berkeley, CA), 1981.

Standing by Words: Essays, North Point Press (Berkeley, CA), 1983, reprinted, Shoemaker & Hoard (Washington, DC), 2005.

(Editor, with Wes Jackson and Bruce Colman) *Meeting the Expectations of the Land: Essays in Sustainable Agriculture and Stewardship,* North Point Press (Berkeley, CA), 1984.

Home Economics: Fourteen Essays, North Point Press (Berkeley, CA), 1987.

The Landscape of Harmony, Five Seasons (Madley, Hereford, England), 1987.

Traveling at Home, wood engravings by John DePol, Bucknell University (Lewisberg, PA), 1988.

Harland Hubbard: Life and Work, University Press of Kentucky (Lexington, KY), 1990.

What Are People For? Essays, North Point Press (Berkeley, CA), 1990.

Sex, Economy, Freedom, and Community: Eight Essays, Pantheon (New York, NY), 1993.

Another Turn of the Crank, Counterpoint Press (Washington, DC), 1995.

A World Lost, Counterpoint Press (Washington, DC), 1996.

(With William Kittredge, Susan Griffin, Montague, and Mark Dowie) *Waste Land: Meditations on a Ravaged Landscape,* photographs by David T. Hanson, Aperture (New York, NY), 1997.

Life Is a Miracle: An Essay against Modern Superstition, Counterpoint Press (Washington, DC), 2000.

The Art of the Commonplace: Agrarian Essays of Wendell Berry, Counterpoint Press (Washington, DC), 2002.

Citizenship Papers, Shoemaker & Hoard (Washington, DC), 2003.

Tobacco Harvest: An Elegy, University Press of Kentucky (Lexington, KY), 2004.

The Way of Ignorance, Shoemaker & Hoard (Washington, DC), 2005.

(Editor and author of introduction) *Blessed Are the Peacemakers: Christ's Teachings of Love, Compassion, and Forgiveness,* Shoemaker & Hoard (Emeryville, CA), 2005.

Also author of *Standing on Earth,* 1991. Contributor to books, including *The Blue Grass Region of Kentucky, and Other Kentucky Articles,* edited by James Lane Allen, Books for Libraries, 1972. Contributor to periodicals, including *Nation, New World Writing, New Directions Annual, Prairie Schooner, Contact, Chelsea Review, Hudson Review,* and *Quarterly Review of Literature.* Contributing editor, *New Farm* and *Organic Gardening and Farming.*

ADAPTATIONS: Some of Berry's poems were set to music by David Ashley White and published as *The Peace of Wild Things: For Voice and Piano,* ECS Publishing (Boston, MA), 2004.

SIDELIGHTS: Critics and scholars have acknowledged Wendell Berry as a master of many literary genres, but whether he is writing poetry, fiction, or essays, his message is essentially the same: humans must learn to live in harmony with the natural rhythms of the earth or perish. *The Unsettling of America: Culture and Agriculture,* which analyzes the many failures of modern, mechanized life, is one of the key texts of the environmental movement, but Berry, a political maverick, has criticized environmentalists as well as those involved with big businesses and land development. In his opinion, many environmentalists place too much emphasis on wild lands without acknowledging the importance of agriculture to our society. Berry strongly believes that small-scale farming is essential to healthy local economies, and that strong local economies are essential to the survival of the species and the well-being of the planet. In an interview with *New Perspectives Quarterly* editor Marilyn Berlin Snell, Berry explained: "Today, local economies are being destroyed by the 'pluralistic,' displaced, global economy, which has no respect for what works in a locality. The global economy is built on the principle that one place can be exploited, even destroyed, for the sake of another place."

Berry further believes that traditional values, such as marital fidelity and strong community ties, are essential for the survival of humankind. In his view, the disintegration of communities can be traced to the rise of agribusiness: large-scale farming under the control of giant corporations. Besides relying on chemical pesticides and fertilizers, promoting soil erosion, and causing depletion of ancient aquifers, agribusiness has driven countless small farms out of existence and destroyed local communities in the process. In his *New Perspectives Quarterly* interview Berry commented that such large-scale agriculture is morally as well as environmentally unacceptable: "We must support what supports local life, which means community, family, household life—the moral capital our larger institutions have to come to rest upon. If the larger institutions undermine the local life, they destroy that moral capital just exactly as the industrial economy has destroyed the natural capital of localities—soil fertility and so on. Essential wisdom accumulates in the community much as fertility builds in the soil."

Berry's themes are reflected in his life. As a young man, he spent time in California, Europe, and New York City. Eventually, however, he returned to the Kentucky land that had been settled by his forebears in the early nineteenth century. He taught for many years at the University of Kentucky, but eventually resigned in favor of full-time farming. He uses horses to work his land and employs organic methods of fertilization and pest control; he also worked as a contributing editor to *New Farm Magazine* and *Organic Gardening and Farming,* which have published his poetry as well as his agricultural treatises.

It was as a poet that Berry first gained literary recognition. In volumes such as *The Broken Ground, Openings: Poems, Farming: A Handbook,* and *The Country of Marriage,* he wrote of the countryside, the turning of the seasons, the routines of the farm, the life of the family, and the spiritual aspects of the natural world. Reviewing *Collected Poems, 1957-1982, New York Times Book Review* contributor David Ray called Berry's style "resonant" and "authentic," and claimed that the poet "can be said to have returned American poetry to a Wordsworthian clarity of purpose. . . . There are times when we might think he is returning us to the simplicities of John Clare or the crustiness of Robert

Frost. . . . But, as with every major poet, passages in which style threatens to become a voice of its own suddenly give way, like the sound of chopping in a murmurous forest, to lines of power and memorable resonance. Many of Mr. Berry's short poems are as fine as any written in our time."

It is perhaps Berry's essays that have brought him the greatest broad readership. In one of his most popular early collections, *The Unsettling of America: Culture and Agriculture,* he argues that agriculture is the foundation of America's greater culture. He makes a strong case against the U.S. government's agricultural policy, which promotes practices leading to overproduction, pollution, and soil erosion. *Dictionary of Literary Biography* contributor Leon V. Driskell termed *The Unsettling of America* "an apocalyptic book that places in bold relief the ecological and environmental problems of the American nation."

Another essay collection, *Recollected Essays, 1965-1980,* has been compared by several critics to Henry David Thoreau's *Walden.* Charles Hudson, writing in the *Georgia Review,* noted that, "like Thoreau, one of Berry's fundamental concerns is working out a basis for living a principled life. And like Thoreau, in his quest for principles Berry has chosen to simplify his life, and much of what he writes about is what has attended this simplification, as well as a criticism of modern society from the standpoint of this simplicity."

In *Sex, Economy, Freedom, and Community: Eight Essays,* Berry continues to berate those who carelessly exploit the natural environment and damage the underlying moral fabric of communities. David Rains Wallace observed in the *San Francisco Review of Books:* "There's no living essayist better than Wendell Berry. His prose is exemplary of the craftsmanship he advocates. It's like master cabinetry or Shaker furniture, drawing elegance from precision and grace from simplicity." Wallace allowed that at times, "Berry may overestimate agriculture's ability to assure order and stability," yet he maintained that the author's "attempts to integrate ecological and agricultural thinking remain of the first importance."

Life Is a Miracle: An Essay against Modern Superstition addresses the assumption, held by many, that science will provide solutions to all the world's problems and mysteries. Berry conceived this book as a rebuttal to prominent Harvard University biologist Edward O. Wilson's *Consilience,* which put forth as a thesis the overarching power of science. *Wilson Quarterly* contributor Gregg Easterbrook called Berry's book "a nuanced and thought-provoking critique," while *Washington Monthly* reviewer Bill McKibben observed that "Berry offers a rich variety of responses, never intimidated by the scientific prowess of his rival." Jonathan Z. Larsen suggested in the *Amicus Journal,* though, that perhaps "Wilson has made too convenient a whipping boy," and noted that Wilson and Berry have taken some similar stands, with both voicing great concern about the environment. Larsen also maintained that Berry needs to provide more detailed prescriptions for achieving his ideal society, one filled with reverence for one's land and community. Larsen had praise for the book as well, especially for Berry's writing style, which works at "winning the reader over almost as much through poetry as through logic."

Berry's *Citizenship Papers* characteristically focuses on agrarian concerns, but also turns its attention to the post-9/11 world in several of its nineteen essays. "A Citizen's Response to the New National Security Strategy" focuses on the U.S. government's response to terrorist threats via the Patriotism Act; originally published in the *New York Times,* the four-part statement "probes the definitions of terrorism and security; the role of a government in combating evil; national security based on charity, civility, independence, true patriotism, and rule of law; and the failure of Christianity, Judaism, and Islam to reject war as a vehicle to peace," explained *Sojourners* contributor Rose Marie Berger. In *Booklist* Ray Olson dubbed the author "one of English's finest stylists, as perspicuous as T.H. Huxley at his best and as perspicacious as John Ruskin at his." While Olson maintained that Berry adopts an approach to America's ills "embracing life and community," a *Kirkus* contributor wrote that in the "clangor of worries" echoing in *Citizenship Papers* Berry presents readers with "the antidotes of civility, responsibility, curiosity, skill, kindness, and an awareness of the homeplace."

Farming and community are central to Berry's fiction as well as his poetry and essays. Most of his novels and short stories are set in the fictional Kentucky town of Port William. Like his real-life home town, Port Royal, Port William is a long-established farming community situated near the confluence of the Ohio and Kentucky Rivers. In books such as *Nathan Coulter: A Novel, A Place on Earth: A Novel, The Wild Birds: Six Stories of the Port William Membership,* and *Jayber Crow: The Life Story of Jayber Crow, Barber, of the Port William Membership,* Berry presents the lives of seven generations of farm families. Although *Fidelity: Five Stories* examines Port William in the early 1990s, most of Berry's narratives about the community take place in the first half of the twentieth century; as *Dictionary of Literary Biography* contributor Gary Tolliver explained, "This represents the final days of America's traditional farm communities just prior to the historically critical period when they began to break apart under the influence of technological and economic forces at the end of World War II." Connecting all the stories is the theme of stewardship of the land, which Tolliver said is "often symbolized as interlocking marriages between a man and his family, his community, and the land." What emerges, *Los Angeles Times Book Review* contributor Noel Perrin commented, "is a wounded but still powerful culture."

Jayber Crow, dealing in part with the title character's unrequited love for a married woman, also "strives for something greater, becoming nothing less than a sad and sweeping elegy for the idea of community, a horrifying signal of what we lost in the twentieth century in the name of economic and social progress," related Dean Bakopoulos in the *Progressive. World and I* reviewer Donald Secreast observed that this novel's "basic building block is the recurring metaphor of place as character, a concern that also dominates Berry's nonfiction and poetry. . . . The relationship between landscape and personality is the core concern of Berry's campaign to make people more responsible, more accountable for the effects their lifestyles have on local environments." A flaw Secreast saw in *Jayber Crow* is the sketchy characterization of women and the lack of importance attached to their role in the community. While rural societies have traditionally been male-dominated, Secreast noted, Berry's Port William seems to be less a reflection of rural life as it once existed than a portrayal of rural life as it should be, or should have been. "So if he's not being nostalgic, why should he be bound by the actual dynamics of a real rural community?" Secreast wrote. "Why must Jayber Crow, despite his sensitivity, insist upon his marginalization from the womanhood of Port William?"

On the other hand, *Hannah Coulter: A Novel* centers fully on Port William life from a female perspective. In the style of a memoir, Hannah muses on her life in a countryside that she never expected to change. Hannah's first marriage in 1940 leaves her a widow of World War II and a single mother. Her subsequent marriage to farmer Nathan Coulter ensures, enriching her life with additional children, none of whom remain on the land to work the family farm. Will Nathan's death mark the end of life as Hannah knew it and as she presumed it would remain? A *Publishers Weekly* contributor complimented Berry for his "delicate, shimmering prose" and recommended the novel as "an impassioned, literary vision of American rural life and values." In similar fashion, a *Kirkus Reviews* writer called *Hannah Coulter* "a kind of elegy for the starkly beautiful country life that . . . faded into history, victim of economic and social change."

For a more general overview of life in Port William, readers can immerse themselves in *That Distant Land: The Collected Stories of Wendell Berry*. The stories, which include four not previously published, span a century in the life of the fictional farming community. The locale connects its diverse inhabitants—man, woman, farmer, teacher, lawyer, each struggling in his or her own way to maintain the simple lifestyle of times almost gone by. "Berry is an American treasure," wrote Ann H. Fisher in *Library Journal* review of the collection. A contributor to *Publishers Weekly* observed that the author's "feel for the inner lives of his quirky rural characters makes for many memorable portraits."

Berry's writing style varies greatly from one book to the next. *Nathan Coulter*, for example, is an example of the highly stylized, formal, spare prose that dominated the late 1950s, while *A Place on Earth* was described by Tolliver as "long, brooding, episodic" and "more a document of consciousness than a conventional novel." Several critics have praised Berry's fiction, both for the quality of his prose and for the way he brings his concerns for farming and community to life in his narratives. As Gregory L. Morris stated in *Prairie Schooner*, "Berry places his emphasis upon the *rightness* of relationships—relationships that are elemental, inherent, inviolable. . . . Berry's stories are constructed of humor, of elegy, of prose that carries within it the cadences of the hymn. The narrative voice most successful in Berry's novels . . . is the voice of the elegist, praising and mourning a way of life and the people who have traced that way in their private and very significant histories."

Considering Berry's body of work, Charles Hudson pointed out the author's versatility and commended him for his appreciation of the plain things in life. "In an age when many writers have committed themselves to their 'specialty'—even though doing so can lead to commercialism, preciousness, self-indulgence, social irresponsibility, or even nihilism—Berry has refused to specialize," Hudson wrote in the *Georgia Review*. "He is a novelist, a poet, an essayist, a naturalist, *and* a small farmer. He has embraced the commonplace and has ennobled it."

BIOGRAPHICAL AND CRITICAL SOURCES:

BOOKS

Angyal, Andrew J., *Wendell Berry*, Twayne (New York, NY), 1995.
Contemporary Literary Criticism, Thomson Gale (Detroit, MI), Volume 4, 1975, Volume 6, 1976, Volume 27, 1984, Volume 46, 1988.
Dictionary of Literary Biography, Thomson Gale (Detroit, MI), Volume 5: *American Poets since World War II*, 1980, Volume 6: *American Novelists since World War II*, 1980.
Merchant, Paul, editor, *Wendell Berry*, Confluence (Lewiston, ID), 1991.

PERIODICALS

American Spectator, December, 1990, pp. 51-52.
Amicus Journal, fall, 2000, Jonathan Z. Larsen, review of *Life Is a Miracle: An Essay against Modern Superstition*, p. 34.
Best Sellers, December 1, 1970, pp. 374-375.
Booklist, September 1, 2003, Ray Olson, review of *Citizenship Papers*, p. 28; January 1, 2004, review of *Citizenship Papers*, p. 775.
Boston University Journal, Volume 25, number 3, 1978, pp. 69-72.
Choice, October, 2002, L.S. Cline, review of *The Art of the Commonplace*, p. 298.
Christian Century, June 19, 1996, p. 663.
Christian Science Monitor, March 2, 1984, p. B4; July 3, 1987, pp. B1, B8.
Commonweal, June 6, 1986, pp. 345-346; October 12, 1990, pp. 582-584.
Critique, spring, 2000, Rufus Cook, "The Art of Uncertainty," p. 227.
Georgia Review, winter, 1977-78, pp. 579-581; spring, 1982, pp. 220-223; summer, 1982, pp. 341-347.
Hudson Review, winter, 1986, pp. 681-694; summer, 1993, pp. 395-402.
Iowa Review, winter, 1979, pp. 99-104.
Kirkus Reviews, July 1, 2003, review of *Citizenship Papers*, p. 890; September 15, 2004, review of *Hannah Coulter: A Novel*, p. 880.
Library Journal, April 15, 2004, Ann H. Fisher, review of *That Distant Land: The Collected Stories of Wendell Berry*, p. 128; August 1, 2005, review of *Given: New Poems*, p. 89.
Los Angeles Times Book Review, April 27, 1986, p. 6; November 6, 1988, p. 4; January 10, 1993, p. 8.
Nation, November 9, 1970, pp. 472-474.

National Review, November 14, 1967.

New Perspectives Quarterly, spring, 1992, pp. 29-34.

New York, May 3, 1986, pp. 626-627.

New York Review of Books, June 14, 1990, pp. 30-34.

New York Times Book Review, September 25, 1977; December 20, 1981; December 18, 1983, pp. 8, 16; November 24, 1985, pp. 28-29; April 13, 1986, p. 22; September 27, 1987, p. 30; January 1, 1989, p. 14; November 15, 1992, p. 20; October 17, 1993.

Parabola, fall, 1993.

Parnassus, spring-summer, 1974; fall, 1981, pp. 131-154; January, 1989, pp. 317-330.

Partisan Review, Volume 44, number 2, 1977, p. 317.

Poetry, May, 1974; October, 1985, pp. 40-42; April, 1988, pp. 37-38; April, 1995, p. 38; May, 2000, Henry Taylor, review of *The Selected Poems of Wendell Berry,* p. 96.

Prairie Schooner, fall, 1971, pp. 273-274; winter, 1986, pp. 102-104.

Progressive, December, 2000, Dean Bakopoulos, review of *Jayber Crow: The Life Story of Jayber Crow, Barber, of the Port William Membership As Written by Himself,* p. 41.

Publishers Weekly, April 5, 2004, review of *That Distant Land,* p. 41; October 4, 2004, review of *Hannah Coulter,* p. 66.

Renascence, summer, 1983, pp. 258-268; winter, 2000, Laird Christensen, "Spirit Astir in the World: Wendell Berry's Sacramental Poetry," p. 163.

San Francisco Review of Books, winter, 1988-89, pp. 49-50.

Sewanee Review, summer, 1974.

Shenandoah, autumn, 1969.

Sojourners, May-June, 2003, Rose Marie Berger, "One Citizen's Shining Light," p. 57.

Southern Review, October, 1974, pp. 865-877; October, 1976, pp. 879-890; autumn, 1984, pp. 958-968.

Stand, autumn, 1993, p. 81.

Studies in Short Fiction, winter, 1994, pp. 117-118.

Times Literary Supplement, April 10, 1981, p. 416; June 26, 1987, p. 698.

Village Voice, December 23-29, 1981, p. 47.

Virginia Quarterly Review, spring, 1983, p. 62; spring, 1989, p. 56; summer, 1991, pp. 88-89.

Washington Monthly, June, 2000, Bill McKibben, review of *Life Is a Miracle,* p. 52.

Washington Post Book World, January 1, 1982, p. 5; March 13, 1983, p. 10; November 24, 1993, p. C2.

Whole Earth Review, spring, 1996, p. 75.

Wilson Quarterly, summer, 2000, Gregg Easterbrook, review of *Life Is a Miracle,* p. 131.

World and I, November, 2000, Donald Secreast, "Lessons from a Bootleg Community," p. 249.

BERRY, Wendell Erdman
   See BERRY, Wendell

*   *   *

BETHLEN, T.D.
   See SILVERBERG, Robert

*   *   *

BINCHY, Maeve 1940-

PERSONAL: Born May 28, 1940, in Dalkey, Ireland; daughter of William T. (a lawyer) and Maureen (a nurse; maiden name, Blackmore) Binchy; married Gordon Thomas Snell (a writer and broadcaster), January 29, 1977. *Education:* University College, Dublin, B.A., 1960.

ADDRESSES: Home—Dalkey, Ireland. *Home and office*—P.O. Box 6737, Dun Laoghaire, Dublin, Ireland. *Agent*—Christine Green, 2 Barbon Close, Great Ormond St., London WC1 N3JX, England.

CAREER: Zion Schools, Dublin, Ireland, French teacher; Pembroke School for Girls, Dublin, history and Latin teacher, 1961- 68; *Irish Times,* Dublin, columnist, 1968-2000; writer.

AWARDS, HONORS: International Television Festival Golden Prague Award, Czechoslovak Television, Prague, and Jacobs Award, both 1979, both for *Deeply Regretted By;* Lifetime Achievement Award, British Book Awards, 1999; W.H. Smith Fiction Award, 2001, for *Scarlet Feather.*

WRITINGS:

NOVELS

Light a Penny Candle, Century (London, England), 1982, Viking (New York, NY), 1983.

Echoes, Century (London, England), 1985, Viking (New York, NY), 1986.

Firefly Summer, Century (London, England), 1987, Delacorte Press (New York, NY), 1988.

Silver Wedding, Century (London, England), 1988, Delacorte Press (New York, NY), 1989.

Circle of Friends, Franklin Library (Franklin Center, PA), 1990.

The Copper Beech, Delacorte Press (New York, NY), 1992.

The Glass Lake, Delacorte Press (New York, NY), 1995.

Evening Class, Delacorte Press (New York, NY), 1996.

Tara Road, illustrated by Wendy Shea, Delacorte Press (New York, NY), 1999.

Scarlet Feather, Orion (London, England), 2000, Dutton (New York, NY), 2001.

Quentins, Dutton (New York, NY), 2002.

Two Complete Novels (includes *Circle of Friends* and *The Copper Beech*), Wings Books (New York, NY), 2003.

Nights of Rain and Stars, Dutton (New York, NY), 2004.

STORY COLLECTIONS

The Central Line: Stories of Big City Life (also see below), Quartet (London, England), 1978.

Victoria Line (also see below), Quartet (London, England), 1980.

Maeve Binchy's Dublin Four, Ward River Press (Swords, Ireland), 1982, published as *Dublin Four,* Century (London, England), 1983.

London Transports (contains *The Central Line: Stories of Big City Life* and *Victoria Line*), Century (London, England), 1983.

The Lilac Bus: Stories, Ward River Press, 1984, Delacorte Press (New York, NY), 1991.

This Year It Will Be Different and Other Stories: A Christmas Treasury, Delacorte Press (New York, NY), 1996.

The Return Journey, Delacorte Press (New York, NY), 1998.

Ladies' Night at Finbar's Hotel, edited by Dermot Bolger, Harcourt (New York, NY), 2000.

OTHER

My First Book (journalism), Irish Times (Dublin, Ireland), 1976.

End of Term (one-act play), produced in Dublin, Ireland, at the Abbey Theatre, 1976.

The Half Promised Land (play), produced in Dublin, Ireland, 1979, produced in Philadelphia, PA, at Society Hill Playhouse, 1980.

Deeply Regretted By (television screenplay), Radio Telefis Eireann, 1979, also published as *Deeply Regretted By . . . ,* Arlen House (Galway, Ireland), 2005.

Maeve's Diary (nonfiction), Irish Times (Dublin, Ireland), 1979.

Ireland of the Welcomes (television screenplay), Radio Telefis Eireann, 1980.

Aches & Pains, illustrations by Wendy Shea, Delacorte Press (New York, NY), 2000.

Healing Hands: People Remember Nurses, photography by Ann Henrick, New Island (Dublin, Ireland), 2004.

Contributor to books, including *Portrait of the Artist As a Young Girl,* edited by John Quinn, Methuen (London, England), 1986; *Territories of the Voice: Contemporary Stories by Irish Women Writers,* edited by Louise De-Salvo, Kathleen Walsh D'Arcy, and Katherine Hogan, Beacon Press (Boston, MA), 1989; and *In Sunshine or in Shadow,* edited by Kate Cruise O'Brien and Mary Maher, Delacorte Press, 1998. Some of her plays have been produced by the Peacock Theater in Dublin, Ireland.

ADAPTATIONS: Echoes was made into a miniseries, televised in Great Britain in 1988 and in the United States on Public Broadcasting Service in 1990; *Circle of Friends* was made into a film, produced by Savory Pictures, which starred Chris O'Donnell and Minnie Driver; *Tara Road* was made into a film directed by Gillies McKinnon and produced by Noel Pearson.

WORK IN PROGRESS: Avoid Disappointment, a book of linked short stories.

SIDELIGHTS: Maeve Binchy is a versatile Irish writer who once reported on daily life in London for the *Irish Times.* She lived in London for almost fifteen years before taking up residence outside Dublin with husband and fellow writer Gordon Snell. "We have a lovely room with a long, long desk and two word processors," the novelist once said when asked about living with another writer. "We get on perfectly well sitting beside each other. Just the sound of the keyboard and the printer is all we hear. If one of us doesn't like what the other has said, the rule is ten minutes of sulking time . . . After that the sulks can be construed as being moody or difficult . . . We're not perfect in our judgment of each other's work, but at least we're honest. And normally we're praising—but if we don't like something, we say it straight out."

Binchy's novels, many of them best sellers, have won her critical acclaim and an international following. Set most frequently in rural Ireland, her stories of family life and intimate friendships appeal to a predominantly female audience. She has been praised as thorough in her storytelling and both astute and affectionate in her characterizations. Many of her female protagonists are women who take control of their lives in the midst of coping with such societal ills as alcoholism, adultery, and divorce. Binchy told a *People* magazine reporter that the message within her novels and short stories is that once people take charge of their lives, they can make things work out for the best. "And maybe that's a reassuring idea," she added. "I wouldn't like to be thought of as patting people on the head, but I wouldn't be at all offended by people who think my books are comforting." Critics note that although her writing sometimes lacks profundity, it transcends the superficiality frequently featured in popular romance novels through such subtle feminist undertones. "In 1963 we all played by the rules," commented Binchy to Cathy Edwards of the *San Francisco Review of Books.* "I want to write about people who make their own decisions. Women of my generation were fooled a bit—maybe all women are."

"Binchy's work, though marketed as romances, by no means fits that category precisely," noted a contributor to *Contemporary Novelists.* "Binchy, a longstanding columnist for the *Irish Times,* presents a realistic picture of the lives of women ordered within the rigidities of Catholic orthodoxy that forbid divorce and abortion. In her work, women's survival is predicated on the creation of powerful, though informal, networks of alliance and friendships that survive the vicissitudes of pregnancy, forced marriage, and alcoholism." As a writer for *Contemporary Popular Writers* elaborated, "Her sprawling narratives express a moral but tolerant sensibility." Critics either dismiss or applaud her particular genre as "women's fiction," or even, as Helen Birch of the *Independent* wrote, "600-page doorstoppers, beach books, fireside books." Most reviewers believe Binchy's work transcends these labels. Her accomplished prose contains shrewd, albeit sentimental, social analysis of Irish women's lives in the mid-to-late twentieth century.

Though best known for her novels, Binchy began her fiction-writing career with short stories and plays. As she once commented: "Because the kind of stories I used to write for the *Irish Times* had a fictional or almost dramatic element to them, sometimes I was approached by people in theater or television asking why didn't I try my hand at writing plays. And because I started everything in life a little bit later than everybody else (to be a cub journalist at twenty-eight was very old), I felt, OK, maybe at thirty-five, thirty-six, thirty-

seven I could start to write plays as well." Dublin's Abbey Theatre encouraged new talent and produced Binchy's *End of Term* in 1976.

Although one of her plays, *The Half Promised Land,* was eventually staged as far away as Philadelphia, Pennsylvania, Binchy fared far better with her efforts at writing short fiction. Her collections *London Transports* —originally published in two volumes as *Central Line* and *Victoria Line* —and *Maeve Binchy's Dublin Four* focus on the tedium of city life and the individual plights of female protagonists. In *London Transports,* for example, the women are often dissatisfied with their relationships with men and drawn into the corruption of Binchy's seedy London. *Times Literary Supplement* contributor Helen Harris pointed out that though the themes of *London Transports* are often bleak, Binchy writes with "ease and buoyancy." Harris also declared that the author's "portrayal of the small skirmishes of day-to-day urban survival is enjoyable; her wry observation of the different layers of London life is uncomfortably acute."

Binchy's 1996 collection, *This Year It Will Be Different and Other Stories: A Christmas Treasury,* received mixed assessments. A *Publishers Weekly* critic appraised the volume's stories as "formulaic and superficial." A *Kirkus Reviews* contributor was more positive, however, recommending the "collection of Christmas-centered feel-good tales" as a "bit of sentimentality and a touch of romance, along with humor and hopeful turns to treat . . . the holiday blues." *The Return Journey,* Binchy's 1998 volume, also received uneven, if not unflattering, reviews. A *Publishers Weekly* reviewer declared the work "unimpressive," faulting Binchy for, among other things, "predictable plot mechanisms" and "conclusions [that] are socked home, often in a chirpy manner." "Too many of these finely wrought tales reach their blissful destinations without hitting a single bump in the road," commented Erica Saunders in *People.*

A small rural town is the primary setting of Binchy's first novel, *Light a Penny Candle.* In this work, she depicts the twenty-year friendship of Elizabeth White and Aisling O'Connor. The girls meet when Elizabeth, a ten-year-old Londoner, is sent by her parents to live with the O'Connor family in Ireland at the start of World War II. Together the two friends experience the joys and hardships of growing up, and their close relationship endures despite such ordeals as Elizabeth's difficulties with her uncaring parents once back in London, Aisling's love affair with a onetime boyfriend of Elizabeth's, and both women's failed marriages. As in many of Binchy's stories, the book's male characters are often presented as insensitive, noncommittal, and the source of the women's problems. "It's been a while since I've enjoyed such a loutish, incompetent, drunken, selfish collection of men in one novel," remarked Carol Sternhell in the *Village Voice*. On the other hand, Sternhell found most of the female characters "practical, competent, and loving." Although some critics complained about what one reviewer, writing in *Harper's,* termed a "too heavy-handed and contrived" ending in which "one disaster after another comes crashing down too quickly," the novel received praise. "With its barreling plot and clamorous characters, *Light a Penny Candle* is a lilting book," asserted Dennis Drabelle in the *Washington Post Book World*. Sternhell called the author's effort an "impressive first novel" and proclaimed that "Binchy's strength is in her honesty: she refuses to trim all edges to get us drunk on easy answers."

In *Firefly Summer* Binchy, observed *New York Times Book Review* contributor Michele Slung, "once again gives us rural Ireland, a frequently maddening yet ultimately seductive place that can render problems only in contrasting shades of old and new, past and present, strange and familiar." Patrick O'Neill, the story's main character, is an American millionaire who comes to the Irish town of Mountfern in the 1960s with the goal of converting a dilapidated manor house into a luxury hotel. His experience in a town made up of people who are either eager or reluctant to accept his business venture is the subject of the novel. Slung thought that *Firefly Summer* "is the best Binchy yet . . . Here she does what she does best, which is to manufacture experience in which we fully share."

"With *Silver Wedding,* " noted Robert Plunket in the *New York Times Book Review,* "Binchy tries something a little bit different, and as she does so you can sense a remarkably gifted writer beginning to flex her muscles." Instead of focusing on the dynamics of small-town life, in her fourth novel, Binchy examines the personal conflicts of the members of one family and their friends. In the last chapter of the book, all of the characters unite for Deidre and Desmond Doyle's twenty-fifth wedding anniversary party. The author devotes each of the previous chapters to one individual in the story, ultimately revealing the emotions, resentments, and ambitions of a cast of characters whose lives are all connected in some way. Plunket pointed out that the author's choice of "guilty secrets" as one theme of *Silver Wedding* left him "wish[ing] she'd come up with something a bit more clever," but he acknowledged that "Binchy is a wonderful student of human nature" and described the book as "an effortless pleasure to read."

The importance that Binchy places on a writer's careful observation of people and places was expressed in a "how-to" article the author wrote for the *Writer.* "To get dialogue right, listen to everyone, everywhere—eavesdrop, follow people so you can hear what they are saying. To get a scene right for *Tara Road,* I spent two days watching mothers and teenage daughters buying clothes in a store. Never hang up on a crossed telephone line, watch people in planes and trains, and be vigilant the whole time." Binchy instructs writers to outline and adhere to a general time schedule for each of their books; to think through the story and the characters, making note cards for each; to plan goals for each chapter; and then to begin writing, and when writing to do so at a quick pace. "Don't pause for breath, punctuation, too much analysis," stated Binchy. She advises writers to fully imagine their characters, their appearance, their actions, and reactions: "If you pretend they are real people, they will become so," she said. Among other pointers, Binchy told writers to refrain from analyzing the worth of their writing. "Just keep going," she urged, advocating a style in the manner of a writer's own speech: "I write exactly as I speak; I don't roll each sentence around and examine it carefully before letting it loose. If you speak in your own voice, you can never be accused of being pretentious or showing off; you can just be yourself, and that's a huge advantage in anybody."

Asked by *Writer* interviewer Lewis Burke Frumkes to explain her theory on her wide appeal—Binchy's writing has been translated into numerous languages and her books have outsold literary giants such as James Joyce and William Butler Yeats—Binchy stated that her writing is geared for a mass audience, unlike Joyce and Yeats: "The thing is, if you were going on a journey and you were thinking, I must read something on the plane, and if you had read any of my books before you would think, well, she tells a good story. . . . For some reason I have hit upon a form of story telling that appeals to people in different languages. I suppose they have also felt love and hope and pain, and they have had dreams and had the delight of close families and the more irritating aspects of close families. They have, perhaps, also loved people who haven't loved them in return and also might have wanted to go up to the bright lights of a big city . . . but the principle is the same. You have people who are young and enthusiastic and want to try to achieve their dream, and I think that is why people everywhere like [the characters]."

Circle of Friends also became a best seller. Set in the 1950s, the book revolves around three young women with contrasting personalities who come of age and develop a close friendship while attending University College in Dublin. Although Susan Isaacs suggested in the *New York Times Book Review* that "a cynical reader might reflect [that] this sort of fiction is so commonplace that the characters will be completely fungible," she lauded Binchy for portraying her protagonists as "modern women, each, in her own way, ambitious, intelligent, perceptive." Isaacs summed up the reason for Binchy's immense popularity when she declared that "the author doesn't daze the reader with narrative bombshells (or, for that matter, with brilliant language), but recounts ordinary events . . . with extraordinary straightforwardness and insight."

The Copper Beech, a set of interlinking stories set in the small Irish village during the 1940s and 1950s, "has its share of murder, adultery, alcoholism, unwanted pregnancies and lots more," Anne Tolstoi Wallach commented in the *New York Times Book Review.* "Bad things happen to good people, good things happen to bad people, but because this is the new Maeve Binchy it all comes right in the end." Of *Evening Class,* a *Publishers Weekly* reviewer wrote, "Fans of Binchy's nimble story telling skills, and of her characters, who are always decent without being dull, won't want to change a thing." Jan Blodgett, writing for *Library Journal,* called the book "a complex tale of loves lost, betrayal, loyalty, and renewed courage." For the type of story it is, *Evening Class* is "satisfying," wrote a *Kirkus Reviews* critic, who described the characters as "a flock of middle-and lower- middle [class] worriers, loners, and groaners, all brooding on their peculiar miseries, until an updraft of love or happy coincidences set them free."

Tara Road revolves around two women who swap houses, and to some extent lives, for a summer. Both are mothers: Marilyn is an American living in New England and mourning the death of her teenaged son; Ria is a resident of Dublin who is completely shocked when her husband leaves her for another woman whom he impregnated. A *Kirkus Reviews* contributor declared *Tara Road* "one of Binchy's best." "Once again, Binchy . . . memorably limns the lives of ordinary people caught in the traps sprung by life and loving hearts," stated the critic. Through the course of the story, the women learn about each other as well as themselves. In a *Booklist* review, Brad Hooper called Binchy "a careful writer and a conscientious plotter."

Scarlet Feather was greeted with critical praise and, according to a *Publishers Weekly* reviewer, "Binchy's gift for creating a wide range of characters whose foibles

and challenges make them lovable and real, coupled with her theme that genuine love can transform lives, add up to another crowd- pleaser." Hooper commented: "Binchy writes domestic drama at its most realistic and moving, and her adoring fans will appreciate her latest work." Her fans might have appreciated it more had Binchy not announced that *Scarlet Feather* would be her last novel. According to Christina Cheakalos writing for *People,* after reading the announcement in Binchy's *Irish Times* column, "More than 800 readers wrote in to say don't go." Writing in *Chatelaine,* reviewer Bonnie Schiedel commented, "She's going out on a proverbial high note," calling *Scarlet Feather* "a delicious read."

Regardless of her announcement, Binchy made a surprise return and produced another novel, *Quentins,* which continued with the modern Dublin theme she used in *Tara Road* and *Scarlet Feather.* A *Publishers Weekly* reviewer commented: "Fans of the bestselling Binchy will be grateful that the basic formula is still intact—decent people pulling through hard times—and that some favorite characters from previous novels reappear." This is a story in which the inhabitants are proud of their cosmopolitan attitudes and, as Christine C. Menefee pointed out in *School Library Journal,* "underlying [the characters'] lives and choices are strengths of family and friendship, and a loving kindness, that still confirm the outsider's hopeful expectations about traditional Irish culture."

Binchy delighted readers again with yet another post-retirement novel in 2004. In *Nights of Rain and Stars* a boating accident brings together four vacationing strangers who have arrived in Greece to distance themselves from difficult family situations at home. Carol Haggas, writing for *Booklist,* called the novel "a rich homage to meaningful relationships."

BIOGRAPHICAL AND CRITICAL SOURCES:

BOOKS

Bestsellers 90, Issue 1, Gale (Detroit, MI), 1990, pp. 3-4.
Contemporary Novelists, 6th edition, St. James Press (Detroit, MI), 1996.
Contemporary Popular Writers, St. James Press (Detroit, MI), 1997.
Twentieth-Century Romance and Historical Writers, 3rd edition, St. James Press (Detroit, MI), 1994.

PERIODICALS

Booklist, December 15, 1998, Brad Hooper, review of *Tara Road,* p. 706; December 15, 2000, Brad Hooper, review of *Scarlet Feather,* p. 763; July, 2004, Carol Haggas, review of *Nights of Rain and Stars,* p. 1796.

British Book News, May, 1986, p. 308.

Chatelaine, October, 2000, Bonnie Schiedel, "Tea and Empathy," p. 18.

Chicago Tribune, March 17, 1991, section 6, p. 3; October 27, 1991, section 14, pp. 3, 11.

Cosmopolitan, February, 1995, Chris Chase, review of *The Glass Lake,* p. 18.

Detroit Free Press, December 23, 1990.

Harper's, April, 1983, review of *Light a Penny Candle,* pp. 75- 76.

Independent, May 12, 1995, Helen Birch, interview with Binchy, p. 25.

Kirkus Reviews, August 1, 1996, review of *This Year It Will Be Different and Other Stories: A Christmas Treasury;* January 1, 1997, review of *Evening Class;* December 1, 1998, review of *Tara Road.*

Library Journal, February 1, 1997, Jan Blodgett, review of *Evening Class,* p. 104; February 1, 1999, Carol J. Bissett, review of *Tara Road,* p. 118; September 1, 1999, Barbara Valle, review of *Tara Road,* p. 252; September 13, 1999, Daisy Maryles, "Irish Eyes Are Smiling," p. 20; March 1, 2000, review of *Aches and Pains,* p. S10; August, 2004, Carol J. Bissett, review of *Nights of Rain and Stars,* p. 63.

Los Angeles Times, February 6, 1986; January 14, 1991, p. E3.

New York Times Book Review, January 12, 1986, Kiki Olson, review of *Echoes,* p. 20; September 18, 1988, Michele Slung, review of *Firefly Summer,* p. 13; September 10, 1989, Robert Plunket, review of *Silver Wedding,* p. 18; December 30, 1990, Susan Isaacs, review of *Circle of Friends,* p. 8; December 8, 1991, John Kenny Crane, review of *The Lilac Bus,* p. 22; December 29, 1992, p. 16.

People, December 14, 1992, pp. 34-35; March 30, 1998, Erica Saunders, review of *The Return Journey,* p. 31; August 28, 2000, Christina Cheakalos, "A Novel Retirement," p. 147.

Publishers Weekly, August 26, 1996, review of *This Year It Will Be Different and Other Stories,* p. 74; January 6, 1997, review of *Evening Class,* p. 62; February 16, 1998, review of *The Return Journey,* p. 201; December 21, 1998, review of *Tara Road,* p. 51; April 17, 2000, "June Publications," p. 70; January 8, 2001, review of *Scarlet Feather,* p. 45; September 23, 2002, review of *Quentins,* p. 50.

San Francisco Review of Books, winter, 1992, pp. 6-7.

School Library Journal, February, 2003, Christine C. Menefee, review of *Quentins,* p. 172.

Times Educational Supplement, May 24, 1991, p. 38.

Times Literary Supplement, November 28, 1980, p. 1366; April 1, 1983, p. 324; March 30, 1984, p. 354.

Village Voice, May 17, 1983, Carol Sternhell, review of *Light a Penny Candle,* p. 50.

Washington Post, January 17, 1986; September 11, 1989, p. D3; December 24, 1990, p. C3; November 7, 1991, p. C3.

Washington Post Book World, May 1, 1983, Dennis Drabelle, review of *Light a Penny Candle,* p. 10.

Writer, February, 2000, Maeve Binchy, "Welcome to My Study," p. 12, and Lewis Burke Frumkes, interview with Binchy, p. 14.

ONLINE

Maeve Binchy Home Page http://www.maevebinchy. com/ (February 15, 2006).

*   *   *

BIRD, Cordwainer
See ELLISON, Harlan

*   *   *

BIRDWELL, Cleo
See DeLILLO, Don

*   *   *

BLAIS, Marie-Claire 1939-

PERSONAL: Born October 5, 1939, in Quebec City, Quebec, Canada; daughter of Fernando and Veronique (Nolin) Blais. *Education:* Attended Pensionnat St. Roch in Quebec and Harvard University; studied literature and philosophy at Laval University in Quebec. *Religion:* Catholic.

ADDRESSES: Agent—Agence Goodwin, 839, rue Sherbrooke Est., bureau 200, Montreal, Quebec H2L 1K6, Canada.

CAREER: Full-time writer. Did clerical work, 1956-57.

MEMBER: Academie Royale de la Belgique, Compagnon de l'Order du Canada, Order of Quebec, PEN, Union des Auteurs Dramatiques, Union des Ecrivains, Writers Union of Canada.

AWARDS, HONORS: Prix de la Langue Francaise, L'Academie Francaise, 1961, for *La Belle bete;* Guggenheim fellowships, 1963 and 1964; Le Prix France-Quebec (Paris) and Prix Medicis (Paris), both 1966, for *Une Saison dans la vie d'Emmanuel;* Prix du Gouverneur General du Canada, 1969, for *Les Manuscrits de Pauline Archange,* 1979, for *Le Sourd dans la ville,* and 1996, for *Soifs;* elected member of Order of Canada, 1975; honorary doctorates, York University (Toronto), 1975, and Victoria University; Prix Belgique-Canada (Bruxelles), 1976, for body of work; named honorary professor of humanities, Calgary University, 1978; Prix Athanase-David, 1982, for body of work; Prix de L'Academie Francaise, 1983, for *Visions d'Anna;* Prix Wessim Habif, Academie Royale de langue et de litterature francaises de Belgique, 1990, for body of work; honorary doctorate, University of Victoria (British Columbia), 1990; Commemorative Medal of the 125th Anniversary of the Confederation of Canada, 1992; Elue a L'Academie Royale de langue et de litterature francaises de Belgique, 1993; Ordre National du Quebec, 1995; Prix du Gouverneur General du Canada, 1996, for *Soifs;* W.O. Mitchell Literary Prize, 2000, for body of work.

WRITINGS:

FICTION

La Belle bete (novel), Institut Litteraire du Quebec, 1959, translation by Merloyd Lawrence published as *Mad Shadows,* Little, Brown (Boston), 1961.

Tete Blanche (novel), Institut Litteraire du Quebec, 1960, translation by Charles Fullman, Little, Brown, 1961.

Le Jour est noir (novella), Editions du Jour (Montreal), 1962, translated by Derek Coltman as *The Day Is Dark,* Farrar, Strauss (New York City), 1966.

Pays voiles (poems), Garneau (Quebec), 1964.

Existences (poems), Garneau, 1964.

Une Saison dans la vie d'Emmanuel (novel), Editions du Jour, 1965, translation by Derek Coltman published as *A Season in the Life of Emmanuel,* introduction by Edmund Wilson, Farrar, Straus, 1966.

Les Voyageurs sacres (novella; also see below), HMH Hurtubise (Montreal), 1966, translated by Coltman as *The Three Travelers,* Farrar, Strauss, 1966.

L'Insoumise (novel), Editions du Jour, 1966, translation by David Lobdell published as *The Fugitive,* Oberon (Toronto), 1978.

The Day Is Dark [and] *The Three Travelers,* Farrar, Straus, 1967.

David Sterne (novel), Editions du Jour, 1967, translation by David Lobdell, McClelland & Stewart (Toronto), 1972.

Pays voiles et Existences (poems), Les Editions de l'Homme (Montreal), 1967.

Les Manuscrits de Pauline Archange (novel), Editions du Jour, 1968, translation by Coltman published with translation of *Vivre! Vivre!: La Suite des Manuscrits de Pauline Archange* (also see below) as *The Manuscripts of Pauline Archange,* Farrar, Straus, 1970.

Vivre! Vivre!: La Suite des Manuscrits de Pauline Archange (novel), Editions du Jour, 1969.

Les Apparences (novel), Editions du Jour, 1971, translation by Lobdell published as *Duerer's Angel,* McClelland & Stewart, 1974.

Le Loup (novel), Editions du Jour, 1972, translation by Sheila Fischman published as *The Wolf,* McClelland & Stewart, 1974.

Un Joualonais sa Joualonie (novel), Editions du Jour, 1973, published as *A Coeur joual,* Robert Laffont, 1977, translation by Ralph Manheim published as *St. Lawrence Blues,* Farrar, Straus, 1975.

Une Liaison parisienne (novel), Editions Stanke/Quinze (Montreal), 1975, translation by Fischman published as *A Literary Affair,* McClelland & Stewart, 1979.

Les Nuits de l'underground (novel), Les Editions Internationales Alain Stanke (Montreal), 1978, translation by Ray Ellenwood published as *Nights in the Underground: An Exploration of Love,* General Publishing (Toronto), 1979.

Le Sourd dans la ville (novel), Les Editions Internationales Alain Stanke, 1979, translation by Carol Dunlop published as *Deaf to the City,* Lester & Orpen Dennys (Toronto), 1980.

(Editor with Richard Teleky) *The Oxford Book of French-Canadian Short Stories,* Oxford University Press (Toronto), 1980.

Visions d'Anna (novel), Les Editions Internationales Alain Stanke, 1982, translation by Fischman published as *Anna's World,* Lester & Orpen Dennys, 1985.

Pays voiles-Existences, Stanke, 1983, translation by Michael Harris published as *Veiled Countries* in *Veiled Countries* [and] *Lives,* Vehicule Press, 1984.

Pierre ou la guerre du printemps 81, Primeur (Montreal), 1984, translation by David Lobdell and Philip Stradford, Oberon, 1993.

L'Ange de la Solitude, VLB Editeur (Montreal), 1989, translation by Laura Hodes published as *The Angel of Solitude,* Talonbooks (Vancouver), 1993.

L'Exile (short stories; sequel to *Les Voyageurs sacres*), Bibliotheque Quebecoise (Montreal), 1992, translation by Nigel Spencer published as *The Exile & The Sacred Travellers,* Ronsdale Press (Vancouver, Canada), 2000.

Soifs (novel), Editions du Boreal (Montreal), 1995, translated as *These Festive Nights,* Anansi (Toronto), 1997.

L'instant fragile, Humanitas, 1995.

Oeuvre poetique, Editions du Boreal, 1997.

Thunder and Light, translation by Nigel Spencer, House of Anansi Press (Toronto, Canada), 2001.

PLAYS

La roulotte aux poupees, produced in Quebec, 1960, translation televised as *The Puppet Caravan,* 1967.

Eleanor, produced in Quebec, 1962.

L'execution (two-act; produced at Theatre du Rideau Vert, Montreal, 1968), Editions du Jour, 1968, translation by David Lobdell published as *The Execution,* Talonbooks, 1976.

(With Nicole Brossard, Marthe Blackburn, Luce Guilbeault, France Theoret, Odette Gagnon, and Pol Pelletier) *Marcelle* in *La nef des sorcieres* (produced at Theatre du Nouveau Monde, 1976), Quinze Editeurs, 1977, translation by Linda Gaboriau published as *A Clash of Symbols,* Coach House Press (Toronto), 1979.

Sommeil d'hiver, Editions de la Pleine Lune (Montreal), 1986, translated as *Wintersleep,* Ronsdale (Vancouver), 1998.

L'ile (produced at Theatre l'Eskabel, 1988), VLB Editeur (Montreal), 1988, translated as *The Island,* Operon (Vancouver), 1991.

(Collection) *Theatre,* Editions du Boreal, 1998.

Also author of *Fiere,* 1985, and *Un Jardin dans la tempete* (broadcast in 1990), translated by David Lobdell as *A Garden in the Storm.*

RADIO PLAYS

Le disparu, Radio-Canada, 1971.

L'envahisseur, Radio-Canada, 1972.

Deux destins, Radio-Canada, 1973.

Fievre, Radio-Canada, 1973.

Une autre Vie, Radio-Canada, 1974.

Fievre, et autres textes dramatiques: theatre radiophonique (includes *L'envahisseur, Le disparu, Deux destins,* and *Un couple*), Editions du Jour, 1974.

Un couple, Radio-Canada, 1975.

Une femme et les autres, Radio-Canada, 1976.

L'enfant-video, Radio-Canada, 1977.

Murmures, Radio-Canada, 1977.

L'ocean suivi de Murmures (produced by Radio-Canada, 1976), Quinze (Montreal), 1977, translation of *L'ocean* by Ray Chamberlain published as *The Ocean,* Exile, 1977, translation of *Murmures* by Margaret Rose published in *Canadian Drama/L'art dramatique Canadien,* fall, 1979.

Journal en images froides, Radio-Canada, 1978.

L'exile, L'escale, Radio-Canada, 1979.

Le fantome d'une voix, Radio-Canada, 1980.

Textes radiophoniques, Boreal, 1999.

OTHER

Voies de peres, voix de filles, Lacombe, 1988.

Parcours d'un ecrivain notes americaines (autobiographic notebooks), VLB Editeur, 1993, translated as *American Notebooks: A Writer's Journey,* Talonbooks, 1996.

Des rencontres humaines (biography), Editions Trois-Pistoles (Paroisse Notre-Dame-des-Neiges, Quebec, Canada), 2002.

A collection of Blais's manuscripts is housed in the National Library of Canada, Ottawa.

ADAPTATIONS: Une Saison dans la vie d'Emmanuel, directed by Claude Weisz, 1968; *Le Sourd dans la ville,* directed by Mireille Dansereau, 1987; *L'Ocean* was adapted for television, directed by Jean Faucher, Radio-Canada, 1971.

SIDELIGHTS: Marie-Claire Blais, according to Edmund Wilson in *O Canada: An American's Notes on Canadian Culture,* is "a writer in a class by herself." Although each of her novels is written in a different style and mood, "we know immediately," writes Raymond Rosenthal, "that we are entering a fully imagined world when we start reading any of her books." In 1964 Wilson wrote that Blais is a "true 'phenomenon'; she may possibly be a genius. At the age of twenty-four, she has produced four remarkable books of a passionate and poetic force that, as far as my reading goes, is not otherwise to be found in French Canadian fiction."

When Wilson read *A Season in the Life of Emmanuel* in 1965, he compared the novel to works by J.M. Synge and William Faulkner.

A Season in the Life of Emmanuel is "a particularly Canadian work of art," writes David Stouck, "for the sense of winter and of life's limitations (especially defined by poverty) are nowhere felt more strongly. Yet . . . these physical limitations serve to define the emotional deprivation that is being dramatized. That eroding sense of poverty is never externalized as a social issue, nor is the harshness of the Quebec landscape seen as an existentialist 'condition.' Rather, in the oblique and relentless manner of her writing Miss Blais remains faithful stylistically to the painful vision of her imagination and in so doing has created both a fully dramatic and genuinely Canadian work of art."

Writing in the *New York Times Book Review,* Robertson Davies claims that *The Day Is Dark* and *Three Travelers* are "less substantial than *A Season in the Life of Emmanuel,*" but, he adds, "all the writing of this extraordinary young woman is so individual, so unlike anything else being written on this continent, that admirers of her poetic vision of life may find them even more to their taste." Laurent LeSage, writing in *Saturday Review,* says of the two novellas: "Although the basic structures of fiction are still recognizable, they have been weakened and distorted to prevent any illusion of realistic dimension or true-to-life anecdote from distracting us from the author's intention. Without warning the narrative shifts from one character to another, chronology is jumbled, events are sometimes contradictory, and the fancied is never clearly separated from the real. By a series of interior monologues Mlle. Blais works along the lower levels of consciousness, and only rarely does she come to the surface. The world of her revery is the somber, shadowy one of primitive urges and responses. . . . Each [character] obeys a force that resembles a tragic predestination, leading [him] in a lonely quest through life to [his] final destruction." The novellas are actually prose poems, similar in some respects to works by Walter de la Mare. Rosenthal defines the genre as "a piece of prose that should be read more than once, preferably several times. If after reading it in the prescribed fashion," says Rosenthal, "the work assumes depth and color and value it did not have at the first reading, then the author has written a successful prose poem. In a prose poem each word counts and Mlle. Blais generally doesn't waste a syllable."

Rosenthal emphasizes that Blais has done much to "put Canada on the literary map." He says of her work: "Mlle. Blais leaves out a great deal, almost all the fa-

miliar furniture of fiction, and yet her characters have a tenacious life and her themes, though often convoluted and as evanescent as the mist that dominates so much of her imagination, strike home with surprising force." "With *David Sterne,*" writes Brian Vincent, "Mlle. Blais has placed herself firmly and uncompromisingly in the literary tradition of the French moralists leading back through Camus, Genet and Gide to Baudelaire. The book deals in one way or another with many of the themes explored by these writers, and this makes it somewhat derivative. It owes most, perhaps, to the more abstract and less sensational works of Jean Genet, in which the passionate existential wranglings, the rebellion, the life of crime and sensation are so prominent." The critic adds: "The confessional and didactic style of the book will also strike echoes in the reader's mind. But *David Sterne* survives and transcends these comparisons. What allows it to do so is the immense compassion and tenderness Mlle. Blais displays for her characters in their whirlwind of struggle and suffering. The hard cold eye she casts on the cruel world of *Mad Shadows* has grown into one full of pity and profound sadness for the fate of men condemned to do battle with themselves."

In 1979 Blais saw publication of *Deaf to the City,* a novel told in one book-length paragraph. "Blais," Marjorie A. Fitzpatrick explains in the *French Review,* "brings to life—and then to death—the inhabitants of the gloomy little Montreal hotel that serves as the novel's setting. Like voices in a fugue or threads in a well-made tapestry, their lives weave in and out through each other to form a harmonious (though depressing) whole." Writing in the *Dictionary of Literary Biography,* Eva-Marie Kroeller states that *Deaf to the City* "fuses prose and poetry even more radically than Blais's earlier works." Fitzpatrick concludes that "If Blais can sustain in future works the combination of human authenticity and tight technical mastery that she found in [*A Season in the Life of Emmanuel*] and has achieved again in [*Deaf to the City*], she may well come to stand out as one of the most powerful fiction writers of French expression of this generation."

A *Virginia Quarterly Review* writer concludes that Blais's novels are "to be read slowly and carefully for the unusual insights they present in often difficult but provocative images and sometimes demanding but intriguing technical innovations. This is a serious, talented and deeply effective writer." Kroeller calls Blais "one of the most prolific and influential authors of Quebec's literary scene since the late 1950s." Blais, Kroeller believes, "has firmly established an international reputation as a writer who combines strong roots in the literary tradition of her province with an affinity to existentialist fiction of Western Europe and the United States."

BIOGRAPHICAL AND CRITICAL SOURCES:

BOOKS

Contemporary Authors Autobiography Series, Volume 4, Thomson Gale (Detroit), 1986.
Contemporary Literary Criticism, Thomson Gale, Volume 2, 1974, Volume 4, 1975, Volume 6, 1976, Volume 13, 1980, Volume 22, 1982.
Dictionary of Literary Biography, Volume 53: *Canadian Writers since 1960, First Series,* Thomson Gale, 1986.
Fabi, Therese, *Le Monde perturbe des jeunes dans l'oeuvre romanesque de Marie-Claire Blais: sa vie, son oeuvre, la critique,* Editions Agence d'Arc (Montreal), 1973.
Feminist Writers, St. James Press (Detroit), 1996.
Gay and Lesbian Literature, St. James Press, 1994.
Goldmann, Lucien, *Structures mentales et creation culturelle,* Editions Anthropos (Paris), 1970.
Green, Mary Jean, *Marie-Claire Blais,* Twayne, 1995.
Marcotte, Gilles, *Notre roman a l'imparfait,* La Presse (Montreal), 1976.
Meigs, Mary, *Lily Briscoe: A Self-Portrait,* Talonbooks, 1981.
Meigs, *The Medusa Head,* Talonbooks, 1983.
Nadeau, Vincent, *Marie-Claire Blais: le noir et le tendre,* Presses de l'Universite de Montreal, 1974.
Oore, Irene, and Oriel C.L. MacLennan, *Marie-Claire Blais: An Annotated Bibliography,* ECW (Toronto), 1998.
Stratford, Philip, *Marie-Claire Blais,* Forum House, 1971.
Tilby, Michael, editor, *Beyond the Nouveau Roman,* Berg, 1990.
Wilson, Edmund, *O Canada: An American's Notes on Canadian Culture,* Farrar, Straus, 1965.

PERIODICALS

Books Abroad, winter, 1968.
Books in Canada, February, 1979, pp. 8-10.
Book Week, June 18, 1967.
Canadian Literature, spring, 1972.
Chatelaine, August, 1966.
Cite libre, July-August, 1966.
Coincidences, May-December, 1980.
Culture, March, 1968.
Dalhousie Review, summer, 1995, pp. 1-9; spring, 1997, pp. 143-52.
La Dryade, summer, 1967.
Etudes, February, 1967.
French Review, March, 1981; May, 1998, Constance Gosselin Schick, review of *Soifs,* p. 1088.
Globe and Mail (Toronto), March 30, 1985.
Journal of Canadian Fiction, Volume 2, number 4, 1973; number 25-26, 1979, pp. 186-98.
Journal of Popular Culture, winter, 1981, pp. 14-27.
La Revue de Paris, February, 1967.
Lettres Quebecoises, winter, 1979-80.
Livres et Auteurs Quebecois, 1972.
Los Angeles Times, September 18, 1987.
New Statesman, March 31, 1967.
New York Times Book Review, April 30, 1967; November 16, 1980, review of *A Season in the Life of Emmanuel,* p. 47; October 20, 1985, C. Gerald Fraser, review of *The Day Is Dark* and *Three Travelers,* p. 60; September 20, 1987, Paul West, *Death to the City,* p. 12.
Nous, June, 1973.
Novel, autumn, 1972, pp. 73-78.
Observer (London), April 2, 1967.
Quebec Studies, number 2, 1984.
Recherches Sociographiques, September-December, 1966.
Revue de l'Institut de Sociologie, Volume 42, number 3, 1969.
Romance Notes, autumn, 1973.
Saturday Review, April 29, 1967.
Sphinx, number 7, 1977.
Times Literary Supplement, March 30, 1967.
Virginia Quarterly Review, autumn, 1967.
Voix et Images, winter, 1983.
Weekend Magazine, October 23, 1976.
World Literature Today, autumn, 1997, Chantal Zabus, review of *Soifs,* p. 745.

*   *   *

BLADE, Alexander
See SILVERBERG, Robert

*   *   *

BLISS, Frederick
See CARD, Orson Scott

BLOCK, Francesca Lia 1962-

PERSONAL: Born December 3, 1962, in Hollywood, CA; daughter of Irving Alexander (a painter) and Gilda (a poet; maiden name, Klein) Block; married Chris Schuette (an actor), December 5, 1998; children: Jasmine Angelina, Samuel Alexander. *Education:* University of California—Berkeley, B.A., 1986. *Politics:* Democrat.

ADDRESSES: Home—Los Angeles, CA. *Agent*—Lydia Wills Artists Agency, 230 W. 55th Street, Ste. 29D, New York, NY 10019.

CAREER: Author and screenwriter.

MEMBER: Authors Guild, Authors League of America, Writers Guild of America, Phi Beta Kappa.

AWARDS, HONORS: Shrout Fiction Award, University of California—Berkeley, 1986; Emily Chamberlain Cook Poetry Award, 1986; Best Books of the Year citation, American Library Association (ALA), Best of the 1980s designation, *Booklist,* YASD Best Book Award, and Recommended Books for Reluctant Young Adult Readers citation, all 1989, all for *Weetzie Bat;* Recommended Books for Reluctant Young Adult Readers citation, 1990, for *Witch Baby;* ALA Best Books of the Year citation, Recommended Books for Reluctant Young Adult Readers citation, Best Books citation from the *New York Times,* and Best Fifty Books citation from *Publishers Weekly,* all 1991, all for *Cherokee Bat and the Goat Guys;* Best Books of the Year citations from *School Library Journal* and ALA, and Recommended Books for Reluctant Young Adult Readers, all 1993, all for *Missing Angel Juan;* Margaret A. Edwards Award, 2005, for lifetime contribution in writing for young adults; numerous other awards.

WRITINGS:

NOVELS

Weetzie Bat, HarperCollins (New York, NY), 1989.
Witch Baby, HarperCollins (New York, NY), 1990.
Cherokee Bat and the Goat Guys, HarperCollins (New York, NY), 1991.
Missing Angel Juan, HarperCollins (New York, NY), 1993.

The Hanged Man, HarperCollins (New York, NY), 1994.
Baby Be-Bop, HarperCollins (New York, NY), 1995.
Dangerous Angels: The Weetzie Bat Books, HarperCollins (New York, NY), 1998.
I Was a Teenage Fairy, HarperCollins (New York, NY), 1998.
Violet and Claire, HarperCollins (New York, NY), 1999.
Echo, Joanna Cotler Books (New York, NY), 2001.
Wasteland, Joanna Cotler Books (New York, NY), 2003.
Beautiful Boys: Two Weetzie Bat Books (includes *Missing Angel Juan* and *Baby Be-Bop*), HarperCollins (New York, NY), 2004.
Goat Girls: Two Weetzie Bat Books (includes *Witch Baby* and *Cherokee Bat and the Goat Guys*), HarperCollins (New York, NY), 2004.
Necklace of Kisses, HarperCollins (New York, NY), 2005.

OTHER

Moon Harvest (poetry), illustrated by father, Irving Block, Santa Susanna Press (Northridge, CA), 1978.
Season of Green (poetry), illustrated by Irving Block, Santa Susanna Press (Northridge, CA), 1979.
Ecstasia (novel), New American Library (New York, NY), 1993, Penguin (New York, NY), 2004.
Primavera (novel; sequel to *Ecstasia*), New American Library (New York, NY), 1994, Penguin (New York, NY), 2004.
Girl Goddess #9: Nine Stories, HarperCollins (New York, NY), 1996.
(With Hillary Carlip) *Zine Scene,* Girl Press, 1998.
Nymph, Circlet Press, 2000.
The Rose and the Beast: Fairy Tales Retold, HarperCollins (New York, NY), 2000.
Guarding the Moon: A Mother's First Year (autobiography), HarperCollins (New York, NY), 2003.

Contributor of short stories to anthologies, including *Am I Blue?*, edited by Marion Dane Bauer, 1994; *When I Was Your Age,* edited by Amy Ehrlich, 1994; and *Soft Tar,* 1994. Developer of soap operas for USA and MTV networks.

Block's books have been translated into seven languages, including French, Italian, German, and Japanese.

SIDELIGHTS: Only a few years after her first publication, Francesca Lia Block had carved out a unique piece of literary turf for herself and the characters she has created. With the publication of *Weetzie Bat,* she set the agenda for a new direction in young adult novels for the 1990s: stories of the Los Angeles subculture replete with sex, drugs, and rock 'n' roll—stories for adults and young adults alike. With a cast of characters ranging from Weetzie Bat, a punk princess in pink, to her lover, My Secret Agent Lover Man, and her best friend Dirk and *his* boyfriend, to their common offspring, Witch Baby and Cherokee, Block's novels create postmodernist fairy tales where love and art are the only cures in a world devoid of adult direction. Praised and criticized for her edgy tales of urban adventure, Block was somewhat in awe of her instant success and of the stir her books created. "I wrote *Weetzie Bat* as a sort of valentine to Los Angeles at a time when I was in school in Berkeley and homesick for where I grew up," the author once commented. "It was a very personal story. A love letter. I never expected people to respond to it the way they have. I never imagined I could reach other people from such a very personal place in me."

But reach people her stories have. Block's "technicolor lovesong to Los Angeles," as *Publishers Weekly* commentator Diane Roback described *Weetzie Bat,* sold steadily through several printings and has been translated into seven languages, including French, Italian, German, and Japanese. There have been several sequels to that original novel, each one focusing on a different character and exploring new variations on the theme of the curative power of love and art. "The whole experience is magical," Block said of the success of her series.

And there is something a little magical about Block's life as well. Born in Hollywood, the center of the modern fairy-tale industry, she was exposed to the power of art and creativity from an early age. Her parents were both artists: her father, who died in 1986, was a well-known painter and teacher and one-time special-effects technician and writer for Hollywood studios; her mother is a poet who once wrote a children's poetry book. "My parents taught me that you could be creative in this world. That it was possible," Block once remarked. Books were always part of her life. "I can't remember not having books. There were trips to the library for books and there were books all around our home. It feels like I was always able to read." In addition to traditional childhood favorites such as Charlotte Zolotow's *Mr. Rabbit and the Lovely Present,* Randall Jarrell's *Animal Family,* and Maurice Sendak's *Where the Wild*

Things Are, Block was also greatly influenced by Greek mythology and legend. "My father used to tell me bits of the *Odyssey* for my nighttime story," she once recalled. "It was an incredibly rich upbringing."

A teenager in the late 1970s, Block and her friends were fond of going into Hollywood after school. "When I was seventeen years old, my friends and I used to drive through Laurel Canyon after school in a shiny blue vintage Mustang convertible," Block wrote in the *Los Angeles Times Book Review.* "The short distance of the canyon separating us from Hollywood made that city a little enchanted." Once in Hollywood they would hang out at Schwab's soda fountain, check out the street scene with all the punk costumes, cruise Sunset Strip, or frolic at the Farmer's Market. It was on one such trip that Block first saw the prototype of Weetzie: "A punk princess with spiky bleached hair, a very pink '50s prom dress and cowboy boots," as she described her. It was a momentary glimpse of a hitchhiker that stayed with her over the years, and later a name came with the apparition, for she saw a pink Pinto on the freeway with a driver who looked like that hitchhiker and with a license plate spelling "WEETZIE." The character of this punk princess would ferment for another six years before coming to full bloom in Block's first novel. She continually made up stories about Weetzie and drew her innumerable times: Block came to know Weetzie long before she first wrote about her in a novel.

"I lived a little bit of the Weetzie lifestyle in those years," Block once said in an interview. "Being around creative people, a little bit on the edge, listening to bands like X, being a part of the punk scene because it was something different and expressive." But soon the punk scene took on a violent edge with beatings at concerts and punks wearing swastikas, and the specter of AIDS had appeared. Block left Los Angeles to attend college in Berkeley, California, where she fell in love with the modernist poetry of H.D. (Hilda Doolittle) and the magic realism of Colombian novelist Gabriel García Márquez. "College was a very intense time. I took a course with Jayne Walker in modernist poetry my first year and loved its mix of concrete images and classical references." She also took a poetry workshop with Ron Loewinsohn, developing her poetry into short-short stories and then longer short stories, all with a minimalist influence to them. "And then came my father's illness, and I got increasingly homesick for L.A. and stressed out at school," Block remembered. "I started to write *Weetzie* at that time. It's a nostalgic look at that time and place. A sort of therapy for me."

The therapy worked. Block graduated from the University of California and weathered her father's death. She returned to Los Angeles, took a job in a gallery, lived alone, and wrote. It was a very productive time for Block, during which she completed the manuscripts of two novels, as well as several pieces of short fiction. Of course, Block did not think about the "young adult" genre at the time. "I just wrote," she once explained. "I wanted to tell a story and let it find its readers."

In 1989, a friend at the gallery where Block worked, children's illustrator Kathryn Jacobi, read the manuscript of *Weetzie Bat,* was impressed, and sent it off to the writer and editor Charlotte Zolotow at HarperCollins. Zolotow liked the book and told Block she wanted to publish it as a young adult title. She also encouraged Block to go further with the characters, that there seemed to be more stories there. "I was incredibly lucky that the manuscript went to Charlotte," Block said. "I loved her work as a child and here *she* was responding to mine in return."

Weetzie Bat tells the story of Weetzie and her gay friend Dirk—the only person who seems to understand her—who set up house together in a cottage Dirk's grandmother has left him in Los Angeles. Soon they fill it with a loving extended family. Dirk finds the surfer Duck, Weetzie finds My Secret Agent Lover Man, and even their dog finds a mate. Together they make underground movies and much more. Soon a baby they name Cherokee is born, and the extended family take it as natural that it should belong to all of them. Even the abandoned Witch Baby, reminder of a dalliance My Secret Agent Lover Man once had, is taken in as one of the family. Love is the connecting rod here, the one thing that makes life possible. "I hear that rats shrivel up and die if they aren't like, able to hang out with other rats," Duck says at one point. And this band of punk, hip youth learn that lesson well. "I don't know about happily ever after," Weetzie muses at the end of the book, "but I know about happily."

A modern fairy tale, *Weetzie Bat* blends Block's love of modernist poetry with magical realism—there's a genie granting three wishes and an evil witch—to come up with a potent narrative of love and loyalty in an age of pessimism and AIDS. Using a mixture of L.A. slang and inventive personal hip talk, Block created an "offbeat tale that has great charm, poignancy, and touches of fantasy," wrote Anne Osborn in *School Library Journal. New York Times Book Review* contributor Betsy Hearne also praised the author's style: "Block's far-ranging free association has been controlled and shaped into a story with sensual characters. The language is inventive California hip, but the patterns are compactly folkloristic and the theme is transcendent."

In spite of such glowing reviews, the book still caused a minor uproar among other reviewers and some librarians. Patrick Jones, writing in *Horn Book,* summed up and put such criticism into context: "It is not that the sex [in Block's books] is explicit; it is not. It is just that Block's characters *have* sex lives. . . . In the age of AIDS—whose ugly shadow appears—anything less than a 'safe sex or no sex' stance is bound to be controversial." Jones pointed out that the homosexual relationship between Dirk and Duck is also hard for some reviewers to deal with, as is the communal rearing of the baby, Cherokee. This alternate family lifestyle, so validating for teenager readers whose own lives seldom fit the "Father Knows Best" model, became a sore spot for some. But Block recounted the story of one such critic in her *Los Angeles Times Book Review* article. Having heard of this purportedly perverse book, Frances V. Sedney of the children's department of the Harford, Maryland, County Library read it, then wrote a letter in the novel's defense: "This short novel epitomizes the 'innocent' books where the *reader's* mind and experience make all the crucial difference." *Weetzie Bat* went on to be short-listed for the ALA Best Book of the Year as well making the Recommended Books for the Reluctant Young Adult Reader list.

Following the advice of her editor, Block went on to enlarge the stories of other characters from *Weetzie Bat.* In 1990 she published *Witch Baby,* a novel "reminiscent of a music video," Maeve Visser Knoth wrote in *Horn Book.* "Scenes and sensory images flash across the page; characters speak in complicated slang and create a safe haven for themselves in the midst of a shifting, confusing world." Witch Baby stumbles and sometimes crashes through the book, searching for her own identity, trying to understand her place in the scheme of things, looking for an answer to her own poetic question: "What time are we upon and where do I belong?" Witch Baby, endowed with tilted purple eyes and a Medusa head of black hair, collects newspaper clippings of tragedies in an attempt to understand the world. Ultimately Witch Baby is able to find her real mother and then can deal with her place in the extended family of Weetzie Bat. Ellen Ramsay noted in *School Library Journal,* Block is "a superior writer and has created a superior cast of characters," and in *Witch Baby* she "explores the danger of denying life's pain." This assessment mirrors what the author herself says about her work. "My books talk about tolerance," Block once explained, "though I never consciously think of themes like that as I write. I guess my general theme is the value of love and art as healers. That you must face the darkness, acknowledge it and still have hope. I think that is what is important in life."

With the next installment of the Bat family saga, Block further pursued the theme of family loyalty and the importance of love and a balance of spiritual powers in the world. *Cherokee Bat and the Goat Guys* opens with the adults, Weetzie Bat and others, off on a filming expedition in South America. Teenage Cherokee and Witch Baby are left under their own direction, and soon they team up with Raphael Chong Jah-Love and Angel Juan Perez to form a rock band, the Goat Guys. These four receive and depend on powerful gifts from a Native-American family friend, Coyote, to perform. They are an instant hit, but quickly the euphoria goes to their heads and "everything begins to fly apart in wild and outrageous ways," according to Gail Richmond in *School Library Journal,* as the band loses itself in sex and drugs. "The group descends into the bacchanalian hell of the nightclub scene with tequila and cocaine, skull lamps and lingerie-clad groupies drenched in cow's blood," noted Patty Campbell in a *New York Times Book Review* article. When Angel Juan slashes himself while performing, Cherokee figures it is time to turn in their magic totem gifts to Coyote and "be cleansed of the pain and guilt," according to Campbell. A *Publishers Weekly* reviewer observed: "This latest effort provides yet another delicious and deeply felt trip to Block's wonderfully idiosyncratic corner of California."

It is this idiosyncratic nature of much of Block's work that has also prompted some criticism. Ramsay praised the quality of Block's work but wondered if she is not "just a tad too Southern California cool for broad appeal." Campbell, in *Horn Book,* argued, however, that "many novels are set in New York, and . . . no one thinks those books are strange or labels them as depicting 'an alternate lifestyle' because the characters ride to work on the subway or shop at Bloomingdale's. . . . Why should the second largest city in the United States be perceived so differently? It is doubly puzzling considering that America sees Los Angeles every night on television."

Block moved the action of *Missing Angel Juan* to New York when Witch Baby's boyfriend, Angel Juan, takes off on his own musical career in the Big Apple. Witch Baby misses him and soon follows Angel Juan to New York, and the book is about her search for him—aided by the ghost of Weetzie's father—through the nightmare world of Manhattan. Her search ultimately takes her into the subways of New York, with "strong echoes of Orpheus' descent into Hades," as Michael Cart noted in *School Library Journal.* But in the end, Witch Baby realizes she has to leave Angel Juan to find his own way, as she must find hers. "Love will come," she muses, "because it always does, because why else would it exist, and it will make everything hurt a little less. You just have to believe in yourself." Like its predecessors, *Missing Angel Juan* is "an engagingly eccentric mix of fantasy and reality, enhanced—this time—by mystery and suspense," Cart remarked. And Judy Sasges, writing in *Voice of Youth Advocates,* likewise called the story "imaginative, mystical, and completely engaging."

In *The Hanged Man* Block looks at the "descent of a woman into madness of a sort," as the author stated. Set in the same L.A. club scenes as the "Weetzie" books, *The Hanged Man* is about the darker side of life. The story deals with a young woman named Laurel who is struggling with her emotions in the wake of the death by cancer of her father, with whom she has had an incestuous relationship. "Block's prose moves like a heroin trip through the smog and wet heat, heavy flowers, and velvet grunge of Hollywood," reviewer Vanessa Elder wrote in *School Library Journal.* "There is lots of fairy tale imagery," Block once said of the work, "but there is also an ominous side. It's about obsession and being haunted by the past. This time the cure, the healing power, is much more art than love. In that sense I feel I am in a sort of transition in my writing. So much of my earlier stuff was about searching for love, and in fact love was missing in my own life. But now that exists for me. The result is less of a yearning tone in my books."

In 1995, Block returned to the world of Weetzie Bat with the novel *Baby Be-Bop.* This book is actually a prequel to those earlier ones in that it tells the story of Weetzie's friend Dirk, and of how he deals with the realization that he is gay. "What might seem didactic from lesser writers becomes a gleaming gift from Block," a *Publishers Weekly* reviewer wrote. "Her extravagantly imaginative settings and finely honed perspectives remind the reader that there is magic everywhere."

Block's *Girl Goddess #9* and *I Was a Teenage Fairy* deal with similar themes: young people fighting to come to grips with a rapidly changing world and their place in it. *Girl Goddess #9* is a collection of nine short stories about girls, with the stories arranged chronologically; the first tales are about toddlers, while the last one concerns a young woman entering college. The stories are written in Block's "funky, richly sensual style," Dorie Freebury of *Voice of Youth Advocates* noted, and the characters "are painfully real, facing the challenges of life that can make or break one's spirit."

The novel *I Was a Teenage Fairy* is a modern-day fairy tale about a girl named Barbie who is being pushed into modeling by her mother. The appearance of an acid-tongued, finger-sized fairy named Mab changes Barbie's life and eventually helps her overcome the emotional trauma of being molested by a well-known photographer whose crime was ignored by the girl's mother. According to a critic in *Publishers Weekly*, Block's "prose, less obviously lush than in previous books, sustains steady crescendos of insight. This fairy tale is too pointedly a social critique to be entirely magical, but its spell feels real."

Block's novel *Violet and Claire* is the story of the friendship that develops between two teenage girls as different as night and day. Seventeen-year-old Violet is an aspiring screenwriter and filmmaker and an outsider at her high school. Past depression and a suicide attempt have left her hard-edged and isolated; she devotes her time to studying the films she loves and to writing her own screenplay. Then she meets Claire, a poet with glittering gauze fairy wings sewn on the back of her Tinker Bell T-shirt, and the two become fast friends. As the novel unfolds, the friendship between Violet and Claire is tested as the girls are divided by personal ambition and the intrusion of the outside world. Violet is willingly seduced by a rock star who gets her a job with a screen agent, while Claire enrolls in a poetry workshop and becomes attached to the instructor. The action reaches its peak at a wild party the girls attend after Violet sells a screenplay. Claire flees into the desert, and Violet follows in search of her. "Block excels in depicting strong and supportive friendships between teen girls," wrote Debbie Carton in *Booklist*, "and *Violet and Claire* is at its best when the two protagonists reach past their own pain to help each other." According to a *Kirkus Reviews* critic, "Fans of the author's previous works will take to this one; newcomers will be captured by the rainbow iridescence of Block's prose."

"I hope my work is poetic," Block once said. "I want my books to be contemporary fairy tales with edge. And I love the magical realism in my work. It's not as if you can escape the world. You're in the world. You're part of it. But there is solace and hope through the magic. There is something of another world. Hope, but in a grounded way." It is exactly this sense of hope that Block has given her readers and that has led to her success. She validates their experience by writing about it. "One of the things about *Weetzie Bat* is that it has given readers freedom to take their own contemporary culture and write about it themselves seriously as fiction or poetry," Block once noted. "In letters from my readers, I

see that I have done something of the same service as my mother did for me writing down my early stories. I have made this other culture real and worthy. My readers discover it's okay to write about whatever is important to them and do it in a poetic way. Writing has saved my life in a way. Being able to express myself creatively was the way I could survive at certain parts of my life. If I can give others that message, that their lives and experiences are worth writing about, I would be very happy."

BIOGRAPHICAL AND CRITICAL SOURCES:

BOOKS

Block, Francesca Lia, *Weetzie Bat,* HarperCollins (New York, NY), 1989.

Block, Francesca Lia, *Witch Baby,* HarperCollins (New York, NY), 1990.

Block, Francesca Lia, *Missing Angel Juan,* HarperCollins (New York, NY), 1993.

Children's Literature Review, Volume 33, Thomson Gale (Detroit, MI), 1994.

PERIODICALS

Booklist, August, 1992, Hazel Rochman, review of *Cherokee Bat and the Goat Guys,* p. 2004; October 1, 1996, Debbie Carton, review of *Girl Goddess #9,* p. 340; September 1, 1999, Debbie Carton, review of *Violet and Claire,* p. 122.

Bulletin of the Center for Children's Books, December, 1993, p. 115; September, 1994, p. 6; October, 1996, p. 49; September, 1999, p. 5.

English Journal, December, 1990, Alleen Pace Nilsen and Ken Donelson, review of *Weetzie Bat,* p. 78; October, 1991, Rich McDonald, review of *Weetzie Bat,* pp. 94-95.

Five Owls, January-February, 1999, p. 66.

Horn Book, January-February, 1992, Maeve Visser Knoth, review of *Witch Baby,* pp. 78-79; September-October, 1992, p. 587; November-December, 1992, Patrick Jones, "People Are Talking about . . . Francesca Lia Block," pp. 697-701; January-February, 1993, Patty Campbell, "People Are Talking about . . . Francesca Lia Block," pp. 57-63.

Kirkus Reviews, September 15, 1999, review of *Violet and Claire,* p. 1497.

Los Angeles Times Book Review, July 26, 1992, Francesca Lia Block, "Punk Pixies in the Canyon," pp. 1, 11; November 12, 1995, p. 4.

New Yorker, November 25, 1991, p. 148.

New York Times Book Review, May 21, 1989, Betsy Hearne, "Pretty in Punk," p. 47; January 19, 1992, p. 24; September 20, 1992, Patty Campbell, review of *Cherokee Bat and the Goat Guys,* p. 18; February 26, 1995, Jim Gladstone, review of *The Hanged Man,* p. 21.

Publishers Weekly, March 10, 1989, review of *Weetzie Bat,* p. 91; December 22, 1989, Diane Roback, "Flying Starts: Francesca Lia Block," p. 27; July 20, 1992, review of *Cherokee Bat and the Goat Guys,* p. 251; July 18, 1994, review of *The Hanged Man,* pp. 246-247; July 31, 1995, review of *Baby Be-Bop,* p. 82; September 21, 1998, review of *I Was a Teenage Fairy,* p. 86.

School Library Journal, April, 1989, Anne Osborn, review of *Weetzie Bat,* pp. 116-117; September, 1991, Ellen Ramsay, review of *Witch Baby,* p. 277; September, 1992, Gail Richmond, review of *Cherokee Bat and the Goat Guys,* p. 274; October, 1993, Michael Cart, review of *Missing Angel Juan,* p. 148; December, 1993, p. 24; September, 1994, Vanessa Elder, review of *The Hanged Man,* p. 238; December, 1998, Carolyn Lehman, review of *I Was a Teenage Fairy,* p. 118; September, 1999, Kathleen Isaacs, review of *Violet and Claire,* p. 218.

Voice of Youth Advocates, December, 1993, Judy Sasges, review of *Missing Angel Juan,* p. 287; December, 1995, Dorie Freebury, review of *Girl Goddess #9,* pp. 297-298; February, 1997, p. 326.

ONLINE

Francesca Lia Block Home Page, http://www.francesca liablock.com/ (July 24, 2004).

*   *   *

BLOOM, Amy 1953-

PERSONAL: Born June 18, 1953, in New York, NY; daughter of Murray (a journalist and author) and Sydelle (a writer, teacher, and group therapist) Bloom; married Donald Moon (a professor), August 21, 1977; children: Alexander (stepson), Caitlin, Sarah. *Education:* Wesleyan University, B.A., 1975; Smith College, M.S.W., 1978.

ADDRESSES: Agent—Phyllis Wender, Rosenstone/ Wender, 38 East 29th St., New York, NY 10016.

CAREER: In private practice of psychotherapy, Middletown, CT, 1981—; writer.

AWARDS, HONORS: National Book Award nomination, 1993, for *Come to Me;* O. Henry Award, 1994, for story "Semper Fidelis"; National Book Critics Circle Award nomination, 2000, for *A Blind Man Can See How Much I Love You.*

WRITINGS:

Come to Me (short stories), HarperCollins (New York, NY), 1993.

Love Invents Us (novel), Random House (New York, NY), 1996.

A Blind Man Can See How Much I Love You (short stories), Random House (New York, NY), 2000.

Normal: Transsexual CEOs, Crossdressing Cops, and Hermaphrodites with Attitude (nonfiction), Random House, 2002.

Work represented in anthologies, including *Best American Short Stories, 1991,* edited by Alice Adams, Houghton Mifflin (Boston, MA), 1991; *Best American Short Stories, 1992,* edited by Robert Stone and Katrina Kenison, Houghton Mifflin (Boston, MA), 1992; *Here Lies My Heart: Essays on Why We Marry, Why We Don't, and What We Find There,* Beacon Press (Boston, MA), 1999; *Best American Short Stories, 2000,* edited by E.L. Doctorow, 2000; and *The Secret Self: A Century of Short Stories by Women.* Contributor of columns and articles to periodicals, including *New Yorker, Antaeus, Story, Mirabella, Self, Vogue,* and *Atlantic.*

WORK IN PROGRESS: Another collection of stories.

SIDELIGHTS: Amy Bloom demonstrates her knowledge of the human condition in stories and novels that celebrate "the human need to connect, no matter how awkwardly, how painfully, or how late," commented Susan Balee in the *Philadelphia Inquirer.* A practicing psychotherapist who began writing short stories in her spare time, Bloom creates characters who must face life's most difficult moments—ill health, the death of a spouse, lover, or child, the working-through of family trauma. As Dottie Enrico put it in *USA Today,* "One gets the sense that Bloom embraces life's disappointments and imperfections and does her best, through her writing, to create a world in which people prevail over those disappointments with honesty and acceptance." Consistently praised for the precision and verisimilitude of her observations, Bloom displays "a compelling emotional intelligence at work," according to John Martin in the *Bloomsbury Review. Austin Chronicle* contributor Marion Winik wrote: "Her easygoing empathy for . . . situations and the characters who inhabit them make her stories an epiphany to read—and her unfailing wit makes them a pleasure."

Bloom received a National Book Award nomination for her first book, *Come to Me*, a collection of twelve short stories. In *Come to Me* she delves into the emotional states and mental illnesses of her characters, ranging from Rose, a schizophrenic woman whose family tries to come to terms with her illness in "Silver Water," to an adulterous pianist whose story is related in "The Sight of You." "Although her stories may be full of tragic implications, Ms. Bloom's characters possess extraordinary dignity that lifts them beyond pity," Barbara Kaplan Lane noted in the *New York Times*. "Those whom circumstances might otherwise define as victims or villains reveal heroic potential in the author's skillful, empathic hands." "What Bloom manages to do in story after story is vary her voice . . . alternate the point of view, change the cadence," declared Ruth Coughlin in the *Detroit News*. "But throughout—always, always—she is able to maintain an extraordinarily high level of emotion and a piercingly sharp intelligence." According to *New York Times Book Review* contributor Anne Whitehouse, Bloom "has created engaging, candid and unorthodox characters, and has vividly revealed their inner lives." Coughlin called *Come to Me* "a remarkable collection, an exhilarating display of a talent both large and luminous." Elizabeth Benedict, reviewing the collection in the *Los Angeles Times Book Review*, concluded that *Come to Me* "is so rich, moving and gracefully written, it's hard to believe [Bloom] hasn't been doing this all her life."

Bloom's first novel, *Love Invents Us*, emerged in part from a story that appeared in the collection *Come to Me*. The longer fictional format enabled the author to develop her characters in greater detail and explore their lives over a longer span of time, without losing what Donna Seaman described in the *Chicago Tribune* as "her arresting economy and pointed poignancy." In the novel, the protagonist Elizabeth Taube tells her story in her own words, the story of an unattractive, awkward child searching for love and affection long denied. Her urban Jewish parents are cold and distant, her classmates hostile and cruel. "To compensate for this agonizing combination of indifference and malice," wrote Gary Krist in the *Washington Post Book World*, "Elizabeth is forced to find warmth wherever she can." Not surprisingly, the lonely child does not always make the wisest choices.

Among Elizabeth's discoveries is Mr. Klein, the furrier from the story "Light Breaks Where No Sun Shines,"

who encourages her to model his furs in her underwear in the back room of his shop and gives Elizabeth the esteem-building praise and warmth that was missing from her life. Another discovery is Mrs. Hill, an elderly, disabled member of a black church who engages Elizabeth's services as a companion and caretaker, and whose genuine interest in the young woman provides a parent-substitute that inspires Elizabeth's "loyalty unto death," as Winik commented in the *Los Angeles Times Book Review*. A more "unhealthy" discovery, according to Krist, is English teacher Max Stone, "a pitiful character, a married father tortured by his scandalous desire for a girl who could be his daughter."

These encounters prepare Elizabeth for her own true love, who turns out to be a black high school basketball player. With Huddie Lester, Krist wrote, "Elizabeth gets her first glimpse of a passion unmuddied by complexities and shame, and it's in these scenes that *Love Invents Us* truly comes into its own." Seaman commented: "Elizabeth narrates . . . in a voice as notable for its matter-of-factness in the face of trauma as for its nimble wit, a style that makes each complex scene shimmer."

If the first part of the novel represents discovery, then the second acknowledges loss. Huddie's father exiles him to Alabama, and Mrs. Hill dies. Max, who has become less a lover and more a friend, is afflicted by a series of tragedies that ruin his ability to proffer the love that Elizabeth continues to seek. Huddie's long-delayed return proves anticlimactic. As Winik reported, "it seems the characters are helpless against the assaults of destiny." The final part of the book suggests reconciliation. Winik maintained that "things are turning out . . . not perfectly, but hopefully, with . . . the suggestion, if not the assurance, of a happy ending."

Critics found much to praise in Bloom's first novel. Winik wrote: "It is a quiet book . . . you almost don't notice how brave it is." Seaman concluded: "Bloom's precise, sensual and heartbreaking tale reminds us that the most exquisite of pleasures can be wedded to the most searing of sorrows" and "we are both scarred and strengthened by the ordeal." Krist summarized: "Although her book is not flawless . . . its intelligence and passion never flag." The reviewer concluded that Bloom has shown her readers "that while love may take many different and surprising forms, there's never enough of it to go around."

Death looms large in many of the stories collected in *A Blind Man Can See How Much I Love You*, as Bloom's protagonists suffer from breast cancer, Parkinson's disease, or the loss of their children. *Santa Monica Mirror* correspondent Kate Cooney deemed the work "a catalog of characters in the midst of the hard stuff of life." Cooney added: "We don't often think about paradise as a destination we have to row toward but Bloom shows us time and again that the pleasure and pain of life are intrinsically intertwined." Bloom details her characters' behavior in the face of life-altering experiences, noting the tendency to behave badly and then feel guilty in response to dire circumstance. "Exotic intimacies color the sharply wrought stories in Amy Bloom's fine new collection. And they reveal themselves hauntingly as these tales unfold," stated Janet Maslin in the *New York Times*. "In a set of stories whose characters find themselves bridging various chasms—medical, sexual, racial—and casually breaking assorted taboos, Ms. Bloom writes warmly and astutely, with arresting precision, about the various adjustments that they make." Martin observed: "This is not a brand of storytelling easily imitated or duplicated. It requires a writer of sure abilities and deep intuition." In an online review for *NewCityNet*, Shelly Ridenour concluded: "These stories are the backbone of modern, nontraditional family life: families broken and disjointed and pieced together, proving that blood may be thicker than water, but it's still not as strong as hope—or blind determination. Truly, a work of real literary entertainment."

Bloom grew up in Long Island, New York, and spent a great deal of her time in her local library. After earning a degree in government and theater, she received her master's degree in social work and went into private practice. "I became a therapist because I am not judgmental," Bloom explained to Lane. "People have always liked to tell me their stories. Even when I was seventeen, taking the Long Island Railroad to a summer job, the conductor sat down to tell me his life story." Developing her skills as a listener and interviewer through her career, Bloom has also channeled it into her writing, resulting in the book *Normal: Transsexual CEOs, Crossdressing Cops, and Hermaphrodites with Attitude*. In this nonfiction work, based on interviews, she "introduces members of three very different groups who challenge common definitions of gender and sexuality," as noted by Ina Rimpau in *Library Journal*. Specifically, Bloom presents the reader with female-to-male transsexuals, heterosexual crossdressers, and the intersexed. This last category, as described by Andrea Dworkin in *New Statesman and Society*, are people who are "sometimes called hermaphrodites, whose genitalia and reproductive organs are configured at birth in a variety of atypical ways." In the book, readers meet a variety of sexually ambiguous men and women, such as cross-dressing cops and a seemingly normal middle-class guy

with an unusual genital abnormality that places him far out of the sexual mainstream. Bloom also pays close attention not only to those whose sexuality is considered abnormal by many but also to their families, including a mother who used her life savings to help her daughter make the transition from a girl to boy.

Commenting on Bloom's encounters with transsexuals, Julia M. Klein wrote in the *Nation* that, "In meeting these postoperative transsexuals, Bloom keeps gauging her own reactions, just as the reader might: Do they look male? Act male? Is the chemistry she feels the same as she'd feel with other men? What do their parents and their romantic partners say about them?" A *Publishers Weekly* contributor also commented that Bloom is very interested in why she and others struggle with "gender and sexual experiences we do not share." The reviewer added, "Fascinating without being prurient, detailed without being overly scientific, the book opens new ways of viewing not only gender but our own inability to accept difference." Writing in *Booklist*, Donna Seaman commented, "Beautifully done, Bloom's fascinating and enlightening disquisition greatly extends our perception of humanness."

BIOGRAPHICAL AND CRITICAL SOURCES:

PERIODICALS

Austin Chronicle, August 25, 2000, Marion Winik, "A Blind Man Can See What a Good Writer Amy Bloom Is."
Belles Lettres, winter, 1993, p. 28.
Bloomsbury Review, September-October, 2000, John Martin, review of *A Blind Man Can See How Much I Love You,* p. 23.
Booklist, December 15, 1996, p. 708; September 1, 2002, Donna Seaman, review of *Normal: Transsexual CEOs, Cross-Dressing Cops, and Hermaphrodites with Attitude,* p. 25.
Chicago Tribune, January 26, 1997, Donna Seaman, review of *Love Invents Us,* p. 14.
Detroit News, August 4, 1993, Ruth Coughlin, review of *Come to Me,* p. 3F.
Harper's Bazaar, January, 1997, p. 54.
Hudson Review, winter, 1994, pp. 770-771.
Library Journal, January, 1994, p. 200; December, 1996, p. 141; August, 2002, Ina Rimpau, review of *Normal,* p. 123.
Los Angeles Times Book Review, June 13, 1993, Elizabeth Benedict, review of *Come to Me,* pp. 3, 12; January 12, 1997, p. 8.

Nation, December 2, 2002, Julia M. Klein, review of *Normal,* p. 33.

New Statesman and Society, April 15, 1994, p. 38; September 22, 2003, Andrea Dworkin, review of *Normal,* p. 53.

New York Times, June 20, 1993, Barbara Kaplan Lane, "A Therapist-Author Shuns the Limelight," section CN, p. 14; August 16, 1993, p. C18; July 24, 2000, Janet Maslin, "How Do I Love Thee? Count the Unusual Ways."

New York Times Book Review, July 18, 1993, p. 16; January 19, 1997, p. 23; September 10, 2000, Joan Smith, "Role Reversals," p. 24.

People, February 24, 1997, p. 32.

Philadelphia Inquirer, July 30, 2000, Susan Balee, review of *A Blind Man Can See How Much I Love You.*

Publishers Weekly, June 5, 2000, review of *A Blind Man Can See How Much I Love You,* p. 69; July 1, 2002, review of *Normal,* p. 64.

Santa Monica Mirror, September 13-19, 2000, Kate Cooney, "The Life Stories of Amy Bloom."

Studies in Short Fiction, fall, 1994, p. 694.

USA Today, September 8, 2000, Dottie Enrico, "'Blind Man' Opens Eyes to Female Psyche."

U.S. News and World Report, January 27, 1997, p. 69.

Voice Literary Supplement, December, 1993, p. 10.

Washington Post Book World, February 23, 1997, Gary Krist, review of *Love Invents Us,* p. 3.

ONLINE

NewCityNet, http://www.weeklywire.com/ (August 8, 2000), Shelly Ridenour, "'Blind' Leading."

New York Post Online, http://www.nypost.com/ (November 7, 2000), Nan Goldberg, review of *A Blind Man Can See How Much I Love You.*

*   *   *

BLOUNT, Roy Alton, Jr.
   See BLOUNT, Roy, Jr.

*   *   *

BLOUNT, Roy, Jr. 1941-
(Roy Alton Blount, Jr., Noah Sanders, C.R. Ways)

PERSONAL: Surname rhymes with "punt"; born October 4, 1941, in Indianapolis, IN; son of Roy Alton (a savings and loan executive) and Louise (Floyd) Blount; married Ellen Pearson, September 6, 1964 (divorced, March, 1973); married Joan Ackerman, 1976 (separated); children: (first marriage) Ennis Caldwell, John Kirven. *Education:* Vanderbilt University, B.A. (magna cum laude), 1963; Harvard University, M.A., 1964. *Politics:* "Dated white Southern liberalism, with healthy undertones of redneckery and anarchism; nostalgia for Earl Long." *Religion:* "Lapsed Methodist."

ADDRESSES: Home—Mill River, MA; and New York, NY. *Agent*—c/o Crown Publicity, 1745 Broadway, New York, NY 10019.

CAREER: Journalist, author, and broadcaster. *Decatur-DeKalb News,* Decatur, GA, reporter and sports columnist, 1958-59; *Morning Telegraph,* New York, NY, reporter, summer, 1961; *New Orleans Times-Picayune,* New Orleans, LA, reporter, summer, 1963; *Atlanta Journal,* Atlanta, GA, reporter, editorial writer, and columnist, 1966-68; *Sports Illustrated,* New York, NY, staff writer, 1968-74, associate editor, 1974-75; freelance writer, 1975—. Occasional performer for American Humorists' Series, American Place Theatre, 1986 and 1988, and has appeared on *A Prairie Home Companion, The CBS Morning Show, The Tonight Show, The David Letterman Show, Austin City Limits, All Things Considered, Mark Twain, The Main Stream, Wait Wait Don't Tell Me,* and many other radio and television programs. Instructor at Georgia State College, 1967-68. Member of usage panel, *American Heritage Dictionary.* Has lectured at Manhattan Theatre Club, San Diego Forum, Washington State University, Wyoming Bar Association, and others. *Military service:* U.S. Army, 1964-66; became first lieutenant.

MEMBER: Phi Beta Kappa.

WRITINGS:

About Three Bricks Shy of a Load, Little, Brown (Boston, MA), 1974, revised edition published as *About Three Bricks Shy—and the Load Filled Up: The Story of the Greatest Football Team Ever,* Ballantine (New York, NY), 1989.

Crackers: This Whole Many-Sided Thing of Jimmy, More Carters, Ominous Little Animals, Sad-Singing Women, My Daddy and Me, Knopf (New York, NY), 1980.

One Fell Soup; or, I'm Just a Bug on the Windshield of Life, Little, Brown (Boston, MA), 1982.

What Men Don't Tell Women, Atlantic-Little, Brown (New York, NY), 1984.

Not Exactly What I Had in Mind, Atlantic Monthly Press (New York, NY), 1985.

It Grows on You: A Hair-Raising Survey of Human Plumage, Doubleday (New York, NY), 1986.

Roy Blount's Happy Hour and a Half (one-man show), produced Off-Broadway at American Place Theatre, January 22-February 7, 1986.

Soupsongs/Webster's Ark (double book of verse), Houghton Mifflin (Boston, MA), 1987.

(Contributor) *The Baseball Hall of Fame 50th Anniversary Book,* Prentice Hall Press (Englewood Cliffs, NJ), 1988.

Now, Where Were We?, Villard (New York, NY), 1989.

First Hubby, Villard (New York, NY), 1990.

Camels Are Easy, Comedy's Hard, Villard (New York, NY), 1991.

Roy Blount's Book of Southern Humor, Norton (New York, NY), 1994.

(With Dave Marsh, Kathi Kamen Glodmark, and G. Shields) *The Great Rock 'n' Roll Joke Book,* St. Martin's Press (New York, NY), 1997.

If Only You Knew How Much I Smell You: True Portraits of Dogs, photographed by Valerie Shaff, Bulfinch Press (New York, NY), 1998.

The Wit & Wisdom of the Founding Fathers: Benjamin Franklin, George Washington, John Adams, Thomas Jefferson, edited by Paul M. Zall, Ecco Press (New York, NY), 1998.

Be Sweet: A Conditional Love Story (memoir), Knopf (New York, NY), 1998.

(Author of introduction) E.W. Kemble, *Mark Twain's Library of Humor,* Modern Library (New York, NY), 2000.

I Am Puppy, Hear Me Yap: Ages of a Dog, photographs by Valerie Shaff, HarperCollins (New York, NY), 2000.

Am I Pig Enough for You Yet? Voices of the Barnyard, photographs by Valerie Shaff, HarperCollins (New York, NY), 2001.

Robert E. Lee: A Penguin Life, Lipper/Viking (New York, NY), 2003.

I Am the Cat, Don't Forget That: Feline Expressions, photographs by Valerie Shaff, HarperCollins (New York, NY), 2004.

Feet on the Street: Rambles Around New Orleans, Crown Journeys (New York, NY), 2005.

Also author of two one-act plays produced at Actors Theater of Louisville, KY, November, 1983, and fall, 1984. Contributor to numerous anthologies, including *The Best of Modern Humor,* 1983, *Laughing Matters,* 1987, *The Norton Book of Light Verse,* 1987, *The Oxford Book of American Light Verse, The Ultimate Baseball Book, Classic Southern Humor,* and *Sudden Fic-*

tion. Author of preface for *New Stories from the South: The Year's Best, 2003.* Columnist, *Atlanta Journal,* 1967-70; for the *Oxford American.* Contributor of articles, short stories, poems, crossword puzzles, and drawings, sometimes under pseudonyms Noah Sanders and C.R. Ways, to numerous periodicals, including *Sports Illustrated, New Yorker, Atlantic, New York Times, Magazine, Esquire, Playboy, Rolling Stone, GQ, Conde Nast Traveler, Spy,* and *Antaeus.* Contributing editor, *Atlantic,* 1983—.

ADAPTATIONS: Now, Where Were We? was adapted for audiocassette by sound Editions (Holmes, PA), 1989.

SIDELIGHTS: Roy Blount, Jr. is an author, humorist, sportswriter, performer, lecturer, dramatist, lyricist, television talking head, film actor, radio panelist, and usage consultant to the *American Heritage Dictionary.* He has entertained the American public not only through his multitudinous magazine publications and his books, but also through other media—he has performed on radio and television shows ranging from Minnesota Public Radio's *A Prairie Home Companion* to TV's *David Letterman Show.* "The unceasing drip-drip-drip of bizarre images, intricate wordplay, droll asides and crazy ideas disorients the reader," stated Patrick F. McManus in the *New York Times Book Review,* "until Mr. Blount finally has him at his mercy."

Blount's books, said Leslie Bennetts in the *New York Times,* "attest to the breadth of his interests, from *One Fell Soup, or I'm Just a Bug on the Windshield of Life* (which is also the name of one of the original songs Mr. Blount sings 'unless I'm forcibly deterred') to *What Men Don't Tell Women* to *It Grows on You,* a volume about hair." His first book, *About Three Bricks Shy of a Load,* "did for the Pittsburgh Steelers roughly what Sherman did for the South," stated Donald Morrison in *Time. New York Times Book Review* contributor Robert W. Creamer called *About Three Bricks Shy of a Load* "a terrific book," and he concluded, "I have never read anything else on pro football, fiction or nonfiction, as good as this."

With his second book, *Crackers: This Whole Many-Sided Thing of Jimmy, More Carters, Ominous Little Animals, Sad-Singing Women, My Daddy and Me,* Blount established his reputation as a humorist. *Crackers* examines the presidency of Jimmy Carter, a Georgian like Blount, and concludes that what the Carter administration needed was a more down-to-earth, redneck approach to the business of governing the country. "If *Crackers* reveals an overarching thesis, it is that contemporary America, like its president, is too emotionally constrained, too given to artifice, too Northern," explained Morrison. The book was a critical success. Blount has also achieved success in collections of his magazine articles, including *One Fell Soup; or, I'm Just a Bug on the Windshield of Life, What Men Don't Tell Women, Not Exactly What I Had in Mind, It Grows on You: A Hair-Raising Survey of Human Plumage,* and *Now, Where Were We?* Gathered from sources as diverse as *Esquire,* the *New Yorker,* and *Eastern Airlines Pastimes,* the collections prove Blount's "ability to be amusing on a diversity of topics," according to Beaufort Cranford of the *Detroit News.* After all, he asked, "what other source can prove the existence of God by considering the testicle?"

Although some critics—like *Los Angeles Times* contributor Taffy Cannon, who called Blount's stories "considerably funnier in a bar at midnight than spread at meandering and pointless length across the printed page"—found that Blount's later works aren't as successful as his earlier ones, many others celebrated his collections. Ron Givens, writing in *Newsweek,* declared, "It's downright refreshing, then, to read somebody who has taste, intelligence, style and, oh, bless you, wit— qualities that Roy Blount, Jr. . . . [has] in abundance."

Blount has also attracted attention as a versifier and songwriter. Despite his claims to be "singing impaired," Blount has performed both his stories and his verses in his one-man show, *Roy Blount's Happy Hour and a Half,* and on radio programs such as *A Prairie Home Companion.* A collection of the comic's verse, *Soupsongs/Webster's Ark,* "contains odes to beets, chitlins, barbeque sauce, catfish and grease ('I think that I will never cease / To hold in admiration grease')," explained Bennetts, "along with a 'Song against Broccoli' that reads in its entirety: 'The neighborhood stores are all out of broccoli, / Loccoli.'" "Blount's verses may resemble Burma Shave's more than Byron's," declared the *Chicago Tribune*'s Jim Spencer, "but they are bodaciously funny."

Blount continued to strike literary gold with a string of well-reviewed books published in 1989, 1990, and 1991— *Now, Where Were We?, First Hubby,* and *Camels Are Easy, Comedy's Hard,* respectively. The first and most lauded of these, *Now, Where Were We?,* is a collection of the author's previously published essays. "The genre of earnest, plain- spoken bumpkinhood," wrote Deborah Mason in the *New York Times Book Re-*

view, "forms one of the primal pools of American humor . . . . These pieces are brilliantly loopy, reassuringly subversive, and they put Mr. Blount in serious contention for the title of America's most cherished humorist." Indeed, *Washington Post Book World* contributor Jonathan Yardley went so far as to say that "a half dozen [of the essays] are likely to cause guttural eruptions, five are moderately dangerous to one's health—and one may be, for those with weak constitutions, terminally fatal."

Blount's debut novel, *First Hubby,* was generally considered a credible first effort in the longer genre. The story hinges on a major political event: the first female vice-president of the United States becomes president after the elected chief executive is killed by a huge falling fish. The narrator of *First Hubby* is none other than the frustrated writer-husband of the nation's new president, and he expounds upon his life and times with familiar Blountian humor. "Dialogue, internal and external, is Blount's forte," stated Christopher Hitchens in the *Washington Post Book World.*

Blount delights in confounding expectations in his book production as much as he does in magazine markets. He served as an anthologizer and contributor for *Roy Blount's Book of Southern Humor.* Blount chose short southern writings from over one hundred artists— Flannery O'Connor, Edgar Allan Poe, Alice Walker, Lyle Lovett, Davy Crocket, and Louis Armstrong among them—and the resulting volume received warm praise from critics. According to Mark Bautz in *People,* "Some of the best selections are from people you wouldn't expect to find in such a tome." A critic for *Publishers Weekly* thought that this "generous volume" would be a good gift for the "eclectic—or Dixie-minded— reader."

Critics have tried to define with varying success the sources of Blount's sense of humor. One contributing factor, suggested Givens, "derives from his off-center perceptions." Kenneth Turan, writing in *Time,* called Blount's work "in the tradition of the great curmudgeons like H.L. Mencken and W.C. Fields." And the comic "is not of the punch-line school of humor writing," declared McManus. "His humor is cumulative in effect, like Chinese water torture. When you can bear it no longer, you collapse into a spasm of mirth, often at a line that taken by itself would provoke no more than a smile."

Reaching his mid-fifties made Blount introspective; in his 1998 memoir *Be Sweet: A Conditional Love Story,* he "plumbs the depths" of his youth in Georgia, according to *People* 's Thomas Fields-Meyer. Such a child-hood was greatly informed by his domineering mother, whose continual admonition of "Be sweet" is used as the title of the book. A reviewer for *Publishers Weekly* observed that Blount "lays bare a Mother-complex that seems obsessive." Still, even with such potentially dark material, Blount provides an "achingly funny anecdote" on almost every page, according to Fields-Meyer.

Blount supplied a learned introduction to the year 2000 Modern Library *Mark Twain's Library of Humor,* and then made another change of direction for his 2003 bi-ography, *Robert E. Lee.* Written for the Penguin Life series of concise biographies, the latter book is much like that of the life of Lee himself, noted a contributor for *Publishers Weekly:* "valiant, honorable and surpris-ingly successful with limited resources." Blount uses the perspective of his own southern heritage to detail the life of the Confederate general from his lonely child-hood (abandoned by his once heroic but alcoholic fa-ther) to his appointment to West Point, his career under General Winfield Scott in the Mexican War, his Civil War career leading the Confederacy, and the postwar years when Lee, in failing health, was a strong propo-nent of reconciliation between the former enemy sides. The same reviewer further praised Blount's chronicling of these postwar years as the "most moving part of the book" and went on to comment that *Robert E. Lee* is a "literate and balanced introduction." Nathan Ward, re-viewing the biography in *Library Journal,* similarly found it to be a "vibrant introduction." Ward also felt that Blount managed to "humanize his portrait," and found the detailing of Lee's childhood "surprisingly moving." For Ward, Blount "succeeds" in presenting a multifaceted portrait of Lee, a man at once "flawed, brilliant, but recognizable." Chuck Leddy, writing in the *Denver Post,* similarly thought that Blount "largely suc-ceeds in humanizing the man behind the myth" in his biography. Leddy went on to conclude that Blount's book was an "excellent, concise biography." David Wal-ton, in the *New York Times Book Review,* observed that Blount's biography was primarily a "series of specula-tions and appendixes," but also allowed that the book was "witty, lively and wholly fascinating." Cameron McWhirter, in a review for the *Atlanta Journal-Constitution,* felt that "long after finishing the book, readers will be haunted by Lee." And a critic for *Kirkus Reviews* thought that "Blount honors Lee without slip-ping into hagiography."

In 2004, before Hurricane Katrina devastated the city the following year, Blount published his book *Feet on the Street: Rambles Around New Orleans.* The trave-logue covers the many facets of the city, including "his-

tory, location, weather, food, people, sex, and the au-thor's own experiences," stated John McCormick, a reviewer for *Library Journal.* McCormick also noted that Blount "wittily describes the ambiance of the city."

Blount once commented: "Raised in South by Southern parents. Couldn't play third base well enough so be-came college journalist. Ridiculed cultural enemies. Boosted integration. Decided to write, teach. Went to Harvard Graduate School. Didn't like it. Went back to journalism. Liked it. Got a column. Ridiculed cultural enemies. Wrote limericks. Boosted integration. Wanted to write for magazines. Took writing job at *Sports Illus-trated.* Have seen country, met all kinds of people, heard all different kinds of talk. Like it. Ready now to write a novel that sums it all up."

BIOGRAPHICAL AND CRITICAL SOURCES:

BOOKS

Brown, Jerry Elijah, *Roy Blount, Jr.,* Twayne (Boston, MA), 1990.
Be Sweet: A Conditional Love Story, Knopf (New York, NY), 1998.

PERIODICALS

American Heritage, August-September, 2003, review of *Robert E. Lee,* p. 18.
Atlanta Journal, May 18, 2003, Cameron McWhirter, review of *Robert E. Lee,* p. C4.
Booklist, February 1, 2005, review of *Feet on the Street: Rambles Around New Orleans,* p. 931.
Chicago Tribune, December 24, 1987, Jim Spencer, "Let Us Now Praise Not-So-Lean Cuisine," p. 3.
Denver Post, May 25, 2003, Chuck Leddy, review of *Robert E. Lee,* p. EE3.
Detroit News, October 17, 1982.
Kirkus Reviews, March 1, 2003, review of *Robert E. Lee,* p. 355.
Library Journal, April 1, 2003, Nathan Ward, review of *Robert E. Lee,* p. 108; May 1, 2003, Nathan Ward, "Reckoning with Robert E. Lee," p. 137; February 15, 2005, John McCormick, review of *Feet on the Street,* p. 149.
Los Angeles Times, December 13, 1985, Taffy Cannon, "Even One-Liners Can't Save a Humor Theme," p. 44.
Newsweek, September 17, 1984, Ron Givens, review of *What Men Don't Tell Women,* p. 82.

New York Times, January 25, 1988, Leslie Bennetts, review of *Roy Blount's Happy Hour and a Half,* p. 20.

New York Times Book Review, December 1, 1974, Robert W. Creamer, review of *About Three Bricks Shy of a Load*; November 17, 1985, Patrick F. McManus, review of *Not Exactly What I Had in Mind,* p. 14; April 2, 1989, Deborah Mason, review of *Now, Where Were We?,* p. 9; May 11, 2003, David Walton, review of *Robert E. Lee,* p. 20.

People, November 21, 1994, Mark Bautz, review of *Roy Blount's Book of Southern Humor,* p. 41; June 15, 1998, Thomas Fields-Meyer, review of *Be Sweet: A Conditional Love Story,* p. 49.

Publishers Weekly, September 5, 1994, review of *Roy Blount's Book of Southern Humor,* p. 88; May 1, 1998, review of *Be Sweet,* p. 59; March 10, 2003, review of *Robert E. Lee,* pp. 61-62.

Time, October 20, 1980, Donald Morrison, review of *Crackers: This Whole Many- Sided Thing of Jimmy, More Carters, Ominous Little Animals, Sad-Singing Women, My Daddy and Me,* p. E-2.

Washington Post Book World, February 19, 1989, Jonathan Yardley, review of *Now, Where Were We?,* p. 3; June 17, 1990, Christopher Hitchens, review of *First Hubby,* p. 9.

ONLINE

Atlantic Monthly Online, http://www.theatlantic.com/unbound/blount/rbbio.htm/ (October, 22, 2003).

Roy Blount, Jr., Web site, http://www.royblountjr.com/ (October, 22, 2003).

*　　*　　*

BLUE, Zachary
See STINE, R.L.

*　　*　　*

BLUME, Judy 1938-
(Judy Sussman Blume)

PERSONAL: Born February 12, 1938, in Elizabeth, NJ; daughter of Rudolph (a dentist) and Esther (Rosenfeld) Sussman; married John M. Blume (an attorney), August 15, 1959 (divorced, 1975); married third husband, George Cooper (a writer), June 6, 1987; children: (first marriage) Randy Lee (daughter), Lawrence Andrew; (third marriage) Amanda (stepdaughter). *Education:* New York University, B.S., 1961. *Religion:* Jewish.

ADDRESSES: Home—New York, NY. *Agent*—c/o Author Mail, Atheneum, 1230 Avenue of the Americas, New York, NY 10020. *E-mail*—judyb@judyblume.com.

CAREER: Writer of juvenile and adult fiction. Founder and trustee of KIDS Fund, 1981.

MEMBER: Society of Children's Book Writers and Illustrators (member of board), PEN, Authors Guild (member of council; vice president, 2002—), National Coalition Against Censorship (member of board).

AWARDS, HONORS: New York Times best books for children list, 1970, Nene Award, 1975, Young Hoosier Book Award, 1976, and North Dakota Children's Choice Award, 1979, all for *Are You There God? It's Me, Margaret;* Charlie May Swann Children's Book Award, 1972, Young Readers Choice Award, Pacific Northwest Library Association, and Sequoyah Children's Book Award of Oklahoma, both 1975, Massachusetts Children's Book Award, Georgia Children's Book Award, and South Carolina Children's Book Award, all 1977, Rhode Island Library Association Award, 1978, North Dakota Children's Choice Award, and West Australian Young Readers' Book Award, both 1980, United States Army in Europe Kinderbuch Award, and Great Stone Face Award, New Hampshire Library Council, both 1981, all for *Tales of a Fourth Grade Nothing;* Golden Archer Award, 1974; Arizona Young Readers Award, and Young Readers Choice Award, Pacific Northwest Library Association, both 1977, and North Dakota Children's Choice Award, 1983, all for *Blubber;* South Carolina Children's Book Award, 1978, for *Otherwise Known As Sheila the Great;* Texas Bluebonnet List, 1980, Michigan Young Readers' Award, and International Reading Association Children's Choice Award, both 1981, First Buckeye Children's Book Award, Nene Award, Sue Hefley Book Award, Louisiana Association of School Libraries, United States Army in Europe Kinderbuch Award, West Australian Young Readers' Book Award, North Dakota Children's Choice Award, Colorado Children's Book Award, Georgia Children's Book Award, Tennessee Children's Choice Book Award, and Utah Children's Book Award, all 1982, Northern Territory Young Readers' Book Award, Young Readers Choice Award, Pacific Northwest Library Association, Garden State Children's Book Award, Iowa Children's Choice Award, Arizona Young Readers' Award, California Young Readers' Medal, and Young Hoosier Book Award, all 1983, all for *Superfudge;* American Book Award nomination, Dorothy Canfield Fisher Children's Book Award, Buckeye Children's Book Award, and California

Young Readers Medal, all 1983, all for *Tiger Eyes;* Today's Woman Award, 1981; Eleanor Roosevelt Humanitarian Award, Favorite Author—Children's Choice Award, Milner Award, and Jeremiah Ludington Memorial Award, all 1983; Carl Sandburg Freedom to Read Award, Chicago Public Library, 1984; Civil Liberties Award, Atlanta American Civil Liberties Union, and John Rock Award, Center for Population Options, Los Angeles, both 1986; D.H.L., Kean College, 1987; South Australian Youth Media Award for Best Author, South Australian Association for Media Education, 1988; Most Admired Author, Heroes of Young America Poll, 1989; National Hero Award, Big Brothers/Big Sisters, 1992; Dean's Award, Columbia University College of Physicians and Surgeons, 1993; Margaret A. Edwards Award for Outstanding Literature for Young Adults, American Library Association, 1996, for lifetime achievement writing for teens; honorary degree from Holyoke College, 2003; Writers for Writers Award, Poets and Writers, 2004.

WRITINGS:

JUVENILE FICTION

The One in the Middle Is the Green Kangaroo, Reilly & Lee, 1969, revised edition, Bradbury (New York, NY), 1981, second revised edition, with new illustrations, 1991.

Iggie's House, Bradbury (New York, NY), 1970.

Are You There God? It's Me, Margaret, Bradbury (New York, NY), 1970.

Then Again, Maybe I Won't (also see below), Bradbury (New York, NY), 1971.

Freckle Juice, Four Winds (New York, NY), 1971.

Tales of a Fourth Grade Nothing, Dutton (New York, NY), 1972.

Otherwise Known As Sheila the Great (also see below), Dutton (New York, NY), 1972.

It's Not the End of the World (also see below), Bradbury (New York, NY), 1972.

Deenie (also see below), Bradbury (New York, NY), 1973.

Blubber, Bradbury (New York, NY), 1974.

Starring Sally J. Freedman As Herself, Bradbury (New York, NY), 1977.

Superfudge, Dutton (New York, NY), 1980.

Tiger Eyes, Bradbury (New York, NY), 1981.

The Pain and the Great One, Bradbury (New York, NY), 1984.

Just As Long As We're Together, Orchard (New York, NY), 1987.

Fudge-a-Mania, Dutton (New York, NY), 1990.

Here's to You, Rachel Robinson, Orchard (New York, NY), 1993.

Double Fudge, Dutton (New York, NY), 2002.

A Judy Blume Collection: Three Novels by Best-selling Author Judy Blume: Deenie; It's Not the End of the World; Then Again, Maybe I Won't, Atheneum (New York, NY), 2003.

OTHER

Forever. . . (young-adult novel), Bradbury (New York, NY), 1975.

Wifey (adult novel), Putnam (New York, NY), 1977.

The Judy Blume Diary, Dell (New York, NY), 1981.

Smart Women (adult novel), Putnam (New York, NY), 1984.

Letters to Judy: What Your Kids Wish They Could Tell You (nonfiction), Putnam (New York, NY), 1986.

The Judy Blume Memory Book, Dell (New York, NY), 1988.

(And producer with son, Lawrence Blume) *Otherwise Known As Sheila the Great* (screenplay; adapted from her novel), Barr Films, 1988.

Summer Sisters (adult novel), Delacorte (New York, NY), 1998.

(Editor) *Places I Never Meant to Be: Original Stories by Censored Writers,* Simon & Schuster (New York, NY), 1999.

(With others) *Author Talk: Conversations with Judy Blume (and Others),* Simon & Schuster (New York, NY), 2000.

Some of Blume's papers are housed in the Kerlan Collection, University of Minnesota.

ADAPTATIONS: Forever. . . was adapted as a television film, CBS-TV, 1978; *Freckle Juice* was adapted as an animated film by Barr Films, 1987.

SIDELIGHTS: In the nearly thirty years since she published her first book, Judy Blume has become one of the most popular and controversial authors writing for children. Her accessible, humorous style and direct, sometimes explicit treatment of youthful concerns have won her many fans—as well as critics who sometimes seek to censor her work. Nevertheless, Blume has continued to produce works that are both entertaining and thought-provoking. "Blume has a knack for knowing what children think about and an honest, highly amusing way of writing about it," Jean Van Leeuwen stated in the *New York Times Book Review.*

Many critics attribute Blume's popularity to her ability to discuss openly, realistically, and compassionately the subjects that concern her readers. Her books for younger children, such as *Tales of a Fourth Grade Nothing, Blubber,* and *Otherwise Known As Sheila the Great,* deal with problems of sibling rivalry, establishing self-confidence, and social ostracism. *Tales of a Fourth Grade Nothing* introduces Manhattanite Peter Warren Hatcher and his little brother Fudge. In the book's most memorable scene, Peter learns that his brother Fudge has swallowed his pet turtle. This book won numerous awards from organizations throughout the United States and continues to be a favorite with children. As Mark Oppenheimer noted in the *New York Times Book Review,* by 1996, the title "had sold over six million copies." Blume continued the story begun in *Tales of a Fourth Grade Nothing* with *Superfudge.* In this book, the Hatcher family has moved to Princeton, New Jersey, and Fudge is ready to enter kindergarten. Fudge is still a problem for Peter: he keeps Peter out of the bathroom, sticks stamps all over the baby, and kicks his kindergarten teacher. "No one knows the byways of the under-twelves better than Blume," commented Pamela D. Pollack in *School Library Journal.* Brigitte Weeks of the *Washington Post Book World* remarked that the book demonstrates Blume's ability to create "good clean fun," adding, "Blume's books for younger readers are funny . . . important to children is the clear knowledge that Blume is on their team." In *Double Fudge,* Fudge develops such an obsession with money that his family decides to take him to the mint in Washington, DC, to show him how it is made. There, they run into relatives from Hawaii who end up barging in to stay with them. While the twins Fauna and Flora insist on singing at Fudge's school, their brother enjoys acting like a dog. Peter narrates the humorous events with an appropriate tone of frustration. Terrie Dorio in the *School Library Journal* believed that "Peter is a real twelve-year-old with all the insecurities and concerns of that age." The critic for *Publishers Weekly* praised "the sprightly clip of this cheerful read." Gillian Engberg in *Booklist* found that "Blume's humor and pitch-perfect ear for sibling rivalry and family dynamics will have readers giggling with recognition."

Blume's books for young adults, such as *Are You There God? It's Me, Margaret, Deenie,* and *Just As Long As We're Together* consider matters of divorce, friendship, family breakups, and sexual development, while *Forever. . .* specifically deals with a young woman's first love and first sexual experience. But whatever the situation, Blume's characters confront their feelings of confusion as a start to resolving their problems. In *Are You There God? It's Me, Margaret,* for example, the young protagonist examines her thoughts about religion and speculates about becoming a woman. The result is a book that uses "sensitivity and humor" in capturing "the joys, fears and uncertainty that surround a young girl approaching adolescence," Lavinia Russ wrote in *Publishers Weekly.*

"Blume's books reflect a general cultural concern with feelings about self and body, interpersonal relationships, and family problems," Alice Phoebe Naylor and Carol Wintercorn remarked in the *Dictionary of Literary Biography.* Blume has taken this general concern further, the critics continued, for "her portrayal of feelings of sexuality as normal, and not rightfully subject to punishment, [has] revolutionized realistic fiction for children." Blume's highlighting of sexuality reflects her ability to target the issues that most interest young people; when she first began writing, she "knew intuitively what kids wanted to know because I remembered what I wanted to know," she explained to John Neary of *People Weekly.* "I think I write about sexuality because it was uppermost in my mind when I was a kid: the need to know, and not knowing how to find out. My father delivered these little lectures to me, the last one when I was ten, on how babies are made. But questions about what I was feeling, and how my body could feel, I *never* asked my parents."

Nowhere is Blume's insight into character more apparent than in her fiction for adolescents, who are undeniably her most loyal and attentive audience. As Naomi Decter observed in *Commentary,* "There is, indeed, scarcely a literate girl of novel-reading age who has not read one or more Blume books." Not only does Blume address sensitive themes, she "is a careful observer of the everyday details of children's lives and she has a feel for the little power struggles and shifting alliances of their social relationships," R.A. Siegal commented in *The Lion and the Unicorn.* This realism enhances the appeal of her books, as Walter Clemons noted in a *Newsweek* review of *Tiger Eyes:* "No wonder teen-agers love Judy Blume's novels: She's very good. . . . Blume's delicate sense of character, eye for social detail and clear access to feelings touches even a hardened older reader. Her intended younger audience gets a first-rate novel written directly to them."

Blume reflected on her ability to communicate with her readers in a *Publishers Weekly* interview with Sybil Steinberg: "I have a capacity for total recall. That's my talent, if there's a talent involved. I have this gift, this memory, so it's easy to project myself back to certain stages in my life. And I write about what I know is true of kids going through those same stages." In addition, Blume enjoys writing for and about this age group. "When you're twelve, you're on the brink of adulthood," the author told Joyce Maynard in the *New York Times Magazine,* "but everything is still in front of you, and you still have the chance to be almost anyone you want. That seemed so appealing to me. I wasn't even thirty when I started writing, but already I didn't feel I had much chance myself." As a result, "whether she is writing about female or male sexual awakening, and whatever other adolescent problems, Judy Blume is on target," Dorothy M. Broderick asserted in the *New York Times Book Review.* "Her understanding of young people is sympathetic and psychologically sound; her skill engages the reader in human drama without melodrama."

Blume's style also plays a major role in her popularity; as Adele Geras remarked in *New Statesman,* Blume's books "are liked because they are accessible, warm hearted, often funny, and because in them her readers can identify with children like themselves in difficult situations, which may seem silly to the world at large but which are nevertheless very real to the sufferer." "It's hard not to like Judy Blume," Carolyn Banks elaborated in the *Washington Post Book World.* "Her style is so open, so honest, so direct. Each of her books reads as though she's not so much writing as kaffeeklatsching with you." In addition, Siegal observed that Blume's works are structured simply, making them easy to follow. "Her plots are loose and episodic: they accumulate rather than develop," the critic states. "They are not complicated or demanding."

Another way in which Blume achieves such a close affinity with her readers is through her consistent use of first-person narratives. As Siegal explained: "Through this technique she succeeds in establishing intimacy and identification between character and audience. All her books read like diaries or journals and the reader is drawn in by the narrator's self-revelations." "Given the sophistication of Miss Blume's material, her style is surprisingly simple," Decter similarly commented. "She writes for the most part in the first person: her vocabulary, grammar, and syntax are colloquial; her tone, consciously or perhaps not, evokes the awkwardness of a fifth grader's diary." In *Just As Long As We're Together,* for instance, the twelve-year-old heroine "tells her story in simple, real kid language," noted Mitzi Myers in the *Los Angeles Times,* "inviting readers to identify with her dilemmas over girlfriends and boyfriends and that most basic of all teen problems: 'Sometimes I feel grown up and other times I feel like a little kid.'"

Although Blume's work is consistently in favor with readers, it has frequently been the target of criticism.

Some commentators have charged that the author's readable style, with its focus on mundane detail, lacks the depth to deal with the complex issues that she raises. In a *Times Literary Supplement* review of *Just As Long As We're Together,* for example, Jan Dalley claimed that Blume's work "is all very professionally achieved, as one would expect from this highly successful author, but Blume's concoctions are unvaryingly smooth, bland and glutinous." Critical reaction to Blume's young-adult novel *Here's to You, Rachel Robinson* follows a similar theme. The novel's plot concerns the conflicts and eventual reconciliation experienced by thirteen-year-old Rachel and her troubled and self-destructive older brother Charles. Critics noted that while this book maintains the author's tradition of treating the problems of adolescence with empathy and humor, the novel as a whole suffers from a slight superficiality.

Beryl Lieff Benderly believed that the author's readability sometimes masks what some critics call her "enormous skill as a novelist," as she wrote in a *Washington Post Book World* review of *Here's to You, Rachel Robinson.* "While apparently presenting the bright, slangy, surface details of life in an upper-middle class suburban junior high school, she's really plumbing the meaning of honesty, friendship, loyalty, secrecy, individuality, and the painful, puzzling question of what we owe those we love."

Other reviewers have taken exception to Blume's tendency to avoid resolving her fictional dilemmas in a straightforward fashion, for her protagonists rarely finish dealing with all their difficulties by the end of the book. Many critics, however, think that it is to Blume's credit that she does not settle every problem for her readers. One such critic, Robert Lipsyte, in a *Nation* review maintained that "Blume explores the feelings of children in a nonjudgmental way. The immediate resolution of a problem is never as important as what the protagonist . . . will learn about herself by confronting her life." Lipsyte explained that "the young reader gains from the emotional adventure story both by observing another youngster in a realistic situation and by finding a reference from which to start a discussion with a friend or parent or teacher. For many children, talking about a Blume story is a way to expose their own fears about menstruation or masturbation or death." Countering other criticisms that by not answering the questions they raise Blume's books fail to educate their readers, Siegal likewise suggested: "It does not seem that Blume's books . . . ought to be discussed and evaluated on the basis of what they teach children about handling specific social or personal problems. Though books of this type may sometimes be useful in giving children a vehicle for recognizing and ventilating their feelings, they are, after all, works of fiction and not self-help manuals."

Even more disturbing to some adults is Blume's treatment of mature issues and her use of frank language. "Menstruation, wet dreams, masturbation, all the things that are whispered about in real school halls" are the subjects of Blume's books, related interviewer Sandy Rovner in the *Washington Post*. As a result, Blume's works have frequently been the targets of censorship, and Blume herself has become an active crusader for freedom of expression. She has answers to those who would censor her work for its explicitness. "The way to instill values in children is to talk about difficult issues and bring them out in the open, not to restrict their access to books that may help them deal with their problems and concerns," she said in a Toronto *Globe and Mail* interview with Isabel Vincent. And, as she revealed to Peter Gorner in the *Chicago Tribune,* she never intended her work to inspire protest in the first place: "I wrote these books a long time ago when there wasn't anything near the censorship that there is now," she told Gorner. "I wasn't aware at the time that I was writing anything controversial. I just know what these books would have meant to me when I was a kid."

Others similarly defend Blume's choice of subject matter. For example, Natalie Babbitt asserted in the *New York Times Book Review:* "Some parents and librarians have come down hard on Judy Blume for the occasional vulgarities in her stories. Blume's vulgarities, however, exist in real life and are presented in her books with honesty and full acceptance." And those who focus only on the explicit aspects of Blume's books are missing their essence, Judith M. Goldberger proposed in the *Newsletter on Intellectual Freedom.* "Ironically, concerned parents and critics read Judy Blume out of context, and label the books while children and young adults read the whole books to find out what they are really about and to hear another voice talking about a host of matters with which they are concerned in their daily lives. The grownups, it seems, are the ones who read for the 'good' parts, more so than the children."

Blume, too, realizes that the controversial nature of her work receives the most attention. That causes concern for her beyond any censorship attempts. As the author explained to Maynard: "What I worry about is that an awful lot of people, looking at my example, have gotten the idea that what sells is teenage sex, and they'll exploit it. I don't believe that sex is why kids like my books. The impression I get, from letter after letter, is

that a great many kids don't communicate with their parents. They feel alone in the world. Sometimes, reading books that deal with other kids who feel the same things they do, it makes them feel less alone." The volume of Blume's fan mail seems to reinforce the fact that her readers are looking for contact with an understanding adult. Hundreds of letters arrive each week not only praising her books but also asking her for advice or information. As Blume remarked in *Publishers Weekly,* "I have a wonderful, intimate relationship with kids. It's rare and lovely. They feel that they know me and that I know them."

In 1986 Blume collected a number of letters from her readers and published them, along with some of her own comments, as *Letters to Judy: What Your Kids Wish They Could Tell You.* The resulting book, aimed at both children and adults, "is an effort to break the silence, to show parents that they can talk without looking foolish, to show children that parents are human and remember what things were like when they were young, and to show everyone that however trivial the problem may seem it's worth trying to sort it out," wrote Geras. "If parents and children alike read *Letters to Judy,*" advice columnist Elizabeth Winship likewise observed in the *New York Times Book Review,* "it might well help them to ease into genuine conversation. The book is not a how-to manual, but one compassionate and popular author's way to help parents see life through their children's eyes, and feel it through their hearts and souls." Blume feels so strongly about the lack of communication between children and their parents that she used the royalties from *Letters to Judy,* among other projects, to help finance the KIDS Fund, which she established in 1981. Each year, the fund contributes approximately 45,000 dollars to various nonprofit organizations set up to help young people communicate with their parents.

Over the years, Blume's writing has matured and her audience has expanded with each new book. Her first adult novel, *Wifey,* deals with a woman's search for more out of life and marriage; the second, *Smart Women,* finds a divorced woman trying to deal with single motherhood and new relationships. Although these books are directed at a different audience, they share with her juvenile fiction two characteristics: an empathy for the plights and feelings of her characters and a writing style that is humorous and easy to read. Interestingly enough, even in Blume's adult fiction "the voices of the children ring loudest and clearest," Linda Bird Francke declared in a *New York Times Book Review,* praising Blume's *Smart Women* in particular for its portrayal of "the anger, sadness, confusion and disgust children of divorce can feel."

One reason children play such a role in Blume's "adult" fiction may be due to the author's reluctance to direct her works solely toward a narrow audience, as she disclosed in her interview with Steinberg: "I hate to categorize books. . . . I wish that older readers would read my books about young people, and I hope that younger readers will grow up to read what I have to say about adult life. I'd like to feel that I write for everybody. I think that my appeal has to do with feelings and with character identification. Things like that don't change from generation to generation. That's what I really know." "I love family life," the author added in her interview with Gorner. "I love kids. I think divorce is a tragedy, traumatic and horribly painful for everybody. That's why I wrote *Smart Women.* I want kids to read that and to think what life might be like for their parents. And I want parents to think about what life is like for their kids."

Banks commended Blume not only for her honest approach to issues, but for her "artistic integrity": "She's never content to rest on her laurels, writing the same book over and over as so many successful writers do." For instance, *Tiger Eyes,* the story of Davey, a girl whose father is killed in a robbery, is "a lesson on how the conventions of a genre can best be put to use," Lipsyte claimed. While the author uses familiar situations and characters, showing Davey dealing with an annoying younger sibling, a move far from home, and a new family situation, "the story deepens, takes turns," the critic continued, particularly when Davey's family moves in with an uncle who works for a nuclear weapons plant. The result, Lipsyte stated, is Blume's "finest book—ambitious, absorbing, smoothly written, emotionally engaging and subtly political." And even when Blume returns to familiar characters, as she does in the series starting with *Tales of a Fourth Grade Nothing* and *Superfudge,* her sequels "expand on the original and enrich it, so that [the] stories . . . add up to one long and much more wonderful story," Jean Van Leeuwen remarked in a *New York Times Book Review* article about *Fudge-a-Mania.*

"Blume is concerned to describe characters surviving, finding themselves, growing in understanding, coming to terms with life," John Gough noted in *School Librarian.* While the solutions her characters find and the conclusions they make "may not be original or profound," the critic continued, "neither are they trivial. The high sales of Blume's books are testimony to the fact that what she has to say is said well and is well worth saying." While her "willingness to recognize children's serious thoughts about sex, religion and class made her a

figure of controversy twenty-five years ago," as Mark Oppenheimer commented in the *New York Times Book Review,* "Blume has become an icon, as famous for those who tried to cleanse libraries of her books as for the books themselves." Faith McNulty concluded in the *New Yorker:* "I find much in Blume to be thankful for. She writes clean, swift, unadorned prose. She has convinced millions of young people that truth can be found in a book and that reading is fun. At a time that many believe may be the twilight of the written word, those are things to be grateful for."

BIOGRAPHICAL AND CRITICAL SOURCES:

BOOKS

Children's Literature Review, Thomson Gale (Detroit, MI), Volume 2, 1976, Volume 15, 1988.
Contemporary Literary Criticism, Thomson Gale (Detroit, MI), Volume 12, 1980, Volume 30, 1984.
Dictionary of Literary Biography, Volume 52: *American Writers for Children since 1960: Fiction,* Thomson Gale (Detroit, MI), 1986.
Fisher, Emma, and Justin Wintle, *The Pied Pipers,* Paddington Press, 1975.
Gleasner, Diana, *Breakthrough: Women in Writing,* Walker, 1980.
Lee, Betsey, *Judy Blume's Story,* Dillon Press, 1981.
Rees, David, *The Marble in the Water: Essays on Contemporary Writers of Fiction for Children and Young Adults,* Horn Book (Boston, MA), 1980, pp. 173-184.
Weidt, Maryann, *Presenting Judy Blume,* Twayne (New York, NY), 1989.
Wheeler, Jill C., *Judy Blume,* Abdo and Daughters (Edina, MN), 1996.

PERIODICALS

Booklist, September 15, 2002, Gillian Engberg, "Fudge Is Back!," p. 235.
Boston Globe, January 30, 1971.
Bulletin of the Center for Children's Books, April, 1970, Zena Sutherland, review of *The One in the Middle Is the Green Kangaroo,* p. 125; May, 1975, Zena Sutherland, review of *Blubber,* p. 142; October, 1993, review of *Here's To You, Rachel Robinson,* p. 39.
Chicago Tribune, September 24, 1978; March 15, 1985.
Christian Science Monitor, May 14, 1979; March 14, 1984.
Commentary, March, 1980.

Commonweal, July 4, 1980.

Detroit Free Press, February 26, 1984.

Detroit News, February 15, 1985.

Detroit News Magazine, February 4, 1979.

English Journal, September, 1972; March, 1976.

Entertainment Weekly, October 11, 2002, Rebecca Ascher Walsh, "The 'Fudge' Report: Are You There, Readers? It's Me, Judy Blume, with a New Children's Book . . . Finally," p. 77.

Five Owls, November-December, 1993, pp 37-38.

Globe and Mail (Toronto, Ontario, Canada), November 17, 1990.

Horn Book, November-December, 2002, Jennifer M. Brabander, review of *Double Fudge,* p. 748.

Kirkus Reviews, September 1, 1973, p. 965; March 15, 1998; September 1, 2002, review of *Double Fudge,* p. 1304.

Lion and the Unicorn, fall, 1978, R.A. Siegal, "Are You There, God? It's Me, Me, Me!: Judy Blume's Self-Absorbed Narrators," pp. 72-77.

Los Angeles Times, December 26, 1987.

Los Angeles Times Book Review, October 5, 1980; August 31, 1986.

Nation, November 21, 1981.

NEA Today, October, 1984, p. 10.

Newsletter on Intellectual Freedom, May, 1981.

New Statesman, November 5, 1976; November 14, 1980; October 24, 1986.

Newsweek, October 9, 1978; December 7, 1981; August 23, 1982.

New Yorker, December 5, 1983; December 13, 1993, pp. 116-7.

New York Times, October 3, 1982; February 21, 1984.

New York Times Book Review, May 24, 1970; November 8, 1970; December 9, 1970; January 16, 1972; September 3, 1972; November 3, 1974; December 28, 1975; May 25, 1976; May 1, 1977; November 23, 1980; November 15, 1981; February 19, 1984; June 8, 1986; November 8, 1987, p. 33; November 11, 1990; December 19, 1993, p. 16; November 16, 1997, Mark Oppenheimer, "Why Judy Blume Endures," pp. 44-45; July 19, 1998, p. 18.

New York Times Magazine, December 3, 1978; August 23, 1982.

People Weekly, October 16, 1978; August 16, 1982; March 19, 1984; March 7, 1994, p. 38.

Publishers Weekly, January 11, 1971; October 8, 1973; April 17, 1978; June 24, 2002, review of *Double Fudge,* p. 57; August 12, 2002, Sally Lodge, "The Return of Fudge: Thirty Years On, Judy Blume's Popular Character Is Forever Feisty, Forever Five," p. 150.

Saturday Review, September 18, 1971.

School Librarian, May, 1987.

School Library Journal, August, 1980, Pamela D. Pollack, review of *Superfudge,* pp. 60-61; September, 2002, Terrie Dorio, review of *Double Fudge,* p. 181.

Time, August 23, 1982.

Times Literary Supplement, October 1, 1976; April 7, 1978; January 29-February 4, 1988.

U.S. News and World Report, October 14, 2002, Vicky Hallett, "She Can't Say Farewell to Fudge," p. 12.

Voice of Youth Advocates, December, 1993, p. 287.

Washington Post, November 3, 1981.

Washington Post Book World, August 14, 1977; October 8, 1978; November 9, 1980, Brigitte Weeks, review of *Superfudge,* p. 12; September 13, 1981; February 12, 1984; November 8, 1987.

Wilson Library Bulletin, January, 1994, p. 119.

ONLINE

Judy Blume Web site, http://www.judyblume.com/ (November 6, 2003).

* * *

BLUME, Judy Sussman
 See BLUME, Judy

* * *

BLY, Robert 1926-
 (Robert Elwood Bly)

PERSONAL: Born December 23, 1926, in Madison, MN; son of Jacob Thomas (a farmer) and Alice (Aws) Bly; married Carolyn McLean, June 24, 1955 (divorced, June, 1979); married Ruth Counsell, June 27, 1980; children: Mary, Bridget, Noah Matthew Jacob, Micah John Padma. *Ethnicity:* "Caucasian." *Education:* Attended St. Olaf College, 1946-47; Harvard University, A.B., 1950; University of Iowa, M.A., 1956. *Politics:* Democrat. *Religion:* Lutheran.

ADDRESSES: Home—308 First St., Moose Lake, MN 55767. *Office*—1904 Girard Ave. Minneapolis, MN 55403. *Agent*—c/o Author Mail, George Borchardt, 136 East 57th St., New York, NY 10022. *E-mail*—odinhouse@earthlink.net.

CAREER: Poet, translator, and editor. Fifties (became Sixties, Seventies, Eighties, then Nineties) Press, Moose Lake, MN, founder, publisher, and editor, 1958—. Conductor of writing workshops. *Military service:* U.S. Navy, 1944-46.

MEMBER: American Academy and Institute of Arts and Letters, Association of Literary Magazines of America (executive committee), American Poets against the Vietnam War (founder member; cochair).

AWARDS, HONORS: Fulbright grant, 1956-57; Amy Lowell travelling fellowship, 1964; Guggenheim fellowship, 1964, 1972; American Academy grant, 1965; Rockefeller Foundation fellowship, 1967; National Book Award, 1968, for *The Light around the Body;* nomination for poetry award from *Los Angeles Times,* 1986, for *Selected Poems.*

WRITINGS:

POEMS

(With William Duffy and James Wright), *The Lion's Tail and Eyes: Poems Written Out of Laziness and Silence,* Sixties Press (Madison, MN), 1962.
Silence in the Snowy Fields, Wesleyan University Press (Middletown, CT), 1962.
(Compiler, with David Ray) *A Poetry Reading against the Vietnam War,* Sixties Press (Madison, MN), 1966.
The Light around the Body, Harper (New York, NY), 1967.
Chrysanthemums, Ox Head Press (Menomonie, WI), 1967.
Ducks, Ox Head Press (Menomonie, WI), 1968.
The Morning Glory: Another Thing That Will Never Be My Friend (twelve prose poems), Kayak Books (San Francisco, CA), 1969, revised edition, 1970, complete edition, Harper (New York, NY), 1975.
The Teeth Mother Naked at Last, City Lights (San Francisco, CA), 1971.
(With William E. Stafford and William Matthews) *Poems for Tennessee,* Tennessee Poetry Press, 1971.
Christmas Eve Service at Midnight at St. Michael's, Sceptre Press (Rushden, Northamptonshire, England), 1972.
Water under the Earth, Sceptre Press (Rushden, Northamptonshire, England), 1972.
The Dead Seal Near McClure's Beach, Sceptre Press (Rushden, Northamptonshire, England), 1973.
Sleepers Joining Hands, Harper (New York, NY), 1973.
Jumping Out of Bed, Barre (Barre, MA), 1973.
The Hockey Poem, Knife River Press, 1974.
Point Reyes Poems, Mudra, 1974, new edition, Floating Island (Point Reyes Station, CA), 1989.
Old Man Rubbing His Eyes, Unicorn Press (Greensboro, NC), 1975.

The Loon, Ox Head Press (Marshall, MN), 1977.
This Body Is Made of Camphor and Gopherwood (prose poems), Harper (New York, NY), 1977.
Visiting Emily Dickinson's Grave and Other Poems, Red Ozier Press (Madison, WI), 1979.
This Tree Will Be Here for a Thousand Years, Harper (New York, NY), 1979.
The Man in the Black Coat Turns, Doubleday (New York, NY), 1981.
Finding an Old Ant Mansion, Martin Booth (Knotting, Bedford, England), 1981.
Four Ramages, Barnwood Press, 1983.
The Whole Moisty Night, Red Ozier Press (Madison, WI), 1983.
Out of the Rolling Ocean, Dial Press (New York, NY), 1984.
Mirabai Versions, Red Ozier Press (Madison, WI), 1984.
In the Month of May, Red Ozier Press (Madison, WI), 1985.
A Love of Minute Particulars, Sceptre Press (Rushden, Northamptonshire, England), 1985.
Selected Poems, Harper (New York, NY), 1986.
Loving a Woman in Two Worlds, Perennial/Harper (New York, NY), 1987.
The Moon on a Fencepost, Unicorn Press, 1988.
The Apple Found in the Plowing, Haw River Books, 1989.
Angels of Pompeii, Ballantine (New York, NY), 1991.
What Have I Ever Lost by Dying?: Collected Prose Poems, HarperCollins (New York, NY), 1992.
Gratitude to Old Teachers, BOA Editions (Brockport, NY), 1993.
Meditations on the Insatiable Soul: Poems, HarperPerennial (New York, NY), 1994.
Morning Poems, HarperCollins (New York, NY), 1997.
Holes the Crickets Have Eaten in Blankets: A Sequence of Poems (Boa Pamphlets, No 9), Boa Editions (Rochester, NY), 1997.
Snowbanks North of the House, HarperCollins (New York, NY), 1999.
The Night Abraham Called to the Stars, HarperCollins (New York, NY), 2001.

EDITOR

The Sea and the Honeycomb, Sixties Press (Madison, MN), 1966.
(With David Ray) *A Poetry Reading against the Vietnam War,* Sixties Press (Madison, MN), 1967.
Forty Poems Touching Upon Recent History, Beacon Press (Boston, MA), 1970.
Leaping Poetry, Beacon Press (Boston, MA), 1975.

David Ignatow, *Selected Poems,* Wesleyan University Press (Middletown, CT), 1975.

News of the Universe: Poems of Twofold Consciousness, Sierra Books (San Francisco, CA), 1980.

Ten Love Poems, Ally Press (St. Paul, MN), 1981.

(With William Duffy) *The Fifties and the Sixties* (ten volumes), Hobart and William Smith, 1982.

The Winged Life: The Poetic Voice of Henry David Thoreau, Yolla Bolly Press (Covelo, CA), 1986.

Selected from Twentieth-Century American Poetry: An Anthology, New Readers Press, 1991.

(With James Hillman and Michael Meade) *The Rag and Bone Shop of the Heart: Poems for Men,* Harper-Collins (New York, NY), 1992.

William Stafford, *The Darkness around Us Is Deep: Selected Poems of William Stafford,* HarperPerennial (New York, NY), 1993.

(With Roy U. Schenk, John Everingham, and Gershen Kaufman), *Men Healing Shame: An Anthology,* Springer Publishing (New York, NY), 1995.

The Soul Is Here for Its Own Joy: Sacred Poems from Many Cultures, Ecco Press (Hopewell, NJ), 1995.

Eating the Honey of Words: New and Selected Poems, HarperFlamingo (New York, NY), 1999.

The Best American Poetry 1999, Scribner (New York, NY), 1999.

TRANSLATOR

Hans Hvass, *Reptiles and Amphibians of the World,* Grosset (New York, NY), 1960.

(With James Wright) Georg Trakl, *Twenty Poems,* Sixties Press (Madison, MN), 1961.

Selma Lager, *The Story of Gosta Berling,* New American Library (New York, NY), 1962.

(With James Knoefle and James Wright) César Vallejo, *Twenty Poems,* Sixties Press (Madison, MN), 1962.

Knut Hamsun, *Hunger* (novel), Farrar, Straus (New York, NY), 1967.

(With Christina Paulston) Gunnar Ekeloef, *I Do Best Alone at Night,* Charioteer Press (Washington, DC), 1967.

(With Christina Paulston) Gunnar Ekeloef, *Late Arrival on Earth: Selected Poems,* Rapp & Carroll (London, England), 1967.

Wang Hui-ming, *Woodcut* (limited edition), Epoh Studio (Amherst, MA), 1968.

(With James Wright) Pablo Neruda, *Twenty Poems,* Sixties Press (Madison, MN), 1968.

(With others) Yvan Goll, *Selected Poems,* Kayak, 1968.

Issa Kobayashi, *Ten Poems,* privately printed, 1969.

(And editor) Pablo Neruda and César Vallejo, *Selected Poems,* Beacon Press (Boston, MA), 1971.

Kabir, *The Fish in the Sea Is Not Thirsty: Versions of Kabir,* Lillabulero Press (Northwood Narrows, NH), 1971.

Tomas Tranströmer, *Night Vision,* Lillabulero Press (Northwood Narrows, NH), 1971.

Tomas Tranströmer, *Twenty Poems,* Seventies Press (Madison, MN), 1972.

Rainer Maria Rilke, *Ten Sonnets to Orpheus,* Zephyrus Image (San Francisco, CA), 1972.

Basho, *Basho,* Mudra, 1972.

Tomas Tranströmer, *Elegy; Some October Notes* (limited edition), Sceptre Press (Rushden, Northamptonshire, England), 1973.

Federico Garcia Lorca and Juan Ramon Jimenez, *Selected Poems,* Beacon Press (Boston, MA), 1973.

Friends, You Drank Some Darkness: Three Swedish Poets—Martinson, Ekeloef, and Tranströmer, Beacon Press (Boston, MA), 1975.

Kabir, *Grass from Two Years,* Ally Press (Denver, CO), 1975.

Kabir, *Twenty-eight Poems,* Siddha Yoga Dham, 1975.

Kabir, *Try to Live to See This!,* Ally Press (Denver, CO), 1976.

Rainer Maria Rilke, *The Voices,* Ally Press (Denver, CO), 1977.

Kabir, *The Kabir Book: Forty-four of the Ecstatic Poems of Kabir,* Beacon Press (Boston, MA), 1977.

Rolf Jacobsen, *Twenty Poems of Rolf Jacobsen,* Eighties Press (Madison, MN), 1977.

Antonio Machado, *I Never Wanted Fame,* Ally Press (St. Paul, MN), 1979.

Antonio Machado, *Canciones,* Toothpaste Press (West Branch, IA), 1980.

Tomas Tranströmer, *Truth Barriers,* Sierra Books (San Francisco, CA), 1980.

Rainer Maria Rilke, *I Am Too Alone in the World: Ten Poems,* Silver Hands Press (New York, NY), 1980.

(And editor) Rainer Maria Rilke, *Selected Poems of Rainer Maria Rilke: A Translation from the German, and Commentary,* Harper (New York, NY), 1981.

Rumi, Jalal al-Din, *Night and Sleep,* Yellow Moon Press (Cambridge, MA), 1981.

Goran Sonnevi, *The Economy Spinning Faster and Faster,* SUN, 1982.

Antonio Machado, *Times Alone: Selected Poems,* Wesleyan University Press (Middletown, CT), 1983.

Windows That Open Inward: Images of Chile, photographs by Milton Rogovin, poems by Pablo Neruda, edited by Dennis Maloney, introduction by Pablo Neruda, White Pine Press (Buffalo, NY), 1985.

Rumi, Jalal al-Din, *When Grapes Turn to Wine,* Yellow Moon Press (Cambridge, MA), 1986.

Olav H. Hauge, *Trusting Your Life to Water and Eternity,* Milkweed Editions (Minneapolis, MN), 1987.

Ten Poems of Francis Ponge [and] *Ten Poems of Robert Bly Inspired by the Poems of Francis Ponge,* Owl's Head Press (Riverview, New Brunswick, Canada), 1990.

Lorca and Jimenez: Selected Poems, Beacon Press (Boston, MA), 1997.

(With Sunil Dutta) Ghalib, *The Lightning Should Have Fallen on Ghalib: Selected Poems of Ghalib,* Ecco Press (Hopewell, NJ), 1999.

(With Roger Greenwald and Robert Hedin) *The Roads Have Come to an End Now: Selected and Last Poems of Rolf Jacobsen,* Copper Canyon Press (Port Townsend, WA), 2001.

Tomas Tranströmer, *The Half-Finished Heaven: The Best Poems of Tomas Tranströmer,* Graywolf Press (St. Paul, MN), 2001.

Tomas Tranströmer, *Air Mail: Brev 1964-1990,* Bonnier (Stockholm, Sweden), 2001.

Kabir, *Kabir: Ecstatic Poems,* Beacon Press (Boston, MA), 2004.

The Winged Energy of Delight, HarperCollins (New York, NY), 2004.

Also translator of such volumes as *Forty Poems of Juan Ramon Jimenez,* 1967, and, with Lewis Hyde, *Twenty Poems of Vincente Alexandre,* 1977.

OTHER

A Broadsheet against the New York Times Book Review, Sixties Press (Madison, MN), 1961.

(Contributor) *Ten Songs for Low Man's Voice and Piano,* Mobart (Hillsdale, NY), 1978.

What the Fox Agreed to Do: Four Poems, Croissant (Athens, OH), 1979.

Talking All Morning: Collected Conversations and Interviews, University of Michigan Press (Ann Arbor, MI), 1980.

The Eight Stages of Translation, Rowan Tree (Boston, MA), 1983, 2nd edition, 1986.

The Pillow and the Key: Commentary on the Fairy Tale "Iron John," Ally Press (St. Paul, MN), 1987.

A Little Book on the Human Shadow, edited by William Booth, Harper (New York, NY), 1988.

American Poetry: Wildness and Domesticity, Harper (New York, NY), 1990.

Iron John: A Book about Men, Addison-Wesley (Reading, MA), 1990.

Remembering James Wright, Ally Press (St. Paul, MN), 1991.

(With Jacob Boehme) *Between Two Worlds,* music by John Harbison, G. Schirmer (New York, NY), 1991.

The Spirit Boy and the Insatiable Soul, HarperCollins (New York, NY), 1994.

The Sibling Society, Addison-Wesley Publishers (Reading, MA), 1996.

(With Marion Woodman) *The Maiden King: The Reunion of Masculine and Feminine,* Henry Holt (New York, NY), 1998.

ADAPTATIONS: Bly appears on the recordings *Today's Poets 5,* Folkways, and *For the Stomach: Selected Poems,* Watershed, 1974; Bly appears on the videocassettes *On Being a Man,* 1989, *A Gathering of Men,* 1990, and *Bly and Woodman on Men and Women,* 1992.

WORK IN PROGRESS: The Winged Energy of Delight: Selected Translations.

SIDELIGHTS: Robert Bly is one of America's most respected and influential poets. Since the 1960s, Bly has practiced a poetry that is nonacademic, based in the natural world, the visionary, and the realm of the irrational. In addition to his verse, he has drawn attention for his theories on the roots of social problems, and his efforts to help men reclaim their masculinity and channel it in a positive direction. Believing that modern man has become lost with his primitive roots, he often focuses on the hidden connections between the natural world and the human mind, and their surreal interactions. Bly's poetry is often categorized as part of the deep image school of writing, in which the poet employs a system of private imagery; however, Bly's wish is not to create a personal mythology, but rather to describe modern American life through powerful metaphors and intense imagery. Two of his major inspirations in this regard have been Spanish-language writers César Vallejo and Federico Garcia Lorca. Hugh Kenner, writing in the *New York Times Book Review,* remarked that "Bly is attempting to write down what it's like to be alive, a state in which, he implies, not all readers find themselves all the time."

Born in western Minnesota, Bly grew up in that state in a community dominated by the culture of Norwegian immigrant farmers. After two years in the navy, he attended St. Olaf College in Minnesota for one year, then transferred to Harvard University. There he associated with other graduates who went on to make their name as writers, including Donald Hall, Adrienne Rich, John

Ashbery, John Hawkes, George Plimpton, and Kenneth Koch. After his graduation in 1950, Bly spent some time in New York City before studying for two years at the University of Iowa Writers Workshop, along with W.D. Snodgrass and Donald Justice. In 1956, he traveled on a Fulbright grant to Norway, where he translated Norwegian poetry into English. Translation would continue to be an important activity for him throughout his career. While in Norway, he discovered the work of many poets who would influence him greatly, including Neruda, Vallejo, and Gunnar Ekeloef. He founded his literary magazine and publishing house, *The Fifties* (which later changed its name to reflect the passing decades), as a forum for translated poetry. Returning to Minnesota, he took up residence on a farm there with his wife and children.

Bly's first widely acclaimed collection was *Silence in the Snowy Fields.* In an author's note, Bly stated that he is "interested in the connection between poetry and simplicity. . . . The fundamental world of poetry is an inward world. We approach it through solitude." He added that the poems in this volume "move toward that world."

In 1966, Bly cofounded American Writers against the Vietnam War and led much of the opposition among writers to that war. After winning the National Book Award for *The Light around the Body,* he contributed the prize money to the antiwar effort. The 1970s were a prolific decade for him, in which he published eleven books of poetry, essays, and translations, celebrating the power of myth, Indian ecstatic poetry, meditation, and storytelling. He was strongly influenced by the work of Robert Graves, and his poetry showed his interest in mythology and pre-Christian religion.

In 1979, Bly and his wife divorced, an event which precipitated a serious crisis of the soul for the poet. His emotional journey through this time eventually led him to begin leading men's seminars, in collaboration with James Hillman and Michael Meade. Participants were encouraged to reclaim their male traits and to express their severely repressed feelings through poetry, stories, and other rites. During these seminars, Bly was quoted as saying in *Newsweek,* the emotions can run high. "On the first night of a seminar," he explained, "I may simply put out a question like, 'Why are you having such trouble in relationships with women, or your father?' And the amount of grief and loneliness that pours out is tremendous. So sometimes by the third day there'll be a lot of weeping."

Bly's work in this area led to the character of "Iron John," based on a fairy tale by the Brothers Grimm; it came to stand for an archetype that could help men connect with their psyches. It is Bly's belief that modern men are greatly damaged by an absence of intergenerational male role models and initiation rituals. In his preface to *Iron John: A Book about Men,* he wrote, "The grief in men has been increasing steadily since the start of the Industrial Revolution and the grief has reached a depth now that cannot be ignored." Some critics found Bly's work in this vein to be anti-feminist; he replied by acknowledging and denouncing the dark side of male domination and exploitation. Bly posits a "Wild Man" inside of each male, an archetypical figure who leads men into their full manhood. Not an advocate of machoism or destructive behavior, Bly emphasizes that true masculinity contains such virtues as courage, strength, and wisdom. Still, some feminists continued to argue that Bly was advocating a return to traditional gender roles for both men and women, and other critics assailed what they saw as Bly's indiscriminate, New Age-influenced salad of tidbits from many traditions. Others found great value in the book, stressing its importance to contemporary culture's ongoing redefinition of sexuality. As Deborah Tannen put it in the *Washington Post Book World,* "This rewarding book is an invaluable contribution to the gathering public conversation about what it means to be male—or female." Bly's poetic style comes through in his prose as well. "To be sure, Bly's quirky style of argumentation does not follow a linear model from Point A to Point B," Dan Cryer noted in the *Detroit News.* "When he uses poems to make a point, clarity sometimes suffers. And his metaphorical language no doubt will put off some readers. Once a reader catches on, though, the rewards are plentiful." *Iron John* was at the top of the New York Times best-seller list for ten weeks and stayed on the list for more than a year. A related videocassette, *A Gathering of Men,* was an equally phenomenal success.

Bly put forth more "timely and important" ideas on social ills in his 1997 book *The Sibling Society.* In it, he contends that North Americans are like a race of perpetual adolescents; that young children grow up too quickly, yet never quite finish the process to become full-fledged adults. The result is a world full of people who lack empathy or sympathy, whose lives are self-serving and detrimental to the human race as a whole. The root of these problems, in Bly's opinion, is the erosion of respect for authority of all sorts. As Andres Rodriguez wrote in *National Catholic Reporter,* the poet finds that "consumer capitalism, in other words, has created a savage society where greed and desire extend almost limitlessly on the horizontal plane, while the vertical plane (for example, tradition, religion, devotion) is nearly totally absent." John Bemrose, reviewing *The Sibling Society* in *Maclean's,* remarked that while Bly is not the first person to present the ideas found in his book, "he brings a unique ability to bear on the subject as an interpreter of folktales and great literature," and explains the way "a constant bombardment of advertising keeps the hunger for new goods raging, and as corporations convince politicians that they must be allowed to do what they like (essentially taking over the leadership of society), people succumb to an infantile need for instant gratification." The poet "makes a convincing stab at defining maturity, championing such traditional virtues as self-discipline and a concern for others, as well as less obvious qualities, including a deeper respect for the gifts of the dead to the living. Bly's cranky and often brilliant jeremiad is not going to please apologists for the consumer society. But that alone should be enough to recommend it."

Throughout his career, Bly has maintained his devotion to translating the world's visionary poetry, in part as an effort to furthering multicultural understanding. His collection *The Night Abraham Called to the Stars* reflects his interest in other cultures; the poems in it are stylized versions of a Middle Eastern lyric known as the ghazal. Though traditionally a love-poem, the ghazal also regularly shifts its focus to touch on politics, myth, and philosophy. As such, it was a natural choice for Bly, and his best work in the form is "simple in diction and understated in effect," wrote a *Publishers Weekly* reviewer.

Michiko Kakutani observed in the *New York Times,* "What has remained constant in his work, . . . is Mr. Bly's interest in man's relationship with nature, and his commitment to an idiom built upon simplified diction and the free associative processes of the unconscious mind." Peter Stitt of the *New York Times Book Review* also emphasized the importance of free association in Bly's poetry. "Bly's method," Stitt wrote, "is free association; the imagination is allowed to discover whatever images it deems appropriate to the poem, no matter the logical, literal demands of consciousness." M.L. Rosenberg, writing in *Tribune Books,* noted in Bly's work a blending of European and South American influences with a decidedly American sensibility: "Bly is a genius of the elevated 'high' style, in the European tradition of Rilke and Yeats, the lush magical realism of the South Americans like Lorca and Neruda. Yet Bly's work is truly American, taking its atmosphere of wide empty space from the Midwest, and its unabashed straightforward emotionalism and spiritualism." "The energy with which the Minnesota poet Robert Bly unreservedly gives himself to his ideas, or in some cases, his preju-

dices," James F. Mersmann commented in his *Out of the Vietnam Vortex: A Study of Poets and Poetry against the War,* "makes him both one of the most annoying and most exciting poets of his time."

BIOGRAPHICAL AND CRITICAL SOURCES:

BOOKS

Bly, Robert, *Silence in the Snowy Fields,* Wesleyan University Press (Middletown, CT), 1962.

Contemporary Literary Criticism, Thomson Gale (Detroit, MI), Volume 1, 1973, Volume 2, 1974, Volume 5, 1976, Volume 10, 1979, Volume 15, 1980, Volume 38, 1986.

Contemporary Poets, St. James Press (Detroit, MI), 2001.

Daniels, Kate and Richard Jones, editors, *On Solitude and Silence: Writings on Robert Bly,* Beacon Press (Boston, MA), 1982, pp. 146-152.

Davis, William Virgil, *Understanding Robert Bly,* University of South Carolina Press (Columbia, SC), 1989.

Davis, William Virgil, *Robert Bly: The Poet and His Critics,* Camden House (Columbia, SC), 1994.

Dictionary of Literary Biography, Volume 5: *American Poets since World War II,* Thomson Gale (Detroit, MI), 1980.

Friberg, Ingegard, *Moving Inward: A Study of Robert Bly's Poetry,* Acta University Gothoburgensis, 1977.

Heep, Hartmut, *A Different Poem: Rainer Maria Rilke's American Translators Randall Jarrell, Robert Lowell, and Robert Bly,* Peter Lang (New York, NY), 1996.

Howard, Richard, *Alone with America: Essays on the Art of Poetry in the United States since 1950,* Atheneum (New York, NY), 1969, revised edition, 1980.

Lacey, Paul A., *The Inner War: Forms and Themes in Recent American Poetry,* Fortress Press, 1972.

Lensing, George S., and Ronald Moran, *Four Poets and the Emotive Imagination: Robert Bly, James Wright, Louis Simpson, and William Stafford,* Louisiana State University Press (Baton Rouge, LA), 1976.

Malkoff, Karl, *Escape from the Self: A Study in Contemporary American Poetry and Poetics,* Columbia University Press (New York, NY), 1977.

Mersmann, James F., *Out of the Vietnam Vortex: A Study of Poets and Poetry against the War,* University Press of Kansas (Lawrence, KS), 1974, pp. 113-157.

Molesworth, Charles, *The Fierce Embrace: A Study of Contemporary American Poetry,* University of Missouri Press (Columbia, MO), 1979.

Nelson, Howard, *Robert Bly: An Introduction to the Poetry,* Columbia University Press (New York, NY), 1984.

Newsmakers 1992, Thomson Gale (Detroit, MI), 1992.

Ossman, David, *The Sullen Art,* Corinth, 1963.

Peseroff, Joyce, editor, *Robert Bly: When Sleepers Awake,* University of Michigan Press (Ann Arbor, MI), 1984.

Poems for Young Readers, National Council of Teachers of English, for the Houston Festival of Contemporary Poetry, 1966.

Roberson, William H., *Robert Bly: A Primary and Secondary Bibliography,* Scarecrow (Lanham, MD), 1986.

St. James Encyclopedia of Popular Culture, St. James Press (Detroit, MI), 2000.

Shaw, Robert B., editor, *American Poetry since 1960: Some Critical Perspectives,* Dufour, 1974, pp. 55-67.

Smith, Thomas R., editor, *Walking Swiftly: Writings and Images on the Occasion of Robert Bly's Sixty-fifth Birthday,* Ally Press (St. Paul, MN), 1992.

Stepanchev, Stephen, *American Poetry Since 1945: A Critical Survey,* Harper (New York, NY), 1965, pp. 185-187.

Sugg, Richard P., *Robert Bly,* Twayne (Boston, MA), 1986.

PERIODICALS

America, September 28, 1996, William J. O'Malley, review of *The Sibling Society,* p. 34.

American Dialog, winter, 1968-69.

Antioch Review, summer, 2002, John Taylor, review of *The Roads Have Come to an End Now,* p. 535.

Book, January-February, 2002, Stephen Whited, review of *The Night Abraham Called to the Stars,* p. 70.

Booklist, October 15, 1994, Ray Olson, review of *Meditations on the Insatiable Soul,* p. 395; April 1, 1996, Ray Olson, review of *The Sibling Society,* p. 1322; May 1, 1999, Ray Olson, review of *Eating the Honey of Words: New and Selected Poems,* p. 1573.

Boundary 2, spring, 1976, pp. 677-700, 707-725.

Carleton Miscellany, Volume XVIII, number 1, 1979-80, pp. 74-84.

Chicago Review, Volume 19, number 2, 1967.

Chicago Tribune Book World, May 3, 1981; February 28, 1982, p. 2.

Christian Science Monitor, January 23, 1963.

Commonweal, July 23, 1971, pp. 375-380.

Detroit News, December 5, 1990, p. 3D.

English Studies, April, 1970, pp. 112-137.

Explicator, fall, 1999, Tom Hansen, review of *Surprised by Evening,* p. 53.

Far Point, fall-winter, 1969, pp. 42-47.

Globe and Mail (Toronto, Ontario, Canada), April 4, 1987; December 8, 1990, p. C10.

Harper's Magazine, August, 1968, pp. 73-77; January, 1980, p. 79.

Hollins Critic, April, 1975, pp. 1-15.

Hudson Review, autumn, 1968, p. 553; spring, 1976; spring, 1978; summer, 1987.

Iowa Review, summer, 1972, pp. 78-91; spring, 1973, pp. 111-126; fall, 1976, pp. 135-153.

Lamp in the Spine, number 3, 1972.

Library Journal, October 15, 1994, p. 62; July, 1996, Terry McMaster, review of *The Sibling Society,* p. 140; June 1, 1997, Fred Muratori, review of *Morning Poems,* p. 103; October 1, 1998, Mary Ann Hughes, review of *The Maiden King: The Reunion of Masculine and Feminine,* p. 118; June 1, 1999, Frank Allen, review of *Eating the Honey of Words: New and Selected Poems,* p. 118.

Listener, June 27, 1968.

London, December, 1968.

Los Angeles Times Book Review, May 18, 1980, p. 9; December 29, 1985, p. 11; October 26, 1986, p. 4; November 30, 1986, p. 11; December 2, 1990.

Maclean's, July 22, 1996, John Bemrose, review of *The Sibling Society,* p. 61.

Michigan Quarterly Review, spring, 1981, pp. 144-154.

Minneapolis-St. Paul Magazine, January, 1994, p. 38.

Modern Language Quarterly, March, 2001, Margaret Bruzelius, "The Kind of England . . . Loved to Look upon a Man," p. 19.

Modern Poetry Studies, winter, 1976, pp. 231-240.

Moons and Lion Tailes, Volume II, number 3, 1977, pp. 85-89.

Nation, March 25, 1968, pp. 413-414; November 17, 1979, pp. 503-504; October 31, 1981, pp. 447-448; November 26, 2001, Ian Tromp, review of *Stargazing and Sufi Poetics,* p. 54, review of *The Night Abraham Called to the Stars,* p. 54.

National Catholic Reporter, February 7, 1997, Andres Rodriguez, review of *The Sibling Society,* p. 23.

National Review, May 20, 1996, Florence King, *The Sibling Society,* p. 66.

New Republic, November 14, 1970, pp. 26-27; January 3, 1994, p. 31A; September 16, 1996, David Bromwich, review of *The Sibling Society,* p. 31.

New Statesman, November 15, 1996, Kirsty Milne, review of *The Sibling Society,* p. 47.

Newsweek, November 26, 1990, pp. 66-68.

New York Review of Books, June 20, 1968; November 28, 1996, Diane Johnson, review of *The Sibling Society,* p. 22.

New York Times, May 3, 1986; May 16, 1996.

New York Times Book Review, September 7, 1975; January 1, 1978; March 9, 1980, p. 8; April 26, 1981; February 14, 1982, p. 15; January 22, 1984, p. 1; October 13, 1985, p. 15; May 25, 1986, p. 2; February 22, 1987, p. 34; September 30, 1990, p. 29; December 9, 1990, p. 15; May 29, 1994, Richard Tillinghast, review of *The Darkness around Us Is Deep: Selected Poems of William Stafford,* p. 10; December 31, 1995, Bruno Maddox, review of *The Soul Is Here for Its Own Joy: Sacred Poems from Many Cultures,* p. 8; October 11, 1998, Karen Lehrman, review of *The Maiden King: The Reunion of Masculine and Feminine,* p. 11; November 18, 2001, Noah Isenberg, review of *The Half-Finished Heaven,* p. 68.

New York Times Magazine, February 3, 1980, p. 16.

Ohio Review, fall, 1978.

Partisan Review, Volume XLIV, number 2, 1977.

Poetry, June, 1963; March, 1996, Ben Howard, review of *Meditations on the Insatiable Soul,* p. 346; April, 2002, John Taylor, review of *The Night Abraham Called to the Stars,* p. 45.

Prairie Schooner, summer, 1968, pp. 176-178.

Publishers Weekly, May 9, 1980, pp. 10-11; October 12, 1990; March 25, 1996, review of *The Sibling Society,* p. 70; September 14, 1998, review of *The Maiden King,* p. 61; March 29, 1999, review of *Eating the Honey of Words,* p. 97; July 26, 1999, review of *The Best American Poetry 1999,* p. 84; April 23, 2001, review of *The Night Abraham Called to the Stars,* p. 73.

Rocky Mountain Review of Language and Literature, number 29, 1975, pp. 95-117.

San Francisco Review of Books, July-August, 1983, pp. 22-23.

Schist I, fall, 1973.

Sewanee Review, spring, 1974.

Shenandoah, spring, 1968, p. 70.

Star Tribune, December 2, 2001, John Habich, *Weird Elation,* p. E1.

Texas Quarterly, number 19, 1976, pp. 80-94.

Times Literary Supplement, March 16, 1967; February 20, 1981, p. 208.

Tribune Books (Chicago, IL), April 12, 1987, p. 5.

TWA Ambassador, December, 1980.

U.S. News & World Report, June 24, 1996, John Leo, review of *The Sibling Society,* p. 24.

Utne Reader, May-June, 1996, interview with Robert Bly, p. 58.

Virginia Quarterly Review, winter, 1963.

Washington Post, October 23, 1980; February 3, 1991, p. F1.

Washington Post Book World, April 1, 1973, p. 13; January 5, 1986, p. 6; December 14, 1986, p. 9; November 18, 1990, p. 1.

Western American Literature, spring, 1982, pp. 66-68; fall, 1982, pp. 282-284.

Win, January 15, 1973.

Windless Orchard, number 18, 1974, pp. 30-34.

World Literature Today, autumn, 1981, p. 680; spring, 1994, Ashley Brown, review of *Gratitude to Old Teachers,* p. 378; winter, 2000, Michael Leddy, review of *The Best American Poetry, 1999,* p. 172.

ONLINE

Menweb, http://www.menweb.org/ (July 5, 2003), Bert H. Hoff, interview with Robert Bly.

PBS Web site, http://www.pbs.org/ (July 5, 2003), "No Safe Place: Violence against Women" (interview with Robert Bly).

Robert Bly Home Page, http://www.robertbly.com/ (July 5, 2003), Frances Quinn, interview with Robert Bly.

*   *   *

BLY, Robert Elwood
  See BLY, Robert

*   *   *

BOLAND, Eavan 1944-
  (Eavan Aisling Boland)

PERSONAL: Born September 24, 1944, in Dublin, Ireland; daughter of Frederick (a diplomat) and Frances (a painter; maiden name, Kelly) Boland; married Kevin Casey (a novelist), 1969; children: two daughters. *Education:* Trinity College, Dublin, B.A., 1966.

ADDRESSES: Home—Dundrum, Ireland. *Office*—Department of English, Stanford University, 450 Serra Mall, Stanford, CA 94305. *E-mail*—boland@stanford.edu.

CAREER: Trinity College, Dublin, Ireland, lecturer; School of Irish Studies, Dublin, lecturer; Stanford University, Stanford, CA, Bella Mabury and Eloise Mabury Knapp Professor in Humanities and director of creative writing program. Has taught at University College, Dublin, at Bowdoin College, Brunswick, ME, at the University of Utah, and as Hurst Professor at Washington University, St. Louis, MO, 1993. Participated in University of Iowa International Writing Program, 1979.

MEMBER: Irish Academy of Letters.

AWARDS, HONORS: Irish Arts Council Macauley fellowship, 1967, for *New Territory;* Irish American Cultural Award, 1983; Poetry Book Society Choice, 1987, for *The Journey,* 1990, for *Outside History,* and 1994, for *In a Time of Violence;* Lannan Award for Poetry, 1994; American Ireland Fund Literary Award, 1994; Lawrence O'Shaughnessy Award for Poetry, Center for Irish Studies, University of St. Thomas, 1997; Bucknell Medal of Merit, 2000; *New York Times* notable book designation, 2001, for *Against Love Poetry;* John William Corrington Award for Literary Excellence, Centenary College of Louisiana, 2002; Frederick Nims Memorial Prize, *Poetry,* 2002; Smartt Family Prize, *Yale Review,* for poems in *Against Love Poetry.* Honorary degrees from University College, Dublin, 1997; Strathclyde University, 1997; Colby College, 1998; and Holy Cross College, 2000.

WRITINGS:

POETRY

23 Poems, Gallagher (Dublin, Ireland), 1962.
Autumn Essay, Gallagher (Dublin, Ireland), 1963.
New Territory, Allen Figgis & Co. (Dublin, Ireland), 1967.
The War Horse, Gollancz (London, England), 1975.
In Her Own Image, Arlen House (Dublin, Ireland), 1980.
Introducing Eavan Boland, Ontario Review Press (New York, NY), 1981.
Night Feed, M. Boyars (Boston, MA), 1982.
The Journey, Deerfield Press (Deerfield, MA), 1983.
The Journey and Other Poems, Carcanet Press (Manchester, England), 1987.
Selected Poems, Carcanet Press (Manchester, England), 1989.
Outside History: Selected Poems, 1980-1990, Norton (New York, NY), 1990.
In a Time of Violence, Norton (New York, NY), 1994.
A Dozen Lips, Attic Press (Dublin, Ireland), 1994.

A Christmas Chalice, State University of New York at Buffalo (Buffalo, NY), 1994.
Collected Poems, Carcanet Press (Manchester, England), 1995, published as *An Origin like Water: Collected Poems, 1967-1987,* Norton (New York, NY), 1996.
Anna Liffey, Poetry Ireland (Dublin, Ireland), 1997.
Limitations, Center for the Book Arts (New York, NY), 2000.
Against Love Poetry, Norton (New York, NY), 2001.
Journey with Two Maps: An Anthology, Carcanet Press (Manchester, England), 2002.
After Every War: Twentieth-Century Women Poets: Translations from the German Princeton University Press (Princeton, NJ), 2004.

Work represented in anthologies, including *The Observer Arvon Poetry Collection,* Guardian Newspapers (London, England), 1994; *Penguin Modern Poets,* Penguin (London, England), 1995; *To Persephone,* Wesleyan University Press/New England Foundation for the Arts (Hanover, NH), 1996; *The Norton Anthology of Poetry,* edited by Margaret Ferguson, Mary Jo Salter, and Jon Stallworthy, Norton (New York, NY), 1998; *American's Favorite Poems,* edited by Robert Pinsky and Maggie Dietz, Norton, 1999; *The Norton Anthology of English Literature,* edited by M.H. Abrams and Stephen Greenblatt, Norton, 1999; *The Body Electric: America's Best Poetry from the American Poetry Review,* edited by Stephen Berg, David Bonanno, and Arthur Vogelsang, Norton, 2000; *The Longman Anthology of Women's Literature,* edited by Mary K. Deshazer, Longman (London, England), 2000; *The Norton Introduction to Literature,* eighth edition, edited by J. Paul Hunter, Alison Booth, and Kelly J. Mays, Norton, 2001; *The Longman Anthology of British Literature: The Twentieth Century,* edited by David Damrosch, Addison-Wesley Longman, 2002; and *Faber Anthology of Irish Verse, Penguin Anthology of Irish Verse, Pan Anthology of Irish Verse,* and *Sphere Anthology of Irish Verse.*

OTHER

(With Michael MacLiammoir) *W.B. Yeats and His World,* Thames & Hudson (London, England), 1971, Thames & Hudson (New York, NY), 1986.
The Emigrant Irish, British Council (London, England), 1986.
A Kind of Scar: The Woman Poet in a National Tradition, Attic Press (Dublin, Ireland), 1989.
(With Aileen MacKeogh and Brian P. Kennedy) *House,* Dublin Project (Dublin, Ireland), 1991.

Gods Make Their Own Importance: The Authority of the Poet in Our Time, Society Productions (London, England), 1994, published as *Object Lessons: The Life of the Woman and the Poet in Our Time,* Norton (New York, NY), 1995.

(With Harriet Levin) *The Christmas Show,* Beacon Press (Boston, MA), 1997.

(Editor, with John Hollander) *Committed to Memory: One Hundred Best Poems to Memorize,* Riverhead Books (New York, NY), 1997.

The Lost Land, Norton (New York, NY), 1998.

(Editor, with Mark Strand) *The Making of a Poem: A Norton Anthology of Poetic Forms,* Norton (New York, NY), 2000.

(Editor, with J.D. McClatchy) Horace, *The Odes,* Princeton University Press (Princeton, NJ), 2002.

(Editor) *Three Irish Poets,* Carcanet Press (Manchester, England), 2003.

Regular contributor to *Irish Times.* Contributor to *Irish Press, Spectator, American Poetry Review,* and *Soundings.*

SIDELIGHTS: Over the course of a career that began in the early 1960s, when she was a young wife in Dublin, Eavan Boland has emerged as one of the foremost female voices in Irish literature. Describing those formative years in an interview with Jody Allen Randolph for *Colby Quarterly* and later included on the Web site of her publisher, Carcanet Press, Boland said, "I began that time watching milk being taken in metal churns, on horse and cart, towards the city center. And I ended it as a married woman, in a flat on Raglan Road, watching this ghostly figure of a man walking on the moon. I suppose I began the decade in a city which Joyce would have recognized, and ended it in one that would have bewildered him."

During this time, Boland honed an appreciation for the ordinary in life, an appreciation reflected in the title of her 2001 collection, *Against Love Poetry.* "So much of European love poetry," she told Alice Quinn of the *New Yorker* Online, "is court poetry, coming out of the glamorous traditions of the court. . . . Love poetry, from the troubadours on, is traditionally about that romantic lyric moment. There's little about the ordinariness of love." Seeking a poetry that would express the beauty of the plain things that make up most people's existence, she found that she would have to create it for herself. It is this "dailiness," as Boland calls it, that reviewers often find, and praise, in her poetry. Frank Allen, in a *Library Journal* review of *Against Love Poetry,* wrote, "This volume . . . dramatizes conflicts be-

tween marriage and freedom ('what is hidden in / this ordinary, aging human love')." In her own words, as quoted in Bruce F. Murphy's review of the book in *Poetry,* Boland wrote *Against Love Poetry* "to mark the contradictions of a daily love."

Although Murphy noted that *Against Love Poetry* "is a book that is often less political than it aims to be," Boland does have a political voice. According to Adrian Oktenberg in *Women's Review of Books,* Boland has "long been acknowledged as an essential political poet." Blending the history of Ireland and its ancient culture, as well as modern politics into her work, she offers a unique perspective on love and marriage, as Oktenberg noted, that is "not merely personal and individual but collective and centuries-long. When she looks at a city, she remembers the forest that preceded it. When she examines couplehood, it is not merely her own and her husband's but those who preceded them by generations, and then further back into legend and myth. When she thinks about politics, it is always in the context of history. . . . However often Boland looks at the 'burdens of a history,' she rejects the notion that things should necessarily or inevitably remain the same."

In a Time of Violence is a work in which Boland "explores her imaginative re-creations of history," according to Richard Rankin Russell in his review for *Explicator.* In the poem "Lava Cameo," Boland entwines her personal history with the history of the time, as she relates the relationship between her grandmother and grandfather, beginning from when they met as he disembarked from a ship in Cork Harbour, until their deaths. As Russell noted of the section depicting the grandparents' meeting, "A close reading of this poem illustrates how its subject, tone, sentence structure, and diction enable Boland to imagine this scene, sympathetically write herself into it, and establish a new relationship with her grandparents and her own personal history."

With the themes of feminism and "conflicts between marriage and freedom" recurring in Boland's work, as Ailbhe Smyth stated in her review of *Object Lessons* for *Women's Review of Books,* "Boland has given women a new place in Irish poetry. . . . This rare work expresses the problems and defiances of a poet as a woman seeking truth in her life and career." In the words of Melanie Rehak in the *New York Times Book Review,* Boland's is a voice "that is by now famous for its unwavering feminism as well as its devotion to both the joys of domesticity and her native Ireland." Boland does not seem to be content, as a poet, to uphold one view of things to the exclusion of all other.

Acknowledgement for Boland's work has been long in coming, but as Randolph noted, that recognition had by the 1990s arrived, and in a big way. Irish students wishing to graduate from secondary school must undergo a series of examinations for what is called the "leaving certificate." The writings of great national poets such as Seamus Heaney are a mandatory part of the leaving exam, and since 1999, would-be graduates are required to undergo examinations in Boland's work as well. Among the more traditional awards Boland has won are the Irish American Cultural Award, the Lannan Award for Poetry, the American Ireland Fund Literary Award, the Lawrence O'Shaughnessy Award for Poetry, the Bucknell Medal of Merit, the Corrington Award for Literay Excellence, the Frederick Nims Memorial Prize, and the Smartt Family Prize.

BIOGRAPHICAL AND CRITICAL SOURCES:

BOOKS

Adams, Henry, *The Education of Henry Adams,* introduction by Edmund Morris, Random House (New York, NY), 1999.

Boland, Eavan, *In a Time of Violence,* Norton (New York, NY), 1995.

Boland, Eavan, *An Origin like Water,* Norton (New York, NY), 1997.

Contemporary Literary Criticism, Thomson Gale (Detroit, MI), Volume 40, 1986, Volume 67, 1992.

Coyne, J. Stirling, and N.P. Willis, *Scenery and Antiquitites of Ireland,* Virtue (London, England), 1840.

Dictionary of Literary Biography, Volume 40: *Poets of Great Britain and Ireland since 1960,* Thomson Gale (Detroit, MI), 1985.

Haberstroh, Patricia Boyle, *Women Creating Women: Contemporary Irish Women Poets,* Syracuse University Press (Syracuse, NY), 1996.

PERIODICALS

American Poetry Review, September, 1999, review of *The Lost Land,* p. 7.

Bloomsbury Review, March, 1998, review of *Object Lessons,* p. 22.

Booklist, March 15, 1994, p. 1322; February 15, 1996, p. 983; October 15, 1998, review of *The Lost Land,* p. 389; March 15, 1999, review of *The Lost Land,* p. 1276.

Commonweal, November 4, 1988, p. 595.

Entertainment Weekly, January 15, 1999, review of *The Lost Land,* p. 58.

Explicator, winter, 2002, Richard Rankin Russell, review of *In a Time of Violence,* p. 114.

Financial Times, November 1, 2003, Ruth Padel, review of *Three Irish Poets: An Anthology,* p. 32.

Hudson Review, August, 1999, review of *The Lost Land,* p. 507.

Irish Literary Supplement, fall, 1994, p. 23; fall, 1995, p. 8; spring, 1996, p. 30; spring, 1999, review of *The Lost Land,* p. 15.

Kirkus Reviews, October 15, 1998, review of *The Lost Land,* p. 1492.

Library Journal, November 15, 1990, p. 74; March 1, 1994, p. 90; July, 2001, Frank Allen, review of *Against Love Poetry,* pp. 94-95.

Nation, June 6, 1994, p. 798; April 24, 1995, p. 564.

New Hibernia Review, spring, 2001.

New Statesman & Society, January 26, 1996, p. 40.

New York Review of Books, May 26, 1994, p. 25.

New York Times Book Review, April 21, 1991, p. 40; November 4, 2001, Melanie Rehak, "Map of Love."

Poetry, July, 1990, p. 236; October, 1994, p. 41; February, 1998, review of *An Origin like Water,* p. 282; March, 2003, Bruce F. Murphy, review of *Against Love Poetry,* p. 347.

Publishers Weekly, October 26, 1990, p. 62; December 18, 1995, p. 51; August 31, 1998, review of *The Lost Land,* p. 69.

Southern Review, spring, 1999, review of *The Lost Land,* p. 387.

Times Literary Supplement, August 5, 1994, p. 19; September 8, 1995, p. 28; December 10, 1999, review of *The Lost Land,* p. 23.

Women's Review of Books, September, 1995, Ailbhe Smyth, review of *Object Lessons,* p. 7; April, 1999, review of *The Lost Land,* p. 17; July, 2003, Adrian Oktenberg, review of *Against Love Poetry,* p. 36.

Yale Review, July, 1999, review of *The Lost Land,* p. 167.

ONLINE

Academy of American Poets Web site, http://www.poets.org/ (September 18, 2001), "Eavan Boland."

Carcanet Press Web site, http://www.carcanet.co.uk/ (October 16, 2002), Jody Allen Randolph, "A Backward Look: An Interview with Eavan Boland."

Centanary College of Louisiana, Department of English Web site, http://www.centenary.edu/english/ (July 22, 2004), "Corrington Award."

Galway Arts Center Web site, http://www.galwayarts centre.ie/west47/ (July 23, 2004), Michael S. Begnal, "West 47 Critique/Review, Radical Chic."

New Yorker Online, http://www.newyorker.com/ (October 29, 2001), Alice Quinn, "Q&A: The Stoicisms of Love" (interview with Boland).

Skoool.ie Interactive Learning, http://www.skoool.ie/ (October 16, 2002), "Eavan Boland."

*   *   *

BOLAND, Eavan Aisling
See BOLAND, Eavan

*   *   *

BÖLL, Heinrich 1917-1985
(Heinrich Theodor Böll)

PERSONAL: Born December 21, 1917, in Cologne, Germany; died of complications from arteriosclerosis, July 16, 1985, at his home in Huertgen Forest in the Eifel Mountains, near Bonn, Germany; son of Viktor (a master furniture maker) and Maria (Hermanns) Böll; married Annemarie Cech (a translator), 1942; children: Christoph (died, 1945), Raimund (died, 1982), Rene, Vincent. *Education:* Completed college preparatory school; attended the University of Cologne, 1939. *Religion:* Roman Catholic.

CAREER: Apprentice to a book dealer in Bonn, Germany, 1938; writer, 1947-85. Guest lecturer of poetics, University of Frankfurt, 1964. *Military service:* German Army, 1939-45; American prisoner of war, 1945.

AWARDS, HONORS: Prize from "Group 47," 1951, for short story "The Black Sheep"; Rene Schickele Prize, 1952; Cultural Prize of German Industry; Southern German Radio Prize and German Critics Prize, both 1953, both for radio play *Moench and Raeuber;* French Publishers Prize for best foreign novel, *Tribune de Paris,* 1954; Edward von der Heydt Prize from City of Wuppertal, 1958; Grand Art Prize of North Rhine-Westphalia, 1959; Charles Veillon Prize, 1960; Literature Prize of City of Cologne, 1960; Premio d'Isola d'Elba, 1965; Premio Calabria, 1966; George Buechner Prize, German Academy for Language and Poetry, 1967; Nobel Prize for Literature, 1972, for contributions to "a renewal of German literature in the postwar era"; honorary doctorates from Trinity College, University of Dublin, University of Aston, University of Birmingham, and Brunel University, all 1973; Carl von Ossietzky Medal, International League of Human Rights, 1974; first Neil Gunn fellow, Scottish Arts Council, 1974; named honorary member of American Academy of Arts and Letters, and of American National Institute of Art and Literature, both 1974; named honorary citizen of City of Cologne, 1983; honorary title of professor conferred by North Rhine-Westphalia, 1983.

WRITINGS:

FICTION

Der Zug war puenktlich (also see below; novella), F. Middelhauve (Opladen, Germany), 1949, reprinted, Deutscher Taschenbuch (Munich, Germany), 1973, translation by Richard Graves published as *The Train Was on Time,* Criterion Books (New York, NY), 1956, translation by Leila Vennewitz, Northwestern University Press (Evanston, IL), 1994.

Wanderer, kommst du nach Spa (also see below; short stories; includes "Damals in Odessa"), F. Middelhauve, 1950, reprinted, Deutscher Taschenbuch (Munich, Germany), 1971, translation by Mervyn Savill published as *Traveller, If You Come to Spa,* Arco (New York, NY), 1956, bilingual edition translated and edited by Mervyn Savill and John Bednall, Max Hueber (Munich, Germany), 1956.

Wo warst du, Adam? (also see below; novel), F. Middlehauve, 1951, reprinted, Deutscher Taschenbuch (Munich, Germany), 1972, translation by Mervyn Savill published as *Adam, Where Art Thou?,* Criterion Books (New York, NY), 1955, new translation by Lelia Vennewitz published as *And Where Were You, Adam?,* Northwestern University Press (Evanston, IL), 1994.

Nicht nur zur Weihnachtszeit (also see below; satire), Frankfurter Verlags-Anstalt (Frankfurt, Germany), 1952, expanded edition with other satires published as *Nichtnurzur Weihnachtszeit: Satiren,* Deutscher Taschenbuch (Munich, Germany), 1966, new edition, Kiepenheuer & Witsch (Cologne, Germany), 1981.

Und sagte kein einziges Wort (also see below; novel), Kiepenheuer & Witsch (Cologne, Germany), 1953, reprinted with epilogue by Gerhard Joop, Ullstein (Frankfurt, Germany), 1972, translation by Richard Graves published as *Acquainted with the Night,* Holt (New York, NY), 1954, new translation by Lelia Vennewitz published as *And Never Said a Word,* McGraw (New York, NY), 1978, reprinted, Northwestern University Press (Evanston, IL), 1994.

Haus ohne Hueter (also see below; novel), Kiepenheuer
Witsch (Cologne, Germany), 1954, reprinted, 1974,
translation by Mervyn Savill published as *Tomor-
row and Yesterday,* Criterion Books (New York,
NY), 1957, also published as *The Unguarded
House,* Arco (New York, NY), 1957.

Das Brot der fruehen Jahre: Erzaehlung (also see be-
low; novella), Kiepenheuer & Witsch (Cologne,
Germany), 1955, reprinted, 1980, translation by
Mervyn Savill published as *The Bread of Our Early
Years,* Arco (New York, NY), 1957, new translation
by Lelia Vennewitz published as *The Bread of
Those Early Years,* McGraw (New York, NY),
1976.

So ward Abend und Morgen: Erzaehlungen (stories),
Verlag der Arche (Zurich, Switzerland), 1955.

Unberechenbare Gaeste: Heitere Erzaehlungen (stories), Verlag der Arche, 1956.

Abenteuer eines Brotbeutels, und andere Geschichten
(stories), edited by Richard Plant, Norton (New
York, NY), 1957.

Im Tal der donnernden Hufe: Erzaehlung (also see below; novella), Insel-Verlag (Wiesbaden), 1957.

*Doktor Murkes gesammeltes Schweigen, und andere
Satiren* (also see below; satires; includes *Doktor
Murkes gesammeltes Schweigen* and *Der Wegwerfer*), Kiepenheuer & Witsch (Cologne, Germany),
1958, reprinted, 1977.

Erzaehlungen (contains *Der Zug war puenktlich* and
Wanderer, kommst du nach Spa), F. Middelhauve,
1958.

Billard um halbzehn (also see below; novel), Kiepenheuer & Witsch (Cologne, Germany), 1959, translation by Patrick Bowles published as *Billiards at
Half-Past Nine,* Weidenfeld & Nicolson, 1961,
McGraw (New York, NY), 1962, new translation
by Lelia Vennewitz, Avon, 1975.

Der Bahnhof von Zimpren: Erzaehlungen (stories), Peter List (Munich, Germany), 1959.

Die Waage der Baleks, und andere Erzaehlungen (stories), Union Verlag (Berlin, Germany), 1959.

*Der Mann mit den Messern: Erzaehlungen; mit einem
autobiographischen Nachwort* (stories with an autobiographical epilogue), Reclam (Stuttgart, Germany), 1959, reprinted, 1972.

Nicht nur zur Weihnachtszeit [and] *Der Mann mit den
Messern,* edited by Dorothea Berger, American
Book Company, 1959.

Als der Krieg ausbrach; als der Krieg zu Ende war
(also see below), Insel, 1962, published as *Als der
Krieg ausbrach: Erzaehlungen,* Deutscher Taschenbuch (Munich, Germany), 1966.

Ansichten eines Clowns (also see below; novel),
Kiepenheuer & Witsch (Cologne, Germany), 1963,

translation by Lelia Vennewitz published as *The
Clown,* McGraw (New York, NY), 1965.

*Heinrich Böll, 1947 bis 1951: Der Zug war puenktlich,
Wo Warst du, Adam?, und sechsundzwanzig Erzaehlungen* (also see below) F. Middlehauve, 1963.

*Doktor Murkes gesammeltes Schweigen, and Other Sto-
ries,* edited by Gertrude Seidmann, introduction by
H.M. Waidson, Harrap, 1963.

Entfernung von der Truppe (also see below; novella),
Kiepenheuer & Witsch (Cologne, Germany), 1964.

Fuenf Erzaehlungen (also see below; stories), De Roos,
1964.

Absent without Leave: Two Novellas (translations by
Lelia Vennewitz of *Entfernung von der Truppe* and
Als der Krieg ausbrach; als der Krieg zu Ende war
under the titles *Absent without Leave* and *Enter and
Exit*), McGraw (New York, NY), 1965.

Ende einer Dienstfahrt (also see below; novel), Kiepenheuer & Witsch (Cologne, Germany), 1966, translation by Lelia Vennewitz published as *The End of a
Mission,* McGraw (New York, NY), 1967.

Eighteen Stories (translations by Lelia Vennewitz; contains translation of "Im Tal der donnernden Hufe:
Erzaehlung" published as "In the Valley of the
Thundering Hooves," of "Doktor Murkes gesammeltes Schweigen" published as "Murke's Collected Silences," and of "Der Wegwerfer" published as "The Thrower Away"), McGraw (New
York, NY), 1966.

Absent without Leave, and Other Stories, translated by
Lelia Vennewitz, Weidenfeld & Nicholson, 1967.

Und sagte kein einziges Wort [and] *Haus ohne Hueter*
[and] *Das Brot der fruehen Jahre,* Kiepenheuer &
Witsch (Cologne, Germany), 1969.

Children Are Civilians Too (story translations by Lelia
Vennewitz; contains translation of *Wanderer, kom-
mst du nach Spa,* which includes "Damals in
Odessa" published as "That Time We Were in
Odessa," and selected stories from *Heinrich Böll,
1947 bis 1951*), McGraw (New York, NY), 1970.

Adam, and, The Train: Two Novels (translation by Lelia
Vennewitz of *Wo warst du, Adam?* and *Der Zug
war puenktlich*), McGraw (New York, NY), 1970.

Gruppenbild mit Dame (novel), Kiepenheuer & Witsch
(Cologne, Germany), 1971, translation by Lelia
Vennewitz published as *Group Portrait with Lady,*
McGraw (New York, NY), 1973.

Die Essenholer, und andere Erzaehlungen (stories),
Hirschgraben-Verlag (Frankfurt), 1971.

Fuenf Erzaehlungen (stories), Hyperion-Verlag
(Freiburg), 1971.

Billard um halbzehn [and] *Ansichten eines Clowns*
[and] *Ende einer Dienstfahrt,* Kiepenheuer &
Witsch (Cologne, Germany), 1971.

Erzaehlungen, 1950-1970 (stories), Kiepenheuer & Witsch (Cologne, Germany), 1972.

Die verlorene Ehre der Katharina Blum; oder, wie Gewalt enstehen und wohin sie fuehren kann (novel with epilogue), Kiepenheuer & Witsch (Cologne, Germany), 1974, translation by Lelia Vennewitz published as *The Lost Honor of Katharina Blum: How Violence Develops and Where It Can Lead,* McGraw (New York, NY), 1975, reprinted as *The Lost Honor of Katharina Blum,* Transaction Publishers (New Brunswick, NJ), 2000.

Mein trauriges Gesicht: Humoresken und Satiren, Phillip Reclam (Leipzig, Germany), 1974, 2nd edition, 1979.

Berichte zur Gesinnungslage der Nation (satire), Kiepenheuer & Witsch (Cologne, Germany), 1975.

Fuersorgliche Belagerung (novel), Kiepenheuer & Witsch (Cologne, Germany), 1979, translation by Lelia Vennewitz published as *The Safety Net,* Knopf (New York, NY), 1982.

Du faehrst zu oft nach Heidelberg (stories), Lamuv (Bornheim-Merten), 1979, published as *Du faehrst zu oft nach Heidelberg und andere Erzaehlungen,* Deutscher Taschenbuch (Munich, Germany), 1982.

Gesammelte Erzaehlungen (stories), Kiepenheuer & Witsch (Cologne, Germany), 1981.

Das Vermaechtnis (novel originally written in 1948), Lamuv (Gottingen, Germany), 1982, translation by Lelia Vennewitz published as *A Soldier's Legacy,* Knopf (New York, NY), 1985.

Die Verwundung und andere fruehe Erzaehlungen (stories from 1948-1952), Lamuv (Gottingen, Germany), 1983, translation by Lelia Vennewitz published as *The Casualty,* Farrar, Straus (New York, NY), 1986.

Der Angriff: Erzaehlungen, 1947-1949 (stories), Kiepenheuer & Witsch (Cologne, Germany), 1983.

Die schwarzen Schafe: Erzaehlungen, 1950-1952 (stories), Kiepenheuer & Witsch (Cologne, Germany), 1983.

Veraenderungen in Staech: Erzaehlungen, 1962-1980 (stories), Kiepenheuer & Witsch (Cologne, Germany), 1984.

Frauen vor Flusslandschaft: Roman in Dialogen und Selbstgespraechen (novel), Kiepenheuer & Witsch (Cologne, Germany), 1985, translation by David McLintock published as *Women in a River Landscape: A Novel in Dialogues and Soliloquies,* Knopf (New York, NY), 1989.

The Stories of Heinrich Böll, translated by Lelia Vennewitz, Random House (New York, NY), 1986.

Der Engel Schwieg: Roman, Kiepenheuer & Witsch (Cologne, Germany), 1992, English translation by Breon Mitchell published as *The Silent Angel,* St. Martin's Press (New York, NY), 1994.

The Mad Dog: Stories, translated by Breon Mitchell, St. Martin's Press (New York, NY), 1997.

PLAYS

Die Spurlosen (also see below; radio play), Hans Bredow-Institut (Hamburg, Germany), 1957.

Bilanz [and] *Klopfzeichen: Zwei Hoerspiele* (also see below; radio plays; *Bilanz* first produced, 1957; translation of *Klopfzeichen* produced as *The Knocking,* British Broadcasting Corp., September, 1967), Reclam, 1961.

Ein Schluck Erde (stage play), Kiepenheuer & Witsch (Cologne, Germany), 1962.

Zum Tee bei Dr. Borsig: Hoerspiele (radio plays), Deutscher Taschenbuch (Munich, Germany), 1964.

Die Spurlosen: Drei Hoerspiele (radio plays), Insel-Verlag (Leipzig, Germany), 1966.

Vier Hoerspiele (radio plays), edited by G.P. Sonnex, Methuen, 1966.

Hausfriedensbruch: Hoerspiel [and] *Aussatz: Schauspiel* (radio play and theatre play, respectively; *Aussatz* first produced at Aachen's City Theatre, October 17, 1970), Kiepenheuer & Witsch (Cologne, Germany), 1969.

(With Dorothee Soelle and Lucas Mariz Boehmer) *Politische Meditationen zu Glueck und Vergeblichkeit* (television plays), Luchterhand (Darmstadt, Germany), 1973.

Ein Tag wie sonst: Hoerspiele (radio plays), Deutscher Taschenbuch (Munich, Germany), 1980.

NONFICTION

Irisches Tagebuch, Kiepenheuer & Witsch (Cologne, Germany), 1957, reprinted, 1972, translation by Lelia Vennewitz published as *Irish Journal,* McGraw (New York, NY), 1967, reprinted, Marlboro Press (Evanston, IL), 1998.

Brief an einen jungen Katholiken, Kiepenheuer & Witsch (Cologne, Germany), 1961.

Frankfurter Vorlesungen (lectures), Kiepenheuer & Witsch (Cologne, Germany), 1966.

Hierzulande: Aufsaetze (essays), Deutscher Taschenbuch (Munich, Germany), 1967.

Aufsaetze, Kritiken, Reden (essays, reviews, and speeches), Kiepenheuer & Witsch (Cologne, Germany), 1967.

Neue politische und literarische Schriften (also see below; essays on politics and literature), Kiepenheuer & Witsch (Cologne, Germany), 1973.

Schwierigkeiten mit der Bruederlichkeit: Politische Schriften (selections from *Neue politische und literarische Schriften*), Deutscher Taschenbuch (Munich, Germany), 1976.

Einmischung erwuenscht (selection of essays and speeches published 1971-1976), Kiepenheuer & Witsch (Cologne, Germany), 1977.

Missing Persons and Other Essays (selected essays, reviews, and speeches from 1952-1976), translated by Lelia Vennewitz, McGraw (New York, NY), 1977.

Spuren der Zeitgenossenschaft: Literarische Schriften (selection of literary essays and speeches from 1971-1976), Deutscher Taschenbuch (Munich, Germany), 1980.

Gefahren von falschen Bruedern: Politische Schriften (selection of political essays and speeches from 1971-1976), Deutscher Taschenbuch (Munich, Germany), 1980.

Was soll aus dem Jungen bloss werden? Oder Irgendwas mit Buechern (autobiography), Lamuv (Gottingen, Germany), 1981, translation by Lelia Vennewitz published as *What's to Become of the Boy? Or Something to Do with Books,* Knopf (New York, NY), 1984, published with notes and introduction by J.H. Reid, Manchester University (New York, NY), 1991.

Vermintes Gelaende: Essayistische Schriften 1977-1981 (essays), Kiepenheuer & Witsch (Cologne, Germany), 1982.

Bild, Bonn, Boenisch (political analysis), Lamuv (Gottingen, Germany), 1984.

"HEINRICH BÖLL WERKE" SERIES; OMNIBUS EDITIONS

Heinrich Böll Werke: Romane und Erzaehlungen 1947-1977 (contains all novels, novellas, and stories from 1947-1977), five volumes, edited by Bernd Balzer, Kiepenheuer & Witsch (Cologne, Germany), 1977.

Heinrich Böll Werke: Essayistische Schriften und Reden (contains all essays, reviews, and speeches through 1978), three volumes, edited by Bernd Balzer, Kiepenheuer & Witsch (Cologne, Germany), 1979.

Heinrich Böll Werke: Interviews (contains all interviews and conversations through 1978), edited by Bernd Balzer, Kiepenheuer & Witsch (Cologne, Germany), 1979.

Heinrich Böll Werke: Hoerspiele, Theaterstuecke, Drehbuecher, Gedichte (contains all plays for radio, theater, and film through 1978, and poems through 1972), edited by Bernd Balzer, Kiepenheuer & Witsch (Cologne, Germany), 1979.

OTHER

Aus unseren Tagen, edited by Gisela Stein, Holt (New York, NY), 1960.

Erzaehlungen, Hoerspiele, Aufsaetze (short stories, radio plays, and essays), Kiepenheuer & Witsch (Cologne, Germany), 1961.

(With others) *Der Rat der Welt-Unweisen,* S. Mohn (Guetersloh), 1965.

(Contributor) Albrecht Beckel, *Mensch, Gesellschaft, Kirche bei Heinrich Böll* (contains "Interview mit mir selbst"), Verlag A. Fromm (Osnabruech, Germany), 1966.

Die Spurlosen, by Heinrich Böll [and] *Philemon und Baukis, by Leopold Ahlsen,* Odyssey Press, 1967.

Gespraech mit dem Zauberer (conversation with Alexander Adrion), Olten, 1968.

Mein trauriges Gesicht: Erzaehlungen und Aufsaetze (stories and essays), Verlag Progress (Moscow, Russia), 1968.

Geschichten aus zwoelf Jahren, Suhrkamp, 1969.

Böll fuer Zeitgenossen: Ein kulturgeschichtliches Lesebuch, edited by Ralph Ley, Harper (New York, NY), 1970.

Edition Text [und] *Kritik* (conversation with Heinz Ludwig Arnold), Richard Boorberg (Munich, Germany), 1971.

Gedichte (poetry), Literarisches Colloquium (Berlin, Germany), 1972.

Heinrich Böll: The Novel Prizewinner Reflects on His Career (sound recording; interview by Edwin Newman), Center for Cassette Studies (North Hollywood, CA), c. 1974.

Drei Tage im Maerz (conversations with Christian Linder), Kiepenheuer & Witsch (Cologne, Germany), 1975.

Der Lorbeer ist immer noch bitter: Literarische Schriften, Deutscher Taschenbuch (Munich, Germany), 1976.

(With others) *Die Erschiessung des Georg von Rauch,* Wagenbuch (Berlin, Germany), 1976.

Querschnitte: Aus Interviews, Aufsaetzen und Reden, edited by Viktor Böll and Renate Matthaei, Kiepenheuer & Witsch (Cologne, Germany), 1977.

(Contributor) J. Davis, P. Broughton, and M. Wood, editors, *Literature, Fiction, Poetry, Drama* (contains translation by Denver Lindley of *Nicht nur zur Weihnachtszeit* published as *Christmas Every Day*), Scott Foresman, 1977.

Mein Lesebuch, Fischer-Taschenbuch (Frankfurt), 1978.

(Editor, with Freimut Duve and Klaus Staeck) *Briefe zur Verteidigung der Republik* (letters), Rowohlt (Reinbek bei Hamburg, Germany), 1977.

(Editor, with Freimut Duve and Klaus Staeck) *Briefe zur Verteidigung der burgerlichen Freiheit* (letters, continuation of *Briefe zur Verteidigung der Republik*), Rowohlt (Reinbek bei Hamburg, Germany), 1978.

Einmischung erwunscht: Schriften zur zeit (selected works), Kiepenheuer & Witsch (Cologne, Germany), 1977.

Eine deutsche Erinnerung (translation from the French by Annette Lallenmand of interview with Rene Wintzen), Kiepenheuer & Witsch (Cologne, Germany), 1979.

(Editor, with Freimut Duve and Klaus Staeck) *Kampfen fur die Sanfte Republik: Ausblick auf die achtziger jahre,* Rowohlt (Reinbek bei Hamburg, Germany), 1980.

(Editor, with Freimut Duve and Klaus Staeck) *Zuviel Pazifismus?,* Rowohlt (Reinbek bei Hamburg, Germany), 1981.

Warum haben wir aufeinander geschossen? (conversation with Lew Kopelew), Lamuv (Gottingen, Germany), 1981.

Gedichte mit Collagen von Klaus Staeck (poetry), Lamuv (Gottingen, Germany), 1975, revised edition with poems through 1980, Deutscher Taschenbuch (Munich, Germany), 1981.

Antikommunismus in Ost und West (conversations with Kopelew and Heinrich Vormeg), Bund-Verlag (Cologne, Germany), 1982.

Ueber Phantasie: Siegfried Lenz, Gespraeche mit Heinrich Böll, Guenter Grass, Walter Kempowski, Pavel Kohout (interview), Hoffmann & Campe, 1982.

Das Heinrich Böll Lesebuch, edited by Viktor Böll, Deutscher Taschenbuch (Munich, Germany), 1982.

(Editor, with Freimut Duve and Klaus Staeck) *Verantwortlich fur Polen,* Rowohlt (Reinbek bei Hamburg, Germany), 1982.

Ein-und Zusprueche: Schriften, Reden und Prosa 1981-1983 (essays, speeches, and prose), Kiepenheuer & Witsch (Cologne, Germany), 1984.

(Editor) *Niemandsland,* Lamuv (Bornheim-Merten, Germany), 1985.

Weil die Stadt so fremd geworden ist (conversation with Vormweg), Lamuv (Gottingen, Germany), 1985.

Briefe aus dem Rheinland: Schriften und Reden, 1960-1963 (letters), Deutscher Taschenbuch (Munich, Germany), 1985.

Die Faehigkeit zu trauern: Schriften und Reden, 1983-85, Lamuv (Gottingen, Germany), 1986.

Die Hoffnung ist wie ein wildes Tier: der Briefwechsel zwischen Heinrich Böll und Ernst-Adolf Kunz, 1945-1953, edited by Herbert Hoven, Kiepenheuer & Witsch (Cologne, Germany), 1994.

Der Blass Hund: Erzahlungen, Kiepenheuer & Witsch (Cologne, Germany), 1995.

(Contributor) Thilo Koch, editor, *Portrats zur deutsch-judischen Geistesgeschichte,* DuMont (Cologne, Germany), 1997.

Jochen Schubert, editor, *Briefe aus dem Krieg, 1939-1945* (letters), Kiepenheuer & Witsch (Cologne, Germany), 2001.

Also author of collected work, titled *Novellen; Erzaehlungen; Heiter-satirische Prosa; Irisches Tagebuch, Aufsaetze,* Buchclub Ex Libris. Also author of text for photography books, including several by Hargeshiemer. Also editor of several books. Contributor to other books, including anthologies. Also translator into German, with wife Annemarie Böll, of novels, stories, and plays, including works by J.D. Salinger, Bernard Malamud, George Bernard Shaw, and O. Henry.

ADAPTATIONS: The Lost Honor of Katharina Blum was adapted as a film and released by New World Pictures in 1975.

SIDELIGHTS: When German writer Heinrich Böll died on July 16, 1985, the world press frequently repeated the summation that he represented the conscience of his nation. This definition of Böll as a moralist was not a new formulation; it had originated, in fact, with literary critics who derided him as nothing more than a moral trumpeter. But even as the expression took on more positive meaning, Böll particularly disliked the epithet because this purely ethical assessment of his work, he thought, hindered appreciation of his art. Furthermore, Böll believed that a nation whose conscience was found primarily in its writers instead of in its politicians, its religious leaders, or its people was already a lost land.

Nonetheless, since the end of World War II when Böll's writings first began to appear, critics and ordinary readers alike had sensed in his language a powerful moral imperative. Whatever the genre—novel, story, satire, play, poem, or essay—the dominant force of the work was always the author's Christian ethics. Böll became one of the most important literary phenomena of the postwar era because his writings, regardless of their subject matter, clearly revealed where he stood as author. He was against war, militarism, and all hypocrisy in politics, religion, and human relations. He excoriated the opportunism of Nazis who became overnight democrats after 1945, and he refused to let Germans forget their recent past. He railed against the Catholic church, of which he was a member, for its cooperation in German rearmament and its role in the restoration of German capitalism. He pointed out repeatedly in the 1950s and 1960s the dangers of the Cold War. In the 1960s and 1970s, he supported Willy Brandt's *Ostpolitik* (a program to come to terms with West Germany's Communist neighbors); Böll campaigned for Brandt in the 1972 election—as did other writers like Guenter Grass and Siegfried Lenz. In the 1980s, his practical idealism led him to support the newly formed Green party, a pro-environmental, anti-nuclear group critical of capitalist policies. He was consistently active in the peace movement throughout the postwar era and in the 1980s demonstrated against the deployment of Pershing II's and cruise missiles on German soil.

The Eastern bloc praised Böll for his anti-militarism and his anti-fascism and lauded him as a model proletarian writer. In all the Eastern European countries he was read and admired. He was a best-selling author in East Germany, Poland, Czechoslovakia, Hungary, and especially in the Soviet Union, where sales of his books totaled roughly three million copies during his lifetime. In the West, Böll's death was reported on the first page of most major newspapers. The *New York Times* quoted the words of his Nobel Prize citation, praising him for his contribution "to the renewal of German literature." In France, *Liberation* gave three full pages to Böll's death, and *Le Monde,* comparing him to Albert Camus and Jean-Paul Sartre, praised his morality as an artist, his respect for language, and his responsibility as a writer.

Christian Linder argues in his *Boersenblatt* article that to understand Böll one must understand his youth. Born in the middle of World War I, Böll claimed his earliest memory was of being held in his mother's arms and watching out the family's apartment window while Hindenburg's defeated army marched through Cologne in 1919. By 1923 the inflation caused by Germany's defeat had ravaged the German population worse than the war had done. Böll remembered his father, a master furniture maker, going to the bank to get money in a cart to pay the employees in the family workshop. The money had to be spent immediately because it would be without purchasing power the next day. Böll never forgot the misery brought to his family, friends, and neighbors by the inflation of the 1920s. The stock market crash of 1929 brought the depression and the unemployment of the 1930s, which caused even more suffering. The economic uncertainties of that period also helped fire the flames of hatred in the recently formed National Socialist Party, and Böll witnessed the first Nazi marches through the streets of Cologne and saw how Nazi terror made the once peaceful streets unsafe for ordinary citizens.

Böll's family, like everyone else he knew, lost what financial security they had and with it their faith in an economic-political system that had failed twice in a decade. The fear of social turmoil became part of the psyche of every German. Economic insecurity, the concern for the next meal and a place to stay became the daily worry of a generation. To survive these times when hard work and the occupational skills of Böll's father were not enough, the Bölls relied on family solidarity, mutual help, and religious faith for survival.

Although the setting for Böll's stories became Germany after World War II, the formative experiences of these earlier times essentially determined his oeuvre. The security of love, the values of food and drink, the luxury of a cigarette (things often taken for granted in an affluent world, especially in prosperous, modern West Germany) pervade his work. Never far from the surface of Böll's stories is his distrust of prosperity because he knew that wealth could disappear over night and that it was often the enemy of familial cohesiveness and the foe of social unity when it began to divide people into haves and have-nots.

In 1937, when Böll completed his secondary education, he went to Bonn to begin an apprenticeship to a book dealer. But his training was interrupted during the winter of 1938-1939 by induction into the labor service. After completion of this semimilitary obligation, he enrolled briefly as a student at the University of Cologne where he intended to study philology. But before he could really call himself a student, three months before the Second World War started, he was drafted into the army. In the course of the next six years, he served as an infantryman on the western front in France and on the eastern front in Russia and in other Eastern European countries as the German army retreated before the Russian forces. During these six years, Böll was wounded four times and reached the rank of corporal. Although it was customary for soldiers with his education to be officers, his hatred of the war and army life prevented him from cooperating with the military. At the risk of court martial and summary execution, he frequently forged papers to see his family or, after his marriage to Annemarie Cech in 1942, to visit his wife in the Rhineland. In April of 1945, Böll was taken prisoner by American troops and interred in Allied POW camps until September of 1945. After his release, he immediately returned to Cologne, which lay eighty percent in ruins, to begin his life as a writer. Having chosen his vocation at the age of seventeen, he had written novels and poems before the war; some of these early works remain in the Böll Archive in Cologne.

The conditions for Böll, as for many Germans, when he returned home were reminiscent of the struggles for food and shelter after World War I; now, however, the problems included not only earning money for rent but finding an apartment still standing, not only buying food but finding food at all, not only paying for heat but finding fuel of any kind. In these first years after the war, Böll's wife earned most of the family income as a teacher of English while he took only random jobs; even his reenrollment in the university was merely a strategy to obtain a legal ration card without employment so that he could dedicate the majority of his time to writing.

In these early years, Böll, like other postwar German writers, had to struggle with finding a new German literary language. Under the Nazis, German had become polluted by fascist ideology, and the German literary tradition that had served Böll's older contemporaries belonging to the generation of Thomas Mann no longer seemed valid in a post-Auschwitz age. Böll was fortunate in that he found his own style early, one appropriate for his ideas and suitable to the content of his stories. That style can be described as a kind of Hemingwayesque minimalism—simple words in simple sentences—conveying a plainness appropriate to the Germany of 1945, a time when the expression of truth, to be believable again, had to possess the certainty and simplicity of a mathematical statement, like two plus two equals four. The opening lines of any of the stories written before 1950 illustrate the style. "Damals in Odessa" ("That Time We Were in Odessa") starts with seven words: "In Odessa it was very cold then." The story concludes: "It was cold in Odessa, the weather was beautifully clear, and we boarded the plane; and as it rose, we knew suddenly that we would never return, never." Between the terse opening sentence and the final lines, the story tells of soldiers eating and drinking to forget their fears before going to die. In the history of German literature, Böll's sober language has the place accorded a Shaker chair in the history of American furniture.

In 1947 these first stories began to appear in various periodicals. They were collected in 1950 as *Wanderer, kommst du nach Spa (Traveller, If You Come to Spa)*. In 1983 twenty-two more of these early stories were discovered in the Böll Archive in Cologne and published in the collection *Die Verwundung und andere fruehe Erzaehlungen (The Casualty)*. Of these early stories the twenty-five in *Traveller, If You Come to Spa* can be found in *Children Are Civilians Too*, while those in *Die Verwundung* were later made available in English. The subject matter of these works is the war and the return of soldiers to a homeland morally impoverished and physically destroyed. Containing none of the heroism and gallantry of popular war literature written during the Weimar Republic, Böll's earliest narratives feature men who die without honor for an inhuman cause. Despite the stark realism of war, Böll did not dwell on battle scenes; he more often depicted the boredom of military life and fear of death. In these tales the only haven from despair is love, discovered in momentary encounters between soldiers and women on the periphery of the war.

Two novellas, *Der Zug war puenktlich (The Train Was on Time)* and *Das Vermaechtnis (A Soldier's Legacy)*, and the episodic novel, *Wo warst du, Adam? (And Where Were You, Adam?)*, represent Böll's longer treatment of the war. While they differ from one another in structure, they, like the shorter works, share a fatalism that death is bigger than life and proclaim a Christian optimism that heavenly consolation is greater than suffering. Thus the war narratives acknowledge that God is still in his heaven, although all is not right with the world.

Böll's epigraph for *And Where Were You, Adam?* (which he took from Antoine de Saint-Exupery's *Flight to Arras*) can stand as a motto for all his war stories from this period: "When I was younger, I took part in real adventures: establishing postal air routes across the Sahara and South America. But war is no true adventure; it is only a substitute for adventure. War is a disease just like typhus." In an essay collected in *The Second World War in Fiction*, Alan Bance claims that this apolitical perspective on the war was typical of German literature in the 1940s and 1950s. He even sees a kind of "realism" in this political vagueness because, as he says, "war is not conducive to clear thinking." In Böll's case the unanalytic response to the war (seeing international conflict as a natural illness) was compounded by his feeling of being a lucky survivor, for only one of four German men in his age group returned from battle. His sense of destiny forced Böll to deal subjectively rather than objectively with the suffering of the Hitler years.

This narrow perspective manifests itself in Böll's simplistic division of characters into two groups: victims and executioners, with the victims often being the Germans themselves. A dichotomous view of World War II is understandable and even accurate for someone who was himself an anti-fascist and a sufferer of twelve years of oppression. Still, the result of the dichotomy is that the war stories cannot reveal truly what the war was about because the limited categories of suffering innocents and brutal henchmen are too unrefined to do the job. This kind of dualism, as Walker Sokel calls it in his *In Sachen Böll* essay, is characteristic of Böll's work in this period but disappears from the later stories as they become more sophisticated in their characterizations. Guenter Wirth's indictment, in *Heinrich Böll*, of the early war stories as "timeless irrationalism" is to the point because certainly war is not like typhus or any other sickness that has biological causes. War is not nature's making; it is made by people who have political and economic interests.

In the stories treating conditions following the war, satire became Böll's main weapon in his chastisement of Germany. Certain of these works, such as *Nicht nur zur Weihnachtszeit* (*Christmas Every Day*), "Doktor Murkes gesammeltes Schweigen" ("Murke's Collected Silences"), and "Der Wegwerfer" ("The Thrower Away"), have become classics of postwar German literature. A humorous, bizarre fantasy characterizes these satires of developing West German society. In *Christmas Every Day* a tyrannical old aunt demands daily holidays to avoid confronting the guilt of the Hitler years. In "Murke's Collected Silences" a Ph.D. in psychology, working for a radio station, tries to preserve his sanity by collecting on tape snips of dead air cut from cultural programs. In "The Thrower Away" a fanatical time-study expert makes a place for himself in the business world by systematically destroying junk mail, the surplus production of the advertising industry. Böll's success in this genre, the satirical short story, has led critics such as Erhard Friedrichsmeyer, James Henderson Reid, and Walter Jens to conclude that Böll's acutest artistic sense was his eye for satire. These stories have garnered high critical acclaim because they take to task the shortcomings of all Western democracies even though they are grounded in West German economic and political reality. One recognizes, too, that Böll's satire hits the mark equally as well in the Eastern bloc, where culture is an industry, production often leads to waste, and people avoid confronting the unpleasant past.

Böll's sense of satire was also the high point of many of his novels and raises them in some cases to great literature and in others saves them from the doldrums. For example, in *Ansichten eines Clowns* (*The Clown*), the scene of the penniless clown pantomiming his blindness during the visit of his millionaire industrialist father contains the essence of the novel's political content, and in *Entfernung von der Truppe* ("Absent without Leave"), the narrator's account of his latrine duty in World War II reveals his total alienation from society. In *Ende einer Dienstfahrt* (*End of a Mission*) Böll's choice of a pedantic, objective, understated tone confers on the novel the main feature of its readability; the dry reporting of the events of a trial of a father and son accused of burning an army jeep discloses how the courts and the press keep political protest under control.

And Böll's last novel, *Frauen vor Flusslandschaft: Roman in Dialogen und Selbstgespraechen*, published just after his death in 1985, reaches its high point in a long interior monologue by a disenchanted intellectual whose job requires him to write speeches for a corrupt and stupid Christian Democratic minister. Here the monologue summarizes the novel's political intent by revealing the politician's incompetence and moral emptiness as well as the intellectual's sellout of his ideals.

Beginning with the novel *Und sagte kein einziges Wort* (*And Never Said a Word*), Böll developed a new method for dealing with contemporary reality. He began choosing themes, drawing characters, and selecting events tied directly to current developments in Germany. If you read chronologically, the books treat every significant phase in West German history from the nation's establishment in 1949 to the mid-1980s, including the period of hunger after the war, the restoration of capitalism, the process of rearmament, the achievement of prosperity, the terrorist responses to social and political inequities produced by the economic recovery, and the soul-searching of the 1980s. Treating all these aspects of West German history not as isolated phenomena of the postwar era, but in light of the Hitler years and German history since the turn of the century, Böll's canon not only helped to establish West German literature after the war but also provides a political and social understanding of German development in this century.

In Böll's work, ordinary people become objects of social forces, often victims of the decisions of others. In *Die verlorene Ehre der Katharina Blum; oder, wie Gewahlt enstehen und wohin sie fuehren kann* (*The Lost Honor of Katharina Blum: How Violence Develops and Where It Can Lead*), which takes place during four days of Carnival in Cologne, Böll showed how an unpolitical, law-abiding young woman could be turned into a vengeful murderer by society's toleration of social injustice. The protagonist, Katharina, becomes a "dangerous" person because she finds herself a victim of character assassination perpetrated by those institutions most responsible for a just democratic society: the press, the police, the law.

The philosophical position implied in Böll's assumption that a person is a product of social forces may be called Marxist, except that it is thoroughly religious, lacks Marxist optimism, and never suggests social change through political organization. Social solutions are not found in Böll's work. Implied, however, is the belief that if people in power practiced more compassion in the execution of their offices, society would be more just. In general, a certain sadness about the human condition prevails in Böll's work, even though a mild optimism flourishes within narrow limits. His protagonists always make important decisions regarding their own lives. They are not completely passive; they do not yield to or accept injustice. Their decisions affirm their individual human dignity and assert a militant humanism. Although their actions may not effect significant social change but merely permit them to live with their consciences, their decisiveness symbolically opposes an unjust world and thereby suggests that social awareness and conscious opposition are the way to a better future. The story of Katharina Blum's vengeance neither recommends nor condones murder, but merely illustrates the simple truth that injustice, when tolerated, is often the cause of social violence.

When the Swedish Academy awarded Böll the Nobel Prize in 1972, it singled out the novel *Gruppenbild mit Dame (Group Portrait with Lady)* for special praise, calling that work the summation of Böll's oeuvre. Although the writer continued to publish novels, stories, poems, plays, and essays regularly after 1971, *Group Portrait with Lady* is still regarded as the work that most fully represents the whole of Böll's canon. The book recapitulates his major themes and provides their most masterful formulation.

Böll stated his intention for the novel in an *Akzente* interview with Dieter Wellershoff: "I tried to describe or to write the story of a German woman in her late forties who had taken upon herself the burden of history from 1922-1970." In this story of Leni Gruyten-Pfeiffer, her family, and friends, Böll challenged the norms of West German society with a model of radical socialism and religious humanism. The protagonist Leni synthesizes in her person seeming contradictions. Although she is a simple person, she confounds any attempt at simple explanation. She is a materialist who delights in the senses but also a mystic who penetrates the mystery of the Virgin Birth, an innocent in her heart and a tramp in the eyes of society, a communist by intuition and an embodiment of the fascist ideal of "the German girl." In her, her Russian lover Boris, and their son Lev, Böll created a holy family that proclaims an undogmatic Christian socialism as a gospel for modern times.

Around Leni are grouped more than 125 characters representing all classes of society and various nations: communists and capitalists, industrialists and proletarians, fascists and anti-fascists, Jews and Muslims, Turks and Germans, rich and poor, saints and sinners the whole spectrum of German society from 1922-1970. To

hold the various levels of the story together and to keep Leni in the center of the novel, the work employs two narrative techniques. In the first half of the novel, an unnamed narrator scrupulously relates the events of Leni's life. This half of the book consists of the narrator's meticulous research on Leni and his comments on the accuracy and validity of his findings. Leni's story proceeds chronologically from her birth to March 2, 1945, the day in which a nine-hour Allied raid on Cologne effectively brought the war to an end for the people of that city. After this event, midway through the novel, the narrator relinquishes his role as narrator to assume a role as a member of Leni's circle of friends, and to become an actor in the events of the book. At this point various characters tell their life stories from the day of the terrible bombing to 1970. Since these people have contact with Leni their stories also reveal from various perspectives Leni's own life during this twenty-five year period. Again Böll found a structure that allowed him to come to terms with recent German history and postwar developments.

Group Portrait with Lady, is, in the minds of many critics, the summation of Böll's writing, because it crystalizes the radical message that runs through all of his work since *And Never Said a Word:* Christianity and capitalism are incompatible with each other; their long standing marriage survives only because organized religion continually surrenders its humanistic values to the demands of economics and politics.

Some of Böll's works continued to be published for the first time in English after his death. For example, in 1994 the first novel Böll wrote, *Der Engel Schwieg: Roman,* was published for the first time in English as *The Silent Angel.* In fact, the novel was only published in Germany in 1992, forty years after it was originally rejected by German publishers. Donna Seaman, writing in *Booklist,* noted that few German readers would have wanted to read the book in the 1950s because it is so "staggering in its intensity and evocation of despair and shock" experienced by that country following World War II. The story focuses on Hans, a German soldier who struggles to survive following the war. Despite his homelessness, degradation, and delirium, he shows that he can still love. Seaman called the book's English publication "an occasion for renewing our appreciation for Böll's genius for setting scenes of tremendous emotional dimension and creating characters of great psychological vividness." A *Publishers Weekly* contributor noted, "All of Böll's mature themes are present in this lyrical, spare and somnambulistic tale."

A collection of ten short stories previously unavailable in English were published as *The Mad Dog: Stories* in

1997. Written between 1938 and 1949, the stories are also culled from segments of unfinished novels and other manuscripts by the author. Michael T. O'Pecko commented in *Library Journal* that "the stories cover territory familiar to readers of Böll's early works: the difficulty of maintaining one's moral integrity during war and its aftermath." In the story "Youth on Fire," readers are treated to perhaps Böll's earliest extant fiction work in a story about young people who face the personal and social evils rampant in 1936-1937 pre-war Germany. Despite their difficulties, the story's characters triumph personally in that they do not fall into despair, suicide, cynicism, or crime. A *Publishers Weekly* contributor wrote that "These stories are rougher, less finished than Böll's previously published short fiction, but they are alive with raw emotion." Joseph Hynes, writing in *Commonweal*, noted: "I find fascinating these early traces of Böll's subsequent fullblown achievement; but the present tales and fragments are also a useful introduction to a major writer's blend of anger, love, and hope."

BIOGRAPHICAL AND CRITICAL SOURCES:

BOOKS

Böll, Heinrich, *Wo warst du, Adam?* (also see below; novel), F. Middlehauve, 1951, reprinted, Deutscher Taschenbuch (Munich, Germany), 1972, translation by Mervyn Savill published as *Adam, Where Art Thou?*, Criterion Books (New York, NY), 1955, new translation by Lelia Vennewitz published as *And Where Were You, Adam?*, Northwestern University Press (Evanston, IL), 1994.

Böll, Heinrich, *Children Are Civilians Too* (story translations by Lelia Vennewitz; contains translation of *Wanderer, kommst du nach Spa*, which includes "Damals in Odessa" published as "That Time We Were in Odessa," and selected stories from *Heinrich Böll, 1947 bis 1951*), McGraw (New York, NY), 1970.

Böll, Heinrich, *Heinrich Böll, On His Death: Selected Obituaries and the Last Interview*, translated by Patricia Crampton, Inter Nationes (Bonn, Germany), 1985.

Böll, Rene, Viktor Böll, Karl Heiner Busse, and Markus Schafer, editors, *Heinrich Böll: Leben & Werk*, Heinrich-Böll-Stiftung (Cologne, Germany), 1995.

Böll, Rene, Viktor Böll, Reinhold Neven DuMont, Klaus Staeck, and Robert C. Conard, *Heinrich Böll*, Twayne, 1981.

Böll, Viktor, editor, *Böll und Koln*, Emons (Cologne, Germany), 1990.

Friedrichsmeyer, Erhard, *The Major Works of Heinrich Böll: A Critical Commentary*, Monarch Press (New York, NY), 1974.

Hoven, Herbert, editor, *Die Hoffnung is wie ein wildes Tier: der Briefwechsel zwischen Heinrich Böll und Ernst-Adolf Kunz, 1945-1953*, Kiepenheuer & Witsch (Cologne, Germany), 1994.

Klein, Holger, John Flower, and Eric Homberger, editors, *The Second World War in Fiction*, Macmillan (London, England), 1984.

MacPherson, Enid, *A Student's Guide to Böll*, Heinemann, 1972.

McHugh, John, editor and compiler, *The Heinrich Böll Cottage on Achill Island*, (published to mark the eightieth anniversary of Heinrich Böll's birth), Achill, 1998.

Rademacher, Gerhard, editor, *Heinrich Böll: Auswahlbibliographie zur Primar-und Sekundarliteratur*, Bouvier (Bonn, Germany), 1989.

Reid, James Henderson, *Heinrich Böll: Withdrawal and Re-Emergence*, Wolff (London, England), 1973.

Schwartz, Wilhelm Johannes, *Heinrich Böll, Teller of Tales: A Study of His Works and Characters*, Ungar (New York, NY), 1969.

PERIODICALS

Booklist, June 1, 1994, Donna Seaman, review of *The Silent Angel*, p. 1770; August, 1997, Donna Seaman, review of *The Mad Dog: Stories*, p. 1875.

Commonweal, November 7, 1997, Joseph Hynes, review of *The Mad Dog: Stories*, p. 28.

Germanic Review, summer, 1978; summer, 1984.

German Life and Letters, July, 1959.

German Quarterly, March, 1960; Volume 45, 1972; Volume 50, 1977.

Library Journal, August, 1997, Michael T. O'Pecko, review of *The Mad Dog: Stories*, p. 137.

Modern Fiction Studies, autumn, 1975.

New York Review of Books, February 11, 1965; December 29, 1966; September 14, 1967; March 26, 1970; November 5, 1970; May 31, 1973; March 18, 1982.

Publishers Weekly, March 7, 1994, review of *Irish Journal*, p. 65; April 18, 1994, review of *The Silent Angel*, p. 44.

World Literature Today, summer, 1965; autumn, 1977; summer, 1979; spring, 1980; spring, 1985; spring, 1986.

OBITUARIES:

PERIODICALS

Boston Globe, July 17, 1985.
Chicago Tribune, July 17, 1985.

Le Monde (international edition), July 18-24, 1985.
New York Times, July 17, 1985.
Times (London, England), July 17, 1985.
Toronto Star, July 17, 1985.
Washington Post, July 17, 1985.

*　　　*　　　*

BÖLL, Heinrich Theodor
　　See BÖLL, Heinrich

*　　　*　　　*

BOOT, William
　　See STOPPARD, Tom

*　　　*　　　*

BORGES, Jorge Luis 1899-1986
　　(F. Bustos, B. Lynch Davis, a joint pseudonym, H. Bustos Domecq, a joint pseudonym, B. Suarez Lynch, a joint pseudonym)

PERSONAL: Born August 24, 1899, in Buenos Aires, Argentina; died of liver cancer, June 14, 1986, in Geneva, Switzerland; buried in Plainpalais, Geneva, Switzerland; son of Jorge Guillermo Borges (a lawyer, teacher, and writer) and Leonor Acevedo Suarez (a translator); married Elsa Astete Millan, September 21, 1967 (divorced, 1970); married Maria Kodama, April 26, 1986. *Education:* Attended College Calvin, Geneva, Switzerland, 1914-18; also studied in Cambridge, England, and Buenos Aires, Argentina.

CAREER: Writer. Miguel Cane branch library, Buenos Aires, Argentina, municipal librarian, 1937-46; teacher of English literature at several private institutions and lecturer in Argentina and Uruguay, 1946-55; National Library, Buenos Aires, director, 1955-73; University of Buenos Aires, Buenos Aires, Argentina, professor of English and U.S. literature, beginning in 1956. Visiting professor or guest lecturer at numerous universities in the United States and throughout the world, including University of Texas, 1961-62, University of Oklahoma, 1969, University of New Hampshire, 1972, and Dickinson College, 1983; Charles Eliot Norton Professor of Poetry, Harvard University, 1967-68.

MEMBER: Argentine Academy of Letters, Argentine Writers Society (president, 1950-53), Modern Language Association of America (honorary fellow, 1961-86), American Association of Teachers of Spanish and Portuguese (honorary fellow, 1965-86).

AWARDS, HONORS: Buenos Aires Municipal Literary Prize, 1928, for *El Idioma de los argentinos;* Gran Premio de Honor, Argentine Writers Society, 1945, for *Ficciones, 1935-1944;* Gran Premio Nacional de la Literatura (Argentina), 1957, for *El Aleph;* Premio de Honor and Prix Formentor, International Congress of Publishers (shared with Samuel Beckett), 1961; Commandeur de l'Ordre des Arts et des Lettres (France), 1962; Fondo de les Artes, 1963; Ingram Merrill Foundation Award, 1966; Matarazzo Sobrinho Inter-American Literary Prize, Bienal Foundation, 1970; nominated for Neustadt International Prize for Literature, *World Literature Today* and University of Oklahoma, 1970, 1984, and 1986; Jerusalem Prize, 1971; Alfonso Reyes Prize (Mexico), 1973; Gran Cruz del Orden al Merito Bernardo O'Higgins, Government of Chile, 1976; Gold Medal, French Academy, Order of Merit, Federal Republic of Germany, and Icelandic Falcon Cross, all 1979; Miguel de Cervantes Award (Spain) and Balzan Prize (Italy), both 1980; Ollin Yoliztli Prize (Mexico), 1981; T.S. Eliot Award for Creative Writing, Ingersoll Foundation and Rockford Institute, 1983; Gold Medal of Menendez Pelayo University (Spain), La Gran Cruz de la Orden Alfonso X, el Sabio (Spain), and Legion d'Honneur (France), all 1983; Knight of the British Empire; National Book Critics Circle Award for Criticism, 1999, for *Selected Non-Fictions.* Recipient of honorary degrees from numerous colleges and universities, including University of Cuyo (Argentina), 1956, University of the Andes (Colombia), 1963, Oxford University, 1970, University of Jerusalem, 1971, Columbia University, 1971, and Michigan State University, 1972.

WRITINGS:

POETRY

Fervor de Buenos Aires (title means "Passion for Buenos Aires"), Serantes (Buenos Aires, Argentina), 1923, revised edition, Emecé (Buenos Aires, Argentina), 1969.
Luna de enfrente (title means "Moon across the Way"), Proa (Buenos Aires, Argentina), 1925.
Cuaderno San Martín (title means "San Martin Copybook"), Proa (Buenos Aires, Argentina), 1929.
Poemas, 1923-1943, Losada, 1943, 3rd enlarged edition published as *Obra poética, 1923-1964,* 1964, translation published as *Selected Poems, 1923-1967* (bilingual edition; also includes prose), edited, with an introduction and notes, by Norman Thomas di Giovanni, Delacorte (New York, NY), 1972, enlarged Spanish-language edition published as *Obra poética 1923-1976,* Emecé (Buenos Aires, Argentina), 1977.

Nueve poemas, El Mangrullo (Buenos Aires, Argentina), 1955.

Límites, Francisco A. Colombo (Buenos Aires, Argentina), 1958.

Seis poemas escandinavos (title means "Six Scandinavian Poems"), privately printed, 1966.

Siete poemas (title means "Seven Poems"), privately printed, 1967.

El Otro, el mismo (title means "The Other, the Same"), Emecé (Buenos Aires, Argentina), 1969.

Elogio de la sombra, Emecé (Buenos Aires, Argentina), 1969, translation by Norman Thomas di Giovanni published as *In Praise of Darkness* (bilingual edition), Dutton (New York, NY), 1974.

El Oro de los tigres (also see below; title means "The Gold of Tigers"), Emecé (Buenos Aires, Argentina), 1972.

Siete poemas sajones/Seven Saxon Poems, Plain Wrapper Press (Austin, TX), 1974.

La Rosa profunda (also see below; title means "The Unending Rose"), Emecé (Buenos Aires, Argentina), 1975.

La Moneda de hierro (title means "The Iron Coin"), Emecé (Buenos Aires, Argentina), 1976.

Historia de la noche (title means "History of Night"), Emecé (Buenos Aires, Argentina), 1977.

The Gold of Tigers: Selected Later Poems (contains translations of *El Oro de los tigres* and *La Rosa profunda*), translation by Alastair Reid, Dutton (New York, NY), 1977.

La Cifra, Emecé (Buenos Aires, Argentina), 1981.

Also author of *Los Conjurados* (title means "The Conspirators"), Alianza (Madrid, Spain), 1985.

ESSAYS

Inquisiciones (title means "Inquisitions"), Proa (Buenos Aires, Argentina), 1925.

El Tamano de mi esperanza (title means "The Measure of My Hope"), Proa (Buenos Aires, Argentina), 1926.

El Idioma de los argentinos (title means "The Language of the Argentines"), M. Gleizer (Buenos Aires, Argentina), 1928, 3rd edition (includes three essays by Borges and three by Jose Edmundo Clemente), Emecé (Buenos Aires, Argentina), 1968.

Figari, privately printed, 1930.

Las Kennigar, Francisco A. Colombo (Buenos Aires, Argentina), 1933.

Historia de la eternidad (title means "History of Eternity"), Viau & Zona (Buenos Aires, Argentina), 1936, revised edition published as *Obras completas,* Volume 1, Emecé (Buenos Aires, Argentina), 1953.

Nueva refutacion del tiempo (title means "New Refutation of Time"), Oportet & Haereses (Buenos Aires, Argentina), 1947.

Aspectos de la literatura gauchesca, Número (Montevideo, Uruguay), 1950.

El Lenguaje de Buenos Aires, Emecé (Buenos Aires, Argentina), 1963.

(With Delia Ingenieros) *Antiguas literaturas germanicas,* Fondo de Cultura Economica (Mexico City, Mexico), 1951, revised edition with Maria Esther Vazquez published as *Literaturas germanicas medievales,* Falbo, 1966.

Otras inquisiciones, Sur (Buenos Aires, Argentina), 1952, published as *Obras completas,* Volume 8, Emecé (Buenos Aires, Argentina), 1960, translation by Ruth L.C. Simms published as *Other Inquisitions, 1937-1952,* University of Texas Press (Austin, TX), 1964.

(With Margarita Guerrero) *El "Martín Fierro,"* Columba (Buenos Aires, Argentina), 1953.

(With Bettina Edelberg) *Leopoldo Lugones,* Troquel (Buenos Aires, Argentina), 1955.

(With Margarita Guerrero) *Manual de zoologia fantastica,* Fondo de Cultura Economica (Mexico City, Mexico), 1957, translation published as *The Imaginary Zoo,* University of California Press (Berkeley, CA), 1969, revised Spanish edition published as *El Libro de los seres imaginarios,* Kier (Buenos Aires, Argentina), 1967, translation and revision by Norman Thomas di Giovanni and Borges published as *The Book of Imaginary Beings,* Dutton (New York, NY), 1969.

La Poesia gauchesca (title means "Gaucho Poetry"), Centro de Estudios Brasileiros, 1960.

(With Maria Esther Vazquez) *Introducción a la literatura inglesa,* Columba (Buenos Aires, Argentina), 1965, translation by L. Clark Keating and Robert O. Evans published as *An Introduction to English Literature,* University Press of Kentucky (Lexington, KY), 1974.

(With Esther Zemborain de Torres) *Introducción a la literatura norteamericana,* Columba (Buenos Aires, Argentina), 1967, translation by L. Clark Keating and Robert O. Evans published as *An Introduction to American Literature,* University of Kentucky Press (Lexington, KY), 1971.

(With Alicia Jurado) *Qué es el budismo?* (title means "What Is Buddhism?"), Columba (Buenos Aires, Argentina), 1976.

Nuevos ensayos dantescos (title means "New Dante Essays"), Espasa-Calpe (Madrid, Spain), 1982.

The Library of Babel, translation by Andrew Hurley, David R. Godine (Boston, MA), 2000.

Prólogos de "La Biblioteca de Babel," Alianza (Madrid, Spain), 2001.

Museo: Textos inéditos, Emecé (Buenos Aires, Argentina), 2002.

SHORT STORIES

Historia universal de la infamia, Tor (Buenos Aires, Argentina), 1935, revised edition published as *Obras completas,* Volume 3, Emecé (Buenos Aires, Argentina), 1964, translation by Norman Thomas di Giovanni published as *A Universal History of Infamy,* Dutton (New York, NY), 1972.

El Jardin de senderos que se bifurcan (also see below; title means *Garden of the Forking Paths*), Sur (Buenos Aires, Argentina), 1941.

(With Adolfo Bioy Casares, under joint pseudonym H. Bustos Domecq) *Seis problemas para Isidro Parodi,* Sur (Buenos Aires, Argentina), 1942, translation by Norman Thomas di Giovanni published under authors' real names as *Six Problems for Don Isidro Parodi,* Dutton (New York, NY), 1983.

Ficciones, 1935-1944 (includes *El Jardin de senderos que se bifurcan*), Sur (Buenos Aires, Argentina), 1944, revised edition published as *Obras completas,* Volume 5, Emecé (Buenos Aires, Argentina), 1956, translation by Anthony Kerrigan and others published as *Ficciones,* edited and with an introduction by Kerrigan, Grove Press (New York, NY), 1962, new edition with English introduction and notes by Gordon Brotherson and Peter Hulme, Harrap (London, England), 1976.

(With Adolfo Bioy Casares, under joint pseudonym H. Bustos Domecq) *Dos fantasias memorables,* Oportet & Haereses (Buenos Aires, Argentina), 1946, reprinted under authors' real names with notes and bibliography by Horacio Jorge Becco, Edicom (Buenos Aires, Argentina), 1971.

El Aleph, Losada (Buenos Aires, Argentina), 1949, revised edition, 1952, published as *Obras completas,* Volume 7, Emecé (Buenos Aires, Argentina), 1956, translation and revision by Norman Thomas di Giovanni in collaboration with Borges published as *The Aleph and Other Stories, 1933-1969,* Dutton (New York, NY), 1970.

(With Luisa Mercedes Levinson) *La Hermana de Eloísa* (title means "Eloisa's Sister"), Ene (Buenos Aires, Argentina), 1955.

(With Adolfo Bioy Casares) *Crónicas de Bustos Domecq,* Losada (Buenos Aires, Argentina), 1967, translation by Norman Thomas di Giovanni published as *Chronicles of Bustos Domecq,* Dutton (New York, NY), 1976.

El Informe de Brodie, Emecé (Buenos Aires, Argentina), 1970, translation by Norman Thomas di Giovanni in collaboration with Borges published as *Dr. Brodie's Report,* Dutton (New York, NY), 1971.

El Matrero, Edicom (Buenos Aires, Argentina), 1970.

El Congreso, El Archibrazo (Buenos Aires, Argentina), 1971, translation by Norman Thomas di Giovanni in collaboration with Borges published as *The Congress* (also see below), Enitharmon Press (London, England), 1974, translation by Alberto Manguel published as *The Congress of the World,* F.M. Ricci (Milan, Italy), 1981.

El Libro de arena, Emecé (Buenos Aires, Argentina), 1975, translation by Norman Thomas di Giovanni published with *The Congress* as *The Book of Sand,* Dutton (New York, NY), 1977.

(With Adolfo Bioy Casares) *Nuevos cuentos de Bustos Domecq,* Librería de la Ciudad (Buenos Aires, Argentina), 1977.

Rosa y azul (contains *La Rosa de Paracelso* and *Tigres azules*), Sedmay (Madrid, Spain), 1977.

Veinticinco agosto 1983 y otros cuentos de Jorges Luis Borges (includes interview with Borges), Siruela (Madrid, Spain), 1983.

OMNIBUS VOLUMES

La Muerte y la brujula (stories; title means "Death and the Compass"), Emecé (Buenos Aires, Argentina), 1951.

Obras completas, ten volumes, Emecé (Buenos Aires, Argentina), 1953–67, published in one volume, 1974.

Cuentos (title means "Stories"), Monticello College Press, 1958.

Antologia personal (prose and poetry), Sur (Buenos Aires, Argentina), 1961, translation published as *A Personal Anthology,* edited and with foreword by Anthony Kerrigan, Grove Press (New York, NY), 1967.

Labyrinths: Selected Stories and Other Writings, edited by Donald A. Yates and James E. Irby, New Directions Press (New York, NY), 1962, augmented edition, 1964.

Nueva antologia personal, Emecé (Buenos Aires, Argentina), 1968.

Prólogos, con un prólogo de prólogos, Torres Aguero (Buenos Aires, Argentina), 1975.

(With others) *Obras completas en colaboracion* (title means "Complete Works in Collaboration"), Emecé (Buenos Aires, Argentina), 1979.

Narraciones (stories), edited by Marcos Ricardo Bamatan, Catedra, 1980.

Prose completa, two volumes, Bruguera (Barcelona, Spain), 1980.

Antología poética (1923-1977), Alianza (Madrid, Spain), 1981.

Borges: A Reader (prose and poetry), edited by Emir Rodriguez Monegal and Alastair Reid, Dutton (New York, NY), 1981.

Ficcionario: Una Antologia de sus textos, edited by Rodriguez Monegal, Fondo de Cultura Economica (Mexico City, Mexico), 1985.

Textos cautivos: Ensayos y resenas en "El Hogar" (1936-1939) (title means "Captured Texts: Essays and Reviews in 'El Hogar'"), edited by Rodriguez Monegal and Enrique Sacerio-Gari, Tusquets (Barcelona, Spain), 1986.

El Aleph borgiano, edited by Juan Gustavo Cobo Borda and Martha Kovasics de Cubides, Biblioteca Luis-Angel Arango (Bogota, Colombia), 1987.

Biblioteca personal: Prologos, Alianza (Madrid, Spain), 1988.

Obras completas, 1975-1985, Emecé (Buenos Aires, Argentina), 1989.

Collected Fictions, edited and translated by Andrew Hurley, Viking Press (New York, NY), 1998.

Selected Poems, edited by Alexander Coleman, Viking Press (New York, NY), 1999.

Selected Non-Fictions, edited and translated by Eliot Weinberger, Esther Allen, and Suzanne Jill Levine, Viking Press (New York, NY), 1999.

Jorge Luis Borges, Nextext (Evanston, IL), 2001.

OTHER

(Author of afterword) Ildefonso Pereda Valdes, *Antologia de la moderna poesia uruguaya,* El Ateneo (Buenos Aires, Argentina), 1927.

Evaristo Carriego (biography), M. Gleizer (Buenos Aires, Argentina), 1930, revised edition published as *Obras completas,* Volume 4, Emecé (Buenos Aires, Argentina), 1955, translation by Norman Thomas di Giovanni published as *Evaristo Carriego: A Book about Old-Time Buenos Aires,* Dutton (New York, NY), 1984.

Discusión, Gleizer (Buenos Aires, Argentina), 1932, revised edition, Emecé (Buenos Aires, Argentina), 1976.

(Translator) Virginia Woolf, *Orlando,* Sur (Buenos Aires, Argentina), 1937.

(Editor, with Pedro Henriquez Urena) *Antologia clasica de la literatura argentina* (title means "Anthology of Argentine Literature"), Kapelusz (Buenos Aires, Argentina), 1937.

(Translator and author of prologue) Franz Kafka, *La Metamorfosis,* [Buenos Aires, Argentina], 1938.

(Editor, with Adolfo Bioy Casares and Silvina Ocampo) *Antologia de la literatura fantastica* (title means "Anthology of Fantastic Literature"), with foreword by Bioy Casares, Sudamericana, 1940, enlarged edition with postscript by Bioy Casares, 1965,

translation of revised version published as *The Book of Fantasy,* with introduction by Ursula K. Le Guin, Viking (New York, NY), 1988.

(Author of prologue) Adolfo Bioy Casares, *La Invencion de Morel,* Losada, 1940, translation by Ruth L.C. Simms published as *The Invention of Morel and Other Stories,* University of Texas Press (Austin, TX), 1964.

(Editor, with Adolfo Bioy Casares and Silvina Ocampo and author of prologue) *Antologia poetica argentina* (title means "Anthology of Argentine Poetry"), Sudamericana (Buenos Aires, Argentina), 1941.

(Translator) Henri Michaux, *Un Barbaro en Asia,* Sur (Buenos Aires, Argentina), 1941.

(Compiler and translator, with Adolfo Bioy Casares) *Los Mejores cuentos policiales* (title means "The Best Detective Stories"), Emecé (Buenos Aires, Argentina), 1943.

(Translator and author of prologue) Herman Melville, *Bartleby, el escribiente,* Emecé (Buenos Aires, Argentina), 1943.

(Editor, with Silvina Bullrich) *El Compadrito: Su destino, sus barrios, su mûsica* (title means "The Buenos Aires Hoodlum: His Destiny, His Neighborhoods, His Music"), Emecé (Buenos Aires, Argentina), 1945, 2nd edition, Fabril, 1968.

(With Adolfo Bioy Casares, under joint pseudonym B. Suarez Lynch) *Un Modelo para la muerte* (novel; title means "A Model for Death"), Oportet & Haereses (Buenos Aires, Argentina), 1946.

(Editor with Bioy Casares) Francesco de Quevedo, *Prosa y verso,* Emecé (Buenos Aires, Argentina), 1948.

(Compiler and translator, with Adolfo Bioy Casares) *Los Mejores cuentos policiales: Segunda serie,* Emecé (Buenos Aires, Argentina), 1951.

(Editor and translator, with Adolfo Bioy Casares) *Cuentos breves y extraordinarios: Antologia,* Raigal (Buenos Aires, Argentina), 1955, revised and enlarged edition, Losada, 1973, translation by Anthony Kerrigan published as *Extraordinary Tales,* Souvenir Press (New York, NY), 1973.

(With Adolfo Bioy Casares) *Los Orilleros* [and] *El Paraiso de los creyentes* (screenplays; titles mean "The Hoodlums" and "The Believers' Paradise"; *Los Orilleros* produced by Argentine director Ricardo Luna, 1975), Losada (Buenos Aires, Argentina), 1955.

(Editor and author of prologue, notes, and glossary, with Adolfo Bioy Casares) *Poesia gauchesca* (title means "Gaucho Poetry"), two volumes, Fondo de Cultura Economica (Mexico City, Mexico), 1955.

(Translator) William Faulkner, *Las Palmeras salvajes,* Sudamericana (Buenos Aires, Argentina), 1956.

(Editor, with Adolfo Bioy Casares) *Libro del cielo y del infierno* (anthology; title means "Book of Heaven and Hell"), Sur (Buenos Aires, Argentina), 1960.

El Hacedor (prose and poetry; Volume 9 of *Obras completas;* title means "The Maker"), Emecé, 1960, translation by Mildred Boyer and Harold Morland published as *Dreamtigers,* University of Texas Press (Austin, TX), 1964.

(Editor and author of prologue) *Macedonio Fernandez,* Culturales Argentinas, Ministerio de Educacion y Justicia, 1961.

Para las seis cuerdas: Milongas (song lyrics; title means "For the Six Strings: Milongas"), Emecé (Buenos Aires, Argentina), 1965.

Dialogo con Borges, edited by Victoria Ocampo, Sur (Buenos Aires, Argentina), 1969.

(Translator, editor, and author of prologue) Walt Whitman, *Hojas de hierba,* Juarez (Buenos Aires, Argentina), 1969.

(Compiler and author of prologue) Evaristo Carriego, *Versos,* Universitaria de Buenos Aires (Buenos Aires, Argentina), 1972.

Borges on Writing (lectures), edited by Norman Thomas di Giovanni, Daniel Halpern, and Frank MacShane, Dutton (New York, NY), 1973.

(With Adolfo Bioy Casares and Hugo Santiago) *Les Autres: Escenario original* (screenplay; produced in France and directed by Santiago, 1974), C. Bourgois (Paris, France), 1974.

(Author of prologue) Carlos Zubillaga, *Carlos Gardel,* Jucar (Madrid, Spain), 1976.

Cosmogonias, Librería de la Ciudad (Buenos Aires, Argentina), 1976.

Libro de suenos (transcripts of Borges's and others' dreams; title means "Book of Dreams"), Torres Aguero, 1976.

(Author of prologue) Santiago Dabove, *La Muerte y su traje,* Calicanto, 1976.

Borges-Imagenes, memorias, dialogos, edited by Vazquez, Monte Avila, 1977.

Adrogue (prose and poetry), privately printed, 1977.

Borges para millones, Corregidor (Buenos Aires, Argentina), 1978.

Poesía juvenile de Jorge Luis Borges, edited by Carlos Meneses, José Olañeta (Barcelona, Spain), 1978.

(Editor, with Maria Kodoma) *Breve antología anglosajona,* Emecé (Buenos Aires, Argentina), 1979.

Borges oral (lectures), edited by Martin Mueller, Emecé (Buenos Aires, Argentina), 1979.

Siete noches (lectures), Fondo de Cultura Economica (Mexico City, Mexico), 1980, translation by Eliot Weinberger published as *Seven Nights,* New Directions Press (New York, NY), 1984.

(Compiler) Paul Groussac, *Jorge Luis Borges selecciona lo mejor,* Fraterna (Buenos Aires, Argentina), 1981.

(Compiler and author of prologue) Francisco de Quevedo, *Antologia poetica,* Alianza (Madrid, Spain), 1982.

(Compiler and author of introduction) Leopoldo Lugones, *Antologia poetica,* Alianza (Madrid, Spain), 1982.

Milongas, Dos Amigos (Buenos Aires, Argentina), 1983.

(Compiler and author of prologue) Pedro Antonio de Alarcon, *El Amigo de la muerte,* Siruela (Madrid, Spain), 1984.

(With Maria Kodama) *Atlas* (prose and poetry), Sudamericana (Buenos Aires, Argentina), 1984, translation by Anthony Kerrigan published as *Atlas,* Dutton (New York, NY), 1985.

En voz de Borges (interviews), Offset, 1986.

Libro de dialogos (interviews), edited by Osvaldo Ferrari, Sudamericana (Buenos Aires, Argentina), 1986, published as *Dialogos ultimos,* 1987.

A/Z, Siruela (Madrid, Spain), 1988.

Borges en la Escuela Freudiana de Buenos Aires, Agalma (Buenos Aires, Argentina), 1993.

(Editor, with James F. Lawrence), *Testimony to the Invisible: Essays on Swedenborg,* Chrysalis Books (West Chester, PA), 1995.

Borges en Revista multicolor: Obras, resenas y traducciones ineditas de Jorge Luis Borges: Diario Critica, Revista multicolor de los sabados, 1933-1934, edited by Irma Zangara, Atlantida (Buenos Aires, Argentina), 1995.

Borges: Textos recobrados, 1919-1929, edited by Irma Zangara, Emecé (Buenos Aires, Argentina), 1997.

Borges professor: Curso de literature inglesa en la Universidad de Buenos Aires, edited by Martín Arias and Martín Hadis, Emecé (Buenos Aires, Argentina), 2000.

This Craft of Verse, edited by Calin-Andrei Mihailescu, Harvard University Press (Cambridge, MA), 2000.

Borges en "El Hogar," 1935-1958, Emecé (Buenos Aires, Argentina), 2000.

(With Alvaro Miranda) *Conversaciones, versaciones,* Ediciones del Mirador (Montevideo, Uruguay), 2001.

(With others) *Cuentos de hijos y padres: Estampas de familia,* Editorial Páginas de Espuma (Madrid, Spain), 2001.

Destino y obra de Camoens, Comunidades Portuguesas (Buenos Aires, Argentina), 2001.

(With others) *Cuentos históricos: De la piedra al átomo,* Páginas de Espuma (Madrid, Spain), 2003.

El Círculo secreto: Prólogos y notas, Emecé (Buenos Aires, Argentina), 2003.

Editor, with Adolfo Bioy Casares, of series of detective novels, "The Seventh Circle," for Emecé, 1943-56. Contributor, under pseudonym F. Bustos, to *Critica,* 1933. Contributor, with Bioy Casares, under joint pseudonym B. Lynch Davis, to *Los Anales de Buenos Aires,* 1946-48. Founding editor of *Prisma* (mural magazine), 1921; founding editor of *Proa* (Buenos Aires literary revue), 1921 and, with Ricardo Guiraldes and Pablo Rojas Paz, 1924-26; literary editor of weekly arts supplement of *Critica,* beginning 1933; editor of biweekly "Foreign Books and Authors" section of *El Hogar* (magazine), 1936-39; coeditor, with Bioy Casares, of *Destiempo* (literary magazine), 1936; editor of *Los Anales de Buenos Aires* (literary journal), 1946-48.

ADAPTATIONS: "Emma Zunz," a short story, was made into the movie *Dias de odio* (*Days of Wrath*) by Argentine director Leopoldo Torre Nilsson, 1954, a French television movie directed by Alain Magrou, 1969, and a film called *Splits* by U.S. director Leonard Katz, 1978; "Hombre de la esquina rosada," a short story, was made into an Argentine movie of the same title directed by Rene Mugica, 1961; Bernardo Bertolucci based his *La Strategia de la ragna* (*The Spider's Stratagem*), a movie made for Italian television, on Borges's short story, "El Tema del traidor y del heroe," 1970; Hector Olivera, in collaboration with Juan Carlos Onetti, adapted Borges's story "El Muerto" for the Argentine movie of the same name, 1975; Borges's short story "La Intrusa" was made into a Brazilian film directed by Carlos Hugo Christensen, 1978; three of the stories in *Six Problems for Don Isidro Parodi* were dramatized for radio broadcast by the British Broadcasting Corporation.

SIDELIGHTS: Argentine author Jorge Luis Borges exerted a strong influence on the direction of literary fiction through his genre-bending metafictions, essays, and poetry. Borges was a founder, and principal practitioner, of postmodernist literature, a movement in which literature distances itself from life situations in favor of reflection on the creative process and critical self-examination. Widely read and profoundly erudite, Borges was a polymath who could discourse on the great literature of Europe and America and who assisted his translators as they brought his work into different languages. He was influenced by the work of such fantasists as Edgar Allan Poe and Franz Kafka, but his own fiction "combines literary and extraliterary genres in order to create a dynamic, electric genre," to quote Alberto Julián Pérez in the *Dictionary of Literary Biography.* Pérez also noted that Borges's work "constitutes, through his extreme linguistic conscience and a formal synthesis capable of representing the most varied ideas, an instance of supreme development in and renovation of narrative techniques. With his exemplary

literary advances and the reflective sharpness of his metaliterature, he has effectively influenced the destiny of literature."

In his preface to *Labyrinths: Selected Stories and Other Writings,* French author André Maurois called Borges "a great writer." Maurois wrote that Borges "composed only little essays or short narratives. Yet they suffice for us to call him great because of their wonderful intelligence, their wealth of invention, and their tight, almost mathematical style. Argentine by birth and temperament, but nurtured on universal literature, Borges [had] no spiritual homeland."

Borges was nearly unknown in most of the world until 1961 when, in his early sixties, he was awarded the Prix Formentor, the International Publishers Prize, an honor he shared with Irish playwright Samuel Beckett. Prior to winning the award, according to Gene H. Bell-Villada in *Borges and His Fiction: A Guide to His Mind and Art,* "Borges had been writing in relative obscurity in Buenos Aires, his fiction and poetry read by his compatriots, who were slow in perceiving his worth or even knowing him." The award made Borges internationally famous: a collection of his short stories, *Ficciones,* was simultaneously published in six different countries, and he was invited by the University of Texas to come to the United States to lecture, the first of many international lecture tours.

Borges's international appeal was partly a result of his enormous erudition, which becomes immediately apparent in the multitude of literary allusions from cultures around the globe that are contained in his writing. "The work of Jorge Luis Borges," Anthony Kerrigan wrote in his introduction to the English translation of *Ficciones,* "is a species of international literary metaphor. He knowledgeably makes a transfer of inherited meanings from Spanish and English, French and German, and sums up a series of analogies, of confrontations, of appositions in other nations' literatures. His Argentinians act out Parisian dramas, his Central European Jews are wise in the ways of the Amazon, his Babylonians are fluent in the paradigms of Babel." In the *National Review,* Peter Witonski commented: "Borges's grasp of world literature is one of the fundamental elements of his art."

The familiarity with world literature evident in Borges's work was initiated at an early age, nurtured by a love of reading. His paternal grandmother was English and, since she lived with the Borgeses, English and Spanish were both spoken in the family home. Jorge Guillermo Borges, Borges's father, had a large library of English and Spanish books, and his son, whose frail constitution made it impossible to participate in more strenuous activities, spent many hours reading. "If I were asked to name the chief event in my life, I should say my father's library," Borges stated, in "An Autobiographical Essay," which originally appeared in the *New Yorker* and was later included in *The Aleph and Other Stories, 1933-1969.*

Under his grandmother's tutelage, Borges learned to read English before he could read Spanish. Among the first English-language books he read were works by Mark Twain, Edgar Allan Poe, Henry Wadsworth Longfellow, Robert Louis Stevenson, and H.G. Wells. In Borges's autobiographical essay, he recalled reading even the great Spanish masterpiece, Cervantes's *Don Quixote,* in English before reading it in Spanish. Borges's father encouraged writing as well as reading: Borges wrote his first story at age seven and, at nine, saw his own Spanish translation of Oscar Wilde's "The Happy Prince" published in a Buenos Aires newspaper. "From the time I was a boy," Borges noted, "it was tacitly understood that I had to fulfill the literary destiny that circumstances had denied my father. This was something that was taken for granted. . . . I was expected to be a writer."

Borges indeed became a writer, one with a unique style. Critics were forced to coin a new word—Borgesian—to capture the magical world invented by the Argentine author. Jaime Alazraki noted in *Jorge Luis Borges:* "As with Joyce, Kafka, or Faulkner, the name of Borges has become an accepted concept; his creations have generated a dimension that we designate 'Borgesian.'" In the *Atlantic,* Keith Botsford declared: "Borges is . . . an international phenomenon . . . a man of letters whose mode of writing and turn of mind are so distinctively his, yet so much a revealed part of our world, that 'Borgesian' has become as commonplace a neologism as the adjectives 'Sartrean' or 'Kafkaesque.'"

Once his work became known in the United States, Borges inspired many young writers there. "The impact of Borges on the United States writing scene may be almost as great as was his earlier influence on Latin America," commented Bell-Villada. "The Argentine reawakened for us the possibilities of farfetched fancy, of formal exploration, of parody, intellectuality, and wit." Bell-Villada specifically noted echoes of Borges in works by Robert Coover, Donald Barthelme, and John Gardner. Another American novelist, John Barth, con-

fessed Borges's influence in his own fiction. Bell-Villada concluded that Borges's work paved the way "for numerous literary trends on both American continents, determining the shape of much fiction to come. By rejecting realism and naturalism, he . . . opened up to our Northern writers a virgin field, led them to a wealth of new subjects and procedures."

The foundation of Borges's literary future was laid in 1914 when the Borges family took an ill-timed trip to Europe. The outbreak of World War I stranded them temporarily in Switzerland, where Borges studied French and Latin in school, taught himself German, and began reading the works of German philosophers and expressionist poets. He also encountered the poetry of Walt Whitman in German translation and soon began writing poetry imitative of Whitman's style. "For some time," Emir Rodriguez Monegal wrote in *Borges: A Reader,* "the young man believed Whitman was poetry itself."

After the war the Borges family settled in Spain for a few years. During this extended stay, Borges published reviews, articles, and poetry and became associated with a group of avant-garde poets called Ultraists (named after the magazine, *Ultra,* to which they contributed). Upon Borges's return to Argentina in 1921, he introduced the tenets of the movement—a belief, for example, in the supremacy of the metaphor—to the Argentine literary scene. His first collection of poems, *Fervor de Buenos Aires,* was written under the spell of this new poetic movement. Although in his autobiographical essay he expressed regret for his "early Ultraist excesses," and in later editions of *Fervor de Buenos Aires* eliminated more than a dozen poems from the text and considerably altered many of the remaining poems, Borges still saw some value in the work. In his autobiographical essay he noted, "I think I have never strayed beyond that book. I feel that all my subsequent writing only developed themes first taken up there; I feel that all during my lifetime I have been rewriting that one book."

One poem from the volume, "El Truco" (named after a card game), seems to testify to the truth of Borges's statement. In the piece he introduced two themes that appear over and over again in his later writing: circular time and the idea that all people are but one person. "The permutations of the cards," Rodriguez Monegal observed in *Jorge Luis Borges: A Literary Biography,* "although innumerable in limited human experience, are not infinite: given enough time, they will come back again and again. Thus the cardplayers not only are repeating hands that have already come up in the past. In a sense, they are repeating the former players as well: they are the former players."

Although better known for his prose, Borges began his writing career as a poet and was known primarily for his poetry in Latin America particularly. In addition to writing his own original poetry, he translated important foreign poets for an Argentinian audience. He also authored numerous essays and gave whole series of lectures on poetry and various poets from Dante to Whitman. Observing that Borges "is one of the major Latin American poets of the twentieth century," Daniel Balderston in the *Dictionary of Literary Biography* added that in Latin America, Borges's poetry "has had a wide impact: many verses have been used as titles for novels and other works, many poems have been set to music, and his variety of poetic voices have been important to many younger poets."

Illusion is an important part of Borges's fictional world. In *Borges: The Labyrinth Maker,* Ana Maria Barrenechea called it "his resplendent world of shadows." But illusion is present in his manner of writing as well as in the fictional world he describes. In *World Literature Today,* William Riggan quoted Icelandic author Sigurdur Magnusson's thoughts on this aspect of Borges's work. "With the possible exception of Kafka," Magnusson stated, "no other writer that I know manages, with such relentless logic, to turn language upon itself to reverse himself time after time with a sentence or a paragraph, and effortlessly, so it seems, come upon surprising yet inevitable conclusions."

Borges expertly blended the traditional boundaries between fact and fiction and between essay and short story, and was similarly adept at obliterating the border between other genres as well. In a tribute to Borges that appeared in the *New Yorker* after the author's death in 1986, Mexican poet and essayist Octavio Paz wrote: "He cultivated three genres: the essay, the poem, and the short story. The division is arbitrary. His essays read like stories, his stories are poems; and his poems make us think, as though they were essays." In *Review,* Ambrose Gordon, Jr. similarly noted, "His essays are like poems in their almost musical development of themes, his stories are remarkably like his essays, and his poems are often little stories." Borges's "Conjectural Poem," for example, is much like a short story in its account of the death of one of his ancestors, Francisco Narciso de Laprida. Another poem, "The Golem," is a short narrative relating how Rabbi Low of Prague created an artificial one

To deal with the problem of actually determining to which genre a prose piece by Borges might belong, Martin S. Stabb proposed in *Jorge Luis Borges,* his book-length study of the author, that the usual manner of grouping all of Borges's short fiction as short stories was invalid. Stabb instead divided the Argentinian's prose fiction into three categories which took into account Borges's tendency to blur genres: "'essayistic' fiction," "difficult-to-classify 'intermediate' fiction," and those pieces deemed "conventional short stories." Other reviewers saw a comparable division in Borges's fiction but chose to emphasize the chronological development of his work, noting that his first stories grew out of his essays, his "middle period" stories were more realistic, while his later stories were marked by a return to fantastic themes.

"Funes the Memorious," listed in Richard Burgin's *Conversations with Jorge Luis Borges* as one of Borges's favorite stories, is about Ireneo Funes, a young man who cannot forget anything. His memory is so keen that he is surprised by how different he looks each time he sees himself in a mirror because, unlike the rest of us, he can see the subtle changes that have taken place in his body since the last time he saw his reflection. The story is filled with characteristic Borgesian detail. Funes's memory, for instance, becomes excessive as a result of an accidental fall from a horse. In Borges an accident is a reminder that people are unable to order existence because the world has a hidden order of its own. Alazraki saw this Borgesian theme as "the tragic contrast between a man who believes himself to be the master and maker of his fate and a text or divine plan in which his fortune has already been written." The deliberately vague quality of the adjectives Borges typically uses in his sparse descriptive passages is also apparent: Funes's features are never clearly distinguished because he lives in a darkened room; he was thrown from his horse on a dark "rainy afternoon"; and the horse itself is described as "blue-gray"—neither one color nor the other. "This dominant chiaroscuro imagery," commented Bell-Villada, "is further reinforced by Funes's name, a word strongly suggestive of certain Spanish words variously meaning 'funereal,' 'ill-fated,' and 'dark.'" The ambiguity of Borges's descriptions lends a subtle, otherworldly air to this and other examples of his fiction.

In "Partial Magic in the *Quixote*" (also translated as "Partial Enchantments of the *Quixote*") Borges describes several occasions in world literature when a character reads about himself or sees himself in a play, including episodes from Shakespeare's plays, an epic poem of India, Miguel de Cervantes's *Don Quixote,* and *The One*

Thousand and One Nights. "Why does it disquiet us to know," Borges asked in the essay, "that Don Quixote is a reader of the *Quixote,* and Hamlet is a spectator of *Hamlet?* I believe I have found the answer: those inversions suggest that if the characters in a story can be readers or spectators, then we, their readers, can be fictitious."

That analysis was Borges's own interpretation of what John Barth referred to in the *Atlantic* as "one of Borges's cardinal themes." Barrenechea explained Borges's technique, noting: "To readers and spectators who consider themselves real beings, these works suggest their possible existence as imaginary entities. In that context lies the key to Borges's work. Relentlessly pursued by a world that is too real and at the same time lacking meaning, he tries to free himself from its obsessions by creating a world of such coherent phantasmagorias that the reader doubts the very reality on which he leans." Pérez put it this way: "In his fiction Borges repeatedly utilizes two approaches that constitute his most permanent contributions to contemporary literature: the creation of stories whose principal objective is to deal with critical, literary, or aesthetic problems; and the development of plots that communicate elaborate and complex ideas that are transformed into the main thematic base of the story, provoking the action and relegating the characters—who appear as passive subjects in this inhuman, nightmarish world—to a secondary plane."

For example, in one of Borges's variations on "the work within a work," Jaromir Hladik, the protagonist of Borges's story "The Secret Miracle," appears in a footnote to another of Borges' stories, "Three Versions of Judas." The note refers the reader to the "Vindication of Eternity," a work said to be written by Hladik. In this instance, Borges used a fictional work written by one of his fictitious characters to lend an air of erudition to another fictional work about the works of another fictitious author.

These intrusions of reality on the fictional world are characteristic of Borges's work. He also uses a device, which he calls "the contamination of reality by dream," that produces the same effect of uneasiness in the reader as "the work within the work," but through directly opposite means. Two examples of stories using this technique are "Tlon, Uqbar, Orbis Tertius" and "The Circular Ruins." The first, which Stabb included in his "difficult-to-classify 'intermediate' fiction," is one of Borges's most discussed works. It tells the story, according to Barrenechea, "of an attempt of a group of men to create a world of their own until, by the sheer weight of concentration, the fantastic creation acquires consistency and some of its objects—a compass, a metallic cone—which are composed of strange matter begin to appear on earth." By the end of the story, the world as we know it is slowly turning into the invented world of Tlon. Stabb called the work "difficult-to-classify" because, he commented, "the excruciating amount of documentary detail (half real, half fictitious) . . . make[s] the piece seem more like an essay." There are, in addition, footnotes and a postscript to the story as well as an appearance by Borges himself and references to several other well-known Latin-American literary figures, including Borges's friend Bioy Casares.

"The Circular Ruins," which Stabb considered a "conventional short story," describes a very unconventional situation. (The story is conventional, however, in that there are no footnotes or real people intruding on the fictive nature of the piece.) In the story a man decides to dream about a son until the son becomes real. Later, after the man accomplishes his goal, much to his astonishment, he discovers that he in turn is being dreamt by someone else. "The Circular Ruins" includes several themes seen throughout Borges's work, including the vain attempt to establish order in a chaotic universe, the infinite regression, the symbol of the labyrinth, and the idea of all people being one.

The futility of any attempt to order the universe, seen in "Funes the Memorious" and in "The Circular Ruins," is also found in "The Library of Babel" where, according to Alazraki, "Borges presents the world as a library of chaotic books which its librarians cannot read but which they interpret incessantly." The library was one of Borges's favorite images, often repeated in his fiction, reflecting the time he spent working as a librarian himself. In another work, Borges uses the image of a chessboard to elaborate the same theme. In his poem "Chess," he speaks of the king, bishop, and queen, who "seek out and begin their armed campaign." But, just as the dreamer dreams a man and causes him to act in a certain way, the campaign is actually being planned by someone other than the members of royalty. "They do not know it is the player's hand," the poem continues, "that dominates and guides their destiny." In the last stanza of the poem Borges uses the same images to suggest the infinite regression: "God moves the player, he in turn, the piece. / But what god beyond God begins the round / of dust and time and sleep and agonies?" Another poem, "The Golem," which tells the story of an artificial man created by a rabbi in Prague, ends in a similar fashion: "At the hour of anguish and vague light, / He would rest his eyes on his Golem. / Who can tell us what God felt, / As he gazed on His rabbi in Prague?" Just as there is a dreamer dreaming a man, and beyond that a dreamer dreaming the dreamer who dreamt the man, then, too, there must be another dreamer beyond that in an infinite succession of dreamers.

The title of the story, "The Circular Ruins," suggests a labyrinth. In another story, "The Babylon Lottery," Stabb explained that "an ironically detached narrator depicts life as a labyrinth through which man wanders under the absurd illusion of having understood a chaotic, meaningless world." Labyrinths or references to labyrinths are found in nearly all of Borges's fiction. The labyrinthine form is often present in his poems, too, especially in Borges's early poetry filled with remembrances of wandering the labyrinth-like streets of old Buenos Aires.

In "The Circular Ruins," Borges returns to another favorite theme: circular time. This theme embraces another device mentioned by Borges as typical of fantastic literature: time travel. Borges's characters, however, do not travel through time in machines; their travel is more on a metaphysical, mythical level. Circular time—a concept also favored by Nietzsche, one of the German philosophers Borges discovered as a boy—is apparent in many of Borges's stories, including "Three Versions of Judas," "The Garden of the Forking Paths," "Tlon, Uqbar, Orbis Tertius," "The Library of Babel," and "The Immortal." It is also found in another of Borges's favorite stories, "Death and the Compass," in which the reader encounters not only a labyrinth but a double as well. Stabb offered the story as a good example of Borges's "conventional short stories."

"Death and the Compass" is a detective story. Erik Lonnrot, the story's detective, commits the fatal error of believing there is an order in the universe that he can understand. When Marcel Yarmolinsky is murdered, Lonnrot refuses to believe it was just an accident; he looks for clues to the murderer's identity in Yarmolinsky's library. Red Scharlach, whose brother Lonnrot had sent to jail, reads about the detective's efforts to solve the murder in the local newspaper and contrives a plot to ambush him. The plan works because Lonnrot, overlooking numerous clues, blindly follows the false trail Scharlach leaves for him.

The final sentences—in which Lonnrot is murdered—change the whole meaning of the narrative, illustrate many of Borges's favorite themes, and crystalize Borges's thinking on the problem of time. Lonnrot says to

Scharlach: "'I know of one Greek labyrinth which is a single straight line. Along that line so many philosophers have lost themselves that a mere detective might well do so, too. Scharlach, when in some other incarnation you hunt me, pretend to commit (or do commit) a crime at A, then a second crime at B. . . . then a third crime at C. . . . Wait for me afterwards at D. . . . Kill me at D as you now are going to kill me at Triste-le-Roy.' 'The next time I kill you,' said Scharlach, 'I promise you that labyrinth, consisting of a single line which is invisible and unceasing.' He moved back a few steps. Then, very carefully, he fired."

"Death and the Compass" is in many ways a typical detective story, but this last paragraph takes the story far beyond that popular genre. Lonnrot and Scharlach are doubles (Borges gives us a clue in their names: rot means red and scharlach means scarlet in German) caught in an infinite cycle of pursuing and being pursued. "Their antithetical natures, or inverted mirror images," George R. McMurray observed in his study *Jorge Luis Borges,* "are demonstrated by their roles as detective/criminal and pursuer/pursued, roles that become ironically reversed." Rodriguez Monegal concluded: "The concept of the eternal return . . . adds an extra dimension to the story. It changes Scharlach and Lonnrot into characters in a myth: Abel and Cain endlessly performing the killing."

Doubles, which Bell-Villada defined as "any blurring or any seeming multiplication of character identity," are found in many of Borges's works, including "The Waiting," "The Theologians," "The South," "The Shape of the Sword," "Three Versions of Judas," and "Story of the Warrior and the Captive." Borges's explanation of "The Theologians" (included in his collection, *The Aleph and Other Stories, 1933-1969*) reveals how a typical Borgesian plot involving doubles works. "In 'The Theologians' you have two enemies," Borges told Richard Burgin in an interview, "and one of them sends the other to the stake. And then they find out somehow they're the same man." In an essay in *Studies in Short Fiction,* Robert Magliola noticed that "almost every story in *Dr. Brodie's Report* is about two people fixed in some sort of dramatic opposition to each other." In two pieces, "Borges and I" (also translated as "Borges and Myself") and "The Other," Borges appears as a character along with his double. In the former, Borges, the retiring Argentine librarian, contemplates Borges, the world-famous writer. It concludes with one of Borges's most-analyzed sentences: "Which of us is writing this page, I don't know."

Some critics saw Borges's use of the double as an attempt to deal with the duality in his own personality:

the struggle between his native Argentine roots and the strong European influence on his writing. They also pointed out what seemed to be an attempt by the author to reconcile through his fiction the reality of his sedentary life as an almost-blind scholar with the longed-for adventurous life of his dreams, like those of his famous ancestors who actively participated in Argentina's wars for independence. Bell-Villada pointed out that this tendency is especially evident in "The South," a largely autobiographical story about a library worker who, like Borges, "is painfully aware of the discordant strains in his ancestry."

The idea that all humans are one, which Anderson-Imbert observed calls for the "obliteration of the I," is perhaps Borges's biggest step toward a literature devoid of realism. In this theme we see, according to Ronald Christ in *The Narrow Act: Borges' Art of Illusion,* "the direction in Borges's stories away from individual psychology toward a universal mythology." This explains why so few of Borges's characters show any psychological development; instead of being interested in his characters as individuals, Borges typically uses them only to further his philosophical beliefs.

All of the characteristics of Borges's work, including the blending of genres and the confusion of the real and the fictive, seem to come together in one of his most quoted passages, the final paragraph of his essay "A New Refutation of Time." While in *Borges: A Reader* Rodriguez Monegal called the essay Borges's "most elaborate attempt to organize a personal system of metaphysics in which he denies time, space, and the individual 'I,'" Alazraki noted that it contains a summation of Borges's belief in "the heroic and tragic condition of man as dream and dreamer."

"Our destiny," wrote Borges in the essay, "is not horrible because of its unreality; it is horrible because it is irreversible and ironbound. Time is the substance I am made of. Time is a river that carries me away, but I am the river; it is a tiger that mangles me, but I am the tiger; it is a fire that consumes me, but I am the fire. The world, alas, is real; I, alas, am Borges."

Since his death from liver cancer in 1986, Borges's reputation has only grown in esteem. In honor of the centenary of his birth, Viking Press issued a trilogy of his translated works, beginning with *Collected Fictions,* in 1998. The set became the first major summation of Borges's work in English, and *Review of Contemporary Fiction* writer Irving Malin called the volume's debut

"the most significant literary event of 1998." The collection includes "The Circular Ruins," "Tlon, Uqbar, Orbis Tertius," and the prose poem "Everything and Nothing," along with some of the Argentine writer's lesser-known works. "I admire the enduring chill of Borges," concluded Malin. "Despite his calm, understated style, he manages to make us unsure of our place in the world, of the value of language."

The second volume from Viking was *Selected Poems,* with Borges's original Spanish verse alongside English renditions from a number of translators. *Nation* critic Jay Parini commended editor Alexander Coleman's selections of poems from different periods of Borges's life, praised some of the English translations, and described Borges's work as timeless. "Borges stands alone, a planet unto himself, resisting categorization," Parini noted, adding, "Although literary fashions come and go, he is always there, endlessly rereadable by those who admire him, awaiting rediscovery by new generations of readers."

Selected Non-Fictions, the third in the commemorative trilogy, brings together various topical articles from Borges. These include prologues for the books of others, including Virginia Woolf, and political opinion pieces, such as his excoriating condemnation of Nazi Germany as well as to the tacit support it received from some among the Argentine middle classes. Borges also writes about the dubbing of foreign films and the celebrated Dionne quintuplets, born in Canada in the 1930s. "One reads these," noted Richard Bernstein in the *New York Times,* "with amazement at their author's impetuous curiosity and penetrating intelligence." *Review of Contemporary Fiction* critic Ben Donnelly, like other critics, felt that all three volumes complemented each other, as Borges's own shifts between genres did: "The best essays here expose even grander paradoxes and erudite connections than in his stories," Donnelly noted.

In 2000, Harvard University Press issued *This Craft of Verse,* a series of lectures delivered by Borges at Harvard University in the late 1960s. They languished in an archive for some thirty years until the volume's editor, Calin-Andrei Mihailescu, found the tapes and transcribed them. Micaela Kramer, reviewing the work for the *New York Times,* commented that its pages show "Borges's ultimate gift" and, as she noted, "his unwavering belief in the world of dreams and ideas, the sense that life is 'made of poetry.'" In his essay on Borges, Pérez observed that the author "created his own type of post-avant-garde literature—which shows the process of critical self-examination that reveals the moment in which literature becomes a reflection of itself, distanced from life—in order to reveal the formal and intellectual density involved in writing."

BIOGRAPHICAL AND CRITICAL SOURCES:

BOOKS

Alazraki, Jaime, *Critical Essays on Jorge Luis Borges,* G.K. Hall (Boston, MA), 1987.

Alazraki, Jaime, *Jorge Luis Borges,* Columbia University Press (New York, NY), 1971.

Balderston, Daniel, *Out of Context: Historical References and the Representation of Reality in Borges,* Duke University Press (Durham, NC), 1993.

Barnstone, Willis, *Borges at Eighty: Conversations,* Indiana University Press (Bloomington, IN), 1982.

Barrenechea, Ana Maria, *Borges: The Labyrinth Maker,* translated by Robert Lima, New York University Press (New York, NY), 1965.

Bell-Villada, Gene H., *Borges and His Fiction: A Guide to His Mind and Art,* University of North Carolina Press (Chapel Hill, NC), 1981.

Burgin, Richard, *Conversations with Jorge Luis Borges,* Holt (New York, NY), 1969.

Christ, Ronald J., *The Narrow Act: Borges' Art of Illusion,* New York University Press (New York, NY), 1969.

Contemporary Literary Criticism, Thomson Gale (Detroit, MI), Volume 1, 1973, Volume 2, 1974, Volume 3, 1975, Volume 4, 1975, Volume 6, 1976, Volume 8, 1978, Volume 9, 1978, Volume 10, 1979, Volume 13, 1980, Volume 19, 1981, Volume 44, 1987, Volume 48, 1988.

Cortínez, Carlos, editor, *Borges the Poet,* University of Arkansas Press (Fayetteville, AR), 1986.

Cottom, Daniel, *Ravishing Tradition: Cultural Forces and Literary History,* Cornell University Press (Ithaca, NY), 1996.

Dictionary of Literary Biography, Thomson Gale (Detroit, MI), Volume 113: *Modern Latin-American Fiction Writers, First Series,* 1992, pp. 67-81; Volume 238: *Modern Spanish American Poets, First Series,* 2001, pp. 41-58.

Dictionary of Literary Biography: Yearbook, 1986, Thomson Gale (Detroit, MI), 1987.

Di Giovanni, Norman Thomas, editor, *In Memory of Borges,* Constable (London, England), 1988.

Di Giovanni, Norman Thomas, editor, *The Borges Tradition,* Constable (London, England), 1995.

Friedman, Mary L., *The Emperor's Kites: A Morphology of Borges' Tales,* Duke University Press (Durham, NC), 1987.

Irwin, John T., *The Mystery to a Solution: Poe, Borges, and the Analytic Detective Story,* Johns Hopkins University Press (Baltimore, MD), 1994.

Kinzie, Mary, *Prose for Borges,* Northwestern University Press (Evanston, IL), 1974.

Maier, Linda S., *Borges and the European Avant-Garde,* P. Lang (New York, NY), 1996.

McMurray, George R., *Jorge Luis Borges,* Ungar (New York, NY), 1980.

Molloy, Sylvia, and Oscar Montero, *Signs of Borges,* Duke University Press (Durham, NC), 1994.

Rodriguez Monegal, Emir, *Jorge Luis Borges: A Literary Biography,* Dutton (New York, NY), 1978.

Stabb, Martin S., *Borges Revisited,* Twayne (Boston, MA), 1991.

Stabb, Martin S., *Jorge Luis Borges,* Twayne (Boston, MA), 1970.

Sturrock, John, *Paper Tigers: The Ideal Fictions of Jorge Luis Borges,* Clarendon Press (Oxford, England), 1977.

Woodall, James, *Borges: A Life,* Basic Books (New York, NY), 1997.

PERIODICALS

Americas, January, 2000, Barbara Mujica, review of *Selected Non-Fictions,* p. 60; April, 2000, Barbara Mujica, review of *Collected Fictions,* p. 63.

Atlantic Monthly, January, 1967; August, 1967; February, 1972; April, 1981.

Booklist, April 1, 1999, Donna Seaman, review of *Selected Poems,* p. 1379; August, 1999, Brad Hooper, review of *Selected Non-Fictions,* p. 2010; August, 2000, Ray Olson, review of *This Craft of Verse,* p. 2097.

Commentary, July, 1999, Marc Berley, review of *Collected Fictions* and *Selected Poems,* p. 89.

Cross Currents, summer, 1999, "Editor's Choice," p. 260.

Detroit News, June 15, 1986; June 22, 1986.

Library Journal, August, 2000, Jack Shreve, review of *This Craft of Verse,* p. 102.

Los Angeles Times, June 15, 1986.

Nation, December 29, 1969; August 3, 1970; March 1, 1971; February 21, 1972; October 16, 1972; February 21, 1976; June 28, 1986; May 31, 1999, Jay Parini, "Borges in Another Metier," p. 25.

National Review, March 2, 1973.

New Criterion, November, 1999, Eric Ormsby, "Jorge Luis Borges and the Plural I," p. 14; January, 2001, Alexander Coleman, review of *This Craft of Verse,* p. 79.

New Republic, November 3, 1986.

New Yorker, July 7, 1986.

New York Review of Books, August 14, 1986.

New York Times, June 15, 1986; October 6, 1999, Richard Bernstein, "So Close, Borges' Worlds of Reality and Invention"; October 15, 2000, Micaela Kramer, review of *This Craft of Verse.*

Publishers Weekly, July 4, 1986; March 29, 1999, review of *Selected Poems,* p. 97; July 12, 1999, review of *Selected Non-Fictions,* p. 80.

Review, spring, 1972; spring, 1975; winter, 1976; January-April, 1981; September-December, 1981.

Review of Contemporary Fiction, spring, 1999, Irving Malin, review of *Contemporary Fictions,* p. 175; spring, 2000, Ben Donnelly, review of *Selected Non-Fictions,* p. 192; spring, 2001, Thomas Hove, review of *This Craft of Verse,* p. 209.

Studies in Short Fiction, spring, 1974; winter, 1978.

Time, June 23, 1986.

USA Today, June 16, 1986.

Washington Post, June 15, 1986.

World Literature Today, autumn, 1977; winter, 1984.

Yale Review, October, 1969; autumn, 1974.

*   *   *

BOUCOLON, Maryse
    See CONDÉ, Maryse

*   *   *

BOWLES, Paul 1910-1999
    (Paul Frederick Bowles)

PERSONAL: Born December 30, 1910, in New York, NY; died November 18, 1999; son of Claude Dietz (a dentist) and Rena (Winnewisser) Bowles; married Jane Sydney Auer (a writer), February 21, 1938 (died 1973). *Education:* Studied music with Aaron Copland, 1930-32, and Virgil Thomson, 1933-34; also attended New York School of Design and Liberal Arts and University of Virginia.

CAREER: Writer. Composer for stage, operas, film scores, ballets, songs, and chamber music; musical works include scores for *The Glass Menagerie, Love's Old Sweet Song, My Heart's in the Highlands,* and *Sweet Bird of Youth,* and for ballets *Pastorelas, Yankee Clipper,* and *Sentimental Colloquy.* Visiting professor, San Fernando Valley State College (now California State University, Northridge), 1968.

AWARDS, HONORS: Guggenheim fellowship, 1941; National Institute of Arts and Letters Award in Literature, 1950; Rockefeller grant, 1959; National Endowment for the Arts creative writing fellowship, 1978, and senior fellowship, 1980; American Book Award nomination, 1980, for *Collected Stories of Paul Bowles, 1939-1976.*

WRITINGS:

NOVELS, EXCEPT AS INDICATED

The Sheltering Sky, New Directions (New York, NY), 1949, reprinted, Ecco Press (New York, NY), 2000.

Let It Come Down, Random House (New York, NY), 1952.

The Spider's House, Random House (New York, NY), 1955.

Up above the World, Simon & Schuster (New York, NY), 1966.

Points in Time, Ecco Press (New York, NY), 1982.

Too Far from Home: The Selected Writings of Paul Bowles, introduction by Joyce Carol Oates, Ecco Press (New York, NY), 1993.

(With Mario Vargas Llosa) *Cladio Brave: Paintings and Drawings* (nonfiction), Abberville Press (New York, NY), 1997.

The Sheltering Sky; Let It Come Down; The Spider's House, Penguin (New York, NY), 2002.

SHORT STORIES

The Delicate Prey and Other Stories, Random House (New York, NY), 1950.

A Little Stone, J. Lehmann (Tyne and Wear, England), 1950.

The Hours after Noon, Heinemann (London, England), 1959.

A Hundred Camels in the Courtyard, City Lights (San Francisco, CA), 1962.

The Time of Friendship, Holt (New York, NY), 1967.

Pages from Cold Point and Other Stories, P. Owen (London, England), 1968.

Three Tales, F. Hallman, 1975.

Things Gone and Things Still Here, Black Sparrow Press (Santa Barbara, CA), 1977.

Collected Stories of Paul Bowles, 1939-1976, Black Sparrow Press (Santa Barbara, CA), 1979.

Midnight Mass, Black Sparrow Press (Santa Barbara, CA), 1981.

A Distant Episode: The Selected Stories, Ecco Press (New York, NY), 1988.

Call at Corazon, P. Owen (London, England), 1988.

Unwelcome Words: Seven Stories, Tombouctou Books (Bolinas, CA), 1988.

A Thousand Days for Mokhtar, and Other Stories, P. Owen (London, England), 1989.

The Stories of Paul Bowles, Ecco Press (New York, NY), 2001.

Collected Stories and Later Writings, Penguin (New York, NY), 2002.

POETRY

Scenes, Black Sparrow Press (Santa Barbara, CA), 1968.

The Thicket of Spring: Poems, 1926-1969, Black Sparrow Press (Santa Barbara, CA), 1972.

Next to Nothing, Starstreams, 1976.

TRANSLATOR FROM THE MOGHREBI

Driss ben Hamed Charhadi, *A Life Full of Holes,* Grove (New York, NY), 1963.

Mohammed Mrabet, *Love with a Few Hairs,* P. Owen (London, England), 1967.

Mohammed Mrabet, *The Lemon,* P. Owen (London, England), 1969.

Mohammed Mrabet, *M'Hashish,* City Lights (San Francisco, CA), 1969.

Mohammed Mrabet, *The Boy Who Set the Fire and Other Stories,* Black Sparrow Press (Santa Barbara, CA), 1974.

Mohammed Mrabet, *Hadidan Aharam,* Black Sparrow Press (Santa Barbara, CA), 1975.

Mohammed Mrabet, *Harmless Poisons, Blameless Sins,* Black Sparrow Press (Santa Barbara, CA), 1976.

Mohammed Mrabet, *Look and Move On,* Black Sparrow Press (Santa Barbara, CA), 1976.

Mohammed Mrabet, *The Big Mirror,* Black Sparrow Press (Santa Barbara, CA), 1977.

Five Eyes, Black Sparrow Press (Santa Barbara, CA), 1979.

Mohammed Mrabet, *The Beach Café,* Black Sparrow Press (Santa Barbara, CA), 1980.

Mohammed Mrabet, *The Chest,* Tombouctou Books (Bolinas, CA), 1983.

Marriage with Papers, Tombouctou Books (Bolinas, CA), 1986.

Mohammed Mrabet, *Chocolate Creams and Dollars,* Distributed Art Publishers, 1993.

TRANSLATOR FROM THE FRENCH

Jean-Paul Sartre, *No Exit,* S. French (New York, NY), 1946.

Isabelle Eberhardt, *The Oblivion Seekers,* City Lights (San Francisco, CA), 1975.

Also translator of other works from French.

TRANSLATOR FROM THE ARABIC

Mohamed Choukri, *For Bread Alone,* P. Owen (London, England), 1973.

Mohamed Choukri, *Jean Genet in Tangier,* Ecco Press (New York, NY), 1974.

Mohamed Choukri, *Tennessee Williams in Tangier,* Cadmus Editions (Santa Barbara, CA), 1979.

OTHER

(With Luchino Visconti and Tennessee Williams) *Senso* (screenplay), Domenico Forges Davanzati, 1954.

Yallah (travel essays), McDowell, Obolensky (New York, NY), 1957.

Their Heads Are Green and Their Hands Are Blue (travel essays), Random House (New York, NY), 1963, published as *Their Heads Are Green,* P. Owen (London, England), 1963, reprinted, Abacus/Sphere (New York, NY), 1990.

Paul Bowles in the Land of the Jumblies (screenplay), Gary Conklin, 1969.

Without Stopping: An Autobiography, Putnam (New York, NY), 1972, revised edition, Ecco Press (New York, NY), 1991.

She Woke Me up and So I Killed Her, Cadmus Editions (Santa Barbara, CA), 1985.

(Translator from the Spanish) Rodrigo Rey Rosa, *The Beggar's Knife,* City Lights (San Francisco, CA), 1985.

Two Years beside the Strait: Tangier Journal 1987-1989 (diary), P. Owen (London, England), 1990, published as *Days: Tangier Journal 1987-1989,* Ecco Press (New York, NY), 1991.

Tanger: vues choisies (travel pictorial), photographs by Jellel Gasteli, Editions E. Koehler (Paris, France), 1991.

(Translator) Rodrigo Rey Rosa, *Dust on Her Tongue,* City Lights (San Francisco, CA), 1992.

Conversations with Paul Bowles, edited by Gena Dagel Caponi, University Press of Mississippi (Jackson, MS), 1993.

Morocco (travel pictorial), photographs by Barry Brukoff, Abrams (New York, NY), 1993.

In Touch: The Letters of Paul Bowles, edited by Jeffrey Miller, Farrar, Straus (New York, NY), 1994.

Paul Bowles Photographs, edited by Simon Bischoff, Scalo Publishers (New York, NY), 1994.

The Portable Paul and Jane Bowles, edited by Millicent Dillon, Viking Penguin (New York, NY), 1994.

China after Socialism: In the Footsteps of Eastern Europe or East Asia?, edited by Barrett L. McCormick and Jonathan Unger, M.E. Sharpe (Armonk, NY), 1996.

Dear Paul, Dear Ned: The Correspondence of Paul Bowles and Ned Rorem, Abbeville Press (New York, NY), 1997.

(Translator) Rey Rosa, *The Pelcari Project/Carcel de arboles,* Cadmus Editions (Santa Barbara, CA), 1997.

Desultory Correspondence: An Interview with Paul Bowles on Gertrude Stein, edited by Florian Vetsch, Distributed Art Publishers, 1997.

The Paul Bowles Reader, P, Owen (New York, NY), 2000.

(Coauthor) Cherie Nutting, *Yesterday's Perfume: An Intimate Memoir of Paul Bowles,* Clarkson Potter (New York, NY), 2000.

Paul Bowles on Music, edited by Timothy Mangan and Irene Herrmann, University of California Press (Berkeley, CA), 2003.

ADAPTATIONS: Bowles recorded his short stories "The Delicate Prey" and "A Distant Episode" on an album for Spoken Arts, 1963; *A Hundred Camels in the Courtyard* was recorded for Cadmus Editions, 1981; a film version of *The Sheltering Sky* narrated by Bowles and starring John Malkovich and Debra Winger was released by Warner Bros., 1990.

SIDELIGHTS: Paul Bowles' fiction depicts the frailty of Western rationalism. In the essential Bowles story, American or European travelers visit a civilization they consider vastly inferior to their own, usually in the North African desert. When they enter that more primitive world, however, their Western values quickly disintegrate. Inevitably, contact with the older culture transforms the travelers' world view; not infrequently, it destroys them. Although he remains best known for his novel *The Sheltering Sky,* Bowles also distinguished himself as a composer, short story writer, translator, and poet.

Even as a child Bowles wrote fiction and music; he was sixteen years old when the highly regarded magazine *transition* published his surrealist poetry. A 1931 trip to Paris really marked the beginning of his adult writing career, however, for it was then that he met and became friends with author Gertrude Stein and her companion, Alice B. Toklas. These two women were to give Bowles important direction concerning his literary efforts; Stein was not fond of surrealism, and her criticism of Bowles' poetry was harsh. In a *Dictionary of Literary Biography* essay, Lawrence D. Stewart quoted her as saying to the young writer: "Now Bravig Imbs, for instance, he's just a very bad poet. . . . But you—you're not a poet at all!"

Stein believed that time away from Western culture would help Bowles discover his own style. Toklas, who according to Stewart "had a talent for putting people in a proper setting," suggested Morocco. In so doing, she introduced the young author to the place where he would live for most of his life, and which would serve as the setting for the greater part of his fiction. He rented a house in Tangier, sharing it with composer Aaron Copland, who was then serving as Bowles' musical mentor. Although primarily concerned with his composition at this time, Bowles did send some prose passages to Stein from Tangier, which pleased her much more than had his poetry. Stewart quotes a letter to Bowles in which Stein wrote: "I like your story, I like your descriptions, go on with them."

It was in 1942 that Bowles again became inspired to write fiction. Watching his wife, Jane Auer, at work on her novel *Two Serious Ladies* "was the thing that detonated the . . . explosion," Stewart quoted Bowles as explaining. His stories were soon appearing in such diverse publications as *Harper's Bazaar, View, Mademoiselle,* and *Partisan Review.* When he had collected enough to make up an entire volume, he sent them to a publisher "hoping somehow to bypass the unwritten law which makes it impossible for a writer to publish a book of short stories until after he has published a novel," noted Bowles in an essay for *Contemporary Authors Autobiography Series* (CAAS). He did not succeed in this aim, but after reading his stories, editors at Doubleday were willing to commission a novel. A vivid dream of Morocco convinced Bowles that he must return there to write. Soon he was en route to Fez, and within eight months he had completed *The Sheltering Sky,* a novel so startling that upon receiving the manuscript, Doubleday demanded the return of their advance money, declaring that what Bowles had produced was not a novel at all.

Subsequently published by New Directions, *The Sheltering Sky* has since been praised as a masterpiece of existential literature. Theodore Solotaroff expressed the opinion of many critics in a *New Republic* review, calling it "one of the most beautifully written novels" of the mid-twentieth century "and one of the most shattering. Bowles is not the philosopher that Sartre or Camus were, but he is an existentialist to his fingertips, and beside the emotional concreteness of *The Sheltering Sky,* books like *Nausea, The Age of Reason,* or *The Stranger* seem vague, arbitrary, imaginatively barren."

According to Stewart, Bowles himself described *The Sheltering Sky* as "an adventure story, in which the actual adventures take place on two planes simultaneously: in the actual desert, and in the inner desert of the spirit." The main characters are Port and Kit Moresby, two sophisticated American drifters whose feelings of emptiness are revealed in Port's remark to his wife: "We've never managed, either of us, to get all the way into life." Their wanderings take them to the North African desert. There, wrote *Esquire* contributor Tobias Wolff, "in the silent emptiness of desert and sky, the knowledge of their absolute isolation from other people comes upon them so violently that it subverts their belief in their own reality and in the reality of their connection to each other. Doubting that connection is, of course, prelude to betraying it. And betray it they do, in every way." Port falls mortally ill; Kit abandons her dying husband for another man. Eventually, she becomes the mindlessly contented slave of an Arab named Belqassim. Subjugation brings her such peace that when Belqassim loses interest in her, she searches for another captor. When French colonial authorities finally locate Kit, she has abandoned her identity so completely that she fails even to recognize her own name.

"*The Sheltering Sky* has been called nightmarish; that description lets us off the hook too easily, because it implies a fear of the unreal," believed Wolff. "The power of this novel lies precisely in the reality of what it makes us fear—the sweetness of that voice in each of us that sings the delight of not being responsible. . . . Our failing resistance to . . . attacks on our sense of worth as individuals is the central drama of our time. *The Sheltering Sky* records the struggle with complete fidelity, impassively noting every step in the process of surrender. Like *The Sun Also Rises* and *Under the Volcano,* Bowles' novel enacts a crucial historical moment with such clarity that it has become part of our picture of that moment."

With a critically acclaimed novel to his credit, Bowles was able to publish his collection *The Delicate Prey and Other Stories.* The stories in this volume, wrote Wolff, extend "the perceptions of the novel into even more exotic and disturbing terrain." The title story, for example, delineates a hashish-maddened hunter's murder of three brothers, and the revenge of the slain brothers' tribesmen: after capturing the killer, they bury him up to his neck in sand and abandon him to the elements. In "A Distant Episode," which Tennessee Williams described in the *Saturday Review of Literature* as "a true masterpiece of short fiction," an American linguistics professor, betrayed by his native guide, is seized by a band of hostile nomads. Mutilated and dressed in a suit of flattened tin cans, the professor is then kept as a hideous pet by the tribesmen, who teach him to dance for their amusement. "The curiosity-seeker has himself become a curiosity, comically and ineffectually armored in the detritus of his own culture," noted Wolff. "The story is a tour de force, an ominous parable of the weakening of the individual will to survive." Solotaroff stated that the stories in *The Delicate Prey,* "with their lucid, quiet evocation of mood and motive leading to revelations of scarifying depravity," are so powerful that they make "the nihilism of the early Hemingway seem like a pleasant beery melancholy. . . . These stories . . . make one feel they were written with a razor, so deftly and chillingly do they cut to the bone."

Bowles' later fiction continued to feature the elements that make *The Sheltering Sky* and *The Delicate Prey* unique: exotic locations, existential concerns, and pristine prose. *Let It Come Down* follows a bank clerk as he flees the desolation of his life in New York City for Tangier, where he experiences a rapid disintegration. In *The Spider's House* four expatriate Westerners are caught up in the violence of revolution in Fez. *Up above the World* tells of a jaded American couple traveling across South America; their entanglement with a stranger leads to their brainwashing and murder. The similarities found in Bowles' works have led some critics to suggest that the author made his strongest statement in his first two books and failed to develop artistically thereafter. While admiring the author's stylistic mastery, Bernard Bergonzi in the *New York Review of Books* found "what he does with it very limited and ultimately monotonous. He places his characters before us and then destroys them in an unerring way: it is a remarkable performance, but one expects something more from literature." Francis King concurred in a *Spectator* article that Bowles unfortunately restricted himself to a "constant retreading of the same narrow plot, instead of the exploration of previously untrodden jungle."

Bowles' writing was curtailed when his wife suffered a stroke and, afterward, a long physical decline. "During the latter years of Jane's illness . . . it was impossible for me to write fiction," he once revealed in *CAAS.*

"The periods which I had to myself were of very short duration: fifteen or twenty minutes, instead of several hours. Frequent interruptions destroyed creative impetus." Discovering that "the act of translating did not suffer in any way from being stopped at short intervals," however, Bowles began what he felt was among his most important work: the publication of tales told by his young Arab friends. These tales, often produced when the narrators were high on *kif*—a marijuana-related substance—were tape-recorded, transcribed, and translated by Bowles. They illustrate the manner of thought the American author came to appreciate during his many years in North Africa.

After Jane Auer's death in 1973 Bowles once again turned to fiction. Some critics indicated that the work produced during this period may have been his most distinguished. Wolff described Bowles' 1982 publication *Points in Time* as "a nervy, surprising, completely original performance, so original that it can't be referred to any previous category of fiction or nonfiction." The book's structure reflects Bowles's musical training; it is divided into several sections or "movements." In this way, the author combines legends, historical anecdotes, description, and passages of popular song to create a portrait of Morocco through the years. It is accomplished with "a centered precision that at times reaches perfection and becomes so memorable, it does damage to the eye and the brain of the reader," explained Ben Pleasants in the *Los Angeles Times Book Review*. Wolff agreed that *Points in Time* is "a brilliant achievement, innovative in form, composed in a language whose every word, every pause feels purposeful and right." Conrad Knickerbocker concluded in a *New York Times* article that among American writers, Bowles continued to stand "in the front rank for the substance of his ideas and for the power and conviction with which he expresses his own particular vision, which, if hellish, is totally appropriate to the times."

Points in Time was followed by several short story collections including *A Distant Episode: The Selected Stories, Unwelcome Words: Seven Stories,* and *Call at Corazon.* These collections represent over forty years of Bowles' work and reflect his long-running exploration of themes concerning the acculturation, miscegenation, and syncretism of Westerners as they explore foreign locales. During this exploration, Bowles' characters often encounter—and sometimes participate in—brutal and grotesque acts. In the story "Hugh Harper" from *Call at Corazon,* for example, Bowles' English protagonist has a penchant for drinking the blood of young Muslim boys. In his review of *Unwelcome Words* in the *Times Literary Supplement,* John Ryle concluded that

"the Islamic wonder-tale converges in Bowles's work with the horror story. West and East meet in the act of violence. . . . It is hard to know if he is trying to move you to shiver or shrug or smile—or none of these things."

Bowles' *Two Years beside the Strait: Tangier Journal 1987-1989* was also published during this period. In this diary, Bowles witnesses and records occurrences that often assault the senses, delivering his short tales with an eloquence and distance usually reserved for the snapshot. In one of the entries, for instance, "Bowles describes a 'typical tale of Ramadan violence' in a market," noted Millicent Dillon in the *Times Literary Supplement.* "One Moroccan merchant refuses to allow another to sit close to him. Tired, the second man sits down for a minute; the first one kills him. This story is told without further comment. No judgment is made." Some critics felt Bowles maintained *too* much distance from his subject in *Two Years beside the Strait,* and were disappointed that the journal does not explicate the author's life—long a bone of contention among Bowles' readers. Gerald Nicosia lamented in the *Washington Post Book World* that "it is precisely that withdrawn and detached mode of observation that makes Bowles' journal, *Days,* such a 'humdrum' read—to use his own description in the 'Preface.' Except for a few wonderful passages of natural observation, you could never guess that this was a journal of one of the major writers of our century."

Fans and critics had hoped for more revealing insights from the author in *Conversations with Paul Bowles* and *In Touch: The Letters of Paul Bowles,* published in 1993 and 1994 respectively. Unfortunately, the author "deliberately deceives the interlocutor, offering diverse, ambivalent remarks" in the interviews contained in *Conversations,* Irving Malin contended in *Studies in Short Fiction.* Malin quoted Bowles as saying, "the man who wrote the books didn't exist. No writer exists. He exists in his books and that's all," and observed of Bowles that "by distancing the writer from biographical investigation, he privileges the text, and at the same time adds to his legend as invisible man." More personal and insightful, *In Touch* offers readers a closer look at the author through his correspondences dating back to 1929. The letters present glimpses of such celebrity friends as William Burroughs, Aaron Copland, and Tennessee Williams, as well as a melancholy documentation of Bowles' wife's illness and untimely death. *In Touch* reveals something of the private life of Bowles, but the real worth of this collection is that "the descriptive passages found in the letters often rival those of his novels and stories," according to Michael Upchurch in the

New York Times Book Review. Jack Sullivan, reviewing *In Touch* for the *Washington Post Book World,* remarked that Bowles' "newly published letters—some 400 of them, selected from over 7,000 pages—are a major publishing event and an endless source of fascination." He continued: "these letters can be as ceremoniously formal as Bowles's public persona or as surreal and off-the-wall as his wildest fiction."

For fans of his fiction, Bowles complied in 1993 with *Too Far from Home: The Selected Writings of Paul Bowles.* A collection of previously released work supplemented by the previously unpublished title story, *Too Far from Home,* "at some 15,000 words, . . . is no more a novel than a handkerchief is a bedsheet," asserted Francis King in the *Spectator.* Although new, the story "Too Far from Home" reverts to the theme of Americans trying to adapt to a foreign culture. Through brother and sister Tom and Anita, Bowles illuminates the prejudices and contrasts inherent in acculturation. In a letter to a friend, quoted by James Campbell in the *Times Literary Supplement,* Anita writes, "I am being forced to participate in some sort of communal consciousness that I really hate. I don't know anything about these people. They're all black, but nothing like 'our' blacks back in the States." Her brother Tom is a painter and, in contrast to his sister, is not at all affected by the rigors of Saharan living or Anita's inability to adjust to her new surroundings. Bowles includes horror scenes typical of his past stories and explores supernatural themes as well. Although many critics were disappointed that Bowles' extended hiatus from short fiction did not result in more than *Too Far from Home,* interest in his characteristic subject matter continued. "Right or wrong, beauty and terror go wonderfully well together in his work," stated Madison Smartt Bell in the *Chicago Tribune,* adding that *Too Far from Home* "should increase our awareness that Bowles is one of the most important writers of our times."

In a departure from his previous work, Bowles collaborated with photographer Barry Brukoff to produce the pictorial titled *Morocco* in 1993. Bowles wrote the text to accompany eighty photos by Brukoff that depict scenes from Tangier, Fez, Marrakesh, and the Sahara. In his introduction to the volume Bowles reasserts his commitment to objectivity: "To aid the reader's imagination in its task of seizing the essence of how things were but no longer are, and of how they are now, it is important that a chronicler adhere to a scrupulous honesty in reporting. Any conscious distortion is equivalent to cheating at solitaire: the purpose of the game is nullified."

Bowles died in the late fall of 1999.

BIOGRAPHICAL AND CRITICAL SOURCES:

BOOKS

Aldridge, John W., *After the Lost Generation,* Noonday Press, 1951.

Allen, Walter, *The Modern Novel,* Dutton (New York, NY), 1965.

Bainbridge, John, *Another Way of Living: A Gallery of Americans Who Choose to Live in Europe,* Holt (New York, NY), 1968.

Bertens, Hans, *The Fiction of Paul Bowles: The Soul Is the Weariest Part of the Body,* Humanities (Atlantic Highlands, NJ), 1979.

Bowles, Paul, *Morocco,* photographs by Barry Brukoff, Abrams (New York, NY), 1993.

Caponi, Gena Dagel, *Paul Bowles: Romantic Savage,* Southern Illinois University Press (Carbondale, IL), 1994.

Contemporary Authors Autobiography Series, Volume 1, Thomson Gale (Detroit, MI), 1984.

Contemporary Literary Criticism, Thomson Gale (Detroit, MI), Volume 1, 1973, Volume 2, 1974, Volume 19, 1981.

Dictionary of Literary Biography, Thomson Gale (Detroit, MI), Volume 5: *American Poets since World War II,* 1980, Volume 6: *American Novelists since World War II, Second Series,* 1980.

Dillon, Millicent, *You Are Not I: A Portrait of Paul Bowles,* University of California Press (Berkeley, CA), 1998.

Green, Michelle, *The Dream at the End of the World: Paul Bowles and the Literary Renegades in Tangier,* HarperCollins (New York, NY), 1991.

Hibbard, Allen, *Paul Bowles: A Study of the Short Fiction,* Twayne (New York, NY), 1993.

Lacey, R. Kevin, and Francis Poole, *Mirrors on the Maghrib: Critical Reflections on Paul and Jane Bowles and Other American Writers in Morocco,* Caravan Books (Delmar, NY), 1996.

Miller, Jeffrey, *Paul Bowles: A Descriptive Bibliography,* Black Sparrow Press (Santa Barbara, CA), 1986.

Patteson, Richard F., *A World Outside: The Fiction of Paul Bowles,* University of Texas Press (Austin, TX), 1987.

Pulsifer, Gary, editor, *Paul Bowles by His Friends,* P. Owen (London, England), 1992.

Sawyer-Lauocanno, Christopher, *An Invisible Spectator: A Biography of Paul Bowles,* Weidenfeld & Nicolson (New York, NY) 1989.

Solotaroff, Theodore, *The Red Hot Vacuum and Other Pieces on the Writing of the Sixties,* Atheneum (New York, NY), 1970.

Steen, Mike, *A Look at Tennessee Williams,* Hawthorn (New York, NY), 1969.

Stewart, Lawrence D., *The Illumination of North Africa,* Southern Illinois University Press (DeKalb, IL), 1974.

Stewart, Lawrence D., *The Mystery and Detection Annual,* Donald Adams, 1973.

PERIODICALS

Books and Bookmen, June, 1968.

Boston Globe, June 25, 1989, p. A16; March 4, 1990, p. 15; January 10, 1991, p. 69; January 14, 1991, p. 29.

Chicago Tribune, August 9, 1988, sec. 5, p. 3; June 25, 1989, sec. 14, p. 6; March 4, 1993, pp. 1, 9.

Choice, April, 1994, p. 1291.

Commonweal, March 7, 1952.

Critique, Volume 3, number 1, 1959.

Esquire, May, 1985.

Film Comment, May-June, 1991, pp. 18-20, 22-3.

Harper's, October, 1959.

Hollins Critic, April, 1978.

Library Journal, August, 1997, p. 82.

Life, July 21, 1967.

Listener, February 2, 1967; February 23, 1989, pp. 32-3.

London Magazine, November, 1960; February, 1967; June, 1968.

Los Angeles Times, April 9, 1981; August 13, 1991, p. E5; February 22, 1993, p. E1.

Los Angeles Times Book Review, September 16, 1984; July 17, 1988, p. 14; May 26, 1991, p. 10.

Mediterranean Review, winter, 1971.

Nation, September 4, 1967.

National Observer, July 24, 1967.

New England Review, spring, 1980.

New Republic, September 2, 1967; April 22, 1972; January 7, 1991, p. 33.

New Statesman, January 27, 1967; April 15, 1988, pp. 39-40; February 25, 1994, pp. 40-41; November 4, 1994, p. 40.

New York, October 9, 1995, p. 92.

New York Review of Books, November 9, 1967; May 18, 1972; November 23, 1989, pp. 6-12.

New York Times, March 12, 1966; March 21, 1972; July 24, 1988, section 2, p. 27; October 17, 1989, p. C21.

New York Times Book Review, March 2, 1952; March 9, 1952; August 25, 1963; March 10, 1966; August 6, 1967; April 9, 1972; September 20, 1979; April 7, 1991, p. 7; September 15, 1991, p. 7; June 26, 1994, p. 1; July 6, 1997, p. 15.

Observer (London, England), April 10, 1988, p. 41; February 19, 1989, p. 44.

Ontario Review, spring-summer, 1980.

Opera News, September, 1995, p. 28.

Partisan Review, winter, 1968.

Publishers Weekly, October 4, 1993, p. 63.

Punch, February 8, 1967.

Rolling Stone, May 23, 1974.

San Francisco Review of Books, summer, 1991, pp. 9-10.

Saturday Review of Literature, December 23, 1950; October 20, 1955.

Spectator, March 30, 1985; June 30, 1990, pp. 35-36; March 5, 1994, pp. 34-35.

Studies in Short Fiction, summer, 1994, pp. 531-533.

Time, August 4, 1967; August 27, 1979.

Times (London, England), August 20, 1981; August 11, 1985.

Times Literary Supplement, September 30, 1949; February 2, 1967; May 9, 1968; October 13, 1972; May 13, 1988, p. 526; September 15, 1989, pp. 995-96; March 9, 1990, p. 266; September 7, 1990, p. 938; March 4, 1994, p. 21; December 1, 1995, p. 27; September 13, 1996, p. 8.

Tribune Books (Chicago, IL), February 13, 1994, p. 3; November 19, 1995, p. 8.

USA Today, July 21, 1989, p. D4.

Voice Literary Supplement, April, 1986.

Washington Post Book World, September 9, 1979; August 2, 1981; August 14, 1988, p. 12; June 11, 1989, p. 3; August 4, 1991, p. 11; December 5, 1993, p. 17; August 14, 1994, p. 11.

World Literature Today, autumn, 1989, p. 681.

*   *   *

BOWLES, Paul Frederick
See BOWLES, Paul

*   *   *

BOX, Edgar
See VIDAL, Gore

*   *   *

BOYLE, Mark
See KIENZLE, William X.

*   *   *

BOYLE, T.C.
See BOYLE, T. Coraghessan

BOYLE, T. Coraghessan 1948-
(T.C. Boyle, Thomas Coraghessan Boyle)

PERSONAL: Middle name pronounced "kuh- *ragg-issun*"; born Thomas John Boyle, December 2, 1948, in Peekskill, NY; changed middle name to Coraghessan when he was seventeen; married Karen Kvashay, 1974; children: Kerrie, Milo, Spencer. *Education:* State University of New York at Potsdam, B.A., 1968; University of Iowa Writers' Workshop, M.F.A., 1974, Ph.D., 1977.

ADDRESSES: Office—Department of English, University of Southern California, THH 430, University Park, Los Angeles, CA 90089-0354. *Agent*—Georges Borchardt, 136 E. 57th St., New York, NY 10022.

CAREER: Writer. Professor of English, University of Southern California, Los Angeles, 1977—.

AWARDS, HONORS: Coordinating Council of Literary Magazines Award for fiction, 1977; National Endowment for the Arts fellowship, 1977; St. Lawrence Prize, 1980, for *Descent of Man;* Aga Khan Prize, *Paris Review* magazine, 1981, for excerpts from *Water Music;* National Endowment for the Arts grant, 1983, for *Water Music;* John Train prize, *Paris Review,* 1984, for humor; Commonwealth Club of California, silver medal for literature, 1986, for *Greasy Lake;* Editors' Choice, *NY Times Book Review* 1987; PEN/Faulkner Award, 1988, for *World's End;* Commonwealth Club of California Club Gold medal, 1988, for *World's End;* Guggenheim Fellowship, 1988; O. Henry Award, 1988, for "Sinking House," 1989, for "The Ape Lady in Retirement"; PEN Award for short story, PEN American Center, 1990, for *If the River Was Whiskey;* Prix Passion novel of the year, 1989, for *Water Music;* PEN Center West Literary prize, 1989; Editors' Choice, *New York Times,* 1989; Best American prose excellence, D.H.L., State University of New York, 1991; National Academy of Arts and Letters, Howard D. Vursell Memorial Award, 1993; National Academy of Arts and Letters, 1993; *Prix Medicis Etranger* for best foreign novel published in France, 1997, for *The Tortilla Curtain*; PEN/Malamud Award for short story, 1999; National Book Award nomination for fiction, National Book Foundation, 2003, for *Drop City.*

WRITINGS:

The Descent of Man (stories), Little, Brown (Boston, MA), 1979.
Water Music (novel), Little, Brown (Boson, MA), 1981.

Budding Prospects: A Pastoral (novel), Viking (New York, NY), 1984.
Greasy Lake and Other Stories, Viking (New York, NY), 1985.
World's End (novel), Viking (New York, NY), 1987.
If the River Was Whiskey (stories), Viking (New York, NY), 1990.
East Is East (novel), Viking (New York, NY), 1991.
The Road to Wellville (novel), Viking (New York, NY), 1993.
Without a Hero (stories), Viking (New York, NY), 1994.
The Tortilla Curtain (novel), Viking (New York, NY), 1995.
Riven Rock, Viking (New York, NY), 1998.
T.C. Boyle Stories, Viking (New York, NY), 1998.
A Friend of the Earth, Viking (New York, NY), 2000.
After the Plague (stories), Viking (New York, NY), 2001.
Drop City, Viking (New York, NY), 2003.
The Inner Circle, Viking (New York, NY), 2004.
(Editor, with daughter, Kerrie Kvashay-Boyle) *Doubletakes: Pairs of Contemporary Short Stories,* Thomson/Wadsworth (Boston, MA), 2004.
Tooth and Claw (stories), Viking (New York, NY), 2005.
(As T.C. Boyle) *The Human Fly and Other Stories* (young adult), Speak (New York, NY), 2005.
Talk Talk, Viking (New York, NY), 2006.

Books printed in England under name T.C. Boyle. Contributor of short stories to periodicals, including *Esquire, Paris Review, Atlantic Monthly,* and *Harper's.* Fiction editor of *Iowa Review,* c. early 1970s.

ADAPTATIONS: The Road to Wellville, starring Anthony Hopkins, Matthew Broderick, and Bridget Fonda, was directed by Alan Parker and released by Columbia Pictures in 1994; a film version of *The Tortilla Curtain,* starring Kevin Costner and Meg Ryan, is in production.

SIDELIGHTS: Over the course of the 1980s, T. Coraghessan Boyle, who is also well known as T.C. Boyle, went from being a relatively unknown short-story writer to becoming a best-selling novelist whose works are studied in college classrooms. His wildly imaginative stories filled with quirky characters, lush descriptions, and cynical humor have elicited comparisons to the works of John Barth, Thomas Pynchon, and Evelyn Waugh. *Los Angeles Times Book Review* writer Charles Champlin termed Boyle's prose "a presence, a litany, a symphony of words, a chorale of idioms ancient and modern, a treasury of strange and wondrous place names, a glossary of things, good food and horrendous ills." *Times Literary Supplement* critic Thomas Sutcliffe described the author's style as "punctuated with firecracker metaphors, a showy extravagance with obscurities of language and an easy mediation between hard fact and invention." While Michael Adams, writing in the *Dictionary of Literary Biography Yearbook, 1986,* acknowledged Boyle's debt to the masters of absurdist and experimental fiction—Barth, Pynchon, Franz Kafka, James Joyce—he observed: "For all Boyle's similarities to other artists, no Americans . . . write about the diverse subjects he does in the way he does."

A self-described "pampered punk" of the 1960s, Boyle did not set out to become a writer. A music student at the State University of New York at Potsdam, he began to compose plays and short stories after enrolling in a creative writing course on a whim. He continued to write short fiction after graduation, between his daytime job as a high school teacher (a position he admits he took to avoid serving in Vietnam) and his nightly drug-and-alcohol binges. One of his stories, "The OD and Hepatitis Railroad or Bust," was published in the *North American Review,* giving Boyle the confidence to apply to the respected University of Iowa Writers' Workshop. "The only one I'd ever heard of was Iowa," he explained to Anthony Decurtis in *Rolling Stone,* "so I wrote to them, and they accepted me, because they accept you just on the basis of the work. I could never have gotten in on my record."

In 1981, Boyle published his first novel, *Water Music.* The book tells of two men: Mungo Park, a Scottish explorer who actually existed and led expeditions to Africa in 1795 and 1805, and the fictional Ned Rise, a drunken con-man from the London slums. Much of *Water Music* is concerned with Park's African excursions, and it offers particularly vivid accounts of his adventures with curious natives; Rise, meanwhile, has been involved in such dubious activities as running a sex show, robbing graves, and peddling fake caviar. Together the two protagonists travel down the Niger on the 1805 expedition, from which the real Park never returned. With *Water Music* Boyle strengthened his reputation as a prominent American humorist. Champlin characterized the novel as "dark and sprawling, ribald, hilarious, cruel, language-intoxicated, exotic, and original," and hailed Boyle as "an important new writer." Other critics offered similar praise: Sutcliffe deemed *Water Music* "compendious, funny and compelling" and cited Boyle's "tropically fecund imagination," while Jay Tolson wrote in the *Washington Post Book World* of Boyle's ability to present "his most implausible inventions with wit, a perfect sense of timing, and . . . con-

siderable linguistic gifts." Although most reviewers responded enthusiastically to the humor in *Water Music,* some tempered their praise by questioning the work's flamboyant style. Writing in the *New York Times Book Review,* Alan Friedman decried the novel's prose as "a freewheeling mixture of elegant polysyllabic rhetoric . . . with current colloquialisms" and claimed that it results in merely "an extended occasion for comic-strip pathos."

Like *Water Music, Budding Prospects* received both praise as an invigoratingly funny novel and criticism as a superficial work. Michael Gorra of the *New York Times Book Review* called *Budding Prospects* an "energetically written and very funny" novel and declared that Boyle's "raw ability to make one laugh" is reminiscent of Kingsley Amis and Thomas Berger. But Gorra also contended that Boyle "stops at the surface too often, settling for one-liners . . . rather than working toward a more sustained comic display." Similarly, Eva Hoffman wrote in the *New York Times* that *Budding Prospects* is "often quite hilarious" but argued that it lacks depth; she accused Boyle of failing to sufficiently differentiate and develop the characters and claimed that he writes as if he were "dancing on the edges of language, afraid that if he slowed down for a minute, he might fall into a vacuum." Despite these objections, however, even Hoffman concluded that "Boyle possesses a rare and redeeming virtue—he can be consistently, effortlessly, intelligently funny."

Boyle continued to garner high praise as a humorist with his 1985 collection *Greasy Lake and Other Stories.* As with the earlier *Descent of Man, Greasy Lake* offers bizarre action within seemingly normal settings. Among the many odd tales in the collection are "Ike and Nina," which relates a love affair between President Dwight Eisenhower and the wife of Soviet leader Nikita Khrushchev; "The Hector Quesadilla Story," which depicts an aging baseball player in a never-ending game; and "On for the Long Haul," which concerns a survivalist who moves his family to Montana only to discover that his new neighbor is an even more paranoid survivalist who loathes the newcomer's children and pets. In a *New York Times* review of *Greasy Lake,* Michiko Kakutani commended Boyle's "vigorous and alluring . . . use of language" as well as his ability to move from "the literary to the mundane without the slightest strain." *Detroit News* reviewer Peter Ross hailed the collection as "a triumphantly funny assembly, incredibly diverse in its inspirations and foundations," and numbered Boyle among "the select cadre of great American humorists."

Boyle first began to achieve widespread fame with the 1987 publication of *World's End.* Set in the Hudson

River Valley area of New York where Boyle himself grew up, *World's End* describes the intertwining of three families over ten generations. In 1663, the rich, tyrannical Van Warts own the land tended by the oppressed Van Brunts—land once belonging to the Mohonk family of Indians, until they gave it up to the Van Warts. In 1968, Walter Van Brunt crashes his motorcycle into an historical marker honoring the spot where a group of rebels were hanged, betrayed to the authorities by yet another Van Brunt. Walter's collision is just one instance in which the past and the present meet: as the novel progresses, jumping between past and present, we see dozens of Van Brunts indentured to Van Warts, and we witness the same mistakes made time and time again. Even Walter, in the end, must come to terms with destiny.

Critics hailed *World's End* as a work finally worthy of Boyle's unique prose and fecund imagination. Despite the novel's prodigious length, John Calvin Batchelor wrote in the *Washington Post Book World,* the author "displays a talent so effortlessly satirical and fluid that it suggests an image of the author at a crowded inn of wicked wits in a tale-telling fight for best space at the hearth." The *New Statesman*'s Geoff Dyer remarked: "Word for word Boyle has never been a cost-effective writer. Like a fast car he gets through a lot of fuel, guzzling up words in an amphetamine rush of similes. *World's End* is uneconomic in a very different way. Here he has embarked on such a long haul with such a freight of material that there is no point in hurrying."

The novel is shaped, primarily, by a sense of overwhelming, inescapable predestiny. The history of the Van Warts and Van Brunts was described by John Clute of the *Times Literary Supplement* as "a crushing machine, which limns a world without exit; nowhere in [the novel] does any moment of hilarity or joy or love do more than strengthen the grip of the past." Several critics found Boyle's inescapable destiny to be problematic. The characters "are not only invaded by the past but flattened by it," wrote Richard Eder in the *Los Angeles Times Book Review.* "Or rather, they are flattened by the awkwardness of having three centuries of fatality come to a point in them." "Even Walter's tale begins to sound increasingly contrived," commented Kakutani. "Instead of feeling that he's living out some inexorable family destiny, we end up suspecting that he is just another pawn in the author's elaborate chess game."

After the ambitious reach displayed in *World's End,* a few critics were dissatisfied with *If the River Was Whiskey,* Boyle's 1990 collection of short stories. Though

they found it as quirky and entertaining as his past story collections, some reviewers viewed this new book as the author's way of playing it safe, producing stories filled with his characteristic wit but lacking any real substance. "The writing is evocative, the craft stunning," explained *Village Voice* critic Sally S. Eckhoff. "But it's all wrapped up too tight to explode into the imagination . . . . At every story's end, we don't have much to savor but how good Boyle is." Nicholas Delbanco in *Tribune Books* called the stories at times "simply silly—a five-finger exercise," while Kakutani lamented that Boyle's talents "are used, singly, for showy but shallow effects."

Still, as Delbanco pointed out, "there are worse problems than a prodigality of talent." "What keeps us reading," observed Francine Prose in the *Washington Post,* "are Boyle's humor, his imagination, his narrative gifts: the pleasure of watching a writer make each story more inventive than the last one." Eckhoff, too, happily conceded that in these stories Boyle "is completely in command . . . . On all counts, *If the River Was Whiskey* is impressive."

The critical response to Boyle's 1991 novel *East Is East* was similar to that of *If the River Was Whiskey;* Charles Dickinson of Chicago's *Tribune Books,* for example, called the novel "Boyle Lite. It is better than most fiction being written today, but because of the standard he has set for himself, a disappointment nonetheless." *East Is East* describes the attempts of Japanese-born Hiro Tanaka to find his long-vanished American father. Envisioning the thriving cities of New York, Philadelphia, and Boston, Hiro takes a job on a Japanese freighter, jumping from its bow as it sails near the eastern coast of the United States. He swims to the closest shore, that of Georgia's Tupelo Island—a soggy, insect- and reptile-infested morass with little to offer in the way of food or shelter. At the far end of the island is a writers' colony full of eccentric and neurotic artists, and it is into their midst that Hiro, attempting to evade agents of the Immigration and Naturalization Service, arrives.

Dickinson called *East Is East* "the kind of knowing, cynical farce that Boyle can toss off in his sleep . . . . The writing is seamless and slick, and in a few instances the equal of anything Boyle has yet produced, but without the power that informs his other novels." Julian Loose, writing in the *New Statesman,* observed that the book "is at its funniest when portraying the colony's literati doing battle with writer's block and one another," but that the novel as a whole "singularly fails as an allegory of cultural misunderstanding." "In the final pages Boyle makes a swift and, to me, unconvincing stab at tragedy," observed the *Washington Post* contributor David Payne, "after the prevailing comic tone, this leaves a preservative aftertaste."

Boyle's short-story collection *Without a Hero* received high marks from readers and reviewers alike. Critic Ian Sansom, who in his *New Statesman* review of the collection frequently compared and contrasted Boyle with John Updike, wrote: "While Updike's stories descend with heavenly choirs from the *New Yorker,* Boyle's crawl up out of *Rolling Stone* and *Wig Wag,* yelling prophecies and denunciations . . . . For all [Boyle's] warnings about the road to excess, he is—like Updike—at his best when writing about life's unexpected failures and inevitable defeats." *Knight Ridder/ Tribune News Service* contributor Sandy Bauers similarly offered glowing words: "Boyle is superbly demented. He's the court jester of modern society, tweaking our icons. These are the sort of stories that the kid who flicked spitballs at the blackboard in grade school would write. Only now the kid has grown up; he has more finesse. Boyle's stories are more than funny, better than wicked. They make you cringe with their clarity . . . . [Boyle is] the absolute genius of description."

Boyle's most read and perhaps most controversial work, *The Tortilla Curtain* was described by its publisher as a "*Grapes of Wrath* for the 1990s." Set in southern California and involving the intersection of white, upper-middle-class Americans with poor, homeless Mexican illegals, the novel examines more than border relations and the corresponding struggle between the "haves" and the "have-nots" of the region. Barbara Kingsolver, writing in the *Nation,* explained how the novel "addresses what has probably always been the great American political dilemma: In a country that proudly defines itself as a nation of immigrants, who gets to slam the door on whom?" While acknowledging that "Boyle has his finger firmly on the pulse of an American middle class whose fear of the iron curtain has been replaced by an obsession with one made of tortillas," *New Statesman* reviewer Julie Wheelwright also claimed that "Boyle explores powerful issues through his parallel characters, but they operate just shy of caricature. They are more symbolic figures than real inhabitants of a state wallowing in economic downturn. The Mexicans are naive, but essentially good, while their Anglo counterparts grow increasingly ugly with rage." Despite similar complaints about the novel's characters, Kingsolver concluded: "What Boyle does, and does well, is lay on the line our national cult of hypocrisy. Comically

and painfully he details the smug wastefulness of the haves and the vile misery of the have-nots." *The Tortilla Curtain* received the 1997 Prix Medicis Etranger as the best foreign novel published that year in France.

Set in the early part of the twentieth century in Santa Barbara, California, on an estate called Riven Rock, Boyle's 1998 novel of the same name tells the story of millionaire Stanley McCormick, who suffers from madness and sexual dysfunction. Katherine, his wife, who has not seen him in more than twenty years, remains ever hopeful that he will recover. Michiko Kakutani, writing in the *New York Times,* called *Riven Rock* "a long meandering and fluently written book that has some truly affecting moments but that ultimately reduces two of its three main characters to caricatures." Novelist D.M. Thomas, writing in the *New York Times Book Review,* noted the theme of the dichotomous nature of men's love for women as both madonna and whore, who are conflicted by thoughts of both desire and worship for them. But Thomas, too, concluded that the novel's "promise of intellectual and emotional exploration . . . is not fulfilled."

Boyle's *T.C. Boyle Stories,* an impressive release containing all the stories from his four earlier collections, along with seven new stories, enjoyed considerable admiration upon its 1998 publication. Contending that Boyle's stories "concentrate his talents more powerfully than his seven novels," critic John C. Hawley explained in his *America* review that Boyle "plays with famous stories by Gogol, Kafka, Chekhov and Joyce, and imitates some of the best of his contemporaries— Barthelme, Coover, Lorrie Moore. He is very funny and Dickensian in his clearly drawn characters and in the cornucopia of plots that tumble out into page after fascinating page." Offering similar praise, a *Publishers Weekly* contributor called Boyle "a premier practitioner of short fiction" and praised the collection for its "narrative outtakes that are invariably amusing and, like Boyle's more serious work, mordant, worldly, and irreverent."

The next satiric novel, *A Friend of the Earth,* states the youthful premise of its protagonists early on, that "to be a friend of the earth, you have to be an enemy of the people." Dale Singer in the *St. Louis Post-Dispatch* introduced the book thus: "Tyrone O'Shaughnessy Tierwater is a baby boomer whose family struck it rich in real estate and construction; he becomes an ecoterrorist using any means necessary to stop what he considers the desecration of the land by rampaging development. Take that neat bundle of contradictions, throw in a lot of irony and a heavy dose of fate—at times so heavy it seems contrived—and *A Friend of the Earth* becomes a haunting if occasionally frustrating tale." The story is set in the near future, 2025, and the earth's system has continued to swing out of balance. Tierwater and his family are members of Earth Forever!, a vigilante group devoted to fighting for the earth in any way they can. Singer quoted from the novel to show what Boyle's imagined northern California surroundings have become: "The smog was like mustard gas, burning in his lungs. There was trash everywhere, scattered up and down the off-ramp like the leavings of a bombed-out civilization, cans, bottles, fast-food wrappers, yellowing diapers and rusting shopping carts, oil filters, Styrofoam cups, cigarette butts. The grass was dead, the oleanders were buried in dust." Boyle told Marilyn Bauer of the Environmental News Network (distributed by *Knight Ridder/ Tribune News Service*), "I really feel . . . no matter what we do it's over . . . . I've been depressed for years. And even in cases like Yellowstone, even with the best intentions, we've destroyed the ecosystem. When I go on tour, we don't have Q and A's anymore. Now we pass out hankies, cry and go home."

A *Christian Science Monitor* reviewer noted, "The day I finished reading it, the United Nations weather agency announced they'd recorded the largest-ever hole in the ozone layer. This seems a strange time to satirize the excesses of the environmental movement. But Boyle has always been a writer of complex sympathies." The reviewer continued, "Polemists on both sides of the environmental debate will feel betrayed by the book's pinwheeling satire. The chapters from 1989 depict green fanatics in all their comic excess. But the future Boyle describes in 2025 is a nightmare of environmental destruction. Gosh, it turns out those eco-nuts were right." The form of the book is a to-ing and fro-ing between the 1980s and 90s when Ty and his family are at their most outrageous and 2025 when he has become a zookeeper for a wealthy popstar. An *Austin American-Statesman* reporter wrote, "Boyle uses parallel narratives in alternating chapters. Those dealing with Tierwater's ecotage salad days of the late '80s and early '90s are omniscient, while the ones dealing with events a quarter-century from now are told in the voice of the seventy-five-year-old damp, disillusioned protagonist. The technique allows Boyle to have a global sweep and to bear down on the impact of world events on one man, Tierwater, a character who, in classic Boyle style, is born to fail." Several critics found this structure to be distracting but all found the novel powerful despite it.

To double and triple the turning, Ty's daughter Sierra becomes an even more fanatical rebel than he had been, ironically calling up his protectiveness as a parent:

"Raised on protest, she moves from vegetarian to veganism and finally refuses to disturb even dirt or rocks. What happens when a radical parent loves an even more radical child? Patterned after Julia Butterfly Hill, the young woman who recently completed two years in a giant redwood tree, Sierra beats that record by another twelve months . . . . This quiet treetop refuge captures the poignant interaction of pride and fear inspired by watching your daughter become a martyr to your own beliefs. In the end, Boyle is more interested in human nature than Mother Nature. But for a novelist, that's probably the best way to be a friend of the earth," concluded a *Christian Science Monitor* reviewer. Boyle himself commented to Bauer, "It looks very, very grim." *Salon.com* interviewer Gregory Daurer recorded some of Boyle's reasons for writing this novel: "Like Ty, I'm addicted to my machines too, and I'm just a criminal and enemy of the environment in many ways, even while I love it and want to save it. We're all, in the Western world, suffering from these contradictions. And that's another reason why I've written *A Friend of the Earth*."

The next novel, *Drop City,* is a companion piece to *A Friend of the Earth,* Boyle told Jay MacDonald of the Fort Myers, Florida, *News Press* in a telephone interview. Set in the 1970s—going backward instead of forward to a time when, as Boyle says, "there were only four billion people on earth"—it focuses on a California hippie commune, Drop City, whose members decide to homestead in the Alaskan wilderness in "the ongoing pursuit of free love, free dope and world peace," according to MacDonald. Instead, the communards first find themselves struggling with the overload of their physical possessions and then, once they arrive in Alaska, with surviving the harsh realities of an Arctic winter. Donald Secreast, in the *World and I,* argued that the dominant theme of *Drop City,* is that "spiritual structures must always allow for the weight of bodily needs." The commune hippies and other characters, such as the new wife of their fur trapper neighbor, search for spiritual transcendence but must come to terms with the realities of materiality in order to survive, but also as they are faced with their own unacknowledged consumerism. According to Secreast, Boyle argues that by the mid-twentieth century, we have replaced sublimation via poetry and spirituality with shopping and collecting objects, a theme he has played out in the story, "Filthy with Things."

Michiko Kakutani in the *New York Times* recognized the maturing of Boyle's writing in his development from the "pure satire and rollicking farce" of *Budding Prospects* to "a more subtle and sympathetic brand of comedy" in this novel, his former "manic verbal pyrotechnics" becoming "more sustained storytelling." She praised *Drop City,* commenting, "As might be expected, Mr. Boyle uses his merciless sociological eye and antic sense of humor to send up the self-delusions and flaky pretensions of the Drop City denizens. Though this might sound like shooting fish in a barrel—exposing the sexism that flourishes beneath the talk of sexual freedom and the nostalgia for the comforts of bourgeois life that lurks beneath the commune's self-righteous proselytizing—he manages to make their hypocrisies funny and oddly touching." She maintained that Boyle "has written a novel that is not only an entertaining romp through the madness of the counterculture 70's, but a stirring parable about the American dream as well."

Boyle's tenth novel, *The Inner Circle,* features the narrator John Milk, an undergraduate at Indiana University. Set in 1939, John takes a class taught by infamous sex researcher Alfred C. Kinsey. Kinsey, a true historical figure, was notorious for his ignorance of the emotional element of sex and for his unorthodox research methods. A.O. Scott, writing in *The New York Times Book Review,* noted that "the picture of Kinsey that emerges has an element of creepiness to it." Eventually, Milk must choose between Kinsey, his mentor, and Iris, his beautiful wife. While Scott felt that Boyle's novel had a "blurry, hasty, unfinished quality," Jennifer Reese, writing in *Entertainment Weekly,* noted that "no one . . . is better at capturing a grotesque."

Following *The Inner Circle* Boyle published two collections of short stories, *Tooth and Claw* and *The Human Fly and Other Stories.* In a review of *Tooth and Claw, Booklist* critic Donna Seaman pointed out Boyle's "evocation of visceral detail" and applauded his "great gift for supple social commentary." A *Kirkus Reviews* critic similarly praised *The Human Fly and Other Stories,* stating that the collection gives "young readers a taste of real quality in these seriously thought-provoking selections." Another *Kirkus Reviews* contributor, upon critiquing *Tooth and Claw,* called Boyle "one of our most versatile and prolific writers."

BIOGRAPHICAL AND CRITICAL SOURCES:

BOOKS

Contemporary Literary Criticism, Gale (Detroit, MI), Volume 36, 1986, Volume 55, 1989.

Dictionary of Literary Biography Yearbook, 1986, Gale (Detroit, MI), 1987.
Short Story Criticism, Volume 10, Gale (Detroit, MI), 1992.

PERIODICALS

America, April 23, 1994, p. 20; May 22, 1999, p. 31.
Atlantic Monthly, November, 1987, p. 122; October, 1990, p. 135.
Austin American- Statesman, September 24, 2000, p. L6.
Booklist, June 1, 2005, Donna Seaman, review of *Tooth and Claw,* p. 1711; November 1, 2005, Gillian Engberg, review of *The Human Fly and Other Stories,* p. 37.
Boston Herald, March 9, 2003, p. 56.
Buffalo News, September 16, 2001, p. F4.
Carolina Quarterly, fall, 1979, p. 103.
Christian Science Monitor, September 14, 2000, p. 21.
Denver Post, October 22, 2000, p. G-03; February 23, 2003, p. EE-02.
Entertainment Weekly, September 10, 2004, Jennifer Reese, "Nookie Monster: T.C. Boyle's Novel *The Inner Circle* Gets into Bed with Sex Researcher Alfred Kinsey," p. 166.
Financial Times, November 3, 2001, p. 4.
Herald (Glasgow, Scotland), September 30, 2000, p. 17.
Interview, January, 1988, p. 91.
Irish Times, May 31, 2003, p. 55.
Kirkus Reviews, June 15, 2005, review of *Tooth and Claw,* p. 650; September 15, 2005, review of *The Human Fly and Other Stories,* p. 1021.
Knight Ridder/Tribune News Service, May 25, 1994; March 9, 2001; November 15, 2001, p. K5036.
Library Journal, August, 1996, p. 136.
London Review of Books, January 6, 1994, p. 19.
Los Angeles Times, June 17, 1982; October 7, 1987; April 21, 1988; April 6, 1990; October 3, 1990, p. E1; September 24, 1995, p. 4; September 15, 1996, p. 44; April 28, 2001, David Ferrell, interview with Boyle, p. A-1.
Los Angeles Times Book Review, January 3, 1982; May 6, 1984, p. 3; June 30, 1985; October 11, 1987, p. 3; July 24, 1988, p. 10; May 21, 1989, p. 3; May 30, 1993, p. 2.
Milwaukee Journal Sentinel, September 12, 2001, p. 04.
Nation, April 7, 1979, p. 377; September 1, 1984, pp. 151-153; September 25, 1995, p. 326.
New Republic, February 10, 1979; June 12, 1989, p. 40; October 4, 1993, p. 43.
News Press (Fort Myers, FL), March 16, 2003, p. 8E.

New Statesman, August 26, 1988, p. 36; March 29, 1991, p. 31; October 22, 1993, p. 38; February 10, 1995, p. 44; November 10, 1995, p. 39.

Newsweek, April 19, 1993, p. 62.

New Yorker, January 19, 1998, p. 68.

New York Review of Books, January 17, 1991, p. 31.

New York Times, May 19, 1979; May 22, 1989; September 7, 1990, p. C25; January 20, 1998, p. E10; October 3, 2000, p. E8; February 17, 2003, p. E1; February 17, 2003, p. E1; February 23, 2003, p. 9; March 16, 2003, p. 4.

New York Times Book Review, April 1, 1979, p. 14; December 27, 1981, p. 9; June 6, 1982; July 1, 1984, p. 18; June 9, 1985, p. 15; July 21, 1985; September 27, 1987, Michael Freitag, interview with Boyle, p. 53; December 6, 1987, p. 85; May 14, 1989, Brian Miller, interview with Boyle, p. 33; May 6, 1990, p. 38; September 9, 1990, p. 13; April 25, 1993, Tobin Harshaw, interview with Boyle, p. 28; May 8, 1994, p. 9; September 3, 1995, p. 3; December 3, 1995, p. 78; September 15, 1996, p. 44; February 8, 1998, p. 8; September 2, 2001, p. 5; September 19, 2004, A.O. Scott, "The Joy of Sex Research," p. 8.

New York Times Magazine, March 19, 1989, p. 57; December 9, 1990, p. 50.

Publishers Weekly, October 9, 1987, pp. 71-72; July 3, 1995, p. 47; July 22, 1996, p. 234; September 21, 1998, p. 71.

Review of Contemporary Fiction, summer, 1991, p. 17.

Rocky Mountain News (Denver, CO), March 7, 2003, p. 25D.

Rolling Stone, January 14, 1988, pp. 54-57.

St. Louis Post- Dispatch, September 19, 2000, p. C3.

Saturday Review, March 31, 1979.

Seattle Times, March 23, 2003, p. K12.

Star Tribune (Minneapolis, MN), February 23, 2003, p. 16F.

Time, May 10, 1993, p. 71.

Times (London, England), March 21, 1991.

Times Literary Supplement, June 20, 1980; February 26, 1982; September 14, 1985; January 31, 1986; August 26, 1988, p. 927; March 22, 1991, p. 19; October 27, 1995, p. 25.

Tribune Books (Chicago, IL), October 11, 1987, p. 3; May 21, 1989, p. 7; July 15, 1990, p. 4; September 9, 1990, p. 5.

Village Voice, January 6, 1982, p 39; September 6, 1989.

Voice Literary Supplement, November, 1987.

Wall Street Journal, September 7, 1990, p. A13.

Washington Post, May 23, 1989.

Washington Post Book World, February 7, 1982, p. 10; June 23, 1985; November 1, 1987, p. 4; March 9,

1988; April 20, 1988; September 2, 1990, p. 1; May 9, 1993, p. 5.

World and I, July, 2003, p. 242.

Writer, October, 1999, p. 26.

ONLINE

BookReporter.com, http://www.bookreporter.com/ (November 24, 2000), Jana Siciliano, interview with Boyle.

Salon.com, http://www.salon.com/ (December 11, 2000), Gregory Daurer, interview with Boyle.

T. Coraghessan Boyle Home Page, http://www.tcboyle.com/ (March 28, 2000).

T. Coraghessan Boyle Resource Center, http://www.tcboyle.net/ (March 5, 2004).

*   *   *

BOYLE, Thomas Coraghessan
See BOYLE, T. Coraghessan

*   *   *

BRACKETT, Peter
See COLLINS, Max Allan

*   *   *

BRADBURY, Edward P.
See MOORCOCK, Michael

*   *   *

BRADBURY, Ray 1920-
(D.R. Banat, Ray Douglas Bradbury, Leonard Douglas, William Elliott, Douglas Spaulding, Leonard Spaulding, Brett Sterling)

PERSONAL: Born August 22, 1920, in Waukegan IL; son of Leonard Spaulding and Esther (Moberg) Bradbury; married Marguerite Susan McClure, September 27, 1947 (died, 2003); children: Susan Marguerite, Ramona, Bettina, Alexandra. *Education:* Attended schools in Waukegan, IL, and Los Angeles, CA. *Politics:* Independent. *Religion:* Unitarian Universalist. *Hobbies and other interests:* Painting in oil and water colors, collecting Mexican artifacts.

*ADDRESSES: Home—*10265 Cheviot Drive, Los Angeles, CA 90064. *Agent—*Don Congdon, 156 Fifth Ave.,

No. 625, New York, NY 10010. *E-mail*—Ray Bradbury@harpercollins.com.

CAREER: Newsboy in Los Angeles, CA, 1940-43; full-time writer, 1943—.

MEMBER: Writers Guild of America, Screen Writers Guild, Science Fantasy Writers of America, Pacific Art Foundation.

AWARDS, HONORS: O. Henry Prize, 1947 and 1948; Benjamin Franklin Award, 1953-54, for "Sun and Shadow"; gold medal, Commonwealth Club of California, 1954, for *Fahrenheit 451;* National Institute of Arts and Letters award, 1954, for contribution to American literature; Junior Book Award, Boys' Clubs of America, 1956, for *Switch on the Night;* Golden Eagle Award, 1957, for screenwriting; Academy Award nomination for best short film, 1963, for *Icarus Montgolfier Wright;* Mrs. Ann Radcliffe Award, Count Dracula Society, 1965, 1971; Writers Guild Award, 1974; World Fantasy Award, 1977, for lifetime achievement; D.Litt., Whittier College, 1979, Woodbury University, 2005; Balrog Award, 1979, for best poet; Aviation and Space Writers Award, 1979, for television documentary; Gandalf Award, 1980; Body of Work Award, PEN, 1985; inducted into the University of Kansas Center for the Study of Science Fiction's Science Fiction and Fantasy Hall of Fame, 1999; medal for "Distinguished Contribution to American Letters," National Book Foundation, 2000; Bram Stoker Award nominee in novel category, Horror Writers Association, 2001, for *From the Dust Returned,* and 2003, for *One More for the Road;* the play version of *The Martian Chronicles* won five Los Angeles Drama Critics Circle Awards; Grand Master Nebula Award, Science Fiction and Fantasy Writers of America; star on Hollywood Walk of Fame; National Medal of the Arts, 2004; honorary degree, National University of Ireland, 2005.

WRITINGS:

NOVELS

The Martian Chronicles (also see below), Doubleday (Garden City, NY), 1950, revised edition published as *The Silver Locusts,* Hart-Davis (London, England), 1965, anniversary edition published as *The Martian Chronicles: The Fortieth Anniversary Edition,* Doubleday (New York, NY), 1990.

Fahrenheit 451 (novelette; also see below), Ballantine (New York, NY), 1953, Long Beach Public Library Foundation (Long Beach, CA), 2005.
Dandelion Wine (also see below), Doubleday (Garden City, NY), 1957, Avon (New York, NY), 1999.
Something Wicked This Way Comes (also see below), Simon & Schuster (New York, NY), 1962, Avon (New York, NY), 1999.
Death Is a Lonely Business, Knopf (New York, NY), 1985, Avon (New York, NY), 1999.
A Graveyard for Lunatics: Another Tale of Two Cities, Knopf (New York, NY), 1990.
Quicker Than the Eye, Avon (New York, NY), 1996.
Green Shadows, White Whale, Knopf (New York, NY), 1992, published with a new afterword by the author, Perennial (New York, NY), 2002.
From the Dust Returned: A Family Remembrance, William Morrow (New York, NY), 2001.
Let's All Kill Constance, Morrow (New York, NY), 2003.

STORY COLLECTIONS

Dark Carnival, Arkham (Sauk City, WI), 1947, revised edition, Hamish Hamilton (London, England), 1948, published as *The October Country,* Ballantine (New York, NY), 1955.
The Illustrated Man, Doubleday (Garden City, NY), 1951, revised edition, Hart-Davis (London, England), 1952, Chivers Press (Bath, England), 1999.
Fahrenheit 451 (contains "Fahrenheit 451" [also see below], "The Playground", and "And the Rock Cried Out"), Ballantine (New York, NY), 1953.
The Golden Apples of the Sun (also see below), Doubleday (Garden City, NY), 1953, fortieth anniversary edition with a new foreword by the author, G. K. Hall (Thorndike, ME), 1997.
A Medicine for Melancholy (also see below), Doubleday (Garden City, NY), 1959, revised edition published as *The Day It Rained Forever* (also see below), Hart-Davis (London, England), 1959.
The Ghoul Keepers, Pyramid (New York, NY), 1961.
The Small Assassin, Ace (New York, NY), 1962.
The Machineries of Joy, Simon & Schuster (New York, NY), 1964.
The Vintage Bradbury, Vintage (New York, NY), 1965.
The Autumn People, Ballantine (New York, NY), 1965.
Tomorrow Midnight, Ballantine (New York, NY), 1966.
Twice Twenty-Two (contains *The Golden Apples of the Sun* and *A Medicine for Melancholy*), Doubleday (Garden City, NY), 1966.
I Sing the Body Electric!, Knopf (New York, NY), 1969.

(With Robert Bloch) *Bloch and Bradbury: Ten Master-pieces of Science Fiction,* Tower, 1969 (published as *Fever Dreams and Other Fantasies,* Sphere (London, England), 1970.

(With Robert Bloch) *Whispers from Beyond,* Peacock Press, 1972.

Selected Stories, Harrap (London, England), 1975.

Long after Midnight, Knopf (New York, NY), 1976.

The Best of Bradbury, Bantam (New York, NY), 1976.

To Sing Strange Songs, Wheaton, 1979.

The Stories of Ray Bradbury, Knopf (New York, NY), 1980.

Dinosaur Tales, Bantam (New York, NY), 1983.

A Memory of Murder, Dell (New York, NY), 1984.

The Toynbee Convector, Random House (New York, NY), 1988.

Quicker Than the Eye, Avon (New York, NY), 1997.

Driving Blind, Avon (New York, NY), 1997.

Ray Bradbury Collected Short Stories, illustrated by Robert Court, Peterson Publishing (North Mankato, MN), 2001.

One More for the Road: A New Short Story Collection, Morrow (New York, NY), 2002.

Bradbury Stories: 100 of His Most Celebrated Tales, Morrow (New York, NY), 2003.

The Cat's Pajamas, Morrow (New York, NY), 2004.

(Edited by Donn Albright) *Match to Flame: The Fictional Paths of Fahrenheit 451,* Gauntlet Press (Colorado Springs, CO), 2006.

FOR CHILDREN

Switch on the Night, Pantheon (New York, NY), 1955, illustrated by Leo and Diane Dillon, Knopf (New York, NY), 1993.

R Is for Rocket (story collection), Doubleday (Garden City, NY), 1962.

S Is for Space (story collection), Doubleday (Garden City, NY), 1966.

The Halloween Tree, Knopf (New York, NY), 1972, updated edition, compiled by Donn Albright, edited by Jon Eller, illustrated by Joe Mugnaini, Gauntlet Press (Colorado Springs, CO), 2005.

The April Witch, Creative Education (Mankato, MN), 1987.

The Other Foot, Creative Education (Mankato, MN), 1987.

The Foghorn (also see below), Creative Education (Mankato, MN), 1987.

The Veldt (also see below), Creative Education (Mankato, MN), 1987.

Fever Dream, St. Martin's Press (New York, NY), 1987.

Ahmed and the Oblivion Machines, Avon (New York, NY), 1998.

The Country, illustrated by Joe Mugnaini, Avon (New York, NY), 1999.

PLAYS

The Meadow, produced in Hollywood at the Huntington Hartford Theatre, 1960.

Way in the Middle of the Air, produced in Hollywood at the Desilu Gower Studios, 1962.

The Anthem Sprinters, and Other Antics (play collection produced in Beverly Hills, CA), Dial (New York, NY), 1963.

The World of Ray Bradbury (three one-acts), produced in Los Angeles, CA, at the Coronet Theater, 1964, produced off- Broadway at Orpheum Theatre, 1965.

Leviathan 99 (radio play), British Broadcasting Corp., 1966, produced in Hollywood, 1972.

The New York, NYed Forever (one-act), Samuel French (New York, NY), 1966.

The Pedestrian (one-act), Samuel French (New York, NY), 1966.

Dandelion Wine (based on his novel of same title; music composed by Billy Goldenberg), produced at Lincoln Center's Forum Theatre, 1967.

Christus Apollo (music composed by Jerry Goldsmith), produced in Los Angeles at Royce Hall, University of California, 1969.

The Wonderful Ice-Cream Suit and Other Plays (collection; *The Wonderful Ice-Cream Suit,* produced in Los Angeles at the Coronet Theater, 1965; *The Veldt* [based on his story of same title], produced in London, 1980; includes *To the Chicago Abyss*), Bantam (New York, NY), 1972, published as *The Wonderful Ice-Cream Suit and Other Plays for Today, Tomorrow, and Beyond Tomorrow,* Hart-Davis (London, England), 1973.

Madrigals for the Space Age (chorus and narration; music composed by Lalo Schifrin; performed in Los Angeles, 1976), Associated Music Publishers, 1972.

Pillar of Fire and Other Plays for Today, Tomorrow, and Beyond Tomorrow (*Pillar of Fire,* produced in Fullerton at the Little Theatre, California State College, 1973; *The Foghorn* [based on his story of same title], produced in New York, 1977; includes *Kaleidoscope*), Bantam (New York, NY), 1975.

That Ghost, That Bride of Time: Excerpts from a Play-in-Progress, Squires, 1976.

The Martian Chronicles (based on his novel of same title), produced in Los Angeles, 1977.

Fahrenheit 451 (musical, based on his story of same title), produced in Los Angeles, 1979.

A Device out of Time, Dramatic Publishing (Woodstock, IL), 1986.

Falling Upward (produced in Los Angeles, March, 1988), Dramatic Publishing (Woodstock, IL), 1988.

To the Chicago Abyss, Dramatic Publishing (Woodstock, IL), 1988.

The Day It Rained Forever (musical based on his story of the same title), Dramatic Publishing (Woodstock, IL), 1990.

On Stage: A Chrestomathy of His Plays, Primus (New York, NY), 1991.

SCREENPLAYS

It Came from Outer Space, Universal Pictures, 1953.

The Beast from 20,000 Fathoms (based on his story, "The Foghorn"), Warner Bros., 1953.

Moby Dick, Warner Bros., 1956.

(With George C. Johnson) *Icarus Montgolfier Wright,* Format Films, 1962.

(Author of narration and creative consultant) *An American Journey,* U.S. Government for United States Pavilion at New York World's Fair, 1964.

(Under pseudonym Douglas Spaulding, with Ed Weinberger) *Picasso Summer,* Warner Bros./Seven Arts, 1972.

Something Wicked This Way Comes (based on his novel of same title), Walt Disney, 1983.

Also author of television scripts for *Alfred Hitchcock Presents, Jane Wyman's Fireside Theatre, Steve Canyon, Trouble Shooters, Twilight Zone, Alcoa Premiere,* and *Curiosity Shop* series. Author of television scripts for *Ray Bradbury Television Theatre,* USA Cable Network, 1985-90.

POETRY

Old Ahab's Friend, and Friend to Noah, Speaks His Piece: A Celebration, Roy A. Squires Press (Glendale, CA), 1971.

When Elephants Last in the Dooryard Bloomed: Celebrations for Almost Any Day in the Year (also see below), Knopf (New York, NY), 1973.

That Son of Richard III: A Birth Announcement, Roy A. Squires Press (Glendale, CA), 1974.

Where Robot Mice and Robot Men Run 'Round in Robot Towns (also see below), Knopf (New York, NY), 1977.

Twin Hieroglyphs That Swim the River Dust, Lord John (Northridge, CA), 1978.

The Bike Repairman, Lord John (Northridge, CA), 1978.

The Author Considers His Resources, Lord John (Northridge, CA), 1979.

The Aqueduct, Roy A. Squires Press (Glendale, CA), 1979.

This Attic Where the Meadow Greens, Lord John (Northridge, CA), 1979.

The Last Circus and *The Electrocution,* Lord John (Northridge, CA), 1980.

The Ghosts of Forever (five poems, a story, and an essay), Rizzoli (New York, NY), 1980.

The Haunted Computer and the Android Pope (also see below), Knopf (New York, NY), 1981.

The Complete Poems of Ray Bradbury (contains *Where Robot Mice and Robot Men Run 'Round in Robot Towns, The Haunted Computer and the Android Pope,* and *When Elephants Last in the Dooryard Bloomed*), Ballantine (New York, NY), 1982.

The Love Affair (a short story and two poems), Lord John (Northridge, CA), 1983.

Forever and the Earth, limited edition, Croissant & Co. (Athens, OH), 1984.

Death Has Lost Its Charm for Me, Lord John (Northridge, CA), 1987.

With Cat for Comforter, illustrated by Louise Reinoehl Max, Gibbs Smith (Salt Lake City, UT), 1997.

Dogs Think That Every Day Is Christmas, illustrated by Louise Reinoehl Max, Gibbs Smith (Salt Lake City, UT), 1997.

(With others) *You Are Here: The Jerde Partnership International* (architecture), Phaidon Press Limited (London, England), 1999.

I Live by the Invisible: New and Selected Poems, Salmon (Dublin, Ireland), 2002.

OTHER

(Editor and contributor) *Timeless Stories for Today and Tomorrow,* Bantam (New York, NY), 1952.

(Editor and contributor) *The Circus of Dr. Lao and Other Improbable Stories,* Bantam (New York, NY), 1956.

Sun and Shadow (short story), Quenian Press (Berkeley, CA), 1957.

(With Lewy Olfson) *Teacher's Guide: Science Fiction,* Bantam (New York, NY), 1968.

Zen and the Art of Writing, Capra Press (Santa Barbara, CA), 1973.

(With Bruce Murray, Arthur C. Clarke, Walter Sullivan, and Carl Sagan) *Mars and the Mind of Man,* Harper (New York, NY), 1973.

The Mummies of Guanajuato, Abrams (New York, NY), 1978.

(Author of text) *About Norman Corwin,* Santa Susana Press (Northridge, CA), 1979.

Beyond 1984: Remembrance of Things Future, Targ (New York, NY), 1979.

(Author of text) *Los Angeles,* Skyline Press, 1984.

The Last Good Kiss: A Poem, Santa Susana Press (Glendale, CA), 1984.

(Author of text) *Orange County,* Skyline Press, 1985.

(Author of text) *The Art of "Playboy,"* Alfred Van der Marck (New York, NY), 1985.

The Dragon, B. Munster (Round Top, NY), 1988.

The Fog Horn, Creative Education (Mankato, MN), 1988.

Yestermorrow: Obvious Answers to Impossible Futures, Joshua O'Dell (New York, NY), 1991.

The Smile, Creative Education (Mankato, MN), 1991.

Journey to Far Metaphor: Further Essays on Creativity, Writing, Literature, and the Arts, Joshua O'Dell (New York, NY), 1994.

A Chapbook for Burnt-Out Priests, Rabbis, and Ministers, 2001.

Conversations with Ray Bradbury, edited by Steven L. Aggelis, University Press of Mississippi (Jackson, MS), 2004.

Bradbury Speaks: Too Soon from the Cave, Too Far from the Stars (essays), Morrow (New York, NY), 2005.

Work represented in more than seven hundred anthologies. Contributor of short stories and articles, sometimes under pseudonyms including Leonard Spaulding, to *Playboy, Saturday Review, Weird Tales, Magazine of Fantasy and Science Fiction, Omni, Life,* and other publications.

ADAPTATIONS: *Fahrenheit 451* was filmed by Universal in 1966 and adapted as an opera by Georgia Holof and David Mettere and produced in Fort Wayne, IN, 1988; *The Illustrated Man* was filmed by Warner Bros. in 1969; the story "The Screaming Woman" was filmed for television in 1972; the story "Murderer" was filmed for television by WGBH-TV (Boston, MA), 1976; *The Martian Chronicles* was filmed as a television miniseries in 1980. *Bradbury Theatre* presented adaptations of Bradbury's short stories on the USA Network from 1985 to 1992. Several of Bradbury's short stories have been adapted as comics and included in *The Best of Ray Bradbury: The Graphic Novel,* 2003. Many of Bradbury's works have also been adapted as sound recordings.

SIDELIGHTS: Ray Bradbury is one of the best-known writers of science fiction, thanks to his numerous short stories, screenplays, and classic books such as *The Martian Chronicles, Dandelion Wine, Fahrenheit 451,* and *Something Wicked This Way Comes.* Ironically, Bradbury does not identify himself as a science fiction writer and has proclaimed his aversion to portions of modern technology: he does not drive a car or own a computer. His fiction reflects this mindset, for unlike many of his colleagues, Bradbury deemphasizes gimmicky space hardware and gadgetry in favor of an exploration of the impact of scientific development on human lives. In general, Bradbury warns man against becoming too dependent on science and technology at the expense of moral and aesthetic concerns. Writing in the *Dictionary of Literary Biography,* George Edgar Slusser noted that "to Bradbury, science is the forbidden fruit, destroyer of Eden. . . . In like manner, Bradbury is a fantasist whose fantasies are oddly circumscribed: he writes less about strange things happening to people than about strange imaginings of the human mind. Corresponding, then, to an outer labyrinth of modern technological society is this inner one—fallen beings feeding in isolation on their hopeless dreams."

Bradbury's works have provided a foundation for much of the science fiction written in the twentieth century. James Sallis, in an article for the *Magazine of Science Fiction and Fantasy,* described, "Some artists have a presence so pervasive that we take them wholly for granted; they're the floor we walk on. Ray Bradbury, for instance." In spite of his reputation, Bradbury maintained in *Writer,* "I do not feel like a science fiction writer at all," stating that much of his work is too fantastic to be considered science fiction, which he felt had to be based on possibilities for the future. Regardless of how his work has been classified, whether in his prose, his children's stories, his poetry, his noir mysteries, or his plays, it is clear that his writings have had a profound affect on his audiences. *Writer* contributor Beatrice Cassina summed up what makes Bradbury's work stand out: "In his writing we meet people like us; people who are not all that involved with futuristic machines; human beings who cry, love and sometimes live in doubt. We read about people who are emotionally involved with their lives, and about places and times that everybody can, in some way, recognize and relate to."

Bradbury was born in Waukegan, Illinois, in 1920. "At age six he began reading comic strips," reported David Steinberg in the *Albuquerque Journal.* By the age of eight he was eagerly reading the popular pulp magazines of the time, such as *Amazing Stories.* Steinberg continued, "From there he moved on to reading Edgar

Rice Burroughs' *Tarzan* and *Warlord of Mars* and the novels of H. G. Wells and Jules Verne." He started writing when he was twelve years old, and has been reported to have written a short story every week from then on. In 1934 the Bradbury family moved to Los Angeles, California. Bradbury began to work seriously on his writing at that time, his efforts including attendance at a writing class taught by science fiction master Robert Heinlein. His first published story appeared in an amateur fan magazine in 1938. He continued to work hard on honing his writing craft, and by the 1940s he was publishing in the better magazines and receiving national recognition for his work, winning several important awards and being featured in major anthologies. His first short story collection, *Dark Carnival,* later published by its better-known title *October Country,* features eerie and fantastic short stories, including "The Homecoming," the first tale to introduce the Elliott family, who appear in his later fiction.

In 1950 Bradbury published *The Martian Chronicles,* a cycle of stories chronicling the Earth's colonization of, and eventual destruction of, the planet Mars. The portrayal of the Martians ranged from sympathetic to threatening, but the stories really focus on the Earthling colonists. *The Martian Chronicles* was lavishly praised by such literary standouts as Christopher Isherwood, Orville Prescott, and Angus Wilson, bringing its author a standing as a writer of highest merit. "The book owed much to the American tradition of frontier literature, and quickly consolidated Bradbury's reputation as one of science fiction's leading stylists," commented an essayist for *St. James Guide to Science Fiction Writers.* The book continued to be published throughout the twentieth century and into the twenty-first; a 2000 edition was published with dates pushed back, so that the events take place in 2030 instead of 1999. "I did not change them for any other reason than to encourage (people) to go to Mars," he told Steven G. Reed of the *Sarasota Herald Tribune.* "I didn't want people to read the book and get discouraged, you see." In the years *The Martian Chronicles* has been in print, it has been made into a movie, a miniseries, a radio show, a stage play, and an interactive adventure game on CD-ROM. According to a contributor to the Newark, NJ, *Star Ledger,* on Bradbury's eighty-third birthday, the author made the following wish, "One night, 100 years from now, a youngster will stay up late reading *The Martian Chronicles* with a flashlight under his blanket—on the Red Planet."

The Illustrated Man, which appeared the following year, is another story cycle; in this volume, though, each story represents a tattoo that has come alive. The Mar-

tian setting of the previous book is revisited in a few of the tales, notably "The Fire Balloons," which probes the question of whether or not an alien life form can receive Christian grace. The amoral tendencies of children is the basis of "The Veldt" and "Zero Hour." In "Kaleidoscope," Bradbury dramatized the fate of a crew of astronauts whose spaceship has exploded, and who are drifting through space to slowly meet their deaths. Charles De Lint, reviewing a new edition of the collection published in 1997 for the *Magazine of Science Fiction and Fantasy,* commented that the stories are "still as vibrant and startling and telling" as they were when the book was published, containing "strong characters, fascinating ideas, crisp dialogue."

The novella *Fahrenheit 451* is, along with *The Martian Chronicles,* Bradbury's most famous work. In this story, "firemen" are those who set forbidden books aflame, rather than those who put out fires. Guy Montag, the protagonist, is a fireman himself; however, he begins to question his work when he takes home one of the books he is supposed to have destroyed and reads it. *Fahrenheit 451* is a somewhat simple tale, "as much an attack on mass culture as it is a satire of McCarthy-era censorship," remarked the essayist for *St. James Guide to Science Fiction Writers.* The tale implies that the government-sanctioned illiteracy is the outgrowth of pandering to special interest groups in the mass media, as well as a result of the rise of television. A society of outcasts is the only bastion of great literature; its members dedicate themselves to memorizing the great books of the world. Many commentators note a disturbing similarity between Bradbury's fictional world and our real one. The repressive future world is so vividly depicted in this work that the novella has become as much a staple of political study as George Orwell's *1984.* *Fahrenheit 451* has become both a banned book and a book used in many high school classrooms to discuss the topic of censorship. In 2002 Los Angeles Mayor Jim Hahn used the book as the focus of a citywide reading campaign.

Fahrenheit 451 has an interesting history: the germ of the idea came to Bradbury when he was a teenager, watching a newsreel of Nazis performing a book burning in Berlin. The first draft, published as "The Fireman," introduces Montag for the first time, and was written in nine days on a typewriter that Bradbury rented in the library for ten cents per half hour. At the urging of a publisher, Bradbury expanded the novella into its current form. The title, *Fahrenheit 451,* refers to the temperature at which paper ignites. Robert A. Baker, in an article for the Syracuse, NY, *Post-Standard,* reported that Bradbury explained, "he called several places to get the answer before thinking of the fire department. He asked the fire chief, who left the phone briefly before returning to tell him '451 Fahrenheit.' 'I hope he wasn't lying to me,' Bradbury said." Reviewers of the anniversary edition made a point of acknowledging the book's continued relevance. "It has reminded readers over the past fifty years that books can be dangerous things," wrote a reviewer from Australia's *Canberra Times*.

After the publication of *Fahrenheit 451,* Bradbury moved away from the science fiction genre with which he had become identified. He published other story collections during the 1950s containing a mix of fantasies, stories set in Mexico (a setting which had a lasting fascination for the author), crime stories, and small town tales. In *A Medicine for Melancholy,* Bradbury published his first stories concerning Irish life and character. This interest, sparked during a stay in Ireland in 1954, would be another ongoing concern in his work for years to come. He also continued publishing regularly in magazines, both inside the science fiction genre and in more mainstream publications.

Published in 1962, *Something Wicked This Way Comes* was Bradbury's first full-length novel, and another of his best-known works. This fantasy concerns a malevolent carnival that disrupts life in a small Midwestern town. The action occurs mostly at night and explores the darker parts of humanity. The supernatural powers within the carnival have the power to grant dreams, but also to steal away one's soul. "The merry-go-round, the Hall of Mirrors, the parade and other carnivalesque trappings become truly creepy under Bradbury's skillful pen," noted the writer for *St. James Guide to Science Fiction Writers.*

In the 1960s and 1970s, Bradbury's subject matter became more realistic, and his output slightly less prolific. His themes were frequently rather dark, concerning dysfunctional marriages, fear of aging and death, and more warnings on the dangers of technology. Such stories can be found in *The Machineries of Joy* and *I Sing the Body Electric!* The author also worked on nonfiction, plays, editing of anthologies, and writing children's stories. Many of his plays are adaptations of his short stories, and they have continued to appear on stage over the years and in many incarnations. Bradbury's love of theater began at an early age; he was cast for the first time in a musical when he was twelve years old. "His second love has always been theater," reported Ben P. Indick in *Publishers Weekly.* In 2003 Los Angeles theaters featured no less than four of Bradbury's plays.

Bradbury's children's books have featured elements of his science fiction writing; *Switch on the Night* tells of a boy who is afraid of the darkness until a girl named Dark shows him that there are many things to be experienced at night that can't be seen or heard during the day: the stars, the crickets, the croaking frogs. In 1993 *Switch on the Night* was published with new illustrations by Caldecott Medalists Leo and Diane Dillon. Another of Bradbury's children's tales, *Ahmed and the Oblivion Machines,* tells the story of a young boy who is separated from his family in the desert and rescued by an "old god" who shows him the meaning of life.

In 1985 Bradbury published a long-awaited new novel, a noir mystery titled *Death Is a Lonely Business.* Based loosely on his early years as a writer in the pulp fiction market, it features a protagonist whose optimism works to save him from the strange deaths that are striking down his comrades. Characters introduced in this book are the tough cop Elmo Crumley and the hard-living Constance, both of whom appear in later mysteries; with these two, wrote John Coleman of London's *Sunday Times,* Bradbury has "created a memorable couple of tough, compassionate characters: the match for any Martian."

A Graveyard for Lunatics is another noir tale of a writer, working in Hollywood during the 1950s, who discovers a body, frozen in time, in the graveyard next to the studio that employs him. There are autobiographical threads in this story as well; Bradbury wrote for such popular early television shows as *The Twilight Zone* and the *Alfred Hitchcock* series, and his work in Hollywood included writing the award-winning screen adaptation of Herman Melville's *Moby-Dick.* "Bradbury is at his best when he grants real people and actual events the quality of hallucinations," commented Stefan Kanfer in his *Time* review of *A Graveyard for Lunatics.* Sybil Steinberg, writing for *Publishers Weekly,* pointed out that "Bradbury toes the fine line between reality and illusion."

Using another of his screenwriting experiences, Bradbury developed the novel *Green Shadows, White Whale* around his work adapting *Moby-Dick* as a screenplay in Ireland. In the novel, the director John Huston has a large impact on everything that occurs—reviewers compared Huston in the novel to the white whale in Melville's original tale. Kanfer, again writing for *Time,* called the novel Bradbury's "most entertaining book in a distinguished fifty-year career." A *Publishers Weekly* reviewer noted, "Bradbury's prose is as vibrant and distinctive as the landscape in which these delightful tales are set."

Several of Bardbury's short story collections were released in the late 1990s and early 2000s. *Driving Blind*
features twenty-one new tales by the author. *One More
for the Road* is a collection of short stories and novellas, most of them new to print. Several of Bradbury's
earlier themes appear here as well: nostalgia for childhood, love, and time travel. Dorman T. Shindler of the
St. Louis Post-Dispatch noted that Bradbury's writing
has a "fluid, elegiac style that's impossible to copy." A
Kirkus Reviews contributor considered the collection
"slight, affecting, voluble, exuberant," and Roland
Green, writing for *Booklist,* stated that "Bradbury is
justly considered a master of the short story."

As Bradbury turned eighty-three, he selected one hundred of his stories to be collected in *Bradbury Stories:
100 of His Most Celebrated Tales.* "This will quite
likely go down as grandmaster Bradbury's magnum
opus," commented a critic for *Kirkus Reviews.* Bradbury's 2004 collection *The Cat's Pajamas* combines
new stories with "lost" stories, written early in his career but never before published; "old or new, they are
remarkably of a piece," Ray Olson noted in his *Booklist*
review. Some critics felt that Bradbury's earlier unpublished stories were stronger than the collection's newer
stories. According to Meg Jones in her review for *Knight
Ridder/Tribune News Service,* "Bradbury still writes
great stories, but it's his older tales that shine in this
collection." However, Jessie Milligan, also writing for
the *Knight Ridder/Tribune News Service,* was unabashed
in her praise: "This collection is a true gift from a powerful writing talent who has entertained Americans for
almost sixty years."

With *From the Dust Returned,* Bradbury returns to the
Elliot family of "The Homecoming." The Elliots live in
a Victorian style castle; each of them has a supernatural
ability that makes them something more or less than
human. "Like the members of his Family, Bradbury's
talents are immortal," praised Shindler, this time writing for the *Denver Post.* "The book reads like liquid
poetry while telling the interconnected stories of a number of unusual . . . family members," Rachel Singer
Gordon declared in her *Library Journal* review. Featured family members include Grand-Mere, a mummy
who was once a pharoah's daughter; Uncle Einar, whose
bat wings allow the younger family members to use
him as a kite; Cecy, who enters people's minds and occasionally controls their actions; and Timothy, a human
foundling who is recording the family history.

In 2003 Bradbury penned another mystery with a film
noir flavor: *Let's All Kill Constance.* "When Bradbury
writes stories set during Hollywood's heyday of the

'40s and '50s, the result is a crackerjack tale full of sly
wit and gentle insight," Shindler praised in his review
of the book for the *Austin American Statesman.* In this
tale, the screenwriter/detective who appeared in *Death
Is a Lonely Business* and *A Graveyard for Lunatics* is
asked for help by Constance Rattigan, an aging film
star who seems to be the next prey of a killer. Constance visits the screenwriter in the middle of the night,
producing an old address book of hers and an ancient
phone book, both of which have old contacts and friends
marked with red crucifixes. Once Constance confesses
her fears, she vanishes into the night, leaving the screenwriter to try to pick up her trail—along which there are
plenty of dead bodies. A *Publishers Weekly* reviewer
called the book a "whirlwind of staccato dialogue, puns
and references to old Hollywood," and added that "it's
the author's exuberant voice more than the mystery itself that will have readers hooked." Meg Jones, in a review of the book for *Knight Ridder/Tribune News Service,* concluded, "In Bradbury's breathless and
unbeatable prose, the mystery slowly reveals itself like
a flickering projector in a darkened theater."

*Bradbury Speaks: Too Soon from the Cave, Too Far
from the Stars,* a collection of 37 essays, was published
in 2005. Some essays provide a background for the creation of many of Bradbury's classic stories, and in others the author provides "opinions galore on books, movies, [science fiction] and the people and places in his
life," according to a *Kirkus Reviews* contributor. The
same reviewer called the collection "uneven," stating
that Bradbury sometimes resorts to "preening and rant-
ing." However, a reviewer for *Publishers Weekly*
claimed that in this collection, the author's "enthusiasm
remains as contagious as ever."

Throughout his career, Bradbury has remained an energetic and insightful writer. Damon Knight observed in
his *In Search of Wonder: Critical Essays on Science
Fiction:* "His imagery is luminous and penetrating, continually lighting up familiar corners with unexpected
words. He never lets an idea go until he has squeezed it
dry, and never wastes one. As his talent expands, some
of his stories become pointed social commentary; some
are surprisingly effective religious tracts, disguised as
science fiction; others still are nostalgic vignettes; but
under it all is still Bradbury the poet of twentieth-
century neurosis. Bradbury the isolated spark of consciousness, awake and alone at midnight; Bradbury the
grown-up child who still remembers, still believes." As
Shindler wrote in his *Denver Post* article, "After nearly
six decades of professional publication, Ray Bradbury
could lie back and relax. . . . Yet, instead of resting
on his laurels, Bradbury is riding his third wind into a

creative vortex, hurling out screenplays, stage adaptations, new stories," not to mention new novels. In addition, Bradbury has declared he has no intention of slowing down. He still writes every day. "It is not that I have to," he explained to Beatrice Cassina in *Writer.* "It is just that I feel I need to. Every day, every morning when I wake up. It is nice to be in the twenty-first century. It is like a new challenge. It is really a good and threatening new century to create for!"

BIOGRAPHICAL AND CRITICAL SOURCES:

BOOKS

Adams, Anthony, *Ray Bradbury,* Harrap (London, England), 1975.

Clareson, Thomas D., editor, *Voices for the Future: Essays on Major Science Fiction Writers,* Volume 1, Bowling Green State University Press (Bowling Green, OH), 1976.

Concise Dictionary of American Literary Biography: Broadening Views, 1968-1988, Gale (Detroit, MI), 1989.

Contemporary Literary Criticism, Gale (Detroit, MI), Volume 1, 1973, Volume 3, 1975, Volume 10, 1979, Volume 15, 1980, Volume 42, 1987.

Contemporary Popular Writers, St. James Press (Detroit, MI), 1997.

Dictionary of Literary Biography, Gale (Detroit, MI), Volume 2: *American Novelists since World War II,* 1978; Volume 8: *Twentieth-Century American Science Fiction Writers,* 1981.

Ketterer, David, *New Worlds for Old: The Apocalyptic Imagination, Science Fiction, and American Literature,* Indiana University Press (Bloomington, IN), 1974.

Kirk, Russell, *Enemies of the Permanent Things: Observations of Abnormity in Literature and Politics,* Arlington House (New Rochelle, NY), 1969.

Knight, Damon, *In Search of Wonder: Critical Essays on Science Fiction,* 2nd edition, Advent, 1967.

Moskowitz, Sam, *Seekers of Tomorrow: Masters of Modern Science Fiction,* Ballantine (New York, NY), 1967, pp. 351-370.

Nolan, William F., *The Ray Bradbury Companion,* Gale (New York, NY), 1975.

Platt, Charles, *Dream Makers: Science- Fiction and Fantasy Writers at Work,* Ungar (New York, NY), 1987.

Scribner Encyclopedia of American Lives, Thematic Series: The 1960s, Charles Scribners Sons (New York, NY), 2003.

St. James Encyclopedia of Popular Culture, St. James Press (Detroit, MI), 2000.

St. James Guide to Horror, Ghost & Gothic Writers, St. James Press (Detroit, MI), 1998.

St. James Guide to Science Fiction Writers, 4th edition, St. James Press (Detroit, MI), 1996.

St. James Guide to Young Adult Writers, 2nd edition, St. James Press (Detroit, MI), 1999.

Slusser, George Edgar, *The Bradbury Chronicles,* Borgo Press (San Bernardino, CA), 1977.

Touponce, William F., *Ray Bradbury and the Poetics of Reverie: Fantasy, Science Fiction, and the Reader,* UMI Research Press (Ann Arbor, MI), 1984.

Touponce, William F., *Naming the Unnameable: Ray Bradbury and the Fantastic after Freud,* Starmont House, 1997.

Weller, Sam, *The Bradbury Chronicles,* Morrow (New York, NY), 2005.

Wollheim, Donald, *The Universe Makers,* Harper (New York, NY), 1971.

UXL Encyclopedia of World Biography, volume 2, Gale (Detroit, MI), 2003.

World Literature Criticism, Gale (Detroit, MI), 1992.

PERIODICALS

Albuquerque Journal, November 29, 1998, David Steinberg, "Bradbury Keeps Pounding Both Keys and Pavement," p. F6.

Atlanta Journal- Constitution (Atlanta, GA), August 31, 2003, Gary A. Witte, interview with Bradbury, p. M1.

Austin American- Statesman, February 16, 2003, Dorman T. Shindler, "Bradbury Has Mystery Noir Down to a Science," p. K5.

Back Stage West, July 25, 2002, Dally Margolies, "Bradbury: Past, Present and Future at the Court Theatre," p. 27; April 3, 2003, Jenelle Riley, "What's Up with Ray Bradbury?," p. 4.

Book, September- October, 2003, Eric Wetzel, review of the Fiftieth anniversary hardcover of *Fahrenheit 451,* p. 34.

Booklist, October 1, 1998, Ray Olson, review of *Ahmed and the Oblivion Machines,* p. 312; August, 2001, Candace Smith, review of *From the Dust Returned,* p. 2049; April 1, 2002, Roland Green, review of *One More for the Road,* pp. 1312-1313; November 15, 2002, Connie Fletcher, review of *Let's All Kill Constance,* p. 579; July, 2003, Olson, review of *Bradbury Stories: 100 of His Most Celebrated Tales,* p. 1844; July, 2004, Ray Olson, review of *The Cat's Pajamas,* p. 1796.

Canberra Times, September 26, 2004, "Burning Bright after Fifty Years."

Coventry Evening Telegraph, May 31, 2003, Michael Wood, review of *One More for the Road,* p. 26.

Denver Post, October 7, 2001, Dorman T. Shindler, review of *From the Dust Returned,* p. FF-04; August 10, 2003, Shindler, "Fantasy Genius Bradbury Cranks 'em out at Eighty-three," p. EE- 02.

Hollywood Reporter, May 10, 2005, "Angelica Huston, Author Ray Bradbury, and Merv Griffin Were Conferred Honorary Degrees," p. 16.

Kirkus Reviews, August 15, 2001, review of *From the Dust Returned,* p. 1143; February 15, 2002, review of *One More for the Road,* p. 227; October 15, 2002, review of *Let's All Kill Constance,* p. 1491; June 15, 2003, review of *Bradbury Stories: 100 of His Most Celebrated Tales,* p. 834; June 1, 2004, review of *The Cat's Pajamas,* pp. 504-505; June 1, 2005, review of *Bradbury Speaks: Too Soon from the Cave, Too Far from the Stars,* p. 619.

Kliatt, September, 2002, Bette D. Ammon, review of *From the Dust Returned,* pp. 52-53.

Knight Ridder/Tribune News Service, March 15, 1999, Luaine Lee, "A Conversation with Ray Bradbury," p. K5648; August 23, 2000, John Mark Eberhart, "Fifty Years of Fantasy," p. K151; January 8, 2003, Meg Jones, review of *Let's All Kill Constance,* p. K4394; July 8, 2004, Meg Jones, "Ray Bradbury's Older Work Still Purrs," p. K0626; August 12, 2004, Jessie Milligan, "Ray Bradbury's *Cat's Pajamas* Is Exactly That," p. K5315.

Library Journal, May 1, 1999, Michael Rogers, review of *Death Is a Lonely Business,* p. 118; September 15, 2001, Rachel Singer Gordon, review of *From the Dust Returned,* p. 108; December, 2002, Devon Thomas, review of *Let's All Kill Constance,* p. 174; August, 2003, A. Berger, review of *Bradbury Stories: 100 of His Most Celebrated Tales,* p. 138; November 15, 2003, Michael Rogers, review of the fiftieth anniversary hardcover of *Fahrenheit 451,* p. 103; December 2004, Karen Sokol, review of *The Cat's Pajamas,* p. 174.

Magazine of Fantasy and Science Fiction, October, 1997, Charles De Lint, review of *The Illustrated Man,* p. 41; August, 2003, De Lint, review of *They Have Not Seen the Stars: The Collected Poetry of Ray Bradbury,* p. 34; March, 2005, James Sallis, review of Bradbury biographies, pp. 30-35.

New York Times, October 15, 2000, Emily-Greta Tabourin, review of *Switch on the Night,* p. L31.

New York Times Book Review, December 9, 2001, Mary Elizabeth Williams, review of *From the Dust Returned,* p. 28; January 26, 2003, Marilyn Stasio, review of *Let's All Kill Constance,* p. 20.

New York Times Magazine, November 5, 2000, Mary Roach, interview with Bradbury, p. 21.

Palm Beach Post, March 10, 2002, Scott Eyman, interview with Bradbury, p. J1.

Plain Dealer (Cleveland, OH), February 18, 2003, Karen Sandstrom, "Library Lover Bradbury Shares Burning Passion for Books," p. E1.

Post-Standard (Syracuse, NY), October 6, 2004, Robert A. Baker, " *Fahrenheit 451* Author Discusses Book," p. B1.

PR Newswire, April 22, 2003, "Ray Bradbury to Receive Honorary Degree from Woodbury University."

Publishers Weekly, May 11, 1990, Sybil Steinberg, review of *A Graveyard for Lunatics,* p. 249; April 6, 1992, review of *Green Shadows, White Whale,* p. 52; October 26, 1998, review of *Ahmed and the Oblivion Machines,* p. 49; March 19, 2001, review of *A Chapbook for Burnt-Out Priests, Rabbis, and Ministers,* p. 81; August 27, 2001, review of *From the Dust Returned,* p. 60; October 22, 2001, Ben P. Indick, interview with Bradbury, p. 40; March 11, 2002, review of *One More for the Road,* p. 51; September, 2002, review of *I Live by the Invisible: New and Selected Poems,* p. 54; November 11, 2002, review of *Let's All Kill Constance,* p. 40; March 22, 2004, review of *It Came from Outer Space,* p. 68; June 28, 2004, review of *The Cat's Pajamas,* p. 31; June 6, 2005, review of *Bradbury Speaks,* p. 51; September 26, 2005, review of *The Halloween Tree,* p. 67.

Sarasota Herald Tribune, February 6, 2000, Steven G. Reed, "A Phone Call from Ray Bradbury."

St. Louis Post- Dispatch, June 16, 2002, Dorman T. Shindler, "Bradbury Is Back with a Fascinating New Collection," p. F10.

Star Ledger (Newark, NJ), August 25, 2003, "A Nearly Out-of-This-World Party," p. O26.

Star Tribune (Minneapolis, MN), April 25, 2003, Graydon Royce, "A Suitable Storyteller," p. E8; April 29, 2003, Lisa Brock, " *Ice Cream Suit* Topped with a Sense of Wonder," p. B4.

Sunday Mirror (London, England), May 15, 2005, "History Made in Galway Uni," p. 11.

Sunday Times (London, England), May 25, 1986, John Coleman, review of *Death Is a Lonely Business.*

Time, March 24, 1975; October 13, 1980; August 6, 1990, Stefan Kanfer, review of *A Graveyard for Lunatics,* p. 75; May 25, 1992, Kanfer, review of *Green Shadows, White Whale,* p. 68.

Writer, January, 2003, Beatrice Cassina, "Ray Bradbury's 'Theater of the Morning': When His Characters Come Talk to Him, He Listens," pp. 26-31; December, 2003, "'I Was Never a Science Fiction Writer,' Ray Bradbury Says," p. 11.

Writing!, November- December, 2001, Sarah Kizis, "A Virtual Visit to the Veldt," p. 14.

ONLINE

Ray Bradbury Home Page, http://www.raybradbury.
    com/ (June 5, 2005).
Salon.com, http://www.salon.com/ (July 11, 2003),
    James Hibberd, "Ray Bradbury Is on Fire!"

*   *   *

BRADBURY, Ray Douglas
See BRADBURY, Ray

*   *   *

BRADLEY, Marion Zimmer 1930-1999
(Lee Chapman, John Dexter, Miriam Gardner,
Valerie Graves, Morgan Ives, Elfrida Rivers)

PERSONAL: Born June 3, 1930, in Albany, NY; died
following a heart attack September 25, 1999, in Berkeley, CA; daughter of Leslie Raymond (a carpenter) and
Evelyn (a historian; maiden name, Conklin) Zimmer;
married Robert Alden Bradley, October 26, 1949 (divorced, 1963); married Walter Henry Breen (a numis-
matist), February 14, 1964 (divorced May, 1990); children: (first marriage) David Robert; (second marriage)
Patrick Russell, Moira Evelyn Dorothy. *Education:* Attended New York State College for Teachers (now State
University of New York at Albany), 1946-48; Hardin-
Simmons College, B.A., 1964; additional study at University of California, Berkeley, 1965-67.

CAREER: Writer and musician; editor, *Marion Zimmer
Bradley's Fantasy Magazine.*

MEMBER: Authors Guild, Science Fiction Writers of
America, Mystery Writers of America, Horror Writers
of America, Gay Academic Union, Alpha Chi.

AWARDS, HONORS: Invisible Little Man Award, 1977;
Leigh Brackett Memorial Sense of Wonder Award,
1978, for *The Forbidden Tower;* Locus Award for best
fantasy novel, 1984, for *The Mists of Avalon.*

WRITINGS:

SCIENCE FICTION/FANTASY

The Door through Space (bound with *Rendezvous on
    Lost Planet* by A. Bertram Chandler), Ace (New
    York, NY), 1961.

Seven from the Stars (bound with *Worlds of the Impe-
    rium* by Keith Laumer), Ace (New York, NY),
    1962.
Falcons of Narabedla and *The Dark Intruder and Other
    Stories,* Ace (New York, NY), 1964.
The Brass Dragon (bound with *Ipomoea* by John Rack-
    ham), Ace (New York, NY), 1969.
Hunters of the Red Moon, DAW (New York, NY),
    1973.
The Parting of Arwen (short story), T-K Graphics,
    1974.
The Endless Voyage, Ace (New York, NY), 1975, ex-
    panded edition published as *Endless Universe,*
    1979.
The Ruins of Isis, Donning (Norfolk, VA), 1978.
(With brother, Paul Edwin Zimmer) *The Survivors,*
    DAW (New York, NY), 1979.
The House between the Worlds, Doubleday (New York,
    NY), 1980, revised edition, Del Rey (New York,
    NY), 1981.
Survey Ship, Ace (New York, NY), 1980.
Web of Light (also see below), Donning (Norfolk, VA),
    1982.
The Mists of Avalon, Knopf (New York, NY), 1983.
(Editor and contributor) *Greyhaven: An Anthology of
    Fantasy,* DAW (New York, NY), 1983.
Web of Darkness (also see below), Donning (Norfolk,
    VA), 1983.
The Inheritor, Tor (New York, NY), 1984, 1997.
(Editor) *Sword and Sorceress* (annual anthology), nine-
    teen volumes, DAW (New York, NY), 1984–2002.
Night's Daughter, Ballantine (New York, NY), 1985.
(With Vonda McIntyre) *Lythande* (anthology), DAW
    (New York, NY), 1986.
The Fall of Atlantis (contains *Web of Light* and *Web of
    Darkness*), Baen Books (Riverdale, NY), 1987.
The Firebrand, Simon & Schuster (New York, NY),
    1987.
Warrior Woman, DAW (New York, NY), 1988.
City of Sorcery, DAW (New York, NY), 1988.
The Colors of Space (Reissue), Donning (Norfolk, VA),
    1988.
Witch Hill, Tor (New York, NY), 1990.
The Best of Marion Zimmer Bradley, Mapes Monde
    Editore, 1991.
Black Trillium, Bantam (New York, NY), 1991.
*Jamie and Other Stories: The Best of Marion Zimmer
    Bradley,* Academy Chicago (Chicago, IL), 1993.
The Forest House, Viking (New York, NY), 1994.
Lady of the Trillium, Bantam (New York, NY), 1995.
(With Andre Norton and Mercedes Lackey) *Tiger, Burn-
    ing Bright,* Morrow (New York, NY), 1995.
Ghostlight, Tor (New York, NY), 1995.

(With Holly Lisle) *Glenraven,* Baen Books (Riverdale, NY), 1996.

Witchlight, Tor (New York, NY), 1996.

The Gratitude of Kings, ROC (New York, NY), 1997.

Gravelight, Tor (New York, NY), 1997.

Lady of Avalon, Viking (New York, NY), 1997.

In the Rift (sequel to *Glenraven*) Baen Books (Riverdale, NY), 1998.

(With Diana L. Paxson) *Priestess of Avalon,* Viking (New York, NY), 2001.

"DARKOVER" SCIENCE-FICTION SERIES

The Sword of Aldones and *The Planet Savers,* Ace (New York, NY), 1962.

The Bloody Sun, Ace (New York, NY), 1964, revised edition, 1979.

Star of Danger, Ace (New York, NY), 1965.

The Winds of Darkover (bound with *The Anything Tree* by Rackham), Ace (New York, NY), 1970.

The World Wreckers, Ace (New York, NY), 1971.

Darkover Landfall, DAW (New York, NY), 1972.

The Spell Sword, DAW (New York, NY), 1974.

The Heritage of Hastur (also see below), DAW (New York, NY), 1975.

The Shattered Chain (also see below), DAW (New York, NY), 1976.

The Forbidden Tower, DAW (New York, NY), 1977.

Stormqueen! (also see below), DAW (New York, NY), 1978.

(Editor and contributor) *Legends of Hastur and Cassilda,* Thendara House, 1979.

(Editor and contributor) *Tales of the Free Amazons,* Thendara House, 1980.

Two to Conquer, DAW (New York, NY), 1980.

(Editor and contributor) *The Keeper's Price and Other Stories,* DAW (New York, NY), 1980.

Sharra's Exile (also see below), DAW (New York, NY), 1981.

(Editor and contributor) *Sword of Chaos* (short stories), DAW (New York, NY), 1981.

Children of Hastur (includes *The Heritage of Hastur* and *Sharra's Exile*), Doubleday (New York, NY), 1981, published as *Heritage and Exile,* DAW (New York, NY), 2002.

Hawkmistress! (also see below), DAW (New York, NY), 1982.

Thendara House (also see below), DAW (New York, NY), 1983.

Oath of the Renunciates (includes *The Shattered Chain* and *Thendara House*), Doubleday (New York, NY), 1983.

City of Sorcery (also see below), DAW (New York, NY), 1984.

(Editor and contributor) *Free Amazons of Darkover* (short stories), DAW (New York, NY), 1985.

(With others) *Red Sun of Darkover* (short stories), DAW (New York, NY), 1987.

(With others) *The Other Side of the Mirror and Other Darkover Stories,* DAW (New York, NY), 1987.

(Editor and contributor) *Four Moons of Darkover* (short stories), DAW (New York, NY), 1988.

(Editor) *Domains of Darkover* (short stories), DAW (New York, NY), 1990.

The Heirs of Hammerfell, DAW (New York, NY), 1990.

(Editor and contributor) *Renunciates of Darkover* (short stories), DAW (New York, NY), 1991.

(Editor and contributor) *Leroni of Darkover* (short stories), DAW (New York, NY), 1991.

(With Mercedes Lackey) *Rediscovery: A Novel of Darkover,* DAW (New York, NY), 1993.

(Editor) *Towers of Darkover* (short stories), DAW (New York, NY), 1993.

(Editor) *Snows of Darkover* (short stories), DAW (New York, NY), 1994.

Exile's Song: A Novel of Darkover, DAW (New York, NY), 1996.

The Shadow Matrix, DAW (New York, NY), 1997.

Heartlight (sequel to *The Shadow Matrix*), Tor (New York, NY), 1998.

Traitor's Sun: A Novel of Darkover, DAW (New York, NY), 1999.

(With Deborah J. Ross) *The Fall of Neskaya: Book One of the Clingfire Trilogy,* DAW (New York, NY), 2001.

The Ages of Chaos (includes *Stormqueen!* and *Hawkmistress!*), DAW (New York, NY), 2002.

The Saga of the Renunciates (includes *The Shattered Chain, Thendara House,* and *City of Sorcery*), DAW (New York, NY), 2002.

OTHER

Songs from Rivendell, privately printed, 1959.

(With Gene Damon) *A Complete, Cumulative Checklist of Lesbian, Variant, and Homosexual Fiction,* privately printed, 1960.

Castle Terror (novel), Lancer (New York, NY), 1965.

Souvenir of Monique (novel), Ace (New York, NY), 1967.

Bluebeard's Daughter (novel), Lancer (New York, NY), 1968.

(Translator) Lope de Vega, *El Villano en su Rincon,* privately printed, 1971.

Dark Satanic (novel), Berkley Publishing (New York, NY), 1972.

In the Steps of the Master (teleplay novelization), Tempo Books, 1973.

Men, Halflings, and Hero Worship (criticism), T-K Graphics, 1973.

The Necessity for Beauty: Robert W. Chamber and the Romantic Tradition (criticism), T-K Graphics, 1974.

The Jewel of Arwen (criticism), T-K Graphics, 1974.

A Gay Bibliography, Arno Press, 1975.

Can Ellen Be Saved? (teleplay novelization), Tempo Books, 1975.

(With Alfred Bester and Norman Spinrad) *Experiment Perilous: Three Essays in Science Fiction,* Algol Press (New York, NY), 1976.

Drums of Darkness (novel), Ballantine (New York, NY), 1976.

The Catch Trap, Ballantine (New York, NY), 1979.

(Editor, with Rachel E. Holmen) *Marion Zimmer Bradley's Fantasy Worlds,* M.Z. Bradley Literary Works Trust (Berkeley, CA), 1998.

Also author of novels under undisclosed pseudonyms. Contributor, sometimes under Elfrida Rivers and other pseudonyms, to anthologies and periodicals, including *Magazine of Fantasy and Science Fiction, Amazing Stories,* and *Venture.* Contributor to *Essays Lovecraftian,* edited by Darrell Schweitzer, T-K Graphics, 1976. Author (as Lee Chapman) of *I Am a Lesbian;* (as Morgan Ives) *Spare Her Heaven* and *Knives of Desire,* (as Miriam Gardner) *Twilight Lovers* and *My Sister, My Love;* and (as John Dexter) *No Adam for Eve.*

ADAPTATIONS: The Mists of Avalon was adapted for a TNT television miniseries, 2001. Bradley's "Clingfire" trilogy was completed by Deborah J. Ross.

SIDELIGHTS: Marion Zimmer Bradley was born to an impoverished family in upstate New York at the beginning of the Great Depression. At an early age she fell in love with both books and opera. Before she had learned to write, Bradley was already dictating stories her mother transcribed for her. Her first long work of fiction was written in high school, based on a libretto of the opera *Norma,* and it served as the basis for a novel she would publish nearly fifty year later, titled *The Forest House.* Before Bradley had finished high school she discovered the worlds of science fiction and science-fiction fandom, both of which she would remain close to for the rest of her life.

Bradley's first published stories appeared in the pulp science-fiction magazines of the 1950s. Her novel *Planet Savers* began the popular "Darkover" series, which has

since become one of the best-loved series in science fiction and fantasy. Bradley's "Darkover" novels have not only inspired their own fan magazines, or "fanzines," but also a number of story collections in which other authors set their tales in Bradley's universe. A lost space colony rediscovered after centuries of neglect by Earth's Terran Empire, Darkover has developed its own society and technology, both of which produce internal and external conflicts. Darkover fascinates readers because it is a world of many contradictions; not only do the psychic abilities of the natives contrast with the traditional technologies of the empire, but a basically repressive patriarchal society coexists (however uneasily) with groups such as an order of female Renunciates known as the Free Amazons. Consisting of over twenty books and spanning many years of the world's history, "the Darkover novels test various attitudes about the importance of technology and, more important, they study the very nature of human intimacy," claimed Rosemarie Arbur in *Twentieth-Century Science-Fiction Writers.* The critic explained that "by postulating a Terran Empire the main features of which are advanced technology and bureaucracy, and a Darkover that seems technologically backward and is fiercely individualistic, Bradley sets up a conflict to which there is no 'correct' resolution." The permutations of this basic conflict have provided Bradley with numerous opportunities to explore several themes in various ways.

Reviewer Susan M. Shwartz observed in *The Feminine Eye: Science Fiction and the Women Who Write It* that one theme in particular provides a foundation for the "Darkover" novels: "For every gain, there is a risk; choice involves a testing of will and courage." Unlike some fantasy worlds where struggles are easily decided, "on Darkover any attempt at change or progress carries with it the need for pain-filled choice," Shwartz commented. While Bradley provided her characters with ample avenues of action, Scwartz observed that "in the Darkover books, alternatives are predicated upon two things, sincere choice and a willingness to pay the price choice demands." *The Shattered Chain,* for example, "in terms of its structure, plot, characterization, and context within the series, is about the choices of all women on Darkover and, through them, of all people, male and female, Darkovan and Terran."

The Shattered Chain is one of Bradley's most renowned "Darkover" novels. As Arbur described it in her study *Marion Zimmer Bradley,* the book "is one of the most thorough and sensitive science-fiction explorations of the variety of options available to a self-actualizing woman; not only does it present us with four strong and different feminine characters who make crucial decisions about their lives but its depth of characterizations permits us to examine in detail the consequences of these decisions." The novel begins as a traditional quest when Lady Rohana, a noblewoman of the ruling class, enlists the aid of a tribe of Free Amazons to rescue a kidnapped kinswoman from a settlement where women are chained, to show that they are possessions. But while the rescue is eventually successful, it is only the beginning of a series of conflicts; Rohana's experiences force her to re-evaluate her life, and both the daughter of the woman she rescued and a Terran agent who studies the Amazons find themselves examining the limits of their own situations. "As we see in *The Shattered Chain*," Shwartz concluded, "the payment for taking an oath is the payment for all such choices: pain, with a potential for achievement. In Bradley's other books, too, the price of choice is of great importance."

In coming to this conclusion about the price of choice, Bradley emphasized two other themes, as Laura Murphy stated in the *Dictionary of Literary Biography:* "The first is the reconciliation of conflicting or opposing forces—whether such forces are represented by different cultures or by different facets of a single personality. The second," the critic continued, "closely related to the first, is alienation or exile from a dominant group." While these ideas are featured in Bradley's "Darkover" series, they also appear in the author's first big mainstream best seller, *The Mists of Avalon.* "Colorfully detailed as a medieval tapestry, *The Mists of Avalon* . . . is probably the most ambitious retelling of the Arthurian legend in the twentieth century," Charlotte Spivack maintained in *Merlin's Daughters: Contemporary Women Writers of Fantasy.* Spivack added that this novel "is much more than a retelling. . . . It is a profound revisioning. Imaginatively conceived, intricately structured, and richly peopled, it offers a brilliant reinterpretation of the traditional material from the point of view of the major female characters," such as Arthur's mother Igraine, the Lady of the Lake, Viviane, Arthur's half-sister, the enchantress Morgaine, and Arthur's wife, Gwenhwyfar.

In addition, Bradley presents the eventual downfall of Arthur's reign as the result of broken promises to the religious leaders of Avalon; while Arthur gains his crown with the aid of Viviane and the Goddess she represents, the influence of Christian priests and Gwenhwyfar lead him to forsake his oath. Thus, not only does Bradley present Arthur's story from a different viewpoint, she roots it "in the religious struggle between matriarchal worship of the goddess and the patriarchal institution of Christianity, between what the author calls 'the cauldron and the cross,'" described

Spivack. In presenting this conflict, Bradley "memorably depicts the inevitable passing of times and religions by her use of the imagery of different simultaneous worlds, which move out of consciousness as their day ebbs," remarked Maude McDaniel in the *Washington Post.* Bradley also "compares head-on the pre-Christian Druidism of Britain and the Christianity that supplants it, a refreshing change from some modern writers who tend to take refuge at awkward moments in cryptic metaphysics," McDaniel stated.

Bradley used similar themes and approaches in reworking another classic tale: *The Firebrand,* the story of the fall of Troy and of Kassandra, royal daughter of Troy and onetime priestess and Amazon. As the author remarked in an interview with *Publishers Weekly* reviewer Lisa See, in the story of Troy she saw another instance of male culture overtaking and obscuring female contributions: "During the Dorian invasion, when iron won out over bronze, the female cult died," Bradley explained. "The Minoan and Mycenaean cultures were dead overnight. But you could also look at that period of history and say, here were two cultures that should have been ruled by female twins—Helen and Klytemnestra. And what do you know? When they married Menelaus and Agamemnon, the men took over their cities. I just want to look at what history was really like before the women-haters got hold of it. I want to look at these people like any other people, as though no one had ever written about them before."

Despite this emphasis on female viewpoints in *The Firebrand* and her other fiction, Bradley was not a "feminist" writer. "Though her interest in women's rights is strong," elaborated Murphy, "her works do not reduce to mere polemic." Rosemarie Arbur related in *Twentieth-Century Science-Fiction Writers* that "Bradley's writing openly with increasing sureness of the human psyche and the human being rendered whole prompted Theodore Sturgeon to call the former science-fiction fan 'one of the Big ones' . . . writing science-fiction." Arbur concluded that "Sturgeon's phrase applies . . . to the science-fiction writer Marion Zimmer Bradley . . . , for she has transcended categories." Arbur similarly stated that the author "refuses to allow her works to wander into politics unless true concerns of realistic characters bring them there. Her emphasis is on character, not political themes."

While Bradley passed away in 1999, unfinished manuscripts begun by her but completed by other authors continued to appear. *Priestess of Avalon,* completed by Diana L. Paxson, serves as a prequel to *The Mists of*

Avalon. The story opens in the year 296 when a British princess, Helena, travels to the Isle of Avalon to study "the path of the goddess." Helena falls in love with Flavius Constantius Chlorus, a man destined to become Roman emperor. Helena's Aunt Ganeda, opposed to the union of the two lovers, exiles Helena from Avalon. Yet Helena is already pregnant with Flavius's child. She later joins Flavius, advising him in his political strategies in dealing with the Roman Empire, and eventually makes her own pilgrimage to the Holy Land. A contributor in *Publishers Weekly* praised Paxson's "skill at bringing historical characters and places to vivid life," and also observed that fans of Bradley's *The Mists of Avalon* will embrace the book's "message that all religions call on the same high power."

Another posthumously completed title, *The Fall of Neskaya,* coauthored by Deborah J. Ross and billed as Book One of the "Clingfire" trilogy, continues Bradley's "Darkover" series. In the scheme of Darkover history, the tale is set in the Ages of Chaos when laran telepathic power ruled the planet. Young Coryn Leynier is discovered to possess such power and rises to the position of Keeper of Neskaya Tower. Unknown to Coryn, those who seek the downfall of Darkover have planted a powerful weapon of destruction in his mind. A *Publishers Weekly* reviewer praised *The Fall of Neskaya* as "a competent, fast-paced narrative congruent with . . . [Bradley's] familiar 1960s theme: 'make various kinds of love, but not nuclear war.'" Paula Luedtke, reviewing the novel for *Booklist,* commented that Ross, who planned to complete the trilogy on her own, "succeeds in keeping it true to Bradley's style."

In the 1950s Bradley published several lesbian novels under a variety of pseudonyms, and later, under her own name, two bibliographies of gay and lesbian literature and a gay mainstream novel titled *The Catch Trap.* Writing a remembrance of Bradley in the *Lambda Book Report,* Lawrence Shimmel observed: "While she is best known for her science-fiction and fantasy novels, lesbian and gay readers also know her for her innumerable contributions to gay literature." Essayist Jeanette Smith, writing in *Gay and Lesbian Literature,* took a more detailed look at this aspect of Bradley's career. Although Bradley always avoided the label "feminist" and insisted that literature should entertain rather than serve as propaganda, according to Smith the author's "enthusiasm for women's rights and gay rights is apparent in her works." Smith credited Bradley with being "one of the first science-fiction writers to feature independent female characters" and went on to note that "Bradley peoples her worlds with characters representing many types of gender roles and relationships." *The*

Mists of Avalon, though it dwells primarily on heterosexual relationships, includes love scenes between priestesses Morgraine and Raven. The cultures of Darkover, in contrast to Terran cultures, encompass a wide variety of sexual identities—gay, lesbian, bisexual, virginal, celibate—without prejudice. In the *Heritage of Hastur,* a novel in the "Darkover" series, Lord Regis Hastur acknowledges both his homosexuality and his love for a fellow male schoolmate. On a darker note, some of the "Darkover" books portray the sexual enslavement of women by men and vice versa, as well as necrophilia and child prostitution. Yet on the whole, Smith stated, such negative elements are outweighed by positive ones, and "Bradley's storytelling is a message of acceptance and respect for oneself and for others, an affirmation of human rights and human dignity."

BIOGRAPHICAL AND CRITICAL SOURCES:

BOOKS

Alpers, H. J., editor, *Marion Zimmer Bradley's Darkover,* Corian, 1983.

Arbur, Rosemarie, *Leigh Brackett, Marion Zimmer Bradley, Anne McCaffrey: A Primary and Secondary Bibliography,* G.K. Hall (Boston, MA), 1982.

Arbur, Rosemarie, *Marion Zimmer Bradley,* Starmont House (Mercer Island, WA), 1985.

Darkover Cookbook, Friends of Darkover, 1977, revised edition, 1979.

Dictionary of Literary Biography, Volume 8: *Twentieth Century American Science-Fiction Writers,* Thomson Gale (Detroit, MI), 1981.

Malinowski, Sharon, editor, *Gay & Lesbian Literature,* St. James Press (Detroit, MI), 1994.

Paxson, Diana, *Costume and Clothing as a Cultural Index on Darkover,* Friends of Darkover, 1977, revised edition, 1981.

Roberson, Jennifer, editor, *Return to Avalon: A Celebration of Marion Zimmer Bradley,* DAW (New York, NY), 1996.

Staicar, Tom, editor, *The Feminine Eye: Science-Fiction and the Women Who Write It,* Ungar (New York, NY), 1982.

Twentieth-Century Science-Fiction Writers, St. James Press (Detroit, MI), 1986.

Wise, S., *The Darkover Dilemma: Problems of the Darkover Series,* T-K Graphics, 1976.

PERIODICALS

Algol, winter 1977-1978.

Booklist, February 15, 1993; January 15, 1994; July 2001, review of *The Fall of Neskaya,* Paula Luedtke, p. 1991.

English Journal, January, 1989.

Entertainment Weekly, May 20, 1994, p. 57.

Fantasy Review of Fantasy and Science-Fiction, April, 1984.

Library Journal, August, 1988; May 15, 1993; June 15, 1993; March 15, 1994; June 15, 1994.

Locus, November, 1999.

Los Angeles Times Book Review, February 3, 1983.

Mythlore, spring, 1984.

New York Times Book Review, January 30, 1983; November 29, 1987.

Publishers Weekly, September 11, 1987; October 30, 1987; March 15, 1993; February 28, 1994; June 18, 2001, review of *The Fall of Neskaya,* p. 64; July 30, 2001, Daisy Maryles, "Rising from the Mists," p. 18; April 30, 2002, review of *Priestess of Avalon,* p. 62.

San Francisco Examiner, February 27, 1983.

School Library Journal, October, 1994, p. 158.

Science Fiction Review, summer 1983.

Washington Post, January 28, 1983.

West Coast Review of Books, number 5, 1986.

Writer's Digest, June, 1988.

OBITUARIES:

PERIODICALS

Lambda Book Report, December, 1999, Lawrence Shimmel, "Lawrence Shimmel Remembers the Mistress of Avalon," p. 30.

Los Angeles Times, September 30, 1999, p. A24.

New York Times, September 29, 1999, p. A25.

Washington Post, October 3, 1999, p. C6.

ONLINE

MZB Ltd News Online, http://www.mzbfm.com/ (September 30, 1999), Rachel E. Holman, "Marion Zimmer Bradley: June 3, 1930-Sept. 25, 1999."

                    *   *   *

BRAGG, Rick 1959(?)-

PERSONAL: Born c. 1959, in Possum Trot, AL; son of Margaret Marie Bragg. *Education:* Attended Harvard University.

ADDRESSES: Home—347 Joseph St., New Orleans, LA 70115. *Agent*—c/o Pantheon Books, 201 E. 50th St., New York, NY 10022.

CAREER: Journalist and memoirist. Worked as reporter for various Alabama newspapers; worked as a reporter for *St. Petersburg Times,* St. Petersburg, FL, and *New York Times,* New York, NY.

AWARDS, HONORS: Nieman fellowship, Harvard University; Pulitzer Prize for feature writing, 1996, for coverage of Oklahoma City bombing; American Society of Newspaper Editors Distinguished Writing Award (twice); University of Alabama Clarence Cason Award for Nonfiction Writing, 2004.

WRITINGS:

All Over but the Shoutin', Pantheon (New York, NY), 1997, published as *Redbirds: Memories from the South,* Harville Press (London, England), 1999.

(With Walker Evans) *Wooden Churches: A Celebration,* Algonquin Books (Chapel Hill, NC), 1999.

Somebody Told Me: The Newspaper Stories of Rick Bragg, University of Alabama Press (Tuscaloosa, AL), 2000.

Ava's Man, Knopf (New York, NY), 2001.

(Author of foreword) *Best of the Oxford American: Ten Years from the Southern Magazine of Good Writing,* Hill Street Press (Athens, GA), 2002.

I Am a Soldier Too: The Jessica Lynch Story, Knopf (New York, NY), 2003.

ADAPTATIONS: Ava's Man was recorded on compact disc and released by Random Audio, 2001. *All Over but the Shoutin'* was narrated by Bragg and released as an audiobook produced by Random Audio, 1997.

SIDELIGHTS: In his acclaimed memoir, *All Over but the Shoutin',* Rick Bragg describes his personal journey from harsh childhood to national renown as a prize-winning journalist. A reporter who won a Pulitzer Prize for his coverage of the Oklahoma City bombing, Bragg pays special homage in his memoir to his mother, Margaret, for her heroic efforts to provide her children a good home despite nearly insurmountable hardships.

Bragg grew up in Possum Trot, Alabama, located in the Appalachian foothills on the border between Alabama and Georgia. He was the second of three sons, a fourth having died in infancy. The family was very poor, surviving on a fifty-dollar-per-month Social Security check in addition to what Margaret Bragg made as a field hand. Bragg's father, a Korean War veteran who became a physically abusive alcoholic and died at age forty, was rarely present; when he was, he often beat Margaret. She withstood mistreatment stoically and bestowed a compensating love on her children, which enabled Bragg to find eventual success as a writer. All in all, his childhood, Bragg wrote in *All Over but the Shoutin'*, was "full, rich, original and real," as well as "harsh, hard, mean as a damn snake." "I am not a romantic figure," he added, ". . . but I have not led a humdrum life."

After graduating from high school, Bragg spent six months in college, then landed a job at a local newspaper after the paper's first choice for the job opening decided to remain in a fast-food restaurant position instead. After moving on to the *St. Petersburg Times*, Bragg covered Hurricane Andrew, problems in Haiti, and riots in Miami before spending a year at Harvard University on a Nieman fellowship. Subsequently, he joined the *New York Times*, covering the Susan Smith child murders and the U.S. intervention in Haiti.

In 1996 Bragg's coverage of the Oklahoma City bombing earned him the Pulitzer Prize. He brought his mother to New York City by plane for the awards ceremony; she had not only never been on a plane, or on an escalator, or in New York, but she had not bought a new dress in eighteen years. Bragg describes the prize ceremony in *All Over but the Shoutin'* and the scene is, according to Diane Hartman in the *Denver Post*, "the best in the book." Bragg also memorably recounts his cash purchase, with his prize money and book profits, of a new house for his mother. *Seattle Times* contributor Chris Solomon concluded that *All Over but the Shoutin'* is a "well-received effort to enshrine a saint (his mother), exorcise a demon (his father) and tell his own Horatio Alger story."

Many reviewers have praised Bragg's gripping real-life story, though the enthusiasm has been tempered by some of the story's psychological residue. For Hartman a maudlin tone, born of "survivor's guilt," enters the writing at points—"but Bragg is good and there's no denying it," she concluded. A writer for *Library Journal* recommended *All Over but the Shoutin'* highly for its "honest but unsentimental" style, its "plainspoken and lyrical" effects, and its "telling" details. A *Publishers Weekly* contributor, however, called the book "uneven" and "jolting," referring to it as "a mixture of

moving anecdotes and almost masochistic self-analysis" but nonetheless praising Bragg's "gift for language." Similar admiration was expressed by *Times Literary Supplement* reviewer Charles McNair, who considered the memoir a "heartbreaking, inspiring account" that "is no sentimental, soft-lens nostalgic piece, but an uncomfortably honest portrait of growing up with less than nothing, a memoir fraught with sharp edges and hard truths."

Bragg's prequel to *All Over but the Shoutin'*, titled *Ava's Man*, is, as he told *Book* writer Anthony DeCurtis, a "necessary response to his readers' righteous demands" after reading *All Over but the Shoutin'*. In this book he tells the story of his maternal grandparents, Ava and Charlie Bundrum. Because he knew few details about the lives of his grandparents, he had to reconstruct the story from an oral history he collected from his mother, aunts and uncles, and other family members and friends. These friends and relatives had rich tales to tell about Charlie Bundrum, a man who was much loved and admired. Bragg had never met his grandfather, as he died the year before Bragg's birth, but he did rely on his own recollections of his grandmother Ava, who lived on thirty-six years after her husband's death.

Charlie Bundrum raised his family in the Deep South during the heart of the economic depression of the 1930s, and moved his wife and eight children twenty-one times, determined to do whatever it took to keep his family fed and safe. Bundrum worked as a roofer and general laborer, as well as a bootlegger, for most of his life. While he developed a taste for the illegal corn liquor, which eventually killed him at a young age, he never let alcohol run his life. Bragg depicts his grandfather, in DeCurtis's words, as "a moonshine maker who worked hard and fiercely protected his family; loved to fight, fish, and tell stories, and cared little for any law but the unspoken, unquestioned code of his community."

At one point in Bragg's story, Bundrum gets arrested for vagrancy, based on his appearance, while trying to get home from a fishing trip. This was not an uncommon experience for poor white men living in Appalachia during the 1940s. Anthony Day in the *Los Angeles Times* pointed out that Bragg is one of the first authors to tell the story of poor whites in the south from an insider's perspective, and noted that Bragg writes "honestly and affectionately" regarding this topic. Robert Morgan, in the *New York Times Book Review*, acknowledged that "relatively few authors have truly caught the voice of the Southern working class," and in *Ava's Man* the characters and setting "grab you from the first sentence." Morgan went on to call *Ava's Man* "a kind of sublime testimonial" and added: "Bragg gets the combination of sentiment and independence and fear in this culture just right."

For Bragg, writing *Ava's Man* was an opportunity to acquaint himself with the grandfather he never knew and to build a monument to this beloved man. Though *Orlando Sentinel* writer John Harper found the book "structurally weak," a reviewer for *Publishers Weekly* reported that "Bragg delivers, with deep affection, fierce familial pride, and keen, vivid prose."

In 2003 Bragg was selected by Knopf to write the story of one of the first women to be injured in active duty while serving in the U.S. military. Discussing *I Am a Soldier, Too: The Jessica Lynch Story* with *Publishers Weekly* interviewer Charlotte Abbot, Bragg noted that the appeal of writing the book lay primarily in the "wonderful story" Lynch, a soldier fighting in the War on Terror in Iraq, has to tell. "What happened was unexpected: a nineteen-year-old supply clerk was pressed into driving a truck into a war. It was an unscripted drama. Some people died, others got broken. But at least where Jessie is concerned there's a win. I've written so many stories where there wasn't a win. . . . Jessie wanted to see what was 'on the other side of the holler.' These are people who fight and die and serve their country, and they deserve some good attention, something beyond the sneers of intellectuals."

BIOGRAPHICAL AND CRITICAL SOURCES:

BOOKS

Bragg, Rick, *All Over but the Shoutin'*, Pantheon (New York, NY), 1997.

PERIODICALS

Book, September, 2001, Anthony DeCurtis, "Southern Grit," p. 53.
Booklist, September 15, 1997, p. 182; June 1, 2001, Joanne Wilkinson, review of *Ava's Man,* p. 1795.
Denver Post, October 5, 1997, Diane Hartman, review of *All Over but the Shoutin'*.
Entertainment Weekly, November 21, 2003, Tina Jordan, review of *I Am a Soldier, Too: The Jessica Lynch Story,* p 88.

Geographical, September, 1999, Chris Martin, review of *Redbirds: Memories from the South,* p. 71.
Kliatt, January, 1999, review of *All Over but the Shoutin',* p. 23.
Library Journal, September 15, 1997, p. 81; January 5, 1998; September 1, 1999, Russell T. Clement, review of *Wooden Churches: A Celebration,* p. 186; November 15, 1999, review of *All Over but the Shoutin',* p. 115; May 1, 2000, Pam Kingsbury, review of *Somebody Told Me: The Newspaper Stories of Rick Bragg,* p. 128; June 15, 2001, Pam Kingsbury, review of *Ava's Man,* p. 81; September 1, 2001, Pam Kingsbury, "Building Himself a Grandfather," p. 194.
Los Angeles Times, October 12, 2001, Anthony Day, "An Affectionate Portrait of the South's Poor, Hard-Living Whites," p. E3.
Mississippi Quarterly, winter, 1999, Amy E. Weldon, "When Fantasy Meant Survival," p. 89.
New York Times, September 10, 2001, Theodore Rosengarten, "Hammer-Swinging Roofer, Not a Hillbilly, in Appalachia," p. E6.
New York Times Book Review, June 25, 2000, Ruth Bayard Smith, review of *Somebody Told Me;* September 2, 2001, Robert Morgan, review of *Ava's Man,* p. 9.
Orlando Sentinel, September 19, 2001, John Harper, review of *Ava's Man*.
Publishers Weekly, July 14, 1997, p. 73; August 6, 2001, review of *Ava's Man,* p. 74; September 8, 2003, Charlotte Abbot, "Bragg: Lynch Has a 'Wonderful Story to Tell,'" p. 16.
Rapport, May, 1999, review of *All Over but the Shoutin',* p. 39.
San Francisco Chronicle, September 16, 2001, review of *Ava's Man,* p. 68.
Sarasota Herald Tribune, November 5, 2000, Thomas Becnel, "Bragg Shares What *Somebody Told Me,*" p. E5; November 4, 2001, Susan L. Rife, "Bragg's Portrait of Grandfather Is Revealing and Very Human," p. E5.
Seattle Times, October 30, 1997, Chris Solomon, review of *All Over but the Shoutin'*.
Times Literary Supplement, October 16, 1998, Charles McNair, "The Struggle So Far," p. 34.
Washington Post, August 19, 2001, Fred Chappell, "Hardscrabble," p. T4.

*   *   *

BRASHARES, Ann 1967-

PERSONAL: Born 1967, in Chevy Chase, MD; married Jacob Collins (an artist); children: Sam, Nathaniel, Susannah. *Education:* Graduated from Barnard College.

ADDRESSES: Home—Brooklyn, NY. *Agent*—c/o Author Mail, Delacorte Press, 1540 Broadway, New York, NY 10036.

CAREER: Writer and editor.

AWARDS, HONORS: Best Book for Young Adults citation, American Library Association, and Book Sense Book of the Year, both 2002, both for *The Sisterhood of the Traveling Pants.*

WRITINGS:

The Sisterhood of the Traveling Pants (young adult novel), Delacorte (New York, NY), 2001.
Linus Torvalds: Software Rebel (nonfiction; *"Techies"* series), Twenty-first Century Books (Brookfield, CT), 2001.
Steve Jobs: Think Different (nonfiction; *"Techies"* series), Twenty-first Century Books (Brookfield, CT), 2001.
The Second Summer of the Sisterhood (young adult novel), Delacorte (New York, NY), 2003.
Girls in Pants: The Third Summer of the Sisterhood (young adult novel), Delacorte (New York, NY), 2005.
Keep in Touch: Letters, Notes, and More from The Sisterhood of the Traveling Pants (young adult novel), Delacorte (New York, NY), 2005.
The Sisterhood of the Traveling Pants: The Official Scrapbook, Delacorte (New York, NY), 2005.

ADAPTATIONS: The Sisterhood of the Traveling Pants was adapted for audiocassette by Listening Library, 2002, and adapted for a film directed by Ken Kwapis and released by Warner Brothers, 2005.

SIDELIGHTS: Rule number one: "You must never wash the pants." Rule number two: "You must never double cuff the pants. It's tacky." Thus begin the ten commandments of *The Sisterhood of the Traveling Pants,* a young adult novel penned by first-time novelist Ann Brashares and published in 2001. Rule number ten: "Remember: Pants equal Love. Love your pals. Love yourself." If there is a message in this "feel-good novel with substance," as a critic for *Kirkus Reviews* called the book, it is found in that final rule.

Long-time editor Brashares posits a new kind of sisterhood in her debut fiction bestseller, introducing four teenage girls who agree to send a pair of secondhand jeans from friend to friend the first summer they are to be separated. These traveling pants thus take on a metaphoric quality, uniting the best friends across the thousands of miles separating them.

Brashares, one of four children, grew up in Chevy Chase, Maryland, a very "Plain Jane" sort of place, as she noted in an autobiographical sketch on the Random House Web site. She and her three brothers attended Sidwell Friends, a Quaker school near Washington, DC, and she was an avid reader, enjoying the works of Jane Austen, Charles Dickens, and other nineteenth-century writers. "When I was a kid, I had a scrapbook that I used to write letters in from places I wished I could have gone," Brashares noted on the Random House Web site. "I would imagine being in Argentina and then write about all the incredible things I was seeing there." Attending Barnard College, Brashares majored in philosophy and also met her future husband, artist Jacob Collins.

After graduation, Brashares took a year off before graduate school, planning to save money to pay for tuition. However, the job she took, working as an editor, was such a good fit that she never returned to school and instead made her career in publishing, working in children's books.

As an extension of her editorial work, Brashares gained authorial experience on two nonfiction titles, both published in 2001: *Steve Jobs: Think Different* and *Linus Torvalds: Software Rebel.* These books, Brashares related to Dave Weich in a *Powells.com* interview, "came out of an editing project." Brashares further explained, "I hadn't at any point considered myself an author of nonfiction. It was more a question of who was going to write those books, and I decided to try it. I was wearing a certain hat to do that project, and it was really fun, but I was functioning more as an editor, trying to come up with ideas for children's projects." Part of the "Techies" series for Twenty-first Century Books, Brashares's two nonfiction titles detail in brief format the lives of two computer and software pioneers.

Steve Jobs is a child of the 1960s who has become one of the most successful businessmen in the world, his name synonymous with Apple computers and Macintosh. Brashares traces Jobs's life from his youth traveling around the world in search of himself to his collaboration with Steve Wozniak during which the two made prototype PC's in a garage, to his departure and triumphant return to head Apple Computers. Linus Torvalds is the Finnish mastermind behind the open-source operating system known as Linux. His teamwork approach to programming and the free access he allows to his operating system have caused a revolution in computing. Reviewing *Steve Jobs* in *Voice of Youth Advocates,* Susan H. Levine praised the "breezy style, short length, large font, numerous photographs, and attractive page design" of the series. Similarly, Yapha Nussbaum Mason, writing in *School Library Journal,* found *Linus Torvalds* to be "fairly short and definitely accessible," with "appeal not only to report writers, but also to recreational readers."

While her nonfiction titles proved successful, Brashares always had the desire to write fiction. When she heard an appealing story about a traveling pair of pants, she saw the germ of an idea for a quirky novel. A woman Brashares worked with told her the story of one summer when she and her friends shared a pair of pants. Unfortunately, the pants were ultimately lost in Borneo. "My mind was immediately filled with all sorts of wonderful possibilities," Brashares noted on the Random House Web site. "I think pants have unique qualities, especially in a woman's life. Whatever bodily insecurities we have, we seem to take out on our pants. In high school, my friends would have their skinny pants and their fat pants. I like pants that allow women not to judge their bodies."

Brashares had also had another experience with shared clothing, as she recalled on the *BookBrowse* Web site. When she was planning her marriage, the sister of a friend offered her own bridal gown. Brashares at first turned down the offer, especially as the woman's own marriage had not been successful. Besides, she had envisioned the perfect gown for her and she was determined to find it. Then one night, this persistent donor came by with the wedding dress and Brashares discovered it was the exact dress she had been dreaming of. She wore it at her own wedding, and subsequently loaned it to other friends, creating a sort of "bond of the bridal gown." Taking these experiences together, as well as some of her own teenage angst and problems, Brashares came up with a fictional pair of pants that fit every body type and make the wearer feel loved. Brashares worked up a cast of characters to wear her magic pants, and an outline—a mixture of Greek myth and themes from movies such as *It's a Wonderful Life*—and then took the project to Random House, whose editors liked the idea.

The resulting book recounts the adventures of a group of girls who one summer decide to share a pair of jeans as a way of keeping their friendship alive. Carmen,

Lena, Bridget, and Tibby are fifteen and have been best friends since childhood. Their mothers became friends when they enrolled in the same aerobics class together, and the four girls subsequently became bosom buddies, meeting periodically in the gym where their mothers had their classes. In the summer featured in *The Sisterhood of the Traveling Pants,* the friends will be separated for the first time: Carmen is planning to go to South Carolina and visit her divorced father; Lena is off to Greece to be with her grandparents; Bridget will be working out at a soccer camp in Baja California; and Tibby will stay at home in Washington, DC, working in the local Wallman's drugstore. Before departure, Carmen has purchased a pair of jeans at a local thrift shop for less than four dollars. She decides to toss them, but when Tibby sees them she thinks she'd like them. Lena and Bridget also think they are fabulous. All the friends try on the pants, and they fit each in turn, even Carmen, who thinks she never looks good in anything. The friends decide these must be magic pants, for each of them has a distinctly different body type from the other girls. The night before departure they form the Sisterhood of the Traveling Pants, agreeing to a set of rules and behavior regarding the pants. (Rule number 4: "You must never let a boy take off the pants (although you may take them off yourself in his presence.") Each friend will wear the pants for a week, and then send them on to the next wearer. The pants become a link between the members of the sisterhood.

If the pants seemed magical at first, the four girls soon realize they can not help them solve the problems each encounters that summer; such solutions must come from inner understanding. The pants, however, serve as a reminder that none of the friends are alone. Each learns to deal with individual problems and learn some elemental life lessons. Carmen's dream of spending time alone with her dad is thwarted when she discovers he is on the verge of marrying into a brand new family in South Carolina. Lena in Greece falls for Kostos, a family friend, but their relationship becomes marred when she accuses him, mistakenly, of spying on her while she is skinny dipping. Bridget also has romantic problems, falling in love with one of the counselors, something that is definitely off-limits at the camp. And Tibby, who has stayed home, becomes friends with a young girl, Bailey, who is suffering from leukemia. Together these two are making a documentary film about odd but interesting people, but when Bailey becomes so ill that she must go to the hospital, Tibby is confronted with the specter of death for the first time.

The pants connect the four friends, but they are not magic after all. "The pants are just pants," wrote Frances Bradburn in *Booklist,* "and life is just life, full of joys, sorrows, living, and dying. This is the charm of *The Sisterhood of the Traveling Pants*." Brashares' unique coming-of-age novel won further critical praise from *New York Times* reviewer Christine Leahy, who called the characters "winning and precocious" and praised the narrative pace, noting that the "story zips along, bouncing faster than the jeans from girl to girl." Linda Bindner, reviewing the title in *School Library Journal,* also lauded Brashares's story-telling skills, re-marking that the author "deftly moves from narrative to narrative, weaving together themes from the mundane to the profoundly important." Bindner further felt that Brashares created a "complex book about a solid group of friends." A contributor for *Kirkus Reviews* found that Brashares "renders each girl individual and lovable in her own right," while in *Horn Book,* Jennifer M. Bra-bander praised the life lessons learned in this "breezy feel-good book." Reviewing the novel in *Voice of Youth Advocates,* teen critic Deana Rutherford mentioned that *The Sisterhood of the Traveling Pants* is "enjoyable and meaningful at the same time, and that's sometimes a hard thing to find in YA literature." James Blasingame, writing in *Journal of Adolescent and Adult Literacy,* echoed something the book's sales figures had already established: "Ann Brashares's first fiction attempt is a successful one."

As Brashares noted on the Random House Web site, the characters in her book grew out of different parts of her own personality. "Carmen was the girl who said things I could never say and Bridget was the girl who did things I would never do." Speaking with Weich, Brashares also noted that she wanted to use the idea of the pants as a "repository of friendship—love, hope, challenges, all of those things." She also remarked to Weich that stay-at-home Tibby is the one who seems to grow and learn the most about herself during this one turbulent summer. "She's the one who's shaken up the most," Brashares commented. "The idea that that can happen at home was something I wanted to present." Brashares, the mother of three, has her own favorite pants: red ones that "make me feel loved even through major body transitions (like having a baby!)," as she re-marked on the Random House site.

In a review of *The Sisterhood of the Traveling Pants,* a critic for *Publishers Weekly* called Brashares's novel an "outstanding and vivid book that will stay with readers for a long time." The same reviewer also noted that readers "will hope that Brashares chronicles the sister-hood for volumes to come." Brashares did exactly that, with the 2003 sequel, *The Second Summer of the Sister-hood.* In this take, the four girls are sixteen, and Bridget takes off for Alabama, Lena spends time with Kostos,

Carmen is afraid her mother is going to make a fool of herself over a man, and Tibby takes a film course in-stead of spending another summer at Wallman's. Writ-ing in *Horn Book,* Brabander suggested that "Fans of the first book . . . will eagerly travel with the sister-hood again." Offering warm words for the author's abil-ity to present a realistic, "hopeful book, easy to read and gentle in its important lessons," *Booklist* critic Brad-burn predicted that "readers will want" the girls to re-turn for another season of shared sisterhood.

Like Brashares's earlier title, *The Second Summer of the Sisterhood* takes a lighthearted look at serious top-ics. "I feel as though there are a lot of books trying very hard to deal with social issues—illness or social ills, all kinds of shocking things—and in some part of my mind I knew that I didn't want to do that," the au-thor told Weich. "I wanted to write a book that wasn't insubstantial but wasn't really issues-driven, either. I hope I did that." Writing on the Random House site, Brashares concluded about her "Sisterhood" books that she hopes they are the sort to "stick with [readers] a bit, the way books I liked when I was that age stuck with me. If there's a message, I guess it's just this: love yourself and your friends unconditionally."

The four friends—Tibby, Bee, Lena and Carmen—team up for a third adventure in the 2005 *Girls in Pants: The Third Summer of the Sisterhood.* The book unfolds over the course of the summer following their graduation from high school and before they all go off to different colleges. Claire Rosser, reviewing this installment in *Kliatt,* noted the "bittersweet quality" to the novel be-cause of this imminent separation. The magical pair of pants takes a lesser role in this tale, as each of the young women prepares to go out into the world. Rosser went on to praise the "absolutely believable characters" in this "delightful series." Reviewing the audiobook version of this novel in *Booklist,* Jean Hatfield felt that despite the lesser role the traveling pants play in this title, the "strong bonds of love and friendship remain intact" between each of the girls.

Following a 2005 movie adaptation, Brashares furthered her series with a tie-in, *The Sisterhood of the Traveling Pants: The Official Scrapbook,* filled with stills from the movie and sections of the filming storyboard and production diary. Brashares shared some of the secret of her literary success in an interview for *Writer:* "Don't think of yourself as a young-adult writer. Think of your-self as a writer writing about characters who are teenag-ers (or thereabout)."

BIOGRAPHICAL AND CRITICAL SOURCES:

BOOKS

Brashares, Ann, *The Sisterhood of the Traveling Pants,* Delacorte (New York, NY), 2001.

PERIODICALS

Booklist, August, 2001, Frances Bradburn, review of *The Sisterhood of the Traveling Pants,* p. 2106; January 1, 2002, review of *The Sisterhood of the Traveling Pants,* p. 764; April 15, 2003, Frances Bradburn, review of *The Second Summer of the Sisterhood,* p. 1461; May 1, 2005, Jean Hatfield, review of *Girls in Pants: The Third Summer of the Sisterhood* (audiobook), p. 1598.

Bookseller, March 15, 2002, Jennifer Taylor, "Strong Contenders," p. S31.

Horn Book, November-December, 2001, Jennifer M. Brabander, review of *The Sisterhood of the Traveling Pants,* pp. 741-742; May-June, 2002, Kristi Beavin, review of *The Sisterhood of the Traveling Pants* (audiobook), p. 353; May-June, 2003, Jennifer M. Brabander, review of *The Second Summer of the Sisterhood,* p. 339.

Journal of Adolescent and Adult Literacy, September, 2002, James Blasingame, review of *The Sisterhood of the Traveling Pants,* pp. 87-88.

Kirkus Reviews, August 1, 2001, review of *The Sisterhood of the Traveling Pants,* p. 1117; July, 2002, Barbara Baskin, review of *The Sisterhood of the Traveling Pants* (audiobook), pp. 1866-1867.

Kliatt, January, 2005, Claire Rosser, review of *Girls in Pants,* p. 6.

New York Times, March 10, 2002, Christine Leahy, review of *The Sisterhood of the Traveling Pants,* p. 7.

Publishers Weekly, July 16, 2001, review of *The Sisterhood of the Traveling Pants,* p. 182; October 15, 2001, review of *The Sisterhood of the Traveling Pants* (audiobook), p. 26; December 24, 2001, Diane Roback, "Flying Starts," p. 30; March 25, 2002, Daisy Maryles, "A YA Debut Makes Five," p. 18; September 30, 2002, "Have Pants, Will Travel," p. 30; March 3, 2003, review of *The Second Summer of the Sisterhood,* p. 77; May 9, 2005, "Nice Threads!," review of *The Sisterhood of the Traveling Pants: The Official Scrapbook,* p. 73; May 30, 2005, Diane Roback, "Children's Series and Tie-ins Bestsellers," p. 22.

School Library Journal, August, 2001, Linda Bindner, review of *The Sisterhood of the Traveling Pants,* p. 175; December, 2001, Yapha Nussbaum Mason, review of *Linus Torvalds: Software Rebel,* p. 153; May, 2003, Susan W. Hunter, review of *The Second Summer of Sisterhood,* p. 144.

U.S. News and World Report, May 12, 2003, Holly J. Morris, "Flying by the Seat of Her Pants," p. 8.

Voice of Youth Advocates, August, 2001, Susan H. Levine, review of *Steve Jobs: Think Different;* October, 2001, Deana Rutherford, review of *The Sisterhood of the Traveling Pants.*

Women's Wear Daily, June 6, 2002, Scott Malone and Julee Greenberg, "Denim Dish," p. 9.

Writer, July, 2005, "Ann Brashares Interview," p. 66.

Writing!, January, 2005, "Pf Pants and Pens: A Chat with Ann Brashares," p. 4.

ONLINE

BookBrowse, http://www.bookbrowse.com/ (February 2, 2003), "Ann Brashares."

Powells.com, http://www.powells.com/ (September 7, 2001), Dave Weich, "Author Interviews: Ann Brashares Embarks into Fiction."

Random House Web site, http://www.randomhouse.com/ (February 2, 2003), "Teens@Random: Talking with Ann Brashares about the Sisterhood."

*   *   *

BRESLIN, James
See BRESLIN, Jimmy

*   *   *

BRESLIN, Jimmy 1930-
(James Breslin)

PERSONAL: Born October 17, 1930, in Jamaica, NY; son of James Earl and Frances (a high school teacher and social worker; maiden name, Curtin) Breslin; married Rosemary Dattolico, December 26, 1954 (died, June, 1981); married Ronnie Myers Eldridge (an executive), September 12, 1982; children: (first marriage) James and Kevin (twins), Rosemary, Patrick, Kelly, Christopher; (stepchildren) Daniel, Emily, Lucy Eldridge. *Education:* Attended Long Island University, 1948-50.

ADDRESSES: Office—New York Newsday, 2 Park Ave., New York, NY 10016-5603. *Agent*—Joan Brandt, Sterling Lord Literistic, Inc., 65 Bleecker St., New York, NY 10012-2420.

CAREER: Worked as a copyboy at *Long Island Press,* 1948; sportswriter for several newspapers, including *New York Journal-American,* all in New York, NY, 1950-63; *New York Herald Tribune* (later *New York World Journal Tribune*), New York, NY, began as sportswriter, became columnist, 1963-67; *New York Post,* New York, NY, columnist, 1968-69; author and freelance journalist in New York, NY, 1969—; *New York Daily News,* New York, NY, columnist, 1978-88; *Newsday,* Long Island, NY, columnist, 1988—. Syndicated columnist for *Newsday,* Long Island, NY, *New York Daily News, New York Herald-Tribune,* and *Paris Tribune.* Contributing editor and initiating writer, *New York* magazine, 1968-71, *New Times* magazine, 1973. Commentator, WABC-TV, 1968-69, WNBC-TV, 1973. Host of *Jimmy Breslin's People,* ABC-TV, 1987. Actor in television programs, commercials, and feature film *If Ever I See You Again.* Democratic primary candidate for president of New York City council, 1969; delegate to Democratic National Convention, 1972.

MEMBER: Writers Guild of America, Screen Actors Guild, American Federation of Television and Radio Artists, New York Boxing Writers Association.

AWARDS, HONORS: Best Sports Stories Award, E.P. Dutton & Co., 1961, for magazine piece "Racing's Angriest Young Man"; award for general reporting, Sigma Delta Chi, and Meyer Barger Award, Columbia University, both 1964, both for article on the death of President John F. Kennedy; New York Reporters Association Award, 1964; Pulitzer Prize and George Polk Award, both 1986, both for collected newspaper columns; American Society of Newspaper Editors award, 1988, for commentary-column writing.

WRITINGS:

Sunny Jim: The Life of America's Most Beloved Horseman, James Fitzsimmons (nonfiction), Doubleday (New York, NY), 1962.
Can't Anybody Here Play This Game? (nonfiction), edited by Dick Schapp, Viking (New York, NY), 1963, with introduction by Bill Veeck, Ivan R. Dee (Chicago, IL), 2003.
The World of Jimmy Breslin (collected articles), annotated by James G. Bellows and Richard C. Wald, Viking (New York, NY), 1967.
The Gang That Couldn't Shoot Straight (novel), Viking (New York, NY), 1969.
(With Norman Mailer, Peter Maas, Gloria Steinem, and others) *Running against the Machine: The Mailer-Breslin Campaign* (collected speeches, policy statements, interviews, etc.), edited by Peter Manso, Doubleday (New York, NY), 1970.

World without End, Amen (novel) Viking (New York, NY), 1973.
How the Good Guys Finally Won: Notes from an Impeachment Summer (nonfiction), Viking (New York, NY), 1975.
(With Dick Schaap) *.44* (novel), Viking (New York, NY), 1978.
Forsaking All Others (novel), Simon & Schuster (New York, NY), 1982.
The World according to Breslin (collected columns), annotated by Michael J. O'Neill and William Brink, Ticknor & Fields (New York, NY), 1984.
Collection of Daily News Columns, Viking (New York, NY), 1986.
Table Money (novel), Ticknor & Fields (New York, NY), 1987.
He Got Hungry and Forgot His Manners (novel), Ticknor & Fields (New York, NY), 1987.
Damon Runyon, Ticknor & Fields (New York, NY), 1991.
A Slight Case of Amazing Grace: A Memoir, Little, Brown (Boston, MA), 1996.
I Want to Thank My Brain for Remembering Me: A Memoir, Little, Brown (Boston, MA), 1996.
I Don't Want to Go to Jail, Little, Brown (Boston, MA), 2001.
The Short Sweet Dream of Eduardo Gutierrez (biography), Crown (New York, NY), 2002.
The Church That Forgot Christ, Free Press (New York, NY), 2004.

Contributor to numerous newspapers and magazines, including *Penthouse, Sports Illustrated, Saturday Evening Post, Time,* and *New York.*

ADAPTATIONS: The Gang That Couldn't Shoot Straight was adapted into a feature film.

SIDELIGHTS: For more than two decades, Jimmy Breslin has provided the literary voice for a group that for many years had none: that of the Irish-American working class from New York's Queens neighborhoods, where Breslin himself grew up. As novelist and columnist for various New York newspapers, Breslin encompasses the "New Journalism" ideals that originated in the 1970s, wherein the writer, far from distancing himself from his subject, instead becomes passionately and personally involved in the story. And so Breslin wrote about politics by throwing himself into the political arena in 1969 by running—unsuccessfully—for president of the New York City council under mayoral candidate Norman Mailer. Their platform was to make New York City America's fifty-first state. In 1977 Breslin gained celebrity for a less-humorous reason when accused "Son-of-Sam" serial murderer David Berkowitz made the columnist the sole recipient of letters sent periodically while officials were combing the city for the killer.

A former sportswriter, Breslin uses the native poetry of the street to make his points. His columns often defend the ordinary man against the bureaucracies of government and industry. Breslin "seems to play by different rules than most reporters, which is probably why it took the Pulitzer committee so long to honor him," noted Jonathan Alter in a 1986 *Newsweek* article published just after the Pulitzer prize panel finally awarded the writer. "For years Breslin's fabled ear for dialogue has struck some colleagues as a bit *too* good, too epigrammatic for the way people really speak between quotation marks," Alter continued. To this charge Breslin responds in the *Newsweek* piece that other reporters "take a cop on the beat and make him sound like he's the under secretary of state. *They're* the ones who make up quotes."

The Gang That Couldn't Shoot Straight, the book that marked Breslin's move into fiction, disappointed some critics with what they saw as stereotypical portrayals of comic hoodlums on the make. Thomas Meehan of the *New York Times,* for example, while noting that the book "may be the best first novel written all year by a defeated candidate for President of the City Council," found that Breslin's humor comes mostly from "mayhem—funny, perhaps, to those capable of getting a laugh out of someone being blown up, garroted, or pitched headfirst off a bridge." Though *New York Times Book Review* critic Christopher Lehmann-Haupt was similarly unimpressed overall with *The Gang That Couldn't Shoot Straight,* he shared Meehan's view that Breslin does touch the book with sharply satirical jabs at New York City. "Indeed, the best parts of the novel (and Breslin addicts should agree) are such throwaway details [as Breslin provides]," added Meehan, "again, the sort of thing this author does so well in his magazine and newspaper pieces."

Breslin took account of his own background for his next novel, *World without End, Amen,* the tale of a New York cop of Irish extraction whose racist views and weary existence are challenged when he takes a trip to his mother country and witnesses "The Troubles" ongoing between Catholic and Protestant Irish. "Because [protagonist Dermot Davey's] life is coming apart, the reader might well expect that his visit to the land of his forebears will open up new vistas, not only of social

conscience but of meaning, and that the ruined cop will somehow find himself quixotically in the cause of the Irish Republic," wrote *Washington Post Book World* reviewer Richard Brown. "This is not the author's intent, however, and except for a moving encounter between father and son in a bar in Derry, . . . the found father is of little significance, and the idea of Ireland as homeland is of even less." In the opinion of *Commentary* critic Dorothy Rabinowitz, "There is no hope for the Dermots and their families, Breslin wishes to teach us—not because they are poor or uncultured or incurious (for so are their kin in Ulster), but because they are political reactionaries. That so much of life's worth should be thought to depend on a certain politics might be thought extraordinary in another time than ours. Yet this is a cornerstone of belief for Breslin, as it is for the sensibility he represents."

Harvey Gardner, writing in the *New York Times Book Review,* found a split in the quality of *World without End, Amen.* "In a skillful Breslin style the first third of the book draws the picture of Dermot and the cop world he knows. There is a great deal of grim humor, and where humor fails, one sees a satisfaction in showing succinctly the causes of human inadequacy." However, added Gardner, when the action moves to Northern Ireland, the "New York idiom" Breslin employs "often seems inappropriate. That is something one does not like to say of a writer so much to be valued for his rightness about things on his own turf." A *Times Literary Supplement* reviewer offered a different point of view when he stated: "If the story were merely a moral tale of a victor humanized by being made a victim, it would have little to offer but the pleasure afforded by a just come-uppance. Beyond that, though, *World without End, Amen* is memorable for being an account of Northern Ireland by a thuggish but not wholly unfeeling character who cannot work out whether he is a foreigner, or a stranger, or both, or neither. It is a confusion probably shared by half the people in Britain."

Breslins' 1986 book, *Table Money,* drew cheers as an insightful look at the lives of working-class "sandhogs," the men who dig the vast tunnels that bring water to New York City. Breslin traces the generations of one family of sandhogs, the Morrisons, back to the first immigrant from Ireland in the nineteenth century. But by 1970, when the novel takes place, the latest Morrison man, Owney, newly returned from Vietnam with a Medal of Honor, becomes plagued by self-doubt when his wife Dolores decides to better their station in life by attending medical school. George James, writing in the *New York Times Book Review,* expressed surprise that "the blue-collar bard of the Borough of Queens [would write] a strongly feminist novel," but Breslin's depiction of the strong-willed Dolores, who forges ahead while her husband slips into obscurity, does not surprise her creator. As Breslin told James, *Table Money* was written during a time in his life when "my wife contracted an illness and I wound up for some time taking care of the house [and six children] and getting closer to a woman than I ever had been before—unfortunately so, in illness. I came out of it with a lot of wreckage in my hands, but I learned from it."

Breslin followed *Table Money* with another novel, *He Got Hungry and Forgot His Manners,* which did not receive as much attention, partly because the "deep, bitter, almost Kafkaesque satire," as Lehmann-Haupt called it in a *New York Times* review, did not appeal to as wide an audience. *He Got Hungry and Forgot His Manners* is a tall tale involving events surrounding the controversial racial attacks that occurred at Howard Beach, Queens, in 1986. D'Arcy Cosgrove, a priest dispatched by order of the Vatican to the borough in response to the attacks, believes the incident was sexually motivated. Described in the novel as "a man bristling with celibacy," Cosgrove arrives in Queens accompanied by a seven-foot-tall African cannibal whose idiosyncratic eating habits accounts for the novel's title. To *Time*'s R.Z. Sheppard, "Cosgrove and his giant sidekick are farcical figures meant to illustrate the failures of both church and state when dealing with morality and poverty. . . . The kinks in New York's welfare bureaucracy are authentic and darkly humorous, but the black characters are not developed beyond their jive. Father D'Arcy's mission is unfocused, his misadventures are a blur, and his conversion from guardian of orthodoxy to radical activist unbelievable, even for farce." Lehmann-Haupt also found faults in Breslin's style, but added that "it is easiest to get through such [rough] patches by thinking of the novel as a high-speed animated cartoon."

In his 2001 novel, *I Don't Want to Go to Jail,* Breslin presents a mafia spoof of a mobster and his family and one member, young Fausti, who is trying to stay straight despite a family full of tough guys, including an uncle, Fausti "The Fist" Dellacava, who walks around in a pajamas and robe and megadoses on Thorazine. The novel parallels the decline of the older Fausti and the nephew's trials and tribulations as he tries to establish a life outside of the mob. A *Publishers Weekly* contributor noted that "The lack of narrative structure makes this book a sticky read, but Breslin knows his subject and provides enough entertainment to justify wading through the slow spots." Paul Evans, writing in *Book,*

praised *I Don't Want to Go to Jail,* commenting, "Speedy, sharp and funny, the book lambastes the good-fellas myth by showing how tawdry a bunch these bad guys are."

The Short Sweet Dream of Eduardo Gutierrez, published in 2002, is a biography of a twenty-one-year-old illegal Mexican immigrant who was working in construction in Brooklyn when an accident caused him to drown in a pool of concrete. Writing in the *Library Journal,* Elaine Machleder noted that "author Breslin . . . gives voice and respect to the powerless like Gutierrez." In the book, Breslin recounts the itinerant worker's life, both in Mexico and America, giving the reader a look at the tough and lonely life shared by many immigrant workers. He also looks into the seamy side of builders, employers, and bureaucrats whose actions, according to the journalist, all contributed to the Guiterrez's death. "For Breslin, Gutierrez's story not only typifies the hardships that Mexican migrants face in coming north but shows how harsh the working conditions are when they arrive," wrote Theodore Hamm in the *Nation.* Evans, writing in *Book,* called the book "riveting" and noted that "the author lays bare a political tragedy—here, the heedless U.S. immigration policy and its human cost." In an interview with Edward Nawotka of *Publishers Weekly,* Breslin commented on what Gutierrez represented to him, noting, "Now we just use cheap labor and people make money on their backs, not caring about them at all. When you bring this up in Washington—immigration—all they ever talk about is shooting them, putting up border controls and fences. Then they come up with schemes: guest workers. You're not going to get bothered by Immigration, but you can't join a union. They're not going to get more money. They're getting nothing! I'm writing about the afflicted."

Breslin continued his look at the powerful and how they abuse the peoples' trust with his next book, *The Church That Forgot Christ.* Outraged by the sex-abuse scandals that emerged concerning the Catholic church, Breslin, a life-long Roman Catholic, severed his ties to the church because he could not reconcile his faith with the efforts of the Catholic hierarchy to cover up repeated scandals. When asked why he wrote the book, Breslin told Dermont McEvoy of *Publishers Weekly* that, after talking to many people within the church, he concluded, "They've done nothing. They don't care about America and that's what it comes down to. They don't care at all." While Breslin condemns the church, he distinguishes between the "Church" and the Catholic religion, viewing the situation through the eyes of victims, perpetrators, and the scores of true believers who, like Breslin, also found themselves struggling with the gap between the ideal and the reality. In addition to pointing out the faults and corruption in the Catholic Church, Breslin also discusses a renewed church that would include such changes as married priests and female priests. A *Publishers Weekly* contributor noted that Breslin not only points out the bad but also shows those in the church who have been truly dedicated to helping their parishioners, noting that "he draws wonderful portraits of dedicated clerics." Writing in *Booklist*, Margaret Flanagan commented that Breslin's "soul-wrenching denunciation should make American Catholics sit up, take notice, and begin debating."

In his nonwriting life, Breslin has enjoyed a longtime reputation as an iconoclast. Most notably, he has a unique, and personal, style of giving notice to quit: He puts out ads in the *New York Times* and posts signs on his front lawn. For instance, when in 1986 his television talk show, *Jimmy Breslin's People,* was juggled around the late-night schedule by its network, ABC, and then unceremoniously deposited in the undesirable time-slot of 1:30 a.m., Breslin paid for a front-page *New York Times* ad stating, "ABC Television Network, your services, such as they are, will no longer be required as of 12/20/86," which was the end of his thirteen-week contract. The *Times* ad was a device Breslin had used before, when he informed the *New York Post,* in 1969, that he intended to give up his column, telling his editor: "Robert J. Allen: You are on your own."

In 1995 the iconoclastic Breslin underwent surgery to remove a brain aneurysm, a life-threatening procedure that inspired his 1996 memoir, *I Want to Thank My Brain for Remembering Me.* Breslin uses his near-death experience as a point of departure for an unruly meditation on his life and career, from his days as a copyboy to the present. The operation itself is described in explicit detail from both his own and the surgeon's point of view. Most critics believed the brush with mortality brought out the best in Breslin. "With or without his bulging brain vessel, the man knows how to write," said Mary Carroll in *Booklist*. While conceding that the book is "occasionally disorderly, prideful, and cocky," a critic for *Kirkus Reviews* found it "always distinctive and often affecting." And Christopher Lehmann-Haupt of the *New York Times* thanked Breslin for providing "a dizzying glimpse of great depths, both of his own brain under a microscope and of his gratitude to the medicine that saved his life."

BIOGRAPHICAL AND CRITICAL SOURCES:

BOOKS

Contemporary Literary Criticism, Volume 4, Thomson Gale (Detroit, MI), 1975.
Graauer, Neil A., *Wits & Sages,* Johns Hopkins University Press (Baltimore, MD), 1984.

PERIODICALS

Art in America, July, 1994.
Book, May, 2001, Paul Evans, review of *I Don't Want to Go to Jail,* p. 74; March-April, 2002, Paul Evans, review of *The Short Sweet Dream of Eduardo Gutierrez,* p. 74.
Booklist, August, 1996; July 19, 1996, Mary Carroll, review of *I Want to Thank My Brain for Remembering Me,* p. 1778; July, 2004, Margaret Flanagan, review of *The Church That Forgot Christ,* p. 1795.
Chronicle of Higher Education, February 2, 1994, p. A6.
Commentary, December, 1975, Dorothy Rabinowitz, review of *World without End, Amen.*
Commonweal, August 29, 1975.
Detroit News, August 1, 1982.
Kirkus Reviews, July 1, 1996, review of *I Want to Thank My Brain for Remembering Me.*
Library Journal, January, 2002, Elaine Machleder, review of *The Short Sweet Dream of Eduardo Gutierrez,* p. 132; July, 2004, Anna M. Donnelly, review of *The Church That Forgot Christ,* p. 86.
Los Angeles Times Book Review, July 25, 1982; May 18, 1986.
Nation, June 4, 1990; June 3, 2002, Theodore Hamm, review of *The Short Sweet Dream of Eduardo Gutierrez,* p. 33.
New Republic, July 19, 1982; October 21, 1991; January 24, 1994, p. 27.
Newsweek, August 9, 1982; May 12, 1986, Jonathan Alter, "The Two Faces of Breslin," p. 74; May 26, 1986.
New York Times, November 21, 1969, Thomas Meehan, review of *The Gang That Couldn't Shoot Straight;* May 19, 1975; May 23, 1978; June 16, 1982; October 26, 1984; May 8, 1986; May 5, 1987; January 11, 1988; September 12, 1996, p. B5.
New York Times Book Review, November 30, 1969, Christopher Lehmann-Haupt, review of *The Gang That Couldn't Shoot Straight;* August 26, 1973,

Harvey Gardner, review of *World without End, Amen;* May 11, 1975; June 20, 1982; May 18, 1986; July 24, 1994.

People, June 16, 1986; December 15, 1986; October 7, 1991; October 7, 1996.

Publishers Weekly, October 7, 1991; June 24, 1996; April 2, 2002, review of *I Don't Want to Go to Jail,* p. 37; February 4, 2002, Edward Nawotka, "PW Talks with Jimmy Breslin," p. 65; June 28, 2003, review of *The Church That Forgot Christ,* p. 46; February 4, 2004, review of *The Short Sweet Dream of Eduardo Gutierrez,* p. 66; June 28, 2004, Dermont McEvoy, "Breslin Takes on the Church," p. 48.

Time, June 12, 1975; June 14, 1982; May 5, 1986; January 4, 1988.

Times Literary Supplement, May 14, 1970; May 3, 1974.

Tribune Books (Chicago, IL), October 5, 1986.

Variety, October 21, 1991.

Washington Post Book World, August 12, 1973, Richard Brown, review of *World without End, Amen;* July 4, 1982; June 1, 1986.

*   *   *

BRINK, André 1935-
(André Philippus Brink)

PERSONAL: Born May 29, 1935, in Vrede, Orange Free State, South Africa; son of Daniel (a magistrate) and Aletta (a teacher; maiden name, Wolmarans) Brink; married Estelle Naudé, October 3, 1951 (divorced); married Salomi Louw, November 28, 1965 (divorced); married Alta Miller (a potter), July 17, 1970 (divorced); married Marésa de Beer, November 16, 1990; children: (first marriage) Anton; (second marriage) Gustav; (third marriage) Danie, Sonja. *Education:* Potchefstroom University, B.A., 1955, M.A. (Afrikaans), 1958, M.A. (Afrikaans and Dutch), 1959; postgraduate study at Sorbonne, University of Paris, 1959-61.

ADDRESSES: Home—6 Banksia Rd., Rosebank, Cape Town 7700, South Africa. *Office*—Department of English, University of Cape Town, Rondebosch 7700, South Africa. *Agent*—Ruth Liepman, Maienburgweg 23, Zurich, Switzerland.

CAREER: Author. Rhodes University, Grahamstown, South Africa, lecturer, 1963-73, senior lecturer, 1974-75, associate professor, 1976-79, professor of Afrikaans

and Dutch literature, 1980-90; University of Cape Town, Cape Town, South Africa, professor of English, 1991—. Director of theatrical productions.

MEMBER: South African PEN, Afrikaans Writers' Guild (president, 1978-80).

AWARDS, HONORS: Reina Prinsen Geerligs prize, 1964; Central News Agency award for Afrikaans literature, 1965, for *Olé,* and for English literature, 1979, for *Rumours of Rain,* 1983, for *A Chain of Voices;* prize for prose translation from South African Academy, 1970, for *Alice se Avonture in Wonderland,* and 1982; D.Litt., Rhodes University, 1975, Witwatersrand University, 1985, and University of the Orange Free State, 1997; Central News Agency award for English literature, 1978, for *Rumours of Rain;* Martin Luther King, Jr., Memorial Prize and Prix Médicis Étranger, both 1980, both for *A Dry White Season;* named chevalier de Legion d' Honneur and officier de l'Ordre des Arts et des Lettres, promoted to commandeur, 1992; Premio Mondello, 1997, for *Imaginings of Sand;* honorary doctorate, Rhodes University, 2001.

WRITINGS:

FICTION

Die meul teen die hang, Tafelberg (Cape Town, South Africa), 1958.

Die gebondenes, Afrikaanse Pers (Johannesburg, South Africa), 1959.

Die eindelose weë, Tafelberg (Cape Town, South Africa), 1960.

Lobola vir die lewe (title means "Dowry for Life"), Human & Rousseau (Cape Town, South Africa), 1962

Die Ambassadeur, Human & Rousseau (Cape Town, South Africa), 1963, translated by Brink as *File on a Diplomat,* Longmans, Green (London, England), 1965, revised translation published as *The Ambassador,* Faber (New York, NY), 1985.

Orgie, John Malherbe (Cape Town, South Africa), 1965.

(With others) *Rooi,* Malherbe (Cape Town, South Africa), 1965.

Miskien nooit: 'n Somerspel, Human & Rousseau (Cape Town, South Africa), 1967.

A Portrait of Woman as a Young Girl, Buren (Cape Town, South Africa), 1973.

Oom Kootjie Emmer (short stories), Buren (Cape Town, South Africa), 1973.

Kennis van die aand (novel), Buren (Cape Town, South Africa), 1973, translated by Brink as *Looking on Darkness,* W.H. Allen (London, England), 1974, Morrow (New York, NY), 1975.

Die Geskiedenis van oom Kootjie Emmer van Witgratworteldraai, Buren (Cape Town, South Africa), 1973.

'n Oomblik in die wind, Taurus, 1975, translated as *An Instant in the Wind,* W.H. Allen (London, England), 1976, Morrow (New York, NY), 1977.

Gerugte van Reen (novel), Human & Rousseau (Cape Town, South Africa), 1978, translated as *Rumours of Rain,* Morrow (New York, NY), 1978, published as *Rumors of Rain,* Penguin (New York, NY), 1984,

'n Droe wit seisoen, Taurus, 1979, translated as *A Dry White Season,* W.H. Allen (London, England), 1979, Morrow (New York, NY), 1980.

'n Emmertjie wyn: 'n versameling dopstories, Saayman & Weber (Cape Town, South Africa), 1981.

Houd-den-bek (title means "Shut Your Trap"), Taurus, 1982, translated as *A Chain of Voices,* Morrow (New York, NY), 1982.

Oom Kootjie Emmer en die nuwe bedeling: 'n stinkstorie, Taurus (Johannesburg, South Africa), 1983.

Die Muur van die pes, Human & Rousseau (Cape Town, South Africa), 1984, translated as *The Wall of the Plague,* Summit (New York, NY), 1984.

Loopdoppies: Nog dopstories, Saayman & Weber (Cape Town, South Africa), 1984.

States of Emergency, Penguin, 1988, Summit (New York, NY), 1989.

Die Eerste lewe van Adamastor, Saayman & Weber (Cape Town, South Africa), 1988, translated as *Cape of Storms: The First Life of Adamastor: A Story* (novel), Simon & Schuster (New York, NY), 1993, published as *The First Life of Adamastor,* Secker & Warburg (London, England), 1993.

Mal en ander stories: 'n omnibus van humor, three volumes, Saayman & Weber (Cape Town, South Africa), 1990.

Die kreef raak gewoond daaraan, Human & Rousseau (Cape Town, South Africa), 1991.

An Act of Terror, Secker & Warburg (London, England), 1991, Summit (New York, NY), 1992.

Inteendeel, Human & Rousseau (Cape Town, South Africa), 1993.

On the Contrary: A Novel: Being the Life of a Famous Rebel, Soldier, Traveler, Explorer, Reader, Builder, Scribe, Latinist, Lover, and Liar, Little, Brown (Boston, MA), 1993.

Sandkastele, Human & Rousseau (Cape Town, South Africa), 1995, translated as *Imaginings of Sand,* Harcourt (New York, NY), 1996.

Duiwelskloof, Human & Rousseau (Cape Town, South Africa), 1998, translated as *Devil's Valley,* Harcourt (New York, NY), 1999.

Donkermaan, Human & Rousseau (Cape Town, South Africa), 2000, translated as *The Rights of Desire,* Secker & Warburg (London, England), 2000, Harcourt (New York, NY), 2001.

The Other Side of Silence, Harcourt (Orlando, FL), 2002.

DRAMA

Die band om ons harte (title means "The Bond around Our Hearts"), Afrikaanse Pers (Johannesburg, South Africa), 1959.

Caesar (first produced at Stellenbosch, Cape Province, 1965), Nasionale Boekhandel (Capetown, South Africa), 1961.

(With others) *Die beskermengel en ander eenbedrywe* (title means "The Guardian Angel and Other One-Act Plays"), Tafelberg (Cape Town, South Africa), 1962.

Bagasie: Triptiek vir die toneel (contains *Die koffer, Die trommel,* and *Die tas;* first produced in Pretoria, South Africa, 1965), Tafelberg (Cape Town, South Africa), 1964.

Elders mooiweer en warm (three-act play; title means "Elsewhere Fine and Warm"; first produced in Bloemfontein, South Africa, 1970), John Malherbe, 1965.

Die Rebelle: Betoogstuk in nege episodes (title means "The Rebels"), Human & Rousseau (Cape Town, South Africa), 1970.

Die verhoor: Verhoogstuk in drie bedrywe (first produced in Pretoria, South Africa, 1975), Human & Rousseau (Cape Town, South Africa), 1970.

Kinkels innie kabel: 'n verhoogstuk in elf episodes (adaptation of Shakespeare's *Much Ado about Nothing;* title means "Knots in the Cable"), Buren (Cape Town, South Africa), 1971.

Afrikaners is plesierig (two one-act plays; title means "Afrikaners Make Merry"), Buren (Cape Town, South Africa), 1973.

Bobaas van die Boendoe (adaptation of Synge's *Playboy of the Western World;* first produced in Bloemfontein, South Africa, 1974), Human & Rousseau (Cape Town, South Africa), 1974.

Pavane (three-act play; first produced in Cape Town, 1974), Human & Rousseau (Cape Town, South Africa), 1974.

Die hamer van die hekse (title means "The Hammer and the Witches"), Tafelberg (Cape Town, South Africa), 1976.

Toiings op die langpad (title means "Toiings on the Long Road"), Van Schaik (Pretoria, South Africa), 1979.

Die Jogger, Human & Rousseau (Cape Town, South Africa), 1997.

FOR CHILDREN

Die bende (title means "The Gang"), Afrikaanse Pers (Johannesburg, South Africa), 1961.

Platsak (title means "Broke"), Afrikaanse Pers (Johannesburg, South Africa), 1962.

Die verhaal van Julius Caesar (title means "The Story of Julius Caesar"), Human & Rousseau (Cape Town, South Africa), 1963.

LITERARY HISTORY AND CRITICISM

Orde en chaos: 'n studie oor Germanicus en die tragedies van Shakespeare, Nasionale Boekhandel (Cape Town, South Africa), 1962.

Aspekte van die nuwe prosa (title means "Aspects of the New Fiction"), Academica (Pretoria, South Africa), 1967, revised edition, 1975.

Die Poësie van Breyten Breytenbach, Academica (Pretoria, South Africa), 1971.

Inleiding tot die Afrikaanse letterkunde, onder Redaksie van E. Lindenberg, Academica (Pretoria, South Africa), 1973.

Aspekte van die nuwe Drama (title means "Aspects of the New Drama"), Academica (Pretoria, South Africa), 1974.

Voorlopige Rapport: Beskouings oor die Afrikaanse Literatuur van Sewentig (title means "Preliminary Report: Views on Afrikaans Literature in the 1970s"), Human & Rousseau (Cape Town, South Africa), 1976.

Tweede voorlopige Rapport: Nog beskouings oor die Afrikaanse Literature van sewentig (title means "Second Preliminary Report"), Human & Rousseau (Cape Town, South Africa), 1980.

Why Literature?/Waarom literatuur? (essays), Rhodes University (Grahamstown, South Africa), 1980.

(With others) *Perspektief en profiel: 'n geskiedinis van die Afrikaanse letterkunde,* Perskor, 1982.

Literatuur in die strydperk (essays; title means "Literature in the Arena"), Human & Rousseau (Cape Town, South Africa), 1985.

Vertelkunde: 'n inleiding tot die lees van verhalende tekste, Academica (Pretoria, South Africa), 1987.

The Novel: Language and Narrative from Cervantes to Calvino, New York University Press (New York, NY), 1998.

TRANSLATOR

Pierre Boulle, *Die Brug oor die rivier Kwaï,* Tafelberg (Cape Town, South Africa), 1962.

André Dhôtel, *Reisigers na die Groot Land,* Tafelberg (Cape Town, South Africa), 1962.

Joseph Kessel, *Die Wonderhande,* HAUM (Cape Town, South Africa), 1962.

L.N. Lavolle, *Nuno, die Visserseun,* HAUM (Cape Town, South Africa), 1962.

Léonce Bourliaguet, *Verhale uit Limousin,* Human & Rousseau (Cape Town, South Africa), 1963.

Léonce Bourliaguet, *Die slapende Berg,* Human & Rousseau (Cape Town, South Africa), 1963.

Leonard Cottrell, *Land van die Farao's,* Malherbe (Cape Town, South Africa), 1963.

Michel Rouzé, *Die Bos van Kokelunde,* Malherbe (Cape Town, South Africa), 1963.

Marguerite Duras, *Moderato Cantabile,* HAUM (Cape Town, South Africa), 1963.

Paul-Jacques Bonzon, *Die Goue kruis,* Malherbe (Cape Town, South Africa), 1963.

Leonard Cottrell, *Land van die Twee Riviere,* Malherbe (Cape Town, South Africa), 1964.

C.M. Turnbull, *Volke van Afrika,* Malherbe (Cape Town, South Africa), 1964.

Lewis Carroll, *Alice se Avonture in Wonderland,* Human & Rousseau (Cape Town, South Africa), 1965.

Die mooiste verhale uit die Arabiese Nagte, Human & Rousseau (Cape Town, South Africa), 1966.

James Reeves, *Die Avonture van Don Quixote,* HAUM (Cape Town, South Africa), 1966.

Elyesa Bazna, *Ek was Cicero,* Afrikaanse Pers (Johannesburg, South Africa), 1966.

Jean de Brunhoff, *Koning Babar,* Human & Rousseau (Cape Town, South Africa), 1966.

Colette, *Die Swerfling,* Afrikaanse Pers (Johannesburg, South Africa), 1966.

Miguel Cervantes, *Die vindingryke ridder, Don Quijote de la Mancha,* Human & Rousseau (Cape Town, South Africa), 1966.

Simenon, *Speuder Maigret, Maigret en sy Dooie, Maigret en die Lang Derm,* and *Maigret en die Spook,* four volumes, Afrikaanse Pers (Johannesburg, South Africa), 1966–69.

Charles Perrault, *Die mooiste Sprokies van Moeder Gans,* Human & Rousseau (Cape Town, South Africa), 1967.

Ester Wier, *Die Eenspaaier,* Human & Rousseau (Cape Town, South Africa), 1967.

Graham Greene, *Die Eendstert,* Human & Rousseau (Cape Town, South Africa), 1967.

P.L. Travers, *Mary Poppins in Kersieboomlaan,* Malherbe (Cape Town, South Africa), 1967.

C.S. Lewis, *Die Leeu, die Heks en die Hangkas,* Human & Rousseau (Cape Town, South Africa), 1967.

(With others) *Die groot Boek oor ons Dieremaats,* Human & Rousseau (Cape Town, South Africa), 1968.

(With others) *Koning Arthur en sy Ridders van die Ronde Tafel,* Human & Rousseau (Cape Town, South Africa), 1968.

Lucy Boston, *Die Kinders van Groenkop,* Human & Rousseau (Cape Town, South Africa), 1968.

Lewis Carroll, *Alice deur die Spieël,* Human & Rousseau (Cape Town, South Africa), 1968.

Ian Serraillier, *Die Botsende rotse, Die Horing van Ivoor,* and *Die Kop van de Gorgoon,* four volumes, HAUM (Cape Town, South Africa), 1968.

Dhan Gopal Mukerji, *Bontnek,* HAUM (Cape Town, South Africa), 1968.

Henry James, *Die Draai van die Skroef,* Afrikaanse Pers (Johannesburg, South Africa), 1968.

Oscar Wilde, *Die Gelukkige Prins en ander Sprokies,* Human & Rousseau (Cape Town, South Africa), 1969.

William Shakespeare, *Richard III,* Human & Rousseau (Cape Town, South Africa), 1969.

Charles Perrault, *Die Gestewelde kat,* Human & Rousseau (Cape Town, South Africa), 1969.

Pearl S. Buck, *Die groot Golf,* Human & Rousseau (Cape Town, South Africa), 1969.

Hans Christian Andersen, *Die Nagtegaal,* HAUM (Cape Town, South Africa), 1969.

Albert Camus, *Die Terroriste,* Dramatiese Artistieke en Letterkundige Organisasie (Johannesburg, South Africa), 1970.

Michel de Ghelderode, *Eskoriaal,* Dramatiese Artistieke en Letterkundige Organisasie (Johannesburg, South Africa), 1971.

Nada Curcija-Prodanovic, *Ballerina,* Malherbe (Cape Town, South Africa), 1972.

Anton Chekhov, *Die Seemeeu,* Human & Rousseau (Cape Town, South Africa), 1972.

Synge, *Die Bobaas van die Boendoe,* Human & Rousseau (Cape Town, South Africa), 1973.

Richard Bach, *Jonathan Livingston Seemeeu,* Malherbe (Cape Town, South Africa), 1973.

Henrik Ibsen, *Hedda Gabler,* Human & Rousseau (Cape Town, South Africa), 1974.

Kenneth Grahame, *Die Wind in die Wilgers,* Human & Rousseau (Cape Town, South Africa), 1974.

William Shakespeare, *Die Tragedie van Romeo en Juliet,* Human & Rousseau (Cape Town, South Africa), 1975.

Claude Desailly, *Die Tierbrigade,* Tafelberg (Cape Town, South Africa), 1978.

Claude Desailly, *Nuwe Avontuur van die Tierbrigade,* Tafelberg (Cape Town, South Africa), 1979.

Oscar Wilde, *Die Nagtegaal en die Roos,* Human & Rousseau (Cape Town, South Africa), 1980.

Kenneth Grahame, *Rot op Reis,* Human & Rousseau (Cape Town, South Africa), 1981.

Elizabeth Janet Gray, *Adam van die Pad,* Human & Rousseau (Cape Town, South Africa), 1981.

Charles Perrault, *Klein Duimpie,* Human & Rousseau (Cape Town, South Africa), 1983.

OTHER

Pot-pourri: Sketse uit Parys (travelogue; title means "Pot-pourrie: Sketches from Paris"), Human & Rousseau (Cape Town, South Africa), 1962.

Sèmpre diritto: Italiaanse reisjoernaal (travelogue; title means "Always Straight Ahead: Italian Travel Journal"), Afrikaanse Pers (Johannesburg, South Africa), 1963.

Olé: Reisboek oor Spanje (travelogue; title means "Olé: A Travel Book on Spain"), Human & Rousseau (Cape Town, South Africa), 1966.

Midi: Op reis deur Suld-Frankyrk (travelogue; title means "Midi: Traveling through the South of France"), Human & Rousseau (Cape Town, South Africa), 1969.

Parys-Parys: Return, Human & Rousseau (Cape Town, South Africa), 1969.

Fado: 'n reis deur Noord-Portugal (travelogue; title means "Fado: A Journey through Northern Portugal"), Human & Rousseau (Cape Town, South Africa), 1970.

Portret van di vrou as 'n meisie (title means "Portrait of Woman as a Young Girl"), Buren (Cape Town, South Africa), 1973.

Brandewyn in Suid-Afrika, Buren (Cape Town, South Africa), 1974, translated by Siegfried Stander as *Brandy in South Africa,* 1974.

Dessertwyn in Suid-Afrika, Buren (Cape Town, South Africa), 1974, translated as *Dessert Wine in South Africa,* 1974.

(With others) *Ik ben er geweest: Gesprekken in Zuid-Afrika* (title means "I've Been There: Conversations in South Africa"), Kok (Kampen, South Africa), 1974.

Die Wyn van bowe (title means "The Wine from up There"), Buren (Cape Town, South Africa), 1974.

Die Klap van die meul (title means "A Stroke from the Mill"), Buren (Cape Town, South Africa), 1974.

Jan Rabie se 21, Academica (Cape Town, South Africa), 1977.

(Editor) *Oggendlied: 'n bundel vir Uys Krige op sy verjaardag 4 Februarie 1977,* Human & Rousseau (Cape Town, South Africa), 1977.

(Editor) Top Naeff, *Klein Avontuur,* Academica (Pretoria, South Africa), 1979.

Heildronk uit Wynboer Saamgestel deur AB ter viering van die Blad se 50ste bestaansjaar, Tafelberg (Cape Town, South Africa), 1981.

Die Fees van die Malles: 'n keur uit die humor, Saayman & Weber (Cape Town, South Africa), 1981.

Mapmakers: Writing in a State of Siege (essays), Faber (New York, NY), 1983, revised edition published as *Writing in a State of Siege: Essays on Politics and Literature,* Summit (New York, NY), 1983.

(Editor with J.M. Coetzee) *A Land Apart: A South African Reader,* Faber (London, England), 1986, Viking (New York, NY), 1987.

Latynse reise: 'n keur uit die reisbeskrywings van André P. Brink, Human & Rousseau (Cape Town, South Africa), 1990.

The Essence of the Grape, Saayman & Weber (Cape Town, South Africa), 1993.

(Compiler) *SA, 27 April 1994: An Author's Diary,* Queillerie (Pretoria, South Africa), 1994.

(Compiler) *27 April: One Year Later/Een Jaar later,* Queillerie (Pretoria, South Africa), 1995.

Reinventing a Continent: Writing and Politics in South Africa (essays), Secker & Warburg (London, England), 1996, revised edition, preface by Nelson Mandela, Zoland Books (New York, NY), 1998.

Destabilising Shakespeare, Shakespeare Society of Southern Africa (Grahamstown, South Africa), 1996.

(Compiler) *Groot Verseboek 2000,* Tafelberg (Cape Town, South Africa), 2000.

Jan Vermeiren: A Flemish Artist in South Africa, Lanoo (Tielt, South Africa), 2000.

Author of scenarios for South African films and television series, including *The Settlers.* Contributor to books on Afrikaans literature and to periodicals, including *World Literature Today, Asahi Journal,* and *Theatre Quarterly.* Editor of *Sestiger* magazine, 1963-65; editor of *Standpunte,* 1986-87; editor of weekly book page in *Rapport.*

Brink's manuscripts are housed at the University of the Orange Free State, Bloemfontein, and the National English Literary Museum, Grahamstown, South Africa.

ADAPTATIONS: A Dry White Season was adapted for film by Euzhan Palcy and Colin Welland, directed by Palcy, Metro-Goldwyn-Mayer, 1989.

SIDELIGHTS: As an Afrikaner, novelist, playwright, essayist, and educator André Brink is "a rarity in anti-apartheid literature," Scott Kraft stated in the *Los Angeles Times.* A product of his country's exclusionary white culture, Brink repudiated its policies of apartheid during his studies in Paris in 1960 but was drawn back to the land of his birth to witness and record its turmoil and injustice. Earning both international recognition and governmental censure for his work in the years that followed, "Brink is one of the leading voices in the literary chorus of dissent, and for two decades his tales of black hope and white repression have shamed the nation," remarked Curt Suplee in the *Washington Post.*

Brink writes in both English and Afrikaans, the latter a language derived from that spoken by South Africa's seventeenth-and eighteenth-century Dutch, French, and German settlers. In an interview with *Contemporary Authors, (CA)* Brink once noted: "There is a certain virility, a certain earthy, youthful quality about Afrikaans because it is such a young language, and because, although derived from an old European language like Dutch, it has found completely new roots in Africa and become totally Africanized in the process. . . . One can do almost anything with it. If you haven't got a word for something you want to express, you simply make a word or pluck a word from another language and shape it to fit into yours. Working in this young and very vital language is quite exhilarating, which creates a very special sense of adventure for authors working in it. And if one works in both languages, there is the wonderful experience of approaching the same subject, the same territory, through two totally different media. One is the more or less rigorous English language, the world language, and although one can still do a hell of a lot of new things in it, so much of it has already become standardized: it's almost as if one looks at the African experience through European eyes when one writes English. Through the Afrikaans language, it is a totally different, a more 'immediate,' experience. It's a language that can take much more emotionalism, for instance, whereas English tends toward understatement, Afrikaans is more overt, more externalized, more extroverted in its approach."

Brink translated his 1963 novel *Die Ambassadeur* from Afrikaans into English. Published in England as *File on a Diplomat,* and in the United States as *The Ambassador,* the novel relates a story about a French ambassador to South Africa and his third secretary who become involved with the same young, promiscuous female and are drawn into the wild nightlife of Paris until jealousy destroys them both, reported Savkar Altinel in a *Times Literary Supplement* essay. Fred Pfeil suggested in a *Nation* review that the novel "sets forth Brink's vision of sexual-existential liberation with nary a nod toward any political considerations." Altinel called the novel "an elegantly tidy creation which, with its trinity of somewhat stylized central characters and its economically evoked setting, seems very much the unified product of a powerful initial vision." In a London *Times* review of the revised version of the novel in 1985, Henry Stanhope wrote that, despite "something ever so slightly dated about it," *The Ambassador* "remains a good book, intelligent in its exploration of human behaviour under emotional and political stress."

"In 1968 I left South Africa to settle in Paris with the exiled poet Breyten Breytenbach," Brink once explained to *CA*, "but the nature of the student revolt of that year forced me to reassess my situation as a writer and prompted my return to South Africa in order to accept full responsibility for whatever I wrote, believing that, in a closed society, the writer has a specific social and moral role to fill. This resulted in a more committed form of writing exploring the South African political situation and notably my revulsion of apartheid. My first novel to emerge from this experience was *Kennis van die aand*, which became the first Afrikaans book to be banned by the South African censors. This encouraged me to turn seriously to writing in English in order not to be silenced in my own language. Under the title *Looking on Darkness*, it became an international success, with translations into a dozen languages, including Finnish, Turkish, Japanese, Czechoslovakian, and Russian."

In Brink's *Looking on Darkness*, protagonist Joseph Malan murders his white lover, Jessica Thomson, in a mutual pact and then sits in jail, awaiting execution. Calling the 1973 novel "ambitious and disturbing," Jane Larkin Crain concluded in the *Saturday Review* that "a passionately human vision rules here, informed by an imagination that is attuned at once to complex and important abstractions and to the rhythms and the texture of everyday experience." Noting that the "novel is structured in the form of a confessional," Martin Tucker added in *Commonweal* that its style "is compelling: it is a work that throbs with personal intensity." Because of the novel's explicit treatment of sex, racism, persecution, and the torture of political prisoners in South African jails, C.J. Driver suggested in the *Times Literary Supplement* that it is not difficult to understand why it

was banned; however, Driver concluded that "within its context this is a brave and important novel and in any terms a fine one."

Publication of *Looking on Darkness* in Europe coincided with the Soweto riots of 1976, and the novel became something of a handbook on the South African situation. Regarding racism generally, Brink once told *CA*: "America seems to be slowly working its way through racism; whereas in South Africa it is entrenched in the whole system and framework of laws on which society has had its base. It is not just a matter of sentiment, of personal resentment, of tradition and custom, but these negative aspects of society are so firmly rooted in the framework of laws that it is very, very difficult to eradicate. *Looking on Darkness* elicited much comment because it is one of the first Afrikaans novels to confront openly the apartheid system. This account of an illicit love between a 'Cape Coloured' man and a white woman evoked, on the one hand, one of the fiercest polemics in the history of that country's literature and contributed, on the other, to a groundswell of new awareness among white Afrikaners of the common humanity of all people regardless of color. In numerous letters from readers I was told that for the first time in my life I now realize that 'they' feel and think and react just like 'us.'"

"In *An Instant in the Wind*," Brink once explained to *CA*, "I used essentially the same relationship—a black man and a white woman—but placed it in the midst of the eighteenth century in an attempt to probe the origins of the racial tensions of today. An episode from Australian history in which a shipwrecked woman and a convict return to civilization on foot is here transposed to the Cape Colony with so much verisimilitude that many readers have tried to look up the documentation in the Cape Archives." In the *Spectator*, Nick Totten described the plot further: "A civilised woman, her husband dead, is lost in the wilderness . . . rescued by an escaped black prisoner . . . with whom she experiences for the first time fulfilled sexual love, but whom she betrays after the long trek back to civilisation." Calling it "a frank confrontation with miscegenation in a contemporary South African setting," Robert L. Berner commented in *World Literature Today:* "What Brink has produced is a historical novel with an almost documentary degree of verisimilitude. . . . But more than for its interest as evidence of Brink's artistic development, it is the recognition of the relationship of sex to politics that makes *An Instant in the Wind* a remarkable work of South African literature." R.A. Sokolov suggested in the *New York Times Book Review* that "it is important for political reasons that Brink should be published, but doubtful on the evidence of this book that he will be read for his art as a writer." Richard Cima contended in *Library Journal* that "the subject is important and the novelistic achievement impressive."

"*Rumours of Rain,* set on the eve of the Soweto riots, is placed on a much larger stage," Brink once remarked to *CA* about his 1978 novel. "The apartheid mind is demonstrated in the account given by a wealthy businessman of the one weekend in which his whole familiar world collapsed through the conviction of his best friend for terrorism, the revolt of his son, the loss of his mistress, and the sale of his family's farm. In spite of his efforts to rigorously separate all the elements of his life, he becomes the victim of his own paradoxes and faces an apocalypse." The novel is about Martin Mynhardt, a mining entrepreneur, whose "only principles are money and safety," observed Phoebe-Lou Adams in the *Atlantic,* "and for them he betrays friend, colleague, brother, mother, wife, and mistress, and will eventually betray his son." According to C.G. Blewitt in *Best Sellers,* "Much insight is shed on the life of the Afrikaner, his judicial system and the horrors of apartheid." Similarly, Daphne Merkin commented in *New Republic* that "Brink has taken a large, ideologically-charged premise and proceeds to render it in intimate terms without . . . sacrificing any of its hard-edged 'political' implications." Moreover, Merkin believed that the book "is an ambitious resonant novel that depicts a volatile situation with remarkable control and lack of sentimentality."

"In comparison with the complex structures" of *Rumours of Rain,* Brink once commented to *CA* that his *A Dry White Season* "has a deceptively simple plot: a black man dies while being detained by the security police. In all good faith his white friend tries to find out what really happened, and as a result the whole infernal machinery of the State is turned against him." According to June Goodwin in the *Christian Science Monitor,* "Few novels will speak to the Afrikaner—or to foreigners who want to understand the Afrikaner—as well as this one." *A Dry White Season* is about Afrikaner Ben Du Toit, who helps a black school janitor investigate the questionable circumstances surrounding the death of his son at the hands of the police. Mel Watkins, in a *New York Times Book Review* essay, found that the novel "demonstrates André Brink's continuing refinement of his fictional technique, without sacrificing any of the poignancy that his previous books have led us to expect."

"Brink's writing is built on conviction," remarked Dinah Birch in the London *Times.* "His characters move in a world of absolutes: goodness and truth war with

cruelty and greed, and the reader is never left in any doubt as to which is which." Although not considering Brink "a 'great' writer," Eric Redman pointed out in the *Washington Post Book World* that "he's an urgent, political one and an Afrikaner other Afrikaners can't ignore." Moreover, noting that "big books have sparked change throughout South Africa's recent history," Redman observed that "this much is certain: the era of the trivial South African novel is dead, and courage killed it." Remarking to *CA* that the novel was begun "almost a year before the death in detention of black-consciousness leader Steve Biko in 1976," Brink added: "In fact, the death of Biko came as such a shock to me that for a long time I couldn't go back to writing. I believe that however outraged or disturbed one may be, a state of inner serenity must be obtained before anything meaningful can emerge in writing."

Brink went on to add that in 1982's *A Chain of Voices* he worked to "extend and expand my field of vision. Using as a point of departure a slave revolt in the Cape Colony in 1825, I used a series of thirty different narrators to explore the relationships created by a society shaped by the forces of oppression and suffering. The 'separateness' of the voices haunted me; masters and slaves, all tied by the same chains, are totally unable to communicate because their humanity and their individuality are denied by the system they live by. I tried to broaden and deepen the enquiry by relating the voices, in four successive sections, to the elements of earth, water, wind, and fire."

Many critics consider *A Chain of Voices* to be Brink's best work to date. Suplee labeled it "an incendiary success abroad and a galling phenomenon at home." According to Julian Moynahan in the *New York Times Book Review,* "Like all good historical novels, [it] is as much about the present as the past. . . . Brink searches the bad old times for a key to understanding bad times in South Africa today, and what he sees in the historical record is always conditioned by his awareness of the South African racial crisis now." However, while Jane Kramer suggested in the *New York Review of Books* that "Brink may have an honorable imagination," she believed that "he has written a potboiler of oppression" in which the "voices" of the novel "end up more caricature than character." On the other hand, Moynahan compared the device of telling a story from multiple viewpoints to the novels of William Faulkner in which he "counts the moral cost of white racism, both before and after Emancipation, in terms of the tragic spoliation of all relationships, not merely those between white oppressors and their nonwhite or partially white victims."

In *States of Emergency* Brink tells a story within a story. A writer's attempt to compose an apolitical love story is marred by the reality of racism, violence, and death. When the narrator receives an impressive but unpublishable manuscript from Jane Ferguson, a young writer who subsequently commits suicide by setting herself on fire, he abandons the historical novel he has been writing about South Africa and begins to compose a love story based on Ferguson's manuscript. The novel he writes is centered around a professor of literary theory and a student with whom he has an affair. According to a *Publishers Weekly* contributor, Brink "demonstrates that neither love nor art offers an escape; even the imagination is determined by political realities." Finding intensity between "reality and the author's idea of just what reality best suits his characters," Alfred Rushton commented in the Toronto *Globe and Mail* that the reader becomes aware that "no writer owns his or her characters, just as the state doesn't own people no matter what method is used to justify the attempt."

Not all critics responded positively to *States of Emergency.* For example, *Los Angeles Times* book critic Richard Eder suggested that "it is one thing for contemporary theory to come in afterward and argue that the fiction we have read tells us not about real characters but only about how its text was created. It is another for this reductivism to be applied in the moment of creation. It is literary contraception; nothing emerges alive." However, calling the novel "complicated and forceful" as well as "richly developed," Michael Wood maintained in the London *Observer* that Brink "does depict, with great compassion and authority, the 'weight and madness of the violence' surrounding individuals." And Rushton concluded that the novelist "also successfully challenges those people, writers and artists included, who persist in believing reason will somehow prevail over passion."

In *An Act of Terror* Brink portrays the political tension in South Africa in 1988, a particularly brutal period of police repression. The narrative centers on Thomas Landman, a member of a guerrilla group of blacks and whites who are planning to assassinate the president. When the plan fails, Landman seeks to escape from the police, and revisits the scenes of his past life. Reviewers found much to praise in the work. Adam Hochschild wrote in the *Los Angeles Times Book Review,* "the meal that Brink cooks up is an intricate, fast-moving story that succeeds in keeping us at the table for more than 600 pages of this 834-page behemoth of a book." *Nation* contributor Jenefer Shute similarly praised the novel's ambition, asserting that *An Act of Terror* "soars in its aspiration, its revised creation myth for a race 'conceived and born in lies,' its hope for a history that might open out instead of shutting down." Several critics,

however, judge that the novel's lengthy, oratorical conclusion, in which Landman chronicles his family's presence in South Africa from the first Dutch settlers in the seventeenth century to the present day, compromises the work as a whole. Hochschild maintained that "Brink's skill as a storyteller collapses" in this "interminable" chronicle. Similarly, Randolph Vigne, commenting in the *San Francisco Review of Books,* characterized the conclusion as "a heavy dose of cheap magazine fiction."

Brink returned to historical fiction in his next two novels, *Cape of Storms: The First Life of Adamastor* and *On the Contrary.* In the first of these works, Brink draws on Greek mythology and Renaissance European literature to shape an allegorical commentary on the colonial history of southern Africa. The novel is narrated by T'kama, a Khoi who witnesses the arrival of the first Europeans and inadvertently precipitates an attack on his people by frightening a white woman who has come ashore to bathe. Despite the humorous style of the novel, Brink told Laurel Graeber in the *New York Times Book Review* that "under the humor there's a deep and serious concern with the origins of racial animosities in South Africa and everywhere." In reviewing the novel for that same publication, Mario Vargas Llosa echoed this concern, asserting that "however much we enjoy reading the book, André Brink's beautiful mythological re-creation leaves us anguished over what appear to be its predictions regarding a society where, after a bloody past of injustice and institutionalized racism, different races and cultures are finally preparing to try coexistence under conditions of equality."

In *On the Contrary* Brink again concentrates on the racial tensions of early South Africa by telling the story of the historical figure Estienne Barbier, who emigrated from France to South Africa in the eighteenth century and who was executed by the Dutch East India Company for his role in fomenting rebellion in the Cape in 1739. The novel is presented as a single letter—comprising over three hundred sections interweaving fact and fantasy—that is written to a slave-girl on the eve of the protagonist's execution. Critics gave the work a mixed reception. *New York Times Book Review* contributor Peter S. Prescott, for example, maintained that while the novel is "ambitious and imaginative," it nevertheless suffers from a "serious confusion of styles" and a lack of humor and wit. Boyd Tomkin, writing in the *Observer,* noted that "though he conjures up the sun-dried veldt, Brink's prose gorges on a lush glut of ideas. It leaves its readers as drunk as its hero, addled but inspired."

Brink returns to contemporary political concerns with his 1996 novel *Imaginings of Sand.* This work concentrates on the experiences of Kristien, a disaffected Afrikaner who living in self-imposed exile in England returns to her native land to care for her dying grandmother during the elections that ultimately bring an end to the apartheid system. Critics were divided in their assessment of Brink's handling of female characters in this work. *Spectator* reviewer Barbara Trapido asserted that the main character, "who is offered to the reader as the spirit of defiance, a left-hander, a 'witch,' never really rises above drag act and disappoints with her ordinariness." Amanda Hopkinson maintained in the *New Statesman,* however, that "Brink raises even familiar feminist issues in intelligent ways." Similarly, the quality of the writing itself elicited conflicting responses. Hopkinson found Brink's style "varied and highly accomplished," while *New York Times* reviewer Richard Bernstein characterized *Imaginings of Sand* as "a ramshackle, muddled work always threatening to blow apart by virtue of its very extravagance." *Washington Times* contributor Martin Rubin described the work as Brink's "finest achievement yet. . . . More substantial than Nadine Gordimer's recent novels and more authentically rooted in myth than J.M. Coetzee's work." Alan Cheuse offered similar praise in his review for the *Chicago Tribune,* contending that "Brink presents his kinsmen in the patterns and rhythms of myth and legend, sometimes employing the techniques of magical realism, thus making his novel seem thoroughly African in texture and effect."

Devil's Valley concerns a group of Afrikaner settlers who have been isolated from the rest of the world for some 150 years. Their remote valley is difficult and dangerous for outsiders to visit, while those who leave the valley and talk too much tend to die mysteriously. When crime reporter Flip Lochner finds his way to Devil's Valley, the insular community begins to fall apart. According to Lorna Sage, reviewing the book for the *New York Times, Devil's Valley* "stages a ritual resurrection and reburial of the Afrikaner past."

Translated as *The Rights of Desire, Donkermaan* is a novel about a May-December romance. Ruben Olivier is an aging former librarian who lost his job to a black man after South Africa's white government fell from power. He has retreated into his home, listening to classical music, reading books, and contemplating his life, which includes the loss of his wife in an accident. Olivier's children, who have moved out of the country, urge him to leave, too. Barring that, they ask him to take on a boarder so that there is someone else in the house with him. Ruben takes their advice and brings a young woman named Tessa Butler into his home. Tessa, who seems to be in some sort of trouble and is in need of a

place to stay, is a rather radical figure in Ruben's life. She smokes dope, is promiscuous, and even flirts with Ruben. The two form a bond that is linked in interesting conversations—not just sexual tensions—and Tessa's unique perspective on life forces Ruben to reexamine his past, including his political beliefs, and realize that he is not the man he has convinced himself he is. Into this tale, Brink also throws in Ruben's maid, Margrieta Daniels, whose keen sensibilities prevent Ruben from getting away with anything, even in his own house, and Antje of Bengal, the ghost of a woman who was a slave and accomplice to murder, who was executed for her crime.

While calling *The Rights of Desire* "probably the most intimate one Brink has ever written," Ludo Stynen commented in *World Literature Today* that the author "makes it very clear that writing without politics is impossible as far as he is concerned." The politics of living in South Africa seep into the story inevitably. Stynen added, "Reminiscences and fragments of other texts, historical facts and fiction, the mystery element, and the in fact predictably unpredictable woman make the work an unmistakable Brink novel. It is a well-told story and a valuable contribution to the social debate." Other reviewers, commenting on *The Rights of Desire,* did not rank it with Brink's best efforts. Edward B. St. John, for example, commented in *Library Journal* that "this novel is essentially an old-fashioned and somewhat predictable May-December romance." A *Publishers Weekly* reviewer similarly felt the novel "isn't Brink's best effort"; however, the critic went on to praise Brink as "a consummately professional storyteller, and the voice of his narrator, with its subtle wit and vulnerability, is a welcome one."

In the 2002 novel *The Other Side of Silence* Brink pens an indictment of colonialism and sexism in German South-West Africa, which is modern-day Nambia. Set in the early 1900s, the novel tells the story of Hanna X, an orphan whose ultimate life journey is one of degradation and violence. The first part of the novel focuses on Hanna's life in Germany and the humiliation she suffers working as a domestic in family households, where the husbands typically make sexual advances towards her. Hanna ends up immigrating to South-West Africa as part of a German government-sponsored movement promoting emigration by single women to provide brides for male farmers and traders living in the colony. Hanna's journey is not one to safety, however. She is attacked and mutilated, and her tongue cut out, by a sadistic German officer named Bohlke. Hanna ends up at a terrifying outpost known as the Frauenstein, where unwanted and abused women are kept. For the remainder of the book, Brink details Hanna's escape and trail of revenge as she forms a small vigilante group that murders German soldiers as they hunt for Bohlke.

Writing in the *Washington Times,* Judith Chettle found Brink's characters in *The Other Side of Silence* somewhat stereotypical: "The white men, with rare exceptions, are sexually obsessed brutes, the Africans noble, and the women, especially the heroine Hanna X, helpless victims." Chettle went on to note, "But though the settings are vividly evoked, and the story often compelling, it is too message-driven to completely satisfy." A *Publishers Weekly* contributor also found Hanna to be, at times, a "one-dimensional character" because of the relentless violence depicted. Nevertheless, the reviewer noted that "the imagery from this haunting novel will stay with readers as will the frightening allure of all-consuming hatred." Brendan Driscoll, writing in *Booklist,* maintained that *The Other Side of Silence* "proves provocative by evoking these themes [—violence, memory, and apartheid—] within the unconventional setting of German colonialism." In a review for *Library Journal,* Lawrence Rungren commented, "Brutal in its action while poetic in its language, this is an unflinching portrayal of the savagery just beneath civilization's skin."

Reinventing a Continent: Writing and Politics in South Africa is a collection of Brink's essays concerning apartheid, the Afrikaners who settled his homeland, and the grim chaos of South Africa's struggling democratic government. Throughout the book, Brink focuses on the role of the writer in political matters and asks what role those writers who opposed apartheid for so long can now play in a black-run society. "Brink chronicles," Vanessa Bush noted in *Booklist,* "a 15-year period in the political and social transformation of South Africa." According to a reviewer for *Publishers Weekly,* the novelist presents readers with "a thoughtful and human response to injustice."

Brink turns his attention to the crafting of literature in his nonfiction work *The Novel: Language and Narrative from Cervantes to Calvino,* a survey of fifteen classic novels. While his own novels have been marked by their strong political preoccupations, Brink argues that the genre is really about a play with language. He backs up his argument with examples from such works as *Don Quixote* and Italo Calvino's *If on a Winter Night a Traveller.* Writing in the *New York Times,* Peter Brooks found that "Brink is an alert, enthusiastic and engaging reader, who reports his reading experiences with wit and fluency." Thomas L. Cooksey concluded in *Library Journal* that Brink's text is "marked by clarity, insight, and comprehension."

"Since my tastes in literature are catholic," Brink once remarked to *CA,* "I have never been a disciple of any one school. The most abiding influence on my work, however, has been Albert Camus, notably in his view of man in a state of incessant revolt against the conditions imposed upon him, and reacting creatively to the challenge of meaninglessness. In much of my work this is linked to an element of mysticism derived from the Spanish writers of the seventeenth century. The other most abiding influence on my writing is the study of history. All my work is pervaded with a sense of 'roots,' whether in the collective history of peoples or in the private history of an individual." Brink added, "However close my work is to the realities of South Africa today, the political situation remains a starting point only for my attempts to explore the more abiding themes of human loneliness and man's efforts to reach out and touch someone else. My stated conviction is that literature should never descend to the level of politics; it is rather a matter of elevating and refining politics so as to be worthy of literature."

BIOGRAPHICAL AND CRITICAL SOURCES:

BOOKS

Contemporary Literary Criticism, Thomson Gale (Detroit, MI), Volume 18, 1981, Volume 36, 1986.
Jolly, Rosemary Jane, *Colonization, Violence, and Narration in White South African Writing: André Brink, Breyten Breytenbach, and J.M. Coetzee,* Ohio University Press (Athens, OH), 1995.

PERIODICALS

Atlantic, October, 1978.
Best Sellers, February, 1979.
Booklist, July, 1998, Vanessa Bush, review of *Reinventing a Continent: Writing and Politics in South Africa,* p. 1852; March 15, 1999, review of *Devil's Valley,* p. 1288; May 15, 2003, Brendan Driscoll, review of *The Other Side of Silence,* p. 1637.
Bookwatch, October, 1998, review of *Reinventing a Continent,* p. 9.
Canadian Forum, December, 1983.
Chicago Tribune, September 5, 1995; October 16, 1996; November 24, 1996.
Choice, November, 1998, review of *The Novel,* p. 515.
Christian Science Monitor, March 10, 1980; July 21, 1982; April 10, 1985; June 4, 1986.
Commonweal, September 12, 1975; July 13, 1984.

English Journal, January, 1998, Patricia Faith Goldb-
    latt, review of *Imaginings of Sand,* p. 111.
Globe and Mail (Toronto, Ontario, Canada), August 20,
    1988.
Kirkus Reviews, March 15, 1989; March 1, 1998, re-
    view of *The Novel,* p. 310; July 1, 1998, review of
    Reinventing a Continent, p. 940; January 15, 1999,
    review of *Devil's Valley,* p. 81; January 15, 2001,
    review of *The Rights of Desire,* p. 69.
Library Journal, August, 1975; February 15, 1977;
    April 1, 1985; April 15, 1998, Thomas L. Cooksey,
    review of *The Novel,* p. 78; February 15, 1999, re-
    view of *Devil's Valley,* p. 181; January 1, 2001, Ed-
    ward B. St. John, review of *The Rights of Desire,*
    p. 151; March 1, 2003, Lawrence Rungren, review
    of *The Other Side of Silence,* p. 116.
Listener, October 8, 1987.
London Magazine, June, 1979.
London Review of Books, August 4, 1988.
Los Angeles Times, August 19, 1987; May 18, 1989;
    September 29, 1989; October 7, 1989; October 15,
    1989; April 17, 1990; January 26, 1992; August 29,
    1993.
Los Angeles Times Book Review, March 21, 1999, re-
    view of *Devil's Valley,* p. 2.
Maclean's, May 10, 1982.
Nation, June 21, 1986; April 6, 1992, p. 455.
New Leader, January 14-28, 1985.
New Republic, October 21, 1978; April 30, 1984.
New Statesman, November 17, 1978; October 5, 1979;
    July 8, 1983; September 28, 1984; December 6,
    1985; August 29, 1986; August 27, 1993, p. 37;
    February 23, 1996, p. 45.
Newsweek, December 2, 1974.
New Yorker, August 25, 1975.
New York Review of Books, December 2, 1982; April
    25, 1985.
New York Times, February 2, 1984; March 6, 1984;
    September 17, 1989; September 20, 1989; Septem-
    ber 25, 1989; December 11, 1996; August 2, 1998,
    Peter Brooks, "What Flaubert Knew."
New York Times Book Review, February 27, 1977;
    March 23, 1980; June 13, 1982; March 17, 1985;
    June 29, 1986; January 12, 1992, p. 6; July 25,
    1993, p. 1; August 14, 1994, p. 94; August 2, 1998,
    review of *The Novel,* p. 20; March 21, 1999, Lorna
    Sage, "Escape from Paradise," p. 8.
Observer (London, England), May 15, 1988; August
    29, 1993; August 16, 1998, review of *Devil's Val-
    ley,* p. 15.
Publishers Weekly, March 10, 1989; June 22, 1998, re-
    view of *Reinventing a Continent,* p. 74; January 18,
    1999, review of *Devil's Valley,* p. 326; March 5,
    2001, review of *The Rights of Desire,* p. 60; April
    7, 2003, review of *The Other Side of Silence,* p. 42.

Reference and Research Book News, November, 1998,
    review of *The Novel,* p. 198; February, 1999, re-
    view of *Reinventing a Continent,* p. 35.
San Francisco Review of Books, January, 1992.
Saturday Review, August 23, 1975.
Shakespeare Quarterly, summer, 1998, review of *Desta-
    bilising Shakespeare,* p. 235.
Spectator, September 18, 1976; October 6, 1984; Febru-
    ary 17, 1996.
Studies in the Novel, spring, 2002, Isidore Diala, "His-
    tory and the Inscriptions of Torture as Purgatorial
    Fire in André Brink's Fiction," p. 60; winter, 2002,
    Isidore Diala, "The Political Limits of (Western)
    Humanism in André Brink's Early Fiction," p. 422.
Times (London, England), May 6, 1982; November 14,
    1985; March 3, 1990.
Times Literary Supplement, November 15, 1974; Sep-
    tember 17, 1976; October 20, 1978; May 14, 1982;
    September 16, 1983; October 5, 1984; January 10,
    1986; February 26, 1993; September 3, 1993; Feb-
    ruary 9, 1996; October 2, 1998, review of *The
    Novel,* p. 32.
UNESCO Courier, September, 1993, p. 4.
Voice Literary Supplement, November, 1987.
Washington Post, May 28, 1982; July 13, 1989; Sep-
    tember 22, 1989; September 26, 1989.
Washington Post Book World, January 20, 1980; Febru-
    ary 17, 1985; July 13, 1989; March 15, 1992.
Washington Times, November 24, 1996; June 22, 2003,
    Judith Chettle, review of *The Other Side of Silence,*
    p. B08.
World Literature Today, autumn, 1977; summer, 1984;
    winter, 1985; summer, 1986; spring, 1989; summer,
    1998, Sheila Roberts, review of *Die Jogger,* p. 674;
    autumn, 1998, review of *The Novel,* p. 908; spring,
    1999, review of *Reinventing a Continent,* p. 381;
    spring, 2001, Barend J. Toerien, review of *Groot
    verseboek 2000,* p. 311; summer-autumn, 2001, Ur-
    sula A. Barnett, review of *The Rights of Desire,*
    p. 106, and Ludo Stynen, review of *Donkermaan,*
    p. 123.

*   *   *

BRINK, André Philippus
    See BRINK, André

*   *   *

BRODSKY, Iosif Alexandrovich 1940-1996
    (Joseph Brodsky, Yosif Brodsky)

PERSONAL: Born May 24, 1940, in Leningrad (now
St. Petersburg), U.S.S.R. (now Russia); became naturalized U.S. citizen, 1977; died of heart failure, January

28, 1996, in Brooklyn Heights, New York; son of Alexander I. and Maria M. (Volpert) Brodsky; married wife (an Italian-Russian translator), 1990; children: Andrei, Anna. *Education:* Attended schools in Leningrad until 1956. *Religion:* Jewish

CAREER: Poet. Worked variously as a stoker, sailor, photographer, geologist's assistant on expedition to Central Asia, coroner's assistant, and farm laborer; University of Michigan, Ann Arbor, MI, poet-in-residence, 1972-73, 1974-79; Columbia University, New York, NY, adjunct professor; Mount Holyoke College, South Hadley, MA, educator, became Andrew W. Mellon Professor of Literature, 1990-96.

MEMBER: Bavarian Academy of Sciences (Munich; corresponding member), American Academy of Arts and Sciences, until 1987.

AWARDS, HONORS: D.Litt., Yale University, 1978, Dartmouth College, University of Keele, Amherst College, Uppsala University, University of Rochester, Williams College, Colchester University, and Oxford University; Mondello Prize (Italy), 1979; National Book Critics Circle Award nomination, 1980, for *A Part of Speech,* and award, 1986, for *Less than One: Selected Essays;* New York Institute for the Humanities fellowship; MacArthur fellowship, 1981; Guggenheim fellowship; Nobel Prize in Literature, 1987; Poet Laureate of the United States, 1991; Decorated Legion d'Honneur (France); Knight, Order of St. John of Malta.

WRITINGS:

Stikhotvoreniia i poemy (title means "Longer and Shorter Poems"), Inter-Language (Washington, DC), 1965.

Xol 'mi, translated by Jean-Jacques Marie and published in France as *Collines et autres poemes,* Editions de Seuil, 1966.

Ausgewahlte Gedichte, Bechtle Verlag, 1966.

Velka elegie, Edice Svedectvi (Paris, France), 1968.

Ostanovka v pustyne (title means "A Halt in the Wilderness"), Chekhov (New York, NY), 1970.

Konets prekrasnoi epokhi: Stikhotvoreniia, 1964-1971 (title means "The End of a Wonderful Era: Poems"), Ardis (Ann Arbor, MI), 1977.

Chast' rechi: Stikhotvoreniia, 1972-1976 (title means "A Part of Speech: Poems"), Ardis (Ann Arbor, MI), 1977, translation published as *A Part of Speech,* Farrar, Straus (New York, NY), 1980.

V Anglii (title means "In England"), Ardis (Ann Arbor, MI), 1977.

Verses on the Winter Campaign 1980, translation by Alan Meyers, Anvil Press (London, England), 1981.

Rimskie elegii (title means "Roman Elegies"), [New York, NY], 1982.

Novye stansy k Avguste: Stikhi k M.B., 1962-1982 (title means "New Stanzas to Augusta: Poems to M.B."), Ardis (Ann Arbor, MI), 1983.

Uraniia: Novaia kniga stikhov (title means "Urania: A New Book of Poems"), Ardis (Ann Arbor, MI), 1984, translation published as *To Urania: Selected Poems, 1965-1985,* Farrar, Straus (New York, NY), 1988.

Mramor, Ardis (Ann Arbor, MI), 1984.

(With Gianni Berengo Gardin) *Gli anni di Venezia,* F. Motta (Milan, Italy), 1994.

Isaak I Avraam, Izd-vo M.K. (St. Petersburg, Russia), 1994.

Brodskii o Tsvetaevoi, Nezavisimaia gazeta (Moscow, Russia), 1997.

Pis-mo Goratsiiu, Nash dom-L'age d'Homme (Moscow, Russia), 1998.

Gorbunov i Gorchakov, Pushkinskii fond (St. Petersburg, Russia), 1999.

Predstavlenie, Novoe literaturnoe obozrenie (Moscow, Russia), 1999.

Bol'shaia kniga interv'iu, Zakharov (Moscow, Russia), 2000.

Peremena imperii: stikhotvoreniia, 1960-1996, Nezavisimaia gazeta (Moscow, Russia), 2001.

Iosif Brodskii: Uraniia: Leningrad-Venetsiia-Neiu Iork: 11 aprelia-31 avgusta 2003, [redaktor, IA.A. Gordin], Muzei Anny Akhmatovoi v Fontannom dome: Izd-vo zhurnala "Zvezda" (St. Petersburg, Russia), 2003.

UNDER NAME JOSEPH BRODSKY

Elegy to John Donne and Other Poems, selected, translated, and introduced by Nicholas Bethell, Longmans, Green (London, England), 1967.

Poems, Ardis (Ann Arbor, MI), 1972.

Selected Poems, translated by George L. Kline, Harper (New York, NY), 1973.

(Editor, with Carl Proffer) *Modern Russian Poets on Poetry: Blok, Mandelstam, Pasternak, Mayakovsky, Gumilev, Tsvetaeva* (nonfiction), Ardis (Ann Arbor, MI), 1976.

Less than One: Selected Essays, Farrar, Straus (New York, NY), 1986.

(Editor, with Alan Myers) *An Age Ago: A Selection of Nineteenth-Century Russian Poetry,* Farrar, Straus (New York, NY), 1988.

Marbles: A Play in Three Acts, Farrar, Straus (New York, NY), 1989.

Watermark, Farrar, Straus (New York, NY), 1992.

(With Alexander Liberman) *Campidoglio: Michaelangelo's Roman Capitol,* Random House (New York, NY), 1994.

(Editor) *The Essential Hardy,* Ecco Press (Hopewell, NJ), 1995.

On Grief and Reason: Essays, Farrar, Straus (New York, NY), 1995.

So Forth: Poems, Farrar, Straus (New York, NY), 1995.

(With Seamus Heaney and Derek Walcott) *Homage to Robert Frost,* Farrar, Straus (New York, NY), 1996.

Discovery, Farrar, Straus (New York, NY), 1999.

Collected Poems in English, edited by Ann Kjellberg, Farrar, Straus (New York, NY), 2000.

Nativity Poems, Farrar, Straus (New York, NY), 2001.

Joseph Brodsky: Conversations, edited by Cynthia L. Haven, University Press of Mississippi (Jackson, MS), 2002.

Contributor to *Three Slavic Poets: Joseph Brodsky, Tymoteusz Karpowicz, Djordie Nikoloc,* edited by John Rezek, Elpenor Books, 1975.

Translations of Brodsky's poems appear in James Scully's *Avenue of the Americas,* University of Massachusetts Press, 1971, and in *New Underground Russian Poets: Poems by Yosif Brodsky and others.* Poems have been published in anthologies in twelve languages, and in *Russian Review, New York Review of Books, Nouvelle Revue Française, Unicorn Journal, Observer Review, Kultura, La Fiera Letteraria, New Yorker, New Leader,* and other journals. Author also translated poetry from English and Polish into Russian, and from Russian into Hebrew.

SIDELIGHTS: Iosif Alexandrovich Brodsky was reviled and persecuted in his native Soviet Union, but the Western literary establishment lauded him as one of that country's finest poets. From the time he began publishing his verse—both under his own name, and under the name Joseph Brodsky—which was characterized by ironic wit and a spirit of fiery independence, Brodsky aroused the ire of Soviet authorities; he was also persecuted because he was a Jew. He was brought to trial for "parasitism," and a smuggled transcript of that trial helped bring him to the attention of the West, for he answered his interrogators with courageous and articulate idealism. Brodsky was condemned to a Soviet mental

institution and later spent five years in Arkhangelsk, an Arctic labor camp. A public outcry from American and European intellectuals over his treatment helped to secure his early release. Forced to emigrate, he moved to Michigan in 1972, where, with the help of the poet W.H. Auden, he settled in at the University of Michigan in Ann Arbor as poet-in-residence. He then taught at several universities, including Queens College in New York and Mount Holyoke College in Massachusetts. He continued to write poetry, however, often writing in Russian and translating his own work into English, and eventually winning the Nobel Prize for his work. His predominant themes were exile and loss, and he was widely praised for his hauntingly eloquent writing style.

In many ways, Brodsky had lived as an exile before leaving his homeland. His father had lost a position of rank in the Russian Navy because he was Jewish, and the family lived in poverty. Trying to escape the ever-present images of Lenin, Brodsky quit school and embarked on a self-directed education, reading literary classics and working a variety of unusual jobs, which included assisting a coroner and a geologist in Central Asia. He learned English and Polish so that he would be able to translate the poems of John Donne and Czeslaw Milosz. His own poetry expressed his independent character with an originality admired by poets such as Anna Akhmatova.

According to a *Times Literary Supplement* reviewer, Brodsky's poetry "is religious, intimate, depressed, sometimes confused, sometimes martyr-conscious, sometimes elitist in its views, but it does not constitute an attack on Soviet society or ideology unless withdrawal and isolation are deliberately construed as attack: of course they can be, and evidently were." According to a reviewer in *Time,* the poet's expulsion from Russia was "the culmination of an inexplicable secret-police vendetta against him that has been going on for over a decade." Brodsky said: "They have simply kicked me out of my country, using the Jewish issue as an excuse." The vendetta first came to a head in a Leningrad trial in 1964, when Brodsky was charged with writing "gibberish" instead of doing honest work; he was sentenced to five years hard labor. Protests from artists and writers helped to secure his release after eighteen months, but his poetry still was banned. Israel invited him to immigrate, and the government encouraged him to go; Brodsky, though, refused, explaining that he did not identify with the Jewish state. Finally, Russian officials insisted that he leave the country. Despite the pressures, Brodsky reportedly wrote to Leonid Brezhnev before leaving Moscow, asking to be allowed to stay in Russia and work in Russian literature.

Brodsky's poetry bears the marks of his confrontations with the Russian authorities. "Brodsky is someone who has tasted extremely bitter bread," wrote Stephen Spender in *New Statesman,* "and his poetry has the air of being ground out between his teeth. . . . It should not be supposed that he is a liberal, or even a socialist. He deals in unpleasing, hostile truths and is a realist of the least comforting and comfortable kind. Everything nice that you would like him to think, he does not think. But he is utterly truthful, deeply religious, fearless and pure. Loving, as well as hating."

Brodsky elaborated on the relationship between poetry and politics in his Nobel lecture, "Uncommon Visage," published in *Poets & Writers* magazine. Art teaches the writer, he said, "the privateness of the human condition. Being the most ancient as well as the most literal form of private enterprise, it fosters in a man . . . a sense of his uniqueness, of individuality, or separateness— thus turning him from a social animal into an autonomous 'I.'" Brodsky went on to note, "A work of art, of literature especially, and a poem in particular, addresses a man tete-a-tete, entering with him into direct—free of any go-betweens—relations."

In addition, literature points to experience that transcends political limits. Brodsky observed, "Language and, presumably, literature are things that are more ancient and inevitable, more durable than any form of social organization. The revulsion, irony, or indifference often expressed by literature toward the state is essentially the reaction of the permanent—better yet, the infinite—against the temporary, against the finite. . . . The real danger for a writer is not so much the possibility (and often the certainty) of persecution on the part of the state, as it is the possibility of finding oneself mesmerized by the state's features which, whether monstrous or undergoing changes for the better, are always temporary."

Brodsky went on to say that creative writing is an essential exercise of individual freedom, since the writer must make many aesthetic judgments and choices during the process of composition. He pointed out, "It is precisely in this . . . sense that we should understand Dostoyevsky's remark that beauty will save the world, or Matthew Arnold's belief that we shall be saved by poetry. It is probably too late for the world, but for the individual man there always remains a chance. . . . If what distinguishes us from other members of the animal kingdom is speech, then literature—and poetry, in particular, being the highest form of locution—is, to put it bluntly, the goal of our species."

Even more compelling than the relationship between poetry and politics is the relationship between the writer and his language, Brodsky claimed. He explained in Nobel speech that the first experience the writer has when taking up a pen to write "is . . . the sensation of immediately falling into dependence on language, on everything that has already been uttered, written, and accomplished in it." But the past accomplishments of a language do not impinge on the writer more than the sense of its vast potential. Brodsky added, "There are times when, by means of a single word, a single rhyme, the writer of a poem manages to find himself where no one has ever been before him, further, perhaps, than he himself would have wished for. . . . Having experienced this acceleration once . . . one falls into dependency on this process, the way others fall into dependency on drugs or alcohol."

In keeping with these views, Brodsky's poetry is known for its originality. Arthur C. Jacobs, in the *Jewish Quarterly,* noted that Brodsky is "quite apart from what one thinks of as the main current of Russian verse." A critic in *New Leader* wrote: "The noisy rant and attitudinizing rhetoric of public issues are superfluous to Brodsky's moral vision and contradictory to his craft. As with all great lyric poets, Brodsky attends to the immediate, the specific, to what he has internally known and felt, to the lucidities of observation heightened and defined by thought."

Though many critics agreed that Brodsky was one of the finest contemporary Russian poets, some felt that the English translations of his poetry are less impressive. Commenting on George L. Kline's translation of *Selected Poems, Joseph Brodsky* in the *New Statesman,* Spender wrote: "These poems are impressive in English, though one is left having to imagine the technical virtuosity of brilliant rhyming in the originals. . . . One is never quite allowed to forget that one is reading a second-hand version." In *A Part of Speech,* Brodsky gathered the work of several translators and made amendments to some of the English versions in an attempt to restore the character of the originals. Brodsky's personal style remains somewhat elusive in that collection due to the subtle effects he achieves in the original Russian, Tom Simmons observed in the *Christian Science Monitor.* Brodsky, he said, "is a poet of dramatic yet delicate vision—a man with a sense of the increasingly obscured loftiness of human life. But under no circumstances is his poetry dully ethereal. . . . He can portray a luminous moment or a time of seemingly purposeless suffering with equal clarity."

Czeslaw Milosz felt that Brodsky's background allowed him to make a vital contribution to literature. Writing in the *New York Review of Books,* Milosz stated, "Behind Brodsky's poetry is the experience of political terror, the experience of the debasement of man and the growth of the totalitarian empire. . . . I find it fascinating to read his poems as part of his larger enterprise, which is no less than an attempt to fortify the place of man in a threatening world." This enterprise connected Brodsky to the literary traditions of other times and cultures.

Exile was always difficult for Brodsky. In one poem, he describes an exiled writer as one "who survives like a fish in the sand." Yet despite these feelings, Brodsky was largely unmoved by the sweeping political changes that accompanied the fall of the Soviet Union. He told David Remnick of the *Washington Post* that those changes were "devoid of autobiographical interest" for him, and that his allegiance was to his language. In the *Detroit Free Press,* Bob McKelvey cited Brodsky's declaration from a letter: "I belong to the Russian culture. I feel part of it, its component, and no change of place can influence the final consequence of this. A language is a much more ancient and inevitable thing than a state. I belong to the Russian language."

Shortly before his death, Brodsky completed *So Forth,* a collection of poems he wrote in English, or translated himself from poetry he wrote in Russian. *So Forth* was judged inferior to Brodsky's best work by several critics, including Michael Glover, who in *New Statesman* described the collection as "more failure than success." Glover felt that too often Brodsky "lapses into a kind of swashbuckling slanginess, a kind of raw muscularity that, at its worst, reads like embarrassing doggerel." Yet others found *So Forth* a powerful statement, such as a *Publishers Weekly* contributor who called it "an astonishing collection from a writer able to mix the cerebral and the sensual, the political and the intimate, the elegiac and the comic. . . . Brodsky's death is a loss to literature; his final collection of poems is the best consolation we could ask for."

Collected Poems in English, published posthumously, is a definitive collection of Brodsky's translated work and his original work in English. It is "dramatic and ironic, melancholy and blissful," reported Donna Seaman in *Booklist.* She claimed this volume "will stand as one of the twentieth century's tours de force." *Collected Poems in English* is "a highly accomplished, deft, and entertaining book, with a talent for exploitation of the richness of language and with a deep core of sorrow," commented Judy Clarence in *Library Journal.* It captures Brodsky's trademark sense of "stepping aside and peering in bewilderment" at life, according to Sven

Birkerts in the *New York Review of Books.* Birkerts concluded: "Brodsky charged at the world with full intensity and wrestled his perceptions into lines that fairly vibrate with what they are asked to hold. There is no voice, no vision, remotely like it."

In 2001, a collection of eighteen Christmas poems by Brodsky were published as *Nativity Poems.* According to Paul Mariani, writing in *America,* Brodsky once told an interviewer, "Ever since I took to writing poems seriously . . . I've tried to write a poem for every Christmas—as a sort of birthday greeting. Several times I've missed the opportunity, let it slip by. One or another circumstance blocked the road." The poems range from 1962, when Brodsky was twenty-two, until 1992. They were translated from the original Russian, which appears on the facing pages, by six poets, including Brodsky. Judy Clarence, writing in *Library Journal,* called the collection "enjoyable." Mariani noted that the early Christmas poems, written while Brodsky underwent hardships in the former Soviet Union, were much different than the later poems, commenting that the early poems were "more concerned with surviving the dark turning of the year than about Christ's coming among us. They're brash, angry poems, and you feel Brodsky is simply trying to stay alive in a world where that takes some doing." Mariani went on to comment that the later poems were "in fact Christmas poems. The focus has changed. Brodsky seems to have slowed down, he seems to have more breathing room, and he can begin to ask what Christmas may be all about."

BIOGRAPHICAL AND CRITICAL SOURCES:

BOOKS

Authors in the News, Volume 1, Thomson Gale (Detroit, MI), 1973.

Bethea, David, *Joseph Brodsky and the Creation of Exile,* Princeton University Press (Princeton, NJ), 1994.

Brodsky, Joseph, *A Part of Speech,* Farrar, Straus (New York, NY), 1980.

Contemporary Literary Criticism, Thomson Gale (Detroit, MI), Volume 4, 1975, Volume 6, 1976, Volume 36, 1986, Volume 50, 1988.

Speh, Alice J., *The Poet as Traveler: Joseph Brodsky in Mexico and Rome,* Peter Lang (New York, NY), 1996.

PERIODICALS

Agenda, winter, 1998, review of *On Grief and Reason: Essays* and *So Forth: Poems,* p. 140.

America, December 17, 2001, Paul Mariani, review of *Nativity Poems,* p. 18.

Antioch Review, winter, 1985; spring, 1996, Gerda Oldham, review of *On Grief and Reason: Essays,* pp. 247-248.

Bloomsbury Review, March, 1998, review of *Homage to Robert Frost,* p. 22.

Booklist, July, 1996, Donna Seaman, review of *So Forth,* p. 1797; August, 2000, Donna Seaman, review of *Collected Poems in English,* p. 2100.

Books in Canada, summer, 1996, review of *On Grief and Reason,* p. 12.

Book World, February 11, 1996, review of *On Grief and Reason,* p. 13.

Children's Book Review Service, December, 1999, review of *Discovery,* p. 42.

Choice, April, 1974; September, 1977.

Christian Century, November 11, 1987.

Christian Science Monitor, August 11, 1980, Tom Simmons, review of *A Part of Speech.*

Commonweal, November 5, 1999, review of *Discovery,* p. 24.

Contemporary Review, June, 1997, review of *Watermark,* p. 334.

Detroit Free Press, September 17, 1972; October 23, 1987.

Hungry Mind Review, fall, 1999, review of *Discovery,* p. 33.

Jewish Quarterly, winter, 1968-69, Arthur C. Jacobs.

Kirkus Reviews, July 1, 1996, review of *Homage to Robert Frost,* p. 940; September 15, 1999, review of *Discovery,* p. 1498.

Knight-Ridder/Tribune News Service, March 12, 1996; October 16, 1996.

Library Journal, June 1, 1996, Graham Christian, review of *So Forth,* p. 110; November 15, 1996, Denise S. Sticha, review of *Homage to Robert Frost,* p. 62; January, 1997, review of *So Forth,* p. 48; August, 2000, Judy Clarence, review of *Collected Poems in English,* p. 109; March 1, 2002, Judy Clarence, review of *Nativity Poems,* p. 104.

Los Angeles Times, October 23, 1987; February 15, 1989.

Los Angeles Times Book Review, October 20, 1996, review of *Homage to Robert Frost,* p. 14; November 7, 1999, review of *Discovery,* p. 8.

Nation, October 4, 1980; February 12, 1996, Jessica Greenbaum, review of *On Grief and Reason,* pp. 32-33.

New Leader, December 10, 1973; December 14, 1987; October 31, 1988; September 9, 1996, John Simon, reviews of *So Forth* and *On Grief and Reason,* pp. 14-19; January 13, 1997, Phoebe Pettingell, review of *Homage to Robert Frost,* pp. 14-15.

New Republic, March 4, 1996, Stanislaw Baranczak, review of *On Grief and Reason,* pp. 39-42.

New Statesman, December 14, 1973; December 20, 1996, Michael Glover, reviews of *On Grief and Reason* and *So Forth,* pp. 119-120.

New Statesman and Society, June 19, 1992, p. 24.

Newsweek, November 2, 1987.

New Yorker, July 13, 1992, p. 84; December 16, 1996, review of *So Forth,* p. 107.

New York Review of Books, August 14, 1980, Czeslaw Milosz, review of *A Part of Speech;* January 21, 1988; November 24, 1988; February 1, 1996, J.M. Coetzee, review of *On Grief and Reason,* pp. 28-31; September 17, 2000, Sven Birkerts, review of *Collected Poems in English.*

New York Times, October 31, 1987.

New York Times Book Review, November 8, 1987; May 31, 1992; February 29, 1996, p. 7; March 3, 1996, Seamus Heaney, "The Singer of Tales: On Joseph Brodsky," p. 31; April 14, 1996, Hugh Kenner, review of *On Grief and Reason,* p. 14; September 1, 1996, John Bayley, review of *So Forth,* p. 6; December 8, 1996, review of *So Forth,* p. 82; April 26, 1998, review of *So Forth,* p. 36; November 21, 1999, Deborah Hautzig, review of *Discovery,* p. 57.

Observer (London, England), October 27, 1996, review of *On Grief and Reason,* p. 15; September 28, 1997, review of *On Grief and Reason,* p. 18; January 4, 1998, review of *Homage to Robert Frost,* p. 15.

Partisan Review, fall, 1974.

Poetry, October, 1975; November, 1988; June, 1997, John Taylor, review of *So Forth,* pp. 169-172; April, 2001, F.D. Reeve, review of *Collected Poems in English,* p. 31.

Poets & Writers, March-April, 1988.

Publishers Weekly, June 1, 1996, Graham Christian, review of *So Forth,* p. 110; June 24, 1996, review of *So Forth,* p. 51; July 15, 1996, review of *Homage to Robert Frost,* p. 60; July 21, 1997, review of *Homage to Robert Frost,* p. 199; October 18, 1999, review of *Discovery,* p. 80; June 26, 2000, review of *Collected Poems in English,* p. 71.

School Library Journal, November, 1999, review of *Discovery,* p. 168.

Sewanee Review, April, 1996, review of *On Grief and Reason,* p. 295.

Texas Studies in Literature and Language, number 17, 1975.

Time, June 19, 1972; August 7, 1972; April 7, 1986; November 2, 1987.

Times Literary Supplement, July 20, 1967; January 10, 1997, reviews of *So Forth* and *On Grief and Reason,* p. 6.

Translation Review Supplement, July, 1997, review of *So Forth,* p. 35.

Tribune Books (Chicago, IL), February 11, 1996, review of *On Grief and Reason,* p. 3.

Village Voice Literary Supplement, winter, 1996, review of *So Forth,* p. 8.

Vogue, February, 1988.

Washington Post, October 23, 1987; March 21, 1996, Richard Cohen, "One of Them's a Poet," p. A17.

Washington Post Book World, August 24, 1980.

Wilson Quarterly, autumn, 1996, review of *Homage to Robert Frost,* p. 97.

World Literature Today, spring, 1996, Theodore Ziolkowsky, review of *On Grief and Reason,* p. 479; summer, 1997, Rosette C. Lamont, review of *So Forth,* pp. 592-593; autumn, 1997, William Pratt, review of *Homage to Robert Frost,* p. 801, "Peizazh S Navodneniem," p. 819; winter, 1997, David MacFadyen, "24 May 1996 in St. Petersburg, Russia: The Perceived Significance of Joseph Brodsky's Legacy," pp. 81-86; spring, 1998, "Brodskii o Tsvetaevoi," p. 406; summer-autumn, 2002, Victor Terras, review of *Nativity Poems,* p. 146.

ONLINE

Academy of American Poets, http://www.poets.org/ (August 28, 2004), "Joseph Brodsky."

OBITUARIES:

PERIODICALS

Chicago Tribune, January 29, 1996, p. 6.

Los Angeles Times, January 29, 1996, p. A14.

New Republic, February 19, 1996, pp. 10-11.

New York Times, January 29, 1996, pp. A1, B5.

Washington Post, January 29, 1996, p. B4; January 30, 1996, p. D1.

*   *   *

BRODSKY, Joseph
  See BRODSKY, Iosif Alexandrovich

*   *   *

BRODSKY, Yosif
  See BRODSKY, Iosif Alexandrovich

BROOKNER, Anita 1928-

PERSONAL: Born July 16, 1928, in London, England; daughter of Newson (a company director) and Maude (a singer; maiden name, Schiska) Brookner. *Education:* King's College, London, B.A., 1949; Courtauld Institute of Art, London, Ph.D., 1953; three-year postgraduate scholarship in Paris.

ADDRESSES: Agent—A.M. Heath, 79 St. Martin's Lane, London WC2, England.

CAREER: Writer. University of Reading, Reading, England, visiting lecturer in the history of art, 1959-64; Courtauld Institute of Art, London, lecturer, 1964-77, reader in the history of art, 1977-87 (retired); Cambridge University, Slade Professor of Art, 1967-68, New Hall fellow.

AWARDS, HONORS: Royal Society of Literature fellow, 1983; Booker McConnell Prize, National Book League, 1984, for *Hotel du Lac;* Commander, Order of the British Empire, 1990; Booker Prize, 2002, for *The Next Big Thing.*

WRITINGS:

NONFICTION; ART HISTORY AND CRITICISM

(Translator) Waldemar George, *Utrillo,* Oldbourne Press (London, England), 1960.

(Translator) Jean-Paul Crespelle, *The Fauves,* Oldbourne Press (London, England), 1962.

(Translator) Maximilien Gauthier, *Gauguin,* Oldbourne Press (London, England), 1963.

J.A. Dominique Ingres, Purnell (London, England), 1965.

Watteau, Hamlyn (London, England), 1968.

The Genius of the Future: Studies in French Art Criticism, Phaidon (London, England), 1971, published as *The Genius of the Future: Essays in French Art Criticism,* Cornell University Press (Ithaca, NY), 1988.

Greuze: The Rise and Fall of an Eighteenth-Century Phenomenon, Elek (London, England), 1972, New York Graphic Society (Greenwich, CT), 1974.

Jacques-Louis David: A Personal Interpretation: Lecture on Aspects of Art, Oxford University Press (London, England), 1974, revised edition, Thames & Hudson (New York, NY), 1987.

Jacques-Louis David, Chatto & Windus (London, England), 1980, Harper (New York, NY), 1981, revised edition, Thames & Hudson (New York, NY), 1987.

Soundings: Studies in Art and Literature (essays; art and literature criticism), Harvill Press (London, England), 1997.

Romanticism and Its Discontents, Farrar, Straus & Giroux (New York, NY), 2000.

Also author of *An Iconography of Cecil Rhodes,* 1956. Contributor of essays on Rigaud, Delacroix, Ingres, and Cezanne to a British Broadcasting Corporation (BBC) production on painters, 1980, published as *Great Paintings,* edited by Edwin Mullins, St. Martin's Press, 1981. Contributor to *The Brothers Goncourt and the Nineteenth-Century Novel,* edited by Richard Faber, Boydell (Wolfeboro, NH), 1988. Also contributor to "The Masters" series, Purnell (London, England), 1965-67.

NOVELS

The Debut, Linden Press (New York, NY), 1981, published as *A Start in Life,* J. Cape (London, England), 1981.

Providence, J. Cape (London, England), 1982, Pantheon (New York, NY), 1984.

Look at Me, Pantheon (New York, NY), 1983.

Hotel du Lac, Pantheon (New York, NY), 1984.

Family and Friends, Pantheon (New York, NY), 1985.

A Misalliance, J. Cape (London, England), 1986, published as *The Misalliance,* Pantheon (New York, NY), 1987.

A Friend from England, Pantheon (New York, NY), 1987.

Latecomers, Random House (New York, NY), 1988.

Lewis Percy, J. Cape (London, England), 1989, Pantheon (New York, NY), 1990.

Brief Lives, J. Cape (London, England), 1990, Random House, (New York, NY), 1991.

A Closed Eye, J. Cape (London, England), 1991, Random House (New York, NY), 1992.

Fraud, J. Cape (London, England), 1992, Random House (New York, NY), 1993.

A Family Romance, J. Cape (London, England), 1993, published as *Dolly,* Random House (New York, NY), 1994.

A Private View, J. Cape (London, England), 1994, Random House (New York, NY), 1995.

Incidents in the Rue Laugier, J. Cape (London, England), 1995, Random House (New York, NY), 1996.

Altered States, J. Cape (London, England), 1996, Random House (New York, NY), 1997.

Visitors, J. Cape (London, England), 1997, Random House (New York, NY), 1998.

Falling Slowly, Viking (London, England), 1998, Random House (New York, NY), 1999.

Undue Influence: A Novel, Viking (London, England), 1999, Random House (New York, NY), 2000.

The Bay of Angels, Viking (London, England), 2001, Random House (New York, NY), 2002.

The Next Big Thing, Viking (London, England), 2002, published as *Making Things Better,* Random House (New York, NY), 2003.

The Rules of Engagement, Random House (New York, NY), 2003.

Leaving Home, Viking (New York, NY), 2005.

OTHER

(Author of introduction) *The House of Mirth,* Macmillan (New York, NY), 1987.

(Editor and author of introduction) Edith Wharton, *The Stories of Edith Wharton,* Volume 2, Simon & Schuster (New York, NY), 1988.

(Selector and author of introduction) Edith Wharton, *The Collected Stories of Edith Wharton,* Carroll & Graf (New York, NY), 1998.

(Author of introduction) L.P. Hartley, *Eustace and Hilda: A Trilogy,* New York Review Books (New York, NY), 2001.

Also author of introduction to Margaret Kennedy's *Troy Chimneys,* Virago, 1985, Edith Templeton's *The Island of Desire,* 1985, *Summer in the Country,* 1985, and *Living on Yesterday,* 1986. Contributor of book reviews and articles to periodicals, including *Burlington, London Review of Books, London Standard,* London *Sunday Times, Observer, Spectator, Times Literary Supplement,* and *Writer.*

ADAPTATIONS: An adaptation of *Hotel du Lac* was coproduced in 1985 by the BBC and the Arts and Entertainment Network.

SIDELIGHTS: Anita Brookner is internationally acclaimed for her extensive knowledge and incisive explications of eighteenth-and nineteenth-century French artists and their work. She is an accomplished novelist as well, penning more than twenty novels since 1981, including the Booker McConnell prize-winning *Hotel du Lac.* Critical response to her work has included a great deal of praise, but Phillip Lopate dispelled whatever skepticism a first-time reader might have about the caliber or profusion of Brookner's work in the *New York Times Book Review:* "Yes, she is that good, and she keeps producing quality fiction at a calm, even rate precisely because she knows what she is doing. Each new Brookner novel seems a guarantee of the pleasures of a mature intelligence, felicitous language, quirky humor, intensely believable characters, bittersweet karma and shapely narrative."

Brookner, the first woman to be named Slade Professor of Art at Cambridge University, once referred to herself in a *Saturday Review* interview as a "speculative" art historian rather than a scholar. Her work attempts to position a subject within a larger context. For instance, *The Genius of the Future: Studies in French Art Criticism,* based upon Brookner's Slade lectures during the late 1960s, offers "paradigmatic" presentations of Diderot, Stendhal, Baudelaire, Zola, the Brothers Goncourt, and Huysmans, and identifies each with a principal idea that becomes a "touchstone for her discussion," wrote Robert E. Hosmer, Jr. in the *Dictionary of Literary Biography Yearbook: 1987.* Hosmer considered *The Genius of the Future* "a work of impeccable scholarship, precise, carefully annotated and designed, whose grace and narrative ease enable the discerning reader, whether art historian or layperson, to read it with pleasure and profit." *Greuze: The Rise and Fall of an Eighteenth-Century Phenomenon* grew out of Brookner's doctoral dissertation and sought to restore Jean-Baptiste Greuze to the historical recognition she believes his work warrants, said Hosmer, who called it "intellectually vital and engagingly written." A *New York Times Book Review* contributor similarly remarked that Brookner's "commanding acquaintance with everything and everybody, minor and major, in art, literature, and philosophy . . . is staggering, and the grace with which she organizes the minutiae to give them an air of spontaneity even more so." Brookner's *Jacques-Louis David: A Personal Interpretation,* the published version of her address to the British Academy in 1974, offers a biographical profile of the artist and traces the progress of his work. "Clearly a blueprint" for her lengthy study six years later, commented Hosmer, the work "testifies to Brookner's powers as a critical scholar and her charms as a lecturer: her text displays learning animated by anecdotal wit." In her subsequent major study, *Jacques-Louis David,* Brookner blends biography, history, and criticism to reveal that the artist's shifts in subject matter and style reflect political changes in France from the Revolution to the restoration of the monarchy twenty-five years later. Calling it "a reciprocal reading," Hosmer explained that Brookner demonstrates "how David was both formed by the sociopolitical/cultural context and how he helped to shape the forces creating that context." Praised by Richard Cobb in the *Times Literary Supplement* as "an art historian of great sensitivity and understanding," Brookner "provides a superb show of investigative work, a thorough and intelligent probing of the meaning of a man's art," maintained Celia Betsky in the *New Republic.*

Soundings: Studies in Art and Literature is a collection of essays written over a span of twenty-five years. The collection begins with essays on three nineteenth-century French artists, Gericault, Ingres, and Delacroix, and goes on to discuss the complex history of and tension between French Neoclassicism and Romanticism. Culled from Brookner's contributions to the *Times Literary Supplement* and the *London Review of Books,* the collection was generally well received by critics. "Her style evinces a contagious love of culture," asserted Douglas F. Smith in *Library Journal.* "It's to her credit that many of these reviews, some dating back to 1975, are far less stale than their onetime targets.""Brookner's survey of the last century can't help but provoke a pang of nostalgia for the classical urge manifested by these characters," wrote a *Publishers Weekly* reviewer.

Published in England as *A Start in Life* and in the United States as *The Debut,* Brookner's first novel concerns Ruth Weiss, a literary scholar in her forties who tries to escape a suffocating life of studying literature and coping with the demands of her aging parents. Disillusioned with literary notions that patience and virtue will triumph in the end, Ruth embraces the opportunistic view of the world expressed by Balzac; after the romantic affair she plans misfires, she returns home to care for her dying parents, and resigns herself to a lonely middle age. "As well as the arm's length of wit, there is a great deal of precision and perception" in Brookner's rendering of Ruth's story, commented Anne Duchene in the *Times Literary Supplement.* And although Duchene believed that Brookner goes too far in blaming literature "for the festering resentments of filial dutifulness," this "hardly matters, given the confidence of the telling." Art Seidenbaum remarked in a *Los Angeles Times* review: "The art historian who studied portraiture and landscapes also knows the terrain of the heart. Her heroine is almost historic, tethered to responsibility, but her technique is modern, hard-edged and as uneuphemistic as today."

With her second novel, *Providence,* Brookner "effectively claims her territory as a writer," suggested Frances Taliaferro in *Harper's.* The story focuses on another academic—Kitty Maule, a reserved, elegantly dressed professor of Romantic literature at a small, well-funded British college. Never having known her British father, Kitty was raised in the French traditions by her maternal grandparents—French and Russian immigrants, and feels like a foreigner in her native England. She falls in love with a handsome and clever colleague, Maurice Bishop, whose unshakable self-assurance and Catholic faith further impede her desire to assimilate into British culture. The *New York Times*' Michiko Kakutani, who praised Brookner's "sharp eye for the telling detail" and "graceful, economical way with words," pronounced Brookner a "master at creating miniaturist portraits of attenuated lives." However, because Brookner narrates the novel almost exclusively in terms of Kitty and through her perspective alone, according to Joyce Kornblatt in the *Washington Post,* the reader does not see her in a larger context—its "very strength—the vivid creation of Kitty Maule—becomes its limitation." Nonetheless, Kornblatt called the novel "perfectly observed and quietly witty," and praised its craft: "Each expertly paced scene is brought to life through a fastidious accretion of detail, a fine ear for speech, a narrative diction that is always intelligent and often arresting."

In *Look at Me,* her third novel, Brookner portrays the life of Frances Hinton, a young librarian at a British medical institute. Her dreary job of cataloging and filing pictures of death and disease is relieved only by observing the other staff members who frequent the institute's archives. Upon returning to her apartment, bequeathed by her deceased mother, she spends solitary evenings writing about the day's observations. Nick Fraser, an attractive young doctor at the institute, with his glamorous wife, Alix, befriends Frances and welcomes her into their intimate circle of friends. They introduce her to Nick's colleague James, with whom Frances shares a chaste romance; but when Frances and James try to secure some privacy in their relationship, they exclude Alix, who then abandons Frances. Angered, Frances finds release in writing the novel that becomes *Look at Me.* In a *Washington Post Book World* review, Julia Epstein deemed the book "a nearly impossible achievement, a novel about emptiness and vacancy." Believing that the protagonist's novel is "not so much self-reflexive as self-digesting, its material imaged and converted into prose even as it unfolds in Frances' life," Epstein concluded that *Look at Me* is "simultaneously a tragedy of solitude and loss, and a triumph of the sharp-tongued controlling self."

Brookner's fourth novel, *Hotel du Lac,* won the 1984 Booker McConnell Prize, Britain's most prestigious literary award. Like her three earlier novels, it is about romance and loneliness in the life of a discreet, educated, literary woman with conventional dreams of love and marriage; unlike her earlier novels, it suggests that rewards accompany boldness rather than goodness. The story centers on a thirty-nine-year-old London romance novelist, Edith Hope, who jilts her fiancée on her wedding day. Exiled to an off-season Swiss hotel by her family and friends, she spends her time observing the other guests, involving herself in their personal lives, writing letters to her married lover, and working on her latest novel. Edith's popular novels promote the romantic equivalent of Aesop's fable of the tortoise and the hare—that slow and steady wins the race; however, while Edith publicly acknowledges the falsity of the myth, she privately clings to romantic ideals of perfect love. The *New York Times*' John Gross, who considered Brookner "one of the finest novelists of her generation," called *Hotel du Lac* "a novel about romance, and reality, and the gap between them and the way the need for romance persists in the full knowledge of that gap." What distinguishes this novel from Brookner's previous novels, remarked Anne Tyler in the *Washington Post Book World,* is that in *Hotel du Lac,* "the heroine is more philosophical from the outset, more self-reliant, more conscious that a solitary life is not, after all, an unmitigated tragedy."

A Misalliance returns to a type of character familiar from Brookner's earlier novels—a repressed, intellectual woman who finds herself defined by the man she loves. Rejected by her husband of more than twenty years for his secretary, Blanche Vernon still yearns for his occasional visits and spends time in museums contemplating the two contrasting archetypes of woman she sees in paintings: pleasure-loving nymphs of ancient mythology and dutiful saints who personify emotional martyrdom. According to Kakutani, the character sees herself as the inevitable loser in a contest between women who are "calm, sincere, doting and honest in their dealing with men," and those who are "sly, petulant, manipulative and demanding." *Washington Post Book World* columnist Jonathan Yardley thought that what distinguishes this protagonist from her predecessors, though, "is that she had her chance at love and, much though she wanted to seize it, failed to do so out of misunderstanding and uncertainty." Critical consensus confirms that the novel solidified Brookner's status as a master of prose. Yardley believed that "in writing about these lonely women, she has universal business in mind: the peculiarities and uncertainties of love, the relationship between fate and will, the connections—and disconnections—between art and reality." However, in the *New York Times Book Review,* Fernanda Eberstadt lauded what she thought was the novel's "rather salutary and peculiarly welcome message, namely, that keeping up appearances in hard times is a virtue in itself, that kindness, self-restraint, good housekeeping and a certain cheerful worldliness may after all save the day. To this message, delivered with a lucid and refined intelligence and an invigorating asperity of tone, one can respond only with gratitude and pleasure."

A Friend from England presents a female protagonist who has recovered neither from the loss of her parents nor from a disillusioning love affair with a married man. Part owner of a London bookstore, Rachel lives alone in a bleak apartment and becomes increasingly involved in the sumptuous lifestyle of her accountant's family, the Livingstones, who are recent winners of the football pools. Rachel serves as a companion of sorts to their twenty-seven-year-old daughter, Heather. Although not especially fond of her charge, Rachel encourages her into independence; then, fearful of becoming a surrogate daughter to the Livingstones, reverses herself and tries to persuade Heather to return to her family. Describing Rachel as "repellently cold and cerebral," Deborah Singmaster added in the *Times Literary Supplement* that "she becomes increasingly sinister as the book progresses . . . her blundering insensitivity as she thrusts herself into the disintegrating lives of the Livingstones is mesmerizing." Praising Brookner's "unrivalled eye for the details of appearance and behaviour," Heather Neill added in the *Listener:* "Often she writes like someone describing a painting or a photography. . . . She can take her reader into an environment, conjuring the feel of a place, paying particular attention to light and heat, colour and texture." Although he did not find the novel to be one of Brookner's best, Michael Gorra noted in the *Washington Post Book World* that the beginning of the novel "is as classically elegant as anything Anita Brookner has written and shows why, in its concentration on the limitations of gentility, hers is one of the most characteristically English voices to emerge in the last decade."

Latecomers, considered by critics to be among Brookner's most poignant novels, focuses upon two male characters. Orphaned during the Holocaust, Thomas Fibich and Thomas Hartmann escape Nazi Germany to become schoolmates, friends, and then successful business partners in England. Each character attempts to reconcile himself to the past in a different way, but both rely heavily on the strength and constancy of familial relationships to establish their place in the present. Brookner's "rich, utterly convincing portrayals of Fibich and Hartmann are likely to go a long way in dispelling any labeling of her as a 'women's writer' and in bolstering her reputation for drawing characters with the scrupulousness of a master draftsman," wrote Jocelyn McClurg in the *Los Angeles Times.* Yardley called it "a book not about romantic love but about love in the real world: about accepting and loving people for what they are rather than what one might wish them to be, about the slow, secret ways in which people work themselves so deeply into each other's hearts that extrication is unimaginable, about the acceptance and even celebration of human imperfection."- Suggesting that "few writers can offer better, more specific insight than Anita Brookner," Bonnie Burnard maintained in the Toronto *Globe and Mail:* "Her conclusions seem valid, not arrogantly wise or uptown smart. . . . She is in control and has at her disposal a vast, accessible vocabulary of both spoken words and private thought. She can bring to life, calmly and sharply, place, gesture, attitude, intonation; she has mastered the master strokes." Finding the novel "written with grace and elegance that border on the astonishing,"Yardley concluded, "At her own pace and in her own fashion, Anita Brookner works a spell on the reader; being under it is both an education and a delight."

Lewis Percy traces an inhibited young man's quest for tranquility; or as Carol Shields put it in her Toronto *Globe and Mail* review, it is "a book about finding an appropriate mode of heroism for our times." Lonely following the death of his mother, Lewis marries Tissy, a library coworker, in an attempt to rescue her from a stifling life. When she falsely suspects him of sleeping with Emmy, the wife of a library colleague, "Lewis struggles to act honorably and keep his marriage vows, thereby antagonizing both women," wrote Lopate. The characterization of Lewis recalls that of Ruth in *A Start in Life,* observed Julian Symons in the *Times Literary Supplement:* "Both are immersed in literature, Ruth an authority on Balzac, Lewis working on a thesis about the concept of heroism in the nineteenth-century novel, which in due time becomes a book and brings him a job in the college library. Both find living a trickier business than reading about it." The novel "bears the clear imprint of a painterly quality of mind," wrote Tyler: "The plot derives less from a chain of events than from a juxtaposition of portraits, each more detailed than the last. People we'd be unlikely to notice on our own . . . take on texture and dimension, gradually rising right off the page." Although Isabel Raphael considered the novel "less brilliant and distilled" than Brookner's other writings, she added in her London *Times* review, "but for me, it glowed with a new serenity and reality which gave great pleasure, along with a sense that I will return more happily in future to this tender and sympathetic author."

Brookner's eleventh novel, *Brief Lives,* concerns Fay Langdon, a successful but aging businesswoman. After the death of her husband, Fay becomes the mistress of his law partner, thus betraying his wife and her long-time friend, Julia. In recalling the events of her life, Fay begins to question what Nicola Murphy described in the London *Times* as "her immature and foolish supposition that living would be a happy business." In the *Times Literary Supplement,* Lindsay Duguid described Fay as "an intelligent narrator, who is sensitive and shrinking but always sure of the superiority of her judgment. . . . We follow Fay's flat, pathetic first-person story with interest, keen to find out if she will find happiness, suspecting that she will not." Praising Brookner's "infallible precision," Murphy judged the novel "a fine, poised and pointed examination of stoicism in a woman too marginal to be missed. *Brief Lives* is beautifully written."

In *A Closed Eye* and *Fraud,* Brookner continues the theme of female loneliness. In *A Closed Eye,* Harriet, at her parents' urging, marries Freddie, a rich but dull man who is nearly twice her age. They have a daughter, Imogen, who is killed in a car accident. Harriet has only one friend, Tessa, who also has a daughter, Lizzie. At the novel's close, with all other family and friends either dead or withdrawn from their lives, Harriet and Lizzie end up together. Gabriele Annan found the novel "bleak," but considered it "elegantly constructed." Brookner, as Annan explained in the *New York Review of Books,* is often compared to Jane Austen, and although this reviewer found significant differences between Austen's women and Brookner's women, Annan admitted that "*A Closed Eye* does have its Jane Austen side." Namely, noted Annan, "Brookner is a witty and ironic observer of a society she peoples with sharply described characters." What is more, "Brookner has a particular knack for dealing with the sphere where society and locality overlap," capturing "the psyche of each individual [London] *quartier* as she walks her characters through it or settles them in some wickedly specific abode." In the end, believed Annan, Brookner "is an art historian specializing in eighteenth-and early nineteenth-century French art, and her writing recalls—deliberately or not—the elegant cruelty of certain French novels of the period."

The novel *Fraud* begins as a mystery with the disappearance of a middle-aged spinster named Anna Durrant. Through flashbacks, the reader learns that Anna has spent much of her life caring for her sickly mother, that her mother's death was followed by a grim winter and late spring, and that Anna had a mild flirtation with her mother's doctor. Through these events, *New York Times Book Review* contributor Ursula Hegi noted, Brookner offers "unsettling insights into what can hap-

pen when the boundaries between aging parents and their children dissolve." In *A Family Romance* (published in the United States as *Dolly*) Brookner explores the relationship between the book's narrator, Jane, and Jane's aunt-by-marriage, Dolly. In this novel Brookner examines the characters' differences from several angles—personality, generational, and ethnic. "Brookner's novel tells the story of how this pair . . . finally develop the bonds that make them a family," Carol Kino noted in the *New York Times Book Review.*

In *A Private View,* as with many of her previous novels, Brookner proves that she is both unafraid of and quite adept at exploring the lives of her contemporaries in England, even as they age and retire. "As newly disenfranchised [retired] workers face the prospect of building a life without the familiar routines of a job, profound questions about identity, activity, and purpose arise," commented Marilyn Gardner in the *Christian Science Monitor.* It is this disenfranchisement that Brookner examines in the life of George Bland of *A Private View.* A bachelor by default, Bland has just retired from his only job as a personnel manager in a London manufacturing company. The event was supposed to be celebrated by a trip to Asia with his long-time friend Putnam, another lifelong bachelor, but Putnam has just died of cancer. Now, though comfortable with his own money and that of his departed friend, Bland has nothing to look forward to or to look back on. He attempts to fill the void with Katy Gibb, a flaky young American occupying his neighbor's flat. She lives and breathes the many manifestations of New Age self-help and sees Bland as a source of financial support for her business aspirations, to spread the New Age gospel.

As with *Look at Me,* Brookner uses a character in *Incidents in the Rue Laugier* to write the story that becomes her novel. In this case, however, the character is peripheral to the story of the novel. *Incidents in the Rue Laugier* is the tale of a love triangle and its aftermath involving the narrator's mother, father, and another man reconstructed from a few entries in the mother's journals. The mother, Maud, a young French woman, visits her aunt in the country. There, she meets two young Englishmen, falls in love with one, David Tyler, and eventually marries the other, Edward Harrison. The couple is condemned to live, in the words of *Library Journal* contributor Wilda Williams, "thwarted, empty lives." Joan Thomas, writing in the Toronto *Globe and Mail,* found the disparity between the opening love triangle and the couple's ultimate resignation problematic. "Brookner's romantic premise is disastrous to the novel," she wrote. "Unable to deal with Maud and Edward's adult lives in an interesting way, Brookner has nothing to write about for the last half of the book." Still, Thomas conceded, "Brookner has been getting away with writing the same plot with variations for more than a decade because she is a beautiful stylist, with an almost nineteenth-century formality and a fine wit." And, because of Brookner's style and wit, "the reader turns pages compulsively for a dazzling read in which every sentence seems clairvoyant," noted a *Publishers Weekly* reviewer.

Brookner's 1996 novel, *Altered States,* examines the romantic career of Alan Sherwood, a thoroughly conventional middle-aged London solicitor. Flashbacks reveal Alan's many quashed hopes and unfulfilled erotic longings. The novel's dark musings struck a chord with many critics. Calling the novel "unnervingly morbid," Donna Seaman of *Booklist* wrote that Alan Sherwood's "altered states are all forms of loss and compromise, intrinsic aspects of life that Brookner analyzes with brilliant intensity and surprising suspense." This feeling of discomfort coupled with admiration for the author's words was echoed by other reviewers. "Though impressive for its craftsmanship,"observed Clare McHugh in *People,* "*Altered States* is unremittingly dark."A reviewer for *Publishers Weekly* found the narrative "alive with tension and heartbreak" while lamenting that Brookner's "view of female nature . . . seems essentially uncharitable and extreme."

Brookner's next novel, *Visitors,* covers similar emotional terrain—this time with a female narrator. Dorothea May is an elderly London widow, who, like many Brookner protagonists, sees her settled life disturbed by unforeseen events. This time it is a visit from her cousin's granddaughter and her wedding party, including a dissolute free spirit who prompts Dorothea to reexamine her own life choices. The very typicality of *Visitors* earned praise from many critics. "Brookner remains an exquisitely subtle observer of how manners bear the imprint of psyches," wrote a critic for *Publishers Weekly.* Brigitte Frase of the *San Francisco Chronicle* praised the book for its subdued prose. "Initially seduced by Brookner's urbane and intelligent language, one is coaxed gradually into an ever more disquieting emotional landscape," Frase wrote. Jacqueline Cary of the *New York Times Book Review* summarized *Visitors* as "the book Brookner has spent her life aiming toward."

Falling Slowly is the story of two sisters, Beatrice Sharpe, a pianist, and Miriam Sharpe, a translator, both of whom are experiencing a form of decline—Beatrice, in the form of an illness, and Miriam, in the form of loneliness. Miriam, once married but now divorced, is disillusioned about romantic endeavors; Beatrice, on the other hand, has always expected one day to meet the man of her dreams. "Like George Bland in Brookner's novel *A Private View,* or Dorothea May in *Visitors,* Miriam and Beatrice are ultimately torn between an idealized hankering for connection and, far more powerfully, an almost greedy complacency about their unruffled existence," summarized *New York Times Book Review* critic Claire Messud. "Women whose empty emotional lives are conducted behind a facade of stoic acceptance are Brookner's stock-in-trade," noted a *Publishers Weekly* critic. But here, in her delineation of the Sharpe sisters, Brookner "evokes an almost palpable atmosphere of resigned regret." Critics were largely positive in their assessment of *Falling Slowly.*"Brookner's impeccable craftsmanship and worldly irony make each of her novels memorable, but here her heroines' passivity becomes exasperating," concluded the critic for *Publishers Weekly.* Donna Seaman in *Booklist* called the novel "a richly figured book," referring to Brookner as a "sagacious and elegant novelist." "The ghastly power of Brookner's novels," argued Messud, "arises from their trenchant accuracy, and in this regard *Falling Slowly* is a further testament to its author's gifts."

Undue Influence focuses on a younger woman, Claire Pitt, twenty-nine, highly intelligent and perceptive of the world she sees around her but blind to her own dysfunctions and vulnerability. Cristina Nehring in the *San Francisco Chronicle* described Claire as "the fruit of feminism triumphant: Independent, unsentimental and intellectually confident, she asserts her sexual needs squarely, refuses romantic mystifications, despises her mother's bond to an invalid husband and her friend's loyalty to a married man. 'She deserves better,' she intones." But Claire, we begin to see, is deceiving herself and those around her. In her affair with Martin Gibson (according to Colin Walters of the *Washington Times,* "a discerning, right-on portrait of the masochistic male)," Claire presents herself as invulnerable, distant, and in charge. Nehring continued, "If these assumptions are convenient for the men, they are encouraged by the women. Claire labors to present herself as a hardened vamp with a 'predator's instinct' and a disdain for 'relationships.' It is she, not Martin—she tells us repeatedly—who 'controls' their affair. But it isn't long before we see that if Claire is masterminding anything, she is masterminding her own destruction." Intelligence, added Nehring, is the undoing rather than the saving of many of Brookner's protagonists.

Nehring maintained that Brookner's focus on similar characters and similar problems in her novels ultimately makes her writing "claustrophobic and repetitive." Ka-sia Boddy, however, in the London *Daily Mail* argued, "Anita Brookner's . . . novels have so much in common that, in some ways, to consider one is to consider them all. This is not to say that she retells the same story. . . . The arbitrary nature of human entanglements is a common thread." and Melinda Bargreen of the *Seattle Times* considered Anita Brookner "at her most sly and witty in this new novel." Bargreen concluded, "As always, Brookner's prose style gives us a felicitous turn of phrase in nearly every paragraph. And at the end, when Claire 'dispatch(es) naivete forever, consigning it to a prelapsarian time before doubt had set in,' you know she's on the road to self-knowledge." Walters commended the book: "Of Miss Brookner's novels that I've read, this one may have given the most pleasure." Interesting is the difference between those who find humor and those who find no humor in Brookner's work. For instance, a *Christian Science Monitor* reviewer described "some of the novel's most darkly comic moments," whereas Robert Allen Papinchak in the *Milwaukee Journal Sentinel* called this a "relentlessly somber . . . novel."

The protagonist of *The Next Big Thing* is a man, Julius Herz, who is about to retire from an unfulfilling job at age seventy-three. The question is whether he will take up the remainder of his life with vigor and an adventurous spirit or whether it is only death that will be "the next big thing." Sara Maitland in the *Spectator* had equivocal feelings about Brookner's focus: "One of the central themes of Brookner's novels has been 'resignation': Is it possible? Is it virtuous? Is it desirable? What are its compensations? What are the rewards and costs of realism and good behaviour? . . . My problem with Brookner's novels has always been that I feel that resignation is a pseudo-virtue, a vile diminishment preached to the already marginalized." Julius, wrote Maitland, "has endured a thin life; thinner, he rightly feels, than he deserved. . . . What should he do now? How should he fill in the years that will intervene between now and his death? Should he accept that this is all he is going to get, should he practise resignation? Or should he make one last effort to make life deliver its fruit?"

Having warned that Brookner is getting emotionally no easier to read, Ron Charles of the *Christian Science Monitor* found, "The reasons to pay attention to Anita Brookner grow no less compelling. First, she's one of the great English stylists, an artist of such extraordinary precision that her novels serve as an antidote to the overwritten tomes from so many contemporary writers. Second, in a literary marketplace excited by the bizarre, she remains committed to the mundane. No, she can't

tell us about a hermaphrodite whose grandparents were siblings—for advice in that situation you must go to Jeffrey Eugenides's widely praised *Middlesex,*—but if you're considering the somewhat more common predicament of getting older, Brookner is as wise a guide as you'll find." Brookner presents Julius as a man who has lost himself in serving others, wrote Charles, and the problem considered is whether, now freed from financial worry and from work, he can make something more exciting of his last years. "A chorus of acquaintances offers advice: His cordial ex-wife admonishes him to cheer up, his lawyer suggests travel, his distractingly beautiful neighbor tells him to stop staring. But none of these courses can solve the problem of learning how to live with an abundance of unaccustomed freedom. 'Keeping one's dignity,' he admits, 'is a lonely business. And how one longs to let it go'." As Charles observed, Julius is in danger of already regarding himself as "posthumous," and the reviewer concluded, "This is bitter medicine for sure, but Brookner draws a portrait of despair so perfectly that it might serve a homeopathic purpose for anyone in or slipping toward 'a pale simulacrum of life.' Only a writer of her astonishing wit and insight could get us to swallow it."

Observer contributor Adam Mars-Jones, however, found the thinness of descriptive prose and action in the novel a problem. "In a more dynamic novel, the absence of observation wouldn't matter, but here, in a narrative virtually denuded of incident (Herz makes modest perambulations and rambling peregrinations, he remembers, he surmises, he envisages), the thinness of texture is damaging." Rather than seeing Julius Herz as a figure of pathos, as Charles did, Mars-Jones observed, "Herz, wanting company without liking people, sees himself as a stoic, when, in fact, he floats in an admittedly dilute solution of self-pity from the first page to the last. The problem with the psychology on offer is not that it's negative, but that it's dull," concluding, "Brookner once remarked, quoting Freud, that art was a way of turning strong feelings into weak ones. Judge her on that basis, and her success is remarkable. Every trace of urgency has been effaced."

Brookner continues with *The Rules of Engagement*, which follows the lives of two women friends, Elizabeth and Betsy, both born in 1948 and who go at life in very different ways. Elizabeth chooses safety, marrying a kind man much older than herself. Betsy falls in love with a Parisian revolutionary and stays in Paris. The crossing of the two friends' lives thereafter throws a light on the possibilities offered by such choices and such views on the world—Elizabeth's pragmatic and Betsy's romantic. The *Spectator*'s Anne Chisholm noted,

"It is, perhaps, a measure of Brookner's great gifts as a writer and her achievement in establishing, over twenty-two novels in thirty years, such a powerful message about the plight of women today that occasionally even her admirers want to fight back. . . . All one can say, perhaps, is that some are and that Anita Brookner knows and understands them. . . . There is beauty as well as courage in Brookner's new book."

BIOGRAPHICAL AND CRITICAL SOURCES:

BOOKS

Contemporary Literary Criticism, Thomson Gale (Detroit, MI), Volume 32, 1985, Volume 34, 1985, Volume 51, 1989.

Dictionary of Literary Biography Yearbook: 1987, Thomson Gale (Detroit, MI), 1988.

Malcolm, Cheryl Alexander, *Understanding Anita Brookner,* University of South Carolina Press (Columbia, SC), 2001.

Skinner, John, *The Fictions of Anita Brookner: Illusions of Romance,* Macmillan (London, England), 1992.

Soule, George, *Four British Women Novelists: Anita Brookner, Margaret Drabble, Iris Murdoch, Barbara Pym: An Annotated and Critical Secondary Bibliography,* Scarecrow Press (Lanham, MD), 1998.

Werlock, Abby H.P., and Regina Barreca, editors, *British Women Writing Fiction,* University of Alabama Press (Tuscaloosa, AL), 2000.

PERIODICALS

Albuquerque Journal, February 13, 2000, p. F8.

Atlanta Journal-Constitution, March 2, 2003, p. E6.

Atlantic Monthly, March, 1985, p. 124.

Austin American-Statesman, January 30, 2000, p. K6.

Birmingham Post (Birmingham, England), August 7, 1999, p. 60; January 27, 2001, p. 52.

Booklist, November 1, 1997, p. 434; November 1, 1998, p. 450; November 1, 2003, Donna Seaman, review of *Rules of Engagement,* p. 458.

Boston Globe, March 18, 1992, p. 58; May 4, 1993, p. 59.

Boston Herald, April 29, 2001, p. 051; January 26, 2003, p. A24.

Chicago Tribune, March 30, 1989; March 8, 1990.

Christian Science Monitor, March 1, 1985, p. B3; June 18, 1987, p. 26; June 8, 1988, p. 20; May 10, 1989, p. 13; April 26, 1990, p. 14; July 10, 1992, p. 11;

February 8, 1993, p. 14; February 22, 1994, p. 11; January 26, 1995; February 18, 1998, p. 14; January 7, 1999, p. 20; January 27, 2000, p. 17; p. B3; April 19, 2001, p. 21; January 2, 2003, p. 12.

Cincinnati Post, May 19, 2001, p. 5C.

Commonweal, September 20, 1985, p. 502.

Contemporary Literature, winter, 2001, p. 825.

Courier-Mail (Brisbane, Australia), April 14, 2001, p. M05.

Critique: Studies in Contemporary Fiction, summer, 1998, p. 325.

Daily, June 28, 2003.

Daily Mail (London, England), July 5, 2002, p. 58; July 4, 2003, p. 58.

Daily Telegraph (London, England), January 20, 2001, p. 06; October 20, 2001; June 22, 2002; April 26, 2003; June 28, 2003.

Deep South, Volume 1, number 3, spring, 1995.

Entertainment Weekly, January 23, 1998, p. 58; January 9, 2004, Lisa Swarzbaum, review of *Rules of Engagement,* p. 87.

English Studies: A Journal of Language and Literature, February 2001, p. 44.

English: The Journal of the English Association, summer, 1993, p. 125; spring 2001, p. 47.

Evening Standard (London, England), June 24, 2002, p. 10; June 23, 2003, p. 39.

Express (London, England), June 29, 2002, p. 52.

Financial Times, October 14, 2000, p. 5.

Globe and Mail (Toronto, Ontario, Canada), November 8, 1986; April 7, 1990; January 13, 1996.

Guardian (London, England), July 31, 1999, p. 10; December 23, 2000, p. 10; February 3, 2001, p. 10; October 27, 2002, p. 11; June 22, 2002, p. 28; July 5, 2003, p. 26.

Harper's, April, 1981; July, 1983.

Herald (Glasgow, Scotland), December 16, 2000, p. 16; January 27, 2001, p. 20; July 5, 2003, p. 12.

Hudson Review, autumn, 1993.

Independent (London, England), July 30, 1999, p. 9; September 9, 2000, p. 11; June 29, 2002, p. 18; July 12, 2003, p. 26.

Independent on Sunday (London, England), September 10, 2000, p. 53; January 28, 2001, p. 45; July 6, 2003, p. 17; July 20, 2003, p. 19.

Irish Times (Dublin, Ireland), August 2, 2003, p. 62; August 16, 2003, p. 60.

Journal of Aging Studies, summer, 1989, p. 177.

Journal of Popular Culture, winter, 1994, p. 1.

Kirkus Reviews, November 1, 2003, review of *Rules of Engagement,* p. 1284.

Knight Ridder/Tribune News Service, April 25, 2001, p. K1955; May 16, 2001, p. K2083; January 8, 2003, p. K4392; January 15, 2003, p. K0748.

Library Journal, November 15, 1994, p. 98; April 1, 1997, p. 145; May 1, 1997, p. 145; September 1, 1997, p. 233; November 1, 1997, p. 115; September 1, 1998, p. 236; October 1, 1998, p. 80; December, 1998, p. 152; January, 2004, Barbara Love, review of *Rules of Engagement,* p. 151.

Listener, August 20, 1987, pp. 18-19.

London Review of Books, September 6, 1984, p. 20; September 5, 1985, p. 13; September 4, 1986, p. 20; October 1, 1987, p. 11; September 1, 1988, p. 24; September 14, 1989, p. 19; September 13, 1990, p. 16; August 29, 1991, p. 18; October 8, 1992, p. 12.

Los Angeles Times, March 18, 1981; May 3, 1983; February 8, 1984; December 25, 1989; March 27, 1992, p. E4; January 12, 1993, p. E2; April 15, 2001, p. 11; January 22, 2003, p. E11.

Los Angeles Times Book Review, October 27, 1985, p. 3; March 20, 1988, p. 2; April 30, 1989, p. 3; March 25, 1990, p. 3; July 7, 1991, p. 3; February 13, 1994, p. 10; January 22, 1995, p. 3; February 19, 1995, p. 11; February 9, 1997, p. 4; January 18, 1998.

Mail on Sunday (London, England), February 18, 2001, p. 66.

Milwaukee Journal Sentinel, January 9, 2000, p. 6E; April 15, 2001, p. 06.

Mosaic, spring, 1991, p. 131; June 1995, p. 123.

Ms., June, 1985, p. 62.

Nation, September 9, 1991, p. 274.

New Leader, October 7-21, 1991, p. 20; December 16-30, 1996, p. 28.

New Republic, May 30, 1981; March 25, 1985, p. 37; April 24, 1995, p. 41; February 9, 2004, Deborah Friedell, review of *Rules of Engagement,* p. 32.

News Letter (Belfast, Northern Ireland), July 1, 2002, p. 34.

New Statesman, May 22, 1981; September 7, 1984; September 6, 1985, p. 30; August 22, 1986, p. 26; August 28, 1987, p. 21; August 19, 1988, p. 39; August 25, 1989, p. 26; August 31, 1990, p. 35; August 23, 1991; August 21, 1992, p. 38; July 9, 1993, p. 33; June 24, 1994, p. 40; August 1, 1997, p. 47.

Newsweek, February 25, 1985, p. 87; March 30, 1987, p. 69.

New Yorker, March 23, 1981; April 9, 1984; February 18, 1985, p. 121; March 10, 1986, p. 121; May 18, 1987, p. 115; May 1, 1989, p. 111; August 23, 1990, p. 115; April 27, 1992, p. 106; February 22, 1993, p. 183; April 11, 1994, p. 99; January 30, 1995, p. 89.

New York Review of Books, January 31, 1985, p. 17; June 1, 1989, p. 34; May 14, 1992, p. 25; January 12, 1995, p. 20.

New York Times, July 4, 1983; February 1, 1984; January 22, 1985; October 12, 1985, p. 18; March 25, 1987, p. C23; February 20, 1988; February 24, 1989, p. C31; February 20, 1990, p. C19; April 6, 1990; February 28, 1992, p. C32; February 2, 2003, p. 17 col. 01.

New York Times Book Review, December 3, 1972; March 29, 1981; May 22, 1983; March 18, 1984; February 3, 1985, p. 1; April 28, 1985, p. 38; November 10, 1985, p. 15; March 29, 1987, p. 10; March 20, 1988, p. 9; April 2, 1989, p. 3; March 11, 1990, p. 10; July 21, 1991, p. 14; April 12, 1992, p. 12; January 10, 1993, p. 7; February 20, 1994, p. 12; January 8, 1995, p. 9; January 14, 1996, p. 13; January 26, 1997; January 18, 1998; January 31, 1999, p. 7; January 3, 2000, p. 34; November 19, 2000, p. 70; June 3, 2001, p. 23; October 28, 2001, p. 32; April 28, 2002, p. 24; February 2, 2003, p. 17.

Observer (London, England), December 2, 1984, p. 19; September 8, 1985, p. 21; August 24, 1986, p. 20; August 23, 1987, p. 24; August 14, 1988, p. 41; August 27, 1989, p. 38; August 26, 1990, p. 55; August 25, 1991, p. 51; July 11, 1993, p. 61; June 19, 1994, p. 22; June 11, 1995, p. 14; June 18, 1995, p. 17; July 11, 1999, p. 5; August 1, 1999, p. 12; October 29, 2000, p. 13; January 18, 2001, p. 17; June 30, 2002, p. 17.

People, February 20, 1995, p. 31; January 13, 1997, p. 27; February 23, 1998, p. 33.

Plain Dealer (Cleveland, OH), May 27, 2001, p. 12I; January 26, 2003, p. J12.

Publishers Weekly, September 6, 1985; November 20, 1995, p. 66; November 11, 1996; November 17, 1997, p. 53; September 28, 1998, p. 84; October 26, 1998, p. 42; December 22, 2003, review of *Rules of Engagement,* p. 38.

Rocky Mountain News (Denver, CO), May 18, 2001, p. 25D.

St. Louis Post-Dispatch, January 30, 2000, p. F10.

San Francisco Chronicle, January 9, 2000, p. 1; January 23, 2000, p. 4.

Saturday Review, March-April, 1985; May-June, 1985.

Scotland on Sunday (Edinburgh, Scotland), January 28, 2001, p. 9; June 16, 2002, p. 6.

Scotsman (Edinburgh, Scotland), September 4, 1999, p. 11; July 29, 2000, p. 14; January 27, 2001, p. 10; June 29, 2002, p. 9.

Seattle Times, February 20, 2000, p. M7; July 1, 2001, p. J11; January 12, 2003, p. L9.

Spectator, September 14, 1985, p. 28; August 23, 1986, p. 22; August 22, 1987, p. 27; August 20, 1988, p. 24; August 26, 1989, p. 21; September 8, 1990, p. 33; August 31, 1991, p. 25; August 22, 1992,

p. 20; June 19, 1993, p. 29; June 18, 1994, p. 33; June 17, 1995, p. 43; June 7, 1997, p. 38; June 29, 2002, p. 40; July 5, 2003, p. 36.

Star Ledger (Newark, NJ), March 5, 2000, p. 004; April 29, 2001, p. 004; January 5, 2003, p. 004.

Sunday Herald (Glasgow, Scotland), January 28, 2001, p. 10.

Sunday Mirror (London, England), July 23, 2000, p. 41.

Sunday Telegraph (London, England), January 21, 2001, p. 15; June 30, 2002, p. 15; June 1, 2003; June 22, 2003, p. 16.

Sunday Times (London, England), July 25, 1999, p. 12; August 8, 1999, p. 6; September 3, 2000, p. 35; January 28, 2001, p. 45; June 30, 2002, p. 45; July 6, 2003, p. 47.

Tampa Tribune, February 13, 2000, p. 4.

Time, October 28, 1985, p. 93; March 21, 1988, p. 76; March 19, 1990, p. 83; June 24, 1991, p. 65; February 8, 1993, p. 83; January 30, 1995, p. 83.

Times (London, England), March 21, 1983; March 31, 1983; September 6, 1984; October 20, 1984; August 21, 1986; August 16, 2000, p. 14; September 6, 2000, p. 12; June 26, 2002, p. 21; July 9, 2003, p. 20; August 2, 2003, p. 20.

Times Educational Supplement, August 6, 1993, p. 20.

Times Literary Supplement, November 26, 1971; January 9, 1981; May 29, 1981; May 28, 1982; March 25, 1983; September 14, 1984; April 26, 1985, p. 479; September 6, 1985, p. 973; August 29, 1986, p. 932; August 21, 1987, p. 897; August 12, 1988, p. 891; August 25, 1989, p. 916; August 24-30, 1990, p. 889; August 23, 1991, p. 20; August 21, 1992, p. 17; June 25, 1993, p. 22; June 17, 1994, p. 22; June 2, 1995, p. 21.

Tribune Books (Chicago, IL), March 1, 1987, p. 7; July 14, 1991, p. 6; March 22, 1992, p. 7; February 14, 1993, p. 4; February 13, 1994, p. 6; February 5, 1995, p. 6.

Twentieth Century Literature, spring, 1995, p. 1.

Village Voice, July 5, 1983; June 25, 1991, p. 70.

Vogue, February, 1985.

Voice Literary Supplement, May, 1987, p. 4; April, 1988, p. 11.

Wall Street Journal, March 30, 1992, p. A9; January 20, 1993, p. A10; December 20, 2000, p. A20(E); April 27, 2001, p. W12.

Washington Post, April 28, 1981; March 9, 1984; January 20, 1999, p. A20(E); November 12, 2000, p. X15; June 20, 2001, p. T04.

Washington Post Book World, July 24, 1983; February 10, 1985, p. 1; October 13, 1985, p. 3; March 8, 1987, p. 3; February 28, 1988, p. 5; March 12, 1989, p. 3; February 18, 1990, p. 3; March 22, 1992, p. 6; January 31, 1993, p. 3; January 9, 1994, p. 3; January 15, 1995, p. 8.

Washington Times, February 20, 2000, p. 6; December 10, 2000, p. 6.

Weekend Australian (Sydney, New South Wales, Australia), September 18, 1999, p. R13; April 7, 2001, p. R15; July 27, 2002, p. B08; October 4, 2003, p. B08.

West Virginia University Philological Papers, 2001-2002, p. 92.

Women's Review of Books, July, 1992, p. 30.

World Literature Today, spring, 1993, p. 380; winter, 1995, p. 138; spring, 1998, p. 367.

ONLINE

Contemporary Writers, http://www.contemporary writers.com/ (March 6, 2004), biography of Brookner.

Deep South, http://www.otago.ac.nz/DeepSouth/ (spring, 1995), Giuliana Giobbi, "Blood Ties: A Case of Mother-Daughter Relationships in Anita Brookner, Sara Maitland and Rosetta Roy."

George Soule Home Page, http://www.people.carleton. edu/~gsoule/ (March 21, 2000), George Soule, reviews of *Visitors, Altered States,* and *Falling Slowly.*

Pittsburgh Post-Gazette, http://www.post-gazette.com/ (February 27, 2000), Betsy Kline, review of *Undue Influence.*

*   *   *

BROOKS, Cleanth 1906-1994

PERSONAL: Born October 16, 1906, in Murray, KY; died of cancer of the esophagus, May 10, 1994, in New Haven, CT; son of Cleanth (a Methodist minister) and Bessie Lee (Witherspoon) Brooks; married Edith Amy Blanchard, September 12, 1934 (died, October 1, 1986). *Education:* Vanderbilt University, B.A., 1928; Tulane University, M.A., 1929; Exeter College, Oxford, B.A. (with honors), 1931, B.Litt., 1932. *Politics:* Independent Democrat *Religion:* Episcopalian

CAREER: Louisiana State University, Baton Rouge, 1932-47, began as lecturer, became professor of English, visiting professor, 1970 and 1974; Yale University, New Haven, CT, professor of English, 1947-60, Gray Professor of Rhetoric, 1960-75, professor emeritus, 1975-94. Visiting professor of English at University of Texas, summer, 1941, University of Michigan, summer, 1942, University of Chicago, 1945-46, Kenyon

School of English, summer, 1948 (fellow, 1948-94), University of Southern California, summer, 1953, Breadloaf School of English, summer, 1963, University of South Carolina, 1975, Tulane University, 1976, University of North Carolina, 1977 and 1979, and University of Tennessee, 1978 and 1980; research professor with Bostick Foundation, 1975; Lamar Lecturer, 1984; Jefferson Lecturer, 1985. *Southern Review,* Baton Rouge, LA, comanaging editor, 1932-41, coeditor, 1941-42. Member of advisory committee for Boswell Papers, 1950-94; Library of Congress, fellow, 1953-63, member of council of scholars, 1984-87; American Embassy, London, England, cultural attaché, 1964-66; National Humanities Center, senior fellow, 1980-81.

MEMBER: Modern Language Association of America, American Academy of Arts and Sciences, National Institute of Arts and Letters, American Philosophical Society, American Association of University Professors, Royal Society of Literature, Phi Beta Kappa, Athenaeum (London, England), Fellowship of Southern Writers (chancellor, 1986-91).

AWARDS, HONORS: Rhodes scholar, 1929-32; Guggenheim fellowship, 1953 and 1960; senior fellowship, National Endowment for the Humanities, 1975; Explicator Award, c. 1980, for *William Faulkner: Toward Yoknapatawpha and Beyond.* Honorary D.Litt. from Upsala College, 1963, University of Kentucky, 1963, University of Exeter, 1966, Washington and Lee University, 1968, Tulane University, 1969, University of the South, 1975, Newberry College, 1979, and Indiana State University, 1992; L.H.D. from University of St. Louis, 1968, Centenary College, 1972, Oglethorpe University, 1976, St. Peter's College, 1978, Lehigh University, 1980, Millsaps College, 1983, University of New Haven, 1984, University of South Carolina, 1984, and Adelphi University, 1992.

WRITINGS:

EDITOR

(With others) *An Approach to Literature,* Louisiana State University Press (Baton Rouge, LA), 1936, 5th edition, Prentice-Hall (Englewood Cliffs, NJ), 1975.

(With Robert Penn Warren, and coauthor) *Understanding Poetry,* Holt (New York, NY), 1938, 4th edition, 1975, transcript of tape recording to accompany 3rd edition entitled *Conversations on the Craft of Poetry: Cleanth Brooks and Robert Penn Warren, with Robert Frost, John Crowe Ransom, Robert Lowell, and Theodore Roethke,* Holt (New York, NY), 1961.

(With Robert Penn Warren) *Understanding Fiction,* F.S. Crofts, 1943, 3rd edition, Prentice-Hall (Englewood Cliffs, NJ), 1979, abridged edition published as *The Scope of Fiction,* 1960.

(General editor, with A.F. Falconer and David Nichol Smith) *The Percy Letters,* 1944–88, Volumes 1-6, Louisiana State University Press (Baton Rouge, LA), Volumes 7-9, Yale University Press; special editor of Volume 2: *The Correspondence of Thomas Percy and Richard Farmer* and Volume 7: *The Correspondence of Thomas Percy and William Shenstone.*

(With Robert Heilman) *Understanding Drama,* Holt (New York, NY), 1945.

(With John Edward Hardy) *The Poems of John Milton* (1645 edition), Harcourt (New York, NY), 1951.

(With Robert Penn Warren) *An Anthology of Stories from the "Southern Review,"* Louisiana State University Press (Baton Rouge, LA), 1953.

Tragic Themes in Western Literature: Seven Essays by Bernard Knox (and Others), Yale University Press (New Haven, CT), 1956.

(With Robert Penn Warren and R.W.B. Lewis) *American Literature: The Makers and the Making,* two volumes, St. Martin's Press (New York, NY), 1973, paperbound edition published in four volumes, 1974.

Southern Review, managing editor with Robert Penn Warren, 1935-41, editor with Warren, 1941-42; *Kenyon Review,* member of advisory board, 1942-60.

OTHER

The Relation of the Alabama-Georgia Dialect to the Provincial Dialects of Great Britain, Louisiana State University Press (Baton Rouge, LA), 1935.

Modern Poetry and the Tradition, University of North Carolina Press, 1939.

The Well Wrought Urn, Reynal & Hitchcock, 1947, Harcourt (New York, NY), 1956.

(With Robert Penn Warren) *Modern Rhetoric,* Harcourt (New York, NY), 1949, 4th edition, 1979, abridged edition, 1961.

(With Robert Penn Warren) *Fundamentals of Good Writing,* Harcourt (New York, NY), 1950.

(Contributor) *Humanities: An Appraisal,* University of Wisconsin Press (Madison, WI), 1950.

(With William K. Wimsatt) *Literary Criticism: A Short History,* Knopf (New York, NY), 1957.

Metaphor and the Function of Criticism, Institute for Religious and Social Studies, c. 1957.

The Hidden God: Studies in Hemingway, Faulkner, Yeats, Eliot and Warren, Yale University Press (New Haven, CT), 1963.

William Faulkner: The Yoknapatawpha Country, Yale University Press (New Haven, CT), 1963.

William Faulkner: Toward Yoknapatawpha and Beyond, Yale University Press (New Haven, CT), 1978.

(Contributor) Louis D. Dollarhide and Ann J. Abadie, editors, *Eudora Welty: A Form of Thanks,* University Press of Mississippi (Jackson, MS), 1979.

Cleanth Brooks at the United States Air Force Academy, April 11-12, 1978 (lectures), edited by James A. Grimshaw, Jr., Department of English, U.S. Air Force Academy, 1980.

William Faulkner: First Encounters, Yale University Press (New Haven, CT), 1983.

The Language of the American South, University of Georgia Press (Athens, GA), 1985.

On the Prejudices, Predilections, and Firm Beliefs of William Faulkner, Louisiana State University Press (Baton Rouge, LA), 1987.

Historical Evidence and the Reading of Seventeenth Century Poetry, University of Missouri Press (Columbia MO), 1991.

Community, Religion, and Literature: Essays, University of Missouri Press (Columbia, MO), 1995.

Cleanth Brooks and Robert Penn Warren: A Literary Correspondence, edited by James A. Grimshaw, Jr., University of Missouri Press (Columbia MO), 1998.

Cleanth Brooks and Allen Tate: Collected Letters, 1933-1976, edited by Alphonse Vinh, University of Missouri Press (Columbia, MO), 1998.

Also author of recorded lectures on works by William Faulkner. Contributor of articles and reviews to literary journals.

SIDELIGHTS: From the early 1940s until his death in 1994, Cleanth Brooks was "one of the pillars of the American literary-critical establishment," as noted by Brian Stonehill in the *Los Angeles Times.* Brooks is best remembered as one of the pioneers of the so-called "New Criticism," a scholarly approach that examines literary works to discover internal tensions and abiding ironies that enable them to stand free of personal, religious, and historical circumstances. *Southern Review* essayist Rene Wellek described the erudite Brooks as an "eminently fair-minded, text-oriented, conscientious ex-

aminer of ideas who is rarely openly polemical." Wellek added that Brooks "is convinced that the amalgamation and confusion of literary theory with morals, politics, and religion has been at the root of many difficulties of critical theory."

From his base at Yale University, Brooks wrote and edited a number of volumes that aimed to enlarge a reader's understanding of seminal works of literature. His best-known books, including *The Well Wrought Urn: Studies in the Structure of Poetry* and (with Robert Penn Warren) *Understanding Poetry: An Anthology for College Students* "revolutionized literary pedagogy by employing the criterion of shared aesthetic properties, rather than subject, author, or chronology, to organize poems," according to *Dictionary of Literary Biography* contributor James J. Sosnoski. Long before his retirement from Yale in 1975, Brooks had turned to an indepth examination of William Faulkner's fiction, becoming "*the* most important Faulkner critic," according to a *Washington Post Book World* reviewer.

Sosnoski wrote of Brooks: "Not only was he considered to be *the* critic of his generation of critics but also . . . he was critical of other critics. During the 1940s and 1950s he was widely regarded as the most lucid and instructive close reader of literary texts." Unlike his associates Warren, Allen Tate, and John Crowe Ransom, Brooks wrote little poetry or fiction of his own. Instead he concentrated on criticism, revealing undervalued or unsuspected complexity in poetry from Shakespeare to William Butler Yeats. In *The Possibilities of Order: Cleanth Brooks and His Work,* Monroe K. Spears noted: "Far from being the irresponsible aesthete or technician that his opponents have represented him as (in the polemics of literary journals and seminar rooms), Brooks is . . . distinguished among critics precisely by his strong sense of responsibility. This is not his only distinction; aside from such obvious gifts as perceptiveness, imagination, and intelligence, his critical integrity, his sense of proportion, and his instinct for the centrally human are rare qualities indeed. But responsibility is primary."

Brooks was born in Kentucky in 1906, the son of a Methodist clergyman. During his childhood the family moved often, going from town to town in Tennessee. Brooks's father was a scholarly man who encouraged his son to read works of world literature. Later Brooks attended the McTyeire School, a small classical academy where students became well acquainted with Greek and Latin in addition to a standard curriculum.

In 1924 Brooks entered Vanderbilt University, the seat of an important 1920s literary group known as the Fugitives. The Fugitives—including Ransom, Donald Davidson, Tate, and Warren—wrote and discussed modern literature and "laid the theoretical groundwork for the New Critical movement," according to Sosnoski. Brooks's exposure to the Fugitives changed the direction of his career. He had planned to become a lawyer, but he opted instead to pursue the study of literature. He was quoted in the *Dictionary of Literary Biography* as saying: "The thing that I got most out of Vanderbilt was to discover suddenly that literature was not a dead thing to be looked at through the glass of a museum case, but was very much alive."

After graduating from Vanderbilt in 1928, Brooks continued his studies at Tulane University, receiving his M.A. in 1929. Tulane nominated him for a prestigious Rhodes scholarship that sent him to Exeter College at Oxford University in England. At Exeter he earned another B.A. with honors and was accorded a graduate degree in 1932. He returned to the United States the same year and began teaching literature at Louisiana State University. Robert Penn Warren was also hired by LSU shortly after Brooks arrived, and the two men continued a close personal and professional relationship that had begun in their Vanderbilt days. Together, in 1939, they founded the *Southern Review,* one of the nation's most important critical quarterlies.

As college professors, Brooks and Warren found the existing textbooks for the study of literature grossly inadequate. They determined to develop their own, editing *An Approach to Literature: A Collection of Prose and Verse with Analyses and Discussions; Understanding Poetry;* and *Understanding Fiction.* Sosnoski noted of these works that the editors "tried to deal with what they considered a widespread problem, namely to get students to do a close analyses of the literary works. Therefore, they provided model analyses as well as questions that might provoke students to do their own analyses. This approach was quite controversial." Indeed, some opponents of Brooks's approach accused him of neglecting such "essentials" as the author's background and the poem's place in cultural history. Brooks, on the other hand, saw himself merely as a proponent of a more text-oriented criticism.

In *The Well Wrought Urn,* published in 1947, Brooks applied this text-oriented New Criticism to ten English language poems, some of them centuries old. *New York Times Book Review* correspondent R.P. Blackmur noted of the work: "Mr. Brooks gives us intensive and exciting readings of his chosen poems. . . . He wants to liberate—to bring out into the open air of the poems

themselves—a way in which the poems grow together and grow into life which we can recognize as related to our own practice. His readings suggest something much more important: that, at least from Shakespeare to Yeats, English poetry has an identity of inner or conceptual forms; and that even more important, we can learn the scope of our own practice, and stretch it, too, better from old models than our own."

From works such as *The Well Wrought Urn,* Brooks earned a reputation as a "close reader" of literary texts. In *Southern Renascence: The Literature of the Modern South,* John Edward Hardy remarked of Brooks's method: "Commentary is never allowed to get in the way of the poem. Whatever the other risks involved in the style he has chosen, Brooks avoids the greatest danger that the 'inspired' critic faces, that of having his critique become a rival or substitute poem for the one supposedly being investigated." Sosnoski wrote: "In combining aesthetic formalism with linguistic self-reflexivity, Brooks's readings mark a real turning point in the development of poetic theory, one that (to Brooks's chagrin) could be claimed to lead to deconstructionist practices. On the other hand, Brooks also thus moves even further from the kind of political or social or cultural criticism so many called for in the troubled decades of the 1930s and 1940s."

Like many other writers, Brooks found the labels attached to him—"New Critic," "close reader"—quite confining. In *A Shaping Joy: Studies in the Writer's Craft,* Brooks commented on his position in the academic community. "The pigeonhole assigned to me carries the label 'The New Criticism,'" he wrote. "Now, it is bad enough to live under any label, but one so nearly meaningless as 'The New Criticism'—it is certainly not *new*—has peculiar disadvantages. For most people it vaguely signifies an anti-historical bias and a fixation on 'close reading.'" Brooks calls this reaction to his intentions "an overshadowing generalization."

Brooks moved to Yale University in 1947 and remained there until his retirement in 1975. He also served as a visiting professor at numerous universities and even worked as a cultural attaché at the American embassy in London. As a Southerner himself, Brooks was perhaps inevitably drawn to William Faulkner's fiction, and he spent nearly three decades analyzing Faulkner's difficult but rewarding texts.

Yale University Press published Brooks's *William Faulkner: The Yoknapatawpha Country* in 1963. The book considers Faulkner as a product of his Southern milieu with its particular ethical and religious heritage and then explores the themes and characters in Faulkner's Yoknapatawpha novels. *Yale Review* contributor Joseph Blotner called the work "the best single critical work on the novels of Faulkner's fictional saga," praising Brooks for his "remarkable erudition, broad historical consciousness, penetrating insight, sympathetic sensitivity, blessed common sense, and the ability to express them in a flexible prose that is clear, straightforward, and persuasive." Blotner concluded that Brooks "leads the reader through Faulkner's complexities and intricacies, not only making them more easily understandable but also showing how they function in the novel's ultimate meaning."

In 1978 Brooks published a companion volume, *William Faulkner: Toward Yoknapatawpha and Beyond,* a study of Faulkner's development as a writer with a discussion of novels not set in Yoknapatawpha County. Critics also found favor with a 1983 Brooks work, *William Faulkner: First Encounters.* The volume, intended principally for undergraduates and general readers interested in Faulkner, assists in unraveling the great writer's most difficult novels. *Washington Post* columnist Jonathan Yardley wrote of *First Encounters* that, for the reader coming to Faulkner for the first time, "this slender volume provides the keys to the kingdom." Yardley concluded: "*First Encounters* can be read with profit by the scholar, for it is a distillation of our most important Faulkner critic's views of Faulkner's most enduring work. But the reader who will value it most is the daunted but determined one who wants to gain admission to one of the great bodies of work in the English language."

Many of Brooks's books were inspired by lectures he gave to students over the years. He also published two volumes on Southern dialect and its relationship to speech patterns in the south of England. Spears noted, "Brooks has always seemed to think of his criticism as simply an extension of his teaching, exactly the same in nature and purpose." Spears also said, "It appears never to have occurred to him to think of his criticism as autotelic; assuming its role to be obviously ancillary to that of literature itself but nevertheless vitally important, he has been concerned chiefly with its practical effectiveness upon its audience—mostly students and teachers, with some general readers. Through collaborative textbooks and editing, as well as through reviewing, lecturing, and criticism proper, Brooks has devoted himself single-mindedly to the aim of improving this audience's understanding of literature and hence its power of discrimination."

Sosnoski offered a similar assessment of Brooks's career. "Brooks's accomplishments are considerable," Sosnoski wrote. "He has been in every respect an exemplary literary scholar. Despite his . . . disclaimer, he is important in the history of criticism as a 'close reader' of complex modern literary texts. His two greatest achievements are that he made difficult modern writers accessible to a generation of scholars for whom it was inconceivable that a great writer could exist in the twentieth century, and he taught the next generation of critics how to read closely."

Brooks's death in 1994 inspired additional reflection on his lifelong dedication and highly influential contributions to the study of literature. Former student and friend Judith Farr wrote in a *Dictionary of Literary Biography Yearbook: 1994* tribute to Brooks: "Cleanth's vision was that the critic, however magisterial, however brilliant, essentially served the artist: he was never a rival presence but an adroit commentator, the most willing of willing, informed, knowledgeable readers, prepared to assist the public in achieving the richest possible understanding of the artist's work. There was a modesty implicit in this point of view, and I always felt Cleanth's reverence for true writers, though he could certainly be savage in his controlled fashion to a false or poor one." A London *Times* reviewer noted, "To his students, Brooks appeared a gentle, quietly spoken man, with enormous authority."

Commenting on Brooks's persistent effort to reconcile competing social, political, and historical forces in both literary creation and interpretation, Carol M. Andrews wrote in an essay for *The Vanderbilt Tradition,* "Brooks solves this conflict to his own satisfaction by seeing his traditional values as universal, inhering in human experience itself and therefore quite rightly represented in a work of art that separates itself from historical flux." According to Brooks, as quoted by Spears in the *New York Review of Books,* "Genuine literature . . . 'is not a luxury commodity but neither is it an assembly-line product. It cannot be mass produced. It has to be hand made, fashioned by a genuine craftsman out of honest human emotions and experiences, in the making of which the indispensable material is our common language, in all its variety, complexity, and richness.'"

As Michael L. Hall noted in *Sewanee Review,* "Brooks intends to demonstrate, finally, that his method of historical reading is not antiquarian but serves a larger purpose, and part of that purpose is to remind us why we would want to read these old poems, or any other works of literature, in the first place: 'No one has ever doubted that poems (and novels and plays) are products of the culture out of which they came, and consequently at some level they must reflect that culture. But that fact does not prevent our assessing these literary documents on other levels, including what they can tell us about the universal human condition.'"

In 1998, two books were published focusing on Brooks's correspondence with Allen Tate and Robert Penn Warren. In *Cleanth Brooks and Robert Penn Warren: A Literary Correspondence,* readers can peruse 372 letters between the two men concerning their collaborations on such books as *Understanding Fiction.* The volume also includes essays by colleagues of Brooks and Warren. David Kirby, writing in the *Library Journal* commented that the book "will matter considerably to biographers of two literary giants as well as historians of a critical method that has fallen into disrepute among literary theorists yet that continues to shape reading practices in classrooms today." The volume *Cleanth Brooks and Allen Tate: Collected Letters, 1933-1976* includes some 250 letters between two people who John L. Brown, writing in *World Literature Today,* called "outstanding Southern men of letters of their generation." The letters include personal events of the two men and discussions of literary criticism. Denise J. Stankovics, writing in *Library Journal,* commented, "Their correspondence testifies to their mutual respect and admiration as the stature of each writer grew over time."

While many have continued to debate Brooks's literary theories, few would disparage his ability as a teacher who could articulate his theories clearly. *Southern Review* contributor Joseph Leo Blotner commented, "He helped me to help my students in fundamental ways. When one of them asked me, as often happened during the writing of dissertations or theses, 'What style should I use?,' I would enumerate what were to me the attributes desirable in good scholarly writing. Then I would cite models to follow, exemplars of clarity in form and content. I would have them read Malcolm Cowley; more often, I would tell them to read Cleanth Brooks."

BIOGRAPHICAL AND CRITICAL SOURCES:

BOOKS

Brooks, Cleanth, *A Shaping Joy: Studies in the Writer's Craft,* Harcourt (New York, NY), 1972.
Bryher, Jackson R., editor, *Sixteen Modern American Authors,* Norton (New York, NY), 1973.

Contemporary Literary Criticism, Thomson Gale (Detroit, MI), Volume 24, 1983; Volume 86, 1995.
Crane, R. S., editor, *Critics and Criticism: Ancient and Modern,* University of Chicago Press (Chicago, IL), 1952.
Cutrer, Thomas W., *Parnassus on the Mississippi: The Southern Review and the Baton Rouge Literary Community,* Louisiana State University Press (Baton Rouge, LA), 1984.
Dictionary of Literary Biography, Volume 63: *Modern American Critics, 1920-1955,* Thomson Gale (Detroit, MI), 1988.
Dictionary of Literary Biography Yearbook: 1994, Thomson Gale (Detroit, MI), 1995.
Krieger, Murray, *The New Apologists for Poetry,* University of Minnesota Press, 1956.
Littlejohn, David, *Interruptions,* Grossman (New York, NY), 1970.
Poems and Essays, Vintage (New York, NY), 1955.
Price, Reynolds, *Things Themselves: Essays and Scenes,* Atheneum (New York, NY), 1972.
Pritchard, John Paul, *Criticism in America,* University of Oklahoma Press (Norman, OK), 1956.
Rubin, Louis D., and Robert D. Jacobs, editors, *Southern Renascence: The Literature of the Modern South,* Johns Hopkins University Press (Baltimore, MD), 1953.
Simpson, Lewis P., editor, *The Possibilities of Order: Cleanth Brooks and His Work,* Louisiana State University Press (Baton Rouge, LA), 1975.
Vanderbilt, Kermit, *American Literature and the Academy: The Roots, Growth, and Maturity of a Profession,* University of Pennsylvania Press (Philadelphia, PA), 1986.
Wellek, Rene, *Concepts of Criticism,* Yale University Press (New Haven, CT), 1963.
Wellek, Rene, *Discriminations,* Yale University Press (New Haven, CT), 1970.
Wellek, Rene, *History of Modern Criticism, 1750-1950,* Volume 6, 1986.
Winchell, Mark Royden, editor, *The Vanderbilt Tradition: Essays in Honor of Thomas Daniel Young,* Louisiana State University Press (Baton Rouge, LA), 1991.
Winchell, Mark Royden, *A Blossoming Labor: Cleanth Brooks and the Rise of Modern Criticism,* University Press of Virginia (Charlottesville, VA), 1996.

PERIODICALS

American Scholar, Volume 53, 1983; spring, 1995, p. 257.
Books, July 28, 1963.

Encounter, December, 1971.

Georgia Review, winter, 1973.

Globe and Mail (Toronto, Ontario, Canada), February 25, 1984.

Library Journal, April 15, 1998, David Kirby, review of *Cleanth Brooks and Robert Penn Warren: A Literary Correspondence,* p. 78; January, 1999, Denise J. Stankovics, review of *Cleanth Brooks and Allen Tate: Collected Letters, 1933-1976,* p. 95.

Los Angeles Times, November 18, 1983, Brian Stonehill.

New Republic, February 5, 1940; July 29, 1978.

New York Herald Tribune Books, July 28, 1963.

New York Review of Books, January 9, 1964; May 7, 1987, p. 38; March 7, 1991, p. 48.

New York Times Book Review, June 8, 1947; December 10, 1972; May 21, 1978; November 13, 1983; November 15, 1987.

Sewanee Review, fall, 1947; Volume 87, 1979; spring, 1992.

Southern Review, winter, 1974, Rene Wellek; summer, 1997, Joseph Leo Blotner, "Remembering Cleanth Brooks," p. 628.

Times (London, England), May 16, 1994, p. 19.

Times Literary Supplement, March 30, 1984.

Washington Post, August 31, 1983, Jonathan Yardley, review of *William Faulkner: First Encounters.*

Washington Post Book World, March 10, 1985.

World Literature Today, autumn, 1999, John L. Brown, review of *Cleanth Brooks and Allen Tate: Collected Letters, 1933-1976,* p. 750.

Yale Review, October, 1978.

OBITUARIES:

PERIODICALS

Chicago Tribune, May 12, 1994, p. 11.

Los Angeles Times, May 14, 1994, p. A26.

New York Times, May 12, 1994, p. B14.

Washington Post, May 13, 1994, p. C4.

*   *   *

BROOKS, Gwendolyn 1917-2000

PERSONAL: Born June 7, 1917, in Topeka, KS; died of cancer December 3, 2000, in Chicago, IL; daughter of David Anderson (a janitor) and Keziah Corinne (a teacher; maiden name, Wims) Brooks; married Henry Lowington Blakely, II, September 17, 1939; children: Henry Lowington, III, Nora. *Education:* Graduate of Wilson Junior College, 1936.

CAREER: Poet and novelist. Publicity director, National Association for the Advancement of Colored People (NAACP) Youth Council, Chicago, IL, 1937-38. Taught poetry at numerous colleges and universities, including Columbia College, Elmhurst College, Northeastern Illinois State College (now Northeastern Illinois University), and University of Wisconsin-Madison, 1969; Distinguished Professor of the Arts, City College of the City University of New York, 1971; professor at Chicago State University. Member, Illinois Arts Council.

AWARDS, HONORS: Named one of ten women of the year, *Mademoiselle* magazine, 1945; National Institute of Arts and Letters grant in literature, 1946; American Academy of Arts and Letters Award for creative writing, 1946; Guggenheim fellowships, 1946 and 1947; Eunice Tietjens Memorial Prize, *Poetry* magazine, 1949; Pulitzer prize in poetry, 1950, for *Annie Allen;* Robert F. Ferguson Memorial Award, Friends of Literature, 1964, for *Selected Poems;* Thormod Monsen Literature Award, 1964; Anisfield-Wolf Award, 1968, for *In the Mecca;* named Poet Laureate of Illinois, 1968; Black Academy of Arts and Letters Award, 1971, for outstanding achievement in letters; Shelley Memorial Award, 1976; Poetry Consultant to the Library of Congress, 1985-86; inducted into National Women's Hall of Fame, 1988; Essence Award, 1988; Frost Medal, Poetry Society of America, 1989; Lifetime Achievement Award, National Endowment for the Arts, 1989; Society for Literature Award, University of Thessaloniki (Thessaloniki, Greece), 1990; Kuumba Liberation Award; Aiken-Taylor award, 1992; Jefferson Lecturer award, 1994; National Book Foundation medal for Lifetime Achievement, 1994; Gwendolyn Brooks Elementary School named in her honor, Aurora, IL, 1995; approximately fifty honorary degrees from universities and colleges, including Columbia College, 1964, Lake Forest College, 1965, and Brown University, 1974.

WRITINGS:

POETRY

A Street in Bronzeville (also see below), Harper (New York, NY), 1945.

Annie Allen (also see below), Harper (New York, NY), 1949.

The Bean Eaters (also see below), Harper (New York, NY), 1960.

In the Time of Detachment, In the Time of Cold, Civil War Centennial Commission of Illinois (Springfield, IL), 1965.

In the Mecca (also see below), Harper (New York, NY), 1968.

For Illinois 1968: A Sesquicentennial Poem, Harper (New York, NY), 1968.

Riot (also see below), Broadside Press (Highland Park, MI), 1969.

Family Pictures (also see below), Broadside Press (Highland Park, MI), 1970.

Aloneness, Broadside Press (Highland Park, MI), 1971.

Aurora, Broadside Press (Highland Park, MI), 1972.

Beckonings, Broadside Press (Highland Park, MI), 1975.

Primer for Blacks, Black Position Press (Chicago, IL), 1980.

To Disembark, Third World Press (Chicago, IL), 1981.

Black Love, Brooks Press (Chicago, IL), 1982.

Mayor Harold Washington and *Chicago, The I Will City,* Brooks Press, 1983.

The Near-Johannesburg Boy, and Other Poems, David Co. (Chicago, IL), 1987.

Gottschalk and the Grande Tarantelle, David Co. (Chicago, IL), 1988.

Winnie, Third World Press (Chicago, IL), 1988.

Children Coming Home, David Co. (Chicago, IL), 1991.

In Montgomery, and Other Poems, Third World Press (Chicago, IL), 2003.

COLLECTED WORKS

Selected Poems, Harper (New York, NY), 1963.

(With others) *A Portion of That Field: The Centennial of the Burial of Lincoln,* University of Illinois Press (Urbana, IL), 1967.

The World of Gwendolyn Brooks (contains *A Street in Bronzeville, Annie Allen, Maud Martha, The Bean Eaters,* and *In the Mecca;* also see below), Harper (New York, NY), 1971.

(Editor) *A Broadside Treasury* (poems), Broadside Press (Highland Park, MI), 1971.

(Editor) *Jump Bad: A New Chicago Anthology,* Broadside Press (Highland Park, MI), 1971.

(With Keorapetse Kgositsile, Haki R. Madhubuti, and Dudley Randall) *A Capsule Course in Black Poetry Writing,* Broadside Press (Highland Park, MI), 1975.

Young Poet's Primer (writing manual), Brooks Press (Chicago, IL), 1981.

Very Young Poets (writing manual), Brooks Press (Chicago, IL), 1983.

The Day of the Gwendolyn: A Lecture (sound recording), Library of Congress (Washington, DC), 1986.

Blacks (includes *A Street in Bronzeville, Annie Allen, The Bean Eaters, Maud Martha, A Catch of Shy Fish, Riot, In the Mecca,* and most of *Family Pictures*), David Co. (Chicago, IL), 1987.

The Gwendolyn Brooks Library, Moonbeam Publications, 1991.

OTHER

Maud Martha (novel; also see below), Harper (New York, NY), 1953.

Bronzeville Boys and Girls (poems; for juveniles), Harper (New York, NY), 1956.

Report from Part One: An Autobiography, Broadside Press (Highland Park, MI), 1972.

The Tiger Who Wore White Gloves: Or You Are What You Are (for juveniles), Third World Press (Chicago, IL), 1974, reissued, 1987.

Report from Part Two (autobiography), Third World Press (Chicago, IL), 1996.

Stories included in books, including *Soon One Morning: New Writing by American Negroes, 1940-1962* (includes "The Life of Lincoln West"), edited by Herbert Hill, Knopf (New York, NY), 1963, published as *Black Voices,* Elek (London, England), 1964; and *The Best Short Stories by Negro Writers: An Anthology from 1899 to the Present,* edited by Langston Hughes, Little, Brown (Boston, MA), 1967. Contributor to poetry anthologies, including *New Negro Poets USA,* edited by Langston Hughes, Indiana University Press, 1964; *The Poetry of Black America: Anthology of the Twentieth Century,* edited by Arnold Doff, Harper, 1973; and *Celebrate the Midwest! Poems and Stories for David D. Anderson,* edited by Marcia Noe, Lake Shore, 1991. Author of broadsides *The Wall* and *We Real Cool,* for Broadside Press, and *I See Chicago,* 1964. Contributor of poems and articles to *Ebony, McCall's, Nation, Poetry,* and other periodicals. Contributor of reviews to Chicago *Sun-Times,* Chicago *Daily News, New York Herald Tribune,* and *New York Times Book Review.*

SIDELIGHTS: Gwendolyn Brooks was a highly regarded, much-honored poet, with the distinction of being the first black author to win the Pulitzer Prize. She also was poetry consultant to the Library of Congress—the first black woman to hold that position—and poet laureate of the State of Illinois. Many of Brooks' works display a political consciousness, especially those from the 1960s and later, with several of her poems reflecting the civil rights activism of that period. Her body of work gave her, according to *Dictionary of Literary Bi-*

ography contributor George E. Kent, "a unique position in American letters. Not only has she combined a strong commitment to racial identity and equality with a mastery of poetic techniques, but she has also managed to bridge the gap between the academic poets of her generation in the 1940s and the young black militant writers of the 1960s."

Brooks was born in Topeka, Kansas, but her family moved to Chicago when she was young. Her father was a janitor who had hoped to become a doctor; her mother was a schoolteacher and classically trained pianist. They were supportive of their daughter's passion for reading and writing. Brooks was thirteen when her first published poem, "Eventide," appeared in *American Childhood;* by the time she was seventeen she was publishing poems frequently in the *Chicago Defender,* a newspaper serving Chicago's black population. After such formative experiences as attending junior college and working for the National Association for the Advancement of Colored People, she developing her craft in poetry workshops and began writing the poems, focusing on urban blacks, that would be published in her first collection, *A Street in Bronzeville.*

Her poems in *A Street in Bronzeville* and the Pulitzer Prize-winning *Annie Allen* were "devoted to small, carefully cerebrated, terse portraits of the Black urban poor," commented Richard K. Barksdale in *Modern Black Poets: A Collection of Critical Essays.* Brooks once described her style as "folksy narrative," but she varied her forms, using free verse, sonnets, and other models. Several critics welcomed Brooks as a new voice in poetry; fellow poet Rolfe Humphries wrote in the *New York Times Book Review* that "we have, in *A Street in Bronzeville,* a good book and a real poet," while *Saturday Review of Literature* contributor Starr Nelson called that volume "a work of art and a poignant social document." In *Annie Allen,* which follows the experiences of a black girl as she grows into adulthood, Brooks deals further with social issues, especially the role of women, and experimented with her poetry, with one section of the book being an epic poem, "The Anniad"—a play on *The Aeneid.* Langston Hughes, in a review of *Annie Allen* for *Voices,* remarked that "the people and poems in Gwendolyn Brooks' book are alive, reaching, and very much of today."

In the 1950s Brooks published her first and only novel, *Maud Martha,* which details a black woman's life in short vignettes. It is "a story of a woman with doubts about herself and where and how she fits into the world. Maud's concern is not so much that she is inferior but

that she is perceived as being ugly," related Harry B. Shaw in *Gwendolyn Brooks.* Maud suffers prejudice not only from whites but also from blacks who have lighter skin than hers, something that mirrors Brooks's experience. Eventually, Maud takes a stand for her own dignity by turning her back on a patronizing, racist store clerk. "The book is . . . about the triumph of the lowly," commented Shaw. "Brooks shows what they go through and exposes the shallowness of the popular, beautiful white people with 'good' hair. One way of looking at the book, then, is as a war with . . . people's concepts of beauty." Its other themes, Shaw added, include "the importance of spiritual and physical death," disillusionment with a marriage that amounts to "a step down" in living conditions, and the discovery "that even through disillusionment and spiritual death life will prevail."

David Littlejohn, writing in *Black on White: A Critical Survey of Writing by American Negroes,* found *Martha Maud* "a striking human experiment, as exquisitely written . . . as any of Gwendolyn Brooks's poetry in verse. . . . It is a powerful, beautiful dagger of a book, as generous as it can possibly be. It teaches more, more quickly, more lastingly, than a thousand pages of protest." In a *Black World* review, Annette Oliver Shands noted the way in which *Maud Martha* differs from the works of some black writers: "Brooks does not specify traits, niceties or assets for members of the Black community to acquire in order to attain their just rights. . . . So, this is not a novel to inspire social advancement on the part of fellow Blacks. Nor does it say *be poor, Black and happy.* The message is to accept the challenge of being human and to assert humanness with urgency."

Brooks's later work took a far more political stance. Just as her first poems reflected the mood of their era, her later works mirrored their age by displaying what *National Observer* contributor Bruce Cook termed "an intense awareness of the problems of color and justice." Toni Cade Bambara reported in the *New York Times Book Review* that at the age of fifty "something happened to Brooks, a something most certainly in evidence in 'In the Mecca' and subsequent works—a new movement and energy, intensity, richness, power of statement and a new stripped lean, compressed style. A change of style prompted by a change of mind." "Though some of her work in the early 1960s had a terse, abbreviated style, her conversion to direct political expression happened rapidly after a gathering of black writers at Fisk University in 1967," Jacqueline Trescott reported in the *Washington Post.* Brooks herself noted that the poets there were committed to writing as blacks, about blacks, and for a black audience. If many of her earlier poems had fulfilled this aim, it was not due to conscious intent, she said; but from this time forward, Brooks thought of herself as an African determined not to compromise social comment for the sake of technical proficiency.

Although *In the Mecca* and Brooks's subsequent works have been characterized as tougher and possessing what a *Virginia Quarterly Review* critic called "raw power and roughness," several commentators emphasized that these poems are neither bitter nor vengeful. Instead, according to Cook, they are more "about bitterness" than bitter in themselves. *Dictionary of Literary Biography* essayist Charles Israel suggested that *In the Mecca*'s title poem, for example, shows "a deepening of Brooks's concern with social problems." A mother has lost a small daughter in the block-long ghetto tenement, the Mecca; the long poem traces her steps through the building, revealing her neighbors to be indifferent or insulated by their own personal obsessions. The mother finds her little girl, who "never learned that black is not beloved," who "was royalty when poised, / sly, at the A and P's fly-open door," under a Jamaican resident's cot, murdered. A *Virginia Quarterly Review* contributor compared the poem's impact to that of Richard Wright's fiction. R. Baxter Miller, writing in *Black American Poets between Worlds, 1940-1960*, observed, "*In the Mecca* is a most complex and intriguing book; it seeks to balance the sordid realities of urban life with an imaginative process of reconciliation and redemption." Other poems in the book, occasioned by the death of Malcolm X or the dedication of a mural of black heroes painted on a Chicago slum building, express the poet's commitment to her people's awareness of themselves as a political as well as a cultural entity.

Brooks's activism and her interest in nurturing black literature led her to leave major publisher Harper & Row in favor of fledgling black publishing companies. In the seventies, she chose Dudley Randall's Broadside Press to publish her poetry (*Riot, Family Pictures, Aloneness, Aurora,* and *Beckonings*) and *Report from Part One,* the first volume of her autobiography. She edited two collections of poetry—*A Broadside Treasury* and *Jump Bad: A New Chicago Anthology*—for the Detroit-area press. The Chicago-based Third World Press, run by Haki R. Madhubuti—formerly Don L. Lee, one of the young poets she had met during the sixties—also brought some Brooks titles into print. She did not regret having supported small publishers dedicated to the needs of the black community. Brooks was the first writer to read in Broadside's original Poet's Theatre series and was also the first poet to read in the second opening of the series when the press was revived under new ownership in 1988.

Brooks, however, felt that *Riot, Family Pictures, Beckonings,* and other books brought out by black publishers were given only brief notice by critics of the literary establishment because they "did not wish to encourage Black publishers." Key poems from these books, later collected in *To Disembark,* call blacks to "work together toward their own REAL emancipation," Brooks once indicated. Even so, "the strength here is not in declamation but in the poet's genius for psychological insight," commented J.A. Lipari in *Library Journal.*

Later Brooks poems continue to deal with political subjects and figures, such as South African activist Winnie Mandela, the onetime wife of anti-apartheid leader—and later president of the country—Nelson Mandela. Brooks once told *Contemporary Literature* interviewer George Stavros: "I want to write poems that will be non-compromising. I don't want to stop a concern with words doing good jobs, which has always been a concern of mine, but I want to write poems that will be meaningful . . . things that will touch them." Still, Brooks's work was objective about human nature, several reviewers observed. Janet Overmeyer noted in the *Christian Science Monitor* that Brooks's "particular, outstanding, genius is her unsentimental regard and respect for all human beings. . . . She neither foolishly pities nor condemns—she creates." Overmeyer continued, "From her poet's craft bursts a whole gallery of wholly alive persons, preening, squabbling, loving, weeping; many a novelist cannot do so well in ten times the space." Littlejohn maintained that Brooks achieves this effect through a high "degree of artistic control," further relating, "The words, lines, and arrangements have been worked and worked and worked again into poised exactness: the unexpected apt metaphor, the mock-colloquial asides amid jewelled phrases, the half-ironic repetitions—she knows it all." More important, Brooks's objective treatment of issues such as poverty and racism "produces genuine emotional tension," the critic wrote.

Among Brooks's major prose works are her two volumes of autobiography. When the first, *Report from Part One,* was published in 1972, some reviewers expressed disappointment that it did not provide the level of personal detail or the insight into black literature that they had expected. "They wanted a list of domestic spats," remarked Brooks. Bambara noted that it "is not a sustained dramatic narrative for the nosey, being neither the confessions of a private woman poet or the usual sort of mahogany-desk memoir public personages inflict upon the populace at the first sign of a cardiac. . . . It documents the growth of Gwen Brooks." Other critics praised the book for explaining the poet's new orientation toward her racial heritage and her role as a poet. In a passage she presented again in later books as a definitive statement, Brooks wrote: "I—who have 'gone the gamut' from an almost angry rejection of my dark skin by some of my brainwashed brothers and sisters to a surprised queenhood in the new Black sun—am qualified to enter at least the kindergarten of new consciousness now. New consciousness and trudge-toward-progress. I have hopes for myself. . . . I know now that I am essentially an essential African, in occupancy here because of an indeed 'peculiar' institution. . . . I know that Black fellow-feeling must be the Black man's encyclopedic Primer. I know that the Black-and-white integration concept, which in the mind of some beaming early saint was a dainty spinning dream, has wound down to farce. . . . I know that the Black emphasis must be not *against white* but *FOR Black.* . . . In the Conference-That-Counts, whose date may be 1980 or 2080 (woe betide the Fabric of Man if it is 2080), there will be no looking up nor looking down." In the future, she envisioned "the profound and frequent shaking of hands, which in Africa is so important. The shaking of hands in warmth and strength and union."

Brooks put some of the finishing touches on the second volume of her autobiography while serving as poetry consultant to the Library of Congress. Brooks was sixty-eight years of age when she became the first black woman to be appointed to the post. Of her many duties there, the most important, in her view, were visits to local schools. Similar visits to colleges, universities, prisons, hospitals, and drug rehabilitation centers characterize her tenure as poet laureate of Illinois. In that role, she sponsored and hosted annual literary awards ceremonies at which she presented prizes funded "out of her own pocket, which, despite her modest means, is of legendary depth," Reginald Gibbons related in Chicago *Tribune Books.* She honored and encouraged many poets in her state through the Illinois Poets Laureate Awards and Significant Illinois Poets Awards programs.

Proving the breadth of Brooks's appeal, poets representing a wide variety of "races and . . . poetic camps" gathered at the University of Chicago to celebrate the poet's seventieth birthday in 1987, Gibbons reported. Brooks brought them together, he said, "in . . . a moment of good will and cheer." In recognition of her service and achievements, a junior high school in Harvey, Illinois, was named for her, and she was similarly honored by Western Illinois University's Gwendolyn Brooks Center for African-American Literature.

BIOGRAPHICAL AND CRITICAL SOURCES:

BOOKS

Berry, S. L., *Gwendolyn Brooks,* Creative Education (Mankato, MN), 1993.

Bigsby, C.W. E., *The Second Black Renaissance: Essays in Black Literature,* Greenwood Press (Westport, CT), 1980.

Black Literature Criticism, Thomson Gale (Detroit, MI), 1992.

Children's Literature Review, Volume 27, Thomson Gale (Detroit, MI), 1992.

Concise Dictionary of American Literary Biography: The New Consciousness, 1941-1968, Thomson Gale (Detroit, MI), 1985.

Contemporary Literary Criticism, Thomson Gale (Detroit, MI), Volume 1, 1973, Volume 2, 1974, Volume 4, 1975, Volume 5, 1976, Volume 15, 1980, Volume 49, 1988.

Dictionary of Literary Biography, Thomson Gale (Detroit, MI), Volume 5: *American Poets since World War II,* 1980, Volume 76: *Afro-American Writers, 1940-1955,* 1988, Volume 165: *American Poets since World War II, Fourth Series,* 1996.

Evans, Mari, editor, *Black Women Writers (1950-1980): A Critical Evaluation,* Anchor/Doubleday (New York, NY), 1984.

Gates, Henry Louis, Jr., editor, *Black Literature and Literary Theory,* Methuen (New York, NY), 1984.

Gayles, Gloria Wade, editor, *Conversations with Gwendolyn Brooks,* University Press of Mississippi (Jackson, MS), 2003.

Gibson, Donald B., editor, *Modern Black Poets: A Collection of Critical Essays,* Prentice-Hall (Englewood Cliffs, NJ), 1973.

Gould, Jean, *Modern American Women Poets,* Dodd, Mead (New York, NY), 1985.

Kent, George, *Gwendolyn Brooks: A Life,* University Press of Kentucky (Lexington, KY), 1990.

Kufrin, Joan, *Uncommon Women,* New Century Publications, 1981.

Littlejohn, David, *Black on White: A Critical Survey of Writing by American Negroes,* Grossman (New York, NY), 1966.

Madhubuti, Haki R., *Say that the River Turns: The Impact of Gwendolyn Brooks,* Third World Press (Chicago, IL), 1987.

Melhem, D. H., *Gwendolyn Brooks: Poetry and the Heroic Voice,* University Press of Kentucky (Lexington, KY), 1987.

Melhem, D. H., *Heroism in the New Black Poetry: Introductions and Interviews,* University Press of Kentucky (Lexington, KY), 1990.

Miller, R. Baxter, *Black American Poets between Worlds, 1940-1960,* University of Tennessee Press (Knoxville, TN), 1986.

Mootry, Maria K., and Gary Smith, editors, *A Life Distilled: Gwendolyn Brooks, Her Poetry and Fiction,* University of Illinois Press (Urbana, IL), 1987.

Poetry Criticism, Thomson Gale (Detroit, MI), Volume 7, 1994.

Shaw, Harry B., *Gwendolyn Brooks,* Twayne (New York, NY), 1980.

World Literature Criticism, Thomson Gale (Detroit, MI), 1992.

Wright, Stephen Caldwell, editor, *On Gwendolyn Brooks: Reliant Contemplation,* University of Michigan Press (Ann Arbor, MI), 1996.

PERIODICALS

African American Review, summer, 1992, pp. 197-211.
American Literature, December, 1990, pp. 606-16.
Atlantic Monthly, September, 1960.
Best Sellers, April 1, 1973.
Black American Literature Forum, spring, 1977; winter, 1984; fall, 1990, p. 567.
Black Enterprise, June, 1985.
Black Scholar, March, 1981; November, 1984.
Black World, August, 1970; January, 1971; July, 1971; September, 1971; October, 1971; January, 1972; March, 1973; June, 1973; December, 1975.
Book Week, October 27, 1963.
Book World, November 3, 1968.
Chicago Tribune, January 14, 1986; June 7, 1987; June 12, 1989.
Christian Science Monitor, September 19, 1968.
CLA Journal, December, 1962; December, 1963; December, 1969; September, 1972; September, 1973; September, 1977; December, 1982.
Contemporary Literature, March 28, 1969; winter, 1970.
Critique, summer, 1984.
Discourse, spring, 1967.
Ebony, July, 1968; June, 1987, p. 154.
English Journal, November, 1990, pp. 84-8.
Essence, April, 1971; September, 1984.
Explicator, April, 1976; Volume 36, number 4, 1978.
Houston Post, February 11, 1974.
Jet, May 30, 1994, p. 37.
Journal of Negro Education, winter, 1970.
Kenyon Review, winter, 1995, p. 136.
Library Journal, September 15, 1970.
Los Angeles Times, November 6, 1987; September 14, 1993, p. F3; April 21, 1997.
Los Angeles Times Book Review, September 2, 1984.

Modern Fiction Studies, winter, 1985.
Nation, September, 1962; July 7, 1969; September 26, 1987, p. 308.
National Observer, November 9, 1968.
Negro American Literature Forum, fall, 1967; summer, 1974.
Negro Digest, December, 1961; January, 1962; August, 1962; July, 1963; June, 1964; January, 1968.
New Statesman, May 3, 1985.
New Yorker, September 22, 1945; December 17, 1949; October 10, 1953; December 3, 1979.
New York Times, October 5, 1953; December 9, 1956; October 6, 1963; March 2, 1969; April 30, 1990, p. C11.
New York Times Book Review, November 4, 1945; October 23, 1960; October 6, 1963; March 2, 1969; January 2, 1972; June 4, 1972; December 3, 1972; January 7, 1973; June 10, 1973; December 2, 1973; September 23, 1984; July 5, 1987; March 18, 1990, p. 21.
Phylon, summer, 1961; March, 1976.
Poetry, December, 1945; Volume 126, 1950; March, 1964.
Publishers Weekly, June 6, 1970.
Ramparts, December, 1968.
Saturday Review, February 1, 1964.
Saturday Review of Literature, January 19, 1946; September 17, 1949; May 20, 1950.
Southern Review, spring, 1965.
Southwest Review, winter, 1989, pp. 25-35.
Studies in Black Literature, autumn, 1973; spring, 1974; summer, 1974; spring, 1977.
Tribune Books (Chicago, IL), July 12, 1987.
Virginia Quarterly Review, winter, 1969; winter, 1971.
Voices, winter, 1950, pp. 54-56.
Washington Post, May 19, 1971; April 19, 1973; March 31, 1987.
Washington Post Book World, November 11, 1973; May 4, 1994, p. C1.
Women's Review of Books, December, 1984.
World Literature Today, winter, 1985.

OBITUARIES:

PERIODICALS

Chicago Tribune, December 10, 2000, sec. 4, p. 10.
Los Angeles Times, December 4, 2000, p. B4.
New York Times, December 5, 2000, p. C22.
Times (London), December 21, 2000.
Washington Post, December 5, 2000, p. B7.

BROOKS, Terry 1944-

PERSONAL: Born January 8, 1944, in Sterling, IL; son of Dean Oliver (a printer) and Marjorie Iantha (a homemaker; maiden name, Gleason) Brooks; married Barbara Ann Groth, April 23, 1972 (marriage ended); married Judine Elaine Alba (a bookseller), December 11, 1987; children: (first marriage) Amanda Leigh, Alexander Stephen. *Education:* Hamilton College, A.B., 1966; Washington and Lee University, LL.B., 1969.

ADDRESSES: Home—2850 Southwest Yancy St., P.O. Box 229, Seattle, WA 98126-2577; Hawaii. *Agent*—Anne Sibbald, Janklow & Nesbit Associates, 445 Park Ave., New York, NY 10022.

CAREER: Called to the Bar of the State of Illinois; Besse, Frye, Arnold, Brooks & Miller, P.C. (attorneys), Sterling, IL, partner, 1969-86; writer, 1977—.

MEMBER: Authors Guild, American Bar Association, Trial Lawyers of America, Illinois State Bar Association.

AWARDS, HONORS: Best Young Adult Books citation, American Library Association, 1982, for *The Elfstones of Shannara;* Best Books for Young Adults citations, *School Library Journal,* 1982, for *The Elfstones of Shannara,* and 1986, for *Magic Kingdom for Sale—Sold!*

WRITINGS:

"SHANNARA" SERIES; FANTASY NOVELS

The Sword of Shannara, illustrated by the Brothers Hildebrandt, Random House (New York, NY), 1977, reprinted, Ballantine (New York, NY), 1991, published as *The Sword of Shannara: The Secret of the Sword,* Del Rey (New York, NY), 2003.
The Elfstones of Shannara, Ballantine/Del Rey (New York, NY), 1982.
The Wishsong of Shannara, Ballantine/Del Rey (New York, NY), 1985.
The Sword of Shannara Trilogy, (includes *The Sword of Shannara, The Elfstones of Shannara,* and *The Wishsong of Shannara*), Del Rey (New York, NY), 2002.
The Druid's Keep, Ballantine/Del Rey (New York, NY), 2003.

"SHANNARA" PREQUEL TRILOGY; FANTASY NOVELS

First King of Shannara, Ballantine (New York, NY), 1996.

"HERITAGE OF SHANNARA" SERIES; FANTASY NOVELS

The Scions of Shannara, Ballantine/Del Rey (New York, NY), 1990.
The Druid of Shannara, Ballantine/Del Rey (New York, NY), 1991.
The Elf Queen of Shannara, Ballantine/Del Rey (New York, NY), 1992.
The Talismans of Shannara, Ballantine/Del Rey (New York, NY), 1993.
The Heritage of Shannara, (includes *The Scions of Shannara, The Druid of Shannara, The Elf Queen of Shannara,* and *The Talismans of Shannara*), Ballantine Books (New York, NY), 2003.

"VOYAGE OF THE JERLE SHANNARA" SERIES; FANTASY NOVELS

Ilse Witch, Ballantine (New York, NY), 2000.
Antrax, Del Rey (New York, NY), 2001.
Morgawr, Del Rey (New York, NY), 2002.

"HIGH DRUID OF SHANNARA" SERIES; FANTASY NOVELS

Jarka Ruus, Del Rey (New York, NY), 2003.
Tanequil, Del Rey (New York, NY), 2004.
Straken, Del Rey (New York, NY), 2005.

"MAGIC KINGDOM OF LANDOVER" SERIES; FANTASY NOVELS

Magic Kingdom for Sale—Sold!, Ballantine/Del Rey (New York, NY), 1986.
The Black Unicorn, Ballantine/Del Rey (New York, NY), 1987.
Wizard at Large, Ballantine/Del Rey (New York, NY), 1988.
The Tangle Box, Ballantine/Del Rey (New York, NY), 1994.
Witches' Brew, Ballantine/Del Rey (New York, NY), 1995.

"WORD AND THE VOID" TRILOGY; FANTASY NOVELS

Running with the Demon, Ballantine (New York, NY), 1997.
A Knight of the Word, Del Rey (New York, NY), 1998.
Angel Fire East, Ballantine (New York, NY), 1999.

OTHER

Hook (novelization of film), Fawcett Columbine (New York, NY), 1992.
Star Wars: Episode I, The Phantom Menace (novelization of film), Ballantine (New York, NY), 1999.
(With Teresa Patterson) *World of Shannara* (guidebook to Brooks's fantasy world), illustrated by David Cherry, Ballantine (New York, NY), 2001.
Sometimes the Magic Works: Lessons from a Writing Life (memoir and writing guide), Del Rey (New York, NY), 2003.
Born of Wild Magic ("Pre-Shannara" trilogy), Del Rey (New York, NY), 2006.

ADAPTATIONS: Many of Brooks's works have been adapted as audiobooks. The "Shannara" series has been adapted as a CD-ROM game.

WORK IN PROGRESS: Two more untitled books in a "Pre-Shannara" trilogy; *The Voyage of the Jerle Shannara,* a collection of the "Voyage of the Jerle Shannara" series.

SIDELIGHTS: With his successful multiple-volume "Shannara" series of novels, Terry Brooks has established himself as a fantasy writer who has crossed over into the mainstream. Brooks's debut novel, *The Sword of Shannara,* was the first work of fantasy fiction to appear on the *New York Times* trade paperback best-seller list, and its publication heralded a new era in the popularity of the fantasy genre. Brooks is considered one of the founding fathers of fantasy-adventure, and his titles have sold more than fifteen million copies in the United States and abroad. By mid-2004, nineteen of his novels had hit the *New York Times* best-seller list, proving that Brooks's fiction has appeal to readers who are not necessarily fantasy buffs.

Born and raised in a small town in Illinois, Brooks began writing fiction as a child when he staged imaginative adventures to amuse himself. He also liked to read adventure novels such as those by Alexandre Dumas,

Sir Walter Scott, and Robert Louis Stevenson. In college and later law school, Brooks dabbled in fiction as a hobby. He taught himself to write while working for seventeen years as an attorney at a law firm in his hometown.

When he became more serious about writing, Brooks settled upon the fantasy genre because he wanted to be able to craft an adventure tale that was independent of recorded history. "Fantasy is the only canvas large enough for me to paint on," he explained in an online interview for the Random House Web site. "It lets me capture the magic I felt reading my favorite books, and imagining my own worlds. A world in which elves exist and magic works offers greater opportunities to digress and explore. I think that it gives both the reader and writer more room to play." In an interview published in *Albedo One,* he elaborated: "I don't look at my work as principally fantasy; I look at it as adventure stories. So that my approach to storytelling is from that viewpoint. Now I'm always inclined to do it with fantasy trappings, because that allows me to do things that I can't do otherwise. I'm not pinned to this world. I'm not pinned to this time and place. I'm not pinned to what we know to be absolutely fixed about this world. And I can do metaphorical study much better."

The Sword of Shannara was the first manuscript Brooks ever submitted for publication. The second publisher to see it bought it. That publisher, Lester Del Rey, placed great faith in the book not only as a piece of literature but as a force for creating a bigger market for fantasy. *The Sword of Shannara* "became a Del Rey project to prove that fantasy fiction would sell to a large, commercial, fiction audience," Brooks said in his *Albedo One* interview. "They essentially established *The Sword of Shannara* as the lynchpin for a series of books they were going to publish, that would sell commensurate with any piece of fiction out there." The idea was a sound one: *The Sword of Shannara* became a best-seller, and the "Shannara" series has drawn legions of fans.

Upon its first publication, *The Sword of Shannara* received an ambivalent reception, and although critical reception of his subsequent works has improved, Marilyn Achiron in a *People* interview noted, "most critics ignore his work." Despite this lack of attention—which has traditionally extended to most genre fiction—Brooks's fantasy-adventure stories have been best-sellers, and those reviewers who have taken stock of his work have found his sense of humor and the moral underpinnings of his stories appealing.

Brooks once commented that when he begins to feel jaded with the "Shannara" books, he switches to other projects as a diversion. As a result, "Shannara" has had three incarnations, and Brooks has produced two other well-received series. The "Magic Kingdom of Landover" series began with the idea that a wealthy man might be able to buy his own kingdom from a catalogue. In Brooks's hands, this premise became the foundation of a darkly humorous adventure in which a bored lawyer seeks a more interesting alternate universe. *Magic Kingdom for Sale—Sold!*, the first novel in the series, was praised by Jackie Cassada in *Library Journal* for its "welcome touches of humor" and "endearing characters," while Roland Green, writing in *Booklist*, noted in his review of series sequel *The Tangle Box* that Brooks has a "surer touch with humorous fantasy than with the saga." A *Kirkus Reviews* critic found *The Tangle Box* to be "solid entertainment for series fans, and useful comic relief."

Brooks also found intriguing the idea of setting a fantasy series in a small Midwestern town similar to his own hometown. Thus was born the "Demon" books, in which mortals gifted with magical abilities must vie with supernatural demons who seek to dispatch humankind to a Void. The central character, John Ross, is a "Knight of the Word," a reluctant hero who gains insight into his foes by dreaming of the past and the future. A *Publishers Weekly* reviewer praised Brooks's portrayal of a "hometown of Norman Rockwell blissfulness primed for demonic devastation." In *Library Journal,* Cassada suggested that the series provides a "tale of a courageous man's dedication to a demanding cause." Another *Publishers Weekly* critic felt that the strength of the "Demon" series lies in Brooks's "orchestration of the tale's social issues and personal dramas into a scenario with the resonance of myth."

Myth and morality play important roles in Brooks's fiction. While good and bad are not portrayed in stark shades of black and white, the protagonists generally strive in a mythic-heroic way to control evil, personified in a variety of forms. "I write in a tradition of fairy tales and mythologies in which [a strong moral tone is] indigenous to the writing form," Brooks said in *Albedo One.* "I think that's what's interesting to people, because it's something that we have to come to grips with in our own lives." He added: "If I were writing science fiction, I'd be writing about ideas . . . . But fantasy is about character and about relationship between characters, and there is a strong moral undertone in most fantasy."

In 1999, Brooks announced that he was returning to Shannara for a new series of as many as five more novels. The first of these, *Ilse Witch,* in the "Voyage of the

Jerle Shannara" series, begins 500 years after *The Sword of Shannara,* although some of its characters are introduced in the "Heritage of Shannara" series. As the new saga unfolds, the Druid Walker—the last of his kind—sets off to retrieve an elfin treasure that is also coveted by the deadly and powerful Ilse Witch. A *Publishers Weekly* correspondent called *Ilse Witch* a "lively new adventure . . . with an array of well-defined characters and malevolent beings." Cassada declared in *Library Journal* that with *Ilse Witch,* the Shannara mythology "gains a new level of history and depth."

With the publication of *Jarka Ruus,* Brooks began another series, the "High Druid of Shannara," and in this first installment reintroduces several characters from his "Voyage of the Jerle Shannara" series. C. Caston Jarvis wrote in the *Knight Ridder/Tribune News Service:* "Though one could be forgiven in thinking the Shannara series had about run its course, Brooks is an old hand at these sagas—this book is his twenty-first novel—and he once again finds room in his imaginary land to weave together a compelling story of mystery, adventure and romance. As a result, [*Jarka Ruus*] is sure to leave Brooks's legions of fans restlessly awaiting his next installment."

Tanequil, the second book in the "High Druid of Shannara" series, was welcomed by favorable reviews. A *Publishers Weekly* reviewer noted that "Brooks's efficient pacing, skillful characterizations and suspenseful plotting all bode well for the trilogy's conclusion." That ending, titled *Straken,* was published in 2005. A critic writing in *Kirkus Reviews* called the novel "a satisfying conclusion in the trilogy's climax."

In addition to his imaginative fiction, Brooks has also published two novelizations of films, *Hook* and *Star Wars Episode I: The Phantom Menace.* He found the "Star Wars" title in particular to be both a career-enhancing and creatively stimulating opportunity. "There are some very strong similarities between Shannara and Star Wars: the light and dark sides, flawed family histories impacting future generations, the usage of magical powers," the author explained in *Writer's Digest.* "I was allowed to do a number of chapters that are not in the movie [because] there's a lot of history that's not in the movie just for time and space constraints." Brooks added: "If you're an up-and-coming or midlist writer, this can be an excellent opportunity. Use it as a jumping-off point for your career."

As for his own place in the publishing landscape, Brooks is satisfied that his work sells well and that he can make a living by exercising his imagination. In an online interview for *TheOneRing.net,* he was invited to describe himself. "I'm a solid, workmanlike writer, plain and simple," he replied. "I'm a storyteller with a love of adventure. That's what I am and who I am."

Brooks took advantage of an opportunity to share the secrets of his writing success when he published his memoir and writing guide *Sometimes the Magic Works: Lessons from a Writing Life.* Roland Green, writing for *Booklist,* pointed out that the volume "is more a collection of essays than a connected narrative." He added that "some essays are more worth reading than others." However, a *Publishers Weekly* reviewer concluded that the book is a "succinct and warmhearted autobiographical meditation on the writing life."

BIOGRAPHICAL AND CRITICAL SOURCES:

BOOKS

Sometimes the Magic Works: Lessons from a Writing Life Del Rey (New York, NY), 2003.

PERIODICALS

Albedo One, winter, 1997-98, Robert Neilson, "An Interview with Terry Brooks."

Atlantic, May, 1977.

Booklist, September 15, 1987; September 1, 1988; December 15, 1991; March 15, 1994, Roland Green, review of *The Tangle Box,* p. 1302; July, 1999, Ray Olson, review of *Angel Fire East,* p. 1892; June 1, 2000, Sally Estes, review of *Ilse Witch,* p. 1796; January 1, 2003, Roland Green, review of *Sometimes the Magic Works: Lessons from a Writing Life,* p. 832; June 1, 2004, Sally Estes, review of *Tanequil,* p. 1670; June 1, 2005, Sally Estes, review of *Straken,* p. 1711.

Kirkus Reviews, October 15, 1987; February 1, 1990; January 1, 1992; March 15, 1994; February 1, 1995; July 1, 2005, review of *Straken,* p. 713.

Knight-Ridder/Tribune News Service, May 18, 1999, Jeff Guinn, review of *Star Wars: Episode 1: The Phantom Menace;* September 17, 2003, C. Caston Jarvis, review of *Jarka Ruus.*

Library Journal, February 15, 1990, Jackie Cassada, review of *The Scions of Shannara,* p. 215; February 15, 1992, Jackie Cassada, review of *The Elf Queen of Shannara,* p. 200; April 15, 1994, Jackie Cassada, review of *The Tangle Box,* p. 117; March 15, 1995, Jackie Cassada, review of *Witches' Brew,*

p. 101; October 15, 1999, Jackie Cassada, review of *Angel Fire East,* p. 111; August, 2000, Jackie Cassada, review of *Ilse Witch,* p. 167.

Locus, October, 1992.

New York Times Book Review, April 10, 1977.

People, May 10, 1993, Marilyn Achiron, "Laying Down the Law" (interview), p. 53.

Publishers Weekly, September 25, 1987, review of *The Black Unicorn,* p. 98; August 19, 1988; January 19, 1990, Sybil Steinberg, review of *The Scions of Shannara,* p. 101; December 20, 1991, review of *The Elf Queen of Shannara,* p. 68; January 18, 1993; April 4, 1994, review of *The Tangle Box,* p. 62; February 20, 1995, review of *Witches' Brew,* p. 199; July 28, 1997, review of *Running with the Demon,* p. 57; July 13, 1998, review of *A Knight of the Word,* p. 65; September 13, 1999, review of *Angel Fire East,* p. 65; August 21, 2000, review of *Ilse Witch,* p. 53; December 16, 2002, review of *Sometimes the Magic Works,* p. 52; August 2, 2004, review of *Tanequil,* p. 56.

Washington Post, May 21, 1999, Gene Weingarten, "Instant 'Menace,'" p. C1.

Washington Post Book World, May 1, 1977.

Writer's Digest, June, 1999, Melanie Rigney, "May the Writing Force Be with You," p. 16.

ONLINE

BookBrowser.com, http://www.bookbrowser.com/ (July 25, 2000), Conan Tigard, review of *Ilse Witch.*

Random House Web site, http://www.randomhouse.com/ (July 26, 2001), "The Demon Series: An Interview with Terry Brooks."

Terry Brooks Web site, http://www.terrybrooks.net/ (July 26, 2004).

TheOneRing.net, http://www.theonering.net/ (July 26, 2001), interview with Brooks.

Zealot.com, http://www.zealot.com/ (July 26, 2001), "Luck, Law, and Lester del Rey (Oh, and Shannara, Too): Zealot Interviews Terry Brooks."

*   *   *

BROWN, Dan 1964-

PERSONAL: Born June 22, 1964 in Exeter, NH; son of a math professor and a professional sacred musician; married; wife's name Blythe (an art historian and painter). *Education:* Amherst College, B.A., 1986; studied art history at University of Seville, Spain.

ADDRESSES: Agent—c/o Author Mail, Random House, 1745 Broadway, New York, NY 10019.

CAREER: Author. Formerly an English teacher at Phillips Exeter Academy, Exeter, NH.

AWARDS, HONORS: Book of the Year, British Book Awards, 2005, for *The Da Vinci Code.*

WRITINGS:

Digital Fortress, St. Martin's Press (New York, NY), 1998.
Angels and Demons, Pocket Books (New York, NY), 2000.
Deception Point, Pocket Books (New York, NY), 2001.
The Da Vinci Code, Doubleday (New York, NY), 2003.

Brown's work has been translated into numerous languages.

ADAPTATIONS: Film rights to *The Da Vinci Code* were purchased by Columbia Pictures, Inc.

WORK IN PROGRESS: A sequel to *The Da Vinci Code.*

SIDELIGHTS: Dan Brown's interest in code-breaking and government intelligence agencies developed after one of his students at Phillips Exeter Academy was detained by the U.S. Secret Service following a night of political debate with friends via e-mail. Though the student was never prosecuted, the incident "really stuck with me," Brown told Claire E. White in an interview for *Writers Write.* "I couldn't figure out how the Secret Service knew what these kids were saying in their E-mail." Subsequent research on government organizations and intelligence data resulted in his debut novel, a techno-thriller titled *Digital Fortress.* It is the story of an attack on a government computer known as TRNSLTR, which is supposed to monitor e-mail between terrorists but can also be used to read the mail of civilians. When TRNSLTR discovers a code it cannot break, Susan Fletcher, a government cryptographer, is called upon to help. What she uncovers is a threat to the nation and its government, as well as to her own survival. According to a reviewer for *Publishers Weekly,* "In this fast-paced, plausible tale, Brown blurs the line between good and evil enough to delight patriots and paranoids alike."

In his second novel, *Angels and Demons,* Brown introduces protagonist Robert Langdon, a well-known Harvard symbologist. Langdon is called in to assist Swiss investigators in deciphering the markings left on the body of a murdered scientist and finds himself in the thick of a terrorist plot against a group of Roman Catholic cardinals working at the Vatican. Inspired by Brown's own tour of the tunnels beneath Vatican City, *Angels and Demons* imagines the resurgence of an ancient secret brotherhood known as the Illuminati—the enlightened ones—that desires revenge against the Vatican for crimes against scientists like Galileo and Copernicus. A reviewer for *Publishers Weekly* noted that, "Though its premises strain credulity, Brown's tale is laced with twists and shocks that keep the reader wired right up to the last revelation." Jeff Ayers, in a review for *Library Journal,* called the novel "one of the best international thrillers of recent years," concluding that "Brown clearly knows how to deliver the goods."

Deception Point, Brown's third novel, revolves around NASA's discovery of a meteor in the Arctic circle that may contain proof of extraterrestrial life. The discovery coincides with the mysterious death of an agency scientist, as well as with an important presidential election. *Library Journal's* Jeff Ayers noted, "Brown . . . proves once again that he is among the most intelligent and dynamic of authors in the thriller genre." A *Kirkus Reviews* contributor called *Deception Point* "mostly tedious," but added that Brown's "impressive grasp of his material" makes him "a more astute storyteller than most of his brethren in the technothriller vein." David Pitt, writing for *Booklist,* remarked that the "characters range from inventive to wooden" and that the plot "lies somewhere between bold and ridiculous," but praised Brown's "knack for spinning a suspenseful yarn." A reviewer for *Publishers Weekly* also praised Brown's storytelling skills, calling *Deception Point* an "excellent thriller—a big yet believable story unfolding at breakneck pace, with convincing settings and just the right blend of likable and hateful characters."

Protagonist Robert Langdon returns in Brown's fourth novel, *The Da Vinci Code.* The book, which debuted in early 2003 at number one on the *New York Times* bestseller list, has since been translated into over thirty languages. The story begins with the murder of the chief curator of the Louvre in Paris. When a mysterious riddle is discovered planted near the body, French authorities call Langdon in to investigate. Subsequent clues lead the symbolist to the paintings of Leonardo Da Vinci and, as the story progresses, on a long and dangerous quest for the Holy Grail. *Library Journal* critic Jeff Ayers called *The Da Vinci Code* an "amazing sequel" through which Brown "solidifies his reputation as one of the most skilled thriller writers on the planet." A *Publishers Weekly* reviewer remarked that while "Brown sometimes ladles out too much religious history at the expense of pacing," he "has assembled a whopper of a plot that will please both conspiracy buffs and thriller addicts." Frank Sennett in *Booklist* praised the novel's "brain-teasing puzzles and fascinating insights into religious history and art," adding that "Brown's intricate plot delivers more satisfying twists than a licorice factory." *New York Times* critic Janet Maslin called *The Da Vinci Code* a "gleefully erudite suspense novel" in which Brown "takes the format he has been developing through three earlier novels and fine-tunes it to blockbuster perfection."

Brown spent over a year of research before writing *The Da Vinci Code*. Some critics, such as *Bookpage* reviewer Edward Morris, have attributed the novel's appeal to its "plot-related codes and cryptograms that impel the reader to brainstorm with the protagonists." Jo Ann Heydron in *Sojourners* noted that "the book's narrative drive is all the more remarkable because it contains a skeletal history of a real secret society, of which Leonardo Da Vinci and other icons of Western culture are said to have been members." The novel also stirred some debate due to its treatment of Christian theology and biblical characters, particularly Mary Magdalene. In addition, charges were leveled by veteran novelist Lewis Perdue that Brown's 2003 bestseller too-closely resembles Perdue's 2000 novel, *Daughter of God;* Brown maintained that he was unfamiliar with Perdue's book. Similar claims were made by other writers. In 2006 Brown defended himself in Britain's High Court against appropriation allegations made by Michael Baigent and Richard Leigh, authors of 1982's *Holy Blood and Holy Grail.*

BIOGRAPHICAL AND CRITICAL SOURCES:

PERIODICALS

Booklist, September 15, 2001, David Pitt, review of *Deception Point,* p. 198; March 1, 2003, Frank Sennett, review of *The Da Vinci Code,* p. 1148.
Kirkus Reviews, September 1, 2001, review of *Deception Point,* p. 1232; January 1, 2003, review of *The Da Vinci Code,* p. 5.
Library Journal, November 15, 2000, Jeff Ayers, review of *Angels and Demons,* p. 124; October 1, 2001, Jeff Ayers, review of *Deception Point,* p. 139; February 1, 2003, Jeff Ayers, review of *The Da Vinci Code,* p. 114.

Newsweek, June 9, 2003, "Page-Turner: A Stolen 'Da Vinci'—or Just Weirdness?," p. 57.
New Yorker May 5, 2003, Nick Paumgarten, "Acknowledged," p. 36.
New York Times, March 17, 2003, Janet Maslin, review of *The Da Vinci Code.*
People, March 24, 2003, review of *The Da Vinci Code.*
Publishers Weekly, December 22, 1997, review of *Digital Fortress,* p. 39; May 1, 2000, review of *Angels and Demons,* p. 51; September 10, 2001, review of *Deception Point,* p. 56; January 27, 2003, Charlotte Abbott, "Code Word: Breakout," p. 117; February 3, 2003, review of *The Da Vinci Code,* p. 53; February 9, 2004, Steven Zeitchik, "Riding Along With 'Da Vinci,'" p. 18.
Sojourner, July-August, 2003, Jo Ann Heydron, review of *The Da Vinci Code,* p. 58.
Time, August 11, 2003, David Van Biema, "Mary Magdalene: Saint or Sinner?"

ONLINE

Bookpage.com, http://www.bookpage.com/ (April, 2003), Edward Morris, "Explosive New Thriller Explores Secrets of the Church," p. 11.
Dan Brown Web site, http://www.danbrown.com/ (June 20, 2003).
USA Today Online, http://www.usatoday.htm/ (May 8, 2003), Ayesha Court, review of *The Da Vinci Code.*
Writers Write, http://www.writerswrite.com/ (May, 1998), Claire E. White, interview with Dan Brown.

*   *   *

BROWN, Dee Alexander 1908-2002

PERSONAL: Born February 28, 1908, in Alberta, LA; died December 12, 2002, in Little Rock, AR; son of Daniel Alexander and Lulu (Cranford) Brown; married Sara Baird Stroud, August 1, 1934; children: James Mitchell, Linda. *Education:* Attended Arkansas State Teachers College (now University of Central Arkansas); George Washington University, B.L.S., 1937; University of Illinois, M.S., 1952.

CAREER: U.S. Department of Agriculture, Washington, DC, library assistant, 1934-39; Beltsville Research Center, Beltsville, MD, librarian, 1940-42; U.S. War Department, Aberdeen Proving Ground, Aberdeen, MD, technical librarian, 1945-48; University of Illinois—

Urbana-Champaign, librarian of agriculture, 1948-72, professor of library science, 1962-75. *Military service:* U.S. Army, 1942-45.

MEMBER: Authors Guild, Western Writers of America, Society of American Historians, Beta Phi Mu.

AWARDS, HONORS: Clarence Day Award, American Library Association, 1971, for *The Year of the Century;* Christopher Award, 1971; Buffalo Award, New York Westerners, 1971, for *Bury My Heart at Wounded Knee;* named Illinoisan of the Year, Illinois News Broadcasters Association, 1972; Best Western for young people award, Western Writers of America, 1981, for *Hear that Lonesome Whistle Blow: Railroads in the West;* Saddleman Award, Western Writers of America, 1984.

WRITINGS:

NOVELS

Wave High the Banner (based on the life of Davy Crockett), Macrae Smith, 1942, reprinted, University of New Mexico Press, 1999.
Yellowhorse, Houghton (Boston, MA), 1956.
Calvary Scout, Permabooks, 1958.
They Went Thataway (satire), Putnam (New York, NY), 1960, reprinted as *Pardon My Pandemonium,* August House (Little Rock, AR), 1984.
The Girl from Fort Wicked, Doubleday (New York, NY), 1964.
Creek Mary's Blood, Holt (New York, NY), 1980.
Killdeer Mountain, Holt (New York, NY), 1983.
Conspiracy of Knaves, Holt (New York, NY), 1986.
The Way to Bright Star, Forge (New York, NY), 1998.

NONFICTION

Grierson's Raid, University of Illinois Press (Champaign, IL), 1954.
The Gentle Tamers: Women of the Old Wild West, Putnam (New York, NY), 1958.
The Bold Cavaliers: Morgan's Second Kentucky Cavalry Riders, Lippincott (Philadelphia, PA), 1959.
(Editor) George B. Grinnell, *Pawnee, Blackfoot, and Cheyenne,* Scribner (New York, NY), 1961.
Fort Phil Kearny: An American Saga, Putnam (New York, NY), 1962, published in England as *The Fetterman Massacre,* Barrie & Jenkins, 1972, published as *The Fetterman Massacre,* University of Nebraska Press (Lincoln, NE), 1984.

The Galvanized Yankees, University of Illinois Press (Champaign, IL), 1963.
The Year of the Century: 1876, Scribner (New York, NY), 1966.
Action at Beecher Island, Doubleday (New York, NY), 1967.
Bury My Heart at Wounded Knee: An Indian History of the American West, Holt (New York, NY), 1970, thirtieth-anniversary edition, 2001.
Andrew Jackson and the Battle of New Orleans, Putnam (New York, NY), 1972.
Tales of the Warrior Ants, Putnam (New York, NY), 1973.
The Westerners, Holt (New York, NY), 1974.
Hear That Lonesome Whistle Blow: Railroads in the West (also see below), Holt (New York, NY), 1977, reprinted, University of New Mexico (Albuquerque, NM), 2001.
American Spa: Hot Springs, Arkansas, Rose Publishing (Little Rock, AR), 1982.
Wondrous Times on the Frontier, August House, 1993.
When the Century Was Young: A Writer's Notebook (autobiographical), August House, 1993.
Images of the Old West, with paintings by Mort Kunstler, Park Lane Press, 1996.
(Editor) Stan Banash, *Best of Dee Brown's West: An Anthology,* Clear Light Publishers (Santa Fe, NM), 1997.
Dee Brown's Civil War Anthology, edited by Stan Banash, Clear Light Publishers (Santa Fe, NM), 1998.

Contributor to *Growing Up Western: Recollections,* Knopf (New York, NY), 1990.

WITH MARTIN F. SCHMITT

Fighting Indians of the West (also see below), Scribner (New York, NY), 1948.
Trail Driving Days (also see below), Scribner (New York, NY), 1952.
The Settlers' West (also see below), Scribner (New York, NY), 1952.
The American West (contains *Fighting Indians of the West, Trail Driving Days,* and *The Settlers' West*), Scribner (New York, NY), 1994.

FOR CHILDREN

Showdown at Little Big Horn, Putnam (New York, NY), 1964, reprinted, University of Nebraska Press, 2004 (Lincoln, NE).

Teepee Tales of the American Indians, Holt (New York, NY), 1979, published as *Dee Brown's Folktales of the Native American, Retold for Our Times,* illustrated by Louis Mofsie, Owl Books, 1993.

(With Linda Proctor) *Lonesome Whistle: The Story of the First Transcontinental Railroad* (abridged edition of *Hear That Lonesome Whistle Blow: Railroads in the West*), Holt (New York, NY), 1980.

OTHER

Editor of "Rural America" series, Scholarly Resources, 1973. Contributor of articles to periodicals, including *American History Illustrated, Civil War Times,* and *Southern Magazine.* Editor of *Agricultural History,* 1956-58.

Brown's books have been published in more than twenty languages, including Latvian, Russian, and Icelandic.

SIDELIGHTS: The American West of the nineteenth century figures prominently in the writings of historian and novelist Dee Alexander Brown. His bestseller, *Bury My Heart at Wounded Knee: An Indian History of the American West,* chronicled the settling of the West during the nineteenth century from the viewpoint of the Native Americans. In his novels *Creek Mary's Blood* and *Killdeer Mountain,* Brown dramatized events and characters from Western history, while his many nonfiction works concerned such subjects as the building of the railroads, the massacre at Little Big Horn, and women settlers of the Old West. Throughout his career, Brown showed a consistent compassion for the Native Americans and moral outrage at the injustices they suffered. In the *Los Angeles Times,* Bob Sipchen credited Brown's fictional and nonfictional accounts of Native Americans as pivotal in bringing about a widespread change in attitude toward the legends of the West.

Brown's interest in Native Americans stemmed from his childhood in Arkansas where, as he once told an interviewer for *Publishers Weekly,* "there were quite a few Indians around, people with mixed blood, and at the beginning, I swallowed the old myths. When I began to travel and meet more Indian I began wondering, Why do people think of them as such villains?" The question spurred Brown to investigate Native Americans on his own, reading everything he could about their history and culture. In time this interest led to his writing about the American West. Three of his early books, *Fighting Indians of the West, Trail Driving Days,*

and *The Settlers' West,* were written with Martin F. Schmitt and were based on historic photographs that the two men discovered in the National Archives. Writing their text around these previously unpublished photographs, Brown and Schmitt succeeded in presenting pictorial histories of three great Western subjects that had never before been seen.

After writing a score of books about the Old West, Brown embarked upon his most ambitious and successful historical work, *Bury My Heart at Wounded Knee,* a book that chronicles the settling of the West based on eyewitness reports from the Native Americans who lived there. Brown's reason for writing the book, explained Peter Farb of the *New York Review of Books,* is reflected in his belief that "whites have for long had the exclusive use of history and that it is now time to present, with sympathy rather than critically, the red side of the story."

"The Indians," wrote Helen McNeil in her *New Statesman* review of *Bury My Heart at Wounded Knee,* "knew exactly what was being done to them." Brown used quotes from the Native Americans themselves to present their history of the period. The book, according to J.W. Stevenson in *Library Journal,* is based "largely upon primary source material such as treaty council records, pictographic and translated autobiographical accounts of Indian participants in the events, and contemporary newspaper and magazine interviews, [and it is an] extensively researched history." N. Scott Momaday, in his review of the book for the *New York Times Book Review,* offered a similar assessment. *Bury My Heart at Wounded Knee,* he stated, is "a compelling history of the American West, distinguished not because it is an Indian history . . . but because it is so carefully documented and designed." As Brown told an interviewer for *Publishers Weekly,* "I had a document for everything in the book."

The uniquely Native-American viewpoint of the book was acheived not only through the extensive use of the Native American's own words, but also by the use of the Native-American names for the white historical figures of the period. General Custer, for example, was called "Hard Backsides" by the Native Americans, and is so referred in the book. When the names are "consistently used," wrote R.A. Mohl in *Best Sellers,* "these become creative and effective literary devices which force the reader, almost without his knowing it, into the position of the defeated, retreating Indian."

Bury My Heart at Wounded Knee took Brown over two years to write, and he maintained a consistently Native-American perspective throughout the book. Speaking to

Anne Courtmanche-Ellis in the *Wilson Library Bulletin,* Brown once explained how he did it: "I would tell myself every night, 'I'm a very, very old Indian, and I'm remembering the past. And I'm looking toward the Atlantic Ocean.' And I always kept that viewpoint every night. That's all I did."

The importance of *Bury My Heart at Wounded Knee* to the field of Western history was noted by several reviewers. "Brown," Farb related, "dispels any illusions that may still exist that the Indian wars were civilization's mission or manifest destiny; the Indian wars are shown to be the dirty murders they were. . . . *Bury My Heart* is an extremely ambitious and readable attempt to write a different kind of history of white conquest of the West: from the point of view of the victims, using their words whenever possible." McNeil judged the book to be "a deliberately revisionist history [that tells] the story of the Plains Indians from an amalgamated Indian viewpoint, so that the westward march of the civilized men, 'like maggots,' according to a Sioux commentator, appears as a barbaric rout of established Indian culture." *Bury My Heart,* Cecil Eby wrote in *Book World,* "will undoubtedly chart the course of other 'revisionist' historical books dealing with the Old West."

Bury My Heart at Wounded Knee became a nation-wide top-seller, gaining the number-one spot on the country's bestselling books list and selling well over one million copies. But Brown claimed the most satisfying compliment he ever received for the book came from an old Native-American friend who told him: "You didn't write that book. Only an Indian could have written that book! Every time I read a page, I think: That's the way I feel."

In *Hear That Lonesome Whistle Blow: Railroads in the West,* Brown approached the ruthless setting of the West from a different perspective—the history of the building of the Western railroads, although the author did not intend to write an exposé. Union Pacific was so upset with Brown's manuscript that the company denied him access to its corporate library for further research.

"Brown does a good job with the drama and with the scalawaggery of the great railroad promoters," Tony Hiss commented in the *New York Times Book Review.* Philip French of *New Statesman* also commended Brown's absorbing narrative, but added that "the constant emphasis on shoddy deals serves not merely to qualify almost out of existence the epic nature of the undertaking, but to deny a true complexity to the events

and a full humanity to the participants." But Winifred Farrant Bevilacqua, in the *Dictionary of Literary Biography Yearbook: 1980,* described the book as "an engaging reconstruction of the drama surrounding the advent of the iron horse and a case against railroads."

In his fiction, Brown dramatized many of the historical themes he presented in his nonfiction, creating stories from the actual historical conditions of the nineteenth century. *Creek Mary's Blood,* for instance, is based on a Native-American woman in Georgia who organized an attack on British-held Savannah during the American Revolutionary War. The novel tells her story and that of her descendants as they are pushed farther and farther west by the expanding frontier. Brown told Judy Klemesrud of the *New York Times:* "I tried to make the historical events as accurate as possible, but I did make some changes for dramatic effect. That's something you never do in nonfiction, and I felt guilty about it."

Despite its fictional liberties, *Creek Mary's Blood* is considered to accurately describe Native-American life of the nineteenth century while chronicling the lives of one Native-American family on their westward trek. Interspersed with the family's story are chapters about events of the time that affected all Native Americans. "In this absorbing historical romance," Bevilacqua stated, "Brown skillfully blends fact with fiction but falters in his attempt to confer on his characters an authentic Indian perspective." But Joseph McClellan commented otherwise in the *Washington Post Book World:* "Using fictional characters against a carefully researched historical background, [Brown] combines the attractions of both genres. The major incidents of his story are true, but by inventing fictional participants he is able to give the events a human dimension lacking in the historic record."

"The dominant themes of *Creek Mary's Blood,*" explained Mary Anne Norman of the *Lone Star Book Review,* "are the displacement of the Indians and the treachery of the U.S. government in its dealings with the Indians." Through the misfortunes of Creek Mary's family, Brown outlines the fate of all Native Americans during the course of the nineteenth century. Creek Mary's two husbands, McClellan pointed out, symbolize the two ways that Native Americans sought to deal with the white settlers. Her first husband was an English colonist, "who is related thematically to the effort at accommodation and assimilation," McClellan wrote. Her second husband was a Cherokee warrior, "a leader of the resistance to white encroachment." "Both ways of coping," McClellan concluded, "ultimately proved futile, and in his novel's epic length Dee Brown has leisure to examine the modes of futility in assimilation and in resistance."

Although concerned with the same themes as his earlier works, Brown's novel *Killdeer Mountain* was a stylistic departure from his previous writings. Its disjointed narrative structure presents a number of conflicting versions of the same basic story. Reviewing *Killdeer Mountain* for the *Chicago Tribune Book World,* Robert Gish described it as "perhaps [Brown's] most intriguing book to date." Told by a newspaper reporter who is unraveling the true story of Major Charles Rawley, a Native-American fighter and military hero, the novel contains the differing accounts of people who knew and worked with him. The reporter's attempts to make sense of the ambiguities and contradictions in the stories, and his efforts to discover the truth concerning the major's heroism and supposed death, turn the novel into a kind of mystery story. "The world we view," Brown stated in the novel, "is a complex mirror that tricks us with false images so that what we believe to have happened . . . may or may not have taken place." "We gradually acquire," wrote Michael A. Schwartz of the *Detroit News,* "a complex tangled web of evidence resting upon a shadow. Brown makes the various guises that Major Rawley assumes seem quite real, and in Rawley's manifestations we discover the ambiguous nature of this country's westward expansion."

The strongest aspect of *Killdeer Mountain,* according to several critics, was Brown's narrative ability, which makes adventurous scenes come alive, while the weakest aspect is his use of dialogue. "Brown's gift for strong narrative," Jonathan Coleman of the *New York Times Book Review* believed, "far outweighs his skill at writing dialogue, which, at times, hurts his novel by trivializing it." Using similar terms, C.C. Loomis wrote in the *Washington Post Book World:* "Brown is at his best narrating adventurous episodes within the novel. . . . But most readers want vivid characters in novels as well as vivid narration, and here . . . Brown has only limited success. . . . [His] dialogue is artificial; it flattens his characters." Brown's narrative strength was best used, Schwartz related, in a scene involving the massacre of Sioux Indians, which "shows Brown's mastery as a storyteller and his thorough understanding of these times. . . . It is rendered with such intensity that it becomes a brutally realistic portrait of the Indian wars."

With *Wondrous Times on the Frontier,* Brown returned to nonfiction with a look at the social and cultural history of the nineteenth-century West. Reviewing this collection of anecdotes for the *Washington Post Book World,* Paula Mitchell Marks noted that Brown takes a more benign approach to characterizing life on the frontier than do other recent Western historians: "Brown's key word is 'merriment'—there are 'merry' frontier courtrooms and military expeditions, merry cowboys and gold stampeders and gamblers." James R. Kincaid, writing in the *New York Times Book Review,* pointed out that many of the light-hearted stories that Brown terms "jollity" are, in fact, dismal. Kincaid drew attention to Brown's "odd insensitivity to a running nastiness in these stories and their willingness to find what the author regards as 'merriment' in such things as women's helplessness ('I done left Edna May locked up in a room for twenty-four hours an' I ain't neither fed nor watered her'), the susceptibility of Native Americans to practical jokes, and the fun of spreading lies about 'Injuns on the warpath.'" It is incongruous, continued Kincaid, that the author of "the powerful *Bury My Heart at Wounded Knee* . . . who alerted us to how catastrophic such lies were, should now offer them for fun." Although Marks also faulted the book for glossing "over the complexities of frontier experience in favor of joviality," she acknowledged that may readers will enjoy enjoy the "engaging and well-presented" anecdotes in the book.

The American West, published in 1994, combines the three photography-based histories that Brown produced with Martin F. Schmitt into a single narrative. The result is a detailed chronicle of the mythic West, from the legendary gunfighters and heroic Native-American leaders to the insect plagues and ferocious blizzards that elevated the place and time into America's collective consciousness. Several reviewers praised the volume as a powerful and compelling account that both reinforces the myths of the West and reveals the underlying truth behind those stories.

Brown "reminds us that myths are based on actual events, people, places and concepts, and encourages us to learn the 'true' history of the West 'so we can recognize a myth when we see one,'" commented Donna Seaman in a *Booklist* review of *The American West.* Calling the work "wondrous," *Los Angeles Times Book Review* contributor Larry Watson noted Brown's achievement in documenting the "astonishing swiftness" with which Native-American customs and cultures were transformed. Watson averred, "Brown documents these losses, until, finally, the American West feels more like an elegy than history." Writing in the *Washington Post Book World,* Elliot West criticized Brown for leaving out many important aspects of the frontier experience. "Mountain men and traders, the

Mexican War, the Mormons, Lewis and Clark, missionaries and buffalo hunters are only the merest flickerings in the narrative," commented West. However, West praised Brown's storytelling prowess and his "vivid, straightforward prose," noting that Brown excels at bringing famous events to life by including the perspectives of ordinary men and women who participated in the events.

In book after book, Brown examined the history of the settling of the West and presented the hardships and triumphs of this vast undertaking. In particular, he drew attention to "the destruction of ancient Indian cultures," Bevilacqua stated, "and investigated other aspects of the toll exacted by the nation's western expansion. He has always been recognized as a tireless researcher and a gifted raconteur who narrates his stories in an informative and entertaining matter."

BIOGRAPHICAL AND CRITICAL SOURCES:

BOOKS

Brown, Dee Alexander, *Killdeer Mountain,* Holt (New York, NY), 1983.
Contemporary Authors Autobiography Series, Volume 6, Thomson Gale (Detroit, MI), 1988.
Contemporary Literary Criticism, Thomson Gale (Detroit, MI), Volume 18, 1981, Volume 47, 1988.
Contemporary Southern Writers, St. James Press (Detroit, MI), 1999.
Dictionary of Literary Biography Yearbook: 1980, Thomson Gale (Detroit, MI), 1981.

PERIODICALS

American Historical Review, April, 1955.
American West, March, 1975.
Arkansas Business, September 23, 2002, p. 30.
Atlantic Monthly, February, 1971.
Best Sellers, March 1, 1971.
Booklist, September 1, 1993, p. 27; October 15, 1994, p. 397; May 1, 1998, p. 1477; May 15, 1998, p. 1563.
Book World, February 28, 1971.
Catholic World, August, 1971.
Chicago Tribune Book World, March 2, 1980; March 13, 1983.
Christian Century, February 3, 1971.
Christian Science Monitor, June 21, 1977.
Detroit News, July 13, 1983.

Economist, October 2, 1971; September 10, 1977; December 21, 2002.
Globe and Mail (Toronto, Ontario, Canada), February 14, 1987.
Guardian, September 21, 1974.
Journal of American History, November, 1966.
Library Journal, December 15, 1970; October 15, 1994, p. 73; March 15, 1997, p. 73; November 1, 1998, Randall Miller, review of *Dee Brown's Civil War Anthology,* p. 108; April 15, 2001, Michael Rogers, review of *Bury My Heart at Wounded Knee,* p. 138.
Life, April 2, 1971.
Lone Star Book Review, April, 1980.
Los Angeles Times, July 1, 1987.
Los Angeles Times Book Review, April 3, 1983; January 25, 1987; August 9, 1987; October 2, 1988; December 18, 1994, p. 2.
National Review, March 9, 1971.
New Republic, December 14, 1974.
New Statesman, October 1, 1971; September 30, 1977.
Newsweek, February 1, 1971; May 23, 1977; March 28, 1983.
New York, April 7, 1980.
New Yorker, February 13, 1971.
New York Post, April 22, 1971.
New York Review of Books, December 16, 1971.
New York Times, December 3, 1976; April 13, 1980.
New York Times Book Review, May 3, 1942; March 7, 1971; May 15, 1977, p. 15; April 13, 1980; April 27, 1980; May 25, 1980; April 26, 1981; June 5, 1983; June 17, 1984, p. 20; January 11, 1987; April 21, 1991; February 2, 1992, p. 11.
Pacific Historical Review, November, 1972.
Publishers Weekly, April 19, 1971; March 21, 1980; October 4, 1991; July 26, 1993, p. 54; October 24, 1994, p. 47; April 20, 1998, p. 46.
Time, February 1, 1971.
Times Literary Supplement, December 16, 1977.
Tribune Books (Chicago, IL), January 25, 1987.
Village Voice, August 5, 1971; June 27, 1977.
Voice Literary Supplement, November, 1991.
Washington Post Book World, March 16, 1980; March 14, 1983; January 18, 1987; March 3, 1991; January 5, 1992, pp. 6-7; December 27, 1992; January 8, 1995, p. 9.
Wild West, April, 1997, p. 64; December, 1998, review of *Best of Dee Brown's West: An Anthology,* p. 80.
Wilson Library Bulletin, March, 1978.

OBITUARIES:

PERIODICALS

Chicago Tribune, December 14, 2002, section 2, p. 11.

Los Angeles Times, December 14, 2002, p. B20.
New York Times, December 14, 2002, p. B18.
School Library Journal, February, 2003, p. 19.
Time, December 23, 2002.
Times (London, England), December 17, 2002, p. 28.
Washington Post, December 14, 2002, p. B6.

*   *   *

BROWN, Rita Mae 1944-

PERSONAL: Born November 28, 1944, in Hanover, PA; adopted daughter of Ralph (a butcher) and Julia Ellen (Buckingham) Brown. *Education:* Attended University of Florida; Broward Junior College, A.A., 1965; New York University, B.A., 1968; New York School of Visual Arts, cinematography certificate, 1968; Institute for Policy Studies, Washington, DC, Ph.D., 1973. *Hobbies and other interests:* Polo, fox hunting, horses, gardening.

ADDRESSES: Home—Charlottesville, VA. *Office*—American Artists Inc., P. O. Box 4671, Charlottesville, VA 22905. *Agent*—The Wendy Weil Agency, 232 Madison Ave., New York, NY 10016.

CAREER: Writer. Sterling Publishing, New York, NY, photo editor, 1969-70; Federal City College, Washington, DC, lecturer in sociology, 1970-71; Institute for Policy Studies, Washington, research fellow, 1971-73; Goddard College, Plainfield, VT, visiting member of faculty in feminist studies, beginning 1973. Founder, Redstockings Radical Feminist Group, National Gay Task Force, National Women's Political Caucus; cofounder, Radical Lesbians; member of board of directors of Sagaris, a feminist school. American Artists Inc., Charlottesville, VA, president, 1980—. Member of literary panel, National Endowment for the Arts, 1978-81; Hemingway judge for first fiction PEN International, 1984; blue ribbon panelist for Prime Time Emmy Awards, 1984, 1986.

MEMBER: PEN International.

AWARDS, HONORS: Shared Writers Guild of America award, 1983, for television special *I Love Liberty;* Emmy Award nominations for *I Love Liberty,* 1982, and *The Long Hot Summer,* ABC mini-series, 1985; Literary Lion Award, New York Public Library, 1986; named Charlottesville Favorite Author.

WRITINGS:

(Translator) *Hrotsvitra: Six Medieval Latin Plays,* New York University Press (New York, NY), 1971.
The Hand That Cradles the Rock (poems), New York University Press (New York, NY), 1971.
Rubyfruit Jungle (novel; also see below), Daughters, Inc. (Plainfield, VT), 1973.
Songs to a Handsome Woman (poems), Diana Press (Baltimore, MD), 1973.
In Her Day (novel), Daughters, Inc. (Plainfield, VT), 1976.
A Plain Brown Rapper (essays), Diana Press (Baltimore, MD), 1976.
Six of One (novel), Harper (New York, NY), 1978.
Southern Discomfort (novel), Harper (New York, NY), 1982.
Sudden Death (novel), Bantam Books (New York, NY), 1983.
High Hearts (novel), Bantam Books (New York, NY), 1986.
The Poems of Rita Mae Brown, Crossing Press (Trumansburg, NY), 1987.
Starting from Scratch: A Different Kind of Writer's Manual (nonfiction), Bantam Books (New York, NY), 1988.
Bingo (novel), Bantam Books (New York, NY), 1988.
Venus Envy (novel), Bantam Books (New York, NY), 1993.
Dolley: A Novel of Dolley Madison in Love and War (novel), Bantam Books (New York, NY), 1994.
Riding Shotgun, Bantam Books (New York, NY), 1996.
Rita Will: Memoir of a Literary Rabble-Rouser, Bantam Books (New York, NY), 1997.
Loose Lips, Bantam Books (New York, NY), 1999.
Outfoxed, Ballantine Books (New York, NY), 2000.
Alma Mater (novel), Ballantine Books (New York, NY), 2001.
Hotspur (mystery), Ballantine Books (New York, NY), 2002.
Full Cry (mystery), Ballantine Books (New York, NY), 2003.
The Hunt Ball (novel), Ballantine Books (New York, NY), 2005.

WITH CAT, SNEAKY PIE BROWN

Wish You Were Here (mystery; also see below), Bantam Books (New York, NY), 1990.
Rest in Pieces (mystery; also see below), Bantam Books (New York, NY), 1992.

Murder at Monticello; Or, Old Sins (mystery; also see below), Bantam Books (New York, NY), 1994.

Pay Dirt; Or, Adventures at Ash Lawn (also see below), Bantam Books (New York, NY), 1995.

Murder, She Meowed (mystery; also see below), Bantam Books (New York, NY), 1996.

Murder on the Prowl (also see below), Bantam Books (New York, NY), 1998.

Cat on the Scent, Bantam Books (New York, NY), 1998.

Sneaky Pie's Cookbook for Mystery Lovers, illustrated by Katie Cox Shively, Bantam Books (New York, NY), 1999.

Pawing through the Past, illustrated by Itoko Maeno, Bantam Books (New York, NY), 2000.

Claws and Effect, illustrated by Itoko Maeno, Bantam Books (New York, NY), 2001.

Catch as Cat Can (mystery), Bantam Books (New York, NY), 2002.

The Tail of the Tip-Off (mystery), Bantam Books (New York, NY), 2003.

Wish You Were Here; Rest in Pieces; Murder at Monticello (three "Mrs. Murphy" mysteries in one volume), Wings Books (New York, NY), 2003.

Whisker of Evil (mystery), Bantam Books (New York, NY), 2004.

Pay Dirt; Murder, She Meowed; Murder on the Prowl, (three "Mrs. Murphy" mysteries in one volume), Wings Books (New York, NY), 2005.

Cat's Eyewitness (mystery), Bantam Books (New York, NY), 2005.

Sour Puss (mystery), Bantam Books (New York, NY), 2006.

Also author or coauthor of eight screenplays, including *Rubyfruit Jungle* (based on novel of same title) and *Slumber Party Massacre;* contributor to script of television special *I Love Liberty,* American Broadcasting Companies, Inc. (ABC), 1982, and author of television filmscripts for *The Long Hot Summer,* a mini-series for National Broadcasting Company, Inc. (NBC), 1985, *The Mists of Avalon,* 1986, *The Girls of Summer,* 1989, *Selma, Lord, Selma,* 1989, *Rich Men, Single Women,* 1989, *Home, Sweet Home,* Columbia Broadcasting System, Inc. (CBS), 1990, and *Graceland,* Napello County Productions, 1992.

SIDELIGHTS: With the 1973 publication of her autobiographical novel *Rubyfruit Jungle,* Rita Mae Brown joined the ranks of those in the forefront of the feminist and gay rights movements. Described by *Ms.* reviewer Marilyn Webb as "an inspiring, bravado adventure story of a female Huck Finn named Molly Bolt," *Rubyfruit Jungle* was at first rejected by editors at the major New York publishing companies due to what they believed to be its lack of mass-market appeal. Eventually published by the small feminist firm Daughters, Inc., it sold an unexpected 70,000 copies. The book's popularity soon brought it to the attention of Bantam Books, which acquired the rights to *Rubyfruit Jungle* in 1977 and printed an additional 300,000 copies. Total sales of the novel number more than one million, and in 1988, Bantam released the book for the first time in hardcover form.

As Webb's comment suggests, *Rubyfruit Jungle* is told in a picaresque, Mark Twain-like fashion, an observation shared by *New Boston Review* critic Shelly Temchin Henze. "Imagine, if you will, Tom Sawyer, only smarter; Huckleberry Finn, only foul-mouthed, female, and lesbian, and you have an idea of Molly Bolt," wrote Henze. Though some adopted *Rubyfruit Jungle* as "a symbol of a movement, a sisterly struggle," the critic continued, the plot of the book is basically that of the "classic American success story." Explained Henze: *Rubyfruit Jungle* "is not about revolution, nor even particularly about feminism. It is about standing on your own two feet, creaming the competition, looking out for Number One." The truly original part of the novel, maintained the critic, is Brown's perspective. "While American heroes may occasionally be women, they may not be lesbian. Or if they are, they had better be discreet or at least miserable. Not Molly. She is lusty and lewd and pursues sex with relentless gusto."

Village Voice reviewer Bertha Harris had a few reservations about the authenticity of Brown's portrayal of lesbian life. "Much of Molly's world seems a cardboard stage set lighted to reveal only Molly's virtues and those characteristics which mark her as the 'exceptional' lesbian," remarked Harris. Nevertheless, Harris went on to state, "it is exactly this quality of *Rubyfruit Jungle* which makes it exemplary (for women) of its kind: an American primitive, whose predecessors have dealt only with male heroes. Although Molly Bolt is not a real woman, she is at least the first real *image* of a heroine in the noble savage, leatherstocking, true-blue bullfighting tradition in this country's literature."

Another *Village Voice* critic, Terry Curtis Fox, viewed *Rubyfruit Jungle* in a somewhat different light. Like Henze, Fox found that Brown relies on a well-known theme for her novel, namely, "sensitive member of outside group heads toward American society and lives to tell the tale." Since this portrayal of resilience and triumph in the face of adversity is so familiar and appealing, maintained the reviewer, "you don't have to be gay or female to identify with Molly Bolt—she is one of the outsiders many of us believe ourselves to be." Furthermore, said Fox, Brown "can laugh at herself as well as at others, and make us laugh, too."

Acutely aware of the fact that humor is a quality seldom found in books dealing with homosexual life, Brown attaches special importance to her ability to make readers laugh, regarding it as a means of overcoming offensive stereotypes. "Most lesbians are thought to be ugly, neurotic and self- destructive and I just am not," she explained in a *New York Times* article. "There's no way they can pass me off that way. I'm not passing myself off as gorgeous, and a bastion of sanity, but I'm certainly not like those gay stereotypes of the miserable lesbian, the poor woman who couldn't get a man and eventually commits suicide . . . . I'm funny. Funny people are dangerous. They knock down barriers. It's hard to hate people when they're funny. I try to be like Flip Wilson, who helped a lot of white people understand blacks through humor. One way or another, I'll make 'em laugh, too."

The novel *Six of One* was Brown's second major breakthrough into the mass-market arena. Based once again on the author's own life as well as on the lives of her grandmother, mother, and aunt, *Six of One*—like *Rubyfruit Jungle*—attempts to make its point through ribald humor and an emphasis on the poor and uneducated as sources of practical wisdom. The story chronicles the events in a half- Northern, half-Southern, Pennsylvania-Maryland border town from 1909 to 1980, as viewed through the eyes of a colorful assortment of female residents. John Fludas of the *Saturday Review,* noting that *Six of One* is a "bright and worthy successor" to *Rubyfruit Jungle,* wrote that Brown "explores the town's cultural psychology like an American Evelyn Waugh, finding dignity and beauty without bypassing the zany and the corrupt . . . . If at times the comedy veers toward slapstick, and if there are spots when the prose just grazes the beauty of the human moment . . . , the novel loses none of its warmth."

Both Eliot Fremont-Smith and Richard Boeth felt Brown could have done a better job with her material. Commenting in *Village Voice,* for example, Fremont-Smith admitted that *Six of One* "does have a winning cheerfulness," but concluded that "it's mostly just garrulous. . . . As a novel, it doesn't go anywhere; there's no driving edge; and the chatter dissipates. And as a polemical history (the secret and superior dynamics of female relationships), it gives off constant little back-

fires." *Newsweek* critic Boeth was even less impressed. He stated: "It is a major sadness to report that Brown has made her women [in *Six of One*] not only boring but false . . . . Her only verbal tool is the josh—speech that is not quite witty, sly, wry, sardonic, ironic or even, God help us, clever, but only self-consciously breezy . . . . These aren't human beings talking; it's 310 pages of 'Gilligan's Island.'"

In her *New York Arts Journal* review of *Six of One,* Liz Mednick attributed what some reviewers perceived as characterization problems to Brown's determination "to show how wise, witty, wonderful and cute women really are. Her silent competitor in this game is the masculine standard; her method, systematic oneupmanship. The women in *Six of One* buzz around like furies trying to out-curse, out-class, out-wit, out-smart, out-shout, out-smoke, out-drink, out-read, out-think, out- lech, out-number and outrage every man, dead or alive, in history. Needless to say, ambition frequently leads the author to extremes . . . . As if to insure her success, Brown makes her men as flat as the paper on which they're scrawled. The problem with her men is not even so much that they lack dimension as that they don't quite qualify as male." In short, concluded Mednick, *Six of One* "is less a novel than a wordy costume the author wears to parade herself before her faceless audience. Her heroines are presented not for inspection but as subjects for whom the narrative implicitly demands admiration." *Washington Post Book World* reviewer Cynthia Macdonald, on the other hand, cited *Six of One* as evidence of a welcome change in women's literature. She wrote: "The vision of women we have usually gotten from women novelists is of pain and struggle or pain and passivity; it is seldom joyous and passionate, and almost never funny. And what humor there was has been of the suffering, self-deprecating New York Jewish stand-up comedian type. [This book] is joyous, passionate and funny. What a pleasure! . . . I believe that Brown uses a kind of revisionist history to support her conviction that what was seen in the first half of the twentieth century as the life of women was only what was on the surface, not what was underneath."

Responding to criticism that women of the early 1900s could not possibly have been as liberated—not to mention as raucous—as they are depicted in the novel, Brown told Leonore Fleischer in a *Washington Post Book World* interview: "I grew up with these two almost mythical figures around me, my mother and my aunt, who didn't give a rat's a— what anybody thought. They'd say anything to anybody, and they did as they damn well pleased. We were so poor, who cares what poor people do? Literature is predominantly written by middle-class people for middle-class people and their lives were real different. As a girl, I never saw a woman knuckle under to a man, or a man to a woman, for that matter . . . . The people closest to me were all very dominating characters. The men weren't weak, but somehow the women . . . were the ones you paid attention to."

Though it, too, focuses on the difficulties straight and gay women face in a hypocritical and judgmental society, Brown's novel *Sudden Death* represents what the author herself has termed "a stylistic first for me." Written in an uncharacteristically plain and direct manner, *Sudden Death* examines the "often vicious and cold-blooded" world of women's professional tennis; many readers assume that it more or less chronicles Brown's experiences and observations during her involvement with star player Martina Navratilova. As Brown sees it, however, the book is much more than that: it is the fulfillment of a promise to a dying friend, sportswriter Judy Lacy, who had always wanted to write a novel against the background of women's tennis. Just prior to her death from a brain tumor in 1980, Lacy extracted a reluctant promise from Brown to write such a novel, even though Brown "didn't think sports were a strong enough metaphor for literature." Judy "tricked me into writing it," explained the author to Fleischer in a *Publishers Weekly* column. "She knew me well enough to know how I'd feel about my promise, that it would be a deathbed promise . . . . I thought about her all the time I was writing it. It was strange to be using material that you felt belonged to somebody else. It's really Judy's book."

For the most part, critics felt that *Sudden Death* has few of the qualities that make *Rubyfruit Jungle* and *Six of One* so entertaining. In the *Chicago Tribune Book World,* for instance, John Blades noted that despite the inclusion of "intriguing sidelights on how [tennis] has been commercialized and corrupted by sponsors, promoters and greedy players," *Sudden Death* "lacks the wit and vitality that might have made it good, unwholesome fun. Brown seems preoccupied here with extraliterary affairs; less interested in telling a story than in settling old scores." Anne Chamberlin commented in the *Washington Post:* "If you thought Nora Ephron's *Heartburn* had cornered the market on true heartbreak, thinly veiled, make room for *Sudden Death. . . .* Don't get mad; get even, as the saying goes, and this novel should bring the score to deuce. It not only chops the stars of women's professional tennis down to size; it tackles the whole pro tennis establishment . . . . Having reduced that tableau to rubble, Brown turns her guns on America's intolerance of lesbians. That's a lot of targets for

one bombing run, and all 241 acerbic pages of *Sudden Death* are jammed with as disagreeable a bunch of people doing mean things to each other as you are likely to meet at one time." *Los Angeles Times Book Review* critic Kay Mills felt that the protagonist is characterized so flatly "that one is devoid of sympathy for her when a jealous rival seeks to break her," and Elisabeth Jakab in the *New York Times Book Review* commented that Brown "is not at her best here. The world of tennis does not seem to be congenial terrain for her, and her usually natural and easy style seems cramped . . . . In *Sudden Death* we can almost hear the pieces of the plot clanking into their proper slots." Brown, who says she does not read reviews of her books, is nevertheless aware of the kinds of remarks critics made about *Sudden Death,* to which she responds: "I don't care; it doesn't matter at all; and anyway, I'm already on the next book . . . . I wrote this because Judy asked me to . . . . I learned a lot, but I can't wait to get back on my own territory."

In 1990, Brown attempted a literary departure, of sorts. With the "help" of her cat Sneaky Pie Brown, she wrote a mystery titled *Wish You Were Here.* The plot is rather complicated, full of death by cement and train "squishing." At the center of all the mayhem is postmistress Mary Minor Haristeen, or Harry, and her pets, a cat named Mrs. Murphy and a Welsh Corgi named Tee Tucker. According to See, *Wish You Were Here* is "a carefree canvas for Rita Mae Brown—who remember, has declared independence from the rest of us—to air certain of her own views on the human, feline, and canine condition . . . . Independence is her great thing. And animals, and nature, and a few friends. Not a bad agenda, come to think of it."

Brown and Sneaky Pie continued to pen several more mysteries together, including *Pay Dirt; Or, Adventures at Ash Lawn, Catch as Cat Can,* and *Sour Puss,* to name a few. In *Pay Dirt,* Brown and Sneaky Pie's fourth collaboration, Harry, Mrs. Murphy, and Tee Tucker return for what one *Publishers Weekly* reviewer called "the best Mrs. Murphy adventure yet." The same reviewer praised Brown's "supporting cast of eccentric characters, (both two- and four-legged)."

Claire McNab, writing for *Lambda Book Report,* noted that *Catch as Cat Can* is "definitively in the cozy genre." She went on to say that "the pleasures of *Catch as Cat Can* lie not so much in the mystery being explored, but in the light-hearted, frequently ironic tone that Rita Mae Brown assumes, and in the amusing, sometimes tart, conversations between the animals."

Sour Puss, published in 2006, was met with similar praise. Jenny McLarin, a reviewer for *Booklist* felt that the author becomes increasingly "relaxed and comfortable with her characters in each new adventure, reenergizing a series that could easily have grown stale over time."

Brown resumed her focus on a strong lesbian character in her novel, *Venus Envy.* Although her forthright treatment of lesbianism first attracted many critics to *Rubyfruit Jungle,* reception of *Venus Envy* was somewhat less enthusiastic. Carla Tomaso, who found Frazier to be another of Brown's loveable, "irreverent individualists," suggested in a *Los Angeles Times Book Review* that Brown's tenth novel, focusing as it does on the importance of self-acceptance and self-love, is too didactic, with the author attempting to pull "too many strings . . . . Brown needs to relax and stop worrying that we won't get the message." R.C. Scott of the *New York Times Book Review* goes even further, stating that the book "forsake[s] character for the naive and irksome dogma of guilt-free and munificent sex." Nevertheless, *Book* reviewer Diane Salvatore found Brown still capable of acerbic wit, and noted that the message, if somewhat repetitive, is valid.

Brown's 1994 historical work and a product of extensive research, *Dolley: A Novel of Dolley Madison in Love and War,* renewed critical admiration of Brown. The product of eight years of research, *Dolley* stimulated interest in one of America's still-admired though nearly-forgotten women at a time when the current first lady, Hillary Rodham Clinton, was sparking new debates on the roles and rights of presidential wives. A series of journal entries interspersed with third-person chapters, *Dolley* follows history more closely in some areas than others. The connection between the political power-plays, scandals, and infighting during Madison's presidency and contemporary times was not lost on reviewer Roz Spafford, who noted that Washington, during the War of 1812, is "not unfamiliar." The reviewer stated: "Brown successfully brings to life . . . a woman who up to now has not been redeemed by feminist scholarship . . . [and] persuasively highlights the tensions Dolley Madison must have felt: She was closely connected to her Quaker heritage, yet committed to the war effort, strongly anti-slavery but, through her husband, the owner of slaves." *Library Journal* reviewer Mary Ann Parker commented: "Brown knows how to combine the personal and the political in an attractive picture of Dolley."

In 1997, Brown switched directions once again, penning her autobiography *Rita Will: Memoir of a Literary Rabble-Rouser.* The memoir "affords her readers some insight into who and what propels her fiction," stated Robert A. Pela writing for the *Advocate.* The memoir is an introspective analysis of her life's struggles, including her troubled upbringing and family life, her removal from the University of Florida, and her failed lesbian love affairs. Pela also noted that "nothing escapes her rueful, sympathetic analysis . . . yet all these opinions are tempered by the same generous, homespun language that made her place in the queer literary canon." After reading the memoir, Barbara Levy, reviewing the book for *Women's Review of Books,* was "unprepared" and "delighted" by Brown's "mellower, more thoughtful tone than in her fiction." *Library Journal* reviewer Jeris Cassel concluded that "reading this book is like sitting down and exchanging tales with a good friend or close family member."

Since her initial publication of *Rubyfruit Jungle*—which remains her best known work—Brown's identity as a writer has developed several facets. Despite her commitment to depicting gay women in a positive light, she has balked at being labeled a "lesbian writer." In a *Publishers Weekly* interview, she stated: "Calling me a lesbian writer is like calling [James] Baldwin a black writer. I say no; he is not: he is a great writer and that is that. I don't understand people who say Baldwin writes about 'the black experience'—as if it is so different from 'the white experience' that the two aren't even parallel. That is so insulting . . . and I really hate it."

In an essay written for the *Publishers Weekly* column "My Say," Brown elaborated on her opposition to the use of such labels. "Classifying fiction by the race, sex or sex preference of the author is a discreet form of censorship," she maintained. "Americans buy books by convicted rapists, murderers and Watergate conspirators because those books are placed on the bestseller shelf, right out in front where people can see them. Yet novels by people who are not safely white or resolutely heterosexual are on the back shelves, out of sight. It's the back of the bus all over again. Is this not a form of censorship? Are we not being told that some novels are more 'American' than others? That some writers are true artists, while the rest of us are 'spokespersons' for our group? What group? A fiction writer owes allegiance to the English language only. With that precious, explosive tool the writer must tell the *emotional* truth. And the truth surely encompasses the fact that we Americans are female and male; white, brown, black, yellow and red; young, old and in-between; rich and poor; straight and gay; smart and stupid . . . . On the page all humans really are created equal. All stories are important. All lives are worthy of concern and description . . . . Incarcerating authors into types is an act of treason against literature and, worse, an assault on the human heart." Therefore, concluded Brown in her interview, "next time anybody calls me a lesbian writer I'm going to knock their teeth in. I'm a writer and I'm a woman and I'm from the South and I'm alive, and that is that."

BIOGRAPHICAL AND CRITICAL SOURCES:

BOOKS

Contemporary Literary Criticism, Gale (Detroit, MI), Volume 18, 1981, Volume 43, 1987.

Ward, Carol Marie, *Rita Mae Brown,* Twayne (Boston, MA), 1993.

Brown, Rita Mae, *Rita Will: Memoir of a Literary Rabble-Rouser,* Bantam Books (New York, NY), 1997.

PERIODICALS

Advocate, June 15, 1993, D.B. Atcheson, "Lovely Rita," p. 68; October 14, 1997, Robert A. Pela, review of *Rita Will,* p. 123.

Best Sellers, February, 1979, May, 1982.

Booklist, August, 1992, Barbara Duree, review of *Rest in Pieces,* p. 1997; February 15, 1993, Marie Kuda, review of *Venus Envy,* p. 1011; March 15, 1994, Marie Kuda, review of *Dolly: A Novel of Dolley Madison in Love and War,* p. 1302; October 1, 1994, Barbara Duree, review of *Murder at Monticello; Or, Old Sins,* p. 241; February 1, 1996, Brad Hooper, review of *Riding Shotgun,* p. 898; January 1, 1999, Jenny McLarin, review of *Cat on the Scent,* p. 791; April 15, 1999, Brad Hooper, review of *Loose Lips,* p. 1451; October 15, 1999, Emily Melton, review of *Outfoxed,* p. 394; March 1, 2000, Jenny McLarin, review of *Pawing through the Past,* p. 1147; January 1, 2001, Jenny McLarin, review of *Claws and Effect,* p. 923; October 1, 2001, Whitney Scott, review of *Alma Mater,* p. 268; December 15, 2002, Joanne Wilkinson, review of *The Tail of the Tip-Off,* p. 707; January 1, 2004, Jenny McLarin, review of *Whisker of Evil,* p. 788; July, 2005, Jenny McLarin, review of *The Hunt Ball,* p. 1875; January 1, 2006, Jenny McLarin, review of *Sour Puss,* p. 22.

Chicago Tribune Book World, July 4, 1982; July 3, 1983; June 26, 1994, p. 6.

Christian Science Monitor, November 22, 1978.

Detroit Free Press, May 15, 1983.

Detroit News, May 8, 1983.

Globe and Mail (Toronto, Ontario, Canada), May 28, 1988; November 5, 1988; November 22, 2003, review of *Full Cry,* p. D43.

Kirkus Reviews, January 15, 1996, p. 83; February 1, 1998, review of *Murder on the Prowl,* p. 160; October 1, 2001, review of *Alma Mater,* p. 1379; January 1, 2003, review of *The Tail of the Tip-Off,* p. 27; January 1, 2006, review of *Sour Puss,* p. 17.

Lambda Book Report, May, 1993, pp. 13-14; May, 2002, Claire McNab, review of *Catch as Cat Can,* p. 19.

Library Journal, November 15, 1987, Rosaly Demaios Roffman, "Poems," p. 83; February 1, 1988, Mollie Brodsky, review of *Starting from Scratch: A Different Kind of Writer's Manual,* p. 64; October 15, 1988, Beth Ann Mills, review of *Bingo,* p. 100; November 1, 1990, Rex E. Klett, review of *Wish You Were Here,* p. 128; April 15, 1994, Mary Ann Parker, review of *Dolley,* p. 108; October 15, 1995, Cynthia Johnson, review of *Pay Dirt; Or, Adventures at Ash Lawn,* p. 86; November 15, 1997, Jeris Cassel, review of *Rita Will,* p. 58.

Los Angeles Times, March 10, 1982; April 28, 1986; February 22, 1988; November 10, 1988.

Los Angeles Times Book Review, May 22, 1983; November 27, 1988; April 4, 1993; December 10, 1995, p. 15.

Maclean's, November 13, 1978.

MBR Bookwatch, February, 2005, Harriet Klausner, review of *Cat's Eyewitness.*

Ms., March, 1974; June, 1974; April, 1977.

Nation, June 19, 1982, Alice Denham, review of *Southern Discomfort,* p. 759.

New Boston Review, April-May, 1979.

Newsweek, October 2, 1978.

New York Arts Journal, November-December, 1978.

New York Times, September 26, 1977.

New York Times Book Review, March 21, 1982, Annie Gottlieb, review of *Southern Discomfort,* p. 10; June 19, 1983, review of *Sudden Death,* p. 12; May 17, 1987, Patricia T. O'Conner, review of *High Hearts,* p. 54; December 20, 1987, p. 13; June 5, 1988, p. 13; September 6, 1992, Marilyn Stasio, review of *Rest in Pieces,* p. 17; June 27, 1993, R. C. Scott, review of *Venus Envy,* p. 18; December 8, 1996, Marilyn Stasio, review of *Murder, She Meowed,* p. 50; May 3, 1998, Marilyn Stasio, review of *Murder on the Prowl,* p. 28; March 17, 2002, Marilyn Stasio, review of *Catch as Cat Can,* p. 20.

Omni, April, 1988, Marilyn Long, "Paradise Tossed," p. 36; December 16, 1990, p. 33.

People, April 26, 1982, Karen G. Jackovich, "The Unthinkable Rita Mae Brown Spreads around a Little

'Southern Discomfort,'" p. 75; September 6, 1992, p. 17; June 27, 1993, p. 18.

Publishers Weekly, October 2, 1978; February 18, 1983; July 15, 1983; November 20, 1987, John Mutter, review of *The Poems of Rita Mae Brown,* p. 66; December 11, 1987, review of *Starting from Scratch,* p. 56; September 9, 1988, review of *Bingo,* p. 122; September 21, 1990, review of *Wish You Were Here,* p. 66; June 1, 1992, review of *Rest in Pieces,* p. 54; February 8, 1993, review of *Venus Envy,* p. 76; March 28, 1994, review of *Dolley,* p. 81; August 14, 1995, p. 79; October 16, 1995, review of *Pay Dirt,* p. 44; January 22, 1996, review of *Riding Shotgun,* p. 57; October 14, 1996, "Murder, She Meowed," p. 67; February 1, 1999, review of *Cat on the Scent,* p. 79; May 3, 1999, review of *Loose Lips,* p. 66; December 20, 1999, review of *Outfoxed,* p. 58; March 20, 2000, review of *Pawing through the Past,* p. 74; January 8, 2001, review of *Claws and Effect,* p. 50; March 8, 2004, review of *Whisker of Evil,* p. 55; January 31, 2005, review of *Cat's Eyewitness,* p. 52; July 11, 2005, review of *The Hunt Ball,* p. 62.

Quill and Quire, December, 1990, p. 24.

Saturday Review, September 30, 1978.

School Library Journal, April, 1991, Claudia Moore, review of *Wish You Were Here,* p. 153.

Times Literary Supplement, December 7, 1979.

Village Voice, September 12, 1977; October 9, 1978.

Washington Post, May 31, 1983, Anne Chamberlin, review of *Sudden Death,* p. C2; October 27, 1988, p. 11.

Washington Post Book World, October 15, 1978; May 1, 1994.

Wilson Library Bulletin, January, 1991, Kathleen Maio, review of *Wish You Were Here,* p. 113.

Women's Review of Books, July, 1998, Barbara Levy, review of *Rita Will,* p. 36.

*　　*　　*

BROWN, Sterling Allen 1901-1989

PERSONAL: Born May 1, 1901, in Washington, DC; died of leukemia, January 13, 1989, in Takoma Park, MD; son of Sterling Nelson (a writer and professor of religion at Howard University) and Adelaide Allen Brown; married Daisy Turnbull, September, 1927; children: John L. Dennis. *Education:* Williams College, A.B., 1922; Harvard University, A.M., 1923, graduate study, 1930-31.

CAREER: Virginia Seminary and College, Lynchburg, VA, English teacher, 1923-26; also worked as a teacher

at Lincoln University in Jefferson City, MO, 1926-28, and at Fisk University, 1928-29; Howard University, Washington, DC, professor of English, 1929-69. Visiting professor at University of Illinois, University of Minnesota, New York University, New School for Social Research, Sarah Lawrence College, and Vassar College. Editor on Negro Affairs, Federal Writers' Project, 1936-39, and staff member of Carnegie-Myrdal Study of the Negro, 1939.

MEMBER: Phi Beta Kappa.

AWARDS, HONORS: Guggenheim fellowship for creative writing, 1937; honorary doctorates from Howard University, 1971, University of Massachusetts, 1971, Northwestern University, 1973, Williams College and Boston University, both 1974, Brown University and Lewis and Clark College, both 1975, Harvard University, Yale University, University of Maryland, Baltimore County, Lincoln University (Pennsylvania), and University of Pennsylvania; Lenore Marshall Poetry Prize, 1982, for *The Collected Poems of Sterling A. Brown;* named poet laureate of District of Columbia, 1984.

WRITINGS:

POETRY

Southern Road, Harcourt (New York, NY), 1932, revised edition, Beacon Press (Boston, MA), 1974.

Sixteen Poems by Sterling Brown (sound recording), Folkway Records, 1973.

The Last Ride of Wild Bill, and Eleven Narrative Poems, Broadside Press (Detroit, MI), 1975.

The Collected Poems of Sterling A. Brown, selected by Michael S. Harper, Harper (New York, NY), 1980, reprinted, TriQuarterly Books (Evanston, IL), 1996.

NONFICTION

The Negro in American Fiction (also see below), Associates in Negro Folk Education (Washington, D.C.), 1937, Argosy-Antiquarian (New York, NY), 1969.

Negro Poetry and Drama (also see below), Associates in Negro Folk Education, 1937, revised edition, Atheneum (New York, NY), 1969.

(Editor, with Arthur P. Davis and Ulysses Lee, and contributor) *The Negro Caravan,* Dryden, 1941, revised edition, Arno (New York, NY), 1970.

Negro Poetry and Drama [and] *The Negro in American Fiction,* Ayer (New York, NY), 1969.

(With George E. Haynes) *The Negro Newcomers in Detroit* [and] *The Negro in Washington,* Arno (New York, NY), 1970.

A Son's Return: Selected Essays of Sterling A. Brown, edited by Mark A. Sanders, Northeastern University Press (Boston, MA), 1996.

Also author of *Outline for the Study of the Poetry of American Negroes,* 1930.

CONTRIBUTOR

Benjamin A. Botkin, editor, *Folk-Say,* University of Oklahoma Press (Norman, OK), 1930.

American Stuff: An Anthology of Prose and Verse by Members of the Federal Writers' Project, with Sixteen Prints by the Federal Arts Project, U.S. Government Printing Office (Washington, DC), 1937.

Washington City and Capital, U.S. Government Printing Office (Washington, DC), 1937.

The Integration of the Negro into American Society, Howard University Press (Washington, DC), 1951.

Lillian D. Hornstein, G.D. Percy, and others, editors, *The Reader's Companion to World Literature,* New American Library (New York, NY), 1956.

Langston Hughes and Arna Bontemps, editors, *The Book of Negro Folklore,* Dodd, Mead (New York, NY), 1958.

John Henrik Clarke, editor, *American Negro Short Stories,* Hill & Wang (New York, NY), 1966.

Also contributor to *What the Negro Wants,* 1948. Contributor of poetry and articles to anthologies and journals, including *Crisis, Contempo, Nation, New Republic,* and *Journal of Negro Education.* Contributor of column, "The Literary Scene: Chronicle and Comment" to *Opportunity,* beginning 1931.

SIDELIGHTS: Sterling Allen Brown devoted his life to the development of an authentic black folk literature. A poet, critic, and teacher at Howard University for forty years, Brown was one of the first people to identify folklore as a vital component of the black aesthetic and to recognize its validity as a form of artistic expression. He worked to legitimatize this genre in several ways. As a critic, he exposed the shortcomings of white literature that stereotypes blacks and demonstrated why black authors are best suited to describe the negro experience. As a poet, he mined the rich vein of black

Southern culture, replacing primitive or sentimental caricatures with authentic folk heroes drawn from Afro-American sources. As a teacher, Brown encouraged self-confidence among his students, urging them to find their own literary voices and to educate themselves to be an audience worthy of receiving the special gifts of black literature. Overall, Brown's influence in the field of Afro-American literature was so great that scholar Darwin T. Turner told *Ebony* magazine: "I discovered that all trails led, at some point, to Sterling Brown. His *Negro Caravan* was *the* anthology of Afro-American literature. His unpublished study of Afro-American theater was *the* major work in the field. His study of images of Afro-Americans in American literature was a pioneer work. His essays on folk literature and folklore were preeminent. He was not always the best critic . . . but Brown was and is the literary historian who wrote the Bible for the study of Afro-American literature."

Brown's dedication to his field has been unflinching, but it was not until he was in his late sixties that the author received widespread public acclaim. Before then, he labored in obscurity on the campus of Howard University. His fortune improved in 1968 when the Black Consciousness movement revived an interest in his work. In 1969, two of his most important books of criticism, *Negro Poetry and Drama* and *The Negro in American Fiction,* were reprinted by Argosy; five years later, in 1974, Beacon Press reissued *Southern Road,* his first book of poems. These reprintings stimulated a reconsideration of the author, which culminated in the publication of *The Collected Poems of Sterling A. Brown* in 1980. More than any other single publication, it is this title, which won the 1982 Lenore Marshall Poetry prize, that brought Brown widespread recognition.

Because he had largely stopped writing poetry by the end of the 1940s, most of *Collected Poems* is comprised of Brown's early verse. Yet the collection is not the work of an apprentice, but rather "reveals Brown as a master and presence indeed," in the view of a *Virginia Quarterly Review* critic. While acknowledging that "his effective range is narrow," the critic called Brown "a first-rate narrative poet, an eloquent prophet of the folk, and certainly our finest author of Afro-American dialect." *New York Times Book Review* contributor Henry Louis Gates appreciated that in *Collected Poems,* "Brown never lapses into bathos or sentimentality. His characters confront catastrophe with all of the irony and stoicism of the blues and of black folklore. What's more, he is able to realize such splendid results in a variety of forms, including the classic and standard blues, the ballad, the sonnet and free verse." Despite Brown's relatively small poetic output, *Washington Post* critic Joseph McClellen believed this collection "is enough to establish the poet as one of our best."

After high school, Brown won a scholarship to the predominantly white, Ivy League institution, Williams College. There he first began writing poetry. While other young poets his age were imitating T.S. Eliot, Ezra Pound, and other high modernists, Brown was not impressed with their "puzzle poetry." Instead, he turned for his models to the narrative versifiers, poets such as Edward Arlington Robinson, who captured the tragic drama of ordinary lives, and Robert Frost, who used terse vernacular that sounded like real people talking. At Williams, Brown studied literature with George Dutton, a critical realist who would exert a lasting influence. "Dutton was teaching Joseph Conrad," Brown recalled, as reported in the *New Republic.* "He said Joseph Conrad was being lionized in England . . . [but] Conrad was sitting over in the corner, quiet, not participating. Dutton said he was brooding and probably thinking about his native Poland and the plight of his people. He looked straight at me. I don't know what he meant, but I think he meant, and this is symbolic to me, I think he meant don't get fooled by any lionizing, don't get fooled by being here at Williams with a selective clientele. There is business out there that you have to take care of. Your people, too, are in a plight. I've never forgotten it."

Brown came to believe that one way to help his people was through his writing. "When Carl Sandburg said 'yes' to the American people, I wanted to say 'yes' to my people," Brown recalled in *New Directions: The Howard University Magazine.* In 1923, after receiving his masters degree from Harvard, Brown embarked on a series of teaching jobs that would help him determine what form that "yes" should assume. He moved south and began to teach among the common people. As an instructor, he gained a reputation as a "red ink man," because he covered his students' papers with corrections. But as a poet, he was learning important lessons from students about black Southern life. Attracted by his openness and easygoing manner, they invited him into their homes to hear work songs, ballads, and the colorful tales of local lore. He met ex-coal-miner Calvin "Big Boy" Davis, who became the inspiration for Brown's "Odyssey of Big Boy" and "Long Gone," as well as singer Luke Johnson, whom he paid a quarter for each song Luke wrote down. As Brown began to amass his own folklore collection, "he realized that worksongs, ballads, blues, and spirituals were, at their best, poetical expressions of Afro-American life," wrote Robert O'Meally in the *New Republic.* "And he became

increasingly aware of black language as often ironic, understated and double-edged."

In 1929, the same year his father died, Brown returned to Howard University, where he would remain for the rest of his career. Three years later, Harcourt, Brace published *Southern Road,* a first book of poems, drawn primarily from material he had gathered during his travels south. The book was heralded as a breakthrough for black poetry. Alain Locke, one of the chief proponents of what was then called the New Negro Movement, acknowledged the importance of the work in an essay collected in *Negro Anthology.* After explaining that the primary objective of Negro poetry should be "the poetic portrayal of Negro folk-life . . . true in both letter and spirit to the idiom of the folk's own way of feeling and thinking," he declared that with the appearance of *Southern Road,* it could be said "that here for the first time is that much-desired and long-awaited acme attained or brought within actual reach."

The success of *Southern Road* did not insure Brown's future as a publishing poet. Not only did Harcourt, Brace reject *No Hiding Place* when Brown submitted the manuscript a few years later, they also declined to issue a second printing of *Southern Road,* because they did not think it would be profitable. These decisions had a devastating impact upon Brown's poetic reputation. Because no new poems appeared, many of his admirers assumed he had stopped writing. "That assumption," wrote Sterling Stuckey in his introduction to *Collected Poems,* "together with sadly deficient criticism from some quarters, helped to fix his place in time—as a not very important poet of the past."

Discouraged over the reception of his poems, Brown shifted his energies to other arenas; he continued teaching, but also produced a steady stream of book reviews, essays, and sketches about black life. He argued critically for many of the same goals he had pursued in verse: recognition of a black aesthetic, accurate depiction of the black experience, and the development of a literature worthy of his people's past. One of his most influential forums for dissemination of his ideas was a regular column he wrote for *Opportunity* magazine. There "Brown argued for realism as a mode in literature and against such romantic interpretations of the South as the ones presented in *I'll Take My Stand,* the manifesto of Southern agrarianism produced by contributors to the *Fugitive,* including John Crowe Ransom, Allen Tate, and Robert Penn Warren," wrote R.V. Burnette in the *Dictionary of Literary Biography.* "Although he praised the efforts of white writers like

Howard Odum ('he is a poetic craftsman as well as a social observer'), he was relentless in his criticism of popular works that distorted black life and character."

Brown did not limit his writing to periodicals, but also produced several major books on Afro-American studies. His 1938 works, *Negro Poetry and Drama* and *The Negro in American Fiction,* are seminal studies of black literary history. The former shows the growth of black artists within the context of American literature and delineates a black aesthetic; the latter examines what has been written about the black man in American fiction since his first appearance in obscure novels of the 1700s. A pioneering work that depicts how the prejudice facing blacks in real life is duplicated in their stereotyped treatment in literature, *The Negro in American Fiction* differs "from the usual academic survey by giving a penetrating analysis of the social factors and attitudes behind the various schools and periods considered," Alain Locke noted in the *Dictionary of Literary Biography.*

In 1941, Brown and two colleagues Arthur P. Davis and Ulysses S. Lee edited *The Negro Caravan,* a book that "defined the field of Afro-American literature as a scholarly and academic discipline," according to *Ebony* contributor. In this anthology, Brown demonstrates how black writers have been influenced by the same literary currents that have shaped the consciousness of all American writers—"puritan didacticism, sentimental humanitarianism, local color, regionalism, realism, naturalism, and experimentalism"—and thus are not exclusively bound by strictures of race. The work has timeless merit, according to Julius Lester, who wrote in the introduction to the 1970 revised edition that "it comes as close today as it did in 1941 to being the most important single volume of black writing ever published."

Commenting on Brown's legacy to American literature, Eleanor W. Traylor, R. Victoria Arana, and John M. Reilly, writing in *African American Review,* noted, "He was a pioneer cultural critic, anticipating the trends in recent literary theory that have interconnected anthropology, sociology, folklore, linguistics, race politics, and religion to the study of literature. He anticipated the deconstructionist critique of logocentrism by showing the primacy of the labeling word in American literature and culture. He anticipated the field of Gender Studies by pointing out the ways discourse can structure, prejudice, illuminate, and restructure the same human experiences." Also writing in *African American Review,* Fahamisha Patricia Brown, pointed out that Brown was able to portray blacks as being both distinct

from American mainstream culture and literature while also demonstrating blacks' essential contribution to both. The writer went on to note, "As a student, scholar, and performer of Black poetry, I have found in the work of Sterling A. Brown a subject of study, a critical resource, and a body of texts which translate to the stage to the delight of varied audiences." Brown also added, "I would be remiss if I did not point out how well Brown's poems exemplify his theory. His portraits of Black folk, his tall tales and ballads, his music, and his talk, with its irony, exaggeration, hyperbole, wit, and sophistication, exemplify the suggestions he made for a Negro American literary expression."

BIOGRAPHICAL AND CRITICAL SOURCES:

BOOKS

Brown, Sterling Allen, *The Collected Poems of Sterling A. Brown,* selected by Michael S. Harper, Harper (New York, NY), 1980.

Brown, Sterling Allen, Arthur P. Davis, and Ulysses Lee, editors, *The Negro Caravan,* Dryden, 1941, revised edition, Arno (New York, NY), 1970.

Contemporary Literary Criticism, Thomson Gale (Detroit, MI), Volume 1, 1973; Volume 23, 1983; Volume 59, 1990.

Cunard, Nancy, editor, *Negro Anthology,* Wishart Co. (London, England), 1934.

Davis, Arthur P., *From the Dark Tower: Afro-American Writers, 1900-1960,* Howard University Press (Washington), 1974.

Dictionary of Literary Biography, Thomson Gale (Detroit, MI), Volume 48: *American Poets, 1880-1945, Second Series,* 1986; Volume 51: *Afro-American Writers from the Harlem Renaissance to 1940,* 1987; Volume 63: *Modern American Critics, 1920-1955,* 1988.

Gabbin, Joanne V., *Sterling A. Brown: Building the Black Aesthetic Tradition,* University Press of Virginia (Charlottesville, VA), 1994.

Gayle, Addison, Jr., editor, *Black Expression: Essays by and about Black Americans in the Creative Arts,* Weybright & Talley (New York, NY), 1969.

Mangione, Jerre, *The Dream and the Deal: The Federal Writers' Project, 1935-1943,* Little, Brown (Boston, MA), 1972.

Wagner, Jean, *Black Poets of the United States: From Paul Laurence Dunbar to Langston Hughes,* translated by Kenneth Douglas, University of Illinois Press (Urbana, IL), 1973.

PERIODICALS

African American Review, fall, 1997, Eleanor W. Traylor, R. Victoria Arana, John M. Reilly, "'Runnin'

Space': The Continuing Legacy of Sterling Allen Brown," p. 389; fall, 1997, Ronald D. Palmer, "Memories of Sterling Brown," p. 433; fall, 1997, Fahamisha Patricia Brown, "And I Owe It All to Sterling Brown: The Theory and Practice of Black Literary Studies," p. 449.

Black American Literature Forum, spring, 1980.
Callaloo: A Black South Journal of Arts and Letters, February-May, 1982.
Ebony, October, 1976.
Los Angeles Times Book Review, August 3, 1980.
New Directions: The Howard University Magazine, winter, 1974.
New Republic, February 11, 1978; December 20, 1982.
New York Times, May 15, 1932.
New York Times Book Review, November 30, 1969; January 11, 1981.
Studies in the Literary Imagination, fall, 1974.
Village Voice, January 14, 1981.
Virginia Quarterly Review, winter, 1981.
Washington Post, November 16, 1969; May 2, 1979; September 4, 1980; May 12, 1984.

*   *   *

BROWNMILLER, Susan 1935-

PERSONAL: Born February 15, 1935, in Brooklyn, NY. *Education:* Attended Cornell University, 1952-55, and Jefferson School of Social Sciences. *Hobbies and other interests:* Travel.

ADDRESSES: Home—61 Jane St., New York, NY 10014. *Office*—Grove Weidenfeld, 841 Broadway, New York, NY 10003.

CAREER: Actress in New York, NY, 1955-59; *Coronet*, New York, NY, assistant to managing editor, 1959-60; *Albany Report*, Albany, NY, editor, 1961-62; *Newsweek*, New York, NY, national affairs researcher, 1963-64; *Village Voice*, New York, NY, staff writer, 1965; National Broadcasting Company, Inc. (NBC), New York, NY, reporter, 1965; American Broadcasting Companies, Inc. (ABC), New York, NY, network newswriter, 1966-68; freelance journalist, 1968-70; writer. Lecturer. Organizer of Women against Pornography.

MEMBER: New York Radical Feminists (cofounder).

AWARDS, HONORS: Grants from Alicia Patterson Foundation and Louis M. Rabinowitz Foundation; *Against Our Will: Men, Women, and Rape* was listed among the outstanding books of the year by *New York Times Book Review*, 1975; named among *Time*'s twelve Women of the Year, 1975.

WRITINGS:

Shirley Chisholm: A Biography (for children), Doubleday (New York, NY), 1970.
Against Our Will: Men, Women, and Rape, Simon & Schuster (New York, NY), 1975.
Femininity, Simon & Schuster (New York, NY), 1984.
Waverly Place (novel), Grove (New York, NY), 1989.
Seeing Vietnam: Encounters of the Road and Heart, HarperCollins (New York, NY), 1994.
In Our Time: Memoir of a Revolution, Dial Press (New York, NY), 1999.

Contributor of articles to magazines, including *Newsweek*, *Esquire*, and *New York Times Magazine*.

SIDELIGHTS: Susan Brownmiller was among the first of the politically active feminists in New York City during the 1960s. In 1968 she helped found the New York Radical Feminists, and as a member of that group, she took part in a number of protest demonstrations, including a sit-in at the offices of the *Ladies' Home Journal* opposing the magazine's "demeaning" attitude toward women. Her interest in women's rights surfaced in much of her work as a freelance journalist, and one article she wrote, about Shirley Chisholm, the first black U.S. congresswoman, developed into a biography for young readers. In 1971 Brownmiller helped to organize a "Speak-out on Rape," and in the process, she realized that once again she had the material for a book. She submitted an outline of her idea to Simon & Schuster, they contracted for the book, and Brownmiller began researching the subject of rape. After four years of research and writing, she published *Against Our Will: Men, Women, and Rape.*

Against Our Will explores the history of rape, exploding the myths that, as the author says, influence one's modern perspective. She traces the political use of rape in war from biblical times through Vietnam, explains the origins of American rape laws, and examines the subjects of interracial rape, homosexual rape, and child molestation. Brownmiller asserts that rape "is nothing more or less than a conscious process of intimidation by which *all men* keep *all women* in a state of fear." Supporting her thesis with facts taken from her extensive research in history, literature, sociology, law, psychoanalysis, mythology, and criminology, Brownmiller argues that rape is not a sexual act but an act of power based on an "anatomical fiat"; it is the result of early man's realization that women could be subjected to "a thoroughly detestable physical conquest from which there could be no retaliation in kind."

Against Our Will was serialized in four magazines and became a best-seller and Book-of-the-Month Club selection, and its nationwide tour made Brownmiller a celebrity. Her appearance on the cover of *Time* as one of the twelve Women of the Year and on television talk shows as a frequent guest confirmed the timeliness of her book. Brownmiller herself remarked, "I saw it as a once-in-a-lifetime subject that had somehow crossed my path," and she expressed gratitude to the women's movement for having given her "a constructive way" to use her rage.

In researching and writing *Against Our Will,* Brownmiller was motivated by "a dual sense of purpose," theorized Carol Eisen Rinzler in the *Village Voice,* "a political desire that the book be of value to feminism, and a personal desire to make a lasting contribution to the body of thought." Brownmiller mentions yet another goal in her conclusion to *Against Our Will:* "Fighting back. On a multiplicity of levels, that is the activity we must engage in, together, if we—women—are to redress the imbalance and rid ourselves and men of the ideology of rape. . . . My purpose in this book has been to give rape its history. Now we must deny it a future."

Brownmiller's next book, *Femininity,* is less confrontational in tone than *Against Our Will* but has still provoked mixed reactions. *Femininity* examines the ideal qualities—both physical and emotional—that are generally considered feminine and the lengths women go to conform to those ideals. The controversy arises, Brownmiller told *Detroit News* writer Barbara Hoover, when readers and reviewers "want to know where the blame is—is she blaming men or is she blaming us women? Well," the author explained, "I'm blaming neither. I don't criticize; I just explore the subject."

Brownmiller addresses the subject of child abuse in *Waverly Place,* her first novel. The book is a fictionalized account of the lives of Hedda Nussbaum and her abusive lover, Joel Steinberg, a New York attorney who was accused during the late 1980s of beating to death their illegally adopted daughter. Explaining why she chose to present the story as fiction instead of nonfic-

tion, Brownmiller wrote in her introduction to *Waverly Place:* "I wanted the freedom to invent dialogue, motivations, events, and characters based on my own understanding of battery and abuse, a perspective frequently at variance with the scenarios created by the prosecution or the defense in courts of law." "Brownmiller's effort serves a potentially constructive purpose," assessed reviewer Christopher Lehmann-Haupt in the *New York Times.* "It tries to fill the emotional void created by any incomprehensible human act. It proposes how such a thing could have happened and allows us to participate in the drama of its answer. It offers us an experience of mourning, as well as some reassurance that we ourselves are safe from such disasters. . . . In all these respects," Lehmann-Haupt concluded, "Ms. Brownmiller's novel succeeds very well."

When reviewing *In Our Time: Memoir of a Revolution* for London's *Feminist Review,* Bryony Hoskins commented that—among many other important feminist issues—the book "brings alive" feminist activism in the United States during the late 1960s and 1970s. Hoskins pointed out that this historical and at times autobiographical account of women's second-wave revolution—in which Brownmiller played a pivotal role—"places into overall context the writing of second wave feminist texts. . . . *In Our Time* describes how the women's movement influenced the writing of these texts and the influence that these texts had on the movement." Brownmiller here depicts the "large scale collective action and demonstration, women being angry and standing up to patriarchy at every level of society: from the bedrooms, the law courts and working environments to the government," wrote Hoskins. Brownmiller recounts the rise and fall of many women's organizations, including the birth of the National Organization for Women (NOW) in 1966 and the influence certain agendas—including the New York Radical Feminist consciousness raising session—had on her conversion to feminist action. She also traces how key feminist issues arose during the era: "how to discuss sex and sexuality; women's right to abortion; new ways to understand rape; the acknowledgment and naming of the battery of women, sexual abuse of children and sexual harassment; and finally the divisive understandings of pornography as crime against women," wrote Hoskins, and Brownmiller then discusses "how these notions were used to change the many masculine-dominated cultures in the United States law and society."

In creating *In Our Time,* Brownmiller used what Sara M. Evans, in her review of the book for *Feminist Studies,* called "a wealth of interviews" while also being perfectly clear about her own judgments and points of view. "She endeavors to be fair to those with whom she disagrees," commented Evans, "although she pulls no punches when it comes to some of the most wretched conflicts." In Kathleen Endres's review of the book for *Journalism History,* she noted that *In Our Time* "is not the first book that tells an insider's story of the Women's Liberation Movement of the second half of the twentieth century. However, from the perspective of the journalism historian, it may be one of the best. She provides an insider's perspective of the role journalism played in this extraordinarily important radical reform movement."

BIOGRAPHICAL AND CRITICAL SOURCES:

BOOKS

Brownmiller, Susan, *Against Our Will: Men, Women, and Rape,* Simon & Schuster (New York, NY), 1975.

Brownmiller, Susan, *Waverly Place* (novel), Grove (New York, NY), 1989.

Edwards, Alison, *Rape, Racism, and the White Women's Movement: An Answer to Susan Brownmiller,* Sojourner Truth Organization (Chicago, IL), 1980.

PERIODICALS

Business Review Weekly, October 3, 1994, p. 107.

Commentary, February, 1976.

Commonweal, December 5, 1975.

Detroit News, February 1, 1984.

Far Eastern Economics Review, July 14, 1994, p. 52.

Feminist Review (London, England), 2003, Bryony Hoskins, review of *In Our Time: Memoir of a Revolution,* p. 179.

Feminist Studies, summer, 2002, Sara M. Evans, review of *In Our Time,* p. 258.

Journalism History, spring, 2001, Kathleen Endres, review of *In Our Time,* p. 44.

Nation, November 29, 1975.

National Review, March 5, 1976.

New Leader, January 5, 1976.

New Statesman, December 12, 1975.

New York Review of Books, December 11, 1975.

New York Times, February 2, 1989, Christopher Lehmann-Haupt, review of *Waverly Place,* p. B2.

New York Times Book Review, October, 1975; December 28, 1975; May 15, 1994, Arnold R. Isaacs, review of *Seeing Vietnam: Encounters of the Road and Heart,* p. 11.

Time, October 13, 1975; January 5, 1976.

Village Voice, October 6, 1975.

ONLINE

Susan Brownmiller Web site, http://www.susanbrown miller.com/ (July 24, 2004).

*   *   *

BRUCHAC, Joseph, III 1942-

PERSONAL: Surname is pronounced "*brew*-shack"; born October 16, 1942, in Saratoga Springs, NY; son of Joseph E., Jr. (a taxidermist and publisher) and Marion (a homemaker and publisher; maiden name, Bowman) Bruchac; married Carol Worthen (a director of a non-profit organization), June 13, 1964; children: James Edward, Jesse Bowman. *Ethnicity:* "Native American (Abenaki)/Slovak/English." *Education:* Cornell University, A.B., 1965; Syracuse University, M.A., 1966; graduate study at State University of New York—Albany, 1971-73; Union Institute of Ohio Graduate School, Ph.D., 1975. *Politics:* Liberal Democrat. *Religion:* "Methodist and Native-American spiritual traditions." *Hobbies and other interests:* Gardening, music, martial arts.

ADDRESSES: Home and office—Greenfield Review Press, P.O. Box 308, Greenfield Center, NY 12833; fax: 518-583-9741. *Agent*—Barbara Kouts Agency, P.O. Box 560, Bellport, NY 11713. *E-mail*—nudatlog@earthlink. net.

CAREER: Keta Secondary School, Ghana, West Africa, teacher of English and literature, 1966-69; Skidmore College, Saratoga Springs, NY, instructor in creative writing and African and black literatures, 1969-73; University without Walls, coordinator of college program at Great Meadow Correctional Facility, 1974-81; writer and storyteller, 1981—. Greenfield Review Press, Greenfield Center, NY, publisher and editor of *Greenfield Review,* 1969—; director, Greenfield Review Literary Center, 1981—; musician with Dawn Land Singers, recording stories and music on *Abenaki Cultural Heritage* and *Alnobak,* Good Mind Records. Member of adjunct faculty at Hamilton College, 1983, 1985, and 1987, and State University of New York—Albany, 1987 and 1988; storyteller-in-residence at CRC Institute for Arts in Education, 1989-90, and at other institutions, including Oklahoma Summer Arts Institute, St. Regis

Mohawk Indian School, Seneca Nation School, Onondaga Indian School, Institute of Alaska Native Arts, and Annsville Youth Facility; featured storyteller at festivals and conferences; presents workshops, poetry readings, and storytelling programs. Print Center, member of board of directors, 1975-78; Returning the Gift, national chairperson, 1992; judge of competitions, including PEN Prison Writing Awards, 1977, National Book Award for Translation, 1983, and National Book Award for Poetry, 1995; past member of literature panels, Massachusetts Arts Council, Vermont State Arts Council, Illinois Arts Council, and Ohio Arts Council.

MEMBER: Poetry Society of America, PEN, National Storytelling Association (member of board of directors, 1992-94), Native Writers Circle of the Americas (chairperson, 1992-95), Wordcraft Circle of Native Writers and Storytellers, Hudson Valley Writers Guild, Black Crow Network.

AWARDS, HONORS: Poetry fellow, Creative Artists Public Service, 1973 and 1982; fellow, National Endowment for the Arts, 1974; editors' fellow, Coordinating Council of Literary Magazines, 1980; Rockefeller fellow, 1982; PEN Syndicated Fiction Award, 1983; American Book Award, 1984, for *Breaking Silence;* Yaddo resident, 1984 and 1985; Cherokee Nation Prose Award, 1986; fellow, New York State Council on the Arts, 1986; Publishers Marketing Association, Benjamin Franklin Audio Award, 1992, for *The Boy Who Lived with the Bears,* and Person of the Year Award, 1993; Hope S. Dean Memorial Award for Notable Achievement in Children's Literature, 1993; Mountains and Plains Award, 1995, for *A Boy Called Slow;* Knickerbocker Award, 1995; Paterson Children's Book Award, 1996, for *Dog People; Boston Globe-Horn Book* Honor Award, 1996, for *The Boy Who Lived with the Bears;* Writer of the Year Award, Wordcraft Circle of Native Writers and Storytellers, 1998; Storyteller of the Year Award, Wordcraft Circle of Native Writers and Storytellers, 1998; Lifetime Achievement Award, Native Writers Circle of the Americas, 1999.

WRITINGS:

Indian Mountain (poems), Ithaca House (Ithaca, NY), 1971.
The Buffalo in the Syracuse Zoo (poems), Greenfield Review Press (Greenfield Center, NY), 1972.
The Poetry of Pop (nonfiction), Dustbooks (Paradise, CA), 1973.

Great Meadow Poems, Dustbooks (Paradise, CA), 1973.
The Manabozho Poems, Blue Cloud Quarterly, 1973.
Turkey Brother and Other Iroquois Folk Tales, Crossing Press (Trumansburg, NY), 1975.
Flow (poems), Cold Mountain Press, 1975.
The Road to Black Mountain (fiction), Thorp Springs Press (Austin, TX), 1976.
This Earth Is a Drum (poems), Cold Mountain Press, 1976.
The Dreams of Jesse Brown (fiction), Cold Mountain Press, 1978.
Stone Giants and Flying Heads: Adventure Stories of the Iroquois, Crossing Press (Trumansburg, NY), 1978.
There Are No Trees inside the Prison (poems), Blackberry Press, 1978.
Mu'ndu Wi Go (poems), Blue Cloud Quarterly, 1978.
Entering Onondaga (poems), Cold Mountain Press, 1978.
The Good Message of Handsome Lake (poems), Unicorn Press (Greensboro, NC), 1979.
Translators' Son (poems), Cross-Cultural Communications (Merrick, NY), 1980.
How to Start and Sustain a Literary Magazine, Provision (Austin, TX), 1980.
Ancestry (poems), Great Raven (Fort Kent, ME), 1981.
Remembering the Dawn (poems), Blue Cloud Quarterly, 1983.
Iroquois Stories: Heroes and Heroines, Monsters and Magic, Crossing Press (Trumansburg, NY), 1985.
The Wind Eagle (traditional stories), Bowman Books, 1985.
Walking with My Sons (poems), Landlocked Press, 1985.
Tracking (poems), Ion Books, 1985.
Near the Mountains (poems), White Pine (Buffalo, NY), 1986.
Survival This Way: Interviews with American Indian Poets, University of Arizona (Tucson, AZ), 1987.
The Faithful Hunter and Other Abenaki Stories, Bowman Books, 1988.
The White Moose (fiction), Blue Cloud Quarterly, 1988.
Langes Gedachtnis/Long Memory (poems), OBEMA (Osnabruck, Germany), 1988.
(With Michael Caduto) *Keepers of the Earth,* Fulcrum Press (Golden, CO), 1989.
(With Michael Caduto) *Keepers of the Animals,* Fulcrum Press (Golden, CO), 1990.
Return of the Sun: Native American Tales from the Eastern Woodlands, Crossing Press (Trumansburg, NY), 1990.
Native American Stories, Fulcrum Press (Golden, CO), 1991.

Hoop Snakes, Hide-Behinds, and Sidehill Winders (folk stories), Crossing Press (Trumansburg, NY), 1991.

(With Jonathan London) *Thirteen Moons on Turtle's Back,* Philomel (New York, NY), 1992.

Turtle Meat and Other Stories, Holy Cow! Press (Minneapolis, MN), 1992.

The First Strawberries, Dial (New York, NY), 1993.

Fox Song, Philomel (New York, NY), 1993.

Dawn Land (novel), Fulcrum Press (Golden, CO), 1993.

Flying with the Eagle, Racing the Great Bear (traditional stories), Bridgewater (New York, NY), 1993.

Native American Animal Stories, Fulcrum Press (Golden, CO), 1993.

The Native American Sweat Lodge (traditional stories), Crossing Press (Trumansburg, NY), 1993.

The Great Ball Game, Dial (New York, NY), 1994.

(With Michael Caduto) *Keepers of the Night,* Fulcrum Press (Golden, CO), 1994.

(With Michael Caduto) *Keepers of Life,* Fulcrum Press (Golden, CO), 1994.

(With Gayle Ross) *The Girl Who Married the Moon* (traditional stories), Bridgewater (New York, NY), 1994.

A Boy Called Slow, Philomel (New York, NY), 1995.

The Earth under Sky Bear's Feet, Philomel (New York, NY), 1995.

Gluskabe and the Four Wishes, Cobblehill Books (Boston, MA), 1995.

(With Gayle Ross) *The Story of the Milky Way,* Dial (New York, NY), 1995.

Dog People: Native Dog Stories, Fulcrum Press (Golden, CO), 1995.

Long River (novel), Fulcrum Press (Golden, CO), 1995.

Native Wisdom, HarperSanFrancisco (San Francisco, CA), 1995.

Native Plant Stories, Fulcrum Press (Golden, CO), 1995.

The Boy Who Lived with the Bears: And Other Iroquois Stories, HarperCollins (New York, NY), 1995.

Between Earth and Sky: Legends of Native American Sacred Places, illustrated by Thomas Locker, Harcourt (San Diego, CA), 1996.

The Maple Thanksgiving, Celebration (Nobleboro, ME), 1996.

Children of the Longhouse (novel), Dial (New York, NY), 1996.

Roots of Survival: Native American Storytelling and the Sacred, Fulcrum Press (Golden, CO), 1996.

The Circle of Thanks (traditional stories), Bridgewater (New York, NY), 1996.

Four Ancestors: Stories, Songs, and Poems, Bridgewater (New York, NY), 1996.

(With Michael Caduto) *Native American Gardening,* Fulcrum Press (Golden, CO), 1996.

(With Melissa Fawcett) *Makiawisug: Gift of the Little People,* Little People (Warsaw, IN), 1997.

Many Nations: An Alphabet of Native America, Troll Publications (Mahwah, NJ), 1997.

Bowman's Store (autobiography), Dial (New York, NY), 1997.

Eagle Song (novel), Dial (New York, NY), 1997.

Lasting Echoes: An Oral History of Native American People, Harcourt (New York, NY), 1997.

Tell Me a Tale: A Book about Storytelling, Harcourt (New York, NY), 1997.

The Arrow over the Door (fiction; for children), illustrated by James Watling, Dial (New York, NY), 1998.

Buffalo Boy (biography), illustrated by Baviera, Silver Whistle Books (San Diego, CA), 1998.

The Heart of a Chief: A Novel (for children), Dial (New York, NY), 1998.

The Waters Between: A Novel of the Dawn Land, University Press of New England (Hanover, NH), 1998.

(With James Bruchac) *When the Chenoo Howls: Native-American Tales of Terror* (traditional stories), illustrated by William Sauts Netamu'xwe Bock, Walker (New York, NY), 1998.

No Borders (poems), Holy Cow! Press (Duluth, MN), 1999.

Seeing the Circle (autobiography), photographs by John Christian Fine, R.C. Owen (Katonah, NY), 1999.

The Trail of Tears, illustrated by Diana Magnuson, Random House (New York, NY), 1999.

Trails of Tears, Paths of Beauty, National Geographic Society (Washington, DC), 2000.

(With James Bruchac) *Native American Games and Stories,* illustrated by Kayeri Akwek, Fulcrum Press (Golden, CO), 2000.

Crazy Horse's Vision, illustrated by S.D. Nelson, Lee & Low Books (New York, NY), 2000.

Pushing Up the Sky: Seven Native American Plays for Children, illustrated by Teresa Flavin, Dial (New York, NY), 2000.

Sacajawea: The Story of Bird Woman and the Lewis and Clark Expedition, Silver Whistle (San Diego, CA), 2000.

Squanto's Journey: The Story of the First Thanksgiving, illustrated by Greg Shed, Silver Whistle (San Diego, CA), 2000.

(With James Bruchac) *How Chipmunk Got His Stripes,* illustrated by Jose Aruego and Ariane Dewey, Dial (New York, NY), 2001.

Skeleton Man, HarperCollins (New York, NY), 2001.

The Journal of Jesse Smoke: A Cherokee Boy, Scholastic (New York, NY), 2001.

Seasons of the Circle: A Native American Year, illustrated by Robert F. Goetzel, Bridgewater (New York, NY), 2002.

Navajo Long Walk: The Tragic Story of a Proud People's Forced March from Their Homeland, illustrated by Shonto Begay, National Geographic Society (Washington, DC), 2002.

Foot of the Mountain, Holy Cow! Press (Duluth, MN), 2002.

The Winter People, Dial (New York, NY), 2002.

Our Stories Remember: American Indian History, Culture, and Values through Storytelling, Fulcrum Press (Golden, CO), 2003.

Pocahontas (novel), Silver Whistle (Orlando, FL), 2003.

(With James Bruchac) *Turtle's Race with Beaver: A Traditional Seneca Story,* pictures by Jose Aruego and Ariane Dewey, Dial Books for Young Readers (New York, NY), 2003.

Above the Line (poetry), West End Press (Albuquerque, NM), 2003.

Hidden Roots (novel), Scholastic (New York, NY), 2004.

Jim Thorpe's Bright Path (biography), illustrated by S.D. Nelson, Lee & Low Books (New York, NY), 2004.

(With Thomas Locker) *Raccoon's Last Race: A Traditional Abenaki Story,* pictures by Jose Aruego and Ariane Dewey, Dial Books for Young Readers (New York, NY), 2004.

(With James Bruchac) *Rachel Carson: Preserving a Sense of Wonder,* Fulcrum Press (Golden, CO), 2004.

A Code Talker's Story, Dial Books (New York, NY), 2004.

Dark Pond, illustrated by Sally Wern Comport, HarperCollins (New York, NY), 2004.

Also editor of anthologies, including *The Last Stop: Prison Writings from Comstock Prison,* 1973; *Words from the House of the Dead: Prison Writing from Soledad,* 1974; *Aftermath: Poetry in English from Africa, Asia, and the Caribbean,* 1977; *The Next World: Thirty-two Third World American Poets,* 1978; *Songs from Turtle Island: Thirty-two American Indian Poets,* [Yugoslavia], 1982; *Songs from This Earth on Turtle's Back: Contemporary American Indian Poetry,* 1983; *Breaking Silence: Contemporary Asian-American Poets,* 1983; *The Light from Another Country: Poetry from American Prisons,* 1984; *North Country: An Anthology of Contemporary Writing from the Adirondacks and the Upper Hudson Valley,* 1986; *New Voices from the Long-*

house: *Contemporary Iroquois Writing,* 1989; *Raven Tells Stories: Contemporary Alaskan Native Writing,* 1990; *Singing of Earth,* 1993; *Returning the Gift,* 1994; *Smoke Rising,* 1995; and *Native Wisdom,* 1995. Audiotapes include *Iroquois Stories, Alnobak, Adirondack Tall Tales,* and *Abenaki Cultural Heritage,* all Good Mind Records; and *Gluskabe Stories,* Yellow Moon Press. Work represented in more than a hundred anthologies, including *Carriers of the Dream Wheel; Come to Power; For Neruda, for Chile; New Worlds of Literature;* and *Paris Review Anthology.* Contributor of more than three hundred stories, poems, articles, and reviews to magazines, including *American Poetry Review, Akwesasne Notes, Beloit Poetry Journal, Chariton Review, Kalliope, Mid-American Review, Nation, Poetry Northwest, River Styx,* and *Virginia Quarterly Review.* Editor, *Trojan Horse,* 1964, *Greenfield Review,* 1969-87, *Prison Writing Review,* 1976-85, and *Studies in American Indian Literature,* 1989—; student editor, *Epoch,* 1964-65; member of editorial board, *Parabola, Storytelling Journal, MELUS,* and *Obsidian.* Translator from Abenaki, Ewe, Iroquois, and Spanish. Cross-Cultural Communications, member of editorial board.

ADAPTATIONS: Several of Bruchac's books have been recorded on audio tapes, including *Keepers of the Earth, Keepers of the Animals, Keepers of Life,* and *Dawn Land,* all released by Fulcrum; and *The Boy Who Lived with the Bears,* Caedmon/ Parabola.

SIDELIGHTS: Joseph Bruchac III, according to *Publishers Weekly* contributor Sybil Steinberg, ranks as "perhaps the best-known contemporary Native American storyteller." Bruchac draws on his heritage for his critically acclaimed collections, including *Flying with the Eagle, Racing the Great Bear: Stories from Native North America* and *The Girl Who Married the Moon: Stories from Native North America.* These stories also influence Bruchac's novel *Dawn Land,* about the Abenaki living in the American northeast before the arrival of Columbus. "His stories," Steinberg concluded, "are often poignant, funny, ironic—and sometimes all three at once."

Dawn Land introduced readers to the character of Young Hunter. In a sequel to this novel, 1995's *Long River,* Bruchac again features Young Hunter in a series of adventures, as he battles a wooly mammoth and an evil giant. As with the earlier work, *Long River* incorporates actual myths from the author's Abenaki heritage. Bruchac's children's stories, like his novels, entertain and educate young readers by interweaving Native American history and myth. The biography *A Boy*

Called Slow recounts the story of a Lakota boy named Slow, who would later be known as Sitting Bull. Bruchac's ability to "gently correct" stereotypes of Native-American culture was noted by Carolyn Polese in the *School Library Journal*. In *The Great Ball Game* he relates the importance of ball games in Native-American tradition as a substitute for war, tying neatly together history and ethics lessons in "an entertaining tale," commented Polese. He combines several versions of a Native-American tale in *Gluskabe and the Four Wishes*.

"I was born in 1942, in Saratoga Springs, New York, during October, that month the Iroquois call the Moon of Falling Leaves," Bruchac once explained. "My writing and my interests reflect my mixed ancestry, Slovak on one side and Native American (Abenaki) and English on the other. Aside from attending Cornell University and Syracuse and three years of teaching in West Africa, I've lived all of my life in the small Adirondack foothills town of Greenfield Center in a house built by my grandfather.

"Much of my writing and my life relates to the problem of being an American. While in college I was active in civil rights work and in the anti-war movement. . . . I went to Africa to teach—but more than that, to be taught. It showed me many things. How much we have as Americans and take for granted. How much our eyes refuse to see because they are blinded to everything in a man's face except his color. And, most importantly, how human people are everywhere—which may be the one grace that can save us all.

"I write poetry, fiction, and some literary criticism and have been fortunate enough to receive recognition in all three areas. After returning from Ghana in 1969, my wife, Carol, and I started the *Greenfield Review* and the Greenfield Review Press. Since 1975, I've been actively involved in storytelling, focusing on northeastern Native-American tales and the songs and traditions of the Adirondack Mountains of upstate New York, and I am frequently a featured performer at storytelling gatherings. I've also done a great deal of work in teaching and helping start writing workshops in American prisons. I believe that poetry is as much a part of human beings as is breath—and that, like breath, poetry links us to all other living things and is meant to be shared.

"My writing is informed by several key sources. One of these is nature, another is the Native-American experience (I'm part Indian). . . . I like to work outside, in the earthmother's soil, with my hands . . . but maintain my life as an academic for a couple of reasons: it gives me time to write (sometimes) and it gives me a chance to share my insights into the beautiful and all-too-fragile world of human life and living things we have been granted. Which is one of the reasons I write—not to be a man apart, but to share."

Bruchac has continued to write prolifically. In his 2003 book *Our Stories Remember: American Indian History, Culture, and Values through Storytelling,* he relates stories from many different Indian nations to illustrated their core values and culture. Writing in the *School Library Journal*, S.K. Joiner noted that, "Part cultural lesson, part history, and part autobiography, the book contains a wealth of information," while *Booklist* contributor Deborah Donovan dubbed it a "thought-provoking work, enriched with valuable annotated reading lists." Bruchac has also continued his work in picture books for children, including several biographies of Native Americans and others. In *Rachel Carson: Preserving a Sense of Wonder,* he presents a biography of the author of *Silent Spring* and one of the people credited with inspiring the environmental movement in the 1960s. Writing in *Booklist,* Carolyn Phelan noted that "Bruchac writes lyrically about [Carson's] . . . love of nature, particularly the ocean, and concludes with an appreciation of her impact on the environment." Another 2004 picture-book publication, *Jim Thorpe's Bright Path,* tells of the famed Native-American athlete. *School Library Journal* contributor Liza Graybill noted, "The theme of overcoming personal and societal obstacles to reach success is strongly expressed."

In an interview with Eliza T. Dresang on the Cooperative Children's Book Center Web site, Bruchac noted that he does not expect to run out of things to write about. He told Dresang: "The last thirty years of my life in particular have been blessed with so many . . . experiences and by the generosity of so many Native people who have shared their stories and their understanding of their land with me that I know I can never live long enough to share everything I've learned. But I'll try."

BIOGRAPHICAL AND CRITICAL SOURCES:

PERIODICALS

Alaska, December, 1992, p. 74.
Albany Times Union, June 1, 1980.
Booklist, February 15, 1993, p. 1075; July, 1993, p. 1969; October 15, 1993, p. 397; November 15, 1993, p. 632; December 15, 1993, p. 749; August,

1994, p. 2017; September, 1994, p. 55; October 15, 1994, p. 377; December 15, 1994, p. 756; September 1, 1997, p. 69; September 15, 1997, pp. 234, 237; December 5, 1997, p. 688; February 15, 1998; October 1, 2002, Heather Hepler, review of *Seasons of the Circle: A Native American Year,* p. 316, GraceAnne A. DeCandido, review of *The Winter People,* p. 322; April 15, 2003, Deborah Donovan, review of *Our Stories Remember: American Indian History, Culture, and Values through Storytelling,* p. 1444; September 15, 2003, John Peters, review of *Turtle's Race with Beaver,* p. 244, Ed Sullivan, review of *Pocahontas,* p. 229; July, 2004, Carolyn Phelan, review of *Rachel Carson: Preserving a Sense of Wonder,* p. 1838.

Bulletin, April, 1995, p. 265.

English Journal, January, 1996, p. 87.

Horn Book, January-February, 1994, p. 60; March-April, 1994, p. 209; November-December, 1994, p. 738; March-April, 1995, p. 203; September-October, 1995, p. 617.

Kirkus Reviews, March 15, 1996, p. 445; May 1, 1996, p. 685; December 1, 1996, p. 1734.

Publishers Weekly, March 15, 1993, p. 68; June 28, 1993, p. 76; July 19, 1993, pp. 254, 255; August 29, 1994, p. 79; January 9, 1995, p. 64; July 31, 1995, p. 68; July 14, 1997, p. 83; September 8, 1997, p. 78; November 24, 1997, p. 75; May 31, 2004, review of *Jim Thorpe's Bright Path,* p. 76.

School Library Journal, March, 1993, p. 161; August, 1993, p. 205; September, 1993, pp. 222, 238; February, 1994, p. 78; November, 1994, p. 112; December, 1994, p. 96; February, 1995, p. 104; October, 1995, Carolyn Polese, review of *A Boy Called Slow,* p. 145; July, 2002, Anne Chapman Callaghan, review of *Navajo Long Walk: The Tragic Story of a Proud People's Forced March from Their Homeland,* p. 131; November, 2002, Rita Soltan, review of *The Winter People,* p. 154; July, 2003, S.K. Joiner, review of *Our Stories Remember,* p. 155; May, 2004, Sean George, review of *Pocahontas,* p. 140; June, 2004, Liza Graybill, review of *Jim Thorpe's Bright Path,* p. 124.

Silver Whistle, spring-summer, 2000, p. 67.

Voice Literary Supplement, November, 1991, p. 27.

Wilson Library Bulletin, June, 1993, p. 103; September, 1993, p. 87; April, 1995, p. 110.

ONLINE

Cooperative Children's Book Center Web site, http://www.soemadison.wisc.edu/ccbc/ (October 22, 1999), Eliza T. Dresang, "An Interview with Joseph Bruchac."

Joseph Bruchac Storyteller and Writer, http://www.josephbruchac.com/ (September 16, 2003).

BRYAN, Michael
See MOORE, Brian

*   *   *

BUCKLEY, William F., Jr. 1925-
(William Frank Buckley, Jr.)

PERSONAL: Born November 24, 1925, in New York, NY; son of William Frank (a lawyer and oil man) and Aloise (Steiner) Buckley; married Patricia Austin Taylor, July 6, 1950; children: Christopher Taylor. *Education:* Attended University of Mexico, 1943-44; Yale University, B.A. (with honors), 1950. *Politics:* Republican. *Religion:* Roman Catholic.

ADDRESSES: Office—National Review, Inc., 215 Lexington Ave., New York, NY 10016-6023.

CAREER: Writer. Yale University, New Haven, CT, instructor in Spanish, 1947-51; Central Intelligence Agency (CIA), Washington, DC, worked in Mexico, 1951-52; *American Mercury* (magazine), New York, NY, associate editor, 1952; freelance writer and editor, 1952-55; *National Review* (magazine), New York, NY, founder, president, and editor in chief, 1955-90, editor at large, 1990—, syndicated columnist, 1962—. *Firing Line* (weekly television program), host, 1966-99; Starr Broadcasting Group, Inc., board chair, 1969-78. Conservative Party candidate for mayor of New York City, 1965; U.S. Information Agency, member of Advisory Commission on Information, 1969-72; public member of U.S. delegation to United Nations, 1973. New School for Social Research (now New School University), lecturer, 1967-68; Russell Sage College, Froman Distinguished Professor, 1973. *Military service:* U.S. Army, 1944-46; became second lieutenant.

MEMBER: Council on Foreign Relations, Century Club, Mont Pelerin Society, New York Yacht Club.

AWARDS, HONORS: Freedom Award, Order of Lafayette, 1966; George Sokolsky Award, American Jewish League against Communism, 1966; named best columnist of the year, 1967; Distinguished Achievement Award in Journalism, University of Southern California, 1968; Liberty Bell Award, New Haven County Bar Association, 1969; Emmy Award, National Academy of Television Arts and Sciences, 1969, for *Firing Line;* Man of the Decade Award, Young Americans for Freedom, 1970; Cleveland Amory Award, *TV Guide,* 1974, for best interviewer or interviewee on television; fellow, Sigma Delta Chi, 1976; Bellarmine Medal, 1977; Americanism Award, Young Republican National Federation, 1979; Carmel Award, American Friends of Haifa University, 1980, for journalism excellence; American Book Award, best paperback mystery, 1980, for *Stained Glass;* Creative Leadership Award, New York University, 1981; Lincoln Literary Award, Union League, 1985; Shelby Cullom Davis Award, 1986; Lowell Thomas Travel Journalism Award, 1989; Julius Award for Outstanding Public Service, School of Public Administration, University of Southern California, 1990; Presidential Medal of Freedom, 1991; Gold Medal Award, National Institute of Social Sciences, 1992. Honorary degrees include L.H.D. from Seton Hall University, 1966, Niagara University, 1967, Mount Saint Mary's College, 1969, University of South Carolina, 1985, Converse College, 1988, University of South Florida, 1992, Adelphi University, 1995, and Yale University, 2000; LL.D. from St. Peter's College, 1969, Syracuse University, 1969, Ursinus College, 1969, Lehigh University, 1970, Lafayette College, 1972, St. Anselm's College, 1973, St. Bonaventure University, 1974, University of Notre Dame, 1978, New York Law School, 1981, and Colby College, 1985; D.Sc.O. from Curry College, 1970; Litt.D. from St. Vincent College, 1971, Fairleigh Dickinson University, 1973, Alfred University, 1974, College of William and Mary, 1981, William Jewell College, 1982, Albertus Magnus College, 1987, College of St. Thomas, 1987, Bowling Green State University, 1987, Coe College, 1989, Saint John's University, Northfield, MN, 1989, and Grove City College, 1991.

WRITINGS:

NONFICTION

God and Man at Yale: The Superstitions of "Academic Freedom," Regnery (Washington, DC), 1951.

(With L. Brent Bozell) *McCarthy and His Enemies: The Record and Its Meaning,* Regnery (Washington, DC), 1954.

Up from Liberalism, Helene Obolensky Enterprises (New York, NY), 1959.

Rumbles Left and Right: A Book about Troublesome People and Ideas, Putnam (New York, NY), 1963.

The Unmaking of a Mayor, Viking (New York, NY), 1966.

The Jeweler's Eye: A Book of Irresistible Political Reflections, Putnam (New York, NY), 1968.

Quotations from Chairman Bill: The Best of William F. Buckley Jr., compiled by David Franke, Arlington House (New York, NY), 1970.

The Governor Listeth: A Book of Inspired Political Revelations, Putnam (New York, NY), 1970.

Cruising Speed: A Documentary, Putnam (New York, NY), 1971.

Inveighing We Will Go, Putnam (New York, NY), 1972.

Four Reforms: A Guide for the Seventies, Putnam (New York, NY), 1973.

United Nations Journal: A Delegate's Odyssey, Putnam (New York, NY), 1974.

Execution Eve and Other Contemporary Ballads, Putnam (New York, NY), 1975.

Airborne: A Sentimental Journey, Macmillan (New York, NY), 1976.

A Hymnal: The Controversial Arts, Putnam (New York, NY), 1978.

Atlantic High: A Celebration, Doubleday (New York, NY), 1982.

Overdrive: A Personal Documentary, Doubleday (New York, NY), 1983.

Right Reason, Doubleday (New York, NY), 1985.

Racing through Paradise: A Pacific Passage, Random House (New York, NY), 1987.

On the Firing Line: The Public Life of Our Public Figures, Random House (New York, NY), 1989.

Gratitude: Reflections on What We Owe to Our Country, Random House (New York, NY), 1990.

Windfall: End of the Affair, Random House (New York, NY), 1992.

In Search of Anti-Semitism, Continuum (New York, NY), 1992.

Happy Days Were Here Again, Random House (New York, NY), 1993.

Buckley: The Right Word, edited by Samuel S. Vaughan, Random House (New York, NY), 1996.

Nearer, My God: An Autobiography of Faith, Doubleday (New York, NY), 1997.

Let Us Talk of Many Things: The Collected Speeches of William F. Buckley Jr., Forum (Roseville, CA), 2000.

The Fall of the Berlin Wall, John Wiley (Hoboken, NJ), 2004.

Miles Gone By: A Literary Autobiography, Regnery (Washington, DC), 2004.

Contributor to books, including *Racing at Sea,* Van Nostrand (New York, NY), 1959; *What Is Conservatism?,* edited by F.S. Meyer, Holt (New York, NY), 1964; *Violence in the Streets,* edited by S. Endleman, Quadrangle (New York, NY), 1968; *Spectrum of Catholic Attitudes,* edited by R. Campbell, Bruce Publishing, 1969; and *Essays on Hayek,* edited by Fritz Machlup, New York University Press (New York, NY), 1976; also author of numerous book introductions and forewords. Author of syndicated column "On the Right," 1962—.

Contributor to *Esquire, Saturday Review, Harper's, Atlantic, Playboy, New Yorker, New York Times Magazine,* and other periodicals.

FICTION

The Temptation of Wilfred Malachey (juvenile), Workman Publishing (New York, NY), 1985.
Brothers No More (novel), Doubleday (New York, NY), 1995.
The Redhunter: A Novel Based on the Life of Senator Joe McCarthy, Little, Brown (Boston, MA), 1999.
Spytime: The Undoing of James Jesus Angleton, Harcourt (New York, NY), 2000.
Elvis in the Morning, Harcourt (New York, NY), 2001.
Nuremberg: The Reckoning, Harcourt (New York, NY), 2002.
Getting it Right (novel), Regnery (Washington, DC), 2003.

NOVELS; "BLACKFORD OAKES" SERIES

Saving the Queen, Doubleday (New York, NY), 1976.
Stained Glass, Doubleday (New York, NY), 1978.
Who's on First, Doubleday (New York, NY), 1980.
Marco Polo, if You Can, Doubleday (New York, NY), 1982.
The Story of Henri Tod, Doubleday (New York, NY), 1984.
See You Later, Alligator, Doubleday (New York, NY), 1985.
High Jinx, Doubleday, 1986.
Mongoose, RIP, Random House (New York, NY), 1988.
Tucker's Last Stand, Random House (New York, NY), 1990.
A Very Private Plot, William Morrow (New York, NY), 1994.
The Blackford Oakes Reader, Andrews & McMeel (Kansas City, MO), 1994.
Last Call for Blackford Oakes, Harcourt (Orlando, FL), 2005.

EDITOR

(With others) *The Committee and Its Critics: A Calm Review of the House Committee on Un-American Activities,* Putnam (New York, NY), 1962.
Odyssey of a Friend: Whittaker Chambers' Letters to William F. Buckley Jr., 1954-1961, Putnam (New York, NY), 1970.

Did You Ever See a Dream Walking? American Conservative Thought in the Twentieth Century, Bobbs-Merrill (New York, NY), 1970, revised edition published as *Keeping the Tablets: Modern American Conservative Thought,* Perennial Library (New York, NY), 1988.
The Lexicon: A Cornucopia of Wonderful Words for the Inquisitive Word Lover, Harcourt (New York, NY), 1998.

Beinecke Library at Yale University houses Buckley's correspondence since 1951 and material concerning the *National Review.*

SIDELIGHTS: William F. Buckley, Jr., is one of the most recognized and articulate spokespersons for American political conservatives. As host of his television program *Firing Line,* in the pages of the *National Review,* the magazine he founded, and through the books and syndicated columns he writes, Buckley has argued throughout his career for individual liberty, the free market, and the traditional moral values of Western culture. His eloquence, wit, and appealing personal style have made him palatable even to many of his political opponents.

Buckley's writings are considered instrumental to the phenomenal growth of the U.S. conservative movement in the second half of the twentieth century. In the 1950s, when Buckley first appeared on the scene, conservatism was a peripheral presence on the national political spectrum. But in 1980 conservative voters elected Ronald Reagan, a longtime reader of Buckley's *National Review,* as president of the United States. "When the tide of intellectual and political history seemed headed inexorably leftward," Morton Kondracke wrote in the *New York Times Book Review,* "Mr. Buckley had the temerity to uphold the cause of Toryism. He and his magazine nurtured the movement . . . and gave it a rallying point and sounding board as it gradually gained the strength and respectability to win the Presidency. Conservatism is not far from the dominant intellectual force in the country today, but neither is liberalism. There is now a balance between the movements, a permanent contest, and Mr. Buckley deserves credit for helping make it so."

Buckley first came to public attention in 1951 when he published *God and Man at Yale: The Superstitions of "Academic Freedom,"* an attack against his alma mater, Yale University. The book accuses Yale of fostering values—such as atheism and collectivism—which are an anathema to the school's supporters. Further, Buckley claims that Yale stifles the political freedom of its more conservative students. Those students who spoke out against the liberal views of their professors were often ostracized. The book's charges stemmed from Buckley's own experiences while attending Yale, where his views on individualism, the free market, and communism found little support among liberal academics.

God and Man at Yale raised a storm of controversy as Yale faculty members denounced the charges made against them. Some reviewers joined in the denunciation. McGeorge Bundy, writing in the *Atlantic Monthly,* called the book "dishonest in its use of facts, false in its theory, and a discredit to its author." Peter Viereck agreed with Buckley that "more conservatism and traditional morality" were needed at universities and wrote in the *New York Times* that "this important, symptomatic, and widely held book is a necessary counterbalance. However, its Old Guard antithesis to the outworn Marxist thesis is not the liberty security synthesis the future cries for."

His position as a right-wing spokesperson was strengthened in 1955 when Buckley founded *National Review,* a magazine of conservative opinion. with the growth of the conservative movement, *National Review* eventually boasted a circulation of over 100,000, including some highly influential readers. Former president Ronald Reagan, for example, declared *National Review* his favorite magazine. Speaking at the magazine's thirtieth anniversary celebration in 1985—a celebration attended by such notables as Charlton Heston, Tom Selleck, Jack Kemp, and Tom Wolfe—Reagan remarked: "If any of you doubt the impact of *National Review* 's verve and attractiveness, take a look around you this evening. The man standing before you now was a Democrat when he picked up his first issue in a plain brown wrapper; and even now, as an occupant of public housing, he awaits as anxiously as ever his biweekly edition—without the wrapper."

Buckley presents a fictionalized account of the founding of the *National Review* in his 2003 novel *Getting It Right.* Following the rise of author Ayn Rand and her Objectivism philosophy as it caught fire with many mid-century intellectuals, Buckley also weaves the radical John Birch Society and that organization's response to the Communist scare into a novel that a *First Things* contributor dubbed "fascinating and informative." Noting the novel's strongly factual basis—Buckley footnotes his fiction—*Library Journal* contributor Barbara Conaty recommended *Getting It Right* for followers of

Buckley's novels, adding that the author's "writing is so polished that he could turn the Yellow Pages into a spy novel or the federal budget into a sparkling memoir."

In addition to his writing and editing for the *National Review,* Buckley has also contributed a syndicated column, "On the Right," to at least 250 newspapers two times weekly, as well as articles of opinion for various national magazines. Many of these columns and articles have been published in book-length collections. These shorter pieces display Buckley's talent for political satire. John P. Roche of the *New York Times Book Review,* critiquing Buckley's articles collected in *Execution Eve and Other Contemporary Ballads,* claimed that "no commentator has a surer eye for the contradictions, the hypocrisies, the pretensions of liberal and radical pontiffs . . . even when you wince, reading Buckley is fun."

Happy Days Were Here Again, is a comprehensive primer of Buckley's ideas. It contains more than 120 articles and addresses written between 1985 and 1993. John Grimond commented in the *New York Times Book Review* that Buckley is "eloquent" on the subjects of anti-communism, conservatism, sailing, and illegitimacy. Yet, Grimond continued: "It is a pity his range is not wider. A columnist needs to be able to say something interesting on many more issues than these if he is to delight his readers as much as himself. . . . Especially among the articles in which he is supposedly appreciating others, the self-serving references to himself occur with tedious frequency. The strongest single quality to emerge from this book is not percipience or wit; it is vanity."

Buckley again showed his willingness to confront flaws in the conservative ranks with his book *In Search of Anti-Semitism.* It grew out of a special issue of *National Review*—December 30, 1991—in which he explored the subject of anti-Semitism in depth. Furthermore, he criticized two friends and conservative brethren, Joseph Sobran and Pat Buchanan, for anti-Semitic attitudes and remarks. The book contains Buckley's original article, comment from readers, and additional comment from Buckley. "Leave it to William Buckley to see right to the heart of a complex issue," commented Jacob Neusner in *National Review.* "Instead of assuming that 'we all know' what anti-Semitism is, he takes up the burden of sorting matters out. This he does with wit, insight, common sense—and unfeigned affection for the Jews and appreciation of what the State of Israel stands for. . . . In sorting matters out with the obvious affection and respect for the Jews and Judaism that this book shows, Buckley should win from those most affected . . . the trust that is needed so that people can stop choosing up sides and start sorting out their conflicts— and resolving them." *New York Times Book Review* contributor Nathan Glazer also praised the book as "fascinating reading: some of our most skillful, subtle and elegant conservative analysts of political trends can be read here, often in private correspondence with Mr. Buckley. He evokes very good letters—in part because he is such a good writer and letter-writer himself."

In other books, Buckley turns from politics to his personal life. *Cruising Speed: A Documentary* is a diary-like account of a typical Buckley week. *Overdrive: A Personal Documentary* follows a similar format. Because of the many activities in which he is typically engaged, and the social opportunities afforded by his political connections and inherited wealth, Buckley's life makes fascinating reading. And he unabashedly shares it with his readers, moving some reviewers to criticize him. Nora Ephron, writing in the *New York Times Book Review,* called *Overdrive* "an astonishing glimpse of a life of privilege in America today." She complained that "it never seems to cross [Buckley's] mind that any of his remarks might be in poor taste, or his charm finite." And yet Carolyn See, writing in the *Los Angeles Times,* believed that while the portrait Buckley may desire to paint of himself in *Overdrive* "is a social butterfly, a gadabout, a mindless snob (or so he would have us believe) . . . Buckley shows us a brittle, acerbic, duty-bound, silly, 'conservative' semi-fudd, with a heart as vast and varicolored and wonderful to watch as a 1930s jukebox."

In 1997 Buckley continued in the autobiographical mode with *Nearer, My God: An Autobiography of Faith.* The book represents a return to the subject that occupied the author in his earlier publication, *God and Man at Yale:* the role of religion in American public life. The first chapters are narratives of Buckley's Catholic boyhood, but later chapters turn to a more argumentative mode, asserting that multiculturalism has replaced spirituality, and defending the concept of sin as useful for instilling a sense of social responsibility which Buckley believes U.S. society lacks. The book was received with ideologically polarized reviews. *Houston Chronicle* religion writer Richard Vara called *Nearer, My God* "engaging reading," praising it for the "vigorous questioning and debate that courses throughout." In the *New York Times Book Review* Christopher Lehmann-Haupt wrote, "what best invites the reader's belief is the joy with which Buckley goes about his business in this 'Autobiography of Faith,'" but said that "the problem,

at least for the nonbelieving reader, is that where almost every logical contradiction arises, we are asked simply to accept what we can't understand."

As he neared the age of eighty, Buckley produced *Miles Gone By: A Literary Autobiography,* a task which a *Publishers Weekly* reviewer likened to "sandwiching a selection of fifty essays between a brief preface and epilogue." The essays cover a wide range of topics and, not unexpectedly, many decades of Buckley's life. The reviewer made particular note of essays that illuminated the lives of some of Buckley's "offbeat friends."

When not writing about politics or sailing, Buckley has also found time to pen a series of bestselling espionage novels featuring CIA agent Blackford Oakes. The series, as Derrick Murdoch described it in the Toronto *Globe and Mail,* is set in the cold-war years of the 1950s and 1960s and takes readers behind the scenes of the major political crises of the time. In doing so, the novels provide Buckley with the opportunity to dramatize some of his ideas concerning East-West relations. As Lehmann-Haupt remarked in the *New York Times,* "not only can Buckley execute the international thriller as well as nearly anyone working in the genre . . . he threatens to turn this form of fiction into effective propaganda for his ideas."

Saving the Queen, the first of the "Blackford Oakes" novels, is based in part on Buckley's own experiences in the CIA. Oakes, a thinly disguised version of his creator, also shares Buckley's school years at an English public school and at Yale University. The story concerns a leak of classified information at the highest levels of the British government. Oakes is sent to locate the source of the leak, and his investigation uncovers a treasonous cousin in the royal family. Amnon Kabatchnik of the *Armchair Detective* called *Saving the Queen* "an entertaining yarn, graced with a literate style, keen knowledge and a twinkling sense of humor [that] injected a touch of sophistication and a flavor of sly irony to the genre of political intrigue."

Stained Glass is set in post-World War II Germany and revolves around the efforts of both East and West to prevent the reunification of Germany under the popular Count Axel Wintergrin. Both sides fear that a united Germany would be a military threat to the peace of Europe. Oakes penetrates Wintergrin's political organization disguised as an engineer hired to restore a local church. His restoring of broken church windows contrasts ironically with his efforts to keep Germany divided. "This novel is a work of history," Robin W. Winks of the *New Republic* observed, "for it parallels those options that might well have been open to the West [in the 1950s]. . . . *Stained Glass* is closer to the bone than le Carré has ever cut." Jane Larkin Crain in the *Saturday Review* called Buckley's novel a "first-rate spy story and . . . a disturbing lesson in the unsavory realities of international politics." *Stained Glass* earned its author an American Book Award in 1980.

In building his novels around actual events, Buckley is obliged to include historical figures in his cast of characters. Speaking of *See You Later, Alligator,* Murdoch believed that "the telling personal [details] are helping to make the Blackford Oakes series unique in spy fiction." In his review of *The Story of Henri Tod,* Anatole Broyard suggested in the *New York Times* that "the best part" of the novel is Buckley's "portrait of former President John F. Kennedy. His rendering of Nikita Khrushchev is quite good too, and this tempts me to suggest that Mr. Buckley seems most at home when he projects himself into the minds of heads of state."

A Very Private Plot, Buckley's tenth offering in the "Blackford Oakes" series, takes his hero to the end of the cold war. Commenting on the author's development as a novelist, D. Keith Mano wrote in *National Review,* "He is a better fiction writer now by leagues than he was in 1976, when *Saving the Queen* took off. New directness and clarity jumpstart his prose. He has command of several voices and can modulate each. And, structurally, his later volumes . . . have had an arrow-shaped ease and purpose." Furthermore, in Mano's opinion, "no one, Right or Left, has chronicled the Cold War period with more imagination or authority."

One may never know the answer. As its title suggests, *Last Call for Blackford Oakes* seems to represent the end of an era. Set in 1987 during the terms of Ronald Reagan and Mikhail Gorbachev, Oakes's potentially final assignment takes him to Moscow once again, this time to investigate a threat to Soviet Community party leader Gorbachev. The investigation fades into the background as Oakes becomes infatuated with a Russian physician and embroiled in a confrontation with Kim Philby, real-life double agent and defector from the free world. In typical Buckley fashion, *Last Call for Blackford Oakes* is replete with references to the history of U.S.-Soviet relations and the author's own views on U.S. politics.

Buckley's novel *Brothers No More* finds its author departing from his "Blackford Oakes" series. Described as "an epic saga of doomed Yalies" by Joe Queenan in the

New York Times Book Review, the novel turns on the changing fortunes of two men who share a foxhole during World War II. One becomes a corrupt businessman, the other a tenacious reporter. Years after their initial encounter, their paths cross again in a strange twist of fate. In Queenan's opinion, the novel's plot is flimsy and contrived, the book "best thought of as patrician trash." He went on to say that Buckley's fine writing actually sabotages the novel: "For trash to work, the writing has to be genuinely trashy, as in Jackie Collins, Danielle Steel, Judith Krantz. For trash to work, the writing has to be positively awful." Queenan speculated that Buckley intended *Brothers No More* to be a genuinely serious book, but that it falls far short of that ambition. A *Publishers Weekly* reviewer rated the book as enjoyable, but concluded that "this is just a potboiler, deftly stirred but no match for Buckley's best."

Buckley wrote *McCarthy and His Enemies: The Record and Its Meaning* with L. Brent Bozell in 1954 in support of the Wisconsin senator who, after the conviction of spy Alger Hiss in 1950, led hearings to uncover suspected communists in the United States. He revisits this subject in his 1999 novel *The Redhunter: A Novel Based on the Life of Senator Joe McCarthy.* Caspar W. Weinberger, reviewing the novel in *Forbes,* called *The Redhunter* "one of the year's best books, full of tension, excitement, suspense, and realism." The protagonist is Harry Bontecou, a history professor and McCarthy supporter whose life parallels that of the young Buckley. Terry Teachout wrote in *National Review* that *The Redhunter* "tells us much of what he [Buckley] knows about the anti-Communist movement, and does so in a way that is likely to engage the attention of a great many readers who might not otherwise question the received wisdom regarding Joe McCarthy." *Fortune* reviewer Sam Tanenhaus called the novel "an arresting hybrid of fact and invention" and "a penetrating account of McCarthy's intellectual laziness and lack of discipline, which were heightened by his dependence on both the vodka bottle and the advice of Roy Cohn, his sinister young aide." *Booklist* reviewer Mary Carroll added: "one can only hope readers will understand that Buckley . . . is telling only one side of this very complicated story."

Like the books in Buckley's "Blackford Oakes" series, *Spytime: The Undoing of James Jesus Angleton* is a fictional account of the life of a Yale graduate who served as a spy for the United States in Italy during World War II, then returned to head the counterintelligence operation of the CIA for twenty years. A *Publishers Weekly* reviewer called Buckley's perspective on Angleton's life "perceptive," but added that *Spytime* "suffers from glaring gaps in the master spy's biography." David Pitt wrote in *Booklist* that "readers familiar with Buckley's politics will find much to enjoy here . . . but those looking for a fully formed novel may be a tad disappointed." "This novel successfully explores the enigmatic life of a Cold Warrior," reported Barbara Conaty in *Library Journal*.

Let Us Talk of Many Things, published in 2000, contains about one-third of the speeches Buckley delivered during the last half of the twentieth century. *Booklist* reviewer Ray Olson noted that "scattered throughout are delicious anecdotes, piquant quotations, and much evidence of a keen moral sensibility." "From his earliest efforts in the 1950s to the very last page, Buckley's speeches are alive with wit, conviction, and a lucid, fluent grace few of his contemporaries can match," added Aram Bakshian, Jr., in *National Review.* "And they are as much of a delight on the printed page as from the podium. Patinated rather than rusted, they have stood the severest test of all for public utterances—the test of time."

As columnist, television host, novelist, and magazine editor, Buckley became "one of the most articulate, provocative, and entertaining spokesmen for American conservatism" in the twentieth century, according to Gene M. Moore in his *Dictionary of Literary Biography Yearbook* essay. For his role in the development of the modern conservative movement that fueled the careers of commentators such as George Will and Rush Limbaugh, Buckley "is a man who richly deserves praise," Kondracke argued. "He is generous, erudite, witty and courageous, and he has performed a service to the whole nation, even to those who disagree with him." Summing up Buckley's role in the nation's political life, Moore found that his "flickering tongue and flashing wit have challenged a generation to remember the old truths while searching for the new, to abhor hypocrisy and to value logic, and to join in the worldwide struggle for human rights and human freedom."

BIOGRAPHICAL AND CRITICAL SOURCES:

BOOKS

Cain, Edward R., *They'd Rather Be Right: Youth and the Conservative Movement,* Macmillan (New York, NY), 1963.

Contemporary Literary Criticism, Thomson Gale (Detroit, MI), Volume 7, 1977, Volume 18, 1981, Volume 37, 1986.

Dictionary of Literary Biography Yearbook: 1980, Thomson Gale (Detroit, MI), 1981.

Forster, Arnold, and B.R. Epstein, *Danger on the Right,* Random House (New York, NY), 1964.

Judis, John, *William F. Buckley, Jr.: Patron Saint of the Conservatives,* Simon & Schuster (New York, NY), 1988.

Markmann, Charles L., *The Buckleys: A Family Examined,* William Morrow (New York, NY), 1973.

PERIODICALS

America, January 31, 1998, Thomas M. King, review of *Nearer, My God: An Autobiography of Faith,* p. 32.

Armchair Detective, June, 1976, Amnon Kabatchnik, review of *Saving the Queen.*

Atlantic Monthly, November, 1951, McGeorge Bundy, review of *God and Man at Yale: The Superstitions of "Academic Freedom,".*

Booklist, September 1, 1997, Ray Olson, review of *Nearer, My God,* p. 4; March 15, 1999, Mary Carroll, review of *The Redhunter: A Novel Based on the Life of Senator Joe McCarthy,* p. 1259; April 15, 2000, David Pitt, review of *Spytime: The Undoing of James Jesus Angleton,* p. 1498; May 1, 2000, Ray Olson, review of *Let Us Talk of Many Things,* p. 1639; February 1, 2003, Mary Carroll, review of *Getting It Right,* p. 955.

Christian Century, November 19, 1997, D.G. Hart, review of *Nearer, My God,* pp. 1091-1094.

Christianity Today, November 17, 1997, John Wilson, review of *Nearer, My God,* p. 59.

Commonweal, March 13, 1998, Neil Coughlan, review of *Nearer, My God,* p. 15.

First Things, May, 2003, review of *Getting It Right,* p. 74.

Forbes, August 9, 1999, Caspar W. Weinberger, review of *The Redhunter,* p. 41.

Fortune, June 7, 1999, Sam Tanenhaus, "W.F. Buckley's Auto-Revisionism," p. 48.

Globe and Mail (Toronto, Ontario, Canada), April 13, 1985, Derrick Murdoch, review of *See You Later, Alligator.*

Houston Chronicle, January 9, 1998, Richard Vara, review of *Nearer, My God.*

Kirkus Reviews, November 1, 1996, review of *Buckley: The Right Word;* August 1, 1997, review of *Nearer, My God;* January 15, 2003, review of *Getting It Right,* p. 103; March 15, 2005, review of *Last Call for Blackford Oakes,,* p. 302.

Library Journal, September 15, 1997, Richard S. Watts, review of *Nearer, My God,* p. 79; November 1, 1998, Lisa J. Cihlar, review of *The Lexicon: A Cor-*

nucopia of *Wonderful Words for the Inquisitive Word Lover,* p. 80; June 15, 1999, Barbara Conaty, review of *The Redhunter,* p. 105; May 1, 2000, Barbara Conaty, review of *Spytime,* p. 152; February 1, 2003, Barbara Conaty, review of *Getting It Right,* p. 114.

Los Angeles Times, August 11, 1983, Carolyn See, review of *Overdrive: A Personal Documentary.*

National Catholic Reporter, November 7, 1997, review of *Nearer, My God,* p. 27.

National Review, December 28, 1992, Jacob Neusner, *In Search of Anti-Semitism,* pp. 40-42; February 21, 1994, D. Keith Mano, review of *A Very Private Plot,* pp. 58-60; June 5, 2000, Aram Bakshian, Jr., "Music for Our Ears"; June 14, 1999, Terry Teachout, "McCarthy and His Friends," p. 47; March 10, 2003, Austin Bramwell, review of *Getting It Right;* March 24, 2003, "Objectivist Sex—And Politics" (interview).

New American, March 10, 2003, William Norman Greig, review of *Getting It Right,* p. 25.

New Republic, June 10, 1978, Robin W. Winks, review of *Stained Glass.*

New York Times, November 4, 1951, Peter Viereck, review of *God and Man at Yale;* February 4, 1985, Anatole Broyard, review of *The Story of Henri Tod.*

New York Times Book Review, September 28, 1975, John P. Roch, review of *Execution Eve and Other Contemporary Ballads,;* August 7, 1983, Nora Ephron, review of *Overdrive;* January 5, 1986, Morton Kondracke, "Right Reason," p. 14; September 27, 1992, Nathan Glazer, review of *In Search of Anti-Semitism,* pp. 3, 24; October 3, 1993, John Grimond, review of *Happy Days Were Here Again,* p. 14; September 10, 1995, Joe Queenan, review of *Brothers No More,* p. 16; October 18, 1998, Christopher Lehmann-Haupt, review of *Nearer, My God,* p. 36.

Publishers Weekly, August 7, 1995, review of *Brothers No More,* p. 441; September 29, 1997, review of *Nearer, My God,* p. 84; May 22, 2000, review of *Spytime,* p. 70; June 21, 2004, review of *Miles Gone By: A Literary Autobiography,* p. 57; April 4, 2005, review of *Last Call for Blackford Oakes,* p. 42.

Saturday Review, May 13, 1978, Jane Larkin Crain, review of *Stained Galss.*

Time, November 10, 1997, John Elson, review of *Nearer, My God,* p. 111; June 7, 1999, Lance Morrow, "Alger 'Ales' and Joe: Was McCarthy on the Right Track?," p. 66.

*   *   *

BUCKLEY, William Frank, Jr.
    See BUCKLEY, William F., Jr.

BUECHNER, Carl Frederick
    See BUECHNER, Frederick

*   *   *

BUECHNER, Frederick 1926-
    (Carl Frederick Buechner)

PERSONAL: Born July 11, 1926, in New York, NY; son of Carl Frederick and Katherine (Kuhn) Buechner; married Judith Friedrike Merck, April 7, 1956; children: Katherine, Dinah, Sharman. *Education:* Lawrenceville School, graduated 1943; Princeton University, A.B., 1948; Union Theological Seminary, B.D., 1958.

ADDRESSES: Home—3572 State Route 315, Pawlet, VT 05761-9753. *Office*—P.O. Box 1145, Pawlet, VT 05761. *Agent*—Lucy Kroll Agency, 390 West End Ave., New York, NY 10024 (drama); Harriet Wasserman, 137 East 36th St., New York, NY 10016.

CAREER: Lawrenceville School, Lawrenceville, NJ, teacher of English, 1948-53; instructor in creative writing, New York University, summers, 1953, 1954; East Harlem Protestant Parish, New York, NY, head of employment clinic, 1954-58; ordained minister of the United Presbyterian Church, 1958; Phillips Exeter Academy, Exeter, NH, chair of department of religion, 1958-60, school minister, 1960-67; writer, 1967—. William Belden Noble Lecturer, Harvard University, 1969; Russell Lecturer, Tufts University, 1971; Lyman Beecher Lecturer, Divinity School, Yale University, 1976; Harris Lecturer, Bangor Seminary, 1979; Smyth Lecturer, Columbia Seminary, 1981; Zabriskie Lecturer, Virginia Theological Seminary, 1982; Trinity Institute, lecturer, 1990. Guest preacher and lecturer. Trustee, Barlow School, 1965-71; author. *Military service:* U.S. Army, 1944-46.

MEMBER: National Council of Churches (committee on literature, 1954-57), Council for Religion in Independent Schools (regional chair, 1958-63), Foundation for Arts, Religion, and Culture, Presbytery of Northern New England, PEN, Authors Guild, Authors League of America, Century Association, University Club (New York, NY).

AWARDS, HONORS: Irene Glascock Memorial Intercollegiate Poetry Award, 1947; O. Henry Memorial Award, 1955, for short story "The Tiger"; Richard and Hinda Rosenthal Award, 1959, for *The Return of Ansel*

Gibbs; National Book Award nomination, 1971, for *Lion Country;* Pulitzer Prize nomination, 1980, for *Godric;* American Academy Award, 1982; D.D. from Virginia Theological Seminary, 1983, Lafayette College, 1984, Cornell College, 1988, Yale University, 1990, and Sewanee University; Litt.D. from Lehigh University.

WRITINGS:

NOVELS

A Long Day's Dying, Knopf (New York, NY), 1950, reprinted, Brook Street Press (Saint Simons Island, GA), 2003.

The Seasons' Difference, Knopf (New York, NY), 1952.

The Return of Ansel Gibbs, Knopf (New York, NY), 1958.

The Final Beast, Atheneum (New York, NY), 1965, reprinted, Harper (San Francisco, CA), 1982.

The Entrance to Porlock, Atheneum (New York, NY), 1970.

Lion Country (also see below; first in "Book of Bebb" tetralogy), Atheneum (New York, NY), 1971.

Open Heart (also see below; second in "Book of Bebb" tetralogy), Atheneum (New York, NY), 1972.

Love Feast (also see below; third in "Book of Bebb" tetralogy), Atheneum (New York, NY), 1974.

Treasure Hunt (also see below; fourth in "Book of Bebb" tetralogy), Atheneum (New York, NY), 1977.

The Book of Bebb (contains *Lion Country, Open Heart, Love Feast,* and *Treasure Hunt*), Atheneum (New York, NY), 1979, reprinted, HarperSanFrancisco (San Francisco, CA), 2001.

Godric, Atheneum (New York, NY), 1980.

Brendan, Atheneum (New York, NY), 1987.

Wizard's Tide: A Story, Harper (New York, NY), 1990.

The Son of Laughter, HarperSanFrancisco (San Francisco, CA), 1993.

On the Road with the Archangel, HarperSanFrancisco (San Francisco, CA), 1997.

The Storm, HarperSanFrancisco (San Francisco, CA), 1998.

NONFICTION

The Magnificent Defeat (meditations), Seabury (New York, NY), 1966.

The Hungering Dark (meditations), Seabury (New York, NY), 1969.

The Alphabet of Grace (theological and autobiographical essays), Seabury (New York, NY), 1970.

Wishful Thinking: A Theological ABC, Harper & Row ((New York, NY), 1973.

The Faces of Jesus, photography by Lee Boltin, Riverwood (Croton-on-Hudson, NY), 1974.

Telling the Truth: The Gospel as Tragedy, Comedy, and Fairy Tale, Harper & Row (San Francisco, CA), 1977.

Peculiar Treasures: A Biblical Who's Who, Harper & Row (San Francisco, CA), 1979.

The Sacred Journey: A Memoir of Early Days (autobiography), Atheneum (New York, NY), 1982.

Now and Then: A Memoir of Vocation (autobiography), Atheneum (New York, NY), 1983.

A Room Called Remember: Uncollected Pieces, HarperSanFrancisco (San Francisco, CA), 1984.

Whistling in the Dark: An ABC Theologized, HarperSanFrancisco (San Francisco, CA), 1988.

Telling Secrets, (autobiography), HarperSanFrancisco (San Francisco, CA), 1991.

The Clown in the Belfry: Writings on Faith and Fiction, HarperSanFrancisco (San Francisco, CA), 1991.

Listening to Your Life: Meditations with Frederick Buechner, HarperSanFrancisco (San Francisco, CA), 1992.

The Longing for Home: Recollections and Reflections (autobiography), HarperSanFrancisco (San Francisco, CA), 1996.

The Eyes of the Heart: A Memoir of the Lost and Found, HarperSanFrancisco (San Francisco, CA), 1999.

Speak What We Feel (Not What We Ought to Say): Reflections on Literature and Faith, HarperSanFrancisco (San Francisco, CA), 2001.

Beyond Words: Daily Readings in the ABC's of Faith, HarperSanFrancisco (New York, NY), 2004.

OTHER

Short stories have been anthologized in *Prize Stories 1955: The O. Henry Awards,* edited by Paul Engle and Hansford Martin, Doubleday (New York, NY), 1955. Contributor to numerous periodicals, including *Poetry* and *Lawrenceville Literary Magazine.*

Collections of Buechner's manuscripts have been established at Princeton University and at Wheaton College, Wheaton, IL.

SIDELIGHTS: Frederick Buechner is a novelist and nonfiction writer whose work as a Presbyterian minister informs his writings. Virtually all of Buechner's books, from his novels to his nonfiction theological "meditations," address moral, ethical, and religious themes.

Two years after graduating from Princeton University, Buechner published his first novel, *A Long Day's Dying*. The book "is a strikingly fine first novel, and it seems entirely safe to say that its publication will introduce a new American novelist of the greatest promise and the greatest talent," wrote C.W. Weinberger in the *San Francisco Chronicle*. "In strict accuracy, it is not proper to refer to Mr. Buechner as being a novelist of great promise, for he has already arrived in superlative fashion."

Buechner's *A Long Day's Dying* is generally considered to be an unusually sensitive and insightful study of various relationships. "Buechner has written a perceptive and often astringently witty study of subtle human relationships and delicate tensions," stated C.J. Rolo in *Atlantic*, "a book which continually reaches for the emotional meanings of the moment." And David Daiches wrote in the *New York Times* that "this first novel by a young man of twenty-three is a remarkable piece of work. There is a quality of civilized perception here, a sensitive and plastic handling of English prose and an ability to penetrate to the evanescent core of a human situation."

Buechner's second novel, *The Seasons' Difference*, was not greeted with the same degree of enthusiasm as *A Long Day's Dying*. For example, Oliver La Farge pointed out in *Saturday Review* that *The Seasons' Difference* "starts with promise. Again and again it looks as if the promise were going to be fulfilled. There are moments when it lights up brightly, and one thinks, at last he has hit his stride—but always, somehow, the light goes out again. It is one of those most tantalizing of all things in writing—a near miss." H.L. Roth wrote in *Library Journal* that Buechner's "emphasis is less on plot than on the development of atmosphere but even that emphasis seems to get lost in an arty attempt at developing a feeling of mysticism."

However, Tangye Lean found Buechner's book "brilliant and closely knit both in its rather overloaded descriptive power and its invention." Writing in *Spectator*, Lean remarked that *The Seasons' Difference* "may be recommended as one of the most distinguished novels that has recently come out of America." And a critic for *U.S. Quarterly Book Review* observed that "the arresting quality of this sensitively and elaborately written novel lies in the delineation of its characters, especially the children, and of their interrelations: adult to adult, child to adult, and child to child." Nevertheless, reasoned Horace Gregory in the *New York Herald Tribune Book Review*, "Buechner probably needs more time to

complete his own vision of the world that is glimpsed in certain descriptive passages of [*The Seasons' Difference*]. The promise of his first book is still awaiting its fulfillment."

With his promise not quite fulfilling the initial expectations of critics or readers, Buechner had reached a writer's block. Having moved to New York with two novels completed, he tried to continue writing but found himself considering other careers, according to Philip Yancey in *Books & Culture*. "Uncharacteristically," Yancey wrote, "simply because the building sat a block from his apartment, he began attending the Madison Avenue Presbyterian Church, pastored by the celebrated George Buttrick." Buechner had never attended church regularly until that time, and only occasionally in his childhood. When he heard a sermon delivered in 1952, right around the time of Queen Elizabeth's coronation, Buechner experienced a life-altering revelation. "Buttrick was contrasting Elizabeth's coronation with the coronation of Jesus in the believer's heart, which, he said, should take place among confession and tears," recounted Yancey. Buechner tells the story in *The Alphabet of Grace*: "And then with his head bobbing up and down so that his glasses glittered, he said in his odd, sandy voice, the voice of an old nurse, that the coronation of Jesus took place among confession and tears and then, as God was and is my witness, great laughter, he said. Jesus is crowned among confession and tears and great laughter, and at the phrase great laughter, for reasons that I have never satisfactorily understood, the Great Wall of China crumbled and Atlantis rose up out of the sea, and on Madison Avenue, at 73rd Street, tears leapt from my eyes as though I had been struck across the face." As Yancey pointed out, that was the beginning of Buechner's belief and trust in God. It continued to shape him as an ordained minister, a teacher, and most importantly, as a writer.

"In *The Return of Ansel Gibbs*, Buechner marked a more decisive departure from his earlier manner," wrote Ihab Hassan in *Radical Innocence: Studies in the Contemporary American Novel*. "The book is reasonably forthright; its material, though rich in moral ambiguities, is topical rather than mythic, dramatic more than allusive." An *Atlantic* contributor noted that this book "is quite a departure from [Buechner's] two previous novels, which were open to the charge of preciosity. Now the style is less ornate, the plot straightforward." Richard McLaughlin remarked in the *Springfield Republican* that Buechner's earlier novels "established him as a writer with a distinguished style but a rather narrow range of interests. In [*The Return of Ansel Gibbs*] he explores, with his usual subtlety and feeling for language and moods, a wider, more public domain."

Writing for *Saturday Review,* A.C. Spectorsky commented that "there is a quality of distinction about Frederick Buechner's [*The Return of Ansel Gibbs*] which might best be compared to the gleam of hand-polished old silver. There is about his work some of the charming cultivation of the best of Marquand, and Cozzens' capacity to make each incident—however casual or trivial in appearance—emerge as meaningful and illuminating."

In 1958, the same year Buechner published *The Return of Ansel Gibbs,* he was ordained a minister of the United Presbyterian Church. For the next several years Buechner performed the duties of school minister at Phillips Exeter Academy while continuing to write his novels. As Elizabeth Janeway explained in the *New York Times:* "Part of Frederick Buechner is a writer of imagination and insight. Part of him is a man with a Christian mission so strong that he decided to enter the Presbyterian ministry. There is no reason why the two shouldn't combine to write excellent and powerful novels."

Not all reviewers have shared Janeway's contention that the ministry and the writing of novels is a likely and acceptable combination. A reviewer for *Publishers Weekly* observed that "to a certain number of critics and reviewers, there is something disconcerting about a minister who can write a novel, containing some vivid sex scenes and a four-letter word or two." Buechner, however, sees no conflict with being a minister and a novelist. He explained in a *Publishers Weekly* interview that, to him, "writing is a kind of ministry." As Buechner once elaborated: "As a preacher I am trying to do many of the same things I do as a writer. In both I am trying to explore what I believe life is all about, to get people to stop and listen a little to the mystery of their own lives. The process of telling a story is something like religion if only in the sense of suggesting that life itself has a plot and leads to a conclusion that makes some kind of sense."

Buechner's first literary work written after his ordination was *The Final Beast.* Published seven years after *The Return of Ansel Gibbs, The Final Beast* displays a shift in theme that a number of reviewers, including Gerald Weales, believed would become more prevalent in future Buechner novels. In the *Reporter,* Weales described the theme as "the possibility of spiritual rebirth." A *Choice* reviewer felt the work marked the beginning of Buechner's "concern with religious belief and the religious life." Charles Dollen remarked in *Best Sellers:* "Despite what might sound like heavy drama in the plot, this [book] is a joyous one and its fictional

people are searching for, and finding, real happiness. This is a deeply religious book without the slightest hint of [piety] or sentimentalism."

In 1971 Buechner published *Lion Country,* the first book of a tetralogy that also includes *Open Heart, Love Feast,* and *Treasure Hunt.* Eight years later these four novels were published in one volume titled *The Book of Bebb.* The tetralogy traces the activities and relationships of Leo Bebb, a former Bible salesman, founder of the Church of Holy Love, Incorporated, and of the Open Heart Church, and president of the Gospel Faith College, a religious diploma mill. Buechner did not originally intend to write a follow-up to *Lion Country.* He explained how the series evolved in his introduction to *The Book of Bebb:* "When I wrote the last sentence of *Lion Country,* I thought I had finished with [the characters in the series] for good but soon found out that they were not finished with me. And so it was with the succeeding volumes, at the end of each of which I rang the curtain down only to find that, after a brief intermission, they'd rung it up again."

The Bebb series is considered by some to be Buechner's best work to date. Christopher Lehmann-Haupt wrote in the *New York Times:* "You smile to think how Frederick Buechner keeps getting better with each new novel, for where he was gently amusing in *Lion Country,* he is funny and profound in *Open Heart.*" While numerous elements have been cited as reasons for the popularity of these four novels, most reviewers agree that much of the credit belongs to Buechner's presentation of thought-provoking ideas in a witty manner. A *Times Literary Supplement* contributor commented that Buechner maintains "a strange, serene balancing act which blends successfully satirical talent and the moral purpose." And a *Publishers Weekly* reviewer noted that the way Buechner "writes is special and engaging—serious, comic, with a kind of reverent irreverence for his people and their lives. [He has an] amused and amusing view." Another reviewer for *Publishers Weekly* held up *Lion Country* as a perfect example of a "human comedy of complexity and persuasion." As a *Virginia Quarterly Review* writer remarked: "Urbane, arcane, intelligent, low-keyed comedy is rare enough in these parlous times, but [*Lion Country*] is a choice example certain to appeal to a variety of tastes."

Some reviewers have noted that Buechner's comical sense is especially evident in his handling of religious matters. "This may sound like slapstick [to] suggest that although Mr. Buechner takes bows toward religion he is really more interested in laughs," suggested

Michael Mewshaw in the *New York Times Book Review,* "but throughout the [tetralogy] he is most serious when he is funny, and he has found an inevitable and instructive confusion between wheat and chaff. As the Bible warns, one can't be cut away without injuring the other." And in a review of *Open Heart,* John Skow observed in *Time:* "It is something of a mystery how Buechner has produced a live, warm, wise comic novel. And yet that is exactly what, in all shifty-eyed innocence, he has done. [He] seems to have found an acceptable way to deal with religious mysteries in fiction."

Other reviewers commented similarly that Buechner seems to have mastered a technique for dealing with theological subjects in an entertaining fashion. A *Times Literary Supplement* contributor pointed out: "The fine lucidity of Mr. Buechner's prose, the pure verve of his humour, the grisly authenticity of his characters and settings make this highly elusive, indeed almost deliquescent brand of Christian Philosophy seem not unpalatable but actually convincing." Lehmann-Haupt wrote in the *New York Times* that Buechner's "contrast between the serious and the absurd serves to underline the meaning of both *Love Feast* and the [tetralogy] as a whole: to wit, the message of Jesus Christ may emanate from strange places indeed, but it is the message that matters, not the messenger."

New York Times Book Review contributor Cynthia Ozick believed that the reason the religious messages seem to fit so well into Buechner's novels is that to the author "sacredness lurks effortlessly . . . nearly everywhere; it singles us out." As Buechner himself writes in *The Hungering Dark:* "There is no place or time so lowly and earthbound but that holiness can be there too. And this means that we are never safe, that there is no place where we can hide from God, no place where we are safe from his power . . . to recreate the human heart because it is . . . just where we least expect him where he comes most fully."

"Life is what Buechner is writing about," explained Jonathan Yardley in the *Washington Post Book World.* "Beneath all the antics of Leo Bebb and those who surround him there is a continuing celebration of life and the interrelation of lives. Buechner's people may at first glance seem caricatures, but their robustness is merely humanity magnified." And Thomas Howard remarked in the *New York Times Book Review* that "[Buechner's] vision, then, is that of the poet—the Christian poet. He has articulated what he sees with a freshness and clarity and energy that hails our stultified imaginations."

Another factor contributing to the success of these novels is Buechner's skill at characterization. "What makes [the 'Leo Bebb' novels] succeed is Buechner's deft placing of all these characters," explained Roger Sale in *Hudson Review,* "keeping them funny or impossible when seen from a distance, then making them briefly very moving when suddenly seen from close up." P.A. Doyle stated in *Best Sellers* that Buechner "grasps each figure firmly and forces it to concrete life. A type of Flannery O'Connor vibrant vividness pervades Bebb . . . and the other principals causing them to pop out most fully alive from the novel[s]." And Sale, writing in another issue of *Hudson Review,* singled out Buechner's treatment of the main character, Leo Bebb, and commented: "The word about Bebb is simple—he lights up every page on which he appears, making each one a joy to read and to anticipate, and of all the characters in American literature, only Hemingway's Bill Gorton rivals him in that respect."

Buechner's skillful use of characters did not end with the Bebb series of novels. Reviewers have cited Buechner's following novel, *Godric,* as still another example of how an effective characterization enriches Buechner's novels. In *Godric,* Buechner tells the story of a twelfth-century Anglo-Saxon saint. Francine Cardman illustrated in *Commonweal:* "Peddler, merchant seaman, pilgrim and perhaps pirate, ultimately hermit; roguist, conniving, irascible, repentant, gentle, fierce: Godric is compelling in his struggle for sanctity. Buechner's retelling draws reader/listener into the world of his words, a world and language so strangely and strongly evocative they would seem to be Godric's own." Noel Perrin remarked in the *Washington Post Book World* that "the old saint [Godric] is so real that it's hard to remember this is a novel. I can think of only one other book like this: Thomas Mann's *The Holy Sinner.* That's the story, taken from medieval legend, of another carnal saint."

Buechner's 1993 novel *The Son of Laughter* again showcased the author's penchant for religious themes—in this case, a novelization of the biblical story of Jacob—and moral issues presented in ambiguous, often comic, tones. In presenting the story of Jacob, Buechner deals with numerous well-known biblical tales, including the stories of Abraham, Sarah, and Isaac—whose name means "laughter." Writing in the *New York Times Book Review,* Lore Dickstein remarked: "Buechner has kept intact all the characters and events, the (unknown) biblical time frame, and much of the tone and cadence of biblical prose. He has altered the sequence of the narrative somewhat, using flashbacks and foreshadowing, but he has omitted nothing." Reviewers noted that in this work, as in his previous novels, Buechner does not offer easy solutions to moral questions. Addressing this issue, Brooke Horvath, in the *Review of Contemporary Fiction*, wrote, "The novel's meditative questioning is often moving. It is also often disturbing." "This question of belief is at the heart of Buechner's work," noted Irving Malin in *Commonweal*. "He makes us wonder about how we can find spiritual truth in the comic incident."

In addition to his novels, Buechner has also written works of nonfiction, including several collections of meditations, religious studies, and autobiographies. Critics have noted that these books are similar in many ways to Buechner novels. As Edmund Fuller wrote in the *New York Times Book Review:* "The same stylistic power, subtlety and originality that have distinguished his novels, from *A Long Day's Dying* to *Open Heart,* lift *Wishful Thinking* far above commonplace religion books nearly to the level of C.S. Lewis's *Screwtape Letters.* An artist is at work here in the vineyard of theology, an able aphorist with a natural gift for gnomics, a wit with wisdom." Reviewing *The Alphabet of Grace,* Thomas Howard wrote in the *New York Times Book Review* that Buechner "takes the common, mundane experiences of daily life and reflects on them," he said. "What he does with his material is what the poets do with theirs: he surprises and delights (and—very softly—teaches) us by giving some shape to apparently random experience by uttering it."

"Novelist Buechner writes about as well as anyone we know of, when it comes to Christian themes today," noted a reviewer for *Christian Century*. In an article on *The Alphabet of Grace,* M.M. Shideler observed in another issue of *Christian Century* that "Buechner's style is by turns meditative, narrative and anecdotal. His manner is honest, sensitive and direct." And N.K. Burger observed in the *New York Times Book Review* that in *The Magnificent Defeat* (Buechner's first book of meditations) Buechner "combines high writing skill with a profound understanding of Christian essentials." Tony Stoneburner wrote in *Christian Century* that Buechner's collections of meditations "grant relative value to the world, distinguish Christianity and morality, argue the propriety of poetry for discourse about mystery." Commenting on Buechner's second collection, *The Hungering Dark,* Fuller stated in the *New York Times Book Review* that "the touches that distinguish [this book] spring from the fact that in addition to Buechner's role as Presbyterian minister and sometime chaplain, he is also one of the better literary talents of his generation." Fuller went on to say that, "He has artistic as well as pastoral insights into the human soul and also some distinction of style." Reviewing *Telling*

the Truth: The Gospel as Tragedy, Comedy, and Fairy Tale, Richard Sistek pointed out that "this is the kind of book that asks for reflection, creativity, and response. With continually changing times and a church in transition, human experience and creativity are sorely needed to make sense out of change, and move forward with hope. The author has challenged me."

Perhaps nowhere else does the reader achieve a real understanding of Buechner, the author and minister, than in his autobiographies. In his introduction to *The Sacred Journey,* Buechner writes: "What I propose to do now is to try listening to my life as a whole, or at least to certain key moments of the first half of my life thus far, for whatever of meaning, of holiness, of God, there may be in it to hear. My assumption is that the story of any one of us is in some measure the story of us all." A *Publishers Weekly* reviewer wrote that in *The Sacred Journey,* Buechner "exemplifies his conviction that God speaks to us not just through sounds but 'through events in all their complexity and variety, through the harmonies and disharmonies and counterpoint of all that happens.'"

Reynolds Price remarked in the *New York Times Book Review* that in *The Sacred Journey,* Buechner "isolates and recreates a few powerfully charged incidents ranging from his early childhood to the time of his decision to enter the ministry." "The heart of this book," Julian N. Hart believed, "is a series of encounters for which 'epiphany,' overworked though it may be, is entirely appropriate." Hart wrote in the *Washington Post Book World* that "the persistent core metaphor is 'journey'; in his case a life-process defined, not merely punctuated, by revelations of what he comes to acknowledge of divine goodness and power."

Now and Then, Buechner's sequel to *The Sacred Journey,* "picks up where the first book ends, with the author's experience of having his life turned upside down while listening to a George Buttrick sermon," recounted Marjorie Casebier McCoy in *Christian Century*. "Part I covers Buechner's years at Union Theological Seminary, where he encountered the theologians and biblical scholars who became his mentors. . . . In Part II Buechner recalls his nine years as a minister and teacher of religion at Phillips Exeter Academy, trying to be an apologist for Christianity against its 'cultured despisers' by presenting the faith 'as appealingly, honestly, relevantly and skillfully as I could,'" she quoted. "Part III begins with Buechner's move to Vermont in 1967, chronicles his struggle to minister through full-time writing and speaking, and provides insights into the development of his subsequent novels and nonfiction."

Buechner's novel *On the Road with the Archangel* is based on the Book of Tobit, which is one of the seven biblical books designated as "Deutero-Canonical" by Catholics. Yet Protestants refer to Tobit and other works, including Esdras, Sirach, and Wisdom, as "the Apocryphal Books"; this alone makes Buechner's choice interesting. Tobit itself is, as Alfred Corn wrote in the *New York Times Book Review,* a sort of historical novel, the only extended first-person narrative in the Old Testament. Written in the second century B.C., its setting is some four centuries earlier, when the Assyrians conquered the northern kingdom of Israel and deported its people (the famous "Lost Tribes of Israel") to the Assyrian capital at Nineveh. There a wealthy and generous figure named Tobit undergoes a series of trials that call to mind those of a more well-known Old Testament figure, Job. Tobit prays for death, while in the town of Ectabana, a beautiful girl named Sarah—plagued by a demon who has killed seven would-be husbands—makes the same request. The angel Raphael hears the prayers of both, and intervenes in their affairs, bringing the two together. The tale ends happily, with Sarah's marriage to Tobit's feckless son Tobias.

"No Job-like depths have been plumbed," in Corn's opinion, "but the conclusion's lightly borne sweetness works to justify the ways of God to man by implying that adversities are sometimes remedied, and that curses can never rival the steadying power given us when we praise being." John Mort in *Booklist* described *On the Road with the Archangel* thus: "Not Buechner's best, but entertaining and wise, even so." W. Dale Brown in *Christian Century* held that "We have long relied on Frederick Buechner for a good story, and he does not disappoint." Summing up the book, David Stewart wrote in *Christianity Today:* "What it adds up to is an unforgettably funny and lovely picture of unlikely Providence, portraying with extraordinary empathy ordinary, flawed folk who at any given moment have only the vaguest idea of what they are doing, or of the import of their actions for themselves or others," he noted. In the end, Douglas Auchincloss concluded in *Parabola:* "Buechner blesses his readers with two happy endings—one secular and one theological."

In 1998 Buechner published *The Storm,* his fifteenth novel. While some reviewers found it to be his least successful novel, they continued to offer praise for his thoughtful direction and his penchant for offering his readers "the sinful saint," as Gwenette Orr Robertson observed in the *Christian Century.* Maude McDaniel noted in the *World and I:* "Although his nonfiction has always been more satisfying to me, displaying a depth, feeling, and literary virtuosity I do not always find in

his storytelling, his fiction often does a grand job of understanding the very real inability among intellectual moderns . . . to commit to religious conviction." The story involves two elderly brothers, Kenzie and Dalton Maxwell, estranged for many years due to a mistake Kenzie made as a volunteer social worker in a New York City shelter for runaways. The theme echoes William Shakespeare's *The Tempest,* with Kenzie working hard to come to terms with his past and the tragedies therein, yet continuing to exercise his control over the lives of those around him. As Bill Ott wrote in *Booklist,* "Faith is at the core of this novel, as it is in much of Buechner's work, but it is an oddly ambiguous, utterly human kind of faith—characterized not by certainty but by good-humored irony, even world-weariness, and above all, by a profound sense of quiet. Kenzie's belief in God translates, in the minutely observed dailiness of his life, into a belief in what he calls Tendresse oblige, and it is that remarkable tenderness, toward people and things, that envelops this tempestuous tale in an irresistible circle of calm."

The Eyes of the Heart: A Memoir of the Lost and Found and *Speak What We Feel (Not What We Ought to Say): Reflections on Literature and Faith* offer further reflections by Buechner. A *Presbyterian Record* reviewer reflected on *The Eyes of the Heart:* "Perhaps following his own dictum that all true theology at its heart is autobiographical, he has produced this fourth volume. But, of course, it is more than a memoir. It is Buechner reflecting on life and the possibility of life after death." Bryce Christensen and Gilbert Taylor wrote in *Booklist* that, "Without ever leaving the magic kingdom of his personal library, the acclaimed author of religious fiction, meditation, and criticism transports us in multiple directions: back in time to witness his grandparents' wedding in Maine; around the world to relive an eventful trip with his wife; and deep into his own dark childhood to comprehend the shock of his alcoholic father's suicide in a fume-filled garage." They concluded saying, "For those unfamiliar with Buechner, these reflections can only awaken desires to explore his other work." In a *Los Angeles Times* review of *Speak What We Feel,* Bernadette Murphy wrote, "This book is a fitting celebration of the grace, courage, honesty, and yes, of the sacredness inherent in remarkable literature."

In all of his writings, the collections of meditations, autobiographical studies, and fiction, Buechner has proven to many his ability to successfully maintain a literary career that reflects his dual roles as author and minister. Max L. Autrey concluded in the *Dictionary of Literary Biography Yearbook:* "Early appraisals of Buechner's work have proved accurate. After producing ten novels and volumes of nonfiction writings, he has demonstrated his right to be listed among such contemporary writers as Mailer, Ellison, Updike, and Barth. Although his literary appeal has been primarily to the intelligentsia, he is now widely recognized as a brilliant, inspirational writer and an original voice."

BIOGRAPHICAL AND CRITICAL SOURCES:

BOOKS

Aldridge, John W., *After the Lost Generation: A Critical Study of the Writers of Two Wars,* McGraw-Hill (New York, NY), 1951.

Buechner, Frederick, *The Hungering Dark,* Seabury (New York, NY), 1969.

Buechner, Frederick, *The Alphabet of Grace,* Seabury (New York, NY), 1970.

Buechner, Frederick, *The Book of Bebb,* Atheneum (New York, NY), 1979.

Buechner, Frederick, *The Sacred Journey: A Memoir of Early Days,* Atheneum (New York, NY), 1982.

Buechner, Frederick, *Now and Then: A Memoir of Vocation,* Atheneum (New York, NY), 1983.

Contemporary Literary Criticism, Thomson Gale (Detroit, MI), Volume 2, 1974, Volume 4, 1975, Volume 6, 1976, Volume 9, 1978.

Davies, Marie-Helene, *Laughter in a Genevan Gown: The Works of Frederick Buechner, 1970-1980,* Eerdmans (Grand Rapids, MI), 1983.

Dictionary of Literary Biography Yearbook: 1980, Thomson Gale (Detroit, MI), 1981.

Hassan, Ihab, *Radical Innocence: Studies in the Contemporary American Novel,* Princeton University Press (Princeton, NJ), 1961.

PERIODICALS

America, April 14, 1973; December 14, 1974; March 28, 1998, Patricia Allwin DeLeeux, review of *On the Road with the Archangel,* p. 26.

Antioch Review, fall, 1993, p. 659.

Atlantic, February, 1950; March, 1958; September, 1979; December, 1980.

Best Sellers, February 1, 1965; March 1, 1971; February, 1978; December, 1980; June, 1982.

Booklist, October 1, 1997, p. 291; October 1, 1998, John Mort, review of *On the Road with the Archangel,* p. 290; November 15, 1998, Bill Ott, review of *The Storm,* p. 566; October 1, 1999, Bryce Christensen and Gilbert Taylor, review of *The Eyes of*

the Heart: A Memoir of Lost and Found, p. 315; October 1, 1999, John Mort and Gilbert Taylor, review of *The Storm,* p. 324; June 1, 2000, Joanne Wilkinson, review of *The Wizard's Tide,* p. 1850; July, 2001, Bryce Christensen, review of *Speak What We Feel (Not What We Ought to Say): Reflections on Literature and Faith,* p. 1969.

Books and Bookmen, March, 1973.

Books & Culture, March-April, 1997, p. 57.

Boston Herald, January 9, 2000, Eric Convey, "Bridging Heaven and Earth—Author Brings Secular Edge to Religious Writing," p. 3.

Choice, September, 1971; June, 1978.

Christian Century, February 9, 1966; April 1, 1970; September 19, 1973; October 13, 1982; March 23, 1983; December 17, 1997, pp. 1203-1204; November 18, 1998, Gwenette Orr Robertson, review of *The Storm,* p. 1097; March 8, 2000, David M. May, review of *The Eyes of the Heart,* p. 283; September 11, 2002, Richard A. Kauffman, interview with Buechner, p. 26.

Christianity Today, February 9, 1998, David Stewart, review of *On the Road with the Archangel,* p. 74; March, 2003, Wendy Murray Zoba, review of *Speak What We Feel,* p. 56.

Commonweal, July, 1971; February 26, 1982; July 16, 1993, p. 27.

Hudson Review, winter, 1972-73; winter, 1974-75.

Library Journal, January 1, 1952; April 15, 1979; October 15, 1997, p. 90.

Los Angeles Times, September 12, 1980; November 15, 1999, review of *The Eyes of the Heart,* p. 54; September 8, 2001, Bernadette Murphy, review of *Speak What We Feel,* p. B18.

National Review, December 20, 1974.

New Republic, January 25, 1975; September 17, 1977.

Newsweek, February 22, 1971; November 10, 1980.

New Yorker, October 21, 1974.

New York Herald Tribune Book Review, January 13, 1952.

New York Review of Books, July 20, 1972.

New York Times, January 8, 1950; February 16, 1958; May 19, 1972; September 25, 1974.

New York Times Book Review, February 20, 1966; March 2, 1969; December 6, 1970; February 14, 1971; June 11, 1972; May 13, 1973; September 22, 1974; October 30, 1977; November 23, 1980; April 11, 1982; September 19, 1993, p. 32; October 26, 1997, p. 23.

Parabola, fall, 1998, Douglas Auchincloss, review of *On the Road with the Archangel,* p. 118.

Presbyterian Record, March, 2001, review of *The Eyes of the Heart: A Memoir of the Lost and Found,* p. 46.

Publishers Weekly, December 28, 1970; March 29, 1971; June 27, 1977; February 12, 1982; November 3, 1997, p. 79; November 8, 1999, review of *The Eyes of the Heart,* p. 54; July 30, 2001, review of *Speak What We Feel (Not What We Ought to Say),* p. 80.

Reporter, September 9, 1965.

Review of Contemporary Fiction, summer, 1994, p. 205.

San Francisco Chronicle, January 22, 1950.

Saturday Review, January 19, 1952.

Saturday Review/Society, July 29, 1972.

Saturday Review/World, October 5, 1974.

Sojourners, May, 2004, review of *Daily Readings in the ABC's of Faith,* p. 38.

Spectator, July 25, 1952.

Springfield Republican, May 11, 1958.

Time, April 12, 1971; July 3, 1972.

Times Literary Supplement, December 29, 1972; May 23, 1975; May 12, 1978; June 13, 1981.

U.S. Quarterly Book Review, June, 1952.

Virginia Quarterly Review, summer, 1971; autumn, 1972.

Washington Post, July 27, 1987.

Washington Post Book World, May 28, 1972; November 3, 1974; November 9, 1980; June 6, 1982; December 7, 1997, p. 12.

World and I, May, 1999, Maude McDaniel, "An Elusive Grace," review of *The Storm,* p. 278.

ONLINE

Pulpit.org, http://www.pulpit.org/ (April, 2002), "Preaching on Hope."

Wheaton College Web site, http://www.wheaton.edu/ (March 31, 2002), "Frederick Buechner."

*   *   *

BUKOWSKI, Charles 1920-1994

PERSONAL: Born August 16, 1920, in Andernach, Germany; died of leukemia, March 9, 1994, in San Pedro, CA; immigrated to the United States, 1922; married Barbara Fry, October, 1955 (divorced); married Linda Lee Beighle (a health-food proprietor); children: (with Frances Smith) Marina Louise. *Education:* Attended Los Angeles City College, 1939-41. *Hobbies and other interests:* Playing the horses, symphony music.

CAREER: Writer. Worked as an unskilled laborer, beginning 1941, in various positions, including dishwasher, truck driver and loader, mail carrier, guard, gas station attendant, stock boy, warehouse worker, shipping clerk, post office clerk, parking lot attendant, Red Cross orderly, and elevator operator; also worked in dog biscuit factory, slaughterhouse, cake and cookie factory, and hung posters in New York subways. Former editor of *Harlequin* and *Laugh Literary and Man the Humping Guns;* columnist ("Notes of a Dirty Old Man"), *Open City* and *L.A. Free Press.*

AWARDS, HONORS: National Endowment for the Arts grant, 1974; Loujon Press Award; Silver Reel Award, San Francisco Festival of the Arts, for documentary film.

WRITINGS:

POETRY

Flower, Fist, and Bestial Wail, Hearse Press (Eureka, CA), 1959.

Longshot Poems for Broke Players, 7 Poets Press (New York, NY), 1961.

Run with the Hunted, Midwest Poetry Chapbooks (Chicago, IL), 1962.

Poems and Drawings, EPOS (Crescent City, FL), 1962.

It Catches My Heart in Its Hands: New and Selected Poems, 1955-1963, Loujon Press (New Orleans, LA), 1963.

Grip the Walls, Wormwood Review Press (Stockton, CA), 1964.

Cold Dogs in the Courtyard, Literary Times (Chicago, IL), 1965.

Crucifix in a Deathhand: New Poems, 1963-1965, Loujon Press (New Orleans, LA), 1965.

The Genius of the Crowd, 7 Flowers Press (Cleveland, OH), 1966.

True Story, Black Sparrow Press (Santa Rosa, CA), 1966.

On Going out to Get the Mail, Black Sparrow Press (Santa Rosa, CA), 1966.

To Kiss the Worms Goodnight, Black Sparrow Press (Santa Rosa, CA), 1966.

The Girls, Black Sparrow Press (Santa Rosa, CA), 1966.

The Flower Lover, Black Sparrow Press (Santa Rosa, CA), 1966.

Night's Work, Wormwood Review Press, 1966.

2 by Bukowski, Black Sparrow Press (Santa Rosa, CA), 1967.

The Curtains Are Waving, Black Sparrow Press (Santa Rosa, CA), 1967.

At Terror Street and Agony Way, Black Sparrow Press (Santa Rosa, CA), 1968.

Poems Written before Jumping out of an Eight-Story Window, Litmus (Salt Lake City, UT), 1968.

If We Take . . . , Black Sparrow Press (Santa Rosa, CA), 1969.

The Days Run away like Wild Horses over the Hills, Black Sparrow Press (Santa Rosa, CA), 1969, reprinted, 1993.

Another Academy, Black Sparrow Press (Santa Rosa, CA), 1970.

Fire Station, Capricorn Press (Santa Barbara, CA), 1970.

Mockingbird, Wish Me Luck, Black Sparrow Press (Santa Rosa, CA), 1972.

Me and Your Sometimes Love Poems, Kisskill Press (Los Angeles, CA), 1972.

While the Music Played, Black Sparrow Press (Santa Rosa, CA), 1973.

Love Poems to Marina, Black Sparrow Press (Santa Rosa, CA), 1973.

Burning in Water, Drowning in Flame: Selected Poems, 1955-1973, Black Sparrow Press (Santa Rosa, CA), 1974.

Chilled Green, Alternative Press, 1975.

Africa, Paris, Greece, Black Sparrow Press (Santa Rosa, CA), 1975.

Weather Report, Pomegranate Press, 1975.

Winter, No Mountain, 1975.

Tough Company, bound with *The Last Poem* by Diane Wakoski, Black Sparrow Press (Santa Rosa, CA), 1975.

Scarlet, Black Sparrow Press (Santa Rosa, CA), 1976.

Maybe Tomorrow, Black Sparrow Press (Santa Rosa, CA), 1977.

Love Is a Dog from Hell: Poems, 1974-1977, Black Sparrow Press (Santa Rosa, CA), 1977.

Legs, Hips, and Behind, Wormwood Review Press, 1979.

Play the Piano Drunk like a Percussion Instrument until the Fingers Begin to Bleed a Bit, Black Sparrow Press (Santa Rosa, CA), 1979.

A Love Poem, Black Sparrow Press (Santa Rosa, CA), 1979.

Dangling in the Tournefortia, Black Sparrow Press (Santa Rosa, CA), 1981.

The Last Generation, Black Sparrow Press (Santa Rosa, CA), 1982.

Sparks, Black Sparrow Press (Santa Rosa, CA), 1983.

War All the Time: Poems 1981-1984, Black Sparrow Press (Santa Rosa, CA), 1984.

The Roominghouse Madrigals: Early Selected Poems, 1946-1966, Black Sparrow Press (Santa Rosa, CA), 1988.

Beauti-ful and Other Long Poems, Wormwood Books and Magazines, 1988.

People Poems: 1982-1991, Wormwood Books and Magazines, 1991.

The Last Night of the Earth Poems, Black Sparrow Press (Santa Rosa, CA), 1992.

(With Kenneth Price), *Heat Wave,* Black Sparrow Graphic Arts (Santa Rosa, CA), 1995.

Bone Palace Ballet: New Poems, Black Sparrow Press (Santa Rosa, CA), 1997.

The Captain Is out to Lunch and the Sailors Have Taken over the Ship, illustrated by Robert Crumb, Black Sparrow Press (Santa Rosa, CA), 1998.

What Matters Most Is How Well You Walk through the Fire, Black Sparrow Press (Santa Rosa, CA), 1999.

Open All Night: New Poems, Black Sparrow Press (Santa Rosa, CA), 2000.

The Night Torn Mad with Footsteps: New Poems, Black Sparrow Press (Santa Rosa, CA), 2001.

Sifting Through the Madness for the Word, the Line, the Way: New Poems, Ecco (New York, NY), 2003.

The Flash of Lightning behind the Mountain: New Poems, Ecco (New York, NY), 2004.

Slouching Toward Nirvana: New Poems, Ecco (New York, NY), 2005.

NOVELS

Post Office, Black Sparrow Press (Santa Rosa, CA), 1971.

Factotum, Black Sparrow Press (Santa Rosa, CA), 1975.

Women, Black Sparrow Press (Santa Rosa, CA), 1978.

Ham on Rye, Black Sparrow Press (Santa Rosa, CA), 1982, reprinted, with an introduction by Roddy Doyle, Canongate (Edinburgh, Great Britain), 2001.

Horsemeat, Black Sparrow Press (Santa Rosa, CA), 1982.

Hollywood, Black Sparrow Press (Santa Rosa, CA), 1989.

Pulp, Black Sparrow Press (Santa Rosa, CA), 1994.

SHORT STORIES

Notes of a Dirty Old Man, Essex House (North Hollywood, CA), 1969, 2nd edition, 1973.

Erections, Ejaculations, Exhibitions, and General Tales of Ordinary Madness, City Lights (San Francisco, CA), 1972, abridged edition published as *Life and Death in the Charity Ward,* London Magazine Editions (London, England), 1974, selections edited by Gail Ghiarello published as *Tales of Ordinary Mad-*

ness and *The Most Beautiful Woman in Town, and Other Stories,* two volumes, City Lights (San Francisco, CA), 1983.

South of No North: Stories of the Buried Life, Black Sparrow Press (Santa Rosa, CA), 1973.

Bring Me Your Love, illustrated by R. Crumb, Black Sparrow Press (Santa Rosa, CA), 1983.

Hot Water Music, Black Sparrow Press (Santa Rosa, CA), 1983.

There's No Business, Black Sparrow Press (Santa Rosa, CA), 1984.

OTHER

Confessions of a Man Insane Enough to Live with Beasts, Mimeo Press (Bensenville, IL), 1966.

All the Assholes in the World and Mine, Open Skull Press (Bensenville, IL), 1966.

A Bukowski Sampler, edited by Douglas Blazek, Quixote Press (Madison, WI), 1969.

(Compiler, with Neeli Cherry and Paul Vangelisti) *Anthology of L.A. Poets,* Laugh Literary (Los Angeles, CA), 1972.

Art, Black Sparrow Press (Santa Rosa, CA), 1977.

What They Want, Neville (Santa Barbara, CA), 1977.

We'll Take Them, Black Sparrow Press (Santa Rosa, CA), 1978.

You Kissed Lilly, Black Sparrow Press (Santa Rosa, CA), 1978.

Shakespeare Never Did This, City Lights (San Francisco, CA), 1979.

(With Al Purdy) *The Bukowski/Purdy Letters: A Decade of Dialogue, 1964-1974,* edited by Seamus Cooney, Paget Press (Ontario, Canada), 1983.

Under the Influence: A Charles Bukowski Checklist, Water Row Press (Sudbury, MA), 1984.

You Get so Alone at Times That It Just Makes Sense, Black Sparrow Press (Santa Rosa, CA), 1986.

(Author of preface) Jack Micheline, *River of Red Wine,* Water Row Press (Sudbury, MA), 1986.

Barfly (screenplay based on Bukowski's life), Cannon Group, 1987, published as *The Movie "Barfly": An Original Screenplay by Charles Bukowski for a Film by Barbet Schroeder,* Black Sparrow Press (Santa Rosa, CA), 1987.

A Visitor Complains of My Disenfranchise (limited edition), Illuminati, 1987.

Bukowski at Bellevue (video cassette of poetry reading; broadcast on EZTV, West Hollywood, CA, 1988), Black Sparrow Press (Santa Rosa, CA), 1988.

Septuagenarian Stew: Stories and Poems, Black Sparrow Press (Santa Rosa, CA), 1990.

(Author of preface) John Fante, *Ask the Dust,* Black Sparrow Press (Santa Rosa, CA), 1993.

Run with the Hunted: A Charles Bukowski Reader, edited by John Martin, Harper Collins (New York, NY), 1993.

Screams from the Balcony: Selected Letters 1960-1970 (autobiography), Black Sparrow Press (Santa Rosa, CA), 1994.

(Author of foreword) Steve Richmond, *Hitler Painted Roses,* Sun Dog Press (Northville, MI), 1994.

Confession of a Coward, Black Sparrow Press (Santa Rosa, CA), 1995.

(Editor) Seamus Cooney, *Living on Luck: Selected Letters, 1960s-1970s, Volume 2,* Black Sparrow Press (Santa Rosa, CA), 1995.

Betting on the Muse: Poems & Stories, Black Sparrow Press (Santa Rosa, CA), 1996.

Reach for the Sun: Selected Letters, 1978-1994, edited by Seamus Cooney, Black Sparrow Press (Santa Rosa, CA), 1999.

(With Fernada Pivano) *Charles Bukowski: Laughing with the Gods* (interview), Sun Dog Press (Northville, MI), 2000.

Beerspit Night and Cursing: The Correspondence of Charles Bukowski and Sheri Martinelli, 1960-1967, edited by Steven Moore, Black Sparrow Press (Santa Rosa, CA), 2001.

Sunlight Here I Am: Interviews and Encounters, 1963-1993, edited by David Stephen Calonne, Sun Dog Press (Northville, MI), 2003.

Also author of the short story "The Copulating Mermaids of Venice, California." Work represented in anthologies, including *Penguin Modern Poets 13,* 1969, *Six Poets,* 1979, and *Notes from the Underground,* edited by John Bryan. Also author of a one-hour documentary film, produced by KCET public television, Los Angeles. A collection of Bukowski's papers is housed at the University of California—Santa Barbara.

ADAPTATIONS: Stories from *Erections, Ejaculations, Exhibitions, and General Tales of Ordinary Madness* were adapted by Marco Ferreri, Sergio Amidei, and Anthony Foutz into the film *Tales of Ordinary Madness,* Fred Baker, 1983; a film adaptation of *Love Is a Dog from Hell* was produced in 1988; *The Works of Charles Bukowski,* based upon more than thirty of his works published by Black Sparrow Press, was staged by California State University in Los Angeles, 1988; *Crazy Love,* based on *The Copulating Mermaids of Venice, California,* was filmed in 1989.

SIDELIGHTS: Charles Bukowski was a prolific underground writer who depicted in his poetry and prose the depraved metropolitan environments of the downtrodden in American society. A cult hero, Bukowski relied on experience, emotion, and imagination in his works, often using direct language and violent and sexual imagery. While some critics found his style offensive, others claimed that Bukowski satirized the machismo attitude through his routine use of sex, alcohol abuse, and violence. "Without trying to make himself look good, much less heroic, Bukowski writes with a nothing-to-lose truthfulness which sets him apart from most other 'autobiographical' novelists and poets," commented Stephen Kessler in the *San Francisco Review of Books,* adding: "Firmly in the American tradition of the maverick, Bukowski writes with no apologies from the frayed edge of society, beyond or beneath respectability, revealing nasty and alarming underviews." Michael Lally, writing in *Village Voice,* maintained that "Bukowski is . . . a phenomenon. He has established himself as a writer with a consistent and insistent style based on what he projects as his 'personality,' the result of hard, intense living."

Bukowski had "a sandblasted face, warts on his eyelids and a dominating nose that looks as if it were assembled in a junkyard from Studebaker hoods and Buick fenders," described Paul Ciotti in the *Los Angeles Times Magazine.* "Yet his voice is so soft and bemused that it's hard to take him seriously when he says: 'I don't like people. I don't even like myself. There must be something wrong with me.'" Born in Germany, Bukowski was brought to the United States at the age of two. His father believed in firm discipline and often beat Bukowski for the smallest offenses. A slight child, Bukowski was also bullied by boys his own age, and was frequently rejected by girls because of his bad complexion. "When Bukowski was thirteen," wrote Ciotti, "one of [his friends] invited him to his father's wine cellar and served him his first drink of alcohol. 'It was magic,' Bukowski would later write. 'Why hadn't someone told me?'"

In 1939, Bukowski began attending Los Angeles City College, dropping out at the beginning of World War II and moving to New York to become a writer. The next few years were spent writing and traveling and collecting numerous rejection slips. By 1946 Bukowski had decided to give up his writing aspirations and went on a drinking binge that took him all over the world and lasted for approximately ten years. Ending up near death, Bukowski's life changed and he started writing again. "If a writer must sample life at its most elemental, then surely Bukowski qualifies as a laureate of poetic preparedness," observed Bob Graalman in the *Dictionary of Literary Biography.* Bukowski's many jobs over the years included stock boy, dishwasher, postal

clerk, and factory worker. He did not begin his professional writing career until the age of thirty-five, and like other contemporaries, Bukowski began by publishing in underground newspapers, especially in his local papers, *Open City* and the *L.A. Free Press.* "It is tempting to make correlations between [Bukowski's] emergence in Los Angeles literary circles and the arrival of the 1960s, when poets were still shaking hands with Allen Ginsberg and other poets of his generation while younger activist poets tapped on their shoulders, begging for an introduction," explained Graalman. "Bukowski cultivated his obvious link to both eras—the blackness and despair of the 1950s with the rebellious cry of the 1960s for freedom."

"Published by small, underground presses and ephemeral mimeographed little magazines," described Jay Dougherty in *Contemporary Novelists,* "Bukowski has gained popularity, in a sense, through word of mouth." Many of his fans regarded him as one of the best of the Meat School poets, who are known for their tough and direct masculine writing. "The main character in his poems and short stories, which are largely autobiographical, is usually a down-and-out writer [Henry Chinaski] who spends his time working at marginal jobs (and getting fired from them), getting drunk and making love with a succession of bimbos and floozies," related Ciotti. "Otherwise, he hangs out with fellow losers—whores, pimps, alcoholics, drifters, the people who lose their rent money at the race track, leave notes of goodbye on dressers and have flat tires on the freeway at 3 a.m."

After his first book of poetry was published in 1959, Bukowski wrote more than forty others. Ciotti maintained: "Right from the beginning, Bukowski knew that if a poet wants to be read, he has to be noticed first. 'So,' he once said, 'I got my act up. I wrote vile (but interesting) stuff that made people hate me, that made them curious about this Bukowski. I threw bodies off my porch into the night. I sneered at hippies. I was in and out of drunk tanks. A lady accused me of rape.'"

Flower, Fist, and Bestial Wail, Bukowski's first book of poetry, covers the major interests and themes that occupy many of his works, the most important being "the sense of a desolate, abandoned world," as R.R. Cuscaden pointed out in the *Outsider.* In addition to this sense of desolation, Bukowski also filled his free verse with all the absurdities of life, especially in relation to death. "Bukowski's world, scored and grooved by the impersonal instruments of civilized industrial society, by twentieth-century knowledge and experience, remains essentially a world in which meditation and analysis have little part," asserted John William Corrington in *Northwest Review.* Among the subjects which are used to describe this bleak world are drinking, sex, gambling, and music. The actual style of these numerous poems, however, has its virtues, including "a crisp, hard voice; an excellent ear and eye for measuring out the lengths of lines; and an avoidance of metaphor where a lively anecdote will do the same dramatic work," maintained Ken Tucker in *Village Voice. It Catches My Heart in Its Hands,* published in 1963, collects poetry written by Bukowski between the years of 1955 and 1963. "Individual poems merge to form together a body of work unrivalled in kind and very nearly unequalled in quality by Bukowski's contemporaries," stated Corrington. The poems touch on topics that were familiar to Bukowski, such as rerolling cigarette butts, the horse that came in, a hundred-dollar call girl, and a rumpled hitchhiker on his way to nowhere. *It Catches My Heart in Its Hands* contains poems which "are energetic, tough, and unnerving," related Dabney Stuart in *Poetry.* Kenneth Rexroth asserted in the *New York Times Book Review* that Bukowski "belongs in the small company of poets of real, not literary, alienation."

Subsequent works, such as *Dangling in the Tournefortia,* addressed subjects similar to those in his first collection. "Low-life bard of Los Angeles, Mr. Bukowski has nothing new for us here," observed Peter Schjeldahl in the *New York Times Book Review,* "simply more and still more accounts in free verse of his follies with alcohol and women and of fellow losers hitting bottom and somehow discovering new ways to continue falling." Despite the subject matter, though, Schjeldahl found himself enjoying the poems in *Dangling in the Tournefortia.* "Bukowski writes well," he continued, "with ear-pleasing cadences, wit and perfect clarity, which are all the more beguiling for issuing from a stumblebum persona. His grace with words gives a comic gleam to even his meanest revelations." William Logan, writing in the *Times Literary Supplement,* concluded: "Life here has almost entirely mastered art."

Similar to his poetry in subject matter, Bukowski's short stories also deal with sex, violence, and the absurdities of life. In his first collection of short stories, *Erections, Ejaculations, Exhibitions, and General Tales of Ordinary Madness,* Bukowski "writes as an unregenerate lowbrow contemptuous of our claims to superior being," stated Thomas R. Edwards in the *New York Review of Books.* On the other hand, Peter Ackroyd maintained in the *Spectator,* "A dull character finally emerges, and it is a dullness which spreads through these stories like a stain." Edwards, however, concluded

that "in some of these sad and funny stories [Bukowski's] status as a relic isn't wholly without its sanctity."

The protagonists in the stories in *Hot Water Music,* published in 1983, live in cheap hotels and are often struggling underground writers, similar to Bukowski himself. Bukowski's main autobiographical figure is Henry Chinaski, who appears in a few of these stories and in many of his novels. Among the semi-autobiographical stories in this collection are two which deal with events following the funeral of Bukowski's father. The other stories deal with numerous violent acts, including a jealous wife shooting her husband over an old infidelity, a drunk bank manager molesting young children, a former stripper mutilating the man she is seducing, and a young man who gets over his impotence by raping a neighbor in his apartment elevator. "Lives of quiet desperation explode in apparently random and unmotivated acts of bizarre violence," described Michael F. Harper in the *Los Angeles Times Book Review,* adding: "There is certainly a raw power in these stories, but Bukowski's hard-boiled fatalism seems to me the flip side of the humanism he denies and therefore just as false as the sentimentality he ridicules." Erling Friis-Baastad, writing in the Toronto *Globe and Mail,* concluded, "In his best work, Bukowski comes close to making us comprehend, if not the sense of it all, then at least its intensity. He cannot forget, and he will not let us forget, that every morning at 3 a.m. broken people lie 'in their beds, trying in vain to sleep, and deserving that rest, if they could find it.'"

Bukowski continued his examination of "broken people" in such novels as *Post Office* and *Ham on Rye.* In *Post Office,* Henry Chinaski is very similar to ex-postman Bukowski; he is a remorseless drunk and womanizer who spends a lot of time at the race track. Chinaski also has to deal with his monotonous and strenuous job, as well as a number of harassing supervisors. Eventually marrying a rich nymphomaniac from Texas, Chinaski is inevitably dumped for another man and finds himself back at the post office. "Bukowski's loser's string of anecdotes, convulsively funny and also sad, is unflagging entertainment but in the end doesn't add up to more than the sum of its parts, somehow missing the novelist's alchemy," stated a *Times Literary Supplement* contributor. But Valentine Cunningham, also writing in the *Times Literary Supplement,* saw the novel as a success: "Pressed in by Post Office bureaucrats, their mean-minded regulations and their heaps of paperwork, the misfit [Chinaski] looks frequently like an angel of light. His refusal to play respectability ball with the cajoling, abusive, never-take-no-for-an-answer loops who own the mailboxes he attends . . . can make even this ribald mess of a wretch seem a shining haven of sanity in the prevailing Los Angeles grimnesses."

Ham on Rye, published in 1982, once again features Henry Chinaski as its protagonist. Bukowski travels into new territory with this novel, describing his/Chinaski's childhood and adolescent years. The first part of the book is dominated by Chinaski's brutal and domineering father, focusing more on Henry as he moves into his lonely and isolated adolescent years. Following high school, Chinaski holds a job and attends college for a short period of time before beginning his "real" life of cheap hotels, sleazy bars, and the track. It is also at this time that Henry starts to send stories to magazines and accumulate a number of rejection slips. "Particularly striking is Bukowski's uncharacteristic restraint: the prose is hard and exact, the writer's impulse towards egocentricity repressed," commented David Montrose in the *Times Literary Supplement*. Ben Reuven, writing in the *Los Angeles Times Book Review,* described the "first-person reminiscences" in *Ham on Rye* as being "taut, vivid, intense, sometimes poignant, [and] often hilarious," concluding that Bukowski's "prose has never been more vigorous or more powerful."

Continuing the examination of his younger years, Bukowski wrote the screenplay for the movie *Barfly,* which was released in 1987, starring Mickey Rourke. The movie focuses on three days in the life of Bukowski at the age of twenty-four. As the lead character, Henry Chinaski, Rourke spends most of these three days in a seedy bar, where he meets the first real love of his life, Wanda, played by Faye Dunaway. While this new romance is developing, a beautiful literary editor takes an interest in Chinaski's writings and tries to seduce him with success. Chinaski must then choose between the two women. "At first *Barfly* seems merely a slice of particularly wretched life," observed David Ansen in *Newsweek*. "But under its seedy surface emerges a cunning comedy—and a touching love story." Vincent Canby, writing in the *New York Times,* saw the film as dealing "in the continuing revelation of character in a succession of horrifying, buoyant, crazy confrontations of barflies, bartenders, police and other representatives of the world of the sober." Michael Wilmington concluded in the *Los Angeles Times:* "Whatever its flaws, [*Barfly*] does something more films should do: It opens up territory, opens up a human being. The worst of it has the edge of coughed-up whimsy and barroom bragging. But the best has the shock of truth and the harsh sweet kiss of dreams."

Bukowski's experiences with the making of *Barfly* became the basis of his novel *Hollywood*. Chinaski is now an old man, married to Sarah, a shrewd woman apt to interrupt him during his many repetitive stories. The couple is off hard liquor, but are faithful drinkers of good red wine, and their life is a peaceful one until a filmmaker asks Chinaski to write a screenplay based upon his previous lifestyle; he agrees, figuring that this new venture will leave him enough time to spend at the track. Entering the world of show business, Chinaski finds himself mingling with famous stars, but must also deal with a number of other things, including a tax man (who advises him to spend his advance money before the government can get it). As the project progresses, its funding becomes shaky, the producer threatens to dismember parts of his body if the movie is not made, there are many rewrites, and Chinaski is hit with a terrible sadness. The movie is about what he used to be—a poetic barfly—and covers a time in his life when he feels he did his best writing. An old man now, Chinaski can watch his life being acted out at the movies, but he cannot jump back into it; he is now a successful man leading a respectable life. "The words often jar and Bukowski is better when he lets his dialogue do his griping for him. But this is still a superb snapshot of what filmmaking at the fag-end of the Hollywood dream is all about," said Toby Moore in *Times Literary Supplement*. Gary Dretzka, writing in the *Chicago Tribune,* asserted that "Bukowski offers an often insightful and continually outrageous view of how some movies get made." Dretzka went on to advise: "Have some fun: Read this book, then go out and rent the *Barfly* video. Grab a beer and offer a toast to Charles Bukowski . . . survivor."

Like Dretzka, Kessler also believed in Bukowski's survival abilities, concluding that he "is a soulful poet whose art is an ongoing testimony to perseverance. It's not the drinking and f—ing and gambling and fighting and shitting that make his books valuable, but the meticulous attention to the most mundane experience, the crusty compassion for his fellow losers, the implicit conviction that by frankly telling the unglamorous facts of hopelessness some stamina and courage can be cultivated."

Pulp, published posthumously, is the novel Bukowski worked on just prior to his death in 1994 from leukemia. It is a send-up, Bukowski-style, of the pulp detective novel. His protagonist, not surprisingly a Bukowski-like character, is Nicky Belane, who sometimes wonders if he is Harry Martel. Like any good pulp detective, Belane has a series of clients including Lady Death (looking for Celine, who has been spotted in Los Angeles bookstores), John Barton (looking for the Red Sparrow, which is a play on Bukowski's publisher John Martin of Black Sparrow Press), and a host of others, whose stories come together in the final pages. George Stade commented in the *New York Times Book Review,* "It does not, of course, take much to send up the hard-boiled detective novel. . . . The conventions . . . seem to mock themselves, if you stand back a bit. But *Pulp* does more than stand back from itself." Daniel Woodreli, writing in *Washington Post Book World,* also found Bukowski's reworking of a time-honored form refreshing: "The hard-boiled form as a framework is nicely utilized, with snappy dialogue that is always off-center, and oddly very honest." He continued, "[Bukowski] treats it with a kind of poignant ridicule that somehow works. *Pulp* is comic and bizarre and sad without a trace of self-pity."

Dick Lochte, in the *Los Angeles Times Book Review,* called *Pulp* "a whimsical and oddly charming (a word not often used in describing Bukowski's work) spoof." *Chicago Tribune* contributor John Litweller similarly offered high praise: "Thriller novel realism never got 'down' like Bukowski's writing usually did. The result is more fun than an ordinary parody." Stade found deeper significance in the novel beyond its form, stating that "as parody, *Pulp* does not cut very deep. As a fare-well to readers, as a gesture of rapprochement with death, as Bukowski's send-up and send-off of himself, this bio-parable cuts as deep as you would want." Litweller concluded, "Maybe some readers hung up on the young, low-life Bukowski will be disappointed. . . . For the rest of us, it's masterly stuff from the old master in his old age."

Run with the Hunted is an anthology of Bukowski's stories and poetry, placed chronologically in the periods in which they were set (not published). It provides a solid overview of Bukowski's work and—given its autobiographical nature—his life. "An effective primer for the uninitiated, or a refresher for past readers who, incredibly, have managed to forget," commented a *Publishers Weekly* contributor. Benjamin Segedin, writing in *Booklist,* wrote of Bukowski's works: "Less celebrations of self-destruction than honest self-portraiture, they reveal him in all his ugliness as an outsider on the verge of respectability." Segedin continued, "Here is a collection of blunt, hard-edged angry stuff as uncompromising as you will ever hope to find." Elizabeth Young in *New Statesman & Society* at once lauded and criticized the anthology, saying, "From the vast vat of Bukowski homebrew, John Martin has distilled a cut-glass decanter of one-hundred-proof literary perfection. . . . [He] has done Bukowski a great service—and a sort of disservice too. After such a brilliantly constructed anthology, who is going to read all the books?" Bukowski's previously unpublished work, introduced posthumously by Black Sparrow Press in *Betting on the Muse: Poems & Stories,* shows him to have continued in the same vein with the character Henry Chinaski, as well as with the verse that made him, according to a *Publishers Weekly* contributor, the "original take-no-prisoners poet." Ray Olson, writing for *Booklist,* found his stories and poems to be "effortlessly, magnetically readable, especially if you are susceptible to their bargain-basement existentialist charm."

Bukowski's life via his letters is chronicled in *Screams from the Balcony: Selected Letters 1960-1970.* "The honesty, humor and lack of pretension in these letters make them a must for Bukowski fans and an engaging read for anyone interested in literary lives," wrote a *Publishers Weekly* reviewer. Segedin, in *Booklist,* spoke for occasional readers and fans alike, finding Bukowski "perversely intriguing, attracting the kind of attention one usually reserves for grisly train wrecks." *Screams from the Balcony* was followed by *Reach for the Sun: Selected Letters, 1978-1994,* which covered the last years of the poet's life. In letters to his publishers, editors, friends, and fellow poets, Bukowski railed against critics, praised the writers who first inspired him, and wrote a great deal about three of his favorite subjects: drinking, women, and the racetrack. "Above all, however, they reveal a man dedicated to his craft," noted William Gargan in *Library Journal.*

Still more new work was published posthumously with the poetry collections *What Matters Most Is How Well You Walk through the Fire* and *Open All Night: New Poems.* Reviewing the former, *Booklist* contributor Olson maintained: "If Bukowski's stuff appeals to you at all, [*What Matters Most*] should be gratifying as all get-out." *Open All Night* was judged somewhat less than the poet's best work by Olson in another *Booklist* article, but while he noted that "there are better books for one's first taste of Bukowski," he added that "this one will do fine for connoisseurs." A *Publishers Weekly* reviewer commented similarly: "Nobody will be converted to Bukowski by these verses, but that's hardly the point: like William Burroughs or Jim Morrison, Bukowski in death retains the tenacious (and mostly youthful) fan base he gathered in life."

An intimate look into Bukowski's last days is provided by *The Captain Is out to Lunch and the Sailors Have Taken over the Ship,* a collection of journal entries from the poet's last years. It begins with his usual celebrations and ruminations on gambling, women, and drinking, but takes on "tragic overtones" as the writer comes to terms with his diagnosis of leukemia, reported Gerald Locklin in *Review of Contemporary Fiction.* "These reflections approaching endgame reveal the complex humanity of a too-often caricatured figure who beat seemingly prohibitive odds to achieve the destiny he came to embrace as a world-class writer of uncompromising novels, stories, and poems." *Booklist* contributor Mike Tribby also recommended *The Captain Is out* as a fine portrait of the "cranky, sardonic, insightful master of gritty expression whose roaring public appearances of the '60s triggered the rebirth of poetry as performance."

Although Bukowski once toiled in obscurity, his memory and his works have continued to reach a wide audience. For example, in 2004, a documentary about the author titled *Bukowski: Born Into This,* was made by John Dullaghan. The film followed upon a steady stream of published works and correspondence by the author, including *Beerspit Night and Cursing: The Correspondence of Charles Bukowski and Sheri Martinelli, 1960-1967.* Published in 2001, the volume presents Bukowski's correspondence with the New York editor that he never met face-to-face. A *Publishers Weekly* contributor called the letters "wacky, outrageous, often oddly intellectual" and said the volume was required reading for Bukowski fans. In 2003 and 2004 two new volumes of Bukowski's previously unpublished poems were made available. In a review of *Sifting Through the Madness for the Word, the Line, the Way: New Poems, Booklist* contributor Olson called the poems "the most purely enjoyable entries in the Bukowski canon." In another review in *Booklist* of *The Flash of Lightning behind the Mountain: New Poems,* Olson pointed out that most of the poems seem to have been written very late in Bukowski's life, including a poem about his hospitalization for leukemia. Olson also noted that the poet "rouses the impulse to feel for him, not just laugh with him. This is mellow Buk. Fancy that!"

In an article in *Interview,* Mickey Rourke, who starred in the film *Barfly,* recalled visiting Bukowski in his San Pedro home and learning about the writer's commitment to his art. Rourke was a little surprised that Bukowski lived in such a nice place because of the writer's reputation. But, when Rourke was shown where Bukowski wrote, he was more amazed to find the room literally torn apart. "The floorboards were sticking up, the walls were destroyed," recalled Rourke. "So you've got this pristine house and then you see this tiny little room, which we've all lived in at some point, and it was truly like a shanty. Some people see Charles as a mad genius, but there was also a regimented discipline to him because in doing that to his room, he constructed a place where he could be creative."

BIOGRAPHICAL AND CRITICAL SOURCES:

BOOKS

Brewer, Gay, *Charles Bukowski,* Twayne (New York, NY), 1997.

Cherkovski, Neeli, *Bukowski: A Life,* Steerforth Press (South Royalton, VT), 1997.

Christy, Jim, *The Buk Book: Musings on Charles Bukowski,* ECW Press (Toronto, Ontario, Canada), 1997.

Contemporary Literary Criticism, Thomson Gale (Detroit, MI), Volume 2, 1974, Volume 5, 1976, Volume 9, 1978, Volume 41, 1987, Volume 82, 1994.

Contemporary Novelists, 4th edition, edited by D.L. Kirkpatrick, St. James Press (Detroit, MI), 1986.

Dictionary of Literary Biography, Volume 5: *American Poets since World War II,* Thomson Gale (Detroit, MI), 1980.

Dorbin, Sanford, *A Bibliography of Charles Bukowski,* Black Sparrow Press (Santa Rosa, CA), 1969.

Fox, Hugh, *Charles Bukowski: A Critical and Bibliographical Study,* Abyss Publications, 1969.

Harrison, Russell, *Against the American Dream: Essays on Charles Bukowski,* Black Sparrow Press (Santa Rosa, CA), 1994.

Richmond, Steve, *Spinning off Bukowski,* Sun Dog Press (Northville, MI), 1996.

Sherman, Jory, *Bukowski: Friendship, Fame, and Bestial Myth,* Blue Horse Press, 1982.

Weinberg, Jeffrey, editor, *A Charles Bukowski Checklist,* Water Row Press, 1987.

PERIODICALS

Booklist, February 15, 1993, p. 1010; January 15, 1994, Benjamin Segedin, review of *Screams from the Balcony: Selected Letters, 1960-1970,* p. 893; May 15, 1996, p. 1563; May 15, 1998, Mike Tribby, review of *The Captain Is out to Lunch and the Sailors Have Taken over the Ship,* p. 1587; December 15, 1999, Ray Olsen, review of *What Matters Most Is How Well You Walk through the Fire,* p. 752; December 1, 2000, Ray Olson, review of *Open All Night: New Poems,* p. 689; January 1, 2003, Ray Olson, review of *Sifting through the Madness for the Word, the Line, the Way,* p. 836; December 1, 2003, Ray Olson, review of *The Flash of Lightning behind the Mountain: New Poems,* p. 635.

Bookwatch, July, 1998, review of *The Captain Is out to Lunch and the Sailors Have Taken over the Ship,* p. 1.

Chicago Tribune, July 18, 1989; August 28, 1994, George Litweller, review of *Pulp,* p. 6.

Globe and Mail (Toronto, Ontario, Canada), January 21, 1984.

Interview, June, 2004, Mickey Rourke, brief article, p. 28.

Kliatt, January, 1998, review of *Bone Palace Ballet,* p. 21.

Library Journal, July, 1999, William Gargan, review of *Reach for the Sun: Selected Letters, 1978-1994,* p. 89; January, 2003, Rochelle Ratner, review of *Sifting through the Madness for the Word, the Line, the Way,* p. 114.

Los Angeles Magazine, June, 1994, p. 76.

Los Angeles Times, March 17, 1983; November 3, 1987; November 5, 1987; September 23, 1988.

Los Angeles Times Book Review, October 3, 1982, p. 6; August 28, 1983, p. 6; December 11, 1983, p. 2; March 17, 1985, p. 4; June 4, 1989, p. 4; October 30, 1994, Dick Lochte, review of *Pulp,* p. 11.

Los Angeles Times Magazine, March 22, 1987, pp. 12-14, 17-19, 23.

New Statesman & Society, June 17, 1994, p. 37.

Newsweek, October 26, 1987, David Ansen, review of *Barfly,* p. 86.

New York Review of Books, October 5, 1972, pp. 21-23.

New York Times, September 30, 1987, Vincent Canby, review of *Barfly.*

New York Times Book Review, July 5, 1964, p. 5; January 17, 1982, pp. 13, 16; June 11, 1989, p. 11; November 25, 1990, p. 19; June 5, 1994, George Stade, review of *Pulp,* p. 50; December 26, 1999, review of *What Matters Most Is How Well You Walk through the Fire,* p. 16; January 7, 2001, Kera Bolonik, review of *Open All Night: New Poems,* p. 18.

Northwest Review, fall, 1963, pp. 123-129.

Outsider, spring, 1963, R.R. Cuscaden, pp. 62-65.

People, November 16, 1987, pp. 79-80.

Poetry, July, 1964, pp. 258-264; May, 2001, David Yezzi, review of *Open All Night: New Poems,* p. 105.

Publishers Weekly, March 29, 1993, p. 34; December 20, 1993, p. 62; April 29, 1996, p. 66; April 20, 1998, review of *The Captain Is out to Lunch and the Sailors Have Taken over the Ship,* p. 60; December 6, 1999, review of *What Matters Most Is How Well You Walk through the Fire,* p. 74; November 20, 2000, review of *Open All Night: New Poems,* p. 65; May 28, 2001, review of *Beerspit Night and Cursing: The Correspondence of Charles Bukowski and Sheri Martinelli,* p. 63.

Review of Contemporary Fiction, fall, 1985, pp. 56-59; fall, 1998, Gerald Locklin, review of *The Captain Is out to Lunch and the Sailors Have Taken over the Ship,* p. 237.

San Francisco Review of Books, January-February, 1983, Stephen Kessler, p. 11.

Spectator, November 30, 1974.

Times (London, England), March 3, 1988; July 8, 1989.

Times Literary Supplement, April 5, 1974, p. 375; June 20, 1980, p. 706; September 4, 1981, p. 1000; November 12, 1982, p. 1251; December 3, 1982, p. 1344; May 4, 1984, p. 486; August 11, 1989, p. 877; September 7, 1990, p. 956.

Village Voice, March 26, 1964, pp. 11-12; February 20, 1978, pp. 89-90; March 23, 1982, pp. 42-43.

Washington Post, November 20, 1987.

Washington Post Book World, July 14, 1994, Daniel Woodreli, review of *Pulp,* p. 2.

ONLINE

Books and Writers, http://www.kirjasto.sci.fi/ (February 20, 2001), "Charles Bukowski."

OTHER

Bukowski: Born Into This (documentary), Magnolia Pictures, 2004.

OBITUARIES:

PERIODICALS

Chicago Tribune, March 11, 1994, p. 12.

Entertainment Weekly, March 25, 1994, p. 49.

Facts on File, March 17, 1994, p. 196.

Los Angeles Times, March 10, 1994, p. 1, 24.

New York Times, March 11, 1994, p. B9.

Time, March 21, 1994, p. 26.

Times (London, England), March 11, 1994, p. 23.

Variety, March 14, 1994, p. 67.

Washington Post, March 11, 1994, p. B5.

*   *   *

BULLINS, Ed 1935-
(Kingsley B. Bass, Jr.)

PERSONAL: Born July 2, 1935, in Philadelphia, PA; son of Edward and Bertha Marie (Queen) Bullins; married; wife's name Trixie. *Education:* Attended Los Angeles City College, San Francisco State College (now

University), New York School of Visual Arts, New School Extension, Vista College, and University of California Berkeley Extension; William Penn Business Institute, general business certificate; Antioch University, B.A., 1989; Sonoma State University, B.A. candidate; San Francisco State University, M.F.A., 1994.

ADDRESSES: Home—3629 San Pablo Ave., Emeryville, CA 94608. *Agent*—Helen Merrill, 435 West 23rd St., No. 1A, New York, NY 10011.

CAREER: Black Arts/West, San Francisco, CA, cofounder and producer, 1965-67; Black Arts Alliance, cofounder, Black House (Black Panther Party headquarters in San Francisco), cultural director until 1967, also serving briefly as Minister of Culture of the Party. New Lafayette Theatre, New York, NY, joined, 1967, playwright-in-residence, 1968, associate director, 1971-73; American Place Theatre, playwright in residence, beginning 1973; The Surviving Theatre, producing director, beginning 1974; New York Shakespeare Festival, writers unit coordinator, 1975-82; Berkeley Black Repertory, public relations director, 1982; Magic Theatre, public relations director, 1982-83; Julian Theatre, group sales coordinator, 1983. Instructor in playwriting and black theater at various colleges, universities, and workshops, 1971-79; School for Continuing Education, New York University, instructor, 1979; Dramatic Writing Department, New York University, instructor, 1981; Summer Playwrights Conference, Hofstra University, New York, instructor, 1982; People's School of Dramatic Arts, San Francisco, playwriting teacher, 1983; Bay Area Playwrights Festival, Mill Valley, CA, summer drama workshop leader, 1983; City College of San Francisco, instructor in dramatic performance, play directing, and playwriting, 1984-88; Antioch University, instructor in playwriting and administrative assistant in public information and recruitment, 1986-87; Bullins Memorial Theatre, Emeryville, CA, producer and playwright, 1988; Antioch University, San Francisco, student instructor in playwriting, 1986-87; American Multicultural Studies Department, Sonoma State University, Rohnert Park, CA, lecturer, 1988—; Afro-American Studies Department, University of California—Berkeley, lecturer, 1988—; African American Humanities/Afro-American Theatre, Contra Costa College, instructor, 1989-94; Northeastern University, Boston, MA, professor of theater, 1995—. *Military service:* Served in the U.S. Navy, 1952-55.

MEMBER: Dramatists Guild.

AWARDS, HONORS: American Place Theatre grant, 1967; Vernon Rice Drama Desk Award, 1968, for plays performed at American Place Theatre; four Rockefeller Foundation grants, including 1968, 1970, and 1973; Off-Broadway Award for distinguished playwriting, *Village Voice,* and Black Arts Alliance award, both 1971, both for *The Fabulous Miss Marie* and *In New England Winter;* Guggenheim fellowship for playwriting, 1971 and 1976; National Endowment for the Arts playwriting grant, 1972, 1989; grant from Creative Artists Public Service Program, 1973, in support of playwriting; Off-Broadway Award for distinguished playwriting, and New York Drama Critics Circle Award, both 1975, both for *The Taking of Miss Janie;* third Off-Broadway Award; AUDELCO award, Harlem Theater; Litt.D., Columbia College (Chicago, IL), 1976.

WRITINGS:

PUBLISHED PLAYS

How Do You Do?: A Nonsense Drama (one-act; first produced as *How Do You Do* in San Francisco, CA, at Firehouse Repertory Theatre, August 5, 1965; produced off-Broadway at La Mama Experimental Theatre Club, February, 1972), Illuminations Press, 1967.

(Editor and contributor) *New Plays from the Black Theatre* (includes *In New England Winter* [one-act; first produced off-Broadway at New Federal Theatre of Henry Street Playhouse, January 26, 1971]), Bantam (New York, NY), 1969.

Five Plays (includes: *Goin 'a Buffalo* [three-act; first produced in New York, NY, at American Place Theatre, June 6, 1968], *In the Wine Time* [three-act; first produced at New Lafayette Theatre, December 10, 1968], *A Son, Come Home* [one-act; first produced off-Broadway at American Place Theatre, February 21, 1968; originally published in *Negro Digest,* April, 1968], *The Electronic Nigger* [one-act; first produced at American Place Theatre, February 21, 1968], and *Clara's Ole Man* [one-act; first produced in San Francisco, CA, August 5, 1965; produced at American Place Theatre, February 21, 1968]), Bobbs-Merrill (Chicago IL), 1969, published as *The Electronic Nigger, and Other Plays,* Faber (London, England), 1970.

Ya Gonna Let Me Take You out Tonight, Baby? (first produced off-Broadway at Public Theatre, May 17, 1972), published in *Black Arts,* Black Arts Publishing (Detroit, MI), 1969.

The Gentleman Caller (one-act; first produced in Brooklyn, NY, in *A Black Quartet,* Chelsea Theatre Center at Brooklyn Academy of Music, April 25, 1969), published in *A Black Quartet,* New American Library (New York, NY), 1970.

The Duplex: A Black Love Fable in Four Movements (one-act; first produced at New Lafayette Theatre, May 22, 1970; produced at Forum Theatre of Lincoln Center, New York, NY, March 9, 1972), Morrow (New York, NY), 1971.

The Theme Is Blackness: The Corner, and Other Plays (includes: *The Theme Is Blackness* [first produced in San Francisco, CA, by San Francisco State College, 1966], *The Corner* [one-act; first produced in Boston, MA, by Theatre Company of Boston, 1968, produced off-Broadway at Public Theatre, June 22, 1972], *Dialect Determinism* [one-act; first produced in San Francisco, CA, August 5, 1965; produced at La Mama Experimental Theatre Club, February 25, 1972], *It Has No Choice* [one-act; first produced in San Francisco, CA, by Black Arts/West, spring, 1966, produced at La Mama Experimental Theatre Club, February 25, 1972], *The Helper* [first produced in New York, NY, by New Dramatists Workshop, June 1, 1970], *A Minor Scene* [first produced in San Francisco, CA, by Black Arts/West, spring, 1966; produced at La Mama Experimental Theatre Club, February 25, 1972], *The Man Who Dug Fish* [first produced by Theatre Company of Boston, June 1, 1970], *Black Commercial No. 2, The American Flag Ritual, State Office Bldg. Curse, One Minute Commercial, A Street Play, Street Sounds* [first produced at La Mama Experimental Theatre Club, October 14, 1970], *A Short Play for a Small Theatre,* and *The Play of the Play*), Morrow (New York, NY), 1972.

Four Dynamite Plays (includes: *It Bees Dat Way* [one-act; first produced in London, England, September 21, 1970; produced in New York, NY, at ICA, October, 1970], *Death List* [one-act; first produced in New York, NY, by Theatre Black at University of the Streets, October 3, 1970], *The Pig Pen* [one-act; first produced at American Place Theatre, May 20, 1970], and *Night of the Beast* [screenplay]), Morrow (New York, NY), 1972.

(Editor and contributor) *The New Lafayette Theatre Presents; Plays with Aesthetic Comments by Six Black Playwrights: Ed Bullins, J.E. Gaines, Clay Gross, Oyamo, Sonia Sanchez, Richard Wesley,* Anchor Press (Garden City, NY), 1974.

The Taking of Miss Janie (first produced in New York at New Federal Theatre, May 4, 1975), published in *Famous American Plays of the 1970s,* edited by Ted Hoffman, Dell (New York, NY), 1981.

New/Lost Plays: An Anthology, That New Publishing Co. (Honolulu, HI), 1993.

Also author of "Malcolm: '71 or Publishing Blackness," published in *Black Scholar,* June, 1975. Plays represented in anthologies, including *New American Plays,* Volume III, edited by William M. Hoffman, Hill & Wang (New York, NY), 1970.

UNPUBLISHED PLAYS

(With Shirley Tarbell) *The Game of Adam and Eve,* first produced in Los Angeles, CA, at Playwrights' Theatre, spring, 1966.

(Under pseudonym Kingsley B. Bass, Jr.) *We Righteous Bombers* (adapted from Albert Camus's *The Just Assassins*), first produced in New York, NY, at New Lafayette Theatre, April, 1969.

A Ritual to Raise the Dead and Foretell the Future, first produced in New York, NY, at New Lafayette Theatre, 1970.

The Devil Catchers, first produced at New Lafayette Theatre, November 27, 1970.

The Fabulous Miss Marie, first produced at New Lafayette Theatre, March 5, 1971; produced at Mitzi E. Newhouse Theatre of Lincoln Center, May, 1979.

Next Time . . . , first produced in Bronx, NY, at Bronx Community College, May 8, 1972.

The Psychic Pretenders (A Black Magic Show), first produced at New Lafayette Theatre, December, 1972.

House Party, a Soul Happening, first produced at American Place Theatre, fall, 1973.

The Mystery of Phyllis Wheatley, first produced at New Federal Theatre, February 4, 1976.

I Am Lucy Terry, first produced at American Place Theatre, February 11, 1976.

Home Boy, first produced in New York, NY, at Perry Street Theatre, September 26, 1976.

JoAnne!, first produced in New York, NY, at Theatre of the Riverside Church, October 7, 1976.

Storyville, first produced in La Jolla, CA, at the Mandeville Theatre, University of California, May, 1977.

DADDY!, first produced at the New Federal Theatre, June 9, 1977.

Sepia Star, first produced in New York, NY, at Stage 73, August 20, 1977.

Michael, first produced in New York, NY, at New Heritage Repertory Theatre, May, 1978.

C'mon Back to Heavenly House, first produced in Amherst, MA, at Amherst College Theatre, 1978.

Leavings, first produced in New York, NY, at Syncopation, August, 1980.

Steve and Velma, first produced in Boston, MA, by New African Company, August, 1980.

Boy x Man, first produced at the Samuel Beckett Theater, June, 1997.

Also author of the plays *Blacklist* and *City Preacher.*

OTHER

The Hungered One: Early Writings (collected short fiction), Morrow (New York, NY), 1971.
The Reluctant Rapist (novel), Harper (New York, NY), 1973.

Also author of article "The Polished Protest: Aesthetics and the Black Writer," published in *Contact,* 1963. Editor of *Black Theatre,* 1968-73; editor of special black issue of *Drama Review,* summer, 1968. Contributor to *Negro Digest, New York Times,* and other periodicals.

SIDELIGHTS: Ed Bullins is one of the most powerful black voices in contemporary American theater. He began writing plays as a political activist in the mid-1960s and soon emerged as a principal figure in the black arts movement that surfaced in that decade. First as Minister of Culture for California's Black Panther Party and then as associate director of Harlem's New Lafayette Theatre, Bullins helped shape a revolutionary "theater of black experience" that took drama to the streets. In more than fifty dramatic works, written expressly for and about blacks, Bullins probed the disillusionment and frustration of ghetto life. At the height of his militancy, he advocated cultural separatism between races and outspokenly dismissed white aesthetic standards. Asked by *Race Relations Reporter* contributor Bernard Garnett how he felt about white critics' evaluations of his work, Bullins replied: "It doesn't matter whether they appreciate it. It's not for them." Despite his disinterest, by the late 1960s establishment critics were tracking his work, more often than not praising its lyricism and depth and commending the playwright's ability to transcend narrow politics. As C.W.E. Bigsby pointed out in *The Second Black Renaissance: Essays in Black Literature,* Bullins "was one of the few black writers of the 1960s who kept a cautious distance from a black drama which defined itself solely in political terms." In the 1970s Bullins won three Off-Broadway Awards for distinguished playwriting, a Drama Critics Circle Award, and several prestigious Guggenheim and Rockefeller playwriting grants.

Bullins's acceptance into the theatrical mainstream, which accelerated as the black arts movement lost momentum, presents some difficulty for critics trying to assess the current state of his art. The prolific output of his early years has been replaced by a curious silence.

One possible explanation, according to *Black American Literature Forum* contributor Richard G. Scharine, is that Bullins has faced the same artistic dilemma that confronts Steve Benson, his most autobiographical protagonist: "As an artist he requires recognition. As a revolutionary he dare not be accepted. But Bullins has been accepted. . . . The real question is whether, severed from his roots and his hate, Bullins can continue to create effectively." In a written response published with the article, Bullins answered the charge: "I was a conscious artist before I was a conscious artist-revolutionary, which has been my salvation and disguise. . . . I do not feel that I am severed from my roots."

Bullins's desire to express the reality of ordinary black experience reflects the philosophy he developed during his six-year association with the New Lafayette Theatre, a community-based playhouse that was a showpiece of the black arts movement until it closed for lack of funds in 1973. During its halcyon days, the New Lafayette provided a sanctuary wherein the black identity could be assuaged and nurtured, a crucial goal of Bullins and all the members of that theatrical family. "Our job," former New Lafayette director Robert Macbeth told Jervis Anderson in a *New Yorker* interview, "has always been to show black people who they are, where they are, and what condition they are in. . . . Our function, the healing function of theatre and art, is absolutely vital."

Bullins was born and raised in a North Philadelphia ghetto, but was given a middle-class orientation by his mother, a civil servant. He attended a largely white elementary school, where he was an excellent student, and spent his summers vacationing in Maryland farming country. As a junior high student, he was transferred to an inner-city school and joined a gang, the Jet Cobras. During a street fight, he was stabbed in the heart and momentarily lost his life (as does his fictional alter-ego Steve Benson in *The Reluctant Rapist*). The experience, as Bullins explained to *New York Times* contributor Charles M. Young, changed his attitude: "See, when I was young, I was stabbed in a fight. I died. My heart stopped. But I was brought back for a reason. I was gifted with these abilities and I was sent into the world to do what I do because that is the only thing I can do. I write."

Bullins did not immediately recognize his vocation, but spent several years at various jobs. After dropping out of high school, he served in the U.S. Navy from 1952-55, where he won a shipboard lightweight boxing championship and started a program of self-education through reading. Not much is known about the years he spent in North Philadelphia after his discharge, but in a *Dictionary of Literary Biography* essay, Leslie C. Sanders noted "his 1958 departure for Los Angeles quite literally saved his life. When he left Philadelphia, he left behind an unsuccessful marriage and several children." In California, Bullins earned a GED high school equivalency degree and started writing. He turned to plays when he realized that the black audience he was trying to reach did not read much fiction and also that he was naturally suited to the dramatic form. But even after moving to San Francisco in 1964, Bullins found little encouragement for his talent. "Nobody would produce my work," he recalled of his early days in the *New Yorker.* "Some people said my language was too obscene, and others said the stuff I was writing was not theatre in the traditional sense." Bullins might have been discouraged had he not chanced upon a production of two plays by LeRoi Jones, *Dutchman* and *The Slave,* that reminded him of his own. "I could see that an experienced playwright like Jones was dealing with the same qualities and conditions of black life that moved me," Bullins explained.

Inspired by Jones's example, Bullins and a group of black revolutionaries joined forces to create a militant cultural-political organization called Black House. Among those participating were Huey Newton and Bobby Seale, two young radicals whose politics of revolution would soon coalesce into the Black Panther Party.

Between 1967 and 1973, Bullins created and/or produced almost a dozen plays, some of which are still considered his finest work. He also edited the theater magazine, *Black Theatre,* and compiled and edited an anthology of six New Lafayette plays. During this time, Bullins was active as a playwriting teacher and director as well. Despite Bullins's close ties to the New Lafayette, his plays were also produced off-Broadway and at other community theaters, notably the American Place Theatre, where he became playwright in residence after the New Lafayette's demise.

Bullins's plays of this period share common themes. *Clara's Ole Man,* an early drama that established the playwright's reputation in New York during its 1968 production, introduces his concerns. Set in the mid-fifties, it tells the story of twenty-year-old Jack, an upwardly mobile black who goes to the ghetto to visit Clara one afternoon when her "ole man" is at work. Not realizing that Clara's lover is actually Big Girl, a lesbian bully who is home when Jack calls, he gets bru-

tally beaten as a result of his ignorance. Sanders believes that "in *Clara's Ole Man,* Bullins's greatest work is foreshadowed. Its characters, like those in many of his later plays, emerge from brutal life experiences with tenacity and grace. While their language is often crude, it eloquently expresses their pain and anger, as well as the humor that sustains them."

By and large, Bullins's plays fared well artistically during the early 1970s while being criticized, by both black and white critics, for their ideology. Some blacks objected to what Bigsby called the "reductive view of human nature" presented in these dramas, along with "their sense of the black ghetto as lacking in any redeeming sense of community or moral values." Other blacks, particularly those who achieved a measure of material success, resented their exclusion from this art form. "I am a young black from a middle-class family and well-educated," wrote one person in the *New York Times Magazine* in response to a black arts article. "What sense of self will I ever have if I continue to go to the theatre and movies and never see blacks such as myself in performance?" For the white theater-going community, Bullins's exclusively black drama also raised questions of a cultural elitism that seems "to reserve for black art an exclusive and, in some senses, a sacrosanct critical territory," Anderson believed.

In the 1990s Ed Bullins's presence was once again felt in the theater world. His anthology *New/Lost Plays* made available a number of works from the past decades. In 1997 a new play *Boy x Man*—pronounced "boy times man"—was presented by the Negro Ensemble Company at New York's Samuel Beckett Theater. The play concerns family, class, and memory. Though sometimes difficult to perform, its dialogue, in the words of *New York Times* theater reviewer Anita Gates, contains Bullins's brand of "down-home poetry."

Early in his career Bullins distanced himself from the critical fray, saying that if he had listened to what critics have told him, he would have stopped writing long ago. "I don't bother too much what anyone thinks," he told Anderson. "When I sit down in that room by myself, bringing in all that I ever saw, smelled, learned, or checked out, I am the chief determiner of the quality of my work. The only critic that I really trust is me."

In a career that has spanned four decades, Bullins has written more than ninety plays in all. He has also started theatre companies and been a founding member of several writing workshops. When *Black Masks* contributor

Pamela Faith Jackson asked him in 1997 what the driving force behind his career has been, Bullins replied, "I did it all to keep from being bored I guess. I mean a lot of things needed to be done."

BIOGRAPHICAL AND CRITICAL SOURCES:

BOOKS

Bigsby, C.W.E., *The Second Black Renaissance: Essays in Black Literature,* Greenwood Press (Westport, CT), 1980.
Black Literature Criticism, Thomson Gale (Detroit, MI), 1992.
Contemporary Authors Autobiography Series, Volume 16, Thomson Gale (Detroit, MI), 1992.
Contemporary Literary Criticism, Thomson Gale (Detroit, MI), Volume 1, 1973, Volume 5, 1976, Volume 7, 1977.
Dictionary of Literary Biography, Thomson Gale (Detroit, MI), Volume 7: *Twentieth-Century American Dramatists,* 1981, Volume 38: *Afro-American Writers after 1955—Dramatists and Prose Writers,* 1985.
Gayle, Addison, editor, *The Black Aesthetic,* Doubleday (New York, NY), 1971.
Hay, Samuel A., *Ed Bullins: A Literary Biography,* Wayne State University Press (Detroit, MI), 1997.
Sanders, Leslie C., *The Development of Black Theater in America: From Shadows to Selves,* Louisiana State University Press (Baton Rouge, LA), 1988.

PERIODICALS

Black American Literature Forum, fall, 1979.
Black Creation, winter, 1973.
Black Mask, September 30, 1997, Pamela Faith Jackson, "Ed Bullins: From Minister of Culture to Living Legend," p. 5.
Black World, April, 1974.
CLA Journal, June, 1976.
Dance, April, 1992, p. 86.
Nation, November 12, 1973; April 5, 1975.
Negro Digest, April, 1969.
Newsweek, May 20, 1968.
New Yorker, June 16, 1973, Jervis Anderson, author interview.
New York Times, September 22, 1971; May 18, 1975; June 17, 1977; May 31, 1979; June 3, 1997, Anita Gates, review of *Boy x Man,* p. C16.

New York Times Book Review, June 20, 1971; September 30, 1973.
New York Times Magazine, September 10, 1972.
Plays and Players, May, 1972; March, 1973.
Race Relations Reporter, February 7, 1972.

ONLINE

Ed Bullins Home Page, http://www.edbullins.com/ (August 10, 2004).

*   *   *

BURKE, Ralph
    See SILVERBERG, Robert

*   *   *

BURNS, Tex
    See L'AMOUR, Louis

*   *   *

BUSIEK, Kurt

PERSONAL: Surname is pronounced "BYOO-zik;" married; children: one daughter.

ADDRESSES: Agent—c/o Author Mail, Marvel Enterprises, Inc., 10 East 40th St., New York, NY 10016.

CAREER: Writer. Has worked as an editor and literary agent.

AWARDS, HONORS: Will Eisner Comic Industry Award, for Best Limited Series, 1994, for "Marvels," Best Single Issue, 1996, for "Kurt Busiek's Astro City," number 4, 1997, for "Kurt Busiek's Astro City," Volume 2, number 1, 1998, for "Kurt Busiek's Astro City," Volume 2, number 10, for Best New Series, 1996, for "Kurt Busiek's Astro City," for Best Continuing Series, 1997 and 1998, for "Kurt Busiek's Astro City," for Best Serialized Story, 1998, for "Kurt Busiek's Astro City," Volume 2, numbers 4-9, and for Best Writer, 1999, for "Kurt Busiek's Astro City" and "Avengers;" Harvey Award, for Best Single Issue or Story, 1995, for "Marvels," number 4, 1996, for "Kurt Busiek's Astro City," number 1, for Best New Series, 1996, for "Kurt Busiek's Astro City," Best Graphic Album of Previously Published Work, 1995, for *Marvels,* 1997, for *Kurt Busiek's Astro City: Life in the Big City,* Best Continuing or Limited Series, 1998, for "Kurt Busiek's Astro City," and for Best Writer, 1998, for body of work.

WRITINGS:

COMIC-BOOK COLLECTIONS AND GRAPHIC NOVELS

(Plotter and scripter) *Vampirella: The Dracula War!,* Harris Comics (New York, NY), 1993.

Kurt Busiek's Astro City Volume I: Life in the Big City, illustrated by Brent Eric Anderson, Image Comics (Orange, CA), 1997.

Kurt Busiek's Astro City Volume II: Confession, illustrated by Brent Eric Anderson, Image Comics (Orange, CA), 1997.

Kurt Busiek's Astro City: Family Album, Image Comics (Orange, CA), 1997.

The Wizard's Tale, illustrated by David Wenzel, DC Comics (New York, NY), 1999.

The Morgan Conquest: The Avengers, Marvel Books (New York, NY), 2000.

Kurt Busiek's Astro City: The Tarnished Angel, illustrated by Brent Eric Anderson and Will Blyberg, Homage Comics (La Jolla, CA), 2000.

Marvels, illustrated by Alex Ross, Marvel Books (New York, NY), 2001.

Thunderbolts: Justice Like Lightning, Marvel Books (New York, NY), 2001.

The Avengers, Earth's Mightiest Heroes: Supreme Justice, Marvel Books (New York, NY), 2001.

Avengers: Ultron Unlimited, illustrated by George Perez, Marvel Books (New York, NY), 2001.

The Avengers: Clear and Present Dangers, illustrated by George Perez, Marvel Books (New York, NY), 2001.

The Liberty Project, About Comics, 2003.

Kurt Busiek's Astro City: Local Heroes, illustrated by Brent Eric Anderson, DC Comics (New York, NY), 2004.

Arrowsmith: So Smart in Their Fine Uniforms, illustrated by Carlos Pacheco, DC Comics (New York, NY), 2004.

Superman: Secret Identity, illustrated by Stuart Immonen, DC Comics (New York, NY), 2004.

Shockrockets: We Have Ignition, illustrated by Stuart Immonen, DC Comics (New York, NY), 2004.

Avengers: Living Legends, Marvel Books (New York, NY), 2004.

Conan Volume I: The Frost Giant's Daughter and Other Stories, illustrated by Cary Nord and Thomas Yeates, Dark Horse (Milwaukie, OR), 2005.

Conan Volume II: The God in the Bowl and Other Stories, illustrated by Cary Nord, Dark Horse (Milwaukie, OR), 2005.

Conan Volume III: The Tower of the Elephant and Other Stories, illustrated by Cary Nord and Michael Wm. Kalut, Dark Horse (Milwaukie, OR), 2006.

Author of hundreds of scripts for comic books, graphic novels, and continuing comic book series, including "The Amazing Spider-Man," "Avengers" "Kurt Busiek's Astro City" "Ninjak" "The Liberty Project" "Superman: Secret Identity" "Power Man and Iron Fist" "Spectacular Spider-Man" "Thunderbolts" "Untold Tales of Spider-Man" "TeenAgents" "Victory" "Silver Star" "Vampirella" "Web of Spider-Man" "Conan the Legend," "JLA/Avengers," and "Iron Man."

OTHER

(Editor, with Stan Lee) *Untold Tales of Spider-Man,* Boulevard Books (New York, NY), 1997.

(With Nathan Archer) *Spider-Man: Goblin Moon,* illustrated by Ed Hannigan and Al Milgrom, Putnam (New York, NY), 1999.

Contributor to anthologies, including *Hotter Blood: More Tales of Erotic Horror,* edited by Jeff Gelb, Michael Grant, and Claire Zion, Simon & Schuster (New York, NY), 1991.

SIDELIGHTS: Comic book writer and novelist Kurt Busiek has been widely praised for his work on comics series such as "Marvels" "Thunderbolts" "Avengers," and "Astro City." Unlike many writers steeped in comic book lore from a young age, however, Busiek had to do his early sampling of comics on the sly; his mother, a librarian, "instilled a love of books into all her kids," he said in an interview with Ray Mescallado on the *Comics Journal* online. Busiek and his siblings "weren't allowed to watch TV, except for a minimal number of shows that were preapproved by my parents, so we got in the habit of reading books as our primary recreation." Comic books, however, were not approved at all. "Naturally, comics and TV being taboo simply meant that I'd read comics and watch TV at friends houses," he remarked. The early rationing of comics and TV, however, meant "I'd developed some level of critical faculty—I didn't just consume them indiscriminately" and without evaluation. "It had to be something worth seeking out, instead of just whatever was available."

Busiek came to comics writing via a well-traveled path. He wrote and submitted fan letters and contributed articles to the fan press, all the while writing comics stories with fellow fan Scott McCloud. Busiek's break came when he interviewed DC editor Dick Giordano for a college term paper. While talking to Giordano, Busiek mentioned that he hoped to be a comics writer when he graduated. Giordano invited him to submit some sample scripts, which led to an invitation to pitch ideas for the "Tales of the Green Lantern Corps" backup in DC's "Green Lantern." There, Busiek made his first major professional comics sale, which appeared in "Green Lantern" number 162.

Kurt Busiek's Astro City: Family Album, a collection of individual issues of the "Astro City" series, serves as one element of Busiek's interpretation of super-heroes. It is "more an ode to the myth of superhero lore than an adventure tale," noted Stephen Weiner in *Library Journal,* an extended story more involved with the "humane elements of the superheroic existence" than brash feats of strength and power, Weiner observed. Distinctly human elements mingle with the superhuman, as one of Busiek's characters deals with the conflicts of being a super-hero and an expectant father. "I try to get to the roots of whatever characters I use in *Astro City,* and I expect I do that deliberately and analytically" as a writer, Busiek commented in the *Jack Kirby Collector* interview.

Similarly, "JLA/Avengers" highlights some of the more subtle and sinister aspects of a super-hero's world. In the series, DC Comics' famed Justice League of America, populated by iconic characters such as Superman, Batman, and Wonder Woman, meet Marvel's Avengers, helmed by Captain America, Thor, and Iron Man. In the story, Busiek "offers some deft contrasts between the turmoil-filled Marvel universe, where the visiting Flash is stunned to stumble onto a mutant lynching, and the comparatively rosier world of DC, where the transported Avengers are giddily asked for their autographs," remarked Tom Russo in *Entertainment Weekly.*

In 2004 Busiek published two more graphic novels: *Superman: Secret Identity* and *Shockrockets: We Have Ignition.* In *Superman,* a teenage farm boy with the name

Clark Kent "suddenly discovers that he has powers like those of his fictional namesake," according to Gordon Flagg in *Booklist.* Steve Raiteri, writing for *Library Journal,* noted that Busiek not only shows how different Clark's powers make him, but he also demonstrates "how Clark remains the same inside . . . and how the issues life poses to him . . . are the same ones faced by non-super people."

Alejandro Cruz, the main character in *Shockrockets,* lives in the year 2087 after Earth has survived a war against aliens. He accidentally becomes part of the Shockrocket team, a group of fighter pilots who "fight crime, curb violent rebellions, and even protect civilians during natural disasters," according to a reviewer for *School Library Journal.* The same reviewer concluded that the book "stands to rival many of today's better science-fiction novels." Tina Coleman, writing in *Booklist,* also praised Busiek for creating "an atmosphere of youthful hope and optimism amid a postwar, futuristic world."

Busiek's comics work remains primarily with superheroes. Despite his deep involvement, he still has some difficulty expressing the appeal the genre has for him. "If I could articulate it, I'd probably be able to let it go and go on to other things, but since I can't, I mess with it, exploring the genre until I find out what it is," Busiek commented in his interview with Mescallado. "I could say it's the metaphoric power of these symbolic characters, who stand for something wider, more universal," he said, or it could be "the scope of the entangled, fictional history, maybe it's the way a world of anything-goes peril and danger works as a character crucible, maybe it's something else. I'm still finding out."

BIOGRAPHICAL AND CRITICAL SOURCES:

PERIODICALS

Booklist, November 1, 2004, Tina Coleman, review of *Shockrockets: We Have Ignition,* p. 474; January 1, 2005, Gordon Flagg, review of *Superman: Secret Identity,* p. 835; February 15, 2005, Gordon Flagg, review of *Kurt Busiek's Astro City: Local Heroes,* p. 1070.

Entertainment Weekly, September 5, 2003, Tom Russo, "Super Collider: The Best and Brightest Heroes from Marvel and DC Clash in *JLA/ Avengers,*" p. 20; November 21, 2003, Marc Bernardin, review of *Conan the Legend,* p. 42.

Jack Kirby Collector number 31, March, 2001, Eric Nolen-Weathington and John Morrow, interview with Busiek.

Library Journal, April 15, 1999, Stephen Weiner, review of *Kurt Busiek's Astro City: Family Album,* p. 82; January 1, 2005, Steve Raiteri, review of *Arrowsmith: So Smart in Their Fine Uniforms,* p. 87; May 15, 2005, Steve Raiteri, review of *Superman: Secret Identity,* p. 98; September 15, 2005, Steve Raiteri, review of *Conan Volume I: The Frost Giant's Daughter and Other Stories,* p. 53.

Publishers Weekly, September 27, 2004, review of *Arrowsmith,* p. 39; April 25, 2005, review of *Conan Volume I,* p. 41.

School Library Journal, March, 2005, Matthew L. Moffett, review of *Shockrockets,* p. 239; January, 2006, Jennifer Feigelman, review of *Kurt Busiek's Astro City: Local Heroes,* p. 165.

ONLINE

Comics Journal Online, http://www.tcj.com/ (April 1, 2004), Ray Mescallado, interview with Busiek.

Fantastic Fiction Web Site, http://www.fantasticfiction.co.uk/ (April 1, 2004), bibliography of Kurt Busiek.

Filmforce Web site, http://www.filmforce.ign.com/ (April 1, 2004), Jonathan Alpers, interview with Busiek.

Silver Bullet Comics Web site, http://www.silverbulletcomicbooks.com/ (April 1, 2004), Tim O'Shea, "Kurt Busiek's Superman: Secret Identity—Q&A" (interview).

Spiderfan.org, http://www.spiderfan.org/ (April 1, 2004).

*   *   *

BUSTOS, F.
   See BORGES, Jorge Luis

*   *   *

BUTLER, Octavia E. 1947-2006
   (Octavia Estelle Butler)

PERSONAL: Born June 22, 1947, in Pasadena, CA; died from a head injury sustained during a fall, February 24, 2006, in WA; daughter of Laurice (a shoe shiner) and Octavia Margaret (Guy) Butler. *Education:* Pasadena City College, A.A., 1968; attended California State University, Los Angeles, 1969, and University of California, Los Angeles.

CAREER: Freelance writer, 1970-2006.

MEMBER: Science Fiction Writers of America.

AWARDS, HONORS: Fifth Prize, *Writer's Digest* Short Story Contest, 1967; Creative Arts Achievement Award, Los Angeles YWCA, 1980; Hugo Award, World Science Fiction Convention, 1984, for short story "Speech Sounds"; Hugo Award, and Nebula Award, Science Fiction Writers of America, Locus Award, *Locus* magazine, and award for best novelette, *Science Fiction Chronicle Reader,* all 1985, all for novelette *Bloodchild;* Nebula Award nominations, 1987, for novelette "The Evening and the Morning and the Night," 1994 for *Parable of the Sower;* MacArthur fellowship, 1995; Nebula Award for Best Novel, 1999, for *Parable of the Talents;* Penn Center West Lifetime Achievement Award, 2000.

WRITINGS:

SCIENCE FICTION

Patternmaster (first novel in the "Patternist" series), Doubleday (New York, NY), 1976.

Mind of My Mind (second novel in the "Patternist" series), Doubleday (New York, NY), 1977.

Survivor (third novel in the "Patternist" series), Doubleday (New York, NY), 1978.

Kindred, Doubleday (New York, NY), 1979, second edition, Beacon Press (Boston, MA), 1988, 25th anniversary edition, Beacon Press (Boston, MA), 2003.

Wild Seed (fourth novel in the "Patternist" series), Doubleday (New York, NY), 1980, Warner Books (New York, NY), 2001.

Clay's Ark (fifth novel in the "Patternist" series), St. Martin's Press (New York, NY), 1984.

Dawn: Xenogenesis (first novel in "Xenogenesis" trilogy), Warner Books (New York, NY), 1987.

Adulthood Rites (second novel in "Xenogenesis" trilogy), Warner Books (New York, NY), 1988.

Imago (third novel in "Xenogenesis" trilogy), Warner Books (New York, NY), 1989.

Lilith's Brood, Aspect/Warner Books (New York, NY), 1989.

The Evening and the Morning and the Night, Pulphouse (Eugene, OR), 1991.

Parable of the Sower (first novel in the "Earthseed" series), Warner Books (New York, NY), 1995.

Bloodchild and other Stories, Four Walls Eight Windows (New York, NY), 1995.

Parable of the Talents (second novel in the "Earthseed" series), Seven Stories Press (New York, NY), 1998, republished with Reading Group Guide questions, Warner (New York, NY), 2000.

Fledgling, Seven Stories Press (New York, NY), 2005.

Contributed to anthologies, including *Clarion,* 1970, and *Chrysalis 4,* 1979; contributor to *Isaac Asimov's Science-Fiction Magazine, Future Life, Transmission,* and other publications.

SIDELIGHTS: Concerned with genetic engineering, psionic powers, advanced alien beings, and the nature and proper use of power, Octavia E. Butler's science fiction presents these themes in terms of racial and sexual awareness. "Butler consciously explores the impact of race and sex upon future society," Frances Smith Foster explained in *Extrapolation.* As one of the few African American writers in the science-fiction field, and the only black woman, Butler's racial and sexual perspective was unique. This perspective, however, did not limit her fiction or turn it into mere propaganda. "Her stories," Sherley Anne Williams wrote in *Ms.,* "aren't overwhelmed by politics, nor are her characters overwhelmed by racism or sexism." Speaking of how Butler's early novels dealt with racial questions in particular, John R. Pfeiffer of *Fantasy Review* maintained that "nevertheless, and therefore more remarkably, these are the novels of character that critics so much want to find in science fiction—and which remain so rare. Finally, they are love stories that are mythic, bizarre, exotic and heroic and full of doom and transcendence."

Among Butler's strengths as a writer, according to several reviewers, is her creation of believable, independent female characters. "Her major characters are black women," Foster explained, and through these characters Butler explored the possibilities for a society open to true sexual equality. In such a society Butler's female characters, "powerful and purposeful in their own right, need not rely upon eroticism to gain their ends." Williams also contended that Butler posited "a multiracial society featuring strong women characters." Still, her characters' race and gender were not Butler's primary concerns, according to a 1993 *Publishers Weekly* interview with the author. "I'm just interested in telling a story, hopefully a good one," the author told Lisa See. "If what I wrote helps others understand the world we live in, so much the better for all of us," said Butler in an interview with *Michigan Chronicle*'s Robert E. McTyler. In addition to her unique characters, critics praise Butler's controlled, economical prose style. Writing in the *Washington Post Book World,* Elizabeth A. Lynn described the author's prose as "spare and sure, and even in moments of great tension she never loses control over her pacing or over her sense of story." "Butler," Dean R. Lambe of *Science Fiction Review* similarly attested, "has a fine hand with lean, well-paced prose."

Butler's stories have been well received by science-fiction fans. In 1985 she won three of the genre's top honors—the Nebula Award, the Hugo Award, and the Locus Award—for her novella *Bloodchild,* the story of human males on another planet who bear the children of an alien race. *"Bloodchild,"* Williams explained, "explores the paradoxes of power and inequality, and starkly portrays the experience of a class who, like women throughout most of history, are valued chiefly for their reproductive capacities." The novella was reprinted in 1995's *Bloodchild and Other Stories,* which also includes the remainder of Butler's previously published short fiction, with afterwords, and two essays. The short stories explore some science-fiction themes—"Speech Sounds" and "The Evening and the Morning and the Night," for instance, envision a troubled future in California—and some family ones, as in "Near of Kin," which focuses on a strained mother-daughter relationship. One of the essays deals with Butler's life, the other with her craft. Chicago's *Tribune Books* reviewer Danille Taylor-Guthrie deemed the afterwords to the short stories valuable: "The author's commentaries on her works are as pleasurable to read as the fiction itself." She also finds that the essays contribute much to the volume. *"Bloodchild and Other Stories* is not only vintage Butler, it permits the reader to look beyond the pen," Taylor-Guthrie remarked. Elizabeth Hand, writing in the *Washington Post Book World,* said the collection will provide "a useful signpost" to Butler's novels.

It is through her novels that Butler has reached her largest audience. She is perhaps best known for her books set in the world of the "Patternists," including *Patternmaster, Mind of My Mind, Survivor,* and *Wild Seed.* The "Patternist" series tells of a society dominated by an elite, specially bred group of telepaths who are mentally linked together into a hierarchical pattern. Originally founded by a 4,000-year-old immortal Nubian named Doro who survives by killing and then taking over younger bodies, these telepaths seek to create a race of superhumans. But Doro's plans are repeatedly thwarted in *Wild Seed* by Anyanwu, an immortal woman who does not need to kill to survive. And in *Mind of My Mind* Mary, Doro's daughter, organizes all the other telepaths to defeat him, thus giving the Patternists an alternative to Doro's selfish and murderous reign. As *Dictionary of Literary Biography* contributor Margaret Anne O'Connor observed, "this novel argues for the collective power of man as opposed to individual, self-interested endeavor."

The "Patternist" novels cover hundreds of years of human history. *Wild Seed* takes place in the eighteenth and nineteenth centuries and *Mind of My Mind* is set in a Los Angeles of the near future, but the other books in the series are set in the distant future. *Patternmaster,* like *Mind of My Mind,* addresses the theme of the importance of compassion and empathy between people over the ambitions of the individual. In this tale Butler describes an agrarian society now ruled by the telepaths whose communities are at constant risk of attack from humans who have been monstrously mutated by a genetic disease—just how this disease is brought to Earth by an astronaut is explained in *Clay's Ark.* During one of these raids, a Patternist ruler is wounded and becomes an invalid. His two sons vie for his position, and Butler shows how the younger son, Teray, learns from a woman healer named Amber that compassion is necessary to maintain and control the communal Pattern. By learning—as Mary did in *Mind of My Mind*—the benefits of the community over the individual, Teray defeats his brother and takes his father's place.

Although many of Butler's protagonists in the "Patternist" books are black women, the novelist did not display any particular favoritism towards either African Americans or women. Instead, she emphasized the need for breaking down race and gender barriers by illustrating the inability of those hindered by prejudice and narrow vision to progress and evolve. According to Foster, for "the feminist critic, Octavia Butler may present problems. Her female characters are undeniably strong and independent." But whether, as Joanna Russ insisted in the *Magazine of Fantasy and Science Fiction* is crucial, "the assumptions underlying the entire narrative are feminist," is uncertain, for "who wins and who loses" is less clear than that a compromise has been made which unifies the best of each woman and man. For African American literary critics, Butler can present problems as well, for their attention has been focused upon the assumptions and depictions about the black experience of the past and the present, yet the implications of Butler's vision should be a significant "challenge."

In *Survivor,* another "Patternist" novel, the author used alien beings to help illustrate her themes. The differences between humans and aliens magnifies the issue of cultural misunderstanding and prejudice-inspired antipathy. With *Survivor,* the character Alanna survives on a distant world by learning to understand and love one of the alien Kohns. Butler's "Xenogenesis" books explore the interrelationships between two peoples in greater depth by creating a race called the Oankali, nomadic aliens who interbreed with other sentient species in order to improve their gene pool. Arriving on Earth after a nuclear holocaust has wiped out almost all of humanity, the Oankali offer mankind a second chance through the combination of the best characteristics of both species. They accomplish this through a third sex, which is both male and female, called ooloi, whose function is to manipulate the two races' genes into a new species. Here, according to *Analog* reviewer Tom Easton, "we may have Butler's [main] point: The ooloi are the means for gene transfer between species, but they also come between, they are intermediaries, moderators, buffers, and Butler says that the human tragedy is the unfortunate combination of intelligence and hierarchy."

The "Xenogenesis" series is comprised of the novels *Dawn, Adulthood Rites,* and *Imago.* In *Dawn* humans awake on a space ship after the earth is destroyed by a nuclear war and choose mates. Lilith, the novel's heroine, chooses Joseph. The two also have a physical alliance with Nikanj, an Oankali. Adele S. Newson, in *Black American Literature Forum,* observed that "Joseph and Lilith are not traditional science-fiction heroes. Neither would they be regarded as people likely to form an alliance. This refreshing approach to human relationships makes a good bit of Butler's literature sensuous." Newson went on to say, "Butler is adept at challenging the reader to evaluate his own moral codes. *Dawn* is philosophical in that it asks the reader, by virtue of the circumstances surrounding the human characters, to pose the basic question, 'What does it mean to be human?'"

Adulthood Rites is the second novel in the "Xenogensis" series and picks up with Lilith's son, Akin, the first male child born of a human since the war that destroyed the earth three hundred years ago. In this novel, the earth is restored and Akin is committed to also restoring a wholly human society. In *Foundation* Francis Bonner criticized the book for making promises it doesn't fulfill. "It is indecisive in its characterization. It flirts with developing a relationship between Lilith and Augustino Leal (Tino), which is never realized," she remarked. Bonner also added that the novel "relies too heavily on dialogue." *Imago,* the last book in the series, tells the story of Jodahs, another of Lilith's children.

Dawn, Adulthood Rites, and *Imago* were republished together in 1989 as *Lilith's Brood.* Writing in *Literary Review,* Burton Raffel noted that *Lilith* readers are "initially drawn on by the utterly unexpected power and subtly complex intelligence of her extraordinary trilogy" but are "sustained and even compelled by the rich dramatic textures" and "profound psychological insights." Bonner contended, "One of the more unusual aspects of the trilogy is that it has no triumphal conclusion. Humanity has lost before the story begins, has still lost, and is disappearing as it ends." However, a reviewer on *Times Warner Bookmark* Web site praised the trilogy, describing it as a "profoundly evocative, sensual—and disturbing—epic of human transformation."

Butler's book *Kindred,* has nothing to do with her other series. Like her other books, *Kindred* has a time-travel theme, but it diverges enough from the science-fiction genre that her publisher marketed it as a mainstream novel. *Kindred* concerns Dana, a contemporary African-American woman who is pulled back in time by her great-great-grandfather, a white plantation owner in the antebellum American South. To insure that he will live to father her great-grandmother—and thus provide the means for her own birth in the twentieth century—Dana is called upon to save the slave owner's life on several occasions. "Butler makes new and eloquent use of a familiar science-fiction idea, protecting one's own past, to express the tangled interdependency of black and white in the United States," Joanna Russ wrote in the *Magazine of Fantasy and Science Fiction.* Williams called *Kindred* "a startling and engrossing commentary on the complex actuality and continuing heritage of American slavery."

Parable of the Sower, the first novel in Butler's "Earthseed" series, also deals with the racial and social concerns typical of Butler's work. Set in a dystopian California in the years 2024 and 2025, the 1995 novel is written in the form of a journal by a young black woman named Lauren Olamina. In Butler's horrific future, a dearth of jobs has created such hostility between haves and have-nots that middle-class towns like the one where Lauren lives have become armed fortresses. Lauren's hometown is eventually attacked and destroyed, but she becomes a leader of survivors who seek to establish a society built on a new religion and nontraditional values. The question of whether or not this society will endure is left unresolved.

Critiquing the novel for *Women's Review of Books,* Hoda Zaki noted that there are echoes of the African-American past in Butler's tale of the future. For in-

stance, Zaki observed, "Lauren's band of survivors recalls the Underground Railroad." She adds that the book, in common with Butler's other works, is a "celebration of racial differences and the coming together of diverse individuals to work, live and build community." Some reviewers point out that in this tale of a world gone awry—according to Zaki, "an exaggerated reflection of what is occurring today"—Butler does not take the expected or obvious approach. "Many other science fiction writers would take this setting and spin out an adventure story following the usual schematics," wrote Thomas Wiloch in the *Bloomsbury Review.* "Many already have. Butler turns her story into a character study of a young woman."

Butler followed *Parable of the Sower,* with *Parable of the Talents,* the second book in the same series. In *Parable of the Talents* Lauren Olamina embraces a religious belief called Earthseed, and sees herself as a future leader of this religion. Lauren founds a community, where she teaches people about Earthseed and encourages them to embrace change. A conservative president who wishes to eradicate any religion other than his own threatens the community and Lauren. He is followed by a ban of terrorists who will do whatever it takes to reach their goal, including separating parents from their children. *Parable of the Talents* received the Nebula Award for Best Novel in 1999.

In 2005, Butler published *Fledgling,* another "beautifully written and inclusive" science fiction novel, according to Bernadette Adams Davis in *Black Issues Book Review.* In the story, a vampire named Shoni wakes to discover that she has lost her memory and must re-learn her entire life. Shoni's dark skin works to her advantage in that it blocks the sunlight, yet it's uniqueness and power is also the reason that she is being hunted. Davis called the book "a literary gem . . . accessible to all readers." A *Kirkus Reviews* critic added, "racist fears of miscegenation are also given an interesting spin in a story so convincingly told . . . that one is likely to forget it's about vampires."

Butler's writing has a solid reputation among both readers and critics of science fiction, and Williams noted that her work has a "cult status among many black women readers." She also observed that "Butler's work has a scope that commands a wide audience." Many of her books have been recommended by critics as examples of the best that science fiction has to offer. For example, speaking of *Kindred* and *Wild Seed,* Pfeiffer argued that with these books Butler "produced two novels of such special excellence that critical appreciation of them will take several years to assemble. To miss them will be to miss unique novels in modern fiction." And Easton asserted that with *Dawn* "Butler has gifted SF with a vision of possibility more original than anything we have seen since [Arthur C.] Clarke's *Childhood's End*."

Nevertheless, Foster believed that Butler's novels deserve more recognition because they fill a void in the science fiction genre, which often neglects to explore sexual, familial, and racial relationships. "Since Octavia Butler is a black woman who writes speculative fiction which is primarily concerned with social relationships, where rulers include women and nonwhites," Foster concluded, "the neglect of her work is startling." For her part, Butler did not discount the unique place she occupies as a black female science-fiction writer, but she had no wish to be typecast by her race or gender, or even by her genre. A reviewer on the *Voices from the Gap* Web site quoted Butler as saying, "Every story I write adds to me a little, changes me a little, forces me to reexamine an attitude or belief, causes me to research and learn, helps me to understand people and grow . . . . Every story I create creates me. I write to create myself."

BIOGRAPHICAL AND CRITICAL SOURCES:

BOOKS

Contemporary Black Biography, Volume 8, Gale (Detroit, MI), 1994.

Contemporary Literary Criticism, Volume 38, Gale (Detroit, MI), 1986.

Contemporary Novelists, St. James Press (Detroit, MI), 2001.

Contemporary Popular Writers, St. James Press (Detroit, MI), 1997.

Dictionary of Literary Biography, Volume 33: *Afro-American Fiction Writers after 1955,* Gale (Detroit, MI), 1984.

Encyclopedia of World Biography, Gale (Detroit, MI), 1998.

Newsmakers 1999, Gale (Detroit, MI), 1999.

Notable Black Writers, Gale (Detroit, MI), 1992.

St. James Encyclopedia of Popular Culture, St. James Press (Detroit, MI), 2000.

St. James Guide to Science Fiction Writers, St. James Press (Detroit, MI), 1996.

St. James Guide to Young Adult Writers, St. James Press (Detroit, MI), 1999.

Stevenson, Rosemary, *Black Women in America, An Historical Encyclopedia,* Carlson Publishing (Brooklyn, NY), 1993.

PERIODICALS

African American Review, summer, 1994, pp. 223-35, 259-71.

Analog: Science Fiction and Fact, January 5, 1981; November, 1984; December 15, 1987; December, 1988; September, 1999, review of *Parable of the Talents,* p. 132; December, 2000, Tom Easton, review of *Lilith's Brood,* pp. 132-138.

Black American Literature Forum, summer, 1984; summer, 1989, Adele S. Newson, review of *Dawn* and *Adulthood Rites,* pp. 389-396.

Black Issues Book Review, September, 2000, Sandra Gregg, "Writing out of the Box," p. 50; November/ December 2005, Bernadette Adams Davis, review of *Fledgling,* p. 71.

Black Scholar, March/April, 1986.

Bloomsbury Review, May/June, 1994, p. 24.

Ebony, August, 2000, p. 20.

Emerge, June, 1994, p. 65.

Equal Opportunity Forum, number 8, 1980.

Essence, April, 1979; May, 1989, pp. 74, 79, 132, 134.

Extrapolation, spring, 1982.

Fantasy Review, July, 1984.

Foundation, spring, 1990, Francis Bonner, "Difference and Desire, Slavery and Seduction: Octavia Butler's Xenogenesis," pp. 50-62.

Janus, winter, 1978-79.

Kirkus, August 15, 2005, review of *Fledgling* p. 867.

Library Journal, August 1, 2005, "Blood Vetting," p. 66.

Literary Review, April 1, 1995, Burton Raffel, "Genre to the Rear, Race and Gender to the Fore: The Novels of Octavia E. Butler," p. 454.

Los Angeles Times, January 30, 1981.

Los Angeles Times Book Review, November 26, 1995, p. 14.

Magazine of Fantasy and Science Fiction, February, 1980; August, 1984.

Michigan Chronicle, April 26, 1994, Robert E. McTyre, "Octavia Butler: Black America's First Lady of Science Fiction," p. PG.

Ms., March, 1986; June, 1987.

New York Times Book Review, January 2, 1994, p. 22; October 15, 1995, p. 33; January 3, 1999, Gerald Jones, "Science Fiction," p. 18; June 6, 1999, review of *Parable of the Talent,* p. 42; December 5, 1999, review of *Parables of the Talent,* p. 101; January 1, 2000, Michel Marriott, "We Tend to the

Right Thing when We Get Scared," p. 21; April 7, 2001, review of *Parables of the Talent,* p. 49; April 29, 2001, Gerald Jones, review of *Wild Seed,* p. 18; June 3, 2001, review of *Wild Seed,* p. 31; December 2, 2001, review of *Wild Seed,* p.74.

Poets & Writers, March/April, 1997, pp. 58-69.
Publishers Weekly, December 13, 1993, pp. 50-51.
Salaga, 1981.
Science Fiction Review, May, 1984.
Science Fiction Studies, November, 1993, pp. 394-408.
Thrust: Science Fiction in Review, summer, 1979.
Tribune Books (Chicago, IL), March 31, 1996, p. 5.
Washington Post Book World, September 28, 1980; June 28, 1987; July 31, 1988; June 25, 1989; October 29, 1995, p. 8; January 24, 1999, review of *Parable of the Talent,* p. 9.
Women's Review of Books, July, 1994, pp. 37-38.

ONLINE

Locus Online, http://www.locusmag.com/ (April 23, 2003), "Octavia E. Butler."
Octavia Estelle Butler: An Unofficial Web Page, http://geocities.com/sela_towanda/index.html (April 23, 2003).
Times Warner Bookmark, http://www.twbookmark.com/authors/ (April 23, 2003), "The Authors: Octavia E. Butler;" "The Books: Lilith's Brood."
Voices from the Gap, http://voices.cla.umn.edu/ (April 23, 2003), "Octavia E. Butler."
Xenogenesis Patterns of Octavia Butler, http://www.math.buffalo.edu/ (April 23, 2003).

*   *   *

BUTLER, Octavia Estelle
  See BUTLER, Octavia E.

*   *   *

BUTLER, Robert Olen 1945-
  (Robert Olen Butler, Jr.)

PERSONAL: Born January 20, 1945, in Granite City, IL; son of Robert Olen (a college professor) and Lucille Frances (an executive secretary; maiden name, Hall) Butler; married Carol Supplee, 1968 (divorced, 1972); married Marilyn Geller (a poet), July 1, 1972 (divorced, 1987); married Maureen Donlan, August 7, 1987 (divorced, 1995); married Elizabeth Dewberry, April 23, 1995; children (second marriage): Joshua Robert. *Edu-*

cation: Northwestern University, B.S. (summa cum laude; oral interpretation), 1967; University of Iowa, M.A. (playwriting), 1969; postgraduate study at New School for Social Research (now New School University), 1979-81. *Politics:* Independent. *Religion:* Roman Catholic.

ADDRESSES: Office—Department of English, 411-Williams Building, Florida State University, P.O. 1580, Tallahassee, FL 32306-1580.

CAREER: Electronic News, New York, NY, editor/reporter, 1972-73; high school teacher in Granite City, IL, 1973-74; Chicago, IL, reporter, 1974-75; *Energy User News,* New York, NY, editor-in-chief, 1975-85; McNeese State University, Lake Charles, LA, assistant professor, 1985-93, professor of fiction writing, beginning 1993, then Francis Eppes Professor; Florida State University, Tallahassee, Michael Shaara Chair in Creative Writing. Member of faculty at various writers' conferences, 1988—. *Military service:* U.S. Army, Military Intelligence, 1969-72; served in Vietnam; became sergeant.

MEMBER: PEN.

AWARDS, HONORS: TuDo Chinh Kien Award for Outstanding Contributions to American Culture by a Vietnam Vet, Vietnam Veterans of America, 1987; Emily Clark Balch Award for Best Work of Fiction, *Virginia Quarterly Review,* 1991; Pulitzer Prize for Fiction, Richard and Hilda Rosenthal Foundation Award, American Academy of Arts and Letters, PEN/Faulkner Award nominee, and Notable Book Award, American Library Association, all 1993, all for *A Good Scent from a Strange Mountain;* Guggenheim fellow, 1993; L.H.D., McNeese State University, 1994; National Endowment for the Arts fellow, 1994; Lotos Club Award of Merit, 1996; National Magazine Award for Fiction, 2001.

WRITINGS:

NOVELS

The Alleys of Eden, Horizon Press, 1981.
Sun Dogs, Horizon Press, 1982.
Countrymen of Bones, Horizon Press, 1983.
On Distant Ground, Knopf (New York, NY), 1985.
Wabash, Holt (New York, NY), 1987.
The Deuce, Holt (New York, NY), 1989.

They Whisper, Holt (New York, NY), 1994.
The Deep Green Sea, St. Martin's Press (New York, NY), 1998.
Mr. Spaceman, Grove Press (New York, NY), 2000.
Fair Warning, Atlantic Monthly Press (Boston, MA), 2002.

SHORT STORIES

A Good Scent from a Strange Mountain: Stories, Viking Penguin (New York, NY), 1992.
Tabloid Dreams, Holt (New York, NY), 1996.
Had a Good Time, Grove Press (New York, NY), 2004.

Butler's stories have appeared in *Atlantic Monthly, Esquire, GQ, Harper's, Hudson Review, New Yorker, Paris Review, Ploughshares, Sewanee Review, Virginia Quarterly Review,* and *Zoetrope.*

OTHER

Also author of feature-length screenplays and teleplays for Disney, New Regency, Paramount, Twentieth Century Fox, Universal Pictures Warner Brothers, and Home Box Office.

SIDELIGHTS: Robert Olen Butler is an American writer whose novels and short stories, many of which deal with the legacy of the Vietnam War, have earned the author wide critical acclaim. Butler's first published novel, *The Alleys of Eden,* is the story of an American Army deserter, Cliff, who falls in love with a Vietnamese prostitute, Lanh, and lives with her for four years in the back alleys of Saigon. When Saigon falls to the North Vietnamese in 1975, they manage to escape to the United States, where the contrasts between the American and Vietnamese cultures, as personified by Cliff and Lanh, are brought into focus.

New York Times critic Anatole Broyard praised *The Alleys of Eden,* writing that "Butler seems to have studied and learned from the best masters: his time shifts are reminiscent of Ford Madox Ford." Tom Clark, reviewing in the *Los Angeles Times,* thought: "Butler has an ability to catch tiny shifts of feeling, momentary estrangements, sudden dislocations of mood—a tool as valuable to the novelist as a scalpel to the surgeon." And John Grant, writing in the *Philadelphia Inquirer,* noted that "This excellent novel should be placed alongside such greats as Graham Greene's *The Quiet American.*"

Although set against the background of Vietnam, *The Alleys of Eden* is not primarily a combat novel. The book was described by Marc Leepson in the *Washington Post Book World* as "a unique, haunting story that ultimately serves as a metaphor for the pain and suffering caused by this country's participation in the Vietnam war." Butler's knowledge of Vietnamese culture results from a tour of duty in which he served as a U.S. Army intelligence agent and later, in 1971, as an interpreter for the U.S. advisor to the mayor of Saigon.

The Alleys of Eden, which was written on a lapboard during Butler's daily commutes to work on a train, was rejected twenty-one times before Butler was able to find a publisher who believed it had marketability. One publisher, Methuen, had brought the book as far as the galley stage before getting out of trade-book publishing and canceling its pending list. The book's eventual publication by Horizon Press was greeted by favorable reviews and nominations for respected book awards, including consideration for a Pulitzer Prize.

Sun Dogs, Butler's second novel, centers on the attempts of Wilson Hand, a former prisoner of war turned private investigator, to come to grips with his Vietnam experience and his ex-wife's suicide. Hand, a secondary character in *The Alleys of Eden,* travels to Alaska in search of corporate spies. "It is incredibly exciting to read Butler," reflected Ronald Reed in a *Fort Worth Star-Telegram* review. "Butler is showing himself to be a master stylist. He moves from the most feverish of prose to a flatness and sparseness that is reminiscent of the best of [Raymond] Chandler and [Dashiell] Hammett. And most importantly, he has something to say."

Butler's novel *Countrymen of Bones* "examines the metaphors men find to justify their violence," synopsized *New York Times* critic Broyard. *Countrymen of Bones* relates the efforts of an archaeologist to work an important burial site he has discovered in the New Mexico desert near the end of World War II. The archaeologist is informed by the military and by scientists at Los Alamos that he only has several weeks to complete his work before the site will be destroyed by the testing of the first atomic bomb. "Though *Countrymen of Bones* is a brilliant novel of ideas," added Broyard, "it is never pretentious or didactic. . . . The characters embody and enact—even dance—the author's ideas."

On Distant Ground, published in 1985, concerns an American intelligence officer dealing with the complex moral terrain of the Vietnam War. Captain David Fleming lives by rigid codes and ideals in order to carry out the work of getting information from the enemy. He seems almost an automaton, but one day a prisoner's scrawled graffiti—"hygiene is healthful," written on the wall of the filthy prison—reaches him. Fleming perceives the writer to be a decent and commendable person, and he becomes obsessed with finding and releasing the prisoner, which he eventually does. Taken back to the United States, he is court-martialed. During the proceedings, he realizes that he must have left behind an unborn son in Vietnam. He flees the United States under an assumed name and finds his former lover and his son just a few days before the fall of Saigon.

Butler's fifth novel, *Wabash,* represented a departure for the author, as he turned his attention from the Vietnam War to Depression-era Illinois. Protagonists Jeremy and Deborah Cole struggle to reclaim their marriage in the aftermath of their daughter's death. While attempting to deal with the loss of their child and, seemingly, their love for each other, the Coles engage in fruitless behavior: Jeremy sets out to assassinate the owner of the steel mill where he works, while Deborah writes letters to the rodents inhabiting their house. Eventually, Deborah learns of and then thwarts Jeremy's violent plan, in so doing repairing the physical and emotional link between husband and wife. Reviewers of the novel were mixed in their appraisal of the work, often commending Butler's distinctive prose but calling the plot and character development uneven. Writing in the Chicago *Tribune Books,* Michael Dorris termed the novel "powerful and disturbingly flawed," taking issue in particular with "thin character motivation and a penchant for overblown profundity." A *Publishers Weekly* critic felt that *Wabash* is "beautifully written." Conversely, a *Kirkus Reviews* contributor characterized the plot as "schematic" and "cardboard." While admitting the story's flaws, Dorris concluded that *Wabash* "is a good read, an absorbing, gritty book about people and communities down on their luck."

In his 1989 novel, *The Deuce,* Butler returns to his focus on the Vietnam War. The novel features a sixteen-year-old protagonist, Tony, who is the child of a Vietnamese mother and an American father. Dissatisfied with his sterile suburban life, Tony runs away from his father's New Jersey home to live on the streets of New York City. While trying to come to terms with his life's meaning and direction, Tony has to avoid the clutches of a murderous pederast who is stalking him. As with Butler's previous novels, reviewers called the work ambitious yet flawed. *New York Times Book Review* contributor Scott Spencer, for instance, averred that *The Deuce* is "tensely dramatic." Admitting that Butler

sometimes fails in his effort to relate the story from a teenager's viewpoint, Spencer nevertheless remarked that "at its most lucid, the novel speaks directly to us in a voice that is marvelously convincing." James Park Sloan, writing in the Chicago *Tribune Books,* felt that Butler falls short in this regard, "in the process exposing the many pitfalls of a child-narrator and the extraordinary difficulty of writing from within a culture other than one's own." Nevertheless, Sloan commented that the novel "is an intriguing and ambitious piece of work." Concluded Spencer, Butler "has crafted a work of fiction with real narrative energy and cultural sweep."

After producing six well-received but small-selling novels, Butler managed to enter the arena of front-list writers with his 1992 story collection, *A Good Scent from a Strange Mountain,* which was awarded the 1993 Pulitzer Prize for fiction. Set in southern Louisiana, where Butler had moved after he finished *The Deuce,* the fifteen stories in *Good Scent* feature Vietnamese-American characters adjusting to life in America and dealing with their war-ravaged past. In "Love," a nerdish man who spied for the Americans during the war has to deal for the first time with competition for his beautiful wife. During the war, he was able to vanquish all such competitors by turning them in as Viet Cong sympathizers; now in America, he has no such method at his disposal and so resorts to an outlandish voodoo spell to conquer his opponent for his wife's affections. The title story, called "a brilliantly told story that I will not soon forget" by *New York Review of Books* contributor Robert Towers, portrays an old Vietnamese man on the verge of death who finds that he is being visited by the ghost of Ho Chi Minh. While passing the time with Ho, the old man realizes that his son-in-law and grandson have helped murder a Vietnamese journalist in New Orleans who was calling for acceptance of their former homeland's Communist government. Echoing Towers in his praise for this story, *Los Angeles Times Book Review* critic Richard Eder remarked, "In a collection so delicate and so strong, the title story stands out as close to magical."

They Whisper, Butler's 1994 novel, recounts the narrator's lifelong passion for women. Ira Holloway, the thirty-five-year-old protagonist, describes his numerous sexual liaisons and his never-ending wonder at the joys of the female body. He also relates his current, dysfunctional marriage to a religion-obsessed woman who demands daily sex to counteract her intense jealousy of other women. Ira's marriage finally unravels when Ira falls in love with another woman. "*They Whisper* conveys my deepest feeling about sexuality, the relationships of men and women, the nature of intimacy—in the sense of secular sacrament. The writing was an act of self-exploration as well as expression," Butler told Sybil S. Steinberg in a *Publishers Weekly* interview.

Reviewers offered differing opinions about *They Whisper*. Commenting in the Chicago *Tribune Books*, Julia Glass praised Butler for once "again tackl[ing] the vagaries of language itself" but criticized the author's treatment of the women in the book: "few of the women we meet seem psychologically distinct, and their soliloquies are mostly indistinguishable in tone from Ira's own voice." While expressing her ambivalence about the novel's ultimate power, Jane Smiley, writing in the *New York Times Book Review*, called the novel "complex and intriguing, . . . many-faceted and fascinating." *Washington Post Book World* contributor Josephine Hart likewise termed *They Whisper* "profound, disturbing and important." While critical of some elements of the novel, Glass concluded that the work is "daring" and an important step "in the ongoing career of a brilliant writer."

Butler followed *Good Scent* with a collection of humorous stories, *Tabloid Dreams*, in which he uses sensationalistic newspaper headlines as jumping-off points for stories about ordinary people. In stories such as "Woman Uses Glass Eye to Spy on Philandering Husband," Butler draws upon both high and low culture to explore issues of cultural exile, loss, hope, and the search for one's self in a consumerist culture. Writing in the *New York Times*, Thomas Mallon compared Butler's sensibility to Flannery O'Connor's and noted, "To call this volume . . . a tour de force would be to reduce something deeply accomplished to a stunt."

In *The Deep Green Sea*, Butler tells of the love story between Tien, a multi-racial Vietnamese woman, and Ben, a forty-eight-year-old Vietnam veteran who returns to Vietnam seeking closure. Though Tien is young enough to be Ben's daughter, the two are immediately drawn to one another. The story is told in alternating "he said/she said" chapters, and encompasses the histories of their respective nations as well as their personal histories. Dwight Gardner, in the *New York Times Book Review*, observed that Butler is perhaps "America's most olfactorily minded novelist . . . he'd rather tell you how a character smells than tell you the color of his eyes." Though admitting that *The Deep Green Sea* falls short of its goal, a *Kirkus Reviews* critic nevertheless finds it "an ambitious, lyrical exploration of the lingering wounds of the Vietnamese war."

The short stories in *Had a Good Time* are based on Butler's collection of vintage postcards from the early decades of the twentieth century. Butler finds the voice of the message on the postcard as interesting as the picture and uses that voice to create the first-person narrative. A *Publishers Weekly* contributor notes that the "stories range in tone and substance, from the humor of 'The Ironworkers' Hayride,' in which a man lusts for a sassy suffragette despite her wooden leg ('her mouth is a sweet painted butterfly'), to the melancholy of 'Carl and I,' about a woman who pines for her consumptive husband ('I breathe myself into my husband's life')." According to a *Kirkus Reviews* contributor, "death haunts every tale. . . . Yet there's delightful humor in stories like . . . 'I Got Married to Milk Can,' about a new bride renouncing her romantic dreams of running off with an artist when he proves to be an 'advanced' painter of the Ash Can school."

Butler once explained of his writing: "I write novels to explore for myself—and to reveal to others—my vision of the fundamental patterns inherent in the flux of experience. These patterns concern man's search for love, kinship, connection, God; man's capacity for desertion, violence, and self-betrayal. But I also write novels to tell stories, a primal human impulse since cave-mouth campfires. I believe that art, to be fully realized, must communicate with as wide a public as possible without losing sight of its deepest truths."

BIOGRAPHICAL AND CRITICAL SOURCES:

BOOKS

Contemporary Literary Criticism, Volume 81, Thomson Gale (Detroit, MI), 1994.
Conversations with American Novelists: The Best Interviews from The Missouri Review and the American Audio Prose Library, edited by Kay Bonetti and others, University of Missouri Press (Columbia, MO), 1997.
Trucks, Rob, *The Pleasure of Influence: Conversations with Eleven Contemporary American Male Fiction Writers*, NotaBell Books, 2002.

PERIODICALS

America, May 17, 1997, pp. 8-29.
Antioch Review, spring, 1997, p. 272.
Fort Worth Star-Telegram, November 14, 1982.
Kirkus Reviews, January 15, 1987, p. 74; November 1, 1997; June 1, 2004.
Library Journal, September 1, 1996, p. 212.
London Review of Books, May 12, 1994, p. 24.

Los Angeles Times, February 11, 1982.

Los Angeles Times Book Review, March 29, 1992, p. 3.

Nation, February 27, 1982.

Newsday, March 21, 1982.

New York Review of Books, August 12, 1993, p. 41.

New York Times, November 11, 1981; October 18, 1983; November 3, 1996; January 11, 1998.

New York Times Book Review, January 9, 1983; April 21, 1985; March 15, 1987, p. 16; September 3, 1989, p. 10; February 13, 1994, p. 12.

Philadelphia Inquirer, January 24, 1982.

Publishers Weekly, January 1, 1982; February 11, 1983; December 21, 1984, p. 82; January 16, 1987, p. 62; July 7, 1989, p. 51; January 3, 1994, p. 60; April 12, 2004, p. 34.

St. Louis Post-Dispatch, December 1, 1981.

Times Literary Supplement, December 10, 1993, p. 19; March 18, 1994, p. 14.

Tribune Books (Chicago, IL), March 8, 1987, p. 1; September 24, 1989, p. 7; February 6, 1994, p. 3.

Vogue, February, 1994, p. 122.

Voice of Youth Advocates, December, 1985, p. 318.

Washington Post Book World, April 21, 1985, p. 11; October 1, 1989, p. 6; January 16, 1994, p. 1.

Whole Earth Review, spring, 1994, p. 56.

Writer, April, 1982.

Writer's Digest, January, 1983.

ONLINE

Inside Creative Writing, http://www.fsu.edu/~butler/ (May 9, 2005).

Writers on America, http://usinfo.state.gov/products/pubs/ (August 3, 2004), Robert Olen Butler, *A Postcard from America.*

*   *   *

BUTLER, Robert Olen, Jr.
See BUTLER, Robert Olen

*   *   *

BYATT, Antonia Susan Drabble
See BYATT, A.S.

*   *   *

BYATT, A.S. 1936-
(Antonia Susan Drabble Byatt)

PERSONAL: Born August 24, 1936, in Sheffield, England; daughter of John Frederick (a judge) and Kathleen Marie (Bloor) Drabble; married Ian Charles Rayner Byatt (an economist), July 4, 1959 (divorced, 1969); married Peter John Duffy, 1969; children: (first marriage) Antonia, Charles; (second marriage) Isabel, Miranda. *Education:* Newnham College, Cambridge, B.A. (first class honors), 1957; graduate study at Bryn Mawr College, 1957-58, and Somerville College, Oxford, 1958-59.

ADDRESSES: Home—37 Rusholme Rd., London SW15 3LF, England.

CAREER: University of London, London, England, staff member in extramural department, 1962-71; Central School of Art and Design, London, part-time lecturer in department of liberal studies, 1965-69; University College, London, lecturer, 1972-81, senior lecturer in English, 1981-83, admissions tutor in English, 1980-83, fellow, beginning 1984; writer, 1983—. Associate of Newnham College, Cambridge, 1977-82; British Council Lecturer in Spain, 1978, India, 1981, and in Germany, Australia, Hong Kong, China, and Korea; George Eliot Centenary Lecturer, 1980. Member of panel of judges for Booker Prize, 1973, Hawthornden Prize, and David Higham Memorial Prize; member of British Broadcasting Corp. (BBC) Social Effects of Television advisory group, 1974-77; member of Communications and Cultural Studies Board, Council for National Academic Awards, 1978; member of Kingman Committee on the Teaching of English, 1987-88; member of British Council of Literature advisory panel, 1990-98, and board, 1993-98.

MEMBER: British Society of Authors (member of committee of management, 1984-88; chair of committee, 1986-88), PEN.

AWARDS, HONORS: English-speaking Union fellowship, 1957-58; fellow of Royal Society of Literature, 1983; Silver Pen Award for *Still Life;* Booker Prize, 1990, *Irish Times*-Aer Lingus International Fiction Prize, 1990, and Best Book in Commonwealth Prize, 1991, all for *Possession;* Mythopoeic Fantasy Award for adult literature, Mythopoeic Society, 1998, for *The Djinn in the Nightingale's Eye: Five Fairy Tales;* Commander of the Order of the British Empire, 1990, Dame Commander, 1999; honorary fellow, Newham College, Cambridge, 1999, London Institute, 2000. D.Litt. from University of Bradford, 1987, University of Durham, 1991, University of Nottingham, 1992, University of Liverpool, 1993, University of Portsmouth, 1994, University of London, 1995, Cambridge University, 1999, and Sheffield University, 2000; D.Univ. from University of York, 1991.

WRITINGS:

FICTION

The Shadow of the Sun, Harcourt (London, England), 1964.

The Game, Chatto & Windus, 1967 (London, England), Scribner (New York, NY), 1968.

The Virgin in the Garden (first novel in tetralogy), Chatto & Windus (London, England), 1978, Knopf (New York, NY), 1979.

Still Life (second novel in tetralogy), Chatto & Windus (London, England), 1985, Scribner (New York, NY), 1987.

Sugar and Other Stories, Scribner (New York, NY), 1987.

Possession: A Romance, Random House (New York, NY), 1990.

Angels and Insects: Two Novellas, (contains "Morpho Eugenia" and "The Conjugial Angel"), Chatto & Windus (London, England), 1992.

The Matisse Stories, Chatto & Windus (London, England), 1993, Random House (New York, NY), 1995.

The Djinn in the Nightingale's Eye: Five Fairy Tales, Chatto & Windus (London, England), 1994.

Babel Tower (third novel in tetralogy), Random House (New York, NY), 1996.

Elementals: Stories of Fire and Ice, Chatto & Windus (London, England), 1998, Random House (New York, NY), 1999.

The Biographer's Tale, Chatto & Windus (London, England), 2000, Knopf (New York, NY), 2001.

A Whistling Woman (fourth novel in tetralogy), Knopf (New York, NY), 2002.

Little Black Book of Stories, Knopf (New York, NY), 2004.

OTHER

Degrees of Freedom: The Novels of Iris Murdoch, Barnes & Noble (New York, NY), 1965, published as *Degrees of Freedom: The Early Novels of Iris Murdoch,* Vintage (London, England), 1994.

Wordsworth and Coleridge in Their Time, Nelson (London, England), 1970, Crane, Russak (New York, NY), 1973, published as *Unruly Times: Wordsworth and Coleridge in Their Time,* Hogarth (London, England), 1989.

Iris Murdoch, Longman (London, England), 1976.

(Editor and author of introduction) George Eliot, *The Mill on the Floss,* Penguin (Middlesex, England), 1979.

(Editor) George Eliot, *Selected Essays, Poems and Other Writings,* Penguin (Middlesex, England), 1989.

(Editor) Robert Browning, *Dramatic Monologues,* Folio Society (London, England), 1990.

Passions of the Mind, Chatto & Windus (London, England), 1991.

(Editor with Alan Hollinghurst) *New Writing 4,* Vintage (London, England), 1995.

(With Ignes Sodre) *Imagining Characters: Conversations about Women Writers: Jane Austen, Charlotte Bronté, George Eliot, Willa Cather, Iris Murdoch, and Toni Morrison,* Chatto & Windus (London, England), 1995, Vintage (New York, NY), 1997.

(Editor with others) *New Writing 6,* Vintage (London, England), 1997.

(Editor) *The Oxford Book of English Short Stories,* Oxford University Press (New York, NY), 1998.

On Histories and Stories, Chatto & Windus (London, England), 2000, Harvard University Press (Cambridge, MA), 2001.

Portraits in Fiction, Chatto & Windus (London, England), 2001.

Contributor to books, including Isobel Armstrong, editor, *The Major Victorian Poets Reconsidered,* Routledge (London, England), 1969; Malcolm Bradbury, editor, *The Contemporary English Novel,* Edward Arnold (London, England), 1979; and *Patrick Heron,* Tate Gallery Publications (London, England), 1998. Author of prefaces to books, including Elizabeth Bowen, *The House in Paris,* Penguin, 1976; Grace Paley, *Enormous Changes at the Last Minute,* Virago, 1979; Paley, *The Little Disturbances of Man,* Virago, 1980; Willa Cather, *My Antonia* and *A Lost Lady,* Virago, 1980, and *My Mortal Enemy, Shadow on the Rock, Death Comes to the Archbishop, O Pioneers!* and *Lucy Grayheart;* and George Eliot, *Middlemarch,* Oxford University Press, 1999. Also author of radio documentary on Leo Tolstoy, 1978, and of dramatized portraits of George Eliot and Samuel Taylor Coleridge for National Portrait Gallery. Contributor of reviews to London *Times, New Statesman, Encounter, New Review,* and *American Studies.* Member of editorial board, *Encyclopaedia,* Longman-Penguin, 1989.

ADAPTATIONS: "Morpho Eugenia" was adapted to film as *Angels and Insects; Possession* was adapted for a film by director Neil LaBute, David Henry Hwang, and Laura Jones, starring Gwyneth Paltrow and Aaron Eckhart, USA Films, 2002.

SIDELIGHTS: A.S. Byatt is a widely experienced critic, novelist, editor, and lecturer who "offers in her work an intellectual kaleidoscope of our contemporary world," according to Caryn McTighe Musil in the *Dictionary of Literary Biography*. Musil added: "Her novels, like her life, are dominated by an absorbing, discriminating mind which finds intellectual passions as vibrant and consuming as emotional ones." A celebrated polymath—whose fiction delves into science, the visual arts, Victorian history and sensibilities, and the postmodern concept of writing about writing—the London-based Byatt has attracted a reading audience on both sides of the Atlantic. In *Publishers Weekly* John F. Baker called Byatt "somewhat of a pillar in the English intellectual establishment . . . whose mind is so compendious that deciding what to leave out of her books is more of a problem than an author's usual frantic search for ideas."

Byatt was relatively unknown as a fiction writer until 1990, the year in which she published her bestseller—and Booker Prize-winning novel—*Possession.* Since then she has been in demand not only as a writer, but also as a lecturer and a judge of others' works. Her own fiction seeks to disprove that writing about the academy must necessarily be fraught with intellectual legerdemain. "All through Byatt's writing life, she has reflected on the way we earthly beings dream of spirit," Michael Levenson observed in the *New Republic.* "She is a Realist, a post-Christian, a sometime academic living in skeptical times. . . . For Byatt these are simply the latest natural conditions for our spirit-hunger. It's no use whining. Her point is not to confirm religious truth, but to enlarge the religious sense, which locates value not in the infinite but in the yearning for the infinite, not in God but in the search for God." As Donna Seaman put it in *Booklist,* Byatt is simultaneously "a dazzling storyteller and a keen observer of the power and significance of her medium. . . . She revels, to her readers' considerable delight, in the infinite potential of the storyteller's art."

Byatt grew up in a scholarly family. Her father was a judge, and her sister, Margaret Drabble, also pursued writing. Byatt attended both Cambridge and Oxford, where she studied art and literature, all the while writing fiction as well. Her career progressed relatively slowly—but considering that she raised four children while teaching, she in fact made commendable strides. Byatt has been a full-time writer since 1983, but still pursues scholarly work in the form of literary criticism, edited volumes, and the writing of introductions for new editions of classic fiction. To quote Hilma Wolitzer in the *New York Times Book Review,* Byatt "has always been concerned with the ways in which art and literature inform and transform our lives."

Byatt's first novel, *The Shadow of the Sun,* reflects the author's own struggle to combine the role of critic with that of novelist on the one hand, and the role of mother with that of visionary on the other, according to Musil. The critic wrote that *The Game,* "a piece of technical virtuosity, is also a taut novel that explores with a courage and determined honesty greater than [D. H.] Lawrence's the deepest levels of antagonism that come with intimacy. Widely reviewed, especially in Great Britain, *The Game* established Byatt's reputation as an important contemporary novelist."

Byatt's novel *The Virgin in the Garden* was described by *Times Literary Supplement* reviewer Michael Irwin as a "careful, complex novel." The book's action is set in 1953, the year of the coronation of Queen Elizabeth II, and Irwin reported that "its theme is growing up, coming of age, tasting knowledge." The book "is a highly intellectual operation," pointed out Iris Murdoch in *New Statesman.* "The characters do a great deal of thinking, and have extremely interesting thoughts which are developed at length." "The novel's central symbol," Musil related, "is Queen Elizabeth I, a monarch Byatt sees as surviving because she used her mind and thought things out, unlike her rival, Mary, Queen of Scots, who was 'very female and got it wrong.'" In Musil's opinion, the work initiated "the middle phase" of Byatt's writing career. "Much denser" than her previous novels "and dependent on her readers' erudition, [*The Virgin in the Garden*] achieves a style that suits Byatt. It blends her acquisitive, intellectual bent with her imaginative compulsion to tell stories." *The Virgin in the Garden* is the first in a series of novels featuring the character Frederica Potter, who, like Byatt, has grown up in the north of England, attended Cambridge, and has become a respected—if beleaguered—academician.

With *Babel Tower* and *A Whistling Woman* Byatt completes a fictional quartet that began with *The Virgin in the Garden* and continued with *Still Life. Babel Tower* finds Frederica Potter trying to overcome a soured marriage and make it on her own as a single mother in the tumult of 1960s London. The novel, which continues Byatt's sweeping portrayal of post-World War II England, also serves, in the words of *New York Times Book Review* critic Ann Hulbert, as a "portrait of the reader as a young woman," wherein Byatt questions the value of literature in modern culture. *Time* magazine reviewer Paul Gray deemed Byatt's subject "certainly worthy but perhaps not sufficiently vivid to propel readers through a long, long literary haul." Hulbert assessed this third novel as "bolder" than Byatt's earlier installments in the series. She wrote that in *Babel Tower,* Byatt's "usual impressive command of slippery ideas and the solidest of details . . . mix and move with new energy, even abandon." In his *Maclean's* review, John Bemrose suggested that "what propels *Babel Tower* into a whole new orbit of achievement is Byatt's fresh and keenly intelligent interpretation of the Sixties—an era many would argue has been documented to death." Bemrose styled the work "a brilliant novel of ideas . . . about the courage required to cope with change."

Noting Byatt's characteristic use of embedded narrative threads within her fiction, *World Literature Today* contributor Mary Kaiser commented that in *A Whistling Woman* "there is also a skein of symbolic threads in this intricate narrative tapestry, in which birds and women are linked as singers, spiritual vehicles, and embodiments of beauty." In this fourth novel in the series, Potter—now a thirty-something single mother and working as a teacher—has found a loyal and growing readership for her fiction. As Potter's acclaim and celebrity grows as a result of the publication of her novel *Laminations,* so too do the successes of her creative friends, often at the cost of romantic love. Potter's decision to shift from teaching to hosting a talk show puts her into the center of 1960s culture and the battle between the status quo and a liberation of social and cultural views, a counterpoint being the destructive influence of charismatic cult leader Joshua Ramsden. Potter represents the prototypical feminist of the period: according to a *Publishers Weekly* contributor, a woman who is "literate, shrewd and knowing, a character who could only be the product of centuries of Enlightenment." Ramsden, in contrast, is "dark, ecstatic," a man "whose psychotic episodes begin to bleed into his essential charismatic goodness," according to the critic. Praising Byatt as "Astute and omnipotent," *Booklist* contributor Donna Seaman described the novel's subject as "nothing less than Western civilization and its endless redefining of faith and fact, good and evil, art and science."

The 1990 publication of *Possession* finally brought Byatt into the mainstream in both English and American letters. *Possession* tells the story of Roland Michell and Maud Bailey, two contemporary literary scholars whose paths cross during their research. Roland is an expert on the famous Victorian poet Randolph Henry Ash, while Maud's interest is Christabel LaMotte, an obscure poet of the same period. Roland and Maud discover evidence that the two Victorians were linked in a passionate relationship; their joint investigation into the

lives of the two writers leads to a love affair of their own. Byatt has been widely acclaimed for her skillful handling of this complex story. In a *Spectator* review, Anita Brookner called *Possession* "capacious, ambitious . . . marvelous," and noted that it is "teeming with more ideas than a year's worth of ordinary novels." Danny Karlin declared in the *London Review of Books* that Byatt's romance is "spectacular both in its shortcomings and its successes; it has vaulting literary ambitions and is unafraid to crash."

Much of the plot of *Possession* is conveyed through poetry and correspondence attributed to Ash and LaMotte, and many reviewers marveled at Byatt's sure touch in creating authentic voices for her fictional Victorians. *New York Times Book Review* contributor Jay Parini commented: "The most dazzling aspect of *Possession* is Ms. Byatt's canny invention of letters, poems and diaries from the nineteenth century. She quotes whole vast poems by Ash and LaMotte, several of which . . . are highly plausible versions of [Robert] Browning and [Christina] Rossetti and are beautiful poems on their own." Parini was also enthusiastic about the manner in which the love story of Ash and LaMotte serves as "ironic counterpoint" to the modern affair between Maud and Roland. Parini concluded: "*Possession* is a tour de force that opens every narrative device of English fiction to inspection without, for a moment, ceasing to delight." The literary world's high regard for the novel is reflected in the fact that Byatt won both the prestigious Booker Prize and the *Irish Times*-Aer Lingus International Fiction Prize for *Possession* in 1990.

Critical praise for Byatt's work continued when *Angels and Insects* was published in 1992. This volume contains two novellas set in the Victorian era. The first, "Morpho Eugenia," concerns a biologist who becomes part of a wealthy household with an ugly secret. The second, "The Conjugial Angel," revolves around the Victorian fascination with spiritualism. Marilyn Butler, a reviewer for *Times Literary Supplement,* called *Angels and Insects* "more fully assured and satisfying than *Possession*" and rated it Byatt's "best work to date." *Belles Lettres* contributor Tess Lewis asserted that "Byatt brings vividly to life the divided Victorian soul— split between faith in the intellect and instinct, free will and determinism, and rationalism and spiritualism. . . . The sheer beauty of many scenes as well as Byatt's luxurious, evocative language remain with the reader long after the clever plots and intriguing, but occasionally too lengthy, intellectual constructs have faded. Byatt's writing is masterful."

Byatt's novel *The Biographer's Tale* is the story of Phineas G. Nanson, a graduate student who, tired of postmodern abstractions, turns to biography in an attempt to deal with solid facts. He begins to read a biography of Elmer Bole, a nineteenth-century scholar, and is intrigued; he resolves to write a biography of the biographer. Byatt includes much of what Phineas reads, mimicking the dry voice of the biographer and providing information on the customs of Lapland, discussions of anthropometric measuring equipment, and descriptions of entomology. Through the course of his studies, Phineas is hired at a travel agency and becomes involved with two women, echoing the life of Elmer Bole, who was married to two women. The biography Phineas himself writes becomes something of an autobiography, and his search to find facts reveals itself as a search to find himself.

"Through clever, lively prose, Byatt . . . moves the action along briskly, treating the reader to numerous witty observations on contemporary academic and social mores along the way," wrote Starr E. Smith in the *Library Journal.* Many reviewers, however, were disappointed with the inclusions of the factual texts. As Jean Blish Siers noted in the *Knight Ridder/ Tribune,* "That Phineas should dive into these artifacts is only right. That readers should be forced to read the manuscripts in their entirety is uncalled for." But Lynne Sharon Schwartz, in a review of *The Biographer's Tale* for the *New Leader* praised Byatt's handling of the shifts in narration, writing: "Like a genie rising from a bottle, the novel swirls out of these notes . . . demanding half a dozen voices that Byatt does expertly." A *Publishers Weekly* reviewer concluded, "The book is an erudite joke carried off with verve and humor" and "will appeal to discriminating readers ready for intellectual stimulation."

In Byatt's more recent short fiction, such as the works collected in *The Matisse Stories,* the author adopts a more concrete style. These stories all make some reference to French impressionist painter Henri Matisse. "The lasting impression the reader has of Antonia Byatt's three stories in this collection is of an extravagance of color, a riot of color, venous-blue and fuchsia-red and crimson and orange henna and copper," David Plante related in the *Los Angeles Times Book Review.* "Byatt's fiction . . . is essentially informed by an intelligent, even a scholarly mind, pitched more to interpretation rather than fact in itself, to 'ideas' rather than 'things.' But it is as though in 'The Matisse Stories' Byatt were trying to break out onto another level, that of making art." London *Observer* writer Helen Dunmore voiced a similar opinion: "These stories show us Byatt still advancing in her technique and range. Like Matisse she is excited by the way a vase of flowers, a

white book or a human being stands in the stream of everyday light, and like Matisse she knows how to set down her observations."

In *The Djinn in the Nightingale's Eye* Byatt presents a collection of contemporary and self-reflexive fairy tales, two of the stories having appeared earlier, woven into the plot of *Possession.* The title story, which is the longest of the five, dramatizes literary theories of the fairy tale through the story of a middle-aged narratologist who encounters a djinn, or genie, with the power to grant her the traditional three wishes. Because she is a scholar of fairy tales, she knows all of the pitfalls, and so her wishes are anything but traditional. "The conversations between the genie and the scholar are beyond all praise," wrote Nancy Willard in the *New York Times Book Review,* "and the description of their lovemaking is a gem of exuberant metaphor and linguistic constraint." *Baltimore Sun* writer Susan Reimer claimed that "the scent of sandalwood and myrrh that rose from the pages of this book caused me to wish for my own wishes."

Elementals: Stories of Fire and Ice includes both realistic and fantastic tales which illustrate the deep connections between literature and life. In one of the pieces, a grieving widow begins to confront her personal tragedy during conversations about folktales with a new friend. In another, a princess who must constantly be freezing cold overcomes supernatural odds to marry a glassblower in the desert. A *Publishers Weekly* reviewer deemed the work a "virtuosic and beguiling collection" that reveals "an unfettered imagination, an intense lyricism combined with distilled and crystalline prose, and an astute grasp of the contradictory impulses of human nature." In *Booklist* Veronica Scrol likewise noted that *Elementals* "showcases Byatt's ability to get to the heart of the human condition," while *New York Times Book Review* critic Wolitzer concluded that the tales are "fired by a fierce intelligence and related in shimmering prose." The five tales included in *Little Black Book of Stories* continue the motifs of *Elementals,* creating a collection wherein "the writing is dauntingly precise and realistic, even as it points to something unnatural and bizarre," according to *Spectator* contributor Stephen Abell: "'always aiming,' as Byatt herself has characterised 'good' modern prose, 'at an impossible exactness which it knows it will never achieve.'"

Byatt once commented: "Perhaps the most important thing to say about my books is that they try to be about the life of the mind as well as of society and the relations between people. I admire—am excited by—

intellectual curiosity of any kind (scientific, linguistic, psychological) and also by literature as a complicated, huge, interrelating pattern. I also like recording small observed facts and feelings. I see writing and thinking as a passionate activity, like any other."

BIOGRAPHICAL AND CRITICAL SOURCES:

BOOKS

Contemporary Literary Criticism, Thomson Gale (Detroit, MI), Volume 19, 1981, Volume 65, 1991.

Dictionary of Literary Biography, Volume 14: *British Novelists since 1960,* Thomson Gale (Detroit, MI), 1983.

Kelly, Kathleen Coyne, *A.S. Byatt,* Twayne (New York, NY), 1996.

PERIODICALS

Atlantic, January, 2001, Stephen Amidon, review of *The Biographer's Tale,* p. 84.

Baltimore Sun, January 6, 1998.

Belles Lettres, fall, 1993, pp. 28-29.

Book, January-February, 2003, Penelope Mesic, review of *A Whistling Woman,* p. 69.

Booklist, April, 1996, p. 100; September 1, 1997, Donna Seaman, review of *The Djinn in the Nightingale's Eye,* p. 6; March 1, 1999, Veronica Scrol, review of *Elementals: Stories of Fire and Ice,* p. 1103; January 1, 2000, Karen Harris, review of *Possession,* p. 948; November 15, 2000, Donna Seaman, review of *The Biographer's Tale,* p. 587; November 15, 2002, Donna Seaman, review of *A Whistling Woman,* p. 547.

Books and Bookmen, January 4, 1979.

Chicago Tribune, June 13, 1993, sec. 14, p. 3.

Chicago Tribune Book World, January 12, 1986.

Christian Science Monitor, March 31, 1992, p. 13; May 25, 1993, p. 13; April 20, 1995, p. 12; September 25, 1997, p. B8.

Economist, June 15, 1996, p. 3.

Encounter, July, 1968.

English Journal, March, 1995, p. 92.

Kirkus Reviews, November 1, 2002, review of *A Whistling Woman,* p. 1548; March 15, 2004, review of *Little Black Book of Stories,* p. 237.

Knight Ridder/Tribune, February 21, 2001, p. K6940.

Lancet, November 7, 1998, Gail Davey, "Still Life and the Rounding of Consciousness," p. 1544.

Library Journal, May 1, 1999, Ann H. Fisher, review of *Elementals,* p. 114; June 1, 2000, Nancy R. Ives, review of *Elementals,* p. 230; December, 2000, Starr E. Smith, review of *The Biographer's Tale,* p. 186; January, 2003, Edward Cone, review of *A Whistling Woman,* p. 151.

London Review of Books, March 8, 1990, pp. 17-18.

Los Angeles Times, November 18, 1985.

Los Angeles Times Book Review, October 28, 1990, pp. 2, 13; June 13, 1993, p. 8; April 23, 1995.

Maclean's, July 1, 1996, John Bemrose, review of *Babel Tower,* p. 59.

Ms., June, 1979.

New Criterion, February, 1991, pp. 77-80.

New Leader, April 23, 1979; January, 2001, Lynne Sharon Schwartz, "Not by Facts Alone," p. 26.

New Republic, January 7-14, 1991, pp. 47-49; August 2, 1993, Michael Levenson, review of *Angels and Insects: Two Novellas,* p. 41.

New Statesman, November 3, 1978; May 3, 1996, p. 40; June 12, 2000, Miranda Seymour, "History Lesson," p. 53.

New Statesman & Society, March 16, 1990, p. 38.

New York Review of Books, June 6, 1996, J.M. Coetzee, review of *Babel Tower,* p. 17; June 10, 1999, Gabriele Annan, review of *Elementals,* p. 28.

New York Times, October 25, 1990, Christopher Lehmann-Haupt, "When There Was Such a Thing as Romantic Love"; July 9, 1996, p. C11; January 23, 2001, Michiko Kakutani, "A Bumbling Literary Sleuth Ends up Clueless," p. B9.

New York Times Book Review, July 26, 1964; March 17, 1968; April 1, 1979; November 24, 1985; July 19, 1987; October 21, 1990, pp. 9, 11; June 27, 1993, p. 14; April 30, 1995, p. 9; June 9, 1996, p. 7; September 14, 1997, p. 27; November 9, 1997, Nancy Willard, "Dreams of Jinni," p. 38; May 10, 1999, Hilma Wolitzer, "Secret Sorrow: Fantasy and Parable."

New York Times Magazine, May 26, 1991, Mira Stout, "What Possessed A.S. Byatt?: A British Novelist's Breakthrough Surprises Everyone but the British Novelist," p. 12.

Observer (London, England), March 11, 1990, p. 68; January 2, 1994, p. 17.

People, April 1, 1991, Michelle Green, "After Years in Her Sister's Shadow, Sibling Rival A.S. Byatt Makes Her Best-selling Mark with *Possession,*" p. 87; April 17, 1995, p. 32.

Publishers Weekly, May 20, 1996, John F. Baker, "A.S. Byatt: Passions of the Mind," p. 235; March 29, 1999, review of *Elementals,* p. 89; November 6, 2000, review of *The Biographer's Tale,* p. 70; November 11, 2002, review of *A Whistling Woman,* p. 41.

Spectator, March 3, 1990, p. 35; January 15, 1994, p. 28; November 29, 2003, Stephen Abell, "Making It a Just so Story," p. 58.

Time, May 20, 1996, p. 76.

Times (London, England), June 6, 1981; April 9, 1987; March 1, 1990.

Times Literary Supplement, January 2, 1964; January 19, 1967; November 3, 1978; June 28, 1985; March 2, 1990, pp. 213-214; October 16, 1992, p. 22.

Vogue, November, 1990, pp. 274, 276.

Wall Street Journal, May 6, 1996, pp. A11-A12.

Washington Post, March 16, 1979; November 22, 1985.

Washington Post Book World, March 29, 1992, p. 11; May 2, 1993, pp. 1, 10.

World Literature Today, October-December, 2003, Mary Kaiser, review of *A Whistling Woman,* p. 93.

Writer, May, 1997, Lewis Burke Frumkes, "A Conversation with A.S. Byatt," p. 15.

Yale Review, October, 1993, Walter Kendrick, review of *Angels and Insects: Two Novellas,* pp. 135-137.

ONLINE

A.S. Byatt: An Overview, http://landow.stg.brown.edu/post/uk/ (March 6, 2001).

A.S. Byatt Home Page, http://www.asbyatt.com/ (April 10, 2004).

OTHER

Scribbling (television documentary), BBC-2, 2003.

C

CABRERA INFANTE, G.
See CABRERA INFANTE, Guillermo

*   *   *

CABRERA INFANTE, Guillermo 1929-2005
(G. Cabrera Infante, G. Cain, Guillermo Cain)

PERSONAL: Born April 22, 1929, in Gibara, Cuba; immigrated to London, England, 1966; naturalized British citizen; died of septicemia on February 21, 2005, in London, England; son of Guillermo Cabrera Lopez (a journalist) and Zoila Infante; married Marta Calvo, August 18, 1953 (divorced, October, 1961); married Miriam Gomez, December 9, 1961; children: (first marriage) Ana, Carola. *Ethnicity:* Hispanic *Education:* Graduated from University of Havana, Cuba, 1956. *Politics:* "Reactionary on the left." *Religion:* Catholic. *Hobbies and other interests:* Birdwatching, old movies.

CAREER: Writer. School of Journalism, Havana, Cuba, professor of English literature, 1960-61; Government of Cuba, Cuban embassy, Brussels, Belgium, cultural attaché, 1962-64, charge d'affairs, 1964-65; scriptwriter for Twentieth Century-Fox and Cupid Productions, 1967-72. Visiting professor, University of Virginia, spring, 1982.

AWARDS, HONORS: Así en paz como en la guerra was nominated for Prix International de Literature (France), 1962; unpublished manuscript version of *Tres tristes tigres* won Biblioteca Breve Prize (Spain), 1964, and was nominated for Prix Formentor—International Publishers Prize, 1965; Guggenheim fellowship for creative writing, 1970; Prix du Meilleur Livre Etranger (France), 1971, for *Tres tristes tigres;* Cervantes Prize, 1997.

WRITINGS:

FICTION

Así en la paz como en la guerra: cuentos (title means *"In Peace as in War: Stories"*), Revolución (Havana, Cuba), 1960, translation by John Brookesmith, Peggy Boyers, and Cabrera Infante published as *Writes of Passage,* Faber and Faber (Boston, MA), 1993.

Vista del amanacer en el trópico, Seix Barral (Barcelona, Spain), 1965, translation by Suzanne Jill Levine published as *A View of Dawn in the Tropics,* Harper (New York, NY), 1978.

Tres tristes tigres, Seix Barral (Barcelona, Spain), 1967, translation by Donald Gardner, Suzanne Jill Levine, and the author published as *Three Trapped Tigers,* Harper (New York, NY), 1971.

La Habana para un infante difunto, Seix Barral (Barcelona, Spain), 1979, translation by Suzanne Jill Levine and the author published as *Infante's Inferno,* Harper (New York, NY), 1984.

Vidas para leerlas, Santillana (Madrid, Spain), 1998.

FILM CRITICISM

(Under pseudonym G. Cain) *Un oficio del siglo veinte* (film reviews; originally published in *Carteles;* also see below), Revolución, 1963, translation by Kenneth Hall and Cabrera Infante published as *A Twentieth-Century Job,* Faber, 1991.

Arcadia todas las noches (title means *"Arcadia Every Night"*), Seix Barral (Barcelona, Spain), 1978.

Cine o sardina, Santillana (Madrid, Spain), 1997.

OTHER

(Editor) *Mensajes de libertad: La España rebelde—Ensayos selectos,* Movimiento Universitario Revolucionario (Lima, Peru), 1961.

Vanishing Point (screenplay), Twentieth Century-Fox, 1970.

(Translator into Spanish) James Joyce, *Dublineses (Dubliners),* Lumen (Barcelona, Spain), 1972.

O (essays), Seix Barral (Barcelona, Spain), 1975.

Exorcismos del esti(l)o (title means *"Summer Exorcisms"* and *"Exorcising Style"*; English, French, and Spanish text), Seix Barral (Barcelona, Spain), 1976.

Cuban Writer Guillermo Cabrera Infante Reading from His Work (sound recording; recorded February 26, 1982, for the Archive of Hispanic Literature on Tape), Library of Congress (Washington, DC), 1982.

Holy Smoke (nonfiction; English text), Harper (New York, NY), 1985.

(Author of introduction) Virgilio Pianera, *Cold Tales,* translation by Mark Schafer, revised by Thomas Christensen, Eridanos Press (New York, NY), 1988.

(With others) *Diablesas y diosas: 14 perversas para 15 autores,* Editorial Laertes (Barcelona, Spain), 1990.

Mea Cuba (collection of writings on Cuba), Plaza & Janes (Barcelona, Spain), 1992, translation by Kenneth Hall and the author published as *Mea Cuba,* Farrar, Straus & Giroux (New York, NY), 1994.

(Author of prologue) *La fiesta innombrable: trece poetas cubanos,* Ediciones el Tucan de Virginia (Mexico, DF), 1992.

Vaya papaya!: Ramon Alejandro (exhibition catalog), Le Polygraphe (Paris, France), 1992.

(Author of prologue) Jose Luis Guarner, *Autoretrato del cronista,* Anagrama (Barcelona, Spain), 1994.

Delito por bailar el chachacha, Santillana (Madrid, Spain), 1995, translation by the author published as *Guilty of Dancing the Chachacha,* Welcome Rain (New York, NY), 2001.

(Contributor) *The Borges Tradition,* Constable (London, England), 1995.

Mi musica extremada, Espasa Calpe (Madrid, Spain), 1996.

Ella cantaba boleros, Santillana (Madrid, Spain), 1996.

(Author of prologue) Augusto M. Torres, *Diccionario Espasa cine,* Espasa (Madrid, Spain), 1996.

(Author of text) Claudio Edinger, *Alt-Havana,* Alfaguaa (Madrid, Spain), 1999.

Infanteria (compilation), Fondo de Cultura Economic [Mexico], 1999.

Also author of screenplay, *Wonderwall,* 1968, and of unfilmed screenplay, *Under the Volcano,* based on Malcolm Lowry's novel of the same title. Also translator of stories by Mark Twain, Ambrose Bierce, Sherwood Anderson, Ernest Hemingway, William Faulkner, Dashiell Hammett, J.D. Salinger, Vladimir Nabokov, and others. Work is represented in many anthologies. Contributor to periodicals, including *New Yorker, New Republic, El País* (Spain), and *Plural* (Mexico). *Carteles* (Cuban magazine), film reviewer under pseudonym G. Cain, 1954-60, fiction editor, 1957-60; editor of *Lunes* (weekly literary supplement of Cuban newspaper, *Revolución*), 1959-61.

SIDELIGHTS: Talking about his award-winning first novel *Tres tristes tigres,* translated as *Three Trapped Tigers,* Cuban-born writer Guillermo Cabrera Infante told Rita Guibert in *Seven Voices:* "I would prefer everyone to consider the book solely as a joke lasting about five hundred pages. Latin American literature errs on the side of excessive seriousness, sometimes solemnity. It is like a mask of solemn words, which writers and readers put up with by mutual consent."

As Alastair Reed pointed out in the *New York Review of Books,* Cabrera Infante is a contemporary of Cuban dictator Fidel Castro; his parents were founding members of the Cuban Communist Party. Following Castro's rise to power, Cabrera Infante was appointed editor of *Lunes de Revolución,* the literary supplement to the new regime's mouthpiece, *Revolución.* In this role, he also provided support to his brother's development of a documentary on nightlife in Havana. The documentary was subsequently banned by authorities as counter-revolutionary. Cabrera Infante protested the banning via *Lunes* but was rebuked publicly on his "duties to the Revolution" by Castro in a trial, and *Lunes* was closed down. Noted Reid, "Cabrera Infante found himself in the kind of limbo many Cuban writers of his generation were to inhabit in succeeding years, forbidden to publish. 'Within the Revolution, everything! Against the Revolution, nothing!' as Fidel 'thundered like a thousand Zeuses.'" He was assigned to Brussels as a cultural attaché and returned to Cuba for his mother's funeral in 1965, but faced "the precariousness of any continuing Cuban existence under an imposed silence . . . he accepted the inevitability of exile," concludes Reid. He was expelled from the Union of Writers and Artists of Cuba as a traitor in 1968, following the publishing of *Three Trapped Tigers,* and began to write and speak publicly on Cuba.

In *Three Trapped Tigers,* we hear the voices of a group of friends as they take part in the nightlife of pre-Castro Havana. The friends take turns narrating the story using the colloquial speech of the lower-class inhabitants of that city. Told from many perspectives and using the language of a small group, the narrative is not always easy to follow. Elias L. Rivers explained in *Modern Language Notes:* "While some passages are readily accessible to any reader, others are obscured by Cuban vernaculars in phonetic transcription and by word-plays and allusions of many different kinds. A multiplicity of 'voices' engage in narrative, dialogue and soliloquy. [The novel] is a test which fascinates as it eludes and frustrates; the over-all narrative sense is by no-means obvious."

The importance of spoken language in *Three Trapped Tigers* is apparent even in the book's title, which in its English version repeats only the alliteration found in the Spanish title and not the title's actual meaning. Inside the book, the emphasis on sound continues as the characters pun relentlessly. There are so many puns in the book that *New Republic* contributor Gregory Rabassa maintained that in it Cabrera Infante "established himself as the punmaster of Spanish-American literature." Appearing most often are literary puns, including such examples as "Shame's Choice" used to refer to James Joyce, "Scotch Fizzgerald" for Scott Fitzgerald and "Somersault Mom" for Somerset Maugham. In another example, a bongo player—a member of the group of friends whose exploits are followed in the novel—is called "Vincent Bon Gogh."

If the emphasis on spoken rather than written language makes complete understanding of the novel difficult, it has made translating nearly impossible. Comparison of the Spanish, English, and French editions of the book proves that readers of each language are not reading the same text. "What Cabrera [Infante] has really done," commented Roger Sale in the *New York Review of Books,* "is to write, presumably with the help of his translators, three similar but different novels." Because of the word play, Sale continues, "quite obviously no translation can work if it attempts word-for-word equivalents."

Playing with words is also an important part of Cabrera Infante's next novel, *Infante's Inferno,* and his nonfiction work, *Holy Smoke.* The latter—Cabrera Infante's first book written originally in English—tells the history of the cigar and describes famous smoking scenes from literature and film. Unlike the nearly universal acclaim received for *Three Trapped Tigers,* critics were unable to reach a consensus on these two works. While some praised Cabrera Infante's continued use of puns as innovative, other had grown tired of the Cuban's verbal contortions.

Commenting on *Infante's Inferno* in the *New York Review of Books* Michael Wood complained that Cabrera Infante's relentless punning "unrepentedly mangles language and hops from one tongue to another like a frog released from the throat." Some of the jokes are "terrible," Wood wrote; "others are so cumbersome, so fiendishly worked for, that the noise of grinding machinery deafens all the chance of laughter." *New York Review of Books* contributor Josh Rubins had similar problems with *Holy Smoke.* He comments, "In *Holy Smoke . . .* the surfeit of puns seems to arise not from mania. . . , but from mere tic. Or, worse yet, from a computer program."

Other reviewers were not so harsh in their criticism. In Enrique Fernandez's *Voice Literary Supplement* review of *Infante's Inferno,* for example, the critic observed that the novel is written in "an everyday Cuban voice, unaffected, untrammeled [and], authentic." John Gross of the *New York Times* hailed Cabrera Infante as a master in the use of language. Commenting on *Holy Smoke,* he claimed: "Conrad and Nabokov apart, no other writer for whom English is a second language can ever have used it with more virtuosity. He is a master of idiomatic echoes and glancing allusions; he keeps up a constant barrage of wordplay, which is often outrageous, but no more outrageous than he intends it to be."

Cabrera Infante's *Mea Cuba* is a collection of his writings on Cuba produced after he left the country. Given the nature of his departure, *Mea Cuba* "as opposed to its gleeful predecessors . . . is in a sense a reluctant book, one that he would hardly have chosen to write had it not more or less accrued through time," said Reid. Critics, while recognizing the inherent value of the work, were mixed in their reactions. "For all its essential rectifications, *Mea Cuba* is so overstated, so patently inflamed by spite and thwarted ambition, that it forfeits its place in the rational, non-polarised debate about Cuba that is needed at this time," declared Lorna Scott Fox in the *London Review of Books.* Alma Guillermoprieto, writing in the *New York Times Book Review,* concluded, "Despite the dazzling writing . . . the style sometimes overwhelms the chronicle, and one finds oneself wishing for a respite from the shrill delivery and the endless petty settling of accounts. . . . At his worst, the bombastic punster's salvos are not meaningful but mean. At his best, he provides a moving chronicle of love and despair for the country he lost to Castro." *World Literature Today* critic Will H. Corral found academic significance as well as entertainment in Cabrera Infante's writings, noting "his texts read as the ideal format for what is bandied about the United States as cultural studies. Despite one's differences with his politics, Cabrera Infante's knowledge of Cuban literariness is the broadest, liveliest, and nastiest to date."

In a 1998 essay for *Nation,* Mario Vargas Llosa recalled that Cabrera Infante's lively sense of humor was not limited to the written page. Vargas Llosa, a prize jury member, had "fought like a lion" to ensure that *Tres tristes tigres* would win the Biblioteca Breve prize. Not long after that, Vargas Llosa received an incensed phone call from a man who demanded to know how the literary honor could be bestowed on "that repellent man Cabrera Infante." Vargas Llosa hastily defended his decision to the caller. Of course, the complainer turned out to be Cabrera Infante, who later signed a copy of his latest book for his duped friend, Vargas Llosa.

Vargas Llosa went on to compare Cabrera Infante to the great English-language wordsmiths: Lewis Carroll, James Joyce, and Laurence Sterne. But the Cuban's style is "unmistakably his own, with a sensoriality and eurythmy that, at times, . . . he persists in calling 'Cuban.' As if literary styles had a nationality!"

The author takes his humor seriously, suggested Vargas Llosa. "For the sake of a joke, a parody, a pun, an acrobatic stunt of wit, a verbal ricochet, Cabrera Infante has always been prepared to make all the enemies on earth, to lose his friends and perhaps his life," he said, referring to the political struggles the author has faced. "Because for him," the essayist continued, "humor is not as it is for common mortals, a mere recreation of the spirit, a diversion that relaxes the mind, but rather a compulsive way of challenging the world as it is, of undercutting its certainties and the rationale that holds it up—bringing to light the infinite possibilities for whimsy, surprise and nonsense concealed in it."

Cabrera Infante's wit was on display again in *Guilty of Dancing the Chachacha,* which was translated by the author from his Spanish-language original. The three interrelated stories feature the same man and woman, having lunch in a Havana restaurant during a rainy Friday afternoon. The couple's relationship with one another and their country are revealed through the three scenarios, each of which ends with the woman walking out. A *Publishers Weekly* critic found that the author's "diverting premise is squandered" in part by the male character's tendency toward racist, sexist and homophobic remarks. "By the end of the book," added the reviewer, "his relentless puns become tedious." Lawrence Olszewski of L *ibrary Journal* likewise felt that this work is "not up to par with [the author's] masterpieces,"

Three Trapped Tigers and *Infante's Inferno.* But *Booklist*'s Brad Hooper thought Cabrera Infante proved "ingenious in exploiting the short-story form" in this work.

Three Trapped Tigers established Cabrera Infante's reputation as a writer of innovative fiction, a reputation that some critics find justified by his later work. Cabrera Infante once described his literary beginnings to *CA:* "It all began with parody. If it were not for a parody I wrote on a Latin American writer who was later to win the Nobel Prize, I wouldn't have become a professional writer and I wouldn't qualify to be here at all. My parents wanted me to go to University and I would have liked to become a doctor. But somehow that dreadful novel crossed my path. After reading a few pages (I just couldn't stomach it all, of course) and being only seventeen at the time, I said to myself, 'Why, if that's what writing is all about—*anch'io sono scrittore* [I am also a writer]!' To prove I too was a writer I wrote a parody of the pages I had read. It was a dreadfully serious parody and unfortunately the short story I wrote was taken by what was then the most widely read publication in Latin America, the Cuban magazine, *Bohemia.* They paid me what at the time I considered a fortune and I was hooked: probably hooked by fortune, probably hooked by fame but certainly hooked by writing."

BIOGRAPHICAL AND CRITICAL SOURCES:

BOOKS

Alvarez-Borland, Isabel, *Discontinuidad y ruptura en Guillermo Cabrera Infante,* Hispanamerica, 1982.
Contemporary Literary Criticism, Thomson Gale (Detroit, MI), Volume 5, 1976, Volume 25, 1983, Volume 45, 1987, Volume 120, 1999.
Diaz Ruiz, Ignacio, *Cabrera Infante y otros escritores latinoamericanos,* Universidad Nacional Autonoma de Mexico (Mexico), 1992.
Dictionary of Literary Biography, Volume 113: *Modern Latin-American Fiction Writers, First Series,* Thomson Gale (Detroit, MI), 1992.
Feal, Rosemary Geisdorfer, *Novel Lives: The Fictional Autobiographies of Guillermo Cabrera Infante and Mario Vargas Llosa,* University of North Carolina Press (Chapel Hill, NC), 1986.
Gallagher, David Patrick, *Modern Latin-American Literature,* Oxford University Press (Oxford, England), 1973.

Gil Lopez, Ernesto, *Guillermo Cabrera Infante: La Habana, el lenguaje y la cinematografia,* ACT, Cabildo Insular de Tenerife (Tenerife, Spain), 1991.

Guibert, Rita, *Seven Voices,* Knopf (New York, NY), 1973.

Hernandez-Lima, Dinorah, *Versiones y re-versiones historicas en la obra de Cabrera Infante,* Pliegos (Madrid, Spain), 1990.

Jimenez, Reynaldo L., *Guillermo Cabrera Infante y Tres tristes tigres,* Ediciones Universal (Miami, FL), 1976.

Machover, Jacobo, *El heraldo de las malas noticias: Guillermo Cabrera Infante: ensayo a dos voces,* Ediciones Universal, 1996.[Alana No place here]

Merrim, Stephanie,*Logos and the Word: The Novel of Language and Linguistic Motivation in "Grande Sertao: Veredas" and "Tres tristes tigres,"* [New York, NY], 1983.

Nelson, Ardis L., *Cabrera Infante in the Menippean Tradition,* with prologue by Cabrera Infante, Juan de la Cuesta (Newark, DE), 1983.

Ortega, Julio, and others, *Guillermo Cabera Infante* [Madrid, Spain], 1974.

Pereda, Rosa Maria,*Guillermo Cabrera Infante,* Edaf, D.L. (Madrid, Spain), 1979.

Souza, Raymond D., *Major Cuban Novelists: Innovation and Tradition,* University of Missouri Press (Columbia, MO), 1976.

Souza, Raymond D., *Guillermo Cabrera Infante: Two Islands, Many Worlds,* University of Texas Press (Austin, TX), 1996.

Tittler, Jonathan, *Narrative Irony in the Contemporary Spanish-American Novel,* Cornell University Press (Ithaca, NY), 1984.

Volek, Emil, *Cuatro claves para la modernidad: Aleixandre, Borges, Carpentier, Cabrera Infante,* Gredos (Madrid, Spain), 1984.

PERIODICALS

Americas, July-August, 1995, p. 24.

Antioch Review, fall, 1995, Adan Quan, review of *Mea Cuba,* pp. 494-495.

Booklist, November 1, 1994, p. 475; May 1, 1999, review of *Cine o sardina,* p. 1583; July, 2001, Brad Hooper, review of *Guilty of Dancing the Chachacha,* p. 1977.

Book World, October 3, 1971.

Commonweal, November 12, 1971.

Hispania, May-September, 1993, William Siemens, "Mirrors and Metamorphosis: Lewis Carroll's Presence in *Tres tristes tigres,*" pp. 297-303; March,

1985, Isabel Alvarez-Borland, "*La Habana para un infante difunto:* Cabrera Infante's Self Conscious Narrative," pp. 44-48.

Ideologies and Literature, January-March, 1981, M.-Pierrette Malcuzynski, "*Tres tristes tigres,* or the Treacherous Play on Carnival," pp. 33-56.

Latin American Literary Review, spring/summer, 1976, Kjelal Kadir, "Stalking the Oxen of the Sun and Felling the Sacred Cows," pp. 15-22; fall/winter, 1976, Claudia Cairo Resnik, "The Use of Jokes in Cabrera Infante's *Tres tristes tigres,*" pp. 14-21; fall/ winter, 1977, Phyllis Mitchell, "The Reel against the Real: Cinema in the Novels of Guillermo Cabrera Infante and Manuel Puig, pp. 22-29; spring/summer, 1980, Stephanie Merrim,"A Secret Idiom: The Grammar and Role of Language in *Tres tristes tigres,* "pp. 96-117; July-December, 1985, Lydia Hazera,"Strategies for Reader Participation in the Works of Cortazar, Cabera Infante, and Vargas Llosa, "pp. 25-28.

Library Journal, November 1, 1994, p. 93; September 1, 1998, review of *Infante's Inferno* and *Three Trapped Tigers,* p. 224; July, 2001, Lawrence Olszewski, review of *Guilty of Dancing the Chachacha,* p. 127.

London Review of Books, October 4-17, 1984; February 6, 1986; December 8, 1988, Philip Horne,"Wasps and All, "p. 22; November 24, 1994, Lorna Scott Fox,"Castration, "p. 22.

Los Angeles Times Book Review, June 6, 1984; November 27, 1994, Richard Eder, review of *Mea Cuba,* p. 11; September 30, 2001, Susan Salter Reynolds, review of *Guilty of Dancing the Chachacha,* p. 11.

Modern Language Notes, March, 1977.

Nation, November 4, 1978; January 4, 1993, Gilberto Perez,"It's a Wonderful Life, "pp. 24-28; May 11, 1998, Mario Vargas Llosa,"Touchstone, "p. 56.

New Republic, July 9, 1984.

Newsweek, October 25, 1971.

New Yorker, September 19, 1977.

New York Review of Books, December 16, 1971; June 28, 1984; May 8, 1986; February 2, 1995, Alastair Reed, review of *Mea Cuba,* pp. 14-16.

New York Times, December 9, 2001, Charles Wilson, "Havana Moon. "

New York Times Book Review, October 17, 1971; May 6, 1984; March 2, 1986.

Observer (London), September 2, 1984; October 13, 1985; December 21, 1986; November 27, 1994, Alma Guillermoprieto, review of *Mea Cuba,* p. 9.

Paris Review, spring, 1983.

Publishers Weekly, June 15, 1998, review of *Infante's Inferno* and *Three Trapped Tigers,* p. 44; July 9, 2001, review of *Guilty of Dancing the Chachacha,* p. 45.

Review, January 10, 1972.

Salamagundi, fall, 1993, Regina James,"Speaking with Authority, "pp. 86-96.

Substance, Volume 13, number 1, 1984, Suzanne Jill Levine,"Translating *Infante's Inferno,* "pp. 85-94.

Time, January 10, 1972.

Times Literary Supplement, April 18, 1968; October 12, 1984; August 26, 1986; January 20, 1989, Nicholas Rankin, review of *View of Dawn in the Tropics,* p. 54; March 6, 1992, John King, review of *A Twentieth-Century Job,* p. 17; October 22, 1993, Will Eaves, review of *Writes of Passage,* p. 22; December 30, 1994, David Gallagher, review of *Mea Cuba,* p. 7; August 14, 1998, review of *Cine o sardina,* p. 20.

Village Voice, March 25, 1986.

Voice Literary Supplement, April 18, 1968; October 12, 1984; August 29, 1986.

Washington Post Book World, January 28, 1979; May 27, 1984; June 7, 1998, review of *Infante's Inferno* and *Three Trapped Tigers,* p. 12.

World Literature Today, spring, 1977; autumn, 1978, Ardis Nelson,"Holy Smoke: Anatomy of a Vice, "pp. 590-593; summer, 1981; autumn, 1987, Mary Davis,"The Minds' Isle: An Introduction to Cabrera Infante, "p. 512, Jose Miguel Oviedo,"Nabokov/ Cabrera Infante: True Imaginary Lies," pp. 559-567; spring, 1993, Will Corral, review of *Mea Cuba,* pp. 342-343; autumn, 1996, Cesar Ferreira, review of *Delito por bailar el chachacha,* pp. 921-922.

OBITUARIES:

PERIODICALS

Chicago Tribune, February 23, 2005, section 3, p. 9.
Los Angeles Times, February 23, 2005, p. B7.
New York Times, February 23, 2005, p. C19.
Times (London, England), February 23, 2005, p. 62.
Washington Post, February 25, 2005, p. B7.

*   *   *

CADE, Toni
    See BAMBARA, Toni Cade

*   *   *

CAIN, G.
    See CABRERA INFANTE, Guillermo

CAIN, Guillermo
    See CABRERA INFANTE, Guillermo

*   *   *

CALDWELL, Erskine 1903-1987
(Erskine Preston Caldwell)

PERSONAL: Born December 17, 1903, in White Oak (some sources say Moreland), GA; died of emphysema and lung cancer, April 11, 1987, in Paradise Valley, AZ; son of Ira Sylvester (a minister) and Caroline Preston (a schoolteacher; maiden name, Bell) Caldwell; married Helen Lannigan, March 3, 1925 (divorced); married Margaret Bourke-White (a photographer), February 27, 1939 (divorced, 1942); married June Johnson, December 21, 1942 (divorced, 1955); married Virginia Moffett Fletcher, January 1, 1957; children: (first marriage) Erskine Preston, Dabney Withers, Janet; (third marriage) Jay Erskine. *Education:* Attended Erskine College, 1920-21, University of Virginia, 1922-26, and University of Pennsylvania, 1924.

CAREER: Held various jobs, including mill laborer, cotton picker, cook, waiter, taxicab driver, farmhand, cottonseed shoveler, stonemason's helper, soda jerk, professional football player, bodyguard, stagehand in a burlesque theater, and a hand on a boat running guns to a Central American country in revolt; *Journal,* Atlanta, GA, reporter, 1925; script writer in Hollywood, CA, 1933-34 and 1942-43; newspaper correspondent in Mexico, Spain, Czechoslovakia, Russia, and China, 1938-40; war correspondent in Russia for *Life* magazine, PM, and Columbia Broadcasting System, Inc., 1941; writer.

MEMBER: American Academy and Institute of Arts and Letters (honorary member), Authors League of America, PEN, Phoenix Press Club (life member), San Francisco Press Club (life member), Euphemian Society, Raven Society.

AWARDS, HONORS: Yale Review Award for fiction, 1933, for short story "Country Full of Swedes."

WRITINGS:

The Bastard (novel; also see below), illustrated by Ty Mahon, Heron Press (New York, NY), 1929.

Poor Fool (novel; also see below), illustrated by Alexander Couard, Rariora Press (New York, NY), 1930, Louisiana State University Press (Baton Rouge, LA), 1994.

American Earth (short story collection), Scribner's (New York, NY), 1931, published as *A Swell-Looking Girl,* MacFadden-Bartell, 1965.

Mamma's Little Girl, privately printed, 1932.

Tobacco Road (novel; also see below), illustrated by Margaret Bourke-White, Scribner's (New York, NY), 1932, University of Georgia Press (Athens, GA), 1995.

Message for Genevieve, privately printed, 1933.

God's Little Acre (novel), Viking (New York, NY), 1933, illustrated by Milton Glaser, Farrar, Straus (New York, NY), 1962, illustrated by Harry Schaare, Franklin Library (Franklin Center, PA), 1979, University of Georgia Press (Athens, GA), 1995.

We Are the Living (short story collection), Viking (New York, NY), 1933.

Some American People, R.M. McBride & Co. (New York, NY), 1935.

Tenant Farmer, Phalanx Press (New York, NY), 1935.

Journeyman (novel), Viking (New York, NY), 1935, with a foreword by Edwin T. Arnold, University of Georgia Press (Athens, GA), 1996.

Kneel to the Rising Sun and Other Stories by Erskine Caldwell, Viking (New York, NY), 1935, published as *Kneel to the Rising Sun,* White Lion Publishers (New York, NY), 1973.

The Sacrilege of Alan Kent (novel; also see below), illustrated by Ralph Frizzell, Falmouth Book House (Portland, ME), 1936, reprinted with illustrations by Alexander Calder, Galerie Maeght, 1975, University of Georgia Press (Athens, GA), 1995.

You Have Seen Their Faces (nonfiction), photographs by Margaret Bourke-White, Viking (New York, NY), 1937, with a foreword by Alan Trachtenberg, University of Georgia Press (Athens, GA), 1995.

Southways (short story collection), Viking (New York, NY), 1938.

North of the Danube (nonfiction), photographs by Margaret Bourke-White, Viking (New York, NY), 1939, Da Capo Press (New York, NY), 1977.

Trouble in July (novel; also see below), Duell (New York, NY), 1940, with a foreword by Bryant Simon, University of Georgia Press (Athens, GA), 1999.

Jackpot: The Short Stories of Erskine Caldwell (also see below), Duell (New York, NY), 1940.

Complete Stories, Little, Brown (Boston, MA), 1941.

Say, Is This the U.S.A.? (nonfiction), photographs by Margaret Bourke-White, Duell (New York, NY), 1941, Da Capo Press (New York, NY), 1977.

All Night Long: A Novel of Guerrilla Warfare in Russia, Duell (New York, NY), 1942.

All-out on the Road to Smolensk (nonfiction), Duell (New York, NY), 1942, published as *Moscow under Fire: A Wartime Diary, 1941,* Hutchinson (London, England), 1942.

Russia at War (nonfiction), photographs by Margaret Bourke-White, Hutchinson (London, England), 1942.

Georgia Boy (novel; also see below), Duell (New York, NY), 1943, published as *Georgia Boy and Other Stories,* Avon, 1946, University of Georgia Press (Athens, GA), 1995.

Twenty-two Great Modern Short Stories from Jackpot, Avon (New York, NY), 1944.

Stories by Erskine Caldwell, edited and with a foreword by Henry Seidel Canby, Duell (New York, NY), 1944.

Tragic Ground (novel; also see below), Duell (New York, NY), 1944.

A Day's Wooing and Other Stories, Grosset (New York, NY), 1944.

The Caldwell Caravan: Novels and Stories by Erskine Caldwell, World Publishing (Cleveland, OH), 1946.

A House in the Uplands (novel), Duell (New York, NY), 1946.

The Sure Hand of God (novel; also see below), Duell (New York, NY), 1947, White Lion Publishers (London, England), 1973.

Midsummer Passion and Other Stories from Jackpot, Avon (New York, NY), 1948.

This Very Earth (novel), Duell (New York, NY), 1948.

Where the Girls Were Different and Other Stories, Avon (New York, NY), 1948, published as *Where the Girls Were Different,* MacFadden-Bartell, 1965.

Place Called Estherville (novel), Duell (New York, NY), 1949.

Episode in Palmetto (novel), Duell (New York, NY), 1950.

(Editor) Albert Nathaniel Williams, *Rocky Mountain Country,* Duell (New York, NY), 1950.

The Humorous Side of Erskine Caldwell, edited by Robert Cantwell, Duell (New York, NY), 1951.

Call It Experience: The Years of Learning How to Write, Duell (New York, NY), 1951, published as *Call It Experience,* MacFadden-Bartell, 1966, with a foreword by Erik Bledsoe, University of Georgia Press (Athens, GA), 1996.

The Courting of Susie Brown (short story collection), Duell (New York, NY), 1952, published as *The Courting of Susie Brown and Other Stories,* Pan Books (England), 1958.

A Lamp for Nightfall (novel), Duell (New York, NY), 1952.

Complete Stories, Duell (New York, NY), 1953, published as *The Complete Stories of Erskine Caldwell,* Little, Brown (Boston, MA), 1953.

Love and Money (novel), Duell (New York, NY), 1954.

Gretta (novel), Little, Brown (Boston, MA), 1955.

Gulf Coast Stories, Little, Brown (Boston, MA), 1956.

The Pocket Book of Erskine Caldwell Stories: Thirty-one of the Most Famous Short Stories, Pocket Books (New York, NY), 1957.

Certain Women (short story collection), Little, Brown (Boston, MA), 1957.

Molly Cottontail (for children), illustrated by William Sharp, Little, Brown (Boston, MA), 1958.

Claudelle Inglish (novel), Little, Brown (Boston, MA), 1959, published as *Claudelle,* Heinemann (London, England), 1959.

When You Think of Me (short story collection), illustrated by Louis Macouillard, Little, Brown (Boston, MA), 1959.

Three by Caldwell—Tobacco Road, Georgia Boy, The Sure Hand of God: Three Great Novels of the South, Little, Brown (Boston, MA), 1960.

Men and Women: Twenty-two Stories, edited and with an introduction by Carvel Collins, Little, Brown (Boston, MA), 1961, published as *Men and Women,* MacFadden-Bartell, 1965.

Jenny by Nature (novel), Farrar, Straus (New York, NY), 1961.

Close to Home (novel), Farrar, Straus (New York, NY), 1962.

The Bastard, Poor Fool and The Sacrilege of Alan Kent, Bodley Head (London, England), 1963.

The Last Night of Summer (novel), Farrar, Straus (New York, NY), 1963.

A Woman in the House, MacFadden-Bartell, 1964.

Around about America (nonfiction), illustrated by Virginia M. Caldwell, Farrar, Straus (New York, NY), 1964.

In Search of Bisco, Farrar, Straus (New York, NY), 1965, University of Georgia Press (Athens, GA), 1995.

The Deer at Our House (for children), illustrated by Ben Wohlberg, Collier (New York, NY), 1966.

In the Shadow of the Steeple (also see below), Heinemann (London, England), 1967.

Writing in America, Phaedra Publishers (New York, NY), 1967.

Miss Mamma Aimee (novel), New American Library (New York, NY), 1967.

Summertime Island (novel), World Publishing (New York, NY), 1968.

Deep South: Memory and Observation (nonfiction; Part 1 first published in England as *In the Shadow of the Steeple*), Weybright (New York, NY), 1968, with a

foreword by Guy Owen, University of Georgia Press (Athens, GA), 1980, 1995.

The Weather Shelter (novel), World Publishing (New York, NY), 1969.

The Earnshaw Neighborhood (novel), World Publishing (New York, NY), 1971.

Annette (novel), New American Library (New York, NY), 1973.

Afternoons in Mid-America: Observations and Impressions (nonfiction), illustrated by Virginia M. Caldwell, Dodd (New York, NY), 1976.

Tragic Ground [and] *Trouble in July,* with an introduction by Calder Willingham, New American Library (New York, NY), 1979.

Stories, illustrated by Dennis Lyall, Franklin Library (Franklin Center, PA), 1980.

Stories of Life, North and South: Selections from the Best Short Stories of Erskine Caldwell, edited by Edward Connery Lathem, Dodd (New York, NY), 1983.

The Black and White Stories of Erskine Caldwell, edited by Ray McIver, Peachtree Publications (Atlanta, GA), 1984.

With All My Might (autobiography), Peachtree Publications (Atlanta, GA), 1987.

Conversations with Erskine Caldwell, edited by Edwin T. Arnold, University Press of Mississippi (Jackson, MS), 1988.

(Editor) North Callahan, *Smoky Mountain Country,* Smoky Mountain Historical Society (Sevierville, TN), 1988.

Midsummer Passion and Other Tales of Maine Cussedness, introduction by Upton Birnie, edited by Charles G. Waugh and Martin H. Greenberg, Yankee Books (Camden, ME), 1990.

The Stories of Erskine Caldwell, foreword by Stanley W. Lindberg, University of Georgia Press (Athens, GA), 1996.

Erskine Caldwell: Selected Letters, 1929-1955, edited by Robert L. McDonald, McFarland & Co. (Jefferson, NC), 1999.

Also author of screenplays *A Nation Dances* and *Volcano.* Editor, "American Folkways," twenty-five volumes, 1940-55.

A collection of Caldwell's manuscripts is housed in the Baker Library of Dartmouth College, Hanover, NH.

ADAPTATIONS: Several of Caldwell's novels have been made into films, including *Tobacco Road,* Twentieth Century-Fox Film Corp., 1941, *God's Little Acre,* United Artists Corp., 1958, and *Claudelle Inglish* (under the title *Claudelle*), Warner Brothers, Inc., 1961. *Tobacco Road* was also adapted for the stage by Jack Kirkland and ran on Broadway for more than seven years.

SIDELIGHTS: As one of America's most banned and censored writers, in addition to being one of its most financially successful, Erskine Caldwell was often "patronized or ignored by academic critics and serious readers," according to James Korges, author of a critical study of the man who has been called "the South's literary bad boy." Korges continued: "Younger readers dismiss him as a writer of the old pornography, for how tame, demure, almost tidy seem the passages that were read aloud in courts as evidence of Caldwell's obscenity. . . . Younger critics seem unwilling to read Caldwell with care. . . . That much of [his] work 'grew towards trash' [in the words of William Faulkner] does not alter the fact that Caldwell has produced an important body of work in both fiction and nonfiction." In fact, Faulkner himself ranked Caldwell among America's five leading contemporary writers.

Because his early works reflected the plight of impoverished sharecroppers, Caldwell earned a reputation as a leading proletarian novelist and won a strong following in the Soviet Union. Caldwell defended his frank handling of the seamier aspects of rural poverty as social realism. According to the *Chicago Tribune,* he later recalled that "in those days hunger, disease and lack of education were central factors of life in rural Georgia," where the author was raised. Indeed, although Caldwell was more than just a novelist, his specialty through the years was the fictional depiction of the seamier side of life in the American South—the bigotry, poverty, and misery among small-town "white trash." The son of a Presbyterian minister who made frequent moves from congregation to congregation throughout the South, Caldwell had ample opportunities as a boy to observe the various people and lifestyles of his native region. He often accompanied his father on visits to the homes of his parishioners, for example, and for a time he even drove a country doctor on his rounds. As he once explained to an interviewer: "You learned a lot living in small towns those days before they became smaller versions of the big towns."

Early in his career, Caldwell worked at a variety of odd jobs, including mill laborer, farm hand, and stage hand. He subsequently became a journalist, reporting for the *Atlanta Journal* and serving as a correspondent in Mexico, Spain, Czechoslovakia, and China, as well as a war correspondent in the Soviet Union for *Life* magazine. For several years Caldwell was also a screenwriter in Hollywood. Among his other writings are *Jackpot: The Short Stories of Erskine Caldwell, The Sure Hand of God, The Caldwell Caravan: Novels and Short Fiction,* and the screenplays *A Nation Dances* and *Volcano.* Additionally, he wrote children's books and from 1941 to 1954 served as editor of the twenty-five-volume "American Folkway Series."

Ten of Caldwell's novels—*Tobacco Road, God's Little Acre, Journeyman, Trouble in July, Tragic Ground, A House in the Uplands, The Sure Hand of God, This Very Earth, Place Called Estherville,* and *Episode in Palmetto*—comprise what the author himself referred to as "a cyclorama of Southern life." Unlike Faulkner's mythical Yoknapatawpha County, however, Caldwell's "cyclorama" does not seek to link his characters and events in any kind of overall historical framework; his goal, according to Korges, was to discover "scenes and actions that [embody] themes and types in the present."

Very few, if any, of Caldwell's characters or themes inspire admiration or optimism. His point of view was essentially pessimistic—man is more or less doomed to a life of pain and hurt, subject to the whims of chance and the effects of the actions of others. Virtually everything that happens—whether the results are bad or good—is regarded by Caldwell's characters as a manifestation of the will of God. And though there is room for humor in Caldwell's work, it is of a very bitter variety that only serves to reinforce the author's dark vision of life.

One reviewer, W.M. Frohock, saw this type of humor as Caldwell's greatest strength. "There is a special sort of humor in America," Frohock wrote in *The Novel of Violence in America.* "Its material is the man who has been left behind in the rush to develop our frontiers, the man who has stayed in one place, out of and away from the main current of our developing civilization, so largely untouched by what we think of as progress that his folkways and mores seem to us, at their best, quaint and a little exotic—and, at their worst, degenerate. . . . [This type of humor] has been the main source, as well as the great strength, of Erskine Caldwell's novels."

For the most part, Caldwell's characters exhibit the last quality—degeneracy—far more than quaintness and exoticism. This characteristic has inspired much of the negative reaction against his two best-known novels, *Tobacco Road* and *God's Little Acre.* Southerners in particular have found his graphic descriptions of incest, adultery, lynchings, prostitution, lechery, murder, and the excesses of that "old-time religion" to be extremely offensive. Joseph Wood Krutch observed in *The American Drama since 1918: An Informal History:* "[Of] Mr. Caldwell one may see that the rank flavor of his work is as nearly unique as anything in contemporary literature. . . . His starveling remnant of the Georgia poor-white trash is not only beyond all morality and all sense of dignity or shame, it is almost beyond all hope and fear as well. As ramshackle and as decayed as the moldy cabins in which it lives, it is scarcely more than a parody on humanity." Caldwell succeeds in making comedy out of these people's wretched lives, Krutch continued, "because he manages to prevent us from feeling at any moment any real kinship with the nominally human creatures of the play. . . . [But] his race of curiously depraved and yet curiously juicy human grotesques are alive in his plays whether they, or things like them, were ever alive anywhere else or not . . . and no attempts at analysis can deprive them of their life."

Korges also thought that Caldwell's characters are "alive" and that they personify very real human needs and desires. *Tobacco Road,* he proposed, "is about tenacity in the spirits of men and women deserted by God and man. The book is not about tobacco or Georgia, about sexology, or sociology, but is instead a work of literary art about the animal tug toward life that sustains men even in times of deprivation." However, Korges continued, "The book is also a study in relationships and desertions. Man in this symbolic landscape is frustrated in his relationship to the soil because fertility has deserted the land. The sterile relationship of man to land is paralleled in the sterile [relationships between the main characters]."

Korges discovered this same theme of sterility in the novel he considered Caldwell's masterpiece, *God's Little Acre.* He questioned its reputation as an "'expose' of southern mentality or habits," insisting that it is instead "a novel of rich sexuality, sexuality being in this symbolic landscape . . . the one impressive life-sign. Yet just as the farm produces neither cotton nor gold . . . , so no woman in the novel is pregnant, despite all the sexuality." The theme of sterility also appears in a more general sense in Caldwell's work. Despite appearances to the contrary, the preservation of family values plays an important part in his novels. In a less "somber" manner than someone like John Steinbeck, for example, Caldwell emphasizes the richness of rural family life as opposed to the sterility and brutality of life in the city. Thus, as Korges pointed out, "the emotional poverty of the city folks is set off against the richness of feeling of the impoverished country folk, free from the economic meanness of making good marriages or of charging for sex."

For the most part, critics of the 1930s did not recognize these subliminal shades of meaning in Caldwell's work. Those who were not disgusted by his stories were amused by what they called his "burlesque"-type humor. Commenting on *Tobacco Road,* for example, Horace Gregory of *Books* noted that "Caldwell's humor, like Mark Twain's, has at its source an imagination that stirs the emotions of the reader. The adolescent, almost idiotic gravity of [his] characters produces instantaneous laughter and their sexual adventures are treated with an irreverence that verges upon the robust ribaldry of a burlesque show." A *Forum* critic noted that "Caldwell recites the orgiastic litany calmly and with a serene detachment. Such detachment is not likely to be shared by most readers, who, if they take the book seriously, will probably finish it—if they do finish it—with disgust and a slight retching; but anyone who considers it as subtle burlesque is going to have a fine time."

The *Nation* reviewer, on the other hand, appeared to sense that there was something more to *Tobacco Road* than just entertainment. He wrote: "The notion has gone about that the deliquescent characters, their squalor, their utter placidity, make Caldwell's writing 'primitive'; his sentence structure has made possible the belief that his work is naive; and because the setting is rural and the humors supposedly exaggerated, he is said to resemble Mark Twain and Bret Harte. These false notions have completely obscured what is an original, mature approach to the incongruities existing in a people who ignore the civilization that contains them as completely as the civilization ignores them."

Though *God's Little Acre* also offended some critics, more seemed willing to identify and comment on its literary merits. The *Saturday Review of Literature* critic, after having admitted that it was a novel "that will lift the noses of the sensitive," concluded that it "is nevertheless a beautifully integrated story of the barren Southern farm and the shut Southern mill, and one of the finest studies of the Southern poor white which has ever come into our literature. . . . Mr. Caldwell has caught in poetic quality the debased and futile aspiration of men and women restless in a world of long hungers which must be satisfied quickly, if at all."

A *Forum* reviewer wrote: "There has been considerable genteel ballyhoo in behalf of Erskine Caldwell but this novel is the first thing he has done which seems to this reader to justify in any way the praise the critics have heaped upon him. Despite its faults . . . it is immensely superior to *Tobacco Road* and *American Earth.* This superiority results from the fact that the author has stressed that element in which he is at his best, poor-white rural comedy." Horace Gregory, commenting once again in *Books,* also thought that "as a novel *God's Little Acre* has its faults, and there are flaws that in the work of a less gifted writer would be fatal to his progress. . . . But even as it stands I believe the book is an important step in the development of an important young novelist."

After this 1930s "golden age" came a gradual decline in the quality of Caldwell's work, a decline from which many critics believed the author never really recovered. More and more frequently, noted Korges, Caldwell turned to "sensational plotting and trite characterization . . . mixed with a good deal of superficial psychological comment and superficial motivation." Edward Hoagland of the *New York Times Book Review* declared that Caldwell simply "vegetated." He wrote: "The trouble with Caldwell seems to have been that he was finally lackadaisical. The eye that could distill so narrowly, the decent heart that roamed *Tobacco Road,* . . . rather soon stopped looking for new insights. . . . [In his later works] there is no bite or discipline, no old-pro's vigor of craftsmanship. Even his way with dialogue . . . has fallen off to casual indifference."

Korges, on the other hand, concluded his study of Caldwell on an optimistic note. He wrote: "Caldwell, now in such disrepute among academic critics, will one day be 'discovered,' and his reputation will rest on a few books. . . . Such a selection from the large and uneven body of Caldwell's writing will make clear the strength of his best work in fiction and nonfiction, and will reveal what is now obscured by the very bulk of his output: his is a solid achievement that supports the assertion that he is one of the important writers of our time."

BIOGRAPHICAL AND CRITICAL SOURCES:

BOOKS

Allen, Walter, *The Modern Novel in Britain and the United States,* Dutton (New York, NY), 1965.

Authors in the News, Volume 1, Thomson Gale (Detroit, MI), 1976.

Beach, Joseph Warren, *American Fiction: 1920-1940,* Russell (New York, NY), 1960.

Caldwell, Erskine, *Call It Experience: The Years of Learning How to Write,* Duell (New York, NY), 1951, published as *Call It Experience,* MacFadden-Bartell, 1966, with a foreword by Erik Bledsoe, University of Georgia Press (Athens, GA), 1996.

Caldwell, Erskine, *With All My Might: An Autobiography,* Peachtree Publications (Atlanta, GA), 1987.

Contemporary Authors Autobiography Series, Volume 1, Thomson Gale (Detroit, MI), 1984.

Contemporary Literary Criticism, Thomson Gale (Detroit, MI), Volume 1, 1973, Volume 8, 1978, Volume 14, 1980, Volume 50, 1988.

Contemporary Novelists, 4th edition, St. Martin's Press (New York, NY), 1986.

Dictionary of Literary Biography, Thomson Gale (Detroit, MI), Volume 9: *American Novelists, 1910-1945,* 1981, Volume 86: *American Short-Story Writers, 1910-1945, First Series,* 1989.

Frohock, W. M., *The Novel of Violence in America,* revised edition, Southern Methodist University Press (Dallas, TX), 1957.

Kazin, Alfred, *On Native Grounds: An Interpretation of Modern American Prose Literature,* Reynal (New York, NY), 1942.

Korges, James, *Erskine Caldwell,* University of Minnesota Press (Minneapolis, MN), 1969.

Krutch, Joseph Wood, *The American Drama since 1918: An Informal History,* Random House (New York, NY), 1939.

McDonald, Robert L., editor, *The Critical Response to Erskine Caldwell,* Greenwood Press (Westport, CT), 1997.

Miller, Dan B., *Erskine Caldwell: The Journey from Tobacco Road: A Biography,* Knopf (New York, NY), 1995.

Mixon, Wayne, *The People's Writer: Erskine Caldwell and the South,* University Press of Virginia (Charlottesville, VA), 1995.

Newquist, Roy, *Counterpoint,* Rand McNally (Chicago, IL), 1964.

PERIODICALS

Atlantic, July, 1962; November, 1963; May, 1965; October, 1968.

Best Sellers, September 1, 1968; November 15, 1969.

Books, February 21, 1932, Horace Gregory, review of *Tobacco Road;* February 5, 1933, Horace Gregory, review of *God's Little Acre.*

Books and Bookmen, June, 1968.

Book Week, May 23, 1943.

Book World, March 24, 1967.

Chicago Daily Tribune, March 4, 1933.

Commonweal, August 21, 1964.

Explicator, winter, 1999, Walter Rankin, review of *Tobacco Road,* pp. 110-112.

Forum, May, 1932, review of *Tobacco Road;* March, 1933.

Journal and Constitution (Atlanta, GA), May 13, 1973.

Mississippi Quarterly, spring, 1993, Jay Watson, "The Rhetoric of Exhaustion and the Exhaustion of Rhetoric: Erskine Caldwell in the Thirties," pp. 215-229; winter, 1996, Andrew Silver, "Laughing over Lost Causes: Erskine Caldwell's Quarrel with Southern Humor," pp. 51-58; summer, 2000, Sylvia J. Cook, review of *Erskine Caldwell: Selected Letters, 1929-1955,* p. 473.

Nation, July 6, 1932, review of *Tobacco Road;* October 18, 1933, review of *God's Little Acre;* June 11, 1977, Walton Beacham, profile of Caldwell's work.

National Observer, March 25, 1968.

New Republic, March 23, 1932, review of *Tobacco Road;* February 8, 1933, review of *God's Little Acre;* November 6, 1944.

Newsday, October 11, 1969.

New Statesman, March 17, 1961, August 31, 1962.

Newsweek, April 5, 1965.

New Yorker, May 22, 1965.

New York Herald Tribune Book Review, March 30, 1958; April 5, 1959; June 10, 1962.

New York Times, February 5, 1933; April 25, 1943.

New York Times Book Review, February 23, 1958, March 19, 1961; June 17, 1962; April 4, 1965; January 4, 1970; November 14, 1976.

Playboy, May, 1968.

Punch, May 8, 1968.

Saturday Review, May 2, 1959; May 1, 1965.

Saturday Review of Literature, March 5, 1932; February 18, 1933, review of *God's Little Acre.*

Southern Review, autumn, 2003, Edwin T. Arnold, "Unruly Ghost: Erskine Caldwell at One Hundred," pp. 851-869.

Spectator, August 24, 1962.

Springfield Republican, February 15, 1933.

Time, August 25, 1961; June 19, 1964.

Times Literary Supplement, June 26, 1969.

OBITUARIES:

PERIODICALS

Chicago Tribune, April 13, 1987.

Dallas Times Herald, April 13, 1987.

Detroit Free Press, April 13, 1987.

Los Angeles Times, April 13, 1987.

New York Post, April 13, 1987.

New York Times, April 13, 1987.

Time, April 20, 1987, p. 64.

Washington Post, April 13, 1987.

*   *   *

CALDWELL, Erskine Preston
See CALDWELL, Erskine

*   *   *

CALISHER, Hortense 1911-

PERSONAL: Born December 20, 1911, in New York, NY; daughter of Joseph Henry (a manufacturer) and Hedwig (Lichstern) Calisher; married Heaton Bennet Heffelfinger, September 27, 1935 (divorced); married Curtis Arthur Harnack (a novelist), March 27, 1959; children: (first marriage) Bennet Hughes (daughter), Peter Hughes. *Education:* Barnard College, A.B., 1932.

ADDRESSES: Home—205 West 57th St., New York, NY 10019. *Agent*—Candida Donadio & Associates, Inc., 231 West 22nd St., New York, NY 10011.

CAREER: Social worker for Department of Public Welfare, New York, NY; adjunct professor at Barnard College, New York, NY, 1957, Columbia University, New York, NY, 1968-70, and Columbia University School of the Arts, 1972-73. Visiting professor at Brandeis University, 1963-64, City College of the City University of New York, 1970-71, State University of New York—Purchase, 1971-72, Bennington College, 1978, Washington University, St. Louis, MO, 1979, and Brown University, 1986. Clark Lecturer, Scripps College, 1968. Regents Professor, University of California—Irvine, 1975. Visiting lecturer at University of Iowa, 1957, 1959-60, Stanford University, 1958, Sarah Lawrence College, 1962, 1967, University of Pennsylvania, 1969, in West Germany, Yugoslavia, Romania, and Hungary, 1978, and for the U.S./China Arts Exchange, Republic of China, 1986.

MEMBER: PEN (president, 1986-87), American Academy and Institute of Arts and Letters (president, 1987-90).

AWARDS, HONORS: Guggenheim fellow, 1951-52, 1953-54; American Specialist's Grant, U.S. Department of State, 1958, for visiting Southeast Asia; National

Council of the Arts award, 1967; Academy of Arts and Letters award, 1967; National Book Award nominations, 1962, for *False Entry,* 1973, for *Herself: An Autobiographical Work,* and 1976, for *The Collected Stories of Hortense Calisher;* four O. Henry prize story awards; Hurst fellow, Washington University, 1979; Kafka Prize, University of Rochester, 1986, for *The Bobby-Soxer;* Lifetime Achievement Award, National Endowment for the Arts, 1989. Litt.D., Skidmore College, 1980, Grinnell College, 1986, Adelphi University, 1988.

WRITINGS:

NOVELS

False Entry, Little, Brown (Boston, MA), 1961.
Textures of Life, Little, Brown (Boston, MA), 1963.
Journal from Ellipsia, Little, Brown (Boston, MA), 1965.
The New Yorkers, Little, Brown (Boston, MA), 1969.
Queenie, Arbor House (Westminster, MD), 1971.
Standard Dreaming, Arbor House (Westminster, MD), 1972.
Eagle Eye, Arbor House (Westminster, MD), 1973.
On Keeping Women, Arbor House (Westminster, MD), 1977.
Mysteries of Motion, Doubleday (New York, NY), 1983.
The Bobby-Soxer, Doubleday (New York, NY), 1986.
Age, Weidenfeld & Nicolson (London, England), 1987, published as *Age: A Love Story,* Marion Boyars (New York, NY), 1996.
Kissing Cousins: A Memory, Weidenfeld & Nicolson (London, England), 1988.
In the Palace of the Movie King, Random House (New York, NY), 1993.
In the Slammer with Carol Smith, Marion Boyars (New York, NY), 1997.
Sunday Jews, Harcourt (New York, NY), 2002.
Tattoo for a Slave, Harcourt (Orlando, FL), 2004.

COLLECTIONS

In the Absence of Angels, Little, Brown (Boston, MA), 1951.
Tale for the Mirror: A Novella and Other Stories, Little, Brown (Boston, MA), 1962.
Extreme Magic: A Novella and Other Stories, Little, Brown (Boston, MA), 1964.

The Railway Police [and] *The Last Trolley Ride* (two novellas), Little, Brown, (Boston, MA), 1966.
The Collected Stories of Hortense Calisher, Arbor House (Westminster, MD), 1975.
Saratoga, Hot (short stories), Doubleday (New York, NY), 1985.
The Novellas of Hortense Calisher, Modern Library (New York, NY), 1997.

OTHER

Herself: An Autobiographical Work, Arbor House (Westminster, MD), 1972.
(Editor, with Shannon Ravenel, and author of introduction) *Best American Short Stories, 1981,* Houghton (Boston, MA), 1981.
(With others) *A Century at Yaddo,* Corporation of Yaddo (Saratoga Springs, NY), 2000.

Contributor to numerous anthologies, including *Fifty Best American Short Stories, 1915-1965, Best American Short Stories, 1951, Great American Short Stories, Mid-Century: An Anthology of Distinguished American Short Stories,* and *O. Henry Memorial Award Prize Stories.* Contributor of short stories, articles, and reviews to *New York Times, Evergreen Review, Texas Quarterly, American Scholar, New Yorker, Harper's, Harper's Bazaar, New Criterion, Mademoiselle, Reporter, Charm, New World Writing, Ladies' Home Journal, Saturday Evening Post, Gentleman's Quarterly, Kenyon Review,* and *Nation.*

SIDELIGHTS: Hortense Calisher is "among the most literate practitioners of modern American fiction, a stylist wholly committed to the exploitation of language," wrote a *Saturday Review* contributor. Calisher's first short stories appeared in the *New Yorker* in the 1940s, and in the decades since then she has alternated her story collections with novels and novellas. In addition, Calisher has written an autobiographical memoir titled *Herself: An Autobiographical Work,* that Robert Kiely in the *New York Times Book Review* considered "primarily and at its best a long meditation on the art of writing fiction in America in the second half of the twentieth century." While the body of Calisher's work has consistently garnered praise, her short stories receive the most acclaim. "Calisher not only is best at writing short stories, she is one of *the best,*" wrote Robert Phillips in his *Commonweal* review of *The Collected Stories of Hortense Calisher,* and Calisher's four O. Henry awards seem to support this view.

Reviewers note that Calisher's sometimes masterful short stories deliver the unexpected. "Calisher has always specialized in astonishment. . . . She excels at jamming shocks into deceptively cool narratives," commented Nora Sayre in the *New York Times Book Review.* For Doris Grumbach, also reviewing in the *New York Times Book Review,* "what happens in [Calisher's] stories is what [Calisher] has defined as 'an apocalypse, served in a very small cup.' Sudden awareness, epiphanies of character are her metier . . . [and] the tea cup is the proper vessel for sudden, small visions into the spirit. In a blaze of light, as startling as Paul's Damascan vision, we see, not a string of events, but a tableau, frozen, static, inevitable—and instructive." Thus, according to Sayre, "a dim, fluttering Southern wallflower becomes a Manhattan Communist, achieving apotheosis and an Order of Stalin, second class, after her accidental death in an explosion; . . . a nighttime scream on 57th Street obsesses and even attracts a widow so lonely that she yearns to hear the scream again; . . . at a posh London dinner table, the women all suddenly remove their blouses; and a completely bald woman discards her wig while in an intimate embrace with her lover, only to be shunned for her attempt at total honesty." Calisher's fiction, though varied in tone and theme, is often "sorrowful, for most of her characters suffer from their difference, their isolation, their concern with those terrible needs of the human being which for most of us seem destined never to be fulfilled," offered *New York Times Book Review* critic Gertrude Buckman in her assessment of Calisher's first short story collection, *In the Absence of Angels.* Additionally, Calisher's characters are inclined to reminisce and become nostalgic, and in some way or another they must grapple with failure. In the *Dictionary of Literary Biography,* Carolyn Matalene stated that "perhaps the overriding impulse of [Calisher's] literary style is that her characters' carefully nurtured abstractions perpetually clash with realities."

Calisher's compelling novella *The Railway Police* manifests this idea. In this novella, Calisher writes of a woman who has been dominated for years by her hereditary baldness; she has even aborted the child in her womb for fear of passing on the defect. After witnessing a vagrant's nonchalant reaction to being thrown off of a train by the railway police, the woman, who is never named, attempts to liberate herself from the constraints that have ruled her life. *New York Times Book Review* contributor R.V. Cassill recounted the woman's attempt to marry "a balding gentleman whose anthropological and artistic tastes imply he will accept her ultimate unveiling with joy." Instead, her lover flees, prompting Cassill to label him a representative of "that modern man who yearns for the nudity of the female, but nudity as he has preconceived it, not as the woman in her full hunger for acceptance and revelation knows it must exist." As full of "terror and torment" as Calisher's works sometimes are, Charles Lee stated in *Saturday Review of Literature* that they are "neither without compassion nor, more important, without hope. . . . Calisher seems willing to pin her badly bruised faith on the virtuous potentialities of man." Thus, in *The Railway Police,* "the heroine's baldness, her deformity, is her humanity, and the story asks us to consider what it means to be human," Joan Joffe Hall noted in *Saturday Review.*

A substantial amount of Calisher's writing is semi-autobiographical, drawing on her heritage as the Jewish daughter of a transplanted Southerner and a German immigrant living a comfortable, middle-class existence in New York. According to Matalene, the sister and brother characters Hester and Joe Elkin—who first appear in *In the Absence of Angels*—are both portraits of Calisher, who "grow up and learn about death, about peripheral persons, about female vanity, about the complicity love sometimes requires, and about the burden of parents, whether alive or dead. The Hester stories are, from one point of view, small gems of social history. . . . And, from another point of view, they are quiet and carefully realized fictions of a young woman's growth into loving and remembering and understanding." In addition, Grumbach figured that a third of the entries in *The Collected Stories of Hortense Calisher,* a compilation of Calisher's three previous collections, are about the author's own family: "her father, mother, aunts, family hangers-on, servants, her brother. She is best . . . with them because she allows herself to wander among them, an awkward, undervalued, sensitive child among proud, attractive, transplanted, late Victorian Southerners, living out their well-to-do 'comfortable' lives in New York."

Grumbach further labeled Calisher the "quintessential New Yorker, entirely comfortable on its streets, in its apartments, lovingly, almost patriotically, wrapping the whole island in the elegant tissue of her words." *Washington Post Book World* commentator Anne Tyler explained that while Calisher's settings are often confined to New York, "sometimes it's New York's Fifth Avenue and sometimes the seedy, lead colored warehouse district way, way downtown. And at still other times, it's the closed world of those transplants to the city who have managed, somehow, to bring their natural habitats with them intact." Still, at other times, Calisher, who calls herself a "city bird," is just as at home in the suburbs and small towns or even outer space.

Incorporating Calisher's Jewish heritage, her familiarity with New York, and her understanding of labyrinthine human relationships is her 1969 novel, *The New Yorkers*. In this work Judge Simon Mannix returns home from a banquet held in his honor to the noise of a gunshot. His twelve-year-old daughter, Ruth, at the onset of her first menarche, has killed his wife as she lay in the arms of a lover. The remainder of the novel chronicles Mannix's life-transforming attempt to conceal the tragedy, even from Ruth. A reviewer for the *Times Literary Supplement* felt that in *The New Yorkers,* Calisher "is out to memorialize an institution even closer to the establishment than the Forsytes—the rich, cultured, philanthropic, New York Jewish family. . . . Her weighty saga is filled with the pain and drama that any family (but in particular such a family, such a race) hides behind its elegant front. . . . Calisher knows how to create the pattern of blood-relationships which tug and strain to keep a family together." Christopher Lehmann-Haupt of the *New York Times* found that "among [the book's] many themes—which include the relationships of Jews and Gentiles, Jews and Jews, class behavior, parents and children—the predominant one is the polarity between masculinity and femininity. . . . Consider that opening incident again: a girl who has just become a woman kills her mother . . . after having witnessed her fornicating with a strange man. Ruth's act is sexually ambivalent, to say the least. And, sure enough, the climactic chapter of *The New Yorker;* . . . is Ruth's version of what happened that fatal evening. It is overwhelmingly preoccupied with her search for sexual identity." In the end, on the occasion of Ruth's marriage to a Quaker, "Judge Mannix and his daughter at last manage to put the two halves of their lives together and to affirm both," wrote Matalene.

Apart from its commentary on familial and social relationships, and apart from its treatment of the development of sexual identity, *The New Yorkers* "is a profoundly local novel. Therein lies its real strength; Calisher knows her chosen city as few others do, and her evocations of it are stunning," Matalene commented. On the other hand, though *New York Times Book Review* contributor John Brooks praised Calisher's insight into human relationships, he felt *The New Yorkers* "is another attempt at the always-elusive, never-quite-achieved Great New York Novel. Certainly this brooding and rather overstuffed Gothic tale isn't that. But it has smaller rewards for the reader with patience."

Calisher's novel *In the Palace of the Movie King* examines dislocation and lost heritage through the ordeal of forced emigration. The novel involves filmmaker Paul Gonchev, born to Russian parents, raised in Japan, and employed by the Albanian government to produce travel documentaries. When his Yugoslavian wife arranges for his kidnaping and subsequent exile to the United States, the traumatic event causes Gonchev to lose speaking ability in all languages except Japanese. Despite the attention he receives as a dissident artist in America, Gonchev longs for his wife in Albania and experiences alienation in his unfamiliar new home. *New York Times Book Review* contributor Michael Gorra described the novel as "Calisher's ambitious attempt, after a long and distinguished career, to capture the mood of this last decade of the twentieth century, its glorious postmodern Babel, its wealth of new immigrants." Though noting elements of the story that seem somewhat outdated, Gorra concluded that *In the Palace of the Movie King* "is a kind of love song to an ever-changing America, where to be an exile, both free of and weighted down by one's past, is the national fate."

While many of Calisher's novels deal with issues surrounding personal heritage, *Age* transcends provincial and ethnic sensibilities to explore universal human fears. The novel features a septuagenarian couple who witness their degenerating physical and mental abilities while facing the inevitability of death and the dreadful loneliness that awaits the surviving spouse. To defend against such despair, both husband and wife agree to keep separate journals intended to console the mourning survivor upon the other's death. The novel revolves around their parallel entries as each reflects on life, relationships, family, and the prospect of living without the other. "In a series of short, alternating chapters, we are taken inside the soul and psyche of each partner," wrote Eleanor J. Bader in *Belles Lettres*. A contributor to *Kirkus Reviews* concluded that *Age* is "an amusing, acrid and sharp view of the 'total disease' of life and death, paced by Calisher's own teasing imagination." However, in a *Spectator* review, Francis King noted the nearly indistinguishable voices of husband and wife in the story. According to King, "It is in the uniformity of style that Calisher's novella suffers from its one major flaw." *New York Times Book Review* critic Thomas Mallon found fault in the couple's "morbidly atypical" obsession with death, noting that "one ironic result of *Age* is that it makes one wonder if it isn't better to live as if there's every tomorrow, right up until death brings its unwanted relief." Despite such criticism, as King proclaimed, "That [Calisher] is a marvel no one should doubt after reading this book."

In 2002, at the age of ninety, Calisher published her fifteenth novel, *Sunday Jews*. Like the others, wrote Emily Barton in the *New York Times Book Review,* this work "evinces [the author's] passion for language and commitment to the possibilities of both a long sentence and a well-placed pause." *Sunday Jews* takes place in the mixed-religion marriage of Zipporah Zangwill. A sixty-ish anthropologist, Zipporah describes her background as "lace-curtain Jewish," assimilated into the mainstream American culture. "In Calisher's hands," commented *New Leader* reviewer Tova Reich, "assimilation is good. It fosters diversity and growth, along with a concomitant rejection of narrow orthodoxies and intolerances." Zipporah is married to lapsed Catholic Peter Duffy; they have raised five children while enduring the childhood death of a sixth. The novel's title refers to a weekly get-together of Zipporah's intellectual and conflicted offspring, plus an assortment of spouses, lovers, and friends. The couple's ambiguous spirituality affects the children, including a daughter, Nell, who "unapologetically bears children out of wedlock," noted Barton, "then sends them to every available kind of Sunday school, including Buddhist." The Zangwill-Duffy family faces a crossroads with the advancing senility of Peter; Zipporah sells their Manhattan townhouse and embarks with her husband on a journey of memory to the "exotic places she had visited and studied," according to a *Kirkus Reviews* contributor.

Sunday Jews earned widespread plaudits. Typical of Calisher, the novel's sentences "burst wide open into absolute pandemonium," as Beth Kephart put it in *Book.* Kephart added that beyond the author's athleticism with language, it is her heartfelt scenes of Zipporah's death that "reflects the genius of this most mystifying writer." "It was my great pleasure to discover how beautifully [*Sunday Jews*] is plotted," said Barton. More than one reviewer found traces of the influence of turn-of-the-twentieth-century American writers Henry James and Edith Wharton in Calisher's novel, as if "Wharton had written about assimilated Jews rather than status-conscious WASPS," commented a *Publishers Weekly* contributor. *Booklist*'s Donna Seaman judged *Sunday Jews* as "Jamesian in style and intent," as it "traces the meshing of inner and outer words with voluptuous precision."

If there is any one aspect of Calisher's writing on which reviewers disagree, it is her way with language. Some critics have found her prose "superlative," "exciting," and "gorgeous," while others have described it as "self-congratulatory," "self-indulgent," and even "pretentious." Jean Martin wrote in the *Nation* that for the author, the telling is all: "In Calisher the art lies in all that she puts into a sentence. From a glittering vocabulary she chooses words that bejewel the tiara of sentence structure." *Saturday Review* critic David Boroff, commenting on Calisher's third short-story collection, *Ex-*

treme Magic, likewise considered her "an immaculate stylist, a precisionist of the utmost rigor, and an arresting phrase-maker." Kiely felt that her fiction reads like "the kind of language . . . one might expect from a metaphysical poet."

On the other hand, though he admitted to a fondness for "a rich, even an overripe prose," *New York Times Book Review* critic Anatole Broyard noted in his assessment of Calisher's novel *On Keeping Women* that "all too often . . . [her] rhetoric seems to me to mire her characters as well as the movement of her book. . . . J.D. Salinger said, sentimentality means loving someone more than God loves them, and I think . . . Calisher may be guilty as charged. Or perhaps it is language that she loves more than God does—it is hard to distinguish people from the prose." Hall made a similar statement, noting that in the novella *The Last Trolley Ride,* "Calisher's style is, at its best, witty and ripe with insights; words melt in her mouth like . . . fritters. But she has such an appetite for language, for seasoning in every sentence, that at its worst her style can become opaque, no medium for discovery and elucidation, a risky idiom for narrating events, dangerous for long fiction." On the whole, noted Matalene, "critics are more comfortable with the terse prose of [Calisher's] . . . short story style than with the stylistic exuberances of her novels."

In *Kissing Cousins: A Memory,* an autobiographical memoir that appeared in 1988, Calisher reflects on her friendship with Katie Pyle, a Southern Jewish girl fifteen years her senior. Pyle nursed Calisher when she suffered from childhood diphtheria and remained a lasting influence in her life as an adult role model and supporter. *Kissing Cousins* describes the author's fascination with Pyle's Southern background, which her own father shared, and memorializes Pyle's ceaseless compassion. According to a *Publishers Weekly* reviewer, *Kissing Cousins* is a "brave, deeply affecting memoir" that displays the "gift for sharply drawn characters and gimlet wit" that distinguishes Calisher's fiction. "The entire inspiration of her book is to pay tribute to a woman she loved, a substitute younger mother or older sister you might say, who died at the beginning of the 1980s," wrote Seymour Krim in *Washington Post Book World.* "There is a brooding melancholy that settles over the end of *Kissing Cousins,*" observed *New York Times Book Review* contributor Roy Hoffman. Referring to the Jewish tradition of remembering the dead, Hoffman concluded that "Calisher's deeply personal and touching book is in keeping with this philosophy."

Calisher's memoir *Tattoo for a Slave* opens with Calisher's father telling her that her greatly respected grandparents never kept slaves, only freed servants.

However as times progresses, the author describes a startling and hurtful revelation. It is only after she is fully grown and her parents have died that Calisher discovers a receipt while cleaning out her parents' safe-deposit box, for two insurance policies taken out by her grandfather years before on two of his "servants." The author describes her struggle to come to terms with the reality that her family did indeed keep slaves in "the most lovely language imaginable—Emersonian in its richness, Nabokovian in its evocativeness," according to a *Kirkus Reviews* contributor who referred to *Tattoo for a Slave* as "a dazzling memoir."

While reviewers inevitably comment on Calisher's literary style, she shuns being labeled a "stylist." "When it begins to be said that I have a style, am a 'stylist,' I chafe. Doesn't this mean I have nothing to say comparable to the way I say it—or else that anything I say will all sound the same?" she questions in *Herself.* Calisher further explains in *Kissing Cousins* that she "hears" her prose before she writes it. According to the author, "this makes for a prose that can always be read, often subtly demands that. Sometimes leading to a rhetoric which, loving its own rhythms, may stray too far from sense, or fall into marvelous accident."

That Calisher may at times use overly fancy prose or self-indulgent language stems from her unwillingness to hide behind her writing. Kiely stated that "one of the recurring themes of [Calisher's] memoir and one of the distinctions of her art [is] that she does not write on behalf of New Yorkers, Americans, Jews, women, liberals, or, for that matter, writers. She writes on behalf of herself." Though the "invisible novelist" may be the current vogue, "Calisher has never been a writer who masked her thinking self or disappeared into her subject," commented Morris Dickstein in his *New York Times Book Review* article on *The Bobby-Soxer.* Calisher "belongs to a different tradition descending from Henry James, in which the writer's own complex intelligence—his humming eloquence, his subtle knowingness—becomes essential to his equipment as a storyteller," the contributor added. "Far from holding the mirror up to life, this kind of writer diffracts it through the prism of his sensibility, as if to show how many-faceted it is, how much he himself has made it up." Susan Rochette-Crawley noted in *Reference Guide to Short Fiction* that "while one does not read a Calisher story to see the most recent narrative trends, one does read her stories for their technical perfection and her skill with language."

As Matalene observed in her *Dictionary of Literary Biography* essay, "For Calisher, the act of writing and the act of living tend to be congruent, and perhaps this ac-

counts for the deep feeling of sympathy with those ordinary people which her writing conveys. In the conclusion to *Herself,* she wrote: 'Perhaps my own process is not so much my own as I thought, nor even one that only artists know—but one that we share with other Americans, other *People.* Less and less do I see any gap—in the process of us all.'"

BIOGRAPHICAL AND CRITICAL SOURCES:

BOOKS

Calisher, Hortense, *Herself: An Autobiographical Work,* Arbor House (New York, NY), 1972.
Calisher, Hortense, *Kissing Cousins: A Memory,* Weidenfeld & Nicolson (London, England), 1988.
Contemporary Literary Criticism, Thomson Gale (Detroit, MI), Volume 2, 1974, Volume 4, 1975, Volume 8, 1978, Volume 38, 1986.
Dictionary of Literary Biography, Volume 2: *American Novelists since World War II,* Thomson Gale (Detroit, MI), 1978.
Modern American Literature, 5th edition, St. James Press (Detroit, MI), pp. 186-189.
Newquist, Roy, *Conversations,* Rand McNally (Chicago, IL), 1967.
Reference Guide to American Literature, St. James Press (Detroit, MI), 2000, pp. 139-141.
Reference Guide to Short Fiction, St. James Press (Detroit, MI), 1999, pp. 110-112.
Snodgrass, Kathleen, *The Fiction of Hortense Calisher,* University of Delaware Press (Newark, DE), 1993.

PERIODICALS

American Libraries, February, 1993, review of *Age,* p. 200.
Atlantic, October, 1972.
Belles Lettres, winter, 1989, Eleanor J. Bader, review of *Age,* p. 7.
Best Sellers, January, 1984, review of *Mysteries of Motion,* p. 356; May, 1986, review of *The Bobby-Soxer,* p. 43.
Book, July-August, 2002, Beth Kephart, review of *Sunday Jews,* p. 81.
Booklist, November 1, 1983, review of *Mysteries of Motion,* p. 397; May 15, 1985, review of *Saratoga, Hot,* p. 1293; March 15, 1986, review of *The Bobby-Soxer,* p. 1057; September 15, 1987, review of *Age,* p. 107; September 15, 1988, review of *Kissing Cousins,* p. 113; September 15, 1993, re-

view of *In the Palace of the Movie King,* p. 126; June 1, 1997, review of *In the Slammer with Carol Smith,* p. 1654; December 15, 1997, review of *The Novellas of Hortense Calisher,* p. 684; May 1, 2002, Donna Seaman, review of *Sunday Jews,* p. 1507.

Books, November 4, 1962; April 28, 1963.

Book World, October 1, 1972.

Christian Science Monitor, November 11, 1965; January 18, 1984, review of *Mysteries of Motion,* p. 22; August 8, 1984, review of *The Collected Stories of Hortense Calisher,* p. 25.

Commonweal, May 7, 1976.

Detroit News, December 25, 1983.

Generations, spring, 1993, review of *Age,* p. 83.

Harper's, March, 1971.

Horn Book, June, 1984, review of *Mysteries of Motion,* p. 372.

Kirkus Reviews, September 1, 1983, review of *Mysteries of Motion,* p. 964; April 1, 1985, review of *Saratoga, Hot,* p. 288; February 1, 1986, review of *The Bobby-Soxer,* p. 140; July 15, 1987, review of *Age,* p. 1009; August 1, 1988, review of *Kissing Cousins,* p. 1112; October 1, 1993, review of *In the Palace of the Movie King,* p. 1217; April 1, 1997, review of *In the Slammer with Carol Smith,* p. 320; October 15, 1997, review of *The Novellas of Hortense Calisher,* p. 1553; April 15, 2002, review of *Sunday Jews,* p. 510, July 1, 2004, review of *Tattoo for a Slave,* p. 612.

Library Journal, December 1, 1983, review of *Mysteries of Motion,* p. 2261; June 15, 1985, review of *Saratoga, Hot,* p. 71; May 15, 1986, review of *The Bobby-Soxer,* p. 76; August, 1987, review of *Age,* p. 139; August, 1993, review of *In the Palace of the Movie King,* p. 148; April 1, 1997, review of *In the Slammer with Carol Smith,* p. 122; May 1, 1998, review of *The Novellas of Hortense Calisher,* p. 144.

Listener, April 21, 1966, Anthony Burgess, review of *Journal from Ellipsia,* p. 589.

Los Angeles Times, October 9, 1983, review of *Mysteries of Motion,* p. 1; February 25, 1986; June 2, 2002, Susan Salter Reynolds, "Three Questions for Hortense Calisher," p. R4.

Los Angeles Times Book Review, October 9, 1983; July 21, 1985, review of *Saratoga, Hot,* p. 5; December 13, 1987, review of *Age,* p. 11.

Ms., January, 1974; July, 1984, review of *Mysteries of Motion,* p. 30.

Nation, November 18, 1961; June 29, 1974; December 1, 1997, review of *The Novellas of Hortense Calisher,* and *In the Slammer with Carol Smith,* p. 34.

New Leader, January 19, 1976; June 16, 1986, review of *The Bobby-Soxer,* p. 20; May-June, 2002, Tova Reich, "The Case for Assimilation," p. 36.

New Republic, November 3, 1973, Irving Malin, review of *Eagle Eye,* p. 26; October 25, 1975.

New Statesman, September 13, 1963, Brigid Brophy, review of *Textures of Life,* p. 326.

Newsweek, April 29, 1963; October 16, 1972.

New York Review of Books, June 25, 1964, Eve Auchincloss, review of *Extreme Magic,* p. 17; December 15, 1966.

New York Times, May 12, 1966; April 18, 1969; November 9, 1972; October 13, 1975; November 1, 1977; November 8, 1983.

New York Times Book Review, November 18, 1951; October 29, 1961; May 12, 1963; November 7, 1965; May 22, 1966; April 13, 1969; March 28, 1971; October 1, 1972, Robert Kiley, review of *Herself: An Autobiographical Work,* p. 3; November 11, 1973; October 19, 1975; October 23, 1977; November 6, 1983, review of *Mysteries of Motion,* p. 7; May 20, 1984; June 17, 1984, review of *The Collected Stories of Hortese Calisher,* p. 32; May 26, 1985, review of *Saratoga, Hot,* p. 10; March 30, 1986, Morris Dickstein, review of *The Bobby-Soxer,* p. 5; October 18, 1987, Thomas Mallon, review of *Age,* p. 14; December 18, 1988, Roy Hoffman, review of *Kissing Cousins,* p. 23; February 20, 1994, Michael Gorra, review of *In the Palace of the Movie King,* p. 12; July 27, 1997, review of *In the Slammer with Carol Smith,* p. 17; January 25, 1998, review of *The Novellas of Hortense Calisher,* p. 19; June 2, 2002, Emily Barton, "6 Rms Riv Vu," p. 10.

Partisan Review, number 2, 1980, review of *On Keeping Women,* p. 308.

Publishers Weekly, September 16, 1983, review of *Mysteries of Motion,* p. 116; February 24, 1984, review of *The Collected Stories of Hortese Calisher,* p. 138; April 12, 1985, review of *Saratoga, Hot,* p. 87; February 7, 1985, review of *The Bobby-Soxer,* p. 60; July 31, 1987, review of *Age,* p. 69; July 29, 1988, review of *Kissing Cousins,* p. 218; October 11, 1993, review of *In the Palace of the Movie King,* p. 69; March 17, 1997, review of *In the Slammer with Carol Smith,* p. 74; October 27, 1997, review of *The Novellas of Hortense Calisher,* p. 54; May 6, 2002, review of *Sunday Jews,* p. 35, June 28, 2004, review of *Tattoo for a Slave,* p. 38.

Quill & Quire, February, 1984, review of *Mysteries of Motion,* p. 41.

Reporter, November 17, 1966.

Review of Contemporary Fiction, spring, 1994, review of *In the Palace of the Movie King,* p. 216.

Saturday Review, October 28, 1961, Granville Hicks, review of *False Entry,* p. 17; October 27, 1962; May 2, 1964; December 25, 1965; June 18, 1966;

April 3, 1971; October 14, 1972; October 18, 1975; July-August, 1985, review of *Saratoga, Hot,* p. 76.

Saturday Review of Literature, December 1, 1951.

Sewanee Review, January, 1999, review of *The Novellas of Hortense Calisher,* p. 134.

Southern Review, winter, 1985, review of *Mysteries of Motion,* p. 204.

Spectator, May 25, 1996, Francis King, review of *Age,* p. 32.

Time, October 22, 1965; May 16, 1966; May 19, 1969.

Times Literary Supplement, January 15, 1970.

Virginia Quarterly Review, summer, 1969; spring, 1984, review of *Mysteries of Motion,* p. 55.

Wall Street Journal, June 20, 1997, review of *In the Slammer with Carol Smith,* p. A16.

Washington Post, December 31, 1983.

Washington Post Book World, March 28, 1971; September 18, 1977; November 6, 1977; May 27, 1984, review of *The Collected Stories of Hortense Calisher,* p. 16; June 9, 1985, review of *Saratoga, Hot,* p. 8; January 8, 1989, Seymour Krim, review of *Kissing Cousins,* p. 7.

West Coast Review of Books, January, 1984, review of *Mysteries of Motion,* p. 41; September, 1986, review of *The Bobby-Soxer,* p. 37.

Writer's Digest, March, 1969.

* * *

CALVINO, Italo 1923-1985

PERSONAL: Born October 15, 1923, in Santiago de Las Vagas, Cuba; died following a cerebral hemorrhage September 19, 1985, in Siena, Italy; son of Mario (a botanist) and Eva (a botanist; maiden name, Mameli) Calvino; married Chichita Singer (a translator), February 19, 1964; children: Giovanna. *Education:* University of Turin, graduated, 1947.

CAREER: Writer. Member of editorial staff of Giulio Einaudi Editore, Turin, Italy, 1947-83; lecturer. *Military service:* Italian Resistance, 1943-45.

AWARDS, HONORS: Viareggio prize (Italy), 1957; Bagutta prize (Italy), 1959, for *I racconti;* Veillon prize, 1963; Premio Feltrinelli per la Narrative, 1972; honorary member of American Academy and Institute of Arts and Letters, 1975; German State Prize for European Literature, 1976; *Italian Folktales* named an American Library Association Notable Book, 1980; Grande Aigle d'Or, Festival du Livre de Nice (France), 1982; honorary degree from Mt. Holyoke College, 1984; Premio Riccione (Italy), for *Il sentiero dei nidi di ragno.*

WRITINGS:

FICTION

Il sentiero dei nidi di ragno, Einaudi (Turin, Italy), 1947, translation by Archibald Colquhoun published as *The Path to the Nest of Spiders,* Collins (London, England), 1956, Beacon Press (Boston, MA), 1957, revised edition, Ecco Press (New York, NY), 2000.

Ultimo viene il corvo (short stories; title means "Last Comes the Crow"; also see below), Einaudi (Turin, Italy), 1949.

Il visconte dimezzato (novel; title means "The Cloven Viscount"; also see below), Einaudi (Turin, Italy), 1952.

L'entrata in guerra (short stories; title means "Entering the War"), Einaudi (Turin, Italy), 1954.

Il barone rampante (novel; also see below), Einaudi (Turin, Italy), 1957, translation by Archibald Colquhoun published as *The Baron in the Trees,* Random House (New York, NY), 1959, original Italian text published under original title with introduction, notes and vocabulary by J.R. Woodhouse, Manchester University Press (Manchester, England), 1970.

Il cavaliere inesistente (novel; title means "The Nonexistent Knight"; also see below), Einaudi (Turin, Italy), 1959.

La giornata d'uno scutatore (novella; title means "The Watcher"; also see below), Einaudi (Turin, Italy), 1963.

La speculazione edilizia (novella; title means "A Plunge into Real Estate"; also see below), Einaudi (Turin, Italy), 1963.

Ti con zero (stories), Einaudi (Turin, Italy), 1967, translation by William Weaver published as *T Zero,* Harcourt (New York, NY), 1969, published as *Time and the Hunter,* J. Cape (London, England), 1970.

Le cosmicomiche (stories), Einaudi (Turin, Italy), translation by William Weaver published as *Cosmicomics,* Harcourt (New York, NY), 1968.

La memoria del mondo (stories; title means "Memory of the World"), Einaudi (Turin, Italy), 1968.

La citta invisibili (novel), Einaudi (Turin, Italy), 1972, translation by William Weaver published as *Invisible Cities,* Harcourt (New York, NY), 1974.

Il castello dei destini incrociati, Einaudi (Turin, Italy), 1973, translation by William Weaver published as *The Castle of Crossed Destinies,* Harcourt (New York, NY), 1976.

Marcovaldo ovvero le stagioni in citta, Einaudi (Turin, Italy), 1973, translation by William Weaver published as *Marcovaldo: or, The Seasons in the City,* Harcourt (New York, NY), 1983.

Se una notte d'inverno un viaggiatore (novel), 1979, translation by William Weaver published as *If on a Winter's Night a Traveler,* Harcourt (New York, NY), 1981.

Palomar (novel), Einaudi (Turin, Italy), 1983, translation by William Weaver published as *Mr. Palomar,* Harcourt (New York, NY), 1985.

Cosmicomiche vecchie e nuove (title means "Cosmicomics Old and New"), Garzanti, 1984.

Sotto il sole giaguaro (stories), Garzanti, 1986, translation by William Weaver published as *Under the Jaguar Sun,* Harcourt (New York, NY), 1988.

Numbers in the Dark and Other Stories, Pantheon (New York, NY), 1995.

(Editor and author of introduction) *Fantastic Tales: Visionary and Everyday,* Pantheon (New York, NY), 1997.

Lettere 1940-1985, edited by Luca Baranelli, introduction by Claudio Milanini, A. Mondadori (Milan, Italy), 2000.

Contributor to books, including *Tarocchi,* F.M. Ricci (Parma, Italy), 1969.

OMNIBUS VOLUMES

Adam, One Afternoon and Other Stories (contains translation by Archibald Colquhoun and Peggy White of stories in *Ultimo viene il corvo* and "La formica argentina"; also see below), Collins (London, England), 1957.

I racconti (title means "Stories"; includes "La nuvola de smog" and "La formica argentina"; also see below), Einaudi (Turin, Italy), 1958.

I nostri antenati (contains *Il cavaliere inesistente, Il visconte dimezzato,* and *Il barone rampante*; also see below), Einaudi (Turin, Italy), 1960, translation by Archibald Colquhoun with new introduction by the author published as *Our Ancestors,* Secker & Warburg (London, England), 1980.

The Nonexistent Knight and The Cloven Viscount: Two Short Novels (contains translation by Archibald Colquhoun of *Il visconte dimezzato* and *Il cavaliere inesistente*), Random House (New York, NY), 1962.

La nuvola de smog e La formica argentina (also see below), Einaudi (Turin, Italy), 1965.

Gli amore dificile (contains stories originally published in *Ultimo viene il corvo* and *I racconti*), Einaudi (Turin, Italy), 1970, translation by William Weaver, Archibald Colquhoun, and Peggy Wright published as *Difficult Loves,* Harcourt (New York, NY), 1984,

expanded edition, translation by Weaver and D.C. Carne-Ross (also see below), Secker & Warburg (London, England), 1984.

The Watcher and Other Stories, Harcourt (New York, NY), 1971.

EDITOR

Cesare Pavese, *La letteratura americana e altri saggi,* Einaudi (Turin, Italy), 1951.

(And reteller) *Fiabe italiane: Raccolte della tradizione popolare durante gli ultimi cento anni e transcritte in lingua dai vari dialetti,* Einaudi (Turin, Italy), 1956, selections translated by Louis Brigante published as *Italian Fables,* Orion Press, 1959, translation by George Martin published as *Italian Folktales,* Harcourt (New York, NY), 1980.

Cesare Pavese, *Poesie edite e inedite,* Einaudi (Turin, Italy), 1962.

Cesare Pavese, *Lettere,* Volume I (with Lorenzo Mondo and Davide Lajolo): *1924-1944,* Volume II: *1945-1950,* Einaudi (Turin, Italy), 1966.

Vittorini: Progettazione e letteratura, All'Insegno del Pesce d'Oro (Italy), 1968.

(And reteller) Ludovico Ariosto, *Orlando furioso,* Einaudi (Turin, Italy), 1970.

Jakob Ludwig Karl Grimm and Wilhelm Karl Grimm, *Fiabe,* Einaudi (Turin, Italy), 1970.

L'uccel belverde e altre fiabe italiane, Einaudi (Turin, Italy), 1972, selections translated by Sylvia Mulcahy as *Italian Folk Tales,* Dent (London, England), 1975.

Il principe granchio e altre fiabe italiane, Einaudi (Turin, Italy), 1974.

Racconti fantastici dell'Ottocento, Mondadori (Milan, Italy), 1983, translation published as *Fantastical Tales,* Pantheon (New York, NY), 1994.

Also editor of fiction series "Cento Pagi" for Einaudi. Coeditor with Elio Vittorini of literary magazine, *Il Menabo,* 1959-66.

OTHER

Una pietra sopra: Discorsi di letteratura e societa, Einaudi (Turin, Italy), 1980, translation by Patrick Creagh published as *The Uses of Literature: Essays,* Harcourt (New York, NY), 1986.

Collezione di sabbia: Emblemi bizzarri e inquietanti del nostro passato e del nostro futuro gli og getti raccontano il mondo (articles), Garzanti, 1984.

Six Memos for the Next Millenium (lectures; originally published as *Sulla fiaba*), translation by Patrick Creagh, Harvard University Press, 1988.

The Road to San Giovanni (autobiographical essays; originally published as *ITA*), translation by Tim Parks, Pantheon (New York, NY), 1993.

Album Calvino, edited by Luca Baranelli Ernesto Ferrero, A. Mondadori (Milan, Italy), 1995.

(With Valerio Adami) *Adami: Itinerari dello sguardo* (title means *Adami: Itineraries of the Look*), edited by Julian Zugazagoitia, Electa (Milan, Italy), 1997.

Ali Baba: Progetto di una rivista, 1968-1972 (title means *Ali Baba: Project of a Magazine, 1968-1972*), edited by Mario Barenghi and Marco Belpoliti, Marcos y Marcos (Milan, Italy), 1998.

Why Read the Classics?, translation by Martin McLaughlin, Pantheon (New York, NY), 1999.

Mondo Scritto e Mondo non Scritto (literary essays), Oscar Mondadori (Milano, Italy), 2002.

The Hermit in Paris: Autobiographical Writings, translated from the Italian by Martin McLaughlin, Pantheon (New York, NY), 2003.

Contributor to books, including *Finibusterre,* edited by Antonio Lucio Giannone Nardo, Besa (Lecce, Italy), 1999, and *Il cinema di Folco Quilici,* introduction by Tullio Kezich Venezia, Scuola Nazionale di Cinema, 2000.

SIDELIGHTS: Italian novelist and short story writer Italo Calvino was famous for the fables he wrote and for the monumental collection of Italian fables he edited. Commenting in the *New York Times Book Review,* John Gardner called Calvino "one of the world's best fabulists." Although he wrote in what Patchy Wheatley referred to in the *Listener* as a "dazzling variety of fictional styles," Calvino's stories and novels are fables for adults. Gore Vidal noted in a *New York Review of Books* essay that because Calvino both edited and wrote fables he was "someone who reached not only primary school children . . . but, at one time or another, everyone who reads."

Calvino's theory of literature, established very early in his career, dictated his use of the fable. For Calvino, to write any narrative is to write a fable. In *A Guide to Contemporary Italian Literature: From Futurism to Neorealism,* Sergio Pacifici quoted a portion of Calvino's 1955 essay "Il midollo del leone" ("The Lion's Marrow") in which the novelist wrote: "The mold of the most ancient fables: the child abandoned in the woods or the knight who must survive encounters with beasts and enchantments remains the irreplaceable scheme of all human stories."

To understand Calvino, therefore, one must first understand the fable. Calvino "portrayed the world around him," Sara Maria Adler noted in *Calvino: The Writer as Fablemaker,* "in the same way it is portrayed in the traditional fable. In all his works, the nature of his narrative coincides with those ingredients which constitute the underlying structure of the genre." A traditional fable, Adler explained, is told from a child's point of view and usually has a young protagonist. Although not all of Calvino's protagonists or narrators are young, John Gatt-Rutter maintained in the *Journal of European Studies,* "The childlike psychology is characteristic of all [these characters], whatever their supposed age." The presence of such youthful narrators/protagonists in Calvino's works lends a fanciful touch to his fiction because, according to Pacifici, "only a youngster possesses a real sense of enchantment with nature, a sense of tranquility and discovery of the mysteries of life."

Another aspect of the fable is what Adler called "the basic theme of tension between character and environment." A typical tale might have a child lost in the woods, for example. Such tension is also a constant in Calvino's fiction. As Adler noted, "No matter what the nature of the author's fantasy may be, in every case his characters are faced with a hostile, challenging environment [over] which they are expected to triumph." In "The Argentine Ant," for instance, a family moves to a house in the country only to find it inhabited by thousands of ants. In a more comic example from *Mr. Palomar,* the title character must decide how to walk by a sunbather who has removed her bathing suit top—without appearing either too interested or too indifferent.

Calvino began his career as a fabulist in the late 1940s while still under the influence of the leading writers of postwar Italy. These authors, who had been kept from writing about the world around them by government censorship, now turned wholeheartedly to their everyday life for themes and action for their narratives. Together they formed the neorealist literary movement and, according to Nicholas A. DeMara in the *Italian Quarterly,* dedicated themselves to drawing "material directly from life and . . . reproduce faithfully real situations through traditional methods."

Conceived in this milieu, Calvino's first novel, *The Path to the Nest of Spiders,* and his short-story collections, *Adam, One Afternoon* and *L'entrata in guerra* ("Entering the War"), are all realistic. A *Times Literary Supplement* reviewer noted, for example, that Calvino's narratives are "sometimes based on autobiography, and mainly set against the background of recent Italian history and politics." Even while the three works portray the realities of war, Calvino's imagination was the dominant element.

Following the standard form of a fable, *The Path to the Nest of Spiders* has a young protagonist, an adolescent boy named Pin. According to DeMara and Adler, Calvino's choice of Pin as his protagonist allowed the novelist to add fanciful elements to an otherwise realistic story. In *The Path to the Nest of Spiders*, DeMara stated, "Calvino portrays an essentially realistic world, but through the use of the adolescent figure he is frequently able to inject into the work a sense of fantasy." Pin is nearly a child, and he describes his world as many children do, using a combination of real and imaginary elements. A fable-like quality is added to the novel, Adler observed, because "seen through the boy's own eyes" everything is "infused with a fanciful and spirited attitude toward life. . . . The countryside may be as lyrical as an animated cartoon, while at other times it may assume the proportions of a nightmare."

Calvino's childlike imagination and sense of playfulness fills his work with fantasy but also serves another purpose. According to J.R. Woodhouse in *Italo Calvino: A Reappraisal and an Appreciation of the Trilogy*, "Calvino's description of child-like candour is often a very telling way of pointing to an anomaly, a stupidity in society, as well as providing a new and refreshing outlook on often well-worn themes." In this way Calvino added another fable-like dimension to his work: that of moral instruction.

Young people play prominent roles in all three of the novels in Calvino's *Our Ancestors* trilogy: *The Cloven Viscount, The Baron in the Trees,* and *The Nonexistent Knight.* The tension between the protagonist and his or her environment and the moral intent are also clear in these three works, demonstrating for JoAnn Cannon in *Modern Fiction Studies* that "the fantastic in Calvino is not a form of escapism, but is grounded in a persistent sociopolitical concern."

The narrator of *The Baron in the Trees* is the younger brother of the twelve-year-old baron of the title who ascends into the trees to avoid eating snail soup. In his introduction to *Our Ancestors* Calvino explained the meaning of *The Cloven Viscount,* a narrative about a soldier split in half by a cannonball during a crusade: "Mutilated, incomplete, an enemy to himself is modern man; Marx called him 'alienated,' Freud 'repressed'; a state of ancient harmony is lost, [and] a new state of completeness aspired to."

Calvino's ability to fuse reality and fantasy captured the imagination of critics on both sides of the Atlantic. For example, in the *New York Times Book Review* Alan Cheuse wrote about Calvino's "talent for transforming the mundane into the marvelous," and in the *London Review of Books* Salman Rushdie referred to Calvino's "effortless ability of seeing the miraculous in the quotidian." According to *New York Times* reviewer Anatole Broyard, the books in which Calvino perfects this tendency are three of his more mature works: *Cosmicomics, Invisible Cities,* and *If on a Winter's Night a Traveler.* With their juxtaposition of fantasy and reality, these books led critics such as John Updike and John Gardner to compare Calvino with two other master storytellers noted for using the same technique in their fiction: Jorge Luis Borges and Gabriel García Márquez.

The stories in *Cosmicomics*—as well as most of the stories in *T Zero* and *La memoria del mondo* (*Memory of the World*)—chronicle the adventures of Qfwfq, a strange, chameleon-like creature who was present at the beginning of the universe, the formation of the stars, and the disappearance of the dinosaurs. In a playful scene typical of Calvino—and reminiscent of the comic episodes of García Márquez's *One Hundred Years of Solitude*—Qfwfq describes how time began. According to his story, all the universe was contained in a single point until the day one of the inhabitants of the point, Mrs. Ph(i)Nko, decided to make pasta for everyone. Rushdie explained, "The explosion of the universe outwards . . . is precipitated by the first generous impulse, the first-ever 'true outburst of general love,' when . . . Mrs. Ph(i)Nko cries out: 'Oh, if I only had some room, how I'd love to make some noodles for you boys.'"

Even as his fiction became more and more fantastic in the "Qfwfq" stories, Calvino continued to maintain the moral and social overtones present in his earlier work. In *Science-Fiction Studies* Teresa de Lauretis observed that while Calvino's fiction acquired a science-fiction quality during the 1960s and 1970s due to its emphasis on scientific and technological themes, it was still based on specific human concerns. "The works," she commented, "were all highly imaginative, scientifically informed, funny and inspired meditations on one insistent question: What does it mean to be human, to live and die, to reproduce and to create, to desire and to be?"

In a *New Yorker* review Updike made a similar observation about the seriousness underlying Calvino's fantasies: "Calvino is . . . curious about the human truth as it becomes embedded in its animal, vegetable, historical, and comic contexts; all his investigations spiral in upon the central question of *How shall we live?*"

Invisible Cities is the book Calvino called his "most finished and perfect" in a *Saturday Review* interview with Alexander Stille. It also brought him large-scale international attention. *Invisible Cities* relates an imaginary conversation between thirteenth-century explorer Marco Polo and Mongol emperor Kublai Khan in which Polo describes fifty-five different cities within the emperor's kingdom. Critics applauded the book for the beauty of Calvino's descriptions. In the *New Republic* Albert H. Carter, III, called it "a sensuous delight, a sophisticated literary puzzle," while in the *Chicago Tribune* Constance Markey judged it "a fragile tapestry of mood pieces." Perhaps the most generous praise came from *Times Literary Supplement* contributor Paul Bailey, who observed of *Invisible Cities:* "This most beautiful of books throws up ideas, allusions, and breathtaking imaginative insights on almost every page."

Invisible Cities is another fable with a youthful Marco Polo and a moral to be pondered. Adler explained: "Polo's task is that of teaching the aging Kublai Khan to give a new meaning to his life by challenging the evil forces in his domain and by insuring the safety of whatever is just. . . . [Polo's] observations . . . are a general explanation of the world—a panoramic view where rich and poor, the living and the dead, young and old, are challenged by the complex battles of existence."

In the *Hudson Review*, Dean Flower compared *Invisible Cities* with one of Calvino's subsequent novels, *The Castle of Crossed Destinies,* calling them both "less novels than meditations on the mysteries of fictive structures." This statement could also be applied to Calvino's most experimental novel, *If on a Winter's Night a Traveler. The Castle of Crossed Destinies,* like *The Nonexistent Knight,* is a chivalric tale filled with knights and adventure. *If on a Winter's Night a Traveler,* however, is not only different from Calvino's previous work, it is also marked by a complexity that makes it his least fable-like book.

In *If on a Winter's Night a Traveler* Calvino parodies modern fictional styles in a complicated novel-within-a-novel format. But even this novel includes at least one element of the fable. In *Newsweek* Jim Miller noted that in Calvino's introduction to *Italian Folktales* the novelist wrote, "There must be present" in each tale "the infinite possibilities of mutation, the unifying element in everything: men, beasts, plants, things." While the fable explores mutation in nature, in *If on a Winter's Night a Traveler* Calvino explores the "infinite possibilities of mutation" within the novel.

After her husband's death, Calvino's widow oversaw the issue of new volumes of his work in English. *The*

Road to San Giovanni is a compilation of several essays or "memory exercises" that are the closest Calvino ever came to writing an autobiography. These works span his development as a writer, from his boyhood in San Remo during the 1930s through his work in the Italian Resistance during World War II to his experience as an expatriate in Paris during the 1960s. "The Calvino that emerges here is extremely self-conscious, offering finely observed evocations of the Italian landscape or a Parisian suburb, but also a running metacommentary on the act of writing a biography," wrote Lawrence Venuti in the *New York Times Book Review.* "A Cinema-Goers Autobiography" details Calvino's adolescent obsession with the movies, particularly American movies with their popular movie stars. Movies, for the young Calvino, helped the author satisfy his craving for fantasy, a craving that would show up later in his work. "Memories of Battle" chronicles Calvino's resistance activities during the war, and also the vagaries of memory as he tries to recall this period from his past. The title essay tells of Calvino's rift with his father, who wanted him to continue in the family business of farming. John Updike commented in the *New Yorker* that "through this small, scattered, posthumous book, we draw closer to the innermost Calvino than we have before."

Numbers in the Dark and Other Stories, also published after Calvino's death, gave English-speaking audiences a chance to read some of the author's early short stories, as well as others that had never before been translated into English. These tales span his development from a 1943 story on a communist brigade to a later work about a man who goes to get ice for his whiskey and finds his apartment, upon his return, turned into an icy world. "The earliest stories present a Calvino still preoccupied with the war and the impact of fascism," wrote Aamer Hussein in the *New Statesman.* "He demonstrates his belief—still prevalent among writers resisting dictatorships—in the fable as the best vehicle for veiled protest." Calvino moved from his early interest in communism to later esoteric works in which he conducts imaginary interviews with historical figures such as Montezuma, Henry Ford, and a Neanderthal. "This collection brings American readers a somewhat different Calvino, more the product of his cultural and political origins in Italy, but as ever a writer of fantasies that possess extraordinary precision and beauty," concluded Lawrence Venuti in the *New York Times Book Review.*

Calvino's childlike imagination allowed him to leave the tenets of neorealism behind and opened up infinite possibilities for his fiction. He imaginatively used the traditional fable form to write non-traditional fiction.

Although he was a fabulist, according to Pacifici in *A Guide to Modern Italian Literature,* Calvino's works were "not . . . flights from reality but from the bitter reality of our twentieth century. They are the means—perhaps the only means left to a writer tired of a photographic obsession with modern life—to re-create a world where people can still be people—that is, where people can still dream and yet understand."

Books containing Calvino's nonfiction works have also been published posthumously. In 1999 a collection of Calvino's essays was published as *Why Read the Classics?* Writing in *Contemporary Review,* Stephen Wade commented "that within this large collection of literary essays, Italo Calvino mixes critical judgment with literary history, and reflections on the writer's art with sheer readerly enthusiasm." After opening with an essay discussing what defines a classic work of literature, the book examines well-known classics and their authors, from Ernest Hemingway to lesser-known writers like Giammaria Ortes, whom Calvino greatly admired. While calling the opening essay "outstanding," a *Publishers Weekly* contributor found the book to be "an uneven hodgepodge" and "lackluster." Wade, however, enjoyed the text and noted: "The style is always interesting: allusive, entreatingly digressive and always displaying knowledge easily and without mere show." Rachel Hadas, writing in the *American Scholar,* called *Why Read the Classics?* "charming and stimulating."

Calvino's widow edited a collection of Calvino's ruminations on his own life that was published in English as *Hermit in Paris: Autobiographical Writings.* In addition to essays, the volume includes newspaper and magazine interviews and articles presented in the order Calvino had once filed them. The essays, interviews, and articles deal with a wide range of occurrences in the author's life, from his memories of fascist Italy to his long trip to the United States in 1959—during which he was struck by the country's attempts to deal with issues of civil rights—to his life in Paris in the 1970s. Ali Houissa, writing in the *Library Journal,* called the collection "excellent" but noted that because Calvino does not find himself interesting the volume lacks a thorough account of the writer's own life. A contributor to *Contemporary Review* commented, "These pieces give us a unique insight in the Italian novelist and, in addition, to Italian history of the twentieth century." Donna Seaman, writing in *Booklist,* called *Hermit in Paris* "urbane and observant in even the most casual of pieces" and went on to note that it serves as "a delectable addition to a great writer's shelf."

BIOGRAPHICAL AND CRITICAL SOURCES:

BOOKS

Adler, Sara Maria, *Calvino: The Writer as Fablemaker,* Ediciones Jose Porrua Turanzas, 1979.
Contemporary Literary Criticism, Thomson Gale, Volume 5, 1976, Volume 8, 1978, Volume 11, 1979, Volume 22, 1982, Volume 33, 1984, Volume 39, 1986, Volume 73, 1993.
Gatt-Rutter, John, *Writers and Politics in Modern Italy,* Holmes & Meier, 1978.
Mandel, Siegfried, editor, *Contemporary European Novelists,* Southern Illinois University Press, 1986.
Pacifici, Sergio, *A Guide to Contemporary Italian Literature: From Futurism to Neorealism,* World (New York, NY), 1962.
Re, Lucia, *Calvino and the Age of Neorealism: Fables of Estrangement,* Stanford University Press (Stanford, CA), 1990.
Tamburri, Anthony Julian, *A Semiotic of Re-reading: Italo Calvino's "Snow Job,"* Chancery Press (New Haven, CT), 1998.
Woodhouse, J.R., *Italo Calvino: A Reappraisal and an Appreciation of the Trilogy,* University of Hull (Hull, England), 1968.

PERIODICALS

American Scholar, autumn, 1999, Rachel Hadas, review of *Why Read the Classics?,* p. 137.
Atlantic, March, 1977.
Booklist, March 15, 2003, Donna Seaman, review of *Hermit in Paris: Autobiographical Writings,* p. 1268.
Chicago Tribune, November 10, 1985.
Commonweal, November 8, 1957; June 19, 1981; June 2, 1989, p. 339.
Contemporary Review, November, 1999, Stephen Wade, review of *Why Read the Classics?,* p. 269; April, 2003, review of *Hermit in Paris: Autobiographical Writings,* p. 256.
Globe and Mail (Toronto, Ontario, Canada), July 7, 1984; January 25, 1986.
Hudson Review, summer, 1984.
Italian Quarterly, winter, 1971; winter-spring, 1989, pp. 5-15, 55-63.
Journal of European Studies, December, 1975.
Library Journal, April 1, 2003, Ali Houissa, review of *Hermit in Paris: Autobiographical Writings,* p. 96.
Listener, February 20, 1975; March 17, 1983, p. 24.

London Review of Books, September 30, 1981; March 26, 1992, pp. 20-21.

Los Angeles Times Book Review, November 27, 1983; October 6, 1985; October 20, 1985, p. 15.

Modern Fiction Studies, spring, 1978.

Nation, February 19, 1977; May 23, 1981; December 29, 1984-January 5, 1985.

New Criterion, December, 1985.

New Leader, May 16, 1988, p. 5; January 9, 1989, p. 19.

New Republic, October 17, 1988, pp. 38-43.

New Statesman, April 3, 1987, p. 27; December 1, 1995, p. 38.

New Statesman and Society, February 21, 1992, p. 40.

Newsweek, February 14, 1977; November 17, 1980; June 8, 1981; November 28, 1983; October 8, 1984; October 21, 1985.

New Yorker, February 24, 1975; April 18, 1977; February 23, 1981; August 3, 1981; September 10, 1984; October 28, 1985, pp. 25-27; November 18, 1985; May 30, 1994, p. 105.

New York Review of Books, November 21, 1968; January 29, 1970; May 30, 1974; May 12, 1977; June 25, 1981; December 6, 1984; November 21, 1985; October 8, 1987, p. 13; September 29, 1988, p. 74; July 14, 1994, p. 14.

New York Times, October 11, 1959; August 6, 1968; January 13, 1971; May 5, 1981; November 9, 1983, p. C20; September 25, 1984; November 26, 1984; September 26, 1985.

New York Times Book Review, November 8, 1959; August 5, 1962; August 12, 1968; August 25, 1968; October 12, 1969; February 7, 1971; November 17, 1974; April 10, 1977; October 12, 1980; June 21, 1981; January 22, 1984, p. 8; October 7, 1984; March 20, 1988, pp. 1, 30; October 23, 1988, p. 7; October 10, 1993, p. 11; November 26, 1995, p. 16.

New York Times Magazine, July 10, 1983.

PMLA, May, 1975.

Publishers Weekly, August 30, 1999, review of *Why Read the Classics?,* p. 66.

Saturday Review, December 6, 1959; November 15, 1969; May, 1981; March-April, 1985.

Science-Fiction Studies, March, 1986, pp. 97-98.

Spectator, February 22, 1975; May 14, 1977; August 15, 1981; September 24, 1983, pp. 23-24; November 20, 1993, p. 46.

Time, January 31, 1977; October 6, 1980; May 25, 1981; October 1, 1984; September 23, 1985; November 14, 1988, p. 95.

Times (London, England), July 9, 1981; September 1, 1983; October 3, 1985.

Times Literary Supplement, April 24, 1959; February 23, 1962; September 8, 1966; April 18, 1968; February 9, 1973; December 14, 1973; February 21, 1975; January 9, 1981; July 10, 1981; September 2, 1983; July 12, 1985; September 26, 1986; March 11, 1994, p. 29.

Village Voice, December 16, 1981.

Voice Literary Supplement, October, 1986.

Washington Post, January 13, 1984.

Washington Post Book World, April 25, 1971; October 12, 1980; June 7, 1981; November 18, 1984; September 22, 1985; November 16, 1986.

OBITUARIES:

PERIODICALS

Chicago Tribune, September 21, 1985.

Detroit Free Press, September 20, 1985.

Listener, September 26, 1985, p. 9.

Los Angeles Times, September 21, 1985, part IV, p. 7.

Newsweek, September 30, 1985.

New York Times, September 20, 1985, p. A20.

Observer, September 22, 1985, p. 25.

Times (London, England), September 20, 1985.

Washington Post, September 20, 1985.

*   *   *

CAMP, John 1944-
(John Roswell Camp, John Sandford)

PERSONAL: Born February 23, 1944, in Cedar Rapids, IA; son of Roswell Sandford and Anne (Barron) Camp; married Susan Lee Jones, December 28, 1965; children: Roswell Anthony, Emily Sarah. *Education:* State University of Iowa, B.A., 1966, M.A., 1971. *Religion:* Roman Catholic. *Hobbies and other interests:* Painting, archaeology.

ADDRESSES: Home—Near St. Paul, MN. *Agent*—Esther Newberg, International Creative Management, 40 West 57th St., New York, NY 10019. *E-mail*—js\@johnsandford.org.

CAREER: Miami Herald, Miami, FL, reporter, 1971-78; *St. Paul Pioneer Press,* St. Paul, MN, reporter and columnist, 1978-89; writer 1966—. *Military service:* U.S. Army, 1966-68; served in Korea.

AWARDS, HONORS: Pulitzer Prize nomination, 1980, for series of articles on Native Americans in *St. Paul Pioneer Press Dispatch;* Pulitzer Prize for Feature Writing, 1986, for series of articles on a farming family in *Pioneer Press Dispatch;* Distinguished Writing Award, American Society of Newspaper Editors, 1986.

WRITINGS:

The Eye and the Heart: The Watercolors of John Stuart Ingle (nonfiction), Rizzoli (New York, NY), 1988.
Plastic Surgery: The Kindest Cuts (nonfiction), Holt (New York, NY), 1989.
(As John Sandford) *The Night Crew* (novel), Putnam (New York, NY), 1997.

"JASON KIDD" NOVELS

The Fool's Run, Holt (New York, NY), 1989.
The Empress File, Holt (New York, NY), 1991.
(Under name John Sandford) *The Devil's Code,* Putnam (New York, NY), 2000.
(Under name John Sandford) *The Hanged Man's Song,* Putnam (New York, NY), 2003.

"LUCAS DAVENPORT" NOVELS; AS JOHN SANDFORD

Rules of Prey, Putnam (New York, NY), 1989.
Shadow Prey, Putnam (New York, NY), 1990.
Eyes of Prey, Putnam (New York, NY), 1991.
Silent Prey, Putnam (New York, NY), 1992.
Winter Prey, Putnam (New York, NY), 1993.
Night Prey, Putnam (New York, NY), 1994.
Mind Prey (also see below), Putnam (New York, NY), 1995.
Sudden Prey (also see below), Putnam (New York, NY), 1996.
Secret Prey (also see below), Putnam (New York, NY), 1998.
Certain Prey, Putnam (New York, NY), 1999.
Easy Prey, Putnam (New York, NY), 2000.
Three Complete Novels: Mind Prey, Sudden Prey, Secret Prey, Putnam (New York, NY), 2000.
Chosen Prey, Putnam (New York, NY), 2001.
Mortal Prey, Putnam (New York, NY), 2002.
Naked Prey, Putnam (New York, NY), 2004.
Hidden Prey, Putnam (New York, NY), 2004.

ADAPTATIONS: Rules of Prey was adapted for film by Adam Greenman and released as *Mind Prey,* Jaffe/Braunstein, Ltd., 1999.

WORK IN PROGRESS: More "Lucas Davenport" novels.

SIDELIGHTS: Pulitzer Prize-winning journalist John Camp is a versatile writer who has distinguished himself as an author of both nonfiction and mysteries. He is best known under the pseudonym John Sandford for his "Lucas Davenport" novels, a series of thrillers that all feature the word "Prey" in their titles, as well as for the "Jason Kidd" novels which feature a clever computer expert who operates on the fringe of cyberlaw. Throughout the 1990s and into the first decade of the twenty-first century, Camp—as Sandford—has published the "Lucas Davenport" novels at a rate of almost one per year. A *Publishers Weekly* contributor noted the "vast popularity" of the titles and credited it to the author's "clever plotting, sure pacing and fully rounded villains."

As far back as high school, Camp knew he had a talent for writing. After earning a bachelor's degree from the University of Iowa in 1966, he entered the United States Army, and it was there that he began to train as a journalist. Upon completion of his military service, he returned to the University of Iowa, where he earned a master's degree in journalism. He began his career as a newspaper reporter, eventually earning a Pulitzer Prize for a lengthy investigative series first published in the *St. Paul Pioneer Press* about the difficulties facing one farm family in Minnesota.

Camp's experiences as a reporter inform his earliest books, both fictional and nonfictional. He once told *Publishers Weekly* that "most of the hard information in my books comes from a series I did in a newspaper." That series, in fact, was based on a group of incarcerated murderers who had formed a computer corporation in prison. Camp has since said that the opportunity to interview nearly fifty intelligent men serving life sentences was central to his ability to develop villains for his thrillers.

Camp's first book, *The Eye and the Heart: Watercolors of John Stuart Ingle,* is a catalog of Ingle's works seen in a touring exhibition in the late 1980s. Included in the book, which features an essay by Camp, are more than forty color reproductions of the contemporary painter's meticulously realistic works. Camp's next nonfiction publication, *Plastic Surgery: The Kindest Cuts,* relates his insights about cosmetic and restorative surgery. Camp's observations derive from his time spent with surgeon Bruce Cunningham, who allowed Camp operating-room access. Critics found the book to be an engrossing and frank look at plastic surgery.

Camp began publishing fiction in 1989 with *The Fool's Run,* a suspense novel about an eccentric computer criminal hired to undermine a defense contractor. Kidd, the narrator and hero, is a painter, martial arts student, and occult dabbler who possesses considerable computer wizardry. He is hired to disable an aerospace company's information system. Accordingly, he wreaks havoc on the company's computer programs, but in so doing he also discovers the existence of a formidable foe. Critics praised Camp's first fictional effort, and several described *The Fool's Run* as fast-paced, suspenseful, and engaging. A second novel, *The Empress File,* finds Kidd embroiled in racial conflict. His employer, a black activist, engages him to sabotage a band of racist, corrupt officials in Mississippi. Kidd and his lover/accomplice LuEllen, a skilled burglar, soon manage to infiltrate the group and draw them into a scheme designed to result in their downfall. The officials, however, eventually discover that their operation risks exposure, and they retaliate with violence.

Both *The Fool's Run* and *The Empress File* were originally published by Henry Holt under the author's real name, John Camp. When Camp's agent sold the first "Lucas Davenport" novel, *Rules of Prey,* to Putnam, that publisher wanted to print it under a pseudonym. Putnam felt that the "Lucas Davenport" books would become best-sellers, and the company reportedly did not want Holt to cash in on the success by riding the *Prey* books' coattails. Camp cooperated, choosing his great-grandfather's name, Sandford, as a pseudonym. That name is so widely recognized now that Camp is even using it on sequels to *The Fool's Run* and *The Empress File.*

Rules of Prey, the first novel in the series, presents Lucas Davenport, a resourceful Minneapolis detective determined to apprehend a particularly vicious killer, Maddog, who preys on young women. At the scene of each crime, Maddog leaves a note relating his rules for murder. "Never kill anyone you know," reads one message. "Never carry a weapon after it has been used," reads another. Determined to jar Maddog's sense of gamesmanship, Davenport engages the psychopath in a dangerous cat-and-mouse contest, one with potentially fatal repercussions. *Washington Post Book World* contributor Daniel Woodrell, in his assessment of *Rules of Prey,* deemed it "a big, suspenseful thriller."

In *Shadow Prey,* the next "Lucas Davenport" novel, the detective opposes a terrorist network operated by local Native Americans avenging themselves against their white oppressors. Davenport discovers that one of the group's intended victims is a loathsome FBI director who molests Native-American children. The ensuing action builds to a violent climax. Another book in the series, *Eyes of Prey,* involves a murderous, drug-addicted hospital pathologist, Michael Bekker, and a disfigured actor, Carlo Druze. The two men commit murders for each other, with Bekker killing Druze's theater manager and Druze killing Bekker's wife. By working together, Bekker and Druze are also able to conveniently provide alibis for each other. It is left to Davenport, who is fighting depression and is involved in a rocky love relationship, to apprehend these criminals.

Subsequent "Lucas Davenport" titles have built upon their predecessors without becoming dependent upon one another. Davenport is always present in each story, but in some of them he plays a smaller role. Critics have commended the author for creating, in Davenport, a character whose career choice simultaneously stimulates and depresses him—like an addict, the detective cannot extricate himself from his work no matter how grisly the killings become, not even when they tear apart his relationships with women. It is the author's villains, however, who draw the most praise in the reviews. In *Booklist,* Wes Lukowsky suggested that the series has been sustained "most of all" by its plethora of "great villains." A *Publishers Weekly* correspondent likewise noted that the people Davenport vies against in his labors "are shrewdly conceived originals, cut from fabric way at the back of the bin."

In recent years Camp—again using the Sandford pseudonym—has taken temporary leave of his "Lucas Davenport" series to write independent thrillers featuring other heroes. He brought back Kidd in the novel *The Devil's Code,* a work described by a *Kirkus Reviews* critic as "computer skullduggery on an epic scale." He has also introduced Anna Batory, a video freelancer who speeds around Los Angeles, looking for footage of murder and mayhem that she can sell to the television stations. Batory finds herself a target for violence in *The Night Crew,* a thriller that Pam Lambert commended in *People* as "tough, fiercely intelligent and irresistible." Appealing as the heroine is, Sandford explained in an interview published on his Web site, there will not likely be more more Anna Batory novels, because "Anna is basically a female Lucas, minus the badge. And having two characters that similar, by the same author, is just redundant."

Reviewing *The Hanged Man's Song* in *Library Journal,* Denise Garofolo said, "The fourth installment in Sandford's Kidd series finds Kidd's genius hacker friend

Bobby brutally murdered and Bobby's laptop missing." Together with LuEllen, Kidd travels from Minnesota to Mississippi, and then Washington, DC, in pursuit of the killer, along the way encountering "chases, crooked politicians, identity theft, and plenty of peeks into the worlds of burglary and computer hacking." In an interview posted on John Sandford's Web site, the author differentiated between his two major protagonists. Davenport, he said, "is an amalgam of cops I've known, a couple of movie stars, and the characters in any number of thrillers I've read in the past." He added: "There really aren't any cops like Davenport, because he's just too much like Sherlock Holmes, he's a little over the top." Kidd is hardly less extravagant. His creator described Kidd as "a criminal who does industrial espionage to support his watercolor painting habit."

Camp returned to the "Lucas Davenport" series in 2001 with the publication of *Chosen Prey*. In this, the twelfth installment, Deputy Police Chief Lucas Davenport decides to take matters in his own hands when a serial killer begins murdering young women in Wisconsin and Minnesota. Though distracted with sudden changes in his personal life, Davenport soon links the dead women with a prominent art professor at a local university, James Qatar. However, wrapping up the case before Qatar strikes again proves to be a daunting challenge for Davenport, one that nearly claims his life. The author "is in top form here," claimed a *Publishers Weekly* contributor, "his wry humor . . . lighting up the dark of another grisly investigation."

In *Mortal Prey* Lucas is pitted aginst an old nemesis, Clara Rinker, in a novel a *Booklist* contributor called "among the most ambitious" of Sandford's efforts because he effectively "integrates the mundane domesticity of Davenport's life . . . with the terror of a circling killer." *Naked Prey* finds Davenport now a happily married father. However, commented David Koepple in an *Entertainment Weekly* review, "he's lost none of his powers of deduction" as he delves into two murders and "uncovers a corrupt community in which everyone from a mechanic to an ex-nun is keeping secrets." *Hidden Prey* pairs Davenport with a Russian intelligence agent in order to investigate a murder that might be the work of a supposedly defunct Soviet network "forgotten by the motherland," according to Wes Lukowsky in *Booklist*.

Camp once told a *Publishers Weekly* interviewer that he planned to continue writing books featuring his two popular protagonists, Kidd and Davenport, and was contemplating a new pseudonym under which to write

mainstream novels of a more literary nature. "Those are the kind of strategies that you have to think about," he remarked, adding: "I like to write books that have real stories in them, but I don't know whether a person who writes thrillers, as I do, *can* write literary books; whether critics will accept them." This is not to suggest that Camp does not see his thrillers as legitimate literature. In his online interview, he said: "What I do is really pretty hard, and I appreciate it when people take my effort with some degree of seriousness, as well as enjoying the stories." He concluded: "Readers are the other half of the essential storytelling partnership. What writers do is create the skeleton of a dream, which is dreamt in full by the readers."

BIOGRAPHICAL AND CRITICAL SOURCES:

PERIODICALS

Booklist, March 15, 1996, Wes Lukowsky, review of *Sudden Prey,* p. 1220; March 1, 1997, Emily Melton, review of *The Night Crew,* p. 1069; March 15, 1998, Wes Lukowsky, review of *Secret Prey,* p. 1180; April 15, 1999, Jenny McLarin, review of *Certain Prey,* p. 1484; March 1, 2000, Wes Lukowsky, review of *Easy Prey,* p. 1148; April 1, 2004, review of *Mortal Prey;* May 1, 2004, Wes Lukowsky, review of *Hidden Prey,* p. 1518.

Entertainment Weekly, May 23, 2003, David Koepple, review of *Mortal Prey.*

Globe and Mail (Toronto, Ontario, Canada), April 27, 1991, p. C7.

Kirkus Reviews, August 1, 2000, review of *The Devil's Code,* p. 1067.

Library Journal, April 1, 2000, Jo Ann Vicarel, review of *Easy Prey,* p. 132; April 15, 2000, Michael Adams, review of *Certain Prey,* p. 141; June 1, 2004, Denise Garofolo, review of *The Hanged Man's Song,* p. 196.

New York Times Book Review, June 7, 1998, Marilyn Stasio, review of *Secret Prey,* p. 47.

People, March 31, 1997, Pam Lambert, review of *The Night Crew,* p. 39.

Publishers Weekly, June 29, 1990, pp. 83-84; April 1, 1996, review of *Sudden Prey,* p. 54; March 10, 1997, review of *The Night Crew,* p. 49; April 20, 1998, review of *Secret Prey,* p. 47; April 19, 1999, review of *Certain Prey,* p. 60; March 20, 2000, review of *Easy Prey,* p. 68; September 4, 2000, review of *The Devil's Code,* p. 79; April 23, 2001, review of *Chosen Prey,* p. 49.

Tribune Books (Chicago, IL), July 2, 1989, p. 4.

Washington Post Book World, July 16, 1989, p. 6.
Writer, September, 2000, Lewis Burke Frumkes, p. 26.

ONLINE

Official John Sandford Web site, http://www.john sandford.org/ (August 23, 2004).

*   *   *

CAMP, John Roswell
   See CAMP, John

*   *   *

CAMPBELL, Bebe Moore 1950-

PERSONAL: Born 1950, in Philadelphia, PA; daughter of George Linwood Peter and Doris (a social worker; maiden name, Carter) Moore; married Tiko F. Campbell (divorced); married Ellis Gordon, Jr. (a banker); children: Maia, Ellis Gordon III. *Education:* University of Pittsburgh, B.S. (summa cum laude).

ADDRESSES: Home—Los Angeles, CA. *Agent*—Beth Swofford, William Morris Agency, 151 El Camino Dr., Beverly Hills, CA 90212.

CAREER: Freelance writer. Schoolteacher for five years; commentator on *Morning Edition,* National Public Radio. Guest on television talk shows, including *Donahue, Oprah, Sonya Live,* and *Today,* and numerous radio talk shows.

MEMBER: National Alliance for the Mentally Ill, Alpha Kappa Alpha, Delta Sigma Theta.

AWARDS, HONORS: Body of Work Award, National Association of Negro Business and Professional Women, 1978; National Endowment for the Arts grant, 1980; Golden Reel Award, Midwestern Radio Theatre Workshop Competition, for *Sugar on the Floor;* Certificate of Appreciation, from the mayor of Los Angeles, CA; National Association for the Advancement of Colored People (NAACP) Image Award for outstanding literary work (fiction); National Association for the Mentally Ill (NAMI) Outstanding Literature Award, 2003, for *Sometimes My Mommy Gets Angry.*

WRITINGS:

Successful Women, Angry Men: Backlash in the Two-Career Marriage, Random House (New York, NY), 1986, revised, Berkeley (New York, NY), 2000.
Sweet Summer: Growing Up with and without My Dad (memoir) Putnam (New York, NY), 1989.
Your Blues Ain't Like Mine, Putnam (New York, NY), 1992.
Brothers and Sisters, Putnam (New York, NY), 1994.
Singing in the Comeback Choir, Putnam (New York, NY), 1998.
What You Owe Me, Putnam (New York, NY), 2001.
Sometimes My Mommy Gets Angry, illustrated by E.B. Lewis, Putnam (New York, NY), 2003.
72 Hour Hold (novel), Knopf (New York, NY), 2005.
Stompin' at the Savoy, illustrated by Richard Yarde, Philomel Books (New York, NY), 2006.

Also author of nonfiction work "Old Lady Shoes" and a radio-play adaptation; author of radio play *Sugar on the Floor;* author of play *Even with the Madness.* Contributor to periodicals, including *Ebony, Lear's, Ms., New York Times Book Review, New York Times Magazine, Publishers Weekly, Savvy, Seventeen, Washington Post,* and *Working Mother.* Contributing editor of *Essence.*

ADAPTATIONS: Film rights to *Sweet Summer* were bought by Motown Productions, 1989; film rights to *Brothers and Sisters* were bought by Touchstone Pictures, 1995.

WORK IN PROGRESS: A novel, *Where I Useta Live.*

SIDELIGHTS: Bebe Moore Campbell's fiction and nonfiction have earned her widespread acclaim for the insights on racism and divorce that they contain. Campbell worked as a teacher for several years before turning to a career in freelance journalism following the birth of her daughter. It was an article for *Savvy* magazine that led to the development of her first book, *Successful Women, Angry Men: Backlash in the Two-Career Marriage.* Another article, about Father's Day, prompted the 1989 book, *Sweet Summer: Growing Up with and without My Dad,* her memoir as a child of divorce.

Because her parents separated when she was quite young, Campbell lived a divided existence, spending school years in Pennsylvania with her mother and summers in North Carolina with her father. Campbell draws a sharp contrast between the two worlds. According to *Sweet Summer,* her Philadelphia home was dominated by women—notably her mother, aunt, and grandmother—who urged her to speak well, behave properly, study hard, and generally improve herself. Life with her father, his mother, and his male friends, on the other hand, she describes as a freer one full of cigar and pipe smoke, beer, loud laughter, "roughness, gruffness, awkward gentleness," and a father's abiding love. Wheelchair-bound by a car accident, Campbell's father was nonetheless her hero, a perfect dad who loved her just for herself. When she learned that he was responsible, through speeding, not only for his own crippling accident but also for one that killed a boy, her image of him became tarnished, and Campbell had to come to terms with him as a flawed human being no longer the dream-father she had once idolized.

Critics hailed *Sweet Summer* for its poignant, positive look at a father-daughter relationship and especially for showing such a loving relationship in the black community. *Times Literary Supplement* contributor Adeola Solanke observed that in Campbell's memoir "a black father is portrayed by his daughter as a hero, instead of as the monster stalking the pages of many black American women writers." Similarly, poet Nikki Giovanni, writing in the *Washington Post Book World,* praised the book for providing "a corrective to some of the destructive images of black men that are prevalent in our society." Campbell also earned approval for her treatment of ordinary black life and for the vitality and clarity of her writing. Some reviewers expressed reservations about her work, however, suggesting that she is too hard on women; Martha Southgate, in the *Village Voice,* found "the absolute dichotomy Campbell perceives between men and women . . . disturbing." A few critics pointed out Campbell's lack of emphasis on social context and analysis, which some deemed a drawback, others an advantage. Stated Solanke, "One of the book's main strengths is that the political and social tumult it presents never eclipses the vitality and immediacy of personal experience."

By sharing her story, Campbell gives readers "the opportunity to reflect on our own fathers," mused Melissa Pritchard in Chicago's *Tribune Books,* "to appreciate their imperfect, profound impact on our lives." The importance of fathers and other men in girls' lives is in fact "perhaps the crucial message in her book," related Itabari Njeri in the *Los Angeles Times,* "one still not fully understood by society." As Campbell explained to Njeri, "Studies show that girls without that nurturing from a father or surrogate father are likely to grow up

with damaged self-esteem and are more likely to have problems with their own adult relationships with men." She hoped that reading her book might inspire more divorced fathers to increase their participation in their children's lives. Reflecting on the flurry of Campbell's talk show appearances, the competition for paperback rights, and the interest shown in the book by film producers, Njeri suggested that she was indeed reaching her audience. Noted the critic, "Campbell's gentle, poignant story about her relationship with her father has struck a nerve."

Campbell turned to fiction in 1992 with her novel *Your Blues Ain't Like Mine,* which tells of a young black man murdered in 1955 whose white killer was acquitted by an all-white jury. The novel goes on to trace what happens to the families of the killer and the victim in subsequent years. As Campbell told a *New York Times* reporter: "I wanted to give racism a face . . . . African-Americans know about racism, but I don't think we really know the causes. I decided it's first of all a family problem." The care with which the book's characters are drawn has been cited as one of its greatest strengths. Clyde Edgerton, writing for the *New York Times,* felt that much of the power of the novel "results from Ms. Campbell's subtle and seamless shifting of point of view. She wears the skin and holds in her chest the heart of each of her characters, one after another, regardless of the character's race or sex, response to fear and hate, or need for pity, grace, punishment or peace."

The rioting that broke out in Los Angeles after the 1992 Rodney King trial was the impetus behind Campbell's novel *Brothers and Sisters.* Explained Veronica Chambers in the *New York Times Magazine:* "While many saw the Los Angeles riots as the curtain falling on the myth of racial unity, Campbell . . . saw them as an opportunity to write about race and gender." The setting is a Los Angeles bank during the days after the riots, and the author explores the conflicting loyalties held by two women friends, one black, the other white. In this work the author uses her characters differently than she has previously; *New York Times* reviewer Elizabeth Gleick dubbed the protagonists "a fairly conventional batch," and a *Publisher Weekly* contributor noted that they are "intriguing (if not always three-dimensional)." Instead, *Brothers and Sisters* focuses on the complexities of the characters' relations. *Time* contributor Christopher John Farley praised the work accordingly: "Writing with wit and grace, Campbell shows how all our stories—white, black, male, female—ultimately intertwine." *Ms.* reviewer Retha Powers commended Campbell for her "astute observations about the subtleties of race and race relations in the U.S." The popular success of the novel was proven by its appearance on the *New York Times* best-seller list two weeks after its release. Writing in the *New York Times*, Pamela Newkirk placed Campbell "among a growing number of black women whose writing has mass crossover appeal. One reason for that appeal—to readers as well as to talk show hosts—is that in her characters, and in person, she manages to articulate deftly both black and white points of view."

Campbell's *Sometimes My Mommy Gets Angry* won the National Association for the Mentally Ill's Outstanding Literature Award the same year it was published. As Campbell explained in a preface to the book—a fictional account of a young African-American girl living with a mentally ill mother—she wrote the story "to address the fears and concerns of children who have a parent who suffers from mental illness." Her introductory note to adults discusses bipolar disorder and suggests ways in which the community can play a supportive role for those who suffer from it. In a review for *Publishers Weekly*, a contributor described the picture book narrated from a child's point of view as an "insightful, moving tale." "Most importantly," commented Suzanne Rust in *Black Issues Book Review*, Campbell shows young readers that her young protagonist "is not responsible for her mother's behavior." Anna DeWind Walls added in *School Library Journal* that the book's "multicultural cast is depicted with realistic sensitivity," making *Sometimes My Mommy Gets Angry* a "skillful treatment of a troubling subject."

In 2005 Campbell published her novel titled *72 Hour Hold*. The book tells the story of Keri Whitmore, whose entire life is disrupted when her seventeen-year-old daughter Trina is diagnosed with bipolar disorder. When Trina turns eighteen, her mania escalates but she cannot legally be held in the hospital for more than 72 hours against her will. Keri, now desperate to save her daughter, seeks out help from a group of radical underground health care workers. Eventually, Trina "comes to a truce with treatment even as her parents find sustenance where it's long been found in black culture—in the sharing of the burden among families and a community," commented Ariel Swartley in a review of the book for *Los Angeles Magazine*. Although one *Publishers Weekly* reviewer felt that the novel "reads at times like a heightened procedural," a *Kirkus Reviews* critic stated that "Campbell . . . transforms one mother's heartbreaking dilemma into a compassionate and suspenseful story that reverberates long after the final chapter is over."

BIOGRAPHICAL AND CRITICAL SOURCES:

BOOKS

Campbell, Bebe Moore, *Sweet Summer: Growing Up with and without My Dad,* Putnam (New York, NY), 1989.
Newsmakers 96, Gale (Detroit, MI), 1996, pp. 76-77.

PERIODICALS

African American Review, summer, 1997, Kari J. Winter, review of *Brothers and Sisters,* p. 369.
American Visions, October-November, 1994, T. Andreas Spellman, review of *Brothers and Sisters,* p. 38.
Black Enterprise, February, 1995, Sheryl Hillard Tucker, review of *Brothers and Sisters,* p. 224.
Black Issues Book Review, September-October, 2003, Suzanne Rust, review of *Sometimes My Mommy Gets Angry,* p. 68.
Booklist, June 1, 1994, Donna Seaman, review of *Brothers and Sisters,* p. 1725; December 15, 1997, Donna Seaman, review of *Singing in a Comeback Choir,* p. 666.
Entertainment Weekly, September 9, 1994, Vanessa V. Friedman, review of *Brothers and Sisters,* p. 78.
Kirkus, April 1, 2005, review of *72 Hour Hold,* p. 369.
Library Journal, August, 1994, Marie F. Jones, review of *Brothers and Sisters,* p. 124; December, 1994, Danna C. Bell-Russel, review of *Your Blues Ain't Like Mine,* p. 154; February 15, 1998, Michele Leber, review of *Singing in the Comeback Choir,* p. 169.
Los Angeles Magazine, August, 2005, Ariel Swartley, "Torn in Two: In Bebe Moore Campbell's Latest Novel, *72 Hour Hold,* a Daughter is Laid Low by Mental Illness," p. 369.
Los Angeles Times, July 25, 1989; December 1, 1989.
Ms., September- October, 1994, Retha Powers, review of *Brothers and Sisters,* p. 78.
Newsweek, April 29, 1996, Malcolm Jones, Jr., "Successful Sisters: Faux Terry Is Better Than No Terry," p. 79.
New York Times, November 15, 1995, Pamela Newkirk, "An Expert, Unexpectedly, on Race," p. C6.
New York Times Book Review, June 11, 1989, Bharati Mukherjee, review of *Sweet Summer,* p. 47; September 20, 1992, Clyde Edgerton, "Medicine for Broken Souls," review of *Your Blues Ain't Like Mine,* p. 13; October 16, 1994, Elizabeth Gleick,

review of *Brothers and Sisters*, p. 18; April 12, 1998, Betsy Groban, review of *Singing in the Comeback Choir*, p. 17.

New York Times Magazine, December 25, 1994, Veronica Chambers, "Which Counts More, Gender or Race?," p. 16.

People, November 21, 1994, V. R. Peterson, review of *Brothers and Sisters*, p. 32.

Publishers Weekly, June 30, 1989, Lisa See, "Bebe Moore Campbell; Her Memoir of 'A Special Childhood' Celebrates the Different Styles of Her Upbringing in a Divided Black Family" (interview), pp. 82-83; July 4, 1994, review of *Brothers and Sisters*, p. 51; December 15, 1997, review of *Singing in the Comeback Choir*, p. 49; December, 8, 2003, review of *Sometimes Mommy Gets Angry*, p. 61; May 23, 2005, review of *72 Hour Hold*, p. 56.

School Library Journal, February, 1995, Ginny Ryder, review of *Brothers and Sisters*, p. 134; September, 2003, Anna DeWind Walls, review of *Sometimes Mommy Gets Angry*, p. 175.

Time, October 17, 1994, Christopher John Farley, review of *Brothers and Sisters*, p. 81.

Times Literary Supplement, October 26, 1990, p. 1148.

Tribune Books (Chicago, IL), June 18, 1989, p. 7.

U.S. Catholic, September, 1987, Gerald M. Costello, review of *Successful Women, Angry Men: Backlash in the Two-Career Marriage*, p. 48.

Village Voice, July 4, 1989, p. 63.

Washington Post Book World, June 18, 1989, pp. 1, 8.

ONLINE

Bebe Moore Campbell Home Page, http://www.bebe moorecampbell.com/ (July 24, 2004).

*   *   *

CAPOTE, Truman 1924-1984

PERSONAL: Original name, Truman Streckfus Persons; name legally changed; born September 30, 1924, in New Orleans, LA; died of liver disease complicated by phlebitis and multiple drug intoxication, August 25, 1984, in Los Angeles, CA; son of Archulus Persons (a nonpracticing lawyer) and Lillie Mae (Faulk) Persons Capote; adopted by Joseph G. Capote. *Education:* Attended Trinity School and St. John's Academy, both in New York City, and public schools in Greenwich, CT.

CAREER: Writer. Worked for *New Yorker* magazine as a newspaper clipper and cartoon cataloger, c. 1943-44;

also moonlighted as a filmscript reader and freelance writer of anecdotes for a digest magazine. Appeared in motion picture *Murder by Death*, Columbia, 1976.

MEMBER: National Institute of Arts and Letters.

AWARDS, HONORS: Won first literary prize at age ten in Mobile Press Register contest, for short story, "Old Mr. Busybody"; O. Henry Award, Doubleday & Co., 1946, for "Miriam," 1948, for "Shut a Final Door," and 1951; National Institute of Arts and Letters creative writing award, 1959; Edgar Award, Mystery Writers of America, 1966, and National Book Award nomination, 1967, both for *In Cold Blood;* Emmy Award, 1967, for television adaptation *A Christmas Memory.*

WRITINGS:

Other Voices, Other Rooms (novel), Random House, 1948, reprinted with an introduction by the author, 1968.

A Tree of Night, and Other Stories (also see below), Random House, 1949.

Local Color (nonfiction sketches), Random House, 1950.

The Grass Harp (novel; also see below), Random House, 1951.

The Grass Harp, and A Tree of Night, and Other Stories, New American Library, 1956.

The Muses Are Heard: An Account (first published in *New Yorker*), Random House, 1956 (published in England as *The Muses Are Heard: An Account of the Porgy and Bess Visit to Leningrad,* Heinemann, 1957).

A Christmas Memory (first published in *Mademoiselle,* December, 1956; also see below), Random House, 1966.

Breakfast at Tiffany's: A Short Novel and Three Stories, Random House, 1958 (published in England as *Breakfast at Tiffany's,* Hamish Hamilton, 1959).

(Author of commentary) Richard Avedon, *Observations,* Simon & Schuster, 1959.

Selected Writings, introduction by Mark Schorer, Random House, 1963.

In Cold Blood: A True Account of a Multiple Murder and Its Consequences (nonfiction novel; Book-of-the-Month Club selection; first serialized in *New Yorker*), Random House, 1966.

The Thanksgiving Visitor (first published in *McCall's;* also see below), Random House, 1968, published with illustrations by Beth Peck, Knopf (New York, NY), 1996.

The Dogs Bark: Public People and Private Places, Random House, 1973.

Miriam (first published in *Mademoiselle;* also see below), Creative Education, Inc., 1982.

Music for Chameleons: New Writing, Random House, 1983.

One Christmas (first published in *Ladies Home Journal*), Random House, 1983.

Answered Prayers: The Partial Manuscript (first serialized in *Esquire*), edited by Joseph Fox, Random House, 1986, published as *Answered Prayers: The Unfinished Novel,* Random House, 1987.

I Remember Grandpa, Peachtree, 1987.

"The Thanksgiving Visitor," "One Christmas," "A Christmas Memory," Modern Library (New York, NY), 1996.

A House on the Heights new introduction by George Plimpton, Little Bookroom (New York, NY), 2002.

Breakfast at Tiffany's was also published in serial format in its entirety in the *New York Times'* Metro Section, 2004.

PLAYS

The Grass Harp: A Play (based on novel of the same title; first produced on Broadway at Martin Beck Theatre, March 27, 1952; produced as a musical on Broadway at Martin Beck Theatre, November, 1971), Random House, 1952.

(With Harold Arlen) *The House of Flowers* (libretto; based on short story of the same title; first produced on Broadway at Alvin Theatre, December 30, 1954; rewritten version first produced Off-Broadway at Theater de Lys, January 24, 1968), Random House, 1968.

SCREENPLAYS

(With John Huston) *Beat the Devil,* United Artists, 1954.

(With William Archibald and John Mortimer) *The Innocents* (based on Henry James's novel of the same title), Twentieth Century-Fox, 1961.

(With Eleanor Perry) *Trilogy* (also see below; adapted from Capote's short stories "Miriam," "Among the Paths to Eden," and the novella *A Christmas Memory*), Allied Artists, 1969.

TELEPLAYS

A Christmas Memory (based on novella of same title), American Broadcasting Co. (ABC-TV), December 21, 1966.

The Thanksgiving Visitor (based on book of same title), ABC-TV, November, 1968.

Also author of teleplays *Among the Paths to Eden* (adapted from short story of the same title), first produced in 1967; *Laura,* 1968; *Behind Prison Walls,* 1972; with Tracy Keenan Wynn and Wyatt Cooper, *The Glass House,* 1972; and *Crimewatch,* 1973.

OTHER

(Author of introduction) *The Collected Works of Jane Bowles,* Farrar, Straus, 1966.

(With E. Perry and Frank Perry) *Trilogy: An Experiment in Multimedia,* Macmillan, 1969.

A Capote Reader, Random House, 1987.

Marilyn Monroe: Photographs, 1945-1962 Norton, 1994.

(Essay) *Marlon Brando: Portraits and Film Stills 1946-1995,* edited by Lothar Schirmer, Stewart, Tabori and Chang (New York, NY), 1996.

Also author of *Then It All Came Down: Criminal Justice Today Discussed by Police, Criminals, and Correction Officers, With Comments by Truman Capote,* 1976. Contributor to numerous anthologies, including *Five Modern American Short Stories,* edited by Helmut Tischler, M. Diesterweg, 1962. Author of *Esquire* column "Observations," beginning March, 1983. Contributor to national magazines, including *Vogue, Mademoiselle, Ladies Home Journal, Esquire,* and *New Yorker.* Many of Capote's books have been translated into foreign languages, including French, German, Spanish, and Italian.

ADAPTATIONS: Capote made a sound recording of his short story "Children on Their Birthdays" for Columbia in the 1950s; *Breakfast at Tiffany's* was filmed by Paramount, 1961; *In Cold Blood* was filmed by Columbia Pictures, 1967; "Handcarved Coffins" was sold to Lester Persky Productions, 1980.

SIDELIGHTS: A masterful stylist who took great pride in his writing, Truman Capote was also a well-known television personality, openly obsessed with fame. In addition to literary recognition, the flamboyant, Southern-born writer sought social privilege and public celebrity, objectives he achieved in 1948 with the appearance of his first novel, *Other Voices, Other Rooms.* That book—published with a provocative dust-jacket photo of the author that far overshadowed the literary merit of the work—was the start of what Capote later termed "a certain notoriety" that kept step with him over the years. Believing that fame would not affect his art, Capote cultivated an entourage of rich and celebrated friends, observing their foibles with a watchful eye and inspiring confidences he would later betray. By 1959, he had already embarked on *Answered Prayers*—the never-to-be-finished *roman a clef* that precipitated a personal and professional crisis. Then he decided to put it "temporarily" aside while he explored something more serious—"a theme," as he explained to *Newsweek*'s Jack Kroll, "not likely to darken and yellow with time." His idea was to bring "the art of the novelist together with the technique of journalism" to produce a new genre, the nonfiction novel. Over six years in the making, the resulting book was *In Cold Blood: A True Account of a Multiple Murder and Its Consequences,* not only an enormous critical and commercial success, but also a seminal work of new journalism that remains the highlight of Capote's career.

Though the nonfiction novel was his most original contribution to the literary world, Capote also produced conventional writing of top quality. In short stories, plays, straight reportage, television adaptations, and filmscripts, he demonstrated what *Los Angeles Times* contributor Carolyn See called "the uncanny gift of putting a world or a scene together in a few perfect details." Among his other talents were "his patience for fact-collecting, his faithfulness to the true nature of his subject and his consummate gift as a storyteller," according to *New York Times Book Review* contributor Lis Harris. He was, in, the words of David Remnick in the *Washington Post,* "a writer of brilliance, capable of economical, evocative prose. His technique was mature, professional in the best possible sense."

Though his style of writing evolved over the years, falling into what Capote himself considered four different phases, his poetic voice was distinctive right from the start. "Truman had an odd and personal perspective on experience that only real writers have," poet and novelist James Dickey explained in the *New York Times.* "A lot of writers sweat and labor to acquire that, but Truman Capote had it naturally. He was maybe a little heavy on the Southern gothic side of things, a little bit willfully perverse. . . . But at his best, he had a very great sensitivity and linguistic originality." In the same *New York Times* article, novelist John Knowles expressed a similar view, saying of Capote's voice that "it was like no one else's—precise, clear, sometimes fey, lyrical, witty, graceful."

Capote himself often suggested that his originality was pervasive, influencing not just his writing, but every aspect of his life. "The thing about people like me is that we always knew what we were going to do," Capote

told *New York Times Magazine* contributor Anne Taylor Fleming. "Many people spend half their lives not knowing. But I was a very special person, and I had to have a very special life. . . . I would have been successful at whatever I did. But I always knew that I wanted to be a writer and that I wanted to be rich and famous." According to Fleming, "looking at the boy he must have been, the slender, pretty, high-voiced boy. . . , it seems easy to see, too easy maybe, how the kind of fame he coveted would someday become too heavy."

Born Truman Streckfus Persons in New Orleans, Louisiana, Capote had a childhood that, by all accounts, was difficult. His mother, a former Miss Alabama who later committed suicide, considered herself temperamentally unsuited to motherhood and sent him off to be raised by relatives in Monroeville, a small Alabama town. When he was four, his parents ended their marriage in a bitter divorce: his mother went north to New York, his father south to New Orleans, and young Truman became "a spiritual orphan," in Fleming's words. Though he frequently summered with his father, traveling up and down the Mississippi on the family-owned Streckfus Steam Boat Line, the two were never close, and Capote considered him "a bounder and a cad." The Monroeville years were difficult for Capote, comprising a time when he felt "like a turtle on its back. You see," he explained to Fleming, "I was so different from every one, so much more intelligent and sensitive and perceptive. I was having fifty perceptions a minute to everyone else's five. I always felt that nobody was going to understand me, going to understand what I felt about things. I guess that's why I started writing. At least on paper I could put down what I thought."

His closest friends at this time were an elderly cousin, Miss Sook Faulk, whom Fleming describes as "the archetype of the aging innocent, the best of the simple people with an inarticulate wisdom and a childlike capacity for joy and strange imaginings," and a neighboring tomboy, Harper Lee, who helped young Truman type his manuscripts and eventually became an award-winning author herself, writing *To Kill a Mockingbird.* Both personalities appear in Capote's early fiction, his cousin in autobiographical stories, such as "A Christmas Memory," and his friend in his first novel *Other Voices, Other Rooms.*

His mother, meanwhile, had remarried a Cuban-born New York businessman, Joe Capote, and when, after a series of miscarriages, she realized she could have no more children, she sent for Truman. He was nine years old. Legally adopted by his stepfather, the young author attended school in Manhattan, then enrolled at Trinity, and, at thirteen, was sent to live at St. John's Academy, a military boarding school. "I was lonely and very insecure," Capote told *Playboy* interviewer Eric Norden about his schooling. "Who wouldn't be? I was an only child, very sensitive and intelligent, with no sense of being particularly wanted by *anybody*.... I wasn't neglected financially; there was always enough money to send me to good schools, and all that. It was just a total *emotional* neglect. I never felt I belonged anywhere. All my family thought there was something wrong with me."

His grades were so low that, over the years, his family began to worry that he might be retarded. But when a special group of WPA researchers came to his school to conduct intelligence tests, Capote received the highest score they had ever seen. "I had the highest intelligence of any child in the United States," Capote told *Washington Post* reporter David Remnick, "an IQ of 215." Nonetheless, he had little use for formal schooling and, though he did graduate from high school (a fact which he obscured for many years), Capote told Norden he was "determined never to set foot inside a college classroom. If I was a writer, fine; if I wasn't, no professor on earth was going to make me one."

In place of formal education, Capote substituted experience, landing a job with the *New Yorker* when he was seventeen. "That job wasn't very glamorous, just clipping newspapers and filing cartoons," Capote told Norden, but it marked the beginning of a long association with the magazine that would serialize his best-known work and, to some extent, shape his writing style. Initially, however, his stories were rejected by the magazine. He made his first big sale shortly after leaving the *New Yorker,* when *Mademoiselle* bought a short story, "Miriam," which later garnered an O. Henry Award. According to *Dictionary of Literary Biography* contributor Craig M. Goad, "'Miriam' typifies the early Capote manner. It is a story of isolation, dread, and psychological breakdown told in rich, precisely mannered prose. There is little technical or thematic experimentation in 'Miriam' and the other Capote stories that appeared regularly in the postwar years. The shadow of Edgar Allan Poe floats over the surface of these stories, and their chief aim often seems to be only to produce a mild *frisson*."

"Miriam" caught the attention of Random House editor Robert Linscott, who told Capote that he would be interested in publishing whatever he wanted to write. Capote had already begun work on *Summer Crossing,* "a

spare, objective story with a New York setting," according to Capote, who acknowledged in the preface to the 1968 reprint of *Other Voices, Other Rooms* that "in order to complete the book . . . I took courage, quit my job, left New York and settled with relatives in a remote part of Alabama." But, once arrived, Capote began having doubts about his novel. "More and more," he wrote, "*Summer Crossing* seemed to me thin, clever, unfelt." While walking in the woods one afternoon, Capote was seized with a new vision, one inspired by childhood memories. He returned home, "tossed the manuscript of *Summer Crossing* into a bottom bureau drawer, collected several sharp pencils and a fresh pad of yellow lined paper and with pathetic optimism, wrote: *Other Voices, Other Rooms*—a novel by Truman Capote."

The novel took two years to complete and was published in 1948 to mostly favorable reviews. But it was the book's packaging rather than its literary merit that titillated the public's attention, for the dust-jacket photo portrayed the twenty-three-year-old author reclining on a couch, looking "as if he were dreamily contemplating some outrage against conventional morality," according to a report in the *Los Angeles Times*. Because Capote, an open homosexual, had focused on the developing relationship between an effete transvestite and his young male cousin, "readers at the time suspected that Capote may have identified with the book's protagonist and that 'Other Voices, Other Rooms' was a confession of sexual deviation," continued George Ramos and Laurie Becklund in the *Los Angeles Times*. In retrospect, Capote was able to identify the book's many autobiographical elements—particularly, as he explained in his 1968 preface, the parallels between protagonist Joel Knox's quest for love and his own search for an "essentially imaginary" father—but he did not make the connection at the time. "Rereading it now, I find such self-deception unpardonable," Capote wrote.

What many conservative critics found "unpardonable" was not Capote's self-deception, but rather his aberrant theme. "For all his novel's gifted invention and imagery, the distasteful trappings of its homosexual theme overhang it like Spanish moss," wrote the *Time* contributor. And, writing in the *Nation,* respected literary critic Diana Trilling expressed a similar view: "Even if Mr. Capote were ten or twenty years older than he is, his powers of description and evocation, his ability to bend language to his poetic moods, his ear for dialect and for the varied rhythms of speech would be remarkable. . . . On the other hand, I find myself deeply antipathetic to the whole artistic moral purpose of Mr. Capote's novel. I would freely trade eighty per cent of his technical virtuosity for twenty per cent more value in the uses to which it is put."

Some critics also reacted against the apparent self-consciousness of the writing. "*Other Voices, Other Rooms* is the novel of someone who wanted, with a fixed and single-minded and burning will, to write a novel," wrote Cynthia Ozick in a *New Republic* critique of the twentieth-anniversary edition. "The vision of *Other Voices, Other Rooms* is the vision of capital-A Art—essence freed from existence." What this artistic preoccupation led to, in the eyes of the *Times Literary Supplement* reviewer, was "the temptation to mystify for the sake of mystification." Noted *Saturday Review* contributor Richard McLaughlin: "If he had selected his material more carefully, shown more restraint, and had been less concerned with terrifying us out of our wits, he might have easily made a real and tenderly appealing story out of the experiences of thirteen-year-old Joel Knox and the people he meets during that long and lonely summer of his approaching maturity."

After the publication of *Other Voices, Other Rooms,* Capote moved for a time to Europe, where he traveled widely with novelist Jack Dunphy, "the only man . . . with whom he has ever been in love," according to Fleming in the *New York Times Magazine.* During this ten-year period, which Capote described as the second phase of his development and which ended in 1958, the author experimented with various kinds of writing. There were nonfiction travel essays and portraits (*Local Color, Observations*), short story collections (*A Tree of Night, A Christmas Memory*), adaptations of two earlier fictions into Broadway plays (*The Grass Harp, House of Flowers*), and the scripting of two original films (*Beat the Devil, The Innocents*). There was also "a great deal of factual reportage, most of it for the *New Yorker,*" Capote recalled in the preface to *Music for Chameleons.* His most memorable assignments included a tongue-in-cheek profile of Marlon Brando and a wry account of a black theatrical troupe's production of "Porgy and Bess" in Russia, later published in book form as *The Muses Are Heard.*

Though Capote's version of the "Porgy and Bess" tour of Russia "didn't quite jibe with the way some other observers of the trip remembered it," according to *Washington Post* reporter Tom Zito, *The Muses Are Heard* was a critical success, which "brilliantly utilized the literary forms of a fiction writer to present factual material." To achieve its effect of "deadpan mockery," the book poked gentle fun at a number of people, leaving "almost everyone touched by Mr. Capote's pen looking

a little foolish," according to a review in the *Christian Science Monitor.* But *The Muses Are Heard* had "more to it than entrancing fun," as *Atlantic* contributor C.J. Rolo explained: "While Capote's eye and ear have a radar-like sensitivity to the incongruous and the hilarious, they also dig the significant. What is dingy and nasty in Soviet life is revealed subtly and shrewdly, with a telling selectivity."

That selectivity reflected Capote's approach to his subject. To research his chronicle, he had employed neither tape recorder nor note pad, relying instead upon his photographic memory, which he viewed as the journalist's stock-in-trade. He would write up his impressions at the end of the day, but never during an interview, for he felt note-taking put his subjects on guard. "Taking notes produces the wrong kind of atmosphere," he pointed out to *Newsweek*'s Jack Kroll, explaining how he had trained his memory "by getting a friend to read me the Sears Roebuck catalog. I would have a tape recorder going at the same time. At first I could remember only forty per cent, then after three months sixty per cent. Now I can remember ninety per cent, and who cares about the other ten per cent," he said in 1966.

The Muses Are Heard, which was the first book Capote produced using this method, impressed the *New York Times* reviewer as "a record made by a brilliant writer in a casual, almost flippant manner—but with such freshness, with such light strokes and subtle innuendo, that the book reads like a highly enjoyable, charming story." The technique was so successful that it prompted Capote to envision a new kind of novel—"something on a large scale that would have the credibility of fact, the immediacy of film, the depth and freedom of prose, and the precision of poetry," Capote explained to James Wolcott in the *New York Review of Books.* In his mind, he christened this new genre "the nonfiction novel" and began looking for a suitable theme.

Before Capote found his subject, he published one more conventional novel, *Breakfast at Tiffany's,* later adapted into a popular film starring Audrey Hepburn and George Peppard. The engaging story of Manhattan playgirl Holly Golightly, *Breakfast at Tiffany's* demonstrated a maturity lacking in Capote's early fiction—at least in the opinion of *New Republic* contributor Stanley Kauffmann, who wrote: "It was with *Breakfast at Tiffany's* . . . that . . . Capote began to see enough of life and love to be more interested in his material than himself and to reveal the humor that now seems basic to him." Though Capote conceived of his story as a fiction, he was already drawing heavily from real life incidents, a point not lost on Kauffmann, who observed that "real names might conceivably be affixed to every character in *Breakfast at Tiffany's* and the whole published as a report on Manhattan life in the war years. If this is a restrictive comment, it is not meant to be condemnatory: because from her first appearance Holly leaps to life. Her dialogue has the perfection of pieces of mosaic fitting neatly and unassailably in place. The fey madness and extravagance, character qualities that easily throw fiction off the rails, always seem intrinsic, not contrived. . . . His fiction is strongest, most vital, when it resembles his best non-fiction." In the opinion of the *Times Literary Supplement* critic, the writing in *Breakfast at Tiffany's* "shorn of affection and the too-carefully chosen word," put Capote "in immediate sympathy with his characters" and placed "him at once among the leading American writers of the day."

Capote saw the second phase of his development as a writer come to a close with *Breakfast at Tiffany's*, and, after its publication, he turned his efforts "toward journalism as an art form in itself. I had two reasons," Capote explained in the preface to *Music for Chameleons*. "First, it didn't seem to me that anything truly innovative had occurred in prose writing . . . since the 1920s; second, journalism as an art was almost virgin territory." He began to search in earnest for a suitable subject, experimenting with several different ideas at this time. One project was a Proustian work, according to Baumgold, tentatively entitled *Answered Prayers*. "Capote had the title since the 1950s," wrote Baumgold, and "began in 1958 with notes, a full outline, and an ending." Despite his commitment to the project—which he admittedly envisioned as his masterwork—*Answered Prayers* was "temporarily" shelved when Capote got a brainstorm. "One day," he recalled to Haskel Frankel in the *Saturday Review*, "it suddenly occurred to me that a crime might be an excellent subject to make my big experiment with. . . . Once I had decided on the possibility of a crime . . . I would half-consciously, when looking through the papers, always notice any item that had a reference to a crime."

On November 16, 1959, Capote found what he had been looking for. Briefly noted in a *New York Times* wire story was the multiple murder of a wealthy wheat farmer, his wife, and their two teenage children in a small Kansas town. "Almost instantaneously I thought, well, this is maybe exactly what I want to do, because I don't know anything about that part of the world," Capote told Frankel. "I've never been to Kansas, much less western Kansas. It all seems fresh to me. I'll go without any prejudices. And so I went."

Three days later, Capote arrived in Holcomb, Kansas, accompanied by his childhood friend Harper Lee, who assisted him with the initial research. The town was in the throes of a brutal unsolved slaying, its residents not only traumatized but also deeply suspicious, and the urbane little dandy from New York City was not well received. Capote recalled that it took about a month for his presence to be accepted and that after the killers, Perry Smith and Dick Hickock, were apprehended, people finally began to open up to him. In addition to interviewing the townspeople, murderers, and anyone else even remotely connected to the Clutter case, Capote retraced the killers' flight, journeying south to Miami and Acapulco, renting rooms in the same cheap hotels. He did months of research on the criminal mind and interviewed a number of death row killers, "solely to give me a perspective on these two boys," Capote told George Plimpton in the *New York Times Book Review*. Before he began writing, he had amassed over six thousand pages of notes, explaining, "Eighty per cent of the research I . . . never used. But it gave me such a grounding that I never had any hesitation in my consideration of the subject." All told, the project, which Capote regarded as the third phase of his writing development, consumed almost six years. When it was over, Capote confessed to Frankel, "I would never do it again. . . . If had known what that book was going to cost in every conceivable way, emotionally, I never would have started it, and I really mean that."

Some people attribute Capote's escalating physical and emotional problems to the acute stress he suffered during the project. Fleming reported that this was the period when he "began to take the tranquilizers to which he later became addicted." But, if he paid a high personal price, the financial compensations for *In Cold Blood* were generous, for the story was a commercial success even before it appeared in book form. Serialized in the *New Yorker* in four consecutive issues, *In Cold Blood* boosted the magazine's sales and netted Capote a rumored 70,000 dollars in serialization rights. New American Library paid a reported 700,000 dollars for paperback rights and Columbia Pictures spent almost a million dollars for filming rights. By 1983, according to the *Washington Post, In Cold Blood* had brought the author 2 million dollars in royalties.

The book was also a critical success, described by *New York Times Book Review* contributor Conrad Knickerbocker as "a masterpiece—agonizing, terrible, possessed, proof that the times, so surfeited with disasters, are still capable of tragedy." *In Cold Blood,* according to the *Time* reviewer, "plays a light that illuminates the interior climate of murder with intense fidelity. Capote has invested the victims with a dignity and reality that life hitherto had confined only to the closed circle of their friends, and he has thrust the act of violence itself before the reader as if it were happening before his very eyes." David Remnick deemed certain "passages in it every bit as rhythmically spellbinding as Hemingway's famous opening to 'A Farewell to Arms,'" while F.W. Dupee extolled it as "the best documentary account of an American crime ever written," in the *New York Review of Books.*

Like any experimental literary work, *In Cold Blood* also had its share of detractors. Fellow novelist Norman Mailer, when asked his reaction to Capote's new genre, glibly dismissed it as "a failure of imagination," though as Capote took great pleasure in pointing out, Mailer later employed the same subject and technique in his Pulitzer Prize-winning *The Executioner's Song.* "Now I see that the only prizes Norman wins are for the very same kind of writing," Capote later quipped to the *Washington Post.* "I'm glad I was of some service to him."

Capote, who told Norden that he had "undertaken the most comprehensive and far-reaching experiment to date in the medium of reportage," never doubted the originality of his contribution. But others, like Diana Trilling, were not convinced. "Works of autobiography such as Isak Dinesen's *Out of Africa,* works of history such as Cecil Woodham Smith's *The Reason Why,* works of journalism like James Agee's *Let Us Now Praise Famous Men* are all at least as close to, or far from, proposing a new nonfiction form as Mr. Capote's *In Cold Blood,*" she wrote in the *Partisan Review.* While admitting that "the form is not new or remarkable," the *Times Literary Supplement* reviewer acknowledged that "it is handled here with a narrative skill and delicate sensibility that make this re-telling of a gruesome murder story into a work of art." Capote "did not intend to be merely the novelist-as-journalist, writing diversionary occasional pieces," wrote Conrad Knickerbocker in the *New York Times Book Review.* "In the completer role of novelist-as-journalist-as-artist, he was after a new kind of statement. He wanted the facts to declare a reality that transcended reality."

Capote believed that in order for his nonfiction-novel form to be successful, it must be an objective account in which the author himself did not appear. "Once the narrator does appear," he explained to Plimpton, "he has to appear throughout . . . and the I-I-I intrudes when it really shouldn't." Capote's absence from the story was interpreted as a moral cop-out by some critics, including Cynthia Ozick, who complained that *In Cold Blood* "has excised its chief predicament, the rela-

tion of the mind of the observer to the mind of the observed, and therefore it cannot be judged, it escapes interpretation because it flees its own essential deed." Diana Trilling accused Capote of "employing objectivity as a shield for evasion. This is what is resented . . . the sense shared in some dim way by virtually all of Mr. Capote's audience of having been unfairly used in being made to take on the burden of personal involvement pridefully put aside by Mr. Capote himself. An unpleasant critical charge leveled against *In Cold Blood* is that it is itself written in cold blood, exploiting tragedy for personal gain."

No one familiar with Capote's involvement with the Clutter case leveled this charge, for he made his personal commitment clear. "I had to surrender my entire life to this experience," he told Norden. "Try to think what it means to totally immerse yourself in the lives of two men waiting to be hanged, to feel the passage of hours with them, to share every emotion. Short of actually living in a death cell myself, I couldn't have come closer to the experience." Though his sympathies were divided between one of the killers, Perry Smith, and the head of the investigation, Alvin Dewey, Capote worked openly to have the murderers' death sentences commuted. He became physically ill when they were hanged.

Writing in the *Dictionary of Literary Biography,* Craig M. Goad concluded that "the controversy about the nature and literary status of *In Cold Blood* can never be wholly resolved, for it hinges on the definition of art that the individual reader accepts, but there is little doubt that the book creates a vivid portrait of western Kansas and captures the manners and speech of the people who live there. . . . It explores the irony of the fact that the murder of the Clutters, apparently exactly the sort of crime that a prosecuting attorney can describe as being committed 'in cold blood,' was essentially a crime of passion, a brief explosion of repressed rage and hate, while the executions of Hickock and Smith were carried out cold-bloodedly after years of legal wrangling. Finally, and perhaps most importantly, *In Cold Blood* contains the detailed portraits of Hickock and Smith which continue to fascinate not only those with literary interests, but students of criminal psychology as well."

After the book was finished, Capote orchestrated a major promotional campaign, prompting further charges of impropriety, which he answered with one of his quips: "A boy has to hustle his book," he said, according to the *Los Angeles Times.* He took a long vacation from writing and resumed his fast-paced social life, hosting a fancy dress ball for 540 friends in November, 1966. According to Fleming, "Capote worked on the party as if it were a book, laboring over flowers, colors, seating, food—which alone cost $12,000—scrawling details in a notebook in his tiny hand." Many of those closest to the author believed his quest for social acceptance was pathological, compensating for the emotional neglect of his childhood years. "It was harder to do than was the writing for him," Norman Mailer told Julie Baumgold in *New York* magazine. "His talent was his friend. His achievement was his social life."

In 1966, Capote had taken a $750,000 writing advance in the form of stocks and was supposed to resume work on *Answered Prayers,* the nonfiction novel he had named from a quote by Saint Therese: "More tears are shed over answered prayers than unanswered ones." Instead, Capote wrote in the preface to *Music for Chameleons,* "for four years, roughly from 1968 through 1972, I spent most of my time reading and selecting, rewriting and indexing my own letters, other people's letters, my diaries and journals . . . for the years 1943 through 1965." Finally, in 1972, he resumed work on the book, entering what he viewed as the fourth and final cycle of his writing. He wrote the last chapter first, then produced several more chapters in random order. In 1975 and 1976, four chapters were published in *Esquire* magazine.

Capote's reasons for releasing a work in progress remain unclear. Fleming theorized that it was "to jolt himself out of his sadness." Albin Krebs hypothesized that he did it "to keep alive the public's interest in the promised work," while Norman Mailer speculated that it "may have been Capote's deliberate effort to free himself" from the debilitating influence of his cafe society friends. Whatever his reasons, the results, according to Baumgold were "social suicide."

In the work, which Capote likened to a contemporary version of Marcel Proust's *Remembrance of Things Past,* Capote divulged many of the scandalous secrets he had coaxed from his wealthy and powerful friends. "The first excerpt was called '*La Cote Basque,*' after the New York restaurant frequented by many of society's more celebrated members," wrote Tom Zito in the *Washington Post.* "Many of the whispered stories and innuendoes he had heard over the years he now had the audacity to print, either factually or thinly veiled. It was as if he was metaphorically recreating what Perry Smith had said in '*In Cold Blood*' about the murder of Herbert Clutter: 'I thought he was a very nice gentleman.

Softspoken. I thought so right up to the moment I cut his throat.'" The reprisals were swift and immediate. Many of the circles in which he'd traveled now became closed to him. His telephone calls went unreturned. Invitations fell off. Perhaps the most deeply felt repercussion was the loss of his relationship with Babe Paley, once an almost constant companion and friend.

This social crisis was paralleled by a creative crisis that struck Capote around 1977. Dissatisfied with the texture of his writing, Capote reread every word he had ever published and "decided that never, not once in my writing life, had I completely exploded all the energy and esthetic excitements that material contained. Even when it was good," Capote continued in *Music for Chameleons,* "I was never working with more than half, sometimes only a third, of the powers at my command."

In a 1978 television interview with Stanley Siegel, Capote appeared on the air under the influence of drugs and alcohol, confessing that he frequently mixed "them together like some kind of cocktail." Before the segment was cut, Capote attributed his substance abuse problems to "free-floating anxiety," developed as a child: "My mother was a very beautiful girl and only seventeen years old, and she used to lock me in these rooms all the time, and I developed this fantastic anxiety." He also alluded to his artistic problems with *Answered Prayers,* admitting "I'm pretty anxious about this new book of mine . . . really a great sense of anxiety about it."

A legendary fabricator, Capote may well have been exaggerating the hardships of his childhood, at least according to his aunt Marie Rudisill, who told Baumgold that "he might have locked his mother in rooms." Capote's penchant for exaggeration was also confirmed by the late playwright Tennessee Williams, who once told a reporter for the *Washington Post,* "Truman's a mythologist, baby, you know that. That's a polite way of saying he does fabricate. I love him too much to say he's a liar. That's part of his profession." In the case of *Answered Prayers,* however, the writer's block he alluded to was real.

The crux of the problem, as Capote explained in *Music for Chameleons,* was that "by restricting myself to the techniques of whatever form I was working in, I was not using everything I knew about writing—all I'd learned from film scripts, plays, reportage, poetry, the short story, novellas, the novel. A writer ought to have all his colors . . . available on the same palette for mingling. . . . But how?" The solution, he decided after months of contemplation, was to reverse the process of invisibility he had mastered for *In Cold Blood* and to set himself at "center stage" in his writing. From this vantage point, using dialogue, stage direction, narrative, and a variety of other literary techniques, he would report his tales. This is the approach Capote employed in most of the selections published in his 1980 work, *Music for Chameleons,* the last major book he would write.

A collection of stories and portraits, *Music for Chameleons* has as its centerpiece "Handcarved Coffins"—a 30,000 word "nonfiction account of an American crime." In an interview with *Los Angeles Times* reporter Wayne Warga, Capote attributed his ability to "get that story at that length" to the innovative techniques he was using. "The entire point of this whole book is stylistic compression. I want everything to be minimal," he explained. But in a *Saturday Review* critique of the work, John Fowles found that "despite [Capote's] claims, the technique is (mercifully) innovatory only in one or two superficial and formal ways; in many more important ones it is a brave step back to older literary virtues. He now writes fiction increasingly near fact, and vice versa. In practice this means that he is very skillfully blending the received techniques of several kinds of writing."

Though *Los Angeles Times Book Review* contributor Thomas Thompson dismissed the book as "fast food coated with snake oil," other reviewers reserved their criticisms for Capote's preface, with its self-conscious posturing about capital-A Art, rather than denouncing the work as a whole. As Anthony Quinton put it in the *London Times,* "Where he is a detached, neutral observer, as in the main item in this collection, there is brilliant force and economy to his writing." Less attractive, "and more conspicuous, is a kind of nervous blustering, only an inch away from self-pity that afflicts Capote when occupied with the topic of his own importance and achievements." Writing in the *Village Voice,* Seymour Krim also addressed this issue, noting: "Not one of these first-person vignettes is boring or without its humane and unexpected charm. And practically all the writing, it is true, is unstudied simplicity at its best, often so light that you can blow it around the room like a tissue-paper airplane. But as far as its living up to the burn-your-bridges trumpet call at the beginning of *Music for Chameleons...,* one has to conclude that the ringing peptalk is more important to the author than to the reader."

Like *In Cold Blood, Music for Chameleons* also raised the issue of fact versus fiction. Publicized as a true story, in which names and locations had been changed

to protect identities, "Handcarved Coffins" was particularly scrutinized. "The details are so fuzzy and the murders so far-fetched that you begin to wonder whether fact and fiction aren't bubbling together in the same pot," wrote James Wolcott in the *New York Review of Books.* Writing in the *Times Literary Supplement,* David Lodge attributed his skepticism to "the inherent implausibility of the discrete events narrated" as well as "the very literary 'feel' of the whole text." Asked *Time's* R.Z. Sheppard: "How much of this book can be called documentary truth? How much is a masterly synthesis of all the author has learned as a fiction writer, scenarist and journalist? It is impossible to be sure." According to *Washington Post Book World* contributor Noel Perrin, "the proper response is to ignore [Capote's] pronouncements and read his work. D.H. Lawrence's advice, 'Trust the tale and not the teller,' might have been composed with Capote in mind. . . . Trust these tales. They are brilliant renderings of some of the more bizarre aspects of human reality—and if they happen to be literal word-for-word transcriptions, well, no harm in that. Either way, they are superb reading."

Between the appearance of *Music for Chameleons* in 1980 and the author's death in 1984, Capote wrote some magazine pieces and published *One Christmas,* a twenty-one-page short story, packaged as a book. His personal and health problems persisted, but he spoke frequently of the progress he was making on his masterwork *Answered Prayers,* telling *Publishers Weekly* in January, 1984 that he was "finishing my long-lost novel. . . . I hope it will be published in fall 1984." After his death, however, such remarks turned out to have been a smokescreen. Except for the portions published in *Esquire,* no manuscript of *Answered Prayers* was ever found. So convincing had been Capote's fabrications that several obituaries reported that the author was working on his book just hours before his death. Though the exact nature of that prose—whether magazine article, short story, or memoir—has not been determined, consensus is that it does not belong to *Answered Prayers.*

Because Capote had shown bits and pieces of his work in progress to associates and had actually read unpublished passages to friends over the telephone, some people speculate that Capote destroyed what he had written. Baumgold, for instance, alluded to the possibility of whole chapters being "rewritten out of existence in Capote's obsession with getting his work perfect." His editor, Joseph Fox, even remembered receiving an additional excerpt, which Capote subsequently took back and never returned. When asked about the content of *Answered Prayers: A Partial Manuscript,* a representative for Random House explained, "We are publishing the excerpts as they appeared in *Esquire* because, as I understand it, there's nothing else that goes with it."

A final version of the collected excerpts appeared in 1987 under the title *Answered Prayers: The Unfinished Novel.* The slim volume contains only the three previously published parts as chapters entitled "Unspoiled Monsters," "Kate McCloud," and "La Cote Basque." The narrator of each is P.B. Jones, a struggling writer and sometime male prostitute who rises from humble orphan origins in the South to infiltrate the inner circles of the New York social elite. According to John Melmoth in the *Times Literary Supplement,* "*Answered Prayers* can be read as a historical novel bent on dismantling the glitz and depravity of a crummy *ancien regime* whose way of life was built on inconsequential sexual contacts made tolerable by cocaine and liqueurs and is now threatened by AIDS." Commenting on the unusual harshness of Capote's characterizations, Walter Nash wrote in the *London Review of Books,* "there is little innocent laughter in this book. The prevailing tone is the giggling of the vicious." Despite his egregious authorial indiscretion, as R.Z. Sheppard noted in *Time,* "Capote was on his way to a spectacular best seller, an irresistible piece of malicious mischief inspired by the traditional detective thriller and the *National Enquirer.*"

Speculating on the cause of Capote's difficulty finishing the novel, *New York Times Book Review* contributor Christopher Lehmann-Haupt observed, "What he seems really to have wanted was to tell a deeper, more damning truth about himself and the world, a truth that would brand him a criminal and 'put me in prison for life.'" Sadly, as Charles Trueheart remarked in *Washington Post Book World,* "*Answered Prayers* is a coldly accurate memorial to the writer's worst days. It contains isolated examples of Capote at his keen-eared, storytelling best, and of Capote at his pickle-brained, gossipmongering worst—examples suspended in an aspic of undistinguished other stuff." As Shirley Ann Grau concluded in Chicago *Tribune Books,* "'Answered Prayers' is quirky, annoying, sad, funny, brilliant, exasperating. . . . the sad relic of a talent, a faint echo from the brain of an extraordinary writer."

Despite protestations to the contrary while stalling on *Answered Prayers,* Capote may never have gotten over his writer's block, and that, in turn, may have contributed to his death. According to Norman Mailer, who told Baumgold, "He loved writing so much and had such pride of offering nothing but his best, that when he could no longer deliver, he lost much of his desire to live." Reflecting on Capote's life and work, *Los Angeles Times* contributor Armand S. Deutsch concluded: "The exhausting years of the alcohol and drug battles, the long hospital stays, the illnesses, are behind him. The celebrity, which was such an integral part of him, will soon vanish, but his writing will remain to speak brilliantly and strongly for him."

BIOGRAPHICAL AND CRITICAL SOURCES:

BOOKS

Algeo, Ann M., *The Courtroom as Forum: Homicide Trials by Dreiser, Wright, Capote, and Mailer,* P. Lang (New York, NY), 1996.

Brinnin, John Malcolm, *Truman Capote: Deat Heart, Old Buddy,* Delacourte Press, 1986.

Clarke, Gerald, *Capote: A Biography,* Simon Schuster, 1986.

Contemporary Literary Criticism, Thomson Gale, Volume 1, 1973; Volume 3, 1975; Volume 8, 1978; Volume 13, 1980; Volume 14, 1981; Volume 38, 1986; Volume 58, 1990.

Dictionary of Literary Biography, Volume 2, *American Novelists since World War II,* Thomson Gale, 1978.

Dictionary of Literary Biography Yearbook: 1980, Thomson Gale, 1981.

Grobel, Lawrence, *Conversations with Capote,* New American Library, 1985.

Guest, David, *Sentenced to Death: The American Novel and Capital Punishment,* University Press of Mississippi, 1997.

Hallowell, John, *Between Fact and Fiction: New Journalism and the Nonfiction Novel,* University of North Carolina Press, 1977.

Moates, Marianne M., *A Bridge of Childhood: Truman Capote's Southern Years,* Henry Holt, 1989.

Moates, Marianne M. and Jennings Faulk Carter, *Truman Capote's Southern Years: Stories from a Monroeville Cousin,* University of Alabama Press (Tuscaloosa), 1996.

Nance, William L., *The Worlds of Truman Capote,* Stein Day, 1970.

Plimpton, George, *Truman Capote: In Which Various Friends, Enemies, Acquaintances, and Detractors Recall His Turbulent Career,* Doubleday, 1997.

Rudisill, Marie, and James C. Simmons, *Truman Capote,* William Morrow, 1983.

Short Story Criticism, Thomson Gale, Volume 2, 1989.

PERIODICALS

America, January 22, 1966; October 4, 1980.
American Scholar, winter, 1955-56; summer, 1966.

Atlantic, March, 1948; January, 1957; March, 1966.

Book Week, January 16, 1966.

Canadian Forum, March, 1966.

Chicago Tribune, June 5, 1983; July 5, 1987.

Christian Science Monitor, November 8, 1956.

Commentary, February, 1988, p. 81.

Detroit News, November 27, 1983.

Detroit News Magazine, September 7, 1980.

Esquire, April, 1988, p. 174.

Harper's, February, 1966.

Interview, November, 1989, p. 98.

Listener, March 28, 1968.

London Review of Books, December 18, 1986, p. 19.

Los Angeles Times, August 3, 1980; November 28, 1983; September 2, 1984.

Los Angeles Times Book Review, August 3, 1980.

Nation, February 7, 1966.

New Republic, February 23, 1963; January 22, 1966; January 27, 1973; December 21, 1987, p. 30.

New Statesman, August 30, 1963; March 22, 1968.

Newsweek, January 24, 1966.

New York, October 29, 1984; November 26, 1984.

New Yorker, September 21, 1987, p. 113; November 27, 1989, p. 143.

New York Review of Books, February 3, 1966; September 25, 1980; December 17, 1987, p. 3.

New York Times, December 2, 1956; January 7, 1980; August 5, 1980; September 10, 1987.

New York Times Book Review, January 18, 1948; February 24, 1952; January 16, 1966; October 28, 1973; August 3, 1980; November 13, 1983; September 13, 1987, p. 13.

New York Times Magazine, July 9, 1978; July 16, 1978.

Paris Review, spring-summer, 1957.

Partisan Review, spring, 1966.

Playboy, March, 1968.

Publishers Weekly, January 6, 1984.

Saturday Review, February 14, 1948; February 16, 1963; January 22, 1966; July, 1980.

Spectator, March 18, 1966; March 29, 1968.

Time, January 26, 1948; January 21, 1966; August 4, 1980; September 7, 1987, p. 65.

Times (London), February 19, 1981.

Times Literary Supplement, October 3, 1948; December 19, 1958; March 17, 1966; August 30, 1974; February 20, 1981; December 5, 1986, p. 1369.

Tribune Books (Chicago), October 18, 1987, p. 7.

Village Voice, August 6, 1980; October 20, 1987, p. 57.

Washington Post, December 8, 1973; June 6, 1979; June 7, 1979; March 13, 1983; March 31, 1983; September 20, 1987, p. 1.

Washington Post Book World, July 27, 1980.

Writer's Digest, April, 1990, p. 26.

OBITUARIES:

PERIODICALS

Chicago Tribune, August 27, 1984.

Los Angeles Times, August 26, 1984.

Newsweek, September 3, 1984.

New York Times, August 27, 1984.

Publishers Weekly, September 7, 1984.

Time, September 3, 1984.

Times (London), August 27, 1984.

*   *   *

CARD, Orson Scott 1951-
(Frederick Bliss, Brian Green, P.Q. Gump, Byron Walley)

PERSONAL: Born August 24, 1951, in Richland, WA; son of Willard Richards (a teacher) and Peggy Jane (a secretary and administrator; maiden name, Park) Card; married Kristine Allen, May 17, 1977; children: Michael Geoffrey, Emily Janice, Charles Benjamin (deceased), Zina Margaret, Erin Louisa (deceased). *Education:* Brigham Young University, B.A. (with distinction), 1975; University of Utah, M.A., 1981. *Politics:* Moderate Democrat. *Religion:* Church of Jesus Christ of Latter-Day Saints (Mormon). *Hobbies and other interests:* Computer games.

ADDRESSES: Agent—Barbara Bova Literary Agency, 3951 Gulf Shore Blvd. North #PH1B, Naples, FL 34103-3639.

CAREER: Mormon missionary in Brazil, 1971-73; operated repertory theater in Provo, UT, 1974-75; Brigham Young University Press, Provo, editor, 1974-76; *Ensign,* Salt Lake City, UT, assistant editor, 1976-78; freelance writer and editor, 1978—; Compute! Books, Greensboro, NC, senior editor, 1983; Lucasfilm Games, game design consultant, 1989-92. Instructor at Brigham Young University, University of Utah, University of Notre Dame, Appalachian State University, Clarion West Writers' Workshop, Cape Cod Writer's Workshop, and Antioch Writers' Workshop. Has served as local Democratic precinct election judge and Utah State Democratic Convention delegate.

AWARDS, HONORS: John W. Campbell Award for best new writer of 1977, World Science Fiction Convention, 1978; Hugo Award nominations, World Science Fiction

Convention, 1978, 1979, 1980, for short stories, 1986, for novelette *Hatrack River,* and 1988, for *Seventh Son;* Nebula Award nominations, Science Fiction Writers of America, 1979, and 1980, for short stories; Utah State Institute of Fine Arts prize, 1980, for epic poem "Prentice Alvin and the No-Good Plow"; Hamilton-Brackett Award, 1981, for *Songmaster;* Nebula Award, 1985, and Hugo Award and Hamilton-Brackett Award, both 1986, all for *Ender's Game;* Nebula Award, 1986, and Hugo Award and Locus Award, both 1987, all for *Speaker for the Dead;* World Fantasy Award, 1987, for *Hatrack River;* Hugo Award, and Locus Award nomination, both 1988, both for novella "Eye for Eye"; Locus Award, World Fantasy Award nomination, and Mythopoeic Society Fantasy Award, all 1988, all for *Seventh Son;* Locus Award, 1989, for *Red Prophet;* Hugo Award for nonfiction, 1991, for *How to Write Science Fiction and Fantasy;* Israel's Geffen Award for Best Science Fiction book, 1999, for *Pastwatch: The Redemption of Christopher Columbus;* Grand Prix de L'Imaginaire, 2000, for *Heartfire.*

WRITINGS:

SCIENCE FICTION AND FANTASY

Capitol (short stories), Ace (New York, NY), 1978.
Hot Sleep: The Worthing Chronicle, Baronet, 1978.
A Planet Called Treason, St. Martin's Press (New York, NY), 1979, revised edition, Dell (New York, NY), 1980, published as *Treason,* St. Martin's Press (New York, NY), 1988.
Songmaster, Dial (New York, NY), 1980, reprinted, Orb (New York, NY), 2002.
Unaccompanied Sonata and Other Stories, Dial (New York, NY), 1980.
(Editor) *Dragons of Darkness,* Ace (New York, NY), 1981.
Hart's Hope, Berkley (New York, NY), 1983, reprinted, Orb (New York, NY), 2003.
(Editor) *Dragons of Light,* Ace (New York, NY), 1983.
The Worthing Chronicle, Ace (New York, NY), 1983.
(With others) *Free Lancers,* Baen (New York, NY), 1987.
Wyrms, Arbor House (New York, NY), 1987, reprinted, Orb (New York, NY), 2003.
Folk of the Fringe (short stories), Phantasia Press (Huntington Woods, MI), 1989.
The Abyss (novelization of screenplay by James Cameron), Pocket Books (New York, NY), 1989.
Eye for Eye (bound with *The Tunesmith* by Lloyd Biggle, Jr.), Tor (New York, NY), 1990.

Maps in a Mirror: The Short Fiction of Orson Scott Card (includes stories originally published under pseudonym Byron Walley), Tor (New York, NY), 1990.
Worthing Saga, Tor (New York, NY), 1990.
(Editor) *Future on Fire,* Tor (New York, NY), 1991.
The Changed Man, Tor (New York, NY), 1992.
Cruel Miracles, Tor (New York, NY), 1992.
Flux, Tor (New York, NY), 1992.
Monkey Sonatas, Tor (New York, NY), 1993.
(With Kathryn H. Kidd) *Lovelock* (first novel in "Mayflower" trilogy), Tor (New York, NY), 1994.
(Editor) *Future on Ice* (companion volume to *Future on Fire*), Tor (New York, NY), 1998.
Magic Mirror, illustrated by Nathan Pinnock, Gibbs Smith Publisher (Salt Lake City, UT), 1999.
(Editor) *Masterpieces: The Best Science Fiction of the Century,* Ace Books (New York, NY), 2001.
(Editor, with Keith Olexa) *Empire of Dreams and Miracles: The Phobos Science Fiction Anthology,* foreword by Lawrence Krauss, Phobos Books (New York, NY), 2002.
(Editor with Keith Olexa) *Hitting the Skids in Pixeltown: The Phobos Science Fiction Anthology,* Phobos Books (New York, NY), 2003, Volume 2 also with Christian O'Toole, 2003.
(With Doug Chiang) *Robota: Reign of Machines,* Chronicle Books (San Francisco, CA), 2003.

Also author of novelette *Hatrack River,* 1986. Contributor to *The Bradbury Chronicles: Stories in Honor of Ray Bradbury,* edited by William F. Nolan and Martin H. Greenberg, New American Library (New York, NY), 1991. Contributor to numerous anthologies.

"ENDER" SERIES; SCIENCE FICTION

Ender's Game (also see below), Tor (New York, NY), 1985.
Speaker for the Dead (also see below), Tor (New York, NY), 1986.
Ender's Game [and] *Speaker for the Dead,* Tor (New York, NY), 1987.
Xenocide, Tor (New York, NY), 1991.
Children of the Mind, Tor (New York, NY), 1996.
First Meetings: In the Enderverse (includes "Ender's Game," "The Polish Boy," and "Teacher's Pest"), Tor (New York, NY), 2003.

"HEGEMON" SERIES; SCIENCE FICTION

Ender's Shadow, Tor (New York, NY), 1999.
Shadow of the Hegemon, Tor (New York, NY), 2001.

Shadow Puppets, Tor (New York, NY), 2002.
The Shadow Saga, Orbit (New York, NY), 2003.

"TALES OF ALVIN MAKER" SERIES

Seventh Son, St. Martin's Press (New York, NY), 1987.
Red Prophet, Tor (New York, NY), 1988.
Prentice Alvin, Tor (New York, NY), 1989.
Alvin Journeyman, Tor (New York, NY), 1995.
Heartfire, Tor (New York, NY), 1998.
The Crystal City, Tor (New York, NY), 2003.

"HOMECOMING" SERIES

The Memory of Earth (also see below), Tor (New York, NY), 1992.
The Call of the Earth (also see below), Tor (New York, NY), 1993.
The Ships of Earth (also see below), Tor (New York, NY), 1993.
Earthfall, Tor (New York, NY), 1994.
Homecoming: Harmony (contains *The Memory of Earth, The Call of Earth,* and *The Ships of Earth*), Science Fiction Book Club, 1994.
Earthborn, Tor (New York, NY), 1995.

PLAYS

(And director) *Tell Me That You Love Me, Junie Moon* (adaptation of novel by Marjorie Kellogg), produced in Provo, UT, 1969.
The Apostate, produced in Provo, UT, 1970.
In Flight, produced in Provo, UT, 1970.
Across Five Summers, produced in Provo, UT, 1971.
Of Gideon, produced in Provo, UT, 1971.
Stone Tables, produced in Provo, UT, 1973.
A Christmas Carol (adapted from the story by Charles Dickens), produced in Provo, UT, 1974.
Liberty Jail, produced in Provo, UT, 1975.
Father, Mother, Mother, and Mom (produced in Provo, UT, 1974), published in *Sunstone,* 1978.
Fresh Courage Take, produced in Salt Lake City, UT, 1978.
Elders and Sisters (adaptation of novel by Gladys Farmer), produced in American Fork, UT, 1979.
Barefoot to Zion (book and lyrics), music composed by Arlen L. Card, produced in North Salt Lake City, UT, 1997.

Also author, under pseudonym Brian Green, of *Rag Mission,* published in *Ensign,* July, 1977. Author of *Wings* (fragment), produced in 1982.

OTHER

Listen, Mom and Dad, Bookcraft (Salt Lake City, UT), 1978.
Saintspeak: The Mormon Dictionary, Signature Books (Midvale, UT), 1981.
Ainge, Signature Books (Midvale, UT), 1982.
A Woman of Destiny (historical novel), Berkley (New York, NY), 1983, published as *Saints,* Tor (New York, NY), 1988.
Compute's Guide to IBM PCjr Sound and Graphics, Compute (Greensboro, NC), 1984.
Cardography, Hypatia Press, 1987.
Characters and Viewpoint, Writer's Digest (Cincinnati, OH), 1988.
(Author of introduction) Susan D. Smallwood, *You're a Rock, Sister Lewis,* Hatrack River Publications, 1989.
How to Write Science Fiction and Fantasy, Writer's Digest (Cincinnati, OH), 1990.
Lost Boys, HarperCollins (New York, NY), 1992.
(Editor, with David C. Dollahite), *Turning Hearts: Short Stories on Family Life,* Bookcraft (Salt Lake City, UT), 1994.
Treasure Box (novel), HarperCollins (New York, NY), 1996.
Pastwatch: The Redemption of Christopher Columbus, Tor (New York, NY), 1996.
Stone Tables (novel), Deseret Book Co. (Salt Lake City, UT), 1997.
Homebody (novel), HarperCollins (New York, NY), 1998.
Enchantment, Del Rey (New York, NY), 1999.
Sarah (first novel of "Women of Genesis" series), Shadow Mountain (Salt Lake City, UT), 2000.
Rebekah (second novel of "Women of Genesis" series), Shadow Mountain (Salt Lake City, UT), 2001.
An Open Book (poetry collection), Subterranean Press/Hatrack River Publications (Burton, MI), 2003.
Rachel and Leah (third novel of "Women of Genesis" series), Shadow Mountain (Salt Lake City, UT), 2004.

Also author of audio plays for Living Scriptures; coauthor of animated videotapes. Contributor of regular review columns, including "You Got No Friends in This World," *Science Fiction Review,* 1979-86, "Books to Look For," *Fantasy and Science Fiction,* 1987-94, and

"Gameplay," *Compute!,* 1988-89; contributor of columns and editorials to Web sites *Hauvoo* and *Ornery American.* Contributor of articles and reviews to periodicals, including *Washington Post Book World, Science Fiction Review, Destinies,* and *The Rhinoceros Times* (Greensboro, NC). Author of works under pseudonyms Frederick Bliss and P.Q. Gump.

Card's manuscripts are housed at Brigham Young University. His books have been translated into Catalan, Danish, Dutch, Finnish, French, German, Hebrew, Italian, Japanese, Polish, Portuguese, Romanian, Russian, Slovakian, Spanish, and Swedish.

ADAPTATIONS: Xenocide was adapted as an audiobook read by Mark Rolston, Audio Renaissance, 1991; *Seventh Son* was adapted as an audiobook, read by Card, Literate Ear, Inc., 1991; *Maps in a Mirror* was adapted as an audiobook, Dove Audio (Los Angeles, CA), 1999; audiobook productions of most of Card's novels have been acquired by Blackstone Audiobooks (Ashland, OR). Card's short stories "Clap Hands and Sing," "Lifeloop," and "Sepulcher of Songs" were adapted for the stage as *Posing as People* by Scott Brick, Aaron Johnston, and Emily Janice Card respectively, produced 2004.

WORK IN PROGRESS: Rasputin, in the "Mayflower" trilogy; *Magic Street,* a contemporary fantasy novel.

SIDELIGHTS: Orson Scott Card is the award-winning author of over sixty books of science fiction, fantasy, history, and ghost stories. With the creation of Andrew "Ender" Wiggin, the young genius of *Ender's Game,* Card launched an award-winning career as a science fiction and fantasy writer. Since his debut in the field in 1977, when the short story "Ender's Game" appeared in *Analog* magazine, Card went on to become the first writer to win the genre's top awards, the Nebula and the Hugo, for consecutive novels in a continuing series. These two novels—*Ender's Game* and *Speaker for the Dead*—have been described by *Fantasy Review* contributor Michael R. Collings as "allegorical disquisitions on humanity, morality, salvation, and redemption"—evaluations that many critics have applied to Card's other works as well. Such thematic concerns, in part influenced by Card's devout Mormonism, are what critics feel set him apart from other writers in the science-fiction field. Beyond the "Ender" series, Card's other projects include creating the American fantasy series "Tales of Alvin Maker," a retelling of ancient scripture in the "Homecoming" series, contempo-

rary novels with occult and ghost themes such as *Lost Boys, Treasure Box,* and *Homebody,* and a series with a religious theme, "Women of Genesis," begun with the novels *Sarah* and *Rebekah.*

In many of his works Card focuses on the moral development of young protagonists whose abilities to act maturely and decisively while in challenging situations often determine the future of their communities. Card, a devout Mormon, is intrigued by the role of the individual in society, and credits his solid religious background with instilling in him both a strong sense of community and an affinity for storytelling. "I don't want to write about individuals in isolation," he told Graceanne A. DeCandido and Keith R.A. DeCandido in *Publishers Weekly.* "What I want to write about is people who are committed members of the community and therefore have a network of relationships that define who they are. I think if you're going to write about people, you have to write about storytelling." In his works Card is deeply concerned with his own unresolved moral and philosophical questions as well, and maintains that science fiction affords him the benefit of exploring these issues against a futuristic and imaginative backdrop. "In some of the best SF, you move into a universe where all moral bets are off, where you have a group of aliens, or humans in an alien setting, who live by different rules because some key aspect of life that we take for granted as human beings has been changed radically. . . . After a while we can see ourselves through their eyes and see how bizarre we are. Then you come back and you question everything."

Though a profoundly moral writer, Card dismisses standard black-and-white versions of good and evil. As he told Laura Ciporen of *Publishers Weekly,* such representations are "so boring." Card further explained, "When a character comes upon a case of right and wrong and chooses to do wrong, that shows you he's the kind of jerk who'd do that. My characters wrestle with real moral dilemmas where all the choices have steep prices. If they make the selfish choice, then I show the consequences. I'm not trying to teach that lesson, though it underlies everything I write."

Card was born in 1951, in Richland, Washington, the son of a teacher father and an administrator mother. Card moved often in his youth, growing up in California, Arizona, and finally Utah. As a teenager, both the theater and science fiction captured Card's attention. At only sixteen, he entered Brigham Young University and three years later saw his first play, *Tell Me That You Love Me, Junie Moon,* produced in Provo, Utah. Ten plays and adaptations followed through the seventies, mostly with scriptural or historical themes, but Card's education and writing were put on hold for several years in the early 1970s when Card served as a missionary in Brazil. Returning to Provo, Card founded a theater company and earned his B.A., with honors, in 1975. Thereafter he became an editor at *Ensign* magazine, the official publication of the Church of Jesus Christ of Latter-Day Saints, and also worked for the Brigham Young University Press. There was, however, little money in writing plays. "I was supporting myself on the pathetic wages paid to an editor at a university press—and BYU's wages were even more pathetic than usual," he told the DeCandidos. "I knew there was no hope of paying off my debts through my salary, so I made a serious effort to write fiction as a career."

"All the time that I was a playwright," Card once said, "these science fictional ideas that never showed up in my plays were dancing around in the back of my mind." The genre, he felt, offered him the most expedient way of getting published, since the field thrives on up-and-coming talent and fresh ideas. He also admitted that he chose science fiction because, as he noted, "I knew the genre. While it was never even half my reading, I had read enough to be aware of the possibilities within it. It allowed the possibility of the kind of high drama that I'd been doing with religious plays for the Mormon market. . . . In order to write the kind of intense romantic drama that I wanted to write, I needed the possibilities that science fiction and fantasy offered."

Hoping to break into the field, Card sent "The Tinker," one of his first short stories, to Ben Bova, then editor of the leading science-fiction magazine *Analog*. Bova in turn rejected the work, though he did not crush the aspirations of its author. "Apparently he [Bova] saw some reason to hope that I might have some talent," Card explained to the DeCandidos. "His rejection letter urged me to submit a real science fiction story, because he liked the way I wrote." The real story became "Ender's Game," which, upon its publication, garnered Card the World Science Fiction Convention's John W. Campbell Award for best new writer.

Though Card was thrilled with his sudden success, he later admitted to a *Publishers Weekly* interviewer that he was "not so stupid as to quit my job." He retained his position as editor for *Ensign* and in 1978 began composing audio plays for Living Scriptures. He also continued honing his writing skills and released his first book, *Capitol,* during that same year. A collection of short stories, the work follows the fall of the planet

Capitol and revolves in part around the drug somec, which induces a state of suspended animation in its user and allows him to live for several thousand years. At least one reviewer remarked upon Card's literary skill in *Capitol.* The collection "demonstrates a fine talent for storytelling and characterization," decided a critic for *Publishers Weekly.* Card's 1980 novel *Songmaster* generated praise as well. The lyrical tale, set in a futuristic galactic society that reveres those who sing, focuses on Ansset, a "Songbird" who is summoned to serve the emperor. The work encompasses "personal growth and exploration melded into a tale of interplanetary politics and court intrigue," asserted Richard A. Lupoff in *Washington Post Book World.* "*Songmaster* is a first-class job." Some of Card's other early works, however, including *Hot Sleep* and *A Planet Called Treason,* encountered critical censure for employing standard science fiction elements and for containing what some reviewers considered gratuitous violence. George R.R. Martin in the *Washington Post Book World* especially criticized Card's 1981 work, *Unaccompanied Sonata and Other Stories,* which he found filled "with death, pain, mutilation, dismemberment, all described in graphic detail." The volume includes such unfortunate characters as a malformed infant who is drowned in a toilet and whose body is sliced to pieces, and a woman whose breasts are chopped off and eaten. Apart from these negative evaluations, the general critical consensus of Card's early works was that they display imagination, intelligence, literary aptitude, and promise. "Card is a young, talented, and ambitious writer," conceded Martin.

In 1985 Card released *Ender's Game.* This novel began as a short story, which Card once described as "still the most popular and the most reprinted of my stories, and I still have people tell me that they like it better than the novel. . . . When I started working on the novel that became *Speaker for the Dead,* a breakthrough for me in that story was realizing that the main character should be Ender Wiggin. That made it a kind of sequel, although its plot had nothing to do with the original plot; it was just using a character. . . . I told the publisher, Tom Doherty, that I needed to do a novel version of 'Ender's Game' just to set up *Speaker for the Dead.* That's the only reason 'Ender's Game' ever became a novel."

Ender's Game concerns the training of Ender Wiggin, a six-year-old genius who is the Earth's only hope for victory over invading "bugger" aliens. While this plot appears to be standard science-fiction fare, *New York Times Book Review* critic Gerald Jonas observed that "Card has shaped this unpromising material into an affecting novel full of surprises that seem inevitable once they are explained." The difference, asserted Jonas and other critics, is in the character of Ender Wiggin, who remains sympathetic despite his acts of violence. A *Kirkus Reviews* contributor, for example, while noting the plot's inherent weakness, admitted that "the long passages focusing on Ender are nearly always enthralling," and concluded that *Ender's Game* "is altogether a much more solid, mature, and persuasive effort" than the author's previous work. Writing in *Analog,* Tom Easton noted that *Ender's Game* "succeeds because of its stress on the value of empathy," and *Washington Post Book World* reviewer Janrae Frank concluded that "Card is a writer of compassion."

Following the success of *Ender's Game,* its sequel, *Speaker for the Dead,* was hailed as "the most powerful work Card has produced" by Michael R. Collings in *Fantasy Review.* "*Speaker* not only completes *Ender's Game* but transcends it. . . . Read in conjunction with *Ender's Game, Speaker* demonstrates Card's mastery of character, plot, style, theme, and development." Ender Wiggin, now working as a "Speaker for the Dead," travels the galaxy to interpret the lives of the deceased for their families and neighbors; as he travels, he also searches for a home for the eggs of the lone surviving "hive queen" of the race he destroyed as a child. "Like *Game, Speaker* deals with issues of evil and empathy, though not in so polarized a way," observed Tom Easton in his *Analog* review. Some critics found an extra element of complexity in the "Ender" books; *Washington Post Book World* contributor Janrae Frank, for example, saw "quasi-religious images and themes" in the conclusions of both novels.

With the publication of 1991's *Xenocide,* Card's reputation as an unflinching explorer of both moral and intellectual issues was firmly established. In this novel, Card picks up the story of Ender as he works feverishly with his adopted Lusitanian family to neutralize a deadly virus. Many critics venture that with *Xenocide,* Card relies more on the scientific ruminations of a multitude of contemplative characters rather than on a plot. "The real action is philosophical: long, passionate debates about ends and means among people who are fully aware that they may be deciding the fate of an entire species, entire worlds," observed Gerald Jonas in the *New York Times Book Review.*

In 1996 Card published *Children of the Mind,* the final volume of the "Ender" series. In this novel, Ender is already moving off the stage, playing a relatively minor part in the hectic attempt to avoid destruction of the

planet Lusitania by the Starways Congress. Characters who take a more active role in this episode are Peter and Young Valentine, who are copies of Ender's brother and sister, and both products of Ender's mind. Also instrumental in Ender's current bid to save his adopted planet is Jane, a rather irascible Artificial Intelligence who has the uncanny knack of transcending the light-speed barrier. Together these three must roam the galaxy to find a new home for the three races of Lusitania that may all too soon become refugees. Meanwhile, they also try and convince politicians to halt the Starways Congress from destroying the planet. "Card's prose is powerful here," commented a reviewer for *Publishers Weekly,* "as is his consideration of mystical and quasi-religious themes." The same writer went on to wonder whether this book, "billed as the final Ender novel," would in fact be the last the reader hears of Ender or his world. "[T]his story leaves enough mysteries unexplored to justify another entry."

When Card once again approached that same world it was not from Ender's point of view, but from the perspective of a young orphan named Bean. In the first book in the four-part "Hegemon" series, 1999 *Ender's Shadow,* he again enters his parallel universe. *Library Journal*'s Jackie Cassada noted that "Card returns to the world of his award-winning *Ender's Game* to tell the story of a child's desperate struggle for recognition and self-worth." The superhuman child in question, Bean, is taken from the streets of Rotterdam and sent to the Battle School to learn to fight the insect-like Buggers. Bean wins selection to the Battle School by his understanding of personal motivation—a skill that kept him alive in the mean streets when he was a starving child. At Battle School he learns how to command fleets for the war with the alien Buggers. When he comes into contact with Ender, Bean wants to understand what makes this larger-than-life figure tick. "Thus Bean's story is twofold," wrote a *Publishers Weekly* contributor, "he learns to be a soldier, and to be human." Through Bean the reader learns about the formation of Ender's Dragon army and also about the last of Ender's games. "Everyone will be struck by the power of Card's children," concluded the same reviewer, "always more and less than human, perfect yet struggling, tragic yet hopeful, wondrous and strange." Cassada felt that Card's "superb storytelling and his genuine insight into the moral dilemmas that lead good people to commit questionable actions" blend together to make the novel a "priority purchase."

Questioned by Laura Ciporen in *Publishers Weekly* about his child protagonists, Card observed that, for children, life is very real. "They don't think of themselves as cute or sweet. I translate their thoughts from the language available to children into the language available to adults." For Card, children are every bit as complex as adults, and in fact their thoughts and fears—because they have fewer such to compare with—can be even more real than those of adults. Card's ability to portray young protagonists sympathetically yet not condescendingly is part of what makes him a popular writer for adults and juveniles alike.

The "Hegemon" series continues with *Shadow of the Hegemon* and *Shadow Puppets.* With the wars over and Ender off to colonize a new world, the children of the Battle School become increasingly important to those nations wishing to gobble up their neighbors, and Peter Wiggin rises to the position of hegemon, ruler of the Earth government. In *Shadow of the Hegemon,* Bean is second best of the Battle School children and aide to Wiggin; he is wooed for his powers by Wiggin's nemesis, Achilles, an unbalanced genius who wishes to conquer Earth. In *Shadow Puppet* Bean is forced to confront his mortality—his body grows too quickly, dooming him to an early death—and with his young wife Petra pregnant, he seeks an antidote against a similar fate for his unborn children. "The complexity and serious treatment of the book's young protagonists will attract many sophisticated YA readers," observed a writer for *Publishers Weekly* in a review of *Shadow of the Hegemon,* the reviewer further commenting that Card's "impeccable prose, fast pacing and political intrigue will appeal to adult fans of spy novels, thrillers and science fiction." *Library Journal* reviewer Jackie Cassada dubbed the same novel a "gripping story of children caught up in world-shaking events," while in *Booklist* Sally Estes praised *Shadow Puppets* for Card's ability to maintain "the action, danger, and intrigue levels" of the previous series installments.

Card's storytelling techniques are further displayed in the "Tales of Alvin Maker" series. "This series began as an epic poem I was writing during graduate study at the University of Utah," Card once commented, "when I was heavily influenced by Spenser and playing games with allegory. That epic poem won a prize from the Utah State Institute of Fine Arts, but I realized that there is very little future for an epic poem in terms of reaching an audience and telling a story to real people, so I converted it and expanded it and, I think, deepened and enriched it into something much longer and larger." The series includes the novels *Seventh Son, Red Prophet, Prentice Alvin,* and *The Crystal City.*

The first novel in the "Tales of Alvin Maker" series, *Seventh Son,* "begins what may be a significant recasting in fantasy terms of the tall tale in America," wrote

Washington Post Book World reviewer John Clute. Set in a pioneer America where the British Restoration never happened, where the Crown colonies exist alongside the states of Appalachia and New Sweden, and where folk magic is readily believed and practiced, *Seventh Son* follows the childhood of Alvin Miller, who has enormous magical potential because he is the seventh son of a seventh son. While *Fantasy Review* contributor Martha Soukup admitted that "this could easily have been another dull tale of the chosen child groomed to be the defender from evil," she asserted that Card's use of folk magic and vernacular language, along with strongly realized characters, creates in *Seventh Son* "more to care about here than an abstract magical battle."

"Because we know it is a dream of an America we do not deserve to remember, Orson Scott Card's luminous alternate history of the early 19th century continues to chill as it soothes," Clute explained in a review of *Red Prophet,* the second volume of Alvin's story. The novel traces Alvin's kidnaping by renegade Reds employed by "White Murderer" William Henry Harrison, who wishes to precipitate a massacre of the Shaw-Nee tribe. Alvin is rescued by the Red warrior Ta-Kumsaw, however, and learns of Native American ways even as he attempts to prevent the conflict caused by his supposed capture and murder. While "*Red Prophet* seems initially less ambitious" than its predecessor, covering a period of only one year, a *West Coast Review of Books* contributor commented that, "In that year, Card creates episodes and images that stun with the power of their emotions." Sue Martin, however, believed that the setting was not enough to overcome the plot, which she described in the *Los Angeles Times Book Review* as "yet another tale of Dark versus Light." She conceded, however, that while Alvin "seems almost Christlike" in his ability to heal and bring people together, the allegory is drawn "without the proselytizing." *Booklist* writer Sally Estes summarized, "Harsher, bleaker, and more mystical than *Seventh Son,*" Card's second volume displays his strong historical background, "keen understanding of religious experience, and, most of all, his mastery of the art of storytelling."

In *Prentice Alvin* and *Alvin Journeyman* Card explores Alvin's life during and following his apprenticeship. In the second volume Alvin's bad but similarly talented brother, Calvin, leaves for Europe, hoping to learn the arts of manipulation and domination from Napoleon Bonaparte. Alvin himself is forced to leave Vigor Church after being accused of improprieties by a girl dreaming of his passion. He returns to Hatrack River, his birthplace and the location of his apprenticeship, but has to defend himself in court. Written with the input of Card's fans via online forums, the story could have descended into mediocrity, as Martin Morse Wooster noted in the *Washington Post Book World.* However, Wooster declared, "Card appears to have resisted the encroachments of his admirers because *Alvin Journeyman* is a well-written, engaging entertainment."

Heartfire and *The Crystal City* continue the Alvin Maker adventures. *Heartfire* sees Alvin traveling to New England during Puritan times with historical friends such as John James Audubon, seeking to put an end to anti-witch laws. Meantime Alvin's wife, Peggy, who has the ability to see into the hearts of others, tries to put an end to slavery in the South and to stop Alvin's more malevolent brother, Calvin, from destroying her husband. In *The Crystal City* Alvin's ability to channel Native American and African magic works to his advantage as he works to heal the frontier's ills and create a peaceful utopia he calls the Crystal City. "Card's antebellum settings, dialogue and historical figures seem authentic and thoroughly researched," according to a writer for *Publishers Weekly,* who noted however that in *Heartfire* Card "is as occasionally windy and preachy as ever." Jackie Cassada, reviewing the novel in *Library Journal,* concluded that the fifth installment to the "Tales of Alvin Maker" series "exhibits the same homespun charm of its predecessors." Noting that *The Crystal City* "still enchants," a *Publishers Weekly* contributor commented that "a large part of the appeal" of the sixth "Alvin Maker" installment "lies in the book's homegrown characters using their powers for ordinary purposes."

In 1992 Card introduced his "Homecoming" series with *The Memory of Earth,* a novel many critics found to be a mixture of philosophy, futuristic technology, and biblical lore. *Memory* opens on the planet Harmony, where for forty million years humans have been controlled by Oversoul, a powerful, global computer programmed to prevent humanity from destroying itself through needless wars. David E. Jones, in Chicago's *Tribune Books,* argued that "what Card gives us [in *The Memory of Earth*] is an interaction between supreme intelligence and human mental capability that is at once an intellectual exercise, a Biblical parable and a thoroughly enjoyable piece of storytelling."

Card joined forces with a newer science fiction voice, Kathryn H. Kidd, for the publication of *Lovelock* in 1994. The title shares its name with the central character, a genetically enhanced monkey, who is trained to record the activities of important persons for posterity.

Realizing his own servitude and the indifferent neglect of his masters, *Lovelock* plots his escape. The work was welcomed by several critics as a solid blending of two talents. "Masterful," commented Maureen F. McHugh in the *Washington Post Book World,* who found the character of Lovelock to be, "Clearly as nasty and clever as a genetically enhanced capuchin monkey could be expected to be." McHugh continued, "None of Card's previous tellings has possessed the satirical bite we see here, which makes for a welcome change."

Card concludes his "Homecoming" series with the fourth and fifth novels, *Earthfall* and *Earthborn.* In *Earthfall,* the wandering humans return from Harmony to Earth to continue the species when it appears Harmony is about to self destruct. They meet two new species who have evolved in the absence of humans and must make peace with them. "As in other Card novels, plotting is intricate, characters are multifaceted, and strange creatures co-exist with humans," observed Pam Carlson in *Voice of Youth Advocates. Earthborn* focuses on the three groups from *Earthfall* who are speaking a common language but who differ in their habitat. The sky people are able to fly as angels; the earth people or diggers are treated as slaves; the returned humans from Harmony are known as the middle people. As Gerald Jonas noted in the *New York Times Book Review,* "As in all Mr. Card's novels, the characters spend . . . time talking about what they are going to do and why they are going to do it." The critic continued, "these long philosophical discussions crackle with tension." While several reviewers appreciated the "Homecoming" series, the concluding volume received mixed reviews.

Though firmly established as a successful author of science fiction, Card has not limited himself to that genre, publishing throughout his career numerous works of nonfiction, drama, and, most notably, historical fiction. In *A Woman of Destiny* (later published as *Saints*), for example, he returns to the subject of the life of Joseph Smith, first touched upon in *Seventh Son. A Woman of Destiny* offers an account of the lives of Smith, the founder of Mormonism, and Dinah Kirkham, a (fictional) English woman who is converted to Mormonism and becomes Smith's polygamous wife. When Smith is murdered in 1844, Kirkham escapes with a group of fellow Mormons to Utah, where she becomes a staunch leader as well as one of the wives of Brigham Young, Smith's successor as president of the Mormon Church. *Los Angeles Times Book Review* critic Kristiana Gregory pronounced *Saints* an "engrossing epic," stressing that Card "is a powerful storyteller."

Card's *Treasure Box* is billed as a mainstream novel, yet it contains elements of the supernatural. Quentin

Fears loses his beloved older sister Lizzy as a young boy. However, he continues to confide in her following her death. A millionaire, following his sellout of his computer firm, he meets his true love, Madeleine, at a party and marries her. But there are gaps in her background, and when he finally meets his in-laws at a spooky mansion in upstate New York, events unravel following Madeleine's insistence that Quentin open a box supposedly containing her inheritance. 1998's *Homebody* is another mainstream supernatural fantasy, combining elements of spirituality, the occult, and psychological insight in a haunted house tale. *Homebody* tells the story of Don Lark who, grieving the death of his two-year-old daughter, sets out to renovate the Bellamy House, a grand old Victorian mansion in a terrible state of disrepair. His three elderly neighbors warn him about the house's dark powers, but he goes forward with his project and becomes attached to a squatter who lives there. She is the occult key to the violent history of the house as a brothel and speakeasy. A writer for *Kirkus Reviews* assessed the novel as "solid but undistinguished work, not high in either tension or in depth." A *Publishers Weekly* reviewer found more to like, saying that the novel has "great potential that shines through its superfluous detail," and describing it as "a powerful tale of healing and redemption that skillfully balances supernatural horrors with spiritual uplift."

Card turns from the realms of the haunted to those of fairy tales with *Enchantment,* a blending of the story of Sleeping Beauty with Russian mythology. Ten-year-old Ivan is both frightened by and attracted to a lovely woman frozen in time in the midst of a Russian forest. A decade later and now an up-and-coming track star, Ivan returns to the forest to set this bewitched woman free. Drawn back into the ninth-century world of his princess, Ivan discovers that his modern-day talents do not stand him in good stead in his desperate battle to defeat the mythical witch Baba Yaga and claim his princess. Ivan takes Princess Katerina back to the modern world for a time, and the pair learns each other's powers before returning to battle the witch. A *Publishers Weekly* reviewer felt that Card's "new look at a classic tale is clever . . . [due to] adding attractive whimsical twists and cultural confluences to a familiar story."

In *Stone Tables* Card returns to biblical themes, telling the story of Moses and retelling Exodus in a novel "that exhibits the same profound and compassionate understanding of human nature that marks his best sf and fantasy efforts," according to a contributor to *Publishers Weekly.* Card puts the focus here on the difficult relationship between Moses and his siblings. With *Sarah* Card inaugurated a new series, "Women of Genesis." In

Card's retelling, Sarah is to become a priestess of Asherah until she meets a man named Abram, a mystic and desert wanderer. Sarah realizes that her destiny is tied up with Abram's and she waits eight years for his return, only to have many more years of a childless marriage test her belief in Abram's God. "Card adds depth, understanding, and human frailty to the woman who became known as Sarah," wrote Melanie C. Duncan in a *Library Journal* review. Duncan felt the novel "will attract secular readers as well." A reviewer for *Publishers Weekly* maintained that Card's rendering of Sarah as "a wise and virtuous figure who struggles to have the unflinching faith of Abraham," and his portrait of Biblical life and times, creates a "playfully speculative novel" that "succeeds in bringing Sarah's oft-overlooked character into vivid relief."

In a critique of the author's 1990 story collection, *Maps in a Mirror: The Short Fiction of Orson Scott Card, Analog* reviewer Easton characterized Card as "an intensely thoughtful, self-conscious, religious, and community-oriented writer." In spite of such critical acclaim and the numerous awards his writing has earned, Card seems to prefer a simpler description of himself; as he told the DeCandidos, "I'm Kristine's husband, Geoffrey and Emily and Charlie's dad, I'm a Mormon, and I'm a science fiction writer, in that order." Replying to a query by Ciporen of *Publishers Weekly* as to why he writes mainly science fiction, Card replied: "The truth is, SF is the most powerful genre available right now. Mainstream literature is so stultifyingly rigid. I don't just want to talk to people who believed everything their English teacher told them. I want to reach people who read books for the sheer pleasure of it, because those are the people who are open to having their lives changed by what they read."

BIOGRAPHICAL AND CRITICAL SOURCES:

BOOKS

Collings, Michael R., *Storyteller: Official Guide to the Works of Orson Scott Card,* Overlook Connection Press (Woodstock, CA), 2001.

Collings, Michael R., and Boden Clarke, *The Work of Orson Scott Card: An Annotated Bibliography and Guide,* Borgo Press (San Bernardino, CA), 1995.

Contemporary Literary Criticism, Thomson Gale (Detroit, MI), Volume 44, 1987, Volume 47, 1988, Volume 50, 1988.

Contemporary Popular Writers, St. James Press (Detroit, MI), 1997.

Tyson, Edith S., *Orson Scott Card: Writer of the Terrible Choice,* Scarecrow Press (Lanham, MD), 2003.

PERIODICALS

Analog, July, 1983, p. 103; July, 1985, Tom Easton, review of *Ender's Game,* p. 180; June, 1986, Tom Easton, review of *Speaker for the Dead,* p. 183; mid-December, 1987; September, 1988, p. 179; August, 1989, p. 175; January, 1990, p. 305; March, 1991, p. 184; mid-December, 1991; January, 1996, Tom Easton, review of *Pastwatch,* p. 277; June, 1996, p. 145; February, 2003, Tom Easton, review of *Shadow Puppets,* p. 136.

Booklist, December 15, 1985, p. 594; December 15, 1987, Sally Estes, review of *Red Prophet;* December 1, 1995, p. 586; June 1 & 15, 1996, Roland Green, review of *Pastwatch,* p. 1629; July, 2002, Sally Estes, review of *Shadow Puppets,* p. 1796.

Economist, September 5, 1987, p. 92.

Fantasy Review, April, 1986, Michael R. Collings, "Adventure and Allegory," p. 20; June, 1987, Martha Soukup, review of *Seventh Son;* July/August, 1987.

Kirkus Reviews, December 1, 1980, p. 1542; November 1, 1984, p. 1021; May 1, 1994, p. 594; June 15, 1995, p. 864; June 15, 1996, p. 839; February 2, 1998, review of *Homebody;* June 15, 2002, review of *Shadow Puppets,* p. 846.

Kliatt, April, 1991, p. 15.

Library Journal, February 15, 1989, p. 179; November 15, 1990; September 1, 1991; October 15, 1991; January, 1994, p. 172; June 15, 1994, p. 99; May 15, 1995, p. 99; December, 1995, p. 163; July, 1996, p. 154; April 15, 1998, Jackie Cassada, review of *Stone Tablets,* p. 111; August, 1998, Jackie Cassada, review of *Heartfire,* p. 140; September 14, 1999, Jackie Cassada, review of *Ender's Shadow,* p. 115; November 1, 2000, Melanie C. Duncan, review of *Sarah,* p. 60; December, 2000, Jackie Cassada, review of *Shadow of the Hegemon,* p. 196; September 15, 2003, Jackie Cassada, review of *First Meetings,* p. 96.

Locus, April, 1991, p. 15; February, 1992, pp. 17, 57; May, 1994, p. 48; February, 1995, p. 17.

Los Angeles Times Book Review, September 28, 1980; March 6, 1983; July 22, 1984, Kristiana Gregory, review of *A Woman of Destiny,* p. 8; February 3, 1985; August 9, 1987; February 14, 1988, Sue Martin, "Battling the Natives along the Mississippi"; July 20, 1990.

Magazine of Fantasy and Science Fiction, January, 1980, p. 35.

New York Times Book Review, June 16, 1985, Gerald Jonas, review of *Ender's Game,* p. 18; October 18, 1987, p. 36; September 1, 1991, Gerald Jonas, review of *Xenocide,* p. 13; March 15, 1992; May 8, 1994, p. 25; July 9, 1995, Gerald Jonas, review of *Earthborn,* p. 18.

Publishers Weekly, December 4, 1978, review of *Capitol,* p. 62; January 2, 1981, p. 49; January 24, 1986, p. 64; December 25, 1987, p. 65; September 16, 1988; May 19, 1989, p. 72; August 17, 1990, p. 55; November 30, 1990, interview with Card, pp. 54-55; June 14, 1991, p. 48; June 20, 1994, p. 97; January 30, 1995, p. 89; April 10, 1995, p. 58; August 7, 1995, p. 445; January 22, 1996, review of *Pastwatch,* pp. 61-62; June 24, 1996, review of *Children of the Mind,* pp. 45, 49; August 12, 1996, p. 20; February 2, 1998, review of *Homebody,* p. 79; June 29, 1998, review of *Heartfire,* p. 40; September 28, 1998, p. 77; March 8, 1999, review of *Enchantment,* p. 52; July 5, 1999, review of *Ender's Shadow,* p. 63; November 1, 1999, p. 48; September 11, 2000, review of *Sarah,* p. 71; November 20, 2000, Laura Ciporen, "PW Talks with Orson Scott Card," p. 51, and review of *Shadow of the Hegemon,* p. 50; July 15, 2002, review of *Shadow Puppets,* p. 59; October 27, 2003, review of *The Crystal City,* p. 48.

School Library Journal, January, 1991, p. 123; November, 1991; June, 2001, Jan Tarasovic, review of *Shadow of the Hegemon,* p. 183; January, 2004, Mara Alpert, review of *First Meetings,* p. 124.

Science Fiction and Fantasy Book Review, April, 1979, p. 27; December, 1979, p. 155; June, 1983, p. 21.

Science Fiction Review, August, 1979; February, 1986, p. 14.

SF Chronicle, June, 1988, p. 50.

Tribune Books (Chicago, IL), March 1, 1990; March 1, 1992, David E. Jones, "Trapped in a Serial Universe."

Voice of Youth Advocates, October, 1992, p. 236; August, 1995, Pam Carlson, review of *Earthfall* and *Earthborn,* p. 167.

Washington Post Book World, August 24, 1980, Richard A. Lupoff, "Beasts, Songbirds, and Wizards," p. 6; January 25, 1981, George R.R. Martin, "Scanning the Stars of the Short Story," pp. 9, 11; March 27, 1983; February 23, 1986, Janrae Frank, "War of the Worlds," p. 10; August 30, 1987, John Clute, review of *Seventh Son;* February 28, 1988, John Clute, review of *Red Prophet;* March 19, 1992; September 25, 1994, Maureen F. McHugh, review of *Lovelock,* p. 14; September 24, 1995, Martin Morse Wooster, review of *Alvin Journeyman.*

West Coast Review of Books, March, 1984; July, 1986; no. 2, 1987; no. 4, 1988, review of *Red Prophet.*

Wilson Library Bulletin, February, 1994, p. 70.
Writer's Digest, October, 1986, p. 26; November, 1986, p. 37; December, 1986, p. 32; May, 1989, p. 31.

ONLINE

Fantastic Fiction http://www.fantasticfiction.co.uk/ (September 16, 2003).
Hatrack River (Orson Card Official Web site), http://www.hatrack.com/ (February 9, 2001).
Nauvoo Web site, http://www.nauvoo.com/ (June 28, 2004), Card's Latter-Day Saints site.
Ornery American, http://www.ornery.org/ (June 28, 2004).

*   *   *

CAREY, Peter 1943-

PERSONAL: Born May 7, 1943, in Victoria, Australia; son of Percival Stanley (an automobile dealer) and Helen Jean (an automobile dealer; maiden name, Warriner) Carey; married Alison Margaret Summers (a theater director), March 16, 1985; children: Sam, Charley. *Education:* Attended Monash University, 1961.

ADDRESSES: Office—c/o Rogers, Coleridge and White, Powis Mews, London W11 1JN, England. *Agent*—Amanda Urban, International Creative Management, 40 West 57th St., New York, NY 10019.

CAREER: Writer. Worked part-time in advertising in Australia, 1962-88; also worked as a writing instructor at New York University and Princeton University.

AWARDS, HONORS: New South Wales Premier's Literary Award, 1980, for *War Crimes;* Miles Franklin Award, 1981, New South Wales Premier's Literary Award and National Book Council Award, both 1982, all for *Bliss;* AWGIE Award and awards for best film and best screenplay from the Australian Film Institute, all 1985, all for *Bliss; The Age* Book of the Year Award and nomination for Booker Prize, both 1985, Victorian Premier's Literary Award and National Book Council Award, both 1986, all for *Illywhacker;* Booker Prize, 1988, for *Oscar and Lucinda,* and 2001, for *True History of the Kelly Gang;* Litt.D., University of Queensland, Australia, 1989; Commonwealth Writers Prize, 1998, for *Jack Maggs,* and 2001, for *True History of the Kelly Gang;* Common Wealth Writers Prize, 2004, for *My Life as a Fake.*

WRITINGS:

SHORT FICTION

The Fat Man in History (also see below), University of Queensland Press (St. Lucia, Queensland, Australia), 1974.
War Crimes (also see below), University of Queensland Press (St. Lucia, Queensland, Australia), 1979.
The Fat Man in History, and Other Stories (contains selections from *The Fat Man in History* and *War Crimes*), Random House (New York, NY), 1980, published as *Exotic Pleasures,* Picador Books (London, England), 1981.
Collected Stories, University of Queensland Press (St. Lucia, Queensland, Australia), 1994.

NOVELS

Bliss, University of Queensland Press (St. Lucia, Queensland, Australia), 1981, Harper (New York, NY), 1982, reprinted, Faber & Faber (London, England), 2001.
Illywhacker, Harper (New York, NY), 1985.
Oscar and Lucinda, Harper (New York, NY), 1988.
The Tax Inspector, Faber & Faber (London, England), 1991, Knopf (New York, NY), 1992.
A Letter to Our Son, University of Queensland Press (St. Lucia, Queensland, Australia), 1994.
The Unusual Life of Tristan Smith, University of Queensland Press (St. Lucia, Queensland, Australia), 1994, Knopf (New York, NY), 1995.
The Big Bazoohley, Holt (New York, NY), 1995.
Jack Maggs, University of Queensland Press (St. Lucia, Queensland, Australia), 1997, Knopf (New York, NY), 1998.
True History of the Kelly Gang, Knopf (New York, NY), 2000.
My Life as a Fake, Knopf (New York, NY), 2004.
Wrong about Japan: A Father's Journey with His Son, Knopf (New York, NY), 2005.

OTHER

(With Ray Lawrence) *Bliss* (screenplay; adapted from Carey's novel of the same title), Faber (London, England), 1986.
Thirty Days in Sydney: A Wildly Distorted Account, Bloomsbury (New York, NY), 2001.

Work represented in anthologies, including *The Most Beautiful Lies,* Angus & Robertson (Sydney, Australia).

ADAPTATIONS: *Oscar and Lucinda* was adapted as a film by Fox, 1997, directed by Gillian Armstrong and starring Ralph Fiennes and Cate Blanchett.

SIDELIGHTS: Peter Carey "has built a distinguished career out of offbeat, risk-taking novels," wrote *Time's* Paul Gray. An Australian writer, Carey has earned substantial recognition for his quirky, inventive fiction, including several volumes of short stories and seven highly acclaimed novels. In his first short-story collection, *The Fat Man in History,* published in 1974, he presented a matter-of-fact perspective on bizarre and occasionally grotesque subjects. Included in this book are "Conversations with Unicorns," in which the narrator recalls his various encounters with the extraordinary creatures, and "American Dreams," in which a clerk succumbs to madness and isolates himself from his community. Upon his death, townspeople discover that while he was in seclusion, he constructed a model of their village. More gruesome are "Peeling," in which a character's quirky obsession results in a surreal mutilation, and "Withdrawal," in which the protagonist is a necrophiliac dealer of corpses and severed limbs. Among the curious figures in this tale is a pig who becomes dependent on narcotics after consuming an addict's excrement.

The publication of *The Fat Man in History* quickly established Carey as an important new figure in Australian literature. Carl Harrison-Ford wrote in *Stand* that Carey's first work is "the *succes d'estime* of 1974," and Bruce Bennett declared in *World Literature Written in English* that "Carey's first collection of stories . . . stamps him as the major talent among . . . new writers." Bennett found similarities between Carey's work and that of Kurt Vonnegut and Evelyn Waugh, but he added that "the shaping imagination is Carey's own."

Equally unique is *War Crimes,* Carey's second collection of stories. The volume includes such vividly bizarre accounts as "The Chance," where a man vainly attempts to dissuade his lover from entering a lottery in which the major prize is a repulsive body. In the similarly disturbing title piece, a hippie-turned-businessman kills people threatening his profits from frozen food sales. Like Carey's first collection, *War Crimes* was immensely popular in Australia and received the New South Wales Premier's Literary Award in 1980.

In 1981, Carey published his first novel, *Bliss.* Like his short stories, *Bliss* is fairly surreal, rendering the bizarre as if it were the norm. The novel's protagonist is Harry Joy, an overworked advertising executive who suffers a near-fatal heart attack. Upon recovering from the heart attack and equally life-threatening open-heart surgery, Joy believes that he is in hell. He discovers that his wife is compromising him with a close friend and that his seemingly lethargic son is actually a freewheeling drug dealer who forces his sister—Joy's daughter—to commit incest in return for drugs. Joy eventually forsakes his family for Honey Barbara, a worldly nature lover who supports herself as a drug dealer and prostitute. Around the time he befriends the charge-card accommodating prostitute, Joy also discovers that his advertising company maintains a map indicating cancer density for the area, with accountability traced to the company's clients. Aghast, Joy renounces his work and grows more remote from his family. Eventually, his wife has him committed to a mental institution, where he once again meets Honey Barbara, who has also been incarcerated. Together they escape to her home in a rain forest, where Joy finally finds happiness and fulfillment before meeting an unfortunate demise.

With *Bliss,* Carey gained further acclaim from U.S. and British reviewers. In *British Book News,* Neil Philip referred to the book as "a rich, rewarding novel: crisply written, daringly conceived, brilliantly achieved," while in the *Washington Post Book World,* Judith Chettle wrote that Carey's novel possesses "all the virtues of a modern fable." For Chettle, Carey is "a writer of power and imagination." Even more impressed was *Spectator* critic Francis King. "In both the breadth of his vision of human life," wrote King, "in all its misery and happiness, and in the profundity of his insight into moral dilemmas, Mr. Carey makes the work of most of our 'promising' young and not so young novelists seem tinselly and trivial."

In 1985 Carey published his second novel, *Illywhacker,* a wide-ranging comic work about Herbert Badgery, a 139-year-old trickster and liar. Badgery's life, which parallels the development of Australia following its independence from England, is full of odd adventures, including stints as a pilot, car salesman, and snake handler. His accounts of his escapades, however, are not entirely reliable, and over the course of the novel's six hundred pages, Badgery often revels in tomfoolery and good-natured treachery. But he is hardly the novel's only unusual figure: Molly MaGrath maintains her sanity by periodically shocking herself with an "invigorator belt"; Emma, Badgery's daughter-in-law, lives in a lizard's cage; and an entire village proves gullible enough to cooperate with Badgery in his hastily organized plan to build an Australian airplane. By the novel's end, Badgery has recounted many more mad schemes and regaled the reader with recollections of seemingly countless eccentrics.

Illywhacker, like Carey's previous publications, impressed many critics. In *Encounter,* D.J. Taylor dubbed the novel "a dazzling and hilarious book" and described the narrative as "a vast, diffuse plot chock-full of luminous characters and incident." Curt Suplee, reviewing *Illywhacker* for the *Washington Post Book World,* recommended the novel as "huge and hugely rewarding" and added that it is a "rare and valuable" work of fiction. Howard Jacobson, writing in the *New York Times Book Review,* considered *Illywhacker* "a big, garrulous, funny novel, touching, farcical, and passionately bad-tempered." Jacobson also found *Illywhacker* a uniquely Australian work and contended that the experience of reading it is nearly the equivalent of visiting Australia.

Carey's third novel, *Oscar and Lucinda,* is an extraordinary tale of two compulsive gamblers. The work begins in Victorian England, where the child Oscar endures life under the rigid rule of his intimidating father, a preacher. Later, Oscar breaks from his father and joins the conventional Anglican Church, which he serves as a clergyman. Lucinda, meanwhile, has been raised in Australia by her mother, an intellectual who maintains the farm inherited from her late husband. Upon her mother's death, Lucinda inherits funds from the farm's sale. She also becomes owner of a glassworks and consequently devises construction of a glass cathedral. Eventually, Oscar and Lucinda meet on a ship, where Lucinda reveals her own obsession with gambling. Together, Oscar and Lucinda commence an extensive gambling excursion through Australia while simultaneously attempting to spread Christianity throughout the still-wild country.

Oscar and Lucinda resulted in still further praise for Carey and received the 1988 Booker Prize. Beryl Bainbridge, writing in the *New York Times Book Review,* was particularly impressed with those portions devoted to Oscar's traumatic childhood, though the critic added that the remaining episodes are "racy with characters, teeming with invention and expressed in superlative language." Bainbridge also declared that Carey shares with author Thomas Wolfe "that magnificent vitality, that ebullient delight in character, detail and language that turns a novel into an important book." Even more enthusiastic was *Los Angeles Times* reviewer Carolyn See, who wrote of *Oscar and Lucinda:* "There's so much richness here. The sweetness of the star-crossed lovers. The goodness within the stifled English clergyman. The perfect irrationality of human behavior as it plays itself out in minor characters."

Carey returned to writing about modern-day life with his fourth novel, *The Tax Inspector,* which describes four apocalyptic days in the life of the Catchprice family, proprietors of a crumbling auto dealership in a slummy suburb of Sydney, Australia. "Light-years beyond the merely dysfunctional, they're the Beverly Hillbillies on bad acid," stated Francine Prose in the *New York Times Book Review.* "The Catchprices are the sort of people you'd rather read about than spend time with." Granny Frieda Catchprice is a tough, half-senile widow who carries explosives in her pocketbook; her middle-aged daughter Cathy still dreams of leaving the family business to become a country-western singer; Cathy's brother Mort seems mild-mannered and harmless but has cruelly abused his two sons, as he himself was abused by Granny's late husband. One of Mort's children, sixteen-year-old Benny, listens religiously to "self-actualization" tapes until he comes to believe that he is an angel.

Suspecting that her children are about to put her in a nursing home, Granny reports them to the Australian Taxation Office, which sends Maria Takis—an unmarried, pregnant tax collector—to investigate. Maria's sympathy for Granny draws her into the Catchprices' malevolent vortex. "To summarize the novel's characters or its twisted plot is to risk making the book sound simply cartoonish, quirky and grotesque," warned Prose. "In fact, there's something extremely likable about all this, and especially about the way Mr. Carey gives the combative Catchprices great complexity and depth." Prose asserted that eventually, "the black hole these people call home" is transformed into "a dark mirror for the larger world outside."

Carey's *The Unusual Life of Tristan Smith* is a sprawling tale set in the imaginary country of Efica—a tiny island nation colonized and exploited by Voorstand, a huge world power. Carey supplies a rich background for Efica, including a glossary of Efican dialect. The plot is typically convoluted, involving the Eficans' struggle to retain their own cultural identity. The Voorstanders attack that identity with a high-tech, semi-religious entertainment spectacle known as the Sirkus. The featured players in the Sirkus—Broder Mouse, Oncle Duck, and Hairy Man—bear more than a passing resemblance to three icons of the Walt Disney empire, Mickey Mouse, Donald Duck, and Goofy. The story is narrated by Tristan Smith, whose mother belongs to a radical theater group determined to resist the influence of the Sirkus. Hideously deformed at birth, Tristan finally finds love and acceptance after disguising himself in an electronic Broder Mouse costume.

Writing in the *Chicago Tribune,* Douglas Glover found *The Unusual Life of Tristan Smith* "at once bizarre, comic and nauseating, . . . a deeply melancholy book about the Australia of the human heart. . . . Disturbing, wildly original and terribly sad, *The Unusual Life of Tristan Smith* is a book about the place where nation, myth and the personal intersect." Remarking on the novel's themes and relation to contemporary society, Michael Heyward, writing in the *New Republic,* stated: "If all the world is not a stage now but a themepark, we really are destined to become the residents of Voorstand and Efica. Could there be anything worse, Carey seems to be asking, than a situation in which practically everyone espoused the values of mass culture, especially in societies that did not create them?" The novel's driving force, Heyward continued, is "the savage irony of the provincial who has learned that the metropolis is merely a larger and more powerful province than his own." *Washington Post* contributor See was also enthusiastic, declaring that "Peter Carey has attempted to do about one hundred things in this very ambitious novel and—if I'm correct—has about a ninety percent success rate. This, combined with his always magical, absolutely lovable narrative voice, makes *The Unusual Life of Tristan Smith* an important contribution to contemporary fiction."

After a foray into children's literature with *The Big Bazoohley* in 1995, Carey published another major historical novel, *Jack Maggs,* in 1998. In this work, Carey reworks the Charles Dickens classic *Great Expectations,* giving it a decidedly Australian twist. Carey's protagonist, Jack Maggs, is a variation on Abel Magwitch, the Australian convict in Dickens' novel. Carey narrates the adventures of the exiled man, who has in the meantime become a wealthy landowner in Australia, upon his return to England, where he has come to seek out his long lost son. In the process, Maggs becomes involved with a young writer and mesmerist, Tobias Oates, who is a representation of Dickens himself.

Critics praised *Jack Maggs* for being a page-turner and a richly documented historical novel, as well as a clever postmodern comment on the Dickensian literary tradition. In the *Los Angeles Times Book Review,* Richard Eder credited Carey for "writing Dickens darker." *New York Times Book Review* critic Caryn James maintained that the novel's "bright nineteenth-century surface masks a world-weary twentieth-century heart" and "transforms Dickens's characters and his London into a fable about class, national identity, and art." A reviewer for *Booklist* found the novel's melodramatic conclusion "gripping . . . in the classic Dickens manner," while James described it as surprisingly sentimental, seemingly "rigged by Carey to reinforce Maggs's Australian identity."

Carey won his second Booker Prize in 2001 for *True History of the Kelly Gang,* "a dazzling imaginative re-creation of the life of the bushranger and Australian folk hero, Ned Kelly," according to a reviewer for the *Economist.* "It takes the form of an apologia," the same reviewer commented, "written by Ned for the future benefit of his (wholly fictitious) daughter." The novel "cocks the ear like a pistol with its mesmerizing, dialect-driven narration," added a *Library Journal* contributor. Recalling the tall tales of *Illywhacker* and *Oscar and Lucinda,* as well as the Dickensian overtones of *Jack Maggs,* Carey's *True History* is yet "bolder and more challenging than anything he has tried before," according to Anthony Quinn in the *New York Times.* Quinn felt that Carey's novel is not "merely a historical novel; it's a fully imagined act of historical impersonation."

Kelly confesses all in the pages of *True History of the Kelly Gang,* outlining a life every bit as full of adventure as that of America's Jesse James, but one related with verve and edge. The narrative is purportedly drawn from thirteen parcels the outlaw left behind, and in it the territory of northeast Victory in Australia of the 1860s and 1870s is drawn with precision. Born of immigrant stock, Ned grows up adoring his mother, a hot-tempered woman who has no love for the police. Ned wonders throughout his youth about his father's convict past in Ireland. Mocked at school for his poverty, Ned is soon apprenticed "under duress," according to Quinn, to a bushranger, and essentially kidnapped into a life of crime. When he escapes and returns to his mother, he discovers it is she who sold him into service to begin with. Between spells in prison as a teen, Ned turns his hand to horse stealing and then to bank robbing, founding the Kelly gang with his brother and two friends. Ned plays Robin Hood, as well, and it is for his more selfless deeds that he has gone down in Australian folk history. Quinn noted that once Ned turns rebel, "it becomes impossible for us not to saddle up and ride with him to his terminus as tragic hero," hanged at age twenty-five. Quinn concluded that Carey has "transformed sepia legend into brilliant, even violent, color, and turned a distant myth into warm flesh and blood. Packed with incident, alive with comedy and pathos," Carey's book "contains pretty much everything you could ask for of a novel. It is an adjectival wonder."

Other reviewers shared Quinn's glowing appreciation of *True History.* "Carey has fashioned a prose marvel," wrote *Book* contributor Jeff Ousborne, while the critic for the *Economist* felt that Carey "has found a convincing voice for his hero," and presents a "fully rounded character that we can believe in and—his obvious failings notwithstanding—sympathize with wholeheart-edly." *Newsweek*'s Malcolm Jones noted that it is the "best measure" of Carey's novel that the reader does not worry about the historical veracity of his tale for more than a page of the adventures. "This act of literary ventriloquism is so adroit that you never doubt that it's Kelly's own words you're reading in the headlong, action-packed story," Malcolm further commented. "Thanks to Peter Carey's power and skill as a novelist, Ned Kelly's story now has a chance of being heard, if not believed, by the world," wrote David Coad in *World Literature Today*. For Coad, "Carey's Kelly is convinc-ing, captivating, and one cannot but be impressed by the author's attention to detail," while "historical fiction doesn't get much better than this," in the opinion of Dori DeSpain in *School Library Journal*.

In Carey's award-winning 2004 novel, *My Life as a Fake,* narrator Sarah Wode-Douglass is a literary maga-zine editor for a prestigious London poetry journal that needs saving. After accepting an invitation from an old family friend to accompany him to Malaysia, Sarah stumbles upon what could possibly be her savior. Her fate lies in the hands of Australian writer Christopher Chubb, who is responsible for a well-known 1940s Aus-tralian literary hoax that ultimately ended in the suicide of a magazine editor. While Chubb offers Sarah a poem she knows could possibly save her magazine, she can-not help but be suspicious. While Chubb promises he can produce the poem's source, to attain that book Sa-rah ends up having to go to great lengths. Referred to as "something bewilderingly original and powerful," by a reviewer for *Publishers Weekly,* Carey displays his ability as an "extravagantly gifted writer." Marc Klosze-wski commented in *Library Journal* that, in characteris-tic Carey fashion, *My Life as a Fake* "reads like a shot, and . . . the author peoples his tales with charming and intelligent rogues."

Carey returned to his native Australia during the 2000 Olympics after a seventeen-year absence—most of which was spent in New York—in order to write the second volume of Bloomsbury's "The Writer and the City" series. The result was *Thirty Days in Sydney: A Wildly Distorted Account,* a "desultory, impressionistic love letter to the city," according to a reviewer for *Pub-lishers Weekly.* "While other travelogues may provide more information," the same reviewer continued that Carey's "effort will leave more lasting impressions." Similarly, Brad Hooper wrote in *Booklist* that the "im-pressions [the work] imparts are both meaningful and indelible." Gary Krist, reviewing *Thirty Days in Sydney* for the *New York Times,* noted that the author unfolds

his book in many forms, "through arguments, dreams, anecdotes and tirades." Krist concluded that overall Carey "is remarkably fair to the city he left years ago, acknowledging that the forces that shaped it have pro-duced both monstrosities . . . and triumphs."

BIOGRAPHICAL AND CRITICAL SOURCES:

BOOKS

Contemporary Literary Criticism, Thomson Gale (De-troit, MI), Volume 40, 1986, pp. 127-135, Volume 55, 1989, pp. 112-119, Volume 96, 1997, pp. 19-85.
Encyclopedia of World Literature in the Twentieth Cen-tury, 3rd edition, St. James Press (Detroit, MI), 1999.
Huggan, Graham, *Peter Carey,* Oxford University Press (New York, NY), 1996.
Lamb, Karen, *Peter Carey: The Genesis of Fame,* An-gus & Robertson (Sydney, Australia), 1992.

PERIODICALS

Book, January, 2001, Jeff Ousborne, review of *True History of the Kelly Gang,* p. 80.
Booklist, January 1, 1998, review of *Jack Maggs;* Au-gust, 2001, Brad Hooper, review of *Thirty Days in Sydney: A Wildly Distorted Account,* p. 2078.
Boston Globe, January 12, 1992, p. B43; March 14, 1995, p. 28.
British Book News, February, 1981, Neil Philip, review of *Bliss;* May, 1982.
Chicago Tribune, February 21, 1986; January 5, 1992, sec. 14, p. 1; February 19, 1995, Douglas Glover, review of *The Unusual Life of Tristan Smith,* sec. 14, p. 5.
Christian Science Monitor, February 9, 1989, p. 12; No-vember 12, 1996, p. 14.
Economist, January 20, 2001, "A Wizard from Oz," p. 8.
Encounter, September-October, 1985, D.J. Taylor, re-view of *Illywhacker.*
Entertainment Weekly, November 21, 2003, Gregory Kirschling, review of *My Life as a Fake,* p. 90.
Foundation, number 63, pp. 107-111.
Guardian, October 23, 1994, p. 28.
Lancet, February 3, 2001, Robin Gerster, "The Ned Kelly Myth and Australian Identity," p. 401.
Library Journal, January, 1992, p. 170; August, 2001, Joseph L. Carlson, review of *Thirty Days in Syd-ney,* p. 144; January, 2002, review of *True History of the Kelly Gang,* p. 48; November 1, 2003, Marc Kloszewski, review of *My Life as a Fake,* p. 122.

Listener, March 31, 1988, p. 29.

London Review of Books, April 18, 1985; April 21, 1988, p. 20; September 22, 1994, p. 5.

Los Angeles Times, October 2, 1980; August 29, 1985; February 21, 1986; June 19, 1988, Carolyn See, review of *Oscar and Lucinda;* June 11, 1989, p. B12; November 5, 2001, "Mining a Colonial Past," p. E1.

Los Angeles Times Book Review, December 29, 1991, pp. 3, 8; February 5, 1995, pp. 3, 8.

Maclean's, March 26, 2001, John Bemrose, "Dialogue with a Desperado," p. 48.

Meanjin, September, 2001, Andreas Gaile, review of *True History of the Kelly Gang,* pp. 214-220.

Nation, March 16, 1992, pp. 346-348.

New Republic, April 10, 1995, Michael Heyward, review of *The Unusual Life of Tristan Smith,* pp. 38-41.

New Statesman, October 24, 1980; November 20, 1981; August 19, 1985; April 1, 1988, p. 28; January 8, 2001, D.J. Taylor, review of *True History of the Kelly Gang,* p. 42.

Newsweek, April 19, 1982; January 27, 1992, p. 60; January 29, 2001, Malcolm Jones, "An Outlaw down Under," p. 64.

New York, January 13, 1992, p. 62.

New Yorker, August 23, 1982; November 11, 1985; February 24, 1992, p. 101; March 6, 1995, pp. 124-125; September 25, 1995, p. 54; November 27, 1995, p. 96; January 22, 2001, John Updike, review of *True History of the Kelly Gang,* pp. 80-83.

New York Review of Books, June 25, 1992, pp. 35-36; March 29, 2001, John Banville, review of *True History of the Kelly Gang,* pp. 15-16.

New York Times, May 4, 1986; May 14, 1989; section 7, p. 1; January 28, 1992, pp. C11, C15; January 16, 1992, p. C21; January 7, 2001, Anthony Quinn, "Robin Hood of the Outback," section 7, p. 8; February 15, 2001, Mel Gussow, "Novelist Champions an Australian Rogue," p. B8; September 16, 2001, Gary Krist, "A Month down Under," section 7, p. 34.

New York Times Book Review, October 4, 1985, Howard Jacobson, review of *Illywhacker;* May 29, 1988, Beryl Bainbridge, review of *Oscar and Lucinda;* January 12, 1992, Francine Prose, review of *The Tax Inspector,* p. 1; February 28, 1993, p. 32; June 6, 1993, p. 56; February 12, 1995, p. 7; June 22, 1995, p. 44; February 8, 1998, Caryn James, review of *Jack Maggs.*

Observer (London, England), November 15, 1981; April 14, 1985; March 27, 1988, p. 43; September 11, 1994, p. 18.

Partisan Review, spring, 1992, pp. 282-295.

People, December 15, 2003, Allison Lynn, review of *My Life as a Fake,* p. 49.

Publishers Weekly, May 31, 1985; August 20, 2001, review of *Thirty Days in Sydney,* p. 73; October 13, 2003, review of *My Life as a Fake,* p. 56.

Review of Contemporary Fiction, spring, 2004, Irving Malin, review of *My Life as a Fake,* p. 146.

San Francisco Chronicle, October 18, 2001, Oscar Villalon, "'Kelly Gang' Author Peter Carey Wins Second Booker Prize," p. B3.

Saturday Review, August, 1980.

School Library Journal, April, 2001, Dori DeSpain, review of *True History of the Kelly Gang,* p. 171.

Southerly, December, 1977.

Spectator, December 12, 1981, Francis King, review of *Bliss;* January 13, 2001, John de Falbe, review of *True History of the Kelly Gang,* pp. 35-36; August 25, 2001, Peter Porter, review of *Thirty Days in Sydney,* p. 35.

Stand, Volume 16, number 3, 1975, Carl Harrison-Ford, review of *The Fat Man in History.*

Time, March 17, 1986; January 20, 1992, p. 54; January 22, 2001, Paul Gray, "Sympathy for an Outlaw," p. 82.

Times (London, England), March 20, 1988, pp. 8-9.

Times Literary Supplement, October 31, 1980; November 20, 1981; May 3, 1985; August 30, 1991, p. 21; September 2, 1994, p. 10.

Tribune Books (Chicago, IL), June 19, 1988, pp. 1, 11; December 6, 1992, p. 1; February 19, 1995, p. 5.

Village Voice, February 28, 1995, p. 59.

Voice Literary Supplement, February, 1982.

Washington Post, April 17, 1986; February 17, 1995, Carolyn See, review of *The Unusual Life of Tristan Smith,* p. F7.

Washington Post Book World, May 2, 1982, Judith Chettle, review of *Bliss;* August 18, 1985, Curt Suplee, review of *Illywhacker.*

World and I, June, 2001, Robert Ross, "Heroic Underdog down Under," p. 251.

World Literature Today, spring, 2001, David Coad, review of *True History of the Kelly Gang,* p. 314.

World Literature Written in English, November, 1976, Bruce Bennett, review of *The Fat Man in History.*

ONLINE

Peter Carey Web Site, http://ehlt.flinders.edu.au/ (August 5, 2004).

CARROLL, James P. 1943-

PERSONAL: Born January 22, 1943, in Chicago, IL; married Alexandra Marshall (a novelist), 1977; children: Lizzie, Patrick. *Education:* Attended Georgetown University, 1960-61; studied poetry with Allen Tate at University of Minnesota, 1965.

ADDRESSES: Home—Boston, MA. *Office*—c/o Little, Brown & Co., 34 Beacon St., Boston, MA 02106.

CAREER: Entered Missionary Society of St. Paul the Apostle (Paulists), 1963; ordained Roman Catholic priest, 1969, left the priesthood, 1974; Boston University, Boston, MA, chaplain, 1969-74; full-time writer, 1974—. Playwright-in-residence at the Berkshire Theater Festival, Stockbridge, MA, 1974; visiting fellow, Joan Shorenstein Center on the Press, Politics, and Public Policy at Harvard University's Kennedy School of Government, 1997. Author of weekly op-ed column in *Boston Globe,* teacher at Ploughshares International Fiction Writing Seminar, chairman of PEN/New England.

AWARDS, HONORS: R.O.T.C. Cadet of the Year, Georgetown University, 1960; Awarded National Book Award for Nonfiction, 1996, for *An American Requiem;* National Jewish Book Award, 2002, for *Constantine's Sword: The Church and the Jews: A History.*

WRITINGS:

NOVELS

Madonna Red, Little, Brown (Boston, MA), 1976.
Mortal Friends, Little, Brown (Boston, MA), 1978.
Fault Lines, Little, Brown (Boston, MA), 1980.
Family Trade, Little, Brown (Boston, MA), 1982.
Prince of Peace, Little, Brown (Boston, MA), 1984.
Supply of Heroes, Dutton (New York, NY), 1986.
Firebird, Dutton (New York, NY), 1989.
Memorial Bridge, Houghton (Boston, MA), 1991.
The City Below, Houghton (Boston, MA), 1994.
Secret Father, Houghton Mifflin (Boston, MA), 2003.

RELIGIOUS WORKS

Feed My Lambs: A Beginner's Guide for Parents Who Want to Prepare Their Children for the Eucharist and Penance, Pflaum/Standard (Dayton, OH), 1967.

Tender of Wishes: The Prayers of a Young Priest, Newman Press (Paramus, NJ), 1969.
Wonder and Worship, Newman Press (Paramus, NJ), 1970.
Prayer from Where We Are: Suggestions about the Possibility and Practice of Prayer Today, Pflaum (Dayton, OH), 1970.
Elements of Hope, Pastoral Educational Services (Paramus, NJ), 1971.
Contemplation: Liberating the Ghost of the Church, Churching the Ghost of Liberation, Paulist Press (New York, NY), 1972.
A Terrible Beauty: Conversions in Prayer, Politics, and Imagination, Newman Press (Paramus, NJ), 1973.
The Winter Name of God, Sheed and Ward (New York, NY), 1975.
Constantine's Sword: The Church and the Jews: A History, Houghton Mifflin (Boston, MA), 2001.
Toward a New Catholic Church: The Promise of Reform, Houghton Mifflin (Boston, MA), 2002.

OTHER

Forbidden Disappointments (poems), Paulist Press (New York, NY), 1974.
An American Requiem: God, My Father, and the War That Came between Us (memoir), Houghton (Boston, MA), 1996.
Crusade: Chronicles of an Unjust War (collected columns), Holt (New York, NY), 2004.

Also author of *O, Farrell! Oh, Family!* (drama), produced in New York, NY. Contributor of articles and poetry to journals, including *Catholic World, Poetry,* and *Christian Century.*

SIDELIGHTS: For several years James P. Carroll worked at two jobs: being a priest and being a writer. In 1965, when he went to the University of Minnesota to study poetry with Allen Tate, Carroll had his first inkling that he could not meet the demands of both careers forever. After finishing the poetry course, Carroll requested that Tate autograph a book of his poetry. Tate scrawled across the page: "Inscribed to James Carroll, with best wishes for his two vocations." Then Tate looked up at Carroll and warned him: "You know, you're not going to be able to have them both." Tate's prediction proved to be true: in the mid-1970s Carroll left the priesthood to devote himself to writing.

All of Carroll's writings are infused with religious and moral concerns. *Forbidden Disappointments,* his volume of poetry, deals with the difficulties of being a priest as well as with the problems of maintaining faith in an increasingly secular world. Writing in *Commonweal*, Gerard Reedy praised Carroll's "bursts of power and fresh perception," although he found that some of the poems lack "sustained discipline of thought and form, ironic rejection of stock situations, and attention to certain generally accepted rules of good writing." The tone and style of the poems aroused Frances Sullivan's admiration. "It is an amiable poetry, James Carroll's small book, partly because the language of it is uniformly simple and self-giving, partly because the vision of each poem is like a recovered boyishness with the motes and beams of adult wickedness stuck in its eye," Sullivan commented in *America*.

Ostensibly a suspense novel, *Madonna Red* also examines religious issues, as a contributor to the *New York Times Book Review* emphasizes: *Madonna Red* "is a very up-to-date book about the problems of Catholicism in the modern world; about the role of women in the church; about the obligations of priesthood and the doctrine of unfaltering obedience to the bishop." In writing this novel about the attempted assassination of a British ambassador, Carroll throws a red herring across the reader's path early in the book, a ploy which a commentator in the *New York Times Book Review* found particularly clever: "At the beginning of the book there is as neat a piece of misdirection as one is going to come across in any crime novel anywhere." In contrast, a critic for *Newsweek* was less enthusiastic regarding the misleading clue, writing that "The foundation for this trick is laid early in the book and in such a self-conscious manner that no reader with an IQ above seventy-nine can possibly fail to catch it."

Mortal Friends met with greater critical approval. The novel revolves around the life of Colman Brady, an Irish rebel who is compelled to flee to America with his infant son. Brady lands in Boston, where he becomes involved in a series of shady political intrigues, underworld activities, and bloody schemes for vengeance. Reflecting the favorable opinions of many other critics, Webster Schott noted in the *New York Times Book Review* that *Mortal Friends* "is a serious work of fiction intended for a wide audience. It informs, entertains, and does so without abandoning intellectual standards. James Carroll has observed life carefully, and thought about what he saw." Although Schott complained that the plot too often relies on chance and that the book is humorless, he nonetheless considered *Mortal Friends* an impressive work, and declared Carroll to be "a novelist of consequence."

Carroll's intermingling of historical and fictional characters in *Mortal Friends* was a subject that attracted much comment. Among the real people who appear in the novel are Senator Estes Kefauver, Boston mayor James Michael Curley, Richard Cardinal Cushing, and Joseph, John, and Robert Kennedy. In keeping with Carroll's philosophy that "all historical figures in some way are unsavory, and all in some way merit respect," the depictions of the authentic people are neither entirely flattering nor entirely disparaging.

Themes of defeat, betrayal, and revenge also pervade *Mortal Friends*. In the *New York Times Book Review*, Christopher Lehmann-Haupt compared the novel to a Greek tragedy and asserted that the denouement of the book, in which Colman Brady finally decides to end the cycle of gory retaliation, "is a resolution that was first worked out over two-and-a-half millennia ago in Aeschylus's Oresteian trilogy, but is a lesson that must somehow be impressed on our increasingly archaic contemporary society, where cries for revenge seem to grow louder with each passing day."

Like *Mortal Friends*, *The City Below* is set in working-class Boston and centers on a conflict between good and evil. The novel focuses on two brothers, Terry and Nick Doyle, at four points in their lives: 1960, 1968, 1975, and 1984. Their ever-diverging paths continue to bring them into conflict, with one abandoning the priesthood for politics and then real estate development while the other remains in the old neighborhood, running the family business as a front for the Italian mafia. "While not a very original plot device, Carroll's dramatization of parallel lives of brothers in conflict is skillfully managed to carry the weight of the larger social, political and moral themes," argued Michael Lee in the *National Catholic Reporter*. Like Carroll's earlier novels, *The City Below* features cameo appearances by historical figures, in this case Edward Kennedy and Richard Cardinal Cushing. As Carroll explores the many facets of brotherhood, critics have noted that, once again, he blends the pace of popular fiction with realistic characters and serious themes.

In 1996 Carroll won the National Book Award in the nonfiction category for his memoir of his relationship with his father and how it was permanently altered during the years of the Vietnam War. In *An American Requiem: God, My Father, and the War That Came between Us,* he details the unusual career of his father, who left the seminary before taking the vows that would have made him a priest, then worked in the stockyards while attending law school at night and after graduation was recruited into the Federal Bureau of Investigation. He became the first director of the Defense Intelligence

Agency in 1961, and played a direct role in choosing bombing targets during the Vietnam War. It was in this final role that the elder Carroll came into conflict with his increasingly pacifistic priest son, who had been deeply moved by religious leaders such as Martin Luther King, Hans Küng, and the Berrigan brothers, who preached peace. The book opens with Carroll's first sermon as a priest, into which he inserted the word "napalm" to the dismay of his father and other high-ranking military personnel present; it ends with the funeral mass for his father, whose angry ghost, Carroll told Nicholas A. Basbanes in *Publishers Weekly,* he hoped to lay to rest with this narrative.

"*An American Requiem* is extraordinary—articulate, personal, detailed, insightful, probing, dramatic," wrote Patrick H. Samway in *America.* "I think this book should be proclaimed a minor (dare I say major?) classic." Other reviewers were similarly enthusiastic, deeming Carroll's work a deeply felt, intelligent portrayal of the peace movement of the 1960s, warmed by the nostalgic picture the author paints of growing up in Washington, D.C., during the 1940s and 1950s. "This is a magnificent portrayal of two noble men who broke each other's hearts," concluded Patricia Hassler in *Booklist.*

A columnist with the *Boston Globe* since 1992, Carroll continues to comment on the world around him in addition to continuing his fiction-writing. His writings on the Iraq war were been collected in *Crusade: Chronicles of an Unjust War,* which was published in 2004.

BIOGRAPHICAL AND CRITICAL SOURCES:

BOOKS

Carroll, James P., *The Winter Name of God,* Sheed, 1975.
Contemporary Literary Criticism, Volume 38, Thomson Gale (Detroit, MI), 1986, pp. 102-111.

PERIODICALS

America, May 10, 1975; August 7, 1976; June 8, 1996, p. 24.
Atlantic, July, 1994, pp. 100-107; April, 1996, pp. 76-85.
Bestsellers, September, 1976.
Booklist, March 15, 1994, p. 1302; May 1, 1996, p. 1483.

Christian Science Monitor, May 18, 1978.
Commonweal, March 26, 1976; July 12, 1996, pp. 25-27; May 23, 1997, pp. 6-9, 12-17.
Critic, fall, 1976.
Entertainment Weekly, November 29, 1996, pp. 82-84.
National Catholic Reporter, September 9, 1994, p. 25; May 24, 1996, p. 29.
Newsweek, June 21, 1976; July 3, 1978.
New Yorker, May 22, 1978.
New York Times, May 25, 1978; April 23, 1989, sec. 7, p. 20; July 3, 1994; May 9, 1996.
New York Times Book Review, July 11, 1976; April 30, 1978; August 6, 1978.
Poetry, April, 1976.
Publishers Weekly, April 11, 1994, pp. 54-56; April 1, 1996, p. 63; May 27, 1996, pp. 52-54.
Time, June 12, 1978.
U.S. Catholic, May, 1997, pp. 27-32.
Washington Monthly, July-August, 1996, pp. 57-59.
Washington Post, April 21, 1978.

*   *   *

CARROLL, Jonathan 1949-

PERSONAL: Born January 26, 1949, in New York, NY; son of Sidney (a screenwriter) and June (an actress and lyricist; maiden name, Sillman) Carroll; married Beverly Schreiner (an artist), June 19, 1971; children: Ryder Pierce. *Education:* Rutgers University, B.A. (cum laude), 1971; University of Virginia, M.A., 1973.

ADDRESSES: Home—Vienna, Austria. *Agent*—c/o Author Mail, Tor/St. Martin's Press, 175 Fifth Ave., New York, NY 10010.

CAREER: Writer. North State Academy, Hickory, NC, English teacher, 1971-72; St. Louis Country Day School, St. Louis, MO, English teacher, 1973-74; American International School, Vienna, Austria, English teacher, 1974—.

AWARDS, HONORS: Emily Clark Balch fellowship in creative writing at University of Virginia, 1972; *Washington Post* Book of the Year citation, 1983, for *Voice of Our Shadow;* World Fantasy Award, 1988; British Fantasy Award, 1992; Bram Stoker Award, Horror Writers of America, 1995, for best collection; Imaginaire Award, 2000.

WRITINGS:

NOVELS

The Land of Laughs, Viking (New York, NY), 1980, reprinted, Orb (New York, NY), 2001.

Voice of Our Shadow, Viking (New York, NY), 1983.

Bones of the Moon, Century (London, England), 1987, Arbor House (New York, NY), 1988, reprinted, Orb (New York, NY), 2002.

Sleeping in Flame, Legend (London, England), 1988, Doubleday (New York, NY), 1989, reprinted, Tor (New York, NY), 2004.

A Child across the Sky, Legend (London, England), 1989, Doubleday (New York, NY), 1990.

Black Cocktail, illustrated by Dave McKean, Legend (London, England), 1990, St. Martin's Press (New York, NY), 1991.

Outside the Dog Museum, Macdonald (London, England), 1991, Doubleday (New York, NY), 1992.

After Silence, Macdonald (London, England), 1992, Doubleday (New York, NY), 1993.

From the Teeth of Angels, Doubleday (New York, NY), 1994.

Kissing the Beehive, N.A. Talese/Doubleday (New York, NY), 1998.

The Marriage of Sticks, Tor (New York, NY), 1999.

The Heidelberg Cylinder, Mobius New Media (Wilmington, DE), 2000.

The Wooden Sea, Tor (New York, NY), 2001.

White Apples, Tor (New York, NY), 2002.

OTHER

The Panic Hand (story collection), HarperCollins (London, England), 1995, St. Martin's Press (New York, NY), 1996.

Also author of screenplays, including *The Joker.* Contributor of short stories to periodicals, including *Transatlantic Review, Sport, Cimarron Review, Folio, Christian Science Monitor,* and *Four Quarters,* and of book reviews to *St. Louis Globe-Democrat* and *Cleveland Plain Dealer.*

SIDELIGHTS: Jonathan Carroll has received critical plaudits for his novels of the supernatural. According to Michael Moorcock, writing in the *New Statesman and Society,* "Carroll's books are dangerous. He takes considerable risks and trusts his readers with the nerve and intelligence to follow him. He's a moral visionary whose sturdy, subtle plots are rooted in character, a profound liking for people, a relish for life. Yet he writes about active evil. He uses supernatural fiction to comment upon that evil." Reviewing 1999's *The Marriage of Sticks,* for *Booklist,* Ray Olsen noted that "Carroll realizes characters and settings superbly and propels the story forward compellingly," while a *Publishers Weekly*

critic praised the author's prose as "poetic and magical, dense with a wonderful strangeness reminiscent of Fellini and urgent with inklings of horror."

Writing in the *St. James Guide to Horror, Ghost, and Gothic Writers,* Brian Stableford explained the narrative strategy of Carroll's supernatural novels. His books, noted Stableford, "are set in a distinctive narrative space whose deceptively close resemblances to the reader's world usually break down with the abrupt introduction of some unexpected fantastic motif. These unceremonious intrusions of the supernatural can seem jarring, although they often serve the purpose of rendering brutally explicit a creeping but numinous unease which has possessed the plot since its inception. Carroll has standardized a strategy whereby his books grip the reader with their easy narrative manner and sentimental accounts of rewarding emotional relationships, then spring transformative narrative ambushes which remove everything into a new and exotic context."

Jack Sullivan of the *Washington Post Book World* heralded Carroll's first book, *The Land of Laughs,* as a "beguiling and original novel." Elaborating that Carroll "deftly avoids the clichés of contemporary occult fiction," the critic also observed that the author's "descriptions of his small-town Missouri setting are charming and paradoxically down-to-earth; his characters are engaging, sweet-natured antiquarian oddballs; and his sense of humor is nicely attuned to his fantastic subject matter." Sullivan noted, however, that this "whimsical fantasy" soon develops into a "malevolent horror . . . full of startling juxtapositions and surprises." In a more recent *Washington Post* review, Sullivan called *The Land of Laughs* "probably the most imaginative supernatural novel in ten years."

Carroll explained his purpose in writing *The Land of Laughs* in a *Publishers Weekly* interview. "I have tried to show," he disclosed, "that in literature as well as in life, the very things that delight us may well turn around and hurt or scare us, unendingly."

In *A Child across the Sky,* Carroll tells the story of a filmmaker who searches for lost footage from a horror film made by a deceased friend. He is accompanied by his friend's imaginary playmate from childhood, who has now come to life and claims to be an angel. *A Child across the Sky,* explained Stableford, "is the most complicated of Carroll's works, and the most nakedly horrific; the conscientiously nasty-minded double-twist ending is the most effective of all his climaxes."

From the Teeth of Angels finds four characters confronted by and struggling with the Angel of Death, who appears to them in ominous dreams. "Carroll writes with grace and style," noted Dennis Winters in *Booklist*, "weaving the different strands of his story to their frightening shared climax." Moorcock found that, as the story draws to a close, "we come to realise we have been experiencing a struggle between good and evil as monumental as anything in Milton."

Noting that Carroll's idiosyncratic fiction has gained a loyal following among British and European readers, a *Publishers Weekly* contributor maintained that while he "has yet to achieve commesurate stature on his native shore," novels such as 2001's *The Wooden Sea* would likely attract a greater audience in the United States. In the novel, small-town police chief Frannie McCabe adopts an old stray, only to have the animal die shortly thereafter. When the dead dog turns up in the trunk of a car examined during an across-town police investigation, it sparks a series of surreal connections that ultimately find McCabe confronting his teenaged self and aiding an otherwordly entity solve the puzzle of the universe. "This delightfully eerie story eschews all small-town stereotypes and eludes categorization," wrote *Booklist* contributor Bonnie Johnson, while the *Publishers Weekly* critic dubbed *The Wooden Sea* "wonderfully offbeat."

In Carroll's 2002 novel, *White Apples,* Vincent Ettrich, a divorced philanderer, is summoned back from the dead by his unborn son. It seems Vincent has information about the afterlife essential to maintaining a harmonious balance in the universe. Trouble is, he cannot remember what it is. Vincent struggles to recall what he is supposed to know while dodging agents of chaos determined to stop him. Don McLeese, reviewing *White Apples* in *Book*, noted that "linear logic means little in the imaginative world of Carroll" and that the author's "speculative fables not only resist categorization, they defy paraphrase." A *Publishers Weekly* critic described *White Apples* as "a classic Carroll romp in which personified states of mind achieve independent life, characters interact with quirky incarnations of aspects of themselves, and bizarre metaphors ('When you're dead they teach you how to make a water sandwich') are illuminatingly literalized." In *Library Journal*, Jackie Cassada wrote of Carroll's "simple yet powerful prose," citing in particular "his talent for creating characters that seem both unique and familiar."

BIOGRAPHICAL AND CRITICAL SOURCES:

BOOKS

St. James Guide to Horror, Ghost, and Gothic Writers, St. James Press (Detroit, MI), 1998.

PERIODICALS

Book, September-October, 2002, p. 78.
Booklist, May 1, 1994, p. 1581; December 15, 1997, Ted Leventhal, review of *Kissing the Beehive,* p. 685; August, 1999, Ray Olson, review of *The Marriage of Sticks,* p. 2038; December 15, 2000, Bonnie Johnson, review of *The Wooden Sea,* p. 795; September 15, 2002, p. 211.
Library Journal, March 15, 2001, Jackie Cassada, review of *The Wooden Sea,* p. 110; October 15, 2002, p. 97.
New Statesman and Society, May 6, 1994, p. 36.
Publishers Weekly, June 15, 1980; February 1, 1993, p. 70; March 28, 1994, p. 82; October 7, 1996, p. 60; November 10, 1997, p. 56; July 5, 1999, p. 63; January 8, 2001, review of *The Wooden Sea,* p. 47; September 23, 2002, p. 54.
Washington Post, April 25, 1983.
Washington Post Book World, May 3, 1981.

*   *   *

CARRUTH, Hayden 1921-

PERSONAL: Surname accented on final syllable; born August 3, 1921, in Waterbury, CT; son of Gorton Veeder (an editor) and Margery Tracy Barrow (maiden name, Dibb) Carruth; married Sara Anderson, March 14, 1943; married Eleanore Ray, November 29, 1952; married Rose Marie Dorn, October 28, 1961; married Joe-Anne McLaughlin, December 29, 1989; children: (first marriage) Martha Hamilton; (third marriage) David Barrow. *Education:* University of North Carolina, A.B., 1943; University of Chicago, M.A., 1948. *Politics:* Abolitionist

ADDRESSES: Home—RD 1, Box 128, Munnsville, NY 13409.

CAREER: Poet; freelance writer and editor. *Poetry,* editor-in-chief, 1949-50; University of Chicago Press, associate editor, 1951-52; Intercultural Publications, Inc., project administrator, 1952-53. Poet-in-residence, Johnson State College, 1972-74; adjunct professor, University of Vermont, 1975-78; visiting professor, St. Michael's College, Winooskie, VT. Syracuse University, professor of English, 1979-85, 1986-91, professor emeritus, 1991—; Bucknell University, professor, 1985-86. Owner and operator, Crow's Mark Press, Johnson, VT. *Military service:* U.S. Army Air Forces, World War II; became staff sergeant; spent two years in Italy.

MEMBER: New York Foundation for the Arts (senior fellow, 1993).

AWARDS, HONORS: Vachel Lindsay Prize, 1954, Bess Hokin Prize, 1956, Levinson Prize, 1958, and Morton Dauwen Zabel Prize, 1967, all from *Poetry* magazine; Harriet Monroe Poetry Prize, University of Chicago, 1960, for *The Crow and the Heart;* grant-in-aid for poetry, Brandeis University, 1960; Bollingen Foundation fellowship in criticism, 1962; Helen Bullis Award, University of Washington, 1962; Carl Sandburg Award, *Chicago Daily News,* 1963, for *The Norfolk Poems;* Emily Clark Balch Prize, *Virginia Quarterly Review,* 1964, for *North Winter;* Eunice Tietjens Memorial Prize, 1964; Guggenheim Foundation fellow, 1965 and 1979; National Endowment for the Humanities fellow, 1967; National Foundation on the Arts and Humanities grant, 1967 and 1974; Governor's Medal, State of Vermont, 1974; Shelley Memorial Award, Poetry Society of America, 1978; Lenore Marshall Poetry Prize, 1978, for *Brothers, I Loved You All; The Voice That Is Great within Us: American Poetry of the Twentieth Century* was selected as one of the New York Public Library's Books for the Teen Age, 1981 and 1982; Whiting Writers Award, Whiting Foundation, 1986; honorary degrees from New England College, 1987, Syracuse University, 1993; Sarah Josepha Hale Award, 1988; senior fellowship, National Endowment for the Arts, 1988; Ruth Lilly Poetry Prize, 1990; National Book Critics Circle Award in Poetry, 1993; Pulitzer Prize and National Book Award, both 1996, both for *Scrambled Eggs and Whiskey: Poems 1991-1996.*

WRITINGS:

POETRY

The Crow and the Heart, 1946-1959, Macmillan (New York, NY), 1959.

In Memoriam: G.V. C., privately printed, 1960.

Journey to a Known Place (long poem), New Directions (New York, NY), 1961.

The Norfolk Poems: 1 June to 1 September 1961, Prairie Press (Iowa City, IA), 1962.

North Winter, Prairie Press (Iowa City, IA), 1964.

Nothing for Tigers; Poems, 1959-1964, Macmillan (New York, NY), 1965.

Contra Mortem (long poem), Crow's Mark Press (Johnson, VT), 1967.

For You: Poems, New Directions (New York, NY), 1970.

The Clay Hill Anthology, Prairie Press, 1970.

From Snow and Rock, from Chaos: Poems, 1965-1972, New Directions (New York, NY), 1973.

Dark World, Kayak (Santa Cruz, CA), 1974.

The Bloomingdale Papers, University of Georgia Press (Athens, GA), 1975.

Loneliness: An Outburst of Hexasyllables, Janus Press (Rogue River, OR), 1976.

Aura, Janus Press (Rogue River, OR), 1977.

Brothers, I Loved You All, Sheep Meadow (New York, NY), 1978.

Almanach du Printemps Vivarois, Nadja, 1979.

The Mythology of Dark and Light, Tamarack (Madison, WI), 1982.

The Sleeping Beauty, Harper (New York, NY), 1983, revised edition, Copper Canyon Press (Port Townsend, WA), 1990.

If You Call This Cry a Song, Countryman Press (Woodstock, VT), 1983.

Asphalt Georgics, New Directions (New York, NY), 1985.

Lighter than Air Craft, edited by John Wheatcroft, Press Alley, 1985.

The Oldest Killed Lake in North America, Salt-Works Press, 1985.

Mother, Tamarack Press, 1985.

The Selected Poetry of Hayden Carruth, Macmillan (New York, NY), 1986.

Sonnets, Press Alley, 1989.

Tell Me Again How the White Heron Rises and Flies across the Nacreous River at Twilight toward the Distant Islands, New Directions (New York, NY), 1989.

Collected Shorter Poems, 1946-1991, Copper Canyon Press (Port Townsend, WA), 1992.

Collected Longer Poems, Copper Canyon Press (Port Townsend, WA), 1993.

Selected Essays and Reviews, Copper Canyon Press (Port Townsend, WA), 1995.

Scrambled Eggs and Whiskey: Poems, 1991-1995, Copper Canyon Press (Port Townsend, WA), 1996.

Doctor Jazz: Poems, 1996-2000, Copper Canyon Press (Port Townsend, WA), 2001.

Contributor of poetry to books, including *Where Is Vietnam?: American Poets Respond,* Anchor Books (New York, NY), 1967.

EDITOR

(With James Laughlin), *A New Directions Reader,* New Directions (New York, NY), 1964.

The Voice That Is Great within Us: American Poetry of the Twentieth Century, Bantam (New York, NY), 1970.

The Bird/Poem Book: Poems on the Wild Birds of North America, McCall, 1970.

The Collected Poems of James Laughlin, Moyer Bell (Wakefield, RI), 1994.

(And author of introduction) James Laughlin, *A Commonplace Book of Pentastichs,* New Directions (New York, NY), 1998.

OTHER

Appendix A (novel), Macmillan (New York, NY), 1963.

After "The Stranger": Imaginary Dialogues with Camus, Macmillan (New York, NY), 1964.

Working Papers: Selected Essays and Reviews, edited by Judith Weissman, University of Georgia Press (Athens, GA), 1981.

Effluences from the Sacred Caves: More Selected Essays and Reviews, University of Michigan Press (Ann Arbor, MI), 1984.

Sitting In: Selected Writings on Jazz, Blues, and Related Topics (includes poetry), University of Iowa Press (Iowa City, IA), 1986, expanded edition, 1993.

Suicides and Jazzers, University of Michigan Press (Ann Arbor, MI), 1992.

Reluctantly: Autobiographical Essays, Copper Canyon Press (Port Townsend, WA), 1998.

Beside the Shadblow Tree: A Memoir of James Laughlin, Copper Canyon Press (Port Townsend, WA), 1999.

Listener's Guide: Reading from Collected Shorter Poems and Scrambled Eggs and Whiskey (sound recording), Copper Canyon Press (Port Townsend, WA), 1999.

Letters to Jane, Ausable Press (St. Paul, MN), 2004.

Contributor to *The Art of Literary Publishing,* Pushcart Press (Wainscott, NY), 1980; contributor to periodicals, including *Poetry, Hudson Review, New Yorker,* and *Partisan Review.* Member of editorial board, *Hudson Review,* beginning 1971; poetry editor, *Harper's,* 1977-83.

SIDELIGHTS: "Now and then a poet comes along whose work ranges across wide and diverse territories of form, attitude, and emotion—yet with the necessary intelligence that belies a deep, lifelong engagement with tradition—so that variance never seems mere experimentation or digression, but improvisation," wrote *Midwest Quarterly* contributor Matthew Miller. "Hayden Carruth is such an artist."

The Pulitzer Prize won by Carruth in 1996 for his collection *Scrambled Eggs and Whiskey: Poems, 1991-1995* provided a grace note for a long academic and literary career that has seen the author become known as a proponent of twentieth-century modernism. Though recognized primarily as a critic and editor, Carruth is also, according to a critic in the *Virginia Quarterly Review,* "a poet who has never received the wide acclaim his work deserves and who is certainly one of the most important poets working in this country today. . . . [He is] technically skilled, lively, never less than completely honest, and as profound and deeply moving as one could ask." Characterized by a calm, tightly controlled, and relatively "plain" language that belies the intensity of feeling behind the words, Carruth's poetry elicits praise from those who admire its wide variety of verse forms and criticism from those who find its precision and restraint too impersonal and academic.

Commenting in his book *Babel to Byzantium,* James Dickey speculated that these opposing views of Carruth's work may result from the occasionally uneven quality of his poetry. In a discussion of *The Crow and the Heart, 1946-1959,* for example, Dickey noted "a carefulness which bursts, once or twice or three times, into a kind of frenzied eloquence, a near-hysteria, and in these frightening places sloughing off a set of mannerisms which in the rest of the book seems determined to reduce Carruth to the level of a thousand other poets. . . . [He] is one of the poets (perhaps all poets are some of these poets) who write their best, pushing past limit after limit, only in the grip of recalling some overpowering experience. When he does not have such a subject at hand, Carruth amuses himself by being playfully skillful with internal rhyme, inventing bizarre Sitwellian images, being witty and professionally sharp."

American Poetry Review critic Geoffrey Gardner, who characterized Carruth as "a poet who has always chosen to make his stand just aside from any of the presently conflicting mainstreams," said that such linguistic playfulness is typical of the poet's early work. He attributes it to Carruth's struggle "to restore equilibrium to the soul [and] clarity to vision, through a passionate command of language," a struggle that gives much of his poetry "a Lear-like words-against-the-storm quality." Continued Gardner: "I won't be the first to say Carruth's early work is cumbered by archaisms, forced inversions, sometimes futile extravagances of vocabulary and a tendency of images and metaphors to reify into a top heavy symbolism. . . . But the courage of [his] poems can't be faulted. From the earliest and against great odds, Carruth made many attempts at many kinds of poems, many forms, contending qualities of diction and texture. . . . If the struggle of contending voices and attitudes often ends in poems that don't quite succeed, it remains that the struggle itself is moving for its truthfulness and intensity. . . . Carruth uniformly refuses to glorify his crazies. They are pain and pain alone. What glory there is—and there are sparks of it everywhere through these early poems—he keeps for the regenerative stirrings against the storm of pain and isolation."

In his essay, Miller looked at one major influence on Carruth's poetry. "Carruth's relationship to jazz music has been lifelong," he noted, "and it has expressed itself on many different levels in his work." Carruth produced an essay, "Influences: The Formal Idea of Jazz," in which he described his personal feelings about the musical genre. He did read the prominent poets Ben Johnson, William Yeats, and Ezra Pound, but added that "the real question is not by whom I was influenced, but how." To Miller, Carruth's early grounding in traditional poetic forms prepared him to "improvise" later on, much like the way jazz musicians often study classical music early in their training: "The discipline must precede the rejection of discipline."

In Carruth's poetry, that means using an external, fixed poetic structure upon which to launch improvisation. But even when he works in a spontaneous, "jazz" mode, his "poetic improvisation does not mean the abandonment of form or rhyme," declared Miller, "nor does it limit itself to any particular attitude or emotion. . . . What improvisation ultimately amounts to is structure becoming a function of feeling, whatever that feeling may be." Miller pointed to *Brothers, I Loved You All* as a prime example of Carruth in his spontaneous prime. Noted Alastair Reed in the *Saturday Review:* Carruth's "poems have a sureness to them, a flair and variety. . . . Yet, in their dedication to finding an equilibrium in an alien and often cruel landscape, Vermont, where the poet has dug himself in, they reflect the moods and struggles of a man never at rest. . . . His work teems with the struggle to live and to make sense, and his poems carve out a kind of grace for us."

Like many poets, Carruth often turns to personal experience for inspiration; however, with the possible exception of *The Bloomingdale Papers*—a long poetic sequence the poet wrote in the 1950s while confined to a mental hospital for treatment of alcoholism and a nervous breakdown—he has not indulged in the self-obsessed meditations common among some of his peers. Instead, Carruth turns outward, exploring such "universal opposites" as madness—or so-called madness—and

sanity or chaos and order. He then tries to balance the negative images—war, loneliness, the destruction of the environment, sadness—with mostly nature-related positive images and activities that communicate a sense of stability—the cycle of the seasons, performing manual labor, contemplating the night sky, observing the serenity of plant and animal life. But, as Gardner pointed out, "Carruth is not in the least tempted to sentimentality about country life. . . . [He recognizes] that it can be a life of value and nobility in the midst of difficult facts and chaos." Nor is he "abstractly philosophical or cold," according to the critic. "On the contrary," Gardner stated, "[his poems] are all poems about very daily affairs: things seen and heard, the loneliness of missing friends absent or dead, the alternations of love for and estrangement from those present, the experiences of a man frequently alone with the non-human which all too often bears the damaging marks of careless human intrusion." Furthermore, he said, "Carruth comes to the politics of all this with a vengeance. . . . [His poems] all bear strong public witness against the wastes and shames of our culture that are destroying human value with a will in a world where values are already hard enough to maintain, in a universe where they are always difficult to discover. Carruth does not express much anger in [his] poems. Yet one feels that an enormous energy of rage has forced them to be."

In the 1990s, the appearance of anthologies and collections of Carruth's verse and prose allowed critics to assess his career as a whole. In reviewing *Collected Shorter Poems,* which appeared in 1992, *Poetry* contributor David Barber called attention to the rich diversity of the poet's oeuvre: "Carruth is vast; he contains multitudes. Of the august order of American poets born in the Twenties, he is undoubtedly the most difficult to reconcile to the convenient branches of classification and affiliation, odd man out in any tidy scheme of influence and descent."

Somewhat deceptively titled, Carruth's *Collected Shorter Poems,* which won the 1992 National Book Critics' Circle Award, is not a comprehensive volume but is comprised of selections from thirteen of Carruth's previously published volumes, together with many poems appearing for the first time. Writing in the *Nation,* Ted Solotaroff found the volume to be a welcome opportunity for giving a "full hearing" to "a poet as exacting and undervalued as Carruth generally has been." Solotaroff highlighted two characteristics typifying Carruth's poetic achievement. First, he describes him as a "poet's poet, a virtuoso of form from the sonnet to free verse, from medieval metrics to jazz ones." Secondly, Solotaroff drew attention to the moral seriousness of

Carruth's work as a critic of contemporary poetry, claiming that the poet "has also been, to my mind, the most catholic, reliable and socially relevant critic of poetry we have had in an age of burgeoning tendencies, collapsing standards and a general withdrawal of poets from the public to the private sector of consciousness."

The 1993 volume *Collected Longer Poems* received similar praise from critics, many who felt that this collection contains much of the poet's best work. Anthony Robbins, commenting in *American Book Review,* characterized Carruth's poetry as being "grounded in the traditions of Romance, in *entre-les-guerres* modernism revised in light of mid-[twentieth]-century existentialism, and in his own personal forms of nonviolent anarchism." Both Robbins and *Bloomsbury Review* contributor Shaun T. Griffin called attention to the importance of the volume's opening selection, "The Asylum," which details the poet's experiences of being hospitalized for a breakdown. Griffin judged these "among the most honest and harrowing in the volume," maintaining that "they ring with the compelling voice of despair; the wind floats through them, and the reader finds himself staring at the November landscape, leafless, dark, and dormant."

Winner of both the Pulitzer Prize for poetry and a National Book Award in 1996, Carruth's *Scrambled Eggs and Whiskey* centers on meditations of such themes as politics, history, aging, nostalgia, guilt, and love. Another collection, *Doctor Jazz: Poems, 1996-2000,* written as the poet approached his ninth decade, includes a fifteen-page elegy to the author's daughter, Martha, who died in her forties of cancer. That poem in particular "refuses to release us until its final syllable," wrote *Library Journal* reviewer Fred Muratori. In 1998 Carruth turned to a different form of self-narrative with *Reluctantly: Autobiographical Essays.* These essays—the words of a self-described "old man in his cave of darkness, regretting his arthritis and impotence and failing imagination"—speak frankly of his often troubled life, including treatment for depression, debilitating phobias, and a nearly successful suicide attempt. Peter Szatmary, writing in *Biblio,* found the "fractured" nature of Carruth's life reflected in his prose: "At its best," noted Szatmary, *Reluctantly* "isolates idiosyncratic clarity. At its worst it betrays arbitrary self-indulgence." In a similar vein, "fragmentary" was the word used by Ray Olson of *Booklist* to describe the memoir, though Olsen also characterized the book as a "powerful autobiography." A *Publishers Weekly* critic had a similar impression, saying that *Reluctantly* shows that, "although life is messy and unpredictable, it is possible to survive, to write well and to salvage from the wreckage a redemptive dignity."

Carruth has explained of his work as a writer: "I have a close but at the same time uncomfortable relationship with the natural world. I've always been most at home in the country probably because I was raised in the country as a boy, and I know something about farming and woodcutting and all the other things that country people know about. That kind of work has been important to me in my personal life and in my writing too. I believe in the values of manual labor and labor that is connected with the earth in some way. But I'm not simply a nature poet. In fact, I consider myself and I consider the whole human race fundamentally alien. By evolving into a state of self-consciousness, we have separated ourselves from the other animals and the plants and from the very earth itself, from the whole universe. So there's a kind of fear and terror involved in living close to nature. My poems, I think, exist in a state of tension between the love of natural beauty and the fear of natural meaninglessness or absurdity."

BIOGRAPHICAL AND CRITICAL SOURCES:

BOOKS

Carruth, Hayden, *Reluctantly: Autobiographical Essays,* Copper Canyon Press (Port Townsend, WA), 1998.
Contemporary Literary Criticism, Thomson Gale (Detroit, MI), Volume 4, 1975, Volume 7, 1977, Volume 10, 1979, Volume 18, 1981, Volume 84, 1994.
Dickey, James, *Babel to Byzantium,* Farrar, Straus (New York, NY), 1968.
Dictionary of Literary Biography, Volume 5: *American Poets since World War II,* Thomson Gale (Detroit, MI), 1980.

PERIODICALS

American Book Review, September, 1995, p. 23.
American Poetry Review, May, 1979; January, 1981; July-August, 2004, Christian Thompson, "In Measured Resistance," p. 20.
Antioch Review, fall, 2002, John Taylor, review of *Doctor Jazz: Poems, 1996-2000,* p. 714.
Biblio, April, 1999, Peter Szatmary, review of *Reluctantly: Autobiographical Essays,* p. 60.
Bloomsbury Review, January-February, 1996, p. 18.
Booklist, August, 1998, Ray Olson, review of *Reluctantly,* p. 1953; April 15, 1999, review of *Beside the Shadblow Tree: A Memoir of James Laughlin,* p. 1502; September 1, 2001, Ray Olson, review of *Doctor Jazz,* p. 44.

Chicago Tribune Book World, December 26, 1982.

Georgia Review, spring, 2000, Jeff Gundy, review of *Reluctantly,* p. 142.

Houston Chronicle, June 20, 1999, Robert Phillips, "Poets Carruth, Snodgrass Pen Prose Memoirs," p. 25.

Kirkus Reviews, June 1, 1998, review of *Reluctantly,* p. 788.

Library Journal, September 1, 1990, p. 263; November 1, 1993, p. 95; March 1, 1996, p. 4; July, 1998, David Kirby, review of *Reluctantly,* p. 88; June 15, 1999, review of *Beside the Shadblow Tree,* p. 79; September 1, 2001, Fred Muratori, review of *Doctor Jazz,* p. 184.

Los Angeles Times, December 12, 1986.

Los Angeles Times Book Review, June 3, 1984.

Midwest Quarterly, spring, 1998, Matthew Miller, "A Love Supreme: Jazz and Poetry of Hayden Carruth," p. 294.

Nation, February 15, 1965; October 25, 1971; November 16, 1992, p. 600; December 27, 1993, p. 810.

New York Times, January 3, 1976; October 21, 2001, Ken Tucker, review of *Doctor Jazz.*

New York Times Book Review, May 12, 1963; April 6, 1975; September 2, 1979; May 23, 1982; August 21, 1983; January 22, 1984; July 14, 1985; May 11, 1986; December 27, 1992, p. 2.

Poetry, August, 1963; May, 1974; July, 1993, p. 237; March, 1996, p. 343; March, 2003, Bruce F. Murphy, review of *Doctor Jazz,* p. 329.

Publishers Weekly, January 31, 1994, p. 82; October 9, 1995, p. 80; February 26, 1996, p. 101; June 29, 1998, review of *Reluctantly,* p. 44; April 19, 1999, review of *Beside the Shadblow Tree,* p. 55; August 6, 2001, review of *Doctor Jazz,* p. 87.

Review of Contemporary Fiction, fall, 1999, Amy Havel, review of *Beside the Shadblow Tree,* p. 167.

San Francisco Chronicle, February 13, 2000, Lawrence Ferlinghetti, "Poetry That Is Really Prose in Disguise," p. 2.

Saturday Review, October 27, 1979.

Seneca Review, spring, 1990.

Threepenny Review, spring, 1999, review of *Reluctantly,* p. 8.

Times Literary Supplement, July 23, 1971.

Virginia Quarterly Review, summer, 1963; summer, 1971; summer, 1979.

Washington Post Book World, January 1, 1984; April 13, 1986.

Western American Literature, fall, 1998, review of *Selected Essays and Reviews,* p. 304.

World Literature Today, summer-autumn, 2002, Michael Leddy, review of *Doctor Jazz,* p. 95.

ONLINE

Academy of American Poets Web site, http://www.poets.org/poets/ (January 11, 2002), "Hayden Carruth."

*   *   *

CARTER, Nick
    See SMITH, Martin Cruz

*   *   *

CARVER, Raymond 1938-1988

PERSONAL: Born May 25, 1938, in Clatskanie, OR; died of lung cancer August 2, 1988, in Port Angeles, WA; son of Clevie Raymond (a laborer) and Ella Beatrice (a homemaker; maiden name, Casey) Carver; married Maryann Burk (a teacher), June 7, 1957 (divorced, October, 1983); married Tess Gallagher (a poet), June 17, 1988; children: Christine LaRae, Vance Lindsay. *Education:* Humboldt State College (now California State University, Humboldt), A.B., 1963; University of Iowa, M.F.A., 1966. *Hobbies and other interests:* Travel.

CAREER: Writer. Manual laborer, c. late 1950s-early 1960s; Science Research Associates, Inc., Palo Alto, CA, editor, 1967-70. University of California, Santa Cruz, lecturer in creative writing, 1971-72; University of California, Berkeley, lecturer in fiction writing, 1972-73; Syracuse University, Syracuse, NY, professor of English, 1980-83. Visiting professor of English, Writers Workshop, University of Iowa, 1973-74; member of faculty writing program, Goddard College, 1977-78; visiting distinguished writer, University of Texas at El Paso, 1978-79.

MEMBER: International PEN (member of executive board), American Academy and Institute of Arts and Letters, Authors Guild.

AWARDS, HONORS: National Endowment for the Arts Discovery Award for poetry, 1970; Joseph Henry Jackson Award for fiction, 1971; Wallace Stegner Creative Writing fellowship, Stanford University, 1972-73; National Book Award nomination in fiction, 1977, for *Will You Please Be Quiet, Please?;* Guggenheim fellowship, 1977-78; National Endowment for the Arts Award in fiction, 1979; Carlos Fuentes Fiction Award, for short story "The Bath"; Mildred and Harold Strauss Living Award, American Academy and Institute of Arts and Letters, 1983; O. Henry Award, 1983, for "A Small, Good Thing" and 1988, for "Errand"; National Book Critics Circle Award nomination in fiction, 1984, and Pulitzer Prize nomination for fiction, 1985, both for *Cathedral;* Levinson Prize for poetry, 1985; *Los Angeles Times* book prize, 1986, for *Where Water Comes Together with Other Water;* Creative Arts Award citation, Brandeis University, 1988; National Book Critics Circle Award nomination in fiction, 1988, and Pulitzer Prize nomination for fiction, 1989, both for *Where I'm Calling From: New and Selected Stories;* honorary degree from University of Hartford, 1988.

WRITINGS:

SHORT FICTION

Put Yourself in My Shoes, Capra Press, 1974.
Will You Please Be Quiet, Please?, McGraw (New York, NY), 1976, reprinted, Vintage (New York, NY), 1992.
Furious Seasons, Capra, 1977.
What We Talk about When We Talk about Love, Knopf (New York, NY), 1981.
The Pheasant, Metacom, 1982.
"A Small, Good Thing," Doubleday (New York, NY), 1983.
Cathedral: Stories, Knopf (New York, NY), 1984, reprinted, Wadsworth (Boston, MA), 2003.
If It Please You, Lord John, 1984.
The Stories of Raymond Carver, Picador (London, England), 1985.
Elephant, and Other Stories, Harvill Press (London, England), 1988.
Where I'm Calling From: New and Selected Stories, Atlantic Monthly Press (New York, NY), 1988.
Short Cuts: Selected Stories, Vintage (New York, NY), 1993.

POETRY

Near Klamath, Sacramento State College, 1968.
Winter Insomnia, Kayak, 1970.
At Night the Salmon Move, Capra, 1976.
Two Poems, Scarab Press, 1982.
For Tess, Ewert, 1984.
Where Water Comes Together with Other Water, Random House (New York, NY), 1985.
This Water, Ewert, 1985.

Ultramarine, Random House (New York, NY), 1986.
In a Marine Light: Selected Poems, Harvill (London, England), 1987.
Saints, Random House (New York, NY), 1987.
A New Path to the Waterfall: Poems, introduction by Tess Gallagher, Atlantic Monthly Press (New York, NY), 1989.
All of Us: The Collected Poems, Harvill (London, England), 1998.

OTHER

Fires: Essays, Poems, Stories, 1966-1982, Capra, 1983.
(Author of foreword) John Gardner, *On Becoming a Novelist,* Harper (New York, NY), 1983.
(Editor and author of introduction) William Kittredge, *We Are Not in This Together: Stories,* Greywolf Press (Minneapolis, MN), 1984.
Dostoevsky: The Screenplay, Capra, 1985.
(Editor with Shannon Ravenel) *The Best American Short Stories 1986,* Houghton (Boston, MA), 1986.
My Father's Life, Babcock and Koontz, 1986.
Those Days: Early Writings by Raymond Carver: Eleven Poems and a Story, edited by William L. Stull, Raven Editions, 1987.
(Editor with Tom Jenks) *American Short-Story Masterpieces,* Delacorte (New York, NY), 1987.
Conversations with Raymond Carver, edited by Marshall Bruce Gentry and William L. Stull, University Press of Mississippi, 1990.
Carver Country, Scribner (New York, NY), 1990.
No Heroics, Please: Uncollected Writings, edited by William L. Stull, Random House (New York, NY), 1992.
Call If You Need Me: The Uncollected Fiction and Other Prose, edited by William L. Stull, Vintage (New York, NY), 2001.

Also author, with Michael Cimino, of script "Purple Lake"; author of short story "Errand," 1988. Contributor to anthologies, including *The Best American Short Stories,* 1967, 1982, and 1983, *Short Stories from the Literary Magazines, Best Little Magazine Fiction,* 1970 and 1971, *Prize Stories: The O. Henry Awards,* 1973, 1974, 1975, and 1983, *Pushcart Prize Anthology,* 1976, 1981, 1982, and 1983, *New Voices in American Poetry,* and *The Generation of 2000: Contemporary American Poets.* Contributor of poems and stories to national periodicals, including *Esquire, New Yorker, Atlantic,* and *Harper's,* and to literary journals, including *Antaeus, Georgia Review, Ohio Review, Paris Review,* and *Poetry.* Editor, *Quarry* (magazine), 1971-72; editor, *Ploughshares,* Volume 9, number 4, 1983.

Several of Carver's short stories were adapted for film as *Short Cuts,* directed by Robert Altman.

SIDELIGHTS: Raymond Carver was one of a handful of contemporary American short-story writers credited with reviving what was thought of by the mid-twentieth century as a dying literary form. His stories mainly take place in his native Pacific Northwest region; they are peopled with the type of lower-middle-class characters the author was familiar with while he was growing up. In a *New York Review of Books* article, Thomas R. Edwards described Carver's fictional world as a place where "people worry about whether their old cars will start, where unemployment or personal bankruptcy are present dangers, where a good time consists of smoking pot with the neighbors, with a little cream soda and M & M's on the side. . . . Carver's characters are waitresses, mechanics, postmen, high school teachers, factory workers, door-to-door salesmen. [Their surroundings are] not for them a still unspoiled scenic wonderland, but a place where making a living is as hard, and the texture of life as drab, for those without money, as anywhere else."

Carver's own life paralleled that of one of his characters. Born in an Oregon logging town, the author was married and the father of two before he was twenty years old. Like his characters, Carver also worked at a series of low paying jobs: he "picked tulips, pumped gas, swept hospital corridors, swabbed toilets, [and] managed an apartment complex," according to Bruce Weber in a *New York Times Magazine* profile of the author. Carver's wife at the time, continued Weber, "worked for the phone company, waited tables, [and] sold a series of book digests door-to-door." Not coincidentally, "of all the writers at work today, Carver may have [had] the most distinct vision of the working class," as Ray Anello observed in *Newsweek.* Carver taught creative writing in California and produced two books of poetry before his first book of short stories, *Will You Please Be Quiet, Please?,* was published in 1976.

In introducing readers to the desperation of ordinary people, Carver created tales that are "brief . . . but by no means stark," noted Geoffrey Wolff in his *New York Times Book Review* piece on *Will You Please Be Quiet, Please?* The critic continued: "They imply complexities of action and motive and they are especially artful in their suggestion of repressed violence. No human blood is shed in any of these stories, yet almost all of them hold a promise of mayhem of some final, awful break-ing from confines, and breaking through to liberty." The theme of breaking from confines is central to one of the stories, "Neighbors," in which Bill and Arlene Miller agree to feed their neighbors' cat while the neighbors, the Stones, are on vacation. With access to the Stones' home, the Millers find themselves increasingly taken with their friends' clothes, furniture, and other belongings. Bill and Arlene, in fact, begin to assume the identities of the Stones; "each finds this strangely stimulating, and their sex life prospers, though neither can find anything much to say about it at all," reported Edwards. The end of the story finds the Millers clinging to the Stones' door as their neighbors return, knowing that their rich fantasy life will soon end.

The author's "first book of stories explored a common plight rather than a common subject," noted *New York Times Book Review* critic Michael Wood. "His characters were lost or diminished in their own different ways. The 17 stories in [Carver's third collection, *What We Talk about When We Talk about Love*], make up a more concentrated volume, less a collection than a set of variations on the themes of marriage, infidelity and the disquieting tricks of human affection." "The first few pieces seem thin and perfunctory," Adam Mars-Jones wrote in the *Times Literary Supplement,* "and there is a recurring pattern . . . of endings which lurch suddenly sideways, moving off in a direction that seems almost random." Anatole Broyard found such endings frustrating. In his *New York Times* review of *What We Talk about When We Talk about Love,* Broyard criticized what he calls "the most flagrant and common imposition in current fiction, to end a story with a sententious ambiguity that leaves the reader holding the bag."

"Perhaps there is a reason for this," said Mars-Jones. "Endings and titles are bound to be a problem for a writer like Carver, since readers and reviewers so habitually use them as keys to interpret everything else in a story. So he must make his endings enigmatic and even mildly surrealist, and his titles for the most part oblique. Sometimes he over-compensates." *Newsweek* reviewer Peter S. Prescott felt that all seventeen stories in Carver's third collection "are excellent, and each gives the impression that it could not have been written more forcefully, or in fewer words."

Prescott also noted that the author is concerned "with the collapse of human relationships. Some of his stories take place at the moment things fall apart; others, after the damage has been done, while the shock waves still reverberate. Alcohol and violence are rarely far removed from what happens, but sometimes, in another characteristic maneuver, Carver will nudge the drama that triggers a crisis aside to show that his story has really been about something else all along." "Carver's is not a particularly lyrical prose," said Weber in his *New York Times Magazine* review. He added, "A typical sentence is blunt and uncomplicated, eschewing the ornaments of descriptive adverbs and parenthetical phrases. His rhythms are often repetitive or brusque, as if to suggest the strain of people learning to express newly felt things, fresh emotions. Time passes in agonizingly linear fashion, the chronology of a given scene marked by one fraught and simple gesture after another. Dialogue is usually clipped, and it is studded with commonplace observations of the concrete objects on the table or on the wall rather than the elusive, important issues in the air."

Of Carver's 1984 short-fiction collection, *Cathedral,* "it would be hard to imagine a more dispirited assortment of figures," declared David Lehman in *Newsweek.* In each story a "note of transcendent indifference, beyond resignation or fatigue, is sounded," added Lehman, cautioning, "fun to read they're not." But, the critic stressed, "it's impossible to ignore Carver's immense talent." In *Cathedral* Carver rewrites the ending of one of his most acclaimed stories from *What We Talk about When We Talk about Love.* The original story, "The Bath," is about a mother who orders a special cake for her eight-year-old son's birthday—but the boy is hit by a car on that day and is rushed to the hospital, where he lingers in a coma. The baker, aware only that the parents have not picked up their expensive cake, badgers them with endless calls demanding his money. As the story ends the boy's fate is still unknown, and the desperate parents hear the phone ring again. In *Cathedral* the author retells this story—now titled "A Small, Good Thing"—up to the final phone ring. At this point ambiguity vanishes; Carver reveals that the boy has died, and the call is from the irate baker. But this time the parents confront the baker with the circumstances, and the apologetic man invites them over to his bakery. There he tells the parents his own sad story of loneliness and despair and feeds them fresh coffee and warm rolls, because "eating is a small, good thing in a time like this."

"In revising 'The Bath' into 'A Small, Good Thing,' Carver has indeed gone into [what he describes as] 'the heart of what the story is about,' and in the process has written an entirely new story—has created, if you will, a completely new world," declared Jonathan Yardley in the *Washington Post Book World.* "The first version is beautifully crafted and admirably concise, but lacking in genuine compassion; the mysterious caller is not so

much a human being as a mere voice, malign and characterless. But in the second version that voice becomes a person, one whose own losses are, in different ways, as crippling and heartbreaking as the one suffered by the grieving parents." As Broyard wrote in a *New York Times* review of *Cathedral,* "It is typical of Mr. Carver's stories that comfort against adversity is found in incongruous places, that people find improbable solace. The improbable and the homely are [the author's] territory. He works in the bargain basement of the soul." Yardley maintained that "'The Bath' is a good short story," while "'A Small, Good Thing' comes breathtakingly close to perfection."

Carver's 1988 short-fiction collection *Where I'm Calling From,* released shortly before his death, combines new and previously published stories. The entire volume is colored by Carver's standard themes of alienation, failed relationships, and death, but critics generally considered the newer contributions softer and more rambling than the author's earlier, more intense pieces.

According to *New York Times Book Review* critic Irving Howe, Carver's stories evoke "strong American literary traditions. Formally, they summon remembrances of Hemingway and perhaps Stephen Crane, masters of tightly packed fiction. In subject matter they draw upon the American voice of loneliness and stoicism, the native soul locked in this continent's space. [The author's] characters, like those of many earlier American writers, lack a vocabulary that can release their feelings, so they must express themselves mainly through obscure gesture and berserk display." Paul Gray, writing about *Cathedral* in *Time,* maintained that "Carver's art masquerades as accident, scraps of information that might have been overheard at the supermarket check-out or local beer joint. His most memorable people live on the edge: of poverty, alcoholic self-destruction, loneliness. Something in their lives denies them a sense of community. They feel this lack intensely, yet are too wary of intimacy to touch other people, even with language."

Such appraisals of his writing left Carver a little wary. He once told Weber: "Until I started reading these reviews of my work, praising me, I never felt the people I was writing about were so bad. . . . The waitress, the bus driver, the mechanic, the hotel keeper. God, the country is filled with these people. They're good people. People doing the best they could."

Carver also wrote extensively as a poet. A collection of his poetry, including some works written shortly before his death, was published in *A New Path to the Water-*

fall. Although he had already released a volume of his collected verse, the diagnosis of lung cancer inspired him to write another volume. These poems are characterized by a reliance on sentence-sounds and a structure steeped in storytelling. Edna Longley commented in the *London Review of Books* that "all his writing tends toward dramatic monologue, present-tense soliloquy that wears the past like a hairshirt." He explores tortured marriages and strained familial relationships, all of which lead him bravely into discussing his own terminal illness. Longley praised Carver for his ability to forge solid beginnings and endings: "A Carver poem instantly establishes its presence." Fred Chappell, writing in the *Kenyon Review,* took a much different view of the book. He admitted that he had reservations in reviewing it: "My personal impression has been that Carver desiccated the short story and that his effort to trivialize the form has been as irrelevant as it was unsuccessful. . . . the poems here are pretty bad. In fact, it is difficult to think of these productions as poems; they stand in relation to poetry rather as iron ore does to Giacometti sculpture."

In 1998, all Carver's poems were collected and published as *All of Us: The Collected Poems,* complete with bibliographic notes and indexes. Donna Seaman, writing in *Booklist,* called the collection "direct and lucid." Noting that Carver became especially dedicated to poetry as his death from lung cancer loomed on the horizon, an *Economist* contributor added: "This is confessional poetry at its scrupulous best: neither self-dramatizing nor self-pitying, but penetrating, focused, and unflinching."

In 1992 a collection of Carver's early works was published. *No Heroics, Please: Uncollected Writings* contains poems, essays, book reviews, and other pieces Carver had chosen not to include in any of his other collected works. Several of the short stories included had only been published before in student literary magazines. Of particular interest to Carver scholars is the fact that in these stories Carver uses literary devices such as flashbacks and experimentation with verb tenses—techniques he shunned in his later work. Alan Davis commented in the *Hudson Review* that "the artfulness of Carver, the way he consciously chisels a world out of workaday detail, becomes quickly apparent after perusing his earliest stories."

Several of Carver's previously published short stories received attention when acclaimed film director Robert Altman adapted them as the film *Short Cuts.* Although Altman took some liberties in adapting these stories for the screen, they remained essentially true to Carver's ideas. The filmed stories are also collected into the book *Short Cuts.* In "So Much Water So Close to Home" a wife learns that the source of her marital disharmony is the fact that her husband found a drowned woman while on a fishing trip and took days before reporting his find to the police. "Jerry and Molly and Sam" chronicles the life of a disgruntled husband and father who thinks ditching the family pet will relieve some of his stress.

Carver's widow, Tess Gallagher, discovered three unpublished short stories by her husband in 1999, and two more were later discovered among the author's papers at Ohio State University. These stories were published in 2001 in *Call If You Need Me: The Uncollected Fiction and Other Prose.* Gallagher was reluctant to publish the stories because her husband had not yet finished them enough to consider submitting them for publication. "Ray would sometimes take a story through 30 rewrites," she was quoted as saying by Paul Gray in *Time.* "These stories had been put aside well before that." Nevertheless, the stories reflect Carver's approach to short fiction and, as noted by Daniel Garrett in *World Literature Today,* are still "distinguished." Garrett added, "These are mature stories, the work of a man in command of his talent and in touch with his emotions." As noted by Brad Hooper in *Booklist,* "To a one, they demonstrate the author's characteristic bare-bones style as he placed characters of modest means and resources into the kind of ordinary crises that define ordinary lives." A *Publishers Weekly* contributor commented, "For fans of Carver . . . the five newly discovered stories collected here are like a stash of diamonds stumbled upon in a long-abandoned mine." The collection also includes book reviews of Sherwood Anderson letters, two biographical pieces on Ernest Hemingway, a fragment from a novel, and other assorted essays and reviews. Some reviewers found these additional materials to be merely "padding," according to Troy Patterson in *Entertainment Weekly.* Others looked on the writings more favorably, including the *Publishers Weekly* contributor, who noted that Carver's fans "won't be disappointed by the remainder of the book."

"I never figured I'd make a living writing short stories," Carver told Penelope Moffet in a *Publishers Weekly* interview only a few months before his death in 1988. "How far in this world are you going to get writing short stories? I never had stars in my eyes. I never had the big-score mentality." Astonished by his literary prominence, Carver told Moffet that fame "never ceases to amaze me. And that's not false modesty, either. I'm pleased and happy with the way things have turned out. But I was surprised."

BIOGRAPHICAL AND CRITICAL SOURCES:

BOOKS

Carver, Raymond, *Cathedral,* Knopf (New York, NY), 1984.

Contemporary Literary Criticism, Thomson Gale (Detroit, MI), Volume 22, 1982, Volume 26, 1983, Volume 53, 1989, Volume 55, 1989.

Dictionary of Literary Biography, Volume 130: *American Short-Story Writers since World War II,* Thomson Gale (Detroit, MI), 1993.

Dictionary of Literary Biography Yearbook, Thomson Gale (Detroit, MI), *1984,* 1985, *1988,* 1989.

Gentry, Marshall Bruce, and Stull, William L., editors, *Conversations with Raymond Carver,* University Press of Mississippi, 1990.

Halpert, Sam, *Raymond Carver: An Oral Biography,* University of Iowa Press (Iowa City, IA), 1995.

Lohafer, Susan, *Coming to Terms with the Short Story,* Louisiana State University Press (Baton Rouge, LA), 1983.

Meyer, Adam, *Raymond Carver,* Twayne (New York, NY), 1994.

Nesset, Kirk, *The Stories of Raymond Carver: A Critical Study,* Ohio University Press (Athens, OH), 1995.

Short Story Criticism, Thomson Gale (Detroit, MI), Volume 8, 1991.

Weaver, Gordon, editor, *The American Short Story, 1945-1980,* Twayne (New York, NY), 1983.

PERIODICALS

Akros Review, spring, 1984.
Antioch Review, spring, 1984.
Atlantic, June, 1981.
Booklist, June 1, 1994, p. 1775; September 1, 1998, Donna Seaman, review of *All of Us: The Collected Poems;* November 1, 2000, Brad Hooper, review of *Call if You Need Me: The Uncollected and Other Prose,* p. 518.
Books, March, 1994, p. 13.
Boston Globe, July 17, 1983.
Canto, Volume 2, number 2, 1978.
Chariton Review, spring, 1984.
Chicago Tribune, October 28, 1986.
Chicago Tribune Book World, October 2, 1983.
Commonweal, December 1, 1989.
Contemporary Literature, winter, 1982.
Detroit News, October 2, 1983.

Economist, January 4, 1992; August 15, 1998, review of *All of Us: The Collected Poems,* p. 72.
Entertainment Weekly, January 19, 2001, Troy Patterson, review of *Call if You Need Me,* p. 78.
Eureka Times-Standard (Eureka, CA), June 24, 1977.
Georgia Review, fall, 1982; winter, 1993, pp. 820-821.
Globe and Mail (Toronto, Ontario, Canada), November 24, 1984; July 2, 1988.
Hollins Critic, December, 1987.
Hudson Review, summer, 1976; autumn, 1981; spring, 1984; winter, 1993, pp. 653-658.
Iowa Review, summer, 1979.
Kenyon Review, summer, 1990, pp. 168-179.
Library Journal, September 15, 1998, Graham Christian, review of *All of Us: The Collected Poems,* p. 83; December, 2000, Marc Kloszewski, review of *Call if You Need Me,* p. 194.
London Review of Books, February 2-15, 1984; March 22, 1990, pp. 22-23; March 10, 1994, p. 19.
Los Angeles Times, May 25, 1988.
Los Angeles Times Book Review, May 24, 1981; October 2, 1983; July 28, 1985; October 26, 1986; December 28, 1986; January 31, 1988; June 26, 1988; July 19, 1992, p. 1.
Nation, July, 1981.
New Republic, April 25, 1981; November 14, 1983.
New Statesman & Society, August 19, 1988; February 16, 1990; December 6, 1991.
Newsweek, April 27, 1981; September 5, 1983.
New York, April 20, 1981.
New York Review of Books, November 24, 1983; November 18, 1993, p. 66.
New York Times, April 15, 1981; September 5, 1983; May 11, 1988; May 31, 1988.
New York Times Book Review, March 7, 1976; April 26, 1981; February 9, 1986; June 7, 1987; May 15, 1988; July 19, 1992; January 21, 2001, Claire Dederer, review of *Call if You Need Me,* p. 8.
New York Times Magazine, June 24, 1984.
Paris Review, summer, 1983.
People, November 23, 1987.
Philological Quarterly, winter, 1985.
Poetry, July, 1999, David Orr, review of *All of Us,* p. 231.
Publishers Weekly, May 27, 1988; April 20, 1990, p. 70; August 16, 1993, p. 100; October 30, 2000, review of *Call if You Need Me,* p. 43.
Saturday Review, April, 1981; October, 1983.
Studies in Short Fiction, winter, 1984; summer, 1985; summer, 1986.
Time, April 6, 1981; September 19, 1983; January 15, 2001, Paul Gray, review of *Call if You Need Me,* p. 131.

Times (London, England), January 21, 1982; April 17, 1985; May 16, 1985.

Times Literary Supplement, January 22, 1982; February 17, 1984; May 24, 1985; September 15, 1989; February 28, 1992, p. 16; January 24, 1997.

Tribune Books (Chicago, IL), November 9, 1986; May 8, 1988; September 4, 1994, p. 12.

Village Voice, September 18, 1978.

Washington Post, August 4, 1988.

Washington Post Book World, May 3, 1981; September 4, 1983; May 15, 1988; July 9, 1989; January 27, 1991, p. 15.

World Literature Today, spring, 1999, Lee Oser, review of *All of Us,* p. 333; summer-autumn, 2001, Daniel Garrett, review of *Call if You Need Me,* p. 143.

OBITUARIES:

PERIODICALS

Chicago Tribune, August 3, 1988; August 7, 1988.

Los Angeles Times, August 4, 1988.

New York Times, August 3, 1988.

Times (London, England), August 4, 1988.

Washington Post, August 4, 1988.

*   *   *

CAVALLO, Evelyn
   See SPARK, Muriel

*   *   *

CELA, Camilo José 1916-2002
(Camilo José Cela y Trulock, Matilde Verdu)

PERSONAL: Surname pronounced *Say*-lah; born May 11, 1916, in Iria Flavia, La Coruna, Spain; died of heart disease, January 17, 2002, in Madrid, Spain; son of Camilo (a customs official and part-time writer) and Camila Emmanuela (Trulock Bertorini) Cela; married Maria del Rosario Conde Picavea, March 12, 1944 (divorced, 1989); married Marina Castano, 1991; children: (first marriage) Camilo José. *Education:* Attended University of Madrid, 1933-36 and 1939-43. *Hobbies and other interests:* Collecting wine bottles, stamps, and literary myths.

CAREER: Writer. Publisher of *Papeles de Son Armadans* (literary monthly), 1956-79; appointed to Spanish Senate by King Juan Carlos, 1977. Lecturer in En-

gland, France, Latin America, Belgium, Sweden, Italy, and the United States. *Military service:* Served in Spanish Nationalist Army during Spanish Civil War, 1936-39; became corporal.

MEMBER: Academie du Monde Latin, Real Academia Espanola, Premio Nacional de Literatura, Premio Principe de Asturias, Real Academia Gallega, Royal Academy of Literature (Barcelona, Spain), Royal Galician Language Academy, Hispanic Society of America, American Association of Teachers of Spanish and Portuguese (honorary fellow, beginning 1966), Institute for Cultural Relations between Israel, Latin America, Spain, and Portugal, Society of Spanish and Spanish-American Studies.

AWARDS, HONORS: Premio de la critica, 1955, for *Historias de Venezuela: La Catira;* Spanish National Prize for Literature, 1984, for *Mazurca para dos muertos;* Premio Principe de Asturias, 1987; Nobel Prize for literature, 1989; Cervantes Prize, 1994. Has received honorary doctorates from Syracuse University, 1964, University of Birmingham, 1976, University of Santiago de Compostela, 1979, University of Palma de Mallorca, 1979, John F. Kennedy University (Buenos Aires, Argentina), and Interamericana University (Puerto Rico).

WRITINGS:

IN ENGLISH TRANSLATION

La familia de Pascual Duarte (novel), Aldecoa (Madrid, Spain), 1942, translation by John Marks published as *Pascual Duarte's Family,* Eyre & Spottiswoode, 1946, translation by Anthony Kerrigan published as *The Family of Pascual Duarte,* Little, Brown, 1964, reprinted, Dalkey Archive Press (Normal, IL), 2004, Spanish/English version by Herma Briffault published as *Pascual Duarte and His Family,* Las Americas Publishing, 1965.

Pabellon de reposo (novel; first published serially in *El Espanol,* March 13 to August 21, 1943), illustrations by Suarez de Arbol, Afrodisio Aguado (Madrid, Spain), 1943, Spanish/English version by Herma Briffault published as *Rest Home,* Las Americas Publishing, 1961.

Las botas de siete leguas: Viaje a la Alcarria, con los versos de su cancionero, cada uno en su debido lugar (travel), Revista de Occidente, 1948, published as *Viaje a la Alcarria,* Papeles de Son Armadans, 1958, translation by Frances M. Lopez-Morillos published as *Journey to the Alcarria*, University of Wisconsin Press, 1964.

Caminos inciertos: la colmena (novel), Emece (Buenos Aires, Argentina), 1951, published as *La colmena*, Noguer (Barcelona, Spain), 1955, translation by J.M. Cohen and Arturo Barea published as *The Hive*, Farrar, Straus, 1953, reprinted, Dalkey Archive Press (Normal, IL), 2001.

Mrs. Caldwell habla con su hijo (novel), Destino (Barcelona, Spain), 1953, translation by Jerome S. Bernstein published as *Mrs. Caldwell Speaks to Her Son*, Cornell University Press, 1968.

Visperas, festividad y octava de San Camilo del ano 1936 en Madrid, Alfaguara (Madrid, Spain), 1969, translation by J.H.R. Polt published as *San Camilo, 1936: The Eve, Feast, and Octave of St. Camillus of the Year 1936 in Madrid*, Duke University Press, 1991.

Mazurca para dos muertos, Ediciones del Norte (Hanover, NH), 1983, translation by Patricia Haugaard published as *Mazurka for Two Dead Men*, New Directions (New York, NY), 1992.

Madera de Boj (novel) Espasa (Madrid, Spain), 1999, translation by Patricia Haugaard published as *Boxwood*, New Directions (New York, NY), 2002.

Also author of *Avila* (travel), 1952, revised edition, 1968, translation by John Forrester published under same title, 1956.

NOVELS

Nuevas andanzas y desventuras de Lazarillo de Tormes, y siete apuntes carpetovetonicos (title means "New Wanderings and Misfortunes of Lazarillo de Tormes"; first published serially in *Juventud*, July 4 to October 18, 1944), La Nave (Madrid, Spain), 1944.

Santa Balbina 37: Gas en cada piso (novella; title means "Santa Balbina 37, Gas in Every Flat"), Mirto y Laurel (Melilla, Morocco), 1952, 2nd edition, 1977.

Timoteo, el incomprendido (novella; title means "Misunderstood Timothy"), Rollan (Madrid, Spain), 1952.

Cafe de artistas (novella), Tecnos (Madrid, Spain), 1953.

Historias de Venezuela: La catira (title means "Stories of Venezuela: The Blonde"), illustrations by Ricardo Arenys, Noguer (Barcelona, Spain), 1955, published as *La catira*, 1966.

Tobogan de hambrientos (title means "Toboggan of Hungry People"), illustrations by Lorenzo Goni, Noguer (Barcelona, Spain), 1962.

Oficio de tinieblas 5; o, Novela de tesis escrita para ser cantada por un coro de enfermos (title means "Ministry of Darkness 5; or, Novel with a Thesis Written to Be Sung by a Chorus of Sick People"), Noguer (Barcelona, Spain), 1973.

Cristo versus Arizona (title means "Christ versus Arizona"), Seix Barral (Barcelona, Spain), 1988.

Also author of *Los cipreses creen en Dios* (title means "The Cypresses Believe in God").

STORIES

Esas nubes que pasan (title means "The Passing Clouds"), Afrodisio Aguado, 1945.

El bonito crimen del carabinero, y otras invenciones (stories; title means "The Neat Crime of the Carabiniere and Other Tales"; portions originally published in *Arriba*, April 25, 1946; also see below), José Janes (Barcelona, Spain), 1947, published as *El bonito crimen del carabinero*, Picazo (Barcelona, Spain), 1972.

Baraja de invenciones (title means "Pack of Tales"), Castalia (Valencia, Spain), 1953.

Historias de Espana: Los ciegos, los tontos, illustrations by Manuel Mampaso, Arion (Madrid, Spain), 1958, new enlarged edition published in four volumes as *A la pata de palo* (title means "The Man with the Wooden Leg"), illustrations by Lorenzo Goni, Alfaguara (Madrid, Spain), Volume 1: *Historias de Espana* (title means "Stories of Spain"), 1965, Volume 2: *La familia del Heroe; o, Discurso historico de los ultimos restos; ejercicios para una sola mano*, 1965, Volume 3: *El ciudadano Iscariote Reclus* (title means "Citizen Iscariote Reclus"), 1965, Volume 4: *Viaje a U.S.A.* (title means "Trip to the U.S.A."), 1967, published in one volume as *El tacata oxidado: florilegio de carpetovetonismos y otras lindezas*, Noguer (Barcelona, Spain), 1973.

Los viejos amigos, two volumes, illustrations by Jose Maria Prim, Noguer (Barcelona, Spain), 1960–61, 3rd edition, 1981.

Gavilla de fabulas sin amor (title means "A Bundle of Loveless Fables"), illustrations by Pablo Picasso, Papeles de Son Armadans (Palma de Mallorca, Spain), 1962.

Once cuentos de futbol, illustrations by Pepe, Nacional (Madrid, Spain), 1963.

Toreo de salon: Farsa con acompanamiento de clamor y murga, photographs by Oriol Maspons and Julio Ubina, Editorial Lumen (Barcelona, Spain), 1963.

Izas, rabizas y colipoterras: Drama con acompan-amiento de cachondeo y dolor de corazon, photographs by Juan Colom, Editorial Lumen (Barcelona, Spain), 1964.

Nuevas escenas matritenses (title means "New Scenes of Madrid"), seven volumes, photographs by Enrique Palazuela, Alfaguara (Madrid, Spain), 1965–66, published in one volume as *Fotografias al minuto,* Organizacion Sala (Madrid, Spain), 1972.

La bandada de palomas (for children), illustrations by Jose Correas Flores, Labor, 1969.

Cuentos para leer despues del bano, La Gaya Ciencia (Barcelona, Spain), 1974.

Rol de cornudos, Noguer (Barcelona, Spain), 1976.

El espejo y otros cuentos, Espasa-Calpe, 1981.

TRAVEL

Del Mino at Bidasoa: Notas de un vagabundaje (title means "From the Mino to the Bidasoa: Notes of a Vagabondage"), Noguer (Barcelona, Spain), 1952.

Vagabundo por Castilla (title means "Vagabond in Castile"), Seix Barral (Barcelona, Spain), 1955.

Judios, moros y cristianos: Notas de un vagabundaje por Avila, Segovia y sus tierras (title means "Jews, Moors, and Christians: Notes of a Vagabondage through Avila, Segovia, and Their Surroundings"), Destino (Barcelona, Spain), 1956.

Primer viaje andaluz: Notas de un vagabundaje por Jaen, Cordoba, Sevilla, Huelva y sus tierras (title means "First Andalusian Trip: Notes on a Vagabondage through Jaen, Cordoba, Seville, Huelva, and Their Surroundings"), illustrations by Jose Hurtuna, Noguer (Barcelona, Spain), 1959.

Cuaderno del Guadarrama (title means "Guadarrama Notebook"), illustrations by Eduardo Vicente, Arion (Madrid, Spain), 1959.

Paginas de geografia errabunda (title means "Pages of Wandering Geography"), Alfaguara (Madrid, Spain), 1965.

Viaje al Pirineo de Lerida: Notas de un paseo a pie por el Pallars Sobira, el Valle de Aran y el Condado de Ribagorza, Alfaguara (Madrid, Spain), 1965.

Madrid, illustrations by Juan Esplandiu, Alfaguara (Madrid, Spain), 1966.

Calidoscopio callejero, maritimo y campestre de C.J.C. para el reino y ultramar, Alfaguara (Madrid, Spain), 1966.

La Mancha en el corazon y en los ojos, EDISVEN (Barcelona, Spain), 1971.

Balada del vagabundo sin suerte y otros papeles volanderos, Espasa-Calpe, 1973.

Madrid, color y siluta, illustrations by Estrada Vilarrasa, AUSA (Sabadell, Spain), 1985.

Nuevo viaje a la Alcarria, three volumes, Informacion y Revistas (Madrid, Spain), 1986.

Also author of *Barcelona,* 1970.

OMNIBUS VOLUMES

El molino de viento, y otras novelas cortas (title means "The Windmill and Other Short Novels"; contains "El molino de viento," "Timoteo, el incomprendido," "Cafe de artistas," and *Santa Balbina 37: Gas en cada piso*), illustrations by Lorenzo Goni, Noguer (Barcelona, Spain), 1956.

Mis paginas preferidas (selections), Gredos (Madrid, Spain), 1956.

Nuevo retablo de don Cristobita: Invenciones, figuraciones y alucinaciones (stories; contains "Esas nubes que pasan," "El bonito crimen del carabinero," and part of *Baraja de invenciones*), Destino (Barcelona, Spain), 1957.

Obra completa (title means "Complete Works"), fourteen volumes, Destino (Barcelona, Spain), 1962–83.

Las companias convenientes y otros figimientos y cegueras (stories; title means "Suitable Companions and Other Deceits and Obfuscations"), Destino (Barcelona, Spain), 1963.

Cafe de artistas y otros cuentos, Salvat/Alianza, 1969.

Timoteo el incomprendido y otros papeles ibericos, Magisterio Espanol, 1970.

Obras selectas (includes "La familia de Pascual Duarte," "Viaje a la Alcarria," "La colmena," "Mrs. Caldwell habla con su hijo," "Iazas," "Rabizas y colipoterras," and "El carro de heno; o, El inventor de la guillotina"), Alfaguara (Madrid, Spain), 1971.

Prosa, edited by Jacinto-Luis Guerena with notes and commentaries, Narcea (Madrid, Spain), 1974.

Cafe de artistas y otros papeles volanderos, Alce (Madrid, Spain), 1978.

Galicia, illustrated by Zaxiero and photographs by Vitor Vaqueiro, Vigo (Spain), 1990.

Also author of *Antologia,* 1968.

OTHER

Mesa revuelta (essays) Ediciones de los Estudiantes Espanoles, 1945, expanded edition (includes text of *Ensuenos y figuraciones*), Taurus (Madrid, Spain), 1957.

Pisando la dudosa luz del dia: Poemas de una adoles-cencia cruel (poems; title means "Treading the Un-certain Light of Day"), Zodiaco (Barcelona, Spain), 1945, corrected and expanded edition, Papales de Son Armadans (Palma de Mallorca, Spain), 1963.

(Under pseudonym Matilde Verdu) *San Juan de la Cruz,* [Madrid, Spain], 1948.

El gallego y su cuadrilla y otros apuntes carpetovetoni-cos (title means "The Galician and His Troupe and Other Carpeto-Vettonian Notes"), Ricardo Aguilera (Madrid, Spain), 1949, 3rd edition corrected and enlarged, Destino (Barcelona, Spain), 1967.

Ensuenos y figuraciones, Ediciones G. P., 1954.

La rueda de los ocios (title means "The Wheel of Idle Moments"), Mateu (Barcelona, Spain), 1957.

La obra literaria del pintor Solana: Discurso leido ante la Real Academia Espanola el dia 26 de mayo de 1957 en su recepcion publica por el Excmo. Sr. D. Camilo José Cela y contestacion del Excmo. Sr. D. Gregorio Maranon, Papeles de Son Armadans (Madrid, Spain), 1957.

Cajon de sastre (articles) Cid (Madrid, Spain), 1957.

Recuerdo de don Pio Baroja (title means "Remem-brance of Pio Baroja"), illustrations by Eduardo Vi-cente, De Andrea (Mexico City, Mexico), 1958.

La cucana: memorias (memoirs), Destino (Barcelona, Spain), 1959, portion printed as *La rosa,* Destino (Barcelona, Spain), 1979, reprinted, Espasa (Madrid, Spain), 2001.

(Editor) *Homenaje y recuerdo a Gregorio Maranon (1887-1960),* Papeles de Son Armadans, 1961.

Cuatro figuras del 98: Unamuno, Valle Inclan, Baroja, Azorin, y otros retratos ensayos espanoles, Aedos (Barcelona, Spain), 1961.

El solitario: Los suenos de Quesada (title means "The Solitary One"), illustrations by Rafael Zabaleta, Pa-peles de Son Armadans, 1963.

Garito de hospicianos; o, Guirigay de imposturas y bambollas (articles; title means "Poorhouse In-mates; or, Jargon of Frauds and Sham"), Noguer (Barcelona, Spain), 1963.

(Author of prologue) Tono y Rafael Florez, *Memorias de mi: novela,* Biblioteca ca Nueva (Madrid, Spain), 1966.

(With Cesareo Rodriguez Aguilera) *Xam* (illustrated art commentary), Daedalus (Palma de Mallorca, Spain), 1966.

Maria Sabina (dramatic poem), Papeles de Son Ar-madans, 1967, 2nd edition bound with *El carro de heno; o, El inventor de la guillotina* (play), Alf-aguara (Madrid, Spain), 1970.

Diccionario secreto (title means "Secret Dictionary"), Alfaguara (Madrid, Spain), Volume 1, 1968, Vol-ume 2, 1972.

Poesia y cancioneros, [Madrid, Spain] 1968.

Homenaje al Bosco, I: El carro de heno; o, El inventor de la guillotina, Papeles de Son Armadans, 1969.

Al servicio de algo, Alfaguara (Madrid, Spain), 1969.

La bola del mundo: Escenas cotidianas, Organizacion Sala (Madrid, Spain), 1972.

A vueltas con Espana, Seminarios y Ediciones (Madrid, Spain), 1973.

Cristina Mallo (monograph), Theo (Madrid, Spain), 1973.

Diccionari manual castella-catala, catala-castella, Bib-liograf (Barcelona, Spain), 1974.

Enciclopedia de erotismo (title means "Encyclopedia of Eroticism"), D.L. Sedmay (Madrid, Spain), 1977.

(Adaptor) Fernando de Rojas, *La Celestina puesta res-petuosamente en castellano moderno por Camilo José Cela quien anadio muy poco y quito aun menos* (title means "La Celestina Put Respectfully into Modern Castilian by Camilo José Cela Who Added a Little and Took Out Even Less"), Destino (Barcelona, Spain), 1979.

Los suenos vanos, los angeles curiosos, Argos Vergara (Barcelona, Spain), 1979.

Los vasos comunicantes, Bruguera (Barcelona, Spain), 1981.

Vuelta de hoja, Destino (Barcelona, Spain), 1981.

Album de taller (art commentary), Ambit (Barcelona, Spain), 1981.

(Editor and author of prologue) Miguel de Cervantes Saavedra, *El Quijote,* Ediciones Rembrandt (Ali-cante, Spain), 1981.

El juego de los tres madronos, Destino (Barcelona, Spain), 1983.

El asno de Buridan (articles), El Pais (Madrid, Spain), 1986.

Memorias, entendimientos y voluntades (memoirs), Plaza & Janes (Barcelona, Spain), 1993.

Also author of *San Camilo, 1936,* and, with Alfonso Canales, *Cronica del cipote de Archidona* (first pub-lished as *La insolita y gloriosa hazana del cipote de Archidona*), 1977. Author of poems Himno a la muerte (title means "Hymn to Death"), 1938, and Dos romances de ciego, 1966.

ADAPTATIONS: The Hive was filmed by director Mario Camus; *The Family of Pascual Duarte* was filmed by director Ricardo Franco.

SIDELIGHTS: While not widely known in the United States, 1989 Nobel laureate Camilo José Cela played a pivotal role in twentieth-century Spanish literature. Upon awarding the prize to Cela, the Swedish Academy praised the author "for a rich and intensive prose, which with restrained compassion forms a challenging vision of man's vulnerability," related Sheila Rule for the *New York Times*. In the same article, Rule reported Julio Ortego's statement that "Cela represents the searching for a better literature from the Franco years, through the democratic experiments and into European Spain. At the same time, he remained very Spanish, keeping the cultural traditions of Spanish art and literature in his writing. He did not follow a European literature, but developed his own style, and so, in his way, symbolized Spain's going through a long period of adjustment." Throughout the Franco regime, Cela suffered from heavy governmental censorship. Many of his books were banned outright or removed from the shelves: the second edition of *Pascual Duarte* was seized; the censor found it "nauseating," and *The Hive* was initially published in South America. D.W. McPheeters maintained in *Camilo José Cela* that, in spite of such opposition, Cela "has always had the courage to express himself frankly, even forthrightly, . . . which has led to problems with an overly squeamish censorship."

Cela's stylistic development moved from the more traditional *Pascual Duarte* to the innovative fiction of his later novels. McPheeters saw Cela as "dedicated to a constant trying of various forms . . . of fiction in a search for the one that best suits him and . . . what he has to say concerning the human situation. He [is] an outspoken critic of traditional forms of the novel and the restrictions which [some] would impose upon the creative artist." Cela's first novel, *The Family of Pascual Duarte,* has been called the most widely read Spanish novel since *Don Quixote*. It was published in the early 1940s, a time when "the Spanish novel . . . had virtually ceased to exist as a worthy genre," attests McPheeters. "Almost single-handedly, Cela [gave the genre] new life and international significance." Many critics noted that Cela's national prominence and international fame is a result of the popularity of *The Family of Pascual Duarte* and a later novel, *The Hive*. McPheeters stated that while *Pascual Duarte,* Cela's first novel, "secured a wide foreign acceptance," *The Hive* "assured his place as one of Europe's outstanding novelists."

Pascual Duarte relates the life of a convicted murderer awaiting execution. It is introduced as a prison letter to an old family friend, but the reader soon becomes immersed in a first-person narrative. Pascual responds to a life of poverty and frustration through killing: his dog, his horse, his wife's lover, and finally, his mother, all fall victim to his rage. "A deceptive objectivity masks

the presentation of cruel and monstrous scenes, including murder and matricide," *Michigan Quarterly Review* contributor Francis Donahue described. "In a taut style, with emotion carefully reined, Cela evokes an atmosphere of extreme brutality, one which a nation suffering from the after-effects of a brutal civil war could readily understand and believe." But some reviewers found such intense scenes hinder any identification with the main character. "Pascual Duarte speaks of suffering and ferocity so appalling as to be almost beyond the reach of our sympathy. They stun even more than they horrify," noted *Saturday Review* contributor Emile Capouya.

Some critics, as J.S. Bernstein stated in his introduction to *Mrs. Caldwell Speaks to Her Son,* credit Cela with the invention of "tremendismo," a type of fiction that dwells on the darker side of life—the distasteful, the grotesque, and the vulgar. Although in his prologue to the Spanish version of *Mrs. Caldwell Speaks to Her Son,* Cela denies this paternity, *tremendista* elements are abundant in *Pascual Duarte*. As an example of *tremendismo,* McPheeters translated a portion of the struggle in which Pascual kills his mother: "I was able to bury the blade in her throat. . . . Blood squirted out in a torrent and struck me in the face. It was warm like a belly and tasted the same as the blood of a lamb." Other gruesome incidents fill the pages of the novel; in one scene Pascual's retarded brother's ears are eaten off by a pig. This type of detail—meant to shock the placid reader—is present in a lesser degree or nonexistent in some of Cela's novels, but even so, a *Times Literary Supplement* critic called Cela's works "perversely restricted to a pathology of human decay and loneliness." His *Mazurca para dos muertos,* for example, concludes with a six-page postmortem examination of a cadaver. Even Cela's nonfiction works such as *Enciclopedia de eroticismo* (the title means "Encyclopedia of Eroticism") and *Diccionario secreto,* which contains definitions of vulgar words, are written in defiance of Spain's traditionalist moral code.

The Hive led critics to compare Cela with John Dos Passos, particularly to Dos Passos's novel *Manhattan Transfer,* which characterizes frenetic Manhattan life. Comparisons between the two novels are based on the large number of characters introduced in both works and by the novelists' similarly cinematographic styles. In both novels, the shifting time sequence is similar to the filmmaker's flashback. But while David W. Foster conceded in *Forms in the Work of Camilo José Cela* that an analogy can be made between the two techniques, he noted: "Cela's perspective goes much beyond that of the camera in what it is able to record. It is, in effect, all inclusive, omniscient, and omnipresent."

The Hive is frequently seen as Cela's greatest work. In *Books Abroad,* Jacob Ornstein and James Y. Causey noted that "Spanish criticism has been almost unanimous in acclaiming this novel as Cela's masterpiece, both for its vigorous simplicity and for the author's artistry in evoking the atmosphere of Madrid during the final days of World War II and the years immediately following." *The Hive*'s publication was typical of Cela's struggle with the censors, as it was banned in Spain and printed in Buenos Aires in 1952; William D. Montalbano reported in the *Los Angeles Times* that Cela presents "a bitter chronicle of a bitter time." *Nation* contributor Maxwell Geismar found *The Hive* "suffused with anger and bitterness at society in Madrid."

Mrs. Caldwell contains excerpts from the letters of a mentally disturbed woman to her dead son. McPheeters found that *Mrs. Caldwell* "is about as much an anti-novel as has yet been conceived in Spain." The theme is incest, one ideally suited to Cela's fiction because of its shock value. The form is equally unexpected: although only slightly longer than two hundred pages, it contains two hundred and twelve chapters. There is no connection between the chapters (except for chapters fourteen and sixty) and no reason for ending the novel other than the illegibility of the last of the "Letters from the Royal Hospital for the Insane."

The form and content of *Tobogan de hambrientos, San Camilo, 1936,* and *Oficio de tinieblas 5* are also out of the ordinary. *Oficio de tinieblas,* for example, has no capital letters, while *San Camilo, 1936* has no paragraphs. *Tobogan de hambrientos,* Foster noted in *Forms in the Work of Camilo José Cela,* "employs many of the devices of the new novel, especially in its use of pattern and in the rejection of chronology, definable plot, and unified points of view." The book is divided into two hundred units. These two hundred are in turn divided in half and labeled in ascending, then, at the halfway point, in descending numerical order. Each narrative unit presents a new individual or group of individuals and the characters from the first half of the book reappear in the corresponding chapters of the second half.

Except for the epilogue, *San Camilo, 1936* is a young student's continuous stream of consciousness. Again, in content and form the book is far removed from the traditional novel. The book's opening chapter, for instance, includes a list of Madrid's brothels, complete with addresses and names of proprietresses. A *Times Literary Supplement* reviewer remarked on the novel's unusual style: "[Cela] reinforces his . . . contempt for petit-bourgeois credulity by quoting an enormous variety of patent medicine advertisements, [and] making astonishingly free with his sexual and other carnal references, indeed, the language of [the book] is scabrous." While noting Cela's emphasis on "the erotic, obscene and scatological" in *San Camilo, 1936, Hispania* contributor Robert Louis Sheehan also observed the "stylistic innovations" present in the novel, including "the rhythmic reiteration of names, clauses, [and] phrases," the "use of one-paragraph chapters, run-on sentences, and frequent use of commas in place of periods."

The name of Camilo José Cela is associated with the rebirth of the Spanish novel and with experimentation in its form and content. *Pascual Duarte* is credited with starting a new school of Spanish literature, while *The Hive* brought a new cinematographic technique to literature, which Margaret E.W. Jones in *The Contemporary Spanish Novel, 1939-1975* believed "suggested new possibilities in [the] elasticity of novelistic form." Jones also confirmed the author's sense of exploration, and claimed that "Cela has consistently been at the forefront of new movements in the contemporary novel since the 1940s." And Cela himself summed up his feelings on his favorite genre in the dedication to *Journey to the Alcarria*—which Jones quoted—"Anything goes in the novel, as long as it's told with common sense."

In 1999 at the age of eighty-four, Cela saw his last novel reach Spain's bestseller list. Titled *Madera de Boj* and published as *Boxwood* in English in 2002, the novel, as described by Mark Tursi in the *Review of Contemporary Fiction,* "is a complex adventure that weaves and branches through varying narratives, including traditional wisdom, folklore, history, superstition, seafarers' stories, and autobiography." Set in Cela's native Galicia, the book is about the notorious Coast of Death (Costa de la Muerte) and the many seafarers who have lost their lives there. According to Benjamin Jones, writing in *Europe,* Cela told a reporter, "There is no real plot. It is supposed to be a reflection of life, and life does not have a plot." Tursi praised the book's test as "treasure trove of possibilities and potential discoveries." He also noted, "*Boxwood* represents Cela's fullest realization of *tremendismo,* which combines aspects of existential philosophy and 'brutal realism' with a surreal atmosphere."

In 2002 Cela's biographer, Tomas Garcia Yebra, accused the late author of using ghostwriters extensively throughout his career. Most notably, Yebra named Marcial Suarez and Mariano Tudela as the ghostwriters who provided the plots and characters for two of Cela's prize-winning novels, *The Cross of Saint Andrew* and *Mazurka for Two Dead Men.*

BIOGRAPHICAL AND CRITICAL SOURCES:

BOOKS

Cela, Camilo José, *La familia de Pascual Duarte,* Alde-coa (Madrid, Spain), 1942, translation by John Marks published as *Pascual Duarte's Family,* Eyre & Spottiswoode, 1946, translation by Anthony Kerrigan published as *The Family of Pascual Duarte,* Little, Brown, 1964, reprinted, Dalkey Archive Press (Normal, IL), 2004

Cela, Camilo José, *Mrs. Caldwell habla con su hijo,* Destino (Barcelona, Spain), 1953, translation by Jerome S. Bernstein published as *Mrs. Caldwell Speaks to Her Son,* Cornell University Press, 1968.

Chandler, Richard E., and Kessel Schwartz, *A New History of Spanish Literature,* Louisiana State University Press (Baton Rouge, LA), 1961.

Charlebois, Lucile C., *Understanding Camilo José Cela,* University of South Carolina Press (Columbia, SC), 1997.

Contemporary Authors Autobiography Series, Volume 10, Thomson Gale (Detroit, MI), 1989.

Contemporary Literary Criticism, Thomson Gale (Detroit, MI), Volume 4, 1975, Volume 13, 1980.

Foster, David W., *Forms in the Work of Camilo José Cela,* University of Missouri Press (Columbia, MO), 1967.

Ilie, Paul, *La novelistica de Camilo José Cela,* Gredos (Madrid, Spain), 1963.

Jones, Margaret E. W., *The Contemporary Spanish Novel, 1939-1975,* Twayne, 1985.

Kirsner, Robert, *The Novels and Travels of Camilo José Cela,* University of North Carolina Press, 1964.

McPheeters, D. W., *Camilo José Cela,* Twayne (Boston, MA), 1969.

Santoro, Patricia J., *Novel into Film: The Case of La Familia de Pascal Duarte and Los Santos Inocentes,* University of Delaware Press (Newark, DE), 1996.

PERIODICALS

America, November 7, 1964.
Books Abroad, spring, 1953; winter, 1971.
Choice, May, 1992; March, 1993.
Christian Science Monitor, January 14, 1965.
Europe, March, 2000, Benjamin Jones, "Cela Sows Stories of Spain," p. 42.
Georgia Review, spring, 1996.
Hispania, March, 1965; March, 1966; September, 1966; September, 1967; May, 1972.

Los Angeles Times, November 2, 1989, William D. Montalbano, review of *The Hive.*
Michigan Quarterly Review, summer, 1969, Francis Donahue, review of *Pascual Duarte.*
Modern Language Review, January, 1996.
Nation, November 14, 1953.
New Republic, September 3, 1990.
New Statesman, February 19, 1965.
New Yorker, January 30, 1965.
New York Review of Books, October 8, 1992.
New York Times, October 20, 1989; January 18, 2002.
New York Times Book Review, May 26, 1968; January 5, 1992.
Observer (London, England), February 14, 1965.
Paris Review, summer, 1996.
Review of Contemporary Fiction, summer, 1992; spring, 1993; spring, 2003, Mark Tursi, review of *Boxwood,* p. 137.
Saturday Review, November 23, 1964, Emile Capouya, review of *Pascual Duarte.*
Spectator, February 19, 1965.
Times Literary Supplement, February 2, 1965; February 25, 1965; May 27, 1965; November 11, 1965; February 12, 1970; April 2, 1970; November 5, 1971; February 11, 1972; October 12, 1990.
Washington Post, October 20, 1989.
World Literature Today, autumn, 1977; summer, 1982; autumn, 1984.

OBITUARIES:

PERIODICALS

Chicago Tribune, January 19, 2002, sec. 1, p. 25.
Los Angeles Times, January 18, 2002, p. B15.
New York Times, January 18, 2002, p. A23.
Times (London, England), January 18, 2002, p. 23.
Washington Post, January 19, 2002, p. B7.

*　　　*　　　*

CELA Y TRULOCK, Camilo José
See CELA, Camilo José

*　　　*　　　*

CESAIRE, Aimé 1913-
(Aimé Fernand Cesaire)

PERSONAL: Born June 25, 1913, in Basse-Pointe, Martinique; son of Fernand (a comptroller with the revenue service) and Marie (Hermine) Cesaire; married Suzanne Roussi (a teacher), July 10, 1937; children:

Jacques, Jean-Paul, Francis, Ina, Marc, Michelle. *Education:* Attended Ecole Normale Superieure, Paris; Sorbonne, University of Paris, licencie es lettres.

ADDRESSES: *Office*—Assemblee Nationale, 75007 Paris, France; La Mairie, 97200 Fort-de-France, Martinique, West Indies.

CAREER: Lycee of Fort-de-France, Martinique, teacher, 1940-45; member of the two French constituent assemblies, 1945-46; mayor of Fort-de-France, 1945—; deputy for Martinique in French National Assembly, 1946. Conseiller general for fourth canton (district) of Fort-de-France; president of the Parti Progressiste Martiniquais.

MEMBER: Society of African Culture (Paris, France; president).

AWARDS, HONORS: *Aimé Cesaire: The Collected Poetry* was nominated for the *Los Angeles Times* Book Award, 1984; commander, Order of Merit of Côte d'Ivoire, 2002.

WRITINGS:

(With Gaston Monnerville and Leopold Sedar-Senghor) *Commemoration du centenaire de l'abolition de l'esclavage: Discours pronounces a la Sorbonne le 27 avril 1948* (title means "Commemoration of the Centenary of the Abolition of Slavery: Speeches Given at the Sorbonne on April 27, 1948"), Presses Universitaires de France, 1948.

Discours sur le colonialisme, Reclame, 1950, 5th edition, Presence Africaine (Paris, France), 1970, translation by Joan Pinkham published as *Discourse on Colonialism,* Monthly Review Press, 1972.

Lettre a Maurice Thorez, 3rd edition, Presence Africaine, 1956, translation published as *Letter to Maurice Thorez,* 1957.

Toussaint L'Ouverture: La revolution française et le probleme coloniale (title means "The French Revolution and the Colonial Problem"), Club Français du Livre, 1960, revised edition, Presence Africaine, 1962.

Ouvres completes (title means "Complete Works"), three volumes, Editions Desormeaux, 1976.

(Contributor) *Studies in French,* William Marsh Rice University, 1977.

Culture and Colonization, University of Yaounde, 1978.

La Poesie, (collection), edited by Daniel Maximin and Gilles Carpentier, Seuil (Paris, France), 1994.

Aimee Cesaire: Pour Aujourdhui et Pour Demain, edited by Guy Ossiro Midiohovan, Sepia, 1995.

Anthologie poetique, edited by Roger Toumson, Impr. Nationale Editions, 1996.

Also author of *Textes,* edited by R. Mercier and M. Battestini, French and European Publications.

POETRY

Cahier d'un retour au pays natal, published in the Paris, France, periodical *Volontes,* 1939, published by Presence Africaine, 1956, 2nd edition, 1960, translation by Emil Snyders published as *Return to My Native Land,* Presence Africaine, 1968, translation by John Berger and Anna Bostock published under same title, Penguin Books (New York, NY), 1969, translation by Mireille Rosello and Annie Pritchard published as *Notebook of a Return to My Native Land = Cahier d'un Retour au Pays Natal,* Bloodaxe Books (Newcastle upon Tyne, England), 1995, translated by Clayton Eshleman and Annette Smith as *Notebook of a Return to My Native Land,* Wesleyan University Press, 2001.

Les armes miraculeuses (title means "The Miracle Weapons;" also see below), Gallimard, 1946, reprinted, 1970.

Soleil cou-coupe (title means "Solar Throat Slashed"), K (Paris, France), 1948, reprinted (bound with *Antilles a main armee* by Charles Calixte under title *Poems from Martinique*), Kraus, 1970.

Corps perdu, illustrations by Pablo Picasso, 1949, translation by Clayton Eshleman and Annette Smith published as *Lost Body,* Braziller, 1986.

Ferrements (title means "Shackles;" also see below), Editions du Seuil (Paris, France), 1960.

Cadastre (also see below), Editions du Seuil (Paris, France), 1961, translation by Gregson Davis published as *Cadastre,* Third Press, 1972, translation by Emil Snyders and Sanford Upson published under same title, Third Press, 1973.

State of the Union, translation by Clayton Eshleman and Dennis Kelly of selections from *Les armes miraculeuses, Ferrements,* and *Cadastre,* [Bloomington, IL], 1966.

Moi, Laminaire (title means "I, Laminarian"), first published in 1982, published by French & European Publications, 1991.

Aimé Cesaire: The Collected Poetry, translation and with an introduction by Clayton Eshleman and Annette Smith, University of California Press, 1983.

Non-Vicious Circle: Twenty Poems, translation by Gregson Davis, Stanford University Press, 1985.

Lyric and Dramatic Poetry, 1946-82 (includes English translations of *Et les Chiens se taisaient* and *Moi, laminaire*), translation by Clayton Eshleman and Annette Smith, University Press of Virginia, 1990.

PLAYS

Et les chiens se taisaient: tragedie (title means "And the Dogs Were Silent: A Tragedy"), Presence Africaine, 1956.

La tragedie du roi Christophe, Presence Africaine, 1963, revised edition, 1973, translation by Ralph Manheim published as *The Tragedy of King Christophe,* Grove (New York, NY), 1970.

Une saison au Congo, Editions du Seuil (Paris, France), 1966, translation by Ralph Manheim published as *A Season in the Congo* (produced in New York at the Paperback Studio Theatre, July, 1970), Grove (New York, NY), 1969.

Une tempete: d'apres "le tempete" de Shakespeare. Adaptation pour un theatre negre, Editions du Seuil (Paris, France), 1969, translation by Richard Miller published as *A Tempest,* Ubu Repertory, 1986.

OTHER

Editor of *Tropiques,* 1941-45, and of *L'Afrique.*

SIDELIGHTS: Because of his role in creating and promoting negritude, a cultural movement which calls for black people to renounce Western society and adopt the traditional values of black civilization, Aimé Cesaire is a prominent figure among blacks in the Third World. A native of the Caribbean island of Martinique, where he has served as mayor of the city of Fort-de-France since 1945, Cesaire also enjoys an international literary reputation for his poems and plays. His 1,000-line poem *Return to My Native Land,* a powerful piece written in extravagant, surreal language and dealing with the reawakening of black racial awareness, is a major work in contemporary French-language literature. Cesaire is, Serge Gavronsky stated in the *New York Times Book Review,* "one of the most powerful French poets" of the twentieth century.

At the age of eighteen, Cesaire left his native Martinique, at that time a colony of France, to attend school in Paris. The city was the center for a number of political and cultural movements during the 1930s, several of which especially influenced the young Cesaire and his fellow black students. Marxism gave them a revolutionary perspective, while surrealism provided them with a modernist esthetic by which to express themselves. Together with Leon-Goutran Damas and Leopold Sedar Senghor, who later became president of Senegal, Cesaire founded the magazine *L'Etudiant Noir,* in which the ideology of negritude was first developed and explained. "Negritude . . . proclaimed a pride in black culture and, in turning their contemporaries' gaze away from the notion of things French, these young students began a revolution in attitudes which was to make a profound impact after the war," Clive Wake explained in the *Times Literary Supplement.* The influence of the movement on black writers in Africa and the Caribbean was so pervasive that the term negritude has come to refer to "large areas of black African and Caribbean literature in French, roughly from the 1930s to the 1960s," Christopher Miller wrote in the *Washington Post Book World.*

The first use of the word negritude occurs in Cesaire's poem *Return to My Native Land* (*Cahier d'un retour au pays natal*), first published in the magazine *Volontes* in 1939. In this poem, Cesaire combines an exuberant wordplay, an encyclopedic vocabulary, and daring surreal metaphors with bits of African and Caribbean black history to create an "exorcism . . . of the poet's 'civilized' instincts, his lingering shame at belonging to a country and a race so abject, servile, petty and repressed as is his," Marjorie Perloff wrote in the *American Poetry Review.* Gavronsky explained that the poem "is a concerted effort to affirm [Cesaire's] stature in French letters by a sort of poetic one-upmanship but also a determination to create a new language capable of expressing his African heritage." *Return to My Native Land,* Perloff maintained, is "a paratactic catalogue poem that piles up phrase upon phrase, image upon image, in a complex network of repetitions, its thrust is to define the threshold between sleep and waking—the sleep of oppression, the blind acceptance of the status quo, that gives way to rebirth, to a new awareness of what is and may be."

Written as Cesaire himself was leaving Paris to return to Martinique, *Return to My Native Land* reverberates with both personal and racial significance. The poet's definition of his own negritude comes to symbolize the growing self-awareness of all blacks of their cultural heritage. Judith Gleason, writing in the *Negro Digest,* believed that Cesaire's poetry is "grounded in the historical sufferings of a chosen people" and so "his is an angry, authentic vision of the promised land." Jean Paul Sartre, in an article for *The Black American Writer: Po-*

etry and Drama, wrote that "Cesaire's words do not describe negritude, they do not designate it, they do not copy it from the outside like a painter with a model: they create it; they compose it under our very eyes."

Several critics see Cesaire as a writer who embodies the larger struggles of his people in all of his poetry. Hilary Okam of *Yale French Studies,* for example, argued that "Cesaire's poetic idiosyncracies, especially his search for and use of uncommon vocabulary, are symptomatic of his own mental agony in the search for an exact definition of himself and, by extension, of his people and their common situation and destiny." Okam concluded that "it is clear from [Cesaire's] use of symbols and imagery, that despite years of alienation and acculturation he has continued to live in the concrete reality of his Negro-subjectivity." Writing in the *CLA Journal,* Ruth J.S. Simmons noted that although Cesaire's poetry is personal, he speaks from a perspective shared by many other blacks. "Poetry has been for him," Simmons explaind, "an important vehicle of personal growth and self-revelation, [but] it has also been an important expression of the will and personality of a people. . . . [It is] impossible to consider the work of Cesaire outside of the context of the poet's personal vision and definition of his art. He defines his past as African, his present as Antillean and his condition as one of having been exploited. . . . To remove Cesaire from this context is to ignore what he was and still is as a man and as a poet."

The concerns found in *Return to My Native Land* ultimately transcend the personal or racial, addressing liberation and self-awareness in universal terms. Gleason called *Return to My Native Land* "a masterpiece of cultural relevance, every bit as 'important' as *The Wasteland,* its remarkable virtuosity will ensure its eloquence long after the struggle for human dignity has ceased to be viewed in racial terms." Andre Breton, in *What Is Surrealism?: Selected Writings,* also sees larger issues at stake in the poem. "What, in my eyes, renders this protest invaluable," Breton stated, "is that it continually transcends the anguish which for a black man is inseparable from the lot of blacks in modern society, and unites with the protest of every poet, artist and thinker worthy of the name . . . to embrace the entire intolerable though amendable condition created for *man* by this society."

Cesaire's poetic language was strongly influenced by the French surrealists of the 1930s, but he uses familiar surrealist poetic techniques in a distinctive manner. Breton claimed that Cesaire "is a black man who handles the French language as no white man can handle it today." Alfred Cismaru stated in *Renascence* that Cesaire's "separation from Europe makes it possible for him to break with clarity and description, and to become intimate with the fundamental essence of things. Under his powerful, poetic eye, perception knows no limits and pierces appearances without pity. Words emerge and explode like firecrackers, catching the eye and the imagination of the reader. He makes use of the entire dictionary, of artificial and vulgar words, of elegant and forgotten ones, of technical and invented vocabulary, marrying it to Antillean and African syllables, and allowing it to play freely in a sort of flaming folly that is both a challenge and a tenacious attempt at mystification." Poetic language is seen by some critics as a form of literary violence, with the jarring images and forceful rhythms of the poetry assaulting the reader. Perloff found that Cesaire's "is a language so violently charged with meaning that each word falls on the ear (or hits the eye) with resounding force." Gleason explained this violence as the expression of an entire race, not just of one man: "Cesaire's is the turbulent poetry of the spiritually dislocated, of the damned. His images strike through the net. . . . Cesaire's is the Black Power of the imagination."

This violent energy is what first drew Cesaire to surrealism. The surrealist artists and writers of the 1930s saw themselves as rebels against a stale and outmoded culture. Their works were meant to revive and express unconscious, suppressed, and forbidden desires. Politically, they aligned themselves with the revolutionary left. As Gavronsky explained, "Cesaire's efforts to forge a verbal medium that would identify him with the opposition to existing political conditions and literary conventions [led him to] the same camp as the Surrealists, who had combined a new poetics that liberated the image from classical restraints with revolutionary politics influenced by Marx and his followers." Cesaire was to remain a surrealist for many years, but he eventually decided that his political concerns would best be served by more realistic forms of writing. "For decades," Karl Keller noted in the *Los Angeles Times Book Review,* "[Cesaire] found the surreal aesthetically revolutionary, but in the face of the torture and the suffering, he has pretty well abandoned it as a luxury."

In the late 1950s Cesaire began to write realistic plays for the theatre, hoping in this way to attract a larger audience to his work. These plays are more explicitly political than his poetry and focus on historical black nationalist leaders of the Third World. *The Tragedy of King Christophe* is a biographical drama about King Henri Christophe of Haiti, a black leader of that island nation in the early nineteenth century. After fighting in a successful revolution against the French colonists, Christophe assumed power and made himself king. But his cruelty and arbitrary use of power led to a rebellion in turn against his own rule, and Christophe committed suicide. Writing in *Studies in Black Literature,* Henry Cohen called *The Tragedy of King Christophe* "one of French America's finest literary expressions." *A Season in the Congo* follows the political career of Patrice Lumumba, first president of the Republic of the Congo in Africa. Lumumba's career was also tragic. With the independence of the Congo in 1960, Lumumba became president of the new nation. But the resulting power struggles among black leaders led in 1961 to Lumumba's assassination by his political opponents. The reviewer for *Prairie Schooner* called *A Season in the Congo* "a passionate and poetic drama." Wake remarks that Cesaire's plays have "greatly widened [his] audience and perhaps tempted them to read the poetry." Gavronsky claims that "in the [1960s, Cesaire] was . . . the leading black dramatist writing in French."

Despite the international acclaim he has received for his poetry and plays, Cesaire remains well known on Martinique for his political career. After 1945 he served as mayor of Fort-de-France and as a member of the French National Assembly. For the first decade of his career, Cesaire was affiliated with the Communist bloc of the assembly, then moved to the Parti du Regroupement Africain et des Federalistes for a short time, and then became president of the Parti Progressiste Martiniquais, a leftist political organization. Cesaire's often revolutionary rhetoric is in sharp contrast to his usually moderate political actions. He opposes independence for Martinique, for example, and was instrumental in having the island declared an oversea department of France—a status similar to that of Puerto Rico to the United States. And as a chief proponent of negritude, which calls for blacks to reject Western culture, Cesaire nonetheless writes his works in French, not in his native black language of creole.

But what may seem contradictory in Cesaire's life and work is usually seen by critics as the essential tension that makes his voice uniquely important. A. James Arnold, in his *Modernism and Negritude: The Poetry and Poetics of Aimé Cesaire,* examined and accepted the tension between Cesaire's European literary sources and his black subject matter and between his modernist sensibility and his black nationalist concerns. Miller explained that "Arnold poses the riddle of Cesaire with admirable clarity" and "effectively defuses . . . either a wholly African or a wholly European Cesaire." This uniting of the European and African is also noted by

Clayton Eshleman and Annette Smith in their introduction to *Aimé Cesaire: The Collected Poetry.* They describe Cesaire as "a bridge between the twain that, in principle, should never meet, Europe and Africa. . . . It was by borrowing European techniques that he succeeded in expressing his Africanism in its purest form." Similarly, Sartre argued that "in Cesaire, the great surrealist tradition is realized, it takes on its definitive meaning and is destroyed: surrealism—that European movement—is taken from the Europeans by a Black man who turns it against them and gives it vigorously defined function."

It is because of his poetry that Cesaire is primarily known worldwide, while in the Third World he is usually seen as an important black nationalist theoretician. Speaking of his poetry, Gavronsky explained that Cesaire is "among the major French poets" of his generation. Cismaru believed that Cesaire "is a poet's poet when he stays clear of political questions, a tenacious and violent propagandist when the theme requires it. His place in contemporary French letters . . . is assured in spite of the fact that not many agree with his views on Whites in general, nor with his opinions on Europe, in particular." *Return to My Native Land* has been his most influential work, particularly in the Third World where, Wake notes, "by the 1960s it was widely known and quoted because of its ideological and political significance." To European and American critics, *Return to My Native Land* is seen as a masterpiece of surrealist literature. Cesaire's coining of the term negritude and his continued promotion of a distinctly black culture separate from Western culture has made him especially respected in the emerging black nations. Eshleman and Smith reported that "although Cesaire was by no means the sole exponent of negritude, the word is now inseparable from his name, and largely responsible for his prominent position in the Third World."

BIOGRAPHICAL AND CRITICAL SOURCES:

BOOKS

Aimé Cesaire: Ecrivain Martiniquais, Fernand Nathan, 1967.

Antoine, R., *Le Tragedie du roi Christophe d'Aimé Cesaire,* Pedagogie Moderne, 1984.

Arnold, A. James, *Modernism and Negritude: The Poetry and Poetics of Aimé Cesaire,* Harvard University Press (Cambridge, MA), 1981.

Bhalla, Alok, editor, *Garcia Marquez and Latin America,* Sterling Publishers, 1987, pp. 161-168.

Bigsby, C.W. E., editor, *The Black American Writer: Poetry and Drama,* Volume 2, Penguin Books, 1971.

Black Literature Criticism, Thomson Gale (Detroit, MI), Volume 1, 1992.

Bouelet, Remy Sylvestre, *Espaces et dialectique du heros cesairien,* L'Harmattan, 1987.

Breton, Andre, *What Is Surrealism?: Selected Writings,* edited by Franklin Rosemont, Monad Press, 1978.

Cesaire, Aimé, *The Collected Poetry,* translated and with an introduction by Clayton Eshleman and Annette Smith, University of California Press (Berkeley, CA), 1983.

Contemporary Literary Criticism, Thomson Gale (Detroit, MI), Volume 19, 1981, Volume 32, 1985.

Davies, Gregson, *Aimé Cesaire,* Cambridge University Press, 1997.

Dennis, Philip A., and Wendell Aycock, editors, *Literature and Anthropology,* Texas Tech University Press (Lubbock, TX), 1989, pp. 113-132.

Frutkin, Susan, *Aimé Cesaire: Black between Worlds,* Center for Advanced International Studies: University of Miami, 1973.

Kesteloot, Lilyan, *Aimé Cesaire,* P. Seghers, 1962, new edition, 1970.

Leiner, Jacqueline, *Soleil eclate: Melanges offerts a Aimé Cesaire a l'occasion de son soixante-dixieme anniversaire par une equipe internationale d'artiste et de chercheurs,* Gunter Narr Verlag (Tubingen, Germany), 1985.

Ngal, M., editor, *Cesaire 70,* Silex, 1985.

Owusu-Sarpong, Albert, *Le Temps historique dans l'oeuvre theatrale a'Aimé Cesaire,* Naaman, 1987.

Pallister, Janis L., *Aimé Cesaire,* Twayne (New York, NY), 1991.

Scharfman, Ronnie Leah, *Engagement and the Language of the Subject in the Poetry of Aimé Cesaire,* University Presses of Florida, 1980.

Songolo, Aliko, *Aimé Cesaire: Une Poetique de la decouverte,* Harmattan (Paris, France), 1985.

PERIODICALS

African Journal, spring, 1974, pp. 1-29.

Afro-Hispanic Review, January, 1985, p. 1.

American Poetry Review, January-February, 1984.

Black Images, spring, 1973, pp. 7-15.

Black Renaissance/Renaissance Noire, fall, 2000, p. 166.

Callaloo, February, 1983, pp. 61-136; summer, 1989, p. 612.

Choice, March, 1991, p. 1141.

CLA Journal, March, 1976; September, 1984; December, 1986, pp. 144-153.

Comparative Literature Studies, summer, 1978.

Concerning Poetry, fall, 1984.

Culture et Developpement, Volume 15, number 1, 1983, pp. 57-63.

Diagonales, October 12, 1989, pp. 5-6.

French Review, May, 1949, pp. 443-447; December, 1982, pp. 272-280; February, 1983, pp. 411-423; March, 1983, pp. 572-578; December, 1983, pp. 224-230.

French Studies Bulletin, 1990.

Hemispheres, fall-winter, 1943-44, pp. 8-9.

Journal of Ethnic Studies, spring, 1981, pp. 69-74.

Journal of West Indian Literature, October, 1986; June, 1987.

Kentucky Foreign Language Quarterly, 1967, pp. 71-79.

Kentucky Romance Quarterly, number 3, 1969, pp. 195-208.

La Licorne, number 9, 1985, pp. 153-160.

Le Monde, December, 1981.

L'Esprit Createur, fall, 1970, pp. 197-212; spring, 1992, p. 110.

Los Angeles Times Book Review, December 4, 1983.

Monthly Review, November, 1999, p. 1.

Negro Digest, May, 1968, pp. 53-61; January, 1970.

New Scholar, number 8, 1982, pp. 1-2.

New York Times Book Review, February 19, 1984, p. 14.

Notre Librairie, number 74, 1984, pp. 9-13.

Prairie Schooner, spring, 1972.

Quadrant, November, 1984, pp. 50-53.

Renascence, winter, 1974.

Research in African Literatures, winter, 2001, p. 77; summer, 2002, p. 210.

Revue de Litterature Comparee, April-June, 1986.

Revue Francophone de Louisiane, spring, 1988, p. 1.

San Francisco Review of Books, Volume 15, number 3, 1990, p. 36.

Studies in Black Literature, winter, 1974.

Studies in the Humanities, June, 1984.

Times Literary Supplement, July 19, 1985.

Twentieth Century Literature, July, 1972.

Washington Post Book World, February 5, 1984.

Yale French Studies, number 46, 1971, pp. 41-47; number 53, 1976.

*   *   *

CESAIRE, Aimé Fernand
See CESAIRE, Aimé

CHABON, Michael 1963-

PERSONAL: Surname is pronounced "shay-bahn"; born 1963, in Washington, DC; son of Robert (a physician, lawyer, and hospital manager) and Sharon (a lawyer) Chabon; married Lollie Groth (a poet; divorced, 1991); married Ayelet Waldman (a writer), 1993; children: (second marriage) Sophie, Ezekiel, Rosie. *Education:* University of Pittsburgh, B.A., 1984; University of California—Irvine, M.F.A.

ADDRESSES: Home—Berkeley, CA. *Agent*—Mary Evans, Inc., 242 East 5th Street, New York, NY 10003.

CAREER: Writer and screenwriter.

AWARDS, HONORS: Publishers Weekly best books, *New York Times* Notable Book, both 1995, and Scripter Award, Friends of the University of Southern California Libraries, 2000, all for *Wonder Boys;* O. Henry Award, Third Prize, 1999, for story "Son of the Wolfman"; National Book Critics Circle Award nomination, 2000, short-listed for PEN/Faulkner Award for Fiction, 2001, New York Society Library Award, 2001, Gold Medal, Commonwealth Club of California, 2001, and Pulitzer Prize for fiction, 2001, all for *The Amazing Adventures of Kavalier and Clay;* Mythopoeic Fantasy Award for children's literature, 2003, for *Summerland.*

WRITINGS:

The Mysteries of Pittsburgh (novel), Morrow (New York, NY), 1988.
A Model World, and Other Stories (includes "The Lost World," "The Little Knife," "More Than Human," and "Blumenthal on the Air"), Morrow (New York, NY), 1991.
Wonder Boys (novel), Villard (New York, NY), 1995.
Werewolves in Their Youth (stories), Random House (New York, NY), 1999.
The Amazing Adventures of Kavalier and Clay (novel), Random House (New York, NY), 2000.
Summerland (juvenile novel), Hyperion/Miramax (New York, NY), 2002.
The Final Solution: A Story of Detection, Fourth Estate/HarperCollins (New York, NY), 2004.

Also author of screenplays, including *The Gentleman Host, The Martian Agent,* and *The Amazing Spider-Man,* a 2004 sequel to the original movie. Author of in-troduction to Ben Katchor's *Julius Knipl, Real-Estate Photographer,* Little, Brown (Boston, MA), 1996. Contributor to periodicals, including *Gentlemen's Quarterly, Mademoiselle, New Yorker, New York Times Magazine, Esquire, Playboy, Forward, Paris Review, Civilization,* and *Vogue.* Guest editor of *McSweeney's Mammoth Treasury of Thrilling Tales,* McSweeney's Books (San Francisco, CA), 2002. Contributor to *Fault Lines: Stories of Divorce,* edited by Caitlin Shetterly, Berkley (New York, NY), 2003. Contributor to *Michael Chabon Presents: The Amazing Adventures of the Escapist,* a quarterly comic book based on the character from Chabon's novel *The Amazing Adventures of Kavalier and Clay,* Dark Horse Comics (Milwaukie, OR), 2003.

ADAPTATIONS: Wonder Boys was adapted for film and released by Paramount Studios; *The Amazing Adventures of Kavalier and Clay* has been optioned for a film by Paramount.

WORK IN PROGRESS: A novel, *Hotzeplotz.*

SIDELIGHTS: Michael Chabon is considered by many critics one of the major literary authors of his generation, and with his 2002 novel, *Summerland,* he turned his hand to juvenile fiction, serving up a five-hundred page children's fantasy novel intended to give J.K. Rowling and her "Harry Potter" series a bit of American competition. As Patrick Meanor noted in *Dictionary of Literary Biography,* Chabon "consciously set out to create his own kind of American magical world, combining elements of Native American and Norse myth and folklore." Such a turn to juvenile fiction was all the more surprising, considering that Chabon won the Pulitzer Prize in 2001 for his novel *The Amazing Adventures of Kavalier and Clay,* a book that confirmed the early critical response to his first novel, *The Mysteries of Pittsburgh,* and of his second, the wryly humorous *Wonder Boys.*

Dubbed a "virtuoso" by *Booklist* 's Donna Seaman, and a "master stylist" by *Book*'s James Sullivan, Chabon has achieved "buzz most writers only dream about," according to Rex Roberts, writing in *Insight on the News.* Such "buzz" has made life easier at the Chabon household, where he and his wife, also a writer, of mysteries, share parenting duties of their children. The versatile Chabon has, in addition to his novels, penned two short story collections, *A Model World* and *Werewolves in Their Youth,* as well as television pilots, screenplays, and articles

Chabon was born in Washington, DC, in 1963, the son of Robert and Sharon Chabon. His father was a physician, lawyer, and hospital manager; his mother later became a lawyer. At the age of six, Chabon and his family moved to the city-in-construction of Columbia, Maryland. They were, as Chabon wrote in "Maps and Legends" on his Web site, "colonists of a dream, immigrants to a new land that as yet existed mostly on paper. More than four-fifths of Columbia's projected houses, office buildings, parks, pools, bike paths, elementary schools and shopping centers had yet to be built; and the millennium of racial and economic harmony that Columbia promised to birth in its theoretical streets and cul-de-sacs was as far from parturition as ever." It was in this never-never land of a city-in-the-making that Chabon came of age. "My earliest memories of Columbia are of the Plan," Chabon wrote, indicating the blueprint for the structure and shape of the city. Hanging a copy of this plan, or map of the projected town, on his wall, Chabon took to studying it as closely as he did the map of Walt Disney's new Magic Kingdom, also thumbtacked nearby. "I glanced up at the map at night as I lay in bed, reading *The Hobbit* or *The Book of Three* or a novel set in Oz. And sometimes I would give it a once over before I set out with my black and white friends for a foray into the hinterlands, to the borders of our town and our imaginations. . . . How fortunate I was to be handed, at such an early age, a map to steer by, however provisional."

A second guidance system for young Chabon was the world of comic books. "I was introduced to them pretty early," Chabon told Scott Tobias in an *Onion* interview, "right around the age of six or so, by my father, who had himself been a devoted reader of comics when he was a child." Chabon's paternal grandfather, a typographer in New York, worked in a plant where they printed comic books and would thus bring home loads of the comics to his son, Chabon's father. Repeating this favor, Robert Chabon introduced his own son to the wonders of DC Comics. Chabon remembered, in his interview with Tobias, the "naive, innocent, primary-colored" nature of these comics, "set in a world with very clear distinctions between good and evil." This was the world of Superman, primarily; as he grew older he sought out the "murkier and more ambiguous" world of the heroes found in Marvel comics. However, by the time he was fourteen or fifteen, he had given up the world of comics, science fiction, and fantasy for more adult, literary fiction, "the stuff my parents would recommend to me that they were enjoying," he told Tobias.

Graduating from high school, Chabon attended the University of Pittsburgh where he earned his undergraduate degree, and then attended the University of California—Irvine, ultimately earning a master's degree in creative writing. During his college years, Chabon expanded on his literally encyclopedic reading. The author has noted that as a child he read the dictionary and encyclopedia for fun; later, he adopted a disparate collection of favorite authors, from Thomas Pynchon to Herman Melville. Writing on his Web site, Chabon lists the writers and works that changed his life, including Jorge Luis Borges and his *Labyrinths*, Gabriel Garcia Marquez and his *Love in the Time of Cholera*, John Cheever's collected stories, Edith Wharton's *The Age of Innocence*, Vladimir Nabokov's *Lolita* and *Pale Fire*, Robert Stone's *Children of the Light*, and F. Scott Fitzgerald's *The Great Gatsby*, among fiction works, and nonfiction works such as Robert Graves's *The White Goddess* and Jan Morris's *Among the Cities*. All of these writers have influenced Chabon in a style of writing that avoids popular minimalism. With more similarity to Marcel Proust than Ernest Hemingway, Chabon has developed a writing style at once expansive and lyric. As he explained to Goodman, "I'll start writing a sentence with a general idea. I want to say x about this character, and before I know it, it's 135 words long, and I've broken it up with a few parentheticals and something between dashes, and it just happens that way."

Chabon's first book, *The Mysteries of Pittsburgh,* was actually his master's thesis at the University of California—Irvine. Not only did the novel earn him his degree, but also his instructor thought highly enough of it to send the manuscript to his own agent, who quickly found a publisher for it. Upon the publication of the coming-of-age novel *The Mysteries of Pittsburgh* in 1988, Chabon earned recognition as a promising young fiction writer. The story centers on Art Bechstein, who has recently graduated from college and is about to experience what he perceives as the last summer of his youth.

Chabon followed *The Mysteries of Pittsburgh* with *A Model World, and Other Stories,* which includes tales previously published in the *New Yorker.* Many of the stories in this collection involve unrequited love, and five of the tales—collectively termed "The Lost World"—chart the angst of adolescent Nathan Shapiro as he grows from age ten to sixteen. Among these chronicles is "The Little Knife," showing Nathan agonizing over both his parents' antagonistic relationship and the Washington Senators' imminent demise from major-league baseball. In "More Than Human," another tale focusing on Shapiro, the boy must come to terms with his shattered family after his father leaves home. Another story in *A Model World,* "Blumenthal on the Air," centers on an American narrator who marries an Iranian woman simply to provide her with United States citizenship, then finds himself falling in love with her.

In her *New York Times Book Review* appraisal of *A Model World*, Elizabeth Benedict noted that Chabon sometimes uses his polished style as a means of remaining emotionally aloof from his material. "All too often he keeps his distance," she alleged, but she added that even in tales where Chabon remains reserved, he nonetheless manages to produce "fluent, astonishingly vivid prose." Benedict was particularly impressed with "The Lost World" stories, which she lauded for their "breathtaking" descriptive passages. Other tales in the volume, Benedict noted, recalled *The Mysteries of Pittsburgh*. Such stories, the critic affirmed, "have a kaleidoscopic beauty."

Chabon experienced considerable difficulty in following up the success of *The Mysteries of Pittsburgh* and *A Model World*. While living on a large advance from his publisher, he wrote 1,500 pages of what he intended to be his second novel, *Fountain City*. It was, Chabon told *Los Angeles Times* contributor Erik Himmelsbach, "sort of a map of my brain," and in it, he attempted to express his love for Paris, architecture, baseball, Florida, and more. After four-and-a-half years and four drafts, however, Chabon admitted to himself that he was never going to be able to craft *Fountain City* into a readable book. He explained to Himmelsbach, "Because I had taken that [advance] money, I felt like I couldn't dump the project, even when it was fairly clear to me that it wasn't working."

The *Fountain City* experience was demoralizing, but Chabon eventually turned it to his advantage. In early 1993, he began work on *Wonder Boys* and in less than a year had finished his second novel. *Wonder Boys* is a fast-paced, comic romp that chronicles one long, disastrous weekend in the life of Grady Tripp, a once-lauded writer now burdened with a 2,000-page manuscript he cannot finish. Joseph P. Kahn of the *Boston Globe* called Tripp "an instant classic . . . part Ginger Man, part Garp and altogether brilliantly original." Chabon confided to Lisa See in *Publishers Weekly* that until his wife read the manuscript of *Wonder Boys* and he heard her laughing as she turned the pages, he had no idea that he was writing a comic novel. "To me, Grady has a wry tone, but I felt sad writing about him. In a lot of ways, he is a projection of my worst fears of what I was going to become if I kept working on *Fountain City*." He continued: "To me, the book is about the disappointment of getting older and growing up and not measuring up to what you thought, and the world and the people in it not being what you expected. It's about disillusionment and acceptance." *Wonder Boys* was adapted for a movie starring Michael Douglas as the burnt-out writer.

Library Journal reviewer Joanna M. Burkhardt called the stories in Chabon's 1999 collection *Werewolves in Their Youth* "remarkably crafted." "Brief synopses can't begin to convey the rich texture of Chabon's involved tales," added Donna Seaman in *Booklist*. Failed relationships serve as the recurring theme in the collection's nine stories, all set in the Pacific Northwest. The title story is of two eleven-year-old boys whose games turn extreme. In "The Harris Fetko Story," Harris is a football player in a failing football venture. His father, Norm, a coach who groomed his son to be an athlete, is now selling cars, but dreams of a new sport called "Powerball" that will revive his career. Although father and son have not spoken for years, Norm calls on Harris to be his main attraction. "When faced with difficult family relations, the protagonists in Michael Chabon's new stories, man and boy alike, harden their hearts and draw into their shells," noted Randall Holdridge in the *Tucson Weekly*. "But vulnerability in these male carapaces, a softness in their hearts, yields compassion at moments of crisis. Usually they pay a high cost in self-sacrifice, but they're rewarded by transfiguring new esteem."

Chabon's next tale, *The Amazing Adventures of Kavalier and Clay,* takes readers into the pulp world of the 1930s and 1940s through the experiences of two Jewish cousins. American Sammy Klayman is an opportunistic young fellow with a real knack for plotting pulp fiction, while Josef Kavalier, a Czech who has fled the Nazis, complements this storytelling talent with his own rare, bold drawing style. Together they create a Harry Houdini-like comic character in a series called *The Escapist,* a superhero who battles World War II enemies on the pages of the comic. Quickly, the cartooning duo become a phenomenal success, but Joe continues to be plagued by guilt and grief over the loss of his family. Finally, he leaves Sammy and his lover to join the Navy. Exploring themes from escapist literature to Golems and beyond, Chabon created, during four years of writing, a huge manuscript that he pared down by two hundred pages before publication. The book became the publishing sensation of the 2000 season.

Reviewing the novel in *Commentary,* John Podhoretz noted that it "combines fable, magical realism, boy's adventure storytelling, Horatio Alger, and mordant humor in an exhilarating stew that also attempts something entirely new in the depiction of the European Jewish catastrophe and the guilt suffered by those who succeeded in escaping it." Podhoretz ultimately felt, however, that while *The Amazing Adventures of Kavalier and Clay* was a "wonderful book," it was still, "despite its scope, a small one." Most other critics offered different opinions. *Booklist*'s Seaman thought that Chabon was "equally adept at atmosphere, action, dialogue, and cultural commentary," plumbing the "depths of the human heart" and celebrating "the healing properties of escapism . . . with exuberance and wisdom." Writing in the *World and I*, Tom Deignan called *The Amazing Adventures* a "slam-bang accomplishment, dazzling and profound, cerebral yet wonderfully touching," and went on to proclaim, "Chabon has produced a great and very American novel, which feels both intimate and worldly."

Troy Patterson of *Entertainment Weekly* added to the chorus of praise, noting that Chabon's novel is "a long, lyrical one that's exquisitely patterned rather than grandly plotted, composed with detailed scenes, and spotted with some rapturous passages of analysis." Patterson concluded, "It's like a graphic novel inked in words and starring the author himself in the lead role: Wonder Boy." "Chabon has pulled off another great feat," wrote Susanna Meadows in *Newsweek,* while *Time* critic R.Z. Sheppard characterized the novel as one written with "much imagination, verve and affection." Roberts concluded his review in *Insight on the News* by commenting, "With *Amazing Adventures,* Chabon lives up to his early accolades, and takes a soaring leap into the literary stratosphere." Awards committees offered similar response, as *The Amazing Adventures of Kavalier and Clay* was nominated for both the National Book Award and the PEN/Faulkner Award for fiction before it took the Pulitzer Prize for fiction in 2001.

With his 2002 novel, *Summerland,* Chabon extended his literary ambitions to the world of young-adult literature. The inspiration for this book came from a couple of sources. "It originated in part," Chabon explained to a contributor for *Library Journal,* "with the experience of reading to my kids. . . . A big turning point for me was rereading *Charlotte's Web* and just being blown away again by how beautiful that book is." Combined with this was a youthful ambition he had had to write about American folklore in the same manner as C.S. Lewis and J.R.R. Tolkien had used British folklore as "the backdrops for their works."

Chabon was one of several well-known adult writers to turn his hand to children's books in 2002, and for this "complex, wildly ambitious novel," as *Booklist*'s Brian Wilson described the book, Chabon uses baseball as a symbol or metaphor for life. Eleven-year-old Ethan Feld is perhaps the world's worst baseball player, at least the worst in Clam Island, Washington, where he makes his home. But he and best friends tomboy Jennifer T. Rideout, a Native-American pitcher, and Thor

Wignutt, are pressed into service one summer by the sports-loving faeries, the ferishers, to save the world. Coyote, the Native-American trickster, is out to create "Ragged Rock," or the destruction of the world. To this end, he kidnaps Ethan's father, who has invented a mysterious substance that is a universal solvent; Coyote plans to dissolve the world away. Ethan—whose mother has died of cancer—along with Jennifer, Thor, and the ferishers, set off on a mission to rescue Ethan's father and secure the fate of the universe. The family Saab—held aloft by a blimp—becomes their ship as they sail through various worlds on their rescue mission. These worlds include Winterland, Summerland, the Middling, and the Gleaming. They play baseball in Summerland and are joined by an unlikely cast of characters, including a talking rat, a former ball player from the Negro leagues, and a Sasquatch named Taffy whom they also rescue. In the end, the fate of the world depends on a baseball game between the villains and this bizarre cast of good guys and girls.

Chabon's first venture into children's books was widely reviewed. A contributor for *Publishers Weekly* felt that Chabon "hits a high-flying home run, creating a vivid fantasy where baseball is king." The same critic further commented that the author "unspools an elaborate yarn in a style that frequently crackles with color and surprise." Similarly, Kimberly L. Paone, writing in *School Library Journal,* thought that Chabon's debut foray into juvenile literature "will enchant its audience." Troy Patterson, writing in *Entertainment Weekly,* noted that Chabon's book "is a baseball novel that gives new meaning to the words fantasy league." Yet Patterson also wondered if *Summerland* were really a children's book. "By calling it such," Patterson observed, "Chabon gives himself prosaic license to indulge in open-hearted hokeyness and reflexive nostalgic revelry."

Laura Miller, writing for *Salon.com,* noted that while *Summerland* "is meant for kids, . . . it's just as rangy, eccentric, dreamy, and funky as [Chabon's] books for adults." However, some other reviewers also noted that the contents of the book might go over the heads of young readers. *Booklist*'s Bill Ott felt that even "committed fantasy buffs . . . will have to bring their A-games if they expect to digest this ingredient-rich plot." Robert Lipsyte, writing in the *New York Times Book Review,* felt that "Chabon drops the ball by giving us a nerdy hero who wins a baseball game in a derivative fantasy world." *Horn Book*'s Peter D. Sieruta also mentioned the "diffuse, somewhat baroque plot," but also went on to observe that "much of the prose is beautifully descriptive as Chabon navigates vividly imagined other worlds and offers up some timeless themes."

James Sullivan, reviewing the novel in *Book,* likewise wrote, "Certainly young readers will delight in the author's masterful use of imagery, whatever they make of the story." A critic for *Kirkus Reviews* had less guarded praise for the book, however, declaring that "this raucous, exhilarating, joyful, and above all, fun offering displays an enormous respect for the tradition of great fantasies that come before it."

The versatile Chabon might have a sequel to *Summerland* up his creative sleeve, and most definitely intends to expand his award-winning writing into new directions. As Richard Lacayo noted in *Time* magazine, Chabon wants "literary fiction to enjoy the liberties of fantasy genres like science fiction and horror." Chabon told Lacayo, "I'm not going to become a fantasy writer or a writer of science fiction. But I'm going to ignore the conventions of literary fiction as much as I can. And whatever kind of fiction comes out of that, I'm just going to hope I can bring readers along with me."

BIOGRAPHICAL AND CRITICAL SOURCES:

BOOKS

Contemporary Literary Criticism, Vol. 55, Thomson Gale (Detroit, MI), 1989.

Dictionary of Literary Biography, Volume 278: *American Novelists since World War II, Seventh Series,* Thomson Gale (Detroit, MI), 2003, pp. 81-90.

Newsmakers, Issue 1, Thomson Gale (Detroit, MI), 2003.

PERIODICALS

Advocate, December 19, 2000, p. 62.

Atlanta Journal-Constitution, April 2, 1995, p. M12.

Book, November, 2000, James Sullivan, review of *The Amazing Adventures of Kavalier and Clay,* p. 66; September-October, 2002, James Sullivan, review of *Summerland,* p. 73; November-December, 2002, "Best Children's Book," p. 58.

Booklist, December 15, 1998, Donna Seaman, review of *Werewolves in Their Youth,* p. 726; August, 2000, Donna Seaman, review of *The Amazing Adventures of Kavalier and Clay,* p. 2074; August, 2002, Bill Ott, review of *Summerland,* p. 1884; February 1, 2003, Brian Wilson, review of *Summerland* (audiobook), p. 1006.

Boston Globe, May 14, 1995, Joseph P. Kahn, review of *Wonder Boys,* p. 50; May 22, 1995, p. 30.

Chicago Tribune, April 2, 1995, sec. 14, p. 5.

Commentary, June, 2001, John Podhoretz, review of *The Amazing Adventures of Kavalier and Clay,* p. 68; June, 2003, Sam Munson, "Slices of Life," review of *McSweeney's Mammoth Treasury of Thrilling Tales,* p. 67.

Entertainment Weekly, April 14, 1995, p. 61; September 29, 2000, Troy Patterson, "Comic Genius," p. 123; October 4, 2002, Troy Patterson, "The Natural," p. 146; April 11, 2003, Carina Chocano, "Monster's Ball: Michael Chabon Guest-Edits Dave Eggers' McSweeney's, Producing a Mixed-Bag of Genre Tales," review of *McSweeney's Mammoth Treasury of Thrilling Tales,* p. 80.

Gentlemen's Quarterly, March, 1995, p. 118.

Horn Book, November-December, 2002, Peter D. Sieruta, review of *Summerland,* p. 751.

Insight on the News, February 12, 2001, Rex Roberts, review of *The Amazing Adventures of Kavalier and Clay,* p. 26.

Interview, March, 1988, p. 48.

Kirkus Reviews, November 1, 1998, review of *Werewolves in Their Youth*; September 1, 2002, review of *Summerland,* p. 1305.

Library Journal, January, 1999, Joanna M. Burkhardt, review of *Werewolves in Their Youth,* p. 161; October 15, 2000, p. 100; September 1, 2002, "Ten Books for Fall," pp. 48-52.

Los Angeles Times, June 28, 1988; April 27, 1995, Erik Himmelsbach, "A Life of Wonder and Awe," p. E1; April 17, 2001, p. A16.

Los Angeles Times Book Review, April 17, 1988, Brett Lott, review of *The Mysteries of Pittsburgh,* pp. 1, 11; March 26, 1995, p. 3.

New Republic, June 26, 1995, p. 40.

New Statesman, May 13, 1988, M. George Stevenson, review of *The Mysteries of Pittsburgh,* pp. 34-35.

New Statesman and Society, June 9, 1995, Roz Kaveney, review of *Wonder Boys,* p. 38.

Newsweek, April 10, 1995, pp. 76-77; September 25, 2000, Susannah Meadows, "Golems and Superheroes," p. 69.

New York, April 3, 1988, p. 7; May 2, 1988, p. 30; April 1, 1991, p. 63.

New York Times, March 17, 1995, p. C28; September 21, 2000, p. B10.

New York Times Book Review, April 3, 1988, Alice McDermott, review of *The Mysteries of Pittsburgh,* p. 7; May 26, 1991, Elizabeth Benedict, review of *A Model World, and Other Stories,* p. 7; April 9, 1995, Robert Ward, review of *Wonder Boys,* p. 7; January 31, 1999, p. 10; September 24, 2000, pp. 8, 9; November 17, 2002, Robert Lipsyte, review of *Summerland,* p. 24.

People Weekly, May 1, 1995, p. 32; June 26, 1995, pp. 63-64; October 14, 2002, Francine Prose, review of *Summerland,* p. 53; December 16, 2002, Galina Espinoza, "Author, Author: She Writes. He Writes. And Both Ayelet Waldman and Michael Chabon Raise the Kids," p. 151.

Publishers Weekly, April 10, 1995, Lisa See, "Michael Chabon: Wonder Boy in Transition," pp. 44-45; November 6, 1995, p. 58; November 23, 1998, review of *Werewolves in Their Youth,* p. 57; August 21, 2000, review of *The Amazing Adventures of Kavalier and Clay,* pp. 44, 45; October 9, 2000, p. 22; June 24, 2002, review of *Summerland,* p. 57; February 24, 2003, review of *McSweeney's Mammoth Treasury of Thrilling Tales,* p. 51.

School Library Journal, Kimberly L. Paone, review of *Summerland,* p. 159.

Time, May 16, 1988, p. 95; April 8, 1991, p. 77; April 10, 1995, John Skow, review of *Wonder Boys,* p. 87; September 25, 2000, R.Z. Sheppard, "Biff! Boom! A Super Novel about the Golden Age of Comics," p. 103; September 23, 2002, Richard Lacayo, "Kids Are Us!," p. 68.

Times Literary Supplement, June 17, 1988, p. 680.

U.S. News and World Report, September 25, 2000, Holly J. Morris, "Smells Like Teen Comics," p. 74.

Village Voice, April 19, 1988, p. 60.

Wall Street Journal, September 22, 2000, p. W13.

Washington Post, June 9, 1995, p. B1.

Washington Post Book World, April 24, 1988, p. 5; April 26, 1991, p. 20; March 19, 1995, p. 3; September 17, 2000, p. X15.

World and I, February, 2001, Tom Deignan, "Playing with Kiddie Dynamite," p. 220.

Writer, August, 2001, p. 15; April, 2002, Kelly Nickell, "The WD Interview: Michael Chabon," pp. 20-21.

ONLINE

Michael Chabon Home Page, http://www.michaelchabon.com/ (August 31, 2003).

Onion, http://avclub.theonion.com/ (November 22, 2000), Scott Tobias, interview with Chabon.

Oregon Live, http://www.oregonlive.com/ (February 8, 1999).

Powell's City of Books, http://www.powells.com/ (September 17, 2001), Dave Welch, "Michael Chabon's Amazing Adventures," author interview.

Salon.com, http://www.salon.com/ (February 22, 1999); (October 22, 2002), Laura Miller, "The Lost Adventure of Childhood."

Tucson Weekly, http://www.tucsonweekly.com/ (March 4-10, 1999), Randall Holdridge, review of *Werewolves in Their Youth.*

CHANG, Iris 1968-2004

PERSONAL: Born March 28, 1968, in Princeton, NJ; committed suicide November 9, 2004, in Santa Clara County, CA; daughter of Shau-Jin (a physics professor) and Ying-Ying (a microbiology professor) Chang; married Bretton Lee Douglas (an electrical engineer), August 17, 1991. *Ethnicity:* "Chinese American" *Education:* University of Illinois-Urbana-Champaign, B.S., 1989; Johns Hopkins University, M.S., 1991.

CAREER: Writer. Has worked as a reporter for *Chicago Tribune* and the Associated Press; lecturer on human rights issues and history.

MEMBER: Committee of One Hundred.

AWARDS, HONORS: John D. and Catherine T. MacArthur Foundation Peace and International Cooperation Award; Woman of the Year Award, Organization of Chinese Americans, 1998; honorary doctorates, College of Wooster and California State University—Hayward.

WRITINGS:

Thread of the Silkworm, Basic Books (New York, NY), 1995.

The Rape of Nanking: The Forgotten Holocaust of World War II, Basic Books (New York, NY), 1997.

The Chinese in America: A Narrative History, Viking (New York, NY), 2003.

Contributor to periodicals, including *New York Times, Los Angeles Times,* and *Newsweek. The Rape of Nanking* has been translated into Chinese and numerous other languages.

ADAPTATIONS: Thread of the Silkworm was adapted as an eight-set audiotape, Blackstone Audiobooks, 1998.

SIDELIGHTS: Iris Chang, the granddaughter of immigrants who fled China in 1937, was a full-time author and former journalist who made the issue of human rights, both in China and in the United States, her main focus of research. Her interest in the treatment of the Chinese under the Japanese occupation led to her best-known book, *The Rape of Nanking: The Forgotten Holocaust of World War II.* Chang's grandparents had fled the city shortly before the invasion, narrowly escaping the bloodbath that ensued: Japanese troops, on order that came down from the Imperial family, tortured and killed more than 300,000 civilians over the course of six to eight weeks. They raped 80,000 women, bayoneted babies, beheaded individuals with swords, skinned people alive, and devised several other extremely cruel ways to murder their victims. Yet this incident remained little known except to those who were personally affected by it. Unlike the Holocaust in Europe, which has been extensively documented and studied and for which Germany has publicly acknowledged guilt, the rape of Nanking was all but forgotten. Chang's book on the subject, however, is perceived by commentators as opening Western eyes to the atrocity.

Chang did extensive research for her project, which was the first full account in English of the Nanking massacre. As a girl, Chang wanted to learn more about the story but could find nothing on the subject in her local library. As a college student with access to better research facilities, she discovered that what little information had been published about Nanking was too scholarly to be readable—these reports, she noted in an interview with Ami Chen Mills on the *MetroActive* Web site, were dry compilations of statistics. The frustration she encountered in her quest for information prompted the young writer to begin work on the story of Nanking herself.

In December, 1994, Chang attended the Global Alliance for Preserving the Truth of the Sino-Japanese War, where she first saw photographs of mutilated bodies in Nanking. "I was walking around in a state of shock," she told Mills. She did research at Yale Divinity School and the National Archives and was allowed to interview survivors in China. Chang had access to much previously unpublished material, including the diaries of foreign missionaries living in China at the time who witnessed the Japanese actions and tried to save Chinese civilians. A particularly interesting discovery was the diary of John Rabe, a German businessman in Nanking who set up an "International Safety Zone" to protect victims. Ironically, Rabe was a Nazi, who wore a swastika armband as he traveled through Nanking trying to help Chinese civilians and who was apparently unaware of the similar actions his native country was taking in Europe against Jews. Rabe became known as "the living Buddha of Nanking," and, because of the interest sparked by Chang's book, his diary has now been published in German, Chinese, and Japanese.

The Rape of Nanking, which was denounced in Japan for allegedly inflating the number of casualties, caused an immediate sensation and became an international best-seller. It was published in the United States at a time of renewed interest in World War II, shortly after the fiftieth anniversary of that conflict. By then the aging survivors of the war were starting to make their stories heard. Korean women came forward to reveal that Japanese soldiers had abused them as involuntary prostitutes. Two novels about Japanese atrocities in China, Paul West's *The Tent of Orange Mist* and R.C. Binstock's *Tree of Heaven,* were published in 1995, and a visual account, Shi Young and James Yin's *Rape of Nanking: An Undeniable History in Photographs,* was also available. Yet Chang's book was the first complete narrative on the subject in English.

Many critics deemed the book well researched and important. In a piece in the *New York Times Book Review,* Orville Schell praised the book highly and provided extensive context for the historical neglect of its subject. A *Publishers Weekly* reviewer called the book a "compelling, agonizing chronicle," and a critic for *Booklist* found it "a literary model of how to speak about the unspeakable." *The Rape of Nanking* was featured by the UPI Network and by *Ashi Shimbun,* a Japanese magazine with a large readership. It was also featured on *The NewsHour with Jim Lehrer* on PBS. The book became a *New York Times* notable book and was cited by the *Bookman Review* syndicate as one of the best books of 1997. *Reader's Digest* featured Chang in a cover story in 1998.

Working on *The Rape of Nanking* was emotionally difficult, admitted Chang, whose family fled China for Taiwan and then immigrated to the United States. "It's really frightening how fast you get used to the atrocities," she commented to Mills about her background reading on the subject. "It's very, very easy to just accept these atrocities and almost see them as banal. It really gave me insight into the true nature of evil and how easily we all can become desensitized." Speaking with David Gergen on PBS, Chang said that she was particularly upset to discover that the Nanking atrocities were committed by ordinary people. "Many of them were model citizens from Japan and when they returned became respectable members of the community," she noted. Extreme concentration of power, she concluded from her research, regardless of race or political affiliation, can create conditions under which seemingly normal human beings could commit crimes against humanity. "So it seems as if almost all people have this potential for evil, which would be unleashed only under certain dangerous social circumstances," she concluded.

Chang made it clear in her interview with Mills that, though her book has prompted comparisons with the Nazi Holocaust, it is "not an attempt to show that one ethnic group's suffering was worse than another's." Chang also noted that, after the United States dropped atom bombs on Japanese civilians in Hiroshima and Nagasaki, the shocked international community viewed Japan as a victim of war rather than an aggressor, which contributed to reluctance to hold Japan accountable for war crimes.

In the interview Chang also considered the issue of China's own reluctance to force Japan to offer significant apologies and reparations, because China so desperately needed Japan as an ally after the war. There is also a "tradition of Chinese political apathy in [the United States]," she commented. "Chinese learned from their ancestors and their parents that politics can be deadly." But she emphasized that, in recent years, activism among Chinese Americans is increasing, in part because the younger generation is beginning to enter fields such as filmmaking or literature, which provide wide-based options for communication. A three-day conference on the Nanking massacre, which Chang helped emcee, was held at Stanford University in 1996— evidence of growing political involvement among second-generation Chinese in Silicon Valley. A trend is also beginning that will require American schoolchildren to learn about the rape of Nanking as part of their history curriculum.

In her writings, Chang has also shown a continuing concern for the treatment of Chinese immigrants here in the United States. Her first book, though it attracted less notice than her work on Nanking, was the well-received *Thread of the Silkworm*. It tells the story of Chinese-American space scientist Hsue Shen Tsien, who was unjustly deported from the United States on trumped-up political charges during the McCarthy era. Chang shows in this book how irrational fears for immigrants and their descendants can be very counterproductive to our country. After being interrogated by the FBI, as Chang explained in an online interview with Robert Birnbaum for *Identity Theory,* Tsien was deported to China "against his will . . . because he was swapped for some American POWs. Here is an example of someone who was just a pawn in this whole chess game of international politics. But the story is so compelling because the intent of the government was to heighten and preserve national security, but the irony is that by deporting him they risked national security. Tsien went back and founded the ballistic missile program in China." A *Choice* reviewer called *Thread the Silkworm* "the most complete account of one of the saddest episodes of the Cold War," and the *Washington Post*'s Daniel Southerland said that Chang "writes compellingly."

Chang's theory about how Chinese immigrants are treated in the United States is that it has a lot to do with

economic and political conditions at the time. If times are good, Americans will generally treat people of Chinese descent well. But in other cases, such as during recessions when Americans often saw Chinese immigrants as threats to their jobs, they have met with extreme racism. In her own experience growing up in a liberal university town, Chang did not come up against a great deal of prejudice, and had felt that such racism was something largely in the past. As she told Birnbaum, "I thought racism was soon going to be a relic of the past . . . [until] I saw [anti-Chinese] images explode onto the covers of national magazines in the late '90s."

Curious about the history of the Chinese experience in America, Chang recently researched Chinese immigration over approximately the last 150 years. The result of this research is her third book, *The Chinese in America: A Narrative History.* She explores in these pages the several waves of immigration that have occurred since the mid-nineteenth century, including those who came to America during the Gold Rush years, those who fled Communism in the 1950s, and the recent immigrants of the late-twentieth century who have come to study and find jobs as political tensions between the United States and China eased. *Seattle Times* writer Kimberly B. Marlowe, described the book as "thorough, important and devastating." A *Publishers Weekly* critic admired the way Chang portrayed the "rocky road between identity and assimilation" that Chinese immigrants must endure, concluding that *The Chinese in America* "surpasses even the high level of her best-selling *Rape of Nanking*." And Brad Hooper, writing in *Booklist,* praised Chang for interspersing personal accounts through her books, "making it a much more human account. . . . This is history at its most dramatic and relevant." *The Chinese in America* was selected by the *San Francisco Chronicle* as one of the best books of 2003, and was nominated for the Bay Area Bookreviewers Association Award.

As in the past, the future of how Chinese Americans are treated in the United States will depend on political and economic developments, according to Chang. For example, as China becomes more technologically advanced, more Chinese engineers may take jobs from Americans, causing tensions to rise. On the other hand, many Americans are adopting more Chinese children into their families, which may foster better understanding between cultures. But whether Chang will write about such issues in the future remains to be seen. "I may attempt a novel," she told Birnbaum. "I think that no matter what you write it requires being honest with oneself and you have to pull yourself out of the whirlwind of daily life to meditate upon what you have experienced. That's a very difficult thing."

BIOGRAPHICAL AND CRITICAL SOURCES:

PERIODICALS

Air & Space-Smithsonian, April, 1996, p. 97.

Atlantic Monthly, April, 1998, review of *The Rape of Nanking: The Forgotten Holocaust of World War II,* pp. 110-116.

Book, May-June, 2003, Eric Wargo, review of *The Chinese in America: A Narrative History,* p. 79.

Booklist, December 1, 1997, p. 606; April 1, 2003, Brad Hooper, review of *The Chinese in America,* p. 1354.

Bulletin of the Atomic Scientist, March-April, 1998, Gretchen Kreuter, review of *The Rape of Nanking,* p. 65.

Choice, May 1996, p. 1498.

Christian Science Monitor, May 8, 2003, Terry Hong, "Fu Manchu Doesn't Live Here; The Struggle and Triumph of Chinese-Americans Are an Integral Part of U.S. History," p. 18.

Economist, June 21, 2003, "A Ragged Tale of Riches: Chinese Immigration," p. 76.

Foreign Affairs, May, 1996, p. 139; March-April, 1998, Donald Zagoria, review of *The Rape of Nanking,* p. 163.

Kirkus Reviews, November 1, 1997, p. 1618; March 15, 2003, review of *The Chinese in America,* p. 437.

Library Journal, January, 1998, Steven Lin, review of *The Rape of Nanking,* p. 115; May 15, 1999, Kent Rasmussen, review of *Thread of the Silkworm* (sound recording), p. 144; July, 1999, Kent Rasmussen, review of *The Rape of Nanking,* p. 158; May 1, 2003, Peggy Spitzer Christoff, review of *The Chinese in America,* p. 134.

Los Angeles Times, May 9, 2003, Anthony Day, "The Chinese Immigrant Story, All Part of the American Epic," p. E-26.

Los Angeles Times Book Review, March 24, 1996, p. 10.

National Review, November 10. 1997, p. 57.

Nature, March 14, 1996, p. 117.

New York Times Book Review, December 14, 1997.

Publishers Weekly, October 27, 1997, p. 58; May 5, 2003, review of *The Chinese in America,* p. 216.

Reason, June, 1998, Carl F. Horowitz, review of *The Rape of Nanking,* p. 69; May-June, 2003, review of *The Chinese in America,* p. 216.

San Francisco Chronicle, May 18, 2003, review of *The Chinese in America,* p. M2.

School Library Journal, April, 1998, Judy McAloon, review of *The Rape of Nanking,* p. 160.

Science, April 12, 1996, p. 217.

Science Books & Films, June, 1996, p. 136.

SciTech Book News, March, 1996, p. 55.

Seattle Times, May 18, 2003, Kimberly B. Marlowe, review of *The Chinese in America,* p. K10.

Society, January, 2000, Peter Li, "The Nanking Holocaust Tragedy, Trauma, and Reconciliation," p. 56.

Wall Street Journal, December 29, 1997, p. A9.

Washington Post Book World, January 21, 1996, pp. 1-2.

ONLINE

Identity Theory, http://www.identitytheory.com/ (June 2, 2003), Robert Birnbaum, interview with Iris Chang.

Iris Chang Web Site, http://www.irischang.net/ (February 15, 2004).

MetroActive, http://www.metroactive.com/ (December 12-18, 1996).

Online NewsHour, http://www.pbs.org/newshour/ (February 20, 1998).

OBITUARIES:

PERIODICALS

Chicago Tribune, November 11, 2004, section 3, p. 11.

Los Angeles Times, November 11, 2004, p. B11.

New York Times, November 12, 2004, p. C9.

Times (London, England), November 15, 2004, p. 54.

Washington Post, November 12, 2004, p. B6.

ONLINE

New York Times Online, http://www.nytimes.com/ (November 11, 2004).

*   *   *

CHAPMAN, Lee
  See BRADLEY, Marion Zimmer

*   *   *

CHAPMAN, Walker
  See SILVERBERG, Robert

*   *   *

CHARBY, Jay
  See ELLISON, Harlan

CHÁVEZ, Denise 1948-
(Denise Elia Chávez)

PERSONAL: Born August 15, 1948, in Las Cruces, NM; daughter of Ernesto E. (an attorney) and Delfina (a teacher; maiden name, Rede) Chávez; married Daniel Zolinsky (a photographer and sculptor), December 29, 1984. *Education:* New Mexico State University, B.A., 1971; Trinity University (San Antonio, TX), M.F.A., 1974; University of New Mexico, M.A., 1982. *Politics:* Democrat. *Religion:* Roman Catholic. *Hobbies and other interests:* Swimming, bowling, movies.

ADDRESSES: Home—80 La Colonia, Las Cruces, NM 88005.

CAREER: Northern New Mexico Community College, Espanola, instructor in English, 1975-77, professor of English and theatre, 1977-80; playwright, 1977—; New Mexico Arts Division, Santa Fe, artist in the schools, 1977-83; University of Houston, Houston, TX, visiting scholar, 1988, assistant professor of drama, 1988-91; New Mexico State University, Las Cruces, assistant professor of creative writing, playwrighting, and Chicano literature, 1996—. Instructor at American School of Paris, 1975-77; visiting professor of creative writing at New Mexico State University, 1992-93 and 1995-96; artistic director of the Border Book Festival, 1994—; past member of faculty at College of Santa Fe; teacher at Radium Springs Center for Women (medium-security prison); gives lectures, readings, and workshops throughout the United States and Europe; has given performances of the one-woman show *Women in the State of Grace* throughout the United States. Writer in residence at La Compania de Teatro, Albuquerque, NM, and Theatre-in-the-Red, Santa Fe, NM; artist-in-residence at Arts with Elders Program, Santa Fe and Las Cruces; codirector of senior citizen workshop in creative writing and puppetry at Community Action Agency, Las Cruces, 1986-89.

MEMBER: National Institute of Chicana Writers (founding member), PEN USA, PEN USA West, Authors Guild, Western Writers of America, Women Writing the West, Santa Fe Writers Cooperative.

AWARDS, HONORS: Best Play Award, New Mexico State University, 1970, for *The Wait;* grants from New Mexico Arts Division, 1979-80, 1981, and 1988; award for citizen advocacy, Dona Ana County Human Services Consortium, 1981; grants from National Endowment for the Arts, 1981 and 1982, Rockefeller Foundation, 1984, and University of Houston, 1989; creative writing fellowship, University of New Mexico, 1982; Steele Jones Fiction Award, New Mexico State University, 1986, for short story "The Last of the Menu Girls"; Puerto del Sol Fiction award, 1986, for *The Last of the Menu Girls;* creative artist fellowship, Cultural Arts Council of Houston, 1990; Favorite Teacher Award, University of Houston, 1991; Premio Aztlan Award, American Book Award, and Mesilla Valley Writer of the Year Award, all 1995, all for *Face of an Angel;* New Mexico Governor's Award in literature and *El Paso Herald Post* Writers of the Pass distinction, both 1995; Luminaria Award for Community Service, New Mexico Community Foundation, 1996.

WRITINGS:

PLAYS

The Wait (one-act), 1970, also produced as *Novitiates,* Dallas Theater Center, Dallas, TX, 1971.

Elevators (one-act), produced in Santa Fe, NM, 1972.

The Flying Tortilla Man (one-act), produced in Espanola, NM, 1975.

The Mask of November (one-act), produced in Espanola, NM, 1977.

Nacimiento (one-act; title means "Birth"), produced in Albuquerque, NM, 1979.

The Adobe Rabbit (one-act), produced in Taos, NM, 1979.

Santa Fe Charm (one-act), produced in Santa Fe, NM, 1980.

Si, hay posada (one-act; title means "Yes, There Is Shelter"), produced in Albuquerque, NM, 1980.

El santero de Cordova (one-act; title means "The Woodcarver of Cordova"), produced in Albuquerque, NM, 1981.

How Junior Got Throwed in the Joint (one-act), produced in Santa Fe at Penitentiary of New Mexico, 1981.

(With Nita Luna) *Hecho en Mexico* (one-act; title means "Made in Mexico"), produced in Santa Fe, NM, 1982.

The Green Madonna (one-act), produced in Santa Fe, NM, 1982.

La morenita (one-act; title means "The Dark Virgin"), produced in Las Cruces, NM, 1983.

Francis! (one-act), produced in Las Cruces, NM, 1983.

El mas pequeno de mis hijos (one-act; title means "The Smallest of My Children"), produced in Albuquerque, NM, 1983.

Plaza (one-act), produced in Albuquerque, NM, 1984, also produced in Edinburgh, Scotland, and at the Festival Latino, New York, NY.

Novena narrativas (one-woman show; title means "The Novena Narratives"), produced in Taos, NM, 1986.

The Step (one-act), produced in Houston, TX, at Museum of Fine Arts, 1987.

Language of Vision (one-act), produced in Albuquerque, NM, 1987.

Women in the State of Grace (one-woman show), produced in Grinnell, IA, 1989; produced nationally since 1993.

The Last of the Menu Girls (one-act; adapted from Chávez's short story of the same title), produced in Houston, TX, 1990.

Author of unproduced plays *Mario and the Room Maria,* 1974, *Rainy Day Waterloo,* 1976, *The Third Door* (trilogy), 1979, *Plague-Time,* 1985, and *Cruz Blanca, Story of a Town.*

OTHER

(Editor) *Life Is a Two-Way Street* (poetry anthology), Rosetta Press (Las Cruces, NM), 1980.

The Last of the Menu Girls (stories), Arte Publico (Houston, TX), 1986, reprinted, Vintage Contemporaries (New York, NY), 2004.

The Woman Who Knew the Language of Animals (juvenile), Houghton Mifflin (Boston, MA), 1992.

(Selector) *Shattering the Myth: Plays by Hispanic Women,* edited by Linda Feyder, Arte Publico (Houston, TX), 1992.

Face of an Angel (novel), Farrar, Straus (New York, NY), 1994.

(Author of essays) *Writing down the River: Into the Heart of the Grand Canyon,* photographed and produced by Kathleen Jo Ryan, foreword by Gretel Ehrlich, Northland (Flagstaff, AZ), 1998.

Loving Pedro Infante, Farrar, Straus & Giroux (New York, NY), 2001.

Work represented in numerous anthologies, including *An Anthology of Southwestern Literature,* University of New Mexico Press, 1977; *An Anthology: The Indian Rio Grande,* San Marcos Press, 1977; *Voces: An Anthology of Nuevo Mexicano Writers,* El Norte Publications, 1987; *Iguana Dreams: New Latino Fiction,* HarperCollins, 1992; *Mirrors beneath the Earth,* Curbstone Press, 1992; *Growing Up Latino: Memories and Stories,* Houghton Mifflin, 1993; *New Mexico Poetry Renaissance,* Red Crane Books, 1994; *Modern Fiction*

about Schoolteaching, Allyn & Bacon, 1996; *Mother of the America,* Riverhead Books, 1996; *Chicana Creativity and Criticism: New Frontiers in American Literature,* edited by Maraia Herrera-Sobek and Helena Maraia Viramontes, University of New Mexico Press, 1996; and *Walking the Twilight II: Women Writers of the Southwest,* edited by Kathryn Wilder, Northland, 1996. Contributor to periodicals, including *Americas Review, New Mexico, Journal of Ethnic Studies,* and *Revista Chicano-Riquena.*

SIDELIGHTS: Denise Chávez is widely regarded as one of the leading Chicana playwrights and novelists of the U.S. Southwest. She has written and produced numerous one-act plays since the 1970s; however, she is best known for her fiction, including *The Last of the Menu Girls,* a poignant and sensitive short-story collection about an adolescent girl's passage into womanhood, and *Face of an Angel,* an exploration of a woman's life in a small New Mexico town. With the publication of *Face of an Angel*—and its selection as a Book-of-the-Month Club title in 1994—Chávez gained a national readership for her portraits of Chicanos living in the Mexican-American borderlands.

Born in Las Cruces, New Mexico, Chávez was reared in a family that particularly valued education and self-improvement. The divorce of her father, an attorney, and her mother, a teacher, when Chávez was ten was a painful experience. She spent the rest of her childhood in a household of women that included her mother, a sister, and a half-sister, and has acknowledged that the dominant influences in her life—as well as in her work—have been female. From an early age Chávez was an avid reader and writer. She kept a diary in which she recorded her observations on life and the personal fluctuations in her own life. During high school she became interested in drama and performed in productions. Chávez recalled her discovery of the theater to *Journal North* interviewer Jim Sagel as a revelation: "I can extend myself, be more than myself." She wrote her first play while a senior in college at New Mexico State University. Originally titled *The Wait,* the play was renamed *Novitiates* when it was produced in 1971. A story about several persons in transitional periods in their lives, her play won a prize in a New Mexico literary contest.

Critics have noted that Chávez's plays typically focus on the characters' self-revelation and developing sense of their personal place within their community. *Mario and the Room Maria,* for example, is a play about personal growth: its protagonist, Mundo Reyes, is unable to develop emotionally due to his refusal to confront painful experiences from his past. Likewise, *Si, hay posada* depicts the agony of Johnny Briones, whose rejection of love during the Christmas season is the result of emotional difficulties experienced as a child. While Chávez's plays often concentrate on her characters' inner lives, some deal with external and cultural elements that impede social interaction. Set in Santa Fe, New Mexico, her well-known 1984 play *Plaza* contrasts characters who have different impressions of life in the town square. According to *Dictionary of Literary Biography* contributor Rowena A. Rivera, the theme of *Plaza* "emphasizes the importance of family and friendship bonds as a means by which individuals can recover their personal and cultural heritage."

Many of the themes pervading Chávez's plays are echoed and drawn together in her short-story collection *The Last of the Menu Girls.* Composed of seven related stories, the work explores the coming of age of Rocio Esquibel through high school and college. In the opening story, Rocio goes to work handing out menus in a hospital, where she is exposed to many different people and experiences. Her impressions are shaped, in large part, by the ordinary individuals whom she daily encounters: the local repairman, the grandmother, and the hospital staff, among others.

Reviewers have commented that Chávez interweaves the seven stories that comprise *The Last of the Menu Girls* in order to emphasize the human need for *comunidad,* or community. Although some scholars find her style to be disjointed and flawed, many laud her lively dialogue, revealing characterization, and ability to write with insight. Chávez does not look upon *The Last of the Menu Girls* as a novel, but as a series of dramatic vignettes that explore the mysteries of womanhood. In fact, she envisions all her work as a chronicle of the changing relationships between men and women as women continue to avow their independence. This assertion has led to the creation of non-stereotypical Chicana heroines like Rocio, who *Women's Studies Review* contributor Maria C. Gonzalez described as "an individual who fights the traditional boundaries of identity that society has set up and expects her to follow."

Chávez's ambitious first novel, *Face of an Angel,* centers on the life of Soveida Dosamantes and her relations with her family, coworkers, former husbands, and lovers in the small New Mexico town of Agua Oscura. Soveida has worked as a waitress for more than thirty years and is deeply involved in preparing a handbook, *The Book of Service,* that she hopes will aid other

would-be waitresses. *Face of an Angel* received wide attention for a first novel. Groundbreaking in the Chicana fiction genre due to its nontraditional heroines and frank discussion of sexual matters, the book was generally hailed as the debut of an important new voice in Hispanic American letters. *Belles Lettres* correspondent Irene Campos Carr called *Face of an Angel* "engrossing, amusing, and definitely one to be savored," adding: "The author's mordant wit is pervasive, the language is pithy, blunt, and explicit." Campos Carr concluded: "Chávez has become a fine writer and a great storyteller. With *Face of an Angel,* her second book, her name can be added to the growing list of Chicana authors making their mark in contemporary American fiction."

Chávez once remarked, "I consider myself a performance writer. My training in theater has helped me to write roles that I myself would enjoy acting. My characters are survivors, and many of them are women. I feel, as a Chicana writer, that I am capturing the voice of so many who have been voiceless for years. I write about the neighborhood handymen, the waitresses, the bag ladies, the elevator operators. They all have something in common: they know what it is to love and to be merciful. My work as a playwright is to capture as best as I can the small gestures of the forgotten people, the old men sitting on park benches, the lonely spinsters inside their corner store. My work is rooted in the Southwest, in heat and dust, and reflects a world where love is as real as the land. In this dry and seemingly harsh and empty world there is much beauty to be found. That hope of the heart is what feeds me, my characters."

In her 2001 novel, *Loving Pedro Infante,* Chávez tells the story of a thirty-something teacher's aide named Teresina "Tere" Avila who is divorced and obsessed with a macho Mexican film star named Pedro Infante, despite the fact that he died in 1957. Tere has a married lover who, true to form, makes promises that he never intends to keep. Tere's deep emotional life, however, revolves around the Pedro Infante fan club and her friend Irma, who espouses the movies as one of the best ways to learn about Mexican culture and life in general. In reality, Tere's ability to function in the real world is being compromised by her obsession with the screen icon. *Library Journal* contributor Lee McQueen commented, "Through Tere, Chávez explores femininity and cultural identity." Bill Ott, writing in *Booklist,* noted, "This thoroughly engaging novel walks the delicate line between comedy and pathos perfectly, using laughter to pull us back from pain but never letting us forget that the laughs come with a price."

In an interview with William Clark of *Publishers Weekly,* Chávez commented on what writing means to her, noting, "Writing for me is a healing, therapeutic, invigorating, sensuous manifestation of the energy that comes to you from the world, from everything that's alive. Everything has a voice and you just have to listen as closely as you can. That's what's so exciting—a character comes to you and you can't write fast enough because the character is speaking through you. It's a divine moment."

BIOGRAPHICAL AND CRITICAL SOURCES:

BOOKS

Balassi, William, John Crawford, and Annie Eysturoy, editors, *This Is about Vision: Interviews with Southwestern Writers,* University of New Mexico Press (Albuquerque, NM), 1990.
Dictionary of Literary Biography, Volume 122: *Chicano Writers, Second Series,* Thomson Gale (Detroit, MI), 1992, pp. 70-76.
Kester-Shelton, Pamela, editor, *Feminist Writers,* St. James Press (Detroit, MI), 1996, pp. 94-96.
Saldivar, Jose-David, and Rolando Hinojosa, editors, *Criticism in the Borderlands: Studies in Chicano Literature, Culture, and Ideology,* Duke University Press (Durham, NC), 1991.

PERIODICALS

American Studies International, April, 1990, p. 48.
Americas Review, Volume 16, number 2, 1988.
Belles Lettres, spring, 1995, Irene Campos Carr, review of *Face of an Angel,* p. 35.
Bloomsbury Review, September-October 1993; May-June 1995.
Booklist, April 15, 2001, Bill Ott, review of *Loving Pedro Infante,* p. 1532.
Boston Globe, September 30, 1994, p. 61.
Journal North, August 14, 1982, Jim Sagel, interview with author, p. E4.
Journal of Semiotic and Cultural Studies, 1991, pp. 29-43.
Library Journal, April 1, 2001, Lee McQueen, review of *Loving Pedro Infante,* p. 132.
Los Angeles Times, November 9, 1994, pp. E1, E4.
New York Times Book Review, October 12, 1986, p. 28; September 25, 1994, p. 20.
Performance, April 8, 1983, p. 6.
Publishers Weekly, August 15, 1994, William Clark, "It's All One Language Here" (interview), pp. 77-78.
School Library Journal, September, 2001, Adriana Lopez, "Chávez Hunts for Translator," p. S7.
Village Voice, November 8, 1994, p. 18.
Women's Studies Review, September-October, 1986, Maria C. Gonzalez, review of *The Last of the Menu Girls.*
World Literature Today, autumn, 1995, p. 792.

ONLINE

Desert Exposure, http://www.zianet.com/desertx/ (March, 1998), "An Interview with Denise Chavez."

*   *   *

CHÁVEZ, Denise Elia
    See CHÁVEZ, Denise

*   *   *

CHEEVER, John 1912-1982

PERSONAL: Born May 27, 1912, in Quincy, MA; died of cancer June 18, 1982, in Ossining, NY; son of Frederick (a shoe salesman and manufacturer) and Mary (a gift shop owner; maiden name Liley) Cheever; married Mary M. Winternitz (a poet and teacher), March 22, 1941; children: Susan, Benjamin Hale, Frederico. *Education:* Attended Thayer Academy. *Religion:* Episcopal *Hobbies and other interests:* Sailing and skiing.

CAREER: Novelist and short-story writer. Instructor at Barnard College, New York, NY, 1956-57, Ossining, NY, Correctional Facility, 1971-72, and University of Iowa Writers Workshop, 1973; visiting professor of creative writing, Boston University, 1974-75. Member of cultural exchange program to USSR, 1964. *Military service:* U.S. Army Signal Corps, 1943-45; became sergeant.

MEMBER: National Institute of Arts and Letters, Century Club (New York, NY).

AWARDS, HONORS: Guggenheim fellowship, 1951; Benjamin Franklin Award, 1955, for "The Five Forty-Eight"; American Academy of Arts and Letters award in literature, 1956; O. Henry Award, 1956, for "The Country Husband," and 1964, for "The Embarkment for Cythera"; National Book Award in fiction, 1958, for *The Wapshot Chronicle;* Howells Medal, American Academy of Arts and Letters, 1965, for *The Wapshot Scandal;* Editorial Award, *Playboy,* 1969, for "The Yellow Room"; honorary doctorate, Harvard University, 1978; Edward MacDowell Medal, MacDowell Colony, 1979, for outstanding contributions to the arts; Pulitzer prize in fiction, 1979, National Book Critics Circle Award in fiction, 1979, and American Book Award in fiction, 1981, all for *The Stories of John Cheever;* National Medal for Literature, 1982.

WRITINGS:

NOVELS

The Wapshot Chronicle (also see below), Harper (New York, NY), 1957, reprinted, Perennial (New York, NY), 2003.

The Wapshot Scandal (also see below), Harper (New York, NY), 1964, reprinted, Perennial (New York, NY), 2003.

Bullet Park, Knopf (New York, NY), 1969, reprinted, Vintage (New York, NY), 1991.

Falconer, Knopf (New York, NY), 1977, reprinted, Vintage (New York, NY), 1991.

The Wapshot Chronicle [and] *The Wapshot Scandal,* Harper (New York, NY), 1979.

Oh, What a Paradise It Seems, Knopf (New York, NY), 1982.

SHORT STORIES

The Way Some People Live: A Book of Stories, Random House (New York, NY), 1943.

The Enormous Radio and Other Stories, Funk, 1953.

(With others) *Stories,* Farrar, Straus (New York, NY), 1956, published as *A Book of Stories,* Gollancz (London, England), 1957.

The Housebreaker of Shady Hill and Other Stories, Harper (New York, NY), 1958.

Some People, Places, and Things That Will Not Appear in My Next Novel, Harper (New York, NY), 1961.

The Brigadier and the Golf Widow, Harper (New York, NY), 1964.

Homage to Shakespeare, Country Squire Books, 1965.

The World of Apples, Knopf (New York, NY), 1973.

The Day the Pig Fell into the Well (originally published in the *New Yorker,* October 23, 1954), Lord John Press, 1978.

The Stories of John Cheever, Knopf (New York, NY), 1978, reprinted, Vintage (New York, NY), 2000.

The Leaves, the Lion-Fish and the Bear, Sylvester & Orphanos, 1980.

Angel of the Bridge, Redpath Press, 1987.

Thirteen Uncollected Stories by John Cheever, Academy Chicago Publishers, 1994.

Also author of *Depression Stories by John Cheever: The Apprentice Years, 1931-1945,* Academy Chicago Publishers.

OTHER

Atlantic Crossing: Excerpts from the Journals of John Cheever, Ex Ophidia (Cottondale, AL), 1986.

Conversations with John Cheever, edited by Scott Donaldson, University Press of Mississippi (Jackson, MS), 1987.

The Letters of John Cheever, edited by son, Benjamin Cheever, Simon & Schuster (New York, NY), 1988.

The Journals of John Cheever, Knopf (New York, NY), 1991.

(With John D. Weaver) *Glad Tidings: A Friendship in Letters,* HarperCollins (New York, NY), 1993.

Also author of television scripts, including *Life with Father.* Contributor to numerous anthologies, including *O. Henry Prize Stories,* 1941, 1951, 1956, 1964; contributor to *New Yorker, Collier's, Story, Yale Review, New Republic, Atlantic,* and other publications.

ADAPTATIONS: "The Swimmer" was adapted for film by Columbia, 1968; PBS-TV broadcast "The Sorrows of Gin," "The Five Forty-Eight," and "O Youth and Beauty!," all 1979; film rights to *The Wapshot Chronicle, The Wapshot Scandal, Bullet Park,* and *Falconer* have been purchased. *A Cheever Evening: A New Play Based on the Stories of John Cheever* was written by A.R. Gurney, Dramatists Play Service (New York, NY), 1995.

SIDELIGHTS: John Cheever is considered among the finest American writers of the twentieth century, a master of the short story, and a competent novelist. Best known as a chronicler of suburbia, Cheever won critical acclaim for his humorous, yet compassionate, accounts of privileged communities populated by affluent people living spiritually impoverished lives. A rehabilitated alcoholic and a suburban dweller himself, "Cheever knew," eulogized Peter S. Prescott in *Newsweek,* "that in a world that most people envy there are people who are bravely enduring."

Cheever's long career as a short story writer began at the age of seventeen when he sold his first story to the *New Republic.* He became a regular contributor to the *New Yorker* five years later, a relationship that would last for decades and account for the publication of a majority of his stories. Cheever's short work, at times discounted because it was categorized as *New Yorker* style, earned a wider audience and greater recognition when his collection *The Stories of John Cheever* was awarded the Pulitzer prize in fiction in 1979. The publication of this volume of sixty-one stories, including "The Enormous Radio," "The Country Husband," "The Chimera," and "The Swimmer," "revived singlehanded publishers' and readers' interest in the American short story," in the opinion of *Time* contributor Paul Gray. Commenting on the author's place in American literature, John Leonard wrote in the *Atlantic* during Cheever's lifetime: "I happen to believe that John Cheever is our best living writer of short stories: a[n Anton] Chekhov of the exurbs."

Cheever the novelist was not as widely praised, but even in this role the writer had his champions. Cheever's novels—most notably *The Wapshot Chronicle, Bullet Park,* and *Falconer*—display "a remarkable sensitivity and a grimly humorous assessment of human behavior that capture[s] the anguish of modern man," commented Robert D. Spector in *World Literature Today,* "as much imprisoned by his mind as by the conventions of society."

Cheever drew on the same confined milieu—geographical and social—in creating his five novels and numerous stories. "There is by now a recognizable landscape that can be called Cheever country," Walter Clemons observed in *Newsweek.* It comprises "the rich suburban communities of Westchester and Connecticut," explained Richard Locke in the *New York Times Book Review,* "the towns [the author] calls Shady Hill, St. Botolphs and Bullet Park." In this country Cheever found the source for his fiction: the lives of upwardly mobile Americans, both urban and suburban, lives lacking purpose and direction. His fictional representation of these lives capture what a *Time* reviewer termed the "social perceptions that seem superficial but somehow manage to reveal (and devastate or exalt) the subjects of his suburban scrutiny."

For the most part, the characters represented in Cheever's short stories and novels are white and Protestant; they are bored with their jobs, trapped in their lifestyles, and out of touch with their families. "Cheever's account of life in suburbia makes one's soul ache," Guy Davenport remarked in *National Review.* Added the reviewer: "Here is human energy that once pushed plows and stormed the walls of Jerusalem . . . spent daily in getting up hung over, staggering drugged with tranquilizers to wait for a train to . . . Manhattan. There eight hours are given to the writing of advertisements about halitosis and mouthwash. Then the train back, a cocktail party, and drunk to bed." According to Richard Boeth of *Newsweek,* "what is missing in these people is not the virtue of their forebears . . . but the passion, zest, originality and underlying stoicism that fueled the Wasps' domination of the world for two . . . centuries. Now they're fat and bored and scared and whiny."

A recurring theme in Cheever's work is nostalgia, "the particular melancholia induced by long absence from one's country or home," Joan Didion explained in the *New York Times Book Review.* In her estimation, Cheever's characters have "yearned always after some abstraction symbolized by the word 'home,' after 'tenderness,' after 'gentleness,' after remembered houses where the fires were laid and the silver was polished and everything could be 'decent' and 'radiant' and 'clear.'" Even so, Didion added: "Such houses were hard to find in prime condition. To approach one was to hear the quarreling inside. . . . There was some gap between what these Cheever people searching for home had been led to expect and what they got." What they got, the critic elaborated, was the world of the suburbs, where "jobs and children got lost." As Locke put it, Cheever's characters' nostalgia grows out of "their excruciating experience of present incivility, loneliness and moral disarray."

Throughout his tales of despair and nostalgia, Cheever offers an optimistic vision of hope and salvation. His main characters struggle to establish an identity and a set of values in an absurd world. In his *Dictionary of Literary Biography* essay, Robert A. Morace maintained that "while he clearly recognizes those aspects of modern life which might lead to pessimism, his comic vision remains basically optimistic. . . . Many of his characters go down to defeat, usually by their own hand. Those who survive, . . . discover the personal and social virtues of compromise. Having learned of their own and their world's limitations, they can, paradoxically, learn to celebrate the wonder and possibility of life."

Critics have also been impressed by Cheever's episodic style. In a discussion of the author's first published work, "Expelled," Morace commented: "The opening paragraph lures the reader into a story which, like many of the later works, is a series of sketches rather than a linear narrative. The narrator, who remains detached even while recognizing his own expulsion, focuses on apparently disparate events which, taken together, create a single impression of what life at prep school is like." And in a review of *Bullet Park*, a *Time* critic noted that most of the novel "is composed of Cheever's customary skillful vignettes in which apparent slickness masks real feeling."

Some reviewers have found, however, that although this episodic structure works well in Cheever's short fiction, his novels "flounder under the weight of too many capricious, inspired, zany images," as Joyce Carol Oates remarked in the *Ontario Review*. John Updike offered a similar appraisal in his *Picked-up Pieces*: "In the coining of images and incidents, John Cheever has no peer among contemporary American fiction writers. His short stories dance, skid, twirl, and soar on the strength of his abundant invention; his novels fly apart under its impact." Moreover, Oates contended that though "there are certainly a number of powerful passages in *Falconer,* as in *Bullet Park* and the Wapshot novels, . . . in general the whimsical impulse undercuts and to some extent damages the more serious intentions of the works."

Clemons, among others, drew a different conclusion. He noted that "the accusation that Cheever 'is not a novelist' persists," despite the prestigious awards, such as the Howells Medal and the National Book Award, his novels have received. Clemons suggested that this lack of reviewer appreciation is due to Cheever's long affiliation with the *New Yorker*. "The recognition of Cheever's [work] has . . . been hindered by its steady appearance in a debonair magazine that is believed to publish something familiarly called 'the *New Yorker* story,'" the reviewer wrote, "and we think we know what *that* is." Clemons added: "Randall Jarrell once usefully [defined the novel] as prose fiction of some length that has something wrong with it. What is clearly 'wrong' with Cheever's . . . novels is that they contain separable stretches of exhilarating narrative that might easily have been published as stories. They are loosely knit. But so what?"

Over the years, critical and popular response to Cheever's work has remained overwhelmingly favorable. Although some have argued that his characters are unimportant and peripheral and that the problems and crises experienced by the upper middle class are trivial, oth-

ers, such as *Time*'s Gray, contended that the "fortunate few" who inhabit Cheever's fictional world "are much more significant than critics seeking raw social realism will admit." Gray explained: "Well outside the mainstream, the Cheever people nonetheless reflect it admirably. What they do with themselves is what millions upon millions would do, given enough money and time. And their creator is less interested in his characters as rounded individuals than in the awful, comic and occasionally joyous ways they bungle their opportunities." John Leonard of the *New York Times* found the same merits, concluding that "by writing about any of us, Mr. Cheever writes about all of us, our ethical concerns and our failures of nerve, our experience of the discrepancies and our shred of honor."

In 1991 Cheever's son Benjamin published an edited version of Cheever's journals. Written over a period of thirty-five years, and composing twenty-nine looseleaf notebooks when unedited, the journals were distilled to a hefty 399-page book. *The Journals of John Cheever* is marked by Cheever's woeful reminiscences about life—in particular his addiction to alcohol before he quit drinking in 1975 and his growing dissatisfaction with his marriage. The writer also delves into his awakening sexual identity. As a child, he was considered effeminate by others, and friends and family members speculated that he might be gay. Cheever, himself, hid the fact from others and himself for many years. It was not until he had been with several male lovers that he became more open about his bisexuality.

Critical reaction to *The Journals of John Cheever* was mixed. Scott Donaldson, writing in the Chicago *Tribune Books,* felt that the volume is "exquisitely written" but depressing: "the story these . . . journals tell is almost unrelievedly one of woe." Donaldson concludes that "troubled though the story of [Cheever's] life may be, it is told in the same luminous prose that characterized his stories and novels. He takes us on a journey to the depths, but we could not want a better guide." While Jonathan Yardley in the *Washington Post Book World* also characterized Cheever's writing as exceptional, he pondered the need for the publication of the volume: "it is difficult to see how it contributes anything of genuine importance to our understanding of Cheever's work," Yardley opined.

After Cheever's death, his widow contracted Academy Chicago to publish thirteen of the sixty-eight stories that had remained unpublished at the author's death because their author did not believe they measured up to his later works. The tales included in *Thirteen Uncol-*

lected Stories of John Cheever tread on familiar Cheever ground: the troubles of the East Coast middle class. In "His Young Wife," an older man, upset that his wife is slipping away from him, turns to gambling as a means to ruin his rival and win back her love. "In Passing" visits Saratoga, New York, during its famed racing season as a Marxist organizer upset over the foreclosure on his home finds himself in turmoil over his family's reaction to the tragedy. "Family Dinner" looks at the devices a husband and wife use to fool themselves and each other during their unhappy marriage. "Cheever's sympathetic feelings are liberal, generous and extensive," commented Mark Harris in the Chicago *Tribune Books,* "His command of his craft, on the other hand, had yet to be fully developed."

Sven Birkerts, writing in the *New York Times Book Review,* found that "the stories are competent, solid," but believed that "such a collection would not see the light if it did not have the Cheever name on the cover." John B. Breslin in *America* concluded: "immature some of these stories may be, but not embarrassingly so, and certainly much less 'naked' in their revelations of the writer than the letters and journals that have been published with the approval and participation of his family." Breslin added that collection editor Franklin Dennis "has done Cheever no disservice with this collection and has done his admirers a favor."

Cheever's name often ranks alongside the names of such highly regarded contemporaries as John O'Hara, Saul Bellow, Thomas Pynchon, and Philip Roth. Yet, as Peter S. Prescott noted in a *Newsweek* tribute on the occasion of Cheever's death, "His prose, unmatched in complexity and precision by that of any of his contemporaries . . . is simply beautiful to read, to hear in the inner ear—and it got better all the time." "More precisely than his fellow writers," added Prescott, Cheever "observed and gave voice to the inarticulate agonies that lie just beneath the surface of ordinary lives." In the words of Gray in a *Time* tribute, Cheever "won fame as a chronicler of mid-[twentieth-]century manners, but his deeper subject was always the matter of life and death."

BIOGRAPHICAL AND CRITICAL SOURCES:

BOOKS

Aldridge, John W., *Time to Murder and Create: The Contemporary Novel in Crisis,* McKay (New York, NY), 1966.

Bosha, Francis J., *John Cheever: A Reference Guide,* G.K. Hall (New York, NY), 1981.

Bosha, Francis J., editor, *The Critical Response to John Cheever,* Greenwood Press (Westport, CT), 1994.

Byrne, Michael, *Dragons and Martinis: The Skewed Realism of John Cheever,* Borgo Press (San Bernardino, CA), 1993.

Cheever, Susan, *Home before Dark,* Houghton (Boston, MA), 1984.

Concise Dictionary of American Literary Biography, 1941-1968, Thomson Gale (Detroit, MI), 1987.

Contemporary Literary Criticism, Thomson Gale (Detroit, MI), Volume 3, 1975, Volume 7, 1977, Volume 8, 1978, Volume 11, 1979, Volume 15, 1980, Volume 25, 1983, Volume 64, 1991.

Dictionary of Literary Biography, Thomson Gale (Detroit, MI), Volume 2: *American Novelists since World War II,* 1978, Volume 102: *American Short-Story Writers, 1910-1945, Second Series,* 1991.

Dictionary of Literary Biography Yearbook, Thomson Gale (Detroit, MI), 1980, 1982.

Donaldson, Scott, editor, *Conversations with John Cheever,* University Press of Mississippi (Jackson, MS), 1987.

Donaldson, Scott, *John Cheever: A Biography,* Random House (New York, NY), 1988.

Hassan, Ihab, *Radical Innocence,* Princeton University Press (Princeton, NJ), 1961.

Kazin, Alfred, *Bright Book of Life,* Atlantic-Little, Brown (Boston, MA), 1973.

Meanor, Patrick, *John Cheever Revisited,* Twayne (New York, NY), 1995.

Short Story Criticism, Volume 1, Thomson Gale (Detroit, MI), 1988.

Updike, John, *Picked-up Pieces,* Knopf (New York, NY), 1976.

Waldeland, L., *John Cheever,* G.K. Hall (New York, NY), 1979.

PERIODICALS

America, October 1, 1994, pp. 28, 30-31.

Atlantic, May, 1969; June, 1973; November, 1993, p. 159.

Book Week, January 5, 1964.

Chicago Tribune, February 27, 1989.

Chicago Tribune Magazine, April 22, 1979.

Christian Century, May 21, 1969.

Christian Science Monitor, October 22, 1964.

Commonweal, May 9, 1969.

Critique, spring, 1963.

Detroit News, November 28, 1978.

Guardian, (Manchester, England), January 30, 1959.

Life, April 18, 1969.

Ms., April, 1977.

Nation, December 5, 1988, p. 606.

National Review, June 3, 1969.

New Leader, May 26, 1969.

New Republic, May 25, 1953; June 3, 1957; May 15, 1961; January 25, 1964; April 26, 1969; March 6, 1989, p. 35; December 2, 1991, p. 46.

Newsweek, March 14, 1977; October 30, 1978; June 28, 1982.

New York, April 28, 1969; October 7, 1991, p. 109.

New Yorker, August 19, 1991, p. 26; May 30, 1994, pp. 107-110.

New York Herald Tribune Lively Arts, April 30, 1961.

New York Times, March 24, 1965; August 2, 1965; December 18, 1966; April 29, 1969; March 3, 1977; November 7, 1978.

New York Times Book Review, May 10, 1953; September 7, 1958; January 5, 1964; April 27, 1969; May 20, 1973; March 6, 1977; December 3, 1978; January 28, 1979; December 18, 1988; October 6, 1991, pp. 1, 21-22; March 13, 1994, p. 17.

New York Times Magazine, October 21, 1979.

Ontario Review, fall/winter, 1977-78.

Playboy, December, 1993, p. 36.

Publishers Weekly, November 6, 1987; August 26, 1988.

Ramparts, September, 1969.

San Francisco Chronicle, May 24, 1953; March 25, 1957; April 28, 1961.

Saturday Review, May 27, 1961; April 26, 1969; April 2, 1977.

Time, March 27, 1964; April 25, 1969; February 28, 1977; October 16, 1978; June 28, 1982; November 28, 1988, p. 98; October 17, 1994, p. 78.

Times Literary Supplement, October 9, 1953; October 18, 1957; August 4, 1961; December 6, 1991, p. 6.

Tribune Books (Chicago, IL), September 22, 1991, p. 5; March 20, 1994, p. 3.

Twentieth-Century Literature, January, 1969.

Variety, October 10, 1994, p. 93.

Washington Post, April 29, 1969; October 8, 1979.

Washington Post Book World, March 30, 1980; September 22, 1991, p. 3.

World Literature Today, autumn, 1977.

*   *   *

CHEVALIER, Tracy 1962-

PERSONAL: Born October, 1962, in Washington, DC; married; children: one son. *Education:* Oberlin College, B.A., 1984; University of East Anglia, M.A., 1994.

ADDRESSES: Home—London, England. *Agent*—Jonny Geller, Curtis Brown, Haymarket House, 28/29 Haymarket, London SWIY 4SP, England. *E-mail*—hello@tchevalier.com.

CAREER: Writer.

WRITINGS:

NOVELS

The Virgin Blue, Penguin (London, England), 1997, Dutton (New York, NY), 2003.

Girl with a Pearl Earring, Dutton (New York, NY), 2000.

Falling Angels, Dutton (New York, NY), 2001.

The Lady and the Unicorn, Dutton (New York, NY), 2003.

Contributor of short stories to *Fiction* and various magazines.

EDITOR

Twentieth-Century Children's Writers, preface by Naomi Lewis, St. James Press (Chicago, IL), 1989.

Contemporary Poets, prefaces by C. Day Lewis and Diane Wakoski, 5th edition, St. James Press (Chicago, IL), 1991.

Contemporary World Writers, preface by Susan Bassnett, St. James Press (Detroit, MI), 1993.

Encyclopedia of the Essay, Fitzroy Dearborn (Chicago, IL), 1997.

ADAPTATIONS: Girl with a Pearl Earring was released as a film in 2003. All of Chevalier's novels have been adapted as audiobooks.

SIDELIGHTS: Beginning her career as an editor, Tracy Chevalier has gained a growing following as an author of historical fiction. Her novels include *Girl with a Pearl Earring,* an imagined account of the model who appears in Dutch master Johannes Vermeer's painting of the same title, as well as *The Lady and the Unicorn* and *The Virgin Blue.* Discussing *Girl with a Pearl Earring* in a *Fire and Water* interview, Chevalier noted that the girl in Vermeer's painting is "both universal and specific" and added that "you never really know what she's thinking." In Chevalier's story, the painting depicts an illiterate teenager, Griet, who works as a servant in Vermeer's household. Griet is responsible for maintaining Vermeer's studio, and thus she becomes familiar with the painter's interests and technical concerns. "By the time she sits for her portrait," wrote R.Z. Sheppard in *Time,* "Griet is a budding connoisseur."

Vermeer's wife, who recognizes her own earring as the one worn by Griet in the painting, soon grows to resent the bond that has developed between her husband and the servant. Likewise, Vermeer's mother-in-law suspects that an inappropriate relationship has developed between artist and model. "But the truth is loftier than a studio tryst," noted Sheppard, who described Chevalier's account as "an exquisitely controlled exercise that illustrates how temptation is restrained for the sake of art." Another critic, Ruth Coughlin, summarized *Girl with a Pearl Earring* in the *New York Times Book Review* as "marvelously evocative," and a *Publishers Weekly* reviewer called the novel "a completely absorbing story."

While *Girl with a Pearl Earring* is Chevalier's best-known novel, it was not her first; she began her fiction-writing career with *The Virgin Blue,* a story about an American midwife who moves to France and finds her life circumstances reflected in those of a sixteenth-century ancestor. In *Library Journal,* Jo Manning praised the debut novel as a "marvelous piece of writing" that possesses "fluid language, strong characters, and imaginative plotting." Ted Hipple offered a similar opinion in a *Booklist* interview, noting that Chevalier "demonstrates . . . admirable gifts with language."

The Lady and the Unicorn was inspired by a series of six tapestries that hang in the Cluny museum in Paris, their origins mysterious. In Chevalier's novel, the works are commissioned by a powerful and manipulative French nobleman whose female household ultimately becomes involved with the worldly and opportunistic artisan commissioned to do the work. Over time, the lives of these women become entwined—romantically and otherwise—in that of the artist and the work he creates, which was originally meant to be the battle of Nancy but comes to be something far different.

Praising *The Lady and the Unicorn* as a "luminous tale," *Booklist* contributor Kristine Huntley commended Chevalier for the insight she brings to the historical epoch she describes, as well as for "colorful characters" who "leap off the page." Such praise was echoed by other reviewers, with a *Kirkus Reviews* contributor noting that the book is "marvelously imagined and sharply constructed, with a good feel for the people and the era." "What makes the tale enthralling are the details Chevalier offers," added a *Publishers Weekly* contributor, as well as "the deft way she herself weaves together each separate story strand" to create "a work of genuine power and beauty." In *The Lady and the Unicorn,* Rochelle Ratner added in *Library Journal,* Chevalier continues to develop the theme begun in *Girl with a Pearl Earring:* taking "artworks beautiful beyond words" and creating from them "an enchanting novel."

Chevalier's shift from reference-book editor to novelist came in 1993, when she quit her editorial job and earned her M.A. in creative writing at the University of East Anglia. "I try to put the success of my previous books out of my head when I write," she explained on her Web site. "If I thought about it much I'd be paralyzed with the fear of everyone's expectations of me." However, she has been able to sustain the critical success of *Girl with a Pearl Earring,* as well as juggle motherhood and a host of other responsibilities. "It's kind of like running," the author added: "you feel terrible for those first ten minutes but then it gets better and afterwards you feel great."

BIOGRAPHICAL AND CRITICAL SOURCES:

BOOKS

American Reference Books Annual, Libraries Unlimited, 1998, Bernice Bergup, review of *Encyclopedia of the Essay,* p. 478.

PERIODICALS

Booklist, April 15, 1998, review of *Encyclopedia of the Essay,* p. 1462; September 15, 2003, Ted Hipple, review of *The Virgin Blue,* p. 252; November 1, 2003, Kristine Huntley, review of *The Lady and the Unicorn,* p. 458; April 15, 2004, Joyce Saricks, review of *The Lady and the Unicorn,* p. 1460.
Choice, April, 1998, A.C. Labriola, review of *Encyclopedia of the Essay,* p. 1347.
Cleveland Plain-Dealer, October 24, 2001, Donna Marchetti, "Fed-up Editor Starts Writing Her Own Books," p. E1.
Kirkus Reviews, November 15, 2003, review of *The Lady and the Unicorn,* p. 1325.

Library Journal, October 15, 1999, Barbara Hoffert, review of *Girl with a Pearl Earring,* p. 103; August, 2003, Jo Manning, review of *The Virgin Blue,* p. 127; January, 2004, Kellie Gillespie, review of *The Lady and the Unicorn,* p. 152; June 15, 2004, Rochelle Ratner, review of *The Lady and the Unicorn,* p. 108.

New York Times Book Review, January 23, 2000, Ruth Coughlin, review of *Girl with a Pearl Earring,* p. 20.

People, January 12, 2004, Lee Aitken, review of *The Lady and the Unicorn,* p. 47.

Publishers Weekly, October 11, 1999, review of *Girl with a Pearl Earring;* December 8, 2003, review of *The Lady and the Unicorn,* p. 45.

Reference and User Services Quarterly, fall, 1998, Andrew B. Wertheimer, review of *Encyclopedia of the Essay,* p. 93.

RQ, spring, 1992, Anna M. Donnelly, review of *Contemporary Poets,* p. 435.

St. Louis Post-Dispatch, January 23, 2002, Gail Pennington, review of *Girl with a Pearl Earring,* p. E1.

School Library Journal, April, 2004, Molly Connally, review of *The Lady and the Unicorn,* p. 182.

Time, January 17, 2000, R.Z. Sheppard, "A Portrait of Radiance: Tracy Chevalier Brings the Real Artist Vermeer and a Fictional Muse to Life in a Jewel of a Novel," p. 94.

ONLINE

Fire and Water, http://www.fireandwater.com/ (February 2, 2000).

Tracy Chevalier Web site, http://www.tchevalier.com/ (August 5, 2004).

*   *   *

CHILDRESS, Alice 1920-1994

PERSONAL: Surname is pronounced "*Chil*-dress"; born October 12, 1920, in Charleston, SC; died of cancer, August 14, 1994, in Queens, NY; married second husband, Nathan Woodard (a musician), July 17, 1957; children: (first marriage) Jean (Mrs. Richard Lee). *Education:* Attended public schools in New York, NY.

CAREER: Playwright, novelist, actress, and director. Began career in theater as an actress, with her first appearance in *On Strivers Row,* 1940; actress and director with American Negro Theatre, New York, NY, for eleven years, featured in the plays *Natural Man,* 1941, *Anna Lucasta,* 1944, and *Florence,* which she also wrote and directed, 1949; also performed on Broadway and television; made her film appearance in *Uptight,* in 1968. Lecturer at universities and schools; member of panel discussions and conferences on Black American theater at numerous institutions, including New School for Social Research, 1965, and Fisk University, 1966; visiting scholar at Radcliffe Institute for Independent Study (now Mary Ingraham Bunting Institute), Cambridge, MA, 1966-68. Member of governing board of Frances Delafield Hospital.

MEMBER: PEN, Dramatists Guild (member of council), American Federation of Television and Radio Artists, Writers Guild of America East (member of council), Harlem Writers Guild.

AWARDS, HONORS: Obie Award for best original off-Broadway play, *Village Voice,* 1956, for *Trouble in Mind;* John Golden Fund for Playwrights grant, 1957; Rockefeller grant, 1967; Outstanding Book of the Year, *New York Times Book Review,* Woodward School Book Award, 1974, Jane Addams Children's Book Honor Award for young adult novel, 1974, National Book Award nomination, 1974, Best Young Adult Book of 1975, and Lewis Carroll Shelf Award, University of Wisconsin, 1975, all for *A Hero Ain't Nothin' but a Sandwich;* Sojourner Truth Award, National Association of Negro Business and Professional Women's Clubs, 1975; Virgin Islands film festival award for best screenplay, and first Paul Robeson Award for Outstanding Contributions to the Performing Arts, Black Filmmakers Hall of Fame, both 1977, both for *A Hero Ain't Nothin' but a Sandwich;* "Alice Childress Week" officially observed in Charleston and Columbia, SC, 1977, to celebrate opening of *Sea Island Song;* Paul Robeson Award, 1980; Best Book, *School Library Journal,* 1981, one of the Outstanding Books of the Year, *New York Times,* 1982, notable children's trade book in the field of social studies, National Council for the Social Studies and Children's Book Council, 1982, and honorable mention, Coretta Scott King Award, 1982, all for *Rainbow Jordan;* Radcliffe Graduate Society Medal, 1984; Audelco Pioneer Award, 1986; Lifetime Achievement Award, Association for Theatre in Higher Education, 1993.

WRITINGS:

Like One of the Family: Conversations from a Domestic's Life, Independence Publishers, 1956, reprinted with an introduction by Trudier Harris, Beacon Press (Boston, MA), 1986.

(Editor) *Black Scenes* (collection of scenes from plays written by African Americans), Doubleday (New York, NY), 1971.

A Hero Ain't Nothin' but a Sandwich (novel; also see below), Coward (New York, NY), 1973, reprinted, Puffin (New York, NY), 2000.

A Short Walk (novel), Coward (New York, NY), 1979.

Rainbow Jordan (novel), Coward (New York, NY), 1981.

Many Closets, Coward (New York, NY), 1987.

Those Other People, Putnam (New York, NY), 1989.

PLAYS

Florence (one-act), first produced in New York, NY, at American Negro Theatre, 1949.

Just a Little Simple (based on Langston Hughes's short story collection *Simple Speaks His Mind*), first produced in New York, NY, at Club Baron Theatre, September, 1950.

Gold through the Trees, first produced at Club Baron Theatre, 1952.

Trouble in Mind, first produced off-Broadway at Greenwich Mews Theatre, November 3, 1955, revised version published in *Black Theatre: A Twentieth-Century Collection of the Work of Its Best Playwrights,* edited by Lindsay Patterson, Dodd (New York, NY), 1971.

Wedding Band: A Love/Hate Story in Black and White (first produced in Ann Arbor, MI, at University of Michigan, December 7, 1966; produced off-Broadway at New York Shakespeare Festival Theatre, September 26, 1972; also see below), Samuel French (New York, NY), 1973.

String (one-act; based on Guy de Maupassant's story "A Piece of String"; also see below), first produced off-Broadway at St. Mark's Playhouse, March 25, 1969.

Mojo: A Black Love Story (one-act; also see below), produced in New York, NY, at New Heritage Theatre, November, 1970.

Mojo [and] *String,* Dramatists Play Service (New York, NY) (New York, NY), 1971.

When the Rattlesnake Sounds: A Play (for children), illustrated by Charles Lilly, Coward (New York, NY), 1975.

Let's Hear It for the Queen: A Play (for children), Coward (New York, NY), 1976.

Sea Island Song, produced in Charleston, SC, 1977, produced as *Gullah* in Amherst, MA, at University of Massachusetts, Amherst, 1984.

Moms: A Praise Play for a Black Comedienne (based on the life of Jackie "Moms" Mabley), music and lyrics by Childress and her husband Nathan Woo-

dard, first produced by Green Plays at Art Awareness, 1986, produced off-Broadway at Hudson Guild Theatre, February 4, 1987.

Also author of *Martin Luther King at Montgomery, Alabama,* music by Nathan Woodard, 1969; *A Man Bearing a Pitcher,* 1969; *The Freedom Drum,* music by Nathan Woodard, produced as *Young Man Martin Luther King* by Performing Arts Repertory Theatre, 1969-71; *The African Garden,* music by Nathan Woodard, 1971; and *Vashti's Magic Mirror.*

SCREENPLAYS

Wine in the Wilderness: A Comedy-Drama (first produced in Boston by WGBH-TV, March 4, 1969), Dramatists Play Service (New York, NY), 1969.

Wedding Band (based on her play of the same title), American Broadcasting Companies (ABC-TV), 1973.

A Hero Ain't Nothin' but a Sandwich (based on her novel of the same title), New World Pictures, 1978.

String (based on her play of the same title), Public Broadcasting Service (PBS-TV), 1979.

Also author of "Here's Mildred" column in *Baltimore Afro-American,* 1956-58. Contributor of plays, articles, and reviews to *Masses and Mainstream, Black World, Freedomways, Essence, Negro Digest, New York Times,* and other publications.

SIDELIGHTS: Alice Childress is considered by many to be the "greatest African American woman playwright in the history of this country," according to Susan Koppelman, writing in *Belles Lettres.* But Childress excelled in numerous creative fields. An award-winning actress and playwright, she also was a director and a novelist whose adult and juvenile works earned critical acclaim and the attention of numerous awards committees. Childress's work is noted for its frank treatment of racial issues, its compassionate yet discerning characterizations, and its universal appeal. Because her books and plays often deal with such controversial subjects as interracial relationships and teenage drug addiction, her work has been banned in certain locations. She recalled that some affiliate stations refused to carry the nationally televised broadcasts of *Wedding Band* and *Wine in the Wilderness,* and in the case of the latter play, the entire state of Alabama banned the telecast. In addition, Childress noted that as late as 1973 the novel *A Hero Ain't Nothin' but a Sand-*

wich "was the first book banned in a Savannah, Georgia, school library since *Catcher in the Rye*." Despite such regional resistance, Childress won praise and respect for writings that a *Variety* reviewer termed "powerful and poetic." Koppelman noted that Childress's "ability to personalize social issues such as poverty, racism, addiction, and child abuse mobilized those who saw her plays and read her novels to take action on behalf of social justice."

A talented writer and performer in several media, Childress began her career in the theater, initially as an actress and later as a director and playwright. Although "theater histories make only passing mention of her, . . . she was in the forefront of important developments in that medium," wrote *Dictionary of Literary Biography* contributor Trudier Harris. Rosemary Curb pointed out in another *Dictionary of Literary Biography* essay that Childress's 1952 drama *Gold through the Trees* was "the first play by a black woman professionally produced on the American stage." Moreover, Curb added, "As a result of successful performances of [*Just a Little Simple* and *Gold through the Trees*], Childress initiated Harlem's first all-union off-Broadway contracts recognizing the Actors Equity Association and the Harlem Stage Hand Local."

Partly because of her pioneering efforts, Childress is considered a crusader by many. But she is also known as "a writer who resists compromise," explained Doris E. Abramson in *Negro Playwrights in the American Theatre: 1925-1959.* "She tries to write about [black] problems as honestly as she can," thus, the problems Childress addressed most often were racism and its effects. Her *Trouble in Mind,* for example, is a play within a play that focuses on the anger and frustration experienced by a troupe of black actors as they try to perform stereotyped roles in a play that has been written, produced, and directed by whites. As Sally R. Sommer explained in the *Village Voice,* "The plot is about an emerging rebellion begun as the heroine, Wiletta, refuses to enact a namby-Mammy, either in the play or for her director." In the *New York Times,* Arthur Gelb stated that Childress "has some witty and penetrating things to say about the dearth of roles for [black] actors in the contemporary theatre, the cutthroat competition for these parts and the fact that [black] actors often find themselves playing stereotyped roles in which they cannot bring themselves to believe." And of *Wedding Band,* a play about an interracial relationship that takes place in South Carolina during World War I, Clive Barnes wrote in the *New York Times,* "Childress very carefully suggests the stirrings of black consciousness, as well as the strength of white bigotry."

Both Sommer and the *New York Times*'s Richard Eder found that Childress's treatment of the themes and issues in *Trouble in Mind* and *Wedding Band* gives these plays a timeless quality. "Writing in 1955, . . . Alice Childress used the concentric circles of the play-within-the-play to examine the multiple roles blacks enact in order to survive," Sommer remarked. She found that viewing *Trouble in Mind* years later enables one to see "its double cutting edge: It predicts not only the course of social history but the course of black playwriting." Eder stated: "The question [in *Wedding Band*] is whether race is a category of humanity or a division of it. The question is old by now, and was in 1965, but it takes the freshness of new life in the marvelous characters that Miss Childress has created to ask it."

The strength and insight of Childress's characterizations have been widely commented upon; critics contend that the characters who populate her plays and novels are believable and memorable. Eder called the characterizations of *Wedding Band: A Love/Hate Story in Black and White* "rich and lively." Similarly impressed, Harold Clurman wrote in the *Nation* that "there is an honest pathos in the telling of this simple story, and some humorous and touching thumbnail sketches reveal knowledge and understanding of the people dealt with." In the novel *A Short Walk,* Childress chronicled the life of a fictitious black woman, Cora James, from her birth in 1900 to her death in the middle of the century, illustrating, as *Washington Post* critic Joseph McLellan described it, "a transitional generation in black American society." McLellan noted that the story "wanders considerably" and that "the reader is left with no firm conclusion that can be put into a neat sentence or two." What is more important, he asserted, is that "the wandering has been through some interesting scenery, and instead of a conclusion the reader has come to know a human being—complex, struggling valiantly and totally believable." In her play *Moms,* Childress drew a portrait of real-life comic Jackie "Moms" Mabley, a popular black comedienne of the 1960s and 1970s. Dressed as a stereotypical shopping-bag lady, Moms Mabley was a television staple with her stand-up routine as a feisty woman with a sharp tongue. Childress, Mel Gussow wrote in the *New York Times,* "shrewdly gives Moms center stage and lets her comic sensibility speak for itself."

In several novels aimed at a young adult audience, Childress displayed her talent for believable characterization. In the novel *A Hero Ain't Nothin' but a Sandwich,* the author creates a portrait of a teenaged heroin addict by giving us his story not only from his point of view but from several of his friends and family as well. The

Lion and the Unicorn's Miguel Oritz stated, "The portrait of whites is more realistic in this book, more compassionate, and at the same time, because it is believable, more scathing." In *Those Other People*, Childress tells of a group of young friends who are all outsiders: a homosexual, a wealthy black sister and brother, a teacher who has molested one of his students, and a psychiatric patient who was sexually abused as a girl. Each character tells his or her story in separate chapters. The result is a multifaceted look at a pivotal incident at their school which calls into question matters of race and sexual preference. Kathryn Havris, writing in the *School Library Journal,* called *Those Other People* "a disturbing, disquieting novel that reflects another side to life." A *Publishers Weekly* critic concluded that the novel provides "a penetrating examination of bigotry and racism."

Many have acclaimed Childress's work for its honesty, insight, and compassion. In his review of *A Hero Ain't Nothin' but a Sandwich,* Oritz wrote: "The book conveys very strongly the message that we are all human, even when we are acting in ways that we are somewhat ashamed of. The structure of the book grows out of the personalities of the characters, and the author makes us aware of how much the economic and social circumstances dictate a character's actions." Loften Mitchell concluded in *Crisis:* "Childress writes with a sharp, satiric touch. Character seems to interest her more than plot. Her characterizations are piercing, her observations devastating."

Childress died in 1994, leaving behind a body of work both on the stage and between the covers of books that continues to cast a sharp and penetrating light on aspects of the African-American experience. Writing in *Footsteps,* Marta J. Effinger noted that in Childress's plays, she left behind "a trail of courageous black characters." Effinger further commented that "without a doubt, [Childress's] plays are an important part of theater in American. Her dramas are a testament to brave, yet often forgotten, working women." Similarly, Olga Duncan, writing in the *Journal of African American History,* praised Childress's works for providing "important subject matter for critical evaluation of the history of dramatic literature in the United States." Duncan went on to observe that the author "wrote her plays despite economic conditions that made and continue to make a financially independent black theater nearly impossible to create. . . . Childress know not everyone would listen; but she trusted that those who had ears to hear would."

BIOGRAPHICAL AND CRITICAL SOURCES:

BOOKS

Abramson, Doris E., *Negro Playwrights in the American Theatre, 1925-1959,* Columbia University Press (New York, NY), 1969.

Betsko, Kathleen, and Rachel Koenig, *Interviews with Contemporary Women Playwrights,* Beech Tree Books (Taylors, SC), 1987.

Brown-Guillory, Elizabeth, *Their Place on the Stage: Black Women Playwrights in America,* Greenwood Press (Westport, CT), 1988, pp. 25-49.

Brown, Janet, *Feminist Drama: Definition and Critical Analysis,* Scarecrow Press (Metuchen, NJ), 1979, pp. 56-70.

Children's Literature Review, Volume 14, Thomson Gale (Detroit, MI), 1988.

Contemporary Dramatists, fifth edition, St. James Press (Detroit, MI), 1993.

Contemporary Literary Criticism, Thomson Gale (Detroit, MI), Volume 12, 1980, Volume 15, 1980, Volume 96, 1997.

Dictionary of Literary Biography, Thomson Gale (Detroit, MI), Volume 7: *Twentieth-Century American Dramatists,* 1981, Volume 38: *Afro-American Writers after 1955: Dramatists and Prose Writers,* 1985.

Donelson, Kenneth L., and Alleen Pace Nilson, *Literature for Today's Young Adults,* Scott, Foresman (Glenview, IL), 1980, 2nd edition, 1985.

Drama Criticism, Volume 4, Thomson Gale (Detroit, MI), 1994.

Evans, Mari, editor, *Black Women Writers (1950-1980): A Critical Evaluation,* Doubleday-Anchor (New York, NY), 1984.

Feminist Theatre: An Introduction to Plays of Contemporary British and American Women, Macmillan (London, England), 1984, pp. 22-52.

Hatch, James V., *Black Theater, U.S.A.: Forty-five Plays by Black Americans,* Free Press (New York, NY), 1974.

Jennings, La Vinia Delois, *Alice Childress,* Twayne (New York, NY), 1995.

Miller, R. Baxter, editor, *Black American Literature and Humanism,* University Press of Kentucky (Lexington, KY), 1981, pp. 8-10.

Mitchell, Loften, editor, *Voices of the Black Theatre,* James White (Clifton, NJ), 1975.

Schlueter, June, editor, *Modern American Drama: The Female Canon,* Fairleigh Dickinson University Press (Rutherford, NJ), 1990, pp. 184-197.

Street, Douglas, editor, *Children's Novels and the Movies,* Ungar (New York, NY), 1983.

PERIODICALS

Atlanta Constitution, March 27, 1986, p. 1.
Belles Lettres, fall, 1994, Susan Koppelman, "Alice Childress: An Appreciation," p. 6.
CLA Journal, June, 1977, pp. 494-507.
Crisis, April, 1965.
Daily Worker, November 8, 1955, p. 7.
Footsteps, May, 2001, Marta J. Effinger, "Alice Childress," p. 18.
Freedomways, Volume 14, number 1, 1974.
Horn Book, May-June, 1989, p. 374.
Interracial Books for Children Bulletin, Volume 12, numbers 7-8, 1981.
Journal of African American History, winter, 2002, Olga Duncan, "Telling the Truth: Alice Childress as Theorist and Playwright," p. 146.
Lion and the Unicorn, fall, 1978.
Los Angeles Times, November 13, 1978; February 25, 1983.
Los Angeles Times Book Review, July 25, 1982.
MELUS, winter, 1980, pp. 57-68; fall-winter, 2000, Joyce Meier, "The Refusal of Motherhood in African American Women's Theater," p. 117.
Ms., December, 1979.
Nation, November 13, 1972.
Negro American Literature Forum, fall, 1976, pp. 93-95.
Negro Digest, April, 1967; January, 1968.
New Republic, November 25, 1972, pp. 22, 36.
Newsweek, August 31, 1987.
New York, November 13, 1972, p. 134.
New Yorker, November 4, 1972, p. 105; November 19, 1979.
New York Times, November 5, 1955, p. 23; February 2, 1969; April 2, 1969; October 27, 1972; November 5, 1972; February 3, 1978; January 11, 1979; January 23, 1987; February 10, 1987, p. 16; March 6, 1987; August 18, 1987; October 22, 1987.
New York Times Book Review, November 4, 1973; November 11, 1979; April 25, 1981.
Publishers Weekly, November 25, 1988, p. 67.
Sage, spring, 1987, pp. 66-68.
School Library Journal, February, 1989, p. 99.
Show Business, April 12, 1969.
Southern Quarterly, spring, 1987, pp. 53-62.
Variety, December 20, 1972.
Village Voice, January 15, 1979.
Washington Post, May 18, 1971; December 28, 1979.
Wilson Library Bulletin, September, 1989, p. 14.

OBITUARIES:

PERIODICALS

Jet, September 5, 1994, p. 18.
Time, August 29, 1994, p. 25.

CHOMSKY, Avram Noam
See CHOMSKY, Noam

*   *   *

CHOMSKY, Noam 1928-
(Avram Noam Chomsky)

PERSONAL: Born December 7, 1928, in Philadelphia, PA; son of William (a Hebrew scholar) and Elsie (Simonofsky) Chomsky; married Carol Schatz (a linguist and specialist on educational technology), December 24, 1949; children: Aviva, Diane, Harry Alan. *Education:* University of Pennsylvania, B.A., 1949, M.A., 1951, Ph.D., 1955. *Politics:* Libertarian socialist

ADDRESSES: Home—15 Suzanne Rd., Lexington, MA 02173. *Office*—Room E39-219, Massachusetts Institute of Technology, 77 Massachusetts Ave., Cambridge, MA 02139. *E-mail*—chomsky@MIT.edu.

CAREER: Massachusetts Institute of Technology, Cambridge, assistant professor, 1955-58, associate professor, 1958-62, professor, 1962-65, Ferrari P. Ward Professor of Modern Languages and Linguistics, 1966-76, Institute Professor, 1976—. Visiting professor of linguistics, Columbia University, 1957-58, University of California, Los Angeles, 1966, University of California, Berkeley, 1966-67, and Syracuse University, 1982. Member, Institute of Advanced Study, Princeton University, 1958-59; Harvard Cognitive Studies Center research fellow, 1964-67. John Locke lecturer, Oxford University, 1969; Bertrand Russell Memorial Lecturer, Cambridge University, 1971; Nehru Memorial Lecturer, University of New Delhi, 1972; Huizinga Lecturer, University of Leiden, 1977; Woodbridge Lecturer, Columbia University, 1978; Kant Lecturer, Stanford University, 1979.

MEMBER: National Academy of Sciences, American Academy of Arts and Sciences, Linguistic Society of America, American Philosophical Association, American Association for the Advancement of Science (fellow), British Academy (corresponding fellow), British Psychological Society (honorary member), Deutsche Akademie der Naturforscher Leopoldina, Gesellschaft für Sprachwissenschaft (honorary member), Linguistic Society of America, Royal Anthropological Institute of Great Britain, Royal Anthropological Institute of Ireland, Utrecht Society of Arts and Sciences (honorary member).

AWARDS, HONORS: Junior fellow, Harvard Society of Fellows, 1951-55; named among "makers of the twentieth century" by London *Times,* 1970; Guggenheim fellowship, 1971-72; award for distinguished scientific contribution from American Psychological Association, 1984; Gustavus Myers Center Award, 1986 and 1988; George Orwell Award, National Council of Teachers of English, 1987, 1989; Kyoto Prize in Basic Sciences, 1988; Professional Excellence Award, Association for Education in Journalism and Mass Communication, 1991; James Killian Faculty Award, Massachusetts Institute of Technology, 1992; Lannan Literary Award for Nonfiction, 1992; Joel Seldin Peace Award, Psychologists for Social Responsibility, 1993; Homer Smith Award, New York University School of Medicine, 1994; Loyola Mellon Humanities Award, Loyola University, 1994; Helmholtz Medal, Berlin-Brand- enburgische Akademie Wissenschaften, 1996; United Nation Society of Writers and Artists award, 2004. Honorary degrees include D.H.L., University of Chicago, 1967, Loyola University of Chicago, and Swarthmore College, 1970, Bard College, 1971, University of Massachusetts, 1973, University of Pennsylvania, 1984, Gettysburg College and University of Maine, 1992, and Amherst College, 1995; D.Litt., University of London, 1967, Delhi University, 1972, Visva-Bharati University (West Bengal), 1980, and Cambridge University, 1995.

WRITINGS:

Syntactic Structures, Mouton & Co. (Hague, Netherlands), 1957, reprinted, 1978.

Current Issues in Linguistic Theory, Mouton & Co. (Hague, Netherlands), 1964.

Aspects of the Theory of Syntax, MIT Press (Cambridge, MA), 1965, reprinted, 1986.

Cartesian Linguistics: A Chapter in the History of Rationalist Thought, Harper (New York, NY), 1966.

Topics in the Theory of Generative Grammar, Mouton & Co. (Hague, Netherlands), 1966.

(With Morris Halle) *Sound Patterns of English,* Harper (New York, NY), 1968.

Language and Mind, Harcourt (New York, NY), 1968, enlarged edition, 1972.

American Power and the New Mandarins, Pantheon (New York, NY), 1969.

At War with Asia, Pantheon (New York, NY), 1970.

Problems of Knowledge and Freedom: The Russell Lectures, Pantheon (New York, NY), 1971.

(With George A. Miller) *Analyse formelle des langues naturelles,* Mouton & Co. (Hague, Netherlands), 1971.

Studies on Semantics in Generative Grammar, Mouton & Co. (Hague, Netherlands), 1972.

(Editor with Howard Zinn) *The Pentagon Papers,* Volume 5: *Critical Essays,* Beacon Press (Boston, MA), 1972.

For Reasons of State, Vintage Books (New York, NY), 1973, reprinted, New Press (New York, NY), 2003.

(With Edward Herman) *Counterrevolutionary Violence,* Warner Modular, Inc., 1974.

Peace in the Middle East?: Reflections on Justice and Nationhood, Vintage (New York, NY), 1974, expanded as *Middle East Illusions: Including Peace in the Middle East?: Reflections on Justice and Nationhood,* Rowman & Littlefield (Lanham, MD), 2003.

The Logical Structure of Linguistic Theory, Plenum (New York, NY), 1975.

Reflections on Language, Pantheon (New York, NY), 1975.

Essays on Form and Interpretation, North-Holland (New York, NY), 1977.

Dialogues avec Mitsou Ronat, Flammarion (Paris, France), 1977, translation published as *Human Rights and American Foreign Policy,* Spokesman, 1978.

Language and Responsibility, Pantheon (New York, NY), 1979.

(With Edward Herman) *The Political Economy of Human Rights,* Volume I: *The Washington Connection and Third World Fascism,* Volume II: *After the Cataclysm: Postwar Indochina and the Construction of Imperial Ideology,* South End (Boston, MA), 1979.

Rules and Representations, Columbia University Press (New York, NY), 1980.

Lectures on Government and Binding, Foris, 1981.

Radical Priorities, Black Rose Books (New York, NY), 1982, third edition, edited by C.P. Otero, AK Press (Oakland, CA), 2003.

Toward a New Cold War: Essays on the Current Crisis and How We Got There, Pantheon (New York, NY), 1982.

Noam Chomsky on the Generative Enterprise: A Discussion with Riny Huybregts and Henk van Riemsdijk, Foris, 1982.

(With Jonathan Steele and John Gittings) *Superpowers in Collision: The Cold War Now,* Penguin (New York, NY), 1982.

Some Concepts and Consequences of the Theory of Government and Binding, MIT Press (Cambridge, MA), 1982.

The Fateful Triangle: The United States, Israel, and the Palestinians, South End (Boston, MA), 1983, updated edition, 1999.

Turning the Tide: U.S. Intervention in Central America and the Struggle for Peace, South End (Boston, MA), 1985.

Barriers, MIT Press (Cambridge, MA), 1986.

Knowledge of Language: Its Nature, Origins, and Use, Praeger (New York, NY), 1986.

Pirates and Emperors: International Terrorism in the Real World, Claremont, 1986.

On Power and Ideology: The Managua Lectures, South End (Boston, MA), 1987.

James Peck, editor, *The Chomsky Reader,* Pantheon (New York, NY), 1987.

Language and Problems of Knowledge: The Managua Lectures, MIT Press (Cambridge, MA), 1987.

Language in a Psychological Setting, Sophia University (Tokyo, Japan), 1987.

Generative Grammar: Its Basis, Development, and Prospects, Kyoto University of Foreign Studies (Kyoto, Japan), 1988.

The Culture of Terrorism, South End (Boston, MA), 1988.

(With Edward S. Herman) *Manufacturing Consent: The Political Economy of the Mass Media,* Pantheon (New York, NY), 1988.

Necessary Illusions: Thought Control in a Democratic Society, South End (Boston, MA), 1989.

Deterring Democracy, Verso (New York, NY), 1991.

Terrorizing the Neighborhood: American Foreign Policy in the Post-Cold War Era, Pressure Drop Press (San Francisco, CA), 1991.

Chronicles of Dissent: Interviews with David Barsamian, Common Courage Press (Monroe, ME), 1992.

What Uncle Sam Really Wants, Odonian Press (Berkeley, CA), 1992.

Letters from Lexington: Reflections on Propaganda, Common Courage Press, (Monroe, ME), 1993, updated edition, Paradigm (Boulder, CO), 2004.

(With David Barsamian) *The Prosperous Few and the Restless Many,* Odonian Press (Berkeley, CA), 1993.

Rethinking Camelot: JFK, the Vietnam War, and U.S. Political Culture, South End (Boston, MA), 1993.

Year 501: The Conquest Continues, South End (Boston, MA), 1993.

World Orders, Old and New, Columbia University Press (New York, NY), 1994, revised and expanded edition, 1996.

Language and Thought, Moyer Bell (Wakefield, RI), 1994.

Keeping the Rabble in Line: Interviews with David Barsamian, Common Courage Press (Monroe, ME), 1994.

Secrets, Lies, and Democracy: Interviews with David Barsamian, Odonian Press (Berkeley, CA), 1994.

The Minimalist Program, MIT Press (Boston, MA), 1995.

Class Warfare: Interviews with David Barsamian, Common Courage Pres (Monroe, ME), 1996.

Power and Prospects: Reflections on Human Nature and the Social Order, South End (Boston, MA), 1996.

Media Control: The Spectacular Achievements of Propaganda, Seven Stories Press (New York, NY), 1997.

The Umbrella of U.S. Power: The Universal Declaration on Human Rights and the Contradictions of U.S. Power, Seven Stories Press (New York, NY), 1998.

On Neoliberalism, Seven Stories Press (New York, NY), 1998.

The Common Good, interviews by David Barsamian, Odonian Press (Berkeley, CA), 1998.

Our Knowledge of the Human Language: Current Perspectives, Casa Editora (Havana, Cuba), 1998.

The Umbrella of U.S. Power: The Universal Declaration of Human Rights and the Contradictions of U.S. Policy, Seven Stories Press (New York, NY), 1999.

Profit over People: Neoliberalism and Global Order, Seven Stories Press (New York, NY), 1999.

The New Military Humanism: Lessons from Kosovo, Common Courage Press (Monroe, ME), 1999.

The Architecture of Language, Oxford University Press (Oxford, England), 2000.

Chomsky on Miseducation, Rowman & Littlefield (Lanham, MD), 2000.

A New Generation Draws the Line: Kosovo, East Timor, and the Standards of the West, Verso (New York, NY), 2000.

New Horizons in the Study of Language and Mind, Cambridge University Press (Cambridge, England), 2000.

Rogue States: The Rule of Force in World Affairs, South End Press (Boston, MA), 2000.

(With David Barsamian) *Propaganda and the Public Mind,* South End Press (Boston, MA), 2001.

9-11, Seven Stories Press (New York, NY), 2001.

(With Peter R. Mitchell and John Schoeffel) *Understanding Power: The Indispensable Chomsky,* New Press (New York, NY), 2002.

Radical Priorities, AK Press (Oakland, CA), 2003.

Power and Terror, Post-9-11 Talks and Interviews, edited by John Junkerman and Takei Masakazu, Jacana (Johannesburg, South Africa), 2003.

Chomsky on Democracy and Education, edited by C.P. Otero, Routledge (New York, NY), 2003.

Hegemony or Survival: America's Quest for Global Dominance, Metropolitan Books (New York, NY), 2003.

At War with Asia: Essays on Indochina, AK Press (Oakland, CA), 2004.

Language and Politics, AK Press (Oakland, CA), 2004.

Contributor to books, including *The Cold War and the University: Toward an Intellectual History of the Postwar Years,* New Press (New York, NY), 1997; and *You Are Being Lied To: The Disinformation Guide to Media Distortion, Historical Whitewashes, and Cultural Myths,* Razorfish Studios (New York, NY), 2001; contributor of articles to scholarly and general periodicals.

SIDELIGHTS: "Judged in terms of the power, range, novelty and influence of his thought, Noam Chomsky is arguably the most important intellectual alive today," wrote Paul Robinson in the *New York Times Book Review.* Chomsky, a professor of linguistics at the Massachusetts Institute of Technology, attracted worldwide attention with his ground-breaking research into the nature of human language and communication. As the founder of the "Chomskyan Revolution," the scholar became the center of a debate that transcended formal linguistics to embrace psychology, philosophy, and even genetics. *New York Times Magazine* contributor Daniel Yergin maintained that Chomsky's "formulation of 'transformational grammar' has been acclaimed as one of the major achievements of the [twentieth] century. Where others heard only the Babel of fragments, he found a linguistic order. His work has been compared to the unraveling of the genetic code of the DNA molecule." Yergin further contended that Chomsky's discoveries have had an impact "on everything from the way children are taught foreign languages to what it means when we say that we are human." Chomsky is also an impassioned critic of American foreign policy, especially as it affects ordinary citizens of third-world nations. Many of his books since 1969 concern themselves with "the perfidy of American influence overseas," to quote *Atlantic* essayist James Fallows. In *America* Kenneth J. Gavin found a unifying strain in all of Chomsky's various writings. The author's goal, said Gavin, is "to highlight principles of human knowledge and indicate the priority of these principles in the reconstruction of a society. His efforts leave us with more than enough to think about."

Chomsky was born in Philadelphia on December 7, 1928. His father was a Hebrew scholar of considerable repute, so even as a youngster Chomsky "picked up a body of informal knowledge about the structure and history of the Semitic languages," according to David Cohen in *Psychologists on Psychology.* While still in high school Chomsky proofread the manuscript of his father's edition of a medieval Hebrew grammar. Yergin noted: "This backdoor introduction to 'historical linguistics' had considerable impact in the future; it helped fuel his later conviction that the explanation of how language worked, rather than categories and description, was the business of linguistic study." The young Chomsky was more interested in politics than grammar, however. He was especially passionate about the rebirth of a Jewish culture and society in what later became the state of Israel, and for a time he entertained the idea of moving there. In 1945 he enrolled at the University of Pennsylvania, where he came under the influence of Zellig Harris, a noted professor of linguistics. John Lyons observed in *Noam Chomsky* it was Chomsky's "sympathies with Harris's political views that led him to work as an undergraduate in linguistics. There is a sense, therefore, in which politics brought him into linguistics."

The school of linguistics in which Chomsky took his collegiate training held as its goal the formal and autonomous description of languages without wide reference to the meaning—or semantics—of utterances. Lyons elaborated: "Semantic considerations were strictly subordinated to the task of identifying the units of phonology and syntax and were not involved at all in the specification of the rules or principles governing their permissible combinations. This part of the grammar was to be a purely *formal* study, independent of semantics." Chomsky questioned this approach in his early work in generative grammar as a student at the University of Pennsylvania and broke with it more radically while in the Harvard Society of Fellows from 1951. There he was immersed in new developments in mathematical logic, the abstract theory of thinking machines, and the latest psychological and philosophical debates. These ideas led him to develop further his earlier work on generative grammar and to ask "precise and formal questions about linguistics and language," to quote Justin Leiber in his work *Noam Chomsky: A Philosophical Overview.* Leiber adds: "His results led him to criticize and discard the prevailing views in linguistics."

What Chomsky began to develop in the 1950s was a mathematically precise description of some of human language's most striking features. Yergin contended that the scholar was "particularly fascinated by 'generative systems'—the procedures by which a mathematician, starting with postulates and utilizing principles and inferences, can generate an infinite number of proofs. He thought that perhaps language was 'generated' from a few principles as well." Yergin claimed that this line of reasoning led Chomsky to another salient question: *"How is it possible that, if language is only a learned habit, one can be continually creative and innovative in its use?"* This question—and its explication—would provide a novel and compelling critique of two established fields, traditional structural linguistics and behavioral psychology. Leiber concludes that Chomsky's new theory "explained many features of language that were beyond structuralist linguistics and placed the specific data, and many lower-level generalizations, of the structuralists within a richer theory."

Many of Chomsky's new ideas were published in his first book, *Syntactic Structures,* in 1957. Yergin called the work "the pale blue book . . . which heralded the Chomskyan Revolution." He adds that the volume "demonstrated that important facts about language could not be explained by either structural linguistics or by computer theory, which was then becoming fashionable in the field. In *Syntactic Structures* Chomsky departed from his mentors in stressing the importance of explaining creativity in language and introduced his own transformational grammar as a more 'powerful' explanation of how we make sentences." Webster Schott offered a similar assessment in the *Washington Post Book World.* In *Syntactic Structures,* wrote Schott, "Chomsky [presents] and [seems] to demonstrate the proposition that every human being has an innate ability to acquire language, and this ability to learn language is called into use when one hears, at the right age, language for the first time. He also [offers] a concept—it came to be known as 'generative' or 'transformational-generative' grammar—which [has] made it possible to predict ('generate') the sentence combinations in a language and to describe their structure." Lyons stated that the short and relatively nontechnical *Syntactic Structures* "revolutionized the scientific study of language."

The proofs Chomsky uses for his theories are complex, but his conclusions are readily accessible. Robinson observed that, put as simply as possible, Chomsky's view holds that "the ability to speak and understand a language cannot be explained in purely empirical terms— that is, purely by induction. When we 'learn' a language, he says, we are able to formulate and understand all sorts of sentences that we've never heard before. What we 'know,' therefore, must be something deeper—a grammar—that makes an infinite variety of sentences possible. Chomsky believes that the capacity to master grammatical structures is innate: It is genetically determined, a product of the evolutionary process, just as the organic structures of our bodies are." A strict "stimulus-response" mechanism cannot adequately account for the way young children master language during the first four years of life; the child, to quote Cohen, "learns . . . to extract the more complex rules of grammar needed for speech." Leiber explained that for Chomsky, then, the primary interest of the linguist should be with specifying the "device of some sort" that *generates* an infinite variety of grammatically correct sentences. "This device will specify what is somehow 'internalized' in the competent speaker-hearer of the language," Leiber wrote. "Though the most usual label for Chomsky's general sort of linguistics is 'transformational-generative linguistics,' the most crucial word is 'generative'—as opposed to 'taxonomical'—since the primary concern is with the 'principles and processes by which sentences are constructed in particular languages,' not with the identification and classification of items found in the surface end product of these principles and processes."

One of the mechanisms Chomsky proposes for sentence generation is the "deep structure-surface structure" scenario. According to Yergin, the surface structure "'faces out' on the world and, by certain phonological rules, is converted into the sounds we hear; it corresponds to the parsing of sentences which we all learned from our indefatigable junior high English teachers. The deep structure 'faces inward' toward the hazy region of conceptualization, is more abstract and related to meaning. It expresses the basic logical relations between nouns and verbs." Transformational grammar therefore "consists of a limited series of rules, expressed in mathematical notation, which transform deep structures into well-formed surface structures. The transformational grammar thus relates meaning and sound." Cohen discussed the applications of this concept. "Chomsky has analysed the necessary constituents of the deep structure and the transformations through which this deep structure is turned into the surface structure we recognize and use as sentences. He has, of course, extended his theory from this point into the implications for our knowledge of man that comes from the fact that our knowledge of language is based upon this deep structure, a structure that we cannot guess or divine just from speaking, and upon the necessary transformations."

Chomsky has argued that all natural human languages possess deep and surface structures and cycles of transformations between them. In the *Nation,* Gilbert Harman wrote: "These built-in aspects of grammar will be parts of the grammar of every language. They are, in other words, aspects of 'universal grammar.' We must therefore suppose that people have a specific faculty of language, a kind of 'mental organ' which develops in the appropriate way, given appropriate experience, yielding a knowledge of whatever language is spoken in their community." John Sturrock elaborated in the *New York Times Book Review:* "Chomskyism starts with grammar and finishes in genetics. Drill deep enough into the structure of our sentences, he maintains, and you will come to those ultimate abstractions with which we were born, the grammar of any given language being originally determined by the fairly restricted grammatical possibilities programmed in the brain. . . . DNA sets up to master a syntax, the accident of birth determines which one." Needless to say, not everyone agrees with Chomsky's view. *Psychology Today* contributor Howard Gardner called the human being in Chomsky's formulation "a totally preprogrammed computer, one that needs merely to be plugged into the appropriate outlet." Lyons, conversely, stated that Chomsky "was surely right to challenge 'the belief that the mind must be simpler in its structure than any known physical organ and that the most primitive of assumptions must be adequate to explain whatever phenomena can be observed.'"

Obviously, Chomsky's theory has as much to do with psychology and philosophy as it does with linguistics. For instance, the very premises of the scholar's work have made him one of the most trenchant critics of behaviorism, the view that suggests all human responses are learned through conditioning. Sturrock noted: "Chomsky's case is that . . . that fanatical core known as behaviorism, has a theory of learning, all rote and Pavlovian reinforcement, which is deficient and, in the end, degrading. . . . [Behaviorists], given their sinister theory of learning, must be proponents of the view that human nature is not nature at all, but a social product conditioned from outside. Chomsky finds hope and a decisive guarantee of intellectual freedom in the cognitive structures which sit incorruptibly in the fastness of our brains." Chomsky's work reinforces the philosophical tradition of "rationalism," the contention that the mind, or "reason," contributes to human knowledge beyond what is gained by experience. He is opposed by the "empiricists," who claim that all knowledge derives from external stimuli, including language. In the *Nation,* Edward Marcotte declared: "What started as purely linguistic research . . . has led, through involvement in political causes and an identification with an older philosophic tradition, to no less than an attempt to formulate an overall theory of man. The roots of this are manifest in the linguistic theory. . . . The discovery of cognitive structures common to the human race but only to humans (species specific), leads quite easily to thinking of unalienable human attributes." Leiber concluded: "Mind is the software of human psychology, and thought is individuated as instances of the mind's operations. The behaviorist is seen to be insisting . . . on a very minimal sort of software; the rationalist is out to show that much more powerful and abstract, perhaps

in good measure innate, software has to be involved. One can feel unhappy with Chomsky's particular way of putting, or productively narrowing, the issue, but it is not an unreasonable viewpoint. Chomsky has an interesting and important sense of *know* at hand. He is looking at men in a way that has an established and well-defined sense when applied to thinking devices."

While establishing his academic reputation, Chomsky continued to be concerned about the direction of American politics and ideology. His moral indignation was excited in the 1960s, and he became "one of the most articulate spokesmen of the resistance against the Vietnam war," to quote Jan G. Deutsche in the *New York Times Book Review.* Chomsky attacked the war in articles, in books, and from the podium; in the process he became better known for his political views than for his linguistic scholarship. In a *New York Times* piece written during that era, Thomas Lask observed: "Unlike many others, even those who oppose the war, Noam Chomsky can't stand it and his hatred of what we are doing there and his shame, as well as his loathing for the men who defend and give it countenance, are tangible enough to touch." *Nation* essayist Brian Morton found "nothing exotic about his critique of the U.S. role in Vietnam: He attempted no analysis of arcane economic or political structures. All he did was evaluate our government's actions by the same standards that we apply when we evaluate the actions of other governments."

Chomsky's first book-length work on Vietnam, *American Power and the New Mandarins,* offers "a searing criticism of the system of values and decision-making that drove the United States to the jungles of Southeast Asia," according to Michael R. Beschloss in the *Washington Post Book World.* The book's strongest vitriol is directed toward those so-called "New Mandarins"—the technocrats, bureaucrats, and university-trained scholars who defend America's right to dominate the globe. Deutsch stated that Chomsky's concern "is not simply that social scientists have participated widely in designing and executing war-related projects. What he finds disturbing are the consequences of access to power by intellectuals; the difficulties involved in retaining a critical stance toward a society that makes the reward of power available as well as the need to be 'constructive,' the recognition as problems of only those difficulties that are soluble by the means at hand." Inevitably, Chomsky's volume has drawn scathing criticism from those who oppose his views and high praise from those who agree with him. In the *Nation,* Robert Sklar contended: "The importance of *American Power and the New Mandarins* lies in its power to free our minds from old perspectives, to stimulate new efforts at historical, political and social thought."

Subsequent Chomsky books on American foreign policy have explored other political hotbeds around the world, drawing the conclusion that U.S. interests in human rights, justice, and morality are inevitably subordinated to the needs of big business. Critics point out that a good introduction to Chomsky's views and main themes is provided by *Chronicles of Dissent: Interviews with David Barsamian,* which collects interviews conducted in a variety of settings from 1984 through 1991. As a *Publishers Weekly* reviewer summarized them, the interviews "range all over world history," but focus on standard Chomsky themes, such as American imperialism and the corruption of the media and academic elite. Several of the conversations also touch on autobiographical topics, with Chomsky discussing his childhood and the development of his thought. As Beschloss noted, Chomsky's "is a portrait of corporate executives manipulating foreign policy for profit motives, of Third World peoples devastated for drifting away from the American 'grand area' of influence; of hand-maiden journalists, politicians, and intellectuals shrouding the darker realities of American statecraft under platitudes about idealism and goodwill with an eye toward their flow of rewards from the Establishment." These, in fact, are the very subjects of Chomsky's and Edward S. Herman's book *Manufacturing Consent: The Political Economy of the Mass Media,* in which they examine the various ways news organizations ultimately serve the ideological aims of the government. Chomsky and Herman propose a "propaganda model" of the mass media in the United States; countering the commonly held belief that the mass media tend to respond to rather than create public opinion, the two authors argue that the major American news organizations actively misinform the public about the activities of the United States government. As Philip Green of the *Nation* put it, Chomsky and Herman seek to discover how it is "that the major American mass media manage so often to produce accounts of the world that are largely indistinguishable from what a commissar [of information and cultural affairs] would have commanded." The bulk of the book tests the "propaganda model" against events in recent North and South American history, including the reporting of elections in El Salvador and the coverage given to the murders of Polish priest Jerzy Popieluszko and Salvadoran Archbishop Oscar Romero.

Times Literary Supplement correspondent Charles Townshend observed that Chomsky "sees a 'totalitarian mentality' arising out of the mainstream American belief in the fundamental righteousness and benevolence of the United States, the sanctity and nobility of its aims. The publicly tolerated 'spectrum of discussion' of these aims is narrow." The increasing narrowness of public discussion is the subject of *Deterring Democracy,* a book in which Chomsky examines how, regardless of the facts, the American mass media and the United States government conspire to limit the range of opinions that can be widely expressed. Chomsky discusses, for example, the fact that mainstream public opinion embraced only specific kinds of debates regarding the Sandanista government and the Contras in Nicaragua; he shows that the vast majority of lawmakers and reporters disagreed only as to which methods should be employed to rid that country of its communist leaders—no serious attention was given to the debate about whether the Sandanistas or the U.S.-backed Contras would best serve the people of Nicaragua. Also, regarding the "war on drugs," Chomsky examines the government's propaganda campaign supporting its various "successes" and described the positive news coverage these victories receive; the facts that 1) drug use was declining in the United States before President George Bush announced the start of the "war"; and that 2) the fact that drug use has increased in the meantime receives very little attention. He concludes that no substantial discussion arose about the effects of this war on the countries involved, and he bitterly denounces the ironic policy of the United States government of threatening trade sanctions against those East Asian countries that block the importing of U.S. tobacco, a product that is proven to be deadly. Chomsky himself transcends that narrow spectrum of debate, however, adducing "example after example to illuminate how American policies have led knowingly to large scale human suffering," to quote Beschloss. In the *New York Times Book Review,* Sheldon S. Wolin suggested that the author "is relentless in tracking down official lies and exposing hypocrisy and moral indifference in the high places. . . . Yet the passion of Chomsky's indictment is always controlled, and while he is harsh toward his opponents, he is never unfair or arrogant."

Other critics have been less sanguine about the quality and influence of Chomsky's political views; in fact, some have labeled him a pariah and attempted to discredit him on a number of grounds. "It has been Chomsky's singular fate to have been banished to the margins of political debate," wrote Steve Wasserman in the *Los Angeles Times Book Review.* "His opinions have been deemed so kooky—and his personality so cranky—that his writings no longer appear in the forums . . . in which he was once so welcome." Wolin offered one dissenting view: "Chomsky's political writings are curiously untheoretical, which is surprising in a writer renowned for his contributions to linguistic theory. His apparent assumption is that politics is not a theoretical subject. . . . One gets the impression from reading Chomsky that if it were not urgently necessary to expose lies, immorality and the abuse of power, politics would have no serious claim upon the theoretical mind." *New York Times Book Review* contributor Paul Robinson noted that in Chomsky's case, "the popular or accessible [political] works often seem to belie the intellectual powers unambiguously established in the professional works. . . . Indeed, one might argue that the discrepancy is more extreme in his work than in that of any other important intellectual." Morton felt that the attacks on Chomsky's historical/political scholarship—and more recently the tendency to ignore his work—have affected his level of stridency. "His later tone is that of a man who doesn't expect anything to change," Morton observed. "Chomsky is savagely indignant because the values he cherishes are being strangled. But increasingly, the reasons for his indignation—the values he cherishes—are hard to see in his work. Only the indignation is clear." This is a major characteristic of *Year 501: The Conquest Continues,* in which Chomsky examines what he sees as the U.S. government's shabby behavior toward its neighbors in the hemisphere. His strident denunciations of U.S. imperialism are often conveyed through striking comparisons.

Leiber found an overriding commitment to freedom in the Chomsky's work—"the freedom of the individual to produce and create as he will without the goad of external force, economic competition for survival, or legal and economic restraint on social, intellectual, or artistic experiment; and the freedom of ethnic and national groups to work out their own destinies without the intervention of one or another Big Brother." "From his earliest writings to his latest, Chomsky has looked with astonishment at what the powerful do to the powerless," Morton declared. "He has never let his sense of outrage become dulled. If his voice has grown hoarse over twenty years, who can blame him? And who can feel superior? No one has given himself more deeply to the struggle against the horrors of our time. His hoarseness is a better thing than our suavity." Deutsch wrote: "The most convincing indication of the extent to which Chomsky's wide ranging indictment of United States society and policy must be taken seriously is that a man possessed of these sensibilities should have felt compelled to undertake it." Morton offered a compelling conclusion. "Americans are no longer convinced that our government has the right to destroy any country it wants to," the essayist stated. "And to the extent that this is true, Chomsky, along with others like him, deserves much of the credit. He did his job well."

In 1970 the London *Times* named Chomsky one of the thousand "makers of the twentieth century." According to Yergin, his theory "remains the foundation of linguistics today," and "his vision of a complex universe within the mind, governed by myriad rules and prohibitions and yet infinite in its creative potential, opens up vistas possibly as important as Einstein's theories." Yergin added: "The impact of Chomsky's work may not be felt for years. . . . Yet this beginning has revolutionized the study of language and has redirected and redefined the broad inquiry into intelligence and how it works." Robinson called the scholar's work "a prolonged celebration of the enormous gulf that separates man from the rest of nature. He seems overwhelmed by the intellectual powers that man contains within himself. Certainly nobody ever stated the case for those powers more emphatically, nor exemplified them more impressively in his own work. Reading Chomsky on linguistics, one repeatedly has the impression of attending to one of the more powerful thinkers who ever lived."

Appreciation has likewise attended Chomsky's political writings. According to Christopher Lehmann-Haupt in the *New York Times,* Chomsky "continues to challenge our assumptions long after other critics have gone to bed. He has become the foremost gadfly of our national conscience." Philip Green in the *Nation* wrote that "not to have read his essays . . . is to court genuine ignorance." *New Statesman* correspondent Francis Hope praised Chomsky for "a proud defensive independence, a good plain writer's hatred of expert mystification, a doctrine of resistance which runs against the melioristic and participatory current of most contemporary intellectual life." Hope concluded: "Such men are dangerous; the lack of them is disastrous."

In the new millennium, Chomsky continued to be a leading political voice. His book *Chomsky on Miseducation* does not deal with U.S. schools but rather with the overall miseducation of U.S. citizens in regards to democracy and U.S. foreign policy, which Chomsky continues to assert is tied to the interest of U.S. corporations. In this work, Chomsky focuses mainly on U.S. relations in Central America, claiming, as Terry Christner wrote in *Library Journal,* "that we have condemned the actions of certain factions while condoning similar actions of other factions and have hidden many such things from the American public." Other topics in this book include discussions of the media in terms of news coverage being controlled by a few large corporate companies, which, as Colman McCarthy stated in the *Washington Post,* "have the power not only to slant the news but also to choose what it is." In terms of other types of information, Chomsky also criticizes military officials who control what the public hears about U.S. military involvement in other countries; and he is very much concerned, McCarthy surmised, about "boardroom executives who bankroll the two main political parties so that corporate security equals national security."

After the terrorist attacks on the World Trade Center in New York, Chomsky sat down and wrote the book *9-11,* which was published in 2001 and contains his thoughts on the causes behind the attacks. He puts part of the blame on capitalist globalization; another part on U.S. foreign policy, especially during the Reagan administration in terms of U.S. involvement in Nicaragua. The overall theses of his discussions in this book has carried over into several other books, among them *Middle East Illusions, Hegemony or Survival: America's Quest for Global Dominance,* and *Understanding Power: The Indispensable Chomsky. Understanding Power* is a collection of Chomsky's talks about politics past, present, and future in which he discusses Vietnam, the decline of federally sponsored social programs, and U.S. involvement in the Middle East. Although critical of U.S. government policy and the influence of corporate America in U.S. politics, Chomsky also praises U.S. citizens for their political activism and their skepticism of the information that the media feed them.

"There is a certain exhilaration in reading Chomsky, however depressing his conclusions, because of the vigor of his reasoning, the diversity of his sources and the Voltaire-like energy of his sarcasm," noted *Book* reviewer Penelope Mesic in a review of *Middle East Illusions.* Also written in opposition to U.S. military involvement in the Middle East, *Hegemony or Survival* tracks what Chomsky discerns as a generations-long trend toward U.S. unilateral international shows of force, and, according to *Booklist* contributor Vanessa Bush, "offers a cautionary look" at the "growing threats to world peace and personal freedom" resulting from this trend in U.S. foreign policy. Praising the book as "highly readable and heavily footnoted," as well as "cogent and provocative," a *Publishers Weekly* contributor noted that in bolstering his argument that the United States is a "rogue nation" in the international realm, Chomsky draws on his past works in making *Hegemony or Survival* "an important addition to an ongoing public discussion about U.S. policy."

BIOGRAPHICAL AND CRITICAL SOURCES:

BOOKS

Achbar, Mark, and the Institute of Policy Alternatives, *Manufacturing Consent: Noam Chomsky and the Media: The Companion Book to the Award-winning Film by Peter Wintonick and Mark Achbar,* Black Rose Books (New York, NY), 1994.

Barsky, Robert F., *Noam Chomsky: A Life of Dissent,* MIT Press (Cambridge, MA), 1997.

Botha, Rudolf P., *Challenging Chomsky: The Generative Garden Game,* B. Blackwell (New York, NY), 1989.

Calvin, William, *Lingua ex machina: Reconciling Darwin and Chomsky with the Human Brain,* MIT Press (Cambridge, MA), 2000.

Cohen, David, *Psychologists on Psychology,* Taplinger (New York, NY), 1977.

Cohn, Werner, *Partners in Hate: Noam Chomsky and the Holocaust Deniers,* Avukah Press (Cambridge, MA), 1995.

Contemporary Issues Criticism, Volume 1, Thomson Gale (Detroit, MI), 1982.

Cook, V.J., and Mark Newson, *Chomsky's Universal Grammar,* Basil Blackwell (New York, NY), 1996.

Greene, Judith, *Psycholinguistics: Chomsky and Psychology,* Penguin (New York, NY), 1972.

Haley, Michael C., and Ronald F. Lunsford, *Noam Chomsky,* Twayne (New York, NY), 1994.

Harman, Gilbert, editor, *On Noam Chomsky: Critical Essays,* Anchor Press (New York, NY), 1974.

Harris, Randy Allen, *The Linguistics Wars,* Oxford University Press (New York, NY), 1993.

Huck, Geoffrey J., and John A. Goldsmith, *Ideology and Linguistic Theory: Noam Chomsky and the Deep Structure Debates,* Routledge (New York, NY), 1995.

Kasher, Asa, *The Chomskyan Turn,* Basil Blackwell (New York, NY), 1991.

Kim-Renaud, Young-Key, *Studies in Korean Linguistics,* Hanshin Publishing (Seoul, Korea), 1986.

Leiber, Justin, *Noam Chomsky: A Philosophical Overview,* Twayne (New York, NY), 1975.

Lyons, John, *Noam Chomsky,* 2nd edition, Penguin Books, 1977, third edition, Fontana Press (London, England), 1991.

Mehta, Ved, *John Is Easy to Please,* Farrar, Straus (New York, NY), 1971.

Newmeyer, Frederick J., *Generative Linguistics,* Routledge (New York, NY), 1994.

Osiatynski, Wiktor, *Contrasts: Soviet and American Thinkers Discuss the Future,* Macmillan (New York, NY), 1984.

Otero, Carlos Peregrin, *Noam Chomsky: Critical Assessments,* Routledge (New York, NY), 1994.

Rai, Milan, *Chomsky's Politics,* Verso (New York, NY), 1995.

Rieber, Robert W., editor, *Dialogues on the Psychology of Language and Thought: Conversations with*

Noam Chomsky, Charles Osgood, Jean Piaget, Ulric Neisser, and Marcel Kinsbourne, Plenum (New York, NY), 1983.

Salkie, Raphael, *The Chomsky Update: Linguistics and Politics,* Unwin Hyman (Boston, MA), 1990.

Sampson, Geoffrey, *Liberty and Language,* Oxford University Press (New York, NY), 1979.

Sen Gupta, Kalyan, and Jadavpur University, *Mentalistic Turn, a Critical Evaluation of Chomsky,* K.P. Bagchi & Co./Jadavpur University (Calcutta, India), 1990.

Smith, N. V., *Chomsky: Ideas and Ideals,* Cambridge University Press (New York, NY), 1999.

Smith, N. V., and Deirdre Wilson, *Modern Linguistics: The Results of Chomsky's Revolution,* Penguin Books (New York, NY), 1990.

Thinkers of the Twentieth Century, Thomson Gale (Detroit, MI), 1983.

Wilkin, Peter, *Noam Chomsky: On Power, Knowledge, and Human Nature,* St. Martin's Press (New York, NY), 1997.

Williams, T. C., *Kant's Philosophy of Language: Chomskyan Linguistics and Its Kantian Roots,* E. Mellen Press (Lewiston, NY), 1993.

Winston, Morton Emanuel, *On Chomsky,* Wadsworth/Thomson Learning (Belmont, CA), 2002.

PERIODICALS

America, December 11, 1971; July 15, 1989, p. 42; August 27, 1994, p. 30.

Arena, April, 2001, Ted Wheelwright, review of *Profit of People: Neoliberalism and Global Order,* p. 44.

Atlantic, July, 1973; February, 1982.

Bloomsbury Review, September, 1993.

Book, May-June, 2003, Penelope Mesic, review of *Middle East Illusions,* p. 72.

Booklist, May 1, 2003, John Green, review of *Middle East Illusions,* p. 1567; November 15, 2003, Vanessa Bush, review of *Hegemony or Survival,* p. 551.

Book World, March 23, 1969.

Choice, April, 2000, S.G. Mestrovic, review of *The New Military Humanism: Lessons from Kosovo,* p. 1529; February, 2001, R.M. Stewart, review of *New Horizons in the Study of Language and Mind,* p. 1094; July-August, 2001, F. Cordasco, review of *Chomsky on Miseducation,* p. 2008.

Christian Century, July 23, 1969.

Christian Science Monitor, April 3, 1969; May 14, 1970.

Chronicle of Higher Education, May 12, 1982.

Commentary, May, 1969.

Dissent, January-February, 1970.

East Timor and the Standards of the West, Brendan Simms, review of *A New Generation Draws the Line: Kosovo,* p. 28.

Economist, November 29, 1969.

Globe and Mail (Toronto, Ontario, Canada), June 16, 1984; July 5, 1986.

Guardian, January 20, 2001, Maya Jaggi, "Noam Chomsky," p. 6.

Harvard Education Review, winter, 1969.

Horizon, spring, 1971.

Humanist, November-December, 1990, p. 8.

International Affairs, January, 1971; May, 2003, Bill Hayton, review of *Power and Terror,* pp. 659-660.

Journal of Contemporary Asia, August, 2001, Frederic F. Clairmont, review of *Rogue States: The Rule of Force in World Affairs,* p. 421.

Journal of Linguistics, March, 1998, Jan-Wouter Zwart, review of *The Minimalist Program,* pp. 213-226.

Library Journal, September 1, 1999, Michael Rogers, review of *Fateful Triangle: The United States, Israel, and the Palestinians,* p. 238; October 15, 2000, Terry Christner, review of *Chomsky on Miseducation,* p. 83.

London Review of Books, August 20, 1992.

Los Angeles Times Book Review, December 27, 1981; June 8, 1986; August 30, 1987.

Maclean's, August 18, 1980; March 22, 1993.

Nation, September 9, 1968; March 24, 1969; May 17, 1971; May 8, 1976; March 31, 1979; February 16, 1980; December 22, 1984; December 26, 1987-January 2, 1988; May 7, 1988; May 15, 1989, p. 670.

National Post, January 6, 2001, Christopher Hitchens, "The Importance of Speaking Truth to Noam Chomsky," p. B9.

National Review, June 17, 1969; July 8, 1991, p. 40.

New Republic, April 19, 1969; October 26, 1974; March 13, 1976; February 17, 1979; September 6-13, 1980; March 24, 1982; March 23, 1987; January 9, 1989, p. 34.

New Statesman, November 28, 1969; August 17, 1979; April 25, 1980; July 17, 1981; August 14, 1981; September 11, 1981; January 21, 1983; March 12, 1993, p. 14; April 16, 1993, p. 38; June 3, 1994, p. 22.

New Statesman & Society, July 5, 1991, p. 35; November 27, 1992, p. 43.

Newsweek, March 24, 1969.

New Yorker, November 11, 1969; May 8, 1971.

New York Review of Books, August 9, 1973; January 23, 1975; November 11, 1976; October 23, 1980; February 1, 1996, p. 41.

New York Times, March 18, 1969; August 2, 1973; February 5, 1979; March 8, 1982.

New York Times Book Review, March 16, 1969; January 17, 1971; January 9, 1972; September 30, 1973; October 6, 1974; February 15, 1976; February 25, 1979; October 19, 1980; March 21, 1982; April 13, 1986.

New York Times Magazine, May 6, 1968; December 3, 1972.

Observer (London, England), June 23, 1991.

Progressive, December, 1982; October, 1991, p. 39; October, 1993, p. 41; January, 1995, p. 39.

Psychology Today, July, 1979.

Publishers Weekly, July 24, 2000, review of *Rogue States: The Rule of Force in World Affairs,* p. 76; May 5, 2003, Christopher Dreher, "The Accidental Bestseller," p. 19; October 13, 2003, review of *Hegemony or Survival,* p. 65.

Rolling Stone, May 28, 1992, p. 42.

Saturday Review, May 31, 1969.

Science and Society, spring, 1970.

Scientific American, May, 1990, p. 40.

Sewanee Review, winter, 1977.

Theoria, December, 2003, p. 147.

Times Higher Education Supplement, April 7, 2000, Jacques B.M. Guy, review of *New Horizons in the Study of Language and Mind,* p. 23; May 25, 2001.

Times Literary Supplement, March 27, 1969; March 31, 1972; December 21, 1973; December 12, 1975; September 10, 1976; November 21, 1980; February 27, 1981; July 23, 1982; July 15-21, 1988.

Utne Reader, November-December, 1993, p. 120.

Village Voice, June 18, 1980; June 23, 1980; July 13, 1982.

Virginia Quarterly Review, summer, 1969.

Washington Post, March 4, 2001, Colman McCarthy, review of *Chomsky on Miseducation,* p. T10.

Washington Post Book World, March 11, 1979; March 7, 1982; February 21, 1988.

Whole Earth, summer, 1999, review of *Profit over People: Neoliberalism and Global Order,* p. 24.

ONLINE

Noam Chomsky Archive, http://www.zmag.org/chomsky/ (November 27, 2001).

*   *   *

CISNEROS, Sandra 1954-

PERSONAL: Born December 20, 1954, in Chicago, IL. *Education:* Loyola University, B.A.,1976; University of Iowa Writers' Workshop, M.F.A., 1978.

ADDRESSES: Office—Alfred A. Knopf Books, 201 East 50th St., New York, NY, 10022. *Agent*—Susan Bergholz Literary Services, 17 West 10th St. #5, New York, NY 10011.

CAREER: Writer. Latino Youth Alternative High School, Chicago IL, teacher, 1978-80; Loyola University of Chicago, Chicago, IL, college recruiter and counselor for minority students, 1981-82; Foundation Michael Karolyi, Vence, France, artist-in-residence, 1983; Guadalupe Cultural Arts Center, San Antonio, TX, literature director, 1984-85; guest professor, California State University, Chico, 1987-88, University of California, Berkeley, 1988, University of California, Irvine, 1990, University of Michigan, Ann Arbor, 1990, and the University of New Mexico, Albuquerque, 1991.

MEMBER: PEN, Mujeres por la paz (member and organizer).

AWARDS, HONORS: National Endowment for the Arts fellow, 1982, 1988; American Book Award, Before Columbus Foundation, 1985, for *The House on Mango Street;* Paisano Dobie Fellowship, 1986; Lannan Foundation Literary Award, 1991; H.D.L, State University of New York at Purchase, 1993; MacArthur fellow, 1995; first and second prize in Segundo Concurso Nacional del Cuento Chicano, University of Arizona.

WRITINGS:

The House on Mango Street (novel), Arte Publico (Houston, TX), 1984.

Woman Hollering Creek and Other Stories, Random House (New York, NY), 1991.

Hairs: Pelitos (juvenile; bilingual), illustrated by Terry Ybanez, Knopf (New York, NY), 1994.

Caramelo (novel), Knopf (New York, NY), 2002, Thorndike (Waterville, ME), 2003.

Vintage Cisneros, Vintage (New York, NY), 2004.

POEMS

Bad Boys, Mango Publications (San Jose, CA), 1980.

The Rodrigo Poems, Third Woman Press (Berkeley, CA), 1985.

My Wicked, Wicked Ways, Third Woman Press (Berkeley, CA), 1987.

Loose Woman, Knopf (New York, NY), 1994.

Author of introduction to *The Future Is Mestizo: Life Where Culture Meets,* by Virgilio Elizondo, University Press of Colorado (Boulder, CO), 2000. Contributor to periodicals, including *Imagine, Contact II, Glamour, New York Times, Los Angeles Times, Village Voice* and *Revista Chicano-Riquena.*

SIDELIGHTS: With only a handful of poetry and short story collections, Sandra Cisneros has garnered wide critical acclaim as well as popular success. Drawing heavily upon her childhood experiences and ethnic heritage as the daughter of a Mexican father and Chicana mother, Cisneros addresses poverty, cultural suppression, self-identity, and gender roles in her fiction and poetry. She creates characters who are distinctly Latina/o and are often isolated from mainstream American culture by emphasizing dialogue and sensory imagery over traditional narrative structures. Best known for *The House on Mango Street,* a volume of loosely structured vignettes that has been classified as both a short story collection and a series of prose poems, Cisneros seeks to create an idiom that integrates both prosaic and poetic syntax. "Cisneros is a quintessentially American writer, unafraid of the sentimental; avoiding the clichés of magical realism, her work bridges the gap between Anglo and Hispanic," remarked Aamer Hussein in the *Times Literary Supplement.*

Born in Chicago, Cisneros was the only daughter among seven children. Concerning her childhood, she recalled that because her brothers attempted to control her and expected her to assume a traditional female role, she often felt like she had "seven fathers." The family frequently moved between the United States and Mexico. Cisneros periodically wrote poems and stories throughout her childhood and adolescence, but it was not until she attended the University of Iowa's Writers' Workshop in the late 1970s that she realized her experiences as a Latina woman were unique and outside the realm of dominant American culture.

Following this realization, Cisneros decided to write about conflicts directly related to her upbringing, including divided cultural loyalties, feelings of alienation, and degradation associated with poverty. Incorporating these concerns into *The House on Mango Street,* a work that took nearly five years to complete, Cisneros created the character Esperanza, a poor, Latina adolescent who longs for a room of her own and a house of which she can be proud. Esperanza ponders the disadvantages of choosing marriage over education, the importance of writing as an emotional release, and the sense of confusion associated with growing up. In the story "Hips,"

for example, Esperanza agonizes over the repercussions of her body's physical changes: "One day you wake up and there they are. Ready and waiting like a new Buick with the key in the ignition. Ready to take you where?" Written in a simple style that makes each section of the book sound like a prose poem, the pieces in *The House on Mango Street* won praise for their lyrical narratives, vivid dialogue, and powerful descriptions.

Woman Hollering Creek and Other Stories is a collection of twenty-two narratives revolving around numerous Mexican-American characters living near San Antonio, Texas. Ranging from a few paragraphs to several pages, the stories in this volume contain the interior monologues of individuals who have been assimilated into American culture despite their sense of loyalty to Mexico. In "Never Marry a Mexican," for example, a young Latina begins to feel contempt for her white lover because of her emerging feelings of inadequacy and cultural guilt. And in the title story, a Mexican woman deluded by fantasies of a life similar to that of American soap operas ventures into Texas to marry an American. When she discovers that her husband and marriage share little in common with her TV dreams, she is forced to reappraise her life.

Reviewers have praised the author's vivid characters and distinctive prose in *Woman Hollering Creek and Other Stories.* Noting Cisneros's background as a poet, *Los Angeles Times Book Review* contributor Barbara Kingsolver remarked that "Cisneros has added length and dialogue and a hint of plot to her poems and published them in a stunning collection." Writing in the *Nation,* Patricia Hart claimed that "Cisneros breathes narrative life into her adroit, poetic descriptions, making them mature, fully formed works of fiction." Hart also commended Cisneros's "range of characters" as "broad and lively." Kingsolver, who stated that "nearly every sentence contains an explosive sensory image," concluded that Cisneros "takes no prisoners and has not made a single compromise in her language." Similarly, Bebe Moore Campbell, discussing the work in the *New York Times Book Review,* felt that "the author seduces with precise, spare prose and creates unforgettable characters we want to lift off the page and hang out with for a little while."

Eighteen years after the publication of *The House on Mango Street,* Cisneros published her second novel, *Caramelo.* In what one *Publishers Weekly* contributor considered to be a "major literary event," this novel, like her first, is heavily autobiographical; it also took nine years for her to write. Although much of it draws on her own life, Cisneros uses other people's stories as a resource, too. As she explained to Adriana Lopez in *Library Journal,* "I did a lot of research on people, like an ethnographer. . . . Much of my book is based on real things. Even if I made things up, I could never match what happens in real life." The main character is a teenager named Celaya Reyes, or "Layla," who is the only daughter of eight siblings just like Cisneros. The story is framed by a trip from Chicago to Mexico City, where the family is going to visit Layla's grandparents in a large reunion involving three generations of Reyes. The narrative goes back and forth between past and present as Layla thinks about her own life—and her desire to assert her true identity within her huge family—and the story of her grandmother, Soledad, who was abandoned as a young girl and who eventually becomes the bitter woman Layla thinks of as "Awful Grandmother." The tales are tied together by a *rebozo caramelo,* a shawl that has passed down through the generations from the grandmother's mother down to Layla. Whenever Layla touches her lips to the tassels, the smell and taste of it evokes strong memories in her of a family that has experienced both great joy and great tragedy. Critics of *Caramelo* were impressed with Cisneros's descriptive powers and realistic bilingual dialogue. For example, a *Kirkus Reviews* critic praised "Cisneros' keen eye [which] enlivens descriptions of everything from Chicago's famed Maxwell Street flea market to Soledad's sun-stroked house on Destiny Street"; the reviewer also enjoying the "casually bilingual text." Lopez appreciated the depiction of Mexico City back in the 1920s "when it was the 'Paris of the New World.'" Although a *Publishers Weekly* contributor felt that the scenes of "cross-generational trauma and rapture" might seem "repetitive" at times, the reviewer asserted that the novel is "a landmark work." Lauding *Caramelo* for being "raucous, spirited, and brimming with energy," *Library Journal* contributor Barbara Hoffert particularly enjoyed the way Cisneros weaves all of the elements of her story together "like the fabric in the caramelo."

Cisneros is primarily known for her fiction, but her poetry has also gained recognition. *My Wicked, Wicked Ways* is a collection of sixty poems. "Cisneros's poems are intrinsically narrative, but not large, meandering paragraphs," explained Gary Soto in the *Bloomsbury Review.* "She writes deftly with skill and idea, in the 'show-me-don't-tell-me' vein, and her points leave valuable impressions." Writing in *Belles Lettres,* Andrea Lockett commented that "particularly alluring here are the daring, perceptive, and sometimes rough-hewn expressions about being a modern woman." In her 1994 poetry collection, *Loose Woman,* Cisneros offers a portrait of a fiercely proud, independent woman of Mexican heritage. "Cisneros probes the extremes of perceptions and negotiates the boundary regions that define the self," remarked Susan Smith Nash in a *World Literature Today* review of the collection. Discussing her poetry with David Mehegan of the *Boston Globe,* Cisneros stated that her poetry "is almost a journal of daily life as woman and writer. I'm always aware of being on the frontier. Even if I'm writing about Paris or Sarajevo, I'm still writing about it from this border position that I was raised in."

In all her works, Cisneros incorporates Latino dialect, impressionistic metaphors, and social commentary in ways that reveal the fears and doubts unique to Latinas and women in general. She told Mary B.W. Tabor in a *New York Times* interview, "I am a woman and I am a Latina. Those are the things that make my writing distinctive. Those are the things that give my writing power. They are the things that give it sabor [flavor], the things that give it picante [spice]." However, it was not easy for Cisneros to get to the point where she felt comfortable with asserting herself as a feminist writer because of her upbringing. "I think that growing up Mexican and feminist is almost a contradiction in terms," she told Martha Satz in *Southwest Review.* "For a long time—and it's true for many writers and women like myself who have grown up in a patriarchal culture, like the Mexican culture—I felt great guilt betraying that culture. Your culture tells you that if you step out of line, if you break these norms, you are becoming anglicized, you're becoming the *malinche*—influenced and contaminated by these foreign influences and ideas. But I'm very pleased to be alive among the current generation of women. Many writers are redefining our Mexicanness and it's important if we're going to come to terms with our Mexican culture and our American one as well. . . . I think many of my stories come from dealing with straddling two cultures, and certainly it's something I'm going to deal with in future stories."

BIOGRAPHICAL AND CRITICAL SOURCES:

BOOKS

Chesla, Elizabeth L., *Sandra Cisneros' "The House on Mango Street,"* Research & Education Association (Piscataway, NJ), 1996.

Contemporary Literary Criticism, Thomson Gale (Detroit, MI), Volume 69, 1992, Volume 118, 1999.

Dictionary of Literary Biography, Volume 152: *American Novelists since World War II, Fourth Series,* Thomson Gale, 1995.

Encyclopedia of World Biography, second edition, Thomson Gale (Detroit, MI), 1998.

Herrera-Sobek, María, and Helena María Viramontes, *Chicana Creativity and Criticism: New Frontiers in American Literature,* pp. 233-244.

Horno-Delgado, Asuncion, editor, *Breaking Boundaries: Latina Writing and Critical Reading,* University of Massachusetts Press, 1989, pp. 62-71.

Mirriam-Goldberg, Caryn, *Sandra Cisneros: Latina Writer and Activist,* Enslow (Springfield, NJ), 1998.

Modern American Literature, fifth edition, St. James Press (Detroit, MI), 1999.

Reesman, Jeanne Campbell, *Speaking the Other Self: American Women Writers,* University of Georgia Press, 1997, pp. 278-287.

Reference Guide to American Literature, fourth edition, St. James Press (Detroit, MI), 2000.

Short Story Criticism, Thomson Gale (Detroit, MI), 1999.

Singley, Carol J., and Susan Elizabeth Sweeney, *Anxious Power: Reading, Writing, and Ambivalence in Narrative by Women,* State University of New York Press, 1993, pp. 295-312.

PERIODICALS

America, July 18, 1992, p. 39.

Americas Review, spring, 1987, pp. 69-76.

Belles Lettres, summer, 1993, p. 51; spring, 1995, p. 62.

Bloomsbury Review, July-August, 1988, Gary Soto, review of *My Wicked Wicked Ways,* p. 21.

Boston Globe, May 17, 1994, David Mehegan, p. 73.

Canadian Review of American Studies, fall, 1992, Maria Elena de Valdés, "In Search of Identity in Cisneros' *The House on Mango Street,*" pp. 55-72.

Chicago Tribune, November 19, 1992, Section 5, p. 8; December 20, 1992, Section 2, p. 1.

Chicano-Riquena, fall-winter, 1985, pp. 109-119.

Children's Literature, Volume 23, 1995, Reuben Sánchez, "Remembering Always to Come Back: The Child's Wished-For Escape and the Adult's Self-Empowered Return in Sandra Cisneros's *House on Mango Street,*" pp. 221-241.

Christian Science Monitor, March 12, 1993, p. 12.

Glamour, November, 1990, pp. 256-57.

Horn Book, November-December, 1994, p. 716.

Kirkus Reviews, July 15, 2002, review of *Caramelo,* p. 972.

Library Journal, May 15, 1994, p. 76; September 15, 2002, Barbara Hoffert, review of *Caramelo,* p. 88; September 15, 2002, Adriana Lopez, "Caramel-colored Prose: Sandra Cisneros's *Caramelo,*" p. 90.

Los Angeles Times, May 7, 1991, p. F1.

Los Angeles Times Book Review, April 28, 1991, Barbara Kingsolver, review of *Woman Hollering Creek and Other Stories,* p. 3.

MELUS, summer, 1996, Harryette Mullen, "'A Silence Between Us Like a Language': The Untranslatability of Experience in Sandra Cisneros' *Woman Hollering Creek,*" pp. 3-20.

Mester, fall, 1993, Juan Daniel Busch, "Self-Baptising the Wicked Esperanza: Chicana Feminism and Cultural Contact in *The House on Mango Street,*" pp. 123-134.

Midwest Quarterly, autumn, 1995, Thomas Matchie, "Literary Continuity in Sandra Cisneros's *The House on Mango Street,*" pp. 67-79.

Mirabella, April, 1991, p. 46.

Nation, May 6, 1991, Patricia Hart, review of *Woman Hollering Creek,* p. 597.

Newsweek, June 3, 1991, p. 60.

New York Times, January 7, 1993, Mary B.W. Tabor, interview with Sandra Cisneros, p. C10.

New York Times Book Review, May 26, 1991, Bebe Moore Campbell, review of *Woman Hollering Creek,* p. 6.

Publishers Weekly, March 29, 1991, pp. 74-75; April 25, 1994, p. 61; August 12, 2002, review of *Caramelo,* p. 275.

Quill & Quire, May, 1991, p. 30.

School Library Journal, August, 1994, p. 181.

Southern Review, spring, 1997, "Returning to One's House: An Interview with Sandra Cisneros," pp. 166-185.

Southwest Review, spring, 1997, Martha Satz, "Returning to One's House: An Interview with Sandra Cisneros," pp. 166-185.

Times Literary Supplement, August 13, 1993, Aamer Hussein, p. 18.

Tulsa Studies in Women's Literature, fall, 1995, Jean Wyatt, "On Not Being La Malinche: Border Negotiations of Gender in Sandra Cisneros's 'Never Marry a Mexican' and 'Woman Hollering Creek,'" pp. 243-271.

Washington Post Book World, June 9, 1991, p. 3.

World Literature Today, winter, 1995, Susan Smith Nash, review of *Loose Woman,* p. 145.

*   *   *

CIXOUS, Hélène 1937-

PERSONAL: Surname is pronounced "Seek-sue"; born June 5, 1937, in Oran, Algeria; daughter of Georges (a physician) and Eva (a midwife; maiden name, Klein) Cixous; married, 1955 (divorced, 1964); children: Anne

Berger, Pierre-François Berger. *Education:* Received Agregation d'Anglais, 1959, and Docteur es Lettres, 1968.

ADDRESSES: Office—Université de Paris VIII, 2 rue de la Liberte, 93526 St. Denis Cedex 02, France; Éditions des Femmes, 6 rue de Mezieres, 75006 Paris, France.

CAREER: University of Bordeaux, Bordeaux, France, assistante, 1962-65; University of Paris (Sorbonne), Paris, France, maitre assistante, 1965-67; University of Paris X, Nanterre, France, maitre de conference, 1967-68; cofounder of experimental University of Paris VIII, Vincennes (then St. Denis), France, 1968, professor of English literature, beginning 1968, founder and director of Centre de Recherches en Etudes Feminines and doctoral program in women's studies, beginning 1974; cofounder of *Revue de Theorie et d'Analyse Litteraire: Poetique,* 1969. Visiting professor and lecturer at numerous universities, including Columbia University, Cornell University, Dartmouth College, Harvard University, New York University, Northwestern University, State University of New York at Binghamton and Buffalo, Swarthmore University, University of Wisconsin—Madison, University of California at Berkeley, and universities in Austria, Canada, Denmark, England, Greece, India, Italy, Japan, Norway, Tunisia, and Spain.

AWARDS, HONORS: Prix Medicis, 1969, for *Dedans;* Southern Cross of Brazil, 1989; Legion d'Honneur, 1994; Prix des Critiques for best theatrical work, 1994, for *La Ville parjure, ou le reveil des Erinyes;* Doctor Honoris Causa, Queen's University, Canada, 1991, Edmonton University, Canada, 1992, York University, England, 1993, Georgetown University, 1995, and Northwestern University, 1996; Amb of Star Awards, Pakistan, 1997; Officier, Ordre Nationale du Merite, 1998.

WRITINGS:

FICTION

Le prenom de dieu (stories), Grasset et Fasquelle (Paris, France), 1967.

Dedans, Grasset et Fasquelle (Paris, France), 1969, 2nd edition, Femmes (Paris, France), 1986, translation by Carol Barko published as *Inside,* Schocken (New York, NY), 1986.

Le troisiéme corps, Grasset et Fasquelle (Paris, France), 1970, translation by Keith Cohen published as *The Third Body,* Northwestern University Press (Chicago, IL), 1999.

Les commencements, Grasset et Fasquelle (Paris, France), 1970.

Un vrai jardin (poetic short story), L'Herne (Paris, France), 1971.

Neutre, Grasset et Fasquelle (Paris, France), 1972, translated and with an introduction by Lorene M. Birden published as *Neuter,* Bucknell University Press (Lewisburg, PA), 2004.

Portrait du soleil, Denoël (Paris, France), 1973.

Tombe, Seuil (Paris, France), 1973.

Revolutions pour plus d'un Faust, Seuil (Paris, France), 1975.

Souffles, Femmes (Paris, France), 1975.

La, Gallimard (Paris, France), 1976, 2nd edition, Femmes (Paris, France), 1979.

Partie, Femmes (Paris, France), 1976.

Angst, Femmes (Paris, France), 1977, translation by Jo Levy published as *Angst,* Riverrun Press (New York, NY), 1985.

Preparatifs de noces au dela de l'abime, Femmes (Paris, France), 1978.

Ananke, Femmes (Paris, France), c. 1979.

Vivre l'orange/To Live the Orange (bilingual edition), English translation by Ann Liddle and Sarah Cornell, Femmes (Paris, France), 1979.

Illa, Femmes (Paris, France), 1980.

With; ou, l'art de l'innocence, Femmes (Paris, France), 1981.

Limonade tout etait si infini, Femmes (Paris, France), 1982.

Le livre de Promethea, Gallimard (Paris, France), 1983, translation by Betsy Wing published as *The Book of Promethea,* University of Nebraska Press (Lincoln, NE), 1991.

La bataille d'Arcachon (tale), Trois (Laval, Quebec, Canada), 1986.

Manne aux Mandelstams aux Mandelas, Femmes (Paris, France), 1988, translation by Catherine A.F. MacGillivray published as *Manna: For the Mandelstams for the Mandelas,* University of Minnesota Press (Minneapolis, MN), 1993.

Jours de l'an, Femmes (Paris, France), 1990, translated by Catherine A.F. MacGillivray as *First Days of the Year,* University of Minnesota Press (Minneapolis, MN), 1997.

L'ange au secret, Femmes (Paris, France), 1991.

Deluge, Femmes (Paris, France), 1992.

Beethoven à jamais; ou, l'existence de dieu, Femmes (Paris, France), 1993.

The Hélène Cixous Reader, Routledge (New York, NY), 1994.

La fiancée juive; ou, de la tentation, Femmes (Paris, France), 1995.

Messie, Femmes (Paris, France), 1996.

Or: les lettres de mon père, Femmes (Paris, France), 1997.

Osnabruck, Femmes (Paris, France), 1999.

Le jour; ou, je n'etais pas la, Galilee (Paris, France), 2000, translation by Beverley Bie Brahic published as *The Day I Wasn't There,* Northwestern University Press (Evanston, IL), 2004.

Veils, translated by Geoffrey Bennington, with drawings by Ernest Pignon-Ernest, Stanford University Press (Stanford, CA), 2001.

Rêve je te dis (fiction collection), Galilée (Paris, France), 2003.

ESSAYS

L'exil de James Joyce; ou, l'art du remplacement (doctoral thesis), Grasset et Fasquelle (Paris, France), 1968, translation by Sally A.J. Purcell published as *The Exile of James Joyce,* D. Lewis (New York, NY), 1972.

Prenoms de personne, Seuil (Paris, France), 1974.

(With Catherine Clement) *La jeune nee,* Union Generale, 1975, translation by Betsy Wing published as *The Newly Born Woman,* introduction by Sandra M. Gilbert, University of Minnesota Press (Minneapolis, MN), 1986.

Un K incomprehensible: Pierre Goldman, Bourgois, 1975.

(With Madeleine Gagnon and Annie Leclerc) *La venue a l'ecriture,* Union Generale, c. 1977.

Entre l'ecriture, Femmes (Paris, France), c. 1986.

L'heure de Clarice Lispector: precede de vivre l'orange (literary criticism), Femmes (Paris, France), 1989, translation by Verena Andermatt Conley published as *Reading with Clarice Lispector,* University of Minnesota Press (Minneapolis, MN), 1990.

"Coming to Writing," and Other Essays, translation by Sarah Cornell and others, Harvard University Press (Cambridge, MA), 1991.

Readings: The Poetics of Blanchot, Joyce, Kafka, Kleist, Lispector, and Tsvetaeva (literary criticism), translated, edited, and with an introduction by Verena Andermatt Conley, University of Minnesota Press (Minneapolis, MN), 1992.

Three Steps on the Ladder of Writing (lectures), translation by Sarah Cornell and Susan Sellers, introduction by Jacques Derrida, Columbia University Press (New York, NY), 1993.

(With Mireille Calle-Gruber) *Hélène Cixous: Photos de racines,* Femmes (Paris, France), 1994, translation by Eric Prenowitz published as *Hélène Cixous, Rootprints: Memories and Life Writing,* Routledge (New York, NY), 1997.

Stigmata: Surviving Texts, Routledge (New York, NY), 1998.

Les rêveries de la femme sauvage: scènes primitives, Galilee (Paris, France), 1999.

Benjamin à Montaigne: il ne faut pas le dire, Galilee (Paris, France), 2001.

Manhattan: lettres de la préhistoire (autobiography), Galilee (Paris, France), 2002.

Portrait de Jacques Derrida en jeune saint juif, [France], translation by Beverley Bie Brahic published as *Portrait of Jacques Derrida as a Young Jewish Saint,* Columbia University Press (New York, NY), 2003.

Author of manifesto "Le rida de la Meduse" (title means "The Laugh of the Medusa"). Work represented in anthologies, including *New French Feminisms,* edited by Elaine Marks and Isabelle de Courtivron, University of Massachusetts Press (Amherst, MA), 1980, and *The Future of Literary Theory,* edited by Ralph Cohen, 1987. Contributor to numerous periodicals.

PLAYS

La Pupille, Gallimard (Paris, France), 1972.

Portrait de Dora (produced in Paris, France, 1976), Femmes (Paris, France), 1976, translation by Anita Barrow published as *Portrait of Dora,* in *Benmussa Directs,* Riverrun Press, 1979.

La Prise de l'ecole de Madhubai (produced in Paris, France, 1983), translation by Deborah Carpenter published as *The Conquest of the School at Madhubai* in *Women and Performance 3,* 1986.

L'Histoire terrible mais inachevee de Norodom Sihanouk, roi du Cambodge (produced in Paris, France, at Theatre du Soleil, 1985), translation by Juliet Flower MacCannell and others published as *The Terrible but Unfinished Story of Norodom Sihanouk, King of Cambodia,* University of Nebraska Press (Lincoln, NE), 1994.

Theatre (collection), Femmes (Paris, France), 1986.

L'Indiade; ou, L'inde de leurs reves, produced in Paris, France, at Theatre du Soleil, 1987.

On ne part pas, on ne revient pas, introduction by Jacques Derrida, Femmes (Paris, France), 1991.

(Translator and author of introduction) *Les Eumenides d'Eschyle,* produced in Paris, France, 1992.

La Ville parjure; ou, Le reveil des Erinyes, produced in Paris, France, 1994.

Voile noir voile blanche/Black Sail White Sail (bilingual; English translation by Catherine A.F. MacGillivray produced in London, England, 1994), New Literary History (Minnesota), 1994.

L'Histoire qu'on ne connaitra jamais (produced in Paris), Femmes (Paris, France), 1994.

Tambours sur la digue, produced in Paris, France, at Theatre du Soleil, 1999.

Rouen, la treintième nuit de mai '31, Galilee (Paris, France), 2001.

Selected Plays, Routledge (New York, NY), 2003.

Also author of teleplay with Ariane Mnouchkine, *La Nuit miraculeuse,* 1989; author of radio play *Amour d'une delicatesse,* 1982.

OTHER

Le nom d'Oedipe: chant du corps interdit (libretto), music by Andre Boucourechliev, Femmes (Paris, France), 1978, translation by Christiane Makward and Judith Miller published as *The Name of Oedipus* in *Out of Bounds: Women's Theatre in French,* University of Michigan Press (Ann Arbor, MI), 1991.

Contributor to books, including Russel Banks, *Le voyage en Palestine de la délégation du Parlement International des Écrivains en Réponse à un Appel de Mahmoud Darwish: suivi de l'appel pour la paix en Palestine du 6 mars 2002,* Climats (Castelnau-le-Lez, France), c. 2002.

SIDELIGHTS: Hélène Cixous, a professor at the University of Paris and the founder and director of France's only doctoral program in women's studies, won the 1969 Prix Medicis for her first novel, *Dedans,* translated as *Inside. La jeune nee,* which she wrote in 1976 with Catherine Clement and which was translated ten years later as *The Newly Born Woman,* was deemed a "ground-breaking feminist tract" by a *New York Times Book Review* critic. Cixous also received wide acclaim for her doctoral thesis, published in 1968 as *L'exil de James Joyce; ou, L'art du remplacement* and translated in 1972 as *The Exile of James Joyce.* Although she supports and writes women's literature, Cixous once noted that she eschews the label "feminist" because of the politically restrictive and unanalyzed overtones the term has gained in its French context. She related to Stella Hughes in the *Times Higher Education Supplement:* "'Feminist' has an extremely precise meaning: It is a reformist demand in terms of equality and not at all in terms of difference." Cixous prefers the concept and the practice of what she calls the "poetics of sexual difference," and is one of the best-known and most influential advocates of *ecriture feminine,* or feminine writing—a form she notes may include works by both male and female writers. "This writing is dedicated to exploding the binary oppositions on which Western thinking rests," explained Marianne Hirsch in the *New York Times Book Review,* "which relegate woman to the side of silence, of otherness."

Cixous, like other French feminist writers, emphasizes "the place of 'woman' in language and the question of a feminine relation to language that [has] relatively little currency within Anglophone feminist thought," explained translator Annette Kuhn in *Signs.* Some critics find Cixous's writings an attempt to negate the male/female distinction through puns and word manipulations. According to Cixous, her aim is to defuse the violence of fixed sexual hierarchy without negating the infinite richness of sexual difference, by engaging all the resources of language, subverting standard usages or pushing them further than their conventionally fixed forms allow. She plays with the apparent rigidity of the grammatical gender that marks the French language, which, unlike English, has "masculine" and "feminine" words. Her aim is not to replace one rigid linguistic system with another, in a reformist shuffle, but rather to use the possibilities of language to take readers beyond their own self-imposed boundaries.

The English translation of Cixous's award-winning first novel was published as *Inside* in 1986, seventeen years after the original French edition appeared. The highly metaphoric work is commonly regarded as an autobiography, although the author did not introduce the book as such. The main character, like Cixous, was born of a North African Jewish father and a German Jewish mother and was raised in Algeria. The novel depicts the daughter's intense love for her father and the grief she suffers when he dies young, as Cixous's father did. "It dwells on a sense of enclosure and entrapment," Hirsch described. "The nameless narrator . . . is inside a family romance where her father is God, the owner of all the words, and where her German-speaking mother offers no access to knowledge." After her father dies, the daughter imagines his death ceaselessly, trying to understand it. Finally, related Hirsch, "she gains the means to write from [her father's] overwhelming bodily closeness and from his empowering mental gifts in life."

Some feminists decried the importance of the father's role in *Inside* as defeating the purpose of feminism, and a *Kirkus Reviews* critic deemed the "densely compact philosophical narrative" simply "intellectual passion from the school of radical French narrative, by turns brilliant and boring." Hirsch, however, offered high praise for the "series of reflections on identity, death and writing." The reviewer noted that *Inside* was timely as well as poignant, calling it a "moving and disturbing experimental work written at the moment of emergence of feminist consciousness—both for the author herself and for a broader intellectual and political movement whose important representative she would become."

Cixous maintains her "special and elusive style" in *Angst,* according to Lorna Sage in the London *Observer.* The novel, first published in 1977, was translated into English in 1985. "The writing is dense, direct, often lurid with metaphor as it records a woman's reflections on her life and her attempt to create mental order out of the chaos she finds," wrote Sage. Nicole Irving, in the *Times Literary Supplement,* praised Cixous's innovative prose style as well as the "loving" translation by Jo Levy, despite calling much of the book "incomprehensible." The reviewer noted that Cixous's "text has a rhythmic pattern, moving from obscurity to relative clarity, from the bodily (erotic and otherwise) to the sometimes punning metaphysical, from violence to calm and occasional tenderness, and at the end, 'she' [the main character] reaches a wholeness." As Sage observed: "The writing is alive even at its oddest."

Like Hirsch and Schneider, Olga Prjevalinskaya Ferrer observed in her *World Literature Today* review of the 1976 novel *Partie* that "Cixous's works most certainly voice a protest against the very strict rules of French intellectual thought and its expression through speech and writing." Perhaps as a protest against even the traditional appearance of books, Ferrer speculated, Cixous presented the work as a wide book divided into two sections, each upside down in relation to the other, with pages meeting in the middle of the volume. Commenting on the difficulty of classifying *Partie* in terms of genre, Ferrer stated that, although Cixous's "writings are, most of the time, poetic, her originality and freedom have surpassed any poetic thought, any poetic trends." The author's freedom of expression, the reviewer asserted, provides *Partie* with "an enchanting depth."

In *Osnabruck* Cixous creates yet another unique work of fiction. She is well known for her experimentation with words, coining new phrases, and taking eccentric liberties with her writing, and this novel is no exception. But, as Pamela A. Genova noted in *World Literature Today,* "*Osnabruck* distinguishes itself from Cixous's earlier works [because it] delves deeply into the realm of the personal, into Cixous's private musings on her own family history." Set against the backdrop of the German community of Osnabruck, a town with a turbulent political history, the author frames her personal reflections on family within the greater context of human history. As Cixous related to Stuart Jeffries in the *Guardian,* "We live in realistic circumstances and desperately need poetic expression and passion. I always want to express my views ethically and politically."

Even though the feminist movement that brought Cixous to the fore lost momentum by the late twentieth century, she has continued to strengthen her reputation as a highly inventive writer. Her publications included literary criticism, dramas, essays, and books that many reviewers consider unclassifiable. *Modern Language Review* contributor Clare Hanson commented on Cixous's *Reading with Clarice Lispector,* an analysis of the late Latin-American author: "Cixous's approach to Lispector mirrors that capacity to mark difference without recourse to binary, hierarchical oppositions which distinguishes Lispector's texts." The reviewer also noted: "What emerges is a reading . . . which is both powerful and delicate, in which Cixous holds in balance her own theoretical sophistication and the different economies, drives, and trajectories of Lispector's texts." Cixous discussed her own writing, and more, in her 1991 publication *L'ange au secret.* Patricia M. Gathercole stated in *World Literature Today* that the book contains "observations about human life and [Cixous's] own struggles in writing a book" and added, "The volume is . . . written in a highly imaginative style . . . [and] offers a powerful account of her own feelings and thoughts, her reflections on her identity as a writer."

On ne part pas, on ne revient pas was also published in 1991. *World Literature Today* reviewer Bettina L. Knapp called the work "perhaps one of Helen Cixous's finest and most powerful works," noting that the book "deals with death, love, sorrow, escape, violence—and music. As is true of many of Cixous's writings, it may be read on many levels. The work is a drama written in free verse, cadenced and stressed in keeping with the magma of sought-for meanings." *Three Steps on the Ladder of Writing,* also released by Cixous in 1991, contains the text of a lecture series she delivered at the University of California—Irvine. In his introduction to this work, Jacques Derrida commented: "Cixous is today, in my view, the greatest writer in what I will call my language, the French language if you like. And I am weighing my words as I say that. For a great writer must be a poet-thinker, very much a poet and a very thinking poet."

In 1993 Cixous reached a new level of creativity, according to Genova. Reviewing *Beethoven à jamais; ou,*

L'existence de dieu for *World Literature Today,* Genova marveled at Cixous's skill in weaving together many styles of writing. *Beethoven a jamais* "combines elements from several styles of writing, weaving together such forms as free verse, interior monologue, spoken dialogue, and third-person narrative prose," noted Genova. "This experimentation seems appropriate in a book whose central personality is that of Beethoven, present in all his forms: the man, the musical genius, the lover. Instead of merely describing the life or work of Beethoven, Cixous constructs a textual framework that reflects his talent and stands as a hymn to Beethoven and his music."

With; ou, L'art de l'innocence is about woman's multiplicity. "Cixous's sinuous prose poem is a conversation between various aspects of her person," explained Rosette C. Lamont in *World Literature Today.* Although the author's various selves are disparate, Lamont observed, "the many voices of Cixous's novel-poem blend into a single interrogation about freedom, a multilingual existence in *l'ecriture* and the mystery of being woman." Moving from a women's-eye view of the world to a broader perspective, her 2001 work *Benjamin à Montaigne: Il ne faut pas le dire* focuses on the history of the German people during the Holocaust. The story of Cixous's mother, who translates the events around her through an outsider's French-language perspective, the book is also a vehicle for Cixous to reflect on broader issues. As Genova noted in *World Literature Today,* "The problem of shame and disgrace, of the possibly unattainable desire for redemption and salvation, colors the often poetic passages in which Cixous offers her thoughts on issues of national identity and the development of a new nation-state."

Attempting another autobiographical work in 1997, Cixous published *Hélène Cixous, Rootprints: Memory and Life Writing.* The book reflects on her childhood in Algeria where she grew up in a city with heavy French, Arabic, and Spanish influences. Her parents, Jewish, chose to live in a non-European neighborhood. Cixous remembers feeling a distinct lack of identity while growing up, and she mixes these memories with historical references to the French colonial rule in Algeria. Jeffries, in the *Guardian,* called this collection of reflections "a fascinating life story," but he also felt that Cixous's "fractured allusive writing" makes the narrative incoherent at times.

In 1998 Cixous published two texts that revisit and rearrange her earlier ideas about women's writing and the body. *First Days of the Year,* written in essay form, examines the connection between writing and the female character. *Stigmata* is a collection of essays about topics ranging from sexual issues, to postcolonial and literary theory, to life and love. Nicole Cooley, in the *Review of Contemporary Fiction,* remarked that "Cixous's subversion of genre distinction is endlessly fascinating."

The author's fiction and nonfiction works continue to be translated into English, including *Le Jour; ou, Je n'etais pas la,* translated as as *The Day I Wasn't There,* and *Portrait of Jacques Derrida as a Young Jewish Saint.* In the *The Day I Wasn't There,* Cixous presents a memoir-novel in which the narrator tells about the premature death of her first-born child, who was a Down's syndrome baby. As she tells the story, the narrator explores the narrator's family history, including her mother, who was a Nazi Germany refugee, her dead father, and a brother who is a medical student. The story ultimately ties into the baby's death as the meaning of the title becomes agonizingly clear. *Portrait of Jacques Derrida as a Young Jewish Saint* is Cixous's look at the roles that Jewishness and non-Jewishness play in the life and works of her lifelong friend and renowned philosopher. In the process of creating a comprehensive portrait of Derrida, Cixous discusses everything from family relationships to the influence of writers and philosophers such as Celan, Rousseau, and others.

"Cixous tells us that she always wished she were a painter, and that this accounts for the way she writes," mused Peter Baker in an *American Book Review* piece on Cixous's *"Coming to Writing" and Other Essays.* "Somehow she manages to paint with words in such a way as actually to bring about an insight into what this might mean. Like the mimosa, which overwhelms the senses but recedes, sensitive to the touch, Cixous overwhelms the written word with layers of thought and sense-description, while withdrawing any possible center or point. As she says: 'And the lesson is: one does not paint ideas. One does not paint *a subject.* And in the same way: no writing ideas. There is no subject. There are only mysteries.'"

BIOGRAPHICAL AND CRITICAL SOURCES:

BOOKS

Calle-Gruber, Mireille, editor, *On the Feminine,* Humanities Press (Atlantic Highlands, NJ), 1996.
Cixous, Hélène, *On ne part pas, on ne revient pas,* introduction by Jacques Derrida, Femmes (Paris, France), 1991.

Conley, Verena Andermatt, *Writing the Feminine,* University of Nebraska Press (Lincoln, NE), 1984, expanded edition, 1991.

Conley, Verena Andermatt, *Hélène Cixous,* University of Toronto Press (Toronto, Ontario, Canada), 1992.

Dictionary of Literary Biography, Volume 83: *French Novelists since 1960,* Thomson Gale (Detroit, MI), 1989, pp. 52-61.

Kim, C.W. Maggie, and others, editors, *Transfigurations: Theology and the French Feminists,* Fortress Press (Minneapolis, MN), 1993.

Moi, Toril, *Sexual/Textual Politics: Feminist Literary Theory,* Methuen (New York, NY), 1985.

Nordquist, Joan, *French Feminist Theory: Luce Irigaray and Hélène Cixous: A Bibliography,* Reference and Research Services (Santa Cruz, CA), 1990.

Penrod, Lynn, *Hélène Cixous,* Twayne (New York, NY), 1996.

Sellers, Susan, *Hélène Cixous: Authorship, Autobiography, and Love,* Blackwell (Cambridge, MA), 1996.

Shiach, Morag, *Hélène Cixous: A Politics of Writing,* Routledge (London, England), 1991.

Stambolian, George, and Elaine Marks, editors, *Homosexuality and French Literature,* Cornell University Press (Ithaca, NY), 1979.

Wilcox, Helen, editor, *The Body and the Text: Hélène Cixous,* St. Martin's Press (New York, NY), 1990.

PERIODICALS

American Book Review, June-July, 1992, pp. 16, 18-19.

College Literature, winter, 2003, Lynn Penrod, "Algeriance, Exile, and Hélène Cixous," p. 135.

Contemporary Literature, summer, 1983.

French Forum, fall, 2001, Cynthia Running-Johnson, "Cixous's Left and Right Hands of Writing in *Tambours sur la digue* and *Osnabruck,*" p. 111; spring, 2003, Mairead Hanrahan, "Of Three-legged Writing," p. 99.

French Review, March, 1999, p. 719; May, 1999, p. 1142; March, 2002, Laurence Enjolras, review of *Le Jour; ou, Je n'etais pas la,* p. 823.

French Studies, April, 2001, Miread Hanrahan, review of *Le Livre de Promethea,* p. 195.

Guardian (London, England), October 29, 1997, Stuart Jeffries, "A Bit of the Other" (interview with Cixous), p. 4.

Hypatia, fall, 2002, Laura Camille Tuley, "On Cardiac Rhythms," p. 218.

Kirkus Reviews, September 1, 1986, review of *Inside.*

Library Journal, June 15, 1993, p. 19; June 1, 1994, p. 106; September 1, 1997, Marilyn Gaddis Rose, review of *Hélène Cixous, Rootprints: Memory and Life Writing,* p. 181; July, 1998, Ali Houissa, review of *First Days of the Year,* p. 89; January, 1999, Robert T. Ivey, review of *Stigmata,* p. 95; September 1, 1999, Amy Irvine, review of *The Third Body,* p. 231.

Modern Language Review, October, 1993, pp. 934-936; January, 1998, Mairead Hanrahan, review of *Portrait de Dora,* p. 48.

New York Times, June 8, 1994, p. C13.

New York Times Book Review, February 11, 1973; August 24, 1986; December 7, 1986.

Observer (London, England), January 12, 1986; April 3, 1994, p. 22.

Publishers Weekly, March 21, 1994, pp. 55-56; July 12, 1999, review of *The Third Body,* p. 88.

Quebec Studies, fall-winter, 2003, Edith Vandervoort, "When They Were Young: Adolescent Representations in *Les fous de Bassan,*" p. 69.

Review of Contemporary Fiction, spring, 1998, Mary Lydon, review of *Hélène Cixous, Rootprints,* p. 234; summer, 1999, Nicole Cooley, review of *First Days of the Year,* p. 135; spring, 2000, Tara Reeser, review of *The Third Body,* p. 181.

Romanic Review, November, 1999, Mairead Hanrahan, "Hélène Cixous's Improper Name," p. 481.

Signs, autumn, 1981.

Theatre Journal, March, 1994, pp. 31-44.

Theatre Research International, autumn, 1998, Sandra Freeman, "Bisexuality in Cixous's 'Le nom d'Oedipe,'" p. 242.

Times Literary Supplement, April 24, 1969; February 12, 1971; March 21, 1986; January 31, 1992, p. 24; December 24, 1993, p. 18; August 13, 1999, Elizabeth Fallaize, review of *Stigmata,* p. 24.

Triquarterly, fall, 1997, pp. 259-279.

Women's Review, May, 1985.

World Literature Today, winter, 1977; spring, 1977; summer, 1977; spring, 1981; summer, 1982; winter, 1984; summer, 1992, p. 482; winter, 1993, pp. 148-149; winter, 1994, p. 76; autumn, 1999, Pamela A. Genova, review of *Osnabruck,* p. 694; spring, 2002, Pamela A. Genova, review of *Benjamin à Montaigne,* p. 121.

ONLINE

Erratic Impact, http://www.erraticimpact.com/ (June 17, 2004).

Stanford Presidential Lectures Web site, http://prelectur.stanford.edu/ (June 17, 2004).

*   *   *

CLANCY, Thomas L.
See CLANCY, Tom

CLANCY, Tom 1947-
(Thomas L. Clancy)

PERSONAL: Born 1947, in Baltimore, MD; son of a mail carrier and a credit employee; married Wanda Thomas (an insurance agency manager), August, 1969 (divorced, 1998); married; wife's name Alex; children: (first marriage) Michelle, Christine, Tom, Kathleen. *Education:* Graduated from Loyola College, Baltimore, MD, 1969. *Politics:* Conservative. *Religion:* Roman Catholic.

ADDRESSES: Home—P.O. Box 800, Huntingtown, MD 20639- 0800. *Agent*—c/o Author Mail, Putnam Berkley Group, 200 Madison Ave., New York, NY 10016.

CAREER: Writer. Insurance agent in Baltimore, MD, and Hartford, CT, until 1973; O.F. Bowen Agency (insurance company), Owings, MD, agent, beginning 1973, owner, beginning 1980. *Military service:* U.S. Army Reserve Officers Training Corps.

WRITINGS:

NOVELS

The Hunt for Red October, Naval Institute Press (Annapolis, MD), 1984.
Red Storm Rising (also see below), Putnam (New York, NY), 1986.
Patriot Games (also see below), Putnam (New York, NY), 1987.
The Cardinal of the Kremlin (also see below), Putnam (New York, NY), 1988.
Clear and Present Danger (also see below), Putnam (New York, NY), 1989.
The Sum of All Fears (also see below), Putnam (New York, NY), 1991.
Red Storm Rising; The Cardinal of the Kremlin: Two Complete Novels, Putnam (New York, NY), 1993.
Without Remorse, Putnam (New York, NY), 1994.
Debt of Honor, Putnam (New York, NY), 1994.
Three Complete Novels: Patriot Games, Clear and Present Danger, The Sum of All Fears, Putnam (New York, NY), 1994.
Executive Orders, Putnam (New York, NY), 1996.
Rainbow Six, Putnam (New York, NY), 1998.
The Bear and the Dragon, Putnam (New York, NY), 2000.
Red Rabbit, Putnam (New York, NY), 2002.
The Teeth of the Tiger, Putnam (New York, NY), 2003.

Also creator of novel series written by others, including (with Steve Pieczenik) "Op-Center," (with Martin Greenberg) "Power Plays," (with Pieczenik) "Net Force," and (with David Michaels) "Splinter Cell," all published by Berkley.

NONFICTION

Submarine: A Guided Tour inside a Nuclear Warship, Putnam (New York, NY), 1993, revised edition, written with John Gresham, Berkley (New York, NY), 2003.
Armed Cav: A Guided Tour of an Armored Calvary Regiment, Putnam (New York, NY), 1994.
Fighter Wing: A Guided Tour of an Air Force Combat Wing, Berkley (New York, NY), 1995.
Reality Check: What's Going On out There?, Putnam (New York, NY), 1995.
Marine: A Guided Tour of a Marine Expeditionary Unit, Berkley (New York, NY), 1996.
Airborne: A Guided Tour of an Airborne Task Force, Berkley Books (New York, NY), 1997.
Carrier: A Guided Tour of an Aircraft Carrier, Berkley (New York, NY), 1999.
(With Martin Greenberg) *SSN: Strategies of Submarine Warfare,* Berkley (New York, NY), 2000.
(With John Gresham) *Special Forces: A Guided Tour of U.S. Army Special Forces,* Berkley (New York, NY), 2001.
(With John Gresham) *Submarine: A Guided Tour Inside a Nuclear Warship,* Berkely (New York, NY), 2003.

NONFICTION; "COMMANDERS" SERIES

(With General Fred Franks, Jr.) *Into the Storm: A Study in Command,* Putnam (New York, NY), 1997.
(With General Chuck Horner) *Every Man a Tiger,* Putnam (New York, NY), 1999.
(With General Carl Stiner and Tony Koltz) *Shadow Warriors: Inside the Special Forces,* Putnam (New York, NY), 2002.
(With General Tony Zinni and Tom Koltz), *Battle Ready,* Putnam (New York, NY), 2004.

Contributor to *Fighting Chance: Journeys through Childhood Cancer,* Woodholme House (Baltimore, MD), 1998. Also author of foreword to *Silent Chase: Submarines of the U.S. Navy,* by Steve Kaufman, Thomasson-Grant, 1989, and *Future War: Non-Lethal Weapons in Modern Warfare,* by John B. Alexander, St. Martin's Press (New York, NY), 1999.

ADAPTATIONS: The Hunt for Red October was adapted as a film for Paramount, directed by John Mc-Tiernan and starring Sean Connery and Alec Baldwin, 1990; *Patriot Games* was adapted as a film for Paramount, directed by Phillip Noyce and starring Harrison Ford and Anne Archer, 1992; *Clear and Present Danger* was adapted as a film for Paramount, directed by Phillip Noyce and starring Harrison Ford and Willem Dafoe, 1994; *The Sum of All Fears* was adapted for a film from Paramount starring Ben Affleck and Morgan Freeman, 2002, and as a video game by Michael Knight, Prima Games (Roseville, CA), 2002. Several of Clancy's novels have been adapted as audio books.

SIDELIGHTS: Tom Clancy has single-handedly created a new thriller genre; franchised his name into audio, movies, and computer games; and sold over a hundred million copies of his military and espionage thrillers worldwide. One of only a select group of authors whose hardcover releases are launched with multimillion-copy printings, Clancy is, according to Jeff Zaleski in *Publishers Weekly,* "more than an author. Just as Walt Disney was more than an animator. He is the producer of a distinctive and innovative body of work, a brand name much as Disney is."

Known for his hugely successful, detailed novels about espionage, the U.S. military, and advanced military technology, Clancy was proclaimed "king of the techno-thriller" by Patrick Anderson in the *New York Times Magazine.* Since the 1984 publication of his first novel, the acclaimed *Hunt for Red October,* all of his books have become best-sellers. As Rich Cohen wrote in *Rolling Stone,* "Indeed, Clancy seems to have saturated the national consciousness, creating a new American style, a hybrid of rugged individualism and high technology." Although popular with armed forces personnel as well as with the public, Clancy's work has also received more negative attention from officials who have found his extrapolations from declassified information uncomfortably close to top-secret reality. Reviewers have also criticized his characterizations and too-perfect weaponry. Still, sales in the millions and constant best-seller status attest to Clancy's continued popularity as "novelist laureate of the military-industrial complex," as Ross Thomas described him in the *Washington Post Book World.*

While Clancy was writing insurance policies for a living, he became a military history buff, specializing in naval history and ultimately becoming something of an expert in military history and weapons technology. Gradually, Clancy put these interests together and be-

gan writing a novel in his spare time. "Writing a novel is murderously hard work—worse than I can say," Clancy wrote in a letter to friends in 1983, toward the end of the creation of *The Hunt for Red October,* when he was still balancing full-time work as an insurance broker, being the father of four children, and attempting to become a novelist.

When Clancy finished his massive first novel, he sent the manuscript off to many publishing houses. After receiving rejections from them, he learned that the Naval Institute Press, which had published only nonfiction for over a century, was going to begin publishing fiction. Clancy sent the book off to them and they bought it for $5,000, subsequently selling off paperback rights to Berkley Books, an imprint of Putnam, for almost $50,000. His first novel also won him the sponsorship of a young agent, Robert Gottlieb, who helped to steer Clancy's career into a mega-star of thriller writers.

The Hunt for Red October, which describes the race between U.S. and Soviet forces to get their hands on a defecting Russian submarine captain and his state-of-the-art vessel, marked a number of firsts. It was the first best-seller for both author and publisher, and it became the first of Clancy's books to be made into a motion picture. Conceived before the author had ever set foot on a submarine, it is "a tremendously enjoyable and gripping novel of naval derring-do," according to *Washington Post Book World* critic Reid Beddow. The book contains descriptions of high-tech military hardware so advanced that former Navy Secretary John Lehman, quoted in *Time,* joked that he "would have had [Clancy] court-martialed: the book revealed much that had been classified about antisubmarine warfare. Of course, nobody for a moment suspected him of getting access to classified information." The details were actually based on unclassified books and naval documents, Clancy's interviews with submariners, and his own educated guesses, the author asserts. Admitting that "neither characterization nor dialogue are strong weapons in Clancy's literary arsenal," Richard Setlowe in the *Los Angeles Times Book Review* nonetheless expressed an opinion shared by other reviewers: "At his best, Clancy has a terrific talent for taking the arcana of U.S. and Soviet submarine warfare, the subtleties of sonar and the techno-babble of nuclear power plants and transforming them into taut drama."

In Clancy's second novel, *Red Storm Rising,* a U.S.-Soviet conflict escalates toward world war. Crippled by a Muslim terrorist attack on a major Siberian oil refinery, the Soviet Union plots to defeat the countries in the

North Atlantic Treaty Organization (NATO) so that it can dominate oil-rich Arab nations unhindered. The novel covers military action on land and in the air as well as on submarines; its complicated narrative prompted *Chicago Tribune Book World* reviewer Douglas Balz to note that Clancy's "skill with the plot . . . is his real strength." Balz and other critics faulted Clancy's characterization, although in the *New York Times Book Review,* Robert Lekachman deemed the problem irrelevant to the book's merits as a "rattling good yarn" with "lots of action" and the "comforting certainty that our side will win." John Keegan, writing in the *Washington Post Book World,* called *Red Storm Rising* "a brilliant military fantasy—and far too close to reality for comfort."

Patriot Games tells how former Marine officer Jack Ryan, a key figure in *The Hunt for Red October,* accidentally places himself between a particularly fanatical branch of the Irish Republican Army and the British royal family. Several reviewers criticized it for lack of credibility, lags in the action, simplistic moral lines and, again, poor characterization, conceding nevertheless that it should appeal to fans of the earlier books. Anderson voiced another perspective: "*Patriot Games* is a powerful piece of popular fiction; its plot, if implausible, is irresistible, and its emotions are universal." Pointing out Clancy's authentic detail, powerful suspense, and relevance to current history, James Idema suggested in a Chicago *Tribune Books* review that "most readers [will] find the story preposterous yet thoroughly enjoyable."

Ryan appears again in *The Cardinal of the Kremlin,* which returns to the theme of conflict between the United States and the Soviet Union. In this episode, regarded by critics such as Lekachman as "by far the best of the Jack Ryan series" to date, Clancy focuses on the controversial laser-satellite "strategic defense systems" also known as "Star Wars." According to Lekachman: "The adventure . . . is of high quality. And while [Clancy's] prose is no better than workmanlike . . . the unmasking of the title's secret agent, the Cardinal, is as sophisticated an exercise in the craft of espionage as I have yet to encounter." Remarked *Fortune* contributor Andrew Ferguson, Clancy "aims not only to entertain but also to let his readers in on the 'inside story,' meanwhile discussing with relish the strategic and technological issues of war and peace." Concluded Ferguson, "It is refreshing to find a member of the literati who is willing to deal with [defense policy] in a manner more sophisticated than signing the latest disarmament petition in the *New York Times.*"

With the fall of the Soviet Union, Clancy had to search for new enemies to engine his novels. In *Clear and*

Present Danger, Ryan, in league with the Central Intelligence Agency (CIA), joins the fight against the powerful South American organizations that supply illegal drugs to the U.S. market. After the director of the Federal Bureau of Investigation (FBI) is murdered on a trip to Colombia, the fight becomes a covert war, with foot soldiers and fighter planes unleashed on targets suspected of drug involvement. Reviewing the novel in the *Wall Street Journal,* former Assistant Secretary of State Elliott Abrams wrote, "What helps to make *Clear and Present Danger* such compelling reading is a fairly sophisticated view of Latin politics combined with Mr. Clancy's patented, tautly shaped scenes, fleshed out with colorful technical data and tough talk." Abrams commended Clancy's awareness of the ethical dilemmas that complicate such covert military operations. Some reviewers echoed earlier criticisms of Clancy's characterizations, focus on technology, and prose style but, as Evan Thomas noted in *Newsweek,* "It doesn't really matter if his characters are two dimensional and his machines are too perfect. He whirls them through a half dozen converging subplots until they collide in a satisfyingly slam-bang finale." Thomas called the book "Clancy's best thriller since his first," and "a surprisingly successful cautionary tale."

Patrick O'Brian commented in the *Washington Post Book World* that *The Sum of All Fears* "is about four times the length of the usual novel and deals with at least four times the usual number of themes." In the novel, Jack Ryan is Deputy Director of the CIA, a Middle East peacemaker, and out of favor with the White House. Not all of the factions accept the peace he negotiates. Palestinian terrorists and other radicals obtain a nuclear weapon that they explode at the Super Bowl hoping to cause an all-out war between the United States and the Soviet Union. "The scenes of deployment and nuclear hell at the Super Bowl are truly chilling," wrote Les Standford in his review of the novel in the Chicago *Tribune Books.* Standford added, "Ryan's subsequent attempts to calm a crackpot president and avert a global nuclear war are harrowing. It's just a shame we couldn't get to the plot a bit sooner." Morton Kondracke remarked in the *New York Times Book Review* that among Clancy's talents is his ability to "keep several sub-plots and sub-sub-plots in the air at the same time. In this book he has outdone himself."

In *Without Remorse* former Navy SEAL John Kelly, who appeared in several previous Clancy novels, becomes something of a vigilante, tracking down and killing the drug-smuggling pimps who are after the prostitute he has befriended following the deaths of his wife and unborn child. In addition, the U.S. government dispatches him on a special mission to Vietnam to liberate POWs. In the *Washington Post Book World,* Marie Arana-Ward declared, "What Clancy manages to deliver to us armchair warriors . . . is a different kind of virtuosity: a meticulous chronicle of military hardware, a confident stride through corridors of power, an honest-to-God global war game, and a vertiginous plot that dutifully tracks dozens of seemingly disparate strands to a pyrotechnic finish." Gene Lyons, writing in *Entertainment Weekly,* commented, "given his turgid style and psychological absurdities, Clancy still knows how to tell a tale, and millions of would-be warriors who make up his loyal readership will no doubt find themselves thrilled to their toes."

In *Debt of Honor* a Japanese financier who blames the United States for his parents' deaths during World War II seeks revenge in the economic markets and through military means. Ryan, now White House national security adviser, becomes vice president as a result of the way he handles the crisis, and ascends to the presidency when a Japanese airman attacks the U.S. capitol with a Boeing 747, killing the president. *Los Angeles Times Book Review* contributor John Calvin Batchelor remarked, "Clancy's passion is overwhelming. His sense of cliffhanging is state of the art. The close of this book is a five-run homer." *Executive Orders* picks up where *Debt of Honor* concludes, with Ryan facing the burden of running a government, most of whose power holders are now dead. He also is being assailed by domestic and foreign political and military challenges. Of the author's weighty ninth novel, Gina Bellafante observed in *Time* that *Executive Orders* "is another doozy of laborious plot, bombastic jingoism and tedious detail."

Clancy's 1998 best-seller, *Rainbow Six,* a sequel to *Executive Orders,* achieved record-setting first-week sales. The work again features John Kelly as its central character, while Ryan sits in the White House. Kelly heads the Rainbow Six group, a counter-terrorist unit working under the auspices of NATO. The London-based Operation Rainbow rescues hostages and possesses weaponry that can vaporize terrorists. Kelly works with his son-in-law, Domingo "Ding" Chavez, from *Clear and Present Danger* and *Without Remorse,* and the novel's action begins when they foil an airplane hijacking. From London they head to Switzerland, where a bank is under siege by terrorists. The plot includes a planned bio-apocalypse engineered by a group of radical environmentalists related to a biotech billionaire named John Brightling. *Booklist* reviewer Roland Green counted "four counterterrorist actions as grippingly depicted as anything Clancy has ever done—set pieces guaranteed to keep thriller readers flipping pages" late at night. A

contributor to *Publishers Weekly* also praised the action sequences as "immensely suspenseful, breathtaking combos of expertly detailed combat and primal emotion," though the reviewer faulted Clancy's characterization of Kelly, calling him a less intriguing hero than Ryan. Writing in *People,* J.D. Reed liked the "jolting denouement" and commended the author's "elaborate descriptions of the latest techno-gadgetry and his bolt-action mayhem."

Considered a popular lay expert on military technology issues, Clancy also writes nonfiction works as well as novels, among them *Into the Storm: A Study in Command,* written with Army general Fred Franks, Jr., and *Every Man a Tiger,* written with fighter pilot Chuck Horner, the top air commander for Desert Shield/Desert Storm. A *Publishers Weekly* reviewer described *Every Man a Tiger* as "less about the Gulf War than about the making of a modern fighter general and the remaking of a modern air force." Clancy also wrote the foreword to *Future War: Non-Lethal Weapons in Modern Warfare* with John B. Alexander, a military veteran who formerly worked with the Los Alamos National Laboratory. The book details future weapons, including a sticky foam that immobilizes the enemy, and beams that induce vomiting.

Clancy has also penned seven books in the "Guided Tours" series, each focusing on a key institution in the U.S. military, from submarines to airborne. In *Special Forces,* written with John Gresham, he looks at these "snake eaters," as they are known in the military, examining aspects from training to specific operations they have been involved in. A *Publishers Weekly* contributor felt that despite the "jargon" Clancy occasionally slips into, the author "remains a consummate storyteller, and this book is no exception to his oeuvre." With his *Shadow Warriors: Inside the Special Forces,* written with Carl Stiner and Tony Koltz, Clancy probes deeper into this elite fighting force. "Clancy has turned his prodigious output to documenting the new face of war making," noted Mel D. Lane in a *Library Journal* review, "and for students of the military, this book is welcome."

In *The Bear and the Dragon* Clancy gives readers a new Jack Ryan thriller. Like his other works, this eleventh Clancy blockbuster was scheduled for a first printing of two million copies, a publishing industry high mark which only John Grisham thrillers and J.K. Rowling's "Harry Potter" books achieve. The thousand-page novel depicts an ominous political situation: a potential showdown between China and Russia. China is in severe economic trouble and needs resources in Eastern Siberia to save it. As U.S. president Ryan works overtime to find a solution, antiterrorist expert Clark helps out, as does a well-connected Chinese woman who is recruited to spy. *Entertainment Weekly* writer Bruce Fretts found some anti-Asian prejudice in the prose, but stated that "Clancy deserves credit for developing a number of compelling African-American characters," including his vice president. Fretts also remarked that " *The Bear and the Dragon* starts draggin' when Clancy shoehorns in an antiabortion subplot, yet it eventually builds to an excitingly cinematic climax as Ryan toils to bring the world back from the brink of nuclear war." A contributor to *Publishers Weekly* commented on the numerous subplots in the lengthy novel. "Each thread carries a handbook's worth of intoxicating, expertly researched—seemingly inside—information, about advanced weapons of war and espionage, about how various governments work," the critic stated, adding that while Clancy's latest offering seemed a veritable "sea of words," it is an enjoyable read nonetheless, "because that sea glitters with undeniable authority."

In *Red Rabbit,* Clancy takes Ryan on his tenth adventure, yet this is not the Ryan of the presidency or the head of the CIA. Here Clancy follows the timeline back to 1981, shortly after Ryan saved the life of Prince Charles from IRA assassins in *Patriot Games.* Knighted by the queen and relocated by the CIA to London to work with British intelligence services, Ryan now becomes involved in the attempt to prevent the assassination of Pope John Paul II. Based on an actual 1981 attempt on the pope's life, probably mounted by the KGB, Clancy's story finds Ryan discovering that top Soviet officials—including then KGB head Yuri Andropov—are plotting to kill the pontiff. Ryan must sift through the information to confirm such a plot, and then battle to foil it. His attempts are aided by a KGB major who does not agree with the assassination plot and wants to stop it by defecting. Ryan, a CIA analyst new to the job, must get this defector and his family out of Moscow and do everything in his power to save the pope while also maintaining the stability between the United States and the Soviet Union.

"There is much to admire in *Red Rabbit,*" noted Patrick Anderson in the *Washington Post.* Anderson praised Clancy's ability to "move skillfully among a large cast of characters" as well as his insider information about "how spy agencies operate." Anderson also felt that Clancy's writing "has improved since the clunky prose and robotic dialogue" of his first novels. However, the same critic also found "maddening" problems in the "repetitious" mention of Clancy's political stance and

favorite phrases, and the "gratuitous profanity" his protagonist uses. Anderson concluded though, that on the whole, the book was in some ways "an impressive achievement" and among the author's "better efforts." Less laudatory was a review by Todd Seavey in *People,* which found the novel lacking in tension. "The only suspense," Seavey wrote, "lies in wondering whether something will happen before the book runs out of pages." A contributor for *Publishers Weekly* also complained that the "suspense is minimal" in this "lumbering" novel, while Bruce Fretts, writing in *Entertainment Weekly,* felt it is a mistake for Clancy to write in the past and thereby deny himself "his trademark obsession with gadgets." For Fretts this "low-tech, action starved" book "lacks any semblance of suspense."

Unprecedented knowledge of military technology, plots of rousing adventure and taut suspense, and themes that address current international concerns have combined to make Clancy "one of the most popular authors in the country," in the estimation of *Washington Post Book World* writer David Streitfeld. He is so well liked by military personnel, in particular, that he has been invited to military bases and given tours of ships. Evan Thomas in *Newsweek* reported, "Bluntly put, the Navy realized that Clancy was good for business." Cohen drew the similarities between Clancy and his popular character Jack Ryan. He wrote, "In a way, Tom Clancy has become Jack Ryan: He lectures at the FBI; he dines at the White House; he has been asked on numerous occasions to run for public office; he gives his thoughts on world affairs; he hosts fund-raisers for his friend Oliver North; he attends meetings at the CIA; and like his friends there, he seems almost comically obsessed with leaks and the flow of information." Some critics even credit the author with helping to banish the negative opinion of the military that arose after the United States' controversial involvement in the Vietnam War.

How wide-ranging Clancy's influence really is may be debatable, but his fan base cannot be questioned. In September, 2003, his novel *The Teeth of the Tiger* roared onto the best- seller list's number-one spot. This time, Clancy writes about Ryan's son, also named Jack, and two of Jack's cousins, the twins Dominic and Brian Caruso, a former FBI agent and U.S. marine, respectively. After describing the trio's recruitment and training by Hendley Associates, a vigilante organization out to fight terrorists and others that threaten America, Clancy then introduces an Islamic terrorist plot involving Colombian drug dealers and a plan to kill people in four shopping malls in America's heartland. Writing in the *Washington Times,* Joseph C. Goulden noted that the story of the terrorists' plot and their coming to

America "is told in the exquisite attention to tradecraft detail that makes Mr. Clancy . . . well, terrifyingly good reading, for his scenarios are not far removed reality." *Entertainment Weekly* contributor Marc Bernardin found the book contained too much of Clancy's "ham-fistedly repetitive passages" and added that "even his vaunted plotting is getting creaky." A *People* reviewer enjoyed the novel far more, writing that "Clancy's look at counterterrorism is educational as well as visceral."

In 2004 Clancy published *Battle Ready,* as part of his nonfiction "Commanders" series. The book, written with retired General Tony Zinni and ghostwriter Tony Koltz, was met with mixed reviews. Joseph C. Goulden, writing for *World and I,* wrote that the book is "perhaps the most alarming critique of the U.S. military I've read in years." "Although he identifies himself as a 'soldier/diplomat' because of his post-military work, Zinni does not hesitate to slice, with a very sharp tongue, what he considers to be nitwit ideas," Goulden added. Philip Caputo, reviewing the book for the *New York Times Book Review,* found fault with the style of the book. He noted, "the writer and the warrior [trade] places like a tag team . . . . The result is neither biography nor autobiography, but a mishmash." Caputo concluded that the book is "curiously lifeless, dulled by abstract discussions of military doctorine and crippled by a lavish use of bewildering bureaucratic abbreviations and acronyms." However, a *Publishers Weekly* reviewer felt that although *Battle Ready* is "often too detailed for nonenthusiasts," it's General Zinni's "closing statement . . . that will sell the book to nonbuff civilians, summing up his service and the ways in which he feels his generation's legacy is in jeopardy."

Jason Cowley, a writer for the *New Statesman,* stated that Americans are addicted to catastrophic narratives, and that Clancy gives them what they want. "Through reading Clancy, Americans have lived vicariously with a sense of an ending, simultaneously embracing what they most fear and perhaps most desire, the ruin of cities, the collapse of nations, the vanquishing of alien peoples," mused Cowley. The author's fiction proved disturbingly prescient in light of the September 11, 2001, attacks on the World Trade Center towers in New York City. In *The Sum of All Fears* Clancy had created a scenario involving militant Arabs who use commercial airliners as weapons of terror. Cowley maintained: "It is no exaggeration to describe Clancy as the novelist who comes closest to understanding and animating the modern American psyche: paranoid, deluded, isolated and aggressively confrontational."

As for criticism of his work, Clancy admitted in a *Washington Post* article: "I'm not that good a writer. I do a good action scene. I handle technology well. I like to think that I do a fair—fairer—job of representing the kind of people we have in the Navy . . . . portraying them the way they really are. Beyond that, I'll try to . . . improve what needs improving." The secrets of his success as an entertainer, concluded Anderson, are "a genius for big, compelling plots, a passion for research, a natural narrative gift, a solid prose style, a hyperactive . . . imagination and a blissfully uncomplicated view of human nature and international affairs."

BIOGRAPHICAL AND CRITICAL SOURCES:

BOOKS

Bestsellers 89, Issue 1, Gale (Detroit, MI), 1989.
Bestsellers 90, Issue 1, Gale (Detroit, MI), 1990.
Contemporary Literary Criticism, Volume 45, Gale (Detroit, MI), 1987.
Greenberg, Martin H., editor, *The Tom Clancy Companion,* Berkley Books (New York, NY), 1992, revised edition, Berkley Books (New York, NY), 2005.
Newsmakers 1998, Gale (Detroit, MI), 1998.

PERIODICALS

American Legion, December, 1991, p. 16.
Barron's, September 17, 2001, "Eerie Parallels: Clancy Novel Anticipated Kamikaze Attack with a Commercial Airliner," p. 28.
Book, March-April, 2002, Chris Barsanti, review of *Shadow Warriors: Inside the Special Forces,* p. 72.
Booklist, August, 1998, Roland Green, review of *Rainbow Six,* p. 1920; February 1, 1999, Roland Green, review of *Carrier: A Guided Tour of an Aircraft Carrier,* p. 946; September 15, 2001, Jeanette Larson, review of *The Bear and the Dragon,* p. 241; January 1, 2004, Candace Smith, review of *The Teeth of the Tiger,* p. 891.
Chicago Tribune Book World, September 7, 1986, Douglas Balz, review of *Red Storm Rising.*
Detroit News, January 20, 1985.
Economist, March 17, 1990, p. 87.
Entertainment Weekly, August 6, 1993, pp. 50-51; September 1, 2000, Bruce Fretts, "Spy vs. Spy," p. 73; August 23, 2002, Bruce Fretts, "Just Say Nyet," p. 136; September 5, 2003, Marc Bernardin, review of *The Teeth of the Tiger,* p. 79.
Foreign Affairs, May, 1999, Eliot A. Cohen, review of *Future War: Non-Lethal Weapons in Modern Warfare,* p. 130.

Fortune, July 18, 1988, Andrew Ferguson, review of *The Cardinal of the Kremlin;* August 26, 1991.

Globe and Mail (Toronto, Ontario, Canada), September 2, 1989.

In Style, February 1, 2000, Jim Jerome, "The Tom of Her Life," p. 256.

Kirkus Reviews, December 15, 2001, review of *Shadow Warriors,* pp. 1731-1732.

Kliatt, November, 1995, p. 6.

Library Journal, May 1, 1999, Ray Vignovich, review of *Rainbow Six,* p. 129; March 15, 2002, Mel D. Lane, review of *Shadow Warriors,* p. 95.

Los Angeles Times, July 16, 1989.

Los Angeles Times Book Review, December 9, 1984, Richard Setlowe, review of *The Hunt for Red October;* July 26, 1987; August 21, 1994, John Calvin Batchelor, review of *Debt of Honor,* pp. 1, 9.

Magazine of Fantasy and Science Fiction, December, 1991, p. 73.

National Review, April 29, 1988.

New American, July 1, 2002, William Norman Grigg, "*Sum* Doesn't Add Up," pp. 28-30.

New Republic, June 24, 2002, Stanley Kauffmann, "Truth and Inconsequences," p. 26.

New Statesman, September 24, 2001, Jason Cowley, "He Is the Most Popular Novelist on Earth, Whose Images of Catastrophe Animate the Modern American Psyche," p. 28.

Newsweek, August 17, 1987; August 8, 1988; August 21, 1989, Evan Thomas, review of *Clear and Present Danger,*

New Yorker, September 16, 1991, p. 91.

New York Times, July 17, 1986; August 12, 1986; February 25, 1990; March 1, 1990; August 18, 2002, Thomas Vinciguerra, "Word for Word: The Clancy Effect," p. 7.

New York Times Book Review, July 27, 1986, Robert Lekachman, review of *Red Storm Rising;* August 2, 1987; July 31, 1988; August 13, 1989; July 28, 1991, Morton Kondracke, review of *The Sum of All Fears,* pp. 9-10; August 22, 1993, pp. 13-14; October 2, 1994, pp. 28-29; July 11, 2004, Philip Caputo, "The Writer and the Warrior," p. 7.

New York Times Magazine, May 1, 1988.

People, September 8, 1986; September 12, 1988; September 5, 1994, p. 34; August 17, 1998, J. D. Reed, review of *Rainbow Six,* p. 37; September 9, 2002, Todd Seavey, review of *Red Rabbit,* p. 43; September 8, 2003, review of *The Teeth of the Tiger,* p. 47.

Publishers Weekly, August 8, 1986; July 1, 1988; July 25, 1994, pp. 34-35; August 5, 1996, p. 433; July 13, 1998, Jeff Zaleski, "The Hunt for Tom Clancy," p. 43, John Zinsser, "Clear and Present Sounds," p. 51, and Daisy Maryles, "The Cardinal of the Lists," p. 52; July 27, 1998, review of *Rainbow Six,* p. 55; August 17, 1998, Daisy Maryles, "Clancy's Latest Victory," p. 20; January 4, 1999, review of *Carrier;* April 19, 1999, review of *Every Man a Tiger,* p. 50; August 21, 2000, review of *The Bear and the Dragon,* p. 51; September 4, 2000, Daisy Maryles, "Clancy Does It Again," p. 24; January 1, 2001, review of *Special Forces: A Guided Tour of U.S. Army Special Forces,* p. 79; January 21, 2002, review of *Shadow Warriors,* p. 78; July 29, 2002, review of *Red Rabbit,* p. 51; August 11, 2003, review of *The Teeth of the Tiger,* p. 257; May 10, 2004, review of *Battle Ready,* p. 49.

Reason, May, 1999, Mike Godwin, "Truthless.com," p. 50.

Rolling Stone, December 1, 1994, p. 114.

Saturday Evening Post, September-October, 1991, p. 16.

School Library Journal, June, 1995, p. 143.

Time, March 4, 1985; August 11, 1986; August 24, 1987; July 25, 1988; August 21, 1989; March 5, 1990; March 12, 1990; September 2, 1996, Gina Bellafante, review of *Executive Orders,* p. 61; July 29, 2002, Lev Grossman, "Ten Questions for Tom Clancy," p. 8.

Tribune Books (Chicago, IL), July 5, 1987, James Idema, review of *Patriot Games;* August 11, 1991, Les Standford, review of *The Sum of All Fears,* p. 7.

Wall Street Journal, October 22, 1984; August 16, 1989, Elliott Abrams, review of *Clear and Present Danger.*

Washington Post, January 29, 1985; March 17, 1989; March 2, 1990; August 8, 1993, pp. 1, 14; August 18, 2002, Patrick Anderson, review of *Red Rabbit,* p. T6.

Washington Post Book World, October 21, 1984, Reid Beddow, review of *The Hunt for Red October;* July 27, 1986, John Keegan, review of *Red Storm Rising;* May 14, 1989; August 13, 1989; July 28, 1991, Patrick O'Brian, review of *The Sum of All Fears,* pp. 1-2.

Washington Times, November 9, 2003, Joseph C. Goulden, review of *The Teeth of the Tiger,* p. B06.

Weekly Tribune Plus, September 16, 1994, p. 8.

West Coast Review of Books, November-December, 1984.

World and I, November, 2000, Robert R. Selle, "Technothriller Creator and Freedom Advocate," p. 50; September, 2004, Joseph C. Goulden, "An Outspoken Retired General Critiques Iraq War Planning," p. I9.

Writer's Digest, October, 1987.

ONLINE

Becoming Tom Clancy Web site, http://www.geocities.
com/everwild7/clancy/ (November 13, 2002), "Letters from Tom: The First, 2/5/83."
Penguin Putnam Web site, http://www.penguinputnam.
com/ (November 13, 2003), "Tom Clancy."

*   *   *

CLARK, Carol Higgins 1956(?)-

PERSONAL: Born c. 1956; daughter of Warren (an airline executive) and Mary (a writer; maiden name, Higgins) Clark. *Education:* Mt. Holyoke College, B.A.

ADDRESSES: Home—New York, NY. *Agent*—c/o
Scribner Publicity Department, Simon & Schuster, Inc.,
1230 Avenue of the Americas, New York, NY 10020.
E-mail—chc4rr@aol.com.

CAREER: Actress and novelist. Appeared off-Broadway, and in television films and miniseries, including
Fatal Charm, Night of the Fox, and *A Cry in the Night.*

AWARDS, HONORS: Agatha Award nomination, 1992,
for *Decked;* AudioFile Earphone Award, 2002, for
Jinxed.

WRITINGS:

"REGAN REILLY" SERIES; MYSTERY NOVELS

Decked, Warner Books (New York, NY), 1992.
Snagged, Warner Books (New York, NY), 1993.
Iced, Warner Books (New York, NY), 1995.
Twanged, Warner Books (New York, NY), 1998.
Fleeced, Scribner (New York, NY), 2001.
Jinxed, Scribner (New York, NY), 2002.
Popped, Scribner (New York, NY), 2003.
Burned, Scribner (New York, NY), 2005.
Hitched, Scribner (New York, NY), 2006.

WITH MOTHER, MARY HIGGINS CLARK

Deck the Halls, Simon & Schuster (New York, NY),
2000.

He Sees You When You're Sleeping, Simon & Schuster
(New York, NY), 2001.
The Christmas Thief, Simon & Schuster (New York,
NY), 2004.

SIDELIGHTS: Some authors have writing in their
blood. Such a writer is Carol Higgins Clark, who has
penned a series of popular mystery novels featuring
sleuth Regan Reilly, beginning with *Decked.* Clark is
the daughter of best-selling suspense novelist Mary
Higgins Clark, whose own titles include *A Stranger Is
Watching, The Cradle Will Fall,* and *Remember Me.*
Carol Higgins Clark is also an actress. Among other
roles, she starred in the television version of one of her
mother's books, *A Cry in the Night.*

Clark grew up with four siblings, all of whom, like
their mother, were interested in storytelling. She recalled for Michael A. Lipton and Ann Guerin in *People*
magazine: "If anyone told a boring story in my family,
he or she was promptly cut off." Clark's father died
when she was still a young child, and her mother began
writing, eventually penning the novels that would send
Carol and her brothers and sisters to college. After college, Carol Higgins Clark began acting, adding her
mother's maiden name to her own at the insistence of
an acting agent. She did both off-Broadway productions
and television work, but between acting roles she
worked typing her mother's manuscripts.

Though she learned much from her mother, critics have
noted that the younger Clark's novel-writing style is
different: lighter and more humorous than that of her
mother. "Her books are scarier," Clark noted of her
mother's novels in an interview with *Philadelphia Inquirer* contributor Thomas J. Brady. "She's known for
being the queen of suspense, as they say, whereas mine
are funny . . . . I'm glad, because I'd rather have my
own voice than to try and do the same thing that my
mother is doing."

Decked, Clark's first effort, introduces sleuth Regan
Reilly, whose mother is a suspense writer. The story
starts with Reilly's visit to Oxford University for a reunion with classmates who had once joined her in
spending a semester abroad. During the reunion, the
body of Athena, a Greek student who Reilly and her
comrades thought had run away years before, is discovered. The corpse is found on the estate of one of
Regan's professors, and in the course of Reilly's investigation, she must accompany the professor's eccentric
aunt on a cruise across the Atlantic Ocean. As a *Pub-*

lishers Weekly reviewer noted, "Clark deftly ties the plot playing out on the ocean liner to Athena's murder in a suspenseful climax." Susan Toepfer, writing in *People,* hailed the book as "a sharp and satisfying mystery." She predicted that the character of Reilly could "easily carry a dozen more books."

Snagged concerns possible murder attempts on a man who has invented a type of virtually indestructible pantyhose. Reilly and her parents are at a hotel in Miami that is hosting two conventions—one for funeral directors (her father's profession) and one for the pantyhose industry. Clark attended a hosiery business convention in order to do research for her novel, where "They kept telling me to say 'hosiery,'" she told Sarah Booth Conroy of the *Washington Post.* Stacy Pober, reviewing *Snagged* for *Library Journal,* cited the author's "fine talent for giving many of the characters distinctive voices." Glenna Whitley, in *New York Times Book Review,* applauded the novel as "upbeat" and "fast-paced."

In *Iced* Clark allows Reilly to travel to Aspen, Colorado, where the sleuth has recommended a friend—who is an ex-con—for a house-sitting job. When her friend and some paintings disappear, others jump to conclusions, but Reilly sets out to clear his name. Several other possible art thieves are on the local scene, including a mysterious figure known as the Coyote. "Clark's tone is as chipper as ever in her third Regan Reilly book," observed a *Publishers Weekly* critic. Emily Melton, in *Booklist,* declared the novel to be "solidly entertaining, mostly clever, occasionally funny, and always fun." *Iced* was also recommended for younger readers by Claudia Moore in the *School Library Journal,* who affirmed it as "a good choice for teens, who will enjoy the wit."

Southampton socialites are Clark's satirical target in *Twanged.* In this novel, Reilly goes to Long Island to protect up-and-coming country music star Brigid O'Neill from the clutches of Chappy Tinka, a wealthy buffoon who wants to steal Brigid's fiddle. The instrument was a gift from legendary Irish fiddler Malachy Sheerin and is believed to bring good luck to its owner; Chappy believes that, if only he possessed the magic fiddle, he could become a major star, and his efforts to get his hands on the instrument set in motion a series of events reviewers have described as more zany than suspenseful. A *Publishers Weekly* contributor enjoyed the book's "promising screwball-comedy plot," but added that *Twanged* suffers from some "clumsy" writing. Alice DiNizo was more enthusiastic about the work, dubbing it in *Library Journal* a "light but well-composed" mystery.

Taking time out from their successful solo writing careers, mother and daughter have collaborated in *Deck the Halls,* a Christmas-themed mystery that critics noted would please both writers' fans. Revolving around a plot to kidnap Reilly's father, Luke, and featuring both Reilly and Mary Higgins Clark's amateur detective, Alvirah Meehan, as investigators, the novel combines suspense and comedy in a mix that *Booklist* critic Stephanie Zvirin found seamless but "lightweight." A reviewer for *Publishers Weekly* expressed a similar opinion, deeming the book a "middling" effort that would nevertheless appeal to the Clarks' loyal readers.

Clark and her mother went on to pen two more Christmastime mysteries together, *He Sees You When You're Sleeping,* and *The Christmas Thief.* The latter book tells the story of a con man's efforts to steal the Rockefeller Christmas tree which, unbeknownst to the public, secretly holds diamonds in its branches. *The Christmas Thief* was not received well by critics. Amy Waldman, writing in *People,* called the plot "as musty as last year's tinsel." A *Publishers Weekly* reviewer had a similar opinion, stating that "there's no mystery concerning who's doing what or why and little sense of menace or suspense." The reviewer concluded that Clark's fans "will be disappointed."

In Clark's seventh solo "Regan Reilly" novel, *Popped,* the detective flies to Las Vegas to help an old school chum, Danny Madley, who is producing a reality TV show pilot where three couples battle for a chance to renew their wedding vows and win one million dollars. At the same time, Madley and his show compete with a sitcom producer for a slot on the Hot Air Balloon Channel. However, someone is trying to sabotage the show before Danny can shoot the final scene at the Albuquerque International Balloon Fiesta. "Clark's latest 'Regan Reilly' mystery," according to a *Booklist* reviewer, "has all the substance of cotton candy, but as a poolside diversion, it's perfectly amiable." "The writing," added the critic, "hovers on the edge of cliche, and there is no suspense to speak of, but the silliness of it all delivers a kind of mindless good time." According to a writer in *Publishers Weekly, Popped* "takes aim at all sorts of eminently spoofable targets, including reality TV shows, advice columnists, and screen actors." The result is "zany, if not particularly brilliant, fun in the desert, with an ending series fans will love."

In 2005, Clark published *Burned,* another "Regan Reilly" mystery. In the story, Regan travels to Hawaii for a vacation but ends up working an investigation of a body washed ashore. The plot thickens as it is discovered that a priceless shell lei, stolen from a museum, is wrapped around the dead woman's neck. A reviewer writing in *MBR Bookwatch* commented, "there is so much action . . . readers will feel that they have taken a ride on the world's fastest roller coaster." Mary Frances Wilkens, writing for *Booklist,* stated "what Clark . . . lacks in style, she makes up for in entertaining storytelling."

BIOGRAPHICAL AND CRITICAL SOURCES:

PERIODICALS

Booklist, May 15, 1995, p. 1611; November 1, 2000, Stephanie Zvirin, review of *Deck the Halls,* p. 492; September 15, 2003, review of *Popped,* p. 180; March 15, 2005, Mary Frances Wilkens, review of *Burned,* p. 1269.
Library Journal, July, 1992, p. 131; September 1, 1993, p. 242; June 1, 1995, p. 170; February 1, 1998, Alice DiNizo, review of *Twanged,* p. 116.
MBR Bookwatch, April, 2005, review of *Burned.*
New York Times Book Review, October 17, 1993, p. 42.
People, August 31, 1992, p. 31; November 2, 1992, pp. 79, 82; December 6, 2004, Amy Waldman, review of *The Christmas Thief,* p. 58.
Philadelphia Inquirer, April 19, 1998, Thomas J. Brady, interview with Carol Higgins Clark.
Publishers Weekly, May 18, 1992, pp. 60-61; June 14, 1993, p. 64; May 29, 1995, p. 70; December 22, 1997, review of *Twanged,* p. 41; March 6, 2000, "Move for Higgins Clark Jr.," p. 14; October 30, 2000, review of *Deck the Halls,* p. 47; September 8, 2003, review of *Popped,* p. 60; October 25, 2004, review of *The Christmas Thief,* p. 31.
School Library Journal, January, 1996, p. 138.
USA Today, May 18, 1995, p. D14.
Washington Post, September 28, 1993, p. C1.

ONLINE

Book Reporter.com, http://www.bookreporter.com/ (January 12, 2001), interview with Clark.

* * *

CLARK, Curt
See WESTLAKE, Donald E.

* * *

CLARK, John P.
See CLARK BEKEDEREMO, J.P.

CLARK, John Pepper
See CLARK BEKEDEREMO, J.P.

* * *

CLARK, J.P.
See CLARK BEKEDEREMO, J.P.

* * *

CLARK, Mary Higgins 1929(?)-

PERSONAL: Born December 24, 1929 (some sources say 1931), in New York, NY; daughter of Luke Joseph (a restaurant owner) and Nora C. (a buyer; maiden name, Durkin) Higgins; married Warren F. Clark (an airline executive), December 26, 1949 (died September 26, 1964); married Raymond Charles Ploetz (an attorney), August 8, 1978 (marriage annulled); married John J. Conheeney (in business), November 30, 1996; children: Marilyn, Warren, David, Carol, Patricia. *Education:* Attended Villa Maria Academy, Ward Secretarial School, and New York University; Fordham University, B.A. (summa cum laude), 1979. *Politics:* Republican. *Religion:* Roman Catholic. *Hobbies and other interests:* Traveling, skiing, tennis, playing piano.

ADDRESSES: Home—Saddle River, NJ; and 210 Central Park South, New York, NY 10019. *Agent*—c/o Publicity Department, Simon & Schuster, Inc., 1230 Avenue of the Americas, New York, NY 10020.

CAREER: Writer. Remington Rand, New York, NY, advertising assistant, 1946; Pan American Airlines, flight attendant, 1949-50; Robert G. Jennings, radio scriptwriter and producer, 1965-70; Aerial Communications, New York, NY, vice president, partner, creative director, and producer of radio programming, 1970-80; David J. Clark Enterprises, New York, NY, chair of board and creative director, 1980—. Chair, International Crime Writers Congress, 1988.

MEMBER: Mystery Writers of America (president, 1987; member of board of directors), Authors Guild, Authors League of America, American Academy of Arts and Sciences, American Society of Journalists and Authors, American Irish Historical Society (member of executive council).

AWARDS, HONORS: New Jersey Author Award, 1969, for *Aspire to the Heavens,* 1977, for *Where Are the Children?* and 1978, for *A Stranger Is Watching;* Grand

Prix de Litterature Policiere (France), 1980; Women of Achievement Award, Federation of Women's Clubs in New Jersey; Irish Woman of the Year Award, Irish-American Heritage and Cultural Week Committee of the Board of Education of the City of New York; Gold Medal of Honor Award, American-Irish Historical Society; Spirit of Achievement Award, Albert Einstein College of Medicine of Yeshiva University; Gold Medal in Education, National Arts Club; Horatio Alger Award, 1997; thirteen honorary doctorates, including Villanova University, 1983, Rider College, 1986, Stonehill College and Marymount Manhattan College, 1992, Chestnut Hill, Manhattan College, and St. Peter's College, 1993; named Dame of the Order of St. Gregory the Great, Dame of Malta, and Dame of the Holy Sepulcher of Jerusalem.

WRITINGS:

Aspire to the Heavens: A Biography of George Washington, Meredith Press (New York, NY), 1969.

Where Are the Children? (also see below), Simon & Schuster (New York, NY), 1975, 30th anniversary edition, Pocket Books (New York, NY), 2005.

A Stranger Is Watching (also see below), Simon & Schuster (New York, NY), 1978.

The Cradle Will Fall (also see below), Simon & Schuster (New York, NY), 1980.

A Cry in the Night, Simon & Schuster (New York, NY), 1982.

Stillwatch, Simon & Schuster (New York, NY), 1984.

(With Thomas Chastain and others) *Murder in Manhattan,* Morrow (New York, NY), 1986.

Weep No More, My Lady, Simon & Schuster (New York, NY), 1987.

(Editor) *Murder on the Aisle: The 1987 Mystery Writers of America Anthology,* Simon & Schuster (New York, NY), 1987.

While My Pretty One Sleeps (also see below), Simon & Schuster (New York, NY), 1989.

The Anastasia Syndrome and Other Stories, Simon & Schuster (New York, NY), 1989.

Loves Music, Loves to Dance (also see below), Simon & Schuster (New York, NY), 1991.

All around the Town (also see below) Simon & Schuster (New York, NY), 1992.

Missing in Manhattan: The Adams Round Table, Longmeadow Press (Stamford, CT), 1992.

Mists from Beyond: Twenty- two Ghost Stories and Tales from the Other Side, New American Library/ Dutton (New York, NY), 1993.

I'll Be Seeing You, Simon & Schuster (New York, NY), 1993.

Remember Me, Simon & Schuster (New York, NY), 1994.

The Lottery Winner: Alvirah and Willy Stories, Simon & Schuster (New York, NY), 1994.

Silent Night: A Novel, Simon & Schuster (New York, NY), 1995.

Mary Higgins Clark: Three Complete Novels (includes *A Stranger Is Watching, The Cradle Will Fall,* and *Where Are the Children?*), Wings Books (New York, NY), 1995.

Let Me Call You Sweetheart, Simon & Schuster (New York, NY), 1995.

Moonlight Becomes You: A Novel, Simon & Schuster (New York, NY), 1996.

Mary Higgins Clark, Three New York Times Bestsellers (includes *While My Pretty One Sleeps, Loves Music, Loves to Dance,* and *All around the Town*) Wings Books (New York, NY), 1996.

My Gal Sunday, Simon & Schuster (New York, NY), 1996.

Pretend You Don't See Her, Simon & Schuster (New York, NY), 1997.

(Editor) *The Plot Thickens,* Pocket Books (New York, NY), 1997.

All through the Night, Simon & Schuster (New York, NY), 1998.

You Belong to Me, Simon & Schuster (New York, NY), 1998.

We'll Meet Again, Simon & Schuster (New York, NY), 1999.

Before I Say Goodbye, Simon & Schuster (New York, NY), 2000.

(With daughter, Carol Higgins Clark) *Deck the Halls,* Simon & Schuster (New York, NY), 2000.

On the Street Where You Live, Simon & Schuster (New York, NY), 2001.

(With daughter, Carol Higgins Clark) *He Sees You When You're Sleeping,* Simon & Schuster (New York, NY), 2001.

Kitchen Privileges (memoir), Simon & Schuster (New York, NY), 2002.

Daddy's Little Girl, Simon & Schuster (New York, NY), 2002.

Mount Vernon Love Story, Simon & Schuster (New York, NY), 2002.

The Second Time Around, Simon & Schuster (New York, NY), 2003.

Nighttime Is My Time, Thorndike Press (Waterville, ME), 2004.

(With daughter, Carol Higgins Clark) *The Christmas Thief,* Simon & Schuster (New York, NY), 2004.

No Place Like Home, Simon & Schuster (New York, NY), 2005.

Two Little Girls in Blue, Simon & Schuster (New York, NY), 2006.

Contributor to books, including *The Best "Saturday Evening Post" Stories,* 1962; *I, Witness,* Times Books (New York, NY), 1978; and *The International Association of Crime Writers Presents Bad Behavior,* Harcourt Brace (San Diego, CA), 1995. Author of syndicated radio dramas. Writer, with John Rutter, of the television story *Haven't We Met Before?* in 2002. Contributor of stories to periodicals, including *Saturday Evening Post, Redbook, McCall's,* and *Family Circle.*

ADAPTATIONS: A Stranger Is Watching was filmed by Metro-Goldwyn-Mayer in 1982; *The Cradle Will Fall* was shown on CBS-TV as a "Movie of the Week" in 1984; *A Cry in the Night* was filmed by Rosten Productions in 1985; *Where Are the Children?* was filmed by Columbia in 1986; *Stillwatch* was broadcast on CBS-TV in 1987; Ellipse, a French production company, produced *Weep No More My Lady, A Cry in the Night* (starring Clark's daughter Carol), and two stories from *The Anastasia Syndrome.* Many of Clark's books have been adapted as sound recordings. Filmed adaptations of *Lucky Day, Loves Music, Loves to Dance, You Belong to Me, All around the Town, Pretend You Don't See Her,* and *Haven't We Met Before?* were released as *Mary Higgins Clark Mystery Movie Collection,* Lion's Gate Home Productions, 2004. Simon & Schuster planned to rerelease all of Clark's works in e-book format.

SIDELIGHTS: "You can set your bestseller clock each spring for a new Mary Higgins Clark winner," observed *Publishers Weekly* contributor Dick Donahue in 2001. The prolific mystery author began her writing career as a newly widowed mother of five and has instilled her passion for suspense stories in her children, including daughter Carol, also a best-selling novelist. Clark's stories have proven so popular that her publisher, Simon & Schuster, signed her to a then-record-breaking $11.4 million contract in 1989 to produce four novels and a short story collection and in 1992 to a $35 million contract for five novels and a memoir. By 2000, Clark had over fifty million titles in print and enjoyed bestseller status around the world.

Clark had always intended to become a writer. "When I was fifteen I was picking out clothes that I would wear when I became a successful writer," she told *Powells.com* interviewer Dave Welch. "I was sure I'd make it." For the first nine years of her first marriage, Clark wrote short stories. "The first one was rejected for six years," she confided to Welch. "Then it sold for $100." Confronted with the daunting task of supporting five young children after the early death of her husband, Clark

turned to suspense novels. Her first, *Where Are the Children?,* became a bestseller in 1975, earning more than $100,000 in paperback royalties. She followed that with another thriller, *A Stranger Is Watching,* which earned more than $1 million in paperback rights and was filmed by Metro-Goldwyn-Mayer in 1982. For Clark, this meant financial security. Her writing earnings "changed my life in the nicest way," she told Bina Bernard in *People.* "It took all the choking sensation out of paying for the kids' schools."

The key to Clark's popularity, according to several critics, is her technique. Jean M. White of the *Washington Post* maintained that Clark "is a master storyteller who builds her taut suspense in a limited time frame," noting that *Where Are the Children?* takes place in one day and *A Stranger Is Watching* in three. Carolyn Banks, moreover, pointed out in the *Washington Post* that there is a kind of "Mary Higgins Clark formula" that readers both expect and enjoy: "There are no ambiguities in any Clark book. We know whom and what to root for, and we do. Similarly, we boo and hiss or gasp when the author wants us to. Clark is a master manipulator." Although Clark wants to provide her readers with entertainment and romance, she once commented: "I feel a good suspense novel can and should hold a mirror up to society and make a social comment."

Clark's style is to write about "terror lurking beneath the surface of everyday life," observed White. She "writes about ordinary people suddenly caught up in frightening situations as they ride a bus or vacuum the living room," such as the characters in *Loves Music, Loves to Dance,* who encounter a murderer when they agree to participate in an experiment involving newspaper personal ads. Other stories play on readers' fears of unfamiliar or undesirable situations. For example, Clark explores mental illness in *Loves Music, Loves to Dance,* in which the killer's behavior is caused by a personality disorder, and in *All around the Town,* in which the main character is afflicted with a multiple personality disorder attributed to severe sexual abuse in her childhood. In *I'll Be Seeing You* Clark's characters find themselves victimized by villains more knowledgeable than they in the issues of genetic manipulation and in-vitro fertilization. Many of the events and details of Clark's stories come from the lives of her friends and family, news events, and even her own experiences. Clark told *New York Times* interviewer Shirley Horner that the burglary the heroine interrupts in *Stillwatch* was based on break-ins Clark herself had endured. "Everything that a writer experiences goes up in the mental attic," she told Horner.

In Clark's more recent novels, nice people vanquish the powers of darkness with great flair. In *Moonlight Be-*

comes You, Maggie Holloway, a young photographer and amateur sculptor, visits her deceased stepmother's home in Newport, Rhode Island, in order to investigate the woman's mysterious death. Maggie's search leads her to a nursing home plagued by a series of sudden deaths, and she begins to suspect that she, too, is being targeted by the killer who does not want her to expose his diabolical plot. A reviewer for *Booklist* acknowledged that, "though this is not her finest book, Clark's popularity will surely put *Moonlight* on the lists."

In her short-story collection *My Gal Sunday,* Clark introduces a new detective team. Henry Parker Britland, IV, is a former U.S. president enjoying an early retirement, and his wife, Sandra—nicknamed "Sunday"—has just been elected to Congress and appointed the darling of the media. Henry and Sunday specialize in solving crimes that occur among their friends in political society. In one story, when Henry's former secretary of state is indicted for the murder of his mistress, Henry and Sunday determine he is willing to take the fall for a crime of passion he did not commit.

In *Pretend You Don't See Her* Clark takes on the federal witness protection program. While working as a real estate agent in Manhattan, Lacey Farrell witnesses a client's murder and is given a new name and a new identity by the government. However, merely changing her name does not protect her from the web of danger and deceit that surrounds the crime. As new clues emerge, Lacey realizes that a link exists between her family and the murder. In the meantime, romance enters her life and leads her to embark on a perilous journey to reclaim her old identity. A *Booklist* reviewer found the story "briskly paced," though with few surprises. Kimberly Marlowe noted in the *New York Times Book Review* that in her fifteenth novel, Clark covers "a lot of ground . . . life, death threats and the perfect date."

By the late 1990s some critics began to suggest that Clark's writing was growing rather stale. In a review of *You Belong to Me* a *Publishers Weekly* contributor commented that the book gives fans "the page-flipping perils they expect without challenging them . . . one whit." However, Clark's popularity remained as strong as ever among her fans. *We'll Meet Again,* in which a greedy head of a Connecticut H.M.O. is murdered, shot straight to the top of bestseller lists after just one week. *New York Times Book Review* contributor Marilyn Stasio appreciated "the diabolical plot that Clark prepares so carefully and executes with such relish," while *Booklist* reviewer Jenny McLarin deemed *We'll Meet Again* "first-rate entertainment." *Before I Say Goodbye,*

also an immediate top-seller, was hailed as one of Clark's "page-turning best" by *Booklist* contributor Kristine Huntley. And *On the Street Where You Live,* Clark's third novel in a row to capture the number- one slot in its first week, intrigued critics with its premise: that a serial killer from a century past might be stalking young women in a present-day New Jersey resort town. "Clark's prose ambles as usual," commented a reviewer for *Publishers Weekly,* "but it takes readers where they want to go—deep into an old-fashioned tale of a damsel in delicious distress."

When reviewing *The Second Time Around* for *Booklist,* Mary Frances Wilkens commented: "Clark isn't the subtlest crime writer, but she knows how to spin an intriguing tale." A *Publishers Weekly* reviewer echoed that sentiment: "There's something special about Clark's thrillers, and it's not just the gentleness with which the bestselling writer approaches her often lurid subject matter . . . Special above all is the compassion she extends to her characters—heroines, villains and supporting cast alike."

In 2004, Clark published *Nighttime Is My Time.* In the story, members of the high school popular crowd become the targets of a serial killer as they attend their twentieth reunion. The murderer, whose alter ego "The Owl" developed due to his nighttime killing preference, is one of many former geeks seeking revenge. "The final revelation is anticlimactic," noted one *Publishers Weekly* contributor, "but Clark's multitude of fans will be happy enough . . . to participate in the guessing game." Mary Frances Wilkens, a reviewer for *Booklist,* found some of the characters to be "relatively shallow," but she concluded that "fans will enjoy the comfort of watching the Clark formula unwind yet again."

Clark followed *Nighttime Is My Time* with *No Place Like Home.* Celia Foster Nolan's past comes back to haunt her when she is given a new house by her husband as a birthday present. Little does he know that Celia is the grown-up little girl Liza Barton, who, at ten years old, shot both of her parents in the very same house. Mystery ensues as incidents, such as the death of their real estate agent, surround the couple as they move in. Marilyn Stasio, writing in the *New York Times Book Review,* complimented Clark's "intuitive grasp of the anxieties of everyday life that can spiral into full-blown terror."

Writing has become a family affair for the Clarks. Daughter Carol Higgins Clark's first novel, *Decked,* appeared on the paperback bestseller list at the same time as her mother's *I'll Be Seeing You* was departing the hardcover list after seventeen weeks. Reacting to critics who suggest that Clark may have contributed to her daughter's books, Sarah Booth Conroy noted in the *Washington Post* that Clark "writes deadly serious novels about the sort of chilling fears that come to women in the middle of the night" while her daughter "spoons in a bit of bawdy, a soupçon of slapstick." Carol Higgins Clark has, however, exerted some influence on her mother's writing: she is responsible for restoring to readers two of Clark's most popular characters, Alvirah, a cleaning woman who wins the lottery, and Alvirah's husband, Willy. When they first appeared in a short story, Alvirah was poisoned and Clark planned to finish her off, until Carol convinced her mother to allow Alvirah to recover. The two have since become recurring characters and are featured in *The Lottery Winner: Alvirah and Willy Stories,* published in 1994.

Mother and daughter took their literary bond to a further level with *Deck the Halls,* a mystery novel they co-wrote that featured both Alvirah and Carol Higgins Clark's popular sleuth, Regan Reilly. Since then, the duo has published two more Christmas-themed novels together, *He Sees You When You're Sleeping,* and *The Christmas Thief.*

BIOGRAPHICAL AND CRITICAL SOURCES:

BOOKS

Bestsellers '89, number 4, Gale (Detroit, MI), 1989.
Newsmakers 2000, Gale (Detroit, MI), 2000.
St. James Guide to Young Adult Writers, second edition, St. James Press (Detroit, MI), 1999.

PERIODICALS

Best Sellers, December, 1984.
Booklist, October 15, 1994, p. 371; April 15, 1996; April, 1998, Mary Frances Wilkens, review of *You Belong to Me,* p. 1277; September 15, 1998, Kathleen Hughes, review of *All Through the Night,* p. 172; April 15, 1999, Jenny McLarin, review of *We'll Meet Again,* p. 1468; April 15, 2000, Kristine Huntley, review of *Before I Say Goodbye,* p. 1500; November 1, 2000, Stephanie Zvirin, review of *Deck the Halls,* p. 492; April 15, 2001, Kristine Huntley, review of *On the Street Where You Live,* p. 1508; May 1, 2003, Mary Frances Wilkens, re-
view of *The Second Time Around,* p. 1538; April 1, 2004, Mary Frances Wilkens, review of *Nighttime is My Time,* p. 1330.
Chicago Tribune, September 20, 1987; July 31, 1989.
Cosmopolitan, May, 1989.
English Journal, December, 1979, p. 80.
Good Housekeeping, November, 1996, pp. 23-24.
Kirkus Review, November 1, 2000, review of *Deck the Halls,* p. 1519.
Newsweek, June 30, 1980.
New Yorker, August 4, 1980; June 27, 1994, p. 91.
New York Times, January 22, 1982; December 6, 1989; May 18, 1997.
New York Times Book Review, May 14, 1978; November 14, 1982; May 2, 1993, p. 22; December 15, 1996; May 5, 1996; April 19, 1998, Marilyn Stasio, review of *You Belong to Me,* p. 30; June 29, 1997; May 23, 1999, Marilyn Stasio, review of *We'll Meet Again;* April 16, 2000, Marilyn Stasio, review of *Before I Say Goodbye,* p. 32; April 10, 2005, Marilyn Stasio, "Blues Clues," p. 27.
Observer (London, England), May 7, 1978, p. 34.
People, March 6, 1978; May 9, 1994, p. 35; December 16, 1996, pp. 54-56.
Progressive, May, 1978, p. 45.
Publishers Weekly, May 19, 1989; October 14, 1996, pp. 28-29; March 30, 1998, review of *You Belong to Me,* p. 70; September 14, 1998, review of *All through the Night,* p. 52; October 30, 2000, review of *Deck the Halls,* p. 47; April 2, 2001, review of *On the Street Where You Live,* p. 41; April 30, 2001, "Clark's Spark Marks," p. 20; April 7, 2003, review of *Second Time Around,* p. 47; March 22, 2004, review of *Nighttime is My Time,* p. 62; March 28, 2005, review of *No Place Like Home,* p. 56.
Tribune Books (Chicago, IL), June 8, 1980.
Wall Street Journal, May 29, 1996, p. A16; December 7, 1998, Tom Nolan, review of *All through the Night,* p. A28; December 11, 2000, Tom Nolan, review of *Deck the Halls,* p. A38.
Washington Post, May 19, 1980; July 17, 1980; October 18, 1982; August 10, 1987.

ONLINE

Powells.com, http://www.powells.com/ (January 12, 2001), "Mary Higgins Clark Reveals."
Writers Write, http://www.writerswrite.com/ (January 12, 2001), "A Conversation with Mary Higgins Clark."

*   *   *

CLARK BEKEDEREMO, Johnson Pepper
See CLARK BEKEDEREMO, J.P.

CLARK BEKEDEREMO, J.P. 1935-
(Johnson Pepper Clark Bekederemo, J.P. Clark, John P. Clark, John Pepper Clark)

PERSONAL: Born Johnson Pepper Clark Bekederemo, April 6, 1935, in Kiagbodo, Nigeria; son of Clark Fuludu (an Ijaw tribal leader) and Poro Clark Bekederema; married Ebun Odutola; children: three daughters, one son. *Education:* University of Ibadan, B.A. (with honors), 1960.

ADDRESSES: Agent—Andrew Best, Curtis Brown Ltd., 162-168 Regent St., London W1R 5TB, England.

CAREER: Poet, playwright, and filmmaker. Nigerian Federal Government, information officer, 1960-61; *Daily Express,* Lagos, Nigeria, head of features and editorial writer, 1961-62; University of Lagos, Lagos, research fellow, 1964-66, professor of African literature and instructor in English, 1966-85.

MEMBER: Society of Nigerian Authors (founding member).

AWARDS, HONORS: Institute of African Studies research fellow, 1961-62, 1963-64; Parvin fellow, Princeton University, 1962-63; honorary degree from University of Benin, 1991; Nigerian National Merit Award for literary excellence, 1991.

WRITINGS:

(As John Pepper Clark) *Song of a Goat* (play; produced at Ibadan University, 1961), Mbari (Ibadan, Nigeria), 1961, new edition edited by Ebun Clark, University Press (Ibadan, Nigeria), 1993.

(As John Pepper Clark) *Poems,* Mbari (Ibadan, Nigeria), 1962.

(As John Pepper Clark) *The Raft* (play), produced at University of Ibadan Arts Theatre, Ibadan, Nigeria, 1964.

Three Plays: Song of a Goat, The Masquerade, The Raft, Oxford University Press (Oxford, England), 1964.

(As John Pepper Clark) *America, Their America* (nonfiction), Deutsch (London, England), 1964, Africana Publishing (New York, NY), 1969.

(As John Pepper Clark) *A Reed in the Tide,* Longmans (London, England), 1965, 2nd edition published as *A Reed in the Tide: A Selection of Poems,* Humanities Press (New York, NY), 1970.

(As John Pepper Clark) *Ozidi: A Play,* Oxford University Press (Oxford, England), 1966.

(As John Pepper Clark) *Casualties: Poems, 1966-68,* Africana Publishing (New York, NY), 1970.

Tides of the Delta: The Saga of Ozidi (screenplay), Colour Film Services (London, England), 1975.

(Translator) Okabou Ojobolo, *The Ozidi Saga,* University Press (Ibadan, Nigeria), 1977.

The Hero as a Villain, University of Lagos Press (Lagos, Nigeria), 1978.

The Boat, produced at University of Lagos Auditorium, Lagos, Nigeria, 1981.

A Decade of Tongues: Selected Poems 1958-1968, Longmans (London, England), 1981.

The Wives' Revolt, produced at PEC Repertory Theatre, Lagos, Nigeria, 1984.

The Return Home, produced at PEC Repertory Theatre, Lagos, Nigeria, 1985.

The Bikoroa Plays (contains *Full Circle, The Return Home,* and *The Boat*) Oxford University Press (Oxford, England), 1985.

State of the Union, Longmans (London, England), 1985.

Mandela and Other Poems, Longman Nigeria (Ikeja, Nigeria), 1988.

The Ozidi Saga, Howard University Press (Washington, DC), 1991.

Collected Plays, 1964-1988, Howard University Press (Washington, DC), 1991.

Collected Plays and Poems, 1958-1988, Howard University Press (Washington, DC), 1991.

Collected Poems, 1958-1988, Howard University Press (Washington, DC), 1991.

The Wives' Revolt, University Press (Ibadan, Nigeria), 1991.

A Lot from Paradise, Malthouse Press (Ikeja, Nigeria), 1997.

The Poems, 1958-1998, Longman Nigeria (Lagos, Nigeria), 2002.

Contributor to *Seven African Writers,* edited by Gerald Moore, Oxford University Press (Oxford, England), 1962, *West African Verse: An Anthology,* Longmans (London, England), 1967, and *A Book of African Verse,* edited by John Reed and Clive Wake, Heinemann (London, England), 1964. Scriptwriter, director, and producer of documentary films *The Ozidi of Atazi* and *The Ghost Town.* Founder and editor, *Horn* (literary magazine); coeditor, *Black Orpheus,* 1968—. Contributor of literary criticism to *Presence Africaine, Nigeria, Transition, African Forum, Black Orpheus,* and other journals. Contributor to anthologies, including *The Example of Shakespeare: Critical Essays on African Literature,* 1970, and *The Philosophical Anachronism of William Godwin,* 1977.

SIDELIGHTS: Nigerian-born J.P. Clark Bekederemo has been called one of the central figures of West African drama, and he is equally well known as one of his country's foremost poets. In both roles he combines classical Western style and structure with stories, characters, and themes rooted in his native Ijaw tradition to create a body of work that is both universal and culturally unique. In a discussion with university students in 1970 included in *Palaver: Interviews with Five African Writers in Texas,* Clark Bekederemo commented on the cross-cultural fusion in his work, noting, "In a new nation like Nigeria which cuts across several groups of people, or rather which brings together several peoples speaking different languages, you've got to have a *lingua franca,* and this is the role that English is playing in the absence of one widely spoken Nigerian language. . . . I belong to the new community of Nigerians who have undergone a new system of education and therefore share a new kind of culture, a synthetic one which exists alongside the traditional one to which fortunately I also belong."

Like the life he has led, the new Nigerian culture Clark Bekederemo references is a bridging of two worlds, African and European. Clark Bekederemo's father was an Ijaw tribal leader in a fishing village in Eastern Nigeria. The author attended local elementary school and the Government College in Ughelli before pursuing a bachelor's degree in English from University College in Ibadan, a branch of the University of London, and a partially completed fellowship at Princeton University in the United States.

Critics have found ample evidence of Clark's bifurcated background in his plays and poetry, noting the presence of Ijaw myths, legends, and religion, masks, pantomimes, drumming, and dancing alongside poetic dialogue that seems distinctly Shakespearean, within epic tragedies styled after Sophocles or Euripides. Commenting in *English Studies in Africa,* T.O. McLoughlin observed, "The interesting point about John Pepper Clark is that his awareness of what he calls 'traditional' and 'native' influences has come to dominate what he has learned from western literature."

Clark Bekederemo's first dramatic work was the 1960 play *Song of a Goat,* about Zifa, a fisherman, whose sexual impotence causes his wife, Ebiere, to seek advice from the village Masseur. The Masseur, a sort of doctor-mystic, suggests that Zifa's younger brother, Tonye, should, as a practical matter, assume the husband's duties. Both husband and wife reject the idea, but eventually Ebiere's frustration drives her to seduce Tonye. Zifa uncovers the truth and attempts to murder his brother. Though Tonye escapes his brother's wrath, his guilt is too heavy and he hangs himself. Zifa walks into the sea to drown and Ebiere is left pregnant, setting the stage for *The Masquerade,* Clark Bekederemo's 1964 sequel to this tragic family drama.

African-American playwright LeRoi Jones asserted in *Poetry:* "[*Song of a Goat*] is English, but it is not. The tone, the references . . . belong to what I must consider an African experience. The English is pushed . . . past the immaculate boredom of the recent Victorians to a quality of experience that is non-European, though it is the European tongue which seems to shape it, externally." Acknowledging that cultural background affects how an audience experiences *Song of a Goat,* Clark Bekederemo once told a group of American students, "The idea of sacrifice is a universal one, but the theme of impotence is something that doesn't have the same kind of cultural significance for you as it has for me. The business of reproduction, of fertility, is a life and death matter in my home area. If a man doesn't bear, he has not lived. And when he is dead, nobody will think of him."

The Masquerade is a lyrical, fairy-tale tragedy that has been compared to Shakespeare's *Romeo and Juliet.* In the play Ebiere's son, Tufa, is a grown man who woos Titi, a popular village girl who has refused all other suitors. Through lavish presents and attention he wins the favor of Titi and her father, Diribi, and an extravagant wedding is arranged. Prior to the nuptials, however, the groom's family history is discovered. Everyone, including the innocent Tufa, is surprised to learn he is the son of his father's brother and that his conception caused the deaths of all his parents. As the plot hurtles to a climax, Diribi shoots and kills his daughter in a furious rage, then is forced by the despondent Tufa to end his life as well.

Critic William Connor praised *The Masquerade* in *World Literature Written in English,* saying, "I can think of no other modern play which in its compactness, the power of its tragic irony and the neatness of its resolution comes as close to duplicating the achievement of Clark's models, the classical Greek tragedies." Nevertheless, the play was generally dismissed by other critics as second-rate, unbelievable storytelling, and what began in the playwright's mind as a classically modeled tragic trilogy was never completed.

Instead, Clark Bekederemo wrote *The Raft,* a tragedy about four lumbermen attempting to earn money by delivering a load of logs downriver to a wealthy buyer.

Although *The Raft* has often been described as a political drama foretelling the fate of Nigeria at the time of its Civil War, the playwright himself insists he was not trying to write a "political thesis," but instead was "trying to create a human condition which I knew existed not only in Nigeria but elsewhere."

Through much of the 1960s, Clark Bekederemo continued to write plays, culminating in his 1966 adaptation of the sprawling Ijaw epic, *Ozidi,* one of the tribe's masquerade serial plays which are told in seven days, and which incorporate music, dance, and mime. After *Ozidi,* however, the author turned from drama to poetry and did not write another play for nearly twenty years.

The intervening decades saw the publication of a handful of volumes of poetry, including *A Reed in the Tide,* the first international publication of Clark Bekederemo's verse, *Urhobo Poetry, Mandela and Other Poems,* and *Collected Poems, 1958-1988.* According to *Research in African Literatures* contributor Dan S. Izevbaye, *Collected Poems, 1958-1988* "effectively carries across Clark-Bekederemo's literary burden—his apprehension of the potentially tragic experience of the Ijo in their riverine home, and its imaginative impact on the sensitive psyche of the poetry. The collection enables the reader to follow the evolution of the poet's sensibility and his quest for an adequate medium for expressing personal and communal themes, as he reaches for the simplicity and clarity of good prose in his poetry."

Like his drama, Clark Bekederemo's poetry reflects both African and European cultures, describing the author's surroundings and experiences in his native country and abroad in a style that has been likened to the English poet Gerard Manley Hopkins. While he was not writing plays Clark Bekederemo also published criticism in magazines, journals, and books, including *The Example of Shakespeare: Critical Essays on African Literature* and *The Philosophical Anachronism of William Godwin.*

1985's "Bikoroa" plays, which include *The Boat, The Return Home,* and *Full Circle,* marked Clark Bekederemo's return to playwriting and his renewed interest in familiar themes. Family conflict, revenge, and hereditary suffering play prominent parts in this epic trilogy about two quarreling brothers who kill each other, and pass their strife along to their sons and their grandsons. This cycle of plays "seems a more unified attempt to explore the notion of the tragic from a purely African perspective" than the author's earlier plays, wrote Osita

Okagbue in *African Writers.* The Bikoroa plays also differ in style, having been written in prose, not verse. Still, Clark Bekederemo is a writer with a poet's penchant for simile, metaphor, and turn-of-phrase; for instance, an angry man in a hurry is described as "a whirlwind with a lot of dust in its eye."

The 1997 collection *A Lot from Paradise* "comprises poems of memory, nostalgia, and passion, qualities that enhance lyricism," wrote *World Literature Today* contributor Tanure Ojaide. The poems in *A Lot from Paradise,* including "Two Loves," "The Last Call," and "Land of Paradise," focus on the people of the Niger Delta. Clark Bekederemo "is working on familiar literary terrain in *A Lot from Paradise,* which marks his return to the land of his nativity, whose water, crops, and atmosphere nourished him physically, spiritually, and creatively," Ojaide stated. "In these poems as in his early verse, there is a strong sense of place, a local specificity of the Niger Delta that gives not only local color but also spiritual color to the poetry."

When asked about the artist's role in society, Clark Bekederemo's first response is typically a practical one. "I think that the writer—whether African, European or American—is just like a lawyer, a doctor, a carpenter, a janitor, one type of citizen within society," he insisted before a student audience. "He has his work as has everyone with a job to do." And what is the writer's job? Clark Bekederemo suggested, "The commitment to produce something beautiful, and perhaps functional as well—this is the business of the artist as an interpreter, as a maker, as a creator, as a constant renewer of life."

BIOGRAPHICAL AND CRITICAL SOURCES:

BOOKS

African Writers, Volume 1, Scribner (New York, NY), 1997.

Black Literature Criticism, Thomson Gale (Detroit, MI), 1992.

Contemporary Black Biography, Volume 44, Thomson Gale (Detroit, MI), 2004.

Contemporary Dramatists, 6th edition, St. James Press (Detroit, MI), 1999.

Contemporary Literary Criticism, Volume 38, Thomson Gale (Detroit, MI), 1986.

Contemporary Poets, 7th edition, St. James Press (Detroit, MI), 2001.

Dictionary of Literary Biography, Volume 117: *Twentieth-Century Caribbean and Black African Writers, First Series,* Thomson Gale (Detroit, MI), 1992.

Drama Criticism, Volume 5, Thomson Gale (Detroit, MI), 1995.

Drama for Students, Volume 13, Thomson Gale (Detroit, MI), 2001.

King, Bruce, editor, *Post-Colonial English Drama,* St. Martin's Press (New York, NY), 1992.

Laurence, Margaret, *Long Drums and Cannons: Nigerian Dramatists and Novelists,* Macmillan (London, England), 1968.

Lindforth, Bernth, and others, editors, *Palaver: Interviews with Five African Writers in Texas,* University of Texas Press (Austin, TX), 1972.

Pieterse, Cosmo, and Dennis Duerden, editors, *African Writers Talking,* Africana Publishing (New York, NY), 1972.

Smith, Rowland, editor, *Exile and Tradition: Studies in African and Caribbean Literature,* Longmans (Harlow, England), 1976.

PERIODICALS

Concerning Poetry, fall, 1984.

English Studies in Africa, March, 1975, pp. 31-40.

Ibadan, June, 1966.

Literary Criterion, volume 23, numbers 1-2, Isaac I. Elimimian, "J.P. Clark as Poet," pp. 30-58.

Literature East and West, March, 1968, pp. 56-67.

Modern Drama, May, 1968, pp. 16-26.

Poetry, March, 1964.

Research in African Literatures, spring, 1994, Dan S. Izevbaye, "J.P. Clark-Bekederemo and the Ijo Literary Tradition," pp. 1-21; summer, 2001, Luke Eyoh, "African Musical Rhythm and Poetic Imagination," p. 105; spring, 2002, Titi Adepitan, "Between Drama and Epic," pp. 120-133; fall, 2003, Isidore Okpewho, "The Art of the Ozidi Saga," pp. 1-26.

World Literature Today, spring, 1993, Aderemi Bamikunle, "The Poet and His Art," pp. 315-319; autumn, 2000, Tanure Ojaide, review of *A Lot from Paradise,* p. 796.

World Literature Written in English, November, 1976, pp. 297-304; November, 1979, pp. 278-286; autumn, 1987; spring, 1988.

*   *   *

CLARKE, Arthur C. 1917-
(Arthur Charles Clarke, E.G. O'Brian, Charles G. Willis)

PERSONAL: Born December 16, 1917, in Minehead, Somersetshire, England; son of Charles Wright (a farmer) and Nora (Willis) Clarke; married Marilyn Mayfield, June 15, 1953 (divorced, 1964). *Education:* King's College, London, B.Sc. (first-class honors), 1948. *Hobbies and other interests:* "Observing the equatorial skies with a fourteen-inch telescope," table-tennis, scuba diving, and "playing with his Chihuahua and his six computers."

ADDRESSES: Home—25 Barnes Place, Colombo 7, Sri Lanka; Dene Court, Bishop's Lydeard, Taunton, Somerset TA4 3LT, England; fax: (94-1) 698730. *Agent*—David Higham Associates, 5-8 Lower John St., Golden Square, London W1R 4HA, England; Scouil, Chichak, Galen Literary Agency, 381 Park Avenue, New York, NY 10016.

CAREER: British Civil Service, His Majesty's Exchequer and Audit Department, London, England, auditor, 1936-41; Institution of Electrical Engineers, *Science Abstracts,* London, assistant editor, 1949-50; freelance writer, 1951—. Underwater explorer and photographer, in partnership with Mike Wilson, on Great Barrier Reef of Australia and coast of Sri Lanka, 1954-64. Has appeared on television and radio numerous times, including as commentator with Walter Cronkite on Apollo missions, Columbia Broadcasting System, Inc. (CBS), 1968-70, and as host of television series *Arthur C. Clarke's Mysterious World,* 1980, and *Arthur C. Clarke's World of Strange Powers,* 1984. Acted role of Leonard Woolf in Lester James Peries's film *Beddagama* (based on Woolf's *The Village in the Jungle*), 1979. Director of Rocket Publishing Co., United Kingdom; founder, director, and owner, with Hector Ekanayake, of Underwater Safaris (scuba-diving business), Sri Lanka; founder and patron, Arthur C. Clarke Centre for Modern Technologies, Sri Lanka, 1984—. Chancellor of University of Moratuwa, Sri Lanka, 1979—; chancellor, International Space University, 1987—; Vikram Sarabhai Professor, Physical Research Laboratory, Ahmedabad, India, 1980; trustee, Institute of Integral Education, Sri Lanka. Fellow, Franklin Institute, 1971, King's College, 1977, and Carnegie-Mellon University Institute of Robotics, 1981. Lecturer, touring United States and Britain, 1957-74. Board member of National Space Institute, United States, Space Generation Foundation, United States, International Astronomical Union (Search for ExtraTerrestrial Intelligence) Commission 51, and Planetary Society, United States. Chair, Second International Astronautics Congress, London, 1951; moderator, *Space Flight Report to the Nation,* 1961. *Military service:* Royal Air Force, radar instructor, 1941-46; became flight lieutenant.

MEMBER: International Academy of Astronautics (honorary fellow), International Science Writers Association, International Council for Integrative Studies, World

Academy of Art and Science (academician), British Interplanetary Society (honorary fellow; chairperson, 1946-47, 1950-53), Royal Astronomical Society (fellow), British Astronomical Association, Association of British Science Writers (life member), British Science Fiction Association (patron), Royal Society of Arts (fellow), Society of Authors (council member), American Institute of Aeronautics and Astronautics (honorary fellow), American Astronautical Society (honorary fellow), American Association for the Advancement of Science, National Academy of Engineering (United States; foreign associate), Science Fiction Writers of America, Science Fiction Foundation, H.G. Wells Society (honorary vice president), Third World Academy of Sciences (associate fellow), Sri Lanka Astronomical Society (patron), Institute of Engineers (Sri Lanka; honorary fellow), Sri Lanka Animal Welfare Association (patron), British Sub-Aqua Club.

AWARDS, HONORS: International Fantasy Award, 1952, for *The Exploration of Space;* Hugo Award, World Science Fiction Convention, 1956, for "The Star"; Kalinga Prize, UNESCO, 1961, for science writing; Junior Book Award, Boys Club of America, 1961; Stuart Ballantine Gold Medal, Franklin Institute, 1963, for originating concept of communications satellites; Robert Ball Award, Aviation-Space Writers Association, 1965, for best aerospace reporting of the year; Westinghouse Science Writing Award, American Association for the Advancement of Science, 1969; Second International Film Festival special award, and Academy Award nomination for best screenplay (with Stanley Kubrick), Academy of Motion Picture Arts and Sciences, both 1969, both for *2001: A Space Odyssey; Playboy* editorial award, 1971, 1982; Hon. D.Sc., Beaver College, 1971, University of Moratuwa, 1979; Nebula Award, Science Fiction Writers of America, 1972, for "A Meeting with Medusa"; Nebula Award, 1973, and Hugo Award, John W. Campbell Memorial Award, Science Fiction Research Association, and Jupiter Award, Instructors of Science Fiction in Higher Education, all 1974, all for *Rendezvous with Rama;* Aerospace Communications Award, American Institute of Aeronautics and Astronautics, 1974; Bradford Washburn Award, Boston Museum of Science, 1977, for "contributions to the public understanding of science"; Galaxy Award, 1979; Nebula and Hugo Awards, both 1980, both for *The Fountains of Paradise;* special Emmy Award for engineering, National Academy of Television Arts and Sciences, 1981, for contributions to satellite broadcasting; "Lensman" Award, 1982; Marconi International fellowship, 1982; Centennial Medal, Institute of Electrical and Electronics Engineers, 1984; E.M. Emme Astronautical Literature Award, American Astronautical Soci-

ety, 1984; Grand Master Award, Science Fiction Writers of America, 1986; Vidya Jyothi Medal (Presidential Science Award), 1986; Charles A. Lindbergh Award, 1987; Third World Academy of Sciences associate fellow, 1987; named to Society of Satellite Professionals Hall of Fame, 1987; D.Litt., University of Bath, 1988; named to International Aerospace Hall of Fame, 1989; named to International Space Hall of Fame, 1989; Special Achievement Award, Space Explorers Association, Riyadh, 1989; R.A. Heinlein Memorial Award, National Space Society, 1990; Freeman of Minehead, 1992; Lord Perry Award for distance education, 1992; Nobel Peace Prize nomination, 1994; Distinguished Public Service Medal, NASA, 1995; Space Achievement Medal and Trophy, BIS, 1995; Mohamed Sahabdeen Award for Science, 1996; Von Karman Award, IAA, 1996; asteroid 4923 named 'Clarke,' IAU, 1996; Presidential Award, University of Illinois, 1997; knighted by Queen Elizabeth, 1998 (invested, 2000); European satellite, launched in April, 2000, named after Clarke in recognition of his contribution to the development of global communication networks. The Arthur C. Clarke Awards bestow annual prizes for writers in fifteen categories and are organized by the Space Frontier Foundation.

WRITINGS:

NONFICTION

Interplanetary Flight: An Introduction to Astronautics, Temple, 1950, Harper (New York, NY), 1951, 2nd edition, 1960.

The Exploration of Space, Harper, 1951, revised edition, Pocket Books (New York, NY), 1979.

The Young Traveller in Space, Phoenix, 1953, published as *Going into Space,* Harper, 1954, revised edition (with Robert Silverberg) published as *Into Space: A Young Person's Guide to Space,* Harper (New York, NY), 1971.

The Exploration of the Moon, illustrated by R.A. Smith, Harper (New York, NY), 1954.

The Coast of Coral, Harper (New York, NY), 1956.

The Reefs of Taprobane: Underwater Adventures around Ceylon, Harper (New York, NY), 1957.

The Scottie Book of Space Travel, Transworld Publishers (London, England), 1957.

The Making of a Moon: The Story of the Earth Satellite Program, Harper (New York, NY), 1957, revised edition, 1958.

Voice across the Sea, Harper (New York, NY), 1958, revised edition, 1974.

(With Mike Wilson) *Boy beneath the Sea,* Harper (New York, NY), 1958.

The Challenge of the Spaceship: Previews of Tomorrow's World, Harper (New York, NY), 1959.

(With Mike Wilson) *The First Five Fathoms: A Guide to Underwater Adventure,* Harper (New York, NY), 1960.

The Challenge of the Sea, Holt (New York, NY), 1960.

(With Mike Wilson) *Indian Ocean Adventure,* Harper (New York, NY), 1961.

Profiles of the Future: An Inquiry into the Limits of the Possible, Harper (New York, NY), 1962, revised edition, Holt (New York, NY), 1984.

The Treasure of the Great Reef, Harper (New York, NY), 1964, new edition, Ballantine (New York, NY), 1974.

(With Mike Wilson) *Indian Ocean Treasure,* Harper (New York, NY), 1964.

(With the editors of *Life*) *Man and Space,* Time-Life (Alexandria, VA), 1964.

Voices from the Sky: Previews of the Coming Space Age, Harper (New York, NY), 1965.

(Editor) *The Coming of the Space Age: Famous Accounts of Man's Probing of the Universe,* Meredith (New York, NY), 1967.

The Promise of Space, Harper (New York, NY), 1968.

(With Neil Armstrong, Michael Collins, Edwin E. Aldrin, Jr., Gene Farmer, and Dora Jane Hamblin) *First on the Moon,* Little, Brown (Boston, MA), 1970.

Report on Planet Three and Other Speculations, Harper (New York, NY), 1972.

(With Chesley Bonestell) *Beyond Jupiter,* Little, Brown (Boston, MA), 1972.

The View from Serendip (autobiography), Random House (New York, NY), 1977.

(With Simon Welfare and John Fairley) *Arthur C. Clarke's Mysterious World* (based on television series), A & W Publishers, 1980.

Ascent to Orbit: A Scientific Autobiography: The Technical Writings of Arthur C. Clarke, Wiley (New York, NY), 1984.

1984: Spring—A Choice of Futures, Del Rey (New York, NY), 1984.

(With Simon Welfare and John Fairley) *Arthur C. Clarke's World of Strange Powers,* Putnam (New York, NY), 1984.

(With Peter Hyams) *The Odyssey File,* Fawcett (New York, NY), 1985.

Arthur C. Clarke's July 20, 2019: Life in the Twenty-first Century, Macmillan (New York, NY), 1986.

Arthur C. Clarke's Chronicles of the Strange and Mysterious, edited by Simon Welfare and John Fairley, Collins (London, England), 1987.

Astounding Days: A Science Fictional Autobiography, Bantam (New York, NY), 1989.

How the World Was One: Beyond the Global Village, Bantam (New York, NY), 1992.

By Space Possessed, Gollancz (London, England), 1993.

Frontline of Discovery: Science on the Brink of Tomorrow, National Geographic Society (Washington, DC), 1994.

The Snows of Olympus: A Garden on Mars, Norton (New York, NY), 1995.

Arthur C. Clarke & Lord Dunsany: A Correspondence, edited by K.A. Daniels, Anamnesis Press (San Francisco, CA), 1998.

Greetings, Carbon-Based Bipeds!: Collected Essays, 1934-1998, edited by I.T. Macauley, St. Martin's Press (New York, NY), 1999.

FICTION

The Sands of Mars, Sidgwick & Jackson (London, England), 1951.

Prelude to Space, World Editions (New York, NY), 1951, published as *Master of Space,* Lancer Books (New York, NY), 1961, published as *The Space Dreamers,* Lancer Books (New York, NY), 1969.

Islands in the Sky, Winston, 1952, new edition, Penguin Books (New York, NY), 1972.

Childhood's End, Ballantine (New York, NY), 1953.

Against the Fall of Night, Gnome Press (New York, NY), 1953.

Expedition to Earth (short stories), Ballantine (New York, NY), 1953.

Earthlight, Ballantine (New York, NY), 1955.

Reach for Tomorrow (short stories), Ballantine (New York, NY), 1956.

The City and the Stars (based on novel *Against the Fall of Night*), Harcourt (New York, NY), 1956.

The Deep Range (also see below), Harcourt (New York, NY), 1957.

Tales from the White Hart, Ballantine (New York, NY), 1957.

The Other Side of the Sky (short stories), Harcourt (New York, NY), 1958.

Across the Sea of Stars (anthology; includes *Childhood's End* and *Earthlight*), Harcourt (New York, NY), 1959.

A Fall of Moondust, Harcourt, (New York, NY), 1961, abridged edition, University of London Press (London, England), 1964.

From the Oceans, from the Stars (anthology; includes *The Deep Range* and *The City and the Stars*), Harcourt (New York, NY), 1962.

Tales of Ten Worlds (short stories), Harcourt (New York, NY), 1962.

Dolphin Island: A Story of the People of the Sea, Holt (New York, NY), 1963.

Glide Path, Harcourt (New York, NY), 1963.

Prelude to Mars (anthology; includes *Prelude to Space* and *The Sands of Mars*), Harcourt (New York, NY), 1965.

An Arthur C. Clarke Omnibus (contains *Childhood's End, Prelude to Space,* and *Expedition to Earth*), Sidgwick & Jackson (London, England), 1965.

(Editor) *Time Probe: The Science in Science Fiction,* Dial (New York, NY), 1966.

The Nine Billion Names of God (short stories), Harcourt (New York, NY), 1967.

A Second Arthur C. Clarke Omnibus (contains *A Fall of Moondust, Earthlight,* and *The Sands of Mars*), Sidgwick & Jackson (London, England), 1968.

(With Stanley Kubrick) *2001: A Space Odyssey* (screenplay), Metro-Goldwyn-Mayer, 1968.

2001: A Space Odyssey (based on screenplay), New American Library, 1968, published with a new introduction by Clarke, ROC (New York, NY), 1994.

The Lion of Comarre; and, Against the Fall of Night, Harcourt (New York, NY), 1968.

The Lost Worlds of 2001, Gregg Press (Boston, MA), 1972.

The Wind from the Sun (short stories), Harcourt (New York, NY), 1972.

(Editor) *Three for Tomorrow,* Sphere Books (London, England), 1972.

Of Time and Stars: The Worlds of Arthur C. Clarke (short stories), Gollancz (London, England), 1972.

Rendezvous with Rama, Harcourt (New York, NY), 1973, adapted edition, Oxford University Press (Oxford, England), 1979.

The Best of Arthur C. Clarke, edited by Angus Wells, Sidgwick & Jackson (London, England), 1973, published as two volumes, Volume 1: *The Best of Arthur C. Clarke: 1937-1955,* Volume 2: *The Best of Arthur C. Clarke: 1956-1972,* 1977.

Imperial Earth: A Fantasy of Love and Discord, Gollancz (London, England), 1975, Harcourt (New York, NY), 1976.

Four Great Science Fiction Novels (contains *The City and the Stars, The Deep Range, A Fall of Moondust,* and *The Fountains of Paradise*), Harcourt (New York, NY), 1979.

(Editor, with George Proctor) *The Science Fiction Hall of Fame,* Volume 3: *The Nebula Winners,* Avon (New York, NY), 1982.

2010: Odyssey Two, Del Rey (New York, NY), 1982.

The Sentinel: Masterworks of Science Fiction and Fantasy (short stories), Berkeley Publishing (Berkeley, CA), 1983.

Selected Works, Heinemann (London, England), 1985.

The Songs of Distant Earth, Del Rey (New York, NY), 1986.

2061: Odyssey Three, Del Rey (New York, NY), 1988.

(With Gentry Lee) *Cradle,* Warner Books (New York, NY), 1988.

A Meeting with Medusa (bound with *Green Mars* by Kim Stanley Robinson), Tor Books (New York, NY), 1988.

(With Gentry Lee) *Rama II,* Bantam (New York, NY), 1989.

(With Gregory Benford) *Beyond the Fall of Night,* Putnam (New York, NY), 1990.

The Ghost from the Grand Banks, Bantam (New York, NY), 1990.

Tales from the Planet Earth, illustrated by Michael Whelan, Bantam (New York, NY), 1990.

(With Gentry Lee) *The Garden of Rama,* Bantam (New York, NY), 1991.

The Hammer of God, Bantam (New York, NY), 1993.

(With Gentry Lee) *Rama Revealed,* Bantam (New York, NY), 1994.

(With Mike McQuay) *Richter 10,* Bantam (New York, NY), 1996.

3001: The Final Odyssey, Ballantine (New York, NY), 1997.

(With Michael Kube-McDowell) *The Trigger,* Bantam (New York, NY), 1999.

(With Stephen Baxter) *The Light of Other Days,* Tor (New York, NY), 2000.

The Collected Stories of Arthur C. Clarke, Tor (New York, NY), 2001.

OTHER

Opus 700, Gollancz (London, England), 1990.

Rama: The Official Strategy Guide, Prima Pub. (Rocklin, CA), 1996.

Also author of introduction to *Inmarsat History.* Contributor to books, including *Mars and the Mind of Man,* Harper, 1973. Author of foreword for Paul Preuss's books *Breaking Strain,* Avon, 1987, and *Maelstrom,* Avon, 1988. Also author of television series *Arthur C. Clarke's World of Strange Powers* and a movie treatment based on *Cradle.* Contributor of more than 600 articles and short stories, occasionally under pseudonyms E.G. O'Brian and Charles Willis, to numerous magazines, including *Harper's, Playboy, New York Times Magazine, Vogue, Holiday,* and *Horizon.*

Clarke's works have been translated into Polish, Russian, French, German, Spanish, Serbo-Croatian, Greek, Hebrew, Dutch, and over twenty other languages.

ADAPTATIONS: In 1984, *2010: Odyssey Two* was made into a motion picture titled *2010: The Year We Make Contact,* directed by Peter Hyams, who also authored the screenplay. The book *Arthur C. Clarke's Mysterious World* was adapted as a series for television by Yorkshire Television, 1980. The short story "The Star" was adapted for an episode of *The New Twilight Zone* by (CBS) in 1985. The following works have been optioned for movies: *Childhood's End,* by Universal; *The Songs of Distant Earth,* by Michael Phillips; *The Fountains of Paradise,* by Robert Swarthe; and *Cradle,* by Peter Guber. Sound recordings include *Arthur C. Clarke Reads from his 2001: A Space Odyssey,* 1976; *Transit of Earth; The Nine Billion Names of God;* and *The Star,* 1978; *The Fountains of Paradise,* 1979; *Childhood's End,* 1979; and *2010: Odyssey Two.* A full-length recording of *A Fall of Moondust* was made by Harcourt in 1976.

SIDELIGHTS: Renowned not only for his science fiction, which has earned him the title of Grand Master from the Science Fiction Writers of America, Arthur C. Clarke also has a reputation for first-rate scientific and technical writing. Perhaps best known in this field for "Extraterrestrial Relays," the 1945 article in which he first proposed the idea of communications satellites, Clarke has also published works on such diverse topics as underwater diving, space exploration, and scientific extrapolation. Nevertheless, it is Clarke's science fiction which has secured him his reputation, with such novels as *Childhood's End* and *Rendezvous with Rama* acknowledged as classics in their field. In addition, his story "The Nine Billion Names of God" was named to the science fiction "Hall of Fame," while the movie *2001: A Space Odyssey,* written with director Stanley Kubrick, has been called the most important science-fiction film of the twentieth century.

The Exploration of Space, one of Clarke's first novels, broke ground in explaining scientific ideas to a popular audience. As H.H. Holmes described in the *New York Herald Tribune Book Review,* in "the realm of speculative factual writing . . . Clarke's new book will serve as the most important yet in its field. Not that it says much that is new," explained Holmes, but because "it is precisely calculated to bring our present knowledge of space travel before a whole new public." What enables the book to reach such an audience is a "charm and magnetism" that is due to "Clarke's ability to reduce complex subjects to simple language and his steadfast avoidance of fantasy as a substitute for factual narration," observed Roy Gibbons in the *Chicago Sunday Tribune.*

Although most speculative science texts are soon outdated, Clarke's work has withstood years of technical progress. In *The Promise of Space,* published in 1968 to "replace" *The Exploration of Space,* Clarke "is able to show the manner in which many of his predictions have been fulfilled," noted a *Times Literary Supplement* contributor. But rather than simply cataloging recent discoveries, Clarke's work incorporates them into new ideas: "All through the book Clarke not only recounts what has been done during the last two decades," explained Willy Ley in the *New York Times Book Review,* "but has his eye on both the immediate results and the future."

Although much of Clarke's early fiction reinforced the idea that space travel was an eventuality, *Childhood's End,* his first successful novel, is "Clarke's only work—fiction or nonfiction—in which 'The stars are not for Man,'" suggested Thomas D. Clareson in *Voices for the Future: Essays on Major Science Fiction Writers.* The novel relates the appearance of the Overlords, a race of devil-shaped aliens who have come to guide Earth to peace and prosperity. Beginning by eliminating all individual governments and thus ending war, the Overlords use their superior technology to solve the problems of poverty, hunger, and oppression. The cost of this utopia is that most scientific research is set aside as unnecessary, and the exploration of space is forbidden. The motives of the Overlords become clear as the youngest generation of humans develops extrasensory powers; the children of Earth are to join the Overmind, a collective galactic "spirit" that transcends physical form. The need for science, technology, and space is eliminated with humanity's maturation, and the Earth itself is destroyed as her children join the Overmind.

Some critics view *Childhood's End* as the first manifestation of the theme of spiritual evolution that appears throughout Clarke's fiction. John Huntington, writing in the critical anthology *Arthur C. Clarke,* believed the novel to be Clarke's solution to one of the problems posed by technological progress: how spiritual development can keep pace with scientific development when by making man comfortable, science often takes away man's curiosity and drive. *Childhood's End* solves the problem with a stage of "transcendent evolution," and Huntington proposes that "it is its elegant solution to the problem of progress that has rightly earned *Childhood's End* that 'classic' status it now enjoys."

Clarke's best-known work, *2001: A Space Odyssey,* was the result of four years' work on both the film version and the subsequent novel. The collaboration between Clarke and director Stanley Kubrick began when the filmmaker sought a suitable basis for making the "proverbial good science fiction movie," as he has frequently described it. The two finally settled upon Clarke's 1951 short story "The Sentinel," and developed it "not [into] a script, which in [Kubrick's] view does not contain enough of the visual and emotional information necessary for filming, but a prose version, rather like a novel," related Michel Ciment in *Focus on the Science Fiction Film*. The result "was of more help to him in creating the right atmosphere because it was more generous in its descriptions," added Ciment.

The film and the novel have the same basic premise: a large black monolith has been sent to Earth to encourage the development of man. First shown assisting in the "dawn of man" four million years ago, a monolith is next uncovered on the moon, and upon its unveiling sends a strong radio signal toward the outer planets. As a result the spaceship *Discovery,* operated by the intelligent computer HAL 9000, is sent in the direction of the signal to investigate. However, while the human crew is kept ignorant of the ship's true assignment, the HAL 9000 begins to eliminate what it sees as obstacles in the way of the mission—including all of the crew. First captain Dave Bowman manages to survive, however, and upon his arrival at a moon of Saturn (Jupiter in the film) encounters yet a third monolith which precipitates a journey through the infinite, "into a world where time and space are relative in ways beyond Einstein," described Penelope Gilliatt in the *New Yorker.* Bowman is transformed during this journey, and subsequently arrives at a higher plane of evolution as the Star Child.

"Clarke's *2001: A Space Odyssey* was an extraordinary development in fiction, a novel written in collaboration with the director who was simultaneously filming it," wrote Colin Greenland of the *Times Literary Supplement. New Statesman* contributor Brenda Maddox found the book lacking beside the movie. She claimed that the novel "has all the faults of the film and none of its virtues. The characters still have the subtlety of comic-strip men and, lacking the film's spectacular visual gimmickry . . . the story must propel itself with little gusts of scientific explanation." In contrast, Eliot Fremont-Smith asserted in the *New York Times* that "the immense and moving fantasy-idea of *2001* . . . is an idea that can be *dramatically* envisioned only in the free oscillations of the delicately cued and stretched mind." The critic added that the film "is too direct for this, its wonders too unsubtle and, for all their majesty, too confining." And where the movie may have been obscure, "all of it becomes clear and convincing in the novel. It is indeed an odyssey, this story, this exhilarating and rather chilling science fiction fantasy." Nevertheless, in comparing the visual genius of the film with

the clarity of the book, Clarke himself admits in *Focus on the Science Fiction Film* that both versions "did something that the other couldn't have done."

Although for several years Clarke—and others—insisted that a sequel to *2001* would be impossible, in 1982 Clarke published *2010: Odyssey Two*. Incorporating elements of both the film and novel versions, as well as new information from the *Voyager* probes of Jupiter, in *2010* "Clarke sensibly steps back down to our level to tell the story of a combined Russian and American expedition to salvage Bowman's deserted ship, the *Discovery,* and find out what happened," related Greenland. Although the expedition finds the remains of the ship and repairs the HAL 9000, the purpose of the black monolith mystifies them. While some critics find this an adequate approach to a sequel, others criticize Clarke for even attempting to follow up a "classic." *Science Fiction Review* writer Gene DeWeese believed a large problem is that *2010* "is not so much a sequel to the original book, which was in many ways superior to the movie, but a sequel to and an explanation of the movie. Unfortunately, many of these explanations already existed [in the novel of *2001*.]" *Washington Post Book World* contributor Michael Bishop similarly noted a tendency to over-explain: "Ponderous expository dialogue alternates with straightforward expository passages in which Heywood Floyd . . . or the author himself lectures the reader." And Gerald Jones of the *New York Times Book Review* complained that *2010* "violates the mystery [of the original] at every turn."

Despite the various criticisms, *2010* still "has its share of that same sense of wonder, which means that it is one of the dozen or so most enjoyable SF books of the year," observed DeWeese. "Clarke deftly blends discovery, philosophy, and a newly acquired sense of play," stated *Time* contributor Peter Stoler, creating a work that will "entertain" readers.

2061: Odyssey Three is the next chapter in the saga of the black monolith. The year 2061 marks the year of the next appearance of Halley's comet; *Odyssey Three* follows Heywood Floyd on a survey of the object. While en route, the survey party is redirected to rescue a ship that has crashed on the Jovian moon of Europa— the one celestial object the monoliths have warned humans against visiting. Some critics have been skeptical of a second sequel, such as the *Time* reviewer who found that "the mix of imagination and anachronism is wearing as thin as the oxygen layer on Mars." Although Jones also observed that "Clarke's heart is obviously not in the obligatory action scenes that advance the plot," he conceded that the author "remains a master at describing the wonders of the universe in sentences that combine a respect for scientific accuracy with an often startling lyricism." Clarke "is not to be measured by the same standards we apply to a mundane plot-smith," asserted David Brin in the *Los Angeles Times*. "He is, after all, the poet laureate of the Space Age. He is at his best making the reader feel, along with Heywood Floyd," continued Brin, "how fine it might be to stand upon an ancient comet, out under the stars, knowing that it is those dreams that finally come true that are the best dreams of all."

Clarke's faith in the human spirit is evident in his non-fiction book *The Snows of Olympus: A Garden on Mars.* Published in 1995, at a time when NASA struggled with massive budget cutbacks, this book nevertheless looks optimistically toward a future when humans will visit and colonize the planet Mars. Clarke asserts that if money were no object, human beings could walk on Mars early in the twenty-first century. He outlines a three-part mission to Mars, beginning with robot probes, which would locate needed resources on the planet and choose suitable landing sites. Unmanned space freighters would follow with equipment and supplies, intended to support the third part of the mission: the landing of a human crew. Clarke predicts that once a human colony is established, work will begin to alter the environment of Mars to make it habitable by unprotected human beings. He even believes that it is possible to create oceans and large-scale agricultural projects there. *The Snows of Olympus* is illustrated with computer-generated art depicting the transformation of Mars. Clarke created the pictures himself, beginning with maps of the planet generated by NASA's *Voyager* probe.

Clarke told John F. Burns of the *New York Times Book Review* that in the years when he was not writing, he felt like Frank Poole after he had his air supply cut off by HAL. Thus, Clarke has done what he long insisted was impossible: write the fourth installment of his "Odyssey series," *3001: The Final Odyssey.* In *3001* another manned space voyage finds the deep-frozen Poole, long presumed dead, and revives him with fourth-millennium technology. Poole masters the use of the "braincap" and other gadgets, learns about Star City, and studies a thousand years of history he has slept through. During his long sleep, a monolith has exploded Jupiter, turning it and its moons into a secondary solar system. One moon, Europa, has been colonized by a monolith that monitors human behavior and influences the plantlike beings beneath the surface to grow. Poole is alarmed to learn that his old colleague, Dave Bowman, and HAL have both become absorbed by the

monolith and that the black slab's superiors are intent on doing something unthinkable to the humans that they have enslaved. Writing in the *New York Times Book Review,* John Allen Paulos found that while the plot hangs together "reasonably well," much of the enjoyment comes from Clarke's ruminations on high technology, Freudian therapy, computer security, terrorism, and religious mania. Ian Watson of the *Times Literary Supplement* suggested that what makes *3001* compelling reading is the way in which he "retrofits" earlier episodes "so that they blend with the new future and the now ex-future."

Clarke released two novels near the turn of the twenty-first century: *The Trigger,* written with Michael Kube-McDowell, and *The Light of Other Days,* written with Stephen Baxter. *The Trigger* depicts a time in the future when weapons using gunpowder are rendered obsolete. A device called the "Trigger" causes them to self-destruct. When the Trigger falls into the wrong hands, questions of ethics arise. According to *Booklist*'s Roland Green, "The discovery's potential for good and evil is enormous." Jackie Cassada of *Library Journal* described the book as a "thought-provoking, suspenseful tale."

Set in the mid-2300s as the last outdated rocket-boosted spaceship is launched in Russia, *The Light of Other Days* tells the tale of scientist Heram Patterson, who unveils wormhole technology, which allows people to view others anywhere in the world. It is soon discovered that this technology can be used to see into the future, and Patterson's son discovers that it can be used to view the past as well. The technology renders privacy nonexistent and reveals the earth's destruction by an asteroid in 500 years. *Booklist*'s Sally Estes noted that "The stories' inter-relationships have a soap-opera quality," but described the book as a "sweeping, mind-boggling read."

The *Collected Stories of Arthur C. Clarke,* published in 2001, contains over one hundred science-fiction tales and nearly 1,000 pages. Most stories in the collection date from 1946 to 1970, but a few are earlier and several are more recent. Jackie Cassada of *Library Journal* remarked that the book displays Clarke's "enthusiasm for both good storytelling and impeccable science." *Booklist*'s Roland Green concluded that *Collected Stories* "may be the single-author science-fiction collection of the decade."

BIOGRAPHICAL AND CRITICAL SOURCES:

BOOKS

Agel, Jerome, editor, *The Making of Kubrick's 2001,* New American Library, 1970.

Aldiss, Brian W., *Trillion Year Spree: The History of Science Fiction,* Atheneum (New York, NY), 1986.

Bleiler, E.F., editor, *Science Fiction Writers: Critical Studies of the Major Authors from the Early Nineteenth Century to the Present Day,* Scribner (New York, NY), 1982.

Clareson, Thomas D., editor, *Voices for the Future: Essays on Major Science Fiction Writers,* Bowling Green University Press (Bowling Green, OH), 1976.

Contemporary Literary Criticism, Thomson Gale (Detroit, MI), Volume 1, 1973, Volume 4, 1975, Volume 13, 1980, Volume 16, 1981, Volume 18, 1981, Volume 35, 1985.

Contemporary Novelists, 7th edition, St. James Press (Detroit, MI), 2001.

Encyclopedia of Occultism and Parapsychology, 5th edition, Thomson Gale (Detroit, MI), 2001.

Hollow, John, *Against the Night, the Stars: The Science Fiction of Arthur C. Clarke,* Harcourt, 1983, expanded edition, Ohio University Press (Athens, OH), 1987.

Johnson, William, editor, *Focus on the Science Fiction Film,* Prentice-Hall (Englewood Cliffs, NJ), 1972.

Ketterer, David, *New Worlds for Old: The Apocalyptic Imagination, Science Fiction, and American Literature,* Indiana University Press (Bloomington, IN), 1974, pp. 43-49.

Knight, Damon, *In Search of Wonder: Essays on Modern Science Fiction,* Advent (Chicago, IL), 1967, pp. 177-205.

Magill, Frank N., editor, *Survey of Science Fiction Literature,* Volumes 1-5, Salem Press (Englewood Cliffs, NJ), 1979.

Malik, Rex, editor, *Future Imperfect,* Pinter, 1980.

McAleer, Neil, *Arthur C. Clarke: The Authorized Biography,* Contemporary Books (Chicago, IL), 1992.

Moskowitz, Sam, *Seekers of Tomorrow: Masters of Science Fiction,* World Publishing, 1966.

Of Time and Stars: The Worlds of Arthur C. Clarke, Gollancz (London, England), 1972, pp. 7-10.

Olander, Joseph D., and Martin Harry Greenburg, editors, *Arthur C. Clarke,* Taplinger (New York, NY), 1977.

Platt, Charles, *Dream Makers: The Uncommon Men and Women Who Write Science Fiction,* Volume II, Berkeley Publishing, 1983.

Rabkin, Eric S., *Arthur C. Clarke,* Starmont House, 1979.

Reid, Robin Anne, *Arthur C. Clarke: A Critical Companion,* Greenwood Press (Westport, CT), 1997.

St. James Encyclopedia of Popular Culture, St. James Press (Detroit, MI), 2000.

St. James Guide to Young Adult Writers, St. James Press (Detroit, MI), 1999.

Samuelson, David N., *Arthur C. Clarke: A Primary and Secondary Bibliography,* G.K. Hall (Boston, MA), 1984.

Short Story Criticism, Volume 3, Thomson Gale (Detroit, MI), 1989.

Slusser, George Edgar, *The Space Odysseys of Arthur C. Clarke,* Borgo (San Bernadino, CA), 1978.

Wollheim, Donald A., *The Universe Makers,* Harper (New York, NY), 1971.

PERIODICALS

Algol, November, 1974.

Analog Science Fiction and Fact, September, 2000, Tom Easton, review of *The Light of Other Days,* pp. 135-141; May, 2001, Tom Easton, "The Reference Library," pp. 132-138.

Atlantic, July, 1952; April, 1963, p. 152.

Best Sellers, October 1, 1973; May, 1979; May, 1984, pp. 75-76; December 24, 1953, p. 13.

Booklist, October 1, 1995, pp. 239-240; January 1-15, 1997, p. 778; August, 1999, Ray Olson, review of *Greetings, Carbon-Based Bipeds! Collected Essays, 1934-1998,* p. 2003; September 15, 1999, Roland Green, review of *The Trigger,* p. 196; February 1, 2000, Sally Estes, review of *The Light of Other Days,* p. 996; September 15, 2000, Leah Sparks, review of *The Light of Other Days,* p. 259; January 1, 2001, Roland Green, review of *The Collected Stories of Arthur C. Clarke,* p. 928.

Book World, June 30, 1968, pp. 1, 3; December 19, 1971, p. 6.

Chicago Sunday Tribune, July 13, 1952.

Chicago Sunday Tribune Magazine of Books, February 16, 1958, p. 7.

Chicago Tribune, December 30, 1990, section 14, p. 6; January 30, 1994, section 14, p. 6.

Christian Science Monitor, February 26, 1963; February 10, 1972, p. 10; August 8, 1973, p. 9; December 3, 1982, p. B3; November 26, 1993, p. 15.

Commonweal, May 3, 1968.

Detroit News, November 28, 1982.

Discover, May, 1997, pp. 68-69.

Economist, April 12, 1997, p. 85.

Extrapolation, winter, 1980, pp. 348-360; summer, 1987, pp. 105-129; spring, 1989, pp. 53-69.

Guardian, January 20, 2001, Andrew Rissik, "Magic among the Stars."

Kirkus Reviews, November 1, 1987.

Library Journal, March 1, 1990, p. 98; November 1, 1995, pp. 101-102; February 15, 1997, p. 164; September 1, 1999, William Baer, review of *Greetings, Carbon-Based Bipeds!,* p. 226; December, 1999,

Jackie Cassada, review of *The Trigger,* p. 192; March 15, 2001, Jackie Cassada, review of *The Collected Stories of Arthur C. Clarke,* p. 110; September 15, 2001, Michael Rogers, "The Fountains of Paradise," p. 188; September 15, 2001, Michael Rogers, "The City and the Stars and the Sands of Mars," p. 118.

Locus, November, 1993, p. 27; February, 1994, p. 75.

Los Angeles Times, December 1, 1982; January 24, 1992, pp. E1, E4; February 12, 1995, p. M4; January 29, 1996.

Los Angeles Times Book Review, December 19, 1982; March 4, 1984; December 6, 1987; December 9, 1990, p. 10; February 3, 1991, p. 10; January 24, 1992, p. E1; August 8, 1993, p. 11; March 10, 1996.

Magazine of Fantasy and Science Fiction, September, 1979, pp. 25-26; October, 1999, Robert K.J. Killheffer, review of *Greetings, Carbon-Based Bipeds!,* p. 36.

Nation, March 5, 1983.

National Review, November 20, 1962, pp. 403-404; May 14, 1976.

New Republic, May 4, 1968; March 20, 1976; March 24, 1979.

New Scientist, April 12, 1997, p. 44.

Newsday, April 4, 1968; April 20, 1968.

New Statesman, December 20, 1968, pp. 877-878; January 26, 1979.

Newsweek, October 30, 1961.

New Yorker, April 24, 1965; May 27, 1967; April 13, 1968; September 21, 1968; August 9, 1969, pp. 40-65; December 13, 1982; December 20, 1982.

New York Herald Tribune Book Review, July 13, 1952; August 10, 1952; August 23, 1953; March 2, 1958, p. 6.

New York Times, May 29, 1968; July 5, 1968; August 22, 1973, p. 35; February 26, 1985; April 7, 1993, pp. C13, C19; November 28, 1994, p. A4; April 1, 1997; April 11, 1997.

New York Times Book Review, March 14, 1954; July 15, 1956, p. 20; April 14, 1963, pp. 22, 24; August 25, 1968, p. 10; September 23, 1973; January 18, 1976; October 30, 1977, p. 12; March 18, 1979; January 23, 1983, p. 24; March 6, 1983; May 11, 1986; December 20, 1987; May 6, 1990, p. 22; July 8, 1990, p. 22; February 3, 1991, p. 33; September 1, 1991, p. 13; June 13, 1993, p. 22; March 13, 1994, p. 30; January 28, 1996; March 9, 1997; December 26, 1999, Gerald Jones, review of *Greetings! Carbon-Based Bipeds!,* p. 14.

New York Times Magazine, March 6, 1966.

Observer, January 21, 2001, Robin McKie, "Master of the Universe."

Omni, March, 1979.

People, December 20, 1982.

Playboy, July, 1986.

Popular Science, October, 2001, Nicole Foulke, "The Banyan Trees of Mars," p. 42.

Publishers Weekly, September 10, 1973; June 14, 1976; January 6, 1984, p. 75; January 27, 1984, p. 72; September 18, 1995, pp. 121-122; January 22, 1996, p. 61; July 26, 1999, review of *Greetings, Carbon-Based Bipeds!,* p. 74; December 6, 1999, review of *The Trigger,* p. 58; January 31, 2000, review of *The Light of Other Days,* p. 86.

Reader's Digest, April, 1969.

Saturday Review, July 5, 1952; April 20, 1968.

Science, August 30, 1968, pp. 874-875.

Science Fiction Review, March-April, 1979; August, 1981; February, 1983, p. 15; May, 1984; fall, 1984, p. 26; summer, 1986.

Science-Fiction Studies, July, 1979, pp. 230-231; November, 1997, pp. 441-458.

Scientific American, December, 1999, review of *Greetings, Carbon-Based Bipeds!,* p. 143.

Time, July 19, 1968; November 15, 1982; January 11, 1988.

Times (London, England), November 25, 1982.

Times Higher Education Supplement, Andrew Robinson, review of *Greetings, Carbon-Based Bipeds!,* p. 21.

Times Literary Supplement, July 15, 1968; January 2, 1969; December 5, 1975; June 16, 1978, p. 662; January 21, 1983; October 31, 1986; March 21, 1997; January 28, 2000, Oliver Morton, review of *Greetings, Carbon-Based Bipeds!,* p. 12; March 2, 2001, Edward James, *The Collected Stories,* p. 23.

Tribune Books (Chicago, IL), January 30, 1994, section 14, p. 6.

Virginia Quarterly Review, winter, 1974.

Voice Literary Supplement, November, 1982, pp. 8-9.

Washington Post, February 16, 1982; November 16, 1982.

Washington Post Book World, December 26, 1982, p. 6; March 25, 1984, p. 6; November 25, 1990, p. 8; March 9, 1992, p. B1.

West Coast Review of Books, number 1, 1986.

Western Folklore, number 28, 1969, pp. 230-237.

Wilson Library Bulletin, March, 1990, pp. 110-111.

World Press Review, April, 1985.

ONLINE

Arthur C. Clarke Unauthorized Homepage, http://www.lsi.usp.br/~rbianchi/clarke/ (November 16, 2003).

CLARKE, Arthur Charles
See CLARKE, Arthur C.

*   *   *

CLARKE, Austin C. 1934-
(Austin Chesterfield Clarke)

PERSONAL: Born July 26, 1934, in St. James, Barbados; son of Kenneth Trothan (an artist) and Gladys (a hotel maid) Clarke; married Betty Joyce Reynolds, 1957 (divorced); children: Janice, Loretta, Jordan (also known as Mphahlele). *Education:* Attended secondary school at Harrison College in Barbados; studied economics and politics at Trinity College, University of Toronto, beginning in 1955.

ADDRESSES: Home—62 McGill St., Toronto, Ontario M5B 1H2, Canada. *Agent*—Phyllis Westberg, Harold Ober Associates, 425 Madison Ave., New York, NY 10017.

CAREER: Coleridge-Parry Primary School, St. Peter, Barbados, teacher, 1952-55; newspaper reporter in Timmins and Kirkland Lake, Ontario, Canada, 1959-60; Canadian Broadcasting Corp., Toronto, Ontario, Canada, producer and freelance broadcaster, beginning 1963; Barbados Embassy, Washington, DC, cultural and press attaché, 1974-76; Caribbean Broadcasting Corp., St. Michael, Barbados, general manager, 1975-76. Also has worked as a freelance journalist for *Toronto Globe and Mail* and Canadian Broadcasting Corp. Yale University, New Haven, CT, Hoyt fellow, 1968, visiting professor of Afro-American literature and creative writing, 1968-71; Brandeis University, Waltham, MA, Jacob Ziskind Professor of Literature, 1968-69; Williams College, Williamstown, MA, Margaret Bundy Scott Visiting Professor of Literature, 1971; Duke University, Durham, NC, lecturer, 1971-72; University of Texas, Austin, visiting professor, 1973-74; Concordia University, Montreal, Quebec, writer in residence, 1977; University of Western Ontario, writer in residence, 1978. Rhode Island School of Design, Providence, member of board of trustees, 1970-75; Ontario Board of Censors, vice-chairperson, 1983-85; Immigration and Refugee Board of Canada, member, 1988-93.

MEMBER: Writers Guild, Writers' Union of Canada (founding member), Yale Club (New Haven).

AWARDS, HONORS: President's Medal for best story, University of Western Ontario, 1966; Belmont Short Story Award, 1965, for "Four Stations in His Circle";

Canada Council, senior arts fellowships, 1968, 1970, 1974, grant, 1977; Indiana University School of Letters, Bloomington, fellow, 1969; Cuba's Casa de las Americas Literary Prize, 1980; Toronto Arts Award for lifetime achievement in literature, 1993; Toronto Pride Achievement Award, 1995; Rogers Writers Trust Prize, 1997, for *The Origin of Waves;* Lifetime Achievement Award, Frontier College, Toronto, 1997; Order of Canada, 1998; W.O. Mitchell Literary Prize, 1999; Writer's Trust of Canada, 1999; Martin Luther King, Jr. Award for excellence in writing, 1999; Giller Prize, 2002, Commonwealth Writers Prize for the best overall book, 2003, Trillium Prize, and Regional Commonwealth Writers Prize for the best book in Canada and the Caribbean, all for *The Polished Hoe*. Also received honorary doctorates from Brock University, 1998, and University of Toronto, 1999.

WRITINGS:

NOVELS

The Survivors of the Crossing, McClelland & Stewart (Toronto, Ontario, Canada), 1964.
Amongst Thistles and Thorns, McClelland & Stewart (Toronto, Ontario, Canada), 1965.
The Prime Minister, General Publishing (Don Mills, Ontario, Canada), 1977.
Proud Empires, Gollancz (London, England), 1986, Viking-Penguin (Markham, Ontario, Canada), 1988.
The Origin of Waves, McClelland & Stewart (Toronto, Ontario, Canada), 1997.
The Question, McClelland & Stewart (Toronto, Ontario, Canada), 1999.
The Polished Hoe, Thomas Allen (Toronto, Ontario, Canada), 2002, Amistad (New York, NY), 2003.

NOVELS; "THE TORONTO TRILOGY"

The Meeting Point, Macmillan (Toronto, Ontario, Canada), 1967, Little, Brown (Boston, MA), 1972.
Storm of Fortune, Little, Brown (Boston, MA), 1973.
The Bigger Light, Little, Brown (Boston, MA), 1975.

SHORT STORY COLLECTIONS

When He Was Free and Young and He Used to Wear Silks, Anansi (Toronto, Ontario, Canada), 1971, revised edition, Little, Brown (Boston, MA), 1973.

When Women Rule, McClelland & Stewart (Toronto, Ontario, Canada), 1985.

Nine Men Who Laughed, Penguin (New York, NY), 1986.

In This City, Exile Editions (Toronto, Ontario, Canada), 1992.

There Are No Elders, Exile Editions (Toronto, Ontario, Canada), 1993.

Choosing His Coffin: The Best Stories of Austin Clarke, Thomas Allen (Toronto, Ontario, Canada), 2003.

Author of *Short Stories of Austin Clarke,* 1984.

OTHER

(Contributor) Lloyd W. Brown, editor, *The Black Writer in Africa and the Americas,* Hennessey & Ingalls (Los Angeles, CA), 1973.

Growing up Stupid under the Union Jack: A Memoir, McClelland & Stewart (Toronto, Ontario, Canada), 1980.

The Confused Bewilderment of Martin Luther King & the Idea of Non-Violence As a Political Tactic, Watkins (Burlington, Ontario, Canada), 1986.

Charlotte Stewart, compiler, *The Austin Clarke Collection,* Mills Memorial Library, McMaster University (Hamilton, Ontario, Canada), 1982.

A Passage Back Home: A Personal Reminiscence of Samuel Selvon, Exile Editions (Toronto, Ontario, Canada), 1994.

Barry Callaghan, editor, *The Austin Clarke Reader,* Exile Editions (Toronto, Ontario, Canada), 1996.

Pigtails 'n Breadfruit: The Rituals of Slave Food: A Barbadian Memoir, Random House Canada (Toronto, Ontario, Canada), 1999, published as *Pig Tails 'n Breadfruit: A Culinary Memoir,* New Press (New York, NY), 1999.

Also author of *Myths and Memories, African Literature,* and other film scripts for Educational Television (ETV), Toronto, beginning in 1968. Managing editor of *Contrast,* a newspaper devoted to Toronto's black community. Launched *McGill Street,* a literary journal. Contributor to periodicals, including *Studies in Black Literature* and *Canadian Literature.* Manuscript collection held at McMaster University, Hamilton, Ontario.

SIDELIGHTS: Austin C. Clarke's childhood in colonial Barbados and his experiences as a black immigrant to Canada have provided him with the background for most of his fiction. His writing is almost exclusively concerned with the cultural contradictions that arise when blacks struggle for success in a predominantly white society. Clarke's "one very great gift," in the words of a *New Yorker* critic, is the ability to see "unerringly into his characters' hearts," and this ability is what makes his stories memorable. Martin Levin wrote in the *New York Times Book Review,* "Mr. Clarke is plugged into the fixations, hopes, loves and dreams of his characters. He converts them into stories that are charged with life." In the *Reference Guide to Short Fiction,* Allan Weiss labeled Clarke "unquestionably the most important black Canadian writer." Whether writing novels, short stories, or memoirs, Clarke has a knack for capturing the dialect, the troubles, the emotions, and the thoughts of his individual characters, and through them relays a larger picture to his readers.

Among Clarke's short-story collections are *When He Was Free and Young and He Used to Wear Silks, When Women Rule, Nine Men Who Laughed,* and *In This City.* According to a *Short Story Criticism* contributor, "Clarke's short stories are fueled by his experience of cultural alienation as a West Indian and his analysis of how racism and colonialism impact the daily lives of Caribbean immigrants. Clarke's frequently anthologized short stories are populated by portraits of complex individuals navigating the difficult terrain of cultural adjustment and assimilation." The stories in the collection *When Women Rule* are about immigrants, both white and black, from a variety of cultural origins, who share similar anxieties and fears for the future. Lloyd Brown remarked in *Contemporary Novelists,* "It is the central irony of this collection that the very idea of a Canadian mosaic, with its implicit promise of social harmony and individual success, binds Clarke's diverse Canadians together by virtue of its failure, rather than its fulfillment." In his introduction to the collection *Nine Men Who Laughed,* according to Victor J. Ramraj in the *Dictionary of Literary Biography,* the author "rails against the Canadian system that perpetually perceives the West Indian immigrant as an outsider," and he also criticizes the immigrant who finally succeeds, then "becomes tolerant of abuses." These stories, Ramraj concluded, "show Clarke honing his skills as a short-story writer. Most of the stories achieve an ironic control, discipline, and aesthetic distance not evident in [his] earlier work." The *Short Story Criticism* contributor commented, "Clarke is often criticized for letting his political agenda interfere with the narrative of his later works, thereby alienating the reader. Many scholars, however, emphasize that while these stories present a world rife with despair, they are ultimately underpinned by an idealized vision of a more equitable society."

Clarke's memoir, *Growing up Stupid under the Union Jack,* is an example of the author's typical theme and style. The narrator, Tom, is a young man from a poor village in Barbados. Everyone in the village is proud that Tom is able to attend the Combermere School, for it is run by a "real, true-true Englishman"—an ex-British army officer who calls his students "boy" and "darky" and who flogs them publicly. The students eagerly imitate this headmaster's morals and manners, for to them he represents "Mother England"; they are unaware that in England he would be looked down upon as a mere working-class soldier. The book is "a personal, captivating, provoking, and often humorous record of ignorance, inhumanity and lowly existence under colonial imperialism in World War II Barbados. . . . With its major emphasis on education and childhood, *Growing up Stupid under the Union Jack* continues to draw attention to one of the chief preoccupations of the anticolonial Anglo-Caribbean novel," wrote Robert P. Smith in *World Literature Today*. "The colonial situation is the essence of the absurd because it both causes and symbolizes the condition of being isolated from one's self, one's cultural and personal roots," explained Brown, who maintained, "the most central, and universal, of all [Clarke's] themes [is] alienation." The theme is well rendered in what Darryl Pinckney called in the *New York Review of Books* Clarke's "tender, funny, unpolemical style." This style emphasizes what Ramraj described as "his immense talent for capturing the feel and flow of Barbadian speech and his adeptness at creating hilariously comic scenes."

Some of Clarke's novels are also "set in Barbados and they explore the twin evils of colonial self-hatred and Caribbean poverty," Brown commented. *The Survivors of the Crossing* describes the attempts of Rufus, a worker at a white-owned sugar plantation, to lead a labor strike. He fails because the powerful white owners and the middle-class black islanders ally themselves against him, and even the poor working-class laborers eventually thrust him from their midst. Rufus's inspiration to incite rebellion came from his perception of the American dream, in this case, the power of the working class in Canada. *Amongst Thistles and Thorns* is the story of a nine-year-old runaway who finds his birth father, spends a weekend with him, then returns home still alienated from his current lot in life, but filled with stories about the American land of opportunity, in particularly New York City's Harlem. As Ramraj summarized, "What North America, in particular Canada, actually holds for the black migrant is not so pleasant, however, which is the concern of Clarke's next three novels, the Toronto trilogy."

The trilogy, which is perhaps Clarke's best-known work, details the lives of the Barbadian blacks who immigrate to Toronto hoping to better their lot. In these novels,

The Meeting Point, Storm of Fortune, and *The Bigger Light,* "it is as if the flat characters of a Dickensian world have come into their own at last, playing their tragicomic roles in a manner which owes much to Clarke's extraordinary facility with the Barbadian dialect," commented Diane Bessai in *Canadian Literature.* Bessai also expressed eagerness for Clarke to "continue to create his Brueghel-like canvasses with their rich and contrasting detail and mood." "The sense of defeat among the poor islanders is enlivened by the humour of the characters and their glowing fantasies about the presumed wealth of relatives and friends who make it big in the fatlands of the United States or Canada," remarked John Ayre in *Saturday Night.* The reality for such immigrants, according to Brown, is that "West Indians must choose between being integrated into a strange culture—at the cost of their cultural uniqueness and racial integrity—or being so dedicated to maintaining their black, West Indian identity that they risk being cultural and economic outsiders in their adopted homeland."

The first two novels dwell mostly on Bernice Leach, a live-in maid at a wealthy Toronto home, and her small circle of fellow immigrants. The *New York Times Book Review*'s Martin Levin praised, "Mr. Clarke is masterful at delineating the oppressive insecurities of Bernice and her friends, and the claustrophobic atmosphere that envelops such a mini-minority" as the Caribbean blacks in Toronto. In *The Meeting Point,* Ramraj wrote, "these characters have to contend with inner as well as outer conflicts as they try to retain their black pride and identity and come to grips with self-hatred and beckoning materialism." In *Storm of Fortune,* he continued, some of the group have increased their "measure of economic success and feel they deserve acceptance into the system [but] now have to cope with more sharply felt social alienation."

The third novel, *The Bigger Light,* explores the life of Boysie, the most successful of this immigrant group, and his wife, Dots. Boysie has at last realized the dream that compelled him to leave Barbados; he owns a prosperous business and his own home. However, in the process of realizing his goals, he has become alienated from his wife and his community. "His economic successes have not protected him from emotional failure," explained Brown. Now he searches for a greater meaning to his life—a "bigger light." "*The Bigger Light* is a painful book to read," claimed David Rosenthal in the *Nation.* It is "a story of two people with many things to say and no one to say them to, who hate themselves and bitterly resent the society around them. . . . Certain African novelists have also dealt with the isolation of self-made blacks, but none with Clarke's bleak intensity." A *New Yorker* writer praised the book further, citing Clarke's strong writing skill as the element that lifts the book beyond social comment: "The universal longings of ordinary human beings are depicted with a simplicity and power that make us grateful for all three volumes of this long and honest record."

Clarke has also written works that attack political corruption in his native Barbados. These include the novel *The Prime Minister* which, according to some critics, bears striking comparisons to Clarke's own experiences and observations in Barbados in 1975, when he served briefly as the general manager of the Caribbean Broadcasting Corporation. The novel *Proud Empire,* set in the 1950s, examines political corruption and middle-class values from the perspective of a teen-aged boy not yet tainted by the reality of island politics. It follows Boy through graduation, a period of study in Canada, and a return to Barbados, after which he enters politics himself, though now reluctant and with open eyes. "The novel confirms," Ramraj explained, "that Clarke's strength as a novelist lies not so much in his probing the psyche and inner development of his protagonists as in capturing the subtleties of the social and political behavior of his Barbadian characters, whether at home or abroad."

In 1997 Clarke published the novel *The Origin of Waves* which, according to John Bemrose in *Maclean's,* "contains some of Clarke's best writing ever." It follows a chance reunion of two old friends, of an age similar to that of the author, who have not seen each other since childhood. The two reminisce for hours in a local bar, enabling Clarke, through their stories, to express what Bemrose called "a gentle melancholy and, finally, a spark of hopefulness" about the lot of the immigrant in Canadian society.

Pig Tails 'n Breadfruit: Rituals of Slave Food: A Barbadian Memoir, also published as *Pig Tails 'n Breadfruit: A Culinary Memoir,* is Clarke's remembrance of the classic Barbadian cuisine of his youth, mixed with a dash of family tales, a hint of island culture, and a sprinkle of his own cooking stories. The book explains how to prepare traditional Barbadian dishes, such as Breadfruit Cou-Cou with Braising Beef, Pepperpot, Souse, Bakes, and other "slave food." In addition, the reader is offered a heaping spoonful of insights on the culture of Barbados. *Library Journal's* John Charles reported, "The colorful cuisine of Barbados is the star of this book, and readers will find themselves immersed in the food and culture of that vibrant country." *Booklist's*

Mark Knoblauch noted, "Clarke's marvelous ability to set down the unique Barbadian dialect and make it accessible sparkles throughout these essays." Knoblauch continued, "Clarke's recipes for ham hocks and lima beans and split pea soup illustrate how slave cooks drew the most flavor out of the simplest staples." One complaint critics had about *Pig Tails 'n Breadfruit* is the lack of measurements in the recipes, but as Clarke points out in the book, "To be caught reading a cookbook would suggest that the wife, daughter, or maid does not know how to cook, does not know how to take care of her man." Charles explained, "Cooks there are expected to rely more on taste and touch." *Kola's* Anthony Joyette dubbed *Pig Tails 'n Breadfruit* "a masterpiece," and noted that Clarke is "humorous, witty, and direct."

Clarke's next novel, *The Question,* focuses on a West Indian judge in Toronto who attends a party and meets a young white woman with whom he eventually goes home, even though his girlfriend intends to pick him up at the end of the party. The judge, who was taught by his mother never to discuss his personal problems in public, is intensely private with his thoughts and feelings. The result, according to Neil Querengesser of the *Canadian Ethnic Studies Journal,* is that "he has throughout his adult life construed as public . . . virtually everything and everyone outside himself. Consequently he carries on an intense and very revealing monologue only within his own mind, which Clarke adroitly relays to the reader." The judge's relationship with the new woman, explained Querengesser, provides "deeper and deeper insight into his psychosexual makeup." Readers soon realize that, though the judge has attained a prestigious place in society, his insecurities with women and inability to communicate effectively with them have robbed him of any form of prestige or power.

"Clarke develops his central character masterfully. . . . The judge draws us into his thoughts, almost effortlessly it seems, so interesting are his insights and so effective his means of expression," wrote Querengesser. The critic praised Clarke for his "vivid and insightful portrayals" of the characters in the novel, writing, "His fictional characters inhabit a compellingly realistic world, their lives shaped by a complex mixture of racial, cultural, sexual, political, geographic, linguistic, and economic influences." Querengesser remarked, "Clarke skillfully weaves an absorbing tale of a man impelled by these influences of his past into a strange and uncertain future."

Clarke's *The Polished Hoe,* published first in Canada and then in the United States, has received much praise from critics and has won several awards. The novel is set in the 1940s on the island of Bimshire (a nickname for Barbados). "In a twenty-four-hour time span," noted Denolyn Carroll of the *Black Issues Book Review,* "the novel's main character, Mary Mathilda, giving a statement to authorities about a crime she has committed, unwittingly dissects the evils of slavery and its legacy of colonialism." Mary Mathilda, former field worker and mistress of Mr. Bellfeels, a plantation owner, and the mother of Bellfeels's only son, exacted revenge on the man that dominated her life for so many years, killing him with a hoe she spent years obsessively polishing. *Library Journal*'s Faye A. Chadwell explained, "The twenty-four-hour saga begins after Mary has murdered Mr. Bellfeels and [police sergeant Percy Stuart] must record her all-night confession, an obligation complicated by his lifelong love for Mary."

A *Publishers Weekly* critic praised the work, saying, "Most of the story . . . unfolds through brilliantly written dialogue, a rich, dancing patois that fills out the dimensions of the island's painful history and its complex caste system." *Kola*'s H. Nigel Thomas commented, "[The Polished Hoe] focuses our gaze on an ugly aspect of Caribbean reality which many of us have been unwilling to examine." Donna Bailey Nurse of *Publishers Weekly* reflected, "Through horror and humor, and this dazzling vernacular, Clarke conjures an idiosyncratic people clinging doggedly to their humanity." *Booklist*'s Brad Hooper felt the novel was "creatively executed" and Chadwell called it "a tragic, complex story" that "deftly reveals an abominable state of sexual oppression and racist tyranny and the revenge both can invoke." A *Kirkus Reviews* contributor dubbed the novel "a scorching indictment of the island's power elite" that is "warmed and softened by Clarke's celebration of Bimshire life: its foods, plants, rum shops, and the fortitude of its regular folks as they laugh and curse in cadences that Clarke catches so expertly."

Clarke has been writing in one form or another for several decades, but when asked by Linda Richards of *January Magazine Online* why he chose to write *The Polished Hoe,* he responded, "I felt the freedom for the first time that I needed as an author to deal with this subject. I did not know the subject was going to be this. But I felt the freedom and the liberation from all of the things that could influence the writing of a book negatively. I was not anxious for anything. I was in a very good mood. I was healthy. I was cheerful. And I had retained my sense of humor. And I thought, if not at the time, certainly now reflecting on it because of your question, that they are the ingredients that an author must experience and realize if he or she is going to write something that is great and good."

BIOGRAPHICAL AND CRITICAL SOURCES:

BOOKS

Algoo-Baksh, Stella, *Austin C. Clarke: A Biography,* Press of the University of West Indies [Barbados], 1994.

Brown, Lloyd, *El Dorado and Paradise: A Critical Study of the Works of Austin Clarke,* Center for Social and Humanistic Studies, University of Western Ontario (London, Ontario, Canada), 1989.

Clarke, Austin C., *Pig Tails 'n Bread Fruit: A Barbadian Memoir,* Random House Canada (Toronto, Ontario, Canada), 1999, published as *Pig Tails 'n Breadfruit: A Culinary Memoir,* New Press (New York, NY), 1999.

Contemporary Authors Autobiography Series, Volume 16, Thomson Gale (Detroit, MI), 1992.

Contemporary Black Biography, Volume 32, Thomson Gale (Detroit, MI), 2002.

Contemporary Literary Criticism, Thomson Gale (Detroit, MI), Volume 8, 1978, Volume 53, 1989.

Contemporary Novelists, 7th edition, St. James Press (Detroit, MI), 2001.

Dictionary of Literary Biography, Thomson Gale (Detroit, MI), Volume 53: *Canadian Writers since 1960, First Series,* 1986, Volume 125: *Twentieth-Century Caribbean and Black African Writers, Second Series,* 1993.

Gibson, Graeme, *Eleven Canadian Novelists,* Anansi (Toronto, Ontario, Canada), 1973, pp. 33-54.

Modern Black Writers, 2nd edition, Thomson Gale (Detroit, MI), 2000.

Reference Guide to Short Fiction, 2nd edition, St. James Press (Detroit, MI), 1998.

Short Story Criticism, Volume 45, Thomson Gale (Detroit, MI), 2001.

PERIODICALS

Black Issues Book Review, November-December, 2003, Denolyn Carroll, "Austin Clarke on Honing His Craft: An Island Epic Is a Capstone on a Distinguished Literary Career," review of *The Polished Hoe,* p. 64.

Booklist, February 15, 2000, Mark Knoblauch, review of *Pig Tails 'n Breadfruit: A Culinary Memoir,* p. 1067; May 15, 2003, Brad Hooper, review of *The Polished Hoe,* p. 1637.

Bookseller, February 20, 2004, "Austin Clarke," p. 27.

Books in Canada, October, 1986, pp. 20-21.

Canadian Book Review Annual, 1999, review of *Pig Tails 'n Breadfruit,* p. 140; 2000, review of *The Question,* p. 141.

Canadian Ethnic Studies Journal, summer, 2000, Neil Querengesser, review of *The Question,* p. 164.

Canadian Forum, August, 1999, Judy Schultz, "A Barbadian Memoir Centered in the Kitchen," review of *Pig Tails 'n Breadfruit,* p. 39.

Canadian Literature, summer, 1974; autumn, 1981, pp. 136-38; winter, 1982, pp. 181-85; spring, 2000, Dorothy Lane, review of *The Origin of Waves,* p. 150; autumn-winter, 2001, Maureen Moynagh, review of *Pig Tails 'n Breadfruit,* p. 193.

College Language Association Journal, September, 1985, pp. 9-32; December, 1992, pp. 123-33.

Essence, July, 2003, Diane Patrick, "Take Note," review of *The Polished Hoe,* p. 106.

Globe and Mail (Toronto, Ontario, Canada), April 24, 1999, review of *Pig Tails 'n Breadfruit,* p. E10; October 30, 1999, review of *The Question,* p. D22; November 27, 1999, review of *The Question,* p. D49.

Journal of Caribbean Studies, fall, 1985-spring, 1986, pp. 71-78.

Journal of Commonwealth Literature (Leeds, England), July, 1970.

Kirkus Reviews, May 1, 2003, review of *The Polished Hoe,* p. 624.

Kola, fall, 1999, Anthony Joyette, review of *Pig Tails 'n Breadfruit,* p. 73; winter, 2003, H. Nigel Thomas, review of *The Polished Hoe,* p. 47, and "The Montreal Black Community Congratulates," p. 53.

Library Journal, February 1, 2000, John Charles, review of *Pig Tails 'n Breadfruit,* p. 96; May 15, 2003, Faye A. Chadwell, review of *The Polished Hoe,* p. 122.

Listener, June 15, 1978.

M2 Best Books, November 8, 2002, "Austin Clarke Awarded Canada's Giller Book Prize"; May 12, 2003, "Commonwealth Writers Prizes Awarded."

Maclean's, April 21, 1997, p. 62; November 18, 2002, "Passages," p. 17, "ScoreCard," p. 13; July 1, 2003, Brian Bethune, "Austin Clarke: 'I Feel That My Feet Are Planted Here in This Landscape,'" brief biography of Austin Clarke.

Nation, November 1, 1975.

New Yorker, February 24, 1975.

New York Review of Books, May 27, 1982.

New York Times Book Review, April 9, 1972; December 9, 1973; February 16, 1975; August 23, 1987; April 9, 2000, Laura Shapiro and Michael Sragow, "Cover-She-Down," review of *Pig Tails 'n Breadfruit,* p. 38.

Publishers Weekly, March 6, 2000, review of *Pig Tails 'n Breadfruit,* p. 92; April 21, 2003, review of *The*

Polished Hoe, p. 36; August 11, 2003, Donna Bailey Nurse, "Austin Clarke: A Barbadian Abroad," interview with Austin Clarke, p. 250.

Quill & Quire, December, 1999, review of *The Question,* p. 32.

Saturday Night, October, 1971; June, 1975.

Times Literary Supplement, May 11, 1967, p. 404.

World Literature Today, winter, 1982.

World Literature Written in English, spring, 1986, pp. 115-127.

ONLINE

Athabasca University Canadian Writers Web site, http://www.athabascau.ca/writers/ (June 21, 2004), "Austin Clarke," brief biography.

Bukowski Agency Web site, http://www.thebukowski agency.com/ (February 7, 2003), description of *Pig Tails 'n Breadfruit.*

January Magazine Online, http://www.january magazine.com/ (November, 2002), Linda Richards, interview with Austin Clarke.

Northwest Passages Web site, http://www.nwpassages. com/ (June 21, 2004), "Author Profiles: Austin Clarke," brief biography.

*　　*　　*

CLARKE, Austin Chesterfield
See CLARKE, Austin C.

*　　*　　*

CLAVELL, James 1925-1994
(James duMaresq Clavell)

PERSONAL: Born October 10, 1925, in Australia; immigrated to United States, 1953; naturalized, 1963; died of complications from cancer, September 6, 1994, in Vevey, Switzerland; son of Richard Charles (a captain in the British Royal Navy) and Eileen (Collis) Clavell; married April Stride, February 20, 1951; children: Michaela, Holly. *Education:* Attended University of Birmingham, 1946-47. *Hobbies and other interests:* Sailing, flying helicopters.

CAREER: Worked as a carpenter, 1953; screenwriter, director, and producer, 1954-94; director of television programs, beginning 1958; novelist, 1962-94. *Military service:* Served as captain with the Royal Artillery, 1940-46; taken prisoner of war by Japanese.

MEMBER: Writers Guild, Authors League of America, Producers Guild, Dramatists Guild, Directors Guild.

AWARDS, HONORS: Writers Guild Best Screenplay Award, 1963, for *The Great Escape;* honorary doctorates from the University of Maryland and the University of Bradford.

WRITINGS:

NOVELS

King Rat (also see below), Little, Brown (Boston), 1962, reprinted as *James Clavell's "King Rat,"* Delacorte (New York, NY), 1983.
Tai-Pan: A Novel of Hong Kong (also see below), Atheneum (New York, NY), 1966, reprinted, Delacorte (New York, NY), 1983.
Shogun: A Novel of Japan, Atheneum (New York, NY), 1975.
Noble House: A Novel of Contemporary Hong Kong, Delacorte (New York, NY), 1981.
The Children's Story, Delacorte (New York, NY), 1981.
James Clavell's "Whirlwind," Morrow (New York, NY), 1986.
James Clavell's "Thrump-o-moto," illustrated by George Sharp, Delacorte (New York, NY), 1986.
James Clavell's Gai-Jin: A Novel of Japan, Delacorte (New York, NY), 1993.
Two Complete Novels (includes *Tai-Pan* and *King Rat*), Wings Books (New York, NY), 1995.

SCREENPLAYS

The Fly, Twentieth Century-Fox, 1958.
Watusi, Metro-Goldwyn-Mayer, 1959.
(And producer and director) *Five Gates to Hell,* Twentieth Century-Fox, 1959.
(And producer and director) *Walk Like a Dragon,* Paramount, 1960.
(And producer and director) *The Great Escape,* United Artists, 1963.
633 Squadron, United Artists, 1964.
The Satan Bug, United Artists, 1965.
(And producer and director) *Where's Jack?,* Paramount, 1968.
(And producer and director) *To Sir with Love,* Columbia, 1969.
(And producer and director) *The Last Valley,* ABC Pictures, 1969.

OTHER

Countdown to Armageddon: E=mc2 (play), produced in Vancouver, British Columbia, Canada, at Vancouver Playhouse Theatre, 1966.
(Author of introduction) *The Making of James Clavell's "Shogun,"* Dell (New York, NY), 1980.
(Editor and author of foreword) Sun Tzu, *The Art of War,* Hodder & Stoughton (London, England), 1981, Delacorte (New York, NY), 1983.

Also author of poetry ("published and paid, by God").

ADAPTATIONS: King Rat was produced by Columbia, 1965; *Tai-Pan* was produced by De Laurentis Entertainment Group, 1986. *Shogun* was produced as a television miniseries, 1980 (Clavell was executive producer); *The Children's Story* was produced as a Mobil Showcase television special, 1982; *Noble House* was produced as a television miniseries under the title *James Clavell's "Noble House,"* 1988; a television miniseries based on *King Rat* and one based on *Whirlwind* are planned. *Shogun* was produced for the stage at the Kennedy Center in Washington, DC, and on Broadway in 1990.

SIDELIGHTS: James Clavell, who called himself an "old-fashioned storyteller," was one of the twentieth century's most widely read novelists. His sagas of the Far East—*Tai-Pan: A Novel of Hong Kong, Shogun: A Novel of Japan,* and *Noble House: A Novel of Contemporary Hong Kong*—each sold millions of copies and dominated bestseller lists for months, while his Iran-based adventure, *James Clavell's "Whirlwind,"* commanded a record-setting five million dollar advance from its publisher. In the *Los Angeles Times,* an industry insider described Clavell as "one of the very few writers . . . whose names have marquee value. Clavell's name on the cover sells enormous quantities of books." As James Vesely noted in the *Detroit News,* the author "always does one thing right: he is never boring." Indeed, Clavell combined action, intrigue, cultural conflicts, and romance to produce "event-packed books with the addictive appeal of popcorn," asserted *Detroit News* correspondent Helen Dudar. Although critics generally found that Clavell's blockbusters did not approach literary greatness, they many thought that his works are backed with the sort of research and detail rarely found in so-called "popular novels." In *National Review,* Terry Teachout called Clavell a "first-rate novelist of the second rank," the kind of writer "who provides genuinely stimulating literary entertainment without insulting the sensibilities."

Washington Post contributor Cynthia Gorney described the main theme of Clavell's novels as being "the enormous gulf between Asian and Occidental views of the world." Against exotic backgrounds, the books explore a human obsession in various forms: waging war, cornering power, or forming giant corporations. International espionage, skulduggery, and forbidden romance often round out the picture. "Each of [Clavell's] novels involves an enormous amount of research and enough plot for a dozen books," wrote Ann Marie Cunningham in the *Los Angeles Times.* "All describe strategic thinking during wartime: Teams of tough British boys try to extract themselves from tight spots, . . . often in parts of the former empire." Webster Schott, in the *New York Times Book Review,* noted that Clavell was "neither literary psychoanalyst nor philosophizing intellectual. He reports the world as he sees people—in terms of power, control, strength. . . . He writes in the oldest and grandest tradition that fiction knows." Likewise, *Chicago Tribune* correspondent Harrison E. Salisbury claimed that the author "gives you your money's worth if you like suspense, blood, thunder, romance, intrigue, lust, greed, dirty work—you name it—and pages. He is a generous man." Clavell "sprayed his prose in machine-gun fashion, strafing targets the size of billboards," commented Paul King in *Maclean's.* "Still, he has learned the art of structuring convoluted plots that would have dazzled even Dickens. Above all, with lengthy tales of gut wrenching suspense, Clavell has mastered the technique of keeping readers turning pages until dawn."

"The people I write about are mostly doers," Clavell told the *Washington Post.* "They're not people who sit on their tails in New York, who are concerned about their place in life or should they get a divorce." His epics, he related to *Publishers Weekly,* concern "ordinary people placed in extraordinary circumstances and exposed to danger. They have to do something to extract themselves from this situation, and what you have, then, are heroics and a good read." In the *New York Times Magazine,* Paul Bernstein compared Clavell's characters to those of Charles Dickens. "Dickens's big-hearted orphans become Clavell's larger-than-life men of action," wrote Bernstein, "Dickens's hard-hearted villains, Clavell's hard-hearted business or political adversaries. The social commentary of Dickens becomes in Clavell cross-cultural education and reactionary political warnings." Schott wrote in the *Washington Post Book World* that some of Clavell's characters are romantic stereotypes. The critic added, however, that "others are troubled outsiders, wondering who they are and what their lives mean. Some of his villains and contemporary courtesans have distant cousins in Marvel Comics. But

others are men and women painfully compromised into evil because they do not know how to fight evil without becoming it." In the same review, Schott offered further praise for Clavell: "The riches of his imagination and the reach of his authority are only the start. James Clavell tells his stories so well . . . that it's possible to miss the tough-minded intelligence at work. . . . Clavell knows people and what motivates them. He understands systems and how they work and fail. He remembers history and sees what technology has wrought. . . . James Clavell does more than entertain. He transports us into worlds we've not known, stimulating, educating, questioning almost simultaneously."

Clavell's life was almost as eventful as one of his books. He was born in Australia in 1925, the son of a British Royal Navy captain who traveled to ports all over the world. As a child, Clavell relished the swashbuckling sea tales—most of them fictional—recounted by his father and grandfather, both career military men. A career in the service seemed a natural choice for Clavell, too, and after his secondary schooling was completed, he joined the Royal Artillery in 1940. A year later, he was sent to fight in the Far East and was wounded by machine-gun fire in the jungles of Malaysia. For several months he hid in a Malay village, but he was eventually captured by the Japanese and sent to the notorious Changi prison near Singapore. The conditions at Changi were so severe that only 10,000 of its 150,000 inmates survived incarceration—and Clavell was there three and a half years. He told the *Guardian:* "Changi was a school for survivors. It gave me a strength most people don't have. I have an awareness of life others lack. Changi was my university. . . . Those who were supposed to survive didn't." The experience invested Clavell with some of the same verve and intensity which characterize his fictional protagonists. Calling Changi "the rock" on which he built his life, he said: "So long as I remember Changi, I know I'm living forty borrowed lifetimes."

Released from captivity after the war, Clavell returned to Great Britain to continue his military career. A motorcycle accident left him lame in one leg, however, and he was discharged in 1946. He attended Birmingham University briefly, considering law or engineering as a profession, but when he began to visit movie sets with his future wife, an aspiring actress, he became fascinated with directing and writing for films. He entered the movie industry on the ground floor as a distributor, gradually moving into production work. In 1953 he and his wife immigrated to the United States, where, after a period in television production in New York, they moved to Hollywood. There Clavell bluffed his way into a screenwriting contract ("They liked my accent, I suppose," he told the *Washington Post*) and set to work in the field that would bring him his first success. His first produced screenplay, *The Fly,* was based on a science fiction story about an atomic scientist whose experiments cause an exchange of heads with a housefly. The movie made a four million dollar profit in two years and has since become a classic genre film in its own right and the source of several sequels and remakes. Clavell won a Writers Guild Best Screenplay Award for the 1963 film *The Great Escape,* also a box-office success. Of the films the author produced, directed, and wrote, perhaps the most notable remains the 1969 hit *To Sir with Love,* starring Sidney Poitier. Produced on a budget of 625,000 dollars, the movie about a black teacher's efforts to mold a class of tough British delinquents grossed fifteen million dollars. Both Clavell and Poitier had contracted for percentages of the profits, so the project proved lucrative.

A Hollywood screenwriters' strike brought a fortuitous change to Clavell's career in 1960. Simultaneously sidelined from his regular employment and haunted by returning memories of Changi, he began to work on a novel about his prison experiences. The process of writing released many suppressed emotions for Clavell; in twelve weeks he had completed the first draft of *King Rat.* Set in Changi, the novel follows the fortunes of an English prisoner of war and his ruthless American comrade in their struggles to survive the brutal conditions. *New York Times Book Review* contributor Martin Levin observed, "All personal relationships [in the work] pale beside the impersonal, soul-disintegrating evil of Changi itself which Mr. Clavell, himself a Japanese P.O.W. for three years, renders with stunning authority." Some critics maintained that the book lost some of its impact because it was aimed at a popular audience, but Paul King of *Maclean's* called *King Rat* the work of "a sensitive craftsman." A *New York Herald Tribune Books* reviewer concluded that *King Rat* is "at once fascinating in narrative detail, penetrating in observation of human nature under survival stress, and provoking in its analysis of right and wrong." In the *Christian Science Monitor,* R.R. Bruun also noted that by virtue of his careful plotting, "Mr. Clavell manages to keep the tension wound up to the snapping point through much of the book." A bestseller, *King Rat* was adapted for film in 1965.

Clavell was still primarily a screenwriter when he penned *Tai-Pan,* a sweeping fictional account of the founding of Hong Kong. A historical novel set in 1841, the story recounts the adventures of Dirk Struan, first tai-pan, or merchant overlord, of the Noble House trading company. Struan builds his empire on the nearly deserted peninsula of Hong Kong, convinced that a British colony there would provide a power base for the growing empire. *New York Times* reviewer Orville Prescott claimed that in *Tai-Pan,* Clavell "holds attention with a relentless grip. *Tai-Pan* frequently is crude. It is grossly exaggerated much of the time. But seldom does a novel appear so stuffed with imaginative invention, so packed with melodramatic action, so gaudy and flamboyant with blood and sin, treachery and conspiracy, sex and murder." A *Time* critic labeled the work "a belly-gutting, god-rotting typhoon of a book" and added: "Its narrative pace is numbing, its style deafening, its language penny dreadful. . . . It isn't art and it isn't truth. But its very energy and scope command the eye." Since its publication in 1966 and its forty-four-week stay on the bestseller lists, it has sold more than two million copies. It too has been made into a motion picture, released in 1986.

According to the *Washington Post*'s Gorney, Clavell's best-known novel, *Shogun,* began almost by accident. She wrote, "James Clavell, his imagination awash with plans for the modern-day Asian chronicle that was to be his third novel, picked up one of his nine-year-old daughter's school books one afternoon in London, and came upon an intriguing bit of history." He read the following sentence from the text: "In 1600, an Englishman went to Japan and became a Samurai." Fascinated by that possibility, Clavell began to read everything he could find about medieval Japan and Will Adams, the historical figure in question. The research led Clavell into the story of *Shogun,* but it also gave him a new understanding of the culture that had kept him in captivity during the Second World War. "I started reading about Japan's history and characteristics," he told the *New York Times,* "and then the way the Japanese treated me and my brothers became clearer to me." After a year of research in the British Museum and several visits to Japan, Clavell created the tale of John Blackthorne, an Elizabethan sailor cast upon the shores of Japan during a period of internal conflict between rival warlords. Bringing in a variety of elements of seventeenth-century Japanese society, the adventure recounts Blackthorne's transformation from a European "barbarian" into a trusted adviser to the powerful Shogun Toranaga.

Most critics have praised *Shogun* for its historical detail as well as for its riveting plot. "Clavell offers a wide-ranging view of feudal Japan at a time of crisis," stated Bruce Cook in the *Washington Post Book World,* adding, "Scene after scene is given, conversation after conversation reported, with the point not merely of advancing the narrative (which does somehow grind inexorably forward), but also of imparting to us the peculiar flavor of life in feudal Japan and the unique code of conduct (*bushido*) which dominated life there and then." Other reviewers have cited the story itself as the source of *Shogun*'s appeal. Gorney of the *Washington Post* described it as "one of those books that blots up vacations and imperils marriages, because it simply will not let the reader go," and *Library Journal* contributor Mitsu Yamamoto deemed it "a wonderful churning brew of adventure, intrigue, love, philosophy, and history." "Clavell has a gift," contended Schott in the *New York Times Book Review*. "It may be something that cannot be taught or earned. He breathes narrative. It's almost impossible not to continue to read *Shogun* once having opened it. The imagination is possessed by Blackthorne, Toranaga and medieval Japan. Clavell creates a world: people, customs, settings, needs and desires all become so enveloping that you forget who and where you are."

Critics have also praised *Noble House,* Clavell's 1981 bestseller about financial power struggles in modern Hong Kong. *Washington Post* correspondent Sandy Rovner informed readers of the mass of the novel—"1,207 pages long, two-and-one-half inches (not counting covers) thick and three pounds and thirteen ounces"—but noted that *Noble House* must be carried around nonetheless, since "you can't put it down." Henry S. Hayward commented on the book's mass as well in the *Christian Science Monitor.* "James Clavell is a master yarn-spinner and an expert on detail," Hayward asserted. "Indeed, one sometimes feels overwhelmed with the masses of information and wishes a firmer editing pencil had been applied. But the author, nevertheless, is in a class with James Michener and Robert Elegant in his ability to handle a massive cast and hold your attention through the intricacies of a 1,200 page plot." *National Review*'s Teachout remarked that one "races through *Noble House* like a fire engine, torn between savoring each tasty bit of local color and wanting to find out as soon as possible what new outrage [the hero] will put down next." In the *New York Times Book Review,* Schott concluded that the novel "isn't primarily about any particular story or character or set of characters. It's about a condition that's a place, Hong Kong. Mr. Clavell perceives that city to be a unique setting for extremes of greed and vengefulness, international intrigue and silky romance." Commenting on Clavell's plotting, *New York Times* columnist Christopher Lehmann-Haupt opined: "Curiously enough, its staggering complexity is one of the things that the novel has going for it. Not only is *Noble House* as long as life, it's also as rich with possibilities. . . . There are so many irons in the fire that almost anything can plausibly happen."

Noble House, the Far East trading company featured in *Tai-Pan* and *Noble House,* is also a part of *James Clavell's Gai-Jin.* Set in Japan in the 1860s, *Gai-Jin* offers a fictional chronicle concentrating on early Yokohama, Japan, and its turbulent history. It was based on events which actually happened in the late 1800s. *Gai-Jin* introduces Malcolm Struan, twenty-year-old heir to the Far East English shipping firm Noble House. The novel received mixed reviews. Lehmann-Haupt observed, "At the start of *Gai-Jin,* which means foreigner in Japanese, *Tai-Pan* crashes into *Shogun.*" He referred in part to the intermixing of characters and action between the three novels. Lehmann-Haupt added, "At its best, *Gai-Jin* achieves a grand historical perspective that makes us feel we're understanding how today's Japan came into being with its ambivalence toward outsiders." The critic questioned the inclusion of stereotypical English pronunciations by Japanese characters, comparing this aspect of the story to a "World War I comic book." Lehmann-Haupt concluded that the thousand-page tome "is in the mainstream of a great and enduring storytelling tradition, full of rich characters and complicated action. It's just that modernism makes such fiction seem unreal."

Reviewer F.G. Notehelfer commented in the *New York Times Book Review,* "*Gai-Jin* is not without interest. Many of the period's colorful characters are here in thin disguise, and so are many episodes from the early days of Yokohama." Yet the critic described the plot and action as "a kind of comic-book portrait of Yokohama and its people," pointing out several instances of a "gap between fiction and reality." Notehelfer concluded that "such reservations do not detract from what is a welltold story, but I feel obliged to mention them because Mr. Clavell prefaces his book with the remark that his tale 'is not history but fiction,' adding that works of history 'do not necessarily always relate what truly happened.'"

Clavell's successes with his novels were not limited to the sales of books. As Teachout noted in the *National Review,* "Even non-readers have gotten pleasure out of his lucrative knack for telling an appealing story." Through movies and television miniseries, Clavell's works have reached audiences estimated in the hundreds of millions. The best known of these efforts are *King Rat,* a film produced in 1965; *Shogun,* which aired on television in 1980; *Tai-Pan,* a 1986 movie; and *James Clavell's "Noble House,"* a 1988 television miniseries. Clavell, who served as executive producer for the *Shogun* and *Noble House* miniseries, expressed approval for the use of his work in that medium. "Television keeps you current, and so do movies," he told *Publishers Weekly.* "People are seeing your name regularly enough that they remember you. . . . In a way, it makes me almost a brand name."

The publishing industry seemed to concur that Clavell's name alone was quite appealing to book buyers. An auction of his 1986 novel *Whirlwind* brought Clavell an unprecedented five million dollar advance from the William Morrow Company, which had based its bid on a preview of only ten percent of the manuscript. Morrow also ordered a first printing of 950,000 hardcover copies, another unprecedented move. Set in Iran during the hectic weeks after the overthrow of the Shah, *Whirlwind* charts the activities of a group of helicopter pilots trying to move their precious machinery out of the country before the new Islamic fundamentalist government can seize it. Dorothy Allison described the work as "1147 pages of violence, passion, cutthroat business, religious obsession, and martyrdom—exactly what his readers expect and want along with their exotic settings." Although *Whirlwind* received mixed reviews, it was also a bestseller.

In various interviews, Clavell discussed both his aims as a writer and his methods of putting a book together. He told the *Los Angeles Times:* "I look at storytelling in picture form," he explained. "I watch the story happen, and I describe what I see. When you write a screenplay, you write only what you can photograph and what you can hear. As a result, my books have no fat, no purple prose, and they're very visual." Writing a lengthy novel, he told the *Washington Post,* requires "pertinacity, you know, grim determination. And a marvelous selfishness to finish, to exclude everything. I begrudge the time spent away from my novel. . . . I've got this need to finish, to find the last page." Clavell mentioned in the *National Review* that his basic goal was entertainment—for himself as well as his readers. "I'm not a novelist, I'm a storyteller," he contended. "I'm not a literary figure at all. I work very hard and try to do the best I can; and I try and write for myself, thinking that what I like, other people may like."

Many critics held that Clavell achieved his goal as an entertaining writer. Teachout declared: "To call Clavell a 'popular novelist' is an understatement: incredibly, he is . . . among the most widely read authors of the century." *New York Times* contributor William Grimes summarized: "Although historians sometimes disputed the historical accuracy of Mr. Clavell's novels, no one doubted his gifts as a storyteller, or his ability to draw the reader into a faraway time and place." And *National Review*'s William F. Buckley opined: "[Clavell] was the supreme storyteller."

BIOGRAPHICAL AND CRITICAL SOURCES:

BOOKS

Contemporary Literary Criticism, Thomson Gale (Detroit, MI), Volume 6, 1976, Volume 25, 1983, Volume 87, 1995.

MacDonald, Gina, *James Clavell: A Critical Companion,* Greenwood Press (Westport, CT), 1996.
The Making of James Clavell's "Shogun," Dell, 1980.

PERIODICALS

Best Sellers, July 15, 1966; October, 1981.
Chicago Tribune, April 12, 1981; February 18, 1982; November 21, 1986.
Christian Science Monitor, August 9, 1962; June 24, 1981, May 12, 1993, p. 13; May 13, 1994, p. 12.
Detroit News, May 3, 1981; May 12, 1993, p. 13.
Fantasy Review, June, 1987, p. 42.
Far Eastern Economic Review, May 20, 1993, p. 46.
Globe and Mail (Toronto, Ontario, Canada), January 4, 1986.
Guardian (London, England), October 4, 1975.
History Today, October, 1981, pp. 39-42.
Los Angeles Times, November 7, 1986; December 11, 1986.
Maclean's, May 11, 1981; November 24, 1986.
National Review, October 12, 1982, pp. 23-24; November 12, 1982, pp. 1420-1422.
New Republic, July 4, 1981.
New Statesman, November 21, 1975.
Newsweek, November 10, 1986, p. 84.
New York Herald Tribune Books, August 5, 1962.
New York Review of Books, September 18, 1975; December 18, 1986, pp. 58-60.
New York Times, May 4, 1966; April 28, 1981; May 17, 1981; February 18, 1982; December 28, 1985; January 7, 1986; January 11, 1986; November 1, 1986; November 7, 1986; November 17, 1986; May 24, 1993, p. C16.
New York Times Book Review, August 12, 1962; May 22, 1966; June 22, 1975; May 3, 1981; April 18, 1993, p. 13.
New York Times Magazine, September 13, 1981.
Observer, July 4, 1993, p. 62.
People, May 10, 1993, pp. 27, 29.
Poe Studies, June, 1983, p. 13.
Publishers Weekly, October 24, 1986; March 22, 1993, p. 69.
Saturday Review, August 11, 1962.
Time, June 17, 1966; July 7, 1975; July 6, 1981.
Times (London, England), November 2, 1986, pp. 41, 43-44.
Times Literary Supplement, December 5, 1986; December 26, 1986.
Village Voice, September 2, 1981, p. 37; December 16, 1986.
Wall Street Journal, October 7, 1986, p. 30.

Washington Post, February 4, 1979; May 5, 1981; November 11, 1986.

Washington Post Book World, July 13, 1975; October 26, 1986; December 7, 1986, p. 4.

OBITUARIES:

PERIODICALS

Current Biography, November, 1994, p. 58.
Facts on File, September 15, 1994, p. 672.
National Review, October 10, 1994, p. 23.
Newsweek, September 19, 1994, p. 75.
New York Times, September 8, 1994, p. D19.
Time, September 19, 1994, p. 27.
Times (London, England), September 9, 1994, p. 21.
U.S. News & World Report, September 19, 1994, p. 24.
Variety, September 12, 1994, p. 67.
Washington Post, September 8, 1994, p. D4.

* * *

CLAVELL, James duMaresq
See CLAVELL, James

* * *

CLEARY, Beverly 1916-
(Beverly Atlee Bunn Cleary)

PERSONAL: Born 1916, in McMinnville, OR; daughter of Chester Lloyd and Mable (Atlee) Bunn; married Clarence T. Cleary, October 6, 1940; children: Marianne Elisabeth, Malcolm James (twins). *Education:* University of California—Berkeley, B.A., 1938; University of Washington, Seattle, B.A., 1939. *Hobbies and other interests:* Travel, needlework.

ADDRESSES: Home—CA. *Agent*—c/o Author Mail, William Morrow/ HarperCollins, 10 East 53rd St., 7th Floor, New York, NY 10022.

CAREER: Public Library, Yakima, WA, children's librarian, 1939-40; U.S. Army Hospital, Oakland, CA, post librarian, 1942-45; writer for young people, 1950—.

MEMBER: Authors Guild, Authors League of America.

AWARDS, HONORS: Young Readers' Choice Award, Pacific Northwest Library Association, 1957, for *Henry and Ribsy,* 1960, for *Henry and the Paper Route,* 1968, for *The Mouse and the Motorcycle,* 1971, for *Ramona the Pest,* and 1980, for *Ramona and Her Father;* Dorothy Canfield Fisher Memorial Children's Book Award, 1958, for *Fifteen,* 1961, for *Ribsy,* and 1985, for *Dear Mr. Henshaw;* Notable Book citation, American Library Association, 1961, for *Jean and Johnny,* 1966, for *The Mouse and the Motorcycle,* 1978, for *Ramona and Her Father,* and 1984, for *Dear Mr. Henshaw;* South Central Iowa Association of Classroom Teachers' Youth Award, 1968, Hawaii Association of School Librarians/ Hawaii Library Association Nene Award, 1971, New England Round Table of Children's Librarians Honor Book Award, 1972, Sue Hefley Award from Louisiana Association of School Librarians, 1972, and Surrey School Book Award from Surrey School District, 1974, all for *The Mouse and the Motorcycle;* Nene Award from Hawaii Association of School Librarians and Hawaii Library Association, 1968, for *Ribsy,* 1969, for *Ramona the Pest,* 1972, for *Runaway Ralph,* and 1980, for *Ramona and Her Father;* William Allen White Award, Kansas Association of School Libraries and Kansas Teachers' Association, 1968, for *The Mouse and the Motorcycle,* and 1975, for *Socks;* Georgia Children's Book Award, College of Education, University of Georgia, 1970, Sequoyah Children's Book Award, Oklahoma Library Association, 1971, and Massachusetts Children's Book Award nomination, 1977, all for *Ramona the Pest;* New England Round Table of Children's Librarians Honor Book Award, 1972, for *Henry Huggins;* Charlie Mae Simon Award, Arkansas Elementary School Council, 1973, for *Runaway Ralph,* and 1984, for *Ramona Quimby, Age Eight;* Distinguished Alumna Award, University of Washington, 1975; Laura Ingalls Wilder Award, American Library Association (ALA), 1975, for substantial and lasting contributions to children's literature; Golden Archer Award, University of Wisconsin, 1977, for *Socks* and *Ramona the Brave;* Children's Choice Election Award, second place, 1978; *Ramona and Her Father* appeared on *Horn Book*'s honor list, 1978; Mark Twain Award, Missouri Library Association and Missouri Association of School Librarians, 1978, for *Ramona the Brave;* Newbery Honor Book Award from ALA and *Boston Globe-Horn Book* Honor Award, both 1978, both for *Ramona and Her Father;* People Honor Book Award, International Board on Books for Young People, Tennessee Children's Book Award, Tennessee Library Association, Utah Children's Book Award, Children's Library Association of Utah, and Garden State Award, New Jersey Library Association, all 1980, for *Ramona and Her Father;* Regina Medal from Catholic Library Association, 1980, for "continued distinguished contributions to literature"; Land of Enchantment Children's Award and Texas Bluebonnet Award, both 1981, for *Ramona and Her Father*; American Book Award, 1981, for *Ramona and Her Mother*; *Ramona Quimby, Age Eight* was included on *School Library Journal*'s "Best Books 1981" list; de Grummond Award, University of Mississippi and medallion, University of Southern Mississippi, both 1982, for distinguished contributions to children's literature; *Ralph S. Mouse* was included on *School Library Journal*'s "Best Books 1982" list; Newbery Honor Book Award, ALA and American Book Award nomination, both 1982, for *Ramona Quimby, Age Eight*; Garden State Children's Choice Award, New Jersey Library Association, 1982, for *Ramona and Her Mother*, 1984, for *Ramona Quimby, Age Eight*, and 1985, for *Ralph S. Mouse*; *Dear Mr. Henshaw* was included on *School Library Journal*'s "Best Books of 1983" list, named *New York Times* Notable Book of 1983, and noted on *Horn Book*'s honor list, 1984; English Award, California Association of Teachers of English, and Golden Kite Award, Society of Children's Book Writers, both 1983, for *Ralph S. Mouse*; Christopher Award, 1983, for *Dear Mr. Henshaw*; Charles Near Simon Award from Arkansas Elementary School Council, Michigan Young Readers Award, and Buckeye Children's Book Award, all 1984, for *Ramona Quimby, Age Eight*; Iowa Children's Choice Award, Iowa Educational Media Association, 1984, for *Ralph S. Mouse*; Newbery Medal, ALA, Commonwealth Silver Medal, Commonwealth Club of California, Dorothy Canfield Fisher Children's Book Award, and *New York Times* notable book citation, all 1984, for *Dear Mr. Henshaw*; U.S. author nominee for Hans Christian Andersen award, 1984; Buckeye Children's Book Award, 1985, for *Ramona and Her Mother*; *Everychild* honor citation, 1985, for thirty-five year contribution to children's literature; Ludington Award, Educational Paperback Association, 1987; honor book citation, Hawaii Association of School Librarians and the Children and Youth Section of Hawaii Library Association, 1988; honorary doctorate, Cornell College, 1993; National Medal of Arts, 2003. Cleary's books have received more than thirty-five state awards based on the direct votes of her young readers.

WRITINGS:

Henry Huggins, Morrow (New York, NY), 1950, fiftieth anniversary edition, with foreword by Cleary, Harper Collins (New York, NY), 1999.

Ellen Tebbits, Morrow (New York, NY), 1951.

Henry and Beezus, Morrow (New York, NY), 1952.

Otis Spofford, Morrow (New York, NY), 1953.

Henry and Ribsy, Morrow (New York, NY), 1954.

Beezus and Ramona, Morrow (New York, NY), 1955.

Fifteen (teen), Morrow (New York, NY), 1956.

Henry and the Paper Route, Morrow (New York, NY), 1957.

The Luckiest Girl, Morrow (New York, NY), 1958.

Jean and Johnny (teen), Morrow (New York, NY), 1959.

The Real Hole (preschool), Morrow (New York, NY), 1960, revised edition, 1986.

Hullabaloo ABC (preschool), Parnassus (New York, NY), 1960, new edition, with new illustrations, Morrow (New York, NY), 1998.

Two Dog Biscuits (preschool), Morrow (New York, NY), 1961, revised edition, 1986.

Emily's Runaway Imagination, Morrow (New York, NY), 1961.

Henry and the Clubhouse, Morrow (New York, NY), 1962.

Sister of the Bride, Morrow (New York, NY), 1963.

Ribsy, Morrow (New York, NY), 1964.

The Mouse and the Motorcycle, Morrow (New York, NY), 1965.

Mitch and Amy, Morrow, 1967, new edition, illustrated by Bob Marstall, Morrow (New York, NY), 1991.

Ramona the Pest (also see below), Morrow (New York, NY), 1968.

Runaway Ralph, Morrow (New York, NY), 1970.

Socks, Morrow (New York, NY), 1973.

The Sausage at the End of the Nose (play), Children's Book Council, 1974.

Ramona the Brave, Morrow (New York, NY), 1975.

Ramona and Her Father (also see below), Morrow (New York, NY), 1977.

Ramona and Her Mother (also see below), Morrow (New York, NY), 1979.

Ramona Quimby, Age Eight (also see below), Morrow (New York, NY), 1981.

Ralph S. Mouse, Morrow (New York, NY), 1982.

Dear Mr. Henshaw, Morrow (New York, NY), 1983.

Cutting Up with Ramona!, Dell (New York, NY), 1983.

Ramona Forever (also see below), Morrow (New York, NY), 1984.

The Ramona Quimby Diary, Morrow (New York, NY), 1984.

Lucky Chuck, Morrow (New York, NY), 1984.

Beezus and Ramona Diary, Morrow (New York, NY), 1986.

The Growing-Up Feet, Morrow (New York, NY), 1987.

Janet's Thingamajigs, Morrow (New York, NY), 1987.

A Girl from Yamhill: A Memoir, Morrow (New York, NY), 1988.

Meet Ramona Quimby (includes *Ramona and Her Father*, *Ramona and Her Mother*, *Ramona Forever*,

Ramona Quimby, Age Eight, and *Ramona the Pest*),
Dell (New York, NY), 1989.

Muggie Maggie, Morrow (New York, NY), 1990.

Strider, Morrow (New York, NY), 1991.

Petey's Bedtime Story, illustrated by David Small, Morrow (New York, NY), 1993.

My Own Two Feet: A Memoir, Morrow (New York, NY), 1995.

Ramona's World, illustrated by Alan Tiegreen, Morrow (New York, NY), 1999.

Lucky Chuck, illustrated by J. Winslow Higginbottom, HarperCollins (New York, NY), 2002.

Also author of *Ramona and Her Friends* (an omnibus edition), and *Leave It to Beaver* (adapted from television scripts). Contributor to periodicals, including *Woman's Day.*

ADAPTATIONS: Pied Piper produced recordings and filmstrips of *Henry and the Clubhouse,* 1962, and *Ribsy,* 1964. Miller-Brody produced recordings, some with accompanying filmstrips, of *Ramona and Her Father,* 1979, *Beezus and Ramona,* 1980, *Henry Huggins,* 1980, *Henry and Ribsy,* 1980, *Ramona and Her Mother,* 1980, *Ramona the Brave,* 1980, *Ramona Quimby, Age Eight,* 1981, *Henry and Beezus,* 1981, *Ralph S. Mouse,* 1983, and *Dear Mr. Henshaw,* 1984. A six-episode series based on *The Mouse and the Motorcycle, Runaway Mouse,* and *Ralph S. Mouse* was produced by Churchill Films for American Broadcasting Companies, Inc. (ABC-TV); *Ramona,* a ten-part series based on Cleary's character Ramona Quimby, was broadcast on the Public Broadcasting Service (PBS) in 1988; television programs based on the "Henry Huggins" books have appeared in Japan, Sweden, and Denmark. Many of the stories have been adapted for the stage.

SIDELIGHTS: Beverly Cleary's humorous, realistic portraits of American children have rendered her among the most successful writers for young readers. Books were important to Cleary from an early age, for her mother established the first lending library in the small town of McMinnville, Oregon, where Cleary was born. "It was in this dingy room filled with shabby leather-covered chairs and smelling of stale cigar smoke that I made the most magic of discoveries," Cleary recalled in *Top of the News.* "There were books for children!"

Cleary eagerly anticipated attending school and learning to read. Once she became a student, however, she found herself stifled by the rigid teaching methods of that time. "We had no bright beckoning book with such words as 'fun,' 'adventure,' or 'horizon' to tempt us on. . . . Our primer looked grim," she remembered in a *Horn Book* article. "Its olive-green cover with its austere black lettering bore the symbol of a beacon light, presumably to guide us and to warn us of the dangers that lay within. . . . The first grade was soon sorted into three reading groups: Bluebirds, Redbirds, and Blackbirds. I was a Blackbird, the only girl Blackbird among the boy Blackbirds who had to sit in the row by the blackboard. . . . To be a Blackbird was to be disgraced. I wanted to read, but somehow I could not. I wept at home while my puzzled mother tried to drill me on the dreaded word charts."

But under the guidance of her second-grade teacher, Cleary eventually learned "to plod through [the] reader a step or two ahead of disgrace," and she even managed to regain her original enthusiasm for books. She found, however, that the books available to her were ultimately unsatisfactory, for they bore no relation to the life she knew as a middle-class child in Portland, Oregon. Instead of reflecting Cleary's own experiences, the books told of "wealthy English children who had nannies and pony carts or books about poor children whose problems were solved by a long-lost rich relative turning up in the last chapter," she explained in a speech reprinted in *Horn Book.* "I had had enough. . . . I wanted to read funny stories about the sort of children I knew and decided that someday when I grew up I would write them." Cleary has achieved just that, and her books are now common fare in elementary school curricula and individual teachers' lessons plans.

Cleary wrote her funny stories, setting most of her books on or around Klickitat Street, a real street near her childhood home. The children in her books face situations common in real children's lives—finding a stray dog, forgetting to deliver newspapers, the horror of having to kiss in a school play. They misbehave, and they discover that adults are not always fair. In a speech reprinted in *Catholic Library World,* Cleary noted that one of her books, *Otis Spofford,* generated considerable controversy upon publication in 1953, and was even rejected by some libraries, merely because "Otis threw spitballs and did not repent."

Perhaps the most endearing and popular of Cleary's characters is Ramona Quimby, a spunky little girl who would make fairly regular appearances in Cleary's books after Henry Huggins began appearing in the 1950s. But it was not until 1968, with the publication of *Ramona the Pest,* that Ramona had assumed the position of heroine in one of Cleary's publications. Critics, as well as readers, responded enthusiastically to this expansion of Ramona's character, and ensuing works about Ramona would be met with almost unqualified praise. A critic in *Young Readers' Review* commented: "As in all her books about the boys and girls of Klickitat Street, Mrs. Cleary invests [*Ramona the Pest*] with charm, humor, and complete honesty. There are some adults who can remember many incidents from their early childhood; there are few who can remember how they felt about things and why; there are fewer who can communicate these feelings. And fewer still who can retain the humorous aspects. Mrs. Cleary is one of those rare ones. . . . Even boys and girls who dislike stories about children younger than themselves enjoy the incidents in which Ramona makes a pest of herself. . . . Ramona has never been funnier and has never been so sympathetic a character. . . . As usual, this is standard Cleary first-rate entertainment." Polly Goodwin of *Book World* called Ramona "a wonderfully real little girl trying hard to express herself, to understand and be understood in a bewildering world."

The sequel to *Ramona the Pest,* titled *Ramona the Brave,* was equally well received. A reviewer in the *Bulletin of the Center for Children's Books* wrote that it is "diverting [and] written with the ebullient humor and sympathy that distinguish Cleary's stories. Ramona is as convincing a first-grader as a fictional character can be." A *Growing Point* reviewer called it "straight domestic writing at its liveliest and most skillful."

Cleary told *CA* that the books about Ramona reflect a "child's relationship with adults." This is evident in *Ramona and Her Father,* in which Mr. Quimby loses his job and begins to smoke too much, prompting Ramona to start a ferocious no-smoking campaign in order to save her father's life. A critic in *Booklist* wrote: "With her uncanny gift for pinpointing the thoughts and feelings of children right down to their own phraseology—while honoring the boundaries of clean, simple writing—the author catches a family situation that puts strain on each of its members, despite their intrinsic strength and invincible humor. . . . [The resulting story is] true, warm-hearted, and funny." A reviewer in *Growing Point* noted that "the humorous tone of these neatly particularized domestic situations is never flippant, and behind it a picture is built up of a stable and sensible American family, in which that wayward individualist Ramona is able to develop in happy security." *Times Literary Supplement* contributor Peter Hunt further praised Cleary for her skill in pulling off "the difficult trick of keeping to a second-grader's viewpoint without being condescending or 'cute.'"

Katherine Paterson analyzed Cleary's brand of humor in a *Washington Post Book World* article. "When I was

young there were two kinds of funny—funny ha-ha and funny peculiar," Paterson wrote. "A lot of funny ha-ha things happen in Cleary's books, but her real specialty is another kind of funny, which is a cross between funny ha-ha and funny ahh. Cleary has the rare gift of being able to reveal us to ourselves while still keeping an arm around our shoulder. We laugh (ha ha) to recognize that funny, peculiar little self we were and are and then laugh (ahhh) with relief that we've been understood at last. . . . Cleary is loved because she can describe simply the complex feelings of a child. But even more, Cleary is able to sketch clearly with a few perfect strokes the inexplicable adult world as seen through a child's eyes."

After publishing *Ramona Forever* in 1984, Cleary allowed fifteen years to pass before she revived the Ramona series with *Ramona's World,* which finds the plucky child in fourth grade. In this tale Ramona gamely endeavors to win a best friend while tolerating the arrival of a baby into her family. During the course of the book, Ramona attempts to vacuum a cat, and while playing in a friend's attic she manages to plunge through the thin ceiling and hang suspended over a dining area. A *Publishers Weekly* critic reported that "most of Ramona's triumphs and traumas are timeless and convincingly portrayed." A *Booklist* reviewer, meanwhile, concluded that "for the most part, this is just what readers have been waiting for: vintage Ramona."

Rosemary Herbert in a 1999 *Boston Herald* article found that Cleary's books were reappearing in the children's sections of bookstores. She asked, "Do you feel as if you've entered a time warp when you browse the children's section of your favorite bookstore? Look around. Here's Ludwig Bemelmans' Madeline. There's Beverly Cleary's Ramona. . . . What brought these plucky girls of the '20s, '30s, '50s and '60s back into print?" Interviewing several publishers provided the answer: "Mindful that parents hold the purse strings, [publishers are] marketing nostalgia to adults rather than books to kids." But in the case of Ramona, Cathryn Mercier, associate director of the Center for the Study of Children's Literature at Simmons College in Boston, assured Herbert, "The release of *Ramona's World*—the first Ramona book to be written by the character's creator in fifteen years—is not clouded in controversy. Like Eloise, Madeline, and Hitty, Ramona remains appealing because she 'exhibits independence of thought and action.'"

The ability to portray the world of adults through a child's perspective is a strength of Cleary's nonfiction as well as her fiction. In her two volumes of autobiographical writing—*A Girl from Yamhill: A Memoir,* which appeared in 1988, and *My Own Two Feet: A Memoir,* which was published in 1995—Cleary "immediately makes one understand why [her] books are perennial favorites," according to Mary M. Burns in *Horn Book.* Recounting Cleary's childhood in Portland, Oregon, during the Great Depression, *A Girl from Yamhill* reveals the real Klickitat Street and shows that the roots of many of the fictional episodes of Ramona Quimby were based on her creator's own life. Praising Cleary's choice of topics—which include the emotional difficulties in moving to a new town, dealing with an overly demonstrative male relative, a less expressive mother whose affection was channelled into molding her children to her own designs, and dealing with the pangs of adolescent first love—Lillian N. Gerhardt wrote in *School Library Journal,* "As with her fiction, readers are likely to want her memoir to go on when they read her last page."

A Girl from Yamhill ends in 1934, as Cleary begins her college education in Southern California. *My Own Two Feet* takes up the story where its predecessor left off, with the future author on a Greyhound bus bound from Oregon to California, ready to begin her life as an independent adult. *My Own Two Feet* "is a Depression story and then a World War II home-front story," explained Perri Klass in the *New York Times Book Review,* "but most remarkably it is a story about craving independence and craving education." From college, where she studied library science, Cleary obtained a job as a children's librarian in Washington. The children she met there would inspire her early attempts at fulfilling her childhood dream of becoming a writer of books for young readers. In between attending college and publishing her first book in 1950, Cleary experienced courtship and marriage, the financial stresses caused by making a living during the Depression years, and an emotional confrontation with a strong-willed, controlling mother. Cleary's "vivid recollections" of the many small events that figured in her journey as a student and young wife "are continued evidence of this author's ability to convince readers," maintained Ruth K. MacDonald in *School Library Journal.* "It's all in the details."

While her autobiographies reveal that many of her books had their basis in her own life, Cleary has also written on topics with which she has not had first-hand experience. Publication of the 1983 volume *Dear Mr. Henshaw,* for example, marked Cleary's response to many letters asking for a book about a child of divorce. In this book, protagonist Leigh Botts's letters to his favorite author reveal his loneliness and confusion following his parents' separation. While Cleary's characteristic humor is still present, *Dear Mr. Henshaw* represents a change in her style and tone, and it is probably the author's most serious work. She remarked in a speech reprinted in *Horn Book:* "When I wrote *Dear Mr. Henshaw,* I did not expect every reader to like Leigh as much as Ramona. Although I am deeply touched that my books have reached two generations of children, popularity has never been my goal. If it had been, I would have written *Ramona Solves the Mystery of the Haunted House and Finds a Baby Brother* or something like *Henry and Beezus Play Doctor,* instead of a book about the feelings of a lonely child of divorce."

Some critics have questioned the role that Cleary's characters (especially Ramona) play in pressuring children to adapt to school homogenization. Linda Benson in *Children's Literature in Education* asked whether "the dominant culture manipulates the character of Ramona, who, if not silenced or entirely subdued by the end of the series, is at least much more civilized according to the norms of the classroom."

But many critics and children alike responded enthusiastically to Cleary's efforts. Natalie Babbitt declared in the *New York Times Book Review:* "Beverly Cleary has written many very good books over the years. This one is the best. It is a first-rate, poignant story. . . . There is so much in it, all presented so simply, that it's hard to find a way to do it justice. Mrs. Cleary knows the voice of children. Dialogue has always been one of the strongest parts of her work. And here, where all is dialogue, that strength can shine alone and be doubly impressive. . . . What a lovely, well-crafted, three-dimensional work this is. And how reassuring . . . to see that a 27th book can be so fresh and strong. Lots of adjectives here; she deserves them all."

Cleary told *CA:* "I doubt if my dear, encouraging high-school English teachers would approve of my writing process today. Fifty years ago, when I began to write, I dutifully tried to outline a story, a task I found so tiresome I quickly abandoned it and simply wrote. I often begin a book in the middle and work out a beginning and an end. This method leads to untidy manuscripts. Revising, however, is the part of writing I enjoy most, and when I can reduce a page to a paragraph, I know my story is headed in the right direction.

"I write in longhand on yellow, lined paper. I write on every third line to leave room for additions. When the manuscript is finished, I fight my enemy, the typewriter, to produce a legible copy for a good typist."

BIOGRAPHICAL AND CRITICAL SOURCES:

BOOKS

Arbuthnot, May Hill, *Children and Books,* 3rd edition, Scott, Foresman, 1964.

Berg, Julie,*Beverly Cleary,* Abdo & Daughters (Edina, MN), 1993.

Books for Children, 1960-65, American Library Association (Chicago, IL), 1966.

Carlsen, R. Robert, *Books and the Teen-Age Reader,* Harper (New York, NY), 1967.

Chambers, Mary, editor, *The Signal Review I: A Selective Guide to Children's Literature,* Thimble Press, 1983.

The Children's Bookshelf, Child Study Association of America, 1965.

Children's Literature Review, Thomson Gale (Detroit, MI), Volume 2, 1976, Volume 8, 1985.

Cullinan, Bernice E., and others, *Literature and the Child,* Harcourt (New York, NY), 1981.

Dictionary of Literary Biography, Volume 52: *American Writers for Children since 1960: Fiction,* Thomson Gale (Detroit, MI), 1986.

Dreyer, Sharon Spredemann, *The Bookfinder: A Guide to Children's Literature about the Needs and Problems of Youth Aged 2-15,* American Guidance Service, 1977.

Eakin, Mary K.,*Good Books for Children: A Selection of Outstanding Children's Books Published, 1950-65,* University of Chicago Press (Chicago, IL), 1966.

Egoff, Sheila A., *Thursday's Child: Trends and Patterns in Contemporary Children's Literature,* American Library Association (Chicago, IL), 1981.

Gannon, Susan R., and Ruth Anne Thompson, editors, *Proceedings of the Thirteenth Annual Conference of the Children's Literature Association,* University of Missouri-Kansas City, May 16-18, 1986, Purdue University Press (West Layfayette, IN), 1988.

Hopkins, Lee Bennett, *More Books by More People,* Citation Press, 1974.

Huck, Charlotte S., and Doris Young Kuhn, *Children's Literature in the Elementary School,* 2nd edition, Holt (New York, NY), 1968.

Kelly, Joanne, *The Beverly Cleary Handbook,* Teacher Ideas Press (Englewood, CO), 1996.

Larrick, Nancy, *A Teacher's Guide to Children's Books,* Merrill (Cincinnati, OH), 1966.

Pflieger, Pat, *Beverly Cleary,* Twayne (Boston, MA), 1991.

Rees, David, *The Marble in the Water: Essays on Contemporary Writers of Fiction for Children and Young Adults,* Horn Book (Boston, MA), 1980.

Sadker, Myra Pollack, and David Miller Sadker, *Now upon a Time: A Contemporary View of Children's Literature,* Harper (New York, NY), 1977.

Sebesta, Sam Keaton, and William J. Iverson, *Literature for Thursday's Child,* Science Research Associates, 1975.

Sutherland, Zena, and others, *Children and Books,* 6th edition, Scott, Foresman, 1981.

Townsend, John Rowe, *Written for Children: An Outline of English-Language Literature,* Horn Book (Boston, MA), 1981.

PERIODICALS

Atlantic Monthly, December, 1953; December, 1964.

Booklist, September 1, 1953; September 1, 1954; October 1, 1977; May 1, 1979; September 1, 1981; September 1, 1983; September 1, 1984; April 15, 1998, p. 1460; November 15, 1998, p. 598; June 1, 1999.

Book Window, spring, 1981.

Book World, September 8, 1968.

Boston Herald, December 13, 1999, Rosemary Herbert, "The Girls Are Back!," p. 37.

Buffalo News, November 13, 2000, p. D1.

Bulletin of Bibliography, December 1999, p. 219.

Bulletin of the Center for Children's Books, September, 1959; September, 1961; October, 1963; May, 1967; July, 1975; December, 1977; June, 1979; September, 1982; May, 1984; September, 1984.

Catholic Library World, February, 1980; July-August, 1981.

Children's Book Review, spring, 1975.

Children's Literature Association Quarterly, fall, 1998, p. 131.

Children's Literature in Education, June, 1991, p. 97; March, 1999, p. 9.

Christian Science Monitor, September 6, 1951; November 27, 1957; November 15, 1962; October 15, 1979; May 14, 1982; June 6, 1983.

Cincinnati Post, September 25, 2000, p. 1B.

Detroit News, August 10, 1983.

Early Years, August-September, 1982.

Elementary English, November, 1967.

Entertainment Weekly, May 7, 1993, p. 66; August 20, 1993, p. 73.

Five Owls, July-August, 1990, pp. 106-107; September-October, 1991, p. 18; February, 1994, p. 58.

Growing Point, March, 1963; January, 1976; September, 1978; July, 1980; January, 1983; May, 1983.

Horn Book, December, 1951; December, 1959; October, 1962; October, 1963; December, 1964; June, 1969; August, 1970; August, 1975; December, 1977; October, 1982; December, 1982; October, 1983; August, 1984; September, 1984; May-June, 1988, pp. 369-370; November-December, 1990, p. 738; September-October, 1991, p. 595; May-June, 1995, p. 297; December, 1995, p. 775.

Language Arts, January, 1979.

Library Journal, September 15, 1950; October 15, 1952; September 15, 1957; September 15, 1962.

Lion and the Unicorn: A Critical Journal of Children's Literature, June, 1988, p. 111; December, 1990, p. 58.

Los Angeles Times Book Review, May 22, 1988, p. 11.

New York Herald Tribune Book Review, October 14, 1951; October 12, 1952; September 27, 1953; November 6, 1955; November 18, 1956; November, 1959.

New York Times, December 1, 1999, pp. B2, E2.

New York Times Book Review, September 14, 1952; October 4, 1953; September 26, 1954; September 16, 1956; October 9, 1960; December 26, 1965; October 14, 1979; November 1, 1981; October 23, 1983; November 11, 1984; November 10, 1985; September 9, 1990, p. 17; November 10, 1991, p. 33; November 12, 1995, p. 40; November 21, 1999, p. 28.

Oklahoma Librarian, July, 1971.

Pacific Northwest Library Association Quarterly, April, 1961.

Pacific Sun Literary Quarterly, May 14, 1975.

Parenting, October, 1995, p. 130.

Publishers Weekly, August 4, 1951; August 15, 1953; July 10, 1954; August 13, 1955; September, 1961; April 3, 1967; April 15, 1968; May 14, 1970; March 31, 1975; February 23, 1976; October 1, 1977; July 30, 1979; July 10, 1981; March 2, 1984; July 12, 1993, p. 80; July 17, 1995, p. 138; June 7, 1999, p. 83; November 22, 1999; January 10, 2000, p. 24.

St. Louis Globe-Democrat, February 13, 1984.

Saturday Review, November 17, 1956; October 28, 1961; March 18, 1967; May 9, 1970.

Saturday Review of Literature, November, 1950; November 10, 1951.

School Librarian, June, 1974; June, 1981.

School Library Journal, May, 1988, p. 115; June, 1990, p. 98; February, 1994, p. 78; September, 1995, pp. 222-223; July 1998, p. 71; February 1999, p. 130; August 1999, p. 131; December, 2003, "Beverly Cleary Wins National Medal of Art," p. 25.

Signal, January, 1981.

Southeastern Librarian, fall, 1968.

Times Literary Supplement, July 7, 1978; July 2, 1980; January 13, 1984; November 20, 1984; February, 1985.

Top of the News, December, 1957; April, 1975; winter, 1977.

Tribune Books (Chicago, IL), September 13, 1987.

Washington Post, May 31, 1983; January 10, 1984.

Washington Post Book World, October 9, 1977; July 12, 1981; September 12, 1982; August 14, 1983; September 9, 1984; May 8, 1988; December 10, 1995, p. 20.

Wilson Library Bulletin, October, 1961.

Writers Digest, January, 1983.

Young Readers' Review, November, 1965; February, 1966; May, 1968.

ONLINE

Beverly Cleary Home Page, http://www.beverlycleary. com/ (March 6, 2004).

BookPage, http://www.bookpage.com/ (August, 1999), Miriam Drennen, interview with Cleary.

OTHER

Meet the Newbery Author: Beverly Cleary (filmstrip), Random House/Miller Brody.

*   *   *

CLEARY, Beverly Atlee Bunn
See CLEARY, Beverly

*   *   *

CLIFTON, Lucille 1936-
(Thelma Lucille Clifton)

PERSONAL: Born June 27, 1936, in Depew, NY; daughter of Samuel Louis, Sr. (a laborer) and Thelma (a laborer; maiden name, Moore) Sayles; married Fred James Clifton (an educator, writer, and artist), May 10, 1958 (died, November 10, 1984); children: Sidney, Fredrica, Channing, Gillian, Graham, Alexia. *Education:* Attended Howard University, 1953-55, and Fredonia State Teachers College (now State University of New York College—Fredonia), 1955.

ADDRESSES: Office—Division of Arts and Letters, St. Mary's College of Maryland, Montgomery Hall #126, St. Mary's City, MD 20686. *Agent*—Marilyn Marlow, Curtis Brown Ltd., 10 Astor Pl., New York, NY 10003. *E-mail*—lclifton@.smcm.edu.

CAREER: New York State Division of Employment, Buffalo, claims clerk, 1958-60; U.S. Office of Education, Washington, DC, literature assistant for Central Atlantic Regional Educational Laboratory, 1969-71; Coppin State College, Baltimore, MD, poet-in-residence, 1974-79; Jirry Moore Visiting Writer, George Washington University, 1982-83; University of California, Santa Cruz, professor of literature and creative writing, 1985-89; St. Mary's College of Maryland, St. Mary's City, MD, Distinguished Professor of Literature, 1989-91, Distinguished Professor of Humanities, 1991—; Hilda C. Landers Chair in the Liberal Arts; Duke University, Durham, NC, Blackburn Professor of Creative Writing; visiting writer, Columbia University School of the Arts, 1995-99; visiting teacher, Memphis State University; visiting poet, St. Edward's University, School of Humanities (Austin, TX), 2000. Woodrow Wilson and Lila Wallace/*Readers Digest* visiting fellowship to Fisk University, Alma College, Albright College, Davidson College, and others. Trustee, Enoch Pratt Free Library, Baltimore. Has made television appearances, including *The Language of Life, The Today Show, Sunday Morning with Charles Kuralt,* Bill Moyers' series, *The Power of the Word,* and *Nightline.*

MEMBER: International PEN, Academy of American Poets (chancellor, 1999—), Poetry Society of America, American Cancer Society, Global Forum Arts Committee, Authors Guild, Authors League of America.

AWARDS, HONORS: Discovery Award, New York YW-YMHA Poetry Center, 1969; *Good Times: Poems* was cited as one of the year's ten best books by the *New York Times,* 1969; Creative Writing Fellowships and awards, National Endowment for the Arts, 1969, 1970, 1972, and 1973; Poet Laureate of the State of Maryland, 1974-85; Juniper Prize, University of Massachusetts Press, 1980; Pulitzer Prize nominations for poetry, 1980, 1987, 1988, and 1991; Coretta Scott King Award, American Library Association, 1984, for *Everett Anderson's Goodbye;* Shestack Poetry Prize, American Poetry Review, 1988; Charity Randall Citation, International Poetry Forum, 1991; Shelley Memorial Prize, Poetry Society of America, 1992; named a "Maryland Living Treasure" and inducted into the Maryland Women's Hall of Fame, 1993; Andrew White Medal, Loyola College of Baltimore, 1993; Cannan Literary Award for Poetry, 1996; National Book Award nomination, 1996, and Lannan Literary Award for poetry, 1997, both for *The Terrible Stories;* inducted into National Literature Hall of Fame for African American Writers, 1998; Lenore Marshal Poetry Prize and *Los Angeles Times* poetry award, both 1998; Phi Beta Kappa, 1998; Lila Wallace/*Readers Digest* Award, 1999; National

Book Award for poetry, 1999, for *Blessing the Boats: New and Selected Poems, 1988-2000;* Emmy Award, American Academy of Television Arts and Sciences; Fellow, American Academy of Arts and Sciences, 1999; selected as a Literary Lion, New York Public Library; recipient of honorary degrees from Colby College, University of Maryland, Towson State University, Washington College, and Albright College.

WRITINGS:

POETRY

Good Times, Random House (New York, NY), 1969.

Good News about the Earth: New Poems, Random House (New York, NY), 1972.

An Ordinary Woman, Random House (New York, NY), 1974.

Two-Headed Woman, University of Massachusetts Press (Amherst, MA), 1980.

Good Woman: Poems and a Memoir, 1969-1980, BOA Editions (Brockport, NY), 1987.

Next: New Poems, BOA Editions (Brockport, NY), 1987.

Ten Oxherding Pictures, Moving Parts Press (Santa Cruz, CA), 1988.

Quilting: Poems 1987-1990, BOA Editions (Brockport, NY), 1991.

The Book of Light, Copper Canyon Press (Port Townsend, WA), 1993.

The Terrible Stories, BOA Editions (Brockport, NY), 1998.

Blessing the Boats: New and Selected Poems, 1988-2000, BOA Editions (Brockport, NY), 2000.

Mercy: Poems, BOA Editions (Brockport, NY), 2004.

FOR CHILDREN

The Black BCs (alphabet poems), illustrations by Don Miller, Dutton (New York, NY), 1970.

Good, Says Jerome, illustrations by Stephanie Douglas, Dutton (New York, NY), 1973.

All Us Come 'cross the Water, pictures by John Steptoe, Holt (New York, NY), 1973.

Don't You Remember?, illustrations by Evaline Ness, Dutton (New York, NY), 1973.

The Boy Who Didn't Believe in Spring, pictures by Brinton Turkle, Dutton (New York, NY), 1973.

The Times They Used to Be, illustrations by Susan Jeschke, Holt (New York, NY), 1974.

My Brother Fine with Me, illustrations by Moneta Barnett, Holt (New York, NY), 1975.

Three Wishes, illustrations by Stephanie Douglas, Viking (New York, NY), 1976, illustrations by Michael Hays, Delacorte, 1992.

Amifika, illustrations by Thomas DiGrazia, Dutton (New York, NY), 1977.

The Lucky Stone, illustrations by Dale Payson, Delacorte (New York, NY), 1979, Yearling Books Random House (New York, NY), 1986.

My Friend Jacob, illustrations by Thomas DiGrazia, Dutton (New York, NY), 1980.

Sonora Beautiful, illustrations by Michael Garland, Dutton (New York, NY), 1981.

Dear Creator: A Week of Poems for Young People and Their Teachers, illustrations by Gail Gordon Carter, Doubleday (Garden City, NY), 1997.

Clifton's works have been translated into Spanish.

"EVERETT ANDERSON" SERIES; FOR CHILDREN

Some of the Days of Everett Anderson, illustrations by Evaline Ness, Holt (New York, NY), 1970.

Everett Anderson's Christmas Coming, illustrations by Evaline Ness, Holt (New York, NY), 1971, illustrations by Jan Spivey Gilchrist, Holt (New York, NY), 1991.

Everett Anderson's Year, illustrations by Ann Grifalconi, Holt (New York, NY), 1974.

Everett Anderson's Friend, illustrations by Ann Grifalconi, Holt (New York, NY), 1976.

Everett Anderson's 1 2 3, illustrations by Ann Grifalconi, Holt (New York, NY), 1977.

Everett Anderson's Nine Month Long, illustrations by Ann Grifalconi, Holt (New York, NY), 1978.

Everett Anderson's Goodbye, illustrations by Ann Grifalconi, Holt (New York, NY), 1983.

One of the Problems of Everett Anderson, illustrations by Ann Grifalconi, Holt (New York, NY), 2001.

OTHER

(Compiler, with Alexander MacGibbon) *Composition: An Approach through Reading,* Harcourt (New York, NY), 1968.

Generations: A Memoir (prose), Random House (New York, NY), 1976.

Lucille Clifton Reading Her Poems with Comment in the Montpelier Room, October 24, 2002 (sound recoring), Archive of Recorded Poetry and Literature, Library of Congress (Washington, DC), 2002.

The Poet and the Poem from the Library of Congress. Lucille Clifton (sound recording), Archive of Recorded Poetry and Literature, Library of Congress (Washington, DC), 2002.

Contributor to *Poetry of the Negro, 1746-1970,* edited by Langston Hughes and Arna Bontemps, Doubleday (New York, NY), 1970; (with Marlo Thomas and others) *Free to Be . . . You and Me,* McGraw-Hill (New York, NY), 1974; *Free to Be a Family,* 1987; Robert Kapilow's *03: This New Immense Unbound World* (printed music), G. Schirmer (New York, NY), 2003; and other anthologies, including *Norton Anthology of Literature by Women, Coming into the Light,* and *Stealing the Language.* Has made numerous additional sound and video recordings of poetry readings. Contributor of poetry to the *New York Times.* Contributor of fiction to *Negro Digest, Redbook, House and Garden,* and *Atlantic.* Contributor of nonfiction to *Ms.* and *Essence.*

SIDELIGHTS: Poet Lucille Clifton "began composing and writing stories at an early age and has been much encouraged by an ever-growing reading audience and a fine critical reputation," wrote Wallace R. Peppers in a *Dictionary of Literary Biography.* "In many ways her themes are traditional: she writes of her family because she is greatly interested in making sense of their lives and relationships; she writes of adversity and success in the ghetto community; and she writes of her role as a poet."

Clifton's work emphasizes endurance and strength through adversity. Ronald Baughman suggested in his *Dictionary of Literary Biography* essay that Clifton's "pride in being black and in being a woman helps her transform difficult circumstances into a qualified affirmation about the black urban world she portrays." A *Publishers Weekly* critic noted that Clifton "redeems the human spirit from its dark moments. She is among our most trustworthy and gifted poets." Clifton is a Distinguished Professor of Humanities at St. Mary's College of Maryland and a Chancellor of the Academy of American Poets. In addition to her numerous poetry collections, her work is included in many anthologies, and she has written many children's books. Not surprising, Clifton has won numerous literary awards and was the first author to have two books of poetry chosen as finalists for the Pulitzer Prize, *Good Woman: Poems and a Memoir, 1969-1980* and *Next: New Poems.* She served as the state of Maryland's poet laureate from 1974 until 1985, and won the prestigious National Book Award in 1999 for *Blessing the Boats: New and Selected Poems, 1988-2000.* Her poetry has been translated into Norwegian, Spanish, French, Japanese, Hebrew, and other languages.

Clifton is noted for saying much with few words. In a *Christian Century* review of Clifton's work, Peggy Rosenthal noted, "The first thing that strikes us about Lucille Clifton's poetry is what is missing: capitalization, punctuation, long and plentiful lines. We see a poetry so pared down that its spaces take on substance, become a shaping presence as much as the words themselves. . . . She has chosen a minimalist mode that clears out human society's clutter, the mess we've made by identifying ourselves in contending genders, ethnicities, nations. Lightly, as if biting her tongue, with a wise smile, she shows us a radically egalitarian world where no one or no capitalized word lords it over others." In an *American Poetry Review* article about Clifton's work, Robin Becker commented on Clifton's lean style. "Clifton's poetics of understatement—no capitalization, few strong stresses per line, many poems totaling fewer than twenty lines, the sharp rhetorical question—includes the essential only."

Clifton's first volume of poetry, *Good Times,* which was cited by the *New York Times* as one of 1969's ten best books, was described by Peppers as a "varied collection of character sketches written with third person narrative voices." Baughman noted that the poems "attain power not only through their subject matter but also through their careful techniques; among Clifton's most successful poetic devices . . . are the precise evocative images that give substance to her rhetorical statements and a frequent duality of vision that lends complexity to her portraits of place and character." Calling the book's title "ironic," Baughman stated: "Although the urban ghetto can, through its many hardships, create figures who are tough enough to survive and triumph, the overriding concern of this book is with the horrors of the location, with the human carnage that results from such problems as poverty, unemployment, substandard housing, and inadequate education."

In Clifton's second volume of poetry, *Good News about the Earth: New Poems,* "the elusive good times seem more attainable," remarked Baughman, who summarized the three sections into which the book is divided: the first section "focuses on the sterility and destruction of 'white ways,' newly perceived through the social upheavals of the early 1970s"; the second section "presents a series of homages to black leaders of the late 1960s and early 1970s"; and the third section "deals with biblical characters powerfully rendered in terms of the black experience." Harriet Jackson Scarupa noted in *Ms.* that after having read what Clifton says about blackness and black pride, some critics "have concluded that Clifton hates whites. [Clifton] considers this a misreading. When she equates whiteness with death, black-

ness with life, she says: 'What I'm talking about is a certain kind of white arrogance—and not all white people have it—that is not good. I think airs of superiority are very dangerous. I believe in justice. I try not to be about hatred.'" Writing in *Poetry,* Ralph J. Mills, Jr., said that Clifton's poetic scope transcends the black experience "to embrace the entire world, human and non-human, in the deep affirmation she makes in the teeth of negative evidence."

An Ordinary Woman, Clifton's third collection of poems, "abandons many of the broad racial issues examined in the two preceding books and focuses instead on the narrower but equally complex issues of the writer's roles as woman and poet," according to Baughman. Peppers likewise commented that "the poems take as their theme a historical, social, and spiritual assessment of the current generation in the genealogical line" of Clifton's great-great-grandmother, who had been taken from her home in Dahomey, West Africa, and brought to America in slavery in 1830. Peppers noted that by taking an ordinary experience and personalizing it, "Clifton has elevated the experience into a public confession" which may be shared, and "it is this shared sense of situation, an easy identification between speaker and reader, that heightens the notion of ordinariness and gives . . . the collection an added dimension." Helen Vendler declared in the *New York Times Book Review* that Clifton "recalls for us those bare places we have all waited as 'ordinary women,' with no choices but yes or no, no art, no grace, no words, no reprieve." "Written in the same ironic, yet cautiously optimistic spirit as her earlier published work," observed Peppers, *An Ordinary Woman* is "lively, full of vigor, passion, and an all-consuming honesty."

In *Generations: A Memoir,* "it is as if [Clifton] were showing us a cherished family album and telling us the story about each person which seemed to sum him or her up best," described a *New Yorker* contributor. Calling the book an "eloquent eulogy of [Clifton's] parents," Reynolds Price wrote in the *New York Times Book Review* that, "as with most elegists, her purpose is perpetuation and celebration, not judgment. There is no attempt to see either parent whole; no attempt at the recovery of history not witnessed by or told to the author. There is no sustained chronological narrative. Instead, clusters of brief anecdotes gather round two poles, the deaths of father and mother." Price believed that *Generations* stands "worthily" among the other modern elegies that assert that "we may survive, some lively few, if we've troubled to *be* alive and loved." However, a contributor to *Virginia Quarterly Review* thought that the book is "more than an elegy or a personal memoir.

It is an attempt on the part of one woman to retrieve, and lyrically to celebrate, her Afro-American heritage."

In a review of Clifton's work for *Southern Literary Journal,* Hilary Holladay remarked about how Clifton addresses her "ancestral South." "Although she does not have the intimate knowledge of the region that her father and mother had, her feelings about the region are nevertheless complicated and passionate. The South we encounter in her poems is a conceit enabling her to address two subjects, the first concrete and the second abstract, that have been equally important to her poetry for many years: 1) slavery and its seemingly endless impact on American life, and 2) the all-powerful role of language in determining our knowledge of ourselves and others. In her poems with southern settings, we don't see much of the region's landscape, but we do see how language . . . can either obliterate or validate one's identity."

Clifton's books for children are designed to help them understand their world. *My Friend Jacob,* for instance, is a story "in which a black child speaks with affection and patience of his friendship with a white adolescent neighbor . . . who is retarded," observed Zena Sutherland in the *Bulletin of the Center for Children's Books.* "Jacob is Sam's 'very very best friend' and all of his best qualities are appreciated by Sam, just as all of his limitations are accepted. . . . It is strong in the simplicity and warmth with which a handicapped person is loved rather than pitied, enjoyed rather than tolerated." Critics felt that Clifton's characters and their relationships are accurately and positively drawn in *My Friend Jacob.* Ismat Abdal-Haqq noted in *Interracial Books for Children Bulletin* that "the two boys have a strong relationship filled with trust and affection. The author depicts this relationship and their everyday adventures in a way that is unmarred by the mawkish sentimentality that often characterizes tales of the mentally disabled." And a contributor to *Reading Teacher* stated that, "in a matter-of-fact, low-keyed style, we discover how [Sam and Jacob] help one another grow and understand the world."

Clifton's children's books also facilitate an understanding of black heritage specifically, which in turn fosters an important link with the past. *All Us Come 'cross the Water,* for example, "in a very straight-forward way . . . shows the relationship of Africa to Blacks in the U.S. without getting into a heavy rap about 'Pan-Africanism,'" stated Judy Richardson in the *Journal of Negro Education.* Richardson added that Clifton "seems able to get inside a little boy's head, and knows how to represent that on paper."

An awareness of one's origins figures also in *The Times They Used to Be.* Called a "short and impeccable vignette—laced with idiom and humor of rural Black folk," by Rosalind K. Goddard in *School Library Journal,* the book was described by Lee A. Daniels in the *Washington Post* as a "story in which a young girl catches her first glimpse of the new technological era in a hardware store window, and learns of death and life." "Most books that awaken adult nostalgia are not as appealing to young readers," maintained Sutherland in the *Bulletin of the Center for Children's Books,* "but this brief story has enough warmth and vitality and humor for any reader."

In addition to quickening an awareness of black heritage, Clifton's books for children frequently include an element of fantasy as well. In *Three Wishes,* for example, a young girl finds a lucky penny on New Year's Day and makes three wishes upon it. Christopher Lehmann-Haupt, in the *New York Times Book Review,* called the book "an urbanized version of the traditional tale in which the first wish reveals the power of the magic object . . . the second wish is a mistake, and the third undoes the second." Lehmann-Haupt added: "Too few children's books for blacks justify their ethnicity, but this one is a winning blend of black English and bright illustration." *The Lucky Stone,* in which a lucky stone provides good fortune for all of its owners, was described by Ruth K. MacDonald in *School Library Journal* as "Four short stories about four generations of Black women and their dealings with a lucky stone. . . . Clifton uses as a frame device a grandmother telling the history of the stone to her granddaughter; by the end, the granddaughter has inherited the stone herself."

Barbara Walker wrote in *Interracial Books for Children Bulletin* that Clifton "is a gifted poet with the greater gift of being able to write poetry for children." But in a *Language Arts* interview with Rudine Sims, Clifton indicated that she does not think of it as poetry especially for children. "It seems to me that if you write poetry for children, you have to keep too many things in mind other than the poem. So I'm just writing a poem," she said.

Some of the Days of Everett Anderson is a book of nine poems, about which Marjorie Lewis observed in *School Library Journal:* "Some of the days of six-year-old 'ebony Everett Anderson' are happy; some lonely—but all of them are special, reflecting the author's own pride in being black." In the *New York Times Book Review,* Hoyt W. Fuller thought that Clifton has "a profoundly simple way of saying all that is important to say, and we know that the struggle is worth it, that the all-important battle of image is being won, and that the future of all those beautiful black children out there need not be twisted and broken." *Everett Anderson's Christmas Coming* concerns Christmas preparations in which "each of the five days before Everett's Christmas is described by a verse," observed Anita Silvey in *Horn Book.* Silvey added: "The overall richness of Everett's experiences dominates the text." Jane O'Reilly suggested in the *New York Times Book Review* that "Everett Anderson, black and boyish, is glimpsed, rather than explained through poems about him." *Everett Anderson's Year* celebrates "a year in the life of a city child . . . in appealing verses," according to Beryl Robinson in *Horn Book.* Robinson felt that "mischief, fun, gaiety, and poignancy are a part of his days as the year progresses. The portrayals of child and mother are lively and solid, executed with both strength and tenderness."

Language is important in Clifton's writing. In answer to Sims's question about the presence of both black and white children in her work, Clifton responded specifically about *Sonora Beautiful,* which is about the insecurities and dissatisfaction of an adolescent girl and which has only white characters: "In this book, I *heard* the characters as white. I have a tendency to *hear* the language of the characters, and then I know something about who the people are." However, regarding objections to the black vernacular she often uses, Clifton told Sims: "I do not write out of weakness. That is to say, I do not write the language I write because I don't know any other. . . . But I have a certain integrity about my art, and in *my* art you have to be honest and you have to have people talking the way they really talk. So all of my books are not in the same language."

In her interview with Sims, she was asked whether or not she feels any special pressures or special opportunities as a black author. Clifton responded: "I do feel a responsibility. . . . First, I'm going to write books that tend to celebrate life. I'm about that. And I wish to have children see people like themselves in books. . . . I also take seriously the responsibility of not lying. . . . I'm not going to say that life is wretched if circumstance is wretched, because that's not true. So I take that responsibility, but it's a responsibility to the truth, and to my art as much as anything. I owe everybody that. . . . It's the truth as I see it, and that's what my responsibility is."

In Clifton's 1991 title, *Quilting: Poems 1987-1990,* the author uses a quilt as a poetic metaphor for life. Each poem is a story, bound together through the chronicles of history and figuratively sewn with the thread of experience. The result is, as Roger Mitchell in *American Book Review* described it, a quilt "made by and for people." Each section of the book is divided by a conventional quilt design name such as "Eight-pointed Star" and "Tree of Life," which provides a framework within which Clifton crafts her poetic quilt. Clifton's main focus is on women's history; however, according to Mitchell, her poetry has a far broader range: "Her heroes include nameless slaves buried on old plantations, Hector Peterson (the first child killed in the Soweto riot), Fannie Lou Hamer (founder of the Mississippi Peace and Freedom Party), Nelson and Winnie Mandela, W.E.B. DuBois, Huey P. Newton, and many other people who gave their lives to [free] black people from slavery and prejudice."

Enthusiasts of *Quilting* included critic Bruce Bennett in the *New York Times Book Review,* who praised Clifton as a "passionate, mercurial writer, by turns angry, prophetic, compassionate, shrewd, sensuous, vulnerable and funny. . . . The movement and effect of the whole book communicate the sense of a journey through which the poet achieves an understanding of something new." Pat Monaghan, in *Booklist,* admired Clifton's "terse, uncomplicated" verse, and judged the poet "a fierce and original voice in American letters." Mitchell found energy and hope in her poems, referring to them as "visionary." He concluded that they are "the poems of a strong woman, strong enough to . . . look the impending crises of our time in the eye, as well as our customary limitations, and go ahead and hope anyway."

Clifton's 1993 poetry collection, *The Book of Light,* examines "life through light in its various manifestations," commented Andrea Lockett in a *Belles Lettres* review of the collection. Among the poetic subjects of the collection are bigotry and intolerance, epitomized by a poem about controversial U.S. Senator Jesse Helms; destruction, including a poem about the tragic bombing by police of a MOVE compound in Philadelphia in 1985; religion, characterized by a sequence of poems featuring a dialogue between God and the devil; and mythology, rendered by poems about figures such as Atlas and Superman. "If this poet's art has deepened since . . . *Good Times,* it's in an increased capacity for quiet delicacy and fresh generalization," remarked *Poetry* contributor Calvin Bedient. Bedient criticized the poems in the collection that take an overtly political tone, taking issue with "Clifton's politics of championing difference—except, of course, where the difference opposes her politics." However, Bedient commended the more personal poems in *The Book of Light,* declaring that when Clifton writes without "anger and sentimentality, she writes at her remarkable best." Lockett concluded that the collection is "a gift of joy, a truly illuminated manuscript by a writer whose powers have been visited by grace."

Political messages are present in other Clifton works, including "Jasper Texas 1998," about an African-American man who was dragged to death from the back of a truck by three white men in Texas, and "Stop," which calls on people to take action. Clifton recited and discussed these poems at a Folger Shakespear Library reading, which Adrienne Ammerman reviewed for *Off Our Backs.* Ammerman noted, as did Sims, that Clifton has a desire to be truthful, "even if it's not currently the 'correct' thing to do." Responding to a critic who was disappointed that Clifton "played the race card," the writer remarked, "It's not a game and I'm not playing." "Stop" is about Nkosi Johnson, the noted twelve-year-old South African victim of AIDS, in which Clifton "calls for people to stop what they are doing, to stop what they are not doing, to pay attention, and to act." Ammermen noted that Clifton takes you to that "sticky place where we are scared to face an exhausting reality, but where we know we can't reconcile ourselves to ignorance." Citing great respect for Clifton's work, the reviewer indicated that the poet "defies the mores of political correctness and is candid about her feelings on race in many of her poems. By putting voice to her experiences, Clifton creates a public space within which politics may take place. By putting voice to the experience of others, she exercises her verbal privilege as a talented writer by enabling others to weld their personal lives with the lives of those different from themselves."

The Terrible Stories and *Blessing the Boats: New and Selected Poems, 1988-2000* shed light upon women's survival skills in the face of ill health, family upheaval, and historic tragedy. *Blessing the Boats* is a compilation of four other Clifton books, plus nineteen new poems, which, Becker noted in her review for *American Poetry Review,* "shows readers how the poet's themes and formal structures develop over time." Among the pieces collected in these volumes are several about the author's breast cancer, but she also deals with juvenile violence, child abuse, biblical characters, dreams, the legacy of slavery, and a shaman-like empathy with animals as varied as foxes, squirrels, and crabs. She also speaks in a number of voices, as noted by Becker, including "angel, Eve, Lazarus, Leda, Lot's Wife, Lucifer, among others . . . as she probes the narratives that undergird western civilization and forges new ones."

In a *Booklist* review of *Blessing the Boats,* Donna Seaman found the poems "lean, agile, and accurate, [with] a beauty in their directness and efficiency." A *Publish-*

ers Weekly reviewer likewise concluded that the collection "distills a distinctive American voice, one that pulls no punches in taking on the best and worst of life." During the National Book Awards ceremony for this book, Renee Olson reported for another *Booklist* article that "Clifton was cited for evoking 'the struggle, beauty, and passion of one woman's life with such clarity and power that her vision becomes representative, communal, and unforgettable.'" In *Mercy,* Clifton's twelfth book of poetry, the poet writes about the relationship between mothers and daughters, terrorism, prejudice, and personal faith.

Speaking to Michael S. Glaser during an interview for the *Antioch Review,* Clifton commented about being inducted into American Academy of Arts and Sciences. Addressing her colleagues as "scholars of the mind, scholars of the heart, and scholars of the spirit," she remarked: "So often people think that intelligence is just about the mind, but, you know—especially in the humanities, you do have to explore both the mind and the heart. Nobody is just mind. Absolutely nobody. Balance is the law of the universe, to balance the inside and the outside of people. It's important." In relaying a story about a reading, Clifton quipped, "A guy came up and he said, 'I really enjoyed that. Of course, I'm not into poetry because I'm a historian, and so I study the history of people.' And I said, 'So do I. You study the outside of them. I just study inside.'"

In Clifton's interview with Glaser, the poet reflected that she continues to write, because "writing is a way of continuing to hope . . . perhaps for me it is a way of remembering I am not alone." How would Clifton like to be remembered? "I would like to be seen as a woman whose roots go back to Africa, who tried to honor being human. My inclination is to try to help."

BIOGRAPHICAL AND CRITICAL SOURCES:

BOOKS

Beckles, Frances N., *Twenty Black Women,* Gateway Press (Baltimore, MD), 1978.
Black Literature Criticism, Thomson Gale (Detroit, MI), 1992.
Children's Literature Review, Volume 5, Thomson Gale (Detroit, MI), 1983.
Contemporary Literary Criticism, Thomson Gale (Detroit, MI), Volume 9, 1981, Volume 66, 1991.
Dictionary of Literary Biography, Thomson Gale (Detroit, MI), Volume 5: *American Poets since World War II,* 1980, Volume 41: *Afro-American Poets since 1955,* 1985.

Dreyer, Sharon Spredemann, *The Bookfinder: A Guide to Children's Literature about the Needs and Problems of Youth Aged 2-15,* Volume 1, American Guidance Service (Circle Pines, MN), 1977.

Evans, Mari, editor, *Black Women Writers (1950-1980): A Critical Evaluation,* Doubleday-Anchor (New York, NY), 1984.

PERIODICALS

America, May 1, 1976.

American Book Review, June, 1992, Roger Mitchell, review of *Quilting: Poems 1987-1990,* p. 21.

American Poetry Review, November-December, 2001, Robin Becker, review of "The Poetics of Engagement," p. 11.

Antioch Review, summer, 2000, interview by Michael S. Glaser, p. 310.

Belles Lettres, summer, 1993, Andrea Lockett, review of *The Book of Light,* p. 51.

Black Scholar, March, 1981.

Black World, July, 1970; February, 1973.

Booklist, June 15, 1991, p. 1926; May 1, 1997, p. 1506; August, 1996, Patricia Monaghan, review of *The Terrible Stories,* p. 1876; March 15, 2000, Donna Seaman, review of *Blessing the Boats: New and Selected Poems, 1988-2000,* p. 1316; January 1, 2001, p. 874.

Book World, March 8, 1970; November 8, 1970.

Bulletin of the Center for Children's Books, March, 1971; November, 1974, Zena Sutherland, review of *Times They Used to Be;* March, 1976; September, 1980, Zena Sutherland, review of *My Friend Jacob.*

Christian Century, January 30, 2002, p. 6.

Christian Science Monitor, February 5, 1988, p. B3; January 17, 1992, p. 14.

Horn Book, December, 1971, Anita Silvey, review of *Everett Anderson's Christmas Coming;* August, 1973; February, 1975; December, 1975; October, 1977; March, 1993, p. 229.

Interracial Books for Children Bulletin, Volume 5, numbers 7 and 8, 1975; Volume 7, number 1, 1976; Volume 8, number 1, 1977; Volume 10, number 5, 1979; Volume 11, numbers 1 and 2, 1980; Volume 12, number 2, 1981.

Journal of Negro Education, summer, 1974, Judy Richardson, review of *All Us Come 'cross the Water.*

Journal of Reading, February, 1977; December, 1986.

Kirkus Reviews, April 15, 1970; October 1, 1970; December 15, 1974; April 15, 1976; February 15, 1982.

Language Arts, January, 1978; February 2, 1982.

Library Journal, April 15, 2000, Louis McKee, review of *Blessing the Boats,* p. 95.

Ms., October, 1976, Harriet Jackson Scarupa, review of *Good News about the Earth.*

New Yorker, April 5, 1976, review of *Generations: A Memoir.*

New York Times, December 20, 1976.

New York Times Book Review, September 6, 1970; December 6, 1970; December 5, 1971; November 4, 1973; April 6, 1975, Helen Vendler, review of *An Ordinary Woman;* March 14, 1976, Reynolds Price, review of *Generations: A Memoir;* May 15, 1977, Christopher Lehmann-Haupt, review of *Three Wishes;* February 19, 1989, p. 24; March 1, 1992, Bruce Bennett, "Preservation Poets"; April 18, 1993, David Kirby, review of *The Book of Light,* p. 15.

Off Our Backs, July, 2001, p. 11.

Poetry, May, 1973, Ralph J. Mills, Jr., review of *Good News about the Earth;* March, 1994, Calvin Bedient, review of *The Book of Light,* p. 344.

Publishers Weekly, July 22, 1996, review of *The Terrible Stories,* p. 236; April 17, 2000, review of *Blessing the Boats,* p. 71.

Reading Teacher, October, 1978; March, 1981, review of *My Friend Jacob.*

Redbook, November, 1969.

Saturday Review, December 11, 1971; August 12, 1972; December 4, 1973.

School Library Journal, May, 1970; December, 1970; September, 1974, Rosalind K. Goddard, review of *Times They Used to Be;* December, 1977; February, 1979, Ruth K. MacDonald, review of *Lucky Stone;* March, 1980.

Southern Literary Journal, spring, 2002, p. 120.

Tribune Books (Chicago, IL), August 30, 1987.

Virginia Quarterly Review, fall, 1976, review of *Generations: A Memoir;* winter, 1997, p. 41.

Voice of Youth Advocates, April, 1982.

Washington Post, November 10, 1974, Lee A. Daniels, review of *Times They Used to Be;* August 9, 1979.

Washington Post Book World, November 11, 1973; November 10, 1974; December 8, 1974; December 11, 1977; February 10, 1980; September 14, 1980; July 20, 1986; May 10, 1987; February 13, 1994, p. 8.

Western Humanities Review, summer, 1970.

World Literature Today, autumn, 2000, Adele S. Newson-Horst, review of *Blessing the Boats,* p. 817.

ONLINE

Academy of American Poets Web site, http://www.poets.org/ (April 23, 2001).

Modern American Poetry Web site, http://www.english.
uiuc.edu/maps/poets/ (July 28, 2004), Jocelyn K.
Moody, "About Lucille Clifton."

Poetry Society of America Web site, http://www.
literature-awards.com/ (July 28, 2004), "PSA
Awards Winners."

St. Mary's College Web site, http://www.smcm.edu/
english/ (July 28, 2004), "Lucille Clifton, Disting-
ished Professor of the Humanities."

University of Buffalo Web site, http://www.math.buffalo.
edu/ (July 28, 2004), "Lucille Clifton."

University of Illinois English Department Web site,
http://www.english.uiuc.edu/ (April 23, 2001),
"Modern American Poetry: About Lucille Clifton."

Voices from the Gaps: Women Writers of Color, http://
voices.cla.umn.edu/ (April 23, 2001).

Washington Post Online, http://www.washingtonpost.
com/ (November 23, 2002), Steven Gray, "A Quiet
Poet Gains the Spotlight, National Book Award
Recognizes Work of St. Mary's College Professor."

*   *   *

CLIFTON, Thelma Lucille
See CLIFTON, Lucille

*   *   *

CLINTON, Dirk
See SILVERBERG, Robert

*   *   *

CLOWES, Daniel 1961-

PERSONAL: Born April 14, 1961, in Chicago, IL; son
of an auto mechanic mother and a race car driver father; married (wife's name, Erika). *Education:* Graduated from Pratt Institute (Brooklyn, NY).

ADDRESSES: Home—Berkeley, CA. *Office*—c/o Fantagraphics Books, 7563 Lake City Way, NE, Seattle, WA
98115.

CAREER: Cartoonist. Worked for *Cracked* magazine.

AWARDS, HONORS: Harvey Award, 1990, for best
single issue or story (*Eightball* no. 1) and for best new
series, 1991, for best single issue or story (*Eightball* no.
3), 1992, for best continuing/limited series, 1997, for

best writer and for best letterer, 1998, for best single issue or story (*Eightball* no. 18), 2002, for best cartoonist, and 2003, for best graphic album of original work
(*Twentieth Century Eightball*); Ignatz Award, 1997, for
outstanding comic (*Eightball* no. 17), 1998, for outstanding story (*Ghost World*), 1999, for outstanding
story (*David Boring*), and 2002, for outstanding comic
(*Eightball* no. 22); Eisner Award, 2000, for best writer/
artist, and 2002, for best single issue (*Eightball* no. 22);
Academy Award nomination in category for screenplay
based on material previously produced or published,
2002, for *Ghost World.*

WRITINGS:

Eightball (comic book series), Fantagraphics (Seattle,
WA), c. 1980s—.
Lout Rampage, Fantagraphics (Seattle, WA), 1992.
Like a Velvet Glove Cast in Iron, Fantagraphics (Seattle,
WA), 1993.
*The Manly World of Lloyd Llewellyn: A Golden Trea-
sury of His Complete Works,* Fantagraphics (Se-
attle, WA), 1994, published as *The Official Lloyd
Llewellyn Collection,* Fantagraphics (Seattle, WA),
1997.
Pussey, Fantagraphics (Seattle, WA), 1995.
Orgy Bound, Fantagraphics (Seattle, WA), 1996.
Ghost World, Fantagraphics (Seattle, WA), 1998, re-
vised edition, *Ghost World: The Film Edition,*
2001.
Caricature, Fantagraphics (Seattle, WA), 1998.
David Boring, Pantheon (New York, NY), 2000.
(With Terry Zwigoff) *The Ghost World Screenplay,* Fan-
tagraphics (Seattle, WA), 2001.
(With Jessica Abel) *Twentieth-Century Eightball,* Fanta-
graphics (Seattle, WA), 2001.

Contributor to publications, including *Details, New
Yorker, Blab!, Cracked, World Art, Newsweek, Village
Voice, Time, Esquire,* and *Vogue.* Author of cartoon se-
ries "Ghost World," beginning 1990. Author of "Art
School Confidential."

ADAPTATIONS: "Art School Confidental" was optioned as a major motion picture; *Ghost World* was
adapted as a motion picture and released in 2001.

SIDELIGHTS: Daniel Clowes is a cartoonist and creator of the alternative comic *Eightball,* which has been
published quarterly since the 1980s. Clowes is the acknowledged successor to the master of the genre, Rob-

ert Crumb. With his *Zap,* Crumb was the first to publish underground comics during the 1960s. Others followed, including Bill Griffith with *Zippy the Pinhead,* Art Spiegelman with *Maus,* Jaime and Gilbert Hernandez with *Love and Rockets,* and Chester Brown with *Yummy Fur.* Many of Clowes' serialized stories from *Eightball* have been published as collections or single-story books that combine "stunning visual art and carefully crafted narrative, thus creating comic books that are as compelling and estimable as any of the more 'traditional' art forms," to quote Winda Benedetti of the *Seattle Post-Intelligencer.* Ken Tucker wrote in *Entertainment Weekly* that Clowes "specializes in stylized moroseness—he makes abject despair funny," and for his part Clowes admitted to Benedetti, "I think the humor was something I developed early on as a sort of defense mechanism. I guess that's the way I've always dealt with the darkness and the melancholy."

When he was young, Clowes was sent by his auto mechanic mother to live with his grandparents in Chicago after his stepfather, a race car driver, was killed. Clowes told *Newsweek* reviewer Sarah Van Boven that his grandparents "bought all of their stuff right after the war, down to the canned food and Perry Como records, and basically never bought new stuff. I felt like I was living in the past my whole life." Clowes attended art school, which he considered of little value, and worked for a period at *Cracked* magazine. In 1986 he created a strip called *Lloyd Llewellyn,* about a 1950s-style detective, but it was canceled. His *The Official Lloyd Llewellyn Collection* was published, went out of print, and was reprinted in 1997 by Fantagraphics.

Clowes then began writing *Eightball,* and the first collection of *Eightball* stories was published as *Lout Rampage* in 1992. *Booklist* reviewer Gordon Flagg commented that Clowes offers "visuals that range from the blunt to the sophisticated and a genuine mastery of narrative," and called the comic book artist's work "the cutting edge of popular culture." Clowes' *Like a Velvet Glove Cast in Iron* was first serialized in ten installments in *Eightball.* The protagonist is Clay Loudermilk, who becomes involved in the making of a snuff film. In reviewing the book, Flagg noted the comparison between the work of Clowes and that of filmmaker David Lynch, creator of the now-defunct television series *Twin Peaks,* which still has a cult following. Flagg commented that while Lynch's work "plays for viewer acceptance . . . *Velvet Glove* is unremittingly bleak; any laughs spring from the reader's discomfort or surprise." Flagg felt the story is more powerful and coherent as a book than it was as a serial. In a further comparison of *Twin Peaks* with *Velvet Glove, Entertainment Weekly* reviewer Ty Burr cited *Velvet Glove* as better, "more rigorous in its use of dream logic, and Clowes' scratchy, warts-and-all drawing style gets to you like a sliver under the skin." A *Publishers Weekly* reviewer called the comic a "faux-existentialist, slapstick, sci-fi sitcom" produced by Clowes' "stream-of-warped-consciousness" and noted that of the comic artists of the 1980s, Clowes is "one of the most talented."

Another book by Clowes, *Orgy Bound,* is a collection that begins with the story of a boy who has a romantic interest in insects. In July of 1998, a work by Clowes titled "Green Eyeliner" was featured in *Esquire* magazine's annual fiction issue. The Clowes concoction *Caricature,* a limited-edition hardcover, includes "Green Eyeliner" as well as "MCMLXVI," "Gold Mommy," "Glue Destiny," and "Gynecology." The book features new covers, end papers, title pages, and graphics.

The graphic novel *David Boring* revolves around the efforts of nineteen-year-old security guard David Boring to understand his absentee father, about whom he has little information. In pursuit of his past and a mysterious ideal woman named Wanda, Boring leads anything put a mundane life, getting shot and being marooned on an island. *David Boring* marked a milestone in the evolution of the comic book for it was published in hardcover and represents a new height of quality. As Flagg remarked, the work is "intense, poetic, and intriguing . . . an expressive slice of graphic surrealism." While a *Publishers Weekly* reviewer found the work to be "sometimes enticing, sometimes baffling," it is "never boring." "Subtle as it is, the work of these two young talents [Daniel Clowes and Chris Ware] can be more powerful than a locomotive," punned *Book* commentator James Sullivan. "Few examples of modern literature can leap so many tall buildings in a single bound."

Robert Crumb had read Clowes' graphic novel *Ghost World* and recommended it to Terry Zwigoff, director of the documentary *Crumb.* The novel is the story of teenage girls Becky Doppelmeyer and Enid Coleslaw (an anagram of Clowes' own name), who hang out together but apart from the outside world. They frequent diners, make fun of their friends, and criticize television programs and magazines like *Sassy.* Flagg said the book accurately portrays teens but found most impressive the book's sympathy, "evident not only in deep understanding of the young protagonists but also an affinity for the supporting characters."

Clowes completed the live-action screenplay version of his graphic novel *Ghost World* and looked forward to the production of the film with Zwigoff. Clowes predicted that *Ghost World* would appeal to a broad audience. "We don't want it to have a John Waters or David Lynch feel where every single actor is out of central casting from Barnum & Bailey," Clowes explained in an interview with Joey Anuff in *Addicted to Noise* online. "We want it to look like the harsh reality you see on Mission and Twenty-fourth Street in San Leandro. People in ill-fitting jumpsuits that say 'Chicago Bulls' on the front, the grim hyper-reality that actually exists. Terry has a good sense for that. He's a very oversensitive guy who's not happy with the way things are, and he has a real sense of why that is and how to show it." In 2001 Clowes published *The Ghost World Screenplay,* which includes the unedited screenplay, several new comic strips, and photographs of the moviemaking, as well as putting out a new edition of the original *Ghost World* graphic novel.

The year 2001 also saw the publication of selected humor strips from the *Eightball* series originally published between 1988 and 1996. *Twentieth-Century Eightball* included such favorites as "I Hate You Deeply," "Sexual Frustration," "Ugly Girls," "Why I Hate Christians," "Message to the People of the Future," "Paranoid," "My Suicide," "Art School Confidential," "On Sports," and "Chicago."

Anuff asked the comic book artist about the future of comics. Clowes noted that, although Crumb experienced huge sales in the 1960s—"Every hippy in the world had a copy"—he himself has trouble finding *Ghost World,* even in Berkeley and San Francisco. "It's incredibly frustrating. . . . People have a bias against comics for, I think, a good reason. Most of what they've seen is really awful." "I just hate the idea of the Internet being comics' final resting place," Clowes added. "I think paper and pulp and that flat surface is the perfect medium," he said, adding that "I think the notion of comics on a screen is backwards." What is Clowes trying to achieve with his work? He told Benedetti, "I'm trying to do something that will hold my interest for the incredibly tedious amount of time it takes to draw a comic book." And in pleasing himself, he is pleasing his audience as well.

BIOGRAPHICAL AND CRITICAL SOURCES:

PERIODICALS

Book, January, 2001, James Sullivan, review of *David Boring,* p. 66.

Booklist, March 1, 1992, Gordon Flagg, review of *Lout Rampage,* p. 1190; May 1, 1993, p. 1562; September 1, 1997, Gordon Flagg, review of *Ghost World,* p. 47; November 15, 2000, Gordon Flagg, review of *David Boring,* p. 598.

Entertainment Weekly, June 26, 1992, Ken Tucker, "Cool Cartoonist: Daniel Clowes," p. 76; May 21, 1993, Ty Burr, "Dread and Laughter," p. 44.

Guardian (London, England), June 2, 1997, Nick Hasted, "Mr. Clowes and His Comic Cult," pp. T10-11.

Library Journal, March 15, 1999, Stephan Weiner, review of *Caricature: Nine Stories,* p. 74.

Newsweek, April 27, 1998, Sarah Van Boven, "Daniel Clowes Wows 'Em with 'Ghost World,'" p. 70.

New York Times Book Review, November 26, 2000, Dave Eggers, "After Wham! Pow! Shazam! Comic Books Move beyond Superheroes to the World of Literature," p. 10.

Print, July-August, 1998, Rhonda Rubinstein, "Creepy, Cool, and Collected," pp. 90-95.

Publishers Weekly, April 12, 1993, review of *Like a Velvet Glove Cast in Iron,* p. 59; October 11, 1993, p. 54; October 20, 1997, Calvin Reid, "Hardcover to Film," p. 14; September 4, 2000, review of *David Boring,* p. 86.

School Library Journal, February, 1999, Francisca Goldsmith, review of *Ghost World,* p. 146.

Seattle Post-Intelligencer, May 11, 2001, Winda Benedetti, "Comic Book Art Earns Respect at Hands of Clowes and Ware," p. 28.

Voice Literary Supplement, October, 1990, p. 17.

ONLINE

Addicted to Noise, http://www.addict.com/ (December 11, 1999), Joey Anuff, "Behind the *Eightball:* Comic Book Creator Daniel Clowes."

Fantagraphics Books Web site, http://www.fantagraphics.com/ (August 16, 2004), "Dan Clowes."